KU-168-833

THE LAWS
OF SCOTLAND

———•———

STAIR MEMORIAL
ENCYCLOPAEDIA

Consolidated Index

This volume contains the consolidated title indexes from Volumes 1–25

THE LAWS
OF SCOTLAND

———•———

STAIR MEMORIAL
ENCYCLOPAEDIA

Consolidated Index

The Law Society of Scotland
Butterworths

Edinburgh   1997

The Law Society of Scotland
The Law Society's Hall, 26 Drumsheugh Gardens, EDINBURGH EH3 7YR

Butterworths

United Kingdom	Butterworths, a Division of Reed Elsevier (UK) Ltd, 4 Hill Street, EDINBURGH EH2 3JZ Halsbury House, 35 Chancery Lane, LONDON WC2A 1EL
Australia	Butterworths, SYDNEY, MELBOURNE, BRISBANE, ADELAIDE, PERTH, CANBERRA and HOBART
Canada	Butterworths Canada Ltd, TORONTO and VANCOUVER
Ireland	Butterworth (Ireland) Ltd, DUBLIN
Malaysia	Malayan Law Journal Sdn Bhd, KUALA LUMPUR
New Zealand	Butterworths of New Zealand Ltd, WELLINGTON and AUCKLAND
Singapore	Reed Elsevier (Singapore) Pte Ltd, SINGAPORE
South Africa	Butterworths Publishers (Pty) Ltd, DURBAN
USA	Michie, Charlottesville, VIRGINIA

All rights reserved. No part of this publication may be reproduced in any material form (including photocopying or storing it in any medium by electronics means and whether or not transiently or incidentally to some other use of this publication) without the written permission of the copyright owner except in accordance with the provisions of the Copyright, Design and Patents Act 1988 or under the terms of a licence issued by the Copyright Licensing Agency Ltd, 90 Tottenham Court Road, London, England WC1P 9HE. Applications for the copyright owner's written permission to reproduce any part of this publication should be addressed to the publisher.

Warning: The doing of an unauthorised act in relation to a copyright work may result in both a civil claim for damages and criminal prosecution.

First published 1997

© Reed Elsevier (UK) Ltd 1997

ISBN 0406 995427

Typeset in England by Data Management Services, Frome
Printed in England by Clays Ltd, Bungay

This index prepared and edited by

Ann Barrett
Member, the Society of Indexers

Margaret Cherry LLB

Based on the indexes to volumes 1-25 compiled by

The late Congreve Banwell, Member, the Society of Indexers (vol 2)

Ann Barrett, Member, the Society of Indexers (vols 3, 6-8, 10-13, 15, 16, 18, 19, 21, 24)

Alexandra Corrin LLB, Barrister (vol 1)

Elizabeth J M Ingham ALA, Member, the Society of Indexers (vols 4, 5, 9, 14, 17, 20, 23, 25)

Patricia Vasey BA, Dip Soc Stud, Barrister (vol 22)

This volume contains tables for the following titles:

Volume 1
Accountants, Accounting and
    Auditing
Administrative Law
Admiralty
Advertising
Agency and Mandate
Agriculture

Volume 2
Alcoholic Liquor
Animals
Arbitration
Armed Forces
Associations and Clubs
Aviation and Air Transport
Banking and Financial Institutions
Bankruptcy
Betting, Gaming and Lotteries

Volume 3
Building Contracts
Building Controls
Building Societies
Burial and Cremation
Carriage
Cautionary Obligations and
    Representations as to Credit
Charities
Children and Young Persons
Churches and Other Religious
    Bodies

Volume 4
Civil Jurisdiction
Commercial Paper
Companies
Competition Law

Volume 5
Compulsory Acquisition
Constitutional Law
Consumer Credit

Volume 6
Consumer Protection
Contempt of Court
Conveyancing
Courts and Competency

Volume 7
Criminal Law
The Crown
Customs and Excise

Volume 8
Deposit
Diligence and Enforcement of
    Judgments
Donation
Education

Volume 9
Employment
Energy
Entertainment
Environment

Volume 10
European Community Law and
    Institutions
Evidence
Family Law
Fire Services
Firearms and Explosives

Volume 11
Fisheries
Food, Dairies and Slaughterhouses
Forestry
Fraud
Game
General Legal Concepts
Guardianship
Harbours
Health Services
Heraldry
Hotels and Tourism
Housing

Volume 12
Human Rights in Europe
Immigration and Extradition
Industrial and Provident Societies,
    Credit Unions and Friendly Societies
Insurance
Interest
Interpretation of Statutes, Deeds and
    Other Documents
Investor Protection

Volume 13
Judicial and Other Remedies
Landlord and Tenant
Lawburrows
Legal Aid
Legal Profession
Libraries, Museums and Galleries
Liferent and Fee
Loan

Volume 14
Local Government
Location: Leasing and Hire of
    Moveables
Medical and Allied Professions
Medicines, Poisons and Drugs
Meetings
Mental Health
Messengers-at-Arms and Sheriff
    Officers
Mines and Quarries
Money and Means of Exchange
Nationality and Citizenship
Nuisance

Volume 15
Obligations
Parliamentary and Other Elections

Volume 16
Partnership
Passports and Other Travel
    Formalities
Peerages
Penal Establishments
Personal Bar
Police
Posts and Telecommunications
Precedence
Prescription and Limitation

Volume 17
Press and Broadcasting
Private International Law
Prize
Procedure

Volume 18
Property

Volume 19
Provisional Orders and Private
    Legislation
Public Corporations
Public Health
Public International Law
Public Registers and Records
Railways, Canals and Tramways
Recreation and Sport
Registration of Births, Deaths and
    Marriages
Revenue

Volume 20
Rights in Security
Road Traffic
Roads
Sale and Exchange

Volume 21
Sea and Continental Shelf
Shipping and Navigation
Social Security

Volume 22
Social Work
Sources of Law (Formal)
Sources of Law (General and Historical),
    Legal Method and Reform
Time

Volume 23
Town and Country Planning
Trade Unions and Trade Disputes
Tribunals and Inquiries

Volume 24
Trusts, Trustees and Judicial Factors
Udal Law
Valuation for Rating

Volume 25
Valuations
Veterinary Surgery
Water and Water Rights
Water Supply
Wills and Succession

Publisher's Note

The Consolidated Index is an index to the law as stated in the twenty-five volumes of *The Laws of Scotland: Stair Memorial Encyclopaedia* and does not take account of changes made subsequent to the publication of each volume. The effect of such changes is set out in the Cumulative Supplement and the Current Service, and reference should always be made to these publications after reading the text to which the Consolidated Index has directed attention.

Subsequent reissues of main volumes will be served by their own indexes, which will supersede the relevant entries in the Consolidated Index.

An index is, by its nature, subjective. No two people will agree on what should or should not be included in an index, and in what way index entries should be phrased. It is hoped, however, that this volume which contains the revised and merged title indexes of the twenty-five published volumes of the *Stair Memorial Encyclopaedia* will assist readers to find their way round the volumes, and to cross refer with greater ease. References are to volume and paragraph numbers. Volume numbers are printed in bold type.

BUTTERWORTHS
EDINBURGH
June 1997

A

A coelo usque ad centrum **principle**
generally, **18**, 196, 198, 647
law of the tenement, **18**, 228
separate tenements, and, **18**, 198, 207
Abandoned property
See PROPERTY
Abandonment
animal of, *see* ANIMAL
child, of, *see* CHILD-CHILDREN
renunciation distinguished, **13**, 438
Abduction
assault, **7**, 215
child, of, *see* CHILD-CHILDREN
Aberdeen
county of city, **14**, 39
educational provision, **14**, 36
feu-ferme charter, **14**, 11
police court, former operation of, **6**, 1157, 1158
population, **14**, 64
transport undertakings, operation of, **14**, 414, 419
Abode
right of, **12**, 107
British citizens, **16**, 1207
British citizenship, acquisition of, **14**, 1906
British Overseas citizenship, **14**, 1942
British subject, **14**, 1950
categories of entrant without—
EU law, **12**, 219–239
EU law, not under, **12**, 240–328
certificate of entitlement, **16**, 1208, 1242
Channel Islands or Isle of Man, entry to UK
via, **12**, 123
Commonwealth citizens, **12**, 118, 118*n*; **16**, 1208
entry clearance, **12**, 151, 153
European Union law, **12**, 117
exclusion order, **12**, 107
generally, **12**, 107; **16**, 1207
immigration, **14**, 1903
meaning, **12**, 117
patrials, **12**, 118*n*
polygamous wives and widows, **12**, 118*n*
children of, **12**, 118*n*
proof, **16**, 1207, 1208
statutory nature, **12**, 118*n*
who has, **12**, 118
Abortion
Abortion Act 1967—
aim and effect, **7**, 283, 286
situation prior to, **7**, 283
attempt to procure, **7**, 169
authorised, **7**, 256
availability, **7**, 283
Chief Medical Officer, notification, **7**, 286
common law, **7**, 283, 284, 285
'conscience clause', **7**, 286
crime of, generally, **7**, 256
death during course of, **7**, 270
documentation, **7**, 286
'eugenic ground', **7**, 287

Abortion—*continued*
European Convention on Human Rights, **12**, 25
failed, duty of care, **15**, 305, 306
father's rights, **10**, 1032
grounds for, **7**, 287
Human Fertilisation and Embryology Act 1990
…, **7**, 284, 289
immediate necessity, circumstances of, **7**, 286
legal, **10**, 1032
legal protection of fetus, **7**, 283
medical approval, requirement for, **7**, 283, 286
nurse, performed by, **7**, 286
post-coital contraception, **7**, 288
premature delivery of fetus, causing, **7**, 285
procuring, Roman Catholic Church, *latae
sententiae* offence, **3**, 1658
protection of children, generally, **10**, 1029, 1030,
1032
right to procure, **11**, 1095
statute law, **7**, 283, 284, 286
supply of information, art and part liability, **7**, 185
therapeutic, **7**, 283
Abrogation
class rights, of, **4**, 349
Absolute discharge
court's power to grant, **17**, 806
Absolute disposition
debtor under, as lessor, **13**, 161, 164
Absolute liability
See STRICT LIABILITY
Absolute privilege
See DELICT
Absolutism
principle of, **5**, 340
Academic freedom
tenure, and, **8**, 1020
university education, **8**, 985
ACAS
See ADVISORY, CONCILIATION AND ARBITRATION
SERVICE
Acceptance
bill of exchange, of, **4**, 139
offer generally, of, *see* OFFER
offer to purchase property, of, *see* MISSIVES
Acceptilation
See CONTRACT
Acceptor
bill of exchange, party to, **4**, 132
Access
child to, *see* CHILD-CHILDREN
Access funds
further education, award to student in, **8**, 945
meaning, **8**, 945
Secretary of State's powers as to, **8**, 945
Accession
accessorium principale sequitur rule, **18**, 570, 589
accessory—
compensation, payment in respect of by owner
of principal, **18**, 574, 577, 676

Accession—*continued*
accessory—*continued*
  extinction of existing title, **18**, 574
  heritable—
    becoming, **18**, 574
    definition, **18**, 579
  meaning, **18**, 570
  moveables to moveables, **18**, 590
  owner—
    compensation, right of, **18**, 574, 577, 586
    severance, right of, **18**, 586
  principal—
    becoming part of, **18**, 574
    subsequent separation from, **18**, 574, 574*n*
alluvion, *see* land to land *below*
annexer, intention of, **18**, 583
  actual, **18**, 583
  deemed, **18**, 583
artificial, **18**, 577
buildings, **18**, 578
  tenements, where building divided into, **18**, 578*n*, 585
chronology, importance of, **18**, 573
commixtion compared, **18**, 571*n*, 588
common property, original acquisition, **18**, 22*n*
confusion compared, **18**, 571*n*, 588
constructive, **18**, 576, 576*n*
contract, law of, relationship with, **18**, 576
corporeal, property must be, **18**, 570
crops, **18**, 595, 596
death, gifts made on, **18**, 576
definition, **18**, 570
derivative, **18**, 574*n*
effects—
  accessory becoming part of principal, **18**, 574, 575
  existing title of accessory extinguished, **18**, 574, 575
  heritable nature of accessory, on, **18**, 574, 575
  rules, application of, **18**, 575
elements—
  functional subordination, **18**, 571, 579
    moveables to land, **18**, 579, 581
  permanence or quasi-permanence, **18**, 571, 579
    moveables to land, **18**, 579, 582
  permanent attachment—
    indissoluble union, where requirement for, **18**, 589
  physical attachment, **18**, 571, 579
    moveables to land, **18**, 579, 580
  sufficiently present, must be, **18**, 571, 572
English law compared, **18**, 2
feudal law, and, **18**, 574, 587
fittings, **18**, 578, 578*n*
fixtures, *see* moveables to land *below*
fruits, by, **18**, 570
  crops, **18**, 595, 596
  meaning of fruits, **18**, 595, 595*n*
  severance, effect of, **18**, 596
functional subordination, element of, **18**, 571, 579
  moveables to land, **18**, 579, 581
generally, **18**, 1

Accession—*continued*
indissoluble union—
  meaning, **18**, 589
  where requirement for, **18**, 589
industrial, **18**, 577
instruction for performance—
  owner of accessory, from, **18**, 577
  owner of principal, from, **18**, 577
  third party, from, **18**, 577
intention, role of, **18**, 583
intestate succession, questions arising on, **18**, 576
land to land (alluvion)—
  advance of waters, **18**, 594
  alvei mutatio, **18**, 594
  avulsion compared, **18**, 592
  generally, **18**, 570, 592
  islands, formation of, **18**, 594
  meaning of alluvion, **18**, 592
  non-tidal waters, retreat, **18**, 594
  reclamation by human act, **18**, 593
  requirements for, **18**, 592
  tidal waters, retreat, **18**, 594
  transmission of soil from one bank to another, **18**, 594
lifetime gifts, **18**, 576
machinery, **18**, 576
mechanical nature of operation, **18**, 572, 572*n*
motor vehicles, **18**, 576
moveables to land, **18**, 570
  annexer, intention of, **18**, 583
  custom, whether affecting, **18**, 584
  definition of heritable accessories, **18**, 579
  feudal law, and, **18**, 587
  fixtures, meaning, **18**, 578, 582
  functional subordination, **18**, 579, 581
  generally, **18**, 578, 584
  intention, role of, **18**, 583
  interior decoration, **18**, 580, 581
  machinery, **18**, 580, 581, 582
  mobile homes, **18**, 584
  moveable property as accessory, **18**, 578
  permanence or quasi-permanence, **18**, 579, 582
  physical attachment, **18**, 579, 580
  rateable value, and, **18**, 578, 578*n*
  separate tenements, no accession across, **18**, 585
  severance, right of, **18**, 586
moveables to moveables, **18**, 570, 571*n*
  accessory, identification, **18**, 590
  generally, **18**, 588
  indissoluble union, need for, **18**, 588
  principal, identification, **18**, 590
  Scottish Law Commission recommendations, **18**, 591
natural, **18**, 577
nemo dat quod non habet rule, **18**, 676
original, **18**, 574*n*
original acquisition, as, **18**, 597
permanence or quasi-permanence, element of, **18**, 571, 579
  moveables to land, **18**, 579, 582
permanent attachment, element of—
  indissoluble union, where requirement for, **18**, 589

Accession—*continued*
physical attachment, element of, **18**, 571, 579
  moveables to land, **18**, 579, 580
principal—
  accessory—
    becoming part of, **18**, 574
    subsequent separation from, **18**, 574, 574*n*
  feudal land, **18**, 574
  heritable, where, **18**, 574
  meaning, **18**, 570
  moveables to moveables, **18**, 590
  owner—
    accessory as property of, **18**, 574, 586
    compensation, obligation to pay, **18**, 574, 577
    two or more, where, **18**, 574
  sale, **18**, 574
  subsidiary right created over, **18**, 574
Roman law, influence of, **18**, 570
sale, law of, relationship with, **18**, 576
severance—
  accession by fruits, and, **18**, 596
  right of, **18**, 586
specificatio (specification) compared, **18**, 571*n*, 588
subjective factors, rejection of, **18**, 572, 572*n*
tenant, fixtures fitted by, **18**, 574, 574*n*, 575, 582, 586
tenements, cannot operate across separate, **18**, 578*n*, 585
unitary law of, concept of, **18**, 575, 576*n*

Accession Declaration
monarch, made by, **7**, 708, 709

Accident
aircraft, *see* AIRCRAFT
disablement benefit, *see* DISABLEMENT BENEFIT
electricity, in connection with, *see* ELECTRICITY
fatal, *see* FATAL ACCIDENT INQUIRIES
industrial injuries benefits, *see* INDUSTRIAL INJURIES BENEFITS
major hazard, control of, **9**, 533
meaning, **12**, 844
mining, **14**, 1621, 1659
notifiable, inspection by safety representative following, **9**, 474
railway, *see* RAILWAYS
road, *see* ROAD ACCIDENT

Accommodation
Commissioner for Local Administration, of, **14**, 135
countryside, provision in, **14**, 680
hostel, for probationers, **22**, 34
hotel, *see* HOTEL
mentally handicapped person, community sheltered, **22**, 31
person in need, temporary accommodation for, **22**, 13
remand centre, committal of young person to, **22**, 32, 33
secure, child, for—
  local authority duty to provide, **22**, 16
  registration by Secretary of State, **22**, 33
tourist, registration of, **11**, 1811
trade descriptions, **6**, 126, 142
trust, provision of residential accommodation for beneficiary of, **24**, 202
See also HOMELESSNESS; HOUSING; RESIDENTIAL CARE

Accommodation agency
Accommodation Agencies Act 1953 ..., **13**, 695
restriction on advertising, **1**, 527
Accommodation bill
bill of exchange, **3**, 830
holder, rights of, **4**, 150
nature of, **4**, 135
Accommodation party
generally, **3**, 830
liability, **4**, 166
Accountancy
associations, integration of, **1**, 11
Consultative Committee of Accountancy Bodies, **1**, 12
origins, **1**, 4
profession—
  characteristics, **1**, 18
  development of, **1**, 19
  role of, **1**, 5
  Scotland, in, **1**, 6
  social background, **1**, 17
  unification of, **1**, 14
  United Kingdom, in, **1**, 5
professional societies, **1**, 5
See also ACCOUNTANT; ACCOUNTANT IN BANKRUPTCY; ACCOUNTANT OF COURT; ACCOUNTING; ACCOUNTS
Accountant
auditing, carrying out, **1**, 5
bankruptcy, in, *see* ACCOUNTANT IN BANKRUPTCY
chartered, *see* CHARTERED ACCOUNTANT
court, appointment by, **1**, 105
Court, of, *see* ACCOUNTANT OF COURT
criminal liability, **1**, 100
delivery of tax documents by, **19**, 1551
duty of care, **15**, 278
early professional organisations, **1**, 7
function, expansion of, **1**, 21
general duty of care, **1**, 24
Inland Revenue, dealing with, **1**, 100
insurance intermediary, **12**, 811
legal obligations of, **1**, 78
meaning, **1**, 2
negligence of, redress for, **1**, 25
office, holding, **1**, 78
partnership, number of partners allowed, **16**, 1011, 1112
penalty, liable to, **1**, 100
professional discipline—
  Appeal Committee, **1**, 28, 32
  Chartered Institute of Public Finance and Accountancy, by, **1**, 36
  Committee of Inquiry, **1**, 28, 30
  decisions relating to, **1**, 31
  disciplinary action, liability for, **1**, 26
  Discipline Committee, **1**, 28, 31
  ethical guidance, **1**, 33
  inefficiency and incompetence, including, **1**, 27
  Institute of Cost and Management Accountants, by, **1**, 35
  Investigation Committee, **1**, 28, 29
  Joint Disciplinary Scheme—
    administration of, **1**, 28
    arrangements outside Scotland, **1**, 34

Accountant—*continued*
professional discipline—*continued*
  Joint Disciplinary Scheme—*continued*
    firms, extending to, **1**, 27
    objectives of, **1**, 27
  non-accountants, role of, **1**, 28
  student, decisions on, **1**, 31
remit, role in, **1**, 105
reports—
  guidance on, **1**, 55
  securities market, for, **1**, 54
societies, **1**, 9
standard of care, **1**, 97, 98
tax adviser, as, **1**, 102
taxpayer client, duty to, **1**, 101
trust, appointment of, **24**, 190
valuation, arbiter in, **1**, 103
valuer, as, **1**, 104
work of, **1**, 1

Accountant in Bankruptcy
court orders to be sent to, **2**, 1339
directions by, to trustee, **2**, 1315
discharge of interim trustee, **2**, 1345
Edinburgh Gazette copy for, **2**, 1341
fees payable to, **2**, 1305
final statement for, **2**, 1348
functions, **2**, 1305
matters to be notified to, **2**, 1339
notice to—
  interim trustee appointment, of, **2**, 1310
  potential sequestration of, **2**, 1305
office of—
  creation, **2**, 1304
  merger of, **2**, 1304
petition, copy of, to be sent to, **2**, 1339
register to be kept by, **2**, 1339
  See also INSOLVENCY
report by interim trustee to, **2**, 1344
report to be made by, **2**, 1305
statutory meeting, notice of, **2**, 1346
supervisory duties, **2**, 1305

Accountant of Court
application for appointment of new trustee, **24**, 160
appointment, **6**, 937
curator bonis, communication with, **11**, 1234
duties, **6**, 937
establishment of office, **6**, 937
exempted person under Financial Services Act 1986, as, **12**, 1323
judicial factors—
  control and supervision of, **24**, 242, 243, 255
  role and duties with respect to, **24**, 237, 246, 250, 253, 255, 265
office, merger of, **2**, 1304

Accounting
Accounting Standards Committee—
  creation of, **1**, 13
  development of, **1**, 44
  Statements of Standard Accounting Practice, issuing, **1**, 45
computers, effect of, **1**, 56

Accounting—*continued*
European Community law—
  Eighth Directive, **1**, 66, 69
  Fourth Directive, **1**, 66, 67
  Seventh Directive, **1**, 66, 68
historical cost, **1**, 50, 51
information system, as, **1**, 56
international character of, **1**, 70
international harmonisation, **1**, 20, 70
management, *see* MANAGEMENT ACCOUNTING
nature of, **1**, 20
obligation of, prescription, **16**, 2116
officer—
  appointment of, **5**, 593
  responsibilities, **5**, 593
origins, **1**, 4
records—
  audit of, **1**, 58
  investment business, duty to keep, **12**, 1404, 1408
standards—
  European Institutions, influence of, **1**, 77
  government, influence of, **1**, 76
  international, **1**, 73–77
  professional bodies, influence of, **1**, 75
  UN groups on, **1**, 76
theory and practice, **1**, 20

Accounting reference period
meaning, **4**, 451

Accounts
agent, of, **1**, 634
appropriation, **5**, 594
building societies, **1**, 88
  See also BUILDING SOCIETIES
company—
  accounting records, maintenance, **4**, 450
  accounting reference period, **4**, 451
  administrator, duties of, **4**, 631
  annual—
    annual general meeting, considered at, **4**, 388
    approval, **4**, 452
    meeting of members, considered at, **4**, 388
  circulation, **4**, 455
  disclosure, **16**, 1005
  dormant companies, **4**, 457
  financial year, **4**, 451
  group, **4**, 453, 454
  medium-sized company, **4**, 454
  publication, **4**, 455
  receiver, duties, **4**, 698
  small company, **4**, 454
  statutory provisions, **4**, 449
  voluntary arrangement, supervisor of, **4**, 597
  See also limited companies, of *below*
corporations, of, **1**, 91
direct labour organisation, **14**, 910
employers' association, of, **1**, 95
European Accounting Association, **1**, 77
final settlement, distribution of assets, **16**, 1105
Fourth Directive, **1**, 66, 67
friendly societies, of, **1**, 89
housing association, of, **1**, 94
industrial and provident societies, of, **1**, 90
inflation, taking notice of, **1**, 51
legislative regulation, not subject to, **1**, 38

Accounts—*continued*

limitations of, **1**, 51
limited companies, of—
   Accounting Standards Committee, development
      of, **1**, 44
   audited, to be, **1**, 40
   group, **1**, 40
      Seventh Directive on, **1**, 66, 68
   historical requirements, **1**, 41
   standard of reporting, **1**, 67
   statutory requirements, **1**, 40
   'true and fair view'—
      concept of, **1**, 42, 43, 67
local authority—
   abstract of, **1**, 46
   audit of, **1**, 87; **14**, 886
   Commission for Local Authority Accounts in
      Scotland, **1**, 48
   defined authority, **14**, 918
   form and preparation of, **1**, 46
   generally, **1**, 87; **14**, 882
   making up and balancing, **14**, 887
   non-statutory guidance, **1**, 47
   objection to accounts, right of, **14**, 889
   objectives of, **1**, 47
   other bodies, application of provisions to, **14**, 896
   public inspection, open to, **1**, 87; **14**, 888
   repayment, order for, **14**, 893
   Secretary of State's powers, **14**, 895
   special report on, **1**, 87
   Statements of Standard Accounting Practice
      applying to, **1**, 47
   statutory regulation, **1**, 46
medium-sized company, of, **1**, 83
partner refusing to keep proper, **16**, 1090
partners refused access, **16**, 1090
partnership whose members are all limited
   companies, **16**, 1003
public corporations, of, **1**, 91
publication, **16**, 1003
regulation of, **1**, 37, 39
Seventh Directive, **1**, 66, 68
small company, of, **1**, 83
solicitors', **1**, 92
special category companies, of, **1**, 82
trade union, of, **1**, 95
trust accounts, audit of, **24**, 195
trustee savings bank, of, **1**, 93
trustee's duty, **24**, 195, 221
unrealised profits, effect of, **1**, 50
value changes, recognition of, **1**, 49

Accretion

back-dating acquisition of title, **18**, 677
basis of doctrine, **18**, 677
contract of deposit, **8**, 5
conveyancing—
   heritable property, **6**, 590
   limitations on doctrine of, **6**, 590
   protection of purchaser by, **6**, 566
historical development, **18**, 677
legacy—
   class—
      ascertaining, **25**, 844
      gifts, **25**, 843

Accretion—*continued*

legacy—*continued*
   conditio si institutus sine liberis decesserit, **25**, 838,
      842
   destination over, **25**, 839
   futurity, words of, **25**, 845
   principle, **25**, 838
   shares—
      conditio si institutus, taken as result of, **25**, 842
      equal, **25**, 841
      joint, **25**, 840
legal fiction, working by, **18**, 677
meaning, **18**, 677
moveable property, **18**, 678
nemo dat quod non habet rule exception—
   generally, **18**, 672
   heritable property, **18**, 677
   moveable property, **18**, 678
ratification by principal of transfer by agent, **18**,
   679
retrospective ownership, fiction of, **18**, 677
sequestration preventing, **18**, 677
subordinate real right, creation, **18**, 677
territory, of, **19**, 670

Accumulation and maintenance trust

discretionary trust, as, **24**, 17
inheritance tax, **19**, 1533
See also TRUST

Accumulation of trust income

beginning—
   on or after death of granter, **24**, 42, 43
   during lifetime of granter, **24**, 40
charitable trusts, **24**, 110
choice of period, **24**, 40–43
condition directing, **25**, 868
debts, for payment of, **24**, 74
definition, **24**, 47, 48
   exceptions, **24**, 48
   matters falling outwith, **24**, 47
directions to accumulate, **24**, 38
equitable compensation, **25**, 804
generally, **24**, 34–48
illegal, **24**, 38
income tax, **24**, 38
inter vivos deeds, **24**, 40, 41
limitation of, **25**, 767
minorities, periods involving, **24**, 36
one accumulation period, **24**, 39
prescribed periods for, **24**, 34, 35–37; **25**, 768, 769
residue clause, **24**, 46
specific gift, **24**, 45
   where no, **24**, 46
statutory prohibition, **24**, 35, 47, 48
   contravention of, **24**, 44–46
vesting, acceleration of, **25**, 956

Accusatorial system

nature of, **17**, 564

Accused

absence of, **17**, 736, 769
address, change of, **17**, 635
appearance in private—
   examination, **17**, 642–644
   full committal, **17**, 645
   generally, **17**, 641

Accused—*continued*
apprehension of, **17**, 543
body corporate as, **17**, 737
bringing before court, **17**, 624
citation of, **17**, 711
evidence for, **17**, 759
immoral lifestyle of, irrelevancy, **7**, 94
intimidation of, **7**, 496
judicial examination, **17**, 546
no case to answer, **17**, 758
presumptions relating to, **10**, 754
recovery of, proceedings on, **17**, 901
rights of—
    bail, **17**, 551
    generally, **17**, 549
    legal representation, **17**, 550
    pardons, **17**, 554
    special defences, **17**, 553
    undue delay, prevention of, **17**, 552
trial in absence of, **17**, 721
unrepresented, plea bargaining, **17**, 733
Achievement of arms
badges and insignia of office, **11**, 1610
banners and flags, **11**, 1609
chapeau, **11**, 1607
components of, generally, **11**, 1603
coronet, **11**, 1607
crest, **11**, 1606
helmet, **11**, 1605
mantling, **11**, 1605
motto, **11**, 1611
shield, **11**, 1604
supporters, **11**, 1608
wreath, **11**, 1605
Acquiescence
age of pursuer, **16**, 1616
annulment of voidable obligation barred by, **15**, 672
applicability, extent and period, **16**, 1620
buildings, to erection of, **16**, 1616, 1617, 1620
company barred by, **16**, 1616
consent—
    inference, **16**, 1615
    parties whose consent binds, **16**, 1616
contract, construing, **16**, 1619
corporation bound by, **16**, 1616
debts, application to payment of, **16**, 1620
dominant tenement, by, **16**, 1616
double, doctrine of, **16**, 1616
duration, **16**, 1620
extent, **16**, 1620
factor, of, whether binding principal, **16**, 1616
feu charter, contravention, **16**, 1618
heir bound by, **16**, 1616
heir of entail bound by, **16**, 1616
heritage—
    objection to use of, bar by acquiescence, **16**, 1614
    transfer, **16**, 1614
implied consent, as, **16**, 1615
knowledge, **16**, 1615
landed proprietor, double acquiescence, doctrine of, **16**, 1616
liferenter, by, **16**, 1616

Acquiescence—*continued*
limits, **16**, 1618
mora, interaction with, **16**, 1613
    abandonment, presumption, **16**, 1624
    culpable delay, **16**, 1621
    delay alone insufficient, **16**, 1622
    division of judicial opinion, **16**, 1623
    heritable title, **16**, 1625
    mora, meaning, **16**, 1621
    taciturnity, **16**, 1621–1625
nuisance, **16**, 1617
operation or act discovered only after committal, **16**, 1617
parties whose consent binds, **16**, 1616
personal bar, as aspect of, **16**, 1613
pollution, **16**, 1617
prevention, person aggrieved must have powers of, **16**, 1617
rei interventus, interaction with, **16**, 1613
representation essentially tacit, **16**, 1613
right of ways, establishing, **16**, 1616
road, public use of, **16**, 1616
servitude, contravention, **16**, 1616
silence, whether person barred by, **16**, 1620
singular successor bound by, **16**, 1616, 1616*n*
time, necessity for, **16**, 1613
Acquired Immune Deficiency Syndrome (AIDS)
legislation as to, **19**, 508, 509
Acquirenda
inhibition, **8**, 156
meaning, **8**, 156
not arrestable, **8**, 265
Acquisata
inhibition, **8**, 156
meaning, **8**, 156
Acquisition
common property, original acquisition—
    accession, **18**, 22*n*
    commixtion, **18**, 22*n*
    confusion, **18**, 22*n*
    specification, **18**, 22*n*
derivative, transfer of property as, **18**, 597
derivative modes of, **11**, 1103
meaning, **4**, 536
See also CORPOREAL MOVEABLE PROPERTY
Acquisition of Land (Authorisation Procedure) (Scotland) Act 1947
application of, **5**, 36
common land, **5**, 39
compulsory purchase orders, **5**, 37
Lands Clauses Acts, incorporation of, **5**, 40
National Trust land, **5**, 38
open spaces, **5**, 39
Railways Clauses Act, incorporation of, **5**, 41
rights of way, **5**, 42
statutory undertakers, land acquired by, **5**, 43
See also COMPULSORY ACQUISITION
Act of Adjournal
documentary evidence, as, **10**, 576
regulation of procedure by, **6**, 861, 930; **22**, 187, 520, 528
statutory instruments, when, **22**, 187
subordinate legislation, **22**, 187

Act of God
carrier not liable for, **15**, 145; **21**, 603
damage caused to harbour by, **11**, 1327
fires, **15**, 414
floods, **15**, 413
hotelkeeper not liable for, **11**, 1746; **15**, 148
land, escape of dangerous agencies from, **15**, 193
meaning, **21**, 603
negligence, as defence against, **15**, 412–415
statutory duty, breach of, **15**, 175

Act of Parliament
citation, **22**, 169
commencement, enactment distinguished, **22**, 155
continuing Acts, **22**, 166
copyright, **18**, 1000
duration, **22**, 156
enabling Acts, **5**, 35
enactment—
    commencement distinguished, **22**, 155
    formula, **22**, 153
    legal validity, effect, **22**, 153
European Communities legislation—
    implementation by, **22**, 221
    precedence, **22**, 214
expiry—
    continuing Acts, **22**, 166
    effect, **22**, 165
incorporation by, **4**, 303, 314
involuntary transfer of ownership by, **18**, 665
judicial notice, as public Act, **22**, 168
operation, generally, **22**, 153–170
parent legislation, as, *see* LEGISLATION; STATUTORY
    INSTRUMENT
partnership does not require, **4**, 302
preamble, **22**, 154
presumption of application to Scotland, **22**, 170
private—
    objects clause cannot be altered without,
        4, 322
    See also PRIVATE BILL; PRIVATE LEGISLATION
promulgation, **22**, 167
proof, **22**, 168
publication, **7**, 731
repeal—
    effect—
        accrued rights etc, on, **22**, 161
        common law, on, **22**, 163
        Interpretation Act 1978 ..., **22**, 159
        repealing enactment, repeal of, **22**, 164
        subordinate legislation, on, **22**, 160, 183
        substitute provisions for enactment repealed,
            22, 164
    express, **22**, 156, 157
    implied, **22**, 156, 158
    re-enactment following, **22**, 164
    repealing enactment, of, **22**, 162
Scotland, application to, **22**, 170
territorial extent, **22**, 170
See also LEGISLATION; STATUTE

Act of Sederunt
documentary evidence, as, **10**, 576
generally, **22**, 187
publication as statutory instrument, **19**, 816*n*
registration procedure, **19**, 816

Act of Sederunt—*continued*
regulation of procedure by, **6**, 861, 930
See also DELEGATED LEGISLATION; STATUTORY
    INSTRUMENT

Act of Union
See UNION AGREEMENT OF 1707

Actio de effusis vel dejectis
application in Scotland, **15**, 152
case law, **15**, 153
institutional writers, **15**, 152
meaning, **15**, 151
proof of fault not required, **15**, 151
quasi-delict, as, **15**, 217

Actio de positis vel suspensis
application in Scotland, **15**, 152
case law, **15**, 153
institutional writers, **15**, 152
meaning, **15**, 151
proof of fault not required, **15**, 151

Actio de in rem verso
unjust enrichment, **15**, 83, 84

Actio mandati
Roman law and development of law of Caution, **3**, 808

Actio popularis, **1**, 309

Actio quanti minoris
protection of purchaser by, **6**, 566

Actio redhibitoria
protection of purchaser by, **6**, 566

Action *in rem*
maritime lien executed by, **1**, 414

Actions
law of, **18**, 1

Actor
employment of, **9**, 1051

Actuary
partnership, number of partners allowed, **16**, 1011

Actus non facit reum nisi mens sit rea
principle in Scots criminal law, **7**, 28, 61

Actus reus
acting to another's detriment, **7**, 44
aggravations, **7**, 36
assault, **7**, 211
attempted crime, **7**, 162, 163
capacity, **7**, 112
circumstances of crime, **7**, 35
common law, **7**, 30
conduct-crimes, **7**, 32
conspiracy, **7**, 171
contract, duty derived from, **7**, 42
danger, duty derived from creation of, **7**, 43
examples, **7**, 30
failure to prevent others committing, **7**, 39
full *actus reus*—
    factors comprising, source, **7**, 31
    must be fulfilled, **7**, 31
incest, **7**, 315
indictment, **7**, 31
injury or death, failure to protect from, **7**, 40
involuntary events, **7**, 34
mental element, **7**, 34
motive, relevancy, **7**, 92
nature, acts of, **7**, 34

Actus reus—continued
omission—
  as *actus reus*, **7**, 45
  effecting *actus reus*, **7**, 39–44
  generally, **7**, 38
reflex actions, **7**, 34
relationship, duty implied by, **7**, 41
requirement for, **7**, 29, 61
result-crimes, **7**, 32, 38
Scots criminal law, generally, **7**, 28, 29, 61
states of affairs, **7**, 33
statute law, **7**, 30
voluntary conduct, **7**, 34
what constitutes, **7**, 30
width of term, **7**, 37

Ad factum praestandum
appeal against interlocutor for making, **17**, 1258

Addict
drug, *see* DRUGS

Additaments
heraldic, grant of, **11**, 1610, 1621
particular dignities, **11**, 1621
succession to, **11**, 1621

Additional Convention
international carriage of goods by rail, **3**, 704

Additives
food—
  advertisement of food containing, **11**, 376
  cream, **11**, 476
  flavouring, **11**, 476
  labelling, **11**, 385, 387
  milk, **11**, 442

Ademption
specific legacy subject to, **25**, 848, 854

Adherence
Court of Session's jurisdiction in action of, **4**, 5
husband and wife, **10**, 839
sheriff court's jurisdiction in action of, **4**, 5

Adjournment
sentence, prior to, **17**, 786
solemn trial procedure, **17**, 558
trial diet, of, **17**, 738

Adjudger
adjudication on a *debitum fundi*, **8**, 373
decree for payment, must hold, **8**, 190
discharge of debtor, **8**, 207
effect of adjudication, **8**, 201
landlord's hypothec, **13**, 514
legal, the, **8**, 204, 205, 206
prescription, **8**, 205
ranking of adjudications *inter se*, **8**, 208
real right vested in adjudicator, **8**, 160
rights of, **8**, 202
sale, no power of, **8**, 203
third party—
  rights, **8**, 209
  sale, **8**, 206

Adjudication
abbreviate, **8**, 193
action of declarator of expiry of the legal, conversion into, **8**, 189
action of, **8**, 191
  defences to, **8**, 192
adjudger, *see* ADJUDGER

Adjudication—continued
apprising replaced by, **8**, 189
company administration, and, **8**, 213
completion of title, **8**, 194
  uncompleted title, **8**, 196
  unregistered property, **8**, 195
contra hereditatem jacentem, **8**, 216
Court of Session jurisdiction, **4**, 7
death of debtor, effect, **8**, 127
debitum fundi, on, *see* DEBITUM FUNDI
debtor rendered apparently insolvent by, **8**, 201
declaratory, **8**, 216
decree of, effect on lease, **13**, 158
decree for payment, adjudger must hold, **8**, 190
defences to action of, **8**, 192
diligence—
  adjudication as, **8**, 101
  effect of winding up on, **4**, 844
discharge of debtor, **8**, 207
divestitive and non-divestitive, **8**, 201
dominium utile, **8**, 197
effect, **8**, 189
expenses—
  action, of, **8**, 215
  completion of title, attendant on, **8**, 215
expiry of the legal, action of declarator of, **8**, 189
extract, **8**, 193
grounds for, **8**, 190
heritable property, **18**, 13
  dominium utile, **8**, 197
  generally, **8**, 197, 199
  heritable securities, **8**, 197, 199
  leases, **8**, 197, 198
    excluding assignees, **8**, 197
  reversions, **8**, 197
  superiorities, **8**, 197
  voluntary alienation, capable and not capable of, **8**, 197
implement, in, **8**, 216; **18**, 664
judicial conveyance, as, **18**, 664
judicial heritable security, as, **8**, 201
leases, **8**, 197, 198; **13**, 184
  excluding assignees, **8**, 197
legal, the, **8**, 204, 205, 206, 216
liquidation, and, **8**, 211
moveable property, **8**, 197, 200
prescription, **8**, 205
procedure, **8**, 189
ranking inter se, **8**, 208
real, *see* DEBITUM FUNDI (adjudication on)
real right vested in adjudger, **8**, 160
receivership, and, **8**, 212
reversions, **8**, 197
security, in, **8**, 216
sequestration, and, **8**, 210
sheriff court jurisdiction, **4**, 7
superiorities, **8**, 197
third party—
  rights, **8**, 209
  sale, **8**, 206
time to pay direction, and, **8**, 214
time to pay order, and, **8**, 214
uncompleted title, debtor holding, **8**, 201

Adjudication—*continued*
unfeudalised, debtor's title, **8**, 196, 196*n*
voluntary alienation, capable and not capable of,
    8, 197
Adjudication officer
appeal against decision of, **21**, 1162, 1175
Chief Adjudication Officer, **21**, 1148
    advice and guidance of, adjudication officers
        act under, **21**, 1162
    annual report, **21**, 1162
    duties, **21**, 1162
generally, **21**, 1141, 1148
independent nature of actions by, **21**, 1162
powers and functions, **21**, 1152, 1162
review of decision by, **21**, 1171
social security appeal tribunal, referral of cases to,
    21, 1162
Administration
administration order—
    application for—
        circumstances in which made, **4**, 606
        petition—
            company, by, **4**, 607
            court's powers on hearing, **4**, 610
            directors, by, **4**, 607
            effect of, **4**, 609
            independent person, report by, **4**, 607
            notice of, **4**, 607
            statutory purposes, **4**, 608
        statutory purposes, **4**, 608
    Cork Report, **4**, 603
    court—
        administrator, appointment of, **4**, 615
        petition, powers on hearing, **4**, 610
    creditors—
        committee, **4**, 644
        preferential, **4**, 633
        protection of interests of, **4**, 645
    deficiencies, **4**, 605
    diligence, and—
        adjudication, **8**, 213, 375
        arrestments, **8**, 296
        inhibition, **8**, 183
        judicial discretion, **8**, 126
        maills and duties, **8**, 399
        poinding, **8**, 371
        real poinding, **8**, 371
        sequestration for rent, **8**, 390
    discharge of, **4**, 646
    effect of, **4**, 611
        examples, **4**, 611
    introduction of new concept of, **4**, 307
    management of affairs, **4**, 611
    meaning, **4**, 611
    members, protection of interests of, **4**, 645
    moratorium, **4**, 611
    notification of, **4**, 616
    purposes specified in, proposals for achieving,
        4, 627
    receiver vacating office, **4**, 614, 636
    variation of, **4**, 617, 646
    White Paper, **4**, 604
administrator—
    additional statutory powers, **4**, 620

Administration—*continued*
administrator—*continued*
    appointment of—
        contract of employment, effect on, **4**, 624
        court, by, **4**, 615
        England and Wales, in, **4**, 621
    bill of exchange, powers relating to, **4**, 127
    company may not be appointed, **4**, 319
    contract—
        employment, of, effect of appointment on, **4**,
        624
        entered into by administrator, **4**, 622
        pre-existing, **4**, 623
    death, **4**, 641
    directors, relationship with, **4**, 635
    duties of—
        abstract of receipts and payments, **4**, 631
        general, **4**, 625
        payments, abstract of, **4**, 631
        preferential creditors, provision for, **4**, 633
        proposals—
            creditors' meeting to approve, **4**, 628
            report of meeting, **4**, 629
            revision of, **4**, 630
            statement of, **4**, 627
        receipts, abstract of, **4**, 631
        sederunt book, maintenance of, **4**, 632
        statement of affairs, relating to, **4**, 626
        VAT bad debt certificates, **4**, 634
    guidelines for, **4**, 613
    liquidator, relationship with, **4**, 638
    powers—
        additional statutory, **4**, 620
        generally, **4**, 618
        secured property, over, **4**, 619
    pre-existing contract, **4**, 623
    receiver, relationship with, **4**, 636, 708
    removal of, **4**, 642
    remuneration, **4**, 639
    resignation of, **4**, 640
    secured property, powers over, **4**, 619
    supervisor under voluntary arrangement,
        relationship with, **4**, 637
    vacation of office—
        death, **4**, 641
        filling of vacancy, **4**, 643
        removal from office, **4**, 642
        resignation, **4**, 640
    voluntary arrangement proposed by—
        administrator as nominee, **4**, 585
        another insolvency practitioner as nominee,
        4, 586
    winding up petition by, **4**, 730, 738
    See also administration order *above*
Atlantic Computer case, **4**, 612, 613
borrowing, **4**, 438
business stationery, **4**, 436
charges—
    defective particulars, **4**, 443
    overseas company, registration by, **4**, 448
    registrable, **4**, 440
    registration of—
        generally, **4**, 439

Administration—*continued*
charges—*continued*
  registration of—*continued*
    notice, registration as, **4**, 442
    procedure for, **4**, 441
  satisfaction of, **4**, 444
  sums secured becoming repayable, **4**, 447
company seal, **4**, 437
company secretary, appointment of, **4**, 434
documents, execution of, **4**, 437
liquidation, comparison with, **4**, 612
liquidator following, **4**, 761
loan capital, **4**, 438
meaning, **4**, 611
order, *see* administration order *below*
receiver, appointment of, **4**, 445
registered office, **4**, 435
responsibility for, **4**, 402
securities, **4**, 439
third party rights, **4**, 611
Administration of estate
administrative powers and *ultra vires* doctrine, **1**, 215
administrative records, whether public records, **19**, 845
administrator, appointment of, **25**, 637
authority to deal with estate, **17**, 349
building societies' powers, **3**, 376
choice of law rules, **17**, 129, 349, 350
completion, **25**, 981, 997
confirmation, **19**, 1642
  obtaining, procedure for—
    additional confirmation—
      ad non executa, **25**, 1093
      ad omissa vel male appretiata, **25**, 1092
    caution for actings—
      amount of, **25**, 1087
      cautioners, **25**, 1088
      generally, **25**, 1086, 1089
    historical development, **25**, 1066–1069
    inventory—
      additional, **25**, 1090
      break-down of estate, **25**, 1073
      corrective, **25**, 1091
      documents to be produced with, **25**, 1078
      estate duties, **25**, 1069
      estates to be included in, **25**, 1068
      executry estate, title restricted to, **25**, 1071
      forms of, **25**, 1081
      generally, **25**, 1067, 1070
      historical development, **25**, 1067–1069
      lodging, **25**, 1080
      oaths, **25**, 1075–1077
      revenue function, **25**, 1079
      special destinations, **25**, 1072
      value of estate, **25**, 1074
    small estate—
      applicant, qualification of, **25**, 1085
      confirmation, application for, **25**, 1084
      generally, **25**, 1082
      identity, proof of, **25**, 1085
      limits of value, **25**, 1083
  ownership before—
    deceased's estate, vesting of, **25**, 1060
    generally, **25**, 1059

Administration of estate—*continued*
confirmation—*continued*
  partial, executor-creditor's power to expede, **25**, 1052
  title or payment or both without—
    confirmation not required to be exhibited, **25**, 1094
    nomination—
      amount nominated, **25**, 1098
      generally, **25**, 1095
      ineffective, to take effect as will, **25**, 1100
      intimation, **25**, 1097
      nominee, payment to, **25**, 1099
      revocation, **25**, 1097
      validity of, **25**, 1096
    privilege, **25**, 1101
    ultimus haeres, **25**, 1102
death and distribution, estate between—
  co-ownership—
    France, **25**, 639
    Germany, **25**, 639
    generally, **25**, 638
    indivision, **25**, 642
    joint tenancy, England, **25**, 640
    partition, **25**, 642
    statutory trust, **25**, 641
excepted estates, **19**, 1643
executors, *see* EXECUTOR
generally, **19**, 1642–1648; **25**, 634
heritable estate—
  historical development, **25**, 1037, 1038
  moveable estate, distinction between, abolition of, **25**, 1038
historical development, **25**, 1034–1038
income arising during—
  beneficiaries, payments to, **25**, 980
  completion, **25**, 981
  executors' expenses, **25**, 979
  foreign estate, **25**, 982
  generally, **25**, 974
  investment income, **25**, 978
  receipts—
    deceased's employment, attributable to, **25**, 975
    deceased's profession, attributable to, **25**, 976
    deceased's trade, attributable to, **25**, 976
    post-cessation, **25**, 977
income tax, completion for purposes of, **19**, 1648
intestate estate, **25**, 1036
meaning, **25**, 1033
moveable estate—
  heritable estate, distinction between, abolition of, **25**, 1038
  historical development, **25**, 1035, 1038
nomination—
  amount nominated, **25**, 1098
  effect of, **25**, 733
  examples, **25**, 733
  friendly society, **12**, 722–724
  industrial and provident society, **12**, 613, 620, 626–629
  ineffective, to take effect as will, **25**, 1100
  intimation, **25**, 1097
  meaning, **25**, 733, 1095

Administration of estate—*continued*
nomination—*continued*
  nominee, payment to, **25**, 1099
  revocation of, **25**, 733, 1097
  testamentary, **25**, 1095–1100
  validity of, **25**, 1096
orders concerning—
  Commonwealth grants of representation, recognition, **8**, 553
  UK reciprocal enforcement scheme, **8**, 484, 552
right to administer, **17**, 349
small estates—
  confirmation—
    application for, **25**, 1084
    generally, **19**, 1644; **25**, 1082
    identity, proof of, **25**, 1085
    limits of value, **25**, 1083
    qualification of applicant, **25**, 1085
succession distinguished from, **17**, 350
taxation, liability to, **19**, 1642–1648
taxation of receipts—
  deceased's employment, **25**, 975
  deceased's profession or trade, **25**, 976
  post-cessation, **25**, 977
transmission—
  administrator, liability of, **25**, 637
  England, **25**, 635
  France, **25**, 636
  Germany, **25**, 636
  heir, liability of, **25**, 637
  personal representative, liability of, **25**, 637
  See also EXECUTOR; SUCCESSION
vitious intromission, *see* VITIOUS INTROMISSION
See also SUCCESSION
Administration of justice
offences against—
  common law, **7**, 489
  contempt of court, *see* CONTEMPT OF COURT
  document, false statement in, **7**, 518
  ends of justice, attempt to defeat, **7**, 493, 496
  evidence, giving or procuring false, *see* EVIDENCE; PERJURY
  False Oaths (Scotland) Act 1933 ..., **7**, 516–520
  generally, **7**, 489
  hindering the course of justice, **7**, 493
  interference with course of justice, **7**, 490
    bribery, **7**, 547
    corruption, **7**, 547
    custody, escape from, *see* CUSTODY, ESCAPE FROM
    evading police, **7**, 542
    false accusation—
      accused, to, **7**, 525
      authorities, to, **7**, 525
      circulating allegations, **7**, 525
      danger of prosecution, putting victim in, **7**, 527
      generally, **7**, 524
      historical background, **7**, 524–526
      mental element, **7**, 528
      verbal information, not restricted to, **7**, 524
      verbal injury, **7**, 525
    false statement, making, **7**, 536–538

Administration of justice—*continued*
offences against—*continued*
  interference with course of justice—*continued*
    harbouring, **7**, 562
    mental element, **7**, 528
    oppression, **7**, 548–551
    police, false reporting to—
      generally, **7**, 529, 533
      mental element, **7**, 531
      setting investigation in motion, **7**, 529, 532
      wasting police time, **7**, 530
    prison breaking, *see* PRISON BREAKING
    resisting or obstructing officers of law, **7**, 539–542
    Road Traffic Act—
      failure to stop, **7**, 544
      false information under, **7**, 537, 538
  obstructing administration of justice, **7**, 493
  overlap with other categories of crime, **7**, 489, 490
  perjury, *see* PERJURY
  pervert course of justice, attempt to—
    attempt, use of term, **7**, 494
    completed crime, **7**, 494
    conduct amounting to, **7**, 496
    course of justice, **7**, 495
    false statements, **7**, 533, 538
    firearm or imitation firearm possessed during, **10**, 1565
    generally, **7**, 491; **16**, 1811
    historical background, **7**, 491
    mental element, **7**, 497
    separate crime, existence as, **7**, 492
    terminology, **7**, 493
    threatening witness, **7**, 496, 523
    registration, false declaration in relation to, **7**, 519
  statute law, **7**, 489
  statutory declaration, false, **7**, 516, 518
Administrative Accompanying Document (AAD)
European Union customs documentation, **7**, 1124
Administrative county
England and Wales, **14**, 60
Administrative functions
classification of, **1**, 209
sheriff exercising, **1**, 208, 210
Administrative law
administrative actions, control of, *see* ADMINISTRATIVE POWERS
administrative functions, **1**, 210
  classification of, **1**, 207, 208, 209
  judicial functions, **1**, 210
  licensing, **1**, 211
  quasi-judicial, **1**, 211
audi alteram partem rule, *see* NATURAL JUSTICE
bias, *see* NATURAL JUSTICE
constitutional law, relationship with, **1**, 201
development of, **1**, 202
discretion, *see* ADMINISTRATIVE POWERS
error of law, *see* ERROR OF LAW
judicial functions, *see* ADMINISTRATIVE POWERS
judicial remedies, *see* JUDICIAL REMEDIES
judicial review, *see* JUDICIAL REVIEW

Administrative powers
bias, in exercising, *see* NATURAL JUSTICE
central government—
    personal bar, subject to, **1**, 296
    powers, delegation of, **1**, 225
certiorari, error of law corrected by, **1**, 285
common law, powers derived from, **1**, 202
Council on Tribunals, *see* COUNCIL ON TRIBUNALS
court, function in administrative law, **1**, 210
Court of Session, *see* COURT OF SESSION
Crown, The, *see* CROWN, THE
decision—
    administrative, revocation of, **1**, 297
    illegality, defence of, **1**, 331
    no evidence to support, **1**, 289
    reasons for—
        adequacy of, **1**, 292
        adequate, failure to give, **1**, 293
        appeal, stated on, **1**, 290
        desirability of giving, **1**, 290
        discretion, in exercising, **1**, 293
        order for, **1**, 293
        right to know, **1**, 281
        tribunals and inquiries giving, **1**, 291
        unclear, where, **1**, 293
delegated legislation, *see* DELEGATED LEGISLATION
discretion in exercising—
    bad faith, exercised with, **1**, 239
    error of law in exercising, **1**, 286
    fettering, **1**, 241
    improper exercise of, **1**, 233, 237
    improper purposes, exercised for, **1**, 238
    individual circumstances, taking notice of, **1**, 241
    intention of Parliament, exercised in accordance with, **1**, 237
    judicial review of—
        extent of, **1**, 234
        grounds for, **1**, 236
        relevant considerations, on basis of, **1**, 237
        unreasonableness, on grounds of, **1**, 240
    legal, nature of, **1**, 233
    legal duty, related to, **1**, 235
    malice, exercised with, **1**, 239
    meaning, **1**, 233
    reasons for exercising, giving, **1**, 293
    unreasonableness, on grounds of, **1**, 240
error of law, *see* ERROR OF LAW
fairness, natural justice, and, **1**, 249, 283
inquiry, *see* INQUIRY—
    public inquiry
interest to sue, *see* TITLE AND INTEREST TO SUE
judicial control of—
    characteristics of law of, **1**, 213
    courts, role of, **1**, 204
    delegated legislation, *see* DELEGATED LEGISLATION
    exercise of, **1**, 303
    grounds of, **1**, 213
    Parliament, reinforcing authority of, **1**, 201
    superior court, intervention by, **1**, 304
judicial functions—
    nature of, **1**, 210
    quasi-judicial, use of term, **1**, 212
    sheriff, **1**, 210

Administrative powers—*continued*
judicial remedies, *see* JUDICIAL REMEDIES
judicial review of, *see* JUDICIAL REVIEW
legitimate expectation of exercise of, **1**, 267
local authorities, of, *see* LOCAL AUTHORITY
Lord Advocate—
    public interest, acting in, **1**, 323
    specific performance of statutory duty, applying for, **1**, 336
natural justice, *see* NATURAL JUSTICE
Parliamentary Commissioner for Administration, *see* PARLIAMENTARY COMMISSIONER FOR ADMINISTRATION
personal bar, *see* PERSONAL BAR
procedural requirements—
    compliance, importance of, **1**, 228
    defects in, **1**, 231, 232
    delegated legislation, in respect of, **1**, 229
    error of law, *see* ERROR OF LAW
    failure to comply, review of decision on grounds of, **1**, 341
    fairness, arising from, **1**, 230
    mandatory and directory, **1**, 228
    natural justice, *see* NATURAL JUSTICE
public authority, *see* PUBLIC AUTHORITY
quasi-judicial functions, use of term, **1**, 212
right to be heard, *see* NATURAL JUSTICE
subordinate bodies—
    categorisation of, **1**, 208
    classification of functions, **1**, 208–209
    constitutional safeguards, **1**, 207
    decision-making, status of, **1**, 209
    judicial control, **1**, 208
title and interest to sue, *see* TITLE AND INTEREST TO SUE
tribunal, *see* TRIBUNAL
Administrative receiver
concept of, **4**, 671
See also RECEIVER
Administrative removal
appeal against, **12**, 201
challenging, **12**, 201
detention for, **12**, 199
European Union citizens, **12**, 195
illegal entry as ground for, **12**, 198
judicial review, **12**, 194, 201
liability for, **12**, 195
meaning, **12**, 194
member of Parliament, representation by, **12**, 376
procurement for, **12**, 200
refusal of leave to enter as, **12**, 197
ship and aircraft crews, **12**, 195, 196
what constitutes, **12**, 194
Administrator
company, of, *see* ADMINISTRATION
Admiral
Admirals-depute, **7**, 816
Judge Admirals, **7**, 816
Lord High Admiral, **7**, 812, 816
Vice-Admirals, **7**, 816
Admiralty
actions *in rem*, maritime lien executed by, **1**, 414
Admiral of Scotland, office of, **1**, 403

Admiralty—*continued*
arrestment—
  jurisdiction based on, **4**, 79
  diligence of, **8**, 322
board, **2**, 603
bottomry—
  maritime cause, as, **1**, 411
  maritime lien, as, **1**, 413
collision—
  maritime cause, as, **1**, 411
  maritime lien, giving rise to, **1**, 413
  preliminary act procedure, **1**, 415
  special rules of jurisdiction, **1**, 416
Court of Admiralty—
  abolition of, **1**, 404; **4**, 2; **6**, 859; **21**, 102, 102*n*
  Admiral of Scotland, exercising functions of, **1**, 403
  Court of Session, and, **1**, 404; **4**, 2; **6**, 909, 916; **22**, 519, 609, 635
  High Court of Justiciary, and, **1**, 405; **6**, 859; **22**, 519, 609, 635
  jurisdiction, **1**, 404, 405, 406; **6**, 909, 916; **17**, 504; **21**, 101, 102, 102*n*
  prize jurisdiction, **1**, 406
  procedure, **1**, 403
  salvage jurisdiction, **21**, 440, 440*n*
  sheriff court, jurisdiction merged with, **4**, 2
  sovereign judicature, as, **1**, 404
  transfer of functions of, **6**, 859; **22**, 519, 609, 635
Court of Session—
  admiralty causes, definition of, **1**, 411
  Court of Admiralty, relationship with, **1**, 404; **6**, 909, 916
  maritime cause, determining, **1**, 411
  maritime civil cases, jurisdiction in, **1**, 407
damages—
  division of, **1**, 411
  preliminary act procedure, **1**, 415
derivation of term, **1**, 401
English Court of Admiralty, **22**, 519, 635
fishing vessels, casualties and incidents, procedure for, **1**, 408
High Court of Admiralty, *see* Court of Admiralty *above*
High Court of Justiciary, **1**, 405; **6**, 859; **22**, 519, 609, 635
hovercraft—
  legislation for, powers of, **1**, 410
  maritime lien, giving rise to, **1**, 413
  ships, treated as, **1**, 410
Judge Admiral, office of, **1**, 403
jurisdiction—
  arrestments, where, **4**, 79
  courts with, **1**, 407; **22**, 519, 635
limitation of liability under, **1**, 418
maritime cause—
  cases constituting, **1**, 411
  maritime law applying to, **1**, 411
maritime law—
  Court of Admiralty applying, **1**, 403
  general and international nature, effect of, **1**, 402
maritime lien—
  action *in rem*, executed by, **1**, 414
  matters giving rise to, **1**, 413

Admiralty—*continued*
maritime lien—*continued*
  meaning, **1**, 413
  ranking, **1**, 413
  vessels subject to, **1**, 413
meaning, **1**, 401
pilotage, maritime lien, whether giving rise to, **1**, 413
prize, jurisdiction in,, **1**, 406
  See also PRIZE
procedure—
  collision cases, in, **1**, 407
  Court of Session Rules applying to, **1**, 412
  specialities of, **1**, 412
respondentia bond, maritime lien, as, **1**, 413
salvage—
  maritime cause, as, **1**, 411
  maritime lien, as, **1**, 413
sea, common law of, **1**, 402
sheriff court, maritime jurisdiction, **1**, 407; **22**, 635
ship—
  arrestment of, **1**, 417
  detention of, **1**, 417
shipowner, limitation of liability of, **1**, 418
shipping casualty—
  jurisdiction over, **1**, 408
  meaning, **1**, 408*n*
ship's officers, conduct or fitness, inquiries into, **1**, 409
special drawing rights, concession of, **1**, 418
towage—
  maritime cause, as, **1**, 411
  maritime lien, whether giving rise to, **1**, 413
Admiralty courts
See ADMIRALTY
Admiralty, High Court of, *see* ADMIRALTY
Admissibility of evidence
character, of—
  the accused, **10**, 638–645
    common law, **10**, 638
    cross-examination of, **10**, 642
    good character, evidence of, **10**, 641
  co-accused, evidence against, **10**, 646
  generally, **10**, 628
  parties, civil cases, **10**, 629
  persons not present in court, **10**, 637
  victim or complainer—
    criminal cases, **10**, 632–634
    rape and other sexual offences, **10**, 634
  witnesses, **10**, 635, 636
    civil cases, **10**, 630, 631
    criminal cases, **10**, 632, 635, 636
    evidence in rebuttal, **10**, 631
credibility, as to—
  generally, **10**, 628
  parties, civil cases, **10**, 629
  victim or complainer—
    criminal cases, **10**, 632–634
    rape and other sexual offences, **10**, 634
  witnesses, **10**, 630–632, 635–637
    civil cases, **10**, 630, 631
    criminal cases, **10**, 632, 635, 636
    evidence in rebuttal, **10**, 631

Admissibility of evidence—*continued*
credibility, as to—*continued*
  witnesses—*continued*
    facts relevant to, **10**, 623
    weight of evidence, **10**, 779
debate on, civil procedure, **17**, 1181
extra-judicial admissions—
  generally, **10**, 513, 722
  implied, **10**, 725
  improperly obtained, **10**, 727
  pleading, **10**, 729
  proof and probative value, **10**, 723
  statements in another cause, **10**, 724
  vicarious, **10**, 726
facts, of—
  character, credibility and previous convictions, **10**, 628
  civil cases—
    evidence in rebuttal, **10**, 631
    parties, **10**, 629
    witnesses, **10**, 630
  criminal cases—
    the accused, **10**, 638–646
    generally, **10**, 632
    persons not present in court, **10**, 637
    victim or complainer, **10**, 633, 634
    witnesses, **10**, 635, 636
  crime for which conviction not sought, evidence of, **10**, 627
  exclusionary rules, **10**, 505, 622
  facts extrinsic to document, **10**, 704
  generally, **10**, 505, 622
  identification, evidence of—
    body fluids, **10**, 622
    body tissues, **10**, 662
    DNA profiling, **10**, 662
    dock identification, **10**, 664
    fingerprint evidence, **10**, 662
    foot-print evidence, **10**, 662
    generally, **10**, 657
    genetic fingerprinting, **10**, 662
    handwriting, **10**, 662
    identification parades, **10**, 666
    indirect, **10**, 660
    photograph, by, **10**, 667
    prior identification, evidence of, **10**, 665
    scientific, **10**, 662
    sufficiency of, **10**, 661
    teeth-marks, **10**, 662
    visual identification, **10**, 658
      reliability of, **10**, 659
    voice identification, **10**, 663
  illegally or irregularly obtained evidence—
    civil cases, **10**, 701–703
      criminal cases distinguished, **10**, 691
      Rattray v Rattray, decision in, **10**, 702
    criminal cases—
      civil cases distinguished, **10**, 691
      conflicting interests, **10**, 693
      ease of rectification of irregularity, **10**, 699
      general rule, **10**, 692
      good faith, **10**, 697
      gravity of offence, **10**, 694
      nature of irregularity, **10**, 696

Admissibility of evidence—*continued*
facts, of—*continued*
  illegally or irregularly obtained evidence—*continued*
    criminal cases—*continued*
      stage of investigation, **10**, 700
      status of investigators, **10**, 698
      urgency, **10**, 695
    generally, **10**, 690
  opinion, evidence of—
    assessors, **10**, 654
    court experts, **10**, 655
    expert's reports, exchange of, **10**, 655
    foreign law, **10**, 653
    generally, **10**, 647, 648
    handwriting, **10**, 652
    skill, men of, **10**, 654
    witnesses, **10**, 649
      expert, **10**, 650, 651
  privilege—
    confidentiality—
      clergyman and penitent, communications between, **10**, 685
      communications relative to litigation, **10**, 681–684
      generally, **10**, 676
      professional obligations of confidentiality, **10**, 686
      spouses, communications between, **10**, 677–680
    definition, **10**, 668
    general principles, **10**, 669
    incrimination—
      adultery, **10**, 675
      criminal offences, **10**, 671–674
      generally, **10**, 670
      prosecution furth of Scotland, liability to, **10**, 674
      spouse, of, **10**, 673
      statutory restrictions on privilege, **10**, 672
    public policy—
      classes of documents, **10**, 688
      generally, **10**, 687
      law enforcement agencies, **10**, 689
  relevancy, **10**, 505, 622–627
    definition, **10**, 623
    intention, **10**, 624
    knowledge, **10**, 624
    motive, **10**, 624
    opportunity, **10**, 624
    similar facts, evidence of—
      civil cases, **10**, 625
      criminal cases, **10**, 626
  facts relevant to, **10**, 623
  hearsay, of—
    civil cases, **10**, 714–718
      procedure, **10**, 718
      statutory provisions, **10**, 716–718
    common law—
      civil cases, **10**, 714, 715
      criminal cases, **10**, 706–713
    de recenti statements, criminal cases, **10**, 707
    deceased persons, statements by, criminal cases, **10**, 711

Admissibility of evidence—*continued*
hearsay, of—*continued*
  exceptions to rule, **10**, 715
    criminal cases, **10**, 709–712
  extra-judicial statements—
    admissions—
      generally, **10**, 722
      implied, **10**, 725
      improperly obtained, **10**, 727
      pleading, **10**, 728
      proof and probative value, **10**, 723
      statements in another cause, **10**, 724
      vicarious, **10**, 726
    confessions—
      determination of admissibility, **10**, 745
      different charge, statements in relation to, **10**, 743
      generally, **10**, 722, 736
      implied, **10**, 725
      intercepted documents, statements in, **10**, 740
      judicial examination, statements made at, **10**, 742
      overheard statements, **10**, 739
      police, statements made to, **10**, 729–735
      previous malice, statements inferring, **10**, 744
      prison officers, statements made to, **10**, 737
      private persons, statements made to, **10**, 738
      proof and probative value, **10**, 723
      public officials, statements made to, **10**, 737
      statements in another cause, **10**, 724
      trial-within-a-trial, **10**, 745
      unconscious, expressions uttered while, **10**, 741
      vicarious, **10**, 725
    generally, **10**, 719
    self-serving statements, **10**, 720, 721
  general rules, **10**, 705–708
  insane persons, statements by, **10**, 711
  original evidence—
    civil cases, **10**, 714
    criminal cases, **10**, 706–708
  presence of accused, statements in, **10**, 712
  previous statements—
    civil cases, **10**, 717
    criminal cases, **10**, 707, 708
  prisoners of war, statements by, **10**, 711
  res gestae, statements forming part of, **10**, 710
  self-serving statements—
    civil trials, **10**, 721
    criminal trials, **10**, 720
  judicial adjudication as to, **10**, 508
Adoption
abandoned child, of, **10**, 1209
access to records of, **19**, 879
access under adoption order, **10**, 1303
Adopted Children Register, **10**, 1216; **19**, 1414, 1469, 1470
  amendment, revocation or cancellation of adoption orders, **19**, 1470

Adoption—*continued*
Adopted Children Register—*continued*
    correction of errors, **19**, 1422*n*, 1423*n*, 1424*n*
    evidence of adoption, as, **19**, 1420
    index, **19**, 1419
advertising, regulation of, **1**, 528; **17**, 45
agencies—
    approved, **10**, 1200
    local authority, **10**, 1199
    relationship with applicants, **10**, 1201
    report of placement, **22**, 19
aliment, obligation to adopted children, **10**, 1240–1242
application for—
    agencies—
      approved, **10**, 1200
      local authority, **10**, 1199
      relationship with applicants, **10**, 1201
    consent of child, information on which based, **10**, 1197
    general requirements, **10**, 1193
      child, in respect of, **10**, 1196
    natural parent—
      alone, application by, **10**, 1194
      spouse, and, **10**, 1195
    relative, by, **10**, 1195
    scrutiny of adoption arrangements, **10**, 1198
British citizenship, acquisition of, **14**, 1910
British Dependent Territories citizenship, acquisition of, **14**, 1934
children's hearing, attendance of parents at, **3**, 1321
choice of law in, **17**, 243
citizenship, and, **10**, 1191; **14**, 1910
consanguinity and capacity to marry, **10**, 817
consent of child, **10**, 1196, 1197
    capacity to consent, **3**, 1209, 1211
    order freeing child for adoption, **3**, 1209
court proceedings, **10**, 1215
Court of Session procedure, **17**, 1427
custody of adopted children, **10**, 1279
decree of, reduction, **13**, 42
domicile and nationality, **10**, 1223
    domicile of adoptive parents, **10**, 1193, 1193*n*
exceptions to general rule, **10**, 1191
expenses of adoption proceedings, **17**, 1192
fosterage, **10**, 1188, 1189
freeing order—
    criterion for, **10**, 1204
    effect, **10**, 1204
    generally, **22**, 18
    parental agreement, and, **10**, 1203, 1204
generally, **11**, 1617; **25**, 713
guardian's allowance where adoptive parents dead or missing, **21**, 954
Hague Convention adoptions, **10**, 1193, 1193*n*; **17**, 243
history of, **10**, 1188–1190
illegitimate child, **10**, 1191
incest in adoptive relationships, **7**, 314, 315; **10**, 1191, 1227
jurisdiction, **17**, 242
legal recognition of adopted child, **10**, 1147, 1188
local authority, role, **22**, 19

Adoption—*continued*
marriage, prohibited degrees, **10**, 1219
married person, by, **10**, 1193, 1193*n*
minor, of, **10**, 1196
natural child of adoptive parent, as, **12**, 1268
natural parent, by, **10**, 1194, 1195, 1214
natural parent's estate, **10**, 1191
nature of, **10**, 1190
order—
    conditions attached to, **10**, 1216
    convention, **17**, 243
    Court of Session jurisdiction, **4**, 5
    deed executed after making of, **25**, 713
    exclusion from scope of Judgments Convention, **8**, 432
    foreign, recognition in Scotland—
        common law, recognised at, **8**, 537
        convention adoption order, **8**, 536
        effect of recognition, **8**, 538
        order made elsewhere in British Isles, **8**, 535
        overseas adoptions, **8**, 536
        types recognised, **8**, 534
    Northern Ireland, made in, **8**, 535
    previous adoption, effect of, **25**, 714
    procedure leading to, **10**, 1213–1216
    range of, **10**, 1216
    refusal, **10**, 1216
    revocation, **10**, 1216
    sheriff court jurisdiction, **4**, 5
    testamentary writing affected by, **12**, 1218
panel, decisions of, **22**, 19
parental agreement, **10**, 1202
    freeing orders and, **10**, 1203, 1204
    parent or guardian—
        abandoning or neglecting child, **10**, 1209
        failing to discharge parental duties, **10**, 1208
        incapable of agreeing, **10**, 1206
        not found, **10**, 1206
        persistently ill-treating child, **10**, 1210
        seriously ill-treating child, **10**, 1211
        withholding agreement unreasonably, **10**, 1207
    power to dispense with, **10**, 1205
    protection of child from abuse or neglect, **10**, 1212
pension, child entitled to, **10**, 1191
placement for, **22**, 19
private international law, in, **17**, 242–243
procedural aspects, **10**, 1214–1216
prohibited degrees of marriage—
    adoptive family, **10**, 1191
    natural parents, **10**, 1191
property conveyance to adopted child, **12**, 1218
prospective adopter, **10**, 1213
    removal of child from, by parent or guardian, **10**, 1213
    protection of child, **10**, 1213
pupil, of, **10**, 1196
range of orders, **10**, 1216
recognition, **17**, 242
records of, access to, **19**, 879
registration, **10**, 1216
relative, by, **10**, 1195, 1214
removal of child by parent or guardian, **10**, 1213
reports for court, **22**, 19

Adoption—*continued*
Scottish custody order freeing child for, **8**, 508
Scottish order, recognition, **8**, 508
scrutiny of arrangements, **10**, 1198
separated person, by, **10**, 1193, 1193*n*
services, generally, **22**, 19
settlement, family reunion or creation by, **12**, 279
sheriff's duties in respect of, **6**, 1046
single person, by, **10**, 1193, 1193*n*
social context, **10**, 1192
social worker, role, **22**, 18
status, action relating to, **4**, 68
step-parents, **10**, 1217
subsequent adoption order, **10**, 1196
succession, **12**, 1218
    by adopted persons, **25**, 713, 714
        natural parent's estate, **10**, 1191
timescales, procedures, absence, **22**, 18
United Kingdom citizenship, **10**, 1191
voluntary organisations, role, **22**, 19
welfare of child, **22**, 18, 19
who may be adopted, **10**, 1196

Adpromissor
Roman law and development of law of caution, **3**, 805, 806

Adultery
child of parents who have committed, **10**, 1167
findings of, as evidence, **10**, 502
as ground for irretrievable breakdown of marriage, *see* DIVORCE
intimation in case of, **17**, 1225
privilege against incrimination, **10**, 675
provocation, as, in homicide cases, **7**, 273

Advance corporation tax
See CORPORATION TAX

Advertisement
accommodation agency, regulation of, **1**, 527
actionable wrong, leading to, **1**, 505
adoption, involving, **1**, 528
Advertising Advisory Committee, **1**, 522
advertising agency—
    contract with client, **1**, 512
    number of, **1**, 502
    placing of advertising by, **1**, 512
advertising industry—
    scale of, **1**, 502
    self-regulation, **6**, 9
Advertising Standards Authority, *see* ADVERTISING STANDARDS AUTHORITY
advocate, by, **13**, 1298, 1324
aerial advertising, regulation of, **1**, 525
aerodrome, displays at, **2**, 951
amusements, of, **1**, 531
ancillary credit business, in relation to, **5**, 830
auction, of, **1**, 504
banknote, reproduction of, **1**, 530
betting office, of, **1**, 531
binding obligation, giving rise to, **6**, 75
boards—
    electric or neon signs, **24**, 551
    generally, **24**, 550
    heritable, **24**, 550, 551
    temporary, **24**, 550
    valuation for rating, **24**, 550–552

Advertisement—*continued*
bond and disposition in security, calling-up, **20**, 118, 119
British Code of Advertising Practice, **1**, 545; **17**, 45
  alcohol and cigarette advertisements, **6**, 93
  children, advertisements directed at, **6**, 93
  complaints, **6**, 91
  generally, **6**, 29, 90, 92
  health claims, **6**, 93
  mail order advertisements, **6**, 93
  sanctions, **6**, 91, 93
  voluntary nature, **6**, 93
broadcast—
  advisory committees and panels, **6**, 88
  cable programmes, in, **1**, 523
  child audience, rules for, **1**, 522
  codes of practice, **6**, 89
  direct broadcasting by satellite services, in, **1**, 524
  frequency and duration of advertisements, **6**, 87
  generally, **6**, 85, 86
  IBA Code, subject to, **1**, 519
  products and services not accepted, **1**, 522
  programmes, separate from, **1**, 522
  rules on, **1**, 522
  spot advertising, **1**, 522
  subliminal, **1**, 522
  time, limitation on, **1**, 522
  type of programme, limitation on, **1**, 522
building, on, **14**, 335
building societies, by, **1**, 533; **3**, 444
business disclosure, **6**, 83
care and maintenance of child, arrangements for, **1**, 528
cars, for, **1**, 532
cars for sale, details displayed on, **6**, 82
child care, relating to, **1**, 528; **17**, 45
circus, of, **9**, 1033
Code of Advertising Practice Committee, **1**, 545, 546
Code of Advertising Standards and Practice of the Independent Broadcasting Authority, **1**, 519, 522
comparative advertising—
  defamation, action for, **1**, 516
  fraud, **1**, 517
  malicious falsehood in, **1**, 515
  meaning, **1**, 513
  misleading, **1**, 517
  slander of goods, action for, **1**, 515
  trade mark, infringing, **1**, 514
consumer credit, **1**, 533; **5**, 827–831; **6**, 80; **14**, 1050
content of, **5**, 829
  exempt, **5**, 828
  form of, **5**, 829
  meaning, **5**, 827
contract, advertising, **1**, 511
control of advertising—
  Advertising Standards Authority, *see* ADVERTISING STANDARDS AUTHORITY
  appeals, **23**, 197
  area of special control, **23**, 201

Advertisement—*continued*
control of advertising—*continued*
  common law, **6**, 74, 75
  compensation, **23**, 200
  consent, **23**, 194, 196
  discontinuance notice, **23**, 195
  enforcement, **23**, 198
  extent of, **23**, 193
  generally, **6**, 73; **14**, 1212
  material change of use, as, **23**, 86
  medicinal products, **14**, 1211, 1212
  offences, **23**, 199
  purchase notice, may give rise to, **23**, 311
  statutory, **6**, 73, 76–81
control of, defensive tactics in takeover bid, **4**, 553, 556
copyright protection, **1**, 509
course of trade or business, indicating sale in, **1**, 510
credit, relating to—
  infringement of regulations, **13**, 1769
  minor, documents sent to, **13**, 1767
  misleading, **13**, 1768
criminal liability, giving rise to, **1**, 510
delictual aspects of, **1**, 506
discriminatory, **9**, 374
election campaign, **15**, 1242
endorsements in—
  actio injuriarum, doctrine of, **1**, 521
  Code of Practice, rules in, **1**, 519
  confidence, breaching obligation of, **1**, 521
  defamatory, **1**, 521
  passing off, action in, **1**, 521
  regulation of, **1**, 518
  trade description, constituting, **1**, 520
experiment on animals, of, **1**, 529
false, **11**, 350
false statement, in—
  medicinal products, **14**, 1212
  when communicated, **6**, 124
false trade description in, **1**, 510
food, of—
  additives, food containing, **11**, 376
  early legislation, **11**, 304
  generally, **1**, 534; **6**, 73, 77
  injurious food, **11**, 341, 341*n*
  meaning, **11**, 341*n*
  misleading descriptions, **11**, 394
  preservatives, **11**, 377
  restrictions on, **1**, 534; **6**, 73, 77; **17**, 45
  specific foods, **11**, 359–370
fraud, **1**, 510, 517
fraudulent misrepresentation in advertising, **6**, 74
gaming, of, **1**, 531
historical background of advertising, **1**, 501
indecent material in, **1**, 537
information to be given in, **6**, 125
insurance broker, by, **1**, 533
insurance company, by, **1**, 533
insurance services, for, **12**, 810
investor protection, *see* INVESTOR PROTECTION
invitation to treat, as, **1**, 503
land, on, **14**, 335
local authority trading standards department, **6**, 95

Advertisement—*continued*
lotteries, of, **1**, 531
mail order—
  information in, **1**, 535
  transactions, **6**, 84
meaning, **11**, 341*n*; **23**, 86*n*
medical procedures and products, for, **1**, 536
medicinal product, of, **6**, 73, 79; **14**, 1211, 1212
milk, **11**, 469, 480
misleading—
  definition, **6**, 95
  European Community directive, **6**, 94, 95
  medicinal products, **14**, 1212
misrepresentation in, **1**, 505
obscenity in, **1**, 537
offences relating to advertising, **5**, 831; **14**, 1212
offer, as, **1**, 503
offer and invitation to treat, **15**, 624
order, making of, **25**, 516
outdoor, regulation of, **1**, 526
passing off, **1**, 507, 521
  comparative advertising, **18**, 1394
  generally, **18**, 1381
  insert advertising, **18**, 1383, 1393
petrol price marking, **1**, 538
pirate radio, for, **1**, 539
political, **1**, 540, 545
price—
  comparisons in, **1**, 510
  marking, **6**, 81
  misleading, **6**, 141, 142
printer and publisher, obligations of, **1**, 511
professional services, for, **1**, 541
promotional literature not given contractual
  force, **6**, 74
publication, restrictions on, **17**, 45
regulation of, **1**, 501; **14**, 1050
representation, amounting to, **1**, 505
reward, offering, **1**, 503
royal approval, false statement of, **1**, 520
securities for, **1**, 533
self-regulatory control, **1**, 543–547
serious professional misconduct, as, **14**, 1124
simplex commendatio non obligat, **6**, 74
solicitor, by, **13**, 1201
standard security, exercise of power of sale, **20**,
  202
statutory meeting, of, **14**, 1311
structure plan, of, examination in public of, **23**,
  34
subliminal, advertising, **6**, 89
taxation of income from advertising appearances,
  19, 1306, 1311
tobacco, of, **1**, 547
trade descriptions in, **6**, 105, 123, 124, 135, 142
trade mark, infringing, **1**, 508
unaesthetic sight, as, **14**, 2084
valuation for rating, advertisement boards, **24**,
  550–552
vehicle, on, **14**, 335
weights and measures, **1**, 534; **6**, 73, 78
Advertising Standards Authority
complaints procedure, **1**, 546
constitution, **1**, 544

Advertising Standards Authority—*continued*
control by, **1**, 543
functions of, **1**, 544
funding, **1**, 544
**Advisory Committee on Restrictive
Practices and Monopolies**
functions, **4**, 1340
**Advisory, Conciliation and Arbitration
Service (ACAS)**
Certification Officer, relationship with, **23**, 788
codes of practice, issue of, **9**, 10; **23**, 749, 752
collective bargaining, assistance for, **9**, 7
disclosure of information, **23**, 749, 751
discrimination, in case of, **9**, 377
industrial tribunal, referral of claim by, **9**, 315
recognition issue referred to, **23**, 712, 743
time off, code of practice on, **23**, 752
unfair dismissal, exclusion following action, **9**,
  212
**Advisory Council of Messengers-at-Arms
and Sheriff Officers**
composition, **14**, 1504
establishment of, **14**, 1504
functions, **14**, 1504
Advocate
abandonment of pursuer's claim, **13**, 1354
absolute privilege, **13**, 1327; **15**, 520
accommodation, **13**, 1294, 1295
admission—
  Faculty, to, *see* FACULTY OF ADVOCATES
  office of, to, declaration of allegiance, **13**, 1314,
    1314*n*
  public office, to, **13**, 1304
advertising by, **13**, 1298, 1324
Advocate Depute—
  Crown, appearing against, **13**, 1344
  House of Lords, ineligibility for membership,
    13, 1329
advocates' clerk, **13**, 1292
  employment and supervision, **13**, 1320
Advocates' Library, **13**, 1254, 1258, 1267
  creation, **13**, 1251
  financial cost, **13**, 1275–1277, 1287
  purpose, **13**, 1251
  transfer to National Library of Scotland, **13**,
    1287, 1288
appeals, duty as to, **13**, 1368
audience, rights of, **13**, 1325
authority to act in court, **13**, 1354
bar, *see* BAR (LEGAL PROFESSION)
business address, **13**, 1319
canonical procedure, **13**, 1130, 1131
client—
  advocate refusing to examine, **13**, 1354
  co-accused, acting for, **13**, 1365
  confession by, **13**, 1364, 1366
  duty towards—
    duty to attend interests of client to end of
      proceedings, **13**, 1367
    generally, **13**, 1321, 1380
    hearing, at, **13**, 1359
    interview before hearing, **13**, 1357
    pleas, advocate's duties in relation to, **13**, 1363
    privilege of confidentiality, waiver by, **13**, 1355

Advocate—*continued*
client—*continued*
  relationship with—
    authority to act in court, **13**, 1354
    generally, **13**, 1352
    mandate, contract of, **13**, 1353
    retainer paid by, **13**, 1349–1351
collective identity, historical background, **13**, 1242
College of Justice, foundation, **13**, 1241
conduct in criminal cases—
  at trial, **13**, 1366
    attendance in court, **13**, 1367
    confession by accused to legal advisers, **13**, 1366
    cross-examination of witnesses, **13**, 1366
    personal belief in innocence of accused must not be expressed, **13**, 1366
  before trial—
    co-accused, acting for, **13**, 1365
    confessions, **13**, 1364
    pleas, **13**, 1363
conduct of litigation—
  at hearing—
    attendance at court, **13**, 1358
    counsel failing to attend, **13**, 1358
      no counsel attending on either side, **13**, 1358
    ex parte statements made at bar, **13**, 1360
    generally, **13**, 1359
    matters of fact, **13**, 1360, 1362
    matters of law, **13**, 1361
    witnesses, relationship with, **13**, 1362
  before hearing—
    client, interview, **13**, 1357
    witnesses, interviewing, **13**, 1357
    written pleadings, **13**, 1356
conduct of proceedings, discretion as to, **13**, 1354
confidentiality, duty of, **13**, 1355
conflict of interests, **13**, 1321, 1355
corporate organisation—
  independence and, **13**, 1247
  recognition of, **13**, 1245
court dress, **13**, 1323
direct professional access to, **13**, 1387
disabilities, **13**, 1329
discipline—
  admonition, **13**, 1373
  advocate practising furth of jurisdiction, where, **13**, 1370
  censure, **13**, 1373
  complaints in relation to legal services, **13**, 1378
  conduct complaint, **13**, 1378
  Disciplinary Tribunal, **13**, 1375–1377
  duty of disclosure, **13**, 1372
  excessive fees, **13**, 1388
  explanation of professional conduct, **13**, 1372
  Faculty of Advocates—
    Dean's powers, **13**, 1371–1377
    Disciplinary Rules, **13**, 1371
    powers, **13**, 1369
    statutory control, **13**, 1378
  handling complaint, **13**, 1378
  investigating committee, **13**, 1374

Advocate—*continued*
discipline—*continued*
  publicity, **13**, 1379
  removal from office, **13**, 1379
    interim, **13**, 1379
    publicity, **13**, 1379
  repayment of fees, order for, **13**, 1373
  reprimand, **13**, 1373
  Scottish Legal Services Ombudsman, **13**, 1378
disclosure, duties relating to, **13**, 1355
dress of, **13**, 1323
education—
  historical background, **13**, 1260–1262
  Roman law, **13**, 1261
ex parte statements made at bar, **13**, 1360
expenses, **13**, 1387
extra-judicial settlement, **13**, 1354
Faculty of Advocates, *see* FACULTY OF ADVOCATES
Faculty Services Ltd, *see* FACULTY OF ADVOCATES
fees—
  action for recovery, **13**, 1381
  adjudication, **13**, 1385
  collection, Faculty Services Ltd, **13**, 1293, 1383, 1386
  direct professional access, on, **13**, 1387
  entitlement to, **13**, 1381
  excessive, **13**, 1388
  expenses covered by, **13**, 1387
  honoraria, as, **13**, 1381
  instructing solicitor receiving from client, **13**, 1381
  legally aided cases, **13**, 1384, 1386, 1390
  negotiation, **13**, 1385
  pactum de quota litis, **13**, 1382
  procedure for payment, **13**, 1386
  proportional, **13**, 1382
  repayment to client, **13**, 1381
  retainers—
    general, **13**, 1349, 1351
    meaning, **13**, 1349
    non-recoverable from opponent on taxation, **13**, 1349
    purpose, **13**, 1349
    special, **13**, 1349, 1350
  Scheme for Accounting and Recovery of Counsel's Fees, **13**, 1383–1386
  solicitor—
    amount of counsel's fees questioned by, **13**, 1385
    obligations of, **13**, 1384, 1386
  speculative arrangements, **13**, 1382
  timescale for payment, **13**, 1386
gentleman, designation as, **16**, 2023
giving up defence, **13**, 1354
herald as, dress, **13**, 1323
indemnity insurance, **13**, 1322
independence, **13**, 1318
  corporate structure and, **13**, 1247
  defiance of judges, **13**, 1252
  historical background, **13**, 1246–1248
  learning and, **13**, 1248
instructions—
  acceptance—
    determining considerations, **13**, 1337

Advocate—*continued*
instructions—*continued*
  acceptance—*continued*
    obligations as to, **13**, 1330
    professional commitment, **13**, 1336
  Advocate Depute, **13**, 1343
  advocate who is also a Member of Parliament, **13**, 1345
  advocate who is also a peer, **13**, 1346
  attendance at court, obligations as to, **13**, 1358, 1367
  'cab-rank' rule, **13**, 1330, 1354
  co-accused, acting for, **13**, 1365
  competing, **13**, 1338
  conflict of interests, **13**, 1355, 1365
  Dean's Ruling, **13**, 1341
  fee, acceptance dependent upon, **13**, 1381
  Law Officer of the Crown, **13**, 1342
  mandate, contract of, **13**, 1353
  multiple, **13**, 1335
  non-Scottish solicitor, by, **13**, 1347, 1348
  passing on, **13**, 1339
  person other than practising solicitor, by, **13**, 1298, 1348
  professional body, by member of recognised, **13**, 1298, 1348, 1348n
  racial discrimination, **13**, 1347
  refusal—
    case unstable, where, **13**, 1333
    exceptions to, **13**, 1331
    fee inadequate, where, **13**, 1334
    general rule, **13**, 1330
    personal interest, where, **13**, 1332
  senior counsel, **13**, 1340
  sex discrimination, **13**, 1347
  sheriff principal, **13**, 1344
 joint minute agreeing matters in dispute or settling action, **13**, 1354
 judges, defiance of, **13**, 1252
 judicial appointments, **13**, 1259
 junior, **13**, 1317
  dress, **13**, 1323
 jury service, ineligibility for, **13**, 1329
 King's Counsel, **13**, 1317
 Law Officer of Crown, preclusion from private practice, **13**, 1342
 Legal Civil Service in, code of conduct, **13**, 1398
 legal education—
  historical background, **13**, 1102
  modern, **13**, 1106
 Legal Secretaries to the Lord Advocate, **13**, 1403, 1404
 legally aided cases—
  exclusion of counsel by Faculty of Advocates, **13**, 1389
  fees, **13**, 1390
  relationship between client and counsel not affected by, **13**, 1389
  selection of counsel, **13**, 1389
 liability—
  duty of care, **13**, 1380
  immunity, **13**, 1380
 man of skill, remit, **13**, 1354
 matriculation, **13**, 1306

Advocate—*continued*
 matters of fact, duty as to, **13**, 1360, 1362
 matters of law, duty as to, **13**, 1361
 Member of Parliament, advocate who is also, **13**, 1345
 negligence, immunity, **13**, 1380
 Officer of State, **7**, 790, 792
 pacta de quota litis, **15**, 769
 Parliament House Chambers, **13**, 1294
 parliamentary inquiry, right of audience, **13**, 1325
 peer, advocate who is also, **13**, 1346
 perjured evidence, **13**, 1362
 practice rules—
  advocate's clerks, **13**, 1320
  business address, **13**, 1319
  client, duty to, **13**, 1321
  conflict of interests, **13**, 1321
  dress, **13**, 1323
  indemnity insurance, **13**, 1322
  independence, **13**, 1318
  other occupations, **13**, 1321
 practising furth of Scotland, discipline, **13**, 1370
 precedence—
  bar, at—
    historical background, **13**, 1271, 1272
    Queen's Counsel, **13**, 1273, 1274
    senior counsel, **13**, 1273, 1274
  generally, **16**, 2020
 privilege, **13**, 1327
 procurators of the council, **13**, 1241
 pupillage, **13**, 1310
  Admission Days, **13**, 1312
  Admission Intervals, **13**, 1312
  exemption, **13**, 1311
  master—
    duties of, **13**, 1312
    master's report, **13**, 1312
    more than one during pupillage, **13**, 1312
  period, calculation of, **13**, 1312
  racial discrimination, **13**, 1312
  removal from Roll of Intrants, **13**, 1312
  sex discrimination, **13**, 1312
 Queen's Counsel, **13**, 1273, 1274, 1317
  application to become, **13**, 1317
  dress, **13**, 1323
 questions—
  leading, **13**, 1362
  matters of fact, **13**, 1362
 remuneration, *see* fees *above*
 retainers—
  general, **13**, 1349, 1351
  meaning, **13**, 1349
  non-recoverable from opponent on taxation, **13**, 1349
  purpose, **13**, 1349
  special, **13**, 1349, 1350
 rights and privileges—
  absolute privilege, **13**, 1327
  audience, rights of, **13**, 1325
  establishment, rights within European Community, **13**, 1328
  plead, entitlement to, **13**, 1325
  protection of, Dean's function as to, **13**, 1302
  writ, signature, **13**, 1326

Advocate—*continued*
Roman law, knowledge of, **13**, 1250, 1251, 1256
Scottish Parliamentary Counsel, **13**, 1403, 1404
senior counsel, **13**, 1317
    unaccompanied appearance by, **13**, 1298
silk, **13**, 1317, 1323
solicitor acting on opinion of counsel, **13**, 1188
submission to arbitration by, **2**, 409
two counsel rule, **13**, 1317
value added tax, liability, **13**, 1391
wig and gown, **13**, 1323, 1323*n*
witnesses, relationship with, **13**, 1357, 1362
women, eligibility for membership of Faculty, **13**, 1268, 1296
writ, duties as to signature of, **13**, 1326
written pleadings, **13**, 1356
See also COUNSEL; FACULTY OF ADVOCATES
Advocate depute
absolute privilege, **15**, 444, 449, 526
appointment of, **17**, 579
functions, **17**, 579
judiciary, relationship to, **17**, 583
pacta de quota litits, **15**, 769
Advocates-general
functions of, **5**, 674
Advocates' Library
transfer to National Library of Scotland, **13**, 1501
Advocation
appropriateness, **17**, 881
background, **17**, 880
bill of—
    disposal of, **6**, 865; **17**, 882
    hearing of, **17**, 882
    meaning, **6**, 871
competency, **17**, 881
generally, **17**, 880
remedy of, **17**, 831
review, as mode of, **13**, 68
Advocatus Pauperum
appointment of, **6**, 905
Aemulatio vicini
active use, applicable to, **14**, 2033*n*
conduct causing invasion, **14**, 2070
damnum absque injuria, remedy in case of, **14**, 2034
doctrine of, **14**, 2007, 2008
modern Scots law, in, **14**, 2034
privacy, defence of maintaining, **14**, 2036
spite fence, **14**, 2036
survival of, **14**, 2033
underground water, abstraction of, **14**, 2034, 2035
Aerodrome
abandoned vehicles at, **2**, 937
acts of violence, protection from, **2**, 1037
advertisement displays, **2**, 951
aviation fuel installation—
    deliveries to, **2**, 974
    records, operator to keep, **2**, 974
charges, *see* AIRPORT
consultations concerning, facilities for, **2**, 944
customs and excise airport—
    designation as, **2**, 940
    landing at, **2**, 940
emergency powers as to, **2**, 902
establishment of, **14**, 449

Aerodrome—*continued*
explosives etc, bringing into, **2**, 1033
facilities for civil aviation, **2**, 914
health control regulations, **2**, 939
inspection etc, powers of, **2**, 959
kites etc, flying near, **2**, 973
licence—
    conditions, contravention of, **2**, 910
    duration of, **2**, 910
    grant of, **2**, 910
licensee, duties of, **2**, 910
licensing—
    necessity for, **2**, 910
    order providing for, **2**, 910, 955
lighting and marking of, **2**, 969
local authority—
    powers, **14**, 448
        See also AIRPORT
    provision of aerodrome by, **2**, 914
maintenance, **14**, 449
meaning, **2**, 909
noise and vibration—
    charges, fixing by reference to, **2**, 1023
    damage caused by, **2**, 1020
    generally, **9**, 1280–1285
    insulation grant schemes, **2**, 1022
    military aerodromes, **2**, 1022
    noise certificates, **2**, 1025
    nuisance by, **2**, 1021
    regulation of, **2**, 933, 1042; **9**, 1283
    sound-proofing buildings near, **2**, 1022; **9**, 1284
obstructions near—
    control powers, **2**, 950
    warning lights etc, **2**, 951
planning controls, **9**, 1285
    environmental impact assessment, **23**, 123
policing of—
    payments for, **2**, 934
    special constables, appointment, **2**, 934
    See also AIRPORT
provision of, by local authorities, **2**, 914
restrictions applying to, **2**, 910
road traffic, control of, **2**, 936
safety—
    general powers as to, **2**, 950
    land use, restriction on, **2**, 949
    securing, compensation provision, **2**, 953
security—
    acts of violence against, **2**, 1037
    annual report as to, **2**, 1046
    directions by Secretary of State—
        general application, for, **2**, 1043
        limitation on scope of, **2**, 1042
        objections to, **2**, 1041
        operation of, **2**, 1044
        restrictions, requiring, **2**, 1039
        searches, for, **2**, 1040
        security measures, to take, **2**, 1041
    information required as to, **2**, 1038
    inspection in respect of, **2**, 1045
    measures to be taken—
        compensation, **2**, 1041
        contracts etc, affecting, **2**, 1044

Aerodrome—_continued_
security—_continued_
  measures to be taken—_continued_
    directions as to, **2**, 1041
    exceptions as to, **2**, 1043
telecommunications apparatus, **2**, 950
theft, prevention of, **2**, 935
trees, height of, control over, **2**, 950
trespassing on, **2**, 911
See also AIRPORT
Aeroplane
See AIRCRAFT
Aerosol products
safety regulations, **6**, 63
weights and measures legislation, **6**, 247
Affidavit
interpretation, **12**, 1262
Affinity
relationship by, capacity to marry, **10**, 817
Affirmation
See OATH
Affirmation of allegiance
Member of Parliament failing to take, **15**, 1060
Affixation to heritage, _see_ HERITABLE PROPERTY
Affreightment, contract of
meaning, **21**, 521_n_
After-care services
health service, **11**, 1410, 1477
mental disorder, person with—
  local authority, duty to provide, **22**, 30
  voluntary organisations, co-operation with local authority, **22**, 30
young offender, for—
  child detained at direction of Secretary of State, **22**, 36
  family placement, **22**, 36
  licence, duration, of, **22**, 36
  mandatory, groups to which applicable, **22**, 36
  planning before offender's release, **22**, 36
  residential unit, **22**, 36
  Secretary of State, notification to, **22**, 36
  social workers' statutory duty, **22**, 36
Age
calculation of, precise moment of birth, **22**, 824
determination of, **19**, 1584
full, person of, construction of wills, **25**, 835
majority, of, **22**, 820, 824, 827
redundancy payment, reduction of, **9**, 190
retirement of judge, **5**, 664
unfair dismissal, applicant for claim for, **9**, 205
voting, lowering of, **5**, 374
Agency
banker as holder, **4**, 209
bill of exchange—
  agent's signature on, **4**, 130
  capacity relating to, **4**, 130
commercial, **4**, 1378
contract—
  alteration of terms, **1**, 630
  formal written, **1**, 604
  nature of, **1**, 601
  no formal written, where, **1**, 605
  power of attorney as, **1**, 604
  termination of, **1**, 663

Agency—_continued_
credit reference agency, _see_ CREDIT REFERENCE AGENCY
employment, **9**, 345
evidence of, **1**, 603
government, **9**, 346
holder holding bill in capacity of agent, **4**, 148
holding out, **16**, 1645
joint purchase, Community aspects, **4**, 1389
joint sales, Commission's view of, **4**, 1370
meaning, **1**, 601
obligation under contract of, **16**, 2116, 2119
permission to act as agent, **16**, 1645
presumption of, **1**, 603
revocation of, **1**, 664
termination of, **1**, 664
where arising, **1**, 605
See also AGENT
Agency of necessity
negotiorum gestio, and, **15**, 94
Agent
accounts of, **1**, 634
authority of—
  acting within, **1**, 626, 650
  actual, **1**, 649
  apparent, **1**, 649
  implied, **1**, 607
  legal proceedings, to take, **1**, 612
  limit on, **1**, 653
  money, authority to borrow, **1**, 608, 615
  ostensible, **1**, 649
  scope, **1**, 649
  usual, acting within, **1**, 626
borrowing money, power of, **1**, 608, 615
capacity of, **1**, 602
commission, right to, **1**, 641
compensation on termination of agency, **1**, 664
corporate personality and, **4**, 318, 319
debt of, retention of principal's property for, **1**, 655
debtor, election as, **1**, 656–658
delegation by, **1**, 633
disburser, expenses, **17**, 1197
discharge, power to give, **1**, 609
discharge on termination of agency, **1**, 664
duties and liabilities of—
  account, to, **1**, 634
  contract, proper conclusion of, **1**, 631
  mandate, performance of, **1**, 630
  principal, effect of behaviour of, **1**, 632
  third parties, to, **1**, 635–639
election, _see_ ELECTION
employment of others by, **1**, 611
entertainer, promotion of, **9**, 1006
fiduciary duty, **24**, 172, 181, 182, 188, 246
fraud by, **1**, 651, 655
implied appointment of, **1**, 606
introduction of business by, **1**, 642
investment advice, **24**, 190
land, functions of, **25**, 136
law, **1**, 613
legal proceedings, power to take, **1**, 612
lessor, as, **13**, 183
lien over principal's goods, **1**, 643

Agent—*continued*
misrepresentation by, **1**, 638
negligence by, **1**, 632, 652
non-resident, of, assessment to tax, **1**, 662
obligations, incurring, **1**, 601
overdraft, incurring, **1**, 608
payment, rights of, **1**, 632
personal advantage, taking, **1**, 634
port, **1**, 614
powers, implied, **1**, 607
price averaging by, **1**, 631
principal, *see* PRINCIPAL
principal and agent, vicarious liability, **15**, 243–246
ratification of acts of—
    act void *ab initio*, **1**, 624
    factor, and, **1**, 629
    knowledge, principal requiring, **1**, 624
    marine insurance, contract of, **1**, 628
    third party rights, not prejudicing, **1**, 624
    undisclosed principal, where, **1**, 625
    usual authority, agent acting within, **1**, 626
receipts, power to give, **1**, 609
remuneration of, **1**, 641
sale, power of, **1**, 610
set-off with third party by, **1**, 621
shipping, **1**, 614
skill and care, exercise of, **1**, 632
state, responsibility for acts of agent, **19**, 645
stockbroker as, **1**, 603, 615
sub-agent, negligence of, **1**, 633
taxation of—
    composite rate tax, **1**, 663
    information, giving to Revenue, **1**, 661
    return, duty to make, **1**, 660
termination of agency—
    compensation on, **1**, 664
    discharge on, **1**, 664
third party—
    liability to—
        disclosed principal, where, **1**, 636
        personal, **1**, 638, 639
        undisclosed principal, where, **1**, 635, 637
    rights against—
        alternative liability, **1**, 644
        losses, claim for, **1**, 646
        party to contract, where, **1**, 647
        principal's losses, claim for, **1**, 645
trust, to, **24**, 190, 202
trustee, as, **24**, 2
ultra vires doctrine, application of, **4**, 324
warrant of authority, breach of, **1**, 639
See also AGENCY; PRINCIPAL
Aggression
breach of the peace, **7**, 216
not aimed at specific person, **7**, 216
Agoraphobia
sickness benefit where claimant suffering from, **21**, 881, 881*n*
Agricultural association, **12**, 614, 617
advances to members, **12**, 623
Agricultural building
exemptions from building regulations, **3**, 209
See also DWELLING HOUSE; VALUATION FOR RATING

Agricultural co-operative
Agricultural and Horticultural Co-operation Scheme, **12**, 617
Agricultural executive committee
close times, powers as to, **11**, 808
ground game, powers as to, **11**, 851
Agricultural holding
assured tenancy, exclusion from, **13**, 636, 642
croft constituting, **1**, 727
decree of removing, **1**, 773
dilapidations, claim for, **1**, 782
dispute, hearings relating to, **6**, 969
disturbance, compensation for, **1**, 739, 750, 783
ejectment, action of, **1**, 773
fixtures, removal of, **1**, 779
grazing lets, **1**, 733
improvements, compensation for, **1**, 727, 775, 780
landlord—
    acquisition of lease, notifying of, **1**, 790
    meaning, **1**, 738
    power of resumption, exercising, **1**, 772
    power to enter, **1**, 766
    rights, reserving, **1**, 766
    violent profits, entitlement to, **1**, 774
lease—
    acquisition, notice to landlord on, **1**, 790
    approval by Secretary of State of short term let, **1**, 734
    breach—
        liquidated damages for, **1**, 767
        obligations, of, **1**, 737, 767
    interest in—
        bequest of, **25**, 719
        decisions in respect of, **25**, 720
        landlord, repossession by, **25**, 718
        succession to, **25**, 716
        termination of, **25**, 717
        vesting of, **25**, 715
    irritancy, **1**, 737
    less than one year, for, **1**, 728, 732
    liferent, **1**, 728, 787
    meaning, **1**, 728
    substantially of agricultural land, to be, **1**, 730
liferent lease, **1**, 728, 787
long lease, standard securities, **20**, 179
meaning, **1**, 729
non-agricultural use, land required for, **1**, 745, 750
notice to quit—
    afforestation, land required for, **1**, 745
    agricultural research, etc, for purposes of, **1**, 746
    arbitration—
        notice requiring, **1**, 743
        reference to, **1**, 748
        tenant requiring, **1**, 756
    bad husbandry, where certified, **1**, 751
    compulsory acquisition, **5**, 185
    counter-notice, **1**, 743
    decision or award, suspension pending, **1**, 743
    defence, lines of, **1**, 756
    disturbance, compensation for, **1**, 739, 750, 783
    duration of, **1**, 738
    executors, defended by, **1**, 795

Agricultural holding—*continued*
notice to quit—*continued*
  fixed equipment, breach relating to, **1**, 755
  form of, **1**, 738
  generally, **5**, 185
  good husbandry, in interests of, **1**, 745
  hardship, consideration of, **1**, 745
  incontestable, arbitration in relation to, **1**, 760
  insolvency of tenant, **1**, 759
  irremediable breach, due to, **1**, 758
  ish date, discrepancy with, **1**, 738
  joint landlords, by, **1**, 738
  Land Court, consent of, **1**, 736, 739, 744, 748*ff*
    See also SCOTTISH LAND COURT
  multiple entry dates, where, **1**, 738
  non-agricultural use, land required for, **1**, 745, 750
  part only of holding, of, **1**, 739
  period shorter than one year, in, **1**, 757
  permanent pasture, relating to, **1**, 749
  possession, fair and reasonable landlord not insisting on, **1**, 746
  reason in, establishment of, **1**, 736
  reason for service of, **1**, 739
  remediable breach, where, **1**, 752
  rent, failure to pay, **1**, 753
  resistance to, **1**, 743
  small landholding, *see* SMALLHOLDING
  sound management, in interests of, **1**, 745
  statement of reasons—
    circumstances in which required, **1**, 739
    form of, **1**, 740
    invalid, effect of, **1**, 740
  subtenants, effect on, **1**, 735
  successor to tenant, on, **1**, 791–794
  term of lease, breach of, **1**, 754
  termination of tenancy by, **1**, 772
  withdrawal of, **1**, 743
record of, **1**, 764
rent, *see* RENT
reorganisation payment, liability for, **1**, 739
right of succession, *see* SUCCESSION
Scottish Land Court jurisdiction, **6**, 969, 970
security of tenure—
  continuation of lease, by, **1**, 736
  exceptions to, **1**, 737
  fixed equipment—
    condition of, recording, **1**, 764
    incorporation of provisions on, **1**, 762
    maintenance and repair—
      breach of condition of, **1**, 755
      tenant, obligations of, **1**, 762
      variation of responsibility for, rent on, **1**, 768
    renewal of, **1**, 762
  legislation on, **1**, 727
  modification to common law, **1**, 761
  rent, provisions on, *see* RENT
  successor to tenant, position of, **1**, 791
  tacit relocation, by, **1**, 736
  See also TENANT-TENANCY
smallholding constituting, **1**, 727
special standard of farming, compensation for, **1**, 781

Agricultural holding—*continued*
statutory small tenancy, amalgamation of, **1**, 860
sublease, granting, **1**, 735
tacit relocation, **13**, 453
tenancy—
  notice to terminate—
    ejectment of tenant, **1**, 742
    executor, by, **1**, 741
    tenant, by, **1**, 738
  partial termination of, **1**, 772
  renouncing, **1**, 772
  security of tenure, *see* security of tenure *above*
  succession, *see* SUCCESSION
  termination of—
    failure to quit on, **1**, 773
    methods of, **1**, 722
    partial, **1**, 722
    violent profits accruing to landlord on, **1**, 774
tenant—
  crop, entitled to reap, **1**, 776
  disturbance, compensation for, **1**, 739, 750, 783
  ejection of, **1**, 742, 743
  failure to quit on termination, **1**, 773
  insolvency of, **1**, 759
  legal person being, dissolution of, **1**, 772
  meaning, **1**, 738
  notour bankruptcy of, **1**, 759
  outgoing, sale of property by, **1**, 778
  planning consent, informing of application for, **1**, 750
  reorganisation payment to, **1**, 784, 785
  security of tenure, *see* security of tenure *above*
  sequestration of estate, **1**, 737
  waygoing claims, *see* WAYGOING CLAIMS
  See also SMALLHOLDING
Agricultural lands and heritages
aggregate of, **1**, 730
agricultural land or crops, meaning, **19**, 1056*n*
agricultural property, meaning, **25**, 1013
amalgamations and boundary adjustments, grants for, **1**, 714
assured tenancy, exclusion from, **13**, 636, 641
break crops, schemes for, **1**, 715
capital gains tax deferral on woodlands, **11**, 654
capital grants for, **1**, 714
control of treatment of—
  good husbandry, responsibility for, **1**, 712
  Secretary of State, directions by, **1**, 712
  soil preservation, **1**, 711
development of—
  blight notice, **23**, 317
  meaning, **23**, 147, 317*n*
  planning application, notification of tenant, **23**, 163
drainage works on, **1**, 716; **25**, 366
  creation of, **25**, 368
  improvement orders, **25**, 369
  maintenance, **25**, 367
dwelling houses, *see* DWELLING HOUSE
fire damage caused by railway engine, **19**, 1056
flood prevention, **25**, 376
improvement order for, **1**, 717
inheritance tax relief, **25**, 1013

Agricultural land and heritages—*continued*
liferent and, **1**, 772; **13**, 1639
meaning, **1**, 729; **23**, 147*n*
non-agricultural land distinguished from, **25**, 365
non-capital improvements, schemes for, **1**, 715
ploughing, schemes for, **1**, 715
size of, **1**, 729
solatium awarded in case of, **5**, 108
use of, **1**, 731; **23**, 88
valuation—
   land agent, functions of, **25**, 136
   other forms, **25**, 137
   other subjects, **25**, 134
   rental valuation, **25**, 133
   statutory claims, **25**, 135
   valuer—
      competent, **25**, 132
      duties of, **25**, 138
valuation for rating—
   abolition of domestic rates, **24**, 561
   agricultural or pastoral purposes, used for, **24**, 558
   allotments, **24**, 560
   buildings, *see* VALUATION FOR RATING
   generally, **24**, 556
   horses, use in respect of, **24**, 559
   market gardens, **24**, 560, 565
   meaning, **24**, 557
   orchards, **24**, 560
   poultry farms, **24**, 560
   reed beds, **24**, 560
   relief, eligibility of lands, **24**, 556, 560, 561
   sawmills, **24**, 560
   sporting purposes, used for, **24**, 561
   woodlands, **24**, 560
Agricultural lease
removings, notice, **13**, 483
See AGRICULTURAL HOLDING
Agricultural levy
fraudulent evasion, **7**, 1162
Agricultural production
beef and veal, **1**, 933
boards for, **1**, 702
   Monopolies and Mergers Commission investigation, **19**, 224
borrowing powers, **1**, 713
cereals, *see* CEREALS
Common Agricultural Policy—
   alternative forms of, **1**, 913
   cereals, in, *see* CEREALS
   common price system, based on, **1**, 902
   Community preference, price structure leading to, **1**, 907
   compatible national legislation, **1**, 967
   competition provisions, effect of, **1**, 887
   deficiency payments by, **1**, 890
   EU Council, powers of, **1**, 977
   financing, **1**, 951
   income, guaranteeing, **1**, 902
   management committees, **1**, 978
   national—
      authorities, conferring powers on, **1**, 964
      export subsidies, not allowing, **1**, 891
      legislation, permitting, **1**, 968

Agricultural production—*continued*
Common Agricultural Policy—*continued*
   national—*continued*
      measures derogating from, **1**, 967
      organisations, replacing, **1**, 884, 969
   non-discrimination, principle of, **1**, 908
   over-production, encouraging, **1**, 916
   pigmeat, **1**, 938
   pre-existing national organisations, replacing, **1**, 969
   price systems, legal effects of, **1**, 966
   quality standards exclusively set by, **1**, 968
   regional impact of, **1**, 906
   rules—
      applying to products without, **1**, 892
      problems raised by, **1**, 965
   single market concept, **1**, 907
   subsidies by, **1**, 890, 922
   sugar, **1**, 939
   techniques used by, **1**, 922
   time limit for, **1**, 885
   transitional period, establishment in, **1**, 884, 885
   underlying concepts, consideration of, **1**, 967
   units of account, prices in, **1**, 952
   See also COMMON AGRICULTURAL POLICY
common market extended to, **1**, 876, 881
competition rules applying to, **1**, 886, 887
countervailing charge on, **1**, 889
EEC Treaty, **1**, 876, 882
   rules in—
      derogation from, **1**, 883, 886
      specific agricultural provisions, precedence of, **1**, 891
      state aids, on, **1**, 888
eggs, *see* EGGS
European Free Trade Association, excluded from, **1**, 881
European Union customs law—
   agricultural levies, **7**, 1038
   Common Agricultural Policy (CAP), **7**, 1014
   definition of agricultural products, **7**, 1014
   duty—
      rates, **7**, 1014
      reliefs, **7**, 1100
   licence—
      export, **7**, 1014
      import, **7**, 1014
first stage processing, products of, **1**, 877
free movement of goods rules, application of, **1**, 888
import charges on, **1**, 881, 886
improvements, assistance for, **1**, 714–717
Intervention Board, **1**, 983, 984; **7**, 1098
lists of, **1**, 876, 878
marketing, compulsory schemes for—
   British Wool Marketing Board, **1**, 703
   committee of investigation, **1**, 709
   consumers' committee, **1**, 709
   discipline, boards exercising, **1**, 708
   financial powers, **1**, 709
   generally, **1**, 974

Agricultural production—*continued*
marketing, compulsory schemes for—*continued*
  making, **1**, 707
  milk marketing boards, **1**, 703
    See also MILK MARKETING BOARDS
  Potato Marketing Board, **1**, 703
  provisions in, **1**, 703
  regulated products, sale of, **1**, 705
  restrictive practices, as, **1**, 704
  sale outside scheme, avoidance of contract for, **1**, 706
  statutory basis, **1**, 703
  trading functions, **1**, 706
meaning, **1**, 876
meaning of products, **1**, 703
milk, *see* MILK
national aid for, **1**, 888
national authorities, powers of, **1**, 964
national protective measures, impermissibility of, **1**, 892
non-agricultural goods with agricultural elements, **1**, 880
not subject to common organisation, principles governing, **1**, 940
pigs, *see* PIGMEAT; PIGS
poultry, *see* POULTRY
processing—
  first stage, products of, **1**, 877
  generally, **1**, 974
producer organisations—
  encouragement of, **1**, 975
  role of, **1**, 985
rennet, exclusive purchasing obligation regarding, **1**, 877
sheepmeat, *see* SHEEP; SHEEPMEAT
state aid, application of rules on, **1**, 888
statutory control, **1**, 710
See also AGRICULTURE
Agricultural vehicle
weight, **20**, 476
See also TRACTOR
Agricultural worker
dwelling house used for, repossession on grounds of, **13**, 736, 743
Agriculture
abstraction of water, **25**, 330
agricultural analyst, appointment of, **14**, 249
agricultural executive committee, **11**, 808, 851
agricultural lease, **6**, 639
agricultural property relief—
  contract of sale, property subject to, **19**, 1556
  controlling shareholding in farming company, **19**, 1555
  inheritance tax, **19**, 1533, 1555–1557, 1597; **25**, 1013
  interest in possession, **19**, 1562, 1563
  liferent, property subject to, **19**, 1562
  minimum period of ownership or occupation, **19**, 1557, 1562
  moveable property, **19**, 1555
  partnerships, **19**, 1558–1560, 1589, 1590
  qualifying period, **19**, 1557

Agriculture—*continued*
agricultural property relief—*continued*
  settled property, **19**, 1560–1563
    relief in respect of, **19**, 1597
    tenancy, *see* AGRICULTURAL HOLDING; TENANCY
  unincorporated farming business, **19**, 1555
agricultural tenant, *see* AGRICULTURAL HOLDING; TENANCY
assistance and grants for, **2**, 1287
Board of, *see* BOARD OF AGRICULTURE
buildings, valuation for rating, *see* VALUATION FOR RATING
co-operative, buildings occupied by, **24**, 568, 569
common agricultural policy, *see* COMMON AGRICULTURAL POLICY
crofts, *see* CROFT; CROFTERS; CROFTERS COMMISSION
cropping and disposal, **1**, 763, 776
crops, prevention of damage to, **11**, 859, 883, 886
derating, **6**, 950
dwelling house, *see* DWELLING HOUSE
European Agricultural Guidance and Guarantee Fund, *see* EUROPEAN AGRICULTURAL GUIDANCE AND GUARANTEE FUND
European Community law—
  breach of, **1**, 863
  directives, implementation of, **1**, 868
  directly enforceable, **1**, 862–865
  European Communities Act, in, **1**, 874
  food, relating to, **1**, 874
  implementation of—
    designation orders, **1**, 873
    directives, **1**, 868
    domestic, requiring, **1**, 866–873
    need for, **1**, 867
    parallel powers of, **1**, 869
    subordinate legislation, by, **1**, 866
  interpretation, principles as guide to, **1**, 911
  national law, conflicting with, **1**, 870
  non-contractual liability, Community incurring, **1**, 912
  permissions under, **1**, 871
  powers under, **1**, 871
  primacy of, **1**, 864
  proportionality, principle of, **1**, 910
  retrospective legislation, liability to issue, **1**, 872
  rights under, **1**, 863, 871
  subordinate legislation—
    implementation by, **1**, 866
    limitations on, **1**, 872
  United Kingdom legislation, effect on, **1**, 874
European Community rules, **1**, 876, 882; **10**, 130
European Economic Community legislation, precedence of, **1**, 891
European Union law—
  agricultural products, **4**, 1392
expenditure programme, **5**, 578
Farm Amalgamation Scheme, **1**, 971
farm amalgamation, repossession of dwelling house in cases of, **13**, 736, 744
Farm and Horticultural Development Schemes, **1**, 971
farm loss payments, **5**, 187; **6**, 1141
farm occupation, repossession of protected tenancy in cases of, **13**, 736, 745

Agriculture—*continued*
growing crops as 'goods', **6**, 112
health and safety at work legislation, **19**, 345
hill farming improvement scheme, **11**, 923
income tax, **19**, 1572, 1573
inorganic fertilisers, sale of, **6**, 239, 246
Lands Valuation Appeal Court cases, **6**, 950
less-favoured areas, in, **1**, 971, 972
liming materials, sale of, **6**, 239
meaning, **1**, 729
muirburning, **11**, 923
pesticides, *see* PESTICIDES
plant and seed protection rights, **6**, 602
pollutants, control of entry into water, **25**, 405
product liability, **6**, 40
production, *see* AGRICULTURAL PRODUCTION
salt, sale of, **6**, 239
Scottish Land Court, agricultural members,
   6, 960
servicemen, emergency employment in, **5**,
   603
sheriff court jurisdiction, **6**, 1076
small tenants, *see* STATUTORY SMALL TENANT
society promoting, **12**, 694*n*
tenancy, *see* TENANT-TENANCY
trade descriptions, **6**, 121
valuation—
   land agent, functions of, **25**, 136
   other forms, **25**, 137
   other subjects, **25**, 134
   rental valuation, **25**, 133
   statutory claims, **25**, 135
   valuer, **25**, 132, 138
wages order, **9**, 403
water rights, acquisition of, **25**, 519
wild birds or animals killed or taken in interests
   of, **11**, 881, 883, 885, 886
Agriculture and Fisheries Department,
   Scottish Office
functions of, **5**, 512
legal services, **13**, 1401
public health matters, **19**, 307*n*
Agriculture, Fisheries and Food, Ministry of
functions of, **5**, 500
Aid
casualty of, feudal law, **18**, 78
Aiding and abetting
mens rea, **7**, 102
use of term, **7**, 102
Air
access to, no natural right to, **14**, 2032
alkali pollution, **19**, 317
clean, **19**, 315–317
inalienable property, as, **18**, 600
navigation, *see* AIR NAVIGATION
res communes, as, **18**, 282
right to, **18**, 5
smoke pollution, **19**, 316
transport of radioactive material by, **9**, 917
weapon, *see* AIR WEAPON
Air, carriage by
agreement between parties, **3**, 740
air transport licensing, *see* CIVIL AVIATION

Air, carriage by—*continued*
air waybill, **3**, 746
   signatures, **3**, 746, 746*n*
Amended Convention carriage, **3**, 741, 744
baggage—
   check, **3**, 745
   destruction, loss or damage, **3**, 751
cargo, destruction, loss or damage, **3**, 751
carriage not wholly by air, where, **3**, 744
carrier, liability—
   death of passenger, **3**, 750
   delay, **3**, 752
   destruction, loss or damage to baggage or
      cargo, **3**, 751
   economic loss by passenger, **3**, 750*n*
   exclusion, **3**, 753
   injury to passenger, **3**, 750
   limitation—
      contributory negligence, where, **3**, 754
      generally, **3**, 755, 756
      more than one carrier, where, **3**, 757
      prescription, **3**, 759
      time limits, **3**, 758
   nervous shock to passenger, **3**, 750*n*
competition law, **4**, 1177
consignee, rights of, **3**, 747, 749
consignor, rights of, **3**, 747, 748
contract of carriage, **3**, 740
contractual documents, **3**, 745, 746
disembarkation, **3**, 750
embarkation, **3**, 750
foreign operators, **2**, 986
   cargo, carriage of, **2**, 986
   passengers, carriage of, **2**, 986
   permits issued to, **2**, 986
generally, **3**, 736
Guadalajara Convention, **3**, 738, 738*n*, 740, 744
Hague Protocol, **3**, 738, 738*n*
international, **3**, 740
law, sources of, **2**, 901
limitation of actions, **16**, 2200
   baggage, destruction, loss or damage, **16**,
      2200
   cargo, loss or damage, **16**, 2200
   passenger, death or personal injury, **16**, 2200
mail or postal packets, **3**, 744
Montreal Protocols, **3**, 739, 739*n*
non-international, **3**, 740, 743
stoppage in transit, **3**, 748
ticket, **3**, 740, 745
Warsaw Convention, **3**, 737, 740, 744
   Amended Convention carriage, **3**, 741, 744
   application, **3**, 744
   high contracting parties, **3**, 741*n*
   limitation of liability, **21**, 758*n*
   scope, **3**, 744
   travaux préparatoires, **12**, 1154
   Warsaw Convention carriage, **3**, 742
waybill, contents and status of, **3**, 746
See also CIVIL AVIATION; PASSENGER
Air-conditioning system
affixation to heritage, **14**, 1071
plant, whether, **14**, 1012

Aircraft
accident—
  aircraft registered outside United Kingdom, **2**, 1018
  inspectors—
    appointment, **2**, 1012
    powers of, **2**, 1012
  inspector's report—
    review of, **2**, 1015
    submission and contents, **2**, 1014
  investigation—
    foreign aircraft, **2**, 1018
    fundamental purposes of, **2**, 1011
    inspector's report, **2**, 1014
    procedure, **2**, 1014
    provision for, **2**, 1011
    public notice of, **2**, 1014
    reopening of, **2**, 1016
  notification of, **2**, 1013
  public inquiry into, **2**, 1017
  review of findings—
    notice of, **2**, 1015
    rehearing of, **2**, 1016
    reopening of, **2**, 1016
  Scotland, in or over, **2**, 1015
action for recovery of possession, **18**, 159
acts of violence, protection from, **2**, 1037
administrative removal, procurement for, **12**, 200
admiralty courts jurisdiction, **2**, 1065
aerial advertising, **2**, 1028
aerial application certificate—
  issue of, **2**, 963
  purposes of, **2**, 963
aerial photography etc by, **2**, 975; **14**, 2086
air force, *see* AIR FORCE
air piracy—
  jurisdiction respecting, **2**, 1035
air traffic control rules, **2**, 969
air transport, *see* AIR TRANSPORT; CIVIL AVIATION
air travel organiser, *see* AIR TRAVEL ORGANISER
airports, *see* AIRPORT
airworthiness, **2**, 959
articles etc, dropping from, **2**, 961
assembly of persons, flying over, **2**, 970
aviation fuel—
  dripping from aircraft, **2**, 1020
  installations on aerodromes, **2**, 974
  venting, regulation of, **2**, 1026
banner towing by, **2**, 1028
births on, registration, **2**, 1064
board, customs officers' power to, **7**, 1240
broadcasting from, suppression of, **17**, 9
certificate of airworthiness, **2**, 959
charter, kinds of, **2**, 1050
choice of law provisions, **17**, 300
civil aviation, **6**, 1046
commander—
  authority of, **2**, 967
  powers of, **2**, 1049
common travel area, journeys outwith, **12**, 133
conduct committed in, extradition procedure, **12**, 515
confiscation by customs officials, **7**, 1225

Aircraft—*continued*
crew—
  drunkenness etc of, **2**, 966
  immigration control, **12**, 129, 195, 196
  meaning, **16**, 1208*n*
  offences by, **2**, 976
  orders respecting, **2**, 960
  UK, entry for temporary shore leave, **16**, 1208
criminal law, application of, **2**, 1047
customs and excise airport, **7**, 1239
customs and excise report, **7**, 1142
damage to property, **2**, 1020
damaging, offences of, **2**, 1031
dangerous—
  articles, carrying, **2**, 1033
  flying, penalty, **2**, 1027
  goods, carriage of, **2**, 965
dangerous occurrences—
  mandatory reporting scheme—
    duties under, **2**, 1019
    objectives of, **2**, 1019
death on, registration, **2**, 1064
delict involving, **17**, 300
deportee, removal by, **12**, 212
design, standards of, **2**, 959
detention, customs' officers power of, **7**, 1240
detention—
  orders providing for, **2**, 954
  patent claims, on, **2**, 1062
  unpaid charges, for, **2**, 1060, 1061
detention of passenger for examination, **12**, 167
diligence against, **8**, 329
dropping of articles etc from, **2**, 961
drunkenness in, **2**, 966
emergency powers as to, **2**, 902
endangering, offence of, **2**, 966
engineers, licensing of, **2**, 959
engines, certification of, **2**, 1026
entry, powers of in relation to Food and Drugs (Scotland) Act 1956 ..., **11**, 340
entry control requirements, **12**, 161
European Union transit procedures, **7**, 1173
examination of goods loaded into, **7**, 1214
explosives, byelaws as to, **10**, 1613
Export of Goods (Control) Order 1994 ..., **7**, 1194
export procedure, clearance outwards, **7**, 1161
firearms and ammunition as part of equipment, **10**, 1541
flight prevention, customs officers' powers, **7**, 1240
flight regulations, **2**, 972
flying—
  dangerous, penalty, **2**, 1027
  minimum height for, **2**, 970
  prohibition or restriction, **2**, 972
foreign operator, carriage by, **2**, 986
fuel, excise duty, **7**, 1067
fuel for, control as to, **2**, 974
goods exported by, time of exportation, **7**, 1155
goods imported by, time of importation, **7**, 1141
Hague Convention on Unlawful Seizure of Aircraft, **12**, 508

Aircraft—*continued*
hijacking, **7**, 362; **19**, 678, 695, 695*n*
　jurisdiction as to, **2**, 1035
　offence of, **2**, 1030
　penalty, **2**, 1030
hunting deer from, **11**, 941
immigrants, entry of, **19**, 510, 512
infectious diseases, regulations as to, **2**, 939; **19**, 491, 492, 494, 497
lease of, **2**, 1050
lights and signals on, **2**, 969
live deer, transport of, **11**, 941
lost or abandoned property on, **16**, 1819*n*
low flying, **2**, 653
　restrictions on, **2**, 970
marine fuel, import, VAT regulations, **7**, 1314
marking of, **2**, 957
military—
　damaging, **2**, 1031
　noise, **9**, 1286
　remains—
　　designation of, **2**, 1071
　　protection of, **2**, 1071
Montreal Convention for the Suppression of Unlawful Acts against the Safety of Civil Aviation, **12**, 508
mortgage—
　bankruptcy of mortgagor, **2**, 1055
　default—
　　circumstances constituting, **2**, 1055
　　powers of sale on, **2**, 1056
　　proceeds of sale, application of, **2**, 1057
　　warrant for possession, **2**, 1058
　generally, **20**, 28
　jurisdiction relating to, **2**, 1059
　power to create, **2**, 1051
　priorities, **2**, 1051
　register—
　　error in, correction, **2**, 1053
　　maintenance of, **2**, 1053
　　rectification, **4**, 81
　registration of, **2**, 1051
　scope of, in Scotland, **2**, 1054
　security, for, **2**, 1051
movements—
　control rules, **2**, 969
　limitation of, **2**, 922
munitions of war, carrying, **2**, 964
navigation, *see* AIR NAVIGATION
noise and vibration, *see* NOISE
nuisance, liability for, **2**, 1020
occupier's liability, **15**, 321
offences—
　acts of violence, **2**, 1037
　air piracy, **2**, 1035
　commander's powers, **2**, 1049
　conventions, created by, **2**, 1029
　criminal law, application of, **2**, 1047
　damaging aircraft, **2**, 1031
　dangerous articles, as to, **2**, 1033
　extradition crimes, **2**, 1036
　firearms etc, carrying, **2**, 1033
　generally, **2**, 653; **6**, 867
　hijacking, **2**, 1030, 1035

Aircraft—*continued*
offences—*continued*
　intended, suspicion of, **2**, 1034
　jurisdiction of courts, **2**, 1035
　offenders, extradition of, **2**, 1048
　powers of commander, **2**, 1049
　restraint of offenders, **2**, 1049
operational ground staff, permit-free employment, **12**, 247
overflight—
　high seas, freedom of, over, **21**, 41
　right of—
　　exclusive economic zone, **21**, 39
　　straits used for international navigation, **21**, 10
owner—
　duties of, **2**, 958
　liability of, **12**, 161
　new, notification of, **2**, 958
　ownership, qualifications for, **2**, 958
parts and equipment, VAT zero-rating, **7**, 1452
passengers, search of, **2**, 1040
patents, infringement of, **2**, 1062
person born on, acquisition of British citizenship, **14**, 1908
persons, dropping of, from, **2**, 962
photography carried on from, **2**, 975; **14**, 2086
piloting, age limit, **3**, 1228
piracy against, **6**, 867
prevention of terrorism powers, **12**, 133
prize jurisdiction extended to, **17**, 401, 402
public transport—
　flights deemed to be, **2**, 982
　operator's certificate, **2**, 983
　orders applying to, **2**, 982
　See also CIVIL AVIATION
registration—
　CAA as authority for, **2**, 958
　charterer, in name of, **2**, 958
　general provisions, **2**, 958
　orders providing for, **2**, 955
　requirement for, **2**, 956
rights in, **2**, 1050
　international recognition, **2**, 1063
safety—
　acts of violence affecting, **2**, 1031, 1037
　byelaws, **2**, 933
　commander's powers, **2**, 1049
　directions by Minister, **2**, 1039
　endangering—
　　articles carried, by, **2**, 1033
　　generally, **2**, 966
　　offence of, **2**, 1031
　　sheriff's jurisdiction, **2**, 1031, 1032
　　suspicion of intent, **2**, 1034
　searches, requirement for, **2**, 1039
　taking or killing wild birds in interests of, **11**, 883
sale of—
　mortgage default, on, **2**, 1056
　unpaid charges, for, **2**, 1060, 1061
salvage provisions, **2**, 1065; **21**, 439
　payment of salvage, **17**, 426
search, customs officers' powers of, **7**, 1228

Aircraft—*continued*
security—
  inspection in respect of, **2**, 1045
  measures for, direction to take, **2**, 1041
seizure, exemption from, **2**, 1062
services in connection with, VAT zero-rating, **7**, 1452
sheriff court jurisdiction, **6**, 1081
smoke emissions, **2**, 1026
smoking in, **2**, 966
smuggling offence, **7**, 1234
stores for—
  surplus stores, import procedure, **7**, 1147
  VAT zero-rating, **7**, 1436
stowaways, **2**, 968
supply, VAT zero-rating, **7**, 1452
surveillance carried on from, **14**, 2086
telecommunications apparatus, **16**, 1928
temporarily within United Kingdom, patented product in, **18**, 865
temporary importation, **7**, 1194, 1315
Tokyo Convention on Offences Committed on Board Aircraft in Flight, **12**, 508; **19**, 695*n*
trades description legislation, **6**, 112
trespass by, liability for, **2**, 1020
unlawful seizure of, *see* hijacking *above*
upholstered fittings for, **19**, 421
vibration—
  operator's duties as to, **9**, 1278
  regulation of, **9**, 1277
weapons, carrying of, **2**, 964
wreck, application of law of, **2**, 1065
wreck from, **18**, 557
Aircraft and Shipbuilding Industries Arbitration Tribunal
Scottish Committee, supervision by, **23**, 911*n*
Air crew
See AIRCRAFT
Airff (inheritance feast)
udal law, **24**, 307, 308
Air Force
Air Force Act 1955—
  persons subject to, **2**, 632
  territorial application, **2**, 613
aliment or maintenance—
  deduction from pay, **2**, 766
  service of process, **2**, 769
arrest—
  outside United Kingdom, **2**, 691
  powers of, **2**, 691
arrested persons, rights of, **2**, 692
authority for, **2**, 602
auxiliary, *see* AUXILIARY AIR FORCE
billeting—
  authority for, **2**, 770
  meaning, **2**, 770
  obstruction etc of, **2**, 772
  offences, **2**, 652
  payment, right to, **2**, 772
  premises liable to, **2**, 771
  procedure, **2**, 771
births etc, registration, **2**, 778
Board, **2**, 603
composition of, **2**, 609

Air Force—*continued*
court-martial, *see* COURTS-MARTIAL
discipline, *see* ARMED FORCES
legal basis, **2**, 609
maintenance orders, **2**, 767
offences, *see* ARMED FORCES
pay, deductions from—
  aliment or maintenance, for, **2**, 767
  court order for, **2**, 766
requisitioning—
  authority for, **2**, 774
  food etc, of, **2**, 775
  offences as to, **2**, 776
  payment for, **2**, 777
  retention of vehicles, **2**, 775
Reserve, *see* AIR FORCE RESERVE
terms of service etc, **2**, 609
wills, validity, **2**, 780
women's services, **2**, 612
See also ARMED FORCES
Air Force Reserve
airmen members, **2**, 748
aliment—
  deduction from pay, **2**, 766
  service of process, **2**, 769
calling out—
  civil duties, for, **2**, 625
  home defence service, for, **2**, 752
  liability for, **2**, 749
  national emergency, in, **2**, 751
civil employment, safeguarding, **2**, 754
civil power, assisting, **2**, 625, 756
composition, **2**, 748
discharge, right to, **2**, 755
legal basis for, **2**, 611
maintenance of, **2**, 748
maintenance orders, **2**, 767
officers, **2**, 748, 750
orders and regulations, **2**, 608
pay, deductions from, **2**, 766–767
permanent service—
  call-out notice, **2**, 753
  duration of, **2**, 755
  liability for, **2**, 751
requisitioning powers, **2**, 775
Volunteer Reserve, **2**, 748
women members, **2**, 748
Air navigation
accidents, *see* AIRCRAFT
Air Traffic Control Board, functions, **2**, 1009
charges—
  liability for payment, **2**, 1010
  services, for, **2**, 1010
  unpaid, sale of aircraft for, **2**, 1061
dangerous occurrences, *see* AIRCRAFT
Eurocontrol—
  damages against, **4**, 82
  functions, **2**, 908
  provision of services by, **2**, 1010
  services, charges for, **2**, 1010
  status of, **2**, 908
installation—
  acts endangering, **2**, 1032
  acts of violence, protection from, **2**, 1037

Air navigation—*continued*
installation—*continued*
  damaging etc, **2**, 1032
  security, measures for, **2**, 1041
National Air Traffic Services—
  manning of, **2**, 1009
  services provided by, **2**, 1009
noise, control of, **9**, 1279
  See also NOISE
orders—
  aerodrome licensing, for, **2**, 910
  appeals under, **2**, 980
  Chicago Convention, giving effect to, **2**, 906, 954
  Crown, application to, **2**, 978
  detention of aircraft by, **2**, 954
  exemptions from, **2**, 978, 979
  extra-territorial effect of, **2**, 977
  matters provided for by, **2**, 954, 955
  particular matters of, **2**, 956–957
  penalties under, **2**, 970
  provisions of, **2**, 955
  public transport flights, for, **2**, 982
  purposes of, **2**, 954
  scope of, **2**, 955
  small aircraft, exemption for, **2**, 981
safety—
  acts endangering, **2**, 1032
  CAA responsibility, **2**, 903
services—
  charges for, **2**, 1010
  costs, defrayment of, **2**, 1008
  duty to provide, **2**, 1008
  Eurocontrol, by, **2**, 1010
  VAT zero-rating, **7**, 1452
United Nations agency for, **2**, 906
Air passenger duty
chargeable aircraft, **7**, 1079
chargeable passenger, **7**, 1079
offences, **7**, 1079
operator of aircraft—
  liability to pay, **7**, 1079
  registration, **7**, 1079
rate of duty, **7**, 1079
Airport
abandoned vehicles, disposal of, **2**, 937
access to, control of, **2**, 933
accommodation, special—
  provision of, **2**, 938
  Treasury grants for, **2**, 938
acquisition of land, *see* CIVIL AVIATION
advertising in, regulation of, **2**, 933
air traffic controllers, licensing, **2**, 971
aircraft movements—
  control rules, **2**, 969
  limitation of, **2**, 922
  orders restricting, **2**, 922
alcoholic liquor, permitted hours, **2**, 8, 23, 941
byelaws—
  contravention of, **2**, 933
  other than Minister, by, **2**, 933
  power to make, **2**, 933
  subject-matters, **2**, 933

Airport—*continued*
capacity—
  directions by Minister as to, **2**, 920
  not fully utilised, **2**, 922
  recommendations concerning, **2**, 920
  schemes for allocating—
    direction to make, **2**, 923
    provisions made by, **2**, 923
    submission for approval, **2**, 923
    variation or revocation, **2**, 923
charges—
  associated companies, in case of, **2**, 927
  complaints as to, **2**, 930
  conditions—
    accounts, as to—
      breach of, **2**, 932
      imposition of, **2**, 927
      mandatory, **2**, 927
      publication of, **2**, 932
      Scottish airports, for, **2**, 927
    breach of—
      criminal proceedings not to lie for, **2**, 931
      investigation by CAA, **2**, 930
      remedy for, **2**, 930
    compliance order—
      application to quash, **2**, 931
      copy for operator, **2**, 930
      effect of, **2**, 931
      enforcement of, **2**, 931
      issue of, **2**, 930
      non-compliance with, **2**, 931
      obligations under, **2**, 931
      requirements of, **2**, 930
      revocation of, **2**, 930
      validity of, **2**, 931
    discretionary—
      discrimination, as to, **2**, 928
      imposition, **2**, 928
      notification to operator of, **2**, 928
    enforcement of, **2**, 926
    imposition, **2**, 925, 926
    mandatory, **2**, 927
    maximum charges, for, **2**, 927
    modification of, **2**, 930
    period for which applied, **2**, 927
  discrimination as to, **2**, 928
  level of, artificially low, **2**, 928
  levy of, by CAA, **2**, 926
  Monopolies Commission, reference to—
    discretionary conditions, as to, **2**, 928
    procedure for, **2**, 929
    questions to be referred, **2**, 927
  noise factor, fixing by reference to, **2**, 1023
  permission to levy—
    application for, **2**, 925
    deemed permission, **2**, 925
    duration of, **2**, 925
    refusal of, **2**, 925
    requirement for, **2**, 924
    responsibility for granting, **2**, 903
  unpaid, sale of aircraft for, **2**, 1060
company, transfer of undertaking to, **14**, 450
constables, power to appoint, **16**, 1818
control areas, **12**, 161

Airport—*continued*
customs and excise, Commissioners' powers in relation to, **7**, 1239
customs and excise airport—
  designation as, **2**, 940
  landing at and departure from, **2**, 940
designated, **12**, 133, 161
  byelaws for, **2**, 933
  policing purposes, for, **2**, 934–936
duty free goods, sale of, **2**, 941
efficiency etc, promotion of, **2**, 903
historical note on, **2**, 912
infectious diseases, regulations as to, **19**, 498
licensing restrictions, exemption from, **2**, 941
liquor licensing, **2**, 8, 23, 941
local authority undertakings—
  acquisition of land for, **2**, 914
  ancillary business at, **2**, 914
  companies to operate—
    formation of, **2**, 914
  transfer schemes—
    compensation etc, provision for, **2**, 914
    direction to formulate, **2**, 914
lost property, custody etc, **2**, 933
meaning, **2**, 909
national security, interests of, **2**, 919
noise and vibration, *see* AERODROME; NOISE
offences—
  aircraft, as to, *see* AIRCRAFT
  bodies corporate, by, **2**, 1067
operational activities—
  byelaws as to, **2**, 933
  directions by Minister, **2**, 919
  limitations as to, **2**, 922
operator—
  acquisition of land—
    authorisation for, **2**, 945
    relevant operators for, **2**, 944
    See also CIVIL AVIATION
  complaints against, **2**, 930
  directions by Minister—
    disclosure, restriction on, **2**, 919
    international obligations, as to, **2**, 919
    national security, as to, **2**, 919
    particular matters, for, **2**, 919
    procedure for giving, **2**, 919
  discrimination by, **2**, 928
  disposal of land by, **2**, 946
  international obligations, discharge of, **2**, 919
ownership, **2**, 912
policing—
  accommodation and facilities for, **2**, 934
  constables for, **2**, 934
  general powers as to, **2**, 935
  payments for, **2**, 934
  stopping and search, **2**, 935
  thefts, prevention, **2**, 935
private security firms, role of, **12**, 138
public airport company—
  activities, control over, **2**, 913
  auditors, appointment, **2**, 917
  capital expenses, **2**, 917
  controlling authority—
    loans by, **2**, 917

Airport—*continued*
public airport company—*continued*
  controlling authority—*continued*
    meaning, **2**, 913
    officers of, restriction on employing, **2**, 915
    securities, power to acquire, **2**, 916
  directors—
    disabilities of, **2**, 915
    requirement as to, **2**, 913
  employees' share scheme, **2**, 916
  financial assistance to, **2**, 917
  formation of, **2**, 914
  investment in, **2**, 916
  loans to, **2**, 917
  meaning, **2**, 913
  property etc vesting in, **2**, 914
  securities—
    disposal etc of, **2**, 916
    transfer, avoidance of restrictions on, **2**, 918
  services for—
    agreement for providing, **2**, 917
    payment for, **2**, 917
  transfer schemes—
    compensation etc under, **2**, 914
    direction to formulate, **2**, 914
  winding up, meeting liability, **2**, 917
road traffic, control of, **2**, 936
safety—
  general powers as to, **2**, 950
  land, restriction on use, **2**, 949
  securing, compensation provision, **2**, 953
  See also AIRCRAFT (safety)
Scottish airports—
  Highlands and Islands Airports, owned by, **2**, 912
  orders relating to, **2**, 1068
  transferred to BAA plc, **2**, 912
security, *see* AERODROME
shops, exemption from restrictions, **2**, 941
stop and search, powers, **2**, 935
theft, prevention of, **2**, 935
traffic distribution rules—
  consultations on making, **2**, 921
  provisions made by, **2**, 921
  purposes of, **2**, 921
transfer of undertaking, **14**, 450
valuation for rating, **24**, 572
vehicular traffic—
  byelaws for, **2**, 933
  control of, **2**, 936
See also AERODROME
Air-raid protection works
relief from rating, **24**, 573
Air services
local authority, powers of, **14**, 451
Airship
aerial advertising, used for, **2**, 1028
flying of, **2**, 973
Air space
a coelo usque ad centrum principle, **18**, 198
high seas, over, **21**, 18
ownership, **18**, 198
sovereignty, **19**, 673
trespass on, **18**, 180
  See also TRESPASS

Air transport
British Railways Board, operation by, **19**, 1005
competition, European Community rules, **10**, 162
See also CIVIL AVIATION
Air travel organiser
air travel reserve fund—
    establishment, **2**, 1007
    funding of, **2**, 1007
    winding up, **2**, 1007
bond—
    fund for supplementing, **2**, 1007
    money, application of, **2**, 1006
    obligation to have, **2**, 1006
legislation, development of, **2**, 1000
licence—
    application for—
        form etc of, **2**, 1001
        procedure for determining, **2**, 1005
    exemption from holding, **2**, 1000
    false information to obtain, **2**, 1001
    refusal of, grounds for, **2**, 1001
    renewal, application for, **2**, 1001
    requirement for, **2**, 1000
    revocation, suspension etc—
        application for, **2**, 1002
        reasons to be stated, **2**, 1005
        unfitness of holder, for, **2**, 1002
    surrender for cancellation, **2**, 1002
    terms of—
        contravention of, **2**, 1000
        matters included in, **2**, 1001
    transfer of—
        circumstances for, **2**, 1004
        refusal of, **2**, 1004
    unfitness to hold—
        appeal against decision, **2**, 1003
        revocation for, **2**, 1002
stranded passengers, repatriation of, **2**, 1006
Air travel reserve fund
See AIR TRAVEL ORGANISER
Air weapon
air guns, **10**, 1521
air pistols, **10**, 1521
air rifles, **10**, 1521
carrying in public place, **10**, 1567
children and young persons—
    possession by, **3**, 1223; **10**, 1551, 1554
    sale to, **3**, 1223
drunk in possession in public place, **10**, 1567
forfeiture and disposal, **10**, 1578
generally, **10**, 1506, 1512
harpoon guns, **10**, 1521
meaning, **10**, 1521
'specially dangerous', **10**, 1521
underwater, designed to be discharged, **10**, 1521
Akrotiri, Sovereign Base Area of
British Dependent Territories citizenship, **14**, 1932
civil jurisdiction, **4**, 23
exclusion for purposes of 1982 Act, **4**, 23
Alba firma
feudal law, generally, **18**, 67
Albania
imports, European Union regulations, **7**, 1029

Alcohol and alcoholic beverages
See ALCOHOLIC LIQUOR
Alcoholic liquor
advertising, **6**, 93
airport—
    liquor licensing, **2**, 8, 23
    permitted hours, **2**, 23, 941
alcoholism, *see* ALCOHOLISM
appeal—
    appealable decisions, **2**, 86
    competent parties to, **2**, 85
    Court of Session, to—
        point of law, on, **2**, 93
        right of, **2**, 85
    disposal of, **2**, 93
    evidence, when heard, **2**, 92
    grounds of—
        error in law, **2**, 88
        generally, **2**, 87
        incorrect material facts, **2**, 89
        natural justice, **2**, 90
        unreasonable exercise of discretion, **2**, 91
    House of Lords, to, **2**, 85
    point of law, on, **2**, 85, 93
    powers of sheriff in, **2**, 93
    procedure as to, **2**, 92
    right of, generally, **2**, 85
    time for lodging, **2**, 92
athletic club, permitted hours, variation of, **2**, 20
betting and gaming—
    licence applications, **2**, 57
    licensed premises, on, **2**, 76
British Code of Advertising Practice, **6**, 93
building control certificate, requirement for, **2**, 45
business—
    categories of, **2**, 8
    wholesale, operation of, **2**, 9
byelaws, **2**, 72
children—
    bars, not allowed in, **2**, 74
    clubs, not allowed in, **2**, 74
    licensed premises, on, **3**, 1227
    purchase by, **10**, 1126
    refreshment places, admittance to, **2**, 14
    supply to, **3**, 1227
    under five, **3**, 1227; **10**, 1135
church—
    licensing objections by, **2**, 49
closure order, *see* licensed premises *below*
club—
    accounts etc, **2**, 30
    age for admission to, **2**, 30
    athletic, **2**, 20
    bona fide, certification, **2**, 27
    category of, **2**, 17
    certification of registration—
        duration of, **2**, 27
        grant by sheriff, **2**, 27
    children not allowed in, **2**, 74
    committee—
        members, liability of, **2**, 31
        rules as to, **2**, 30
    employees, minimum age, **2**, 74

Alcoholic liquor—*continued*
club—*continued*
  licence—
    alteration of, **2**, 32
    registration in lieu of, **2**, 8
  offences, liability for, **2**, 31
  permitted hours, *see* permitted hours *below*
  police powers of entry, **2**, 68
  register of, **2**, 28
  registration—
    application for—
      procedure, **2**, 37
      statement to accompany, **2**, 29
    certification of, **2**, 27
    rules qualifying for, **2**, 30
  rules—
    lodging of, **2**, 29, 30
    requirements as to, **2**, 30
  sale and supply of liquor in, generally, **19**, 1229
  unregistered, sale etc of liquor in, **2**, 80
company, application for licence by, **2**, 41
confectionery, alcoholic liquor in, sale of, **2**, 80
Court of Session, licensing appeals to, **2**, 85, 93
criminal aspects, *see* offences *below*
diluted, **11**, 349
drink driving offences—
  being in charge of motor vehicle under influence, **20**, 417, 417*n*, 419, 420
    defence to charge, **20**, 417
    penalties, **20**, 417
    police powers, **20**, 417
  blood test, *see* BLOOD TESTS
  breath test, *see* BREATH TEST
  careless driving under influence, death caused by, **20**, 416
    obligatory disqualification following conviction, **20**, 453
  in charge, definition, **20**, 420
  disqualification following, **20**, 415, 453
  driver, definition, **20**, 420
  driving or attempting to drive with excess alcohol, **20**, 412, 419
    obligatory disqualification following conviction, **20**, 453
    service personnel, **20**, 432
  driving under influence, **20**, 417, 417*n*
    defence to charge, **20**, 417
    penalties, **20**, 417
    police powers, **20**, 417
  evidence in proceedings—
    back calculation of accused's alcohol level, **20**, 429*n*
    blood and urine specimens, **20**, 429, 431
    detention, **20**, 432
    documentary, **20**, 430
    proportion of alcohol in specimen, **20**, 429, 429*n*
  generally, **20**, 419
  reckless or dangerous driving, causing death by, **20**, 412
  road or other public place—
    being in charge of motor vehicle, **20**, 419, 420
    definition, **20**, 420

Alcoholic liquor—*continued*
drink driving offences—*continued*
  unfitness to drive, test of, **20**, 417
  urine test for, *see* URINE TEST
drunkenness—
  decrease in, **2**, 99
  licence holder, of, **2**, 75
  measures to curb, **2**, 1
  offences relating to, **2**, 75
  See also INTOXICATION
duties, **19**, 1543
entertainment, places of—
  licence, **2**, 15
  meaning, **2**, 15
  noise, control of, **2**, 47, 98
  opening hours restriction order, **2**, 65
  permitted hours, **2**, 15, 18
  six-day licences, **2**, 21
excisable, premises licensed for sale of, tenure, **11**, 1937, 1943
excise law—
  Alcoholic Liquor Duties Act 1979 ..., **7**, 1061
  alcoholic liquor used as an ingredient, **7**, 1061
  beer, **7**, 1061, 1061*n*
    producers, registration, **7**, 1066
  black beer, **7**, 1061*n*
  chocolate, alcohol ingredient in, **7**, 1061
  cider, **7**, 1061, 1061*n*
    producers, registration, **7**, 1066
  compounded spirits, **7**, 1062, 1062*n*
  deferred payment of duty, **7**, 1088
  denatured alcoholic liquor, **7**, 1061
  European Union, **7**, 1035, 1036
  food, alcohol ingredient in, **7**, 1061
  forfeiture, **7**, 1225
  low alcohol beverages, **7**, 1061
  made-wine, **7**, 1061, 1061*n*
    licence to produce, **7**, 1066
  perry, **7**, 1061
  spirits, **7**, 1061, 1061*n*
    licence to manufacture, **7**, 1066
  vinegar, **7**, 1061
  wine, **7**, 1061, 1061*n*
    licence to produce, **7**, 1066
fire safety, provisions for, **2**, 48
food hygiene certificate, requirement for, **2**, 46
goods for domestic production, VAT, **7**, 1445
hotel—
  food hygiene certificate, **2**, 46
  licence—
    offences as to, **2**, 80
    restricted, purposes of, **2**, 12
    sales allowed by, **2**, 11
    See also HOTELKEEPER
  meals, liquor sales as ancillary to, **2**, 12
  meaning, **2**, 11
  occasional licence for, **2**, 25
  permitted hours—
    drinking-up time, **2**, 19
    generally, **2**, 11, 18
  restricted licence, purposes, **2**, 12
  six-day licences, **2**, 21
  sleeping accommodation requirement, **2**, 11
inn, public house, deemed to be, **2**, 9

Alcoholic liquor—*continued*
intoxication *see* INTOXICATION
justice of the peace court legislation, **6**, 1077, 1159
labelling, **11**, 383, 391, 395
legal capacity of person under influence of, **15**, 662
legislation—
  Clayson Commission proposals, **2**, 2
  earliest, **2**, 1
  successful results of, **2**, 99
  war-time, **2**, 1
licence—
  airports, for, **2**, 8, 23
  alterations, application for, **2**, 32
  appeals in respect of, **2**, 58
  application—
    fees, **2**, 6
    renewed, time for, **2**, 61
    See also licensing board *below*
  categories of, **2**, 8
  company name, in, **2**, 41
  complaints, who may make, **2**, 62
  conditions—
    attachment of, **2**, 16, 24, 25
    breach of, **2**, 70
  currency of, **2**, 58
  death, transfer of licence on, **2**, 35
  form of, **2**, 58
  generally, **11**, 315; **16**, 1738
  history of, **2**, 1
  hotel, *see* hotel *above*
  introduction of, **2**, 1
  issue of, **2**, 58
  local authority premises, for, **2**, 95
  objections to, *see* objections *below*
  occasional, *see* occasional licence *below*
  occasional permissions, **2**, 25
  off-sale, *see* off-sale licence *below*
  provisional grant—
    application, purposes of, **2**, 33
    duration of licence, **2**, 58
    finalised licence, duration, **2**, 33
    finality, declaration of, **2**, 33
    grant of, **2**, 34
    simpliciter, application for, **2**, 33
    temporary premises, for, **2**, 34
    transfer of, **2**, 35
  refreshment, *see* refreshment licence *below*
  refusal of—
    appeal against, *see* appeal *above*
    grounds of, **2**, 53
  restaurant, *see* restaurant *below*
  seamen's canteen, *see* seamen's canteen *below*
  seasonal, **2**, 22
  site only licence—
    application for, procedure, **2**, 33
    full licence, becoming, **2**, 33
  six-day licences, **2**, 21
  suitability of premises for, **2**, 43
  suspension, **2**, 62
  transfer of—
    death etc, on, **2**, 35
    duration of licence on, **2**, 58
    forms of, **2**, 35

Alcoholic liquor—*continued*
licence—*continued*
  transfer of—*continued*
    refusal to allow, **2**, 53
    sale of premises, on, **2**, 35
    temporary, duration of, **2**, 61
  types of, **2**, 8
  wrongly obtained, voidance of, **2**, 61
licensed premises, *see* LICENSED PREMISES
licensing—
  authority, **14**, 516
  boards, *see* licensing boards *below*
  certificates, **2**, 1
  Clayson Committee report, **2**, 2
  controls—
    development of, **2**, 1
    relaxation, proposals for, **2**, 2
  development of, **2**, 1
  generally, **11**, 315; **14**, 516
  historical survey of, **2**, 1
  local authority premises, **2**, 95
  offences, *see* offences *below*
licensing boards—
  accommodation to be provided for, **2**, 5
  alteration of premises—
    consent required for, **2**, 36, 64
    control of, **2**, 36
    offences respecting, **2**, 71
    structural, order for, **2**, 64, 71
  applications to—
    building control certificate for, **2**, 45
    club registration, **2**, 37
    companies, by, **2**, 41
    consideration of—
      postponement of, **2**, 56
      procedure, **2**, 57
    contents, **2**, 37
    details of licence required, **2**, 37
    fees payable, **2**, 6, 37
    forms of, **2**, 37
    gaming etc licence, for, **2**, 57
    inspection of, **2**, 40
    list of, publication, **2**, 43
    not entertained, when, **2**, 57
    notice of, **2**, 40
    objection to, *see* objections *below*
    order in which taken, **2**, 57
    plans to be lodged, **2**, 38
    postponement of consideration, **2**, 56
    procedure, **2**, 37
    processing, **2**, 37
    referees, requirement for, **2**, 37
    refusal of—
      extensions, for, **2**, 54
      grounds of, **2**, 53–55
      misconduct, for, **2**, 53
      new application after, **2**, 61
      Sunday opening, **2**, 55
    register of, decisions entered in, **2**, 57
    regulations for, **2**, 39
    suitability of premises for, **2**, 43
    Sunday opening, for, **2**, 40
    types of, **2**, 32–36
    who may lodge, **2**, 37

Alcoholic liquor—*continued*
licensing boards—*continued*
casual vacancy, filling, **2**, 3
chairman, election of, **2**, 3
clerk to, **2**, 3; **13**, 1449
closure orders—
grounds for, **2**, 63
period of, **2**, 63, 67
power to make, **2**, 63
complaints—
notice as to, **2**, 62
substance, without, **2**, 62
who may make, **2**, 62
composition of, **2**, 3
convictions to be notified to, **2**, 81
decisions of—
appeal from, *see* appeal *above*
incorrect facts, based on, **2**, 89
registration of, **2**, 57
written reasons for, **2**, 59
delegation of functions, **2**, 5
error in law by, **2**, 88
expenses, defrayment, **2**, 5
fire authority, consultation with, **2**, 48
hearings in public, **2**, 5, 90
issue of licences, **2**, 58
jurisdiction, **2**, 7
licences for which responsible, **2**, 7
meetings—
adjournment of, **2**, 56
applicant to attend, **2**, 56
complainers may attend, **2**, 62
complaints, to hear, **2**, 62
objections, to hear, **2**, 52
objectors to attend, **2**, 56
periods for holding, **2**, 5, 37
quorum for, **2**, 5
voting at, **2**, 57
members—
allowances to, **2**, 3
canvassing support of, **2**, 69
company shares, holding, **2**, 4, 69
persons disqualified as, **2**, 4, 69
qualification of, **2**, 3
term of office, **2**, 3
objection notice to, **2**, 50
police, consultation with, **2**, 48
proceedings, public, to be in, **2**, 5, 90
regulations, power to make, **2**, 39
statutory provision for, **2**, 3
suspension of licences, **2**, 62
temporary restriction orders, **2**, 66
liquor licence, grant, **16**, 1738
local authority, premises, licensing of, **2**, 95
meaning, **2**, 9
medical advice as to consumption, **11**, 1446
misconduct, **2**, 62
new town, licensed premises, **2**, 17
noise, control of, **2**, 47, 98
objections—
abandoned, when deemed to be, **2**, 52
appeals in respect of, **2**, 86
chief constable, by, **2**, 50
competency to make, **2**, 49

Alcoholic liquor—*continued*
objections—*continued*
frivolous etc, expenses, liability for, **2**, 51
invitations to make, **2**, 49
meetings to consider, **2**, 56
notice—
applicant, to, **2**, 50
lodging of, **2**, 50
time for giving, **2**, 50
unauthorised, liability as to, **2**, 51
occasional licence—
application for, **2**, 24
breach of conditions, **2**, 70
duration of, **2**, 24
effect of, **2**, 25
functions etc for grant of, **2**, 25
hotel or restaurant, for, **2**, 25
one-day occasions, **2**, 24
off-sale licence—
application for, **2**, 38
authorisation given by, **2**, 10
increase in, **2**, 9
permitted hours, **2**, 18, 19
premises—
alterations to, **2**, 36
drinking in, forbidden, **2**, 79
special trading hours for, **2**, 80
Sunday trading barred, **2**, 18
supermarkets, **2**, 10
trading hours, **2**, 18, 80
offences—
administration of Act, as to, **2**, 69
alteration of premises, as to, **2**, 64, 71
byelaws, against, **2**, 72
closure order, against, **2**, 67
clubs, by, **2**, 68
criminal activities in licensed premises, **2**, 76
drink driving, *see* drink driving offences *above*
drinking etc by police officers, **2**, 78
drunkenness, relating to, **2**, 75
frequenters of premises, by, **2**, 62
illegal drinking on premises, **2**, 77
licence conditions, breach of, **2**, 70
miscellaneous, **2**, 79, 80
misconduct of licensee, **2**, 62
name etc, refusal to give, **2**, 68
permitted hours, relating to, **2**, 73
presumption in respect of, **2**, 83
punishment, *see* punitive aspects *below*
sale of drink, relating to, **2**, 79
sales to persons under eighteen, **2**, 74
serious consequences of, **2**, 60
statutory, number of, **2**, 60
trial of, **2**, 81
unauthorised liquor, serving, **2**, 70
under-age drinking, **2**, 74
passenger vessels, sale of liquor on, **2**, 79
permitted hours—
athletic clubs, **2**, 20
consumption outwith, **2**, 19
drinking-up time, **2**, 19
entertainment, places of, **2**, 15
exceptions from, **2**, 20

Alcoholic liquor—*continued*
permitted hours—*continued*
  extension—
    conditions attached, **2**, 24
    differing interpretation as to, **2**, 24
    permitted periods, **2**, 20
  flexibility, proposals for, **2**, 2
  general provisions, **2**, 18
  hotels, **2**, 11, 18; **11**, 1775–1777
  introduction of system, **2**, 1
  licensee entertaining friends outwith, **2**, 19
  limitation of, by board, **2**, 20
  occasional extensions, **2**, 54
  offences respecting, **2**, 73
  outwith—
    sales, **2**, 19
    supply in emergency, **2**, 96
  reduction by licensee, **2**, 18
  regular extension, **2**, 24
    refusal of, **2**, 54
  restriction order—
    appeals respecting, **2**, 65, 86
    application for revocation, **2**, 65
    duration of, **2**, 65
    grounds for, **2**, 65
    group of premises, for, **2**, 65
    power to make, **2**, 65
    procedure as to, **2**, 65
    serious consequences, **2**, 65
    temporary, **2**, 66
  sales outwith, **2**, 19
  seasonal licences, **2**, 22
  Sunday, on, **2**, 18, 55
  tourists etc, catering for, **2**, 24
  variation of, **2**, 20
person under influence of, franchise, **15**, 1082
planning permission, certificate of, **2**, 44
police—
  board consultation with, **2**, 48
  drinking etc in licensed premises, **2**, 78
  entry of licensed premises, **2**, 68
  objection notice by, **2**, 50
police, offences in relation to liquor licensing, **16**, 1812
police discipline code, **16**, 1771
proportion in blood, determination, *see* BLOOD TESTS; BREATH TEST; URINE TEST
public house—
  licence—
    airports allowed to hold, **2**, 8
    auhorisation given by, **2**, 9
    restaurants holding, **2**, 13
  meaning, **2**, 9, 18
  permitted hours, *see* permitted hours *above*
  See also licensed premises *above*
punitive aspects—
  closure orders—
    board, by, **2**, 63
    period of, **2**, 63, 67
    sheriff, by, **2**, 67
  exclusion orders, **2**, 82
  generally, **2**, 61
  penalties, level of, **2**, 84
  police, entry by, **2**, 68

Alcoholic liquor—*continued*
punitive aspects—*continued*
  restriction orders, **2**, 65
  suspension of licence, **2**, 62
  temporary restriction orders, **2**, 66
railways—
  byelaws relating to, **19**, 1272
  designated sporting events, trains from or to, **19**, 1066
refreshment licence—
  effect of, **2**, 14
  introduction of, **2**, 14
  permitted hours, **2**, 18
  premises, **2**, 14
  unpopularity of, **2**, 14
restaurant—
  age for drinking in, **2**, 13
  alcohol licence, **2**, 1
  bars in, **2**, 13
  food hygiene certificate, **2**, 46
  licence, **2**, 13
  occasional licence for, **2**, 25
  permitted hours, **2**, 18
  planning permission, **2**, 44
  public house licence for, **2**, 13
restriction order, *see* permitted hours *above*
revenue trader's premises, powers of entry and search, **7**, 1252
roadside test for, **20**, 418
Royal commission—
  deliberation on law, **2**, 1
sale and supply—
  clubs, in, **19**, 1229
  generally, **11**, 431
  licence for, *see* licensing *above*
  liquor supplied not of kind demanded, **11**, 349
  North Sea limits, within, **11**, 129
  offences relating to, **2**, 79
  passenger vessel, on, **2**, 79
  Sunday, on, **2**, 15
  theatres, in, **2**, 26
seamen's canteen—
  licence—
    breach of conditions, **2**, 70
    conditions, power to attach, **2**, 16
    grant and effect of, **2**, 16
  meaning of canteen, **2**, 16
  permitted hours, **2**, 18
  provision of, **2**, 16
  statutory provision for, **2**, 16
sheriff—
  appeals to, *see* appeal *above*
  closure order by, **2**, 67
  protection from proceedings, **2**, 81
  social policy, effect of, **14**, 1220
sporting events, **19**, 1269–1272
  trains to or from, **19**, 1066
Sunday—
  extension of hours, **2**, 20
  opening, refusal of, **2**, 55
  permitted hours, **2**, 18
  premises permitted to open on, **2**, 1
  sale of liquor, **2**, 15
supermarkets, off-sale licences, **2**, 10

Alcoholic liquor—*continued*
temperance polls, limited provisions as to, **2**, 97
theatre, sale of liquor in, **2**, 26
vehicle or receptacle, delivered from, **11**, 315
voluntary organisations, occasional permissions
for, **2**, 25
weights and measures legislation—
beer, **6**, 196, 255
cider, **6**, 196, 255
generally, **6**, 193
grape must, **6**, 199
made-wine, **6**, 198
prepacked, **6**, 198, 200
spirits, **6**, 197
wine, **6**, 198, 199
yellow wine, **6**, 199
wine—
preservatives in, **11**, 377
sale in off-sales, **2**, 79
tasting, restriction on, **2**, 10
See also ALCOHOL AND ALCOHOLIC BEVERAGES
Alcoholism
arrest or detention, **12**, 29
chronic—
defence of diminished responsibility, **7**, 133
defence of insanity, **7**, 133
nineteenth-century concern as to, **2**, 1
parent or guardian, **3**, 1267
sickness benefit, whether entitlement to, **21**, 879,
888
Alderney
inland bill, nature of, **4**, 120
Alibi
false, concocting, **7**, 496
Alien
accommodation of, **11**, 1723, 1730*n*
allegiance, **14**, 1901
alien outwith realm, **7**, 582
alien within realm, **7**, 581
armorial bearings, grant of, **6**, 1017
British armed forces—
incitement of, **7**, 599
serving in, **7**, 598*n*
Calvo Clause, **19**, 742
creation of trust by, **24**, 14
disqualification from voting in election, **5**, 374
enemy, as partner, **16**, 1014
entry of, see IMMIGRATION
exclusion from membership of House of
Commons, **5**, 379
heritage, acquiring, **6**, 1017
Irish Republic, citizen of, **14**, 1901
land, permitted to hold, **14**, 1901
meaning, **14**, 1956
partner, as, **16**, 1014
political activity of, **12**, 6
prisoner, as—
deportation, **16**, 1430
representative of diplomatic services, visit by,
16, 1460
treatment, **16**, 1430
public office, permitted to take, **14**, 1901
statutory restrictions, **24**, 132
trustee, as, **24**, 132

Alienation
automatism, **7**, 122
Cardle v Mulrainey, **7**, 122
insanity, **7**, 114, 121, 122
Alienum non laedas
maxim, fundamental principle governing nuisance
law, **14**, 2038
Aliment
action for, **6**, 1062; **19**, 1579, 1581
adopted children, **10**, 1240–1242
agreement on, **10**, 851, 1258
alimentary funds, arrestment, **8**, 280
amount—
arbitration as to, **2**, 413
generally, **10**, 849
armed forces, arrangements for, **2**, 766, 769
arrestment, warrants for, **10**, 986
arrestment of earnings, and, **8**, 330
avoidance transactions, order relating to, **10**, 985
child, rights of—
generally, **10**, 951, 1229
independent right, **10**, 968, 969
claims barred by sequestration, **2**, 1414
cohabitee, child of, **10**, 1009, 1217, 1247
debtor, due from, **2**, 1385
deceased person, claims from estate of, **10**, 847,
1250
decree of divorce or separation refused, **10**, 988
deduction from service pay, **2**, 766, 767
defences to claim, **10**, 852, 1254
discharge of obligation—
illegitimate children, **10**, 1236
legitimate children, **10**, 1233
duration of obligation—
illegitimate children, **10**, 1238
legitimate children, **10**, 1232
ex jure representationis obligation, **10**, 1234
executors' obligations, **10**, 1250
extent of obligation, **10**, 1252
factors to be taken into account, **10**, 1253
failure to provide, **3**, 1246
form of award, **10**, 848
generally, **10**, 1248; **17**, 1237; **19**, 1581
husband's obligation, **10**, 847
illegitimate children, **10**, 1177, 1235–1239
imprisonment for debt, **8**, 349
inhibition, warrants for, **10**, 986
inhibition used on dependence of action for, **8**,
136
interim, **10**, 847, 850, 988
legacy for, **25**, 834, 836, 847
legitimate children, **10**, 1230–1234
meaning, **10**, 847
minute relating to, **17**, 1035
mistress, former, payment to, **15**, 767
nature of, **10**, 1249
negotiorum gestor, **15**, 98, 116
obligation of, **10**, 1251; **17**, 1237
orders available, **10**, 1255
parental right of, abolition, **10**, 1259, 1261, 1262
parent's obligations—
generally, **10**, 847, 1250; **15**, 2, 4*n*
illegitimate children, **10**, 1235
legitimate children, **10**, 1230

Aliment—*continued*
pendente lite, **10**, 847
procedural matters, **10**, 1256
process, service of, **2**, 769
quantification, **10**, 1252
   illegitimate children, **10**, 1237
   legitimate children, **10**, 1231
recall of decree, **10**, 853, 1257
relatives' obligations—
   generally, **10**, 1250
   illegitimate children, **10**, 1239
   legitimate children, **10**, 1230
resources, provision of details of, **10**, 987
separation agreements, **10**, 939
sheriff court's jurisdiction in action of, **4**, 5
small amount, of, action for, **17**, 1329
stepchildren, **10**, 1217, 1220, 1243–1246
successors to estate of persons owing, **10**, 847, 1250
surviving spouse's right to, **25**, 711
taxation, **19**, 1579, 1581
trusts—
   alimentary liferent, **24**, 81, 82
   alimentary provisions, **24**, 6, 80, 81
   alimentary rights, **24**, 70, 75
variation of decree, **10**, 853, 1257
wife's obligations, **10**, 847
See also CHILD-CHILDREN; DIVORCE (financial provision on)

Alison, Archibald
authoritative writings—
   Practice of Criminal Law of Scotland, **22**, 441
   Principles of the Criminal Law of Scotland, **7**, 2; **22**, 441

Alkali, *see* POLLUTION

Alleged trustee
title of, **24**, 27

Allegiance
aliens—
   outwith realm, **7**, 582
   within realm, **7**, 581
armed forces, incitement to disaffection, **7**, 598, 598*n*
British citizens, **7**, 579
British subjects not British citizens, **7**, 580
Commonwealth country, citizen of, **14**, 1902
concept of, **14**, 1901
Crown, duty of citizen to, **16**, 1213
generally, **7**, 578
land, power to hold, **14**, 1901
oath or affirmation of, **7**, 706
oath of, evidence, **14**, 1957
public office, power to hold, **14**, 1901

Alley
use of term replaced by road, **20**, 609

Allocation
conveyancing, feudation, of—
   generally, **6**, 529
   methods of obtaining, **6**, 530
   notice of, **6**, 531
   statutory right of, **6**, 531

Allodial ownership
feudal tenure contrasted, **18**, 47
origin of term, **18**, 47*n*

Allodial ownership—*continued*
positive prescription, **16**, 2107
transfer of, **18**, 646
udal law, generally, **18**, 44, 47, 47*n*

Allotment
acquisition of land for purposes of—
   appropriation, **13**, 540
   compulsory acquisition, **13**, 538
   generally, **13**, 537
   land acquired for other purposes, use of, **13**, 540
   lease, **13**, 539
   permanent pasture, **13**, 539
   purchase, **13**, 538
allotment garden—
   crops and manure, compensation for loss of, **13**, 549, 550
   disturbance, compensation for, **13**, 549, 551
   fencing or other erection, removal on termination of tenancy, **13**, 548
   generally, **13**, 532, 533
   lease, **13**, 541
      compensation for depreciation, landlord's entitlement to, **13**, 552
      termination, **13**, 545
         compensation, rights of, **13**, 549
            exclusions, **13**, 554
            set-off, **13**, 553
         fencing or other erection, removal on, **13**, 548
         trees planted by tenant, removal on, **13**, 548
   maximum area held, **13**, 533
   meaning, **13**, 533
   trees planted by tenant, removal on termination of tenancy, **13**, 548
association, **13**, 535
   acquisition of land by, **13**, 539, 540
committee—
   appointment, **13**, 536
   duties, **13**, 536
   membership, **13**, 536
common pasture, and, **13**, 534, 541
lease—
   generally, **13**, 541
   landlord, rights and duties of, **13**, 542
   letting terms—
      making, alteration or revocation, **13**, 541
      matters covered by, **13**, 541
   rent, **13**, 541
   tenant, rights and duties of, **13**, 543
   termination—
      allotment, of, **13**, 544
         rights of parties on, **13**, 546, 547
      allotment garden, of, **13**, 545
         rights of parties on, **13**, 548–554
      compensation, rights of, **13**, 547
local government duties in relation to, **13**, 531
maximum area held, **13**, 532
meaning, **13**, 532
provision—
   generally, **13**, 531
   procedure, **13**, 535
rating relief, **24**, 460, 560

Allotment—*continued*
sheds and buildings, removal on termination of tenancy, **13**, 546
trees planted by tenant, removal on termination of tenancy, **13**, 546
Allotment society
community benefit society, as, **12**, 609
Allowing
mens rea, **7**, 103
use of term, **7**, 103
Alluvion
accession—
generally, **18**, 592
reclamation by human act, **18**, 593
requirements for, **18**, 592
advance of waters, **18**, 594
alvei mutatio, **18**, 594
avulsion compared, **18**, 592
islands, formation of, **18**, 594
meaning, **18**, 592
non-tidal waters, retreat, **18**, 594
tidal waters, retreat, **18**, 594
transmission of soil from one bank to another, **18**, 594
Almoner
office of, **7**, 800, 837, 839
Alms, tenure by
feudal law, generally, **18**, 66*n*
Almshouse
land ownership, income from, **3**, 1134
Altius non tollendi
servitude, **6**, 515
servitude right of, **18**, 486
Alvei mutatio
meaning, **18**, 594
Alveus
alteration in, right to resist, **25**, 31
building on, common interest, and, **18**, 296
common interest, doctrine of, *see* COMMON INTEREST
Crown ownership, where, **18**, 275, 518
loch, ownership, **18**, 275–277, 303, 304
non-tidal loch, **18**, 303, 305
meaning, **18**, 275
navigable water, ownership, **18**, 275
non-tidal river—
ownership of, **25**, 317
non-tidal waters—
loch, **18**, 303, 305
ownership, **18**, 275, 276
presumed pertinent, **18**, 202
operations on—
constraints on, **25**, 318
drought, **25**, 323
flood, **25**, 323
lower riparian, **25**, 319
pollution, **25**, 322
proprietor *ex adverso*, **25**, 320
salmon fisheries, **25**, 321
water supply, control of, **25**, 323
ownership—
a coelo usque ad centrum, **18**, 278, 303
boundary between two estates, river on, **18**, 278
Crown, **18**, 275

Alveus—*continued*
ownership—*continued*
islands, **18**, 278
medium filum, **18**, 278
navigable waters, **18**, 275
non-tidal waters, **18**, 275, 276, 278; **25**, 317
one estate, river within, **18**, 278
private, **18**, 275
riparian proprietor—
meaning, **18**, 278
See also RIVER
several consecutive estates, river within, **18**, 278
tidal waters, **18**, 275, 276, 309
private waters, **18**, 275
classification, generally, **18**, 277
proprietor of bank but not of *alveus*, **18**, 283
public waters, classification, generally, **18**, 277
riparian proprietor—
meaning, **18**, 278
See also RIVER
river, of, interference with, **11**, 6
tidal waters—
meaning, **18**, 276
ownership, **18**, 275, 276
Crown, **18**, 309
Ambassador
foreign, allegiance to British Crown not owed by, **7**, 581
precedence, **16**, 2014
Ambulance
excise duty exemption, **7**, 1073
National Health Service provision, **11**, 1485
Amended Jason clause
See NEW JASON CLAUSE
America
See UNITED STATES OF AMERICA
American Bureau of Shipping, 21, 120
American depositary receipt
negotiable instrument, as, **4**, 103
American Treaty on Pacific Settlement
generally **19**, 698*n*, 720*n*
Ammunition
acquisition, **10**, 1512, 1514
Crown servant, by, **10**, 1580
police officer, by, **10**, 1580
air weapons, forfeiture and disposal, **10**, 1578
blank cartridges, **10**, 1510
borrowed, **10**, 1514
bullets designed to explode on or immediately before impact, **10**, 1517
children and young persons—
gifts to, **10**, 1551, 1578
possession or use by, **3**, 1223
air weapons, ammunition for, **10**, 1551, 1554
restrictions, generally, **10**, 1550, 1552
purchase, acquisition of other form of transfer by, **10**, 1551
supply to, **3**, 1223; **10**, 1551, 1570
component ingredients, **10**, 1510
crime prevention, **10**, 1562–1573
dealers, *see* FIREARM
defective, **10**, 1510
explosive, as, **10**, 1586, 1588

Ammunition—*continued*
export, control over, **10**, 1581
firearm certificates—
    ammunition requiring, **10**, 1519, 1519*n*
    cancellation, **10**, 1578
    exemptions, **10**, 1519
        aircraft, equipment for, **10**, 1541
        antiques and trophies of war, **10**, 1542, 1542*n*
        auctioneers, **10**, 1534
        borrowed rifles on private premises, **10**, 1545
        cadet corps members, **10**, 1538
        carriers, **10**, 1534
        cinematic performances, **10**, 1539
        clubs, **10**, 1538
        Crown servants, **10**, 1543
        export, **10**, 1547
        gun bearers, **10**, 1536
        miniature rifle ranges, **10**, 1539
        museum firearms licence, **10**, 1548
        police officers, **10**, 1543
        police permits, **10**, 1544
        private premises, **10**, 1545
        race meeting starters, **10**, 1537
        registered dealers and their employees, **10**, 1533
        ships, equipment for, **10**, 1541
        shooting galleries, **10**, 1539
        shot guns, **10**, 1520, 1549
        slaughtering instruments, **10**, 1535
        theatrical performances, **10**, 1539
        visitors' permits, **10**, 1531, 1546
        warehousemen, **10**, 1534
    falling outwith, **10**, 1520
    Northern Ireland, granted in, **10**, 1582
    production of, powers to demand, **10**, 1576
    shot guns, **10**, 1520
forfeiture, **10**, 1578
gift, accepted as, **10**, 1514
    child or young person, by, **10**, 1551, 1578
hired, **10**, 1514, 1551
manufacture, **10**, 1512
meaning, **10**, 1510
movement of, control over, **10**, 1581
possession—
    child or young person by, *see* children and young persons *above*
    Crown servant, by, **10**, 1580
    generally, **10**, 1512, 1550–1554
    with intent to injure, **10**, 1563
    meaning, **10**, 1513
    police officer, by, **10**, 1580
    possession, transfer, manufacture, sale and distribution, **10**, 1504
    prohibited persons, by, **10**, 1569
preservation of public safety, **10**, 1562–1573
Prevention of Terrorism Act 1978 ..., **10**, 1563
prohibited—
    acquisition, **10**, 1518
    authority for possession, **10**, 1518
    control of, **10**, 1515
    generally, **10**, 1512
    manufacture, **10**, 1518
    meaning, **10**, 1515, 1517
    possession, **10**, 1518

Ammunition—*continued*
prohibited—*continued*
    purchase, **10**, 1518
    sale, **10**, 1518
    theatrical or cinematic performances, **10**, 1518
    transfer, **10**, 1518
prohibited persons under Firearms Acts 1968–1988 ..., **10**, 1569
    application for removal of prohibition, **10**, 1569
purchase, **10**, 1512
    meaning, **10**, 1514
sale, **10**, 1512, 1606
    child or young person to, **10**, 1551, 1570
    meaning, **10**, 1514
seizure and detention of, **10**, 1574, 1576
stop and search powers, **10**, 1574
supply—
    children and young persons, to, **10**, 1570
transfer, **10**, 1512, 1514, 1606
    child or young person to, **10**, 1551, 1570
    prohibited persons, by, **10**, 1569
warrant, search, **10**, 1574
See also EXPLOSIVES; FIREARM
Amusement arcade
admission to, **9**, 1017
electronic games, **9**, 1016
machines relating to, *see* AMUSEMENTS WITH PRIZES
meaning, **9**, 1008
non-mechanical amusements with prizes, permits for, **9**, 1014
planning controls, **23**, 91, 226
pleasure fairs distinguished from, **9**, 1008
prizes, chance of, **9**, 1008
revenue duties, **9**, 1015
See also AMUSEMENTS WITH PRIZES
Amusement machine
See AMUSEMENTS WITH PRIZES
Amusements
advertising, **1**, 531
non-mechanical, with prizes, permits for, **9**, 1014
park, permitted development, **23**, 159
Amusements with prizes
commercial entertainments, **2**, 1653
conditions for, **2**, 1653
exempt entertainments, **2**, 1652
machines—
    excise duty, **7**, 1080, 1085
    fruit, **9**, 1009
    licence duty, **2**, 1650
    maintenance of, **9**, 1011
    nature of, **2**, 1636
    offences, **9**, 1010
    part 3 machine, **9**, 1010
    permits, *see* permit *below*
    sale of, **9**, 1011
    statutory law, **9**, 1010
    supply of, **9**, 1011
    variety of, **9**, 1009
non-mechanical, permits for, **9**, 1014
permit, **14**, 517
    application for, **2**, 1654; **9**, 1012
    authority responsible for, **2**, 1654
    conditions attached to, **9**, 1012
    death of holder, **2**, 1654

Amusements with prizes—*continued*
permit—*continued*
  duration of, **2**, 1654
  forfeiture of, **2**, 1656
  grant or renewal—
    appeal in respect of, **2**, 1638, 1657; **9**, 1013
    application for, **2**, 1654; **9**, 1012
    discretionary, **2**, 1655
    non-mechanical, **9**, 1014
    refusal of, grounds for, **2**, 1655
    restriction on, **2**, 1656
  not transferable, **2**, 1654

Anaesthetic
administration of, **11**, 1446
dental service, for—
  administered by doctor or other dentist, **11**, 1450, 1456
  fees for providing, **11**, 1450
medicinal product, as, **14**, 1202

Anatomical examination
authorisation, **3**, 507
cremation following, **3**, 559
fatal accident inquiry, where likelihood of, **3**, 507
Her Majesty's Inspector of Anatomy for Scotland, **3**, 507
licensing premises used for, **3**, 507
post-mortem examination, where likelihood of, **3**, 507
records, **3**, 507
specimens, **3**, 507
wishes of deceased, **3**, 507

Anchored vessel
lights and shapes to be displayed, **21**, 368
sound signals, **21**, 374

Anchoring
emergency, in, **21**, 379
innocent passage, right of, **21**, 6
narrow channel or fairway, in, **21**, 347
natural harbours, in, **11**, 1304
navigation rules, **21**, 380
non-tidal river, in, **25**, 307
sheriff, jurisdiction of, **4**, 2
territorial sea, in, **21**, 6

Ancient monuments
Ancient Monuments Board for Scotland, **9**, 1225
compulsory purchase order exemption, **11**, 634
expenditure on, **9**, 1226
generally, **9**, 1217
guardianship of, **9**, 1223
land, information as to interests in, **9**, 1229
legislation concerning, building standards and, **3**, 244
metal detectors, offences, **9**, 1228
offences, **9**, 1221, 1228
preservation of, **9**, 1221
public control, under, public access to, **9**, 1224
scheduled monument consent, **9**, 1222

Ancient Order of Forresters, 12, 679*n*

Ancillary credit business
advertising in relation to, **5**, 830
canvassing, **5**, 833
examples, **5**, 816
meaning, **5**, 816
offences relating to, **5**, 831

Ancillary dental workers
See DENTISTRY

Anglers
representation on district salmon fisheries boards, **11**, 35, 37

Anglican Communion
Scottish Episcopal Church, relationship to, **3**, 1614, 1617

Angling right
not accessory to agricultural tenancy, **11**, 49

Anguilla
British Dependent Territories citizenship, **14**, 1932

Animal
abandoned—
  claim to, time for, **2**, 104
  cruelty, abandonment as, **2**, 247
  detention, **2**, 106, 167
  disposal—
    methods, **2**, 104
    subsequent claim by owner, **2**, 104
  dogs, *see* DOG
  finder, duties of, **2**, 104
  ownership of lost or abandoned animal, **18**, 547*n*, 549
  statutory rules as to, **2**, 104
  straying on land, **2**, 106
  unclaimed—
    disposal of, **2**, 104
    offered to finder, **2**, 104
accession of, **18**, 570, 595, 596
aggressive conduct urged by human handler, **7**, 213
annoyance caused by, **2**, 171
anthrax, **19**, 478
attack by, Criminal Injuries Compensation Scheme, **7**, 8
beneficiary of trust, as, **24**, 115, 118
blood sports, **19**, 1275
boarding establishments, *see* ANIMAL BOARDING ESTABLISHMENT
breeding establishments, *see* ANIMAL BREEDING ESTABLISHMENT
captive, meaning, **9**, 1030
carcases—
  disposal of, **11**, 317
  importation and landing, **11**, 317
  inspection of, **11**, 413
care of, **14**, 1665
cetaceous—
  Slaughter of Animals (Scotland) Act 1980 not applicable to, **11**, 496
child under age of twelve, sale to, **3**, 1222
circuses, **19**, 1295
civil liability for loss etc caused by, *see* injury or damage by *below*
classification, **2**, 102
conveyance of—
  air and sea, by, **2**, 203
    express terms in bill of lading, **21**, 546
  cruelty in course of, **2**, 241
  feeding and watering, **2**, 202
  records in respect of, **2**, 204
  road and rail, by, **2**, 202
  vehicles etc, construction, **2**, 202

Animal—*continued*
cruelty to, **7**, 104, 420
  abandonment as, **2**, 247
  action held to be, **2**, 240
  arrest of persons for, **2**, 250
  badgers, protection for, **2**, 273
  baiting as, **2**, 242
  cockfighting, **2**, 271
  conveyance, in course of, **2**, 241
  conviction of, effect, **2**, 249
  destruction of injured animal—
      court order for, **2**, 249
      veterinary surgeon's direction, **2**, 250
  docking and nicking horses, **2**, 272
  dog, use to draw cart etc, **2**, 244
  exceptions from provisions, **2**, 248
  farrier convicted of, **2**, 158
  fighting animals, **2**, 242
  laws relating to, **2**, 239, 240
  offences—
      disqualification for keeping dog, **2**, 249
      proceedings for, **2**, 250
  offenders, arrest of, **2**, 250
  operations, in—
      permitted, **2**, 246
      prohibited, **2**, 246
      veterinary surgeons, by, **2**, 246
  painful experiments, *see* scientific procedures
      below
  passive capacity, **11**, 1045
  performing animals, **9**, 1031
  permitted operations, **2**, 246
  poisoning, offence of, **2**, 243
  police powers, **2**, 250
  prohibition generally, **2**, 246
  scientific procedures, *see* scientific procedures
      below
  Scottish common law, **2**, 239
  spring traps, use of, **2**, 245
  training, during, **2**, 267
  veterinary surgeon, powers, **2**, 250
  video recordings depicting, **2**, 270
  what constitutes, **2**, 240
damage by, *see* injury or damage by *below*
dangerous or annoying creatures, **19**, 372
dangerous wild animals, keeping, *see* WILD
    ANIMALS
defence against, **13**, 91
defence of, **13**, 91
definition, **2**, 177
destructive—
  importation control, **2**, 218
  offences respecting, **2**, 218
  unlawfully imported, seizure of, **2**, 218
diseases, *see* ANIMAL HEALTH
dogs, *see* DOG
domestic—
  ownership, **2**, 103
  swans, as, **2**, 109
  theft of, **2**, 103
endangered species, *see* ENDANGERED SPECIES
evidence, as, **10**, 620
experiments on, advertising, **1**, 529

Animal—*continued*
exportation—
  animal products, **7**, 1194
  certification for, **25**, 206
  endangered species, **2**, 215–217, 228; **7**, 1197
  examination before, **2**, 219
  farm animals, **2**, 227
  horses, *see* HORSE
  live animals, **7**, 1194
  ponies, *see* PONY
  regulation of, generally, **2**, 219
  restrictions, generally, **7**, 1201
  sheep affected by Chernobyl accident, **2**, 227
  welfare provisions, **2**, 222
feeding stuffs—
  VAT zero-rating, **7**, 1445
  weights and measures legislation, **6**, 243, 246
ferae naturae, **15**, 179, 181
fight—
  animals placed together for purposes of,
      presence where, **7**, 33
  causing, procuring or assisting, **19**, 1274
fodder and feeding stuff, **11**, 311, 317, 319
footpath, footway or cycle track, on, **20**, 706
game, *see* GAME
health, *see* ANIMAL HEALTH
horses, *see* HORSE; RIDING ESTABLISHMENT
importation—
  animal products, **7**, 1194
  conveyances—
      cleansing and disinfection, **2**, 207
      construction and maintenance, **2**, 202
  destructive animals, **2**, 218
  disease—
      finding, **2**, 208
      prevention, **2**, 205
      slaughter of diseased animals, **2**, 208
  dogs, special controls, **2**, 209
  endangered species, *see* ENDANGERED SPECIES
  generally, **7**, 1201; **11**, 317
  goats, import levies, **1**, 936
  hares, **2**, 214
  horses—
      diseased, suspected, **2**, 210
      docked horses, **2**, 212
      generally, **19**, 1294
      Ireland, from, **2**, 211
      licensing, **2**, 210
  illegal, destruction of animals, **2**, 209
  licence, requirement for, **2**, 206
  live animals, **7**, 1194
  orders to control, **2**, 205
  ports etc, designation, **2**, 206
  poultry, **2**, 213
  quarantine—
      detention in, **2**, 209
      period of, **2**, 209
      rabies, prevention of spread, **2**, 209
  restrictions on, **1**, 894; **7**, 1201
  sheep, import levies, **1**, 936
  shipping—
      horses, of, *see* HORSES
      inspector's powers, **2**, 231
      vessels, power to detain, **2**, 233

Animal—*continued*
injurious, control of, **11**, 859–865
injury or damage by—
  Animals (Scotland) Act—
    purposes of, **2**, 165
    strays, detention of, **2**, 167
    strict liability under, **2**, 166. *See also* STRICT
      LIABILITY *below*
  auctioneers, duty of, **2**, 163
  bull on right of way, **2**, 163
  civil liability—
    annoyance, for, **2**, 171
    deliberate wrongdoing, for, **2**, 164
    delictual principles, **2**, 161
    derivation of, **2**, 160
    forms of, **2**, 161
    general principles, **2**, 161, 162; **22**, 662
    law, imposed by, **2**, 161
    rules of law, by, **2**, 160
    strict liability, **2**, 161
  criminal liability, **2**, 169–175
  defences as to, **2**, 161
  duty of care, **2**, 163
  farmer, duties of, **2**, 163
  fault of person injured, due to, **2**, 166
  forms of, **2**, 160
  intentionally causing, **2**, 164
  killing in self-defence, **2**, 168
  livestock, to, **2**, 168, 169
  negligence—
    delictual liability, **2**, 163
    when arising, **2**, 163
  risk of, acceptance of, **2**, 166
  strict liability, *see* STRICT LIABILITY *below*
Law Reform Committee for Scotland 1963
  report, **22**, 662
legislation—
  basis of, **2**, 101
  exclusive to Scotland, **2**, 101
  extent of reform, **22**, 662
licensing of premises, **14**, 524
licensing system, exemption from, **14**, 1203
limitation of hotelkeeper's liability, **11**, 1748
live, are not food, **11**, 311
livestock, *see* LIVESTOCK
livestock attacked by, **2**, 168, 169
lost, *see* abandoned *above*
malicious damage to, **7**, 410, 410*n*
mansuetae naturae, **15**, 179, 181
meaning, **2**, 177; **9**, 1030
medicinal tests on, **14**, 1206
movement of, **2**, 201
  restrictions—
    controls, generally, **2**, 181, 186
    records of movements, **2**, 204
    sea or air, carriage by, **2**, 201
negligence, damage resulting from, common law,
  15, 179, 185
no right of lien over, **11**, 1757
nuisance caused by, **19**, 336
owner, veterinary practice by, **25**, 203
patent not grantable in respect of, **18**, 828
performing, *see* PERFORMING ANIMALS
pet animals, *see* PET ANIMALS

Animal—*continued*
pet shops, *see* PET SHOP
physical damage to, **14**, 2044, 2045
postal packet, living creature enclosed in, **16**,
  1909
projecting load on, **20**, 706
public health legislation, **19**, 305
quarantine provisions, **19**, 1293
rabbits, *see* RABBITS
rabies, **19**, 476
  See also RABIES
real evidence, as, **10**, 620
rearing establishment, licence, **14**, 524
release into wild for sporting purposes, **19**, 1275
road, conveyance by, **3**, 625
road accident—
  caused by, liability, **15**, 185
  involving, **20**, 437
sale to child under age of twelve, **3**, 1222
scientific procedures—
  anaesthetic or analgesic, use of, **2**, 253
  Animal Procedures Committee—
    advisory functions, **2**, 258
    composition etc, **2**, 258
    licences etc, consultation as to, **2**, 259
    research, promotion of, **2**, 258
  breeding establishments—
    animals to be bred at, **2**, 254
    care of animals in, **2**, 256
    certification of, **2**, 256
    fees payable, **2**, 256
  confidential information, disclosure, **2**, 263
  designated establishment—
    certificate of, **2**, 255
    dogs or cats bred at, **2**, 254
    entry and search, **2**, 264
    fees payable, **2**, 255
    specification in licence, **2**, 255
    visitation and report, **2**, 257
  inspectors—
    appointment, **2**, 251, 257
    duties, **2**, 257
    qualifications, **2**, 257
  licences—
    breach of conditions, **2**, 260
    continuance of, **2**, 251
    fraudulently obtaining, **2**, 263
    medicinal tests, **2**, 253
    preliminaries to grant of, **2**, 239
    refusal, notice as to, **2**, 260
    suspension, **2**, 260
    variation etc of, **2**, 260
  neuromuscular blocking agents, use of, **2**, 262
  offences—
    entry and search in respect of, **2**, 264
    false etc statements, **2**, 263
    public exhibitions etc, **2**, 263
    summary proceedings, **2**, 265
  painful experiments—
    formerly called, **2**, 251
    transitional provisions, **2**, 251
  personal licence—
    age for obtaining, **2**, 254
    duration of, **2**, 254

Animal—*continued*
scientific procedures—*continued*
  project licence—
    conditions of, **2**, 254
    considerations for grant of, **2**, 254, 260
    duration of, **2**, 254
    person authorised to receive, **2**, 255
    requirement for, **2**, 254
  protected animals—
    anaesthetic etc, administration, **2**, 253
    day-to-day care of, **2**, 255
    health and welfare, **2**, 255, 256
    killing of—
      direction by inspector, on, **2**, 257
      regulated procedure, as, **2**, 253
      suffering, to prevent, **2**, 261
    meaning, **2**, 252
    re-use of, **2**, 261
  regulated procedure—
    cats or dogs, use of, **2**, 254
    conclusion of, duty on, **2**, 261
    killing animal after, **2**, 254
    meaning, **2**, 253
    pain etc, minimising, **2**, 254
    ringing, tagging etc, **2**, 253
    specification in licence, **2**, 254
Scottish Law Commission review of civil liability
  for loss etc, **22**, 662
sheriff court jurisdiction, **6**, 1078
slaughter—
  confinement and treatment before, **11**, 503
  diseased animals, of, **11**, 317
  early legislation, **11**, 303, 304
  European Community law, **11**, 511
  export, for, **11**, 510
  generally, **11**, 496; **14**, 697
  historical outline, **11**, 497
  hygiene, **11**, 404, 504, 506
  inspection, **11**, 407
    animals to be slaughtered, of, **11**, 413
    carcases, of, **11**, 413
    meat, of—
      animals slaughtered elsewhere, **11**, 508
      animals slaughtered in slaughterhouses, **11**,
        507
  Jewish slaughter, **3**, 1675, 1680; **11**, 503, 513
  knacker's yards, *see* KNACKER
  legislation, **11**, 498
  local authorities, functions of, **11**, 509
  methods of, **11**, 503
  Muslim slaughter, **11**, 503, 513
  research or diagnosis, for, **11**, 503
  sheriff court jurisdiction, **6**, 1078
  See also SLAUGHTERHOUSE
stray dogs, seizure of, **14**, 712
straying on road, **20**, 506, 707
strict liability for injury or damage caused by—
  Animals (Scotland) Act 1987—
    animals covered by, **15**, 184
    contributory negligence, **15**, 186
    damnum fatale, no defence of, **15**, 186
    dangerous wild animals, **15**, 184
    defences, **15**, 186
    disease, transmission of, **15**, 185

Animal—*continued*
strict liability for injury or damage caused by—
  continued
  Animals (Scotland) Act 1987—*continued*
    dogs, **15**, 184
    generally, **15**, 155, 181, 182
    grazing animals, **15**, 184
    injury or damage, requirements as to, **15**, 185
    intervention by third party, **15**, 186
    owner, **15**, 183
      child under sixteen, **15**, 183
    person in possession, **15**, 183
      child under sixteen, **15**, 183
    trespasser, liability towards, **15**, 186
    type of liability, **15**, 182
  common law, **15**, 179, 185
  generally, **15**, 155
  statute law, **15**, 180
testing new products on, **14**, 1206
trade descriptions, **6**, 120
trespass by—
  straying animals—
    damages in respect of, **18**, 190
    detention of, **18**, 188
    generally, **18**, 180, 183, 186
    interdict of, **18**, 187
    killing or injuring, **18**, 189
  troublesome, Slaughter of Animals (Scotland) Act
    1980 not applicable to, **11**, 496
trust, as beneficiary of, **24**, 115, 118
uncontrolled, attack amounting to assault, **7**, 218
urban situation, kept in, **19**, 336*n*
VAT zero-rating, **7**, 1445
veterinary practice—
  agricultural animal owned by, **25**, 203
  owner, by, **25**, 203
  See also VETERINARY SURGEON
veterinary student, examination by, **25**, 203
  farm rights and duties connected with, **25**, 206
wild—
  ownership, **7**, 333
  See also wild animals
wild and tame, abolition of distinction,
  recommendation of, **22**, 662
zoonoses, **19**, 477
zoos, **19**, 1295
See also under names of particular animals
Animal boarding establishment
health etc of animals in, **2**, 132
inspection of, **2**, 134
keeping—
  disqualification from, **2**, 135
  meaning, **2**, 131
licence—
  appeals respecting, **2**, 132; **14**, 119
  exemptions, **2**, 131
  generally, **14**, 524; **19**, 1293
  requirement for, **2**, 131
  transmission on death, **2**, 133
register of animals, **2**, 132
Animal breeding establishment
care of animals in, **2**, 256
death of licensee, **2**, 133
dogs, *see* DOG

Animal breeding establishment—*continued*
licence—
  conditions, subject to, **2**, 132
  duration of, **2**, 132
  generally, **14**, 524
painful experiments, *see* ANIMAL (scientific
  procedures)
Animal health
animal defined, **2**, 177
boarding establishments, in, **2**, 132
conveyance, during, *see* ANIMAL
disease—
  attested areas, declaration of, **2**, 181
  bee diseases, **2**, 189
  bovine, **11**, 447–449
  bovine spongiform encephalopathy, **19**, 477*n*
  brucella, **19**, 477*n*
  carcases—
    disposal of, **2**, 197
    offences relating to, **2**, 199
    seizure of, **2**, 198
  cattle plague, slaughter in case of, **2**, 197
  diagnostic services, **2**, 180
  diseased animals—
    importation of, **2**, 208
    markets, at, **2**, 186
    notification to police, **2**, 183
    persons in contact with, disinfection, **2**, 200
    seizure of, **2**, 198
    separation of, **2**, 183
    suffering, prevention, **2**, 201
    treatment, **2**, 184
  eradication—
    areas, declaration of, **2**, 181
    expenditure on, **2**, 179
  foot-and-mouth disease, **2**, 187
  forms of, **2**, 178
  human health, risk to—
    designation of diseases as, **2**, 188
    information of, duty to give, **2**, 188
    veterinary inspector's powers, **2**, 188
  infected area or place—
    declaration of, **2**, 185
    entry, power to control, **2**, 185
    ministerial powers, **2**, 184
    notice to be displayed, **2**, 185
    order relating to, **2**, 185
  inspectors—
    general powers, **2**, 231
    inspection by, **2**, 179
  markets etc, cleansing, **2**, 200
  meaning of disease, **2**, 178
  milk of diseased cow, **11**, 317
  Ministerial powers, general, **2**, 186
  movement restrictions—
    controls, **2**, 186
    markets, power to licence, **2**, 201
    power to regulate, **2**, 181
    records of movements, **2**, 204
    regulations, **2**, 201
    sea or air, carriage by, **2**, 201
  myxomatosis, **11**, 877
  offences, carcases, as to, **2**, 199

Animal health—*continued*
disease—*continued*
  pleuro-pneumonia—
    poultry, *see* POULTRY
    slaughter of infected cattle, **2**, 197
    special provisions, **2**, 187
  prevention and eradication of, regulations as to,
    11, 317
  rabies, *see* RABIES
  sheep—
    dipping, orders for, **2**, 182
    entry to examine, **2**, 182
  slaughter of diseased animals—
    carcases, disposal of, **2**, 197
    cattle, when compulsory, **2**, 197
    compensation, **2**, 197
    generally, **11**, 317
    imported animals, **2**, 208
    Ministerial powers, **2**, 197
    offences as to, **2**, 199
    seizure for, **2**, 198
  transmission of disease from animal, **19**, 475–
    478
  vaccination, power to require, **2**, 184
  veterinary services, provision of, **2**, 180
    See also VETERINARY SURGEON
  zoonoses, **19**, 447
enforcement of provisions, **2**, 229
exportation control, *see* ANIMAL
importation control, *see* ANIMAL
inspector—
  areas of operation, **2**, 231
  entry of premises, **2**, 231
  general powers, **2**, 231
  inspection by, **2**, 179
  obstruction of, **2**, 234
  poultry, in respect of, **2**, 232
  refusal of admission, **2**, 234
  vessels, power to detain, **2**, 233
licence—
  altering unlawfully, **2**, 237
  blank, issue of, **2**, 235
  failure to produce, **2**, 238
  falsely obtaining, **2**, 234
  falsification, **2**, 234
  offences generally, **2**, 237
local government functions as to, **14**, 711
offences—
  arrest and detention for, **2**, 229
  generally, **2**, 238
  licences, relating to, **2**, 234–237
  police powers, **2**, 229
  seizure of animals for, **2**, 230
poultry—
  diseases of, **2**, 178
  meaning, **2**, 177
statutory provisions generally, **2**, 176
transportation controls, **2**, 201
veterinary services, provision of, **2**, 180
  See also VETERINARY SURGEON
Animus negotia aliena gerendi
negotiorum gestio, **15**, 110–116
Animus pirandi
generally, **7**, 63

Anniversary of event
age, calculation by—
  precise moment of birth, **22**, 824
February 29—
  occurring on, **22**, 811
Annoyance
animals, by, **2**, 171
harm arising from, **14**, 2047
locality, character of, **14**, 2057
materiality, requirement of, **14**, 2050
repossession, as grounds for—
  assured tenancy, **13**, 725, 733
  protected tenancy, **13**, 714, 716
Annual close time
See CLOSE TIME
Annualrent
infeftment, **18**, 112
right of, **20**, 110
sasine, symbols of, **18**, 90
Annuity
alimentary, **12**, 1264
charity, of, tax exemption, **3**, 1103, 1135
deceased's liability to tax, **25**, 969
executors directed to buy, **25**, 837
heritable property, as, **18**, 14
income tax, **25**, 969, 984
liferent distinguished, **13**, 1606
prescription, **16**, 2116
presumption in favour of, **13**, 1620
trust, under, **24**, 54
Annuity policy
advertisement of, **12**, 810
Financial Services Act, application, **12**, 807
friendly society, **12**, 810
Annulment of marriage
custody of children, **10**, 1317
financial provision following—
  declarator of nullity, **10**, 950
  overseas annulment, **10**, 947
  stepchildren, **10**, 1246
meaning, **10**, 943*n*
recognition of decree—
  common law, **10**, 941
  Family Law Act 1986 ... —
    British Islands, decrees granted in, **10**, 943
    generally, **10**, 942
    overseas decrees, **10**, 944–947; **17**, 224
  international law, **17**, 224
See also MATRIMONIAL DECREES
Antarctic region
Antarctic Treaty, **19**, 672
Ante-natal care
See MATERNITY RIGHTS
Anthrax
death by, cremation following, **3**, 565
prevention of infection by, **19**, 478
Anti-Burghers
generally, **3**, 1637*n*
Seceders, **3**, 1636
Anti-competitive practices
See COMPETITION LAW
Anti-freeze
weights and measures legislation, **6**, 244

Anti-War Treaty of Non-Aggression and Conciliation, 19, 698*n*
Antibiotics
medicinal products, distinction between, **14**, 1201
Antioxidants
control of, **11**, 371
Antique
export, **7**, 1194
import, **7**, 1120
VAT margin scheme for used goods, **7**, 1363
Apartheid
crime against humanity, as, **19**, 678
international conventions on, **12**, 5
Apocha trium annorum
debt, termly payments, **15**, 872
rent, application to, **13**, 229
Apostasy
Roman Catholic Church, *latae sententiae* offence, **3**, 1658
Apothecaries
royal household, **7**, 843
Apparatus Supply Company (APC)
generally, **16**, 1944
Apparent insolvency
See INSOLVENCY
Appeal
absence or inadequacy of reasons, raising, **1**, 293
counsel's duty, **13**, 1368
criminal procedure, *see* CRIMINAL PROCEDURE
issue of law, raising, **1**, 288
procurators fiscal, duties, **13**, 1434
reasons for decision to be stated on, **1**, 290
See also under names of individual courts and under subject matter of appeal
Apprehension
accused, of, **17**, 543
wrongful—
  see DETENTION, WRONGFUL
See also ARREST
Apprentice
employer's liability, **15**, 334
Apprenticeship
contract of, minors, **10**, 1078
messenger-at-arms, **14**, 1502
Apprising
adjudication, replacement by, **8**, 189
former registration of, **19**, 841
Appropriation accounts
preparation of, **5**, 594
Aquaeductus
servitude right of, generally, **18**, 490
Aquae educendae
servitude of, **25**, 354
Aquaehaustus
non-tidal river, **18**, 281, 287, 288, 295
servitude of, **6**, 515; **18**, 281, 490; **25**, 352
Aqueduct
construction or alteration, **19**, 19*n*, 24
servitude of, **6**, 515; **18**, 490; **25**, 353
Arable lease
generally, **13**, 215
Arbiter
acceptance of office, **2**, 440
accommodation for, cost of, **2**, 508

Arbiter—*continued*
addressing, by parties, **2**, 446
agreement by—
    failure to reach, **2**, 429, 430
    part of submission, of, **2**, 431
appointment—
    application for, **2**, 428
    court, by, **2**, 426
    Lord Ordinary as, **6**, 927
    preliminary notice requiring, **2**, 422
    statutory provision as to, **2**, 426
    terms too general to effect, **2**, 427
    unnamed person, **2**, 426
architect or engineer as, **2**, 418
assessor, appointment, **2**, 508
award, action to enforce, **1**, 331
award of, *see* ARBITRAL AWARD
bias by, **2**, 417, 477
    rule against, **1**, 252
bribery—
    meaning, **2**, 475
    setting aside award for, **2**, 475
building etc disputes, in, **2**, 418
change of, rules, **2**, 508
claims *ultra vires* of, **2**, 434
clerk—
    appointment—
        procedure for, **2**, 441
        time for making, **2**, 440
    award, duty to prepare, **2**, 457
    dismissal of, **2**, 441
    duties of, **2**, 441
    expenses etc, liability for, **2**, 494, 496
    qualification of, **2**, 441
    remuneration, **2**, 494
    responsibilities of, **2**, 441
    witness, competent as, **2**, 495
commission—
    appointment, rules, **2**, 508
    depositions etc, to take, **2**, 447
consultations by, **2**, 450
contracting parties, one of, as, **2**, 417
corruption—
    allegation, answer to, **2**, 477
    damages, liability for, **2**, 497
    forms of, **2**, 476
    meaning, **2**, 476
    setting aside award for, **2**, 473
    what constitutes, **2**, 477
damages—
    assessment of, **2**, 448
    liability for, **2**, 497, 498
    power to award, **2**, 448
death of, effect of, **2**, 437
decisions—
    challenges, restriction on, **2**, 442
    conclusive nature of, **2**, 470
    condition precedent to enforcement, **2**, 433
    evidence of, **2**, 495
    finality of, **2**, 470
    no power to review, **2**, 470
    reasons to be given, **2**, 463
    time limit for giving, **2**, 435

Arbiter—*continued*
decree arbitral—
    clerk's custody, when in, **2**, 468
    delivery, necessity for, **2**, 485
    directions as to registration, **2**, 457
    enforcement, **2**, 471
    evidence, as, **2**, 495
    foreign—
        enforcement in Scotland, **2**, 507
        validity, **2**, 506
    fraud, obtained by, **2**, 484
    interim, nature of, **2**, 464
    issue of, effect of, **2**, 468
    recall of, **2**, 468
    setting aside, **2**, 460, 481
disqualification to act as—
    exceptions to, **2**, 418
    grounds of, **2**, 417
documents, recovery of, **2**, 447
duties—
    general, **2**, 439
    implied obligations, **2**, 439
    summary of, **2**, 439
    to act strictly within powers, **2**, 439
entitlement to act as, **2**, 416
errors in judgment, **2**, 497, 498
European Court, reference to, **2**, 453
evidence—
    addressing arbiter on, **2**, 446
    decree arbitral as, **2**, 495
    documents, production of, **2**, 447
    generally, **2**, 488
    reference to notes, **2**, 489
examination of, **2**, 488
expenses—
    accommodation, for, **2**, 508
    clause in award, **2**, 457
    matters included in, **2**, 449
    power to grant, **2**, 449
    rules as to, **2**, 508
    taxation of, **2**, 449
failure to agree, **2**, 429, 430
falsehood—
    award set aside for, **2**, 475
    meaning, **2**, 475
fees—
    liability of arbiter for, **2**, 494, 496
firm may act as, **2**, 416
fraud—
    award reducible for, **2**, 477
    punishment of, **2**, 477
    questions of, **2**, 415
general submission to, **2**, 420
havers—
    attendance, no power to compel, **2**, 447
    exhibits of, receiving, **2**, 447
    resident in England, **2**, 447
hearing—
    discretion as to, **2**, 442
    dispensing with, **2**, 444
    general provisions, **2**, 444
    pleadings of claim, **2**, 442
    representation of parties, **2**, 444

Arbiter—*continued*
  requirement for, **2**, 444
  rules as to, **2**, 508
immunity given to, scope of, **2**, 498
impartially, to act, **2**, 402, 439
interdict—
  general rule as to, **2**, 434
  process of, **2**, 472
  reasons for granting, **2**, 434
  refusal of, grounds for, **2**, 434
interest in dispute, having, **2**, 417
interference with, by court, **2**, 434
interpreter, services of, **2**, 508
judicial character of, **2**, 417
jurisdiction—
  failure to comply with, **2**, 470
  limitation of, **2**, 421
layman as, **2**, 440
liability of—
  damages, for, **2**, 497
  fees etc, respecting, **2**, 494, 496
  negligence, for, **2**, 498
litigation, witnesses in, **2**, 495
Lord Ordinary appointed as, **6**, 927
man of skill—
  appointment as arbiter, **2**, 444
  power to consult, **2**, 450
  reference to, **2**, 456
  remuneration of, **2**, 494
meaning, **2**, 416
meetings—
  clerk's duties, **2**, 441
  preliminary, with parties, **2**, 442
minor acting as, **2**, 416
misconduct—
  damages, liability for, **2**, 497
  effect of, **2**, 470, 476
  evidence to disprove, **2**, 488
  examples of, **2**, 483
negligence of, **2**, 406, 498
nomination, party refusing to make, **2**, 427
oversman—
  appointment—
    court, by, **2**, 426, 429
    time for, **2**, 440
  award by, form of, **2**, 457
  death of, effect of, **2**, 437
  declining to act, **2**, 429
  disqualification of, **2**, 429
  duty of, **2**, 429
  nomination of, **2**, 429, 430
  powers and duties, **2**, 429
  prorogation by, **2**, 436
  purpose of appointing, **2**, 429
  remuneration, **2**, 492
  selection, importance of, **2**, 429
  statement of case by, **2**, 451
  submission devolving on—
    part of submission, **2**, 431
    reason for, **2**, 430
pleadings—
  control of, **2**, 508
  form of, **2**, 442

Arbiter—*continued*
points of law—
  guidance on, **2**, 450
powers generally, **2**, 508
procedure—
  advice on, **2**, 441
  regulation of, **2**, 442
  rules of, **2**, 442, 508
proceedings, *see* ARBITRATION
proof—
  allowance of, **2**, 445
  competency and effect, **2**, 446
  conduct of, **2**, 446
  oath etc, witnesses put on, **2**, 446
  power to order, **2**, 445
  refusal to allow, **2**, 445
  relevancy of, **2**, 445
  sufficiency of, **2**, 446
  valuation, of, **2**, 445
proposed findings, issue of—
  desirability of, **2**, 454
  notes, no obligation to issue, **2**, 454
  representations by parties on, **2**, 454
prorogation by, *see* ARBITRATION (submission to)
refusal to act—
  good reason to be shown, **2**, 437
  lapse of submission on, **2**, 437
remuneration—
  former practice as to, **2**, 492
  general rule, **2**, 492
  obligation to pay, **2**, 493
  order to pay, **2**, 493
  stipulation for, **2**, 492
renunciation of office, **2**, 439
rights and liabilities, **2**, 492
Scottish Committee, supervision by, **23**, 911
shorthand writers, services of, **2**, 508
society as, **2**, 416
statement of case—
  court order requiring, **2**, 452
  introduction of procedure, **2**, 401
  obligation as to, **2**, 403
  points of law, on, **2**, 445, 451
  procedure for, **2**, 452
  refusal of, **2**, 452
  refusal to accept court opinion, **2**, 478, 483
  request by party for, **2**, 451, 452
  rules as to, **2**, 452
submission, failure to exhaust, **2**, 481
termination of powers, **2**, 438
valuer distinguished, **2**, 498
witness, as, competency, **2**, 495
witnesses—
  attendance of, **2**, 447
  identity of, disclosure of, **2**, 447
  swearing or affirming, **2**, 446
See also ARBITRAL AWARD; ARBITRATION;
    ARBITRATION AGREEMENT; ARBITRATION
    CLAUSE

Arbitral award
action to enforce, **1**, 331
alteration or correction—
  barred by delivery of award, **2**, 454
  court, by, **2**, 469

Arbitral award—continued
alteration or correction—continued
  end of arbiter's power as to, 2, 469
  time for, 2, 438
alternative awards—
  effect given to, 2, 466
  nature of, 2, 466
ambiguity—
  must be free from, 2, 561
  reducible for, 2, 482
annulment, 2, 472
appeal from, 2, 472
assistance in forming, 2, 450
binding nature of, 2, 402
cancellation of, 2, 438
challenge of—
  common law, as contrary to, 2, 473
  grounds of, 2, 470, 473
  homologation—
    barred by, 2, 456
    plea of, 2, 490
  misconduct by arbiter, 2, 483
  mode of, 2, 472
clauses of, 2, 457
common law, contrary to, 2, 473
conditional—
  enforceability, 2, 467
  nature of, 2, 467
contents of, 2, 457
decree arbitral, see ARBITER
delivery of—
  effect of, 2, 468, 470
  necessity for, 2, 485
  time limit not set, 2, 468
enforcement—
  conditional award, 2, 467
  decree of court for, 2, 471
  foreign award, 2, 507
  prevention of, methods of, 2, 472
  registration with a view to, 2, 471
England, executed in, 2, 456
errors etc, alteration of, 2, 454, 469
evidence as to, see ARBITER
examination of arbiter, 2, 488
exhaustive, must be, 2, 459
failure to agree on, 2, 429–431
finality of, 2, 470
force of, 2, 455
foreign—
  alleged irregularity, 2, 506
  challenge of, 2, 506
  enforcement—
    Convention provisions, 2, 403, 505
    Scotland, in, 2, 507
    United Kingdom, in, 2, 507
  made outside UK, 2, 507
  objection to, 2, 506
  recognition, 2, 403, 507
  validity, 2, 506
form of—
  exceptions to rules, 2, 456
  generally, 2, 456
  holograph instrument, 2, 455, 456
  oversman, by, 2, 457

Arbitral award—continued
form of—continued
  rules as to, 2, 455, 508
  style books, in, 2, 457
  two or more arbiters, where, 2, 456
fraud—
  obtained by, 2, 484
  reducible for, 2, 477
fraudulently concocting, 2, 477
general requirements, 2, 455
general rule as to, 2, 450
hearing before making, see ARBITER
holograph form of, 2, 455, 456
homologation—
  challenging award, bar to, 2, 456
  defects cured by, 2, 490
  generally, 2, 490
  plea of, 2, 490
  reduction, in respect of, 2, 491
impetrated by improper means, 2, 484
impossible of performance, 2, 462
improbative award, 2, 480
improper means, obtained by, 2, 484
inconsistency within, 2, 462
informality in, 2, 456
interdict, see ARBITER
interest on, 12, 1035
interim—
  discretion as to issue of, 2, 464
  final, becoming, 2, 464
  nature of, 2, 464
  power to make, 2, 464
  recall etc, subject to, 2, 464
interpretation of, 2, 461
judicial reference, see ARBITRATION
more than one arbiter, of, 2, 456
obligation to recognise or obtemper, 16, 2116
part award—
  agreement on, 2, 431
  designation as, 2, 465
  nature of, 2, 465
  preparation, responsibility for, 2, 457
proposed, issue of, 2, 460
reasons for giving, note of, 2, 463
recall of, period permitted for, 2, 468
reduction of—
  action for, 2, 472
  ambiguity, for, 2, 482
  application to court for, 2, 472
  arbiter's evidence, 2, 488, 489
  categorised grounds for, 2, 478
  common law, at, 2, 478
  corruption, bribery or falsehood, for, 2, 475
  fraud, for, 2, 477
  grounds for—
    fraud by parties, 2, 484
    generally, 2, 473
    misconduct, 2, 483
    ultra fines compromissi, 2, 480
    ultra vires, 2, 480
  homologation in respect of, 2, 491
  improbative award, 2, 479
  partial, 2, 487
  proof, requirement for, 2, 488

Arbitral award—*continued*
registration—
  enforcement, affecting, **2**, 471
  recall of award before, **2**, 468
res judicata, as, **2**, 402
review, no power to, **2**, 470
self-contained and self-explanatory, should be, **2**, 458
setting aside—
  application to court, **2**, 472
  compromise award, **2**, 486
  ground for, **2**, 473
  misconduct, for, **2**, 476
  submission, failure to exhaust, **2**, 481
sheriff may set aside, **4**, 6
substance of, **2**, 458
suspension of, **2**, 472
terms of submission, bound by, **2**, 460
time limit for giving, **2**, 435
ultra fines compromissi, **2**, 480
ultra vires
  nature of, **2**, 480
  reduction where, **2**, 480
unambiguous, must be, **2**, 455
uncertainty, void for, **2**, 461
validity, rules as to, **2**, 455
Arbitration
abortive, effect of, **2**, 432
agreement, *see* ARBITRATION AGREEMENT
arbiter, *see* ARBITER
Arbitration (International Investment Disputes) Act 1966 ..., **8**, 564
award, *see* ARBITRAL AWARD
Books of Council and Session, registration in, **8**, 559, 562
building contract, *see* BUILDING CONTRACT
Chartered Institute of Arbitrators, **6**, 172
Civil Jurisdiction and Judgments Act 1982 ..., **8**, 555
clauses, *see* ARBITRATION CLAUSE
coast protection works scheme, **25**, 382
common law, enforcement at, **8**, 554
consumer redress, **6**, 172
Court of Session jurisdiction, **6**, 924
damages—
  arbiter's liability, **2**, 497, 498
  assessment of, **2**, 448
  compensation for damage by water authority, **25**, 513
  power to award, **2**, 448
decree conform, **8**, 554, 559
definition, **19**, 719
depositions, taking, **2**, 447
European Court, reference to, **2**, 453
expenses—
  clause in award for, **2**, 457
  grant of, **2**, 449
  rules as to, **2**, 508
  what is included in, **2**, 449
extra-judicial dispute resolution, **6**, 172
Foreign Judgments (Reciprocal Enforcement) Act 1933 ..., **8**, 557
historical background, **2**, 401

Arbitration—*continued*
International Centre for the Settlement of Investment Disputes, **8**, 564
international disputes, **19**, 719, 720
intervention by interdict, **2**, 434
Judgments Convention, exclusion from scope of, **8**, 431, 437
judicial references—
  award, in, **2**, 500
  death of party, effect, **2**, 501
  duration of, **2**, 501
  evidence etc in, **2**, 500
  expenses of, **2**, 502
  generally, **2**, 499
  nature of, **2**, 500
  procedure, **5**, 2
  referee, **2**, 502
  species of arbitration, as, **2**, 405
  subject matter, **2**, 499
law of—
  Act of 1894—
    effect of, **2**, 403
  common law, based on, **2**, 403
  contract, based on, **2**, 402
  development of, **2**, 401
meaning, **2**, 1
Model Rules on Arbitral Behaviour, **19**, 720*n*
nature of, **2**, 401
New York Convention on the Recognition and Enforcement of Foreign Arbitral Awards, **8**, 561–563
non-domestic water, disputes over supply, **25**, 511
non-Scottish judgments—
  Administration of Justice Act 1920 ..., **8**, 556
  Arbitration Act 1950—
    foreign award, conditions for enforcing, **8**, 560
    mode and effect of enforcement, **8**, 559
    scope, **8**, 558
Parliament, prescribed by, **2**, 404
parties—
  bankruptcy of, **2**, 437
  communicating with, **2**, 441
  death, effect of, **2**, 437
  fraud by, **2**, 484
  preliminary meeting with, **2**, 441
partnership agreement, **16**, 1009, 1069, 1079
pleadings and procedure, **2**, 442, 508
proceedings—
  discretion as to, **2**, 442
  initiation, **2**, 440
  minutes of, **2**, 441
  pleadings, **2**, 442, 508
  preliminaries to, **2**, 440
reference to—
  agreement for, *see* ARBITRATION AGREEMENT
  architect, to, **2**, 424
  commercial matters, **2**, 416
  expenses of, **2**, 449
  general provisions, **2**, 419
  illegal matters barred from, **2**, 414
  judicial, *see* judicial reference *above*
  questions referable—
    exceptions from, **2**, 414
    generally, **2**, 413

Arbitration—*continued*
reference to—*continued*
  sequestration, questions arising in, **2**, 408
  submission to arbitration, *see* submission to *below*
  terms of, **2**, 402
  too general, effect, **2**, 427
  unnamed person, to, **2**, 426
representation in, **1**, 279
right to, **2**, 432
right to be heard, **1**, 259
Rules of Law Society—
  adoption by parties, **2**, 443
  arbitration to which applied, **2**, 508
  purposes of, **2**, 443
  text of, **2**, 508
sheriff court jurisdiction, **6**, 1065, 1079
special jurisdiction, **4**, 47
statement made in, absolute privilege, **15**, 524
statutory, **1**, 337
  legal implications, **2**, 404
submission—
  advocates, by, **2**, 409
  agreement for, *see* ARBITRATION AGREEMENT
  ambiguity in, **2**, 421
  ancillary submission—
    categories of, **2**, 423
    construction as, **2**, 423
    meaning, **2**, 422
    operation, bringing into, **2**, 422
    scope of arbitration, **2**, 423
  binding nature of, **2**, 402
  capacity of party for, **2**, 407
  categories of, **2**, 420
  companies, by, **2**, 412
  constituting, method of, **2**, 419
  contract—
    deemed to be, **2**, 402
    parties to, **2**, 407
  contract or deed, by, **2**, 419
  death of party, effect of, **2**, 437
  defects in, cure of, **2**, 490
  devolution of—
    oversman, on, **2**, 430, 431
    prorogation not implied by, **2**, 436
  duration of—
    general rule, **2**, 435
    left blank, where, **2**, 435
  eligible parties, **2**, 407–412
  essential qualities, **2**, 419
  exclusion of court by, **2**, 402
  expiry of, **2**, 435
  forms of, construction of, **2**, 421
  general submission, **2**, 420
  general-special submission, **2**, 420
  heir of entail, by, **2**, 410
  implied conditions in, **2**, 402
  lapsed, **2**, 437
  law agent, by, **2**, 409
  manner of, **2**, 419
  minor's rights as to, **2**, 407
  oversman, devolving on, **2**, 430, 431
  parties to—
    bankruptcy, intimation of, **2**, 437
    death, effect of, **2**, 437

Arbitration—*continued*
submission—*continued*
  parties to—*continued*
    preliminary meeting with, **2**, 441
    prescriptive period, **2**, 435
  prorogation—
    express power required, **2**, 435
    instrument of, form of, **2**, 436
    jurisdiction, act of, as, **2**, 436
    parties themselves, by, **2**, 436
    power not given, where, **2**, 436
    time for executing, **2**, 436
  sisting proceedings on, **2**, 403
  special submission, **2**, 420
  style of, **2**, 508
  termination of—
    death of party etc, by, **2**, 437
    grounds of, **2**, 437
    impossibility of performance, by, **2**, 437
    issue of award, on, **2**, 438
  trustee, by, **2**, 408
  verbal submissions, **2**, 419
tribunals, international law, **19**, 636
UK arbitral awards, reciprocal enforcement, **8**, 555
valid agreement to submit to arbitration, must be outcome of, **8**, 554
valuation, contrasted with, **2**, 406
See also ADVISORY, CONCILIATION AND ARBITRATION SERVICE

Arbitration agreement
capacity to make, **2**, 407
categories of, **2**, 419
clause, *see* ARBITRATION CLAUSE
enforcement by court, **2**, 432
finality of, **2**, 432
holograph, by, **2**, 419
insufficiency of, **2**, 427
private international law, under—
  clauses in, **2**, 503
  foreign awards, *see* ARBITRAL AWARD
  general provisions, **2**, 503
  jurisdiction, Scottish court, **2**, 505
  null and void, effect, **2**, 505
  procedure, law governing—
    alleged irregularity, **2**, 506
    local law, **2**, 504
    Scots law, **2**, 505
  rules governing, **2**, 503
  submission to arbitration—
    enforcement in Scotland, **2**, 503
    validity, **2**, 503
qualified agreement, **2**, 433
style of, **2**, 508

Arbitration clause
ancillary submission—
  categories of, **2**, 423
  construction as, **2**, 423
  meaning, **2**, 422
  operation, bringing into, **2**, 422
  scope of arbitration, **2**, 423
building etc contract, in, **2**, 418, 424
commercial lease, **13**, 558, 574–576
construction by court, **2**, 432

Arbitration clause—*continued*
contract, in, **15**, 718
contracting out of jurisdiction, **2**, 402
contracts, generally found in, **2**, 413
co-partnery contract, in, **2**, 424
frustration etc of contract, effect, **2**, 425
generally, **13**, 234, 241
partnership contract, in, **2**, 413
rules relating to, **2**, 443
scope of, **2**, 422
shipbuilding contract, in, **2**, 424
styles of, **2**, 419
termination of contract, **2**, 425
trade union rules, in, **2**, 433

Arbroath
Declaration of, **19**, 207; **22**, 356

Archaeological areas
archaeological interest, site of, compulsory
    purchase exemption, **11**, 634
designation order, **9**, 1227
generally, **9**, 1217
land, information as to interest in, **9**, 1229
legislation concerning, building standards and, **3**,
    244
metal detectors, offences, **9**, 1228
operations notice, **9**, 1227
preservation of, **9**, 1221

Archdiocese of Glasgow
Roman Catholic Church, **3**, 1655

Architect
administration of contract, **3**, 51
administration of works, **3**, 137
agent, role as, **3**, 130
alteration of building prejudicial to, **3**, 139
appointment, **3**, 56, 127
    architect's appointment form, **3**, 128, 131, 136,
        137
    breach, claim for, prescription, **3**, 174
    failure to appoint, **3**, 56
arbiter, appointment as, **3**, 168
architect's appointment form, **3**, 169
authority of, scope, **3**, 130
building agreement, **3**, 12
claims and dispute resolution, **3**, 168
client, relationship with, **3**, 128
club or association, contract entered into on
    behalf of, **3**, 26
competence, **3**, 56
consultant, use of, **3**, 136
continuing duty, **3**, 135
contract, **3**, 127, 128
contractor, relationship with, **3**, 138
copyright—
    architectural work, **18**, 957, 992
        meaning, **18**, 965
    design document, **18**, 965, 1155
    generally, **3**, 139
    reconstruction of building, **18**, 1132
costs, advice as to, **3**, 134
death, effect, **3**, 130
delay in delivery of drawings etc, **3**, 70
delay in instruction or information by, **3**, 48
delictual liability, **3**, 150

Architect—*continued*
design obligations, **3**, 135
designs provided by third party, where, **3**, 135
direct loss or expense, determination, **3**, 70
discipline, **3**, 140
duties, generally, **3**, 131
employer, relationship with, **3**, 130
employment, **3**, 9
errors, correction, **3**, 135
expert advice, seeking, **3**, 136
extra work or variation requested by, **3**, 41–43
failure to give instructions or information, **3**, 57
fees, dispute as to, **3**, 169
generally, **3**, 2
identification on building, right to, **3**, 139
independent professional, duty to act as, **3**, 130
inspection of works, **3**, 137
law, working knowledge of, **3**, 132
liability, **3**, 130
materials, powers in relation to, **3**, 36
negligence, **3**, 150, 152
new techniques, employment of, **3**, 135
non-designated services, **4**, 1177
payment, **3**, 129
position of, generally, **3**, 127
presence on site, contract providing for, **3**, 53
professional organisation, **3**, 141
professional regulation, **3**, 140
qualifications, **3**, 140
register of, **3**, 140
    removal from, **3**, 140
replacement, **3**, 56
responsibility, **3**, 9
restrictive trade practices, **4**, 1247
schedule of defects, **3**, 39
schools of, **3**, 140
site examination by, **3**, 133
statutory regulation, **3**, 140
sub-contracted, **3**, 127
sub-contractor—
    nomination, **3**, 125
    relationship with, **3**, 138
tendering by, **3**, 130
termination of engagement, **3**, 128
terms of engagement, **3**, 128
under-certfication by, liability, **3**, 138
use of term, restriction on, **3**, 140

**Architects Registration Council of the
    United Kingdom**
generally, **3**, 140

Architectural nuisance
Dean of Guild, jurisdiction of, **14**, 2014

Archives, National Register of, (Scotland)
West Register House, **19**, 829

Archway
construction or alteration, **19**, 19*n*

Arctic region
territorial claims, **19**, 672

Ardmanach, Lord
Sovereign's second son, entitlement to title of, **7**,
    788

Area tourist board
scheme for formation of, **14**, 664

Armed forces

active service—
  meaning, **2**, 629
  offences on, **2**, 629
age limit for employment, minimum, **3**, 1258
alcoholic liquor, sale in canteens, **2**, 784
alien—
  employment in armed forces, **7**, 598*n*
  incitement by, **7**, 599
arrested persons, rights of, **2**, 692
billeting, *see* AIR FORCE; ARMY
births, deaths and marriages, **2**, 778, 779
canteens, sale of liquor in, **2**, 784
civil court—
  court-martial trial, effect of, **2**, 622
  redress in, restriction on, **2**, 615
  relationship with service courts, **2**, 622
civil law, application, **2**, 615
civil powers, assistance to, **2**, 624, 625, 756
civilian employees—
  service law applicable, **2**, 614
  trial outside United Kingdom, *see* STANDING CIVILIAN COURT
colonies, service in, **2**, 620
complaints—
  Defence Council, to, **2**, 637, 638
  investigation, **2**, 637, 638
  redress—
    air force personnel, **2**, 638
    army personnel, **2**, 638
    navy, in, **2**, 637
constitutional authority for, **2**, 601, 602
criminal liability, **2**, 616
Crown—
  proceedings against, **2**, 617
  relationship, **2**, 604
customs and excise, assistance as to, **2**, 625
debtor serving in, **8**, 126
Defence Council—
  complaints to, **2**, 637, 638
  findings, power to review, **2**, 710
  powers of command, **2**, 603
  regulations—
    enlistment etc, for, **2**, 608
    reserve forces, for, **2**, 611
  sentence, power to alter, **2**, 711
  summary findings, review of, **2**, 674
defence establishments, works etc, prohibited places, as, **7**, 629
Defence Organisations, **2**, 787
deserters—
  delivery to service custody, **2**, 623
  offence of desertion, **2**, 649
  powers of arrest, **2**, 623
  waiver of trial, **2**, 667
desertion—
  assisting, **7**, 601
  incitement, **7**, 596
disaffection, incitement, **7**, 598
discipline—
  active service—
    meaning, **2**, 629
    offences committed on, **2**, 629
  arrest of offenders, **2**, 623

Armed forces—*continued*

discipline—*continued*
  attached servicemen, **2**, 633
  auxiliary forces, **2**, 634
  civilians subject to, **2**, 635
  codes—
    application of—
      air force, **2**, 632
      army, **2**, 631
      naval forces, **2**, 630
    basis of, **2**, 626
    duration of, **2**, 605
    law, as part of, **2**, 605
    scope of, **2**, 626
  Commonwealth forces, **2**, 636
  disciplinary proceedings—
    court-martial, *see* COURTS-MARTIAL
    evidence in—
      abstracts and summaries, **2**, 679
      law applied to, **2**, 677
      precognitions, **2**, 679
    jurisdiction—
      place of offence affecting, **2**, 627, 628
    oath, form of, **2**, 680
    Police etc Evidence Act applied, **2**, 678
    provisions common to all services, **2**, 681
    time for beginning, **2**, 628
  navy, *see* NAVY
  persons subject to—
    air force, **2**, 632
    army, **2**, 631
    navy, **2**, 631
  provisions governing, **2**, 626
  re-trial, **2**, 628
  reserve forces, **2**, 634
  scope of legislation, **2**, 639
  Territorial Army, **2**, 634
  visiting forces, **2**, 636
elections, voting at, **2**, 782
emergency temporary employment, **5**, 603
enemy—
  allegiance to British Crown not owed by, **7**, 581
  trading with, **7**, 605–608
enlistment—
  false statements on, **2**, 657
  terms of, **2**, 608, 609
entitlement to vote, **15**, 1122
exempt agreement with members of, **5**, 824
foreign, enlistment in, **7**, 609
freedom of, **12**, 83
homosexual acts between members of, **7**, 313
identity cards, **16**, 1236
immigration control, **12**, 131
  exemption from, **14**, 1905
interference with duty, **7**, 602
jury service, exemption, **2**, 783
justifiable homicide in line of duty, **7**, 254
law applicable, **2**, 601
lessor of protected tenancy member of, repossession, **13**, 736, 747, 748
licensing requirements exemption, **2**, 784
local government office, disqualified for, **2**, 781
Lord Lieutenant, duties in relation to, **5**, 550

Armed forces—*continued*
malingering, aiding, **7**, 603
members—
   appointment, **2**, 604
   civil rights and duties, **2**, 615
   death or injury, action for, **2**, 617
   dismissal of, **2**, 604
   law applicable to, **2**, 605
   Parliamentary disqualification, **2**, 781
   reduction to ranks, **2**, 688
   wills by, **2**, 780
mutiny, incitement, **7**, 597
obstruction, **7**, 602
offences—
   abroad, committed, **2**, 627
   absence without leave, **2**, 649
   active service, on, **2**, 629
   aiding and abetting, **2**, 665
   aircraft, as to, **2**, 653
   assisting enemy, **2**, 640
   billeting, in respect of, **2**, 652
   civil offences—
      commission of, **2**, 664
      meaning, **2**, 664
   civilians abroad, against, **2**, 659
   courts-martial—
      in respect of, **2**, 655
      triable by, **2**, 714
   criminal law, under, **2**, 664
   custody, allowing escape, **2**, 654
   desertion, **2**, 649
   diminished responsibility defence, **2**, 664
   disciplinary, *see* discipline *above*
   disgraceful conduct, **2**, 661
   disobedience—
      command, to, **2**, 646
      standing orders, to, **2**, 648
   disorderly conduct, **2**, 650
   drunkenness, **2**, 650
   duty, neglect of, **2**, 643
   enlistment, false statements on, **2**, 657
   false signals, giving, **2**, 640
   good order and discipline, **2**, 663
   guard duty, as to, **2**, 642
   ill-treatment of inferiors, **2**, 662
   incitement, aiding and abetting, **2**, 665
   information, disclosure of, **2**, 656
   insubordinate behaviour, **2**, 646
   juveniles, punishment limits, **2**, 686
   looting, **2**, 644
   malingering, **2**, 650
   misconduct in action, **2**, 640
   morale, harmful to, **2**, 660
   mutiny, **2**, 645
   obstructing operations, **2**, 640
   official documents, as to, **2**, 658
   Official Secrets Act, under, **2**, 656
   prize, nature of, **2**, 641
   proceedings, time for, **2**, 690, 692
   property, relating to, **2**, 651
   provost officers, obstructing, **2**, 647
   punishments, review of, **2**, 674
   re-trial, **2**, 628
   requisitioning, as to, **2**, 652

Armed forces—*continued*
offences—*continued*
   scandalous conduct, **2**, 661
   Scottish principles as to, **2**, 664
   service property, neglect of, **2**, 651
   ship, hazarding etc, **2**, 653
   specified, **2**, 626
   spying, **2**, 689
   standing civilian court, *see* STANDING CIVILIAN
      COURT
   standing orders, disobeying, **2**, 648
   stealing, **2**, 644
   summary proceedings—
      army and air force—
         delegation of powers, **2**, 670
         disposal of charge, **2**, 671
         further proceedings, **2**, 672
         initial procedure, **2**, 670
         reduction to ranks, **2**, 688
         reference to court-martial, **2**, 672
         subsequent trial, bar to, **2**, 670
         summary punishment, **2**, 688
      navy—
         award of punishment, **2**, 669
         civilians, against, **2**, 668
         election for court-martial, **2**, 668, 687
         evidence etc in, **2**, 669
         jurisdiction, scope of, **2**, 668
         procedure, **2**, 669
         restitution order, **2**, 707
         subsequent trial barred, **2**, 669
         summary punishment, **2**, 687
      review of findings, **2**, 674
officers—
   esquire, entitlement to rank as, **16**, 2022
   gentleman, designation as, **16**, 2023
   summary punishments, **2**, 688
overseas service—
   colonies, in, **2**, 620
   foreign lands, in, **2**, 621
   jurisdiction during, **2**, 618
   NATO countries, in, **2**, 619
physical force in execution of duty, use of, **7**, 238
premises used solely for, fire precautions, **10**, 1470
prisoners of war, assisting escape, **7**, 611
public order, maintaining—
   force used in, **2**, 624
   obligations as to, **2**, 624, 625
   requests for assistance, **2**, 625
racial discrimination, **2**, 604
relevant citizen of the Union, **15**, 1124
residence, **15**, 1081
salvage award, entitlement of member to claim,
   21, 458
sections of, **2**, 601
service passport, **16**, 1236
service qualification, **15**, 1122
sex discrimination, **2**, 604
sheriff court jurisdiction, **6**, 1080
shipbuilding and fitting for foreign state at war, **7**,
   610
standing civilian courts, *see* STANDING CIVILIAN
   COURT
Status of Forces Agreement, **2**, 619

Armed forces—*continued*
statute law, generally, **7**, 600
statutory sick pay provisions, **21**, 920
superior orders, acting under, **7**, 206, 207
temporary employment, **5**, 603
testamentum militare, **25**, 731
visiting—
  customs and excise duty relief, **7**, 1117
  See also VISITING FORCES
wife or husband of serving member, service
  qualification, **15**, 1131
women's services—
  authority for, **2**, 612
  status of, **2**, 612
See also ARMY

Armorial bearing
donated, may not be, **8**, 615
heraldry as study of, **11**, 1601
Lord Lyon, *see* LYON, COURT OF THE LORD
seals of arms, **11**, 1601, 1602
See also ARMS; COAT OF ARMS

Armorial de Gelré, 11, 1602

Armorial records
generally, **11**, 1602

Armour-Bearer
office of, **7**, 820, 824

Arms
achievement of, *see* ACHIEVEMENT OF ARMS
additaments, **11**, 1610, 1621
assumption of, conditions relating to, **25**, 871
cadency, **11**, 1618
coats of, *see* COAT OF ARMS
confirmation of, **11**, 1616
daughters, **11**, 1614
grant of, **11**, 1615
  honorary, **11**, 1625
heirs apparent or presumptive, **11**, 1614
illegal use, **11**, 1633
ladies, **11**, 1604, 1606
law of, **11**, 1622*ff*
legal protection, **11**, 1613
marshalling, **11**, 1626
matriculation, **11**, 1617, 1621
nature of, **11**, 1613
pedigree, proof of, **11**, 1623
penalty for improper use, **11**, 1614, 1633
protection of rights, **11**, 1633
Public Register of, **11**, 1602
recording, **11**, 1614
right to bear or use, **11**, 1614
Rothesay, Duke of, **7**, 787
royal, **7**, 785; **11**, 1632
Scottish and English positions distinguished, **11**,
  1613
seal of, **11**, 1601
shield of, **11**, 1640
  See also SHIELD
Sovereign's eldest son, **7**, 787
study of, **11**, 1601
succession to, **11**, 1619
tailzied, **11**, 1620
transfer of, **11**, 1622

Arm's length
See SALE AT ARM'S LENGTH

Army
Act—
  persons subject to, **2**, 631
  territorial application, **2**, 613
aliment or maintenance—
  deduction from pay, **2**, 766
  service of process, **2**, 769
arrest—
  arrested person, rights of, **2**, 692
  outside United Kingdom, **2**, 691
  powers of, **2**, 691
authority for, **2**, 602, 608
billeting—
  authority for, **2**, 770
  meaning, **2**, 770
  obstruction etc, **2**, 772
  offences, **2**, 652
  payment, right to, **2**, 772
  premises liable to, **2**, 771
  procedure, **2**, 771
births etc, registration, **2**, 778
Board, functions, **2**, 603
composition of, **2**, 608
court-martial, *see* COURTS-MARTIAL
discipline, *see* ARMED FORCES
enlistment—
  conditions of, **2**, 608
  false statements in, **2**, 657
maintenance orders, **2**, 767
offences, *see* ARMED FORCES
pay, deductions from—
  aliment etc, for, **2**, 767
  court order for, **2**, 766
requisitioning—
  authorisation, **2**, 774
  food etc, of, **2**, 775
  offences as to, **2**, 776
  payment for, **2**, 777
  retention of vehicles, **2**, 775
Reserve, *see* ARMY RESERVE
Reserve of Officers, **2**, 750
wills, validity, **2**, 780
women's services, **2**, 612
See also ARMED FORCES

Army Board
functions, **2**, 603

Army Reserve
aliment—
  decrees for, **2**, 769
  deduction from pay, **2**, 766
calling out—
  civil duties, for, **2**, 625
  home defence service, for, **2**, 752
  liability for, **2**, 749
  national emergency, in, **2**, 751
civil employment, safeguarding, **2**, 754
civil power, assisting, **2**, 624, 625, 756
composition, **2**, 748
discharge, right to, **2**, 755
legal basis for, **2**, 611
maintenance of, **2**, 748
maintenance orders, **2**, 767
officers, **2**, 748, 750
pay, deductions from, **2**, 766–767

Army Reserve—*continued*
permanent service—
  call-out notice, **2**, 753
  duration of, **2**, 755
  liability for, **2**, 751
requisitioning powers, **2**, 775
Arrest
charge following, **16**, 1793
child, of, **17**, 891
citizens, police power to call upon assistance of, **16**, 1787
consequences, **16**, 1789
controlled drugs, relating to, **14**, 1252
court, bringing offender before, **16**, 1784
customs officers' powers, **7**, 1232
detention following, **16**, 1788
European Convention on Human Rights, **16**, 1806
explosives, offences in connection with, **10**, 1631
fingerprinting following, **17**, 603, 605
firearm or imitation firearm—
  offences in connection with, **10**, 1576, 1577
  using or attempting to use to resist, **10**, 1564; **16**, 1807
force, use by police, **16**, 1789, 1793
identification parade following, **17**, 603, 606
immigration officer or constable, by, **12**, 168
intimation of custody, right to send, **16**, 1793, 1793*n*
liberation by police, **17**, 609
meaning, **16**, 1789
peer, of, civil action, **16**, 1308
police powers—
  citizens, to call upon assistance of, **16**, 1787
  generally, **16**, 1784, 1787, 1788
police report, **16**, 1784
rights of accused upon, **16**, 1793
salmon fishing offences, **11**, 28
search following, **16**, 1797
six-hour detention power, **16**, 1791, 1794, 1796
solicitor, offender's right to see, **16**, 1793
statement to police after, **10**, 732
suspicion, on, **16**, 1791, 1792
suspicion of crime, on, **15**, 438
terrorism, person suspected of involvement in, **16**, 1801
unlawful, **7**, 550
  consequences of, **17**, 599
  or irregular, **16**, 1788
unreasonable or unnecessary detention following, **16**, 1784, 1788, 1793
warrant, under—
  furth of jurisdiction, **17**, 601
  furth of Scotland, **17**, 602
  generally, **16**, 1790; **17**, 600
warrant for, applicant or holder of passport, of, **16**, 1227
without warrant—
  common law, **16**, 1791
  generally, **15**, 438, **16**, 1790
  police officer, by, **17**, 596
  private citizen, by, **17**, 597
  statute law, **16**, 1792
  statutory offence, for, **17**, 598

Arrest—*continued*
wrongful, *see* DETENTION, WRONGFUL
See also ARREST OR DETENTION
Arrest or detention
alcoholic, of, **12**, 29
compensation for wrongful, **12**, 29
compulsory residence, **12**, 40
drug addict, of, **12**, 29
European Convention on Human Rights—
  general rules, **12**, 29
  lawful, **12**, 29
files, access to, **12**, 36
infectious diseases, to prevent spread of, **12**, 29
legitimate detention, what constitutes, **12**, 29, 30
minor, of, **12**, 29
reasons for, obligation to give, **12**, 29
remand, prolonged detention on, **12**, 32
right to be brought before judicial person or body, **12**, 29, 30
  promptness, **12**, 30, 32
trial within reasonable time, entitlement to, **12**, 32, 46, 47
unauthorised entrants, **12**, 29
unsound mind, persons of, **12**, 29
vagrant, of, **12**, 29
See also ARREST; DETENTION
Arrest of ships
See ARRESTMENT
Arrestment
abuse of process, **15**, 465, 467
acquirenda not arrestable, **8**, 265
ad fundandum jurisdictionem, **8**, 249; **17**, 1119
administrative costs, **8**, 104
Admiralty, **8**, 322
Admiralty causes in so far as jurisdiction is based on, **4**, 79
alimentary funds, of, **8**, 280
arrestee, **8**, 247
  breach by, **8**, 319
  building society as, **8**, 259
  competent, **8**, 259, 260
  corporation as, **8**, 259
  Crown as, **8**, 259, 260
  defences available to, **8**, 312
  execution on, **8**, 258
  liquidator as, **8**, 259
  prohibited from parting with subject arrested, **8**, 284
  trust as, **8**, 259
arrester, **8**, 247
  death of, **8**, 299
arrestment to found jurisdiction, **8**, 249
assignation, competition with, **8**, 289
assurance policy, **8**, 277, 284
attachment theory, **8**, 285
bank account, of, **8**, 272
breach, **8**, 319
  damages, action for, **8**, 319
building society account, of, **8**, 272
cargo, of, **8**, 322, 328; **21**, 482*n*
caveat, **8**, 300
common debtor, defences available to, **8**, 313
common law, **8**, 250
common property, of, **8**, 267

Arrestment—*continued*
company adminstration, and, **8**, 296
competition between two, **8**, 284, 287
completion, **8**, 309
conjoined arrestment order, **8**, 248
constituted debt, of, **8**, 276
contract payment, of, **8**, 275
corporeal moveable property, of, **8**, 247, 248, 281
creditor, **8**, 264
Crown, in hands of, **7**, 747
current maintenance, **8**, 248
damages—
    action for, **21**, 394
    claim for, **8**, 274
death—
    creditor, of, **8**, 253
    debtor, of, **8**, 127, 299
debt assigned, where, **8**, 253
decree for payment, **8**, 119, 253, 253*n*
dependence, on the, **8**, 252, 254, 257; **21**, 137
    maritime lien, priority of, **21**, 392, 479
    mortgagee's rights as to, **21**, 179
    proposed reforms, **8**, 250
    recall, **3**, 997; **8**, 303
    salvage actions, **21**, 482, 482*n*
    towage, action in respect of, **21**, 423
diligence—
    as, **8**, 101
    effect of winding up on, **4**, 845
document of debt, on, **8**, 252, 255
double distress, **8**, 288, 318
earnings, of, *see* EARNINGS
effect of, **8**, 284
equalisation, **8**, 291
    proposed reforms, **8**, 104
error in, **8**, 314
execution, in, **8**, 252, 253
    arrestment on the dependence converted to, **8**, 254
    maritime lien, priority of, **21**, 392
    recall, **8**, 303
executor-creditor, confirmation as, **8**, 356
exempt goods, **8**, 281
expenses, **8**, 317
    arrestment of earnings, **8**, 332
    recall, of, **8**, 306
    storage, of, **8**, 283
extent, **8**, 251
extinction, **8**, 284
floating charges, and, **8**, 295
foreign decree, **8**, 260
foreign insolvency, and, **8**, 298
freight, of, **21**, 482*n*
furthcoming, action of, **8**, 247, 260, 281, 284
    completion by, **8**, 309
    defences available to arrestee, **8**, 312
    defences available to common debtor, **8**, 313
    generally, **8**, 309
    grounds for, **8**, 311
    jurisdiction, **8**, 310
    parties to, **8**, 310
    payment without, **8**, 320
future and contingent debts, of, **8**, 268
future development, **8**, 250

Arrestment—*continued*
generally, **8**, 189
heritable property, of, **8**, 189
in mala fide, used in, **8**, 303
in rem, **21**, 137
    mortgagee's rights as to, **21**, 179
    salvage actions, **21**, 481
inchoate, **8**, 286
incorporeal moveable property, of, **8**, 247, 261
insurance policy, of, **8**, 277
interdict, **8**, 300
interest, problems arising, **8**, 316
international aspects, **8**, 260
    proposed reforms, **8**, 104
joint property, of, **8**, 267
judicial assignation, classification as, **8**, 261
jurisdictionis fundandae causa, **8**, 249
letters of, **8**, 120
limitation fund, establishment, **21**, 763
liquidation, and, **8**, 294
litigiosity, **8**, 286
loosing, **8**, 307
mala fides, made in, **8**, 315
maritime, **8**, 101, 255, 322
meaning, **8**, 189
moveable property, **4**, 42; **8**, 247; **14**, 1812; **17**, 1364; **18**, 13
multiple, ranking, **8**, 284, 287
multiplepoinding, **8**, 284, 318
nature of, **8**, 247
negotiable instrument, of, **8**, 278
nexus, **8**, 285, 286
nimious, **8**, 303
notorial instrument of protest, **8**, 253, 253*n*
officers of court, exercise by, **8**, 105
oppressive, **8**, 303
partnership property, of, **8**, 270
payment without furthcoming, **8**, 320
personal debts, **14**, 1812
poinding, competition with, **8**, 290
possession, nature of required, **8**, 282
prescription, **8**, 308
prior hypothec, **8**, 263
prohibition theory, **8**, 285, 286, 299
ranking, **8**, 287, 289
recall, **8**, 284, 300
    expenses, **8**, 306
    grounds for, **8**, 303
    loosing, and, **8**, 307
    procedure, **8**, 304
    third party, **8**, 304
    title to apply for, **8**, 305
receivership, and, **8**, 295
reduction, **8**, 300
sale—
    action of, **8**, 247
    competition with, **8**, 289
    goods, of, **8**, 281
security, in, **8**, 257
    arrestee, **17**, 1116
    dependence on an action, **17**, 1114, 1297
    execution of warrant for, **17**, 1115
    meaning, **17**, 1113

Arrestment—*continued*
security, in—*continued*
    recall, **8**, 303; **17**, 1118
    subjects of, **17**, 1117
sequestration, and, **8**, 292
    sequestration of creditor, **8**, 253
service—
    generally, **8**, 258
    international aspects, **8**, 260
    special parties, on, **8**, 259
shares, of, **8**, 269, 284
ship, of—
    cargo, **8**, 247, 322, 328; **21**, 482n
    charterparties, **8**, 327
    completion, **8**, 322, 326
    Court of Session jurisdiction, **8**, 322
    damages, action for, **21**, 394
    defender, **8**, 324
    dependence, on the, **21**, 137
        maritime lien, priority of, **21**, 392, 479
        mortgagee's rights as to, **21**, 179
        salvage actions, **21**, 482, 482n
        towage, action in respect of, **21**, 423
    European Union, defender domiciled in, **8**, 322
    execution, in, maritime lien, priority of, **21**, 392
    freight, of, **21**, 482n
    generally, **1**, 417; **8**, 247, 248, 322; **17**, 1119;
        21, 107, 137, 137n, 482n
    grounds for arrest, **8**, 323
    in personam, **8**, 322, 323, 324, 326, 327
    in personam et rem, **8**, 322
    in rem, **8**, 322, 323, 325, 326, 327; **21**, 137
        mortgagee's rights as to, **21**, 179
        salvage actions, **21**, 481
    limitation fund, establishment, **21**, 763
    meaning of ship, **8**, 322
    no arrestee, **8**, 322
    procedure, **8**, 325
    ranking, **8**, 326
    sale, **8**, 356
    Scots and English law, **8**, 322
    shares, division of ship into, **8**, 322
    sheriff court jurisdiction, **8**, 322
    ship, of, generally, **21**, 107, 137, 137n, 482n
    Sunday, on, **8**, 325
    warrant to dismantle, **8**, 325
social security benefits, of, **8**, 280
specially appropriated subject, of, **8**, 279
spes successionis, **8**, 261
state pension, of, **8**, 280
statute law, **8**, 250
storage expenses, **8**, 283
stricti juris rule, **8**, 314
subject matter—
    generally, **8**, 261
    third party, in possession of, **8**, 247
sum consigned to court, of, **8**, 273
summary warrant, on, **8**, 252, 256
tantum et tale rule, **8**, 262, 312
    problems arising, **8**, 263
tax, recovery by arrestment and furthcoming, **19**,
    1550
third party rights, **8**, 266
time to pay direction, and, **8**, 297

Arrestment—*continued*
time to pay order, and, **8**, 297
trust deeds for creditors, **8**, 293
trusts, interaction with, **8**, 271
unintimated assignation defeated by, **20**, 47
unspecified subject matter, **8**, 251
uplifting, as *rei interventus*, **3**, 885
use on dependence of action, **8**, 120
wages, **14**, 1812
warrants—
    arrestment—
        dependence, on the, **8**, 252, 254, 257
        document of debt, on a, **8**, 252, 255
        execution, in, **8**, 252, 253
        summary warrant, on, **8**, 252, 256
    generally, **8**, 119
    letters of arrestment, **8**, 253, 254
    letters of horning, **8**, 253
    precepts of arrestment, **8**, 253, 254
    who may make, **8**, 264
    withdrawal, **8**, 302
    wrongous, **8**, 321
Arrestment on the dependence
See ARRESTMENT
Arrestment or poinding
repeal of remedy, **20**, 870
Arsenic
restriction on use in food, **11**, 380
Arson
Criminal Injuries Compensation Scheme, **7**, 1
See also FIRERAISING
Art
society promoting, **12**, 694n
Art gallery
See MUSEUMS AND GALLERIES
Art gallery authority
generally, **14**, 688
powers and duties, **14**, 689
Art and part liability
concert between accused, **7**, 177, 184, 189
counselling of offence, **7**, 183
forms, **7**, 179ff
generally, **7**, 177, 194
instigation of offence—
    generally, **7**, 179, 183
    withdrawal of instigation, **7**, 184
meaning, **7**, 177
mobbing and rioting, **7**, 438
no prior agreement, where, **7**, 177
participation in commission of offences—
    concert between accused, **7**, 177, 184, 189
    degrees of participation, **7**, 187
        minor differences in, **7**, 188
    pre-involvement actions, **7**, 190
    unintended consequences, liability for, **7**, 191–193
pre-involvement actions, **7**, 190
presence at commission of offence—
    failure in duty to intervene, **7**, 182
    liability by inference, **7**, 181
    mere presence, **7**, 180
requirements to establish, **7**, 177
supply of materials or information, **7**, 185, 186
unintended consequences, liability for, **7**, 191–193
victim, liability of, **7**, 177, 178

Articles and Act of Union
See UNION AGREEMENT OF 1707
Articles Declaratory of the Constitution of the Church of Scotland
adjudication and legislation, Church's rights as to, 3, 1634
Article I, 3, 1502
Article II, 3, 1502, 1504
Article III, 3, 1502, 1504
Article IV, 3, 1502
Article V, 3, 1502, 1504
Article VI, 3, 1502
Article VII, 3, 1502
Article VIII, 3, 1502, 1504
enactment, 3, 1501
generally, 5, 348
interpretation, right of, 3, 1502
modification or addition, 3, 1546
ratification, 3, 1501
Westminster Confession of Faith, 3, 1502
Articles of Agreement
dioceses of Scottish Episcopal Church, 3, 1615
Articles of association
alteration of, 4, 329; 25, 50
copy of, 4, 329
fair value, 25, 68
fixed price transfer, 25, 52
form of, 4, 329
general meetings, right to call, 4, 473
guarantee company, 4, 329
market in shares, restriction on, 25, 50
membership—
  rights and obligations of, 4, 343
  shares—
    class rights—
      generally, 4, 347
      variation of, 4, 348, 349
    disclosure of interests in, 4, 346
    registration of interests in, 4, 346
personal right of shareholder, infringement of, 4, 468
pre-emption rights, 4, 354, 377
proposed, incorporation by registering, 4, 304
registration, incorporation by, 4, 314
shares, company limited by, 4, 329
signing by subscriber of, witness, 4, 314
special resolution—
  alteration by, 4, 329
  approval of changes by, 4, 380
statutory forms of, technical reform relating to, 4, 306
subscriber, signed by, 4, 314
transfer of shares, restrictions on, 25, 63
unlimited company, 4, 329
winding up petition, right of contributory relating to, 4, 504
Articles of Union
See UNION AGREEMENT OF 1707
Articulated vehicle
definition, 20, 408
weight, 20, 476
Artificial harbour
administration, 11, 1306
charter, grant by, 11, 1305

Artificial harbour—*continued*
common law position, 11, 1305
dues, exaction of, 11, 1306
free port, see FREE PORT
generally, 11, 1305
geographical extent, 11, 1305
historical background, 11, 1301
rights implied in grant of, 11, 1305
Artificial insemination
child conceived by, widowed mother's allowance, 21, 896
establishing paternity, 10, 1159
not adultery, 10, 900
See also FERTILITY TREATMENT
Artificial stream
flow, 25, 355
generally, 25, 355
permanent, 25, 356
temporary, 25, 357
Artist
immigration controls—
  change of employment, 12, 256
  entry clearance, 12, 151, 254, 255
  extension of leave, 12, 257
  Immigration Rules, 12, 149
  police registration conditions, 12, 175
  work permit exemption, 12, 154
meaning, 12, 154
personal name, protection by passing off action, 18, 1376, 1397
Artistic craftsmanship, work of
copyright, 18, 957, 966
  design documents, 18, 1155
Artistic expression
freedom of, 12, 73
Arts
art gallery authority, 14, 688, 689
expenditure programme, 5, 585
Arts Council of Great Britain
functions, 14, 62
grant by, tax treatment, 18, 1585
public money provided by, 9, 1007
Ascendant
heritable succession, 25, 679
moveable succession, 25, 682
Ascorbic acid
meat, added to 11, 374n
Ashpit
infectious matter in, 19, 449
public health nuisance, as, 19, 336
Assault
abduction, 7, 215
actus reus, 7, 211
age of victim, 7, 228
aggravated, 19, 1266
aggravations—
  accused, status of, 7, 228
  generally, 7, 224
  intoxication, 7, 228
  mode of attack, 7, 226
  motive, 7, 236
  place of offence, 7, 225
  relationship between accused and victim, 7, 228

Assault—*continued*
aggravations—*continued*
  result of attack, **7**, 227
  victim, status of, **7**, 229
aggressive action undertaken as jape, **7**, 214
aggressive conduct of accused, **7**, 214
alarm, to put victim in state of, **7**, 232
animal urged by human handler, **7**, 213
attack—
  actus reus, constituting, **7**, 211
  constituent elements, **7**, 216
    aggressive conduct, **7**, 214
    injury, **7**, 217
    personal conduct, **7**, 213
    physical conduct, **7**, 215
  meaning, **7**, 212
attempted, **7**, 170, 219
authorities on, **7**, 210
breach of the peace, and, **7**, 447
child, of, **3**, 1246, 1250; **10**, 1137, 1224
  diagnostic techniques, **3**, 1339
  mens rea, **3**, 1339
child under age of criminal responsibility, by, **7**, 213
clothing, damage to, **7**, 216
consent of victim, where, **7**, 220
constructive violence, **7**, 245
corporal punishment, entitlement to use, **7**, 239
corrosive substance, throwing, **7**, 226
court, committed in, **7**, 225
culpable homicide, **7**, 280
death or suicide of victim following, **7**, 227
defences—
  diminished responsibility, **7**, 237, 242
  discipline, duty to keep, **7**, 237, 239
  employment, duty of, **7**, 237, 238
  generally, **7**, 237
  provocation, **7**, 237, 241
  self-defence, **7**, 237, 240
delict, **15**, 255
disease communicated during, **7**, 227
drugging, **7**, 226
evil intent, **7**, 78, 234, 244
failure to act, as, **7**, 218
fear of injury, victim in, **7**, 215, 217
firearm, involving, **7**, 226, 244
frighten, to, **7**, 232, 244
grievous bodily harm, with intent to commit, **7**, 236
hamesucken, **7**, 225
incidence of, control, **7**, 250
indecent, *see* INDECENT ASSAULT
injury to victim, **7**, 215, 217
  actions amounting to injury, **7**, 217
intention, **7**, 232
  cause injury, to, **15**, 255
  constructive, **7**, 233
  evil, **7**, 231, 234, 244
  frighten, to, **7**, 232, 244
  requirement to be intentional, **7**, 130
intoxication of accused, **7**, 128, 130, 228, 231, 234
judge, of, **7**, 545
lawful business, to prevent, **7**, 236
lethal and non-lethal weapons, **7**, 226

Assault—*continued*
malice, **7**, 80
meaning—
  legal, **7**, 209
  ordinary, **7**, 208
medical treatment, as, **7**, 222
mens rea, **7**, 213, 224
  aggravations, **7**, 236
  constructive intention, **7**, 233
  evil intention, **7**, 231, 234, 244
  generally, **7**, 230
  intention, **7**, 232
  proof, **7**, 235
  recklessness, **7**, 234, 249
mode of attack, **7**, 226
motive, aggravation by, **7**, 236
murder, with intent to, **7**, 236
offensive weapon *see* WEAPON
omission as, **7**, 218
other offences, in relation to—
  culpable homicide, **7**, 243, 244
  generally, **7**, 243
  murder, **7**, 243, 244
  preventive offences, related, **7**, 250–252
  rape *see* RAPE
  robbery, **7**, 243, 245
parent, by, **7**, 239
person, must be aimed at, **7**, 216
personal conduct of accused, **7**, 213
physical conduct of accused, **7**, 215
place of offence, **7**, 225
police officer, on, **16**, 1807
political rights, to prevent, **7**, 236
preventive offences, related, **7**, 250–252
private prosecution, **17**, 528
provocative act, as, **7**, 273
rape *see* RAPE
recklessness, **7**, 234, 249
  culpable and reckless—
    endangering of public, **7**, 248, 249
    injury, **7**, 82, 247, 249
related offences—
  culpable and reckless—
    endangering of public, **7**, 248, 249
    injury, **7**, 82, 247, 249
  generally, **7**, 246
  recklessness, **7**, 249
robbery, and, **7**, 215, 359, 360
sexual—
  generally, **7**, 295
  intercourse, **7**, 217
  rape *see* RAPE
significant injury, resulting in, **7**, 227
spitting, **7**, 217
sporting participants, by, **7**, 220, 221; **19**, 1265
status of victim, **7**, 228
supporters, by, **19**, 1266
teacher, by, **7**, 239
verbal attacks, **7**, 208, 209, 215
victim injured while attempting escape, **7**, 227
voluntary, whether, **7**, 213
Assay office
approved hallmarks, **18**, 1416
charges, **18**, 1424

Assay office—*continued*
convention hallmarks, **18**, 1416
list, **18**, 1414, 1414*n*
meaning, **18**, 1414
sponsors' marks, **18**, 1417
unauthorised marks, treatment of, **18**, 1422
Assedation
meaning, **13**, 103
Assembly
intimidation, **14**, 1326
meeting as, **14**, 1301
offences, **14**, 1326
offensive weapon, use of, **14**, 1326
peaceful, right to, **12**, 6
police power to impose conditions, **16**, 1786, 1786*n*
public disorder, resulting in, **14**, 1326
statutory control, **14**, 1326
Assembly hall
water meter charges, **25**, 536
Assessment roll
rates, levying of, **14**, 842
Assets
business—
    capital gains tax, **19**, 1527
    inheritance tax, **19**, 1533
capital, shareholder's rights relating to, **25**, 14
company's financial record, **25**, 32
cover, existence of, **25**, 32
distribution of—
    dividends, **4**, 927
    order of priority of claims, **4**, 926
    pari passu
    ranking, **4**, 925
employees, power to make over to, **4**, 865
execution on, in England and Wales, **4**, 756
finance for acquisition of, **14**, 1005
fixed—
    capital not tied up in, **14**, 1016
    purposes of valuation, **25**, 92
goodwill, **25**, 34
property, valuation of, *see* VALUATION
sale from deceased's estate, relief on, **25**, 1015
security of repayment against, **25**, 14
shareholder has no direct interest in, **25**, 12
surplus, existence of, **25**, 32
trusts of, **24**, 12
valuation of, **25**, 993
    See also VALUATION; VALUER
value—
    break up, **25**, 22
    generally, **25**, 22
    net, **25**, 21
Assignation
assignatus utitur jure auctoris, **12**, 846; **18**, 660, 689
assignee, *see* ASSIGNEE
binding on cedent, when, **18**, 655
cheque as, **4**, 205
constitution, **13**, 367
contract, originating in, **18**, 8
delictual claim, of, **15**, 604
delivered but unintimated, **18**, 658
delivery, **18**, 655
donatio mortis causa, **12**, 847

Assignation—*continued*
execution, **18**, 655
feudal conveyance, **18**, 104
form and wording, **12**, 847; **13**, 366; **18**, 655
general rule, **4**, 102
incorporeal property—
    generally, **18**, 653
inhibition, of, **8**, 186
insurance policy, **12**, 845, 846
intellectual property, **18**, 802
    copyright—
        assignation in security, **18**, 1007
        assignee, dealing by, **18**, 1012
        co-ownership, cases of, **18**, 1011
        exclusive copyright, **18**, 1006
        future copyright, **18**, 1006
        generally, **18**, 1005, 1006
        meaning, **18**, 1005
        partial assignation, **18**, 1006
        restricted acts, in respect of, **18**, 1006
    international aspects, **18**, 1611
intimation—
    necessity for, to insurer, **12**, 847
    without, deposit of, as security, **13**, 1759
lease—
    acceptance by landlord of assignee, **13**, 363
    assignability—
        delectus personae, doctrine of, **13**, 355–357, 583
        diligence, effect, **13**, 184
        exclusion—
            express, **13**, 358–362
            without consent, **13**, 359
        express power to assign, **13**, 364
        generally, **13**, 353, 354
        landlord, consent of, **13**, 345
        legal or judicial assignees, tenant's, **13**, 355
    assignee, *see* ASSIGNEE
    cedent—
        completion between assignee and, **13**, 369
        liability to landlord, **13**, 373
        questions between assignee and, **13**, 374
        rent arrears, **13**, 375
    commercial, **13**, 564, 583
    conditions running with lands, **13**, 239–243
    covert form, in, **13**, 361
    effect—
        cedent and assignee, questions between, **13**, 374
        further assignations, **13**, 376
        liability of cedent to landlord, **13**, 373
        rent arrears, **13**, 375
    express exclusion, **13**, 358–362
        enforceability, **13**, 362
        evasion, **13**, 361
    further assignations, **13**, 376
    intimation, **13**, 370
    landlord, completion between assignee and, **13**, 370
    long lease, **13**, 337
    meaning, **13**, 353
    prohibited, irritancy, **13**, 428
    rent arrears, **13**, 375

Assignation—*continued*
lease—*continued*
sublease—
competition with, **13**, 385
distinguished, **13**, 353
tenant, transfer of interest by, **13**, 353
third parties, completion between assignee and, **13**, 371
title, completion of assignee's, **13**, 369–372
life policy, **12**, 854
nature, **13**, 365
obligation, of, **18**, 662
patent, of, **18**, 811
application for patent by assignee, **18**, 829
registration, **18**, 812
personal rights—
generally, **18**, 8*n*
warrandice, **18**, 717, 718
proof, **13**, 367
protected tenancy, repossession, **13**, 714
real right, of, warrandice, **18**, 718
recording rights, **18**, 1438
registered industrial design, **18**, 1197
retrocession, **18**, 661
right in security created by, *see* RIGHT IN SECURITY
rights in performances, **18**, 1438
sublease—
competition with, **13**, 385
distinguished, **13**, 353
subrogation compared, **12**, 894
title to sue on contract, *see* CONTRACT (assignation; title to sue)
uncompleted, **13**, 368
unregistered design right, **18**, 1227
semiconductor topographies, **18**, 1248
valid, prerequisites of, **12**, 847
warrandice—
clause of, **18**, 655
personal rights, **18**, 717, 718
real rights, **18**, 718
written, must be, **12**, 847
written instrument, creation by, **20**, 46
Assignee
acceptance by landlord, **13**, 363
cedent—
liability to landlord, **13**, 373
questions between assignee and, **13**, 374
commercial lease, **13**, 564
consent, landlord's, unreasonably witheld, **13**, 359
diligence, effect, **13**, 184
express exclusion, **13**, 358–362
enforceability, **13**, 362
evasion, **13**, 361
further assignations, **13**, 376
generally, **13**, 353
landlord's hypothec, **13**, 514
meaning, **13**, 353
removings, action of, **13**, 501
rent arrears, liability for, **13**, 375
title of, completion—
assignees, between, **13**, 372
cedent and assignee, between, **13**, 369
landlord and assignee, between, **13**, 370
third parties and assignee, between, **13**, 371

Assignments and Modifications of Stipends
records of, **19**, 849
Assistance in kind
child under eighteen—
local authority duty, exercise, discretion, **22**, 13
preventing child coming into care, **22**, 13
conditionally given, **22**, 13
emergency, **22**, 13
entitlement, statutory, **22**, 13
home meals service as, **22**, 27
See also HOME MEALS SERVICE
local authority, discretion to provide—
matters required to be considered in exercise, **22**, 13
repayment, local authority, **22**, 13
Assistant chief constable
appointment, **14**, 483
Assisted places scheme
generally, **8**, 817, 818
Associated Presbyterian Churches
generally, **3**, 1636
Association
business, as, **7**, 1295
capital allowances, **19**, 1314
club, *see* CLUB
company distinguished, **2**, 801
contract establishing, **15**, 655
corporation tax, **19**, 1313, 1314
decision of organ of, **4**, 46
defamation, as party to, **15**, 475, 480
discrimination, liability for, **9**, 343
domestic tribunal set up by, **23**, 901, 916
domicile of, **4**, 31
incorporated, **19**, 1228
liability of members, **2**, 814
meaning, **2**, 801
official address of, **4**, 31, 46
partnership, as, **15**, 475
private Bill—
giving powers to, **19**, 91–94
promoted by, **19**, 91–94
relevant service, **14**, 1916
Scots law, treatment in, **2**, 801
seat of, **4**, 46
unincorporated, **19**, 1227
capacity to contract, **3**, 26
corporation tax, **19**, 1519
voluntary churches, **3**, 1632
value added tax, **3**, 1162; **19**, 1315–1318
VAT registration provisions, **7**, 1347
voluntary obligation, capacity to enter, **15**, 663
Association, freedom of
right to, **12**, 6, 73, 75–77
Association of British Insurers (ABI)
Code of Practice for Intermediaries other than Registered Brokers, **12**, 815
Statement of General Insurance Practice, **12**, 816, 861
proposal forms, **12**, 824, 867
materiality, test of, **12**, 867, 872
notification of loss, **12**, 881
warranties, **12**, 873
renewal notices, **12**, 825

Association of British Insurers (ABI)—
continued
Statement of Long-Term Insurance Practice, **12**, 816, 861
  materiality, test of, **12**, 867, 872
  notification of loss, **12**, 881
  proposal forms, **12**, 824, 867
  warranties, **12**, 873
Association of Chief Police Officers
generally, **16**, 1763
Association for Consumer Research
generally, **6**, 9, 26
Association of County Councils in Scotland
replacement by Convention of Scottish Local
  Authorities, **14**, 81
**Association of Lieutenants of Counties and
  Custodes Rotulorum**
committee, **5**, 563
meetings, **5**, 563
Association for Payment Clearing Services
clearing systems established under auspices of, **4**, 200
**Association of Scottish Police
  Superintendents**
generally, **16**, 1763
**Association for the Vindication of Scottish
  Rights**
establishment and aims, **15**, 1016
Assumption of Thirds
records of, **19**, 849
Assurance policy
See INSURANCE
Assured tenancy
conversion of secure tenancy into, **11**, 1936
See TENANT-TENANCY
Assythment
action of, precedent, reasons for not following
  prior decisions—
  cessante ratione cessat ipsa lex, **22**, 354
remedy of, **15**, 215
Astronomer Royal
office of, **7**, 849
Astronomical data
calendar, in, **22**, 801–803
Easter, fixing date of, **22**, 808
Sosigenes, reform, **22**, 803, 804
year, measuring duration, **22**, 811
Asylum
applicant for, removal of, **12**, 318
asylee—
  grant or refusal of leave to enter, **12**, 170
  meaning, **12**, 315
category changed by seeking, **12**, 171
claim for, **12**, 318
eligibility for, **12**, 318
grant of, **12**, 318
Immigration Rules, **12**, 149, 320
leave to enter, **12**, 170, 318
refugee status, and, **12**, 315
water meter charges, **25**, 536
See also REFUGEE
ATC carnet
European Union customs documentation, **7**,
  1124, 1169, 1172
Athens Convention
See SHIPPING

Athletic club
permitted hours, variation of, **2**, 20
Athletic race meetings
starters for, **10**, 1537
Atmospheric pollution
See POLLUTION; SMOKE
Atomic Energy Authority (UK)
buildings belonging to or in occupation of, **3**, 209
Atomic energy and radioactive substances
Chernobyl disaster, food contaminated by **19**,
  491*n*
codes of practice, **9**, 923
common law, **9**, 903–913
competition law, **4**, 1309
Convention on the Physical Protection of
  Nuclear Material, **12**, 508
employers' liability, **9**, 904
Euratom Treaty, *see* EUROPEAN ATOMIC ENERGY
  COMMUNITY
export of atomic product, **7**, 1194
export licences, **9**, 924
export of nuclear product, **7**, 1194
import licences, **9**, 924
legislation relating to, **9**, 1180
liability—
  delictual, to third persons, **9**, 903
  employer, of, **9**, 904
medicinal products, **14**, 1201
mobile apparatus—
  meaning, **9**, 1184
  registration of, **9**, 1187
notes of guidance, **9**, 923
pollution control, **19**, 303
radioactive material—
  meaning, **9**, 1184
  registration of users—
    exemptions from requirement, **9**, 1186
    generally, **9**, 1185
  transport of—
    air, by, **9**, 917
    generally, **9**, 1193
    post, by, **9**, 921
    rail, by, **9**, 919
    road, by, **9**, 920, 1194; **19**, 388, 389
    sea, by, **9**, 918
radioactivity, concern over, **9**, 1179
radiological protection, **9**, 1181, 1182
  international bodies, **9**, 1182
  United Kingdom administrative bodies for, **9**,
    1181
safety regulations—
  educational establishments, **9**, 915
  food, **9**, 916
  ionising radiations at work, **9**, 914
  medicine, **9**, 916
social security, **9**, 922
third person, delictual liability to, **9**, 903
United Kingdom Atomic Energy Authority,
  legislation relating to, **9**, 913
waste—
  disposal of—
    accumulation of waste, **9**, 1191
    authorisation of, **9**, 1189

Atomic energy and radioactive substances—
continued
waste—*continued*
  disposal of—*continued*
    inspectors, **9**, 1192
    local authorities and, **9**, 1190
    methods of, **9**, 1188
    meaning, **9**, 1184
    types of, **9**, 1183
See also ELECTRICITY; NUCLEAR INSTALLATION
Attachment
arrestment as, **8**, 285
inhibition—
  after attachment, **8**, 181
  after floating charge but before attachment, **8**,
    180
poinding as, **8**, 286
Attack
See ASSAULT
Attainder
former use, **7**, 567
House of Lords jurisdiction, **6**, 823
Attainment of majority, *see* MAJORITY
Attempt
actus reus, **7**, 30, 162, 163
assault, **7**, 170, 219
conduct-crime, **7**, 162
conspiracy, attempted, **7**, 170, 173
crimes for which inapplicable, **7**, 170
crminalisation, justifications for, **7**, 161
'final stage' or 'last act' rule, **7**, 164–166
generally, **7**, 161
historical background, **7**, 161
Hume's view, **7**, 161, 162, 164, 168
impossible act, attempt to commit, **7**, 169
  examples, **7**, 169
  factual impossibility, **7**, 169
  legal impossibility, **7**, 169
inchoate crime, as, **7**, 160, 161
incitement, attempted, **7**, 176
instigation, attempted, **7**, 170, 176
Mackenzie's view, **7**, 161, 162, 168
mens rea, **7**, 162, 168
murder, **7**, 168
  capital punishment, **17**, 562
overt act—
  actus reus of completed crime, must be
    proximate to, **7**, 163
  requirement for, **7**, 162
preliminary act criminal, where, **7**, 167
preparation and perpetration, demarcation, **7**,
  164
preventive offences, **7**, 164*n*
recklessness, **7**, 168
remote acts of preparation, **7**, 164
result-crime, **7**, 162
third party involvement, **7**, 166
Attendance allowance
adjudication, **21**, 1162, 1167, 1171
  appeals, **21**, 1167
  review, **21**, 1167, 1168
age of claimant, requirement as to, **21**, 925
day attendance condition, **21**, 925, 926
dialysis treatment, claimant undergoing, **21**, 925

Attendance allowance—*continued*
disability appeal tribunal, **21**, 1180
disability living allowance, interaction with, **21**,
  925
entitlement, **21**, 801, 925
  period of, **21**, 926
  terminally ill claimant, **21**, 927
hospital or other institution, in-patients at, **21**, 926
income support—
  disability premium, **21**, 1074
income support. pensioner premium, **21**, 1074
invalid care allowance and, **21**, 949
local authority member, entitlement to, **14**, 225
night attendance condition, **21**, 925, 926
overlapping benefits, **21**, 999, 1001
rates, higher and lower, **21**, 926
residence and presence in Great Britain—
  claimant absent from Great Britain, **21**, 1025
  requirements as to, **21**, 926
terminally ill claimant, **21**, 927
Attendance order
amendment, **8**, 898
appeal against, **8**, 897; **14**, 119
education authority, powers of, **8**, 894, 896
failure to attend school without reasonable
  excuse, **8**, 894, 895
failure to comply with, **8**, 900
meaning, **8**, 897
period of operation, **8**, 899
prosecution following, **8**, 901
revocation, **8**, 898
Attendance records
exclusion from school, records to be kept, **8**, 907
Attendance registers
contents, **8**, 858
education authority, duty as to, **8**, 858
requirement to keep, **8**, 858
Attested will
formal validity, **25**, 723
signing, **25**, 724
Attorney
lessor, as, **13**, 154, 183
power of, *see* POWER OF ATTORNEY
Attorney-General
England and Wales, reference to Court of Appeal,
  point of law, **22**, 319, 320
litigation, intervention in, **7**, 752
Lord Advocate, analogous powers of reference—
  High Court, on point of law, **22**, 319, 320
precedence, **16**, 2020
Au pair
admission of, **12**, 310
change of category, **12**, 313
entry clearance, **12**, 151
extension of leave, **12**, 312
Immigration Rules, **12**, 149, 291, 310–313
meaning, **12**, 311
police registration conditions, **12**, 175
work permit exemption, **12**, 154
Auction
advertisement of, effect of, **1**, 504
auctioneer's lien, **20**, 896
completion of transaction, **20**, 896
conduct of auction, **20**, 897

Auction—*continued*
generally, **20**, 896
invitation to treat, as, **15**, 625
land, sale of, **20**, 904
mock, **6**, 155, 156; **20**, 898
particulars of sales, requirement as to printer's
    imprint, **17**, 3
reserve price, **20**, 896
retraction of bid, **20**, 896
right to bid expressly reserved, **20**; 896
roup, *see* ROUP
seller's right to withdraw item from sale, **20**, 896
upset price, **20**, 896
Auctioneer
firearms and ammunition, possession of, **10**, 1534
lien, having, **1**, 643
partnership, number of partners allowed, **16**,
    1011, 1112
right of lien, **20**, 78, 87
Auctor in rem suam
judicial factor not to be, **24**, 170, 246
trustee precluded from becoming, **24**, 2
trustees and other fiduciaries, **24**, 175
Audi alteram partem
See NATURAL JUSTICE
Audit
accounting records, of, **1**, 58
agreement, by, **1**, 96
auditing—
    international character of, **1**, 70
    international harmonisation of, **1**, 23, 70
    social value of, **1**, 57
auditor, *see* AUDITOR
building society accounts of, **1**, 88
corporations, of, **1**, 91
Eighth Directive, **1**, 66, 69
employers' association accounts, of, **1**, 95
evidence, evaluation of, **1**, 59, 60
friendly society accounts, of, **1**, 89
function of, **1**, 23
guidelines—
    issue of, **1**, 61
    procedures for applying standards in, **1**, 62
    subject matter of, **1**, 62
housing association accounts, of, **1**, 94
industrial and provident societies, of, **1**, 90
local government—
    auditors, general duties of, **14**, 886
    completion of, **14**, 890
    controller, issues raised with, **14**, 897
    report—
        action by Commission on, **14**, 892
        generally, **14**, 891
meaning, **1**, 57
nature of, **1**, 22, 59
professional opinion, as, **1**, 59
public corporations, of, **1**, 91
responsibility, **1**, 65
scope of, **1**, 23, 79
social function, **1**, 22
standards, *see* AUDITING STANDARDS
trade union accounts, of, **1**, 95
trustee savings bank accounts, of, **1**, 93
use of, **1**, 58

Audit Commission
functions, **14**, 61
Auditing Practices Committee
formation of, **1**, 13
guidance statements by, **1**, 61
Auditing standards
duty of care, relevance to, **1**, 98
issue of, **1**, 61
operational, basic, **1**, 64
principles and practices, prescribing, **1**, 62
public sector, in, **1**, 63
published, **1**, 61–63
Auditor
appointment, **12**, 639, 715, 715*n*
appointment, Securities and Investments Board
    rules, **12**, 1405
building society, *see* BUILDING SOCIETY
company—
    annual accounts, report to members on, **4**, 452
    appointment of, **4**, 449, 456
    company's power to be appointed, **4**, 318
    duties of, **4**, 459
    election of, **4**, 389
    false tax return, submission of, **4**, 459
    independence of, **4**, 458
    liabilities of, **4**, 459
    meeting of members, election at, **4**, 389
    qualification, **4**, 456
    removal of, **4**, 379, 456
    remuneration, **4**, 389
    resignation of, **4**, 456
    rights of, **4**, 459
    status of, **4**, 458
    written resolution, notice of, **4**, 379
contract, liability in, **1**, 97
Court of Session, *see* AUDITOR OF COURT OF
    SESSION
criminal liability, **1**, 99
delict, liability in, **1**, 98
disqualification from appointment as, **12**, 638
duty of care, **1**, 24, 98
functions of, **1**, 79
holding company, of, **1**, 85
incorporated company, of—
    appointment, **1**, 80
    directors' report, considering, **1**, 81
    duties of, **1**, 81
    failure to obtain information, stating, **1**, 81
    information, right to, **1**, 85
    initial accounts, report on, **1**, 84
    removal of, **1**, 86
    report, **1**, 80
    resignation of, **1**, 86
    small and medium-sized, report on, **1**, 83
    special category company, report on, **1**, 82
independence of, **1**, 22, 65
Institute of Internal Auditors, **1**, 10
local authority, of, **1**, 79, 87; **14**, 886
maximum fees chargeable by, **12**, 716
meaning, **1**, 3
negligence of, redress for, **1**, 25
penalty, not liable to, **1**, 100
prospectus, reporting in, **1**, 54
qualifications, **1**, 69

Auditor—*continued*
qualified, meaning, **12**, 637, 715*n*
removal, **12**, 639, 715
report, use of, **1**, 79
report by, **12**, 640
rights and duties, **12**, 716
role of, **1**, 1
sheriff court, *see* AUDITOR OF SHERIFF COURT
statute, liability under, **1**, 99
Auditor of Court of Session
age limit, **6**, 936
appointment, **6**, 936
establishment of office, **6**, 936
functions, **6**, 936
High Court of Justiciary, **6**, 936
remuneration, **6**, 936
Auditor of sheriff court
appointment, **6**, 1035
duties, **6**, 1035
Auld Alliance, **12**, 103
Auld Licht
generally, **3**, 1637
Seceders, **3**, 1636
Auld Session
composition, **6**, 896
erection, **6**, 896
failure of, **6**, 896
jurisdiction, **6**, 896, 902, 915
Aunt
deceased specified relative, as, **15**, 602
marriage to, prohibited, **10**, 817, 1219
settlement, family reunion or creation by, **12**, 289, 290
Australia
constitutional amendments, **5**, 307
Author
copyright, *see* COPYRIGHT
personal name, protection by passing off action, **18**, 1376, 1397
public lending right, tax treatment of payments under, **18**, 1592
Securities and Investments Board Core Conduct of Business Rules, **12**, 1399
Authoritative writings
See INSTITUTIONAL WRITERS; LEGAL LITERATURE
Automatic vending machine
general sale list products, **14**, 1208
Automatism
alienation of reason, **7**, 122
burden of proof, **7**, 153
Cardle v Mulrainey, **7**, 122
concussion, **7**, 151
conditions to be met, **7**, 152
Cunningham v HM Advocate, decision in, **7**, 151, 155
defence of, **7**, 113, 124, 151
diabetes causing, **7**, 151
drug-induced, **7**, 151, 152, 153
  therapeutic drugs, **7**, 132, 154
epilepsy causing, **7**, 151
external factor, mental or pathological condition aggravated by, **7**, 156
generally, **7**, 151

Automatism—*continued*
insane, **7**, 155
intoxication *see* INTOXICATION
mens rea, **7**, 158
mental incapacity due to external factor, **7**, 124
non-insane, **7**, 34, 152, 156
Ross v HM Advocate, decision in, **7**, 151, 152, 153
somnambulism, **7**, 151, 157
Sorley v HM Advocate, decision in, **7**, 153
strict liability, and, **7**, 158
Automobile
See MOTOR VEHICLE
Auxiliary Air Force
additional duties, **2**, 760
aliment, service of process, **2**, 769
associations—
  expenses, **2**, 765
  facilities provided by, **2**, 765
  powers and duties, **2**, 765
billeting powers, **2**, 763
calling out—
  civil power, to aid, **2**, 764
  home defence service, for, **2**, 762
discharge, delivering up property on, **2**, 758
enlistment into, **2**, 757
government etc, **2**, 757
home defence service by, **2**, 762
home service, restricted to, **2**, 757
legal basis for, **2**, 611
maintenance, **2**, 757
orders and regulations, **2**, 609
requisitioning powers, **2**, 763
training—
  annual, **2**, 760
  calling out for, **2**, 760
  notice to attend for, **2**, 761
  preliminary, **2**, 759
Auxiliary Forces
See AUXILIARY AIR FORCE; TERRITORIAL ARMY
Avail of marriage
causality of, feudal law, **18**, 76
Aval
meaning, **4**, 105
Average rule
insured's duty to account, **12**, 903
Averments
agreement or discrepancy with evidence, **10**, 746
Aviation
British Airports Authority, **2**, 904, 912
British Airways Board, **2**, 905
British Airways plc, **2**, 905
Eurocontrol, **2**, 908, 1010
licensing of crew, **19**, 1288
recreational and sporting activities, **19**, 1287–1291
registration, **19**, 1288
restrictions or prohibitions on flying, **19**, 1290
rules for flight, **19**, 1289
See also AERODROME; AIR NAVIGATION; AIRCRAFT; AIRPORT
Aviculture
taking or killing wild birds, **11**, 883
Avulsion
accession not applicable to, **18**, 592
alluvion compared, **18**, 592

B

Babies
food for—
    antioxidants, **11**, 371
    preservatives, **11**, 377
prisoners, of, **16**, 1427, 1441
Baby-sitter
age of, **3**, 1246
duty to protect child, **7**, 42
Back green
See TENEMENT BUILDING
Backhand rent
meaning, **13**, 246
Bad faith
conduct contrary to good faith, **11**, 720
fraud and, **11**, 720
prescription, **16**, 2104
reduction on grounds of, **13**, 44
Badgers
baiting, **19**, 1275
captivity, kept in, **2**, 275
cruelty to, offence of, **2**, 276
dead, offence of possessing, **2**, 274
digging for, **2**, 276
exceptions to provisions, **2**, 278
killing etc—
    damage to crops, to prevent, **2**, 273, 278
    disease, to prevent spread of, **2**, 278
    offence, when, **2**, 273
    suffering, to prevent, **2**, 273
marking, offence of, **2**, 276
offences—
    defences to, **2**, 278
    forfeiture, order for, **2**, 281
offenders—
    requirement to quit land, **2**, 279
    stopping and search, **2**, 280
sale or possession of, **2**, 275
Badges
chivalry, orders of, **11**, 1610
clan members, **11**, 1631
corporations, **11**, 1610
crest, **11**, 1631
eagle's feather, **11**, 1631
form, **11**, 1610
generally, **11**, 1610
identificatory, **11**, 1631
Kingdom of Scotland, **11**, 1610
local authorities, **11**, 1631
Lord High Constable, **11**, 1610
Bag net
salmon fishing by, **11**, 11
Bail
accused —
    address, change of, **17**, 635
    rights of, **17**, 551
administrative removal, detention for, **12**, 199
appeals, **17**, 632
    Lord Justice-Clerk responsible for, **6**, 862, 865
    review of decision, **6**, 865

Bail—*continued*
conditions, **17**, 627
    breach of, **12**, 187
conviction, after, **17**, 636
crimes which are bailable, **17**, 626
general principles, **17**, 625
immigration, passenger detained on arrival, **12**, 169
murder, in case of, **17**, 551
offences, **17**, 634
opposition to, **17**, 628
passport, retention, **16**, 1228
pre-trial diet, **17**, 719
review of, **17**, 633
section 102 committal, **17**, 630
social worker, access to person on—
    condition of bail, as, **22**, 32
    refusal of, **22**, 32
solemn proceedings, **17**, 629
stated case appeal, **17**, 841
summary procedure, **17**, 631, 719
treason, case of, **17**, 551
Bail order
documentary evidence, as, **10**, 588
Bailie
former office of, **6**, 1156, 1157, 1163; **14**, 11
Bailie of the River and Firth of Clyde, Court of
abolition, **6**, 1160
inferior court, as, **6**, 1155
summary procedure, **6**, 1155
Bailiery court
abolition, **17**, 504, 525
former jurisdiction, **6**, 1022; **17**, 523
Bailment
foundation case in England, **14**, 1003
lease as, **14**, 1007
termination on breach, **14**, 1063
Bairn's part
See LEGITIM
Baits
illegal, **11**, 12
powers of Secretary of State, **11**, 23
Bakeries
employment of adult males at night, **9**, 70
Baker's confectionery filling
reheating food containing, **11**, 408, 410
Baking powder
food standard, **11**, 353
Balfour's Practicks
generally, **3**, 812; **22**, 251, 540, 609, 627
Ball games
reparation for damages, action for, **14**, 2085
Ballantynes Bank
debts of, personal liability of Sir Walter Scott for, **4**, 302
Ballast
weights and measures legislation, **6**, 229

Balloons
aerial advertising by, **2**, 1028
Air Navigation Order, exemptions from, **2**, 981
flying of, **2**, 973
generally, **19**, 1287, 1288
Ballot
form, **15**, 1310
secret, introduction, **15**, 1015, 1027
trade union, **15**, 1495
Ballot box
combined poll, **15**, 1363, 1367, 1377
construction, **15**, 1312
issue, **15**, 1312
opening, **15**, 1326
postal voters—
   combined poll, **15**, 1382
   marking, **15**, 1200, 1382
   opening, **15**, 1195–1200, 1239
     attendance at, **15**, 1197, 1211
     generally, **15**, 1211
     notice, **15**, 1199
   provision, **15**, 1200, 1210
sealing—
   close of poll, on, **15**, 1325
   empty boxes, **15**, 1319
Ballot paper
address, application for paper to be sent to
   different, **15**, 1160, 1172, 1173
ballot paper account, **15**, 1325, 1326, 1328
   discrepancies, **15**, 1328
   forwarding or retention of, after count, **15**,
     1355
   verification, **15**, 1326, 1328, 1335
colour, **15**, 1310, 1382
combined poll, **15**, 1363, 1367, 1382
counterfoil, **15**, 1310, 1320, 1325
   combined poll, **15**, 1377
   forwarding or retention of, after count, **15**,
     1355
   opening of sealed packet, order for, **15**, 1357
delivery to voter, **15**, 1320
error in, **15**, 1310
folding, **15**, 1214, 1310, 1320
form and contents, **15**, 1310
forwarding of, after count, **15**, 1355
inspection of, order for, **15**, 1357
issue—
   person, voting in, **15**, 1214
   presiding officers, to, **15**, 1312
marking, **15**, 1214
   back of paper, on, **15**, 1347
   generally, **15**, 1320
   identification of voter from, **15**, 1341, 1344–
     1346
   mark other than cross, **15**, 1341, 1347, 1348
   materials for marking, provision, **15**, 1312
   mode, **15**, 1341
     postal ballot, **15**, 1215
     voting in person, **15**, 1214
   more than one candidate, voting for, **15**, 1341,
     1343
   more than one mark, **15**, 1341
   official mark, *see* official mark *below*
secrecy, **15**, 1320

Ballot paper—*continued*
marking—*continued*
   tick, **15**, 1348
   unconventional marks, **15**, 1341, 1347, 1348
more than one candidate, voting for, **15**, 1341,
   1343
names on, order, **15**, 1310
number, **15**, 1310
official mark, **15**, 1311, 1320
   failure to stamp, **15**, 1342
   instruments for stamping, **15**, 1312
   missing, where, **15**, 1341, 1342
   presiding officer's duty to check, **15**, 1214
   record, **15**, 1311
   voter's duty to check, **15**, 1214
procedure on day of poll, **15**, 1320
rejected—
   adjudication, **15**, 1341–1351
   decision of returning officer, finality, **15**, 1349
   statement as to, **15**, 1350
     forwarding or retention of, after count, **15**,
      1355
   treatment, **15**, 1350
replacement, **15**, 1214, 1315
   postal votes, **15**, 1205, 1213
retention of, after count, **15**, 1355
sealing up counted and rejected papers, **15**, 1354
signature or name on, **15**, 1345
spoilt, **15**, 1325
   combined poll, **15**, 1377
   postal votes, **15**, 1205, 1213, 1239
   reissue, postal votes, **15**, 1205, 1215
   replacement, **15**, 1214, 1315
tendered, **15**, 1310, 1314, 1325
   combined poll, **15**, 1375, 1377
   count, **15**, 1326
United Kingdom Central Council for Nursing,
   Midwifery and Health Visiting election, **15**,
   1503, 1504
unmarked, **15**, 1341, 1347
unused, **15**, 1325
   combined poll, **15**, 1377
void, **15**, 1344–1346
   uncertainty, for, **15**, 1341, 1348
Baltic Exchange
generally, **21**, 120
Baltime Form
charterparty, **21**, 536n, 558n
time charterparty, **21**, 640
Banishment
common law and statutory punishment, **12**, 103,
   105
Bank-banking
accepting houses, **2**, 1105
account—
   arrestment, **2**, 1183; **8**, 272
   attachment of, **2**, 1179
   child's capacity to hold, **3**, 1219
   joint names, in, **2**, 1197, 1260; **19**, 1612
   marriage, property within, **10**, 880
   multiplepoinding, action of, **2**, 1183
   operation by liquidator, **2**, 1178
   partial intestacy, **25**, 708
   powers of attorney, under, **2**, 1259

Bank-banking—*continued*
account—continued
  receivership, effect of, **2**, 1179
  repayment, *see* BANKER
  solicitor's, *see* SOLICITOR
  trustee, *see* TRUSTEE
Acts—
  reasons for, **2**, 1135
  summary of, **2**, 1138
advertisements, regulation of, **2**, 1149
advice by—
  duty of care, **2**, 1214
  investments, as to, **2**, 1215
agency between banks, **2**, 1221
annual accounts, Directive as to, **2**, 1155
arrestee, bank as, **8**, 259
Bank of England, *see* BANK OF ENGLAND
bank notes, *see* BANK NOTE
Bank of Scotland, *see* BANK OF SCOTLAND
banker, *see* BANKER
bankers' books, **10**, 502, 507, 537, 606, 607
bankers' documentary credits, **11**, 772, 773
banker's lien, *see* BANKER
before, **3**, 1979
  advertising control, **2**, 1134
  names, control of, **2**, 1134
  supervision of banks, **2**, 1133
Board of Banking Supervision, **2**, 1144
branches, bank, **4**, 201
British overseas banks, **2**, 1106
building society, services provided by—
  foreign exchange services, **3**, 373
  guarantees, **3**, 373
  money transmission transactions, **3**, 373
  power to provice, **3**, 372, 373
business, days and hours—
  advising customers of, **2**, 1202
  bank holidays, **2**, 1203
  non-business days, **2**, 1203
cards, conditions of use, **2**, 1218
cash withdrawal cards, **4**, 269
charge cards—
  general features of transactions, **4**, 271
  meaning, **4**, 270
cheque, *see* CHEQUE
cheque guarantee cards, **4**, 197, 266, 267, 268
clearing banks—
  names of, **2**, 1103
  nature of, **2**, 1103
  Scottish, **2**, 1104
collapse of, **2**, 1136
Commonwealth banks, **2**, 1106
consortium banks, **2**, 1108
contract—
  jus quaesitum tertio, **15**, 848
  See also BANKER
control, **2**, 1144
credit cards—
  development of, **2**, 1219
  general features of transactions, **4**, 271
  meaning, **4**, 270
  system, operation of, **2**, 1219
crisis of 1973–74, **2**, 1136

Bank-banking—*continued*
customer—
  building society, **2**, 1262
  creditworthiness, **2**, 1211–1213
  death of, **2**, 1176
  duties—
    extension of, notice of, **2**, 1227
    generally, **2**, 1226
  giving advice to, **2**, 1214
  insanity of, **2**, 1177
  meaning—
    bank service purposes, for, **2**, 1223
    different interpretations, **2**, 1224
    generally, **2**, 1220–1221
    importance of determining, **2**, 1224
    Revenue purposes, for, **2**, 1222
  merchant, *see* MERCHANT BANKS
  minor—
    bank account, opening, **2**, 1232
    cautionary obligations, **2**, 1234
    contracts reducible on majority, **2**, 1233
    contractual capacity, **2**, 1232
    curators, appointment, **2**, 1235
    loan to, **3**, 1220
    National Savings account, **2**, 1230
  National Giro Bank, *see* NATIONAL GIRO BANK
  National Savings Bank, *see* NATIONAL SAVINGS
    BANK
  obligations of—
    account, to have, **2**, 1221
    drawing cheques, as to, **2**, 1226
    generally, **2**, 1225
  pupil—
    bank account, opening, **2**, 1229
    cautionary obligations, **2**, 1234
    contracts reducible on majority, **2**, 1233
    contractual capacity, **2**, 1229
    financial obligations, **2**, 1231
    National Savings account, **2**, 1230
    tutor, appointment of, **2**, 1235
  sequestration of, **2**, 1178
  special, *see* special customer *below*
  undue influence over, **2**, 1216
  unilateral act, by, **2**, 1174
debit withdrawal card—
  functions, **4**, 269
deposit receipts—
  meaning, **2**, 1195
  obligation to pay, **2**, 1195
deposit-taking, *see* DEPOSIT-TAKING INSTITUTION
discount houses, **2**, 1112
EEC Directive—
  credit institutions, conditions for, **2**, 1137
  harmonisation of law, for, **2**, 1153
  implementation, **2**, 1137
  objectives of, **2**, 1137
  scope of, **2**, 1153
  Supervision Directive, **2**, 1134
    aims of, **2**, 1153
    application of, **2**, 1154
    controls under, **2**, 1154
EU Directive—
  annual accounts, as to, **2**, 1155
European, *see* EUROPEAN INVESTMENT BANK

Bank-banking—*continued*
finance house, investment in, **14**, 1006
foreign, United Kingdom branches, **2**, 1107
industrial and provient society, **12**, 622, 623
institutions—
 exemption from Moneylenders Acts, **2**, 1131
 growth of, **2**, 1136
 rescue scheme, establishment, **2**, 1136
interest, deceased's liability to tax, **25**, 967
issuing houses, **2**, 1105
Johnson Matthey collapse, **2**, 1138
law, harmonisation of, **2**, 1153
loan—
 minor, to, **3**, 1220
 unrestricted-use credit agreement, as, **5**, 809
loan by—
 bond of cash credit and disposition in security,
  20, 235
 Consumer Credit Act 1974, effect of, **20**, 236
 ex facie disposition in favour of bank, **20**, 234
 generally, **20**, 233
marriage, property within bank account, **10**, 880
meaning, **2**, 1129
merchant banks—
 nature of, **2**, 1105
 Scotland, in, **2**, 1124
 services provided by, **2**, 1105
Minimum Lending Rate, **14**, 1824
name, control of use of, **2**, 1148
National Girobank, **2**, 1111
National Savings Bank, **2**, 1110
notes, *see* BANK NOTE
overdraft—
 disclosure of, **2**, 1205
 loan constituted by, **13**, 1713
person carrying on business of, whether moneylender, **13**, 1770
rescue scheme, establishment, **2**, 1136
safe deposits, **2**, 1217
savings bank, *see* SAVINGS BANK
Scottish—
 bank notes, issue of, **2**, 1104
 banks—
  Adam and Co, **2**, 1119
  Ayr Bank, **2**, 1119
  British Linen Bank, **2**, 1117
  City of Glasgow Bank, **2**, 1119
  Coutts & Co, **2**, 1116, 1124
  merchant banks, **2**, 1124
  Motherwell and District Municipal Bank, **2**,
   1125
  number of, **2**, 1119
 clearing banks, **2**, 1104
 current position as to, **2**, 1119
 Darien Company, **2**, 1115
 development of, **2**, 1114
 earliest forms, **2**, 1114
 framework, **2**, 1128
 goldsmiths, business of, **2**, 1114
 history of, **2**, 1113
 municipal banks, **2**, 1125
 savings banks, *see* SAVINGS BANK
shares, interest in, exclusion relating to, **4**, 346

Bank-banking—*continued*
special customers—
 attorneys etc, **2**, 1259
 building societies, **2**, 1246
 clubs, **2**, 1257
 friendly societies, **2**, 1256
 incorporated bodies—
  authority to act for, **2**, 1245
  companies, **2**, 1244
  generally, **2**, 1249
 insane persons, **2**, 1258
 local authorities, **2**, 1247–1248
 minors, *see* customer *above*
 partnership, **2**, 1250
 provident societies, etc, **2**, 1249
 public bodies, **2**, 1249
 pupils, *see* customer *above*
 solicitors—
  client account—
   bank's liability for, **2**, 1241
   death, operation on, **2**, 1243
   incorporated practice, of, **2**, 1242
   meaning, **2**, 1240
   overdrawing, **2**, 1240
   payments to be made into, **2**, 1240
   striking off etc, effect of, **2**, 1242
 trade unions, **2**, 1255
 trustee—
  fiduciary positions, persons in, **2**, 1239
  liability of bank, **2**, 1238
  payments into, **2**, 1237
 unincorporated bodies, **2**, 1259
 voluntary associations, **2**, 1257
strengthening of, **25**, 324
supervision—
 EEC Directive, **2**, 1154
 Leigh-Pemberton report, **2**, 1139
 recommendations for, **2**, 1139
terrorist funds, disclosure of information as to, **7**,
 623, 624
trustee savings, *see* TRUSTEE SAVINGS BANK
United Dominions Trust case, **2**, 1130
VAT exemptions, **7**, 1424
See also DEPOSIT-TAKING INSTITUTION
Bank of England
bank notes, requirements as to printer's imprint,
 17, 3
Board of Banking Supervision, **2**, 1144
deposit-taking, control of, **2**, 1144
directors, appointment of, **2**, 1102
duties and responsibilities, **2**, 1102
exempted person under Financial Services Act
 1986 ..., **12**, 1321
financial control exercised by, excluded
 agreements, **4**, 1177
formation of, **2**, 1102
Minimum Lending Rate, **14**, 1824
nationalisation, **2**, 1102
notes issued by, as legal tender, **14**, 1816, 1823
Review Committee of Banking Services set up in
 association with, **4**, 105
winding up petition by—
 authorised institution, **4**, 742
 former authorised institution, **4**, 742

Bank note
Carriers Act 1830..., **3**, 610
collectors' item, VAT treatment, **7**, 1424
counterfeit, **7**, 385, 395; **14**, 1836
denomination, **14**, 1820
incorporeal moveable property, as, **14**, 1806
issue of—
　Bank of England, by, **2**, 1102; **17**, 3
　England and Wales, in, **2**, 1126
　monopoly in, **2**, 1126
　Scotland, in, **2**, 1127; **14**, 1817
legal tender, as, **14**, 1816, 1823
marking, **14**, 1820
obligation arising from issue, **16**, 2116
offences—
　counterfeiting, **7**, 385, 397; **14**, 1836
　　possession of counterfeit currency, **14**, 1838
　　possession of counterfeit implements, **14**, 1839
　exportation, **14**, 1843
　generally, **14**, 1834
　importation, **14**, 1843
　passing, **14**, 1837
　reproducing British currency, **14**, 1840
　tendering, **14**, 1837
poinding, **14**, 1812
printer's imprint, requirement not applicable, **17**, 3
reproduction, restrictions on, **1**, 530
sale of, **14**, 1807
Scottish—
　banks authorised to issue, **2**, 1127
　decimalisation, **2**, 1127
　deferred payment, **2**, 1127
　denominations of, **2**, 1127
　history of, **2**, 1127
　irregularities, control of, **14**, 1817
　issue of, **2**, 1104, 1127; **14**, 1817
　legal tender, as, **14**, 1817
　statutory control, **2**, 1127
stolen, restitution not applicable, **15**, 52
VAT zero-rating, **7**, 1455
Bank payment order
proposed introduction, **4**, 191
Bank of Scotland
establishment of, **2**, 1115
former monopoly of, **2**, 1115
functions of, **2**, 1104
fundamental difference from Bank of England, **2**, 1115
public corporation, as, **19**, 211, 217
stock, adjudication, **8**, 200
Banker
Bank of England, *see* BANK OF ENGLAND
Bank of Scotland, *see* BANK OF SCOTLAND
bankers' books, *see* BANKERS' BOOKS
bankers' documentary credits, *see* BANKERS' DOCUMENTARY CREDITS
cheque, *see* CHEQUE
contract with—
　commencement of, **2**, 1172
　nature of, **2**, 1167
　termination of—
　　banker, act of, by, **2**, 1175

Banker—*continued*
contract with—*continued*
　termination of—*continued*
　　company liquidation, on, **2**, 1178
　　customer—
　　　death of, on, **2**, 1176
　　　insanity of, on, **2**, 1177
　　　sequestration of, by, **2**, 1178
　　　unilateral act, by, **2**, 1174
　　generally, **2**, 1173
　　lapse of time, by, **2**, 1180
　　notices as to, **2**, 1174, 1175
　　operation of law, by, **2**, 1176
　　prescription, by, **2**, 1180
　　receivership, on, **2**, 1179
customer relationship—
　agency and trust, **2**, 1169
　cheques, as to, *see* CHEQUE
　confidentiality, **2**, 1169
　contractual relationship, **2**, 1170
　creditor and debtor, as, **2**, 1168, 1170
　customer's obligations, **2**, 1227
　general conclusion as to, **2**, 1171
　judicial opinion as to, **2**, 1168
　legal relationship, **2**, 1167
disclosure of information by—
　authorised by customer, **2**, 1209
　bank's interest, in, **2**, 1208
　company's account, of, **2**, 1206
　compulsion of law by, **2**, 1206
　creditworthiness, as to—
　　duty to customer, **2**, 1213
　　duty to inquirer, **2**, 1212
　　Hedley Byrne case, **2**, 1212
　customer's interests, in, **2**, 1210
　Inland Revenue etc, to, **2**, 1206
　overdraft, concerning, **2**, 1205
　public duty, as, **2**, 1207
　secrecy, implied term as to, **2**, 1205
duty of care, **15**, 278
insurance intermediary, **12**, 811
lien—
　bill of exchange, in relation to, **20**, 83
　conditions for exercise of right of, **20**, 82
　extent and nature of, **20**, 81
　generally, **2**, 1201; **13**, 95
　shares of bank, over, **20**, 85
　third party, securities belonging to, **20**, 84
meaning, **2**, 1229; **4**, 199; **10**, 537
pledge of, **4**, 258
protection of, **2**, 1191
repayment by—
　appropriation of payments, **2**, 1198
　combination of accounts, **2**, 1199
　compensation, pleading, **2**, 1200
　consignment receipts, **2**, 1196
　deposit—
　　accounts, **2**, 1194
　　receipts, **2**, 1195
　joint accounts, **2**, 1197
　lien, affected by, **2**, 1201
　set-off, **2**, 1200
secrecy, obligation of, **2**, 1205
witness, as, **10**, 537

Bankers' books
documentary evidence, as, **10**, 502, 537, 606, 607
meaning, **10**, 537
Bankers' documentary credits
fraudulent, **11**, 773
system of, generally, **11**, 772
third party rights, **15**, 848
Banking Appeal Tribunal
Scottish Committee, supervision by, **23**, 911
Banking partnership
partnership agreement, provisions in, **16**, 1009
professional rules, contravention, **16**, 1017
Bankrupt/Bankruptcy
accountant in, *see* ACCOUNTANT IN BANKRUPTCY
building society director, of, **3**, 403
cautioner, of, **14**, 1502
   creditor's ranking, **3**, 913, 948*ff*
cautioners' rights in—
   insolvency of both principal debtor and some
     or all cautioners, **3**, 953–956
   principal debtor insolvent but cautioners
     solvent, **3**, 951, 952
   principal debtor solvent but cautioners
     insolvent, **3**, 948–950
common law—
   basis of Scots law, **2**, 1301
   principle, derivation of, **2**, 1301
company, winding up insolvent, **17**, 353
computation of time of, **22**, 822, 823
contract, of party to, *see* INSOLVENCY
copyright rights, transmission on, **18**, 1026
Court of Session—
   jurisdiction, **4**, 16; **6**, 924
   procedure, **17**, 1425
creditors, *see* CREDITOR
debt, *see* DEBT
debtor, *see* DEBTOR; DEBTOR'S ESTATE
debts incurred before, **15**, 879
decree arbitral in, **2**, 408
delict, title and interest to sue, **15**, 230
dies inceptus principle, **22**, 822, 823
diligence, distinguished, **8**, 106
   See also DILIGENCE
European Convention on the Calculation of
   Time-Limits, **22**, 827
extortionate credit agreement, **13**, 1771
foreign, interaction with diligence against Scottish
   assets, **8**, 130
foreign decrees, recognition of, **17**, 351
fraud, **2**, 1452; **7**, 379
House of Commons, exclusion of bankrupt from,
   5, 379
judicial factor—
   bankrupt ineligible as, **24**, 241
   See also JUDICIAL FACTOR
jurisdiction, **4**, 16; **6**, 924, 1066; **8**, 431, 435; **17**,
   351; **22**, 645
law—
   assimilation, Scots and English law, **22**, 645
   Bankruptcy (Scotland) Act 1985..., **22**, 678
   Crown preferences, limited retention, **22**, 678
   debt recovery, **22**, 645
   development of, **2**, 1301–1303
   discharge, **22**, 678

Bankrupt/bankruptcy—*continued*
law—*continued*
   reform—
     historical summary, **22**, 629, 633, 645
     private international law, **17**, 354
     Roman Law, modelled on, **22**, 629
     Scottish Law Commission 1982, **22**, 633, 678
legislation—
   development, **2**, 1301–1303
   review and reform of, **2**, 1303
   sequestration, liability to, **2**, 1321
lessee, of, **13**, 185
lessor, of, **13**, 159, 348, 351
licensee, of, **5**, 950
local government candidate, **15**, 1068
Member of Parliament, **5**, 379; **15**, 1059
notice by trustee—
   time/place payment, first dividend—
     time limits, **22**, 822
notour—
   constituting, method of, **2**, 1302
   deed granted in preference to creditors, period
     prior to constitution of, **22**, 822, 823
   legislation, development of, **2**, 1302
   replacement of term, **2**, 930
   See also INSOLVENCY (apparent)
offences—
   common law, at, **2**, 1452
   debtor, by, *see* DEBTOR
   fraudulent bankruptcy, **2**, 1452
other relevant provisions, **17**, 352
partner, of, **16**, 1083, 1098
   joint tenancy, **13**, 192
   limited partner, **16**, 1120
partnership, of—
   apparent insolvency, **2**, 1324
   claims against partners, **2**, 1412; **16**, 1109
   generally, **16**, 1106
   partners remaining solvent, **16**, 1106
   sequestration—
     Court of Session jurisdiction, **2**, 1333
     firm and partners, of, **16**, 1108
     limited partnerships, **2**, 1321, 1486
     petition for, **16**, 1107
   termination of lease by, **13**, 414
personal information, whether part of bankrupt's
   estate, **18**, 1453
preferred debts, *see* PREFERRED DEBTS
principal debtor, of, **3**, 922, 958
promisor or promisee, of, **15**, 616, 653
pursuer in court action, caution for expenses, **3**,
   996
Register of Inhibitions and Adjudications—
   awards recorded in, **2**, 1338, 1340
   entry in, **2**, 1340, 1439
   keeper of, court orders to be sent to, **2**, 1340
   matters to be recorded, **2**, 1340
Register of Insolvencies—
   awards to be registered in, **2**, 1338
   contents, **2**, 1339
   maintenance of, **2**, 1339
   matters to be included in, **2**, 1339
sederunt book, entries in as documentary
   evidence, **10**, 595

Bankrupt/bankruptcy—*continued*
sequestration, *see* SEQUESTRATION
sheriff court jurisdiction, **4**, 16; **6**, 1066; **22**, 645
status diminished by, **11**, 1067
tenant, of—
  debtor's family home, **13**, 417
  generally, **13**, 414
  growing crops, **13**, 422
  irritancy, **13**, 415; **15**, 809
    commercial lease, **13**, 584
  landlord's hypothec, relationship with, **13**, 523
  trust deed for creditors, **13**, 418
  trustee—
    abandonment by, **13**, 421
    acceptance by landlord, **13**, 419
    adoption by, **13**, 420
    vesting in, **13**, 416
Third Party (Rights Against Insurers) Act 1930,
  application of, **12**, 904–910
time limits, procedural, **22**, 822
transfer of estate on, valuation of, **25**, 9
transfer of ownership on, involuntary nature, **18**,
  597, 613, 663
trustee, appointment of bankrupt as, **24**, 130
trustee in—
  insider dealing rules, **12**, 1528
  interim—
    accounts, submission of, **2**, 1312, 1345
    additional powers given to, **2**, 1342
    appointment—
      before sequestration awarded, **2**, 1310
      discretion of court in, **2**, 1310
      notice to Accountant of, **2**, 1310
      objection to, **2**, 1310
      obligation to accept, **2**, 1310
      time for, **2**, 1310, 1342
    bond by—
      amount of, **2**, 1308
      requirement for, **2**, 1308
    carrying on debtor's business, gas etc supplies
      for, **2**, 1484
    concept of, introduction of, **2**, 1306
    debtor's estate—
      delivery up etc of, **2**, 1342
      preservation of, **2**, 1342, 1344
      See also DEBTOR'S ESTATE
    default of, **2**, 1310
    directions to debtor, **2**, 1342
    discharge of—
      application for, **2**, 1345
      certificate, grant or refusal of, **2**, 1345
      claim for remuneration, **2**, 1345
      handing over to permanent trustee, **2**,
        1345
    duties, **2**, 1305, 1306
    functions, general, **2**, 1309
    incapacitated, becoming, **2**, 1310
    information for Accountant, **2**, 1305, 1309
    insolvency practitioners as, **2**, 1307
    list of—
      maintenance of, **2**, 1307
      removal from, **2**, 1307
    offence, suspected of, **2**, 1305
    outlays of, **2**, 1312, 1313

Bankrupt/bankruptcy—*continued*
trustee in—*continued*
  interim—*continued*
    period of office, **2**, 1309
    permanent, becoming, **2**, 1313
    qualifications of, **2**, 1307, 1308
    removal by court, **2**, 1310
    remuneration—
      amount, settlement of, **2**, 1312
      charge on estate for, **2**, 1312
      claim for, **2**, 1345
      estate inadequate to meet, **2**, 1312, 1313
      first charge on assets, **2**, 1417
    report to Accountant, **2**, 1344
    resignation, **2**, 1310
    supervision of, **2**, 1305
  permanent—
    accounts—
      audit, **2**, 1317
      duty to keep, **2**, 1315
      payments out, of, **2**, 1434
      resignation etc, on, **2**, 1372
      submission of, **2**, 1305
    act and warrant for, **2**, 1368
    advice by commissioners to, **2**, 1315, 1367
    agents of, responsibility for, **2**, 1375
    appointment—
      ineligibility for, **2**, 1314
      modified procedure, under, **2**, 1455
      time for making, **2**, 1309
    arbitration, reference to, **2**, 1482
    bank account in name of, **2**, 1379
    bond by, requirement for, **2**, 1308
    composition offer, report on, **2**, 1443
    contracts—
      personal liability for, **2**, 1378
      power to adopt etc, **2**, 1378
    death of—
      election of new trustee, **2**, 1370
      nomination of replacement, **2**, 1305
      procedure on, **2**, 1372
    debtor to co-operate with, **2**, 1481
    debtor's estate—
      taking possession of, **2**, 1375
      title to, proof of, **2**, 1368
      See also DEBTOR'S ESTATE
    debtor's legal rights, claim to, **2**, 1384
    debts, realisation of, **2**, 1376
    default of duty, **2**, 1315
    directions to, **2**, 1315
    discharge of—
      certificate of, **2**, 1372, 1374
      effect, **2**, 1374
      procedure, **2**, 1374
    duties, personal performance, **2**, 1375
    election of—
      confirmation by sheriff, **2**, 1368
      general provisions, **2**, 1345
      new trustee, **2**, 1369
      preliminaries to, **2**, 1368
      report to sheriff of, **2**, 1368
      statutory meeting, at, **2**, 1368
      voting rights, **2**, 1368
    functions, general, **2**, 1315

Bankrupt/bankruptcy—*continued*
trustee in—*continued*
  permanent—*continued*
    handing over to, **2**, 1345, 1368
    heritable property—
      dealing with, **2**, 1376
      title to, **2**, 1383
      vesting of, **2**, 1385
    incapacity to act, **2**, 1371
    insolvency practitioner, to be, **2**, 1314
    interim trustee becoming, **2**, 1313
    legal proceedings, power to continue, **15**, 606
    liability of—
      contracts, as to, **2**, 1378
      losses by estate, for, **2**, 1379
    meetings, power to convene, **2**, 1350
    modified procedure, under—
      accounts, **2**, 1357
      appointment, **2**, 1355
      functions, **2**, 1356
      general provisions, **2**, 1355
      insufficiency of assets, **2**, 1358
      powers and duties, **2**, 1356
      remuneration from public funds, **2**, 1358
      resignation of, **2**, 1355
    money received by, account for, **2**, 1379
    new—
      election of—
        death, on, **2**, 1370
        removal of trustee, on, **2**, 1369
        resignation, on, **2**, 1369
      handing over to, **2**, 1372
    objection to, **2**, 1368
    offence, suspected of, **2**, 1305
    office, aspects of, **2**, 1367
    payments out by, *see* DEBTOR'S ESTATE
    position of defined, **2**, 1367
    powers and duties, **2**, 1375; **4**, 769
    privilege in reports, **2**, 1315
    qualification of, **2**, 1314
    removal of—
      appeal against, **2**, 1371
      application by Accountant for, **2**, 1305, 1315
      election of new trustee, **2**, 1371
      grounds for, **2**, 1371
      procedure on, **2**, 1372
      special meeting for, **2**, 1371
    remuneration—
      account for purposes of, **2**, 1673
      calculation of, **2**, 1373
      determination of, **2**, 1317
      preferential payment, **2**, 1418
    representative capacity, **2**, 1367
    residence qualification, **2**, 1314
    resignation—
      acceptance of, **2**, 1369
      procedure on, **2**, 1372
      restriction on, **2**, 1369
      subject to new appointment, **2**, 1369
    sale of property by, **2**, 1376
    sederunt book—
      contents, **2**, 1380
      duty to maintain, **2**, 1380

Bankrupt/bankruptcy—*continued*
trustee in—*continued*
  permanent—*continued*
    sederunt book—*continued*
      entries in—
        copies of accounts, **2**, 1345
        decrees on unfair preference, **2**, 1392
        examination of debtor, **2**, 1400
      evidence of, **2**, 1380
      inspection, right of, **2**, 1380
    supervision of, **2**, 1317
    unclaimed dividends, **2**, 1478
    utilities, supply by, **2**, 1484
    vesting of property in, **2**, 1381
  undischarged, credit obtained by, **13**, 1764
  VAT-registered person, of, **7**, 1344, 1351, 1352
  winding up, *See* WINDING UP
  See also INSOLVENCY

Banks Committee on the British Patent System
report, **18**, 815, 825

Banks or works on land
constraints on operations on, **25**, 324
prevention of damage by injurious animals or birds, **11**, 859

Bankton, Andrew McDouall, Lord
An Institute of the Laws of Scotland, **18**, 1*n*, 3; **22**, 537
  'authoritative writings'—
    inclusion in canon of, **22**, 441
  condictio causa data causa non secuta, **15**, 33
  on corporeal and incorporeal property, **18**, 11*n*
  custom—
    common law, and, **22**, 368
    formal source of law, as, **22**, 131, 368
    precedent as, **22**, 251
  delict, **15**, 216
  desuetude, doctrine of, **22**, 131
  equity as synonym for law of nature, **22**, 409
  formal source of law, as, **22**, 434
  nobile officium, **22**, 428, 430
  precedent—
    as gloss upon statute, **22**, 136
    as practice or custom, **22**, 251
  real rights, on, **18**, 3*n*
  restitution and recompense, **15**, 59
  special authority of, **22**, 437, 440
  Union legislation as fundamental law, objection to thesis, **22**, 147

Banners
Royal Banner of Scotland, **11**, 1632
shields of arms displayed on, **11**, 1609
signs according to rank, **11**, 1609

Baptism
change of name at, **19**, 1425
parish registers, **19**, 1401
records, transmission of, **19**, 853
Scottish Episcopal Church, **3**, 1629

Bar (legal profession)
European Bars, Faculty of Advocates' links with, **13**, 1299
historical background, **13**, 1102
legal education, historical background, **13**, 1102

Bar (legal profession—*continued*
precedence—
    historical background, **13**, 1271, 1272
    Queen's Counsel, **13**, 1273, 1274
    senior counsel, **13**, 1273, 1274
See also ADVOCATE; FACULTY OF ADVOCATES
Barbed wire fence
dangerous or injurious to person using road, **20**, 697
Barbers' business
Sunday opening by person of Jewish religion, **3**, 1681
Barbiturates
controlled drugs, as, **14**, 1229
Barcelona
free zone, as, **7**, 1164
Bareboat charterparty
generally, **21**, 534*n*
Baron/Barony
barones majores, **16**, 1304, 1306; **18**, 54
barones minores, **18**, 54
barony court—
    abolition, **17**, 504; **22**, 522
    appeal to, **17**, 522
    decline, **22**, 522
    feudal system, **6**, 897
    jurisdiction, **6**, 1022
    pit and gallows, right of, **17**, 522
    procedure *Leges Baronum*, **22**, 512
    restriction of powers, **17**, 525
children of, mode of address, **16**, 1322
jurisdiction, powers, **16**, 1304; **18**, 54
life peerage, **16**, 1312
mode of address, **16**, 1322
original number, **16**, 1304
Parliament, attendance at, **16**, 1304
peer of lowest rank, use of title, **16**, 1322
precedence, **16**, 2021
Scottish Parliament, **15**, 1002, 1003; **16**, 1306
several baronies held by one man, **16**, 1304
title, generally, **16**, 1311
Baronetage-baronetcy
claim to, **11**, 1621
Great Britain, **6**, 1017, 1018
Nova Scotia, of, **6**, 1017, 1018; **11**, 1621
    precedence, **16**, 2005, 2019
official roll, **6**, 1017
precedence, **16**, 2019
    ranking *inter se*, **16**, 2019
Ulster, of, **11**, 1621
United Kingdom, **6**, 1017, 1018
Barratry
acts of, damage caused by, **21**, 551*n*, 554
burden of proof, **21**, 554
meaning, **21**, 554
Barrier, protective
building controls, **3**, 208
Barrier Act
Church of Scotland, **3**, 1546
Barter
bona fides, **6**, 47
caveat emptor, **6**, 47
description of goods, **6**, 47
exclusion clauses, **6**, 101
generally, **6**, 45

Barter—*continued*
incidents of, **6**, 46
money consideration, lack of, **14**, 1802
quality of goods, **6**, 47
rejection, **6**, 48
sale, evolution of, **20**, 801
sale distinguished, **6**, 46
trading in, **6**, 49
See also EXCHANGE
Baselines
See TERRITORIAL SEA
Basic constitution
See CONSTITUTION
Basin
damage to, limitation of liability, **21**, 755
Basis and Plan of Union
Church of Scotland, **3**, 1552
Bath
capacity in excess of 100 gallons, **25**, 506
water fitting, as, **25**, 527
Bathing
canals and inland waterways, in, **19**, 1107
Baton sinister
assignation of, **11**, 1618
Battered woman syndrome
diminished responsibility, **7**, 147
provocation, **7**, 274
Battle cry
See SLUGHORN
Battle of forms
contract, **15**, 636, 636*n*
meaning, **15**, 636
Bays
territorial waters, baseline system, **11**, 78
Beacon
Commissioners of the Northern Lights, **11**, 1322
Bearer bill
order bill distinguished, **4**, 133
Bearer bond
negotiable instrument, as, **4**, 103
regulation of, **14**, 819
Bearer deposit receipt
negotiable instrument, as, **4**, 103
Bearer instrument
coupons issued with or attached to, as negotiable instrument, **4**, 103
Bearer of the National Flag of Scotland
office of, **7**, 820, 826
Bearer of the Royal Banner
office of, **7**, 820, 825
Bearer share
warrants, **4**, 371
Bed and breakfast accommodation
housing benefit, **21**, 1105
secure tenancy, avoidance device, as, **13**, 770
Bedding
disinfection, **19**, 446, 455
Beef
guide prices, **1**, 933
Beer
black, **7**, 1061*n*
excise duty, **7**, 1061, 1061*n*, 1063
    deferred payments, **7**, 1088
producers, registration, **7**, 1066

Bees

diseases, prevention, **2**, 189

property in, **2**, 107

swarming, **2**, 107

valuation for rating, beekeeping, buildings used in connection with, **24**, 571

Beggars

child beggar, **3**, 1247

early provisions concerning, **14**, 34

justice of the peace court jurisdiction, **6**, 1159

Behring Sea Award Act 1894

generally, **11**, 217

Belfast Gazette

documentary evidence, as, **10**, 593

Belgium

competition rules, application, **4**, 1304

European Union customs territory, **7**, 1010

no-passport excursions to, **12**, 132

Bell, Professor George Joseph

Commentaries on the Law of Scotland and on the Principles of Mercantile Jurisprudence, **18**, 814; **22**, 537

'authoritative writings', inclusion in canon of, **22**, 441

intellectual property, on, **18**, 801

Principles of the Law of Scotland, **18**, 1, 1*n*, 12; **22**, 441

property law, treatment, **18**, 1

special authority of writings, **22**, 437, 440, 441

Stair, assessment of, **22**, 440

unjust enrichment, **15**, 13

Bell-ringing

nuisance, as, **14**, 2054

Bend sinister

assignation of, **11**, 1618

Benefice (*beneficium*)

feudal system, **18**, 43, 43*n*

Beneficial interest

granter's intention to constitute, **24**, 63

meaning, **4**, 42

purchase of, **24**, 179

Beneficiary (legal concept)

passive transactional capacity, **11**, 1048–1051

private law, in, **11**, 1048

pure passive capacity, **11**, 1045–1047

Beneficiary (of trust)

action against, **4**, 41

advances—

  capital, **24**, 203

  maintenance, for, **24**, 76

animal as, **24**, 115, 118

approval of variation on behalf of those who cannot assent, **24**, 79

choice of, effect on revocability, **24**, 67

constitution of trusts, **24**, 12

contingent, **24**, 38

defeasible vesting, *see* VESTING

definition, **24**, 9

domiciled outside Scotland, **24**, 216, 217

existence of, **24**, 62

human, **24**, 115

incapable, **24**, 75, 79

incapacity to give consent, **24**, 75

income tax liability, *see* INCOME TAX

Beneficiary (of trust)—*continued*

interest—

  assigned to third party, **24**, 210

  generally, **19**, 1650

jus crediti, **24**, 7, 12

meaning, **24**, 79

minor, *see* MINOR

object of trust, as, **24**, 57

other than human beings, **24**, 115, 118

place or object as, **24**, 115, 118

private trusts, **24**, 86

public trusts, **24**, 86, 89

remedies open to, **24**, 49

residential accommodation, **24**, 202

rights of, **24**, 49–57

  annuities, **24**, 54

  diligence, **24**, 56

  discretionary trusts, **24**, 55

  general nature, **24**, 49

  liferents, **24**, 45, 53

  mixed funds, **24**, 51, 52

  nature, **18**, 10, 14

  particular, **24**, 53–55

  personal right against trustees, as, **18**, 691

  succession to, **24**, 56

  third parties, against, **24**, 187

  to see accounts, **24**, 195, 221

  tracing and recovering his interest, **24**, 115, 123

  transfer of, **24**, 56

  trustee's insolvency, on, **24**, 49–52

  trustees and trust property, against, **24**, 49–52

shortage of qualified, **24**, 110

sole, sole trustee may not be, **24**, 9

termination by, **24**, 70–74

  agreement between beneficiaries, **24**, 70

  principle of *Miller's Trustees v Miller*, **24**, 72, 73

  retention for payment of debts, **24**, 74

  vested provisions, **24**, 71

trustee may be, **24**, 9, 138; **25**, 863

unascertained, **24**, 79, 83

unborn, **24**, 79

vested right to property, **24**, 71

who may be, **24**, 14

Beneficiary (wills and succession)

bequest, generally, *see* LEGACY

certainty of, **25**, 766

competent—

  child conceived but not born at date when benefit vests, **25**, 621

  disclaimer by, **25**, 621

  disposable estate, restriction on size of, **25**, 621

  public policy grounds, statutory exclusion of, **25**, 621

  unworthiness to succeed, **25**, 621

disappointed benificiary cases, **15**, 281–283, 358

disposal to—

  completion of administration, **25**, 997

  death, deemed acquisition on, **25**, 996

  disclaimer, **25**, 998

  variation, **25**, 998

disqualification of—

  common law, **25**, 670

  court's discretion in respect of, **25**, 671

Beneficiary (wills and succession)—*continued*
disqualification of—*continued*
   effect of—
      death of killer, **25**, 673
      generally, **25**, 672
      husband and wife, between, **25**, 674
      statutory provisions, **25**, 669
      unworthy heir, **25**, 668
interest, directions for payment, **25**, 924
non-resident, income tax, **25**, 988
payments to, income tax, **25**, 980
residue, interests in—
   absolute, **25**, 986
   limited, **25**, 985
testator's death, must be known and in existence
   at or prior to, **25**, 934
trustee, acceptance of office as, **25**, 863
See also HEIR; LEGACY
Beneficium cedendarum actionum
rights of cautioner against creditor, **3**, 929, 930
Roman law and development of law of Caution,
   3, 808
Beneficium competentiae
donation, **8**, 644
Beneficium divisionis
See BENEFIT OF DIVISION
Beneficium ordinis vel excussionis
See BENEFIT OF DISCUSSION
Benefit of discussion
cautioner bound as principal and cautioner, **3**, 819
cautioner expressly bound, where, **3**, 818
generally, **3**, 810, 923
Mercantile Law Amendment Act (Scotland) 1856,
   effect, **3**, 818, 818*n*
obligations *ad factum praestandum*, **3**, 916, 923, 925,
   926
origins, **3**, 810
partners, position of, **3**, 825
rights of cautioner against creditor—
   generally, **3**, 923
   limits of benefit of discussion, **3**, 924
   Mercantile Law Amendment Act (Scotland)
      1856, effect, **3**, 925, 926
Benefit of division
cautioner bound as principal and cautioner, **3**, 819
cautioner expressly bound, where, **3**, 818
generally, **3**, 809, 810
meaning, **3**, 927
origins, **3**, 809
partners, position of, **3**, 825
rights of cautioner against creditor—
   improper caution, **3**, 928
   proper caution, **3**, 927
Benefit and testimonial matches
income from, **19**, 1302
Benevolent society
friendly society, **12**, 679*n*, 681, 685
   legislation, **12**, 601
meaning, **12**, 694
valuations exemption, **12**, 717
Benthamism
legal positivism, neglect of equity as result, **22**, 417
Bequest
See LEGACY

Bermuda
British Dependent Territories citizenship, **14**,
   1932
Berth
berth charterparty, **21**, 672
   express terms, **21**, 675
impediment preventing ship's entry, voyage
   charterparty, **21**, 622
nomination, express terms in bill of lading, **21**,
   546
safe, voyage charterparty, **21**, 621
safety, **11**, 1321
Berwick
Court of Four Burghs, **14**, 13
Bestiality
meaning, **7**, 320
penalties, **7**, 320
public morality, offence against, **7**, 295
Beth Din
jurisdiction, **3**, 1675
Betting
advertisements, restrictions on, **17**, 45
   licensed betting office, advertising, **1**, 531; **2**,
      1551
agency permit, *see* BOOKMAKER
appeal to sheriff relating to, **6**, 1082; **17**, 1249
betting transaction—
   age limit, **3**, 1230
   effecting, age limit, **3**, 1230
bookmaker, *see* BOOKMAKER
business, conduct of, **2**, 1514
contract, enforceability, **15**, 768
duties, **19**, 1510, 1543
fixed odds, meaning, **2**, 1512
general betting duty, **7**, 1080, 1081
   collection of, **2**, 1647
   customs and excise powers, **2**, 1647
   liability to, **2**, 1645
   nature of, **2**, 1645
history of, **2**, 1509
horserace betting levy board, *see* HORSERACE
   BETTING LEVY BOARD
Horserace Totalisor Board, **7**, 1081
joint adventure to share winnings, **15**, 768
law—
   controls under, **2**, 1510
   development of, **2**, 1509
licensed betting office—
   admission to, age for, **2**, 1550
   advertising of, **1**, 531; **2**, 1551
   closure, days for, **2**, 1550
   conduct of, **2**, 1550
   drunks etc, expulsion of, **2**, 1550
   employment in, age limit, **3**, 1230
   entry, police powers, **2**, 1550
   facilities provided in, **2**, 1552
   licence, **14**, 517
      appeal respecting—
         conduct of, **2**, 1547
         grounds of, **2**, 1547
         procedure, **2**, 1546
         reasons for allowing, **2**, 1546
      application for, **2**, 57, 1537
      display of, **2**, 1550

Betting—*continued*
licensed betting office—*continued*
  licence—*continued*
    generally, **2**, 1536
    grant or renewal, **2**, 1545
      objection to, **2**, 1538
    preferential grant of, **2**, 1509
    proceedings as to, **2**, 1538
    refusal of—
      grounds for, **2**, 1539
    renewal—
      application for, **2**, 1543
      grounds for refusing, **2**, 1544
    transfer of—
      holders, between, **2**, 1548
      premises, between, **2**, 1549
  licensed premises, on, **2**, 76
  licensing authority, **2**, 1516, 1536
  locality—
    considerations as to, **2**, 1541
    demand in, **2**, 1542
  nature of, **2**, 1536
  premises—
    location, unsuitable, **2**, 1540
    planning control, **2**, 1540
  provision made for, **2**, 1509
  television viewing in, **2**, 1552
  unsuitability of premises, **2**, 1539
  valuation for rating, **24**, 671
licensing board—
  betting agency permit, *see* BOOKMAKER
  betting licences etc, **2**, 1516
  betting office licence, *see* licensed betting office
    above
  bookmaker's permit, *see* BOOKMAKER
locations for—
  restrictions on, **2**, 1517
  unsuitable, **2**, 1540
meaning, **2**, 1511
offshore business, **7**, 1081
places where permitted, **2**, 1517
pool, *see* POOL BETTING
profits from, income tax, **19**, 1297, 1309
sheriff court jurisdiction, **6**, 1082; **17**, 1249
speculation on share or commodity prices, **15**, 768
sponsiones ludicrae, **2**, 1502
statutory control, **2**, 1510
stock market index, on movement of, **15**, 768
street, restriction on, **2**, 1517
track—
  licence—
    application for, **2**, 1559
    cancellation of, **2**, 1561
    death of holder, **2**, 1561
    duration, **2**, 1561
    effect of, **2**, 1558
    grant of, **2**, 1560
    notification of application, **2**, 1559
    objections to grant, **2**, 1559
    refusal of, **2**, 1560
    revocation of, **2**, 1561
    transfer of, **2**, 1561
  meaning, **2**, 1558
  unlicensed, bookmaking on, **2**, 1562

Betting—*continued*
types of, **2**, 1511
VAT exemption, **7**, 1423
Betting and gaming duties, 19, 1510, 1543
Betting Levy Appeal Tribunal
supervision of, **23**, 911
Bias, rule against
arbiter, of, **1**, 252
criteria for finding, **1**, 257
decision-making process, in, **1**, 256
exemption from disqualification for, **1**, 258
generally, **1**, 251
improper procedure, arising from, **1**, 255
interest, arising from, **1**, 251
licensing authority, of, **1**, 254
likelihood of, establishing, **1**, 257
local government matter, in, **1**, 253
minister, application of principle to, **1**, 253
objection to, waiver of, **1**, 258
one member of body, of, **1**, 257
pecuniary interest, **1**, 251
public interest, decisions taken in, **1**, 253
reasonable suspicion of, **1**, 257
Bible
Bible Board, **7**, 731, 851
copyright, **18**, 1002
publication, regulation, **7**, 731, 851
  Master Printer, **7**, 819, 851
source of Scots law, as—
  blasphemy, **22**, 614
  canon law, **22**, 611
  divorce, **22**, 613
  generally, **22**, 611–614
  marriage—
    principles, effect after Reformation, **22**, 612
    prohibited degrees of relationship, **22**, 573, 612
  Reformation, influence on reception, **22**, 611–
    614
  Sunday Observance law, effect, **22**, 614
  witchcraft, **22**, 614
Bicycle
dangerous, reckless or careless cycling, **20**, 413
  prosecution, warning or notice of intended, **20**,
    446
drink or drugs, riding in public place while under
  influence of, **20**, 432
electrically-assisted, **20**, 409
keeper of, must provide information as to rider,
  20, 436
motor, **20**, 407
motor vehicle, not defined as, **20**, 409
police officer, powers in relation to rider of, **20**,
  436
prosecution, warning or notice of intended, **20**,
  446
reckless cycling, charge of, **20**, 413
stand or rack for bicycles, provision of, **20**, 439
See also CYCLE RACING; CYCLE TRACK
Bid
See TAKEOVER
Big ticket lease
belonging, test of, **14**, 1013
contractual terms, **14**, 1055
meaning, **14**, 1025

Bigamy
art and part guilt, **7**, 483
cognitive element, **7**, 79, 90
defences to, **10**, 834
definition, **7**, 477
error of fact and law, **7**, 482
generally, **15**, 596
mens rea, **7**, 481
perjury, former prosecution as, **7**, 477
prior marriage—
    accused believed marriage legally ended, where, **7**, 482
    cohabitation with habit and repute, constituted by, **7**, 478
    irregularly contracted, **7**, 478
    regularly contracted, **7**, 478
    subsisting, must be, **7**, 479
    validity, **7**, 480
    void, **7**, 480
    voidable, **7**, 480
Bill (parliamentary)
amendments to, **5**, 401
committal of, **5**, 400
committee stage of, standing committees for, **5**, 412
consideration on report, **5**, 418, 422
Consolidation, Joint Committee on, **5**, 438, 454
hybrid, *see* HYBRID BILL
money clause, **7**, 766
money resolution, **7**, 766
parliamentary, copyright, **18**, 1001
personal, *see* PERSONAL BILL
Personal Bills Committee, **5**, 460
preparation, role of Office of the Solicitor to the Secretary of State for Scotland, **13**, 1402
private, *see* PRIVATE BILL
public, *see* PUBLIC BILL
Public, Select Committees on, **5**, 459
report of, **5**, 404
report stage, **5**, 418, 422
Royal assent, **7**, 715
Scottish Grand Committee, **5**, 415
security, as, **5**, 908
substituted, **19**, 80
Bill of aids and supplies
House of Lords may not amend, **7**, 768
royal assent, **7**, 768
Bill Chamber
abolition, **6**, 919
Court of Session, **6**, 919
former jurisdiction, **6**, 919
Bill of exchange
acceptance—
    honour, for, **4**, 173
    meaning, **4**, 139
    presentment for, **4**, 153
acceptor, **3**, 829
    holder at maturity, as, **4**, 178
    liability of, **4**, 168
        prior parties *inter se*, **3**, 832
accommodation bill, **3**, 830
accommodation party, **3**, 830
    liability of, **4**, 166
addressed by one person to another, meaning, **4**, 110
alteration of, **4**, 181

Bill of exchange—*continued*
ante-dated, **4**, 112
aval on, full legal recognition given to, **4**, 105
banker's lien in relation to, **20**, 83
bearer, payable to, **4**, 133
Bills of Exchange Act 1882—
    development of law came with passage of, **4**, 104
    negotiable instruments, widening of class of, **4**, 105
build-up of use of, **4**, 104
cancellation, **4**, 180
cautionary obligation compared, **3**, 828
cheque, *see* CHEQUE
classification of, **4**, 119
conflict of laws—
    generally, **4**, 187
    rules, **4**, 188
contract of deposit, **8**, 4
date in relation to, **4**, 112
delivery—
    indorsement completed by, **4**, 143
    meaning, **4**, 137
    transferor by, **4**, 172
deposit of, as security, **13**, 1759
development of rules on, **4**, 104
director, acceptance by, **4**, 127n
discharge of—
    acceptor as holder at maturity, **4**, 178
    alteration of bill, **4**, 181
    cancellation, **4**, 180
    express waiver, **4**, 179
    generally, **4**, 175
    payment in due course, **4**, 176
    payment for honour, **4**, 177
    prescription, **4**, 182
    renunciation, **4**, 179
dishonour—
    non-acceptance, by, **4**, 154
    non-payment, by, **4**, 157
    notice of—
        delay, dispensation from, **4**, 160
        dispensation from giving, **4**, 160
        failure to give, **4**, 158
        generally, **4**, 158
        special circumstances, **4**, 159
        valid, rules for, **4**, 159
dishonoured—
    creditor holding, **8**, 121
    liability for, **3**, 829
documentary evidence, as, **10**, 602
drawee, liability of, **4**, 167
drawer, **3**, 829
    liability of, **4**, 169
earliest reported Scottish case on, **4**, 104
enforcement—
    evidence, **4**, 185
    generally, **4**, 183
    summary diligence, **4**, 116, 184
everyday commercial importance, decline in, **4**, 104
express waiver, **4**, 179
extinction of obligations on creditor's silence, **16**, 1621
form of, **4**, 116
generally, **16**, 1901

Bill of exchange—*continued*
holder—
  action, right of, **4**, 148
  due course, in—
    beneficial position of, **4**, 147
    good faith, required by, **4**, 147
    meaning, **4**, 147
    regularity, requirement for, **4**, 147
    rights of, **4**, 149
  duties of—
    acceptance, presentment for, **4**, 153
    dishonour—
      delay, dispensations from, **4**, 160
      dispensation from giving notice, **4**, 160
      non-payment, by, **4**, 157
      notice of, **4**, 158
      valid notice of, rules for, **4**, 159
    generally, **4**, 152
    non-acceptance, dishonour by, **4**, 154
    noting, **4**, 161
    presentment for payment—
      delay, excuses for, **4**, 156
      non-payment, dishonour by, **4**, 157
      non-presentment, **4**, 156
      rules, **4**, 155
    protest—
      form of, **4**, 163
      nature of, **4**, 161
      place of, **4**, 162
      time of, **4**, 162
  lost bills, rights relating to, **4**, 151
  meaning, **4**, 140, 146
  other, rights of, **4**, 150
  rights of, **3**, 829, 831
  value, for, **4**, 146, 150
impersonal payee, payable to, **4**, 133
inchoate instruments, **4**, 117
indorsement—
  meaning, **4**, 143
  transfer of order bill without, **4**, 142
indorser—
  liability of, **4**, 170
  stranger signing bill as, **4**, 171
instalments, sum payable in, **4**, 113
interest, sum payable with, **4**, 113
interest due *ex lege*, **14**, 1827
issue, **4**, 138
less than 100p, made for, **4**, 113
letter of credit, attached to, negotiation of, **4**, 218
liability—
  dishonoured bill, **3**, 829
  generally, **3**, 829
  holder, towards, **3**, 831
  prior parties *inter se*, **3**, 832
loan—
  constituted by, **13**, 1713
  as evidence of, **13**, 1732
lost, **4**, 151
made on or after 15 February 1971, **4**, 113
meaning, **4**, 106
money, use of term, **14**, 1802
movement of—
  acceptance, **4**, 139
  consideration, **4**, 144

Bill of exchange—*continued*
movement of—*continued*
  delivery, **4**, 137
  issue, **4**, 138
  negotiation, *see* negotiation *below*
transfer, *see* transfer *below*
transmission by operation of law, **4**, 145
value, **4**, 144
negotiable instruments, as, **4**, 103
negotiation—
  drawer, back to, **4**, 140
  means of, **4**, 141
  overdue bill, **4**, 140
  transferability distinguished from, **4**, 140
non-acceptance, dishonour by, **4**, 154
non-essentials, **4**, 115
non-payment, dishonour by, **4**, 157
non-presentment for payment, **4**, 156
obligation under, prescription, **16**, 2116, 2121
order, meaning, **4**, 108
order bill—
  bearer bill distinguished, **4**, 133
parole evidence in questions relating to, **15**, 760
parties to—
  acceptor, **4**, 132
  accommodation party, **4**, 135
  authority of—
    agency, **4**, 130
    capacity distinguished from, **4**, 125*n*
    company, **4**, 127
    corporation, **4**, 127
    executor, **4**, 129
    generally, **4**, 125
    meaning, **4**, 125*n*
    partnership, **4**, 128
    trustee, **4**, 129
  capacity of—
    agency, **4**, 130
    authority distinguished from, **4**, 125*n*
    company, **4**, 127
    corporation, **4**, 127
    executor, **4**, 129
    generally, **4**, 125, 126
    lack of, **4**, 126
    meaning, **4**, 125*n*
    partnership, **4**, 128
    trustee, **4**, 129
  drawee, **4**, 132
  drawer, **4**, 131
  generally, **4**, 121
  indorsee, **4**, 134
  indorser, **4**, 134
  liability of—
    acceptance for honour, **4**, 173
    acceptor, **4**, 168
    accommodation parties, **4**, 166
    delivery, transferor by, **4**, 172
    drawee, **4**, 167
    drawer, **4**, 169
    generally, **4**, 164, 165
    indorser—
      nature of, **4**, 170
      stranger signing bill as, **4**, 171
    more than one party the same, **4**, 136

Bill of exchange—*continued*
parties to—*continued*
  necessary, **4**, 121
  others, **4**, 135
  payee, **4**, 133
  referee in case of need, **4**, 135
  signature—
    corporation, by, **4**, 123
    firm, name of, **4**, 123
    forged, **4**, 124
    form of, **4**, 123
    generally, **4**, 122
    partnership, by, **4**, 123
    pencil, may be in, **4**, 123
    rubber stamp, by, **4**, 123
    unauthorised, **4**, 124
partner, when binding, **16**, 1031
partnership, when binding, **16**, 1031
payment—
  demand, on, or at fixed or determinable future
    time, meaning, **4**, 111
  due course, in, **4**, 176
  honour, for, **4**, 177
  presentment for, *see* presentment for payment
    below
  specified person, to, or to bearer, meaning, **4**,
    114
post, delivery by, **4**, 137
post-dated, **4**, 112
prescription, **4**, 182
presentment for payment—
  delay, excuses for, **4**, 156
  non-payment, dishonour by, **4**, 157
  non-presentment, **4**, 156
  rules, **4**, 155
printer's imprint requirement not applicable, **17**,
  3
promissory notes, *see* PROMISSORY NOTE
protest, **13**, 1223
  form of, **4**, 163
  place of, **4**, 162
  procedure for, **4**, 161
  time of, **4**, 162
quinquennial prescription not applicable, **13**, 1755
rate of exchange, **4**, 113
regularity, **4**, 147
related definitions, **4**, 118
renunciation, **4**, 179
representation re application, **22**, 641
reservation of title, where, **18**, 638
sets, rules as to, **4**, 186
signature—
  negligence relating to, **4**, 122
  See also parties to *above*
stamp duty, abolition, **4**, 116
statutory code relating to, basis of, **4**, 106
sum certain in money, meaning, **4**, 113
summary diligence on, **4**, 116, 184
symbolical delivery, **18**, 621
tax considerations, **4**, 189
taxation of transaction involving, **4**, 189
third party rights, **15**, 848
time in relation to, **4**, 112

Bill of exchange—*continued*
transfer—
  indorsement—
    meaning, **4**, 143
    order bill without, **4**, 142
  negotiation distinguished from, **4**, 140
  transmission by operation of law, **4**, 145
unconditional, meaning, **4**, 107
valuable consideration, **4**, 144
in writing, meaning, **4**, 109
See also MERCANTILE LAW
Bill of lading
acceptor as party to, **4**, 132
advertised timetable, ship running to, **21**, 585
arbitration clause, **21**, 546
berth, nomonation of, express terms, **21**, 546
both to blame collision clause, **21**, 546, 584, 584*n*
breach of contract of carriage, damages for, **21**,
  585
cargo—
  delivery—
    express terms as to, **21**, 546
    failure to take, **21**, 546
      back freight, **21**, 661
    production of bill, on, **21**, 525
    transfer by, **21**, 567
  discharge of, express terms as to, **21**, 546
  express terms as to, **21**, 546
  nature and value of, information as to, **21**, 606
  performance of contract as to, **21**, 585
charterparty—
  bill of lading—
    indorsed by charterer, **21**, 692
    indorsed to charterer, **21**, 693
    received by charterer, **21**, 691
  cesser clause, **21**, 699
  contract, **21**, 695, 695*n*
  demise charterparty, **21**, 691*n*, 694, 695*n*
  generally, **21**, 528, 577*n*, 588, 690
  holder of bill of lading, **21**, 694
  inaccuracy in bill of lading, liability of
    charterer, **21**, 698
  inconsistency between, **21**, 697, 697*n*
  lien clause, **21**, 699
  regulation by terms of, **21**, 696, 696*n*
  relationship with, **21**, 547
  sub-charterparty, **21**, 691, 696*n*
  subject to, **4**, 252
  term incorporating, **21**, 546
choice of law clause, **21**, 546
clause paramount, **21**, 546
clean, **4**, 249; **21**, 525*n*, 564*n*
combined transport bill, **21**, 528*n*
conclusive evidence clause, **21**, 32
construction, rules for, **21**, 539
container bill, **21**, 526*n*
containers, express terms, **21**, 546
contents, **20**, 843
  Hague-Visby Rules, **21**, 595
contract—
  concluded prior to issue of bill, where, **21**, 525
  evidenced by, performance, **21**, 585
  insurance, freight (cif) contract, **21**, 525*n*, 528*n*,
    566

Bill of lading—*continued*
copies of—
  fraud involving, **21**, 569
  generally, **21**, 569
  improper use, **21**, 569
damage to goods, notification, **21**, 598
dangerous goods, express terms as to, **21**, 546
date, **21**, 528, 528n
deck cargo, **21**, 589n
deck storage, providing for, **4**, 252
delivery, **20**, 843
delivery order distinguished, **20**, 12
demise clause, **21**, 546
demurrage, **21**, 585
  clause, **21**, 546
description, **4**, 251
despatch money (despatch), **21**, 689
deviation clause, **21**, 546
disadvantages of using, **21**, 525
document of title, as—
  copies of bills of lading, **21**, 569
  generally, **21**, 525, 566
  indorsement and delivery, **21**, 567–569
  negotiability, **21**, 567
  reform of law, **21**, 566, 572
documentary evidence, as, **10**, 602
effect, **21**, 596
elements of, **21**, 525
employees and contractors, liability, **21**, 560
evidence of contract of carriage, as, **21**, 525
excepted perils, express terms, **21**, 546
exemption clauses, **21**, 546
expenses, express terms as to liability, **21**, 546
express terms, **21**, 525, 525n, 546
form and contents, **21**, 528
freight—
  action in claim for, **21**, 665
  advance, **21**, 653, 659, 659n
  back, **21**, 653n, 656n, 661
  calculation, **21**, 653, 653n, 654, 654n
  damaged cargo, **21**, 657, 657n
  dead, **21**, 653n, 660
  delivery, necessity for, **21**, 656, 656n
  express terms as to, **21**, 546
  generally, **21**, 653
  jurisdiction, **21**, 665
  liability for, **21**, 662
  lump sum, **21**, 653, 655, 655n, 657, 657n
  meaning, **21**, 653n
  non-payment or late payment, **21**, 665
  performance of contract, **21**, 585
  pro rata (freight *pro rata itineris*), **21**, 653, 656n, 658, 658n
  shipowners' lien, **21**, 665
  to whom payable, **21**, 664
  See also SEA, CARRIAGE BY (freight)
general average, **21**, 609
  arbitration clause, **21**, 711
general ship, contract for carriage in, **21**, 540
  contract evidenced by bill of lading, **21**, 521, 524
  express terms, **21**, 546
  generally, **16**, 1901
  goods bought in bulk, **20**, 835

Bill of lading—*continued*
government directions, express terms, **21**, 546
Hague and Hague-Visby Rules, application, **21**, 547n
Himalaya clause, **21**, 546, 560
holder of, meaning, **21**, 572n
importance, **21**, 562
indorsement and delivery—
  effect, **21**, 568
  effectual indorsement where another copy already indorsed, **21**, 569
  personal bar, operation of, **21**, 571n
  transfer by, **21**, 567
  when property not passing on, **21**, 568, 568n
inspection and tallying of goods, **21**, 598
issue, **21**, 562
  Hague-Visby Rules, **21**, 595
jurisdiction clause, **21**, 546
jus quaesitum tertio, **15**, 847
laytime, **21**, 585
leading marks, **21**, 595
  express terms, **21**, 546
  reference to, generally, **21**, 562, 565
liability, exclusion or limitation of, *see* GENERAL SHIP (contract for carriage in, liability of carrier)
lien clause, **21**, 546
limitation of actions, **16**, 2205
live animals and deck cargo, express terms, **21**, 546
loading, express terms as to, **21**, 546
meaning, **20**, 843; **21**, 521n, 525, 528
name of carrier or shipowner, **21**, 546
name of ship, **21**, 546
negligence clause, **21**, 546
negotiability, **21**, 567
New Jason clause, **21**, 546
no bill issued, where, **21**, 525
non-negotiability of, **4**, 103
other requirements, **4**, 252
owners' responsibility clause, **21**, 546
particulars supplied by shipper, **21**, 597
prima facie evidence, as, **21**, 596
printer's imprint requirement not applicable, **17**, 3
receipt—
  acknowledging condition of goods, as, **21**, 562, 564
  acknowledging quantity of goods, as, **21**, 562, 563
  for goods shipped, as, **21**, 525, 562
received for shipment, **4**, 250; **21**, 524n, 526n, 528n, 571n, 572
reservation of title, where, **18**, 638
right in security, symbolical delivery, **20**, 12
salvage, express terms as to, **21**, 546
sea waybill, replacement by, **21**, 521n, 525, 531
set, issue in, **21**, 525
shipowners' lien, **21**, 656, 656n
shipped, **4**, 250; **21**, 524n, 595
shipper, indemnification of carrier by, **21**, 597
ship's delivery order, **21**, 530
short form, **21**, 528
signature, **21**, 528
standard form, **21**, 528

Bill of lading—*continued*
statutory regulation—
  Carriage of Goods by Sea Act, **21**, 586
  generally, **21**, 529
  Hague Rules, **21**, 586
  Hague-Visby Rules, **21**, 587*ff*
    See also SEA, CARRIAGE BY
  Hamburg Rules, **21**, 586, 586*n*
  history, **21**, 586
stowage, express terms, **21**, 546
strikes exception, **21**, 555
sue, title to—
  generally, **21**, 579, 579*n*
  implied contract, **21**, 581
  reform of law, **21**, 572
  transfer of, **21**, 570–572
symbolical delivery, **18**, 621
third party, transfer to, **21**, 596
through, **21**, 528*n*, 695*n*
time charterparty, **21**, 640
time limit for claims, express terms, **21**, 546
transfer from seller to buyer, **21**, 566
transfer of, **20**, 843
  delivery, as equivalent to, **20**, 860
  rights and liabilities—
    assignment of contract, **21**, 573
    Bills of Lading Act 1855..., **21**, 571
    Carriage of Goods by Sea Act 1992..., **21**, 572
    common law, **21**, 570
    meaning, **21**, 571*n*
  security, in, **20**, 19, 19*n*
transhipment clause, **21**, 546
Uniform Customs and Practice for Documentary Credits, rules of, **4**, 248–252
United States law, **21**, 586
voyage charterparty, **21**, 618, 633
war risks, express terms, **21**, 546
'weight and quantity unknown', **21**, 563
'weight, measurement and number unknown', **21**, 563
York-Antwerp Rules, term incorporating, **21**, 546

Bill of Rights
arguments against, **5**, 319
arguments in favour of, **5**, 318
European Convention on Human Rights, adoption of, **5**, 317
generally, **7**, 702*n*, 708, 710
Select Committee of House of Lords on, **5**, 313
taxation, **7**, 764

Bill of sale
ship, of—
  retention by registrar, **21**, 151
  transfer of title, on, **21**, 167

Bingo
cash bingo, **2**, 1611
club—
  employees, age of, **2**, 1610
  guests, admission of, **2**, 1610
  licence, **2**, 1609
  location of, **2**, 1575
  membership requirement, **2**, 1610
commercial gaming, as, **2**, 1573

Bingo—*continued*
duty, **9**, 1015
  exemptions, **7**, 1084*n*
  generally, **7**, 1080, 1084
  rate, **7**, 1084
  unpaid, **7**, 1084
gaming for prizes, **2**, 1614
hall, planning controls, **23**, 98
licence—
  duty—
    rate of, **2**, 1649
    recovery of, **2**, 1649
  requirement for, **2**, 1574
linked bingo—
  legality, **2**, 1613
  maximum stake, **2**, 1613
  nature of, **2**, 1613
meaning, **2**, 1609
method of play, **2**, 1609
multiple—
  maximum prize money, **2**, 1613
  nature of, **2**, 1613
nature of, **2**, 1573
permitted hours for, **2**, 1612
play—
  fees for, **2**, 1611
  method of, **2**, 1609
  minimum age, **2**, 1610
prize bingo, **2**, 1614
sessions, period of, **2**, 1611
stakes, levy on, **2**, 1605

Bings
mineral, value of, **6**, 495
rehabilitation works, **3**, 155
valuation for rating, **24**, 574–577

Biotechnology
European Community legislation, **18**, 1611

Birds
captive—
  cage, insufficient size, **2**, 290
  liberation for shooting, **2**, 291
game, **11**, 878, 878*n*
  pursuing and killing, **19**, 1295
poultry, *see* POULTRY
wild, *see* WILD BIRDS
See also under names of particular birds

Birth
aircraft, on, **2**, 1064
British citizenship, acquisition of, **14**, 1908
British Dependent Territories citizenship, acquisition of, **14**, 1934
legitimacy at, **17**, 239
register of, *see* BIRTHS, REGISTRATION OF
wrongful—
  abortion, failed, **15**, 305, 306
  'consent-based' negligence actions, **15**, 307
  contractual negligence, **15**, 307
  failure to inform, **15**, 307
  generally, **15**, 305
  normal child, damages to compensate for upbringing, **15**, 309
  Scottish position, generally, **15**, 310

Birthbrieves
Court of the Lord Lyon, **6**, 1012, 1018
Public Register of All Genealogies and
 Birthbrieves in Scotland, **6**, 1012
Births, registration of
abandoned children, **19**, 1440
abbreviated birth certificate, **19**, 1430
 authentication, **19**, 1420
 contents, **19**, 1437
certificate, failure to deliver, **19**, 1474
child born in United Kingdom, **14**, 1912
district registrar, **19**, 1406
 attendance at registration offices, **19**, 1408
 returns to be made by, **19**, 1431
 salary, allowances and compensation, **19**, 1407
districts and authorities, **19**, 1405, 1433
 alteration of, **19**, 1405
documentary evidence, register as, **10**, 591
exposed children, **19**, 1440
extracts—
 authentication of, **19**, 1420
 misuse of, **19**, 1474
fees, collection and accounting of, **14**, 588; **19**,
 1410
forged documents, **19**, 1472
General Register Office, **19**, 1402, 1404
generally, **10**, 1048; **19**, 305, 809, 811, 828, 842
historical background, **19**, 1401, 1402
hours fixed for, **19**, 1408
illegitimate children, **19**, 1439, 1443
information, failure to give, **19**, 1474
institutions, children born in, **19**, 1442
journey, child born during course of, **19**, 1441
live births, **19**, 1438–1445
local authority duty, **14**, 588
name, change of, **19**, 1425–1428
offences, **19**, 1477
 certificate, failure to deliver, **19**, 1474
 destruction of entry, **19**, 1473
 duplication of entry, **19**, 1473
 failure to deliver up registers, **19**, 1471
 forged documents, **19**, 1472
 information—
  failure to give, **19**, 1474
  false, **19**, 1472
 misuse of extract certificate, **19**, 1474
organisation, **19**, 1401–1410
parent, duty to give information, **19**, 1435
parish registers, **19**, 1401
records—
 area repositories, **19**, 1409
 safe custody of, **19**, 1408
 transmission of, **19**, 853
registers—
 abandoned children, **19**, 1440
 correction of, **19**, 1414, 1421, 1422–1424
  change of name or status, **19**, 1425–1430
  clerical errors, **19**, 1423
 destruction of entry, **19**, 1402n, 1417, 1473
 documentary evidence, as, **10**, 591
 duplication, **19**, 1415
  of entry, **19**, 1473
 examination, **19**, 1416
 exposed children, **19**, 1440

Births, registration of—*continued*
registers—*continued*
 extracts, **19**, 1420, 1430, 1474
 illegible, **19**, 1402n, 1417
 illegitimate children, **19**, 1439, 1443
 index of, **19**, 1418, 1419
 information required, **19**, 1431, 1432, 1438
 lost, **19**, 1402n, 1417
 mutilated, **19**, 1402n, 1417
 parochial, **19**, 1411–1413
 provision, **19**, 1415
 replacement, **19**, 1417
 reproductions of, **19**, 1416
 statutory control, **19**, 1414
Registrar General, **19**, 1402, 1403
registration—
 authority, **14**, 32
 offices, **19**, 1408
 procedure, **19**, 1433
  abbreviated birth certificate, **19**, 1437
  information—
   district registrar's power to request, **19**,
    1434
   duty to give, **19**, 1435
   three months after birth or finding of child,
    19, 1436
reregistration, **19**, 1443–1445
 applicant for, **19**, 1444
 grounds of, **19**, 1443
 legitimated child, **19**, 1443
 procedure, **19**, 1445
salary, allowances and compensation for officers,
 19, 1407
sex change in later life, **19**, 1424n
sheriff, supervision by, **19**, 1402
sheriff court jurisdiction, **6**, 1127
ship, birth on board, **21**, 226
stillbirths, *see* STILLBIRTHS, REGISTRATION OF
transsexuality and, **12**, 67
Bishop
Roman Catholic—
 authority, **3**, 1655
 Bishops' Conference, **3**, 1655
 dioceses and archdioceses, **3**, 1655
Scottish Episcopal Church, **3**, 1614
 Articles of Agreement, **3**, 1615
 College of Bishops, **3**, 1618, 1619
 designation, **3**, 1619
 eighteenth-century development, **3**, 1615
 Episcopal Synod, **3**, 1618, 1619
 jurisdiction, **3**, 1618
 number, **3**, 1618
 Primus, **3**, 1619
Black fish
meaning, **11**, 2n
Black game
eggs, protection of, **11**, 802, 843
game, as, **11**, 802
Game (Scotland) Act 1832..., **11**, 815
Poaching Prevention Act 1832..., **11**, 843
trespass in search of, **11**, 817
Black Watch
raising of, **2**, 601

Blackmail
extortion by, **7**, 396
Blameworthiness
criminal law, as mental element in, **7**, 64
Blasphemy
crime of, generally, **7**, 476
Blasting materials
blasting powder as explosive, **10**, 1586
compressed air blasting shells, use of, **14**, 1651
maintenance, **14**, 1651
quarry, in, **14**, 1706
use, **14**, 1651
Blazon
function, **14**, 1503
Bleacher
right of lien, **20**, 77, 78n, 79
Bleaching
water unfit for, **14**, 2079
Blench
blenchduties, redemption, **18**, 67
definition, **18**, 67
feudal law, generally, **18**, 67, 67n, 70
survival in Scots law, **6**, 714n; **18**, 68
wardholding converted to, **18**, 64
Blight
notice—
  compensation after, **5**, 104
  effect of, **5**, 103; **23**, 322
  generally, **23**, 315
  interests qualifying for protection, **5**, 99; **23**, 317
  land which may be subject to, **5**, 98; **23**, 316
  Lands Tribunal, reference to, **5**, 102; **23**, 321
  objection to, **23**, 320
  service of, **5**, 100, 101; **23**, 319
  when arising, **5**, 97; **23**, 316
Blind person
bill of exchange, signature on, **4**, 123
disability living allowance, **21**, 934, 936
income support—
  disability premium, **21**, 1074
  pensioner premium, **21**, 1074
postal vote, eligibility on grounds of blindness, **15**, 1160, 1161
proxy vote, eligibility on grounds of blindness, **15**, 1160, 1163, 1176
registered, ophthalmic services, **11**, 1463n
roads authorities' duty of care towards, **20**, 660, 670
talking books—
  provided for, **7**, 1448
  supplied for gratuitous loan to, VAT treatment, **3**, 1163
testator, notarial execution, **25**, 725
training course in use of guide dog, unemployment benefit claimant participating in, **21**, 829n
travel concession, local authority, **20**, 493
voter, **15**, 1214, 1321
  declaration by companion, **15**, 1229
    combined poll, **15**, 1371
  list of blind voters assisted by companion, **15**, 1321
    combined poll, **15**, 1375

Blind person—*continued*
wireless sets—
  provided for, **7**, 1448
  supplied for gratuitous loan to, VAT treatment, **3**, 1163
Block exemption
filling station agreements, *see* COMPETITION
Block storage heaters
rating relief in respect of, **24**, 578
Blockade
close, **17**, 413
neutral ship attempting to break, **17**, 413
purpose of, **17**, 413
restraint of princes, as, **21**, 550
Blood
distribution to food industry, **11**, 416
human—
  donation, age limit, **3**, 1233
  products derived from, VAT exemption, **7**, 1426
supplies of, **11**, 1484
veterinary surgery, blood taken for diagnosis of infectious disease, **25**, 203
Blood relation
meaning, **12**, 1268; **13**, 1627
Blood sports, **19**, 1275
Blood tests
alcohol or drug consumption, for, **20**, 418
  analysis, provision of specimens for, **20**, 424, 425
  back calculation of accused's alcohol level, **20**, 429n
  breath test in relation to, **20**, 425, 426
  defect in procedure, **20**, 429
  defences to action following, **20**, 429
  evidence in proceedings, proportion of alcohol in specimen, **20**, 429
  failure to provide specimen, **20**, 416n, 427
    defence of reasonable excuse, **20**, 427
    disqualification following, **20**, 453
  fear of needle, **20**, 427
  fear of sight of blood, **20**, 427
  hospital patients, safeguards for, **20**, 428
  prescribed limit, **20**, 419
  unfairly or improperly obtained evidence from, **20**, 429
  warning of, failure to give, **20**, 429
  who may take, **20**, 426
evidence, as, **10**, 502
parentage or non-parentage, actions for declarator of, **10**, 1163
Board/Boarder
income from, calculation for income support, **21**, 1077
meaning, **11**, 1710
rent including payments for, **13**, 628, 770
Board of Agriculture
enlargement to Department of Agriculture for Scotland, **6**, 957
former duties, **6**, 957
registration of smallholdings, abortive scheme for, **6**, 957
Board of Banking Supervision
establishment and duties, **2**, 1144

Boarding house
fire certificates, **10**, 1453
hotel distinguished, **11**, 1710
innkeepers' strict liability not applicable to, **15**, 147
liability, **11**, 1742
luggage, for, **11**, 1710
lodging house distinguished, **11**, 1710
meaning, **11**, 1710
water meter charges, **25**, 536
Boat
byelaws controlling boating, **25**, 359
exemptions from explosives regulations, **10**, 1589
gunpowder, byelaws as to, **10**, 1609, 1610
hire, licensing of, **14**, 119, 560
no place to park amounting to homelessness, **11**, 2045, 2048
noise from, **25**, 359
pleasure, navigation of, **25**, 362
See also SHIP
Bodleian Library, Oxford
copy of books published to be delivered to, **17**, 5
Body
dead, *see* DEAD BODY
Body belts
use in penal establishment, rules as to, **16**, 1453
Body corporate
accused, as, **17**, 737
apparent insolvency, **2**, 1324
capacity to contract, **3**, 26
connected, investigation of, **4**, 525
constitution of, **4**, 3
consumer credit—
exempt agreement, **5**, 821
offences, **5**, 961
corporation tax, *see* CORPORATION TAX
data protection, criminal offence in respect of, **18**, 1552
debtor, as, **8**, 128
defamation—
corporate body as defender, **15**, 479
corporate body as pursuer, **15**, 474
generally, **15**, 474
hurt feelings, **15**, 474
patrimonial loss, **15**, 474
what constitutes, **15**, 474
dentistry, prohibition from carrying on business of, **14**, 1133
goods, restrictive agreement as to, **4**, 1137
group company, *see* COMPANY
interconnected, meaning, **4**, 1137*n*
lessee, as, **13**, 190
lessor, as, **13**, 177
limited partner, as, **16**, 1113
dissolution of body corporate, **16**, 1120
offences by, **5**, 961; **11**, 1788
food, in relation to, **11**, 325, 423
health and safety regulations, offences under, **9**, 516
inshore fishing, in relation to, **11**, 143
sea fishing, in relation to, **11**, 153
registered industrial design, offences in relation to, **18**, 1169

Body corporate—*continued*
sequestration—
estate, of, **2**, 1321, 1326
jurisdiction for purposes of, **4**, 72
subscription by, **6**, 417
taxable person for VAT purposes, **7**, 1323, 1348
two or more persons, meaning, **4**, 1137
unfair conduct by, **6**, 18
'usual place of residence', **7**, 1294
VAT registration provisions, **7**, 1348
voluntary obligation, capacity to enter, **15**, 664
Body fluids and tissue
identification by, **10**, 662
police, taken by, **16**, 1797
Body and organs
donation, **8**, 616
Body piercing
age limit, **3**, 1231
Bog
See stagnum
Bogota, Pact of
generally, **19**, 698*n*, 720*n*
Bomb
ammunition, as, **10**, 1510
designed to explode on or immediately before impact, **10**, 1517
security, as, **5**, 908
Bona vacantia
Crown—
disclaimer by, **4**, 931
vesting in, **4**, 930
royal, Crown hereditary revenue derived from, **7**, 769
Bond
ad facta praestandum, **6**, 617
annuity, of, **6**, 619; **20**, 130
bottomry, of, *see* BOTTOMRY
cash credit, **6**, 620; **20**, 131
caution, of, **6**, 621
corroboration, **6**, 624; **20**, 130
fidelity, of, **6**, 623
generally, **6**, 617
meaning, **6**, 617
reduction of, personal bar, **16**, 1605
regulation of, **14**, 816
relief, of, **6**, 625
See also HERITABLE SECURITIES
Book
See PUBLICATION
Book of Common Prayer
copyright, **18**, 1002
Booking tenure
feufarm, merger with, **18**, 65
generally, **18**, 65
meaning, **18**, 65
Bookmaker
agent of—
age limit for, **2**, 1515
authorisation of, **2**, 1515
betting agency permit—
appeal in respect of, **2**, 1535
application for, **2**, 1531
grant of, **2**, 1534; **14**, 517
nature and effect, **2**, 1530

Bookmaker—*continued*
betting agency permit—*continued*
   refusal of—
      appeal against, **2**, 1535
      grounds for, **2**, 1535
   renewal of, **2**, 1533
facilities on tracks, **2**, 1557
levy on, *see* HORSERACE BETTING LEVY BOARD
licensed offices, *see* BETTING
permit—
   age limit, **3**, 1230
   appeal against refusal—
      costs of, **2**, 1529
      disposal of, **2**, 1529
      grounds of, **2**, 1528
      provisions for, **2**, 1527
   application for—
      advertisement of, **2**, 1519
      hearing, **2**, 1519
      partnership, by, **2**, 1519
      procedure, **2**, 1519
   effect of, **2**, 1518
   grant of—
      generally, **2**, 1525
      objections to, **2**, 1519
      renewal, **2**, 1525
   licensing authority for, **2**, 1516; **14**, 517
   minimum age for, **2**, 1518
   proceedings as to, **2**, 1520
   qualifications for obtaining, **2**, 1518
   refusal of—
      discretionary, **2**, 1522
      grounds for, **2**, 1521, 1524
      mandatory, **2**, 1521
      notification of, **2**, 1526
      renewal, of, **2**, 1524
   renewal—
      applications, hearing, **2**, 1523
      objections to, **2**, 1523
      procedure, **2**, 1523
taxation of profits, **19**, 1298
unlicensed tracks, on, **2**, 1562
See also BETTING
Bookmaking partnership
professional rules, contravention, **16**, 1017
Booty
meaning, **17**, 401
prize jurisdiction, **17**, 401
Border
controls, prevention of terrorism powers, **12**, 133
Borders Region
population, **14**, 64
structure, **14**, 64
Bordure company
assignation of, **11**, 1618
Borehole
sinking, procedure for, **25**, 345
Bores
journal of, **3**, 18, 19
Borgathing
Norwegian law code, **24**, 303
Borstal
abolition, **16**, 1404
establishment, **16**, 1404

Botanist, King's
office of, **7**, 846
Bothies
not domestic subject for valuation for rating, **24**, 617
Bottomry
bond of, **20**, 6, 26, 281
   conventional hypothec, as, **21**, 479
   dispute over, **20**, 305
   maritime lien—
      giving rise to, **21**, 392, 479
      priority, **21**, 479n
   security, as, **13**, 1759
jurisdiction, generally, **21**, 101
maritime—
   cause, as, **1**, 411
   lien, as, **1**, 413
Bouncer
failure to prevent crime, **7**, 39
physical force, use of, **7**, 238
Boundary
alteration—
   agreement, by, **18**, 220
   Land Register boundaries, **18**, 219
   March Dykes Act, by, **18**, 221
   Sasine titles, **18**, 219
Boundary Commission, *see* BOUNDARY COMMISSION
bounding charter, **12**, 1239
bounding title, **12**, 1239
common gables—
   alteration, **18**, 225
   generally, **18**, 218, 229
   support, right of, **18**, 233, 272
description—
   particular, **6**, 484; **12**, 1239
   reference to, by, **6**, 485
discrepancy in titles, where, **18**, 197, 220
English practice, **6**, 732
inaccuracy in delineating, **6**, 760
judicially construed, **12**, 1239
land, **24**, 405
lateral, **12**, 1239
legal and occupational, discrepancies between, **6**, 734
march stones, **18**, 214
measurements, **12**, 1240
new, creation of, **12**, 1240
new housing development, **6**, 734
'or thereby' rule, **6**, 732
order by Secretary of State, **14**, 70
physical objects, in relation to, **6**, 735
plans—
   colour, use of, **12**, 1240
   conflicting with boundary, **12**, 1240
   registration, **12**, 1240
Reid Committee, **6**, 732
river or stream on—
   fishing rights, **18**, 280
   ownership, **18**, 278
rivers and roads, **6**, 485
sea-shore, **6**, 485
uncertainty as to, **14**, 2017
valuation areas, between, **24**, 405

Boundary—*continued*
wall or fence—
  accession of things attached, **18**, 223
  ad medium filum ownership, **18**, 223
    alteration of wall or fence, **18**, 225
    common interest, **18**, 359
    maintenance, **18**, 226
  alteration of boundary—
    agreement, by, **18**, 220
    location of boundary, **18**, 219
    March Dykes Act 1669, under, **18**, 221
  common boundary, on, **18**, 217, 223
    consent, requirement for, **18**, 217
    support, right of, **18**, 272
  common gables, *see* COMMON GABLES
  common ownership—
    alteration of wall or fence, **18**, 225
    generally, **18**, 224, 226
    maintenance, **18**, 226
  costs of erection, **18**, 215, 215*n*
    March Dykes Act 1661 ..., **18**, 216
    real burden as to, **18**, 217
  estate, within, **18**, 215, 215*n*, 222
  generally, **6**, 485; **18**, 214
  light, cutting out, **18**, 215, 215*n*
  March Dykes Act 1661 ... **18**, 216
  ownership and maintenance—
    ad medium filum, wall or fence owned, **18**, 226
    agreement, by, **18**, 226
    alteration of boundary wall or fence, **18**, 225
    both sides of boundary, wall or fence on, **18**, 223
    common, wall or fence owned in, **18**, 224–226
    contracting out, **18**, 224
    local authority powers, **18**, 226
    March Dykes Act 1661, under, **18**, 226
    one side of boundary, wall or fence on, **18**, 222
    real burden as to maintenance, where, **18**, 226
  real burdens, where, **18**, 217, 226
  water, in respect of, **24**, 406
  See also HERITABLE PROPERTY; LOCAL GOVERNMENT BOUNDARY COMMISSION
Boundary Commission
establishment, **14**, 65; **15**, 1029
local government constituencies, **14**, 65–71; **15**, 1030, 1039
parliamentary constituencies, **15**, 1037
reports, **15**, 1029
'Bovill's Act'
generally, **16**, 1003
Bovine spongiform encephalopathy (BSE)
public health legislation, **19**, 477*n*
Bow
wild birds or animals taken or killed with, **11**, 880, 884
Bowing
lease, **13**, 219
Bowls
historical background, **19**, 1203
Boxing
injuries, and assault, **7**, 221
licence, **19**, 1238
Queensberry Rules, **19**, 1205, 1264, 1265

Brain tissue
surgical operation for destroying, **14**, 1425
Branch System General (BSG) Licence
apparatus, provisions as to, **16**, 1949
applicatiom, **16**, 1949
electronic mail, provision, **16**, 1949
EU requirements, compliance with, **16**, 1949
generally, **16**, 1948
lift, telephone installed in, **16**, 1949
maintenance services, **16**, 1949
private circuits, **16**, 1949
Brand name
may not be substituted for real name of food, **11**, 384
Breach of confidence
artistic or literary production, **18**, 1452, 1456
business matters, **18**, 1453
case law, **18**, 1451
confidential information—
  bankruptcy, and, **18**, 1453
  becoming public by breach, **18**, 1461, 1473, 1480
  'springboard' doctrine, **18**, 1462, 1480
  business asset, as, **18**, 1453
  court proceedings, obtained during, **18**, 1474
  disclosure, **18**, 1476
    defences, **18**, 1481
  employee, exploitation by, **18**, 1453
  express statement as to confidentiality, **18**, 1463, 1464
  good faith, use or disclosure in, **18**, 1476
  inaccessibility to public, **18**, 1460, 1461
  innocent recipient, **18**, 1453
  licence, **18**, 1453
  manner and circumstances in which information obtained, **18**, 1464
  nature of information, **18**, 1464, 1465
  property, as, **18**, 1453
  protection, generally, **18**, 1451
  recipient—
    agreement as to confidentiality, **18**, 1458
    defences, *see* defences *below*
    information acquired by illegal or improper means, **18**, 1458, 1473
    obligation to maintain confidentiality, **18**, 1463–1465
    reasonable person principle, **18**, 1458, 1459, 1460, 1463, 1473
    state of mind at time of breach, **18**, 1476
    understanding as to confidentiality, **18**, 1458
    See also obligation of confidence *below*
  stopping others seeking to discover, **18**, 1478
  subconscious use of information, **18**, 1476
  subject matter, **18**, 1455
    trivial, **18**, 1455
  third party, disclosure to, **18**, 1475
  trade secrets, **18**, 1455
  use, **18**, 1476
    defences, **18**, 1481
confidentiality, government claiming right to, **18**, 1455, 1477, 1480
copyright, and, **18**, 1452
correspondence, **18**, 1456

Breach of confidence—*continued*
defences—
  authority to disclose, defender having reasonable grounds to believe, **18**, 1481
  generally, **18**, 1481
  prior knowledge, **18**, 1481, 1486
  public interest, **18**, 1481, 1482
    extent, **18**, 1484
    public function, discharge of, **18**, 1485
    testing, **18**, 1483
  public knowledge, **18**, 1481, 1487
detriment flowing from—
  generally, **18**, 1477
  potential, **18**, 1477
doctor and patient, between, **18**, 1466
duration of right, **18**, 1452
employee confidentiality—
  contract, **18**, 1467
  Faccenda Chicken Ltd v Fowler, test in, **18**, 1470
  generally, **18**, 1470
  no express contract term, where, **18**, 1469, 1475
  restrictive covenant, **18**, 1468, 1470
  sales information, **18**, 1470
  trade secrets, **18**, 1470, 1471
English and Scots law compared, **18**, 1451
fidelity, obligation of, compared, **18**, 1470
form in which recorded, relevance, **18**, 1457
freedom of expression, confidentiality, and, **18**, 1454
friends, between, **18**, 1466
general principle against, **18**, 1452
generally, **17**, 44; **18**, 1451; **22**, 674
husband and wife, between, **18**, 1466
innocent infringement, **18**, 1453
intellectual property, as, **18**, 801, 1452
know how, **18**, 1452, 1455
  blacklists clause, **18**, 1458*n*
  whitelists clause, **18**, 1458*n*
legislative reform, whether need for, **18**, 1492
no express contract term, where, **18**, 1469, 1475
obligation of confidence—
  duration, **18**, 1480
  effect, **18**, 1476
  legal relationship between parties, **18**, 1475
  loss on information becoming public—
    generally, **18**, 1461, 1473, 1480
    'springboard' doctrine, **18**, 1462, 1480
  significance, **18**, 1475
  third parties, of, **18**, 1475
  when arising, **18**, 1458
  where no contract exists, **18**, 1475
operation information, **18**, 1452
patent protection legislation—
  compared, **18**, 1452, 1460
  relationship between, **18**, 1452
personal information—
  detriment, and, **18**, 1477
  privacy and confidentiality, **18**, 1456
  whether passing with right-holder's estate, **18**, 1453
press freedom, and, **18**, 1473
privacy and confidentiality, **18**, 1456
public interest—
  disclosure in, defence of—
    extent of public interest, **18**, 1484

Breach of confidence—*continued*
public interest—*continued*
  disclosure in, defence of—*continued*
    generally, **18**, 1481, 1482
    testing public interest, **18**, 1483
  generally, **18**, 1455, 1456, 1477, 1480
public knowledge, defence of, **18**, 1481, 1487
relationship between parties, relevance of, **18**, 1464, 1466
remedies—
  accounting of profits, **18**, 1452, 1490
  damages, **18**, 1452, 1489
  delivery up and destruction, **18**, 1491
  interdict, **18**, 1452, 1478, 1488
sales information, former employee making use of, **18**, 1470
Scots law, generally, **18**, 1451
Scottish Law Commission Report 1984..., **18**, 1451, 1492
silence, right to buy, **18**, 1458
'springboard' doctrine, **18**, 1462, 1480
  duration, **18**, 1462, 1480
technical matters, **18**, 1453
title to sue, **18**, 1479
trade secret—
  generally, **18**, 1470, 1471
  reverse engineering or analysis, **18**, 1472
unrecorded information, **18**, 1457
Breach of contract
See CONTRACT
Breach of the peace
actual disturbance, **7**, 459
actus reus, **7**, 33
aggressive behaviour, **7**, 216
alarm and annoyance, causing, **7**, 443–445
assault, and, **7**, 447
attempt inapplicable, **7**, 170
behaviour constituting—
  actions, **7**, 452
  alarm and annoyance, causing, **7**, 443–445, 455, 456, 459
  breach of public order and decorum, **7**, 443–445, 459
  disorderly conduct, **7**, 446, 447, 448, 455
  duel or fight, challenge to, **7**, 451
  effect of conduct, **7**, 459
  fighting, **7**, 446, 447, 451
  indecent remarks or suggestions, **7**, 453
  language, **7**, 452, 454
  provocative conduct, **7**, 452–454
  sexual theme, conduct with, **7**, 455
  shouting, **7**, 454
  speeches, **7**, 454
  suicide, threatening or attempting, **7**, 255, 455
  violence, threatening, **7**, 446, 447, 452
  wide definition, **7**, 450, 455
breach of public order and decorum, **7**, 443–445
charge, forms, **7**, 446
definitions—
  current position, **7**, 445
  primary, **7**, 443
  twentieth century, **7**, 444
generally, **7**, 442
inconsiderate driving, **7**, 449

Breach of the peace—*continued*
intent, **7**, 460
locus—
  generally, **7**, 456
  private place, **7**, 456, 458
  quasi-private place, **7**, 456, 457
malice, **7**, 80
mens rea, **7**, 460
mobbing and rioting, and, **7**, 429, 432–434, 448, 456
motive, **7**, 460
police preventive powers, **16**, 1785, 1786
provocation of, in public performance of play, **9**, 1046
recklessness, **7**, 460
sports-related violence, **19**, 1268
threats, **7**, 398
Bread
advertisement, **11**, 359
bread rolls and products, labelling, **11**, 388
composition, **11**, 359
emulsifiers and stabilisers, **11**, 373
labelling, **11**, 359
loaves, weight of, **11**, 359
Breath test
alcohol consumption, for, **20**, 418
  analysis, provision of specimens for—
    analysing devices, approved, **20**, 425
    failure to provide—
      disqualification following, **20**, 453
      warning of consequences of, **20**, 424
    generally, **20**, 424
    inability to give breath test, **20**, 425
    priority over blood and urine samples, **20**, 425, 426
    when requirement may be made, **20**, 424
  back calculation of accused's alcohol level, **20**, 429*n*
  blood or urine test—
    following, **20**, 426
    in place of, **20**, 425
  defect in procedure, **20**, 429
  defences to action following, **20**, 429
  failure to provide specimen, **20**, 416*n*, 427
    defence of reasonable excuse, **20**, 427
  first and second specimens, **20**, 425
  generally, **20**, 421
  hospital patients, safeguards for, **20**, 428
  preliminary—
    arrest following, **20**, 422
    failure to provide specimen, **20**, 422
    generally, **20**, 422
    grounds for requiring, **20**, 422, 423
    inability to provide, **20**, 422
    place taken, **20**, 422
    procedure, **20**, 423
    taken after driving has ceased, **20**, 422
    time taken, **20**, 422
    who may require, **20**, 422, 423
  prescribed limit, **20**, 419
  proportion of alcohol in blood, determination, **20**, 421
  unfairly or improperly obtained evidence from, **20**, 429
  warning of, failure to give, **20**, 429

Breathalyser
assemblage and use, **20**, 423
test, **20**, 418
Brehon law
English common law and, **22**, 338
Tanistry Case, **22**, 388
Udal law, comparison, **22**, 388
Bribery
attempted, **7**, 547
electoral malpractice, **7**, 409; **15**, 1444
generally, **7**, 405
judge of, reduction on grounds of, **13**, 50
judicial officers, **7**, 405, 547
judiciary, independence of, **5**, 667
police officer accepting bribe, **16**, 1767
sporting events, **19**, 1273
what constitutes, **15**, 1444
Bridge
access, for, provision by roads authority, **20**, 611
construction—
  alteration, or, **19**, 19*n*, 21
  authority for, **20**, 638
  navigable water, over, **20**, 638, 644
  provision for, **20**, 608
foot, provision of, **20**, 660
history of development—
  eighteenth-century, **20**, 604
  generally, **20**, 601
  medieval, **20**, 602
  nineteenth-century, **20**, 605
  seventeenth-century, **20**, 603
  twentieth-century, **20**, 606
navigable water, over, **20**, 638, 639, 644
as part of road, **20**, 609
privately-owned—
  agreement with owner, **20**, 641
  transfer to Secretary of State, **20**, 642
railway—
  crossing over or under road—
    construction costs, **20**, 645
    liability for, **20**, 645
    not owned by railway operator, where, **20**, 645
  See also RAILWAYS
Railways Board, belonging to, transfer to Secretary of State, **20**, 642
road passing over, generally, **20**, 411
roads authority—
  construction, control over, **20**, 693
  local, responsibility of, **20**, 647
  responsibilities as to, **20**, 611
Secretary of State's powers, **20**, 615
sheriff court jurisdiction, **6**, 1130
special road, on, **20**, 643
swing, discontinuance of operation, **20**, 639
toll, **14**, 33; **20**, 607
  valuation and rating, **20**, 722
trunk road, on ownership, **20**, 642
valuation for rating—
  ancillary structures, **24**, 580
  generally, **24**, 579
  pertinents, **24**, 580
  public road toll bridges, **24**, 580, 581
water diversion to enable building, **20**, 640

Bridge—*continued*
Waterways Board, belonging to, transfer to Secretary of State, **20**, 642
Bridging facilities
building society, *see* BUILDING SOCIETY
Bridleway
conversion of road into, **20**, 676
  revocation order, **20**, 676
development order, affected by, **20**, 654
driving on, **20**, 434
level crossing over, **19**, 1031
meaning, **20**, 610
public right of way, *see* RIGHT OF WAY
railway crossing, **20**, 645
replacement, **20**, 654
sporting event on, **19**, 1284
statutory undertakers' rights, preservation of, **20**, 654
stopping up or diverting road for purposes of, **20**, 657
Brieve system
Anglo-Norman influence on development, **22**, 598, 599
brieve of citation, summons *via*, **22**, 599
decline, **22**, 599
judicial brieve, **22**, 599
origin of brieve, **22**, 599
writ system compared, **22**, 599
British Airports Authority
dissolution of, **2**, 904, 912
permitted development, **23**, 153
British Airways Board
discontinuance of, **2**, 905
British Airways plc
property etc transferred to, **2**, 905
British Antarctic Territory
British Dependent Territories citizenship, **14**, 1932
British Board of Film Censors
powers of, **9**, 1027
British Broadcasting Corporation
charter, regulation by, **17**, 2, 6
election matter, transmission of, **17**, 43
good taste and decency in programme broadcast by, **18**, 1136
government control, **17**, 6
home services—
  finance, **17**, 6
  meaning, **17**, 6*n*
licences, revenue from, **17**, 6
primary duty, **17**, 6
Secretary of State, powers of, **17**, 6
British citizen
abode, right of, **12**, 118; **16**, 1207
burden of proof, **12**, 118, 153
entry into UK, **16**, 1207
passport, **12**, 121
settlement, **12**, 121
UK passport, right to hold, **16**, 1201
British citizenship
acquisition—
  on 1 January, **3**, 1983
    abode, right of, **14**, 1906
    exceptions, **14**, 1906

British citizenship—*continued*
acquisition—*continued*
  after 1 January, **3**, 1983
    adopted child, **14**, 1910
    birth in UK, **14**, 1908
    deprivation—
      generally, **14**, 1929
      procedure, **14**, 1930
      proceedings, **14**, 1931
    descent, **14**, 1911, 1922, 1924
    Falkland Islands—
      child, **14**, 1925
      descent, **14**, 1924
      qualifications, **14**, 1923
      registration, **14**, 1926
    naturalisation—
      requirements for, **14**, 1920
      spouse of British citizen, **14**, 1921
    parent, death of, **14**, 1909
    registration—
      British Dependent Territories, **14**, 1914
      child born in UK, **14**, 1912
      father's citizenship, based on, **14**, 1918
      marriage, **14**, 1917
      minor, **14**, 1913
      relevant employment, **14**, 1916
      renunciation of UK citizenship, following, **14**, 1919
      residence in UK, **14**, 1916
      UK national under EEC treaties, **14**, 1915
    renunciation, **14**, 1927
    resumption, **14**, 1928
    types, **14**, 1907
aircraft, person born on, **14**, 1908
deprivation, **14**, 1929–1931
nationality status, **14**, 1904
naturalisation, requirements for, **14**, 1920
new born infant found abandoned, **14**, 1908
ship, person born on, **14**, 1908
British Coal Corporation
constitution, **14**, 1604
financial directions, **14**, 1604
functions, **14**, 1603
grants, **14**, 1604
licence to work coal, **14**, 1606
minerals, statutory control of rights to work, **14**, 1681
National Coal Board, interests transferred from, **14**, 1603
nationalisation, **19**, 223
opencast coal mining—
  compulsory rights orders, **14**, 1699
  rights of way, suspension of, **14**, 1698
  statutory control, **14**, 1697
planning law, role in, **23**, 19, 169, 231
pneumoconiosis compensation scheme, **14**, 1678
policy, **14**, 1603
prescribed valuation formula, **24**, 547
subsidence damage, obligations in respect of, **14**, 1694
support, right to withdraw, **14**, 1685
British Code of Advertising Practice
advertisements, publication of, **17**, 45
rules in, **1**, 545

British constitution
amendments to, **5**, 307
characteristics of, **5**, 302
common law, fundamental principles depend
entirely on, **5**, 305
comparisons with constitutions of other countries,
5, 303–307
English interpretations of 'constitution', **5**, 351
flexibility of, **5**, 307
judiciary and, **5**, 360
only partly contained in statutes, **5**, 305
single document, not contained in, **5**, 302, 305
unusual characteristics, **5**, 302
British Dependent Territories citizenship
acquisition—
on 1 January 1983, **14**, 1933
after 1 January, **7**, 1983
adoption, by, **14**, 1934
birth, by, **14**, 1934
deprivation, **14**, 1940
descent, by, **14**, 1935, 1941
naturalisation, by, **14**, 1937
registration—
generally, **14**, 1938
minor, of, **14**, 1936
renunciation, **14**, 1939
resumption, **14**, 1938, 1939
deprivation, **14**, 1940
Falkland Islands, **14**, 1923
generally, **14**, 1932
immigration control exemptions, **12**, 132
leave to enter, **12**, 120
meaning, **12**, 107
nationality status, **14**, 1904
passport, **12**, 121
registration, **14**, 1914, 1936, 1938
settlement, **12**, 121
UK passport, right to hold, **16**, 1201
British Excursion document
generally, **16**, 1225
British Film Fund Agency
establishment of, **9**, 1028
winding-up of, **9**, 1028
British Gas Corporation
gas industry under, **9**, 858
privilege, abolition of, **9**, 868
successor company, transfer of rights and liabilities
to, **9**, 867
valuation of lands and heritages, **24**, 415
British Hallmarking Council
establishment, **18**, 1413
functions, **18**, 1415
membership, **18**, 1415
British Indian Ocean Territory
British Dependent Territories citizenship, **14**, 1932
British Linen Bank
acquisition by Bank of Scotland, **2**, 1117
bank notes, issue of, **14**, 1817
British Museum
company donation to, **3**, 1155
tax treatment, **3**, 1166
British National Oil Corporation
establishment, **19**, 211
participation by, **9**, 736

British National (Overseas), **12**, 220n
Hong Kong, connection with, **14**, 1947
immigration control exemptions, **12**, 132
leave to enter, **12**, 120
passport, **12**, 121
settlement, **12**, 121
status—
acquisition of, **14**, 1948
creation of, **14**, 1946
deprivation of, **14**, 1949
generally, **14**, 1904
renunciation of, **14**, 1949
UK passport, right to hold, **16**, 1201
British Overseas citizenship
abode, right of, **14**, 1942
acquisition—
on or after 1 July 1997 ..., **14**, 1944
registration, by, **14**, 1943
future generations, transmissibility to, **14**, 1942
immigration control exemptions, **12**, 132
meaning, **12**, 107
nationality status, **14**, 1904
passport, **12**, 121
registration, **14**, 1914, 1943
renunciation, **14**, 1945
residual category, as, **14**, 1942
returning resident status, **12**, 120
settlement, **12**, 121
UK passport, right to hold, **16**, 1201
British Pharmacopoeia Commission
functions, **14**, 1204
British protected person
appropriate territory, connected with, **14**, 1954
immigration control exemptions, **12**, 132
leave to enter, **12**, 120
registration, **14**, 1914, 1954
UK passport, right to hold, **16**, 1201
British Railways Board
accounts and audit—
auditor, appointment of, **19**, 1012
generally, **19**, 1012
Parliament, laid before, **19**, 1012
air services, operation of, **19**, 1005
borrowing powers, **19**, 1011
British Transport Police, appointment of, **19**,
1058
byelaws—
approval of, **19**, 1016
exhibition of, **19**, 1016
power to make, **19**, 1015
charges, scheme of, **19**, 1013
common carrier, not to be regarded as, **3**, 695,
709; **19**, 1013
Conditions of Carriage of Passengers and their
Luggage, **3**, 709
constitution and status, **19**, 1005–1012
duties, **19**, 1005
duty of care, **3**, 702, 703, 709
passengers, to, **3**, 715
prospective passengers, to, **3**, 710
visitors to Board's premises, to, **3**, 702, 710
employees' share schemes, **19**, 1008
goods, charges for carriage of, **3**, 699
grant, central government, **19**, 1010

British Railways Board—*continued*
land—
    acquisition, **19**, 1018
    additional required, **19**, 1019
    development, **19**, 1018
liability, **19**, 1013
lien, powers in respect of, **3**, 700
loan, central government, **19**, 1010
passengers, carriage of, **3**, 709
position, generally, **3**, 695
powers, **19**, 1005
premises or train, goods left on, **3**, 709
refreshments, provision of, **19**, 1005
regional railway boards, **19**, 1007
road transport, **19**, 1005
Secretary of State for Transport, general
    supervision of, **19**, 1006
stations, *see* RAILWAYS
status as regards Crown, **19**, 1009
sub-contractor, employment by, **3**, 696
subsidiaries, power to dispose of, **19**, 1008
timetables, issue and alteration, **3**, 709
valuation of lands and heritages, **24**, 415
    prescribed formula, **19**, 1001; **24**, 547
British Standard Codes of Practice
building regulations, **3**, 207
British Standards
building regulations, **3**, 207
British Standards Institution
consumer protection, **6**, 28
British subject
leave to enter, **12**, 120
meaning, **12**, 120*n*
nationality status, **14**, 1904, 1950
passport, **12**, 121
registration, **14**, 1914
Republic of Ireland, citizen of, **14**, 1950, 1955
settlement, **12**, 121
UK passport, right to hold, **16**, 1201
See also COMMONWEALTH CITIZEN
British Technology Group
establishment, **19**, 211
British Telecommunications plc (British Telecom)
apparatus—
    production, **16**, 1944
    research and development, **16**, 1944
changes to system or apparatus, duty where, **16**, 1940
charges, notification, **16**, 1941
competitive environment, creation of, provisions as to, **16**, 1940
connection into system by other PTO, **16**, 1934–1936
cross subsidies, prohibition on, **16**, 1942
deregulation, **16**, 1920
equal access, provision of service on basis of, **16**, 1934
exclusive dealing arrangements—
    international services, **16**, 1946
    prohibition, **16**, 1945
hearing-impaired, facilities for, **16**, 1933, 1933*n*
non-discrimination, provisions as to, **16**, 1933, 1933*n*, 1940

British Telecommunications plc (British Telecom)—*continued*
planning privileges, **16**, 1953
preferential treatment, prohibition on, **16**, 1940
price control, **16**, 1947, 1947*n*
private circuits, provision, **16**, 1940
rural areas, provision of services to, **16**, 1933
separate accounts, provision, **16**, 1943
terms and conditions, notification, **16**, 1941
testing apparatus, provisions as to, **16**, 1938
tie-in sales, prohibition, **16**, 1940
transfer of assets to, **16**, 1920, 1920*n*
universal service, provision, conditions as to, **16**, 1932
valuation of lands and heritages, **24**, 415
wiring—
    other telecommunication system, use by, **16**, 1939
    rental, **16**, 1939
    sale, **16**, 1939
British Tourist Authority (BTA)
See TOURISM
British Transport Commission, **19**, 1001
British Transport Police
appointment to, **16**, 1814
constables—
    appointment, **19**, 1058
    oath and declaration, **19**, 1058
    powers, **19**, 1059
constitution of force, **19**, 1058
establishment, **16**, 1814
offences by, **19**, 1067
powers, **16**, 1814
privileges, **16**, 1814
British Visitor's passport
child under eight, **16**, 1224
child under sixteen, **16**, 1224
eligibility to hold, **16**, 1224
entry into UK, **16**, 1207
generally, **16**, 1224
issue, **16**, 1224
    fee, **16**, 1224
purpose, **16**, 1224
British Waterways Board
abstraction of water, **19**, 1105
accounts and audit, **19**, 1114
borrowing powers, supervision of, **19**, 1113
common carrier, not to be regarded as, **19**, 1108
constitution, **19**, 1103
duties, **19**, 1105–1108
    facilities, provision of, **19**, 1105
    services, provision of, **19**, 1105
establishment, **19**, 1103
liability, **19**, 1108–1110, 1124–1126
    exclusion or restriction of, **19**, 1108
port facilities, **19**, 1105
powers, **19**, 1105
    canal byelaws, **19**, 1107
    charges, power to make, **19**, 1105, 1108
    compulsory purchase of land, **19**, 1106
    conditions, power to make, **19**, 1108
    land, purchase of, **19**, 1105, 1106
road, transport of goods by, **19**, 1105
sale of water, **19**, 1105

British Waterways Board—*continued*
supervision by Secretary of State, **19**, 1113
valuation of lands and heritages, **24**, 415
   prescribed formula, **24**, 547
Broadcast
advance programme information, duty to provide,
   18, 1025
British Broadcasting Corporation, *see* BRITISH
   BROADCASTING CORPORATION
broadcasting schedules, European Community
   legislation, **18**, 1663
child, performance by, **9**, 1052
consumer protection, **19**, 240
copyright, **18**, 940, 967, 971, 1024, 1025
   author, meaning, **18**, 979, 982
   cable programme, *see* CABLE PROGRAMME
   copying for private and domestic use, **18**, 1123
   educational establishment, and, **18**, 1112, 1113
   European Community legislation, **18**, 1643, 1644
   generally, **18**, 933, 973
   infringement, **18**, 1055
      playing or showing in public, by, **18**, 1062–
         1064
   needletime, **18**, 1024
   originality, **18**, 948
   ownership rights, **18**, 1005, 1042
   permitted acts, **18**, 1123–1126
   qualification for protection, **18**, 941
   repeats, **18**, 974, 1040
   satellite broadcasts, **18**, 972
   sound broadcasts, **18**, 971
   spoken words, use of, **18**, 1107
   subtitled for the disabled, provision of copies,
      18, 1124
   television broadcasts, **18**, 971
   term of copyright, **18**, 1040
   unauthorised transmissions, dealing in apparatus
      for, **18**, 1083
defamation, *see* DEFAMATION
election campaign, during—
   constraints on, **15**, 1020, 1231, 1449
   expenses, **15**, 1412
European Community legislation, **18**, 1663, 1664
freedom of expression, **12**, 73
illicit recording, **18**, 1438
Independent Broadcasting Authority, *see*
   INDEPENDENT BROADCASTING AUTHORITY
investment advice, publication, **12**, 1307
joint authorship, **18**, 987
licensing, **12**, 73
meaning, **18**, 971
obscene material, **7**, 486
privilege, *see* PRESS AND BROADCASTING
regulation, **17**, 2, 6–8
reports, qualified privilege, **15**, 536
restrictions on publication, *see* PUBLICATION
Sound, Select Committee on, **5**, 444, 466
unauthorised, high seas, from, **21**, 44, 45
See also PRESS AND BROADCASTING
Broadcaster
Securities and Investments Board Core Conduct
   of Business Rules, **12**, 1399
Broadcasting Complaints Commission
function, **17**, 2, 10

Broker
mercantile agent distinguished, **20**, 849
right of lien, **20**, 78
Brothel
child in, **3**, 1244
offences in relation to, **3**, 1239, 1244
residential area, in, **14**, 2083
Brother
deceased specified relative, as, **15**, 602
division of estate on or after 8 December 1986—
   examples, **7**, 25
settlement, family reunion or creation by, **12**,
   289, 290
Brown, E D
international law, writings on, **19**, 611
Brucella
public health legislation, **19**, 477*n*
Brussels Declaration
war conduct, **19**, 707
Bubble Act
contributory factor in passing, **4**, 302
repeal, **4**, 303
reported cases of references to, **4**, 302*n*
Buddhists
personal law, domicile as indicator of, **17**, 188
Budget Day
Ways and Means resolutions, **7**, 765
Budgeting loan
social fund, **21**, 1123, 1124
Buggery
child abuse, as, **7**, 4
generally, **7**, 296
Bugging
police surveillance activities, **16**, 1802
Build, operate, transfer contract
generally, **3**, 9
Builder's skip
See SKIP
Building Agreement
generally, **3**, 12
Building and building controls
accession, **18**, 578
advertising on, **14**, 335
agricultural buildings, **3**, 209
alterations—
   building regulations, **3**, 207
   building warrant, **3**, 220
   plans, examination, passing or rejection, **3**, 203
   unauthorised, **3**, 203
ancient monuments, **3**, 244
archaeological areas, **3**, 244
architectural nuisance, **14**, 2014
authorised, service of purchase notice in case of,
   5, 95
building—
   authorities, **3**, 201; **19**, 350
   contract, *see* BUILDING CONTRACT
   control—
      certificate, liquor licensing, **2**, 45
      meaning, **3**, 203
   extensions—
      building warrant, **3**, 220
      exemptions from building regulations, **3**, 208

Building and building controls—*continued*
building—*continued*
  extensions—*continued*
    local authority control, **3**, 203
    unauthorised, **3**, 203
  operations—
    building, meaning, **23**, 69
    new town development corporation, provided by, **23**, 378
    operational development, **23**, 69
    partial demolition, as, **23**, 73
  regulations, *see* BUILDING REGULATIONS
  warrant—
    additional requirements imposed by, **3**, 222
    alteration or extension of building, **3**, 220
    amendment, **3**, 221
    appeal against refusal, **3**, 236
    application—
      consideration, **3**, 221
      disposal, **3**, 224
      form, **3**, 220
      hearing, **3**, 224
      limited life, for building deemed to have, **3**, 225
        building remaining in construction after expiry of warrant, **3**, 228, 229
      making, **3**, 220
      proposal notice, **3**, 223
      reference to Secretary of State, **3**, 222
    breach of, construction in, **3**, 228, 244
      appeals, **3**, 236
      expenses incurred by local authority, recovery, **3**, 243, 244
    change of use, for, **3**, 220
      appeal against refusal, **3**, 236
    class—
      application, **3**, 216
      certificate of completion, **3**, 218
      designated body, **3**, 216
      enabling provisions, **3**, 216
      failure to implement provisions, **3**, 216, 218
      fee, **3**, 216, 217
      generally, **3**, 216
      issue, **3**, 216
      local authority, role of, **3**, 218
      materials, **3**, 216
      revocation, **3**, 217
      Secretary of State, powers, **3**, 216, 217
      terms and conditions, **3**, 217
      variation, **3**, 217
    completion date, **3**, 226
    construction without, **3**, 228, 230, 244
      appeals, **3**, 236
      expenses incurred by local authority, recovery, **3**, 243, 244
    decision, notification, **3**, 225
    deemed, **3**, 221
    demolition, **3**, 220
      appeal against refusal, **3**, 236
      completion date, **3**, 226
      deemed, **3**, 221
      refusal, **3**, 221
      relaxation, application for, local authority tests, **3**, 239, 241

Building and building controls—*continued*
building—*continued*
  warrant—*continued*
    duration, **3**, 226
    failure to comply with terms—
      civil liability, **3**, 230
      local authority action, **3**, 228, 229
    granted to certain stage, **3**, 221
    inspection of building by local authority, for, **3**, 238
    interest, member of local authority with, **3**, 220
    limited life, building deemed to have, **3**, 222, 225, 244
      appeal against refusal to extend, **3**, 236
    plans, **3**, 220
    proposal notice, **3**, 222, 223
      questions in, **3**, 223
    refusal, **3**, 221
    site inspection, **3**, 237
    style, **3**, 220
    type approval scheme, **3**, 245–247
  building works—
    inspection by local authority, **3**, 203, 237, 238, 241
    obstruction, **3**, 241
    warrant for, **3**, 238
  capital item, building as, **7**, 1380
  certificate—
    self certification of design, **3**, 219
    type approval, **3**, 247
  certificate of completion—
    appeal against refusal, **3**, 236
    application, **3**, 227
    class warrant, where, **3**, 218
    electrical installations, where, **3**, 227
    generally, **3**, 227
    inspection prior to issue, **3**, 203, 237
      obstruction, penalties, **3**, 241
      warrant for, **3**, 238
    issue, **3**, 203
    occupation or use of building, **3**, 227
  change of use—
    building regulations, **3**, 207
    building warrant, **3**, 220
      appeal against refusal, **3**, 236
    Crown building, **3**, 210
    local authority control, **3**, 203
    suspected, where, local authority inspection, **3**, 237
    unauthorised, **3**, 203
    without warrant, civil liability, **3**, 230
  change of use of building, self-supply, **7**, 1306
  charitable building, goods installed in, VAT regulations, **7**, 1449
  classification, building standards, **3**, 205
  common (mutual) gables, *see* COMMON GABLES
  components, **3**, 208
  compulsory acquisition, *see* COMPULSORY ACQUISITION
  conservation of fuel and power, **3**, 208
  construct, meaning, **3**, 204
  construction—
    methods, building regulations, **3**, 205
    VAT zero-rating, **7**, 1449

Building and building controls—*continued*
contract, *see* BUILDING CONTRACT
control, **14**, 629
copyright, **3**, 139
damage caused by, **3**, 230
dangerous buildings, **20**, 696
  access to, prevention, **3**, 232
  adjacent area, prevention of access to, **3**, 232
  civil liability, **3**, 230
  common ownership, property in, **3**, 233
  compulsory purchase, **3**, 235
  Crown buildings, **3**, 210
  demolition—
    appeal against order requiring, **3**, 236
    generally, **3**, 232
    sale of demolished materials, **3**, 234
  local authority powers, **3**, 201, 203
    compulsory purchase, **3**, 235
    demolition, **3**, 232, 234
      sale of demolished materials, **3**, 234
    expenses incurred by local authority, recovery, **3**, 243, 244
    notice—
      execution of order, **3**, 233
      service on owner, **3**, 232
    owner cannot be found, where, **3**, 235
    prevention of access to building and adjacent areas, **3**, 232
    removal of occupants, **3**, 231
  notice as to—
    execution, **3**, 233
    service by local authority, **3**, 232
  occupants, removal, **3**, 231
  owner—
    cannot be found, where, **3**, 235
    generally, **3**, 233
  repairing or securing, order as to, **3**, 232
    appeals, **3**, 236
    execution, **3**, 233
      costs incurred in, **3**, 233
    generally, **3**, 232
  suspected, where, local authority inspection, **3**, 237
death caused by, **3**, 230
demolition, *see* DEMOLITION
detached buildings, exemptions from building regulations, **3**, 209
development, meaning, **19**, 360*n*
  See also TOWN AND COUNTRY PLANNING
disabled, facilities for, **3**, 208, 242
drains, **3**, 208, 209
  See also DRAIN
electrical installations, **3**, 208, 227; **9**, 662–664
encroachment by, generally, **18**, 175
erection, **14**, 324, 639
  acquiescence by land owner, **16**, 1616, 1617, 1620
escalators, **3**, 208
existing building—
  power to require conformity to regulations, **3**, 215
    appeals, **3**, 236
    expenses incurred by local authority, recovery, **3**, 243, 244

Building and building controls—*continued*
existing building—*continued*
  power to require conformity to regulations—*continued*
    local authority—
      inspection, **3**, 237
      power to execute alterations, **3**, 215
    refusal to conform, owner's, **3**, 215
    relaxation, application for, **3**, 215
expenses incurred by local authority, recovery, **3**, 243, 244
fees, prescribed, **3**, 242
feu charter, contravention, **16**, 1618
fire—
  escapes, **3**, 208
  precautions, **3**, 208
  prevention—
    building standards regulations, **10**, 1451, 1464
    firemen's safety to be taken into consideration, **10**, 1475
  resistance, assessment of materials for, **3**, 203
  warning devices, **3**, 208
fire-fighting facilities, **3**, 208
fittings, **3**, 208
flatted property, *see* TENEMENT BUILDING
foundations, undermined by work on another property, **3**, 155
fuel tanks, **3**, 208, 209
functions, **3**, 203
gas—
  installations and tanks, **3**, 208
  regulations relating to, **9**, 879
generally, **3**, 2
glazing, **3**, 208
heating apparatus and storage tanks, **3**, 208
hot water, discharge, **3**, 208
improvement charge, provisional order, **19**, 19
improvement notice, **9**, 500
industrial design, exclusion from registration, **18**, 1173
injury caused by, **3**, 230
inner urban area, in, **14**, 654
inspection, local authority powers—
  generally, **3**, 237
  warrant for, **3**, 238
insurance, **14**, 329
interest in building as capital item, **7**, 1380
legislation, generally, **3**, 201
limited life, intended to have, **3**, 202, 205
luminous tube signs, **19**, 357
materials, *see* BUILDING MATERIALS
meaning, **3**, 202; **23**, 69, 139*n*, 193*n*
Model Building Byelaws, **3**, 201
moisture resistance, **3**, 208
neighbouring, *Maloco v Littlewoods Organisation Ltd*, decision in, **15**, 302, 318
new—
  building goods installed in, VAT regulations, **7**, 1383, 1449
  noise levels for, **9**, 1266
notice requiring works, appeal to sheriff court, **14**, 119
obligation to repair as real condition, **13**, 241
occupation or use, certificate of completion, **3**, 227

Building and building controls—*continued*
occupiers' liability, *see* OCCUPIER'S LIABILITY
oil installations and tanks, **3**, 208
open spaces, private, **19**, 356
owner, entry into building to comply with
    building standards, **3**, 244
partially built, secured against entry, must be, **3**,
    230
passenger conveyors, **3**, 208
people, not frequented by, **3**, 209
pipes, installation through neighbouring property,
    19, 353
plan, passing or rejection, **3**, 203
plant and machinery distinguished, **23**, 69
platforms and raised structures, safety of, **19**, 354
police, **14**, 489
preservation orders, demolition order, **11**, 1983
projection from, **3**, 208
    onto road, **20**, 694, 695
protected building, VAT zero-rating, **7**, 1450
protective barriers, **3**, 208
public health legislation, **19**, 305, 350–360
ramps, **3**, 208
records, **3**, 203
relevant standards, **3**, 207
repairs, **19**, 350
    buildings in need of, **19**, 351
    expenses, **19**, 352
    neighbour's land used to rest ladder or
        scaffolding, **18**, 181
sanitary appliances, **3**, 208
savings for provisions in other Acts concerning,
    14, 325
self certification of design, **3**, 219
servitude rights, and, **18**, 480
sewers, *see* SEWER
sheriff court jurisdiction, **6**, 1083
site, *see* BUILDING SITE
small buildings—
    exemptions from building regulations, **3**, 209
    Small Buildings Guide, **3**, 207
sound insulation, **3**, 208
    grant towards cost of, **9**, 1284
sports grounds and premises, **19**, 358
stairs, **3**, 208
    common, cleansing and painting of, **19**, 355
steam, discharge of, **3**, 208
structural injury to, **14**, 2045
structural strength and stability, **3**, 208
support, right of—
    adjacent support, **18**, 272
    common walls, **18**, 272
    subjacent support, **18**, 271
    where obligation to support, generally, **18**, 260
    See also SUPPORT, RIGHTS OF
surface, safety of, **14**, 1624
temporary building—
    building warrant, **3**, 222, 225
        appeal against refusal to extend, **3**, 236
        building remaining in existence after expiry,
            3, 228, 244
            notice as to, **3**, 228, 229
    demolition date, regulations as to, **3**, 225
    exemptions from building regulations, **3**, 209

Building and building controls—*continued*
temporary building—*continued*
    generally, **3**, 202, 205
temporary structure, **3**, 202
tenement, *see* TENEMENT BUILDING
type approval scheme, **3**, 218
    application for approval, **3**, 246
    buildings to which applicable, **3**, 245
    generally, **3**, 245
    type approval certificate, **3**, 247
unauthorised—
    generally, **3**, 203
    local authority inspection, **3**, 237
unfinished, entry in valuation roll, **24**, 506
unlawful possession of land, action for removal of,
    18, 157
use for a relevant charitable or residential
    purpose, **7**, 1306, 1419, 1449, 1450
VAT input tax, **7**, 1381
ventilation, **3**, 208
waste, storage of, **3**, 208
water supply, **25**, 531
windows, **3**, 208
works, **14**, 324, 325
Building contract
acceptance—
    employer, by, **3**, 24
    offer, must meet, **3**, 24
    qualified, **3**, 24
    what amounts to, **3**, 24
ad hoc, **3**, 9
adjudication, **3**, 171
administration, **3**, 51
agreement, **3**, 14
ambiguous, **3**, 42
approval and certification—
    certifier—
        delictual liability, **3**, 150
        disqualification, **3**, 85
        error in calculation by, **3**, 84
        error of judgment by, **3**, 84
        functions, manner of performance, **3**, 82
        generally, **3**, 80
        independently, obligation to act, **3**, 84, 85
        jurisdiction, **3**, 81
        negligence, **3**, 150
    certifier's duty, **3**, 56
    completion of work, **3**, 38–40
    delay, of, **3**, 78
    delivery, **3**, 79
    disturbance, of, **3**, 78
    employer—
        influence of, **3**, 84
        interference or obstruction by, **3**, 101
    finality of certificate, **3**, 86
        express exclusion, **3**, 86
    form, **3**, 79
    fraud by contractor, where, **3**, 86
    incorrect information supplied to certifier, **3**, 84
    interference with certification process, **3**, 56
    interim certificate, **3**, 86
    oral, **3**, 79
    over-certification, negligent, **3**, 150
    payment linked to, **3**, 62, 65, 78

Building contract—*continued*
approval and certification—*continued*
  requirement for, generally, **3**, 78
  review, **3**, 86
  under-certification, **3**, 138, 150
  written, **3**, 79
approximate quantities—
  inaccuracy in causing delay, **3**, 48
  inaccuracy in causing direct loss and expense,
    3, 70
arbitration—
  arbiter—
    architect or engineer as, **3**, 168
    payment, **3**, 172
    powers, **3**, 172
    selection and appointment, **3**, 172, 173
  clause, **3**, 172, 173
    certification, effect on, **3**, 86
    not all parties covered, where, **3**, 173
  clerk, appointment, **3**, 172
  common law, **3**, 172
  court, reference to, **3**, 173
  fees, dispute as to, **3**, 169
  final award, **3**, 172
  generally, **3**, 166, 172
  interest, award of, **3**, 172
  interim award, **3**, 172
  international commercial, **3**, 172
  partial award, **3**, 172
  prescription, **3**, 174
  witness, architect or engineer as, **3**, 168
architect, *see* ARCHITECT
assignation, **3**, 32
automatic vesting clause, **3**, 163
benefit, assignation, **3**, 32
bill of quantities—
  contract, as part of, **3**, 8
  error or misrepresentation in invitation to
    tender, **3**, 18–20
  preambles or preliminaries, **3**, 30
  Standard form contracts, **3**, 11
  tender, **3**, 21
bings, rehabilitation works, **3**, 155
bores, journal of, **3**, 18, 19
breach of—
  claim under, **3**, 167
  contributory negligence, **3**, 108
  damages—
    aim of award, **3**, 108
    assesment, **3**, 108
    consequential loss, **3**, 109
    contractor, breach by, **3**, 109
    contributory negligence, **3**, 108
    distress and anxiety, in respect of, **3**, 109
    employer, breach by, **3**, 110
    finance charges, **3**, 110
    generally, **3**, 104, 108
    inconvenience, in respect of, **3**, 109
    increased expenditure, **3**, 110
    increased preliminaries, **3**, 110
    interest—
      damages, on, **3**, 113
      head of damages, as, **3**, 114, 115

Building contract—*continued*
breach of—*continued*
  damages—*continued*
    liquidated, **3**, 89, 94, 103, 111
      liquidated damages clause, **3**, 28, 111
      sub-contract, **3**, 111
    loss—
      causal connection with breach, **3**, 108
      productivity, of, **3**, 110
      profit, of, **3**, 110
    managerial time, **3**, 110
    overheads, **3**, 110
    prescription, **3**, 174
    temporary accommodation, costs of, **3**, 109
  guarantee, *see* guarantee *below*
  performance bond, *see* performance bond *below*
  remedies—
    common law—
      generally, **3**, 103, 104
    contractual, **3**, 103
    generally, **3**, 103
    interdict, **3**, 104
    interest—
      damages, on, **3**, 113
      finance charges, claims for, **3**, 114, 115
      head of damages, as, **3**, 114
      late payment, in respect of, **3**, 112
    more than one available, where, **3**, 104
    mutuality principle, **3**, 104
    repudiation, **3**, 104, 105, 107
    rescission, **3**, 104, 106, 107
    retention, **3**, 104
    same remedy available to more than one
      party, where, **3**, 104
    separate but related contracts, **3**, 104
    specific implement, **3**, 104
    two or more parties, breach by, **3**, 104
'build, operate, transfer', **3**, 9
building agreement, **3**, 12
burden, assignation, **3**, 32
capacity to contract, **3**, 26
care, duty of, **3**, 3
cautionary obligation—
  constitution, **3**, 117
  guarantee, **3**, 117
  NHBC house purchaser's agreement, **3**, 116
  performance bond, **3**, 117
circumvention, **3**, 27
civil commotion, loss or damage occasioned by,
  3, 48
claim under, **3**, 167
'Clause 22 peril', loss or damage occasioned by, **3**,
  48
clerk of works, *see* CLERK OF WORKS
collateral warranty—
  claim, prescription, **3**, 174
  generally, **3**, 158
  Standard Form, **3**, 158
common interest, consideration, generally, **3**, 159
common law rights of parties, **3**, 28
completion of work—
  approval by employer, architect or third party,
    3, 38
  certificate, **3**, 38–40

Building contract—*continued*
completion of work—*continued*
  completion, meaning, **3**, 38
  completion date—
    generally, **3**, 47
    ineffectual by agreement, becoming, **3**, 47
    waiver, **3**, 47
  contractor's obligations, **3**, 38–40
  delay, **3**, 106
    employer, caused by, **3**, 59
    second contractor, caused by, **3**, 59
  destruction before, **3**, 61
  extension of time, **3**, 48, 51, 59, 103
    architect refusing to consider, **3**, 48
    contractual provision, **3**, 103
    phased completion, where, **3**, 48
  failure to complete, damages where, **3**, 109
  final, **3**, 39
  payment on—
    amount due, **3**, 66
    when payment due, **3**, 65
  phased, **3**, 11
    extension of time, **3**, 48
  practical, **3**, 39
  sectional, and partial possession, **3**, 40, 53
  slow progress, where, **3**, 49
  sub-contractor delaying, **3**, 58
  time at large, **3**, 47
  time of the essence, where, **3**, 50, 53
conciliation, Institution of Civil Engineers
    procedure, **3**, 170
conclusion—
  acceptance by employer, **3**, 24
  actings subsequent to, **3**, 28
  capacity, **3**, 26
  defect in formation, where, **3**, 27
  formalities, **3**, 25
concurrent liability in delict and, **3**, 153
conflict of interests, **3**, 27
construction law, *see* CONSTRUCTION LAW
contract bills—
  discrepancy or divergence in, **3**, 70
  incorporation into contract, **3**, 30
contract of sale, **3**, 6
contractor—
  adjudication procedure, **3**, 171
  architect, relationship with, **3**, 138
  assignation of benefit, **3**, 32
  assignation of burden, **3**, 32
  breach of contract by, damages, **3**, 109
  building designed or partly designed by,
      standard form contract, **3**, 11
  collateral warranty, **3**, 158
  concealment by, **3**, 86
  contractor's interest, **3**, 32
  corruption, **3**, 100
  death, effect, **3**, 97
  default by, **3**, 99, 100
  delictual duties, **3**, 149
  design team engaged by, **3**, 127
  determination by, **3**, 101, 102
  determination of employment, **3**, 103
  direct loss or expense, payment for, **3**, 66, 70,
      71, 103

Building contract—*continued*
contractor—*continued*
  duty of care letter, **3**, 158
  duty towards employer, *see* employer *below*
  employer's duty towards—
    access to site, **3**, 54
    architect, appointment, **3**, 56
    co-operation, **3**, 52
    employer, works to be done by, **3**, 59, 70
    engineer, appointment, **3**, 56
    information and instructions, supply, **3**, 57
    other contractors, works to be done by, **3**,
        59, 70
    payment, *see* payment *below*
    permissions and consents, obtaining, **3**, 55
    possession of site, **3**, 53
    sub-contractors, nomination, **3**, 58
    suppliers, nomination, **3**, 58
  ex gratia claim by, **3**, 167
  fraud by, **3**, 86
  generally, **3**, 2
  guarantee, **3**, 2
  indemnification of employer, **3**, 87
  insolvency, **3**, 100, 120, 163
  insurance by, **3**, 88, 90
  liability for building, shift from, **3**, 78
  liquidation, **3**, 162*n*
  management—
    Scottish Management Contract, **3**, 11
      Phased Completion Edition, **3**, 11
  materials supplied by, **3**, 162
  more than one, where, **3**, 59, 70
  obligations—
    contract terms, **3**, 33
    defective work, as to, **3**, 46
    design responsibility, **3**, 37
    fitness for purpose, as to, **3**, 37
    generally, **3**, 33
    materials, as to, **3**, 36
    primary, **3**, 33
    time of completion, as to, **3**, 33, 47–50
    variation of agreement, **3**, 41–45
    workmanship, as to, **3**, 35
    works—
      completion, **3**, 38–40
      failure to complete, **3**, 34
      meaning, **3**, 34
      standard of, **3**, 35–37
  payment, *see* payment *below*
  performance bond, **3**, 2
  possession of site, employer obliged to give, **3**, 53
  pre-contract costs, **3**, 23
  receivership, in, **3**, 162*n*
  site, right to be on, **3**, 160
  sub-contract, entitlement to, **3**, 32
  sub-contractor, *see* sub-contractor *below*
  works contractor, *see* sub-contractor *below*
contractual relationship, determination, **3**, 9
copyright and buildings, **3**, 139
cost reimbursable, **3**, 60, 66
costing, architect's duty to advise on, **3**, 134
counter-offers, **3**, 24
court proceedings—
  arbitration, following, **3**, 173

Building contract—*continued*
court proceedings—*continued*
   construction industry disputes, **3**, 173
   partial sist, **3**, 173
damages—
   ascertained damages, **3**, 94
   breach of contract, for, *see* breach of *above*
   managerial time, **3**, 10
   neighbouring property, claim by, **3**, 161
   nuisance, for, **3**, 155
   support, right of, in respect of, **3**, 159
debt, retention in security, **3**, 76
deed, by, **3**, 25
defect in formation, **3**, 27
defects and defective work, *see* works *below*
delay—
   approval and certification, of, **3**, 78
   certification, **3**, 78
   completion of work, in, **3**, 48, 58, 59, 106
   employer, caused by, **3**, 114, 115
   inaccuracy in approximate quantities causing, **3**, 48
   liquidated damages in respect of, **3**, 103
   payment, in, **3**, 106
   site, in access to, **3**, 48
   See also works (completion date) *below*
delectus personae, **3**, 32
design, manage, construct, **3**, 9
design and build, **3**, 9
determination—
   clause, **3**, 98, 105
   contractor, by, **3**, 101, 102
   employer, by, **3**, 100, 102
   extinction by payment, **3**, 74
   JCT'80 conditions, **3**, 99, 100, 102
discharge, *see* obligations (extinction) *below*
dissensus, **3**, 27
disturbance, certification, **3**, 78
documents—
   bill of quantities, **3**, 8
   contract, **3**, 8
   drawings, **3**, 8
   incorporation, **3**, 30
   programme, **3**, 8
   relationship between contract documents, **3**, 30
   schedule of rates, **3**, 8
   specification, **3**, 8
   supply, **3**, 57
drawings—
   contract, as part of, **3**, 8
   copyright, **3**, 139
   delay in receipt, **3**, 70
   discrepancy or divergence in, **3**, 70
   further, request for, **3**, 57
   supply, employer's obligations, **3**, 57
duress, made under, **3**, 27
duty of care letter, **3**, 158
employer—
   acceptance of contract by, **3**, 24
   approval by, **3**, 83
   architect, relationship with, **3**, 130
   assignation of benefit, **3**, 32
   assignation of burden, **3**, 32
   breach of contract by, damages, **3**, 110

Building contract—*continued*
employer—*continued*
   co-operation with contractor, **3**, 52
   compensation, right of, **3**, 76
   contractor's duty towards—
     completion of works, **3**, 33, 38–40
     defective work, **3**, 46
     negligence, **3**, 149
     standard of works, **3**, 33, 35–38
     time taken to complete work, **3**, 33, 47–50
     variations or extra work, where, **3**, 41–45
   death, **3**, 97
   default by, **3**, 99, 101
   delay or disruption caused by, **3**, 114, 115
   delegation by, **3**, 51
   delictual duties, **3**, 148
   design team engaged by, **3**, 127
   determination by, **3**, 100, 102
   determination of contractor's employment, **3**, 103
   duty towards contractor, *see* contractor *above*
   employee, liability for actions of, **3**, 152
     pro hac vice employees, **3**, 152
   extra work or variation requested by, **3**, 41, 43
   finance, **3**, 2
   generally, **3**, 2
   indemnification by contractor, **3**, 87
   information, supply, **3**, 57
   insolvency, **3**, 101
   instructions, supply, **3**, 57
   insurance by, **3**, 90
   liability for building, shift to, **3**, 78
   materials supplied by, **3**, 162
   obligations—
     contractor, towards—
       access to site, **3**, 54
       architect, appointment, **3**, 56
       co-operation, **3**, 52
       engineer, appointment, **3**, 56
       generally, **3**, 51
       information, supply, **3**, 57
       instructions, supply, **3**, 57
       permissions and consents, obtaining, **3**, 55
       possession of site, **3**, 53
       sub-contractors, nomination, **3**, 58, 124
       suppliers, nomination, **3**, 58
       works done by employer, **3**, 59, 70
       works done by other contractors, **3**, 59, 70
   delictual duties, **3**, 148
   failure to perform timeously, **3**, 59
   generally, **3**, 51
   payment—
     adjustment to price at common law, **3**, 72
     changes in cost, **3**, 69
     compensation, **3**, 76
     completion, on, **3**, 65, 66
     direct loss and expense, **3**, 70, 71, 103
     entire contracts, **3**, 61
     failure to pay timeously, **3**, 75
     fluctuations in cost, **3**, 60, 69
     generally, **3**, 51, 60
     instalment, by, **3**, 62–64
     non-material deviations, **3**, 72
     quantum lucratus, **3**, 61, 74, 120

Building contract—*continued*
employer—*continued*
  obligations—*continued*
    payment—*continued*
      quantum meruit, **3**, 73
      retention, **3**, 63, 76
      set-off, **3**, 76, 77, 103
      unjustified enrichment, **3**, 61, 74
      variations and extras, for, **3**, 67, 68
      sub-contractor, towards, **3**, 148
    payment, *see* payment *below*
    presence on site, contract providing for, **3**, 53
    retention, right of, **3**, 76
    sub-contractor, relationship with, **3**, 120
  employment, of, **3**, 6
engineer, *see* ENGINEER (building contracts)
entire—
  meaning, **3**, 61
  payment, **3**, 61
error in, **3**, 27, 28
EU legislation—
  generally, **3**, 3
  public authority, tendering by, **3**, 17
exclusion clause, **3**, 120
  interpretation, **3**, 28
extinction, *see* obligations *below*
extras, *see* works *below*
facility, **3**, 27
failure to comply with terms exactly, **15**, 866
fast-tracking, **3**, 9
fear, made under, **3**, 27
finance charges—
  damages in respect of, **3**, 110
  interest as head of damages, **3**, 114, 115
fitness for purpose, contractor's obligations, **3**, 37
fixed fee prime cost, **3**, 11
flood damage, nuisance, as, **3**, 155
force, made under, **3**, 27
force majeure—
  determination of contract where, **3**, 102
  extension of time where, **3**, 48
form, **3**, 8, 25
formation, **3**, 14
foundations undermined by work on another property, **3**, 155
frustration, **3**, 27
  effect, **3**, 96
  extinction of obligations on, **3**, 95, 96
  payment *quantum meruit*, **3**, 73
funder—
  collateral warranty to, **3**, 158
  interest of, safeguard, **3**, 2
generally, **3**, 3
government intervention, extension of time where, **3**, 48
green book, **3**, 12
guarantee—
  back-to-back obligation, **3**, 116, 118
  cautionary obligation, **3**, 117
  content, **3**, 118
  contractor, taken out by, **3**, 2
  generally, **3**, 116
  guarantor, **3**, 116
  termination date, **3**, 118

Building contract—*continued*
hazardous operation, negligence, liability for, **3**, 148
illegal, **3**, 27
impossibility, involving, **3**, 27
indemnity—
  clause, interpretation, **3**, 28
  death, against, **3**, 87
  existing structures, **3**, 87
  generally, **3**, 87
  insurance, interaction with, **3**, 87
  partial possession, after, **3**, 87
  personal injury, against, **3**, 87
  practical completion, works after, **3**, 87
  property damage, against, **3**, 87
  third parties, property of, **3**, 87
insolvency—
  contractor, of, **3**, 100, 120, 163
  employer, of, **3**, 101
instalment payments, *see* payment *below*
instructions, delay in receipt, **3**, 70
insurance—
  all risks, **3**, 92, 92*n*
  ascertained damages, **3**, 94
  bodily injury, against, **3**, 88
  contractor, by, **3**, 88
    failure to provide adequate cover, **3**, 90
  damage to property, against, **3**, 89–91
    negligent, **3**, 89
  death, against, **3**, 89, 90
  defining risks insured, **3**, 88
  determination of contractor's employment, **3**, 93
  disease, against, **3**, 88
  double, **3**, 88
  employer by, recovery of cost from contractor, **3**, 90, 92
  events for which contractor not liable, **3**, 91
  excepted risks, **3**, 91, 92
  expressly excepted risks, **3**, 89
  extension or alteration of existing structures, contracts for, **3**, 93
  failure to provide adequate cover, **3**, 90
  failure to take out, recovery of cost by other party, **3**, 90, 92
  fees, against, **3**, 92
  full reinstatement value, **3**, 92, 92*n*
  gaps in cover, **3**, 88
  generally, **3**, 2
  good faith, **3**, 88
  indemnity—
    interaction with, generally, **3**, 87
    risks covered by, of, **3**, 87
  insurable interest, **3**, 88
  insurer, approval, **3**, 92
  JCT'80 obligations, **3**, 89
  joint names policy, **3**, 92, 92*n*
  liquidated damages, **3**, 89, 94
  overall project policy, **3**, 88
  personal injury, against, **3**, 89, 90
  review of sum insured, **3**, 92*n*
  site materials, **3**, 92
  specified perils, **3**, 92
  statutory obligation, **3**, 88
  sub-contractor, **3**, 88, 92

Building contract—*continued*
insurance—*continued*
   termination of cover, **3**, 90, 90*n*
   works, against damage to—
      generally, **3**, 89, 92
      procedure, **3**, 93
interdict—
   remedy for breach, **3**, 104
   remedy for nuisance, **3**, 155
interpretation—
   actings subsequent to conclusion, **3**, 28
   case law, **3**, 28
   common law rights of parties, **3**, 28
   contra proferentem rule, **3**, 28
   contract which regulates its own, **3**, 28
   custom of trade, **3**, 28
   deleted words and phrases, **3**, 28
   discrepancies, resolution, **3**, 28
   ejusdem generis rule, **3**, 28
   extrinsic evidence, **3**, 28
   generally, **3**, 28
   interlocking contracts, **3**, 28
   prior communings rule, **3**, 28
   related contract, **3**, 28
   standard form contracts, **3**, 28
   typescript and print, **3**, 28
   vague clause or variation, **3**, 28
invalidity, grounds for, **3**, 27
JCT form, **3**, 10
joint venture, **3**, 9
jus quaesitum tertio, **3**, 120, 138
labour, unforeseeable inability to secure, **3**, 48
land obligations—
   permissions and consents to, responsibility for
      obtaining, **3**, 55
   prescription, **3**, 174
letter of intent—
   effect, **3**, 22
   tendering, in relation to, **3**, 22
   work done by contractor on faith of, **3**, 22, 23
letters, by exchange of, **3**, 25
liability—
   Consumer Protection Act 1987..., under, **3**,
      143, 157, 174
   delictual—
      collateral warranties, **3**, 159
      concurrent liability in contract, **3**, 153
      Consumer Protection Act 1987 ..., under, **3**,
        143, 157, 174
      duty of care letters, **3**, 158
      generally, **3**, 143, 144, 145
      negligence, *see negligence below*
      nuisance, **3**, 143, 155
      solatium, **3**, 146, 153
      statutory duty, breach, **3**, 143, 156
   exclusion, **3**, 31
   limitation, **3**, 31
   liquidated damages, *see* damages *above*
   shift from contractor to employer, **3**, 78
   sub-contraction, contractual chain, **3**, 120
licence, refusal of, frustration of contract by, **3**, 96
light, building work blocking, **3**, 155
liquidated damages, *see* damages *above*
liquidated damages clause, **3**, 28, 111; **15**, 797

Building contract—*continued*
loan security, assignation of contract, **3**, 32
locatio operis faciendi, **3**, 5
location, of, **3**, 5, 6
lump sum, **3**, 60, 61, 66, 72
management contract, **3**, 9
   generally, **3**, 9
   Scottish Management Contract, **3**, 11
      Phased Completion Edition, **3**, 11
manager, generally, **3**, 2
managerial time, damages in respect of, **3**, 110
materials—
   affixed to ground, ownership, **3**, 164
   architect's powers in relation to, **3**, 36
   automatic vesting, **3**, 163
   contractor's obligations, **3**, 36
   fitness for purpose, **3**, 36
   provision, **3**, 162
   substitute, **3**, 41
   supply—
      employer, by, **3**, 59
      exclusion or limitation of liability, **3**, 31
   transfer of ownership, **3**, 162, 164
   unforseeable inability to secure, **3**, 48
   warranty as to, **3**, 36
meaning, dissensus as to, **3**, 27
measured terms, **3**, 11
measurement, **3**, 60, 66
misrepresentation in, **3**, 19, 27
nature of building contracts, **3**, 5
negligence—
   architect, duties owed by, **3**, 150
   certifier, duties owed by, **3**, 150
   clerk of works, by, **3**, 148
   concurrent liability in contract and delict, **3**, 153
   contractor—
      duties owed by, **3**, 149
      employees, liability for, **3**, 152
   delictual liability, as, **3**, 143
   duties owed by particular parties, **3**, 147–151
   duty of care, **3**, 145
   employer—
      duties owed by, **3**, 148
      employees, liability for, **3**, 152
   generally, **3**, 144
   hazardous operations, **3**, 152
   liability, general principles, **3**, 145
   loss—
      duty of care and, **3**, 145
      economic, **3**, 146, 149
      recoverable, **3**, 146
      remoteness, **3**, 145, 146
      solatium, **3**, 146, 153
   professional, duties owed by, **3**, 150
   public authority, duties owed by, **3**, 151
   sub-contractor—
      duties owed by, **3**, 120, 149
      employees, liability for, **3**, 152
   title to sue, **3**, 154
noise, construction work caused by, **3**, 155
non-performance, **3**, 96
nuisance—
   building works, in relation to, **3**, 155
   delictual liability, as, **3**, 143

Building contract—*continued*
nuisance—*continued*
generally, **3**, 155
loss of business, **3**, 155
remedies, **3**, 155
obligations—
cautionary, *see* cautionary obligation *above*
certifier's obligation to act independently, **3**, 84, 85
completion of work, as to, **3**, 38–40
contractor's, *see* contractor *above*
defective work, for, **3**, 46
design responsibility, **3**, 37
drawings and instructions, supply, **3**, 57
extinction—
agreement, by, **3**, 95
confusion, by, **3**, 95
death of contractor, effect, **3**, 97
death of employer, effect, **3**, 97
determination of contract—
contractor, by, **3**, 101, 102
determination clause, **3**, 98
employer, by, **3**, 100, 102
JCT'80 conditions, **3**, 99, 100, 102
express contractual terms as to, **3**, 95
frustration, on, **3**, 95, 96
generally, **3**, 95
novation, by, **3**, 95
performance, by, **3**, 95
prescription, by, **3**, 95
repudiation, by acceptance of, **3**, 95
rescission, by, **3**, 95
waiver, by, **3**, 95
fitness for purpose, as to, **3**, 37
insurance, **3**, 88, 89
inter se, **3**, 3
payment, **3**, 60
probative writ, constituted or evidenced by, prescription, **3**, 174
site access, **3**, 54
site possession, **3**, 53
sub-contractor, of, **3**, 119
workmanship, as to, **3**, 35
offer and acceptance, **3**, 24
oral, **3**, 25
overheads, damages in respect of, **3**, 110
package deal, **3**, 9
parties to—
contractual relationship, determination, **3**, 9
generally, **3**, 2
payment—
approval by employer as precondition, **3**, 83
architect, of, **3**, 129
compensation, right of, **3**, 76, 77
completion, on—
amount due, **3**, 66
certificate, linked to, **3**, 65, 78
when payment due, **3**, 65
construction professional, of, **3**, 129
contractual obligation, **3**, 60
prescription, **3**, 174
cost reimbursable contract, **3**, 60, 66
default by employer, **3**, 101
delay, **3**, 106

Building contract—*continued*
payment—*continued*
employer's obligations, generally, **3**, 60
entire contracts, **3**, 61
estimate, whether binding, **3**, 66
extras, payment *quantum meruit*, **3**, 73
failure to pay timeously, **3**, 75
fluctuation in price, where, **3**, 66, 69
certification, **3**, 78
frustration of contract, where, **3**, 73, 96
instalment payments—
acceptance of work not implied by, **3**, 74
calculation, **3**, 63
certificates, linked to, **3**, 62, 78
contractual retention, **3**, 63, 76
generally, **3**, 62
no implied right to, **3**, 62
payments to account, **3**, 64
stages of contract, on, **3**, 62
stated intervals of time, **3**, 62
stated values of work done, on, **3**, 62
subsequent dispute as to work, **3**, 64
late, interest in respect of, **3**, 112
loss or expense, direct—
determination, **3**, 70
generally, **3**, 66, 70
meaning of direct, **3**, 71
remedies, **3**, 103
lump sum contract, **3**, 60, 61, 66, 72
measurement contract, **3**, 60, 66
not contractually due, **3**, 66
overpayment, **3**, 66
prescription, **3**, 174
price adjustment—
common law, at, **3**, 72
generally, **3**, 60, 66
non-material deviations, **3**, 72
quantum lucratus, **3**, 61, 74, 120
quantum meruit, **3**, 66, 73
reasonable price, ascertainment, **3**, 73
retention—
common law right of, **3**, 76
contractual, **3**, 63, 76
set-off, **3**, 76, 77, 103
sub-contract, provisions in, **3**, 121
sub-contractor—
action by, **3**, 120
express contractual provision, **3**, 120
unjustified enrichment, **3**, 60, 61, 74
variations or extras, for—
certification, **3**, 78
generally, **3**, 60, 66, 67, 69
price fluctuation, where, **3**, 66, 69, 78
valuation of variations, **3**, 68
penalty clause, liquidated damages clause distinguished, **3**, 111
performance bond—
back-to-back obligation, **3**, 116, 118
cautionary obligation, **3**, 117
content, **3**, 118
contractor, taken out by, **3**, 2
generally, **3**, 116
guarantor, **3**, 116
on-demand, **3**, 118

Building contract—*continued*
performance bond—*continued*
  termination date, **3**, 118
  terminus a quo, **3**, 175
  unconditional, **3**, 118
possession—
  employer taking—
    completion, on, **3**, 39
    partial, **3**, 40, 53, 87
  site, of, *see* site *below*
pre-contractual—
  costs, **3**, 23
  negotiations, misrepresentations in, **3**, 153
preliminaries—
  increased, damages in respect of, **3**, 110
  meaning, **3**, 110
prescription, claims and disputes procedure, **3**, 174, 175
price adjustment, *see* payment *above*
prior communings rule, **3**, 28
productivity, loss of, damages in respect of, **3**, 110
programme of work, as part of, **3**, 8
prout de jure, proved, **3**, 25
purchaser—
  collateral warranty to, **3**, 158
  prospective, interests of, **3**, 2
real burden or condition, **3**, 159
rectification, **3**, 28
red book, **3**, 12
Regulations and General Conditions, **3**, 10
rei interitus, frustration by, **3**, 96
repudiation, **3**, 95, 104, 105, 107
rescission, **3**, 95, 104, 106, 107
retention, **3**, 104
rights of way, **3**, 159
risk, passing of, **3**, 165
schedule of rates, **3**, 8, 21
separate contracts co-ordinated by employer, **3**, 9
servitudes, **3**, 159
set-off provisions, **3**, 76, 77, 103
severability, doctrine of, **3**, 27
specific implement,, **3**, 104
specifications, **3**, 8
standard form contract—
  Building Agreement, **3**, 12
  choice of form, **3**, 11
  FIDIC Conditions, **3**, 12
  Fixed Fee Form of Prime Cost Contract for Building Works, **3**, 11
  Form GC/Works/1, **3**, 12, 60
  Form GC/Works/2, **3**, 12
  generally, **3**, 10
  Government Forms, **3**, 12
  green book, **3**, 12
  ICE Conditions, **3**, 12, 23, 27, 60, 124, 168
  interpretation, **3**, 3, 28
  JCT form, **3**, 10, 27, 89, 92, 99, 100, 102, 103, 111, 124
  Model Form of General Conditions of Contract (mechanical and electrical engineering industry), **3**, 12
  red book, **3**, 12

Building contract—*continued*
standard form contract—*continued*
  Scottish Building Contract—
    generally, **3**, 10, 11
    Sectional Completion With Quantities Edition, **3**, 11
    With Approximate Quantities, **3**, 11, 60
    With Contractor's Design, **3**, 11
    With Contractor's Designed Portion With Quantities, **3**, 11
    With Quantities, **3**, 11, 60
    Without Quantities, **3**, 11, 60
  Scottish Management Contract, **3**, 11, 60
    Phased Completion Edition, **3**, 11
  Scottish Measured Term Contract, **3**, 11
  Scottish Minor Works Contract, **3**, 11
  Standard Form of Building Contract, **3**, 10
  yellow book, **3**, 12
statutory requirements, compliance with, **3**, 55
statutory undertaker, provision for, **3**, 53
strike, extension of time where, **3**, 48
sub-contract—
  completion date later than main contract, where, **3**, 58
  contractual chain, **3**, 120
  entitlement of contractor to sub-contract, **3**, 32
  generally, **3**, 119
  guarantee or performance bond, **3**, 116, 118
  interpretation, **3**, 28
    reference to main contract, by, **3**, 121
  JCT form, **3**, 122
  labour-only, **3**, 6
  liquidated damages clause, **3**, 111
  main contract—
    obligations in, **3**, 121
    provisions of incorporated into sub-contract, **3**, 121
    relationship with, **3**, 121
  payment provisions, **3**, 121
  privity of contract, **3**, 120
  terms of main contract, purporting to incorporate, **3**, 30
sub-contractor—
  adjudication procedure, **3**, 171
  architect, relationship with, **3**, 138
  assignation of rights, **3**, 120
  collateral contract with employer, **3**, 120
  contractor treated as agent, where, **3**, 120
  contractual chain, **3**, 120
  contractual provision, **3**, 120
  defective work by, **3**, 120
  delay caused by, **3**, 58
  delictual duties, **3**, 149
  delictual liability, **3**, 120, 149
  design responsibility and fitness for purpose, **3**, 37
  domestic, **3**, 2, 122, 123
  employer—
    paying directly, **3**, 120
    relationship with, **3**, 120
  exclusion clause breaking contractual chain, **3**, 120
  express provision as to, **3**, 120
  failure to complete works, **3**, 34

Building contract—*continued*
sub-contractor—*continued*
  generally, **3**, 2, 119
  guarantee, **3**, 116, 118
  insolvency of contractor, effect, **3**, 120
  insurance, **3**, 88, 92
  JCT form, **3**, 122
  labour-only, **3**, 2, 152
  liability for actions of, **3**, 152
  main contract and sub-contract, relationship, **3**, 121
  main contractor, and, **3**, 9
  materials supplied by, **3**, 162
  named, **3**, 123
  negligence, **3**, 152
  nominated, **3**, 2, 122, 124
    collateral warranty, **3**, 158
    default by, **3**, 124
    delay by, **3**, 48
  nomination, **3**, 58
    procedures and forms, **3**, 125
  objection to by employer, **3**, 58
  obligations, implied, **3**, 119
  payment of—
    action for, **3**, 120
    express contractual provision, **3**, 120
    prescription, **3**, 174
  performance bond, **3**, 116, 118
  renomination, **3**, 58
  Scottish Management Contracts, **3**, 122
  site, right to be on, **3**, 160
  suppliers to, **3**, 126
  tendering, **3**, 123
  workmanship, **3**, 35
  works contractor, **3**, 2
supervening difficulties, **3**, 27
supervisory officer, **3**, 51
supplier—
  domestic, **3**, 2, 126
  materials supplied by, ownership, **3**, 162
  nominated, **3**, 2, 58, 126
    delay by, **3**, 48
  sub-contractor, to, **3**, 126
tenants, **3**, 2, 158
tendering—
  agreement subject to contract, **3**, 22
  agreements between contractors, **3**, 21
  anti-competitive practices, **3**, 21
  architect, by, **3**, 130
  error by contractor, **3**, 21
  error in documentation—
    case law, approach in, **3**, 20
    information warranted to be true, **3**, 18
    misrepresentation, **3**, 19
  invitation to tender, **3**, 14
    contractor's rights, **3**, 14
    error in documentation, **3**, 18–20
    invitation to treat, when, **3**, 14
    offer, when, **3**, 14
    withdrawal, **3**, 14
  letter of intent, **3**, 22, 23
  local authority, by, **3**, 16
  open, **3**, 15
  pre-contractual costs, **3**, 23

Building contract—*continued*
tendering—*continued*
  procedure, **3**, 15
  public authority, by, EC law, **3**, 17
  restricted, **3**, 15
  restrictive trade practices, **3**, 21
  selective, **3**, 15
  serial, **3**, 15
  single-stage, **3**, 15
  sub-contractor, **3**, 123
  tender, meaning, **3**, 21
  two stage, **3**, 15
termination—
  express terms as to, **3**, 95
  terminus a quo, **3**, 175
  See also obligations (extinction) *above*
terms—
  exclusion or limitation of liability, **3**, 31
  express, **3**, 29, 33
    access to site, **3**, 54
    workmanship, as to, **3**, 35
  implied, **3**, 29, 31
    access to site, **3**, 54
    possession of site, **3**, 53
    workmanship, as to, **3**, 35
time at large, **3**, 47
title *see* TITLE (building contract)
trespass, neighbouring property, onto, **3**, 161
turnkey, **3**, 9
types of, **3**, 9
uncertainty in, **3**, 27
variation of works, *see* works *below*
void, **3**, 27
voidable, **3**, 27
watercourse, alteration of natural, **3**, 155
weather conditions, extension of time due to, **3**, 48
workmanship—
  continuing obligation, as, **3**, 35
  contractor's obligations, **3**, 35
  implied or express contract term, **3**, 40
  sub-contractors, **3**, 35
works—
  additional, payment for, **3**, 34
  administration, architect's responsibility, **3**, 137
  approval by employer, architect or third party, **3**, 38
  completion—
    certificate, **3**, 38–40
    delay, **3**, 106
    destruction before, **3**, 61
    failure to complete, damages where, **3**, 109
    final, **3**, 39
    meaning, **3**, 38
    practical, **3**, 39
    sectional, partial possession where, **3**, 40
  completion date—
    delay caused by employer or second contractor, **3**, 59
    extension of time, **3**, 48, 53, 59
      contractual provision, **3**, 103
    generally, **3**, 47
    slow progress, where, **3**, 49
    time at large, **3**, 47
    time of the essence, where, **3**, 50, 53

Building contract—*continued*
works—*continued*
  contractor's obligations, **3**, 34
  defect—
    contractor's obligation for, **3**, 46
    latent, **3**, 39, 46
      terminus a quo, **3**, 175
    rectification period, **3**, 39, 46
    schedule of defects, **3**, 39
  defective work—
    breach of contract, whether, **3**, 106
    contractor's obligation for, **3**, 46
    damages in respect of, **3**, 109
    sub-contractor, by, **3**, 120
  employer, carried out by, **3**, 59
  extra work, where requirement for, **3**, 34
    extra, meaning, **3**, 67
    payment for, **3**, 66–68
  inspection, architect's responsibility, **3**, 137
  insurance against damage to—
    generally, **3**, 89, 92
    procedure, **3**, 93
  meaning, **3**, 34
  other contractor, carried out by, **3**, 59
  postponement, direct loss, causing, **3**, 70
  preparatory, **3**, 59, 73
  standard—
    defective work, *see* defective work *above*
    design responsibility, **3**, 37
    fitness for purpose, **3**, 37
    materials, **3**, 36
    workmanship, **3**, 35
  sub-contractor—
    causing delay, **3**, 59
    failure to complete, **3**, 34
  variation—
    additional extras, **3**, 41, 67
      meaning, **3**, 67
    architect requesting, **3**, 41–43
    automatic, **3**, 45
    certification, **3**, 78
    direct loss or expense caused by, **3**, 70
      remedies, **3**, 103
    employer requesting, **3**, 41, 43
    form, **3**, 44
    generally, **3**, 41
    instructions, **3**, 41, 42
    meaning, **3**, 43, 67
    oral instruction, **3**, 44
    payment for, **3**, 66–68
    procedure, **3**, 44
    substitute materials, **3**, 41
    valuation of variations, **3**, 68
    written instruction, **3**, 44
  written, **3**, 25
  yellow book, **3**, 12
Building Law Reports
generally, **3**, 4
Building lease
generally, **13**, 209
meaning, **13**, 209
Building materials
building regulations, **3**, 205, 208
class warrant, **3**, 216

Building materials—*continued*
durability, assessment for, **3**, 203
European Community standards, **3**, 207
fire resistance, assessment for, **3**, 203
meaning, **7**, 1383*n*, 1449*n*
road, deposit on, **20**, 684
Technical Standards, **3**, 207
testing, local authority powers, **3**, 237, 239
  obstruction, **3**, 239, 241
VAT, charge to, **7**, 1383
Building operations regulations
contravention, civil liability, **3**, 230
generally, **3**, 230
Building regulations
additional requirements imposed by warrant, **3**, 222
application, **3**, 207
civil liability, **3**, 230
classification of buildings, **3**, 205
construction methods, **3**, 205
construction not in accordance with, **3**, 230
criteria, **3**, 205
dispensing with, warrant, **3**, 224
exemptions, **3**, 208, 209
inspection—
  powers as to, generally, **3**, 237
    obstruction, penalties, **3**, 241
  warrant for, **3**, 238
limited life, building intended to have, **3**, 205, 244
materials, **3**, 205
power to make, **3**, 205
principal, **3**, 207
relaxation—
  appeal, **3**, 214
    existing buildings, **3**, 215
  application for, **3**, 203, 212
  building warrant, **3**, 224
  conditional, **3**, 211
  existing building required to conform, where, **3**, 215
  firemaster, notification, **3**, 212
  hearing, **3**, 213
  local authority powers as to, **3**, 211
  powers, generally, **3**, 211
  testing, local authority powers, **3**, 239
  unconditional, **3**, 211
requirements, generally, **3**, 208, 208*n*
testing, materials, of, **3**, 237, 239
  obstruction, **3**, 239, 241
Building site
access to—
  delay in, **3**, 48
  direct loss caused by access to or from site, **3**, 70
  employer's obligations, **3**, 54
  implied terms, **3**, 54
building operations regulations, **3**, 230
contractor's right to be on, **3**, 160
examination, architect's duty as to, **3**, 133
inspection, **3**, 203, 237
limitations on use of, architect's duty in respect of, **3**, 132
materials brought onto, possession, **3**, 160

Building site—*continued*
neighbouring properties—
  amenity of, consideration, **3**, 2
  common interest, **3**, 159
  generally, **3**, 161
  rights of way, **3**, 159
  servitudes, **3**, 159
  support, right of, **3**, 159
possession—
  deferment, **3**, 48, 53
  employer taking, **3**, 53
  employer's obligations, **3**, 53
  extent given to contractor, **3**, 53
  implied terms, **3**, 53
  legal position, **3**, 160
  partial, **3**, 40, 53
  specified date, **3**, 53
preparations, general requirements, **3**, 208
road, separation from, **3**, 230
Building Societies Commission
aggregation notice, associated body, as to, **3**, 370
auditors' reports, **3**, 434
authorisation of building societies, *see* BUILDING
  SOCIETY (authorisation)
building society—
  dispute between member and, **3**, 387
  management, supervision, **3**, 395
chairman and deputy chairman, **3**, 305
constitution, **3**, 305
deposits, authorisation of society to take, **3**, 320,
  321
designated corporate body, **3**, 366, 369
establishment, **3**, 305
expenses, **3**, 305
functions, **3**, 305, 306
  delegation, **3**, 305
funds—
  authorisation of society to raise, **3**, 320, 321
  breach of limits on assets and liabilities, **3**, 440
information—
  confidentiality, **3**, 307
  power to obtain, **3**, 307
inspectors, **3**, 308
investor protection schemes, approval and
  authorisation, **3**, 393, 394
merger or amalgamation, confirmation, **3**, 447,
  452
name of society, approval, **3**, 316, 317
officer, building society, removal, **3**, 407
powers, **3**, 307
  abuse of society's principal purpose, where, **3**,
    441
  advertising, control, **3**, 444
  attendance and assistance, to require, **3**, 446
  authorisation, as to, *see* BUILDING SOCIETY
    (authorisation)
  control of building societies, **3**, 309, 309n
  funds and assets limits, as to, **3**, 440
  inspections, **3**, 445
  interim report, to require, **3**, 446
  prohibition order, to make, **3**, 443
  special meetings, to call, **3**, 445
  unauthorised activities, as to, **3**, 442, 443
prohibition order, power to make, **3**, 343

Building Societies Commission—*continued*
revocation of authorisation by, **3**, 436
statutory instruments, power to make, **3**, 305,
  309, 309n
transfer of business, consent to, **3**, 458
**Building Societies Investor Protection
  Scheme**
borrowing power, **3**, 392
indemnity limit, **3**, 392
introduction, **3**, 392
operation, **3**, 392
powers, generally, **3**, 392
Building society
account (customer)—
  arrestment, **8**, 272
  child, capacity to hold, **3**, 1219
  facility, **3**, 359
  partial intestacy, **25**, 708
accounts (management)—
  accounting records, **3**, 395, 422
  annual, **3**, 381, 404, 423, 436
  auditors' report, **3**, 432
  completion, **3**, 426
  control systems, **3**, 422
  form, **3**, 426
  group, **3**, 424, 426
  income and expenditure, **3**, 426
  inspection and report, **3**, 422
  statement of source and application of funds, **3**,
    426
  subsidiary undertakings, where, **3**, 422, 424
  termination, complaints procedure, **3**, 389
administration of estate, powers as to, **3**, 376
advance—
  bridging facilities, **3**, 338, 355, 357, 361, 378
  class 1—
    advance fully secured on land, as, **3**, 347
    changes in terms on merger, **3**, 447
    complaints procedure, **3**, 389
    linking of services, **3**, 352
    requirements for, **3**, 348
  class 2—
    advance fully secured on land, as, **3**, 347
    changes in terms on merger, **3**, 447
    complaints procedure, **3**, 389
  class 3 assets—
    generally, **3**, 355
  deposit payable for land purchase, **3**, 347
  finance leasing, **3**, 355
  fully secured over land, power to make—
    borrower protection, **3**, 351–353
    class 1 advance, **3**, 347, 348, 352
    class 2 advance, **3**, 347, 349
    generally, **3**, 343, 347
    heritable security, by, **3**, 347
    index-linked capital element, **3**, 347, 348
    land outwith UK, **3**, 354, 354n
    management criteria, **3**, 395
    mortgage, by, **3**, 347
    valuation of security, **3**, 350
  hire purchase arrangement, **3**, 355
  linking of services, **3**, 352
  offer of, **3**, 379

Building society—*continued*
advance—*continued*
  unsecured, **3**, 355
    generally, **3**, 355, 357
    heritable security, **3**, 357
    non-member, to, **3**, 357
    overdraft facilities, **3**, 357
advertising—
  controls on, **1**, 533; **3**, 444
  prohibition, modification or withdrawal order,
    13, 1766
amalgamation—
  cancellation of registration following, **3**, 464
  confirmation, **3**, 452
  generally, **3**, 447, 448, 451
  proposals for, **3**, 453
annual business statement—
  auditors' report, **3**, 432
  generally, **3**, 381, 404, 425, 426
annual general meeting—
  accounts, **3**, 426
  annual accounts, **3**, 404
  auditors, appointment, **3**, 428
  directors, election, **3**, 400
  failure to hold, **3**, 413
  generally, **3**, 413
  rules of society, generally, **3**, 412
arbitration—
  society and member, between, **3**, 386
arrestee, as, **8**, 259
associated body—
  accounts, **3**, 422, 424
  aggregation notice as to assets and liabilities of,
    3, 370
  apparent, **3**, 371
  auditor, access to information, **3**, 435
  commercial assets—
    classification, **3**, 341
    determination, **3**, 341
  complaint as to, **3**, 389
  complaints scheme, membership, **3**, 388
  estate agency work, **3**, 377
  inspection, Building Societies Commission
    powers of, **3**, 445, 446
  investment in or support of—
    generally, **3**, 344, 365
  liabilities of, **3**, 330
    guarantee of discharge, **3**, 365, 370
  meaning, **3**, 308*n*
  resolution, linked by, **3**, 370
  subsidiaries, prohibition against, **3**, 369
  See also corporate body *below*
auditor—
  access to information, **3**, 435
  appointment, **3**, 428
  casual vacancy, **3**, 428
  disqualifications from appointment, **3**, 429
  meetings, attendance at, **3**, 435
  qualifications, **3**, 429
  re-appointment, **3**, 428
  removal, **3**, 430
  reports—
    accounts, **3**, 432
    Building Societies Commission, to, **3**, 434

Building society—*continued*
auditor—*continued*
  reports—*continued*
    transactions with directors, on, **3**, 433
  resignation, **3**, 429, 431
authorisation—
  appeal, right of, **3**, 325, 326
  application for, **3**, 322
  commercial asset limits, and, **3**, 339
  conditional grant, **3**, 324, 436, 438
    appeal, right of, **3**, 326
    imposition of conditions, **3**, 436, 438
    revocation of conditions, **3**, 324
    variation of conditions, **3**, 324
  existing building society, of, **3**, 321
  generally, **3**, 320
  re-authorisation, **3**, 320, 322, 439
  refusal, **3**, 325
    appeal, right of, **3**, 325, 326
  renewal, **3**, 436, 437
  revocation, **3**, 320, 324, 380, 436
    appeal, right of, **3**, 326
  unconditional grant, **3**, 323, 436
bank customer, as, **2**, 1262
banking services—
  foreign exchange services, **3**, 373
  guarantees, **3**, 373
  money transmission transactions, **3**, 373
  power to provice, **3**, 372, 373
bonus payable on merger, **3**, 447, 451
borrower protection—
  advances fully secured over land, **3**, 351–353
  generally, **3**, 351
  linking of services, **3**, 352
  power of sale, **3**, 353
borrowing limit—
  failure to comply with, **3**, 331
  generally, **3**, 329
breach of limits on assets and liabilities, **3**, 440
bridging facilities—
  class 3 assets, as, **3**, 361
  provision, generally, **3**, 338, 355, 361, 378
  requirements for, **3**, 361
  unsecured advances, **3**, 357, 361
business control systems, management criteria, **3**,
  395
capital resources, management criteria, **3**, 395,
  396
'central office'—
  certificate of incorporation, issue, **3**, 310
  duties, **3**, 304
  generally, **3**, 304, 304*n*
chairman, appointment, **3**, 398
chief executive—
  accounts, duty as to, **3**, 426
  appointment, **3**, 407
  function, **3**, 407
  generally, **3**, 398, 406
  officer, as, **3**, 406
  removal, **3**, 407
combined assets of UK societies, **2**, 1262
commercial assets—
  association bodies, of, **3**, 341
  class 1 assets, **3**, 338, 345

Building society—*continued*
commercial assets—*continued*
  class 2 assets, **3**, 338, 345
  class 3 assets, **3**, 337, 338, 355–361, 365
    additional, catgories, **3**, 378
    adoption of power to make, **3**, 344
  classification, **3**, 338
    existing building societies, **3**, 340
    re-classification of advances, **3**, 342
  limits, **3**, 339
    breach, **3**, 440
  management criteria, **3**, 395
  risk element, **3**, 337
commission, building officer etc, paid to, **3**, 408
common seal, name to appear on, **3**, 315
company—
  investment in or support of, **3**, 366
  society member, as, **3**, 379
complaint—
  action outwith UK, as to, **3**, 389
  adjudicators, powers and duties, **3**, 390
  associated bodies, **3**, 388, 389
  Building Society Ombudsman, **3**, 388
  complaints scheme—
    members' right to investigation under, **3**, 388
    membership, generally, **3**, 388
    recognition, **3**, 388
    withdrawal from, **3**, 388
  court, matters already before or decided by, **3**, 389
  determination, effect, **3**, 391
  frivolous or vexatious, **3**, 389
  generally, **3**, 388
  internal complaints procedure, **3**, 389
  matters covered by complaints procedure, **3**, 389
  subsidiaries, **3**, 388, 389
  undue delay in bringing, **3**, 389
connected person—
  disclosure of interests, **3**, 405, 405*n*
  register of transactions, **3**, 405
control—
  Building Societies Commission, *see* BUILDING SOCIETIES COMMISSION
  statutory, **3**, 302, 303
conveyancing services, power to offer, **3**, 344
corporate body—
  account which may be overdrawn, **3**, 355
  ancillary services body, **3**, 369
  apparent associated, **3**, 371
  Building Societies Commission, designated by, **3**, 366, 369
  building society investment in or support of—
    class 3 assets, **3**, 365
    designated bodies, **3**, 369
    generally, **3**, 344, 365
    permitted corporate bodies, **3**, 366
    undesignated European bodies, **3**, 368
    undesignated UK bodies, **3**, 367
  building society shares held by, **3**, 328
  estate agencies body, **3**, 369
  European Community, bodies formed within, **3**, 366, 368
  financial services body, **3**, 369

Building society—*continued*
corporate body—*continued*
  funding body, **3**, 369
  general insurance body, **3**, 369
  holding body, **3**, 369
  housing association, **3**, 369
  housing trust, **3**, 369
  lending body, **3**, 369
  liabilities of associated, guarantees of discharge, **3**, 365, 370
  life insurance body, **3**, 369
  loan to, **3**, 365
  mortgage indemnity insurance body, **3**, 369
  offence by, **3**, 411
  pension body, **3**, 369
  services or property used by, **3**, 365
  subordinate organisation, **3**, 369, 369*n*
credit facility, power to make, **3**, 355
debt—
  facility, *see* facility debt *below*
  factoring, **3**, 373
deceased depositor, representatives of, **3**, 384
deposit-taking powers, **2**, 1246, 1262
deposits, **3**, 303
  authorisation to take, **3**, 320, 321
  breach of limits, **3**, 440
  building society funds, as source of, **3**, 303
  form, **3**, 335
  funds raised by, **3**, 327
  non-retail—
    exclusions, **3**, 328
    failure to comply with limits, **3**, 331
    liabilities of associated bodies, **3**, 330
    meaning, **3**, 327, 328
    percentage of total liabilities, **3**, 328
  withdrawal, minimum period, **3**, 335
directors—
  absence of, **3**, 403
  accounts, **3**, 422, 423, 426
  annual business statement, **3**, 425
  appointment date, **3**, 400
  bankruptcy, **3**, 403
  board vacancy, filling, **3**, 400, 401
  chairman, **3**, 398
  co-opted, **3**, 400, 401
  directors' report, **3**, 404, 425
    auditors' report, **3**, 432
  election, **3**, 400
    postal ballot, **3**, 417
  eligibility, **3**, 399
  executive, **3**, 398
  interests, disclosure, **3**, 405, 405*n*
  liability, **3**, 410
  loans to, **3**, 405, 405*n*
  mergers or transfers, interest in, **3**, 447
  minimum number, **3**, 398
  nomination, **3**, 400
  officer of society, as, **3**, 398, 406
  powers and duties, generally, **3**, 404
  qualifying shareholding, ceasing to hold, **3**, 403
  register of transactions, **3**, 405
  related busines, with, **3**, 409
  removal from office, **3**, 403
  remuneration, **3**, 402

Building society—*continued*
directors—*continued*
  resignation, **3**, 403
  retirement age, **3**, 399, 403
  termination of directorship, **3**, 403
  transactions with—
    auditors' report, **3**, 433
    disclosure, **3**, 405
    offences in relation to, **3**, 405
  valuation of securities by, **3**, 350
disputes—
  building society and member, between—
    arbitration, **3**, 386
    Building Societies Commission, settlement by, **3**, 387
    Court of Session jurisdiction, **3**, 385
dissolution—
  borrowing members, position of, **3**, 460
  cancellation of registration following, **3**, 464
  consent of members, **3**, 460, 461
  deferred shares, **3**, 333
  generally, **3**, 460, 461
  instrument of, **3**, 461
  public file, record in, **3**, 461
  revocation of authorisation, **3**, 436
  void, declared, **3**, 460
election address, refusal to circulate, **3**, 385, 386
establishment, requirements as to, **3**, 310
estate agencies body—
  land services, power to provide, **3**, 377
  power to invest in and support, **3**, 369
executorship services, power to provide, **3**, 372, 376
exempt agreement, **5**, 821
facility debt—
  meaning, **3**, 359
  power to acquire, hold and dispose of, **3**, 359, 378
financial planning advice, **3**, 374
financial services, **2**, 1246
  complaints procedure, **3**, 389
  meaning, **3**, 372*n*
  power to provide, **3**, 344, 372
financial statement, **1**, 88; **3**, 381, 404, 427
foreclosure, land held on, **3**, 338, 364
friendly society, society shares held by, **3**, 328
funding body, power to invest in and support, **3**, 369
funds—
  authorisation to raise, **3**, 320, 321, 343
  borrowing, raised by, **3**, 327
  breach of limits, **3**, 440
  building societies' power to raise, **3**, 345
  deposits, raised by, **3**, 327
  non-retail funds and deposits—
    exclusions, **3**, 328
    failure to comply with limits, **3**, 331
    limits of associated bodies, **3**, 330
    meaning, **3**, 327
    percentage of total liabilities, **3**, 328
  raising, generally, **3**, 337, 343
  share issue, raised by, **3**, 327
  source of, **3**, 303
furniture removal and storage, **3**, 377

Building society—*continued*
hedge, power to, **3**, 336, 344, 345
hire purchase arrangement, power to make, **3**, 338, 355, 358, 378
historical background—
  control, **3**, 302
  establishment, **3**, 301
  modern legislation, **3**, 303
  permanent societies, **3**, 301
  purpose, **3**, 301
  statutory recognition, **3**, 301
  supervision, **3**, 304
  terminating societies, **3**, 301
  unincorporated societies, **3**, 301
historical note, **2**, 1262
housing association, power to invest in and support, **3**, 369
housing trust, power to invest in and support, **3**, 369
incorporation, **3**, 343, 346
  certificate of, **3**, 310
  effect, **3**, 311
  existing society, of, **3**, 312
  memorandum, **3**, 313
industrial and provident society—
  building society member, as, **3**, 379
  investment in or support of, **3**, 366
inspection, Building Societies Commission powers, **3**, 445, 446
insurance—
  body, power to invest in and support, **3**, 369
  intermediary, **12**, 811
  services, power to provide, **3**, 372, 375
interest, deceased's liability to tax, **25**, 967
investment and support, designated bodies, **3**, 369
investor protection—
  Building Societies Investor Protection Scheme, **2**, 1246; **3**, 392
  loans from other building societies, **3**, 394
  protected investments, **3**, 392, 392*n*
  voluntary schemes, **3**, 393
land—
  acquisition by society, **3**, 372
  advance fully secured over—
    borrower protection—
      generally, **3**, 351
      linking of services, **3**, 352
      power of sale, **3**, 353
    class 1 advances, **3**, 347, 348, 352
    class 2 advances, **3**, 347, 349
    deposit for purchase of land, **3**, 347
    generally, **3**, 343, 347
    heritable security, **3**, 347
    index-linked capital element, **3**, 347, 348
    land outwith UK, **3**, 354, 354*n*
    management criteria, **3**, 395
    mortgage, **3**, 347
    valuation of security, **3**, 350
  development, held for, **3**, 338
  investment in, **3**, 303
  power to hold—
    foreclosure, held on, **3**, 338, 364
    purposes of society's business, held for, **3**, 362
    residential development, held for, **3**, 338, 363

Building society—*continued*
land—*continued*
  residential development, acquired and held for,
    3, 344, 363
  services relating to, power to provide—
    generally, **3**, 344, 372, 377
    meaning of services relating to, **3**, 372*n*
land services, building societies' power to
  provide, **3**, 377
leasing facilities—
  finance leasing, **3**, 355
  generally, **3**, 338, 378
  leasing agreements, **3**, 358
lending body, power to invest in and support, **3**,
  369
lending powers, **13**, 1778
linking of services, borrower protection, **3**, 352
liquid assets—
  limits, breach, **3**, 440
  management criteria, **3**, 395, 397
liquidation, **3**, 392
loan—
  advance, *see* advance *above*
  body corporate, to, **3**, 365
  borrowing by society, for, **3**, 335
  commission payable in respect of, **3**, 408
  complaints procedure, **3**, 389
  director, to, **3**, 405, 405*n*
  ex facie dispositions in favour of society, **20**, 227
  form, **3**, 335
  generally, **13**, 1778; **20**, 226
  membership through, **3**, 379
  minor, to, **3**, 1220
  mobile home, *see* mobile home loan *below*
  power to make, generally, **3**, 372
  standard securities taken by, **20**, 228
    deed of variation of standard conditions, **20**,
      229
loans—
  standard securities taken by—
    contents of standard security, **20**, 230
maladministration, **3**, 389
management—
  accounts, **3**, 395
  Building Societies Commission, supervision by,
    3, 395
  business control systems, **3**, 395
  commercial assets, **3**, 395
  liquid assets, **3**, 395, 397
  prudent, criteria for, **3**, 395
  records, **3**, 395
  reserves and capital resources, **3**, 395, 396
managers, **3**, 398, 406
meetings—
  adjourned, **3**, 414
  annual general, *see* annual general meeting
    above
  auditor, attendance at, **3**, 435
  members' rights—
    borrowing member, **3**, 414
    joint members, **3**, 414
    minor, **3**, 414
    notice, to, **3**, 414
    poll, to demand, **3**, 416

Building society—*continued*
meetings—*continued*
  members' rights—*continued*
    proxies, appointment, **3**, 415
    requisition meeting, to, **3**, 412
    resolution, to move, **3**, 412
  notice, **3**, 412, 414
  poll, **3**, 412, 416
  procedure, **3**, 412
  proxies, appointment of, **3**, 415
  resolution, right to move, **3**, 412
  special, Building Societies Commission power
    to call, **3**, 445
  voting rights, **3**, 412, 414
members—
  bonus payable to, merger, on, **3**, 447, 451
  borrowing, **3**, 379
    dissolution or winding up of society,
      position on, **3**, 460
    joint, **3**, 379–381, 414
    resolution, **3**, 417, 418, 420
    voting rights, **3**, 414
  cessation of membership, **3**, 383
  company as, **3**, 379
  complaints procedure, *see* complaint *above*
  deceased, representatives of, **3**, 384
  definition, **3**, 379
  dispute with society—
    arbitration, **3**, 386
    Building Societies Commission,
      determination by, **3**, 387
    jurisdiction, **3**, 385
  industrial and provident society as, **3**, 379
  investing, **3**, 379
  joint borrowing, **3**, 379–381, 414
  joint shareholding, **3**, 379–381, 414
  liability, **3**, 381
    limitation, **3**, 382
  meeting—
    notice, right to, **3**, 414
    poll, right to demand, **3**, 416
    proxies, appointment of, **3**, 415
    resolution, right to move, **3**, 412
    right to requisition, **3**, 412
  members' resolution, **3**, 418, 421
  membership, generally, **3**, 379
  memorandum binding on, **3**, 313, 381
  minor as, **3**, 379, 414
  number of, **3**, 310, 379
  register of, **3**, 380
  rights, **3**, 381
  rules binding on, **3**, 314, 381
  shareholding, **3**, 379
    joint, **3**, 379–381, 414
  trustee as, **3**, 379
memorandum—
  adoption of powers, **3**, 346
  alteration, **3**, 319, 346
  binding nature, **3**, 313
  contents, **3**, 313
  establishment of building society, **3**, 310, 312
  members, binding on, **3**, 381
  name of society, specification, **3**, 313
  name to appear in, **3**, 315

Building society—*continued*
memorandum—*continued*
  persons deemed to have notice of, **3**, 313
  principal office, specification, **3**, 313, 318
merger—
  amalgamation, **3**, 447, 448
  bonuses, payment to members, **3**, 447, 451
  borrowing members' resolution, **3**, 420
  Building Societies Commission, confirmation
    by, **3**, 447, 452
  disproportionate size, societies of, **3**, 419
  existing building society, transfer to, **3**, 447,
    449
  generally, **3**, 447
  loss of office, compensation for, **3**, 447, 451
  new building society, formation, **3**, 447, 448
  partial transfer of engagements, **3**, 450
  procedure, **3**, 447
  proposals for, **3**, 453
  special resolution, **3**, 419
mobile home loan—
  classification, **3**, 338
  complaints procedure, **3**, 389
  form, **3**, 356
  heritable security, **3**, 356
  member, to, **3**, 356
  non-member, to, **3**, 356
  power to make—
    adoption by society, **3**, 344
    generally, **3**, 355, 356
  re-classification of advances, **3**, 342
  requirements to be met, **3**, 356
  security, **3**, 344
money transmission services, **3**, 338, 355, 360,
  373, 378
moneylender, not classed as, **13**, 1770
mutual institution, as, **3**, 327
mutual status, **3**, 303
name—
  approval, **3**, 316, 317
  building society, of, **3**, 310
  change of, **3**, 315, 419
  common seal, **3**, 315
  memorandum, **3**, 315
  misleading, **3**, 316, 317
  registration, **3**, 315
  rules, **3**, 315
  specification in memorandum, **3**, 313
  undesirable, **3**, 315
office—
  generally, **3**, 362
  outwith UK, **3**, 362, 362*n*
  principal—
    change of, **3**, 318
    specification in memorandum, **3**, 313, 318
    specification in rules, **3**, 318
officers—
  chief executive, **3**, 406, 407
  commission, payment to, **3**, 408
  compensation for loss of office, **3**, 447, 451
  director as, **3**, 398, 406
  generally, **3**, 406, 406*n*
  liability, **3**, 410
  managers, **3**, 406

Building society—*continued*
officers—*continued*
  memorandum binding on, **3**, 313
  offence by, **3**, 411
  related business, with, **3**, 409
  removal, **3**, 407
  rules binding on, **3**, 314
  secretary, **3**, 406, 407
overdraft facility, power to make, **3**, 355, 357
overseas activities, **3**, 303
pension body, power to invest in and support, **3**,
  369
pension schemes, **3**, 328, 374
permanent, **3**, 301
personal equity plans, **3**, 328, 374
place of business, **3**, 362
  outwth UK, **3**, 362, 362*n*
  See also office *above*
postal ballot—
  directors, election, **3**, 400
  generally, **3**, 412, 417
  notice, **3**, 417
  procedure, **3**, 417
postponed security, loan on, **3**, 303
power of attorney, forged, **3**, 334
powers, **3**, 303
  activity outwith, society carrying on, **3**, 343
  adoptable, **3**, 344
  adoption, **3**, 343–346
    generally, **3**, 343
  advance fully secured over land, to make—
    borrower protection, **3**, 351–353
    class 1 advances, **3**, 347, 348
    class 2 advances, **3**, 347, 349
    deposit for purchase of land, **3**, 347
    generally, **3**, 343, 347
    heritable security, **3**, 347
    index-linked capital element, **3**, 347, 348
    land outwith UK, **3**, 354, 354*n*
    mortgage, **3**, 347
    valuation of security, **3**, 350
  alteration, **3**, 319, 419
  ancillary to society's purposes, **3**, 343
  availability, **3**, 345
  class 1 advances, to make, **3**, 345, 347, 348
  class 2 advances, to make, **3**, 345, 347, 349
  class 3 advances, to make, **3**, 344, 355–361
  corporate body, investment in and support of,
    3, 344, 365–371
  development, to acquire and hold land for, **3**,
    344
  funds, raising, **3**, 343, 345
  hedging, **3**, 336, 344, 345
  land, to hold, **3**, 362–364
  land outwith UK, advances secured on, **3**, 344
  memorandum, **3**, 346
  mobile home, to make advance in respect of, **3**,
    344
  overdraft facility, power to make, **3**, 355
  rules, **3**, 346
  sale, power of, **3**, 353
  services, to provide, **3**, 344, 372–377
  subsidiary, investment in, **3**, 344, 365
  unauthorised activity, determination, **3**, 442, 443

Building society—*continued*
protected investment, **3**, 392, 392*n*
public file—
    aggregation notice as to liabilities and assets of
        associated body, **3**, 371
    dissolution, record of, **3**, 461
    duty to maintain, **3**, 304
    meaning, **3**, 304*n*
    non-retail funds and deposits, **3**, 328
    opening, **3**, 310
    preparation and maintenance, **3**, 304
    revocation of authorisation, record in, **3**, 436
    transfer of business to commercial company,
        record of, **3**, 459
    winding up, record of, **3**, 462, 463
purpose, **3**, 310
    alteration, **3**, 319, 419
    principal, **3**, 337
        abuse of, **3**, 441
records, management criteria, **3**, 395
registration, cancellation, **3**, 464
reserves, management criteria, **3**, 395, 396
resolution—
    borrowing members', **3**, 417, 418, 420, 449,
        457
    generally, **3**, 418
    members', **3**, 418, 421
    postal ballot, *see* postal ballot *above*
    special, **3**, 418, 419, 449, 462, 463
    transfer, **3**, 418, 457
rules—
    adoption of powers, **3**, 346
    alteration, **3**, 319, 346
    binding nature, **3**, 314
    establishment of building society, **3**, 310
    generally, **3**, 314
    members, binding on, **3**, 381
    name to appear in, **3**, 315
    persons deemed to have notice of, **3**, 314
    principal office, specification, **3**, 313, 318
    void, **3**, 314
secretary—
    appointment, **3**, 407
    generally, **3**, 398, 406, 407
    removal, **3**, 407
security—
    basic—
        meaning, **3**, 342*n*
        security additional to, **3**, 351
    land outwith UK, **3**, 344, 345
    loan without, **3**, 303
    mobile home, **3**, 344
    postponed, **3**, 303, 349
    valuation—
        advance fully secured over land, where, **3**,
        350
        arrangements for, directors' duties as to, **3**,
        350
        financial interest in disposition of property,
        person with, **3**, 350
share subscription, **3**, 303
shares—
    advanced, **3**, 379
    body corporate, held by or for, **3**, 328

Building society—*continued*
shares—*continued*
    charity, held by, **3**, 328
    classes, **3**, 333
    deferred, **3**, 332, 333
    friendly society, held by, **3**, 328
    fully paid up, **3**, 333
    investment, **3**, 333, 379
    membership defined by holding in, **3**, 379
    ordinary investment, **3**, 333
    personal equity plan, held by, **3**, 328
    personal pension scheme, held by, **3**, 328
    preferential, **3**, 333
    retirements benefit scheme, held by, **3**, 328
    share issue—
        authorisation, **3**, 332, 333
        funds raised by, **3**, 327
        generally, **3**, 333
        powers in relation to, **3**, 332
        terms, document containing, **3**, 333
    trade union, held by, **3**, 328
    transfer, **3**, 332
        forged, **3**, 334
        loss arising from, **3**, 334
sheriff court jurisdiction, **6**, 1084
subscription on behalf of, **6**, 417
subsidiary—
    accounts, **3**, 422, 424
    associated body prohibited from having, **3**, 369
    auditor, access to information, **3**, 435
    building society operating through, **3**, 303
    complaint as to, **3**, 389
    complaints scheme, membership, **3**, 388
    discharge of liabilities, guarantee by parent
        company, **3**, 370
    estate agency work, **3**, 377
    inspection, Building Societies Commission
        powers, **3**, 445, 446
    investment in or support of, **3**, 344, 365
    unauthorised activity by, determination, **3**, 442
    See also corporate body *above*
supervision, **3**, 304
taxation advice, provision, **3**, 374
transfer of business—
    cancellation of registration following, **3**, 464
    commercial company, to—
        borrowing members' resolution, **3**, 420
        Building Societies Commission consent, **3**,
        458
        completion, **3**, 459
        generally, **3**, 454
        protective provisions, **3**, 455
        regulated terms, **3**, 456
        special resolution, **3**, 419, 457
        transfer resolution, **3**, 419, 457
transfer of engagement—
    borrowing members' resolution, **3**, 420, 449,
        457
    cancellation of registration following, **3**, 464
    generally, **3**, 449
    partial, **3**, 450
    record of, **3**, 449
    special resolution, **3**, 419, 449
transferable instrument, non-retail funds, **3**, 328

Building society—*continued*
trusteeship services, power to provide, **3**, 372, 376
unauthorised activity by—
    determination, **3**, 442
    prohibition order, **3**, 443
unfair treatment by, **3**, 389
voting rights—
    generally, **3**, 412, 414
    postal ballot, *see* postal ballot *above*
    proxies, appointment, **3**, 415
wills, power to assist in making, **3**, 376
winding up—
    borrowing members, position of, **3**, 460
    cancellation of registration following, **3**, 464
    cessation of membership, **3**, 383
    court, by, **3**, 460, 463
    deferred shares, **3**, 333
    generally, **3**, 460
    public file, record in, **3**, 462, 463
    revocation of authorisation, **3**, 436
    special resolution as to, **3**, 462, 463
    void, declared, **3**, 460
    voluntary, **3**, 460, 462
        special resolution, **3**, 419
Building Society Ombudsman
complaints to, **3**, 388
Building Standards Advisory Committee
appointment, **3**, 206
constitution, **3**, 206
consultation with, **3**, 205
functions, **3**, 206
members' expenses, reimbursement, **3**, 206
Building standards regulations
See BUILDING REGULATIONS
Buildings authority
Dean of Guild Court as, **3**, 201
institution, **3**, 201
jurisdiction and functions, transfer, **3**, 201
powers, **3**, 201
Bulgaria
imports, European Union regulations, **7**, 1029
Bulls
pasturing on rights of way, **2**, 163
performances involving, **2**, 269
wrestling or fighting, **19**, 1274
Bumping
employment lost as result of, **9**, 171
Buoys
harbour authority, duty of, **11**, 1322
Burden of proof
See PROOF
Bureau Veritas, **21**, 120
Burgage tenure
dispone, power to, **18**, 59
feufarm, merger with, **18**, 58, 65
generally, **18**, 65
meaning, **18**, 65
non-entry not applicable to, **18**, 81
sasine, symbols of, **18**, 90
subinfeudation, and, **18**, 58
transfer of land, **6**, 586
watch and ward, obligation as to, **18**, 65
Burgess Oath
voluntary churches, **3**, 1636, 1637, 1637*n*

Burgh
barony, of, **14**, 10
bishop, **14**, 10
building controls, **3**, 201
burghal parish, **15**, 1025
chamberlain—
    appointment of, **14**, 249
    supervision of courts by, **22**, 510
charter, **14**, 10
commerce, privileges centre around, **14**, 12
Convention of the Royal Burghs, **22**, 510
corporate personality, **19**, 216
council, **14**, **14**, 16
courts—
    abolition, **6**, 1160; **17**, 517
    administration of law, powers, **22**, 510
    antecedents of district court, as, **6**, 1155
    appeal from, **14**, 13
    chamberlain, supervision by, **22**, 510
    Court of the Four Burghs, **14**, 13; **22**, 510
    customs of burgh, administration, **22**, 609
    feudal system, as part of, **6**, 898
    former jurisdiction, **6**, 1022; **14**, 13
    generally, **6**, 1156
    geographical jurisdiction, **17**, 518
    history, **17**, 518
    inferior courts, as, **6**, 1155
    maritime custom, administration, **22**, 609
    royal burghs, **6**, 1156
    summary procedure, **6**, 1155
craft, monopoly of, **14**, 12
creation of, **14**, 10
description, **22**, 510
financial liability, **14**, 11
functions, increase in, **14**, 22
history of, **6**, 586*n*
inter-burghal disputes, **14**, 13
juristic personality, **19**, 205
justice of peace, introduction of, **14**, 27
large, reform of, **14**, 39
Laws of the Four Burghs, **22**, 510
local authority elections, **15**, 1021–1023
medieval law, 202*n*, 215; **2**, 216; **19**, 202
merchant guild, **14**, 14
neighbourhood, **14**, 2011
nuisance applied within, **14**, 2012
parliament, representation in, **14**, 15; **15**, 1002, 1007, 1015, 1016
Parliamentary, **15**, 1015, 1023
police, **14**, 21
    'public police', **14**, 2011
powers, **14**, 12
privileges, **14**, 12
public health, responsibility for, **14**, 37
records, **19**, 842, 868
    transmission of, **19**, 853
reform, **14**, 21
regality, of, **14**, 10
Registers, **19**, 864
rise and fall, **14**, 18
royal—
    bailie or magistrate, office of, **6**, 1156
    burgage tenure, **6**, 586
    burgh court, **6**, 1156

Burgh—*continued*
royal—*continued*
  continued existence of, **6**, 1156
  contract of ground annual, **6**, 586
  convention of, **14**, 17
  creation and number of, **6**, 586; **14**, 10; **22**, 510
  exclusive privilege, **18**, 5
  feu-ferme status, **14**, 11
  financial liability, **14**, 11
  parliament, representation in, **14**, 15; **15**, 1002, 1015
  police court, **6**, 1157
  privileges, **14**, 10
  provost, esquire, as, **16**, 2022
  rise and fall, **14**, 18
  trade, monopoly of, **14**, 12, 19
  sanitary inspector, appointment of, **14**, 249
  schools, origins of, **14**, 36
  small—
    meaning, **25**, 502*n*
    reform of 1929, **14**, 39
    statutory regulations, **25**, 502
  status of town as, **22**, 510
  system, effects of, **14**, 20
  town council, **14**, 16
  trade, privileges centre around, **14**, 12
Burgh courts
See BURGH
Burghers
generally, **3**, 1637, 1637*n*
Seceders, **3**, 1636
Burial
authority, *see* BURIAL AUTHORITY
burial ground, *see* BURIAL GROUND
certificate of notice of, **19**, 1455
Christian practice, as, **3**, 501
church—
  right of burial in, **3**, 515
  within, **3**, 1605
cremated ashes, of, **3**, 568
death, certification and registration, **3**, 514
directions of deceased, **3**, 506
disinterment, *see* DEAD BODY
fees and charges, **3**, 525
funeral directors, instructions issued to, **3**, 569
historical background, **3**, 501
land scarcity, **3**, 501
local authority—
  expenses, recovery by—
    deceased estate, **22**, 15
    person liable to maintain, **22**, 15
  payments, discretionary to assist/attend, **22**, 15
  power to arrange, of person in care, **22**, 15
local burial authorities, *see* BURIAL AUTHORITY
no right of burial, in ground where, **3**, 534
parish registers, **19**, 1401
public health considerations, **19**, 463
register, **3**, 529
sea, at, *see* SEA, BURIAL AT
sheriff court jurisdiction, **6**, 1085
statutory regulation, **3**, 502
stillborn child, of, **19**, 1449
transmission of records, **19**, 853
VAT exemption, **7**, 1427

Burial authority
conveyance of bodies, facilitating, **3**, 526
cremation, powers and duties in relation to, **3**, 542
enlargement or extension of burial ground, **3**, 519, 522
fees and charges for burials, **3**, 525
finance, **3**, 528
kirkyard burial grounds, transfer of management to, **3**, 519, 520
land, acquisition, **3**, 519, 521
  Crown lands, **3**, 523
management of burial grounds, **3**, 524
monuments, preservation and maintenance, **3**, 519
mortuary etc, provision, **3**, 526
powers, generally, **3**, 524
register of burials, **3**, 529
vacant and unoccupied, allocation of burial ground as, **3**, 519
Burial ground
burial fees and charges, **3**, 525
burial rights, sale, **3**, 524
chapel, construction, **3**, 524
Church of Scotland General Trustees, management by, **3**, 519
closed, **3**, 522
closure—
  grant of licence for exercise of burial rights, **3**, 532
  Order in Council on grant of interlocutor, **3**, 531, 532
  petition requesting, **3**, 530
compulsory acquisition or use, **19**, 19
construction or extension, **19**, 15
conveyance of body to, **3**, 526
embellishments, **3**, 524
enlargement or extension, **3**, 519, 522
family, **3**, 515
finance, **3**, 528
health, dangerous to, **3**, 515
islands or district council, transfer to, **3**, 1580
Jewish, **3**, 531
kirkyard—
  historical background, **3**, 517
  maintainence, **3**, 517
  management, **3**, 518
  parish councils, transfer of management to, **3**, 520
  provision, responsibility for, **3**, 517
  transfer to local burial authority, **3**, 519
  use for purpose other than burial of dead, **3**, 518
land, acquisition by burial authority, **3**, 519, 521
  Crown lands, **3**, 523
  planning legislation, under, **3**, 533
layout, **3**, 524
local burial authority, *see* BURIAL AUTHORITY
management, **3**, 524
monuments—
  preservation and maintenance, **3**, 519
  right to erect, **3**, 524
new—
  Order in Council on grant of interlocutor, **3**, 531
  petition opposing, **3**, 530
  provision, generally, **3**, 522
  town, in, **23**, 376

Burial ground—*continued*
nuisance, when classed as, **3**, 515
overcrowded, **3**, 515
parish councils, transfer of management to, **3**, 520
private, **3**, 531
  church, right of burial in, **3**, 515
  commercial, **3**, 516
  common law, **3**, 515
  nuisance, when classed as, **3**, 515
public—
  historical background, **3**, 517
  management, **3**, 518
    transfer to local burial authority, **3**, 519
  types, **3**, 517
Quaker, **3**, 531
replacing closed, **3**, 522
tombstones, *see* TOMBSTONES
unaesthetic sight, **14**, 2084
vacant and unoccupied, allocation as, **3**, 519
vault, construction, **3**, 524
See also CEMETERY

Bursary
further education, award to student in—
  amount payable, **8**, 942
  conditions for payment, **8**, 943
  eligibility, **8**, 944
  generally, **8**, 941
university student, award to, **8**, 1029

Bus
conductor, duty of care, **3**, 680
contract carriage, **3**, 684
contract for carriage by, **3**, 601
deregulation, **14**, 422
handholds, **3**, 674
handling, vehicle, **3**, 676
hired, **3**, 684
luggage, **3**, 686
overcrowding, **3**, 675, 681
permit—
  community, **14**, 424
  educational body, use by, **14**, 423
  religious body, use by, **14**, 423
  social welfare, use for, **14**, 423
platform, defect in, **3**, 674
safety of vehicle, **3**, 674
See also PUBLIC SERVICE VEHICLE

Bus shelter
provision of, **20**, 612, 667

Bus station
safety, occupier's duty, **3**, 671

Business
advice in course of carrying on, **25**, 69
ancillary credit, *see* ANCILLARY CREDIT
anti-competitive practices in course of, **4**, 1252
assets—
  capital gains tax, **19**, 1527
  inheritance tax, **19**, 1533
  value added tax—
    charge to, **7**, 1288, 1300
    transfer of disposal, **7**, 1296, 1298
    use of as supply of services, **7**, 1289, 1299
  See also ASSETS
carrying on within UK, meaning, **4**, 1138, 1173*n*
charge, meaning, **12**, 1008, 1011

Business—*continued*
consumer credit, *see* CONSUMER CREDIT
entertainment, VAT and, **7**, 1384
established, meaning, **19**, 374
expansion scheme relief—
  income tax relief, **25**, 48
  withdrawal of, **25**, 970
franchise, transfer of, **9**, 180
hours, **22**, 823, 825, 828
investment, *see* INVESTMENT BUSINESS
meaning, **4**, 31, 1252; **9**, 166, 179; **7**, 1295; **16**, 1006
name—
  changes of, registrar's certificate relating to, **4**, 332
  clause, **4**, 321
  correct company name, use of, **4**, 321
  memorandum of association, form of, **4**, 320
  offence, breach of statutory provisions as, **4**, 321
  re-use of, restriction on, **4**, 866
  registered, **4**, 321
  registered overseas company, **4**, 315
  sheriff court jurisdiction, **6**, 1120
place of, meaning, **4**, 31, 315
premises—
  lease, **13**, 197
  commodities, **13**, 198
  furnishings, **13**, 217
  partners' names and addresses to be displayed, **16**, 1025
  shops, of, **13**, 197
  tenancy not secure, **11**, 1937, 1943
  water meter charges, **25**, 536
profits, liferenter's rights to, **13**, 1643
property—
  inheritance tax relief, **25**, 1012
  meaning, **25**, 1012
provisional closure, fairness of, **12**, 60
slander of, *see* SLANDER
Start-Up Scheme, tax relief, **2**, 1277
stationery—
  business cards, **17**, 3
  information to be stated on, **16**, 1025, 1038, 1096
tenancy, transfer of, **9**, 180
termination, action in connection with, **7**, 1296
transfer of, **9**, 177, 181
value added tax—
  entertainment, **7**, 1384
  liabilities, disposition, **7**, 1296
  meaning of business for, **7**, 1295
  tests for liability to, **7**, 1296
  transfer as going concern, **7**, 1290, 1296, 1350
  transfer to member of group, self-supply, **7**, 1305

Business Statistics Office
disclosure of information to, by Commissioners of Customs and Excise, **7**, 1283

Busking
adult performers, by, **9**, 1040
child, by, **9**, 1040
young person, by, **9**, 1040

Bustard
game, as, **11**, 802
Game Acts, **11**, 496*n*
Game (Scotland) Act 1832..., **11**, 815
trespass in search of, **11**, 817

Butter
advertisement, **11**, 360
composition, **11**, 360
constitution, **11**, 439
early legislation, **11**, 301
labelling, **11**, 360
Buy-back
operating lease, **14**, 1020
Byelaws
amendment, **14**, 287
application of procedure, **14**, 279
authentication, **14**, 280; **22**, 190
boating, control of, **25**, 359
certainty, **14**, 293
children, employment of, **14**, 274
civil action, **14**, 289
commencement, **22**, 190
common property, cleaning of, **14**, 278
confirmation of—
   appeal to sheriff, **14**, 119
   generally, **14**, 109; **22**, 191
   procedure, **14**, 283
   Secretary of State's powers, **14**, 109
confirming authority—
   generally, **14**, 282
   powers, **22**, 189
conservation, relating to, **25**, 390
countryside, **14**, 275, 682
cultural facilities, with regard to, **14**, 277
dairy, **14**, 710
danger, prevention of, **25**, 362
district salmon fisheries boards, enforcement by,
   11, 38
documentary evidence, as, **10**, 578
drought, relating to, **25**, 390
enactment, **22**, 189
enforcement—
   civil action, **14**, 289
   evidence, **14**, 290
   prosecution, **14**, 288
England and Wales, inshore fisheries, **11**, 133
evidence of, **14**, 290
Fishery Acts implemented by, **11**, 117
flood prevention, **14**, 463
Forestry Commission—
   enforcement, **11**, 640
   power to make, **11**, 609
good rule and government, for, **14**, 271
harbour authorities' power to make, **11**, 1317
intra vires, must be, **14**, 291
judicial control of, **1**, 298, 299
leisure facilities, with regard to, **14**, 277

Byelaws—*continued*
local authority power to make, **11**, 1902; **14**, 270–
   278; **22**, 189–193
milk and dairies, in relation to, **11**, 322
navigation, control of, **25**, 307
noise, control of, **25**, 359
notification, **14**, 281
nuisance, prevention of, **25**, 362
objections, **14**, 281
offences against, **2**, 72
police, with regard to, **14**, 272
pollution, control of, **25**, 426, 528
powers to make, **2**, 72; **14**, 270–278; **22**, 189–193
prescribed procedure, **14**, 295
prosecution, **14**, 288
public health, with regard to, **14**, 273
public inspection, **14**, 281
publication of, **14**, 284
publicity, **22**, 190
reasonableness, **14**, 294
recreational facilities, with regard to, **14**, 277, 278
register of, **14**, 286
repugnance to general law, **14**, 292
review, **22**, 193
revision, **14**, 285
revocation, **14**, 287; **22**, 192
seashore, with regard to, **14**, 278
social activities, with regard to, **14**, 277
sporting facilities, with regard to, **14**, 277, 278
ultra vires, **11**, 1317
   challenge not vitiated by confirmation, **22**, 191
   See also ultra vires
validity of—
   certainty, **14**, 293
   generally, **22**, 191
   intra vires, must be, **14**, 291
   prescribed procedure, **14**, 295
   reasonableness, **14**, 294
   repugnance to general law, **14**, 292
water, in relation to—
   access agreements and orders, **25**, 359
   misuse of water, **25**, 527
   water authority powers, **14**, 276
   water development board powers, **14**, 276
See also DELEGATED LEGISLATION
By-election
See ELECTION
Byre
nuisance arising from, **19**, 336
Byssinosis
Pneumoconiosis and Byssinosis Benefit Scheme,
   21, 1002
prescribed diseases regulations, **21**, 992, 997

C

'Cab-rank' rule
instruction of advocates, **13**, 1330, 1354
Cabinet
development of, **5**, 306; **7**, 702
Lord Chancellor as member of, **5**, 370
minister, **5**, 480
Office, **5**, 486
Privy Council replaced as principal organ of executive government by, **5**, 306
Queen, advice on public affairs to, **5**, 306
secretariat, **5**, 487
Cable
burning, environmental pollution by, **9**, 1119
exemptions from building regulations, **3**, 209
overhead, roads authority control over construction, **20**, 693
submarine—
continental shelf, laying and maintenance rights and duties, **21**, 31
exclusive economic zone, laying and maintenance rights, **21**, 39
high seas, freedom to lay in, **21**, 41
navigation rules, **21**, 380
Cable programme
advertising on, **1**, 523; **6**, 95
child, performance by, **9**, 1052
copyright, **18**, 967, 975, 1024, 1025
author, meaning, **18**, 979, 983
copying for private and domestic use, **18**, 1123
educational establishment, and, **18**, 1112, 1113
European Community legislation, **18**, 1643, 1644
generally, **18**, 933, 975
infringement, **18**, 1055
playing or showing in public, by, **18**, 1062–1064
needletime, **18**, 1024
originality, **18**, 948
ownership rights, **18**, 1005, 1042
permitted acts, **18**, 1123–1126
place of transmission, and, **18**, 940
qualification for protection, **18**, 941
spoken words, use of, **18**, 1107
subtitled, for the disabled, provision of copies, **18**, 1124
term of copyright, **18**, 1040
unauthorised transmissions, dealing in apparatus for, **18**, 1083
illicit recording, **18**, 1438
joint authorship, **18**, 987
licensing, **17**, 9
no copyright, where, **18**, 976
special qualified privilege, **17**, 20
Cable television
See CABLE PROGRAMME
Cachet Seal
custody, **7**, 895
generally, **7**, 853, 855, 894, 899
history, **7**, 894

Cachet Seal—*continued*
Register of—
Department of Registers, kept in, **19**, 820
generally, **6**, 459
use, **7**, 894
Cadency
differing systems, **11**, 1618
heirs apparent and presumptive, **11**, 1618
meaning, **11**, 1618
Cadet corps members
possession of firearms, generally, **10**, 1538
Calcium cyanide
special restrictions, **14**, 1216
Calendar
Babylonian, **22**, 802
calendar month, **22**, 813
commencement of year, **22**, 806, 811
definition, **22**, 801
evolution, **22**, 801
Great Britain, in, **22**, 805
Gregorian—
commencement of year, **22**, 806
Easter, fixing date of, **22**, 808
Julian calendar compared, **22**, 804, 805
leap year, **22**, 811
promulgation, **22**, 804
Scotland, introduction to, **22**, 805, 808
Julian—
description, **22**, 803
Easter, fixing date of, **22**, 808
Gregorian calendar compared, **22**, 804, 805
Scotland, introduction to, **22**, 805
lunations, as collection of, **22**, 813
Roman Republican, **22**, 802, 806
Calvo Clause
treatment of aliens under, **19**, 742
Cambridge University Library
delivery of book by publisher to, **17**, 5
Cameron Report
generally, **11**, 112
Cameronians
raising of, **2**, 601
Camp
water meter charges, **25**, 536
Camping site
provision of, **14**, 678
Canada
constitution—
amendments to, **5**, 307
evolution of, **5**, 304
Canals and inland waterways
abstraction of water, **19**, 1105, 1123
accommodation works, **19**, 1112
amenity and recreational facilities, **19**, 1106n
apportionment, **24**, 586
bathing, byelaws as to, **19**, 1107
bridge, negligent management, **19**, 1125
British Waterways Board, *see* BRITISH WATERWAYS BOARD

Canals and inland waterways—*continued*
byelaws, **19**, 1107
Caledonian Canal, **19**, 1103
canals—
  authorisation, **19**, 1103
  byelaws, **19**, 1107
  canal authority, duties, **21**, 382
  canal basins, maintenance of, **19**, 1122
  classification, **19**, 1110
  deterioration of banks, **19**, 1125
  independent companies, **19**, 1104
  inspection of, **19**, 1117
  nationalisation, **19**, 1103
  navigable water, as, **21**, 112
  owner, limitation of liability, **21**, 753*n*, 769, 769*n*
  pilotage, *see* PILOT; PILOTAGE
  railway construction affecting, **19**, 1024
  salvage operations, **21**, 440
  towpaths,*see* towpaths *below*
charges for use of, **19**, 1105, 1108
Clyde Canal, **19**, 1103
commercial waterways, **19**, 1110
conditions as to use, **19**, 1108
construction or alteration, **19**, 19*n*, 1109–1112
  accommodation works, **19**, 1112
  diversion, widening or narrowing, **19**, 24
  drainage works, **25**, 374
control and management, **19**, 1103, 1104
Crinan Canal, **19**, 1103
cruising waterways, **19**, 1110
dangerous goods, conveyance of, **19**, 1107
delay, liability for, **19**, 1109
diversion, **19**, 24
drainage works, **25**, 374
duty to maintain watercourse, order altering, **19**, 1119
explosives, conveyance of—
  byelaws as to, **10**, 1610, 1620
  inspections, generally, **10**, 1621
flooding, **19**, 1125
historical development, **5**, 5
inflammable substances conveyed by, **19**, 392
Inland Waterways Amenity Advisory Council, **19**, 1118, 1119
inquiries, **19**, 1116
liability, **19**, 1108
  delay, for, **19**, 1109
  injury or damage, for, **19**, 1124–1126
  negligence, for, **19**, 1109, 1124, 1125
  statutory limitation, **19**, 1126
maintenance, **19**, 1109–1112
  canal basins, of, **19**, 1122
narrowing, **19**, 24
negligence, **19**, 1124
  alleged, **19**, 1125
  liability for, **19**, 1109
obstructions, **19**, 1107
pollution of, **14**, 2079, **19**, 1125
port facilities, **19**, 1105
prior notification, **19**, 1107
private navigation rights, **19**, 1110
provisional order in connection with, **19**, 15, 26
reclassification orders, **19**, 1111, 1119
rubbish, **19**, 1107

Canals and inland waterways—*continued*
sale of water, **19**, 1105, 1123
Secretary of State for the Environment, powers, **19**, 1103, 1113–1117
sheriff court jurisdiction, **6**, 1125
special Act, **19**, 1103
statutory powers, negligence in operating, **19**, 1124, 1125
supply of water from, **19**, 1105, 1123
support of land purchased for construction, **14**, 1690
tolls, **19**, 1107
towpaths—
  included in canal, **12**, 1239
  passage on, **19**, 1107
unclassified, **19**, 1110
Union Canal, **19**, 1103
valuation for rating—
  apportionment, **24**, 586
  definitions, **24**, 584
  derating, **24**, 585
  formula, valuation by, **24**, 582, 583
    exceptions from, **24**, 583
  generally, **24**, 582
  revenue principle, **24**, 585
vessels—
  abandoned, **19**, 1120
  construction, **19**, 1107
  discharging of, **19**, 1107
  left without consent, **19**, 1121
  liability for loss or damage, **19**, 1126
  loading, **19**, 1107
  marking, **19**, 1107
  mooring, **19**, 1107
  removal of, **19**, 1120, 1121
  size, **19**, 1107
  stranded, **19**, 1120
  sunk, **19**, 1120
water—
  pollution of, **14**, 2079; **19**, 1125
  sale of, **19**, 1105, 1123
  supplying from, **19**, 1123
water sports and recreation, **19**, 1107, 1218, 1280
waterskiing, **19**, 1107
widening, **19**, 24
Cancer
advertisement of treatment for, **1**, 536
Candidate
election, *see* ELECTION
Canine specialist
unregistered person, description by, **25**, 203
Canine surgery
unregistered person, description by, **25**, 203
Cannabis
controlled drug, as, **14**, 1228
criminal behaviour, link with, **14**, 1221
cultivation of, **14**, 1246
legal policy, relaxation of, **14**, 1220
soft drug, as, **14**, 1222
Canned food
preservatives, **11**, 377
Canon law
1983 Code, **22**, 579, 586
apostolic times to the *Decretum* of Gratian (1140), **22**, 560–563

Canon law—_continued_
appellate jurisdiction, **22**, 569–574, 585
archbishoprics in Scotland—
    Glasgow, **22**, 569
    St Andrews, **22**, 569
archival material, **22**, 560, 571–573, 586
canon, meaning, **22**, 558
Clementinae, **22**, 567
Commissary Courts, canonical influence on procedure, **22**, 581
Corpus Iuris Canonici
    consolidation of writings in, **22**, 568
    judicial system for resolution of disputes, **22**, 568
Council of Trent decrees, **22**, 576
Court of Session—
    constitution of—
        Sacra Romana Rota, influence, **22**, 583
    procedure, influence, **22**, 551
decline in influence, **22**, 584
Decretals—
    books of, **22**, 566
diocesan courts—
    appeals, **22**, 568–570
        Sacra Romana Rota to, **22**, 574
    generally, **22**, 569, 570
    judge, appointment, **22**, 570
    jurisdiction, **22**, 570
dioceses—
    creation in Scotland—
        effect on jurisdiction, **22**, 569
        number of, **22**, 570
ecclesiastical precedence, **16**, 2003
ecumenical councils—
    Edict of Milan, **22**, 312, 560, 561
    promulgation of disciplinary laws, **22**, 561
establishment, surviving source material, **22**, 560
Extravagantes, **22**, 567
Gratian to Council of Trent, from, **22**, 564–575
historical source of Scots law, as, **22**, 548, 557–586
ius antiquum, **22**, 564
ius novissimum, **22**, 577
ius novum
    Gratian _Decretum_, **22**, 564, 565
legal representation, **13**, 1130, 1131
local collections of canons—
    adaptation of general canons within framework of general law, **22**, 562
    surviving documents, **22**, 562
marriage—
    influence on post-Reformation Scots law, **22**, 580, 581
    as law of pre-Reformation Scotland, **22**, 580
matrimonial causes—
    Sacra Penitentiaria Apostolica, **22**, 573, 574
    Sacra Romana Rota, **22**, 573, 574, 586
meaning, **22**, 558
nature, **22**, 558, 559
officials' courts—
    abolition, 1560, **22**, 585
    matrimonial jurisdiction transferred to Commissary Courts, **22**, 585
    restoration, 1878, **22**, 585

Canon law—_continued_
Papacy—
    independence from secular authority, **22**, 564
    policy of uniformity, **22**, 563
post-Reformation Scotland—
    indirect influences, **22**, 580, 581
Post-Tridentine—
    Codex Iuris Canonici, **22**, 578
    generally, **22**, 577–579
    Ius Novissimum, **22**, 577
    Sacrae Disciplinae Legis, **22**, 579, 586
printing, effect of invention, **22**, 577
procedural law of Scotland, influence on, **22**, 582
procedure, influence on Scots civil law, **22**, 551, 574
Protestant Revolution—
    Council of Trent, decrees, **22**, 576
relevance to development of Scots law—
    before 1560, **22**, 580
    generally, **22**, 580–586
Roman Catholic Church—
    authority of, **22**, 559
    Scottish hierarchy, restoration of, **22**, 585
    See also Papacy _above_
Roman Curia—
    administration of entire judicial system, **22**, 568, 570
    decretals of Popes, **22**, 566
Roman law—
    admixture, **22**, 549
    derivation from, **22**, 551, 554
    influence on Scots law through, **22**, 551, 554
Romano-canonical procedure—
    reception in Scots law, **22**, 551
Sacra Romana Rota
    description, **22**, 571, 574
    Manualia, **22**, 574
    Scottish litigants, estimated numbers per diocese, **22**, 574
Scottish cases in _Decretals_, **22**, 570
succession—
    testamentary, to moveable property—
        as law of pre-Reformation Scotland, **22**, 580
supreme tribunals of the Church—
    Sacra Penitentiaria Apostolica, **22**, 571, 573, 574
    Sacra Romana Rota, **22**, 571, 574, 577, 582, 583
    Segnatura Iustitiae, **22**, 571, 572
teaching in Scotland, **22**, 552, 575, 580
    See also UNIVERSITY
theology, distinct from, **22**, 563, 564
Tribunal Nationale Scoticanum.1970, **22**, 585
uniformity, Papal policy, **22**, 563
Canteen
food supplied by, **11**, 342_n_
Canton
meaning, **11**, 1617_n_
voided, **11**, 1617, 1618
Capacity
actus reus, **7**, 112
automatism, _see_ AUTOMATISM
buy, to, **20**, 816
child, of, **3**, 1202, 1211, 1215
corporations, of, **11**, 1064–1066
    active, **11**, 1065
    inactive, **11**, 1065

Capacity—*continued*
defences, generally, **7**, 112
domicile of choice, acquisition of, **17**, 203
generally, **7**, 112
incapax—
 rights of, **11**, 1075
insanity, *see* INSANITY
intoxication, *see* INTOXICATION
mens rea, **7**, 112
minor, of, **9**, 25; **10**, 1073, 1144, 1146
natural person, of, **4**, 68
non-age, *see* NON-AGE
passive rights, to have, **11**, 1075
persons, of, *see* PERSONS AND PERSONALITY
pupil, of, **10**, 1051
sell, to, **20**, 816
status, **11**, 1067
trustee, to be, **24**, 128–138
will, to make, **25**, 761
Capercailzie
game, as, **11**, 802
Game Acts, **11**, 496*n*
Game (Scotland) Act 1832..., **11**, 815
trespass in search of, **11**, 817
Capital
assets, shareholder's rights relating to, **25**, 14
concept of money central to, **14**, 1801
encroachment on by judicial factor, **24**, 261
fixed assets, not tied up in, **14**, 1016
freedom of movement within European
 Community, **10**, 149
liferenter, power to encroach to benefit, **25**, 923
limited authority to spend, **14**, 1016
redemption of, mineral properties, **25**, 139
share, conversion of, **25**, 14
sum, power to advance, **25**, 922
Capital allowances
corporation and income tax, **19**, 1314
corporation tax, **19**, 1520
first year capital, **14**, 1009
investment, **14**, 1009
landlord's fixtures, on, **19**, 1615
leisure and recreation businesses, **19**, 1321
lessor, benefit obtained by, **14**, 1011
rental variation clauses, **14**, 1056
writing-down allowance—
 introduction of, **14**, 1010
 plant and machinery, ownership of, **14**, 1013
 taxation, impact of, **14**, 1016
Capital gains tax
accrued gains, **19**, 1524
administration and collection, **19**, 1544*n*
amount chargeable, **19**, 1524
assessment of liability, **19**, 1544
beneficiaries, disposals to—
 completion of administration, **25**, 997
 death, deemed acquisition on, **25**, 996
 disclaimers, **25**, 998
 variation, **25**, 998
business reliefs, **19**, 1527
cautionary obligations, treatment of, **3**, 1002
charities exempt, **3**, 1102, 1157; **19**, 1525

Capital gain tax—*continued*
charity, exemption—
 charitable trusts, property held on, ceasing to
  be, **3**, 1157, 1158, 1160
 generally, **3**, 1102, 1157; **19**, 1525
 gifts to charities, **3**, 1159
 offshore income gains, **3**, 1158
 restrictions, **3**, 1105
clubs, liability of, **2**, 821
death, consequences on—
 assets, valuation of, **25**, 993
 deceased, liability of, **25**, 990
 executors—
  deemed acquisition by, **25**, 991
  property not acquired by, **25**, 992
death, subsequent disposal of assets, **19**, 1526
deceased, liability of, **25**, 990
discrimination, **12**, 86
divorce or separation, transfers following, **10**,
 1000–1002
donations, **8**, 653
executors—
 administration, gains realised during—
  exemptions, **25**, 995
  liability for tax, **25**, 994
  reliefs, **25**, 995
 capital gains realised by, **19**, 1636
 deemed acquisition by, **25**, 991
 property not acquired by, **25**, 992
 realisation by, **19**, 1636
exemptions, **19**, 1525
 annual exempt amounts, **19**, 1524
financial year, **22**, 811
grant of right to fell and remove timber, **11**, 650
held-over gain relief, intellectual property, **18**,
 1600
husband and wife, **10**, 892
inflation, allowance for, **19**, 1528
inheritance tax—
 interaction with, **19**, 1600
 value of asset determined for, **25**, 55
intellectual property rights, payments in respect
 of, **18**, 1600
legal rights, on, **25**, 797
liferenter, on death of, **19**, 1641
losses set against gains, **19**, 1524
main residence exemption, **19**, 1525
maintenance payments and transfers of property
 on divorce—
  after separation, **10**, 1001
  assets other than dwelling house, **10**, 1001
  generally, **10**, 1000
  matrimonial home, **10**, 1002
market value, meaning, **25**, 55
minor's property, **19**, 1583
occupational pension scheme—
 approved, **21**, 1285
 exempt approved, **21**, 1315
ordinarily resident in United Kingdom, persons,
 19, 1529
partnerships, **19**, 1587
 asset-owning ratio, change in, **16**, 1134
 assets, disposal, **16**, 1124, 1133
 composition, change in, **16**, 1135

Capital gains tax—*continued*
partnerships—*continued*
  roll-over relief, **16**, 1133
  share, gift or bequest, **16**, 1124, 1136
professional sportsmen, **19**, 1309
property, transfer of, **19**, 1598, 1600
public bodies exempt, **19**, 1525
pupil's property, **19**, 1582
rate, **19**, 1524
realised gains, **19**, 1524
resident in United Kingdom, persons, **19**, 1529
roll-over relief—
  intellectual property, **18**, 1600
  partnerships, **16**, 1133
scientific research associations, **3**, 1165
sheriff court jurisdiction, **6**, 1109
spouses, disposals between, **19**, 1574
timber, grant of right to fell or remove, **11**, 650
valuations for, **6**, 1141, 1149; **25**, 55
woodlands, **11**, 649; **19**, 1510
Capital punishment
attempted murder, **17**, 562
competent sentence, **17**, 796
murder, **17**, 562
public prosecutor, concurrence of, **17**, 528
sheriff, judicial functions of, **17**, 511, 516
treason, **7**, 567; **17**, 562
Capital Redemption contract
Financial Services Act, application, **12**, 807
Capital transfer tax
Court of Session jurisdiction, **6**, 624, 924; **25**, 56
donations, **8**, 651
entails, **20**, 242
inheritance tax, replacement by, **6**, 624*n*; **25**, 56
  See also INHERITANCE TAX
Captain of the Gentlemen-at-Arms
office of, **7**, 774
Captain of the Guard
office of, **7**, 800
Capture
ship, of, *see* PRIZE
Car
See MOTOR VEHICLE; PRIVATE HIRE CAR
Car park
valuation for rating, **24**, 587, 614
Car-sharing arrangement
exception from public service vehicle definition, **20**, 488
Car tax
See MOTOR VEHICLE (excise duty)
Caravan
action for recovery of possession, **18**, 159
assured tenancy, **13**, 615
caravan sites, *see* CARAVAN SITE
generally, **24**, 588
heritable and moveable distinguished, **24**, 589
holiday rental of, **14**, 1002
lease, **13**, 194
matrimonial home, as, **10**, 857
meaning, **23**, 328
mobile homes, VAT zero-rating, **7**, 1453
site charge, housing benefit, **21**, 1105
tow, under, **23**, 357

Caravan—*continued*
trailer, meaning, **23**, 357
valuation for rating, **24**, 589, 590
Caravan site
code of practice, **23**, 356
compulsory acquisition, displacement from, **5**, 189
crofting counties, **1**, 835
entry, powers of, **23**, 344
existing, special provisions as to, **23**, 342
licence—
  alteration of, **23**, 337
  circumstances where not required, **23**, 332
  conditions of, **23**, 334, 336
  duration of, **23**, 338
  penalties, **23**, 331
  procedure on application for, **23**, 333
  relevant local authorities, **23**, 330
  requirement to obtain, **23**, 329
  transfer of, **23**, 339
  transmission of, by operation of law, **23**, 340
local authority—
  provided by, **14**, 678; **23**, 343
  relevant, **23**, 330
meaning, **23**, 101*n*, 146*n*, 328
model standards, **23**, 335
occupier—
  meaning, **23**, 329*n*
  potential vicarious responsibility of, **23**, 341
  residential, protection of—
    arbiter, jurisdiction of, **23**, 354
    eviction, against, **23**, 347
    eviction order, suspension of, **23**, 3, 48
    generally, **23**, 345, 350
    harassment, against, **23**, 347
    mandatory implied terms, **23**, 352
    procedure, **23**, 353
    succession in title, **23**, 355
    written statement, **23**, 351
permitted development, **23**, 146, 157
planning permission—
  development not requiring, **23**, 101
  requirement to obtain, **23**, 329
problem, **23**, 326
protected—
  meaning, **23**, 345
  minimum standards for, **23**, 349
  owner, meaning, **23**, 352*n*
rating, **23**, 358; **24**, 502, 588
remedy, **23**, 327
residential contract, notice to terminate, **23**, 346
sheriff court jurisdiction, **6**, 1099; **23**, 354
special tenancy, **23**, 341, 345
standards—
  minimum, for protected site, **23**, 349
  model, **23**, 335
Carcases
disposal of, **11**, 317
importation and landing, **11**, 317
inspection of, **11**, 413
Care, duty of
abortion, failed, **15**, 305, 306
accountants, **15**, 278

Care, duty of—_continued_
actual—
  generally, **15**, 259, 268
  neighbourhood, **15**, 268, 269
  proximity, **15**, 269, 278, 279
  reasonable foreseeability, **15**, 269, 278
    actual pursuer, **15**, 270
    circumstances leading to harm, **15**, 272
    type of harm suffered, **15**, 271
affront, **15**, 284
ascertainment of role of person owing, **11**, 1018
bankers, **15**, 278
breach of duty—
  availability of precautions, **15**, 369
  burden of proof, **15**, 376
  common practice, **15**, 370–372
  cost of precautions, **15**, 368
  defender, position, **15**, 365
  employer's liability, **15**, 371
  foreseeability, **15**, 363
  generally, **15**, 362
  inconvenience of precautions, **15**, 368
  probability of injury, **15**, 366
  professional negligence, **15**, 372, 374, 375
  'reasonable man' test, **15**, 362, 363, 364, 370
  res ipsa loquitur, **15**, 376–378
  seriousness of injury, **15**, 367
  skill, activities requiring, **15**, 373
  standard of care, **15**, 363
    determination, **15**, 364
building contract, _ex delicto_, arising, **3**, 3
carelessness, **15**, 256
common law, **14**, 1616
contract, co-existing with, **15**, 587
damage—
  property, to, liability, **15**, 276
  remoteness of, _see_ DAMAGE
defect to property, causing, liability, **15**, 276
defender—
  duty of, **14**, 2076
  standard of care expected of, **15**, 365
delict, and, **15**, 255
distress, **15**, 284
doctor, duty of, **15**, 299, 303
Donoghue v Stevenson, decision in, **15**, 258, 263, 268, 285
economic loss—
  defective property, non-liability for, **15**, 276
  derivative, **15**, 273, 276
  development of law, **15**, 274
  pure, **15**, 273
    Hedley Byrne liability, **15**, 274, 277, 278
    Junior Books liability, **15**, 279
    non-liability for, **15**, 273, 274
      defective property, **15**, 276
      exceptions to rule, **15**, 274, 277–283
  secondary—
    development of law, **15**, 274
    meaning, **15**, 274
    non-liability for, **15**, 275
employee, duty of, **9**, 82
employer's liability, _see_ EMPLOYER
extent, generally, **15**, 362
financial adviser, duty of, **15**, 278, 300

Care, duty of—_continued_
foreseeability, **15**, 269, 271, 278, 362, 363
  actual pursuer, of, **15**, 270
  circumstances leading to harm, **15**, 272
  determining standard of care, **15**, 363, 364
  remoteness of damage, **15**, 383, 384
  type of harm suffered, **15**, 271
fright, **15**, 284
generally, **11**, 1015, 1020; **15**, 255
guardian, of, **15**, 299
harbour authority, duty of, **11**, 1326
Hedley Byrne & Co Ltd v Heller & Partners Ltd, **15**, 274, 277, 278, 300
historical background, **15**, 257
injury, remoteness of damage, _see_ DAMAGE
insurance brokers, **15**, 278
judicial factor, duty of, **24**, 248
landowner's, **18**, 184
lessee, obligations of, **14**, 1047
liability, generally, **15**, 362
manufacturers' duty of, **6**, 37
meaning, **15**, 255, 259
mines and quarries, in, **14**, 1617
negligence, and, **15**, 255, 256
negligent—
  defamation, **15**, 280
  misstatement by defender, **15**, 278, 279, 280
'neighbourhood principle', **15**, 257
nervous shock—
  anxiety, **15**, 287
  defamation, **15**, 284
  definition, **15**, 287
  derivative emotional harm, **15**, 285
  elements, **15**, 287
  foreseeability, **15**, 289, 291, 292, 293, 295
  fright, **15**, 285, 287
  generally, **15**, 284, 288
  McLoughlin v O'Brian, decision in, **15**, 292, 293
  method by which inflicted, **15**, 292, 293
  normal emotional reactions, **15**, 287
  physical injury, arising from, **15**, 285
  physical threat to pursuer, **15**, 289
    where no physical threat, **15**, 290–294
  primary victim, relationship to pursuer, **15**, 292, 293, 294
  proof, **15**, 287
  provable illness, **15**, 287
  proximity, **15**, 291, 292, 293, 295
  pure emotional harm, **15**, 286
  real and substantial, harm must be, **15**, 287
  sudden shock, harm must result from, **15**, 287
  verbal injury, **15**, 284
notional—
  generally, **15**, 259, 260, 268
  meaning, **15**, 259, 260
  no notional duty, cases of, **15**, 261
occupiers' liability, _see_ OCCUPIER'S LIABILITY
omissions—
  acts and, **15**, 296
  assumption of responsibility, **15**, 300
  control over safety of another, **15**, 298
  danger, creation by defender, **15**, 297

Care, duty of—*continued*
omissions—*continued*
  doctor, duty of—
    duty to inform, **15**, 303
    generally, **15**, 299
  financial adviser, duty of, **15**, 300
  foreseeability, **15**, 296, 298, 301
  liability, establishment, **15**, 296
  proximity, **15**, 298, 301, 304
  pure omission, **15**, 296, 304
  rescue, duty to, **15**, 304
  special relationship between pursuer and defender, **15**, 299, 300
  third party, harm by, failure to prevent, **15**, 301, 302
  trustee, duty of, **15**, 299
  whether duty to avoid, **15**, 296
parent, duty of, **15**, 299, 304
private law, in, **11**, 1017
probability of injury, **15**, 366
professional liability, *see* PROFESSIONAL LIABILITY
professional or quasi-professional services, **15**, 278
rail passengers, responsibility for safety of, **15**, 298
'reasonable man' test, **15**, 362, 363, 364, 370
relational economic loss and negligence, **15**, 586–593
remoteness of damage, and, **15**, 257
responsibility, assumption of, **15**, 277
road traffic, application to, **20**, 401
seriousness of injury, **15**, 367
ship's master, liability, **15**, 298, 304
skill, activities requiring, **15**, 373
solicitor, duty of, **15**, 278, 300
special, **11**, 1021, 1022
special skill or knowledge of defender, pursuer reliant upon, **15**, 274, 277, 278
sporting or recreational activities, **19**, 1241, 1242
sterilisation, failed, **15**, 305
surveyors, **15**, 278
tenant's obligation to use care, **13**, 269
threshold—
  Anns, decision in, **15**, 263, 264
  'fair, just and reasonable' test—
    effect, **15**, 266
    generally, **15**, 265
  generally, **15**, 259, 268
  meaning, **15**, 262
  no threshold duty, cases of, **15**, 267
  policy question, as, **15**, 263
trustee, duty of, **15**, 299
unborn or unconceived foetus, **11**, 1032, 1037
underwriting agents, **15**, 278
vicarious liability, **11**, 1056
wrongful birth, **15**, 305
wrongful pregnancy, **15**, 305
Care, standard of
common practice, **15**, 370–372
cost of precautions, **15**, 368
defender, position of, **15**, 365
determination, **15**, 364
employer's liability, **15**, 371
foreseeability and, **15**, 363, 364
generally, **15**, 362
inconvenience of precautions, **15**, 368

Care, standard of—*continued*
practical precautions, availability, **15**, 369
probability of injury, **15**, 366
professional negligence, **15**, 372, 374, 375
'reasonable man' test, **15**, 362, 363, 364, 370
seriousness of injury, **15**, 367
skill, activities requiring, **15**, 373
Care worker
children's hearing, attendance at, **3**, 1327
Careers services
education authorities' duties—
  collection and furnishing of information, **8**, 960
  future role, **8**, 964
  generally, **8**, 958
  part-time students, **8**, 958
  records to be kept, **8**, 961
  vocational advice, **8**, 958
    records of, **8**, 961
    summaries of, **8**, 962
  who may be assisted, **8**, 958, 959
future of, **8**, 964
meaning, **8**, 958
Secretary of State's powers, **8**, 963
Careless cycling
warning or notice of intended prosecution, **20**, 446
Careless driving
charge of, **20**, 413, 414
consideration for other road users, driving without, **20**, 414
death caused by—
  drink or drugs, under influence of, **20**, 416
    obligatory disqualification following conviction, **20**, 453
disqualification following, **20**, 414, 453
drink or drugs, under influence of, **20**, 416
  See also ALCOHOLIC LIQUOR; DRUGS
due care and attention, driving without, **20**, 414
licence, endorsement following, **20**, 414, 456
negligence, **7**, 81
penalties for, **20**, 414
prosecution, warning or notice of intended, **20**, 446
Road Traffic Act 1988, under, **20**, 416*n*
signal, giving misleading, **20**, 414
skids, **20**, 414
what constitutes, **20**, 414
Carelessness
fraud, whether constituting, **11**, 728
negligence and, **15**, 255, 256
Carer
aged less than eighteen, income support, **21**, 1065, 1067
invalid care allowance, *see* INVALID CARE ALLOWANCE
Cargo
abandoned *sine spe revertendi* or *sine spe recuperandi*, **21**, 511
aircraft, of, whether salvage subject, **21**, 439
arrest of, **8**, 248, 322, 328; **21**, 482*n*
arrestment, salvage actions, **21**, 482*n*
bill of lading, *see* BILL OF LADING
bottomry bond, **13**, 1759
care of, Hague-Visby Rules, **21**, 594, 594*n*

Cargo—*continued*
cargo ship, *see* SHIP
cargo-worthiness, *see* worthiness *below*
carriage by sea, *see* SEA, CARRIAGE BY
charterparty, contract by, *see* CHARTERPARTY
container, carriage in—
  bill of lading, express terms, **21**, 546
  generally, **21**, 526
damage to—
  collision, caused by, **21**, 583, 584
    'both to blame clause', **21**, 584*n*
  consequential loss, **21**, 716
  exclusion or limitation of liability, **21**, 547
  freight, **21**, 657, 657*n*
  general average, **21**, 708
    See also GENERAL AVERAGE
  generally, **21**, 383
  notification, **21**, 598
dangerous goods, *see* SEA, CARRIAGE BY (dangerous
  goods)
deck—
  bill of lading, **21**, 589*n*
  express terms, **21**, 546, 546*n*
  Hague-Visby Rules, **21**, 587, 589*n*
  jettison, general average, **21**, 708
  regulations, power to make, **21**, 230
  timber, **21**, 230
delivery—
  delay—
    as breach of contract, **21**, 716
    consequential loss, **21**, 716
  failure to take, **21**, 546
    back freight, **21**, 661
derelict, **21**, 511
destruction, loss resulting from, limitation of
  liability, **21**, 756
discharge, Hague-Visby Rules, **21**, 594
expansion during transit, calculation of freight,
  21, 654*n*
failure to load, **21**, 717
failure to provide, **21**, 717
failure to take delivery, **21**, 546, 661
  back freight, **21**, 661
flotsam, jetsam or lagan, classed as, **21**, 511
formerly on board ship, **21**, 511
freight, *see* FREIGHT
general, **21**, 524, 524*n*
general average, **21**, 708
  See also GENERAL AVERAGE
general ship, carriage by, *see* GENERAL SHIP
grain, carriage of, safety regulations, **21**, 232
handling, Hague-Visby Rules, **21**, 594
harmless, loss resulting from rendering, limitation
  of liability, **21**, 756
inherent defect, quality or vice—
  liability of carrier, **21**, 542, 552
  wastage or other loss or damage resulting from,
    21, 603
insufficiently packed, **21**, 553
jettison, general average, **21**, 708
leading marks, **21**, 595
liability of carrier—
  contracting out, non-negotiable receipts, **21**, 602
  Hague-Visby Rules, *see* HAGUE-VISBY RULES

Cargo—*continued*
liability of carrier—*continued*
  inherent vice, where, **21**, 542, 552
  limitation, in respect of cargo claims, **21**, 753*n*
  prior to loading, **21**, 601
  subsequent to discharge, **21**, 601
lighters, discharge into, **21**, 560, 632, 632*n*
  laytime, **21**, 670*n*
live—
  bill of lading, express terms, **21**, 546
  Hague-Visby Rules, **21**, 587
loading—
  Hague-Visby Rules, **21**, 594
  improper, **21**, 206
  laytime and demurrage, *see* DEMURRAGE;
    LAYTIME
  load lines, **21**, 230, 230*n*
  overloading, **21**, 206
    damages for negligence, **21**, 719*n*
  Plimsoll lines, **21**, 230, 230*n*
  unsafe, **21**, 206
loss of—
  exclusion or limitation of liability, **21**, 547
  general average, *see* GENERAL AVERAGE
  generally, **21**, 383
maritime lien over, **21**, 479
marks, insufficient or inadequate, loss or damage
  as result of, **21**, 603
mate's receipt, **21**, 562
mixed—
  cargos which have become, **21**, 632
  generally, **21**, 526, 526*n*
nature and value of, declaration by shipper before
  shipment, **21**, 606
owner of—
  breach of contract by, **21**, 717
  organisations designed to promote interests of
    owners, **21**, 118
packing—
  defective, liability of carrier, **21**, 542, 553
  insufficient, loss or damage as result of, **21**, 603
particulars supplied by shipper, **21**, 597
persons on board, loss or damage caused to, **21**,
  321, 325
property rights in, danger to, salvage, **21**, 442
re-loading costs, general average, **21**, 710
receiver of wreck, delivery to, **21**, 513
removal, loss resulting from, limitation of
  liability, **21**, 756
respondentia, **13**, 1759
sale by master of voyage charterparty, **21**, 629
salvage—
  generally, **21**, 434, 436
  Lloyd's Standard Form of Salvage Agreement,
    21, 484
salvage operation, put at risk by, **21**, 447
seaworthiness in relation to, **21**, 614, 614*n*
shipowners' lien—
  breach of contract, where, **21**, 719
  demurrage, **21**, 686, 686*n*, 688
  general average contribution, **21**, 711
ships' mortgage not covering, **21**, 176
shrinkage in transit, calculation of freight, **21**,
  654*n*

Cargo—*continued*
stevedores loading and unloading, liability, **21**, 560, 560n
stowage, *see* STOWAGE
time charterparty, express terms, **21**, 640, 643
transhipment, voyage charterparty, **21**, 629, 630
unloading—
    laytime and demurrage, *see* DEMURRAGE; LAYTIME
    voyage charterparty, **21**, 632, 634–637
valuation—
    assessment of salvage award, in, **21**, 469n
    generally, **21**, 606
voyage charterparty—
    bagging bulk, liability for costs of, **21**, 632n
    damage caused by defect in ship's equipment, **21**, 632
    duty to protect, **21**, 630
    express terms, **21**, 618
    generally, **21**, 624–626, 624n
    liability for care of cargo, **21**, 628
    mixed, cargos which have become, **21**, 632
    owner failing to land or take delivery of cargo, **21**, 632, 634
    owner failing to make entry, **21**, 634
    person entitled to delivery, **21**, 633
    sale of cargo, master's powers, **21**, 629
    salvage services rendered to, **21**, 630
    shipowner's lien, preservation and discharge of, for freight, **21**, 635–637
    transhipment, **21**, 629, 630
    unloading—
        equipment, responsibility for provision of, **21**, 632
        Merchant Shipping Act 1894, under, **21**, 634–637
    where cargo cannot be landed, **21**, 632
weight, calculation of freight, **21**, 654, 654n
worthiness—
    generally, **21**, 614n
    time charterparty—
        express terms, **21**, 640, 644
        voyage charterparty, **21**, 618
wreck, classed as, **21**, 511
Cargo liner
meaning, **21**, 524
Caricature
defamatory, **15**, 483
Carnegie Trust for the Universities of Scotland
establishment, **8**, 1003
purpose of, **8**, 1003
special provisions, **8**, 837
Carnival
See PLEASURE FAIR
Carport
exemptions from building regulations, **3**, 209
Carriage
air, by, *see* AIR, CARRIAGE BY
animals, of—
    air and sea, by, **2**, 203
        express terms in bill of lading, **21**, 546
    cruelty in course of, **2**, 241
    feeding and watering, **2**, 202

Carriage—*continued*
animals, of—*continued*
    records in respect of, **2**, 204
    road and rail, by, **2**, 202
    vehicles etc, construction, **2**, 202
bus, by, *see* BUS; PUBLIC SERVICE VEHICLE
carrier, *see* CARRIER
carrier's lien, **3**, 629, 672, 700
cash on delivery, goods consigned, **3**, 629
consignee—
    acceptance by, **3**, 605
    air, carriage by, rights, **3**, 747, 749
    Cash on Delivery terms, payment by, **3**, 629
    delivery to—
        delivery not taken, where, **3**, 635
        domestic carriage of goods, **3**, 633
        duty on taking delivery, **3**, 634
        generally, **3**, 605, 633
        implied contractual liablity, **3**, 606
    freight payable by, **3**, 629
    insolvent, stoppage in transit where, **3**, 641–644
consignment note, *see* CONSIGNMENT NOTE
consignor—
    air, carriage by—
        air waybill, **3**, 746
        disposal, rights of, **3**, 748
        rights, generally, **3**, 747
        stoppage in transit, **3**, 748
    carriage by land, contract of—
        conduct of consignor, **3**, 608
        generally, **3**, 601
    charge, carrier's, liability to pay, **3**, 629
    Convention on the Contract for the International Carriage of Goods by Road (CMR)—
        disposal, rights of, **3**, 650
        responsibilities under, **3**, 648
        stoppage in transit, rights of, **3**, 650
    international carriage of goods by road—
        liability, **3**, 655
    private carrier, contractual relations with, **3**, 619
    stoppage in transit, **3**, 641–644, 650, 748
contract, **3**, 684
air, carriage by, **3**, 740
carrier, *see* CARRIER
charge for carriage, **3**, 629
conditions of carriage, **3**, 615
consignee, *see* consignee *above*
consignor, *see* consignor *above*
contractual liability—
    express, **3**, 606
    implied, **3**, 606
Convention on the Contract for the International Carriage of Goods by Road (CMR), **3**, 646ff
domestic carriage—
    goods by rail, **3**, 695
    goods by road, **3**, 619
    passengers by rail, **3**, 709
    passengers by road, **3**, 670
frustration, **3**, 606
gratuitous carriage, **3**, 616
Hague Rules, *see* HAGUE RULES

Carriage—*continued*
contract—*continued*
  Hague-Visby Rules, *see* HAGUE-VISBY RULES
  insurance of goods in transit, **3**, 628
  international carriage—
    goods by rail, **3**, 704
    goods by road, **3**, 646
    passengers by rail, **3**, 726
    passengers by road, **3**, 687
  jus quaesitum tertio, **15**, 847
  land, carriage by—
    generally, **3**, 601
    locatio mercium vehendarum, as, **3**, 601
    locatio operis faciendi, as, **3**, 601
    nature of, **3**, 601
  limitation of liability by, **3**, 614
  modern division of subject, **3**, 617
  onerous carriage, **3**, 616
  passenger, *see* PASSENGER
  sources of law, **3**, 602
  ticket, *see* TICKET
  unfair contract terms, **3**, 619, 619*n*, 701
crew—
  competent and careful, carrier's liability to provide, **3**, 606, 615, 626
  international carriage of goods by road, **3**, 646, 660
  wilful misconduct or default by, CMR contracts, **3**, 660
damnum fatale, loss attributable to, **3**, 608
driver—
  competent and careful, carrier's liability to provide, **3**, 606, 615, 625
  contract carriage, of, **3**, 684
  domestic carriage of passengers by road, **3**, 676–680
  EU safety code, **3**, 735
  international carriage of goods by road, **3**, 646
  rest periods and time limits for driving, **3**, 626, 735
  train, **3**, 721
  wilful misconduct or default by, **3**, 660
EU legislation—
  transport policy—
    competition rules, **3**, 732
    generally, **3**, 731
    permits, quota, **3**, 734
    prior consultation, systems of, **3**, 731
    rate bracket system, **3**, 733
    rest periods, **3**, 735
    safety code, **3**, 735
fare—
  common carrier's, **3**, 672
  proper fare in legal tender, refusal to pay, **3**, 673
forwarding agent, **3**, 618
goods, of—
  air, carriage by—
    air waybill, **3**, 746
    destruction, loss or damage to, **3**, 751
      contributory negligence, where, **3**, 754
    disposal, consignor's right of, **3**, 748
    stoppage in transit, **3**, 748
  Carriage of Goods by Sea Act 1924 ..., **21**, 586

Carriage—*continued*
goods, of—*continued*
  damage to—
    articles within Carriers Act 1830 ..., **3**, 610
    British Rail, by, **3**, 697
    carrier, presumption against, **3**, 606
    cause, proof, **3**, 608
    consignee's duty on delivery, **3**, 634
    damnum fatale, loss attributable to, **3**, 608
    edictal liability, **3**, 608
    gratuitous carrier, where, **3**, 616
    inevitable accident, **3**, 606, 608
    international carriage—
      rail, **3**, 707
      road, **3**, 653, 654, 656–667
    limitation of liability, **3**, 609, 610, 611
      excluded cases, **3**, 613
      special contract, by, **3**, 614
    nature of goods, due to, **3**, 654
    private carrier, liability, **3**, 615
    proof of value, **3**, 608
    unusual or unexpected causes, where, **3**, 606
  dangerous goods—
    consignor's duty as to, **3**, 623, 648
    domestic carriage by rail, **3**, 698
    justifiable refusal to carry, **3**, 604
  definition, Hague-Visby Rules, **21**, 587, 587*n*, 588
  delivery—
    consignee's duty on taking, **3**, 634
    Contract for the International Carriage of Goods by Road (CMR), **3**, 651, 652, 661
    domestic carriage by road, **3**, 633
    misdelivery, **3**, 633
    not taken, where, **3**, 635
  fragile goods—
    fragile nature concealed from carrier, **3**, 608
    higher carrying charges for, **3**, 629
  inherent vice, **3**, 606, 608, 654
  labelling—
    consignor's duty, **3**, 621, 706
    international carriage of goods by rail, **3**, 706
  loading—
    carrier's liability, **3**, 606
    consignor, by, **3**, 622, 654
    goods tendered too early or too late, **3**, 604
    vehicle fully loaded, where, **3**, 604
  loss—
    air, carriage by, **3**, 751
    articles within Carriers Act 1830), **3**, 610
    British Rail, by, **3**, 697
    cause, proof, **3**, 608
    gratuitous carrier, where, **3**, 616
    international carriage—
      rail, **3**, 707
      road, **3**, 653, 654, 656–667
    limitation of liability, **3**, 609, 610, 611
    nature of goods, due to, **3**, 654
    private carrier, liability, **3**, 615
    proof of value, **3**, 608
  misdelivery, **3**, 633, 640
    British Rail, by, **3**, 697
  packing—
    carrier's liability, **3**, 606

Carriage—*continued*
goods, of—*continued*
packing—*continued*
    consignor's duty, **3**, 621, 648, 654, 706
    inadequate, **3**, 604, 605, 608
    international carriage by rail, **3**, 706
    perishable goods—
        carrier's duty as to, **3**, 624
        consignor's duty as to, **3**, 624
        deterioration, **3**, 608
        higher carrying charges for, **3**, 629
        international carriage by rail, **3**, 707
        international carriage by road, **3**, 669
    stowage—
        consignor, by, **3**, 622, 654
        responsibility for, **3**, 622
    valuable goods—
        articles within Carriers Act 1830 ..., **3**, 610
        declaration of value, **3**, 611, 612, 657
        increased charge for carriage of, **3**, 629
        notice, **3**, 611
        justifiable refusal to carry, **3**, 604
    weather, protection from, **3**, 622
gratuitous, **3**, 616
limitation of actions—
    air, carriage by, **16**, 2200
    generally, **16**, 2134
    rail, carriage by, **16**, 2201
    road, carriage by—
        goods, **16**, 2203
        luggage, **16**, 2202
        passengers, **16**, 2202
    sea, carriage by—
        goods, **16**, 2205
        luggage, **16**, 2204
        passengers, **16**, 2204
locatio conductio rei, contract of, **3**, 601
locatio mercium vehendarum, contract of, **3**, 601
locatio operis faciendi, **3**, 601
luggage, *see* LUGGAGE
onerous, **3**, 616
passengers, *see* PASSENGER
rail, by, *see* RAILWAYS
road, by, *see* ROAD (carriage by)
route—
    carrier's duty as to, **3**, 630
    international carriage of goods by rail, **3**, 706
    terminus—
        no fixed, **3**, 603
        outwith jurisdiction, where, **3**, 603
sea, by, *see* SEA, CARRIAGE BY
speed, contractual liability to carry with reasonable, **3**, 606
stoppage in transit—
    air, carriage by, **3**, 748
    Convention on the Contract for International Carriage of Goods by Road (CMR), **3**, 650
    rescission and resale by seller, **3**, 644
    unpaid seller's right of, **3**, 641–644
taxi, *see* TAXI
unloading, sender or consignee, by, **3**, 654
Carriage by air
See AIR, CARRIAGE BY

Carriage by sea
See SEA, CARRIAGE BY
Carriage of goods
See CARRIAGE
Carriageway
division of, **20**, 660
meaning, **14**, 405; **20**, 501, 610
See also ROAD
Carrick, Earl of
heir to Crown as, **7**, 704, 704*n*, 786
Carrier
act of God, not liable for, **21**, 603
air, carriage by—
    consignee, duty to, **3**, 749
    liability—
        cargo or baggage, destruction, loss or damage, **3**, 751
        death of passenger, **3**, 750
        delay, **3**, 752
        exclusion, **3**, 753
        generally, **3**, 747
        limitation—
            contributory negligence, where, **3**, 754
            generally, **3**, 755, 756
            more than one carrier, where, **3**, 757
            prescription, **3**, 759
            time limits, **3**, 758
        personal injury of passenger, **3**, 750
British Railways Board, position of, **3**, 695
charge—
    Cash on Delivery terms, **3**, 629
    consignor's liability to pay, **3**, 629
common, **21**, 543
domestic carriage—
    goods by road, **3**, 619
    passengers by road, **3**, 670
duty of care, **3**, 670
fares, **3**, 672
    lien for, **3**, 672
goods, **3**, 604
liability—
    articles within Carriers Act 1830 ..., **3**, 610
    contractual, **3**, 606
    edictal, **3**, 608
    extent, **3**, 607
    limitation, **3**, 609, 610, 611
        excluded cases, **3**, 613
        special contract, by, **3**, 614
    when discharged, **3**, 605
    when incurred, **3**, 605
meaning, **3**, 603
not bound to treat all customers equally, **3**, 629
offer to carry, **3**, 603, 604
passenger, *see* PASSENGER
principles applicable to, **3**, 604
private carrier distinguished, **3**, 603
public service vehicle, *see* PUBLIC SERVICE VEHICLE
refusal to carry, justifiable and unjustifiable, **3**, 604
route terminus, **3**, 603
strict liability, **3**, 602
taxi, *see* TAXI
ticket, issue of, **3**, 672, 688

Carrier—*continued*
contract carriage, **3**, 684
Convention on the Contract for the International
    Carriage of Goods by Road (CMR), **3**, 646,
    649
custodier, when becoming, **3**, 635
definition, Hague-Visby Rules, **21**, 587, 587*n*
delay in transit—
    duty as to, **3**, 632
    liability, **3**, 636–639
delivery to—
    generally, **20**, 861, 878
    place of, **3**, 620
    responsibility, generally, **3**, 620
dispatch, duty as to, **3**, 632
duty of care—
    conractual, **3**, 601
    ex lege, **3**, 601
    vehicle safety, **3**, 674
exceptions in favour of, Hague-Visby Rules, **21**,
    603
explosives regulations, exemptions from, **10**, 1589
firearms and ammunition, exemptions in regard
    to, **10**, 1534
forwarding agent, relationship with, **3**, 618
general ship, carriage by, *see* GENERAL SHIP
gratuitous, **3**, 616
haulage contractor, **3**, 619
indemnification by shipper, **21**, 597
international, passenger of, **16**, 1205, 1206, 1238
land, carriage by, **3**, 601
liability—
    Athens Convention, under, **21**, 730, 733
    limitation, **21**, 603, 605–611, 753*n*
    loss of or damage to goods carried, for, **3**, 602,
        605–609
        international carriage of goods by road, **3**,
            653, 654
    personal injury or death of passenger, **3**, 683,
        689
    strict, **3**, 602
        basis in English law, **21**, 544
        basis in Scots law, **21**, 543
lien, **3**, 629, 672, 700; **13**, 95; **20**, 77
local, **3**, 619
meaning, **21**, 727*n*
misdelivery by, **3**, 633, 640
onerous carriage, **3**, 616
performing—
    liability, **21**, 730
    meaning, **21**, 727*n*
private, **21**, 543
    common carrier distinguished, **3**, 603
    conditions of carriage, **3**, 615
    consignor, contractual relations with, **3**, 619
    discrimination by, **3**, 615
    domestic carriage—
        goods by road, **3**, 619
        passengers by road, **3**, 670
    driver, competence and trustworthiness, **3**, 615
    duty of care, **3**, 670
    liability, **3**, 606, 615
    meaning, **3**, 603
    passenger, *see* PASSENGER

Carrier—*continued*
private—*continued*
    request to carry, whether bound to accept, **3**, 615
    roadworthiness of vehicle, **3**, 615
route, duty as to, **3**, 630
stoppage in transit, **20**, 878, 879
stowage, responsibility for, **3**, 622
strict liability, **15**, 144
    Carriers Act 1830, effect, **15**, 146
    common carrier, **15**, 144, 145
        meaning, **15**, 145
    consignor personally barred, where, **15**, 145
    contractual limitation, **15**, 146
    damage unexplained, where, **15**, 145
    damnum fatale, loss due to, **15**, 145
    defences, **15**, 145
        burden of proof, **15**, 145
    exclusion of certain articles, **15**, 146
    hire, carriage must be for, **15**, 145
    inevitable accident, loss due to, **15**, 145
    inherent vice in thing carried, loss due to, **15**,
        145
    land, carrier on, **15**, 144
    packing faulty, where, **15**, 145
    safe carriage of goods, for, **15**, 145
    shipmaster, **15**, 144
    value of goods, duty to declare, **15**, 146
sub-contractor, **3**, 631
    wilful misconduct or default by, CMR
        contracts, **3**, 660
successive carriers, where, **3**, 608
    international carriage of goods by road, **3**, 667
wrongful acceptance by carrier, **3**, 620
Carrier or custodier of goods
insurable interest in goods carried, **12**, 852
Cartel
aggregated rebates, **4**, 1146, 1373
crisis, **4**, 1394
Cartoon
defamatory, **15**, 483
Cartouche
device displayed on, **11**, 1613
Cartridges
blank, **10**, 1510
explosives, as, **10**, 1586
filling—
    licensing exemptions, **10**, 1620
    private use, for, **10**, 1618
private use, for, **10**, 1618
Case law
casebooks, **17**, 116
international law, as source of, **19**, 646
Scots law founded on principles, **11**, 1011
See also JUDICIAL PRECEDENT
Cash advance
See LOAN
Cash and carry
sale by, passing of property, **18**, 630
Cash credit bond and disposition in security
former competency, **20**, 130
object of, **20**, 131
Cash on delivery
goods consigned, **3**, 629
meaning, **16**, 1904*n*

Cash withdrawal card
functions, **4**, 269
Casset Seal
See CACHET SEAL
Casual water
See WATER
Casualties
See FEUDAL LAW
Casus omissus
not to be supplied by courts, **12**, 1107
Catchment area
See SCHOOL
Catechisms
copyright, **18**, 1002
Catering
food and drink supplied in course of, VAT, **7**, 1445
late hours, licensing of, **14**, 119, 564
Catholic security
rights of catholic creditor, **20**, 253
Cats
boarding establishment, **14**, 524
See also ANIMAL; VETERINARY PRACTICE
Cattle
diseases, *see* ANIMAL HEALTH
exportation of, **2**, 227
footpath, footway or cycle track, on, **20**, 706
inspection of, **9**, 492; **11**, 444, 444n.11.445
operations on, **2**, 246
plague, slaughter in case of, **2**, 197
public performances, in, **2**, 269
slaughter of, **14**, 2083
stray, **18**, 547n
trespass by, *see* ANIMAL
watering, **14**, 2079
servitude right, **18**, 469
Cattle grid
bridges and, **20**, 669
bypass or gate at, **20**, 669
gate, replacement of, **20**, 669
notice of proposed, **20**, 669
provision of, **20**, 503, 669
railway tunnel, over or near, **19**, 1029
repair and maintenance, **20**, 618, 669
Cattle insurance society, 12, 693
animals covered by, **12**, 693
death only risk insured, **12**, 693
dissolution, voluntary, **12**, 700
friendly society—
  as, **12**, 679n, 685
  legislation, **12**, 601
investigation of affairs, **12**, 700
recovery of unpaid subscription or fine, **12**, 706
rules, **12**, 700
valuations exemption, **12**, 717
Causal condition
meaning, **15**, 6
Causation
breach of contract, **15**, 423
burden of proof, **15**, 425
'but for' (*sine qua non*) test, **15**, 423, 424
causa causans, **15**, 423
criticism of law, **15**, 423

Causation—*continued*
damages—
  breach, and, **15**, 893
  contract—
    intervening events, **15**, 895
    intervention—
      pursuer, by, **15**, 897
      third party, by, **15**, 896
  delict—
    intervening events, **15**, 898
    intervention—
      pursuer, by, **15**, 901
      third party, by, **15**, 899, 900
  generally, **15**, 422, 893
  multiple causes, where, **15**, 894
  onus of proof, **15**, 893
death, proof of cause of, **7**, 50
directly caused result, **7**, 48
factual—
  'but for' test, **15**, 424
  generally, **15**, 423, 424, 425
  legal causation, and, **15**, 431
  loss of chance, **15**, 430
  material contribution, **15**, 426, 427
  material increase in risk, **15**, 427, 428
  multiple causes, **15**, 429
  subsequent interpretation, **15**, 428
foreseeability, **7**, 48
generally, **7**, 46; **15**, 422, 423
indirectly caused result, **7**, 48
insurance claims, **12**, 879
intentional delicts, **15**, 423, 423n
legal—
  causal responsibility—
    ascription, **15**, 432
    assessment criteria, **15**, 433
  contributory negligence, **15**, 432
  factual causation, and, **15**, 431
  generally, **15**, 423, 431, 432
  negligence, **15**, 432
  novus actus interveniens, **15**, 431, 434
medical treatment, improper, **7**, 54
mens rea, causal link independent of, **7**, 49
multiple causes, **15**, 429
negligence, **15**, 311, 422, 423, 432
novus actus interveniens, **7**, 51, 52, 54–56
omission, **7**, 48, 52
proximate cause, **12**, 879
result-crimes, **7**, 46
sine qua non test, **15**, 423, 424
supervening infection, **7**, 53
susceptibility of victim, **7**, 55
tests of, **15**, 423
third party intervention, **7**, 56
time gap, where, **7**, 47
victim, supervening act or omission by, **7**, 52
Cautio usufructuaria
fiar's right to remedy of, **13**, 1661
Caution
Actings, for—
  amount of caution, **25**, 1087
  cautioners, **25**, 1088
  generally, **25**, 1086, 1089
administration of estates, **25**, 1086–1089

Caution—*continued*
bond of, issue of, **14**, 1502
defended ordinary action, expenses of—
 defender, by, **17**, 1074
 limited company, by, **17**, 1073
 order to find, **17**, 1072
 procedure, **17**, 1075
good behaviour, for, **17**, 801
interim interdict, **17**, 1109
judicial factor, on appointment of, **24**, 242
lawburrows, action of—
 amount, **13**, 907
 Books of Court, acted in, **13**, 907
 crave, **13**, 907
 defender failing to find, **13**, 901, 907
  caption and imprisonment following, **13**, 901, 903, 907, 918
 forfeiture, **13**, 901
 generally, **13**, 901
limited company, by, **17**, 1073
Cautionary obligation
acceptance—
 form, **3**, 884
 necessity for—
  express acceptance, **3**, 883
  generally, **3**, 882
  implied acceptance, **3**, 883
accessory nature—
 continuing existence of principal obligation, **3**, 850
 debtor's defences available to cautioner—
  generally, **3**, 841
  liability—
   reduction of, **3**, 843
   release from, **3**, 842
 effect, **3**, 835
 extent of cautioner's debt must coincide with debtor's, **3**, 847
 generally, **3**, 811, 835, 844
 principal debtor, liability—
  failure *ab initio* of principal obligation, **3**, 836–838
  generally, **3**, 826
  subsequent defects in principal contract, **3**, 840
  termination of principal contract, **3**, 840
  voidable obligations, **3**, 839, 846
 subsequent defect in principal contract, **3**, 840
 termination—
  obligation, of, **3**, 957
  principal contract, of, **3**, 840
actio mandati, **3**, 808
ad factum praestandum, **3**, 801
 benefit of discussion, **3**, 916, 923, 925, 926
adpromissor, **3**, 805, 806
advancement of money to debtor as *rei interventus*, **3**, 885
agent—
 capacity—
  actual express authority, **3**, 860, 861
  actual implied authority, **3**, 860, 862
  generally, **3**, 860
  liability of agent, **3**, 864
  ostensible authority, **3**, 860, 863
 subscription by, **3**, 876

Cautionary obligation—*continued*
ambiguity in, cautioner, must be resolved in favour of, **3**, 909
arrestment on the dependence, recall, **3**, 997
beneficium cedendarum actionum, **3**, 808, 929, 930
beneficium divisionis, *see* BENEFIT OF DIVISION
beneficium ordinis vel excussionis, *see* BENEFIT OF DISCUSSION
benefit of discussion, *see* BENEFIT OF DISCUSSION
benefit of division, *see* BENEFIT OF DIVISION
bill of exchange compared, **3**, 828–832
 See also BILL OF EXCHANGE
breach—
 effect, **3**, 841, 842
 express, **3**, 841
 implied, **3**, 841
building contract, *see* BUILDING CONTRACT
capacity to enter—
 agent, *see* agent *above*
 company, *see* company as party to *below*
 minor, **3**, 859
 partner, **3**, 865
capital gains tax treatment, **3**, 1002
cautioner, *see* CAUTIONER
classification—
 cautioner and debtor, agreements between, **3**, 816, 821
 creditor and cautioner, agreements between, **3**, 816, 833, 834
 creditor, cautioner and debtor, agreements between, **3**, 816, 817–820
 generally, **3**, 816
 primary and secondary liability for same debt, **3**, 816, 822–832
co-cautioners, *see* CAUTIONER
co-extensiveness, principle of, **3**, 918
collateral undertaking, as, **3**, 801
commercial security instruments—
 commercial surety bond, **3**, 988
 first demand guarantee, **3**, 987
 generally, **3**, 987
 guarantee, **3**, 987
  International Chamber of Commerce Model Guarantee, **3**, 991
  performance, **3**, 990
 letter of comfort, **3**, 992
 letter of respectability, **3**, 992
 standby letter of credit, **3**, 989
commercial surety bond, **3**, 988
common law, **3**, 815
company as party to—
 authority to bind company, **3**, 868, 869
 capacity of company to enter, **3**, 867, 868
 director or other acting outwith limitations of powers, **3**, 868
 generally, **3**, 867
 winding up, **3**, 982
company as pursuer in court action, caution for expenses, **3**, 996
concealment—
 cautioner's responsibility, **3**, 897
 creditor's duty of disclosure—
  cautioner's responsibility, **3**, 897
  full disclosure, **3**, 898

Cautionary obligation—*continued*
concealment—*continued*
  creditor's duty of disclosure—*continued*
    generally, **3**, 897
    higher than ordinary, guarantee with, **3**, 899
    limits of right to remain silent, **3**, 898
    misapprehensions of, creditor's duty to correct, **3**, 898
    partial disclosure, **3**, 898
    silence, when amounting to misrepresentation, **3**, 898
    subsequent, **3**, 900
  guarantees, **3**, 899
    fidelity, **3**, 899, 900
  insurance contracts, **3**, 899
constitution—
  common law, at, **3**, 870
  debt, of, **3**, 921
  defect in—
    proof, **3**, 888
  formal attestation, by, **3**, 870
  gratuitous cautionary obligations, **3**, 880
  imperfections of, *rei interventus*, **3**, 885
  in re mercatoria, **3**, 875
  Mercantile Law Amendment Act (Scotland) 1856—
    reform, proposals for, **3**, 879–881
    situation prior to, **3**, 870
  writing, necessity for—
    consequences, **3**, 874
    formal writing, whether required, **3**, 872
    generally, **3**, 871
    in modum probationis, **3**, 871, 874
    proof, constitution of, **3**, 873
    reform, proposals for, **3**, 879–881
    rei interventus doctrine, **3**, 871, 874, 880
  parole, by, **3**, 870
  proof, of, whether writing necessary for, **3**, 873
  reform, proposals for, **3**, 879–881
  Scots and English law, **3**, 804
  subscription—
    foot of writ, whether signature must be at, **3**, 877
    valid, what constitutes, **3**, 876
    who may sign, **3**, 878
  whole debt clause, **3**, 913
contra proferentem rule, **3**, 909
contract—
  alteration, effect—
    fidelity guarantees, **3**, 975
    generally, **3**, 974
    insubstantial alterations, **3**, 974
  conditions—
    on crystallisation of liability, **3**, 908
    duration of obligation, during, **3**, 907
    generally, **3**, 905
    suspensive, **3**, 906
  freedom of parties to establish own terms, **3**, 815
  independent, necessity for, **3**, 801
  principal—
    alteration, giving time as, **3**, 967
    generally, **3**, 801
    termination, consequences, **3**, 840

Cautionary obligation—*continued*
contract, resemblance to, **3**, 882
contractual obligation, as, **3**, 909; **15**, 642
creditor—
  acts prejudicial to cautioner's rights, effect, **3**, 964
    alteration of contract, **3**, 974, 975
    giving time, *see* giving time *below*
    positive act or omission, **3**, 964
  advancement of money to debtor as *rei interventus*, **3**, 885
  agreement between cautioner and debtor only, where, **3**, 821
  assignation, co-cautioner, of, **3**, 943
  bankruptcy of cautioner—
    principal debtor solvent, where, **3**, 948–950
    ranking in case of, **3**, 913, 948*ff*
  bankruptcy of principal debtor, **3**, 951–956
  careless conduct by, **3**, 964
  cautioner bound as principal and cautioner, where, **3**, 819
  cautioners' rights against—
    benefit of discussion—
      generally, **3**, 923
      limits, **3**, 924
      Mercantile Law Amendment Act, effect, **3**, 925, 926
    benefit of division—
      improper caution, **3**, 928
      proper caution, **3**, 927
    debt, right to have proved—
      calling cautioner to account, **3**, 922
      constitution of debt, **3**, 921
    right to be put in creditor's place, **3**, 929
    securities, right to—
      creditor taking further security, **3**, 970
      creditor taking security in respect of further debt, **3**, 931
      duty to preserve securities, **3**, 934
      extent of right, **3**, 930
      other creditors having interest in security subjects, **3**, 932
      partial payment, **3**, 933
  contract with principal debtor, alteration—
    fidelity guarantees, **3**, 975
    generally, **3**, 974
    insubstantial alterations, **3**, 974
  creditor and cautioner, agreements between, **3**, 816, 833, 834
  creditor, cautioner and debtor, agreement between, **3**, 816, 817–820
    cautioner bound as principal and cautioner, **3**, 819
    cautioner expressly bound, **3**, 818
    separate notice of cautionary agreement, **3**, 820
  death, effect, **3**, 982
  debtor failing in obligaton to, **3**, 801
  disclosure, duty of—
    cautioner's responsibility, **3**, 897
    full disclosure, **3**, 898
    generally, **3**, 897
    guarantees, **3**, 899
    higher than ordinary, guarantee with, **3**, 899

Cautionary obligation—*continued*
creditor—*continued*
 disclosure, duty of—*continued*
  insurance contracts, **3**, 899
  limits of right to remain silent, **3**, 898
  partial disclosure, **3**, 898
  silence, when amounting to misrepresentation, **3**, 898
  subsequent, **3**, 900
 failure to press for payment, **3**, 968
 giving time—
  additional security, taking, **3**, 970
  after decree, **3**, 971
  alteration of principal contract, as, **3**, 967
  consent by cautioner, **3**, 973
  creditor's failure to press for payment, **3**, 968
  generally, **3**, 821, 826, 965
  indefinite date of payment, **3**, 969
  meaning, **3**, 965, 967
  operation, **3**, 966
  pactum de non petendo distinguished, **3**, 965, 966
  reservation of rights by creditor, **3**, 972
 giving up securities, effect, **3**, 977
 insanity, effect, **3**, 982
 loss of identity, effect, **3**, 982
 misrepresentation by—
  damages, **3**, 1005
  delict, leading to liability in, **3**, 1006, 1008
  duty of care, **3**, 1006
  fraudulent, **3**, 891, 893, 1005, 1006, 1008
  generally, **3**, 891
  inducement, importance of, **3**, 894
  innocent, **3**, 891, 893, 1005, 1005*n*
  liability, **3**, 1004
  materiality, **3**, 893
  Mercantile Law Amendment Act (Scotland) 1856, effect, **3**, 1008
  nature of representations as to credit, **3**, 1004
  negligent, **3**, 891, 893, 1005, 1006
  pre-contractual representations, **3**, 1004, 1005
  representations and conditions, distinction between, **3**, 892
  silence, when amounting to, **3**, 898
  who may rely on representations, **3**, 1007
 necessity for, **3**, 835
 principal debtor released by act or omission of, **3**, 958
 proceedings against principal debtor, expenses incurred in, **3**, 916
 rights, guarantees under Consumer Credit Act 1974 ..., **3**, 856
damages—
 creditor's remedy against cautioner as, **3**, 918
 measure of, **3**, 918
debt—
 compensation of principal, **3**, 961
 creditor's failure to press for payment, **3**, 968
 extent of cautioner's debt must coincide with debtor's, **3**, 847
 failure *ab initio* of principal obligation, **3**, 836, 837
  problems arising, **3**, 838
 giving time, *see* creditor *above*

Cautionary obligation—*continued*
debt—*continued*
 liability for—
  generally, **3**, 836
  liquid, liability under cautionary obligation, **3**, 921
 novation of principal, **3**, 960
 payment date, indefinite, **3**, 969
 prescription of principal, **3**, 963
 principal debtor's failure to pay, creditor neglecting to give notice of, **3**, 964
 void—
  existence of primary liability, **3**, 846, 852
  initial, **3**, 836–838
  subsequent, **3**, 836
debtor—
 agreement with cautioner, proof, **3**, 889
 cautioner and debtor, agreement between, **3**, 816, 821
  co-obligants bound simply as principals, **3**, 821
  rights of co-obligants *inter se*, **3**, 821
 circumstances of, acertaining by cautioner, **3**, 897
 co-obligants bound simply as principals, **3**, 821
 creditor, cautioner and debtor, agreement between, **3**, 816, 817–820
  cautioner bound as principal and cautioner, **3**, 819
  cautioner expressly bound, **3**, 818
  separate notice of cautionary agreement, **3**, 820
 failure, consequences, **3**, 801
 giving of time to principal, effect, **3**, 826
 meaning, **3**, 801
 misrepresentation by—
  generally, **3**, 895
  limitations to general rule, **3**, 896
 necessity for, **3**, 835
 principal, *see* principal debtor *below*
definition, **3**, 801
del credere agency, **3**, 833
delegation, **3**, 850
development of law—
 Balfour, works by, **3**, 812
 common law, **3**, 815
 legislative developments, **3**, 814
 Roman law, contribution, **3**, 805–811
 Stair's *Institutions*, **3**, 813
disclosure, duty of, *see* concealment *above*
English decisions, authority in Scotland, **3**, 804
English law compared, **3**, 801*n*, 803, 804
equities of caution, **3**, 841
error in—
 diminishing importance, **3**, 901
 uninduced, **3**, 901, 902
etymological origin, **3**, 802
execution, **3**, 855
executor dative, **3**, 995
expenses—
 caution for, **3**, 996
 incurred in claim, liability for, **3**, 916
extent of cautioner's debt must coincide with debtor's, **3**, 847

Cautionary obligation—*continued*
facility and circumvention, doctrine of, **3**, 904
fideiussio indemnitatis, **3**, 811
fidelity guarantee, *see* FIDELITY GUARANTEE
firm party to—
  change in constitution, **3**, 983
  winding up, **3**, 982
first demand guarantee, **3**, 987
form—
  correspondence, **3**, 853
  formal document, **3**, 853
  generally, **3**, 853
  guarantees under Consumer Credit Act 1974—
    generally, **3**, 853–858
    impact of Act, **3**, 853
    writing, instrument to be in, **3**, 855
  series of writings, **3**, 853
  wording, **3**, 853
form of agreement, **3**, 845
freedom of parties to establish own terms, **3**, 815
future transactions, principal obligation extending
  to, **3**, 912
giving time, *see* creditor *above*
gratuitous—
  meaning, **3**, 880
  proposed reforms, **3**, 880
guarantee, **3**, 987
  cautionary obligation compared, **3**, 803
  continuing, cautioner's liability, **3**, 914
  contract of, contract of insurance distinguished,
    3, 849
  duty of disclosure, **3**, 899
  fidelity, *see* FIDELITY GUARANTEE
  International Chamber of Commerce Model
    Guarantee, **3**, 991
  limited, cautioner's liability, **3**, 914
  performance, **3**, 990
  representation as to credit distinguished, **3**,
    1004
    consequences of distinction, **3**, 1004
guarantee under Consumer Credit Act 1974—
  creditor's rights, **3**, 856
  enforcement, **3**, 858
  execution of instrument, **3**, 855
  impact of Act, **3**, 854
  signature of instrument, **3**, 855
  surety's rights, **3**, 857
  writing, instrument to be in, **3**, 855
improper caution, **3**, 819
  cautioners' right of relief, assignation, and, **3**,
    943
  no benefit of division, **3**, 928
in re mercatoria, **3**, 875
income tax, **3**, 1001
inhibition on the dependence, recall, **3**, 997
insolvency—
  cautioner, of, **3**, 948–950, 953–956
  co-cautioner, of, **3**, 942
  practitioner, **3**, 994
  principal debtor, of, **3**, 951–956
institution, granted by—
  generally, **3**, 985
  office, caution granted for, **3**, 986
institutional bond, **3**, 801*n*

Cautionary obligation—*continued*
insurance compared, **12**, 802
interest on debt due—
  cautioner's liability, **3**, 917
  cautioner's right to, **3**, 935
international law, effect, **3**, 815
intrest on debt due, liability for, **3**, 917
judicial bonds of caution—
  arrestment on the dependence, recall, **3**, 997
  executor dative, **3**, 995
  expenses, caution for, **3**, 996
  inhibition on the dependence, recall, **3**, 997
  insolvency practioner, **3**, 994
  judicial factor, **3**, 986, 993
  messenger-at-arms, **3**, 986, 1000
  objection to documents, **3**, 999
  petitions for suspension, **3**, 998
  sheriff officer, **3**, 986, 1000
judicial factor, **3**, 986, 993
legislative development, **3**, 814
letter of comfort, **3**, 992
letter of credit, **3**, 989
letter of respectability, **3**, 992
liability—
  cautioner, of, *see* CAUTIONER
  conditions precedent to, **3**, 916
  expiry of period of, **3**, 979
  factors triggering cautioner's, **3**, 851
limited to certain sum—
  entire debt covered but subject to limit, **3**, 913
  limited part of debt covered, **3**, 913
litis contestatio, **3**, 810
meaning, **3**, 918
messenger-at-arms, **3**, 986, 1000
minor, capacity to enter, **3**, 859
misrepresentation—
  creditor, by—
    fraudulent, **3**, 891, 893
    generally, **3**, 891
    inducement, importance of, **3**, 894
    innocent, **3**, 891, 893
    materiality, **3**, 893
    negligent, **3**, 891, 893
    representations and conditions, distinction
      between, **3**, 892
  debtor, by—
    generally, **3**, 895
    limitations to general rule, **3**, 896
money, payment of, as principal obligation, **3**,
  801
named person, whether guarantee addressed to, **3**,
  915
negotiorum gestor incurring, **15**, 96
novation, **3**, 850
objection to documents, **3**, 999
obligatione literis, establishment without reference
  to writ, **3**, 874
obligations *ad factum praestandum*, benefit of
  discussion, **3**, 916, 925
offer and acceptance, **3**, 882–884
office—
  caution granted for, **3**, 986
  for faithful performance of, **3**, 801

Cautionary obligation—*continued*
other obligations distinguished, **3**, 844–852
    contingent primary liability, **3**, 844
        contract of indemnity, **3**, 844
    generally, **3**, 844
    importance of distinction, **3**, 852
    joint primary liability, **3**, 844
    sole primary liability, **3**, 844
partner—
    capacity to enter cautionary obligation, **3**, 865
    liability for debts of firm—
        benefit of discussion, **3**, 825
        benefit of division, **3**, 825
        caution, partner's relationship with firm as
            one of, **3**, 823
        cautioner and partner contrasted, **3**, 824
        discharge of one partner, where, **3**, 826
        generally, **3**, 822, 823, 827
        giving of time to principal debtor, **3**, 826
partnership—
    undertaken by, **3**, 920
    undertaken for, **3**, 919
    undertaken to, **3**, 919
past transactions, principal obligation extending
    to, **3**, 912
performance bond, **3**, 801*n*
personal right counterpart or correlative to, **20**, 2
petitions for suspension, **3**, 998
principal—
    cautioner bound as principal and cautioner, **3**, 818
    co-obligants bound simply as, **3**, 821
principal debtor—
    actio mandati against, **3**, 935
    bankruptcy, **3**, 922, 958
    cautioner bound as principal and cautioner, **3**,
        818, 819
    cautioners' rights against—
        after debt due, **3**, 937
        before debt due, **3**, 936
        fixed period, obligation for, **3**, 936
        full relief, right to—
            excluded or limited by agreement, **3**, 935
            expenses of defending action, **3**, 935
            express, **3**, 935
            extent, **3**, 935
            implied, **3**, 935
            interest payable, **3**, 935
            nature of, **3**, 935
        future and contingent debt, **3**, 939
        precautionary diligence, **3**, 938
        precautionary measures, right to take, **3**, 938
        right in security, transfer, **3**, 938
        sequestration, **3**, 938
        vergens ad inopiam, where debtor, **3**, 938, 939
    cautioner's undertaking that debtor will
        perform, **3**, 918
    co-obligants bound simply as principals, **3**, 821
    company as, **3**, 958
    compensation of principal debt, **3**, 961
    contract with creditor, alteration—
        fidelity guarantees, **3**, 975
        generally, **3**, 974
        insubstantial alterations, **3**, 974
    creditor's failure to press for payment, **3**, 968

Cautionary obligation—*continued*
principal debtor—*continued*
    death, effect, **3**, 982
    decree obtained against, cautioner's rights, **3**, 921
    discharge, termination of principal obligation
        on—
        absolute discharge, **3**, 959
        act or omission of creditor, debtor released
            by, **3**, 958
        bankruptcy of debtor, **3**, 958
        modes of discharge, **3**, 958
        pactum de non petendo, **3**, 959, 965
    discharge without releasing cautioner, term
        purporting to allow, **3**, 958
    extent of cautioner's debt must coincide with
        debtor's, **3**, 847
    failure in contractual obligations—
        cautioner's undertaking to perform in event
            of, **3**, 918
        effect, **3**, 918
    failure to pay, creditor neglecting to give
        notice of, **3**, 964
    giving time—
        after decree, **3**, 971
        consent by cautioner, **3**, 973
        creditor's failure to press for payment, **3**, 968
        generally, **3**, 821, 826, 965
        indefinite date of payment, **3**, 969
        meaning, **3**, 965, 967
        operation, **3**, 966
        reservation of rights by creditor, **3**, 972
        taking additional security, **3**, 970
    insanity, effect, **3**, 982
    insolvency—
        cautioners insolvent, where, **3**, 953–956
        cautioners solvent, where, **3**, 951, 952
    liability—
        generally, **3**, 836
        void, obligation proving to be, **3**, 836
    liquidation, **3**, 922
    loss of identity, effect, **3**, 982
    novation of principal debt, **3**, 960
    precautionary diligence against, **3**, 938
    prescription of principal debt, **3**, 963
    proceedings against, expenses incurred, **3**, 916
    right in security, transfer by cautioner, **3**, 938
    sequestration by cautioner, **3**, 938
    vergens ad inopiam, **3**, 938, 939
    See also debtor *above*
principal obligation—
    cautionary obligation dependent on existence
        of, **3**, 910
    cautioner's distance from, **3**, 833
    distinction between cautionary obligations and,
        3, 844–852
        importance of, **3**, 852
    existence at time caution undertaken
        unnecessary, **3**, 835
    extinction—
        compensation of principal debt, **3**, 961
        discharge of principal debtor—
            absolute, **3**, 959
            mode, **3**, 958
            pactum de non petendo, **3**, 959, 965

Cautionary obligation—*continued*
principal obligation—*continued*
 extinction—*continued*
  generally, **3**, 957
  illegal, where, **3**, 957
  novation of principal debt, **3**, 960
  prescription of principal debt, **3**, 963
  rule in *Clayton's Case*, **3**, 962
  termination of obligation on, **3**, 957
  unenforceable, where, **3**, 957
 future transactions, extending to, **3**, 912
 illegal, **3**, 957
 money, payment of, as, **3**, 801
 necessity for, **3**, 835
 past transactions, extending to, **3**, 912
 right type, must be of, **3**, 910, 911
 scope of guarantee, must fall within, **3**, 910–912
 time limit, **3**, 910, 912
 unenforceable, **3**, 957
 void, failure due to, **3**, 846
principal transaction, extent of cautioner's interest, **3**, 848
proceedings against principal debtor, expenses incurred in, liability, **3**, 916
promise, resemblance to, **3**, 882
pronunciation, **3**, 801*n*
proof of contract—
 cautioner and debtor, proof of agreement between, **3**, 889
 co-cautioners, proof of agreement between, **3**, 890
 extrinsic evidence, **3**, 888
 oath, by, **3**, 886
 parole evidence, **3**, 888
 rei interventus, doctrine of, **3**, 885
 underlying agreement, proof of, **3**, 886
 writ, by, **3**, 886
 writing—
  contents of, **3**, 887
  whether necessity for, **3**, 873
proper caution, **3**, 818
 benefit of division, **3**, 927
 co-cautioners, mutual relief against, **3**, 940
 principal debtor solvent but cautioner insolvent, **3**, 948
recourse agreement, **3**, 816, 833, 834
rei interventus, doctrine of, *see* REI INTERVENTUS
representations as to credit, *see* CREDIT
revocation on change in partnership constitution, **16**, 1039
reward, undertaken for, **3**, 880
secondary obligation, as, **3**, 844, 846
 continuing existence of principal obligation, **3**, 850
 primary obligation, necessity for, **3**, 846
separate notice of cautionary agreement, where, **3**, 820
sequestration—
 principal debtor, of, **3**, 938, 958
 termination of cautionary obligation, **3**, 958
sheriff officer, **3**, 986, 1000
sixteen or seventeen year old, prejudicial transaction entered by, **3**, 859
sponsio, **3**, 806, 808

Cautionary obligation—*continued*
stamp duty, **3**, 1003
standby letter of credit, **3**, 989
stipulatio, **3**, 806, 809
subscription, *see* SIGNATURE
taxation—
 capital gains tax, **3**, 1002
 income tax, **3**, 1001
 stamp duty, **3**, 1003
termination—
 acts prejudicial to cautioner's rights—
  alteration of contract—
   fidelity guarantees, **3**, 975
   generally, **3**, 974
   insubstantial, **3**, 974
  conduct of creditor, **3**, 964
  generally, **3**, 964
  giving time—
   additional security, taking, **3**, 970
   after decree, **3**, 971
   consent by cautioner, **3**, 973
   creditor's failure to press for payment, **3**, 968
   generally, **3**, 821, 826, 965
   indefinite date of payment, **3**, 969
   meaning, **3**, 965, 967
   operation, **3**, 966
   reservation of rights by creditor, **3**, 972
  giving up securities, **3**, 977
  positive act or omission, **3**, 964
  release of co-cautioner, **3**, 976
 alteration of contract—
  fidelity guarantees, **3**, 975
  generally, **3**, 974
  insubstantial, **3**, 974
 change in firm, effect, **3**, 983
 death—
  cautioner, of, **3**, 982
  creditor, of, **3**, 982
  principal debtor, of, **3**, 982
 discharge of cautioner, by, **3**, 978
 expiry of period of liability, by, **3**, 979
 express terms, breach, **3**, 964
 fidelity guarantee, *see* FIDELITY GUARANTEE
 giving up securities, **3**, 977
 implied terms, breach, **3**, 964
 prescription, by, **3**, 984
 principal obligation—
  extinction—
   compensation of principal debt, **3**, 961
   discharge of principal debtor—
    absolute discharge, **3**, 959
    modes of discharge, **3**, 958
    pactum de non petendo, **3**, 959, 965
    generally, **3**, 957
    novation of principal debt, **3**, 960
    prescription of principal debt, **3**, 963
   illegality, **3**, 957
   rule in *Clayton's Case*, **3**, 962
   unenforceable, **3**, 957
  release of co-cautioner, **3**, 976
 revocation by cautioner—
  fidelity guarantees, **3**, 981
  when permissible, **3**, 980
terminus a quo, **3**, 984

Cautionary obligation—*continued*
undue influence, doctrine of—
　application, generally, **3**, 903
　doctrine of facility and circumvention
　　distinguished, **3**, 904
　dominance, cause of, **3**, 903
　when applicable, **3**, 903
void—
　facility and circumvention, doctrine of, **3**, 904
　misrepresentation—
　　creditor, by, **3**, 891
　　debtor, by, **3**, 896
　undue influence, due to, **3**, 903
whole debt clause, **3**, 913
writing—
　constitution of proof, whether necessary for, **3**,
　　873
　contents of writ—
　　ambiguous wording, **3**, 888
　　creditor's name, **3**, 887
　　essential, **3**, 887
　　unsigned non-holograph writ, **3**, 886
　　wording, **3**, 887
　English legislation, **3**, 873
　formal, whether required, **3**, 872
　instrument not in, enforcement, **3**, 855
　Mercantile Law Amendment Act (Scotland)
　　1856—
　　generally, **3**, 871–874
　　reform, proposals for, **3**, 879–881
　necessity for, **3**, 855, 870
　　ambiguous wording, **3**, 888
　　contents, generally, **3**, 887
　　gratuitous cautionary obligations, **3**, 880
　　lack of signed writ, **3**, 886
　　offer and acceptance, **3**, 882–884
　　proof of underlying agreement, where, **3**, 886
　　rei interventus, doctrine of, **3**, 886
　　subscription, **3**, 876–878
　rei interventus doctrine, **3**, 874, 886
　subscribed by cautioner, necessity for, **3**, 871
See also OBLIGATION
Cautioner
accessory nature of caution—
　debtor's defences available to cautioner, **3**,
　　841–843
　generally, **3**, 835
　liability of principal debtor, **3**, 836–840
actio mandati against principal debtor, **3**, 935
agreement with debtor, proof, **3**, 889
ambiguity must be resolved in favour of, **3**, 909
assignation, right of relief, and, **3**, 943
bankruptcy—
　creditor's ranking, **3**, 913, 948*ff*
　principal debtor insolvent, where, **3**, 953–956
　principal debtor solvent, where, **3**, 948–950
beneficium cedendarum actionum, **3**, 929, 930
benefit of discussion—
　generally, **3**, 818, 923
　renunciation, **3**, 819
benefit of division—
　generally, **3**, 818, 927
　renunciation, **3**, 819
calling to account, **3**, 922

Cautioner—*continued*
cautioner and debtor, agreement between, **3**, 816,
　821
co-obligants bound simply as principals, **3**, 821
rights of co-obligants *inter se*, **3**, 821
co-cautioners—
　agreement between, proof, **3**, 890
　all must subscribe, **3**, 906
　discharge, effect, **3**, 978
　insolvency—
　　generally, **3**, 942
　　principal debtor insolvent, where, **3**, 953–956
　　principal debtor solvent, where, **3**, 948–950
　liability, **3**, 940
　proportionate equality of burden, **3**, 940
　release, effect, **3**, 976
　rights against—
　　assignation and right of relief, **3**, 943
　　cautioners not bound *in solidum*, where, **3**, 941
　　communication of benefits, **3**, 947
　　compensation, **3**, 946
　　debt, payment of, and right of relief, **3**, 944
　　extent, **3**, 940
　　insolvency, effect on mutual relief, **3**, 942
　　precautionary measures, **3**, 945
　　pro rata, cautioners bound, **3**, 940, 941
　　retention of assets, **3**, 946
　　right of relief not available, when, **3**, 941
　　separate instruments, co-cautioners bound
　　　by, **3**, 940
　　sharing in securities, **3**, 947
　rights of, where cautioner *vergens ad inopiam*, **3**,
　　945
contract of, enforcement, **3**, 918
co-obligants bound simply as principals, **3**, 821
creditor, cautioner and debtor, agreement
　between, **3**, 816, 817–820
　separate notice of cautionary agreement, **3**, 820
creditor and cautioner, agreements between, **3**,
　816, 833, 834
creditor's place, right to be put into, **3**, 929
creditor's remedy against, **3**, 918
death, effect, **3**, 982
debtor's circumstances, acertaining, **3**, 897
defences available to—
　generally, **3**, 841
　reduction of liability, **3**, 843
　release from liability, **3**, 842
discharge—
　mode of, **3**, 978
　termination of obligation\on, **3**, 978
distance from principal obligation, **3**, 833
document constituting obligation to pay in
　possession of, **15**, 872
expressly bound as cautioner, where, **3**, 817
extent of interest in transaction, **3**, 848
giving time, consent to, **3**, 973
insanity, effect, **3**, 982
liability—
　acts prejudicial to cautioner's rights, effect—
　　alteration of contract—
　　　fidelity guarantees, **3**, 975
　　　generally, **3**, 974
　　　insubstantial alterations, **3**, 974

Cautioner—*continued*
liability—*continued*
  acts prejudicial to cautioner's rights, effect—
    continued
    generally, **3**, 964
    giving time—
      after decree, **3**, 971
      consent by cautioner, **3**, 965, 973
      failure by creditor to press for payment, **3**,
        968
      generally, **3**, 826, 965
      indefinite date of payment, where, **3**, 969
      meaning, **3**, 965, 967
      operation, **3**, 966
      reservation of rights by creditor, **3**, 972
      taking of additional security, **3**, 970
    giving up securities, **3**, 977
    release of co-cautioner, **3**, 976
  conditions precedent to, **3**, 916
  debt must be constituted, **3**, 921
  discharge of cautioner, effect, **3**, 978
  discharge of co-cautioner, effect, **3**, 978
  expiry of period of, **3**, 979
  extent—
    co-extensiveness, principle of, **3**, 918
    construction of limitations as to amount, **3**,
      913
    continuing guarantee, **3**, 914
    entire debt covered but subject to limit, **3**,
      913
    expenses of proceeding against principal
      debtor, **3**, 916
    interest on debt due, **3**, 917
    limit—
      whether to include expenses, **3**, 916
    limited guarantee, **3**, 914
    limited part of debt covered, **3**, 913
    matter of construction, cautioner's liability
      as, **3**, 909
    partnership—
      undertaking by, **3**, 920
      undertaking for, **3**, 919
      undertaking to, **3**, 919
    principal obligation—
      past or future transactions, extending to, **3**,
        912
      right type, must be of, **3**, 911
      scope of guarantee, must fall within, **3**, 910
    who may recover from the cautioner, **3**, 915
  factors triggering, **3**, 851
  insolvency of one or more cautioners—
    principal debtor insolvent, where, **3**, 953–956
    principal debtor solvent, where, **3**, 948–950
  insolvency of principal debtor—
    cautioners solvent, where, **3**, 951, 952
    some or all cautioners insolvent, where, **3**,
      953–956
  liquid debts, **3**, 921
  new cautioner undertaking, **3**, 978
  reduction, **3**, 843
  release from, **3**, 842
  revocation by cautioner—
    fidelity guarantees, **3**, 981
    when permissible, **3**, 980

Cautioner—*continued*
loss of identity, effect, **3**, 982
meaning, **3**, 801
misapprehensions of, creditor's duty to correct, **3**,
  898
necessity for, **3**, 835
partner compared, **3**, 824
principal, expressly bound as, **3**, 818
  cautioner-debtor relationship, where creditor
    has, **3**, 817
  terms of deed disclose true relationship with
    debtor, where, **3**, 817
principal and cautioner, bound as, **3**, 818, 819
principals, co-obligants bound simply as, **3**, 821
protection, generally, **3**, 801
release of co-cautioner, effect, **3**, 826
revocation of obligation by—
  fidelity guarantees, **3**, 981
  when permissible, **3**, 980
rights of—
  acts prejudicial to—
    alteration of contract—
      generally, **3**, 974
      insubstantial alteration, **3**, 974
    conduct of creditor, **3**, 964
    fidelity guarantees, **3**, 975
    generally, **3**, 964
    giving up securities, **3**, 977
    positive act or omission, **3**, 964
    release of co-cautioner, **3**, 976
  bankruptcy of principal debtor, where, **3**, 922
  co-cautioners, against—
    cautioners not bound *in solidum*, where, **3**,
      941
    pro rata, cautioners bound, **3**, 940, 941, 950
    proportional equality of burden, **3**, 940
    relief, mutual—
      assignation and, **3**, 943
      communication of benefits, **3**, 947
      compensation, **3**, 946
      extent of right to, **3**, 940
      insolvency, effect, **3**, 942
      payment of debt and, **3**, 944
      precautionary measures, **3**, 945
      retention, **3**, 946
      sharing in securities, **3**, 947
      when not available, **3**, 941
    separate instruments, co-cautioners bound
      by, **3**, 940
    vergens ad inopiam, where cautioner, **3**, 945
  creditors, against—
    beneficium cedendarum actionum, **3**, 929, 930
    benefit of discussion—
      generally, **3**, 923
      limits, **3**, 924
      Mercantile Law Amendment Act (Scotland)
        1856, section 8 ..., **3**, 925, 926
    benefit of division—
      improper caution, **3**, 928
      proper caution, **3**, 927
    debt proved, right to have—
      calling cautioner to account, **3**, 922
      constitution of debt, **3**, 921
    liquid debts, **3**, 921

Cautioner—*continued*
rights of—*continued*
  creditors, against—*continued*
    securities—
      creditor giving up, **3**, 977
      creditor taking security in respect of further debt, **3**, 931
      duty to preserve securities, **3**, 934
      extent of right to securities, **3**, 930
      other creditors with interest, **3**, 932
      partial payment, **3**, 933
  decree obtained against principal debtor, where, **3**, 921
  insolvency of cautioner—
    principal debtor insolvent, where, **3**, 953–956
    principal debtor solvent, where, **3**, 948–950
  liquidation of principal debtor, where, **3**, 922
  principal debtor, against—
    after debt due, **3**, 937
    before debt due, **3**, 936
    compensation, **3**, 939
    excluded or limited by agreement, **3**, 935
    expenses of defending action, **3**, 935
    express, **3**, 935
    fixed period, where obligation for, **3**, 936
    full relief, right to—
      extent, **3**, 935
      nature of, **3**, 935
    future and contingent debt, **3**, 939
    implied, **3**, 935
    interest payable, **3**, 935
    precautionary measures, right to take, **3**, 938
    retention of assets, **3**, 939
    vergens ad inopiam, where debtor, **3**, 938, 939
  principal debtor insolvent, where—
    cautioner also insolvent, **3**, 953–956
    cautioner solvent, where, **3**, 951, 952
  relief from obligation, **3**, 936
security held by where all obligants insolvent, **3**, 956
subscription by, **3**, 876
vergens ad inopiam, rights against co-cautioners, **3**, 945

Caveat
arrestment prevented by, **8**, 300
interim interdict, **17**, 1105

Caveat emptor
application in Scotland, **20**, 819, 823
barter, **6**, 47
missives, **6**, 566

Cayman Islands
British Dependent Territories citizenship, **14**, 1932

Cedent
meaning, **20**, 46

Cellar
road, under—
  construction, road authority control, **20**, 683
  maintenance, **20**, 664

Celluloid
legislation, generally, **19**, 412–419
meaning, **19**, 412
raw, meaning, **19**, 412

Celluloid—*continued*
storage premises, **19**, 415–417
  appeals against local authority requirements, **19**, 418
  control of, **19**, 413
  penalties for offences, **19**, 419

Celtic law
brehon, role of, **22**, 503
characteristics, **22**, 503
feu-ferme tenure, origins, **22**, 595
feudalism, effect of, **22**, 504, 505
Ireland, influence of, **22**, 503
marriage customs, **22**, 504
proof by compurgation, **22**, 503
survival of, **22**, 504
tribal customs, **22**, 503

Celtic Sea
continental shelf delimitation agreement, **21**, 30

Cement mortar
ready-mixed, sale of, **6**, 238

Cemetery
commercial, **3**, 516
compulsory acquisition or use, **19**, 19
construction or extension, **19**, 15
disused, **19**, 336n
finance, **3**, 528
firearm, discharge in, **3**, 527
game or sport, playing in, **3**, 527
lairholders' rights, **3**, 516
local government functions in respect of, **14**, 699
nuisance, committing in, **3**, 527
offences, **3**, 527
public health nuisance, as, **19**, 336
valuation for rating, **24**, 591
See also BURIAL GROUND

Censorship
theatre, in, abolition of, **9**, 1042

Census
records, transmission of, **19**, 842
Registrar General, duties of, **14**, 590

Central Arbitration Committee
agricultural wages order, referral of, **9**, 403

Central Council for Education and Training of Social Workers (CCETSW)
establishment, **22**, 11
functions, **22**, 11
Secretary of State, appointment of members, **22**, 11
Younghusband Report, **22**, 11

Central Council for Physical Recreation (CCPR)
generally, **19**, 1209, 1211

Central courts
See COURTS

Central government
administrative departments—
  accounting officer, **5**, 593
  appropriation accounts, **5**, 594
  Cabinet Office, **5**, 486
  Cabinet Secretariat, **5**, 487
  Central Policy Review Staff, **5**, 488
  Central Statistical Office, **5**, 490
  Chancellor of Exchequer, **5**, 495
  Chief Scientific Adviser, **5**, 489

Central government—*continued*
administrative departments—*continued*
  classification of, **5**, 472
  delegation of powers, **5**, 483
  department-related select committees—
    current, **5**, 433
    generally, **5**, 432
    membership, **5**, 435
    reports, debates on, **5**, 434
  different, factors behind origins of, **5**, 475
  generally, **5**, 485
  Historical Section, **5**, 491
  Lords of Treasury, **5**, 494
  Management and Personnel Office, **5**, 492
  ministers of Crown, *see* MINISTERS OF CROWN
  parliamentary authority, **5**, 477
  royal prerogative, **5**, 476
  Secretary of State, controlled by, **5**, 478
  territorial limitations, **5**, 473
  treasury—
    functions of, **5**, 497
    lords of, **5**, 494
    meaning, **5**, 493
    ministers, **5**, 496
    organisation of, **5**, 498
consumer protection, **6**, 11
contributions—
  improvement of amenity grants, **11**, 2034
  improvement grants, **11**, 2034
  repairs grants, **11**, 2034
controls—
  appellate powers, **14**, 112
  approval, **14**, 105
  byelaws, confirmation of, **14**, 109
  consent, **14**, 105
  default powers, **14**, 117
  direct, **14**, 105
  financial, **14**, 114
  generally, **14**, 101
  inspection, powers of, **14**, 113
  intervention, powers of, **14**, 106
  local inquiry, power to order, **14**, 116
  ministerial responsibilities, **14**, 102
  officers—
    appointment of, **14**, 110
    dismissal of, **14**, 110
  regulation-making powers, **14**, 107
  relaxation of, **14**, 115
  removal of, **14**, 115
  veto, powers of, **14**, 108
departments, as public corporations, **19**, 201
early history, **17**, 502
education, responsibility for, **14**, 36
executive authority, **14**, 3
expenditure guidelines, **14**, 875
influence—
  advice, **14**, 104
  generally, **14**, 103
  guidance, **14**, 104
  proposals, powers to comment on, **14**, 111
local government—
  compared with, **14**, 1, 94
  relationship with, **5**, 572, 573
meaning, **5**, 471

Central government—*continued*
organisation of functions of, **5**, 474
Parliament, answerable directly to, **14**, 3
personal bar, subject to, **1**, 296
poor relief, responsibility for, **14**, 34
powers, delegation of, **1**, 225
Central heating system
belonging, test of, **14**, 1013
domestic use, supply of water for, **25**, 506
plant, whether, **14**, 1012
Central institutions
See SCOTTISH CENTRAL INSTITUTIONS
Central Policy Review Staff
functions of, **5**, 488
Central Regional Council
water authority, as, **25**, 505
Central reservation
provision of, **20**, 660
Central Scotland Water Development Board
area, **25**, 539
establishment, **14**, 455; **25**, 502, 539
functions, **25**, 502
history, **25**, 502
principal responsibilities, **25**, 539
valuation of lands and heritages, **24**, 415
Central Statistical Office
responsibilities of, **5**, 490
**Central Transport Consultative Committee
for Great Britain, 19**, 1092, 1093
Cereals
'carry-over' payments, **1**, 915
common organisation in, form of, **1**, 913
export refund, **1**, 914, 921
guarantee threshold system, **1**, 916
import levies—
  advance fixing procedure, **1**, 920
  customs duties, and, **1**, 919
  legal nature of, **1**, 919
  world and Community prices, difference
    between, **1**, 914, 919
intervention—
  offers for, **1**, 918
  price, **1**, 914, 918
price structure—
  basis of, **1**, 916
  calculation, method of, **1**, 917
  generally, **1**, 914
  intervention price, **1**, 914, 918
  timetable, **1**, 917
  transport costs, taking account of, **1**, 917
production refunds, **1**, 915
reference price, **1**, 914
subsidies, **1**, 915
target price, **1**, 914, 917
threshold price, **1**, 914
Ceres Games, 19, 1201
Certainty, legal
principle of in European Community law, **10**, 94,
  96
Certificate of deposit
investment, as, **12**, 1308
negotiable instrument, as, **4**, 103
Certificate of Identity
issue, **16**, 1237

Certification officer
accounts, **23**, 796
annual returns, **23**, 797
audits, **23**, 796
certificate of independence, **23**, 792–795
executive election, enforcement of, **23**, 837
functions, **23**, 789
listing—
    advantages, **23**, 791
    procedure, **23**, 790
origins, **23**, 788
statutory authority, **23**, 788, 789
superannuation schemes, **23**, 797
union merger, powers relating to—
    ballot, **4**, **23**, 801
    complaints, **23**, 803
    form of, **23**, 798
    instrument, **23**, 800, 802
    procedure, **23**, 799
    registration of instrument, **23**, 802
Certiorari
error of law corrected by, **1**, 285
Cession
territory, of, **19**, 669
Cesspool
public health nuisance, as, **19**, 336
Cetaceous animals
Slaughter of Animals (Scotland) Act 1980 not
    applicable to, **11**, 496
Ceylon
emancipation legislation, **5**, 353
Chamberlain
appeal from decision of, **14**, 13
appointment of, **14**, 249
Great Chamberlain, **7**, 813
inter-burghal disputes, **14**, 13
Officer of State, **7**, 790, 800
Chancellor of Exchequer
responsibilities of, **5**, 495
Chancellor of Scotland
abeyance of chancellorship, **7**, 794; **22**, 517
history, **7**, 790, 791, 792, 794
theoretical presidency, Court of Session, **22**, 517
Chancery Division
company meeting, jurisdiction as to, **4**, 476
Chancery in Scotland, Order of
Cachet, **7**, 899
Crown Charters (Scotland) Act 1847 …, **7**, 906
expediency, **7**, 909, 911
generally, **7**, 897
Great Seal, **7**, 897, 898, 902
historical background, **7**, 897
per saltum grants, **7**, 904
Privy Seal, **7**, 897, 898, 901, 905
Quarter Seal, **7**, 897, 903, 905
reforms, **7**, 905–907
Signature, **7**, 897, 898
Signet, **7**, 897, 898, 900
Titles to Land Consolidation (Scotland) Act 1868
    …, **7**, 907
Chancery of the United Kingdom, Order of
early procedure, **7**, 870
Great Seal, authorisation, **7**, 870–872

**Chancery of the United Kingdom, Order
of**—*continued*
modern procedure, **7**, 871
offences, **7**, 872
Chancery Office
Department of the Registers of Scotland, **19**, 850
records of, **19**, 801
Channel Four
Independent Broadcasting Authority, provision
    by, **17**, 7
Channel Islands
adoption order made in, **8**, 535
application of competition rules, **4**, 1304
common travel area, **12**, 122; **16**, 1208
copyright legislation, **18**, 935
deportation order made by, **12**, 123
entry to United Kingdom via, **12**, 123
EU—
    customs territory, **7**, 1010
    law rights, **12**, 220
exclusion for purposes of 1982 Act, **4**, 23
exports to, **7**, 1194
Immigration Act, application to, **12**, 123
imports to United Kingdom, customs duty relief,
    7, 1105
Independent Broadcasting Authority, functions
    of, **17**, 7
mentally ill patient absent without leave, custody
    of, **14**, 1423
overseas company, **4**, 315
service Acts applying, **2**, 613
territorial sea, **11**, 76
visiting forces in, **2**, 786
Channel Islands cattle
milk, regulations as to, **11**, 466
Chapeau
colour rules, **11**, 1607
feudal barons entitled to, **11**, 1607
generally, **11**, 1607
Chapel
qualified, Scottish Episcopal Church, **3**, 1616,
    1616*n*, 1617, 1631
right to erect, **3**, 524
valuation for rating, **24**, 592
Chapel of ease
sale of congregational properties and endowments,
    3, 1607
Chapel Royal
Dean of, **3**, 1551
foundation, **3**, 1551
Palace of Holyrood, **3**, 1551
Chaplains in Ordinary
royal household, **7**, 837
Character merchandising
artistic copyright, limitation, **18**, 1157
goodwill, **18**, 1366
passing off, **18**, 1382
Charge card
consumer sale using, passing of property, **18**, 631
general features of transactions, **4**, 271
meaning, **4**, 270
Chargé d'affaire
precedence, **16**, 2014

Charitable
meaning in Scots law, **3**, 1101
Charitable arrangement
contract as to, *jus quaesitum tertio*, **15**, 842
Charitable collection
See PUBLIC CHARITABLE COLLECTION
Charitable purpose
artistic taste, education of, **3**, 1119
arts, promotion and pursuit, **3**, 1119, 1131
benefits conferred on members of society, effect,
　　3, 1121, 1128
classes, **3**, 1116, 1117
education, advancement of—
　　artistic taste, education of, **3**, 1119
　　arts, promotion and pursuit of, **3**, 1119
　　association of persons for mutual, not public,
　　　　improvement, **3**, 1119, 1130
　　charitable purpose, as, **3**, 1108, 1116, 1119
　　closed scholarships, **3**, 1119
　　commercial education, **3**, 1119
　　free schools, maintenance, **3**, 1119
　　institutions diffusing particular type of
　　　　knowledge, **3**, 1119
　　orphans, education and preferment, **3**, 1119
　　professional education, **3**, 1119
　　schools, maintenance, **3**, 1119
　　technical education, **3**, 1119
　　university scholars, maintenance, **3**, 1119
foundations, **24**, 118, 124
free school, maintenance, **3**, 1119
income applied only to, **3**, 1133
meaning—
　　English law, **3**, 1107, 1116
　　　　application in Scotland—
　　　　　　effect, **3**, 1110
　　　　　　generally, **3**, 1109, 1111, 1113, 1116
　　　　　　limits, **3**, 1112
　　Scots law, **3**, 1108, 1109
mutual improvement function, body with, **3**,
　　1119, 1130
objects of body not confined to, where, **3**, 1129
political purpose not classed as, **3**, 1121
poverty, relief of, **3**, 1108, 1116, 1118
public benefit, test, **3**, 1121, 1128
public trusts, **24**, 87, 90, 91
religion, advancement of, **3**, 1632, 1633*n*
　　activities which are not purely religious,
　　　　income spent on, **3**, 1120
　　generally, **3**, 1116, 1120
　　gifts for religious purpose, **3**, 1120
　　missionary work, **3**, 1120
　　repair of churches, gifts for, **3**, 1120
　　Roman Catholic charities, **3**, 1670
　　soundness of religious doctrine, **3**, 1120
school, maintenance, **3**, 1119
shop run for, **3**, 1123
tax advantages, **24**, 87
university, maintenance of scholar in, **3**, 1119
Charitable status
ancillary powers which are not charitable, effect,
　　3, 1115
change in, assets, **4**, 322
charitable purposes, generally, **3**, 1116
construction of documents, **3**, 1115

Charitable status—*continued*
establishment, **3**, 1101
friendly society, **3**, 1118
generally, **3**, 1114
Inland Revenue statement as to, **3**, 1167
more than one purpose, trust with, **3**, 1114
public school, **3**, 1134
public trust, charity as, **3**, 1101, 1114
'recognised body', **3**, 1101
'Scottish charity', **3**, 1101
tax exemption, and, **3**, 1101
Charitable trust
accumulation of income, **24**, 110
ancillary powers which are not charitable, effect,
　　3, 1115
benign treatment, **24**, 101
charitable—
　　public trusts and, **3**, 1101, 1114
　　purposes at common law, **24**, 93
　　status, generally, **3**, 1114
coal industry beneficiaries, representation for, **14**,
　　1677; **24**, 115
cy-près, doctrine of, **24**, 101–111
　　approval of, **24**, 111
　　approximation and, **24**, 111
descriptive words, **24**, 94–98
destructive phraseology, **24**, 99
educational, meaning, **24**, 95
failure—
　　ab initio, **24**, 106
　　after taking effect, **24**, 108
　　of purpose, **24**, 105
　　initial or subsequent, **24**, 109
　　insufficiency of funds, **24**, 110
　　intermittent performance, **24**, 110
　　less than absolute, **24**, 110
meaning, of charitable, **24**, 10, 91–94
more than one purpose, with, **3**, 1114
mortifications, **24**, 3
motive, **24**, 107
proceedings in relation to, **6**, 924
public trusts, **3**, 1101, 1114; **24**, 102
religious purposes, **24**, 96
scientific purposes, **24**, 96
scope of, **24**, 7
variation, **24**, 104
Charity
bequest to, avoidance of intestacy, **25**, 822
building society shares held by, **3**, 328
capital gains tax—
　　charitable trusts, property held on, ceasing to
　　　　be, **3**, 1157, 1158, 1160
　　exemption—
　　　　generally, **3**, 1102, 1157; **19**, 1525
　　　　gifts to charities, **3**, 1159
　　　　offshore income gains, **3**, 1158
　　　　restrictions, **3**, 1105
charitable purpose, *see* CHARITABLE PURPOSE
charitable status, *see* CHARITABLE STATUS
commercial venture, *see* trade carried on by *below*
company—
　　donation to—
　　　　close company, by, **3**, 1155, 1156
　　　　corporation tax, **3**, 1155

Charity—*continued*
company—*continued*
  donation to—*continued*
    income tax, **3**, 1155
    qualifying, **3**, 1155
    tax relief, qualification for, **3**, 1155
  limited by guarantee, formation of, **4**, 312
  shares held by, **3**, 1103
  third party, protection of, **4**, 414
  ultra vires doctrine, **4**, 327
corporation tax—
  company donations, **3**, 1155
  covenanted donation, **3**, 1141, 1147
  tax exemption, restrictions, **3**, 1106
  trading profits of charitable body, **3**, 1132
covenanted donation or payment, *see* COVENANTED
  PAYMENT
distribution, tax exemption, **3**, 1103, 1135
dividend income, tax exemption, **3**, 1103, 1135
enclosed religious community, **3**, 1643
English law, application in Scotland—
  Court of Session, duty of, **3**, 1111
  effect, **3**, 1110
  generally, **3**, 1109, 1113, 1116
  limits, **3**, 1112
exempt agreement, **5**, 821
fiscal privileges, **3**, 1632
friendly society qualifying as, **12**, 681
gift aid, **3**, 1154
gifts to—
  capital gains tax treatment, **3**, 1159
  generally, **25**, 1010
  local government contributions, **14**, 313
income tax—
  covenanted payment or donation to charity, **3**,
    1137, 1147, 1149
    annual payments, as, **3**, 1136–1138
    company, by, **3**, 1139, 1147, 1149
    generally, **3**, 1139
    gross and net payments, **3**, 1144
    husband and wife, independent taxation, **3**,
      1140
  discretionary trust, payment for charitable
    purposes, **3**, 1152
  donation to charity by company, **3**, 1155
  exemption for charity, restrictions, **3**, 1104
  gift aid—
    income or gains not subject to income tax,
      3, 1154
    payment by donor, **3**, 1154
    recovery by charity, **3**, 1154
  income and gains not less than £10,000, where,
    3, 1104
  investment income, charity, of, **3**, 1102
  partnership, covenanted payment by, **3**, 1150
  payroll deduction scheme, **3**, 1153
  Schedule A—
    British Museum and other bodies, **3**, 1166
    charitable tax exemption, **3**, 1103, 1134
  Schedule B, charitable tax exemption, **3**, 1103
  Schedule C, charitable tax exemption, **3**, 1103,
    1135
  Schedule D—
    British Museum and other bodies, **3**, 1166

Charity—*continued*
income tax—*continued*
  Schedule D—*continued*
    Case I—
      annual profits or gains of trade, **3**, 1122
      covenanted donation to charity, **3**, 1147
      covenanted payment—
        partnership by, **3**, 1150
        sole trader by, **3**, 1151
    Case II—
      covenanted payment—
        partnership by, **3**, 1150
        sole trader by, **3**, 1151
    Case III, **3**, 1135, 1137, 1138
    charitable tax exemption, **3**, 1103, 1127,
      1135
  Schedule E, payroll deduction scheme, **3**, 1153
  Schedule F, charitable tax exemption, **3**, 1103,
    1135
  sole trader, covenanted payment by, **3**, 1151
  tax avoidance, two or more charities acting in
    concert, **3**, 1104
  trading profits—
    destination, **3**, 1126
    generally, **3**, 1122
    mutual improvement as object of body, **3**,
      1130
    profit and loss, computation, **3**, 1122, 1123
    purpose to which applied, **3**, 1124
    tax exemption—
      beneficiaries of charity, work mainly
        carried out by, **3**, 1131
      generally, **3**, 1127
      objects of body not confined to charitable
        purposes, where, **3**, 1129
      trade exercised as primary purpose of
        charity, where, **3**, 1128
    taxable trading by charities, **3**, 1123
    trade, meaning, **3**, 1122
    whether trade being carried on, **3**, 1125
  See also trading profits *below*
inheritance tax—
  charity, transfer of value to, **3**, 1161
    conditions to be met, **3**, 1161
  close company, gift made by, **3**, 1161
  exemption, **19**, 1533
  transfers of capital after death, **3**, 1161
  trust, gift made to, **3**, 1161
interest, income from, **3**, 1103, 1135
investment income, taxation, **3**, 1102
meaning—
  English law, **3**, 1107
  generally, **3**, 1117
  Scots law, **3**, 1108, 1109
offshore income gains, tax treatment, **3**, 1158
passing off action brought by, **18**, 1363
payroll deduction scheme, **3**, 1153
purpose of—
  charitable *see* CHARITABLE PURPOSE
  and charitable status, *see* CHARITABLE STATUS
rates, relief from, **14**, 861
religious bodies, **3**, 1632
rental income, **3**, 1103, 1134
Roman Catholic, **3**, 1670

Charity—*continued*
stamp duty, exemption from liability, **3**, 1164
supplies made by, VAT zero-rating, **7**, 1459
tax avoidance, two or more charities acting in
  concert, **3**, 1104
tax treatment—
  charitable status, **3**, 1101
  English law, application in Scotland—
    Court of Session, duty of, **3**, 1111
    effect, **3**, 1110
    generally, **3**, 1109, 1113, 1116
    limits, **3**, 1112
  exemption—
    claims for, **3**, 1101
      Inland Revenue statement, **3**, 1167
    establishment of charitable status, **3**, 1101
    generally, **3**, 1102
    income and gains not less than £10,000,
      where, **3**, 1104
    land ownership, income from, **3**, 1103, 1134
    restrictions, **3**, 1104–1106
    special exemptions, **3**, 1103
    stamp duty, **3**, 1164
  See also capital gains tax; corporation tax;
    income tax; inheritance tax *above*; value
    added tax *below*
trade carried on by—
  annual profits or gains of trade, **3**, 1122
  beneficiaries of charity, work mainly carried
    out by, **3**, 1131
  body whose objects not confined to charitable
    purposes, by, **3**, 1129
  carnivals, gymkhanas and other displays, **3**,
    1132
  charitable function, **3**, 1130
  charitable purposes only, income applied to, **3**,
    1133
  competition with other traders, **3**, 1132
  corporation tax, **3**, 1132
    trading profits, **3**, 1132
  extra-statutory concession, **3**, 1132
  income applied to charitable purposes only, **3**,
    1133
  income tax—
    generally, **3**, 1122
    taxable trading, what constitutes, **3**, 1123
    See also trading profits *below*
  jumble sales, bazaars etc., **3**, 1132
  mutual improvement, **3**, 1130
  profit and loss, computation, **3**, 1122, 1123
  public support, reason for, **3**, 1132
  regular trading, **3**, 1132
  taxation—
    generally, **3**, 1102, 1103, 1122
    taxable trading, what constitutes, **3**, 1123
  test of trade being carried on, **3**, 1125
  trade primary purpose of charity, where, **3**,
    1128
  trading profits—
    beneficiaries of charity, work mainly carried
      out by, **3**, 1131
    body whose objects not confined to
      charitable purposes, **3**, 1129
    charitable function, society with, **3**, 1130

Charity—*continued*
trade carried on by—*continued*
  trading profits—*continued*
    destination, **3**, 1126
    extra-statutory concession, **3**, 1132
    income applied to charitable purposes only,
      3, 1133
    mutual improvement function, society with,
      3, 1130
    primary purpose of charity, trade exercised
      as, **3**, 1127, 1128
    profit and loss, computation, **3**, 1122, 1123
    purpose to which applied, **3**, 1124
    tax exemption, generally, **3**, 1127
  transactions treated as supplies, VAT zero-rating,
    7, 1311
  trust, voluntary church, for purpose of, **3**, 1643
  ultra vires act by, **4**, 413
  value added tax—
    charity—
      business carried on by, **3**, 1162
      goods, importation into UK, **3**, 1162
      goods or services, making taxable supplies, **3**,
        1162
      registration for value added tax, **3**, 1162
    input tax, recovery, **3**, 1162
    output tax, **3**, 1162
    patriotic nature, body with objects of, **3**, 1162
    philanthropic nature, body with objects of, **3**,
      1162
    philosophical nature, body with objects of, **3**,
      1162
    political nature, body with objects of, **3**, 1162
    religious nature, body with objects of, **3**, 1162
    subscription to society or other body, **3**, 1162
    zero-rated supplies, charitable items, **3**, 1163
  See also VOLUNTARY ORGANISATIONS

Charity Commissioners
disclosure of information to, by Customs and
  Excise Commissioners, **7**, 1283
registration with not required by Scots charities,
  3, 1101, 1101*n*, 1167

Chart
copyright, **18**, 958

Charter
burgh, of, **14**, 10
Crown, **14**, 10
feu-ferme, **14**, 11

Charter by progress
Great Seal, passed under, **7**, 874
types, **7**, 874

Chartered accountant
disciplinary arrangements, **1**, 26–33
education and training, **1**, 15
institutes, amalgamation of, **1**, 8
meaning, **1**, 2
practical experience, requirement of, **1**, 16
public practice, training in, **1**, 8
See also ACCOUNTANT

**Chartered Association of Certified
Accountants**
authorisation by, **12**, 1313
disciplinary arrangements, **1**, 34
generally, **1**, 9

Chartered corporation
acting contrary to terms of charter, **19**, 229
Chartered Institute of Public Finance and Accountancy
audit standards, publishing, **1**, 63
disciplinary arrangements, **1**, 36
generally, **1**, 9
local authority accounts, issuing guidance on, **1**, 47
Chartered surveyor
building contracts, generally, **3**, 142
role of in purchase and sale of land, **25**, 72
Charterer
breach of contract by, **21**, 717
liability, limitation, *see* SEA, CARRIAGE BY (limitation of liability)
salvor, as, **21**, 444, 446
Charterparty
ASBATIME Form, **21**, 536n
Baltime Form, **21**, 536n, 558n
bareboat charterparty, **21**, 534n
berth charterparty, **21**, 672
bill of lading, **21**, 577n
  cesser clause, **21**, 699
  contract, **21**, 695, 695n
  demise charterparty, **21**, 691n, 694, 695n
  generally, **21**, 528, 546, 588, 690
  holder of, **21**, 694
  inaccuracy in, liability of charterer, **21**, 698
  inconsistency between, **21**, 697, 697n
  indorsed by charterer, **21**, 692
  indorsed to charterer, **21**, 693
  lien clause, **21**, 699
  received by charterer, **21**, 691
  regulation by terms of charterparty, **21**, 696, 696n
  relationship with charterparty, **21**, 547
  sub-charterparty, **21**, 691, 696n
  through bill of lading, **21**, 695n
  time charterparty, generally, **21**, 640
  voyage charterparty, generally, **21**, 618, 633
both to blame collision clause, **21**, 584, 584n, 618, 640
charterer, *see* CHARTERER
collision damage—
  both to blame collision clause, **21**, 640
  liability, **21**, 321
  title to sue, **21**, 320
construction, rules for, **21**, 539
contract—
  generally, **21**, 533
  services and custody, for, **21**, 613, 613n
dangerously unsafe ship, **21**, 206
demise charterparty—
  bill of lading, **21**, 691n, 694, 695n
  charterer, position of, **21**, 534
  freight, **21**, 664
  fuel, provision of, **21**, 534
  hire—
    generally, **21**, 653
    meaning, **21**, 653n
  hire purchase, ship being acquired on, **21**, 534n
  intention of parties, **21**, 534
  master and crew—
    position of, **21**, 534
    provision of, **21**, 534, 534n

Charterparty—*continued*
demise charterparty—*continued*
  meaning, **21**, 534
  option to purchase, containing, **21**, 534n
  responsibility for, **21**, 534
  salvage earned by, **21**, 534
  shipowner, position of, **21**, 534, 534n
  shipper's right to sue charterer, **21**, 578
  stores, provision of, **21**, 534
  towage contract, **21**, 403
  usage, **21**, 534n
disponent owner, **21**, 538
dock charterparty, **21**, 672
fixtures, **21**, 533
form and contents, **21**, 536
Gencon Form, **21**, 536n, 558n
general average, arbitration clause, **21**, 711
Hague-Visby Rules—
  application, **21**, 591
  clause paramount, **21**, 591n, 618
head charterparty, **21**, 538
laytime (lay days), *see* LAYTIME
liability—
  collision damage, for, **21**, 321
  exclusion or limitation—
    cargo, loss of or damage to, **21**, 547
    damnum fatale, **21**, 542, 548
    deviation, unjustified, **21**, 547
    employees and contractors, **21**, 560
    excepted perils, **21**, 547
    exceptions clauses, **21**, 547
    generally, **21**, 547
    negligence, **21**, 547
    owners' responsibility clause, **21**, 558
    perils of the sea, **21**, 551
    Queen's enemies, damage caused by, **21**, 549
    strikes exception, **21**, 555
    Unfair Contract Terms Act 1977 ...561
    unseaworthiness, **21**, 547, 627
loss of or damage to ship, damages for lost future engagements, **21**, 385, 385n, 387, 387n
meaning, **21**, 521, 533
net charterparty, **21**, 534n
NYPE Form, **21**, 536n
oral, **21**, 536
penalty clause, **15**, 799
port charterparty, **21**, 672
sale of ship which is subject to existing contract, **21**, 718
sea waybill, **21**, 690
ship's delivery order, **21**, 690
shipbroker, role of, **21**, 533
shipper's right to sue owner, **21**, 578, 578n
sub-charterparty—
  bill of lading, **21**, 691
  freight, **21**, 664
  generally, **21**, 538
time charterparty—
  arbitration clause, **21**, 640
  Baltime Form, **21**, 640
  bill of lading, *see* bill of lading *above*
  both to blame collision clause, **21**, 640
  breach of contract, **21**, 640
  breakdown, offhire, **21**, 649

Charterparty—*continued*
time charterparty—*continued*
  cancelling clause, **21**, 640, 645
  cargo, express provisions as to, **21**, 640
  cargo-worthiness, **21**, 640, 644
  choice of law clause, **21**, 640
  clause paramount, **21**, 640
  dangerous goods, express and implied terms, **21**, 639, 643
  delivery of ship to charterer, **21**, 645
  description of vessel, **21**, 640, 641
  deviation, **21**, 615n, 639
  employment and indemnity clause, **21**, 640, 650
  exemption or exceptions clause, **21**, 640
  express terms, **21**, 640
  extension, **21**, 648
  frustration, **21**, 652
  fuel, **21**, 640, 647
    consumption as consideration, **21**, 638, 640
  generally, **21**, 534, 535, 638
  Hague Rules, **21**, 640
  Hague-Visby Rules, **21**, 640
  harbour dues, **21**, 640
  hire, **21**, 638
    charge, **21**, 640
    damages, **21**, 648
    generally, **21**, 653
    loss of ship, **21**, 652, 652n
    meaning, **21**, 653n
    non-payment or late payment, **21**, 638, 640, 651, 651n
    payment—
      express terms, **21**, 651
      generally, **21**, 640, 653
    rate, **21**, 651, 651n
  ice clause, **21**, 640
  implied terms, **21**, 639
  jurisdiction clause, **21**, 640
  legitimate last voyage, **21**, 648
  lien clause, **21**, 640
  loading, **21**, 643
    costs, **21**, 640
  logs, **21**, 640
  loss of ship—
    express terms, **21**, 640
    generally, **21**, 652, 652n
  loss of time, offhire, **21**, 649
  maintenance of ship, apparel and equipment, **21**, 640, 646
  meaning, **21**, 535
  New Jason clause, **21**, 640
  NYPE Form, **21**, 640
  offhire clause, **21**, 640, 649
  owners' responsibility clause, **21**, 640
  period of charterparty, **21**, 648
  pilotage dues, **21**, 640
  preliminary voyage to port, **21**, 640
  provisions etc, costs of, **21**, 640
  reasonable despatch, **21**, 639, 640
  redelivery of ship, express provisions, **21**, 640, 648
  safe ports, implied terms, **21**, 639, 640
  seaworthiness, **21**, 639, 640, 644, 645

Charterparty—*continued*
time charterparty—*continued*
  ship's disbursements, **21**, 640
  shipping agents, appointment and responsibility, **21**, 640
  speed, **21**, 638, 640
  stowage, responsibility for, **21**, 640
  sub-chartering, **21**, 640
  trading limits, **21**, 640, 642
  unloading, **21**, 643
    costs, **21**, 640
  voyage delayed, **21**, 648
  war clause, **21**, 640
  withdrawal clause, **21**, 651, 651n
  withdrawal of vessel following non-payment of hire, **21**, 651, 651n
  York-Antwerp Rules, **21**, 640
title to sue—
  collision damage, for, **21**, 320
  shipowner, **21**, 577
towage contract expressed as, where, **21**, 403, 403n
voyage charterparty—
  advance freight, **21**, 612
  arbitration clause, **21**, 618
  berth—
    discharge, **21**, 631
    impediment preventing ship's entry, **21**, 622
  berth charterparty, **21**, 672
  bill of lading, *see* bill of lading *above*
  both to blame collision clause, **21**, 618
  cancelling clause, **21**, 618, 619, 619n
  cargo—
    alternative, **21**, 624
    care of, liability for, **21**, 628
    charterer refusing to load, **21**, 624
    delivery, shipowner's duty, **21**, 632
    discharge, **21**, 612
    express terms, **21**, 618
    full and complete—
      charterer's duty to provide, **21**, 625
      meaning, **21**, 625
    loading, **21**, 612, 626
      costs, **21**, 618
      equipment, provision of, **21**, 626
    master's power to sell, **21**, 629
    mixed, cargos which have become, **21**, 632
    owner failing to land or take delivery of cargo, **21**, 632, 634
      back freight, **21**, 661
    owner failing to make entry, **21**, 634
    protection of, duty as to, **21**, 630
    provision of, generally, **21**, 624
    receipt and delivery, who takes, **21**, 632, 633
    salvage services rendered to, **21**, 630
    stowage, **21**, 626
      liability for improper, **21**, 626
      re-stowage during voyage, **21**, 626
    time limit for loading, **21**, 624
    transhipment, **21**, 629, 630
    unloading—
      costs, **21**, 618
      Merchant Shipping Act 1894, under, **21**, 634–637

Charterparty—*continued*
voyage charterparty—*continued*
  cargo—*continued*
    unloading—*continued*
      port and berth, **21**, 631
      shipowner's duty, **21**, 632
      where cargo cannot be landed, **21**, 632, 661
  cargo-worthiness, **21**, 614*n*, 618
  cesser clasue, **21**, 618
  choice of law clause, **21**, 618
  clause paramount, **21**, 618
  completion of voyage, duty as to, **21**, 630
  consecutive, **21**, 535
  contract evidenced by, performance, **21**, 585
  damages for detention, **21**, 612, 624*n*, 633
    See also SEA, CARRIAGE BY (damages for detention)
  dangerous goods, implied terms, **21**, 617, 617*n*
  delay, master's powers of, **21**, 629
  demurrage, **21**, 612, 618, 624*n*, 633, 666
  despatch money (despatch), **21**, 689
  deviation—
    clause, **21**, 618
    implied terms, **21**, 615, 615*n*
    master's powers in relation to, **21**, 629
  dock charterparty, **21**, 672
  exceptions clauses, **21**, 618
  express terms, **21**, 618
  freight, **21**, 612, 633
    action in claim for, **21**, 665
    advance, **21**, 653, 659, 659*n*
    back, **21**, 653*n*, 656*n*, 661
    calculation, **21**, 653, 653*n*, 654, 654*n*
    damaged cargo, **21**, 657, 657*n*
    dead, **21**, 612, 625, 653*n*, 660
    delivery, necessity for, **21**, 656, 656*n*
    express terms, **21**, 618
    generally, **21**, 653
    jurisdiction, **21**, 665
    liability for, **21**, 663
    lump sum, **21**, 653, 655, 655*n*, 657, 657*n*
    meaning, **21**, 653*n*
    non-payment or late payment, **21**, 665
    pro rata (freight *pro rata itineris*), **21**, 653, 656*n*, 658, 658*n*
    shipowners' lien, **21**, 665
    to whom payable, **21**, 664
    See also SEA, CARRIAGE BY (freight)
  generally, **21**, 535, 612
  Hague Rules, **21**, 618
  Hague-Visby Rules, **21**, 618
  ice clause, **21**, 618
  implied terms, **21**, 613–617
  indemnity clause, **21**, 618
  jurisdiction clause, **21**, 618
  law of flag ship, **21**, 629
  lay/can spread, **21**, 619*n*
  laytime (lay days), *see* LAYTIME
  lien clause, **21**, 618
  liquidated damages clause, **21**, 618
  loading cargo, *see* cargo *above*
  London clause, **21**, 632*n*
  loss, master's power to incur, **21**, 629
  lump sum freight, **21**, 612

Charterparty—*continued*
voyage charterparty—*continued*
  master's authority, **21**, 629
  meaning, **21**, 535, 612
  New Jason clause, **21**, 618
  owner's responsibility clause, **21**, 618
  port—
    discharge, **21**, 631
    impediment preventing ship's entry, **21**, 622
    loading—
      delay in naming, **21**, 620
      preliminary voyage to, **21**, 618, 619
    provisions as to ports, generally, **21**, 618–621
  port charterparty, **21**, 672
  preliminary voyage to loading port, **21**, 618, 619
  readiness to load or unload, responsibility for, **21**, 623
  reasonable despatch—
    express terms, **21**, 617
    generally, **21**, 618, 619
    implied terms, **21**, 616
  repairs, delay or transhipment due to, **21**, 629, 630
  safe berths, express terms as to, **21**, 618, 621
  safe ports, express terms as to, **21**, 618, 621
  salvage agreement, master's power to enter, **21**, 629
  seaworthiness, **21**, 618, 627
    implied terms, **21**, 614, 614*n*
  shipowners'—
    credit, master raising money by pledging, **21**, 629
    lien, **21**, 612, 618, 632, 656, 656*n*
      preservation and discharge of, for freight, **21**, 635–637
  stevedores, express terms, **21**, 618
  stowage, express terms, **21**, 618
  strike clause, **21**, 618
  transhipment, **21**, 618
  unloading cargo, *see* cargo *above*
  war clause, **21**, 618
  York-Antwerp Rules, **21**, 618
written, **21**, 536
Chattel leasing agreement
administrator, powers of, **4**, 619
meaning, **4**, 619
Chattels
gift of, **19**, 1610
Chattels mortgage
finance lease as, **14**, 1007
plant and machinery, ownership of, **14**, 1013
Cheese and cheese products
advertisement, **11**, 361
composition, **11**, 361
emulsifiers and stabilisers, **11**, 373
labelling, **11**, 361
mineral hydrocarbons, treatment with, **11**, 375
preservatives, **11**, 377
Chemist
See PHARMACEUTICAL CHEMIST
Cheque
account payee, legal status given to words, **4**, 191

Cheque—*continued*
alteration of—
  authenticated, **2**, 1186
  not apparent, effect of, **2**, 1186
assignation, as, **4**, 205
bank payment order, proposal for introduction of,
  4, 191
banker—
  collecting—
    duties generally, **4**, 208
    holder, as, **4**, 209
    statutory protection, **4**, 212, 213
  customer, relationship with, **4**, 199
  meaning, **4**, 199
  obligations of, **2**, 1188
  paying—
    assignation, cheque as, **4**, 205
    authority, termination of, **4**, 204
    crossed cheques, duties as to, **4**, 207
    duty to honour cheques, **4**, 202
    failure to honour cheques, **4**, 203
    mistake, payment by, **4**, 206
    statutory protection, **4**, 211
  protection of—
    collecting banker, **4**, 212, 213
    paying banker, **4**, 211
bar to payment—
  arrestment, **2**, 1183
  breach of trust, **2**, 1184
  countermand as, **2**, 1185
  forgery as, **2**, 1187
  insufficient funds, **2**, 1182
  material alteration, **2**, 1186
  unauthorised signature, **2**, 1187
bill of exchange distinguished, **4**, 192
branches of banks, **4**, 201
breach of trust, drawn in, **2**, 1184
cash, payable to, **4**, 192
certified, **4**, 196
cheque guarantee cards—
  consumer credit legislation, **4**, 268
  contractual relationship, **4**, 267
  generally, **4**, 197, 266
clearing system, **4**, 200
collecting banker, **2**, 1192
  See also banker *above*
countermand—
  effect of, **2**, 1185
  notice of, failure to implement, **2**, 1204
crossed—
  additions to crossing, **4**, 195
  alterations to, **4**, 195
  banker's duties as to, **4**, 207
  generally or specially, **4**, 195
  not negotiable, **4**, 195
  origins of crossing, **4**, 195
crossed, payment of, **2**, 1191
customer—
  banker, relationship with, **4**, 199
  duties of, **4**, 210
  meaning, **4**, 199
dishonoured on presentment for payment, **4**, 193
documentary evidence, as, **10**, 602
duty to honour, **4**, 202

Cheque—*continued*
executory estate, drawn on, **2**, 1184
failure to honour, **4**, 203
features—
  certified cheques, **4**, 196
  cheque cards, **4**, 197
  crossed cheques, **4**, 195
  generally, **4**, 192
  payment by cheque, **4**, 198
  presentment for payment, **4**, 193
  transfer of cheques, **4**, 194
forged, **11**, 768
fraud, **7**, 367
gaming, used in—
  acceptance of, **2**, 1607
  statutory protection, **2**, 1503
gift made by, **19**, 1606
honouring—
  failure in, damages on, **2**, 1190
  general obligation, **2**, 1189
  protection of banker, **2**, 1191
indorsed, not evidence of loan, **13**, 1735
insurance premium payment by, **12**, 833
loan constituted by, **13**, 1713
mandate to banker to pay, as, **4**, 190
mistake, payment by, **4**, 206
money, use of term, **14**, 1802
negotiable instrument—
  cheque as, **4**, 103, 190
  See also NEGOTIABLE INSTRUMENT
origins, **4**, 190
overdue, **4**, 194
parole evidence in questions relating to, **15**, 760
partner, signature by, **16**, 1031
paying banker, *see* banker *above*
payment by, **4**, 198
post-dated, not irregular, **4**, 147
presentation of, assignation, operates as, **2**, 1182
presentment for payment, **4**, 193, 202
reform, proposals for, **4**, 191
signature on, **4**, 192
signing etc, provisions in partnership agreement,
  16, 1009
sum certain in money, for, **4**, 192
summary diligence not competent on, **4**, 184, 192
termination of banker's authority, **4**, 204
third party rights, **15**, 848
transfer of, **4**, 194
true owner of, **4**, 207
wages, payable to, **4**, 192
  See also NEGOTIABLE INSTRUMENT
Cheque guarantee card
consumer credit legislation, **4**, 268
contractual relationship, **4**, 267
fraud, **7**, 367
generally, **4**, 197, 266
Chewing gum
food for purposes of Food and Drugs Act, **11**, 311
Chicago Convention
agency established by, **2**, 906
giving effect to, in UK, **2**, 906
Chief constable
accountability, **16**, 1736
amalgamation scheme, where, **16**, 1757, 1757*n*

Chief constable—*continued*
annual report, **14**, 485; **16**, 1727
appointment, **14**, 110, 249, 483; **16**, 1730, 1736, 1747
assistant—
    appointment, **14**, 483; **16**, 1730, 1737, 1747
    complaint against, **16**, 1778–1780
    dismissal, **16**, 1730
    enforced retirement, **16**, 1730
    generally, **16**, 1743
    rank structure, **16**, 1742
    resignation, **16**, 1730
    suspension, **16**, 1772
Association of Chief Police Officers, **16**, 1763
business interests, **16**, 1748
cadets, powers as to, **16**, 1737, 1746
child appearing in adult court, duties as to, **22**, 33
collaboration agreements, powers in relation to, **16**, 1738
complaint against—
    hearing, **16**, 1779
    investigation, **16**, 1778
    punishment, **16**, 1780
criminal statistics—
    duty to report, **16**, 1729, 1738
    statement of, **16**, 1738
deputy—
    appointment, **14**, 110, 249, 483; **16**, 1730, 1737, 1747
    complaint against, **16**, 1778–1780
    complaints book, **16**, 1772
    discipline book, **16**, 1772
    dismissal, **14**, 110; **16**, 1730
    enforced retirement, **16**, 1730
    function and responsibilities, **16**, 1743
    more than one, inclusion of, **16**, 1743
    rank structure, **16**, 1742
    resignation, **16**, 1730
    suspension, **16**, 1772
disciplinary authority, **16**, 1737, 1773
discipline, **16**, 1736
dismissal, **14**, 110; **16**, 1730
duty of care to constables, **16**, 1769
enforced retirement, **16**, 1730
firearms—
    certificates, issue, **16**, 1738
    dealers, registration, **16**, 1738
    issue, **16**, 1738
functions—
    appointment and promotions, **16**, 1737
    establishment, in relation to, **16**, 1737
    general, **14**, 484
    operational control, **16**, 1702, 1739
    operational matters, **16**, 1738
    other enactments, under, **14**, 486
independence, **16**, 1736
mutual aid, power to request, **16**, 1738
powers, **16**, 1738, 1741
proceedings against, **16**, 1765
property of persons in custody, functions in relation to, **16**, 1821
public prosecutors, directions from, **16**, 1740
qualifications, **16**, 1748
rank structure, **16**, 1742

Chief constable—*continued*
removal, **16**, 1736
reports, **14**, 485; **16**, 1738
    police authority, to, **16**, 1715
    Secretary of State, to, **16**, 1727
resignation, **16**, 1730
responsibility, **16**, 1736
sheriff principal, directions from, **16**, 1740
suspension, **16**, 1772
temporary constables, powers as to, **16**, 1737
watching of premises under agreement with occupier, **16**, 1738
wrongdoing by constable, liability for, **16**, 1765
Chief education officer
appointment, **8**, 714
Chief Inspector of Prisons
See HER MAJESTY'S CHIEF INSPECTOR OF PRISONS
Chief Rabbi
jurisdiction, **3**, 1675
Chief Registrar of Friendly Societies, 3, 304
Chief Scientific Adviser
role of, **5**, 489
Child–children
abandonment, **3**, 1246; **10**, 1137, 1224
    adoption of abandoned child, **10**, 1209
    new-born infant, **14**, 1908
    parental rights, assumption by local authority, **3**, 1267
    registration of birth of abandoned child, **19**, 1440
abduction of—
    European Convention on Recognition and Enforcement, **10**, 1325–1329
    Hague Convention on the Civil Aspects of International Child Abduction, **8**, 530; **10**, 1330–1341
    international, **10**, 1313
    plagium, **10**, 1225, 1342
    private international law, **10**, 1313
    Scotland, to, **10**, 1321
    sexual purposes, for, **3**, 1239, 1244
    taking child out of UK without appropriate consent, **10**, 1343
    United Kingdom, custody orders made in, **10**, 1322–1324
abortion, **10**, 1029, 1030, 1032
    relevance of, **10**, 1029
abuse, *see* CHILD ABUSE
abuse of trust, **10**, 1137
    sexual offence, where, **7**, 318
access to—
    adoption order, under, **10**, 1303
    child's views, **10**, 1302
    counterclaim for, **17**, 1233
    dispute over, **17**, 1235
    Hague Convention on the Civil Aspects of International Child Abduction, **10**, 1341
    history of right of, **10**, 1294–1297
    how applications arise, **10**, 1298
    Law Reform (Parent and Child) (Scotland) Act 1986—
        under, **10**, 1298–1302
    nature of right, **10**, 1293

Child-children—*continued*
access to—*continued*
  welfare of child—
    assessment of, **10**, 1299
    emotional, **10**, 1301
    physical, **10**, 1300
adoption, *see* ADOPTION
after-born *conditio* a presumption for benefit of, **25**, 752
after-care supervision, release after detention at direction of Secretary of State, **22**, 36
age, relevance of—
  abuse of trust, **10**, 1137
  child offender, **10**, 1138
  criminal law, **10**, 1134–1140
  date of birth, **10**, 1047
  delict—
    child as defender, **10**, 1124
    child as pursuer, **10**, 1121
    contributory negligence, **10**, 1122
    parent as defender, **10**, 1123
  determining age, **10**, 1045
  infancy, **10**, 1050
  majority, age of, **10**, 1041, 1049
  minority—
    actings of minors and curators, **10**, 1105–1109
    apprenticeship, contracts of, **10**, 1078
    business, contracts in course of, **10**, 1079
    curator—
      actings of minors and curators, **10**, 1105–1109
      appointment by court, **10**, 1095
      control of minor's person by, **10**, 1117–1120
      father as, **10**, 1084–1086
      generally, **10**, 1083
      illegitimate children, **10**, 1085
      married children, **10**, 1086
      minor's choice of, **10**, 1092, 1093
      mother as, **10**, 1088, 1089
      parents as curators, **10**, 1090
      role of, **10**, 1073, 1096
      termination of curatory, **10**, 1097
      testamentary, **10**, 1087, 1091, 1094
      See also CURATOR
    employment, contracts of, **10**, 1078
    enorme lesion, and, **10**, 1110–1115
    forisfamiliation, **10**, 1098–1104
    fraudulent misrepresentation by minor, **10**, 1116
    generally, **10**, 1049
    legal capacity of minors, **10**, 1073, 1107, 1144–1146
    legal relations, minor's capacity to enter, **10**, 1074, 1083
    marriage, **10**, 843, 1040, 1080, 1100
    obtaining necessaries, **10**, 1075, 1076, 1077
    reform of law, **10**, 1082, 1141–1146
    scope of doctrine, **10**, 1077
    trade, contracts in course of, **10**, 1079
    wills, **10**, 1081
  modern position, **10**, 1140
  modern reproductive techniques, **10**, 1047

Child-children—*continued*
age, relevance of—*continued*
  nonage, *see* NONAGE
  proof of birth, **10**, 1046
  protection of children—
    care, *see* CHILD IN CARE
    reporter, role of, **10**, 1129
    specific statutory protection, **10**, 1126
  pupillarity—
    beneficial transactions, **10**, 1052
    generally, **10**, 1049
    legal incapacity, **10**, 1051
    modern context, relevance in, **10**, 1055
    necessaries, liability for, **10**, 1054
    reciprocity, **10**, 1053
    reform of law, **10**, 1141–1146
    tutor—
      administration of pupil's estate, **10**, 1071
      control of pupil's person, **10**, 1070
      factors *loco tutoris*, **10**, 1069
      functions of, **10**, 1056
      history of tutory, **10**, 1057
      parents as, **10**, 58, 59, 1060
      role of, **10**, 1070, 1071
      termination of tutory, **10**, 1072
      testamentary, **10**, 1015, 1061–1063
      tutor at law, **10**, 1064–1066
      tutor dative, **10**, 1065, 1067–1069
      See also TUTOR
    See also PUPIL
  registration of birth, **10**, 1048
  sexual offences, **10**, 1136
  victim, child as, **10**, 1135
  See also MINOR
aliment—
  adopted child, **10**, 1240–1242
  agreements on, **10**, 1258
  child living in same household as person from whom claimed, **10**, 1254
  child over sixteen, **10**, 1254
  cohabitee, child of, **10**, 1217, 1247
  conduct of defender, **10**, 1253
  deceased person, claims from estate of, **10**, 847, 1250
  education and training, during, **10**, 1249
  executors, obligations as to, **10**, 1250
  extent of obligation, **10**, 1252
  factors to be taken into account, **10**, 1253
  failure to provide, **3**, 1246
  handicapped child, **10**, 1249
  independent right to, **10**, 968, 969
  legitimate child—
    alimentary debtor, succession to, **10**, 1230
    discharge of obligation, **10**, 1233
    duration of obligation, **10**, 1232
    ex jure representationis obligation, **10**, 1234
    generally, **10**, 1230
    parents, **10**, 1230
    quantification, **10**, 1231
    relatives other than parents, **10**, 1230
  life-long right to, abolition of, **10**, 1249
  nature of right, **10**, 1249
  orders, nature of available, **10**, 1255
  parental obligation, **10**, 1250; **15**, 2, 4*n*

Child-children—*continued*
aliment—*continued*
 persons owing obligation, **10**, 1250, 1251
  defences to, **10**, 1254
 procedural matters, **10**, 1256
 provision by *negotiorum gestor*, **15**, 98
 quantification, **10**, 1252
 recall of decree, **10**, 853, 1257
 relatives, obligations as to, **10**, 1250, 1251
 right to, generally, **10**, 1229, 1248
 stepchildren, **10**, 1217, 1243–1246
 successors to estate of person owing alimentary
  obligation, **10**, 847, 1250
 taxation of, **19**, 1579, 1581
 variation of decree, **10**, 853, 1257
 See also ALIMENT
alimentary liferent, *see* LIFERENT
ante-natal situation, removal of child on account
 of, **10**, 1027
antenuptial trust, **24**, 62
appointment, power of, **3**, 1202, 1211
apprenticeship, contract of, **10**, 1078
arbiter, acting as, **3**, 1202
arrest, **17**, 891
artificial insemination, **10**, 900, 1159
assault by, instigated by adult, **7**, 213
assault of, **3**, 1246, 1250; **10**, 1137, 1224
 diagnostic techniques, **3**, 1339
 mens rea, **3**, 1339
assistance in kind—
 local authority, duty to exercise discretion, **22**, 13
 preventing child coming into care, **22**, 13
babysitter, age of, **3**, 1246
bad associations, falling into, **3**, 1330
bank account, capacity to hold, **3**, 1219
bank loan to, **3**, 1220
bars, not allowed in, **2**, 74
begging, **3**, 1247
birth—
 friendly society payments on, **12**, 686
 parents' duty to obtain assistance at, **7**, 41, 48,
  292
 registration of, **10**, 1048; **14**, 1912
 revocation of gift following, **8**, 645
bodily injury to, Schedule 1 offences, **3**, 1250
born in United Kingdom who are not British, **12**,
 127
 entry clearance, **12**, 151
 Immigration Rules, **12**, 149
 settlement, family reunion or creation by, **12**,
  284
British Visitor's passport, **16**, 1224
broadcast, performance in, **9**, 1052
brothels, offences in relation to, **3**, 1239, 1244
building society account held by, **3**, 1219
business, contract in course of, **10**, 1078
busking, **9**, 1040
cable programme service, performance in, **9**, 1052
care—
 advertising relating to, **1**, 528; **17**, 45
 arrangements for, **17**, 1234
 committal to, **12**, 64
 exclusion from scope of Judgments Convention,
  8, 432

Children-children—*continued*
care—*continued*
 generally, **10**, 1125, 1133; **17**, 236
 parental access and visitation rights, **12**, 64
 reception into, *see* CHILD IN CARE
 separation of siblings, **12**, 64
 termination of care order, promotion of
  parent-child relationship, **12**, 64
chastisement of, **3**, 1246; **10**, 1312
child benefit, *see* CHILD BENEFIT
Child Support Agency, **21**, 1070
children's hearing, *see* CHILDREN'S HEARING
cinema—
 children's cinema, **9**, 1026
 performance in film, **9**, 1052
circus performance by—
 dangerous, **9**, 1035
 illegal, **9**, 1035
 training for, **9**, 1035
class gift, **25**, 843
classification, generally, **10**, 1012, 1013
close support unit, **3**, 1375
cohabitee, of, **10**, 1003, 1005
 aliment, **10**, 1217, 1247
compulsory care—
 child requiring—
  children's hearing system, **3**, 1275, 1285, 1287
  decision, power to make, **3**, 1285
  Schedule 1 offences, **3**, 1243
  child of same household, **3**, 1243
  sexual intercourse by girl under sixteen,
   following, **3**, 1235
compulsory removal—
 procedure, **22**, 18
 social worker, evidence, **22**, 18
concealment of pregnancy, **10**, 1031
 art and part guilt, **7**, 293
 Concealment of Birth (Scotland) Act 1809 …,
  7, 291
 elements of crime, **7**, 292
 generally, **7**, 290
consent to intentional delict, **15**, 393n, 396
contributory negligence by, **15**, 406
conviction—
 detention at direction of Secretary of State—
  placement, local authority function, **22**, 33
corporal punishment, **12**, 26, 90, 91
court—
 adult, appearance in, **22**, 33
 brought before, notification of local authority,
  16, 1788
criminal capacity—
 child under eight, **3**, 1218
 children's hearing, disposal of case by, **3**, 1218
 courts' powers in relation to, **3**, 1218
 detention, sentence of, **3**, 1218
 detention of child before trial, **3**, 1218
 murder conviction, where, **3**, 1218
 prosecution, **3**, 1218
 trial, **3**, 1218
Criminal Injuries Compensation Scheme—
 applications, generally, **7**, 1, 2
 dangerous game, injury sustained during, **7**, 10
 family, violence within, **7**, 1, 4, 5

Child-children—*continued*
Criminal Procedure (Scotland) Act 1975,
  sentenced under, **16**, 1432
criminal registers of cases concerning, access to,
  19, 879
cruelty towards, **3**, 1246
curator, *see* CURATOR
curatory, order relating to, **8**, 508
custodial sentence, imposition, **3**, 1218
custody, **10**, 1259
  application for by social work department, **22**,
    20
  counterclaim for, **17**, 1048, 1233
  court powers in relation to, **10**, 1318
  Court of Session—
    jurisdiction, **4**, 5, 69
    procedure, **17**, 1427
  dispute over, **17**, 1235
  foreign decrees, recognition and enforcement—
    abduction to Scotland, **10**, 1321
    child abduction, criminal law aspects, **10**,
      1342, 1343
    child wrongfully removed from or retained
      in Scotland, **10**, 1334, 1335
    domicile and habitual residence, **10**, 1319
    European Convention on Recognition and
      Enforcement, **10**, 1325–1329
      application of contracting state, **10**, 1326
      decisions outside United Kingdom, **10**,
        1327
      refusal of recognition, **10**, 1328, 1329
    Hague Convention on the Civil Aspects of
      International Child Abduction, **10**,
      1330–1341
    United Kingdom decrees, **10**, 1322–1324
      interim orders, **10**, 1324
      registration of order, **10**, 1323
    welfare of child, **10**, 1320
  illegitimate children, **10**, 1178
  interim order, **17**, 1128
  intimation, where order may be made, **17**, 1226
  matrimonial proceedings, **10**, 1317
  messenger-at-arms, duties as to, **14**, 1504
  order—
    in relation to, **4**, 69
    See also CUSTODY ORDER
  parental rights—
    adopted children, **10**, 1279
    assessing child's welfare, **10**, 1284
    behaviour of applicant, **10**, 1291
    child's views, **10**, 1287
    criteria for resolution, **10**, 1283
    emotional welfare of child, **10**, 1286
    gender of child, **10**, 1289
    illegitimate children, **10**, 1277, 1278
    imaginative custody decisions, **10**, 1292
    Law Reform (Parent and Child) (Scotland)
      Act 1986—
        under, **10**, 1281–1292
    legitimate children, **10**, 1275, 1276
    nature of, **10**, 1274
    physical welfare of child, **10**, 1285
    procedural issues, **10**, 1281
    spiritual welfare of child, **10**, 1290

Child-children—*continued*
custody—*continued*
  parental rights—*continued*
    statutory intervention, **10**, 1276, 1278
    stepchildren, **10**, 1280
    tender years doctrine, **10**, 1288
    third persons, applications by, **10**, 1282
  physical possession of child, and, **10**, 1306
  private international law—
    common law jurisdiction, **10**, 1314, 1315
    Court of Session jurisdiction, **10**, 1314
    generally, **10**, 1313; **17**, 237
    sheriff court jurisdiction, **10**, 1315
    statutory jurisdiction, **10**, 1316, 1317
  sheriff court, jurisdiction of, **4**, 5, 69
dangerous performance, participation in, **3**, 1249
day care, **3**, 1259; **22**, 21
  See also DAY FACILITIES
death—
  child born dead, where, **15**, 600
  injuries sustained *in utero*, as result of, **15**, 600
decision-making, parental rights as to—
  chastisement of child, **10**, 1312
  education, **10**, 1307, 1308
  generally, **10**, 1304
  naming child, **10**, 1305
  physical possession of child, **10**, 306
  religion, **10**, 1309–1311
delict—
  ante-natal injuries, **10**, 1021–1026
  child as defender, **10**, 1124
  child as pursuer, **10**, 1121
  contributory negligence, **10**, 1122
  mother, liability of, **10**, 1026
  parent as defender, **10**, 1123
  posthumous child, **10**, 1021
  principle, generally, **10**, 1021
  wrongful birth actions, **10**, 1025
  wrongful life actions, **10**, 1024
delict committed by, **15**, 242, 603
delivery order, **8**, 514
dependant, **12**, 264
  social security payment increases, **21**, 1015, 1016
deportation of parent, **12**, 208
detention—
  direction of Secretary of State, **22**, 33
  generally, **17**, 891
  placement after conviction, local authority
    function, **22**, 33
  principles, **22**, 33
  sentence of, **3**, 1218
  sexual purposes, for, **3**, 1239, 1244
disclosure of whereabouts, order for, **8**, 515
divorce, *see* DIVORCE
domicile and nationality, **10**, 1223
  adopted children, **10**, 1193, 1193n, 1223
  dependence, domicile of, **17**, 201
  illegitimate children, **10**, 1186, 1223
  origin, domicile of, **17**, 198
  reforms to law, **17**, 208
donor-parent, of, access to databank information,
  18, 1541
Draft Convention on the Rights of the Child, **10**,
  1012

Child-children—*continued*
drug abuse by mother, **10**, 1027
economic and social protection, **12**, 7
education—
  failure to attend school, **3**, 1330, 1379
  parental duties, **10**, 1307, 1308
  religious instruction in local authority schools,
    10, 1311
  See also EDUCATION; SCHOOL
employment of—
  byelaws relating to, **14**, 274
  contract of, **10**, 1078
  entertainment industry, in, **3**, 1256
  schoolchildren, of, *see* SCHOOLCHILDREN
enticement to leave family, **15**, 596
European Social Charter, **12**, 7
European Union law, 'primary right' holder, of,
  12, 223
exercise of rights by, **10**, 1013
expectant and nursing mothers, care of, **11**, 1478
exposure, **3**, 1246
  danger, to, **10**, 1224
  registration of birth, **19**, 1440
  suffering or injury to health, to, **10**, 1137
Falkland Islands, born in, **14**, 1925
family credit, *see* FAMILY CREDIT
family relationships, **11**, 1063, 1068
female prisoner, of, **16**, 1427, 1441
fiduciary fees trusts, **24**, 32
film, performance in, **9**, 1052
firearms and ammunition—
  possession or use by—
    air weapons, **10**, 1551, 1554
    general restrictions, **10**, 1550, 1552
    prohibited weapons, **10**, 1552
    purchase, acquisition and other forms of
      transfer, **10**, 1551
    shot guns, **10**, 1553
  supply to, **10**, 1570
foetus, protection of, **10**, 1030–1033
food for—
  antioxidants, **11**, 371
  preservatives, **11**, 377
forisfamiliation, *see* MINOR
foster parent, *see* FOSTER PARENT
fosterage, **10**, 1188, 1189
  advertising relating to, **1**, 528; **17**, 45
  legal origins, **22**, 361
  local authority duties in relation to, **3**, 1260
  meaning of of foster child, **3**, 1260
fraudulent misrepresentation by minor, **10**, 116
friendly society account held by, **3**, 1219
futurity, words of, **25**, 845
gender, relevance of, **10**, 1013
  change of gender—
    generally, **10**, 1036
    Human Rights Convention, **10**, 1037
    other legal systems, under, **10**, 1038
  child offenders, **10**, 1042
  determining gender, **10**, 1034
  error in relation to gender, **10**, 1035
  hermaphrodites, **10**, 1034
  heterosexual offence, child victim, **10**, 1043, 1044
  majority, age of, **10**, 1041

Child-children—*continued*
gender, relevance of—*continued*
  minority, **10**, 1039
    marriage during, **10**, 1040
  pupillarity, **10**, 1039
gift over to, distinguished from gift over to heir,
  25, 918
gifts, class, **25**, 843
guardian, *see* GUARDIAN-GUARDIANSHIP
guardian's allowance, *see* GUARDIAN'S ALLOWANCE
gunpowder, sale to, **10**, 1604
handicapped, wrongful birth, **15**, 305
hearing, *see* CHILDREN'S HEARING
horror comics, access to, **17**, 39
hotchpot, principle of, **25**, 611
identity of—
  children's hearings, **17**, 37
  civil proceedings, **17**, 36
  criminal proceedings, **17**, 35
  fatal accident inquiries, **17**, 38
ill-treatment, **3**, 1246; **10**, 1137, 1224
  adoption of ill-treated child, **10**, 1210, 1211
illegitimate, *see* ILLEGITIMACY
immediate family, as, **15**, 601
imprisonment—
  educational provision, **16**, 1456
  unruly or depraved child, **16**, 1431
incest, *see* INCEST
income support, **21**, 1069, 1070
  family premium, **21**, 1074
  lone parent premium, **21**, 1074
  personal allowance, **21**, 1072
indecent acts with, **7**, 309, 310
infancy, **10**, 1050
infanticide, **7**, 258
institution, born in, **19**, 1442
insurance relating to death of child under ten, **12**,
  692, 724
interdict preventing removal—
  Scotland, from, **8**, 516
  UK, from, **8**, 516
interim interdict, proceedings concerning, **17**, 1112
journey, born during course of, **19**, 1441
judicial discretion, applicant for, **25**, 616
legal aid in proceedings relating to, **13**, 1070
legal capacity, **10**, 1144–1146; **11**, 1053, 1054, 1067
  adoption, **3**, 1209
  age limit, where express, **3**, 1210, 1213, 1221
  general rule, **3**, 1202
  medical procedures, **3**, 1207
  passive, **3**, 1203, 1219
  residual, **3**, 1206
  testamentary capacity, **3**, 1208
  transaction—
    age limit, where express, **3**, 1210, 1213
    arbiter, acting as, **3**, 1202
    civil proceedings, **3**, 1202
    consent, giving, **3**, 1202
    definition, **3**, 1202
    fraudulent misrepresentation, party induced
      by, **3**, 1211
    guardian of child, made by, **3**, 1205
    person under age of sixteen, capacity to
      enter, **3**, 1202, 1206

Child-children—*continued*
legal capacity—*continued*
  transaction—*continued*
    power of appointment, **3**, 1202
    pre-25 September 1991, made, **3**, 1202
    prejudicial—
      court's power to set aside, **3**, 1211, 1212
      meaning, **3**, 1211
      ratification, **3**, 1211, 1212
    ratification—
      applicant after attaining age of eighteen, **3**, 1211
      court, by, **3**, 1211, 1212
    testamentary capacity, exercise, **3**, 1202
    trustee, acting as, **3**, 1202
    unilateral, **3**, 1202
legal custody, child in, disentitlement to child benefit, **21**, 962
legal personality, **10**, 1014
legitim—
  claim for, interest on sum, **12**, 1031
    sum advanced during lifetime of deceased, **12**, 1031
  division of, **25**, 700
  illegitimate child, right of, **25**, 699
  representation in, **25**, 700
legitimacy—
  adultery of parents, **10**, 1167
  generally, **10**, 1147, 1148, 1165
  legitimation—
    adopted child, **10**, 1191
    generally, **10**, 1171; **17**, 240
    letters of, **10**, 1172
    per subsequens matrimonium, **10**, 1173
  presumption of, **10**, 1166
  putative marriages, children of, **10**, 1168
  rape, children conceived as result of, **10**, 1169
  void marriages, children of, **10**, 831, 1168
  voidable marriages, children of, **10**, 831, 1170
  See also LEGITIMACY
legitimate—
  aliment, **10**, 1230–1234. *See also* aliment *above*
  custody—
    at common law, **10**, 1275
    statutory intervention, **10**, 1276
  domicile and nationality, **10**, 1223
  marriage, prohibited degrees, **10**, 1219
  succession, **10**, 1220
lessee, as, **13**, 188
lessor, as, **13**, 168
liability to maintain, **21**, 1070
liferent property, destination to—
  allernarly liferent, **13**, 1629
  Dobie's table, **13**, 1622
  generally, **13**, 1626
  legatees, descriptive terms, **13**, 1627
  unascertainable heir, **13**, 1628, 1629
  unborn children, **13**, 1628, 1629
live birth, **25**, 662
local authority—
  assistance in kind or cash, **3**, 1261
  care, *see* CHILD IN CARE; LOCAL AUTHORITY (residential care facilities)
  travel concession, **20**, 493

Child-children—*continued*
maintenance for, counterclaim for, **17**, 1048
maintenance order, **21**, 1070
majority, age of, **10**, 1041, 1049
marriage—
  consanguinity and affinity, relationships of, **10**, 817, 1219
  minor, of, **10**, 1080
married child, whether entitled to child benefit, **21**, 962
maternity, establishing, **10**, 1149–1154
meaning, **4**, 69; **12**, 279, 1268; **13**, 1627; **17**, 37, 887
minor, *see* age, relevance of *above*—
minor
modern reproductive techniques—
  artificial insemination, **10**, 900, 1159
  conception—
    death of both genetic parents, after, **10**, 1019
    death of father, after, **10**, 1018
    divorce or separation of genetic parents, after, **10**, 1020
  date of birth, **10**, 1047
  nasciturus principle, **10**, 1017
  ovum donation, **10**, 1150
moral danger, exposed to, **3**, 1330
mother—
  drug abuse by, **10**, 1027
  protective measures taken against, **10**, 1028
murder—
  child or foetus, of, **10**, 1030
murder, convicted of, **16**, 1432
name of—
  change of, **19**, 1425, 1426
  parental rights as to, **10**, 1305
nasciturus principle
  application to succession, **10**, 1016
  condictio si testator sine liberis decesserit, **10**, 1016
  death of both genetic parents, child conceived after, **10**, 1019
  death of father, child conceived after, **10**, 1018
  direct benefit to child, **10**, 1015
  divorce or separation of genetic parents, child conceived after, **10**, 1020
  generally, **10**, 1015, 1033
  indirect benefit to child, **10**, 1015
  meaning, **10**, 1015
  modern reproductive techniques, **10**, 1017
  posthumous child, **10**, 1016
  succession, application of principle to, **10**, 1016
national savings account held by, **3**, 1219
nationality, **10**, 1223
neglect of, **3**, 1246; **10**, 1137, 1224
  adoption of neglected child, **10**, 1209, 1212
  compulsory measures of care, **10**, 1128
  McBoyle Committee recommendations, **22**, 4
  reporter, role of, **10**, 1129
new born infant found abandoned, **14**, 1908
nonage, *see* NONAGE
offences against, increase in referrals, **3**, 1278
offender—
  child under eight, where, **3**, 1336
  child under thirteen, where, **3**, 1378
  gender of, **10**, 1042
  nonage, **10**, 1139, 1140

Child-children—*continued*
offender, prosecution of—
  court procedure, **17**, 890
  general guidelines, **17**, 888
  generally, **3**, 1330; **10**, 1138; **17**, 887
  notification, **17**, 889
  standard of proof, **10**, 761
offender—
  serious offence, Lord Advocate's Direction, **3**, 1285
  young, **3**, 1379–1381
officer, *see* CHILDREN'S OFFICER
ophthalmic services, **11**, 1463*n*
over sixteen, legal capacity, **11**, 1245
ovum donation, **10**, 1150
panel, *see* CHILDREN'S PANEL
parent, *see* PARENT
parentage—
  action affecting, **17**, 1023
  blood test evidence, **10**, 1163
  corroboration by false denial, abolition of, **10**, 1160
  declarator of, action for, **10**, 1160–1164
  disputes over, **10**, 1160
  DNA fingerprinting, **10**, 1164
  establishing maternity, **10**, 1149–1154
  establishing paternity—
    artificial insemination, **10**, 1159
    pater   est   quem   nuptiae   demonstrant presumption, **10**, 1155
      rebuttal of, **10**, 1156
    real evidence, **10**, 620
    registration as father of child, **10**, 1158
    statutory presumptions, **10**, 1157
  gestation periods, **10**, 1161
  non-parentage, action for declarator of, **10**, 1160–1164
  ovum donation, **10**, 1150
  physical resemblance, **10**, 1162
  surrogacy, **10**, 1151
    custody of surrogate child, **10**, 1154
    maternity in, **10**, 1152
    surrogacy contracts, **10**, 1153
parental—
  care, lack of, **3**, 1330, 1338
  control, beyond, **3**, 1330
  duties—
    duty of care, **15**, 299, 304
    duty to protect, **7**, 41, 48, 182
    duty to rescue, **15**, 304
  rights, *see* PARENTAL RIGHTS
parents, relationship with—
  adopted children, **10**, 1147
  legitimacy and illegitimacy, **10**, 1147, 1148
parents' insurable interest in life of, **12**, 853
paternity—
  adultery cases, **10**, 932
  establishing, **10**, 1155–1159
  findings of, **10**, 502
  proof of, **10**, 846
  real evidence, questions as to, **10**, 620
person in need, as, Social Work (Scotland) Act 1968 ..., **22**, 13
personality, **10**, 1014

Child-children—*continued*
physical chastisement, **3**, 1246
physical force against to keep discipline—
  entitlement to use, **7**, 239, 306
  indecent assault, **7**, 306
physical possession of, parental rights as to, **10**, 1306
picture book for, VAT zero-rating, **7**, 1447
place of safety—
  committal by court to, **22**, 33
  custody in, **17**, 892
  interim detention in—
    abscondment, **3**, 1372–1374
    appeals, **3**, 1366, 1368
    assessment order, proposals for, **3**, 1371
    change, proposals for, **3**, 1363, 1369–1371
    child protection order, proposed, **3**, 1369
    emergency hearing, **3**, 1290
    exclusion order for suspected abuser, proposals for, **3**, 1370
    failure to attend children's hearing, following, **3**, 1368
    generally, **3**, 1363, 1366, 1367
    grounds for, **3**, 1364
    harbouring absconder, **3**, 1374
    hearing, bringing child to, **3**, 1366, 1367
    legal challenge, proposed changes in procedure, **3**, 1369
    limits on, **3**, 1365
    procedure following, **3**, 1287
    recall, application for, **3**, 1369
    release, **3**, 1287
    reporter to be informed, **3**, 1364
    taking child to place of safety, **3**, 1364
    variation, application for, **3**, 1369
    warrant for apprehension of child, **3**, 1368
    warrant for continued detention, **3**, 1367
      renewal, **3**, 1367
plagium, **3**, 1242; **10**, 1225, 1342
polygamous wives and widows, of, **12**, 118*n*
pornography, child, **7**, 311
posthumous—
  benefit to child, **25**, 661
  generally, **25**, 660
  live birth, **25**, 662
  nasciturus principle, **10**, 1016
priority housing needs, **11**, 2051, 2053
prison—
  child in, disentitlement to child benefit, **21**, 962
  sole surviving parent in, **21**, 953, 956
private international law—
  adoption, **17**, 242–243
  custody, **17**, 237
  generally, **17**, 236
  legitimacy, **17**, 239–241
  property, **17**, 238, 241
  rights, **17**, 236–237
pro-curator, **15**, 92
pro-tutor, **15**, 92
protection of—
  caretaker, absence of adequate, **10**, 1224
  criminal sanctions, **10**, 1224
  local authority care, **10**, 1224
  protective legislation, generally, **10**, 1027

Child-children—*continued*
punishment, infliction of, **10**, 1224
pupil, *see* age, relevance of *above*; PUPIL
reckless supply of substances to, **7**, 13
refreshment places, admittance to, **2**, 14
registration of birth, *see* BIRTHS, REGISTRATION OF
Rehabilitation of Offenders Act 1974, effect, **3**, 1337
relationship with particular adults, **10**, 1013
release, Secretary of State, recommendations, **22**, 33
religion—
  child's views, **10**, 1310
  choice of, parental rights, **10**, 1309
  instruction in local authority schools, **10**, 1311
removal from family, unjustified, **15**, 596
removal from United Kingdom, unlawful, **10**, 1226
reporter, role of, **10**, 1129
rescue, duty to, **15**, 304
reset of child, **7**, 393
residence, place of, parental rights as to, **10**, 1306
residential care, **22**, 13, 17, 36
  See also RESIDENTIAL CARE
restriction on movements of, **15**, 437
rights of—
  generally, **10**, 1228; **11**, 1075; **17**, 236
  international conventions on, **12**, 5
rights and protection, benefit from, **10**, 1013
risk, at, McBoyle Committee recommendations, **22**, 4
  marriage contract trust, under, **24**, 18, 69
running away from home, **3**, 1373
safeguarder, *see* SAFEGUARDER
Schedule 1 offences—
  abandonment, **3**, 1246
  accidental conduct, **3**, 1246
  alleged offender—
    effect of prosecution, **3**, 1341
    naming, **3**, 1340
  assault, **3**, 1246
  begging, **3**, 1247
  bodily injury, offence involving, **3**, 1250
  child under seventeen, committed against, **3**, 1243
  compulsory measures of care inferred by, **3**, 1243
  cruelty, **3**, 1246
  dangerous performance, child taking part in, **3**, 1249
  drunk in public place with child under ten, being, **3**, 1252
  exposure, **3**, 1246
  generally, **3**, 1242, 1243, 1246–1249
  grounds for referral to children's hearing, as, **3**, 1330
  homosexual offences, **3**, 1244
  ill-treatment, **3**, 1246
  interim detention in place of safety, as ground for, **3**, 1364
  lewd, indecent or libidinous practices, **3**, 1251
  neglect, **3**, 1246
  open fire, offence in relation to, **3**, 1248
  physical chastisement, **3**, 1246

Child-children—*continued*
Schedule 1 offences—*continued*
  same household—
    child of, effect on, **3**, 1243
    meaning, **3**, 1342
    sexual offences, **3**, 1244
  suffocation of child while in bed with drunken person, **3**, 1246
  unattended, child left, **3**, 1246
school, failure to attend, **3**, 1330, 1379
schoolchildren, *see* SCHOOLCHILDREN
secure accommodation, registration with Secretary of State, **22**, 33
selection of doctor for, **11**, 1436
separation agreements, **10**, 939
settled Commonwealth citizen, of, **12**, 125
settlement, family reunion or creation by, *see* SETTLEMENT (IMMIGRATION)
severe disablement allowance, child entitled to, disentitlement to child benefit, **21**, 962
sex, unlawful, with under-age, consent, **15**, 393n
sexual activities—
  boy over fourteen, **3**, 1235
  boy under fourteen, **3**, 1235
  child, with, as result of abuse of trust, **3**, 1244
  children and young persons, protection of, generally, **3**, 1241
  consent by girl under sixteen, **3**, 1235
  girl under sixteen, **3**, 1235, 1236, 1240, 1244
  girl under thirteen, **3**, 1235, 1244
  girl under twelve, **3**, 1235
  homosexual—
    female, **3**, 1236
    male, **3**, 1237, 1240
  incest, **3**, 1238
  indecent behaviour, **3**, 1244
  lewd, indecent and libidinous practices, **3**, 1235, 1236, 1251
  marriage, age limit, **3**, 1235, 1241
  procuring and related activities, **3**, 1239, 1244
  puberty, age of, **3**, 1234
  Schedule 1 offences, **3**, 1244
  shameless indecency, **3**, 1235, 1236
  unlawful sexual intercourse, **3**, 1235
sexual offences—
  age of child, **10**, 1136
  defences to, **10**, 1136
  generally, **7**, 301, 304, 308–310
sheriff court jurisdiction, **6**, 1086
social work department, duties to child—
  care provision, **22**, 17
  generally, **22**, 17–22
  rights of department, **17**, 1236
  supervision by social worker, **22**, 21
  See also CHILD IN CARE
status—
  concept of, **11**, 1068, 1071
  valid marriage, **10**, 846
stepchildren—
  aliment, **10**, 1217, 1220, 1243–1246
  custody of, **10**, 1280
  marriage to step-parent, **10**, 1217
  succession, **10**, 1220

Child-children—*continued*

step-parents—
    aliment, **10**, 1217, 1220, 1243–1246
    legal significance, **10**, 1217
    marriage to stepchild, **10**, 1217
    meaning, **10**, 1217
    parental rights, application for, **10**, 1217
    rights and responsibilities, **10**, 1217
    sexual relations with stepchild, **10**, 1217
    step-relationship, generally, **10**, 1217
stillborn—
    burial of, **19**, 1449
    register of, *see* STILLBIRTHS, REGISTRATION OF
student, *see* STUDENT
succession—
    child conceived but not born at date when benefit vests, **25**, 33
    class gifts, **25**, 843
    division of estate on or after 8 December 1986 ..., **25**, 704
    gift over to, **25**, 918
    nasciturus principle, application of, **10**, 1016
    stepchildren, **10**, 1220
supervision order, child subject to, moving to Scotland, **3**, 1384
supervision requirement, *see* SUPERVISION REQUIREMENT
surrogate child—
    advertisements relating to arrangements, **17**, 45
    custody of, **10**, 1154
    generally, **10**, 1151
    maternity in surrogacy cases, **10**, 1152
    nasciturus principle, **10**, 1019
    surrogacy contracts, **10**, 1153
taxation of income, **19**, 1517
theatre, in—
    education, **9**, 1052
    licence, **9**, 1052
    safety, **9**, 1052
    school plays, **9**, 1052
    welfare, **9**, 1052
theft of, **3**, 1242; **7**, 328
trade, contract in course of, **10**, 1078
tutor, *see* TUTOR
tutory, order relating to, **8**, 508
unattended, left, **3**, 1246
unborn, **24**, 18, 32
    contingent right in, **24**, 70, 75, 76
    killing, **7**, 256
    no provision for, **24**, 67
under—
    seventeen, local authority duty to provide care, **22**, 17
    sixteen—
        legal capacity, **11**, 1244
        unlawful attempt to take out of UK, **16**, 1227
under-age girl, sexual intercourse with, **7**, 301, 304, 308
undue influence, **25**, 764
United Kingdom citizenship—
    adopted children, **10**, 1191
    illegitimate children, **10**, 1186
United Kingdom passport, **16**, 1220, 1221
unruly certificate, **17**, 893

Child-children—*continued*

unruly or depraved, imprisonment, **16**, 1431
variation of trust on divorce, **24**, 84
vicarious liability for actions of, **11**, 1056
victims, as—
    criminal offences, **10**, 1135
    heterosexual offences, **10**, 1043
    homosexual offences, **10**, 1044
violence used against, **10**, 1224
volatile substance, misuse of, **3**, 1330, 1331
voluntary—
    obligation, capacity to enter, **15**, 660
    organisation, child living with, child benefit, **21**, 963, 965
    supervision, **3**, 1287, 1287n
welfare, **10**, 1320; **22**, 1, 18, 19, 20
will—
    capacity to make, **25**, 761
    interpretation—
        conditio si institutus sine liberis decesserit, **12**, 1265
        conditio si testator sine liberis decesserit, **12**, 1265
        legal rights, **12**, 1264
    revocation of, **17**, 348
witness, as, **10**, 502
    admissibility, **3**, 1216
    commissioner, proceedings before, **3**, 1217
    criminal trial, at, **3**, 1217
    evidence, taking, **3**, 1217
    identification in court, **10**, 552
    live television link, use of, **3**, 1217
    memorandum of guidance, **3**, 1217
    oath and affirmation, **10**, 548
    questions as to credibility of, **10**, 636
works likely to corrupt, importation, **7**, 1203
wrongful birth, **15**, 305
wrongful pregnancy—
    case law, **15**, 306
    'consent-based' negligence actions, **15**, 307
    generally, **15**, 305
    negligent failure to warn, **15**, 308
    normal child, damages to compensate for upbringing, **15**, 309
    Scottish position, generally, **15**, 310
See also MINOR; YOUNG PERSON

Child abuse

acts constituting, **7**, 4
assessment, level of risk, social worker, **22**, 1
children's hearing, time limit for, place of safety warrant, after, **22**, 22
co-ordination of services to protect children, **22**, 22
compulsory measures of care, **10**, 1128
Criminal Injuries Compensation Scheme, **7**, 2, 3, 4
criticisms of social work intervention, **22**, 1
place of safety, application for warrant, **22**, 22
protection from, adoption of child, **10**, 122
risk, social worker's duty to investigate, **22**, 22
sexual abuse, removal of child at birth, **10**, 1027
social worker—
    discretion, problems in exercise, **22**, 1
    intervention, generally, **22**, 1, 22

Child benefit

adjudication, **21**, 1149
advanced education, person receiving, **21**, 959, 959n

Child benefit—*continued*
child, meaning, **21**, 959
claim to be made in prescribed manner, **21**, 958
disentitlement, **21**, 962
elder or eldest child, **21**, 965
entitlement, **21**, 801
  generally, **21**, 958
  one parent benefit, **21**, 964
  persons entitled deemed not entitled, circumstances where, **21**, 1015
  priority between two or more persons, **21**, 961
    overlapping benefits, **21**, 1006
  where legislation provides benefit not payable, **21**, 1015
full-time education, person receiving, **21**, 959
income support, child receiving, **21**, 959
legal custody, child in, **21**, 962
local authority care, child in, **21**, 962
married child, **21**, 962
one parent benefit, **21**, 964
  disqualification for, **21**, 964
  overlapping benefits, **21**, 1005
only child, **21**, 965
overlapping benefits, **21**, 1005
  priority between persons entitled to increase of benefit, **21**, 1006
person responsible for child—
  benefit payable to, **21**, 958, 961
    priority between two or more persons, **21**, 961
  meaning, **21**, 960
prison, child in, **21**, 962
rates, **21**, 965
severe disablement allowance, child receiving, **21**, 962
single parent, **21**, 964, 1005
  cohabiting, **21**, 964
supervision requirement, child under, **21**, 962
two families living together, where, **21**, 965
voluntary organisations' right to, **21**, 963, 965
youth training scheme, trainee engaged in, **21**, 959
Child guidance service
education authorities' duty to provide, **8**, 864
Child in care
after-care facilities, **3**, 1274
assistance in kind, as alternative to, **22**, 13
boarding out facilities, provision of, **22**, 17
child benefit, entitlement, **21**, 962
compulsory measures for, **3**, 1128
criteria for reception into, **3**, 1262–1264; **22**, 17
historical background, **22**, 1, 2
local authority duties to—
  adoption services, **22**, 19. *See also* ADOPTION
  assessment of child's needs, **22**, 18
  boarding out facilities, provision, **22**, 17
  delegation to voluntary organisations, **22**, 10, 13, 16, 28
  foster carers, assessment of, **22**, 17. *See also* FOSTER PARENT
  generally, **3**, 1263; **22**, 17–22
  residential homes, provision of, **3**, 1261; **22**, 16, 17. *See also* RESIDENTIAL CARE
  welfare principle, upholding, **22**, 18

Child in care—*continued*
National Health Service, duties of, **11**, 1478
registration, **22**, 16, 28
religious considerations, **3**, 1263
review, **3**, 1272
visits from parent etc to child, **22**, 15, 17
welfare principle, primacy of, **22**, 18
Child minder
duty to protect child, **7**, 42
inspection of premises, **3**, 1259
registration, **3**, 1259; **22**, 2
regulation, **3**, 1259
statutory provisions, **22**, 2
what constitutes a child minder, **3**, 1259
Child protection order
proposals for, **3**, 1369
Child Support Agency
parentage, disputes as to, **21**, 1070
powers, **21**, 1070
Child support appeal tribunal
statement made in, absolute privilege, **15**, 524
Child support liability order
deductions from earnings order, **8**, 34
inhibition—
  generally, **8**, 134
poinding, **8**, 217
Childbearing
presumption as to age of, **24**, 70, 210
Children's centres
local authority duty as to, **22**, 13
Children's hearing
adjudication, discrete nature, **3**, 1275
adult court, appearance by young person while on supervision from, powers of adult court to remit etc, **22**, 33
age of child, ascertainment, **3**, 1319
appeal—
  child and parents must be informed of rights as to, **3**, 1353
  Court of Appeal, to, **3**, 1300
  Court of Session, to, **3**, 1360, 1361
  legal aid, entitlement to, **3**, 1353, 1361
  procedural irregularity as grounds, **3**, 1314
  reconsideration by hearing after, **3**, 1359
  right of, generally, **3**, 1275
  sheriff, to, **3**, 1358, 1361
  sheriff court, to, **3**, 1299, 1362
appeal, time limits, **22**, 822
attendance at, **3**, 1346
  child, **3**, 1319, 1320
    responsibility for securing, **3**, 1320
  child failing to attend, detention following, **3**, 1368
  Council on Tribunals representatives, **3**, 1325
  discretion of chairman, at, **3**, 1327
  obligation to attend, **10**, 1130
    parties with, **3**, 1318–1326
  panel members, **3**, 1318
  parents, **3**, 1321, 1344
    exclusion from proceedings, **3**, 1320
  police constables, **3**, 1324
  press, **3**, 1326
  prison officers, **3**, 1324
  reporter, **3**, 1318

Children's hearing—*continued*
attendance—*continued*
  representatives, **3**, 1322
  safeguarder, **3**, 1323, 1362
  statutory right to attend, parties with, **3**, 1318–
    1326
  who may attend, **3**, 1316; **10**, 1224
authentication of documents, **3**, 1298
care worker, attendance, **3**, 1327
changing nature of referrals, **3**, 1285, 1286
child—
  expenses, reimbursement, **3**, 1322
  representation of, **3**, 1322
  views of, **3**, 1344
child in all his circumstances, principle of, **3**, 1345
child failing to attend, detention following, **3**,
  1368
children's panel, *see* CHILDREN'S PANEL
compulsory removal of child, requirement to
  produce evidence, **22**, 18
conditions of referral, *see* grounds of referral *below*
confidentiality, **3**, 1316
conflict between interests of child and parent,
  where, **3**, 1362
consensus, aim to achieve, **3**, 1344
constitution, **3**, 1318
convening—
  emergency hearing, **3**, 1288, 1290
  notification to children, **3**, 1289, 1290
  notification to panel members, **3**, 1288
  notification to parents, **3**, 1291
Council on Tribunals, attendance by
  representative of, **3**, 1325
documents, entitlement to receive, **3**, 1288
court, remit of cases from, **3**, 1378
criminal capacity of child, **3**, 1218
decision—
  appeal against, *see* appeal *above*
  discharge of referral, **3**, 1347
  further information, continuing hearing for, **3**,
    1348
  implementation, **3**, 1355
  minority, panel member expressing, **3**, 1354
  no further action, to take, **3**, 1347
  notification, **3**, 1294, 1295
  range available, **3**, 1347–1349
  relaying, **3**, 1353, 1354
  statement of reasons, **3**, 1294
  supervision requirement, *see* SUPERVISION
    REQUIREMENT
  written statement of reasons for, **3**, 1353, 1354
discharge of case, **3**, 1333
discussion—
  child in all his circumstances, principle of, **3**,
    1345
  disclosure of substance, **3**, 1346
  generally, **3**, 1344, 1353
disposal, discrete nature, **3**, 1275
disposal of case, **10**, 1132
documents—
  authentication, **3**, 1298
  child and parents not entitled to see, **3**, 1289
  confidentiality, **3**, 1288, 1316
  disclosure of substance, **3**, 1346

Children's hearing—*continued*
documents—*continued*
  panel members, to be passed to, **3**, 1288
  parents' and child's rights as to, **3**, 1316, 1346
  return to reporter, **3**, 1316
  safeguarder's entitlement to receive, **3**, 1362
educational psychologist, attendance, **3**, 1327
emergency, **3**, 1288, 1290
England, Wales or Northern Ireland—
  child moving from, **3**, 1384
  child moving to, **3**, 1383
establishment, **3**, 1281
European Convention on Human Rights,
  compliance with, **3**, 1344
expenses incurred by attendance at, **3**, 1322
Finlayson Report, **3**, 1286
generally, **3**, 1275, 1276; **10**, 1130
grounds of referral—
  acceptance or denial by child or parent, **3**, 1330
    explanation of consequences, **3**, 1332
    procedure following, **3**, 1333
  application to sheriff for finding as to, **3**, 1293,
    1333, 1334
  assault, **3**, 1339
  child incapable of understanding, **3**, 1333
  explanation to child and parents, **3**, 1332, 1333
  failure to attend school, **3**, 1330, 1343, 1379
  framing, **3**, 1292
  generally, **3**, 1330
  incomprehension by parent or child, **3**, 1333
  lack of parental care, **3**, 1330, 1338
  reform proposals, **3**, 1331
  Schedule 1 offences, **3**, 1330, 1340–1342
  Social Work (Scotland) Act, referral in
    pursuance of, **3**, 1330
  statement of, **3**, 1288, 1292, 1320
    copies to be sent to child and parents, **3**,
      1292
  supporting facts, explanation, **3**, 1332, 1339
historical background, **3**, 1277–1281
identity of child, **17**, 37
initial investigation of case, **3**, 1287
introductions, **3**, 1328
judicial reference, **3**, 1288
jurisdiction, **3**, 1319
Kilbrandon Committee recommendations, **3**,
  1278–1280, 1380; **22**, 5
legal aid, **10**, 1130
local authority duty—
  implementation of decision by, **3**, 1355
  panel, establishment of, **22**, 21
  reference, **3**, 1288
  report, **3**, 1288
  reporter, appointment of, **22**, 21
membership, **3**, 1318; **10**, 1130
notification, **3**, 1319
obligation to attend, **10**, 1130
parent—
  attendance by, **3**, 1321, 1344
    adopted child, parent of, **3**, 1321
    desirability, **3**, 1280
    guardian, **3**, 1321
    illegitimate child, parent of, **3**, 1321
    non-attendance, offence, as, **3**, 1321

Children's hearing—*continued*
parent—*continued*
  attendance by—*continued*
    persons believed by child to be parents, **3**, 1321
    presence dispensed with, where, **3**, 1321
    unmarried parents, **3**, 1321, 1322
    who qualifies as parent, **3**, 1321
  attendance of, **6**, 317
  behavioural problem, with, **3**, 1350
  conflicting interests of child and, **3**, 1362
  expenses, reimbursement, **3**, 1322
  involvement in system, **3**, 1279
  no power to impose conditions on, **3**, 1350
  notification, **3**, 1291
  parental co-operation, enlisting, **3**, 1279
  representation of, **3**, 1322
  right of appeal, **3**, 1358
  right to be present, **3**, 1321, 1344
  sanctions against, rejection, **3**, 1279
  views of, **3**, 1344
persistent offender, **3**, 1379, 1380
place of safety, interim detention in, *see* CHILD-CHILDREN
place of safety warrant, time limit after, **22**, 22
placement—
  household outwith child's own home, in, **3**, 1351
  residential establishment, in, **3**, 1352
police constable, attendance by, **3**, 1324
police stand-by, **3**, 1346
preliminary business meeting, **3**, 1320
premises for sittings, generally, **3**, 1280, 1283, 1303, 1303*n*, 1320
press, attendance by, **3**, 1326
prison officer, attendance by, **3**, 1324
privacy of proceedings, **3**, 1316
privileges relating to, **17**, 17
procedure—
  acceptance or denial of grounds of referral, following, **3**, 1333
  average time scheduled for hearing, **3**, 1314
  chairman, selection, **3**, 1315
  confidentiality, **3**, 1316
  decision, *see* decision *above*
  discussion, **3**, 1344–1346, 1353
  generally, **3**, 1314
  grounds of referral, explanation, **3**, 1332, 1333
  informality, **3**, 1314
  introductions, **3**, 1328
  irregularity in as grounds for appeal, **3**, 1314
  privacy, **3**, 1316
  purpose of hearing, explanation, **3**, 1329
  selection of panel members, **3**, 1315
  sheriff, referral to, **3**, 1333, 1334
  standard of proof—
    generally, **3**, 1335
    offence by child cases, **3**, 1336
psychiatrist, attendance, **3**, 1327
purpose, explanation, **3**, 1329
records, **3**, 1297
referral to, **10**, 1131, 1224; **17**, 894; **22**, 13
  generally, **3**, 1218, 1280, 1287
  grounds, *see* grounds of referral *above*

Children's hearing—*continued*
Rehabilitation of Offenders Act, effect, **3**, 1337
remission of case from adult court to—
  social work report, **22**, 33
  young person on supervision, **22**, 33
reporter—
  appointment, **22**, 21
  child abuse, notification of risk by social worker, **22**, 22
  Kilbrandon Committee recommendations, **22**, 5
  staff, **22**, 21
  See also CHILDREN'S PANEL (reporter to)
reports examining, **3**, 1275, 1286
representation at, **3**, 1322
representative—
  child, of, **3**, 1322
  disruptive behaviour by, **3**, 1322
  expenses, refund, **3**, 1322
  parent, of, **3**, 1322
  solicitor as, **3**, 1322
  views of, **3**, 1344
review, local authority power to recommend, **22**, 8
Review Group report, **3**, 1275
safeguarder, *see* SAFEGUARDER
seating arrangements, **3**, 1324, 1346
secure accommodation, child or young person, placement in—
  close support units, **3**, 1375
  criteria for, **3**, 1376
  duration of warrant, **3**, 1377
  emergency hearing, **3**, 1290
  generally, **3**, 1375
  home leave, **3**, 1376
  objective, **3**, 1375
  open unit, discretion to move child to, **3**, 1376
  outings, **3**, 1376
  power to authorise, **3**, 1377
  protective measure, where, **3**, 1375
  review, **3**, 1290, 1377
  suicide or self-harm, to prevent, **3**, 1375
  transfer from one place to another, **3**, 1290
secure accommodation—
  meaning, **3**, 1376
  reform proposals, **3**, 1380
  residence in, review, **3**, 1357
sheriff, appeal to, **3**, 1275
'silent child', **3**, 1344
sixteen to eighteen years, offenders aged, **3**, 1379–1381
social work department report, consideration, **3**, 1344
social worker—
  application for compulsory removal of child, requirement to produce evidence, **22**, 18
  attendance by, **3**, 1327
  compulsory care application reports, **22**, 21
  supervision of child requiring care, **22**, 21
standard of proof—
  generally, **3**, 1335
  offence by child cases, **3**, 1336
statement made in, absolute privilege, **15**, 524
statutory tribunal, as, **23**, 902

Children's hearing—continued
student, attendance, **3**, 1327
subsequent hearing, **3**, 1348
supervision of, **23**, 911
supervision requirement, see SUPERVISION
   REQUIREMENT
teacher, attendance, **3**, 1327
transfer of case to another hearing, **3**, 1382
venue, **22**, 21
violence, where possibility of, **3**, 1324, 1346
welfare of child as basis of, **3**, 1275, 1280
who may attend, **10**, 1224
young offenders, dealing with, **3**, 1379–1381
See also CHILDREN'S PANEL
Children's Hearing Chairmen's Group, 3,
  1313
Children's Hearing Representative Group
  (CHRG)
meetings, **3**, 1313
membership, **3**, 1313
Children's officer
Kilbrandon Committee recommendations, **22**, 5
local authority duty to appoint, **22**, 2
Children's panel
accommodation and facilities for, provision, **3**,
  1303
administrative responsibility, **3**, 1282
chairman—
  appointment, **3**, 1305, 1306
  Children's Hearing Chairmen's Group, **3**, 1313
  duties, **3**, 1305n, 1315
    explanation of grounds of referral, **3**, 1332
    introductions, **3**, 1328
    purpose of hearing, explanation, **3**, 1329
    safeguarder, appointment, **3**, 1362
  powers—
    who may attend hearing, as to, **3**, 1327
  selection, **3**, 1315
  who may attend hearing, discretion as to, **3**,
    1327
depute chairman—
  appointment, **3**, 1305, 1306
  duties, **3**, 1305n
  generally, **3**, 1305
documents to be sent to members, **3**, 1288
institution, **3**, 1280
jurisdiction, **3**, 1280
lay body, as, **3**, 1280, 1303
local authority duty to form, **3**, 1303, 1305
members—
  appointment, **3**, 1305
  expenses, reimbursement, **3**, 1303
  generally, **3**, 1280, 1303, 1304
  lay persons, as, **3**, 1280, 1303
  monitoring, **3**, 1306
  names and addresses, publication, **3**, 1303
  organisations on which views of represented, **3**,
    1313
  period of office, **3**, 1305, 1305n
  reappointment, **3**, 1305n, 1306, 1310
  recruitment, **3**, 1306
  removal, **3**, 1305
  reporter, relationship with, **3**, 1317
  selection for hearings, **3**, 1315

Children's panel—continued
members—continued
  selection for membership, **3**, 1306
  suitability, **3**, 1303
  survey of, **3**, 1304
  training—
    audit, **3**, 1308
    compulsory, when, **3**, 1310
    continuing, **3**, 1310
    core curriculum, **3**, 1310
    distance learing, **3**, 1311
    evaluation, **3**, 1310
    generally, **3**, 1307
    local, **3**, 1307
    national school, **3**, 1308, 1308n
    new members, **3**, 1310
    pre-service, **3**, 1310
    reform proposals, **3**, 1312
    regional, **3**, 1307
  training committees, **3**, 1309
  training organisers, **3**, 1308, 1308n
  voluntary nature of membership, **3**, 1303
notification of hearing, **3**, 1288
powers, **3**, 1280
reporter to—
  accommodation and facilities, provision, **3**,
    1283
  administrative responsibility, **3**, 1282
  appeal to Court of Session, **3**, 1300
  appointment, **3**, 1283; **14**, 110, 249
  career structure, **3**, 1286
  children's hearing, attendance at, **3**, 1318
  children's panel, relationship with, **3**, 1286,
    1317
  deputy, appointment, **3**, 1283
  detention of child in place of safety, duty
    where, **3**, 1364, 1365
  dismissal, **14**, 110
  duties—
    appeals, as to, **3**, 1299–1301
    authentication of documents, **3**, 1298
    child's attendance at hearing, duty to secure,
      3, 1320
    convening hearing, **3**, 1288–1291
    criminal offence committed by child, where,
      3, 1218
    future, proposals for, **3**, 1302
    grounds of referral—
      application to sheriff to find, **3**, 1293
      framing, **3**, 1292
      statement of, **3**, 1292
    initial investigation, **3**, 1287
    notification of hearing decision, **3**, 1294,
      1295
    place of safety, where child detained in, **3**,
      1364, 1365
    records, duty to keep, **3**, 1297
    review of supervision requirements, **3**, 1296
    secure accommodation, as to child in, **3**,
      1377
  explanation of role at hearing, **3**, 1328
  Finlayson Report recommendations, **3**, 1286,
    1287
  generally, **3**, 1282

Children's panel—*continued*
reporter to—*continued*
  legal knowledge, necessity for, **3**, 1286
  national reporters' service, proposed, **3**, 1286
  no further action required, procedure where, **3**, 1287
  police—
    meetings with, **3**, 1285
    report, **3**, 1287
  powers, **3**, 1317
    advice, guidance and assistance of child and family, referral for, **3**, 1287
    discretionary, **3**, 1285
    release of child, power to order, **3**, 1287
  Principal Reporter, proposed, **3**, 1302
  procurator fiscal, meetings with, **3**, 1285
  qualifications, **3**, 1283
  records, duty to keep, **3**, 1287
  referral to, **3**, 1287
  referrals to children's hearing, generally, **3**, 1280, 1282, 1285, 1287
  removal from office, **3**, 1283
  resignation, **3**, 1283
  school report, **3**, 1287
  sheriff court, right to conduct proceedings before, **3**, 1284
  skills required by, **3**, 1286
  social work report, **3**, 1287
  staff, provision, **3**, 1283
  training, **3**, 1286
rota, **3**, 1305*n*, 1315
Scottish Association of Children's Panels (SACP), **3**, 1313
sexes, ratio of, **3**, 1304, 1315
training, **3**, 1327
Children's Panel Advisory Committee
children's hearing, attendance by chairman or member, **3**, 1327
function, **3**, 1306
local authority obligation to form, **3**, 1306
training, **3**, 1306
Children's Panel Advisory Group
functions, **3**, 1306
Child's special allowance
claimant absent from Great Britain, **21**, 1023
Chiltern Hundreds
appointment to stewardship of, **5**, 379
Chimney
domestic building, of, defence to charge of emitting smoke from, **9**, 1124
height of, **9**, 1132
law of the tenement, **18**, 230, 236
order *ad factum praestandum*, **14**, 2157
China, People's Republic of
imports, European Union regulations, **7**, 1029
Chinese wall
Securities and Investments Board Core Conduct of Business Rules, **12**, 1358, 1395
Chiropodist
Council for Professions Supplementary to Medicine, **15**, 1516–1521
discipline, statutory regulation of, **23**, 917
employment of, **11**, 1500
non-designated services, **4**, 1177*n*

Chiropodist—*continued*
private practice, health service facilities used for, **11**, 1496
Chivalry
orders of, badges, **11**, 1610
Chlorate mixture
explosive, as, **10**, 1588
Chocolate
See COCOA AND CHOCOLATE PRODUCTS
Choice of law
adoption, in, **17**, 243
bill of lading, clause in, **21**, 546
clause, contract, in, **15**, 736, 751
companies, application of ordinary rules, **17**, 357
connecting factor—
  domicile, *see* DOMICILE
  flexible, **17**, 125
  interpreting—
    law of country, **17**, 147
    meaning, **17**, 110
    process of, **17**, 146
  location of, **17**, 146
  nature of, **17**, 122
current approaches, **17**, 129
dissolution of marriage, on, **17**, 235
evolution of rules—
  alternative reference, rules of, **17**, 126
  complexity, growth in, **17**, 127
  developing subject, conflict as, **17**, 123
  flexible connecting factors, **17**, 125
  fragmentation, **17**, 124
  general trends, **17**, 124
  vested rights approach, **17**, 124
external public policy rule, **17**, 172
foreign decrees, recognition of, relationship between, **17**, 135, 137
  alternative reference, rules of, **17**, 126
foreign expropriatory claim, **17**, 329
general rule, **17**, 133
harmonisation, need for, **17**, 113
internal rules—
  compatibility of, **17**, 131
  distinction between, **17**, 130
  statutory provisions, spheres of operation, **17**, 132
jurisdiction, relationship with rules of, **17**, 135, 136
legal rights, **17**, 341
multilateral rule, **17**, 133
nature of—
  connecting factor, **17**, 122
  examples of rules, **17**, 120
  juridical category, **17**, 121
particular provision, **17**, 133
polygamous marriage and, **17**, 219
renvoi, see renvoi
rules, **17**, 104
succession—
  intestate, **17**, 342
  legal rights, **17**, 341
time charterparty, clause in, **21**, 640
uncertainty as to, **17**, 145
unilateral provisions—
  choice of law clause distinguished from, **17**, 133
  generally, **17**, 133

Choice of law—*continued*
unilateral provisions—*continued*
  incompatible, **17**, 134
  meaning, **17**, 110
  overriding statutes, **17**, 134
  self-denying statutes, **17**, 134
voyage charterparty, clause in, **21**, 618
See also LEX CAUSAE; PRIVATE INTERNATIONAL LAW

Cholera
death by, cremation following, **3**, 565
infection, fear of, **14**, 2082

Christmas
date, **22**, 805, 808
Glastonbury thorn, legend, **22**, 805
shooting of game on Christmas Day, **11**, 804n

Church
burgh—
  district council rights, provision for, **3**, 1588
  historic position, **3**, 1587
  post-1925 position, **3**, 1588
  sale, pre-emptive rights of district council, **3**, 1588
burial or deposit of cremated remains within, **3**, 1605
burial in, right of, **3**, 515
Church of Scotland—
  New Parishes (Scotland) Act 1844, erected under, **3**, 1591
  quoad omnia parish—
    historical position, **3**, 1578, 1591
    New Parishes (Scotland) Act 1844, erected under, **3**, 1591
    post-1925 position, **3**, 1580, 1591
    See also PARISH
  quoad sacra parish—
    historical position, **3**, 1583
    non-statutory endowments, **3**, 1586
    post-1925 position, **3**, 1584
    statutory endowments, **3**, 1585
    See also PARISH
  repairs, **3**, 1580
  See also CHURCH OF SCOTLAND
church wardens, **19**, 219n
churchyard, *see* CHURCHYARD
courts, *see* CHURCH COURTS
education, shifting relationship with state over, **5**, 346
fire certificate, exemption from, **14**, 503
licensing objections by, **2**, 49
maintenance, **3**, 1606
marriage in, **19**, 1461
minister, use by, **3**, 1605
new town, in, **23**, 376
parliamentary—
  churchyard, **3**, 1590
  historical position, **3**, 1589
  post-1925 position, **3**, 1590
planning controls, **3**, 1671
property, **5**, 694
  and endowments—
    generally, **5**, 694
    non-statutory, sale, **3**, 1607
    sale of congregational properties and endowments, **3**, 1607–1609

Church—*continued*
rates, **3**, 1671
  valuation for rating, **24**, 592
repair of, gifts for, **3**, 1120
sale of congregational properties and endowments, **3**, 1607–1609
seat, pertinent as, **12**, 1242
separation of powers, **5**, 624
state, and, *see* CHURCH AND STATE
use, **3**, 1605
valuation roll, **3**, 1671
voluntary, *see* VOLUNTARY CHURCHES
wardens in English law, **19**, 219n

Church and state
church property, **5**, 694
courts, *see* CHURCH COURTS
Crown, role of, **5**, 705
disestablishment—
  Ireland, in, **5**, 688
  Wales, in, **5**, 688
establishment—
  challenge to, **5**, 689–691
  inroads into, **5**, 690
  legislation, amendment of, **5**, 687
  monarchy, relations with, **5**, 686
  union, effect of, **5**, 684, 685
historical introduction, **5**, 679–683
patronage, **5**, 691
pre-Reformation, **5**, 680
Reformation, **5**, 681
Reformed Church, **5**, 682
separation of, **5**, 689
seventeenth-century Church, **5**, 683
voluntary religious bodies, **5**, 701–704
Westminster Confession, status of, **5**, 698–700

Church courts
commissary courts, and, **6**, 918
deeds presented in, **19**, 836
description, **22**, 511
exclusive powers, **22**, 511
jurisdiction, **5**, 692
marriage questions, **22**, 511
non-established Churches, **5**, 693
notarial instruments, **19**, 831
obligations, registration of, **19**, 836
professional lawyers, participation, **22**, 511
property of Church, **5**, 694
registration in, **19**, 836
statement made in, absolute privilege, **15**, 524
status, questions of, **22**, 511
See also CANON LAW

Church of Christ Scientist
nursing homes, **11**, 1531

Church of England
bishops, nomination, **7**, 709, 709n
clergy—
  disqualification for parliamentary election, **15**, 1061
  exclusion from membership of House of Commons, **5**, 379
Coronation Oath, requirements of, **7**, 708
Crown and, **7**, 708, 709
Lords Spiritual, **5**, 366; **16**, 1307, 1307n
  precedence, **16**, 2016

Church of England—*continued*
Measure of the General Synod, copyright, **18**, 1000, 1035
measure to secure, **5**, 361
proposals to disestablish, **5**, 348
royal assent to laws, **7**, 709
Scottish Episcopal Church, relationship to, **3**, 1617
Sovereign must be in communion with, **7**, 703*n*
Thirty-nine Articles, **3**, 1627
Church of Scotland
accounts, kirk session, annual attestation, **3**, 1512
Act of 1921 ..., **5**, 695–697
Act for Settling the Quiet and Peace of the Church, **3**, 1611
Articles Declaratory, *see* ARTICLES DECLARATORY OF THE CONSTITUTION OF THE CHURCH OF SCOTLAND
Barrier Act, **3**, 1546
Basis and Plan of Union, **3**, 1552
beadle, direction by minister, **3**, 1565
buildings, *see* property and endowments *below*
choirmaster—
    direction by minister, **3**, 1565
    salary, **3**, 1515, 1565
church officer—
    appointment and dismissal, **3**, 1510, 1565
    direction by minister, **3**, 1565
    salary, **3**, 1515
clergy of, exclusion from membership of House of Commons, **5**, 379
committees of management, **3**, 1517
Communion Roll—
    annual attestation, **3**, 1512
    annual revision, **3**, 1508
    keeping, **3**, 1508
    restoration of name to, **3**, 1508
    Supplementary Roll, **3**, 1508
congregation—
    assessors, appointment, **3**, 1523
    changed circumstances, where, **3**, 1529
    dissolution, **3**, 1528
    elders, election, **3**, 1507
    jus devolutum, **3**, 1526, 1558
    minister, election, **3**, 1504, 1511, 1557, 1558
    minister's stipend, **3**, 1562
        See also RELIGION, MINISTER OF (Church of Scotland)
    Model Deed of Constitution, **3**, 1508, 1515, 1563
    qualified chapels, **3**, 1616, 1616*n*, 1617, 1631
    superintendence committee, **3**, 1523
    union and linking, **3**, 1527
    unsatisfactory state, in, **3**, 1523, 1524
    vacant, **3**, 1525, 1557, 1558
        pulpit supply, **3**, 1511, 1570
    visitation, **3**, 1523
congregational board—
    constitution, **3**, 1515
    functions, **3**, 1515
    officials, **3**, 1515
Courts—
    judicial review, **3**, 1505
    status, **3**, 1634

Church of Scotland—*continued*
Crown and, **7**, 709
deacons' courts, **3**, 1516
Dean of the Chapel Royal, **3**, 1551
Dean of the Order of the Thistle, **3**, 1551
Declaratory Articles, **5**, 348
    See also ARTICLES DECLARATORY OF THE CONSTITUTION OF THE CHURCH OF SCOTLAND
dignitaries, **3**, 1551
discipline, **3**, 1508, 1512
disruption, **3**, 1633, 1636
doctrinal operational independence of state, **5**, 348
elder, *see* ELDER
endowments, *see* property and endowments *below*
episcopacy, rejection, **3**, 1610, 1611, 1635
Formula, subscription to—
    elders, **3**, 1507
    ministers, **3**, 1556
Fund for the Maintenance of the Ministry, **3**, 1562
fundamental law, issue of, **5**, 348
General Assembly, *see* GENERAL ASSEMBLY OF THE CHURCH OF SCOTLAND
glebe lands, *see* GLEBE
government—
    adjudication, **3**, 1502
    civil authority, and, **3**, 1502
    Courts—
        generally, **3**, 1502, 1505
        See also individual courts
    legislation, **3**, 1502
        early, **3**, 1501
    membership, **3**, 1502
    office, **3**, 1502
    presbyterian form, generally, **3**, 1501, 1502
    Union Agreement, **3**, 1501
    Westminster Confession of Faith, **3**, 1501
heritors—
    duties, **3**, 1578–1580
    meaning, **3**, 1578
Holy Catholic or Universal Church, as part of, **3**, 1501, 1502
hours of worship, fixing, **3**, 1508
jurisdiction—
    Ballantyne v Wigtown Presbytery, decision in, **3**, 1504
    civil law, interaction with, **3**, 1504
    generally, **3**, 1502, 1504, 1634
    presbytery, **3**, 1522
    sheriff court, **6**, 1087
kirk sessions, *see* KIRK SESSION
Lord High Commissioner to the General Assembly, **7**, 709, 709*n*
    precedence, **16**, 2006
manse, minister's right to occupy, **3**, 1560
marriages, solemnisation, **3**, 1564
membership—
    adjudication, **3**, 1502
minister, *see* RELIGION, MINISTER OF (Church of Scotland)
Model Constitution, **3**, 1508, 1515, 1563
Moderator of the General Assembly, precedence, **16**, 2006, 2016

Church of Scotland—*continued*
national church, as, **3**, 1502
national institution, as, **5**, 348
office-bearers—
   adjudication over, **3**, 1502
   election, **3**, 1502
order, maintenance of, **3**, 1508
organist—
   appointment and dismissal, **3**, 1510
   direction by minister, **3**, 1510, 1565
   salary, **3**, 1515, 1565
overtures, **3**, 1546, 1546*n*
parish, *see* PARISH
precentor—
   appointment and dismissal, **3**, 1510
   direction by minister, **3**, 1510, 1565
   presbytery, as official of, **3**, 1520
   salary, **3**, 1565
prelacy, abolition, **3**, 1611
presbyterian government, establishment, **3**, 1610,
   1611, 1635
presbyteries, *see* PRESBYTERY, CHURCH OF SCOTLAND
prison chaplains, **16**, 1411, 1417, 1458
   appointment, **3**, 1668
property and endowments—
   alienation, **3**, 1508
   burgh churches—
      historical position, **3**, 1587
      post-1925 position, **3**, 1588
   church halls—
      provision, **3**, 1578
      sale, **3**, 1607
   Church of Scotland General Trustees, **3**, 1576
   Church of Scotland Trust—
      constitution, **3**, 1604
      origins, **3**, 1603
      powers, **3**, 1604
   churches—
      quoad omnia parishes, **3**, 1578, 1580, 1591,
      1607
      New Parishes (Scotland) Act 1844, erected
         under, **3**, 1591
      quoad scara parishes, **3**, 1583–5186
      See also ecclesiastical buildings *below*
   churchyards, islands or district council, transfer
      to, **3**, 1580
   Clauses for Congregation Titles, **3**, 1600
   congregational, sale, **3**, 1607–1609
      current position, **3**, 1609
      pre-1929 Church of Scotland, originating in,
         3, 1607
   debt, burden with, **3**, 1508
   ecclesiastical buildings—
      fabric committee, **3**, 1523, 1606
      maintenance, **3**, 1606
      use, **3**, 1605
      See also churches *above*
   Free Church of Scotland, originating in—
      Churches (Scotland) Act 1905, effect, **3**, 1599
      Clauses for Congregation Titles, **3**, 1600
      pre-1900 ... 1598
      pre-1929 ... 1600
   generally, **3**, 1574
   glebe lands, *see* GLEBE

Church of Scotland—*continued*
property and endowments—*continued*
   improvements or alterations, **3**, 1508
   insurance, **3**, 1508
   lease, **3**, 1508
   maintenance, **3**, 1508, 1606
   manses—
      quoad omnia parishes, **3**, 1579, 1580, 1591
      New Parishes (Scotland) Act 1844, erected
         under, **3**, 1591
      quoad scara parishes, **3**, 1583–5186
   ownership, **3**, 1508
   parliamentary churches and manses—
      historical position, **3**, 1589
      post-1925 position, **3**, 1590
      pre-1929 Church of Scotland, originating in, **3**,
         1574, 1575*ff*
      pre-1929 United Free Church, originating in,
         3, 1608
   presbytery fabric committee, **3**, 1523, 1606
   protection of, title to sue, **3**, 1522
   quoad omnia parishes, **3**, 1578–1582
      glebes—
         historical position, **3**, 1581
         post-1925 position, **3**, 1582
      historical position, **3**, 1578, 1579, 1591
      New Parishes (Scotland) Act 1844, churches
         and manses erected under, **3**, 1591
      post 1925-position, **3**, 1580, 1591
   quoad scara parishes, **3**, 1583–5186
   repair, **3**, 1508
   Scottish Ecclesiastical Commissioners, **3**, 1577
   stipends, *see* RELIGION, MINISTER OF (Church of
      Scotland)
   teinds, *see* TEINDS
   tenure, **18**, 47, 68, 70
   United Free Church of Scotland, originating
      in, **3**, 1600
   United Original Secession Synod, originating
      in, **3**, 1602
   United Presbyterian Church, originating in, **3**,
      1597
   use, **3**, 1605
   vidication, title to sue, **3**, 1522
property registers, annual attestation, **3**, 1512
pulpit supply, arrangements for, **3**, 1511, 1570
reader, supervision, **3**, 1534
records held by Scottish Record Office, **19**, 849, 862
reformed, **3**, 1501
registers of baptisms, annual attestation, **3**, 1512
religious and moral condition of parish,
   superintendance, **3**, 1508
Revolution Settlement, **3**, 1610, 1611
rolls of baptised persons, annual attestation, **3**, 1512
Seceders, **3**, 1636
separations, **3**, 1501
services—
   Baptism, choice of time for administering, **3**,
      1508
   number held, **3**, 1508
   Sacrament of Lord's Supper—
      appointment of time and place for, **3**, 1508
      distribution of elements, **3**, 1508
      right administration, oversight, **3**, 1522

Church of Scotland—*continued*
sheriff court jurisdiction, **6**, 1087
sovereign, position of, **3**, 1501
spiritual oversight of members, **3**, 1508, 1522
status, **3**, 1501
stipends, *see* RELIGION, MINISTER OF (Church of Scotland)
students of divinity—
    examination and licensing, **3**, 1522, 1532
    nomination and supervision, **3**, 1522, 1532, 1553
Supplementary Roll, **3**, 1508
synods, provincial, abolition, **3**, 1541
teinds, *see* TEINDS
temporal affairs, administration, **3**, 1514–1517
Union Agreement 1707:, **3**, 1501, 1502, 1634; **7**, 739
union with other churches, obligation to seek and promote, **3**, 1502
United Free Church, union with, **3**, 1503
voluntary churches' position compared, **3**, 1634
Westminster Confession of faith—
    attitudes to, **5**, 348
    See also WESTMINSTER CONFESSION OF FAITH
See also KIRK; KIRKLANDS; KIRKYARD
Church of Scotland General Trustees
churchyards, right of access to, **3**, 1580
ecclesiastical buildings vested in, **3**, 1508
functions, **3**, 1576
incorporation, **3**, 1576
members, **3**, 1576
powers, **3**, 1576
Church of Scotland Trust
constitution, **3**, 1604
origins, **3**, 1603
powers, **3**, 1604
trustee, exempted person under Financial Services Act 1986, as, **12**, 1323
Churchyard
allodial land, as, **18**, 47, 646
burial rights, sale, **3**, 524
compulsory acquisition or use, **19**, 19
felling trees in, **11**, 617
functions in respect of, **14**, 699
islands or district council, transfer to, **3**, 1580
parliamentary church, **3**, 1590
public health nuisance, as, **19**, 336
transfer of ownership, **18**, 646
See also BURIAL GROUND; KIRKYARD
Churning
meaning, **12**, 1385
Securities and Investments Board Core Conduct of Business Rules, **12**, 1385
Cider
excise duty, **7**, 1061, 1061n, 1065
    deferred payments, **7**, 1088
producers, registration, **7**, 1066
Cigar
duty on, *See* TOBACCO
Cigarette
duty on, *See* TOBACCO
sale—
    person under age of sixteen, to, **3**, 1225
    pre-packed quantities, to be in, **3**, 1225
    vending machine, from, **3**, 1225

Cinema
British Board of Film Censors, **9**, 1027
British Film Fund Agency, **9**, 1028
censorship, **9**, 1027
children—
    admission of, **9**, 1026
    club, show promoted by, **9**, 1026
    health of, **9**, 1026
    local authority, consent to use of premises, **9**, 1026
    regulations in respect of, **9**, 1021
    safety of, **9**, 1026
    welfare of, **9**, 1026
cinematograph film, *see* CINEMATOGRAPH FILM; CINEMATOGRAPH FILMS COUNCIL; FILM
commercial—
    licensing provisions, **9**, 1020
    non-commercial distinguished from, **9**, 1018, 1023
    public supervision, **9**, 1019
controls over, **9**, 1018
exempted exhibitions, **9**, 1023
licence, appeals to sheriff court, **14**, 119
licensing, **12**, 73
mobile, **9**, 1020
non-commercial—
    commercial distinguished from, **9**, 1018, 1023
    generally, **9**, 1022
private gain, film show promoted for, **9**, 1025
public money for, **9**, 1028
quasi-commercial, **9**, 1024
safety, regulations in respect of, **9**, 1021
sheriff court jurisdiction, **6**, 1098, 1124; **14**, 119
Use Classes Order, **23**, 98
valuation for rating, **24**, 745
Cinematograph film
censorship, **9**, 1027
child—
    performance by, **9**, 1052
    protection by licensing system, **3**, 1242
club, as exempted organisation, **9**, 1023
copyright, *see* FILM
film exhibition—
    licensing of premises, **14**, 523
    meaning, **9**, 1019
    video game as, **9**, 1016
home-movie, **9**, 1023
licensing, **3**, 1242
meaning, **18**, 969; **19**, 412
private gain, shows promoted for, **9**, 1025
public health legislation, **19**, 412–419
storage premises, **19**, 415–417
    appeals against local authority requirements, **19**, 418
    control of, **19**, 413
    penalties for offences, **19**, 419
See also FILM
Cinematograph Films Council
abolition of, **9**, 1028
establishment of, **9**, 1028
Circuits
early history, **17**, 507
numbers of, **17**, 507

Circumcision
religious grounds, on, **11**, 1450
Circumstantial evidence
See EVIDENCE
Circumvention
delict, **15**, 216
donation, reduction of, **8**, 647
Circus
advertising, **9**, 1033
licence for, **9**, 1034; **19**, 1295
parades, **9**, 1033
performers—
　child, **9**, 1035
　employment of, **9**, 1032
　equity, membership of, **9**, 1032
performing animals—
　cruelty to, **9**, 1031
　protection from, **9**, 1029
　protection of, **9**, 1030
Cistern
public health nuisance, as, **19**, 336
water fitting, as, **25**, 527
Citation
See SERVICE OF DOCUMENTS
Citizen
See PRIVATE CITIZEN
Citizens Advice Bureaux
expansion of, **6**, 9
Citizenship
acquisition—
　naturalisation, by, **12**, 121
　registration, by, **12**, 121
acquisition of, common law principles, **14**, 1901
adopted children, of, **10**, 1191; **14**, 1910
British, *see* BRITISH CITIZENSHIP
British Dependent Territories, *see* BRITISH
　DEPENDENT TERRITORIES CITIZENSHIP
British Overseas, *see* BRITISH OVERSEAS CITIZENSHIP
Commonwealth, *see* COMMONWEALTH CITIZEN
illegitimate children, **10**, 1186
marriage, **10**, 836
new legal category, creation of, **14**, 1902
registration—
　British Dependent Territories, **14**, 1914, 1936,
　　1938
　British National, **14**, 1914
　British Overseas citizen, **14**, 1914, 1943
　British protected person, **14**, 1914, 1954
　British subject, **14**, 1950
　child born in United Kingdom, **14**, 1912
　Falkland Islands, **14**, 1926
　father's citizenship, based on, **14**, 1918
　renunciation of citizenship following, **14**, 1919
　stateless person, **14**, 1914, 1952
renunciation of, **14**, 1927*ff*
status of, **11**, 1069
　matched with immigration law rights, **14**, 1903
Citrus fruit
preservatives in, **11**, 377
City of London
functions, **14**, 60
Civic code
licences, *see* LICENCES
public procession, **14**, 573

Civil aviation
accidents, *see* AIRCRAFT
administration of, **2**, 902
aerodrome, *see* AERODROME
air services, **14**, 451
air traffic controllers, licensing, **2**, 971
air transport licence—
　application for, **2**, 988
　CAA duties as to, **2**, 998
　considerations as to grant of, **2**, 998
　contravention of terms of, **2**, 985
　death of holder, **2**, 996
　decisions on, publication of, **2**, 999
　environmental cases, **2**, 987
　exemptions, grant of, **2**, 985
　grant of, **2**, 988, 991
　hearings—
　　notice of, **2**, 993
　　procedure at, **2**, 993
　　record of proceedings, **2**, 993
　　right to be heard, **2**, 993
　law relating to, **2**, 984
　objections to grant, **2**, 992
　objectives of, **2**, 998, 999
　policies as to, publication of, **2**, 999
　refusal of, **2**, 988
　renewal of, **2**, 989
　representations as to, **2**, 992
　requirement for, **2**, 985
　revocation, suspension etc—
　　appeal against, **2**, 994
　　application for, **2**, 991
　　CAA, by, **2**, 994
　　grounds for, **2**, 994
　tariff provisions of, **2**, 997
　terms of, **2**, 997
　transfer of, **2**, 996
airport, transfer of undertaking, **14**, 450
authority, *see* CIVIL AVIATION AUTHORITY
carriage by air, *see* AIR, CARRIAGE BY
carriage by air—
　foreign operators, **2**, 986
　law, sources of, **2**, 901
development of, responsibility for, **2**, 903
facilities at aerodromes, **2**, 914
flight information officers, **2**, 971
highways—
　acquisition of land for, **2**, 952
　stopping up or diversion, **2**, 952
land—
　acquired, disposal of, **2**, 946
　acquisition of—
　　compensation to undertakers, **2**, 945
　　displacement of persons by, **2**, 945, 950
　　powers as to, **2**, 945
　　relevant operators for, **2**, 944
　consecrated land and burial grounds, **2**, 945
　controls by Minister, **2**, 950
　entry for survey purposes, **2**, 947
　rights over—
　　extinguishment, **2**, 950
　　grant of, by agreement, **2**, 947
　　servitude rights, creation of, **2**, 948
law, source of, **2**, 901

Civil aviation—*continued*
orders applying to Scotland, **2**, 1068
services—
    competition in, **2**, 998
    securing provision of, **2**, 903
stopping up or diverting road for purposes of, **20**, 657
travel organisers, *see* AIR TRAVEL ORGANISER
See also AIRCRAFT; AIR NAVIGATION
Civil Aviation Authority
acquisition of land, *see* CIVIL AVIATION
air travel licensing, *see* AIR TRAVEL ORGANISER
airport capacity, recommendations as to, **2**, 920
appeals from decisions of, **2**, 980
certificates of airworthiness, **2**, 959
duties of, **2**, 902
general objective of, **2**, 903
investigation of complaints by, **2**, 930
navigation services—
    charges for, **2**, 1010
    duty to provide, **2**, 1008
    See also AIR NAVIGATION
official Record of, **2**, 901
permitted development, **23**, 153
publications of, **2**, 901
responsibilities of, **2**, 903
Secretary of State's duties in relation to, **2**, 902
status etc, **2**, 903
supervision of, **23**, 911
Civil aviation constabulary
power to appoint, **16**, 1818
Civil commotion
building contract affected by, extension of time where, **3**, 48
loss or damage resulting from, carrier not liable, **21**, 603
Civil defence
care and maintenance basis, **5**, 621
district council, functions of, **14**, 506, 508
fire brigade manpower and equipment, **10**, 1435
generally, **5**, 617
islands council, functions of, **14**, 506, 507
legislation in 1939–45 war, **5**, 618
post-war developments, **5**, 620
reform, **14**, 49
regional council, functions of, **14**, 506, 507
schemes, suspension in 1945 ..., **5**, 619
Civil imprisonment
debt, for, **8**, 101
officers of court, exercise by, **8**, 105
Civil jurisdiction
admissibility, examination as to jurisdiction and, **4**, 64
appeal, tribunal, decision of, excluded jurisdiction, **4**, 85
co-defenders, **4**, 49, 50
conflicts of jurisdiction—
    admissibility, examination as to, **4**, 64
    examination as to jurisdiction, **4**, 64
    lis pendens, **4**, 65
    protective measures, **4**, 66
    provisional measures, **4**, 66
    related actions, **4**, 65
    sequestration, **4**, 76

Civil jurisdiction—*continued*
contracting states—
    exclusive jurisdiction, **4**, 60
    international jurisdiction of courts of, **4**, 21
    meaning, **4**, 22
conventions—
    generally, **4**, 26
    judicial notice of, **4**, 22
    meaning, **4**, 22
decrees, suspension, **4**, 13
defender—
    action with none, excluded jurisdiction, **4**, 86
    domicile of, **4**, 86
domestic jurisdiction—
    generally, **4**, 21
    Scottish courts, **4**, 21, 24
domicile, *see* DOMICILE
elements of civil jurisdiction—
    contracting states, international jurisdiction of courts of, **4**, 21
    domestic jurisdiction, **4**, 21
    international jurisdiction, **4**, 21
    United Kingdom, allocation of jurisdiction within, **4**, 21
exclusions—
    Admiralty causes, **4**, 79
    aircraft mortgages, rectification of register of, **4**, 81
    Civil Aviation (Eurocontrol) Act 1962 ..., **4**, 82
    commissary proceedings, **4**, 80
    companies, proceedings relating to, **4**, 71, 75
    custody, **4**, 69
    general, **4**, 67
    judicial arrangements or composition, **4**, 74
    judicial factors, **4**, 70
    no defender, action with, **4**, 86
    Oil and Gas (Enterprise) Act 1982 ..., **4**, 83
    other conventions, **4**, 87
    Protection of Trading Interests Act 1980 ..., **4**, 84
    sequestration, *see* SEQUESTRATION
    status, action relating to, **4**, 68
    tribunal, decision of—
        appeal from, **4**, 85
        decision of, **4**, 85
    winding up, *see* WINDING UP
exclusive jurisdiction—
    1968 Convention, **4**, 58
    Act of 1982—
        Schedule 4 ..., **4**, 59
        Schedule 8 ..., **4**, 60
    contracting state, **4**, 60
    designs, **4**, 58, 59, 60
    form of agreement, **4**, 62, 63
    patents, **4**, 58, 59, 60
    primary, **4**, 61
    secondary rule of, **4**, 61
    trade marks, **4**, 58, 59, 60
    validity of agreement, **4**, 61
grounds of jurisdiction—
    Act of 1982
        purpose of, **4**, 25
        scope of, **4**, 26
    consumer contract, *see* CONTRACT

Civil jurisdiction—*continued*
grounds of jurisdiction—*continued*
  domicile, *see* DOMICILE
  elements of civil jurisdiction, **4**, 21
  exclusive jurisdiction, *see* exclusive jurisdiction
    above
  generally, **4**, 20, 28, 53
  insurance contract, **4**, 57
  international factor, **4**, 22
  prorogation, *see* PROROGATION
  purpose of 1982 Act, **4**, 25
  scope of 1982 Act, **4**, 26
  Scottish courts, domestic jurisdiction, **4**, 24
  special jurisdiction, *see* SPECIAL JURISDICTION
  treatment, **4**, 27
  United Kingdom, allocation of jurisdiction
    within, **4**, 23
international factor, **4**, 22
international jurisdiction as element of, **4**, 21
mere personal defences, meaning, **4**, 150
place, meaning of, **4**, 28
prorogation, **4**, 8, 61, 62, 63
protective measures—
  conflicts of jurisdiction, **4**, 66
  granting, **4**, 28
  interim interdict, **4**, 44
purpose of, **4**, 25
related actions, conflicts of jurisdiction, **4**, 65
rescissory action, **4**, 6
restitution, claim for, **4**, 38
rules of jurisdiction—
  Act of 1982
    purpose of, **4**, 25
    scope of, **4**, 26
  elements of civil jurisdiction, **4**, 21
  generally, **4**, 20, 28
  international factor, **4**, 22
  purpose of 1982 Act, **4**, 25
  scope of 1982 Act, **4**, 26
  Scottish courts, domestic jurisdiction of, **4**, 24
  treatment, **4**, 27
  United Kingdom, allocation of jurisdiction
    within, **4**, 23
  See also grounds of jurisdiction *above*
scope, **4**, 26
special jurisdiction—
  agency, **4**, 40
  arbitration, **4**, 47
  association, decision of organ of, **4**, 46
  branch, agency or other establishment, **4**, 40
  co-defenders, **4**, 49, 50
  contract, **4**, 36
  corporation, decision of organ of, **4**, 46
  counterclaims, **4**, 49, 52
  criminal proceedings, civil claim in, **4**, 38
  debts secured over heritage, **4**, 45
  delict, **4**, 37
  designs, **4**, 48
  generally, **4**, 34
  heritable property, situation of, **4**, 42
  heritage, debts secured over, **4**, 45
  interdict, **4**, 44
  itinerancy, **4**, 35
  maintenance, **4**, 39

Civil jurisdiction—*continued*
special jurisdiction—*continued*
  moveable property—
    arrestment of, **4**, 42
    disposal of, **4**, 43
    rights therein, **4**, 43
    situation of, **4**, 42
  patents, **4**, 48
  third party procedure, **4**, 49, 51
  trade marks, **4**, 48
  trust, **4**, 41
subject matter—
  adjudication, **4**, 7
  consistorial proceedings, **4**, 5
  generally, **4**, 3
  inhibition, **4**, 8
  nobile officium, **4**, 4
  proving tenor, **4**, 11
  reduction, **4**, 6
  special cases, **4**, 10
  trusts, **4**, 9
territorial, **4**, 2
value of—
  bankruptcy, **4**, 16
  death, presumption of, **4**, 17
  generally, **4**, 12
  judicial factors, **4**, 14
  liquidation, **4**, 15
  maritime proceedings, **4**, 18
  sheriff court, private jurisdiction of, **4**, 19
  suspension, **4**, 13
Civil liberty
principle of, **11**, 1012
Civil List
generally, **7**, 770
Civil ministries
military aid to, *see* MILITARY AID
**Civil and Political Rights, International
  Covenant on**
generally, **19**, 694
Civil prisoner
meaning, **16**, 1426, 1426*n*
medical or dental practitioner of own choice, **16**,
  1464
negligent officer, liability of, **14**, 1507
privileges, **16**, 1466
restriction direction, subject to, **14**, 1468
restrictions on association, **16**, 1426
transfer direction, subject to, **14**, 1468
treatment, **16**, 1426, 1432
visits to, **16**, 1459
See also PRISONER
Civil Servant
Crown servant, as, **7**, 757
meaning, **7**, 757, 757*n*
Civil Service
lawyers in—
  Home Civil Service, **13**, 1392, 1393
  Legal Civil Service, *see* LEGAL CIVIL SERVICE
procurator fiscal service, assimilation into, **17**, 536
Scottish Office, **5**, 521
special legal powers, **11**, 1062
unfair dismissal from, **9**, 211

Civil Service Superannuation Scheme
tax treatment, **21**, 1287
Claim of Right
effect, **6**, 809
generally, **7**, 702n, 703n, 710
lawburrows and, **13**, 914
taxation, **7**, 764
Claims, Court of
Lord Lyon King of Arms, and, **6**, 1011
Clams
early legislation, **11**, 118
Clan
membership and badges, **11**, 1631
Clan chief
precedence, **16**, 2021, 2022
Clare constat
feudal conveyance, **18**, 108, 109
writ of, **6**, 605
Class gifts
ascertaining membership of class, **25**, 844
generally, **25**, 843
Class rights
See SHARES
Classification societies
generally, **21**, 120
'Clause 22 peril'
building contract affected by, extension of time
  where, **3**, 48
Clause paramount
bill of lading, **21**, 546
charterparty, **21**, 591n, 618, 640
Clauses Acts
historical development, **5**, 10
land, *see* LANDS CLAUSES CONSOLIDATION
  (SCOTLAND) ACT
railways, *see* RAILWAYS CLAUSES CONSOLIDATION
  (SCOTLAND) ACT
Clayton's Case
rule in—
  form precluding, **3**, 962
  termination of cautionary obligation by, **3**, 962
Clean air
licensing, **14**, 526
smoke, *see* SMOKE
Cleaning materials
weights and measures legislation, **6**, 243, 244
Cleansing
meaning, **9**, 1172
public health, **14**, 706
road, **14**, 411
Clearing house
function, **12**, 1322
recognised—
  application for recognition order, **12**, 1322
register, **12**, 1415
Clergy
clergyman and penitent, privilege in relation to
  communications between, **10**, 685
European Parliament, **15**, 1065
exclusion from membership of House of
  Commons, **5**, 379
Member of Parliament, disqualification for
  election as, **15**, 1061

Clergy—*continued*
Scottish Parliament, representation in, **15**, 1002,
  1003
See also (RELIGION) MINISTER OF
Clerk of Parliaments
status, **7**, 757
Clerk of the Crown in Chancery
United Kingdom parliamentary elections—
  'Election Writ and Return', **15**, 1353
  name of candidate elected, return to, **15**, 1352,
    1353
  record of returns, **15**, 1353
Clerk of the House of Commons
status, **7**, 757
Clerk of the peace
appointment of, **6**, 1164
Clerk of the Rolls
Lord Clerk Register, origins of, **19**, 802
Officer of State, **7**, 790
Clerk of works
appointment, **3**, 127
architect's responsibility, and, **3**, 137
generally, **3**, 2
negligence by, **3**, 148
presence on site, contract providing for, **3**, 53
Clerk Register
Officer of State, **7**, 790, 792, 800
Clerks to the Signet
College of Justice, **6**, 904
Clinic
charges for goods supplied at, **11**, 1515
Clinical medicine
qualifications, **14**, 1106
Clinical trial
acceptability of product, **14**, 1206
licensing system, exemption from, **14**, 1203
meaning, **14**, 1207
Clock
mechanical, evolution of, **22**, 801
public, maintenance or illumination, **14**, 701
Clog on redemption
whether unlawful, **13**, 1762
Close relative
conditio si institutus sine liberis decesserit, application
  of, **25**, 896
Close season
deer, **11**, 930, 933
North-East Atlantic Fisheries Commission powers,
  11, 95
possession of game, **11**, 841
sale of game, **11**, 840
See also CLOSE TIME
Close support unit
generally, **3**, 1375
Close time
agricultural executive committee powers, **11**, 808
annual, **11**, 14, 15, 32
  buying salmon, **11**, 16
  cruives and other equipment, **11**, 16
  obstruction of fish, **11**, 19
  offences relating to, **11**, 16
  order, **11**, 15
  River Esk, **11**, 46
  River Tweed, **11**, 42, 43

Close time—*continued*
annual—*continued*
  Secretary of State's powers, **11**, 15, 23
  selling salmon or exposing for sale, **11**, 16
  shipping or exporting salmon, **11**, 16
  trout, **11**, 53
seal fishing, **11**, 216, 217
weekly, **11**, 14, 17, 32
  introduction of principle, **11**, 2
  River Esk, **11**, 46
  River Tweed, **11**, 42, 43
  Secretary of State's powers, **11**, 23
wilful destruction of game during, **11**, 806
See also CLOSE SEASON
Closed agreement
nature of, **4**, 1379
Closed circuit television
single set of premises, within, **16**, 1928
Closed shop agreement
code of practice as to, **9**, 241
freedom of association, **12**, 77
Closing order
acquisition, local authority powers of, **11**, 1987
appeal against, **11**, 1986
consequences of generally, **11**, 1988
demolition order—
  replaced by, **11**, 1983
  substitution of, **11**, 1987
effect of, **11**, 1982
food premises, **11**, 422
generally, **11**, 1982, 1983
power to make, **14**, 305
renewal, **11**, 1984
revocation, **11**, 1984
service, **11**, 1985
suspension, **11**, 1984
using or permitting use of building for human
  habitation, **11**, 1988
vacation, notice requiring, **11**, 1988
Closure order
See LICENSED PREMISES
Clothes
communal washing of, **19**, 447
disinfection of, **19**, 446, 455
VAT, zero-rating, **7**, 1460
Club
accounts etc, **2**, 30
age for admission to, **2**, 30
alcoholic liquor, supply of—
  offences as to, **2**, 824
  permitted hours, **2**, 824
  registration for, **2**, 823
  sale on club premises, **19**, 1229
  unregistered, sale in, **2**, 80
bank account, **2**, 1257
bona fide, certification, **2**, 27
business, as, **7**, 1295
capacity to contract, **3**, 26
capital allowances, **19**, 1314
capital gains tax, **2**, 821
category of, **2**, 17
certification of registration—
  duration of, **2**, 27
  grant by sheriff, **2**, 27

Club—*continued*
child or young person in bar, **3**, 1227
children not allowed in, **2**, 74
committee—
  borrowing by, **2**, 805, 813
  credit dealings, **2**, 816
  delict, liability in, **2**, 805
  liability—
    for actions of, **2**, 804
    generally, **2**, 816
    members, of, **2**, 31
  pledging members' credit, **2**, 813
  powers and duties, **2**, 805
  rules as to, **2**, 30
  scope of authority, **2**, 813
  surrender of powers to, **2**, 804
community benefit society, as, **12**, 609
constitution, **2**, 804
contracts, liability for, **2**, 816
corporation tax, **2**, 821; **19**, 1313, 1314
court actions—
  Court of Session, in, **2**, 818
  generally, **2**, 817
  restrictions, **2**, 817
  sheriff court, in, **2**, 819
courts—
  intervention by, **2**, 804
  jurisdiction of, **2**, 804
dangerous activities, promoting, **2**, 814
data held by, protection, **18**, 1518
dissolution—
  division of assets on, **2**, 811
  resolution for, **2**, 811
domestic tribunal set up by, **23**, 901, 916
employees, minimum age, **2**, 74
food supplied by, **11**, 342*n*
formation, **2**, 804
funds—
  committee powers as to, **2**, 805
  damages payable from, **2**, 814
  insufficiency of, **2**, 813
gaming, *see* BINGO; GAMING
gaming machines, use of, **2**, 825
incorporated, **2**, 803; **19**, 1228
investment, nature of, **2**, 801
liability of members—
  contracts, for, **2**, 816
  contractual obligations, **2**, 813
  damages, for, **2**, 814
  delictual liability, **2**, 814
  general, **2**, 812
  pro rata, **2**, 813
  vicarious, **2**, 814
  work done, for, **2**, 813
licence—
  alteration of, **2**, 32
  registration in lieu of, **2**, 8
management, **2**, 805
members—
  admission of, **2**, 806
  associate, **2**, 809
  contractual obligations, **2**, 813

Club—*continued*
members—*continued*
  expulsion—
    court action as to, **2**, 808
    grounds for, **2**, 808
    remedy for, **2**, 808
  inter se, position of, **2**, 815
  number reduced to one, **18**, 35
  payments on admission, **2**, 806
  payments by, **2**, 804
  property, rights in, **2**, 810
  refusal of membership, **2**, 806
  regulation by constitution, **2**, 804
  requirements for membership, **2**, 806
  resignation—
    liability, to avoid, **2**, 807
    procedure, **2**, 807
  sue on contracts, right to, **2**, 813
  types of, **2**, 809
  women, **2**, 806
name, passing off, **18**, 1377
negligence, action for, **2**, 814
offences, liability for, **2**, 31
permitted hours, *see* ALCOHOLIC LIQUOR
police powers of entry, **2**, 68, 824
private, distribution of publications at, **6**, 306
private meeting, **14**, 1303
property—
  beneficial interest in, **18**, 34
  joint ownership, generally, **18**, 536
  joint property, as, **18**, 34, 34*n*
    characteristics of joint property, **18**, 35
    management, rules of, **18**, 36, 36*n*
    resignation or death of member, **18**, 35
    See also CO-OWNERSHIP
  ownership, **2**, 810
  title to, **18**, 34
  vesting of, **2**, 805
proprietary—
  constitution, **2**, 826
  delictual liability, **2**, 832
  dissolution, **2**, 831
  management committee, **2**, 828
  members—
    liability of, **2**, 832
    position of, **2**, 826
    rights of, **2**, 827
  nature of, **2**, 802, 826
  property, ownership, **2**, 830
  proprietor—
    ownership of property, **2**, 830
    powers etc, **2**, 832
  taxation liability, **2**, 821
purposes, alteration of, **2**, 804
racial discrimination, **2**, 806
register of—
  duty to keep, **2**, 28
  entries in, **2**, 28
registered club, Sunday opening, **22**, 817
registration—
  application for—
    generally, **2**, 823
    procedure, **2**, 37
    statement to accompany, **2**, 29

Club—*continued*
registration—*continued*
  certification of, **2**, 27, 823
  effect of, **2**, 823
  Gaming Act, under—
    refusal of, **2**, 825
    use of gaming machines, for, **2**, 825
  grounds for refusing, **2**, 823
  objection to, **2**, 823
  renewal, time for, **2**, 823
  rules qualifying for, **2**, 30
  sheriff's duties, **2**, 823
  withdrawing certificate of, **2**, 824
rules—
  alteration, power to make, **2**, 804
  changes, allowing, **2**, 804
  dissolution, provision for, **2**, 811
  duty to abide by, **2**, 806
  lodging of, **2**, 29, 30
  membership, for, **2**, 806
  requirements as to, **2**, 30
  submission by committee, **2**, 805
secretary, oversight of, **2**, 805
sheriff court jurisdiction, **6**, 1067
staff, power to employ, **2**, 805
subscriptions—
  conveyancing, **6**, 417
  increase of, **2**, 804
  liability for, **2**, 806, 812
taxation—
  direct—
    forms of, **2**, 820
    liability for, **2**, 821
  indirect, **2**, 822
  value added tax, **2**, 822; **19**, 1315–1318
trustees—
  composition, **2**, 810
  property rights and duties, **2**, 805
types of, **2**, 802
unincorporated—
  formation, **2**, 804
  generally, **19**, 1227
  nature of, **2**, 803
unregistered, sale etc of liquor in, **2**, 80
VAT, **3**, 1162
  liability, **2**, 822; **19**, 1315–1318
  registration provisions, **7**, 1347
voluntary obligation, capacity to enter, **15**, 663
water meter charges, **25**, 536
winding up, **2**, 811; **18**, 35
Clyde Report
proposals, **3**, 1369
Clydesdale Bank
current position of, **2**, 1119
formation of, **2**, 1118
functions etc, **2**, 1104
Coal
heating fuel, VAT rating, **7**, 1461
mined, **18**, 12
mines, *see* MINES
rights to, separate tenement, as, **18**, 209, 211, 212
seam, in, **18**, 12
stoop and room mining, **18**, 252

Coal—*continued*
support, right of—
   generally, **18**, 252
   See also SUPPORT, RIGHTS OF
Coal industry
Coal Industry Social Welfare Organisation—
   functions, **14**, 1677
   local welfare committees, transfer of functions, **14**, 1677
competition law, **4**, 858, 1149, 1165, 1308
consumer protection, 241*n*; **6**, 162; **19**, 240
Crown ownership of coal, **6**, 491
Domestic Coal Consumers' Council, **6**, 162
licence to work coal, **14**, 1606
sheriff court jurisdiction, **6**, 1119
See also BRITISH COAL CORPORATION; MINES
Coal tar
excise duty, **7**, 1067, 1067*n*
Coast
coastal waters—
   infectious diseases, regulations as to, **19**, 491
   meaning, **19**, 491*n*
protection of, *see* COAST PROTECTION
Coast protection
authority—
   functions, **14**, 470
   general powers and duties, **14**, 471
generally, **19**, 325; **25**, 380
proposals—
   approval, **14**, 472
   objections, **14**, 472
regional councils, unified approach to, **25**, 380
repair, general powers of, **14**, 474
scheme, **14**, 473
sheriff court jurisdiction, **6**, 1088
unified approach to, **25**, 380
works—
   compensation, **25**, 388
   consent to, **25**, 386
   grants, **25**, 388
   land, powers in respect of, **25**, 384
   maintenance, **14**, 474; **25**, 387
   notice to carry out, **25**, 386
   powers relating to, **25**, 381
   repair, **25**, 387
   schemes—
      appeal, **25**, 382
      arbitration, **25**, 382
      carrying out, **25**, 385
      charges, **25**, 382
      compulsory powers, **25**, 382
      confirmation of, **25**, 383
Coastguard
arrest, powers of, **7**, 1232
British sea-fisheries officer, as, **11**, 126*n*
coastguard service, responsibility for, **21**, 113
disciplinary provision, **2**, 607
emergency, service in, **2**, 746
management and control, **2**, 746
salvage award, entitlement to claim, **21**, 459
signals connected with smuggling, powers in relation to, **7**, 1234

Coastwise traffic
meaning, **7**, 1241
regulation, **7**, 1241
Coat of arms
achievement, component of, **11**, 1603
   See also ACHIEVEMENT OF ARMS
badges, **11**, 1610
banner, use as, **11**, 1609
cadency, **11**, 1618
chapeau, **11**, 1607
colours, heraldic, **11**, 1604*n*
confirmation of, **11**, 1616
control over use, **11**, 1601
coronet, **11**, 1607
crest, **11**, 1606
cumulo coat, **11**, 1628
derivation of, **11**, 1601
devices amounting to, **11**, 1613
fief annoblissant, as, **11**, 1613
foreign, use of, **11**, 1614
helmet, **11**, 1605
heraldry as study of, **11**, 1601
heritable property, as, **11**, 1613
impalement, **11**, 1627
inescutcheon, **11**, 1629
insignia of office, **11**, 1610
ladies, **11**, 1604, 1606
mantling, **11**, 1605
metals, heraldic, **11**, 1604*n*
motto, **11**, 1611
quartering, **11**, 1629
recording of, **11**, 1614
separate and distinct, **11**, 1614
shield, **11**, 1604
status conferred by, **11**, 1613
supporters, **11**, 1608
transfer of, **11**, 1622
wreath, **11**, 1605
wrongful use of, **11**, 1633
Coble
meaning, **11**, 3*n*
net and coble, *see* NET AND COBLE
Cocaine
controlled drug, as, **14**, 1226
drug abuse, patterns of, **14**, 1222
Cockfield White Paper, 10, 24, 28, 111
Cockfighting
instruments, possession of, **2**, 271; **19**, 1274
Cocks
water fittings, as, **25**, 527
Cocoa and chocolate products
advertisement, **11**, 362
composition, **11**, 362
emulsifiers and stabilisers, **11**, 373
labelling, **11**, 362
Code of Advertising Practice Committee
complaints procedure, **1**, 546
control by, **1**, 545
Code of Advertising Standards and Practice of the Independent Broadcasting Authority
broadcast advertisements subject to, **1**, 519
principles in, **1**, 522

Code of Canon Law
Roman Catholic Church—
    attempts, **3**, 1658
    Book VI (*De Sanctionibus in Ecclesia*), **3**, 1658
    Book VII (*De processibus*), **3**, 1658
    collaboration, **3**, 1658
    culpa, **3**, 1658
    diminished imputability, **3**, 1658
    dolus, **3**, 1658
    insanity, **3**, 1658
    offences, **3**, 1658
    penalties, **3**, 1658
    revision, **3**, 1657
Code of Canons
Scottish Episcopal Church—
    generally, **3**, 1615
    implementation, **3**, 1620
Code of Magnus 'the Law-Mender' (Gulathing law)
common land, **24**, 306
fishings, **24**, 315
foreshore, **24**, 306
landownership, **24**, 307
St Ninian's Isle Treasure case, **24**, 304, 313
scat, **24**, 309
udal law, **24**, 301, 303, 308, 318, 321, 325
whether surviving to modern times, **24**, 304
Codes of practice
advertising, **6**, 90–93
Advisory, Conciliation and Arbitration Service, issue by, **9**, 10; **23**, 749, 752
broadcasting, **6**, 89
caravan site, **23**, 356
Commission for Racial Equality, of, **9**, 389
consumer protection, contravention of, **6**, 144
development procedures, **23**, 263, 264
documentary evidence, as, **10**, 598
employment law in, **9**, 9–12, 241; **22**, 199
Equal Opportunities Commission, of, **9**, 387
fair trading, **6**, 23, 72, 158
health and safety at work—
    approval, **9**, 536
    contravention, **9**, 537; **22**, 200
    role, **9**, 535
Highway Code, **10**, 598; **22**, 197, 198
Manpower Services Commission, of, **9**, 11
noise, for minimising, **9**, 1270
occupational noise, **9**, 1289
packaged goods, **6**, 260
safety representative, right to time off, **9**, 480
statutory—
    formula, **22**, 197, 199
    functions, **22**, 196
    promulgation, **22**, 197
    self-regulation by, **22**, 196
    status, generally, **22**, 197
    statutory guidance for, **22**, 201
    subordinate legislation, whether, **22**, 195
supply of services, **6**, 72
Codicil
date of will modified by, **25**, 887
Coercion
defence of—
    crimes for which defence unavailable, **7**, 202

Coercion—*continued*
defence of—
    defence of excuse, as, **7**, 198
    generally, **7**, 202
    Hume's view, **7**, 202
    necessity compared, **7**, 198
external public policy rule, **17**, 171
treaty invalidated by, **19**, 629
Coffee and coffee products
advertisement, **11**, 363
colouring matter not permitted, **11**, 372
composition, **11**, 363
labelling, **11**, 363
Coffin
cremation, **3**, 569
sea, burial at, **3**, 540
unlawful removal of whole or part, **3**, 505
Cohabitation
agreements, **10**, 1011
aliment payable to child of cohabitee, **10**, 1009, 1217, 1247
children, protection of, **10**, 1003, 1005
cohabitation with habit and repute, marriage by, **10**, 811, 814, 819
    legal capacity to marry, parties must have, **10**, 814
    when inapplicable, **10**, 814
compellability and competency, **10**, 1010
criminal offences, **10**, 1010
damages, cohabitant as claimant, **22**, 676
division and sale, actions for, **10**, 1005
exclusion orders, **10**, 1005
financial provision, **10**, 1007
husband and wife, as—
    widow's payment, effect on, **21**, 895, 896
    widow's pension ceasing on, **21**, 897
    widowed mother's allowance ceasing on, **21**, 896
legal status in Scotland, **10**, 1003
matrimonial home—
    rights relating to, **10**, 870; **17**, 1124
    tenancy, succession of cohabitee, **10**, 1005
meaning, **10**, 911, 1003, 1004
moveables, **10**, 1006
parents, status of, **10**, 801*n*
property rights, **10**, 801*n*
rape cases, **10**, 1010
regulatory orders, **10**, 1005
reset, **10**, 841
separate property rule, **10**, 1005–1007
sexual intercourse does not constitute, **10**, 911
taxation, **10**, 1003, 1008
tenancy, succession of cohabitee, **10**, 1005
violence—
    prevention of, **10**, 1003
    protection from, **10**, 870
Cohabitee
immediate family, as, **15**, 601
Cohen Committee
recommendations, adoption by Parliament, **4**, 304, 471
unfair prejudice remedy, history of, **4**, 478

Coin
Carriers Act 1830 ..., **3**, 610
coinage—
    creation of, **6**, 173
    standards, **6**, 181
collectors' item, **7**, 1424
counterfeit, **7**, 385, 395
denomination, **14**, 1820
gold, **14**, 1832
Krugerrands, **14**, 1808
legal tender, as, **14**, 1816, 1822
marking, **14**, 1820
offences—
    breaking up, **14**, 1842
    coining, **14**, 1834
    counterfeit currency, possession of, **14**, 1838
    counterfeit implements, possession of, **14**, 1839
    counterfeiting, generally, **14**, 1836
    exportation, **14**, 1843
    generally, **14**, 1834
    importation, **14**, 1843
    issuing without authority, **14**, 1841
    making without authority, **14**, 1841
    melting down, **14**, 1842
    passing, **14**, 1837
    reproducing British currency, **14**, 1840
    tendering, **14**, 1837
poinding, **14**, 1812
protected, meaning, **14**, 1835
quantities which are legal tender, **14**, 1822
sale of, **14**, 1807
standard of, **14**, 1821
stolen, restitution not applicable, **15**, 52
Cold store
local authority provision, **11**, 405
Cold weather payment
social fund, **21**, 1123, 1129
Collage
copyright, **18**, 957, 958, 963
Collateral warranty
claim, prescription, **3**, 174
generally, **3**, 158
Standard Form, **3**, 158
Collation
doctrine of, **25**, 808
inter haeredes
    heir-at-law, **25**, 683
    meaning, **25**, 683
Collecting society
audit, **12**, 715
meaning, **12**, 682
meetings, **12**, 713
registration, **12**, 680*n*
rules, preparation of, **12**, 701
Collective agreement
conflict between, **23**, 740
contract, as, **23**, 736
contract of employment, effect on, **9**, 32
incorporation, **23**, 737, 738
Industrial Relations Act 1971 ..., **23**, 732
legal effect, **23**, 734
legal status, **23**, 731
provision in, classification of status of, **9**, 34
rebutting presumption, **23**, 735

Collective agreement—*continued*
termination of, **23**, 741
terms—
    incorporation, **23**, 737
    suitability of, **23**, 739
    variation of, **23**, 742
TINA LEA clauses, **23**, 732
Trade Union and Labour Relations Act 1974 ...,
    23, 733
variation of terms, **23**, 742
Collective bargaining
agreement, *see* COLLECTIVE AGREEMENT
content of, **23**, 730
continuing process of, **9**, 34
development of, **9**, 7
general, **23**, 728
International Labour Organisation Convention,
    23, 717, 743
legal support for—
    consultation, right to—
        general, **23**, 757
        redundancy, **23**, 763–766
        safety representatives, **23**, 758
        transfer of undertaking, **23**, 759–762
    facilities for trade union—
        complaints, **23**, 751
        disclosure of information, **23**, 749, 750
        general, **23**, 748
        time off, **23**, 743–747
levels of, **23**, 729
meaning, **23**, 750, 763
record, Certification Officer's test, **23**, 794
voluntarist system of, **9**, 3
Collective investment scheme
criminal acts by, **12**, 1330
establishment, **12**, 1307
European Community member state, from,
    authorisation, **12**, 1315, 1318, 1328
excluded investment categories, **12**, 1325
intervention by Securities and Investments Board,
    12, 1329
investigation, **12**, 1330
    confidentiality, **12**, 1330
    criminal acts, discovery, **12**, 1330
meaning, **12**, 1325
open-ended investment company, **12**, 1325
    See also OPEN-ENDED INVESTMENT COMPANY
operation, **12**, 1307
promotion, **12**, 1326
recognised, **12**, 1328
    promotion, **12**, 1326
    types, **12**, 1328
Securities and Investments Board powers, **12**, 1328
    interventions, **12**, 1329
    investigations, **12**, 1330
single property scheme, promotion, **12**, 1326
Undertakings for Collective Investment in Trans-
    ferable Securities (UCITS), **12**, 1328, 1399
unit in as investment, **12**, 1308
unit trust schemes, **12**, 1325
    See also UNIT TRUST SCHEME
winding up, **12**, 1307
Collective redundancies
EEC law, influence of, **9**, 15

Collective resale price maintenance
See RESALE PRICE MAINTENANCE

Collector-General of the thirds of benefices
Officer of State, **7**, 791

College
valuation for rating, **24**, 733
See also FURTHER EDUCATION

College council
See EDUCATION

College of Justice
canonically-based procedure, **22**, 551
clergy, participation of, **22**, 551
Clerks to the Signet, **6**, 904
Court of Session, **6**, 904
   See also COURT OF SESSION
establishment, **6**, 807, 901, 904; **13**, 1129
formation, **22**, 515
foundation, **13**, 1241
history of, **5**, 627
jurisdiction, **6**, 904
macers, **6**, 904
membership, **6**, 904
modern constitution of, **5**, 628
permanent bench of professional judges, **6**, 904
precedence, **16**, 2020
privileged and unprivileged summonses, **6**, 904
Privy Council, and, **6**, 904
rules ratified by king, **6**, 904
Sederunt, Acts of, purported powers conferred on
   judges of Court of Session, **22**, 187
Senator—
   appointment, **7**, 883
   precedence, **16**, 2020
   See also SENATORS OF THE COLLEGE OF JUSTICE

Collision at sea
maritime cause, as, **1**, 411
maritime lien, giving rise to, **1**, 413
preliminary act procedure, **1**, 415
special rules of jurisdiction, **1**, 416

Colonial territory
conduct committed in, extradition procedure, **12**,
   515
   designated colony, **12**, 520
forces serving in, **2**, 620
prerogative powers, **7**, 724

Coloured fires
explosives, as, **10**, 1586

Colouring matter
food, in, **11**, 372
   milk, **11**, 442

Colours
heraldic, **11**, 1604*n*

Combat
trial by, **17**, 541

Combined Nomenclature (CN)
European Union Common Customs Tariff, **7**,
   1015, 1038

Comfort letter
UK and EU law, conflict between, **4**, 1117

Comic
horror, falling into hands of child, **17**, 39
bankruptcy law, **22**, 822, 823

Commencement of period
civilis computatio, **22**, 820, 821, 822

Commencement of period—*continued*
'commencing from (date)', **22**, 822
   See also DAY; DATE
dies inceptus principle, **22**, 822, 823
exceptions to general rule, **22**, 822
exclusion *dies a quo* and *dies ad quem*, **22**, 819, 821,
   822
inclusion *dies a quo* and *dies ad quem*, **22**, 819, 821
naturalis computatio, **22**, 820, 821
prescriptive period—
   legislation, **22**, 823

Commerce
burgh, privileges of, **14**, 12
commercial—
   contract, **17**, 254
   enterprise, public corporation, as, **19**, 201
   law, *see* COMMERCIAL LAW
   transactions—
      nature of, **25**, 7
      shares, valuation of, **25**, 7
   trusts, purpose of, **24**, 115
   vehicle, contract hire, **14**, 1022
   waste, collection of, **9**, 1168
enterprise zone, *see* ENTERPRISE ZONE
financial assistance to, **14**, 312
industry, *see* INDUSTRY
loan—
   building, erection of, **14**, 639
   interest, **14**, 639
   land, acquisition of, **14**, 639
   security for advance, **14**, 639

Commercial agency
nature of, **4**, 1378

Commercial law
custom and precedent, influence, **22**, 260
precedent—
   reasons for not following prior decisions—
      cessante ratione cessat ipsa lex, **22**, 354
      Commerzbank case, **22**, 354
      Miliangos case, **22**, 354

Commercial lease
See LEASE-LEASING

Commercial letter of credit
See LETTER OF CREDIT

Commercial paper
capacity, **4**, 125
electronic transfer of funds—
   applications of, **4**, 260
   automated teller machines, **4**, 260
   clearing systems, **4**, 200
   contract—
      application of law of, **4**, 264
      provider of facility and user, between, **4**, 262
      purchaser, vendor and provider of facility,
         between, **4**, 263
   generally, **4**, 259
   home banking, **4**, 260
   legal regulation, **4**, 261
   point of sale terminals, **4**, 260
   provider of facility—
      purchaser, contract with, **4**, 263
      user, contract with, **4**, 262
      vendor, contract with, **4**, 263
European, US, may not be transferred to, **4**, 103

Commercial paper—*continued*
foreign bill—
  classification, **4**, 119, 120
  inland bill distinguished, **4**, 120
  noting and protest, **4**, 161
  summary diligence on, **4**, 104
grovelling, excess held to disqualify instrument, **4**, 108*n*
inland bill—
  classification of bills, **4**, 119, 120
  foreign bill distinguished, **4**, 120
  noting and protest, **4**, 161
  summary diligence on, **4**, 104
letter of credit, *see* LETTER OF CREDIT
meaning, **4**, 101
negligence—
  collecting banker acting without, **4**, 213
  paying banker acting without, **4**, 211
negotiable instrument, see NEGOTIABLE INSTRUMENT
rate of exchange, **4**, 113
scope of title, **4**, 101
title to bill, defective, **4**, 150
Commercial surety bond
generally, **3**, 988
use, **3**, 988
Commissary courts
abolition, **6**, 918
appellate jurisdiction, **22**, 519
assimilation by Court of Session and sheriff courts, **6**, 918; **22**, 519, 630
canonical procedures retained in post-Reformation courts, **22**, 581, 584
Commissary Court of Edinburgh, **6**, 918, 1022; **22**, 519, 585
confirmation of testaments, **22**, 519
ecclesiastical courts, and, **6**, 918
establishment, **6**, 918
former jurisdiction, **6**, 918, 1022
local—
  jurisdiction, **22**, 519
  sheriff court, absorption by, **22**, 519, 630
marriage, jurisdiction as to, **22**, 519, 585
officials' courts, **22**, 585
post-Reformation foundation, **22**, 519
registration of deeds abolished, **19**, 839*n*
status, exclusive jurisdiction in causes of, **22**, 519
succession, moveable property, canonical influence, **22**, 581
transmission of, **19**, 859
Commission for Local Authority Accounts in Scotland
accounts, **14**, 885
audit standards, issuing, **1**, 63
designated body, **14**, 136
expenses, **14**, 885
  functions, **1**, 48; **14**, 884
hearings, **14**, 894
issues raised with, **14**, 897
membership, **14**, 883
powers, **14**, 884
report to—
  action on, **14**, 892
  generally, **14**, 891
Secretary of State, action by, **14**, 895

Commission for Racial Equality
codes of practice issued by, **9**, 10, 389
duties of, **9**, 388
formal investigations, **9**, 390
non-discrimination notices, **9**, 391
powers of, **9**, 388
sheriff court, application to, **17**, 1253
Commission of Industrial Relations
collective bargaining, assistance for, **9**, 7
Commission of inquiry
international disputes, settlement by, **19**, 714, 717
Commission of supply
duties, **14**, 29
establishment, **19**, 208
highways, responsibility for, **14**, 33
quasi-corporation, as, **19**, 208, 218
rating valuations, appeal against, **6**, 940
sheriff depute, role of, **14**, 29
Commissioner for Local Administration in Scotland
accommodation, **14**, 135
annual report, **14**, 134
appointment, **14**, 133
complainant, **14**, 140
designated body, **14**, 136
disqualification from appointment, **14**, 133
expenses, **14**, 135
findings, implementation of, **14**, 147
generally, **14**, 61; **19**, 242
Health Service Commissioner, consultation with, **14**, 145
investigation—
  authorities subject to, **14**, 137
  complaint initiating, **14**, 141
  defamation, **14**, 144
  disclosure of information, **14**, 144
  formal, procedure in, **14**, 142
  matters subject to, **14**, 138
  report, **14**, 143
merits of decision not to be questioned, **14**, 139
Parliamentary Commissioner, consultation with, **14**, 145
pension, **14**, 133
planning decision, appeal to, **23**, 282
public corporations, **19**, 239, 242
remuneration, **14**, 133
report—
  annual, **14**, 134
  investigation, of, **14**, 143
  review of, **14**, 146
review, **14**, 134
staff, **14**, 135
term of office, **14**, 133
Commissioner for the Regalia
office of, **19**, 805, 807
Commissioners of Customs and Excise
administration, **7**, 1204
appointment, **7**, 1204
customs officers and appointees, appointment, **7**, 1204
disclosure of information by, **7**, 1283
European obligations, **7**, 1205
generally, **7**, 1282
obstruction, **7**, 1207

Commissioners of Customs and Excise—
continued
offences concerning office of, **7**, 1207
official seal of, interference with, **7**, 1237
powers and duties—
  bonds and security, power to require, **7**, 1242,
    1243
  cancellation, **7**, 1242
  civil penalties, **7**, 1408–1412
  coastwise traffic, in relation to, **7**, 1241
  confidence, duty of, **7**, 1206
  control area, **7**, 1239, 1240
  customs and excise control areas, in relation to,
    7, 1239, 1240
  directions, power to make, **7**, 1283, 1283n
  entry of premises or article, as to, **7**, 1246–1248
  excise licence, in relation to, **7**, 1245
  facilities and appliances, power to require, **7**,
    1243
  generally, **7**, 1155, 1166, 1204, 1211
  hovercraft, control over movements, **7**, 1240
  inquiries, power to hold, **7**, 1213
  legal proceedings, as to, **7**, 1265–1271
  mitigation of penalty, power to, **7**, 1275
  obtaining information, **7**, 1402
  overclaims, in relation to, **7**, 1404
  pipe-lines, control over movement of goods in,
    7, 1240
  records, issue of notice requiring, **7**, 1283
  registered excise dealers and shippers, power to
    regulate, **7**, 1244, 1244n
  rulings on liability matters, power to issue, **7**,
    1283
  smuggling, powers to combat, **7**, 1233
  trader's compliance, securing, **7**, 1403
  underdeclarations, in relation to, **7**, 1404
  VAT assessments, **7**, 1405–1407
  warehousing, in relation to, **7**, 1176, 1178,
    1179
property of, interference with, **7**, 1237, 1238
remuneration, **7**, 1204
VAT, powers in relation to, **7**, 1283
See also CUSTOMS AND EXCISE, DEPARTMENT OF
Commissioners of Inland Revenue
administration and collection of taxes, **19**, 1544
appeals from, **19**, 1502
charitable tax exemption, claim for, **3**, 1101
Committee for Privileges (House of Lords)
House of Lords, **5**, 367, 455
pedigrees, acception of proof of, **11**, 1623
proof, generally, **11**, 1623
See also COMMITTEE OF PRIVILEGES (HOUSE OF
  COMMONS)
Committee on Dental and Surgical Materials
functions, **14**, 1204
**Committee of English Parliament in
  Conference with Deputies from Scotland**
bill of exchange, reference in report to, **4**, 104
**Committee of Experts for the Improving of
  Procedures for the Protection of
  Human Rights**, **12**, 13
Committee of Inquiry
appointment, **7**, 728
call to serve on, **7**, 728

**Committee of Inquiry into Functions and
  Powers of Islands Council of Scotland**
See MONTGOMERY COMMITTEE
**Committee of Inquiry into Local
  Government in Scotland**
See STODART COMMITTEE
Committee of London Clearing Bankers
certified cheques, use of, **4**, 196
Committee of Ministers
composition, **12**, 10n
European Commission of Human Rights, report
  by, **12**, 15
European Convention on Human Rights—
  application of, **12**, 10
  petitions alleging violation—
    Commission reports, **12**, 15
    decisions on, **12**, 15
    referral to Court of Human Rights, **12**, 15
  supervision of application, **12**, 13
European Court of Human Rights, execution of
  judgment of, **12**, 20
**Committee of Permanent Representatives
  (COREPER)**
Economic and Social Committee, observers at,
  10, 441
function, **10**, 39
generally, **10**, 402, 409
organisation, **10**, 403
working parties, **10**, 404
**Committee of Privileges (House of
  Commons)**
functions, **5**, 439
House of Commons, **5**, 439
terms of reference, **5**, 439
See also COMMITTEE FOR PRIVILEGES (HOUSE OF
  LORDS)
Committee of Selection
functions of, **5**, 446
membership, **5**, 446
nominations by, **5**, 446
Committee on Consumer Credit
See CROWTHER COMMITTEE
Committee on Review of Medicines
functions, **14**, 1204
Committee on Safety of Medicines
functions, **14**, 1204
licence, granting of, **14**, 1204
**Committee on Tariff and Statistical
  Nomenclature**
European Union Common Customs Tariff, **7**,
  1015
Commixtion
accession compared, **18**, 571n
common property, original acquisition, **18**,
  22n
corporeal moveable property, **18**, 539, 564
meaning, **18**, 564
original acquisition, as, **18**, 597
ownership, principles governing, **18**, 564
Commodatum
agreement of lender and borrower, **13**, 1784
constitution of contract, **13**, 1786
contract *bonae fide*, as, **13**, 1702
contract of, deposit, **8**, 17

Commodatum—*continued*
definition, **13**, 1705
delivery to borrower, **13**, 1784, 1786
duration of contract, **13**, 1787
essential elements, **13**, 1784
gratuitous contract, as, **13**, 1701
locatio conductio rei, **13**, 1706, 1783
meaning, **13**, 1701, 1783
mutuum compared, **13**, 1702
obligations of borrower, **13**, 1784, 1789
obligations of lender, **13**, 1788
precarium compared, **13**, 1791
prescription, **13**, 1792
proof—
　contract, of, **13**, 1786
　parole evidence, by, **13**, 1786
real contract, as, **13**, 1702
Roman law, **13**, 1702
sequestration of borrower's estate, **13**, 1789
subject matter, **13**, 1785
　delivery, contract completed by, **13**, 1703
　deterioration of, **13**, 1789
　fungible property, **13**, 1785
　misuse by borrower, **13**, 1789
unfair contract terms, **13**, 1790
Commodity
foreign currency treated as, **14**, 1809, 1829
francs as, **14**, 1809
lease, **13**, 198
market, origin and development, **2**, 1279
money as purchasing power in terms of, **14**, 1804
sale of money as, enforcement of contract for, **14**, 1814
Commodity transaction
VAT zero-rating, **7**, 1432
Common Agricultural Policy
accession compensation, **1**, 962, 963
administration of—
　EC Commission, role of, **1**, 978, 979
　EC Council, role of, **1**, 977
　European Agricultural Guidance and Guarantee Fund, control of, **1**, 979–982. *See also* EUROPEAN AGRICULTURAL GUIDANCE AND GUARANTEE FUND
　management committee system, **1**, 977, 978
　national agencies, **1**, 983–985
　national authorities, by, **1**, 951
　producer organisations, **1**, 983–985
agricultural structures, improving efficiency of, **1**, 971
Community preference, **1**, 907
conversion rates—
　establishment of, **1**, 956
　legality of, **1**, 958
customs duties and, **7**, 1014
customs warehousing, **7**, 1174
equality, judicial consideration of breach of, **1**, 908, 909
express objectives of, **1**, 901
factors in working out, **1**, 906
fair standard of living, securing, **1**, 904
financing, **1**, 951
fisheries, including, **1**, 879, 942, 944
generally, **2**, 1291; **6**, 31

Common Agricultural Policy—*continued*
green currencies, use of, **1**, 957
health, protection of—
　animals, restriction on import, **1**, 894
　Community health measures, **1**, 895
　inspections—
　　charges, **1**, 899, 900
　　external frontier, at, **1**, 900
　　harmonisation of laws, **1**, 899
　　inspection charges, **1**, 899, 900
　　inspections under, **1**, 896
　　reasonableness of, **1**, 898
　　rules on, **1**, 896
　　safeguards in, **1**, 894
　　seriously considered health policy, constituting, **1**, 897
integrated development projects, **1**, 976
introduction of, **1**, 861
levies, collection of, **1**, 986
markets, stabilising, **1**, 905
monetary compensatory amounts—
　advance fixing, **1**, 961
　calculation of, **1**, 955
　conversion rates, introduction of, **1**, 956
　derived products, and, **1**, 960
　disturbances in trade, preventing, **1**, 959
　elimination, intended, **1**, 957
　green currencies, use of, **1**, 957
　intervention arrangements, on products subject to, **1**, 959
　Intervention Board, payment to, **1**, 983
　introduction of, **1**, 955
　legitimate expectation of traders, and, **1**, 961
　market, partitioning, **1**, 958
　monetary gap, filling, **1**, 957
　positive and negative, **1**, 957
　snake currencies, **1**, 956
non-discrimination, principle of, **1**, 908
outward processing, **7**, 1188
payments due to trader, recovery of, **1**, 987
productivity, aiming to increase, **1**, 903
proportionality, principle of, **1**, 910
reasonable prices, assuring, **1**, 905
single prices—
　exceptions, **1**, 953
　exchange rates, effect of, **1**, 954
　problems with system of, **1**, 954
　units of account, in, **1**, 952
structural policy, **1**, 971
supplies, assuring, **1**, 905
units of account, prices in, **1**, 952, 953
Common Commercial Policy (CCP)
Commons Customs Tariff, interaction with, **7**, 1017
establishment, **7**, 1017
generally, **7**, 1017, 1023
implementation, **7**, 1025, 1026
purpose, **7**, 1017
Common Customs Tariff (CCT)
accessories delivered with equipment, **7**, 1046
ad valorem duties, **7**, 1015
Annexes, **7**, 1015
application, **7**, 1015
classification of goods, **7**, 1038

Common Customs Tariff (CCT)—*continued*
Combined Nomenclature, **7**, 1015, 1038
Committee on Tariff and Statistical Nomenclature
    (Nomenclature Committee), **7**, 1015
Common Commercial policy, interaction with, **7**,
    1017
derogations from, **7**, 1016
EFTA, preferential trade agreements, **7**, 1016
establishment, **7**, 1015
fixed sum duties, **7**, 1015
GATT, interaction with, **7**, 1009, 1015
Generalised System of Tariff Preferences, **7**, 1016
generally, **7**, 1004, 1011, 1015
Harmonized Description and Coding System
    (HS), **7**, 1015
implementation, **7**, 1025, 1026
Lomé Convention signatories, preferential trade
    agreement, **7**, 1016
mixed duties, **7**, 1015
NIMEXE (statistical nomenclature), **7**, 1015
origin of goods—
    determination, **7**, 1046
    proof, **7**, 1047
rates of duty, expression, **7**, 1015
reliefs from duties, **7**, 1099
spare parts delivered with equipment, **7**, 1046
Taric, **7**, 1015, 1015*n*
tariff—
    ceiling, **7**, 1016
    quota, **7**, 1016
    suspension, **7**, 1016
third countries, unified tariffs applicable to, **7**, 1015
tools delivered with equipment, **7**, 1046
valuation of goods, **7**, 1046
Common Fisheries Policy
access to British fisheries, **11**, 131, 132
Cameron Report, **11**, 112
completion of, **1**, 941
conflict with national measures, **11**, 113
generally, **1**, 893, 941; **11**, 65, 70, 76, 81, 112–
    115, 117
inshore fishing, **11**, 135
relation with United Nations Convention on the
    Law of the Sea, **11**, 105
Common gables
alteration, **18**, 225
destruction, rebuilding costs, **18**, 218
law of the tenement, **18**, 229
meaning, **18**, 218
ownership, **18**, 218
right of support, **18**, 233, 272
town or city, applicable to land in, **18**, 218
Common good
disposal of land forming part of, **14**, 321
Common grazing
croft, appertaining to, *see* CROFT
ground game, **11**, 858
landholders, pertaining to subjects tenanted by, **1**,
    853
regulation, **6**, 959, 963, 967
Common interest
doctrine of—
    boundary walls, **18**, 359
    burden on ownership of others, as, **18**, 357

Common interest—*continued*
doctrine of—*continued*
    common property, and, **18**, 26, 356, 362
    constitution, **18**, 358
    content, rules as to, **18**, 348
    dominant proprietor—
        ownership, interest falling short of, **18**, 363
        reciprocity of obligation, **18**, 360
        remedies available to, **18**, 366
        title and interest to enforce, **18**, 363
        two or more, where, **18**, 363, 365
    dominant tenement—
        division, **18**, 365
            feudal, **18**, 365
        generally, **18**, 350
        physical changes affecting, **18**, 372
        servient and dominant tenement coming into
            single ownership, **18**, 371
    drainage, **18**, 359
    express creation, **18**, 358
    extension of doctrine, **18**, 361
    extinction—
        acquiescense, by, **18**, 369
        dominant and servient tenements coming
            into single ownership, **18**, 371
        express consent, by, **18**, 368
        generally, **18**, 367
        implied consent, by, **18**, 369
        mutuality principle, **18**, 373
        negative prescription, by, **18**, 370
        physical changes affecting either tenement,
            18, 372
        variation and discharge by Lands Tribunal,
            18, 374
    flatted properties, **18**, 350
    gardens in common ownership, **18**, 359
    implication of law, arising by, **18**, 358
    incidence, **18**, 359
    liability in obligation, **18**, 364
    meaning, **18**, 354
    mutuality principle, **18**, 373
    non-tidal loch, **18**, 305, 307, 359
    non-tidal river—
        alteration in course, **18**, 284, 285
        alveus, building on, **18**, 296
        artificially introduced water, **18**, 286
        common interest as natural servitude, **18**, 355
        development of doctrine, generally, **18**, 282
        dominant and servient proprietors, **18**, 283
        enforcement, **18**, 290
        generally, **18**, 359
        mineral rights, **18**, 282
        natural flow—
            meaning, **18**, 285
            preservation, **18**, 284, 289, 291–294, 295
        pollution, **18**, 299
        primary purposes, water consumption for,
            18, 287
        real right, as, **18**, 290
        res communes, running water as, **18**, 282
        riparian ownership, obligations, generally,
            18, 281
        river, meaning, **18**, 286
        scope, **18**, 284

Common interest—*continued*
doctrine of—*continued*
  non-tidal river—*continued*
    secondary purposes, water consumption for,
      18, 288
    sources feeding into, **18**, 286
    variation and discharge, **18**, 290
    weir or dam, construction of, **18**, 296
  physical changes affecting either tenement,
    extinction by, **18**, 372
  proprietary nature, **18**, 362
  real condition, as, **18**, 7, 282, 344, 357, 362,
    375
  real right, whether, **18**, 362
  reciprocity of obligation, **18**, 360
  repair, access for, **18**, 359
  road, buildings on public, right to light, **18**,
    359, 359*n*
  salmon fishings, **18**, 326, 359
  servient proprietor—
    liability in obligation, **18**, 364
    reciprocity of obligation, **18**, 360
    two or more, where, **18**, 365
  servient tenement—
    division, **18**, 365
    feudal, **18**, 365
    physical changes affecting, **18**, 372
    servient and dominant tenement coming into
      single ownership, **18**, 371
  servitude, as natural, **18**, 355
  servitude rights compared, **18**, 357, 445
  several ownership, single thing in, **18**, 359
  support, right of, **18**, 254, 255, 258
  tenants—
    no liability, **18**, 364
    no title to enforce, **18**, 364
  tenement building—
    common interest as natural servitude, **18**, 355
    generally, **18**, 355, 357*n*, 359, 361
    implication of law, arising by, **18**, 358
    See also TENEMENT BUILDING, LAW OF
  title and interest to enforce—
    infeft, proprietor must be, **18**, 363
    more than one dominant proprietor, where,
      18, 363
    praedial, interest must be, **18**, 363
  variation and discharge by Lands Tribunal, **18**,
    374
  wall owned *ad medium filum*, **18**, 359
former use of term, **18**, 354
loch, *see* non-tidal loch *below*
river, *see* non-tidal river *above*
Common land
acquisition of, **5**, 21
committee of those with interest in, **5**, 21
purchase of land forming part of, **5**, 39
udal law, **24**, 306
Common law
abandonment at, **17**, 1080
allegiance, concept of, **14**, 1901
artificial harbours, **11**, 1305
atomic energy and radioactive substances, **9**, 903–
  913
Bankton, custom as common law, **22**, 368

Common law—*continued*
beneficiary of will, disqualification under, **25**, 670
berths, safety of, **11**, 1321
British constitution depends on, **5**, 305
care, duty of, **14**, 1616
citizenship, acquisition of, **14**, 1901
coining, punishment of offence, **14**, 1834
Coke, Sir Edward, description of common law,
  22, 358
collation *inter haeredes*, **25**, 683
contempt of court—
  conduct in court, **6**, 319
  court order, failure to obey, **6**, 322
  generally, **6**, 318
  mens rea, **6**, 323
  slander of judge, **6**, 320
  witness, by, **6**, 321
contributory fault, **14**, 2129
Craig, Sir Thomas, sources of English law, **22**, 364
criminal law—
  circumstances of crime, **7**, 35
  generally, **7**, 1, 15, 37
  innominate crime, **7**, 24
  mala in se, **7**, 25
  nominate crime, **7**, 24
  terms denoting *mens rea*, **7**, 76–84
custom as formal source in Scotland—
  Bankton's view, **22**, 368
  displacement by sixteenth century, **22**, 362
  generally, **22**, 355–359, 375, 376
death, presumption of, **25**, 647
Declaratory Power *see* DECLARATORY POWER
desuetude, doctrine of, **22**, 376
  See also DESUETUDE, DOCTRINE OF
displacement of custom as source of law by, **22**,
  362
disqualification of beneficiary under, **25**, 670
drainage works, relating to, **25**, 364
eighteenth century change in terminology,
  custom, relationship to, **22**, 369
emergence distinctively in Scotland, **22**, 359, 362
enforcement, **22**, 362
English—
  Coke's description, **22**, 358
  custom and usage as source, **22**, 372, 374, 389,
    390
  'from time immemorial', **22**, 372, 373
  Tanistry Case, **22**, 388
  test of antiquity, **22**, 372, 373
equity and, absence of distinction between, **6**, 908
fitness for purpose, exclusion of obligations as to,
  14, 1059
free port, **11**, 1306
fundamental law, acceptance as, **5**, 339
heritable estate—
  ascendants, **25**, 679
  collaterals, **25**, 679
  descendants, **25**, 678
  general scheme, **25**, 676
  moveable estate distinguished from, **25**, 682
  special destination, **25**, 677
  surviving spouse, **25**, 680
  ultimus haeres, **25**, 681
  vesting, **25**, 684

Common law—_continued_
hire contract, _see_ HIRE CONTRACT
identification parade, **17**, 606
industrial tribunal, jurisdiction of, **9**, 305
initiating proceedings, **17**, 696
intention of succession law, **25**, 603
interest due _ex lege_, **14**, 1827
intestate succession—
    generally, **25**, 675–685
    reform of, **25**, 686, 687
King and Parliament, enforcement by, **22**, 362
law and order, preservation of, **5**, 608
law of arbitration based on, **2**, 403
lease, _see_ LEASE
lessor, liability as to delivery, **14**, 1058
lex et consuetudo, **22**, 356
    local custom still a valid source of law, **22**, 377
march, right to take part in, **14**, 1325
mental disorder, meaning, **14**, 1401
mercantile usage, incorporation into, **22**, 375, 390
modern developments, **25**, 301
modern Scots law—
    desuetude, doctrine of, **22**, 376, 381
    England, contrasting reception of custom as, **22**, 375
    general custom as common law, **22**, 375, 376
moveable estate—
    ascendants, **25**, 682
    collaterals, **25**, 682
    descendants, **25**, 682
    heritable estate distinguished from, **25**, 682
    surviving spouse, **25**, 680
    ultimus haeres, **25**, 681
    vesting, **25**, 685
natural harbours, **11**, 1304
next of kin, **25**, 1045
notice, termination of contract by, **9**, 134
nuisance, **9**, 1107
overseas migration of English common law, **5**, 713
pollution, control of, **25**, 395
powers derived from, **1**, 202
prescription of crime, **17**, 569
presumption against alteration by statute, **12**, 1126
prevalence over other laws and customs, **22**, 362
private piers, **11**, 1307
procession, right to take part in, **14**, 1325
public meeting, right to attend, **14**, 1325
repeal of statute, effect, **22**, 162
revival, by repeal of statute, **22**, 162
Stair—
    custom as common law, **22**, 366
    custom as source of law, **22**, 366
survivance, proof of, **25**, 656
'time immemorial', **22**, 372, 373, 379, 380, 381, 385
tract of time, Scots and English law contrasted, **22**, 379–382
unfair dismissal, scope of, **9**, 204
vesting—
    heritage, **25**, 684
    moveable succession, **25**, 685
wages, payment of—
    accrual of, **9**, 52
    forfeiture of, **9**, 53

Common law—_continued_
wages, payment of—_continued_
    generally, **9**, 51
    late, **9**, 55
    non-payment, **9**, 55
    sickness of employee, during, **9**, 54
    withholding, **9**, 57
    work not available, when, **9**, 56
Common nuisance
meaning, **14**, 2015
Common passage and stair
See TENEMENT BUILDING
Common pasture
islands or district council, acquisition of land for use as, **13**, 534, 541
Common Pleas, Court of
emergence of, **6**, 803
Common property
See CO-OWNERSHIP
Common seal
building society name to appear on, **3**, 315
standing orders, **14**, 1319
Common Services Agency
accounts, **11**, 1508
expenses, **11**, 1506
functions and duties, **11**, 1411
investigation of complaints as to, **11**, 1426, 1522–1524
liabilities, **11**, 1413
management committee, **11**, 1401, 1411
membership, **11**, 1411
privilege of, **11**, 1413
rights, **11**, 1413
Common travel area
exclusions from, Secretary of State's powers, **12**, 122
journeys outwith—
    leave to enter, **12**, 119
    prevention of terrorism powers, **12**, 133
    ships and aircraft, **12**, 133
local journeys, **12**, 122
meaning, **12**, 122; **16**, 1208
Commons, House of
See HOUSE OF COMMONS
Commonty
co-ownership, **18**, 18
compulsory acquisition or use, **19**, 12, 19
distinctive features, **18**, 37
division, **6**, 1062; **18**, 37
inseparable pertinent, as, **18**, 37
meaning, **18**, 37; **19**, 12_n_
udal law, **24**, 310, 320
Commonwealth
abode, right of, **14**, 1903
ascertainment of law, **17**, 163
citizen, _see_ COMMONWEALTH CITIZEN
citizenship laws, **14**, 1902
common allegiance, **14**, 1902
Crown, and—
    British Dependent Territories, **7**, 779
    executive powers, exercise, **7**, 777
    Independence Acts, **7**, 782
    Privy Council, appeals to, **7**, 778
    Queen's title in, **7**, 775

Commonwealth—*continued*
Crown, and—*continued*
   Statute of Westminster, **7**, 781, 782
   succession to throne, alteration, **7**, 776
   UK and colonial law, **7**, 780
extradition from—
   generally, **12**, 579, 580
   procedure, **12**, 542
   'own nationals' exemption not applicable, **12**, 549
extradition to—
   ad hoc extradition, **12**, 524
   authentication of documents, **12**, 566
   designated Commonwealth countries, **12**, 520
   extradition crime, definition, **12**, 522
   international law, **12**, 518
   liability for, **12**, 521
   municipal law, **12**, 519
   restrictions on, **12**, 523
   review, **12**, 571
forces, *see* VISITING FORCES
High Commissioner, precedence, **16**, 2014
Independence Acts, **7**, 782
Ireland, separation of, **14**, 1901
list, **25**, 204
members listed, **7**, 775*n*
monarchies, **7**, 775*n*
register of veterinary surgeons, **25**, 204
Secretariat, precedence, **16**, 2014
Commonwealth citizen
abode, right of, **12**, 118, 118*n*
citizenship laws, **14**, 1902
deportation, with protection against, **12**, 125, 126
designation of, **14**, 1953
East African dependencies, asian population, **12**, 107
employment—
   conditions, **12**, 174
   vouchers, **12**, 107
entry clearance, **12**, 151, 261; **16**, 1238
entry into UK, **16**, 1208
immigration rights, **12**, 101, 102; **14**, 1902, 1903
   appeals system, **12**, 329
   control exemptions, **12**, 132
   employment vouchers, **12**, 107
   Immigration Rules, **12**, 149
   statute law, **12**, 107
   statutory restrictions, **12**, 107
leave to enter—
   employment conditions, **12**, 174
   extension, **12**, 262
meaning, **16**, 1208, 1208*n*
nationality status, **14**, 1904
polygamous wives and widows, **12**, 118*n*
   children of, **12**, 118*n*
prisoner, as—
   deportation, **16**, 1430
   treatment, **16**, 1430
protected rights of entry, with, **12**, 125
right of abode in UK—
   with, **16**, 1208
   without, **16**, 1211
settled—
   children, **12**, 127
   wives, **12**, 127

Commonwealth citizen—*continued*
settlement, **12**, 121
United Kingdom ancestry, with—
   employment, taking or seeking, **12**, 261
   entry clearance, **12**, 261
young, on working holiday, **12**, 149, 151, 154, 174, 241, 263
Communal housing
residential establishments, **24**, 610*n*, 615
sheltered housing, **24**, 610*n*, 615
Communicant
Church of Scotland, discipline, **3**, 1512
Communicants' Roll
Scottish Episcopal Church, **3**, 1629
Communication pipes
escape of water from, compensation for damage, **25**, 513
meaning, **25**, 524
wholesome water, supply of, **25**, 508
Communications
interception—
   Commissioner—
      appointment, **16**, 1964
      functions, **16**, 1964
      reports, **16**, 1964
   consent to, where reason to believe, **16**, 1961
   disclosure of intercepted messages, **16**, 1960
   evidence, exclusion, **16**, 1965
   generally, **7**, 733; **16**, 1961
   post, transmission by, **16**, 1963
   regulation, **16**, 1961
   safeguards, **16**, 1963
   statutory basis, **7**, 733
   telecommunications operator, by, **16**, 1960
   telephone tapping, **12**, 68
      police surveillance activities, **16**, 1802
   tribunal—
      appeal, not subject to, **16**, 1963
      investigation by, **16**, 1963
   unlawful, **16**, 1960
   warrant, **7**, 733
      expiry, **16**, 1962
      external communications, **16**, 1962
      generally, **16**, 1961, 1962
      issue, **16**, 1962
      modification, **16**, 1962
postal, *see* POST OFFICE; POSTAL CARRIER; POSTAL NETWORK; POSTAL PACKET
telecomunications, *see* PUBLIC TELECOMMUNI-CATIONS OPERATOR; TELECOMMUNICATIONS
Communion plate
Church of Scotland, alienation by sale or gift, **3**, 1508
Communion Roll
Church of Scotland—
   annual attestation, **3**, 1512
   annual revision, **3**, 1508
   keeping, generally, **3**, 1508
   restoration to Roll, **3**, 1508
   Supplementary Roll, **3**, 1508
Community benefit society, **12**, 609
committee, **12**, 613
requirements of, **12**, 609
See also INDUSTRIAL AND PROVIDENT SOCIETY

Community care grant
social fund, **21**, 1123, 1125, 1126
Community charge
arrears, recovery of, **14**, 874
collection, **14**, 873
collective, **14**, 869; **25**, 534
community charges register, transmission of records, **19**, 853
date from which effective, **24**, 402
deaths, district registrar's returns, **19**, 1431
domestic rates replaced by, **19**, 1538
domestic subjects, continuing need for valuation, **24**, 402
fixing of, **14**, 7
generally, **14**, 866; **19**, 1538
income support, claimant of, **21**, 1073, 1082
levying, **14**, 873
personal, **14**, 867; **25**, 534
poll tax, as form of, **19**, 1538
register of, **14**, 871
appeal, **14**, 872
officer, **14**, 870
reserved functions, **14**, 236
sheriff court jurisdiction, **6**, 1126
standard, **14**, 868; **25**, 534
sums not due, repayment of, **14**, 874
tax system, as integral part of, **19**, 1510
winding up, **6**, 924, 1069
Community council
election to, age limit, **3**, 1214
elections, **14**, 75
functions of, **14**, 72
loans to, **14**, 73n
resources, **14**, 73
schemes for—
amendment of, **14**, 76
establishment of, **14**, 57, 74
status of, **14**, 72
Community Customs Code
appeal, right of, **7**, 1276
free zones, **7**, 1164
generally, **7**, 1008, 1025, 1026
repayment and remission of duty, **7**, 1089
import procedure, **7**, 1129
origin of goods, determination, **7**, 1046
valuation of goods, **7**, 1048
See also CUSTOMS AND EXCISE DUTIES; EUROPEAN UNION
Community medicine specialist
employment of, **11**, 1498
meaning, **11**, 1498n
Community Patent Convention
See EUROPEAN COMMUNITY
Community service expenditure
health board contributions to, **11**, 1507
Community service order
appointment of supervisor, **22**, 38
breach, **22**, 38
competent sentence, **17**, 802
consent of offender, **22**, 38
description, **22**, 38
eligibility, offender, **22**, 38
failure to comply, **22**, 38
financing, **22**, 38

Community service order—*continued*
hours of work, maximum/minimum, **22**, 38
local authority duty, appointment of supervisor, **22**, 38
non-custodial penalties, **17**, 563
report on suitability by social worker before, **22**, 38
Secretary of State, annual report to, **22**, 38
social work department—
discretion to initiate proceedings, **22**, 38
supervision by, **22**, 34
supervision—
appointment of supervisor, **22**, 38
contrast with probation supervision, **22**, 38
Companies (Beneficial Interests) Act
technical amendments effected by, **4**, 305
Company
accounting data, exemption from registration in data protection register, **18**, 1520
accounts, *see* ACCOUNTS
acquiescence, whether bound by, **16**, 1616
actions, *see* ordinary actions *below*
address, **4**, 435
administration, *see* ADMINISTRATION
advance corporation tax, **19**, 1521
affairs—
investigation, *see* investigation *below*
meaning, **4**, 483
unfairly prejudicial conduct, effect of, **4**, 483
agreement—
members, of, **4**, 401
transfer of shares, to, **4**, 373
airport, transfer of undertaking, **14**, 450
amalgamation—
reconstruction distinguished, **4**, 558
scheme of arrangement used to effect, **4**, 988
ancillary document, **4**, 668
annual general meeting—
elective resolution to dispense with, **4**, 392
holding of, **4**, 387
annual return—
fees, **4**, 334
registrar, filed with, **4**, 332, 334
application for liquor licence by, **2**, 41
arbiter, as, **2**, 416
articles of association, *see* ARTICLES OF ASSOCIATION
assets, *see* ASSETS
associate, *ultra vires* doctrine, application, **4**, 328
associated bodies, **4**, 420
auditor, *see* AUDITOR
bank transactions—
authority to act in, **2**, 1245
capacity to enter into, **2**, 1244
bankruptcy, transmission of copyright on, **18**, 1026
bid, *see* TAKEOVER
bill of exchange—
authority relating to, **4**, 127
capacity relating to, **4**, 127
bills etc, powers as to, **2**, 1244–1245
board meeting, precedence, **16**, 2002
borrowing powers, **4**, 438; **13**, 1774

Company—*continued*

building society—
  investment in or support of, **3**, 366
  member, as, **3**, 379
bus undertaking, transfer of, **14**, 429
calls—
  contributories, on—
    enforcement of, **4**, 782
    power to make, **4**, 781
  generally, **4**, 824
  power to make, **4**, 361
  procedure for making, **4**, 361
capital, **25**, 13
  loan, power to borrow, **4**, 438
  reduction of, petition for, *see* petition *below*
  share, *see* SHARE CAPITAL
  uncalled, may be used as security, **4**, 438
cautionary obligation, as party to—
  authority to bind company, **3**, 868, 869
  capacity of company to enter, **3**, 867, 868
  director or other acting outwith limitations of
    powers, **3**, 868
  generally, **3**, 867
  winding up, **3**, 982
chairman—
  meeting of members, of, **4**, 395
  voting rights, **4**, 397
charges—
  floating, *see* FLOATING CHARGE
  non-registration, effect of, **4**, 443
  public register of, creation of, **4**, 304
  registrable, **4**, 440
  registration of—
    defective particulars, **4**, 443
    generally, **4**, 439
    notice, as, **4**, 442
    overseas company, by, **4**, 448
    procedure for, **4**, 441
    ranking, affecting, **4**, 446
    registrar's certificate relating to, **4**, 332
  satisfaction of, **4**, 444
  suspension of, **4**, 13
charitable, *see* CHARITABLE COMPANY
charity—
  donation to—
    close company, by, **3**, 1155, 1156
    corporation tax, **3**, 1155
    covenanted, *see* COVENANTED DONATION
    income tax, **3**, 1155
    qualification for tax relief, **3**, 1155
    qualifying donations, **3**, 1155
  shares held by, **3**, 1103
circular, **4**, 385
close, **19**, 1523
  charity, gift to, **3**, 1155, 1156
  inheritance tax treatment, **3**, 1161
  meaning, **3**, 1156
'company in question', meaning of, **4**, 462*n*
company let as avoidance device, **13**, 773
compensation, entitlement to, **4**, 318
competent authority—
  insolvency practitioner, authorisation of, **4**, 951
  meaning, **4**, 951
concert party, *see* CONCERT PARTY

Company—*continued*

consortia, **19**, 1522
constitution—
  director, powers of, **4**, 413
  meaning, **4**, 413*n*, 414
  meeting of members, of, **4**, 394
contingent liabilities, **25**, 33
contributories—
  arrest, power of, **4**, 783
  bankrupt, **4**, 821
  calls on—
    enforcement of, **4**, 782
    power to make, **4**, 781
  debts due from, **4**, 780
  deceased, **4**, 821
  first meeting of, **4**, 760
  liability, prescription of, **4**, 822
  list of, **4**, 823
  meaning, **4**, 498*n*, 816, 942
  reports to, **4**, 833
  settlement of list of, **4**, 779
  winding up, *see* WINDING UP
corporation tax, **19**, 1519
court proceedings, cannot appear personally, **4**,
    318
Court of Session jurisdiction, **17**, 1422
credit union, convertion to, **12**, 673
creditor—
  administrator's proposals, meeting to approve,
    4, 628, 644
  committee of, receiver's duties relating to, **4**, 700
  contingent, position relating to winding up
    petition, **4**, 504, 732
  directors' duties to, **4**, 430
  first meeting of, **4**, 760
  not proving in time, power to exclude, **4**, 785
  preferential—
    administrator, duties of, **4**, 633
    floating charge, ranking of, **4**, 666
    voluntary arrangement, approval of, **4**, 593
  prospective, **4**, 732
  protection of interests of, **4**, 645
  reports to, **4**, 833
  schemes of arrangement with, **4**, 979
  subsidiary, of, cannot claim against parent, **4**,
    319
  voluntary winding up, *see* WINDING UP
  winding up, *see* WINDING UP
criminal act by, state of mind of company,
    determination, **4**, 318
customers, **25**, 35
defamation—
  business reputation, protection against, **4**, 318
  employee, deliberate wrongful act of, liability,
    4, 318
  officer, deliberate wrongful act of, liability, **4**,
    318
delict, title and interest to sue, **15**, 228
directors—
  administrator, relationship with, **4**, 635
  advice of, unfairly prejudicial conduct and, **4**,
    489
  agents, as, **1**, 606
  alternate, status, **4**, 403, 406

Company—*continued*
directors—*continued*
  appointment of—
    generally, **4**, 404
    invalid, effect of, **4**, 409
    qualifications, **4**, 405
    Registrar of Companies, filing with, **4**, 404
  associate director, status, **4**, 403
  associated bodies, **4**, 420
  bill of exchange, acceptance of, **4**, 127
  body corporate as, **12**, 1506
  breach of fiduciary duty, reduction on grounds
    of, **13**, 44
  building society, *see* BUILDING SOCIETY
  cautionary obligation, capacity to enter on
    behalf of company, **3**, 868, 869
  communications, qualified privilege, **15**, 528
  Companies Act 1976, provisions of, **4**, 305
  company as legal personality separate from, **4**,
    318
  company secretary—
    appointment of, **4**, 434
    sole director cannot act as, **4**, 404, 434
  competence, **4**, 415
  conduct of, receiver's report on, **4**, 699
  connected persons, **4**, 420
  constitutional powers of, **4**, 413
  contracts—
    between company and, **3**, 27
    pre-incorporation, **4**, 432
    restrictions on, **4**, 421
    service, **4**, 422
  correct company name, use of, **4**, 321
  court order, disqualification by, **4**, 411
  credit transactions for, **4**, 427
  creditors, duties relating to, **4**, 430
  dealings with company generally, **4**, 418
  debentures, dealings in, **4**, 425
  directorship fees, income tax treatment, **16**,
    1130
  disclosure, duty of, **4**, 419
  disqualification of—
    court order, by, **4**, 411
    liability, *see* WINDING UP
    petition for, **4**, 997
  duties of—
    creditors, relating to, **4**, 430
    employees, relating to, **4**, 429
    procedural aspects of, **4**, 433
  election of, **4**, 391
  employee—
    directors not classed as, **4**, 403
    duties relating to, **4**, 429
  employment of, **14**, 1002
  fiduciary duty, **4**, 416; **24**, 172, 181, 183, 188
  fraudulent misrepresentation in prospectus,
    liability as to, **11**, 783
  indemnity for liabilities, **4**, 417
  insider dealing, prohibition on, **12**, 1505, 1506,
    1507
  invalid appointment, effect of, **4**, 409
  knowledge of as knowledge of company, **16**,
    1616

Company—*continued*
directors—*continued*
  liabilities—
    indemnity for, **4**, 417
    petition granting relief to, **4**, 995
    third parties, to, **4**, 431
  loans—
    generally, **4**, 426
    public company, **4**, 427
    quasi-loans, **4**, 427
  managing, **4**, 412
  meeting of members—
    calling of, **4**, 381
    election at, **4**, 391
    requisitioning of, **4**, 474
  members—
    admission to register, control of, **4**, 344
    liability, enforcement of, **4**, 343
  negligence of, where self-serving, **4**, 467
  non-cash benefits, **19**, 1514
  non-executive director, status of, **4**, 403
  ordinary action, **4**, 957
  passing off, personal liability, **18**, 1401
  payments—
    service contracts, related to, **4**, 422
    transfer of property to company, arising
      from, **4**, 423
  pensions, **4**, 418
  personal liability of, **4**, 901, 903
  pre-incorporation contract, **4**, 432
  primary insiders, as, **12**, 1501
  private debts, **15**, 879
  property—
    payments arising from transfers of, **4**, 423
    substantial transactions, **4**, 424
  protection of third parties, **4**, 414
  public company, of, credit transactions for, **4**,
    427
  qualification to be appointed as, **4**, 405
  quasi-loans, **4**, 427
  receiver, relationship with, **4**, 706
  register of, **4**, 404
  related company, of, **12**, 1505, 1506
  removal of—
    generally, **4**, 410
    term of office, before expiry of, **4**, 379
  remuneration—
    approval by company, **4**, 408
    no automatic right to, **4**, 391, 408
    whether excessive, **4**, 488
  resignation, **4**, 410
  retiral, **4**, 410
  sales director, status of, **4**, 403
  Schedule E, **25**, 57
  secret profit, duty not to make, **16**, 1059
  securities for, **4**, 426
  service contracts—
    generally, **4**, 422
    payments related thereto, **4**, 422
  shadow director, meaning, **4**, 403, 407
  shares—
    dealings in, **4**, 425
    interests in, **4**, 428
  skill, **4**, 415

Company—*continued*
directors—*continued*
  status of, **4**, 403
  third parties—
    liabilities to, **4**, 431
    protection of, **4**, 414
  transfers—
    property, of, payments arising from, **4**, 423
    restrictions on, **4**, 421
  trust concept applied to, **24**, 11
  ultra vires doctrine, application of, **4**, 328
  unlimited liability of, **4**, 819
  vacation of office, **4**, 410
  voluntary arrangement proposed by—
    nominee, notice to, **4**, 582
    report to court, **4**, 583
    summoning of meetings, **4**, 584
  voluntary winding up, powers relating to, **4**, 811
  winding up—
    court, by, powers relating to, **4**, 757
    disqualified director, liability of, *see* WINDING UP
    petition—
      position relating to, **4**, 504
      presentation of, **4**, 730, 731
  working, status of, **4**, 403
  wrongful trading, personal liability for, **4**, 306
disclosure—
  director's duty of, **4**, 419
  petition relating to—
    generally, **4**, 991
    restrictions, application for lifting of, **4**, 992
    shares, order for sale of, **4**, 993
  shares, interests in, **4**, 346
  takeover bid, steps before making of, **4**, 544
dissolved, reinstatement of, **4**, 929
distributable profits, meaning, **4**, 367
distributions—
  kind, in, **4**, 460
  making, **1**, 84
  meaning, **4**, 460
  profits available for, **4**, 460
  taxation of, **19**, 1521
dividends, *see* DIVIDENDS
documents—
  ancillary document, meaning, **4**, 668
  as evidence, **10**, 592
  execution of, **4**, 437
  investigation of company, conduct of, **4**, 527
  letters of credit, *see* LETTER OF CREDIT
  probative, **4**, 437
  registered name shown on, **4**, 321
  registrar, retained by, public inspection of, **4**, 332
  registration, how effected, **4**, 314
  requisition of general meeting, in, **4**, 474
domicile, **17**, 356
dormant—
  auditor, provisions relating to, **4**, 456
  nature of, **4**, 457
  published accounts, **4**, 457
draft order—
  altering constitution, **19**, 27
  conferring powers, **19**, 27
earnings, **25**, 20

Company—*continued*
economic background, **25**, 31
Edinburgh Gazette, publication of information in, **4**, 333
elective regime—
  accounts, circulation of, **4**, 455
  private company, procedure for, **4**, 301
elective resolution—
  giving effect to, **4**, 380
  private company, modifying or dispersing with procedural requirements by,, **4**, 380
  shares, authority for issue of, **4**, 353
employee—
  company cannot act except through, **4**, 318
  delictual act by, liability, **4**, 318
  director's duties relating to, **4**, 429
  individual, statutory definition only applicable to, **4**, 318
  shares, class rights, **4**, 347
  ultra vires doctrine, application, **4**, 324
  voluntary arrangement, approval, **4**, 594
  winding up, position on, *see* WINDING UP
  wrongful act, deliberate liability, **4**, 318
employment protection not applicable to, **4**, 318
European Community, free movement of persons and services within, **10**, 131
  financial services, **10**, 147
European (*Societas Europaea*), proposed, **16**, 1004
excluded jurisdiction, **4**, 75
expenses—
  creditable testimony, meaning, **4**, 1002
  generally, **4**, 1003
  investigation, of, **4**, 523, 530
  pursuer, where company is, **4**, 1002
  voluntary arrangement, supervisor of, **4**, 599
fiduciary duty of directors, **24**, 172, 181, 183, 188
financial information, disclosure, **4**, 554, 556
financial record, **25**, 32
floating charges, *see* FLOATING CHARGE
flotation—
  capital profits, leading to, **25**, 41
  hope value, **25**, 23
formation—
  corporate personality, **4**, 317
  foreign company, **4**, 315
  guarantee, company limited by, **4**, 312
  island company, **4**, 315
  overseas company, **4**, 315
  piercing veil, **4**, 317
  private company, **4**, 313
  promotion of company, **4**, 316
  public company, **4**, 313
  registration, incorporation by, **4**, 314
  shares, company limited by, **4**, 312
  unlimited company, **4**, 312
fraudulent trading, *see* FRAUDULENT TRADING
friendly society conversion into, **12**, 726, 731
general meeting, *see* meeting (members, of) *below*
goodwill, **25**, 34
governor, use of term, **4**, 403
gratuitous alienation, *see* GRATUITOUS ALIENATION
group—
  accounts, **4**, 453, 454
  business transferred to member of group, **7**, 1305

Company—*continued*

group—*continued*

  equity capital, meaning, **4**, 370

  generally, **19**, 1522

  holding company, meaning, **4**, 370

  parent, meaning, **4**, 370

  share capital, **4**, 370

  subsidiary, meaning, **4**, 370

  supplies between group companies, **7**, 1290

  ultimate holding company, meaning, **4**, 370

  wholly owned subsidiary, meaning, **4**, 370

growth potential, **25**, 37

holding, **4**, 370

illegal act, minority shareholders, rights of, **4**, 464, 465

incorporated, audit of, *see* AUDITOR

incorporation, *see* INCORPORATION

individual factors, assessment of, **25**, 43

industrial and provident society—

  conversion from, **12**, 650

  conversion into, **12**, 651

injury, conviction for offence involving, **4**, 318

insider dealing, *see* INSIDER DEALING

insolvency—

  fraud, **7**, 380

  proprietor, of, standard securities, **20**, 165

  solicitor's lien, **20**, 100

  winding up, *see* BANKRUPTCY

International Court of Justice claims, **19**, 743

investigation—

  administrative process, as, **4**, 523

  conduct of—

    agents, meaning, **4**, 527*n*

    documents, production of, **4**, 527

    evidence to inspectors, **4**, 527

    inspectors, powers of, **4**, 526

    officers and agents, meaning, **4**, 527*n*

  connected body corporate, of, **4**, 525

  expenses, **4**, 523, 530

  Fair Trading Act 1973, under, **4**, 562

  general comments, **4**, 523

  inspectors—

    appointment of—

      department declining to appoint, **4**, 523

      public announcement of, **4**, 523

      statutory criteria pursuant to, **4**, 524

    conduct of investigation, **4**, 526

    documents, production of, **4**, 527

    evidence to, **4**, 527

    ownership, investigation into, **4**, 532

    report—

      consequences stemming from, **4**, 529

      requirement to make, **4**, 528

  interests in shares, into, right to requisition—

    concert party agreement, **4**, 515

    generally, **4**, 515

    minorities, rights of, **4**, 516

    notice, failure to comply with, **4**, 518

    preparation or report, **4**, 517

  ownership—

    alternative methods of ascertaining, **4**, 533

    inspectors, powers of, **4**, 532

    Secretary of State's power to investigate, **4**, 531

Company—*continued*

investigation—*continued*

  private, **4**, 526

  shares, restrictions on, **4**, 534

  Vetting Section, consideration by, **4**, 523

  witnesses, **4**, 526

investigation under Fair Trading Act, **4**, 562

judicial factor on estate of, **24**, 276

knowledge of director as knowledge of, **16**, 1616

labour, **25**, 36

law, *see* COMPANIES ACTS; COMPANY LAW

Law Reform Committee for Scotland report, **22**, 658

legislation, **17**, 358

lessee, as, **13**, 190

lessor, as, **13**, 177, 773

limited—

  accounts of, *see* ACCOUNTS

  alteration of unlimited company to, **4**, 340

  caution by, **17**, 1073

  floating charges over assets of, **6**, 638

  guarantee, by—

    articles of association, form of, **4**, 329

    formation, **4**, 312

    member, admission as, **4**, 344

    memorandum of association, form of, **4**, 320

    name clause, **4**, 321

    nature of, **4**, 312

    registration, incorporation by, **4**, 314

    share capital, function of, **4**, 350

  ineligible as judicial factor, **24**, 241

  liquidation or receivership, **6**, 417

  memorandum of association, **4**, 312

  partner, as—

    accounts, publication, **16**, 1003

  partnership whose members are all limited companies, **16**, 1003

  re-registration, **4**, 339, 340

  register of members as deed of trust, **24**, 27

  share capital, reduction of, **4**, 359

  shares, by—

    articles of association, form of, **4**, 329

    formation, **4**, 312

    memorandum of association, form of, **4**, 320

    nature of, **4**, 312

    paid-up shares, **4**, 351

    registration, incorporation by, **4**, 314

    share capital, **4**, 351

  subject to trades description legislation, **6**, 109

  subscription by, **6**, 417

  unlimited company, alteration to, **4**, 339

limited liability—

  share capital, function of, **4**, 350

liquidation, *see* LIQUIDATION

loan capital—

  meaning, **4**, 438

  power to borrow, **4**, 438

loan to, **13**, 1774

mailing list, exemption from registration in data protection register, **18**, 1519

management, **25**, 39

  deadlock in, winding up petition based on just and equitable rule, **4**, 511

  responsibility for, **4**, 402

Company—*continued*
management—*continued*
  takeover, position on, **4**, 539
  See also administration *above*
meaning, **4**, 302, 370
meeting—
  adjournment, **4**, 398
  annual general, **4**, 387, 392
  members, of—
    adjournment of, **4**, 398
    agreements of members, **4**, 401
    annual accounts, consideration of, **4**, 388
    annual general meeting—
      elective resolution to dispense with, **4**, 392
      holding of, **4**, 387
    attendance, **4**, 393
    auditors—
      election of, **4**, 389
      remuneration, **4**, 389
    calling of, **4**, 381
    chairman of, **4**, 395
    circulars, **4**, 385
    conduct of, **4**, 396
    constitution of, **4**, 394
    convene, meaning, **4**, 475
    corporate representatives, **4**, 393
    directors—
      calling of meeting by, **4**, 381
      election of, **4**, 391
      remuneration, **4**, 391
    dividend, declaration of, **4**, 390
    elective resolution, **4**, 380
    extraordinary resolution, **4**, 380
    general—
      members' right to call, **4**, 473
      requisition of, **4**, 474
    members' resolutions and circulars, **4**, 385
    minority shareholders, rights of—
      convene, meaning, **4**, 475
      general meeting—
        requirements relating to, **4**, 472
        requisition of, **4**, 474
        right to call, **4**, 473
      requisitioning meeting—
        resolutions, circulation of, **4**, 477
        rights relating to, **4**, 476
        statements, circulation of, **4**, 477
    minutes, **4**, 400; **10**, 595
    notice of—
      form of, **4**, 382
      minority shareholders, rights of, **4**, 472
      period of, **4**, 384
      right to receive, **4**, 383; **25**, 13
    ordinary resolution, **4**, 380
    proxy, **4**, 393
    publication of resolutions, **4**, 401
    quorum, **4**, 394
    remuneration—
      auditors, of, **4**, 389
      directors, of, **4**, 391
    reports, consideration of, **4**, 388
    requirement to hold, **4**, 472

Company—*continued*
meeting—*continued*
  members, of—*continued*
    requisitioning of—
      convene, meaning, **4**, 475
      documents, **4**, 474
      members, by, **4**, 474
      other aspects of, **4**, 476
      resolutions, circulation of, **4**, 477
      statements, circulation of, **4**, 477
      time limit, **4**, 475
      writing, in, **4**, 474
    resolutions—
      alternatives, **4**, 379
      circulation, **4**, 477
      elective, **4**, 380, 392
      extraordinary, **4**, 380
      members' of, **4**, 385
      ordinary, **4**, 380
      publication, **4**, 401
      written, **4**, 379
    role of, **4**, 378
    shareholders' agreement, **4**, 401
    special notice, **4**, 386
    statements, circulation of, **4**, 477
    statute, failure to hold within time fixed by, **4**, 473
    time for convening, **4**, 475
    types of, **4**, 380
    voting—
      procedure, **4**, 399
      rights, **4**, 397
      written resolutions, *see* written resolutions *below*
  minutes as documentary evidence, **10**, 595
  voluntary arrangement, relating to, *see* voluntary arrangement *below*
  winding up, relating to, *see* WINDING UP
members—
  admission as, **4**, 344
  circulars, **4**, 385
  class rights—
    articles, provision in, **4**, 347
    class, meaning, **4**, 347
    equity capital, rights relating to, **4**, 347
    memorandum, no provision made in, **4**, 347
    ordinary shares, rights relating to, **4**, 347
    variation of—
      issued shares, **4**, 349
      unissued shares, **4**, 348
  company as legal person separate from, **4**, 317
  debts of company, liability for, **4**, 319
  employee shares, nature of, **4**, 347
  expectations of, unfairly prejudicial conduct and, **4**, 485
  full contractual capacity, does not have to be person of, **4**, 344
  interest of, unfairly prejudicial conduct and, **4**, 484
  legal personality distinct from company, **4**, 317
  meaning, **4**, 524*n*
  meetings of, *see* meeting *above*
  preference shares, rights relating to, **4**, 347

Company—*continued*
members—*continued*
  redeemable preference shares, rights relating to,
    4, 347
  register of—
    index, **4**, 345
    maintenance of, **4**, 345
    Northern Ireland, company carrying on
      business in, **4**, 345
    overseas branch register, **4**, 345
    petition to rectify, **4**, 989
    registered office, maintained at, **4**, 345
  resolutions, **4**, 385
  schemes of arrangement with, **4**, 980, 986
  shares—
    interests in—
      concert parties, arrangements for notifying,
        4, 346
      disclosure of, **4**, 346
      exclusions, **4**, 346
      interest, meaning, **4**, 346
      notifiable interest, **4**, 346
      registration of, **4**, 346
  status of Company—
    membership—
      articles, determined by, **4**, 343
      memorandum, determined by, **4**, 343
  voluntary winding up, *see* WINDING UP
  winding up, *see* WINDING UP
  See also SHAREHOLDER
memorandum of association, *see* MEMORANDUM OF
  ASSOCIATION
name, passing off, **18**, 1377
nationality of, **19**, 743
net worth, **25**, 13
nominee, second member as, **4**, 302
non-profit purposes, incorporation for, **4**, 302
non-registration, effect, **4**, 443
objects—
  clause—
    alteration, right to object to—
      court, powers of, **4**, 520
      minority's right to object, **4**, 519
    charitable company, **4**, 322
    legal capacity limited by terms of, **4**, 318
    private Act of Parliament, cannot be altered
      without, **4**, 322
    purposes of company restricted by, **4**, 322
    special resolution to approve changes in, **4**,
      380
    statutory formula, not necessary to use, **4**, 322
  main, **4**, 322
  memorandum of association, form of, **4**, 320
offence by—
  death, involving, company's conviction for, **4**,
    318
  injury, involving, company's conviction for, **4**,
    318
  insider dealing, of, creation, **4**, 305
  liquidator, appointment of, corrupt inducement
    affecting, **4**, 922
  market manipulation, **4**, 541
  name, breach of statutory provisions relating to,
    4, 321

Company—*continued*
offence by—*continued*
  prosecution of, **4**, 921
  shares, interest in, failure to observe
    notification provisions, **4**, 346
office-holder—
  investigative powers—
    application of provisions as to, **4**, 868
    co-operation, duty relating to, **4**, 869
    dealings of company, inquiry into, **4**, 870
  meaning, **4**, 868
officer—
  company cannot act except through, **4**, 318
  correct company name, use of, **4**, 321
  deliberate wrongful act of, company's liability
    for, **4**, 318
  public examination of, **4**, 773
  ultra vires delictual act of, company's liability,
    for, **4**, 318
  ultra vires doctrine, application of, **4**, 324
ordinary actions—
  directors, **4**, 957
  opposing shareholders, **4**, 956
  proper defender, **4**, 955
  pursuer, company as, **4**, 954
  remedies in—
    damages, **4**, 963
    declarator, **4**, 959
    generally, **4**, 958
    interdict, **4**, 962
    miscellaneous, **4**, 964
    payment, **4**, 964
    reduction, **4**, 960
    specific implement, **4**, 961
ordinary choice of law rules, application of, **17**,
  357
ordinary resolution, **4**, 380
overseas—
  Channel Islands, **4**, 315
  established place of business, **4**, 315
  formation, **4**, 315
  Isle of Man, **4**, 315
  merger with, **4**, 1285
  name, **4**, 315
  nature of, **4**, 315
  Northern Ireland, **4**, 315
  registration, **4**, 315; **13**, 1223
  registration of charges by, **4**, 448
overseas branch register, maintenance, **4**, 345
ownership—
  alternative methods of ascertaining, **4**, 533
  inspectors, powers of, **4**, 532
  Secretary of State's power to investigate, **4**, 531
Panel on Takeovers and Mergers, *see* PANEL ON
  TAKEOVERS AND MERGERS
parent—
  creditors of subsidiary cannot claim against, **4**,
    319
  meaning, **4**, 370
partner, as, **16**, 1006, 1015
  limited companies, **16**, 1003
  tax treatment, **16**, 1143
partnership company, **4**, 312
partnership distinguished, **4**, 302

Company—*continued*
payments—
  ordinary action, remedy in, **4**, 964
  service contract, relating to, **4**, 422
  transfer of property to company, arising from, **4**, 423
payroll data, exemption from registration in data protection register, **18**, 1520
personality of, **17**, 355
petition—
  administration order, for, *see* administration order *above*
  administrative law remedies, **4**, 1001
  aggrieved, petition by, **4**, 996
  capital, reduction of—
    answers to petition, **4**, 971
    capital redemption reserve, reduction of, **4**, 977
    decision to reduce capital, **4**, 967
    general, **4**, 966
    hearing, **4**, 974
    lost assets, **4**, 969
    no repayment of capital, **4**, 975
    opposed petition, **4**, 972
    repayment of capital, reduction involving, **4**, 970, 976
    reporter, remitting to, **4**, 973
    scheme of arrangement, other than as part of, **4**, 968
    share premium account, reduction of, **4**, 977
  default order, application for, **4**, 998
  directors—
    disqualification of, **4**, 997
    liability, relief from, **4**, 995
  disclosure, relating to—
    generally, **4**, 991
    restrictions, application for lifting of, **4**, 992
    sale of shares, order for, **4**, 993
  general procedure, **4**, 965
  judicial factor, appointment of, **4**, 999
  nobile officium, application to, **4**, 1000
  register of companies, restoration of, **4**, 994
  register of members, to rectify, **4**, 989
  scheme of arrangement—
    amalgamation, schemes for, **4**, 988
    approval, **4**, 981
    arrangement, meaning, **4**, 978
    creditors, with, **4**, 979
    debenture holders, petition involving, **4**, 985
    general procedure, **4**, 987
    identification, **4**, 981
    members, with—
      generally, **4**, 980
      reduction of capital in scheme involving, **4**, 986
    reduction other than as part of, petition for, **4**, 968
    shareholder as petitioner, **4**, 984
    statement on effect of, **4**, 982
  shareholders—
    aggrieved, **4**, 996
    liability, petition granting relief from, **4**, 995
    petition, as, **4**, 984
  takeover, relating to, **4**, 990
  winding up, *see* WINDING UP

Company—*continued*
place of business—
  meaning, **4**, 315
  overseas company, **4**, 315
political background, **25**, 31
powers of, **17**, 355
pre-incorporation contract, **4**, 432
principal, corporate personality and, **4**, 318
private Bill—
  giving powers to company, **19**, 91–94
  promoted by company, **19**, 91–94
private company—
  alteration of public company to, **4**, 338
  borrowing, **4**, 438
  compulsory acquisition of assets, **19**, 223
  directors, *see* COMPANY
  elective regime procedure, **4**, 301
  elective resolution, procedural requirements modified by, **4**, 380
  exempt, abolition of, **4**, 306, 313
  institutional investment in, **25**, 48
  introduction of concept of, **4**, 304
  limited partnership compared, **16**, 1110
  main distinctive features, **4**, 313
  marketability of shares, **25**, 49
    lack of, **25**, 49
  name clause, **4**, 321
  pre-emption rights, exclusion of, **4**, 354
  public company—
    alteration to, **4**, 337
    distinction between, **4**, 313
    subsidiary of, as, **4**, 313*n*
  public company distinguished from, **25**, 20
  re-registration, **4**, 337, 338
  status of, **4**, 313
  subsidiary of public company, as, **4**, 313*n*
  upper limit of fifty members, **4**, 302
  written resolution procedure, **4**, 301, 379
private meeting, **14**, 1303
profits—
  distributable profits, meaning, **4**, 367, 460
  distribution, available for, **4**, 460
  effect on share value, **25**, 1
  generally, **19**, 1519, 1520; **25**, 13
  partnership must be carried on with view to, **4**, 302
  secret, made by promoter, **4**, 316
promoter—
  fiduciary obligations to company, **4**, 316
  promotion of company by, **4**, 316
  secret profit made by, **4**, 316
  trust concept applied to, **24**, 11
property—
  disposition of, winding up by court, **4**, 753
  distribution of, voluntary winding up, **4**, 812
  floating charge, attachment of, **4**, 660
  getting in, **4**, 768
  heritable, situation of, **4**, 42
  heritable security, subject to, sale of, **4**, 850
  natural person's power to acquire, **4**, 318
  payments arising from transfers to company, **4**, 423
  power to acquire, **4**, 318

Company—*continued*
property—*continued*
receiver, disposal of interest by—
authority to dispose, **4**, 711
effect of, **4**, 710
remaining vested in company, winding up by
court, **4**, 754
secured, administrator's powers over, **4**, 619
substantial transactions, **4**, 424
proposal, *see* voluntary arrangement *below*
prospectus—
form and content, **4**, 541
fraudulent misrepresentation in—
directors, liability of, **11**, 783
generally, **11**, 782, 783
listed securities, **11**, 783
unlisted securities, **11**, 783
investor misled by, protection for, **4**, 304
promoter, powers of, **4**, 316
provisional order—
as promoter of, **19**, 27
relating to, 23*n*; **19**, 23
public company—
alteration of private company to, **4**, 337
authorised minimum share capital, **4**, 355
borrowing, **4**, 438
commencement of business, registrar's
certificate relating to, **4**, 332
directors, *see* COMPANY
larger, quasi-partnership distinguished from, **4**,
487
main distinctive features, **4**, 313
memorandum of association, form of, **4**, 320
minimum size for, **4**, 302*n*
old, grounds for winding up by court, **4**, 724
own shares, purchase of, **4**, 366
pre-emption rights, exclusion of, **4**, 354
private company—
alteration to, **4**, 338
distinction between, **4**, 313
subsidiary of public company, as, **4**, 313*n*
private company distinguished, **25**, 20
promoter, common law principles relating to,
4, 316
re-registration, **4**, 337, 338
period, **4**, 313
share capital, *see* SHARE CAPITAL
shares, *see* SHARES
public limited company—
divisions, amendment of Companies Act 1985
in respect of, **4**, 306
generally, **16**, 1004
mergers, amendment of Companies Act 1985 in
respect of, **4**, 306
name clause, **4**, 321
share capital, function of, **4**, 350
public registers, access to, **25**, 13
public transport, **14**, 430
purchase of trust property by, **24**, 177
pursuer, as—
expenses, **4**, 1002
ordinary action, **4**, 954
pursuer in court action, caution for expenses, **3**,
996

Company—*continued*
quasi-partnership, **25**, 15
receiver, *see* RECEIVER
receivership, irritancy following, **13**, 584
reconstruction, amalgamation distinguished, **4**,
558
redemption, **25**, 13
reduction, ordinary action, remedy in, **4**, 960
redundancy, impending, consultation in respect
of, **4**, 863
register of members, rectification, **13**, 71
registered, acting contrary to memorandum of
association, **19**, 229
registered office—
address, **4**, 435
memorandum of association, form of, **4**, 320,
435
register of members, maintenance of, **4**, 345
registered name shown at, **4**, 321
Registrar of Companies, powers of, **4**, 331
situation of, **4**, 320
Registrar of Companies, *see* REGISTRAR OF
COMPANIES
registration—
charges, of—
defective particulars, **4**, 443
generally, **4**, 439
notice, as, **4**, 442
overseas company, by, **4**, 448
procedure for, **4**, 441
ranking, registration affecting, **4**, 446
registrar's certificate relating to, **4**, 332
company name, of, **4**, 321
floating charge, of, *see* FLOATING CHARGE
how effected, **4**, 314
incorporation by, **4**, 314
non-registration, effect of, **4**, 443
overseas company, **4**, 315
overseas territory, in, **4**, 1223
shares, interests in, **4**, 346
transfer of shares, of, refusal of, **4**, 377
relative prospects, **25**, 40
relevant service, **14**, 1916
remedies—
administrative law, **4**, 1001
ordinary actions, in—
damages, **4**, 963
declarator, **4**, 959
generally, **4**, 958
interdict, **4**, 962
miscellaneous, **4**, 964
payment, **4**, 964
reduction, **4**, 960
specific implement, **4**, 961
unfairly prejudicial conduct, for, **4**, 492
remuneration—
administrator, of, **4**, 639
auditor, of, **4**, 389
director, of, *see* directors *above*
employees, of, as preferential debt, **4**, 857
liquidator, of, **4**, 775, 814
provisional liquidator, of, **4**, 749
voluntary arrangement, supervisor of, **4**, 599
reorganisation, meaning, **4**, 558

Company—*continued*
report—
    contributories, to, **4**, 833
    creditors, to, **4**, 833
    independent person, by, in support of administration order, **4**, 611
    inspector, of—
        consequences stemming from, **4**, 529
        requirement to make, **4**, 528
    interests in shares, investigation into, **4**, 517
    meeting of members, considered at, **4**, 388
    voluntary arrangement, relating to, *see* voluntary arrangement *below*
re-registration—
    alteration of status of company by—
        generally, **4**, 336
        limited company—
            alteration to unlimited company, **4**, 339
            unlimited company altered to, **4**, 340
        private company—
            altered to public company, **4**, 337
            public company altered to, **4**, 338
        public company—
            alteration to private company, **4**, 338
            period for, **4**, 313
            private company altered to, **4**, 337
        registrar's certificate, **4**, 332, 341
        unauthorised, **4**, 342
        unlimited company—
            alteration of limited company to, **4**, 339
            limited company, alteration to, **4**, 340
residence, **17**, 356
resolutions—
    circulation, **4**, 477
    elective, *see* elective resolution *above*
    member, of, **4**, 385
    publication, **4**, 401
    written, *see* written resolutions *below*
    See also meetings (members, of) *above*
retention of title agreement—
    administrator, powers of, **4**, 619
    meaning, **4**, 619
reversionary, loan by, **20**, 232
royal charter—
    incorporation by, **4**, 303, 314
    partnership does not require, **4**, 302
royalties paid to, tax treatment, **18**, 1572, 1572*n*
salade helmet granted to (heraldry), **11**, 1605
sale of property to, by company promoters, **24**, 180
sales director, status, **4**, 403
Scottish Law Commission recommendations, **22**, 680
seal—
    obligation to have, **4**, 437
    registered name shown on, **4**, 321
secretary—
    appointment, **4**, 434
    joint, appointment, **4**, 434
    register of, **4**, 434
    sole director cannot act as, **4**, 404, 434
    statutory duties, **4**, 434
Secretary of State—
    correct company name, use of, **4**, 321

Company—*continued*
Secretary of State—*continued*
    ownership of company, power to investigate, **4**, 531
    shares, interests in, restrictions relating to, **4**, 346
    sheriffdoms, powers relating to, **4**, 2
    unfairly prejudicial conduct, petition to court relating to, **4**, 491
    winding up petition by—
        companies generally, **4**, 739
        insurance company, **4**, 740
        investment business, bodies carrying on, **4**, 741
securities—
    directors, for, **4**, 426
    fixed, ranking of floating charges, **4**, 665
    ranking, registration affecting, **4**, 446
    statutory powers of trustees, **24**, 202
sederunt book—
    administration, maintenance in relation to, **4**, 632
    insolvency proceedings, relating to, **4**, 839
    receiver, duties of, **4**, 703
    voluntary arrangement, maintained by supervisor of, **4**, 598
sequestration, *see* SEQUESTRATION
shamelessly indecent conduct by, **7**, 471
share capital, *see* SHARE CAPITAL
shareholder, *see* SHAREHOLDER
shareholding, *see* SHAREHOLDING
shares, *see* SHARES
shares, limited by, *see* limited *above*
situation—
    meaning, **4**, 320*n*
    registered office, of, **4**, 320
size, **25**, 38
    maximum, **4**, 302
    private company, **4**, 302
small, accounts of, **1**, 83
solicitors practising as, **13**, 1201
special category, accounts of, **1**, 82
special notice, resolution, of, **4**, 386
special resolution—
    articles of association, alteration of, **4**, 329
    company name changed by, **4**, 321
    memorandum of association, alteration of, **4**, 320
state of mind, determining, **4**, 318
statement of affairs—
    administrator, duties of, **4**, 626
    liquidator's requirement relating to, **4**, 772
statements, requisition and circulation, **4**, 477
stationery, **4**, 321, 436
status—
    re-registration, alteration by, *see* RE-REGISTRATION
    unauthorised changes of, **4**, 342
stock or estate, common interest in, **16**, 1001
striking off defunct, *see* WINDING UP
submission to arbitration, **2**, 412
subrogation, **12**, 905
subscription clause, subscribers' agreement to become members evidenced by signature to, **4**, 344

Company—*continued*
subsidiary—
   meaning, **4**, 370
   parent, creditors cannot claim against, **4**, 319
   wholly owned, meaning, **4**, 370
substratum, failure of, **4**, 510
successor, following gas privatisation, **9**, 867
suppliers, **25**, 35
takeover, *see* TAKEOVER
third party—
   company name, restraint of name of, **4**, 321
   constructive notice, doctrine of, **4**, 326
   corporate personality and, **4**, 318
   directors' liabilities to, **4**, 431
   fraud on, **4**, 150
   protection of, **4**, 414
   special jurisdiction, **4**, 49, 51
   ultra vires doctrine, European Communities Act
     1972 and, **4**, 325
trading, borrowing powers, **13**, 1774
transfer of friendly society engagements to, **12**,
   728
transfer of ownership, capacity, **18**, 599
transfer of undertaking, consultation prior to, **4**,
   864
trust property purchased by, **24**, 177
trustee—
   company as, **24**, 134
   powers of, **24**, 202
   resignation of, effect, **24**, 166
types—
   corporate personality, **4**, 317
   foreign company, **4**, 315
   guarantee, company limited by, **4**, 312
   island company, **4**, 315
   overseas company, **4**, 315
   piercing veil, **4**, 319
   private company, **4**, 313
   promotion of company, **4**, 316
   public company, **4**, 313
   registration, incorporation by, **4**, 314
   shares, company limited by, **4**, 312
   unlimited company, **4**, 312
ultra vires doctrine, application, **4**, 324
unfair preference, *see* UNFAIR PREFERENCE
unfair prejudice—
   concept of, **4**, 482
   history of remedy, **4**, 478
   Jenkins Report—
     case law since, **4**, 480
     implementation of, **4**, 481
     recommendations, **4**, 479
   just and equitable rule, company to be wound
     up under, **4**, 478
   meetings of members—
     calling of, **4**, 381
     conduct of, **4**, 396
   membership, status of, **4**, 343
   minority shareholders, rights of, **4**, 471
   oppression, meaning, **4**, 478*n*, 479
   pre-emption rights, allotment relating to, **4**, 354
   unfairly prejudicial conduct—
     affairs of company, resulting from, **4**, 483
     business venture, other forms of, **4**, 486

Company—*continued*
unfair prejudice—*continued*
   unfairly prejudicial conduct—*continued*
     directors' advice, **4**, 489
     expectations of members, **4**, 485
     interest of member, **4**, 484
     jurisdiction, extent of, **4**, 493
     other members' rights, **4**, 488
     petitioner, conduct of, **4**, 495
     quasi-partnership—
       effect on, **4**, 486
       receiver, appointment of, **4**, 487
     relief, types of, **4**, 494
     remedies for, **4**, 492
     Secretary of State's right to petition court, **4**,
       491
     share issues as, **4**, 490
     unconstitutional propriety, acts involving, **4**,
       482
     unfairly prejudicial, meaning, **4**, 479, 482
     valuation of shares—
       date of, **4**, 497
       generally, **4**, 496
unincorporated, contract between promoter and,
   4, 316
unlimited, **16**, 1004
   alteration of limited company to, **4**, 339
   articles of association, form of, **4**, 329
   limited company, alteration to, **4**, 340
   memorandum of association, form of, **4**, 320
   nature of, **4**, 312
   registration, incorporation by, **4**, 314
   re-registration, **4**, 339, 340
   share capital, function of, **4**, 350
unregistered—
   meaning, **4**, 936
   winding up, *see* WINDING UP
valuer, task of, **25**, 30
vicarious liability, **4**, 318
voluntary arrangement—
   approval—
     binding effect, **4**, 591
     employees, **4**, 594
     fraud in obtaining, **4**, 592
     preferential creditors, **4**, 593
   completion of—
     final notice, **4**, 602
     report, **4**, 602
   Cork Report, **4**, 579
   court—
     applications to—
       challenge of decisions, **4**, 600
       other, **4**, 601
     report to, **4**, 583
   Insolvency Act 1986 Part I, application of, **4**,
     581
   introduction of new concept of, **4**, 307
   liquidator following, **4**, 761
   meetings—
     decisions of, **4**, 587
     procedure, **4**, 588
     report of, **4**, 590
     summoning of, **4**, 584
     voting at, **4**, 589

Company—*continued*
voluntary arrangement—*continued*
  notice—
    final, **4**, 602
    nominee, to, **4**, 582
  proposal—
    administrator, by—
      administrator as nominee, **4**, 585
      another insolvency practitioner as
        nominee, **4**, 586
    directors, by—
      court, report to, **4**, 583
      nominee, notice to, **4**, 582
      summoning of meetings, **4**, 584
    liquidator, by—
      another insolvency practitioner as nominee,
        4, 586
      liquidator as nominee, **4**, 585
    nominee—
      administrator as, **4**, 585
      another insolvency practitioner as, **4**, 586
      liquidator as, **4**, 585
      notice to, **4**, 582
  report—
    completion, on, **4**, 602
    court, to, **4**, 583
    meetings, of, **4**, 590
    supervisor, of, **4**, 597
  supervisor—
    accounts, **4**, 597
    administrator, relationship with, **4**, 637
    costs, **4**, 599
    expenses, **4**, 599
    functions of, **4**, 595
    powers of, **4**, 595
    remuneration, **4**, 599
    replacement of, **4**, 596
    reports, **4**, 597
    sederunt book, maintenance of, **4**, 598
    vacancies in office of, **4**, 596
    winding up petition by, **4**, 730, 738
  White Paper, **4**, 580
voting—
  procedure, **4**, 399
  rights—
    chairman, of, **4**, 397
    members, of, **4**, 397
    weighted, **4**, 397
winding up, *see* BANKRUPTCY; WINDING UP
written resolution—
  auditor, notice to, **4**, 379
  minute book, must be recorded in, **4**, 400
  new procedural requirement, **4**, 379
  own shares, purchase by company, **4**, 366
  private company, procedure for, **4**, 301, 379
  shares—
    authority for issue of, **4**, 353
    financial assistance for acquisition, **4**, 369
    funding purchase, **4**, 367
    own, purchase by company, **4**, 366
    See also meetings (members, of) *above*
yield, selection of, **25**, 19
See also CORPORATION

Company law
before 1856 ..., **4**, 303
European Communities Act 1972 ..., **4**, 311
from 1856 to 1948 ..., **4**, 304
from 1948 to 1985 ..., **4**, 305
Insolvency Act 1976 ..., **4**, 305
See also COMPANIES ACTS
Company Law Committee
establishment, **4**, 471
Company secretary
See COMPANY
Company-owned filling station
See OIL (marketing)
Compensation
accommodation works, in lieu of, **19**, 1042
blight, **5**, 104; **6**, 1141, 1149
canals, private navigation rights, **19**, 1110
'cleared site value', **6**, 1141
coast protection works, **25**, 388
compensatory award, *see* UNFAIR DISMISSAL
compulsory purchase, *see* COMPULSORY
  ACQUISITION; COMPULSORY PURCHASE
conservation, relating to, **25**, 393
Criminal Injuries Compensation Scheme, *see*
  CRIMINAL INJURIES COMPENSATION SCHEME
damage relating to fisheries, for, **11**, 176
death or injury caused by railway accident, **19**,
  1073
defaulter, imprisonment—
  generally, **16**, 1433*n*
  treatment, **16**, 1428
depreciation in land value, **6**, 1141
development of land previously acquired, **6**, 1141
discontinuance of use of land, order for, **6**, 1141
disputed, determined by Lands Tribunal for
  Scotland, **5**, 195
disturbance payments, *see* COMPULSORY ACQUISITION
drainage works, damage caused by, **25**, 370
drought, relating to, **25**, 393
electricity, land compulsorily purchased for use,
  9, 657
extinction of contractual obligation by—
  concursus debiti et crediti, **15**, 879
  decree, after, **15**, 877
  generally, **15**, 865, 877
  liquid debts, **15**, 878
felling licence, for refusal to grant, **11**, 618
flood prevention operation, land depreciated by,
  14, 466; **25**, 378
game, for damage by, **11**, 889–894
general vesting declaration, **6**, 1141
harbours, dredging of, **6**, 1141
housing legislation, under, **6**, 1141
injurious affection, *see* INJURIOUS AFFECTION
judges, liability of, **17**, 886
land, **14**, 2115
  noise, nuisance caused by, **9**, 1295
  railway, additional land required for, **19**,
    1019
Lands Tribunal for Scotland, **6**, 1141, 1149
  See also LANDS TRIBUNAL FOR SCOTLAND
listed building, **6**, 1141
minerals, controls relating to, **23**, 218
mining, **6**, 1141; **14**, 1683, 1689, 1700

Compensation—*continued*
miscarriage of justice, for, **17**, 836
notice of entry—
  agricultural tenants, **6**, 1141
  crofters, **6**, 1141
offender required to pay, **17**, 803
oil pollution damage, international fund for, **9**, 1216
opencast coal mining, **14**, 1700
orders, **6**, 171; **17**, 800
'owner occupier's supplement', **6**, 1141
payment by one local authority to another, **14**, 323
planning—
  entitlement, **23**, 305
  permission, revocation or modification of, **6**, 1141; **23**, 176
pneumoconiosis, for, **14**, 1678
positive requirement to compensate, **5**, 106
private international law, **17**, 360
quarrying stopped by planning authority, **6**, 1141
radiation, injury from, **9**, 1198
railway—
  accident, **19**, 1073
  construction, **19**, 1024
  contract, discharge of, **17**, 275
restitution distinguished from, **17**, 803
restrictions on new developments, for, **6**, 1141
roads and land taken by railway company, **19**, 1020
severance, *see* COMPULSORY ACQUISITION
sewage, relating to, **25**, 439
short tenancy, *see* SHORT TENANCY
stop notice ceases effect, **6**, 1141
trees, removal by railway undertaker, **19**, 1038
unfair dismissal, *see* UNFAIR DISMISSAL
water authorities, duties of, **25**, 513
water supply, **25**, 513
wrongful capture, for, **17**, 417
wrongful conviction and detention, for, **7**, 730
Compensation order
enforcement, **4**, 38
generally, **7**, 2
meaning, **7**, 2*n*
Compensatory award
See UNFAIR DISMISSAL
Competition and Choice: Telecommunications Policy for the 1990s, **White Paper**
generally, **16**, 1924
Competition law
administrative law remedies—
  practice and procedure, **4**, 1001
agreement—
  Commission's report, consequences of, **4**, 1243
  court undertaking to abandon, **4**, 1131
  information—
    goods, as to, *see* goods *below*
    services, as to, **4**, 1127, 1178
  meaning, **4**, 1129, 1133, 1173*n*
  registrable, *see* RESTRICTIVE TRADE PRACTICES ACT
  restrictive—
    goods, as to, *see* goods *below*
    services, as to, *see* services *below*

Competition law—*continued*
agriculture, **4**, 1165, 1310
allocative efficiency—
  achievement of, **4**, 1102
  meaning, **4**, 1102
anti-competitive practices—
  business, course of, **4**, 1252
  case law, **4**, 1265
  conduct, course of, **4**, 1253
  cost, perfect competition, effect of, **4**, 1102
  Director General, preliminary investigation by—
    formal, **4**, 1259
    informal, **4**, 1258
    undertakings in consequence of, **4**, 1260
  distorting competition, **4**, 1256
  divisions of functions, **4**, 1257
  exclusionary tactics, **4**, 1267
  exclusions, **4**, 1255
  general, **4**, 1250
  investigations—
    number of, **4**, 1263
    outcome of, **4**, 1264
  meaning, **4**, 1251
  notice reference, **4**, 1261
  orders, **4**, 1262
  practices, **4**, 1254
  preventing competition, **4**, 1256
  proposed list of, **4**, 1290
  report, **4**, 1262
  report reference, **4**, 1261
  restrictive competition, **4**, 1256
  selective distribution, **4**, 1266
  undertakings, **4**, 1262
appeals, White Paper 1989, proposals in, **4**, 1294
bargaining power, inequality, **4**, 1107
bilateral agreement, **4**, 1306
boycotts, prohibition, **4**, 1374
cartel—
  aggregated rebates, **4**, 1146, 1373
  crisis, **4**, 1394
case law, **4**, 1265
closed agreement, **4**, 1379
comfort letter, **4**, 1117
commercial agency, nature of, **4**, 1378
complaints—
  infringement, application for finding of, **4**, 1343
  third parties, by, procedure in, **4**, 1365
concerted practices, **4**, 1321
crossover problem, registrable agreements, **4**, 1179
de minimis, **4**, 1291, 1323
decision-making, location of, **4**, 1109
defence against bid under, **4**, 555
Director General's statement on, **9**, 821
disregarded provisions, *see* goods (restrictive agreement as to) *below*
distribution—
  selective, **4**, 1266, 1383
distribution agreement—
  closed agreement, **4**, 1379
  commercial agency, **4**, 1378
  exclusive distribution, **4**, 1380

Competition law—*continued*
distribution agreement—*continued*
  exclusive purchasing, **4**, 1384
  export ban, **4**, 1379
  extraterritoriality, problems of, **4**, 1381
  franchising, **4**, 1385
  general, **4**, 1377
  resale price maintenance, **4**, 1382
  selective distribution, **4**, 1383
dominant position, **4**, 1329, 1330, 1333
dumping, **4**, 1396; **7**, 1024, 1050
Economic Commission, inquiries by, **4**, 1346
economic equity, **4**, 1106
economics of—
  generally, **4**, 1101
  monopoly, competition contrasted with, **4**, 1103
  theory of competition, **4**, 1102
efficiency—
  allocative, *see* allocative efficiency *above*
  merger, impact of, **4**, 1286
  productive, *see* productive efficiency *below*
European Commission—
  administrative file, **4**, 1354
  Council of Ministers, delegation of enforcement powers of, **4**, 1111
  decisions of—
    exemptions, **4**, 1361
    infringement, termination of, **4**, 1360
    negative clearance, **4**, 1359
  fines imposed by, **4**, 1362, 1364
  hearings, **4**, 1350
  information, request for, **4**, 1344
  interim measures by—
    power to take, **4**, 1356
    protective measures, **4**, 1357
    restrictions on, **4**, 1358
  investigatory powers, **4**, 1345
  limitation of actions, **4**, 1355
  notification—
    exemption from, **4**, 1342
    requirement of, **4**, 1341
  Office of Fair Trading, liaison with, **4**, 1121
  publicity, **4**, 1352
  reasoning, **4**, 1353
  sector inquiries, **4**, 1346
European Community rules—
  air transport agreements, **10**, 162
  complementarity of treaty provisions, **10**, 153
  concentrations, **10**, 165
  dominant position, abuse of, **10**, 164
  dumping, **10**, 152
  exclusive distribution agreements, **10**, 162
  exclusive purchasing agreements, **10**, 162
  filling station agreements, **9**, 822–833
    See also filling station agreements *below*
  franchising, **10**, 162
  generally, **10**, 151, 152, 163; **19**, 243
  know-how agreements, **10**, 162
  mergers, **10**, 165
  motor vehicle distribution and servicing agreements, **10**, 162
  patent licensing agreements, **10**, 162
  prohibitions, **10**, 157

Competition law—*continued*
European Community rules—*continued*
  public undertakings, **10**, 166
  Reports on Competition Policy, **10**, 460
  research and development agreements, **10**, 162
  sex discrimination, **10**, 154
  specialisation agreements, **10**, 162
  state aid, **10**, 152, 167
  undertakings, rules applying to, **10**, 152
    enforcement, **10**, 158
    exemption, **10**, 159–162
    generally, **10**, 155, 163
    meaning of undertakings, **10**, 156
European Union—
  administrative procedure—
    administrative file, **4**, 1354
    hearings, **4**, 1350
    information, request for, **4**, 1344
    investigatory powers, **4**, 1345
    legal privilege, **4**, 1347
    limitation of actions, **4**, 1355
    notification of decisions, **4**, 1351
    publicity, **4**, 1352
    reasoning, **4**, 1353
    sector inquiries, **4**, 1346
    service, **4**, 1349
    statement of objection, **4**, 1348
  agriculture—
    agricultural products, **4**, 1392
    application of rules to, **4**, 1310
  atomic energy, application of rules to, **4**, 1309
  automatic nullity, **4**, 1324
  Bankruptcy Convention, **4**, 311
  bilateral agreements, **4**, 1306
  coal and steel, application of rules to, **4**, 1308
  complaints—
    infringement, application for finding of, **4**, 1343
    third party, by, **4**, 1365
  concentration—
    Continental Can case—
      decision of Commission in, **4**, 1335
      position after, **4**, 1336
    generally, **4**, 1334
  concerted practices, **4**, 1321
  conflicts between UK law and—
    Articles 85 and 86, non-application of, **4**, 1116
    block exemption, **4**, 1115
    comfort letters, **4**, 1117
    generally, **4**, 1112
    individual exemption, **4**, 1114
    mergers, **4**, 1118
    prohibition, **4**, 1113
    UK authorities, attitude of, **4**, 1119
  crisis cartels, **4**, 1394
  de minimis rule, **4**, 1323
  decision-making, location of, **4**, 1109
  direct effects, **4**, 1303
  distribution agreement, *see* specific issues *below*
  dominant position—
    abuse of—
      general nature of, **4**, 1332
    general, **4**, 1329

Competition law—*continued*
European Union—*continued*
  dominant position—*continued*
    one or more undertakings, **4**, 1330
  DTI bulletin on progress in company law
    proposals, **4**, 311*n*
  European Communities Act 1972 ..., **4**, 311
  extra-territoriality, **4**, 1305
  firms, arrangements between—
    different member states, in, **4**, 1316
    same member state, in, **4**, 1317
  foundations of, **4**, 1298
  group exemption, **4**, 1328
  individual exemption, **4**, 1327
  infringement—
    application for finding of, **4**, 1343
    termination of, **4**, 1360
  market integration, **4**, 1108
  member states, concept of trade between—
    firms, arrangements between—
      different member states, in, **4**, 1316
      same member state, in, **4**, 1317
    generally, **4**, 1314
    trade, meaning, **4**, 1315
  non-application of, **4**, 1116
  object or effect, **4**, 1322
  objectives of—
    foundations of EU, **4**, 1298
    policy of EU, **4**, 1298
    principles, **4**, 1297
  offending clauses, severability of, **4**, 1326
  outline of competition law, **4**, 1111
  permitted co-operation, *see*specific issues *below*
  policy of, **4**, 1298
  preface, **4**, 1296
  procedural aspects—
    administrative, *see*administrative procedure
      above
    complaints—
      infringement, application for finding of, **4**,
        1343
      third party, by, **4**, 1365
    decisions of Commission—
      exemptions, **4**, 1361
      infringement, termination of, **4**, 1360
      negative clearance, **4**, 1359
    deemed validity of certain agreements, **4**,
      1367
    infringement, application for finding of, **4**,
      1343
    interim measures by Commission—
      power to take, **4**, 1356
      protective measures, **4**, 1357
      restrictions on, **4**, 1358
    judicial review, powers of Court of Justice,
      4, 1366
    national authorities—
      Advisory Committee on Restrictive
        Practices and Monopolies, **4**, 1340
      jurisdiction, **4**, 1338
      legislative powers, **4**, 1337
      liaison, **4**, 1339
      negative clearance, application for, **4**, 1341,
        1342

Competition law—*continued*
European Union—*continued*
  procedural aspects—*continued*
    notification—
      exemption from, **4**, 1342
      requirement of, **4**, 1341
    opposition procedure, **4**, 1367
    penalties, *see* sanctions and penalties *below*
    sanctions and penalties—
      Article 15(6) of Regulation 17 ..., **4**, 1364
      double jeopardy, **4**, 1363
      fines, **4**, 1362
  prohibited horizontal agreements, *see* specific
    issues *below*
  provisional validity, **4**, 1325
  public undertakings, application of rules to, **4**,
    1312
  relevant market—
    common market, **4**, 1331
  Restrictive Practices Court, agreements not
    referred to, **4**, 1181
  scope—
    field of application—
      agriculture, **4**, 1310
      atomic energy, **4**, 1309
      coal and steel, **4**, 1308
      extent of coverage, **4**, 1307
      public undertakings, **4**, 1312
      temporal, **4**, 1313
      transitional provisions, **4**, 1313
      transport, **4**, 1311
    geographical—
      application within territory, **4**, 1304
      bilateral agreements, **4**, 1306
      extra-territoriality, **4**, 1305
    temporal, **4**, 1313
    transitional provisions, **4**, 1313
  Second Directive—
    implementation, **4**, 303
    reforms, **4**, 305
  shared competence of law, **4**, 1302
  single member company, proposal for, **4**, 302*n*
  specific issues—
    agricultural products, **4**, 1392
    crisis cartels, **4**, 1394
    distribution agreement—
      closed agreement, **4**, 1379
      commercial agency, **4**, 1378
      exclusive distribution, **4**, 1380
      exclusive purchasing, **4**, 1384
      export bans, **4**, 1379
      extra-territoriality, problems of, **4**, 1381
      franchising, **4**, 1385
      general, **4**, 1377
      resale price maintenance, **4**, 1382
      selective distribution, **4**, 1383
    dumping, **4**, 1396
    permitted co-operation—
      exhibitions, **4**, 1390
      fairs, **4**, 1390
      general, **4**, 1386
      joint purchase agency, **4**, 1389
      joint research and development agreement,
        4, 1388

Competition law—*continued*
European Union—*continued*
  specific issues—*continued*
    permitted co-operation—*continued*
      joint ventures, **4**, 1391
      specialisation agreement, **4**, 1387
    prohibited horizontal agreements—
      aggregated rebate cartels, **4**, 1373
      boycotts, **4**, 1374
      collective exclusive reciprocal dealing, **4**, 1372
      information agreement, **4**, 1371
      joint price fixing, **4**, 1369
      joint sales agencies, **4**, 1370
      market sharing, **4**, 1368
      restrictive covenants, **4**, 1376
      voluntary restraints, **4**, 1375
    public undertakings, **4**, 1393
    state intervention, **4**, 1395
  supremacy of law, **4**, 1301
  trade, meaning, **4**, 1315
  transport, application of rules to, **4**, 1311
  Treaty framework—
    detailed provisions, **4**, 1300
    objectives, **4**, 1299
    tasks, **4**, 1299
  ultra vires doctrine, European Communities Act 1972, and, **4**, 325
  undertakings, **4**, 1318
    agreements between, **4**, 1319
    associations of, decisions by, **4**, 1320
exclusive distribution agreement—
  exemption, **4**, 1159, 1176, 1380
  restraint of trade doctrine, scope, **4**, 1212
exclusive purchasing agreement, **4**, 1384
exclusive reciprocal dealing, **4**, 1372
export agreements, **4**, 1161, 1176, 1180
export ban nature of, **4**, 1379
exports, **4**, 1224–1226
Fair Trading Act 1973 ..., **4**, 1268
fiduciary, by, **24**, 182
filling station agreements, application of EC law to—
  article 85—
    application of, **9**, 822
    block exemption—
      general principles, **9**, 823
      regulations, **9**, 824
      withdrawal of, **9**, 832
    duration of agreements, **9**, 826
    general provisions, application of, **9**, 831
    permitted restrictions, **9**, 829
    prohibited restrictions, **9**, 830
    regulation 1984/83
      four Titles in, **9**, 827
      scope of, **9**, 825
      service station agreements covered by, **9**, 828
    transitional provisions, **9**, 833
functions—
  advancing other policies, **4**, 1107
  consumer protection, **4**, 1105
  decision-making, location of, **4**, 1109
  economic equity, **4**, 1106
  generally, **4**, 1101, 1104

Competition law—*continued*
functions—*continued*
  market integration, **4**, 1108
goods—
  behavioural monopolies in relation to, **4**, 1222
  generally, **4**, 1127
  information agreement as to—
    agreements covered, **4**, 1170
    control of, **4**, 1171
    generally, **4**, 1169
  restrictive agreement as to—
    agreement, meaning, **4**, 1129, 1133
    arrangements, meaning, **4**, 1130, 1131
    carrying on business within UK, meaning, **4**, 1138
    disregarded provisions—
      approved standards, **4**, 1152
      coal producers, **4**, 1149
      extension of, **4**, 1155
      financing terms, **4**, 1154
      generally, **4**, 1148
      judicial decisions, **4**, 1151
      restrictive labour practices, **4**, 1153
      steel producers, **4**, 1149
      vertical restraints, **4**, 1150
    exempt agreements—
      agriculture, agreement affecting, **4**, 1165
      coal, agreement affecting, **4**, 1165
      Crown agreement, **4**, 1167
      duration irrelevant, **4**, 1168
      exclusive distribution agreement, **4**, 1159
      export agreement, **4**, 1161
      express authorisation, **4**, 1157
      fisheries, agreement affecting, **4**, 1165
      forestry, agreement affecting, **4**, 1165
      generally, **4**, 1156
      industrial rationalisation schemes, **4**, 1158
      intellectual property, licensing of, **4**, 1160
      merger investigation, undertaking following, **4**, 1166
      monopoly investigation, undertaking following, **4**, 1166
      prices, agreement to keep down, **4**, 1163
      section 29 agreement, **4**, 1162
      steel, agreement affecting, **4**, 1165
      wholesale co-operative agreements, **4**, 1164
    legislation, **4**, 1128
    recent decisions, **4**, 1132
    restrictions—
      implied, **4**, 1135
      leases, meaning of restriction in, **4**, 1136
      markets, division of, **4**, 1144
      meaning, **4**, 1134, 1136
      price fixing, **4**, 1140
      prices, agreement to recommend, **4**, 1141
      range of production, on, **4**, 1143
      section 6, relating to matters specified in, **4**, 1139
      terms and conditions, agreement relating to, **4**, 1142
      volume of production, on, **4**, 1143
    supplementary provisions—
      compliance, benefits for, **4**, 1146
      generally, **4**, 1145

Competition law—*continued*
goods—*continued*
  restrictive agreement as to—*continued*
    supplementary provisions—*continued*
      non-compliance, penalties for, **4**, 1146
      trade associations, **4**, 1147
      time element, **4**, 1168
      two or more persons—
        bodies corporate, **4**, 1137
        partnerships, **4**, 1137
      two persons carrying on business, **4**, 1138
    structural monopolies in relation to, **4**, 1221
Green Paper 1988—
  Restrictive Trade Practices Act 1976, review
    of, **4**, 1110, 1289
  UK authorities, attitude of, **4**, 1119
horizontal agreement, *see* HORIZONTAL AGREEMENT
inflation, capacity of competition to dampen, **4**,
  1107
Information—
  agreement—
    European Commission's attitude to, **4**, 1371
information, services, as to, **4**, 1178
infringement—
  application for finding of, **4**, 1343
  termination, **4**, 1360
institutions, generally, **4**, 1120
international competition, failure to take into
  account, **4**, 1282
international sea transport, **4**, 1177
investigation—
  European Commission, powers of, **4**, 1345
  merger, of, *see* MONOPOLIES AND MERGERS
    COMMISSION
  monopoly, of, *see* MONOPOLIES AND MERGERS
    COMMISSION
  Restrictive Trade Practices Act 1976, under, **4**,
    1196
labour practices, restrictive, **4**, 1235
lawyers—
  non-designated services, **4**, 1177
  restrictive trade practices, **4**, 1247
local authority, provisions for—
  accounts, **14**, 918
  defined activity, meaning, **14**, 915
  defined authorities, meaning, **14**, 915
  financial objectives, **14**, 918
  functional work, **14**, 917
  local authority company, **14**, 920
  reports, **14**, 918
  sanctions, **14**, 919
  works contract, **14**, 916
market sharing, **4**, 1368
markets—
  single market integration, role of competition
    law in achieving, **4**, 1108
  structure, **4**, 1244
meaning of competition, **4**, 1102
merger, *see* MERGER
monopolies, *see* MONOPOLIES AND MERGERS
  COMMISSION
Monopolies and Mergers Commission, *see*
  MONOPOLIES AND MERGERS COMMISSION
monopoly, *see* MONOPOLIES

Competition law—*continued*
national authorities, jurisdiction of, **4**, 1338
non-compliance, penalties for, **4**, 1146
oil marketing—
  exclusive retail outlets secured by acquisition,
    9, 820
  exclusive tie agreements, inducements offered
    by suppliers for, **9**, 813
  filling station agreements, *see* filling stations *above*
  selective price support—
    complex monopoly, **9**, 815
    contractual effects of, **9**, 818
    generally, **9**, 814
    in practice, **9**, 817
    public interest, not against, **9**, 816
  undertakings—
    1968 review, **9**, 809
    1976 review, **9**, 810
    petrol retailers, application to supplies to, **9**,
      807
    retail petrol suppliers, regarding, **9**, 855
penalties—
  double jeopardy, **4**, 1363
  fines, **4**, 1362, 1364
  non-compliance, for, **4**, 1146
  White Paper 1989, proposals in, **4**, 1294
perfect competition, effect, **4**, 1102
permitted co-operation—
  exhibitions, **4**, 1390
  fairs, **4**, 1390
  generally, **4**, 1386
  joint purchase agencies, **4**, 1389
  joint research and development agreement, **4**,
    1388
  joint ventures, **4**, 1391
  specialisation agreement, **4**, 1387
price, discrimination between retailers as to, **9**, 812
procedural aspects—
  evidence, **4**, 1004
  expenses—
    generally, **4**, 1003
    pursuer, where company is, **4**, 1002
production—
  range of, restrictions on, **4**, 1143
  volume of, restrictions on, **4**, 1143
productive efficiency—
  achievement of, **4**, 1102
  meaning, **4**, 1102
  monopoly, objection to, **4**, 1103
public interest, *see* PUBLIC INTEREST
public undertakings, **4**, 1312, 1393
reasonableness—
  parties, between, **4**, 1210
  public interest, in, **4**, 1211
reform, **4**, 1289, 1290–1295
regional policy, as instrument of, **4**, 1107
registrable agreements, *see* RESTRICTIVE TRADE
  PRACTICES ACT 1976
remuneration, restrictive labour practices, **4**, 1153
report reference—
  meaning, **4**, 1261
  See also anti-competitive practices *below*
resale price maintenance, *see* RESALE PRICE
  MAINTENANCE

Competition law—*continued*
research and development agreement, joint,
    Community aspects, **4**, 1388
restriction—
    meaning, **4**, 1134, 1136, 1173*n*
    relevant restrictions, meaning, **4**, 1197*n*
restrictive agreement—
    goods, as to, *see* goods *above*
    services, as to, *see* services *below*
restrictive covenant—
    Commission's view of, **4**, 1376
    competitive business, as to, **16**, 1060
    generally, **4**, 1376
    partnership agreement, in, **16**, 1009
    third party rights, **15**, 849
    trade secret, protection of, **18**, 1468, 1470
    unenforceability of contracts, **15**, 763
Restrictive Practices Court, *see* RESTRICTIVE
    PRACTICES OURT
Restrictive Trade Practices Act 1976, *see*
    RESTRICTIVE TRADE PRACTICES ACT 1976
section 29 agreement, exemption, **4**, 1162
services—
    behavioural monopolies in relation to, **4**, 1223
    control—
        agreement brought under, **4**, 1173
        agreement potentially subject to, **4**, 1178
        generally, **4**, 1127
    information agreement as to, **4**, 1127, 1178
    order relating to, **4**, 1177
    place of supply, **4**, 1223
    restrictive agreement as to—
        control, agreement brought under, **4**, 1173
        disregarded provisions, **4**, 1175
        exemptions, **4**, 1176
        generally, **4**, 1172
        services order, **4**, 1177
        supplementary provisions, **4**, 1174
    restrictive trade practices, **4**, 1247
    structural monopolies in relation to, **4**, 1223
severance, public interest, restrictions contrary to,
    4, 1188
specialisation agreement, **4**, 1387
standardisation, **4**, 1175
third party—
    complaints by, procedure in, **4**, 1365
    restraint of trade doctrine, scope of, **4**, 1214
UK and EU law, conflict between—
    European Union—
        Articles 85 and 86, non-application of, **4**, 1116
        block exemption, **4**, 1115
        individual exemption, **4**, 1114
        prohibition, **4**, 1113
        generally, **4**, 1112
        mergers, **4**, 1118
    United Kingdom—
        attitude of authorities, **4**, 1119
        domestic authorisation, **4**, 1113
        domestic prohibition, **4**, 1114, 1115, 1116
        generally, **4**, 1112
voluntary restraints, **4**, 1375
White Paper 1989, proposals in, **4**, 1290–1295
wholesalers, sales promotion schemes by, **9**, 819

Composer
copyright, *see* COPYRIGHT
Composition
alioquin successorus (alioqui successurus), **18**, 80
casualty of, feudal law, generally, **18**, 80
charter of, **18**, 80
propulsion of the fee, **18**, 80
taxed, **18**, 80
Compound interest
contractual stipulation, **12**, 1002
generally, **12**, 1038
Comptroller and Auditor General
control of expenditure, **7**, 766
functions of, **1**, 78; **5**, 436
Officer of State, **7**, 790, 791, 792
Public Accounts Committee, **19**, 224
Comptroller of the Household
office of, **7**, 774
Comptroller of Patents
See PATENT
**Comptroller-General of Patents, Designs
    and Trade Marks**
supervision of, **23**, 911*n*
Compulsory acquisition
acquiring authority, **5**, 2
    advance payment by, **5**, 2
    increasing burden on, **5**, 125
    short tenancy, powers in respect of, **5**, 185
    taking possession of land before payment of
        compensation, interest payable, **5**, 194
Acquisition of Land Act, **3**, 1947
    See also ACQUISITION OF LAND (AUTHORISATION
        PROCEDURE) (SCOTLAND) ACT
advance payment, **5**, 193
agreement, purchase of land by, **5**, 15
allotment, of land for use as, **13**, 538
assessment of compensation—
    general principles, **5**, 105
    heads of claim—
        depreciation, **5**, 106, 107
        value of land, **5**, 106, 107
    injurious affection, **5**, 172, 182
    measure to be applied—
        1845 ..., **5**, 107
        financial equivalence, **5**, 110
        generally, **5**, 105
        today, **5**, 110
    over-generous, **5**, 108
    procedures for, **5**, 105
    rules of—
        disturbance, safeguarding of right to
            compensation for, **5**, 109
        owner, value to, **5**, 109
        replacement value preferred to market value,
            5, 109
        solatium, prohibition of payment of, **5**, 109
        willing seller, value to, **5**, 109
    severance, **5**, 172
    solatium—
        award of, **5**, 108
        meaning, **5**, 108
        prohibition of payment, **5**, 109
authority for, **5**, 2
bibliography, **5**, 203

Compulsory acquisition—*continued*
blight, *see* BLIGHT
British Waterways Board, by, **19**, 1106
causation, disturbance claim, **5**, 163
certificates of appropriate alternative development—
  appeals to Secretary of State, **5**, 147
  application for, **5**, 145
  generally, **5**, 130, 144
  issue of, **5**, 146
  physical factors, **5**, 132
  planning policies, application of, **5**, 131
  right of challenge in courts, **5**, 148
compensation for—
  advance payment, **5**, 193
  assessment of, *see* assessment of compensation
    above
  bibliography, **5**, 203
  blight notice, **5**, 104
  claim for—
    disturbance, *see* disturbance compensation
     below
    farm loss payment, **5**, 187
    home loss payment, **5**, 186
    injurious affection, *see* INJURIOUS AFFECTION
    legislation upon which founded, **5**, 106
    solatium, **5**, 108, 109, 133
    statutory authority to support, **5**, 106
  code, **5**, 105
  dispossession, **5**, 165
  disputed, determined by Lands Tribunal for
    Scotland, **5**, 195
  disturbance, *see* disturbance compensation *below*
  earliest legislation dealing with, **5**, 105
  expropriation, for, **5**, 106
  farm loss payment, **5**, 187; **6**, 1141
    See also FARM LOSS PAYMENT
  home loss payment, **5**, 186
    See also HOME LOSS PAYMENT
  injurious affection, *see* INJURIOUS AFFECTION
  intention to take property away without, **5**, 106
  interest on, **5**, 194
  Lands Clauses Act, under, **5**, 17
  notification as to, **5**, 47
  persons entitled to claim—
    generally, **5**, 111
    heritable creditors, **5**, 114
    lessees, **5**, 113
    owner or owners, **5**, 112
    servitude, effect of, **5**, 115
  severance—
    basis of assessment, **5**, 172
    generally, **6**, 1141
    injury to land, **5**, 171
    land taken and land retained, link
      between, **5**, 170
    Lands Tribunal for Scotland, **6**, 1146
    notice of objection to, protection of
      person entitled to serve, **5**, 51
    other injurious affection distinguished
      from, **5**, 169
    proposed compulsory acquisition involves,
      5, 51
    short tenancy, **5**, 185
  short tenancy, **5**, 185

Compulsory acquisition—*continued*
compensation for—*continued*
  persons entitled to claim—*continued*
    unfit house, **5**, 190, 191
    valuation, *see* VALUATION
  servitude, existence of, **5**, 115
  statutory authority to support, **5**, 106
  well-maintained payment, **5**, 190, 191
compulsory purchase procedure, *see* COMPULSORY
  PURCHASE
confirmation, *see* COMPULSORY PURCHASE
conveyance, **5**, 18, 31
corporate veil, piercing of, **4**, 317
croft of, **1**, 832
development—
  appropriate alternative—
    appeals to Secretary of State, **5**, 147
    application for, **5**, 145
    generally, **5**, 130, 144
    issue of, **5**, 146
    physical factors, **5**, 132
    planning policies, application of, **5**, 131
    right of challenge in courts, **5**, 148
  assumptions as to—
    development plan, derived from, **5**, 143
    development for which land acquired, **5**, 142
    existing use development, **5**, 141
    generally, **5**, 140
  existing use, **5**, 141
  meaning, **14**, 614
  plan, assumptions derived from, **5**, 143
  potential, establishment of, **5**, 139
  regulation of—
    compensation, generally, **5**, 197
    development order, planning permission
      granted by—
      modification of, **5**, 201
      withdrawal of, **5**, 201
    discontinuance order, **5**, 200
    established development value, unexpended
      balances of, **5**, 198
    existing use, restrictions on, **5**, 199
    expropriation distinguished from, **5**, 197
    new development—
      development not constituting, **5**, 202
      meaning, **5**, 198
    revocation order, **5**, 200
  value—
    certificates of appropriate alternative
      development—
      application for, **5**, 145
      courts, right of challenge in, **5**, 148
      development potential establishment of, **5**,
        139
      generally, **5**, 144
      issue of, **5**, 146
      nature of, **5**, 138
      Secretary of State, appeals to, **5**, 147
  See also TOWN AND COUNTRY PLANNING
disturbance compensation—
  avoidable loss, **5**, 168
  causation, **5**, 163
  claimant, **5**, 166, 167
  dispossession, consequences of, **5**, 165

Compulsory acquisition—*continued*
disturbance compensation—*continued*
 disturbance payment distinguished, **5**, 188
 entitlement, **5**, 160
 ill-health of claimant, loss due to, **5**, 166
 remoteness, **5**, 164
 safeguarding of right to, **5**, 109
 scope of claim, **5**, 162
disturbance payment—
 amount of, **5**, 188
 disturbance compensation distinguished from, **5**, 188
 entitlement to, **5**, 188
 generally, **6**, 1141
 interest on, **5**, 194
 lawful possession of land, requirement of, **5**, 188
 removal expenses, **5**, 188
electricity, in connection with, **9**, 656
expropriation and regulation distinguished, **5**, 197
farm loss payment, *see* FARM LOSS PAYMENT
fire authority, by, **10**, 1421; **14**, 502
gas, in connection with, **9**, 874
general vesting declaration—
 compensation, notification of, **5**, 47
 entry, right of, **5**, 49
 expedited procedure, replacement of, **5**, 46
 introduction of, **5**, 46
 Lands Clauses Acts, application of, **5**, 48
 Railways Clauses Acts, application of, **5**, 48
 statement of effects of, **5**, 47
 taking title by—
  alteration of area of land, **5**, 90
  effects of, **5**, 90
  generally, **5**, 81
  number of declarations, use of, **5**, 90
  schedule, **5**, 90
  style, **5**, 90
 valuation date, **5**, 121
 vesting of land, **5**, 49
generally, **5**, 518; **6**, 1089, 1141; **14**, 307, 502; **25**, 518
historical developments—
 canals, **5**, 5
 Clauses Acts, **5**, 10
 estuaries, **5**, 4
 generally, **5**, 3
 harbours, **5**, 4
 private enterprise, **5**, 8
 private legislation, **5**, 9
 railways, **5**, 6
 roads, **5**, 5
 water supply, **5**, 7
home loss payment, *see* HOME LOSS PAYMENT
injurious affection, *see* INJURIOUS AFFECTION
interest payable, **5**, 194
jurisdiction, **6**, 1141
land—
 acquisition of, **3**, 1947
 acquisition of, *see* ACQUISITION OF LAND (AUTHORISATION PROCEDURE) (SCOTLAND) ACT
 agricultural, solatium awarded in case of, **5**, 108
 blight, subject to, *see* BLIGHT

Compulsory acquisition—*continued*
land—*continued*
 burial ground, for, **3**, 521
 Clauses Act, **6**, 1845
 Clauses Act, *see* LANDS CLAUSES CONSOLIDATION (SCOTLAND) ACT
 common, *see* COMMON LAND
 compensation for loss, *see* compensation for *above*
 depreciation, head of claim for compensation, as, **5**, 106, 107
 entry on—
  Lands Clauses Act, under, **5**, 19
  right of, **5**, 49
 interests in—
  fixing, **5**, 117
  injury to, **5**, 171
  omission to be purchased, **5**, 26
  valuation, *see* VALUATION
 intersected, **5**, 20
 leases, subject to, **5**, 25
 mortgage, in, **5**, 22
 motorway service area, for, **20**, 628
 National Trust, **5**, 38
 purchase of—
  agreement, by, **5**, 15
  otherwise than by agreement, **5**, 16
 regulation of development, *see* TOWN AND COUNTRY PLANNING
 rentcharges, subject to, **5**, 24
 roads authority, by, **20**, 708, 712
 special road, for, **20**, 626
 statutory undertakers, acquired by, **5**, 43, 55
 superfluous, sale of, **5**, 27
 trunk road, for provision of buildings or facilities to service or construct, **20**, 620
 valuation, *see* valuation *below*
 value of, head of claim for compensation, as, **5**, 106, 107
 vesting of, **5**, 49
Lands Tribunal for Scotland, jurisdiction, **6**, 1141
legislation—
 compensation, dealing with, **5**, 105, 106
 current—
  acquisition of land, **5**, 1947
   See also ACQUISITION OF LAND (AUTHORISATION PROCEDURE) (SCOTLAND) ACT
  enabling Acts and provisions, **5**, 35
 early—
  clauses Acts, generally, **5**, 10
  land, **9**, 1845
  land, *see* LANDS CLAUSES CONSOLIDATION (SCOTLAND) ACT
  railways, **0**, 1845
  railways, *see* RAILWAYS CLAUSES CONSOLIDATION (SCOTLAND) ACT
  enabling Acts and provisions, **5**, 35
  private, historical development of, **5**, 9
light railway construction, for, **19**, 1086
listed building consent, **5**, 95
local authority, by, **11**, 1907; **14**, 317
meaning, **5**, 1
mining code, *see* MINING CODE
National Trust for Scotland, relating to, **5**, 38

Compulsory acquisition—*continued*
nature of, **5**, 1
open spaces, **5**, 21, 39
owner, entitlement to claim compensation, **5**, 112
owner-occupier—
  home loss payment, entitlement to, **5**, 186
  meaning, **5**, 189n
  supplement—
    first owner, payment to, **5**, 192
    unfit house, paid in respect of, **5**, 190, 192
    well-maintained payment, effect of payment,
      5, 191
penalties, recovery of, **5**, 29
person aggrieved—
  compulsory purchase order challenged by, **5**, 79
  meaning, **5**, 79
planning permission, *see* PLANNING PERMISSION
procedure for assessment of compensation, **5**, 105
provisional orders, for, **7**, 19, 25; **19**, 12, 12n, 15
public local inquiry, *see* PUBLIC LOCAL INQUIRY
public rights of way, whether extinguishible, **18**,
  511
public telecommunications operator, by, **16**,
  1917, 1956
purchase notice, *see* PURCHASE NOTICE
rehousing, obligation to, **5**, 189
reorganisation payment on, **1**, 785
reverse, *see* REVERSE COMPULSORY ACQUISITION
servitudes—
  creation, **18**, 448, 463
  loss on, **18**, 479
severance—
  basis of assessment, **5**, 172
  injury to land, **5**, 171
  land taken and land retained, link between, **5**,
    170
  notice of objection to, **5**, 51
  other injurious affection distinguished, **5**, 169
  proposed compulsory acquisition involves, **5**,
    51
  short tenancy, **5**, 185
sheriff court jurisdiction, **6**, 1089
sheriff's duties in respect of, **6**, 1046
short tenancy, **5**, 185
statutory conveyance, *see* STATUTORY CONVEYANCE
statutory undertakers, by, **5**, 42, 43, 45
title, *see* TITLE (to property)
Town and Country Planning (Scotland) Act 1972
  ..., **8**, 1972
  See also TOWN AND COUNTRY PLANNING
    (SCOTLAND) ACT
treat, notice to, *see* TREAT, NOTICE TO
valuation—
  additional rules—
    depreciation—
      development value, in, **5**, 151
      use value, in, **5**, 151
      value of land, in, disregard of, **5**, 150
    generally, **5**, 149
    increase or decrease in value—
      disregard of, **5**, 152
      identification of scheme, **5**, 155
      Pointe Gourde principle, **5**, 153, 154
      value of land, effect of scheme on, **5**, 156

Compulsory acquisition—*continued*
valuation—*continued*
  arrangement of section, **5**, 118
  date—
    fixing, for, **5**, 117
    general rule, **5**, 119
    general vesting declarations, **5**, 121
    Lands Tribunal cases, **5**, 120
    meaning, **5**, 117
    relevant, importance of, **5**, 117
  depreciation—
    development value, in, **5**, 151
    set-off—
      adjoining land, increase in value of, **5**, 157
      double, avoidance of, **5**, 159
      increases disallowed, **5**, 158
    use value, in, **5**, 151
    value in land, in, disregard of, **5**, 150
  determination of interests to be valued—
    acquiring authority, increasing burden on, **5**,
      125
    change in nature of interest distinguished
      from change in value, **5**, 123
    generally, **5**, 122
    interests to be valued, **5**, 124
    scheme, interests in land and, **5**, 123
  development value—
    assumptions as to development—
      development plan, derived from, **5**, 143
      development for which land acquired, **5**,
        142
      existing use development, **5**, 141
      generally, **5**, 140
    certificates of appropriate alternative
      development, **5**, 144–148
    See also development *above*
    development potential, establishment of, **5**, 139
    nature of, **5**, 138
  physical and planning circumstances—
    certificates of appropriate alternative
      development, **5**, 130–132
    generally, **5**, 126
    physical factors, **5**, 127
    statutory rules and assumptions, **5**, 129
    town planning circumstances, **5**, 128
  scheme—
    identification of, **5**, 155
    increases or decreases in value due to—
      disregard of, **5**, 152
      identification of scheme, **5**, 155
      Pointe Gourde principle, **5**, 153–154
    interests in land and, **5**, 123
    value of land, effect on, **5**, 156
  value of land to be taken—
    equivalent reinstatement, reasonable cost of,
      5, 137
    open market, amount realised on, **5**, 134
    potential of land—
      generally, **5**, 135
      one purchaser only, **5**, 135
      public bodies as only purchasers, **5**, 135
      statutory powers, exercise of, achieved
        through, **5**, 135
    rules, generally, **5**, 133

Compulsory acquisition—*continued*
valuation—*continued*
  value of land to be taken—*continued*
    solatium, prohibition of payment of, **5**, 133
    use, proportion of market value resulting
      from, **5**, 136
Compulsory care order
child, *see* CHILD IN CARE
elderly person, **22**, 29
Compulsory labour
See FORCED LABOUR
Compulsory purchase
advance payment, **5**, 193
compulsory acquisition, *see* COMPULSORY
  ACQUISITION
confirming authority—
  decision, issue of, **5**, 74
  submission of order to, **5**, 62
dangerous building, **3**, 235
electricity, land used in connection with—
  compensation for, **9**, 657
  generally, **9**, 656
expropriation—
  entitlement to compensation for, **5**, 106
  regulation distinguished from, **5**, 197
involuntary transfer of ownership, as, **18**, 597,
  613, 663, 665
judicial review of, **1**, 296
land, of—
  compensation, **6**, 1141
  public telecommunications operator, by, **16**,
    1917, 1956
    disputes, **16**, 1956
    scat, **24**, 309
land which has passed through, position in feudal
  law, **18**, 68*n*, 70
Lands Clauses Acts, incorporation into modern
  code, **5**, 40
order—
  application to quash, **1**, 340–342
  confirmation of—
    confirming authority, submission to, **5**, 62
    generally, **5**, 75
    notice of, **5**, 76
  draft, **5**, 58
  making of—
    generally, **5**, 58
    notice of—
      generally, **5**, 60
      service of, **5**, 61
  mining code incorporated in, **5**, 34
  objections to—
    absence of, procedure in, **5**, 65
    generally, **5**, 63
    grounds for, **5**, 64
    receipt of, procedure after, **5**, 65
  occupier's liability where, **15**, 319
  recording, **5**, 82
  resolution to make, **5**, 57
  right of challenge—
    exercise of, **5**, 78
    grounds of, **5**, 77
    method of challenge, **5**, 77
    persons aggrieved, **5**, 79

Compulsory purchase—*continued*
order—*continued*
  Secretary of State, consent of, **14**, 105
  style of, **5**, 59
person aggrieved, **5**, 79
procedure—
  basic principle, **5**, 37
  common land, **5**, 39
  entry, **5**, 80
  exceptions, **5**, 37
  generally, **5**, 56
  Lands Clauses Acts, incorporation of, **5**, 40
  National Trust land, **5**, 38
  open space, **5**, 39
  Railways Clauses Act, incorporation of, **5**, 41
  regulation, **5**, 36
  rights of way, **5**, 42
  statutory undertakers, land acquired by, **5**, 43
public local inquiry—
  evidence at, **5**, 70
  expenses, **5**, 72
  government representation, **5**, 69
  holding of, **5**, 66
  new material, **5**, 71
  procedure at, **5**, 67
  report of, **5**, 73
  right to be heard, **5**, 68; **23**, 921
Railways Clauses Act, incorporation into modern
  code, **5**, 41
  general vesting declaration, application to, **5**,
    48
  generally, **5**, 32
  injurious affection, compensation for, **5**, 33
  mining code, **5**, 34
real burdens, effect on, **18**, 436
rights of way, order extinguishing, **5**, 42
short tenancies, **5**, 185
statutory undertakers—
  land acquired by, **5**, 43
  rights of way, consent to order extinguishing,
    5, 42
sub-standard housing, **6**, 1141
tenant at will, rights of, **18**, 72
time limit, **5**, 25
Compulsory residence
European Convention on Human Rights, **12**, 40
Compurgation
trial by, **17**, 541
Computer
capital item for VAT, **7**, 1380
counterfeiting of, **6**, 118
data protection, *see* DATA PROTECTION
fraud, **7**, 387
hacking, **7**, 387
meaning, **18**, 1502*n*
semiconductor topographies, *see* SEMICONDUCTOR
  TOPOGRAPHIES
value added telecommunications services, **16**,
  1950
word processing, data protection in relation to,
  18, 1502
Computer bureau
meaning, **18**, 1504
occasional basis, conduct of activities on, **18**, 1504

Computer bureau—*continued*
registration—
amendment, **18**, 1510
application, **18**, 1510
fee, **18**, 1510
information to be supplied, **18**, 1510
renewal, **18**, 1510
requirement for, **18**, 1509
See also DATA PROTECTION (DATA PROTECTION REGISTER)
Computer generated work
copyright—
author—
meaning, **18**, 979
problems arising, **18**, 993
moral rights, **18**, 1134, 1136
evidence, in, **10**, 607
unregistered design right—
author, **18**, 1221
semiconductor topographies, **18**, 1247
Computer industry
growth of, **14**, 1006
leasing terms, **14**, 1006
operating leasing, **14**, 1020
Computer program
copyright, **18**, 931, 1023
adaptation, **18**, 1065
infringement—
problems arising, **18**, 1051
transient copies, **18**, 1052
literary work, computer program as, **18**, 950, 954
moral rights, **18**, 1134, 1136
originality, **18**, 941
rental rights, **18**, 1059
See also LITERARY WORK
European Community legislation, **18**, 1611
patent may not be granted in respect of, **18**, 825
translation, meaning, **18**, 1065
Concealment
active, fraudulent misrepresentation by, **11**, 711
Concealment of pregnancy
art and part guilt, **7**, 293
birth, neglect to obtain assistance at, **7**, 291, 292
concealment, what constitutes, **7**, 292
Concealment of Birth (Scotland) Act 1809 ..., **7**, 291
elements of crime, **7**, 292
general, **10**, 1031
historical background, **7**, 290
length of pregnancy, **7**, 292
mens rea, **7**, 292
pregnancy must be shown to have occured, **7**, 292
Concentrations
European Community rules on competition, **10**, 165
Concert
accused, between, art and part liability, **7**, 189
Concert party
arrangements for notifying, **4**, 346
company investigation, **4**, 515
Takeover Panel, judicial review of decisions of, **4**, 542
Concessionary travel
See PUBLIC TRANSPORT

Conciliation
conciliation commissions, settlement of international disputes by, **19**, 714, 718
divorce, action for, **17**, 1215
Institution of Civil Engineers procedure, **3**, 170
See also ADVISORY, CONCILIATION AND ARBITRATION SERVICE
Concrete
ready-mixed, sale of, **6**, 238
Concussion
automatism, as cause of, **7**, 151
Condemnation
decree of, **17**, 428
enforcement, **17**, 428
restraint of princes, as, **21**, 550
sentence, effect of, **17**, 427
Condescendence
articles of, **17**, 1374
writ, prescribed form of, **17**, 1009
Conditio causa data causa non secuta
restitution, **15**, 45, 46
See also REPETITION
Condictio indebiti
restitution, **15**, 45, 46
See also REPETITION
Conditio si institutus sine liberis decesserit
accretion considered subject to, **25**, 838, 842
after-born child, for benefit of, **25**, 752
application of, **25**, 753
close relatives, **25**, 896
deeds, **25**, 895
direct descendants, outside, **25**, 897
generally, **25**, 894
factors unfavourable—
generally, **25**, 898
original share, issue take only, **25**, 901
relationship, bequest must be motivated by, **25**, 900
testator's intention, **25**, 899
principle, **25**, 751
rebuttal of presumption, **25**, 754
share taken as result of, **25**, 842
Condition of the right
See REAL BURDEN
Conditional obligation
casual conditions, **15**, 6
meaning, **15**, 5
mixed conditions, **15**, 6
potestative conditions, **15**, 6
purification, **15**, 6
resolutive condition, **15**, 5
suspensive condition, **15**, 5
Conditional sale agreement
assignation of rights under, **7**, 1290
buyer disposing of property under, **20**, 855
capital allowances, **14**, 1011
court, special powers of, **5**, 929
goods subject to, entry to repossess, **5**, 892
health and safety, **14**, 1051
heritable property, recovery of possession of, **5**, 893
lease distinguished from, **14**, 1007
meaning, **5**, 805
motor vehicle subject to, sale, **15**, 52

Conditional sale agreement—*continued*
motor vehicle under, *nemo dat quod non habet* rule,
  exception to, **18**, 683
protected goods, recovery of, **5**, 891
repeal of legislation, **5**, 801
restricted-use credit agreement, as, **5**, 809
termination by debtor—
  landlord's hypothec, operation of, **5**, 903
  liability on, **5**, 902
  right to terminate, **5**, 901
Conditions, deeds of
construction and interpretation, **12**, 1260
Conduct
approval and disapproval of, **11**, 1007
dismissal, reason for, **9**, 245
disorderly, exclusion from local authority meeting
  due to, **14**, 1334
employer-employee relationship, **9**, 245
fraudulent, nature of, **11**, 708, 723–729
  carelessness, effect of, **11**, 728
  fraudulent misrepresentation, **11**, 723, 724
  mens rea of fraud, **11**, 725–729
law as guide, **11**, 1006
lawful and unlawful, **11**, 1006–1013
legally wrongful, **11**, 1010
local government code of conduct, **14**, 232
rights in regard to, **11**, 1073–1090
  personal conduct, **11**, 1081
statements as to future, trade descriptions, **6**, 130
unreasonableness, **11**, 728
values, plurality of, **11**, 1008
virtue and vice distinguished, **11**, 1007
Confectionery
alcoholic liquor in, sale of, **2**, 80
baker's confectionery filling, **11**, 408, 410
labelling, **11**, 383, 387
mineral hydrocarbons, treatment with, **11**, 375
Conference of European Post and
  Telecommunications Administrations
  (CEPT)
generally, **16**, 1974
Conference on Security and Co-operation
  in Europe
human rights and fundamental freedoms, respect
  for, **12**, 4
Confession
advocate's duties as to, **13**, 1364, 1366
co-accused by, **10**, 726
corroboration, **10**, 770
extra-judicial, admissibility of—
  circumstances and manner of questioning, **10**,
    733
  determination of, **10**, 745
  different charge, statements made in relation to,
    10, 743
  generally, **10**, 722, 729
  implied, **10**, 725
  inadmissible confession, evidence obtained as
    result of, **10**, 734
  initial investigation, **10**, 730
  intercepted documents, statements in, **10**, 740
  judicial admissions distinguished, **10**, 513
  judicial discretion, **10**, 508
  overheard statements, **10**, 739

Confession—*continued*
extra-judicial, admissibility of—*continued*
  previous malice, statements inferring, **10**, 744
  prison officers, statements made to, **10**, 737
  private persons, statements made to, **10**, 738
  proof and probative value, **10**, 723
  public officials, statements made to, **10**, 737
  stage of suspicion, **10**, 731
  statements in another case, **10**, 724
  statements made after arrest, **10**, 732
  tape-recorded police interviews, **10**, 735
  trial-within-a-trial, **10**, 745
  unconscious, statements made while, **10**, 741
  unfairness, **10**, 505
  vicarious, **10**, 726
Confession of Faith
copyright, **18**, 1002
Confessor (Roman Catholic Church)
violation of seal of, **3**, 1658, 1667
Confidence, breach of
See BREACH OF CONFIDENCE
Confidential information
breach of confidence, *see* BREACH OF CONFIDENCE
intellectual property, and, **18**, 1452
property, as, **18**, 1453
protection, generally, **18**, 1451
restraint of trade, protectable interests, **15**, 773
Confidentiality
advocate, duty of, **13**, 1355
medical practitioner, owed by, **14**, 1131
privilege—
  accountants, **10**, 686
  bankers, **10**, 686
  business advisers, **10**, 686
  clergyman and penitent, **10**, 685
  doctor and patient, **10**, 686
  general rules, **10**, 676
  litigation, communications concerning—
    generally, **10**, 681
    legal adviser and client, **10**, 682
    negotiations for settlement, privileges in aid
      of, **10**, 684
    post litem motam made, **10**, 683
  marital intercourse, concerning, **10**, 680
  professional personal advisers, **10**, 686
  public policy, evidence excluded for reasons of,
    10, 687–689
  spouses, communications between—
    civil proceedings, **10**, 678
    criminal proceedings, **10**, 679
    generally, **10**, 677
Confinement
See MATERNITY RIGHTS
Confirmation
charter of—
  feudal conveyance, **18**, 58, 94, 99, 103, 393
executor-creditor, as, *see* EXECUTOR-CREDITOR
grant of, to executor-creditor, unintimated
  assignation defeated by, **20**, 47
papers to found or oppose application,
  unqualified person drawing or preparing, **13**,
  1182, 1184
solicitor's role, **13**, 1184
See also ADMINISTRATION OF ESTATES

Confirmation Bill
introduction of—
  notice of, **19**, 69
  proceedings on, **19**, 70
joint committee—
  not referred to, **19**, 74
  proceedings after, **19**, 77
  proceedings in, **19**, 76
  referred to, **19**, 75
private business—
  as, **19**, 64
  deferred, **19**, 66
  House of Lords, **19**, 68, 72
  opposed, **19**, 67
  unopposed, **19**, 65
provisional order—
  opposed, **19**, 73–77
  unopposed, **19**, 71, 72
Confiscation
foreign expropriatory claims, **17**, 329
Confiscation order
drug trafficking, relating to, **14**, 1255
Conflict of laws
private international law as term for, **19**, 604
See also PRIVATE INTERNATIONAL LAW
Confusion
accession compared, **18**, 571*n*
common property, original acquisition, **18**, 22*n*
contractual obligation extinguished by, **15**, 865, 876
corporeal moveable property, **18**, 539, 564
doctrine of, loss of real right through, **18**, 9
meaning, **18**, 564
original acquisition, as, **18**, 22*n*, 597
ownership, principles governing, **18**, 564
Conies
See RABBITS
Conjoined arrestment order
See EARNINGS
Connected person
building societies—
  disclosure of interests, **3**, 405, 405*n*
  register of transactions, **3**, 405
meaning, **4**, 420
Conquest
feudal law, generally, **18**, 56
meaning, **18**, 56
territory, of, **19**, 668, 700*n*
Consanguinity
relationship by, capacity to marry, **10**, 817, 1219
  half-blood, **10**, 817
  illegitimacy, **10**, 817
Conscience, freedom of
European Convention on Human Rights, **12**, 6, 72
restrictions on, **12**, 78–84
Universal Declaration of Human Rights, **12**, 4, 4*n*
Consensus in idem
dissensus, **11**, 705
fraud preventing, **11**, 705
lease, as cardinal element of, **13**, 104, 105
test for, **11**, 705

Consent
acquiescence—
  implied consent, as, **16**, 1615
  inferred from, **16**, 1615
  parties whose consent binds, **16**, 1616
fraud as factor vitiating, **11**, 707–714
  active concealment, **11**, 711
  conduct, nature of, **11**, 708
  false statements, **11**, 709
  material error, inducement of, **11**, 713
  non-disclosure, **11**, 712
  positive acts, **11**, 710
  remedies, **11**, 714
medical treatment, to, **14**, 1130
pollution, consent system, *see* POLLUTION
private international law—
  contract, in, **17**, 269
  marriage, requirement of, **17**, 229
Conservancy authority
limitation of liability, **21**, 753*n*, 769, 769*n*
meaning, **21**, 769*n*
wreck, removal of, **21**, 514
Conservation
ancient monuments, *see* ANCIENT MONUMENTS
archaeological areas, *see* ARCHAEOLOGICAL AREAS
Conservation of Seals Act 1970 …, **11**, 220
countryside, **9**, 1232
  See also COUNTRYSIDE
deer, **11**, 929
forestry, advisory committees, **11**, 612
Forestry Commission, duty of, **11**, 606, 607
fuel and power, of, building controls, **3**, 208
generally, **19**, 303, 1106; **25**, 389
high seas, fish stocks in, **11**, 89, 90
historic buildings, *see* HISTORIC BUILDINGS
international fishery commissions, **11**, 67
landing of foreign-caught fish, **11**, 144, 150
making and maintaining shellfish beds, **11**, 157
nets and gear, regulations and conventions, **11**, 89, 146
rural environment, of, *see* COUNTRYSIDE
salmon—
  act or omission relating to salmon, salmon roe or salmon eggs, **11**, 13, 43
  Convention for the Conservation of Salmon in the North Atlantic Ocean, **11**, 103
  North Atlantic, **11**, 67, 101–105
  North Atlantic Salmon Conservation Organisation, **11**, 67, 104, 105
  stocks of, **11**, 89, 90
scientific research, **11**, 68
sea fish, of, **11**, 144–154
  bodies corporate, offences by, **11**, 153
  enforcement, **11**, 154
  European Community measures, **11**, 67
  exclusive economic zone, **11**, 107
  exploration and exploitation interfering with, **11**, 85
  foreign-caught sea fish, regulation of landing, **11**, 144, 150
  high seas, stocks in, **11**, 89, 90
  increase or improvement of marine resources measures for, **11**, 151
  restrictions on fishing for sea fish, **11**, 148

Conservation—*continued*
sea fish, of—*continued*
  scientific research, **11**, 68
  Sea Fish (Conservation) Act 1967 …, **11**, 144
  size limits for fish, **11**, 144, 145
  trans-shipment of fish, prohibition on, **11**, 44, 147, 149
seals, **11**, 220
shellfish fisheries, **11**, 161, 162
trans-shipment of fish, **11**, 144, 147, 149
United Nations Convention on the Law of the Sea, **11**, 82, 84, 106–109
urban, **9**, 1217
water—
  byelaws, **25**, 390
  compensation for interference with supply, **25**, 393
  misuse of water, prevention of, **25**, 525, 527
  prohibition of use, **25**, 391
  restriction of use, **25**, 391
  Secretary of State, duties of, **25**, 503
wild birds or animals killed or taken in interests of, **11**, 881, 883, 885, 886
wrecks—
  dangerous, prohibition on approaching, **9**, 1231
  historic, protection of sites of, **9**, 1230
Conservation area
advertisement, control of, **23**, 201
consent, Crown land, **23**, 107
demolition of building in, **23**, 73, 283
designation of, **23**, 189
enhancement of, **23**, 191
grants, **23**, 192
meaning, **23**, 142*n*, 189*n*
planning application, publicity for, **23**, 164
protection in, **23**, 190
satellite antenna, installation of, **23**, 142
simplified planning zone scheme, exclusion from, **23**, 119
tree, in, **23**, 190
Conservative Party
annual conference, **5**, 392
constituency association, **5**, 392
executive committee, **5**, 392
functions of, **5**, 392
organisation of, **5**, 392
work of, **5**, 392
Conservatory
exemptions from building regulations, **3**, 209
Consideration
Scots and English law, **3**, 804
Consignations
arrestment, **8**, 273
Consignment note
British Rail General Conditions, **3**, 696
Convention on the Contract for the International Carriage of Goods by Road (CMR), **3**, 647, 648, 649
  declaration of value, **3**, 657
international carriage of goods by train, **3**, 706
requirement for, **3**, 619
Consistorial causes
divorce, *see* DIVORCE
expenses, **17**, 1193

Consistorial causes—*continued*
jurisdiction—
  Court of Session, **4**, 5
  sheriff court, **4**, 5; **6**, 1060
procedure—
  Court of Session, **17**, 1392, 1406
  sheriff court, **17**, 1222–1233
Consolidated Fund
expenditure from, **7**, 766
judicial salaries charged on, **6**, 863
payment into, **7**, 766
Consolidated Fund Bill
House of Lords may not amend, **7**, 768
royal assent, **7**, 768
Consolidated loans fund
establishment of, **14**, 813
Consolidation
feudal conveyance, generally, **18**, 98
Consolidation Acts
interpretation and construction of statutes, **12**, 1148, 1158
Conspiracy
actus reus, **7**, 171
attempted, **7**, 170, 173
criminalisation, objective, **7**, 173
definition, **7**, 171
economic delict of—
  generally, **15**, 581
  lawful means, **15**, 582
  unlawful means, **15**, 583
generally, **7**, 171
impossible objective, where, **7**, 174
inchoate crime, as, **7**, 160
mens rea, **7**, 171
prior agreement, **7**, 171, 172
state, offence against, **7**, 594
  sedition, and, **7**, 594
two or more persons, as agreement of, **7**, 171
types, **7**, 172
Constable
appointment of, **14**, 28
duties, **14**, 28
Officer of State, **7**, 790
Constabulary courts
jurisdiction, **6**, 1022
Constituency
boundaries—
  Boundary Commission, **15**, 1029, 1037
  historical background, **15**, 1028, 1029
  burgh, **15**, 1002, 1007, 1015, 1016, 1037
  county, **15**, 1015, 1016, 1037
distinct communities, as, **5**, 373
European Parliament, **15**, 1036, 1038
  number, **15**, 1038
franchise, *see* FRANCHISE
general review of, **5**, 373
meaning, **15**, 1037
number of, **5**, 373
polling districts, **15**, 1304
redistribution of seats, **5**, 373
register of electors, supply to, **15**, 1114
representation, **5**, 373

Constituency—*continued*
United Kingdom Parliament, **15**, 1032, 1036, 1037
  boundary reviews, **15**, 1037
  number, **15**, 1037
university, **15**, 1016, 1028
Constitution
British, *see* BRITISH CONSTITUTION
Canadian, *see* CANADA
conventions of, **5**, 306
flexible, **5**, 307
French, *see* FRANCE
peerage as part of, **16**, 1301
rigid, **5**, 306, 307
single document, generally in, **5**, 303
United States, of, *see* UNITED STATES OF AMERICA
West German, **5**, 303
Constitutional law
administrative law, and, **1**, 201
Bill of Rights, **5**, 317–319
  See also BILL OF RIGHTS
British constitution, characteristics of, **5**, 302, 305
church and state, **5**, 679–705
constitutions of other countries, **5**, 303–307
devolution, repealed proposals for, **5**, 332–337
European Communities Acts 1972—
  effect of, **5**, 310
European Community, accession to, **5**, 320–329
  See also EUROPEAN COMMUNITY LAW
executive, **5**, 471–621
fundamental law, **5**, 338–360
human rights, **5**, 213–216
judicial review, **5**, 330, 331
judiciary, **5**, 622–674
Parliament—
  generally, **5**, 361–387
  self-limitation by, **5**, 352–354
  sovereignty of, **5**, 308–312, 342
  See also HOUSE OF COMMONS; HOUSE OF LORDS
political parties in Scotland, **5**, 388–396
pretensions of English law as 'imperial law', **5**, 711–719
Principality of Scotland, **5**, 706–710
retrospective legislation, **5**, 311
separation of powers, **5**, 341
Union Agreement of 1707, *see* UNION AGREEMENT OF 1707
***Constitutum possessorium* (possessory declaration or agreement)**
concept of, **18**, 532
Construction
deed, of, *see* DEED
statute, of, *see* STATUTE
Construction law
case law, **3**, 3, 4
claims and dispute resolution, **3**, 166*ff*
  prescription and time limits, **3**, 174, 175
  terminus a quo, **3**, 175
custom, **3**, 4
equity, **3**, 4
generally, **3**, 3
historical introduction, **3**, 1
institutional writings, **3**, 4
law reports, **3**, 4
periodicals, **3**, 4

Construction law—*continued*
reference works, **3**, 4
sources, **3**, 4
statute law, **3**, 4
Construction services
self-supply, **7**, 1301, 1304
  VAT input tax, **7**, 1374
Construction work
construction or maintenance work, meaning, **14**, 903
construction site—
  noise on—
    appeal against notice as to, **9**, 1254
    generally, **9**, 1253
  prior consent for work on—
    appeal as to, **9**, 1256
    generally, **9**, 1255
extra policing where, **14**, 492; **16**, 1738
house required for, **13**, 749, 755
sanctions imposed by Secretary of State, **14**, 913
See also BUILDING CONTRACT; BUILDING AND BUILDING CONTROLS
Constructive notice
doctrine of, **4**, 326
Constructive trust
See TRUST
Constructive violence
generally, **7**, 245
Consul
family of, **12**, 130
immigration control, **12**, 130
precedence, **16**, 2014, 2015
Consular relations
Convention on Special Missions, **19**, 684
immunities and privileges of consular staff, **19**, 684
severance of, between parties to treaty, **19**, 632
Vienna Conventions on, **19**, 684
Consultative Committee of Accountancy Bodies
creation of, **1**, 12
Consultative Council of the Bars and Law Societies of the European Community
Faculty of Advocates, affiliation with, **13**, 1302
Consumer
meaning, **4**, 54, 56
sovereignty of, **4**, 1102
welfare—
  perfect competition, maximised in conditions of, **4**, 1102
  short-term benefits outweighed by long-term harm to, **4**, 1105
Consumer contract
meaning, **6**, 33; **14**, 1052; **15**, 727, 730
Unfair Terms in Consumer Contracts Regulations 1994, **15**, 738–752
See also CONTRACT
Consumer credit
Act of 1974, *see* CONSUMER CREDIT ACT
advertising, **1**, 553; **6**, 80; **17**, 45
agreement, *see* CONSUMER CREDIT AGREEMENT
business—
  ancillary credit, *see* ANCILLARY CREDIT BUSINESS
  consumer, disclosure of information, alternative procedure for, **5**, 958

Consumer credit—*continued*
business—*continued*
 licensing of, *see* licensing *below*
 seeking—
  advertising—
   advertisements—
    content of, **5**, 829
    exempt, **5**, 828
    form of, **5**, 829
    ancillary credit business, in relation to, **5**,
     830
    generally, **5**, 827
    offences relating to, **5**, 831
   brokerage fees, recovery of, **5**, 840
   business regulations, conduct of, **5**, 839
   canvassing—
    ancillary credit business, **5**, 833
    consumer hire agreement, **5**, 832
    debtor-creditor agreement, **5**, 832
    debtor-creditor-supplier agreement, **5**, 832
    minor, circular to, **5**, 834
    off trade premises, **5**, 832
    unsolicited credit-token, **5**, 835
   display of information, **5**, 838
   quotations—
    content of, **5**, 837
    form of, **5**, 837
    provision of, **5**, 836
   statutory control generally, **5**, 826
 charge card, nature of, **4**, 270
 cheque guarantee card, nature of, **4**, 268
 consumer protection generally, **6**, 1, 9
 credit, generally, *see* CREDIT
 credit brokerage, **5**, 816
 credit card, nature of, **4**, 270
 credit reference agency, *see* CREDIT REFERENCE
  AGENCY
 credit transaction, *see* CREDIT TRANSACTION
 credit-sale agreement, **5**, 805, 809
 credit-token, *see* CREDIT TOKEN
 creditor, *see* CREDITOR
 debtor, *see* DEBTOR
 debtor-creditor agreement, **5**, 810, 832
 debtor-creditor-supplier agreement, **5**, 810, 832
 default, *see* CREDITOR
 enforcement—
  authorities, **5**, 959
  defences, **5**, 964
  further sanctions, **5**, 962
  offences—
   bodies corporate, **5**, 961
   generally, **5**, 960
   penalties for, **5**, 965
  onus of proof, **5**, 963
  order, **5**, 925
  security, **5**, 922
  unlicensed trader, agreements made by, **5**, 953
 extortionate credit bargain—
  nature of, **5**, 932
  reopening of agreement, **5**, 933
 statutory contracts, **14**, 1050
 federal credit union, exempt agreement, **5**, 531
 fees—
  brokerage, recovery of, **5**, 840

Consumer credit—*continued*
 fees—*continued*
  Director General of Fair Trading, **5**, 803
  register, in respect of, **5**, 951
 financial relief, on repossession of goods, **5**, 928
 fixed-sum credit—
  information, right to, **5**, 873
  meaning, **5**, 808
  running-account credit distinguished, **5**, 808
 foreign connection, exempt agreement with, **5**,
  824
 friendly society, exempt agreement, **5**, 821
 goods—
  cancellation, consequences of, **5**, 869–870
  entry in order to repossess, **5**, 892
  part exchange, given in, **5**, 870
  protected, recovery of, **5**, 891
  repossession, **5**, 891, 892, 928
  return of, **5**, 869
  whereabouts, information on, **5**, 879
 heritable property—
  exempt agreement relating to, **5**, 821
  prospective agreement secured on, withdrawal
   from, **5**, 861
  recovery of possession on, **5**, 893
 hire-purchase agreement, *see* HIRE-PURCHASE
  AGREEMENT
 hirer, *see* HIRER
 hypothec, *see* HYPOTHEC
 information—
  display of, **5**, 838
  pre-contract disclosure, **5**, 846
  right to—
   consumer credit, **5**, 873
   fixed-sum credit, **5**, 873
   running-account credit, **5**, 873, 874
  security instrument, relating to, provision of, **5**,
   910
  whereabouts of goods, on, **5**, 879
  See also CREDIT REFERENCE AGENCY
 judicial control—
  conditional sale agreement, special powers in
   relation to, **5**, 929
  extortionate credit bargain—
   nature of, **5**, 932
   reopening of agreement, **5**, 933
  generally, **5**, 923
  hire-purchase agreement, special powers in
   relation to, **5**, 929
  jurisdiction, **5**, 924
  orders—
   conditions, imposition of, **5**, 930
   enforcement, **5**, 925
   protection, **5**, 927
   suspension of operation of, **5**, 930
   time, **5**, 926
  parties—
   declaration of rights of, **5**, 931
   generally, **5**, 924
  reposession of goods, financial relief for hirer,
   5, 928
 land improvement company, exempt agreement,
  5, 821

Consumer credit—*continued*
legal regulation of—
Consumer Credit Act 1974, *see* CONSUMER CREDIT ACT
Director General of Fair Trading, **5**, 803
general law of contract, application of, **5**, 802
generally, **5**, 801–803
judicial control, *see* judicial control *above*
repeal of legislation, **5**, 801
legislation, **6**, 73
licensing—
generally, **5**, 934
licence—
application for, **5**, 939
classification of, **5**, 936–938
determination of applications, **5**, 944
fitness to hold, **5**, 941
group—
generally, **5**, 937
issue of, **5**, 943
issue of—
group licence, **5**, 943
standard licence, **5**, 940
renewal, **5**, 946
requirement of, **5**, 935
revocation, **5**, 948
specific activities, authorisation of, **5**, 938
standard—
generally, **5**, 936
issue of, **5**, 940
misleading trading name, **5**, 942
suspension—
application to end, **5**, 949
compulsory, **5**, 948
variation—
compulsory, **5**, 948
request, on, **5**, 947
licensee—
bankruptcy, **5**, 950
conduct of business by, **5**, 945
death of, **5**, 950
linked transactions—
early settlement, effect of, **5**, 900
meaning, **5**, 815
security, transactions for provision of, exclusion, **5**, 815
local authority, exempt agreement, **5**, 821
multiple agreement—
exclusion from operation of Act, **5**, 814
form and content, **5**, 851
meaning, **5**, 814
notice—
before taking certain actions, duty to give, **5**, 880
cancellation, **5**, 865–866
rescission, **5**, 906
offences—
advertising, relating to, **5**, 831
circulars to minors, **5**, 834
enforcement, relating to—
bodies corporate, **5**, 961
defences, **5**, 964
generally, **5**, 960
penalties, **5**, 965
unsolicited credit-tokens, **5**, 835

Consumer credit—*continued*
orders—
enforcement, **5**, 925
protection, **5**, 927
time, **5**, 926
overdraft facility as unrestricted-use credit agreement, **5**, 809
owner, variation by, **5**, 809
part exchange, goods given in, **5**, 870
personal credit agreement, **5**, 806, 808
personal loan as unrestricted-use credit agreement, **5**, 809
pledge—
generally, **5**, 912
pawn—
agreement to take article in, **5**, 913
delivery of, **5**, 917
failure to redeem, consequences of, **5**, 918
realisation of, **5**, 919
receipt, loss of, **5**, 916
redemption—
period, **5**, 914
procedure, **5**, 915
security, as, **5**, 908
professional rules, contravention, **16**, 1017
protected goods, **5**, 891
protection order, **5**, 927
rebate on early settlement—
calculation of, **5**, 899
entitlement to, **5**, 898
generally, **5**, 897
register—
changes, duty to notify, **5**, 952
fees, **5**, 951
maintenance of, **5**, 951
matters required to be registered, **5**, 951
unlicensed trader, enforceability of agreements made by, **5**, 953
restricted-use credit agreement, **5**, 809
running-account credit, **5**, 808, 873, 874
security—
content of, **5**, 909
enforcement of, **5**, 922
evasion of Consumer Credit Act 1974 by use of, prohibition of, **5**, 911
form of, **5**, 909
instrument—
information relating to, provision of, **5**, 910
negotiable—
non-compliance, consequences of, **5**, 921
restrictions on use of, **5**, 920
supply of copy of, **5**, 877
meaning, **5**, 908
pledge, *see* pledge *above*
realisation of, **5**, 922
settlement—
early, **5**, 896–900
statement, **5**, 875
sheriff court jurisdiction, **6**, 1107
small agreement, **5**, 813
standard licence, **5**, 936, 940
statement—
periodic, **5**, 874

Consumer credit—*continued*
statement—*continued*
  settlement, **5**, 875
  termination, **5**, 907
supplier—
  breach of contract by, **5**, 871, 872
  misrepresentation by, **5**, 871, 872
surety—
  information, right to, **5**, 878
  meaning, **5**, 908
termination—
  creditor, by, non-default cases, **5**, 895
  debtor, by—
    landlord's hypothec, operation of, **5**, 903
    liability of, **5**, 902
    right to terminate, **5**, 901
  default distinguished from, **5**, 888
  hirer, by—
    liability on, **5**, 905
    right to terminate, **5**, 904
  statement, **5**, 907
time order, **5**, 926
Tribunal, functions, **23**, 902
unrestricted-use credit agreement, **5**, 809
variation of agreement, **5**, 882, 883
workers' organisation, exempt agreement, **5**, 821
See also CONSUMER CREDIT AGREEMENT; CONSUMER
  HIRE AGREEMENT
Consumer Credit Act 1974
background to, **5**, 801
comprehensive review of law preceding, **5**, 801
credit transaction, types of—
  agreement—
    consumer credit, **5**, 806
    consumer hire, **5**, 812
    credit-token, **5**, 811
    debtor-creditor, **5**, 810
    debtor-creditor-supplier, **5**, 810
    multiple, **5**, 814
    restricted-use credit, **5**, 809
    small, **5**, 813
    unrestricted-use credit, **5**, 809
  ancillary credit business, **5**, 816
  credit—
    fixed-sum, **5**, 808
    meaning, **5**, 807
    restricted-use, **5**, 809
    running-account, **5**, 808
    unrestricted-use, **5**, 809
  linked transactions, **5**, 815
  main types, distinctions between, **5**, 805
default—
  creditors' remedies for, restrictions on—
    entry in order to repossess goods, **5**, 892
    heritable property, recovery of possession of,
      5, 893
    interest on default, **5**, 894
    protected goods, recovery of, **5**, 891
  interest on, **5**, 894
  notice—
    content of, **5**, 890
    form of, **5**, 890
    need for, **5**, 889
  termination distinguished from, **5**, 888

Consumer Credit Act 1974—*continued*
entry into agreement—
  consumer credit, *see* CONSUMER CREDIT
    AGREEMENT
  consumer hire, *see* CONSUMER HIRE AGREEMENT
exempt agreements—
  consumer hire, **5**, 825
  foreign connection, with, **5**, 824
  generally, **5**, 820
  heritable property, relating to, **5**, 821
  number of payments, exempt by reference to,
    5, 822
  total charge for credit, exempt by reference to
    rate of, **5**, 823
judicial control—
  quotations—
    content, **5**, 837
    form, **5**, 837
    provision of, **5**, 836
law extensively reformulated by, **5**, 801
Part V, scope of—
  ancillary credit agreement, **5**, 845
  antecedent negotiations, **5**, 847
  exempt agreements, **5**, 843
  future agreement, agreement to enter into, **5**,
    844
  generally, **5**, 842
  pre-contract disclosure, **5**, 846
provisions, when operational, **5**, 802
quotations—
  content, **5**, 837
  form, **5**, 837
  provision of, **5**, 836
register—
  changes, duty to notify, **5**, 952
  fees, **5**, 951
  maintenance of, **5**, 951
  matters required to be registered, **5**, 951
  unlicensed trader, enforceability of agreements
    made by, **5**, 953
rights in security, transactions Act applicable to—
  cancellation of agreement, **20**, 40
  creditor, extent of benefit to, **20**, 40
  failure to comply with requirements, **20**, 38
  generally, **20**, 36
  information, creditor's duty to give, **20**, 39
  negotiable instruments, **20**, 22
  pledges, **20**, 21
  related securities, **20**, 40
  requirements as to, **20**, 37
  termination of agreement, **20**, 40
scope of, **5**, 802
security—
  content of, **5**, 909
  enforcement of, **5**, 955
  evasion of Consumer Credit Act 1974 by use
    of, **5**, 911
  form of, **5**, 909
  instrument—
    negotiable—
      consequences of non-compliance, **5**, 921
      restrictions on use of, **5**, 920
    provision of information relating to, **5**, 920
    supply of copy of, **5**, 877

Consumer Credit Act 1974—*continued*
security—*continued*
  meaning, **5**, 908
  pledge, *see* PLEDGE
  realisation of, **5**, 922
seeking business, **5**, 839
  advertising—
    ancillary credit business, in relation to, **5**, 830
    content of advertisements, **5**, 829
    exempt advertisements, **5**, 828
    form of advertisements, **5**, 829
    generally, **5**, 827
    offences relating to, **5**, 831
  brokerage fees, recovery of, **5**, 840
  business regulations, conduct of, **5**, 839
  canvassing—
    ancillary credit business, **5**, 833
    consumer hire agreement, **5**, 832
    debtor-creditor agreement, **5**, 832
    debtor-creditor-supplier agreement, **5**, 832
    minor, circular to, **5**, 834
    off trade premises, **5**, 832
    unsolicited credit-tokens, **5**, 835
  display of business, **5**, 838
  quotations—
    content of, **5**, 837
    form of, **5**, 837
    provision of, **5**, 836
  statutory control generally, **5**, 826
subordinate legislation, **5**, 802
termination—
  creditor, by, non-default cases, **5**, 895
  debtor, by—
    landlord's hypothec, **5**, 903
    liability of, **5**, 902
    right to terminate, **5**, 901
  default distinguished, **5**, 888
  hirer, by—
    liability on, **5**, 905
    right to terminate, **5**, 904
    statement, **5**, 907
terminology generally, **5**, 804
terms of, **5**, 801
total charge for credit—
  computation of—
    annual percentage rate, **5**, 819
    generally, **5**, 818
    tables, **5**, 819
generally, **5**, 8
Consumer credit agreement
agreement regulations, **5**, 849
ancillary credit agreement, **5**, 845
armed forces, exempt agreement with member of, **5**, 824
bank loan as unrestricted-use credit agreement, **5**, 809
body corporate—
  exempt agreement, **5**, 821
  offences by, **5**, 961
breach of contract—
  supplier, by—
    creditor, liability of, **5**, 872
    generally, **5**, 871
brokerage fees, recovery of, **5**, 840

Consumer credit agreement—*continued*
building society, exempt agreement, **5**, 821
cancellation of—
  cancellable agreements, **5**, 863
  consequences of—
    credit, repayment of, **5**, 868
    debtor, recovery of payments by, **5**, 867
    goods—
      part exchange, given in, **5**, 870
      return of, **5**, 869
    hirer, recovery of payments by, **5**, 867
  cooling-off period within, **5**, 862–866
  generally, **5**, 862
  notice of—
    effect of, **5**, 866
    generally, **5**, 865
  rights, duty to give notice of, **5**, 857
canvassing—
  ancillary credit business, **5**, 833
  circulars to minors, **5**, 834
  consumer hire agreement, **5**, 832
  debtor-creditor agreement, **5**, 832
  debtor-creditor-supplier agreement, **5**, 832
  off trade premises, **5**, 832
  statutory controls, **14**, 1050
  unsolicited credit-token, **5**, 835
computation—
  total charge for credit, of—
    annual percentage rate, **5**, 819
    generally, **5**, 818
conditional sale agreement, *see* CONDITIONAL SALE AGREEMENT
Consumer Credit Act 1974 ..., **2**, 1974
Consumer Credit Act 1974, *see* CONSUMER CREDIT ACT
credit facilities, liability for misuse of, **5**, 884–885
credit tokens, new, issue of, **5**, 886
debtor, death of, **5**, 887
early settlement by debtor—
  linked transactions, effect on, **5**, 900
  rebate on—
    calculation of, **5**, 899
    entitlement to, **5**, 898
    generally, **5**, 897
  right to effect, **5**, 896
entry into—
  cancellation, **5**, 862–870
  execution, **5**, 853–859
  form of, **5**, 848–852
  Part V of Consumer Credit Act 1974 ..., **5**, 842–847
  parties to agreement, **5**, 841
  withdrawal, **5**, 860–861
European Economic Community Draft Directive, **5**, 801
execution of—
  cancellation rights, duty to give notice of, **5**, 857
  content of, **5**, 848–852
  copies—
    duty to supply, **5**, 855
    scope of regulations relating to, **5**, 856
  credit-tokens, acceptance of, **5**, 859
  generally, **5**, 853

Consumer credit agreement—*continued*
execution of—*continued*
  improper, consequences of, **5**, 858
  signature, **5**, 854
exempt—
  consumer hire, **5**, 825
  foreign connection, with, **5**, 824
  generally, **5**, 820
  heritable property, relating to, **5**, 821
  number of payments, exempt by reference to, **5**, 823
  total charge for credit, exempt by reference to rate of, **5**, 823
foreign connection, exempt agreement with, **5**, 824
form and content of—
  agreements regulations, **5**, 849
  documents, proper execution of, **5**, 850
  generally, **5**, 848
  legibility, **5**, 852
  multiple agreements, **5**, 851
generally, **5**, 841
hirer, death of, **5**, 887
information, right to, **5**, 873–881
  periodic statement, **5**, 874
  settlement statement, **5**, 875
matters arising during currency of, **5**, 871–887
meaning, **5**, 806; **13**, 1746*n*
misrepresentation—
  creditor, liability of, **5**, 872
  generally, **5**, 871
modifying, **5**, 883
multiple agreement—
  exclusion from operation of Act, **5**, 814
  form and content, **5**, 851
  meaning, **5**, 814
Part V of Consumer Credit Act, **1**, 1974
  ancillary credit agreement, **5**, 845
  antecedent negotiations, **5**, 847
  exempt agreements, **5**, 843
  future agreement, agreement to enter into, **5**, 844
  generally, **5**, 842
  pre-contract disclosure, **5**, 846
parties to, **5**, 841
payments—
  agreement exempt by reference to number of, **5**, 822
  appropriation of, **5**, 881
  cancellation, recovery of, **5**, 867
  variation of, **5**, 882
proof of loan, **13**, 1746
prospective, withdrawal from, **5**, 860, 861
protection order, **5**, 927
regulated agreement, as, **5**, 806
restricted-use credit agreement, **5**, 809
running-account credit, **5**, 808
  information, right to, **5**, 873, 874
small agreements, **5**, 813
supplier, breach of contract by—
  creditor, liability of, **5**, 872
  generally, **5**, 871
surety, **5**, 878, 908
unlicensed trader, made by, **5**, 953

Consumer credit agreement—*continued*
unrestricted-use credit agreement, **5**, 809
variation of—
  creditor, by, **5**, 882
  modifying agreement, **5**, 883
  owner, by, **5**, 882
whereabouts of goods, information on, **5**, 879
withdrawal from prospective agreement—
  generally, **5**, 860
  heritable property, secured on, **5**, 861
See also CONSUMER CREDIT; HIRE PURCHASE AGREEMENT
Consumer goods
meaning, **6**, 52
Consumer hire agreement
cancellation of—
  cancellable agreements, **5**, 863
  consequences of—
    credit, repayment of, **5**, 868
    debtor, recovery of payments by, **5**, 867
    goods—
      part exchange, given in, **5**, 870
      return of, **5**, 869
    hirer, recovery of payments by, **5**, 867
  cooling-off period, **5**, 864
  generally, **5**, 862
  notice of—
    effect of, **5**, 866
    generally, **5**, 865
canvassing, **5**, 832
credit facilities, liability for misuse of, **5**, 884–885
credit-tokens, new, issue of, **5**, 886
debtor, death of, **5**, 887
entry into—
  cancellation, **5**, 862–870
  execution, **5**, 853–859
  form of, **5**, 848–852
  Part V of Consumer Credit Act 1974 ..., **5**, 842–847
  parties to agreement, **5**, 841
  withdrawal, **5**, 860–861
execution of—
  cancellable rights, duty to give notice of, **5**, 857
  content of, **5**, 848–852
  copies—
    duty to supply, **5**, 855
    scope of regulations relating to, **5**, 856
  credit-tokens, acceptance of, **5**, 859
  generally, **5**, 853
  improper, consequences of, **5**, 858
  signature, **5**, 854
exempt, **5**, 825
form and content of—
  agreements regulations, **5**, 849
  documents, proper execution of, **5**, 850
  generally, **5**, 848
  legibility, **5**, 852
  multiple agreements, **5**, 851
generally, **5**, 841
goods subject to, entry to repossess, **5**, 892
hirer, death of, **5**, 887
information, right to, **5**, 873–881
matters arising during currency of, **5**, 871–887
meaning, **5**, 812; **13**, 1746*n*; **14**, 1050

Consumer hire agreement—*continued*
misrepresentation—
 creditor, liability of, **5**, 872
 generally, **5**, 871
Part V of Consumer Credit Act—
 ancillary credit agreement, **5**, 845
 antecedent negotiations, **5**, 847
 exempt agreements, **5**, 843
 future agreement, agreement to enter into, **5**, 844
 generally, **5**, 842
 pre-contract disclosure, **5**, 846
parties to, **5**, 841
proof of loan, **13**, 1746
regulated agreement when not exempt agreement, as, **5**, 812
repossession of goods, financial relief, **5**, 928
statutory controls, **14**, 1050
supplier, breach of contract by—
 creditor, liability of, **5**, 872
 generally, **5**, 871
termination by hirer—
 liability on, **5**, 905
 right to terminate, **5**, 904
variation of, **5**, 882–883
withdrawal from prospective agreement—
 generally, **5**, 860
 heritable property, secured on, **5**, 861
Consumer protection
administrative control, **6**, 9
Advisory Committee, **6**, 15
building contracts, **3**, 3, 143, 157
central government, **6**, 11
civil law, **6**, 6
class actions, **6**, 170
codes of practice, **6**, 23, 72
compensation orders, **6**, 171
conduct detrimental to consumers' interests, **6**, 16
consumer programmes, basic rights, **6**, 31
consumer redress, *see* CONSUMER REDRESS
control—
 common law, **6**, 98
 excluding or restricting liability, meaning, **6**, 100
 generally, **6**, 1, 7, 9, 97, 103
 Unfair Contract Terms Act 1972 ..., **6**, 99–101
 where liability can not be excluded, **6**, 101
criminal law, **6**, 6
customs and excise—
 detention of goods, **7**, 1216
 disclosure of information, **7**, 1218
defective product, damage caused by, **15**, 155, 196
 common law, **15**, 196
 delictual liability, **15**, 196
Donoghue v Stevenson, decision in, **15**, 196
European Community—
 obligation, product defect attributable to compliance with, **15**, 212
 product liability directive, **15**, 197, 198
European institutions, **6**, 30, 31
exclusion clauses, **6**, 1, 7, 9
gas, **6**, 161; **19**, 241
generally, **4**, 1105; **11**, 1779–1789

Consumer protection—*continued*
guarantee, **6**, 36, 101, 154
historical background, **6**, 2
independent and voluntary organisations, **6**, 25–29
institutional structure, **6**, 10–31
liability—
 EC directive, **6**, 39
 exclusion clauses, **6**, 97–103
 manufacturer, *see* manufacturer *below*
licensing system, **6**, 21
local government, **6**, 12
manufacturer, liability of—
 agricultural products, **6**, 40
 damaged products, **6**, 43
 dangerous or defective products, **6**, 37, 39, 41, 43, 44
 defences, **6**, 42
 development risk defence, **6**, 42
 economic loss, claim for, **6**, 38
 guarantees, **6**, 36
 limitation of actions, **6**, 44
 prescription of obligations, **6**, 44
meaning, **6**, 1
misleading information, *see* TRADE DESCRIPTIONS
Molony Report 1962 ..., **6**, 8, 9, 51, 104, 111, 126, 159
national and European Union law, where disparity between, **7**, 1021
Office of Fair Trading, *see* OFFICE OF FAIR TRADING
prescription, **16**, 2128
product safety legislation, **6**, 51
public policy, developments, generally, **15**, 197
purity of goods, **6**, 4
reasonableness test, **6**, 7, 10
repair, goods undergoing, **6**, 70
role of the courts, **6**, 7
Secretary of State's powers, **6**, 11
self-regulation, **6**, 9
services, provision of, **6**, 64, 67–72
statutory duty, breach—
 generally, **15**, 155, 196
strict liability—
 amount recoverable, **15**, 205
 breach of contract, and, **15**, 199
 business use, defective product used for, **15**, 205
 circumstances of case to be considered, **15**, 203
 Consumer Protection Act 1987, **15**, 199
 damage—
  death or personal injury, **15**, 204
  economic loss, **15**, 204
  excluded, **15**, 205
  meaning, **15**, 204
  must be caused by defect, **15**, 199, 206
  product itself, to, **15**, 205
  pursuer must suffer, **15**, 199, 204
 death, **15**, 204
 defect—
  constituent product, in, **15**, 212
  product must contain, **15**, 199
  what constitutes, **15**, 202
 defences, **15**, 211, 212
 EC obligation, product defect attributable to compliance with, **15**, 212
 EC product liability directive, **15**, 197, 198

Consumer protection—*continued*
strict liability—*continued*
  economic loss, **15**, 204
  excluded products, **15**, 201
  generally, **15**, 197
  get-up, effect, **15**, 203
  importer, liability, **15**, 208
  instructions or warnings, manufacturer's, **15**, 203
  joint and several liability, **15**, 210
  limitation or exclusion not permitted, **15**, 199
  marketing, effect, **15**, 203
  negligence, and, **15**, 199
  negligence or fault need not be proven, **15**, 199
  non-manufactured products or substances, **15**, 207
  'own brand' product, **15**, 210
  personal injury, **15**, 204
  private use, defective product used for, **15**, 205
  producer—
    brand name, use of, **15**, 208
    imported as, **15**, 208
    liability, **15**, 207
    what constitutes, **15**, 207, 208
  product, meaning, **15**, 200
  psychiatric injury, **15**, 204
  pursuer's right of action under other legal rules, **15**, 199
  reasonable use of product, **15**, 203
  repair or replacement costs, **15**, 205
  requirements for, **15**, 199
  scientific and technical knowledge, state of, **15**, 212
  supplier, liability, **15**, 207, 209, 210
  supply, meaning, **15**, 212
  time product supplied, **15**, 203
  trade mark etc, use of, **15**, 208
  type of liability, **15**, 199
  who is liable, **15**, 199, 207, 208
supply of services, **6**, 71
trades and vocations, **6**, 69
uncompetitive practices, **6**, 15
weights and measures legislation, *see* FOOD—
  weights and measures
Consumer Protection Advisory Committee
reference to, **6**, 15
Consumer redress
class actions, **6**, 170
compensation orders, **6**, 171
costs, **6**, 168
Court of Session, actions in, **6**, 168
extra-judicial dispute resolution, **6**, 172
generally, **6**, 31, 167
Hughes Report, **6**, 168
legal aid, **6**, 168
mail order transactions, **6**, 84
sheriff court, actions in, **6**, 168, 169
small claims, **6**, 31, 169
Consumer safety
detention of goods in interest of, **7**, 1216
disclosure of information concerning, **7**, 1218
Consumers' Association, **6**, 9, 26
Container
carriage by, generally, **21**, 526
carriage by sea, express terms in bill of lading, **21**, 546

Container—*continued*
food, **11**, 350, 350n
load, dimensions, **20**, 475
poison, supply of, **14**, 1217
Contamination
food, protection of, **9**, 1205
Contemporanea expositio
ancient statutes, **12**, 1112
modern statutes, **12**, 1113
Contempt of court
administration of law, as aspect of, **6**, 301
apology, remission of penalty on, **6**, 302
avoiding giving evidence, **7**, 522
broadcasting, effect on activities of those concerned with, **17**, 1
challenging findings of, **6**, 325
civil contempt, **6**, 322
committal for, treatment of prisoner, **16**, 1426
common law, **7**, 499
  aspects of behaviour covered by, **6**, 303, 318
  conduct in court, **6**, 319
  court order, failure to obey, **6**, 322
  mens rea, **6**, 323
  slander of judges, **6**, 320
  witness, offences by, **6**, 321
conduct amounting to, **7**, 499
corruption or oppression by public official, **7**, 499
Court of Session procedure, **17**, 1464
criminal investigations, publications liable to prejudice, **6**, 304
critcism of law or decision not amounting to, **7**, 546
custody order, in relation to, **8**, 518
defaming judges, **7**, 546
defences, **17**, 30
Employment Appeal Tribunal, **6**, 986
evidence, interference with, **7**, 499
flouting court's authority, **7**, 499
generally, **7**, 498
historical background, **6**, 301
interdict, breach of, **6**, 322
interference with evidence, **7**, 521
intoxication, **6**, 319; **7**, 502
jurisdiction, when taking effect, **6**, 304
Lands Tribunal for Scotland, **6**, 1151
legal aid in respect of, **13**, 1020, 1071
  appeal against decision, **13**, 1071
meaning, **6**, 303
mental element, **7**, 500
modern development of law, **6**, 304
nature of, **7**, 501
non-disclosure, **17**, 23
offence *sui generis*, as, **6**, 302
other crimes, relationship with, **7**, 501, 502
penalties—
  fines, **6**, 324
  maximum, **6**, 324
  prison, committal to, **6**, 324
  remission of, **6**, 302
  Scottish proceedings, meaning, **6**, 324n
perjury, and, **7**, 501
Phillimore Committee report, **6**, 304, 305
press, effect on activities of those concerned with, **17**, 1

Contempt of court—*continued*
prosecutions, guidelines in relation to, **6**, 314
publication in, **17**, 33
publications, by, **7**, 499, 502
quasi-criminal, nature of contemptuous proceedings, **6**, 302
refusal to answer questions, **10**, 550, 563
selective law reforms, **6**, 304
self-induced incapacity of witness, **10**, 532
standard of proof, **6**, 302
statement or action prejudicing outcome of trial, **7**, 499
statute law, main purposes, **6**, 304
statutory—
    active proceedings, necessity for, **6**, 307
    appellate proceedings, **6**, 310
    civil proceedings at first instance, **6**, 309
    criminal proceedings at first instance, **6**, 308
    existing law, saving of, **6**, 314
    fair and accurate reports, **6**, 312
    generally, **6**, 305
    information, disclosure of sources, **6**, 316
    innocent publication or distribution, **6**, 311
    jury deliberations, **6**, 315
    public affairs, discussion of, **6**, 313
    strict liability rule, **6**, 303, 306; **17**, 28
    tape recordings, **6**, 315
    test, **6**, 306
    witnesses, offences by, **6**, 317
strict liability rule, **6**, 303, 306; **17**, 28
trader in breach of court order, **6**, 19
wilful, **7**, 500, 502
witness, by, **10**, 550, 563; **17**, 756
    refusal to answer questions, **10**, 550, 563
    reluctant witness, **10**, 563
    self-induced incapacity through drink or drugs, **10**, 532
witness, interference with, **7**, 499
Contiguous zone
claimed, must be, **21**, 37
coastal state powers, **21**, 36
Convention of the Territorial Sea and the Contiguous Zone, **21**, 2, 35, 36
    passage, right to deny and suspend, **21**, 8
evolution of concept, **21**, 35
extent, **21**, 36, 37
generally, **11**, 77, 78
'hovering' Acts, **21**, 35
incoming vessels, **21**, 36
outgoing vessels, **21**, 36
Continental jurists
influence of, **17**, 111
Continental Shelf
coastal state—
    'exclusive sovereign rights', **21**, 18
Convention on the Continental Shelf, **21**, 2, 13
    conflicts with other uses of the sea, **11**, 85
    continental shelf installations, rights and duties with respect to, **21**, 32–34
    definition of continental shelf in, **21**, 20
    delimitation of continental shelf, **21**, 23, 24, 26, 28
    developments subsequent to, **21**, 17
    generally, **11**, 82; **21**, 17, 30

Continental Shelf—*continued*
Convention on the Continental Shelf—*continued*
    legal character of continental shelf, **21**, 18, 19
    natural resources, rights to, **11**, 83, 84
    submarine cables and pipelines, provisions as to, **21**, 31
Court of Session, territorial limits of, **4**, 2
definition, **21**, 20–23
    geological and legal, dissimilarities between, **21**, 15, 23
    UNCLOS III, **21**, 23
delimitation, **21**, 4
    adjacent states, **21**, 26, 29
    agreement, by, **21**, 30
    Convention on the Continental Shelf, **21**, 23, 24, 26, 28
    customary international law, **21**, 27
    equidistance principle, **21**, 28
    generally, **21**, 21
    'natural prolongation' concept, **21**, 21, 27
    opposite states, **21**, 26, 29
    straddle fields, **21**, 30
    transboundary oil fields, **21**, 30
    Truman Proclamation, **21**, 27
    UK position, **21**, 22
    UK practice, **21**, 30
    UNCLOS III, **21**, 29, 30
doctrine of, **19**, 639, 639*n*, 642
employees on, social security benefits, **21**, 1026
extra-territorial jurisdiction, **6**, 867
generally, **21**, 13
installations constructed on, **11**, 85
    abandoned or disused, **21**, 33
    coastal state control and jurisdiction, **21**, 32, 34
islands, of, **21**, 25
jurisdiction over, **21**, 13
legal status, **21**, 15
licensed areas, exclusion from rating, **24**, 670
natural resources—
    Convention on the Continental Shelf, **11**, 83, 84
    exploitation, **21**, 18
    jurisdiction over, **21**, 13
    meaning, **21**, 19
    Truman Proclamation, **21**, 15
origins of legal status, **21**, 13, 14
outer limit, **11**, 82; **21**, 20–25
products taken from—
    United Kingdom import duty relief, **7**, 1106
rights in, legal character of, **21**, 18, 19
sea bed—
    natural resources, rights in, **21**, 19
    Truman Proclamation, **21**, 15
sedentary species, rights in, **21**, 19
sheriff court, territorial limits of, **4**, 2
submarine cables and pipelines, **21**, 31
subsoil—
    exploitation by tunnelling, **21**, 18
    legal status, **21**, 18
    natural resources, rights in, **21**, 19
    Truman Proclamation, **21**, 15
superjacent waters, legal status, **21**, 18
Truman Proclamation—
    generally, **21**, 15, 18
    significance, **21**, 16

Contingencies Fund
public corporation recourse to, **19**, 224
Contingent liability transaction
customer agreements, **12**, 1375
meaning, **12**, 1375*n*
Securities and Investments Board Core Conduct
of Business Rules, **12**, 1386
Contingent obligation
See CONDITIONAL OBLIGATION
Continuous employment
See EMPLOYMENT
Contra proferentem **rule**
building contracts, **3**, 28
Contraband
neutral goods as, **17**, 419
penalty for carrying, **17**, 414
Contraception
post-coital, **7**, 288
See FAMILY PLANNING
Contract
absurd construction resisted, **15**, 756
accelerated payment clause, **15**, 811
acceptance—
  agreement, and, **15**, 619
  agreement without offer and acceptance, **15**,
    655
  battle of forms, **15**, 636
  communication—
    contract of cautionry, **15**, 642
    late, **15**, 645
    need for, **15**, 641
    post or telegram, by, **15**, 644, 648
    what amounts to, **15**, 643
  conduct, implied from, **15**, 631, 633, 638, 641
  counter-offer, **15**, 635
  cross-offers, identical, **15**, 634
  definition, **15**, 631
  express, **15**, 631
  generally, **15**, 627, 631
  ignorance of offer, in, **15**, 633
  implied, **15**, 631, 633, 638
  mode prescribed by offeror, **15**, 637
  qualified, **15**, 635, 636
  silence—
    acceptance, amounting to, **15**, 640
    not implied from, **15**, 639
  'subject to contract', **15**, 635, 656
  time of communication, **15**, 628
  time limit for, **15**, 628, 648
  what constitutes, **15**, 631–640
  who may accept, **15**, 632
  words, in, **15**, 631
acceptilation—
  extinction of contractual obligation by, **15**, 865,
    873
  fitted accounts, **15**, 873
  gratuitous discharge, **15**, 873
  implied discharge, **15**, 873
  meaning, **15**, 873
  several debts incurred to same debtor, **15**, 873
acquiescence in construing, **16**, 1620
acquiescence, *mora* and taciturnity, annulment of
  voidable obligation barred by, **15**, 672

Contract—*continued*
addressee of offer—
  class as, **15**, 627
  general public as, **15**, 627
  individual as, **15**, 627
adhesion, of, **22**, 107, 108
administrator, entered into by, **4**, 622
advertising, promotion literature as, **6**, 74
agreement, **15**, 4, 611
  dependence on, **15**, 619
  without offer and acceptance, **15**, 655
annulment, **15**, 671, 672
  goods delivered, where, **15**, 46, 50
  recompense, **15**, 66
  See also invalidity, grounds of *below*
arbitration clause, **15**, 718
assignation—
  agreement to transfer rights, **15**, 857
  assignatus utitur jure auctoris, **15**, 864
  assignee, **15**, 855
  cedent, **15**, 855
  contract to transfer rights, **15**, 857
  conveyance of rights, **15**, 857
  damages following ineffective, **15**, 863
  debtor—
    consent, **15**, 861
    defences available to, **15**, 864
    intimation to, **15**, 862
  defences, **15**, 864
  delectus personae, **15**, 855, 856, 859, 862, 863
  delegation, **15**, 856
  effect, **15**, 855
  form, **15**, 857
  generally, **15**, 853, 855
  historical background, **15**, 854
  ineffective, **15**, 862
    cedent's damages following, **15**, 863
  intimation, **15**, 815, 858
  jus quaesitum tertio compared, **15**, 824
  liabilities, contractual, **15**, 856
  payment, for, **15**, 855
  performance, for, **15**, 855
  prohibition, contractual, **15**, 860, 862, 863
  sub-contracting, **15**, 856
bankers' documentary credits, **15**, 848
banking, *jus quaesitum tertio*, **15**, 848
bargaining power, inequality, **15**, 677
barter, **6**, 46
battle of forms, **15**, 636, 636*n*
betting and wagering, **15**, 768
bill of lading—
  jus quaesitum tertio, **15**, 847
  See also BILL OF LADING
breach—
  action, **21**, 719
  arbitration, referable to, **2**, 413
  building contract, *see* BUILDING CONTRACT
  cargo owner, by, **21**, 717
  charterer, by, **21**, 717
  conditio causa data, **15**, 34, 38, 39, 42
  consumer credit, supplier by, **5**, 871–872
  damages, **21**, 714
    exclusion or limitation of liability, **21**, 714

Contract—*continued*
breach—*continued*
  damages—*continued*
    generally, **21**, 585
    statutory controls, **21**, 714
  damages in respect of—
    causation, **15**, 893
    multiple causes of breach, **15**, 894
    See also damages *below*; DAMAGES
  English law compared, **21**, 715
  frustration of contract, where, **21**, 714
  fundamental—
    doctrine of, **15**, 721
    exclusion clause, **15**, 721
  generally, **15**, 576
  hotelkeeper, by, **11**, 1727
  inducing, **15**, 576; **18**, 1478
  interest as damages for, **12**, 1018–1020
  litigation, with regard to, **15**, 460
  materiality, **15**, 720, 780
    immaterial breach, **15**, 779; **21**, 715
    material breach—
      definition, **15**, 780
      effect, **15**, 780; **21**, 715
  money, non-payment of, **15**, 791
  multiple causes, **15**, 894
  mutuality, **15**, 779
  non-material, **21**, 715
  obligation arising from, prescription, **16**, 2116
  procuring, **15**, 576
  recompense, **15**, 67
  remedies, *see* remedies *below*
  ship subject to existing contract, sale of, **21**, 718
  shipowner, by, **21**, 716
  terms and representations distinguished, **15**, 699–701
  trivial, **15**, 779, 780, 791
breach of confidence, *see* BREACH OF CONFIDENCE
broadcasting, effect on activities of those concerned with, **17**, 1
building—
  liquidated damages clause, **15**, 797
  performance, **15**, 866
  See also BUILDING CONTRACT
capacity to enter voluntary obligation, *see* voluntary obligation, capacity to enter *below*
carriage of goods, for, *jus quaesitum tertio*, **15**, 847
carriage of goods, for, services and custody, **21**, 613, 613*n*
cautionry, of, **15**, 642
charitable arrangement, *jus quaesitum tertio*, **15**, 842
charterparty—
  meaning, **15**, 799
  penalty clause, **15**, 799
  See also CHARTERPARTY
cheque guarantee card, relationships in play, **4**, 267
choice of law clause, **15**, 736, 751
co-obligants, status, **15**, 760
coercive force, **15**, 789
collateral agreements, **15**, 701, 760
commencement at specified hour, **22**, 822

Contract—*continued*
commercial, custom and precedent, **22**, 260
communication, *see* acceptance *above*; OFFER
company promoters, **15**, 834
company's power to enter into, **4**, 318
concealing another transaction, **15**, 760
concurrent and cumulative liability, **15**, 9
condictio causa data causa non secuta—
  generally, **15**, 34
  operation outwith contract, **15**, 34, 35
condictio indebtiti, **15**, 16
conditions—
  common understanding, **15**, 708
  notice of, **15**, 704–706
  previous dealings, effect, **15**, 707
  See also CONDITIONAL OBLIGATION
confidential information, **18**, 1452
confusion, **15**, 876
consensus in idem, **15**, 691, 692
consent—
  enforced simulation, **15**, 674
  reluctant expression, **15**, 675
constitution, formalities, **15**, 666–669
construction—
  penalties and liquidated damages clauses, **15**, 786, 787
  terms, of, *see* terms *below*
  time of making contract, of, **15**, 788
  written contracts, of, **15**, 747, 748
consumer contract, **15**, 727, 730
  1968 Convention, **4**, 54
  agreement to prorogate jurisdiction where there is, **4**, 54
  consumer, meaning, **4**, 54, 56
  counterclaim proceedings not affected by jurisdiction over, **4**, 54
  generally, **4**, 4, 8, 55, 56
  goods, supply of, **4**, 54
  instalment credit terms, sale of goods on, **4**, 54
  instalments, loan repayable by, **4**, 54
  insurance, **6**, 99
  insurance contract, **4**, 55, 56, 57
  meaning, **6**, 33; **13**, 1710, 1763, 1790; **14**, 1052
  services, for, **4**, 54; **6**, 67
  unfair contract terms, **13**, 1763
  Unfair Terms in Consumer Contracts Regulations 1994, **15**, 739–752
  work and materials for, **6**, 66
contents—
  arbitration clause, **15**, 718
  choice of law clause, **15**, 736, 751
  collateral agreements, **15**, 701, 760
  'core' contract provisions, **15**, 742, 743
  demurrage clause, **15**, 718
  exception clause, **15**, 702, 718
  exclusion clause, *see* exclusion clause *below*
  exemption clause, **15**, 702, 718
  express terms, *see* terms *below*
  force majeure clause, **15**, 718
  generally, **15**, 696
  implied terms, *see* terms *below*
  indemnity clause, **15**, 718, 726
  limitation clause, **15**, 718
  pre-contractual statements, **15**, 698, 699

Contract—*continued*
contents—*continued*
  reference, terms incorporated by, **15**, 702–710
  representations, **15**, 699
  terms, *see* terms *below*
conveyance, preceding, **18**, 606
covenants in restraint of trade, **19**, 1235
credit, implied terms as to, **12**, 1011
criminal or immoral act, securing performance of, **13**, 1760
Crown, resile by, **7**, 746
damage, remoteness of—
  foreseeability—
    ordinary course of events, in, **15**, 905
    special circumstances, of, **15**, 906
    standard of, **15**, 904
  generally, **15**, 902, 903
  Hadley v Baxendale, decision in, **15**, 903, 905
  test of remoteness, **15**, 902
damages—
  causation, *see* CAUSATION
  certainty of, **15**, 909
  generally, **15**, 892
  inconvenience and trouble, in respect of, **15**, 912
  measure of—
    defective performance, where, **15**, 911
    obligation to supply property, breach, **15**, 911
    pecuniary losses—
      alternative methods of performance, where, **15**, 914
      feelings, injury to, **15**, 913
      generally, **15**, 910
      nominal damages, **15**, 912
      personal injury, **15**, 913
      reputation, injury to, **15**, 913
      types, **15**, 911
  mitigation, **15**, 925, 927
  provisional, **15**, 932
  See also DAMAGES
debt, *see* DEBT
defects or vices of consent, **15**, 670
delectus personae, **15**, 818–820, 855, 856, 859, 862, 863
delivery, **15**, 618, 629
demurrage clause, **15**, 718
dependent upon another contract, **15**, 760
director, with, *see* COMPANY (directors)
domestic arrangement, *jus quaesitum tertio*, **15**, 842
double grant, 'offside goals', rule against, **18**, 697
duration, European Convention on the Calculation of Time Limits, **22**, 827, 828
duties, **15**, 612
duty to protect implied by, **7**, 42
economic relationship, injury to, *see* ECONOMIC RELATIONSHIP
electronic transfer of funds, relating to, *see* ELECTRONIC TRANSFER OF FUNDS
employment, *see* CONTRACT OF EMPLOYMENT
enforceability, **15**, 771
English and Scots law compared, **15**, 612
enorm lesion, **11**, 1205
error—
  ambiguity, **15**, 693
  common, **15**, 690

Contract—*continued*
error—*continued*
  dissensus, **15**, 691, 692
  essential, **15**, 688
  expression, of, **15**, 686
  generally, **15**, 686
  intention, of, **15**, 686, 688
  known, **15**, 694
  motive, in, **15**, 686, 688, 690
  mutual, **15**, 691
  substantials, in, **15**, 687–690
  transaction, in, **15**, 686, 688, 689, 690
European Community actions in respect of liability, **10**, 237, 238
European Convention on Contractual Obligations—
  background, **17**, 278
  evasion, prevention of, **17**, 284
  generally, **17**, 285
  governing system, ascertainment of, **17**, 280
  presumption, advantages and disadvantages of, **17**, 283
  proper law, **17**, 281, 282
  scope, **17**, 279
exception clause, **15**, 702, 718
exchange, of, *see* EXCHANGE
exclusion clause—
  anti-avoidance provisions, **15**, 735
  breach of duty, liability, **15**, 728
  choice of law clause, **15**, 736, 751
  construction, **15**, 719
  definition, **15**, 718
  fairness and reasonableness—
    generally, **15**, 731
    judicial decision, nature of, **15**, 734
    judicial guidelines, **15**, 733
    statutory guidelines, **15**, 732
  forms, **15**, 725
  fundamental breach, and, **15**, 721
  generally, **15**, 702
  jus quaesitum tertio, **15**, 846
  negligence, excluding liability for, **15**, 720
  standard form contract, **15**, 730
  statutory control, **15**, 722–737
  third party, in favour of, **15**, 846
  unreasonable, control, **15**, 729
exemption clause, **15**, 702, 718; **22**, 670
extinction of obligations—
  acceptilation, **15**, 865, 873
  compensation, **15**, 865, 877–879
  confusion, by, **15**, 865, 876
  delegation, by, **15**, 865, 875
  effluxion of time, by, **15**, 890
  frustration, **15**, 865, 880–889
  generally, **15**, 865
  novation, **15**, 865, 874
  prescription, **15**, 865, 890
facility and circumvention, **15**, 678
family arrangement, *jus quaesitum tertio*, **15**, 842
feu contracts—
  irritancy—
    conventional, **15**, 806
    declarator, action of, **15**, 804
    effect, **15**, 804

Contract—*continued*
feu contracts—*continued*
  irritancy—*continued*
    feuing conditions, breach, **15**, 806
    generally, **15**, 802, 803, 804
    legal, **15**, 805
    non-payment of feuduty, **15**, 805, 806
    ob non solutem canonem, **15**, 805
    obligation *ad factum praestandum*, breach, **15**, 806
    purge, **15**, 804–806
    sopiting the superiority, **15**, 804
  tinsel of the feu, action of, **15**, 804
force and fear, coercion by, **15**, 673–677
force majeure clause, **15**, 718
formation—
  acceptance—
    communication, **15**, 641–645
    what constitutes, **15**, 631–640
    See also acceptance *above*
  addressee of offer, **15**, 627
  agreement, **15**, 619
  communication—
    acceptance, **15**, 641–645
    offer, **15**, 628–630
  generally, **15**, 619
  intention to create legal relations, **15**, 656–658
  offers and invitations to treat, **15**, 620–626
  termination of offer, **15**, 646–654
  See also OFFER
fraud, contractual remedies for, **11**, 721
fraudulent misrepresentation—
  induced by, **11**, 707–714; , **15**, 585
frustration—
  condictio causa data, **15**, 34, 36, 37, 42
  contracting out of doctrine, **15**, 883
  destruction of subject, **3**, 96
  effect, **15**, 889
  fault and frustration, **15**, 882
  foresight and frustration, **15**, 881
  generally, **15**, 865, 880
  illegality of performance, **15**, 888
  impossibility, **15**, 885
  impracticality of performance, **15**, 887
  meaning, **15**, 880
  nature of contract, changes in, **15**, 884
  purpose for making contract no longer exists, **15**, 886
  rei interitus, **15**, 885
  risk allocation, **15**, 880
gaming, **13**, 1761
good faith, and, **11**, 1129–1131
government, **22**, 234–235
gratuitous, **15**, 612
  English and Scots law compared, **15**, 612
heritable conveyancing—
  consideration, **6**, 476
  excambion, **6**, 587
  ground annual, **6**, 586
heritable property, regarding—
  agreement to lease, form of writing, **13**, 124
  articles of lease, form of writing, **13**, 125
  bilateral, form of writing, **13**, 123

Contract—*continued*
heritable property, regarding—*continued*
  constitution and proof—
    generally, **13**, 122
    writing, form of, **13**, 123–126
  lease, *see* LEASE-LEASING
  obligationes literis, as, **13**, 122
  probative unilateral obligations, **13**, 126
  writing, necessity for, **13**, 122
heritage, sale of, *see* HERITABLE PROPERTY
hire-purchase—
  irritancy, **15**, 810
  penalty clause, **15**, 798
holograph, **15**, 666
homologation, **15**, 666, 669, 672
illegal, **13**, 1760
  See also pacta illicita below
illegal means, performance by, **15**, 764
illegal provision, **13**, 1760
illegal term in, **15**, 764
implied terms, **22**, 670
inaccurately recorded, **15**, 695
incapax entering into, **13**, 1780
incorporeal property, transfer, **18**, 653
indemnity clause, **15**, 718, 726
informally constituted, **15**, 666, 667
insurance as, **12**, 802
insurance contract, *see* INSURANCE
intention, contractual, **15**, 656–658
interest stipulated by, **12**, 1001
  agreed rate, where, **12**, 1037
  courts, enforcement by, **12**, 1002
  credit, implied terms as to, **12**, 1011
  express contract, **12**, 1002
  fluctuating interest rates, **12**, 1004
  general law, implication by, **12**, 1007
  implied contract terms, **12**, 1005
    credit, as to, **12**, 1011
    heritage, sales of, **12**, 1010
    sale, contract of, **12**, 1009
    types of, **12**, 1005
  interest rates, **12**, 1002
    legal rate or contract rate of interest, **12**, 1003
  loans, **12**, 1008
  mutuality, **12**, 1013
  particular facts, implication on basis of, **12**, 1006
  sale, contract of, **12**, 1007, 1009
    heritage, sales of, **12**, 1009, 1010
    implied contract terms, **12**, 1009
    moveable property, **12**, 1009
interference with—
  delict, **15**, 255
  intent to cause injury, **15**, 255
interpretation—
  extrinsic evidence, **13**, 144–146
  generally, **13**, 144
  parole evidence, **13**, 144–146, 147
  prior communings, **13**, 146
invalidity, grounds of—
  annulment, conditions of, **15**, 672
  challenge, consequences of successful, **15**, 671
  defective expression, **15**, 695

Contract—*continued*
invalidity, grounds of—*continued*
    defects or vices of consent, **15**, 670
    error, *see* error *above*
    facility and circumvention, **15**, 678
    force and fear, **15**, 673–677
    inaccurately recorded obligation, **15**, 695
    misrepresentation, **15**, 680–685
    position of trust, abuse of, **15**, 679
    rectification, **15**, 695
    successful challenge, consequences, **15**, 671
    undue influence, **15**, 679
    weak-mindedness, **15**, 678
invitations to treat—
    advertisements, **15**, 624
    auction sales, **15**, 625
    generally, **15**, 620
    offer distinguished, **15**, 620
    quotations, **15**, 626
    self-service displays, **15**, 622
    shop window displays, **15**, 621
    tenders, **15**, 626
    vending machines, **15**, 623
irritancies—
    conventional, **15**, 802, 805, 809
    effect, **15**, 802
    feu contracts, **15**, 802, 803, 804–806
    generally, **15**, 782, 802
    hire-purchase contracts, **15**, 810
    historical background, **15**, 803
    leases, **15**, 802, 803, 807–809
    legal, **15**, 802, 805, 808
    meaning, **15**, 802
    oppression, **15**, 802
    penal and non-penal, **15**, 803
    purgeable, **15**, 802
joint creditors, status, **15**, 760
jus quaesitum tertio—
    applications, **15**, 841–852
    assignation, **15**, 815, 824
    banking, **15**, 848
    bills of lading, **15**, 847
    Carmichael v Carmichael's Executrix, decision in,
      15, 829–831, 842
    categories of case under, **15**, 831
    charitable arrangements, **15**, 842
    co-disponees, **15**, 850
    co-feuars, **15**, 833, 850
    co-lessees, **15**, 850
    commercial applications, **15**, 842, 845
    company promoters' contracts, **15**, 834
    competing claims, **15**, 832
    debtor, and, **15**, 825, 827, 832
    delict, interaction with, **15**, 838
    delivery, **15**, 831, 832
    domestic arrangements, **15**, 842
    establishing existence, **15**, 824
    exclusion clause, **15**, 846
    existence of third party at time contract made,
      15, 834
    generally, **15**, 814, 824
    historical background, **15**, 826
    identification of third party, **15**, 833
    illegal contracts, **15**, 839

Contract—*continued*
jus quaesitum tertio—*continued*
    insurance contracts, **15**, 841
    intention to benefit third party, **15**, 835, 837
    intimation, **15**, 815
    irrevocability, **15**, 829–832
    liability, imposition on third party, **15**, 840
    meaning, **15**, 824
    nature of, **15**, 815
    null and void, **15**, 839
    obligation amounting to gift, **15**, 831
    partnerships, **15**, 851
    principal contract—
      frustration, **15**, 839
      illegal, **15**, 839
      relationship with third party's claim, **15**, 839
      void or voidable, **15**, 839
    promise, as, **15**, 827, 828
    reforms, proposed, **15**, 852
    remedies of third party, **15**, 837
    restrictive covenants, **15**, 849
    shipping, **15**, 847
    solicitors, claims against, **15**, 843, 844
    stipulator, **15**, 825, 827
    sub-contracts, **15**, 836
    sui generis, as, **15**, 828
    terminology, **15**, 825
    theoretical basis, **15**, 827, 828
    trusts compared, **15**, 832
    unenforceable contracts, **15**, 839
    use of term, **15**, 824
    validity of original contract, **15**, 815
    void or voidable, **15**, 839
    wills, contracts to make, **15**, 843
land, for use or occupation of, categories, **13**, 102
lease as, **13**, 101, 103, 104
    arbitration clauses, **13**, 234
    bilateral contract, form of writing, **13**, 123
    choice of law, **13**, 228
    confusion, **13**, 231
    consent, **13**, 222
    construction, principles of, **13**, 227
    error, **13**, 223
    frustration, **13**, 226
    generally, **13**, 221
    homologation, **13**, 224
    illegality, **13**, 225
    jurisdiction, **13**, 228
    management conditions, **13**, 237, 238
    misrepresentation, **13**, 223
    mutuality, **13**, 232
    penalties, **13**, 238
    personal bar, **13**, 224
    prescription, **13**, 230
    rent, payment of, **13**, 229
    resolutive conditions, **13**, 236
    suspensive conditions, **13**, 236
    unity of contract, **13**, 233
    warrandice, **13**, 235
leasing—
    breach on—
      damages for, **14**, 1065–1068
      insolvency of lessees, **14**, 1063
      lessor, by, **14**, 1063

Contract—*continued*
leasing—*continued*
  breach on—*continued*
    minimum hiring clause, **14**, 1063
    remedies, **14**, 1063
    rent, proceedings for sequestration, **14**, 1063
    repossession, **14**, 1064
  collateral contract, **14**, 1087
  duration, **22**, 827
  nominate consensual contract, **14**, 1004
  pre-lease, **14**, 1032
  standard form, **14**, 1052
  statutory controls, **14**, 1049–1054
  termination, **14**, 1060–1062
  See also LEASE-LEASING
legal relations, intention to create—
  lack of, **15**, 656
  patrimonial interest, infringement, **15**, 658
  'personal' agreements, unenforceability, **15**, 657, 658
legislation, and, **22**, 103–105
liability, assignation, **15**, 856
licence to occupy—
  English law, **13**, 596, 626
  meaning, **13**, 596
life assurance contracts, *jus quaesitum tertio*, **15**, 841
limitation clause, **15**, 718
liquidated damages clause—
  building contracts, **15**, 797
  construction at time of contract, **15**, 788
  effect, **15**, 795
  English law, **15**, 784
  essence of, **15**, 793
  generally, **15**, 782, 785, 789, 790, 793
  historical background, **15**, 783–785
  intention, **15**, 793
  leases, **15**, 801
  modern law, **15**, 785
  penalties distinguished, **15**, 786–788, 795, 796
  pre-estimation of loss, **15**, 793, 794
  purpose, **15**, 793
  rules of construction, **15**, 786
  standard form contract, **15**, 793
  terminology not conclusive, **15**, 787
liquidation, effect of—
  no automatic termination, **4**, 859
  repudiation, right of, **4**, 860
  rescission, right of, **4**, 860
loan, of, *see* COMMODATUM; LOAN; MUTUUM; PRECARIUM
location, of, lease as, **13**, 103
loss must lie where it falls, **15**, 765
meaning, **15**, 4
minors, **10**, 1078, 1079, 1233
  curator, acting with, **11**, 1204
  reduction and, **11**, 789, 1205
misrepresentation, inducement to enter by—
  fraudulent misrepresentation, **15**, 683
  generally, **15**, 589, 680
  inaccurate representation of fact, **15**, 681
  innocent misrepresentation, **15**, 685
  method of representation, **15**, 682
  negligent misrepresentation, **15**, 589, 684
missives of sale, *see* MISSIVES OF SALE

Contract—*continued*
model terms and conditions, **22**, 108
multipartite agreements, **15**, 655
mutuality, **15**, 779
natural person's power to enter into, **4**, 318
naturalia as part of agreement, **12**, 1215
negligence, exclusion of liability for, **15**, 720
negligent—
  interference, **15**, 592, 593
  misrepresentation, **15**, 589, 684
  performance, **15**, 590, 593
non-contractual notices, avoidance of liability by, **15**, 737
non-disclosure, **15**, 585
null and void, **15**, 671, 765
  performance—
    acts amounting to, **15**, 866
    assignee or sub-contractor, by, **15**, 866
    building contracts, **15**, 866
    contract terms, **15**, 866
    delectus personae, **15**, 866
    effect, **15**, 865
    good or better standard, to, **15**, 866
    manner rendered, **15**, 866
    onus of proof, **15**, 866
    sale, contracts of, **15**, 866
  prescription, **15**, 865, 890
  remedies, **15**, 765
obligation, as, **11**, 1031
obligations literis, **15**, 666, 669
obligations and property, distinctions between, **11**, 756
offer, *see* OFFER
offeree—
  acceptance, *see* acceptance *above*
  bankruptcy, **15**, 616, 653
  death, **15**, 616, 651
  delivery to address of, sufficiency, **15**, 629
  insanity, **15**, 616, 652
  mode of acceptance prescribed by, **15**, 637
offeror—
  acceptance, communication to, **15**, 641
  bankruptcy, **15**, 616, 653
  death, **15**, 616, 651
  insanity, **15**, 616, 652
  mode of acceptance prescribed by, **15**, 637
pacta illicita—
  betting and wagering contracts, **15**, 768
  effect of illegality, **15**, 764
  enforceability, **15**, 771
  equal wrongdoing, parties in, **15**, 764
  illegal activity, promotion, **15**, 764
  illegality not obvious, where, **15**, 766
  in pari delicto, **15**, 764
  jus quaesitum tertio, **15**, 839
  meaning, **15**, 763
  null and void contracts, **15**, 765
  pacta de quota litis, **15**, 769
  parties to, **15**, 764
  performance by illegal means, **15**, 764
  pleading, **15**, 766
  problems arising, **15**, 764
  protection of class, **15**, 764
  remedies denied where, **15**, 765

Contract—*continued*
pacta illicita—*continued*
  restraint of trade, agreements in, **15**, 763, 770–772
    ambit, **15**, 774
    duration, **15**, 774
    extent, **15**, 774
    interpretation of terms, **15**, 777
    parties accepting, **15**, 774
    protectable interests, **15**, 773
    reasonableness, **15**, 772
      onus of proof, **15**, 776
      parties, between, **15**, 774
      public, with regard to, **15**, 775
    severability, **15**, 778
  sexual immorality, promoting, **15**, 763, 767
  sponsiones ludicrae contracts, **15**, 768
  statutory illegality, **15**, 765
pacta de quota litis, **15**, 769
Part VII, *See* TENANT-TENANCY
parties to—
  assignation, *see* assignation *above*
  death, **15**, 817, 818
    offeree, **15**, 616, 651
    offeror, **15**, 616, 651
  delectus personae, **15**, 818, 819, 820, 855, 856, 859, 862, 863
  determination, **15**, 816
  different status, seeking, **15**, 760
  generally, **15**, 814
  insolvency, **15**, 817, 819–823
    administrators, **15**, 823
    effect, **15**, 819
    liquidators, **15**, 822
    trustee in sequestration, **15**, 820
  legitimate intention of, giving effect to, **15**, 814
  offeree, *see* offeree *above*
  offeror, *see* offeror *above*
  profiting from own wrong, construction against, **15**, 759
  representatives of, **15**, 817
  successors of, **15**, 817
  third party, imposing liability on, **15**, 840
  third party rights, *see jus quaesitum tertio above*
  title to sue, *see* title to sue *below*
partnership, **16**, 1007
  dissolution of, effect, **16**, 1040, 1098
  rights and obligations between partners, **16**, 1056
  third party rights, **15**, 851
patrimonial interest, infringement, **15**, 658
payment for—
  agent, to, **15**, 869
  ascription, **15**, 868
  burden of proof, **15**, 872
  creditor's duty, generally, **15**, 867
  debtor's duty, generally, **15**, 867
  discharge—
    generally, **15**, 873
    implied, **15**, 873
    several debts, where, **15**, 873
  fitted accounts, **15**, 873
  gratuitous discharge, **15**, 873
  lesser sum sent 'in full and final settlement', **15**, 870

Contract—*continued*
payment for—*continued*
  method, **15**, 871
  'on demand', debts payable on, **15**, 867
  part, **15**, 870
  termly, *apocha trium annorum*, **15**, 872
  to whom made, **15**, 869
penalties—
  charterparties, **15**, 799
  construction at time of contract, **15**, 788
  effect, **15**, 796
  employment, contracts of, **15**, 800
  English law, **15**, 784
  essence of, **15**, 789
  extravagant and unconscionable, **15**, 789, 790
  generally, **15**, 782, 785, 789
  greater than original sum, **15**, 791
  hire-purchase contracts, **15**, 798
  historical background, **15**, 783–785, 803
  intention, **15**, 789
  liquidated damages clause distinguished, **15**, 786–788, 795, 796
  modern law, **15**, 785
  punishment, **15**, 789
  purpose, **15**, 789
  rules of construction, **15**, 786
  several different events, applicable to, **15**, 792
  terminology not conclusive, **15**, 787
  unenforceable, **15**, 789
performance—
  acts amounting to, **15**, 866
  alternative methods, contract permitting, **15**, 914
  assignee or sub-contractor, by, **15**, 866
  building contract, **15**, 866
  contract terms, **15**, 866
  defective, damages in respect of, **15**, 911
  delectus personae, **15**, 866
  effect, **15**, 865
  good or better standard, to, **15**, 866
  illegal means, by, **15**, 764
  illegality, **15**, 888
    See also pacta illicita above
  impossibility, **15**, 885
  impracticality, **15**, 887
  manner rendered, **15**, 866
  onus of proof, **15**, 866
  payment for, *see* payment for *above*
  sale, contract of, **15**, 866
  shortfall or excess of goods, **15**, 866
  wrongful interference with, **15**, 577
'personal' agreements, unenforceability, **15**, 657, 658
personal bar, **16**, 1601
post or telegram, communication by, **15**, 644, 647, 648
pre-contractual expenditure, damages in respect of, **15**, 911
pre-contractual statements, **15**, 698, 699
pre-existing, administrator and, **4**, 623
previous dealings, effect, **15**, 707
private international law—
  alternative reference, rules of, **17**, 126
  characterisation, **17**, 360

Contract—*continued*
private international law—*continued*
  choice of law distinguished from unilateral
    choice of law provision, **17**, 133
  commercial, formation of, **17**, 254
  conflict rules, **17**, 109
  connecting factor, **17**, 122, 125
  construction, **17**, 270
  current approach, evolution of, **17**, 246
  discharge of, **17**, 274–277
  European Convention on Contractual
    Obligations, *see above*
  formation of—
    agreement, **17**, 269
    capacity, **17**, 254, 255
    consent, **17**, 269
    formal validity—
      formalities, **17**, 256
      lex fori, mandatory rules of, **17**, 259
      lex loci contractus, application of, **17**, 257
      proper law, application of, **17**, 258
    legality—
      external public policy rule, **17**, 259
      foreign law, general rules excluding, **17**, 261
      foreign revenue claim, **17**, 264
      penal claim, **17**, 264
      unlawful contract, specific rules on, **17**, 265
      unlawfulness, **17**, 260, 262, 266, 267
    residual category, **17**, 268
  fragmentation of rules, **17**, 124
  general approach, **17**, 245
  interpretation of, **17**, 270
  most closely connected system, **17**, 252, 253
  parties, obligations of, **17**, 271–273
  proper law of—
    autonomy approach, **17**, 249
    evasion, **17**, 250
    formal validity, **17**, 258
    implied choice of, **17**, 251
    most closely connected system, **17**, 252, 253
    parties, selection by, **17**, 249
    putative, **17**, 248
    relevance of, **17**, 248
  scope, **17**, 244
  self-denying statutes, **17**, 134
  specific—
    ascertaining proper law, **17**, 290
    divisibility, **17**, 287
    examples, **17**, 286
    international conventions, governed by, **17**,
      288
    legislation, governed by, **17**, 289
  transfer of property *inter vivos*, **17**, 320
  unlawful, specific rules on, **17**, 265
probative, **15**, 667
promise compared, **15**, 611, 613
promoter and unincorporated company, between,
  4, 316
property and obligations, distinctions between,
  11, 756
prospective—
  inducing, **15**, 589
  preventing, **15**, 591
  wrongful interference with, **15**, 578

Contract—*continued*
protectable interests, **15**, 773
prout de jure, **15**, 666
pupils, **10**, 1052, 1053, 1055; **11**, 1203; **13**, 1779
purpose for making no longer in existence, **15**,
  886
recompense not competent where parties'
  relations are regulated by, **13**, 83
recompense in relation to, **15**, 66, 67, 70
reduction, **15**, 760
rei interitus, **15**, 885
rei interventus, **15**, 666, 669; **16**, 1619
  See also REI INTERVENTUS
relational economic loss—
  duty of care, **15**, 586, 588
  existing contract—
    negligent interference, **15**, 592
    negligent performance, **15**, 590
  fraud, and, **15**, 585
  generally, **15**, 594
  Junior Books Ltd v Veitchi Co Ltd, decision in,
    15, 593
  negligence, and, **15**, 586–594
  prospective contract—
    inducing, **15**, 589
    preventing, **15**, 591
remedies—
  available by virtue of—
    compensation, **13**, 96
    damages for breach—
      nominal, **13**, 74
      penalty for, **13**, 75
      pre-estimated loss, **13**, 75
    division and sale, **13**, 97
    lien, **13**, 95
    rescission, **13**, 93
    retention, **13**, 94
  contractually stipulated—
    accelerated payment clause, **15**, 811
    forfeiture of monies already paid, **15**, 812
    generally, **15**, 782
    irritancies, *see* irritancies *above*
    liquidated damages clause, *see* liquidated
      damages clause *above*
    occurence of events other than breach, **15**,
      813
    penalties, *see* penalties *above*
  defensive, **15**, 781
  judicial, **15**, 781
  money, for non-payment of, **15**, 791
  negative, **15**, 781
  null and void contracts, **15**, 765
  pacta illicita, remedies denied where, **15**, 765
  positive, **15**, 781
  rules of construction, **15**, 786
  self-help, **15**, 781
representation—
  collateral agreements, **15**, 701
  term distinguished, **15**, 699–701
resiling, personal bar, **15**, 669; **16**, 1605
restraint of trade, agreements in, **15**, 763, 770–772
  protectable interests, **15**, 773
  reasonableness, **15**, 772
restrictive covenants, **15**, 763

Contract—*continued*

right in, incorporeal property, as, **18**, 11, 652

rights, **15**, 612

sale, of *see* SALE AND SUPPLY OF GOODS

Scots law, generally, **18**, 606

Scottish Law Commission recommendations, **22**, 670–671

self-evidencing, **15**, 667

sexual gratification, for, **11**, 1009

sexual immorality, promoting, **15**, 763, 767

ship, sale of, **21**, 131

special jurisdiction, **4**, 36

specialised concept of law, as, **11**, 1005

specific implement—

    decree of, **13**, 8

      alternative remedies, **13**, 10

      exceptions, **13**, 9

speculative actions, **15**, 769

sponsiones ludicrae, **15**, 768

sport, in—

    dismissal, **19**, 1237

    freedom of, **19**, 1236

standard form contract, **15**, 730

sub-contracts—

    jus quaesitum tertio, **15**, 836

    terms, **15**, 709

'subject to contract', **15**, 635, 656

supply of goods—

    advertising, **6**, 74

    manufacturer's guarantee, **6**, 36

    trading in, **6**, 49

surrogacy, **10**, 1153

technical terms, construction, **15**, 754

termination, at specified hour, **22**, 823

terminology, penalties and liquidated damages clauses, **15**, 787

terms—

    awareness of, **15**, 749

    construction—

      absurd, **15**, 756

      against party profiting from own wrong, **15**, 759

      contra proferentem rule, **15**, 719, 758

      ejusdem generis rule, **15**, 753

      exclusion clause, **15**, 719

      expressio unius est exclusio alterius rule, **15**, 753

      extrinsic evidence as aid to, **15**, 760, 761

      general rules, **15**, 753

        results of applying, **15**, 757

      rectification, **15**, 762

      technical terms, **15**, 754

      as a whole, contract to be construed, **15**, 755

      words, meaning to be given to, **15**, 753

      written contracts, of, **15**, 747, 748

    'core' contract provisions, **15**, 742, 743

    express, **15**, 866

      collateral agreements, **15**, 701, 760

      form, **15**, 697

      generally, **15**, 697

      oral, **15**, 697

      pre-contractual statements, **15**, 698

      reference, incorporated by—

        common understanding, **15**, 708

        conditions, when given, **15**, 704

Contract—*continued*

terms—*continued*

    express—*continued*

      reference, incorporated by—*continued*

        contractual nature, whether document of, **15**, 703

        course of dealing, **15**, 707

        generally, **15**, 697, 702

        other contracts, **15**, 709

        sub-contracts, **15**, 709

        sufficiency of notice, **15**, 705, 706

        terms not apt to be, **15**, 710

        writing, in, **15**, 697

    generally, **15**, 697

    illegal, **15**, 764

    implied, **15**, 866

      business efficacy, **15**, 716

      courts, devised by, **15**, 711, 713

      custom or usage, **15**, 717

      every contract, terms implied in, **15**, 714

      generally, **15**, 697, 711

      'officious bystander' principle, **15**, 715

      presumed to reflect parties' intentions, **15**, 711, 715–717

      statute, by, **15**, 711, 712

      types, **15**, 711

    individually negotiated, **15**, 740

    interdependence, **15**, 779

    mutuality principle, **15**, 779

    notice of, **15**, 704–706

    other contracts, of, **15**, 709

    performance, and, **15**, 866

    previous dealings, effect, **15**, 707

    reciprocity, **15**, 779

    representations distinguished, **15**, 699–701

    restraint of trade, agreements in, **15**, 777

    statutory control—

      exclusion clause, **15**, 722–737

    sub-contracts, **15**, 709

    unfair—

      illustrations of, **15**, 745, 746

      meaning, **15**, 744

      preventing continued use, **15**, 750

    Unfair Contract Terms Act 1977, **15**, 722–737, 738

      anti-avoidance provisions, **15**, 735

      breach of duty, liability, **15**, 728

      choice of law clause, **15**, 736

      excluded contracts and provisions, **15**, 724

      fairness and reasonableness, **15**, 731–734

      forms of exclusion clause, **15**, 725

      generally, **15**, 722, 738

      indemnity clause, **15**, 726

      non-contractual notice, avoidance of liability, **15**, 737

      scope, **15**, 723

      standard form contract, **15**, 730

      terms of art, **15**, 727

      unreasonable exclusion clause, **15**, 729

    Unfair Terms in Consumer Contracts Regulations 1994—

      awareness of term, **15**, 749

      choice of law clause, **15**, 751

      construction of written contracts, **15**, 747, 748

Contract—*continued*
terms—*continued*
  Unfair Terms in Consumer Contracts
    Regulations 1994—*continued*
    contracts covered by, **15**, 739
    'core' contract provisions, exclusion, **15**,
      742, 743
    EC Council Directive 93/13, **15**, 752
    effect, **15**, 742
    excluded contracts, **15**, 741
    fairness, **15**, 748, 749
    generally, **15**, 738
    individually negotiated terms, **15**, 740
    unfair terms—
      illustrations of, **15**, 745, 746
      meaning, **15**, 744
      preventing continued use, **15**, 750
  third party interests, **15**, 760
  third party rights, *see jus quaesitum tertio above*
  tickets, **15**, 703
  title to sue—
    administrators, **15**, 823
    assignation, *see assignation above*
    co-disponees, **15**, 850
    co-feuars, **15**, 833, 850
    co-lesses, **15**, 850
    death, effect, **15**, 818
    delegation, **15**, 856
    generally, **15**, 814
    insolvency, effect, **15**, 819–823
    jus quaesitum tertio, *see jus quaesitum tertio above*
    liquidators, **15**, 821
    parties to contract, who are, **15**, 816
    receivers, **15**, 822
    representatives of contracting parties, **15**, 817
    successors of contracting parties, **15**, 817
    third party rights, *see jus quaesitum tertio above*
    trustees in sequestration, **15**, 820
  transfer of ownership—
    contract, and, generally, **18**, 606
    conveyance, preceding, **18**, 608
    failure of contract—
      abstract basis of transfer, **18**, 608–612
      causal basis of transfer, **18**, 608–612
      conveyance, on, **18**, 608
      corporeal moveable property, **18**, 609
        Sale of Goods Act 1979, under, **18**, 610
      incorporeal property, **18**, 612
      justa causa traditionis, **18**, 608
      land, **18**, 611
  transport, of, **4**, 56
  tug and tow, *see* TOW
  uberrimae fidei, non-disclosure, **15**, 585
  ultra vires, personal bar, **16**, 1606
  undue influence as ground of annulment, **15**, 679
  unfair contract terms, **13**, 1763
    commodatum contracts, **13**, 1790
    mutuum contracts, **13**, 1710
    precarium contracts, **13**, 1790
  Unfair Contract Terms Act 1977—
    anti-avoidance provisions, **15**, 735
    breach of duty, liability, **15**, 728
    choice of law clause, **15**, 736
    contracts covered by, **15**, 723

Contract—*continued*
  Unfair Contract Terms Act 1977—*continued*
    excluded contracts and provisions, **15**, 724
    exclusion clause—
      forms, **15**, 725
      unreasonable, control, **15**, 729
    fairness and reasonableness, **15**, 722, 731–734
    generally, **15**, 722
    indemnity clause, **15**, 726
    non-contractual notice, avoidance of liability
      by, **15**, 737
    standard form contract, **15**, 730
    terms of art, **15**, 727
  validity—
    challenge, **15**, 670
      consequences of successful, **15**, 671
    grounds of invalidity, *see* invalidity, grounds of
      above
  variation, formalities, **15**, 667
  void, **15**, 671, 690, 765
    conditio causa data, **15**, 34, 40
    goods delivered under, **15**, 50
    jus quaesitum tertio, **15**, 839
    recompense, **15**, 66
    remedies, **15**, 765
  voidable, **15**, 671, 672, 699; **18**, 607
    conditio causa data, **15**, 34, 40
    jus quaesitum tertio, **15**, 839
  warrandice—
    generally, **18**, 701
    See also WARRANDICE
  whole, to be construed as a, **15**, 755
  will, to make, *jus quaesitum tertio*, **15**, 843
  winding up by court, consequences of, **4**, 758
  words, meaning to be given to, **15**, 753
  writing, in, **15**, 666, 667, 668
    construction, **15**, 747, 748
  wrongful interference—
    business, with, **15**, 579
    performance of contract, with, **15**, 577
    prospective contract, with, **15**, 578
  wrongful witholding of sums due under, interest
    payable on, **12**, 1012
Contract, insurance, freight (cif) contract
  bill of lading, **21**, 525*n*, 528*n*, 566
  meaning, **21**, 524*n*
Contract of employment
  acquiescence, **9**, 36
  appointment of receiver, effect of, **4**, 624
  authorities, weight attached to, **9**, 17
  breach of, remedies for, **9**, 194
  capacity, **9**, 25
  certainty, rules relating to, **9**, 26
  change in constitution of firm, effect, **16**, 1040
  changing conditions, **9**, 34
  collateral, **9**, 27
  collective agreements, **9**, 32
  content of—
    acquiescence, **9**, 36
    changes in terms, refusal to accept, dismissal as
      result of, **9**, 259
    changing conditions, **9**, 34
    collective agreements, **9**, 32
    express terms, **9**, 31

Contract of employment—*continued*
content of—*continued*
  implied terms, **9**, 31
  other statutory sources, **9**, 37
  sources, generally, **9**, 29
  written statement—
    generally, **9**, 30
    incorporation, whether taking place, **9**, 35
    relevance of, **9**, 33
continuous employment, effect of re-engagement, **9**, 50
contract for services distinguished from, **9**, 18
control, presence of, **9**, 19
dissolution of partnership, effect, **16**, 1098
distinctive features, **9**, 19
duration, **22**, 827
duty to protect implied by, **7**, 42
economic independence, test of, **9**, 19
European Convention on the Calculation of Time Limits, **22**, 827
existence of, effect on jurisdiction of industrial tribunal, **9**, 308
express terms, **9**, 31
fixed-term contracts—
  expiry without renewal, **9**, 217
  industrial tribunal, effect on jurisdiction of, **9**, 311
  meaning, **9**, 209
  unfair dismissal, effect on, **9**, 209, 217
football contract, *see* FOOTBALL
formalities of, **9**, 20
generally, **3**, 6
holidays and holiday pay, **22**, 818
illegality, **9**, 23
implied terms, **9**, 22, 31
judicial review, application for, **9**, 40
liquidated damages clause, **15**, 800
lump labour, **3**, 6
master and servant, *see* MASTER AND SERVANT
minors, **10**, 1078
multiple test for identifying, **9**, 19
mutual obligation, test of, **9**, 19
natural justice, application of, **9**, 39
nominate consensual, **14**, 1004
offer and acceptance, rules relating to, **9**, 26
other doctrines, **9**, 26
other statutory sources, **9**, 37
plant, equipment and materials, **9**, 78
premises occupied under, **11**, 2043, 2057
  tenancy not secure, **11**, 1937, 1938, 1947
proper law of, **9**, 28
receiver, appointment, effect, **4**, 624
restrictive covenants, third party rights, **15**, 849
rights and duties within—
  continuous employment, *see* EMPLOYMENT
  employee, of, *see* EMPLOYEE
  employer, of, *see* EMPLOYER
  hours of work, *see* HOURS OF WORK
  remuneration under statute, *see* REMUNERATION
  wages, payment of, *see* WAGES
seaman, **21**, 241, 261
separate identity of, **9**, 18
services, contract for, distinguished, **9**, 18
services to employer under, **6**, 142
sources, **9**, 29

Contract of employment—*continued*
statutory rights and duties—
  action short of dismissal, *see* DISMISSAL
  criminal law—
    conspiracy, **9**, 122
    generally, **9**, 121
    malicious mischief, **9**, 123
    particular employments, **9**, 125
    protection of property, **9**, 122
    workplace occupations, **9**, 124
  disabled employees—
    generally, **9**, 119
    quotas, **9**, 120
  employee's invention—
    copyright, **9**, 128
    made after May 1978 ..., **9**, 127
    made before June 1978 ..., **9**, 126
  industrial action—
    criminal law, **9**, 131
    different forms, **9**, 132
    generally, **9**, 129
    go-slow, **9**, 132
    remedies, **9**, 133
    statutory rules, **9**, 130
    strike, **9**, 132
    working to rule, **9**, 132
  maternity, *see* MATERNITY RIGHTS
  rehabilitation of offenders, **9**, 118
  time off, *see* EMPLOYMENT
statutory written particulars, relevance of, **9**, 21
Sunday work, **9**, 24
termination of—
  benefits, recoupment of—
    calculation, method of, **9**, 299
    future loss, **9**, 301
    general principles, **9**, 298
    regulations, effect of, **9**, 300
  dismissal, statement of reasons for, right to, **9**, 143
  insolvency, *see* INSOLVENCY
  non-dismissal, **9**, 221
  notice, by—
    common law, **9**, 134
    statutory provisions, **9**, 135
    valid notice, requirements of, **9**, 136
  notice, without—
    frustration, **9**, 138
    partnership, dissolution of, **9**, 139
    passage of time, **9**, 141
    performance, **9**, 141
    repudiation, **9**, 137
    sequestration, **9**, 140, 145–146
    special employments, **9**, 142
    winding up, **4**, 861; **9**, 140
  redundancy, *see* REDUNDANCY
  resignation, by, **9**, 224
  self-dismissal, by, **9**, 223
  unfair dismissal, *see* UNFAIR DISMISSAL
  wrongful dismissal, *see* WRONGFUL DISMISSAL
unemployment benefit, effect on—
  allocation of wages, **21**, 809
  commission, worker paid by, **21**, 806
  default in payment of wages where, **21**, 807
  generally, **21**, 803, 805

Contract of employment—_continued_
unemployment benefit, effect of—_continued_
  no work no wages rule, **21**, 806
  part-time teacher, position of, **21**, 812
  partial payment of wages, where, **21**, 808
  succession of short-term contracts, where, **21**, 812
  termination of employment, **21**, 812
  trade dispute, termination of contract during, **21**, 868
  worker on call, **21**, 825
winding up, effect of, **4**, 861; **9**, 140
written statement—
  contents of, **9**, 30
  incorporation, whether taking place, **9**, 35
  relevance of, **9**, 21, 33
Contract of sale
See SALE AND SUPPLY OF GOODS
Contract-tort fallacy
generally, **15**, 9
Contracting out
unfair dismissal rights, effect on, **9**, 207
Contractor
building contract, _see_ BUILDING CONTRACT
Crown—
  Crown privileges and immunities, application, **7**, 741, 763
  liability of Crown for actings of, **7**, 763
  status, **7**, 763
independent—
  delict committed by, liability, **15**, 242, 243, 251
  employer's liability, **15**, 331, 336
  liability for nuisance created by, **14**, 2138
  vicarious liability, **15**, 242, 243, 251
owner, as, **14**, 1602
strict liability, **15**, 159
tunnelling, required to employ support rules, **14**, 1637
valuation, principal method of, **25**, 71
Contractor's principle
capital value, calculation of effective, **24**, 542
decapitalisation rate, **24**, 544
deductions and allowances, **24**, 543
factories and workshops, valuation of, **24**, 628
modification of, **24**, 545
valuation method, **24**, 527, 542–545
Contributory negligence
See DELICT
Control of pollution
See POLLUTION
Control visit
VAT records, inspection and verification, **7**, 1401
Controlled tenancy
generally, **13**, 603
Controlled waste
See WASTE
Controlled waters
meaning, **20**, 271; **25**, 400n
oil platform within, **20**, 271
Contumacy
extradition rules on, **12**, 536, 537
Convalescence
sickness benefit, **21**, 886

Convene
meaning, **4**, 475
Convention
interpretation—
  statute of, use in, **12**, 1153
  travaux préparatoires, **12**, 1154
Convention Against Illicit Traffic in Narcotic Drugs and Psychotropic Substances
generally, **21**, 42
Convention and Protocol Relating to the Status of Refugees, **12**, 116, 314
Convention concerning International Carriage by Rail (COTIF)
generally, **3**, 705, 727
limitation of actions, **16**, 2201
Uniform Rules, **3**, 706, 727
Convention for Regulating Police of North Sea Fisheries, **11**, 124
British sea-fisheries officers' powers, **11**, 126
Convention for the European Patent for the Common Market (Community Patent Convention), **18**, 815, 815n, 902, 1611, 1611n
Convention for the Prevention and Punishment of the Crime of Genocide
extradition agreement, **12**, 508
Convention for the Protection of Human Rights and Fundamental Freedoms
See EUROPEAN CONVENTION FOR THE PROTECTION OF HUMAN RIGHTS AND FREEDOMS
Convention for the Protection of Individuals with regard to the Automated Processing of Personal data (1981), **18**, 1501
Convention for the Protection of New Varieties of Plants (1961), **18**, 911
Convention for the Unification of Certain Rules relating to International Carriage by Air (The Warsaw Convention), **16**, 2200, 2200n; **21**, 758n
Convention of Royal Burghs
replacement by Convention of Scottish Local Authorities, **14**, 81
role, **14**, 17
Convention of Scottish Local Authorities (COSLA)
advice, **14**, 86
Association of County Councils in Scotland, replacement of, **14**, 81
committee—
  ex officio members, **14**, 84
  Executive, **14**, 83
  office-bearers, **14**, 85
  procedure, **14**, 83
  representation at, **14**, 84
  Standing, **14**, 83
Convention of Royal Burghs, replacement of, **14**, 81
District Councils Association for Scotland, replacement of, **14**, 81
effect of, **14**, 88
finance, **14**, 87

Convention of Scottish Local Authorities (COSLA)—*continued*
meetings—
  procedure, **14**, 83
  quorum, **14**, 84
  representation at, **14**, 84
objects, **14**, 82
office-bearers, **14**, 85
Scottish Counties of Cities Association, replacement of, **14**, 81
sport, regulation of, **19**, 1222
staffing, **14**, 86
Convention on a Code of Conduct for Liner Conferences
generally, **21**, 118
Convention on Conduct of Fishing Operations in the North Atlantic 1967
generally, **11**, 173
Convention on Harmonized Commodity Description and Coding
European Union Common Customs Tariff, **7**, 1015
Convention on International Bills of Exchange and International Trade Law
entry into force, **4**, 105
predecessors to, **4**, 105
Convention on Law applicable to Trusts and their Recognition 1985
provision for ratification of, **24**, 127, 127*n*
Convention on Liability for Death and Personal Injury to Passengers, **3**, 704
Convention on Limitation of Liability for Maritime Claims (London Convention)
See SEA, CARRIAGE BY (limitation of liability)
Convention on Long-range Transboundary Air Pollution
generally, **19**, 687
Convention on Special Missions
generally, **19**, 684
Convention on the Contract for the International Carriage of Goods by Road (CMR)
application, **3**, 646
contrary stipulations, **3**, 668
generally, **3**, 646; **20**, 500
jurisdiction, **3**, 662, 663
limitation of actions, **16**, 2203
Convention on the Contract for the International Carriage of Passengers by Road (CVR)
application, **3**, 687
contrary stipulations, **3**, 694
generally, **3**, 687
jurisdiction, **3**, 692
Convention on the Contract for the International Carriage of Passengers and Luggage by Road, **20**, 493
limitation of actions, **16**, 2202
Convention on the Grant of European Patents (European Patent Convention), **18**, 891, 1611*n*
Convention on the Physical Protection of Nuclear Material, **12**, 508

Convention relating to a Uniform Law on the Formation of Contracts for the International Sale of Goods
generally, **20**, 892*n*
Convention relating to a Uniform Law on the International Sale of Goods
generally, **20**, 892*n*
Convention relating to the Carriage of Passengers and their Luggage by Sea (Athens Convention)
See SHIPPING
Convention respecting the Liquor Traffic in the North Sea, **11**, 129
Conventions of the constitution
generally, **5**, 306
Conversion
legal rights, **25**, 816
reconversion, **25**, 816
Conveyance (deed)
animals, of, *see* CARRIAGE
conflict of interests, solicitor's obligations, **13**, 1188
conveyancer, *see* CONVEYANCER
conveyancing services, meaning, **13**, 1228*n*
feu writ, **12**, 1237, 1244
implied terms, **12**, 1235
individual performing own, **13**, 1183
interpretation—
  a coelo usque ad centrum principle, **12**, 1243
  boundaries, description of, **12**, 1239
    bounding charter, **12**, 1239
    bounding title, **12**, 1239
    measurements, **12**, 1240
    new boundaries, creation of, **12**, 1240
    plans, **12**, 1240
    sea, **12**, 1239
    See also BOUNDARY
  disposition, **12**, 1237
    description of subjects conveyed, **12**, 1238
    dispone, meaning, **12**, 1237
  feuduty—
    imposition of, **12**, 1249
    redemption, **12**, 1249
  incorporeal rights, conditions involving, **12**, 1244
  minerals, **12**, 1242, 1243
  pertinents, **12**, 1242
  plans, **12**, 1240
    boundaries, conflict with, **12**, 1240
    colours used in, **12**, 1240
    measurements, **12**, 1240
    registration, **12**, 1240
  real burdens and conditions—
    constitution, principles for, **12**, 1246
    creation, **12**, 1245
    enforcement, **12**, 1248
    generally, **12**, 1245
    interpretation, **12**, 1247
    real burden, meaning, **12**, 1245
    real condition or restriction, meaning, **12**, 1245
  reddendo, **12**, 1249
  servitudes, of, **12**, 1242
  statutory descriptions, **12**, 1241

Conveyance (deed)
interpretation—*continued*
  subjects conveyed, description of, **12**, 1238
  warrandice, **12**, 1250, 1255
notary public, **13**, 1220
pre-emption clause, **12**, 1244
redemption clause, **12**, 1244
reduction, **13**, 37
restriction on, **13**, 1182, 1183, 1185
Scottish Conveyancing and Executry Services
  Board—
  appointments to, **13**, 1224
  constitution, **13**, 1224
  expenses, **13**, 1225
  functions, **13**, 1225
  powers, **13**, 1225
  register of qualified conveyancers, **13**, 1227
  regulation of independent qualified
    conveyancers, **13**, 1230
  regulatory responsibilities, **13**, 1236–1238
where no term of entry specified, **12**, 1218
Conveyance (transport)
See MOTOR VEHICLE; PUBLIC TRANSPORT
Conveyancer
Conveyancing and Executry Services Board,
  powers of intervention, **13**, 1237
disclosure of documents, **13**, 1238
inadequate professional services provided by, **13**,
  1236
professional misconduct, **13**, 1236
qualified—
  client's money, holding of, **13**, 1230
  commissions, disclosure of and accounting for,
    13, 1230
  conflict of interest, **13**, 1230
  generally, **13**, 1226
  independent, **13**, 1229
    regulation, **13**, 1230
  offences, **13**, 1231
  practice as, **13**, 1228
  pretending to be, **13**, 1231
  register, **13**, 1227
  rules for, **13**, 1227
  who may become, **13**, 1226
Conveyancing
a me, **18**, 88, 93
a me vel de me, **18**, 99, 100
accretion, **18**, 677
assignation, *see* MOVEABLE PROPERTY
bonds, *see* BOND
boundary, *see* BOUNDARY
break-off, **18**, 197, 205
  mineral rights, right of support, **18**, 264
building society offering service, **3**, 344
burden, real—
  title sheets, **6**, 707, 711
  whether entitled to, **6**, 763
consent of transferor and transferee, **18**, 613, 614
contract preceding, **18**, 606
  failure of, effect, **18**, 608
creation, generally, **18**, 388
custom and precedent, **22**, 260
de me, **18**, 88, 93
death, transmission of property on, *see* DEATH

Conveyancing—*continued*
deeds—
  classification, **6**, 471, 472
  definition, **6**, 401
  delivery of, **6**, 444–446
  error in, authentication of, **6**, 422–426
  execution of, **6**, 430–432
  generally, *see* DEED
  privileged writings, *see* DEED
  probative writings, *see* DEED
  registration of, *see* DEED
  stamp duty, **6**, 447
disposition, *see* DISPOSITION
extinction of rights and obligations—
  discharge generally, **6**, 614
  general discharges, **6**, 616
  specific discharges, **6**, 615
feu grants, *see* FEU GRANTS
feudal law, **18**, 88
  a me, **18**, 93
  de me, **18**, 93
  inter vivos—
    adjudication, charter of, **18**, 94, 95
    assignation of unfeudalised title, **18**, 104
    clare constat, **18**, 94
    confirmation, charter of, **18**, 94, 103
    consolidation, **18**, 98
    Crown specialities, **18**, 105
    disposition, **18**, 99
      a me vel de me, **18**, 99, 100
    infeftment without entry, **18**, 102
    investiture, renewal, **18**, 94, 106
    modern usage, **18**, 107
    novodamus, charter of, **18**, 94, 95
    original charter, **18**, 94
    precepts of sasine, **18**, 101
    progress, charter by, **18**, 94
    resignation, **18**, 97
      charter of, **18**, 94, 103
    subinfeudation, **18**, 96
  investiture, renewal, **18**, 94, 106, 108
  mortis causa—
    clare constat, **18**, 109
    courtesy, **18**, 110
    destination, **18**, 111
    generally, **18**, 108
    heir-at-law, **18**, 108
    heir-of-line, **18**, 108
    heir of provision, **18**, 111
    heir of tailzie, **18**, 111
    heirs portioner, **18**, 108
    intestate, owner dying, **18**, 108
    service, **18**, 109
    tailzie, **18**, 111
    terce, **18**, 110
feuduty, *see* FEUDUTY
floating charge, *see* FLOATING CHARGE
forms of, **5**, 18, 31
fraud, effect of, **11**, 756
generally, **18**, 701
ground annual, *see* GROUND ANNUAL
Halliday and Henry Reports—
  land transfers prior to 1835, **6**, 405
  Law Commission, 1838 report, **6**, 406

Conveyancing—*continued*
Halliday and Henry Reports—*continued*
  legislation subsequent to, **6**, 410
  registration of title, **6**, 411
  statutory reforms, **6**, 408, 409
  titles to land, consolidation of law, **6**, 407
heritable, *see* HERITABLE CONVEYANCING
heritable property, law of, relationship to law of
  conveyancing, **18**, 1, 1*n*
heritage, sale of, **20**, 903, 904
historical development—
  charters, development of, **6**, 404
  early history, **6**, 402
  feudal system in Scotland, **6**, 403, 473*n*
  generally, **6**, 401
horizontal limits of estate, **18**, 197
intention as part of—
  consent of transferor and transferee, **18**, 613
  error, **18**, 614, 617
  force and fear, **18**, 614, 615
  fraud, **18**, 614, 616
  real vices, **18**, 614
  theft, **18**, 618
  vices of consent, **18**, 614
law of obligations and property distinguished, **11**,
  756
law reform—
  generally, **22**, 629, 647
  nineteenth century, **22**, 647
lease, *see* LEASE
Lord Advocate's Conveyancing Committee, **22**,
  647
minerals, *see* MINERALS
minute of waiver, **18**, 426
missives, *see* MISSIVES
modern, statutory foundations, **6**, 407
negative prescription, reduction of period, **22**,
  647
obligations—
  ad facta praestandum, **6**, 622
  annuity, bonds of, **6**, 619
  bond granted without security, **6**, 617–625
  cash credit, bonds of, **6**, 620
  caution, bonds of, **6**, 621
  corroboration, bonds of, **6**, 624
  fidelity, bonds of, **6**, 623
  law of, and law of property distinguished, **11**, 756
  personal bonds, **6**, 618
  purchaser, of, **6**, 640
  relief, bonds of, **6**, 625
  seller, of, **6**, 640
  standard security, **6**, 633
overriding interests, *see* OVERRIDING INTERESTS
pertinents—
  generally, **18**, 199, 199*n*
  See also PERTINENT
positive prescription, **22**, 647
real burden created in, **18**, 386, 387, 388
  only principal deed may be consulted, **18**, 388
  placing of burdens in document, **18**, 388
  repetition in subsequent conveyance, **18**, 396
  servient tenement, condition must relate to, **18**,
  388
  See also HERITABLE CONVEYANCING

Conveyancing—*continued*
real conditions, *see* HERITABLE CONVEYANCING
Register of Charges, **6**, 469
registration of title, **22**, 647
  See also REGISTRATION OF TITLE
Roman law, **6**, 402, 404
royal commission 1937 ..., **22**, 647
sasine—
  new form of precept, **22**, 647
  registration, **22**, 629, 647
  superfluity under Titles to Land (Scotland) Act
    1858 ..., **22**, 647
  See also SASINES
Scots law, generally, **18**, 606
seller, obligations of, **6**, 641
servitude, creation, **18**, 450
sheriff court jurisdiction, **6**, 1090
shooting rights, **11**, 897
simplification, procedures, **22**, 647
stamp duty, exemption of charitable bodies, **3**, 1164
standard conditions, **6**, 634, 635
  See also STANDARD SECURITY
standard security, *see* STANDARD SECURITY
statutory conveyance, *see* STATUTORY CONVEYANCE
subinfeudation—
  generally, **18**, 88
  See also FEUDAL LAW
symbolic delivery, **6**, 402
tenendas clause, **18**, 199, 199*n*
title, *see* TITLE (to property)
title, registration of, *see* REGISTRATION OF TITLE
title sheet, *see* LAND REGISTER OF SCOTLAND
traditionibus non nudis pactis dominia rerum
  transferuntur rule, **18**, 606
transfer of ownership by—
  generally, **18**, 606
transferee, consent of, **18**, 613, 614
transferor, consent of, **18**, 613, 614
uninfeft proprietor, land, of, **18**, 645, 645*n*
voidable title, where, **18**, 607
warrandice, *see* WARRANDICE
Conveyancing practice
as aid to interpretation of statute, **12**, 1161
Conveyancing services
building societies' power to offer, **3**, 344
Convicium
defamation, as, **16**, 2173
definition, **16**, 2173
incorrect use of term, **15**, 558, 558*n*
limitation of actions, **16**, 2173
public hatred, contempt and ridicule, **15**, 558
Convicted person
domicile, **4**, 30
membership of House of Commons, exclusion
  from, **5**, 379
prisoner, *see* PRISONER
voting in election, disqualification from, **5**, 374
Conviction
wrongful, compensation for, **7**, 730
Cookery
society promoting, **12**, 694*n*
Cooking
facilities, tolerable standard, **11**, 1979
ship on, regulations as to, **21**, 245, 247

Cooking—*continued*
water supply—
  domestic use, for, **25**, 506
  unfit, **14**, 2079
Cooling-off period
consumer credit agreement, **5**, 862–866
insurance contract, **12**, 819–821
investor protection, **12**, 1336
Co-operative Development Agency
status of, **12**, 607
Co-operative housing associations, 11, 1924, 1927
occupancy dependent upon, **11**, 2043, 2057
premises occupied under, tenancy not secure, **11**, 1937, 1938, 1947
Co-operative society
agricultural, forestry or fishing associations, **12**, 614
Agricultural and Horticultural Co-operation Scheme, **12**, 617
choice as business medium, **16**, 1004
committee, managers and officers, **12**, 613
conduct of business, **12**, 607
democratic control, **12**, 607
distribution of economic results, **12**, 607
general principles, **12**, 607
housing, **12**, 617
inter-society co-operation, **12**, 607
meaning, **12**, 607
meetings, **12**, 613
membership, **12**, 607
  restriction on, **12**, 607
profits, **12**, 607
registration, cancellation, **12**, 607
restrictive trade practices, **12**, 614, 617
share capital, **12**, 607
trade association, exclusion, **4**, 1147, 1164
wholesale, **12**, 614
See also INDUSTRIAL AND PROVIDENT SOCIETY
Co-ownership
common ownership, concept of, **18**, 531, 536, 537
common passage and stair, **18**, 18, 24, 26
  See also TENEMENT BUILDING
common property—
  acquisition, **18**, 22, 22*n*
  alienation of *pro indiviso* share, **18**, 23
  alterations, **18**, 25
    consent of each co-owner required, **18**, 25
    unanimity rule, **18**, 23
  cleaning of, byelaws relating to, **14**, 278
  co-proprietors, use made of property by, **18**, 23, 24
  common interest, doctrine of, **18**, 26, 356, 357
  common passage and stair, **18**, 18, 24, 26
    clean or paint, requirement to, **14**, 278, 278*n*
  constitution, **18**, 22
  court action against third party, unanimity rule, **18**, 23
  definition, **18**, 357
  derivative acquisition, **18**, 22
  disagreement between co-proprietors—
    judicial factor, appointment of, **18**, 31
    judicial regulations, **18**, 31

Co-ownership—*continued*
common property—*continued*
  division and sale—
    co-owner's right to pursue for, **18**, 20
    contract as to, effect, **18**, 32
    entitlement, **18**, 32, 32*n*
    generally, **6**, 1062; **13**, 97; **18**, 23, 536
    indivisible property, **18**, 33
    matrimonial home, **18**, 27, 27*n*, 32
    personal bar, where, **18**, 32
    private bargain, sale by, **18**, 33
    procedure, **18**, 33, 33*n*
    property which may not be divided or sold, **18**, 32
    roup, sale by, **18**, 33
  exclusive possession maintained by one co-owner, **18**, 24
  generally, **18**, 17, 19
  in re communi melior est conditio prohibentis, **18**, 23
  inhibition, **8**, 158
  joint property—
    common property distinguished, **18**, 20
    relationship with, **18**, 19
    whether common property convertible to, **18**, 34
  judicial factor, appointment of, **18**, 31
  judicial factor appointed on, **24**, 278
  judicial regulation, **18**, 23, 30
  juristic acts, **18**, 28
  lease, grant of, **18**, 28, 28*n*
    unanimity rule, **18**, 23
  management, **18**, 23, 537
    consent of all *pro indiviso* owners, **18**, 23
    judicial factor, appointment of, **18**, 31
    judicial regulation, **18**, 23, 30
    majority views, **18**, 23, 23*n*
    title to sue, **18**, 28
  matrimonial home, **18**, 23
    alteration or repair—
      co-owner's right to carry out, **18**, 27
      expenditure, apportionment, **18**, 27
    conveyance to third party of *pro indiviso* share, **18**, 27
    definition, **18**, 27
    division and sale, **18**, 27, 27*n*, 32
    generally, **18**, 27
    occupancy rights, court order as to, **18**, 27
    standard security or other dealing in, grant in relation to *pro indiviso* share, **18**, 27
  nemo dat quod non habet rule, **18**, 28
  non-possessory right in security, subject of, **18**, 28
  original acquisition, **18**, 22, 22*n*
  pledge, grant of, **18**, 28
  prevention of changes to property, co-owner's rights, **18**, 20
  pro indiviso ownership, as, **18**, 17
  pro indiviso shares—
    acts beyond powers of single *pro indiviso* owner, **18**, 28
    generally, **18**, 28
    nemo dat quod non habet rule, **18**, 28
    non-possessory right in security, **18**, 28
    subdivision, **18**, 28
      disposal of subdivided shares, **18**, 28

Co-ownership—*continued*
common property—*continued*
  pro indiviso shares—*continued*
    survivorship destination, **18**, 28
    title to sue, **18**, 28
    transfer—
      inter vivos, **18**, 28
      mortis causa, **18**, 28
  profits, share of, **18**, 24
  real burdens, **18**, 23, 26
  real conditions, **18**, 23, 26
  repairs—
    generally, **18**, 25
    matrimonial home, **18**, 27
    unanimity rule, **18**, 23
  rights of co-owners, **18**, 20
  servitudes, **18**, 23, 26, 28
  shares—
    different sizes, where, **18**, 22
    equality, presumption as to, **18**, 22
    pro indiviso, see pro indiviso shares *above*
  sheriff court jurisdiction, **6**, 1062
  standard security, subject of, **18**, 28
  tenement building, **18**, 24, 26
  title to sue, **18**, 29
  use—
    co-proprietor's rights as to, **18**, 23, 24
    excessive benefit, on proprietor obtaining, **18**, 24
    majority decisions as to, **18**, 23
    ordinary and extraordinary, **18**, 24
commonty, **18**, 18
  distinctive features, **18**, 37
  division, **18**, 37
  inseparable pertinent, as, **18**, 37
  meaning, **18**, 37
conjunct property, **18**, 17
corporate property, **18**, 18*n*
feudal system, generally, **18**, 51
generally, **18**, 1, 17
heirs portioner, **18**, 18, 55, 108
joint property—
  alienation of property, **18**, 35
  beneficial interest, **18**, 34
  characteristics, **18**, 35
  club, property of, **18**, 34, 34*n*
  common property—
    joint property distinguished, **18**, 20, 34
    relationship with joint property, **18**, 19
    whether convertible to joint property, **18**, 34
  corporation, property of, **18**, 34*n*
  destruction of property, **18**, 35
  division and sale, no entitlement to, **18**, 35
  generally, **18**, 17, 19, 531, 536, 537
  juristic act, **18**, 36, 36*n*
  majority decisions, **18**, 36, 36*n*
  management, **18**, 36, 36*n*, 537
  no separate shares, **18**, 17, 20
  number of trustees or association members reduced to one, **18**, 35
  ownership passing on death or resignation, **18**, 20
  pro indiviso ownership, as, **18**, 17, 20
  resignation of death of trustee or association member, **18**, 35

Co-ownership—*continued*
joint property—*continued*
  title, **18**, 34
  trust property, **18**, 20, 538
    generally, **18**, 34
  unincorporated association, property of, **18**, 20, 34*n*
    generally, **18**, 34
  unity of title, **18**, 20, 35
  winding up of trust or association, **18**, 35
jus possidendi, pro indiviso holders of same right to, **18**, 118, 130
part ownership, **18**, 17
partnership property, **18**, 18, 18*n*
pro indiviso ownership—
  common property as, **18**, 17
  defining characteristics, **18**, 17
  joint property as, **18**, 17
ship, **18**, 18
tenement building, **18**, 18
terminology, **18**, 17
timeshare agreement, **18**, 39
trust property, **18**, 18, 39
Copenhagen
free zone, as, **7**, 1164
Copyright
abridgements, **18**, 1054
action relating to, defences, **17**, 26
adaptations—
  computer programs, **18**, 1066
  generally, **18**, 942, 1049
  literary, dramatic or musical works, **18**, 1065
  ownership rights, **18**, 1005, 1042
advertisement, in, **1**, 509
aesthetic or intellectual quality, no requirement for, **18**, 941, 943
agreement, bilateral agreement for exchange of, **4**, 1160
anonymous works—
  generally, **18**, 995, 996
  term of copyright, **18**, 1032
anthologies for educational use, **18**, 1111
architectural works, **3**, 139; **18**, 957, 965, 992
  commissioned, implied licence, **18**, 1010
  design documents, **18**, 1155
  reconstruction of building, **18**, 1128
archives, permitted acts in, **18**, 1115–1120
artistic craftsmanship, works of, **18**, 957, 966
  design documents, **18**, 1155
artistic works, **18**, 957
  anonymous or pseudonymous, **18**, 995, 996, 1032
  character merchandising, and, **18**, 1157
  Crown copyright, term of, **18**, 1034, 1037
  design documents, **18**, 1155
  incidental inclusion, **18**, 1108
  industrial designs—
    generally, **18**, 1153, 1154
    transitional provisions, **18**, 1161
  industrial production, copyright limited where, **18**, 1156
  marketed, copyright limited where, **18**, 1156
  moral rights, *see* moral rights *below*
  originality, **18**, 1153

Copyright—*continued*
artistic works—*continued*
    parliamentary copyright, term of, **18**, 1036, 1037
    permitted acts, **18**, 1128
    quality, no requirement of—
        aesthetic or intellectual quality, **18**, 941, 943
        artistic quality, **18**, 957, 964, 1153
    term of copyright, **18**, 1029, 1030
    three- or two-dimensional reproduction, **18**, 942
    typefaces, **18**, 1160
assignation, **6**, 600; **20**, 55
    assignee, dealing by, **18**, 1012
    co-ownership, cases of, **18**, 1011
    exclusive, **18**, 1006
    expenses incurred following, **18**, 1588
    future copyright, of, **18**, 1006
    generally, **18**, 1005, 1006
    meaning, **18**, 1005
    partial, **18**, 1006
    restricted acts, in respect of, **18**, 1006
    security, in, **18**, 1007
    writing, must be in, **18**, 1006
assignment, **3**, 139
author—
    anonymous works, **18**, 995, 996
    collective works, **18**, 988
    commissioned works, **18**, 997
    compilations, **18**, 989
    computer-generated works, **18**, 993
    death, *post mortem auctoris*, **18**, 1029
    division of copyright rights, **18**, 994
    employment by another, work made in course of, **18**, 997–999
    endurance of copyright beyond author's lifetime, **18**, 978
    expenses, tax treatment, **18**, 1588
    false attribution of authorship, **18**, 1130, 1138
    folklore, works of, **18**, 996
    infringement, co-author may sue alone, **18**, 985
    joint—
        collective works distinguished, **18**, 988
        compilations distinguished, **18**, 989
        generally, **18**, 937, 985
        infringement, co-author may sue alone, **18**, 985
        later editions, **18**, 986
        management of common property, **18**, 985
        media copyrights, **18**, 987
        presumption of authorship, **18**, 985
        term of copyright, **18**, 1033
        test, **18**, 986
        title, passing, **18**, 985
    journalist, employee, **18**, 997
    later editions, **18**, 986
    lump sum payments to—
        backward spreading, **18**, 1586
        forward spreading, **18**, 1587
        tax treatment, **18**, 1585–1589
    meaning, **18**, 979, 980
    moral rights, *see* moral rights *below*
    originator of idea and actual author, positions of, **18**, 990–992

Copyright—*continued*
author—*continued*
    ownership by, **18**, 978, 979
    paternity as moral right, **18**, 1130
    presumption of authorship, **18**, 985
    pseudonymous works, **18**, 995
    qualification for protection, **18**, 936
    royalties—
        foreign, **18**, 1589
        tax treatment, **18**, 1585
    spiritual world, communications from, **18**, 991
    tax treatment—
        lump sum payments, **18**, 1585
        non-resident author, **18**, 1589
        royalties, **18**, 1585
    where no longer owner, artistic works, **18**, 1128
automatic creation, **18**, 979
Berne Convention for the Protection of Literary and Artistic Works 1886 ..., **18**, 804, 890, 931, 1151
Bible, **18**, 1002
Book of Common Prayer, **18**, 1002
breach of confidence, and, **18**, 1452
breach of trust and confidence, and, **18**, 1129
British colonies, **18**, 935
broadcasting, effect on activities of those concerned with, **17**, 1
broadcasts, **18**, 933, 948, 1024, 1025
    advance programme information, duty to provide, **18**, 1025, 1663
    author, meaning, **18**, 979, 982
    copying for private and domestic use, **18**, 1123
    educational establishment, recording made by, **18**, 1113
    educational establishment playing, **18**, 1112
    European Community legislation, **18**, 1643, 1644
    generally, **18**, 973
    infringement, generally, **18**, 1055, 1062–1064
    joint authorship, **18**, 987
    meaning, **18**, 971
    neighbouring rights, as, **18**, 967, 971
    ownership rights, **18**, 1005, 1042
    place of transmission, **18**, 940
    repeats, **18**, 974, 1040
    satellite, **18**, 972
    sound, **18**, 971
    spoken words, use of, **18**, 1107
    subtitled, for the disabled, provision of copies, **18**, 1124
    television, **18**, 971
    term of copyright, **18**, 1040
    unauthorised transmissions, dealing in apparatus for, **18**, 1083
building, in, **3**, 139
cable programmes—
    author, meaning, **18**, 979, 983
    copying for private and domestic use, **18**, 1123
    educational establishment, recording made by, **18**, 1113
    educational establishment showing, **18**, 1112
    European Community legislation, **18**, 1643, 1644
    generally, **18**, 933, 948, 975, 1024, 1025

Copyright—*continued*
cable programmes—*continued*
  infringement—
    generally, **18**, 1055
    playing or showing in public, by, **18**, 1062–
      1064
  joint authorship, **18**, 987
  neighbouring rights, as, **18**, 967, 975
  no copyright, where, **18**, 976
  ownership rights, **18**, 1005, 1042
  place of transmission, **18**, 940
  spoken words, use of, **18**, 1107
  subtitled, for the disabled, provision of copies,
    18, 1124
  term of copyright, **18**, 1040
  unauthorised transmissions, dealing in apparatus
    for, **18**, 1083
calculations, **18**, 1153
capital gains tax, **18**, 1600
Catechisms, Longer and Shorter, **18**, 1000, 1035
Channel Islands, **18**, 935
charts, **18**, 958
Church of England Synod, Measures of, **18**, 1000,
  1035
collages, **18**, 957, 958, 963
collection of rights, as, **18**, 994
collective works, **18**, 988
  moral rights, **18**, 1136
commercial publication—
  meaning, **18**, 1137
  moral rights, and, **18**, 1137
commissioned works, **18**, 997
  implied licence, **18**, 1010
compilations, **18**, 989
composer, *see* author *above*
computer, material stored on, **18**, 1153
computer programs—
  adaptation, infringement by, **18**, 1066
  generally, **18**, 931, 1023
  infringement, **18**, 1051
    transient copies, **18**, 1052
  literary works, as, **18**, 950, 954
  rental rights, **18**, 1059
  translation, meaning, **18**, 1065
computer-generated works—
  author, meaning, **18**, 979
  authorship, **18**, 993
  term of copyright, **18**, 1031
Confession of Faith, **18**, 1002
copies, issue of—
  infringement by, *see* infringement *below*
  ownership rights, **18**, 1005, 1042, 1057
copy-protection, dealing in devices designed to
  circumvent, **18**, 1082
Copyright, Designs and Patents Act 1988—
  application, **18**, 935
  extent, **18**, 935
  generally, **18**, 932
Copyright Licensing Agency, **18**, 1013
Copyright Tribunal, *see* COPYRIGHT TRIBUNAL
criminal offences in relation to—
  conspiracy to defraud, **18**, 1098
  delivery up, order for, **18**, 1095
  generally, **18**, 1093

Copyright—*continued*
criminal offences in relation to—*continued*
  penalties, **18**, 1094
  piracy, repression, **18**, 1099
  prohibited goods, treatment of infringing
    copies as, **18**, 1097
  search warrant, issue of, **18**, 1096
  video film, renting illicit copy, **18**, 1098
Crown copyright, **18**, 979
  Acts of Parliament, **18**, 1000
    term of copyright, **18**, 1035
  duration, **18**, 1000
  films, **18**, 1039
  generally, **18**, 1000
  literary, dramatic, musical or artistic works—
    transitional provisions, **18**, 1037
  meaning, **18**, 1000
  Measures of the General Synod of the Church
    of England, **18**, 1000
    term of copyright, **18**, 1035
  moral rights, **18**, 1134, 1136
  officer or servant of—
    works made after retirement, **18**, 1000
    works made in course of duties, **18**, 1000
  reproduction of copyright material, permission
    for, **18**, 1028
  sound recordings, **18**, 1039
  term of copyright—
    Acts and Measures, **18**, 1035
    literary, dramatic, musical and artistic works,
      18, 1034
Crown prerogative, **18**, 1002
current events, report of—
  generally, **18**, 1106
  moral rights, and, **18**, 1136
  spoken words, **18**, 1107
databases, **18**, 953, 993
  infringement—
    transient copies, **18**, 1052
death, transfer on, **18**, 1005
deceased's liability to tax, **25**, 971
derivative works, **18**, 946, 1053
derogatory treatment of works, *see* moral rights
  (integrity) *below*
design documents, **18**, 1154
  artistic work, **18**, 1155
  definition, **18**, 1154
diagrams, **18**, 958
direct copying, **18**, 1153, 1154
division, **18**, 994
dramatic work—
  generally, **18**, 949
dramatic works, **18**, 931, 942, 955
  adaptation, **18**, 1065
  anonymous or pseudonymous, **18**, 995, 996, 1032
  author, meaning, **18**, 980
  copyright not applicable, **18**, 1431
  Crown copyright, term of, **18**, 1034, 1037
  educational establishment performing, showing
    or playing, **18**, 1112
  European Community legislation, **18**, 1643
  infringement by public performance, **18**, 1060,
    1061
  meaning, **18**, 955

Copyright—*continued*
dramatic works—*continued*
 moral rights, *see* moral rights *below*
 musical elements in, **18**, 955
 parliamentary copyright, term of, **18**, 1036, 1037
 public readings and recitations, **18**, 1127
 published editions, **18**, 933, 936, 948, 977, 984, 1056, 1104
  term of copyright, **18**, 1041
 term of copyright, **18**, 1029, 1030, 1041
drawings, **18**, 931, 957, 958, 959, 1153
 plan, or, **3**, 139
duration, *see* term *below*
editions, neighbouring rights, as, **18**, 967, 977
education, permitted acts in, **18**, 1109–1114
educational establishment, photocopies taken by, **18**, 1103
electronic form, copy of works in, **18**, 1023
electronic retrieval system, publication through, **18**, 939
elevations, **3**, 139
employee, invention or work by, **9**, 128; **18**, 830*n*, 997–999
endurance beyond author's lifetime, **18**, 978
engravings, **18**, 931, 958, 962
entrepreneurial, **18**, 933
European Community legislation, **18**, 931, 932, 1611
 broadcasting, **18**, 1664
  schedules, **18**, 1663
 collecting societies, **18**, 1661
 commercial exploitation of copyright, **18**, 1643
 disparity in national laws, **18**, 1634
 exhaustion of rights, **18**, 1633
 film distribution, **18**, 1664
 free movement of goods, **18**, 1632–1636
 generally, **18**, 1615, 1616, 1618
 import from outside European Community, **18**, 1636
 licensing, **18**, 1660
 right to reward, **18**, 1635
 services, free provisions of, **18**, 1643–1645
  free movement of goods, and, **18**, 1645
 specific subject matter, **18**, 1632
examinations, educational, setting and answering questions, **18**, 1110
exhaustion of rights, European Community legislation, **18**, 1633
expiry, **19**, 881
false attributions, right to prevent, *see* moral rights *below*
films, **18**, 933
 author, meaning, **18**, 979, 981
 commissioners' right to privacy, **18**, 1130, 1139
 copying for private and domestic use, **18**, 1123
 Crown copyright, **18**, 1039
 distribution, European Community legislation, **18**, 1664
 educational establishment showing, **18**, 1112
 European Community legislation, **18**, 1643, 1664
 generally, **18**, 948
 infringement—
  generally, **18**, 1055
  public showing, by, **18**, 1062–1064
  supply of copies, **18**, 1081

Copyright—*continued*
films—*continued*
 joint authorship, **18**, 987
 moral rights, *see* moral rights *below*
 neighbouring rights, as, **18**, 967, 969
 overlap with other copyright works, **18**, 970
 permitted acts, **18**, 1126
 rental rights, **18**, 1059
 term of copyright, **18**, 1038, 1039
folklore, **18**, 996
franchising schemes, **18**, 802
free speech, must not be used to restrain, **18**, 1105
future—
 assignation, **18**, 1006
 licence, grant of, **18**, 1008
General Agreement on Trade and Tariffs (GATT), **18**, 931
graphic works, **18**, 957, 958, 959
history, **18**, 931
holograms, **18**, 960
ideas and impressions, **18**, 941, 942, 1059
independent but similar works, **18**, 947
indirect copying, **18**, 1153, 1154
industrial and commercial property, as, **18**, 801
industrial designs—
 artistic character, articles of, **18**, 1158
 artistic works—
  character merchandising, and, **18**, 1157
  industrial process, manufacture by, **18**, 1156
  marketing of product, effect, **18**, 1156
 calculations, **18**, 1153
 computer, material stored on, **18**, 1153
 corresponding registered design, where, **18**, 1193
 design documents, **18**, 1154
 drawings, **18**, 1153
 European Community legislation, and, **18**, 1618
 exclusion of certain articles from limitation, **18**, 1158
 generally, **18**, 1151
 literary character, articles of, **18**, 1158
 models, **18**, 1153, 1154
 no infringement where thing done in reliance on registration, **18**, 1159
 surface decoration applied to industrial product, **18**, 1155
 transitional provisions, **18**, 1161
 typefaces, **18**, 1160
 verbal ideas, **18**, 1153
 when copyright exists, **18**, 1153
infringement—
 adaptation, by—
  generally, **18**, 1065
 apparatus for receiving visual images or sounds conveyed by electronic means, use of apparatus for, **18**, 1063
 authorisation—
  claims of, defences against, **18**, 1069
  generally, **18**, 1067, 1068
  infringement must have occured, **18**, 1067
 copying work, by—
  abridgements, **18**, 1054
  adaptation, **18**, 1049
  broadcasts, **18**, 1055
  cable programmes, **18**, 1055

Copyright—*continued*
infringement—*continued*
  copying work, by—*continued*
    causal connection between works, **18**, 1046
    common source material, **18**, 1053
    computer programs, **18**, 1051, 1052
    databases, **18**, 1052
    derivative works, **18**, 1053
    films, **18**, 1055
    generally, **18**, 1045
    ideas and impressions, **18**, 1050
    knowledge, relevance of, **18**, 1047
    parodies, **18**, 1054
    similarity, problems arising, **18**, 1048
    sound recordings, **18**, 1055
    transient copies, **18**, 1052
    typographical arrangement of published editions, **18**, 1056, 1104
  criminal offences—
    conspiracy to defraud, **18**, 1098
    delivery up, **18**, 1095
    generally, **18**, 1093
    penalties, **18**, 1094
    piracy, repression, **18**, 1099
    prohibited goods, treatment of infringing copies as, **18**, 1097
    search warrant, order for, **18**, 1096
    video film, rental of illicit copy, **18**, 1098
  forms—
    adaptation, **18**, 1065–1069
    broadcasting, **18**, 1064
    copying, **18**, 1045–1056
    issuing, **18**, 1057–1059
    playing or showing, **18**, 1062, 1063
    public performance, **18**, 1060, 1061
  generally, **18**, 1042, 1045
  importation of infringing copies, prevention, **18**, 1097
  incidental inclusion, **18**, 1108
  issue of copies to public, by—
    generally, **18**, 1057
    meaning of issuing to public, **18**, 1057, 1058
    rental rights, and, **18**, 1059
  joint authorship, in case of, **18**, 985
  literary, musical or artistic work, **18**, 1065
  moral right, of—
    consent may be given to, **18**, 1130
    count, reckoning and payment, **18**, 1140
    damages, **18**, 1140
    delivery up, order for, **18**, 1140
    interdict, **18**, 1140
    remedies, **18**, 1140
  part of work, taking, **18**, 1043
  permitted acts, *see* permitted acts *below*
  primary, general principles, **18**, 1043, 1044
  prohibited goods, treatment of infringing copies as, **18**, 1097
  remedies—
    civil, **18**, 1084–1092
    count, reckoning and payment, **18**, 1086, 1091, 1140
    criminal offences, **18**, 1094–1099
    damages, **18**, 1086, 1088, 1140
     additional, **18**, 1090

Copyright—*continued*
infringement—*continued*
  remedies—*continued*
    damages—*continued*
     innocent infringement, no damages where, **18**, 1089
    delivery up, **18**, 1092, 1095, 1140
    generally, **18**, 1086, 1140
    interdict, **18**, 1086, 1087, 1140
    sue—
     title to, **18**, 1084
     who may be sued, **18**, 1085
  reprography, **18**, 1020, 1114
  restricted acts, **18**, 1042
    directly or indirectly, doing, **18**, 1044
  secondary, **18**, 1042
    copy-protection, dealing in circumventing device, **18**, 1082
    dealing in infringing copies, **18**, 1072
    film used to infringe copyright, supply, **18**, 1081
    generally, **18**, 1070
    import of infringing copies, **18**, 1073–1077, 1097
    knowledge of infringement, degree and amount of, **18**, 1070, 1071
    meaning, **18**, 1070
    primary infringement distinguished, **18**, 1071
    provision of apparatus for infringing performance, **18**, 1080
    provision of means to make infringing copies, **18**, 1078
    provision of venue for infringing performance, **18**, 1079
    secondary infringement distinguished, **18**, 1070
    sound recording used to infringe copyright, supply, **18**, 1081
    transmission, unauthorised, dealing in device for, **18**, 1083
  similarity of works, establishment of, **18**, 1045, 1048
  who may sue, **18**, 978
  whole work, taking, **18**, 1043
infringing copies, import restrictions, **7**, 1199
integrity, *see* moral rights *below*
intellectual property, as, **18**, 801
international framework, **18**, 931
international institutions, **18**, 1004
international organisations, vested in, **18**, 979, 980
international recognition—
  Berne Convention, **18**, 890
  Rome Convention, **18**, 931
Isle of Man, **18**, 935
issue of copies, rights as to, **18**, 1042
libraries, permitted acts in, **18**, 1115–1120
licence, grant of—
  certified licensing scheme, reprography, and, **18**, 1022, 1114
  co-ownership, in cases of, **18**, 1011
  collective licensing, **18**, 1013
  compulsory—
    reprography—**18**, 1022
  duration, **18**, 1008

Copyright—*continued*
licence, grant of—*continued*
 exclusive, **18**, 1009
  writing, must be in, **18**, 1008
 future copyright, in respect of, **18**, 1008
 generally, **18**, 1005, 1008
 implied, **18**, 1008, 1010
  commissioned works, **18**, 1010
 licensee, dealing by, **18**, 1012
 licensing schemes—
  monitor by Copyright Tribunal, **18**, 1015
  refusal or delay by operator, **18**, 1016
  unreasonable exclusion from scheme, **18**, 1016
 oral, **18**, 1008, 1010
 otherwise than in pursuance of licensing scheme, **18**, 1016
 repairs and replacements, **18**, 1010
 reprography—
  certified licensing schemes, **18**, 1021, 1114
  generally, **18**, 1020, 1114
  licences of right, **18**, 1022
  meaning, **18**, 1020
 restricted acts, in respect of, **18**, 1008
 rights in performance, interaction with, **18**, 1437
 territorial limitation, imposition, **18**, 1008
 writing, expression in, **18**, 1008
literary works—
 adaptation, **18**, 1065
 aesthetic or intellectual quality, no requirement for, **18**, 941, 943
 anonymous or pseudonymous, **18**, 995, 996, 1032
 author, meaning, **18**, 980
 computer programs, **18**, 950
 copyright not applicable, **18**, 1431
 Crown copyright, term of, **18**, 1034, 1037
 databases, **18**, 953
 definition, **18**, 950
 educational establishment performing, showing or playing, **18**, 1112
 examples, **18**, 951
 generally, **18**, 931, 949
 infringement by public performance, **18**, 1060, 1061
 moral rights, *see* moral rights *below*
 parliamentary copyright, term of, **18**, 1036, 1037
 public readings and recitations, **18**, 1127
 published editions, **18**, 933, 936, 948, 977, 984, 1056, 1104
  term of copyright, **18**, 1041
 spoken or sung works, **18**, 950
 tables and compilations, **18**, 950, 952, 953
 term of copyright, **18**, 1029, 1030
lump sum payments in respect of, tax treatment, **18**, 1585
maps, **18**, 958
matter protected by, **17**, 26
media, **18**, 933
 term of copyright, **18**, 1029
models, **3**, 139; **18**, 1153, 1154
monarch, entitlement of, **18**, 1000

Copyright—*continued*
moral rights—
 derogatory treatment, **18**, 1140
 droit de suite, no British recognition of, **18**, 1130
 false attribution of authorship—
  generally, **18**, 1130, 1138
  right to prevent, **18**, 1130
   term of right, **18**, 1130
 films, commissioners' right to privacy, **18**, 1130, 1139
 generally, **18**, 1130
 infringement—
  consent to, **18**, 1130
  remedies for, **18**, 1140
 integrity, **18**, 1130
  commercial publication, and, **18**, 1137
  current events, report of, **18**, 1136
  generally, **18**, 1135
  limits on right, **18**, 1136
  term of right, **18**, 1130
 introduction of concept, **18**, 1130
 not assignable, **18**, 1130
 paternity, **18**, 1130
  asserted by author, right must be, **18**, 1132
  commercial publication, and, **18**, 1137
  limitation of right, **18**, 1134
  limits on authors' and directors' rights of identification, **18**, 1134
  persons bound by assertion, **18**, 1132
  public exhibition of artistic works, in, **18**, 1133
  term of right, **18**, 1130
  See also author *above*
 photographs, rights of commissioner, **18**, 1130, 1139
 succession, **18**, 1141
 transfer on death, **18**, 1130
 waiver, grant of, **18**, 1130
moveable property, as, **18**, 14
musical works—
 adaptation, **18**, 1065
 anonymous or pseudonymous, **18**, 995, 996, 1032
 author, meaning, **18**, 980
 copyright not applicable, **18**, 1431
 Crown copyright, term of, **18**, 1034, 1037
 educational establishment performing showing or playing, **18**, 1112
 European Community legislation, **18**, 1643
 folksongs, **18**, 996
  archive recordings, **18**, 1120
 generally, **9**, 1037; **18**, 931, 949, 956
 incidental inclusion, **18**, 1108
 infringement by public performance, **18**, 1060, 1061
 meaning, **18**, 956
 moral rights, *see* moral rights *above*
 parliamentary copyright, term of, **18**, 1036, 1037
 published editions, **18**, 933, 936, 948, 977, 984, 1056, 1104
  term of copyright, **18**, 1041
 term of copyright—
  generally, **18**, 1029, 1030, 1041

Copyright—*continued*
neighbouring rights—
    generally, **18**, 933
    meaning, **18**, 933, 967
'no derogation from the grant' principle, **18**, 1129
offences relating to, **17**, 26
Organisation of American States, **18**, 1004
originality—
    adaptations, **18**, 942
    broadcasts, **18**, 948
    cable programmes, **18**, 948
    derivative works, **18**, 946
    effort, skill and labour invested in work, test of, **18**, 941, 944
    films, **18**, 948
    generally, **18**, 941
    ideas, no copyright in, **18**, 941, 942
    independent but similar works, **18**, 947
    meaning in relation to copyright, **18**, 941
    quality or merit, no requirement of—
        aesthetic or intellectual quality, **18**, 941, 943
        artistic quality, **18**, 957
    sound recordings, **18**, 948
    typographical arrangements of published editions, **18**, 948
    infringement, **18**, 1056
    term of copyright, **18**, 1041
    'what is worth copying is worth protecting' concept, **18**, 941, 945, 1151
originator of idea and actual author, positions of, **18**, 990–992
ownership—
    author, by, **18**, 978, 979
    bankruptcy of owner, **18**, 1026
    co-ownership, assignation or licensing, **18**, 1011
    dealings in copyright—
        assignation, **18**, 1005
        assignee, by, **18**, 1012
        broadcasts, **18**, 1024, 1025
        collective licensing, **18**, 1013
        Copyright Tribunal, *see* COPYRIGHT TRIBUNAL
        Crown copyright, **18**, 1028
        formal methods—
            assignation, **18**, 1006, 1007
                dealings by assignees, **18**, 1012
            licensing, *see* licence, grant of *above*
            security over, creation, **18**, 1007
        generally, **18**, 1005
        licensee, by, **18**, 1012
        parliamentary copyright, **18**, 1028
        royalties, **18**, 1005
        transmission of rights—
            bankruptcy, on, **18**, 1026
            death, on, **18**, 1027
    dealings in—
        assignee, dealing by, **18**, 1012
        licensee, dealing by, **18**, 1012
    death of owner, transmission on, **18**, 1027
    first, **18**, 978*ff.*
        anonymous works, **18**, 995, 996
        Crown copyright, **18**, 1000
        Crown prerogative, **18**, 1002
        employment, works made during course of, **18**, 997–999

Copyright—*continued*
ownership—*continued*
    first—*continued*
        folklore and folksongs, **18**, 996
        international organisations, **18**, 1003
        parliamentary copyright, **18**, 1001
        pseudonymous works, **18**, 995
        universities' copyright, **18**, 1003
        See also author *above*
    generally, **18**, 978
    infringement, right to sue, **18**, 978
    moral rights, *see* moral rights *above*
    prospective, **18**, 1008
    registration, no requirement for, **18**, 979
    rights—
        conferred by—
            generally, **18**, 1005, 1042
            issue of copies to public, **18**, 1057
        transfer from author, term of copyright where, **18**, 1029
paintings, **18**, 931, 958
Parliament, Acts of, **18**, 1000
parliamentary—
    generally, **18**, 979, 980, 1001
    literary, dramatic, musical or artistic works—
        transitional provisions, **18**, 1037
    moral rights, **18**, 1134, 1136
    reproduction of copyright material, permission for, **18**, 1028
parodies, **18**, 1054
patent, relationship with, **18**, 826
paternity, *see* moral rights *below*
performance of works, rights as to, **18**, 1005, 1042
performances, no copyright in, **18**, 1431
Performing Right Society, **18**, 1013
Performing Right Tribunal, *see* COPYRIGHT TRIBUNAL
permitted acts—
    acts authorised by Act of Parliament, **18**, 1122
    archives, *see* libraries and archives *below*
    broadcasts, **18**, 1123–1126
    cable programmes, **18**, 1123–1126
    confidential documents, **18**, 1105
    criticism or review, copying for purposes of, **18**, 1101, 1105
    Crown, material communicated to in course of public business, **18**, 1122
    education, in—
        broadcasts, **18**, 1113
        cable programmes, **18**, 1113
        copies—
            method of taking, **18**, 1110, 1114
            number, **18**, 1110, 1114
            who may take, **18**, 1110
        examinations, setting and answering questions, **18**, 1110
        generally, **18**, 1109, 1110
        instruction, use in, **18**, 1109, 1110
        performing, playing or showing work, **18**, 1112
    fair dealing, **18**, 1101
    generally, **18**, 1100
    incidental inclusion, **18**, 1108
    judicial proceedings, **18**, 1122

Copyright—*continued*
permitted acts—*continued*
libraries and archives—
  archival purposes, recording for, **18**, 1120
  export condition, copies required to be made by, **18**, 1119
  generally, **18**, 1115
  making and supplying copies to other librarians, **18**, 1118
  replacement copies, making, **18**, 1119
  research and private study—
    making copies of published material, **18**, 1116
    making copies of unpublished material, **18**, 1117
    supplying copies of published material, **18**, 1116
    supplying copies of unpublished material, **18**, 1117
material open to public inspection, making copies of, **18**, 1122
parliamentary proceedings, **18**, 1122
public administration, in, **18**, 1122
public inspection, information open to by statutory requirement, **18**, 1122
public readings and recitations, **18**, 1127
public records, **18**, 1122
report of current events, copying for purposes of, **18**, 1101, 1106
research and private study—
  copying by person other than researcher or student, **18**, 1102
  educational establishments, in, **18**, 1103
  generally, **18**, 1101, 1102
  libraries and archives, copies made by, **18**, 1116, 1117
  folksongs, archival recordings, **18**, 1120
  meaning, **18**, 1102
  multiple copies, no justification for, **18**, 1102
  typographical arrangement of published editions, **18**, 1104
royal commission, proceedings before, **18**, 1122
scientific articles, abstracts of, **18**, 1121
spoken words, use of notes or recordings of, **18**, 1107
statutory inquiry, proceedings before, **18**, 1122
study aids do not qualify, **18**, 1102, 1105
technical articles, abstracts of, **18**, 1121
typographical arrangement of published editions, **18**, 1104
perpetual, rejection of notion, **18**, 931
Phonographic Performance Limited, **18**, 1013, 1024
photographs—
  commissioners' right to privacy, **18**, 1130, 1139
  generally, **18**, 931, 933, 957, 958, 959, 960
  preventing publication of, **1**, 521
plans, **18**, 958
press, effect on activities of those concerned with, **17**, 1
printed works, **18**, 958, 962
Psalms, metrical version, **18**, 1002
pseudonymous works—
  generally, **18**, 995
  term of copyright, **18**, 1032

Copyright—*continued*
public interest and, **18**, 1129
public readings and recitations, **18**, 1127
public records, **19**, 881
publication—
  definition, **18**, 939
  electronic retrieval system, through, **18**, 939
  first, country of, **18**, 938
  simultaneous, in more than one country, **18**, 938
published and unpublished work, **19**, 881
publishers' rights, reprography, **18**, 1020
qualification for protection—
  author, through, **18**, 936
  broadcasts, **18**, 941
  cable programmes, **18**, 941
  Convention county, in, **18**, 934
  Copyright, Designs and Patents Act 1988, extent and application, **18**, 935
  first publication, by, **18**, 938
  joint ownership, where, **18**, 937
  qualifying person, who is, **18**, 936
  United Kingdom, in, **18**, 934
quality or merit, no requirement of, **18**, 941, 943, 957, 964, 1153
radio broadcasts, *see* broadcasts *above*
recording rights, European Community legislation, **18**, 1643
registration—
  former requirement for, **18**, 931
  no requirement for, **18**, 979
rental rights, fixing payment for, **18**, 1019
restricted acts—
  generally, **18**, 1042
  permitted acts, and, generally, **18**, 1100
right to reward, European Community legislation, **18**, 1635
rights in security, **20**, 43
royal family, members of, **18**, 1000
royalties, **18**, 1005
  fixing, **18**, 1019
  tax treatment, **18**, 1585, 1591
    foreign royalties, **18**, 1589
    non-resident, payment to, **18**, 1589
  variation, **18**, 1019
sale or transfer, **18**, 978
satellite broadcasts, **18**, 972
sculptures, **18**, 931, 957, 958, 959
showing works, rights as to, **18**, 1042
sound recordings, **18**, 933, 948, 1024, 1025
  author, meaning, **18**, 979, 981
  Crown copyright in, **18**, 1039
  educational establishment playing, **18**, 1112
  European Community legislation, **18**, 1643
  infringement, **18**, 1055
    playing in public, by, **18**, 1062–1064
    supply of copies, **18**, 1081
  joint authorship, **18**, 987
  needletime, **18**, 1024
  neighbouring rights, as, **18**, 967, 968
  permitted acts, **18**, 1126
  rental rights, **18**, 1059
  term of copyright, **18**, 1038, 1039
  specific subject matter, European Community legislation, **18**, 1632

Copyright—*continued*
spoken words—
  current events, report of, **18**, 1107
  recordings of, **18**, 1107
  written recordings of, **18**, 1107
subject matter, **18**, 931, 933
surface decoration applied to industrial product, **18**, 1155
taking and using, **7**, 345
technical article, accompanying abstract, **18**, 1121
television broadcasts, *see* broadcasts *above*; cable programmes *above*
term—
  anonymous works, **18**, 1032
  broadcasts, **18**, 1040
  cable programmes, **18**, 1040
  computer-generated works, **18**, 1031
  Crown copyright, **18**, 1035
  fifty-year period, **18**, 1029
  films, **18**, 1038, 1039
  generally, **18**, 1029
  joint authorship, where, **18**, 1033
  media copyrights, **18**, 1029
  pseudonymous works, **18**, 1032
  sound recordings, **18**, 1038, 1039
  where transfer of ownership from author, **18**, 1029
trade-related aspects of intellectual property (TRIPS), **18**, 931
transfer of ownership, **18**, 653
  death, on, **18**, 1005
transient copies, **18**, 1052
transmission of rights—
  bankruptcy, on, **18**, 1026
  death, on, **18**, 1027
  testamentary disposition, **18**, 1027
Tribunal, *see* COPYRIGHT TRIBUNAL
typefaces, **18**, 1134, 1154, 1155, 1160
typographical arrangement of published editions—
  generally, **18**, 933, 936, 977, 984, 1056
  originality, **18**, 948
  permitted acts, **18**, 1104
  term of copyright, **18**, 1041
United Nations and its Specialised Agencies, **18**, 1004
Universal Copyright Convention 1952 ..., **18**, 931
universities and other educational institutions, **18**, 1003
university student's right of, **8**, 1023
university teacher's right of, **8**, 1022
unregistered design right, interaction with, **18**, 1233
value added tax, **18**, 1602
verbal ideas, **18**, 1153
video recordings—
  generally, **18**, 969
  making for private and domestic use, **18**, 1123
  See also films *above*
'what is worth copying is worth protecting' concept, **18**, 941, 945
writ or pleading, **13**, 1326
writing, meaning, **18**, 949

Copyright Licensing Agency, 18, 1013
Copyright Tribunal
appeal from, **18**, 1014
attendance of witnesses, powers as to, **18**, 1014
constitution, **18**, 1014
examination of witnesses, **18**, 1014
factors to be taken into account by, **18**, 1018
functions—
  licensing schemes—
    entilements to licence under, consideration, **18**, 1016
    monitor of, **18**, 1015
    review of licences granted otherwise than by licensing scheme, **18**, 1017
  generally, **18**, 1013, 1014
jurisdiction, **18**, 1014
production of documents, powers as to, **18**, 1014
recording rights, jurisdiction, **18**, 1436
rental rights—
  fixing of payments for, **18**, 1019
  variation of payments for, **18**, 1019
rights in performances, jurisdiction, **18**, 1436
supervision of, **23**, 911
COREPER
See COMMITTEE OF PERMANENT REPRESENTATIVES
Cork Committee
accepted recommendations, **4**, 574
administration order, recommendations relating to, **4**, 603
liquidation of assets, adoption of expression, **4**, 717
unaccepted recommendations, **4**, 575
voluntary arrangements, on, **4**, 579
wrongful trading, concept of, introduction of, **4**, 900
Cornwall, Duchy of
parliamentary Bill affecting prerogative or interest, **7**, 744
Coronation
homage, Peerage, by, **7**, 706
Oath, **7**, 708, 709
Stone of Destiny, **7**, 709*n*
Coronation of Scottish kings
Lord Lyon King of Arms' duties, **6**, 1010, 1011
Coroner
inquest in England and Wales, **17**, 975
See also FATAL ACCIDENT INQUIRIES
Coronet
generally, **11**, 1607
local authorities, **11**, 1607
Scottish and English forms, **11**, 1607
special designs, **11**, 1607
Corporal punishment
abolition of, **17**, 562
child, of, **3**, 1246
entitlement to use, **7**, 239, 306
European Convention on Human Rights, **12**, 26, 90, 91
former forms of, **17**, 562
school education—
  generally, **8**, 903
  grant-aided schools, **8**, 820
Corporate actings
firms, **11**, 1042
personality, and, **11**, 1041–1043

Corporate body
See BODY CORPORATE
Corporate liability
crime only punishable by imprisonment, where, **7**, 110
fictions relative to, **7**, 111
generally, **7**, 109
limitations on criminal liability, **7**, 110
mens rea, **7**, 110, 111
Corporate personality
common law, remedy against, **19**, 229
corporate actings, **11**, 1041–1043
imputing to corporate groups, **11**, 1043
legal, **11**, 1044
See also PERSONS AND PERSONALITY
Corporation
accounts of, **1**, 91
acquiescence, bound by, **16**, 1616
actings or knowledge of promoters, personal bar, **16**, 1607
arrestee, as, **8**, 259
badges granted to, **11**, 1610
bill of exchange—
 signature on, **4**, 123
capacity of, **11**, 1064–1066
 active, **11**, 1065
 passive, **11**, 1065
capax doli, **11**, 1054
corporate status, **11**, 1072
decision of organ of, **4**, 46
delict—
 title and interest to sue, **15**, 228
 vicarious liability, **15**, 228
display of arms, **11**, 1614
domicile of, **4**, 31
grant of arms to, **11**, 1604
heritable security granted by, **20**, 222
meaning, **4**, 29
official address of, **4**, 31, 46
partner, as, **16**, 1015
persona, **16**, 1026
powers of, **11**, 1064*n*
precedence, **16**, 2025
property, co-ownership, **18**, 18*n*, 34*n*
property of, whether joint property, **18**, 34*n*
public authority, creation by, **14**, 2
salade helmet granted to company, **11**, 1605
seat of, **4**, 46
specialised concept of law, as, **11**, 1005
tax, *see* CORPORATION TAX
trade marks, recording, **11**, 1614
transfer of ownership, capacity, **18**, 599
vassal, as, **18**, 61
voluntary churches, legal status, **3**, 1638, 1638*n*
See also COMPANY
Corporation tax
accounting period, **19**, 1519
administration and collection, **19**, 1544*n*
advance corporation tax (ACT), **19**, 1521
 consortia and groups of companies, **19**, 1522
assessment of liability, **19**, 1544
bodies corporate, **19**, 1519
capital allowances, **19**, 1314, 1520

Corporation tax—*continued*
charity—
 company donations, **3**, 1155
 covenanted donations, **3**, 1141, 1147
 tax exemption for, restrictions, **3**, 1106
 trading profits of charitable body, **3**, 1132
close companies, **19**, 1523
clubs, liability of, **2**, 821; **19**, 1313, 1314
company distributions, **19**, 1521
company profits, **19**, 1519, 1520
consortia, **19**, 1522
date due for payment, **19**, 1519, 1521
donations, **8**, 654
enterprise zone, **14**, 647
financial year, **22**, 811
friendly societies, exemption, **12**, 687, 689, 690
income tax and capital gains tax principles, application of, **19**, 1520
land valuation assessments, **6**, 1149
leisure and recreation businesses, **19**, 1319–1321
life assurance policy, taxation of gain under, **21**, 1329
rate, **19**, 1519
royalties, **18**, 1572, 1575
sheriff court jurisdiction, **6**, 1109
small companies rate, **19**, 1519
sports clubs and associations, **19**, 1313, 1314, 1510
standard rate, **19**, 1519
trading losses, **19**, 1520
unincorporated associations, **19**, 1519
unit trusts, **19**, 1519
Corporeal heritable property
accession, *see* ACCESSION
generally, **18**, 11
meaning, **18**, 12
transfer of ownership, *see* TRANSFER OF OWNERSHIP
warrandice, *see* WARRANDICE
See also LAND
Corporeal moveable property
accession, *see* ACCESSION
acquisition, *see* ownership *below*
alienation—
 inter vivos, **18**, 533, 535
 mortis causa, **18**, 533, 535
 ownership, as right of, **18**, 531, 533, 535
 trust property, **18**, 535
arrestment, **8**, 247, 248, 281
commixtion, **18**, 539, 564
 accession compared, **18**, 571*n*
confusion, **18**, 539, 564
 accession compared, **18**, 571*n*
constitutum possessorium (possessory declaration or agreement), **18**, 532
damage to, public telecommunications operator, by, **16**, 1956
defence of possession—
 applicable rules, **18**, 192
 generally, **18**, 191
definition, **20**, 805
deposit, contract of, **8**, 4
disposal, owner's right of, **18**, 531
document relating to, contract of deposit, **8**, 4

Corporeal moveable property—*continued*
dominium, **11**, 762
  effect of fraud on transfer of, **11**, 763
  less than, transferred, **11**, 764
donation, **18**, 116
  delivery, **8**, 635
    independent custodier, property held by, **8**, 634
    necessity for, **8**, 634
    proving, **8**, 634
    third party, to, **8**, 634
ejusdem generis, **25**, 825
generally, **6**, 591; **11**, 761; **25**, 825
gift of, **19**, 1610
hire, owner retaining title and civil possession, **18**, 534
inferior real rights, charge or burden with, **18**, 531
influences on Scots law, **18**, 530
insolvency, **11**, 778
liferent—
  generally, **18**, 534
  subordinate real right, as, **18**, 534
  See also LIFERENT
loan, owner retaining title and civil possession, **18**, 534
meaning, **6**, 591
money as, **14**, 1804, 1805
Natural law, influence of concept, **18**, 530
natural possession, protection of, **18**, 138
obligations and property, laws of distinguished, **11**, 762
occupatio (occupancy), appropriation, **18**, 541
ownership—
  abandoned property, **18**, 541
  abandonment, **18**, 9, 568
  absolute right, as, **18**, 531
  accession, *nemo dat quod non habet* rule, **18**, 676
  acquisition—
    accession, **18**, 676
    appropriation, **18**, 541
    commixtion, **18**, 564
      accession compared, **18**, 571*n*
    confusion, **18**, 564
      accession compared, **18**, 571*n*
    derivative, **18**, 539
    game and game legislation, **18**, 541, 544, 545
    lost and abandoned property, **18**, 547–552, 676
    nemo dat quod non habet rule, *see* TRANSFER OF OWNERSHIP
    occupatio (occupancy), **18**, 540–546
      international law, **18**, 558
    original, **18**, 539
    royal fish, **18**, 541, 542, 543
    specificatio (specification), **18**, 559–563, 564
      accession compared, **18**, 571*n*, 588
    specification, **18**, 676
    things which can be acquired, **18**, 542–546
    treasure, **18**, 553
    wildlife conservation, **18**, 546
    wreck, **18**, 554–557
  alienation, **18**, 533, 535
    inter vivos, **18**, 533, 535
    mortis causa, **18**, 533, 535
    owner's right of, generally, **18**, 531

Corporeal moveable property
ownership—*continued*
  commixtion, **18**, 539, 564
    accession compared, **18**, 571*n*
  common, *see* CO-OWNERSHIP
    See also joint or common *below*
  confusion, **18**, 539, 564
    accession compared, **18**, 571*n*
  content of right of, **18**, 533
  Crown, ownership falling to, **18**, 9
  definition, **18**, 531
  destruction, **18**, 568
  disposal, owner's right of, **18**, 531
  English law compared, **18**, 531, 531*n*
  extinction, **18**, 568
  floating charge, where, **18**, 534
  hire-purchase agreement, where, **18**, 534
  hired goods, of, **18**, 534
  inferior real rights, right to charge or burden with, **18**, 531
  joint or common—
    generally, **18**, 531, 536
    management of property in, **18**, 537
    See also CO-OWNERSHIP
  loaned articles, of, **18**, 534
  lost and abandoned property, **18**, 568
    abandoned property, definition, **18**, 547
    appeals as to, **18**, 551
    care and custody of, **18**, 548
    claimant, rules as to, **18**, 549
    disposal, **18**, 549
    employer of finder, duty of, **18**, 548
    finder, duty of, **18**, 548
    living creatures, **18**, 547*n*, 549
    lost property, definition, **18**, 547
    motor vehicle, abandoned, **18**, 552
    negotiorum gestor, **18**, 547, 547*n*
    nem dat quod non habet rule, **18**, 676
    owner of land where property discovered, duty of, **18**, 548
    public sector housing tenant, property abandoned by, **18**, 552
    quod nullius est fit domini regis, **18**, 540, 547
    records, chief constable's duty to keep, **18**, 550
    stray dogs, **18**, 552
    title to, **18**, 550
    transport services, property found on premises of, **18**, 552
    waifs and strays, **18**, 547*n*
  multiple—
    joint or common ownership, *see* CO-OWNERSHIP
      See also joint or common *above*
    management of property in, **18**, 537
    trust, ownership in, **18**, 538
  nature of right, **18**, 531
  occupatio (occupancy), **18**, 539
    appropriation, **18**, 541
    definition, **18**, 540
    game and game legislation, **18**, 541, 542, 544, 545
    international law, **18**, 558
    royal fish, **18**, 541, 542, 543
    scope, **18**, 540
    things which can be acquired, **18**, 542

Corporeal moveable property—*continued*
ownership—*continued*
  occupatio (occupancy)—*continued*
    wildlife, **18**, 542
      conservation, **18**, 546
  owner's entitlement to claim property, **18**, 531
  possession, and, **18**, 531, 565
    positive prescription, **18**, 539, 565, 566
    See also possession *below*
  prescription—
    generally, **18**, 565
    loss of rights by, **18**, 569
    negative, **18**, 567, 569
    positive, **18**, 565, 566, 569
  presumption of, **18**, 531, 565
  relationship between owner and thing owned, as, **18**, 531
  renunciation, **18**, 9
  reputed, **18**, 532
  rights bestowed by, **18**, 531
  Scots law, generally, **18**, 531
  specificatio (specification), **18**, 539, 559
    accession compared, **18**, 571*n*, 588
    case law, **18**, 562
    definition, **18**, 559
    institutional writers, **18**, 561
    nemo dat quod non habet rule, **18**, 676
    Roman law, **18**, 560
    Scottish Law Commission proposals, **18**, 563
  subordinate rights, grant of, **18**, 533, 534
    contractual right, **18**, 534
    personal right, **18**, 534
    real rights, **18**, 534
  things never owned, **18**, 540
  things once owned but no longer having owner, **18**, 540
  treasure, **18**, 553
  trust, ownership in, **18**, 538
  wreck—
    aircraft, from, **18**, 557
    common law, **18**, 554
    Crown rights and donatories, **18**, 554, 556, 557
    hovercraft, from, **18**, 557
    Merchant Shipping Acts, **18**, 555, 556
    ownerless or abandoned property, as, **18**, 554
    person finding or taking possession, duty of, **18**, 555
    receivers of wreck—
      appointment, **18**, 555
      duties, **18**, 555, 556
  See also OWNERSHIP
pledge, **18**, 5
poinding, **8**, 217, 229
possession—
  constitutum possessorium (possessory declaration or agreement), **18**, 532
  contractual right, holder of, as possessor, **18**, 534
  defence of, **18**, 174
  delivery and redelivery, **18**, 532
  detention, **18**, 119
  English law compared, **18**, 531, 531*n*
  owner parting with natural, effect, **18**, 531
  ownership, and, **18**, 531, 565
  positive prescription, **18**, 539, 565, 566

Corporeal moveable property—*continued*
possession—*continued*
  presumption of ownership arising from, **18**, 114
  proof of right of—
    defence of possession, actions in, **18**, 149
    generally, **18**, 141, 148
    recovery of possession, actions for, **18**, 150, 151
  recovery founded on right to—
    action of delivery, **18**, 158
    ejection, **18**, 159
    interdict, **18**, 159
    self-help, **18**, 160
    spuilzie, **18**, 160
  reputed ownership, and, **18**, 532
  Roman law, **18**, 531
  sale and rehire of property, **18**, 532
real conditions, **18**, 353
recovery of, action for, generally, **18**, 150, 151
repetition, **15**, 16, 31, 31*n*
res nullius, **18**, 531
restitution, **15**, 14
right in security, subordinate real right, as, **18**, 534
rights in—
  liferent, **18**, 534
  ownership, *see* ownership *above*
  security rights, **18**, 534
  subordinate, **18**, 533, 534
Roman law, influence of, **18**, 2, 530
sale and rehire, **18**, 532
security rights, **18**, 534
ship as, **21**, 101, 131
spuilzie, **18**, 161
  spuilzied property, protection of natural possession, **18**, 140
succession, **18**, 535
transfer of ownership, *see* TRANSFER OF OWNERSHIP
  accretion, **18**, 678
  common law—
    brevi manu, delivery, **18**, 619, 622
    constitutum possessorium, **18**, 619, 623
    longa manu, delivery, **18**, 619, 620
    modus transferendi, **18**, 619
    symbolical, **18**, 619, 621
treasure—
  Crown's right to, **18**, 553
    regalia, as, **18**, 553
  definition, **18**, 553
  disposal, **18**, 553
  finder—
    duty of, **18**, 553
    reward, payment to, **18**, 553
  ownership of, **18**, 553
  valuation, **18**, 553
trust property—
  alienation, **18**, 535
  ownership, **18**, 536, 538
use, right of—
  contractual right, grant of, **18**, 534
  damage caused by use, **18**, 533
  licensing system, where, **18**, 533
  restrictions, **18**, 533
warrandice, *see* WARRANDICE
writing, on requirement for, **18**, 8

Corporeal property
corporeal heritable property, **18**, 11
   meaning, **18**, 12
   See also CORPOREAL HERITABLE PROPERTY; LAND
corporeal moveable property, **18**, 11
   attachment to land, **18**, 12
   meaning, **18**, 12
   See also CORPOREAL MOVEABLE PROPERTY
incorporeal property distinguished, **18**, 11
meaning, **18**, 11
Corpses
See DEAD BODY
Corrections Etc, Register of
death—
   investigation by procurator fiscal, **19**, 1458
   precognition as to, **19**, 1430
divorce, decree of, **19**, 1430
general, **19**, 1414, 1421
illegitimacy, **19**, 1439
   decree of declarator, **19**, 1430
legitimacy, decree of declarator, **19**, 1430
marriage, dissolution of, **19**, 1430
name, change of, **19**, 1428
paternity—
   decree of, **19**, 1430
   statutory declaration acknowledging, **19**, 1430
status, change of, **19**, 1429
Corroboration
civil cases, evidence in—
   abolition of rule, **10**, 766, 772
      effect of, **10**, 773
   consistorial proceedings, **10**, 775
   how corroboration obtained, **10**, 774
confessions, of, **10**, 770
consistorial proceedings, **10**, 775
   criteria of, **10**, 673
criminal cases, evidence in—
   circumstantial evidence, **10**, 767
   confessions, of, **10**, 770
   crucial facts (*facta probanda*), **10**, 767, 768
   essential facts, **10**, 767
   evidential facts, **10**, 767
   facts which must be corroborated, **10**, 767
   generally, **10**, 766; **17**, 566
   how corroboration obtained, **10**, 768
   incidental facts, **10**, 767
   material facts, **10**, 767
   mutual corroboration where separate crimes charged, **10**, 769
   procedural facts, **10**, 767
   statutory exceptions to rule, **10**, 771
definition, **10**, 766
divorce, action for, **17**, 1219
false denial, by, **10**, 1160
general rule, **10**, 766
how obtained, **10**, 768, 774
objective of, **10**, 766
requirement of, **17**, 566
statutory exceptions, **10**, 771
Corrosive substance
assault with, **7**, 226
Corruption
bribery, **7**, 405, 547
common law, **7**, 405

Corruption—*continued*
electoral malpractices, **5**, 374, 377; **7**, 409
individuals, agents of, **7**, 407
judge or judicial officer, **7**, 547
local authority members, **7**, 408
local or public bodies, **7**, 406
person convicted of, exclusion from House of Commons, **5**, 379
private bodies, agents of, **7**, 407
statute law, **7**, 406–409
Corruption of blood
former use, **7**, 567
COSLA
See CONVENTION OF SCOTTISH LOCAL AUTHORITIES
Cottar
conveyance of site of dwelling house, right to, **1**, 829
conveyance of subject, right to, **1**, 827
dwelling house occupied by, **6**, 967
financial assistance to, **1**, 819
house, rating and valuation of, **1**, 834
landlord's interest, acquisition of, **13**, 335
meaning, **1**, 824
overriding interests of, **6**, 741
permanent improvements, compensation for, **1**, 824
planning blight, protection from, **1**, 833
site of dwelling house, heritable security for acquisition of, **1**, 831
spouse, transfer of tenancy to, **1**, 824
Council
burgh, **14**, 14, 16
community, *see* COMMUNITY COUNCIL
county, *see* COUNTY COUNCIL
district, *see* DISTRICT COUNCIL
islands area, *see* ISLANDS AREA
regional, *see* REGIONAL COUNCIL
Council for National Academic Awards (CNAA)
central institutions, degrees awarded by, **8**, 976
degrees awarded by, **8**, 994
Council for Professions Supplementary to Medicine
boards, **15**, 1518
   membership, **15**, 1519
function, **15**, 1517
generally, **15**, 1516, 1521
investigatory and disciplinary proceedings, **15**, 1517
membership, **15**, 1518
registers of practitioners, **15**, 1517
tenure of office, **15**, 1520
Council of Europe
Committee of Ministers, **12**, 10*n*
Consultative Assembly, **12**, 10*n*
Convention for the Protection of Individuals with regard to the Automated Processing of Personal data 1981 ..., **18**, 1501
establishment, **12**, 6*n*
European Community, relations with, **10**, 299
European Convention for the Protection of Human Rights and Freedoms, **5**, 315; **12**, 6*n*
generally, **10**, 4
international law, as source of, **19**, 649*n*
members, **12**, 6*n*

Council of Europe—continued
Organisation for Economic Co-operation and Development, relations with, **10**, 299
Council of Ministers
agenda—
'A' and 'B' items on, **10**, 400, 407, 409
items where agreement reached by COREPER, **10**, 407
annual report to European Parliament, **10**, 370
blocking of proposals by member state, **10**, 413
budgetary powers, **10**, 427
approval of budget, **10**, 386, 387
draft budget, **10**, 427
collegiality, **10**, 417
Commission proposals, consideration of, **10**, 326, 408
composition—
determination by individual member states, **10**, 390
European Council, **10**, 393
assimilation, **10**, 395
criticised by European Parliament, **10**, 394
foreign ministers—
attendance by, **10**, 391
European Council, **10**, 393
general meetings, **10**, 391
generally, **10**, 36, 390
intergovernmental nature, **10**, 389
ministers attending, **10**, 391
permanent under-secretaries, whether eligible to attend, **10**, 390
President, role of, **10**, 396
reform, proposals for, **10**, 392
specialised meetings, **10**, 391
variation, **10**, 391
contribution to Community system, **10**, 428
COREPER (Committee of Permanent Representatives), **10**, 39, 39n
generally, **10**, 402, 409
items where agreement reached, **10**, 407
organisation, **10**, 403
working parties, **10**, 404
Correspondents' Group, **10**, 406
Court of Auditors, appointments to, **10**, 450
Court of Justice of the European Communities, may sue and be sued before, **10**, 37
decisions, enforcement in UK, **8**, 565
delegates to, **10**, 390, 391
Directorates-General, **10**, 37, 405
Economic and Social Committee—
consultation of, **10**, 440, 441
powers in relation to, **10**, 438
'empty chair' policy, **10**, 414
European Commission—
Commission proposals, action on, **10**, 326, 425
Council's failure to act, **10**, 338
delegation of enforcement powers to, **4**, 1111
instigation of Commission action, **10**, 421
relationship with, **10**, 418, 419
European Council—
assimilation, **10**, 395
criticised by European Parliament, **10**, 394
foreign ministers, attendance at, **10**, 393
function, **10**, 393

Council of Ministers—continued
European Parliament—
questioning by, **10**, 369
relation with, **10**, 368, 388
reports of Council to, **10**, 370
failure to act, European Commissioner's powers, **10**, 338
foreign ministers, attendance by, **10**, 391
European Council, **10**, 393
foreign policy matters, **10**, 422
functions, **10**, 35
decisions, power to take, **10**, 417
policy formulation—
co-ordination of national economic policies, **10**, 417, 418, 420
ECSC Treaty, under, **10**, 418
EEC Treaty, under, **10**, 419
foreign policy matters, **10**, 423
instigating Commission action, **10**, 421
responsibility, extent of, **10**, 422
policy implementation—
budgetary powers, **10**, 427
Commission proposals, acting on, **10**, 425
decision-making powers, **10**, 424
treaties, conclusion of, **10**, 426
general meetings, **10**, 391
generally, **10**, 308
interests of member states, **10**, 415
intergovernmental composition, **10**, 389
Legal Service, **10**, 37
legislative procedure, **10**, 41
majority decision-making, **10**, 410, 412
meetings—
agenda, **10**, 400
attendance at, **10**, 399
convening, **10**, 398
in camera, **10**, 401
meetings of governments, status of, **10**, 394
ministers attending—
general meetings, **10**, 391
specialised meetings, **10**, 391
national interests, defence of, **10**, 389
negative role of, **10**, 389
officials other than ministers, attendance by, **10**, 399
organisation—
COREPER, see coreper above
Correspondents' Group, **10**, 406
in camera, meetings held in, **10**, 401
Political Committee, **10**, 406
President, see president below
rules governing, **10**, 396
Secretariat, **10**, 405
Political Committee, **10**, 406
powers of, **10**, 40
President, **10**, 38, 38n
agenda fixed by, **10**, 400
attendance at meetings, **10**, 399
functions, **10**, 397
meetings convened by, **10**, 398
rotation of office, **10**, 396
questioning by European Parliament, **10**, 369
reforms, proposed, **10**, 392, 409, 416
responsibility, extent of, **10**, 422

Council of Ministers—*continued*
Secretariat, **10**, 37, 405
Secretary General, **10**, 405
specialised meetings, **10**, 391
treaties—
    conclusion of, **10**, 426
    treaty negotiations, authorisation of, **10**, 410*n*
unanimity, **10**, 412, 414
veto, within, **10**, 42, 416
voting—
    majority decisions, **10**, 410, 413
    procedure, generally, **10**, 42
    qualified majorities, **10**, 412
    unanimity, **10**, 412, 414
    weighted, **10**, 411
Council of the Pharmaceutical Society of Great Britain
constitution, **15**, 1514
elections, **15**, 1514
functions, **15**, 1514
generally, **15**, 1514
Council of the Royal College of Veterinary Surgeons
functions, **15**, 1531
Council on Tribunals
advisory powers, **23**, 908
chairman, **23**, 910
children's hearing, attendance at, **3**, 1325
consultative powers, **23**, 908, 914
Director General of Fair Trading, supervision of, **5**, 803
establishment of, **1**, 207; **23**, 908
Franks Committee, recommendations of, **23**, 908, 913, 919
functions, **23**, 909
membership, **23**, 910
objectives of, **23**, 913
Parliamentary Commission for Administration as member of, **23**, 263
planning, supervision in public examination, **23**, 263
public corporations, **19**, 239
tribunals under supervision of, **23**, 911
visits to tribunals by members of, **23**, 915
See also SCOTTISH COMMITTEE
Councillor
code of conduct, **14**, 232
disqualification for office—
    appeal to sheriff, **14**, 119
    bankruptcy, **15**, 1068
    by-election, **15**, 1067
    citizenship, **15**, 1066
    common law, **15**, 1071
    legal incapacity, **15**, 1066, 1071
    Local Government (Scotland) Act, under, **15**, 1069
    office, by virtue of, **15**, 1069, 1070
    sequestration, **15**, 1068
    statutory, **15**, 1066–1070
election, *see* ELECTIONS
personal liability, **14**, 223
qualification for office, **15**, 1066
register of electors, supply to, **15**, 1114

Counsel
advice and assistance provided by, **13**, 1021
fees, payment, burden of proof, **15**, 872
legal aid—
    choice of counsel, **13**, 1072
    civil cases, employment of expert, **13**, 1045
    criminal cases, **13**, 1052
        sanction for, **13**, 1064
    exclusion from selection, **13**, 1072
    fees and expenses, **13**, 1074
        regulation, **13**, 1074
    refusal to act, **13**, 1072
See also ADVOCATE
Counselling services
probation hostel, in, **22**, 34
psychiatric hospital team, in, **22**, 30
voluntary organisations, **22**, 13
Counsellors of State
choice of, **7**, 705
circumstances requiring, **7**, 705
functions exercised by, **7**, 705
Count, reckoning and payment
copyright, infringement, **18**, 1086, 1091, 1140
Counterclaim
consumer contract, proceedings not affected by jurisdiction over, **4**, 54
Court of Session procedure, **17**, 1390
sheriff court procedure—
    abandonment, where lodged, **17**, 1047
    access to child, for, **17**, 1048, 1233
    Civil Jurisdiction Convention, under, **17**, 1049
    custody of child, for, **17**, 1048, 1233
    lodging, **17**, 1046
    maintenance for child, for, **17**, 1048, 1233
    summary causes, **17**, 1308
special jurisdiction, **4**, 49, 52
Counterfeit
currency, possession of, **14**, 1838
document, customs and excise, in connection with, **7**, 1257
implements, possession of, **14**, 1839
notes and coins, **7**, 385, 395
Counterfeiting
commercial, trade descriptions, **6**, 118
offence, generally, **14**, 1836
Counties of cities
reform in 1929 ..., **14**, 39
Counting agent
appointment, **15**, 1052, 1333
    notice, **15**, 1227, 1229, 1244
    notification, **15**, 1333
count—
    attendance, **15**, 1326, 1330, 1330*n*, 1333
    conduct at, **15**, 1326, 1332
income tax, liability to, **15**, 1403
national insurance contributions, liability for, **15**, 1402
'political functions', **15**, 1335
role, **15**, 1335
substitute, **15**, 1229
time and place of count, notification, **15**, 1245, 1246, 1334

Country park
provision of, generally, **9**, 1239; **14**, 676; **25**, 360
regional, **9**, 1240; **14**, 677
Countryside
access—
 agreement, **9**, 1236; **14**, 673
 local government powers, **14**, 673
 order, **9**, 1236
 public, **9**, 1235
accommodation, local government provision of, **14**, 680
byelaws, **14**, 275, 682
camping sites, **14**, 678
caravan sites, **14**, 678
Commission for Scotland, **14**, 672
conservation, generally, **9**, 1232
country parks, *see* COUNTRY PARK
entry, powers of, **14**, 685
environmentally sensitive areas, **9**, 1238
inland waters, control of, **14**, 686
long-distance routes, planning and provision of, **9**, 1239; **14**, 675
management agreement, **14**, 679
meals, local government provision of, **14**, 680
nature reserves, **9**, 1237; **14**, 671
parking places, **14**, 681
public paths, **9**, 1239; **14**, 674
recreation—
 open air, improvement of waterways for, **14**, 683
 water authority, provision of facilities by, **14**, 684
reform, **14**, 46
refreshments, local government provision of, **14**, 680
seashore and adjacent water, control of, **14**, 686
special scientific interest, sites of—
 generally, **9**, 1241
 special protection for, **9**, 1242
wildlife, protection of, **9**, 1243
Countryside Commission for Scotland
functions of, **9**, 1233
notified of planning application, **23**, 166
County
administrative, England and Wales, **14**, 60
borough, England and Wales, **14**, 60
clerk, appointment of, **14**, 249
council, *see* COUNTY COUNCIL
counties of cities, **14**, 39
functions, **14**, 23
justice of peace, introduction of, **14**, 27
local authority elections, **15**, 1021, 1024, 1025
origins, **14**, 23
reform of 1929, **14**, 39
sanitary inspector, appointment of, **14**, 249
sheriff, functions of, **14**, 23, 26
sheriffdoms, creation of, **14**, 23
treasurer, appointment of, **14**, 249
County council
establishment, **14**, 30; **15**, 1024
franchise, **15**, 1024
functions, **14**, 30
highways, responsibility for, **14**, 33
public health, responsibility for, **14**, 37

County council—*continued*
reform, **14**, 30
standing joint committee, **14**, 30
statutory regulation, **25**, 501, 502
Coups
foreshore used as, **24**, 593
valuation for rating, **24**, 593
Course of justice
interference with, *see* ADMINISTRATION OF JUSTICE (offences against)
Court
Admiralty, *see* ADMIRALTY
auditors, of, *see* COURT OF AUDITORS
body constituting, **1**, 210
burgh, *see* BURGH
child brought before, notification of local authority, **16**, 1788
Church, *see* CHURCH COURTS
contempt of, *see* CONTEMPT OF COURT
Court of First Instance, *see* COURT OF FIRST INSTANCE
Court of Session, *see* COURT OF SESSION
courts-martial appeals, *see* COURTS-MARTIAL APPEAL COURT
Criminal Appeal, *see* CRIMINAL APPEAL, COURT OF
criminal courts, *see* CRIMINAL COURTS
district, *see* DISTRICT COURT
documents of, printers' imprint, **17**, 3
exchequer, *see* COURT OF EXCHEQUER
Four Burghs, of, **14**, 13; **22**, 510
franchise, *see* FRANCHISE COURT
functions of, **1**, 210
hearing, right to fair and public, *see* HUMAN RIGHTS
High Court of Justiciary, *see* HIGH COURT OF JUSTICIARY
House of Lords, *see* HOUSE OF LORDS
human rights, *see* EUROPEAN COURT OF HUMAN RIGHTS
international and national, decisions as evidence of state practice, **19**, 642
Judicial Committee of Privy Council, *see* PRIVY COUNCIL
judicial review, *see* JUDICIAL REVIEW
jurisdiction—
 generally, **5**, 714
 statute ousting or adding to, **12**, 1128–1130
Justice, of, *see* COURT OF JUSTICE OF THE EUROPEAN COMMUNITIES
Lands Tribunal for Scotland, *see* LANDS TRIBUNAL FOR SCOTLAND
Lyon Court, *see* LYON, COURT OF THE LORD
meaning, **4**, 6n
peer's right to sit covered, **16**, 1308
penal affairs, intervention in, **16**, 1486, 1494–1496
police, *see* POLICE COURT
privileges relating to proceedings, **17**, 16
records—
 access to, **19**, 879
 commissary records, **19**, 859
 Court of Session, **19**, 856
 disposal of, **19**, 866, 869
 High Court, **19**, 856
 justice of the peace records, **19**, 859

Court—_continued_
records—_continued_
  origin of public registers, **19**, 830
  Scottish Land Court, **19**, 858
  Scottish Record Office, **19**, 849
  sheriff court, **19**, 855, 859
  Teind Court, **19**, 858
  transmission of, **19**, 855
Referees, Court of, **5**, 448
right of access to, **12**, 44
Scottish Courts Administration, **13**, 1406
Scottish Land Court, _see_ SCOTTISH LAND COURT
sentence, _see_ SENTENCE
sheriff, _see_ SHERIFF COURT
Sovereign, participation of, **5**, 624
sovereign power, authority derives from, **4**, 1
Union Agreement of 1707, **5**, 349; **7**, 739
voluntary arrangement, powers relating to, _see_
  COMPANY (voluntary arrangement)
voluntary winding up, powers relating to, **4**, 815
winding up by, _see_ WINDING UP
Court of Admiralty
See ADMIRALTY
Court of Appeal
Jenkins Report, case law since, **4**, 480
unfair prejudice remedy, history of, **4**, 478
Court of Auditors
allocation of membership, **10**, 450
annual report, **10**, 453
composition, **10**, 450
contribution of, **10**, 454
control of policy implementation, **10**, 449–454
decisions of, **10**, 451
drawbacks to, **10**, 455
establishment, **10**, 71, 499
functions, **10**, 71, 452
generally, **10**, 29, 71
membership, **10**, 71
  appointment of members, **10**, 450
organisation, **10**, 451
policy decisions questioned by, **10**, 452
President, **10**, 451
revenue and expenditure, examination by, **10**,
  452
status of, **10**, 429
Court of Claims
Lord Lyon King of Arms, and, **6**, 1011
Court of Common Pleas
emergence of, **6**, 803
Court of Criminal Appeal
See CRIMINAL APPEAL, COURT OF
Court of Exchequer
abolition, **7**, 905
Exchequer Causes, **19**, 1548
institution, **22**, 322
jurisdiction, **5**, 714
precedent—
  Court of Session decisions, **22**, 322
  House of Lords, Scottish appeals—
    binding decisions, **22**, 322
  own decisions, **22**, 322
  strictness of doctrine, **22**, 322
Seal, **7**, 885

Court of First Instance (EU)
action wrongly raised in, **10**, 61
actions, forms of, **10**, 62
advocate appearing before, dress, **13**, 1323
advocate's right of audience, **13**, 1325
advocate-general, member performing task of, **10**,
  194
appeal to Court of Justice—
  by party not involved in Court of First Instance
    proceedings, **10**, 246
  decisions which may be appealed, **10**, 245
  effect of bringing, **10**, 249
  expenses, **10**, 292
  generally, **7**, 197; **10**, 61, 61_n_.194
  grounds of, **10**, 247
  powers of Court of Justice on, **10**, 250
  procedure—
    generally, **10**, 287
    ill-founded appeals, dismissal of, **10**, 286
    initiation of appeal, **10**, 281
    intervention in, **10**, 285
    oral procedure, **10**, 284
    responding to appeal, **10**, 282
    subsequent written pleadings, **10**, 283
  refusal of application to intervene, against, **10**,
    246
  time limit, **10**, 248
  title to bring, **10**, 246
application to intervene refused, **10**, 245
breach of procedure, appeal on grounds of, **10**,
  247
Chambers, sittings in, **10**, 61, 194
competition cases, **10**, 194
European Coal and Steel Community, cases
  under, **10**, 194
function, **10**, 194
generally, **10**, 61, 61_n_
infringement of Community law, appeal on
  grounds of, **10**, 247
jurisdiction, **10**, 61, 194, 197
lack of competence of, appeal on grounds of, **10**,
  247
membership, **10**, 61, 194
plenary sessions, **10**, 61, 194
referral of action—
  Court of Justice, from, **10**, 194
  Court of Justice, to, **10**, 194
Registrar and Registry, **10**, 61
remit to, **17**, 864
rules of procedure, **10**, 61
staff cases, **10**, 66, 194
**Court of Justice of the European
  Communities**
admissibility of action, objections to, **10**, 270
advertisement of proceedings, **10**, 256
advocates-general—
  first Advocate-General, **10**, 191
  functions, **5**, 674; **10**, 60, 191
  generally, **10**, 57
  opinions, **10**, 60, 251
appeal against reference to, **17**, 832, 884
appellate jurisdiction—
  application refused by Court of First Instance,
    10, 245

Court of Justice of the European Communities—*continued*
appellate jurisdiction—*continued*
  by party not involved in Court of First Instance proceedings, **10**, 246
  decisions disposing of procedural issue, **10**, 245
  decisions disposing of substantive issues in part only, **10**, 245
  decisions which may be appealed, **10**, 245
  effect of bringing, **10**, 249
  expenses—
    appeals, **10**, 292
    court fees, **10**, 288
    direct actions, **10**, 289
    legal aid, **10**, 293
    preliminary rulings, **10**, 291
    recoverable, **10**, 290
    taxation, **10**, 290
  final decisions, **10**, 245
  grounds of, **10**, 247
  powers, **10**, 250
  procedure—
    allocation to Chambers, **10**, 287
    costs or expenses, **10**, 287
    ill-founded appeals, dismissal of, **10**, 286
    initiation of appeal, **10**, 281
    interim measures, application for, **10**, 287
    interpretation of judgment, **10**, 287
    intervention in appeals, **10**, 285
    joining of cases, **10**, 287
    Judge Rapporteur, preliminary report of, **10**, 287
    judgments, **10**, 287
    legal aid, **10**, 287
    new issues, restriction on introduction of, **10**, 287
    oral, **10**, 284, 287
    pleadings, service of, **10**, 287
    responding to appeal, **10**, 282
    revision of judgment, **10**, 287
    subsequent written pleadings, **10**, 283
    third party proceedings for review of judgment, **10**, 287
  refusal of application to intervene, against, **10**, 246
  time limit, **10**, 248
  title to bring, **10**, 246
arbitration cases, **10**, 196
case law, treatment in, **22**, 268
Chambers—
  composition, **10**, 188
  Presidents of, **10**, 190
  referral of case to full court, **10**, 188
  sessions in, **10**, 59
citizen and member state, between, **10**, 239
Clerk of Justiciary, responsibilities, **6**, 868
collegiality, **10**, 59, 59*n*
Community legislation, precedence of, **22**, 213
competence—
  additional, under other instruments, **10**, 185
  founding treaties, under, **10**, 184
  generally, **10**, 195
composition of court, **10**, 187
constitution, **5**, 670

Court of Justice of the European Communities—*continued*
Council of Ministers may sue and be sued, **10**, 37
court fees, **10**, 288
Court of First Instance—
  action wrongly raised in, **10**, 61
  actions, forms of, **10**, 620
  appeal from, **10**, 194, 197
  decisions of, **1**, 865
  generally, **10**, 61, 61*n*
  See also COURT OF FIRST INSTANCE
decisions of, **22**, 205, 329
direct actions, **10**, 62–67, 196
  act adversely affecting applicant, **10**, 235
  annulment, actions for, **6**, 93, 207; **10**, 64, 64*n*, 85
    acts susceptible to, **10**, 209, 210
    ECSC Treaty, under, **10**, 210, 213
    EEC Treaty, under, **10**, 209, 211
    effects of, **10**, 215
    grounds for, **10**, 213
    illegality pled by way of exception, **10**, 216
    nature of remedy, **10**, 208
    time limit, **10**, 214
    who may bring, **10**, 211, 212
  Community institution, against, **10**, 196, 207–216
  contractual liability, in respect of, **10**, 237, 238
    national law, **10**, 237
    prorogation, **10**, 238
  damages, of, **10**, 67
  entitlement to bring, **10**, 233
  expenses, liability for, **10**, 289
  failure to act, action for, **10**, 65, 217–221
  failure to fulfil obligation, for, **10**, 63, 63*n*, 198–163*n*, 206
  indemnity, of, **10**, 67
  member state, against, **10**, 196, 198–206
    ECSC Treaty, under—
      Commission, at instance of, **10**, 204
      enforcement of decisions by Commission, **10**, 205
      member state, by, **10**, 206
    EEC Treaty, under—
      Commission, actions by, **10**, 200
      court's powers, **10**, 202
      member state, by, **10**, 201
      voluntary submission of disputes, **10**, 203
    failure by member state, concept of, **10**, 199
  failure to act, for, **10**, 217–221
    definition by institute of its position, **10**, 220
    ECSC Treaty, under, **10**, 217, 219
    EEC Treaty, under, **10**, 217, 218
    nature of remedy, **10**, 217
    time limit, **10**, 221
    generally, **10**, 198
  nature of remedy, **10**, 232
  parties entitled to bring, **10**, 198
  pre-action internal procedure, **10**, 234
  procedure, **10**, 251
    ordinary procedure, **10**, 258–268
      application, **10**, 258
      defence, **10**, 259

Court of Justice of the European Communities—*continued*
direct actions—*continued*
  procedure—*continued*
    ordinary procedure—*continued*
      experts' reports, **10**, 265
      joining of cases, **10**, 261
      judgment, **10**, 268
      oral evidence, **10**, 264
      oral procedure, **10**, 267
      preliminary report by Judge Rapporteur, **10**, 262
      preparatory inquiries, **10**, 263–265
      rejoinder, **10**, 260
      reply, **10**, 260
    special forms of, **10**, 269–277
      default, judgment by, **10**, 269
      interim measures, **10**, 271
      interpretation of judgment, **10**, 276
      objections to admissibility, **10**, 270
      procedural issues, **10**, 270
      rectification of judgment, **10**, 274
      review of judgment, third party proceedings for, **10**, 273
      revision of judgment, **10**, 277
      supplementing the judgment, **10**, 275
      third parties, intervention by, **10**, 272
  reparations in respect of non-contractual liability, for—
    causal link, **10**, 229
    fault, liability for, **10**, 225
    generally, **10**, 222–231
    grounds, **10**, 223
    maladministration, **10**, 226
    national authorities, against, **10**, 230
    nature of remedy, **10**, 222
    necessity of loss, **10**, 228
    time limit, **10**, 231
    without fault liability, **10**, 224
    wrongful legislative measures, **10**, 227
  staff cases, **10**, 66, 232–236
  time limits, **10**, 236
documents—
  advice on documentation, **10**, 254*n*
  service of, **10**, 255
enforcement of Community rights, **10**, 85
establishment under founding treaties, **10**, 184
expenses—
  court fees, **10**, 288
  direct actions, **10**, 289
  legal aid, **10**, 293
  liability—
    appeals, **10**, 292
    direct actions, **10**, 289
    preliminary rulings, **10**, 291
  recoverable, **10**, 290
  taxation, **10**, 290
experts' reports, **10**, 265
forms of action, **10**, 62, 195–238
full court, **10**, 188
functions, **5**, 671; **10**, 56, 56*n*, 195
generally, **10**, 12, 308
illegality, plea of, **10**, 62, 69
interim or interlocutory decisions, **10**, 59

Court of Justice of the European Communities—*continued*
interim measures by, **10**, 271
international agreements to which member states party, **10**, 74
interpretation service, **10**, 193
invalid, acts declared, **10**, 85
Judge Rapporteur's report, **10**, 251, 262
  preliminary ruling, request for, **10**, 279
judges, **10**, 57
  nomination, **10**, 57
judgments—
  deliberation, **10**, 268
  delivery, **10**, 268
  enforcement, **8**, 565; **10**, 268
  individual opinions, no provision for, **10**, 268
  interpretation of, **10**, 276
  language of, **2**, 253; **10**, 59*n*, 96
  majority decision, **10**, 268
  precedent, **10**, 80
  preliminary ruling, request for, **10**, 280
  publication of, **10**, 59
  reasons for, **10**, 268
  rectification of, **10**, 274
  report for the hearing, **10**, 268
  review of, third party proceedings for, **10**, 273
  revision of, **10**, 277
  source of Community law, as, **10**, 74
  supplementing, **10**, 275
  suspension, **8**, 568
judicial review, **4**, 1366
jurisdiction, **5**, 673; **10**, 56, 196
  appellate, **10**, 197
jurisprudence as source of Community law, **10**, 74
jurisprudence of, supremacy of EU law over national law reflected in, **4**, 1112
language of case, **10**, 253
lawyer, entitlement to practice before, **10**, 252
legal aid, **10**, 293; **13**, 1034, 1052
library and research directorate, **10**, 193
limitation of action, **4**, 1355
members, **10**, 57, 189
  cabinets of, **10**, 193
  immunity from legal proceedings, **10**, 189
opinions, **10**, 62
  compatibility of proposed agreements, as to, **10**, 70
organisation, **10**, 187–194
precedence--
  Community legislation, **22**, 213
  flexibility, **22**, 268
  Scottish courts, **22**, 269
  United Kingdom recognition of, **22**, 214
preliminary ruling—
  after lodging of, **10**, 279
  questions which may be referred, **10**, 240
  authority in Scottish case in which reference arose, **22**, 267
  generally, **5**, 672
  references for—
    Community institutions, validity and interpretation of acts, **10**, 240
    courts entitled to request, **10**, 241
    criteria for making request, **10**, 242

Court of Justice of the European Communities—*continued*
preliminary ruling—*continued*
  references for—*continued*
    effects of, **10**, 244
    entitlement to request, **10**, 241
    expenses, **10**, 291
    function, **10**, 239
    generally, **10**, 62, 68, 196
    interpretation of EEC Treaty, **10**, 240
    interpretation of statutes, **10**, 240
    Judge Rapporteur's report, **10**, 279
    legal representation in, **10**, 252
    national court, to assist, **10**, 239
    nature of, **10**, 239
    obligation to request, **10**, 242, 243
    private parties, between, **10**, 239
    procedure—
      generally, **10**, 251
      judgment, **10**, 280
      oral hearing, **10**, 280
      written observations, **10**, 278
    tribunals entitled to request, **10**, 241
preparatory inquiry—
  closure of, **10**, 266
  experts' reports, **10**, 265
  generally, **10**, 263
  oral evidence, **10**, 264
President, **10**, 58, 190
  interim or interlocutory decisions, **10**, 59
press and information service, **10**, 193
private parties, **10**, 196, 239, 252
privileges, **10**, 189
procedure—
  advertisement of proceedings, **10**, 256
  agent, representation by, **10**, 252
  audience, rights of, **10**, 252
  direct actions, **10**, 251
    ordinary procedure, **10**, 258–268
      application, **10**, 258
      defence, **10**, 259
      experts' reports, **10**, 265
      joining of cases, **10**, 261
      judgment, **10**, 268
      oral evidence at preparatory inquiry, **10**, 264
      oral procedure, **10**, 267
      preliminary report by Judge Rapporteur, **10**, 262
      preparatory inquiries, **10**, 263–266
      rejoinder, **10**, 259
      reply, **10**, 259
    special forms, **10**, 269–277
      admissibility, objections to, **10**, 270
      default, judgment by, **10**, 269
      interim measures, **10**, 271
      interpretation of judgment, **10**, 276
      procedural issues, **10**, 270
      rectification of judgment, **10**, 274
      review of judgment, third party proceedings for, **10**, 273
      revision of judgment, **10**, 277
      supplementing judgment, **10**, 275
      third parties, intervention by, **10**, 272

Court of Justice of the European Communities—*continued*
procedure—*continued*
  documents, service of, **10**, 255
  generally, **10**, 251
  institutions, representation of, **10**, 252
  judgment, **10**, 251
  language of case, **10**, 253
  lawyers—
    entitlement to practice before Court of Justice, **10**, 252
    parties represented by, **10**, 252
  member states, representation of, **10**, 252
  minutes, **10**, 253
  oral, **10**, 251, 267
    Advocate-General, delivery of opinion, **10**, 251
    appellate procedure, **10**, 284
    argument and submissions on behalf of parties, **10**, 251
    language, **10**, 253
    preliminary ruling, **10**, 280
    preparatory enquiries, **10**, 251, 264
    reading of Judge-Rapporteur's report, **10**, 251
  preliminary rulings, **10**, 251, 278–280
  private parties, representation of, **10**, 252
  representation, **10**, 252
  Rules of, **10**, 56, 186
  time limits, **10**, 257
  written, **10**, 251
    appellate procedure, **10**, 283
    language, **10**, 253
    preliminary ruling, references for, **10**, 278, 279
  written pleadings—
    general rules, **10**, 254
    service of, **10**, 255
reference to—
  appeal against, **17**, 832, 884
  Court of Session procedure, **17**, 1401
  generally, **2**, 453
Registrar and Registry, **10**, 61, 192
retrospectiveness of legislation, **22**, 217
Rules of Procedure, **10**, 56, 186
Scottish courts, precedent in, **22**, 269
Selected Instruments relating to the organisation, jurisdiction and procedure of the Court, **10**, 56
staff, **10**, 193
Statutes of, **10**, 56
  Protocol on, **10**, 186
third party—
  intervention by, **10**, 272
  review of judgment, third party proceedings for, **10**, 273
time limits, **10**, 257
translation service, **10**, 193
United Kingdom recognition of precedence, **22**, 214
validity of regulations, preliminary ruling by Court of Justice, **10**, 93
Whole Court sessions, **10**, 59
written pleadings, **10**, 254
  service of, **10**, 255

Court of Referees
functions of, **5**, 448
membership, **5**, 448
Court of Session
Act of Sederunt, *see* ACT OF SEDERUNT
adjudication, **8**, 189
administration, generally, **6**, 934
admiralty causes, and, **1**, 411; **4**, 2; **6**, 916; **22**, 519, 609, 635
advocate—
    admission to public office, **13**, 1304
        petition to court, **13**, 1305
    appearing before, dress, **13**, 1323
    audience, right of, **13**, 1325
appeal from—
    House of Lords, to, **5**, 637; **6**, 801, 810–812, 818, 825, 829, 836, 920; **13**, 1326; **22**, 602, 635
    Scots Parliament, to, before, 1707 ..., **5**, 638; **22**, 602
appeal to—
    abandonment of, **17**, 1286
    appellate jurisdiction generally, **17**, 1353, 1434
    contempt of court, on, **17**, 1464
    Employment Appeal Tribunal, from, **6**, 924
    generally, **1**, 248, 339; **5**, 625; **6**, 924; **17**, 1280; **22**, 518
    Inner House, appellate jurisdiction of, **17**, 1434–1436, 1451
        report for ruling, **17**, 1465
    Lands Tribunal for Scotland, **6**, 924, 1154
    licensing decisions, on, **2**, 85, 93
    Lyon Court, from, **6**, 1020
    Pensions Appeal Tribunal, from, **6**, 924
    planning decisions, on, **6**, 924; **23**, 270–279
    procedure—
        motion for new trial, **17**, 1449–1451
        reclaiming motion—
            competency, **17**, 1438
            effect of, **17**, 1446
            enrolled out of time, **17**, 1443
            generally, **17**, 1437
            grounds, **17**, 1448
            hearing, **17**, 1447
            interlocutor, **17**, 1439–1442, 1444
            procedure, **17**, 1445
        stated case, appeal by way of—
            application for, **17**, 1455
            competency, **17**, 1454
            form of, **17**, 1456
            generally, **17**, 1453
            grounds, **17**, 1458
            procedure on, **17**, 1457
    sheriff court, from, **17**, 1280–1286, 1334, 1463
    single bills, **17**, 1435
    Social Security Commissioners, from, **6**, 924
    statutory bodies from—
        generally, **17**, 1452
        stated case, by, **17**, 1453–1458
        statutory appeal, **17**, 1459–1462
    summar roll, **17**, 1435
    tribunals, generally, from, **1**, 248, 339; **6**, 924
    value added tax tribunals, from, **6**, 924
    verdict, application to enter, **17**, 1466

Court of Session—*continued*
arrest of ship, jurisdiction, **8**, 322
arrestment, service of, **8**, 258
audience—
    advocate's right of, **13**, 1325
    solicitors' right of, **13**, 1152, 1180
authentic instruments, enforcement, **8**, 474
Bill Chamber, and, **6**, 919
Books of Council and Session, *see* BOOKS OF COUNCIL AND SESSION
borrowing process from, restriction, **13**, 1181
canon law, *see* CANON LAW
children's hearing—
    appeal against decision of, **3**, 1300, 1360, 1361
    nobile officium, application, **3**, 1386
composition of—
    Divisions of, **5**, 632; **6**, 862, 911, 926
    Inner House, *see* INNER HOUSE
    Outer House, *see* OUTER HOUSE
constitution of, **6**, 807
custody order—
    Custody Orders Register, **8**, 511, 512
    enforcement in other parts of UK, **8**, 511
    interdict—
        interim, **8**, 516
        power to grant, **8**, 516
education authority, supervisory jurisdiction, **8**, 836
evolution of—
    absorption of other courts, **6**, 915–918; **22**, 519, 635
    College of Justice, **5**, 627, 628; **6**, 904; **22**, 515
    early sessions, **6**, 922
    Lords of Council and Session, **6**, 903
    nineteenth century restructuring, **6**, 910–912; **22**, 254, 518, 635
first instance—
    court of, as, **22**, 518
    proceedings at, civil legal aid, **13**, 1034
historical antecedents—
    Advocatus Pauperum, **6**, 905
    Auld Session, **6**, 896, 902, 915
    barony courts, **6**, 897
    Courts of Regality, **6**, 897
    Curia Regis, **6**, 898–900; **22**, 515
    See also Curia Regis
    'Haill Fifteen', **6**, 910, 911
investor protection—
    interdict granted by, **12**, 1324, 1410, 1413
    restitution order, grant, **12**, 1324, 1411, 1413
judges—
    appointment, **5**, 629; **6**, 906, 929
    College of Justice, **6**, 904
    disqualification, **6**, 932
    functions, **6**, 807, 932
    Inner House, **6**, 926
    Insolvency Judge, **6**, 927
    judicial title, **6**, 929
    Lord Justice-Clerk, **6**, 862, 923, 926, 929–931; **22**, 520
        See also LORD JUSTICE-CLERK
    Lord Justice-General, **6**, 903, 911, 923; **22**, 520
    Lord President, **6**, 903, 911, 913, 923, 926, 927, 929, 930, 934
        See also LORD PRESIDENT

Court of Session—*continued*
judges—*continued*
  Lords of Council and Session, **6**, 903, 904
  Lords Ordinary, **6**, 911, 923
    Exchequer Causes, **6**, 917, 927
    Teind Causes, **6**, 921, 927
  number of, **5**, 630; **6**, 911, 923
  Outer House, **6**, 927
  Patent Judge, **6**, 927
  qualification of, **5**, 629
  removal, **6**, 929
  retirement, **6**, 906*n*, 929
  Senators of the College of Justice, **1**, 929; **6**, 906*n*, 923
  specialist, **6**, 932
  status, **6**, 930
  Vacation Judge, **6**, 932, 933
  wives, title, **6**, 929
judicial precedent, doctrine of—
  collegiate nature of Court of Session, effect of, **22**, 286–289
  development of, **22**, 249–256, 539–544
  Divisions, binding decisions of, **22**, 291, 293
  Extra Division, decisions, of, **22**, 294
  Fuller Court, decisions of, **22**, 289, 291
  House of Lords, and, **22**, 255, 257, 602
  Inner House, decisions of, **22**, 290
  Outer House, decisions of, **22**, 295
  Whole Court, decisions of, **22**, 289, 291, 292
  See also JUDICIAL PRECEDENT
judicial review, *see* JUDICIAL REVIEW
judgment—
  enforcement—
    foreign judgment, of, **8**, 455
    furth of Scotland, **8**, 427, 473
  registration—
    EU judgments, **8**, 566, 567
    foreign judgment, **8**, 419
    furth of Scotland, **8**, 453
  UK—
    reciprocal scheme, setting aside registration, **8**, 490
jurisdiction—
  adjudication, **4**, 7
  admiralty, **4**, 2
  appellate, **17**, 1353, 1434. *See also* appeal *above*
  arbitration, *see* ARBITER; ARBITRATION
  bankruptcy, **4**, 16
  building society and member disputes, **3**, 385
  competent actions, **6**, 924
  consistorial proceedings, **4**, 5
  consumer protection, **6**, 168
  contempt of court, **6**, 309; **17**, 1464
  death, presumption of, **4**, 17
  divorce, **17**, 897; **17**, 1376. *See also* DIVORCE
  election petitions, **6**, 829
  Exchequer Causes, **6**, 924
  excluded, **17**, 1351, 1359, 1365
  exclusive, **17**, 1352, 1359. *See also* NOBILE OFFICIUM
  factors, *see* JUDICIAL FACTORS
  first instance, at, **17**, 1350
  generally, **4**, 12; **6**, 924; **17**, 508, 1349, 1354–1355, 1357

Court of Session—*continued*
jurisdiction—*continued*
  heritage, questions relating to, **6**, 908
  inhibition, **4**, 8; **8**, 133
  judicial review, *see* JUDICIAL REVIEW
  licensing appeals, *see* ALCOHOL
  liquidation, **4**, 15
  lis alibi pendens, **17**, 1360
  maritime causes, *see* ADMIRALTY
  matters outwith, **6**, 925
  meaning, **4**, 1
  messengers-at-arms, **17**, 1506
  nobile officium, see NOBILE OFFICIUM
  other courts and tribunals contrasted, **4**, 1
  patents, **6**, 924; **18**, 861–865
  planning appeals, **1**, 340–342; **23**, 270–279
  prorogation, **17**, 1360
  proving tenor, **4**, 11; **6**, 924
  rating valuation appeals, **24**, 500
  reduction, **4**, 6; **6**, 92, 1060
  remedies, **17**, 135, 1355
  sequestration, **2**, 133, 1335; **6**, 924. *See also* SEQUESTRATION
  sheriff court, review of, **4**, 19
  special cases, **4**, 10; **17**, 1358
  supervisory—
    application to, **1**, 346
    errors, correcting, **1**, 247
    errors of law, correcting, **1**, 285
    exclusion of, **1**, 306
    exclusive, **1**, 245
    exercising, **1**, 243
    failure to act, over, **1**, 302
    grounds for exercising, **1**, 246
    meaining, **1**, 348
    substitution of decision, not extending to, **1**, 248
    See also JUDICIAL REVIEW
  suspension, **3**, 998
  territorial, **4**, 2
  trusts and trustees, *see* TRUSTS AND TRUSTEES
  winding-up, **4**, 655
lawburrows, **13**, 902, 903, 906
legal aid—
  adjustment of, powers in relation to, **13**, 1084, 1084*n*
  appellate proceedings in, **13**, 1034
mails and duties, action of, **8**, 397
maintenance order, registration, **8**, 572, 573
nobile officium. See also NOBILE OFFICIUM
notary public, application for admission as, **13**, 1217
officers—
  Accountant of Court, **6**, 937
  appointment of, **6**, 934, 935
  Auditor of the Court, **5**, 628; **6**, 936
  central office, **6**, 934
  Clerks to the Signet, **6**, 904
  Deputy Principal Clerks of Session, **6**, 934
  Keeper of the Rolls, **6**, 934
  macers, **6**, 904, 935
  Principal Clerk of Session and Justiciary, **6**, 934
  Principal Extractor, **6**, 934
  training, **6**, 934

Court of Session—*continued*
patent proceedings, **18**, 861–865
  patent application, appeal in relation to, **18**, 854
  Patent Office inquiry, order for, **18**, 861
  revocation of patent, application for, **18**, 863
peerage claims, **16**, 1318
petition, signature, **13**, 1326
petition for suspension, **3**, 998
procedure—
  appeal, *see* appeal *above*
  consistorial action, procedure, **17**, 1392, 1406
  interim decree, **17**, 1394
  multiplepoinding, **17**, 1408
  petition, procedure on—
    bankruptcy, **17**, 1424
    children, adoption and custody of, **17**, 1427
    companies, **17**, 1422
    documents, recovery of, **17**, 1421
    general form of petition, **17**, 1414
    generally, **17**, 1367, 1413
    incapax, appointment of *curator bonis* to, **17**, 1423
    interdict, **17**, 1420
    judicial factor, appointment of, **17**, 1424
    judicial review, **17**, 1419
      See also JUDICIAL REVIEW
    lodging petition, **17**, 1415
    opposed, **17**, 1417
    particular forms, **17**, 1418–1427
    property, recovery of, **17**, 1421
    suspension, **17**, 1420
    trusts, **17**, 1420
    unopposed, **17**, 1416
  proof, conduct of, re-examination, **17**, 1169
  protestation, **17**, 1385
  reparation, action for, **17**, 1375, 1405
  special case—
    form of, **17**, 1429
    generally, **1**, 344; **17**, 1428
    procedure on, **17**, 1430
  stated case, appeal by way of, *see* appeal *above*
  petition, procedure on—
    bankruptcy, **17**, 1424
    children, adoption and custody of, **17**, 1427
    companies, **17**, 1422
    documents, recovery of, **17**, 1421
    general form of petition, **17**, 1414
    generally, **17**, 1367, 1413
    incapax, appointment of *curator bonis* to, **17**, 1423
    interdict, **17**, 1420
    judicial factor, appointment of, **17**, 1424
    judicial review, **17**, 1419
      See also JUDICIAL REVIEW
    lodging petition, **17**, 1415
    opposed, **17**, 1417
    particular forms, **17**, 1418–1427
    property, recovery of, **17**, 1421
    suspension, **17**, 1420
    trusts, **17**, 1420
    unopposed, **17**, 1416
  proof, conduct of, re-examination, **17**, 1169
  protestation, **17**, 1385
  reparation, action for, **17**, 1375, 1405

Court of Session—*continued*
procedure—*continued*
  special case—
    form of, **17**, 1429
    generally, **1**, 344; **17**, 1428
    procedure on, **17**, 1430
  stated case, appeal by way of, *see* appeal *above*
  summary trial—
    arbitration, procedure similar to, **2**, 405
    generally, **17**, 1431
    petition, form of, **17**, 1432
    procedure, **17**, 1433
  summons, procedure on—
    additional parties, **17**, 1400
    address, **17**, 1371
    adjustment roll, **17**, 1402
    appearance, failure to enter, **17**, 1388
    calling, lodging summons for, **17**, 1383
    charge, **17**, 1371
    commercial action, **17**, 1377, 1407
    commission, **17**, 1397
    conclusions, **17**, 1373
    condescendence, articles of, **17**, 1374
    consistorial causes, **17**, 1392, 1406
    counterclaims, **17**, 1390
    decree, **17**, 1394, 1396
    defences, **17**, 1387, 1388
    development of, **17**, 913
    diligence, **17**, 1397
    documents, inspection of, **17**, 1397
    European Court of Justice, reference to, **17**, 1401
    foreign problems, **17**, 1398
    general form, **17**, 1369
    generally, **17**, 1367, 1368
    hearings, **17**, 1409–1412
    instance, **17**, 1370
    interim damages, **17**, 1394
    motions, **17**, 1393
    multiplepoinding, **17**, 1408
    patent proceedings, **18**, 861–865
    pleas-in-law, **17**, 1374
    presentation of summons, **17**, 1378
    process, **17**, 1379, 1380
    proof essential, action where, **17**, 1389
    protestation, **17**, 1385
    records—
      closing the record, **17**, 1403
      commercial actions, **17**, 1407
      consistorial actions, **17**, 1406
      multiplepoinding, **17**, 1408
      open record and adjustment roll, **17**, 1402
      procedure following closing of, **17**, 1404
      reparation action, **17**, 1405
    registration, **17**, 1381
    reparation action, **17**, 1375, 1405
    service, **17**, 1382
    signeting, **17**, 1381
    simplified divorce procedure, **17**, 1376
    summary decree, **17**, 1396
    third party procedure, **17**, 1391
    time to pay directions, **17**, 1384
    warrant required, **17**, 1372
    written statements, **17**, 1399

Court of Session—*continued*
procedure—*continued*
  third party procedure, time to pay direction,
    17, 1384
public right of way, proceedings relating to, **18**, 513
recall of arrestment on dependence, caution,
  requirement for, **3**, 997
recall of inhibition on dependence, caution,
  requirement for, **3**, 997
records of—
  access to, **19**, 879
  Books of Council and Session, **19**, 839
  disposal of, **19**, 867, 869
  retransmissions, **19**, 872
  transmission, **19**, 856, 860
reduction—
  decree, of, **13**, 38
  generally, **13**, 28
  granted as step towards practical remedy, **13**, 28
  judicial review, application for, **13**, 28
  ope exceptionis, **13**, 29
  principal action, brought as, **13**, 28
Royal Commission on the Court of Session, **13**,
  1297
rule-making powers, **6**, 930
Rules of, **6**, 930; **22**, 187, 528
  See also ACT OF SEDERUNT
Saturday sittings, former, **13**, 1298
Scottish judgment, enforcement in overseas
  contracting state, **8**, 473
Seal, **7**, 885
servitude rights, actions concerning, **18**, 480
solicitor—
  controls over, **13**, 1160, 1171, 1199
  process, restrictions on borrowing, **13**, 1181
  right of audience, **13**, 1152, 1180
summonses, **7**, 883, 884
UK civil judgments, reciprocal enforcement
  scheme—
  setting aside registration, **8**, 490
Union Agreement of 1707, **7**, 739
Court of Teinds
powers, **3**, 1592
Court of the Lord Lyon
See LYON, COURT OF THE LORD
Courtesy
feudal law, generally, **18**, 110
legal liferent, as, **18**, 74
obligation to satisfy, **16**, 2116
Courts-martial
advocate appearing before, dress, **13**, 1323
advocate's right of audience, **13**, 1325
army and air force—
  accused—
    defending officer for, **2**, 722
    fitness to stand trial, **2**, 726
    interests of, protection, **2**, 722
    petitioning rights, **2**, 733
    plea by, **2**, 726
    presence of, **2**, 723
  acquittal, release on, **2**, 730
  appeal, *see* COURTS-MARTIAL APPEAL COURT
  arrest, proof of, **2**, 683
  charge referred to, **2**, 672

Courts-martial—*continued*
army and air force—*continued*
  compensation, order to pay, **2**, 732
  constitution, **2**, 714
  contempt proceedings, **6**, 308
  convening, **2**, 714
  death sentence, **2**, 737
  district, constitution, **2**, 714
  election for trial by, **2**, 673, 688
  evidence—
    admissibility of statements, **2**, 683
    calling, **2**, 726
    computer records, from, **2**, 683
  field general—
    constitution, **2**, 714
    nature of, **2**, 714
  finality of trial, **2**, 719
  findings—
    announcement of, **2**, 729
    confirmation of, **2**, 734
    insanity, of, **2**, 728
    not guilty, **2**, 730
    petitioning rights, **2**, 733
    revision of, **2**, 734
  general, constitution, **2**, 714
  guilty, plea of, **2**, 726
  insanity—
    finding of, **2**, 728
    petitioning as to, **2**, 733
  instruments, authentication of, **2**, 683
  Judge Advocate—
    appointment, **2**, 714, 716
    duties, **2**, 727
    summing up by, **2**, 727
  members—
    appointment, **2**, 715
    objection by accused, **2**, 724
    other services from, **2**, 715
    restrictions regarding, **2**, 714
    women eligible, **2**, 715
  mental disorder, questions as to, **2**, 726
  nature of, **2**, 714
  oaths, administration, **2**, 724
  offences triable by, **2**, 714
  officer, dismissal of, **2**, 684
  official documents, proof of, **2**, 683
  pleadings, **2**, 726
  post-trial matters, **2**, 733
  President, duties, **2**, 727
  proceedings, record of, **2**, 751
  prosecutor, appointment, **2**, 722
  punishments, scale of, **2**, 684
  restitution order, **2**, 732
  rules of procedure—
    compliance, exceptions, **2**, 720
    procedure before trial, **2**, 721
    provisions of, **2**, 720
  sentence—
    commencement and duration, **2**, 736
    death, of, execution of, **2**, 737
    promulgation, **2**, 734
    remission, **2**, 736
    review of, **2**, 735
    suspended, **2**, 736

Courts-martial—*continued*
army and air force—*continued*
  sentencing procedure, **2**, 731
  sitting—
    open court, in, **2**, 723
    place of, **2**, 717
  summing up, **2**, 726
  trial—
    finality of, **2**, 719
    order, where two accused, **2**, 725
    preparations for, **2**, 722
    procedure, **2**, 721, 726
    types of, **2**, 714
  witnesses—
    examination of, **2**, 726
    immunities and privileges, **2**, 724
civil offences, trial of, **2**, 627
civilians—
  contempt of court by, **2**, 718
  punishments, **2**, 685
  sentencing of, **2**, 685
contempt of, **2**, 655
evidence, laws of, **2**, 677, 678
fines, amount of, **2**, 629
jurisdiction, scope of, **2**, 627
juveniles, punishment limits, **2**, 686
naval—
  accused—
    fitness to plead, **2**, 701
    friend to assist, **2**, 698
    objection by, **2**, 701
    representation of, **2**, 698
    rights of, **2**, 700, 703
  alternative offences, conviction of, **2**, 705
  appeals, *see* COURTS-MARTIAL APPEAL COURT
  circumstantial letter—
    application to be made by, **2**, 699
    reading to court, **2**, 702
  clerk, appointment, **2**, 696
  closing speeches, **2**, 704
  compensation, order for, **2**, 707
  constitution, **2**, 693
  convening officer, duties, **2**, 694
  defence, case for, **2**, 703
  election for trial by, **2**, 668, 687
  evidence—
    admissibility of statements, **2**, 682
    official documents as, **2**, 682
  findings—
    general provisions, **2**, 705
    review of, **2**, 710
  guilty, plea of, **2**, 702
  Judge Advocate, *see* JUDGE ADVOCATE
  jurisdiction—
    challenge of, **2**, 701
    time and place, as to, **2**, 693
  legal aid, provision for, **2**, 698
  members—
    number, **2**, 693
    objection to, **2**, 701
    swearing of, **2**, 701
  misconduct in proceedings, **2**, 708
  offences triable, **2**, 693
  officers, appointment, **2**, 695

Courts-martial—*continued*
naval—*continued*
  open court, sitting in, **2**, 701
  ordering of, **2**, 694
  pleading to the charge, **2**, 702
  post-trial matters, **2**, 709
  procedure and practice, **2**, 693
  proceedings—
    misconduct in respect of, **2**, 708
    record of, **2**, 709
  prosecutor—
    appointment, **2**, 697
    opening speech, **2**, 702
    provost marshal, duty of, **2**, 696
  punishments—
    disrating, **2**, 684
    scale of, **2**, 684
  reference of charge to, **2**, 668
  restitution, order for, **2**, 707
  retrial, power to authorise, **2**, 712
  sentence—
    alteration of, **2**, 711
    announcement of, **2**, 706
    death, power to commute, **2**, 711
    remit, power to, **2**, 711
    review of, **2**, 710
  summing up, **2**, 704
  time and place, appointment, **2**, 694
  trial by—
    application for, **2**, 699
    election for, **2**, 687
    preliminaries, **2**, 701
    procedure before, **2**, 699
  witnesses—
    calling, **2**, 700
    examination of, **2**, 704
oath, form of, **2**, 680
persons sentenced by, treatment in detention, **16**, 1429
provisions common to all services, **2**, 681
punishments—
  detention, period of, **2**, 684
  list of, **2**, 684
statement made in, absolute privilege, **15**, 524
supervision of, **2**, 622
trial by—
  bar to civil trial, **2**, 622
  right to elect—
    army or air force, **2**, 673
    civilians, **2**, 739
    naval personnel, **2**, 668
    withdrawal of election, **2**, 673
Courts-Martial Appeal Court
advocate appearing before, dress, **13**, 1323
advocate's right of audience, **13**, 1325
appeal from, **2**, 712
appeals—
  abandonment of, **6**, 886
  application for, **6**, 885
  civilian, by, **6**, 884, 889
  courts-martial held abroad, **6**, 885
  defence of, **6**, 885
  disposal of, **6**, 888
  hearing of, **6**, 888

Courts-Martial Appeal Court—*continued*
appeals—*continued*
  insanity, cases of, **6**, 890
  right of, **6**, 883, 884, 885
  to House of Lords, **6**, 884, 893
  unfitness to plead, where, **6**, 891
constitution, **6**, 883
courts-martial held abroad, **6**, 885
Defence Council, petition to, **2**, 712
documents, production of, **6**, 887
establishment, **6**, 883
evidence, **6**, 887
expenses, **6**, 894
  witnesses, **6**, 894
House of Lords, appeal to, **2**, 712
insanity—
  finding, appeal against, **2**, 728
  petitioning as to, **2**, 733
judges, quorum of, **6**, 883
judgment of, **2**, 712
leave to appeal, **2**, 712, 733
legal aid, **6**, 895
order authorising re-trial, **6**, 892
petition of appeal, **2**, 733
place for sitting, **6**, 883, 895
purpose, **6**, 883
reference to—
  Judge Advocate General, by, **2**, 676
  Judge Advocate of Fleet, by, **2**, 675
  who may make, **2**, 712, 733
retrial, power to authorise, **2**, 712
right of appeal, **2**, 712, 726
right of audience, **6**, 895
royal prerogative and, **6**, 883
rules, **6**, 883
Scotland, sitting in, **2**, 712
sentence, power to quash, **2**, 712
substitution of court-martial findings and
  sentence, **6**, 889
witnesses, **6**, 894
Cousin
deceased specified relative, as, **15**, 602
Covenanted payment
annual payment—
  capital payment, must not be, **3**, 1136, 1147
  disqualification from classification as, **3**, 1142
  ejusdem generis with interest and annuity,
    construed, **3**, 1136
  as form of, **3**, 1136, 1141
  imposed involuntarily, **3**, 1136
  inducements or conditions, effect, **3**, 1142
  legal agreement, must be made under, **3**, 1136
  meaning, **3**, 1136
  payee's income, must form part of, **3**, 1136
  pure income profit in hands of payee, must be,
    3, 1136, 1138, 1142
  recurrence essential, **3**, 1136, 1137
annuity, **3**, 1136
capital, payment must not be charged to, **3**, 1136,
  1147
charges on income, **3**, 1148
charity, to, meaning, **3**, 1141, 1143
company, payment must ultimately be borne by,
  3, 1147

Covenanted payment—*continued*
conditions attached to, **3**, 1142
corporation tax, **3**, 1141, 1147
deed of covenant—
  deposited covenant, **3**, 1146
  execution, **3**, 1145
  loan/covenant arrangement, **3**, 1146
  signature, **3**, 1145
  witnesses, **3**, 1145
deposited covenant, **3**, 1146
discretionary trust, by, **3**, 1152
distribution, not regarded as, **3**, 1147
English charity, Scots covenant to, **3**, 1145
generally, **3**, 1136
gross payments, **3**, 1144
group relief, surrendering and claimant
  companies, **3**, 1148
income tax, **3**, 1137, 1147
  annual payments, as, **3**, 1136–1138
  company, payment by, **3**, 1139
  deduction, **3**, 1149
  donation must be made under deduction of, **3**,
    1147
  generally, **3**, 1139
  gross and net payments, **3**, 1144
  husband and wife, independent taxation, **3**,
    1140
  Schedule D, Case III, **3**, 1137
inducements attached to, **3**, 1142
interest, **3**, 1136
joint, by husband and wife, **3**, 1140
loan/covenant arrangement, **3**, 1146
net payments, **3**, 1144
partnership, by—
  authority to execute, **3**, 1150
  change of partners, where, **3**, 1150
  tax treatment, **3**, 1150
sole trader, by, **3**, 1151
statutory test, **3**, 1147
sum must be paid, **3**, 1147
Covenanters
lawburrows used against, **13**, 913, 914
Cover note
broker with authority to supply, **12**, 825
cancellation, **12**, 825
indemnity insurance, **12**, 818, 825
insurance contracts, **12**, 825
oral, **12**, 825
policy terms—
  requiring immediate notice, **12**, 825
  unusual, **12**, 825
renewable indemnity insurance, **12**, 825
retrospective cover, **12**, 825
temporary cover, **12**, 825
Covered area
exemptions from building regulations, **3**, 209
Cows
diseases, notifiable, **11**, 447
milk from, **11**, 438, 443–451
  bottles and cap colouring, **11**, 471
  children, milk prepared for, depots for sale of,
    11, 451
  consigning authority, compliance with
    legislation, **11**, 446

Cows—*continued*
milk from—*continued*
    customers, list of, **11**, 450
    disease—
        persons suffering from, **11**, 448
        precautions against spread of, **11**, 447–450
    inspection of cattle—
        dairies, in, **11**, 444, 444n
        elsewhere, **11**, 445
    meaning, **11**, 443
    stoppage of milk supplies, **11**, 449
    suppliers, list of, **11**, 450
    urban situation, kept in, **19**, 336n

Crabs
continental shelf, on, rights of coastal state, **21**, 19
prohibition on taking and sale, **11**, 168
size limits, **11**, 145n

Craft
burgh, monopoly of, **14**, 12

Craftsmanship
artistic, works of, copyright, **18**, 957, 966
    design documents, **18**, 1155

Craig, James
Edinburgh New Town plan, **18**, 376, 377, 379

Craig of Riccarton, Sir Thomas
authority of writings, **22**, 437
classification of sources of civil law in Scotland, **22**, 364
custom—
    as a source of law, **22**, 360, 364
    statute, relationship, **22**, 364
De Unione Regnorum Britanniae Tractatus, **22**, 628
desuetude, acceptance of doctrine, **22**, 364
English law, sources, **22**, 364
Jus feudale, **18**, 44; **22**, 535, 537, 542
    Bracton's *De Legibus* contrast, **22**, 251
    canon of 'authoritative writing', **22**, 441
    judicial precedent, **22**, 251
Regiam Majestatem, attitude to, **22**, 360

Crane
motor vehicle fitted with, **20**, 408

Crave
pecuniary, interest on, **17**, 1185
writ, prescribed form of, **17**, 1008

Cream
clotted, **11**, 474
composition, **11**, 475
description, **11**, 475
flavouring, **11**, 476
heat treatment, **11**, 355, 479
ingredients, **11**, 476, 478
labelling, **11**, 478
meaning, **11**, 439, 443, 474
pasteurised, **11**, 474
preservatives, **11**, 377
records of purchases and sales, **11**, 479
sterilised, **11**, 474
substitutes for, **11**, 477
ultra heat-treated, **11**, 474
untreated, **11**, 474, 479

Credit
agreement, *see* CONSUMER CREDIT AGREEMENT
brokerage, *see* CREDIT BROKERAGE
cancellation, repayment on, **5**, 868

Credit—*continued*
cards, *see* CREDIT CARD
concept of money central to, **14**, 1801
consumer, *see* CONSUMER CREDIT ACT; CONSUMER CREDIT AGREEMENT
credit sale agreement, **5**, 805, 809; **14**, 1809
    See also CREDIT SALE AGREEMENT
credit token, *see* CREDIT TOKEN
documentary, *see* BANKERS' DOCUMENTARY CREDITS
facilities, misuse of, **5**, 884–885
fixed sum, meaning, **5**, 808
granting, VAT exemption, **7**, 1424
implied contract terms as to, **12**, 1011
instalment credit finance, **7**, 1424
licensee—
    bankruptcy, **5**, 950
    conduct of business by, **5**, 945
    death of, **5**, 950
licensing of business—
    application for, **5**, 939
    classification of, **5**, 936–938
    determination of applications, **5**, 944
    fitness to hold, **5**, 941
    generally, **5**, 934
    group, generally, **5**, 937
    issue of—
        group licence, **5**, 943
        standard licence, **5**, 940
    renewal, **5**, 946
    requirement of, **5**, 935
    revocation, **5**, 948
    specific activities, authorisation of, **5**, 938
    standard—
        generally, **5**, 936
        issue of, **5**, 940
        misleading trading name, **5**, 942
    suspension—
        application to end, **5**, 949
        compulsory, **5**, 948
    variation, **5**, 948
        request, on, **5**, 947
limit, meaning, **5**, 808
meaning, **5**, 807
minor—
    advancement to, **3**, 1220
    soliciting for business with, **3**, 1220
reference agency, *see* CREDIT REFERENCE AGENCY
representations as to—
    continuing mandate, when, **3**, 1004
    general statement as to creditworthiness, **3**, 1004
    guarantee distinguished, **3**, 1004
        consequences of distinction, **3**, 1004
    liability for inaccuracy, **3**, 1004
    meaning, **3**, 1004
    Mercantile Law Amendment Act (Scotland) 1856, effect, **3**, 1008
    misrepresentation—
        damages, **3**, 1005
        delict, **3**, 1006, 1008
        fraudulent, **3**, 1005, 1006, 1008
            prerequisite of fraud, **3**, 1006
        innocent, **3**, 1005, 1005n
        negligent, **3**, 1005, 1006
    nature of, **3**, 1004

Credit—*continued*
representations as to—*continued*
pre-contractual, **3**, 1004, 1005
specifically addressed, **3**, 1007
statements of fact, **3**, 1004
who may rely upon, **3**, 1007
total charge for—
agreement exempt by reference to rate of, **5**, 823
computation of—
annual percentage rate, **5**, 819
generally, **5**, 818
tables, **5**, 819
generally, **5**, 817
transaction—
ancillary credit business, *see* ANCILLARY CREDIT BUSINESS
conditional sale agreement, *see* CONDITIONAL SALE AGREEMENT
consumer credit agreement, *see* CONSUMER CREDIT AGREEMENT
consumer hire agreement, *see* CONSUMER HIRE AGREEMENT
debtor-creditor, *see* DEBTOR-CREDITOR AGREEMENT
debtor-creditor-supplier, *see* DEBTOR-CREDITOR-SUPPLIER AGREEMENT
fixed-sum credit, *see* FIXED-SUM CREDIT
hire-purchase agreement, *see* HIRE-PURCHASE AGREEMENT
linked transactions, **5**, 815
main types, distinctions between, **5**, 805
multiple agreement, **5**, 814
personal credit agreement, **5**, 806
restricted-use credit, *see* RESTRICTED-USE CREDIT AGREEMENT
running-account credit, *see* RUNNING-ACCOUNT CREDIT
small agreement, **5**, 813
unrestricted-use credit, *see* UNRESTRICTED-USE CREDIT AGREEMENT
union, *see* CREDIT UNION
Credit Accumulation and Transfer Scheme (CATS), **8**, 976
Credit bargain
extortionate, **13**, 1771
meaning, **13**, 1771
Credit brokerage
ancillary credit business, as, **5**, 816
fees, recovery of, **5**, 840
Credit card
consumer sale using, passing of property, **18**, 631
development of, **2**, 1219
fraud, **7**, 367, 369
general features of transactions, **4**, 271
meaning, **4**, 270
system, operation of, **2**, 1219
Credit note
VAT purposes, validity for, **7**, 1360
Credit reference agency
databank information, limitation on access to, **18**, 1535
denial of access to credit facilities, **18**, 1501
generally, **5**, 954

Credit reference agency—*continued*
information—
business consumer, alternative procedure for disclosure, **5**, 958
filed, duty of agency to disclose, **5**, 956
wrong, correction of, **5**, 957
particulars of, duty of creditor to disclose, **5**, 955
use of information detrimental to subject's interests, where, **18**, 1501
See also DATA PROTECTION
Credit sale agreement
currency sold on, **14**, 1809
meaning, **5**, 805
restricted-use credit agreement, as, **5**, 809
Credit token
agreement, **5**, 811
meaning, **5**, 811
misuse of, **5**, 885
new, issue of, **5**, 886
offences, **5**, 835
unsolicited, **5**, 835
Credit union
accounts, display of, **12**, 671
amalgamations, **12**, 672
borrowings, **12**, 666
breach of borrowing limit, **12**, 666n
cancellation, **12**, 677
co-operative movement, affiliations with, **12**, 656
committee members, **12**, 668
company, convertion to credit union, **12**, 673
current legislation, **12**, 603
deposits, **12**, 666
meaning, **12**, 666n
distributions, **12**, 670
dividends, **12**, 670
tax exemption, **12**, 659
employees, insurance against loss attributable to, **12**, 668
general reserve fund, **12**, 670
guarantee arrangements, **12**, 668
heritable property, rules as to, **12**, 667
historical development, **12**, 602, 656
Industrial and Provident Societies Act 1965, application, **12**, 657
inspectors, appointment of, **12**, 675
insurance against loss, **12**, 668
interest earned by, tax exemption, **12**, 659
international credit union movement, **12**, 656
investments, **12**, 666
lending powers, **13**, 1777
limited liability, **12**, 601, 662, 663
liquidation, **12**, 677
loans—
members, to—
interest earned on, **12**, 659, 661, 669
rebates on, **12**, 670
rules as to, **12**, 669
other credit union, to, **12**, 666
meaning, **12**, 601, 656, 661
meeting, registrar's power to call, **12**, 675
membership, **12**, 664
maximum, **12**, 664
minimum, **12**, 664

Credit union—*continued*
membership—*continued*
    qualification for, **12**, 664
    security of members, **12**, 656
name, rules as to, **12**, 663
nature of, **2**, 1263
offences, **12**, 678
    defence to, **12**, 678
officers, **12**, 668
    insurance against loss attributable to, **12**, 668
operation, **12**, 665–671
profits—
    accumulation, **12**, 670
    application of, **12**, 670
    calculation, **12**, 670
    distribution, **12**, 670
    payments from, postponement, **12**, 670
    social, cultural or charitable purposes, use for, **12**, 670
protective insurance, **12**, 663
registrar—
    cancellation of registration by, **12**, 677
    information, power to require, **12**, 674
    inspectors, power to appoint, **12**, 675
    meeting called by, **12**, 675
    operations, suspension by, **12**, 676
    suspension of credit union by, **12**, 677
    winding up, powers as to, **12**, 677
registration, **12**, 656, 662
    before 1979 Act, **12**, 658
    qualification for, **12**, 662
registration area, **12**, 605
rules, **12**, 663
scope of title, **12**, 660
shares, **12**, 665
    transferrable, when, **12**, 665
    withdrawals, **12**, 665
statutory control, **2**, 1263
statutory objects, **12**, 661
structure, **12**, 656
surplus funds, **12**, 666, 666*n*
    investment, **2**, 1263
suspension, **12**, 677
tax concessions, **12**, 659
taxation, **12**, 659
transfer of engagements, **12**, 672
unregistered, **12**, 656
winding up, **12**, 677
See also INDUSTRIAL AND PROVIDENT SOCIETY

Creditor
agency, particulars of, duty to disclose, **5**, 955
amendment of pleadings not to prejudice, **17**, 1094
cautionary obligation, *see* CAUTIONARY OBLIGATION
claims by—
    acceptance—
        effect of, **2**, 1401, 1406
        test for, **2**, 1405
    adjudication of—
        appeal in respect of, **2**, 1406
        interim trustee, by, **2**, 1347
        submission for, **2**, 1401
    arbitration, reference to, **2**, 1403
    contingency, subject to, **2**, 1409

Creditor—*continued*
claims by—*continued*
    conversion into sterling, **2**, 1405
    creditor outside UK, **2**, 1402
    discount, deduction of, **2**, 1408
    evidence supporting, **2**, 1403
    falsification, **2**, 1349, 1404
    foreign currency, in, **2**, 1402
    form of, **2**, 1402
    increase or decrease of, **2**, 1402
    invitation to submit, **2**, 1346
    partners, against, **2**, 1412
    rejection—
        effect of, **2**, 1406
        notification of, **2**, 1405
        reasons to be given, **2**, 1405
    submission of—
        effect of, **2**, 1401
        necessity for, **2**, 1401
        purposes of, **2**, 1401
company, *see* COMPANY
concursus debiti et crediti, **15**, 879
confusion, **15**, 876
credit-token, duty on issue of, **5**, 886
Crown, ranking of, **7**, 747
Customs and Excise as, **8**, 128
death, effect of, **8**, 127
debt due—
    amount of, **2**, 1330
    evidence of, **2**, 1331
debtor's debtor, cannot sue, **15**, 7
default, remedies for, restrictions on—
    entry in order to repossess goods, **5**, 892
    heritable property, recovery of possession of, **5**, 893
    interest on default, **5**, 894
    protected goods, recovery of, **5**, 891
diligence of taken over by Crown, **8**, 129
dividends, unclaimed, **2**, 1479
executor dative as, **25**, 1056
executor nominate as, **25**, 1056
executor-creditor, *see* EXECUTOR
foreign currency, **4**, 827
gold clause, **14**, 1823
heritable, compensation, entitlement to, **5**, 114
heritable security, succession, **20**, 145
impartiality between, **14**, 1504
indexation, protection by, **14**, 1824
Inland Revenue as, **8**, 128
instructions, acknowledgment of receipt of, **14**, 1504
interest due to, *see* INTEREST
interest payable to, *see* INTEREST
judical interruption of prescription by, **16**, 2124
legal tender, payment in, **14**, 1823
liability of, breaches by supplier, for, **5**, 872
mails and duties, rights in action of, **8**, 398
meetings—
    adjournment, **2**, 1351
    chairman, **2**, 1350
    commissioner may call, **2**, 1317, 1350
    minutes of, **2**, 1351
    obligation to convene, **2**, 1350
    permanent trustee may call, **2**, 1350

Creditor—*continued*
meetings—*continued*
  procedure, **2**, 1351
  removal of trustee, for, **2**, 1371
messenger-at-arms, liability of, **14**, 1507
oath by—
  administration, **2**, 1331
  form, **2**, 1331
obligee, as, **11**, 1029
offences by, **2**, 1404
payment in foreign currency, **2**, 1349
petitioning, expenses of, **2**, 1420
poinding of the ground, *see* POINDING OF THE
  GROUND
qualified, meaning, **2**, 1330
ranking of, **25**, 1055
rating authority as, **8**, 128
secured—
  personal rights, and, **18**, 693
  power of sale, **18**, 667
sequestration, involvement in, **2**, 1326
sequestration petition by—
  cases for, **2**, 1327
  limitation of time, **2**, 1332
  oath, form of, **2**, 1331
  qualification to present, **2**, 1330
  statement of debt, **2**, 1331
  time for presenting, **2**, 1332
sheriff officer, liability of, **14**, 1511
special, **8**, 128
statement of claim, **2**, 1349
statutory meeting—
  adjournment of, **2**, 1346, 1351
  business at, **2**, 1348
  chairman, **2**, 1347
  claim to vote—
    evidence to accompany, **2**, 1349
    necessity to submit, **2**, 1349
    offence as to, **2**, 1349
    overseas creditors, **2**, 1349
  conclusion, statement on, **2**, 1348
  dividend, information as to, **2**, 1348
  duties of interim trustee, **2**, 1346
  election of permanent trustee, **2**, 1348
  interim trustee's duties, **2**, 1344
  minutes of, **2**, 1351
  notification to creditors, **2**, 1346
  permanent trustee's election, *see* BANKRUPTCY
  procedure, **2**, 1351
  proxy voting, **2**, 1351
  quorum at, **2**, 1351
  record of proceedings, **2**, 1347
  report of, to sheriff, **2**, 1348
  time for calling, **2**, 1346
summary diligence, when open to use by, **8**, 121
termination by, non-default cases, **5**, 895
transactions in fraud of, **11**, 779
trust deeds for behoof of, **8**, 177
trustee's final statement for, **2**, 1344
trustees for, as lessor, **13**, 175
trusts for, **24**, 16, 20
under heritable security as proprietor, **24**, 444
unsecured, **18**, 667
  personal rights, and, **18**, 694

Creditor—*continued*
valuation of claims—
  alimentary debts, **2**, 1414
  contingent debts, **2**, 1409
  co-obligants, **2**, 1413
  debts under a composition, **2**, 1410
  deductions, **2**, 1408
  general principles, **2**, 1408
  interest, deduction of, **2**, 1415
  partnership debt, **2**, 1412
  purposes of, **2**, 1407
  secured debts, **2**, 1411
variation by, **5**, 882
voluntary arrangements with—
  generally, **2**, 1456
  non-protected trust deed—
    accession of creditors—
      effect of, **2**, 1458
      procedure, **2**, 1460
    common form of, **2**, 1458
    discharge of debtor, **2**, 1462
    form and contents, **2**, 1459
    generally, **2**, 1458
    nature of, **2**, 1458
    non-acceding creditors, **2**, 1460
    trustee's powers and duties, **2**, 1461
  protected trust deeds—
    administration of estate, **2**, 1466
    benefits of, **2**, 1465
    constitution, requirements for, **2**, 1464
    introduction of, **2**, 1463
  voluntary trust deeds—
    generally, **2**, 1456
    proposals for reform, **2**, 1457
See also OBLIGEE
Creek
sheriff, jurisdiction of, **4**, 2
Cremation
anatomical examination, following, **3**, 559
application for—
  death furth of Scotland, **3**, 562
  human remains, **3**, 546, 555
ashes, disposal, **3**, 546, 568, 569
  crematorium, by, **3**, 568
  interment, **3**, 546
  removal from crematorium, **3**, 568
  scattering, **3**, 568
  sea, at, **3**, 539
ashes, disposal within church, **3**, 1605
authorisation—
  medical referee—
    certificate, **3**, 560
    examination of body by, **3**, 561
    given by, **3**, 560
    refusal to authorise cremation, **3**, 561
burial, **3**, 568
burial authority—
  charges and fees, **3**, 545
  powers and duties, **3**, 542
cardiac pacemaker or other implant, **3**, 567
certificate, **3**, 546
  false, **3**, 548
Christian acceptance, **3**, 501
Code of Cremation Practice, **3**, 569

Cremation—*continued*
coffin, **3**, 569
crematorium, *see* CREMATORIUM
death, certification and registration, **3**, 514
  production of death certificate, **3**, 556
death furth of Scotland, **3**, 562
directions of deceased, **3**, 506
disinterment, following, **3**, 564
false representation in relation to, **3**, 548
fees and charges, **3**, 545
funeral directors, instructions issued to, **3**, 569
historical background, **3**, 501
infectious disease, following death by, **3**, 565
local Acts, **3**, 549
local authority, disposal of body by, **3**, 512
local burial authority, *see* BURIAL AUTHORITY
medical certificate, **3**, 557, 558
  cardiac pacemaker or other implant, **3**, 567
  confirmatory—
    generally, **3**, 558
    where unnecessary, **3**, 559
    who may give, **3**, 558
medical referee—
  authority to cremate given by, **3**, 560
  cremation where death by infectious disease, **3**, 565
  generally, **3**, 552
  refusal to authorise cremation, **3**, 561
notice of, **3**, 546
offences in relation to, **3**, 548
percentage of disposal by, in Great Britain, **3**, 501
personal Acts, **3**, 549
post-mortem examination, following, **3**, 559
procurator fiscal, permission given by, **3**, 559
public health considerations, **19**, 463
refusal where death sudden, accidental or suspicious, **3**, 513
register of cremations, **3**, 546, 547, 553
regulations, power to make, **3**, 546
religious objection to, **3**, 501
religious persuasion of deceased, **3**, 512
requirements preliminary to, **3**, 555–567
sheriff court jurisdiction, **6**, 1085
statutory regulation, **3**, 502, 541
stillborn child, of, **3**, 566
VAT exemption, **7**, 1427
See also BURIAL
Cremation authority
meaning, **3**, 550*n*
Crematorium
closure, cremation authority, by, **3**, 550
condition to be kept in, **3**, 550
construction or extension, **19**, 15
disused, **19**, 336*n*
documents, preservation, **3**, 554
functions in respect of, **14**, 699
inquiry into management etc, **3**, 546
inspection, **3**, 546, 551
maintenance, **3**, 546, 569
meaning, **3**, 543
medical referee, *see* CREMATION
new—
  approval of site, **3**, 544
  restrictions on, **3**, 544

Crematorium—*continued*
rates, valuation, **3**, 543
register of cremations, **3**, 546, 547, 553
staff, conduct, **3**, 569
taxation, **3**, 543
valuation for rating, **24**, 591
Crest
badges, **11**, 1631
clergymen, **11**, 1606
generally, **11**, 1606
incorrect use of term, **11**, 1606*n*
ladies, **11**, 1606
Crew agreement
See SEAMAN
Cricket club
third party liability, **2**, 814
Crime
actus non facit reum nisi mens sit rea, **7**, 28
actus reus, *see* ACTUS REUS
aggravations, **7**, 36
attempted, *see* ATTEMPT
bailable, **17**, 626
causation, *see* CAUSATION
circumstances of, **7**, 35
conduct-crime, **7**, 32
  attempted, **7**, 162
contract, duty derived from, **7**, 42
criminal offence, use of term, **7**, 23
danger, creation of, duty derived from, **7**, 43
defences, *see* DEFENCES
direct and indirect causes, **7**, 48
duty to intervene, failure, **7**, 182
elements—
  actus reus, *see* ACTUS REUS
  animus pirandi, **7**, 63
  blameworthiness, **7**, 64
  corporate liability, *see* CORPORATE LIABILITY
  criminal responsibility, **7**, 64
  dole, *see* DOLE
  generally, **7**, 28
  guilt, types of, **7**, 67
  intent—
    types of, **7**, 68
    use of term, **7**, 78
  malice, **7**, 69
  malus animus, **7**, 69
  mens rea, *see* MENS REA
  mental element *see* MENS REA; MENTAL ELEMENT
  omissions—
    actus reus, and—
      generally, **7**, 38
      omission as *actus reus*, **7**, 45
      omission effecting *actus reus*, **7**, 39–44
    contract, duty derived from, **7**, 42
    danger, duty derived from creation, **7**, 43
    failure to prevent *actus reus* by others, **7**, 39
    failure to protect others from injury or death, **7**, 40
    failure to refrain from acting, **7**, 44
    generally, **7**, 38, 48
    licensing offences, **7**, 45
    meaning, **7**, 38
    official status of omitter, **7**, 39
    relationship, duty implied by, **7**, 41

Crime—*continued*
elements—*continued*
 omissions—*continued*
  result-crimes, **7**, 32, 38
  road traffic accidents, **7**, 45
  terrorist acts, **7**, 45
  victim, by, **7**, 52
 strict liability, *see* STRICT LIABILITY
 supervening act or omission by victim, **7**, 52
 terminology, **7**, 62–84
 wilfulness, **7**, 70
elements, causation, *see* CAUSATION
entrapment, *see* ENTRAPMENT
failure to protect from injury or death, **7**, 40
failure to refrain from acting to another's detriment, **7**, 44
false accusation of—
 accused, to, **7**, 525
 authorities, to, **7**, 525
 circulating allegations, **7**, 525
 danger of prosecution, putting victim in, **7**, 527
 generally, **7**, 524
 historical background, **7**, 524–526
 interference with course of justice, **7**, 524–528
 mental element, **7**, 528
 verbal information, not restricted to, **7**, 524
 verbal injury, **7**, 525
inchoate—
 attempt, *see* ATTEMPT
 conspiracy, *see* CONSPIRACY
 generally, **7**, 160
 incitement, *see* INCITEMENT
 instigation, **7**, 160
 meaning, **7**, 160
 mens rea, **7**, 162, 168
 preliminary act criminal, where, **7**, 167
 stages, **7**, 160
innominate, **7**, 24
instigation, *see* INSTIGATION
interpretation by prosecutor, **7**, 26
investigation of—
 generally, **23**, 949
 police powers, generally, **16**, 1787
involuntary conduct, **7**, 34
mala prohibita, **7**, 25
mala in se, **7**, 25
meaning, **17**, 501
mens rea, *see* MENS REA
mental element, *see* MENS REA; MENTAL ELEMENT
motive, relevancy, **7**, 92
nature of, **7**, 3
nomen juris, identification by, **7**, 74
nominate, **7**, 24
offence, use of term, **7**, 23
offence distinguished, **12**, 1140
omission, *see* elements *above*
overt act—
 attempted crime, **7**, 162, 163
 dependence on, **7**, 29
 voluntary conduct, **7**, 34
parties to—
 ancillary or supporting role, **7**, 177
 art and part liability, *see* LIABILITY (art and part)

Crime—*continued*
parties to—*continued*
 generally, **7**, 177
 liability by participation, *see* LIABILITY (participation, by)
 one person acting alone, **7**, 177
 preparatory role, **7**, 177
 two or more persons acting together, **7**, 177
 vicarious liability, *see* LIABILITY (vicarious)
prescription of, **17**, 569
presence during, **7**, 39
 art and part liability, **7**, 180–182
private, **7**, 26
private prosecution, **7**, 26
prosecution policy, **7**, 26
public, **7**, 26
public prosecutors, **7**, 26
relationship, duty implied by, **7**, 41
result-crime, **7**, 32, 38, 46
 attempted, **7**, 162
thought, criminal or anti-social, **7**, 29
time gap between crime and its result, **7**, 47
voluntary conduct, **7**, 34
Crimen dolo contrahitur
principle of, **7**, 61
Criminal Appeal, Court of
appeals to, **6**, 874
disposal of appeal, **6**, 874
High Court of Justiciary sitting as, **6**, 874
miscarriage of justice as ground of appeal, **6**, 874
point of law, opinion on, **6**, 874
quashing or substitution of sentence, **6**, 874
supplemental powers, **6**, 874
Criminal attempt
See ATTEMPT
Criminal courts
Ayres, **17**, 507
Bailiary court, **17**, 504, 523, 525
Barony Court, *see* BARONY COURT
Burgh court, *see* BURGH COURT
circuits, **17**, 507
district court, *see* DISTRICT COURT
franchise court, *see* FRANCHISE COURT
generally, **17**, 504
jurisdiction, **17**, 508
justice of the peace court, *see* JUSTICE OF THE PEACE COURT
origin, **17**, 505
personnel, **17**, 506
police court, *see* POLICE COURT
regality court, *see* REGALITY, COURTS OF
See also HIGH COURT OF JUSTICIARY; SHERIFF COURT
Criminal Injuries Compensation Board
establishment under prerogative power, **7**, 729
judicial review, **7**, 729
Tariff Scheme, **7**, 729
Criminal Injuries Compensation Scheme
1990 Scheme—
 generally, **7**, 1
accidents, **7**, 7
administration, **7**, 1
alcohol and drug related incidents, **7**, 1, 8
animals, attacks by, **7**, 8

Criminal Injuries Compensation Scheme—
continued
applications for compensation, **7**, 6
  deciding, *see* deciding claim *below*
  standard of proof, **7**, 2
arson, **7**, 1
assessment of compensation—
  accommodation costs, **7**, 5
  child conceived as result of rape etc, **7**, 7, 11
  fatal cases, **7**, 1–6
  future wage loss, **7**, 3
  generally, **7**, 1
  medical care, **7**, 6
  multiple injuries, **7**, 10
  necessary services, provision, **7**, 4
  nursing care, **7**, 5
  patrimonal loss, **7**, 1
  property, damage to, **7**, 8
  rape, cases of, **7**, 7, 11
  sexual offences, cases of, **7**, 7, 11
  solatium, **7**, 1, 2
  Tariff Scheme, **7**, 1, 9–12
attempted crimes, **7**, 5
background, **7**, 2, 3
child—
  applications on behalf of, **7**, 1, 2
  dangerous game, injury sustained during, **7**, 10
  family, violence within, **7**, 1, 4, 5
child abuse, **7**, 2, 3, 4
'close relationship of love and affection', **7**, 6, 8
compensation order, where, **7**, 6
contributory negligence, **7**, 1
crime of violence, **7**, 1, 2, 3
Criminal Injuries Compensation Authority, **7**, 1, 3, 5
Criminal Injuries Compensation Board—
  abolition, **7**, 3, 5
  constitution, **7**, 5
  delegation of decisions, **7**, 1, 5
  establishment, **7**, 5
  jurisdiction, **7**, 6
  powers and duties, **7**, 1, 3, 4
damages awarded, where, **7**, 6
deciding claim—
  challenging award, **7**, 4
  generally, **7**, 1
  judicial review, **7**, 4, 7
  procedure, **7**, 3
  standard of proof, **7**, 2
  Tariff Scheme, **7**, 5, 6
deductions from award, **7**, 1–6
directly attributable—
  definition, **7**, 2
  foreseeability, **7**, 3
  injuries not immediately attributable, **7**, 3
  injury must be, **7**, 1
  mental injuries, **7**, 6, 9
  pre-existing medical condition, where, **7**, 4
  property, crimes against, **7**, 5
  railway employees, **7**, 3, 10
  reasonable fear of immediate physical harm, **7**, 6, 7
  secondary victims, **7**, 8
  sexual offences, **7**, 7, 9

Criminal Injuries Compensation Scheme—
continued
disability, persons under, applications on behalf of, **7**, 1, 3
double compensation, avoidance, **7**, 1
eligibility—
  assistance in connection with application, giving, **7**, 5
  co-operation in bringing offender to justice, **7**, 1–4
  conduct of applicant, **7**, 1, 6–10
  criminal convictions, applicants with, **7**, 1, 11
  'deserving' victims, **7**, 1
  fatal cases, *see* fatal injuries *below*
  foreign nationals, **7**, 6
  generally, **7**, 1
  natural persons, **7**, 1
  person responsible must not benefit, **7**, 12
  territorial basis, **7**, 6
ex gratia basis, **7**, 3, 4
exceptional risk rule, **7**, 12, 13
excluded offences, **7**, 2, 3
family, violence within, **7**, 1–5
  child, application on behalf of, **7**, 1, 4, 5
  fraudulent or collusive applications, **7**, 1
  generally, **7**, 1
  person responsible must not benefit, **7**, 1, 12
fatal injuries—
  character and conduct of applicant, **7**, 2
  death after time lapse, **7**, 3
  extraneous causes, victim dying from, **7**, 4
  funeral expenses, **7**, 1, 6
  generally, **7**, 1
  pension accruing as result, where, **7**, 4
  relatives, qualifying, **7**, 1
  relatives of victim, application by, **7**, 1
  Tariff Scheme, **7**, 1, 5
fighting, **7**, 1, 7
fraud, safeguards against, **7**, 2
funding, **7**, 3
generally, **7**, 1, 2
harassment, **7**, 5
immoral conduct by victim, **7**, 8
insurance payment, where, **7**, 3
interim awards, **7**, 1
judicial review, **7**, 4, 7
justification for, **7**, 2
law enforcement activities, injury attributable to, **7**, 1, 11
  exceptional risk rule, **7**, 12, 13
legal basis, **7**, 4
mental injury, **7**, 1, 2, 6
minimum level of award, injuries assessed at, **7**, 1
motor vehicle, injuries sustained by—
  driver untraced, where, **7**, 9
  weapon, vehicle used as, **7**, 9
nervous shock, **7**, 2
other authorities, payments from, **7**, 5
payment of awards, **7**, 1, 2
pension accruing as result of injury, where, **7**, 4
personal injury, **7**, 1
poisoning, **7**, 1
pre-existing medical condition, where, **7**, 4
property, offences against, **7**, 2, 5, 8

Criminal Injuries Compensation Scheme—
continued
provocative behaviour, **7**, 1, 7
qualifying incidents, **7**, 1–14
qualifying injuries, **7**, 1, 2
railway, trespass on, injury sustained through, **7**, 1, 3, 14
   railway employees, **7**, 3, 10, 14
rape, **7**, 7
   child conceived as result of, **7**, 1, 7, 11
re-opening case, powers as to, **7**, 2, 3
regulatory offences, **7**, 6
reviews and amendments, **7**, 3
sexual offences, **7**, 2, 4, 9, 11
social security benefits, and, **7**, 2
statutory scheme, proposed, **7**, 3
Tariff Scheme—
   administration, **7**, 1
   appeal under, **7**, 6
   assessment of compensation, **7**, 1, 9–12
   deciding claim, **7**, 1
   exceptional risk rule, **7**, 12
   fatal award, **7**, 1, 5
   funeral expenses, **7**, 1
   generally, **7**, 1
   introduction, **7**, 3
   review under, **7**, 5
   time limits for application, **7**, 1
   ultra vires, as, **7**, 1, 3, 5
territorial basis, **7**, 6
threats to commit crime, **7**, 5
time limits for application—
   civil claim pursued, where, **7**, 4
   function, **7**, 1
   generally, **7**, 1
   ignorance of Scheme, where, **7**, 4
   impaired ability, applicants of, **7**, 1, 2
   injuries not immediately attributable to incident, **7**, 1, 3
   Tariff Scheme, **7**, 1
   waiver, **7**, 1
undeserving applicants, rejection, **7**, 3
unlawful conduct by victim, **7**, 9
victim—
   condition worsening after award, where, **7**, 2, 3
   conduct of, **7**, 1, 6–10
   eligibility, *see* eligibility *above*
   fatal injuries, *see* fatal injuries *above*
   pre-existing medical condition, with, **7**, 4
   secondary, **7**, 8
Criminal intent
use of term, **7**, 68, 70
Criminal law
actus non facit reum nisi mens sit rea, **7**, 28
actus reus, *see* ACTUS REUS
authoritative writings—
   influence, **22**, 440
   works included in canon of, **22**, 441
capacity, *see* CAPACITY
coercive system, as, **7**, 161
common law, **7**, 1, 15, 37
   mala in se, **7**, 25
   terms denoting *mens rea*, **7**, 76–84
conspiracy, **22**, 122

Criminal law—*continued*
consumer protection, as means of, **6**, 6
contempt of court, **6**, 302
contractual duties, and, **9**, 121–125
courts, *see* CRIMINAL COURTS
criminal code, lack of, **7**, 1, 3
de minimis non curat lex, principle of, **7**, 27
Declaratory Power—
   Alison's *Principles*, **7**, 6, 8, 11
   Cockburn's principles, **7**, 9–11, 13
   early nineteenth century cases, **7**, 7
   generally, **7**, 5, 6, 15
   Greenhuff, **7**, 8, 13
   Hume's *Commentaries*, **7**, 6–9, 11, 12
   Macdonald's *Criminal Law*, **7**, 6, 13
   maximum certainty, principle of, **7**, 11
   post-*Greenhuff*, **7**, 11
   real injury, general principle of, **7**, 13
   refusal to declare, **7**, 14
   twentieth century cases, **7**, 12–14
   'wide general principle', **7**, 11, 13
designation of action as criminal, **22**, 424, 425
diligence used in, **8**, 132
English decisions, **22**, 302, 304, 318
English and Scots compared, **7**, 1
equity, development of, **22**, 420–425
Hume's writings on, **22**, 423, 424
industrial action, application of rules, **9**, 131
Kames, natural law as criterion of criminality, **22**, 422
legality, principle of, **7**, 4*n*
Lord Advocate, reference to High Court on point of law, **22**, 319
Mackenzie, crime and natural or positive law distingushed, **22**, 421
male in se and *male prohibita* distinguished, **22**, 420
malicious mischief, **9**, 123
maximum certainty, principle of—
   Declaratory Power, **7**, 11
   generally, **7**, 4, 5
mens rea, *see* MENS REA
moral and judicial criminal behaviour, **22**, 420
non-retroactivity—
   Declaratory Power, **7**, 5–15
   generally, **7**, 4, 5
nullum crimen sine lege principle, **7**, 3, 4
particular employments, **9**, 125
precedent, operation of, **22**, 302–320
   See also JUDICIAL PRECEDENT
prescription, **16**, 2131
property, protection of, **9**, 122
prospectivity, **7**, 4
real injury, general prinicple of, **7**, 13
retroactivity, protection against, **12**, 6, 61
Scots law founded on principles, **11**, 1011
seventeenth-century administration, **22**, 520
statute law, **7**, 1, 16
   mala prohibita, **7**, 25
   strict construction—
      ambiguity, **7**, 21
      analogy, interpretation by, **7**, 20
      common sense, **7**, 18, 22
      consideration of policy, interpretation by, **7**, 20

Criminal law—*continued*
statute law—*continued*
  strict construction—*continued*
    generally, **7**, 4, 16, 18
    Scottish construction, **7**, 17
    ultra-strict interpretation, **7**, 19
  text writings, **7**, 2
  mens rea, **7**, 58–61, 74
Thomson Committee on Criminal Appeals in Scotland, **22**, 319
workplace occupations, **9**, 124
Criminal letters
bill for, **6**, 865
private prosecution upon issue of, **6**, 872
Criminal offence
See OFFENCE
Criminal procedure
accusatorial system, as, **17**, 564
accused, *see* ACCUSED
Act of Adjournal, *see* ACT OF ADJOURNAL
advocation, bill of, *see* ADVOCATION
appeal—
  compensation, **17**, 886
  conviction and sentence, against, *see* SENTENCE
  European Court of Justice, **17**, 832, 884
  generally, **17**, 813
  High Court of Justiciary—
    generally, **17**, 576, 588, 814
    quorum of judges, **6**, 865; **17**, 815
  legal aid, **17**, 816
  nobile officium, petition to, **6**, 865, 870; **17**, 883
  pardons, **17**, 885
  sentence, against, *see* SENTENCE
  solemn procedure, arising from, *see* SOLEMN PROCEDURE
  summary procedure, arising from, *see* SUMMARY PROCEDURE
arrest—
  unlawful, consequences of, **17**, 599
  warrant, under, **17**, 600–602
  without warrant, **17**, 596–598
bail, *see* BAIL
civil claims, **4**, 38
corroboration, **17**, 566
criminal courts—
  barony courts, **17**, 504
  burgh courts, **17**, 504
  district court, *see* DISTRICT COURT
  High Court of Justiciary, *see* HIGH COURT OF JUSTICIARY
  regality courts, **17**, 504
  sheriff court, *see* SHERIFF COURT
custody, person in, *see* CUSTODY
defence—
  plea bargaining, **17**, 729–733
    See also PLEA BARGAINING
  preparation of—
    Crown productions, examination of, **17**, 657
    documents, recovery of, **17**, 658, 701
    generally, **17**, 654, 700
    identification parade, **17**, 655
    intermediate diets, **17**, 703
    post mortems, **17**, 656
    preliminary pleas, **17**, 704

Criminal procedure—*continued*
defence—*continued*
  preparation of—*continued*
    witness—
      examination of, **17**, 657
      precognoscing, **17**, 659
      summary procedure, **17**, 702
      See also WITNESS
  requirements of—
    generally, **17**, 671
    productions, **17**, 672–674
    rights of defence, **17**, 715
    special defences, **17**, 716
    witness—
      Crown objections to, **17**, 675
      lists of, **17**, 672
  special, *see* special defence *below*
detention—
  generally, **17**, 593
  nature of, **17**, 595
  right to detain, **17**, 594
early procedure in Scotland, **17**, 502, 541
evidence—
  competency and relevancy of, **17**, 567
  oral testimony, **17**, 568
  See also EVIDENCE
fingerprinting, **17**, 603, 605
general principles of—
  accusatorial system, as, **17**, 564
  corroboration, **17**, 566
  evidence—
    competency and relevancy, **17**, 567
    oral testimony, **17**, 568
  prescription of crime, **17**, 569
  proof, burden and standard of, **17**, 565
High Court of Justiciary, *see* HIGH COURT OF JUSTICIARY
historical background—
  accused—
    apprehension of, **17**, 543
    bail, **17**, 551
    legal representation, **17**, 550
    rights of, generally, **17**, 549
    royal pardon, **17**, 554
    special defences, **17**, 553
    undue delay, prevention of, **17**, 552
  bail, *see* BAIL
  judicial examination, **17**, 546
  jury trial, development of, **17**, 542
  legal representation, **17**, 550
  police force, setting up of, **17**, 543
  police investigation, **17**, 547
  pre-trial investigations, **17**, 544
  precognitions, **17**, 545
  royal pardon, **17**, 554
  sentence, **17**, 561–563
    See also SENTENCE
  seventeenth century onwards, **17**, 503
  solemn procedure, **17**, 555–559
    See also SOLEMN PROCEDURE
  special defences, **17**, 553
  summary procedure, **17**, 560
    See also SUMMARY PROCEDURE

Criminal procedure—*continued*
historical background—*continued*
taking up dittay, **17**, 548
trial, delay in bringing, **17**, 552
identification parades, **17**, 603, 606
institution of proceedings—
court, by, **17**, 586
High Court of Justiciary, by, **6**, 872
private individual, by, **17**, 585
public bodies, by, **17**, 587
public officials, by, **17**, 587
investigation—
police, by, **17**, 547
pre-trial, **17**, 544
jurisdiction of criminal courts—
appellate, **17**, 588
extra-territorial, **17**, 590
multiple, **17**, 591
original, **17**, 588
subject matter, **17**, 592
territorial, **17**, 589
jury, *see* JURY
meaning, **17**, 501
mentally disordered person, and, *see* MENTALLY
DISORDERED PERSON
penalties, *see* PENALTIES; SENTENCE
plea bargaining, *see* PLEA BARGAINING
prescription of crime, **17**, 569
procurator fiscal, *see* PROCURATOR FISCAL
proof, burden and standard of, **17**, 565
prosecution, *see* title to prosecute *below*
public prosecutor, *see* PUBLIC PROSECUTOR
regulation of, **6**, 882
See also ACT OF ADJOURNAL
search—
generally, **17**, 603
person, of, **17**, 604
premises, of, **17**, 607
sentence, *see* PENALTIES; SENTENCE
sheriff court, *see* SHERIFF COURT
solemn procedure, *see* SOLEMN PROCEDURE
special defence—
fair notice, requirement of, **17**, 678
insanity—
generally, **17**, 895
time of offence at, **17**, 902
lodging of, **17**, 676
meaning, **17**, 677
pre-trial procedure, **17**, 553
summary proceedings, **17**, 716
withdrawal of, **17**, 679
summary procedure, *see* SUMMARY PROCEDURE
suspension, bill of, *see* SUSPENSION, BILL OF
taking up dittay, **17**, 548
title to prosecute—
Crown Agent, **17**, 539–540
See also CROWN AGENT
Crown Office, **17**, 539–540
See also CROWN OFFICE
Lord Advocate, *see* LORD ADVOCATE
procurator fiscal, *see* PROCURATOR FISCAL
public prosecutor, *see* PUBLIC PROSECUTOR
Solicitor-General for Scotland, *see* SOLICITOR-
GENERAL FOR SCOTLAND

Criminal procedure—*continued*
trial, *see* TRIAL
Criminal record
refusal of leave to enter country due to, **12**, 171
Criminal registers
access to, **19**, 879
Criminal responsibility
age of, **3**, 1277; **7**, 159, 159n; **11**, 1202n
use of term, **7**, 64
Criminal statistics
reporting—
chief constable, by, **16**, 1729, 1738
Secretary of State's powers as to, **16**, 1729
Criminality, imputations of
defamation, **15**, 491
Crimping
restrictions on, **21**, 249
Crisis loan
social fund, **21**, 1123, 1125
Croft
agricultural holding, constituting, **1**, 727
assignation of, **1**, 805
bequest of, **1**, 807
common grazings—
acquisition, order authorising, **1**, 828
apportionment of, **1**, 820, 822
fencing repairs, payment for, **1**, 804, 821
grazings committee, **1**, 821
regulated, **1**, 821
Scottish Land Court jurisdiction, **6**, 959, 963,
967
subtenant, rights of, **1**, 826
unregulated, **1**, 821
compensation—
additional items, for, **1**, 811
compulsory acquisition, on, **1**, 832
conveyance, where order made, **1**, 830
deterioration and damage, for, **1**, 814
improvements, for, **1**, 811, 813
compulsory acquisition of, **1**, 832; **6**, 967, 1141
constitution of, original, **1**, 799
conveyance of land—
compensation, effect on, **1**, 830
consideration for, **1**, 828
duration of order, **1**, 830
Land Court—
authorising, **1**, 828
powers of, **1**, 830
landlord under disability, where, **1**, 830
National Trust for Scotland, by, **1**, 830
shooting and fishing rights, landlord leasing, **1**,
828
cottars, occupation by, **6**, 967
counties—
caravan sites, licensing of, **1**, 835
generally, **6**, 953
ground game, **11**, 858
meaning, **1**, 797
smallholding in, **1**, 836
Crofter, *see* CROFTER
Crofters Commission, *see* CROFTERS COMMISSION
decrofting, **6**, 967
development value, crofter's right to share in, **6**
967

Croft—*continued*
early records, **6**, 957, 967
entry and inspection, rights of, **1**, 823
house, rating and valuation of, **1**, 834; **24**, 594
    acquisition of, **1**, 798, 817, 829, 830, 831; **6**,
    967
land—
    conveyance of, *see* conveyance of land *above*
    disposal within five years of acquisition, **1**, 828
    right to acquire, **1**, 827, 828
lease, interest in—
    decisions in respect of, **25**, 720
    landlord, repossession by, **25**, 718
    succession to, **25**, 716
    termination of, **25**, 717
    vesting of, **25**, 715
legislation relating to, **6**, 955
long lease, standard securities, **20**, 179
meaning, **1**, 799
new, provisions for establishing, **1**, 799
notice of entry compensation, **6**, 1141
parishes, **6**, 953
permanent improvement to—
    compensation for, **1**, 811, 813
    meaning, **1**, 812
    value of, **1**, 813
planning blight, protection from, **1**, 833
questions of fact and law, **6**, 967
record of holding, **1**, 803
register of, **1**, 800
registration, **1**, 800; **6**, 967
rent—
    alteration, **1**, 802
    fair, Land Court fixing, **1**, 802
    yearly, **1**, 802
renunciation of, **1**, 804
resettlement schemes, **6**, 957
resumption by landlord, **1**, 809; **6**, 967
    authorisation, **6**, 959, 963
    compensation, **6**, 959, 967
    de-crofting compared, **6**, 967
sheriff court jurisdiction, **6**, 1076
site of dwelling house, acquisition of—
    cessation of crofting tenure, **1**, 817
    heritable security, loan secured by, **1**, 831
    part remaining subject to tenancy, fair rent for,
    1, 830
    peats, right to cut and take, enjoyment of, **1**, 830
squatters, occupation by, **6**, 967
subdivision of, **1**, 806
subletting, **1**, 826
succession to, **1**, 808
supervision of, **23**, 911
tenancy, transfer of, **1**, 808
tenure—
    cessation of, **1**, 817
    introduction of, **1**, 797
    land brought into, **1**, 799
    Land Court, jurisdiction of, **1**, 825
    original constitution of, **1**, 799
    principles of, **1**, 801
    removal of subjects from, **1**, 798
    statutory conditions, **1**, 801
    vacant, dealing with, **1**, 816

Crofter
absentee, **1**, 818
compensation on resumption, **1**, 809
conveyance, right to, **1**, 827, 828
croft, *see* CROFT
Crofters Commission, *see* CROFTERS COMMISSION
death of, procedure on, **1**, 807
executors, rights vested in, **1**, 811
financial assistance to, **1**, 819
land or dwelling house—
    acquisition of, **1**, 798, 817, 829, 830, 831; **6**,
    967
    right to conveyance of, **1**, 829
    valuation for rating, **1**, 834; **24**, 594
landholder, renamed as, **6**, 956
landlord's interest, acquisition of, **13**, 335
meaning, **1**, 798, 799
overriding interests of, **6**, 741
removal of, **1**, 810
replacement of term, **1**, 797
rights, agreement depriving of, **1**, 801
Secretary of State, transfer of right to
    compensation to, **1**, 810
See also LANDHOLDER
Crofters Commission
absentee crofter, terminating tenancy of, **1**, 818
administrative duties, **6**, 955, 967
annual report of, **1**, 815
appeal from, **1**, 815
assignation of croft, approving, **1**, 805
bequest, determining validity of, **1**, 807
cessation of croft, directing, **1**, 817
change of ownership, notifying of, **1**, 830
constitution, **13**, 1414
    functions, and, **6**, 955
crofting counties and parishes, **6**, 953
decrofting applications, **6**, 967
establishment, **6**, 955
fair rents, **6**, 955
function, **13**, 1414
information, furnishing to, **1**, 815
judicial review, **6**, 968
landholders, crofters renamed as, **6**, 956
members, **1**, 815
newly constituted (1955), **6**, 966
Ombudsman system, **19**, 242
powers and duties of, **1**, 815
procedure, **1**, 815
references of fact or law to, **6**, 967
registration of crofts, **1**, 800; **6**, 967
right of entry and inspection, **1**, 823
Scottish Land Court replaces, **6**, 956, 958
solicitor's duties, **13**, 1414
    Red Deer Commission, in relation to, **13**, 1415
subdivision of croft, approving, **1**, 806
subletting, consent to, **1**, 826
supervision of, **23**, 911
township reorganisation schemes, preparing, **1**, 820
vacant croft, dealing with, **1**, 816
Cromwellian period
unification proposals, **22**, 628
Crop
accession by fruits, **18**, 570, 595, 596
agricultural, meaning, **19**, 1056*n*

Crop—*continued*
break crops, **1**, 715
fire damage caused by railway engine, **19**, 1056
growing, bankruptcy of tenant, **13**, 422
industrial growing—
    goods, as, **20**, 805
    meaning, **20**, 805
    moveable property, as, **18**, 12
    ownership, **18**, 596
pesticides, *see* PESTICIDES
prevention of damage to, **11**, 859, 883, 886
See also AGRICULTURAL PRODUCTION; AGRICULTURE
Cropping and disposal
freedom of, **1**, 763, 776
Cross-border leasing
conflict of laws, **14**, 1095
double-dip lease, **14**, 1096
exchange control, **14**, 1096
huge market in, **14**, 1094
leveraged lease, **14**, 1096
non-recourse financing, **14**, 1096
satellites, **14**, 1095
'Shogun lease', **14**, 1094
space, **14**, 1095
taxation, **14**, 1096
triple-dip lease, **14**, 1096
Cross-examination
proof, conduct of, **17**, 1167
See also WITNESS (examination in court)
Crossbow
carrying or being drunk in possession in public
    place, **10**, 1567*n*
deer, killed with, **11**, 940
wild birds or animals taken or killed with, **11**,
    880, 884
Crown
Agent, *see* CROWN AGENT
air navigation orders applied, **2**, 978
allegiance to, duty of, **16**, 1213
alveus, ownership of—
    generally, **18**, 275
    tidal waters, **18**, 275, 276
appointments, **5**, 705
armed forces, relationship with, **2**, 604, 617
arrestee, as, **8**, 259, 260
arrestment, **7**, 747
bailies, appointment of, **14**, 11
bankruptcy, preferences, **7**, 747; **22**, 678
body, *see* CROWN BODY
bona vacantia—
    disclaimer, **4**, 931
    vesting of, **4**, 930
building owned by, **3**, 210
    building operations regulations, **3**, 230
case—
    close of, **17**, 780
    trial diet, **17**, 779, 780
central and local government, essential difference
    between, **14**, 94
charter, **14**, 10
Commissioner for Local Administration in
    Scotland, appointment of, **14**, 133
Commissioner of Police of Metropolis,
    appointment of, **14**, 62

Crown—*continued*
Commonwealth, and, *see* COMMONWEALTH
contract, resile, **7**, 746
contract enforced against, **3**, 26
contractor, *see* CONTRACTOR (Crown)
copyright—
    Acts of Parliament—
        term of copyright, **18**, 1035
    Crown prerogative, **18**, 1002
    generally, **18**, 979, 1000
    literary, dramatic, musical or artistic works, **18**,
        1034, 1037
    transitional provisions, **18**, 1037
    Measures of the General Synod of the Church
        of England—
        term of copyright, **18**, 1035
    moral rights, **18**, 1134, 1136
    reproduction of copyright material, permission
        for, **18**, 1028
corporate personality, **19**, 208
counsel, *see* CROWN COUNSEL
Counsellors of State, **7**, 705
Crown property, passport as, **16**, 1216, 1228
debt, poinding in respect of, **14**, 1812
debtor, as, exemption from diligence, **8**, 128
declaratory orders in relation to, **13**, 5
decree against, **7**, 747
    special provision in, **17**, 1032
delict—
    Crown liability, exclusions, **15**, 225
    defender, Crown as, **15**, 224
    representation in Scotland, **15**, 223
    title and interest to sue, **15**, 223
diligence, preferences, **7**, 747
diligence may not be executed against, **7**, 747
domicile of, **4**, 32
droits of, **17**, 407
duty upon, **7**, 763
employment, *see* CROWN EMPLOYMENT
enactments, application to, **12**, 1212
equitable, jurisdiction, **22**, 547
executive function, **7**, 702, 716–719
exempt agreements, **4**, 1167
exercise of powers by, **1**, 215
Extraordinary Lords, nomination of, **22**, 517
feudal law, position, **22**, 591, 592, 596
feudal system—
    dominium eminens, **18**, 38, 42, 47, 49
    generally, **18**, 38, 42
    ultimate superior, Crown as, **18**, 42
flood prevention scheme, rights relating to, **14**,
    469
harbour, rights of, granted by, **11**, 1301
immunity, **19**, 233–237
    patent rights, and, **18**, 887
interdict or interim interdict against, **1**, 328; **13**,
    23
judicial function, **7**, 702, 716–719
judicial role, original, **22**, 523
Kindly Tenants of Lochmaben, **13**, 212
land, *see* CROWN LAND
lands, feufarm, **18**, 68
law, subjugation to, **7**, 702, 702*n*
Law Officers of, **5**, 535, 536

Crown—*continued*
lawburrows, action of—
   contravention action, **13**, 901
   forfeiture of half caution to, **13**, 901
legal corporate personality as prerogative of, **4**, 303
legislative function, **7**, 702, 716–719
lessee, overriding interests of, **6**, 743
lessor, as, **13**, 181
liability, generally, **7**, 746
litigation involving, *see* LITIGATION
lost and abandoned property, ownership of, **18**, 540, 547
material communicated to in course of public business, copyright, **18**, 1122
minerals passing automatically to, **6**, 491
mines royal, **13**, 200
national sovereignty, as focus of, **7**, 701
nobile officium Crown's equitable jurisdiction, **22**, 547
nullius est fit domini regis, doctrine of, **18**, 540
Officers of, *see* OFFICERS OF THE CROWN
Officers of State, *see* OFFICERS OF STATE
official and private capacity, **19**, 203, 204, 207
Orkney, Scottish Crown's claim to, **24**, 302
overseas service, person in, **15**, 1131
ownership of land falling to, **18**, 9
pardons, **17**, 554
patented invention, Crown use of—
   compensation for, **18**, 888
   disputes relating to, **18**, 877
   emergency powers, **18**, 889
   rights of proprietor, **18**, 887
personal bar—
   pled against, **16**, 1610
   subject to, **1**, 296
personal property or interests, parliamentary Bill affecting, **7**, 744
petition to, for declaration of precedency, **16**, 2004
petroleum, rights in respect of, **9**, 724
plant breeders' rights, infringement, **18**, 914
plea bargaining, **17**, 731
pleas of, *see* PLEAS OF CROWN
positive prescription against, **16**, 2102, 2107
powers—
   exercise, **7**, 718, 719
   prerogative, *see* PREROGATIVE POWERS
   statutory executive, **7**, 719, 723
preferences, **8**, 128, 129
premises—
   emission of smoke from, **9**, 1137
   occupier's liability, **15**, 330
prerogative legislation, **22**, 171–175, 523
prerogative powers—
   common law, based on, **1**, 202
   review of exercise of, **1**, 234
prisoner, petition by, **16**, 1470
privilege, **10**, 668; **19**, 236
   hearsay evidence, **10**, 707
proceedings, **6**, 1060
productions, examination of, **17**, 657
property—
   fire precaution regulations, **10**, 1470
   granted to university, **24**, 595

Crown—*continued*
property—*continued*
   infectious diseases, notification of, **19**, 490
   rating, exemption from, **24**, 595
     waiver of, **24**, 596
   valuation roll, entry in, **24**, 597
   protection, duty of, **16**, 1212, 1213
   public corporation, as, **19**, 201, 213
   quod nullius est fit domini regis principle—
     generally, **18**, 9
     lost and abandoned property, **18**, 540, 547
     treasure, **18**, 553
   refusal or revocation of passport by, **16**, 1216, 1227, 1232
     EU law, **16**, 1233
regalia, treasure as, **18**, 553
regalian rights, **18**, 207, 210, 213, 213*n*
Regency, **7**, 705
registered industrial design, use of, **18**, 1201
   royalties, **18**, 1201
   third party rights in respect of, **18**, 1202
restraints on power of monarchy, *see* SOVEREIGN (RESTRAINTS ON POWER)
Revolution Settlement, **19**, 207
royal commission, appointment of, **22**, 637
royal family, **7**, 704, 704*n*
royal household, *see* ROYAL HOUSEHOLD
Royal Marriages Act, **7**, 704, 704*n*
royal prerogative, **5**, 476
royal style and titles—
   consent to, **7**, 703, 703*n*
   heir to Crown, **7**, 704, 704*n*
   present, **7**, 703, 703*n*
   Scottish, **7**, 704, 704*n*
salmon fishing—
   provision binding on, **11**, 39
   rights—
     acquisition by subject proprietors, **18**, 322–325
     catching salmon vested in Crown, **11**, 3, 3*n*
     generally, **18**, 322
     grant of, **11**, 4
salvage award, entitlement to claim, **21**, 457
sasine, **18**, 48
scat payable to, **24**, 309
Scots and English law, **19**, 208
Scots law, **1**, 203
Scottish, claim to Orkney and Shetland, **24**, 302
seabed—
   claim to, **24**, 316
   proprietary right to vested in, **11**, 61
   rights in, **11**, 1304
   within territorial sea, property rights, **21**, 11
seals, *see* SEAL
seat of, **4**, 32
servant, *see* CROWN SERVANT
servants and agents of, immunity, **7**, 741, 763
service, *see* CROWN SERVICE
set-off by or against, **4**, 841
sheriff depute, payment of, **17**, 514
sheriff officer as local officer of, **14**, 1508
Shetland, Scottish Crown's claim to, **24**, 302
sovereign, *see* SOVEREIGN
state power, **7**, 702

Crown—*continued*
statutory authority upon, **7**, 763
statutory enactments, application—
   advantage of, Crown's right to take, **7**, 742
   Crown immunity, questions of, **7**, 740, 740*n*
   EC law, **7**, 743
   English and Scots law compared, **7**, 740
   general rule, **7**, 740
   prerogative or interest, Bill affecting, **7**, 744
   servants and agents of Crown, immunity, **7**, 741
   taxing statutes, **7**, 740
succession—
   Act of Settlement, **7**, 783
   alteration—
      Act of Parliament, by, **7**, 703, 703*n*, 783
      concurrence of Commonwealth countries, **7**, 776
   attempting to hinder, **7**, 569
   heredity, **7**, 703, 703*n*
   primogeniture, **7**, 703*n*
   Scots, history, **7**, 703*n*, 783
   seals, new, **7**, 896
   sisters, position of, **7**, 783
tenancy, assured tenancy status, exclusion from, **13**, 636, 646
territorial waters, rights in, **11**, 1304
tidal areas and rivers, Crown rights in, **25**, 310, 312
tidal waters, ownership of—
   adjacent proprietors, rights of, **18**, 312
   alienation to subject proprietors, **18**, 311
   nature of ownership, **18**, 310
   presumption as to, **18**, 309
title to, statutory basis, **7**, 703, 703*n*
treason, protection by law of, **7**, 704
treasure, right to, **18**, 553; **24**, 313, 324, 329
trustee, as, **24**, 136
udal law, **24**, 306
ultimus haeres, **13**, 411; **18**, 48, 48*n*; **25**, 681
unity, underlying, **7**, 717
unregistered design right, right to use, **18**, 1228
vessel owned by, no maritime lien over, **21**, 479, 479*n*
water pollution, rights as to, **14**, 2079
witnesses—
   examination of, **17**, 753
   objections to, **17**, 753
wreck, rights as to, **21**, 512
wrongful capture, compensation for, **17**, 417
Crown Agent
appointments to, **17**, 580
function, **13**, 1410
functions, **17**, 539, 580
procurator fiscal service, supervision of, **17**, 540
public prosecutor, as, **17**, 580
solicitor to Lord Advocate, as, **17**, 539
solemn procedure, duties, **13**, 1432
staff, **17**, 580
Crown body
bodies which are and are not, **7**, 754
delegation of powers, **7**, 755, 756
enactments not applicable to Crown, **7**, 753
executive agencies, **7**, 755

Crown body—*continued*
interdict against, **7**, 748, 753
licences, requirements as to, **7**, 753
Next Step Agencies, **7**, 755
officers and servants, **7**, 753, 754, 756
privatisation, **7**, 756
rates and taxes, **7**, 753
state, relationship with, **7**, 753
status as, significance, **7**, 753
trading funds, **7**, 756
Crown charter
Great Seal of Scotland, **7**, 874
Crown counsel
appointment of, **17**, 579
Crown Office, instruction by, **13**, 1410
functions, **17**, 537
Crown employment
health and safety, **9**, 409
industrial tribunal, exclusion from, **9**, 331
office holder, **9**, 38
statutory sick pay, **21**, 920
Crown estate
administration, **7**, 769
hereditary revenues, **7**, 769
Crown Estate Commissioners
interest in foreshore of, **6**, 778
Crown Grants
Register of, **6**, 463; **19**, 820
Crown land
burial ground, designation as, **3**, 523
Crown estate, **7**, 769, 772
development of—
   agreement on, **23**, 108
   appropriate authority, meaning, **23**, 105
   consultation regarding, **23**, 106
   planning permission, **23**, 100, 105, 107
meaning, **23**, 105
planning permission, **7**, 742, 753, 753*n*
private revenues, **7**, 772
Roads (Scotland) Act 1984, application of, **20**, 719
status of, **23**, 105
Crown Office
appeals, consideration of, **13**, 1434
Crown Agent, **13**, 1410
function, **5**, 509; **13**, 1410
lawyers, role, **13**, 1410
legal staff, **13**, 1410
procurator fiscal service, supervision of, **17**, 540
solicitors to Lord Advocate, **17**, 539
sudden, suspicious or unexplained death, report by procurator fiscal, **13**, 1435
Crown proceedings
exclusion from sheriff court jurisdiction, **6**, 1060
Crown revenues
annual supply, **7**, 764, 765
Bill of aids and supplies—
   House of Lords may not amend, **7**, 768
   royal assent, **7**, 768
Civil List, **7**, 770
Consolidated Fund, **7**, 766
Consolidated Fund Bill—
   House of Lords may not amend, **7**, 768
   royal assent, **7**, 768

Crown revenues—*continued*
expenditure—
  control, **7**, 764, 766
  Sovereign's recommendation, on, **7**, 767
Finance Bill, **7**, 765
hereditary revenues, **7**, 764, 769
  Civil List, **7**, 770
  Privy Purse, **7**, 771
National Loans Fund, **7**, 766
parliamentary control—
  annual supply, **7**, 765
  Bill of aids and supplies, **7**, 768
  Consolidated Fund Bill, **7**, 768
  development, **7**, 764
  expenditure, **7**, 766, 767
payment of tax by monarch, **7**, 773
private revenues of Crown, **7**, 772
Privy Purse, **7**, 771
taxation and other government receipts, **7**, 764
Ways and Means resolutions, **7**, 765
Crown servant
acquisition and possession of firearms by, **10**, 1543, 1580
action arising from wrongs of, **7**, 745, 746
British subject, **14**, 1950
Civil Service, **7**, 757
conditions of service, **7**, 758
contract of employment, **7**, 761
Crown body, officers and servants of, **7**, 753, 754, 756
delict—
  action against Crown, **7**, 757
  title and interest to sue, **15**, 226
descent, citizenship by, **14**, 1911
driving offence by, **20**, 412
executive agencies, **7**, 755
naturalisation, requirements for, **14**, 1920
Next Step Agencies, **7**, 755
pension, **7**, 762
police constables, **7**, 757
privatisation of Crown body, **7**, 756
relevant service, **14**, 1916
salvage award, entitlement to claim, **21**, 458
some purposes only, for, **7**, 757
status of, significance, **7**, 757
status in relation to Crown, **7**, 758
superannuation, **7**, 757, 762
terms of service, **7**, 759
  changes in, **7**, 760
  contract of employment, **7**, 761
unfair dismissal, **7**, 759, 760
Crowther Committee on Consumer Credit
recommendations, **14**, 1007
review of law undertaken by, **5**, 801
total charge for credit, on, **5**, 817
Cruelty
animal, to, **7**, 104, 420
child, towards, **3**, 1246
mens rea, **7**, 104
use of term, **7**, 104
Cruives
annual close time, **11**, 16
byelaws relating to, failure to comply with, **11**, 19
charter rights, **11**, 11

Cruives—*continued*
generally, **18**, 326
meaning, **11**, 2*n*
prohibition in tidal waters, **11**, 2
regulations as to, **11**, 32
salmon fishing rights, exercise of, **18**, 326
Secretary of State's powers, **11**, 23
when permitted, **11**, 11
Crystallisation
floating charge, recognition of validity of, **4**, 305
Culpa
meaning, **15**, 254
necessity for, **14**, 2005
obligation arising from, **15**, 3
proximate cause of injury, as, **11**, 1019
unintentional injury and fault, **15**, 254
See also LIABILITY
Culpable
culpably, use of term, **7**, 75
culpably and recklessly, **7**, 82
  endangering public, **7**, 248, 249
  injury, causing, **7**, 82, 247, 249
diminished responsibility, and, **7**, 136, 278
Culpable homicide
adultery as provocation, **7**, 273
assault—
  not involving, **7**, 281
  through, **7**, 243, 244, 280
attempt inapplicable, **7**, 170
automatism, **7**, 34
categories, **7**, 271
concealment of pregnancy, *see* CONCEALMENT OF PREGNANCY
consent of victim, where, **7**, 93
contractual obligation, failure to perform, **7**, 279
criminal homicide, as, **7**, 253
death caused by driving, **20**, 412, 453
death or suicide of victim following assault, **7**, 227
diminished responsibility, **7**, 135, 138, 139, 149, 150, 253, 278
forseeability, **7**, 193
intoxication, grounds for plea of, **7**, 271
involuntary, **7**, 282
  assault, culpable homicide by, **7**, 280
  lawful act, as result of, **7**, 271, 282
  omission, culpable homicide by, **7**, 279
  unlawful act, as result of, **7**, 271, 279–281
meaning, **7**, 253
medical help, failure to obtain, **7**, 279
mens rea, **7**, 34
negligence, where, **7**, 279, 282
novus actus interveniens, **7**, 51
omission, by, **7**, 279
penalties, **7**, 253, 253*n*
person charged with, duty solicitor, **13**, 1053
prior actings, as result of, **7**, 279
proof of cause of death, **7**, 50
provocation, **7**, 253
  accused engaging in unlawful act, where, **7**, 276
  degree of provocation required, **7**, 275
  immediacy, **7**, 274
  intention to kill, **7**, 272
  physical assault, **7**, 273
  self-defence, and, **7**, 277

Culpable homicide—*continued*
reckless ignorance, **7**, 82
recklessness, **7**, 82
result-crime, as, **7**, 46
voluntary, **7**, 271
wilfully, **7**, 84
See also HOMICIDE
Cultural activity
national and European Union law, disparity
    between, **7**, 1021
Cultural facilities
byelaws, **14**, 277
district council, powers and duties of, **14**, 690–692
island council, powers and duties of, **14**, 690–692
regional council, financial contributions by, **14**, 693
Cultural goods
export licence, requirement for, **7**, 1200
national and European Union law, disparity
    between, **7**, 1022
Cultural life
right to participation in, **12**, 4*n*
Culverting
artificial stream, creation of, **25**, 355
Cumulative legacy
generally, **25**, 857
more than one deed, **25**, 858
one deed, **25**, 859
Cumulo penalties
imposition of, **17**, 791
Curator
actings of minors, **10**, 1105, 1108, 1109
ad litem
    adoption proceedings, **11**, 1227
    advocate as, **11**, 1227
    appointment, **3**, 1215; **11**, 1226; **24**, 83
    conduct of proceedings, **11**, 1228
    divorce or separation, in cases of, **11**, 1227
    dominus litis, as, **11**, 1228
    expenses, **11**, 1228
    generally, **11**, 1226
    personal injury, as pursuer in action relating to,
        16, 2150, 2168
    proceedings commenced without consent of,
        11, 1226
    remuneration, **11**, 1228
    rights of, limitation, **11**, 1226
administration by, **10**, 1096; **11**, 1222, 1224
application for curatory, **10**, 1316
appointment of, **10**, 1095; **11**, 1220; **24**, 9, 13
bonis—
    Accountant of Court, communication with, **11**,
        1234
    administration by, **11**, 1224
    administrative costs, **11**, 1236
    appointment, **11**, 1233
        mental impairment as reason for, **11**, 1232
        more than one, **11**, 1233
        petition for, **11**, 1233, 1478; **17**, 1423
    caution, finding of, **11**, 1233
    death of, **11**, 1235
    delict—
        defender, as, **15**, 234
        title and interest to sue, **15**, 234
    discharge of, **11**, 1235

Curator—*continued*
bonis—*continued*
    duties, **11**, 1234
    exercise of office, problems with, **11**, 1236
    foreign *incapax* with property in Scotland, **11**,
        1233
    generally, **11**, 1226
    incapax, acting for, **13**, 1780
    incapax to, **17**, 1423; **24**, 239, 265, 271
    inventory, lodging of, **11**, 1234
    jurisdiction of court, **11**, 1233
    medical certification of ward's inability to
        manage affairs, **11**, 1233
    mental impairment as reason for appointment,
        11, 1232
    mentally disorderd person, and, *see* MENTALLY
        DISORDERED PERSON
    minor, to, **24**, 239, 265, 270
    payments or transfers of property to, divorce
        cases, **10**, 955
    problems in exercise of office—
        cost, **11**, 1236
        lack of power over ward, **11**, 1236
        social security benefits, in relation to, **11**, 1236
    proposed reform, **11**, 1237
    reappointment, **11**, 1235
    recovery of ward, **11**, 1235
    special powers, **24**, 253
    substitute, appointment of, **11**, 1235
breach of fiduciary duty, reduction on grounds of,
    13, 44
contracts of minor who has curator, **11**, 1204
control of minor's person—
    education, **10**, 1118
    generally, **10**, 1117, 1120
    medical treatment, **10**, 1119
death, **10**, 1097
death of parent, on, **11**, 1211
deed by minor who has, **12**, 1229
deed *in liege poustie*, **11**, 1220
duties and responsibilities, **11**, 1224
father as, **10**, 1084–1087
fiduciary duty, **24**, 172
generally, **10**, 1083; **11**, 1202, 1219, 1222
guardian of minor child, as, **11**, 1202
illegitimate child, of, **10**, 1085, 1089
legal rights, potential claimant for, **25**, 790
legitimate child, of, **10**, 1084
lessee, as, **13**, 187
lessor, as, **13**, 167
liability, **11**, 1225
marriage, consent not required, **10**, 1080
married child, of, **10**, 1086
minor as trustee, **24**, 129
minor's choice of, **10**, 1092
    statutory erosion of, **10**, 1093
minor's petition for, **11**, 1220
mother as, **10**, 1088, 1089
order relating to child, **8**, 508
parent as, **10**, 1090; **11**, 1209
'pro curator', **11**, 1217
    meaning of, **15**, 92
    negotiorum gestio and pro-curatory distinguished,
        15, 92

Curator—*continued*
property management by, **11**, 1220
proposal to abolish office, **11**, 1243
proprietor, as, **24**, 444
removings, action of, **13**, 497
resignation, **10**, 1097
role of, **10**, 1096
  respective roles of tutor and, **10**, 1073
Roman law as basis of office, **11**, 1202
statute law, effect of, **11**, 1202
termination of curatory, **10**, 1097; **11**, 1221
testamentary—
  appointment by father, **10**, 1087
  appointment by parents, **10**, 1091
  generally, **10**, 1094
trustee, as, **24**, 2, 128
tutor's functions distinguished, **10**, 1056, 1073, 1083; **11**, 1207

Curator of the Historical Department
generally, **19**, 810, 810n

***Curia Regis* (King's Council)**
composition, **6**, 898
court of appeal, as, **6**, 898
deficiencies as court, **6**, 900
development of Privy Council, **6**, 898
generally, **22**, 506
jurisdiction, **6**, 850, 898, 902
Parliament, and, **6**, 802, 803
possessory remedies, **6**, 898
procedure, **6**, 899
Scotland, **6**, 804
summons, method of serving, **6**, 899

Curling
historical background, **19**, 1203
sports-governing institutions, **19**, 1205

Currency
counterfeit—
  illegal importation, **7**, 1151
  possession of, **14**, 1838
credit sale agreement, sale on, **14**, 1809
depreciation, indexation as protection against, **14**, 1824
foreign, *see* FOREIGN CURRENCY
note, meaning, **14**, 1835
reproducing, **14**, 1840
Scottish—
  abolition, **14**, 1818
  references to, **14**, 1818
  table, **14**, 1818
See also BANK NOTES; COINS; MONEY

Current maintenance arrestment
See EARNINGS

Curtilage
house within curtilage of certain other buildings, **11**, 1937, 1945
meaning, **24**, 714

Custodial penalties
child, **3**, 1218
terms of, **17**, 563
young person, **3**, 1218

Custodial sentence
first offenders, of, restrictions, **16**, 1435
objectives, **16**, 1436

Custodial sentence—*continued*
setting off time in custody against, **12**, 34
young offenders, of, restrictions, **16**, 1435

Custodier
civil possession by, **18**, 121

Custody
appearance in court from, **17**, 610
appellant in, **17**, 852
assisting escape of person in, **16**, 1807
child, in, **17**, 892
child, of, *see* CHILD-CHILDREN
escape from—
  absconding from legal custody, **7**, 557, 558
  assisting escape, **7**, 559
  police custody, from, **7**, 560, 561
  prison breaking—
    civil prisoner, **7**, 554
    definition, **7**, 553
    escape, means of, **7**, 555
    generally, **7**, 552
    lawfully confined, prisoner must be, **7**, 553, 554
    prison, meaning, **7**, 556
    remand, prisoner on, **7**, 554
intimation of, right to send, **16**, 1793, 1793n
legal, person in, residence, **15**, 1081
liberation by police, **17**, 609
lien distinguished, **20**, 70
mentally disordered person, of, *see* MENTALLY DISORDERED PERSON
order, *see* CUSTODY ORDER
police powers, **16**, 1788
property in possession of persons taken into, **16**, 1821
rights of person in, **17**, 608
time limits—
  eighty-day rule, **17**, 662
  extension of, **17**, 664
  generally, **17**, 660
  hundred-and-ten-day rule, **17**, 661
  one-year rule, **17**, 663
unreasonable or unnecessary detention in, **16**, 1784, 1788, 1793
whether individual is in, **16**, 1789

Custody order
common law, recognition and enforcement at—
  principles followed by Scottish courts, **8**, 532
contempt of court, enforcement by means of, **8**, 518
European Convention on Recognition and Enforcement, within scope of—
  access, decisions relating to, **8**, 528
  application for recognition or enforcement, **8**, 524
  cancellation of registered decision, **8**, 531
  central authorities, Scottish, **8**, 520
  enforcement—
    central authorities—
      duties of, **8**, 524
      establishment of, **8**, 524
    registration, effect, **8**, 529
  general principles of Convention, **8**, 520
  geographical extent of Convention, **8**, 522

Custody order—*continued*
European Convention on Recognition and Enforcement, within scope of—*continued*
  improper removal of child across international frontier, **8**, 530
  interim powers, **8**, 527
  recognition of Convention decisions, **8**, 523
  registration—
    enforcement, **8**, 529
    procedure, **8**, 525
    refusal, grounds for, **8**, 526
  scope of Convention, **8**, 521
  variation of registered decision, **8**, 531
Hague Convention on the Civil Aspects of International Child Abduction, **8**, 530
Judgments Convention, exclusion from scope of, **8**, 432
sequestration of income, **8**, 518
UK orders, reciprocal recognition and enforcement—
  application for enforcement, **8**, 519
  delivery orders, **8**, 514
    ad factum praestandum, **8**, 514
  disclosure of child's whereabouts, order for, **8**, 515
  dismissal of proceedings, **8**, 519
    application for, **8**, 519
  enforcement, **8**, 513, 518, 519
  England and Wales, orders made in, **8**, 506
  Family Law Act 1986, governed by, **8**, 505
  generally, **8**, 504
  interdict to prevent removal of child from UK, **8**, 516
  interim order, **8**, 519
  Northern Ireland, orders made in, **8**, 507
  orders made prior to commencement of Family Law Act 1986 ..., **8**, 509
  Part I orders—
    enforcement, **8**, 513, 518, 519
    generally, **8**, 509
    recognition, generally, **8**, 510
    registration, **8**, 511
      cancellation or variation, **8**, 512
  procedure, **8**, 519
  Scottish orders, **8**, 505, 508
  sisting proceedings, **8**, 519
    application for, **8**, 519
    recall of sist, **8**, 519
  warrant to search for and take possession of child, **8**, 517
welfare of child, consideration, **8**, 533

Custom
'ancient and immemorial'—
  Stair's view, **22**, 532
ancient and recent, **22**, 533
authoritative writing, **22**, 358
binding, **22**, 530
Brehon law, English common law and, **22**, 388
case law, **22**, 358
Celtic law, based on, **22**, 361
certainty, test, **22**, 383
common law, relationship with—
  England, in, **22**, 370–374, 388
  meaning, **22**, 369

Custom—*continued*
common law, relationship with—*continued*
  modern Scots law, doctrine of desuetude, **22**, 376, 381
    incorporation of custom into, **22**, 375
    legal custom and, **22**, 377
    See also DESUETUDE, DOCTRINE OF
  narrowing ambit of customary law—
    distinctive Scottish development, **22**, 359
    early Scots law, **22**, 359, 362
    England, thirteenth century, **22**, 358
compilations of customary law—
  Leges Quatuor Burgorum, **22**, 360
  Quoniam Attachiamenta, **22**, 360
  Regiam Majestatem, **22**, 360
constituent element of Scots law, as, **22**, 529
conveyancing practice, **22**, 260
Court of Session—
  role in clarification, **22**, 532
  uniform decisions as customary law, **22**, 367
'custom of the realm'—
  England, **22**, 363
derogation from statute—
  contrary custom, principle, **22**, 357, 376
diminution of role, **22**, 357, 359
England, in—
  'custom of the realm', **22**, 363
  legality, test, **22**, 378
  local variation of general law, as, **22**, 371, 385
  reasonableness, **22**, 373
  tests, **22**, 372, 378
  'time immemorial', **22**, 372
  usage, distinction, **22**, 372, 374
equitable, **22**, 532
  rules becoming customary rules, **22**, 414
erosion as source of law, **22**, 531
Erskine's view, **22**, 367, 529–532
'essential'—
  Erskine's view, **22**, 532
European background—
  common law of England, relationship with, **22**, 358
  diminishing role, later Middle Ages, **22**, 357
  early Scots law, **22**, 359–361
  France, written and unwritten law, **22**, 356
  lex et consuetudo, **22**, 356
  narrowing ambit, **22**, 358
  source of customary rules, **22**, 363
feudal custom as source of law, **22**, 363
formal source of law, as, **22**, 501, 529–533
  England, in, **22**, 370–374
  Scots law—
    modern, **22**, 375–393
    pre-nineteenth century, **22**, 355–369
fosterage, Celtic legal origin, **22**, 361
French customary law, influence of, **22**, 604
fundamental legal principle and, **22**, 377, 378
general acceptance, test, **22**, 384
historical background—
  diminishing role in later Middle Ages, **22**, 357
  early Scots law, **22**, 359–361
  lex et consuetudo, **22**, 356
  narrowing ambit, **22**, 358
  source of customary rules, **22**, 363

Custom—*continued*
institutional writers, in—
  Bankton, **22**, 368
  Craig, **22**, 360, 364
  Erskine, **22**, 367
  generally, **22**, 364–369
  Mackenzie, **22**, 365
  Stair, **22**, 366
'institutional' writers, juristic treatment, **22**, 532, 533
  See also 'INSTITUTIONAL' WRITERS
international law, as source of, **19**, 603
judicial authority—
  development of 'learned' custom, **22**, 440
  source of law in own right, effect of theory on custom, **22**, 418
judicial precedent, particular example of customary law, **22**, 257, 260
Kames's *Principles of Equity*, **22**, 414
King's court, practices as source of custom, **22**, 363
'learned', **22**, 440
legal, differing from general common law, **22**, 377
  local, **22**, 530
  test of legality, **22**, 378
  universal, **22**, 530
legal systems as source of, **22**, 363, 366–368
legal treatises, development through, **22**, 532
legislation and custom contrasted, **22**, 109
lex et consuetudo
  early Scots law, **22**, 359
  eighteenth century change in terminology, **22**, 369
  European law, **22**, 356, 363
  lex and *consuetudo* compared, **22**, 356
  medieval recognition as twin sources—
    Stair, sources of civil law in Scotland, **22**, 366
local usage—
  distinction, in England, **22**, 372, 374
  source, **22**, 363–368
marine, **22**, 608, 609
marriage, secular, Celtic legal origin, **22**, 361
meaning, **22**, 530
mercantile usage as source, **22**, 363
modern, **22**, 533
notorious, **22**, 533
origins, **22**, 363
Orkney and Shetland—
  Udal law, **22**, 366, 367, 368, 387, 530
practice, and, *see* CUSTOM AND PRACTICE
precedent and, **22**, 543
prescription and, **22**, 391
primacy as source of law over statute, **22**, 129
reasonableness, test—
  Bruce v Smith, **22**, 385–388
  English law, **22**, 373, 388
  Scots law, modern, **22**, 385–388
  Tanistry Case, **22**, 388
recent, **22**, 533
Reformation, effect, **22**, 532
rights of way, **22**, 380, 391, 393
Scots law—
  early—
    Celtic law, based on, **22**, 361
    common law, emergence of, **22**, 359

Custom—*continued*
Scots law—*continued*
  early—*continued*
    compilations of customary law, **22**, 360
    feudal law and custom, **22**, 359
    generally, **22**, 359–369
    local or regional custom, survival into medieval period, **22**, 361
    pre-feudal law, survival into medieval period, **22**, 361
  modern—
    common law, custom as, **22**, 375
    desuetude, doctrine of, **22**, 376
      See also DESUETUDE, DOCTRINE OF
    distinct source of law, custom as, **22**, 377, 378
    tests—
      certainty, **22**, 383
      general acceptance, **22**, 384
      reasonableness, **22**, 385–388
      tract of time, **22**, 379–382
social consensus and custom, **22**, 385, 386
sources of Scottish customary law—
  canon law, **22**, 532
  civil law, **22**, 532
  feudal law, **22**, 532
Stair's *Institutions*, **22**, 529, 532, 533
statute and, **22**, 129, 357
'time immemorial'
  desuetude, statute since, **22**, 381
  English customary law, **22**, 372, 379
  meaning, **22**, 380, 385
  public right of way, **22**, 380, 391, 393
tract of time—
  English doctrine of immemorial antiquity contrasted, **22**, 379
  as factor testing existing, **22**, 379
  leading cases, **22**, 381
  relative in Scots law, **22**, 382
  'time immemorial', **22**, 372, 379, 380
Udal law, **22**, 366, 367, 368, 387, 530
usage—
  distinction in English law, **22**, 372, 374, 389
  local, **22**, 363, 366–368
  Scots law, **22**, 363, 366–368, 389, 390
validity, proof of, **22**, 533
written, medieval development, **22**, 356
Customs and excise
agricultural levy, fraudulent evasion, **7**, 1162
agricultural product—
  Common Agricultural Policy (CAP), *see* COMMON AGRICULTURAL POLICY
  European Union customs law—
    agricultural levies, **7**, 1038
    Common Agricultural Policy (CAP), **7**, 1014
    definition of agricultural products, **7**, 1014
    duty—
      rates, **7**, 1014
      reliefs, **7**, 1100
    export licence, **7**, 1014
    import licence, **7**, 1014
  Intervention Board of Agriculture, **7**, 1098
air passenger duty—
  chargeable aircraft, **7**, 1079
  chargeable passenger, **7**, 1079

Customs and excise—*continued*
air passenger duty—*continued*
  offences, **7**, 1079
  operator of aircraft—
    liability to pay, **7**, 1079
    registration, **7**, 1079
  rate of duty, **7**, 1079
alcohol and alcoholic beverages, *see* ALCOHOL AND ALCOHOLIC BEVERAGES
amusement machine licence, *see* AMUSEMENT MACHINE LICENCE
animal, import or export, *see* ANIMAL
antiques, **7**, 1120, 1194
Commissioners, Administration of Food and Drugs (Scotland) Act, **11**, 329
copyright law, right to restrict import of infringing copies, **18**, 1077, 1097
customs duties, *see* CUSTOMS DUTIES
customs officers, *see* CUSTOMS OFFICERS
enterprise zone, **14**, 647
European Union, in—
  ad valorem duties, **7**, 1015, 1048
  agricultural products, **7**, 1014, 1038
  Common Commercial Policy (CCP), *see* COMMON COMMERCIAL POLICY
  Common Customs Tariff (CCT), *see* COMMON CUSTOMS TARIFF
  Community Customs Code, *see* COMMUNITY CUSTOMS CODE
  Community customs duty, meaning, **7**, 1048*n*
  conformity with, **7**, 1108
  customs authorities, representation before, **7**, 1208
  customs control, processing under, **7**, 1186
  customs debt—
    deferred payment of customs duty, **7**, 1043
    exportation, on, **7**, 1041
    extinction, **7**, 1042
    failure to pay, **7**, 1044
    importation, on, **7**, 1040
    incurrence, **7**, 1039
    meaning, **7**, 1039
    payment, **7**, 1039, 1043
    security for, **7**, 1045
  customs documentation, **7**, 1124
  customs duty—
    charge to, **7**, 1037
    repayment and remission, **7**, 1089
  customs territory, **7**, 1010
    importation of goods into, **7**, 1130
    treatment of goods entering, **7**, 1131
  decisions, **7**, 1003
  deflections of trade, **7**, 1023
  destruction of non-Community goods, **7**, 1167
  directives, **7**, 1003
  disparities between national laws, **7**, 1021
  dumping, on, **7**, 1024, 1050
  duty suspension arrangements, **7**, 1053, 1056, 1057, 1058
  'equally applicable measures', **7**, 1019
  equivalent effect, duties and charges having, **7**, 1012, 1013
  excise duty point—
    Community excise goods, **7**, 1053
    duty suspension arrangements, **7**, 1053

Customs and excise—*continued*
European Union, in—*continued*
  excise duty point—*continued*
    introduction, **7**, 1052
    meaning, **7**, 1052*n*, 1053
    occasional importer, goods consigned to, **7**, 1053
    REDS, goods consigned to, **7**, 1053
  excise law, **7**, 1032–1036
  export procedure, *see* EXPORT PROCEDURE (european community law)
  export restrictions, **7**, 1030, 1031
    quantitative, **7**, 1020
  external trade effects, **7**, 1004
  free circulation—
    member state, in, goods in, **7**, 1011, 1168
    release of goods for, **7**, 1168
  free zones, *see* FREE ZONE
  General Agreement on Tariffs and Trade (GATT), *see* GENERAL AGREEMENT ON TARIFFS AND TRADE
  import procedure, *see* IMPORT PROCEDURE (european community law)
  internal taxation and customs duties, **7**, 1013
  internal trade effects, **7**, 1004
  'local grab' measures, **7**, 1020
  mandatory requirements, national, **7**, 1021
  national safeguards against free movement of goods, **7**, 1021–1023
  non-preferential trade agreements, **7**, 1046
  non-tariff barriers to internal trade, **7**, 1004, 1018–1020
  occasional importer, **7**, 1053, 1056, 1058
  origin of goods—
    determination, **7**, 1046
    proof, **7**, 1047
  outward processing, **7**, 1188–1191
  preferential trade agreements, **7**, 1016, 1025, 1026, 1046, 1047
  primary legislation, **7**, 1003, 1011–1024
  quantitative restrictions, **7**, 1018–1020
    equivalent effect, measures having, **7**, 1018–1020
  registered excise dealer and shipper (REDS), *see* REGISTERED EXCISE DEALER AND SHIPPER
  regulations, **7**, 1003
  reliefs from duties—
    end-use relief, **7**, 1101
    export duties, **7**, 1100
    generally, **7**, 1099
    import duties, **7**, 1100
    inherited property, **7**, 1100, 1113, 1116
    inward processing relief, **7**, 1099, 1102, 1182–1191
    outward processing relief, **7**, 1099, 1182–1191
    personal property, **7**, 1100
    returned goods, **7**, 1102
    sea, products taken from, **7**, 1103
    sea-fishing, products of, **7**, 1103
    system of reliefs, **7**, 1100
    temporary importation relief, **7**, 1099, 1187
  secondary legislation, **7**, 1003, 1007, 1025–1031
  service for benefit of importer, charge for, **7**, 1012

Customs and excise—*continued*
European Union, in—*continued*
Single Market, **7**, 1005, 1052, 1152, 1193
tariff barriers—
free movement of goods, to, **7**, 1012
internal trade, to, **7**, 1004
third countries, goods originating in, **7**, 1011,
1015, 1017
transit procedure—
EFTA countries, with, **7**, 1171
external, **7**, 1169, 1170, 1173
internal, **7**, 1172, 1173
treaties, **7**, 1003, 1011–1024
Treaty on European Union, **7**, 1007
United Kingdom law, interaction with, **7**,
1003, 1052
valuation of goods—
determination of value, **7**, 1049
generally, **7**, 1048
warehousing, customs, *see* WAREHOUSE
excise duty, *see* EXCISE DUTY
food unfit for human consumption, **11**, 401
forfeiture—
aircraft, **7**, 1225
detention, seizure and condemnation of goods
liable to, **7**, 1226
drug trafficking, proceeds of, **7**, 1231
motor vehicle, **7**, 1225
ship or vessel, **7**, 1225
smuggling offences, **7**, 1233
spirits, **7**, 1225
generally, **19**, 1510, 1543
goods—
condemnation, customs officers' powers, **7**,
1226
customs officer's powers in relation to, *see*
CUSTOMS OFFICERS
customs-approved treatments or uses,
assignment, **7**, 1192
destruction or sale, customs officers' powers, **7**,
1217
forfeiture, customs officers' powers, **7**, 1225
free circulation—
Community member state, in, **7**, 1011, 1168
release for, **7**, 1168
inward processing procedure, **7**, 1182
movement, customs officers' power to restrict,
7, 1240
samples, **7**, 1298
temporary importation, **7**, 1290
transit, in, export, **7**, 1194
inward processing—
authorisation, **7**, 1183
compensating products, **7**, 1182
customs declaration, **7**, 1183
drawback, **7**, 1094, 1182, 1885
free circulation, goods released for, **7**, 1182
generally, **7**, 1099, 1102, 1182
operation, **7**, 1184
prior exportation system, **7**, 1182
processing operation, meaning, **7**, 1182
purpose of procedure, **7**, 1182
re-exportation, **7**, 1182
suspension, **7**, 1182, 1184, 1185

Customs and excise—*continued*
legal proceedings and penalties—
appeal provisions, **7**, 1276, 1277
Customs and Excise Acts, under—
civil proceedings, **7**, 1267
conduct of proceedings, **7**, 1271
generally, **7**, 1267
institution of proceedings, **7**, 1268
judicial review, **7**, 1278
jurisdiction in proceedings, **7**, 1270
limitation of commencement of proceedings,
7, 1269
penalties—
generally, **7**, 1273
mitigation, powers as to, **7**, 1275
non-payment, imprisonment for, **7**, 1271
proof, matters of, **7**, 1269
summons, **7**, 1265
Finance Act 1994, under—
civil penalties, **7**, 1260
outward processing—
authorisation, **7**, 1189
declarations, **7**, 1189
duration, **7**, 1190
excluded goods, **7**, 1188
generally, **7**, 1188
import duties, **7**, 1188
local clearance procedure, **7**, 1189
operation, **7**, 1190
prior importation, **7**, 1191
purpose, **7**, 1188
rate of yield, **7**, 1190, 1190*n*
re-importation, **7**, 1189, 1190
repairs, to enable, **7**, 1190
standard exchange system, **7**, 1191
preferential debts, **4**, 854
records—
revenue traders, **7**, 1252
trades or businesses connected with import and
export goods, **7**, 1255
search of premises, **17**, 607
special powers, **8**, 128
tax evasion, possession of or dealing in goods, **7**,
395
transit procedure—
EFTA and European Union countries,
between, **7**, 1171
external transit, **7**, 1169, 1170, 1173
internal transit, **7**, 1172, 1173
value added tax, administration of, **19**, 1542
Customs and Excise, Department of
Computer Services Division, **7**, 1282
constitution, **7**, 1282
generally, **7**, 1282
Internal Taxation Directorate, **7**, 1282
Investigation Division, **7**, 1282
Solicitor's Office, **7**, 1282
VAT Central Unit, **7**, 1282
VAT Directorate, **7**, 1282
See also COMMISSIONERS OF CUSTOMS AND EXCISE
Customs duties
ad valorem duties, **7**, 1015, 1048
allowance, examination of goods, **7**, 1214
avoidance, attempted, **7**, 1151

Customs duties—*continued*
cancellation, **7**, 1145
charge to—
 classification of goods, **7**, 1038
 customs debt—
  deferred payment, **7**, 1043
  exportation, on, **7**, 1041
  extinction, **7**, 1042
  failure to pay, **7**, 1044
  importation, on, **7**, 1040
  incurrence, **7**, 1038
  payment, **7**, 1038
  security for, **7**, 1045
 European Union, **7**, 1037
 generally, **7**, 1037
collection—
 Commissioners of Customs and Excise, *see*
  COMMISSIONERS OF CUSTOMS AND EXCISE
 customs officers, *see* CUSTOMS OFFICERS
 generally, **7**, 1204, 1210
Commissioners of Customs and Excise, *see*
 COMMISSIONERS OF CUSTOMS AND EXCISE
correction, **7**, 1145
customs authorities, representation before, **7**,
 1208
customs control, processing under, **7**, 1186
customs debt—
 customs control, processing under, **7**, 1186
 deferred payment, **7**, 1043, 1174
 exportation, on, **7**, 1041
 extinction, **7**, 1042
 failure to pay, **7**, 1044
 importation, on, **7**, 1040
 incurrence, **7**, 1039
 interest on late payment, **7**, 1044
 legal proceedings to recover—
  civil, **7**, 1267
  conduct, **7**, 1271
  generally, **7**, 1267
  institution, **7**, 1268
  jurisdiction, **7**, 1270
  limitation of commencement, **7**, 1269
  penalties, **7**, 1273
   mitigation, powers of, **7**, 1275
   non-payment, imprisonment for, **7**, 1274
  proof, matter of, **7**, 1272
 meaning, **7**, 1039
 payment, **7**, 1039
 security for, **7**, 1045
  additional or replacement, **7**, 1045
  compulsory, **7**, 1045
  form, **7**, 1045
  part release, **7**, 1045
customs officers, *see* CUSTOMS OFFICERS
damaged goods, destruction, **7**, 1092
declarations—
 acts equivalent to, **7**, 1127
 amendment, **7**, 1125
 cancellation, **7**, 1125
 computerised, **7**, 1127
 customs debt, **7**, 1039
 generally, **7**, 1123, 1125
 invalidated, where, **7**, 1089
 oral, **7**, 1127

Customs duties—*continued*
declarations—*continued*
 requirement for, **7**, 1125
 simplified, **7**, 1126
 Single Administrative Document (SAD), **7**, 1125
 untrue, **7**, 1257
 verification, **7**, 1125
 who may make, **7**, 1125
deferred payment, **7**, 1043
denatured goods, **7**, 1091, 1096
destination, **7**, 1051
destroyed goods, **7**, 1092, 1096
documentation—
 European Union—
  Administrative Accompanying Document
   (AAD), **7**, 1124
  ATA carnet, **7**, 1124, 1169, 1172
  data-processing techniques, **7**, 1124
  generally, **7**, 1124
  Single Administrative Document (SAD), **7**,
   1124
  Supplementary Statistical Declaration (SSD),
   7, 1124
  T1, **7**, 1170
  T5, **7**, 1124
  TIR carnet, **7**, 1124, 1169, 1172
 generally, **7**, 1123
donations *mortis causa*, **8**, 657
drawback—
 calculation, **7**, 1095
 claims for, **7**, 1095
 denatured goods, **7**, 1096
 examination of goods for which claim made, **7**,
  1214
 generally, **7**, 1094
 goods system applicable to, **7**, 1185
 inward processing procedure, **7**, 1094, 1182,
  1185
 lost or destroyed goods, **7**, 1096
 meaning, **7**, 1094
 offences in relation to, **7**, 1098, 1162
 time limit for applications, **7**, 1185
dumping, against, **7**, 1024, 1050
European Community assets and revenues,
 exemption from, **10**, 296
European Union law—
 agricultural products, **7**, 1014, 1038
 Common Commercial Policy (CCP), *see*
  COMMON COMMERCIAL POLICY
 Common Customs Tariff (CCT), *see* COMMON
  CUSTOMS TARIFF
 Community Customs Code, *see* COMMUNITY
  CUSTOMS CODE
 Community customs duty, meaning, **7**, 1048*n*
 customs authorities, representation before, **7**,
  1208
 customs debt—
  deferred payment of customs duty, **7**, 1043,
   1174
  exportation, on, **7**, 1041
  extinction, **7**, 1042
  failure to pay, **7**, 1044
  importation, on, **7**, 1040
  incurrence, **7**, 1039

Customs duties—*continued*
European Union law—*continued*
  customs debt—*continued*
    meaning, **7,** 1039
    payment, **7,** 1039, 1043
    security for, **7,** 1045
  customs territory, **7,** 1010
    importation of goods into, **7,** 1130
    treatment of goods entering, **7,** 1131
  customs union, **7,** 1011
  deferred payment, **7,** 1043, 1174
  deflections of trade, **7,** 1023
  dumping, on, **7,** 1024, 1050
  'equally applicable measures', **7,** 1019
  equivalent effect, duties and charges having, **7,**
    1012, 1013
  European Economic Area Agreement (EEA), **7,**
    1006
  European Union practices, conformity with, **7,**
    1109
  export restrictions, **7,** 1030, 1031
    quantitative, **7,** 1020
  external trade, **7,** 1004
  free circulation in member state, goods in, **7,**
    1011, 1168
  free zones, **7,** 1010
  generally, **7,** 1037
  interaction with United Kingdom law, **7,** 1003
  internal and external trade effects, **7,** 1004
  internal taxation and customs duties, **7,** 1013
  'local grab' measures, **7,** 1020
  mandatory requirements, national, **7,** 1021
  national safeguards against free movement of
    goods, **7,** 1021–1023
  non-preferential trade agreements, **7,** 1046
  non-tariff barriers to internal trade, **7,** 1004,
    1018–1020
  origin of goods—
    determination, **7,** 1046
    proof, **7,** 1047
  outward processing, **7,** 1188–1191
  preferential trade agreements, **7,** 1016, 1025,
    1026, 1046, 1047
  primary legislation, **7,** 1011–1024
  quantitative restrictions, **7,** 1018–1020
    equivalent effect, measures having, **7,** 1018–
      1020
  reliefs—
    agriculturally related property, **7,** 1100
    community system of, **7,** 1100
    end-use relief, **7,** 1101
    export duties, **7,** 1100
    generally, **7,** 1099
    import duties, **7,** 1100
    inward processing, **7,** 1099, 1102, 1182–1191
    negligible value, consignments of, **7,** 1100
    outward processing, **7,** 1099, 1182–1191
    personal property, **7,** 1100
    returned goods, **7,** 1102
    sea, products taken from, **7,** 1103
    sea-fishing, products of, **7,** 1103
    temporary importation relief, **7,** 1099, 1187
  repayment and remission, **7,** 1089
  secondary legislation, **7,** 1025–1031

Customs duties—*continued*
European Union law—*continued*
  service for benefit of importer, charge for, **7,** 1012
  Single Market, **7,** 1005, 1152
  tariff barriers—
    free movement of goods, to, **7,** 1012
    internal trade, to, **7,** 1004
  third countries, goods originating in, **7,** 1011,
    1015, 1017
  Treaty on European Union, **7,** 1007
  valuation of goods—
    determination of value, **7,** 1049
    generally, **7,** 1048
evasion, **7,** 1258
  preparatory steps for, taking, **7,** 1263
free zones, *see* FREE ZONE
General Agreement on Tariffs and Trade (GATT),
  see GENERAL AGREEMENT ON TARIFFS AND TRADE
gifts, **8,** 657
internal taxation—
  distinguished, **7,** 1013
  interaction with, **7,** 1013
international obligations, conformity with, **7,** 1108
lost goods, **7,** 1092, 1096
meaning, **7,** 1001
offences—
  corporate body, committed by, **7,** 1266
  counterfeiting documents, **7,** 1258
  customs officer, removal, **7,** 1265
  evasion—
    fraudulent, **7,** 1259
    preparatory steps for, taking, **7,** 1263
  generally, **7,** 1256, 1266
  handling goods subject to unpaid duty, **7,** 1262
  outlying provisions of Acts, under, **7,** 1266,
    1266*n*
  scales, use of false or unjust, **7,** 1264
  untrue declaration, **7,** 1257
payment, procedure, **7,** 1148
postponed payment, **7,** 1143
re-exported goods, **7,** 1094
rebate, examination of goods, **7,** 1214
reliefs—
  antiques, **7,** 1120
  Channel Islands, imports from, **7,** 1105
  continental shelf produce, **7,** 1106
  diplomats, for, **7,** 1117
  directions or discretion, by virtue of, **7,** 1118
  end-use, **7,** 1101, 1110
  European Union, *see* European Union law
    above
  European Union practices—
    conformity with, **7,** 1108
    referable to, **7,** 1109
  examination, goods imported for, **7,** 1118
  false statement in application for, **7,** 1122
  forfeiture of goods subject to, **7,** 1121
  inherited property, **7,** 1100, 1116
  international obligations, conformity with, **7,**
    1108
  prizes and honours awarded abroad, **7,** 1120
  sea produce, **7,** 1106
  statutory orders, under, **7,** 1108–1110
  temporary importation, **7,** 1187

Customs duties—*continued*
reliefs—*continued*
  testing, goods imported for, **7**, 1118
  trade samples, **7**, 1119
  United Kingdom law, **7**, 1104–1106
  visiting forces, for, **7**, 1117
remission—
  denatured goods, **7**, 1091
  destroyed goods, **7**, 1092
  error, made in, **7**, 1089
  European Union law, **7**, 1089
  examination of goods, **7**, 1214
  lost goods, **7**, 1092
  meaning, **7**, 1089
  offences in relation to, **7**, 1098
  post-clearance recovery, **7**, 1089
repayment—
  denatured goods, **7**, 1091
  destroyed goods, **7**, 1092
  error, made in, **7**, 1089
  European Union law, **7**, 1089
  examination of goods, **7**, 1214
  lost goods, **7**, 1092
  meaning, **7**, 1089
  offences in relation to, **7**, 1098
  post-clearance recovery, **7**, 1089
  security for duty, of, **7**, 1090
  United Kingdom provisions 1090*ff*
revenue trader, *see* REVENUE TRADER
security for, repayment, **7**, 1090
stores, goods shipped as, **7**, 1094
surplus goods, destruction, **7**, 1092
suspension, inward processing procedure, **7**, 1182
United Kingdom law, **7**, 1002
  interaction with European Union law, **7**, 1003
valuation of goods—
  computed value, **7**, 1048
  deductive value, **7**, 1048
  determination, **7**, 1049
  generally, **7**, 1048
  transaction value, **7**, 1048
Customs officers
appointment, **7**, 1204
British sea-fisheries officers, as, **11**, 126*n*
facilities and appliances, power to require, **7**, 1243
obstruction, **7**, 1207
offences concerning office of, **7**, 1207
powers and duties—
  access to information, right of, **7**, 1220
  aircraft, flight prevention, **7**, 1240
  arrest, power of, **7**, 1232
  boarding, power of, **7**, 1240
  coastwise traffic, in relation to, **7**, 1241
  consumer safety, in matters of, **7**, 1216, 1218
  controls deemed necessary, power to carry out,
    7, 1212
  destruction of goods, **7**, 1217
  detention, powers of—
    goods, detention of, **7**, 1216
    means of transport, detention of, **7**, 1240
    person, detention of, **7**, 1229, 1230
  drugs, in relation to, **7**, 1230, 1231
  evidence, power to require, **7**, 1224
  examination of goods, **7**, 1214

Customs officers—*continued*
powers and duties—*continued*
  export, goods solely intended for, **7**, 1221
  forfeiture, in relation to, **7**, 1225–1227
  generally, **7**, 1204, 1211
  goods, in relation to, **7**, 1214–1217
  information, in relation to, **7**, 1218–1224
  movement of goods, power to restrict, **7**, 1240
  questioning, powers of, **7**, 1229
  recorded information, in relation to, **7**, 1223
  records, duty to keep, **7**, 1219
  removal of information, **7**, 1220
  revenue traders, in respect of, **7**, 1251–1253
  sale of goods, **7**, 1217
  samples, power to take, **7**, 1215
  search and entry, powers of, **7**, 1228
  smuggling, in relation to, **7**, 1230, 1233–1236
    taking account of goods, **7**, 1214
  travellers' possessions, in relation to, **7**, 1222
removal without consent, **7**, 1265
suspension, **7**, 1204
VAT records, inspection and verification, **7**, 1401
Customs procedure
customs authorities, representation before, **7**, 1208
customs control, processing under, **7**, 1186
customs rules, application, decisions on, **7**, 1209
declarations, *see* CUSTOMS DECLARATION
destruction of non-Community goods, **7**, 1167
documentation, *see* CUSTOMS DOCUMENTATION
economic impact, with, **7**, 1137, 1187, 1188
export procedure, *see* EXPORT PROCEDURE
free circulation, release for, **7**, 1168
free zones, *see* FREE ZONE; WAREHOUSE (free)
generally, **7**, 1128
import procedure, *see* IMPORT PROCEDURE
inward processing, *see* INWARD PROCESSING
outward processing, **7**, 1188–1191
  See also OUTWARD PROCESSING
placement under, **7**, 1136
re-exportation, **7**, 1153, 1154, 1163, 1165
records, customs officers' duty to keep, **7**, 1219
release of goods for, **7**, 1128
temporary importation, **7**, 1149, 1187
transfer between customs-approved treatments or
  uses, **7**, 1192
transit—
  EFTA countries, within, **7**, 1171
  external, **7**, 1169, 1170, 1173
  internal, **7**, 1172, 1173
warehousing, customs, *see* WAREHOUSE
Customs warehouse
See WAREHOUSE
Cut
construction or alteration, **19**, 19*n*, 24
Cy-près
approval of scheme, **24**, 111, 198
approximation and, **24**, 111
doctrine of, **24**, **7**, 110–111
variation of charitable trust, **24**, 104
Cycle
See BICYCLE
Cycle racing
regulations as to, **19**, 1284
conversion of footpath from or to, **20**, 616

D

Dairies
byelaws, **11**, 322, 492; **14**, 710
  model, **11**, 492, 493
cattle, inspection of, **2**, 449, 492; **11**, 444, 444*n*,
  445
cleansing, **11**, 493
dairyman—
  meaning, **11**, 444*n*
  registration, **11**, 494
drainage, **11**, 493
floors, **11**, 493
historical background, **11**, 441
inspection of, **11**, 489
  reports to Secretary of State, **11**, 490
leased, alterations to, **11**, 491
licensing, **14**, 526
lighting, **11**, 493
meaning, **11**, 440, 488
public health considerations, **19**, 305
refuse, removal of, **11**, 493
registration, **11**, 494
regulations, power to make, **11**, 306
ventilation, **11**, 493
wall coverings, **11**, 493
water supply, **11**, 493
See also MILK
Dairy produce
early legislation, **11**, 301, 302
regulations, power to make, **11**, 306
Dairy Produce Quota Tribunal
functions, **23**, 902
supervision of, **23**, 911*n*
Dam
building, enlarging or extending, **19**, 22
construction on *alveus*, common interest, and, **18**,
  296
construction of, **25**, 329
examination of, **11**, 25
flow of water, interference with, **25**, 328, 329
meaning, **11**, 25*n*
obstruction of passage of salmon, **11**, 19
Secretary of State's powers, **11**, 23
servitude of damhead, **18**, 295; **25**, 353
Damage, remoteness of
certainty of damage, **15**, 909
concept, generally, **15**, 257
contract—
  certainty of damage, **15**, 909
  foreseeability—
    ordinary course of events, in, **15**, 905
    special circumstances, of, **15**, 906
    standard of, **15**, 904
  generally, **15**, 902, 903
  Hadley v Baxendale, decision in, **15**, 903, 905
delict—
  certainty of damages, **15**, 909
  foreseeability—
    Re Polemis and Furness, Withy & Co Ltd,
      decision in, **15**, 907

Damage, remoteness of—*continued*
delict—*continued*
  foreseeability—*continued*
    Scots law, **15**, 908
    The Wagon Mound, decision in, **15**, 907
  generally, **15**, 902
duty of care—
  assessment of damages, **15**, 381
  extra losses arising, **15**, 390
  foreseeability, **15**, 383, 384
  further harm from another source, **15**, 387
  generally, **15**, 379
  'grand rule', **15**, 382, 384
  initial harm spreading, **15**, 386
  injury, remoteness of, **15**, 380
  intentionally inflicted harm, **15**, 391
  naturalness and directness as test, **15**, 382, 383
    application of test, **15**, 385–391
  pursuer's response—
    harm caused by, **15**, 388
    initial item of harm, to, **15**, 388
  'reasonable and probable consequence' rule, **15**,
    379
  reasonableness, **15**, 384
  relationship with, **15**, 257
  taking victim as found, **15**, 385
Damages
aggravated, **13**, 74
alternative method of performance, where
  contract permits, **15**, 914
antenatal injury, liability, **10**, 1021–1026; **22**,
  675
arbiter—
  assessment of, **2**, 448
  award of, by, **2**, 448
  liability for, **2**, 497, 498
assessment—
  currency used in, **13**, 81
  See also measure of *below*
assignation of claim, **15**, 605
assythment, **15**, 215
averred losses, **19**, 1243
breach by landlord, as remedy against, **13**, 284
breach by tenant, as remedy against, **13**, 276
breach of contract, for, interest as, **12**, 1018–1020
breach of obligations under missives, **6**, 575, 576
British Waterways Board liability, **19**, 1108, 1109,
  1124–1126
building contract, in, *see* BUILDING CONTRACT
canal undertakers' liability, **19**, 1124–1126
capital gains tax, **19**, 1309
causation, *see* CAUSATION
certainty of damage, **15**, 909
civil claim for, **4**, 38
claim for, arrestment, **8**, 274
cohabitant as claimant, personal injuries action,
  22, 676
common interest, breach of, **18**, 366
compensatory object, **13**, 73

Damages—*continued*
compromise, **15**, 607
concept of money central to, **14**, 1801
confidence, breach of, **18**, 1452, 1489
  obligation of, **17**, 44
contemptuous, **13**, 74
contractual breach, **13**, 73
  nominal damages, **13**, 74
  penalty, **13**, 75
  pre-estimated loss, **13**, 75
contributory negligence—
  defence of, **15**, 403
  generally, **15**, 929
  reduction due to, **13**, 80
copyright, infringement—
  additional damages, **18**, 1090
  generally, **18**, 1086, 1088
  innocent infringement, no damages for, **18**, 1089
  moral rights, **18**, 1140
criminal and civil liability, **15**, 214, 215
Criminal Injuries Compensation Scheme, *see* CRIMINAL INJURIES COMPENSATION SCHEME
Crown, action against, **7**, 746
currency rendered in, **15**, 940
death—
  executors, claims by, **15**, 934
  interim damages, **15**, 933
  Law Reform Committee Report, **22**, 660
  relative, of—
    death of claiming relative, **15**, 934
    derivative claims, **15**, 935
    funeral expenses, **15**, 937
    immediate family, **15**, 936
    loss of support, **15**, 937
defamation, in respect of—
  aggravation of damages, **15**, 552
  assessment, **15**, 550, 551
  generally, **15**, 550
  mitigation of damages, **15**, 553
  resulting from publication, **17**, 25
  review, **15**, 554
defective performance, where, **15**, 911
definition of damages as legal remedy, **13**, 72
delict—
  children's rights, **10**, 1021–1026
  reasonable foreseeability of damages sustained, **13**, 73
  restitutio in integrum, **13**, 73
  spouse, proceedings against, **10**, 844
  See also DELICT
detention, for, *see* SEA, CARRIAGE BY
diligence, wrongous execution of, **14**, 1507
discharge, **15**, 607
earnings, loss of, **19**, 1243
economic delict, in respect of, **15**, 584
ejection, **15**, 215
employer's right to recover—
  injury to employee, **22**, 661
  Law Reform Committee for Scotland 1963 report, **22**, 660
employment, loss of, **15**, 922
enforcement of statutory duty by, **1**, 334
Eurocontrol, against, **4**, 82

Damages—*continued*
European Community Law, **10**, 67
exemplary, **13**, 74
external public policy rule, **17**, 170
factors reducing, *see* reduction, factors causing *below*
feelings, in respect of injury to, **15**, 913
firedamp, explosion occurring after, **14**, 1656
general and special distinguished, **13**, 76
generally, **15**, 891
'grand rule', **15**, 382, 383, 384
hotelkeeper's refusal to receive traveller, following, **11**, 1753
inconvenience and trouble, in respect of, **15**, 912
injuries causing death—
  Law Reform Committee for Scotland 1960 report, **22**, 660
  parents of deceased illegitimate child, right to sue in respect of child, **22**, 660
  rights to sue for solatium and loss of support, **22**, 660
intellectual property, infringement, generally, **18**, 803
interest due *ex mora* compared with, **14**, 1828
interest on, **15**, 938
  date allowable from, **12**, 1032
  death or personal injury, awarded for, **12**, 1034
  discretion of court, **12**, 1032
  generally, **12**, 1032
  interest on interest, **12**, 1032
  Law Reform Committee for Scotland 1957 report, **22**, 653
  lump sum damages, **12**, 1033
  past or future loss, **12**, 1032
  taxation of, **12**, 1034
interference with honour and reputation, *see* HONOUR AND REPUTATION, INTERFERENCE WITH
interim, **15**, 933
  Court of Session procedure, **17**, 1394
  grant of, **17**, 1066
investor, action for damages by, **12**, 1412
lead poisoning, **25**, 508
leasing contract—
  breach of, remedy for, **14**, 1063
  liquidate damages clauses, **14**, 1068
  termination of, **14**, 1065, 1066, 1067
liquidated, **15**, 941
  clause, *see* CONTRACT
loss of earnings, **19**, 1243
loss must be caused by act or omission of defending party, **13**, 79
maritime causes, in, **1**, 411, 415
measure of, **13**, 78
  contract, in—
    alternative method of performance, where contract permits, **15**, 914
    feelings, in respect of injury to, **15**, 913
    nominal damages, **15**, 912
    pecuniary losses—
      generally, **15**, 910
      pre-contractual expenditure, **15**, 911
      types, **15**, 911
    personal injury, in respect of, **15**, 913

Damages—*continued*
measure of—*continued*
  contract, in—*continued*
    provisional damages, **15**, 932
    reputation, in respect of injury to, **15**, 913
  delict, in—
    destruction of property, **15**, 915
    misrepresentation, where, **15**, 915
    pecuniary loss, **15**, 916
    personal injury—
      actuarial tables, calculation of loss by, **15**, 917
      benefit, loss, **15**, 918
      earnings, loss, **15**, 918
      expenses, **15**, 919
      generally, **15**, 915, 916
      pecuniary loss, **15**, 916
      relative—
        services rendered by, **15**, 920, 920*n*
        services rendered to, **15**, 921
    property and economic interests, **15**, 915
    provisional damages, **15**, 932
    solatium—
      employment, loss of, **15**, 922
      generally, **15**, 922
      loss of amenity, **15**, 924
      pursuer's awareness, relevance, **15**, 923
    wrongful interference with economic interests, where, **15**, 915
  difficulty in, **15**, 909
medical costs, **19**, 1243
mines—
  fall into working place, **14**, 1633
  injury in, **14**, 1619
  redundancy payments, effect of, **14**, 1679
  subsidence damage, for, **14**, 1694
  support, loss of, **14**, 1686
mining, fall into working place, **14**, 1633
misstatement, economic loss caused by, **15**, 555, 556
mitigation—
  contract, **15**, 925, 927
  delict, **15**, 925
  generally, **15**, 925
  limitations on principle, **15**, 926
  onus of proof, **15**, 925
  steps taken in which avoid loss, **15**, 928
nominal, **13**, 74; **15**, 912
non-pecuniary loss, **13**, 73
nuisance, for, **14**, 2151, 2153, 2155; **19**, 1245
  economic loss, **14**, 2153
  intangible harm, assessment in case of, **14**, 2151
  nominal, **14**, 2154
  past, **14**, 2150
  personal injury, **14**, 2080, 2152
  prospective, **14**, 2150
obligation to supply property, where breach, **15**, 911
ordinary action, remedy in, **4**, 963
passing off, intellectual property, **18**, 1400
patent, infringement, **18**, 858, 867, 868, 870
pecuniary loss, **13**, 73
personal injury—
  parties who may claim, **22**, 676

Damages—*continued*
personal injury—*continued*
  in respect of—
    contract, **15**, 913
    death, transmission of claim on, **15**, 934
    delict, **15**, 915–921
    interim damages, **15**, 933
    provisional damages, **15**, 932
  Scottish Law Commission report, **22**, 676
plant breeders' rights, infringement, **18**, 915
power to award, **1**, 333
private international law, characterisation of, **17**, 360
procedural reforms, action for, **22**, 676
provisional, **13**, 82; **15**, 932
public authorities, against, European Community law, **10**, 88
pupils and minors, for, appointment of judicial factor, **24**, 279
purpose, **15**, 892, 910, 915
pursuer cannot recover more than he has suffered, **15**, 928
railways, offences committed on, **19**, 1065
real burden, breach of, **18**, 423
recovery of possession, action for, **18**, 170
reduction, factors causing—
  contributory negligence, **15**, 929
  mitigation, principle of—
    contract, factors peculiar to, **15**, 927
    duty to mitigate loss, **15**, 925
    generally, **15**, 925
    limitations on, **15**, 926
    onus of proof, **15**, 925
    steps taken which avoid loss, **15**, 928
  pension or benefit payable, **15**, 930
  personal injuries, awards in respect of, **15**, 930
  recoupment of benefits, **15**, 931
  remuneration or earnings, **15**, 930
registered industrial design, infringement, **18**, 1209
reparation, as, **15**, 550
reputation, in respect of injury to, **15**, 913
restoration, principle of, **15**, 892, 910, 915
rights in performance, infringement, **18**, 1438
rights in respect of, **11**, 1073
Roman law—
  actio injuriarum, **15**, 214
  actio legis aquiliae, **15**, 214
Scottish practice, **19**, 1243
sea fisheries offence, **4**, 38
services, loss of, admissibility of claims, **22**, 676
servitude right, breach of, **18**, 482
settlement, **15**, 607
shareholder, infringement of personal right of, **4**, 468
sheriff officer, liability of, **14**, 1511
single action, recovery in, **13**, 77
small, **13**, 74
social security bnefits, recoupment, **15**, 930
solatium, **19**, 1243
  death, transmission on, **15**, 934
  delict, where, **15**, 922–924
special, **13**, 76
sporting disasters, **19**, 1244

Damages—*continued*
spuilzie, **15**, 215
substitutory redress, as, **15**, 891
support, right to, breach of, **18**, 262
taxation, **15**, 939
    Law Reform Committee for Scotland 1959
        report, **22**, 656
tenant's right to sue third party, **13**, 290
trading interests, protection of, **4**, 84
transfer of claim—
    bankruptcy, on, **15**, 606
    death, on, **15**, 605
    liquidation, on, **15**, 606
unlawful eviction, in respect of, **13**, 704–707
unregistered design right, infringement, **18**, 1234
vaccine damage, *see* VACCINATION AND
        IMMUNISATION
wrongful dismissal, for—
    benefits arising on breach, effect of, **9**, 200
    generally, **9**, 196
    loss, mitigation of, **9**, 198
    measure of, **9**, 197
    taxation, incidence of, **9**, 199
wrongous inhibition, for, **8**, 188
Damnum absque injuria
aemulatio vicini remedy in case of, **14**, 2034
Damnum fatale
carrier not liable for, **21**, 603
loss attributable to, carriage, **3**, 608
meaning, **21**, 548
See also ACT OF GOD
Damnum injuria datum
fault, and, **15**, 252
Damp
tolerable standard, **11**, 1979
Danger
creation of, duty derived from, **7**, 43
highway, on, **14**, 2165
mines and quarries—
    fall, duty to avoid, **14**, 1702
    hours of work, **14**, 1668
    official, duty to report to, **14**, 1657
    overhang, duty to avoid, **14**, 1702
    removal of, **14**, 1657
    workman, withdrawal of, **14**, 1657, 1707
nature of operation, inherent in, **14**, 2138
trees felled to prevent, **11**, 617
water, from, **25**, 362
Dangerous agencies escaping from land
Law Reform Committee for Scotland 1964
    report, **22**, 663
Dangerous animals
See ANIMAL; WILD ANIMALS
Dangerous building
See BUILDING AND BUILDING CONTROLS
Dangerous controlled waste
See WASTE
Dangerous cycling
offence of, **20**, 413
warning or notice of intended prosecution, **20**, 446
Dangerous driving
causing death by, **20**, 412
    disqualification following conviction, **20**, 412,
        413, 453

Dangerous driving—*continued*
causing death by—*continued*
    licence, endorsement of, **20**, 412, 413
    obligatory disqualification following conviction,
        20, 453
meaning, **20**, 412
motoring event, participation in, **20**, 413
offence of, to replace reckless driving, **7**, 82*n*; **20**,
    412, 413
penalties for, **20**, 413
prosecution, warning or notice of intended, **20**, 446
Dangerous goods
control of, **6**, 39, 41, 43, 44, 51, 58, 61
imported, **6**, 58
sea, carriage by, *see* SEA, CARRIAGE BY
suspension notices, **6**, 56
See also HAZARDOUS SUBSTANCES; INFLAMMABLE
        SUBSTANCES; NOXIOUS SUBSTANCES
Dangerous occurrence
health and safety at work regulations—
    inspection by safety representative following, **9**,
        474
    reporting of, **9**, 534
Dangerous performance
child participating in, **3**, 1249
Dangerous substance
reckless supply, **7**, 13, 30, 85
    indirect causal route, **7**, 48
See also DANGEROUS GOODS; HAZARDOUS
        SUBSTANCES; INFLAMMABLE SUBSTANCES;
        NOXIOUS SUBSTANCES
Darien Company, 19, 211, 217
Dark smoke
See SMOKE
Data processing system
patent not grantable in respect of, **18**, 825
Data protection
civil liability, generally, **18**, 1522
codes of practice—
    encouragement of development, **18**, 1523, 1544
    nature, **18**, 1544
    voluntary status, **18**, 1544
computer, meaning, **18**, 1502*n*
computer bureau—
    meaning, **18**, 1504
    occasional basis, conduct of activities on, **18**,
        1504
    registration, **18**, 1509
        amendment, **18**, 1510
        application, **18**, 1510
        fee, **18**, 1510
        information to be supplied, **18**, 1510
        renewal, **18**, 1510
        See also data protection register *below*
controls, generally, **18**, 1501
Convention for the Protection of Individuals with
        regard to the Automated Processing of
        Personal Data 1981 ..., **18**, 1501
credit reference agency, databank information,
        limitation on access to, **18**, 1535
crime, prevention or detection of—
    access to information principle, exception, **18**,
        1530
    non-disclosure principle, exception, **18**, 1526

Data protection—_continued_
criminal offences in relation to—
  corporate body, by, **18**, 1552
  generally, **18**, 1522, 1549–1553
  government department, by, **18**, 1553
  intentional obstruction of execution of search
    warrant, **18**, 1550
  penalties, **18**, 1549, 1551
  summary prosecution, **18**, 1549, 1550
Data Protection Act—
  application, **18**, 1502
  background to, **18**, 1501
  computer bureau, definition, **18**, 1504
  data protection principles, **18**, 1521
  data subjects, concept, **18**, 1505
  data users, definition, **18**, 1503
  principles, **18**, 1523
  scope, **18**, 1502–1505
data protection register—
  amendment of register entry, wilful or reckless
    provision of false or misleading
    information, **18**, 1550, 1553
  application for registration, **18**, 1510
    multiple, **18**, 1511
    processing, **18**, 1512
    single, **18**, 1511
  computer bureaux, **18**, 1510
  data users, **18**, 1510
  de-registration notice, **18**, 1522
  enforcement notice, **18**, 1522
    failure to comply with provisions, **18**, 1551
  failure to register, **18**, 1551
  fee for entry copies, **18**, 1513
  generally, **18**, 1513
  procedure, **18**, 1510
  registration fee, **18**, 1510
  removal of entries, Registrar's power to order,
    18, 1545
  renewal of registration, **18**, 1510
  requirement to register, **18**, 1509
    exemptions—
      accounting data, **18**, 1520
      domestic purposes, data held for, **18**, 1516,
        1517
      generally, **18**, 1514
      incorporated members' club, data held for,
        18, 1518
      limited purposes, data held for, **18**, 1516
      mailing lists, **18**, 1519
      national security, **18**, 1515
      payroll and accounts, **18**, 1520
  small-scale data users, **18**, 1510
  wilful or reckless failure to conform with scope
    of entry, **18**, 1551
  wilful or reckless provision of false or
    misleading information, **18**, 1550, 1553
Data Protection Registrar—
  appeal from, **18**, 1507, 1542
  appointment, **18**, 1506
  complaints to, **18**, 1556
  compliance, power to order, **18**, 1545
  data protection register, _see_ data protection
    register _above_
  de-registration notice, **18**, 1542, 1545, 1548

Data protection—_continued_
Data Protection Registrar—_continued_
  duties, **18**, 1507
  enforcement notice, **18**, 1542, 1545, 1546
  establishment, **18**, 1506
  functions, **18**, 1506
  powers, **18**, 1522, 1545–1548
    investigatory, **18**, 1554, 1555
  public corporation as, **19**, 209
  removal of entries from register, power to
    order, **18**, 1545
  staff, **18**, 1506, 1506n
  transfer prohibition notice, **18**, 1545, 1547
Data Protection Tribunal—
  appeal to, **18**, 1507, 1542
  case law, **18**, 1543
  constitution, **18**, 1507
  establishment, **18**, 1506
  jurisdiction, **18**, 1507
  supervision of, **23**, 911n
data subject—
  civil action brought by, **18**, 1522
  databank information on, use detrimental to,
    18, 1501
  identifiable, **18**, 1502
  meaning, **18**, 1505
  personal data, _see_ personal data _below_
  protection, **18**, 1501
data user—
  meaning, **18**, 1503
  registration—
    amendment, **18**, 1510
    application—
      generally, **18**, 1510
      multiple, **18**, 1511
      processing, **18**, 1512
      single, **18**, 1511
      small-scale users, **18**, 1510
    fee, **18**, 1510
    information to be supplied, **18**, 1510
    procedure, **18**, 1510
    renewal, **18**, 1510
    requirement for, **18**, 1509
    See also data protection register _above_
  requirement to comply with data protection
    principles, **18**, 1521
  small-scale, **18**, 1510
de-registration notice, **18**, 1522, 1542, 1545, 1548
enforcement notice, **18**, 1522, 1542, 1545, 1546
  failure to comply with provisions, **18**, 1551
European Community legislation, **18**, 1611
examination results, **18**, 1528
financial services, regulation, limitation on access
  to data held in connection with, **18**, 1534
health of data subject, information as to physical
  or mental, limitation on access to, **18**, 1531
human embryos, information on, limitation on
  access to, **18**, 1541
infertility treatment, information on, limitation
  on access to, **18**, 1541
information held in databank—
  access—
    action for, **18**, 1557

Data protection—*continued*
information held in databank—*continued*
  compensation—
    disclosure of data, for, **18**, 1561
    generally, **18**, 1559
    inaccuracy of data, for, **18**, 1560
    loss of data, for, **18**, 1561
  correction, **18**, 1501
  data to be held for specified and lawful
    purpose, **18**, 1521, 1524
  disclosure in manner incompatible with purpose
    for which held, **18**, 1521, 1524, 1525, 1526
    exceptions to principle, **18**, 1526
  fairly and lawfully, must be obtained and
    processed, **18**, 1521, 1524
  false or misleading, rectification or erasure, **18**,
    1558
  historical purposes, used for, **18**, 1524
  international access, **18**, 1501
  personal data, *see* personal data *below*
  research purposes, used for, **18**, 1524
  security precautions, **18**, 1521, 1524
  specified and lawful purpose, must be held for,
    18, 1521, 1524
  statistical purposes, use for, **18**, 1524
  subject's rights to information and access—
    definition of subject access, **18**, 1527
    exceptions, **18**, 1529–1541
    generally, **18**, 1521, 1524, 1527
      procedures for access, **18**, 1528
    Order of Secretary of State as to, **18**, 1537
    replacement data, **18**, 1538
    self-incrimination, **18**, 1540
    statistical data, **18**, 1539
    time limit for access, **18**, 1528
  use detrimental to subject's interests, where,
    18, 1501
  verification, **18**, 1501
intellectual property, in relation to, **18**, 801
international law, **18**, 1501
judicial appointments, data held in connection
  with, limitation on access to, **18**, 1532
lawyer-client confidentiality, **18**, 1533
legislation, generally, **18**, 1501
national security, data held for purpose of
  safeguarding, **18**, 1515
offender, apprehension or prosecution of—
  access to information principle, exception, **18**,
    1530
  non-disclosure principle, exception, **18**, 1526
ovum donor, information on, limitation on access
  to, **18**, 1541
personal data—
  accurate, must be, **18**, 1521, 1524
  adequate, must be, **18**, 1521
  disclosure in manner incompatible with
    purpose for which held, **18**, 1521, 1524,
    1525, 1526
    exceptions to principle, **18**, 1526
  duration of storage, **18**, 1521
  excessive to purposes for which held, must not
    be, **18**, 1521

Data protection—*continued*
personal data—*continued*
  health of data subject, information as to
    physical or mental, limitation on access to,
    18, 1531
  information to be obtained and processed fairly
    and lawfully, **18**, 1521, 1524
  knowing or reckless disclosure other than with
    data user's instructions, **18**, 1551
  lawyer-client confidentiality, **18**, 1533
  meaning, **18**, 1502
  process—
    data must be processed, **18**, 1502
    meaning of processed, **18**, 1502
    word processing, exclusion, **18**, 1502
  relevant, must be, **18**, 1521
  security precautions, **18**, 1521, 1524
  Social Work Order, limitation of access to
    information on grounds of, **18**, 1531
  specified and lawful purpose, must be held for,
    18, 1521, 1524
  subject's rights to information and access—
    definition of subject access, **18**, 1527
    exceptions, **18**, 1529–1541
    generally, **18**, 1521, 1524, 1527
    Order of Secretary of State as to, **18**, 1537
    procedures for access, **18**, 1528
    replacement data, **18**, 1438
    self-incrimination, **18**, 1540
    statistical data, **18**, 1539
    time limit for access, **18**, 1528
  trivial information, **18**, 1502
police records, **16**, 1803
principles—
  compliance, Registrar's power to order, **18**,
    1545
  failure to comply with, **18**, 1522
  generally, **18**, 1521, 1524
  interpretation, **18**, 1523
    statutory guidance, **18**, 1524
  Registrar's duty to promote observance, **18**,
    1554
privacy, right to, **18**, 1501
public, information available to, limitation on
  rights of access, **18**, 1536
public records, **19**, 847, 875
replacement data, restriction on access to, **18**,
  1538
search warrant—
  intentional obstruction of execution, **18**, 1550
  Registrar's power to apply for, **18**, 1555
self-incrimination, data user not obliged to
  comply with access request where in danger
  of, **18**, 1540
sheriff court jurisdiction, **6**, 1128
Social Work Order, limitation on access to
  information on grounds of, **18**, 1531
sperm donor, information on, limitation on access
  to, **18**, 1541
statistical data, restriction on access to, **18**, 1539
tax or duty, collection or assesment of—
  access to information principle, exception, **18**,
    1530
  non-disclosure principle, exception, **18**, 1526

Data protection—*continued*
transfer prohibition notice, **18**, 1545
unauthorised disclosure of information, **16**, 1803
word processing, questions arising, **18**, 1502
Data Protection Registrar
See DATA PROTECTION
Data Protection Tribunal
See DATA PROTECTION
Data user
See DATA PROTECTION
Database
American Legal Realism, application of
  precedent, **22**, 263
computerised law reporting, effect on application
  of precedent, **22**, 263
copyright, **18**, 953, 993
House of Lords, views on changing attitudes to
  precedent caused by, **22**, 263
Lexis inclusion of Scottish material, **22**, 263
Date
appropriate date, meaning, **4**, 182
'at a date', **22**, 822
'at which date', **22**, 822
'beginning with the date of', **22**, 822
bills of exchange, in relation to, **4**, 112
clear days, meaning, **22**, 822, 823, 826
'commencing from' a specified date, **22**, 826
fixing and valuing interests, *see* VALUATION
'from' a specified date, **22**, 826
meaning, **22**, 822
'time' distinguished, **22**, 822
valuation for rating, of, **24**, 512, 513
will, of, *see* WILL
See also DAY
Daughter
ancestral land, share in, **25**, 608
class gift, **25**, 843
corporeal items bequeathed to, **25**, 825
heritable succession, **25**, 678
Daughter-in-law
immediate family, as, **15**, 601
Dawn raid
takeover bid, steps before, **4**, 544
Day
'after' a specified day, **22**, 826
'at least (so many) days', **22**, 823
'by' a specified day, **22**, 826
clear days, meaning, **22**, 822, 823, 826
common law, at, **22**, 815
dies ad quem, definition, **22**, 828, 829
dies a quo, definition, **22**, 828, 829
dies inceptus pro completo habetur, **22**, 828
division, origin, **22**, 801
duration, determination, **22**, 801, 815
European Convention on the Calculation of
  Time-Limits—
  dies ad quem, **22**, 828, 829
  dies a quo, **22**, 828, 829
first, exclusion/inclusion, computation of period,
  22, 819–822
intercalation, pattern to construct coherent
  calendar, **22**, 802, 803
intervening, disregarded calculating periods
  numbered in days, **22**, 815

Day—*continued*
last—
  exclusion/inclusion, computation of period, **22**,
    819–823, 825
  part *dies inceptus* pro completo habetur, **22**, 819,
    822, 823
legislation coming into force on particular day,
  time of commencement, **22**, 815
less than a day, **22**, 816, 822
natural day, **22**, 815
'not earlier than' a specified number of days, **22**,
  826
'not exceeding 28 days from date of ...', **22**, 822
'not less than (so many) clear days', **22**, 822, 823
'not less than' a specified number of days, **22**, 826
'on' a specified day, **22**, 826
Scotland, common law, **22**, 815
solar—
  accurate measurement, **22**, 801
  incompatibility with solar day/tropical year, **22**,
    801, 802
statutory provisions, **22**, 815
Day facilities
central government expenditure, **22**, 16
child, referral from children's panel, **22**, 21
elderly persons, **22**, 28
handicapped persons, **22**, 24, 31
local authority duty to provide, **22**, 13, 16, 21, 24,
  28
mentally handicapped persons, **22**, 24, 31
promotion of social welfare, **22**, 13
registration, **14**, 521
regulations by Secretary of State, **22**, 16
standard, **22**, 16
voluntary organisations—
  local authority assistance to, **22**, 10
  local authority duty, delegation to, **22**, 16, 28
young child, for, regulation, **3**, 1259
Daylight saving
historical background, **22**, 810
legislation, **22**, 810
Dazzling device
wild birds or animals taken or killed with, **11**,
  880, 884
De minimis non curat lex
principle of, **7**, 27
De minimus non curat praetor
meaning, **12**, 1170
***De recenti* statements**
hearsay evidence, as, **10**, 707
Deacon/deaconess
Church of Scotland—
  discipline, **3**, 1512
  election, **3**, 1516
  presbytery, membership, **3**, 1519
  supervision, **3**, 1534
commissioners to General Assembly, **3**, 1543
Scottish Episcopal Church—
  generally, **3**, 1614
Deacons' court
Church of Scotland, **3**, 1516
Dead body
anatomical examination, *see* ANATOMICAL
  EXAMINATION

Dead body—*continued*
articles buried with, unlawful removal, **3**, 505
cardiac pacemaker or other implant, containing, **3**, 567
conveyance—
    burial ground, to, **3**, 526
    infectious body, **3**, 511
    mortuary, to, **3**, 526
decomposed, removal, **3**, 504
disinterment—
    application for authority, **3**, 535
    common law, **3**, 534
    cremation following, **3**, 564
    crime involved or suspected, where, **3**, 537
    examples of cases where authority given, **3**, 536
    petition for authority, **3**, 535
disposal of—
    directions of deceased, **3**, 506
    executor's entitlement to arrange, **3**, 503, 506
    legal obligations, **3**, 503
    local authority duty, **3**, 512
        recovery of costs from deceased's estate, **3**, 512
    methods—
        choice, **3**, 506
        generally, **3**, 501, 502*n*
    next of kin's entitlement to arrange, **3**, 503, 506
    relative's entitlement to arrange, **3**, 503
    responsibility for, **3**, 503
    statutory restrictions, generally, **3**, 502
embalmed—
    burial at sea not authorised, **3**, 538
    theft, **3**, 504
exhumed, theft, **3**, 504
human organ transplant, offences in relation to, **3**, 509
infectious disease, death by—
    disposal, **19**, 463
    removal, **19**, 461
    retention, **19**, 460
    transport of, **19**, 462
    See also DISEASE
interred, removal, **3**, 504
medical education, use for, **3**, 508
part of, removal, **3**, 508
possession, person lawfully in—
    anatomical examination, authorisation, **3**, 507
    medical purposes, authorisation of use for, **3**, 507
    research purposes, authorisation of use for, **3**, 507
    therapeutic purposes, authorisation of use for, **3**, 507
preserved, unlawful removal, **3**, 504
property in, whether right of, **3**, 504
removal, unlawful, **3**, 504
    after interrment, **3**, 504
    decomposed body, **3**, 504
    exhumed body, **3**, 504
    preserved body, **3**, 504
    violating sepulchres, offence of, **3**, 504
research purposes, use for, **3**, 508
theft, **3**, 504
therapeutic purposes, use for, **3**, 508

Deaf or deaf mute witness
generally, **10**, 533
interpretation for, **10**, 551
Deafness
disability living allowance, **21**, 934, 936
occupational—
    definition, **21**, 993
    disablement benefit, **9**, 1291, **21**, 995
    prescibed diseases regulations, **21**, 992
    prescribed occupations, **21**, 992, 993, 994
    social security benefit for, **9**, 1291
    time limit for claims, **21**, 996
Dealer, registered excise
See REGISTERED EXCISE DEALER AND SHIPPER (REDS)
Dealing
insider, *see* INSIDER DEALING
meaning, **12**, 1510
publication, ahead of, **12**, 1384
Dean of Guild
architectural nuisance, **14**, 2014
buildings authority, as, **3**, 201
jurisdiction and functions, **3**, 201
Model Building Byelaws, **3**, 201
neighbourhood, **14**, 2011
procurator fiscal, powers of, **14**, 2161
public police, **14**, 2011
reparation action, jurisdiction over, **14**, 2017
Dean of the Chapel Royal
designation, **3**, 1551
generally, **3**, 1551
office of, **7**, 837, 838
Dean of the Order of the Thistle
designation, **3**, 1551
generally, **3**, 1551
office of, **7**, 837
Death
accidental, fatal accident inquiry, **3**, 513
administrator, of, **4**, 641
agricultural tenant, of, **19**, 1564–1567
aircraft, on, **2**, 1064
ascertainment of, **11**, 1039
beneficiary deemed to acquire on, **25**, 996
British Railways Board liability, **19**, 1013
capital gains tax, *see* CAPITAL GAINS TAX
careless driving under influence of drink or drugs, caused by, **20**, 416, 453
cautioner, of, **14**, 1502
certificate, *see* DEATH CERTIFICATE *and* registration *below*
certification, **3**, 514
company's conviction for offence involving, **4**, 318
context of passing property, *see* property passing on *below*
contract, party of, **15**, 817, 818
copyright rights, transmission on, **18**, 1027
culpable homicide, charge of, **20**, 412, 453
damages in respect of—
    executors, claims by, **15**, 934
    family member or relative, of—
        death of claiming relative, **15**, 934
        deceased's claim, **15**, 599
        derivative claims, **15**, 935
        funeral expenses, **15**, 937

Death—*continued*
damages in respect of—*continued*
  family member or relative, of—*continued*
    generally, **15**, 598
    immediate family, **15**, 601, 936
    loss of support, **15**, 937
    relatives dependent claim, **15**, 598, 599, 600
    specified relatives, **15**, 602
  interest on, **12**, 1034
  interim damages, **15**, 933
dangerous driving, causing by, **20**, 412, 453
date of—
  actual, **25**, 620
  legal rights on property owned at—
    inter vivos trust, reversionary right in, **25**, 784
    valuation—
      actual realised, **25**, 794
      capital gains tax, **25**, 797
      generally, **25**, 793
      income tax, **25**, 796
      interest, **25**, 795, 796
  presumed, **25**, 620
deathbed expenses, **24**, 193
debtor, of, **5**, 887
debts due to deceased, **25**, 1064
declarator of, **6**, 1062; **10**, 819, 833, 834; **13**, 7; **25**, 651, 652
delict, caused by, title to sue, **15**, 220, 232
devolution on, *see* SUCCESSION
discrimination, provisions in relation to, **9**, 349
domicile at, *see lex ultimi domicilii*
exclusion from scope of Judgments Convention, **8**, 432
fact of, rules for establishing, **25**, 620
factors determining, **7**, 257
failure to protect others from, **7**, 40
fatal accident inquiries, *see* FATAL ACCIDENT INQUIRY
friendly society payments on, **12**, 686, 723, 724
furth of Scotland, cremation, **3**, 562
guardian, of, **14**, 1445
hirer, of, **5**, 887
homicide, *see* HOMICIDE
hotelkeeper's liability, **11**, 1738
industrial and provident society member, of, **12**, 627, 628
infectious disease, from, **19**, 460–463, 465, 466
inheritance tax, *see* INHERITANCE TAX
institution, in, **19**, 1459
journey, during, **19**, 1457
judge, of, **17**, 741
landlord's interest, transfer on, **13**, 348, 350
licensee, of, **5**, 950
liferent, termination on, **13**, 1647, 1648, 1654*n*, 1655
meaning, **7**, 257; **25**, 644
nomination, *see* NOMINATION
nuisance, cause of action in, **14**, 2044
obligation, transmission on, **11**, 1030
offeree or offeror, of, effect, **15**, 616, 651
open market valuation on, **25**, 52
parent, of, status at time of, **14**, 1909
partner, of, joint tenancy, **13**, 192
partnership tenancies, **19**, 1569, 1570

Death—*continued*
passing of property on, background to, **25**, 604
  See also property passing on *below*
patent holder, of, **18**, 811
penalty, *see* CAPITAL PUNISHMENT
precognition as to, **19**, 1430
presumption of, **6**, 759; **19**, 1460; **22**, 669; **25**, 647
  Court of Session jurisdiction, **4**, 17
  effect of decree of court furth of Scotland, **8**, 542
  sheriff court jurisdiction, **4**, 17
procurator fiscal, investigated by, **19**, 1458
promisor or promisee, of, **15**, 616
proof of—
  background to legislation, **25**, 649
  common law, presumption of death under, **25**, 647
  life expectancy, **25**, 648
  method of proving, **25**, 645
  missing person—
    background to legislation, **25**, 649
    common law, presumption under, **25**, 647
    declarator of death—
      jurisdiction, **25**, 652
      seven-year rule, **25**, 651
    generally, **25**, 646
    life expectancy, **25**, 648
    reappearance of—
      information, disclosure of, **25**, 654
      property rights order, **25**, 653
      variation order, **25**, 653
    seven-year rule, **25**, 651
    statutory provisions, **25**, 650
  need to prove, **25**, 643
  statutory provisions, **25**, 650
property passing on—
  competent beneficiaries, **25**, 621
  distribution, **25**, 605
  family property, **25**, 608
  future property, **25**, 622
  generally, **25**, 604, 606, 619
  identification, **25**, 605
  presumptions, **25**, 620
  reassembly of estates—
    English law, **25**, 611
    French law, **25**, 609
    German law, **25**, 610
  species of property, distinction of, **25**, 607
  transmission of—
    '1964 method', **6**, 611
    clare constat, writ of, **6**, 605
    disposition, **6**, 610
    executor's title, completion of, **6**, 608
    general service, decree of, **6**, 607
    generally, **6**, 603
    heirs title of heritage, completion of, **6**, 604
    notice of title, **6**, 613
    owners domiciled outwith Scotland, **6**, 612
    special service, decree of, **6**, 606
    trustees, conveyance to, **6**, 609
qualifying sale of shares, **25**, 56
reckless driving, causing by, **20**, 412, 453
registration of—
  certificate—
    causes of death, of, **19**, 1454

Death—*continued*
registration of—*continued*
  certificate—*continued*
    failure to deliver, **19**, 1474
    notice of burial, **19**, 1455
    registration of death, of, **19**, 1455
  district registrar, **19**, 1406
    attendance at registration offices, **19**, 1408
    returns, **19**, 1431
    salary, allowances and compensation, **19**, 1407
  districts and authorities, **19**, 1405
  documentary evidence, register as, **10**, 591
  extracts—
    authentication, **19**, 1420
    misuse of, **19**, 1474
  fees, collection and accounting of, **14**, 588; **19**, 1410
  forged documents, **19**, 1472
  General Register Office, **19**, 1402, 1404
  generally, **3**, 514; **19**, 305, 809, 811, 828, 842
  historical background, **19**, 1401, 1402
  hours fixed for, **19**, 1408
  information—
    district registrar's powers to request, **19**, 1451
    duty to give, **19**, 1452
    failure to give, **19**, 1474
  institution, death in, **19**, 1459
  journey, death during course of, **19**, 1457
  late registration, **19**, 1453
  local authority duty, **14**, 588
  local organisation, **19**, 1405–1410
  offences, **19**, 1477
    certificate, failure to deliver, **19**, 1474
    destruction of entry, **19**, 1473
    duplication of entry, **19**, 1473
    false information, **19**, 1472
    forged documents, **19**, 1472
    information, failure to give, **19**, 1474
    misuse of extract certificate, **19**, 1474
    registers, failure to deliver up, **19**, 1471
  organisation, **19**, 1401–1410
  parish registers, **19**, 1401
  presumed deaths, **19**, 1460
  procedure, **19**, 1450–1455
  procurator fiscal, investigation by, **19**, 1458
  records, safe custody of, **19**, 1408
    area repositories, **19**, 1409
  registers, **19**, 1456
    authentication of extracts, **19**, 1420
    correction of, **19**, 1414, 1421, 1422–1424
      change of name or status, **19**, 1425–1430
      clerical errors, **19**, 1423
    destroyed, **19**, 1402*n*, 1417
    destruction of entry, **19**, 1473
    duplication, **19**, 1415
      of entry, **19**, 1473
    examination, **19**, 1416
    failure to deliver up, **19**, 1471
    illegible, **19**, 1402*n*, 1417
    indexes of, **19**, 1418, 1419
    information required from, **19**, 1431, 1432
    information to be entered, **19**, 1456
    lost, **19**, 1402*n*, 1417

Death—*continued*
registration of—*continued*
  registers—*continued*
    mutilated, **19**, 1402*n*, 1417
    parochial, **19**, 1411–1413
    provision, **19**, 1415
    Registrar General, **19**, 1402, 1403
    replacement, **19**, 1417
    reproductions of, **19**, 1416
    statutory control, **19**, 1414
  registration—
    authority, **14**, 32
    offices, **19**, 1408
  salary, allowances and compensation for officers, **19**, 1407
  sheriff court jurisdiction, **6**, 1127; **19**, 1402
  ship, death on board, **21**, 226
retailer, of, **9**, 773
right of fee, termination on, **13**, 1663
seven years before, transfers within, **25**, 1000
sheriff depute, of, effect on sheriff substitute, **17**, 515
simultaneous, proof of, **25**, 658
spouse, of, rights on, **25**, 602
sudden, **17**, 960
  fatal accident inquiry, **3**, 513
  suspicious or unexplained, **13**, 1435
survivorship, destination of assets, **19**, 1577
suspicious, fatal accident inquiry, **3**, 513
tax consequences of, **19**, 1616; **25**, 962
tenant, of, *delectus personae*, doctrine of, **13**, 355
testator, of, beneficiary must be known and in existence at or prior to, **25**, 934
transfer of ownership on, **18**, 613, 663
  involuntary transfer, as, **18**, 597
transmission of—
  delictual claim on, **15**, 605
  property on, *see* property passing on *above*
  records, **19**, 853
trustee, of, **24**, 162
VAT registered person, of, **7**, 1344
whole life policy, **12**, 804
See also DECEASED

Death certificate
causes of death, of, **19**, 1454
cremation, requirement to produce certificate before, **3**, 556
failure to deliver, **19**, 1474
generally, **3**, 514; **25**, 645
notice of burial, **19**, 1455
proof of death, as, **25**, 645
registration of death, of, **19**, 1455

Debenture
bond—
  repayment, notarial functions, **13**, 1223
convertible, **4**, 438
insider dealing, *see* INSIDER DEALING
investment, as, **12**, 1308
loan constituted by, **13**, 1713
meaning, **4**, 438
savings for—
  dwelling house included in subject, heritable security in relation to, **20**, 255

Debenture—*continued*
savings for—*continued*
  standard security provisions, debenture conditions unaffected by, **20**, 254
security, as, **5**, 908
Debenture holder
director's dealings in, **4**, 425
scheme of arrangement, petition for, **4**, 985
trustee for, **24**, 11
Debenture stock
investment, as, **12**, 1308
Debit withdrawal card
functions, **4**, 269
Debitor non praesumitur donare
generally, **8**, 624
Debitum fundi
adjudication on—
  advantage over ordinary adjudication, **8**, 374
  company administration, during, **8**, 375
  competence, **8**, 373
  enforcement of secured debts, **8**, 101
  generally, **8**, 216
  ground annual, adjudication for, **8**, 376
  liquidation, and, **8**, 375
  nature of, **8**, 372
  ordinary adjudication, ranking, **8**, 375
  poinding of the ground, following, **8**, 373
  procedure, **8**, 373
  ranking, **8**, 374, 375
  sequestration, and, **8**, 375
  subjects, **8**, 374
  title, completion of, **8**, 373
holder of, maills and duties, action of, **8**, 394
Debt
amount, calculation of, **2**, 1330
arrestment, **14**, 1812
assignation, **4**, 102; **6**, 595
cautionary obligation, *see* CAUTIONARY OBLIGATION
cessio for civil debt, **22**, 645
collection, **14**, 1512
company member's liability for, **4**, 319
compensation—
  concursus debiti et crediti, **15**, 879
  generally, **15**, 865, 877
  liquid debts, **15**, 878
composition, under, **2**, 1410
concept of money central to, **14**, 1804
consigned, arrestment, **8**, 268
constituted, arrestment, **8**, 276
contingent, **4**, 828
  valuation, **2**, 1409
contractual—
  creditor's duty, generally, **15**, 867
  debtor's duty, generally, **15**, 867
  'on demand', debts payable on, **15**, 867
  payment—
    acceptilation, **15**, 865, 873
    agent, to, **15**, 869
    apocha trium annorum, **15**, 872
    ascription, **15**, 868
    burden of proof, **15**, 872
    compensation, **15**, 865, 877–879
    confusion, **15**, 865, 876
    delegation, **15**, 865, 875

Debt—*continued*
contractual—*continued*
  payment—*continued*
    discharge—
      gratuitous, **15**, 873
      several debts, where, **15**, 873
      fitted accounts, **15**, 873
      frustration, **15**, 865, 880–889
      lesser sum sent 'in full and final settlement', **15**, 870
      method, **15**, 871
      novation, **15**, 865, 874
      part, **15**, 870
      prescription, **15**, 865, 890
      termly, *apocha trium annorum*, **15**, 872
      to whom made, **15**, 869
contributory, due from, **4**, 780
Crown, poinding in respect of, **14**, 1812
debitum fundi, adjudication on, **8**, 101
  See also debitum fundi
debt-adjusting as ancillary credit business, **5**, 816
debt-collecting as ancillary credit-business, **5**, 816
debt-counselling as ancillary credit-business, **5**, 816
debtor, *see* DEBTOR, DEBTOR'S ESTATE
deceased, due to, **25**, 1064
diligence—
  forming basis of, **25**, 1054
  See also DILIGENCE
document of—
  arrestment on, **8**, 255
  inhibition on, **8**, 134
  meaning, **8**, 134
documents in debtor's possession, **15**, 872
dominus negotii—
  due by, **15**, 96, 97
  due to, **15**, 96, 133
evidence of, **2**, 1331
executory estate, due by, **24**, 212
extinction—
  confusion, by, **15**, 876
  effect on right in security, **20**, 1
  novation, by, **15**, 874
fraudulent preference, payment by, **11**, 781
future—
  arrestment, **8**, 268
  generally, **4**, 828
  voluntary, inhibition, **8**, 159, 161–165, 167
generally, **25**, 665
gratuitous alienation, **11**, 780
heir, liability of, **25**, 637
heritable, **25**, 667
heritable security, secured by—
  adjudication on a *debitum fundi*, **8**, 372
heritage, secured over, **4**, 45
imprisonment for, **2**, 1302; **22**, 645
  abolition, **8**, 347, 348
  aliment, non-payment of sums decerned for, **8**, 348, 349
  competence, **8**, 347, 349
  death duties, for non-payment of, **8**, 348
  dependence, on the, **8**, 347
  generally, **8**, 101
  historical background, **8**, 347

Debt—*continued*
imprisonment for—*continued*
  Holyrood Park, debtors within bounds of, **8**, 347
  length of imprisonment, **8**, 348
  procedure, **8**, 347
  purchase tax, for non-payment of, **8**, 348
  rates, for non-payment of, **8**, 348
  re-imprisonment, **8**, 349
  taxes, for non-payment of, **8**, 348
inability to pay, grounds for winding up by court, **4**, 727
incapax, owing to, recovery of, **11**, 1225
inheritance tax, **25**, 847, 1008
inhibition—
  assignation of, **8**, 186
  contracted after, **8**, 133
  passing automatically with, **8**, 186
inhibition in security, **8**, 135
insolvency and bankruptcy, **11**, 776–781
interest on, **4**, 832
justice of the peace court jurisdiction, **6**, 1159
law reform, Debtor's (Scotland) Act 1880 ..., **22**, 645
leasehold securities—
  creditor's remedies, **13**, 331
  effect of registration, **13**, 330
  generally, **13**, 328
  writs registrable, **13**, 329
legal rights, **25**, 782, 791, 792
legal tender, payment in, **14**, 1823
liquid—
  compensation, **15**, 878
  meaning, **15**, 878
maills and duties, **8**, 101
  See also MAILLS AND DUTIES
maritime arrestment *in rem*, **8**, 101
moveable, **25**, 667
next of kin, of, **25**, 1058
novation, **15**, 865, 874
open account, **12**, 1011
partners, liability—
  bankruptcy of partner, where, **16**, 1037
  death of partner, where, **16**, 1037
  existence of partnership, determination, **16**, 1020
  generally, **16**, 1035
  incoming partners, **16**, 1036
  joint and several liability, **16**, 1035
  retirement, obligations incurred after, **16**, 1038
  retiring partners, **16**, 1037
payment of, **25**, 666, 847
pledge retained for, **20**, 16
poinding of the ground, **8**, 101
  See also POINDING OF THE GROUND
police constable refusing or neglecting to discharge, **16**, 1749
preference of, *see* PREFERENTIAL PAYMENTS; PREFERRED DEBTS; WINDING UP (debts)
privileged, **25**, 666, 847
refusal to act, **14**, 1511
restriction direction, civil prisoner subject to, **14**, 1468
retention for payment of, **24**, 74

Debt—*continued*
retention in security, **3**, 76
revalorisation, **14**, 1823
right in security, **20**, 43
  See also RIGHT IN SECURITY
Sale of Goods Act, not covered by, **20**, 805
secured, **4**, 829
securities over commercial lease, **13**, 585
security for, passport may not be used as, **16**, 1228
sequestration for rent and feuduty, **8**, 101
several incurred to same debtor, ascription of payments, **15**, 868
sheriff court jurisdiction, **22**, 645
time to pay order and direction—
  judicial discretion, **8**, 126
transactions in fraud of creditors, **11**, 779
transfer direction, civil prisoner subject to, **14**, 1468
transfer of, **4**, 102
trustees' powers, **24**, 202
truster's, **24**, 193, 202
unit of account, incurred in, **14**, 1804
unregistered company unable to pay, **4**, 940
Debtor
adjudication—
  apparent insolvency following, **8**, 201
  defences to action of, **8**, 192
aliment payments, **2**, 1385
armed forces, serving in, **8**, 126
assurance policies effected by, **2**, 1389
body corporate, **8**, 128
books of, not evidence of loan, **13**, 1738
business carried on by trustee, **2**, 1311, 1342
cancellation, recovery of payments on, **5**, 867
cautionary obligation, *see* CAUTIONARY OBLIGATION
co-operation, duty of, **2**, 1481
co-ownership of property, **8**, 110
composition offer—
  acceptance or rejection, **2**, 1444
  approval of—
    discharge of debtor on, **2**, 1446
    recall of, **2**, 1447
    sheriff, by, **2**, 1445
  default in payment, **2**, 1447
  making, procedure, **2**, 1443
  meaning, **2**, 1442
  procedure, **2**, 1443
  rejection, effect of, **2**, 1445
  report by trustee on, **2**, 1443
  trustee's duties as to, **2**, 1445
concealment of assets, **2**, 1452
concursus debiti et crediti, **15**, 879
confirmation as executor-creditor, **8**, 101
confusion, **15**, 876
Crown as, **8**, 128
death of, **5**, 887
  confirmation as executor-creditor, **8**, 101
debt contracted after inhibition, **8**, 133
debtor-creditor agreement, *see* DEBTOR-CREDITOR AGREEMENT
debtor-creditor-supplier agreement, *see* DEBTOR-CREDITOR-SUPPLIER AGREEMENT
debtor's debtor, creditor cannot sue, **15**, 7
debtor's life insured by creditor, **12**, 854

Debtor—*continued*

deceased—
    basis of diligence, **25**, 1054
    exclusion of diligence, **25**, 1053
    inhibition, **8**, 153
default by, sale by secured creditor as involuntary transfer of ownership, **18**, 667
delegation, **15**, 875
demand for payment by creditor, doctrine of acquiescence, **16**, 1620
designation, error in, **8**, 125
diligence, *see* DILIGENCE
directions by interim trustee, **2**, 1342
discharge—
    automatic—
        effect of, **2**, 1441
        introduction of, **2**, 1438
        transitional provisions, **2**, 1440
    certificate of, **2**, 1438
    composition, on—
        acceptance of, **2**, 1442
        availability of, **2**, 1443
        effect of, **2**, 1446
    deferment—
        period of, **2**, 1439
        procedure, **2**, 1439
    early legislation, under, **2**, 1438
    liabilities remaining after, **2**, 1441
    methods of, **2**, 1459
    sheriff's order, on, **2**, 1446
    three years, after, **2**, 1438
    voluntary arrangement, by, **2**, 1462
    wrongfully obtained, **2**, 1448
discharge of inhibition by, **8**, 146
document constituting obligation to pay in possession of, **15**, 872
domestic tenancy, rent for, **8**, 126
early settlement by—
    linked transactions, effect on, **5**, 900
    rebate on—
        calculation of, **5**, 899
        entitlement to, **5**, 898
        generally, **5**, 897
    right to effect, **5**, 896
embezzlement, detecting, **2**, 1388
estate of, *see* DEBTOR'S ESTATE
examination of—
    generally—
        arrest of examinee, **2**, 1400
        debtor's family included in, **2**, 1397
        documents, production of, **2**, 1400
        mandatory, is not, **2**, 1397
        oath, taken on, **2**, 1400
        procedure, **2**, 1400
        record of, **2**, 1400
        refusal to answer, **2**, 1400
        request by trustees for, **2**, 1398
    modified procedure, under, **2**, 1356
    private—
        application for, **2**, 1398
        discretion of sheriff, **2**, 1398
        failure of examinee to appear, **2**, 1398
        order of sheriff for, **2**, 1344
        procedure, **2**, 1398

Debtor—*continued*

examination of—*continued*
    private—*continued*
        questioners at, **2**, 1400
        time for, **2**, 1398
    public—
        application for order, **2**, 1305, 1399
        default in appearance, **2**, 1399
        Gazette notice of, **2**, 1399
        importance of, **2**, 1397
        other persons, of, **2**, 1399
        time for, **2**, 1399
expenses, liability for, **8**, 131
extra-judicial composition contracts—
    breach of, **2**, 1470
    caution for, **2**, 1475
    definition of, **2**, 1467
    evidence of, **2**, 1469
    terms of, **2**, 1468
extrajudicial interruption of prescription by, **16**, 2124, 2125
family—
    home—
        disposal of, **2**, 1377
        powers of trustee in sequestration, **13**, 417
    maintenance of, **2**, 1385
foreign state as, **8**, 128
formal demand for payment, **12**, 1014–1017
fraudulent bankruptcy, **2**, 1452
gratuitous alienation, *see* DEBTOR'S ESTATE
heritable security, succession, **20**, 144
income after sequestration date, **2**, 1385
insolvency of, right in security as safeguard against, **20**, 1
interest—
    as compensation paid by, **12**, 1001
    See also INTEREST
intimation to, **12**, 1014, 1016
judicial demand for payment, **12**, 1014, 1015
lessor, as—
    debtor under bond and disposition in security, **13**, 162, 164
    debtor under *ex facie* absolute disposition, **13**, 161, 164
    debtor under standard security, **13**, 163, 164
list of assets and liabilities—
    copy to Accountant, **2**, 1344
    default in respect of, **2**, 1343
    delivery to trustee, **2**, 1343
    preparation of, **2**, 1343
maintenance of, provision for, **2**, 1385
matrimonial home—
    occupancy rights, **2**, 1377
    protection of, **2**, 1377
meaning, **2**, 1319
messenger-at-arms, liability of, **14**, 1507
no title to property, where, **8**, 109
obligor, as, **11**, 1029
offences—
    code of, **2**, 1453
    common law, **2**, 1452
    credit, obtaining, **2**, 1454
    duty to report, **2**, 1305
    general, **2**, 1454

Debtor—*continued*
offences—*continued*
  leaving Scotland, **2**, 1454
  non-compliance with directions, **2**, 1342
  procedure and penalties, **2**, 1455
  statutory, **2**, 1453
  suspected, report of, **2**, 1315
petition by, for sequestration, **2**, 1322, 1326
poinding, apparent insolvency following, **8**, 221
poinding of the ground against goods of, **8**, 361, 365
salary, treatment of, **2**, 1385
sheriff court jurisdiction, **6**, 1097
sheriff officer, liability of, **14**, 1511
spouse—
  joint owner of heritable property, **2**, 1385
  occupancy rights, **2**, 1361
  protection of interests of, **2**, 1377
statement of affairs by, **2**, 1343
termination by—
  landlord's hypothec, operation of, **5**, 903
  liability on, **5**, 902
  right to terminate, **5**, 901
third party, dealings with, **2**, 1386
trade union, **8**, 128
trustee for creditors, as, **2**, 1388
trusts for creditors, **24**, 16, 20
unfair preference—
  challenge of—
    common law, at, **2**, 1388, 1391
    exempt transactions, **2**, 1391, 1392
    jurisdiction as to, **2**, 1392
    limitation of time, **2**, 1391
    method of, **2**, 1391
    right of, **2**, 1391, 1392
    statute, under, **2**, 1392
    successful, effect of, **2**, 1391
  essential proofs, **2**, 1391
  introduction of term, **2**, 1391
  meaning, **2**, 1392
  principle as to, **2**, 1388
  third party, interest of, **2**, 1391
voluntary arrangements, *see* CREDITORS
wrongful withholding of sum, due to—
  intimation to debtor, **12**, 1014, 1016
  judicial demand for payment, **12**, 1014, 1015
See also OBLIGOR
Debtor-creditor agreement
canvassing, **5**, 832
debtor-creditor-supplier agreement distinguished from, **5**, 810
meaning, **5**, 810
Debtor-creditor-supplier agreement
canvassing, **5**, 832
debtor-creditor agreement distinguished from, **5**, 810
meaning, **5**, 810
Debtor's estate
additional, acquisition of, **2**, 1384
claims on, *see* CREDITORS
co-obligants, **2**, 1413
deceased debtor's estate—
  administration expenses, **2**, 1419
  generally, **4**, 72

Debtor's estate—*continued*
deceased debtor's estate—*continued*
  gratuitous alienation, **2**, 1450
  judicial factor—
    administration by, **2**, 1451
    application for, **2**, 1451
    appointment, **2**, 1449
    jurisdiction as to, **2**, 1450
  sequestration—
    creditor's petition, on, **2**, 1332
    procedure, **2**, 1450
    provision for, **2**, 1449
diligence, *see* DILIGENCE
distribution of—
  accounting periods, **2**, 1432
  equitable manner, in, **2**, 1416
  estate available, **2**, 1416
  order of, **2**, 1416
  ordinary debts, **2**, 1422
  postponed debts, **2**, 1424
  surplus, payment over, **2**, 1425
documents etc, recovery of, **2**, 1375
family home, protection of, **2**, 1377
gratuitous alienation—
  challenge by judicial factor, **2**, 1318
  common law challenge—
    Bell's statement on, **2**, 1388
    considerations which may defeat, **2**, 1389
    essential proofs, **2**, 1389
    fraud, no need to prove, **2**, 1389
    generally, **2**, 1388
    judicial comments on, **2**, 1388
    right to challenge, **2**, 1389
  common law remedies, **2**, 1387
  company, by, **2**, 1390
  deceased debtor, **2**, 1450
  divorce, payments on, **2**, 1390
  early legislation, **2**, 1302
  statutory challenge—
    absolute insolvency, proof of, **2**, 1390
    limitation of time, **2**, 1390
    normal mode of, **2**, 1390
    when possible, **2**, 1390
    who may challenge, **2**, 1390
  statutory provisions, **2**, 1387
  value of, gifts etc excluded, **2**, 1390
  wife's rights, **2**, 1390
heritable property—
  decree of adjudication, **2**, 1383
  spouse joint owner, **2**, 1385
  trustee's title to, **2**, 1383
  vesting of, **2**, 1385
instructions for dealing with, **2**, 1376
interim safeguard, **2**, 1309
management of, **2**, 1376
moveable property, **2**, 1382
offences, *see* DEBTOR
payments—
  accounts by trustee, **2**, 1434
  administration expenses, **2**, 1432
  claims—
    adjudication on, **2**, 1435
    adjustment of, **2**, 1436
    appeal as to, **2**, 1433

Debtor's estate—*continued*
payments—*continued*
  claims—*continued*
    submission, **2**, 1433
    timetable for, **2**, 1435
  dividend—
    deposit of funds for, **2**, 1437
    submission of claims, **2**, 1433
    times for, **2**, 1432
    timetable as to, **2**, 1435
  interim trustee, to, **2**, 1432
possession of, taking, **2**, 1375
preferential payments—
  common law, at, **2**, 1419
  executor's expenses, **2**, 1419
  pension contributions, **2**, 1430
  petitioning creditor's expenses, **2**, 1420
  remuneration—
    interim trustee, of, **2**, 1417
    permanent trustee, of, **2**, 1418
  statutory, **2**, 1416
preferred debts—
  categories, **2**, 1426
  common law, at, **2**, 1426
  Crown debts, **2**, 1426
  customs and excise, **2**, 1426
  employees' remuneration, **2**, 1431
  funeral etc expenses, **2**, 1419
  gaming duties, **2**, 1428
  generally, **2**, 1426
  inadequate funds to meet, **2**, 1426
  Inland Revenue debts, **2**, 1427
  ordinary debts, ranking, **2**, 1422
  post-sequestration interest, **2**, 1423
  social security contributions, **2**, 1429
  statutory, ranking of, **2**, 1421
  taxes, **2**, 1427
  value added tax, **2**, 1428
property—
  additional, acquisition of, **2**, 1384
  comprising, **2**, 1381
  fraudulently acquired, **2**, 1385
  held on trust, **2**, 1385
  outwith Scotland, **2**, 1381
purchase by trustee, **2**, 1376
salary, division of, **2**, 1385
sale, power of, **2**, 1376
spouse's estate, **2**, 1384
third parties, protection, **2**, 1386
vesting of—
  absolute nature of, **2**, 1381
  date of, **2**, 1381
  disputed property, **2**, 1384
  exclusions from, **2**, 1385
  heritable property, **2**, 1383, 1385
  moveable property, **2**, 1382
  special situations, **2**, 1384
  statutory provisions, **2**, 1381
  third party claims affecting, **2**, 1386
what constitutes, **2**, 1381
Decapitalisation rate
contractor's principle, **24**, 544
Decency
employment discrimination, **9**, 362

Declaration concerning Friendly Relations and Co-operation
generally, **19**, 685, 700, 700*n*
Declaration of Arbroath
lex et consuetudo, recognition, **19**, 207; **22**, 356
Declaration of human rights, *see* HUMAN RIGHTS
Declaration of Identity
issue, **16**, 1237
Declaration of Identity for Visa Purposes
generally, **16**, 1211, 1239
Declarator
action of, **6**, 1062
  dissolution of partnership, for, **16**, 1093
  mortgagee's right to make, **21**, 179
  void or null deeds or writings, **13**, 35
bastardy, of, **4**, 5
Crown—
  action for, **7**, 746
  orders in relation to, **13**, 5
death, of, **6**, 1062; **10**, 819, 833, 834; **13**, 7; **25**, 651, 652
enforcement of statutory duty by, **1**, 334
expiry of the legal, **13**, 6
further remedies following, **13**, 4
future and contingent rights, **13**, 4
generally, **1**, 326; **13**, 3
grant, effect of, **13**, 4
hypothetical questions, **13**, 4
interdict, appropriate remedy in lieu of, **14**, 2149
judicial declaration of rights, **13**, 3
live practical importance to party, issue must be of, **13**, 4
marriage, of, **13**, 4
negative prescription of objection by way of, **14**, 2123
ordinary action, remedy in, **4**, 959
patent, concerning, **18**, 858
  non-infringement, declarator of, **18**, 875, 877
remedy, as, **13**, 2
rights of travellers, of, action for, **11**, 1752
tenant's right to sue third party, **13**, 290
trade union membership, as to, **13**, 4
will, holograph, **13**, 7
wrongful dismissal, action in case of, **9**, 195
Declaratory Acts
retrospectivity, **12**, 1193
Declaratory Articles
doctrinal operational independence achieved by, **5**, 348
generally, **5**, 696
Westminster Confession, and, **5**, 348, 698–700
See also ARTICLES DECLARATORY OF THE CONSTITUTION OF THE CHURCH OF SCOTLAND
Declaratory Power
Alison's *Principles*, **7**, 6, 8, 11
Cockburn's principles, **7**, 9–11, 13
early nineteenth century cases, **7**, 7
generally, **7**, 5, 6, 15
Greenhuff, **7**, 8, 13
Hume's *Commentaries*, **7**, 6–9, 11, 12
Macdonald's *Criminal Law*, **7**, 6, 13
maximum certainty, principle of, **7**, 11
non-retroactivity, **7**, 5

Declaratory Power—*continued*
post-*Greenhuff*, **7**, 11
real injury, general principle of, **7**, 13
refusal to declare, **7**, 14
twentieth century cases, **7**, 12–14
'wide general principle', **7**, 11, 13
Declinature, trustees
express, **24**, 144, 145
implied, **24**, 146
resignation distinguished, **24**, 144*n*
Decoy
live bird or animal used as, **11**, 880, 884
Decree
arbitral, partial reduction, **13**, 63
date from which due, **12**, 1032
discretion of court, **12**, 1032
foreign, *see* JUDGMENTS
interest on, **12**, 1032
matrimonial, *see* MATRIMONIAL DECREE
reduction, **13**, 38
 decree in absence, **13**, 40
 decree of adoption, **13**, 42
 decree *in foro*, **13**, 41
 effect, **13**, 64
 extracted decree, **13**, 39
 grounds for—
  action dismissed *ex proprio motu*, **13**, 47, 48
  auctor in rem suam, **13**, 52
  court acting in excess of jurisdiction, **13**, 48
  error or omission by party or agent, **13**, 47
  exceptional circumstances, **13**, 47
  fraud on the court, **13**, 50
  irregularities in original process, **13**, 49
  res judicata, **13**, 45, 50
  res noviter, **13**, 51
  review, reduction as mode of, **13**, 46, 47
  ultra vires, court acting, **13**, 47, 48
 partial, **13**, 63
 prescription, barred by, **13**, 61
 void or voidable decree, **13**, 35
 void or voidable—
  reduction, **13**, 35
  third party rights, **13**, 56, 57
Decreet of Ranking
peerage, precedence, **16**, 2010, 2018
Decreet of transumpt
notarial instruments, **19**, 831
Deduction from earnings order
See EARNINGS
Deed or writing
access to public registers, **19**, 878
bilateral, **6**, 471
blanks in, **6**, 426
 material part, **12**, 1228
change of name required by, **19**, 1428
classification, **6**, 471
coming into operation before 8 June 1968 ..., **25**, 883
conditio si institutus sine liberis decesserit, application of, **25**, 895
constitution, of, **6**, 471
court, construction by, **25**, 907
date of entry left blank, **12**, 1228

Deed or writing—*continued*
Deeds and Probative Writs, Register of, **6**, 454; **19**, 820
Deeds Office, **19**, 850
deletion in, **6**, 424
delivered but not yet registered, **18**, 14
delivery—
 constructive or implied, **6**, 445
 exception to rules as to, **6**, 446
 generally, **6**, 444
discharge, of, **6**, 471
drafting, **6**, 412*n*
erasures in, **6**, 425
error in, authentication, **6**, 422–426
execution, **6**, 430–432
family arrangement, of, **25**, 1028
feu grants, **6**, 473, 474
foreign, **6**, 417, 442
 privilege, **6**, 442
foreign person, by, **6**, 417
form of records, **19**, 846
future voluntary, inhibition, **8**, 159, 161–165, 167
generally, **6**, 412
granter reserving interest, **6**, 446
heritable conveyancing, *see* HERITABLE CONVEY- ANCING
holograph writings, *see* HOLOGRAPH WRITINGS
incapax, granted by, **12**, 1229
instrument of sasine as, **16**, 2109
inter vivos, **6**, 471
interpretation and construction—
 adoption order, effect, **12**, 1218
 affidavit, **12**, 1262
 alterations, **12**, 1227
  pencil, in, **12**, 1230
 ambiguity, **12**, 1215, 1223
 blanks, **12**, 1228
 capacity, **12**, 1229
 clerical errors, **12**, 1233
 co-partnership, contract of, **12**, 1261
 conditions, deed of, **12**, 1260
 construction as a whole, **12**, 1221
 contra proferentem construction, **12**, 1232
 conveyance, *see* CONVEYANCE
 creditor's voluntary trust deed, **12**, 1262
 ejusdem generis, **12**, 1224
 entail, deed of, **12**, 1262
 error—
  clerical, **12**, 1233
  rectification, **12**, 1234
 extrinsic evidence, **12**, 1225
 factory and commission or power of attorney, **12**, 1262
 family arrangement, deed of, **12**, 1262
 floating charge, **12**, 1262
 foreign language, **12**, 1217
 generally, **12**, 1213, 1262
 ground annual, contract of, **12**, 1262
 holograph writings, **12**, 1218
 implied terms, **12**, 1235, 1236
  inappropriate implication, **12**, 1236
 ink, written in, **12**, 1230
 intention, ascertainment, **12**, 1216
 inter vivos settlements, **12**, 1214, 1262

Deed or writing—*continued*
interpretation and construction—*continued*
  invalidating or defeating agreement, **12**, 1215
  judicially defined, **12**, 1219
  land certificate, **12**, 1259
  lease, *see* LEASE
  majority, reference to, **12**, 1218, 1231
  marriage, contract of, **12**, 1262
  meaning of terms which adverse party understood, **12**, 1215
  minority, reference to, **12**, 1218, 1231
  naturalia of particular contract, **12**, 1215
  overriding interests, **12**, 1218
  parole evidence, **12**, 1222, 1225, 1251
  pencil—
    alterations written in, **12**, 1230
    deed written in, **12**, 1230
  popular sense of words, **12**, 1215
  power of attorney, **12**, 1262
  prior communications, **12**, 1215, 1222
  purpose of, **12**, 1214
  renunciation, minute of, **12**, 1262
  rules, general, **12**, 1214–1234
  sense giving validity and effect to agreement, **12**, 1215
  servitude, of, **12**, 1262
  statute, effect of, **12**, 1218
  statutory declaration, **12**, 1262
  statutory meanings, **12**, 1231
  technical terms, **12**, 1215, 1217
  testing clause, use of, **12**, 1226, 1228
  trade usage, **12**, 1215
  typewritten, **12**, 1230
  usage, **12**, 1215, 1220
  waiver, minute of, **12**, 1262
  will, *see* WILL
  words, generally, **12**, 1215, 1219
judicial decree as, **16**, 2109
land, conveying interest in—
  implied terms, **12**, 1235
  See also CONVEYANCE
language, **6**, 412
later words, authentication, **12**, 1228
local authority, execution by, **14**, 2, 260
minor, granted by, **12**, 1229, 1231
mortis causa, **6**, 471; **11**, 736
multilateral, **6**, 471
mutual, **6**, 446
natural keeper, granter as, **6**, 446
nonage, capacity of person in, **12**, 1229, 1231
not truly of granter, onus of proof, **6**, 415
notarial protocol and notarial instrument, **13**, 1221; **16**, 2109
  compulsory acquisition of land, **5**, 81, 89
notice of title as, **16**, 2109
partnership, whether binding on, **16**, 1031
parts of, **6**, 472
pencil, written or altered in, **12**, 1230, 1263
plans annexed to, **6**, 729
positive prescription founded on, **16**, 2106, 2107, 2109
positive servitude, **16**, 2111
prescription, **13**, 61
presentation in Court of Session, **19**, 836

Deed or writing—*continued*
printed form, problems arising from use of, **12**, 1228
printer's imprint, requirement not applicable, **17**, 3
prior title, land certificate and, **6**, 713
privileged writings—
  deeds not of great importance, **6**, 435
  'envelope cases', **6**, 441
  foreign deeds, **6**, 442
  generally, **6**, 443
  holograph writings, **6**, 436–440
  statute, privileged by, **6**, 434
  writings *in re mercatoria*, **6**, 443
probative writings—
  authentication of errors, **6**, 422–426
  blanks, **6**, 426; **12**, 1228
  deletions, **6**, 424
  erasures, **6**, 425
  essentials, **6**, 414
  evidence, admissible in, **10**, 600
  execution, **6**, 430–432
  marginal additions, **6**, 423
  meaning, **6**, 413
  minor alterations, **6**, 422
  nature of, **6**, 413
  signature, *see* subscription *below*
  subscription, *see* subscription *below*
  testing clause, **6**, 427–429
  witnesses, **6**, 414, 420, 421
pupil, granted by, **12**, 1229
rectification—
  case, establishment of, **13**, 69
  company's register of members, of, **13**, 71
  generally, **13**, 69
  Land Register of Scotland, of, **13**, 71
  reduction at common law, by, **13**, 70
  statutory provisions, **13**, 71
  testamentary writings, recommended extension to, **13**, 71
reduction of, **6**, 924; **13**, 63, 64
registration, **19**, 821, 836, 837
  Books of Council and Session, **6**, 454; **19**, 839
  Burgh, **19**, 839*n*
  Cachet Seal, Register of, **6**, 459
  Chancery Office Register, **6**, 457–463
  Charges Register, **6**, 469
  consent for, **6**, 548
  Crown Grants, Register of, **6**, 462
  Deeds and Probative Writs, Register of, **6**, 454; **19**, 820
  English and Irish Judgments, **6**, 456
  Entails, Register of, **6**, 466
  execution, for, **6**, 450, 548
  Great Seal, Register of, **6**, 458
  Hornings, Register of, **6**, 464
  Housing Office Register, **6**, 464–470
  Inhibitions and Adjudications, Register of, **6**, 465, 707, 766
  Land Register, *see* LAND REGISTER OF SCOTLAND
  legal fiction, as, **19**, 837
  preservation, for, **6**, 448, 548
  Prince's Seal, Register of, **6**, 461
  Protests, Register of, **6**, 455
  publication, for, **6**, 449, 548
  Quarter Seal, Register of, **6**, 460

Deed or writing—*continued*
registration—*continued*
    Register of Deeds and Probative Writs, **6**, 454
    Registers of Scotland, **6**, 451, 459
    registration—
        publication, for, **6**, 449
    Sasine Office Register, *see* SASINES
    Service of Heirs, Register of, **6**, 457
    Sheriff court books, **6**, 468
    Sheriffs' Commissions, Register of, **6**, 463
    title, of, *see* REGISTRATION OF TITLE
    warrant of, **6**, 551
seal, use of, **14**, 260
signature, of, *see* subscription *below*
spouses, and, **10**, 876
stamp duty, **6**, 447
subscription, of—
    attorney, by, **6**, 417
    blind persons, **6**, 418
    building societies, on behalf of, **6**, 417
    clubs, on behalf of, **6**, 417
    corporate bodies, **6**, 417
    factor, by, **6**, 417
    illiterate persons, **6**, 418
    limited companies, **6**, 417
    meaning, **6**, 416
    mode of, **6**, 418
    necessity for, **6**, 415
    partnership, **6**, 417
    peers of the realm, **6**, 417
    position of, **6**, 419
    probative writings, **6**, 414
    regional, islands or district council, **6**, 417
    Subscription of Deeds Act 1584 ..., **19**, 838
    trade unions, on behalf of, **6**, 417
    wills and testamentary documents, **6**, 415
Sunday, execution on, **12**, 1229
superiorities, dealing with, **6**, 585
tenements, dealing with, **6**, 584
testamentary, **6**, 446
testing clause—
    details, **6**, 427
    errors in, **6**, 429
    nature of, **6**, 427
    timing, **6**, 428
    wills and testamentary documents, **6**, 416
transfer, of, **6**, 471
trust deed, *see* TRUST
unilateral, **6**, 471, 579
validity of, **14**, 2
warrandice, implied terms, **12**, 1235
witnesses, incompetent, **12**, 1229
Deed of condition
attestation, **18**, 388
bilateral, **18**, 388
creation, generally, **18**, 388
granter, infeft or uninfeft, **18**, 388
improperly executed, **18**, 388
real burden created in, **18**, 386, 387, 388
    only principal deed may be consulted, **18**, 388
    servient tenement, condition must relate to, **18**, 388
unilateral, **18**, 388

Deed of covenant
See COVENANTED PAYMENT
Deer
aircraft—
    hunting from, **2**, 301; **11**, 941
    offences involving, **2**, 301
    transport in, **11**, 941
authorisation of taking or killing, **2**, 297, 301
calf, fawn or kid deprived of its mother, **11**, 935
carcases—
    removal of, **11**, 938
    sale or disposal, **2**, 298
    unlawfully removing, **2**, 301
close season, **11**, 930
    control during, **11**, 933
    meaning, **2**, 300
common law restriction on killing, **11**, 926
conservation, **11**, 929
    responsibility for, **2**, 296
control schemes, **11**, 931–937
    enforcement—
        expenses of, **2**, 298
        search and seizure, **2**, 302
    failure to comply with, **2**, 298
    institution of, **2**, 298
crossbow, killing with, **11**, 940
dogs, hunting with, **11**, 940
enclosed lands, taking or killing on, **11**, 830
fallow, conservation of, **11**, 929
false information, giving, **2**, 296
farms, **11**, 930
firearms etc—
    cancellation of certificates, **2**, 304
    permitted arms and ammunition, **11**, 937
    seizure, **2**, 302
    unlawful use to kill or injure deer, **11**, 943
forests, valuation for rating, **11**, 906, 915; **24**, 737, 740
forfeiture of, **11**, 961
game, as, **11**, 802, 927
Game Acts, **11**, 496*n*
injured or diseased, prevention of suffering by, **11**, 935
legislation, **11**, 928
marauding, **2**, 297; **11**, 932, 935
night—
    killing or injuring during, **2**, 301; **11**, 940
    shooting during, **11**, 934–936
offences—
    arrest for, **2**, 303
    defences to, **2**, 301
    generally, **2**, 301
    suspects, search of, **2**, 302
poaching, **11**, 938
    gang poaching, **11**, 939
red, **11**, 860*n*
    conservation, **11**, 929
    game, as, **11**, 926
Red Deer Commission, **11**, 929
    carcases, power to sell, **2**, 298
    constitution, **2**, 296; **13**, 1415
    creation of, **11**, 929
    entry on land, powers, **2**, 299
    expenses, **2**, 298

Deer—*continued*
Red Deer Commission—*continued*
  functions, **13**, 1415
  marauding deer, **11**, 932, 935
  night shooting, **11**, 935
  powers and duties, **2**, 296
  venison dealers' licences, **11**, 947
regulations as to preparation and sale as food, **11**, 312
requirement notice to control, **11**, 860–863
roe, conservation of, **11**, 929
sika, **11**, 860*n*
  conservation, **11**, 929
snaring, **11**, 940
taking or killing—
  authorisation of, **2**, 297, 301
  damage, to prevent, **2**, 297, 298, 301
  offences as to, **2**, 301
  returns of, **2**, 296
  unlawful, *see* unlawful taking and killing *below*
trapping, **11**, 940
unlawful possession, **11**, 943
unlawful taking and killing, **2**, 301; **11**, 938–942
  arrest, powers of, **11**, 958
  attempting or preparing to commit offence, **11**, 956
  cancellation of firearms certificate, **11**, 959
  exempted persons, **11**, 942
  search and seizure, powers of, **11**, 957
vehicles, driving deer with, **11**, 941, 942
vehicles etc, search of, **2**, 302
venison, *see* VENISON

Defamation
Act of 1952 generally, **17**, 20
action—
  damages for, conviction as documentary evidence, **10**, 584
  generally, **15**, 483, 496
  solicitor's communications, confidentiality, **13**, 1190
amends, offer of, unintentional defamation, in cases of, **15**, 504–506
broadcasting, effect on activities of those concerned with, **17**, 1
business reputation, protection against, **4**, 318
calumnious statements, **15**, 486
caricatures, **15**, 483
cartoons, **15**, 483
character, attack on, **15**, 471, 472
circumstances of statement, **15**, 495
civil legal aid not available, **13**, 1034
Commissioner for Local Administration, investigation by, **14**, 144
communication of idea—
  actions, by, **15**, 483, 496
  defamatory nature—
    criminality, imputations of, **15**, 491
    examples, **15**, 489
    financial unsoundness, imputations of, **15**, 493
    generally, **15**, 486
    matters of fact and law, **15**, 488
    moral character, imputations on, **15**, 490
    objective test, **15**, 487

Defamation—*continued*
communication of ideas—*continued*
  defamatory nature—*continued*
    professional competence or conduct, imputations against, **15**, 492
    public character, aspersions against, **15**, 494
  foreign language, **15**, 496
  method, **15**, 483
  pursuer alone, to, **15**, 484
  repetition, **15**, 485
  requirements as to, **15**, 483
  visual methods, by, **15**, 483
  words, by, **15**, 483
comparative advertising, in, **1**, 516
convicium, **15**, 558
criminality, imputations of, **15**, 491
damages, award of—
  aggravation of damages, **15**, 552
  assessment, **15**, 550, 551
  generally, **15**, 550
  mitigation of damages, **15**, 553
  reparation, as, **15**, 550
  review, **15**, 554
defamatory, statement must be, **15**, 470
defamatory matter, publication of, **17**, 25
defamatory statement, meaning, **15**, 486
defences—
  absolute privilege, **15**, 516–526
  fair comment, **15**, 539–545
  fair retort, **15**, 547
  in rixa, statements made, **15**, 546
  innocent dissemination, **15**, 549
  qualified privilege, **15**, 527–538
  unintentional defamation, **15**, 500–506
  veritas, **15**, 507–515
  vulgar abuse, **15**, 548
defender—
  child, **15**, 482
  corporate body, **15**, 479
  denial of defamatory content, **15**, 512
  partnership, **15**, 480
  veritas as defence, *see veritas* as defence *below*
  voluntary association, **15**, 481
definition, **15**, 470, 486; **16**, 2173
delict, as, **15**, 255, 280, 470
demeaning statements, **15**, 486, 487
disparaging statements, **15**, 486, 487
dissemination, innocent, **15**, 549
effigies, **15**, 483
elements, **15**, 470
employee, committed by, **4**, 318; **15**, 479
endorsement being, **1**, 521
examples, **15**, 489–494
fair comment—
  facts, on, **15**, 540, 541
  facts truly stated, **15**, 540, 542
  generally, **15**, 539
  hidden facts, **15**, 542
  onus of proof, **15**, 540
  public interest, matters of, **15**, 539, 540, 544
  rebutting defence, **15**, 545
fair retort, **15**, 547
false, statement must be, **15**, 470
falsity, **15**, 507, 508

Defamation—*continued*
financial unsoundness, imputations of, **15**, 493
foreign language, **15**, 496
generally, **17**, 18
gestures, **15**, 483
historical background, **15**, 471
honour, attack on, **15**, 471, 472
in rixa, statements made, **15**, 546
innocent dissemination, **15**, 549
innuendo—
  circumstances of statement, **15**, 495
  definition, **15**, 495
  examples, **15**, 499
  foreign language, **15**, 496
  generally, **15**, 495
  matters of fact and law, **15**, 498
  pursuer's onus, **15**, 496
  reasonable man test, **15**, 497
intent to cause injury, **15**, 255
intentional delict, as, **15**, 472
judge, of, **7**, 546
judicial slander, **15**, 523, 529, 535
jurisdiction, **15**, 471
justification, *see veritas* as defence *below*
legal advice and assistance, **13**, 1024
legal aid, denial, **15**, 471
legal persons, **15**, 472, 474, 479
limitation of actions—
  accrual of right of action, **16**, 2174
  application of provisions, **16**, 2173
  commencement of action, **16**, 2172, 2174
  death of defamed party, **16**, 2174
  disregard provisions, **16**, 2175
  executor as pursuer, **16**, 2174
  legal disability, defamed party under, **16**, 2175
  limitation period—
    computation, **16**, 2172, 2175
    generally, **16**, 2172
    judicial discretion to override, **16**, 2176–2185
  nonage, **16**, 2172, 2175
loss, **15**, 470
  patrimonial, **15**, 470
malice—
  damages, award of, **15**, 552
  statement must be made maliciously, **15**, 470, 479
  unintentional defamation, **15**, 500
matters of fact and law, **15**, 488
  innuendo, **15**, 498
moral character, imputations on, **15**, 490
more than one individual defamed, where, **15**, 473
natural persons, **15**, 472
negligent, duty of care, **15**, 280
nervous shock, duty of care, **15**, 284
non-disclosure, **17**, 23
officer, deliberate wrongful act of, liability, **4**, 318
onus of proof, **15**, 470, 508, 513
parliamentary papers, **17**, 19
Parliamentary reports, **15**, 525
parties to—
  generally, **15**, 472
  See also defender *above*; pursuer *below*
pictures, **15**, 483

Defamation—*continued*
press, effect on activities of those concerned with, **17**, 1, 18, 19
presumption of falsity, **15**, 508
privilege—
  absolute—
    aim, **15**, 516
    circumstances in which applicable, **15**, 516
    generally, **15**, 516
    judicial proceedings, statements in—
      advocates, **13**, 1327; **15**, 520
      civil actions, **15**, 518, 523
      court officers, **15**, 528
      generally, **15**, 518
      judges, **15**, 519
      judicial slander, **15**, 523, 529, 535
      jurors, **15**, 522
      pleaders, **15**, 520
      solicitors, **15**, 520
      witnesses, **15**, 521
      written pleadings, **15**, 520
    meaning, **15**, 516
    Parliamentary reports, **15**, 525; **17**, 19
    Parliamentary statements, **15**, 517
    qualified privilege distinguished, **15**, 516
    quasi-judicial proceedings, statements made in, **15**, 524
    tribunals, statements made in, **15**, 524
    witnesses, **15**, 521, 524
  qualified—
    absolute privilege distinguished, **15**, 516
    aim, **15**, 527
    circumstances of, **15**, 528–536
    duty or interest, **15**, 528–531
    extent of protection, **15**, 531; **17**, 22
    generally, **15**, 527
    judicial proceedings, reports of, **15**, 533, 534
    judicial slander, **15**, 529, 535
    law, as matter of, **15**, 527
    malice—
      generally, **15**, 527, 537
      proof of, **15**, 538
    matters enjoying, **17**, 21
    newspapers and broadcasts, statutory protection, **15**, 536; **17**, 20–22
    Parliamentary proceedings, reports of, **15**, 532
    protection of interest, **15**, 529
    reciprocity of interest, **15**, 530
    recklessness, **15**, 537
    reports enjoying, **17**, 21
professional competence or conduct, imputations against, **15**, 492
provocation, **15**, 553
public character, aspersions against, **15**, 494
puppets, **15**, 483
pursuer—
  communication to pursuer alone, **15**, 484
  corporate body, **15**, 474
  department of state, **15**, 477
  executor, **15**, 478
  government or government body, **15**, 477
  individual, **15**, 473
  local authority, **15**, 477

Defamation—*continued*
pursuer—*continued*
more than one individual defamed, where, **15**, 473
onus of proof, **15**, 470, 496, 513
partnership, **15**, 475
provocation, **15**, 553
trade union, **15**, 476
two or more charges against, defence of *veritas*, **15**, 511
voluntary association, **15**, 475
quasi-judicial proceedings, statements made in, **15**, 524
reparation, obligation to make, **16**, 2116
repetition, **15**, 485
reputation, attack on, **15**, 471, 472
Roman law, **15**, 214
signs, **15**, 483
'sting', proof, **15**, 510
test of, **15**, 486, 487
innuendo, **15**, 497
tribunals, statements made in, **15**, 524
unintentional—
amends, offer of—
acceptance, **15**, 505
generally, **15**, 504
rejection, **15**, 506
defence under Defamation Act 1952, **15**, 502, 503
innocent publication, **15**, 502, 503
liability for, **15**, 500
Scottish cases, **15**, 501
verbal injuries, generally, **15**, 555
veritas as defence—
counter issue—
generally, **15**, 514
relevancy, **15**, 515
Defamation Act 1952, **15**, 511
denial of defamatory content, **15**, 512
generally, **15**, 507
historical background, **15**, 507
onus of proof, **15**, 508, 513
presumption of falsity, **15**, 507, 508
proving *veritas*, **15**, 509, 510
two or more charges against pursuer, where, **15**, 511
vulgar abuse, **15**, 548
words, **15**, 483
Defeasance
vesting subject to, *see* VESTING
Defecation
public health nuisance, as, **19**, 370
Defective product
See CONSUMER PROTECTION
Defence
case, conduct of trial, **17**, 781
See also CRIMINAL PROCEDURE
civil, *see* CIVIL DEFENCE
confidential information as to, disclosure, **7**, 638
Court of Session procedure, **17**, 1387, 1388
establishments, works etc, prohibited places, as, **7**, 629
regulations, **5**, 616

Defence, Ministry of
creation of, **5**, 501
functions of, **5**, 501
Defence organisations
immunity and privileges, **2**, 787
visiting forces provisions applied, **2**, 787
Defence Police Federation
generally, **16**, 1816
Defences
automatism, *see* AUTOMATISM
capacity, *see* CAPACITY
coercion, **7**, 198, 202
defence of excuse, as, **7**, 198
diminished responsibility, *see* DIMINISHED RESPONSIBILTY
due diligence, **7**, 197
duress, *see* coercion *above*
entrapment—
Scots law, **7**, 205
substantive defence, as, **7**, 204
theoretical basis, **7**, 203
error of fact, **7**, 95, 97
excuse, of, **7**, 198
insanity, *see* INSANITY
intoxication, *see* INTOXICATION
justification, of, **7**, 198
motive, **7**, 92
necessity—
defence of justification, as, **7**, 198
generally, **7**, 198, 199
limits of defence, **7**, 201
nature of defence, **7**, 198
Scots law, **7**, 200
non-age, *see* NON-AGE
strict liability, where, **7**, 108
superior orders—
case law, **7**, 207
Hume's views, **7**, 206
Deferred payment
money as standard for, **14**, 1803
Deferred purchase agreement
avoidance device, as, **13**, 772
Deforcement
generally, **7**, 491, 540
High Court of Justiciary jurisdiction, **6**, 867
Del credere agency
cautionary obligation, whether, **3**, 833
Delectus personae
doctrine of—
commercial lease, **13**, 583
generally, **13**, 354, 355, 358
when implied, **13**, 356
when not implied, **13**, 357
Delegated legislation
Act of Adjournal, *see* ACT OF ADJOURNAL
Act of Sederunt, *see* ACT OF SEDERUNT
byelaws, *see* BYELAW
consultation on—
allowing, **1**, 263
failure of, **1**, 300
debates in House on, **5**, 424
exercise of, control over, **1**, 207
illegality, pleading, **1**, 301

Delegated legislation—*continued*
judicial control of—
  negative procedure, instrument subject to, **I**, 301
  procedural *ultra vires*, **I**, 300
  process of making, during, **I**, 301
  substantive *ultra vires*, **I**, 299
  supervisory jurisdiction, under, **I**, 298
  validity, review of, **I**, 301
procedural requirements, complying with, **I**, 229
review, reasons for, **I**, 299
Standing Committees on, **5**, 425
statutory instruments, procedure for, **I**, 300
  See also STATUTORY INSTRUMENT
Delegation
contractual obligation extinguished by, **15**, 865, 875
Delict
absolute privilege—
  advocate, **15**, 520
  advocate depute, **15**, 444, 449, 526
  aim, **15**, 516
  circumstances in which applicable, **15**, 516
  foreign embassy officials, communications between, **15**, 526
  generally, **15**, 516
  judge, **15**, 519
  judicial proceedings, statements in—
    civil actions, **15**, 523
    generally, **15**, 518, 533
    judge, **15**, 519
    judicial slander, **15**, 523
    juror, **15**, 522
    pleader, **15**, 520
    witnesses, **15**, 521
  judicial slander, **15**, 523
  juror, **15**, 522
  Lord Advocate, **15**, 444, 448, 449, 526
  meaning, **15**, 516
  military officer, official report by, **15**, 526
  minister of the Crown, **15**, 526
  officer of state, **15**, 526
  Parliamentary reports, **15**, 525
  Parliamentary statements, **15**, 517
  pleader, **15**, 520
  police officers, communications between, **15**, 526
  procurator fiscal, **15**, 444, 448, 449, 450, 526
  public prosecutor, **15**, 444, 448, 449
  qualified privilege distinguished, **15**, 516
  quasi-judicial proceedings, statements made in, **15**, 524
  solicitor, **15**, 520
  tribunals, statements made in, **15**, 524
  verbal injuries, **15**, 556, 559
  witness, **15**, 521, 524
  written pleadings, **15**, 520
actio de effusis vel dejectis, **15**, 217
actio popularis, **15**, 229
administrative official, committed by, **15**, 242
assignation, **15**, 604
assault, **15**, 255
assythment, **15**, 215
breach of contract, **15**, 3
breach of trust, **15**, 3
carelessness, **15**, 256

Delict—*continued*
causation, *see* CAUSATION
children—
  ante-natal injuries, **10**, 1021–1023
  child as defender, **10**, 1124
  child as pursuer, **10**, 1121
  committed by, **15**, 242
  contributory negligence, **10**, 1122
  in utero child, **10**, 1021
  mother, liability to, **10**, 1026
  parent as defender, **10**, 1123
  posthumous child, **10**, 1021
  wrongful birth actions, **10**, 1025
  wrongful life actions, **10**, 1024
circumvention, *see* FRAUD
compensation, element of, **15**, 219
compromise, **15**, 607
concurrent and cumulative liability, **15**, 9
confidential information, **18**, 1452
consumer protection, **15**, 196
contract, interference with, **15**, 255
contractor, independent—
  delict committed by, **15**, 242, 243, 251
  vicarious liability, **15**, 242, 243, 251
contractual right arising under, generally, **18**, 3
Crown—
  Crown servant, neglect or default must be by, **7**, 757
  litigation involving, **7**, 745
culpa, *injuria* committed with, **15**, 216
culpa tenet suos auctores—
  exceptions to maxim, **15**, 243
  generally, **15**, 242
damage, remoteness of, **15**, 902, 907, 908
  test of remoteness, **15**, 902
  See also DAMAGE; CARE, DUTY OF
damages—
  certainty of, **15**, 909
  generally, **15**, 892
  measure of—
    actuarial tables, calculation of loss by, **15**, 917
    benefit, loss, **15**, 918
    destruction of property, **15**, 915
    earnings, loss, **15**, 918
    generally, **15**, 915, 916
    misrepresentation, where, **15**, 915
    pecuniary loss, **15**, 916
    personal injury—
      actuarial tables, calculation of loss by, **15**, 917
      benefit, loss, **15**, 918
      earnings, loss, **15**, 918
      expenses, **15**, 919
      generally, **15**, 916
      pecuniary loss, **15**, 916
    property and economic interests, **15**, 915
    relative—
      services rendered by, **15**, 920, 920*n*
      services rendered to, **15**, 921
    solatium—
      employment, loss of, **15**, 922
      generally, **15**, 922
      loss of amenity, **15**, 924
      pursuer's awareness, relevance, **15**, 923

Delict—*continued*
damages—*continued*
  measure of—*continued*
    wrongful interference with economic
      interests, where, **15**, 915
    mitigation, **15**, 925
    provisional, **15**, 932
    See also DAMAGES
damnum sine injuria, **15**, 221
death, title to sue in respect of, **15**, 220, 232
defamation, *see* DEFAMATION
defences—
  common law authority, **15**, 417
  consent by pursuer, **15**, 393
    child, where pursuer, **15**, 393*n*, 396
  contractual limitation, **15**, 392
  contributory negligence—
    agony rule, **15**, 408
    appeal, reconsideration on, **15**, 409
    apportionment, **15**, 409, 410
    causation, **15**, 403, 407, 408, 432
      inevitable accident, **15**, 415
      test, **15**, 403
    child, by, **15**, 406
    common law authority, **15**, 417
    criminal conduct, pursuer participating in,
      15, 411
    damnum fatale, **15**, 412–415
    dilemma principle, **15**, 408
    disabled, by, **15**, 406
    employment cases, **15**, 404
    ex turpi causa non oritur actio, **15**, 411
    exceptions, **15**, 408
    fires, **15**, 414
    floods, **15**, 413
    foreseeability, **15**, 407
    generally, **15**, 403
    inevitable accident, **15**, 415
    infirm, by, **15**, 406
    instinctive behaviour, principle on, **15**, 408
    justification, **15**, 418
    meaning, **15**, 403*n*
    multiple defenders, where, **15**, 410
    necessity, **15**, 420, 421
    novus actus interveniens, **15**, 403*n*, 407
    onus of proof, **15**, 403
    provocation, **15**, 419
    self-defence, **15**, 420
    standard of care, **15**, 403, 404
    statutory authority, **15**, 416
    two acts of negligence not simultaneous,
      where, **15**, 407
    volenti non fit injuria, **15**, 403*n*
  duty of care, **15**, 392
  exclusion of liability, **15**, 392
  extinction, **15**, 392
  fact, issues of, **15**, 392
  generally, **15**, 392, 393, 396
  inevitable accident, **15**, 415
  justification, **15**, 418
  limitation of actions, **15**, 392
  mental capacity to accept risk, **15**, 396
  necessity, **15**, 420, 421
  prescription, **15**, 392

Delict—*continued*
defences—*continued*
  provocation, **15**, 419
  questions of fact and law, **15**, 392
  self-defence, **15**, 420
  statutory authority, **15**, 416
  title and interest to sue, **15**, 392
  transfer, **15**, 392
  volenti non fit injuria—
    duty of care, **15**, 395
    employment cases, **15**, 395, 396, 398
    generally, **15**, 394
    landlord and tenant, **15**, 395, 396, 397
    meaning, **15**, 394
    passengers, **15**, 395, 402
    property cases, **15**, 395, 396, 397
    requisites of defence, **15**, 396
    'rescuer' cases, **15**, 395, 396, 401
    sporting events—
      participants, **15**, 395, 400
      spectators, **15**, 395, 399
defender—
  Crown as, **15**, 223, 224
  executor as, **15**, 231
  joint and several liability, **15**, 238–241, 243
  judicial factor as, **15**, 234
  multiple defenders, **15**, 238–241
  multiple wrongs by same, **15**, 237
  parties not called as, title to defend, **15**, 222
  title to defend and counterclaim, **15**, 222
  trustee as, **15**, 233
  vicarious liability, *see* vicarious liability *below*
Department of Trade and Industry, *see* trade and
  industry, department of
deterrence, element of, **15**, 219
discharge, **15**, 607
duty of care—
  actual, **15**, 259, 268–272
  category of persons, owed to, **15**, 220
  defender must owe to pursuer, **15**, 220
  generally, **15**, 255
  meaning, **15**, 255, 259
  negligent misstatement by defender, **15**, 278,
    279, 280
  notional, **15**, 259–261
  threshold, **15**, 259, 262–267
  See also CARE, DUTY OF
economic—
  breach of contract—
    inducing, **15**, 576
    procuring, **15**, 576
  conspiracy—
    generally, **15**, 581
    lawful means, **15**, 582
    unlawful means, **15**, 583
  damages, **15**, 584
  generally, **15**, 575, 584
  intentional harm as essential element, **15**, 584
  intimidation, **15**, 580
  loss, **15**, 584
  wrongful interference—
    business, with, **15**, 579
    performance of contract, with, **15**, 577
    prospective contract, with, **15**, 578

Delict—*continued*
economic relationship—
  generally, **15**, 547
  injury to—
    competition, legitimate, **15**, 573
    controversial nature of law as to, **15**, 574
    derivative or parasitic economic loss, **15**, 574
    economic delicts—
      breach of contract—
        inducing, **15**, 576
        procuring, **15**, 576
      conspiracy—
        generally, **15**, 581
        lawful means, **15**, 582
        unlawful means, **15**, 583
      damages in respect of, **15**, 584
      generally, **15**, 575, 584
      intentional harm as essential element, **15**, 584
      intimidation, **15**, 580
      loss, **15**, 584
      wrongful interference—
        business, with, **15**, 579
        performance of contract, with, **15**, 577
        prospective contract, with, **15**, 578
    economic loss, **15**, 574
      non-relational, **15**, 574
      relational—
        fraud, and, **15**, 584
        negligence, and, **15**, 586–594
      See also ECONOMIC LOSS
      generally, **15**, 574
      pure economic loss, **15**, 574
    wealth, constituting part of, **15**, 547
  ejection, **15**, 215
  employer, committed by, **15**, 242
  employer and employee, vicarious liability, **15**, 243, 247–251
  enticement, **15**, 596
  extinction, **15**, 604–607
  fame and honour, injury to, **15**, 216
  family relationship, injuries to, *see* FAMILY RELATIONSHIP
  fault—
    culpa, **15**, 254
    definition, **15**, 252
    dolus, **15**, 253
    generally, **15**, 252
    intentional injury, **15**, 253
    unintentional injury, **15**, 254
  foreseeability—
    Polemis and *The Wagon Mound*, decisions in, **15**, 907
    Scots law, **15**, 908
  forgery, **15**, 216
  foster parent, committed by, **15**, 242
  fraud as—
    bad faith, fraud and, **11**, 720
    contractual and delictual remedies, **11**, 721
    delictual liability, **11**, 785
    development of law, **11**, 719
    generally, **15**, 216, 255, 585
    procedural and evidential aspects, **11**, 722

Delict—*continued*
function of law, **15**, 219
generally, **15**, 11, 213–219
historical background—
  early Scots law, **15**, 215
  English law, **15**, 213
  generally, **15**, 213
  institutional writers, **15**, 215, 216
  negligence, **15**, 217
  Roman law, **15**, 213, 214
  statute law, **15**, 218
imperial law, English law as, **5**, 718
incorporeal property, as, **18**, 11
injuria sine damno, **15**, 221
injury caused by, title to sue, **15**, 220
intentional, **15**, 253, 255
interest—
  nature of, **15**, 221
  scale of, **15**, 221
interest to sue, *see* title and interest to sue *below*
interference with honour and reputation, *see* HONOUR AND REPUTATION, INTERFERENCE WITH
judicial official, committed by, **15**, 242
jus quaesitum tertio, interaction with, **15**, 838
lawburrows, contravention, **15**, 216
liability—
  defences to, **15**, 392*ff*
  parties and types, **15**, 220*ff*
liberty, injury to, **15**, 216
limitation, **15**, 608
loss and wrongfulness, interaction between notions of, **15**, 219
meaning of delictual liability, **15**, 219
molestation, **15**, 216
multiple wrongs, where, **15**, 237
nautae, caupones, stabularii edict, **15**, 217
negligence, **15**, 217, 255, 256
nervous shock, **15**, 284
  See also CARE, DUTY OF
object of affection, injury to, **15**, 216
partners, vicarious liability, **15**, 246
passing off, **15**, 255
person, injury to, **15**, 216
Praetorian edicts, **15**, 217
prescription, **15**, 608
  building contracts, **3**, 174
principal and agent, vicarious liability, **15**, 243–246
private international law—
  aircraft, involving, **17**, 300
  alternative reference, rules of, **17**, 126
  characterisation of, **17**, 360
  choice of law for, **17**, 126
  double delict rule—
    defences, **17**, 295
    English law, differences with, **17**, 293
    general rule, **17**, 292
    limitation, **17**, 297
    matters of substance in delict, **17**, 296
    place of delict, **17**, 298
    prescription, **17**, 297
    proper law exceptions, **17**, 294
  evolution of choice of law rules, **17**, 123

Delict—continued
private international law—*continued*
  flexible connecting factors, **17**, 125
  Law Commission's memoranda on, **17**, 301
  reforms—
    anomalies in present law, **17**, 302
    case for, **17**, 301–306
    forum shopping, **17**, 305
    injustice, present law leads to, **17**, 303
    proposed, **17**, 307–309
    uncertainty of present law, **17**, 304
  sea, at, **17**, 299
  separate treatment of conflict rules, reasons for, **17**, 109
pro hac vice employment, vicarious liability, **15**, 249
professional liability, *see* PROFESSIONAL LIABILITY
property, injury to, **15**, 216
  interest in property, where, **15**, 220
  title to sue where transfer of ownership, **15**, 220
public nuisance or danger, action to prevent, **15**, 229
public rights, defence of, **15**, 229
pursuer—
  multiple pursuers, **15**, 236
  multiple wrongs to, **15**, 237
  title and interest to sue, *see* title and interest to sue *below*
quasi-delict, **15**, 217
recovery of possession, action for, claim by party recovering possession, **18**, 170
reparation, **15**, 216
representations as to credit, **3**, 1006, 1008
retribution, element of, **15**, 219
right in, incorporeal property, as, **18**, 652
risk re-allocation and spreading, element of, **15**, 219
sea, at, **17**, 299
settlement, **15**, 607
shipping—
  avoidance action, damage caused by, **21**, 311
  cargo damage, damages in respect of, **21**, 391, 391*n*
  collisions at sea, **21**, 311, 312
    See also SHIPPING (collision)
  commercial maritime activity, application to, generally, **21**, 101
  title to sue shipowner, **21**, 580
  towage contract, implied terms, **21**, 404
  tug and tow, generally, **21**, 401
special jurisdiction, **4**, 37
specialised concept of law, as, **11**, 1005
spouse, committed by, **15**, 242
spuilzie, **15**, 215
state of mind of company, means of determining, **4**, 318
support, right of, **18**, 254, 256, 258
tenant, committed by, **15**, 242
title and interest to sue—
  actio popularis, **15**, 229
  assignation, **15**, 220
  bankrupts, **15**, 230
  corporations, **15**, 228

Delict—continued
title and interest to sue—*continued*
  counterclaim, **15**, 222
  court officials, **15**, 227
  Crown, **15**, 223
    defender, as, **15**, 223, 224
    liability, exclusions, **15**, 225
    representation in Scotland, **15**, 223
  Crown servants, **15**, 226
  deceased—
    delicts of, liability, **15**, 231
    killed as result of another's delict, relatives of, **15**, 220, 232
    loss or injury to deceased or estate of, **15**, 231
  defend, title to, **15**, 222
  executors, **15**, 231
  injuries, in respect of, **15**, 220
  interest, generally, **15**, 221
  joint and several liability—
    apportionment, **15**, 241
    generally, **15**, 239, 243
    satisfaction of decree, **15**, 240
    vicarious liability, **15**, 243
  judges, **15**, 227
  judicial factors, **15**, 234
  liquidators, **15**, 230
  local authority, **15**, 223
  mandataries, **15**, 235
  ministers and executive officers, **15**, 226
  multiple defenders, **15**, 238
  multiple pursuers, **15**, 236
  multiple wrongs, **15**, 237
  property, damage to, **15**, 220
  prosecutors, **15**, 227
  public corporation, **15**, 223
  public departments, bodies or boards, **15**, 223
  public rights, defence of, **15**, 229
  receivers, **15**, 230
  Secretary of State for Scotland, **15**, 223
  title, generally, **15**, 220
  trustees, **15**, 233
  trustees in bankruptcy, **15**, 230, 231
  unincorporated associations, **15**, 229
transfer, **15**, 604–607
  bankruptcy, on, **15**, 606
  death, on, **15**, 605
  liquidation, on, **15**, 606
trustees' liability, **24**, 231
unintentional, **15**, 254
unjust enrichment, **15**, 11
use of term, **15**, 2, 3
verbal injuries, *see* DEFAMATION; VERBAL INJURY
vicarious liability—
  contractor, independent, **15**, 242, 243, 251
  culpa tenet suos auctores, **15**, 242, 243
  employer and employee, **15**, 243, 247–251
  generally, **15**, 242
  partners, **15**, 246
  principal and agent, **15**, 243–246
  pro hac vice employment, **15**, 249
wrongful act causing no loss or damage, **15**, 221
wrongful civil proceedings—
  abuse of process—
    breach of contract, **15**, 460

Delict—*continued*
wrongful civil proceedings—*continued*
  abuse of process—*continued*
    diligence—
      generally, **15**, 465
      heritage, against, **15**, 468
      moveable property, against, **15**, 467
      person, against, **15**, 466
    generally, **15**, 457
    interdict—
      generally, **15**, 461
      interim—
        continuing possession, **15**, 464
        inverting possession, **15**, 463
        perpetual, **15**, 462
    litigation, **15**, 458–460
    malice and want of probable cause, **15**, 457, 459
    sequestration, **15**, 469
wrongful detention, *see* DETENTION, WRONGFUL
wrongous diligence, **8**, 124
See also LEX LOCI DELICTI COMMISSI
Delivery
actual, **18**, 619
bill of exchange, symbolical delivery, as, **18**, 621
bill of lading, symbolical delivery, as, **18**, 621
brevi manu, **18**, 619, 622
constitutum possessorium, **18**, 619, 623
constructive, **18**, 619
contract of deposit constituted by, **8**, 8
corporeal moveable property—
  action for delivery founded on right to possession, **18**, 158
  defences, **18**, 158
  jurisdiction, **18**, 158
  actual delivery, **18**, 619
  brevi manu, delivery, **18**, 619, 622
  constitutum possessorium, **18**, 619, 623
  constructive delivery, **18**, 619
  fictitious delivery, **18**, 619
  longa manu, delivery, **18**, 619, 620, 620n
  modus transferendi, **18**, 619
  symbolical delivery, **18**, 621, 621n
  tracing person to whom delivery should be made, **18**, 158
  where required, **18**, 619
feudal law, **18**, 640
fictitious, **18**, 619
goods, of, *see* SALE AND SUPPLY OF GOODS
indorsement completed by, **4**, 143
longa manu, **18**, 619, 620, 620n
meaning, **4**, 137; **20**, 837n
modus transferendi, **18**, 619
moveable property, right in security—
  actual delivery, **20**, 9, 10
  appropriate to security subject, chosen method must be, **20**, 9
  attempted evasion of requirement of, **20**, 13
  bill of lading, **20**, 12
  constructive delivery, **20**, 9, 11
  physically impossible, where, **20**, 10
  pledge, **20**, 14
  symbolical delivery, **20**, 9, 12
natural possession, protection of, **18**, 138

Delivery—*continued*
possession, recovery of, **18**, 140
post, by, **4**, 137
recovery of possession, action for, **18**, 151
rei vindicatio, **18**, 158
symbolic—
  feudal law, **18**, 640
  generally, **18**, 621, 621n
  possession, and, **18**, 119, 119n
thing delivered but not actually received, **18**, 620
thing to be delivered in hands of third party, **18**, 620
transferor, delivery *longa manu*, **18**, 620
where required, **18**, 619
Delivery up, order for
intellectual property—
  breach of confidence, **18**, 1452, 1491
  copyright infringement, **18**, 1140
  generally, **18**, 1092, 1095, 1234
  registered industrial design, infringement, **18**, 1209
Delors Commission, **10**, 24
Democracy
local, as objective of reform, **14**, 44
local government grew from, **14**, 1
Demolition
'actual state' rule, **24**, 506
building operations regulations, **3**, 230
dangerous building—
  local authority powers—
    appeals against order requiring demolition, **3**, 236
    compulsory purchase, **3**, 235
    generally, **3**, 232
    sale of demolished materials, **3**, 234
house required for, repossession of assured tenancy, **13**, 749, 755
housing action areas, **11**, 1996, 1998
limited life, building deemed to have, **3**, 225
local authority control, **3**, 203
order—
  appeal against, **11**, 1986
  building preservation order, **11**, 1983
  closing order in place of, **11**, 1983
  compulsory acquisition of site, **11**, 1988
  consequences of, **11**, 1988
  demolition by local authority, **11**, 1988
  expenses, recovery of, **11**, 1988
  generally, **11**, 1983
  listed buildings, **11**, 1983
  local authority powers, **11**, 1983, 1987
  obstructive buildings, **11**, 1989
  offences with regard to, **11**, 1988
  power to make, **14**, 305
  requirements, **11**, 1983
  revocation, **11**, 1984
  service, **11**, 1985
  substitution for closing order, **11**, 1987
  suspension, **11**, 1984
  time for demolition, **11**, 1988
  vacation, notice requiring, **11**, 1988
partially demolished building, secured against entry, must be, **3**, 230
valuation for rating, **24**, 506

Demolition—*continued*
warrant, **3**, 220, 221
  appeal against refusal, **3**, 236
  completion date, **3**, 226
  deemed, **3**, 221
  failure to comply, civil liability, **3**, 230
  refusal, **3**, 221
  relaxation, application for, local authority tests, **3**, 239, 241
Demurrage
bill of lading, performance of contract, **21**, 585
calculation, **21**, 683
clause—
  bill of lading, express terms, **21**, 546
  contract, in, **15**, 718
conditions preventing accrual, **21**, 666
damages for detention, **21**, 682
delay caused by shipowner, **21**, 684, 684*n*
deviation, **21**, 615
exceptions—
  clauses, **21**, 547*n*
  to running, **21**, 684
fixed period, expiry, **21**, 685
generally, **21**, 682
liability—
  action, **21**, 688
  charterparty, **21**, 686
  general ship, **21**, 687
  lien, **21**, 686, 686*n*, 688
meaning, **21**, 666, 682
no provision for, where, **21**, 682, 685
not fixed, where, **21**, 682*n*
shipowner taking action to enable earlier end, **21**, 682
unreasonable length, running for, **21**, 682
voyage charterparty, **21**, 612, 618, 624*n*, 633
Denmark
civil jurisdiction, contracting state, as, **4**, 22
competition rules, application, **4**, 1304
European Union customs territory, **7**, 1010
Denomination
coins, of, **14**, 1820
notes, of, **14**, 1820
Treasury approval, **14**, 1823
Dentist
absences, **11**, 1458
anaesthetic administered by doctor or other dentist, **11**, 1450, 1456
application to, for general dental services, **11**, 1455
assistants, **11**, 1458, 1458*n*
capitation arrangements, provision of services under, **11**, 1453, 1461
  meaning of capitation arrangement, **11**, 1461*n*
  patients' records, **11**, 1461
clinical trial, **14**, 1207
complaints against, **11**, 1520
controlled drugs, use of, **14**, 1258
criminal offence by, **14**, 1139
dental list—
  application for inclusion in, **11**, 1454
  copies of, **11**, 1454
  reinstatement, application for, **11**, 1521
  removal from, **11**, 1454, 1521

Dentist—*continued*
dental list—*continued*
  Tribunal, inquiry by, **11**, 1425
  withdrawal from, **11**, 1454
dentistry, *see* DENTISTRY
deputies, **11**, 1458, 1458*n*
discipline, statutory regulation of, **23**, 917
disqualification of, **11**, 1521
fees, **11**, 1459, 1462
immigration rules—
  change of category, **12**, 298
  entry requirements, **12**, 295
  extension of leave, **12**, 300
  postgraduate training, **12**, 292
legal control, scope of, **14**, 1101
limited treatment, **11**, 1456
non-designated services, **4**, 1177
overseas practitioner, **14**, 1136
partners, **11**, 1458
partnership as business medium, **16**, 1004
patients, dental services to, **11**, 1456
poison, sale of, **14**, 1215
prescription, medicinal products supplied by, **14**, 1209
preventative treatment, **11**, 1456
professional misconduct, **14**, 1140
professional rules, partnership contravening, **16**, 1017
qualifications, supervising of grant of, **14**, 1135
records, duties as to, **11**, 1457, 1461
  capitation arrangements, dentist providing services under, **11**, 1461
  salaried dentists, **11**, 1460
registered—
  criminal offences by, **14**, 1139
  registration, generally, **14**, 1134
  serious professional misconduct, **14**, 1140
regulation of profession, **14**, 1132
remuneration, **11**, 1459, 1510
  Statement of Dental Remuneration, **11**, 1462
salaried, **11**, 1453, 1460
  meaning, **11**, 1460*n*
  records, duty to keep, **11**, 1460
surgeries, **11**, 1457
terms of service, **11**, 1453
  capitation arrangement, dentist working under, **11**, 1461
  salaried dentists, **11**, 1460
use of health service premises, goods or services, **11**, 1492
veterinary practice by, **25**, 203
waiting rooms, **11**, 1457
See also DENTISTRY
Dentistry
committee structure, *see* GENERAL MEDICAL COUNCIL
criminal offences, **14**, 1139
dental authority, **14**, 1134
dental auxiliaries—
  categories of, **14**, 1145
  committee, **14**, 1132, 1146
  dental hygienist, **14**, 1145
  dental therapist, **14**, 1145
  enrolment of, **14**, 1144

Dentistry—*continued*
dental auxiliaries—*continued*
  meaning, **14**, 1143
  training, **14**, 1144
dental hygienist, **14**, 1143, 1145
dental practice board, *see* SCOTTISH DENTAL
  PRACTICE BOARD
dental services, VAT exemption, **7**, 1426
dental therapist, **14**, 1143, 1145
dentist, *see* DENTIST
education, defects in course of, **14**, 1135
European Economic Community, national of
  member state, **14**, 1135
General Dental Council, *see* GENERAL DENTAL
  COUNCIL
general dental services—
  accommodation, health service provision, **11**,
    1476
  administrative authorities, **11**, 1402
  anaesthetics, provision of—
    dental practitioner, for, **11**, 1450, 1456
    fees for, **11**, 1450
  application for, **11**, 1455
  area dental committee, **11**, 1423
  arrangements for, **11**, 1452
  charges for dental appliances and treatment, **11**,
    1514, 1516
  complaints, **11**, 1520
  dental auxiliary, treatment by, **11**, 1456
  dental list, *see* DENTIST
  dental service committee, **11**, 1520
  dentist, *see* DENTIST
  executive councils, **11**, 1402
  fees, **11**, 1459
  health boards, administration by, **11**, 1410
  obtaining general dental services, **11**, 1455
  private practice, health service facilities used
    for, **11**, 1496
  records, **11**, 1457
  schools, provision in, **11**, 1479
  Scottish Dental Practice Board, *see* SCOTTISH
    DENTAL PRACTICE BOARD
  Statement of Dental Remuneration, **11**, 1462
  surgeries, **11**, 1457
  treatment must be completed with reasonable
    expedition, **11**, 1456
  waiting rooms, **11**, 1457
overseas practitioner, **14**, 1136
penalties, **14**, 1141
practice of—
  corporate body, by, **14**, 1133
  meaning, **14**, 1133
  offences, **14**, 1133
  restrictions on, **14**, 1133
serious professional misconduct, **14**, 1140
  penalties, **14**, 1141
Dépeçage
meaning, **17**, 110
Dependant
immigration—
  entry clearance requirement, **12**, 264, 265
  extension of leave, **12**, 266
  meaning, **12**, 264
  settlement in UK, application for, **12**, 266

Dependant—*continued*
inadequate provision in will for, **25**, 611
meaning void through uncertainty, **13**, 1627
term too vague to receive effect in will, **12**, 1268
Deportation
alternatives to, **12**, 215
appeal against, **12**, 202, 211, 335
breach of conditions, following, **12**, 205
British citizen, deportee becoming, **12**, 214
Channel Islands, order made by, **12**, 123
Commonwealth citizen, **12**, 126
compassionate circumstances, **12**, 202, 210
control of departure decisions, limits on appeals
  relating to, **12**, 342
court recommendation, **12**, 202, 204, 206, 209
  general principles, **12**, 206, 209
court's discretion to recommend, **17**, 809
curtailment of stay as alternative to, **12**, 215
decision, **12**, 202
  appeal against, **12**, 202, 211, 335
  consistency in, **12**, 202, 210
  general considerations, **12**, 209
  grounds for, **12**, 204
  notification of, **12**, 211
    detention permitted by, **12**, 211, 213
    unsuccessful service, **12**, 211
detention prior to, **12**, 38
European Union national, **12**, 203
family of deportee, **12**, 204, 208
  voluntary departure, **12**, 215
grounds for—
  breach of conditions, **12**, 186
  overstaying, **12**, 186
immigration control, exempt groups, **12**, 132
Immigration Rules, **12**, 149
imprisonment, conviction of offence punishable
  by, **12**, 206
indefinite leave to enter or remain, **12**, 120, 177
Isle of Man, order made by, **12**, 123
liability for, **12**, 203
marriages of convenience, **12**, 207
meaning, **12**, 147, 202
member of Parliament, representation by, **12**, 376
notice, **12**, 202
order, **12**, 212
  detention pending, **12**, 211, 213
  effect of, **12**, 212
  lapse, **12**, 214
  person subject to, refusal of leave to enter, **12**,
    171
  revocation, **12**, 214
    appeal against refusal, **12**, 214
    no entitlement to enter conferred by, **12**,
      214
overstaying as ground for, **12**, 204, 205
protected status, **12**, 126
public good, **12**, 204, 207
public interest, **12**, 202, 210
refugees, **12**, 203, 321, 322
regulations, Secretary of State's powers as to, **12**,
  138
Republic of Ireland, citizen of, **12**, 126
right to be heard before, **1**, 264, 265
Secretary of State, order by, **12**, 202

Deportation—*continued*
'security' deportation cases, **12**, 335
supervised departure as alternative to, **12**, 215
See also ADMINISTRATIVE REMOVAL
Deposit
candidate in election, payment by—
  acceptance, **15**, 1288
  forfeiture, **15**, 1290
  form, **15**, 1287, 1288
  holding, **15**, 1289
  requirement for, **15**, 1287
  return, **15**, 1290
  time provisions, **15**, 1227
  whether paid, determination, **15**, 1258
contract of—
  accessories, **8**, 5
    restoration, depositary's duty as to, **8**, 14
  accretions, **8**, 5
  agreed period, deposit for, **8**, 11
  bill of exchange, **8**, 4
  bonds, **8**, 4
  commodatum, contract of, **8**, 17
  computerised information, **8**, 4
  consent, based on, **8**, 2, 22
  delivery, constituted by, **8**, 8
  depositary, *see* DEPOSITARY
  depositer, *see* DEPOSITOR
  depositor, *see* DEPOSITOR
  donation, defence of, **8**, 10
  executory contract not, **8**, 8
  gratuitous nature, **8**, 3, 3*n*
  heritage may not be subject of, **8**, 4
  improper deposit, **8**, 7
  indemnified, depositary must be, **8**, 12, 12*n*
  lien, and, **8**, 15, 15*n*
  locatio custodiae, contract of, **8**, 3
  locatio operis faciendi, contract of, **8**, 3
  nature of, **8**, 1
  obligations of parties—
    depositary, **8**, 13–17, 13*n*
    depositor, **8**, 11, 12, 12*n*
  parole evidence, proved by, **8**, 10
  possession, transfer of, **8**, 9
  property, concealed in property lawfully deposited, **8**, 2, 6
  prout de jure, proved, **8**, 10
  remuneration or reward accepted by depositary, **8**, 3
  Roman law, origins in, **8**, 1
  subject matter—
    accretions and accessories, deposit of, **8**, 5
    alienation of thing deposited, **8**, 16
    bill of exchange, **8**, 4
    bonds, **8**, 4
    computerised information, **8**, 4
    contents, deposit of, **8**, 6
    contents of thing deposited, **8**, 2, 6
    corporeal moveables, **8**, 4
    damage to, liability for, **8**, 14
    dangerous, **8**, 12*n*
    delivery of, **8**, 8
    depositary must not use, **8**, 17
    depositor must take back, **8**, 11
    excluded property, **8**, 4

Deposit—*continued*
contract of—*continued*
  subject matter—*continued*
    fungibles, deposit of, **8**, 7
    heritage, document relating to, **8**, 4
    incorporeal moveables—
      document relating to, **8**, 4
      may not be subject, **8**, 4
    money, **8**, 7, 10
    possession, not ownership, transferred, **8**, 9
    reasonable care of property deposited, depositary's duty to take, **8**, 13
    restoration, **8**, 14, 15
      depositary claiming goods already returned, **8**, 13
      depositary's failure to restore, **8**, 13
    retention by depositary, **8**, 15
    third party—
      obtaining possession, **8**, 15
      responsibility for acts of, **8**, 13
    title, document of, **8**, 4
    unabandoned property, position of finder, **8**, 2
    wrongful interference with thing deposited, **8**, 17
deposit of—
  subject matter—
    repair or other work to be done on, **8**, 3
deposit-taking institution, *see* DEPOSIT-TAKING INSTITUTION
depositum ex necessitate, concept of, **8**, 2, 22
goods held on, restitution, **15**, 46, 49
onerous, **8**, 3, 3*n*
payment of, **13**, 693
property on, negative prescription, **18**, 566
reward, for, **8**, 3
trust compared, **24**, 6, 9
unsolicited goods, recipient of, **8**, 2, 2*n*
Deposit receipt
donation, **8**, 637
donation *mortis causa*, **8**, 630
reduction, **13**, 37
Deposit-taking institution
accounts, EEC Directive, **2**, 1155
authorisation of—
  appeals respecting, **2**, 1144
  application for, **2**, 1143
  assets, minimum, for, **2**, 1139, 1143
  criteria for, **2**, 1143
  exemption as to, **2**, 1142
  information required for, **2**, 1144
  partnership, in case of, **2**, 1143
  requirement for, **2**, 1140
  revocation or restriction, **2**, 1144
authorised—
  annual list of, **2**, 1144
  bodies deemed to be, **2**, 1141
Bank of England, control by, **2**, 1144
banks, **2**, 1103
Board of Banking Supervision, control by, **2**, 1144
deposit advertisements—
  meaning, **2**, 1149
  misleading, **2**, 1150
  regulation of, **2**, 1149

Deposit-taking institution—*continued*
Deposit Protection Board—
  continuance of, **2**, 1145
  contributions, determination of, by, **2**, 1146
Deposit Protection Fund—
  bank account for, **2**, 1145
  continuance of, **2**, 1145
  contributions to, **2**, 1146
  protected deposit, amount, **2**, 1139, 1147
  purpose of, **2**, 1147
deposit receipts—
  meaning, **2**, 1103
  obligation to pay, **2**, 1195
deposit-taking business—
  exempted transactions, **2**, 1142
  meaning, **2**, 1141
deposits—
  fraudulently inducing, **2**, 1151
  meaning, **2**, 1140
  protection, amount of, **2**, 1139
  unsolicited calls to procure, **2**, 1152
EEC Directive, *see* BANK-BANKING
investigation of, **2**, 1144
name, control of use of, **2**, 1148
statutory provisions, **2**, 1139
supervision, recommendations for, **2**, 1139
unsolicited calls by, **2**, 1152
winding up, **2**, 1144
Depositary
alienation of thing deposited, **8**, 16
claiming deposited goods already restored to
  depositor, **8**, 13
damages, liability for, **8**, 14
delivery of subject into possession of, **8**, 8
edictal liability, **8**, 1*n*
expenses, claiming, **8**, 3*n*, 12, 12*n*, 15
indemnified by depositor, must be, **8**, 12, 12*n*
involuntary, **8**, 2
meaning, **8**, 1
meddling with goods, **8**, 2*n*
must not use thing deposited, **8**, 17
possession transferred to, **8**, 9
reasonable care of property deposited, duty to
  take, **8**, 13
remuneration or reward accepted by, **8**, 3
request for deposit to be removed, **8**, 11
restoration of subject matter—
  burden of proof, **8**, 14
  duty as to, **8**, 14
  refusal to restore, **8**, 14
  wrongful retention of thing deposited, **8**, 15
retention, has no right of, **8**, 15
servant of, acts or ommissions by, **8**, 13
sub-depositary, acts or omissions of, **8**, 13, 13*n*
third parties, responsibility for acts of, **8**, 13
unsolicited goods, as recipient of, **8**, 2, 2*n*
wrongful interference with thing deposited, **8**, 17
Deposition
contract of, *see* DEPOSIT
Depositor (depositer)
meaning, **8**, 1
obligations of—
  depositary must be indemnified, **8**, 12, 12*n*
  taking back thing deposited, **8**, 11

Depreciated replacement cost
property assets, valuation of, **25**, 94
Depression
diminished responsibility, **7**, 147
Deputy Clerk Register
creation of office, **19**, 805, 808
decline of office, **19**, 811
duties, **19**, 808, 809
history of office, **19**, 808–811
rights, **19**, 809
Derelict
danger to navigation, master's duty to report, **21**,
  210
meaning, **21**, 511
wreck—
  compared, **21**, 511
  when classed as, **21**, 511
Derivative action
minority shareholders, rights of, **4**, 470
Desborough Committee
report, **16**, 1708, 1708*n*
Descendant
direct, application of *conditio* outside, **25**, 897
heritable succession, **25**, 678
moveable succession, **25**, 682
Descent
British citizenship, acquisition of, **14**, 1911, 1922,
  1924
British Dependent Territories citizenship, **14**,
  1935, 1941
Falkland Islands, **14**, 1924
Desertion
armed forces by—
  assisting, **7**, 601
  incitement, **7**, 597
irretrievable breakdown of marriage, *see* DIVORCE
Design
exclusive jurisdiction, **4**, 58, 59, 60
industrial, *see* INDUSTRIAL DESIGN, PROTECTION OF
meaning, **18**, 1214
registered, *see* INDUSTRIAL DESIGN, PROTECTION OF
  (REGISTERED DESIGNS)
registration of, assignation, **6**, 602
rights—
  Comptroller-General of Patents, Designs and
    Trade Marks, **18**, 814
  intellectual property, as, **18**, 801
  International Convention for the Protection of
    Industrial Property (Paris Convention)
    (1883), **18**, 801, 865, 865*n*, 891, 1151
  transfer of ownership, **18**, 653
special jurisdiction, **4**, 48
unregistered, *see* INDUSTRIAL DESIGN, PROTECTION
  OF (UNREGISTERED DESIGN RIGHT)
Design and build contract, **3**, 9
Design document
copyright—
  artistic works, **18**, 1155
  restriction, **18**, 1154
definition, **18**, 1154
reproduction as infringement of unregistered
  design right, **18**, 1230, 1231
three-dimensional article copied from two-
  dimensional design document, **18**, 1154

Design, manage, construct contract, 3, 9
Design responsibility
architect's design obligations, **3**, 135
contractor's obligations, **3**, 37
Designation order
local authority power to make, **14**, 304
smoke control area, relating to, **14**, 304
Designs Registry
generally, **18**, 1162
Despatch money (despatch)
bill of lading, **21**, 689
laytime, **21**, 689
meaning, **21**, 666
Destination
feudal law, generally, **18**, 111
heir of provision, **18**, 111
moveable property, conversion to heritable
property, **18**, 15
over, *see* VESTING
special, *see* SPECIAL DESTINATION
Destructive animals
regulations with regard to, **2**, 218
Desuetude, doctrine of
Bankton—
sovereign's tacit consent, notion of, **22**, 131
statute and custom as sources of law, **22**, 131
contrary custom, derogation from statute, **22**, 376
Craig, **22**, 364
Erskine, **22**, 130
generally, **22**, 129–133, 256
law reform, contribution to, **22**, 626
Mackenzie, **22**, 130
pre-Union legislation, **22**, 376, 526, 626
redundancy in modern context, extent, **22**, 133
retention of principle in modern Scots law, **22**,
376, 381
Stair, **22**, 129
time immemorial, statute in desuetude since, **22**,
381
udal law, whether applicable to, **24**, 304
Detention
arrest distinguished, **16**, 1788
centre—
offenders under twenty-one, for, **16**, 1404
persons committed to, **22**, 32
custody, **16**, 1788
customs officers' powers—
goods, detention of, **7**, 1216
means of transport, detention of, **7**, 1240
person, detention of, **7**, 1229
drug smuggling offence, relating to, **7**, 1230
damages for, *see* SEA, CARRIAGE BY
deportation, prior to, **12**, 38
end of detention period, what constitutes, **12**, 32
European Convention on Human Rights, **16**, 1806
extradition, prior to, **12**, 37
fingerprints, taking, **16**, 1796
firearm, using or attempting to use to resist, **16**,
1807
force, use of, **16**, 1796
freedom from, European Convention on Human
Rights, **12**, 6, 85, 86
further detention on same grounds disallowed, **16**,
1796

Detention—*continued*
indeterminate length, **12**, 35
lawfulness to be decided speedily, **12**, 33
legalised police cells, in, **16**, 1822
meaning, **16**, 1788
minors, of, **12**, 39
parole, life prisoners, **12**, 35
period of, **16**, 1796
police powers—
common law, **16**, 1794
force, use of, **16**, 1795
generally, **16**, 1787, 1788; **17**, 594
individual not under arrest, **16**, 1794
'on the street' search, **16**, 1795
statute law, **16**, 1795
police station, individual taken to, **16**, 1795
possession, and, *see* POSSESSION
questioning, for, **16**, 1796
questions, whether legal obligation to answer, **16**,
1796
record of, **16**, 1796
rights of detainee, **16**, 1796
search, for, **16**, 1796, 1797
See also ARREST OR DETENTION
setting off against custodial sentence, **12**, 34
six-hour detention power, **16**, 1791, 1794, 1796
property of persons in detention, **16**, 1821
solicitor, right of detainee to inform, **16**, 1796
terrorism, person suspected of involvement in, **16**,
1801
unlawful, **7**, 550
irregular, or, **16**, 1788
unreasonable or unnecessary, **16**, 1784, 1788,
1793
unsound mind, persons of, **12**, 41
vagrancy, **12**, 42
voluntary surrender to, **12**, 42
without trial, **12**, 32
witness, of, **16**, 1795
wrongful—
beyond that authorised, **15**, 445
child's movements, restriction of, **15**, 437
compensation for, **7**, 730
damages in respect of, **15**, 435
detention, what constitutes, **15**, 436
European Convention on Human Rights, **15**,
435
generally, **15**, 435
imprisonment for debt, **15**, 466
intentional delict, as, **15**, 437
judges, liability, **15**, 441–443
judicial order, detention by, **15**, 441
detention beyond authorisation, **15**, 445
legal protection of liberty, generally, **15**, 435
length, **15**, 436
liability, **15**, 441, 442
malice—
generally, **15**, 439
jurisdiction, **15**, 443
prosecuting agencies, liability, **15**, 444
malicious prosecution, following, **15**, 447
personal injury, **15**, 435
prosecuting agencies, liability, **15**, 444
statute, detention authorised by, **15**, 437

Detention—*continued*
wrongful—*continued*
  suspicion of crime, detention on, **15**, 438
  threats of physical violence, by, **15**, 436
  time limit for actions, **15**, 435
  unjustified further procedures, **15**, 440
  unknowing detention, **15**, 437
  voluntary limitation of freedom, **15**, 437
  want of probable cause—
    generally, **15**, 439
    jurisdiction, **15**, 443
    prosecuting agencies, liability, **15**, 444
  wrongful, what amounts to, **15**, 437

Detonators
explosives, as, **10**, 1586

Development
See COMPULSORY ACQUISITION; TOWN AND COUNTRY PLANNING

Development corporation
allocation of houses, **11**, 1935
landlord, as, assured tenancy status excluded, **13**, 636, 647
reduction of powers, **11**, 1920

Development of the Common Market for Telecommunications Services and Equipment, **Green Paper**
generally, **16**, 1966, 1967, 1973

Development of the Single Market Postal Services, **Green Paper**
generally, **16**, 1913

Development order
road affected by, stopping up and diversion, **20**, 654

Devolution, succession
See SUCCESSION

Devolution of Scotland and Wales
devolved matters, **5**, 335
formal machinery contrasted with effective powers, **5**, 334
Scotland Act, **9**, 1978
  background to, **5**, 333
  provisions, **5**, 332
Wales, in, **5**, 332

Dhekelia, Sovereign Base Area of
British Dependent Territories citizenship, **14**, 1932
civil jurisdiction, **4**, 23

Diabetes
automatism, as cause of, **7**, 151
diagnosis of, **11**, 1467
hypoglycaemic episode, offence committed during, **7**, 113
mental condition, relevance, **7**, 114
person suffering from, ophthalmic services, **11**, 1463*n*

Diagram
copyright, **18**, 958

Dialysis
attendance allowance where claimant receiving, **21**, 925
disability living allowance where claimant receiving, **21**, 932
sickness benefit where claimant receiving, **21**, 880

Dicey, A V
Parliamentary sovereignty, dogma, **22**, 120
Union legislation as fundamental law, objection to thesis, **22**, 148

Dies a quo
meaning, **22**, 828

Dies ad quem
meaning, **22**, 828

Diesel engine
EEC directives on, **9**, 1143

Diet
See TRIAL

Dietitian
Council for Professions Supplementary to Medicine, **15**, 1516–1521
employment of, **11**, 1500

Diffuse mesothelioma
prescribed diseases regulations, **21**, 992, 997

Dignity
donated, may not be, **8**, 615

Diligence
abuse of process—
  arrestment, **15**, 465, 467
  diligence as of right, **15**, 465
  generally, **15**, 465
  heritage, diligence against, **15**, 468
  inhibition on the dependence, **15**, 546
  liability, **15**, 465
  malice and want of probable cause, **15**, 465, 468
  moveable property, diligence against, **15**, 467
  person, diligence against, **15**, 466
  poinding, **15**, 465
  requirements for, **15**, 465
  warrant, requirement for, **15**, 465
adjudication, *see* ADJUDICATION
administration distinguished, **8**, 106
advantages of procedure, **8**, 106
aircraft, against, **8**, 329
apprising, replacement by adjudication, **8**, 189
arrestment, *see* ARRESTMENT
bankruptcy, and, **8**, 106
beneficiaries' rights, **24**, 56
breach by tenant, as remedy against, **13**, 275
Child Support Act (1991), Secretary of State's privileges under, **8**, 128
common law, **8**, 103
confirmation as executor-creditor, *see* EXECUTOR-CREDITOR
Court of Session procedure, **17**, 1397
creditor, *see* CREDITOR
criminal law, use in, **8**, 132
Crown immunity, **7**, 747
Crown preferences, **7**, 747; **8**, 128
  taxes, **8**, 129
death of debtor, effect, **8**, 127
debitum fundi, adjudication on, *see* DEBITUM FUNDI
debt—
  civil imprisonment for, **8**, 101
  debitum fundi, adjudication on, **8**, 101
  enforcement of secured, **8**, 101
  mails and duties, *see* MAILLS AND DUTIES
  maritime arrestment *in rem*, **8**, 101

Diligence—*continued*
debt—*continued*
  poinding of the ground, *see* POINDING OF THE
    GROUND
  sequestration for rent and feuduty, **8**, 101
debt arrangement schemes, proposals omitted
    from draft legislation, **22**, 679
debtor, *see* DEBTOR
deceased debtor—
  basis of diligence, **25**, 1054
  exclusion of diligence, **25**, 1053
decree—
  use without, **8**, 101
  without, **8**, 120
    summary warrant, **8**, 121
decree of registration, **8**, 122
dependence, on—
  expenses, **17**, 1200
  expenses, liability for, **8**, 131
  judicial disrection, **8**, 126
  proposed reforms, **8**, 104
designation, error in, **8**, 125
earnings, against, *see* EARNINGS
effect of, **8**, 115, 116
equalisation of—
  arrestments and poindings, **2**, 1394
  deceased debtor's estate, **2**, 1395
  during sequestration, **2**, 1396
  outwith sequestration, **2**, 1394
  upon sequestration, **2**, 1395
equivalent to formal intimation of assignation, as,
    20, 49
error in designation, **8**, 125
execution of, **17**, 1150
expenses, **8**, 131
feuduty, *see* FEUDUTY
floating charge, attachment of, **4**, 663
foreign bankruptcy, interaction with diligence
    against Scottish assets, **8**, 130
foreign judgment, on, *see* JUDGMENTS
forms of, **2**, 1393
generally, **15**, 465
goods not belonging to debtor, **22**, 664
heritable property, **18**, 13
heritable securities, competition with rights
    acquired by, **20**, 248
  adjudger, rights of, **20**, 251
  inhibitor, rights of, **20**, 251
historical background, **8**, 102
improper, **14**, 1507
inchoate, **8**, 286
incorporeal property, **18**, 13
inhibition, *see* INHIBITION
introductory note, **2**, 1393
irregular, **15**, 465
judicial direction, **8**, 126
judicial factor's duty of, **24**, 248
jus in re aliena, where, **8**, 111
Law Reform Committee for Scotland 1964
    report, **22**, 664
legislation, **2**, 1302; **22**, 679
lessee, effect on, **13**, 184
lessor, effect on, **13**, 158
letters of, **7**, 883

Diligence—*continued*
letters staying or prohibiting, **7**, 883
lex situs, **8**, 130
liquidation distinguished, **8**, 106
litigiosity, **8**, 116
maills and duties, *see* MAILLS AND DUTIES
maritime arrestment *in rem*, **8**, 101
meaning, **8**, 101
messenger-at-arms—
  liability, improper diligence, **14**, 1507
  remuneration for, **14**, 1505
  wrongous diligence, **14**, 1507
money, against, **14**, 1812
moveable property, **18**, 13
nature, **8**, 101
nexus, **8**, 115
nullifying effect of, **2**, 1395
officers of court, exercise by, **8**, 105
partnership property, **8**, 128
pension, against, *see* PENSION
personal, **8**, 118
poinding, *see* POINDING; POINDING OF THE GROUND
power of sale, where conferred, **18**, 667
preference by, avoidance of, **2**, 1394
principal debtor, against, by cautioner, **3**, 938
prior tempore potier jure rule, **8**, 106
private international law, **8**, 130
property law, and—
  catholic securities, **8**, 117
  co-ownership, **8**, 110
  generally, **8**, 107
  jura in re aliena, **8**, 111
  litigiosity, **8**, 116
  nexus, **8**, 115
  personal diligence, **8**, 118
  personal rights, **8**, 112
  real diligence, **8**, 118
  secondary securities, **8**, 117
  third party rights, **8**, 108
  trust rights, **8**, 113, 114
  where debtor has no title, **8**, 109
public policy restrictions, **8**, 126
railway stock and plant, **19**, 1101
real, **8**, 118
receivership distinguished, **8**, 106
recovery by, **17**, 1149
reforms—
  proposed, **8**, 104
  statutory, **8**, 103
right, as matter of, **8**, 126
Scottish Law Commission consultative memoranda,
    22, 679
sequestration—
  decree, effect, **2**, 1395
  distinguished, **8**, 106
  rent, for, *see* SEQUESTRATION FOR RENT
  rent and feuduty, for, **8**, 101
sheriff court procedure—
  diligence, expenses of, **17**, 1200
  execution of, **17**, 1150
  recovery by diligence, **17**, 1149
  sisting of diligence, **17**, 1030
  summary causes, **17**, 1330
  supersession of, **17**, 1184

Diligence—*continued*
ship, against, *see* ARRESTMENT
ship as subject, **21**, 107
sisting of, **17**, 1030
summary—
    meaning, **8**, 122
    registration, time limit, **8**, 121
    remedy against, **8**, 121
    where applicable, **8**, 121
summary causes, **17**, 1330
supersession of, **17**, 1184
suspension to stay, **13**, 15
third party—
    jus in re aliena, **8**, 111
    personal rights of, **8**, 112
    property owned by, **8**, 107
    right in property, owning, **8**, 108
    trust rights, interaction with, **8**, 113, 114
UK civil judgments, reciprocal enforcement scheme, *see* JUDGMENTS (non-Scottish)
unincorporated voluntary association, **8**, 128
use of term, **8**, 101
vitiations—
    error in designation, **8**, 125
    wrongous diligence—
        defensive measures, **8**, 123
        reparation, **8**, 124
warrant for—
    generally, **8**, 119; **15**, 465
    summary, **8**, 121
winding up, effect on—
    adjudications, **4**, 844
    apparent insolvency, effect of, **4**, 848
    arrestments, **4**, 845
    bankruptcy rules, application of, **4**, 843
    Cross-Border provisions, **4**, 847
    inhibitions, **4**, 844
    poindings, **4**, 845, 846
    taxes, **4**, 849
wrongous, **14**, 1507; **15**, 465
    defensive measures, **8**, 123
    delict, amounting to, **8**, 124
    reparation, **8**, 124
Diligence Register
generally, **8**, 141*n*
Diminished responsibility
alcoholism, **7**, 133, 138
assault, mitigatory plea in case of, **7**, 237, 242
battered woman syndrome, **7**, 147
Brennan v HM Advocate, **7**, 128
burden of proof, **10**, 747, 756
culpability, and, **7**, 136
culpable homicide, **7**, 135, 138, 139, 149, 150, 253, 278
depression, **7**, 147
doctrine in Scots law, **7**, 137–140, 278
    modern, **7**, 140
early use of term, **7**, 137
generally, **7**, 114
HM Advocate v Savage, decision in, **7**, 140, 141
homicide, **7**, 253
housebreaking, **7**, 150
intoxication, **7**, 128–130, 133, 135, 148

Diminished responsibility—*continued*
mental disease—
    proof, **7**, 142
    requirement of, **7**, 140, 141
    strict legal formula, application, **7**, 143
murder cases, **7**, 135, 136, 138, 139, 149, 150
personality disorders, **7**, 144, 145
pre-menstrual syndrome, **7**, 146
psychopathy, **7**, 144, 145
requirements for plea of, **7**, 140
strict legal formula, application, problems arising, **7**, 143
test for, **7**, 139
theft, **7**, 150
Diocese
Roman Catholic Church, **3**, 1655
Diphtheria
vaccination against, **11**, 1446
Diplomacy
diplomatic correspondence, **19**, 642
diplomatic immunity—
    agents and mission personnel, **19**, 682
    choice of law, current approach to, **17**, 129
    consular staff, **19**, 684
    evidence, and, **10**, 526
    International Court of Justice judges, **19**, 722
    mission premises, **19**, 683
    naturalisation, requirements for, **14**, 1920
    ordinarily resident, meaning, **14**, 1905; **19**, 679, 681–684
diplomatic mission—
    immigration control, **14**, 1905
    immunity of premises, **19**, 683
    offences against, **19**, 695*n*
diplomatic relations—
    cessation of, **19**, 661*n*
    customary international law, **19**, 681
    initiation of, **19**, 661*n*
    severance of, **19**, 632
    Vienna Convention on, **19**, 681
diplomatic service—
    diplomatic agent, meaning, **19**, 682*n*
    non-national servants, **19**, 682*n*
Diplomat
customs and excise duty relief, **7**, 1117
family of, **12**, 130
foreign—
    allegiance to British Crown not owed by, **7**, 581
    official secrets legislation, application, **7**, 627
goods imported for, **7**, 1314
immigration control, **12**, 130
inland purchases by, **7**, 1290
passport of, **16**, 1236
precedence, **16**, 2014
protection—
    Crown's duty as to, **16**, 1212
    passport as aid in seeking, **16**, 1203
servants and staff, **12**, 247
UK, right to enter, **16**, 1208
Diplomatic asylee
see ASYLUM

Diplomatic Service
lawyers in, generally, **13**, 1392, 1393
representative of, visits to foreign prisoner, **16**, 1460
Direct broadcasting
satellite, by, **17**, 7
Direct debit
insurance premium payment by, **12**, 833
Direct effect, doctrine of
European Community law, **10**, 81, 83
Director
company, of, *see* COMPANY
Director General of Fair Trading
annual report, **4**, 1119, 1988
anti-competitive practices, *see* COMPETITION LAW
appointment and dismissal, **6**, 14
Channel Tunnel Act 1987, powers under, **4**, 1121
Companies Act 1989, powers under, **4**, 1121
competition, statement on, **9**, 821
confidential guidance by, **4**, 1273
consumer protection, public corporations, **19**, 241
Council on Tribunals, supervision by, **5**, 803
creation of post, **6**, 13
discretion of, **4**, 1268
export agreements, particulars of, **4**, 1180
Fair Trading Act 1973, investigation under, **4**, 562
fees, **5**, 803
Financial Services Act 1986, powers under, **4**, 1121
functions, **4**, 1121; **5**, 803
mergers, powers relating to, **4**, 1121
monopoly reference may be made by, **4**, 1233
monopoly situations, powers relating to, **4**, 1121, 1232
register, maintenance of—
    changes, duty to notify, **14**, 952
    fees, **14**, 951
    maintenance of, **14**, 951
    matters required to be registered, **14**, 951
    unlicensed trader, enforceability of agreements made by, **14**, 953
Registrar of Restrictive Trading Agreements, transfer of functions of, **4**, 1126
registration of agreements, **4**, 1180
role of, **4**, 1273
scope of functions, **6**, 15, 16
Scottish Committee, supervision by, **23**, 911*n*
tribunal, as, **5**, 803
UK authorities, attitude of, **4**, 1119
See also OFFICE OF FAIR TRADING
Director General of Telecommunications
appointment, **16**, 1922
functions and duties, **16**, 1922, 1923, 1926
generally, **6**, 165
incapacity or misbehaviour, **16**, 1922
Office of Telecommunications (OFTEL), **16**, 1923
regulatory agency, as, **16**, 1921
removal, **16**, 1922
Directorate-General for Telecommunications, Information Industries and Innovation (DG XIII)
generally, **16**, 1966

Directory information telecommunications services
regulatory control, **16**, 1923
telecommunications service, as, **16**, 1924
Disability appeal tribunal
appeal to, generally, **21**, 1162
constitution, **21**, 1174
member, invalidity benefit, **21**, 896
organisation, **21**, 1174
proceedings before, **21**, 1180
referral of cases to, **21**, 1180
Social Security Commissioner, appeal to, **21**, 1182
Disability living allowance
absent from Great Britain, claimant, **21**, 1025
adjudication, **21**, 1152, 1162, 1167, 1168, 1171
    appeals, **21**, 1167
    review, **21**, 1167, 1168
age of claimant—
    over pensionable age, **21**, 928
    under sixteen, **21**, 929
appeal to—
    generally, **21**, 1180
    notice of, **21**, 1180
    time limit, **21**, 1180
attendance allowance, interaction with, **21**, 925
care component—
    adjudication, **21**, 1167
    attention in connection with bodily functions, **21**, 929, 931
    awarded alone or together with mobility component, **21**, 928
    claim, generally, **21**, 933
    continual supervision test, **21**, 930
    cooked main meal, inability to prepare, **21**, 929
    entitlement—
        conditions of, **21**, 929
        generally, **21**, 933
    generally, **21**, 928
    hospitalisation of claimant, effect, **21**, 932
    mental disablement, **21**, 929
    night care, requirement for, **21**, 929
    physical disablement, **21**, 929
    rates, **21**, 929
    renal dialysis, claimant undergoing, **21**, 932
    severely disabled physcally or mentally, **21**, 929, 931
    terminally ill claimant, **21**, 933
chairman, powers of, **21**, 1180
disability appeal tribunal, **21**, 1152, 1162, 1180
entitlement—
    care component, **21**, 929, 933
    generally, **21**, 801, 928
    mobility component, **21**, 934
    period of, **21**, 928
income support—
    disability premium, **21**, 1074
    pensioner premium, **21**, 1074
invalid care allowance and, **21**, 949
member absent, where, **21**, 1180
mental disablement, **21**, 929
mobility component—
    adjudication, **21**, 1168
    age, requirement as to, **21**, 934

Disability living allowance—*continued*
mobility component—*continued*
  awarded alone or together with care
    component, **21**, 928
  blind and deaf claimant, **21**, 934, 936
  entitlement—
    conditions of, **21**, 934
    generally, **21**, 934, 939
  generally, **21**, 928
  inability to walk, **21**, 934, 935
  outdoors without guidance or support, **21**, 934,
    938
  rates, **21**, 940
  severely mentally impaired claimant, **21**, 934,
    937, 939
overlapping benefits, **21**, 999, 1001
physical disablement, **21**, 929
rates—
  care component, **21**, 929
  mobility component, **21**, 940
residence and presence in Great Britain,
  requirement as to, **21**, 928
Disability working allowance
adjudication, **21**, 1152, 1162, 1168, 1171
  appeals, **21**, 1168
  review, **21**, 1168
calculation, **21**, 1100
capital limits, **21**, 1100
definition, **21**, 1097
disability appeal tribunal, **21**, 1152, 1162, 1180
entitlement conditions, **21**, 1099
family credit, interaction with, **21**, 1090, 1100
income support—
  disability premium, **21**, 1074
  pensioner premium, **21**, 1074
introduction, **21**, 1097
legislation, **21**, 1098
purpose, **21**, 1097
qualification, **21**, 1100
Disabled person
attendance allowance, *see* ATTENDANCE ALLOWANCE
constant attendance needed, disablement benefit,
  21, 983
contributory negligence by, **15**, 406
Criminal Injuries Compensation Scheme,
  applications, **7**, 1, 3
day-care facilities, **22**, 10, 24
  See also DAY FACILITIES
disability appeal tribunal, *see* DISABILITY APPEAL
  TRIBUNAL
disability living allowance, *see* DISABILITY LIVING
  ALLOWANCE
disability working allowance, *see* DISABILITY
  WORKING ALLOWANCE
disablement benefit, *see* DISABLEMENT BENEFIT
driving licence application, declaration in, **20**, 450
employee, as—
  contract of employment, rights and duties
    under, **9**, 119–120
  quotas of, **9**, 120
facilities for, building controls, **3**, 208, 242
home help, **22**, 24
housing, adaptation, **22**, 9, 24

Disabled person—*continued*
income support, disability premium, **21**, 1074
  severe, **21**, 1074
invalid care allowance, *see* INVALID CARE
  ALLOWANCE
invalid carriages, provision of, **11**, 1486
invalidity allowance, *see* INVALIDITY ALLOWANCE
invalidity benefit, *see* INVALIDITY BENEFIT
invalidity pension, *see* INVALIDITY PENSION
lack of services, local authority duty to explain,
  22, 24
laundry service, **22**, 14, 24
local authority duties—
  day-care facilities, provision, **22**, 24
  generally, **22**, 23, 24
  lack of provision, duty of explain, **22**, 24
  practical assistance, **22**, 24
  residential care, provision, **22**, 10, 24
meaning, **16**, 1922n; **21**, 984
medical appeal tribunal, referral of cases to, **21**,
  1179
mental, *see* MENTALLY DISORDERED PERSON
occupational therapist, visits, **22**, 24
person caring for, provision of laundry care, **22**,
  14, 24
person in need, as, **22**, 13, 23
public conveniences for disabled persons, **19**, 369
rates, relief from, **14**, 863; **24**, 748
residential care, **22**, 10, 24
roads authorities' duty of care towards, **20**, 660,
  670
severe disablement allowance, *see* SEVERE
  DISABLEMENT ALLOWANCE
sickness benefit, **21**, 878, 879
  See also SICKNESS BENEFIT
statutory sick pay, **21**, 908
talking books supplied for gratuitous loan to,
  VAT treatment, **3**, 1163
telecommunications apparatus for use by—
  development, **16**, 1922
  lift, apparatus installed in, **16**, 1949
  PTO licence provisions, **16**, 1933, 1933n
training, rehabilitation and resettlement, **12**, 7
travel concession, local authority, **20**, 493
vaccine damage, disablement due to, **19**, 502–507
voluntary organisations, co-ordination, statutory
  services, **22**, 24
Disablement benefit
byssinosis, **21**, 992, 997
constant attendance needed, increase where, **21**,
  983
deafness, occupational, **21**, 995
diffuse mesothelioma, **21**, 997
disablement—
  assessment, **21**, 984
  dual causation, **21**, 980, 985
  extent, **21**, 980, 984
  meaning, **21**, 984
  mental, **21**, 980
  physical, **21**, 980
  pre-existing injury or disease, where, **21**, 986
  subsequent injury or disease, **21**, 987
employed earner, **21**, 980

Disablement benefit—*continued*
entitlement—
  assessment, **21**, 980, 984
    multiple injuries, **21**, 984
    provisional, **21**, 980
  change in condition of claimant, **21**, 980
  constant attendance needed, where, **21**, 983
  employed earner's, **21**, 980
  generally, **21**, 801, 966, 980
  percentage of disablement, **21**, 980, 984
    100 per cent, **21**, 988
form, **21**, 980
generally, **21**, 980
imprisonment of claimant, **21**, 1020
industrial injury, generally, **21**, 966
loss of faculty—
  cause, **21**, 982
    dual causation, **21**, 985
  definition, **21**, 981
  disablement, meaning, **21**, 984
  disablement need not result, **21**, 984
  doctrine of remoteness, **21**, 982
  mental faculty, **21**, 980
  physical faculty, **21**, 980
  pre-existing injury or disease, where, **21**, 986
  subsequent injury or disease, **21**, 987
mental faculty, loss of, **21**, 980
onus of proof, **21**, 980
period for which payable, **21**, 980
personal injury, **21**, 980
physical faculty, loss of, **21**, 980
pneumoconiosis, **21**, 992, 997
rate, **21**, 980
tuberculosis, **21**, 992
Disaster
expenditure, **14**, 327
grants, **14**, 327
homelessness as result of, **11**, 2055
loans, **14**, 327
material for countering effect of—
  temporary importation, **7**, 1187
Disc
documentary evidence, as, **10**, 572, 607
Discharge grant
prisoner, to, **16**, 1481
Disclamation
casualty of, feudal law, **18**, 83
Discomfort
damage distinguished from, **14**, 2048, 2049
harm arising from, **14**, 2047
materiality, requirement of, **14**, 2050
sensible and personal, **14**, 2050
Discotheque
See ENTERTAINMENT, PLACES OF
Discours particulier d'Escosse
summary of early laws of Scotland, **6**, 850
Discretion
See ADMINISTRATIVE POWERS
Discretionary enactment
cases where found not to be mandatory, **12**, 1180
generally, **12**, 1179
whether mandatory enactment may be, **12**, 1175
Discretionary trust
See TRUST

Discrimination
European Convention on Human Rights, **12**, 6,
  85, 86
international conventions on, **12**, 5
nationality, on grounds of, European Union law,
  12, 221
public telecommunications operator, by, **16**,
  1933, 1933*n*, 1940
racial, *see* RACIAL DISCRIMINATION
religion or belief, on grounds of, **12**, 6, 72
sex, *see* SEX DISCRIMINATION
See also EMPLOYMENT
Disease
Acquired Immune Deficiency Syndrome (AIDS),
  19, 508, 509
animals, transmitted from, **19**, 475–478
  See also ANIMAL HEALTH
anthrax, prevention of infection by, **19**, 478
assault, communicated during, **7**, 227
bovine, **11**, 488
  cow milked by diseased person, **11**, 448, 449
  milk taken from diseased cow, **11**, 447, 449
  precautions, generally, **11**, 450
bovine spongiform encephalopathy (BSE), **19**,
  477*n*
brucella, **19**, 477*n*
byelaws, **11**, 488
carriers, medical examination of, **19**, 479–481
cleansing and disinfection of premises and
  contents, **19**, 448
communal washing of clothes, regulations as to,
  19, 447
control in fish farms—
  inland farms, **11**, 60
  marine farms, **11**, 61
control of spread, **19**, 444–457
death by—
  conveyance of infectious bodies, **3**, 511
  cremation following, **3**, 565
  removal by local authority, **3**, 510
  storage of deceased's body, **3**, 510
  unclaimed body, **3**, 510
disinfection of bedding and clothing, **19**, 446, 455
Human Immunodeficiency Virus (HIV), **19**, 508,
  509
immunisation, *see* VACCINATION AND IMMUNISATION
incapacity for work due to, statutory sick pay, **21**,
  908
industrial injuries benefits, *see* INDUSTRIAL
  INJURIES BENEFITS
infected houses—
  ceasing to occupy, **19**, 451
  letting of, **19**, 450
infected persons, **19**, 452–457
  conveyance of, **19**, 458, 459
  hospital, detention in, **19**, 453
    removal to, **19**, 452
  medical examination, **19**, 479–481
  work place, attendance at, **19**, 457
infection, fear of, **14**, 2082
infectious—
  aircraft, **19**, 494, 497
  airports, **19**, 498
  blood taken for diagnosis, **25**, 203

Disease—*continued*
infectious—*continued*
  carrier of, sickness benefit, **21**, 886
  control of spread, **11**, 1483
  corpses, **19**, 460–463
  Crown property, **19**, 490
  enforcing authorities, **19**, 493
  entry, powers of, **19**, 494
  exposure of infected persons and things, **19**, 455
  food, regulations as to, **19**, 473
  food poisoning, **19**, 491
  houses of reception, **19**, 464
  immigrants, entry of, **19**, 510–512
  laboratories, provision of, **19**, 499
  lodging houses, regulation of, **19**, 469–472
  meaning, **19**, 445
  medicine, regulations as to, **19**, 473
  mortuaries, provision of, **19**, 465
  multiple occupation, houses in, **19**, 467
  penalties for offences, **19**, 495
  post-mortem examination, provision of premises for, **19**, 466
  prevention of spread, **19**, 491–499
  school—
    attendance of infected child at, **19**, 456
    infected teacher or other employee, **19**, 457
  Secretary of State, regulations made by, **19**, 491–495
  services for control of, **19**, 499
  ships, **19**, 494, 496
  slaughterhouses, regulations as to, **19**, 474
  treatment of, **19**, 491–499
  underground dwellings, **19**, 468
  vaccination, *see* VACCINATION AND IMMUNISATION
  vessels, **19**, 490
infectious matter thrown into ashpit, **19**, 449
meaning, **21**, 879
medical examination of infected persons, **19**, 479–481
medical officer, powers of entry, **19**, 481
medicinal purpose, meaning, **14**, 1202
notifiable, **19**, 306, 482–490
  certificate or form of notification, **19**, 485
  confidentiality of notification, **19**, 487
  duty of notification, **19**, 485
  food poisoning, **19**, 484
  locally notifiable, **19**, 483
  meaning, **19**, 482*n*
  medical officer, duties of, **19**, 486
  occupational diseases, **19**, 489
  punishment of offences, **19**, 488
  who must notify, **19**, 485, 485*n*
occupational, **19**, 489
pests, destruction of, **19**, 326
prescribed, *see* PRESCRIBED DISEASES
prevention and mitigation of, **19**, 302, 306, 444–481
rabies, **19**, 476
  See also RABIES
reporting of, **9**, 534
schoolchildren, medical examination of, **19**, 480
sickness benefit, entitlement to, **21**, 878, 879
  See also SICKNESS BENEFIT

Disease—*continued*
taking or killing wild birds or animals to prevent spread of, **11**, 883, 886
vermin, control of, **19**, 444
zoonoses, **19**, 477
Disembarkation
meaning, **12**, 146
Disestablishment
See CHURCH AND STATE
Disinterment, *see* DEAD BODY
Dismissal
action short of—
  employee's remedy, **9**, 91
  generally, **9**, 87
  meaning, **9**, 90
  trade union—
    independent, appropriate time and activities of, **9**, 89
    membership and activities, **9**, 88
fair, **9**, 234
health and safety regulations, breach of, **9**, 466
manner of, loss arising from, **9**, 280
non-dismissal, **9**, 221
pregnancy, as reason for—
  automatically unfair dismissal, **9**, 115
  generally, **9**, 114
  incapability, **9**, 116
  remedy, **9**, 117
procedures agreement, **9**, 208
reasons for—
  capability, **9**, 244
  conduct, **9**, 245
  enactment, contravention of, **9**, 247
  general considerations, **9**, 243
  generally, **9**, 242
  incompetency, **9**, 254
  other, **9**, 248
  pregnancy, *see* pregnancy as reason for *above*
  qualifications, **9**, 244
  redundancy, **9**, 246
redundancy payment, entitlement to, *see* REDUNDANCY
self-dismissal, **9**, 223
statement of reasons for, right to, **9**, 143
unfair, *see* UNFAIR DISMISSAL
written statement of reasons for, **6**, 999
wrongful, *see* WRONGFUL DISMISSAL
wrongous, **19**, 1237
Disorderly conduct
breach of the peace, **7**, 446, 447, 448, 455
exclusion from meeting due to, **14**, 1334
Disponee
co-disponees, *jus quaesitum tertio*, **15**, 850
Disposal of waste
See WASTE
Disposition
absolute, **18**, 112
  landlord's hypothec, **13**, 514
ancillary rights, assignation of, **18**, 642
bond and diposition in security, **18**, 112
contract, originating in, **18**, 8
contractual clauses, **18**, 642
death of transferee, where, **18**, 649
death of transferor, where, **18**, 648

Disposition—*continued*
deceased person's estate, of, **6**, 609
delivered but not yet registered, **18**, 14
dispositive clause, **6**, 582
dominium utile, **18**, 642
exception to rules regarding, **6**, 579
execution and delivery, **18**, 642
   evaluation, **18**, 644
feudal conveyance—
   a me, **18**, 99
   a me vel de me, **18**, 99, 100
form, **6**, 580; **18**, 642
formal attestation, **18**, 642
functions, **18**, 642
General Register of Sasines—
   land registered in, **18**, 642
   registration in, **18**, 643
generally, **6**, 579
insolvency of transferee, where, **18**, 649
insolvency of transferor, where, **18**, 648
interpretation, **12**, 1237
Land Register of Scotland—
   land registered in, **18**, 642
   registration in, **18**, 643
meaning, **18**, 640
missives normally superseded by, **6**, 579
narrative clause, **6**, 581
non-supersession clause, **18**, 641
recording, in Sasines or Land Register, **6**, 579
registration, **18**, 640
   death of transferee, where, **18**, 649
   death of transferor, where, **18**, 648
   effect, **18**, 643
   evaluation, **18**, 644
   generally, **18**, 643
   insolvency of transferee, where, **18**, 649
   insolvency of transferor, where, **18**, 648
special, **6**, 579
stamp duty, **18**, 643
subordinate clauses, **6**, 583
taking title by way of, **5**, 81
unilateral deed, as, **6**, 579
unregistered, **18**, 645
warrandice, **18**, 702, 708
   assignation, **18**, 642
   delivery, date of, **18**, 710
   enforcement, **18**, 710, 712
   extinction, **18**, 714
   missives kept in force beyond disposition, where, **18**, 710, 714
writ, assignation of, **18**, 642
Dispossession
natural and reasonable consequences of, **5**, 165
Disrepair
tenant's failure to abide by lease, due to, fair rent decisions, **13**, 661, 663
Disruption
Church of Scotland, **3**, 1633, 1636
Distance, measurement of
Interpretation Act 1978 rules as to, **12**, 1209
Distance sales
excise duty, **7**, 1054
VAT, relevant supplies, **7**, 1328

Distance selling arrangement
meaning, **7**, 1054*n*
Distress for rent
railway stock and plant, **19**, 1102
Distress signal
shipping, **21**, 209, 220, 331, 375, 376
Distributable profits
meaning, **4**, 367
Distribution
administration of estate prior to, *see* SUCCESSION
competition, European Community rules, **10**, 162
distributing main, requisition for laying down, **9**, 674
distributive wholesale business—
   commencement of distribution, **24**, 642
   exclusion from industrial derating, **24**, 642
electricity boards, duties regarding, **9**, 619
food in transit, examination of, **11**, 401
innocent, publisher, by, **6**, 311
meat, of, hygiene regulations, **11**, 416, 417
succession, **25**, 605
   executor, duties of, **25**, 1105
   partial intestate estate, remainder of, **25**, 709
   See also SUCCESSION
systems, tariff for use of, **9**, 717
District
local authority elections, **15**, 1021, 1025, 1039
District and islands councils
district courts, responsibility for, **13**, 1448
foreshore, duties in relation to, **18**, 524
right of way, creation of public, **18**, 502
District council
aerodrome, powers relating to, *see* AERODROME
allocation of functions, **14**, 402
art gallery authority, **14**, 688, 689
buildings, water supply to, **25**, 531
burgh churches, rights in relation to, **3**, 1588
byelaws, *see* BYELAWS
civil defence, **14**, 506, 508
community council, scheme for establishing, **14**, 57, 74
compensation, **25**, 513
concerted action, **14**, 80
Convention of Scottish Local Authorities, representation on, **14**, 84
District Councils Association for Scotland, **14**, 81
drainage works, **25**, 373
education authority, as, **8**, 712
Food and Drugs (Scotland) Act, administration of, **11**, 329
functions—
   concurrent, **14**, 79
   sole, **14**, 78
harbour, acquisition of, **14**, 445
housing, *see* HOUSING
industrial promotion, **14**, 634
inter-authority relationships—
   concerted action, **14**, 80
   concurrent functions, **14**, 79
   generally, **14**, 77
   sole functions, **14**, 78
library authority, **14**, 687, 689
licences, powers relating to, *see* LICENCE
litigation, **14**, 118

District council—*continued*
museum authority, **14**, 688, 689
name, change of, **14**, 71
new structure, **14**, 64
pier, acquisition of, **14**, 445
private legislation, promotion of, **14**, 306
public health matters, **19**, 308
public transport, *see* PUBLIC TRANSPORT
registration, powers relating to, *see* REGISTRATION
social work function, **14**, 608
tourism, promotion of, **14**, 662
wards, **15**, 1036, 1039
See also LOCAL AUTHORITY

District court
advocate appearing before, dress, **13**, 1323
antecedents, **6**, 1155–1159
clerk, **6**, 1164; **13**, 1448
clerk of the peace, **6**, 1164
closure, Secretary of State's powers, **6**, 1164
commission areas, **6**, 1160, 1162, 1164
constitution, **17**, 574
contempt of court, **6**, 324
creation of, **17**, 517
crime committed outside area of jurisdiction, **6**, 1161
criminal legal aid, **13**, 1052
establishment of, **5**, 655; **6**, 1155; **14**, 509
expenses, **14**, 514
fixed penalty offences, **6**, 1165
foundation of, **6**, 1160
generally, **5**, 655; **17**, 504
hybrid nature, **6**, 1160
jurisdiction, **5**, 655; **6**, 1161; **14**, 511; **17**, 517
justices of the peace, **6**, 1162, 1163; **14**, 513
lawburrows, action of, **13**, 906
lay justices, **13**, 1448
lay magistracy, **6**, 1160–1168
legal aid, **6**, 1157
legal assessor, **13**, 1448
nature of, **6**, 1163
new, power to open, **6**, 1164
officers, appointment of, **14**, 512
personnel, **6**, 1162, 1163
powers, **17**, 575
practice, local divergence in, **6**, 1163
precedent, operation, **22**, 302
predecessors—
     burgh court, **17**, 517, 518
     justice of peace court, **17**, 517, 519
     police court, **17**, 517, 518
prosecuting function, **6**, 1163
public prosecutor in, **17**, 538
reputation, **6**, 1167
responsibility for, **13**, 1448
sentencing powers, **6**, 1161
stipendiary magistrates, **13**, 1448
     appointment of, **6**, 1164; **14**, 512
workload, **6**, 1166

District salmon fishery boards, **11**, 35
application for changes in legislation, **11**, 38
byelaws, enforcement of, **11**, 38
clerk, appointment of, **11**, 38
defect in appointment or qualification of member, **11**, 39

District salmon fishery boards—*continued*
duties, **11**, 38
election procedure, **11**, 35
financial powers and duties, **11**, 38
fishery assessments, **11**, 38
generally, **11**, 32, 32*n*
heritable property, purchase of, **11**, 38
mandatories, **11**, 37
maximum number of members, **11**, 35
may sue and be sued, **11**, 38
powers, **11**, 38
proprietors, **11**, 35
report, **11**, 38
salmon anglers, **11**, 35
statement of accounts, **11**, 38
tenant netsmen, **11**, 35
vacancies, **11**, 35, 39
water bailiffs, appointment of, **11**, 38
where no salmon in district, **11**, 39

Disturbance compensation
See COMPULSORY ACQUISITION

Disturbance payment
See COMPULSORY ACQUISITION

Ditch
cleansing of, **19**, 367
danger caused by, **20**, 698
public health nuisance, as, **19**, 336
unauthorised reopening, **20**, 698
water pollution, **14**, 2079

Dittay
brieve of, **6**, 853; **17**, 548
meaning, **6**, 853
points, **6**, 849
taking up, **6**, 853; **17**, 548

Dividends
cash, *prima facie* dividends payable in, **4**, 461
cash, shareholder's right to receive in, **4**, 468
company, advance corporation tax, **19**, 1521
company's financial record, **25**, 32
cover, **25**, 32
'cum div', **4**, 461
deceased's liability to tax, **25**, 969
declaration of, **4**, 390, 461
distribution, profits available for, **4**, 460
distribution of assets, **4**, 927
minority shareholder, rights of, **25**, 28
payments, generally, **1**, 84; **4**, 461; **19**, 1521; **25**, 18
preference shares, special rights in relation to, **4**, 461
prima facie, **4**, 461
quantum of, considered in petition by minority shareholders, **4**, 487
shareholder's right to receive dividend in cash, **4**, 468
stability, **25**, 32
unclaimed, **4**, 461, 928
valuation by reference to, **25**, 18
warrants—
     negotiable instruments, as, **4**, 103
     printer's imprint, requirement not applicable, **17**, 3
yield, selection of, **25**, 19

Dividing society
friendly society, as, **12**, 682
meaning, **12**, 682
Diving operation, vessel engaged in
restricted manoeuvrability, vessel with, lights and
   shapes to be diplayed, **21**, 365
Divinity, student of
Church of Scotland, **3**, 1522, 1532
preparation for ministry, *see* RELIGION, MINISTER
   OF (Church of Scotland)
Division
electoral, **15**, 1036, 1039
   polling districts, **15**, 1040, 1304
   register of electors, **15**, 1106
Division and sale
common property, of, **15**, 104
remedy of, **13**, 97
ship in co-ownership, **21**, 137, 138
Divorce
adultery—
   after raising of action, **10**, 899
   artificial insemination, **10**, 900
   before the marriage, **10**, 899
   collusion, **10**, 922
   condonation, **10**, 918–920
   evidentiary matters, **10**, 932
   generally, **10**, 840
   as ground for irretrievable breakdown of
      marriage, **10**, 840, 898
   intimation, **17**, 1225
   lenocinium, **10**, 917
   liability, abolition—
      Scottish Law Commission recommendation—
         legislative implementation, **22**, 686
   paternity of children, **10**, 932
   physical requirements, **10**, 900
   polygamous marriage, **10**, 899
   previous decrees, **10**, 931
   venereal disease, **10**, 932
   what constitutes, **10**, 899
affidavit—
   evidence, **17**, 1213
   notary public, taken before, **13**, 1223
   preparation of, **17**, 1231
   procedure on, **17**, 1230
   use of, **17**, 1229
aliment, *see* ALIMENT
antenuptial or postnuptial marriage settlements,
   24, 60
application, advice and assistance in cases of, **13**,
   1024
Bible, law of, **22**, 613
British Isles, granted in, *see* MATRIMONIAL DECREES
canonical law, **22**, 613
capacity to remarry, **17**, 224
child—
   access—
      counterclaim for, **17**, 1233
      dispute over, **17**, 1235
   arrangements for care of, **17**, 1234
   custody, **10**, 1317
      counterclaim for, **17**, 1233
      dispute over, **17**, 1235
      intimation, **17**, 1226

Divorce—*continued*
child—*continued*
   fair sharing of economic burden of children
      following—
         accommodation, provision of suitable, **10**, 969
         age and health of child, **10**, 969
         caring for child leading to loss of earnings,
            10, 969
         child-care facilities, considerations with
            regard to, **10**, 969
         educational factors, **10**, 969
         generally, **10**, 968
         orders available, **10**, 970
      financial provisions for, **10**, 948, 951
         personal tax allowance, **10**, 991
      social work departments, right of, **17**, 1236
civil legal aid, when not available, **13**, 1034
cohabitation, meaning, **10**, 911
conciliation, **17**, 1215
consistorial action—
   access, counterclaim for, **17**, 1233
   affidavit—
      preparation of, **17**, 1231
      procedure on, **17**, 1230
      use of, **17**, 1229
   appeal, **17**, 1223
   custody, counterclaim for, **17**, 1233
   defender, late appearance by, **17**, 1223
   generally, **10**, 897
   initial writ, **17**, 1222
   intimation—
      adultery, **17**, 1225
      custody order made, where, **17**, 1226
      homosexuality, **17**, 1225
      polygamy, **17**, 1225
      sodomy, **17**, 1225
      transfer of property order sought, where, **17**,
         1227
   maintenance, counterclaim for, **17**, 1233
   minute by defender, **17**, 1232
   non-cohabitation, notice in case of, **17**, 1228
   rules applicable only in, **17**, 1224
Court of Session—
   jurisdiction, **4**, 5
   simplified divorce procedure, **17**, 1376
decree—
   absence, in, undefended actions, **17**, 1203
   variation of—
      procedure, **17**, 1242
      subsequent order, **17**, 1243
defences and bars—
   acquiescence, **10**, 924
   collusion, **10**, 922
   condonation, **10**, 918
      adultery, **10**, 918–920
      desertion, **10**, 918, 919, 921
      reconciliation provisions, **10**, 920
      requirements for, **10**, 919
   grave financial hardship, **10**, 923
   lenocinium, **10**, 917
   mora, **10**, 924
desertion—
   act of, **10**, 906
   cohabitation, meaning of, **10**, 911

Divorce—*continued*
desertion—*continued*
  computing the period, **10**, 905
  condonation, **10**, 918, 919, 921
  establishment of, **10**, 905
  five years, **10**, 924
    grave financial hardship as bar, **10**, 923
  genuine and reasonable offer to adhere, refusal
    of, **10**, 904, 912
  as ground for irretrievable breakdown of
    marriage, **10**, 898
  meaning, **10**, 905
  parties' intentions, **10**, 907
  previous court decrees affecting, **10**, 913
  pursuer must be willing to adhere, **10**, 905
  reconciliation provisions, **10**, 904
  relevant desertion, **10**, 904
  two years' continuous non-cohabitation
    without a genuine and reasonable offer to
    adhere, **10**, 904, 909
  while residing at same house, **10**, 906
  'without reasonable cause', **10**, 904, 908
Divorce (Scotland) Act 1976 ..., **10**, 896
domicile of parties, **22**, 693
  existence of forty-day rule, **4**, 30
enticement of spouse—
  Scottish Law Commission recommendation—
    legislative implementing, **22**, 686
evidence in divorce actions—
  action must be proved, **10**, 925
  adultery cases, **10**, 932
  best evidence, **10**, 929
  burden of proof, **10**, 927
  compellability of witness, **10**, 930
  competency of witness, **10**, 930
  corroboration, **10**, 928
  generally, **10**, 925
  marital intercourse, as to, **10**, 930
  marriage, proof of, **10**, 933
  previous decrees, **10**, 931
  standard of proof, **10**, 926
exclusion orders, **10**, 902
expenses—
  general rule, **17**, 1244
  specific cases, **17**, 1245
financial provision on—
  age, health and earning capacity of dependent
    partner, **10**, 974, 976
  agreements on—
    generally, **10**, 983
    later reconciliation of parties, **10**, 983
  aliment, award of, *see* ALIMENT
  ancillary orders, **10**, 955
  arrestment, **10**, 986
  avoidance transactions, orders relating to, **10**,
    985
  capital gains tax, **10**, 1000–1002
  capital sum, order for payment of, **10**, 952, 953
  children, **10**, 948
  clean break, **10**, 954
  conduct of party claiming provision, **10**, 969,
    973, 976
  court's discretion, **10**, 948, 949
  court's powers, **10**, 952

Divorce—*continued*
financial provision on—*continued*
  criteria for, **10**, 982
  death of payer, **10**, 954
  dependent partner, adjusting to loss of
    support—
    age, health and earning capacity of
      dependent partner, **10**, 973
    duration and extent of dependence, **10**, 973
    education or training, intentions of
      dependent party, **10**, 973
    factors to be taken into account, **10**, 973
    general principle regarding, **10**, 971, 978
    meaning of dependency, **10**, 972
    orders available, **10**, 974
  Divorce (Scotland) Act, **9**, 1976
    generally, **10**, 979
    periodical allowance after decree of divorce,
      10, 979, 980
      variation, **10**, 891, 979
  duration of marriage, **10**, 973, 976
  economic advantages and disadvantages,
    account taken of, **10**, 963–967
    assessing imbalance, **10**, 966
    contributions, meaning, **10**, 964
    economic advantage, meaning, **10**, 964
    utility of principle, **10**, 967
  economic burden of children, fair sharing of—
    accommodation, provision of, **10**, 969
    age and health of child, **10**, 969
    educational factors, **10**, 969
    factors to be taken into account, **10**, 969
    loss of earnings due to caring for child, **10**,
      969
    orders available, **10**, 970
    principle, generally, **10**, 968
  fair sharing of net value of matrimonial
    property—
    conduct of parties, **10**, 962
    generally, **10**, 957, 961
    meaning of matrimonial property, **10**, 960
    meaning of net value, **10**, 958
    property acquired before marriage, **10**, 960
    relevant date, **10**, 959, 960
  Family Law (Scotland) Act 1985 ..., **10**, 984
    children, for, **10**, 951
    generally, **10**, 949
    scope, **10**, 950
  financial provision order, **17**, 1238
  foreign divorce, **10**, 947; **22**, 686
  generally, **10**, 948, 949
  incidental order, **10**, 952, 955
    when made, **10**, 955
  inheritance tax—
    capital transfers, **10**, 999
    lump sums, **10**, 998
    periodical payments, **10**, 998
  inhibition, **10**, 986
  legislation implementation, Scottish Law
    Commission recommendation, **22**, 684,
    685
  matrimonial home and contents, incidental
    order as to, **10**, 955
  nature of, **10**, 952–955

Divorce—*continued*
financial provision on—*continued*
overseas decree, **10**, 947; **22**, 686
partner likely to suffer hardship—
  principle, generally, **10**, 975, 978
payment made to *curator bonis* or trustee, **10**, 955
periodical allowance, order for, **10**, 952, 954
  death or remarriage of payee, **10**, 954
  Divorce (Scotland) Act (1976)—
    under, **10**, 979–982
    variation, **10**, 981, 982
principles, **10**, 956–978
  application of, **10**, 956
  dependent partner, adjusting to loss of support, **10**, 971–974
  economic advantages and disadvantages, **10**, 963–967
  economic burden of children, fair sharing of, **10**, 968–970
  fair sharing of net value of matrimonial property, **10**, 957–962
  partner likely to suffer hardship, **10**, 975–978
property—
  declarator as to ownership of disputed, **10**, 955
  incidental order for valuation of, **10**, 955
  order for sale of, **10**, 955
  transfer to *curator bonis* or trustee, **10**, 955
resources of parties, **10**, 952
  provision of details of, **10**, 987
Scottish Law Commission recommendation, **22**, 684, 685
security for, **10**, 955
transfer of property, order for, **10**, 952, 953
financial provision orders, **17**, 1238; **22**, 685, 693
foreign—
  financial provision after recognition—
    Hague Convention, **22**, 685, 693
grounds for, **22**, 649, 683
  establishing, **10**, 898
  meaning, **10**, 898
habitual residence of parties, **22**, 693
  additional ground of jurisdiction in, **4**, 39
Hague Convention on Recognition of Divorces and Legal Separations, **22**, 693
inheritance tax, effect upon, **19**, 1578
inhibition used on dependence of action for, **8**, 136
irretrievable breakdown of marriage, **10**, 898
  adultery as grounds, **10**, 840
  establishing, **10**, 898
  single ground, as, **22**, 683
judicial discretion, exercise of, **25**, 617
judicial separation, *see* JUDICIAL SEPARATION
jurisdiction—
  continuing proceedings, in, **17**, 1218
  domicile, **17**, 1217
    in Scotland, **10**, 897
  general, **10**, 897; **17**, 1216
  residence in Scotland, **10**, 897
  sheriff court, **6**, 1062
legal advice and assistance, **13**, 1028, 1033
lenocinium, **10**, 917

Divorce—*continued*
liferent, termination on, **13**, 1658
maintenance following, **19**, 1578
  See also ALIMENT
marriage, proof of, **10**, 933
matrimonial decrees, *see* MATRIMONIAL DECREES
matrimonial home, *see* MATRIMONIAL HOME
non-cohabitation—
  with defender's consent, **10**, 898, 914, 915
  five years, **10**, 898, 916, 924
    grave financial hardship as bar, **10**, 923
  two years, **10**, 898, 914, 915
overseas, granted, *see* MATRIMONIAL DECREES
parents as guardians, where, **11**, 1210, 1211
post-Reformation church law, **22**, 613
pre-1976 situation, **10**, 895
previous decrees, **10**, 931
  desertion, and, **10**, 913
procedural reforms, nineteenth century, **22**, 649
proof of ground, **10**, 925–927
publication of matter derived from divorce proceedings, **17**, 41
re-marriage—
  capacity as to, **17**, 224
  Church of Scotland minister, by, **3**, 1564
recognition of decree—
  common law, **10**, 940
  Family Law Act (1986)—
    British Islands, decrees granted in, **10**, 943
    generally, **10**, 942
    overseas, decrees granted, **10**, 944–947
reconciliation, **17**, 1215
reforming legislation, **22**, 649
registration—
  change of status recorded in, **19**, 1429
  evidence of divorce, as, **19**, 1420
  generally, **19**, 1467, 1468
  Register of Corrections, **19**, 1430
  Register of Divorces, **19**, 857, 1414
    index of entries, **19**, 1419, 1468
revocation on, proposed reform, **25**, 1117
Royal Commission on Divorce 1850 ..., **22**, 649
Scottish Law Commission recommendations, **22**, 683, 684
second marriage, marriage notice, **10**, 805
separation—
  with defender's consent, **10**, 914, 915
  five years, **10**, 898, 916
  as ground for irretrievable breakdown of marriage, **10**, 898
  proceedings, restriction on publication of matter derived from, **17**, 41
  two years, **10**, 898, 914, 915
  undefended action of, **17**, 1023
Service Divorce Department, **13**, 1002
sexual intercourse, refusal of, **10**, 906
sheriff court jurisdiction, **4**, 5
sheriff court procedure—
  affidavit—
    evidence, **17**, 1213
    procedure, **17**, 1229–1231
  agreements between parties, alteration of, **17** 1239

Divorce—*continued*
sheriff court procedure—*continued*
child—
    access, **17**, 1233, 1235
    arrangements for care of, **17**, 1234
    custody—
        counterclaim for, **17**, 1233
        dispute over, **17**, 1235
        intimation, **17**, 1226
    consistorial action, *see* consistorial action *above*
    expenses, **17**, 1244, 1245
    financial provision order, **17**, 1238
    procedural rules, **17**, 1214
    simplified procedure—
        appeal in action under, **17**, 1275
        citation in, **17**, 1019
        form of application, **17**, 1220
        generally, **17**, 1213, 1221
    undefended action of, **17**, 1023
simplified procedure—
    Court of Session, in, **17**, 1375
    sheriff court, in, **17**, 1019, 1213, 1219–1221, 1275
status, action relating to, **4**, 68
taxation consequences—
    capital gains tax, **10**, 1000–1002
    inheritance tax, **10**, 998, 999
    personal allowances—
        additional personal allowance, **10**, 991
        children, additional personal relief in respect of, **10**, 991
        married couple's, **10**, 990
        remarriage, **10**, 991
        single person's, **10**, 989
    separate taxation of husband and wife, **10**, 989
terms of agreements between parties, alteration of, **17**, 1239
transaction designed to defeat claims on, reduction, **13**, 44
transfer of property on, **19**, 1578
trustees' liability, where reduced, **24**, 210
undefended action of, **17**, 1023
unreasonable behaviour—
    examples, **10**, 903
    generally, **10**, 840, 901
    as ground for irretrievable breakdown of marriage, **10**, 898
    meaning of behaviour, **10**, 902
    mental element, **10**, 901, 902
    passive behaviour, **10**, 902
    single incident sufficient, **10**, 902
variation of trust on, **24**, 84
Divorcee
state retirement pension scheme, **21**, 1207
Divot
servitude right of—
    extent, **18**, 464
    generally, **18**, 483, 489
    restriction of area to which access allowed, **18**, 469
DNA profiling
evidence, as, **10**, 502
identification by, **10**, 662
parentage or non-parentage, actions for declarator of, **10**, 1164

Docks
charges or dues, damages claim, **21**, 386
constables, undertaker's power to appoint, **16**, 1818
construction or alteration, **19**, 19*n*
dock charterparty, **21**, 672
dock owner, limitation of liability, **21**, 753*n*, 769, 769*n*
dock worker, jurisdiction of industrial tribunals, **9**, 331
dockyard port, *see* DOCKYARD PORT
dry, meaning, **11**, 1303
dry docking expenses, damages claim, **21**, 386
explosives, byelaws as to, **10**, 1611
graving, meaning, **11**, 1303
meaning, **11**, 1303; **21**, 769*n*; **24**, 599
pilotage, *see* PILOT; PILOTAGE
sheriff court jurisdiction, **6**, 1106
valuation for rating—
    apportionment of net annual value, **24**, 606
    derating relief, **24**, 602
    dock purposes, **24**, 603, 604
    dock undertaking, **24**, 605
    generally, **24**, 415, 598, 601
    meaning, **24**, 599
    prescribed valuation formula, **24**, 547
    private, **24**, 605
wet, meaning, **11**, 1303
Dockyard port
definition, **11**, 1319
harbour master, powers of, **11**, 1319
meaning, **11**, 1319
regulations, making of, **11**, 1319
Scotland, in, **11**, 1319
Doctor
absence of, **11**, 1447, 1449
accident, provision of immediate treatment for, **11**, 1445
advice as to general health given by, **11**, 1446
anaesthetics, administration of, **11**, 1446
assignment of persons to, **11**, 1437
assistants, **11**, 1447, 1447*n*
breach of confidence, **18**, 1466
budgets, health boards, set by, **11**, 1401
change of, **11**, 1440
    application for, **11**, 1440
    death of doctor, **11**, 1440, 1441
    temporary arrangements, **11**, 1441
    withdrawal or removal from medical list, **11**, 1440, 1441
clinical trial, **14**, 1207
complaints against, **11**, 1520
consultants, **11**, 1498
consultations, **11**, 1446
consulting room accommodation, regulations as to, **11**, 1446
controlled drugs, use of, **14**, 1258
deputies, **11**, 1447, 1449
disability, **11**, 1449
disqualification of, **11**, 1521
doctors' lists—
    applications for acceptance on, **11**, 1436
    limitation of persons in, **11**, 1439
    removal from, **11**, 1438, 1443

Doctor—*continued*
doctors' lists—*continued*
   revision, **11**, 1438
   schools and residential institutions, **11**, 1443
   temporary residents, **11**, 1442, 1445
   transfers, **11**, 1438
drugs and other substances, *see* DRUGS
duties and obligations, **11**, 1447
duty of care—
   duty to inform, **15**, 303, 307, 308
   generally, **15**, 299
   wrongful birth, **15**, 305
     See also BIRTH
   wrongful pregnancy, **15**, 305
     See also PREGNANCY
elderly or infirm, relief from certain duties, **11**, 1437
emergency treatment, **11**, 1445
   fees for, **11**, 1450
exchange of practices, **11**, 1434
experience, **14**, 1128
   qualifications of, **14**, 1108
   resident medical capacity, in, **14**, 1108
fees, when acceptable, **11**, 1450
fund-holding practice, application for recognition as, **11**, 1401
general practitioners' drugs budgets, **11**, 1401
hospital care, purchase of, **11**, 1401
legal control, scope of, **14**, 1101
licensing system, exemption from, **14**, 1203
maternity medical services, **11**, 1446
medical list—
   application for inclusion, **11**, 1429, 1431
     appeal against decision, **11**, 1429
     consideration of, **11**, 1415
     refusal of, **11**, 1429
   contraceptive services, willingness to provide, **11**, 1430
   copies, availability of, **11**, 1430
   English, necessary knowledge of, **11**, 1429
   maternity medical services, willingness to provide, **11**, 1430
   reinstatement, application for, **11**, 1521
   removal from, **11**, 1432, 1521
     appeals, **11**, 1432
   revision, **11**, 1430
   Tribunal, inquiry by, **11**, 1425
   withdrawal from, **11**, 1432
medical service committee, **11**, 1520
non-designated services, **4**, 1177
ophthalmic treatment, **11**, 1464
   ophthalmic list, **11**, 1465
   recommendation of patient for, **11**, 1446
partners, **11**, 1447, 1447*n*
partnership as business medium, **16**, 1004
patients, obligations with regard to, **11**, 1445, 1446
payments to, **11**, 1451
physical examination by, **11**, 1446
poison, sale of, **14**, 1215
postgraduate training, in, immigration rules, **12**, 292
   change of category, **12**, 298
   entry requirements, **12**, 295
   extension of leave, **12**, 300
practice area, **11**, 1448

Doctor—*continued*
practice funds, **11**, 1401
prescription, medicinal products supplied by, **14**, 1209
privilege in relation to, **10**, 686
professional liability, *see* PROFESSIONAL LIABILITY
professional rules, partnership contravening, **16**, 1017
records, requirement to keep, **11**, 1446
referral to other services, **11**, 1446
sale of practices prohibited, **11**, 1435
selection of, by patients, **11**, 1436
ship's—
   medical treatment and supplies where no doctor on board, **21**, 268
   regulations as to, **21**, 245, 247
social work services, advice as to, **11**, 1446
standard of care, **14**, 1128
temporary residents, **11**, 1442, 1445
terms of service, **11**, 1428
   alteration of, **11**, 1444
   rights and obligations under, **11**, 144
trainee medical practitioner, **11**, 1447*n*
treatment, requirement to given personally, **11**, 1447
treatment not within scope of doctor's obligations, **11**, 1446
undue influence, **25**, 764
vacant medical practice, succession to, **11**, 1433
vaccination and immunisation by, **11**, 1446
veterinary practice by, **25**, 203
waiting room accommodation, regulations as to, **11**, 1446
Working for Patients White Paper, **11**, 1401
See also MEDICAL PRACTITIONER
Document
forgery, *see* FORGERY
prescribed form, **12**, 1178
uttering false, *see* UTTERING
Documentary credits
fraudulent, **11**, 773
system of, generally, **11**, 772
Documentary evidence
bankers' books, **10**, 607
bankruptcy proceedings, **10**, 595
classification, **10**, 573
codes of practice, **10**, 598
computer statements, **10**, 607
copies, **10**, 610–612
definition, **10**, 572
discs, **10**, 607
extracts, **10**, 613
films, **10**, 607
foreign judgment as, **10**, 587
generally, **10**, 522
Highway Code, **10**, 598
identification by witness, **10**, 572
intercepted documents, admissibility of statement in, **10**, 740
judicial records—
   absence, decrees in, **10**, 586
   bail orders, **10**, 588
   civil proceedings, **10**, 585
     decrees and verdicts in, **10**, 585

Documentary evidence—*continued*
judicial records—*continued*
  criminal convictions, **10**, 584
  criminal proceedings, **10**, 584
  foreign courts, decrees in, **10**, 587
  generally, **10**, 582
  judicial warrants, **10**, 589
  notes of evidence, **10**, 590
  previous acquittal, **10**, 584
  subsequent proceedings, use in, **10**, 583
meaning, **10**, 503
microfilm, **10**, 607
official documents, **10**, 596
official *Gazettes*, **10**, 593
Parliamentary journals, **10**, 594
photographs, **10**, 607
private documents—
  bankers' books, **10**, 606
  business records, **10**, 603, 605, 608
  civil proceedings, **10**, 607–609
  correspondence, **10**, 603
  criminal proceedings, **10**, 605, 606
  diaries, **10**, 603
  generally, **10**, 573, 599, 603
  holograph writings, **10**, 601
  informal documents, **10**, 603
  maps, **10**, 604, 607
  plans, **10**, 604, 607
  privileged writings, **10**, 600–602
  probate writs, **10**, 600
  statutory provisions, **10**, 605–609
  telegrams, **10**, 603
  trade documents, **10**, 605
  writings *in re mercatoria*, **10**, 602
privilege to withhold, **10**, 668
public documents, **10**, 591–598
  byelaws, **10**, 578
  Community instruments, **10**, 581
  foreign official and governmental documents, **10**, 580
  foreign statutes, **10**, 579
  generally, **10**, 573, 574
  governmental documents, **10**, 575–581
  presumption in favour of genuineness, **10**, 574
  regulations, **10**, 578
  royal proclamations, **10**, 577
  statutes—
    Commonwealth, **10**, 579
    foreign, **10**, 579
    public general, **10**, 575
  statutory instruments, **10**, 576
public registers—
  births, deaths and marriages, register of, **10**, 591
  company documents, **10**, 592
  electoral roll, **10**, 592
  shipping documents, **10**, 592
  Valuation Roll, **10**, 592
sound recordings, **10**, 607
statutory bodies, minutes of, **10**, 595
statutory certificates, **10**, 597
tape recordings, **10**, 607
Dodgems
See PLEASURE FAIR

Dog
accommodation, refusal of, **11**, 1723
aggressive conduct urged by human handler, **7**, 213
attack by, Criminal Injuries Compensation Scheme, **7**, 8
blind persons, licence exception, **2**, 111
boarding establishment, **14**, 524; **19**, 1293
breeding etc establishment—
  death of licensee, **2**, 116
  diseases, prevention and control, **2**, 115
  disqualification for keeping, **2**, 118
  entry of, officers' powers, **2**, 117
  inspection, **2**, 117
  licence—
    conditions attached to, **2**, 115
    duration of, **2**, 115
    grant, generally, **14**, 524
    refusal to grant, **2**, 115
    requirement for, **2**, 115
  protection in emergency, **2**, 115
  suitability of, **2**, 115
canine specialist, **25**, 203
canine surgery, **25**, 203
collars to be worn by, **2**, 174
dangerous, **2**, 170; **11**, 1723, 1739
deer hunting with, **11**, 940
deliberately setting on someone, **2**, 164
disqualification for keeping, **2**, 249
dog fighting, **19**, 1274
finder of—
  duties of, **2**, 105
  permission to keep dog, **2**, 105
fouling footways etc, **2**, 172; **19**, 371
game licence, **19**, 1293
guard, *see* GUARD DOG
guide dogs, **2**, 111
hotelkeeper's liability for acts of guest's dog, **11**, 1739, 1739*n*
importation, special controls, **2**, 209; **19**, 1293
injured in road accident, driver's duties, **20**, 437
licence—
  abolition of, **19**, 1293
  duration of, **2**, 112
  exceptions from, **2**, 111
  failure to have, **2**, 111
  issue of, **14**, 524; **19**, 1293
  offences, **2**, 111
  register of, **2**, 111
  requirement as to, **2**, 111
livestock, worrying, **2**, 169
malicious damage to, **7**, 410, 412
police dog, use of, **2**, 164
quarantine provisions, **19**, 1293
rabies, *see* RABIES
rearing establishment, **14**, 524
registration schemes, **14**, 524; **19**, 1293
road, on—
  control of, **2**, 173
  straying, **20**, 506, 707
  without lead, **20**, 439
savage or dangerous, **2**, 170; **11**, 1723, 1739
sheep, worrying, **7**, 412
sheep dogs, **2**, 111

Dog—*continued*
sheriff court jurisdiction, **6**, 1078
Slaughter of Animals (Scotland) Act (1980) not
    applicable to, **11**, 496
stray, **16**, 1819*n*, 1820*n*
    address on collar, effect, **2**, 105
    detention of, **2**, 106, 167
    ownership, **18**, 552
    seizure of, **2**, 105; **14**, 712
    trespass by, *see* ANIMAL (trespass by)
    unclaimed, disposal of, **2**, 105
straying on road, **20**, 506, 707
surgery, unregistered person, **25**, 203
unsuitable, **11**, 1723
use for drawing cart etc, **2**, 244
See also ANIMAL
Dog racecourse
pool betting on, **2**, 1564
Dole
mens rea—
    generally, **7**, 58, 61, 66
    Gordon on, **7**, 59
    Hume on, **7**, 58, 60
use of term, **7**, 73
See also MENS REA
Dolphin
royal fish, as, **18**, 543*n*
Dolus
capacity for, **11**, 1054
intentional injury and fault, **15**, 253
meaning, **15**, 253
obligation arising from, **15**, 3
Domestic animals
dogs, *see* DOG
ownership, **2**, 103
swans as, **2**, 109
theft of, **2**, 103
Domestic building
chimney of, defence to charge of emitting smoke
    from, **9**, 1124
Domestic Coal Consumers' Council
duties, **14**, 1605
Domestic law
European Convention on Human Rights, **19**,
    652, 656
international law, relationship with,
    conflicting legislation, **19**, 655
    dualist approach, **19**, 652
    'Fitzmaurice Compromise', **19**, 652–656
international law, relationship with—
    monist approach, **19**, 652, 652*n*
    treaty law, **19**, 605, 656
international law compared, **19**, 602, 603, 613
polygamous marriage and, **17**, 216
recognition of state, effect, **19**, 663
state practice, as evidence of, **19**, 642
treaties, **19**, 656
    when binding on, **19**, 605
Domestic rates
See RATES
Domestic service
immigration of private servant, **12**, 247
industrial tribunal, exclusion from, **9**, 331
redundancy payment, **9**, 184

Domestic subjects
See VALUATION FOR RATING
Domestic violence
Criminal Injuries Compensation Scheme, *see*
    CRIMINAL INJURIES COMPENSATION SCHEME
Domicile
adult, of, **17**, 209
association, of—
    generally, **4**, 31
child, of—
    adopted children, **10**, 1193, 1193*n*, 1223
    custody, **10**, 1319
    dependence, of, **17**, 201
    domicile and nationality, **10**, 1223
    generally, **10**, 1223
    illegitimate, **10**, 1186, 1223
    origin, domicile of, **17**, 198
    reforms, **17**, 208
choice, of—
    acquisition of, **17**, 202, 205
    capacity, **17**, 203
    indefinite residence, intention as to, **17**, 205
    loss of, **17**, 206
    nature of, **17**, 192
    permanent residence, intention as to, **17**, 205
    residence, **17**, 204
commissary proceedings, **4**, 80
company, of, **17**, 356
convict, of, **4**, 30
corporation, of, **4**, 31
Crown, of, **4**, 32
death, at, *see* LEX ULTIMI DOMICILII
defender, of, **4**, 86
dependence, of, **4**, 30, 68
    generally, **4**, 30, 68
    married woman, **17**, 200
    nature of, **17**, 192
    pupil, **17**, 201
divorce, action for, **17**, 1217
enemy character, means of determining, **17**, 410
every person must have, at all times, **17**, 193
evolution of choice of law rules, **17**, 123
exclusion from scope of Judgments Convention,
    8, 432
federal, **17**, 195
fields in which used, **17**, 191
foundling, of, **17**, 193
individual, of, **4**, 30
lodgings, residence in, **4**, 30
marriage, and, **10**, 837
marriage notice, **10**, 805
married woman, of, **17**, 197, 200
meaning, **17**, 196; **19**, 1516*n*
mentally ill person, of, **4**, 30
military personnel, **4**, 30
more than one, no one can have, **17**, 195
nationality, **17**, 189
only one kind of, **17**, 196
origin, of—
    acquisition of, **17**, 198
    change of, **17**, 199
    nature of, **17**, 192
    rendered dormant, **17**, 199
    revival, **17**, 199

Domicile—*continued*
personal law—
    generally, **17**, 187
    indicators of, **17**, 188, 190
pre-existing, presumed still to exist, **17**, 194
principal ground of jurisdiction, as, **4**, 29
reforms, **17**, 207–209
Scots law, determined by, **17**, 197
state, **17**, 195
status, action relating to, **4**, 68
trust, of, **4**, 33, 41
types of, **17**, 192
See also LEX DOMICILII
Dominium
definition, **18**, 5
directum, **6**, 473
generally, **18**, 3
irritancy, **18**, 9
jus utendi, fruendi, abutendi, **18**, 5
no fixed term, **18**, 6
ownership may not be owned, **18**, 652
passing of property, **18**, 625, 628, 637
plenum, **6**, 473
real right, as, **18**, 5
subordinate real rights distinguished, **18**, 6
utile, **6**, 473; **8**, 197
See also FEUDAL LAW; OWNERSHIP
Dominus litis
allegation of, confidentiality rule, **13**, 1190
Dominus negotii
absence, **15**, 95, 107–109
administration must not be authorised by, **15**, 95,
    105
age, **15**, 137, 141
death of—
    completion of *gestio*, **15**, 130
    transmissibility of actions, **15**, 124
debts due by, discharge by *gestor*, **15**, 96, 97
debts due to, collection by *gestor*, **15**, 96
express wishes of, actions against, **15**, 137, 138, 139
failure to object to *gestor's* management, **15**, 109
health, preservation of, **15**, 102
ignorance, **15**, 95, 107–109
incapacity, **15**, 95, 107–109, 122, 137, 141
life or limb, rescue of, **15**, 102
litigation, intervention by *gestor*, **15**, 96, 101
management of another's affairs—
    both *dominus* and *gestor* interested, where, **15**,
        104
    generally, **15**, 95, 103
meaning, **15**, 87
minor as, **15**, 137, 141
obligation to *gestor*, **15**, 90
presumable wishes of, **15**, 122
pupil as, **15**, 137, 141
rights of *gestor* against—
    generally, **15**, 125
    indemnity of *gestor*, **15**, 126
    possessory lien, *gestor's*, **15**, 128
    relief from obligations, **15**, 127
rights of—
    auctor in rem suam, **15**, 134, 135
    completion of *gestio*, **15**, 129, 130
    fault in *gestor's* management, liability, **15**, 136

Dominus negotii—*continued*
rights of—*continued*
    gains, surrender by *gestor*, **15**, 129, 133
    generally, **15**, 129
    gestor's duty not to commence new business or
        affair, **15**, 131
    gestor's duty to account for intromissions, **15**,
        129, 132
    negative duties of *gestor*, **15**, 134, 135
    restoration of property, **15**, 129, 133
suicide attempt by, **15**, 102*n*
unjustified enrichment, **15**, 137–141
Donatio mortis causa
generally, **8**, 630
meaning, **25**, 735
origin, **25**, 735
substituted will, as, **25**, 735
See also DONATION
Donation
acceptance by donee, **8**, 629
alleged, circumstances of, **8**, 622
animus donandi—
    circumstances of alleged donation, **8**, 622
    debitor non praesumitur donare, **8**, 624
    generally, **8**, 619
    husband and wife, **8**, 626
    money in bank or deposit receipt, **8**, 637
    mortis causa, **8**, 630
    presumed gift, **8**, 627
    presumption against donation, **8**, 619, 620
    proof of, **8**, 620
    relationship between parties, **8**, 623
    subject matter of donation, **8**, 625
ante nuptias, **8**, 602
beneficium competentiae, **8**, 605, 644
capacity—
    generally, **8**, 610
    legal persons, **8**, 612
    natural persons, **8**, 611
    non-existent donee, **8**, 614
    reduction, donations open to, **8**, 613
    trusts, **8**, 612
    unincorporated associations, **8**, 612
    void donations, **8**, 613
child or grandchild, to, *beneficium competentiae*, **8**,
    605
competing interests, **8**, 607, 649
conditions—
    impossible, immoral or illegal, **8**, 641
    non-fulfilment, **8**, 642
    resolutive, **8**, 640
    suspensive, **8**, 640
consequences of, **8**, 639
conveyance—
    form of delivery, **8**, 633
    in implement of, **8**, 605
    whether necessary, **8**, 628, 630
corporeal moveable property, delivery, **8**, 634, 635
customs duty, **8**, 657
debitor non praesumitur donare, **8**, 624
defence of, **8**, 10
delivery—
    corporeal moveables, **8**, 634
        special types, **8**, 635

Donation—*continued*
delivery—*continued*
  deposit receipts, **8**, 637
  donation *inter vivos*, **8**, 628
  donation *mortis causa*, **8**, 628–630
  form, **8**, 633
  general rule, **8**, 628
  incorporeal moveable property, **8**, 636
  independent custodier, property held by, **8**, 634
  land, **8**, 638
  meaning, **8**, 628
  money in bank, **8**, 637
  mortis causa donation, **8**, 630
  ownership, presumption of following possession, **8**, 634
  proving, **8**, 634
  third party, to, on donee's behalf, **8**, 634
  traditio brevi manu, **8**, 634
  traditio longa manu, **8**, 634
  traditionibus non nudis pactis dominia rerum transferuntur, **8**, 628
  trust, donations by means of, **8**, 629, 631
deposit receipt, **8**, 630, 637
donatio non praesumitur, **8**, 620
donee, *see* DONEE
donor, *see* DONOR
entail, heirs of, **8**, 618
evidence of, reliability, **8**, 621
gratuitous acts, **8**, 601
historical background—
  Roman law, **8**, 602
  Scots law, **8**, 603
husband and wife, between, **8**, 602, 603, 604, 608, 645
  presumption against donation, **8**, 626
incorporeal moveable property, **8**, 636
inter virum et uxorem, **8**, 602, 604, 608
inter vivos—
  minor's incapacity to make, **8**, 611
inter vivos transactions, **8**, 601, 606
  animus donandi—
    generally, **8**, 619
  capital transfer tax, **8**, 651
  conditional, **8**, 606
  conflict between donees, **8**, 628
  constitution, **8**, 606
  conveyance necessary to, **8**, 628, 630
  delivery, **8**, 628
  inheritance tax, **8**, 652
  presumption against, **8**, 620, 621
  revocation, **8**, 643, 645
  Roman law, **8**, 602
  Scots law, **8**, 603
land, **8**, 638
lesion, **8**, 611
meaning, **8**, 601, 604
minority, challenge on grounds of, **8**, 611
mortis causa, **8**, 601, 606, 607; **25**, 735
  animus donandi, **8**, 630
    generally, **8**, 619
  capital gains tax exemption, **8**, 653
  capital transfer tax, **8**, 651
  competing interests, **8**, 649

Donation—*continued*
mortis causa—*continued*
  conditio si institutus sine liberis decesserit, whether applicable to, **8**, 607
  conveyance, whether necessary, **8**, 628, 630
  customs duties, **8**, 657
  delivery, **8**, 628–630
  deposit receipts, **8**, 630
  function, **8**, 607
  impossible, immoral or illegal conditions, **8**, 641
  inheritance tax, **8**, 652
  legacy compared, **8**, 607
  meaning, **8**, 607
  minor's capacity, **8**, 611
  money in bank or deposit receipt, **8**, 637
  postponed to claims of deceased's creditors, **8**, 607
  predecease of donor by donee, **8**, 607
  presumption against, **8**, 620, 621
  revocation, **8**, 607, 632, 643, 646
    automatic, **8**, 646
    donor, by, **8**, 646
  Roman law, **8**, 602
  Scots law, **8**, 603
  traditio longa manu, **8**, 634
  uplift of sum deposited, **8**, 630
negotiorum gestio, and, **15**, 116
obligations to give, **8**, 605
presumed gift, **8**, 627
presumption against, **8**, 619, 620
  circumstances of alleged donation, **8**, 622
  evidence of, reliability, **8**, 621
  relationship between parties, **8**, 623
proof of, **8**, 605
property, transfer of, **8**, 601
  obligation to transfer, **8**, 601
propter nuptias, **8**, 602
purpose, non-fulfilment of, **8**, 642
reduction, **13**, 36
  circumvention, **8**, 647
  competing interests, **8**, 649
  facility, **8**, 647
  gratuitous transactions or transactions on favourable terms, **8**, 647
  grounds for, **8**, 647
  insolvency of donor, **8**, 648
  open to, **8**, 613
  undue influence, **8**, 647
relationship between parties, **8**, 623
remuneratory, **8**, 606, 608
revocation—
  child, on subsequent birth of, **8**, 645
  donation *inter vivos*, **8**, 643, 645
  donation *mortis causa*, **8**, 607, 632, 643, 646, 649
  generally, **8**, 643
  implications of, **8**, 643
  trust, donation by means of, **8**, 632
social security benefits, effect on, **8**, 658
statement of intention to give, **8**, 605
sub modo, **8**, 640; **24**, 6
subject matter—
  animus donandi, **8**, 625

Donation—*continued*
subjects of—
  commercio property, **8**, 615
  human body and organs, **8**, 616
  illegality, **8**, 617
  inalienable property, **8**, 615
  limited interests, **8**, 618
taxation—
  capital gains tax, **8**, 653
  capital transfer tax, **8**, 651
  corporation tax, **8**, 654
  customs duties, **8**, 657
  generally, **8**, 650
  income tax, **8**, 654
  inheritance tax, **8**, 652
  stamp duty, **8**, 655
  value added tax, **8**, 656
  testamentary provisions, **8**, 601, 609
title, and, **8**, 619
trust, by means of—
  delivery, **8**, 631
  revocability, **8**, 632
trust, constituted by means of—
  delivery, **8**, 629
unjust enrichment, and, **15**, 16, 29
void, **8**, 613
warrandice, **8**, 639; **18**, 716
Donee
acceptance of donation by, **8**, 629
conflict between donees *inter vivos*, **8**, 628
conveyance to, whether necessary, **8**, 628, 630
delivery to third party on donee's behalf, **8**, 634
donation *mortis causa*, **8**, 607
  revocation, **8**, 646
gift taken *cum onere*, **8**, 639
immoral or illegal purpose, donation made for, **8**, 641
inheritance tax, **8**, 652
mortis causa, competing interests, **8**, 649
non-existent, **8**, 614
predecease of donor by, donation *mortis causa*, **8**, 607
sum deposited, uplift, **8**, 630
Donor
donation *mortis causa*, **8**, 607
donation *mortis causa*, revocation, **8**, 646
immoral or illegal purpose, donation made for, **8**, 641
inheritance tax, **8**, 652
insolvency, **8**, 648
liability, **8**, 639
predecease by donee, donation *mortis causa*, **8**, 607
survival of particular danger, donation *mortis causa*, **8**, 607
Donor (sperm or ovum)
databank information on, limitation on access to, **18**, 1541
Door
obstruction of road by, **20**, 695
Double contingency rule
See VESTING
Double-depreciation lease
cross-border leasing, **14**, 1096

Double-dip lease
cross-border leasing, **14**, 1096
reverse, **14**, 1096
Double taxation agreements, **19**, 1516, 1534
Douglas Earls of Angus
precedence, **16**, 2006
Dower
abolition of, **25**, 611
uses to bar, **25**, 611
Dracone
meaning, **21**, 362*n*
towed or pushed, lights, **21**, 362
Dragging
salmon fishing by, **11**, 11*n*
Drain
building controls, **3**, 208, 209
installation through neighbouring property, **19**, 353
law of the tenement, **18**, 239
local authority duties and powers, **19**, 330
matter or substance prejudicial to health, **19**, 334
owner, drainage works carried out by, **25**, 363
owners and occupiers rights and duties, **19**, 331
public health considerations, **19**, 305, 336
Secretary of State's powers, **25**, 371
See also SEWER
Drainage
common interest, doctrine of, **18**, 359
construction or alteration, **19**, 19*n*
land, *see* LAND
loch, of, **25**, 338
owner, drainage works carried out by, **25**, 363
percolating water, **25**, 343
regional councils, works by, **25**, 373
road, of—
  alteration, **20**, 662
  cleansing drains, **20**, 662
  flood prevention works, roads authority contributions towards, **20**, 681
  interference with, **20**, 662
  notice of works of, **20**, 662
  obstruction, **20**, 662
  offences in relation to, **20**, 662
  roads authority duty as to, **20**, 662, 681
servitude of, prescription, creation by, **18**, 460
surface water, **25**, 343
  common law, **18**, 340
  statute law, **18**, 341
tolerable standard, **11**, 1979
water running naturally off superior land, obligation to receive, **18**, 337, 339, 342, 359, 442
Drainage work
agricultural land—
  creation of drains, **25**, 368
  generally, **1**, 716; **25**, 366
  improvement order, **25**, 369
  maintenance of drains, **25**, 367
common law, **25**, 364
damage—
  compensation, **25**, 370
  repair of, **25**, 370
generally, **25**, 363
government agencies, schemes by, **25**, 363, 374

Drainage work—_continued_
improvement—
  grants in respect of cost, **25**, 372
  orders, **25**, 369
landholder, carried out by, **25**, 363
non-government agencies, powers of, **25**, 374
permitted development, **23**, 150
schemes for drainage generally, **1**, 716
Secretary of State, powers of, **25**, 371
sheriff court jurisdiction, **6**, 1110
statutory authority, carried out under, **25**, 363
statutory control, **25**, 365
water authorities, powers of, **25**, 373
water development board, powers of, **25**, 373

Dramatic work
anonymous or pseudonymous, **18**, 995, 996, 1032
author—
  meaning, **18**, 980
  See also COPYRIGHT
copyright, **18**, 931, 933, 955
  adaptation, **18**, 1065
  audio-visual recording, **18**, 949
  computer, storage on, **18**, 949
  Crown copyright, term of, **18**, 1034, 1037
  educational establishment performing, showing
    or playing, **18**, 1112
  employment by another, work made in course
    of, **18**, 997–999
  European Community legislation, **18**, 1643
  generally, **18**, 949
  moral rights, _see_ COPYRIGHT (MORAL RIGHTS)
  musical elements, **18**, 955
  originality, **18**, 941
  parliamentary, term of, **18**, 1036, 1037
  public performance, infringement by, **18**, 1060,
    1061
  public reading or recitation, **18**, 1127
  published editions, **18**, 933, 936, 977, 984
    infringement, **18**, 1056
    originality, **18**, 948
    term of copyright, **18**, 1041
  quality and merit, **18**, 942
  recording—
    without permission, **18**, 949
    work must be recorded, **18**, 949
  tape-recording, **18**, 949
  term of copyright, **18**, 1029, 1030
  writing, meaning, **18**, 949
meaning, **18**, 955
performance—
  amateur, **9**, 1048
  obscene, **9**, 1044
  professional, **9**, 1048
  prosecutions in respect of, **9**, 1048
  rights, _see_ PERFORMANCE
  school, **9**, 1052
record of performance of, offence relating to, **9**,
  1006
See also PLAY; THEATRE

Drawback
See CUSTOMS DUTY

Drawing
copyright, **18**, 931, 957, 958, 959, 1153

Dredging
artificial stream, creation of, **25**, 355
non-tidal river, **25**, 315
tidal river, **25**, 312
vessel engaged in, **21**, 365

Dried fruit
mineral hydrocarbons, treatment with, **11**, 375

Drink
alcoholic liquor, _see_ ALCOHOLIC LIQUOR
drink driving offences, _see_ ALCOHOLIC LIQUOR
drinking water—
  consumption of water, **25**, 334
  domestic use, supply for, **25**, 506
  fluoridation, _see_ FLUORIDATION
  supply of, **14**, 1664
  water unfit for, **14**, 2079
food for statutory purposes, **11**, 311
soft—
  composition, **11**, 368
  diabetic, **11**, 368
  labelling, **11**, 368
  low calorie, **11**, 368
  vending machine, sale from, **11**, 368
VAT zero-rating, **7**, 1445

Drinking fountain
closure, **25**, 526

Drinking trough
charge for supply, **25**, 537
provision of, **25**, 526

Drive, private
road, whether, **20**, 411

Driver/Driving
accident, _see_ BREATH TEST; ROAD ACCIDENT
careless driving, _see_ CARELESS DRIVING
dangerous driving, _see_ DANGEROUS DRIVING
definition, **20**, 410
  drink driving offences, in relation to, **20**, 420
disqualification, **20**, 459
  appeals, **20**, 454
  application for removal, **20**, 454, 455
  careless driving, following, **20**, 414, 453
  consecutive basis, may not be imposed on, **20**,
    453
  deception to avoid, **20**, 457
  discretionary, **20**, 456, 457
  driving while disqualified, **20**, 455
  endorsement on driving licence, **20**, 456
    See also DRIVING LICENCE
  fine or prison sentence, in connection with, **20**,
    453
  fixed penalties and conditional offers in relation
    to, **20**, 458
  generally, **20**, 453
  obligatory, **20**, 453
  obtaining licence while disqualified, **20**, 455
  penalty, as, **20**, 453
  period of, **20**, 453, 453n
    indefinite disqualification not allowed, **20**
      453
    life, for, **20**, 453
    start, **20**, 453
  personal circumstances of driver, **20**, 453
  previous disqualifications, effect of, **20**, 457
  totting-up, **20**, 457

Driver/Driving
eyesight, defective, **20**, 450
following another, duty of, **20**, 414
foreign—
    goods or public service vehicle, **20**, 499
    licensing, **20**, 451
goods vehicle, of, *see* GOODS VEHICLE
inconsiderate, **7**, 449
information as to, keeper of vehicle must provide, **20**, 436
instruction, **20**, 452
licence, *see* DRIVING LICENCE
misleading signal given by, **20**, 414
night driving, **20**, 414
offence by, fixed penalty or conditional offer, **20**, 458
parking—
    darkness, during hours of, **20**, 443
    illegally, obstructively or dangerously parked vehicles—
        immobilisation, **20**, 439
        removal of, **20**, 439
    meters, **20**, 439
    offences in relation to, **20**, 439
    places, provision of, **20**, 439
        countryside, in, **14**, 681
    servitude rights and, **18**, 491
    traffic warden, powers and duties, **20**, 510
    See also CAR PARK
police powers in relation to, **20**, 436
private hire car licence, **14**, 552
reckless driving, *see* RECKLESS DRIVING
taking and driving away motor vehicle without consent, **20**, 444
taxi licence, **14**, 552
test—
    conduct of, complaints as to, **20**, 449
    grant of, generally, **20**, 449
    regulations governing, **20**, 449
traffic directions and signs, compliance with, **20**, 435
    failure, prosecution over, **20**, 446
unfit, while, **20**, 416*n*
    unfitness to drive, test of, **20**, 417
without due care and attention, **20**, 414
See also ROAD ACCIDENT; ROAD TRAFFIC
Driving instruction
paid, Register of Approved Instructors, **20**, 452
Driving licence
age limits, **20**, 448, 455
agricultural tractor, **20**, 447
causing or permitting another person to drive without, **20**, 447, 447*n*
disabilities precluding holding, **20**, 450
disqualification, *see* DRIVER
disqualified driver obtaining, **20**, 455
driving without, onus of proof, **20**, 447
endorsement—
    careless driving, following, **20**, 414, 456
    court's powers to refrain from, **20**, 456
    deception to avoid, **20**, 457
    obligatory, **20**, 456, 458
    penalty points, **20**, 456, 457
    prima facie evidence, as, **20**, 456

Driving licence—*continued*
endorsement—*continued*
    production of licence, **20**, 457
    reckless or dangerous driving, following, **20**, 412, 413
exchangeable, **20**, 447*n*
false statement concerning, **20**, 472
falsification, **20**, 472
foreign, **20**, 447*n*
foreign driver, **20**, 451
inability to read, declaration as to, **20**, 450
issue of, false statement or documents, **20**, 472
material information, withholding, **20**, 472
police power to demand production, **20**, 436
provisional, **20**, 449
refused on medical grounds, local authority travel concession to person, **20**, 493
requirement for—
    exceptions to, **20**, 447, 447*n*
    generally, **20**, 447
revocation, **20**, 453
test, **20**, 449
validity, **20**, 450
Droits
Admiralty, of, **17**, 407
Crown, of, **17**, 407
Drought
alveus, operations on, **25**, 323
byelaws, **25**, 390
compensation, **25**, 393
generally, **25**, 389
obtaining supplies during, **25**, 392
spray irrigation, restrictions on, **25**, 331
water—
    prohibition of use, **25**, 391
    restriction of use, **25**, 391
    supply during, generally, **25**, 530
Drug abuse
addict as double offender, **14**, 1220
cannabis, *see* CANNABIS
cocaine, *see* COCAINE
controlled drugs, *see* DRUGS
criminal law, regulation by, **14**, 1234
dealers—
    heroin, **14**, 1220
    sentencing, **14**, 1220
hard and soft drugs compared, **14**, 1222
heroin, *see* HEROIN
internal hostility to, **14**, 1220
legal control, development of, **14**, 1233
non-controlled drugs—
    alcohol, **14**, 1231
    nicotine, **14**, 1231
    solvents, **14**, 1232
parent or guardian who is addict, **3**, 1267
pregnancy, during, **10**, 27
regulations, **14**, 1258–1261
social policy, effect of, **14**, 1220
substances resorted to, **14**, 1222
suppression of, arguments for, **14**, 1221
Drugs
abuse, *see* DRUG ABUSE

Drugs—*continued*
administration with intent to enable or assist a
   crime—
   firearm or imitation firearm possessed during,
      10, 1565
advertisements, restrictions on, **17**, 45
assault, drugging as, **7**, 226
automatism induced by, **7**, 151, 152, 153
cannabis, *see* CANNABIS
cocaine, *see* COCAINE
confiscating orders, offences in relation to, **14**,
   1255
controlled—
   addict—
      notification of, **14**, 1261
      supply to, **14**, 1261
   administering, supply of articles for, **14**, 1249
   amphetamines, **14**, 1227
   barbiturates, **14**, 1229
   cannabis, **14**, 1228, 1246
   classification, **14**, 1235, 1259
   cocaine, **14**, 1226
   control, concept of, **14**, 1244
   dentist, use by, **14**, 1258
   doctor, use by, **14**, 1258
   exportation, **14**, 1236
   generally, **14**, 1223
   hallucinogens, **14**, 1225
   importation, **14**, 1236
   nature of substance, knowledge of, **14**, 1243
   offences—
      arrest, **14**, 1252
      attempt, **14**, 1250
      cannabis, cultivation of, **14**, 1246
      conspiracy, **14**, 1251
      control, concept of, **14**, 1244
      exportation, **14**, 1236
      forfeiture, **14**, 1253
      importation, **14**, 1236
      incitement, **14**, 1250
      possession—
         consumption, after, **14**, 1241
         generally, **14**, 1238
         intent to supply, with, **14**, 1245
         legitimate, **14**, 1239
         minute quantities, in, **14**, 1240
         requirements of, **14**, 1242
      premises, use of drugs in, **14**, 1247
      production, **14**, 1237
      prosecution, **14**, 1254
      punishment, **14**, 1254
      search, **14**, 1252
      substance, knowledge of nature of, **14**, 1243
      supply, **14**, 1237
   opiates, **14**, 1224
   opium offences, **14**, 1248
   pharmacist, use by, **14**, 1258
   possession—
      consumption, after, **14**, 1241
      generally, **14**, 1238
      intent to supply, with, **14**, 1245
      legitimate, **14**, 1239
      minute quantities, in, **14**, 1240
      requirements of, **14**, 1242

Drugs—*continued*
controlled—*continued*
   premises, use in, **14**, 1247
   preparation, supply of articles for, **14**, 1249
   production, **14**, 1237
   regulations, **14**, 1258–1261
   safe custody, **14**, 1260
   supply of, **14**, 1237
   tranquillisers, **14**, 1230
   veterinary practitioner, use by, **14**, 1258
   veterinary surgeon, use by, **14**, 1258
criminal activity, connection with, **14**, 1221
death following supply of, **7**, 281
driving offences related to—
   being in charge of vehicle under influence, **20**,
      417, 417n
      defence to charge, **20**, 417
      penalties, **20**, 417
      police powers, **20**, 417
      service personnel, **20**, 432
   blood test, *see* BLOOD TESTS
   careless driving under influence, death caused
      by, **20**, 416, 453
   disqualification following, **20**, 415, 453
   driving or attempting to drive under influence,
      20, 417, 417n
      defence to charge, **20**, 417
      obligatory disqualification following, **20**, 453
      penalties, **20**, 417
      police powers, **20**, 417
   evidence in proceedings—
      back calculation of level in accused's blood,
         20, 429n
      blood and urine specimens, **20**, 431
      detention, **20**, 432
      documentary, **20**, 430
   solvents, as, **20**, 417
   specimen, failure to provide, **20**, 416n
   unfitness to drive, test of, **20**, 417
   urine test, *see* URINE TEST
exportation offences, **7**, 1162
forcible drugging to achieve theft, **7**, 358
fraud, **7**, 383
general enforcement, **14**, 708
hard, distinguished from soft drugs, **14**, 1222
heroin, *see* HEROIN
illegal importation, **7**, 1151
infringement of patent rights, **18**, 865
intoxication, *see* INTOXICATION
legal capacity of person under influence of, **15**, 662
legal control—
   medicinal purposes, **14**, 1220
   non-therapeutic purposes, **14**, 1220
meaning, **11**, 311
medical—
   charges for, **11**, 1512
   checking amount supplied, **11**, 1472
   chemist, *see* PHARMACEUTICAL CHEMIST
   Drug Tariff, **1**, 1474, 1475; **11**, 1446n, 1472
   general practitioners' drugs budgets, **11**, 1401
   listed, **11**, 1472, 1472n
   restrictions on supply, **11**, 1446, 1446n, 1472
   scheduled, **11**, 1446, 1472, 1472n
   standards or formulas, **11**, 1472

Drugs—*continued*
medical—*continued*
    supply to patients, **11**, 1472
    testing quality, **11**, 1472
    See also PHARMACEUTICAL SERVICES
medicinal, VAT zero-rating, **7**, 1456
offences in relation to, **14**, 1255
    See also controlled drugs *above*
person under influence of, franchise, **15**, 1082
pregnancy, abuse during, **10**, 1027
prescribed—
    confiscation order, **7**, 1195
    importation or exportation, **7**, 1195
    proceeds of drug trafficking, seizure, detention
        or forfeiture, **7**, 1231
    smuggling offences, detention relating to, **7**, 1230
public analyst, **14**, 709
sampling, **14**, 708
sheriff court jurisdiction, **6**, 1117
social policy, effect of, **14**, 1220
soft, distinguished from hard drugs, **14**, 1222
therapeutic—
    automatism induced by, **7**, 132, 154
    intoxication by, **7**, 132
trafficking—
    confiscation order, **14**, 1255
    Convention Against Illicit Traffic in Narcotic
        Drugs and Psychotropic Substances, **21**, 42
    enforcement, **14**, 1257
    high seas, jurisdiction over, **21**, 45
veterinary, *see* VETERINARY PRACTICE
Vienna Convention against Illicit Narcotic Drugs
    and Psychotropic, **12**, 508
Drunkenness
alcoholic liquor, generally, *see* ALCOHOLIC LIQUOR;
    INTOXICATION
capacity to buy and sell, **20**, 816
child suffocated while in bed with drunken
    person, **3**, 1246
decrease in, **2**, 99
drunk in public place while in charge of child
    under ten, **3**, 1242, 1252
intoxication, **14**, 1220, 1221
licence holder, of, **2**, 75
measures to curb, **2**, 1
offences relating to, **2**, 75
police powers as to, **16**, 1787
sporting event, at, **19**, 1271
Dry dock
meaning, **11**, 1303
Ducie Island
British Dependent Territories citizenship, **14**, 1932
Duck
slaughter of, **11**, 516
wild—
    duck decoys, **11**, 882
    game, as, **11**, 802
    trespass in search of, **11**, 817
Due diligence
defence of—
    product safety, **6**, 57
    trade descriptions, **6**, 135, 136, 137
    weights and measures, **6**, 252
litigation regarding, **6**, 137

Duelling
challenge to duel, as breach of peace, **7**, 451
criminal activity, as, **7**, 221
Duke
daughter, mode of address, **16**, 1322
eldest son, courtesy title, **16**, 1311
mode of address, **16**, 1322
Scottish Parliament, representation in, **15**, 1003
title, generally, **16**, 1311
younger son, mode of address, **16**, 1322
Dumbarton Castle
keeper of, **7**, 830, 835
Dumfries and Galloway Region
population, **14**, 64
structure, **14**, 64
Dumper vehicle
whether motor vehicle, **20**, 405
Dumping
anti-dumping duty, **7**, 1050
competition law, **4**, 1396
European Union regulations, **7**, 1024, 1050
United Kingdom legislation, **7**, 1050
Dunblane Cathedral
provisions relating to, **13**, 1514
Dunconnel Castle
keeper of, **7**, 830
Dundee
county of city, **14**, 39
Dundee Police Court, former operation of, **6**,
    1157, 1158
educational provision, **14**, 36
population, **14**, 64
transport undertakings, operation of, **14**, 414, 419
Dungpit
public health nuisance, as, **19**, 336
Dunstaffnage Castle
keeper of, **7**, 830
Durability
contract of sale for moveable property, **20**, 827
Duress
See COERCION; FORCE AND FEAR
Dust
furnace, emission from, arrestment equipment—
    exemption from requirement, **9**, 1131
    generally, **9**, 1129
    provision of, **9**, 1130
mines and quarries in—
    accumulation of, **14**, 1658
    control of, **14**, 1658
    generally, **14**, 1706
temporary interference caused by, **14**, 2052
Dustbin
household waste, collection of, **9**, 1166
Duty
breach of—
    constitutional reasons, for, **11**, 1024
    embezzlement, **11**, 1015
    gives rise to remedy, **11**, 1023
    obligations of reparation, **11**, 1032–1034
care, of, *see* CARE, DUTY OF
civil liability, and, **11**, 1016
criminal liability, and, **11**, 1015
culpa as proximate cause of injury, **11**, 1019

Duty—*continued*

employment contracts, within, *see* CONTRACT OF
    EMPLOYMENT
enforcement of duties, **11**, 1022
imposition of requirements, as, **11**, 1025
injured party, remedial action by, **11**, 1023
judiciary, **11**, 1024
legal subject, **11**, 1014
meaning, **11**, 1014
Ministers of the Crown, **11**, 1024
moral agent, **11**, 1014
obligation, and, **11**, 1028, 1034
public duties, enforcement of, **11**, 1024
public interest, imposed in, **11**, 1029
rights depend on relevant, **11**, 1074
statutory, breach, *see* STRICT LIABILITY

Dwelling house

closing order, **14**, 305
cottar, occupied by, **6**, 967
debenture where subject includes, heritable
    security in relation to, **20**, 255
demolition order, **14**, 305
domestic rates, abolition of, **24**, 610–617
domestic water rates, **25**, 533
existing, meaning, **23**, 140*n*
factory, used as, **19**, 336*n*
fire certificate, **14**, 503
holiday let, **13**, 604
industrial purposes, used for, **24**, 639
intestate succession—
    prior rights, **25**, 690
    value, dispute as to, **25**, 692
land let with, protected tenancy status affected by,
    13, 635
landlord's hypothec, **13**, 513
lease—
    generally, **13**, 595
    long—
        limitations on residential use, **13**, 339–347
licence to occupy, **13**, 596, 626
meaning, **11**, 1901, 1901*n*, 1982*n*, 2001*n*; **13**, 606;
    19, 366*n*; **24**, 608; **25**, 690*n*
multiple occupation, meaning, **23**, 140*n*

Dwelling house—*continued*

nature of, **20**, 178
number, **14**, 410
occupied by spouse, as heritable security, **20**, 221
order relating to, appeal to sheriff court, **14**, 119
original, meaning, **23**, 140*n*
overcrowding, **19**, 336
partial residences, **24**, 611
permitted development—
    alteration of, **23**, 140
    curtilege, erection within, **23**, 141
    generally, **23**, 139
    oil storage tank, erection of, **23**, 143
    satellite antenna, installation of, **23**, 142
private—
    lease, security over, **20**, 261
    meaning, **13**, 341
    protection on leasehold subjects, standard
        securities, **20**, 177, 178, 181, 182
protected tenancy, **13**, 605–607
protection of private sector residential tenant, *see*
    TENANT-TENANCY
public health nuisance, **19**, 336
railway property, **24**, 721
rateable values, **24**, 618–624
removings, notice, **13**, 483
rents, **14**, 827
residential and non-residential uses, **24**, 639
servant of the Crown, occupied by, **24**, 595
tenements and flats, **24**, 609
terrace house, meaning, **23**, 140*n*
trades descriptions legislation, **6**, 112, 126
udal law, **24**, 308
valuation for rating, **24**, 621–623
    adjustment of rate for, **24**, 624
    comparative principle, **24**, 621, 622
    schemes of, **24**, 623
    See also VALUATION FOR RATING
water meter charges, **25**, 536
See also HOUSING

Dynamite

explosive, as, **10**, 1586

E

Eadem sonans **rule**
application, **6**, 430
Eady levy
termination of, **9**, 1028
Ear piercing
age limit, **3**, 1231
Earl
daughter, mode of address, **16**, 1322
eldest son, courtesy title, **16**, 1311
mode of address, **16**, 1322
original number, **16**, 1304
Scottish Parliament, representation in, **15**, 1003
territory, association with, **16**, 1303, 1304
title, generally, **16**, 1311
use of term, **16**, 1303
younger son, mode of address, **16**, 1322
Earl Marischal
Officer of the Crown, as, **7**, 812, 815
Earnings
alimentary, **8**, 330
arrestment of, **8**, 248, 330
  amount arrestable, **8**, 335
  death of debtor, effect, **8**, 127
  disbursement by sheriff clerk, **8**, 344
  effect, **8**, 334
  execution, **8**, 333
  expenses, **8**, 332
  grounds for, **8**, 332
  interaction of arrestments, **8**, 341
  interest, **8**, 332
  principal sum, **8**, 332
  review, **8**, 336
  termination, **8**, 336
  what can be arrested, **8**, 331
bonus payments as, **8**, 331
commissions as, **8**, 331
company, **25**, 20
conjoined arrestment order, **8**, 330
  generally, **8**, 342
  operation, **8**, 343
  review, **8**, 345
  termination, **8**, 345
  variation, **8**, 345
current maintenance arrestment—
  amount arrestable, **8**, 339
  commencement, **8**, 338
  generally, **8**, 337
  interaction of arrestments, **8**, 341
  review, **8**, 340
  termination, **8**, 340
damages, effect on scale of, **15**, 930
deduction from earnings order—
  child support liability order, **8**, 346
  employer, earnings must be paid by, **8**, 346
  employer's failure to comply, **8**, 346
  generally, **8**, 330, 346
  priority over other diligences, **8**, 346
  sequestration of debtor, and, **8**, 346
  sheriff court powers, **8**, 346

Earnings—*continued*
diligence against, generally, **8**, 330
fees as, **8**, 331
meaning, **8**, 331
per share, **25**, 20
social security regulations, *see* SOCIAL SECURITY
valuation based on, **25**, 20
yield, substitution for dividend yield, **25**, 20
See also REMUNERATION; WAGES
Earthcloset
public health nuisance, as, **19**, 336
Easement
servitude compared, **18**, 440, 440*n*
See also SERVITUDE
East African dependencies
Asian population, **12**, 107
  special vouchers, **12**, 158
Easter
Church of England, Book of Common Prayer, **22**, 808
description, **22**, 808
Eastern churches, **22**, 808
etymology, **22**, 808
fixing date, **22**, 804, 808
Gregorian calendar, **22**, 808
Julian calendar, **22**, 808
legislation governing date, **22**, 808
Scotland, fixing date in, **22**, 808
Scottish Episcopal Church, Prayer Book, **22**, 808
Second Vatican Council, **22**, 808
summer time, effect on calculation, **22**, 810
Western churches, **22**, 808
Eavesdrop
servitude right of, **6**, 515; **18**, 485
Ecclesiastical arbiter
functions, **22**, 511
Ecclesiastical buildings, *see* CHURCH; CHURCH OF SCOTLAND (property and endowments); SYNAGOGUE
Ecclesiastical courts
See CHURCH COURTS
Ecclesiastical precedence
generally, **16**, 2003, 2016
Lords Spiritual, **16**, 2016
Economic development
generally, **14**, 630
industrial, *see* INDUSTRIAL DEVELOPMENT
inner urban area, *see* INNER URBAN AREA
North Board, by, **9**, 624
tourism, *see* TOURISM
urban development area, *see* URBAN DEVELOPMENT AREA
urban development corporation, *see* URBAN DEVELOPMENT CORPORATION
Economic loss
competition, legitimate, **15**, 575
damages for, **14**, 2153
derivative or parasitic, **15**, 574
duty of care, *see* CARE, DUTY OF

Economic loss—*continued*
non-relational, **15**, 574
pure, **15**, 574
relational—
fraud, and, **15**, 585
negligence, and—
duty of care, **15**, 586, 588
existing contract—
interference, negligent, **15**, 593
performance, negligent, **15**, 590
general duty, **15**, 587
generally, **15**, 586, 588, 594
Henderson v Merrett Syndicates Ltd, decision in, **15**, 586, 587
Junior Books Ltd v Veitchi Co Ltd, decision in, **15**, 593, 594
misrepresentation, negligent, **15**, 589
prospective contracts—
inducing, **15**, 589
preventing, **15**, 591
Economic, Social and Cultural Rights, International Covenant on
generally, **19**, 694
Edinburgh
county of city, **14**, 39
Court of Four Burghs, **14**, 13
Edinburgh Police Court—
composition, **6**, 1156
former operation of, **6**, 1156–1158
educational provision, **14**, 36
Festival fringe, temporary public entertainment licence, **9**, 1004
feu-ferme charter, **14**, 11
Incorporation of Goldsmiths of the City of Edinburgh, **18**, 1412
New Town plan, effect on development of real burdens, **18**, 376–379, 381*n*
population, **14**, 64
transport undertakings, operation of, **14**, 414, 419
Edinburgh Castle
Governor of, office of, **7**, 834
Edinburgh Gazette
documentary evidence, as, **10**, 593
notification in—
application to remove trustee, **2**, 1371
companies, information as to, **4**, 333
composition offer, **2**, 1444
conservation area, of, **23**, 189
environmental statement, publicity for, **23**, 128
examination of debtor, **2**, 1399
petition for recall, **2**, 1360
provisional orders, **19**, 7, 13
sequestration notice, **2**, 1341
territorial designations listed in, **6**, 1018
Education
academic freedom, university education, **8**, 985, 1020
access funds, **8**, 945
ad hoc authorities, **14**, 36
advancement of, charitable status, *see* CHARITABLE PURPOSE
advisory council—
establishment, **8**, 710
purpose, **8**, 710

Education—*continued*
Appeal Committee, supervision of, **23**, 911
attendance order, *see* ATTENDANCE ORDER
attendance registers, **8**, 858
authority—
appointment committee, powers and duties, **8**, 821
attendance order, *see* ATTENDANCE ORDER
attendance registers, requirements as to, **8**, 858
books and equipment, provision of, **8**, 847
careers service—
collection and furnishing of information, **8**, 960
duties, generally, **8**, 958
future role, **8**, 964
records to be kept, **8**, 961
Secretary of State's powers, **8**, 963
vocational advice—
records of, **8**, 961
summaries of, **8**, 962
who may be assisted, **8**, 958, 959
catchment areas, *see* SCHOOL
chief education officer, appointment, **8**, 714
child guidance service, duty to provide, **8**, 864
cleanliness, power to ensure, **8**, 862
closure of schools on medical advice, **8**, 863
clothing, provision of, **8**, 848
pupils' right over clothing provided, **8**, 848
school uniforms, **8**, 849
colleges, maintenance of, **8**, 730
colleges of further education, **8**, 701
college council, *see* college council *below*
compulsory testing in primary schools, requirements as to, **8**, 859
consultation and consent, requirement for—
catchment area, alteration of, **8**, 724
generally, **8**, 724
more than one proposal made, **8**, 724
new school, provision of, **8**, 724
notification to parents, **8**, 724
special classes, changes concerning, **8**, 724
transfer from primary to secondary school, changes concerning, **8**, 724
curriculum, publication of details of, **8**, 843
delegation to school boards, **8**, 725
dental care, duty to provide, **8**, 861
director of education—
appointment, **8**, 714
discharge of functions, **14**, 597
discretionary payment of allowances, **8**, 846
discrimination in educational services, **9**, 366
district councils, **8**, 712
duties—
enforcement, Secretary of State's powers, **8**, 706
failure to discharge, **8**, 701
generally, **8**, 701, 713
principal duty, **8**, 713
education committee—
appointment, **8**, 715
composition, **8**, 717
discharge of functions, **8**, 721
dismissal of teachers, **8**, 723
joint committees, **8**, 722

Education—*continued*
authority—*continued*
  education committee—*continued*
    religious education, promotion, **8**, 718
    remit, **8**, 716
    teachers' nominees, **8**, 719
    voting rights, **8**, 720
  educational endowment, reorganisation of, **8**, 838
  educational provision, schemes for, **8**, 711
  employment of schoolchildren, duties in relation to, **8**, 866–873
  equipment, provision, **8**, 847
  fees, power to charge, **8**, 844
  financial assistance for student in further education—
    access funds—
      conditions for payment, **8**, 945
      generally, **8**, 945
      Secretary of State's powers as to, **8**, 945
    bursary, **8**, 941
      amount payable, **8**, 942
      conditions for payment, **8**, 943
      eligibility, **8**, 944
    course outwith Scotland, for, **8**, 941
    generally, **8**, 941
  food, provision of, **8**, 850
  free education, duty to provide, **8**, 844
  further education—
    approval of schemes by Secretary of State, **8**, 927
    college councils—
      casual vacancies, **8**, 931
      company, formation of, **8**, 939
      delegation schemes, **8**, 928, 936, 937
        suspension of, **8**, 937
      disapplication of requirement for, **8**, 940
      duty to establish, **8**, 928
      generally, **8**, 925
      meetings, **8**, 933
      membership, **8**, 929
        conflict of interests, **8**, 934
        disqualification from, **8**, 932
      powers, generally, **8**, 935
      proceedings, **8**, 930
      supply of goods and services, **8**, 938
    duty to provide, **8**, 925
    proposed reforms, **8**, 925
  general functions, **14**, 595, 603
  grant to—
    Secretary of State's powers, **8**, 708
  health and safety, duties in relation to, **8**, 734
  health service joint liaison committees, **11**, 1412
  homework—
    duties as to, generally, **8**, 860
    policy on, publication of, **8**, 843, 860
  hostel, duty to provide, **8**, 729
  houses and hostels for teachers or officials, duties in relation to, **8**, 731
  information to be made available by, **8**, 843
  islands councils, **8**, 701, 712
  judicial review—
    subject to, **8**, 836
    when available, **8**, 836

Education—*continued*
authority—*continued*
  local government reorganisation, generally, **8**, 712
  meaning, **8**, 701
  medical and dental services, duty in connection with, **11**, 1479
  medical care, duty to provide, **8**, 861
  mentally handicapped person, duty of authority—
    to inform parent, **22**, 31
    to inform social work department, **22**, 31
  milk, provision of, **8**, 850
  physical education and training, provision for, **8**, 843
  placing policy, publication of details of, **8**, 843
  placing request, *see* PLACING REQUEST
  playground supervision, duty as to, **8**, 865
  progress records, requirements as to, **8**, 858
  property owned by, reversion of title, **8**, 735, 839
  proposals by—
    Secretary of State's consent, when required, **8**, 726
    denominational education—
      deterioration in position, **8**, 728
      withdrawal of, **8**, 727
    provision of schools, buildings and equipment, **8**, 729–735
    Secretary of State's consent to construction work, **8**, 732
  public examinations, publication of details of entrants, **8**, 843
  recreation and sport, duties as to, **19**, 1224, 1225
  regional councils, **8**, 701, 712
  religious instruction, duty as to, **8**, 856, 857
  reports and returns, duty to make, **8**, 705
  scholarships, power to award, **8**, 844
  school boards—
    co-operation with, **8**, 736
    delegation of functions to, **8**, 725, 776
    duties in relation to, **8**, 747
    funding, **8**, 777
    partial transfer of powers to, **8**, 701
    supply of information and reports to, **8**, 770
  school education, role generally, **8**, 843
  school health service, **11**, 1410, 1450, 1479
  school uniform—
    clothing grants, **8**, 849
    policy on, **8**, 849
  Scottish Joint Negotiating Committee for Teaching Staff in School Education, representation on, **8**, 832
  Secretary of State's powers in relation to, **8**, 701
  self-governing school—
    benefits or services provided to, **8**, 807
    duties on closure of, **8**, 804
    educational endowments, administration of, **8**, 807
    financing, **8**, 798
    interaction with, **8**, 807
    self-governing status—
      effect of initiating procedure for, **8**, 793–797
      school attaining, **8**, 701

Education—*continued*
authority—*continued*
  social, cultural and recreative education and facilities, provision of, **8**, 843, 925
  special educational needs, provision for children with—
    duties as to, generally, **8**, 909
    publication of arrangements for, **8**, 843
    See also SPECIAL EDUCATION
  special needs, functions in relation to children and young persons with—
    appeal procedure, **8**, 916–920
    assessment procedure, **8**, 911
    children who cease to be of school age, **8**, 922, 923
    provision outwith UK, **8**, 924
    record of needs, **8**, 912–915, 923
    review of recording decisions, **8**, 921
    See also SPECIAL EDUCATION
  student records—
    access to—
      duties as to, **8**, 946
      refusal of, **8**, 946
    erasure of information contained in, **8**, 946
    information which need not be disclosed, **8**, 946
    rectification, **8**, 946
      refusal, review of decision, **8**, 946
  teachers, appointment of, **8**, 821
  transport, provision of, **8**, 851–855
  travel arrangements, publication of, **8**, 843
  unauthorised property deals by, reduction or prevention, **8**, 802, 803
  voluntary organisations, discretion to assist, **22**, 10
  welfare of pupils, duties as to, **8**, 861–865
bus—
  permit for use of, **14**, 423
  school, use to carry fare-paying passenger, **14**, 438
careers services, *see* CAREERS SERVICES
catchment areas, *see* CATCHMENT AREA
central institutions, *see* SCOTTISH CENTRAL INSTITUTIONS
charitable status, *see* CHARITABLE PURPOSE
child, rights of, **17**, 236
child in theatre, of, **9**, 1052
church and state, shifting relationship of, **5**, 346
clinical training and research, **11**, 1487
college council—
  disqualification, **14**, 600
  duty to appoint, **14**, 598
  generally, **8**, 701
  membership, **14**, 599
committee—
  appointment, **8**, 715
  composition, **8**, 717
    religious education, promotion of, **8**, 718
  dismissal of teachers, **8**, 723
  disqualification, **14**, 600
  functions, discharge of, **8**, 721
  joint committees, **8**, 722
    sub-committees, appointment of, **8**, 722
  membership, **14**, 596

Education—*continued*
committee—*continued*
  powers, **14**, 36
  remit, **8**, 716
  special provisions, **14**, 241
  teachers' nominees, **8**, 717, 719, 720
  voting rights, **8**, 720
copyright, permitted acts—
  anthologies for educational use, **18**, 1111
  broadcasts, **18**, 1113
  cable programmes, **18**, 1113
  copies—
    method of making, **18**, 1110
    number, **18**, 1110
    photocopies, **18**, 1110
    reprographic, **18**, 1114
    Roneo or Gestetner copies, **18**, 1110
    who may make, **18**, 1110
  exam questions, setting and answering, **18**, 1110
  generally, **18**, 1109
  instruction, in, generally, **18**, 1110
  performing, playing or showing work, **18**, 1112
  research and private study, **18**, 1102, 1103
corporal punishment, **8**, 820, 903; **12**, 26, 90, 91
curriculum, education authority policy, **8**, 843
denominational—
  appointment of teachers, **8**, 761, 826
  deterioration in position of, representations to Secretary of State, **8**, 728
  proposed withdrawal, Secretary of State's consent, **8**, 727
  provision of, educational authorities' duty to provide, **8**, 729
  religious instruction, education authorities' duties as to, **8**, 857
development of service, **14**, 36
director of, **14**, 249, 601
  appointment, **8**, 714
  school board appointment committee, role in, **8**, 765
educational, meaning, **24**, 95
educational and scientific materials—
  European Union import duty relief, **7**, 1100
  temporary importation, **7**, 1187
educational charitable trusts, **24**, 95, 96
  nomination of trustees, **24**, 157
educational establishments—
  inspection, **8**, 701, 709
  meaning, **8**, 709*n*
  radioactive materials, safety regulations as to, **9**, 915
equipment, provision, **8**, 729–735, 847
examinations—*continued*
  educational authority policy, **8**, 848
  result, data protection of, **18**, 1528
  University and academic performance, **8**, 1026
expenditure programme, **5**, 584
fees—
  discretionary payment of allowances by education authority, **8**, 846
  education authorities' power to charge, **8**, 844
forisfamiliation by, **10**, 1103
free, education authorities' duty to provide, **8**, 844

Education—*continued*
further, *see* FURTHER EDUCATION
General Teaching Council for Scotland, *see*
   GENERAL TEACHING COUNCIL FOR SCOTLAND
grant—
  education authority, to, **8**, 708
  educational research, to carry out, **8**, 708
  educational service, for provision of, **8**, 708
  managers of educational establishment, to, **8**, 708
  student, to, Secretary of State's powers, **8**, 701,
    708
  university, to, **8**, 708
headteacher, *see* HEADTEACHER
health, provisions as to, **8**, 861; **11**, 1482; **19**, 305
heritors of parish, duties of, **19**, 208
historical background, **8**, 701
independent, *see* INDEPENDENT SCHOOL
Independent Schools Tribunal, **6**, 1046
Inner London Education Authority—
  elections, **14**, 62
  functions, **14**, 60
international conventions on, **12**, 5
legal, *see* LEGAL EDUCATION
linguistic considerations, **12**, 89
local inquiry—
  appointment of officials, **8**, 707
  notification, **8**, 707
  requirement to attend, **8**, 707
  Secretary of State's power to hold, **8**, 707
migrants, children of, **8**, 893
minor, of, curator's control, **10**, 1118
parental convictions, **12**, 89, 90, 92
parental rights and duties—
  attendance at school—
    commencement—
      dates for, **8**, 890
      generally, **8**, 889
    exemption from, **8**, 892
    leaving date, **8**, 891
    migrants, children of, **8**, 893
    non-attendance, *see* non-attendance *below*
    travelling persons, children of, **8**, 893
  choice of school—
    generally, **8**, 874
    parents' wishes, **8**, 874
    school placement—
      catchment area, **8**, 875
      placing requests, **8**, 875
      refusal—
        appeals, **8**, 877–887
        grounds for, **8**, 876
        related cases, review of, **8**, 888
  duty to educate, **8**, 874
  non-attendance—
    enforcement procedures—
      attendance order, **8**, 897
        amendment, **8**, 898
        failure to comply with, **8**, 900
        period of operation, **8**, 899
        revocation, **8**, 898
      education authorities' powers, **8**, 896
      prosecution, **8**, 901
    failure to attend school without reasonable
      excuse, **8**, 894, 895

Education—*continued*
parental rights and duties—*continued*
  parents' wishes, generally, **8**, 874
  to determine education, **11**, 1208
penal establishments, educational provision, **16**, 1456
  young prisoner, **16**, 1456
physical education and training, **8**, 843
placing request
  appeal to sheriff, **14**, 119
  more than one school mentioned in, **8**, 875
  parental rights, **8**, 875
  refusal—
    appeal against, **8**, 877
      appeal committee, **8**, 878
        decisions of, **8**, 885
          appeal to sheriff, **8**, 887
          deemed, **8**, 886
        matters which may be referred, **8**, 879
      combined hearings, **8**, 883
      education authority, deemed decisions of,
        8, 886
      jurisdiction, **8**, 879
      persons entitled to be present, **8**, 884
      procedure, **8**, 882
      self-governing school, **8**, 880
    grounds for, **8**, 876
  review of related cases, **8**, 888
  school level approach, **8**, 876
  single child approach, **8**, 876
  special educational needs, child with, **8**, 916,
    919, 920
  specified school, **8**, 875
  under-age, **8**, 876
public health, **19**, 305
punishment of children, **10**, 1224
reform, **14**, 47
religious instruction, *see* RELIGIOUS INSTRUCTION
religious observance in, right to withdraw from,
  3, 1679
right to—
  European Community consumer programmes,
    6, 31
  generally, **12**, 87, 89–92
  Universal Declaration of Human Rights, **12**, 4*n*
Roman Catholic, state-supported school, *see* SCHOOL
Royal College of Veterinary Surgeons, powers of,
  25, 201
school, *see* SCHOOL; SCHOOL EDUCATION
school council—
  disqualification, **14**, 600
  duty to appoint, **14**, 598
  membership, **14**, 599
school outfits and scholastic material, import duty
  relief, **7**, 1100, 1113
Scottish central institutions, *see* SCOTTISH CENTRAL
  INSTITUTIONS
secondary, **14**, 36
Secretary of State for Scotland, powers and
  duties—
  access funds, award of, **8**, 945
  advisory councils, **8**, 710
  consent of, educational proposals for which
    required, **8**, 726–728
  construction work, consent to, **8**, 732

Education—_continued_
Secretary of State for Scotland, powers and duties—_continued_
  denominational education—
    deterioration in position of, consultation over, **8**, 728
    proposed withdrawal, consultation over, **8**, 727
  directions, power to make, **8**, 704
  educational endowments, register of, **8**, 837
  enforcement, powers of, **8**, 706
  funding, as to, **8**, 701
  further education schemes, approval, **8**, 927
  generally, **8**, 701, 702
  grant-aided colleges, funding, **8**, 947
  grants, power to make, **8**, 701, 708
  independent school, notice of complaint regarding, **8**, 812
  industrial scholarship, award of, **8**, 708
  inspection, powers of, **8**, 709
  local inquiry, power to hold, **8**, 707
  regulations, power to make, **8**, 703
  reports, power to make, **8**, 705
  returns, power to make, **8**, 705
  schemes for educational provision, power to require submission, **8**, 711
  Scottish Examination Board—
    powers as to, generally, **8**, 948
    report by, **8**, 952
  self-governing school—
    board of management, powers in relation to, **8**, 792
    closure of, **8**, 804–806
    financing, **8**, 798
    powers in relation to applications for self-governing status, **8**, 783
    recurrent grants, **8**, 798
  special educational needs, record of children with, decisions on, **8**, 918
  university degrees, in relation to, **8**, 1013
services, non-designated, **4**, 1177n
sex, **12**, 92
sheriff court jurisdiction, **6**, 1093
society promoting, **12**, 694n
special, _see_ SPECIAL EDUCATION
sub-committee, disqualification for membership, **14**, 600
teachers, **14**, 602
  See also HEADTEACHER; TEACHER
technology academy, _see_ TECHNOLOGY ACADEMY
travel concession to person undergoing full-time, **20**, 493
university, _see_ UNIVERSITY EDUCATION
VAT and, **7**, 1425
wild birds or animals taken or killed in interests of, **11**, 883, 886
See also SCHOOL
Education and Science, Department of
functions of, **5**, 502
Educational endowment
See ENDOWMENT
Educational establishment
copyright, permitted acts—
  generally, **18**, 1109

Educational establishment—_continued_
copyright, permitted acts—_continued_
  research and private study, **18**, 1102, 1103
  See also EDUCATION
landlord, as—
  repossession, **13**, 736, 740, 749, 753
  student let, tenancy status, **13**, 630, 633, 636, 643
meaning, **18**, 1109
photocopies taken by, **18**, 1103
Eels
freshwater fish, as, **11**, 5n
fry, **11**, 5n
Effective capital value
valuation for rating, **24**, 527
Effigy
defamatory, **15**, 483
Effluent
sewage, _see_ SEWAGE
trade, _see_ TRADE EFFLUENT
Eggs
accession compensatory amounts, **1**, 937
cereal market, parallel legislation to, **1**, 937
export refunds, **1**, 938
mineral hydrocarbons, treatment with, **11**, 375
pasteurisation of, **11**, 356
sluice-gate price, **1**, 938
Eidsivathing **law**
Norwegian law code, **24**, 303
Eire
see REPUBLIC OF IRELAND
Ejection
availability of remedy, **18**, 153, 154
corporeal moveable property, action for recovery of possession, **18**, 159
intrusion, and, remedy of, **15**, 215
jurisdiction, **18**, 154
land, recovery of founded on right to possession, **18**, 152, 153, 154
  interdict as subsidiary crave, **18**, 155
meaning, **13**, 467
natural possession, protection of, **18**, 138
procedure, **18**, 154
recovery of possession, **18**, 140
removing distinguished, **13**, 467; **18**, 153
service tenancy, **13**, 469
spuilzie, **18**, 154, 161
standard security, enforcement of, **18**, 154
vi clam aut precario, defender possessing, **18**, 154
violent profits, **13**, 505, 508, 512
wrongous, damages, **13**, 471
Ejusdem generis **rule**
statute, use in construction of—
  generally, **12**, 1166, 1167
  where inapplicable, **12**, 1168
Elder
Church of Scotland—
  admission, form of, **3**, 1507
  appointment, **3**, 1507
  commissioners to General Assembly, **3**, 1543
  congregational board, **3**, 1515
  discipline, **3**, 1512
  elect, **3**, 1507
  election, **3**, 1507
  Formula, subscription to, **3**, 1507

Elder—*continued*
Church of Scotland—*continued*
  kirk session, as member of, **3**, 1507
  minister, dissatisfaction with, **3**, 1512
  minister as, **3**, 1507
  moving to another congregation, **3**, 1507
  number required, **3**, 1507
  objections to life or doctrine of, **3**, 1507
  presbytery, membership, **3**, 1519
  resignation, **3**, 1507
  roll of elders, **3**, 1507
  ruling, **3**, 1507
  Sacrament of Lord's Supper, distribution of
    elements, **3**, 1508
  teaching, **3**, 1507
Elderly person
assistance in kind to facilitate person living at
  home, **22**, 13
compulsory care—
  circumstances warranting removal, **22**, 29
  procedure, **22**, 29
  revocation, application, **22**, 29
  summary proceedings—
    order, time limits of detention, **22**, 29
    parties entitled to be heard, **22**, 29
counselling services, voluntary organisations, **22**,
  13
day facilities, **22**, 28
financial residential care in privately owned
  home, **22**, 28
home-help service, **22**, 26
home meals service, **22**, 27
laundry service ancillary to home help, **22**, 26
local authority duty to—
  general, **22**, 25
  social work services, duty to provide, **22**, 25–29
  specific, **22**, 26–28
persons in need, as, **22**, 13
property, local authorities' duty to protect—
  expenses, right to recover, **22**, 29
  person subject to compulsory care order, **22**, 29
residential care, **22**, 25, 28
Election
absent voting, *see* VOTE
address, **15**, 1019, 1020
agent—
  appointment, **15**, 1051, 1231
    notification, **15**, 1240
    public notice of, **15**, 1232
    revocation, **15**, 1051, 1052, 1231
    statutory provisions, **15**, 1493
    time provisions, **15**, 1220, 1231
  candidate acting as own, **5**, 377; **15**, 1019,
    1051, 1245, 1246, 1317, 1420
  corrupt or illegal practice by—
    criminal consequences, **15**, 1463
    finding by election court, **15**, 1455
    illegal payment, employment or hiring, **15**,
      1462
    incapacity for voting, **15**, 1466
    void, election, **15**, 1469
  count—
    attendance, **15**, 1330, 1336
    role at, **15**, 1326, 1336

Election—*continued*
agent—*continued*
  counting agents, appointment, **15**, 1333
  death, **15**, 1051, 1231
  deemed, public notice of, **15**, 1232
  deputy (sub-agent)—
    appointment—
      notification, **15**, 1240
      statutory provisions, **15**, 1493
      time provisions, **15**, 1220
    county and burghal constituencies, **15**, 1037
    election expenses returns and declarations,
      15, 1427
    generally, **15**, 1053
    office of, **15**, 1054
  duties and powers, **5**, 377; **15**, 1052
    timetable in respect of, **15**, 1237, 1238
  election expenses—
    corrupt practices, **15**, 1447
    duties as to, **15**, 1231
    false declaration, **15**, 1426, 1447
    functions in relation to, **15**, 1409, 1410
    illegal practices, **15**, 1456
    incurred with authority of, **15**, 1425
    incurred by, **15**, 1411
    returns and declarations, **15**, 1420, 1423
  European parliamentary election—
    generally, **15**, 1051
    timetable, **15**, 1226, 1227, 1231
  expenses, duties as to, **15**, 1231
  illegal payment, employment or hiring by, **15**,
    1462
  local government election—
    generally, **15**, 1051
    timetable, **15**, 1228–1231
  name and address, declaration, **15**, 1051
  office, **15**, 1054
  personal expenses, **15**, 1407
  petty expenses, statement as to, **15**, 1231
  polling agent, appointment and assistance, **15**,
    1308
  postal ballot, issue and receipt (opening), **15**,
    1197
  prior, election expenses returns and
    declarations, **15**, 1427
  public notice of name, address and office
    address, **15**, 1245, 1246
  re-count, right to request, **15**, 1336, 1338
  requirement for, **15**, 1019, 1020, 1051
  secrecy, maintenance of, **15**, 1318
  statutory requirements, **5**, 377
  sub-agent, *see* deputy *above*
  substitute—
    appointment, **15**, 1231
    death, **15**, 1231
    public notice of name, address and office
      address, **15**, 1245
    public notice of, **15**, 1232
  United Kingdom parliamentary election, **15**,
    1051
    timetable, **15**, 1225, 1227, 1231
  written intimation as to, **15**, 1231
ballot, *see* BALLOT
ballot box, *see* BALLOT BOX

Election—*continued*
ballot paper, *see* BALLOT PAPER
Boundary Commission, *see* BOUNDARY COMMISSION
bribery, **7**, 409
Burgh Police etc (Scotland) Acts, **15**, 1023
Burghs and Police (Scotland) Act 1833 ..., **15**, 1023
by-election—
  European Parliament, *see* EUROPEAN PARLIAMENT (election to)
  member taking seat after, **5**, 383
  United Kingdom Parliament, *see* PARLIAMENT (election to)
campaign, *see* ELECTION CAMPAIGN
candidate—
  accommodation expenses, **15**, 1407
  corrupt or illegal practice by, **15**, 1235
    criminal consequences, **15**, 1463
    election expenses, **15**, 1426
    finding by election court, **15**, 1455
    illegal payment, employment or hiring, **15**, 1462
    incapacity for re-election, **15**, 1465
    incapacity for voting, **15**, 1466
    void, election, **15**, 1467
  count—
    attendance, **15**, 1330, 1336
    role at, **15**, 1336
  counting agents, appointment, **15**, 1333
  statutory provisions, **15**, 1493
  death, **15**, 1258, 1290, 1340
    poll countermanded or abandoned, **15**, 1417
    combined poll, **15**, 1387
  declaration of candidate elected, **15**, 1230, 1245, 1246, 1352
  determination of election, **15**, 1485
  disparaging, **15**, 1411
  disqualification—
    confirmation of, source, **15**, 1256
    European parliamentary election, **15**, 1440
    local government election, **15**, 1440
    nomination papers invalid where, **15**, 1251
    questioning election on grounds of, **15**, 1440
    statutory provisions, **15**, 1493
    United Kingdom parliamentary election, **15**, 1440
  election agent—
    appointment, **15**, 1051
    candidate acting as own, **15**, 1019, 1051, 1245, 1246, 1317, 1420
    deputy, **15**, 1037
    name and address, declaration, **15**, 1062, 1245, 1246
    requirement for, **15**, 1019, 1020, 1051
  election expenses—
    candidate, meaning, **15**, 1406
    corrupt practices, **15**, 1447
    county and burghal constituencies, **15**, 1037
    election agent, duties, **15**, 1052, 1231
    exemptions, **15**, 1412
    false declaration, **15**, 1426, 1447
    generally, **15**, 1411
    illegal practices, **15**, 1456
    limitation, **15**, 1018–1020, 1413

Election—*continued*
candidate—*continued*
  election expenses—*continued*
    maximum amounts—
      abandonment of poll, on, **15**, 1417
      calculation, **15**, 1415
      countermandment of poll, on, **15**, 1417
      demise of Crown, on, **15**, 1418
      generally, **15**, 1414
      joint candidates, **15**, 1419
      variation, **15**, 1416
    meaning, **15**, 1405
    payment—
      conditions of, **15**, 1409
      meaning, **15**, 1408
    personal expenses, **15**, 1407, 1409
    persons employed for payment, **15**, 1410
    statutory provisions, **15**, 1493
    time provisions, **15**, 1220, 1231
    who may incur, **15**, 1411
    written statement as to, **15**, 1231, 1245
  European parliamentary election—
    citizenship, **15**, 1065, 1065*n*
    disqualification, **15**, 1065
      questioning election on grounds of, **15**, 1440
    generally, **15**, 1050
    incapacity for re-election, **15**, 1465
    relevant citizen of the Union—
      declaration and certificate, **15**, 1291
    timetable, **15**, 1226, 1227, 1231
  false statement as to, **15**, 1451
  General Medical Council, for, **15**, 1509
  illegal payment, employment or hiring by, **15**, 1462
  incapacity for re-election, **15**, 1465
  joint, election expenses, **15**, 1419
  local government election—
    citizenship, statutory, **15**, 1066
    declaration of candidate elected, **15**, 1230
    disqualification—
      bankruptcy, **15**, 1068
      by-elections, **15**, 1067
      common law, **15**, 1071
      legal incapacity, **15**, 1066, 1071
      Local Government (Scotland) Act, under, **15**, 1069
      mental disability, **15**, 1071
      non-age, **15**, 1066
      office, by virtue of, **15**, 1069, 1070
      questioning election on grounds of, **15**, 1440
      sequestration, **15**, 1068
      statutory, **15**, 1066–1070
    generally, **15**, 1050
    incapacity for re-election, **15**, 1465
    notice of poll, **15**, 1303
    qualification, **15**, 1066
    timetable, **15**, 1228–1231
  meaning, **15**, 1050
    election expenses, in relation to, **15**, 1406
  nomination—
    abuse of right of, **15**, 1251

Election—*continued*
candidate—*continued*
  nomination—*continued*
    adjournment of proceedings—
      riot, **15**, 1301
      violence, **15**, 1301
    consent to—
      attestation, **15**, 1286
      content, **15**, 1285
      generally, **15**, 1227, 1229, 1284
    deposit, requirement for, **15**, 1287–1290
    disqualification, **15**, 1227
    invalid, **15**, 1246
    irregularities, **15**, 1254
    more than one paper, by, **15**, 1293
    multiple, **15**, 1290, 1292
    notice of poll, **15**, 1303
    objections to—
      European parliamentary elections, **15**, 1227
      United Kingdom parliamentary elections, **15**, 1227
    obvious unreality, **15**, 1251
    proceedings, attendance at, **15**, 1297
    relevant citizen of the Union—
      declaration and certificate, **15**, 1291
    returning officer, role, **15**, 1250–1258
    statement of persons nominated, **15**, 1302
    time for, publication, **15**, 1245
    whether candidate stands nominated, determination, **15**, 1250, 1257
    withdrawal, **15**, 1258, 1298
  nomination paper—
    address of candidate—
      generally, **15**, 1266
      home address, **15**, 1269
      local government elections, **15**, 1274
      misnomer or inaccurate description, effect of, **15**, 1273
      per register, as, **15**, 1270
      sufficiency of address, **15**, 1268
      true address, **15**, 1267
    alteration, **15**, 1283
    assenters, **15**, 1276
    clerical error, **15**, 1255
    completion, **15**, 1282
    constituency, omission of name, **15**, 1281
    contents, **15**, 1265–1272
    delivery, **15**, 1258
      generally, **15**, 1261
      local government elections, **15**, 1228
      place of, **15**, 1263
      time provisions, **15**, 1264
      United Kingdom parliamentary elections, **15**, 1225
      who may make, **15**, 1262
    description of candidate, **15**, 1271, 1272
      misnomer or inaccurate description, effect of, **15**, 1273
    electoral area, omission of name, **15**, 1281
    errors, miscellaneous, **15**, 1281
    European parliamentary election, **15**, 1226
    examination, **15**, 1229
    form and substance, **15**, 1253, 1255, 1259, 1260

Election—*continued*
candidate—*continued*
  nomination paper—*continued*
    inspection, **15**, 1300
    invalid—
      disqualification of candidate, where, **15**, 1256
      irregularities, **15**, 1254
      language, **15**, 1260
      more than one for each candidate, **15**, 1261, 1293
    name of candidate, **15**, 1259, 1265
      contractions, **15**, 1265
      initials, **15**, 1265
      local government elections, **15**, 1274
      misnomer or inaccurate description, effect of, **15**, 1273
    non-delivery, **15**, 1258
    objections—
      European parliamentary elections, **15**, 1226
      generally, **15**, 1294
      nature of, **15**, 1296
      United Kingdom parliamentary elections, **15**, 1225
      who may make, **15**, 1295
    proposer, **15**, 1276
    seconder, **15**, 1276
    separate paper for each candidate required, **15**, 1259
    signature, **15**, 1253, 1255
    subscription—
      elector, meaning, **15**, 1277
      electoral numbers of subscribers, **15**, 1280
      meaning, **15**, 1275
      persons subscribing, **15**, 1276
      restrictions, **15**, 1278
      valid signatures, **15**, 1279
    substitution of different candidate, **15**, 1283
    surname, **15**, 1259, 1265
    validity—
      abuse of right of nomination, **15**, 1251
      determination, **15**, 1250–1258
      notice of decision to candidate, **15**, 1299
      obvious unreality, **15**, 1251
      procedure on decisions, **15**, 1299
      returning officer, role, **15**, 1250–1258, 1299
    who may complete, **15**, 1282
  notice of poll—
    local government elections, **15**, 1303
  personal character or conduct, false statement as to, **15**, 1451
  personal expenses, meaning, **15**, 1407
  polling agent, **15**, 1308
  postal ballot, issue and receipt (opening), **15**, 1197
  powers and duties—
    timetable in respect of, **15**, 1237, 1238
  public notice of candidate elected, **15**, 1352
  public notice of candidates, **15**, 1245
  qualification, statutory provisions, **15**, 1493
  re-count, right to request, **15**, 1336, 1338
  register of electors, supply to, **15**, 1114

Election—*continued*
candidate—*continued*
  return name of candidate elected, **15**, 1352, 1353
  sitting or voting where no expenses returns or declarations delivered, **15**, 1430
  specialists, supply of copies to, **15**, 1193
  statement of persons nominated—
    European parliamentary elections, **15**, 1226, 1302
    United Kingdom parliamentary elections, **15**, 1225, 1302
  travelling expenses, **15**, 1407
  United Kingdom Central Council for Nursing, Midwifery and Health Visiting, **15**, 1499–1501
  United Kingdom parliamentary election—
    disqualification—
      affirmation of allegiance, failure to make, **15**, 1060
      bankruptcy, **15**, 1059
      citizenship, **15**, 1058
      clergy, **15**, 1061
      common law, **15**, 1055
      mental disability, **15**, 1055
      non-age, **15**, 1056
      oath of allegiance, failure to make, **15**, 1060
      office, by virtue of, **15**, 1064
      peerage, **15**, 1062
      prisoners, **15**, 1063
      questioning election on grounds of, **15**, 1440
      sequestration, **15**, 1059
      sitting member ineligible for any other, **15**, 1057
      statutory, **15**, 1056–1064
  'Election Writ and Return', **15**, 1353
  generally, **15**, 1050
  incapacity for re-election, **15**, 1465
  record of returns, **15**, 1353
  timetable, **15**, 1225, 1227, 1231
  withdrawal, **15**, 1298
    delivery of notice—
      European parliamentary elections, **15**, 1226
      local government elections, **15**, 1228
      United Kingdom parliamentary elections, **15**, 1225
    determination, **15**, 1258
    false statement as to, **15**, 1451
    inducing, **15**, 1459
    nomination, of, **15**, 1258, 1298
canvasser—
  conduct, **15**, 1020
  corrupt or illegal practice, **15**, 1074
  paid, employment, **15**, 1461
capacity to stand for public office, **11**, 1069
capacity to vote, **11**, 1069
combined poll—
  abandonment of poll, effect of, **15**, 1387
  death of candidate, **15**, 1387
  ancillary proceedings, discretionary combination, **15**, 1362

Election—*continued*
combined poll—*continued*
  ballot boxes, **15**, 1367, 1377
  ballot papers, **15**, 1367
    counterfoils, **15**, 1377
    spoilt, **15**, 1377
    tendered, **15**, 1377
    unused, **15**, 1377
  blind voters assisted by companions, list, **15**, 1375
  close, parcelling of documents on, **15**, 1377
  combined functions—
    generally, **15**, 1363
    responsibility for, **15**, 1364
  common documents and action, **15**, 1375
  count—
    procedure, **15**, 1384, 1385
    returning officer, **15**, 1384, 1385
  countermandment of poll, effect of, **15**, 1387
  declaration by companion of blind voter, **15**, 1371
  direction for guidance of voters, **15**, 1370
  discretionary, **15**, 1361
  disposal of documents, after count, **15**, 1378, 1386
  financial aspects—
    accountability, **15**, 1388
    apportionment of costs, **15**, 1390, 1391
    control of costs, **15**, 1389
    count, matters arising at, **15**, 1393
    poll, matters arising at, **15**, 1392
  hours of poll, **15**, 1366
  list of proxies, **15**, 1375
  mandatory, **15**, 1360
  parcelling of documents on close, **15**, 1377
  poll cards, **15**, 1362
    elector's official, **15**, 1372
    proxy's official, **15**, 1372
  polling agents, notice of appointment, **15**, 1373
  polling stations—
    description of voters entitled to vote at, **15**, 1363, 1368
    generally, **15**, 1365
    situation, notification, **15**, 1363, 1368
  postal voting—
    absent voters lists, marking, **15**, 1381
    agents, notice of appointment, **15**, 1380
    amendments to documentation, **15**, 1382
    ballot boxes, labelling of, **15**, 1382
    ballot papers, **15**, 1382
    declarations of identity, **15**, 1215, 1381, 1382
    envelopes, **15**, 1382
    generally, **15**, 1196, 1215, 1362, 1363, 1379–1383
    postal proxies voters lists, marking, **15**, 1381
    procedure, **15**, 1383
    receptacle, labelling of, **15**, 1382
  questions to be put to voters, **15**, 1374
  register of electors, **15**, 1375
  returning officer, **15**, 1363, 1378, 1384, 1385, 1388
  riot, adjournment of poll, notice, **15**, 1376
  statutory provisions, **15**, 1493
  tendered votes list, **15**, 1375

Election—*continued*

combined poll—*continued*

    violence, adjournment of poll, notice, **15**, 1376

    votes marked by presiding officer, list, **15**, 1375

    voting compartment notice, **15**, 1363, 1369

committee room—

    hire on behalf of election candidate, **15**, 1410

    illegal hire, **15**, 1458

community council member, age limit, **3**, 1214

conduct of proceedings, statutory provisions, **15**, 1493

constituency, *see* CONSTITUENCY

contested—

    declaration of result, **15**, 1352

    public notice, **15**, 1352

corrupt practices at, convicted person disqualified from voting, **5**, 374

count—

    admission card—

        generally, **15**, 1244

    attendance, **15**, 1330, 1336, 1337

    ballot boxes, opening, **15**, 1326, 1335

    ballot paper account, **15**, 1326, 1328

        discrepancies, **15**, 1328

        verification, **15**, 1326, 1328, 1335

    ballot papers—

        back of paper, marked on, **15**, 1347

        counting and recording number, **15**, 1326, 1335

        decision of returning officer, finality, **15**, 1349

        doubtful, **15**, 1335

        face to be shown, **15**, 1326, 1335

        identification of voter from writing or mark, **15**, 1341, 1344–1346

        invalid, **15**, 1341–1351

        mixing, **15**, 1326, 1335, 1384, 1385

        more than one candidate, voting for, **15**, 1341, 1343

        official mark missing, where, **15**, 1341, 1342

        other than cross, **15**, 1341, 1347, 1348

        rejected—

            adjudication, **15**, 1341–1351

            decision of returning officer, finality, **15**, 1349

            election petition, **15**, 1349

            statement as to, **15**, 1350

            treatment, **15**, 1350

        signature or name on, **15**, 1345

        sorting according to candidate, **15**, 1326, 1335

        ticked, **15**, 1348

        unconventional marks, **15**, 1341, 1347, 1348

        unmarked, **15**, 1341, 1347

        void, **15**, 1344–1346

            uncertainty, for, **15**, 1341, 1348

    breaks in, **15**, 1335

    candidate, role at, **15**, 1336

    clerks, **15**, 1337

    combined poll—

        procedure, **15**, 1384, 1385

        returning officer, **15**, 1384, 1385

    counting agent—

        role, **15**, 1335

Election—*continued*

count—*continued*

    death of candidate, effect, **15**, 1340

    declaration of result, **15**, 1352

    disposal of documents, after, **15**, 1354–1359

        combined poll, **15**, 1378, 1386

    election agent—

        presence, **15**, 1326

        role, **15**, 1336

    equality of votes, decision by lot, **15**, 1339

    European parliamentary election—

        attendance at count, **15**, 1330

        first and second counts, **15**, 1326, 1329

        generally, **15**, 1326

        verifying officers, **15**, 1326, 1326*n*, 1328, 1337

    expulsion from, **15**, 1332

    first, **15**, 1326

        attendance, **15**, 1330

        combined poll, **15**, 1384

        counting agents' role, **15**, 1335

        time provisions, **15**, 1329

    food, drink and tobacco, consumption, **15**, 1332

    local government election—

        attendance at count, **15**, 1330

        generally, **15**, 1230, 1326

    media coverage, **15**, 1332, 1332*n*

    notification of time and place, **15**, 1245, 1246

    order, maintenance, **15**, 1332

    postal ballot papers, **15**, 1326

    premises, selection and layout, **15**, 1327

    procedure, generally, **15**, 1326

    re-count—

        bundle check, **15**, 1338

        full, **15**, 1338

        further re-counts, **15**, 1338

        provisions as to, **15**, 1338

        refusal, **15**, 1338

        right to request, **15**, 1336

    sealing up ballot papers, after, **15**, 1354

    second, **15**, 1326

        attendance, **15**, 1330

        counting agents' role, **15**, 1335

        time provisions, **15**, 1329

    secrecy, requirement as to, **15**, 1331

    staff employed or required by returning officer, **15**, 1337

    statutory notice, **15**, 1331

    tendered ballot papers, **15**, 1326

    time provisions, **15**, 1329

        local government election, **15**, 1230

    United Kingdom Central Council for Nursing, Midwifery and Health Visiting election, **15**, 1505

    United Kingdom parliamentary election—

        attendance at count, **15**, 1330

        generally, **15**, 1326

court, *see* ELECTION COURT

declaration, reduction of, **13**, 37

decision, reduction of, **13**, 37

documents, procedure after count—

    combined poll, **15**, 1378, 1386

    forwarding of documents, **15**, 1355

Election—*continued*
documents, procedure after count—*continued*
  inspection of ballot papers, order for, **15**, 1357
  opening of sealed packets, order for, **15**, 1357
  production of retained documents, order for,
      15, 1357, 1358
    evidence of vote, **15**, 1359
  public inspection of retained documents, **15**, 1356
  retention of documents, **15**, 1355, 1356
  sealing up of ballot papers, **15**, 1354
Election of Commissioners Act 1681 ..., **15**,
    1005, 1006, 1010
elector, *see* ELECTOR
electoral areas, *see* ELECTORAL AREAS
electoral malpractices, **7**, 409
  See also illegal practices *below*
electoral register, *see* ELECTORAL REGISTER
electoral registration officer—
  appointment of, **14**, 249
  electoral register compiled by, **5**, 374
electoral system—
  post-Union—
    constitutional significance, **5**, 467–470
    context, **5**, 467
    effect of Union generally, **5**, 468
    freeholders as guardians of terms, **5**, 470
    representation in Parliament, **5**, 469
  proportional representation, **5**, 378
  reform of, **5**, 378
  relative majority, **5**, 378
  simple majority, **5**, 378
European Parliament, to, **10**, 21, 31, 351–353
  principles governing, **10**, 354
  United Kingdom, in, **10**, 355
  See also EUROPEAN PARLIAMENT (election to)
expenditure, **5**, 377
expenses, *see* ELECTION EXPENSES
financial aspects—
  candidates' election expenses—
    candidate, meaning, **15**, 1406
    meaning, **15**, 1405
    payment—
      conditions of, **15**, 1409
      meaning, **15**, 1408
    personal expenses, **15**, 1407
    persons employed for payment, **15**, 1410
    who may incur, **15**, 1411, 1412
  combined poll—
    accountability, **15**, 1388
    apportionment of costs, **15**, 1390
      matters arising from, **15**, 1391
    control of costs, **15**, 1389
    count, matters arising at, **15**, 1393
    poll, matters arising at, **15**, 1392
  local government election, **15**, 1397, 1398
  returning officer, **15**, 1394–1401
    advance on account of charges, **15**, 1396
    consideration in respect of writ, **15**, 1394
    income tax, liability to, **15**, 1403
    listed items, **15**, 1401
    national insurance contributions, **15**, 1402
    recovery of charges, **15**, 1395
    rendering accounts, **15**, 1401
    superannuation, **15**, 1400

Election—*continued*
financial aspects—*continued*
  returning officer—*continued*
    taxing of accounts, **15**, 1399
    value added tax, **15**, 1404
  writ for United Kingdom parliamentary
      election, **15**, 1394
franchise, *see* FRANCHISE
free, right to, **12**, 87, 93
General Council (Convention), role, generally,
    15, 1002
holiday, person enabled to vote when on, **5**, 374
illegal practices—
  agent, by, *see* agent *above*
  canvasser, by, **15**, 1074
  election expenses, **15**, 1456
  generally, **7**, 409
  paid canvassers, employment of, **5**, 377
  person convicted of—
    membership of House of Commons,
        exclusion from, **5**, 379
    voting in election, disqualification from, **5**, 374
  unlawful election expenses, **5**, 377
local—
  act or omission in breach of election law, **15**,
      1441
  ballot paper, **14**, 90
  Boundary Commission, **15**, 1039
  burghal, former category, **15**, 1021–1023
  by-election—
    expenses, maximum amount, **15**, 1415
    qualification for candidature, **15**, 1067
    timing, **15**, 1045, 1219
  candidate, political affiliation of, **14**, 90
  combined poll, **15**, 1360
  community council, elections to, **14**, 75
  constituency boundaries, **15**, 1030
  corrupt or illegal practice—
    candidate guilty of, **15**, 1072–1074
    election agent, duties, **15**, 1052
    election petition, **15**, 1234
  corrupt or illegal practices, **7**, 409
  count, *see* COUNT
  county, former category, **15**, 1021, 1024, 1025
  disposal of documents, after count, *see*
      ELECTION (documents)
  district, **15**, 1021, 1030, 1039
  election agent, **15**, 1051
  election court, **15**, 1472
  election expenses—
    election agent, duties, **15**, 1052
    maximum amount, **15**, 1414
    meaning, **15**, 1405
    personal expenses, **15**, 1407
    returning officer, role, **15**, 1435
  election petition, **15**, 1475
    amendment, **15**, 1234
    presentation, **15**, 1234
  elector, meaning, **15**, 1277
  electoral areas, **14**, 203
  electoral divisions, **15**, 1036, 1039
  financial aspects—
    advances, **15**, 1398
    combined poll, **15**, 1388–1393

Election—*continued*
local—*continued*
  financial aspects—*continued*
    expenditure, **15**, 1397
    superannuation, **15**, 1400
  franchise, **14**, 201; **15**, 1021, 1026, 1077, 1078
  generally, **15**, 1035
  illegal practice, *see* corrupt or illegal practice
    above
  joint candidates, **15**, 1419
  local authority meeting before, **14**, 1309
  meaning, **15**, 1032
  municipal elections until 1832 ..., **15**, 1022
  nineteenth-century reforms, **15**, 1023
  nomination paper, **14**, 90
  notification—
    form, **15**, 1243
    generally, **15**, 1240, 1241, 1244
    statutory, **15**, 1246–1248
      mode, **15**, 1248
  parish, **15**, 1021, 1025
  parliamentary elections compared with, **14**, 6
  patient's declaration, **15**, 1128
  personal expenses of candidate, **15**, 1407
  political influence, visibility of, **14**, 90
  poll, notice of, **15**, 1228, 1303
  polling districts, **15**, 1040
  proper officer of the council, **15**, 1352, 1355–
    1358
  public notice—
    generally, **15**, 1240, 1241
    meaning, **15**, 1240
  questioning—
    generally, **15**, 1436
    method, **15**, 1439
  register of electors, **15**, 1104, 1105
  returning officer, **15**, 1047
  review of arrangements, **14**, 67
  riot or violence, **15**, 1229, 1316
  secret ballot, **15**, 1027
  service declaration, **15**, 1137
  statutory documentation, **14**, 90
  statutory notices, **15**, 1246, 1247
    misnomer or inaccurate description, **15**, 1249
    mode, **15**, 1248
  time, provisions as to—
    after completion of poll, **15**, 1230
    generally, **15**, 1217–1222
    up to completion of poll, **15**, 1228, 1229
  timing, **14**, 202; **15**, 1045
  uncontested, **15**, 1228, 1246
    declaration of result, **15**, 1352
  uniform franchise, introduction, **15**, 1021
  voting—
    modes, **15**, 1152
    person, in, **15**, 1153
  wards, **15**, 1030, 1036, 1039
    polling districts, **15**, 1040
local authority meeting before, **14**, 1309
local authority member, age limit, **3**, 1214
meeting—
  conduct, **15**, 1020
  disruption, **15**, 1454
Member of Parliament, age limit, **3**, 1214

Election—*continued*
Municipal Elections (Scotland) Act 1868 ..., **15**,
  1023
nomination—
  consent to, **5**, 375
  day, poll takes place on tenth day after, **5**, 375
  rejection of paper, **5**, 375
  validity of paper, **5**, 375
nomination paper, subscription, *see* SUBSCRIPTION
notice of, publication—
  European parliamentary elections, **15**, 1226,
    1245
  local government elections, **15**, 1228, 1246
  United Kingdom parliamentary elections, **15**,
    1225, 1245
paid canvassers, employment of, **5**, 377
paid employees, **15**, 1410
Parliamentary, *see* PARLIAMENT
Parliamentary Burghs (Scotland) Act 1833 ..., **15**,
  1023
Parliamentary Elections Act 1742 ..., **15**, 1010
patient's declaration—
  attestation, **15**, 1126
  cancellation, **15**, 1129
  content, **15**, 1125
  effect, **15**, 1127
  electors lists, **15**, 1088, 1090, 1100
    preparation, **15**, 1113
  local government elections, **15**, 1125
  notification requirements, **15**, 1130
  register of electors—
    generally, **15**, 1121
  requirements, generally, **15**, 1125
  United Kingdom parliamentary elections, **15**,
    1128
personation, **7**, 409
  aiding, abetting, counselling or procuring, **15**,
    1443
  corrupt practice, as, **15**, 1443
  criminal proceedings, **15**, 1471
  detection, **15**, 1308
  questioning election, **15**, 1443
  voter, by, challenge to, **15**, 1227, 1229, 1323
petition—
  abatement on death of petitioner, **15**, 1490
  adjournment of trial, **15**, 1484
  amendment—
    local elections, **15**, 1234
    parliamentary elections, **15**, 1233
  'at issue', **15**, 1480
  civil legal aid not available, **13**, 1034
  determination of court, **15**, 1485
    execution, **15**, 1486, 1487
  diet of trial, **15**, 1484
  European parliamentary election, **15**, 1438,
    1474
  evidence—
    admissibility, **15**, 1482, 1484
    lodging and intimating in advance, **15**, 1481
    not lodged in advance, leave to use, **15**, 1482
    trial, at, **15**, 1482
  expenses, **15**, 1492
  form, **15**, 1474, 1475
  generally, **15**, 1438

Election—*continued*
petition—*continued*
  grounds—
    act or omission in breach of election law, **15**,
      1441
    bribery, **15**, 1444
    broadcast, illegal practice in relation to, **15**,
      1449
    corrupt practices, **15**, 1443–1447, 1476
      mens rea, **15**, 1443
    disqualification of candidate, **15**, 1440
    disruption of election meeting, **15**, 1454
    election expenses—
      corrupt practices in relation to,, **15**, 1447
      illegal practice in relation to, **15**, 1456
    employments, illegal, **15**, 1457–1463
    false documents, **15**, 1450
    false statements, **15**, 1451
    hirings, illegal, **15**, 1457–1463
    illegal practices, **15**, 1448–1456, 1476
      hirings, payments and employments, **15**,
        1457–1463
    incompetent votes, scrutiny and re-count,
      15, 1442
    inducing withdrawal of candidate, **15**, 1459
    name and address of printer and publisher,
      omission, **15**, 1453
    payments—
      conveyance of voters, for, **15**, 1455, 1457
      exhibition of notices, for, **15**, 1452
      illegal, **15**, 1457–1463
      illegal purposes, providing money for, **15**,
        1460
    personal character, false statement as to, **15**,
      1451
    personal conduct, false statement as to, **15**,
      1451
    personation, **15**, 1443
    treating, **15**, 1445
    undue influence, **15**, 1446
    void votes, scrutiny and re-count, **15**, 1442
    voting illegally, **15**, 1448
  grounds for presenting, **5**, 376
  hearing of, **5**, 376
  local government election, **15**, 1439, 1475
  lodging, **15**, 1474, 1475
  notice of trial, **15**, 1480
  order cannot affect proceedings on, **5**, 379
  parties to, **15**, 1473–1475
  petitioner—
    death, **15**, 1490
    substitute, **15**, 1489
    who may be, **5**, 376
    withdrawal, **15**, 1488, 1489
  place of trial—
    fixing, **15**, 1480
    intimation, **15**, 1480
  postponement, **15**, 1480
  presentation, **15**, 1474, 1475
    local elections, **15**, 1234
    parliamentary elections, **15**, 1233
    time limits, **15**, 1476
  procedure, **15**, 1235, 1480–1492

Election—*continued*
petition—*continued*
  rejection of nomination paper, questioning, **5**,
    375
  requirement as to, **15**, 1478, 1478*n*
  respondent—
    ceasing to hold office, **15**, 1484
    withdrawal, **15**, 1491
  security for expenses—
    objections to, **15**, 1479, 1479*n*
    types, **15**, 1478
  service, **15**, 1477
  signature, **15**, 1474, 1475
  time of trial—
    fixing, **15**, 1480
    intimation, **15**, 1480
  time provisions, **15**, 1220, 1235
  timing of, **5**, 376
  United Kingdom parliamentary election, **15**,
    1438, 1474
  withdrawal, **15**, 1488
    substitution of new petitioner, **15**, 1489
  witnesses—
    citation, **15**, 1483
    examination, **15**, 1483
    expenses, **15**, 1483
physical incapacity—
  voter incapacitated by, **15**, 1214, 1321
poll—
  abandonment of—
    combined poll, **15**, 1387
    election expenses where, **15**, 1417
  countermandment of—
    combined poll, **15**, 1387
    election expenses, **15**, 1417
  date of, notification, **15**, 1245, 1246
poll card—
  combined poll, **15**, 1362, 1372
  dispatch, **15**, 1309
  form of official, **15**, 1309
  imitation, **15**, 1019, 1020, 1309, 1450
  issue—
    European parliamentary election, **15**, 1227
    United Kingdom parliamentary election, **15**,
      1227
polling
  statutory timetable—
    European parliamentary elections, **15**, 1226
    local government elections, **15**, 1228
    United Kingdom parliamentary elections, **15**,
      1225
polling agent—
  appointment, **15**, 1052, 1308, 1410
    notice, **15**, 1227, 1229
      combined poll, **15**, 1373
  death or incapacity, **15**, 1308
  duties, **15**, 1308
  number, **15**, 1308
  paid, **15**, 1308, 1410
  polling station, admittance to, **15**, 1308
  secrecy, maintenance of, **15**, 1318
  substitute, **15**, 1229
  unpaid, **15**, 1308

Election—*continued*
polling clerk—
  duties, **15**, 1214
polling district—
  alteration, **15**, 1305
  complaints as to, **15**, 1305
  division, **15**, 1245
  European parliamentary election, **15**, 1304
  generally, **15**, 1304
  informality in, **15**, 1305
  local government election, **15**, 1304
  meaning, **15**, 1040
  polling place, **15**, 1040
  register of electors, **15**, 1106
  statutory provisions, non-compliance, **15**, 1305
  United Kingdom parliamentary election, **15**, 1304
polling place—
  generally, **15**, 1304
  informality in, **15**, 1305
  meaning, **15**, 1040, 1307
  multi-station room, **15**, 1306
  polling station distinguished, **15**, 1155, 1307
  rooms, provisions for use of, **15**, 1306
  statutory provisions, non-compliance, **15**, 1305
polling station—
  allotment, **15**, 1155
    combined poll, **15**, 1363
  allotted—
    generally, **15**, 1155
    voting elsewhere than, **15**, 1156
    voting procedure, **15**, 1214
  ballot box, **15**, 1312
    combined poll, **15**, 1363
  clerks, **15**, 1317
  combined poll, **15**, 1363, 1365
  description of voters entitled to vote at, **15**, 1227, 1229, 1240, 1245, 1246
    combined poll, **15**, 1363, 1368
  designation, **15**, 1245
  directions for guidance of voters, **15**, 1313
    combined poll, **15**, 1370
  equipment, **15**, 1312
    combined poll, **15**, 1363
  expenses incurred, **15**, 1306
  multi-station room or hall, **15**, 1328
  number of voters admitted, **15**, 1324
  polling place distinguished, **15**, 1155, 1307
  presiding officer, **15**, 1317
    combined poll, **15**, 1363
  register of electors, **15**, 1312
  regulation of voters in, **15**, 1324
  secrecy, officers' etc duty as to, **15**, 1318
  situation, notice of, **15**, 1227, 1229, 1240, 1245, 1246
    combined poll, **15**, 1363, 1368
  special lists, **15**, 1312
  staffing, **15**, 1317
  unoccupied house, use of, **15**, 1306
  verifying officer, **15**, 1317
  voter's duty to leave, **15**, 1214
  voting compartment notice—
    combined poll, **15**, 1363, 1369
postal vote, *see* VOTE

Election—*continued*
presiding officer—
  ballot paper, duties in respect of, **15**, 1320
  ballot paper account, **15**, 1325
  challenge of voter, **15**, 1323
  close of poll, duties on, **15**, 1325
  combined poll, **15**, 1363
  duties, **15**, 1214
  list of votes marked by—
    combined poll, **15**, 1375
    forwarding or retention of, after count, **15**, 1355
  regulation of voters, **15**, 1324
  secrecy, maintenance of, **15**, 1318
procedure, **14**, 6
propaganda, control of, **5**, 377
proportional representation, **15**, 1028, 1343
proxy, *see* VOTE
proxy vote, *see* VOTE
public meetings to advance candidacy, **5**, 375
publication—
  exhibition, illegal payment for, **15**, 1452
  printer's name and address, **15**, 1242
    omission, **15**, 1453
  publisher's name and address, **15**, 1242
    omission, **15**, 1453
questioning—
  corrupt practices, **15**, 1443–1447
    consequences, **15**, 1464–1471
    criminal proceedings, **15**, 1471
    mens rea, **15**, 1443
    relief from consequences, **15**, 1470
  election petition—
    generally,, **15**, 473
  European parliamentary election, **15**, 1436, 1438
  generally, **15**, 1436
  grounds—
    breach of election law, **15**, 1441
    bribery, **15**, 1444
    broadcasting, offences in relation to, **15**, 1449
    corrupt practices, **15**, 1443–1447
      consequences, **15**, 1464–1471
      criminal proceedings, **15**, 1471
      relief from consequences, **15**, 1470
    disqualification of candidate, **15**, 1440
    disruption of election meeting, **15**, 1454
    election expenses—
      corrupt practices in relation to,, **15**, 1447
      illegal practices in relation to, **15**, 1456
    false documents, **15**, 1450
    false statements, **15**, 1451
    illegal practices, **15**, 1448–1456
      consequences, **15**, 1464–1471
      criminal proceedings, **15**, 1471
      relief from consequences, **15**, 1470
    incompetent votes, scrutiny and re-count, **15**, 1442
    name and address of printer and publisher, omission, **15**, 1453
    payments—
      canvasser, to, **15**, 1461
      committee room, in relation to, **15**, 1458

Election—_continued_
questioning—_continued_
  grounds—_continued_
    payments—_continued_
      conveyance of voters, for, **15**, 1455, 1457
      criminal consequences, **15**, 1463
      employments, illegal, **15**, 1457–1463
      exhibition of notices, for, **15**, 1452
      hirings, illegal, **15**, 1457–1463
      illegal purposes, providing money for, **15**, 1460
      inducing withdrawal of candidate, **15**, 1459
      personal character or conduct, false statements as to, **15**, 1451
      personation, **15**, 1443
      treating, **15**, 1445
      undue influence, **15**, 1446
      void votes, scrutiny and re-count, **15**, 1442
      voting illegally, **15**, 1448
  historical background, **15**, 1437
  illegal practices, **15**, 1448–1456
    consequences, **15**, 1464–1471
    criminal proceedings, **15**, 1471
    relief from consequences, **15**, 1470
  local government election, **15**, 1436, 1439
  methods—
    European parliamentary election, **15**, 1438
    local government election, **15**, 1439
    United Kingdom parliamentary election, **15**, 1438
  time provisions, **15**, 1220
  United Kingdom parliamentary election, **15**, 1436, 1438
questioning return, **15**, 1438_n_
Redistribution of Seats Act 1885 ..., **15**, 1017
register of electors, _see_ REGISTER OF ELECTORS
registration officer, _see_ REGISTRATION OFFICER
Representation of the People Act 1884 ..., **15**, 1918, 1948, 1949
  generally, **15**, 1020
  local government elections, **15**, 1026
  municipal elections, **15**, 1017, 1023
  parliamentary elections, **15**, 1017, 1018, 1019, 1028
Representation of the People (Equal Franchise) Act 1928—
  generally, **15**, 1018
  local government elections, **15**, 1026
  parliamentary elections, **15**, 1018
Representation of the People (Scotland) Acts—
  burgh members, **15**, 1014, 1015, 1023
  county members, **15**, 1013, 1015
  disputes, provisions as to, **15**, 1015
  entitlement to vote—
    burghs, **15**, 1014
    counties, **15**, 1013
  generally, **15**, 1012, 1012_n_, 1016
  local government elections, **15**, 1023
  Scottish representation in Parliament, **15**, 1028
result, public notice, **15**, 1240, 1245, 1246, 1352
returning officer, **5**, 374; **14**, 204
  See also RETURNING OFFICER
riot or violence, adjournment of poll, **15**, 1229, 1316

Election—_continued_
Royal Burghs (Scotland) Act 1833 ..., **15**, 1023
school room—
  count premises, use as, **15**, 1327
  election campaign, free use during, **15**, 1321
  polling station, use as, **15**, 1306
secrecy of ballot, **5**, 374
service declaration—
  attestation, **15**, 1135
  cancellation, **15**, 1137
  contents, **15**, 1133
  effects, **15**, 1136
  electors lists, **15**, 1088, 1090, 1110, 1113
  local government elections, **15**, 1137
  notification requirements, **15**, 1139
  register of electors, **15**, 1122
  requirements, generally, **15**, 1134
  service qualification, **15**, 1131
    postal vote, eligibility, **15**, 1176
    proxy vote, eligibility, **15**, 1176
  supplementary provisions as to, **15**, 1132
  who has, **15**, 1122
  United Kingdom parliamentary elections, **15**, 1137
sheriff court jurisdiction, **6**, 1094
Sheriff Principal, responsibilities of, **5**, 374
staff—
  council employees, **15**, 1317
  income tax, liability to, **15**, 1403
  offences, **15**, 1317
  polling station, **15**, 1317
statutory provisions, **15**, 1493
swallow voter, measures against, **15**, 1018
tendered votes list—
  combined poll, **15**, 1375
  forwarding or retention of, after count, **15**, 1355
  generally, **15**, 1314
time, provisions as to—
  absent voting—
    applications, **15**, 1217, 1222
    generally, **15**, 1217, 1221
    notices, **15**, 1217, 1222
  candidate, duties and powers, **15**, 1237
  computation—
    European parliamentary elections, **15**, 1219
    generally, **15**, 1216
    local government elections, **15**, 1218, 1219
    statutory provisions, **15**, 1217
    United Kingdom parliamentary elections, **15**, 1219
  count, **15**, 1329
  dies non, **15**, 1219–1222
  election agent—
    appointment, **15**, 1220
    duties and powers, **15**, 1237
  election petition—
    presentation, **15**, 1476
    procedure on, **15**, 1220
  electoral registration, **15**, 1221
  European parliamentary elections—
    by-elections, **15**, 1219, 1226
    statutory provisions, **15**, 1217, 1219
    statutory timetable, **15**, 1226

Election—*continued*
time, provisions as to—*continued*
  inconsistency, **15**, 1223
  local government elections, **15**, 1217–1219
  questioning of elections, **15**, 1220
  registration officer, duties and powers, **15**,
    1236, 1237
  Representation of the People Act 1983 ..., **15**,
    1220, 1231–1235
  Representation of the People (Scotland)
    Regulations 1986 ..., **15**, 1221, 1236–1239
  scope of timetables, **15**, 1224
  United Kingdom parliamentary elections—
    by-elections, **15**, 1219, 1225
    statutory provisions, **15**, 1217, 1219
    statutory timetable, **15**, 1225
Town Councils (Scotland) Act 1900 ..., **15**, 1023
trade union—
  executive membership, for, **15**, 1495
  independent scrutineer, eligibility as, **15**, 1495
  independent scrutiny, **15**, 1495
treating, **15**, 1445
uncontested—
  declaration of result, **15**, 1352
  public notice, **15**, 1240, 1246, 1352
United Kingdom Parliament, *see* PARLIAMENT
  (election to)
verifying officer—
  appointment and function, **15**, 1326, 1326*n*,
    1328, 1329
  count, attendance, **15**, 1330, 1337
violence—
  adjournment of nomination proceedings, **15**,
    1301
  adjournment of poll, **15**, 1229, 1316
    combined poll, **15**, 1376
void—
  agent guilty of corrupt or illegal practices,
    where, **15**, 1469
  candidate guilty of corrupt or illegal practices,
    where, **15**, 1467
  determination, **15**, 1485
  general corruption, for, **15**, 1468
voting for more than one constituency, **5**, 374
See also VOTE
Election agent
See ELECTION
Election campaign
broadcasts—
  constraints on, **15**, 1020, 1231, 1449
  expenses, **15**, 1412
disturbances during, **15**, 1231
exhibition of notices, illegal payment for, **15**,
  1452
meeting rooms, free use of, **15**, 1231
newspaper or periodical, publications in, **15**, 1412
publications, requirements as to, **15**, 1242
timetable—
  candidate, **15**, 1231
  election agent, **15**, 1231
  returning/appropriate officers, **15**, 1232
Election court
adjournment of trial, **15**, 1484
constitution, **6**, 928; **15**, 1472

Election court—*continued*
corrupt and illegal practices, candidate reported,
  15, 1072–1074
determination, **15**, 1485
  difference of opinion between judges, **15**, 1485
  European parliamentary election, **15**, 1487
  execution, **15**, 1486, 1487
  United Kingdom parliamentary election, **15**,
    1486
diet of trial, **15**, 1484
expenses, **15**, 1472, 1484
finding by, **15**, 1464
generally, **6**, 928; **15**, 1472
order for inspection of ballot papers, **15**, 1357
shorthand writer, **15**, 1484
Election expenses
abandonment of poll, where, **15**, 1417
by-election, **15**, 1414
candidates'
  meaning of candidate, **15**, 1406
  meaning of election expenses, **15**, 1405
  payment—
    conditions of, **15**, 1409
    meaning, **15**, 1408
  personal expenses, **15**, 1407, 1409
    meaning, **15**, 1407
  persons employed for payment, **15**, 1410
  statutory provisions, **15**, 1493
  who may incur, **15**, 1411, 1412
corrupt practices in relation to, **15**, 1447
countermandment of poll, where, **15**, 1417
county and burghal constituencies, **15**, 1037
declarations—
  appropriate officer, role, **15**, 1435
  authority of election agent, incurred with, **15**,
    1425
  election agent, role, **15**, 1423
  failures in respect of—
    authorised excuses for, **15**, 1431–1434
    consequences, **15**, 1426–1428
    jurisdiction, **15**, 1431
    non-delivery, **15**, 1430
    relief, application for, **15**, 1431–1434
  false, **15**, 1426, 1447
  generally, **15**, 1423
  inspection, **15**, 1231, 1232, 1245
  no requirement for, where, **15**, 1429
  non-delivery, consequences, **15**, 1430
  persons before whom made, **15**, 1424
  requirement for, **15**, 1456
  returning officer, role, **15**, 1435
demise of Crown, where, **15**, 1418
election agent, **15**, 1407
  duties, **15**, 1231, 1425
European parliamentary election, **15**, 1405
  personal expenses, **15**, 1407
illegal practices in relation to, **15**, 1456, 1460
limitation—
  generally, **15**, 1018–1020, 1413
  maximum amounts—
    abandonment of poll, where, **15**, 1417
    by-election, **15**, 1414
    calculation, **15**, 1415
    countermandment of poll, where, **15**, 1417

Election expenses—*continued*
limitation—*continued*
  maximum amounts—*continued*
    demise of Crown, on, **15**, 1418
    generally, **15**, 1414
    joint candidates, **15**, 1419
    providing money in excess of, **15**, 1460
    specified, **15**, 1414
    variation, **15**, 1416
  local government election, **15**, 1405
  personal expenses, **15**, 1407
meaning, **15**, 1405
pecuniary reward, meaning, **15**, 1408
personal expenses, **15**, 1407
  who may incur, **15**, 1411, 1412
petty, **15**, 1231
returns—
  appropriate officer, role, **15**, 1435
  authority of election agent, incurred with, **15**, 1425
  content, **15**, 1421
  declarations, *see* declarations *above*
  delivery, **15**, 1420
  election agent, role, **15**, 1420
  failures in respect of, **15**, 1431–1434
    authorised excuses for, **15**, 1431–1434
    consequences, **15**, 1426–1428
    jurisdiction, **15**, 1431
    non-delivery, **15**, 1430
  form, **15**, 1421
  inspection, **15**, 1231, 1232, 1245
  no requirement for, where, **15**, 1429
  non-delivery, consequences, **15**, 1430
  paid under leave of court, where, **15**, 1422
  requirement for, **15**, 1456
  returning officer, role, **15**, 1435
statutory provisions, **15**, 1493
time provisions, **15**, 1220, 1231
United Kingdom parliamentary election, **15**, 1405
Election Petition Court
See ELECTION COURT
Election (succession)
injurious election, **25**, 802
judicial factor, by, **25**, 256
legal rights, **25**, 777
'Election Writ and Return'
United Kingdom parliamentary elections, **15**, 1353
Elective dictatorship
entrenchment, and, **5**, 355
Elector
absent voting, *see* VOTE
blind—
  declaration by companion, **15**, 1229
  postal vote, **15**, 1161
  proxy vote, **15**, 1163, 1176
  voting procedure, **15**, 1214, 1321
bribery, **15**, 1444
challenge by presiding officer, **15**, 1323
conveyance—
  hiring vehicle for, **15**, 1457
  paying for, **15**, 1455
corrupt or illegal practice by—
  incapacity following conviction, **15**, 1235
  incapacity for voting, **15**, 1466

Elector—*continued*
corrupt or illegal practice by—*continued*
  personation, **15**, 1443
  treating, **15**, 1445
death, **15**, 1095
drink or drugs, under influence of, **15**, 1082
electors lists, *see* ELECTORS LISTS
entitlement to vote, statutory provisions, **15**, 1493
European parliamentary, **15**, 1076
  disqualification, **15**, 1082
  generally, **15**, 1077
  overseas electors' declaration, **15**, 1146, 1147
  peers, **15**, 1076
    overseas electors, as, **15**, 1146, 1147
  relevant citizens of the Union, **15**, 1076, 1090
    declaration, **15**, 1148
  right to be registered, **15**, 1120
  United Kingdom parliamentary electors, **15**, 1076
General Medical Council, **15**, 1509
legal incapacity, under, **15**, 1082
local government, **15**, 1077
  disqualification, **15**, 1082
  generally, **15**, 1077
  right to be registered, **15**, 1120
meaning—
  European parliamentary election, **15**, 1277
  local government election, **15**, 1277
  United Kingdom parliamentary election, **15**, 1277
mental capacity, lacking sufficient, **15**, 1149
  lucid intervals, **15**, 1149
overseas—
  declaration, **15**, 1035, 1088
    attestation, **15**, 1142
    cancellation, **15**, 1144
    content, **15**, 1141
    effect, **15**, 1143
    European parliamentary, **15**, 1147
    evidential value, **15**, 1143
    notification requirements, **15**, 1145
    qualification as overseas elector, **15**, 1140
    requirements, generally, **15**, 1141
  electors lists—
    amendment, **15**, 1237
    claims and objections, **15**, 1110
    misnomer or misdescription, effect of, **15**, 1096
    preparation, **15**, 1088, 1090, 1091, 1113
    publication, **15**, 1092, 1097, 1237
    supply, **15**, 1093
  generally, **15**, 1035
  peers, **15**, 1123
  postal vote, **15**, 1176
  proxy vote, **15**, 1176
  register of electors, **15**, 1123
  right to register, **15**, 1123
  United Kingdom parliamentary elections, **15**, 1075
personation, **15**, 1227, 1229, 1308, 1323, 1443
  criminal proceedings, **15**, 1471
physical incapacity—
  postal vote, eligibility on grounds of, **15**, 1160, 1161

Elector—*continued*
physical incapacity—*continued*
    proxy vote, eligibility on grounds of, **15**, 1160, 1163, 1164, 1176
physically incapacitated—
    postal vote, **15**, 1161
    proxy vote, **15**, 1163, 1164, 1176
    voting procedure, **15**, 1214, 1321
polling station, allotment, **15**, 1155
postal vote, *see* VOTE
proxy, *see* VOTE
proxy vote, *see* VOTE
questions which may be put to, **15**, 1322
register of electors, *see* REGISTER OF ELECTORS
registration—
    European parliamentary elections, **15**, 1076, 1084
    local government elections, **15**, 1077, 1084
    peers, **15**, 1084
    publication of registers, **15**, 1084
    registration officer, appointment and functions, **15**, 1083–1085
    right to be registered—
        generally, **15**, 1120
        mental disorder, persons suffering from, **15**, 1149
        overseas electors, **15**, 1123, 1140–1147
        relevant citizens of the Union, **15**, 1124, 1148
        service qualification, persons with, **15**, 1122, 1131–1139
        voluntary mental patients, **15**, 1121, 1125–1130
    statutory provisions, **15**, 1493
    time provisions, **15**, 1221
    United Kingdom parliamentary elections, **15**, 1075, 1084
relevant citizen of the Union—
    application, **15**, 1148
    declaration, **15**, 1148
residence—
    armed forces, **15**, 1081
    disqualification, **15**, 1082
    generally, **15**, 1079, 1080
    legal custody, detention in, **15**, 1081
    local government elections, **15**, 1077
    mental disorder, detention due to, **15**, 1081
    mental patient, voluntary, **15**, 1081
    merchant seaman, **15**, 1081
    qualifying date, **15**, 1078, 1079
    statutory position, **15**, 1079, 1081
    tent, bender or vehicle, in, **15**, 1080
signing of electoral documents—
    rubber stamp, by means of, **15**, 1151
    valid signature, what constitutes, **15**, 1151
treating, corrupt practice, as, **15**, 1445
undue influence to prevent free franchise of, **15**, 1446
United Kingdom parliamentary—
    disqualification, **15**, 1082
    generally, **15**, 1075
    overseas elector, **15**, 1075
    right to be registered, **15**, 1120
voluntary mental patients, **15**, 1081, 1121, 1125–1130
voting illegally, **15**, 1448

Electoral areas
electoral divisions, **15**, 1036, 1039
European parliamentary, **15**, 1036, 1038
generally, **15**, 1036
local government, **15**, 1036, 1039
polling districts, **15**, 1040
polling places, **15**, 1040
United Kingdom parliamentary, **15**, 1036, 1037
wards, **15**, 1036, 1039
Electoral law
boundary changes, **15**, 1028–1030
case law, **15**, 1033
generally, **15**, 1001
historical background—
    local government elections, **15**, 1021–1026
    parliamentary elections, **15**, 1002–1020
modern, **15**, 1031*ff*
secret ballot, introduction, **15**, 1015, 1027
Electoral register
annual compilation, **5**, 374
conditions for inclusion in, **5**, 374
disqualified persons, **5**, 374
documentary evidence, as, **10**, 592
draft, **5**, 374
dual registration, **5**, 374
electoral registration officer, **5**, 374; **14**, 249
multiple registration, **5**, 374
offences, **5**, 374
residence, **5**, 374
See also ELECTORS LISTS
Electors lists
alterations, **15**, 1094
claims, **15**, 1237
    generally, **15**, 1098
    hearing, **15**, 1101
    notice, **15**, 1097
    preliminary disposal, **15**, 1101
    procedure, **15**, 1101
    time for, **15**, 1100
corrections, **15**, 1095, 1237
    objections to, **15**, 1237
deletions from, **15**, 1095
generally, **15**, 1088
inaccurate description, effect of, **15**, 1096
information, requirement to supply, **15**, 1090
list of proxies, **15**, 1084, 1188
misnomer, effect of, **15**, 1096
objections, **15**, 1237
    form, **15**, 1099
    hearing, **15**, 1101
    notice, **15**, 1097
    preliminary disposal, **15**, 1101
    procedure, **15**, 1101
    time for, **15**, 1100
overseas electors, **15**, 1088, 1090, 1091, 1113
    amendment, **15**, 1237
    claims and objections, **15**, 1100
    publication, **15**, 1092, 1097, 1237
    supply, **15**, 1093
patient's declaration, **15**, 1088, 1090, 1100
postal voters list, **15**, 1084, 1188
preparation, **15**, 1088–1090
publication, **15**, 1090, 1092, 1097
    date of, **15**, 1103

Electors lists—*continued*
service declaration, **15**, 1088, 1090, 1100
special—
  polling stations, supply to, **15**, 1312
  sealing, **15**, 1203, 1239
structure and arrangement, **15**, 1089
supply, **15**, 1093
See also ELECTORAL REGISTER
Electricity
accidents in connection with—
  liability for, **9**, 679
  notification of, **9**, 682
boards, *see* ELECTRICITY BOARDS
building control—
  electrical installations, **9**, 664
  large substations, **9**, 663
  legislation generally, **9**, 662
consultative councils, **6**, 160; **9**, 612, 613
definitions relating to, **24**, 627
early suppliers of, **9**, 602
electric motors for trade or industry, **24**, 708
electrical apparatus—
  access to, **14**, 1650
  installation, **9**, 677; **14**, 1650
  testing, **9**, 681
  underground, **9**, 654
  use, **14**, 1650
  working space, adequacy of, **14**, 1650
electrical device—
  fishing with prohibited, **11**, 12
  illegal use in trout fishing, **11**, 54
  wild birds or animals taken or killed with, **11**, 880, 884
electrical installations, **9**, 664; **14**, 1012, 1650
electrical luminous tube signs, **10**, 1466
generating stations—
  consent to, **9**, 631
  construction of, procedure before, **9**, 627
  extension of—
    procedure before, **9**, 627
    provisions relating to, **9**, 628
  Fisheries Committee functions, **11**, 10
  gas fired, **9**, 630
  hydro-electric development—
    consent of Secretary of State to, **9**, 711
    constructional schemes, **9**, 633
    diversion of water, **25**, 327
    fisheries, protection of, **9**, 635
    notices, **9**, 634
    objections to, **9**, 637
    obstruction of salmon by, **11**, 19
    planning authorities, notification to, **9**, 636
    reservoir, constructon of, **9**, 640
    scheme—
      confirmation of, **9**, 638
      constructional, **9**, 633
      existing works, minor extensions of, **9**, 639
    statutory control generally, **9**, 632
  nuclear generation—
    construction of, **9**, 641
    European Community directorate, **6**, 30
    operation of, consent of Secretary of State to, **9**, 712

Electricity—*continued*
generating stations—*continued*
  nuclear generation—*continued*
    statutory control of—
      generally, **9**, 641
      international conventions, reflection of, **9**, 642
    objections to, **9**, 629
    obstruction of salmon, **11**, 19
    oil-fired, **9**, 630
    public inquiries into, **9**, 629
    Secretary of State, consent of, **9**, 631, 711, 712
heritable nature of equipment, **24**, 625
historical background—
  early suppliers, **9**, 602
  generally, **9**, 601
  nationalisation, **9**, 605
  Scottish boards, establishment of, **9**, 606
  Weir Report, **9**, 604
  Williamson Report, **9**, 603
inflammable gas, prevention of ignition, **14**, 1650
inquiries, **9**, 658
insulation, **14**, 1650
land used in connection with—
  compensation, **9**, 657
  compulsory purchase, **9**, 656
  generally, **24**, 620
  surveys, **9**, 655
  valuation of, **24**, 415
lighting, electric, whether plant, **14**, 102
lines—
  compulsory rights, **9**, 648
  heritable rights, **9**, 644
  meaning, **9**, 643
  overhead—
    consent to erect, **9**, 646
    proposed erection, public notice in respect of, **9**, 647
    regulations, **9**, 653
  roads, in, **9**, 652
  service lines, meaning, **9**, 643
  tenements, supply to, **9**, 651
  tree cutting, **9**, 650
  underground—
    apparatus, records of, **9**, 654
    permitted development, **9**, 645
  wayleave agreement—
    consent embodied in, **9**, 644
    retention of rights, **9**, 649
local committees, **6**, 160
meters—
  accuracy of, dispute over, **9**, 690
  certification of, **9**, 686
  connection of, notice of intention, **9**, 689
  disconnection of, notice of intention, **9**, 689
  installation of, **9**, 688
  maintenance of, **9**, 688
  private supplier, use by, **9**, 720
  public institution, meter charges, **25**, 536
  reading, **9**, 691
  resold electricity, **9**, 705
  uncertified, **9**, 687

Electricity—*continued*
meters—*continued*
use of—
   generally, **9**, 685
   statutory control, **9**, 684
planning—
  legislation generally, **9**, 659
  permitted developments, **9**, 660
  Secretary of State, development requiring, **9**, 661
private supplier—
  duty to supply to, **9**, 715
  meter, use of, **9**, 720
  premises of, right to enter, **9**, 719
quarry, in, **14**, 1705
resale of—
  maximum charge for, **9**, 703
  meters, **9**, 705
  purchasers, **9**, 704
safety—
  atmospheric emissions, **9**, 668
  Factories Act 1961—
    effect of, **9**, 665
  Health and Safety at Work etc Act 1974—
    effect of, **9**, 667
  regulations, **9**, 666
Scottish boards, *see* ELECTRICITY BOARDS
service lines, **9**, 643
space heating, **24**, 578
station, construction of, **19**, 15
substations, **9**, 663
suppliers, prescribed valuation formula, **24**, 547
supply of—
  accidents—
    liability for, **9**, 679
    notification of, **9**, 682
  apparatus, testing of, **9**, 681
  board, duty of, **9**, 670
    See also ELECTRICITY BOARDS
  charges—
    public institution, to, **25**, 536
    recovery of, **9**, 695
    security for payment, **9**, 697
    special agreements, **9**, 696
    tariff—
      discrimination, must not show, **9**, 694
      fixing, **9**, 692
      included in, **9**, 693
      preference, must not show, **9**, 694
  commercial basis, on, **9**, 672
  damage, liability for, **9**, 679
  disconnect, right to—
    arrears, in respect of, **9**, 701
    circumstances where applicable, **9**, 700
    costs, **9**, 702
    insolvency, in respect of, **9**, 701
  distribution main, requisition for laying down, **9**, 674
  injuries, liability for, **9**, 679
  maintenance of—
    constant, **9**, 678
    equipment, installation of, **9**, 677
    generally, **9**, 676
    sufficient, **9**, 678

Electricity—*continued*
supply of—*continued*
  notice by person requiring, **9**, 671
  offences, **9**, 709
  penalties, **9**, 709
  private generator or supplier, to, **9**, 715
  private person, by—
    Energy Act 1983, before, **9**, 710
    generating station—
      nuclear, **9**, 712
      other, **9**, 713
    hydro generation, **9**, 711
    local authorities, **9**, 714
    meters, **9**, 720
    premises, right to enter, **9**, 719
  private supplier, to, **9**, 715
  privatisation, **4**, 1125, 1226
  provisional orders as to, **19**, 19
  reconnection, costs of, **9**, 702
  rectifying defects, **9**, 683
  refusal of, **9**, 673
  safety of, **9**, 675
  statutory control, **9**, 669
  tariffs for, **9**, 692, 693
  temporary, payment for, **9**, 708
  termination of—
    consumer quitting premises, **9**, 706
    procedure, **9**, 707
  testing, **9**, 681
  type of, notice to consumer of, **9**, 680
  winding up, position relating to, **4**, 867
theft, **7**, 327
use, **14**, 1650
valuations for rating, **24**, 625–627
VAT rating, **7**, 1461
waste, from, **9**, 1171
wiring, affixation to heritage, **14**, 1071
Electricity bill
income support direct payments, **21**, 1082
Electricity boards
additional powers, **9**, 620
annual reports, **9**, 611
bulk supplies, transfer of, **9**, 621
constitution, **9**, 609
dam, construction of, **25**, 329
disputes, **9**, 718
districts of, **9**, 607
documents, execution of, **9**, 610
duties of—
  distribution, with regard to, **9**, 619
  environment, preservation of, **9**, 616
  general, **9**, 615, 670
  principal, **9**, 614
  revenues sufficient to meet outgoings, **9**, 617
  tariffs—
    discrimination not to be shown in fixing, **9**, 618, 694
    preference not to be shown in fixing, **9**, 618, 694
economic development by, **9**, 624
electricity purchased by, tariff for, **9**, 716
entry, rights of—
  generally, **9**, 698
  procedure, **9**, 699

Electricity boards—*continued*
establishment of, **9**, 606
finance, **9**, 625
functions of, **9**, 608
heat, schemes for production and use of, **9**, 623
lands and heritages occupied by, **24**, 620
valuation of, **24**, 415
North Board, economic development by, **9**, 624
power, schemes for production and use of, **9**, 623
railways, supply to, **9**, 622
rates, **9**, 626
reservoir, construction of, **25**, 329
returns, **9**, 611
statistics, **9**, 611
tariffs—
electricity, purchase of, **9**, 716
transmission and distribution system, for use of, **9**, 717
taxes, **9**, 626
valuation of lands and heritages, **24**, 415
Electrified fence
dangerous or injurious to person using road, where, **20**, 697
Electro-convulsive therapy
consent to, **14**, 1425
Electronic games
video games, **9**, 1016
Electronic mail
Branch System General (BSG) Licence, **16**, 1949
Emancipation legislation
Ceylon, **5**, 353
generally, **5**, 353
judiciary and, **5**, 359
Mauritius, **5**, 353
Embankment
artificial stream, creation of, **25**, 355
construction or alteration, **19**, 19*n*
Embargo
restraint of princes, as, **21**, 550
Embarkation
card, requirements as to, **12**, 192
meaning, **12**, 147
place and manner of, requirements as to, **12**, 192
Embezzlement
actus reus, **7**, 352
appropriation as element of, **7**, 351, 352
breach of duty, **11**, 1015
breach of trust, **7**, 352
business ineptitude, and, **7**, 352
claim of right, **7**, 96
corporate body, by, **7**, 355
definition, **7**, 351, 354
duty as element of, **7**, 351, 352
executor, by, **7**, 352
fraud, and, **7**, 350
generally, **7**, 350
goods, **7**, 354
mens rea, **7**, 353
money, **7**, 354
natural person, by, **7**, 355
proof of intent, **7**, 88
solicitor, by, **7**, 352, 356
temporary removal of funds, **7**, 352

Embezzlement—*continued*
theft, and, **7**, 350, 352
theft distinguished, **7**, 356
what can be embezzled, **7**, 354
white collar crime, as, **7**, 356
Emblements
goods, as, **20**, 805
meaning, **20**, 805
Embryo
Human Fertilisation and Embryology Act (1990), **7**, 284, 289
See also FETUS
Emergency
compulsory care order, **22**, 29
expenditure, **14**, 327
grants, **14**, 327
homelessness as result of, **11**, 2055
hospital, admission of mental health patient to, **14**, 1417; **22**, 30
loans, **14**, 327
powers, *see* EMERGENCY POWERS
proclamation of, **5**, 599, 600
public—
derogation from European Convention on Human Rights in times of, **12**, 31
meaning, **12**, 31
state of, *see* EMERGENCY POWERS
Emergency powers
civil defence, *see* CIVIL DEFENCE
drought, during, **25**, 530
general war, *see* WAR
generally, **5**, 597
hours of work, exemption from control, **14**, 1668
law and order, *see* LAW AND ORDER
military aid to civil ministries, *see* MILITARY AID
prerogative powers of Crown, **7**, 726
regulation of supply and distribution of food, **11**, 320
Secretary of State, powers of, **25**, 530
standing orders, **14**, 1319
state of emergency, proclamation of—
generally, **5**, 599; **7**, 857
parliamentary consideration of, **5**, 600
Emergency telecommunications services, provision
regulatory control, **16**, 1923
Emigration
number of emigrants, **12**, 101
Employee
action short of dismissal, remedy in case of, **9**, 91
breach of confidence by, **18**, 1455, 1467
express statement as to confidentiality, where, **18**, 1463, 1464
nature of information, **18**, 1465
restrictive covenant, **18**, 1468, 1470
trade secrets, **18**, 1470, 1471
where no express contract term, **18**, 1469
See also BREACH OF CONFIDENCE
characteristics of, effect on jurisdiction of tribunal, **9**, 309
company cannot act except through, **4**, 318
competition law, disregarded provisions, **4**, 1175
continuous employment, *see* EMPLOYMENT
contributory negligence by, **15**, 405

Employee—*continued*
copyright of work made in course of employment, **18**, 997–999
death, breach of statutory duty, action for, **3**, 156, 174
defamation committed by, liability, **15**, 479
delictual act by, liability, **4**, 318
director's duties relating to, **4**, 429
directors not classed as, **4**, 403
disability working allowance, *see* DISABILITY WORKING ALLOWANCE
disabled—
   generally, **9**, 119
   quotas, **9**, 120
duties of—
   care, **9**, 82
   competence, **9**, 82
   express terms, **9**, 86
   fidelity, **9**, 84
   fiduciary duty, **24**, 181, 182
   implied term, **9**, 85
   obedience, **9**, 83
   respect, **9**, 83
   restrictive covenants, **9**, 86
duty of care towards, **19**, 1241
employer's liability, *see* EMPLOYER (liability)
ex-employee as assured tenant, repossession, **13**, 725
family credit, *see* FAMILY CREDIT
food and accommodation supplied to, **7**, 1358
health and safety, *see* HEALTH AND SAFETY AT WORK
hired out to work for others, strict liability, and, **15**, 159
house required by landlord for, as ground for repossession, **13**, 714, 721
individual, statutory definition only applicable to, **4**, 318
industrial designs by, ownership, **18**, 1163, 1221
injury to, employer's right to recover damages, **22**, 661
invention by—
   compensation, grant of, to employee, **18**, 830
   copyright, **18**, 830*n*
   patent, **18**, 829, 830
   semiconductor topographies, **18**, 1245, 1246
   special duty to further best interests of employer, employee with, **18**, 830
invention of—
   copyright, **9**, 128
   made after May 1978 ..., **9**, 127
   made before June 1978 ..., **9**, 126
itemised pay statement, entitlement to receive, **9**, 66
payroll deduction scheme—
   generally, **3**, 1153
   meaning of employee in relation to, **3**, 1153
personal circumstances of, reasonableness of dismissal, **9**, 253
possession through, **16**, 2108
redundancy, *see* REDUNDANCY
Redundancy Fund, access to, **9**, 154
references, passing between employers, **15**, 528
safety, liability for, **15**, 298
Schedule E, **25**, 57

Employee—*continued*
service occupancy—
   ejection, action of, **13**, 469
   generally, **13**, 599
   lease compared, **13**, 115, 601
shares, class rights, **4**, 347
sickness of, wages during, **9**, 54
soliciting information from, **18**, 1478
statements as to, qualified privilege, **15**, 528, 529
termination of contract by, **9**, 218
terrorist funds, disclosure of information as to, **7**, 623, 624
ultra vires doctrine, application, **4**, 324
unfair dismissal, of, *see* UNFAIR DISMISSAL
vicarious admission or confession by, **10**, 726
vicarious liability of employer, **7**, 194–197
voluntary arrangement, approval, **4**, 594
wages, *see* WAGES
water authority, land acquired for erection of housing for, **25**, 518
winding up, position on, *see* WINDING UP
wrongful act, deliberate liability, **4**, 318
See also EMPLOYMENT
Employee share scheme
collective investment scheme categorisation, exclusion from, **12**, 1325
Employer
building contract, *see* BUILDING CONTRACT
deduction from earnings order, failure to comply with, **8**, 346
delict committed by, liability, **15**, 242
delictual liability, **15**, 395, 396, 398, 405
   statutory duty, breach, **15**, 405
different, employment with, effect on continuous employment, **9**, 47
discrimination, liability for, **9**, 342
duties of—
   competent staff, selection of, **9**, 77
   environment, as to, **9**, 443, 444
   equipment, as to, **9**, 78
   health and safety, as to, *see* HEALTH AND SAFETY AT WORK
   materials, as to, **9**, 78
   miscellaneous, **9**, 81
   plant, as to, **9**, 78
   safety, **9**, 75
   work—
      provision of, **9**, 80
      safe place of, **9**, 79
      safe system of, **9**, 76
employers' association—
   accounts, **1**, 95
   discrimination, liability for, **9**, 343
employers' organisation, exempt agreement, **5**, 821
health and safety at work legislation, **19**, 304
instructions, acknowledgment of receipt of, **14**, 1504
liability—
   activities outwith employment, **15**, 334
   apprentice, duty owed to, **15**, 334
   circumstances, questions arising, **15**, 337
   codes of practice, duty to follow, **15**, 338
   common employment, doctrine of, **15**, 332

Employer—*continued*

liability—*continued*

  common practice and standard of care, **15**, 371

  competent staff, duty to engage, **15**, 349

  contractor, independent, use of, **15**, 331, 336

  contractual, **15**, 333

  delict committed by employer, **15**, 242

  delictual, **15**, 333

  elements of duty—

    equipment, plant and materials, **15**, 346

    generally, **15**, 344

    place of work, **15**, 345

  employee, duty owed to, **15**, 334

  equipment, plant and materials—

    duty in respect of, **15**, 346

    Employers' Liability (Defective Equipment) Act 1969, **15**, 347

  foreseeability, **15**, 340

  generally, **15**, 331

  'in the course of employment', **15**, 334

  information and warnings, duty to give employees, **15**, 348

  instructions, duty to give employees, **15**, 348

  insurance—

    approved policies, **15**, 351

    generally, **15**, 350

  job rotation, **15**, 348

  magnitude of risk, questions arising, **15**, 341

  negligence of another employee, injury caused by, **15**, 331, 332

  place of work, duty in respect of, **15**, 345

  posture, poor, **15**, 348

  pro hac vice employee, duty owed to, **15**, 336

  repetitive work, injuries due to, **15**, 348

  risk-reducing procedures, practicability, **15**, 343

  safety of employees, for, **15**, 298

  safety equipment, provision, **15**, 346, 347, 348

  seconded employee, duty owed to, **15**, 336

  self-employed worker, duty owed to, **15**, 335

  standard of duty owed—

    circumstances, questions arising, **15**, 337

    codes of practice, **15**, 338

    Health and Safety Executive etc guidance, **15**, 338

    magnitude of risk, **15**, 341

    practical considerations, **15**, 343

    probability, **15**, 340

    reasonable care, questions arising, **15**, 339

    'reasonable employer', **15**, 338

    up to date, keeping, **15**, 338

    value of activity, **15**, 342

  system of work, **15**, 344

  temporary employee, duty owed to, **15**, 336

  up to date, duty to keep, **15**, 338

  value of activity, questions arising, **15**, 341

  vicarious, **15**, 243, 247–251

  work method, planning, **15**, 344

liability of, **9**, 904; **14**, 1507

medical services supplied to, fees for, **11**, 1450

payroll deduction scheme—

  generally, **3**, 1153

  meaning of employer in relation to, **3**, 1153

standard of duty owed—

  common practice and standard of care, **15**, 371

Employer—*continued*

termination of contract by, **9**, 216

vicarious admission or confession by employee, **10**, 726

vicarious liability, **7**, 194–197

Employer's association

authorisation, **12**, 807

Employment

absence due to pregnancy, *see* MATERNITY RIGHTS

accidents, **9**, 474, 533

actors, of, **9**, 1051

adult males, of—

  mining, in, **9**, 68

  night bakeries, in, **9**, 70

  sheet glass works, in, **9**, 70

  transport, in, **9**, 69

Advisory, Conciliation and Arbitration Service, *see* ADVISORY, CONCILIATION AND ARBITRATION SERVICE

age—

  redundancy payment, reduction of, **9**, 190

  unfair dismissal, applicant to claim for, **9**, 205

age limit, minimum, stipulation, **3**, 1258

agency, liability for discrimination, **9**, 345

armed services, age limit, **3**, 1258

articles—

  safety in use of, **9**, 436, 437

  work, used at, duty of manufacturer—

    article for use at work—

      installation, **9**, 460

      meaning, **9**, 456

    generally, **9**, 455

    information, provision of, **9**, 459

    research, **9**, 458

    supplier, **9**, 457

    supply, **9**, 462

    transfer of responsibility, **9**, 461

    user, **9**, 457

balanced distribution of, Monopolies and Mergers Commission regard for, **4**, 563

bond status, abolition, **22**, 632

breach of confidence, **18**, 1455, 1467

casual—

  meaning, **21**, 822

  termination, **21**, 822

charity, trade carried on by, beneficiaries of charity, work mainly carried out by, **3**, 1131

child, of—

  byelaws relating to, **3**, 1254; **14**, 274

  entertainment industry, **3**, 1256

  factory, in, **3**, 1257

  generally, **3**, 1253

  heavy lifting, involving, **3**, 1254

  hours of work, **3**, 1254

  mine or quarry, in, **3**, 1257

  street trading, **3**, 1255

  Sunday, on, **3**, 1254

circus performer, of, **9**, 1032

codes of practice—

  Commission for Racial Equality, of, **9**, 389

  development of, **9**, 9

  Equal Opportunities Commission, of, **9**, 387

  functions of, **9**, 12

Employment—*continued*
codes of practice—*continued*
  health and safety at work—
    approval, **9**, 536
    contravention, **9**, 537; **22**, 200
    role, **9**, 535
    issue of, **9**, 10
    Manpower Services Commission, of, **9**, 11
    safety representative, right to time off, **9**, 480
    trade union, **9**, 241; **23**, 200, 749
  collateral contracts, **9**, 27
  collective agreements, **9**, 32, 34
    See also COLLECTIVE AGREEMENT
  collective bargaining, **9**, 3, 7, 34
    See also COLLECTIVE BARGAINING
  collective redundancies, **9**, 15
  common, doctrine of, **15**, 332
  common law—
    industrial tribunal, jurisdiction of, **9**, 305
    notice, termination of contract by, **9**, 134
    unfair dismissal, scope of, **9**, 204
    wages, payment of—
      accrual of, **9**, 52
      forfeiture of, **9**, 53
      generally, **9**, 51
      late, **9**, 55
      non-payment, **9**, 55
      sickness of employee, during, **9**, 54
      withholding, **9**, 57
      work not available, when, **9**, 56
  condition relating to, **25**, 869
  conditions of, regulation, **11**, 1791
  continuous—
    different employers, employment with, **9**, 47
    general provisions, **9**, 42
    industrial dispute, effect of, **9**, 46
    industrial tribunal, effect on jurisdiction of, **9**, 310
    interruption of, **9**, 44
    liquidation, effect of, **9**, 49
    qualifying period, **9**, 45
    re-engagement, effect on, **9**, 50
    receivership, effect of, **9**, 49
    statutory rights conditional on existence of period of, **9**, 41
    transfer of undertakings, **9**, 48
    unfair dismissal claim, effect on, **9**, 206
    weeks which count, **9**, 43
  contract of, *see* CONTRACT OF EMPLOYMENT
  contracting out, effect on unfair dismissal rights, **9**, 207
  contravention of enactment as reason for dismissal, **9**, 247
  copyright of employee's invention, **9**, 128
  criminal law—
    conspiracy, **9**, 122
    contractual duties and, **9**, 121–125
    industrial action, application of rules to, **9**, 131
    malicious mischief, **9**, 123
    particular employments, **9**, 125
    protection of property, **9**, 122
    workplace occupations, **9**, 124
  criminal offence, dismissal for reason of, **9**, 256

Employment—*continued*
Crown—
  health and safety, **9**, 409
  industrial tribunal, exclusion from, **9**, 331
  office holder, **9**, 38
damages, wrongful dismissal for, *see* DAMAGES
dangerous, **15**, 398
deceased, of, receipts attributable to, **25**, 975
delictual liability—
  defences, **15**, 395, 396, 398
  statutory duty, breach, **15**, 405
  statutory liability, breach, **15**, 405, 405*n*
director, of, **14**, 1002
disabled employees, **9**, 119, 120
disablement benefit, *see* DISABLEMENT BENEFIT
discrimination—
  advertising, **9**, 374
  complaints and appeals relating to, **6**, 994, 996
  condition, **9**, 336
  detriment—
    generally, **9**, 339
    subjection to, **9**, 359
  direct, **9**, 334
  electricity supply, tariffs, **9**, 618, 694
  enforcement—
    conciliation, **9**, 377
    generally, **9**, 375
    remedies, **9**, 378
    time limit, **9**, 376
  European Community law, **10**, 97, 109
  exemptions—
    death, provisions in relation to, **9**, 349
    private households, **9**, 348
    retirement, provisions in relation to, **9**, 349
    special categories, **9**, 351
    territorial jurisdiction, **9**, 350
  generally, **9**, 352
  genuine occupational qualification, defence of—
    decency, **9**, 362
    education services, **9**, 366
    generally, **9**, 360
    living-in employment, **9**, 364
    physiology, **9**, 361
    privacy, **9**, 362
    private home, work in, **9**, 363
    racial group, membership of, **9**, 370
    special care, **9**, 365
    spouses, joint appointment of, **9**, 369
    statutory restrictions, **9**, 367
    welfare services, **9**, 366
  indirect, **9**, 335
  industrial action, *see* INDUSTRIAL ACTION
  justifiable, **9**, 338
  liability—
    association, of, **9**, 343
    employer, of, **9**, 342
    employment agency, of, **9**, 345
    generally, **9**, 341
    government agency, of, **9**, 346
    partnership, of, **9**, 343
    qualifying body, of, **9**, 344
    trade union, of, **9**, 343
    vocational training body, of, **9**, 344

Employment—*continued*
discrimination—*continued*
  nationality, based upon, European Community
    rules, **10**, 137
  offer of employment—
    deliberate omission of, **9**, 355
    refusal of, **9**, 355
    terms of, **9**, 354
  persons protected, **9**, 347
  persons to be employed, **9**, 353
  practices, **9**, 373
  promotion, access to, **9**, 356
  proportion who can comply, **9**, 337
  purpose of legislation, **9**, 333
  questionnaire—
    evidence, as, **9**, 372
    information, to obtain, **9**, 371
  race, *see* RACIAL DISCRIMINATION
  requirement, **9**, 336
  scope, **9**, 332
  sex, based upon, European Community rules,
    9, 14; **10**, 154, 171, 172
    See also SEX DISCRIMINATION
  training, access to, **9**, 356
  transfer, access to, **9**, 356
  victimisation, **9**, 340
dismissal, *see* DISMISSAL; UNFAIR DISMISSAL;
  WRONGFUL DISMISSAL
domestic service, *see* DOMESTIC SERVICE
employee, *see* EMPLOYEE
employer, *see* EMPLOYER
Employment Appeal Tribunal, *see* EMPLOYMENT
  APPEAL TRIBUNAL
entertainer, of, **9**, 1006
environment, working, **9**, 443, 444
Equal Opportunities Commission, *see* EQUAL
  OPPORTUNITIES COMMISSION
equal pay, *see* EQUAL PAY
expenditure programme, **5**, 579
fire services—
  appointments—
    establishment schemes, **10**, 1438
    fire brigade, **10**, 1437
  discipline, **10**, 1439, 1440
  Firemen's Pension Scheme, **10**, 1442–1450
  generally, **10**, 1436
  military aid, **10**, 1441
functional work—
  meaning, **14**, 904
  regulation of, **14**, 907
health and safety at work, *see* HEALTH AND SAFETY
  AT WORK
holidays—
  holiday pay, **22**, 818
  statutory requirements, **22**, 818
hours of work, *see* HOURS OF WORK
housing benefit, *see* HOUSING BENEFIT
human rights—
  children and young persons, **12**, 7
  collective bargaining, **12**, 7
  European Social Charter, **12**, 7
  health and safety, **12**, 7
  international conventions on, **12**, 5
  maternity rights, **12**, 7

Employment—*continued*
human rights—*continued*
  migrant workers, **12**, 7
  organisations for protection of workers'
    interests, **12**, 7
  remuneration, **12**, 7
  territory of other contracting national, in, **12**, 7
  vocational guidance and training, **12**, 7
  women, **12**, 7
immigration and, *see* IMMIGRATION
industrial action, *see* INDUSTRIAL ACTION
industrial injuries benefits, *see* INDUSTRIAL
  INJURIES BENEFITS
industrial relations, *see* INDUSTRIAL ACTION;
  INDUSTRIAL RELATIONS; INDUSTRIAL TRIBUNAL
information—
  articles for use at work, on, **9**, 459
  employee's duty of confidence, **9**, 85
  Equal Opportunities Commission—
    disclosure, restrictions on, **9**, 383
    power to obtain, **9**, 382
  health and safety, as to, **9**, 438, 439, 492
  questionnaire to obtain, **9**, 371
  safety representative, right to, **9**, 475
insolvency, *see* INSOLVENCY
inspection—
  health and safety, *see* HEALTH AND SAFETY AT
    WORK
  Health and Safety Commission inspector, by, **9**,
    417
  safety representative, by—
    dangerous occurrence, following, **9**, 474
    documents, of, **9**, 475
    notifiable accident, following, **9**, 474
    notifiable disease, following, **9**, 474
    workplace, of, **9**, 473
law reform, **22**, 632
living-in, discrimination, genuine occupational
  qualification as defence to, **9**, 364
maternity rights, *see* MATERNITY RIGHTS
mining industry, women and young persons, **9**,
  71; **14**, 1666
National Health Service staffing, *see* NATIONAL
  HEALTH SERVICE
national insurance contributions, *see* NATIONAL
  INSURANCE CONTRIBUTIONS
naturalisation, requirements for, **14**, 1920
occupational diseases, notification of, **19**, 489
offshore, *see* OFFSHORE EMPLOYMENT
part-time, unemployment benefit, entitlement to
  21, 816
place of, *see* PLACE OF WORK
plant and machinery—
  employer's duty as to, **9**, 78, 430–433
  fencing of—
    civil action, causation and, **9**, 547
    construction of, **9**, 548
    duty to fence—
      generally, **9**, 539
      nature of, **9**, 545
    exceptions, **9**, 550
    extraneous objects, dangers arising from, **9**,
      542
    foreseeability, questions of, **9**, 544

Employment—*continued*
plant and machinery—*continued*
  fencing of—*continued*
    maintenance of, **9**, 548
    materials—
      dangers arising out of use of, **9**, 541
      ejection of, **9**, 543
      in motion or use, meaning, **9**, 549
      part of any machinery, meaning, **9**, 540
      safe to every person, meaning, **9**, 546
    maintenance of, **9**, 432
    meaning, **9**, 433
    provision of, **9**, 431
    unfenced, **9**, 551–600
pro hac vice, vicarious liability, **15**, 249
questions of, legal advice and assistance, **13**, 1028
redundancy, *see* REDUNDANCY
registration, application for, **14**, 1916
remuneration, *see* REMUNERATION
renewal, effect on redundancy payment, **9**, 172
restrictive labour practices, **4**, 1153
safety, *see* SAFETY
schoolchildren, of, *see* SCHOOLCHILDREN
Secretary of State for, *see* SECRETARY OF STATE FOR
  EMPLOYMENT
self-dismissal, **9**, 223
self-employed, *see* SELF-EMPLOYED
servicemen, temporary employment of, **5**, 603
sheriff court jurisdiction, **6**, 1095
shift work, reorganisation involving introduction
  of, **9**, 170
short time, **9**, 165
sickness benefit, *see* SICKNESS BENEFIT
sickness of employee, wages during, **9**, 54
standard contract of, **9**, 1006
strikes, *see* INDUSTRIAL ACTION; STRIKE
subsidiary, unemployment benefit, calculation of
  entitlement to, **21**, 815
substances—
  dangerous—
    classification of, **9**, 532
    labelling of, **9**, 532
    road, conveyance by, **9**, 529
  hazardous, notification of installations handling,
    9, 530
  safety in use of, **9**, 436, 437
  work, used at, duty of manufacturer—
    generally, **9**, 455
    information, provision of, **9**, 459
    research, **9**, 458
    substance for use at work, meaning, **9**, 456
    supplier, **9**, 457
    supply, **9**, 462
    transfer of responsibility, **9**, 461
    user, **9**, 457
Sundays, restrictions on, **3**, 1682; **22**, 817
suspension, **21**, 822
temporary, for unemployed, **14**, 630
termination, **21**, 822
time off—
  generally, **9**, 92
  looking for work, **9**, 95
  public duties, for, **9**, 94
  remedies, **9**, 98

Employment—*continued*
time off—*continued*
  safety representatives, **9**, 97, 479–481
  trade union duties and activities, for, **9**, 93; **23**,
    755
  training, arrangement of, **9**, 95
trade unions, *see* TRADE UNION
training—
  access to, discrimination as to, **9**, 356
  time off to arrange, **9**, 95
  unemployed, for, **14**, 630
unfair dismissal, *see* UNFAIR DISMISSAL
unilateral change in employment terms, resignation
  following, effect on unemployment benefit,
  21, 844
wages, *see* WAGES
wages councils, **22**, 818
wrongful dismissal, *see* WRONGFUL DISMISSAL
young person over school leaving age, of, **3**, 1258
See also HOURS OF WORK; TRADE UNION; WORK
Employment, Department of
creation of, **5**, 503
functions of, **5**, 503
Employment Appeal Tribunal
appeal—
  award on, **6**, 986
  Court of Session, to, **6**, 924
  generally, **6**, 992*ff*
appointment of members, **6**, 984
civil legal aid, **13**, 1034
compensation for trade union exclusion or
  expulsion, **6**, 1008
constitution, **6**, 984
contempt of, **6**, 986
court of record, as, **6**, 985
decision on appeal, **6**, 986
delay in proceedings, **6**, 991
directions, **6**, 987
documents—
  inspection of, **6**, 986
  production of, **6**, 986, 988
employers' representatives, **6**, 985
employment protection, **6**, 995
enforcement of orders, **6**, 986
establishment, **6**, 984
expenses, **6**, 991
general powers, **6**, 986
hearings, **6**, 989
industrial tribunal, appeal from, **9**, 326
judges, **6**, 984
jurisdiction—
  dismissal, written statement of reasons for, **6**,
    999
  equal pay, claims relating to, **6**, 993
  guarantee payments, **6**, 999
  industrial tribunals, appeals from, **6**, 992
  pregnancy, right to return to work after, **6**, 999
  racial discrimination, **6**, 996
  redundancy, **6**, 995, 998
  secret ballots, **6**, 1001
  sex discrimination, **6**, 994
  suspension from work on medical grounds, **6**,
    999
  time off work, **6**, 999

Employment Appeal Tribunal—*continued*
jurisdiction—*continued*
    trade union membership and activities, **6**, 999, 1001, 1002, 1008
    unfair dismissal, **6**, 997
    written particulars of employment, **6**, 999
lay members, **6**, 984
mistake or omission in order, **6**, 990
National Industrial Relations Court as basis of, **6**, 981, 982
oath, evidence on, **6**, 989
official seal, **6**, 985
order—
    mistake or omission in, **6**, 990
    review of, **6**, 990
organisation, **6**, 985
origin, **6**, 981–983
precedent, binding authority, **22**, 328, 329
President, **6**, 984
private proceedings, **6**, 989
procedure—
    answer and cross-appeals, **6**, 1007
    appeals, generally, **6**, 992*ff*
    incompetent appeals, rejection of, **6**, 1005
    interlocutory applications, **6**, 1009
    rules, **6**, 1003
    trade union exclusion or expulsion compensation, **6**, 1008
'protective award', **6**, 995
review, **6**, 990
rules, **6**, 986, 1003
Senator of the College of Justice, **6**, 923
sittings, **6**, 985
witnesses, **6**, 986, 988
workers' representatives, **6**, 985
Employment Medical Advisory Service
advisers, **9**, 422
establishment of, **9**, 421
functions of, **9**, 421
Emptio venditio
contract of, **20**, 801
Emulsifiers
food, in, **11**, 373
Enabling Acts
provisions, and, **5**, 35
Encroachment
neighbouring property, onto, **3**, 161
possession, defence of, **18**, 140, 141*n*
Endangered species
import and export restrictions, **7**, 1197
importation—
    generally, **7**, 1197
importation and exportation—
    licensing, **2**, 216
    prohibition, **2**, 228
    quarantine provisions, **2**, 216
    restrictions on, **2**, 215
international trade convention, **2**, 215
offences in respect of, **2**, 217
trading in—
    licence for, **2**, 216
    offences respecting, **2**, 217
    scientific advice as to, **2**, 215
    statutory control, **2**, 215

Endowment
Carnegie Trust, **8**, 837
Church of Scotland, *see* CHURCH OF SCOTLAND (property and endowments)
educational—
    education authority powers, **8**, 838
    governing body—
        information to be supplied by, **8**, 837
        meaning, **8**, 837
    individuals, interests of, **8**, 841
    joint educational and non-educational, **8**, 840
    meaning, **8**, 837
    register of, **8**, 837
    reorganisation schemes, **8**, 838, 842
    School Sites Act (1841), **8**, 839
    self-governing schools, when payable to, **8**, 807
theological, **8**, 837
university, **8**, 837
Endowment policy
See LIFE ASSURANCE
Enemy
enemy alien—
    capacity to contract, **3**, 26
    partner, as, **16**, 1014
enemy character—
    domicile, effect of, **17**, 410
    ship's flag, determined by, **17**, 411
enemy goods—
    capture, **17**, 418
    droits of Crown, as, **17**, 407
enemy ship—
    capture, **17**, 411
    droits of Crown, as, **17**, 407
public—
    act of, carrier not liable for, **21**, 603
    trading with, barratry, **21**, 554*n*
sovereign's hotelkeeper not liable for acts of, **11**, 1747
See also SPYING; WAR
Energy
atomic, *see* ATOMIC ENERGY AND RADIOACTIVE SUBSTANCES
electricity, *see* ELECTRICITY
expenditure programme, **5**, 579
gas, *see* GAS
oil, *see* OIL
radioactive substances, *see* ATOMIC ENERGY AND RADIOACTIVE SUBSTANCES
sheriff court jurisdiction, **6**, 1096
Energy, Department of
creation of, **5**, 504
functions of, **5**, 504
Enforcement of judgments
See JUDGMENTS
Engagement
to be married, *see* MARRIAGE
Engineer
building contracts—
    administration of contract, **3**, 51
    appointment, **3**, 56, 127
        failure to appoint, **3**, 56
    arbiter, appointment as, **3**, 168
    building contracts—
        position of, generally, **3**, 127

Engineer—*continued*
building contracts—*continued*
  chemical, standard form contract, **3**, 12
  claims and dispute resolution, **3**, 168
  competence, **3**, 56
  consultant, **3**, 2
  contract, **3**, 127
  disputes, conciliation procedure, **3**, 170
  electrical, standard form contract, **3**, 12
  FIDIC Conditions, **3**, 12
  generally, **3**, 2
  ICE Conditions, **3**, 12, 23, 27, 60, 124, 168
  mechanical, standard form contracts, **3**, 12
  Model Form of General Conditions of
    Contract, **3**, 12
  replacement, **3**, 56
  sub-contracted, **3**, 127
consultant—
  partnership, number of partners allowed, **16**,
    1011
non-designated services, **4**, 1177*n*

England and Wales
administrative counties, **14**, 60
corporate personality, **19**, 215
corporation sole, concept of, **19**, 206, 208
county boroughs, **14**, 60
county district—
  rural, **14**, 60
  urban, **14**, 60
designated milk brought from, **11**, 465
double delict law, **17**, 293
early reference to bills in use in, **4**, 104
English and Irish Judgments, Register of, **6**, 456;
  19, 820
execution on assets in, **4**, 756
Greater London—
  council, abolition of, **14**, 62
  two-tier system, **14**, 60
influence of—
  Anglo-Norman era, **22**, 597, 598
  brieve system, **22**, 598, 599
    See also BRIEVE SYSTEM
  forms of action in Scots law, **22**, 598, 599
  generally, **17**, 111
  historical development of Scots law, **22**, 597–
    602
  House of Lords, appellate jurisdiction, **22**, 602
    See also HOUSE OF LORDS
  mercantile law, development after the Union,
    22, 600
  treason, law, **22**, 601
  Union of 1707, effect, **22**, 597, 600–602
    See also UNION AGREEMENT OF 1707
limited divergences in Scots law, **4**, 301
ministerial responsibility, **14**, 62
negotiable instruments, overlap between law on,
  4, 104
prize court, law applied by, **17**, 406
reform, **14**, 61
rural borough, **14**, 60, 62
rural district functions, **14**, 62
rural parishes, **14**, 60, 62
Secretary of State, meaning, **14**, 62
status of Englishman in Scotland, **14**, 1901

England and Wales—*continued*
Union with Scotland Act 1706 ..., **4**, 1707
  See also UNION AGREEMENT OF 1707
United Kingdom, as part of, **4**, 28
urban district functions, **14**, 62
VAT customs union, **7**, 1281
wills and succession, *see* WILL
English and Irish Judgments
Register of, **6**, 456; **19**, 820
English personages and officials
ranking with Scots, **16**, 2011, 2012
Scotland, in, status of, **14**, 1901
Enorm lesion
exclusion of plea, **10**, 1114
generally, **10**, 1110
meaning, **11**, 1205
onus of proof, **10**, 1112
presumption of, **10**, 1113
quadriennium utile, **10**, 1111
reduction of minor's contract on proof of, **11**, 1205
reform of law, **10**, 1115
to whom plea available, **10**, 1110
Enrichment
unjust, *see* UNJUST ENRICHMENT
Ensigns armorial
heraldry as study of, **11**, 1601
Entail, law of
Aberdeen Act 1824 ..., **22**, 646
abolition, power of entail, **22**, 646
arbitration, submission to by heir of, **2**, 410
assimilation of Scots and English law, **22**, 646
clauses irritant and resolutive, **18**, 424*n*
economic problems resulting from, **22**, 646
Entail (Scotland) Act 1914 ..., **22**, 646
executor, vesting in, **25**, 1109
extended powers to entailed proprietor, **22**, 646
feudal origins, **22**, 646
heir of entail, *see* HEIR OF ENTAIL
interpretation of deed of entail, **12**, 1262
land acquired for public recreation from heir to,
  14, 322
Lord Advocate's Conveyancing Committee, **22**,
  637, 646, 647
meaning, **22**, 646
Montgomery Act 1770 ..., **22**, 646
origins, **24**, 4
perpetuities, proposed abolition, **22**, 634
primogeniture, dependent on, **22**, 646
prohibition of new entails, **22**, 634
Register of, **6**, 466; **19**, 820
statutory limitation, **13**, 1630
tailzie, **22**, 646
  See also TAILZIE
Entailed estate
disposition of land to local authority for
  recreation, **20**, 246
improvements, provisions for, **20**, 238, 241
securities over—
  bond of annual rent, **20**, 237, 244
    improvements, for, **20**, 238, 241
  bond of disposition in security, **20**, 237, 244
    debts, provision for, **20**, 239
    improvements, for, **20**, 238
    wife and children, provision for, **20**, 239

Entailed estate—continued
securities over—continued
  capital transfer tax, **20**, 242
  creditor's power to burden entailed estate with
    his debt, **20**, 245
  estate duty, **20**, 242
  historical background, **20**, 237
  permanent debt, burdening estate with, **20**, 240
  standard security, exclusion of, **20**, 244
  transfer of charge from one estate to another,
    20, 243
Enter, leave to
See IMMIGRATION
Enterprise
meaning, **4**, 1271
Enterprise zone
corporation tax, **14**, 647
customs and excise, **14**, 647
designation of area, **14**, 643; **23**, 114
generally, **14**, 641; **23**, 113
government assistance, **2**, 1288
income tax, **14**, 647
industrial training board, payment of levy to, **14**,
  647
planning aspects, **14**, 645; **23**, 115
rates, exemption from, **14**, 646
scheme—
  generally, **14**, 642
  modifications of, **14**, 644
  road affected by, stopping up and diversion, **20**,
    654
statistical information, **14**, 647
Entertainer
agent, promotion by, **9**, 1006
employment of—
  payment for work done, **9**, 1006
  standard contract, **9**, 1006
  working conditions, **9**, 1006
Entertainment, places of
amusement arcades, see AMUSEMENT ARCADES—
  amusement with prizes
cinemas, see CINEMA
circuses, see CIRCUS
dancing, see MUSIC AND DANCING
licence—
  conditions, power to impose, **2**, 15
  generally, **11**, 1761n
  premises eligible for, **2**, 15
  public entertainment licence distinguished, **9**,
    1005
  sale of liquor under, **2**, 15
  six-day licence, **2**, 21
  meaning, **2**, 15; **9**, 1001
music, see MUSIC AND DANCING
noise, control of, **2**, 47, 98
opening hours restriction order, **2**, 65
permitted hours, **2**, 15, 18
public entertainment, see PUBLIC ENTERTAINMENT
sheriff court jurisdiction, **6**, 1098
theatres, see THEATRES
Entertainment industry
child employed in, **3**, 1256
Enticement
delict of, **15**, 596

Entrapment
defence of—
  English law, **7**, 204
  generally, **7**, 203
  Scots law, **7**, 205
  substantive defence, as, **7**, 204
  theoretical basis, **7**, 203
  United States law, **7**, 204
generally, **15**, 596
Entry
feudal law, meaning in, **18**, 93
Entry, powers of
countryside, **14**, 685
electricity boards, rights of—
  generally, **9**, 698
  private supplier, premises of, **9**, 719
  procedure for, **9**, 699
entry on land—
  Lands Clauses Act, under, **5**, 19
  notice of, **5**, 80
  right of, **5**, 49
flood prevention, **14**, 465
Food and Drugs (Scotland) Act 1956—
  in relation to, **11**, 339
  ships, aircraft, vehicles etc, **11**, 340
  warrant for, **11**, 339
health and safety inspector, by, **9**, 417, 490
local authority licences, in relation to, **14**, 545
public gas supplier, powers of, **9**, 892
public health officers, **19**, 338
repossession of goods, for, **5**, 892
salmon fishing offences, **11**, 25
sports ground, **14**, 580
water authority, powers of, **25**, 517, 525
Entry, right of
See IMMIGRATION
Entry certificate
application procedure, **16**, 1239
entry clearance, as, **12**, 150; **16**, 1238
See also IMMIGRATION
Environment
air pollution, see POLLUTION
conservation of, see CONSERVATION
development of environmental law, **9**, 1102, 1103
duties of state as to, **19**, 687
electricity boards' duties, **9**, 616
environmental law, meaning, **9**, 1101
expenditure on services for, **5**, 582
general control, **19**, 303, 315–329
international awareness of need to preserve, **9**, 1104
litter, **19**, 327, 328
noise pollution, **19**, 303, 318
  See also NOISE
nuisance—
  generally, **9**, 1107
  statutory, **9**, 1108
pests, destruction of, **19**, 326
pollution, see POLLUTION
proper working, employer's duty to provide, **9**,
  443, 444
roads and, see ROAD
sheriff court jurisdiction, **6**, 1099, 1124
Stockholm Declaration on the Human
  Environment, **19**, 687

Environment—*continued*
telecommunications, and, **16**, 1958
water—
    coast protection, **19**, 325
    flood prevention, **19**, 324–325
    fluoridation, **19**, 320
    provision of, **19**, 319
    river pollution, **19**, 321–323
    See also WATER
working, employer's duties to provide proper, **9**,
    443, 444
Environment, Department of
creation of, **5**, 505
functions of, **5**, 505
provisional order, copies of, **19**, 20
Scottish Office, Legal Civil Service, **13**, 1401
Environmental health
animals, **14**, 711
drugs, *see* DRUGS
food, *see* FOOD
plants, **14**, 711
public health, *see* PUBLIC HEALTH
reform, **14**, 50
stray dog, seizure of, **14**, 712
use of term, **19**, 301
water authorities, powers of, **25**, 526
Environmental impact assessment, *see* TOWN
    AND COUNTRY PLANNING
Envoy
precedence, **16**, 2014
Epilepsy
driving licence application, declaration in, **20**, 450
offence committed during seizure, **7**, 34, 113
    automatism, **7**, 151, 155
Episcopacy
abolition, **16**, 1306
Episcopal Church of Scotland
See SCOTTISH EPISCOPAL CHURCH
Equal opportunities
discrimination, *see* EMPLOYMENT
equal pay, *see* EQUAL PAY
Equal Opportunities Commission
appeals, **9**, 386
codes of practice issued by, **9**, 10, 387
duties of, **9**, 379
formal investigation—
    power to conduct, **9**, 380
    terms of reference for, **9**, 381
information—
    disclosure of, restrictions on, **9**, 383
    power to obtain, **9**, 382
non-discrimination notices, **9**, 385
powers of, **9**, 379
recommendations, **9**, 384
reports, **9**, 384
Equal pay
Act of 1970 ..., **9**, 393
agricultural wages orders, **9**, 403
EEC law, influence of, **9**, 14, 392
equality clauses, **6**, 993; **9**, 394
    claims arising from, **6**, 993
exclusions, **9**, 402
industrial tribunal, procedural stages of claim, **9**, 327
material difference, **9**, 400

Equal pay—*continued*
material factor—
    generally, **9**, 399
    genuine, **9**, 398
time limits, **9**, 401
work—
    equal value, of, **9**, 397
    like, **9**, 395
    rated as equivalent, **9**, 396
Equality before the law
Universal Declaration of Human Rights, **12**, 4*n*
Equipment Leasing Association
figures published by, **14**, 1006
formation, **14**, 1006
membership, responsibilities of, **14**, 1006
Equitable interest
English law, in, **21**, 133*n*
Equities of caution
meaning, **3**, 841
Equity
appeal to higher justice as theme, **22**, 394, 396
authority of—
    expediency of equal authority in Scots law, **22**,
        406
    legal positivism, undermining effect, **22**, 417
    limited, in Scots law, **22**, 406
    natural law, paramount, **22**, 406
    Stair's *Institutions*, **22**, 406
Bankton's *Institutes*
    nobile officium, **22**, 428, 430
    positive and natural law, **22**, 409
breach of confidence, English law, **18**, 1451, 1452
canon law, relevance, **22**, 583
civil law—
    generally, **22**, 400–419
    Stair's jurisprudence—
        equity as source of Scots law, **22**, 400–408
common law, relationship with, **6**, 908; **22**, 546
Court of Session, equitable jurisdiction—
    extraordinary or special, **22**, 426–431
    nobile officium, **22**, 426–431, 547, 583
    ordinary or general, **22**, 426, 427
creative function, whether extant, **22**, 432
criminal law—
    declaratory power of court to designate actions
        criminal, **22**, 423–425
    Hume, David—
        declaratory power, **22**, 423, 424
    Kames—
        natural law as criterion of criminality, **22**,
            422
    Mackenzie—
        crime against natural or positive law,
            distinction, **22**, 421
    mala in se and *mala prohibita* distinction, natural
        law approach, **22**, 420
    moral and juridical criminal behaviour, **22**, 420
    part in development, generally, **22**, 420–425
dispensing power as theme, **22**, 394, 397
downgrading of, **22**, 417–419
English law, comparison, **22**, 546
equitable and legal remedies, no ranking in Scots
    law, **15**, 68
equitable rules becoming customary rules, **22**, 414

Equity—*continued*
Erskine's *Institute*
   nobile officium, **22**, 430
   positive and natural law, **22**, 410
formal source of law, as—
   generally, **22**, 394–432, 501, 546, 547
   Stair's *Institutions*, **22**, 404
formalisation in English law, **22**, 398
High Court of Justiciary, special equitable
   jurisdiction, **22**, 547
individualisation of adjudication as theme, **22**,
   394, 395
international law, contribution to, **19**, 645
judicial authority, **22**, 418
Kames's *Principles of Equity*, **22**, 411–416, 422,
   429, 537, 546
legal positivism, **22**, 417–419
limits of, Kames's jurisprudence, **22**, 415
meaning, **19**, 645
modern role in Scots law, **22**, 432
natural justice, tacit identification with, **22**, 396
natural law—
   criminal law and, **22**, 420–425
   positive law, distinction, **22**, 402
   principles, same as those of equity, **22**, 401
   Stair's *Institutions*, **22**, 401
   tacit identification with, **22**, 396
neglect in nineteenth century, **22**, 417
nobile officium, **22**, 426–431
   Court of Session, special equitable jurisdiction,
   22, 547, 583
positive law—
   criminal law and, **22**, 420–425
   natural law, distinction, **22**, 402
   Scots law as, **22**, 403
   Stair's *Institutions*, **22**, 402–405
   theological foundation, **22**, 405
principles of, **19**, 645
Scots law—
   equitable in content, **22**, 407
   historical development, **22**, 399
   modern—
     role, **22**, 432
     as source of law, **22**, 399
   Roman law as parallel, **22**, 399
sociological conceptions to salvage modern, **22**, 432
Stair—
   Bankton compared, **22**, 409
   nobile officium, **22**, 427, 430
   positive and natural law, distinction, foundation
     of equity as source of law, **22**, 400–408
strictum ius, contrast, **22**, 395
subjective character, **22**, 419
theory of, **22**, 394
unjust enrichment, **15**, 11, 68
Equity capital
class rights, **4**, 347
meaning, **4**, 370
Equity security
meaning, **4**, 354
pre-emption rights, **4**, 354
Error
reckless, generally, **7**, 98
reduction on grounds of, **13**, 44

Error of fact
defence, as, **7**, 95, 97
error of law, whether distinction between—
   eighteenth-century law, **15**, 17, 18
   generally, **15**, 17, 25
   ignorantia juris maxim, **15**, 17–20
   nineteenth-century position, **15**, 19
recompense, in relation to, **15**, 61–63
unjustified enrichment, **15**, 17
Error of judgment
negligence, as, **14**, 1127
Error of law
correction of—
   certiorari, by, **1**, 285
   Court of Session, by, **1**, 285
   generally, **17**, 835
   superior courts, by, **1**, 285
decision-making process, in, **1**, 287
discretion, in exercising, **1**, 286
error of fact, whether distinction between—
   eighteenth-century law, **15**, 17, 18
   generally, **15**, 17, 25
   ignorantia juris maxim, **15**, 17–20
   nineteenth-century position, **15**, 19
generally, **7**, 95, 96
illustrations of, **1**, 288
jurisdiction not exceeded by, **1**, 285
no evidence supporting decision, where, **1**, 289
reasons for decision, absence or inadequacy of, **1**,
   293
recompense, in relation to, **15**, 61–63
ultra vires, and, **1**, 286
unjustified enrichment, **15**, 17
Erskine, Professor John
custom, meaning, **22**, 530, 532, 533, 543
custom as formal source of law, **22**, 132, 367, 375,
   382, 383
delict, **15**, 216
desuetude, doctrine of, **22**, 132
equity—
   nobile officium, **22**, 430
   positive and natural law, relationship, **22**, 410
Institutes of the Law of Scotland, **18**, 1n; **22**, 537, 590
   formal source of law, as, **22**, 434
   special authority of, **22**, 437, 440
municipal law of Scotland, description of, **22**, 529
on ownership, **18**, 5
precedent, use of, **22**, 251
Principles of the Law of Scotland, **22**, 441, 537
real and personal rights distinguished, **15**, 1
special authority of writings, **22**, 437, 440
Stair, assessment, **22**, 440
Erucic acid
restriction on use in food, **11**, 381
Erythorbic acid
meat, added to, **11**, 374n
Escalator
building controls, **3**, 208
Escheat
casualty of, feudal law, **18**, 84
liferent, **18**, 84
right of, Great Seal, passed under, **7**, 874
Esk
See RIVER ESK

Espionage
See SPY-SPYING
Esquire
ranking, **16**, 2022
    entitlement to, **16**, 2022
statutory recognition of term, **16**, 2022
Establishment
See CHURCH AND STATE
Estate
administration of, *see* ADMINISTRATION OF ESTATE
co-ownership, **25**, 639
conservation, judicial factor's duty, **24**, 243, 247
debtor's, *see* DEBTOR'S ESTATE
deceased person, of, appointment of judicial
    factor, **24**, 274
disposable, restriction on size, **25**, 621
entailed, *see* ENTAILED ESTATE
excepted, **25**, 1019
foreign, income tax, **25**, 982, 989
free, *see* FREE ESTATE
heritable, *see* HERITABLE ESTATE
ingathering, judicial factor's duty, **24**, 244
legal and equitable, doctrine not recognised in
    Scots law, **24**, 2, 7
loan secured on, **24**, 202
meaning, **19**, 1614
moveable, *see* MOVEABLE ESTATE
partnership, of, appointment of judicial factor, **24**,
    274
reassembly of, **25**, 609–611
residue of—
    abatement, **25**, 856
    beneficiaries' interests in—
        absolute, **25**, 986
        limited, **25**, 985
    intestacy of, **25**, 706
    nature of legacy, **25**, 851
    thrown in with specific items, **25**, 848
sale of, **24**, 202
sequestration, *see* SEQUESTRATION
transmission—
    England, **25**, 635
    France, **25**, 636
    Germany, **25**, 636
variation of distribution, **19**, 1639
    capital gains consequences, **25**, 998
Estate agent
negative licensing, operation of, **6**, 22
partnership, number of partners allowed, **16**,
    1011, 1112
professional rules, partnership contravening, **16**,
    1017
solicitors and incorporated practices, **6**, 22
warning orders, issue of, **6**, 22
Estate Bill, **19**, 5, 111
meaning, **19**, 5*n*
Estate Duties Investment Trust
business of, **2**, 1276
Estate duty
heir of entail in possession, **20**, 242
inventory and, **25**, 1069
Estate manager
partnership, number of partners allowed, **16**,
    1011, 1112

Estonia
imports, European Union regulations, **7**, 1029
Estoppel
English law of, **16**, 1602; **18**, 680
equitable principle of, **19**, 645
negotiability by, **16**, 1608
personal bar compared, **16**, 1602
planning law, in, **1**, 295
public law, in, **1**, 294
res judicata, **16**, 1602
statutes, applicability to, **16**, 1609
waiver and, **16**, 1632
See also PERSONAL BAR
Estuary
development of, **5**, 4
estuary limits order, **11**, 23
limits, fixing of, **11**, 23
obstruction of, Secretary of State's powers, **11**, 23
pilotage, *see* PILOT; PILOTAGE
sheriff, jurisdiction of, **4**, 2
Eton College
copyright rights conferred on, **18**, 1003
Eurocontrol (Air Navigation)
damages against, **4**, 82
functions, **2**, 908
navigation services—
    charges for, **2**, 1010
    provision of, **2**, 1010
status of, **2**, 908
European Accounting Association
generally, **1**, 77
**European Agricultural Guidance and
    Guarantee Fund**
agricultural expenditure, liability for, **1**, 980–982
control functions of, **1**, 979, 982
establishment of, **1**, 951
funds, use of, **1**, 971
Guidance Section—
    fisheries, aid to, **1**, 973
    funds, receiving, **1**, 970
    less-favoured areas, aid to farming in, **1**, 971
    mountain and hill farming, aid to, **1**, 971
    procedures, **1**, 971
    processing and marketing, aid for, **1**, 974
    Western Isles, aid for, **1**, 976
European Assembly
See EUROPEAN PARLIAMENT
European Association
proposed, **16**, 1004
**European Atomic Energy Commission
    Arbitration Committee**
decisions, enforcement in UK, **8**, 565
**European Atomic Energy Community
    (EAEC; Euratom)**
accession of United Kingdom, **5**, 320
Economic and Social Committee, *see* EUROPEAN
    UNION
Euratom Treaty—
    generally, **4**, 1111
    policy formulation under, **10**, 324
forms of Community legislation under, **10**, 90, 91
functions of, **9**, 925
generally, **10**, 1, 8
legal personality, **10**, 294

European Bank for Reconstruction and Development
exempted person under Financial Services Act 1986, as, **12**, 1323
European Centre for the Development of Vocational Training
policy implementation, **10**, 443
European Coal and Steel Community (ECSC)
Consultative Committee—
  accession of United Kingdom, **5**, 320
  appointment of members, **10**, 430, 431
  composition, **10**, 431
  consultation by, **10**, 434
  drawbacks to, **10**, 455
  establishment, **10**, 430
  European Commission, attachment to, **10**, 430
  European Commission objectives and programmes, submission for consultation, **10**, 434
  functions, **10**, 432
  'own initiative' opinions, **10**, 433
  publication of proceedings, **10**, 435
  standing committees, **10**, 431
development and nature of, **10**, 6
ECSC Treaty—
  annulment, action for, **10**, 208, 210, 212
  Consultative Committee, **10**, 430
  policy formation under, **10**, 324
food, provisions as to, **11**, 437
  compliance with, **11**, 321
  European Communities Act 1972 ..., **11**, 305
  fruit and vegetables, grading of, **11**, 432
forms of Community legislation under, **10**, 89, 91
general decisions, **22**, 205, 211, 215
generally, **10**, 1, 6, 7
harmonisation of laws, **22**, 625
High Authority, **10**, 12
individual decisions, **22**, 211
legal personality, **10**, 294
recommendations, **22**, 209
UK authorities, attitude of, **4**, 1119
European Commission
Advisory Committee on Transport, **10**, 327
advisory committees, **10**, 327
agricultural management committees, **10**, 335
amendments to proposals after consultation with European Parliament, **10**, 375
annual report to European Parliament, **10**, 364, 460
autonomy, **10**, 43
budget—
  draft, **10**, 427
  European Parliament, powers shared with, **10**, 367
  implementation, **10**, 340
  proposals, **10**, 330
cabinets, **10**, 321
censure, **10**, 48
collegiality, **10**, 46, 318, 319, 322
'comitology', **10**, 4
Commissioners—
  appointment, **10**, 317
  cabinets, **10**, 321

European Commission—*continued*
Commissioners—*continued*
  choice of, **10**, 311
  collegiality, **10**, 318, 319
  delegation powers, **10**, 320
  independence, **10**, 313, 319
  national governments, relations with, **10**, 316
  nationality, **10**, 312
  number of, **10**, 310
  political activity, **10**, 315
  responsibilities of, **10**, 47, 50
  specialisation of, **10**, 319
  termination of appointment, **10**, 314
committees—
  advisory, **10**, 327
  constitutionality of committee system, **10**, 337
  consultative, **10**, 327
  regulatory, **10**, 336
common position, rejection or amendment by European Parliament to, **10**, 379
compelling Commission to act, **10**, 346
competition law, *see* COMPETITION LAW
composition—
  Commissioners—
    choice of, **10**, 311
    independence, **10**, 313
    national governments, relations with, **10**, 316
    nationality, **10**, 312
    number of, **10**, 310
    political activity, **10**, 315
    termination of appointment, **10**, 314
  reform, proposals for, **10**, 317
consolidated estimates, **10**, 382
consultative committees, **10**, 327, 332
Council of Ministers, relationship with, **10**, 418, 419
  action on proposals of Commission, **10**, 425
  instigation of Commission action, **10**, 421
decision-making powers, **10**, 339
Directorates, **10**, 50
Directorates-General, **10**, 50, 321
discretion, **10**, 344, 345
Divisions, **10**, 50
Dooge Report, **10**, 322
Economic and Social Committee, consultation of, **10**, 440, 441
enforcement powers and functions, **10**, 54
European Community law—
  actions against violations of, **10**, 342, 343, 344
  ensuring application of, **10**, 341
European Parliament—
  annual report to, **10**, 364
  budgetary powers shared with, **10**, 367
  power of, with respect to Commission, **10**, 34
  questioning by, **10**, 363
  vote of confidence in Commission, **10**, 366
executive of Community, as, **5**, 326
functions—
  common interest of Community, promotion of, **10**, 323
  policy formulation, **10**, 323
    advisory committees, **10**, 327
    budget proposals, **10**, 330
    consultative committees, **10**, 327

European Commission—*continued*
functions—*continued*
  policy formulation—*continued*
    ECSC Treaty, **10**, 324
    EEC Treaty, **10**, 324
    Euratom Treaty, **10**, 324
    legislative proposals, submission of, **10**, 329
    national governments, consultation with, **10**, 328, 329
    policy documents, **10**, 325
    proposals to Council, **10**, 326
    treaties, negotiation of, **10**, 331
    under different treaties, **10**, 324
  policy implementation, **10**, 323
    agricultural management committees, **10**, 335
    application of Community law, ensuring, **10**, 341
    budget, implementation of, **10**, 340
    Commission discretion, **10**, 344
      limitation on, **10**, 345
    compelling Commission to act, **10**, 346
    constitutionality of committee system, **10**, 337
    decision-making powers, **10**, 339
    delegated rule-making powers, **10**, 334
    international agreements, **10**, 333
    powers if Council fails to act, **10**, 338
    reasoned opinions, **10**, 343
    regulatory committees, **10**, 336
    rule-making powers, **10**, 332
    violation of Community law, actions against, **10**, 342
  generally, **10**, 10, 12, 29, 308, 309
harmonisation of action by Council of Ministers, **10**, 418
instigation of action by Council of Ministers, **10**, 421
internal organisation, **10**, 50
international agreements, **10**, 333
judgments, enforcement in UK, **8**, 565
Legal Service, **10**, 51
legislation, powers and functions as to, **10**, 52
  subordinate legislation, **10**, 53
legislative power delegated to, **5**, 326
legislative proposals, submission of, **10**, 329
membership, **10**, 44
membership of, **5**, 326
mixed performance, **10**, 347
Monetary Committee, **10**, 327
national governments, consultation with, **10**, 328, 329
nationality, balance of, **10**, 321
objectives and programmes, consultation with ECSC Consultative Committee, **10**, 434
organisation—
  cabinets, **10**, 321
  collegiality, **10**, 318, 319, 321
  Commissioners, appointment of, **10**, 317
  delegation powers, **10**, 320
  determination of, **10**, 318
  Directorates-General, **10**, 321
  Divisions, **10**, 321
  nationality, balance of, **10**, 321
  reform, proposals for, **10**, 322

European Commission—*continued*
organisation—*continued*
  specialisation of Commissioners, **10**, 319
  written procedure, **10**, 320
policy documents, **10**, 325
Presidency, **10**, 45
proposals of, consideration by Council of Ministers, **10**, 408
public service lawyers, **13**, 1419, 1421
questioning by European Parliament, **10**, 363
reform, proposals for, **10**, 317, 322
rule-making powers, **10**, 332
  delegated, **10**, 334
Scientific and Technical Committee, **10**, 327
Secretariat-General, **10**, 51
services of, **10**, 49
Spierenberg Report, **10**, 322
staff, **10**, 321
supranational institution, whether, **10**, 309
technical issues, policy formulation, **10**, 320
'Three Wise Men'—
  Report of, **10**, 322
treaties, negotiation by, **10**, 331
Vice-Presidents, **10**, 45
European Commission of Human Rights
advocate's right of audience, **13**, 1325
Chambers—
  establishment and composition, **12**, 14
  sittings in, **12**, 14
citizens' preference for determination by British judges, **5**, 357
Commissioners—
  election to office, **12**, 11
  nationality, **12**, 11
  part-time nature of office, **12**, 11
  qualifications for office, **12**, 11
committees—
  establishment and composition, **12**, 14
  sittings in, **12**, 14
composition, **12**, 11
decisions taken by, **12**, 15
East African Asians, **12**, 107
establishment of, **5**, 315, 676
European Convention on Human Rights—
  application of, **12**, 10
  petitions alleging violation, **12**, 14
    application form, **12**, 15n
    friendly settlements, **12**, 15
    inadmissibility, **12**, 15, 15n
    indivdual, **12**, 14
    inter-state, **12**, 14
    lawyer, instruction of, **12**, 15
    legal aid, **12**, 15
    lodging, **12**, 15
    official languages, **12**, 15n
    report, **12**, 15
  supervision of application, **12**, 13
European Court of Human Rights, functions in relation to, **12**, 18
High Contracting Party, written representations on admissibility of application, **12**, 19n
individual's right of direct access, **7**, 737
law as 'European' law, **10**, 2, 2n
legal aid, **12**, 15, 19

European Commission of Human Rights—
continued
meetings, in camera, **12**, 15
official languages, **12**, 11, 15*n*
plenary session, **12**, 14
proposed merger with European Court, **12**, 13, 13*n*
rules of procedure, **12**, 11, 15, 15*n*
seat, **12**, 11
supremacy, as constraint on, **5**, 363
workload, **12**, 16
See also HUMAN RIGHTS
European Company
proposed, **16**, 1004
European Convention on Recognition and Enforcement of Decisions Concerning Custody of Children
access, questions relating to, **8**, 528
central authorities—
　duties, **8**, 524
　establishment, **8**, 520, 524
　Scottish, **8**, 520
enforcement, initial stages, **8**, 524
general principles, **8**, 520
geographical extent, **8**, 522
improper removal of child, **8**, 530
interim powers, **8**, 527
operation, **8**, 520
recognition of Convention decisions, **8**, 523
　refusal of, **8**, 523
registration—
　cancellation of registered decisions, **8**, 531
　effect, **8**, 529
　procedure, **8**, 525
　refusal, grounds for, **8**, 526
　variation of registered decisions, **8**, 531
scope, **8**, 521
European Co-operative Society
proposed, **16**, 1004
European Council of Ministers
generally, **5**, 324; **10**, 19, 29, 30
public service lawyers, **13**, 1419, 1422
European Court of Human Rights
advocate's right of audience, **13**, 1325
Chamber—
　ad hoc judges, **12**, 17
　composition, **12**, 17
　'national' judges, **12**, 17
　oral proceedings, **12**, 17
　plenary jurisdiction, **12**, 17
　written procedure, **12**, 17
citizens' preference for determination by British judges, **5**, 357
composition, **12**, 12
constitution, **5**, 676
contempt of court, judgment on, **6**, 305
decisions of, **5**, 678
establishment of, **5**, 315, 676
European Commission—
　functions in relation to Court, **12**, 18
　proposed merger with, **12**, 13, 13*n*
European Convention on Human Rights—
　advisory opinions on interpretation, **12**, 23
　interpretation and application, **12**, 10, 17

European Court of Human Rights—
continued
European Convention on Human Rights—
continued
　petitions alleging violation—
　　referral to Court, **12**, 15
　set up under, **5**, 675
　supervision of application, **12**, 13
judges—
　election to office, **12**, 12
　nationality, **12**, 12
　part-time nature of office, **12**, 12
　qualifications for office, **12**, 12
judgment, **12**, 20
　compensation, award of, **12**, 21
　costs and expenses, award of, **12**, 21
　execution, **12**, 20
　final nature of, **12**, 20
　just satisfaction afforded by, **12**, 20, 21
　reasons must be given for, **12**, 20
　revision, **12**, 20
　separate judicial opinions, **12**, 20
jurisdiction, **5**, 677; **12**, 17
jurisprudence, **12**, 24
legal aid, **12**, 19
official languages, **12**, 18
parties to proceedings, **12**, 18
　individual applicants, **12**, 18
　legal aid, **12**, 19
　legal representation, **12**, 18
　official languages, **12**, 18
　presentation of own case, **12**, 18
penal affairs, intervention in, **16**, 1495
prisoner, action brought by, **16**, 1470
Rules of Court, **12**, 12
Rules of Procedure, **12**, 18
seat, **12**, 12
statistics, **12**, 22, 24
supremacy, as recent constraint on, **5**, 363
who may bring case, **12**, 17
European Court of Justice
See COURT OF JUSTICE OF THE EUROPEAN COMMUNITIES
European Economic Area Agreement (EEA)
generally, **7**, 1006
European Economic Community (EEC)
See EUROPEAN UNION
European Economic Interest Grouping
choice as business medium, **16**, 1004
European Foundation for the Improvement of Living and Working Conditions
policy implementation, **10**, 443
European Free Trade Association (EFTA)
Common Customs Tariff, preferential trade agreement, **7**, 1016
European Economic Area Agreement (EEA), **7**, 1006
Lugano Convention, **8**, 429
Parallel Convention, **8**, 429
transit of goods between European Union and, **7**, 1171
European Investment Bank
autonomous nature, **10**, 443

European Investment Bank—*continued*
Board of Directors, **10**, 443, 444
Board of Governors, **10**, 443, 444
capital of, **10**, 446
  loans raised by, **10**, 446
constitution, **2**, 1293
drawbacks to, **10**, 445
establishment, **10**, 73
financial position, **2**, 1294
functions of, **2**, 1292; **10**, 73, 447
generally, **10**, 29, 73
guarantees granted by, **10**, 447
legal personality of, **2**, 1293; **10**, 443
loans granted by, **2**, 1295; **10**, 447
Management Committee, **10**, 443, 445
non-profit-making basis, **10**, 447
policy implementation, **10**, 443
privileges and immunities, **2**, 1293
regional imbalances, harmonisation of, **10**, 447
relations with Community institutions, **10**, 448
status, **10**, 429
European Monetary System (EMS), **10**, 20
European Currency Unit (EUU), **10**, 20
Exchange Rate Mechanism (ERM), **10**, 20
European Mutual Society
proposed, **16**, 1004
European Parliament
advisory functions and powers, **5**, 327; **10**, 362
budget—
  budgetary and legislative action, **10**, 386
  budgetary powers, generally, **10**, 18, 33, 367, 385
  budgetary reforms, **10**, 380, 380*n*, 381
  compulsory and non-compulsory expenditure, **10**, 385, 385*n*, 386
  conciliation procedure, **10**, 387
  Council approval, **10**, 386, 387
  draft, **10**, 382
    debate on, **10**, 383
    modifications to, **10**, 384
  draft preliminary, **10**, 382
  financing from own resources, **10**, 381
Bureau, **10**, 359
Co-operation Procedure, **10**, 32, 378
Committees of, influence, **10**, 32
composition, **10**, 349–355
Conciliation Procedure, **10**, 32
consultation—
  accession or association agreements, **10**, 371
  consultative role, generally, **10**, 32
  prior to enactment of regulations or directives, **10**, 371
  prior to international agreements, **10**, 371
  procedure, **10**, 372
Council of Ministers—
  common position of rejected or amended by, **10**, 379
  questions to, **10**, 369
  relations with, **10**, 368, 388
  reports of, **10**, 370
Court of Auditors, appointments to, **10**, 450
defects in position of, **10**, 362
Directorates-General, **10**, 359
duration, **15**, 1043

European Parliament—*continued*
Economic and Social Committee, observers at, **10**, 441
elected body, as, **5**, 327
elections to—
  act or omission in breach of election law, **15**, 1441
  arrangements for, **10**, 353
  by-election—
    expenses, maximum amount, **15**, 1414
    statutory timetable, **15**, 1226
    timing, **15**, 1044, 1219
  combined poll, **15**, 1360
  corrupt or illegal practice—
    candidate guilty of, **15**, 1072–1074
    election agent, duties, **15**, 1052
    election petition, **15**, 1233
  count, *see* COUNT
  counting agent, **15**, 1244
  deposit, payment by candidate, **15**, 1287
  disposal of documents, after count, *see* ELECTION (documents)
  disqualification, **15**, 1065
  election agent, **15**, 1051
    sub-agent, **15**, 1053
  election court, **15**, 1472
  election expenses—
    election agent, duties, **15**, 1052
    maximum amount, **15**, 1414
    meaning, **15**, 1405
    personal expenses, **15**, 1407
    returning officer, role, **15**, 1435
  election petition, **15**, 1438, 1474
    amendment, **15**, 1233
    presentation, **15**, 1233
  elector, meaning, **15**, 1277
  financial aspects—
    advance on account of charges to returning officer, **15**, 1396
    combined poll, **15**, 1388–1393
    recovery of charges by returning officer, **15**, 1395
    rendering accounts, **15**, 1401
    superannuation, **15**, 1400
    taxing of accounts, **15**, 1399
  franchise, **15**, 1076, 1078
  generally, **6**, 928; **10**, 21, 31, 351, 352; **15**, 1032, 1035
  illegal practice, *see* corrupt or illegal practice *above*
  notification, **15**, 1240, 1241, 1247
  personal expenses of candidate, **15**, 1407, 1409
  principles governing, **10**, 354
  public notice—
    form, **15**, 1243
    generally, **15**, 1240, 1241, 1244
    meaning, **15**, 1240
    statutory, **15**, 1245
  questioning—
    election petition, **15**, 1438
    generally, **15**, 1436
    method, **15**, 1438
  register of electors, **15**, 1104, 1105
  returning officer, **15**, 1049

European Parliament—*continued*
elections to—*continued*
  statutory notices and notifications—
    misnomer or inaccurate description, **15**, 1249
    mode, **15**, 1248
      registration officer, by, **15**, 1247
      returning officer, by, **15**, 1245
    statutory timetable, **15**, 1226
    time, provisions as to, generally, **15**, 1217, 1219–1222
    timing, **15**, 1043
    United Kingdom, in, **10**, 355
    verifying officers, **15**, 1326, 1326n, 1328, 1329, 1337
    voting, person, in, **15**, 1153
    voting modes, **15**, 1152
electoral malpractices, **7**, 409
European Commission—
  annual reports of, discussion of, **10**, 364
  budgetary powers shared with, **10**, 367
  censure motion on activities of, **10**, 365
  powers with respect to, **10**, 34
  proposals of, amendments to, **10**, 375
  questions to, **10**, 363
  vote of confidence in, **10**, 366
functions, **10**, 362–370
  policy formulation, **10**, 371–387
  policy implementation, control of, **10**, 363
  problems arising, **10**, 362
generally, **10**, 10, 12, 18, 29, 31–34, 308; **15**, 1032
introduction of, **10**, 348
legislation, powers with respect to, **10**, 32
Members of (MEPs)—
  administrative and financial matters concerning, **10**, 359
  citizenship, **15**, 1065, 1065n
  customs and exchange controls, **10**, 357
  differentiation in treatment between nationalities, **10**, 357
  disqualification, **15**, 1065
  division between member states, **10**, 350
  election of, **10**, 351–355
  financial status, **10**, 357
  freedom of movement, **10**, 357
  generally, **10**, 31
  immunities from prosecution, **10**, 357
  number of, **10**, 350
  privileges and immunities, **10**, 296, 357
  register of electors, supply to, **15**, 1114
  naming of, **10**, 349
officers, **10**, 359
Official Journal, **10**, 460
opinions—
  adequate opportunity to deliver, **10**, 374
  effect of, **10**, 373
  not legally binding, **10**, 374
  urgent and non-urgent cases, **10**, 374
organisation, **10**, 356–361
parliamentary papers, **10**, 460
parliamentary questions as source of law, **10**, 75
political groups, **10**, 361
  minimum numbers, **10**, 361
political power, **10**, 373
political weakness, **10**, 388
President, **10**, 359

European Parliament—*continued*
privileges and immunities, **10**, 357
procedural rules, **10**, 359
public service lawyers, **13**, 1419, 1422
quaestors, **10**, 359
reform, proposals for, **10**, 376–378
  Draft Treaty of European Union, **10**, 377
  Vedel Report, **10**, 376
Schuman Plan, **10**, 6, 6n, 9, 348, 348n
Secretariat, **10**, 359
Secretary-General, **10**, 359
sessions, **10**, 358
  annual session, **10**, 358
  election years, **10**, 358
  extraordinary, **10**, 358
  length, **10**, 358
  need not be convened, **10**, 358
  part sessions, **10**, 358
Solemn Declaration, **10**, 378
standing committees—
  camera, sittings in, **10**, 360
  'own initiative' reports, **10**, 360
  role of, **10**, 360
sub-committees, **10**, 360
supervisory functions and powers, **5**, 327; **10**, 362
'Three Wise Men'—
  Report of, **10**, 378
Tindemans Report, **10**, 378
Vedel Report, **10**, 376
Vice-Presidents, **10**, 359
European Patent Convention (1973)
See PATENT (international law)
European Social Charter
declaration of aims, as, **12**, 7
social end economic rights, **12**, 7
European Union/European Economic Comminity
accession to, **5**, 320, 354, 363; **10**, 182
accession or association agreements, **10**, 371
advertising, directive on misleading, **6**, 94, 95
agriculture, *see* COMMON AGRICULTURAL POLICY
anti-dumping measures, **10**, 176
approximation of laws, **10**, 103, 151
association agreements, **10**, 300
Banking Directive, *see* BANKING
Branch System General (BSG) Licence, **16**, 1949
budget—
  budgetary and legislative action, **10**, 386
  budgetary powers, generally, **10**, 385
  budgetary reforms, **10**, 380, 380n, 381
  compulsory and non-compulsory expenditure, **10**, 385, 385n, 386
  conciliation procedure, **10**, 387
  Council approval, **10**, 386, 387
  Council of Ministers, powers of, **10**, 427
  draft, **10**, 382
    Council of Ministers, **10**, 427
    debate on, **10**, 383
    modifications to, **10**, 384
  draft preliminary, **10**, 382
  financing from own resources, **10**, 381
  goods, free movement within EU, *see* GOODS
  implementation, **10**, 340
  proposals, **10**, 330

European Union—*continued*
budget—*continued*
building works, technical specifications as to, **3**, 207
capital, free movement within, **10**, 112, 149
citizen of—
  abode, right of, **12**, 117
  administrative removal, **12**, 195
  citizenship by descent, **14**, 1911
  Community national, meaning, **12**, 222
  depart, right to, **12**, 224
  deportation, **12**, 203
  employment, right to remain after, **12**, 239
  enter, right to, **12**, 225
  entry by, **12**, 101, 102
    refusal of, legal remedies, **12**, 234
  establishment, right of, **12**, 226
  EU law—
    direct effect of, **12**, 114
    relationship with United Kingdom law, **12**, 219, 235
    See also EUROPEAN UNION LAW
  European Convention on, **12**, 509
  exclusion order, **12**, 171
  expulsion, legal remedies, **12**, 234
  family of, **12**, 134
    right of entry, **12**, 236
  foreign state, to—
    political offences, **12**, 516, 531–535
    restrictions on, **12**, 516
    speciality, **12**, 516
  free movement of, **12**, 114, 221
  immigration by, **12**, 101
  Immigration Rules, **12**, 114, 134, 149, 221
  legal remedies of, **12**, 234
  medical reasons, refusal of leave to enter due to, **12**, 171
  nationality, **12**, 222
    EU law rights, and, **12**, 220, 220*n*
  permanent incapacity for work, right to remain after, **12**, 239
  police registration, **12**, 236
  'primary right' holder, **12**, 222
    family of, **12**, 223
      residence permits, **12**, 230
      right to remain, **12**, 228
    residence permit, **12**, 230
    right to depart and return, **12**, 224
    right to enter, **12**, 225, 236
    right to reside, **12**, 226
      termination, **12**, 227, 238
  Republic of Ireland, entry to United Kingdom via, **12**, 124
  reside, right to, **12**, 226
    termination, **12**, 227, 238
  residence permit—
    refusal of issue or renewal, legal remedies, **12**, 234
  retirement, right to remain after, **12**, 239
  return, right to, **12**, 224
  right to remain after employment, **12**, 228
    termination, **12**, 229

European Union—*continued*
citizen of—*continued*
  rights of—
    alteration, **12**, 134
    public policy proviso, **12**, 232
      procedural limits, **12**, 234
      substantive limits, **12**, 233
  'secondary right' holders, **12**, 223
    right to depart and return, **12**, 224
    right to enter, **12**, 225, 236
    right to reside, **12**, 226
      termination, **12**, 238
  self-employed, **12**, 222
  services, providers and recipients of, **12**, 222
    right to reside, **12**, 226
  travel document—
    expiry, **12**, 233
    failure to hold, **12**, 233
  workers—
    educational, training and residential facilities, **12**, 231
    equality of treatment, right to, **12**, 231
    frontier, **12**, 222
      right to remain, **12**, 228
    meaning, **12**, 222
    permanent incapacity for work, **12**, 228
    primary right holders, **12**, 222
    retirement of, **12**, 228
    right to remain after employment, **12**, 228
    seasonal, **12**, 222
    spouses and children, **12**, 231
    temporary, **12**, 222
    trade union membership, **12**, 231
commercial policy, **10**, 175
Common Agricultural Policy, *see* COMMON AGRICULTURAL POLICY
Common Customs Tariff, *see* COMMON CUSTOMS TARIFF
Common Fisheries Policy, *see* COMMON FISHERIES POLICY
common market—
  article 3, application of, **10**, 107
  Cockfield White Paper, **10**, 111
  creation and functions, **10**, 104, 105
  single internal market, **10**, 106, 111
  third countries, **10**, 106
competition, *see* COMPETITION
construction products, technical specificcations as to, **3**, 207
Consultative Council of the Bars and Law Societies of the EU, affiliation, **13**, 1302
consumer protection programme, **6**, 30, 31
contractual liability, **10**, 179
Council of Ministers, *see* COUNCIL OF MINISTERS
Court of Auditors, *see* COURT OF AUDITORS
Court of First Instance, *see* COURT OF FIRST INSTANCE
Court of Justice, *see* COURT OF JUSTICE OF THE EUROPEAN COMMUNITIES
customs and excise, *see* CUSTOMS AND EXCISE
customs union, **10**, 113
dental practitioner, **14**, 1135

European Union—*continued*
directives—
  binding force, **22**, 206
  consultation prior to enactment, **10**, 371
  implementation, **10**, 93; **13**, 87; **22**, 207, 216
  national courts, enforcement in, **10**, 93
  non-implementation, **22**, 208
  United Kingdom, implementation in, **10**, 93
dumping between member states, **10**, 152
economic policy, **10**, 173, 417, 418, 420
Economic and Social Committee—
  advisory status, **10**, 72
  agricultural section, **10**, 438
  allocation of seats, **10**, 437
  appointment, **10**, 72
    members of, **10**, 72, 437
  Chairman, **10**, 437, 439
  composition, **10**, 72, 437
  consultation with, **10**, 440, 441
  COREPER observers, **10**, 441
  Council of Ministers, and, **10**, 438, 440, 441
  drawbacks to, **10**, 455
  Employers' Group, **10**, 439
  establishment, **10**, 430, 437
  European Commission, consultation by, **10**, 440, 441
  European Parliament observers, **10**, 441
  functions, **10**, 72, 440
  General Interests' Group, **10**, 439
  membership, **10**, 72, 437
  officers, **10**, 437
  organisation, **10**, 438
  'own initiative' opinions, **10**, 29, 72, 440
  Praesidium, **10**, 439
  rules of procedure, **10**, 438
  specialised sections, **10**, 438
  transport section, **10**, 438
  Vice-Chairmen, **10**, 439
  Workers' Group, **10**, 439
ECSC Consultative Committee, *see* EUROPEAN COAL AND STEEL COMMUNITY
employment—
  collective redundancies, **9**, 15
  equality of treatment, **12**, 231
  right to remain after, **12**, 228, 239
    termination, **12**, 229
  right to reside for purposes of, **12**, 226
environmental policy, **9**, 1104
equal pay, **9**, 14, 392
European Agricultural Guidance and Guarantee Fund, *see* EUROPEAN AGRICULTURAL GUIDANCE AND GUARANTEE FUND
European assembly, *see* EUROPEAN PARLIAMENT
European Atomic Energy Community, *see* EUROPEAN ATOMIC ENERGY COMMUNITY
European Coal and Steel Community, *see* EUROPEAN COAL AND STEEL COMMUNITY
European Commission, *see* EUROPEAN COMMISSION
European Investment Bank, *see* EUROPEAN INVESTMENT BANK
European Parliament, *see* EUROPEAN PARLIAMENT
European Patent Convention, *see* PATENT
expenditure, examination of, **10**, 452

European Union—*continued*
federalism and confederalism—
  characteristics, **10**, 306
  generally, **10**, 305
filling station agreements, **9**, 822–833
food rules—
  fruit and vegetables, grading, **11**, 432
  generally, **11**, 305, 321, 437
  harmonisation, **10**, 336
foreign policy matters, Council of Ministers, **10**, 423
foundations of, **10**, 102, 112
General Agreement on Tariffs and Trade, relations with, **10**, 299
goods, free movement of, *see* GOODS
hybridity, **10**, 307
identity card, **16**, 1206
immigration rights, **12**, 220. *See also* IMMIGRATION
import and export quotas, **10**, 120
indirect taxation, harmonisation, **7**, 1033, 1034
industrial air pollution, **9**, 1121
industrial property rights, **10**, 127
insider dealing, directive on, **12**, 1536
institutions of, **10**, 308
intellectual property legislation, *see* INTELLECTUAL PROPERTY
international agreements, **10**, 300, 333, 371
international capacity, **10**, 297
international law, as source of, **19**, 649*n*
international organisations, relations with, **10**, 299
investment business, **12**, 1315, 1318, 1320, 1328
judgments, enforcement of, *see* JUDGMENTS
laissez-passer, **16**, 1236
law, *see* EUROPEAN UNION LAW
lawyers, exchange schemes, **13**, 1424
legal capacity, **10**, 295, 295*n*
legal personality, **10**, 178, 294, 294*n*, 295, 296*n*, 302
legal translators, **13**, 1423
legislation, interpretation, **12**, 1205
Luxembourg Compromise, **10**, 14, 17
maladministration, action for, **10**, 226
medical practitioner, **14**, 1109
metrication, **6**, 176
national, of—
  discrimination on grounds of nationality, **12**, 221
  entry to other member state, right of, **16**, 1206, 1208
  generally, **10**, 303
  residence in other member state, right of, **16**, 1206, 1208
national authorities, administration by, **10**, 230
national interests, defence of, **10**, 389
national sovereignty, and, **5**, 328, 329; **10**, 304, 305, 307; **12**, 219
natural gas, information on, **9**, 902
noise, measures of, **9**, 1299
non-discrimination, **10**, 109
objects of, generally, **5**, 329
obligations of membership, **10**, 108, 112
official communications and documents, privilege, **10**, 296
Organisation for Economic Co-operation and Development, relations with, **10**, 299
overseas countries, special relations with, **10**, 300

European Union—*continued*
Parliament, *see* EUROPEAN PARLIAMENT
passport, eligibility for, **16**, 1218, 1233
persons and services, free movement of, **10**, 112,
    131–150; **12**, 221; **14**, 1903
  beneficiaries, **10**, 134
  Community national, meaning, **10**, 134
  companies, **10**, 147
  directive 64/221, **10**, 142
  enforcement in national courts, **10**, 133
  entry, **10**, 136
  equal treatment, **10**, 137
  establishment, right of, **10**, 143
  families, **10**, 139
  financial services, **10**, 147
  legal persons, **10**, 131
  matters internal to member state, **10**, 140
  natural persons, **10**, 131
  persons and services distinguished, **10**, 131, 132
  qualifications, mutual recognition, **10**, 144
  residence, **10**, 136
  restrictions dealt with, **10**, 133
  restrictions on, **10**, 141
  self-employed individuals, **10**, 131
  services, scope of free movement of, **10**, 145
  services and the public interest, **10**, 146
  Single European Act, **10**, 148
  social security benefits, **10**, 139
  workers, **10**, 131, 132, 135
policing, co-operation on, **16**, 1805
policy formulation—
  Economic and Social Committee, **10**, 430, 437–
    442
  ECSC Consultative Committee, **10**, 430–437,
    442
population, **10**, 303
Postal, Telegraph and Telephone administrations
    (PTT), **16**, 1966, 1966*n*
postal services, competition rules, **16**, 1913
privileges and immunities—
  members and servants, **10**, 296, 296*n*
  missions of third countries, **10**, 298
product liability, **6**, 39; **15**, 197, 198
product safety, **6**, 52
professional qualifications, harmonisation and
    mutual recognition, **10**, 144. *See also under
    names of individual professions*
public corporation—
  effect of EU law on, **19**, 243
  enactment of rules contrary to, **19**, 246
  EU as, **10**, 294
  exemptions for, **19**, 248, 249
public health regulations, **19**, 307
refugees, **12**, 222
regional imbalances, harmonisation, **10**, 447
regulations—
  consultation prior to enactment, **10**, 447
  direct effect, **10**, 81, 83, 93
  immediate legislative effect, **10**, 93
  lawfulness, questions of, **10**, 93
  validity of, preliminary ruling on, **10**, 93
representation in third countries, **10**, 298
residence, right of, **12**, 226
  termination, **12**, 227, 238

European Union—*continued*
rights in performances, **18**, 1433
safeguard measures, **10**, 176
sea fishing, rules and controls, **11**, 178–182. *See also*
    FISHING
seccession from, **10**, 183
services, free movement of, **10**, 112, 131–148
sex discrimination, **9**, 14; **10**, 154, 171, 172; **19**, 247
shipping policies, generally, **21**, 114
social policy, **10**, 174
staff, actions at instance of—
  act adversely affecting applicant, **10**, 235
  entitlement to bring, **10**, 233
  nature of remedy, **10**, 232
  pre-action internal procedure, **10**, 234
  time limits, **10**, 236
state aid, restrictions on grant of, **19**, 244
stateless person, **12**, 222
taxation—
  customs duties, **10**, 118, 119
  exemptions from EU assets and revenues, **10**, 296
  fiscal barriers to trade, **10**, 170
  generally, **10**, 151
  rules as to, **10**, 168, 169
technical standards, harmonisation, **10**, 336
telecommunications, *see* TELECOMMUNICATIONS
territorial dimension, **10**, 303
time, harmonisation, **22**, 810
transport, free movement within, **10**, 150
treaties—
  conclusion of, **10**, 426
  negotiation by European Commission, **10**, 331
  meaning or validity, **22**, 267
  powers to make, **10**, 301
undertakings, rules relating to, **10**, 155–166
  dominant position, abuse of, **10**, 164
  enforcement, **10**, 158
  exemption, **10**, 159, 160, 162
  mergers and concentration, **10**, 165
  notification, **10**, 161
  prohibitions, **10**, 157
  public undertakings, **10**, 166
  transfer of, **9**, 16
United Nations and its agencies, relations with,
    10, 299, 302
VAT, proceedings for recovery, **7**, 1283
veterinary rules, harmonisation, **10**, 336
veto—
  Council of Ministers, **10**, 42, 416
  Luxembourg Compromise, **10**, 14, 17
voice telephony, policy on, **16**, 1924, 1924*n*
wrongful legislative measure, action for, **10**, 227
See also under individual subject headings
European Union law
Annual Report, **10**, 460
annulment, actions for—
  ECSC Treaty, under, **10**, 208, 210, 212
  EEC Treaty, under, **10**, 208, 209, 211
  effects of, **10**, 215
  generally, **10**, 64, 64*n*, 209, 210
  grounds for, **10**, 213
  illegality pled by way of exception, **10**, 216
  nature of remedy, **10**, 208
  time limit, **10**, 214

European Union law—*continued*
application of, **10**, 93
    ensuring, **10**, 341
authority, **22**, 212–214
autonomy, **10**, 79
binding legislation, **22**, 523
Bulletin, **10**, 460
Cockfield White Paper, **10**, 24, 28, 111
Commission, *see* EUROPEAN COMMISSION
common market, creation and functions, **10**, 104, 105
Common Market Law Reports, **10**, 459
Community, customary meaning, **10**, 13
Community institutions, Court of Justice actions against—
    annulment, actions for, **10**, 208–216
    contractual liability, actions in respect of, **10**, 237, 238
    failure to act, actions for, **10**, 217–221
    generally, **10**, 207
    non-contractual liability, actions for reparations, **10**, 222–231
    staff cases, **10**, 232–236
Community national, meaning, **10**, 134
competence, **22**, 212
competition, *see* COMPETITION
conventions, **10**, 74
    member states, between, **10**, 74
Council, European, **10**, 19, 29, 30
Council, majority voting in, **10**, 11
Council of Justice, **10**, 10
Council of Ministers, *see* COUNCIL OF MINISTERS
Council of the Communities, **10**, 10, 12
Court of First Instance, *see* COURT OF FIRST INSTANCE
Court of Justice, *see* COURT OF JUSTICE OF THE EUROPEAN COMMUNITIES
Crown, application to, **7**, 743
Crown, remedies against, **7**, 748
customs duties, **10**, 118
customs union, **10**, 113, 114, 117
damages, actions of, **10**, 67
    public authorities, against, **10**, 88
decisions, binding force, **22**, 210, 215
Delors Commission, **10**, 24
development and nature of—
    Assembly, **10**, 10, 12, 18, 18*n*
        See also EUROPEAN PARLIAMENT
    budgetary reform, **10**, 18
    Cockfield White Paper, **10**, 24, 28, 111
    Commission, **10**, 10, 12
        See also EUROPEAN COMMISSION
    Council of Europe, **10**, 4
    Council of Justice, **10**, 10
    Council of the Communities, **10**, 10, 11
    Court of Justice, **10**, 12
    Delors Commission, **10**, 24
    Draft Treaty on European Union, **10**, 23
    economic co-operation, **10**, 5
    entry into force, generally, **22**, 215–217
    European Atomic Energy Community, **10**, 1, 8–10, 12
        See also EUROPEAN ATOMIC ENERGY COMMUNITY

European Union law—*continued*
development and nature of—*continued*
    European Coal and Steel Community, **10**, 1, 6, 7, 8–10; **22**, 205, 208, 209, 211, 215
        See also EUROPEAN COAL AND STEEL COMMUNITY
    European Council, **10**, 19
    European Defence Community, attempt to establish, **10**, 8
    European Monetary System, **10**, 20
    European Parliament, **10**, 18*n*, 21, 18
        See also EUROPEAN PARLIAMENT
    European Political Community, attempt to establish, **10**, 8
    European Union, **10**, 1, 8–10
        See also EUROPEAN UNION
    Fontainebleau Summit, **10**, 23
    form, **22**, 202, 203
    Genscher-Colombo Plan, **10**, 22
    Luxembourg Compromise, **10**, 14, 17
    Luxembourg Conference, **10**, 24
    majority voting, **10**, 27
    Merger Treaty, **10**, 12
    Messina Conference, **10**, 8
    Milan Summit, **10**, 24
    political co-operation, **10**, 5, 19, 26
    Schuman Declaration, **1**, 348; **10**, 6, 6*n*, 9
    Single European Act, **10**, 25–27, 29, 74
    Solemn Declaration of Stuttgart, **10**, 22
    Treaties of Rome, **10**, 8
    treaty amendment, **10**, 26
    United Kingdom membership, **10**, 14–16
    veto, **10**, 14, 17, 42, 416
direct effect, doctrine of, **10**, 81, 83, 93
Draft Treaty on European Union, **10**, 23
EEC Treaty, forms of legislation under, **10**, 90, 91
enforcement of Community rights, **10**, 85–87
    Court of Justice, before, **10**, 85
    methods, **10**, 87
    national courts, before, **10**, 86
equality of treatment, principle of, **10**, 94, 98
establishment, rights of, **10**, 112
European Assembly, *see* EUROPEAN PARLIAMENT
European Commission, *see* EUROPEAN COMMISSION
European Convention on Human Rights, relationship to, *see* EUROPEAN CONVENTION ON HUMAN RIGHTS
European Council, **10**, 19, 29, 30
European Court and Commission on Human Rights, relationship to, **10**, 2, 2*n*
European Court Reports, **10**, 459
European Investment Bank *see* EUROPEAN INVESTMENT BANK
'European' law distinguished, **10**, 2
European Monetary System, **10**, 20
European Parliament, *see* EUROPEAN PARLIAMENT
European Union, *see* EUROPEAN UNION
failure of member state to fulfil obligations, Court of Justice actions, **10**, 198–206
    concept of failure by member state, **10**, 199
    ECSC Treaty, under, **10**, 204–206
    EU Treaty, under, **10**, 200–203
failure to act, action for, **10**, 65
Fontainebleau Summit, **10**, 23

European Union law—*continued*
form and substance, **10**, 92
founding treaties, **10**, 74
four freedoms, **10**, 112–150
Free Trade Agreements, **10**, 74
fundamental human rights, **10**, 94, 95
Gazetteer of European Law, **10**, 459
general principles, **10**, 94
   applicability, **10**, 99
   equality of treatment, **10**, 94, 98
   fundamental human rights, **10**, 94, 95
   legal certainty, **10**, 94, 96
   non-discrimination, **10**, 94, 98
   proportionality, **10**, 94, 97
Genscher-Colombo Plan, **10**, 22
goods, free movement of, *see* GOODS
House of Lords Select Committee on the European Communities, **10**, 75
human right, principle of, **10**, 94, 95
implementation in United Kingdom—
   Act of Parliament, by, **22**, 221
   Community objects and obligations, **22**, 222
   subordinate legislation, **22**, 221
indemnity, action of, **10**, 67
interests of member states, **10**, 415
interpretation, methods of, **10**, 76
judicial review of acts of Community institutions, **10**, 85
language, communication of decision, **10**, 59*n*, 96, 253
law reports, **10**, 459
legal capacity of Community within member states, **10**, 295, 295*n*
legal certainty, principle of, **10**, 94, 96
legal personality of Community, **10**, 294, 294*n*
legally binding acts, creation of, **10**, 93
legislation—
   directives, **5**, 324
   generally, **5**, 324
   parliamentary control of—
      defects in, **5**, 326
      generally, **5**, 325
   regulations, **5**, 324
legislative and other binding acts, of, **10**, 78
Lomé Convention, **10**, 74
Luxembourg Compromise, **10**, 14, 17, 42
Luxembourg Conference, **10**, 24
member states, general obligations, **10**, 108
mercantile law, assimilation, **22**, 625
Merger Treaty, **10**, 12, 74
Messina Conference, **10**, 8
Milan Summit, **10**, 24
nature, **10**, 81–84
non-discrimination, principle of, **10**, 94, 98, 109
notification, **22**, 219
obligation, action for failure to fulfil, **10**, 63, 63*n*
participation, **22**, 218
persons and services, free movement of, **10**, 112, 131–150
political co-operation, **10**, 19
precedence—
   Community standpoint, **22**, 213
   United Kingdom standpoint, **22**, 214

European Union law—*continued*
precedent, **10**, 80, 82, 83
   European Court of Justice, **22**, 268
   generally, **22**, 266–269
   preliminary rulings, **22**, 267
   Scottish courts, **22**, 269
preliminary ruling by Court of Justice—
   courts or tribunals entitled to request, **10**, 241
   criteria for making request, **10**, 242
   effects of, **10**, 244
   function, **10**, 239
   nature of, **10**, 239
   obligation to request, **10**, 242, 243
   questions which may be referred, **10**, 240
prerogative powers of Crown, and, **7**, 738
primacy, doctrine of, **10**, 82, 83
privileges and immunities of Community, **10**, 296, 296*n*
promulgation, **22**, 218
proportionality, principle of, **10**, 94, 97
protocols, **10**, 74
public corporations, and, **19**, 243–249
publication, **22**, 219
reference to, procedure for, **6**, 868
regulations—
   binding force, **22**, 204, 215
   repeal, **22**, 220
   retrospectiveness, **22**, 217
repeal, **22**, 220
Reports on Competition Policy, **10**, 460
Schuman Declaration, **10**, 6, 6*n*, 9, 348
Select Committee on European Legislation, **5**, 426, 458
services, rights in relation to, **10**, 112
Single European Act, **10**, 25–27, 29, 74
   majority voting under, **10**, 27
Solemn Declaration of Stuttgart, **10**, 22
sources, **10**, 74, 75
   ancillary, **10**, 75
   guide to, **10**, 457–461
   interpretation of, **10**, 76
   learned opinion, **10**, 75
   parliamentary questions, **10**, 75
   policy, statements of, **10**, 75
sources of legislation, generally, **10**, 458
staff of Community institutions, disputes concerning, **10**, 66, 232–236
Standing Committee on European Community Documents, **5**, 426
status—
   generally, **10**, 83
   United Kingdom, within, **10**, 84
statutes of bodies established by Council, interpretation of, **10**, 240
Summits, **10**, 19
supranationalism and integration, **10**, 456
supremacy, **5**, 322, 363
taxation, *see* TAXATION
third countries, agreements with, **10**, 70, 74
treaties—
   contractual nature of, **10**, 77
   sources, generally, **10**, 457
Treaties of Accession, **10**, 74
Treaties of Rome, **10**, 8

European Union law—_continued_
United Kingdom, application and enforcement in, **10**, 1, 1_n_
United Kingdom law, interaction, **7**, 738
veto—
  Council of Ministers, **10**, 42, 416
  Luxembourg Compromise, **10**, 14, 17
violation of, actions against, **10**, 342–344
workers, rights of, **10**, 112
Europol
establishment, **16**, 1805
Euthanasia
European Convention on Human Rights, **12**, 25
homicide, as, **7**, 259
Eventide home
hotel distinguished, **11**, 1714
Eviction
judicial, warrandice, in cases of, **18**, 707, 707_n_, 714
protection of tenant against, **13**, 598
unlawful, **13**, 472
  damages in respect of, **13**, 704, 705
    amount, **13**, 707
    defences to damages action, **13**, 706
  generally, **13**, 704
  landlord, by—
    generally, **13**, 698, 700
    residential occupier, meaning, **13**, 690
Evidence
accused, for, **17**, 759
additional, **17**, 760, 826, 849
  civil cases, **10**, 561
  criminal cases, **10**, 564
admissibility, _see_ ADMISSIBILITY OF EVIDENCE
adultery, findings of, **10**, 502
affirmation, **7**, 505; **10**, 548
agreement or discrepancy between averments or libel and, **10**, 746
alteration, **7**, 521
ambiguities in, **10**, 560
assessors, opinion of, **10**, 654
averments, agreement or discrepancy with, **10**, 746
avoiding giving, **7**, 522
bankers' books, entries in, **10**, 502, 537
blood group tests, **10**, 502
burden of proof, _see_ PROOF
business practices, **10**, 512
business records, **10**, 502, 603, 605, 608
calendar, facts relating to, **10**, 512
character and credibility, as to—
  civil cases, **10**, 628
    evidence in rebuttal, **10**, 631
    parties, **10**, 629
    witnesses, **10**, 630
  criminal cases—
    the accused—
      attempt to set up character, **10**, 644
      co-accused, evidence against, **10**, 646
      common law as to, **10**, 638
      cross-examination of, **10**, 642
      good character, evidence of, **10**, 641
      nature or conduct of offence, **10**, 645
      previous convictions, **10**, 639

Evidence—_continued_
character and credibility, as to—_continued_
  criminal cases—_continued_
    the accused—_continued_
      proof of guilt, **10**, 643
      substantive charge, evidence in support of, **10**, 640
    general rule, **10**, 632
    persons not present in court, **10**, 637
    victim or complainer, as to, **10**, 633, 634
    witnesses—
      child, **10**, 636
      generally, **10**, 635
      opinion evidence, **10**, 636
  general rule, **10**, 628
child, compulsory removal of, evidence at hearing, **22**, 18
child witness, credibility of, **10**, 636
circumstantial—
  facts relevant to facts in issue, **10**, 623
  generally, **10**, 767, 777
  weight of evidence, **10**, 777
co-accused, competence as witness, **10**, 502, 726
coherence of evidence, **10**, 780
coinage, **10**, 512
commission, on—
  conduct of, **17**, 1156
  form of, **17**, 1155
  generally, **17**, 1154
  solemn procedure, **17**, 757
competency, **10**, 506; **17**, 567, 1143
computer statements, **10**, 607
conduct of witness, cross-examination as to, **10**, 555
confessions, _see_ CONFESSION
conflicting opinions, **10**, 650
conscience, witness refusing to answer on grounds of, **10**, 508
corroboration, _see_ CORROBORATION
credibility of witness, cross-examination as to, **10**, 554
crime for which conviction not sought—
  evidence of, **10**, 627
  relevancy, **10**, 627
criminal convictions, as, **10**, 502
criminal proceedings—
  additional evidence, **10**, 564
  copies of documents, **10**, 611
  documentary evidence, **10**, 584, 605, 606
  evidence in replication, **10**, 565
  examination of witnesses in court, **10**, 547
  generally, **10**, 502
  judicial admissions, **10**, 513, 518, 519
  objections to evidence, **10**, 567
  oral evidence, **10**, 539–546; **17**, 568
  privilege, **10**, 671–674
  recall of witnesses, **10**, 563
  similar facts, evidence of, **10**, 626
  written statement in lieu of oral evidence, **10**, 517
cross-examination, _see_ WITNESS, EXAMINATION IN COURT
Crown privilege, **10**, 668
de recenti statements, **10**, 707

Evidence—*continued*
debate on—
  admissibility, **17**, 1181
  amendment of record, **17**, 1174
  conclusion on, **17**, 1186
  correlation of productions to, **17**, 1180
  counsel, certification of, **17**, 1177
  diligence, supersession of, **17**, 1184
  expenses, **17**, 1176
  experts, certification of, **17**, 1179
  extract, supersession of, **17**, 1184
  generally, **17**, 1173
  incidental matters at, **17**, 1175
  interim orders, **17**, 1183
  pecuniary craves, interest on, **17**, 1185
  pleas-in-law, **17**, 1182
  relevance, **17**, 1181
  witnesses, certification of, **17**, 1178
deceased, statements by, **10**, 711
declaration, given under, **7**, 505
definition, **10**, 501
destruction, **7**, 521
development of law, **10**, 502
diplomatic immunity, **10**, 526
direct, **10**, 777
  weight of evidence, **10**, 777
discs, as, **10**, 572, 607
divorce cases—
  adultery cases, **10**, 932
  best evidence, **10**, 929
  burden of proof, **10**, 927
  compellability of witness, **10**, 930
  competency of witness, **10**, 930
  corroboration, **10**, 928
  generally, **10**, 925
  marriage, proof of, **10**, 933
  previous decrees, **10**, 931
  standard of proof, **10**, 926
DNA tests, **10**, 502, 662
documentary, *see* DOCUMENTARY EVIDENCE
documents, use to refresh memory, **10**, 566
effect of—
  civil cases—
    fact, presumptions of, **10**, 751
    final decision, **10**, 752
    generally, **10**, 749, 752
    rebuttable presumptions of law, **10**, 750
  criminal cases—
    diminished responsibility, **10**, 756
    facts peculiarly within knowledge of accused, **10**, 755
    general rules, **10**, 753
    insanity, **10**, 756
    presumptions, **10**, 754
    statutory burden on accused, **10**, 757
  evidential, **10**, 748
  generally, **10**, 747
  persuasive, **10**, 748
  shifting, **10**, 748
  tactical, **10**, 748
election petition court, **15**, 1481, 1482, 1484
Employment Appeal Tribunal, **6**, 986
examination-in-chief, *see* WITNESS, EXAMINATION IN COURT

Evidence—*continued*
exclusion of, **10**, 505
  irrebuttable presumptions, **10**, 520
  judicial admissions, **10**, 513–519
  judicial knowledge, **10**, 510–512
  means of, **10**, 509
  public policy, on grounds of, **10**, 668
  res judicata, **10**, 521
exculpatory evidence at own trial, perjury resulting from, **7**, 26
expert, **10**, 650
  assessors, **10**, 654
  corroboration of, **17**, 162
  court experts, **10**, 655
  disagreement between experts, **17**, 162
  exchange of expert's reports, **10**, 655, 656
  foreign law, **10**, 653
    establishment of fact, **10**, 653
    proof of, **17**, 160, 162
  handwriting, **10**, 652
  meaning, **10**, 647
  men of skill, **10**, 654
  special features, **10**, 651
extra-judicial statements—
  admissibility of, *see* ADMISSIBILITY OF EVIDENCE
  generally, **10**, 719
  self-serving—
    civil cases, **10**, 721
    criminal cases, **10**, 720
extrinsic, interpretation of contract, **13**, 144–146
eye-witness, visual identification by, **10**, 658–661
facts, admissibility of, *see* ADMISSIBILITY OF EVIDENCE
facts in issue, **10**, 504, 623, 746
facts relevant to, **10**, 623
false—
  perjury, **7**, 510
  sanction for giving, **10**, 548
False Oaths (Scotland) Act (1933)—
  generally, **7**, 516
false reporting to police, *see* POLICE (false reporting to)
false statement in course of investigation, **7**, 533, 535–538
  inducing another to make, **7**, 534
false statement on oath, **7**, 517
  art and part liability, **7**, 520
  document, false statement in, **7**, 518
  false statutory declatation, **7**, 516, 518
  registration, false declaration in relation to, **7**, 519
fatal accident inquiry, **17**, 957, 968
films, **10**, 572, 607
foreign law, establishment of fact, **10**, 653
Forestry Commission documents, **11**, 604
generally, **10**, 746
  standard of proof—
    civil cases, **10**, 760
    criminal cases, **10**, 759
    generally, **10**, 758, 759
  sufficiency of evidence—
    averment and proof, correspondence between—
      civil cases, **10**, 764
      criminal cases, **10**, 765

Evidence—*continued*
generally—*continued*
  sufficiency of evidence—*continued*
    corroboration—
      civil cases—
        abolition of rule, **10**, 766, 772, 773
        consistorial proceedings, **10**, 775
        how obtained, **10**, 774
      criminal cases—
        confessions, of, **10**, 770
        definition, **10**, 766
        facts which may be corroborated, **10**, 767
        general rule, **10**, 766
        how obtained, **10**, 768
        mutual, where separate similar crimes charged, **10**, 769
        statutory exceptions, **10**, 771
      criteria, **10**, 763
    weight, and, **10**, 762
    weight of—
      circumstantial evidence, **10**, 777
      coherence of evidence, **10**, 780
      credibility of witnesses, **10**, 779
      direct evidence, **10**, 777
      generally, **10**, 776
      primary evidence, **10**, 778
      questions of, on appeal, **10**, 781
      reliability of witnesses, **10**, 779
      secondary evidence, **10**, 778
geographical facts, **10**, 512
guilty, plea of, **10**, 517
health and safety regulations, offences under, **9**, 517
hearsay, *see* HEARSAY EVIDENCE
hire-purchase agreements, **10**, 512
historical facts, **10**, 512
history of law, **10**, 502
identification, of—
  body fluids, **10**, 662
  body tissues, **10**, 662
  DNA profiling, **10**, 502, 662
  dock identification, **10**, 664
  essential to establish, **10**, 657
  fingerprint evidence, **10**, 662
  foot-print evidence, **10**, 662
  generally, **10**, 657
  genetic fingerprinting, **10**, 662
  handwriting, **10**, 652, 662
  identification parades, **10**, 666
  indirect, **10**, 660
  ordinary witnesses, **10**, 649
  photograph, by, **10**, 667
  prior, **10**, 665, 713
  scientific evidence, **10**, 662
  sufficiency of, **10**, 661
  teeth-marks, **10**, 662
  visual identification, **10**, 658
    reliability of, **10**, 659
  voice identification, **10**, 663
illegally or irregularly obtained—
  civil proceedings, **10**, 691, 701–703
    Rattray v Rattray, decision in, **10**, 702

Evidence—*continued*
illegally or irregularly obtained—*continued*
  criminal proceedings, **10**, 691
    conflicting interests, **10**, 693
    ease of rectification of irregularity, **10**, 699
    general rule, **10**, 692
    good faith, **10**, 697
    gravity of offence, **10**, 694
    nature of irregularity, **10**, 696
    stage of investigation, **10**, 700
    status of investigators, **10**, 698
    urgency, **10**, 695
  generally, **10**, 690; **16**, 1802
in retentis, to lie, **17**, 1153
inadmissible, objections to, **10**, 567
inadmissible confession, evidence obtained as result of, **10**, 734
incompetent, **10**, 567
industrial tribunal, to, **9**, 322
insane, statements by, **10**, 711
intention, of, **10**, 624
intentionality, presumption of, **10**, 754
interception of communications, to obtain, **16**, 1802
interference with, **7**, 499, 501, 521
interpreter, given through, **10**, 551
intimidation of witnesses, **10**, 637
irrebuttable presumptions, **10**, 520
irrelevant, **10**, 567
judicial admissions—
  absence of challenge, **10**, 519
  civil cases, **10**, 513–517
  confessions distinguished, **10**, 513
  consistorial cases, **10**, 513
  criminal cases, **10**, 513, 518, 519
  divorce applications, **10**, 513
  extra-judicial admissions distinguished, **10**, 513
  guilty, plea of, **10**, 517
  minute, by, **10**, 515
    criminal cases, **10**, 518
  nature and forms of, **10**, 513
  obligatio literis, **10**, 513
  oral admissions at bar, **10**, 516
    civil cases, **10**, 516
    criminal cases, **10**, 518
  record, on, **10**, 514
judicial discretion, **10**, 508
judicial knowledge, **10**, 510–513
language of court, **10**, 551
law of Scotland as judicial knowledge, **10**, 511
legal adviser and client, communications between, **10**, 505
lex fori governs matters of, **17**, 359
loan, proof of, *see* LOAN
lodging and proof of documents used in cross-examination, **10**, 557
management rules, of, **14**, 299
marital intercourse, as to, **10**, 930
mens rea, **10**, 624
mental or physical illness affecting reliability of witness, **10**, 636
microfilm, **10**, 607
misconduct, of, **14**, 1506
national security, prejudice to, **10**, 512

Evidence—*continued*
nationality, **14**, 1957
no fair notice given on record, **10**, 567
note of case averred on record, **10**, 567
notes of, documentary evidence, as, **10**, 590
oath, **7**, 505
  reference to, **10**, 621
  taking false, **7**, 512
objections to—
  examination-in-chief, **10**, 552
  generally, **10**, 567; **17**, 778, 844, 1170
  noting of, **10**, 567
onus of proof (*onus probandi*), **10**, 746
opinion, of—
  admissibility generally, **10**, 647, 648
  assessors, **10**, 654
  court experts, **10**, 655
  expert's reports, exchange of, **10**, 656
  foreign law, **10**, 653
  general rule, **10**, 648
  generally, **10**, 647, 648
  handwriting, **10**, 652
  Lands Tribunal for Scotland, **6**, 1152
  men of skill, **10**, 654
  witnesses—
    expert, **10**, 650–652
    ordinary, **10**, 649, 651, 652
oral, *see* ORAL EVIDENCE
oral testimony, principle of, **17**, 568
original—
  civil cases, **10**, 714
  criminal cases, **10**, 706–708
parole, *see* PAROLE EVIDENCE
paternity, findings of, **10**, 502
perjured, advocate's duty as to, **13**, 1362
perjury, *see* PERJURY
personal bar, **16**, 1601
photographs, **10**, 607
Poaching Prevention Act 1832 ..., **11**, 846
police, **16**, 1784
  fabrication by, **7**, 496
precognitions, **7**, 509; **17**, 545
prejudice, **10**, 505
preparation of, **17**, 1141–1143
presumption of death, Scottish Law Commission
  recommendation, **22**, 669
presumptions of law—
  adverse inferences, **10**, 754
  criminal cases, **10**, 754
  innocence, **10**, 754
  intentionality, **10**, 754
  rebuttable—
    burden of proof, **10**, 748, 750
    business habits, arising from, **10**, 750
    criminal cases, **10**, 754
    innocence, in favour of, **10**, 750
    life, in favour of, **10**, 750
    mental powers, in favour of, **10**, 750
    misconduct, against, **10**, 750
    parentage, as to, **10**, 750
    physical powers, in favour of, **10**, 750
    regularity, in favour of, **10**, 750
    res ipsa loquitur, **10**, 750
    validity, in favour of, **10**, 750

Evidence—*continued*
presumptions of law—*continued*
  recent possession, **10**, 754
  sanity, **10**, 754
previous conviction, as to, **10**, 639–643
  admissibility of evidence, **10**, 627, 628, 631,
    635
previous inconsistent statements, **10**, 707, 708
prima facie rule—
  extradition, **12**, 544–547
primary, **10**, 778
prisoners of war, statements by, **10**, 711
privilege—
  adultery, **10**, 675
  confidentiality—
    accountants, **10**, 686
    bankers, **10**, 686
    clergyman and penitent, **10**, 685
    doctor and patient, **10**, 686
    general rules, **10**, 676
    legal adviser and client, **10**, 682
    litigation, communications relative to, **10**, 681
    marital intercourse, concerning, **10**, 680
    negotiations for settlement, privileges in aid
      of, **10**, 684
    post litem motam,communications made, **10**,
      683
    professional business and personal advisers,
      10, 686
    spouses, communications between, **10**, 677
      civil proceedings, **10**, 678
      criminal proceedings, **10**, 679
      marital intercourse, **10**, 680
  definition, **10**, 668
  general principles, **10**, 669
  incrimination, **10**, 670
    criminal offences, **10**, 671–674
    furth of Scotland, liability to prosecution,
      10, 674
    spouse, incrimination of, **10**, 673
    statutory restrictions, **10**, 672
  public policy, for reasons of, **10**, 687–689
    classes of documents, **10**, 688
    law enforcement agencies, **10**, 689
procedural aspects, **4**, 1004
professional practices, **10**, 512
proof, *see* PROOF
public local inquiry, at, **5**, 70
questions—
  double, **10**, 550
    objections to, **10**, 567
  hypothetical, **10**, 550, 567
  leading, **10**, 550
    cross-examination, **10**, 553
    examination-in-chief, **10**, 552
    objections to, **10**, 567
    re-examination, **10**, 558
  objectionable, **10**, 550, 567
  through the court, **10**, 559
  usurping function of court, **10**, 550
    objections to, **10**, 567
  witness bound to answer, **10**, 508, 550
rape cases, **10**, 502
  See also RAPE

Evidence—continued
re-examination, see WITNESS, EXAMINATION IN COURT
real—
  animate objects, **10**, 620
  best evidence rule, **10**, 617
  definition, **10**, 614
  destroyed, **10**, 616
  examination by jury, **10**, 619
  generally, **10**, 522
  item typical example of class, **10**, 617
  judge and jury may leave court to view, **10**, 618
  meaning, **10**, 503
  oral evidence in lieu, **10**, 616, 617
  perception of, **10**, 615
  photographs in lieu, **10**, 617
  plan or model in lieu, **10**, 617
  presentation of, **10**, 614, 615
  production of, **10**, 614, 616
  reasonable practicability to produce, **10**, 616
reasonable tolerability, **14**, 2042
recall of witnesses—
  civil cases, **10**, 560
  criminal cases, **10**, 563
recording, **17**, 1161
registration, **14**, 1957
relationship to party, **10**, 502
relevancy—
  civil procedure, **17**, 1143
  crime for which conviction not sought, evidence of, **10**, 627
  criminal procedure, **17**, 567
  definition, **10**, 623
  facts relevant to admissibility of evidence, **10**, 623
  facts relevant to facts in issue, **10**, 623
  generally, **10**, 504, 505, 622
  intention, **10**, 624
  knowledge, **10**, 624
  motive, **10**, 624
  opportunity, **10**, 624
  sheriff court—
    commission, on, **17**, 1154–1156
    debate, on, see debate *above*
  similar facts, evidence of—
    civil cases, **10**, 625
    criminal cases, **10**, 626
reliability of witness, cross-examination as to, **10**, 554
remoteness, **10**, 505
replication, in—
  civil cases, **10**, 562
  criminal cases, **10**, 565; **17**, 761
res gestae, statements forming part of, **10**, 710
res judicata, **10**, 521
right to know, **1**, 276
rules, observation of, **1**, 280
scientific facts, **10**, 512
scope of law—
  admissibility, **10**, 505
  competency, **10**, 506
  definition, **10**, 501
  development of law, **10**, 501, 502

Evidence—continued
scope of law—*continued*
  exclusion of evidence—
    irrebuttable presumptions, **10**, 520
    judicial admissions, **10**, 513–519
    judicial knowledge, **10**, 510–513
    means of exclusion, **10**, 509
    res judicata, **10**, 521
    judicial discretion, **10**, 508
    relevance, **10**, 504
    weight of evidence, **10**, 507
secondary, **10**, 778
self-incriminating statements, **10**, 502
sexual offences, **10**, 502
  Scottish Law Commission recommendation, **22**, 668
sheriff court—
  commission, on, **17**, 1154–1156
  debate, on, see debate *above*
similar facts, of—
  civil cases, **10**, 625
  criminal cases, **10**, 626
social worker, by—
  decision relating to child, **22**, 18
  probation order, breach, **22**, 34
solemn trial procedure, **17**, 556
spouse—
  spouse of party to action as witness, see SPOUSE
  spouses, communications between, see SPOUSE
standard of proof, **10**, 746
  child, offence committed by, **10**, 761
  civil cases, **10**, 760, 761
  criminal cases, **10**, 759, 761
  fatal accident inquiries, **10**, 761
  generally, **10**, 758
state of mind, of, **10**, 624
subornation of perjury, see PERJURY (subornation)
sufficiency of, **10**, 746
  averment and proof, correspondence between, **10**, 764, 765
  corroboration, **10**, 766–775
  criteria of, **10**, 763
  weight of evidence compared, **10**, 762
suppression, **7**, 521
tape recordings, **10**, 572, 607
threatening witness, **7**, 523
to lie *in retentis*, **17**, 1153
trade and business records, **10**, 502, 603, 605, 608
tribunals, whether bound by rules of, **10**, 501*n*
uncorroborated, in action for damages for personal injury, **10**, 502
unfair, **10**, 505
unlawfully intercepting communications, exclusion of evidence, **16**, 1965
unlawfully obtained, **12**, 60
vote, of, **15**, 1359
weight of, **10**, 746
  appeal, questions of weight on, **10**, 781
  circumstantial evidence, **10**, 777
  coherence of evidence, **10**, 780
  direct evidence, **10**, 777
  generally, **10**, 776
  meaning, **10**, 507
  primary, **10**, 778

Evidence—*continued*
weight of—*continued*
    secondary, **10**, 778
    sufficiency of evidence compared, **10**, 762
    witnesses, reliability and credibility of, **10**, 779
weights and measures, **10**, 512
will, interpretation in, **25**, 829
witness, *see* WITNESS
words, meaning of, **10**, 512
written statement—
    oral evidence, in lieu of, **10**, 569–571
    See also WRITTEN STATEMENT
Evil intent
assault, **7**, 231, 234, 244
Ex lege
trusts arising, **24**, 115
Ex turpi causa non oritur actio
delict, defence to, **15**, 411
Excambion
contract of, **20**, 921
real warrandice, **18**, 701*n*
trustees' power of, **24**, 202
Exchange
contract of—
    breach of, remedies, **20**, 901
    contract of sale distinguished, **20**, 801, 899
    ownership, transfer of, **20**, 900
    performance of, **20**, 901
    reform, proposals for, **20**, 902
    risk, transfer of, **20**, 900
control, cross-border leasing, **14**, 1096
money consideration, lack of, **14**, 1802
money as medium of, **14**, 1803, 1804
Exchequer
aggregate grant, **14**, 830
causes, jurisdiction in, **6**, 924, 1060
decrees, sheriff's duties in respect of, **6**, 1046
dues payable to Court of the Lord Lyon, **6**, 1014
flood prevention scheme, grant for, **14**, 468
procurator fiscal and, **13**, 1436
Exchequer bill
negotiable instrument, as, **4**, 103
Exchequer Court
Articles of Union, **6**, 814
assimilation by Court of Session, **6**, 814, 917
Barons of the Exchequer, **6**, 917
House of Lords appellate jurisdiction, **6**, 814
House of Lords jurisdiction over, **6**, 810
independent existence, **6**, 909
jurisdiction, **6**, 917
origins, **6**, 917
Excisable liquor
See ALCOHOLIC LIQUOR
Excise dealer, registered
regulation, **7**, 1244
Excise duty
alcohol and alcoholic beverages, *see* ALCOHOLIC
    LIQUOR
aviation gasoline, **7**, 1067
avoidance, attempted, **7**, 1151
betting duties, **7**, 1080–1082
bingo duty, **7**, 1080, 1084
cancellation, **7**, 1145

Excise duty—*continued*
collection—
    Commissioners of Customs and Excise, *see*
        COMMISSIONERS OF CUSTOMS AND EXCISE
    customs officer, *see* CUSTOMS OFFICER
    generally, **7**, 1204, 1210
Commissioners of Customs and Excise, *see*
    COMMISSIONERS OF CUSTOMS AND EXCISE
correction, **7**, 1145
customs control, processing under, **7**, 1186
deferment arrangement, **7**, 1055
deferred payments, **7**, 1088
    security for deferred duty, **7**, 1088
destination, **7**, 1051
destroyed goods, repayment on, **7**, 1093
distance selling arrangement, **7**, 1054, 1054*n*
drawback—
    calculation, **7**, 1094
    claims for, **7**, 1095
    generally, **7**, 1094, 1097
    hydrocarbon oil, **7**, 1070
    inward processing procedure, **7**, 1094, 1182,
        1185
    offences in relation to, **7**, 1098, 1162
duty suspension arrangements, **7**, 1053, 1056,
    1057, 1058
European Union law—
    alcohol and alcoholic beverages, **7**, 1035, 1036
    cigarettes, **7**, 1036
    Community Customs Code, *see* COMMUNITY
        CUSTOMS CODE
    Completing the Internal Market (1985), **7**, 1034
    EU Treaty, art 95, taxation and, **7**, 1032
    excise duty point—
        Community excise goods, **7**, 1053
        exceptions to, **7**, 1053
        introduction, **7**, 1052
        meaning, **7**, 1052*n*, 1053
        time to pay duty, **7**, 1055
    General Arrangements, **7**, 1035
    harmonisation of excise duty structure, **7**, 1036
    harmonisation of indirect taxes, proposals for,
        7, 1033, 1034
    interaction with United Kingdom law, **7**, 1003
    manufactured tobacco, **7**, 1035, 1036
    mineral oils, **7**, 1035, 1036
    outward processing, **7**, 1188–1191
    Single Market, **7**, 1052, 1152
evasion, **7**, 1259
    civil penalties, **7**, 1260
    preparatory steps for, taking, **7**, 1263
excise licence duty, generally, **7**, 1001
export of goods subject to, **7**, 1422
free zones, *see* FREE ZONE
game licence, **7**, 1087
gaming licence duty, **7**, 1080, 1083
gaming machines, **7**, 1080, 1085
General Agreement on Tariffs and Trade
    (GATT), *see* GENERAL AGREEMENT ON TARIFFS
    AND TRADE
general betting duty, **7**, 1080, 1081
hydrocarbon oil—
    deferred payments, **7**, 1088
    drawback, **7**, 1070

Excise duty—*continued*
hydrocarbon oil—*continued*
    duty-free oil, **7**, 1068
    Hydrocarbon Oil Duties Act (1979), **7**, 1067
    meaning, **7**, 1067*n*
    mixed oils, **7**, 1067
    rebates and reliefs of duty, **7**, 1069
    regulations, power to make, **7**, 1071
  importer, liability, **7**, 1054
  legal proceedings and penalties, *see* LEGAL
    PROCEEDINGS AND PENALTIES
  licence duty, **7**, 1001
  lottery duty, **7**, 1080, 1086
  manufactured composite articles, **7**, 1059
  meaning, **7**, 1001, 1001*n*
  mechanically propelled vehicles—
    alteration of vehicle or use, **7**, 1076
    exemptions from duty, **7**, 1073
    false or misleading declaration in relation to, **7**, 1077
    forgery or fraudulent alteration of licence, **7**, 1077
    generally, **7**, 1073
    offences, generally, **7**, 1077
    proceedings in relation to excise duty, **7**, 1078
    rates, **7**, 1073
    temporary licence, **7**, 1074
    trade licence, **7**, 1074
    unexpired period, rebate on, **7**, 1074
    using or keeping vehicle without licence, **7**, 1075
    vehicle excise licence, **7**, 1074
  National Lottery, **7**, 1080, 1086
  occasional importer, **7**, 1053, 1056, 1058
  offences—
    corporate body, committed by, **7**, 1266
    counterfeiting documents, **7**, 1258
    customs officer, removal, **7**, 1265
    evasion—
      fraudulent, **7**, 1259
      preparatory steps for, taking, **7**, 1263
    generally, **7**, 1256, 1266
    handling goods subject to unpaid duty, **7**, 1262
    outlying provisions of Acts, under, **7**, 1266, 1266*n*
    scales, use of false or unjust, **7**, 1264
    untrue declaration, **7**, 1257
  payment, procedure, **7**, 1148
  point, *see* EXCISE DUTY POINT
  pool betting, **7**, 1080, 1082
  postponed payment, **7**, 1143
  re-imported goods, relief on, **7**, 1107
  REDS, liability, **7**, 1054, 1056, 1057
  reliefs—
    antiques, **7**, 1120
    cross-border shopping, **7**, 1111, 1111*n*
    diplomats, entitlement to, **7**, 1117
    false statement in application for, **7**, 1122
    forfeiture of goods subject to, **7**, 1121
    Her Majesty's ships, goods supplied to, **7**, 1115
    hydrocarbon oil, **7**, 1069
    inherited property, **7**, 1113, 1116

Excise duty—*continued*
reliefs—*continued*
  personal—
    permanently imported goods, **7**, 1113
    traveller from Community member state, **7**, 1111
    traveller from outwith European Union, **7**, 1112
    prizes and honours awarded abroad, **7**, 1120
    re-imported goods, **7**, 1107
    temporary importation, **7**, 1187
    testing, goods imported for, **7**, 1114
    trade samples, **7**, 1119
    United Kingdom law, **7**, 1104, 1107
    visiting forces, for, **7**, 1117
  repayment on returned or destroyed goods, **7**, 1093
  restrictions on movement of excise goods, **7**, 1056
  returned goods, repayment on, **7**, 1093
  revenue trader, *see* REVENUE TRADER
  Single Market, United Kingdom legislation and, **7**, 1052, 1152
  suspension, inward processing procedure, **7**, 1182
  time to pay, **7**, 1055
  tobacco, manufactured—
    European Union law, **7**, 1035, 1036
    Tobacco Products Duty Act (1979), **7**, 1072
  United Kingdom legislation 1002—
    1060*ff*
    interaction with European Union legislation, **7**, 1003, 1052
  VAT zero-rating on goods subject to, **7**, 1443
  warehousekeeper, liability, **7**, 1054
Excise duty point
  Community excise goods, **7**, 1053
  duty suspension arrangements, **7**, 1053
  introduction, **7**, 1052
  meaning, **7**, 1052*n*, 1053
  non-Community goods, **7**, 1053
  occasional importer, goods consigned to, **7**, 1053
  REDS, goods consigned to, **7**, 1053
  time to pay duty, **7**, 1055
Excise licence
  death of holder, **7**, 1245
  form and content, **7**, 1245
  generally, **7**, 1245
  issue, **7**, 1245
  partners in trade, **7**, 1245
  payment for, **7**, 1245
  premises, where change of, **7**, 1245
  regulation, **7**, 1245
  renewal, **7**, 1245
  requirement for, **7**, 1245
  trade, **7**, 1245
  transfer, **7**, 1245
  See also MOTOR VEHICLE
Excise shipper, registered
  regulation, **7**, 1244
Exclusion (immigration control)
  meaning, **12**, 147
Exclusion order
  breach of, **12**, 134
  civil legal aid, urgency, situation of, **13**, 1048
  cohabitees, **10**, 1005

Exclusion order—*continued*
land or premises, management rules of persistently contravened, **14**, 30
matrimonial home, **17**, 1122, 1241
occupancy rights, **10**, 863–865
prevention of terrorism powers, **12**, 107, 117, 122, 134
refusal of leave to enter, **12**, 171
representations against, **12**, 134
revocation, **12**, 134
unreasonable behaviour, **10**, 902
violence, protection from, **10**, 863, 864

Exclusive economic zone
atribution of rights, resolution of conflicts as to, **21**, 39
customary law, **21**, 4
evolution of concept, **21**, 38
exclusive fishery zone, **11**, 80, 81, 92, 107, 116
fisheries, **11**, 107, 116
high seas, and, **11**, 86
international legal regime, **21**, 4
jurisdiction—
    conflicts, resolution, **21**, 39
    Convention Against Illicit Traffic in Narcotic Drugs and Psychotropic Substances, **21**, 42
    EC Declaration, **21**, 40
legal status, **21**, 18
navigation, freedom of, **21**, 39
overflight, right of, **21**, 39
submarine cables and pipelines, rights as to, **21**, 39
third states, rights and duties, **21**, 39
UK claim, **21**, 38
UK position, **21**, 40

Excommunication
Roman Catholic Church, **3**, 1658

Executive
Cabinet as principal organ of, **5**, 306
central government, *see* CENTRAL GOVERNMENT
civil defence, *see* civil defence
elective dictatorship, use of, **5**, 355
emergency powers, *see* EMERGENCY POWERS
Law Officers of Crown, *see* LAW OFFICERS OF CROWN
lieutenancy, *see* lieutenancy
ministers of Crown, *see* MINISTERS OF CROWN
public expenditure, *see* PUBLIC EXPENDITURE
separation of powers, **5**, 341, 623

Executor
acceptance by, **25**, 637
annuity, directions to buy, **25**, 834, 837
appointment of—
    executor dative, **25**, 1044–1050
    executor nominate, **25**, 1040–1043
    executor-creditor, **25**, 1051–1058
    generally, **25**, 1039
bill of exchange, party to, **4**, 129, 130
building society as, **3**, 372, 376
body, entitlement to arrange disposal of, **3**, 503, 506
capital gains realised by, **19**, 1636
    See also CAPITAL GAINS TAX
confirmation of executors, judicial conveyance, as, **18**, 664
damages claimed by, **15**, 934
defamation, executor as pursuer, **15**, 478

Executor—*continued*
delict—
    defender, as, **15**, 231
    title and interest to sue, **15**, 231
discharge of, **19**, 1647; **25**, 1027
duties and functions—
    adopted person, **25**, 1106
    distribution, **24**, 3; **25**, 1105
    fiduciary duty, **24**, 169, 172
    generally, **24**, 169; **25**, 1103
    illegitimate person, **25**, 1106
    meeting liabilities, **25**, 1104
    trustees, application of principles applying to, **25**, 1107
eadem persona cum defuncto, as, **24**, 169
embezzlement by, **7**, 352
executor-creditor—
    administrative appointment, as, **25**, 1047
    appointment, **25**, 1051–1058
        generally, **25**, 1044–1050
        order of preference, **25**, 1050
    competition for office of, **25**, 1049
    confirmation as—
        arrestment and, **8**, 356
        assets furth of Scotland, **8**, 355
        competition, **8**, 356
        domicile of defunct, **8**, 351
        eiking the excess, **8**, 354
        generally, **8**, 101
        grounds, **8**, 352
        immoveables, **8**, 355
        judicial right in security, confirmation as, **8**, 355
        jurisdiction, **8**, 351
        moveables, **8**, 355
        nature of, **8**, 350
        next of kin, creditor of, **8**, 358
        notice in *Edinburgh Gazette*, **8**, 353
        ordinary executor as creditor, **8**, 359
        overvaluation by creditor, **8**, 354
        partial confirmation, **8**, 354
        power of sale, **8**, 355
        procedure, **8**, 353
        property law aspects, **8**, 355
        sequestration—
            advantages over, **8**, 350
            effect, **8**, 357
        two executor-creditors confirmed, **8**, 355, 356
        undervaluation by creditor, **8**, 354
        valuation, **8**, 354
        whether executor-creditor trustee, **8**, 355
    creditor, as, **25**, 1056
    debts—
        diligence, forming basis of, **25**, 1054
        next of kin, of, **25**, 1058
        preference of, **25**, 1057
    diligence—
        debts which form basis of, **25**, 1054
        exclusion of, **25**, 1053
        generally, **24**, 169; **25**, 1044, 1051
        next of kin, common law concept, **25**, 1045
        partial confirmation, power to expede, **25**, 1052
        ranking of creditors, **25**, 1055

Executor—*continued*
executor-creditor—*continued*
  surviving spouse, **25**, 1046
  trustee, as, **24**, 128
executor dative—
  caution—
    regulations, generally, **3**, 995
    requirement for, **3**, 995
  removings, action of, **13**, 497
executor nominate—
  appointment—
    assumed, **25**, 1042
    constructive, **25**, 1042
    express, **25**, 1041
    generally, **25**, 1040
    implied, **25**, 1041
  generally, **24**, 2, 165; **25**, 1040
  order of preference, **25**, 1043
  removings, action of, **13**, 497
expenses, **25**, 979
gains realised by—
  capital gains, **19**, 1636
  exemptions, **25**, 995
  liability for tax, **25**, 994
  reliefs, **25**, 995
  See also CAPITAL GAINS TAX
history of office, **24**, 3
income tax, liability for, **25**, 963
inheritance tax, *see* INHERITANCE TAX
legal rights, possibility of claiming, intimation of, **25**, 774
lessee, as, **13**, 187
lessor, as, **13**, 166
liability, **19**, 1645
obligation, death of party to, **15**, 7
personal injury, as pursuer in action relating to, **16**, 2150, 2168
  judicial discretion to override time limits, **16**, 2177
  nature of rights, **16**, 2165
  product liability defect, case arising from, **16**, 2192, 2195
powers, privileges and immunities, **24**, 169
public trusts, **24**, 89
reference to arbitration by, **2**, 408
surviving spouse's right to be appointed as, **25**, 694
tax liability, **19**, 1645
title of, proprietorial nature, **24**, 169
trustee, as, **24**, 2, 165
trustee compared, **24**, 3, 169
vesting in—
  entailed property, **25**, 1109
  special destination, **25**, 1109
  title, protection of persons acquiring, **25**, 1110
  whole estate, **25**, 1108
Executory contract
not contract of deposit, **8**, 8
Executry funds
interest on, **12**, 1031
Executry petition
expenses, **17**, 1191
Executry practitioner
application for registration, **13**, 1233
disclosure of documents, **13**, 1238

Executry practitioner—*continued*
generally, **13**, 1233
inadequate professional service, providing, **13**, 1236
intervention powers of Conveyancing and Executry Services Board, **13**, 1237
offences, **13**, 1234
professional misconduct, **13**, 1236
register of, **13**, 1232, 1233
unqualified person pretending to be, **13**, 1234
Executry services
executry practitioner, *see* EXECUTRY PRACTITIONER
meaning, **13**, 1233*n*
recognised financial institution, by, **13**, 1235
Scottish Conveyancing and Executry Services Board—
  appointments to, **13**, 1224
  constitution, **13**, 1224
  functions, **13**, 1225
  powers, **13**, 1225
    intervention, of, **13**, 1237
  register of executry practitioners, **13**, 1232
  regulatory responsibilities—
    disclosure of documents, **13**, 1238
    inadequate professional services, **13**, 1236
    professional misconduct, **13**, 1236
unqualified person offering, **13**, 1234
Exemption clause
contract, in, **15**, 702, 718
Exhibit
meaning, **9**, 1030
Exhibitions
community aspects, **4**, 1390
exempted, **9**, 1023
goods for display or use at, temporary importation, **7**, 1187
Exhibitor
meaning, **9**, 1030
Exile
arbitrary, freedom from, **12**, 4*n*
Expectant and nursing mothers
care of, **11**, 1478
Explicit lifetime discharge
See LEGAL RIGHTS
Explosives
accidents—
  inquiries and investigations, **10**, 1624
  notification of, **10**, 1623
administration—
  local, **10**, 1622
  national, **10**, 1621
ammunition, *see* AMMUNITION
amount to be kept in store or registered premises, **10**, 1617
armed forces, for use of, exemptions to regulations, **10**, 1589
Behring Sea Award Act 1894 ..., **11**, 217
care of, **14**, 1652
carriage by rail, **19**, 1015
cartridges, *see* CARTRIDGES
causing explosion likely to endanger life or injure property, **10**, 1565
classification, **10**, 1588
conveyance of, **6**, 1617; **10**, 1589, 1589*n*, 1595 **14**, 1651

Explosives—*continued*
dangerous fireworks, **10**, 1634
endangering life or injuring property, **10**, 1565, 1629
exemptions from regulations, **10**, 1589
Explosive Substances Act (1883)—
　proceedings under, **10**, 1636
Explosives Act (1875)—
　proceedings under, **10**, 1635
export, **7**, 1196
factories and magazines—
　accidental destruction, **10**, 1623
　application of gunpowder provisions to other explosives, **10**, 1617
　dangerous acts, **10**, 1627
　licensing, **10**, 1592, 1593
　　exemptions, **10**, 1620
　trespass, **10**, 1626
fire certificate for storage premises, **10**, 1457, 1467
fireworks, *see* FIREWORKS
fishing with, **11**, 12, 21
　trout fishing, **11**, 54
gunpowder, *see* GUNPOWDER
gunpowder provisions, application to other explosives, **10**, 1617
importation, **10**, 1617
labelling, **10**, 1617
legal proceedings, **10**, 1635, 1636
legislation, generally, **10**, 1585
licensing, **14**, 520
making or possessing, **7**, 413
making under suspicious circumstances, **10**, 1565
malicious mischief caused by, **7**, 413
manufacture, licensing exemptions, **10**, 1620
meaning, **7**, 413; **10**, 1586, 1587
mines or quarries, for use in, **10**, 1620
offences in relation to—
　arrest without warrant, powers of, **10**, 1631
　dangerous acts, **10**, 1627
　enforcement, **10**, 1631–1634
　forfeiture, powers of, **10**, 1633
　generally, **10**, 1625, 1628
　penalties under health and safety regulations, **10**, 1630
　search, powers of, **10**, 1632
　trespass, **10**, 1626
packaging, **10**, 1617
possessing under suspicious circumstances, **10**, 1565
postal packet, enclosed in, **16**, 1909
prescribed, **10**, 1620
private use, maximum amount to be kept for, **10**, 1617
refuse, receptical or place appropriated for, explosives deposited in, **10**, 1628
refuse collector or dustman, handing explosives to, **10**, 1628
registered premises—
　application of gunpowder provisions to other explosives, **10**, 1617
　licensing exemptions, **10**, 1620
rules or documents displayed in pursuance of Explosives Act 1875 ..., **10**, 1595, 1628
safety fuses, special powers in relation to, **10**, 1590

Explosives—*continued*
sale—
　exposure for, **10**, 1617
　packaging and labelling, **10**, 1605, 1617
　person under age of sixteen, to, **3**, 1223
　records of, **10**, 1607
shell, prohibited ammunition, as, **10**, 1517
sheriff court jurisdiction, **6**, 1102
special powers as to, **10**, 1590
specially dangerous, **10**, 1619
statutory control, **14**, 1651
storage, **14**, 1651
stores—
　application of gunpowder provisions to other explosives, **10**, 1617
　dangerous acts, **10**, 1627
　licensing exemptions, **10**, 1620
　trespass, **10**, 1627
use, **14**, 1652
visiting forces, for use of, exemptions to regulations, **10**, 1589
wild birds or animals taken or killed with, **11**, 880, 884
Export
agreement—
　Director General of Fair Trading, particulars to, **4**, 1180
　exemption, **4**, 1161, 1176
　meaning, **4**, 1161
animal products, **7**, 1194
animals, **7**, 1201
　endangered species, **7**, 1197
　live, **7**, 1194
　See also animals
antiques, **7**, 1194
atomic and nuclear products, **7**, 1194
　export licence relating to, **9**, 924
ban, nature of, **4**, 1379
chemical equipment, **7**, 1194
controlled drugs, **14**, 1236
cultural goods, **7**, 1200
customs duty, charge to, generally, **7**, 1001, 1041
drug, prescribed, **7**, 1195
EEC mark, **6**, 262
electrical equipment, **7**, 1194
European Union export restrictions, **7**, 1030, 1031
　quantitative, **7**, 1020
explosives, **7**, 1196
Export of Goods (Control) Order (1994), **7**, 1194
export refund—
　advance fixing, **1**, 921
　complaints from trading partners on, **1**, 921
　differential, **1**, 921
　goatmeat, on, **1**, 936
　milk products, for, **1**, 923
　pigmeat, poultry and eggs, on, **1**, 938
　sheepmeat, on, **1**, 936
　world and Community prices, difference between, **1**, 914
firearms, of, **7**, 1194; **10**, 1581
firearms acquired for, firearms certificate exemption, **10**, 1547
foodstuffs, **7**, 1201

Export—*continued*
free zones, *see* FREE ZONE
goods to be exported outwith European Union,
    work carried out on, **7**, 1451
goods in transit, **7**, 1194
house, VAT zero-rating, **7**, 1438
licence, **7**, 1194, 1202
    cultural goods, requirement for, **7**, 1200
    validity, **7**, 1200
'local grab' measures, **7**, 1020
meat, inspection of, **11**, 417
military equipment, **7**, 1194
monopoly situation in relation to—
    behavioural monopoly, **4**, 1226
    generally, **4**, 1224
    structural monopoly, **4**, 1225
offence, **14**, 1843
poison, **14**, 1215
postal packet, **7**, 1198
procedure, *see* EXPORT PROCEDURE
prohibited goods, generally, **7**, 1194
re-exportation, **7**, 1163, 1165
    examination of goods entered for, **7**, 1214
    inward processing procedure, **7**, 1182
    temporary importation, **7**, 1187
services arranging, VAT treatment, **7**, 1451
ship's stores, **7**, 1194, 1436
slaughterhouses, **11**, 510, 511
VAT, charge to, conditional relief, **7**, 1315
VAT zero-rating, **7**, 1457
    another Community member state, goods
        removed to, **7**, 1442–1444
    excise duty, goods subject to, **7**, 1443
    export house, supplies to, **7**, 1438
    freight containers, **7**, 1437
    motor vehicles, **7**, 1441, 1444
    overseas person, supplies to, **7**, 1439
    person departing from Community member
        states, supplies to, **7**, 1440, 1441
    person taxable in another Community member
        state, supplies to, **7**, 1442
    place outwith European Union, export to, **7**,
        1434–1441
    ship, aircraft or hovercraft, stores for, **7**, 1436
    supplier, export by, **7**, 1435
weights and measures regulations, **6**, 184
Export procedure
air, goods exported by, **7**, 1155
aircraft, clearance outwards, **7**, 1161
clearance outwards, **7**, 1161
Commissioners of Customs and Excise, powers,
    7, 1155
community customs document, **7**, 1156
Community goods, **7**, 1154
Community transit goods, meaning, **7**, 1155*n*
Customs and Excise Management Act (1979), **7**,
    1155
customs office of export, **7**, 1154
date, export, **7**, 1156
determination of levy, **7**, 1156
documentation, **7**, 1154, 1155, 1156
dutiable goods, **7**, 1155
entry outwards, **7**, 1155, 1156
    cancellation, **7**, 1159

Export procedure—*continued*
entry outwards—*continued*
    corrected, **7**, 1158
    exportation without, **7**, 1157
    failure to export following, **7**, 1159
    incomplete, **7**, 1158
    ships, **7**, 1160
European Union law—
    Community customs document, **7**, 1156
    Community goods, **7**, 1154
    customs office of export, **7**, 1154
    documentation, **7**, 1154
    export declaration, **7**, 1154
    exporter, who is considered to be, **7**, 1154
    generally, **7**, 1153
    non-Community goods, **7**, 1154, 1163
    re-exportation, **7**, 1153, 1154, 1163
    simplified declaration procedure, **7**, 1154
    Single Administrative Document (SAD), **7**,
        1154
export declaration, **7**, 1154
exporter, who is considered to be, **7**, 1154
failure to export, **7**, 1159
free zone, exportation from, **7**, 1165
land, goods exported by, **7**, 1155
loading etc, regulations as to, **7**, 1155
non-Community goods, **7**, 1154, 1163
offences, **7**, 1162
passenger embarkation, regulations as to, **7**, 1155
pipe-line, goods exported by, **7**, 1155
re-exportation, **7**, 1153, 1154, 1163, 1165
    examination of goods entered for, **7**, 1214
    inward processing procedure, **7**, 1182
    temporary importation, **7**, 1187
restricted goods, **7**, 1155
sea, goods exported by, **7**, 1155
ship—
    clearance outwards, **7**, 1161
    outward entry, **7**, 1160
Single Administrative Document (SAD), **7**, 1154
Single Market, effect of completion, **7**, 1152
time of export, determination, **7**, 1155
unloading, unauthorised, **7**, 1162
Express revocation
See WILL
Express terms
contract, in, *see* CONTRACT (terms)
Express trust
private trust, as, **24**, 16
Expressio unius exclusio alterius
meaning, **12**, 1165
Expression, freedom of
European Convention on Human Rights, **12**, 6,
    73, 74
'prescribed by law', meaning, **12**, 79
restrictions on, **12**, 78–84
Universal Declaration of Human Rights, **12**, 4*n*
Expulsion clause
partnership agreement, in, **16**, 1061
External public policy rule
exceptions to choice of law rules, **17**, 172
formulation of, **17**, 174
generally, **17**, 168
legality of contract, **17**, 263

External public policy rule—*continued*
penal rule and, **17**, 178
purpose of, **17**, 169
relative nature of test, **17**, 171
transfer of property *inter vivos*, **17**, 324
See also PRIVATE INTERNATIONAL LAW

Extortion
analogous statutory offences—
    harassment, **7**, 403
    maritime offences, **7**, 404
    tenancy, in relation to, **7**, 403
    unsolicited goods and services, **7**, 402
attempted, **7**, 396
blackmail, **7**, 396
defences, **7**, 401
definition, **7**, 396
firearm or imitation firearm possessed during, **10**, 1565
protection racket, **7**, 396
robbery distinguished, **7**, 397
tallymen, **7**, 396
threat, as element of—
    generally, **7**, 396, 397, 398
    kind of threat necessary, **7**, 399
wheel-clamping, **7**, 400

Extortionate credit transaction
court order—
    circumstances in which made, **4**, 892
    content of, **4**, 894
extortionate, meaning, **4**, 893

Extra commercium
right to recover property, **16**, 2126
subjects, **24**, 511

Extradition
ad hoc, **12**, 517, 524, 577
aircraft, conduct committed in, **12**, 515
alternatives to—
    deterritorialisation of criminal jurisdiction, **12**, 503
    terrorism, **12**, 503
    trial *in forum deprehensionis*, **12**, 505
    trial *in absentia*, **12**, 505
arrangements, **12**, 511
    general, **12**, 510, 511
    special, **12**, 510, 511
capital punishment, **12**, 26
colony, conduct committed in, **12**, 515
Commonwealth country, to—
    ad hoc extradition, **12**, 524
    authentication of documents, **12**, 566
    designated Commonwealth countries and colonies, **12**, 520, 566
    extradition crime, definition, **12**, 522
    international law, **12**, 518
    liability for, **12**, 521
    municipal law, **12**, 519
    restrictions on, **12**, 523
    review, **12**, 571
    Secretary of State's order to surrender or return, **12**, 575
contumacy, **12**, 536, 562
    conviction *in absentia*, **12**, 536, 562
    Republic of Ireland, in relation to, **12**, 537

Extradition—*continued*
contumacy—*continued*
    injustice in conviction, **12**, 536
    Republic of Ireland, in relation to, **12**, 537
Convention for the Prevention and Punishment of the Crime of Genocide, **12**, 508
Convention on the Physical Protection of Nuclear Material, **12**, 508
definition, **12**, 501
dependency, conduct committed in, **12**, 515
detention prior to, **12**, 37
double-punishability, **12**, 515, 548
European Convention on, **12**, 509, 517
European Convention on the Suppression of Terrorism, **12**, 508, 532
extradition crime—
    definition by list method, **12**, 513
    double-punishability, **12**, 515, 548
foreign state—
    from, ad hoc, **12**, 577
    meaning, **12**, 512
    to—
        1870 procedure, **12**, 514, 517, 532
            restictions on return to foreign state, **12**, 516, 532
        1989 procedure, **12**, 515, 516, 517, 532
        ad hoc, **12**, 517
        arrangement, **12**, 517
        England, conduct committed in, where conduct offence in Scotland but not in England, **12**, 515*n*
        extra-territorial offences, **12**, 515
        international law, **12**, 506
        irrespective of where offence took place, **12**, 515
        opportunities to challenge surrender, **12**, 516
        political offences, **12**, 531
        United Kingdom, priority of unrelated crimes committed in, **12**, 516
fugitive criminals, **12**, 513
genocide, **12**, 532
habeas corpus, application for writ of, **12**, 562, 568, 575
Hague Convention on Unlawful Seizure of Aircraft, **12**, 508
historical background, **12**, 502–504
hovercraft, conduct committed in, **12**, 515
in absentia trials, **12**, 505, 536, 537, 562
injustice in conviction, **12**, 536, 537
inordinate delay or abuse of process, **12**, 562
International Convention against the Taking of Hostages, **12**, 508, 532
International Convention for the Suppression of the White Slave Traffic, **12**, 508
international law, **12**, 503, 506
    See also INTERNATIONAL LAW
judicial review, **12**, 568–573
legislative authority, **12**, 511
list method, definition by, **12**, 513
military law, offences under, **12**, 516, 534
Montreal Convention for the Suppression of Unlawful Acts against the Safety of Civil Aviation, **12**, 508
municipal law, **12**, 504, 510

Extradition—*continued*
nationality, trials which may be prejudiced by, **12**, 516, 532, 534
New York Convention on Crimes against Internationally Protected Persons, **12**, 508
'own nationals' exemption, **12**, 549, 562
   meaning of 'own nationals', **12**, 549
persecuton, request made for purpose of, **12**, 516
political offences, **12**, 516
   1870 procedure, **12**, 532
   1989 procedure, **12**, 533
      variations under, **12**, 534
   general exemption, **12**, 531, 562
   Republic of Ireland, in relation to, **12**, 535
   terrorism, **12**, 532, 532*n*
political opinion, trials which may be prejudiced by, **12**, 516, 532, 534
previous acquittal or conviction, where, **12**, 516, 538
   Republic of Ireland, in relation to, **12**, 539
prima facie rule—
   1870 procedure, **12**, 545
   1989 procedure, **12**, 546
   Republic of Ireland, in relation to, **12**, 547
   traditional requirement, **12**, 544
purposes, **12**, 505
race, trials which may be prejudiced by, **12**, 516, 532, 534
religion, trials which may be prejudiced by, **12**, 516, 532, 534
Republic of Ireland, **12**, 510
   authority to proceed, **12**, 555
   contumancy, **12**, 537
   double punishability, **12**, 548
   extradition crime, **12**, 528
   from United Kingdom—
      authentication of documents, **12**, 567
      executing warrant, **12**, 561
      hearing and committal, **12**, 564
      order by Secretary of State, not applicable, **12**, 576
      provisional warrants, **12**, 558
      review, **12**, 572, 573
   international law, **12**, 525
   liability for, **12**, 527
   municipal law, **12**, 526
   'own nationals' exemption not applicable, **12**, 549
   political offence exemption, **12**, 535
   previous acquittal or conviction, **12**, 539
   prima facie rule, **12**, 547
   restrictions, **12**, 529
   speciality, **12**, 543
   to United Kingdom, **12**, 581, 582
restrictions on, **12**, 516
   contumacy, **12**, 536, 537
   double criminality, principle of, **12**, 548
   politcal offences, **12**, 531–535
   previous acquittal or conviction, where, **12**, 538, 539
   prima facie rule, **12**, 544–547
   race, religion, nationality or political opinion, trials which may be prejudiced by, **12**, 516, 532, 534
   speciality, **12**, 540–543

Extradition—*continued*
speciality, **12**, 516
   1870 procedure, **12**, 541
   1989 procedure, **12**, 542
   arrangement with, **12**, 541, 541*n*, 542
   Commonwealth countries, **12**, 543
   general rule, **12**, 540, 562
   Republic of Ireland, in relation to, **12**, 543
terrorism—
   deterritorialism of criminal jurisdiction, **12**, 503
tholed his assize, person claiming to have, **12**, 538, 562
to United Kingdom, **12**, 504, 530
Tokyo Convention on Offences Committed on Board Aircraft in Flight, **12**, 508
treaties—
   absence of, **12**, 517
   bilateral, **12**, 503, 531, 577
      expired or lapsed, **12**, 507
      states signatory to, **12**, 507
   expired or lapsed, **12**, 507
   multilateral, **12**, 503, 505, 508, 531, 577
United Kingdom, from, **12**, 504, 506–529
   authenticaton of documents—
      1870 procedure, **12**, 565
      1989 procedure, **12**, 566
      Republic of Ireland, in relation to, **12**, 567
   authority to proceed—
      1870 procedure, **12**, 553
      1989 procedure, **12**, 554
      Republic of Ireland, in relation to, **12**, 555
   burden of proof, **12**, 562–564
   committal, **12**, 562–564
   defences to, **12**, 562, 563
   evidence, production of, **12**, 562
   hearing and committal—
      1870 procedure, **12**, 562
      1989 procedure, **12**, 563
      Republic of Ireland, in relation to, **12**, 564
   informal requisition or request, **12**, 556–558
   inordinate delay or abuse of process, **12**, 562
   Order of the Secretary of State, **12**, 551
   'own nationals' exemption, **12**, 549
   provisional warrants—
      1870 procedure, **12**, 556
      1989 procedure, **12**, 557
      Republic of Ireland, in relation to, **12**, 558
   requisition—
      1870 procedure, **12**, 550
      1989 procedure, **12**, 550
   review—
      1870 procedure, **12**, 568, 569
      1989 procedure, **12**, 570, 571
      Republic of Ireland, in relation to, **12**, 572, 573
   Secretary of State's order to surrender or return—
      1870 procedure, **12**, 574
      1989 procedure, **12**, 575
      Republic of Ireland, not applicable to, **12**, 576
   warrants—
      executing—
         1870 procedure, **12**, 559
         1989 procedure, **12**, 560
         Republic of Ireland, in relation to, **12**, 561

Extradition—*continued*
United Kingdom, from—*continued*
  warrants—*continued*
    production of, **12**, 562
    provisional, **12**, 556–558
United Kingdom, to, **12**, 530
  1870 procedure, **12**, 577
    priority of unrelated crimes committed in, **12**, 516
  1989 procedure, **12**, 577
  Commonwealth countries, from, **12**, 579, 580

Extradition—*continued*
United Kingdom, to—*continued*
  Republic of Ireland, from, **12**, 581, 582
  foreign states, from, **12**, 577, 578
vessel, conduct committed in, **12**, 515
Vienna Convention against Illicit Narcotic Drugs and Psychotropic Substances, **12**, 508
Extrajudicial interruption
prescription, of, **16**, 2124, 2125
Eyrislands
udal law, **24**, 311

F

Facility and circumvention
capacity of testator, **25**, 763
circumvention—
    fraud and, generally, **11**, 736
    meaning, **11**, 736
dishonest advantage, proof of, **11**, 736
doctrine of, application, **3**, 904
facility, meaning, **11**, 734
lesion, **11**, 735
mortis causa deed, plea raised in action for, **11**, 736
plea of, generally, **11**, 733
reduction on grounds of, **8**, 647; **13**, 44
remedies—
    reduction, **11**, 737
    rescission, **11**, 737
    restitutio in integrum impossible, where, **11**, 737
undue influence and, distinguished, **25**, 764
Factor
acquiescence by, whether binding principal, **16**, 1616
agency, ratification and, **1**, 629
attorney as, **13**, 183
damages, administration of award of, **11**, 1226
debarred from profiting by office, **24**, 7
eases, communication of, **24**, 7
judicial, *see* JUDICIAL FACTOR
lessor, as, **13**, 154, 167, 183
lien—
    exclusion, **20**, 89
    extent of, **20**, 86
    goods *in transitu*, **20**, 88
    meaning of factor in relation to, **20**, 87
    mercantile agent, meaning, **20**, 87
    nature of, **20**, 86
    possession, **20**, 88
    principal's bankruptcy, **20**, 88
    retention of goods after satisfaction received, **20**, 88
    right of, **13**, 95
    waiver, **20**, 89
loco tutoris—
    administration by, **11**, 1222, 1223
    appointment, **11**, 1215, 1216
    generally, **10**, 1069; **24**, 239, 269
    pupil of, attaining minority, **11**, 1216
    tutor dative, in place of, **11**, 1216
subscription by, **6**, 417
Factory
child employed in, **3**, 1257
cleansing of, **19**, 366n
fire certificates, **10**, 1454
health and safety at work legislation, **19**, 343
house used as, **19**, 336n
Inspectorate, objectives of, **9**, 487
lease, **13**, 197
    landlord's hypothec, **13**, 513
    See also LEASE-LEASING
local authority functions, **14**, 705
machinery, *see* PLANT AND MACHINERY

Factory—*continued*
meaning, **19**, 336n
occupational noise, **9**, 1290
public health nuisance, as, **19**, 336
safety legislation, justice of the peace court powers, **6**, 1159
valuation for rating—
    closure of factory, **24**, 508
    comparative principle, **24**, 529, 628
    contractors' principle, **24**, 628
    depression, reduction during, **24**, 628
    generally, **24**, 628
    industrial derating—
        apportionment, **24**, 648–651
        generally, **24**, 523, 629
        onus of proof, **24**, 631
        qualification of premises, **24**, 630
        road vehicles, housing and maintenance of, **24**, 637, 646, 647
        stables, **24**, 637, 646
        use as factory, **24**, 632–636
            excepted purposes, **24**, 637–645
    ironworks, **24**, 669
young person in, **9**, 72
Factual nuisance
legal nuisance distinguished from, **14**, 2004
Faculty of Advocates
accommodation, **13**, 1294, 1295
admission—
    application for, **13**, 1313
    changes in requirements, **13**, 1301
    control, **13**, 1249
    declaration of allegiance, **13**, 1314, 1314n
    Diploma in Legal Practice, **13**, 1301, 1307, 1308
        exemption, **13**, 1309
    England and Wales, barrister from, **13**, 1301, 1306, 1307, 1308, 1309, 1310, 1311
    entry money, **13**, 1250, 1301, 1313
    European Community, legal practitioner from, **13**, 1301, 1306, 1307, 1309, 1310, 1311
    examinations, **13**, 1256, 1301, 1306, 1307
        exemption, **13**, 1308
    generally, **13**, 1304, 1313
    historical background—
        character of intrants, **13**, 1263
        control over, **13**, 1249
        educational requirements, **13**, 1262
            BL and LLB degrees, **13**, 1282, 1308
        entry money, **13**, 1250, 1262
        examination of intrants, **13**, 1262, 1278, 1279
            attempted reforms, **13**, 1266
        idle year, **13**, 1280
        politics and ethics, **13**, 1264, 1269
        reform of regulations, **13**, 1279
    idle year, **13**, 1280, 1301
    legal scholarship, **13**, 1307
    LLB standard, **13**, 1301, 1308
    matriculation, **13**, 1306
        fee, **13**, 1306

Faculty of Advocates—*continued*
admission—*continued*
  Northern Ireland, barrister from, **13**, 1301,
    1306, 1307, 1308, 1309, 1310, 1311
  objections to, **13**, 1313
  professional training, **13**, 1301, 1310
    exemptions, **13**, 1311
  pupillage, **13**, 1310, 1312
    Admission Days, **13**, 1312
    Admission Intervals, **13**, 1312
    calculation of period, **13**, 1312
    exemption, **13**, 1311
    master—
      duties of, **13**, 1312
      master's report, **13**, 1312
      more than one during pupillage, **13**, 1312
      who may be, **13**, 1312
      racial discrimination, **13**, 1312
      sex discrimination, **13**, 1312
  Roll of Intrants, removal from, **13**, 1312
  scholarship fund, **13**, 1301
  solicitor, of, **13**, 1301
  thesis, abolition of requirement for, **13**, 1301
  women, **13**, 1296
advocates' clerks, **13**, 1292, 1320
advocates depute, criminal prosecution in
  Scotland, functions as to, **13**, 1430
Bills of Exchange Act 1882—
  representations for application to Scotland, **22**,
    641
Clerk, **13**, 1253, 1265, 1302
Collector and Clerk, **13**, 1265
constitution, draft, **13**, 1253
Consultative Council of the Bars and Law
  Societies of the European Community,
  affiliation with, **13**, 1302
corporate structure, **13**, 1254, 1302
curators, **13**, 1253
Dean, **13**, 1253, 1270, 1290, 1302
  baton of office, **13**, 1302
  Dean's Rulings, **13**, 1302
  development of office, **13**, 1269
  election, **13**, 1269
  functions, **13**, 1302
  precedence, **13**, 1271, 1302
  Standing Committee, **13**, 1302
decision taking, **13**, 1302
disciplinary powers—
  admonition, **13**, 1373
  advocate practising furth of Scotland, where,
    13, 1370
  advocate's duty, **13**, 1369, 1372
  censure, **13**, 1373
  conduct complaint, **13**, 1378
  Dean's powers, **13**, 1371–1377
  Dean's Rulings, **13**, 1302
  Disciplinary Rules, **13**, 1371
  Disciplinary Tribunal—
    constitution, **13**, 1375
    objection to admission, referral to, **13**, 1313
    penalties imposed by, **13**, 1377
    procedure, **13**, 1376
  generally, **13**, 1369
  handling complaint, **13**, 1378

Faculty of Advocates—*continued*
disciplinary powers—*continued*
  investigating committee, **13**, 1374
  penalties, **13**, 1373
    Disciplinary Tribunal, imposition by, **13**,
    1377
  removal of advocate from office, **13**, 1379
    interim, **13**, 1379
    publicity, **13**, 1379
  repayment of fees, order for, **13**, 1373
  reprimand, **13**, 1373
  Scottish Legal Services Ombudsman, **13**, 1378
  statutory control, **13**, 1378
  written or oral representation by advocate, **13**,
    1373
education—
  historical background—
    educational requirements, **13**, 1261
    generally, **13**, 1260
    professional, **13**, 1262
    Roman law, **13**, 1261
elections, **13**, 1253, 1291
emergence, **22**, 552
entail law reform, role, **22**, 634
entry money, **13**, 1302, 1313
  instalments, payment by, **13**, 1313
European Bars, links with, **13**, 1299
examiners, **13**, 1253
Faculty Collection, reports, **22**, 545
Faculty Decisions, reports, **22**, 545
Faculty Services Ltd—
  advocate's clerks, employment and supervision,
    13, 1320
  collection of fees by, **13**, 1293, 1383, 1386
  creation, **13**, 1303
  establishment, **13**, 1293
  function, **13**, 1303
  income, **13**, 1303
  purpose, **13**, 1293
financial position—
  historical background, **13**, 1275–1277
Forbes, William, **22**, 545
growth, **13**, 1286, 1289
historical background, **13**, 1102, 1103, 1239*ff*
  accommodation, **13**, 1294, 1295
  admission to Faculty, **13**, 1249
    entry money, **13**, 1250
    reform, **13**, 1279
    requirements for, changes in, **13**, 1301
  Advocates' Library, **13**, 1251, 1258, 1264, 1267,
    1277
  character of intrants to Faculty, **13**, 1263
  clerks, **13**, 1292
  collective identity, **13**, 1242
  corporate organisation, **13**, 1245, 1254
  draft constitution for Faculty, **13**, 1253
  early pleaders, **13**, 1240
  education, **13**, 1257, 1260–1262
    education requirements, **13**, 1278
    university legal education, **13**, 1244, 1257,
      1278, 1281–1283
  Europe and the Faculty, **13**, 1299
  examinations, **13**, 1256, 1278
  Faculty elections, **13**, 1291

Faculty of Advocates—*continued*
historical background—*continued*
Faculty officers, **13**, 1290
Faculty Services Ltd, **13**, 1293
financial position of Faculty, **13**, 1275–1277
generally, **13**, 1239, 1244, 1247, 1254, 1267, 1268, 1284–1289, 1292, 1298
idle year, **13**, 1280
independence, **13**, 1246–1248
judges, defiance of, **13**, 1252
judicial appointments, **13**, 1259
Lord Chancellor, appointment from, **13**, 1300
office bearers, **13**, 1265, 1270
Parliament House Chambers, **13**, 1294
politics and ethics and the Faculty, **13**, 1264, 1269
precedence at the Bar, **13**, 1271–1273
procurators of the council, **13**, 1241
Queen's Council, Scottish roll, **13**, 1273, 1274
royal commisson reports, **13**, 1297
social background of advocates, **13**, 1243
social status of intrants to Faculty, **13**, 1266
social structure of Faculty, **13**, 1255
women members, **13**, 1268, 1296
Home Advocate Depute, **13**, 1302
income, **13**, 1302
independence, **13**, 1302
judicial appointments, **13**, 1259
junior advocate, **13**, 1317
Keeper of the Library, **13**, 1265, 1302
King's Counsel, **13**, 1317
Library—
Dutch legal scholarship in collection, **22**, 606
French legal scholarship in collection, **22**, 606
interchange of books with National Library of Scotland, **13**, 1502
public access to, **13**, 1502
Library Curators, **13**, 1253
Library Keeper (Bibliothecarius), **13**, 1253
Lord Advocate, **13**, 1269, 1270, 1290, 1302
precedence, **13**, 1271
membership, **13**, 1302
admission to, *see* admission *above*
generally, **13**, 1304
Honorary Members, **13**, 1302, 1316
levies, **13**, 1302
resignation from, **13**, 1315
Sovereign Honorary Member, **13**, 1316
motto, **13**, 1302
office bearers, **13**, 1270
officers, **13**, 1290
officials, **13**, 1302
election, **13**, 1302
Parliament House Chambers, **13**, 1294
practice rules, *see* ADVOCATE
precedence, **16**, 2020
precedence at Bar, **13**, 1302
Dean, **13**, 1271, 1302
historical background, **13**, 1271, 1272
Lord Advocate, **13**, 1271
Queen's Counsel, **13**, 1273, 1274, 1317
resignation and readmission, **13**, 1315
senior counsel, **13**, 1273, 1274
Solicitor General, **13**, 1271
professional conduct, Dean's Rulings, **13**, 1302

Faculty of Advocates—*continued*
professional élite, as, **13**, 1266
Queen's Counsel, **13**, 1273, 1274, 1317
application to become, **13**, 1317
precedence at Bar, **13**, 1273, 1274, 1317
resignation, **13**, 1315
readmission, **13**, 1315
role, examination by royal commissions, **13**, 1297
Roll of Intrants, removal of name from, **13**, 1312, 1313
Roman law, knowledge of, **13**, 1250, 1251, 1256
Roman law, reception in Scotland, influence of advocates, **22**, 553
Sale of Goods Bills 1893—
revision, **22**, 643
Scheme for Accounting and Recovery of Counsel's Fees, **13**, 1383–1386
Scottish Law Commission, proposals for reform to, **22**, 666
senior counsel, **13**, 1317
social structure, **13**, 1243, 1255, 1266
Solicitor General, precedence, **13**, 1271
Treasurer, **13**, 1253, 1270, 1302
two counsel rule, **13**, 1317
Vice-Dean, **13**, 1265, 1270, 1302
women members, **13**, 1268, 1296
See also ADVOCATE
Fair
community aspects, **4**, 1390
right to hold—
regalian right, as, **18**, 210
separate tenement, as, **18**, 210
Fair comment
defamation, as defence against—
essentials of plea, **15**, 540
facts, comment of, **15**, 540, 541
facts truly stated, **15**, 540, 542
fair, meaning, **15**, 545
generally, **15**, 539
hidden facts, **15**, 542
onus of proof, **15**, 540
public interest, matters of, **15**, 539, 540, 544
rebutting defence, **15**, 545
Fair Isle Channel
innocent passage, right of, **21**, 10
Fair retort
defamation, as defence to, **15**, 547
Fair trading
company, investigation, **4**, 562
Director General, *see* DIRECTOR GENERAL OF FAIR TRADING
generally, **4**, 1110, 1268
monopoly control, *see* MONOPOLY CONTROL
Office of, *see* OFFICE OF FAIR TRADING
sheriff court jurisdiction, **6**, 1135
See also COMPETITION LAW
Fair value
shares, valuation of, **25**, 8
valuer's judgment and responsibility, **25**, 68
Fairness
natural justice, and, **1**, 249, 283
Fairway (shipping)
collision regulations, **21**, 347
duty of harbour and other authorities, **21**, 382

Fairway (shipping)—*continued*
fishing vessel in, **21**, 347
meaning, **21**, 347*n*
overtaking in, **21**, 351
turning in, **21**, 347*n*
Falconry
taking or killing wild birds, **11**, 883
Falkland Islands and Dependencies
British citizenship—
    acquisition of, **14**, 1923
    descent, by, **14**, 1924
British Dependent Territories citizenship, **14**, 1932
child born in, **14**, 1925
registration, **14**, 1926
Falkland Palace
keeper of, **7**, 830
Falsa demonstratio non nocet
construction, **25**, 824
False statements and representations
fraudulent misrepresentation by, **11**, 709, 717
offence, **14**, 1479
sale of food, with regard to, **11**, 346
tax offences, **19**, 1552
trade descriptions, in, **6**, 124
Falsing the doom
appeal to Parliament by, **6**, 806, 808, 850, 898, 902
Family
child of, *see* CHILD-CHILDREN
family life, right to, **12**, 6, 62
    access to confidential personal records, **12**, 63
    child care, **12**, 64
    'illegitimate' family, **12**, 62
    immigration, **12**, 65
    restrictions on rights, **12**, 78–84
relationships—
    capacity and status, and, **11**, 1068
    injury to—
        bigamy, **15**, 596
        child—
            death of, **15**, 600
            enticement to leave family, **15**, 596
            unjustified removal, **15**, 596
        death of family member, **15**, 598–602
        destroying relationship, **15**, 598–602
        disenhancing relationship, **15**, 597
        enticement, **15**, 596
        entrapment, **15**, 596
        generally, **15**, 595
        immediate family, meaning, **15**, 601
        recognition of family interests, **15**, 595
        relative, meaning, **15**, 597
        spouse, enticement to leave, **15**, 596
        undermining relationship, **15**, 596
right to found—
    European Convention on Human Rights, **12**, 6
    Universal Declaration of Human Rights, **12**, 4*n*
right to marry, **12**, 6, 71
settlement—
    family relationship on grounds of, *see* SETTLEMENT (immigration)
    family reunion or creation by, *see* SETTLEMENT (immigration)

Family—*continued*
social, legal and economic protection, **12**, 7
spouse, *see* SPOUSE
title to sue, **15**, 603
water unfit for family use, **14**, 2079
wills and succession—
    arrangement, deed of, **25**, 1028
    discretionary provision, **25**, 1114
    head of family, curb of excessive individualism, **25**, 611
    inadequate provision for, **25**, 611
    meaning, **25**, 876
    property—
        England, **25**, 608
        France, **25**, 608
        Germany, **25**, 608
        reserved, *see* WILL
    protection, *see* WILL
    provision—
        discretionary, **25**, 1114
        freedom of testation, restriction on, **25**, 601
Family credit
adjudication, **21**, 1096, 1149
applicable amount, **21**, 1095
application for—
    first, **21**, 1091
    subsequent, **21**, 1091, 1096
award, duration, **21**, 1091
calculation—
    applicable amount, **21**, 1095
    average weekly earnings, calculation—
        employed, **21**, 1092
        self-employed, **21**, 1093, 1094
        generally, **21**, 1095
    period of assessment, **21**, 1092
capital—
    child, of, **21**, 1089
    limits, **21**, 1089
    personal possessions and family home, **21**, 1089
    tariff income, **21**, 1090
change in family circumstances, **21**, 1096
charitable or voluntary work, claimant undertaking, **21**, 1087
child, claimant or claimant's partner must be responsible for, **21**, 1088
child or young person leaving household, **21**, 1096
definition, **21**, 1083
determination of claim, **21**, 1096
disability working allowance, interaction with, **21**, 1090, 1100
entitlement conditions—
    capital limits, **21**, 1089
    child, responsibility for, **21**, 1088
    connection with Great Britain, **21**, 1086
    income limits, **21**, 1090
    presence and residence in Great Britain, **21**, 1086
    working for remuneration, **21**, 1087
family income supplement replaced by, **21**, 1084
income—
    calculation, **21**, 1090
    child, of, **21**, 1090
    expenses, **21**, 1090

Family credit—*continued*
income—*continued*
  income tax, **21**, 1090
  maintenance payments, **21**, 1090
  national insurance contributions, **21**, 1090
  social security benefits, **21**, 1090
  student loan, **21**, 1090
  tariff, **21**, 1090
legislation, **21**, 1085
means-tested benefit, as, **21**, 1083
overpayments, **21**, 1014
purpose, **21**, 1083
student, **21**, 1090
tax-free benefit, as, **21**, 1083
work, conditions as to, **21**, 1087
  holidays, **21**, 1087
Family income supplement
family credit, replaced by, **21**, 1084
Family law
aliment, *see* ALIMENT
children, *see* CHILD–CHILDREN
di＿rce, *see* DIVORCE
husband and wife, *see* HUSBAND AND WIFE;
  MARRIAGE; SPOUSE
international law, in, *see* PRIVATE INTERNATIONAL
  LAW
law reform—
  children, custody of, **22**, 692
  divorce, **22**, 649, 683–685
  financial provision on divorce, **22**, 657, 684, 685
  illegitimacy, **22**, 690
  incest, **22**, 695
  international law, in, **22**, 685, 693
  jurisdiction in family law actions, **22**, 682
  legitimation, **22**, 691
  marriage, **22**, 649
  married woman, **22**, 648
    domicile, **22**, 682
    policies of assurance, **22**, 689
  matrimonial home, **22**, 687
marriage, *see* HUSBAND AND WIFE; MARRIAGE
matrimonial home, *see* MATRIMONIAL HOME
matrimonial property, *see* MATRIMONIAL PROPERTY
spouse, *see* HUSBAND AND WIFE; MARRIAGE; SPOUSE
Family planning
contraceptive substances and appliances, supply
  of, **11**, 1471, 1481
medicinal purposes, meaning, **14**, 1202
provisions as to, **11**, 1481
Family Practitioner Committee
functions, **23**, 902
Fare
common carrier's, **3**, 672
proper fare in legal tender, refusal to pay, **3**, 673
Farm
arable, date of entry, **13**, 246
lease—
  date of entry, **13**, 244, 245, 246
    arable farm, **13**, 246
    pastoral farm, **13**, 246
  delectus personae, doctrine of, **13**, 356
pastoral—
  apportionment, **13**, 246
  date of entry, **13**, 246

Farm—*continued*
rent—
  apportionment, **13**, 247
  backhand and forehand, **13**, 246
rural lease, **13**, 213–215, 217
steelbow, **13**, 217, 220
See also AGRICULTURE
Farm Amalgamation Scheme
implementation of Directive 72/160 by, **1**, 971
**Farm and Horticultural Development
  Schemes**
implementation of Directive 72/159 by, **1**, 971
Farm loss payment
amount of, **5**, 187
claim for, **5**, 187
generally, **6**, 1141
meaning, **5**, 187
qualification for, **5**, 187
reduction of, **5**, 187
Farmer
VAT flat-rate scheme, **7**, 1353
Farrier
competence etc, standards, **2**, 151
conviction of cruelty, **2**, 158
Disciplinary Committee—
  appeals to, **2**, 157
  powers of, **2**, 158
offences by, **2**, 159
professional misconduct, **2**, 158
register—
  parts of, **2**, 152–155
  removal from, **2**, 158
registration—
  acknowledgment of, **2**, 156
  appeals as to, **2**, 157
  certificate of, **2**, 156
  Council responsible for, **2**, 151
  fraudulently obtaining, **2**, 159
  parts of register, in, **2**, 152–155
  suspension of, **2**, 158
statutory control, **2**, 151
unregistered, farriery by, **2**, 159
Fast-tracking contract
building contracts, **3**, 9
Fatal accident inquiry
accidental death, **3**, 513
Act of 1906..., **17**, 959–960
Act of 1976..., **17**, 961–973
Act of 1895—
  history, **17**, 951
  scope, **17**, 952
anatomical examination not allowed where
  likelihood of, **3**, 507
application for, **3**, 513; **17**, 965
assessors, **17**, 970
child, identity of, **17**, 38
conduct of, **17**, 956
coroners' inquests, England and Wales, **17**, 975
discretionary, **17**, 964
documents, service of, **17**, 972
evidence, **17**, 957, 968
holding of, **17**, 954, 967
investigation of death elsewhere, **17**, 976
jury, **17**, 955, 959

Fatal accident inquiry—*continued*
mandatory—
  generally, **3**, 513; **17**, 962
  waiver of, **17**, 963
notification of, **17**, 966
petition for, **17**, 953
procurator fiscal, investigation by, **17**, 965
sheriff—
  determination, **17**, 971
  rules, power to dispense with compliance with,
    17, 973
sheriff court jurisdiction, **6**, 1070
standard of proof, **10**, 761
sudden death, **3**, 513; **17**, 960
suspicious death, **3**, 513
systems in other countries, **17**, 974–976
verdict, **17**, 958
young people, protection of, **17**, 969
Father
British Dependent Territories citizenship, **14**, 1938
division of estate on or after 8 December 1986—
  examples, **25**, 704
moveable succession, **25**, 682
registration based on citizenship of, **14**, 1918
Fault
culpa, **15**, 254
damnum injuria datum, **15**, 252
delict, generally, **15**, 252
dolus, **15**, 253
duty of care, *see* CARE, DUTY OF
intentional injury, in relation to, **15**, 253
negligence—
  elements, **15**, 311
  generally, **15**, 252
obligation arising from, **15**, 1, 3
occupiers' liability, *see* OCCUPIER'S LIABILITY
reparation, as fundamental principle of, **15**, 252
unintentional injury, in relation to, **15**, 254
Feal
servitude right of, **18**, 489
Fealty
alien cannot own land in Scotland, **18**, 53, 53*n*
desuetude, **18**, 53
generally, **18**, 53, 53*n*
homage, and, **18**, 53
one man owning land of two or more lords, **18**,
  53, 60
transfer of superiority, and, **18**, 60
vassalage, generally, **18**, 53
Federal credit union
exempt agreement, **5**, 824
Fee
feudal law, meaning in, **18**, 93
in pendente, **13**, 1629
  judicial factor where, **24**, 281
meanings, **13**, 1603
transmission of right of, **13**, 1663
Feeding stuff
importation, **1**, 725
material sold for use as, **1**, 725
sample, analysis of, **1**, 726
warranty as to, **1**, 725
Feloniously
use of term, **7**, 75

Fence
barbed wire, **20**, 697
boundary, *see* BOUNDARY
electrified, **20**, 697
maintenance of, **11**, 904
nuisance, and, **14**, 2036
obligation to repair as real condition, **13**, 241
privacy, maintenance of, **14**, 2036
railways, **19**, 1040
road, provision on, **20**, 660
wilful damage to, **20**, 704
Fenwick Weavers Society
generally, **12**, 608*n*
Ferrules
water fittings, as, **25**, 527
Ferry
construction or alteration, **19**, 19*n*
lease, **13**, 206
local authority, rights vested in, **14**, 441
maintenance of, **14**, 33
meaning, **14**, 441*n*
powers in relation to, **14**, 442
right of—
  acquisition, **18**, 334
  land ownership, and, **18**, 335
  legal separate tenement, as, **18**, 334
  obligations of, **18**, 335
  public rights as to, **18**, 529
  regalian right, as, **18**, 210
  rights conferred by, **18**, 335, 336
  sasine, symbols of, **18**, 90
  separate legal tenement, as, **18**, 210, 319
valuation for rating, **24**, 652, 653, 693
Fertiliser
importation, **1**, 725
material sold for use as, **1**, 725
sample, analysis of, **1**, 726
Festivals
calendar, inclusion, **22**, 801
Christmas, *see* CHRISTMAS
Easter, *see* EASTER
ecclesiastical, **22**, 801, 804
Passover, **22**, 808
See also HOLIDAY
Fetus
abortion, *see* ABORTION
Human Fertilisation and Embryology Act (1990),
  7, 284, 289
murder of, **10**, 1030
premature delivery, causing, **7**, 285
unborn or unconceived, **11**, 1032, 1037
Feuar
co-feuars, *jus quaesitum tertio*, **15**, 833, 850
liability of, **14**, 2141
servitude, exercise of, **18**, 464
Feudal law
abolition, **18**, 41, 113; **22**, 596
absolute disposition, **18**, 112
accession, and, **18**, 574, 587
administration of justice, theoretical basis, **22**, 506
aid, casualty of, **18**, 78
alba firma, **18**, 67
alienation, **18**, 59, 59*n*
  a me, **18**, 80, 82

Feudal law—*continued*
alienation—*continued*
  objections to, **18**, 59
  prohibitions on, **18**, 382
  vassal, alienation more than one-half of land held, **18**, 82
  without consent of superior, **18**, 82, 82*n*
allodial ownership contrasted, **18**, 47
alms, tenure by, **18**, 66*n*
annualrent, **18**, 90, 112
assignation, **18**, 59
  unfeudalised title, of, **18**, 104
Auld Session, **6**, 896
avail of marriage, **18**, 76
barony—
  baro major, **18**, 54
  baro minor, **18**, 54
  generally, **16**, 1304; **18**, 54, 54*n*
  jurisdiction, **18**, 54
barony courts, **6**, 897
benefice (*beneficium*)—
  merger with vassalage, **18**, 43
  origins of feudalism, **18**, 43, 43*n*
benefice of vassal, meaning, **22**, 588
bequest of heritage, **18**, 42, 79, 108
  objections to, **18**, 59
blench tenure, **18**, 67, 68, 70; **22**, 594, 596
  wardholding converted to, **18**, 64
bond and diposition in security, **18**, 112
Book of the Feus, **18**, 44
booking tenure—
  feufarm, merger with, **18**, 65
  generally, **18**, 65
  meaning, **18**, 65
burgage tenure, **18**, 109; **22**, 594
  dispone, power to, **18**, 59
  feufarm, merger with, **18**, 58, 65
  generally, **18**, 65
  meaning, **18**, 65
  non-entry not applicable to, **18**, 81
  subinfeudation, and, **18**, 58
  symbols of sasine, **18**, 90
  watch and ward, obligation to, **18**, 65
burgh law, **22**, 510
  See also BURGH
casualties—
  aid, **18**, 78
  avail of marriage, **18**, 76
  composition, **18**, 61, 79, 80
  disclamation, **18**, 83
  escheat, **18**, 84
  generally, **18**, 382
  irritancy, **18**, 85
  jus primae noctis, **18**, 77
  marriage, **18**, 76
  meaning of casualty, **18**, 63, 63*n*
  non-entry, **18**, 81
  purpresture, **18**, 83
  recognition, **18**, 82
  relief, **18**, 61, 79, 80
  tinsel, **18**, 85
    superiority, of, **18**, 86
  ward, **18**, 64, 75
Celtic custom, effect, **22**, 505

Feudal law—*continued*
church courts, **22**, 511
civil possession, **18**, 121
commercialisation, **18**, 45, 75
composition—
  alioquin successorus (alioqui successurus), **18**, 80
  casualty of, **18**, 61, 79, 80
  charter of, **18**, 80
  propulsion of the fee, **18**, 80
  taxed, **18**, 80
compulsory purchase, land which has passed through, **18**, 68*n*, 70
confirmation—
  charter of, **18**, 58, 94, 99, 103, 393
  entry by, **18**, 99
consolidation, **18**, 98, 432
conveyance—
  a me, **18**, 58, 93
  adjudication, charter of, **18**, 94, 95
  assignation, **18**, 104
  clare constat, **18**, 94, 109
  confirmation, charter of, **18**, 94, 103
  consolidation, **18**, 98
  courtesy, **18**, 110
  Crown specialities, **18**, 105
  de me, **18**, 93
  destination, **18**, 110
  disposition, **18**, 99
    a me vel de me, **18**, 99, 100
  feu contract, **18**, 94
  feu disposition, **18**, 94
  generally, **18**, 88
  heir-at-law, **18**, 55, 108
  heir-of-line, **18**, 55, 108
  heir of provision, **18**, 110
  heir of tailzie, **18**, 110
  heirs portioner, **18**, 18, 55, 108
  infeftment without entry, **18**, 102
  inter vivos, **18**, 94–107
  investiture, renewal, **18**, 94, 106, 108
  modern usage, **18**, 107
  mortis causa, **18**, 108–111
  novodamus, charter of, **18**, 94, 95, 426
  original charter, **18**, 94
  precepts of sasine, **18**, 101
  progress, charter by, **18**, 94
  resignation, **18**, 94, 97, 103
  service, **18**, 109
  subinfeudation, **18**, 96
  tailzie, **18**, 110
  terce, **18**, 110
  unfeudalised title, **18**, 104
courtesy, **18**, 74, 110
Crown—
  dominium directum, ultimate, **18**, 193; **22**, 591, 592
  dominium eminens, **18**, 38, 42, 47, 49
  sasine of, **18**, 48
  specialities, feudal conveyance, **18**, 105
Curia Regis, **6**, 898; **22**, 506, 511, 512
  See also CURIA REGIS; ROYAL COURTS
decline, **18**, 45, 46, 46*n*
destination, **18**, 111
development in Scotland, **22**, 505

Feudal law—*continued*
disclamation, **18**, 83
disposition—
 a me, **18**, 58, 59, 99
 a me vel de me, **18**, 99, 100
 destination *et assignatis suis*, **18**, 59
 feu, **18**, 94
 generally, **18**, 99
 objections to, **18**, 59
 power to dispone, **18**, 59
 superiority, of, **18**, 60
dominium—
 dominium directum, **18**, 38, 49, 51, 51*n*, 193, 640
  transfer, **18**, 640
 dominium eminens, **18**, 38, 42, 47, 49
 dominium plenum, **18**, 49
 dominium utile, **18**, 38, 49, 51, 51*n*, 52, 193,
  193*n*, 640
  consolidation, **18**, 98
  divided, feuduty, **18**, 69
  ownership of, generally, **18**, 194
  transfer, **18**, 640
 fragmented nature, **18**, 193
 generally, **18**, 43, 193
 liferent, and, **18**, 74
 post-medieval position, **18**, 50, 50*n*
 Scots law, generally, **18**, 51, 51*n*
 terminology, origin of, **18**, 49, 49*n*
earl, **16**, 1303
emphyteusis, **18**, 68
enforcement of condition, **18**, 382
England, **18**, 45
entry, meaning, **18**, 93
escheat, **18**, 84
essential characteristic, **22**, 588, 590
fealty—
 alien cannot own land in Scotland, **18**, 53
 desuetude, **18**, 53
 generally, **18**, 53, 53*n*
 homage, and, **18**, 53
 one man owning land of two or more lords,
  18, 53, 60
 transfer of superiority, and, **18**, 60
fee—
 fee must be full, rule as to, **18**, 87
 fiduciary fee, doctrine of, **18**, 87
 meaning, **18**, 93
 use of term, **18**, 51, 51*n*
ferry, right of. *See also* FERRY
feu charter, **18**, 58, 96
feu contract, **18**, 58
 interpretation, **12**, 1237, 1249
 irritancy—
  conventional, **15**, 806
  declarator, action of, **15**, 804
  effect, **15**, 804
  feuing conditions, breach, **15**, 806
  generally, **15**, 802, 803, 804
  legal, **15**, 805
  non-payment of feuduty, **15**, 805, 806
  ab non solutem canonem, **15**, 805
  obligation *ad factum praestandum*, breach, **15**,
   806
  purge, **15**, 804–806

Feudal law—*continued*
feu contract—*continued*
 irritancy—*continued*
  sopiting the superiority, **15**, 804
  tinsel of the feu, action of, **15**, 804
feu disposition, **18**, 58
feu-ferme tenure
 church land, pre-Reformation, **22**, 595
 Crown land, **22**, 595
 fiscal advantage to tenant, **22**, 595
 grassum, **22**, 595
 Jacobite Risings, after, **22**, 596
 origins, **22**, 595
 survival, **22**, 596
feu grants—
 clauses, **6**, 474
 Edinburgh New Town plan, **18**, 376–379
 enforcement, express rights, **18**, 405
 form, **6**, 474
 generally, **24**, 202
 infeftment, **6**, 475
 interest in land, **6**, 714
 negative prescription and, **18**, 431
 periodical payment under, prescription, **16**, 2116
 stamp duty, **6**, 475
 types of, **6**, 473
 See also DEED
feuar, **18**, 193
feudal conveyancing techniques, **24**, 5
feudal ownership, generally, **18**, 38
feudalism, meaning, **22**, 587
feudi firma, **18**, 68
feudum burgale, **18**, 65
feudum militare, **18**, 64; **22**, 588, 593
feuduty, *see* FEUDUTY
feufarm (feuferme)—
 booking tenure merged with, **18**, 65
 burgage tenure merged with, **18**, 58, 65
 Church lands, **18**, 68; **22**, 595
 Crown lands, **18**, 68; **22**, 595
 feudal law, generally, **18**, 70, 71
 meaning, **18**, 68
 pseudo-feudal nature, **18**, 46
 quasi-feudal tenure, as, **18**, 68
 relief, casualty of, **18**, 79
 subinfeudation, and, **18**, 58
 survival in Scots law, **18**, 68; **22**, 596
 tacks, conversion to feus, **18**, 68
fiar, meaning, **18**, 93
fiduciary fee, doctrine of, **18**, 87
fief—
 conditions of succession to, **22**, 589
 heritable, **22**, 589
 meaning, **22**, 588
 primogeniture, male—
  rule of succession, **22**, 589
fishings, **18**, 90
freeholder, **16**, 1304
glebes, **18**, 68*n*, 70
grassum, **18**, 58; **22**, 595
guardianship, right of, **18**, 75
heir-at-law, **18**, 55, 108
heir-of-line, **18**, 55, 108
heir of provision, **18**, 111

Feudal law—*continued*
heir of tailzie, **18**, 111
heirs portioner, **18**, 18, 55, 108
hereditary development, **18**, 43
heritable bond and diposition in security, **18**, 112
heritable property, importance in relation to, **18**, 1
heritable security—
  history, **18**, 112
  meaning, **18**, 112
  sources of, **18**, 112
heritage—
  aliens acquiring, **6**, 1017
  bequest, **18**, 42, 79, 108
    objections to, **18**, 59
  transmissibility of feu, **18**, 56
historical source of Scots law, as, **22**, 507–509, 587–596
history, **18**, 1, 41–46
homage—
  abolition, **18**, 53
  fealty, and, **18**, 53
  generally, **18**, 53, 53*n*
  one man owning land of two or more lords, **18**, 53
  Scotland as vassal of God, **18**, 42
  wardholding, and, **18**, 53
hosting and hunting, *reddendo* of, **18**, 64
House of Lords, origin of, **6**, 802
Hume's *Lectures*, **18**, 1
immixtio manuum, **18**, 42
infeftment—
  meaning, **18**, 93
  public, **18**, 93
  without entry, **18**, 93, 102
inherent conditions of the feu, **18**, 393, 393*n*
investiture—
  generally, **18**, 53
  improper, **18**, 96
  liferent, **18**, 74
  meaning, **18**, 93
  proper, **18**, 96
  renewal, **18**, 94, 106
irritancy—
  casualty or remedy, classification as, **18**, 85
  extinction by, **18**, 432
  generally, **18**, 82, 83, 424
  lessee, in favour of, **18**, 85
  recognition, **18**, 82
  superior, in favour of, **18**, 85
irritation of feu, **18**, 382
jurisdiction—
  barony, **18**, 54, 54*n*
  landownership, implied by, **18**, 42
  regality, **18**, 54, 54*n*
  symbols of sasine, **18**, 90
jus primae noctis, casualty of, **18**, 77
justiciar, role, **22**, 507
kenning, **18**, 74, 110
kindly tenants, **18**, 72, 72*n*
king, role, **6**, 901; **22**, 506
king in Parliament, **6**, 901
kirklands, **18**, 66, 68*n*, 70

Feudal law—*continued*
land—
  inalienable property, whether, **18**, 600
  land right as personal right, **18**, 42
land tenure—
  administration of justice—
    entitlement of lord to hold courts, **22**, 509
  general description, **22**, 587, 588
  military service, in return for, **22**, 588, 593
  reddendo in return for grant of land, **22**, 588, 593
  transformation by, **22**, 505, 506
landownership—
  capacity, **18**, 599
  concept absent from feudalism, **18**, 42
  generally, **18**, 193
legal literature, **22**, 512
  See also LEGAL LITERATURE
lessee, in favour of, **18**, 85
liability—
  contract, by, **18**, 393
  tenure, by, **18**, 393
liberum maritagium, **18**, 73
Libri Feudorum, **22**, 590
liferent—
  beneficial liferenter, **18**, 93
  escheat, **18**, 84
  generally, **18**, 74, 74*n*
  improper, **18**, 93
  See also LIFERENT
local administration, **22**, 507
local courts, **6**, 897, 908
lord—
  administration of justice, **22**, 509
  vassal, relationship—
    duration, **22**, 589
    heritable fief, development, **22**, 589
    personal, through oath of fealty, **22**, 588, 589
manrent, **18**, 43*n*
manses, **18**, 68*n*, 70
marriage, casuality of, **18**, 76
military tenure—
  description, **22**, 588, 593
  fiscal advantages, **22**, 593
  prestations attached to, **22**, 593
military tenure and obligations, **18**, 53, 64, 71, 75
  corporation as vassal, where, **18**, 61
mill, symbols of sasine, **18**, 90
more burgi, **18**, 65, 109
mortification, **18**, 66, 68*n*, 70; **22**, 594
  tenure, **22**, 594
mortmain, **18**, 66*n*
nature of, **18**, 41, 42
non-entry, casualty of, **18**, 81
novodamus, charter of—
  extinction of grant by, **18**, 426
  generally, **18**, 94, 95
  new burden imposed by, **18**, 426
  registration, **18**, 426
one man owning land of two or more lords, **18**, 53, 60
origin of feudalism, **18**, 43
Orkney and Shetland, introduction to, **24**, 308
ownership—
  capacity, **18**, 599

Feudal law—*continued*
ownership—*continued*
  divided ownership, theory of, **18**, 50, 52
  multiple ownership, feudalism as, **18**, 51
  transfer of—
    delivery—
      requirement for, **18**, 640
      symbolical, **18**, 640
      generally, **18**, 640
      substitution, as, **18**, 640
    See also landownership *above*
Parliament—
  Curia Regis, contrast, **22**, 506
  generally, **6**, 802, 850
  judicial role, **22**, 506
patronage, **18**, 90
personal service, **18**, 382
prescription, **16**, 2121
primogeniture, male, **22**, 589, 646
private and public law, concept of absent from
  feudalism, **18**, 42
purpresture, **18**, 83
real burdens, and, **18**, 351, 376–379, 380, 382,
  385, 385n, 393
real condition, feudal condition as model for, **18**,
  393
recognition, casualty of, **18**, 82
reddendo—
  generally, **12**, 1249; **18**, 63, 382; **22**, 588, 593
  hosting and hunting, **18**, 64
  military tenure, **22**, 588, 593
  mortification tenure, **22**, 594
regality—
  generally, **18**, 54, 54n
  jurisdiction, **18**, 54
regional differences, **18**, 44
relevium, **18**, 79
relief, casualty of, **18**, 61, 79, 80
religion, feudalisation, **18**, 42
resignation—
  ad remanentiam perpetuam, **18**, 97
  charter of, **18**, 94, 99, 103
  entry by, **18**, 99
  generally, **18**, 97
  in favorem, **18**, 97
  instrument of, **18**, 99
  procuratory of, **18**, 99
sale of land, **18**, 42
sasine—
  ceremony of, **18**, 89
  clare constat, **18**, 108, 109
  Crown, of, **18**, 48
  fealty, oath of, **18**, 89
  generally, **18**, 89, 99
  investiture, **18**, 89
  meaning, **18**, 89, 93
  mortuus sasit vivum, **18**, 108
  notarial instrument of, **18**, 89, 89n, 92, 99
  precept of, **18**, 96, 101, 109
  recording, **18**, 99
  registration, **18**, 91
  service, **18**, 108, 109
  symbols of, **18**, 90
  title, notice of, **18**, 92

Feudal law—*continued*
Scotland, **6**, 403; **13**, 1129
  charters, survival, **22**, 591
  growth, **22**, 591
Scots property law, as source of, **18**, 2
sheriff, role of, **22**, 507, 508
  See also SHERIFF
socage (soccage), **18**, 70
sovereignty and landownership, **18**, 42
spread of feudalism, **18**, 44
spread in Western Europe, **22**, 590
subinfeudation—
  burgage tenure, **18**, 58
  confirmation, charter of, **18**, 58
  consent of lord to, **22**, 592
  consent of superior, **18**, 58
  conveyance *de me*, **18**, 93
  description, **22**, 592
  double manner of holding, whether breach, **18**,
    58
  express prohibition, where, **18**, 58
  feu charter, **18**, 58
  feu contract, **18**, 58
  feu disposition, **18**, 58
  feudal conveyance, generally, **18**, 88, 96
  feufarm, **18**, 58
  grant *de me*, as, **18**, 58
  grassum, **18**, 58
  meaning, **18**, 57
  midsuperior, **18**, 57, 58
  mortification, **18**, 58
  pre-emption clause, **18**, 58
  prohibition, **12**, 1244; **18**, 382
    clause in tenant's charter, **22**, 592
  Statute of *Quia Emptores*, curtailment by, **22**,
    592
  substitution replacing, **22**, 592
  transfer of ownership, and, **18**, 650
  wardholding, **18**, 58
superior, **18**, 38
  compensation, entitlement to, **5**, 115
  Crown as ultimate, **18**, 42; **22**, 591, 592
  dominium directum, **18**, 49, 51, 193, 640
  entitlement to identifiable vassal, **18**, 87
  liability of, **14**, 2141
  mid-superior, **18**, 49, 57, 58
  obligations burdening, **18**, 382, 394, 394n
  obligations of vassal to, **18**, 382
  remedies of, **6**, 532–534
  right of, tenure and contract, founded on, **18**,
    393
superiority—
  burden, as, **18**, 52
  congregational properties and endowments, sale
    of, **3**, 1069
  corporeal right, classification as, **18**, 51
  deeds dealing with, **6**, 585
  disposition, conveyance by, **18**, 51
  division, **18**, 60
  dominant interests, **18**, 351
  investment, treatment as, **18**, 60
  irritancy, **18**, 85
  liferenter, **18**, 74
  mineral rights, reservation of, **18**, 60

Feudal law—*continued*
superiority—*continued*
 pro indiviso ownership, **18**, 60
 real burdens in, grant of feu, **18**, 351
 real condition, as, **18**, 351
 servitude, whether qualifying for, **18**, 443
 tinsel of, **18**, 86
 transfer—
  inter vivos, **18**, 60
  mortis causa, **18**, 60
survival in Scotland, **18**, 45, 46, 68
tailzie, **18**, 111
taxation, **18**, 42
teind, **18**, 90
tenant at will, **18**, 72
tenent, **18**, 47
terce, **18**, 74, 110
 kenning, **18**, 110
thirlage, **18**, 90, 90*n*
tinsel, **18**, 85
 superiority, of, **18**, 86
title—
 completion, **18**, 93
 feudalisation, **18**, 93
tocher, **18**, 76
transmissibility of feu—
 alienation, **18**, 59, 62
 assignation, **18**, 59
 casualty, **18**, 63
 conquest, **18**, 56
 disposition, **18**, 59
  superiority, of, **18**, 60
 heritage, **18**, 56
 inheritability, **18**, 55
 liferent, reservation, **18**, 55
 reddendo, **18**, 63
 sanctions for breach, **18**, 62
 subinfeudation, *see* subinfeudation *above*
 superior, power of, **18**, 60
 vassal, who could be, **18**, 61
trust doctrine, development of, **24**, 5
udal law compared, **24**, 306, 307
urban areas, **18**, 65
variations in Europe, **22**, 590
vassal—
 alienation, unlawful, **18**, 62, 82
 civil possession by, **18**, 121
 corporation as, **18**, 61
 death—
  conveyance *mortis causa*, **18**, 108–111
  non-entry, **18**, 81
 dominium utile, **18**, 49, 51, 193, 640
 fealty, **18**, 53, 53*n*
 female, **18**, 55, 61, 75
 generally, **18**, 38, 47
 heir-at-law, **18**, 55, 108
 heir-of-line, **18**, 55, 108
 heirs portioner, **18**, 55, 108
 homage, **18**, 53, 53*n*
 inter vivos transfer of superiority, objection to, **18**, 60
 investiture, **18**, 53
 military tenure and obligations, **18**, 53, 64, 71, 75

Feudal law—*continued*
vassal—*continued*
 minor, **18**, 75
 oath of fealty, **22**, 588
 obligations to superior, **18**, 382
 one, owning land of two or more lords, **18**, 53, 60
 position of, generally, **18**, 43
 prescriptive possession through, **16**, 2108
 pupil, **18**, 75
 subinfeudation, *see* subinfeudation *above*
 trustees as vassals, **18**, 61
  casualty of composition, **18**, 61
  casualty of relief, **18**, 61
 ultimate, **18**, 38
 who could be, **18**, 61
vassalage—
 burden, whether, **18**, 50, 51
 casualty, *see* casualty *above*
 corporeal right, classification as, **18**, 51
 disposition, conveyance by, **18**, 51
 inheritability, **18**, 55
 merger with benefice, **18**, 43
 origins of feudalism, **18**, 43, 43*n*
 ownership, as, **18**, 50, 51
 personal, **18**, 43, 43*n*
 survival in Scotland, **18**, 45
 usufruct, as species of, **18**, 43, 50
wadset, **18**, 112
ward, casualty of—
 black ward, **18**, 75
 disappearence, **18**, 75
 donatar, **18**, 75
 generally, **18**, 64
 taxed, **18**, 75
 ward-upon-ward, **18**, 75
 wardholding, and, **18**, 64
wardholding—
 abolition, **18**, 53, 64, 75; **22**, 596, 630
 aid, casualty of, **18**, 78
 avail of marriage, **18**, 76
 blench, conversion to, **18**, 64
 feudum militare, **18**, 64
 fiscal advantages, **22**, 593
 homage, and, **18**, 53
 hunting and hosting, *reddendo* of, **18**, 64
 liberum maritagium, **18**, 73
 military feu, as, **18**, 53, 64
 recognition, casualty of, **18**, 82
 relief, casualty of, **18**, 79, 80
 subinfeudation, and, **18**, 58
 taxed, **18**, 64, 75
 true feudal tenure, as, **18**, 64
 ward, casualty of, **18**, 64, 75
wardship, commercialisation, **18**, 45
watch and ward, obligation as to, **18**, 65
Feudal ownership
See FEUDAL LAW
Feudal tenure
See FEUDAL LAW
Feudi firma
meaning, **18**, 68
Feudum burgale
meaning, **18**, 65

Feudum militare
meaning, **18**, 64
Feuduty
abolition, **18**, 69
adjudication on a *debitum fundi*, **8**, 372
allocated and unallocated, **6**, 529, 1142, 1149
arrears, moveable property, as, **18**, 14
bond and disposition in security—
    liability of creditor for, **20**, 116
clause of obligation of relief, implied terms, **12**,
    1235
cumulo, **18**, 69
debitum fundi, as, **18**, 69
dominium utile divided, where, **18**, 69
enforcement, **18**, 69
enforcement of secured debts, **8**, 101
heritable securities, competition with, **20**, 248
heritage, sale of, **20**, 917
implied terms, **12**, 1249
imposition of, **12**, 1249
irritancy, **18**, 69
kind, payment in, **18**, 69
lease, **13**, 206
meaning, **18**, 69
military service, **18**, 69
money, payment in, **18**, 69
personal service, **18**, 69
prescription, **16**, 2116
redemption of, **6**, 535–537; **12**, 1249; **18**, 69
sequestration for, **8**, 392
statement of, in missives, **6**, 562
superior's hypothec for, **14**, 1812
survival in Scots law, **18**, 69
unallocated, **18**, 69
Feuferme
See FEUDAL LAW
Fiancé/Fiancée
entry clearance, **12**, 151
settlement, family reunion or creation by, *see*
    SETTLEMENT (IMMIGRATION)
Fiar
acquiescence by liferenter, where, **16**, 1616
damages, remedy of, **13**, 1661
destinations, Dobie's table of, **13**, 1622
feuduty, rights to, **13**, 1639
fiduciary, lessor as, **13**, 170
jus disponendi, **13**, 1619
lessor, as, **13**, 171
meaning, **13**, 1603; **18**, 93
proper liferent, **13**, 1608
proprietor, as, **24**, 444
real right of, **13**, 1603, 1608
remedies open to, **13**, 1660–1662
rights of—
    cautio usufructuaria, **13**, 1661
    generally, **13**, 1659
    proper fiar, **13**, 1660
    transmission of right of fee, **13**, 1663
    trust fiar, **13**, 1662
simple proper liferent, **13**, 1614
trust liferent, **13**, 1609
Fiars Courts
abolition, **24**, 309
scat, **24**, 309

Fiars' prices
determination, **3**, 1592
Fideicommissum
heir, executor as species of, **24**, 3
marriage contracts, **24**, 4
root of trust law, as, **24**, 4, 112
Fideiussio
accessory nature, **3**, 811
advantages, **3**, 806
fideioussio indemnitatis, **3**, 811
Roman law and development of law of Caution,
    3, 806
Fidelity guarantee
alteration of contract, effect, **3**, 975
death or insanity of party to, **3**, 982
disclosure, duty of, **3**, 899, 900
loss of identity of party to, **3**, 982
restrictive nature, **3**, 911
revocation by cautioner, termination by, **3**, 981
uberrimae fidei contract, as, **12**, 802
Fidepromissio
Roman law and development of law of Caution,
    3, 806, 808
FIDIC Conditions
building contracts, **3**, 12
Fiduciary
ad hoc relationships, **24**, 172
auctor in rem suam, precluded from becoming, **24**,
    2, 170
breach of trust—
    consent, **24**, 173
    consequences, **24**, 171, 186–188
    defences to, generally, **24**, 173
    other defences not recognised, **24**, 174
    remedies for, **24**, 186
    specific authorisation, **24**, 173
categories of, **24**, 172
damages for, **24**, 186
duty, ratepayers, owed to, **14**, 132
extent of, **24**, 175
fee trust—
    creation, **24**, 10, 29
    meaning, **24**, 10, 32
fundamental principle, **24**, 170
personal interest not to conflict with, **24**, 170
scope of fiduciary relationship, **24**, 175
    agents, **24**, 188
    directors, **24**, 188
transactions affected by non-profit rule—
    beneficial interests, purchase of, **24**, 179
    companies, purchase of trust property by, **24**,
        177
    competition with trust business, **24**, 182
    confidential information, **24**, 184
    contracts involving fiduciaries, **24**, 180
    fiduciaries, purchase of trust property by, **24**,
        178
    information acquired in fiduciary capacity, **24**,
        185
    relatives, purchase of trust property by, **24**, 177
    third parties, **24**, 181, 182
    trustee purchasing trust property, **24**, 176
    unauthorised remuneration, **24**, 183
trustees, duty of, **11**, 751

Fife Region
population, **14**, 64
structure, **14**, 64
Fight
agreement to, relevancy, **7**, 93
breach of the peace, **7**, 446, 447, 451
Files
access to, **12**, 36
Filleted agreement
Restrictive Practices Court, not referred to, **4**, 1183
Filling station
See OIL (MARKETING)
Film
cinematograph, **18**, 969
copyright, **18**, 933, 967, 969
author, meaning, **18**, 979, 981
commissioners' right to privacy, **18**, 1130, 1139
copying for private and domestic use, **18**, 1123
Crown copyright, **18**, 1039
educational establishment showing, **18**, 1112
European Community legislation, **18**, 1643
infringement, **18**, 1055
public showing, by, **18**, 1062–1064
supply of copies, **18**, 1081
moral rights, *see* COPYRIGHT (MORAL RIGHTS)
originality, **18**, 948
overlap with other copyright works, **18**, 970
permitted acts, **18**, 1126
rental rights, **18**, 1059
term of copyright, **18**, 1038, 1039
distribution, European Community legislation, **18**, 1664
evidence, as, **10**, 572, 607
joint authorship, **18**, 987
live performance, of, **18**, 1432
meaning, **18**, 969
photographs, and, **18**, 970
trade descriptions, **6**, 122
video, **18**, 969
See also CINEMA; CINEMATOGRAPH FILM
Finance Acts
annual amendment, **19**, 1503, 1543
customs and excise law, generally, **7**, 1002
imposition, **19**, 1503–1505
passage through Parliament, **19**, 1503
Finance house
bank investment in, **14**, 1006
leasing, development of, **14**, 1006
Finance lease
asset, acquisition of, **14**, 1005
building society facilities, **3**, 355
chattels mortgage, as, **14**, 1007
contractual terms—
big-ticket lease, **14**, 1055
delivery, **14**, 1058
fitness for purpose, **14**, 1059
generally, **14**, 1055
implied terms, **14**, 1055
insurance, **14**, 1057
rent variation clause, **14**, 1056
standard form, **14**, 1055
full pay-out lease, as, **14**, 1005
fundamental basis of, **14**, 1005

Finance lease—*continued*
model, **14**, 1005
primary period, **14**, 1005
product of leasing industry, **14**, 1019
secondary period, **14**, 1005
security instrument, as, **14**, 1007
subject matter, range of, **14**, 1012
termination—
breach, on—
contract, termination of, **14**, 1063
damages—
lessee entitled to, **14**, 1065
lessor entitled to, **14**, 1066
liquidate damages clause, **14**, 1068
hiring, termination of, **14**, 1063
lessor—
common law rights, **14**, 1067
damages, entitled to, **14**, 1066
repossession, **14**, 1064
normal course, in—
early, **14**, 1061
expiry of hire period, **14**, 1060
proceeds of sale, **14**, 1062
Financial institutions
commodity markets, **2**, 1279
future markets, **2**, 1280
governmental assistance for, **2**, 1282
kinds of, **2**, 1261
nature etc of, **2**, 1264
recognition by Bank, **2**, 1261
See also particular financial bodies
Financial Intermediaries, Managers and Brokers Regulatory Association (FIMBRA)
promotion and marketing of insurance products, **12**, 809
recognised self-regulating organisation, as, **12**, 1312
regulation of insurance intermediaries, **12**, 812
Financial law
imperial law, English law as, **5**, 717
Financial management
meaning, **1**, 52
securities market, regulation of, **1**, 54
standards, **1**, 52
Financial reporting
government attitude to, **1**, 39
limitations of, **1**, 51
regulation of, **1**, 37
reports—
regulation, not subject to, **1**, 38
style, format and content of, **1**, 37
'true and fair view'—
concept of, **1**, 42, 43
See also ACCOUNTS
Financial services
advertising—
authorised person, by, **12**, 1366
collective investment scheme, promotion of, **12**, 1326
DIE advertisements, **12**, 1367
direct offer, **12**, 1367, 1367*n*
exempt, **12**, 1367, 1367*n*
image, **12**, 1367
investment advertisement, meaning, **12**, 1337*n*

Financial services—*continued*
advertising—*continued*
  investment business, of—
    extra-territorial application, **12**, 1337
    restrictions on, **12**, 1337
      exceptions to, **12**, 1337
  investors' remedies, **12**, 1410
  issue and approval of, **12**, 1367
    overseas person, for, **12**, 1368
  meaning of advertisement, **12**, 1337*n*
  non-private customers, directed towards, **12**, 1367
  off-the-page, **12**, 1363, 1367
  overseas business, **12**, 1366, 1370
    private UK customers, for, **12**, 1369
  private customers, directed towards, **12**, 1367, 1369
  short form, **12**, 1367
  SIB Core Conduct of Business Rules, **12**, 1366–1370
    application, **12**, 1400
    information about packaged products, **12**, 1363
    off-the-page, **12**, 1363
  takeover, **12**, 1367, 1367*n*
  third-tier rules, **12**, 1367
advice—
  conduit, **12**, 1360
  packaged products, SIB Core Conduct of Business Rules, **12**, 1365
adviser—
  agent on behalf of client, **12**, 1353, 1362
  principal dealing with clients, **12**, 1353, 1362
  SIB statement of principle, **12**, 1353
allocation—
  SIB Core Conduct of Business Rules—
    fair allocation, **12**, 1383
    timely allocation, **12**, 1382
appointed representative—
  exempted person, as, **12**, 1323
  meaning, **12**, 1361
  prohibitions on, SIB powers of as to, **12**, 1414
  SIB Core Conduct of Business Rules, **12**, 1361, 1378
authorisation of investment business, *see* INVESTMENT BUSINESS
authorised person—
  advertising by, **12**, 1366
  automatic authorisation—
    collective investment scheme from EC member state, **12**, 1318
    EC national carrying on investment business in EC member state, **12**, 1320
    generally, **12**, 1315
    insurance company, **12**, 1316
    registered friendly society, **12**, 1317
  collective investment scheme, promotion, **12**, 1326
  compliance orders, **12**, 1314
  conduct, **12**, 1342
  conduct of investment business, *see* INVESTMENT BUSINESS
  Core Conduct of Business Rules, **12**, 1356, 1399
  disqualification direction, **12**, 1338

Financial services—*continued*
authorised person—*continued*
  exempted person, *see* exempted person *below*
  fiduciary duties, **12**, 1354
  financial standing, **12**, 1342
  generally, **12**, 1301
  misconduct by, public statement as to, **12**, 1339
  necessity for authorisation, **12**, 1306
  prohibitions on, Securities and Investments Board powers as to, **12**, 1414
  recognised professional body, authorisation by, **12**, 1309, 1313, 1314
  register, **12**, 1415
  routes to authorisation, **12**, 1309
  Secretary of State, authorisation by, **12**, 1319
  Securities and Investments Board, authorisation by, **12**, 1309, 1310
    refusal, withdrawal or suspension, **12**, 1311
  Securities and Investments Board statements of principle, **12**, 1342
  self-regulating organisation, member of, **12**, 1309, 1312, 1314
  withdrawal or suspension of authorisation, **12**, 1311, 1342*n*, 1414
care, SIB statement of principle, **12**, 1344
charges—
  fairness, SIB Core Conduct of Business Rules, **12**, 1374
  information to be given, **12**, 1363
Chinese walls, **12**, 1358, 1395
churning—
  meaning, **12**, 1385
  SIB Core Conduct of Business Rules, **12**, 1385
clearing house—
  function, **12**, 1322
  recognised—
    exempted person under Financial Services Act 1986, as, **12**, 1322
  register, **12**, 1415
cold-calling—
  agreement entered after, effect of, **12**, 1334
  dealing restriction, **12**, 1335
  investors' remedies, **12**, 1410
  marketing restriction, **12**, 1335
  misconduct, public statement as to, **12**, 1339
  permitted, **12**, 1335
  prohibition on, **12**, 1333
    extra-territorial application, **12**, 1333
    power to lift, **12**, 1335
  regulations, **12**, 1335
  SIB rules, **12**, 1340
collective investment scheme, *see* COLLECTIVE INVESTMENT SCHEME
commission—
  fairness, **12**, 1374
  information to be given, **12**, 1363
  soft—
    Core Conduct of Business Rules, **12**, 1359, 1362
    meaning, **12**, 1359
compensation—
  claims for, **12**, 1422
  fund, establishment of, SIB rules, **12**, 1340
  SIB scheme, **12**, 1408, 1420, 1421

Financial services—*continued*
complaints, SIB Core Conduct of Business Rules,
    12, 1394
conflict of interest—
    SIB statements of principle, **12**, 1348, 1355
contingent liability transaction, **12**, 1375, 1375*n*,
    1386
    customer agreements, **12**, 1375
    meaning, **12**, 1375*n*
    SIB Core Conduct of Business Rules, **12**, 1386
cooling-off period, **12**, 1336
Core Conduct of Business Rules—
    see SECURITIES AND INVESTMENTS BOARD
Court of Session—
    interdict granted by, **12**, 1324, 1410, 1413
    restitution order, grant, **12**, 1324, 1411, 1413
customer—
    assets, SIB statement of principle, **12**, 1349
    classes of, SIB Core Conduct of Business
      Rules, **12**, 1398
    clients' money regulations, **12**, 1409
    dealing with, SIB Core Conduct of Business
      Rules—
      best execution, **12**, 1359, 1381
      churning, **12**, 1385
      dealing ahead of publication, **12**, 1384
      fair allocation, **12**, 1383
      order priority of customers, **12**, 1379
      switching, **12**, 1385
      timely allocation, **12**, 1382
      timely execution, **12**, 1380
    information about, SIB statement of principle,
      12, 1346
    information for, SIB statement of principle, **12**,
      1347
    investments, safeguarding, SIB Core Conduct
      of Business Rules, **12**, 1391
    non-private—
      advertising directed towards, **12**, 1367
      private customer treated as, **12**, 1398
      SIB Core Conduct of Business Rules, **12**, 1362
    order priority, **12**, 1379
    private, meaning, **12**, 1360*n*
    relationship with, SIB Core Conduct of
      Business Rules—
      appointed representatives, **12**, 1361, 1378
      charges, fairness of, **12**, 1374
      confirmations and information to customers,
        12, 1377
      customer agreements, **12**, 1375
      customers' rights, **12**, 1376
      customers' understanding, **12**, 1372
      fair and clear communications, **12**, 1371
      remuneration, fairness of, **12**, 1374
      suitability of recomendation or transaction to
        customer's requirements, **12**, 1373
    remedies available to, *see* investors' remedies
      below
damages, action for, **12**, 1412
database information access to, **18**, 1534
dealing—
    insider, *see* INSIDER DEALING
    meaning, **12**, 1510
    publication, ahead of, **12**, 1384

Financial services—*continued*
diligence, investment firms duty to act with due,
    12, 1344
EU legislation—
    collective investment scheme, authorisation,
      12, 1315, 1318, 1328
    insider dealing, directive on, **12**, 1536
    member state—
      collective investment scheme from, **12**, 1315,
        1318, 1328
      national from, authorised to run investment
        business in that state, **12**, 1315, 1320,
        1320*n*
    Undertakings for Collective Investment in
      Transferable Securities (UCITS), **12**, 1328,
      1399
execution—
    SIB Core Conduct of Business Rules—
      best execution, **12**, 1359, 1381
      timely execution, **12**, 1380
exempted person—
    Accountant of Court, **12**, 1323
    appointed representatives, **12**, 1323
      Securities and Investments Board Core
        Conduct of Business Rules, **12**, 1361
    Church of Scotland Trust, trustee, **12**, 1323
    European Bank for Reconstruction and
      Development, **12**, 1323
    Financial Services Act 1986, under, **12**, 1301,
      1306, 1321
    General Synod of the Scottish Episcopal Church,
      12, 1323
    meaning, **12**, 1321
    money market institution, **12**, 1321
    partnership, winding up, **12**, 1323
    recognised clearing house, **12**, 1322
    recognised investment exchange, **12**, 1322
    Scottish Enterprise, **12**, 1323
    Scottish Nuclear Ltd, **12**, 1323
    Scottish Tourist Board, **12**, 1323
    sheriff clerk, **12**, 1323
    trustee in sequestration, **12**, 1323
Financial Intermediaries Managers and Brokers
    Regulatory Association (FIMBRA), **12**, 1312
Financial Services Tribunal, *see* FINANCIAL
    SERVICES TRIBUNAL
generally, **12**, 1301, 1423
independence—
    SIB Core Conduct of Business Rules—
      appointed representatives, **12**, 1361
      generally, **12**, 1362
      inducements, **12**, 1357, 1362
      material interest, **12**, 1358, 1362
      polarisation, **12**, 1360
      soft commission, **12**, 1359, 1362
inducements—
    SIB Core Conduct of Business Rules, **12**, 1357,
      1362
    volume overriders, **12**, 1357
information and advice—
    records and reporting, requirements as to, **12**,
      1404, 1406
    SIB Core Conduct of Business Rules, **12**, 1365
      investment busines, advice on, **12**, 1364

Financial services—*continued*
information and advice—*continued*
 SIB Core Conduct of Business Rules—*continued*
  packaged products, information on, **12**, 1363
  periodic information, provision of, **12**, 1377
insider dealing, *see* INSIDER DEALING
integrity, SIB statement of principle, **12**, 1343
investment business, *see* INVESTMENT BUSINESS
investor protection under the Financial Services
 Act 1986—
 generally, **12**, 1301, 1423
 regulatory structure, **12**, 1306–1324
 scope, **12**, 1302, 1303
investors' remedies—
 agreements with unauthorised or unexempted
  person, **12**, 1413
 compensation, **12**, 1420–1422
 damages, action for, **12**, 1412
 interdict, **12**, 1410, 1413
 intervention, SIB powers, **12**, 1414
 investigation and information, SIB powers as
  to, **12**, 1415
 restitution order, **12**, 1411, 1413
 winding up, Securities and Investments Board
  powers as to, **12**, 1413
off-market deals—
 insider dealing, **12**, 1502, 1523, 1524
  deals outside Great Britain, **12**, 1525
 off-market dealer, meaning, **12**, 1524
own account transactions—
 investment business, excluded from, **12**, 1307
 Securities and Investments Board Core
  Conduct of Business Rules, **12**, 1390
packaged product—
 information and advice on, Securities and
  Investments Board Core Conduct of
  Business Rules, **12**, 1363, 1365
 meaning, **12**, 1360*n*
 polarisation, **12**, 1360
personal representative—
 insider dealing rules, **12**, 1532
 investment transactions arranged by or for, **12**,
  1307
prospectus, investor misled by, **4**, 304
public servant—
 insider dealing, **12**, 1502, 1519–1522
 primary insider, as, **12**, 1501
 tippee rules, **12**, 1522
 meaning, **12**, 1520
recognised professional body (RPB)—
 investment business, relations with, **12**, 1352
 register, **12**, 1415
regulatory systems, compliance with, **12**, 1393
 SIB Core Conduct of Business Rules, **12**, 1393
reportable transactions, SIB Core Conduct of
 Business Rules, **12**, 1390
restitution order—
 Court of Session powers, **12**, 1411, 1413
 investment business carried on by unauthorised
  or unexempted person, where, **12**, 1324
 misleading statement or practice, following, **12**,
  1333
Securities and Investments Board (SIB), *see*
 SECURITIES AND INVESTMENTS BOARD

Financial services—*continued*
self-regulating organisation (SRO), *see* SELF-
 REGULATING ORGANISATION
skill, SIB statement of principle, **12**, 1344
stabilisation—
 insider dealing rules, **12**, 1531
 SIB Core Conduct of Business Rules, **12**, 1388
statute, by, **4**, 305
switching, SIB Core Conduct of Business Rules,
 12, 1385
takeovers—
 insider dealing, **12**, 1502, 1514, 1515
 Panel on Takeovers and Mergers, members
  and staff of, **12**, 1520
transaction—
 contingent liability, **12**, 1386
 insider dealing, *see* INSIDER DEALING
 investment, *see* INVESTMENT
 material interest in, SIB Core Conduct of
  Business Rules, **12**, 1358
 own account, **12**, 1307, 1390
 reportable, **12**, 1390
Undertakings for Collective Investment in
 Transferable Securities (UCITS), **12**, 1328,
 1399
volume overrider—
 meaning, **12**, 1357
 SIB Core Conduct of Business Rules, **12**, 1357
Financial services body
building society's power to invest in and support,
 3, 369
Financial Services (Cancellation) Rules 1988
generally, **12**, 819, 821
Financial Services Tribunal
constitution, **12**, 1416
counsel or solicitor, appointment, **12**, 1416
hearings, **12**, 1418
investigation by, **12**, 1418
reference to, **12**, 1417
refusal of authorisation, referral to in cases of, **12**,
 1311
reports by, **12**, 1419
supervision of, **23**, 911*n*
Financial unsoundness, imputations of
defamation, **15**, 493
Financial year
accounting reference date, beginning with, **4**, 451
meaning, **12**, 1171
Financing terms
disregarded provisions, **4**, 1175
goods, restrictive agreement as to, **4**, 1154
Fine
defaulter, imprisonment—
 generally, **16**, 1433*n*
 treatment, **16**, 1428
fixed penalty, *see* FIXED PENALTY
generally, **17**, 799
Fingerprints and other impressions
arrest, taken following, **17**, 603, 605
identification by, **10**, 662
personal search, **16**, 1797
police officer, of—
 destruction, **16**, 1755
 register, **16**, 1752

Fingerprints and other impressions—
continued
prisoner, of, requirement to take, **16**, 1441
taking, **16**, 1752, 1796
warrant to take, **16**, 1794
Finlayson Report
recommendations, generally, **3**, 1286, 1287
Fire
act of God, caused by, **11**, 1746; **15**, 414
building controls—
assessment of fire resistant materials, **3**, 203
fire escape, provision of, **3**, 208
carrier, liability for, **3**, 608; **21**, 603
certificate, *see* FIRE CERTIFICATE
child under seven left in room with, **3**, 1248; **10**, 1135
damnum fatale, **11**, 1746; **15**, 414
homelessness as result of, **11**, 2055
inflammable material, storage, **14**, 1661
insurance—
friendly society, by, **12**, 686
indemnity insurance, as, **12**, 804
reinstatement clause, **12**, 890
mines and quarries, in, **14**, 1660, 1661, 1662
precautions—
building controls for, **3**, 208
hotelkeeper's duty as to, **11**, 1732, 1736, 1738
mines and quarries, **14**, 1660, 1661
sub-surface railway stations, **19**, 1057
railway engine, caused by, **19**, 1055, 1056
road, lighting at or near, **20**, 506, 704
Fire authority
acts or omissions committed by, **10**, 1474
business activities of, charges for, **10**, 1418
discharge of fire authority's functions by another fire authority, **10**, 1410
duties, **10**, 1427–1435
advisory arrangements, **10**, 1433
answering calls for assistance, **10**, 1430
civil defence, in relation to, **10**, 1435
damage, prevention or mitigation of, **10**, 1432
fire-fighting, **10**, 1427–1433
generally, **10**, 1411, 1474
information, arrangements for obtaining, **10**, 1431
non-fire-fighting, **10**, 1434
services, securement of, **10**, 1428
training, **10**, 1429
water supply, regarding, **10**, 1422
functions, **14**, 502–504
generally, **10**, 1407, 1408; **14**, 497
heritable property, powers in relation to, **10**, 1419–1421
landlord, as, **11**, 1937, 1944
negligence by fireman, liability for, **10**, 1474, 1475
reinforcement schemes, **10**, 1411
water authorities, relationship with, **10**, 1422–1426; **14**, 502
Fire certificate
appeals, **10**, 1461
application for, **10**, 1458
boarding houses, **10**, 1453
cancellation, **10**, 1463

Fire certificate—*continued*
contents, **10**, 1459
Crown premises, **10**, 1470
designation of buildings or part of buildings, **10**, 1453–1455
exemptions, **10**, 1456
dwellings, **10**, 1457
explosives or flammable materials kept on premises, **10**, 1457, 1467
factories, **10**, 1454
false statements as to, **10**, 1462
falsification of documents, **10**, 1462
hotels, **10**, 1453
inspection of premises, **10**, 1463
offences, **10**, 1460, 1462
offices, **10**, 1454
railway premises, **10**, 1454
requirement, generally, **10**, 1452
shops, **10**, 1454
use of building, **10**, 1452
Fire escape
building regulations, **3**, 208
grant for—
amount, **11**, 2029
generally, **11**, 2028
procedural and other provisions, **11**, 2030
provision, maintenance, etc, **10**, 1463
standard of, **10**, 1464
Fire-fighting
advisory arrangements, **10**, 1433
breathing apparatus, **14**, 1662
calls for assistance, arrangements for, **10**, 1430
damage, prevention or mitigation of, **10**, 1432
facilities—
building regulations, **3**, 208
fire-fighting purposes—
meaning, **10**, 1474
provision for, **10**, 1474
generally, **10**, 1427
information required for purposes of, **10**, 1431
injury in course of, liability, **15**, 401
local acts, adaptation of, **10**, 1409
regulations, power to make, **10**, 1463
reinforcement schemes, **10**, 1411
direction of Secretary of State, **10**, 1411
variation or revocation, **10**, 1411
securing services, **10**, 1428
training, **10**, 1429
See also FIRE SERVICES
Fire services
administration—
authorities, *see* FIRE AUTHORITY
central control, **10**, 1412–1415
finance, **10**, 1416–1418
Fire Services Act 1947..., **10**, 1407
fire-fighting function, discharge of, **10**, 1409–1411
generally, **10**, 1407, 1408
heritable property, **10**, 1419–1421
Local Government (Scotland) Act (1973), **10**, 1408
reinforcement schemes, **10**, 1411
water authorities, relationship with, **10**, 1422–1426

Fire services—*continued*
central control, **10**, 1412–1415
central rescue station, **14**, 1662
certificates, *see* FIRE CERTIFICATE
charges—
  business activity of fire authority, for, **10**, 1418
  general rule, **10**, 1434
  non-fire-fighting services, **10**, 1434
  services, for, **10**, 1418, 1418*n*
  value added tax, **10**, 1418
chief fire officer, appointment, **14**, 249
civil defence, arrangements for, **10**, 1435
civil liberty, aspects of, **10**, 1474–1476
combined areas, **14**, 498
committees, **14**, 499
compulsory acquisition of land by fire authority, **10**, 1421
employment in—
  discipline, **14**, 501
    caution, **10**, 1440
    conditions of service, **10**, 1439
    dismissal, **10**, 1440
    investigations into, **10**, 1440
    necessity for, **10**, 1440
    pay stoppages, **10**, 1440
    reduction in rank, **10**, 1440
    regulations as to, **10**, 1440
    reprimand, **10**, 1440
    requirement to resign, **10**, 1440
    standard of proof, **10**, 1440
  establishment schemes, **10**, 1438
  fire brigade appointments, **10**, 1437
  Firemen's Pension Scheme—
    contents, **10**, 1445
    development of, **10**, 1444
    Fire Brigade Pensions Act 1925 ..., **10**, 1442
    generally, **10**, 1443
    injury awards, **10**, 1448
    ordinary pensions, **10**, 1446
    review, **10**, 1449
    state benefits, relationship to, **10**, 1450
    widow's pensions, **10**, 1447
  generally, **10**, 1436
  military aid, **10**, 1441
  promotion, **10**, 1437
  qualifications, **10**, 1437
  safety of employees, responsibility for, **10**, 1474
  strikes, **10**, 1441
establishment schemes, **14**, 500
finance—
  central government assistance, **10**, 1417
  generally, **10**, 1416
fire escapes, *see* FIRE ESCAPE
fire hydrants, **10**, 1424
fire precautions—
  building standard regulations, **10**, 1451, 1464
  concept of, **10**, 1451
  Crown property, **10**, 1470
  enforcement, **10**, 1468
  fire certificates, **10**, 1452–1462
  legislative background, **10**, 1451
  liquor licensing, **10**, 1473
  local authority loans, **10**, 1469

Fire services—*continued*
fire precautions—*continued*
  regulations, **10**, 1463–1467
    building standards, **10**, 1451, 1464
    common stairs, **10**, 1465
    electrical luminous tube signs, **10**, 1466
    persons other than occupiers, **10**, 1463
    prohibition notices, **10**, 1467
    Secretary of State's powers in relation to, **10**, 1463
  sports venues, **6**, 1098; **10**, 1471, 1472; **19**, 1253
fire-fighting, *see* FIRE-FIGHTING
firemaster—
  appointment, **14**, 110, 501
  discipline, **14**, 501
  dismissal, **14**, 110
functions—
  fire certificate, **14**, 503
  fire precautions, **14**, 503, 504
  fire-fighting, **14**, 502
  land, compulsory purchase of, **14**, 502
  means of escape, **14**, 503, 504
  water authority, agreement with, **14**, 502
heritable property, fire authorities' powers in relation to, **10**, 1419–1421
historical background—
  Auxiliary Fire Service, **10**, 1404
  Fire Brigades Act 1938..., **10**, 1403
  Fire Services Act 1947..., **10**, 1406, 1407
  National Fire Service, **10**, 1405
  nineteenth and twentieth centuries, **10**, 1402
  pre-nineteenth century, **10**, 1401
inspectorate, **10**, 1414, 1468
joint committee, powers as to heritable property, **10**, 1420
London, **14**, 62
negligence, liability for, **10**, 1474, 1475
  fire services vehicles, injuries caused by, **10**, 1476
non-fire-fighting, **10**, 1434
  charges for, **10**, 1434
occupier of premises—
  liability for fire, **10**, 1475
  liability to firemen, **10**, 1475
officer—
  appointment of, **14**, 249
  charge, in, **10**, 1426
    water supply, duties in relation to, **10**, 1426
other ranks, appointment of, **14**, 249, 501
premises, firemen's safety to be taken into consideration, **10**, 1475
reform, **14**, 49
reinforcement schemes, **10**, 1411
Scottish Central Fire Brigades Advisory Council, **10**, 1415
Scottish Home and Health Department, role of, **10**, 1413
Secretary of State for Scotland, role of, **10**, 1411, 1413, 1463; **14**, 505
sheriff court jurisdiction, **6**, 1098, 1101
traffic lights and direction arrows, exemption from compliance with, **10**, 1475
training, **10**, 1429

Fire services—*continued*
water authorities, relationship with—
    agreement with water authorities, **10**, 1423
    duties on fire authorities, **10**, 1422
    fire hydrants, **10**, 1424
    officer in charge, duties in relation to, **10**, 1426
water supply, **25**, 536
    compensation payable for use of, **10**, 1425
    officer in charge, duties in relation to, **10**, 1426
    persons other than water authorities, **10**, 1425
    water authorities, relationship with, **10**, 1422–1426
See also FIRE-FIGHTING

Firearm
accessory, as, **10**, 1505
    meaning of accessories, **10**, 1508
acquisition, **10**, 1512, 1514
    children and young persons, by, **10**, 1551
    Crown servant, by, **10**, 1580
    police officer, by, **10**, 1580
air weapons, *see* AIR WEAPON
alarm guns, **10**, 1506
ammunition, *see* AMMUNITION
antiques and trophys of war, **10**, 1511, 1519
    firearm certificate exemptions, **10**, 1520, 1542, 1542*n*
appeal to sheriff relating to, **17**, 1250
arrest—
    powers of, in relation to firearms offences, **10**, 1576, 1577
    use of firearm to resist, **10**, 1564
assault involving, **7**, 226, 244
Behring Sea Award Act 1894..., **11**, 217
borrowed, **10**, 1514
cadet corps members, possession of firearms by, **10**, 1538
cannon, **10**, 1506
carrying with criminal intent, **10**, 1566
cartridges, *see* CARTRIDGES
cemetery, discharge in, **3**, 527
certificate, *see* FIREARM CERTIFICATE
children and young persons—
    gifts to, **10**, 1551, 1578
    hire to, **3**, 1223
    owned by, **10**, 1126
    possession or use by—
        air weapons and ammunition, **10**, 1551, 1554
        prohibited weapons, **10**, 1552
        purchase, acquisition of other form of transfer by, **10**, 1551
        restrictions, generally, **3**, 1223; **10**, 1550, 1552
        shot guns, **10**, 1553
    sale to, **3**, 1223
    supply to, **10**, 1551, 1570
cinematic performances, used in, **10**, 1518, 1518*n*, 1540
clubs—
    inspection of premises, **10**, 1575
    members of, **10**, 1538
codification of Firearms control, **10**, 1503
component part, **10**, 1505
    meaning, **10**, 1507
conversion, **10**, 1507, 1519, 1572
crime prevention, **10**, 1562–1573

Firearm—*continued*
de-activated, **10**, 1509
dealers—
    employees of, firearm or shot gun certificates, **10**, 1532
    firearm or shot gun certificates, **10**, 1532
    future disqualification, **10**, 1559
    inspection of premises, **10**, 1575
    non-registered dealers, transactions with, **10**, 1561
    Northern Ireland, registration in, **10**, 1582
    register of transactions, **10**, 1560
        exemptions, **10**, 1560
        false entries, **10**, 1560*n*
        inspection of, **10**, 1575
        non-compliance, **10**, 1560*n*
        non-registered dealers, transactions with, **10**, 1561
    registration—
        appeals, **10**, 1558
        application, **10**, 1555
        chief constables' role, **16**, 1738
        court order, imposed by, **10**, 1559
        designated place of business, removal from register, **10**, 1557
        generally, **10**, 1555
        grounds for refusal, **10**, 1556
        new places of business, **10**, 1555
        Northern Ireland, in, **10**, 1582
        removal from register, **10**, 1557
        appeals, **10**, 1558
distribution, control of, **10**, 1504
drunk in possession of, in public place, **10**, 1567
drunk or of unsound mind, persons, supply to, **10**, 1571
dummy, **10**, 1507, 1507*n*
electrical stun devices, **10**, 1506, 1516
enforcement powers, **10**, 1574–1578
explosives, *see* EXPLOSIVES
export, **7**, 1194; **10**, 1547, 1581
Firearm Acts 1968–1988..., **10**, 1504, 1562
Firearms Consultative Committee, **10**, 1584, 1584*n*
forfeiture, **10**, 1578
game laws, **10**, 1583
gift, accepted as, **10**, 1514
Gun Barrel Proof Acts 1868–1978..., **10**, 1579
gunpowder, **10**, 1510
harpoon guns, **10**, 1521
hired, **10**, 1514
    child or young person, by, **10**, 1551, 1570
historical development of law, **10**, 1501–1503
imitation, **10**, 1505
    antique Firearm, **10**, 1511
    arrest, used to resist, **10**, 1564
    carrying with criminal intent, **10**, 1566
    conversion of, **10**, 1507, 1572
    Fire Arms Acts 1968–1988..., **10**, 1504
    meaning, **10**, 1509
    possession while committing criminal activity, **10**, 1565
    prohibited weapons, **10**, 1516
    using or attempting use to resist or prevent arrest or detention, **16**, 1807

Firearm—*continued*
imported, proving, **10**, 1579
industrial tools, **10**, 1506
issue, chief constables' role, **16**, 1738
legislation, generally, **10**, 1501
lethal barrelled weapon, **10**, 1505
  accessory to, **10**, 1505, 1508
  component part, **10**, 1505, 1507
  meaning, **10**, 1506
  shot gun as, **10**, 1520
line-throwing purposes, used for, **10**, 1516
machine guns and pistols, **10**, 1516
  weapons capable of adaptation to, **10**, 1516
manufacture, control of, **10**, 1504, 1512
meaning of firearm, **10**, 1505
miniature rifle clubs, **10**, 1538
miniature rifle ranges, **10**, 1539
mortars, **10**, 1516
movement of, control over, **10**, 1581
museum firearms licences, **10**, 1548
nail guns, **10**, 1506
Night Poaching Acts, **11**, 810, 813
night shooting of ground game, **11**, 872
noxious liquid or gas, discharge of, **10**, 1516
offensive weapons, as, **10**, 1506
owner's art and part liability, **7**, 182
pawned, Firearm requiring certificates may not
  be, **10**, 1519, 1520, 1555*n*
pistols—
  machine, **10**, 1516
  pistol clubs, **10**, 1538, 1575
  prohibited weapons, as, **10**, 1506*n*
possession—
  committing criminal activity, while, **10**, 1565
  control of, generally, **10**, 1504, 1512
  intent to injure, with, **10**, 1563
  meaning, **10**, 1513
  police officer, by, **10**, 1580
  prohibited persons, by, **10**, 1569
preservation of public safety, **10**, 1562–1573
Prevention of Terrorism Act 1978..., **10**, 1563
prohibited persons under Firearms Acts 1968–
  1988..., **10**, 1569
  application for removal of prohibition, **10**, 1569
prohibited weapons—
  acquisition, **10**, 1518
  aerosol sprays, **10**, 1516
  authority for possession, **10**, 1518
  children and young persons, possession by, **10**,
    1552
  control of, generally, **10**, 1505, 1512, 1515
  conversion of, **10**, 1516
  flame throwers, **10**, 1516
  gas sprays, **10**, 1516
  imitation, **10**, 1516
  manufacture, **10**, 1518
  meaning, **10**, 1515, 1516
  possession, **10**, 1518
  purchase, **10**, 1518
  sale, **10**, 1518
  theatrical or cinematographic performances, **10**,
    1518, 1518*n*
  transfer, **10**, 1518

Firearm—*continued*
proving, **10**, 1519, 1579
  counterfeit marks, **10**, 1579
public place—
  carrying in, **10**, 1567
  drunk in possession in, **10**, 1567
pump-action, 1516*n*; **10**, 1516
purchase—
  children and young persons, by, **10**, 1551
  generally, **10**, 1512
  meaning, **10**, 1514
pyrotechnical purposes, used for, **10**, 1516
reckless discharge, **7**, 80, 82, 82*n*; **10**, 1573
repairs, **10**, 1519
revolvers, **10**, 1516, 1516*n*
rifle, **10**, 1516, 1538, 1539
rifle clubs, **10**, 1538, 1575
rocket launchers, **10**, 1516
rocket signal devices, **10**, 1506
sale, control of, **10**, 1504, 1512, 1514
search, powers of, **10**, 1574, 1575
seizure and detention of, **10**, 1574, 1576
  control over movement of firearms and
    ammunition, **10**, 1581
self-loading, **10**, 1516, 1516*n*
semi-automatic, **10**, 1516
sheriff court jurisdiction, **6**, 1102
ship, transport to, **10**, 1581
shooting galleries, firearm certificates, **10**, 1539
shortening, **10**, 1572, 1577*n*
shot guns, *see* SHOT GUN
signalling apparatus, **10**, 1516
starting pistol, **10**, 1507*n*
stop and search powers, **10**, 1574
supply—
  children and young persons, to, **10**, 1570
  drunk or of unsound mind, persons, to, **10**, 1571
  prohibited persons, to, **10**, 1569
testing, **10**, 1519, 1579
theatrical performances, used in, **10**, 1518, 1518*n*,
  1540
toy, **10**, 1506
transfer, **10**, 1512, 1514
  children and young persons, by, **10**, 1551
  control of, **10**, 1504
  prohibited persons, by, **10**, 1569
trespass with, **10**, 1568, 1583
two or more missiles discharged without repeated
  trigger pressure, **10**, 1516
unlawfully used to kill or injure deer, **11**, 943
using or attempting use to resist or prevent arrest
  or detention, **16**, 1807
visitors' permits, **10**, 23, 1531, 1546
  group applications, **10**, 23
warrant, search, **10**, 1575
wild birds or animals taken or killed with, **11**,
  880, 884
Firearm certificate
age limit, **3**, 1223
air weapons, **10**, 1521
ammunition, *see* AMMUNITION
applications, **10**, 1522
  details to be included, **10**, 1522
  photographs may be required, **10**, 1522

Firearm certificate—*continued*
cancellation—
  generally, **10**, 1578
  offences under Deer (Scotland) Act 1959..., **11**, 959
chief constable, functions of, **10**, 1523–1528
conditions prescribed, **10**, 1522
exemptions, **10**, 1519
  aircraft, equipment for, **10**, 1541
  antique guns and trophys of war, **10**, 1520, 1542, 1542*n*
  auctioneers, **10**, 1534
  borrowed rifles on private premises, **10**, 1545
  cadet corps members, **10**, 1538
  carriers, **10**, 1534
  cinematic performances, **10**, 1540
  club members, **10**, 1538
  Crown servants, **10**, 1543
  dealers and their employees, **10**, 1555
  export, firearms acquired for, **10**, 1547
  generally, **10**, 1532
  gun bearers, **10**, 1536
  miniature rifle ranges, **10**, 1539
  museum firearm licences, **10**, 1548
  police officers, **10**, 1543
  police permits, **10**, 1544
  private premises, **10**, 1545, 1549
  race meeting starters, **10**, 1537
  registered dealers and their employees, **10**, 1533
  ships, equipment for, **10**, 1541
  shooting galleries, **10**, 1539
  slaughtering instruments, **10**, 1535
  theatrical performances, **10**, 1540
  visitors' permits, **10**, 1531, 1546
  warehousemen, **10**, 1534
false, **10**, 1519, 1520
firearms requiring, **10**, 1512
generally, **10**, 1519, 1519*n*
grant, **10**, 1522
issue, chief constables' role, **16**, 1738
Northern Ireland, granted in, **10**, 1582
personation of person to whom made, **10**, 1519, 1520
production of, powers to demand, **10**, 1576
refusal, **10**, 1523
  challenge of decision, **10**, 1524
renewal, **10**, 1522
repairing, testing or proving Firearm, **10**, 1519
revocation, **10**, 1523, 1524
sheriff, functions of, **10**, 1524–1528
shot guns, **10**, 1520
signature, **10**, 1522
visitors' permits, **10**, 1531, 1546
Firemaster
relaxation of building regulations, notification of application for, **3**, 212
Fireplace
grant to adapt, **9**, 1138
Fireraising
actus reus, **7**, 416
barratry, **21**, 554*n*
criminal jurisdiction, **17**, 516
culpable and reckless, **7**, 415
death during course of, **7**, 270

Fireraising—*continued*
defences, **7**, 419
firearm or imitation firearm possessed during, **10**, 1565
generally, **7**, 415
insurers, to defraud, **7**, 418
malice, **7**, 80
malicious mischief, and, **7**, 415, 417
mens rea, **7**, 417
negligent, **7**, 417
reckless, **7**, 82, 88
wilful, **7**, 82, 84, 88, 89, 415, 417
Fireworks
conveyance of, **10**, 1616
dangerous, special powers in relation to, **10**, 1634
explosives, as, **10**, 1586, 1588
sale of, **10**, 1615
  person under age of sixteen, to, **3**, 1223
small fireworks factory licence, **10**, 1614
throwing, casting or setting alight in road or public place, **10**, 1628
See also EXPLOSIVES
Firm
See PARTNER-PARTNERSHIP
First calling
summary causes, **17**, 1305
First demand guarantee
meaning, **3**, 987
use, **3**, 987
First-party cover
meaning, **12**, 805
Firth
sheriff, jurisdiction of, **4**, 2
Fiscal
meaning, **17**, 530
See also PROCURATOR FISCAL
Fish
close seasons—
  buying, selling or exposing for sale during, **11**, 312
fisheries, *see* FISHERIES
fishings, *see* FISHINGS
food, preparation and sale as, **11**, 312
freshwater—
  fishing, regulation of, **11**, 10–30
    electricity generating stations, **11**, 10
    fish farmers, concessions to, **10**, 12*n*; **11**, 10
    net, **11**, 11
    permitted methods of fishing, **11**, 11
    poaching, **11**, 10
    River Tweed, **11**, 10
    rod and line, **11**, 11
    Solway Firth, **11**, 10
    statutory basis, **11**, 10
    trap, **11**, 11
    unlawful methods, **11**, 12
  meaning, **11**, 5*n*
  poaching, **11**, 10, 11
  salmon fishing rights and, **11**, 5
obstructing passage of, **19**, 22
ownership, **7**, 333
products—
  cakes, **11**, 353
  composition, **11**, 366

Fish—*continued*
products—*continued*
   fish content, declaration of, **11**, 366
   ingredients, list of, **11**, 366
   labelling, **11**, 366
res nullius, as, **18**, 280
royal, **18**, 543
Slaughter of Animals (Scotland) Act 1980 not
   applicable to, **11**, 496
Fish farm
buildings—
   marine fish farm, **11**, 61
   planning permission, **11**, 59
concessions to, **11**, 10, 12*n*
derating of, **11**, 64; **24**, 654
   extent of relief, **24**, 656
disease control, **11**, 60
exceptions and exemptions for, **11**, 63
exemptions from prosecution, **11**, 13
farmed salmon, ownership, **18**, 320
financial assistance for, **11**, 214
fish farming, meaning, **11**, 214*n*
inland, **11**, 57, 59, 60
   regulation, **11**, 60
lease, **13**, 205
marine, **11**, 57, 61
   lease, **11**, 61
   licence for, **11**, 61
meaning, **11**, 57; **24**, 655
natural harbour, in, **11**, 1304
planning permission, **11**, 59
pollution control, **11**, 62
rating relief and derating, **11**, 64; **24**, 654, 656
registration of businesses, **11**, 60
River Tweed, **11**, 43
salmon, **11**, 5*n*, 58
   farming rights included in salmon fishing rights,
      18, 321
   unclean or unseasonable salmon, **11**, 18
shellfish, **11**, 57, 60
statutory regulation, **11**, 60
trout, **11**, 58
   brown, **11**, 58
   close time, **11**, 53
   rainbow, **11**, 58
weekly close time, **11**, 17
Fish hatchery
diversion of water, **25**, 327
Fish pass
preventing passage of salmon through, **11**, 19
Fisheries
access to, United Nations Convention on the
   Law of the Sea, **11**, 109
act or omission exempted by Secretary of State,
   11, 13, 18
allowable catch, **11**, 95
assessments, district salmon fisheries boards'
   powers, **11**, 38
British, access to, **11**, 131, 132
brown trout, *see* TROUT
bull trout, *see* TROUT
byelaws, fisheries Acts implemented by, **11**, 117
closed areas, **11**, 95

Fisheries—*continued*
closed seasons, **11**, 95
   See also CLOSE TIME
Common Agricultural Policy, within scope of, **1**,
   879, 942, 944
Common Fisheries Policy, *see* COMMON FISHERIES
   POLICY
competition law, **4**, 1165
conservation measures—
   bilateral relations, **1**, 949
   Conservation of Seals Act 1970..., **11**, 220
   Council rules determining, **1**, 944
   definition, **11**, 90
   European Community, **1**, 947; **11**, 67
   exclusive zones, **1**, 946; **11**, 107
   exploration and exploitation of natural
      resources interfering with, **11**, 85
   high seas, fish stocks in, **11**, 89, 90
   international commitments, Community making,
      1, 948
   international fishery commissions, **11**, 67
   landing of foreign-caught fish, **11**, 144, 150
   making and maintaining shellfish beds, **11**, 157
   member states not having competence in, **1**, 946
   nets and gear, regulations and conventions, **11**,
      89, 146
   salmon—
      act or omission relating to salmon, salmon
         roe or salmon eggs, **11**, 13, 43
      Convention for the Conservation of Salmon
         in the North Atlantic Ocean, **11**, 103
      North Atlantic, **11**, 67, 101–105
      North Atlantic Salmon Conservation
         Organisation, **11**, 67, 104, 105
      stocks of, **11**, 89, 90
   scientific research, **11**, 68
   sea fish, of, **11**, 144–154
      bodies corporate, offences by, **1**, 153
      enforcement, **11**, 154
      foreign-caught sea fish, regulation of landing,
         11, 144, 150
      high seas, stocks in, **11**, 89, 90
      increase or improvement of marine resources,
         measures for, **11**, 151
      restrictions on fishing for sea fish, **11**, 148
      size limits for fish, **11**, 144, 145
      trans-shipment of fish, prohibition on, **11**,
         44, 147, 149
   Sea Fish (Conservation) Act 1967..., **11**, 144
   seals, **11**, 220
   shellfish fisheries, **11**, 161, 162
   trans-shipment of fish, **11**, 144, 147, 149
   United Nations Convention on the Law of the
      Sea, **11**, 82, 84, 106–109
continental shelf, *see* CONTINENTAL SHELF
Convention for Regulating the Police of the
   North Sea Fisheries, **11**, 124, 126
crabs, *see* CRABS
district salmon fishery boards, *see* DISTRICT
   SALMON FISHERY BOARDS
European Community—
   Common Fisheries Policy, **11**, 65, 70, 76, 81,
      112–115, 117
   access to British fisheries, **11**, 131, 132

Fisheries—*continued*
European Community—*continued*
Common Fisheries Policy—*continued*
Cameron Report, **11**, 112
conflict with national measures, **11**, 113
inshore fishing, **11**, 135
relation with United Nations Convention on the Law of the Sea, **11**, 106
enforcement of rules and control measures, **11**, 178–182
conservation measures, **11**, 180
quota measures, **11**, 181
third countries, fishing by, **11**, 182
exclusive economic zone, **11**, 107, 116
exclusive fishery zone, **11**, 80, 81, 92, 107, 116; **19**, 608
interference with fishing operations within, **11**, 172
sea-fishery officers' powers within, **11**, 172
expenditure programme, **5**, 578
exploration and exploitation of natural resources interfering with fishing, **11**, 85
external Community competence, **1**, 948, 949
Fisheries Committee, functions of, **11**, 39
Fisheries Convention 1964..., **11**, 81
fishery products—
common organisation—
introduction of, **1**, 942
price system, **1**, 942
quotas jeopardising system of, **1**, 945
fish farms, *see* FISH FARM
fishing boats, *see* FISHING BOATS
foreign-caught fish, landing, **11**, 144, 150
freshwater fish, *see* FISH
grants and loans for, **2**, 1289
harbours, dredging, **6**, 1141
hatchery, diversion of water, **25**, 327
herring, *see* HERRING
high seas, *see* HIGH SEAS
inshore—
bodies corporate, offences by, **11**, 143
England and Wales, **11**, 133, 134
byelaws, **11**, 133
fishery officers, **11**, 133
local fisheries committees, **11**, 134
illegally caught fish, discarding, **11**, 137
Inshore Fishing (Scotland) Act 1984..., **11**, 135
nets, prohibitions concerning, **11**, 138
offences and penalties, **11**, 140
prohibition of sea fishing in specified areas, **11**, 136
salmon nets, prohibition of fishing near, **11**, 139
sea-fishery officers, powers of, **11**, 141
Secretary of State's powers, **11**, 135
internal Community competence—
1978—
after, **1**, 946
until, **1**, 945
source of, **1**, 944
international legal framework—
Common Fisheries Policy, **11**, 70
See also COMMON FISHERIES POLICY
conservation, **11**, 67, 68, 101–105

Fisheries—*continued*
international legal framework—*continued*
development of, **11**, 70
European Community, *see* European Community *above*
exclusive economic zone, **11**, 116
jurisdictional zones, **11**, 66
migratory species, **11**, 65
need for, **11**, 65
resolution of conflicts, **11**, 69
scientific research, **11**, 68
territorial limits, *see* TERRITORIAL SEA
United Nations Conferences on the Law of the Sea, **11**, 65, 70, 73, 76, 80
United Nations Convention on the Law of the Sea, **11**, 82, 84, 106–109
waters off Scotland, **11**, 92–96
landing of foreign-caught fish, **11**, 144, 150
legislation, changes or variation in, **11**, 38
licensing—
after 1983..., **11**, 115
before 1983..., **11**, 114
pressure stocks, **11**, 115
limits, **1**, 943; **11**, 130–132
marine mammals, *see* MARINE MAMMALS
migratory species, **11**, 65
mussels, *see* MUSSELS
natural resources—
Convention on the Continental Shelf, **11**, 82–85
exploration and exploitation interfering with navigation, fishing or conservation, **11**, 85
meaning, **11**, 84
rights to, **11**, 83
nets—
bag, **11**, 17*n*
Behring Sea Award Act 1894 ..., **11**, 217
drift, **11**, 12
fly, River Tweed, **11**, 43
freshwater fishing by, **11**, 11
gill, 12*n*; **11**, 12
inshore fishing, **11**, 138
mesh size, **6**, 32; **11**, 12; **12***n*, 23
high seas, **11**, 89
North-East Atlantic Fisheries Commission powers, **11**, 95
sea fishing, **11**, 144, 146
paidle—
meaning, **11**, 45
Solway Firth, **11**, 45
prohibited use, **11**, 12, 42
prohibition of fishing near, **11**, 139
proposed review of salmon net fishing, **11**, 39
River Tweed, **11**, 42, 43
seine, **11**, 12
stake, River Tweed, **11**, 43
trawl, **11**, 12
wild birds, catching in, **11**, 880, 882
North-East Atlantic Fisheries Commission, **11**, 92–96
Northwest Atlantic Fisheries Commission, **11**, 92, 97–100
obstructing passage of fish, document authorising, **19**, 22

Fisheries—*continued*
open access to high seas fisheries, problems of, **11**,
   89
over exploitation, **11**, 65
oysters, *see* OYSTERS
poaching—
   brown trout, **11**, 51
   forfeiture of fish or other articles, **11**, 27
   freshwater fish, **11**, 10
   salmon, **11**, 10, 11
poinding and sale of boat, gear or catch, **11**, 174
pollution—
   discharge of pollutants into river, **11**, 6
   fish farms, **11**, 62
pressure stocks, **11**, 115
protection and conservation measures, **1**, 944; **6**,
   1159
protection and conservation measures 1.944—
   hydro-electric developments, **9**, 635
   protection orders, **11**, 55, 56
quotas, European Community, **11**, 181
regulation of conduct of operations—
   compensation for damage, **11**, 176
   fine in relation to, **11**, 174
regulations, power to make, **11**, 23
restrictions, **11**, 144
river, *see* RIVER
roe, buying, selling or possessing, **11**, 20
salmon, *see* SALMON-SALMON FISHERIES
scientific purpose—
   unclean or unseasonable salmon, taking or
     fishing for, **11**, 18
   whaling, permits for, **11**, 230, 238
sea, *see* SEA FISHERIES
sea-fishery officers, *see* SEA FISHERIES
seals, *see* SEALS
Secretary of State, powers of, **11**, 24, 30, 142
shellfish, *see* SHELLFISH
sheriff court jurisdiction, **6**, 1103
size limits for fish, **11**, 144, 145
spears, fishing with, **11**, 12
statutory instruments, fisheries Acts implemented
   by, **11**, 117
structural measures, **1**, 973
territorial jurisdiction, **4**, 2
territorial sea, *see* TERRITORIAL SEA
timeshare schemes, **11**, 34
total allowable catches, observation of, **1**, 947
trans-shipment of fish, **11**, 144, 147, 149
   unqualified fishing boats, **11**, 183
trout, *see* TROUT
unilateral measures, approval for, **1**, 945
United Kingdom laws—
   access to British fisheries, **11**, 131, 132
   bodies corporate, offences by, **11**, 143, 153
   Cameron Report, **11**, 112
   conservation of sea fish, **11**, 144–154
   consolidating legislation, need for, **11**, 116
   Convention for Regulating the Police of the
     North Sea Fisheries, **11**, 124
   early legislation, **11**, 118–129
   European Community measures, conflict with,
     11, 113
   fisheries Acts, implementation of, **11**, 117

Fisheries—*continued*
United Kingdom laws—*continued*
   fishery limits, **11**, 130–132
   foreign-caught sea fish, regulations on landing,
     11, 150
   general purposes and objectives, **11**, 110
   inshore fisheries—
     bodies corporate, offences by, **11**, 143
     discarding of illegally caught fish, **11**, 137
     England and Wales, **11**, 133, 134
     police powers, **11**, 142
     prohibitions, **11**, 136, 138, 139
     Scotland, **11**, 135–143
     sea-fishery officer's powers, **11**, 141
     water bailiff's powers, **11**, 142
   licensing—
     after 1983..., **11**, 115
     before 1983..., **11**, 114
   marine resources, increase or improvement of,
     11, 151
   purposes and objectives, **11**, 110
   regulatory techniques, **11**, 111
   sea fisheries, **11**, 169–182
   shellfish, **11**, 155–168
   size limits for fish, **11**, 145
   trans-shipment of fish, prohibition on, **11**, 147,
     149
water bailiff, *see* WATER BAILIFF
water rights, acquisition of, **25**, 519
Welwod (Welwood)'s writings on, **19**, 608
whales, *see* WHALES
white fish, *see* WHITE FISH
wild birds or animals killed or taken in interests
   of, **11**, 881, 883, 885, 886
See also FISHING
Fishery Board for Scotland, 11, 32
Fishing
boundary, river or stream on, fishing rights, **18**,
   280
canals and inland waterways, **19**, 1106*n*
fishings, *see* FISHINGS
methods of, **11**, 11, 12
non-tidal loch, fishing rights, **18**, 306, 307
rights—
   lease, in, **13**, 194, 202
   landlord's hypothec, **13**, 513
   real right, as, **13**, 296, 297; **18**, 5, 7
   sasine, symbols of, **18**, 90
   servitude rights, whether constituting, **18**, 492
   valuation for rating, **24**, 657–661
riparian proprietor, rights of, **18**, 279, 280
royal fish, occupancy, no right of acquisition by,
   18, 543, 543*n*
salmon fishing rights, *see* SALMON-SALMON
   FISHERIES
udal law—
   salmon fishings, **24**, 315, 320
   sea fishings, **24**, 315
white fish and shellfish, public right to take—
   ancillary rights, **18**, 525
   foreshore, **18**, 524, 525
   generally, **18**, 494, 514
   navigation rights, and, **18**, 515
   salmon fishing, must not interfere with, **18**, 515

Fishing—*continued*
white fish and shellfish, public right to take—
  continued
  shellfish, meaning, **18**, 521
  waters not navigable, where, **18**, 521
  white fish, meaning, **18**, 521
See also FISHERIES; SALMON-SALMON FISHERIES;
  TROUT
Fishing association
advances to members, **12**, 623
generally, **12**, 614, 617
Fishing boats
abandoned at sea, **11**, 198
accidents, reporting, **11**, 207
anchor, under, **21**, 364
casualties and incidents, procedure for, **1**, 408
certificates, **11**, 201
collision regulations, **21**, 356
construction rules, **11**, 202
damages for loss of profits, assessment, **21**, 389
equipment requirements, **11**, 203
fines, **11**, 187
fishing vessel, meaning, **11**, 188*n*
foreign, meaning, **11**, 196*n*
fuel, excise duty relief, **7**, 1069
gear lost or abandoned at sea, **11**, 198
injury to boat or gear, inquiry into, **11**, 199
joint ownership, **11**, 128
jurisdiction of flag state over, **11**, 88
letters and numbers on, **11**, 197
licensing, **11**, 195
life-saving appliances, **11**, 202
lights and shapes to be displayed, **21**, 364
loading and unloading, **11**, 208
lost at sea, **11**, 198
meaning, **11**, 195*n*
medical stores, **11**, 206
mortgaging, **11**, 128
narrow channel or fairway, collision regulations,
  21, 347
offences, **11**, 187
  committed on fishing boat, **6**, 867
official papers, **11**, 123, 196
qualification, conditions for, **11**, 184
radios, **11**, 205
register of fishing vessels, **21**, 131*n*
registered vessel or share—
  mortgage of, **11**, 194
  transfer of or of interest in, **11**, 192, 193
registration, **11**, 188–190
  application, **11**, 190
  eligibility, **11**, 189
  exclusion from, **11**, 188
  full, **11**, 188
  Secretary of State's powers, **11**, 188–190
  separate, **11**, 188
  simple, **11**, 188
safety measures, **11**, 200–208
  accidents, report of, **11**, 207
  construction rules, **11**, 202
  equipment requirements, **11**, 203
  fishing vessel certificates, **11**, 201
  generally, **11**, 200
  life-saving appliances, **11**, 202, 203, 203*n*

Fishing boats—*continued*
safety measures—*continued*
  loading and unloading vessels, **11**, 208
  medical stores, **11**, 206
  radios, **11**, 205
  training, **11**, 204
Sea Fishing Boats (Scotland) Act 1886..., **11**, 128
sea-fishery officers' powers, **11**, 126, 185, 186
sea-fishing boat, meaning, **11**, 125*n*
shares in, **11**, 128
sound signals, **21**, 374
traffic separation scheme, **21**, 348
trawling, lights and shapes to be displayed, **21**,
  364
unqualified, **11**, 183
unregistered, **11**, 191
  British nationality, **21**, 141
Fishing vessels
See FISHING BOATS
Fishpond
meaning, **23**, 147*n*
trout taken from, **11**, 47
Fitness for purpose
building contract, contractor's obligations, **3**, 37
common law obligations, exclusion from, **14**,
  1059
contract for sale of moveable property—
  implied terms—
    generally, **20**, 823–827
    acceptable or satisfactory quality, **20**, 827
    onus of proof, **20**, 825
    reform, proposals for, **20**, 826
  merchantable quality, **20**, 824
lessor, obligations of, **14**, 1042
Fittings
accession, **18**, 578, 578*n*
  See also ACCESSION
building regulations, **3**, 208
meaning, **18**, 578
plant, whether, **14**, 1012
'Fitzmaurice Compromise'
domestic and international law, between, **19**, 652
Fixed assets
valuation, purposes of, **25**, 92
Fixed engine
salmon fishing rights, exercise of, **18**, 326
Fixed penalty
fixed penalty offences—
  'conditional offer', **6**, 1165
  district courts, **6**, 1165
  generally, **17**, 810
prosecutor's discretion to offer, **17**, 620
Fixed-sum credit
information, right to, **5**, 873
meaning, **5**, 808
running-account credit distinguished from, **5**, 808
Fixtures
accession, *see* ACCESSION
commercial lease, **13**, 588
constructive, doctrine of, **18**, 15
landlord's, capital allowances on, **19**, 1615
meaning, **18**, 578, 582
plant and machinery, *see* PLANT AND MACHINERY
trade, commercial lease, **13**, 566

Fixtures—*continued*
valuation for rating, **24**, 441
See also HERITABLE PROPERTY
Flag
shipping—
 discrimination, policy formulation as to, **21**,
  113
 requirement to fly, **21**, 140, 140*n*
 two flags, ship sailing under, **21**, 140
Flag of convenience, **21**, 43
policy formulation as to, responsibility for, **21**,
 113
Flare signal pen
firearm certificate, **10**, 1506*n*
Flat
meaning, **23**, 97*n*
public health nuisance in, **19**, 341
valuation for rating, **24**, 609
See also TENEMENT (law of)
Fleet Reserve
calling out, **2**, 745
composition, **2**, 743
Floating charge, **22**, 658, 680
absence of clear definition of, **4**, 652
alteration of—
 execution, **4**, 669
 instrument of alteration, **4**, 668
 registration, **4**, 670
arrestment and, **8**, 295
attachment of—
 acquirenda, **4**, 662
 diligence, effect on, **4**, 663
 effect of, **4**, 661
 general principles, **4**, 659
 property attached, **4**, 660
 receivership, on, **4**, 662
 winding up, on, **4**, 662
chargeholder, appointment of receiver by, **4**, 674
company assets, creation over, **6**, 638
conditions in, real conditions, as, **18**, 353
constitution of—
 companies which Court of Session has
  jurisdiction to wind up, **4**, 655
 other companies, **4**, 656
creation of right in security, **20**, 28
crystallisation, **6**, 638
discharge of, **6**, 745
English law, **4**, 651
fresh consideration, requirement for, **4**, 889
further reform, **4**, 649
generally, **4**, 439; **6**, 638
holder, circumstances justifying appointment of
 receiver by, **4**, 672
industrial and provident society, **12**, 641
inhibition and, **8**, 178
 inhibition after floating charge but before
  attachment, **8**, 180
 inhibition prior to floating charge, **8**, 179
Insolvency Act 1986 ..., **4**, 888
interpretation, **12**, 1262
introduction into Scots law, **6**, 638
maills and duties, and, **8**, 399
voting of, **6**, 775
old law, **4**, 887

Floating charge—*continued*
overriding interest—
 floating charge as, **6**, 775
 holder, of, **6**, 745
personal right, when, **18**, 8
poinding and, **8**, 240
position after 1961 and before 1972..., **4**, 64
position before 1961..., **4**, 647
possession and ownership of goods, **18**, 534
ranking of—
 express provisions, **4**, 664
 fixed securities arising by operation of law, **4**,
  665
 general rule, **4**, 667
 preferential creditors, **4**, 666
real right, when, **18**, 8
reform of law relating to, **4**, 308
registration, **18**, 8
registration of, **6**, 469, 745
 alteration, effect of, **4**, 670
 Companies Registration Office, at, **4**, 657
 company's own register, in, **4**, 658
relevant time, creation at, **4**, 890
right in security, as, **18**, 5
Scottish position, **4**, 652
securing obligations by, **4**, 439, 654; **13**, 1759
security of creditor in jeopardy, grounds for
 winding up by court, **4**, 729
sequestration for rent, and, **8**, 389
solvency test, **4**, 891
title sheet, **6**, 710
uncalled capital, **4**, 653
unintimated assignation defeated by, **20**, 47
validity, recognition of, **4**, 305
Floating rate note
negotiable instrument, as, **4**, 103
Floating sheriffs
appointment, **6**, 1048
Flood
alveus, operations on, **25**, 323
barriers, construction of, **25**, 378
coast protection, *see* COAST PROTECTION
contributory negligence, **15**, 413
control—
 generally, **25**, 375
 powers, **25**, 377
damage, nuisance as, **3**, 155
damnum fatale, **15**, 413
homelessness as result of, **11**, 2055
non-tidal river, of, barrier, **18**, 297
prevention—
 byelaws, **14**, 463
 compensation, **14**, 466
 Crown rights, **14**, 469
 entry, powers of, **14**, 465
 generally, **19**, 324; **25**, 376
 grant—
  exchequer, **14**, 468
  local authority, **14**, 467
 islands councils powers, **25**, 378
 land, acquisition of, **14**, 464
 local authority—
  contributions to and by, **14**, 467
  functions, **14**, 459

Flood—*continued*
prevention—*continued*
  local authority—*continued*
    generally, **14**, 459–469
    powers, **14**, 460
  powers, **25**, 377
  reform, **14**, 46
  road, prevention works, **20**, 660, 681
  scheme—
    confirmation, **14**, 105, 461, 462
    generally, **25**, 378
    operation, **14**, 462
    validity, **14**, 462
single interference caused by, **14**, 2053
warning system, **19**, 324; **25**, 379
Floodlight
road, at or near, **20**, 697
Floor
overloading, commercial lease, **13**, 269, 588
Flora and fauna
protection of—
  generally, **25**, 422
  polluting material—
    disposal of, **25**, 424
    removal of, **25**, 424
  review of consent, **25**, 423
Flotilla
command, **21**, 408
manned or unmanned, **21**, 408
relationship to third parties, **21**, 401
Flotsam
meaning, **21**, 511
wreck, when classed as, **21**, 511
Flour
advertisement, **11**, 359
composition, **11**, 359
emulsifiers and stabilisers not permitted, **11**, 373
labelling, **11**, 359
self-raising, food standard, **11**, 353
Fluoracetic acid
special restrictions, **14**, 1216
Fluoridation
domestic use, supply of water for, **25**, 506
harmful effects, **25**, 509
health authority powers as to, **19**, 320
interdict against addition, grounds for, **25**, 509
supplies abroad, **25**, 509
Flying freehold
belonging, test of, **14**, 1013
Fodder and feeding stuff
importation and landing, **1**, 725; **11**, 317
not food, **11**, 311
pesticides, powers as to import, sale and use of, **11**, 319
Foetus
See FETUS
Fog signals
explosives, as, **10**, 1586
licensing exemption, **10**, 1589, 1620
Fontainebleu Summit, **10**, 23
Food
additives, **11**, 371–379
  identification on label, **11**, 385
  milk, **11**, 442

Food—*continued*
administration of provisions—
  administrative authorities, **11**, 329
  central, **11**, 327
  local authority—
    acquisition of land by, **11**, 332
    default of, **11**, 331
  public analysts, **11**, 330
  Scottish Food Hygiene Council, abolition of, **11**, 328
advertisement, *see* ADVERTISEMENT
alcoholic liquor, *see* ALCOHOLIC LIQUOR
analysis of samples, **11**, 333–338
  certificates—
    evidence of, **11**, 424
    generally, **11**, 333
    offences in relation to, **11**, 427
  division and disposal of samples, **11**, 338, 423
  Government Chemist, by, **11**, 425
  manufacturer or packer, notification of, **11**, 338
  milk, **11**, 336, 338, 338*n*, 464
  proceedings following, **11**, 423–430
  procuring of samples, **11**, 334
  public analyst, *see* PUBLIC ANALYST
  vending machine, purchased from, **11**, 338*n*
  who may submit samples, **11**, 333, 334
antioxidants, **11**, 371
arsenic, restriction on use of, **11**, 380
brand names, **11**, 384
cognate law, **11**, 325, 326
  conditions of sale, implied, **11**, 326
  offences, **11**, 325
colouring matter, **11**, 372
  in milk, **11**, 442
Community law provisions, **1**, 874
composition—
  early legislation, **11**, 301, 304
  regulations, **11**, 352
    power to make, **11**, 306
  specific foods, **11**, 359–370
condemnation, **11**, 398
consumer protection, **6**, 1, 10, 11
containers, **11**, 350, 350*n*, 408, 409
contamination—
  designated areas and incidents, **11**, 318
  emergency orders on, **11**, 318
  protection from, **9**, 1205
dairies, **14**, 710
  See also DAIRIES
delivery of, **11**, 407
description of, power to make regulations, **11** 306
drugs, *see* DRUGS—
  medicine
durability, indication of, **11**, 383, 386
education authorities' duties in relation to, **8**, 850
emergency, state of, **11**, 320
emulsifiers, **11**, 373
erucic acid, restriction on use of, **11**, 381
European Community provisions—
  European Communities Act 1972..., **11**, 305
  generally, **11**, 321, 437
  harmonisation of rules, **10**, 336
  vegetables and fruit, grading of, **11**, 432

Food—*continued*
expenditure programme, **5**, 578
extraneous matter, **11**, 343, 349
fancy names, **11**, 384
food business, meaning, **11**, 409*n*
food poisoning, **11**, 406; **19**, 491
   meaning, **19**, 484
   notifiable disease, as, **19**, 484
fruit and vegetables, grading of, **11**, 432
general enforcement, **14**, 708
generally, **11**, 1779
handlers, hygiene regulations, **11**, 408, 415
heat treatment, **11**, 354, 355
history of legislation, **11**, 301
hygiene—
   alterations of premises, apportionment of
      expenses, **11**, 435
   certificate, **2**, 46
   cold stores, **11**, 405
   contamination, prevention of risk of, **11**, 410
   early legislation, **11**, 304
   equipment and utensils, **11**, 408, 409
   exportation, inspection of meat for, **11**, 417
   food poisoning, **11**, 406
   handlers, food, **11**, 408, 415
   imported food, **11**, 414
   meat—
      distribution of, **11**, 415, 416
      exportation, for, inspection of, **11**, 417
      handlers, **11**, 415
      markets, **11**, 412
      poultry, **11**, 418
      preparation for human consumption, **11**, 413
   poultry meat, **11**, 418
   premises where food prepared or sold, **11**, 408–
      410
   refuse, disposal of, **11**, 408, 410
   regulations—
      generally, **11**, 1780
      power to make, **11**, 306
      provisions in, **11**, 407–418
   reheating food, **11**, 408, 410
   shellfish, cleansing of, **11**, 403
   slaughter of animals, **11**, 404
      inspection of animals, **11**, 413
      inspection of carcases, **11**, 413
   stalls, **11**, 411
   statutory provisions, **11**, 403–406
   storage, **11**, 408, 409
   vehicles, **11**, 411
importation, **11**, 407
infestation, **11**, 317; **19**, 326
ingredients—
   control of substances used as, **11**, 317–379
   list of, **11**, 383, 385
   meat and fish products, **11**, 366
   restrictions on use of certain, **11**, 380–382
   Secretary of State's powers to obtain particulars
      of, **11**, 351
   water, **11**, 385
injurious—
   advertisement of, **11**, 341, 341*n*
   cumulative effect of multiple consumption, **11**,
      341

Food—*continued*
injurious—*continued*
   exposure for sale, **11**, 341
   offering for sale, **11**, 341
   preparation, **11**, 341
   sale, **11**, 341
   supplied otherwise than by sale, **11**, 342, 342*n*
irradiation, **11**, 357
labelling, **6**, 77; **11**, 359–370, 383–396, 1779
   additives, **11**, 387
   alcoholic drinks, **11**, 383, 391, 395
   colouring matter, **11**, 372
   conditions of use, **11**, 383
   durability of food, indication of, **11**, 383, 386
   early legislation, **11**, 304
   EEC Council Regulations, **11**, 383
   false, **11**, 350
   fancy confectionery, **11**, 383
   generally, **6**, 12, 77
   Her Majesty's forces or visiting forces, food for
      consumption of, **11**, 383
   immediate consumption, food for, **11**, 383, 388
   ingredients, list of, **11**, 383, 385
      low content of particular ingredient, **11**, 383
   instructions for use, **11**, 383, 386
   manner of, **11**, 392
   meat, **11**, 432
   milk, *see* MILK
   milk products, *see* MILK PRODUCTS
   mineral water, **11**, 383
   misleading, **11**, 383, 394
   name and address of manufacturer, packer or
      seller, **11**, 383
   names required by law, **11**, 384
   offences, **11**, 396
   place of origin, **11**, 383
   prepacked in special materials, **11**, 383
   prepared meals, **11**, 388
   preservatives, food containing, **11**, 377
   prohibited and restricted claims, **11**, 393
   regulation of, **11**, 383
      power to make regulations, **11**, 306
   small packages, **11**, 383, 389
   specific foods, of, **11**, 359–370
   storage instructions, **11**, 383
   unprepacked food, **11**, 383, 387
   vending machine, food sold from, **11**, 383, 388,
      390, 396
   wine, word used in composite name, **11**, 393,
      395
lead, restriction on use of, **11**, 382
legislation—
   byelaws, **11**, 322
   cognate law, **11**, 325, 326
   Crown, application to, **11**, 307
   early, **11**, 301–303
   emergency powers, **11**, 320
   European Communities Act 1972..., **11**, 305
   local, alteration of, **11**, 308–310
   milk, **11**, 302
   principal regulations, **11**, 306
   saving for pre-1956 subordinate legislation, **11**,
      323
   Scottish, **11**, 304–307

Food—*continued*

legislation—*continued*
  Secretary of State's powers, **11**, 321
  slaughterhouses, **11**, 303
  subordinate, **11**, 321–334
    regulations and orders, procedure for
      making, **11**, 324
manufacture—
  drainage and sanitation, **11**, 408
  equipment and utensils, **11**, 408, 409
  infested food, **11**, 317
  refuse, disposal of, **11**, 408
manufacturer or packer, notification of sampling,
  11, 338
meaning, **11**, 311
  excluded items, **11**, 311
milk, *see* MILK; MILK MARKETING BOARDS
mineral hydrocarbons, **11**, 375
names required by law, **11**, 384
not of kind demanded, sale of, **11**, 343–349
  extraneous matter, **11**, 343
  false representation, **11**, 346
  nature, substance or quality of food, **11**, 343
  notice to purchaser, **11**, 345
  question of fact, **11**, 347
  sale to prejudice of purchaser, **11**, 344
  standard of quality, **11**, 348
  statutory defences, **11**, 349
noxious ingredients, **11**, 325
offences relating to sale of, **11**, 1779
packaging, **11**, 407
  See also labelling *above*
pesticides, powers as to import, sale and use of,
  11, 319
premises—
  alteration, apportionment of expenses of, **11**,
    435
  closing order, **11**, 422
  control of, generally, **11**, 1781
  drainage, **11**, 419
  first aid equipment, **11**, 419
  forecourts and yards, **11**, 419
  hygiene regulations, **11**, 407, 408, 419–422
  infestations, **11**, 419
  lighting, **11**, 419
  registration, **11**, 420, 421
  sanitary provisions, **11**, 419
  sinks or other washing facilities, **11**, 419
  sleeping places or bedrooms, **11**, 419
  storage, **11**, 419
  ventilation, **11**, 419
  water supply, **11**, 419
  where prepared, **11**, 407, 420, 421
  where sold or offered, **11**, 407, 420, 421
preparation—
  apparatus, **11**, 407
  early legislation, **11**, 304
  infected person, by, **19**, 457, 491, 491*n*
  premises, regulation of, **11**, 407
preservatives, **11**, 377
  early legislation, **11**, 301
prevention of damage by injurious animals or
  birds, **11**, 859

Food—*continued*

price—
  marking regulations, **6**, 81; **11**, 314
  subsidies to reduce, limit or prevent increase
    of, **11**, 314
prize or reward, offered as, **11**, 400
prosecutions and penalties, **11**, 423–430
  act or default of other person, contravention
    due to, **11**, 428
  certificates of analysis, evidence of, **11**, 424
  Government Chemist, analysis by, **11**, 425
  nature of, **11**, 423
  offences in relation to, **11**, 427
  place of, **11**, 423
  presumptions, **11**, 429
  warranty—
    as defence, **11**, 426
    offences in relation to, **11**, 427
public analyst, *see* PUBLIC ANALYST
public health regulations, **19**, 305, 473
purchaser—
  false representation to, **11**, 346
  notice to, **11**, 345
  sale to prejudice of, **11**, 344
quality, standard of, **11**, 348
radioactive substances, safety regulations, **9**, 916
regulations—
  appeal against, **11**, 434
  composition or treatment of food, as to, **11**,
    352, 354–358
  food standards, **11**, 353
  power to make, **11**, 306
reheating, **11**, 408, 410
safety regulations, **6**, 63
  early legislation, **11**, 304
sale of—
  advertisement, *see* ADVERTISEMENT
  clothing of persons selling, **11**, 407
  cognate law, **11**, 326
  early legislation, **11**, 304
  emergency powers, **11**, 320
  excisable liquor, **11**, 315
  exposure for, **11**, 407
  false representation, **11**, 346
  fish, close seasons, **11**, 312
  food not of proper nature, substance or quality,
    11, 343
  food supplied not of kind demanded, **11**, 343–
    349
  game, **11**, 312
  hares, **11**, 312
  implied conditions of, **11**, 326
  infested food, **11**, 317
  injurious food, **11**, 341
  measures, by, **11**, 313
  notice to purchaser, **11**, 345
  number, by, **11**, 313
  pesticides, **11**, 319
  prejudice of purchaser, to, **11**, 344
  premises where sold or offered, **11**, 407
  price control, **11**, 314
  prosecutions and penalties, **11**, 423–430
  salmon, **11**, 312
  sea trout, **11**, 312

Food—*continued*
sale of—*continued*
  Secretary of State's powers to obtain particulars
    of, **11**, 351
  shellfish, **11**, 312, 403, 407
  trade descriptions, **11**, 316
  trout, **11**, 312
  unfit for human consumption, **11**, 397–402
  unsound food, **11**, 399
  value added tax, **11**, 314
  venison, **11**, 312
  weight, measure or number, by, **11**, 313
  wild birds, **11**, 312
sampling officer—
  authorisation of, **11**, 334
  authority of, **11**, 337; **14**, 708
  direction to take samples, **11**, 335
  division and disposal of samples, **11**, 338
  duty, **11**, 333, 334
  milk, sampling of, **11**, 336
Secretary of State's powers, **11**, 321, 351, 407
shellfish, **11**, 407
  cleansing of, **11**, 312, 403
sheriff court jurisdiction, **6**, 1104
solvents, containing, **11**, 378
stabilisers, **11**, 373
standards requirements, **6**, 12
statutory sources, **11**, 301–303
  Scottish legislation, **11**, 304–307
statutory standard of quality, **11**, 348, 353, 359–
    370
storage, **11**, 407, 408
  infested food, **11**, 317
supplied otherwise than by sale, **11**, 342, 342*n*
sweeteners, **11**, 379
trade descriptions, **6**, 121; **11**, 316
trade marks, **11**, 384
transit, in, examination of, **11**, 401
transport of, **11**, 317, 407
treatment of, regulations as to, **11**, 352, 354–358
unfit for human consumption, **11**, 397–402
  condemnation, **11**, 398
  examination of, **11**, 397
    food in transit, **11**, 401
  meat, **11**, 407
  prize or award, food offered as, **11**, 400
  seizure, **11**, 397
  suspected food, **11**, 402
  unsound food, sale of, **11**, 399
unwholesome food, **11**, 325
value added tax, **11**, 314
VAT zero-rating, **7**, 1445
vending machine, sale from—
  analysis of samples, **11**, 338*n*
  labelling, **11**, 383, 383*n*, 388, 390, 396
  soft drinks, **11**, 368
weights and measures legislation—
  biscuits, wafer biscuits and shortbread, **6**, 208
  bread, **6**, 209, 259
  caseins and caseinates, **6**, 219
  cereal breakfast foods, **6**, 210
  cheese, **6**, 201, 202
  chocolate products, **6**, 211
  cocoa products, **6**, 212

Food—*continued*
weights and measures legislation—*continued*
  coffee and chicory products, **6**, 213
  containers, permitted weights, **6**, 201, 205
  countable produce, **6**, 205
  deficiency of quantity, **6**, 253
  edible fats and oils, **6**, 215
  excess of quantity, **6**, 253
  exempted foods, **6**, 206
  fish, **6**, 201, 203
  flour, **6**, 216
  fruit and vegetables—
    dried, **6**, 214
    fresh, **6**, 201, 205
    soft fruit, **6**, 205
  generally, **6**, 193
  grains, **6**, 207
  honey, **6**, 217
  jam and marmalade, **6**, 218
  meat, poultry and sausage meat, **6**, 201, 204
  milk and preserved milk, **6**, 219
  miscellaneous provisions, **6**, 228
  molasses, syrup and treacle, **6**, 220
  multipacks, **6**, 206
  oat products, **6**, 221, 243
  pasta, **6**, 222
  potatoes, **6**, 223
  prepacked and sold by number, **6**, 205, 227,
    228, 253
  sale by weight, measure or number, **11**, 313
  salt, **6**, 224
  sugar, **6**, 225
  tea, **6**, 226
welfare food and milk, **11**, 432, 432*n*
wrappers, **11**, 350
  See also labelling *above*; REFRESHMENTS
Food poisoning
notification by medical practitioner, **11**, 406
Food Safety Tribunal
Scottish Committee, supervision by, **23**, 911*n*
Football
alcohol and related offences, **19**, 1269–1272
clubs, incorporation, **19**, 1228
contracts of employment, **19**, 1231–1237
  covenants in restraint of trade, **19**, 1235
  dismissal, **19**, 1237
  extra-contractual relationship, **19**, 1232
  freedom of contract, **19**, 1236
  inducement of breach, **19**, 1234
  interference with performance of, **19**, 1234
  minors, **19**, 1233
  retention and transfer system, **19**, 1235, 1236
designated sporting events, trains from or to, **19**,
  1066
historical background, **19**, 1202
postponement of match, **19**, 1278
public safety, **19**, 1278
sports-governing institutions, **19**, 1205
sports-related violence, **19**, 1266–1268
transfer fees, **19**, 1236
Footpath-footway
building works adjoining, **3**, 230
conversion of cycle track from or to, **20**, 616
conversion of road into, **20**, 676

Footpath-footway—*continued*
development order, affected by, **20**, 654
driving, **20**, 434
fouling by dogs, **19**, 371
horse, on, **20**, 706
level crossing over, **19**, 1031; **20**, 645
local roads authority taking over responsibility
for, **20**, 648
long distance route forming part of, **14**, 405
maintenance and improvement, **20**, 660
meaning, **14**, 405; **20**, 501, 610
occupier's liability, **15**, 321
public—
creation by planning authority, **14**, 405
Night Poaching Acts, **11**, 810
public right of way, *see* RIGHT OF WAY
replacement, **20**, 654
road, included in definition of, **20**, 411
sporting event on, **19**, 1284
statutory undertakers' rights, preservation of, **20**,
654
stopping up or diverting road for purposes of, **20**,
657
vehicle crossing, **20**, 705
vehicle on, **20**, 705
verge, **20**, 411
warranty as to, **6**, 563
See also ROAD
Foot-prints
identification by, **10**, 662
Footwear
VAT zero-rating, **7**, 1460
Force, use or threat of
collective, United Nations, through, **19**, 704
Declaration concerning Friendly Relations and
Co-operation, **19**, 685
defence of persons or property, in, **13**, 90
permissible use, **19**, 701–705
public meeting, stewards at, **14**, 1343
regional security arrangements, **19**, 703
reprisals, **19**, 702*n*
self-defence, **19**, 702
state's entry into, **19**, 617
United Nations Charter, **19**, 699–702
use prohibited by international law, **19**, 697
Force and fear
defects of title, **4**, 150
holder of bill, rights of, **4**, 150
reduction of actings, deeds etc on grounds of, **13**,
44
transfer of ownership, in, **18**, 614, 615
Force majeure **clause**
building contracts—
determination of contract where, **3**, 102
extension of time where, **3**, 48
effect of invoking, **9**, 777
examples of, **9**, 776
generally, **15**, 718
Forced labour
European Convention on Human Rights, **12**, 6, 28
international conventions on, **12**, 5
meaning, **12**, 28
menace of penalty, **12**, 28
rehabilitation programmes, **12**, 28

Forced sale value
meaning, **25**, 73
Foreclosure
action of, public sale as necessary preliminary, **20**,
118
land held on, **3**, 338, 364
Foregift
meaning, **13**, 103
Forehand rent
meaning, **13**, 246
Foreign and Commonwealth Office
external relations, **5**, 506
functions, **13**, 1417
functions of, **5**, 506
lawers in generally, **13**, 1392, 1393
recruitment to, **13**, 1416
nationality requirements, **13**, 1416
Foreign company
nature of, **4**, 315
Foreign Compensation Commission
Scottish Committee, supervision by, **23**, 911*n*
Foreign court
decrees, *see* FOREIGN DECREES
renvoi, **17**, 157
See also renvoi
Foreign court theory, **17**, 157
Foreign currency
claim, proceedings raised in Scotland, **14**, 1829
commodity, treated as, **14**, 1829
creditors, claims of, **4**, 827
European currency unit, **14**, 1833
Law Commission, consideration by, **14**, 1831
Miliangos/Commerzbank rule, **14**, 1830
money of account, **14**, 1829
payment in, **17**, 273
sale of, **14**, 1809
Scottish Law Commission, consideration by, **14**,
1831
special drawing rights, **14**, 1832
sterling, conversion into, **14**, 1829
Foreign heritage
Scottish trust of, **24**, 15
Foreign judgment
See JUDGMENTS
Foreign national
right to leave United Kingdom, **16**, 1205
state's duty to, **19**, 686
Foreign relations law
meaning, **19**, 605
Foreign state
debtor, as, exemption from diligence, **8**, 128
extradition to—
bilateral treaties, **12**, 507
fugitive criminals, **12**, 513
international law, generally, **12**, 506
multilateral agreements, **12**, 508
See also EXTRADITION
meaning, **12**, 512, 517
recognition, **7**, 724
Foreign title
use in Scotland, **16**, 1301, 1301*n*
Foreseeability
test of, **7**, 48

Foreshore
access to, **18**, 524
access to exercise salmon fishing right, **11**, 8
adjacent land—
  adjacent proprietor, rights of, **18**, 312
  herring fisheries, use of uncultivated land for, **18**, 527
  public rights over, generally, **18**, 494
alienation of, **25**, 310
alteration in location or extent, **18**, 313
artificial barriers against sea, erection, **18**, 318
bathing, public right of, **18**, 526
boundary description as, **6**, 485
Crown, vested in, **20**, 268
Crown Estate Commissioners, interest in, **6**, 788
extent, determination, **18**, 313
  England and Wales, in, **18**, 313, 313*n*
fishings, **24**, 315
jurisdiction of sheriff, **4**, 2; **6**, 1056
lease, **13**, 194, 205
local authorities' duties in relation to, **14**, 278, 686; **18**, 524
meaning, **6**, 485; **12**, 1239; **18**, 313; **24**, 314
mineral rights, **18**, 318
mussels as separate legal tenement, **18**, 318
natural harbours, **11**, 1304
navigation, public right of, **18**, 318, 524, 525
  ancilliary rights, **18**, 520
oil platform on, **20**, 268
ownership—
  a coelo usque ad centrum principle, **18**, 318
  acquisition—
    generally, **18**, 314
    owner, by grant of, **18**, 314, 315
    prescriptive possession, by, **18**, 314, 316
  adjacent proprietor, rights of, **18**, 312
  artificial barriers against sea, erection, **18**, 318
    damage caused by, **18**, 318
  Crown—
    public rights, subject to, **18**, 524
    subject proprietor, acquisition by, **18**, 314–316
  Orkney, **18**, 310, 317
  positive prescription, **16**, 2102, 2107
  private, public rights, subject to, **18**, 524
  servitudes, burdened by, **18**, 318
  Shetland, **18**, 310, 317
  udal law, **18**, 310, 317
  use, restrictions as to, **18**, 318
oysters as separate legal tenement, **18**, 318
passage, public right of, **18**, 526
proprietor, rights of, **20**, 268
public rights—
  generally, **18**, 5, 318, 494, 514, 524; **20**, 268
  recreation, of, **18**, 318, 526
regalia minora, as part of, **24**, 314
registration of interests in, **6**, 778
riding, public right of, **18**, 526
rock or sand outcrops in sea, **18**, 313
salmon as separate legal tenement, **18**, 318
sand for ballast, whether public right to take, **18**, 525
sea-greens not considered part of, **18**, 313
sea-ware, right to gather, **18**, 526

Foreshore—*continued*
seaweed, **24**, 314
shooting, public right of, **20**, 268
shotguns, public right to discharge, **18**, 526
udal law, **24**, 306, 310, 314, 320
valuation for rating, **24**, 593
walking, public right of, **16**, 2126; **18**, 526
water sports and recreation, **19**, 1280
white fish and shellfish, public right to take, *see* FISHING
wreck and ware, servitude of, **18**, 318
wrecks, **24**, 314

Forestry
agricultural land, capital gains tax deferral on woodlands, **11**, 654
ancient monument, compulsory purchase order exemption, **11**, 634
archaeological interest, site of, compulsory purchase order exemption, **11**, 634
byelaws—
  Forestry Commission—
    enforcement, **11**, 640
    power to make, **11**, 609
capital gains tax—
  grant of right to fell and remove timber, **11**, 650
  woodlands, **11**, 649
churchyard, felling trees in, **11**, 617
Committee, supervision of, **23**, 911*n*
compensation, felling licence, for refusal to grant, **11**, 618
competition law, **4**, 1165
conservancy—
  Home Grown Timber Advisory Committee, **11**, 612
  meaning, **11**, 612
conservation, Forestry Commission, duty of, **11**, 606, 607
court, **17**, 504
danger, trees felled to prevent, **11**, 617
dedication agreements—
  ancillary provisions, **11**, 614
  compulsory purchase exemption, **11**, 634
  effect of, **11**, 613, 614
  existing agreements, continuation of, **11**, 614
  form, **11**, 614
  generally, **11**, 613, 614
  grant schemes replacing, **11**, 615
  meaning, **11**, 614
  recording of, **11**, 614
  release from, **11**, 614
  trustees' powers, **24**, 202
evidence, Forestry Commission documents, **11**, 604
felling of trees—
  danger, to prevent, **11**, 617
  enforcement of provisions as to—
    committee of reference, **11**, 629
    compliance notice, **11**, 628
    expenses of, **11**, 630
    identification of trees, **11**, 631
    service of documents, **11**, 632

Forestry—*continued*
felling of trees—*continued*
  felling directions—
    agricultural interests to be considered, **11**, 623
    committee of reference, **11**, 629
    farm or dwelling house, interests to be considered, **11**, 623
    Forestry Commission's power to direct, **11**, 623
      restrictions of, **11**, 624
    identification of trees, **11**, 631
    interests to be considered, **11**, 623
    persons adversely affected by, **11**, 626
    proceedings in respect of, **11**, 627
    review of, **11**, 625
    Secretary of State's powers, **11**, 624–626
    statement of grounds to be given, **11**, 623
  felling licence—
    application for, **11**, 616
    committee of reference, **11**, 629
    conditional, **11**, 619
      review of conditions, **11**, 619
    enforcement, **11**, 628–632
    exemption from requirement, **11**, 617
    felling without authority of, **11**, 622
    generally, **11**, 612, 616
    identification of trees, **11**, 631
    preservation orders, trees subject to, **11**, 621
    public open space, trees growing on, **11**, 617
    refusal to grant—
      compensation for, **11**, 618
      deterioration of timber after, **11**, 618
      review of, **11**, 621
    nuisance, to abate, **11**, 617
    obstruction, to remove, **11**, 617
    restocking notice, *see* restocking notice *below*
    unauthorised, **11**, 622
Forestry Commission, *see* FORESTRY COMMISSION
forestry dedication agreement, compulsory purchase exemption, **11**, 634
Forestry Fund, *see* FORESTRY FUND
forestry grant scheme—
  dedication scheme replaced by, **11**, 615
  procedure, **11**, 615
fruit trees, felling of, **11**, 617
garden, felling trees in, **11**, 617
gift, Forestry Fund, to, **11**, 636
hares, prevention of damage by, **11**, 866, 867
hedges, laying of, licence not required, **11**, 617
Home Grown Timber Advisory Committee—
  consultation with, **11**, 609, 612
  maintenance by Forestry Commissioners, **11**, 612
  regional advisory committees, **11**, 612
income tax—
  woodlands, **11**, 642–648
    abolition of previous system, **11**, 644
    capital allowances, **11**, 646
    election to be charged under Schedule D, **11**, 643
    former taxation under Schedule B, **11**, 642
    transitional provisions, **11**, 645

Forestry—*continued*
income tax—*continued*
inheritance tax—
  woodlands, **11**, 651–654
    deferral of tax, **11**, 651
      advantages of, **11**, 653
      agricultural land, **11**, 654
      subsequent disposal, **11**, 652
land—
  acquisition of—
    compulsory purchase, **11**, 634
      exceptions, **11**, 634
      proximity, land in, **11**, 634
    generally, **11**, 633
    Secretary of State's powers, **11**, 633–635
  disposal of, **11**, 635
  management of, **11**, 635
  use of, **11**, 635; **23**, 88
Lands Tribunal for Scotland, disputed compensation claims, **11**, 618
lopping, licence not required, **11**, 617
National Trust for Scotland—
  land held inalienably by—
    compulsory purchase order exemption, **11**, 634
    felling directions and, **11**, 623
nuisance, trees felled to abate, **11**, 617
obstruction, trees felled to remove, **11**, 617
orchard, felling trees in, **11**, 617
permitted development, **23**, 188
pests, protection of trees and forest products from, **11**, 608, 608n
preservation order, **11**, 620; **23**, 203
proof, Forestry Commission documents, **11**, 604
public open space—
  meaning, **11**, 617n
  trees growing on, felling licence not required, **11**, 617
rabbits, prevention of damage by, **11**, 866, 867
restocking notice—
  acquisition of land, powers as to, **11**, 633–635
  committee of reference, **11**, 629
  compliance with, **11**, 628
  contents, **11**, 622
  expenses in connection with, **11**, 630
  felling directions, powers as to, **11**, 624–626
  review, reference for, **11**, 622
  service, **11**, 622
right of, **18**, 213
royal forest, **18**, 197
sport and recreation, Forestry Commission, provision of facilities by, **11**, 610
standing timber, purchase of, **11**, 608
taxation—
  forestry, income from—
    abolition of previous system, **11**, 644
    capital allowances, **11**, 646
    election to be charged under Schedule D, **11**, 643
    former taxation under Schedule B, **11**, 642
    transitional provisions, **11**, 645
  Forestry Commission exempt from, **11**, 641
  grant of right to fell and removed timber, **11** 650

Forestry—*continued*
taxation—*continued*
    woodlands—
        death of owner, **11**, 651
        inheritance tax deferment, **11**, 652–654
        purchase and sale of, **11**, 647
            capital gains tax, **11**, 649
            income tax, **11**, 648
        See also capital gains tax; income tax; inheritance tax *above*
    timber—
        deterioration after refusal of felling licence, **11**, 618
        meaning, **11**, 608*n*
        ownership of, **11**, 608
        right to fell and remove, grant of, **11**, 650
        sale, **11**, 608
        standing, purchase of, **11**, 608
        utilisation, **11**, 608
    topping trees, licence not required, **11**, 617
    tourism, Forestry Commission, provision of facilities by, **11**, 610
    valuation, entry of, **11**, 906
    vermin, prevention of damage by, **11**, 866, 867
    wild birds or animals killed or taken in interests of, **11**, 881, 883, 885, 886
    woodlands—
        broadleaved, grants for, **11**, 644*n*
        capital allowances, **11**, 646
        commercial, profits and losses arising from, **11**, 644, 645
        death of owner, **11**, 651
        deferral of inheritance tax, **11**, 651–654
        Forestry Commission schemes, **11**, 644
        purchase and sale, taxation on, **11**, 647
            capital gains tax, **11**, 649
            income tax, **11**, 648
Forestry association
    advances to members, **12**, 623
    generally, **12**, 614, 617
Forestry Commission
    byelaws—
        enforcement, **11**, 640
        power to make, **11**, 609
    committees—
        advisory, **11**, 611
        appointment of, **11**, 611
        central, **11**, 611
        regional, **11**, 611
    conservation, **11**, 606
        national interest and, **11**, 607
    constitution, **11**, 603
    documents, **11**, 604
        proof of, **11**, 604
        receipt in evidence, **11**, 604
    entry and enforcement, powers of, **11**, 640
    establishment, **11**, 602
    general duty, **11**, 606
    government department, as, **11**, 603
    grant schemes, approval of, **11**, 615
    grants by, **2**, 1290
    grants and loans, *see* FORESTRY FUND
    Home Grown Timber Advisory Committee, **11**, 609, 612

Forestry Commission—*continued*
    management of forestry land, **11**, 608
    membership, **11**, 603
    obstruction of officers or servants of, **11**, 640
    official seal, **11**, 603
    Ombudsman system, **19**, 242
    prevention of damage by rabbits, hares and vermin, **11**, 866, 867
    proceedings, **11**, 603
    quorum, **11**, 603
    regulations, powers to make, **11**, 609, 612, 616, 617
    sporting or recreational facilities, provision of, **11**, 610
    staff, **11**, 605
    statute law, generally, **11**, 601, 602
    statutory functions, exercise and discharge of, **11**, 606
    taxation, exemption from, **11**, 641
    tourist facilities, provision of, **11**, 610
Forestry court
    minor criminal jurisdiction, **17**, 504
Forestry Fund
    generally, **11**, 608
    gifts to, **11**, 636
    payments into, **11**, 636
    payments out of, **11**, 637
    regulation, **11**, 638
    report and accounts, **11**, 639
Forfeiture
    controlled drugs, relating to, **14**, 1253
    court's power to order, **17**, 807
    criminal penalty, as, judicial conveyance, **18**, 664
    deer, of, **11**, 961
    former use, **7**, 564, 567
    game, of, **11**, 809, 822
    illegally taken fish, **11**, 3, 22
    legacy, of, **25**, 872
    legal rights, **25**, 801
    pension, **21**, 1205
    powers of seizure, **11**, 27
    provision in will, of, **25**, 780
    salmon and freshwater fish poaching, **11**, 11
    social security benefits, and, **21**, 1169, 1186
    tackle or gear, **11**, 22
    unsafe goods, **6**, 59
    weights and measures equipment, **6**, 190
Forgery
    appeal limited by, **12**, 337
    article, false, **7**, 375
    assignation cannot operate by means of, **4**, 205
    bill of exchange, signature on, **4**, 124
    cheques, **11**, 768
    counterfeit notes and coins, **7**, 385, 395
    definition, **7**, 373
    delict, **15**, 216
    fraud, and, **7**, 372
    generally, **7**, 372
    marriage schedule, **19**, 1475
    negotiable instruments, **11**, 767
    paintings etc, **7**, 375
    passport, of, **16**, 1226, 1226*n*
    reduction on grounds of, **13**, 44

Forgery—*continued*
registration of births, marriages and deaths, in
    relation to, **19**, 1472
tickets, **19**, 1273
uttering, *see* UTTERING
what can be forged, **7**, 374, 375
what constitutes, **7**, 373
Forisfamiliation
See MINOR
Formal sources of law
custom, generally, **22**, 501
    See also CUSTOM
definition, **22**, 501
enumeration, **22**, 501
equity, generally, **22**, 501
    See also EQUITY
'institutional' writers, generally, **22**, 501
    See also 'INSTITUTIONAL' WRITERS
legislation, generally, **22**, 501
    See also LEGISLATION
precedent, generally, **22**, 501
    See also JUDICIAL PRECEDENT
Forth Bridge
valuation roll, entry on, **24**, 406
Forthwith
meaning, **12**, 1174
Forum non conveniens
jurisdiction declined on ground of, **4**, 26, 28
Forum shopping
discouragement of, **17**, 305
Forwarding agent
generally, **3**, 618
liability, **3**, 618
meaning, **21**, 524*n*
Foss v Harbottle, **rule in**
See SHAREHOLDER
Foster parent
child in care—
    local authority duty to assess, **22**, 17
    visiting, regulation, **22**, 17
delict committed by, liability, **15**, 242
disqualified persons, **3**, 1260
duties, **3**, 1260
inspection of foster parent's premises, **3**, 1260
local authority powers in relation to, **3**, 1260
removal of child from, **3**, 1260
remuneration, **22**, 9
Fosterage
See CHILD–CHILDREN
Foundling
domicile of, **17**, 193, 198
Fowl
Jewish ritual slaughter, **3**, 1680
slaughter of, **11**, 516
Fowling rights
servitude rights, whether constituting, **18**, 492
Foxes
hunting—
    Day Trespass Act, application of, **11**, 821
    generally, **19**, 1275
requirement notice to control, **11**, 860–863
France
application of competition rules, **4**, 1304
civil jurisdiction, contracting state, **4**, 22

France—*continued*
constitution—
    amendments to, **5**, 307
    fundamental statutes, **5**, 303
European Union customs territory, **7**, 1010
no-passport excursions to, **12**, 132
succession law in—
    acceptance to act, **25**, 637
    active succession, **25**, 614
    co-ownership, **25**, 639
    death, property passing on—
        competent beneficiaries, **25**, 621
        future property, **25**, 622
        generally, **25**, 619
        presumptions, **25**, 620
    devolution, **25**, 606
    distribution of property, **25**, 605
    family property, **25**, 608
    freedom of testation, **25**, 601
    holograph, **25**, 628
    identification of property, **25**, 605
    intestate succession, **25**, 632
    joint will, **25**, 628
    mutual will, **25**, 628
    partition, **25**, 642
    private will, **25**, 628
    privileged will, **25**, 628
    public will, **25**, 628
    reassembly of estate, **25**, 609
    reserved property—
        calculation of estate, **25**, 625
        generally, **25**, 623
        gift—
            purposes of, **25**, 627
            valid, formalities required for, **25**, 628
        voluntary provision, **25**, 624
        voluntary and statutory devolution, balance
            between, **25**, 629
        will—
            purposes of, **25**, 627
            valid, formalities required for, **25**, 628
    secret will, **25**, 628
    separation of property, **25**, 602
    sources of private international law, **17**, 111
    species of property, distinction of, **25**, 607
    transmission, **25**, 636
Franchise (business)
business, transfer of, **9**, 180
capital gains tax, **18**, 1600
collective investment scheme excluded from, **12**,
    1325
European Community rules—
    block exemption, **18**, 1659
    competition, **4**, 1385; **10**, 162
    spare parts supply, **18**, 1662
    trade mark licensing, and, **18**, 1658
goodwill—
    foreign franchise, **18**, 1368
    passing off, and, **18**, 1368, 1371
intellectual property in relation to, **18**, 802
Franchise (electoral)
business premises qualification, **15**, 1018, 1019
drink or drugs, person under influence of, **15**,
    1082

Franchise (electoral)—*continued*
European parliamentary elections, **15**, 1076, 1082
household, **15**, 1017
local government elections, **15**, 1021, 1026, 1077, 1082
lodger, **15**, 1017
peers, **15**, 1023
person's exercise of, conditions for, **5**, 374
plural voting, **15**, 1018
property owners, prejudice in favour of, **15**, 1018
qualifying date, **15**, 1078, 1079
Redistribution of Seats Act 1885..., **15**, 1017
register of parliamentary electors, **15**, 1019
Representation of the People Act 1884..., **15**, 1017
Representation of the People Act 1949..., **15**, 1020
Representation of the People (Scotland) Act 1868..., **15**, 1016
residence—
    determination, **15**, 1020
    qualification, **15**, 1018, 1019
    United Kingdom parliamentary elections, **15**, 1075
service, **15**, 1017
spare parts, supply, European Community legislation, **18**, 1662
twentieth-century reforms, **15**, 1018–1020
undue influence to prevent free, **15**, 1446
United Kingdom parliamentary elections, **15**, 1075, 1078, 1082
university qualification, **15**, 1018, 1019
voting age, lowering of, **5**, 374
women, **15**, 1016–1018, 1023, 1024, 1026
See also ELECTORAL REGISTER
Franchise clause
meaning, **12**, 892
Franchise court
abolition, **17**, 504, 520, 525
bailiery court, **17**, 523
barony court, **17**, 522
generally, **17**, 520
jurisdiction, **17**, 520
regality court, **17**, 521
replegiation, **17**, 524
stewartry court, **17**, 523
Francis Committee Report 1971
generally, **13**, 593, 667
Frankpledge
lawburrows compared, **13**, 908
Franks Committee
Council on Tribunals, recommendations on, **23**, 908, 913, 919
recommendations, **23**, 906
Fraser, Sir William, 16, 1302, 1302*n*
Fraud
advertising, **1**, 510, 517; **6**, 74
agent, by, **1**, 651, 655
antecedent obligations, effect on, **11**, 757
appropriation, **7**, 369
arbitration, as to—
    award obtained by, **2**, 484
    consideration of, by arbiter, **2**, 415
    punishment of, **2**, 477

Fraud—*continued*
arbitration, as to—*continued*
    questions of, **2**, 415
    reduction of award for, **2**, 477
averring fraud, **11**, 704
bad faith, and, **11**, 720
bankers' documentary credits, **11**, 772, 773
bankruptcy, **7**, 379
bankruptcy, *see* INSOLVENCY
barratry, **21**, 554*n*
bill, rights of holder, **4**, 150
bill wrongly dated in order to deceive, **4**, 112
case of, relevant facts, **10**, 624
causal connection, **7**, 370
causation, **11**, 730
cautionary obligations induced by, **11**, 774
    duty of disclosure, **11**, 775
cheque card fraud, **7**, 367
cheque fraud, **7**, 367
cheques, **11**, 768
circumvention—
    facility as separate plea, **11**, 733
    loss or harm suffered by facile person as result, **11**, 735
    meaning, **11**, 736
    remedies, **11**, 737
company—
    insolvency, **7**, 380
    prospectuses, **11**, 782
        liability in respect of, **11**, 783
comparative advertising, in, **1**, 517
computer, **7**, 387
consensus—
    prevention of, **11**, 705
    text for, **11**, 706
consent, fraud as factor vitiating, **11**, 707–714
    active concealment, **11**, 711
    false statements, **11**, 709
    material error, inducement of, **11**, 713
    non-disclosure, **11**, 712
    positive acts, **11**, 710
    relevant fraudulent conduct, nature of, **11**, 708
    remedies, **11**, 714
constitution of an obligation, fraud as factor preventing, **11**, 705, 706
contract, effect on, **11**, 756
conveyance, effect on, **11**, 756, 758
corporeal moveables, transfer of ownership, **11**, 761–764
counterfeit notes and coins, **7**, 385, 395
court, on the, reduction on grounds of, **13**, 50
credit card fraud, **7**, 367, 369
creditors, transactions in fraud of, **11**, 779
deception as element of, **7**, 365
defects of title, **4**, 150
definition, **7**, 365
delict—
    contractual and delictual remedies, **11**, 721
    development of law, **11**, 719
    fraud as, **11**, 719–731
    fraud and bad faith, **11**, 720
    generally, **15**, 216, 255
    procedural and evidential aspects, **11**, 722
delictual liability resulting from, **11**, 785

Fraud—*continued*
dissolution of partnership for, distribution of
  assets, **16**, 1100
documents of title, **11**, 769
dominium, effect on transfer of, **11**, 763
effect of, generally, **11**, 702
elements, **16**, 1226*n*
embezzlement, and, **7**, 350
employee, deliberate wrongful act of, company's
  liability for, **4**, 318
facility—
  annulment of voluntary juristic acts, **11**, 733
  circumvention as separate plea, **11**, 733
  lesion, **11**, 735
  mental weakness, as state of, **11**, 734
  remedies, **11**, 737
  See also FACILITY AND CIRCUMVENTION
false character, taking on, **7**, 366, 370
false pretence—
  appropriation by, **7**, 369
  examples, **7**, 366, 368, 369
  fraud as, **7**, 365
  generally, **7**, 366, 371
  knowledge that making, **7**, 85
fireraising to defraud insurer, **7**, 418
food and drugs, **7**, 383
forgery, *see* FORGERY
fraudulent—
  intent, **7**, 78
  misrepresentation—
    inducement to enter contract by, **15**, 683
    See also MISREPRESENTATION
  preferences, **11**, 781
future promises, **7**, 368
gratuitous alienations, **11**, 780
heritable bonds, **11**, 770
heritable property, transfer of ownership, **11**,
  755–760
  See also HERITABLE PROPERTY
incorporeal property, transactions concerned with,
  11, 765–771
innocent misrepresentation—
  fact, statement must be of, **11**, 717
  material error, **11**, 716
  reduction or rescission for, **11**, 715, 718
insolvency, effect of, *see* INSOLVENCY
intent—
  cause injury, to, **15**, 255
  deceive, to, **7**, 365
international law, **19**, 615
investments, in relation to, **7**, 381
juristic acts, in relation to—
  averration of fraud, **11**, 704
  consensus
    prevention of, **11**, 705
    test for, **11**, 706
  consent, vitiation of, **11**, 707–714
  generally, **11**, 701, 702
  material error, inducement of, **11**, 713
  meaning and effect of fraud, **11**, 702
  misrepresentation, *see* MISREPRESENTATION
  obligation, fraud as factor preventing
    constitution of, **11**, 705, 706
  voluntary obligations, **11**, 703–718

Fraud—*continued*
lease obtained by, **13**, 469
marriage—
  entrapment, **11**, 787
  fraudulently inducing, **11**, 787
  generally, **11**, 788
  null, **11**, 788
  void, fraudulently inducing, **11**, 787
meaning, **11**, 702
mens rea of—
  capacity, **11**, 1054
  carelessness, **11**, 728
  Derry v Peek, **11**, 726, 728
  fraudulent misrepresentation, **11**, 729
    See also FRAUDULENT MISREPRESENTATION
  generally, **7**, 85, 365, 371; **11**, 725–729
  good faith, statements made in, **11**, 728
  proof of fraud, **11**, 726
  requisite mental element, **11**, 726
  statement made without belief in its truth, **11**,
    727
  trade descriptions, **6**, 128
  unreasonableness, **11**, 728
minority shareholders, rights of, **4**, 464, 467
minors, **11**, 789
more than one mental element, where, **7**, 85
nature of fraudulent conduct, **11**, 708, 723–729
negligent misrepresentation, *see* MISREPRESENTATION
negotiable instruments, **11**, 767
no entitlement to indemnity, **6**, 769
obligations, law of, and law of property, **11**, 762
officer, deliberate wrongful act of, company's
  liability for, **4**, 318
'offside goals', rule against, **18**, 695, 695*n*
omission, arising by, **7**, 366
partner, by—
  dissolution of firm, as grounds for, **16**, 1089
  liability, **16**, 1043
passing off, whether fraud essential element, **18**,
  1387
passport in relation to, **16**, 1226
personal nature, **11**, 722
personation, **7**, 388
police court jurisdiction, **6**, 1157
power, fraud on a, **11**, 702, 754
practical result, **7**, 369
present intention, **7**, 368
private prosecution, **7**, 26
proof of, **11**, 726
property, dispositions by fraudulent seller, **11**, 760
pupils, **11**, 789
reduction on grounds of, **13**, 44
relational economic loss and, **15**, 585
relevant fraudulent conduct, nature of, **11**, 708
remedies, **11**, 731, 737
result-crime, as, **7**, 32, 46
road traffic, in relation to, **7**, 386
seduction, **11**, 786
share certificates, **11**, 771
solicitor and client, communications between, **13**,
  1190
sporting events, **19**, 1273
statutory, **7**, 378–388

Fraud—*continued*
succession, in relation to, **11**, 743–748
  discharge, **11**, 746
  election, **11**, 747
  heirs, impersonation of, **11**, 748, 759
  legal rights, **11**, 745
  legatees, impersonation of, **11**, 748, 759
  wills, **11**, 744
tax loss due to—
  partnerships, **19**, 1594
taxpayer, by, **19**, 1544
third party, on, **4**, 150
trade descriptions, **6**, 128; **7**, 382
transfer of ownership, in, **18**, 614, 616
treaty invalidated by, **19**, 628
trusts and trustees, **11**, 749–754
  See also TRUSTS
ultra vires doctrine, application, **4**, 324
undue influence, **11**, 738–742
  independent advice, absence of, **11**, 741
  material or gratuitous benefit, **11**, 740
  parties, relationship between, **11**, 739
  remedies, **11**, 742
uttering, *see* UTTERING
voluntary arrangement, obtaining approval for, **4**, 592
voluntary obligations, **11**, 703–718
  assignation of, **11**, 766
  averring fraud, **11**, 704
  consensus, prevention of, **11**, 705
  consent, fraud as factor vitiating, **11**, 707–714
  constitution of an obligation, fraud as factor preventing, **11**, 705, 706
weights and measures, **7**, 384
wills, **11**, 744
winding up, relating to, **4**, 920
Fraudulent misrepresentation
See MISREPRESENTATION
Fraudulent preference
generally, **11**, 781
unfair preference, replaced by, **11**, 781*n*
Fraudulent trading
Companies Act 1981, provisions of, **4**, 305
insolvency, liability of shareholder participating in management on, **4**, 319
judicial interpretation, **4**, 898
liability of persons party to, **4**, 897
supplementary provisions, **4**, 899
Fraudulently
use of term, **7**, 76, 77
Free Church of Scotland
Church of Scotland properties and endowments originating in, **3**, 1598, 1599
formation, **3**, 1636
See also VOLUNTARY CHURCHES
Free estate
calculation of, **25**, 625
France, **25**, 625
Germany, **25**, 626
meaning, **25**, 625
Free movement of persons and services
European Convention on Human Rights, **12**, 114
European Union law, **12**, 114, 221; **14**, 1903
See also ERUOPEAN UNION; HUMAN RIGHTS

Free port
artificial harbour, position of, **11**, 1306
common law, **11**, 1306
dangers, duty to warn of, **11**, 1306
dues, exaction of, **11**, 1306
maintenance, duty of, **11**, 1306
piers, construction and use, **11**, 1306
revenue, surplus, **11**, 1306
Free Presbyterian Church of Scotland
formation, **3**, 1636
Free school
maintenance, charitable purpose, as, **3**, 1119
Free zone
administration, **7**, 1164
Commissioners of Customs and Excise, powers, **7**, 1166
Common Agricultural Policy, goods covered by, **7**, 1165
Community goods, **7**, 1165
consumption or use of goods in, **7**, 1040
custom debt on importation from, **7**, 1040
Customs and Excise Management Act (1979), **7**, 1166
designation, application for, **7**, 1164
documentation of goods entering or leaving, **7**, 1164
duration of deposit in, **7**, 1164
eligibility, **7**, 1164
entry or departure, checks on, **7**, 1164
entry into, **7**, 1136
European Union, within, **7**, 1164
examination of goods in, **7**, 1214
exportation of goods leaving, **7**, 1165
free warehouse, *see* WAREHOUSE (free)
generally, **7**, 1164
goods which may be placed in, **7**, 1164
meaning, **7**, 1164
non-Community goods, **7**, 1165
permitted actions in respect of goods in, **7**, 1164
presentation of goods to customs authorities, **7**, 1164, 1164*n*
re-exportation of goods leaving, **7**, 1165
stock records, **7**, 1164
United Kingdom, free zones in, **7**, 1164*n*
Freedom
principle of equity, as, **11**, 1125
rights contrasted, **11**, 1085
See also HUMAN RIGHTS
Freehold
flying, **14**, 1013
meaning, **19**, 1614
Freeholders
legislative policies, opportunity to approve, **22**, 630
Michaelmas head courts, **22**, 630
Freight
sea, carriage by, *see* SEA, CARRIAGE BY
Freight container
export, VAT zero-rating, **7**, 1437
Freight forwarder
meaning, **21**, 524*n*
Freight transport services
VAT zero-rating, **7**, 1452

Freight-transport lands and heritages
valuation for rating—
  derating, **24**, 523, 729
  dock undertakings, **24**, 605, 606
  railways, **24**, 729
  valuation roll, **24**, 432
French foreign legion
identity card, **16**, 1236
Freshwater fish
See FISH
Friendly society
accounting year, **12**, 714
accounts, **1**, 89; **12**, 714
  rules as to, **12**, 699
advertisement by, **12**, 810
agriculture, promotion of, **12**, 694*n*
amalgamation, **12**, 726, 727
  offences in relation to, **12**, 744
annual return, **12**, 718
art, society promoting, **12**, 694*n*
Assistant Registrar for Scotland, **12**, 604
  duties, **12**, 604
assistant registrars, **12**, 604
audit, **12**, 699, 714, 715
  display of, **12**, 714
  exempt societies, **12**, 715
auditor—
  appointment, **12**, 715
  rights and duties, **12**, 716
authorisation, **12**, 807
  automatic, **12**, 1315, 1317
balance sheet, **12**, 714
  display of, **12**, 714
bank customer, as, **2**, 1256
benefit conditions, rules as to, **12**, 699
benefits, maximum limits, **12**, 690
benevolent societies, **12**, 679*n*, 681, 685, 694, 717
birth, insurance payments on, **12**, 686
books, inspection of, **12**, 699
borrowing, **12**, 721
branch, conversion into, **12**, 729
branches, societies with—
  audit, **12**, 715
  meaning of branch, **12**, 697
  registration procedure, **12**, 697
  rules—
    amendment of, **12**, 703*n*
    preparation of, **12**, 701
building society shares held by, **3**, 328
categories, **12**, 679, 679*n*
cattle insurance societies, **12**, 679*n*, 685, 693, 706, 717
  rules, **12**, 700
Central Area, business carried on in, **12**, 696
central body, rules as to, **12**, 699
charitable, when regarded as being, **3**, 1118
charity, qualification as, **12**, 681
Chief Registrar, **12**, 604
child, account held by, **3**, 1219
child under ten years, insurance relating to death of, **12**, 692, 724
closed, **12**, 679
collecting societies, **12**, 680*n*, 682

Friendly society—*continued*
committee of management, **12**, 709
  meetings, **12**, 713
  rules as to, **12**, 699
company—
  conversion into, **12**, 726, 731
  transfer of engagements to, **12**, 728
cookery, society promoting, **12**, 694*n*
costs, recovery from, **12**, 742
current legislation, **12**, 603, 683
  proposed reform, **12**, 684
death, insurance payments on, **12**, 686
death of member—
  certification, **12**, 724
  distribution, rules as to, **12**, 723
  nomination, **12**, 722–724
disputes—
  Court of Session, opinions on questions of law,
    12, 725
  internal affairs of society, **12**, 725
  meaning, **12**, 725*n*
  registrar, referral to, **12**, 725
  rules, mandatory provisions, **12**, 725
disputes, settlement of, **12**, 699
disputes—
  sheriff court, settlement by, **12**, 725
dissolution—
  award, by, **12**, 739
  methods, **12**, 737
  offences in relation to, **12**, 744
  voluntary, **12**, 700, 737, 738
dividing societies, **12**, 682
  rules as to, **12**, 700
documents—
  inspection, **12**, 732, 733
    members' requisition, by, **12**, 732
  production, **12**, 734
  registrar, by, **12**, 733
education, society promoting, **12**, 694*n*
employees, performance of duties, guarantee of,
  12, 686
endowment life assurance, **12**, 686
exempt agreement, **5**, 821
expenses, recovery from, **12**, 742
finance, **12**, 719–721
  borrowing by society, **12**, 721
  investments by society, **12**, 719
  lending by society, **12**, 720
Financial Services Act 1986 …, **12**, 691
fire assurance, **12**, 686
funeral expenses, insurance payments for, **12**, 686
historical development, **12**, 602, 679
illness, insurance against, **12**, 686
industrial and provident society, incorporation as,
  12, 684
insurance benefits offered by, **12**, 686
  restrictions on, **12**, 687
interest, accumulation of, **12**, 702
investigation of affairs, **12**, 700
investment of funds in society with different
  object, **12**, 702
investments, **12**, 719
Jewish burial societies, **12**, 694*n*

Friendly society—*continued*
Jewish confined mourning, registered to secure
    payments during, **3**, 1686
juvenile, **12**, 729
land and buildings, powers as to, **12**, 702
legal proceedings by or against—
    costs or expenses, recovery of, **12**, 742
    enforcement, **12**, 741–745
    fines, recovery of, **12**, 741
    offences, **12**, 744
        prosecution of, **12**, 743
    penalties, **12**, 744
    property, recovery of, **12**, 745
    service, **12**, 741
lending powers, **12**, 720; **13**, 1775
liquidation, **12**, 740
literature, society promoting, **12**, 694n
loan fund for members, establishment of, **12**, 702
manager, **12**, 707, 712
marriage, endowments on, **12**, 686
meaning, **12**, 601, 679, 686
meetings—
    general, **12**, 713
    rules as to, **12**, 699, 713
    special, **12**, 713
    special resolutions, **12**, 713, 713n
member-owned premises, repair and decoration
    of, **12**, 694n
membership—
    corporations, **12**, 704
    eligibility, **12**, 704
    expulsion of members, **12**, 705
        irregular or unjustified, **12**, 705
    honorary, **12**, 704
    liabilities of members, **12**, 706
    maximum, **12**, 704
    military service affecting, **12**, 705, 705n
    minimum, **12**, 704, 704n
    minors, **12**, 704
    non-payment of subscription or fine, **12**, 706
    questions of, disputes as to, **12**, 725n
    rules, conditions for set out in, **12**, 704, 705
    termination, **12**, 705
    terms of admission, rules as to, **12**, 699
    voluntary dissolution by, **12**, 737, 738
music, society promoting, **12**, 694n
name, rules as to, **12**, 699
nomination—
    certification, **12**, 724
    marriage, effect of, **12**, 722
    payment on death, **12**, 723
    power to nominate, **12**, 722
    revocation, **12**, 722
objects of, rules as to, **12**, 699
offences—
    penalties, **12**, 744
    prosecution of, **12**, 743
officers—
    appointment, **12**, 707
    committee of management, **12**, 709
    death of, prior claim of friendly society, **12**, 707
    election, **12**, 707
    fidelity bondng, **12**, 694n
    management by, **12**, 707

Friendly society—*continued*
officers—*continued*
    manager, **12**, 707, 712
    money, in receipt or charge of, **12**, 707
    performance of duties, guarantee of, **12**, 686
    removal of, **12**, 707
    resignation, **12**, 707
    rules as to, **12**, 699
    secretary, **12**, 711
    security given by, **12**, 702
    treasurer, **12**, 710
old people's home societies, **12**, 679n, 685, 694,
    717
penalties, rules as to, **12**, 699
pension business, taxation of, **12**, 689
property, recovery of, **12**, 745
property of—
    investment, **12**, 718
    trustees, vested in, **12**, 718
purposes of, **12**, 601, 686
reforms, proposed, **12**, 684
registered office, address, rules as to, **12**, 699
registrar, supervisory functions, **12**, 691
    transfer of, **12**, 691
registration, **12**, 683
    application for, **12**, 695
    area, **12**, 605
    branches, societies with, **12**, 697
    cancellation of, **12**, 736
    procedure, **12**, 695–697
    recording rules, **12**, 696
    refusal of, appeal against, **12**, 695
    registrable societies, **12**, 685
    restrictions on, **12**, 688
    rules confirmed by, **12**, 698
    suspension of, **12**, 736
Registry of, **12**, 604
reinsurance of society's risks, **12**, 702
rest centre, provision of, **12**, 694n
returns, annual, **12**, 699
rules—
    amendment of, **12**, 703
    applicable to all societies, **12**, 699
    cattle insurance societies, **12**, 700
    conduct of business, **12**, 691
        chief registrar, powers as to, **12**, 691
    confirmation, **12**, 698
    dividing societies, **12**, 700
    model, **12**, 698
    officers and trustees, **12**, 707
    powers under, **12**, 702
    preparation, **12**, 701
    society constitution formed by, **12**, 698
science, society promoting, **12**, 694n
secretary, **12**, 707, 711
Securities and Investments Board Core Conduct
    of Business Rules, **12**, 1399
self-regulating organisations—
    conduct of business rules, **12**, 691
    control over, **12**, 691
    recognition of, **12**, 691
sheriff court jurisdiction, **6**, 1105
shop clubs, **12**, 680n

Friendly society—*continued*
specially authorised, **12**, 679*n*, 685, 702
  meaning, **12**, 694
  recovery of unpaid subscription or fine, **12**, 706
  valuations exemption, **12**, 717
sport, society promoting, **12**, 694*n*
supervisory functions, **12**, 604
suspension, **12**, 735
  registration, of, **12**, 736
tax exempt business, **12**, 687, 689
  annual limits, **12**, 690, 690*n*
tax exempt status, **12**, 679
taxation, **12**, 687, 689, 690
thrift and savings societies or clubs, **12**, 680*n*, 694*n*
transfer of engagements, **12**, 726, 728
  offences in relation to, **12**, 744
treasurer, **12**, 710
trustees, **12**, 707, 708
  appointment, **12**, 708
  corporation as, **12**, 708
  death, **12**, 708
  duties, **12**, 708
  removal, **12**, 708
  resignation, **12**, 708
unemployed members, assistance to, **12**, 694*n*
unemployment, insurance against, **12**, 686
unincorporated nature, **12**, 679
unregistered, **12**, 680
valuation, **12**, 717
  appointment of actuary or valuer, **12**, 717
  exemptions from, **12**, 717
  periodic, **12**, 700
  required frequency, **12**, 717
working men's clubs, **12**, 679, 679*n*, 685, 694, 717
Frostathing
Norwegian law code, **24**, 303, 315
Fruit machines
provision of, **9**, 1009
Fruit trees
felling of, **11**, 617
Frustration
extinction of contractual obligation by—
  advance payments made, where, **15**, 889
  contracting out of doctrine, **15**, 883
  effect of frustration, **15**, 889
  fault and frustration, **15**, 882
  foresight and frustration, **15**, 881
  generally, **15**, 865, 880
  illegality of performance, **15**, 888
  impossibility, **15**, 885
  impracticality of performance, **15**, 887
  meaning, **15**, 880
  nature of contract, changes in, **15**, 884
  purpose for making contract no longer exists, **15**, 886
  rei interitus, **15**, 885
  risk allocation, **15**, 880
lease, of, **13**, 226
repetition, **13**, 85
termination of contract of employment by, **9**, 138, 222
Fuel
car, private use, available for, Class 1A national insurance contributions, **21**, 1036

Fuel—*continued*
fuel, feal and divot, *see* FUEL, FEAL AND DIVOT
heating, VAT rating, **7**, 1461
liquid, weights and measures legislation, **6**, 237
non-smokeless unauthorised, use in smoke control area, **9**, 1139
servitude right of—
  extent, **18**, 464
  generally, **18**, 483, 489
  restriction of area to which access allowed, **18**, 469
solid—
  byelaws, **6**, 233
  carriage by road or rail, **6**, 236
  damping of, **6**, 234
  meaning, **6**, 230
  sales from vehicles, **6**, 232
  weighing at buyer's request, **6**, 235
  weights and measures legislation, **6**, 231–236
wood, **6**, 240
Fuel, feal and divot
servitude, **6**, 515
Fugitive criminal
extradition to foreign state, **12**, 513
meaning, **12**, 513
Full fee
gift of, ambiguity of deed, **13**, 1618, 1619
Full pay-out lease
meaning, **14**, 1005
Fulton, Thomas Wemyss
international law, writings on, **19**, 611
Fumes
See NOXIOUS FUMES
Fun palace
See AMUSEMENT ARCADE
Fund-raising event
VAT exemption, **7**, 1431
Fundamental rights, remedy against violation of
right to—
  European Convention on Human Rights, **12**, 6
  Universal Declaration of Human Rights, **12**, 4*n*
Funeral
church service, prohibition during, **3**, 519
directions as to, **25**, 604
director, instruction of, **3**, 569
disturbance of, **3**, 527
expenses, **24**, 193
  damages, claim for, **15**, 937
  distribution of net estate after payment of, **25**, 665
  friendly society payments, **12**, 686
  inheritance tax, **25**, 1008
  payment of, **25**, 847
  social fund payment, **21**, 1123, 1128
  procession, **3**, 526
  transport, international, **20**, 500
Funfair
See PLEASURE FAIR
Fungible property
commodatum contract, **13**, 1785
contract of deposit, **8**, 7
liferent, may not be subject of, **13**, 1604
meaning, **13**, 1707, 1785

Fungible property—*continued*
mutuum contract, **13**, 1706, 1707
specific legacy, **25**, 848
Furious person
meaning, **14**, 1401
mental disorder, meaning, **14**, 1401
Furnace
dust, emission of—
  arrestment equipment—
    exemption from requirement, **9**, 1131
    provision of, **9**, 1130
  generally, **9**, 1129
fuel, excise duty on, **7**, 1069
grit, emission of—
  arrestment equipment—
    exemption from requirement, **9**, 1131
    provision of, **9**, 1130
  generally, **9**, 1129
smoke from, **9**, 1128
worker, hours of work, **14**, 1667
Furnished house
delectus personae, doctrine of, **13**, 356
lease, **13**, 194, 195
  degree of possession, **13**, 250
  services, provision of, **13**, 195, 219
Furniture and furnishings
business premises, **13**, 217
deterioration in—
  fair rent decisions, unaffected by, **13**, 661, 665
  grounds for repossession—
    assured tenancy, **13**, 725, 732, 734
    protected tenancy, **13**, 714, 717, 718
excessive price charged for, **13**, 692
fair rent decisions, whether affected by, **13**, 664, 668, 669
insurance, **14**, 329
intestate succession—
  prior rights, **25**, 691
  value, dispute as to, **25**, 692
lease, **13**, 195, 217
local authority housing, provision of furniture, fittings and conveniences in, **11**, 1906
meaning of furniture, **25**, 691*n*
rag flock and other filling materials—
  aircraft, fittings for, **19**, 421
  cleanliness, standards of, **19**, 426–430
  control, system of, **19**, 420
  defences against prosecution, **19**, 438–443
  enforcement of regulations, **19**, 431–443
  flock from unlicensed sources, **19**, 424
  materials included, **19**, 425
  premises, registration or licence of, **19**, 420–424
  public health legislation, **19**, 420–443
  rag flock, definition, **19**, 425
  railway carriage fittings, **19**, 421
  records to be kept, **19**, 436
  remaking or reconditioning articles, **19**, 421
  road vehicle fittings, **19**, 421
  ships, fittings for, **19**, 421
  storage, **19**, 422
  unclean flock on licensed premises, **19**, 423
removal and storage as land service, **3**, 377
specific legacy, **25**, 848

Furs
carriage of, **3**, 610
Furthcoming, action of
arrestment, **8**, 247, 260, 281
  completion by, **8**, 309
  defences available to arrestee, **8**, 312
  defences available to common debtor, **8**, 313
  extinction, **8**, 284
  generally, **8**, 309
  grounds for, **8**, 311
  jurisdiction, **8**, 310
  parties to, **8**, 310
  payment without, **8**, 320
expenses, **17**, 1201
summary causes, **17**, 1324
Further education
approval of schemes by Secretary of State, **8**, 927
college—
  education authorities' duty to provide, **8**, 729
  maintenance, responsibility for, **8**, 730
college councils, **8**, 701
  committee, discharge of functions by, **8**, 928
  delegation of powers from education authority to, **8**, 928, 936, 937
  delegation schemes, **8**, 936
    suspension, **8**, 937
  establishment, **8**, 928
  generally, **8**, 925
  management company, formation, **8**, 939
  meetings, **8**, 933
  membership, **8**, 929
    appointment, **8**, 701
    casual vacancies, **8**, 931
    conflict of interests, **8**, 934
    disqualification from, **8**, 932
  powers, **8**, 701, 935
  proceedings, **8**, 930
  requirement for, **8**, 928
    disapplication of, **8**, 940
  supply of goods and services, **8**, 938
Credit Accumulation and Transfer Scheme (CATS), **8**, 976
directly funded establishments, **8**, 701
financial assistance for students—
  access funds—
    conditions for payment, **8**, 945
    generally, **8**, 945
    payment of, **8**, 945
    Secretary of State's powers as to, **8**, 945
  bursary—
    amount payable, **8**, 942
    conditions of, **8**, 943
    education authorities' power to grant, **8**, 941
    eligibility, **8**, 944
    course outwith Scotland, for, **8**, 941
freestanding corporate bodies, proposals for, **8**, 925
funding, **8**, 1015
Gaelic, teaching, **8**, 926
grant-aided colleges, **8**, 947
management company, formation to run college of, **8**, 939
meaning, **8**, 926
proposed reforms, **8**, 925

Further education—*continued*
provision—
  approval of schemes by Secretary of State, **8**, 927
  education authorities' duty as to, **8**, 925–927
  generally, **8**, 925
Scottish central institutions, *see* SCOTTISH CENTRAL INSTITUTIONS
Scottish Credit Accumulation and Transfer Scheme (SCOTCATS), **8**, 976
Scottish Vocational Education Council (SCOTVEC), **8**, 927
social and recreational education, provision for, **8**, 925
student records—
  access to—
    generally, **8**, 946
    information which need not be disclosed, **8**, 946
    parental request for, **8**, 946
    refusal, **8**, 946
    student's request, at, **8**, 946
  erasure of information contained in, **8**, 946
  rectification, **8**, 946
    refusal, review of decision, **8**, 946
supply of goods and services, **8**, 938

Furtum usus
theft, and, **7**, 337, 344
Fuses
explosives, as, **10**, 1586
Future acquirenda
right to, **24**, 12
Future markets
evolution of, **2**, 1280
trading in 'futures', **2**, 1281
Future obligation
meaning, **15**, 5
Future property
transfer of—
  England, **25**, 622
  France, **25**, 622
  Germany, **25**, 622
Futures
generally, **12**, 1303
investment, as, **12**, 1308
London International Financial Futures Exchange, **12**, 1322
Securities and Futures Association (SFA), **12**, 1312
VAT zero-rating, **7**, 1433
Futurity
words of, **25**, 845

G

Gable
common (mutual), *see* COMMON GABLES
Gaelic
promotion of, **8**, 701
teaching, **8**, 926
use of—
    Crofters Commission, **6**, 955
    Scottish Land Council, **6**, 960
Gaffs
fishing with, **11**, 12
Game
agricultural executive committee powers, **11**, 808
black game, *see* BLACK GAME
breeding purposes, catching for, **11**, 882
bustard, *see* BUSTARD
capercailzie, *see* CAPERCAILZIE
Christmas Day, shooting on, **11**, 804*n*
close seasons, *see* CLOSE SEASON—
    close time
common law game rights, **11**, 803
conservation—
    deer, **11**, 929
    wild birds or animals killed or taken in interests
      of, **11**, 881, 883, 885, 886
custody of, by unqualified person, **11**, 807
damage by, **1**, 765
    compensation for, **11**, 889–894
    game from neighbouring land, **11**, 894
    increase of game, **11**, 889
Day Trespass Act, **11**, 815–824
    apprehension of trespassers, **11**, 820
    assault, **11**, 823
    daytime, meaning, **11**, 816
    disguise or blackened face, **11**, 817
    forfeiture of game, **11**, 822
    hunting, application to, **11**, 821
    obstruction, **11**, 823
    prosecutions, **11**, 824
    tenant farmers, position of, **11**, 818
    trespass—
      meaning, **11**, 819
      in search of game, **11**, 817
dazzling devices, **11**, 880, 884
decoy, live bird or animal used as, **11**, 880, 884
deer, *see* DEER
disease, taking or killing wild bird or animal in
    interests of, **11**, 883, 886
ducks, *see* DUCK
electrical devices, **11**, 880, 884
explosives, **11**, 880, 884
firearms, game laws in relation to, **10**, 1583
    See also FIREARM
food, preparation and sale as, **11**, 312
forfeiture by poacher—
    Game (Scotland) Act 1772..., **11**, 809
    Game (Scotland) Act 1832..., **11**, 822
    Night Poaching Acts, **11**, 809
frozen game, possession of, **11**, 841

Game—*continued*
game laws, **11**, 803, 805–858
    Game Act 1831..., **11**, 829–842
    Game Laws (Scotland) Amendment Act
      1877..., **11**, 848
    Game Licences Act 1860..., **11**, 829–842
    Game (Scotland) Act 1772..., **11**, 805–809
    Game (Scotland) Act 1832..., **11**, 815–824
    Ground Game Act 1880..., **11**, 849–858
    Hares Preservation Act 1892..., **11**, 825–828
    Hares (Scotland) Act 1848..., **11**, 825–828
    Night Poaching Acts 1828 and 1844..., **11**,
      810–814
    Poaching Prevention Act 1832..., **11**, 843–847
gas, wild bird or animal taken or killed with, **11**,
    880, 884
ground game, *see* HARES; RABBITS
grouse, *see* GROUSE
hares, *see* HARES
heath fowl, **11**, 806, 807
heath game, **11**, 815, 817
historical background to law, **11**, 801, 805
innkeeper, sale by, **11**, 836
landlord and agricultural tenant, relationship
    between—
    common law, **11**, 887–889
    increase of game, **11**, 889
    landlord's rights, **11**, 887
    tenant's right to compensation, **11**, 890–894
landrail, **11**, 802
legislation relating to, **11**, 496
licence, generally, **7**, 1087; **14**, 525
licence to deal in, **11**, 833–842
    application to person licensed to kill game, **11**,
      835
    buying and selling on behalf of licensed dealer,
      11, 838
    close times, **11**, 840, 841
    employee of licensed dealer, **11**, 838
    frozen game, **11**, 841
    grant of, **11**, 834; **14**, 525
    innkeepers, **11**, 836
    offences, **11**, 837
    prohibited periods for sale, **11**, 840
    prosecutions, **11**, 839
    two or more persons in partnership, **11**, 834
licence to kill, **11**, 829–832
    exceptions and exemptions, **11**, 830
    ground game, **11**, 856
    person authorised under control provisions, **11**,
      865
    production of, **11**, 831
    valid throughout United Kingdom, **11**, 829
    void on conviction, **11**, 832
lighting, artificial, used to take or kill wild birds
    or animals, **11**, 880, 884
meaning, **11**, 802
    compensation, for purposes of obtaining, **11**,
      891

Game—*continued*
meaning—*continued*
  deer, **11**, 927
  Poaching Prevention Act 1832..., **11**, 843
moor game, *see* MOOR GAME
muir fowl, **11**, 806, 807
muirburning, *see* MUIRBURNING
neighbouring land, damage caused by game from,
  11, 894
night poaching, *see* POACHING
partridge, *see* PARTRIDGE
patent may not be granted in respect of, **18**, 825
pheasant, *see* PHEASANT
physical damage caused by, **14**, 2045
poaching, *see* POACHERS; POACHING
poison, killing with, **11**, 864, 880, 884
private prosecution relating to, **17**, 531
property in, **18**, 541, 542, 544, 544*n*, 545
ptarmigan, *see* TARMAGAN
pursuing and killing, **19**, 1295
pursuit of, entry of land of another in, **11**, 803,
  817
quail, *see* QUAIL
rabbits, *see* RABBITS
recreation and sport involving, **19**, 1275
res nullius, **11**, 803
sale of—
  frozen game, of, **11**, 841
  prohibited periods, for, **11**, 840
shooting, *see* SHOOTING LEASE; SHOOTING RIGHTS
sighting devices, **11**, 880, 884
smoke, taking wild birds or animals with, **11**, 880,
  884
snares, **11**, 880, 884, 940
snipe, *see* SNIPE
stultifying or stupifying substances, **11**, 880, 884
Sunday, shooting on, **11**, 804
tarmigan, *see* TARMAGAN
tenant, *see* TENANT-TENANCY
traps, *see* TRAP
trespass in pursuit of, **18**, 182
  damage cause by, **11**, 803
  landowners' remedies, **11**, 803
  meaning of trespass, **11**, 819
  See also TRESPASS
venison dealer's licence, *see* VENISON
wild animals, *see* WILD ANIMALS
wild birds, **11**, 878, 878*n*
  See also WILD BIRDS
wilful destruction during close season, **11**, 806
woodcock, *see* WOODCOCK
Game rights
lease, **13**, 194, 202
Gamekeeper
royal family, to, **11**, 830
seizure, powers of, **11**, 812
Gaming
advertisement of, **1**, 531; **17**, 45
age limit, **3**, 1230
amusements with prizes, **14**, 517
appeal to sheriff relating to, **17**, 1249
betting, *see* BETTING
bingo, *see* BINGO

Gaming—*continued*
casino gaming—
  AWP machines in, **2**, 1639
  charges for, **2**, 1605
  cheques, acceptance, **2**, 1607
  credit gaming, **2**, 1607
  forms of, **2**, 1573
  games permitted, **2**, 1604
  licence, **2**, 1574, 1587
  live entertainment, restriction, **2**, 1590, 1608
  minimum age for, **2**, 1603
  nature of, **2**, 1573
  permitted areas, **2**, 1575
  permitted hours, **2**, 1606
  persons eligible for, **2**, 1603
  staff—
    age for employment, **2**, 1610
    certificate of approval—
      application for, **2**, 1616
      duration of, **2**, 1617
      revocation, **2**, 1617
  statistics, **2**, 1575
certificate of consent, *see* GAMING LICENCE
charges for play—
  exemption from restrictions, **2**, 1572
  power to make, **2**, 1605
  restrictions on, **2**, 1571, 1620
cheque—
  acceptance of, **2**, 1607
  statutory protection, **2**, 1503
chips, payment for, **15**, 768
club—
  credit gaming, **2**, 1621
  gaming in—
    age for, **2**, 1619
    restrictions on, **2**, 1620
  registration—
    application for—
      consideration of, **2**, 1623
      procedure, **2**, 1622
    cancellation of, **2**, 1627
    eligibility for, **2**, 1618
    grant or renewal, **2**, 1626
    machines, to use, **2**, 1632
    privileges given by, **2**, 1618
    proprietary clubs, **2**, 1634
    refusal of, **2**, 1624
    renew, refusal to, **2**, 1625
commercial, types of, **2**, 1573
common law rule, **2**, 1502
contract—
  sponsiones ludicrae, **13**, 1761
  whether enforceable, **2**, 1505; **13**, 1761; **15**,
    768
contracts for difference, **2**, 1504
control of, **2**, 1569
courts, attitudes of, **2**, 1502
credit, prohibition of, **2**, 1607
discouragement of, **9**, 1010
domestic occasions, **2**, 1572
excise licence requirement, **2**, 1648
extent of, in UK, **2**, 1508

Gaming—*continued*
facilities, demand for—
    proof of, **2**, 1589
    requirements as to, **2**, 1588
games of chance, **9**, 1010
history of, **2**, 1501
hostels etc, in, **2**, 1572
hotels etc, in, **2**, 1572
income tax, gambling profits, **19**, 1297
joint adventure to share winnings, **15**, 768
law—
    earliest, **2**, 1501
    first Scottish Act, **2**, 1501
    judicial decisions, **2**, 1507
licence, *see* GAMING LICENCE
licensed premises—
    advertising—
        outwith Great Britain, **2**, 1598
        restrictions on, **2**, 1598
    conviction of owner etc, effect, **2**, 1599
    disqualification order, **2**, 1599
    gaming machines on, **2**, 1601
    generally, **14**, 517
machine, by, *see* GAMING MACHINE
meaning, **2**, 1570; **9**, 1010
miners' welfare institute—
    charges for play, **2**, 1572
    credit gaming in, **2**, 1621
    gaming in—
        minimum age for, **2**, 1619
        restrictions on, **2**, 1620
    gaming machines, *see* GAMING MACHINE
registration—
    application for, **2**, 1622, 1623
    cancellation of, **2**, 1627
    eligibility for, **2**, 1618
    grant or renewal, **2**, 1626
    refusal of, **2**, 1624
    renewal, refusal of, **2**, 1625
offences, bodies corporate, by, **2**, 1576
pactum illicitum
    doctrine seldom invoked, **2**, 1505
    meaning, **2**, 1505
premises generally—
    contributions by local authority, **2**, 1600
prizes, for, **2**, 1573
public place, in, **2**, 1571
residual powers of Minister, **2**, 1602
restrictions—
    exempted premises, **2**, 1572
    general, **2**, 1571
sheriff court jurisdiction, **6**, 1067, 1082
stakes, levy on, **2**, 1605
unenforceable contracts, **2**, 1505
VAT exemption, **7**, 1423
winnings, taxation, **2**, 1644
Gaming Board
appeal from decisions of, **2**, 1592
certificate of consent, *see* GAMING LICENCE
establishment, **2**, 1574
licences, *see* GAMING LICENCE
local lottery, registration, **2**, 1673
powers and duties, **2**, 1574

Gaming licence
appeals in respect of—
    Court of Session, to, **2**, 1595
    grounds for, **2**, 1593
    hearing of, **2**, 1594
    powers of sheriff in, **2**, 1594
    procedure, **2**, 1592
    sheriff, to, **2**, 1592
application for—
    advertisement of, **2**, 1584
    authorities to be notified, **2**, 1584
    certificate to accompany, **2**, 1584
    hearing of, **2**, 1585
    procedure, **2**, 1584
cancellation—
    application for, **2**, 1506
    grounds for, **2**, 1506
casino licences, **2**, 1574, 1587
certificate of consent—
    application for, **2**, 1577
    Board's duties as to, **2**, 1578
    conditions for issue of, **2**, 1579
    contents, **2**, 1581
    information required for, **2**, 1577
    issue, discretion as to, **2**, 1580
    minimum age for, **2**, 1579
    refusal, grounds of, **2**, 1580
    requirement for, **2**, 1584
    residence for purposes of, **2**, 1579
    revocation—
        effect on licence, **2**, 1582
        grounds for, **2**, 1582
    suitability of applicant, **2**, 1579
demand for facilities—
    proof of, **2**, 1589
    requirements as to, **2**, 1588
duty, rates of, **2**, 1648
generally, **2**, 1583; **7**, 1080, 1083
grant of—
    inference for, **2**, 1586
    objections to, **2**, 1585
licensing authority, **14**, 517
licensing sessions, **2**, 1583
machines, for, **2**, 1601, 1650
new premises, for, **2**, 1597
offences, **7**, 1083
refusal, grounds for, **2**, 1587
renewal—
    annual, **2**, 1591
    refusal of, **2**, 1591
restricted, *see* BINGO
restrictions, attachment of, **2**, 1590
transfer of, **2**, 1597
unpaid duty, **7**, 1083
unrestricted licence—
    charges permitted under, **2**, 1605
    games permitted under, **2**, 1604
Gaming machine
amusements, at, *see* AMUSEMENTS WITH PRIZES
bingo clubs, in, **2**, 1601
casino, AWP machines in, **2**, 1639
clubs, operated in, **2**, 825
forms of, **2**, 1573

Gaming machine—*continued*
jackpot machine—
    nature of, **2**, 1630
    non-commercial entertainments, at, **2**, 1635
    premises for, **2**, 1631
    prizes from, **2**, 1630
licence—
    duty, charge of, **2**, 1650; **9**, 1015
    machines permitted under, **2**, 1601
maintenance, certificate for—
    issue of, **2**, 1642
    requirement for, **2**, 1641
meaning, **2**, 1628; **9**, 1010
permit for, **14**, 517
proprietary clubs, in, **2**, 1634
registration of premises—
    application for, **2**, 1632
    cancellation of, **2**, 1633
    proprietary clubs, **2**, 1634
    refusal, grounds for, **2**, 1633
sale or supply—
    certificate by Board for—
        issue of, **2**, 1642
        requirement for, **2**, 1640
    control of, **2**, 1640
    restrictions on, **2**, 1643
types of, **2**, 1629
value added tax, **9**, 1015
Garage
liability of hotel keeper, **11**, 1742
proprietor, liability, **15**, 150
valuation for rating, **24**, 663
Garden
allotment, *see* ALLOTMENT
back green, *see* TENEMENT (law of)
common ownership, in, common interest, **18**, 359
drought, water supply during, **25**, 530
felling trees in, **11**, 617
hosepipes, power to restrict use, **25**, 529
tenement buildings, common interest, **18**, 359
watering, supply for, **25**, 506
Garter King of Arms
Lord Lyon King of Arms, and, jurisdiction and
    questions of title, **6**, 1011, 1017
Gas
apparatus—
    construction, **14**, 1647
    installation, **14**, 1647
    maintenance, **14**, 1647
authorisation to supply—
    British Gas Corporation privilege, abolition of,
        9, 868
    information, restriction on use of, **9**, 872
    modification of, **9**, 871
    other persons, of, **9**, 873
    public gas suppliers, of, **9**, 870
    unauthorised supply, prohibition on, **9**, 869
British Gas Corporation, *see* BRITISH GAS
    CORPORATION
buildings, **9**, 879
carrier (ship), construction and survey, **21**, 212,
    212*n*
charges, **9**, 886, 887
consumer protection, generally, **6**, 161; **19**, 241

Gas—*continued*
conveyance of, **19**, 390
Director General of Gas Supply, **6**, 161; **9**, 864
Gas Consumers' Council, **6**, 161; **9**, 865
generating station, gas-fired, **9**, 630
heating fuel, VAT rating, **7**, 1461
historical background, **9**, 857–858
inflammable, *see* INFLAMMABLE SUBSTANCES OR
    MATERIALS
information—
    generally, **9**, 862
    restrictions on use of, **9**, 872
jurisdiction, **4**, 83
land—
    acquisition of, **9**, 874
    development of, **9**, 877
levy—
    imposition of, **9**, 898
    payment of, **9**, 899
natural—
    flaring of, consent to, **9**, 900
    information under EEC legislation, **9**, 902
    methane drainage licence, **9**, 730
    offshore, consent for liquefaction of, **9**, 901
notices, **9**, 862
offences, **9**, 863
offshore natural gas, **9**, 901
oil—
    sulphur dioxide from—
        EEC direction on, **9**, 1146
        UK regulations to control, **9**, 1147
operational safety of gas heating, **3**, 208
organisation of industry—
    Director General of Gas Supply, **9**, 864
    Gas Consumers' Council, **9**, 865
    gas suppliers, **9**, 866
    successor company, **9**, 867
pipes—
    generally, **9**, 876
    maintenance of, **9**, 882
    unauthorised connection, **9**, 891
    unauthorised disconnection, **9**, 891
pollution, **9**, 878
privatisation of gas industry, **6**, 161
public gas supplier—
    authorisation of, **9**, 870
    generally, **9**, 866
    meaning, **9**, 870
public health, **9**, 878
rig or platform, **21**, 108*n*, 110
roads, power to break up, **9**, 875
statutes, **9**, 860
storage tank, **3**, 208
subordinate legislation, **9**, 861
supply of—
    authorisation to supply, *see* authorisation to
        supply *above*
    charge to VAT, **7**, 1320
    charges—
        generally, **9**, 886
        recovery of, **9**, 887
    code, **9**, 881
    entry, powers relating to, **9**, 892
    fittings, injury to, **9**, 889

Gas—*continued*
supply of—*continued*
  generally, **9**, 880
  improper use, **9**, 888
  meters, **9**, 885
  pipes, maintenance of, **9**, 882
  poinding, **9**, 893
  privatisation of, **4**, 1125, 1126
  public code, **9**, 881
  quality of, **9**, 883
  safety, **9**, 884
  sequestration, **9**, 893
  supplier's duties, enforcement of, **9**, 894
  unauthorised—
    connection, **9**, 891
    disconnection, **9**, 891
    restoration, **9**, 890
  winding up, position relating to, **4**, 867
underground storage of—
  authorised order—
    application for, **9**, 896
    generally, **9**, 895
  protective areas, operations in, **9**, 897
  storage areas, operations in, **9**, 897
wild birds or animals taken with, **11**, 880, 884
works, *see* GASWORKS
See also INFLAMMABLE SUBSTANCES OR MATERIALS
Gasworks
construction, **19**, 15
valuation for rating—
  generally, **24**, 664
  pipes as part of, **24**, 664
  prescribed valuation formula, **24**, 547, 664
  valuation of lands and heritages, **24**, 415, 665
Gate
obstruction of road by, **20**, 695
snow, provision of, **20**, 503, 666
GATT
See GENERAL AGREEMENT ON TARIFFS AND TRADE
Gearing
company's financial record, **25**, 32
Geese
Game Acts, **11**, 496*n*
slaughter of, **11**, 516
Gelatine
reheating food containing, **11**, 408, 410
Gelré Herault d'Armes
roll of arms by, **11**, 1602
Gender
change of—
  children of trans-sexual, succession by, **11**, 1038
  generally, **10**, 1036
  Human Rights Convention, under, **10**, 1037
  marriage after, **10**, 818; **11**, 1038
  other legal systems, under, **10**, 1038
  personality, **11**, 1038
  private life, respect for, **12**, 67
  registers, no change in respect of, **10**, 1035; **19**, 1424*n*
child offender, of, **10**, 1042
child victim—
  heterosexual offences, **10**, 1043
  homosexual offences, **10**, 1044
criminal law, **10**, 1042–1044

Gender—*continued*
determination of, **10**, 1034
error in relation to, **10**, 1035
hermaphrodites, **10**, 1034
Interpretation Act 1978 rules as to, **12**, 1207
minority, **10**, 1039–1041
pupillarity, **10**, 1039, 1049
Genealogies
Court of the Lord Lyon, **6**, 1012, 1018
Public Register of All Genealogies and Birthbrieves in Scotland, **6**, 1012
General Act for the Pacific Settlement of International Disputes
generally, **19**, 720*n*
General Agreement on Tariffs and Trade (GATT)
aims, **7**, 1009*n*
Common Customs Tariff (CCT), **7**, 1009
copyright, legislation as to, **18**, 931
Customs Valuation Code, **7**, 1048
dumping, **4**, 1396
European Coal and Steel Community (ECSC) schedule, **7**, 1009
European Economic Community schedule, **7**, 1009
European Union, and, **7**, 1009
GATT 1994…, **7**, 1009
intellectual property, **18**, 804
internal taxes, provisions as to, **7**, 1009
non-tariff barriers, provisions as to, **7**, 1009
relation of European Community with, **10**, 299
tariff concessions, extension to other members, **7**, 1009
TRIPS, semiconductor topographies, protection of design rights, **18**, 1253
General Assembly of the Church of Scotland
administrative body, as, **3**, 1542
  administrative functions, **3**, 1550
advocate appearing before, dress, **13**, 1323
Assembly Council, **3**, 1550
Board of Practice and Procedure, **3**, 1545, 1548
Clerks, Principal and Depute, **3**, 1545
Commission—
  appointment, **3**, 1548
  functions, **3**, 1548
commissioners—
  elders, **3**, 1543
  ministerial, **3**, 1543, 1563
Committee on the Maintenance of the Ministry ('the Committee'), **3**, 1562
Committee on Returns to Overtures, **3**, 1546
corresponding membership, **3**, 1543
Declaratory Articles, ratification, **3**, 1501
establishment, **3**, 1501
generally, **3**, 1501, 1502, 1505
Judicial Commission, **3**, 1549
judicial functions, **3**, 1547
jurisdiction—
  extraordinary equitable, **3**, 1547
  sheriff courts, entitlement to invoke assistance of, **3**, 1547, 1634
Law Agent, **3**, 1545
legislation, **3**, 1546, 1546*n*

General Assembly of the Church of Scotland—*continued*

legislature of Church, as, **3**, 1542, 1634

meetings, **3**, 1542

membership, **3**, 1543

Moderator, **3**, 1545

  appointment, **3**, 1544

  designation, **3**, 1551

  duties, **3**, 1544

  Ex-Moderators, designation, **3**, 1551

  precedence, **3**, 1551

Moderator-Elect, **3**, 1545

officials, **3**, 1545

other churches, delegates from, **3**, 1543

overtures, **3**, 1546, 1546*n*

presbyteries, creation, **3**, 1518

Procurator, **3**, 1545

quorum, **3**, 1543

Standing Orders, **3**, 1547

status, **3**, 1542

supreme court, as, **3**, 1542

witnesses, attendance, **3**, 1547, 1634

General average

action, **21**, 711

adjustment, **21**, 713

arbitration clause, subject to, **21**, 711

bill of lading, **21**, 609, 711

cargo, shipowners' lien, **21**, 711

charterparty, **21**, 711

common adventure, **21**, 701, 703

contribution, **21**, 701

  calculation, **21**, 705

  liability for, **21**, 712

    limitation, **21**, 757

danger as element of, **21**, 701, 702, 702*n*

  categories of losses and expenditure, **21**, 707–710

  consequences of danger need not have transpired, **21**, 702

  real and imminent, danger must be, **21**, 702, 702*n*

  whole maritime adventure, must be to, **21**, 702, 702*n*

definition, **21**, 701

deviation, sacrifice or expenditure as result of, **21**, 704, 704*n*

dispute over, **20**, 305

English law, **21**, 701*n*

expenditure, **21**, 701, 704

  categories, **21**, 707, 710

  success in objective, whether necessity for, **21**, 705

fault, where, **21**, 704, 704*n*

generally, **21**, 700

harbour dues, **21**, 710

history of rule, **21**, 700

initiation of act, **21**, 704

Jason clause, **21**, 704*n*

legislation, generally, **21**, 102*n*

lien, **21**, 711

loss, **21**, 701

  categories, **21**, 707–709

  consequence of deliberate act, where, **21**, 706

  deliberately inflicted or incurred, **21**, 706

General average—*continued*

loss—*continued*

  reasonably foreseeable, **21**, 706

  remoteness, **21**, 706

maritime adventure, interests in, **21**, 700*n*, 701

master, act initiated by, **21**, 704

meaning, **21**, 700

new (amended) Jason clause, **21**, 704*n*

owner, act initiated by, **21**, 704

passengers' luggage, **21**, 712

pilotage fees, **21**, 710

re-loading costs, **21**, 710

remoteness of consequences, **21**, 706

repair costs, **21**, 710

sacrifice, **21**, 701, 704

  cargo, **21**, 707, 708

  freight, **21**, 707, 708

  ship, **21**, 707, 709

  success in objective, whether necessity for, **21**, 705

salvage services, costs of, **21**, 710

stranger, act initiated by, **21**, 704

tug and tow, **21**, 703

voluntary, act must be, **21**, 704

wages, **21**, 710, 712

warehousing costs, **21**, 710

York-Antwerp Rules, **21**, 700, 700*n*, 704, 704*n*

  salvage services, costs of, **21**, 710

General Chiropractic Council

establishment, **15**, 1522–1524

membership, **15**, 1523

  chairman, **15**, 1529

  education members, **15**, 1527

  elected members, **15**, 1525

  lay members, **15**, 1526

  Secretary of State, member appointed by, **15**, 1528

General Commissioners (of Inland Revenue)

appeal to, **19**, 1544, 1547

appointment, **19**, 1546

meaning, **19**, 1544*n*

supervision of by Scottish Committee, **23**, 911*n*

General Council of Solicitors in Scotland

establishment, **13**, 1140

General Dental Council

constitution, **14**, 1132; **15**, 1510

Dental Auxiliaries Committee, **14**, 1132, 1146

Education Committee, **14**, 1132

elections, **15**, 1510, 1511

functions, **15**, 1510

generally, **15**, 1507, 1510

Health Committee, **14**, 1132, 1142

Preliminary Proceedings Committee, **14**, 1132, 1137

President, **15**, 1510

Professional Conduct Committee, **14**, 1132, 1138

register maintained by, **14**, 1132

statute, established by, **14**, 1132

statutory committees, **14**, 1132

General legal concepts

act or abstain from acting, capacity to, **11**, 1058

animals, laws against cruelty to, **11**, 1045

capacity-responsibility, **11**, 1054–1058

civil liberty, principle of, **11**, 1012

General legal concepts—*continued*
civil remedies, **11**, 1009
conduct, lawful and unlawful, **11**, 1006–1013
contracts, unenforceable, **11**, 1009
duties and breach of duty, **11**, 1014–1026
enforcement—
   coercive, **11**, 1009
   direct, **11**, 1009
freedom, **11**, 1085
good faith, **11**, 1125–1136
injunctions, **11**, 1009
institutive rules, **11**, 1118
interdicts, **11**, 1009
law—
   abstract things, place of, **11**, 1096
   body of rules, as, **11**, 1009
   case law, **11**, 1011
   conduct, as guide to, **11**, 1006
   good faith, place of, **11**, 1135
   legal subject, **11**, 1014
   legal system as normative system, **11**, 1003
   meaning of, **11**, 1001
   positive, **11**, 1004, 1005
   precedent, **11**, 1011
   principles, Scots law founded on, **11**, 1011, 1012
   private, duty, **11**, 1015, 1017
   rules and principles, **11**, 1119–1124
   rules of recognition, **11**, 1002
   specialised concepts, **11**, 1005
   statutory provisions, **11**, 1011
   systematic quality of legal concepts, **11**, 1002
   validity of, **11**, 1002
legal frameworks, **11**, 1116
legal powers—
   elements necessarily involved in conferment, **11**, 1061
   special, **11**, 1062
   valid legal effects of exercise, **11**, 1060
liberty, **11**, 1085
nulla poena sine crimine, nullum crimen sine lege, **11**, 1012
obligations and the obligatory, **11**, 1027–1034
persons and personality, **11**, 1035–1044
   active capacity, **11**, 1052–1058
   corporate, **11**, 1041–11044
   passive capacity, **11**, 1045–1051
   transactional capacity, **11**, 1059–1063
principles, **11**, 1123
   good faith as element of, **11**, 1134
   rules, interaction with, **11**, 1124
privilege, **11**, 1085
punishments and penalties, **11**, 1009
rights, **11**, 1073–1112
rules—
   arbitrary nature, **11**, 1121, 1122
   certainty and clarity, **11**, 1120
   good faith as element of, **11**, 1134
   necessity for, **11**, 1119
   principles, interaction with, **11**, 1124
status, **11**, 1067–1071
   corporate, **11**, 1072
terminative rules, **11**, 1117, 1118
things and institutions, **11**, 1113–1118

General legal concepts—*continued*
time—
   existence of entities through, **11**, 1113
   human arrangements and, **11**, 1114
   legal arrangements and, **11**, 1115
values, plurality of, **11**, 1008
virtue and vice distinguished, **11**, 1007
General Medical Council
committees appointed by, **14**, 1102
constitution, **15**, 1508
elected members, **15**, 1508, 1509
elections, **15**, 1508
electors, qualifications, **15**, 1509
establishment of, **14**, 1102
functions, **14**, 1102; **15**, 1508
generally, **15**, 1507, 1508
Health Committee—
   appeal, **14**, 1117
   functions, **14**, 1102, 1111
   immediate suspension, **14**, 1116
   Preliminary Proceedings Committee, reference from, **14**, 1113
   procedure, **14**, 1112
   unfitness to practice, finding of, **14**, 1115
membership, **14**, 1102
Preliminary Proceedings Committee—
   functions, **14**, 1102, 1111, 1113
   Health Committee, reference to, **14**, 1113
   procedure, **14**, 1112
   Professional Conduct Committee, reference to, **14**, 1113
Professional Conduct Committee—
   advertising, **14**, 1124
   appeal, **14**, 1117
   burden of proof, **14**, 1129
   care, standard of, **14**, 1126, 1128
   causation, **14**, 1129
   confidentiality, **14**, 1131
   criminal convictions, **14**, 1114, 1119
   dishonesty, **14**, 1124
   errors of judgment, **14**, 1127
   experience, **14**, 1128
   functions, **14**, 1102, 1111
   immediate suspension, **14**, 1116
   informed consent, **14**, 1130
   matters before, **14**, 1118
   misdiagnosis, **14**, 1127
   neglect of duty, **14**, 1123
   negligence, **14**, 1125
   Preliminary Proceedings Committee, reference from, **14**, 1113
   procedure, **14**, 1112
   serious professional misconduct, **14**, 1114, 1120
   sexual involvement with patient, **14**, 1122
   unethical behaviour, **14**, 1121
qualifications, refusal to register, appeal against, **14**, 1105
Review Board for Overseas Qualified Practitioners, **14**, 1109
statutory regulation of, **23**, 617
General ophthalmic services
See OPHTHALMIC SERVICES

General Optical Council
constitution, **15**, 1512
elections, **15**, 1513
functions, **15**, 1512
generally, **15**, 1507, 1512
General Orders
dispensation with, **19**, 31
Private Business, relating to, **19**, 11
General Osteopathic Council
establishment, **15**, 1522–1524
membership, **15**, 1523
  chairman, **15**, 1529
  education members, **15**, 1527
  elected members, **15**, 1525
  lay members, **15**, 1526
  Secretary of State, member appointed by, **15**, 1528
General practitioner
See DOCTOR; MEDICAL PRACTITIONER
General Register House for Scotland
Register House, **19**, 828
General Register Office
establishment of, **19**, 809, 1402, 1404
General Register of Sasines
access to, **19**, 878
adjudication—
  record of, **8**, 189
  registration in, **8**, 194
back volumes microcopied, **19**, 846
boundaries, alteration, **18**, 219
burgh registers of sasines, **19**, 864
coast protection works scheme, **25**, 383
competing titles, rule as to, **18**, 684, 684*n*
Crown title, no record of, **18**, 48
disposition, registration of, **18**, 640, 643
drainage works, agreements relating to, **25**, 373
duplicate plans, retention of, **19**, 846
extracts from, **19**, 880
generally, **6**, 405, 452, 703; **18**, 91, 91*n*
historical background, **19**, 835
inhibitions not recorded in, **8**, 144
land recorded in—
  determination of ownership, **18**, 194
  horizontal limits of estate, **18**, 197
  possession, proof of right of, **18**, 141, 142
    derivative right, where, **18**, 142, 144
    independent right, defender averring, **18**, 142, 145
    no right averred by defender, where, **18**, 142, 143
    seven-year possessory judgment, **18**, 145, 146
Land Register—
  contrasted with, **6**, 452, 706
  operation in tandem with, **6**, 452, 703
  supersedes, **6**, 703, 705
  See also REGISTRATION OF TITLE
lease, registration of—
  generally, **13**, 318–327
  history of, **13**, 101
  See also LEASE–LEASING
multiple occupation control orders, recording in, **11**, 2009
non-payment of stamp duty, **19**, 1536
origin of, **19**, 834

General Register of Sasines—*continued*
Particular Register of Sasines, **6**, 405
real burden, registration of, **18**, 386, 389
real condition, registration of, **18**, 349
real and personal rights, registration, **18**, 657
register of deeds, as, **16**, 2105, 2109
registration in, **24**, 22, 23
  effect of, **6**, 452; **18**, 640, 643, 644
  procedure, regulation of, **19**, 816
  process of, **6**, 453
regulations prescribing methods of operation, **19**, 846
searches in, **19**, 851
  fees, **19**, 851
servitudes, registration in—
  generally, **18**, 451, 477
  variation or discharge by Lands Tribunal, **18**, 477
uninfeft proprietors, **18**, 645
warrant of registration for, **6**, 551; **13**, 1229
See also SASINES
General ship
contract for carriage in—
  advertised timetable, ship running to, **21**, 585
  bill of lading, contract evidenced by, **21**, 521, 524, 540
    See also BILL OF LADING
  cargo owner, performance of contract, **21**, 585
  collision, loss or damage caused by—
    cargo claims, **21**, 583
      both to blame collision clause, **21**, 584, 584*n*
      restrictions on extent of, **21**, 584
  container, carriage by, generally, **21**, 526
  damage to goods, **21**, 542
  demurrage, **21**, 585
  express terms—
    commonplace, **21**, 546
    generally, **21**, 540, 542
    negligence, liability for expressly excluded, **21**, 544
    where no—
      generally, **21**, 540, 541
      implied terms, **21**, 545
      strict liability, basis of, **21**, 543, 544
  general average, law of, **21**, 541
  generally, **21**, 521
  implied, title to sue, **21**, 581
  implied terms—
    generally, **21**, 541, 545
    where no express terms, **21**, 545
  laytime, **21**, 585
  liability—
    carrier, of, generally, **21**, 542
    common carrier, **21**, 543, 543*n*
    deviation, unjustified, **21**, 542, 547
    exceptions to, **21**, 542
    exclusion or limitation—
      acts of Queen's enemies, damage caused by, **21**, 542, 549
      damnum fatale, **21**, 542, 548
      deviation, unjustified, **21**, 542, 547
      employees and contractors, **21**, 560
      excepted perils, **21**, 547

General ship—*continued*
contract for carriage in—*continued*
  liability—*continued*
    exclusion or limitation—*continued*
      exceptions clauses, **21**, 547
      fire damage, **21**, 557
      generally, **21**, 543, 547
      Himalaya clause, **21**, 560
      insufficiency of packing, **21**, 553
      limitation of liability, generally, **21**, 559
      negligence, **21**, 544, 547, 557
      perils of the sea, **21**, 550*n*, 551
      restraints of princes, **21**, 550
      strikes exception, **21**, 555
      Unfair Contract Terms Act 1977 ...561
      unseaworthiness, **21**, 542, 547
      valuables, loss of or damage to, **21**, 557
    Hague or Hague-Visby Rules, **21**, 543
      See also HAGUE RULES; HAGUE-VISBY RULES
    inherent vice of cargo, **21**, 542, 552
    jettison to avoid danger, where, **21**, 542
    private carrier, **21**, 543
    seaworthiness of vessel, **21**, 542
    strict—
      basis in English law, **21**, 544
      basis in Scots law, **21**, 543
  lost goods, **21**, 542
  non-delivery of goods, **21**, 542
  performance of contract, **21**, 585
  rights and obligations of parties, **21**, 540, 542
  time for making, **21**, 540
  title to sue, **21**, 576–582
  transfer of rights and liabilities—
    bills of lading, **21**, 570–573
    sea waybills, **21**, 575
    ship's delivery orders, **21**, 574
operation, generally, **21**, 526
tramp, **21**, 526, 526*n*
General Teaching Council for Scotland
Disciplinary Committee—
  appeals from decisions of, **8**, 828
  powers and duties, **8**, 828
duties, **8**, 827
establishment, **8**, 827
Investigating Committee—
  dismissal of teachers, **8**, 829
  powers and duties, **8**, 828
register, **8**, 827
  removal from, **8**, 827, 828
Genetic fingerprinting
identification by, **10**, 662
Genocide
Convention for the Prevention and Punishment
  of the Crime of Genocide, **12**, 508
customary international law, **19**, 678
Genocide Convention, **19**, 698
international conventions on, **12**, 5
political offence, not regarded as, **12**, 532
Genscher-Colombo Plan, **10**, 22
Gentry
armigerous, **16**, 2023
gentleman of blood, **16**, 2023
heraldic entitlement, **11**, 1604
office, gentle by virtue of, **16**, 2023

Geographer Royal
former office of, **7**, 844
German Democratic Republic
identity papers and travel documents, **16**, 1236, 1236*n*
Germanischer Lloyd, **21**, 120
Germany
civil jurisdiction, contracting state, **4**, 22
competition rules, application, **4**, 1304
European Union customs territory, **7**, 1010
lease, classification of, **14**, 1007
sources of private international law, **17**, 111
wills and succession—
  acceptance to act, **25**, 637
  active succession, **25**, 614
  co-ownership, **25**, 639
  death, property passing on—
    competent beneficiaries, **25**, 621
    future property, **25**, 622
    generally, **25**, 619
    presumptions, **25**, 620
  devolution, **25**, 606
  distribution of property, **25**, 605
  family property, **25**, 608
  freedom of testation, **25**, 601
  identification of property, **25**, 605
  intestate succession, **25**, 633
  partition, **25**, 642
  reassembly of estate, **25**, 610
  reserved property—
    free estate, **25**, 626
    generally, **25**, 623
    gift—
      purposes of, **25**, 627
      valid, formalities required for, **25**, 628
    heirs, rights of, **25**, 626
    voluntary provision, **25**, 624
    voluntary and statutory devolution, balance
      between, **25**, 629
    will—
      purposes of, **25**, 627
      valid, formalities required for, **25**, 628
  separation of property, **25**, 602
  species of property, distinction of, **25**, 607
  transmission, **25**, 636
Gestor
See NEGOTIORUM GESTOR
Gibraltar
British Dependent Territories citizenship, **14**, 1932
civil jurisdiction, **4**, 23
European Union customs territory, special status, **7**, 1010
European Union law, **12**, 220, 220*n*
Gift
cash, made by, **19**, 1606
charity, to, **25**, 1010
class, **25**, 843, 961
condition attached to, **25**, 913
customs duties, **8**, 657
debitor non praesumitur donare, **8**, 624
donation, *see* DONATION
English law, **8**, 601
exempt transfers, **25**, 999

Gift—*continued*
Forestry Fund, to, **11**, 636
goodwill gift, excise duty relief, **7**, 1113
immoral or illegal purpose, made for, **8**, 641
inheritance tax, **8**, 652
  See also INHERITANCE TAX
insured, to, from party responsible for loss, **12**, 902
inter vivos
  completion, time of, **19**, 1601
  foundations, to, **24**, 118
  interest in estate takes priority over, **25**, 601
  will substitute, as, **25**, 729
lifetime—
  will distinguished, **6**, 416*n*
  See also INHERITANCE TAX
local authority, to, **14**, 232
mortis causa, **25**, 735
outright lifetime, avoidance of legal rights, **25**, 812
presumed, **8**, 627
public body, to, **25**, 1010
purpose, made for, non-fulfilment of condition, **8**, 642
purposes of, **25**, 627
reservation, subject to, **25**, 1001
revocable, **8**, 643
Scots law, **8**, 601
spouses, between, **10**, 873, 876
sub modo, **24**, 4
taxation of, **19**, 1601–1610
testamentary provisions, **8**, 601, 609
valid, formalities required for, **25**, 628
VAT relief, **7**, 1314
vesting, *see* VESTING
whether donation, **8**, 605
Gift aid
certificate, **3**, 1154
conditions to be met, **3**, 1154
income tax—
  income or gains not subject to, **3**, 1154
  payment by donor, **3**, 1154
  recovery by charity, **3**, 1154
one-off gift, as, **3**, 1154
Gladstone Report
generally, **16**, 1491
Glasgow
county of city, **14**, 39
educational provision, **14**, 36
housing, **14**, 609
police court, **6**, 1157, 1158
population, **14**, 64
transport—
  passenger area, **14**, 415
  undertakings, operation of, **14**, 414, 419
underground railway, **24**, 415
Glasgow Polytechnic
structure and powers, **8**, 981
Glass
carriage of, **3**, 610, 610*n*
Glaucoma
diagnosis of, **11**, 1467
ophthalmic services for sufferers, **11**, 1463*n*

Glazing
building controls, **3**, 208
collision with, as potential hazard, **3**, 208
Glebe
allodial land, whether, **18**, 47
feudal law, generally, **18**, 68*n*, 70
generally, **3**, 1579
lease, **13**, 204
quoad omnia parish—
  entitlement to glebe, **3**, 1581
  historical position, **3**, 1581
  post-1925 position, **3**, 1582
sale of congregational properties and endowments, **3**, 1607–1609
See also CHURCH OF SCOTLAND (property and endowments)
Glider-Gliding
generally, **19**, 1287, 1288, 1291
launching, **2**, 973
licensing, **19**, 1291
piloting, age limit, **3**, 1228; **19**, 1291
towing, **19**, 1291
Global accounting system
VAT margin scheme for used goods, **7**, 1363
Go-slow
contractual rights and duties, **9**, 132
Goatmeat
export refunds, **1**, 936
import levies, **1**, 936
Goats
Games Acts, **11**, 496*n*
meat, *see* GOATMEAT
milk, **11**, 438
Going concern value
mineral undertaking, **25**, 141
property assets, valuation of, **25**, 95
Gold
articles or coin, Carriers Act (1830), **3**, 610
coins—
  VAT regulations—
    importation, **7**, 1314
    supply to Central Bank, **7**, 1454
false trade description, **18**, 1418, 1418*n*.
hallmarking, *see* HALLMARKING
mines royal, **13**, 200
as standard of currency, **14**, 1832
VAT regulations—
  importation, **7**, 1314
  supply to Central Bank, **7**, 1454
Gold clause
creditor, use by, **14**, 1823
Krugerrands, **14**, 1808
validity of, **14**, 1823
Goldsmiths Company
Trial of Pyx, **14**, 1821
Golf
club professionals, **19**, 1231
courses, whether entitled to rating relief, **24**, 561
historical background, **19**, 1202, 1204
Royal and Ancient Golf Club, **19**, 1204
sports-governing institutions, **19**, 1204, 1205

Gong
motor vehicle equipped with, **20**, 481
ship, on, **21**, 372
Good faith
action justified by, **11**, 1126
   qualification of principle, **11**, 1127
actus non facit reum nisi mens sit rea, **11**, 1132
American Restatement, **11**, 1130
bona fide possession, *see* POSSESSION
collecting banker acting in, **4**, 213
conduct contrary to, **11**, 720
contracts—
   consumer, **11**, 1131
   generally, **11**, 1129–1132
conventional obligations and, **11**, 1129
debt revalorised on principle of, **14**, 1823
engagement as principle of equity, **11**, 1125
fraudulent misrepresentation by non-disclosure,
   11, 712
freedom as principle of equity, **11**, 1125
holder in due course, position of, **4**, 147
litiscontestation, loss at, **18**, 137
meaning, **18**, 132
negotiable instruments, **11**, 767
obedience as principle of equity, **11**, 1125
partnership—
   compete with firm, duty not to, **16**, 1060
   duty of disclosure, **16**, 1058
   expulsion clauses, **16**, 1061
   private profit, duty not to make, **16**, 1059
   requirement of good faith, generally, **16**, 1057
   retired partners, **16**, 1060
   separate business run by partner or former
      partner, **16**, 1060
paying banker acting in, **4**, 211
personal bar, and, **11**, 1133
place in law, **11**, 1135
precondition, as, **11**, 1128
principles requiring, **11**, 1132
principles and rules, as element of, **11**, 1134
recovery of possession, action for, **18**, 151
rights, acquisition of, **11**, 1128, 1132
statements made in, **11**, 728
termination, **18**, 137
third party, protection of, **4**, 414
violent profits, in relation to, **13**, 511
Goods
carriage, *see* CARRIAGE; SEA, CARRIAGE BY
definition, Hague-Visby Rules, **21**, 587
delivered by mistake, restitution, **15**, 46, 48
enemy, *see* ENEMY GOODS
free movement within European Economic
   Community—
   agriculture, **10**, 130
   article 36—
      application of, **10**, 122
   Common Customs Tariff, **10**, 129
   customs duties, **10**, 118
      internal taxation, and, **10**, 119
   customs union, **10**, 113, 114, 117
   derogation, **10**, 121
   difference between national standards, **10**, 123
   exports, **10**, 120, 126
   free circulation, **10**, 115

Goods—*continued*
free movement within European Economic
   Community—*continued*
   industrial property rights, **10**, 127
   Mandatory Requirement, **10**, 123
   meaning of goods, **10**, 113
   quantitative restrictions, **10**, 120
   restrictions on, **10**, 120, 121
   reverse discrimination, **10**, 125
   Rule of Reason, **10**, 123
   state monopolies of commercial character, **10**,
      128
   tariff and non-tariff barriers, **10**, 116
   technical barriers to trade, harmonisation of,
      10, 124
   transport, **10**, 150
Krugerrands as, **14**, 1808
lost, restitution, **15**, 46, 47
meaning, **10**, 113; **14**, 1802
mislaid, restitution, **15**, 46, 47
money not, **14**, 1808
ownership, **17**, 421
receipts for, printer's imprint, **17**, 3
repetition, **15**, 16, 31, 31*n*
repossession of, **5**, 891, 892, 928
requisition, **17**, 415
restitution, **15**, 14, 46–48
sale of, *see* SALE AND SUPPLY OF GOODS
salvage, payment of, **17**, 426
slander of, *see* SLANDER
straying, restitution, **15**, 46, 47
trade-in, **14**, 1802
Goods test certificate
police powers to require production of, **20**, 436
Goods vehicle
definition, **20**, 408
driver—
   hours of work—
      domestic drivers' hours code, **20**, 497
      foreign vehicles, **20**, 499
      international agreements, **20**, 498, 499
      offences in relation to, **20**, 497
      recording equipment (tachograph), **20**, 497,
         498
      records, **20**, 498
         inspection, **20**, 498
      regulations, generally, **20**, 497
foreign, **20**, 499
international carriage of goods by road, generally,
   20, 500
international road haulage permit—
   requirement for, **20**, 500
      exceptions to, **20**, 500
large goods vehicles driver's licence, **20**, 495
maintenance, inspection to secure proper, **20**, 496
medium-sized, age limit for licence, **20**, 448
operator's licence—
   licensing authority, **20**, 494
   requirement for, **20**, 494
   restricted, **20**, 494
   standard, **20**, 494
plating certificate, **20**, 496
sale, relevant certificates must accompany, **20**, 496
small, age limit for licence holder, **20**, 448

Goods vehicle—*continued*
tachograph, requirement for, **20**, 497
    exemption from, **20**, 497, 498
testing certificate, **20**, 496
Goodwill
assignation, **6**, 598; **20**, 55
cessation of business, effect, **18**, 1370
character merchandising, **18**, 1366
company, valuation practice, **25**, 34
customers, existence of, **18**, 1365
device, in, **18**, 1366
duration, **18**, 1366
foreign, **18**, 1367
franchise, foreign, **18**, 1368
heritable or moveable property, whether, **18**, 14
individual trading under firm name, **16**, 1010
licensed premises, **24**, 671
meaning, **18**, 1365; **24**, 520; **25**, 34
modern valuation practice, **25**, 34
partnership agreement, provisons in, **16**, 1009
partnership property, as, **16**, 1074, 1076
passing off, and—
    actual damage to goodwill, necessity to show,
        18, 1362
    attraction of custom by defender, **18**, 1372
    calculation to injure, **18**, 1362
    damage to goodwill, **18**, 1372
        prospective, **18**, 1362, 1366, 1373
    device, goodwill in, **18**, 1366
    loss of custom by plaintiff, actual or potential,
        18, 1372
    misrepresentation, **18**, 1383
    presence of goodwill, necessity to show, **18**,
        1362, 1363, 1365
    product goodwill, **18**, 1365
    shared goodwill, **18**, 1365, 1366, 1371
payments for, consideration other than rent, **24**,
    520
product goodwill, **18**, 1365
product launch, prior to, **18**, 1366
regional, **18**, 1369
restraint of trade, protectable interests, **15**, 773
rights in security, **20**, 43
sale—
    dissolution of firm, on, **16**, 1076
    firm name, effect on choice of, **16**, 1024
    payment by share in future profits, **16**, 1023
shared goodwill, **18**, 1365, 1366, 1371
transfer of business, effect, **18**, 1370
Gordon, Gerald H
The Criminal Law of Scotland, **7**, 2, 58, 59, 70
Government
administration distinguished from, **14**, 1
byelaws for, **14**, 271
central, *see* CENTRAL GOVERNMENT
constitutional monarchy, **7**, 701, 702
defamation, title to sue, **15**, 477
departmental, **19**, 210
executive function, **7**, 702, 716–719
grant, *see* GRANT
judicial function, **7**, 702, 716–719
legislative function, **7**, 702, 716–719
local, *see* LOCAL GOVERNMENT
rate-capping power, **14**, 7

Government—*continued*
recognition of, **19**, 660
Scotland, of, *see* SCOTTISH OFFICE; SECRETARY OF
    STATE FOR SCOTLAND
unity, underlying, **7**, 717
unrecognised, *see* UNRECOGNISED GOVERNMENT
**Government Communications Headquarters
(GCHQ)**
statutory basis, **7**, 732
Government department
Crown body, as, **7**, 754
data protection, criminal offence in respect of, **18**,
    1553
enforcement of contract against, **3**, 26
explanatory memoranda issued by, as aid to
    interpretation of statute, **12**, 1149
See also CENTRAL GOVERNMENT
Government securities
interest on, deceased's liability to tax, **25**, 967
Gower Report
generally, **4**, 309
proposals, **12**, 1304, 1305
publication, **12**, 1304, 1305
Grágás
Icelandic law code, **24**, 303
Grampian Region
population, **14**, 64
structure, **14**, 64
transport undertakings, operation of, **14**, 419
Grampus
occupancy, no right of acquisition by, **18**, 543*n*
Grandchild
collation, **25**, 808
deceased specified relative, as, **15**, 602
division of estate on or after 8 December 1986—
    examples, **25**, 704
Grandfather clause
European Union prohibition between member
    states, **7**, 1019, 1019*n*
Grandparent
deceased specified relative, as, **15**, 602
incest, **7**, 315; **10**, 1227
marriage, prohibited degree, **10**, 817
Grant
amenities, to improve, **11**, 2033
British Coal Corporation, to, **14**, 1604
central government, **11**, 2034
coast protection works, **25**, 388
educational, *see* EDUCATION
fire escapes, to install, **11**, 2028–2030
housing support grants, **11**, 1910–1914
improvement, *see* IMPROVEMENT GRANT
industrial equipment, acquisition of, **14**, 1006
investment, taxation, **14**, 1009
land drainage, **25**, 372
leasing, disadvantage of, **14**, 1017
local government—
    aggregate Exchequer, **14**, 830
    capital, **14**, 809
    commercial undertakings, **14**, 640
    disaster, relating to, **14**, 327
    emergency, relating to, **14**, 327
    fireplace, adaptation of, **9**, 1138

Grant—*continued*
local government—*continued*
  flood prevention—
    exchequer, **14**, 468
    local authority, **14**, 467
  generally, **14**, 829
  housing support, **14**, 833
  industrial undertakings, **14**, 640
  inner urban area, *see* INNER URBAN AREA
  police, **14**, 496
  public passenger transport—
    facilities, **14**, 436
    rural areas, **14**, 437
    services, **14**, 436
  rate support, *see* RATES
  specific, **14**, 831
  urban programme, eligibility for, **14**, 661
rental variation clauses, capital grant, **14**, 1056
repair, *see* REPAIRS GRANT
Scottish Arts Council, provided by, **9**, 1007
Scottish Homes, power to make, **11**, 1923
sound-proofing, towards cost of, **9**, 1284
thermal insulation, for, **11**, 2035, 2036
Grant-aided college
funding, **8**, 947
meaning, **8**, 947, 947*n*
recurrent and non-recurrent grants, **8**, 947
Grant-aided school
assisted places scheme, **8**, 817, 818
  regulations, **8**, 818
corporal punishment, **8**, 820
denominations, must be open to all, **8**, 856
fees, **8**, 818
meaning, **8**, 817
St Mary's Music School, aided places, **8**, 819
Grass
land kept in, freedom of cropping not extending
  to, **1**, 763
planting alongside road, **20**, 672, 674
Grass-cutting machine
driver's seat, with, **20**, 409
pedestrian, operated by, **20**, 409
Grassum
amounting to *rei interventus*, **13**, 140
meaning, **13**, 103; **18**, 58; **22**, 595; **24**, 520
tenant's failure to pay, **13**, 151
Gratuitous alienation
abuse of power, **4**, 878
burden of proof, **4**, 875
challenge, effect of, **4**, 877
challenging, alteration of rules for, **4**, 307
common law, **4**, 873
excess of power, **4**, 878
Insolvency Act 1986..., **4**, 874
old law, **4**, 872
property, of, **11**, 780
statutory provisions, application of, **4**, 876
Gravestones
See TOMBSTONES
Graving dock
meaning, **11**, 1303
Grazing let
portion of year, for, **1**, 733

Grazing rights
taxation of payments for, **19**, 1573
Grazings
common—
  regulation, **6**, 959, 963, 967
  resumption, **6**, 967
Great Chamberlain
Officer of the Crown, as, **7**, 812, 813
Great Seal of Scotland
abolition, **7**, 873
Act of Union, effect, **7**, 785, 873
design, **7**, 875
forfeiture, decrees of, **7**, 874
generally, **7**, 855, 897, 898, 902
heritable property, grant, **7**, 874, 907
history, **7**, 873
Keeper, **5**, 370; **7**, 877
location, **7**, 877
present use, **7**, 874
testimonial of, *see* QUARTER SEAL
Titles to Land Consolidation (Scotland) Act
  (1868), **7**, 907
uses, **7**, 873, 874
Great Seal of the United Kingdom
authorisation, Order of Chancery, **7**, 870–872
generally, **7**, 855, 856
history, **7**, 856
instruments passed under, **7**, 856–861
international treaties, instruments relating to, **7**,
  856, 860
letters patent, **7**, 856, 859, 871
Lord Keeper, **7**, 804, 805, 864
physical characteristics, **7**, 862
proclamations, **7**, 856, 857
wafer version, **7**, 863
writs, **7**, 856, 858
Great Seal Register
generally, **6**, 458; **7**, 876; **16**, 1310; **19**, 820
Great Stewardship of Scotland
heir to Crown holding, **7**, 704, 704*n*, 786, 812
Officer of the Crown, as, **7**, 812
Greater London
Council, abolition, **14**, 62
Residuary Body, establishment of, **14**, 62
two-tier system, **14**, 60
Greece
application of competition rules, **4**, 1304
European Union customs territory, **7**, 1010
Green Rod, Usher of the
office of, **7**, 829
Greenhouse
agricultural building, as, **24**, 565
exemptions from building regulations, **3**, 209
Greenock Police Court
former operation of, **6**, 1157, 1158
Greenwich Mean Time
basis of calculation, **22**, 809
legal time, as, **22**, 809, 810
overriding summer time as legal time, **22**, 810
summer time defined in terms of, **22**, 810
Grenade
ammunition, as, **10**, 1510
designed to explode on or immediately before
  impact, **10**, 1517

Greyhound racing
licence, **19**, 1238
Grievous bodily harm
assault with intent to commit, **7**, 236
Grilse
River Tweed, **11**, 40
Grit
furnace, emission from—
arrestment equipment—
exemption from requirement, **9**, 1131
provision of, **9**, 1130
generally, **9**, 1129
Gross and shameless indecency
homosexual acts, **7**, 312
Grotius, Hugo
mare liberum advocated by, **11**, 72
Natural law, as leading exponent of, **18**, 530
unjust enrichment, **15**, 11, 75
Ground annual
adjudication, **20**, 265
debitum fundi, on a, **8**, 376
assignation, form of, **20**, 264
bilateral, must be, **20**, 265
building conditions created by, **20**, 265
burgage tenure, **6**, 586
congregational properties and endowments, sale, **3**, 1609
contract of, **6**, 586
interpretation, **12**, 1262
pecuniary real burden, as, **18**, 383, 383n
creditor, **20**, 265
remedies competent to, **20**, 265
deed, form of, **6**, 586
discharge, form of, **20**, 264
extinction, **20**, 265
feuduties distinguished, **6**, 586
generally, **20**, 263
grant of security by way of, **6**, 714
holder's remedies, **20**, 265
indemnity, whether creditor entitled to, **6**, 768
mails and duties, action of, **20**, 265
meaning, **20**, 263
periodical payment under contract of, prescription, **16**, 2116
poinding the ground, **20**, 265
prescription, negative, extinction by, **20**, 265
prohibition on creation, **20**, 264
redemption, **20**, 264
restriction, form of, **20**, 264
standard security, **20**, 150
statutory provisions, **20**, 264
Ground game
See HARES; RABBITS
Ground lease
generally, **13**, 209
meaning, **13**, 209
Group company
VAT registration provisions, **7**, 1349
Groupe d'etudes
accounting standards, influence on, **1**, 77
Grouse
eggs, protection of, **11**, 802, 843
game, as, **11**, 802
Game (Scotland) Act 1832..., **11**, 815

Grouse—*continued*
Games Acts, **11**, 496n
Poaching Prevention Act 1832..., **11**, 843
trespass in pursuit of, **11**, 817
Guadalajara Convention
air, carriage by, **3**, 738, 738n, 740, 744
Guarantee
building contract, *see* BUILDING CONTRACT
contract, as, **6**, 36
definition, **6**, 36
manufacturers', **6**, 36, 101, 154
manufacturers', insurance compared, **12**, 802
purchaser's statutory rights not affected by, **6**, 154
security, as, **5**, 908
undertakings, by, **14**, 640
Guarantee payment (employment protection)
eligibility for, **9**, 60
Employment Appeal Tribunal, **6**, 999
guarantee fund, *see* REDUNDANCY FUND
lay-off, recourse to, **9**, 60
remedy for failure to pay, **9**, 60
workless day, in respect of, **9**, 60
Guard dog
handler to be in control of, **2**, 175
kennels—
licence—
conditions, subject to, **2**, 149
duration, **2**, 149
refusal of, **2**, 149
requirement for, **2**, 148
meaning, **2**, 148
offences, **2**, 150
use of, warning notice, **2**, 175
Guardian-guardianship
access, rights of, where child in local authority care, **3**, 1270
alcoholic, **3**, 1267
appointment of guardian—
directions as to, **25**, 604
generally, **3**, 1205
child appearing in adult court, social worker's duty to provide report to, **22**, 32
children's hearing, attendance at, **3**, 1321
Court of Session jurisdiction, **4**, 5
debts owing to *incapax*, recovery of, **11**, 1225
disability, with, **3**, 1267
duty of care, **15**, 299
gratuitous nature of, **11**, 1214
guardian's allowance, *see* GUARDIAN'S ALLOWANCE
lessor, guardian as, **13**, 167
liability of, **11**, 1225
litigation, pursuance on behalf of child, **3**, 1215
local authority as, **11**, 1229–1231
management by, standard of, **11**, 1225
medical procedure, consent on behalf of child, **3**, 1207
mental disorder, with, **3**, 1267
mentally disordered person, of—
age limit, **11**, 1238
appointment, **11**, 1240; **22**, 31
community care, as aspect of, **11**, 1240
death of guardian, **14**, 1445

Guardian-guardianship—*continued*
mentally disordered person, of—*continued*
  discharge—
    generally, **14**, 1448
    local authority, order made by, **14**, 1449
    Mental Welfare Commission, order made by,
      14, 1449
    nearest relative, order made by, **14**, 1451
    responsible medical officer, order made by,
      14, 1449
    sheriff, order made by, **14**, 1450
  duration of authority for—
    custody, patient in, **14**, 1447
    medical officer, duties of, **14**, 1446
    patient absent without leave, **14**, 1447
    time limits, **14**, 1446
  duties, **11**, 1240, 1241; **22**, 31
  generally, **11**, 1238–1241
  hospitalised patients, 1240*n*; **11**, 1240
  incapacity of, **14**, 1445
  local authority—
    duties of, **14**, 1441, 1476
    duties to, **11**, 1241
    reception, application for, **14**, 1435
  mentally handicapped person over 16 years—
    application to sheriff, **22**, 31
    medical recommendations, **22**, 31
    mental health officer, procedural role, **22**, 31
    review of order, **22**, 31
  order—
    appeal against, **17**, 906
    court's power to make, **14**, 1452
    mental disorder, person suffering from, **17**,
      904
    review, **22**, 31
  patient—
    absence without leave, **14**, 1443
    transfer of, **14**, 1444
  reception into—
    application—
      defective, **14**, 1440
      local authority, addressed to, **14**, 1435
      medical recommendations accompanying—
        defective, **14**, 1440
        mental health officer, by, **14**, 1437
        prescribed form, **14**, 1436
        requirements, **14**, 1436
      mental health officer, by, **14**, 1435
      nearest relative, by, **14**, 1435
      sheriff, approval by, **14**, 1438
      successful, effect of, **14**, 1439
    grounds for, **14**, 1434
    procedure, **14**, 1434
  retention under, duration of authority, **14**,
    1446
parent as guardian, **11**, 1208–1213
powers, **3**, 1205
proposed reforms—
  children over sixteen, legal capacity, **11**, 1245
  children under sixteen, legal capacity, **11**, 1244
  common law, of, **11**, 1242–1246
  curator, abolition of office, **11**, 1243
  curatories, in respect of, **11**, 1237
  generally, **11**, 1242, 1246

Guardian-guardianship—*continued*
proposed reforms—*continued*
  minors, classification of, **11**, 1243
  pupils, classification of, **11**, 1243
  tutor, abolition of office, **11**, 1243
right of, feudal law, **18**, 75
sheriff court jurisdiction, **4**, 5
transaction entered on child's behalf, **3**, 1205
undue influence, **25**, 764
who is, **3**, 1205
writs and titles owing to *incapax*, recovery of, **11**,
  1225
Guardian's allowance
absent from Great Britain, claimant, **21**, 1020,
  1023
entitlement, **21**, 801, 953
generally, **21**, 953
husband and wife as guardians, payment of
  allowance, **21**, 957
imprisonment of claimant, **21**, 1020
overlapping benefits, **21**, 1002
parent—
  adoptive child, of, **21**, 954
  both parents dead, where, **21**, 953
  divorced parents, position of, **21**, 954
  missing parent, discovery of, **21**, 955
  prison, in, **21**, 953, 956
  step, **21**, 954
  whereabouts unknown, **21**, 953, 955
prison, surviving parent in, **21**, 953, 956
residence, conditions as to, **21**, 953
Guernsey
inland bill, nature of, **4**, 120
Guernsey cattle
milk, regulations as to, **11**, 466
Guidons
grant of, **11**, 1609
Guinea fowl
slaughter of, **11**, 516
Gulathing
See CODE OF MAGNUS 'THE LAW-MENDER'
Gun
See FIREARM
Gun-cotton
explosive, as, **10**, 1586
Gunpowder
ammunition, **10**, 1510
application of provisions to other explosives, **10**,
  1617
chemical experiment, manufacture for purposes
  of, **10**, 1591
consumer stores—
  construction, **10**, 1598
  death, incapacity or bankruptcy of occupier,
    10, 1602
  employees in—
    age of, **10**, 1598
    working clothes, **10**, 1598
  general rules, **10**, 1598
  licensing, **10**, 1597
  lightning conductors, **10**, 1598
  Orders in Council, provisions as to, **10**, 1598
  prevention of accidents by fire or explosion,
    10, 1602

Gunpowder—*continued*
consumer stores—*continued*
   repairs to, **10**, 1598
   smoking prohibited in, **10**, 1598
control of—
   conveyance—
      aircraft byelaws, **10**, 1613
      canal byelaws, **10**, 1610
      factories and magazines, **10**, 1595
      harbour authority byelaws, **10**, 1609
      marking, **10**, 1608
      merchant shipping byelaws, **10**, 1613
      packing, **10**, 1608
      railway byelaws, **10**, 1610
      road byelaws, **10**, 1612
      wharves and docks, byelaws, **10**, 1611
manufacture, **10**, 1591
sale—
   ammunition, **10**, 1606
   children, to, **3**, 1223; **10**, 1604
   hawking, **10**, 1603
   packaging and labelling, **10**, 1605
   records, **10**, 1607
   registration and regulation of premises for,
      10, 1600, 1601
     prevention of accidents by fire or
      explosion, **10**, 1602
special powers in relation to, **10**, 1590
special rules, **10**, 1599
storage, **10**, 1592

Gunpowder—*continued*
explosive, as, **10**, 1586, 1588
factories and magazines—
   construction, **10**, 1595
   conveyance within, **10**, 1595
   employees in—
      age of, **10**, 1595
      working clothes, **10**, 1595
   ingredients—
      regulations as to, **10**, 1595
      sifting, **10**, 1595
   licensing, **10**, 1592, 1593
   lightning conductors, **10**, 1595
   prevention of accidents by fire or explosion,
      10, 1602
   prohibited materials, **10**, 1595
   quantity allowed in building, statements as to,
      10, 1595
   regulation, **10**, 1594–1596
   repairs to, **10**, 1595
   smoking prohibited in, **10**, 1595
fireproof safe, storage in, **10**, 1601
private use, kept for, **10**, 1592
provisions as to, application to other explosives,
   10, 1617
statutory control, **14**, 1651
Guthrie Committee
criminal legal aid, recommendations as to, **13**, 1005
Gutter
public health nuisance, as, **19**, 336

H

Habeas corpus
writ of, extradition cases, **12**, 562, 568, 575
Haberdashery
goods to be sold by length, **6**, 242
Hacking
computer fraud, **7**, 387
Hackney carriage
sign to be displayed by, **20**, 466
Haemodialysis
sickness benefit where regular weekly treatment
    for, **21**, 880
Hall
valuation for rating, **24**, 666
Halliday Committee Report
allocation, recommendations as to, **6**, 531
feudation, redemption of, **6**, 535
legislation subsequent to, **6**, 410
subscription of deeds, **6**, 415, 419
unrecorded title, **6**, 589
Hallmarking
alteration or repair of articles, **18**, 1418n, 1421
ancient marks, treatment of, **18**, 1422, 1422n
approved hallmarks, **18**, 1416
assay office—
    approved hallmarks, **18**, 1416
    Birmingham, **18**, 1414, 1414n
    charges, **18**, 1424
    convention hallmarks, **18**, 1416
    Edinburgh, **18**, 1414, 1414n
    London, **18**, 1414, 1414n
    meaning, **18**, 1414
    Sheffield, **18**, 1414, 1414n
    sponsors' marks, **18**, 1417
    unauthorised marks, treatment of, **18**, 1422
British Hallmarking Council, **18**, 1413, 1415
carats, **18**, 1416
charges, **18**, 1424
convention hallmarks, **18**, 1416
counterfeit die, making, **18**, 1420
counterfeit mark, making, **18**, 1420
dealer, duty to exhibit notices as to hallmarks, **18**,
    1423
die, counterfeit, **18**, 1420
Dublin, hallmark struck in, **18**, 1416
enforcement of provisions, **18**, 1425
fineness—
    false trade description, **18**, 1418
    minimum, **18**, 1416
    standards of, **18**, 1416
gold, **18**, 1413
    plated articles, **18**, 1419
    rolled, **18**, 1419
Hallmarking Act 1973 ... 1413
hallmarks, notices as to, **18**, 1423
history, **18**, 1411
improper alteration, article subject to, **18**, 1418n
Incorporation of Goldsmiths of the City of
    Edinburgh, **18**, 1412
medals, **18**, 1413

Hallmarking—*continued*
permitted descriptions, **18**, 1419
platinum, **18**, 1413
    plated articles, **18**, 1419
prohibited descriptions, **18**, 1419
recoated articles, **18**, 1421
silver, **18**, 1413
    plated articles, **18**, 1419
sponsors' marks, **18**, 1417, 1418n
    meaning, **18**, 1417n
unauthorised marks, treatment of, **18**, 1422
unhallmarked articles, prohibited description, **18**,
    1418, 1418n
Hallucinogens
controlled drug, as, **14**, 1225
criminal behaviour, link with, **14**, 1221
Hamburg
free zone, as, **7**, 1164
Hamburg Rules
shipping, **21**, 586, 586n
Hamesucken
assault as alternative charge, **7**, 225
generally, **7**, 225
Hamilton
population, **14**, 64
Handcuffs or other restraints
unjustified use, **15**, 440
use in penal establishment, rules as to, **16**, 1453
Handicapped person
See DISABLED PERSON; MENTALLY DISORDERED
    PERSON; MENTALLY HANDICAPPED PERSON
Handling goods
unpaid excise duty, subject to, **7**, 1262
Handwriting
expert evidence, **10**, 652
Hang gliding, 19, 1287
Hansard
reports, absolute privilege, **15**, 525
Harassment
Criminal Injuries Compensation Scheme, **7**, 5
intention, **13**, 702
landlord, by—
    generally, **13**, 698, 701
    residential occupier, meaning, **13**, 690
meaning, **13**, 701
peace and comfort of occupier, acts likely to
    interfere with, **13**, 702, 703
penalties for, **13**, 702, 703
protected tenancy, repossession, **13**, 709
protection of tenant against, **13**, 593, 598
residential occupier, of, **7**, 403
services, withholding, **13**, 701, 702
single act amounting to, **13**, 701
threats and intimidation, **13**, 702
unlawful, generally, **13**, 472
Harbour
acquisition of—
    district council, by, **14**, 445
    islands council, by, **14**, 444

Harbour—*continued*
acquisition of—*continued*
  regional council, by, **14**, 444
anchorage in natural harbours, **11**, 1304
approaches—
  buoys, **11**, 1322
  depth, **11**, 1322
  leading lights, **11**, 1322
  obstruction, **11**, 1322
artificial, *see* ARTIFICIAL HARBOUR
authority, *see* HARBOUR AUTHORITY
beacons, **11**, 1322
berths, safety of, **11**, 1321
British Waterways Board facilities, **19**, 1105
buoys, **11**, 1322
byelaws, **11**, 1317
care, harbour authorities' duty of, **11**, 1326
charges, **11**, 1318
charters, **11**, 1301
constables, undertaker's power to appoint, **16**, 1818
construction or alteration, **19**, 19*n*
Crown grants, **11**, 1301
damage to—
  Act of God, caused by, **11**, 1327
  liability for, **21**, 755
development of, **11**, 1316; **23**, 153
dock, **11**, 1303
dockyard port, **11**, 1319
dredging of, compensation for, **6**, 1141
dry dock, **11**, 1303
dues—
  damages claim, **21**, 386
  general average contribution, **21**, 710
  time charterparty, **21**, 640
empowerment order, *see* HARBOUR EMPOWERMENT ORDER
explosives, byelaws as to, **10**, 1609, 1620
free port, **11**, 1306
graving dock, **11**, 1303
historical background to law, **5**, 4; **11**, 1301
inflammable substances, byelaws, **19**, 394
local authority, powers of, **14**, 443, 447
master, *see* HARBOUR MASTER
meaning, **11**, 1303; **24**, 599
moorings, **11**, 1304
natural, *see* NATURAL HARBOUR
oil, discharge of, **9**, 1212; **11**, 1327
pilotage, *see* PILOT; PILOTAGE
planning authorities, power of, **11**, 1316; **23**, 153
quays and wharves, **24**, 599
railway property, **24**, 727
regional and islands councils, compulsory powers, **11**, 1316
reorganisation scheme—
  generally, **11**, 1315
  object of, **11**, 1315
revision order—
  application for, **11**, 1312
  generally, **11**, 1312
  objects for which made, **11**, 1312
  special parliamentary procedure, **11**, 1314
sheriff court jurisdiction, **4**, 2; **6**, 1106

Harbour—*continued*
valuation of, **24**, 415, 598, 601
  prescribed formula, **24**, 547
water sports and recreation, **19**, 1283
wet dock, **11**, 1303
wharf, **11**, 1303
wreck, removal of, **11**, 1319, 1322
Harbour, right of
See PORT, RIGHT OF
Harbour authority
acquisition and development of land by, **11**, 1316
approach to harbours, **11**, 1322
beacons, **11**, 1322
berths, safety of, **11**, 1321
buoying of channels, **11**, 1322
byelaws, power to make, **11**, 1317
care, duty of, **11**, 1326
charges levied by, **11**, 1318
compulsory purchase of land by, **11**, 1316
constitution, **11**, 1309
dangerous state of harbour, liability for, **11**, 1325
delict committed by pilot, liability, **15**, 242
dockyard ports, **11**, 1319
duties, **21**, 382
duties and liabilities, **11**, 1320–1326
generally, **11**, 1309
licensing of works, **11**, 1310
lighthouses, **11**, 1322
lighting, **11**, 1322
limitation of liability, **11**, 1324; **21**, 751, 753*n*, 769, 769*n*
  Convention on, **11**, 1324
loans to, **11**, 1309; **14**, 446
meaning, **21**, 293*n*, 769*n*
membership, **11**, 1309
movement of ships within harbour limits, **11**, 1323
pilotage, **21**, 291, 293–297
possessory lien exercised by, **20**, 298
powers and responsibilities, **21**, 114
reorganisation scheme, **11**, 1315
revision order, **11**, 1312
statute law, **11**, 1308, 1326
statutory, **19**, 394, 394*n*
trust as, **11**, 1309
vicarious liability, **11**, 1321
wreck, removal of, **21**, 514
Harbour empowerment order
application for, **11**, 1313
objects of, **11**, 1313
special parliamentary procedure, **11**, 1314
Harbour master
directions, giving of, **11**, 1320
generally, **11**, 1320
Queen's, **11**, 1319
statutory powers, **11**, 1320
unserviceable vessels, removal of, **11**, 1320
Harbouring
criminal, **7**, 562
spy, **7**, 636
Hard labour
abolition of, **17**, 563
Hares
agricultural tenant, permission to kill given by, **11**, 818

Hares—*continued*
annual game certificate, **11**, 826
authorisation to kill, **11**, 830
common grazing, **11**, 858
common law right to kill, **11**, 854
concurrent right to take and kill, **11**, 852
control of, **11**, 859–865
coursing, **11**, 830; **19**, 1275
    Day Trespass Act, application to, **11**, 821
custody of, by unqualified person, **11**, 807
forests, prevention of damage to, **11**, 866, 867
game, as, **11**, 802
Game Acts, **11**, 496*n*
Game (Scotland) Act 1832…, **11**, 815
Hares Preservation Act 1892…, **11**, 825–828
Hares (Scotland) Act 1848…, **11**, 825–828
importation control, **2**, 214
imported, sale of, **11**, 827
killing, **11**, 826
land occupier's right to take and kill, **11**, 850
legal proceedings, who may institute, **11**, 857
moorland, **11**, 853
night shooting, **11**, 828, 872
no close season, **11**, 825
Poaching Prevention Act 1832…, **11**, 843
poisoning prohibited, **11**, 828
regulations as to preparation and sale as food, **11**, 312
requirement notice to control, **11**, 860–863
selling and exposing for sale, **11**, 827
shooting—
    by night, **11**, 828, 872
    lease, clauses in, **11**, 900
spring traps—
    approved, **11**, 874
    inspection of, **11**, 875
    open trapping, **11**, 876
    use, sale and possession of, **11**, 873
trespass in search of, **11**, 817
unenclosed land, **11**, 853
Harm (Nuisance)
adjoining property, caused by, **14**, 2167
extent of—
    degree, matters of, **14**, 2051
    interference—
        single, **14**, 2053
        temporary, **14**, 2052
    materiality, **14**, 2050
    time of day, **14**, 2054
gravity of, relevant factors in evaluating, **14**, 2043
infection, fear of, **14**, 2082
intangible, assessment in case of, **14**, 2151
intentional, **14**, 2105
liability, *see* LIABILITY—
    nuisance
locality, character of—
    changes in, **14**, 2059
    extra sensitivity, **14**, 2058
    generally, **14**, 2056
    industrial area, **14**, 2056
    other annoyance, presence of, **14**, 2057
    residential area, **14**, 2056
negligent, **14**, 2106

Harm (Nuisance)—*continued*
protective measures, burden of taking—
    extent of, **14**, 2066
    generally, **14**, 2064
    want of, **14**, 2065
sensitivity to—
    extra, **14**, 2058
    generally, **14**, 2060
    person, of, **14**, 2061
    property, of, **14**, 2062
    rationale, **14**, 2063
social value, **14**, 2055
type of—
    annoyance, **14**, 2047
    damage distinguished, **14**, 2048, 2049
    damage distinguished from discomfort, **14**, 2048, 2049
    discomfort, **14**, 2047
    enjoyment of land, interference with, **14**, 2046
    generally, **14**, 2044
    inconvenience, **14**, 2047
    physical damage, **14**, 2045
    use of land, interference with, **14**, 2046
unintentional, comparison of Scots and English law, **14**, 2021
Harmful emissions
atmosphere, into, duty of persons in control of premises, **9**, 453, 454
Harmonized Description and Coding System (HS)
European Union Common Customs Tariff (CCT), **7**, 1015
Haughing
criminal offence, as, **11**, 497*n*
Haulage contractor
domestic carriage of goods by road, **3**, 619
private carrier, as, **3**, 619
Havers
citation of, in summary causes, **17**, 1315
Hawking
gunpowder, of, **10**, 1603
Hazardous operation
negligence, liability for, **3**, 148, 152; **14**, 2138
Hazardous substances
classification of, **9**, 532
Crown land, on, **23**, 107
drugs, *see* DRUGS
EC directives, **9**, 1204
food, protection from contamination, **9**, 1205
generally, **9**, 1200
importation, restrictions on, **6**, 58; **9**, 1203
industrial plants handling, **9**, 1201
labelling of, **9**, 532, 851
legislation, **9**, 1180
notification of installations handling, **9**, 530
packaging of, **9**, 851
pesticides—
    EEC directive on, **9**, 1207
    UK legislation on, **9**, 1206
petroleum, *see* PETROLEUM-PETROLEUM-SPIRIT
planning permission, **23**, 219, 220
pollution control, **19**, 303
supply, restrictions on, **9**, 1203
transport of, **9**, 529, 1202

Hazardous substances—_continued_
use, restrictions on, **9**, 1203
Use Classes Order, operation of, **23**, 91
See also DANGEROUS GOODS; INFLAMMABLE SUB-
  STANCES OR MATERIALS; NOXIOUS SUBSTANCES
  and under names of particular substances

Headlease
meaning, **13**, 103

Headteacher
appointment, **8**, 821
  appointment committee, **8**, 760, 762
assistant—
  appointment, **8**, 821
    appointment committee, **8**, 760, 763
deputy—
  appointment, **8**, 821
    appointment committee, **8**, 760, 763
purchase of books and materials, powers of school
  board, **8**, 769
self-governing school board of managment,
  membership of, **8**, 787

Health
accommodation which may endanger, **11**, 2045,
  2049
animal, _see_ ANIMAL HEALTH
authority, local, **11**, 1403
child attending film show, of, **9**, 1026
council, local, **11**, 1420, 1421
education, provision of, **11**, 1482
environmental expenditure programme, **5**, 586
fluoridation, **19**, 320; **25**, 509
injury to, **14**, 2044
insurance, **12**, 60
matter or substance prejudicial to, **19**, 334
National Health Service, _see_ NATIONAL HEALTH
  SERVICE
protection of, EU customs law, **7**, 1021, 1022
public, _see_ PUBLIC HEALTH
service, sheriff court jurisdiction, **6**, 1132
statutory controls, **14**, 1051
suspension from work on medical grounds, **6**, 999
water rights, acquisition of, **25**, 519
wholesome water, duty to provide, **19**, 319_n_; **25**,
  508

Health and safety at work
Act of, **6**, 1974
  civil liability, **9**, 408
  Crown, application to, **9**, 409
  effect of, **9**, 667
  general purposes of, **9**, 425
  nature of, **9**, 407; **19**, 304
  prosecution policy, **9**, 412
  scope of, **9**, 411
  territorial application, **9**, 410
administration—
  Employment Medical Advisory Service, **9**, 421
  Health and Safety Commission, _see_ HEALTH AND
    SAFETY COMMISSION
  Health and Safety Executive, **9**, 419, 420
  licensing provisions, appeals in connection
    with, **9**, 424
  sanctions—
    improvement notice—
      appeal against, _see_ appeal _below_

Health and safety at work—_continued_
administration—_continued_
  sanctions—_continued_
    improvement notice—_continued_
      buildings, and, **9**, 500
      generally, **9**, 498, 499
      provisions common to prohibition notice
        and, **9**, 502
      service of, **9**, 503
    prohibition notice—
      appeal against, _see_ appeal _below_
      generally, **9**, 498, 501
      provisions common to improvement
        notice and, **9**, 502
      service of, **9**, 503
agriculture, **19**, 345
appeal against improvement/prohibition notices—
  burden of proof, **9**, 508
  effect of, **9**, 507
  industrial tribunal, **9**, 504, 509
  judicial review, **9**, 510
  procedure, **9**, 505
  relevant factors, **9**, 506
articles used at work, duty of manufacturer—
  generally, **9**, 455
  information, provision of, **9**, 459
  installation of, **9**, 460
  research, **9**, 458
  safety in use of, **9**, 436, 437
  supply and supplier, **9**, 457, 462
  transfer of responsibility, **9**, 461
  user, **9**, 457
assistance, power to require, **9**, 492
charge levying on employee prohibited, **9**, 468
civil liability—
  causation and, **9**, 547
  existing statutory provisions, breach of, **9**, 538
  generally, **9**, 408
civil proceedings specifically excluded, **15**, 155, 155_n_
codes of practice—
  approval of, **9**, 536
  contravention of, **9**, 537
  role of, **9**, 535
duties—
  employee at work, of—
    dismissal, **9**, 466
    generally, **9**, 463, 465
    prosecution policy, **9**, 464
  employer, of—
    generally, **9**, 429
    health, to ensure, **9**, 427
    information, provision of, **9**, 438, 439
    instruction, provision of, **9**, 438, 439
    persons other than employees, to, **9**, 445–447
    plant—
      generally, **9**, 430
      maintenance of, **9**, 432
      meaning, **9**, 433
      provision of, **9**, 431
      safety, **9**, 435
    policy statements, **9**, 440
    proper working environment, provision of
      9, 443, 444
    reasonably practicable, meaning, **9**, 428

Health and safety at work—*continued*
duties—*continued*
  employer, of—*continued*
    safety—
      articles, use of, **9**, 436, 437
      ensuring, **9**, 427
      meaning, **9**, 435
      place of work, of, **9**, 441, 442
      substances, use of, **9**, 437
    supervision, provision of, **9**, 438, 439
    systems of work—
      generally, **9**, 430
      maintenance of, **9**, 432
      meaning, **9**, 434
      provision of, **9**, 431
      safety, **9**, 435
    training, provision of, **9**, 438, 439
    welfare, to ensure, **9**, 427
  generally, **9**, 426
  manufacturers, of, as to articles for use at work—
    generally, **9**, 455
    information, provision of, **9**, 459
    installation of articles for use at work, **9**, 460
    meaning of 'articles for use at work', **9**, 456
    research, **9**, 458
    responsibility, transfer of, **9**, 461
    substance for use at work, meaning, **9**, 456
    suppliers, **9**, 457
    supply, meaning, **9**, 462
    users, **9**, 457
  premises—
    persons concerned with, of—
      bearers of duty, **9**, 450
      nature of duty, **9**, 448
      non-domestic premises, **9**, 449
      recipients of duty, **9**, 451
      relationship between section 3 and section 4..., **9**, 452
    persons in control of, as to harmful emissions—
      best practicable means, meaning, **9**, 454
      generally, **9**, 453
  safety equipment, misuse of, **9**, 467
  self-employed, of, to persons other than employees, **9**, 445–447
education authorities' duties, **8**, 734
employer, obligations primarily enforced against, **15**, 159
enforcing authorities—
  duty of, **9**, 484
  generally, **9**, 482
  local authority, default of, **9**, 485
  responsibility, transfer of, **9**, 483
existing statutory provisions—
  breach of, **9**, 538
  factory machinery, duty to fence—
    causation, **9**, 547
    dangers—
      extraneous objects, arising from, **9**, 542
      materials, arising out of, **9**, 541
    exceptions, **9**, 550

Health and safety at work—*continued*
existing statutory provisions—*continued*
  factory machinery, duty to fence—*continued*
    fencing—
      construction of, **9**, 548
      maintenance of, **9**, 548
    foreseeability, questions of, **9**, 544
    generally, **9**, 539
    materials—
      dangers arising out of use of, **9**, 541
      ejection of, **9**, 543
    in motion or use, meaning, **9**, 549
    nature of, **9**, 545
    part of any machinery, **9**, 540
    safe to every person, meaning, **9**, 546
    unfenced machinery, **9**, 551–600
factories, **19**, 343
generally, **19**, 304, 342–345
history of legislation, **9**, 404
hotel trade, **11**, 1737
inspectorates—
  entry, inspection and disclosure of information, **9**, 417
  factory, objectives of, **9**, 487
  generally, **9**, 486
  inspectors—
    appointment of, **9**, 488
    general powers, **9**, 489
    indemnity, **9**, 494
    powers of—
      assistance, as to, **9**, 492
      detention, **9**, 491
      entry, **9**, 490
      examination, **9**, 490
      information, as to, **9**, 492
      investigation, **9**, 490
      sampling, **9**, 491
      seizure, **9**, 493
      testing, **9**, 491
islands and district councils' powers, **19**, 342
legislation, generally, **19**, 304
  See also Act of 1974 *above*
licensing provisions, appeals in connection with, **9**, 424
mines, **19**, 344
misuse of safety equipment, **9**, 467
notices, service of—
  generally, **9**, 495
  premises, in respect of, **9**, 497
  proper address for, **9**, 496
offences—
  charge levying on employee, **9**, 468
  corporate body, by, **9**, 516
  court, powers of, **9**, 519
  evidence, **9**, 517
  fault of other person, due to, **9**, 515
  generally, **9**, 511
  jurisdiction, **9**, 514
  onus of proof, **9**, 518
  penalties, **9**, 512
  time limits, **9**, 513
offices, **19**, 343
public health, and, **19**, 304
quarries, **19**, 344

Health and safety at work—*continued*
railway premises, **19**, 343
regulations—
    breach of, **9**, 525
    capacity to make, **9**, 521
    dangerous occurrences, reporting of, **9**, 534
    dangerous substances—
        classification of, **9**, 532
        conveyance by road, **9**, 529
        labelling of, **9**, 532
    diseases, reporting of, **9**, 534
    first-aid, **9**, 528
    further purposes of, **9**, 524
    generally, **9**, 526
    hazardous substances, notification of installations handling, **9**, 530
    Health and Safety Commission, duties of, **9**, 523
    industrial major accident hazards, control of, **9**, 533
    injuries, reporting of, **9**, 534
    lead, control of, **9**, 527
    new substances, notification of, **9**, 531
    proper purposes of, **9**, 522
    Secretary of State, duties of, **9**, 523
    use of, **9**, 520–525
Robens Committee, *see* ROBENS COMMITTEE
safety committee—
    establishment of, **9**, 476, 477
    general functions, **9**, 476
    specific functions, **9**, 478
safety representative—
    appointment of, **9**, 469
    general functions, **9**, 471
    information, right to, **9**, 475
    inspection—
        dangerous occurrence, following, **9**, 474
        documents, of, **9**, 475
        notifiable accident, following, **9**, 474
        notifiable disease, following, **9**, 474
        workplace, of, **9**, 473
    number of, **9**, 470
    specific functions, **9**, 472
    time off for, **9**, 97, 479–481
    workplace, right to inspect, **9**, 473
self-regulation, role of, **9**, 405
shops, **19**, 343
substances for use at work—
    generally, **9**, 455
    information, provision of, **9**, 459
    meaning, **9**, 456
    research, **9**, 458
    supplier, **9**, 457
    supply, **9**, 462
    transfer of responsibility, **9**, 461
    user, **9**, 457
Health and Safety Commission
codes of practice issued by, **9**, 10
constitution, **9**, 413
control of, **9**, 413
discharge of functions, **14**, 1615
functions of, **9**, 413, 414
information, obtaining and disclosure of, **9**, 417, 423

Health and Safety Commission—*continued*
inquiries—
    generally, **9**, 416
    information, disclosure of, **9**, 417
    premises, entry and inspection of, **9**, 417
    witnesses at, **9**, 418
investigation by, **9**, 416
Ombudsman system, **19**, 242
powers of, **9**, 415
regulations, duties as to, **9**, 523
Health and Safety Executive
constitution, **9**, 419
functions of, **9**, 420
Ombudsman system, **19**, 242
planning permission, consultation with, **23**, 169
Health and Social Security, Department of
functions of, **5**, 507
Health and welfare services
VAT exemption, **7**, 1426
Health boards
accounts, **11**, 1508
adequacy of medical services, report on, **11**, 1431
after-care services, for person with mental disorder, co-operation with local authority to provide, **22**, 30
budgets for doctors' practices set by, **11**, 1401
community service expenditure, contributions to, **11**, 1507
complaints as to, investigation of, **11**, 1426, 1522–1524
constitution, **11**, 1410
dental list, preparation of, **11**, 1454
dental services committee, **11**, 1520
doctors, payments to, **11**, 1451
doctors' lists, duties in relation to, **11**, 1438, 1439, 1443
expenses, **11**, 1506
functions, **11**, 1410
fund-holding practice, applications for recognition as, **11**, 1401
general dental services, duties as to, **11**, 1452
general medical services, provision of, **11**, 1427
general ophthalmic services, arrangements as to, **11**, 1463
health visiting, administration of, **11**, 1410
joint liaison committees, **11**, 1412
joint services committee, **11**, 1520
liabilities, **11**, 1413
medical list, preparation of, **11**, 1430
medical service committee, **11**, 1520
membership, **11**, 1410
nursing homes, registration of, **11**, 1527, 1528
ophthalmic list, preparation of, **11**, 1465
ophthalmic services, payments for, **11**, 1468
pharmaceutical service committee, **11**, 1520
pharmaceutical services, duties as to, **11**, 1469
privilege of, **11**, 1413
records of, **19**, 842
rights, **11**, 1413
Scottish Committee, supervision by, **23**, 911*n*
statutory duties, **22**, 2
vacant medical practice, powers as to succession, **11**, 1433

Health boards—*continued*
voluntary organisations, discretion to assist, **22**, 10
See also SCOTTISH HEALTH BOARD
Health Committee
General Dental Council, **14**, 1132, 1142
General Medical Council, *see* GENERAL MEDICAL
    COUNCIL
Health Service Commissioner for Scotland
acting, **11**, 1426
appointment, **11**, 1426
Commissioner for Local Administration,
    consultation with, **14**, 145
complaint to, **11**, 1523, 1524
function, **11**, 1426
jurisdiction, **11**, 1522
Health services
chemist, *see* PHARMACEUTICAL CHEMIST
chiropodist, *see* CHIROPODIST
Common Services Agency—
    accounts, **11**, 1508
    expenses, **11**, 1506
    functions and duties, **11**, 1411
    investigation of complaints as to, **11**, 1426,
        1522–1524
    liabilities, **11**, 1413
    management committee, **11**, 1401, 1411
    membership, **11**, 1411
    privilege of, **11**, 1413
    rights, **11**, 1413
community medicine specialist, **11**, 1498, 1498n
community service expenditure, contributions to,
    11, 1507
contraception, *see* FAMILY PLANNING
dentist, *see* DENTIST; DENTISTRY
designated medical officer, **11**, 1502
dietitian, **11**, 1500
doctor, *see* DOCTOR
drugs, *see* DRUGS
family planning, *see* FAMILY PLANNING
finance, **11**, 1506–1519
General Dental Council, *see* GENERAL DENTAL
    COUNCIL
General Medical Council, *see* GENERAL MEDICAL
    COUNCIL
health boards, *see* HEALTH BOARDS
Health Service Commissioner for Scotland, *see*
    HEALTH SERVICE COMMISSIONER FOR SCOTLAND
health visitor, **11**, 1410, 1499
hospitals, *see* HOSPITAL; PRIVATE HOSPITAL; STATE
    HOSPITAL
immunisation, *see* VACCINATION AND IMMUNISATION
laboratory technician, **11**, 1500
local consultative committees, **11**, 1420, 1423
local health authorities, **11**, 1403
local health council, **11**, 1420, 1421
maternity care, *see* MIDWIFERY, MATERNITY AND
    CHILD CARE
medical supplies, control of prices for, **11**, 1509
National Central Consultative Committee, **11**,
    1419
National Consultative Committee of Scientists in
    Professions Allied to Medicine, **11**, 1419
National Health Service, *see* NATIONAL HEALTH
    SERVICE

Health services—*continued*
nursing, *see* NURSE-NURSING
nursing homes, *see* NURSING HOME
ophthalmic services, *see* OPHTHALMIC SERVICES
optician, *see* OPTICIAN
orthoptist, **11**, 1500
patient, *see* PATIENT
pharmaceutical services, *see* PHARMACEUTICAL
    SERVICES
radiographer, **11**, 1500
remedial gymnast, **11**, 1500
Scottish Health Service Planning Council, *see*
    SCOTTISH HEALTH SERVICE PLANNING COUNCIL
Scottish Medical Practices Committee, *see*
    SCOTTISH MEDICAL PRACTICES COMMITTEE
social work expenditure, contributions towards,
    11, 1507
speech therapist, **11**, 1501
state hospital, *see* STATE HOSPITAL
university liaison committee, **11**, 1420, 1422
    Tribunal, **11**, 1506n
vaccination and immunisation, *see* VACCINATION
    AND IMMUNISATION
voluntary organisations, **11**, 1493
Working for Patients White Paper, **11**, 1401
Health standards
European Social Charter, **12**, 7
Health visitor
employment of, **11**, 1499
health visiting, administration by health boards,
    11, 1410
meaning, **11**, 1499n
qualification, **11**, 1499
    obtained outside UK, **14**, 1152
    United Kingdom, **14**, 1155
register—
    preparation and maintenance of, **14**, 1150
    removal from, **14**, 1158
registration—
    eligibility for, **14**, 1152
    periodic, **14**, 1151
    renewable, **14**, 1151
regulation, framework of, **14**, 1147; **23**, 917
reporter, referral of child to, **3**, 1287
restrictions on practice, **14**, 1156
training of, **14**, 1148, 1149
Hearing Aid Council
members, appointment, **15**, 1507, 1530
Hearing aid dispensers
discipline, **14**, 1172
legal control, scope of, **14**, 1101
organisation of profession, **14**, 1170
registration, **14**, 1171
Hearsay evidence
admissibility of, *see* ADMISSIBILITY OF EVIDENCE
exceptions to rule—
    civil cases, **10**, 715
    criminal cases, **10**, 709–713
Lands Tribunal for Scotland, **6**, 1152
reform of law, **10**, 502
statutory provisions, **10**, 716–718
unreliability, **10**, 505
Heart condition
driving licence application, declaration in, **20**, 450

Heat-Heating
apparatus, safety, **3**, 208
electricity boards, schemes for production and use, **9**, 623
supply, charge to VAT, **7**, 1288, 1320
tolerable standard for housing, **11**, 1979
waste, from, **9**, 1171
Heath fowl
close season, **11**, 806
custody of, by unqualified person, **11**, 807
Heath game
Game (Scotland) Act 1832..., **11**, 815
trespass in search of, **11**, 817
Hebrides
'annual of Norway', **24**, 302
ceded to Scotland, **24**, 302, 304
territorial waters, **11**, 78
Hedge
laying of, licence not required, **11**, 617
overhanging road, **20**, 505, 696
prevention of damage by injurious animals or birds, **11**, 859
Heidsaevisthing law (Eidsivathinglaw)
Norwegian law code, **24**, 303
Heineccius, G
Elementa Juris Civilis Secundum Ordinem Institutionum, **18**, 4, 4*n*
Heir
acquiescence of predecessor, bound by, **16**, 1616
at-law, *see* HEIR-AT-LAW
debts, liability for, **25**, 637
entail, of, *see* HEIR OF ENTAIL
gift over to, distinguished from gift over to child, **25**, 918
impersonation of, **11**, 748, 759
inheritance, remoteness of, **18**, 48*n*
meaning, **12**, 1268; **13**, 1627; **25**, 878
of-line, *see* HEIR-OF-LINE
property passes intact to, **25**, 606
provision in trust, of, **24**, 162
Register of Services of, **6**, 457
right to be served as, **16**, 2126
rights of, Germany, **25**, 626
single, inheritance by, emergence of, **25**, 608
ultimus haeres, Crown as, **18**, 48, 48*n*
unascertainable, **13**, 1628, 1629
unwilling person, burdens cannot be imposed on, **25**, 637
unwillingness to act, **25**, 637
unworthy, **25**, 668
See also BENEFICIARY (WILLS AND SUCCESSION)
Heir-at-law
abolition of concept of, **6**, 479
collation *inter haeredes*, **25**, 683
feudal law, **18**, 55, 108
generally, **24**, 162
heritable succession, **25**, 678, 679
Heir male
peerage granted with destination to, meaning, **16**, 1310
Heir male of the body
peerage granted with destination to, **16**, 1310
extinction, **16**, 1317

Heir of entail
acquiescence of predecessor, bound by, **16**, 1616
donation, **8**, 618
land acquired for public recreation from, **14**, 322
lessor, as, **13**, 172
singular successor, as, **13**, 350
submission to arbitration, effect of, **2**, 410
Heir-of-line
feudal law, **18**, 55, 108
heritable succession, **25**, 678
Heir of provision
feudal law, **18**, 110
Heir of tailzie
feudal law, **18**, 110
Heirs portioner
co-ownership, **18**, 18
feudal law, **18**, 18, 55, 108
Helicopter
environment, provisions affecting, **2**, 987
low flying by, **2**, 970
lowering articles etc from, **2**, 961
Helmet
heraldic rules as to, **11**, 1605
salade, **11**, 1605
Helter-skelter
See PLEASURE FAIR
Henderson Island
British Dependent Territories citizenship, **14**, 1932
Henhouse
urban situation, in, **19**, 366*n*
Henry Committee Report
legislation subsequent to, **6**, 410
registration of title, **6**, 411, 702
Her Majesty's Chief Inspector of Prisons
annual report, **16**, 1423
appointment, **16**, 1423
function, **16**, 1423
Her Majesty's Inspector of Constabulary
See INSPECTOR OF CONSTABULARY
Her Majesty's officers-of-arms
corps of, **14**, 1501
Herald
commission, issue of, **14**, 1501
esquire, entitlement to rank as, **16**, 2022
Her Majesty's officers-of-arms, corps of, **14**, 1501
royal household, as member of, **7**, 833
Heraldry
colours, heraldic, **11**, 1604*n*
conflict of heraldic law, **11**, 1625
heraldic law, *see* LYON, COURT OF THE LORD
meaning, **11**, 1601
metals, heraldic, **11**, 1604*n*
rules of, **11**, 1612
study of, **11**, 1601
Herbal remedies
general sale list products, **14**, 1208
licensing system, exemption from, **14**, 1203
Hereditary peers
See HOUSE OF LORDS; PEERAGE
Hereditary sheriffdom
abolition of, **17**, 512
Heresy
Roman Catholic Church, *latae sententiae* offence, **3**, 1658

Heritable conveyancing
accretion, **6**, 590
allocation, feuduties of, **6**, 529–531
burgage tenure, **6**, 586
death, transmission of property on, **6**, 603–612
    See also DEATH
description of property—
    addenda to, **6**, 489
    area, by, **6**, 487
    boundaries—
        English practice, **6**, 734
        inaccuracy in delineating, **6**, 760
        land, description by reference to, **6**, 485
        legal and occupational, discrepancies between,
            6, 734
        'or thereby' rule, **6**, 732
        physical objects, in relation to, **6**, 735
        reference to, **6**, 485
        Reid Committee, **6**, 732
        rivers and roads, **6**, 485
        seashore, **6**, 485
        trust estate, trustees' power to vary, **24**, 202
        uncertainty as to, **14**, 2017
        valuation areas, between, **24**, 405, 406, 549
        walls, **6**, 485
    extent, error as to, **20**, 907
    generally, **6**, 482, 483
    islands, **6**, 482
    land registration, in, **6**, 489
    parish and county, by, **6**, 488
    particular, **6**, 484
    plan, by reference to, **6**, 486
entry, date of, **6**, 526; **20**, 913
feu grant—
    ancillary cause—
        entry, date of, **6**, 526
        feuduties, **6**, 520–532
            redemption of, 535–538
        remedies—
            irritancy, **6**, 533, 534
            minor, of superior, **6**, 532
        reddendo, **6**, 528
        tenendas, **6**, 527
        warrandice, **6**, 541–547
    form of, **6**, 473
    narrative clause—
        consideration, **6**, 476
        infeftment, requirement of, **6**, 475
        parties to deed, **6**, 477
    obsolescent clauses—
        assignations of the rents, **6**, 539
        assignation of writs, **6**, 538
        obligation of relief, **6**, 540
    operative or dispositive clause—
        addenda to description, **6**, 489
        area, description by, **6**, 487
        boundaries, description by reference to, **6**, 485
        co-disponees, relationship as between, **6**, 507
        co-feuars, relationship as between, **6**, 506
        doctrine of acquiescence, **6**, 509
        general description of land, **6**, 483
        guarantee and destination, **6**, 479
        infeftment, clauses excluding assignees
            before, **6**, 524

Heritable conveyancing—_continued_
feu grant—_continued_
    operative or dispositive clause—_continued_
        irritant clauses, **6**, 525
        ius quaestium tertio, **6**, 506
        land, descriptions of, **6**, 483, 484
        land registration, description in, **6**, 490
        Lands Tribunal, interpretation of tests by, **6**,
            513
        loss of right to enforce real conditions, **6**,
            511
        loss of title or interest, **6**, 508
        mineral bings, **6**, 495
        mineral reservations, **6**, 491–494
        neighbourhood context, in, **6**, 510
        parish and county, description by, **6**, 488
        particular descriptions of land, **6**, 484
        plan, description by reference to, **6**, 486
        pre-emption clauses, **6**, 520
        property, description of, **6**, 482
        qualification of grant, **6**, 491
        real conditions, *see* REAL BURDENS; REAL
            CONDITIONS
        redemption, clauses of, **6**, 520
        registration with time-limit, clauses requiring,
            6, 519
        resolutive clauses, **6**, 525
        revocation of special destination, **6**, 481
        servitudes, *see* SERVITUDES
        special destination, **6**, 480
        subfeuing, **6**, 523
        superior and feuar, relationship between, **6**,
            505
        superiority, reservation of rights to divide, **6**,
            522
        words of conveyance, **6**, 478
    registration, consent for, **6**, 548
    stamp duty certificate, **6**, 549
    testing clause, **6**, 427–429, 550
    warrant of registration, **6**, 551
feuduty, *see* FEUDUTY
fixtures and fittings, **6**, 558
General Register of Sasines, *see* GENERAL REGISTER
    OF SASINES
generally, **6**, 473
irritancy, **6**, 525, 533, 534
land of, scat, **24**, 309
missives, *see* MISSIVES
price, payment of, **20**, 914
    interest on, **12**, 1009, 1010
registration of title, *see* REGISTRATION OF TITLE
standard securities, *see* STANDARD SECURITY
title, production of valid, **20**, 920
vacant possession, **20**, 916
warrandice, *see* WARRANDICE
writing requiring, **15**, 666; **20**, 908–910
    small item exception, **20**, 817
Heritable jurisdiction
abolition, **17**, 513; **22**, 630
commissary courts, inferior, transfer to sheriff
    court on abolition, **22**, 630
feudal law, origin, **22**, 589
right of, abolition, **18**, 213

Heritable property

action for recovery of possession, **17**, 1326

adjudication, **8**, 101

   heritable securities, **8**, 197, 199

   leases, **8**, 197, 198

      excluding assignees, **8**, 197

   reversions, **8**, 197

   superiorities, **8**, 197

   voluntary alienation, capable and not capable of, **8**, 197

affixation to heritage—

   building materials, **3**, 164

   generally, **14**, 1071

   interests of other parties, **14**, 1075

   lessee's obligations, **14**, 1072

   lessor, protection for, **14**, 1076

   relevant factors, **14**, 1073

   trade fixtures, **14**, 1074

agricultural, *see* AGRICULTURAL LANDS AND HERITAGES

annuity, **18**, 14

a..estment, **8**, 189

child's passive capacity, **3**, 1203

coat of arms as, **11**, 1613

compulsory acquisition by fire authority, **10**, 1421

conveyancing law—

   relationship to law of heritable property, **18**, 1, 1*n*

   See also HERITABLE CONVEYANCING

corporeal, *see* CORPOREAL HERITABLE PROPERTY; LAND

credit union, ownership, lease or disposal by, **12**, 667, 678

deposit, may not be subject of contract of, **8**, 4

destination, thing heritable by, **18**, 15

   plant and machinery, **14**, 1013

diligence, **18**, 13

ejection, **18**, 161

equipment becoming heritable—

   lessee's obligations, **14**, 1072

   relevant factors, **14**, 1073

excambion, contract of, **20**, 921

exchange of land, **20**, 921

exclusion from Inland Revenue charge, **19**, 1646

exempt agreement relating to, **5**, 821

feudal law, importance of, **18**, 1

feuduty, redemption of, **6**, 535–537

fire authorities' powers in relation to, **10**, 1419–1421

fraud on transfer of, **11**, 755–760

   antecedent obligation, fraud on, **11**, 757

   conveyance, fraud on, **11**, 758

   dispositions *a non domino*, **11**, 750

   fraudulent seller, dispositions by, **11**, 760

   generally, **11**, 755

   obligations and property, principles of, **11**, 756

friendly society, ownership of, **12**, 702

future time, right with tract of, **18**, 14

generally, **11**, 1097

gifts of, **19**, 1603

goodwill, **18**, 14

grant of, Great Seal, use of, **7**, 874, 907

heritable rights, *see* HERITABLE RIGHTS

heritable security, *see* HERITABLE SECURITY

Heritable property—*continued*

heritage, meaning, **18**, 56

   trespass on, **7**, 345

Hume's *Lectures*, **18**, 1

incorporeal, *see* INCORPOREAL PROPERTY

inhibition, **8**, 101, 155

   future advances, security for, **8**, 174

   heritable creditor, inhibition against, **8**, 175

   heritable security after, **8**, 172

   heritable security prior to, **8**, 172

insurance—

   reinstatement clause, **12**, 890

   subrogation, **12**, 900

joint and common ownership, **6**, 781; **19**, 1611, 1612

land, as, **18**, 11

   See also LAND

landlord's fixtures, capital allowances on, **19**, 1615

lease, *see* HERITABLE SECURITY; LEASE-LEASING

liferent—

   feuduty, rights to, **13**, 1639

   groundannual, rights to, **13**, 1639

   leases, **13**, 1639

   liferenter's rights, **13**, 1638

   rent, rights to, **13**, 1639

   restriction on creation, **13**, 1631, 1632

meaning, **18**, 11

'money'—

   classified as, **14**, 1802

moveable property distinguished, **18**, 11

multiplepoinding—

   inhibition, **8**, 172

mussels, **18**, 331

oysters, **18**, 331

partnership property, **16**, 1072, 1073

pension, **18**, 14

personal right to real right, **18**, 14

prescription, **16**, 2132

   negative, **16**, 2121, 2122

   positive, **16**, 2105

property rights, **11**, 1097

prospective agreement secured on, withdrawal from, **5**, 861

provisional order affecting, **19**, 15

real conditions, **18**, 344, 349

   See also REAL CONDITIONS

recovery of possession, **5**, 893; **17**, 1326

sale of, *see* HERITABLE CONVEYANCING; MISSIVES

Scots and English law compared, **19**, 1597, 1613

security over, *see* HERITABLE SECURITY; STANDARD SECURITY

servitudes, *see* SERVITUDE

simple proper liferent, **13**, 1614

situation of, generally, **4**, 42

standard securities, *see* STANDARD SECURITY

succession, *see* SUCCESSION

terminology, adaptation of English, **19**, 1614

title of honour, **18**, 14

title to—

   actions relating to in sheriff court, **6**, 1062

   inhibition to implement obligation to grant, **8**, 137

   mora, taciturnity and acquiescence, **16**, 1626

trust beneficiary, interest of, **18**, 14

Heritable property—*continued*
trust estate, as part of, **24**, 149
 judicial factor's power to purchase, **24**, 258
 missives for sale of, **24**, 27
valuation of—
 considerations, **25**, 124
 formula for, **25**, 126
 guidance notes, **25**, 131
 history and performance, **25**, 125
 rental growth, **25**, 12
 rental level, **25**, 128
 security of income, **25**, 130
 years' purchase, **25**, 127
water, when classified as, **18**, 273
Heritable rights
meaning, **18**, 14
reduction affecting, **13**, 55, 66
sheriff court, jurisdiction of, **4**, 6; **6**, 1062
Heritable security
absolute disposition—
 back letter, qualified by—
  back letter, destruction of, **20**, 140
  discharge, **20**, 140, 143
  disponee—
   liabilities of, **20**, 142
   possession—
    method of obtaining, **20**, 135
    ousting from, **20**, 135
   proprietor, as, **20**, 135
   relationship with disponer, **20**, 134
   right of absolute property may be
    conferred on, **20**, 140
   rights of, **20**, 135
  disponer—
   possession by, **20**, 135
   relationship with disponee, **20**, 134
   rights of, **20**, 133, 136
  former competency, **20**, 132
  generally, **20**, 132
  nature of, **20**, 133
  prescription, **20**, 140
  recording, effect of, **20**, 137
  reinstatement, **20**, 139
  relationship of parties, **20**, 134
  right of reversion, discharge of, **20**, 140
  security, extent of, **20**, 141
  succession, **20**, 138
 standard security, superseded by, **20**, 148
 terms on which granted, proof of, **20**, 133
adjudication as, **8**, 201
annual rent, right of, **20**, 110
bank, loan by—
 bond of cash credit and disposition in security,
  20, 235
 Consumer Credit Act 1974, effect of, **20**, 236
 ex facie disposition in favour of bank, **20**, 234
 generally, **20**, 233
bond, **20**, 111
bond of annuity and disposition in security, **20**,
 130
bond of corroboration and disposition in security,
 20, 130
bond and disposition in security, **20**, 111
 assignation, **20**, 127

Heritable security—*continued*
bond and disposition in security—*continued*
 bondholder—
  postponed, **20**, 122
  prior, **20**, 122
 calling-up—
  advertisement, **20**, 118, 119
  generally, **20**, 118
  protection of purchasers, **20**, 121
  sale, **20**, 118, 120
 creditor, **20**, 174
  acquisition of subject at sale effected by
   other creditor, **20**, 122
  calling-up, service of notice by, **20**, 118
  claim against trustee in bankruptcy of debtor,
   20, 124
  debtor's position must not be prejudiced by,
   20, 113
  duty to account to debtor, **20**, 123–126
  feuduty, liability for, **20**, 116
  purchase of subject for himself, **20**, 122
  quasi-trustee for debtor, as, **20**, 118
  rates, liability for, **20**, 116
  rights of—
   ejection of proprietor, **20**, 115
   entry, **20**, 114
   insurance, **20**, 114
   maills and duties, **20**, 115
   poinding ground, **20**, 117
   subject, letting of, **20**, 116
  succession of, **20**, 145
 debtor—
  claim against trustee in bankruptcy of, **20**,
   124
  creditor must not be prejudiced by, **20**, 113
  creditor as quasi-trustee for, **20**, 118
  creditor's duty to account to, **20**, 123–126
  default of payment of principal or interest
   by, **20**, 114
  reservation of power to feu, **20**, 124
  rights of, **20**, 113
 debtor under, as lessor, **13**, 162, 164
 discharge, **20**, 128
 disponee—
  completion of title, **20**, 129
 executors—
  completion of title, **20**, 129
 extinguishment, **20**, 128
 feu, reservation by debtor of power to, **20**, 124
 foreclosure, **20**, 118, 122
 generally, **18**, 112; **20**, 111
 heritable, **20**, 111
 interdict against proposed sale, **20**, 122
 letting subjects, creditor's rights, **20**, 116
 poinding ground, creditor's rights, **20**, 117
 power of debtor to grant lease, **13**, 160
 registration for execution, **20**, 126
 standard security, superseded by, **20**, 148
 surplus—
  certificate of no, **20**, 125
  consignation, **20**, 125
 title, completion of, **20**, 129
bond of relief and disposition in security, **20**, 130

Heritable security—*continued*
borrower—
  borrower's title, reduction of, **20**, 218
  capacity of, **20**, 219–225
building society, loan by—
  ex facie dispositions in favour of, **20**, 227
  generally, **3**, 337, 347; **20**, 226
  standard security—
    contents, **20**, 230
    generally, **20**, 228
    standard conditions—
      variation, **20**, 229
  unsecured advances, **3**, 357
cash credit bond and disposition in security, **20**, 130
  object of, **20**, 131
catholic securities, rights of catholic creditor, **20**, 253
charge certificate, **6**, 774
corporation, borrowing powers, **20**, 222
creation by sale and reversion, **24**, 5
creation over a registered interest in land, **6**, 714
creditor—
  catholic, rights of, **20**, 253
  succession, **20**, 145
debentures, savings for—
  dwelling house, debenture where subject includes, **20**, 255
  standard security provisions, debenture conditions unaffected by, **20**, 254
debt occurred by, **6**, 774
debt secured by—
  adjudication on a *debitum fundi*, **8**, 372
  jurisdiction where, **4**, 45
debtor—
  succession, **20**, 144
default, repossession of assured tenancy following, **13**, 749, 751
diligence, competition with rights acquired by, **20**, 248
  adjudger, rights of, **20**, 251
  inhibitor, rights of, **20**, 252
discharge, **6**, 774
entailed estate, over—
  bond of annual rent, **20**, 237, 238
  bond and disposition in security, **20**, 237, 244
    debts, for, **20**, 239
    improvements, for, **20**, 238, 241
    wife and children, to provide for, **20**, 239
  capital transfer tax, **20**, 242
  creditor's power to burden entailed estate with his debt, **20**, 245
  estate duty, **20**, 242
  historical background, **20**, 237
  improvements, estate charged for, **20**, 238, 241
  local authority, disposal of land to, **20**, 246
  permanent debt, burdening estate with, **20**, 240
  standard security excluded, **20**, 244
  transfer of charge from one estate to another, **20**, 243
feuduty, competition with, **20**, 248
foreclosure, action of—
  bond and disposition in security, **20**, 118
  standard security, **20**, 166

Heritable security—*continued*
grant of, **6**, 774
granter—
  reduction of title by, **20**, 218
  title to sue, **13**, 499
ground annual—
  adjudication, **20**, 265
  assignation, form of, **20**, 264
  bilateral, must be, **20**, 265
  building conditions created by, **20**, 265
  creditor, **20**, 265
    remedies competent to, **20**, 265
  discharge, form of, **20**, 264
  extinction, **20**, 265
  holder's remedies, **20**, 265
  interest in land, definition, **20**, 264
  maills and duties, action of, **20**, 265
  meaning, **20**, 263
  poinding the ground, **20**, 265
  prescription, negative, extinction by, **20**, 265
  prohibition on creation, **20**, 264
  redemption, **20**, 264
  restriction, form of, **20**, 264
  statutory provisions, **20**, 264
historical background, **20**, 108–112
income tax relief, **19**, 1518
incomplete title securities granted on, **20**, 247
indemnity, no entitlement where loss, **6**, 770
insurance company, loan by, **20**, 231
interest in land, over, **6**, 707
interpretation and construction—
  bond of cash credit and disposition in security, **12**, 1254
  bond and disposition in security, **12**, 1254
  brevity and uniformity, aim of, **12**, 1255
  charge certificate, **12**, 1256
  discharge, **12**, 1257
  ex facie absolute disposition, **12**, 1254
  Halliday Report, **12**, 1254
  personal obligation, clauses relating to, **12**, 1255
  ranking, clauses relating to, **12**, 1255
  registration for execution, clauses relating to, **12**, 1255
  saving and enabling clauses, **12**, 1258
  standard conditions, **12**, 1255
  standard security, **12**, 1254, 1255
  title deeds, clauses relating to rights to, **12**, 1255
  warrandice, clauses relating to, **12**, 1255
landlord's interest, transfer, **13**, 351
lease—
  debtor's power to grant, **13**, 160
  security over—
    assignment, **20**, 257
    discharge, **20**, 257
    dwelling house, private, exclusion, **20**, 261
    enabling rights, **20**, 257, 258
    land registration, **20**, 262
    poinding the ground, **20**, 259
    possession, **20**, 257
      original necessity, **20**, 256
      recorded lease, prescriptive period, **20**, 260
      recording equivalent to, **20**, 259
      unrecorded lease, prescriptive period, **20**, 260

Heritable security—*continued*
lease—*continued*
  security over—*continued*
    prescription, **20**, 260
    recorded lease, **20**, 257
      effect of recording, **20**, 259
      prescriptive period, **20**, 260
    Registration of Leases (Scotland) Act 1857..., **20**, 257
    renunciation, **20**, 257, 258
    sale, power of, **20**, 258
    translation, **20**, 257
    unrecorded lease, prescriptive period, **20**, 260
   See also HERITABLE SECURITY; LEASE-LEASING
lien, *see* LIEN
local authority, capacity to borrow, **20**, 223
maritime lien, *see* LIEN
married woman, capacity to grant heritable security, **20**, 221
meaning, **3**, 337*n*
minor, capacity to borrow, **20**, 219
mobile home loan, **3**, 356
mortgage, and, **5**, 908
  See also MORTGAGE
oil platform, over—
  common law, **20**, 266–269
  foreshore, on—
    common law, **20**, 268
  generally, **20**, 266, 272
  land, on—
    common law, **20**, 267
    pipelines, servitudes for, **20**, 267
  licences to search for and get petroleum, **20**, 271
  pipeline—
    controlled, meaning, **20**, 271
    land, on, **20**, 267
  sea bed—
    controlled waters, definition, **20**, 271
    nautical mile, definition, **20**, 271
    offshore petroleum, meaning, **20**, 271
    sea, meaning, **20**, 271
    territorial waters—
      meaning, **20**, 271
      outwith, common law, **20**, 270
      within, common law, **20**, 269
  statutory provisions, **20**, 271
operation, **8**, 201
pecuniary real burden, **18**, 375, 383
power of debtor to grant lease, **13**, 160
printed form, issue to debtor, **12**, 1255
private authority, borrowing powers, **20**, 225
public burdens, competition with, **20**, 248
public rates, competition with, **20**, 249
pupil, capacity to borrow, **20**, 219
reduction, **13**, 37
registration, **6**, 774
removings, action of, **13**, 499
restriction, deed of, **20**, 127, 171, 174
reversionary company, loan by, **20**, 232
sale and reversion, creation by, **24**, 5
sale of property subject to, **4**, 850
second securities, notice of, **20**, 146

Heritable security—*continued*
sheriff court jurisdiction, **6**, 1071, 1090
ship—
  mortgage—
    British registered ship, mortgage—
      instrument of, **20**, 287
    discharge of registered, **20**, 288
    dispute over, **20**, 305
    freight, entitlement to, **20**, 294
    mortgagee—
      freight, entitlement to, **20**, 294
      possession, in, **20**, 292–296
      power of sale, **20**, 296
      rights of, **20**, 291–295
      status of, **20**, 290
    priority of mortgages, **20**, 289
    ranking, **20**, 314
    taking possession, **20**, 292
sources, **18**, 112
standard security, *see* STANDARD SECURITY
succession—
  creditor's, **20**, 145
  debtor's, **20**, 144
superior, competition with rights of, **20**, 250
terce, former competition with, **20**, 248
title—
  incomplete, securities granted on, **20**, 247
  reduction by granter, **20**, 218
title sheet, **6**, 707, 710
trustees, grant of security by, **20**, 220
two securities held over same subject, **20**, 248
unfit house, relating to, modification of terms, **5**, 23
urban development corporation, **20**, 224
vessel, possessory lien over, *see* LIEN
wadset, **20**, 109

Heritor
Church of Scotland—
  duties, **3**, 1578–1580
  meaning, **3**, 1578
heritors' records, **19**, 849
public burial grounds, provision of and responsibility for, **3**, 517, 518

Hermaphrodite
law with regard to, **10**, 1034

Heroin
criminal behaviour, link with, **14**, 1221
dealers, sentencing of, **14**, 1220
drug abuse, patterns of, **14**, 1222
hard drug, as, **14**, 1222

Herring
early legislation, **11**, 118–120
Herring Industry Advisory Council, **11**, 210
Herring Industry Board, abolition of, **11**, 210, 211
industry, generally, **11**, 210
Manx fishing licences, **11**, 114
White Herring Fisheries Act 1771..., **11**, 120

Herring fishery
uncultivated land beyond foreshore, use of, **18**, 527

High Constable of Scotland
office of, **16**, 1703

High Court of Admiralty
See ADMIRALTY (Court of Admiralty)

High Court of Chivalry
Earl Marshal of England, **22**, 325
Lyon Court, jurisdiction and precedent
    compared, **22**, 325
High Court of Justiciary
Act of Adjournal, **6**, 861, 930; **22**, 187, 520, 528
adjustments to legal aid, powers in relation to, **13**,
    1084, 1084*n*
administration, **6**, 876
advocate appearing before, dress, **13**, 1323
advocation, bill of, **6**, 865, 871
audience—
    advocate's right of, **13**, 1325
    solicitors' right of, **13**, 1152, 1180
ceremonial, **6**, 879
children's hearing, remit of case to, **3**, 1378
circuit courts, and, **6**, 858; **17**, 507; **22**, 520
composition, **17**, 570
constitution, **6**, 860
criminal conduct, court's power to declare, **6**,
    869; **22**, 424–425
criminal legal aid, **13**, 1052
historical development of—
    absorption of other courts, **22**, 519, 609, 635
    College of Justice, institution of, **6**, 849
    coroner, office of, **6**, 853
    historical background, **5**, 641; **6**, 848–854; **17**,
        504–506
    justice ayres, **6**, 852–853; **17**, 507
    nineteenth century reforms, **6**, 859
    Porteous Roll, **6**, 853
    regality courts, **6**, 854
    royal pardon, abuse of, **6**, 854
    seventeenth century reforms, **6**, 855; **22**, 520
    'taking up dittay', **6**, 853
    Traistes, **6**, 853
    Union Agreement 1707—
        and, **5**, 349
House of Lords—
    decisions of, persuasive authority, **22**, 302
    no appeal to, **5**, 644; **6**, 801, 813, 829
judges, **5**, 641–644; **6**, 861, 923
    appointment in hands of Crown, **6**, 860
    circuit, **6**, 858, 860
    composition of court, **17**, 570
    Justiciars, *see* JUSTICIAR
    Lord Justice-Clerk, *see* LORD JUSTICE-CLERK
    Lord Justice-General, *see* LORD JUSTICE-GENERAL
    Lords Commissioners of Justiciary, **6**, 923; **22**,
        520
    Lords of Session, **6**, 851; **22**, 520
    quorum, **6**, 865
    removal from office, **6**, 860
    retirement, **6**, 860
    robes, **6**, 880
    salaries, **6**, 863
    Senators of College of Justice, **6**, 860
    seniority of rank, **6**, 860
    tenure of office, **6**, 857
judicial precedent, **22**, 302–312
jurisdiction, **1**, 204; **5**, 642; **22**, 520
    appellate, **5**, 643; **6**, 861; **17**, 576, 588
    common law and statutory offences, **6**, 867
    crimes committed partly elsewhere, **6**, 867

High Court of Justiciary—*continued*
jurisdiction—*continued*
    declaratory power to designate action criminal,
        6, 869; **22**, 424–425
    early jurisdiction, **6**, 849
    equitable, special, **6**, 870; **22**, 547
    European Court of Justice, effect of decisions
        of, **6**, 868; **10**, 242
    exclusion by statute, **6**, 867
    exclusive in certain cases, **6**, 867
    generally, **17**, 508
    heritable, abolition of, **6**, 856
    international conventions, **6**, 867
    maritime causes, **1**, 405; **6**, 859; **22**, 519, 609, 635
    nobile officium, **6**, 865, 870; **22**, 547
    offences at sea or on board ship, **6**, 867
    original, **6**, 861; **17**, 588
    origins of, **22**, 520
    Parliamentary privilege, **6**, 867
    piracy, **6**, 867
    precedent, and, **22**, 302–312
    regulation of own procedure, **6**, 861
    review of decisions of inferior courts, **6**, 1155
    sentence, as to, **17**, 571
    subject matter, as to, **17**, 571
    supervisory, **1**, 243; **6**, 861
    territorial, **17**, 570
    treason and piracy, **6**, 867; **17**, 571
    workload and, **6**, 861
lawburrows, warrant of, **13**, 902, 903, 906
macers, **6**, 878, 935
nobile officium, **6**, 865, 870; **22**, 547
presidency of, **6**, 864
procedure, *see* CRIMINAL PROCEDURE
prosecution, conduct and institution of, **6**, 872
quorum of court, **6**, 865
records—
    access to, **19**, 879
    disposal of, **19**, 866, 869
    retransmission of, **19**, 872
    transmission of, **19**, 856
regulation of, **6**, 882
Seal, **7**, 886
solemn procedure, *see* SOLEMN PROCEDURE
summary criminal cases, application for legal aid,
    13, 1057
summary procedure, *see* SUMMARY PROCEDURE
suspension, bill of, *see* SUSPENSION BILL OF
trial—
    generally, **6**, 873
    jury, origins of, **6**, 853
    legal representation at, **17**, 550
    length of, **17**, 555
    See also TRIAL
Union Agreement of 1707, **7**, 739
Whole Court sitting, **6**, 866
workload, **6**, 861
High seas
adjacent to continental shelf, **21**, 18
artificial islands and structures, freedom to
    construct, **21**, 41
conservation of fish stocks, **11**, 89, 90
Convention on Fishing and Conservation of the
    Living Resources of the High Seas, **21**, 2

High seas—*continued*
deep sea bed, *see* SEA BED
definition, **21**, 42
division with territorial sea, origin of, **11**, 71
exclusive economic zone, *see* EXCLUSIVE
   ECONOMIC ZONE
fisheries, open access to, **11**, 89
fishing, freedom of, **21**, 41
fishing vessels, jurisdiction of flag state over, **11**,
   88
freedom of, generally, **21**, 41
Geneva Convention on, **11**, 86, 87, 88; **21**, 2, 41
jurisdiction, **21**, 43
   Convention Against Illicit Traffic in Narcotic
      Drugs and Psychotropic Substances, **21**, 42
   drug traffickers, **21**, 42, 45
   exceptions to general rule, **21**, 44
   flag state of vessel, **21**, 43
   hot pursuit, right of, **21**, 44
   international duties, **21**, 43
   slave trade, ship engaged in, **21**, 44, 45
   terrorist acts, **21**, 44
   warships and other government vessels, **21**, 44
land-locked states, rights of, **11**, 87; **21**, 41
legal status, **11**, 87
living resources, rights of coastal state over, **11**, 91
maritime casualty, power to take avoidance
   measures, **21**, 46
meaning, **11**, 86; **21**, 112
navigation, freedom of, **21**, 41
overflight, freedom of, **21**, 41
piracy, jurisdiction as to, **21**, 44, 45
pollution, power to take avoidance measures, **21**,
   46
right of visit, **21**, 45
safety, environmental and conservation requirements, **21**, 41
salvage operations, **21**, 440
scientific research, freedom to conduct, **21**, 41
ship on, nationality, requirements as to, **21**, 140
submarine cables and pipelines, freedom to lay,
   21, 41
tort on, jurisdiction, **21**, 101
unauthorised broadcasting from, **21**, 44, 45
United Nations Convention on the Law of the
   Sea, **11**, 102
Highland Games
historical background, **19**, 1201
sports-governing institutions, **19**, 1205
Highland Region
population, **14**, 64
structure, **14**, 64
Highlands and Islands Airports Ltd
air services, grants etc for, **2**, 1069
airports owned by, **2**, 912
Highlands and Islands Development Board
assistance provided by, **2**, 1284
functions etc, **2**, 1284
Ombudsman system, **19**, 242
public corporation, as, **19**, 201
Highway
danger on, **14**, 2165
encroachment on or over, **14**, 2164
obstruction on, **14**, 2165

Highway—*continued*
premises in disrepair near, **14**, 2101
public, Night Poaching Acts, **11**, 810
public, public right of way distinguished, **18**, 495
Scots and English law compared, **14**, 2166
use of term replaced by road, **20**, 501, 609
users of, adjoining property causing harm to, **14**,
   2167
See also ROAD
Highway Code
documentary evidence, as, **10**, 598
issue of, **20**, 433
status of, **20**, 433
Hijacking
generally, **19**, 678, 695, 695*n*
jurisdiction in respect of, **2**, 1035
offence of, **2**, 1030; **7**, 362
punishment of, **2**, 1030
Hill farming
aid limits, **1**, 971
EC Directive on, **1**, 971, 972
Himalaya **clause**
bill of lading, express terms, **21**, 546
purpose and usage, **21**, 560
Hindering police
offence of, **16**, 1807
Hindus
personal law, domicile as indicator of, **17**, 188
Hire
See LEASE/HIRE (MOVEABLES)
Hire agreement
consumer, *see* CONSUMER HIRE AGREEMENT
Hire car
passengers sharing fare, **20**, 488
Hire purchase agreement
administrator, powers of, **4**, 619
assignation of rights under, **7**, 1290
building societies' power to make, **3**, 338, 355,
   358, 378
capital allowances, **14**, 1011
collateral contract, existence of, **14**, 1087
conflict of laws, **14**, 1095
control order, **14**, 1053
court, special powers of, **5**, 929
demise charterparty, and, **21**, 534*n*
goods subject to, entry to repossess, **5**, 892
health and safety, **14**, 1051
hirer bound to purchase, where, **20**, 855
hirer disposing of property under, **20**, 855
implied terms, **20**, 819
income support payments towards, **21**, 1075
instalment, payment only possible by, **20**, 35
irritancy, **15**, 810
lease distinguished from, **14**, 1007
lease purchase distinguished from, **14**, 1024
lex fori, application of mandatory provisions of,
   17, 182
lump sum, payment of whole price by, **20**, 35
meaning, **5**, 805; **20**, 813, 855
motor vehicle subject to, sale of, **15**, 52, 64; **18**,
   683; **20**, 35
owner of goods, protection of, **20**, 35
penalty clause, **15**, 798
possession and ownership, **18**, 531, 532, 534

Hire purchase agreement—*continued*
protected goods, recovery of, **5**, 891
purchase option, exercise of, **14**, 1067
questions of, legal advice and assistance, **13**, 1028
repeal of legislation, **5**, 801
resale of goods by buyer, **20**, 35
restricted-use credit agreement, as, **5**, 809
sale, contract of, distinguished, **20**, 34
sale and lease-back, application of, **14**, 1031
termination by debtor—
    hypothec, operation of, **5**, 903
    liability on, **5**, 902
    right to terminate, **5**, 901
theft of hired goods, **7**, 322
title, **20**, 855
See also CONSUMER CERDIT AGREEMENT
Hire purchase company
nature etc of, **2**, 1264
Historic buildings
acquisition of, **9**, 1219
generally, **9**, 1217
Historic Buildings and Monuments Commission
company donation to, **3**, 1155
functions, **14**, 62
listed building, inspection of, **23**, 183
tax treatment, **3**, 1166
Historic Buildings Council for Scotland
functions of, **9**, 1218
Historiographer Royal
office of, **7**, 819, 844, 845
Hobby
whether considered a business, **18**, 1517
Holding
See SMALLHOLDING
Holding company
meaning, **4**, 370
ultimate holding company, meaning, **4**, 370
Holding out
adoption of obligation, **16**, 1645
partner, person representing themselves to be, liability—
    death of partner, effect on constitution of firm, **16**, 1052
    delict, in, **16**, 1054
    firm, liability of, **16**, 1055
    generally, **16**, 1049
    knowingly suffers, generally, **16**, 1049, 1051
    retired partner, position of, **16**, 1053
    words or conduct, by, **16**, 1049, 1050
Holiday
bank holiday—
    payments falling on, obligation to make, **22**, 818
    Scotland, designation, **22**, 818
caravan, rental of, **14**, 1002
contractual agreement, by, **22**, 818
employment contracts—
    designated days, **22**, 818
    holiday pay, **22**, 818
European Convention on the Calculation of Time-Limits, **22**, 830
exclusion, calculating period numbered in days, **22**, 815

Holiday—*continued*
holy days of obligation, origin, **22**, 818
motor car, rental of, **14**, 1002
payment, employee, **22**, 818
person enabled to vote when on, **5**, 374
school board's power to fix, **8**, 774
statutory enactment, by, **22**, 818
termination of period on holiday—
    measured in days, **22**, 825
    qualification to principle of exclusion, **22**, 825
unemployment benefit, day of unemployment, meaning, **21**, 875–877
within a period, calculation, total period, **22**, 825
Holiday let
avoidance device, as, **13**, 769
exclusion from assured tenancy status, **13**, 636, 644
exclusion from protected tenancy status, **13**, 604, 630, 634
off-season, repossession—
    assured tenancy, **13**, 749, 752
    protected tenancy, **13**, 736, 739
possession, recovery of, generally, **13**, 769
working holidays, **13**, 634
Hologram
copyright, **18**, 960
Holograph writings
adoption as holograph, **6**, 439, 440
alterations to, **6**, 436
docquet in notarial execution, **6**, 432
documentary evidence, as, **10**, 601
heritable property, sale of, **20**, 909
meaning, **6**, 436
missives, in, **6**, 554
not probative, **6**, 413
partly holograph, **6**, 438
proof, **6**, 437
subscription, **6**, 416
will, *see* PRIVATE WILL
witnessing not required, **6**, 436
Holy See
international personality, **19**, 664
Holyroodhouse
keeper of, **7**, 830
Homage
abolition, **18**, 53
fealty, and, **18**, 53
generally, **18**, 53, 53*n*
one man owning land of two or more lords, **18**, 53
Scotland as vassal of God, **18**, 42
vassalage, **18**, 53
wardholding, and, **18**, 53
Home Affairs Select Committee
Home Secretary, response to recommendations of, **23**, 974
independent review body, **23**, 973
Home and Health Department
Scottish Office, Legal Civil Service, **13**, 1401
Home Grown Timber Advisory Committee
consultation with, **11**, 609, 612
maintenance by Forestry Commissioners, **11**, 612
regional advisory committees, **11**, 612
Home-Grown Cereals Authority
powers delegated to, **1**, 984

Home Guard
part of armed forces, **2**, 601
status etc, **2**, 611
Home-help service
charge, discretionary, **22**, 14
disabled persons, **22**, 24
elderly persons, **22**, 26
function, **22**, 14
handicapped persons, **22**, 24
laundry services ancillary to, **22**, 14, 24, 26
local authority duty to provide, **22**, 14, 26
persons suffering illness/mental deficiency, **22**, 2
Home loss payment
calculation of, **5**, 186
claim for, **5**, 186
entitlement to, **5**, 186
meaning, **5**, 186
owner-occupier, **5**, 186
tenant, **5**, 186
Urban Motorways Committee, recommendation of, **5**, 186
Home meals service
assistance in kind to person in need, as, **22**, 27
elderly persons, **22**, 27
organisation, **22**, 9
social work department, duty to provide, **22**, 27
Home nursing
health boards, administration by, **11**, 1410
Home Office
functions of, **5**, 508
immigration controls, **12**, 138
Homelessness
access to accommodation, inability to secure, **11**, 2046
accommodation, provision of—
    advice and assistance as to, **11**, 2070
    charges, **11**, 2071
    interim, **11**, 2068
    permanent, **11**, 2069
    protection of property, **11**, 2072
    tenancy not secure, **11**, 1937, 1942
applications for housing, **11**, 2039
bad housing conditions, **11**, 2045, 2049
boat, no place to moor, **11**, 2048
Code of Guidance, **11**, 2037, 2040, 2044, 2053, 2054
disaster, as result of, **11**, 2055
fire, as result of, **11**, 2055
flood, as result of, **11**, 2055
generally, **11**, 2037–2040
homeless, meaning—
    generally, **11**, 2041
    inadequate accommodation for family unit, **11**, 2044
    no right to accommodation, **11**, 2043
    rooflessness, **11**, 2042
    unacceptable accommodation, **11**, 2045–2049
homeless person as person in need, **22**, 13
illness or handicap, **11**, 2040
inquiries by local authority, **11**, 2040
intentional, **11**, 2040
    acts or omissions of applicant, **11**, 2060–2064
    availability of accommodation, **11**, 2058, 2059
    decisions as to, **11**, 2071

Homelessness—continued
intentional—continued
    examples, **11**, 2057
    generally, **11**, 2057
    limitation of local authorities' obligations, **11**, 2057
    local considerations, issues to be considered, **11**, 2066
    review of, **11**, 2066
judicial review of decisions as to, **11**, 2074
legislation, development of, **11**, 2038
local authorities, duties of, **11**, 2037; **22**, 13
local connections, issues to be considered, **11**, 2040, 2066
mobile home, no place to park, **11**, 2048
mortgage arrears, due to, **11**, 2040
obligations in respect of, **11**, 2037
offences with regard to, **11**, 2073
overcrowding, **11**, 2049
preferences, **11**, 2037
priority need—
    dependent children, **11**, 2053
    emergency, as result of, **11**, 2055
    generally, **11**, 2040, 2051, 2056
    mental disability, **11**, 2054
    old age, **11**, 2054
    physical disability, **11**, 2054
    pregnancy, **11**, 2052
    Secretary of State's powers, **11**, 2056
    vulnerability, **11**, 2054
remedies, **11**, 2037, 2038, 2074
temporary accommodation for—
    assured tenancy status excluded, **13**, 636, 648
    secure tenancy status excluded, **11**, 1942
threat of, **11**, 2050
violence, threat of, **11**, 2040, 2053
violence from other resident, probability of, **11**, 2047
Homework
education authorities' duty as to, **8**, 860
publication of policy on, **8**, 843, 860
Homicide
abortion, *see* ABORTION
accidental, **7**, 254
brain death, **7**, 257
Brown v HM Advocate, decision in, **7**, 192, 193
causal, **7**, 254
causation—
    concurrent, **7**, 265
    hastening death, **7**, 259
    malregimen, **7**, 264
    pre-existing conditions, **7**, 261
    subsequent events, **7**, 262
    time gap, where, **7**, 260
    victim, act of, **7**, 263
coma, patient in irretrievable, **7**, 257
concealment of pregnancy, *see* CONCEALMENT OF PREGNANCY
criminal, **7**, 253
culpable—
    death caused by driving, **20**, 412, 453
    person charged with, duty solicitor, **13**, 1053
See also CULPABLE HOMICIDE

Homicide—*continued*
death due to victim's attempted escape, **7**, 263
diminished responsibility, **7**, 253
direct and indirect causes, **7**, 48
duty of care and criminal liability, **11**, 1015
duty as defence, **7**, 254
excusable, **7**, 254
generally, **7**, 259
handicapped infant, treatment of, **7**, 258
human life, protection—
   coma, patient in irretrievable, **7**, 257
   determination of death, **7**, 257
   fetus, destruction, **7**, 256
   generally, **7**, 256
   infanticide, **7**, 258
   unborn child, **7**, 256
infanticide, **7**, 258
intent to kill, **7**, 78, 168, 272
justifiable, **7**, 254
meaning, **7**, 253
medical treatment—
   malregimen, **7**, 264
   negligent, **7**, 264
   non-availability, **7**, 264
   victim's failure to seek, **7**, 263
necessity as defence, **7**, 254
non-criminal, **7**, 253, 254
provocation, **7**, 253
result-crime, as, **7**, 46–48
revenge, acts of, **7**, 272, 274
self-defence, life taken in, **7**, 254
sporting participants, by, **19**, 1264
sports supporters, by, **19**, 1266
suicide, **7**, 255, 263
   aiding, **7**, 255
terminally ill patient, treatment administered to, **7**, 259
'thin skull' rule, **7**, 261
time gap before death, **7**, 47
transplant surgery, **11**, 1039
unborn child, **7**, 256
   damage to, death following birth, **7**, 256
unintended consequences of common plan, liability, **7**, 192, 193
victim's request, killing at, **7**, 255
See also MURDER
Homologation
actings of person acting without authority, of, **16**, 1644
doctrine of, sale of heritage, **20**, 910
lease, right to challenge on grounds of, **13**, 224
legal rights, **25**, 801
perfection of missives by, **6**, 573
See also ARBITRAL AWARD
Homosexuality
armed forces, members of, **7**, 313
consensual, **3**, 1237
decriminalisation, **3**, 1237
females, between, **3**, 1236
gross or shameless indecency, act of, **7**, 312, 485
legal—
   age of parties, **7**, 313
   consent, **7**, 313

Homosexuality—*continued*
legal—*continued*
   generally, **7**, 312, 313
   in private, act must be, **7**, 313
male prostitute, by, **7**, 484, 485
meaning, **3**, 1237
mentally disordered man, person having care or control over, **7**, 312
merchant ship, crew members, between, **7**, 313
more than two persons present, where, **7**, 485
offences, generally, **7**, 294, 295, 485
private, in, **3**, 1237
private life, respect for, **12**, 66
prohibition on promoting, **14**, 337
public lavatory, in, **3**, 1237; **7**, 485
relationship, status, **12**, 269n
Schedule 1 offences, **3**, 1245
sodomy, **3**, 1237; **7**, 312, 485
two or more persons present, where, **3**, 1237
Hong Kong
British Dependent Territories citizenship, **14**, 1932
British Nationality (Hong Kong) Act 1990..., **12**, 107
British Nationals (Overseas), **12**, 220n
connection with, **14**, 1947
immigration by, **12**, 101
Honour and reputation, interference with
abuse of process—
   diligence—
      generally, **15**, 465
      heritage, against, **15**, 468
      moveable property, against, **15**, 467
      person, against, **15**, 466
   forms claimed as of right, **15**, 457
   generally, **15**, 457–469
   interdict—
      generally, **15**, 461
      interim—
         continuing possession, **15**, 464
         inverting possession, **15**, 463
      perpetual, **15**, 462
   litigation—
      breach of contract, **15**, 460
      generally, **15**, 458
      malice and want of probable cause, **15**, 459
   malice and want of probable cause, **15**, 457, 459
   sequestration, **15**, 469
civil proceedings, wrongful, **15**, 457–469
convicium, **15**, 558
criminal proceedings, wrongful, **15**, 447–456
damages, **15**, 446
defamation, *see* DEFAMATION
generally, **15**, 446
legal protection against, **15**, 446
malicious falsehood, **15**, 557, 559
malicious prosecution—
   averments, sufficiency, **15**, 456
   generally, **15**, 447
   liability—
      generally, **15**, 448
      person providing information, of, **15**, 452
      private prosecutors, **15**, 451

Honour and reputation, interference with—
continued
malicious prosecution—*continued*
  liability—*continued*
    prosecuting agencies, **15**, 448–451
    solemn procedure, **15**, 449
    summary procedure, **15**, 450
    malice—
      averments, sufficiency, **15**, 456
      generally, **15**, 453
      meaning, **15**, 454
      requirement to show, **15**, 447
    prosecuting agencies, protection, **15**, 447
    summary procedure, **15**, 450
    want of probable cause—
      averments, sufficiency, **15**, 456
      generally, **15**, 453
      meaning, **15**, 455
    wrongful imprisonment following, **15**, 447
  patrimonial loss, **15**, 446
  public hatred, contempt and ridicule, *see* PUBLIC
    HATRED, CONTEMPT AND RIDICULE
  self-esteem, hurt to, **15**, 446
  slander of title, goods or business, *see* SLANDER
  solatium, **15**, 446, 567, 569, 571
  third party slander, *see* SLANDER
  verbal injuries, *see* VERBAL INJURY
Honour, title of
may not be donated, **8**, 615
recommendations by Lord Lieutenant, **5**, 551
Honour policy
marine insurance, **12**, 848
Horizontal agreement
prohibited—
  aggregated rebate cartels, **4**, 1373
  boycotts, **4**, 1374
  collective exclusive reciprocal dealing, **4**, 1372
  information agreement, **4**, 1371
  joint price fixing, **4**, 1369
  joint sales agencies, **4**, 1370
  market sharing, **4**, 1368
  restrictive covenants, **4**, 1376
  voluntary restraints, **4**, 1375
restraint of trade, doctrine of, **4**, 1216
Horizontal merger
anti-competitive effect, **4**, 1279
Horizontal restraint
goods, restrictive agreement as to, **4**, 1150
Hormone implantation
consent to, **14**, 1425
Horn
motor vehicle, on—
  construction and use regulations, **20**, 481
  two-tone, **20**, 481
Horning
historical note on, **19**, 840
letters of—
  abolition of, **6**, 464
  bill for, **6**, 1021
  issued by Court of the Lord Lyon, **6**, 1021
  Office, **19**, 850
  Register of, **6**, 464; **19**, 820, 840, 843, 860
  Signet of Scotland, **7**, 883

Horse
care of, **14**, 1665
docked, importation, **2**, 212
docking and nicking, prohibition, **2**, 272
employment of, **14**, 1665
exportation—
  aircraft, by, **2**, 225
  breeding purposes, for, **2**, 220
  certificates required for, **2**, 225
  enforcement of provisions, **2**, 226
  examination before, **2**, 222
  generally, **19**, 1294
  restriction on, **2**, 220
  shipper, duties of, **2**, 223
  welfare provisions, **2**, 222
  See also shipment of *below*
farriers, *see* FARRIER
footpath, footway or cycle track, on, **20**, 706
importation, *see* ANIMALS
meaning, **14**, 1665*n*; **24**, 559
mines, employment in, **14**, 1665
public performance involving, **2**, 269
racing, *see* HORSERACE BETTING LEVY BOARD—
  horse racecourse—
    horse racing
reckless, furious or careless driving along road, **20**,
  706
riding, *see* RIDING ESTABLISHMENT
riding deliberately at pedestrian, **2**, 104
shipment of—
  duties of ship owner, **2**, 223
  entry of vessels, right of, **2**, 226
  injury in course of, **2**, 223
  killing instrument to be carried, **2**, 223
  thoroughbreds, **2**, 224
slaughter, **11**, 503
thoroughbred—
  certificate in respect of, **2**, 225
  exemptions for, **2**, 224
water supply for horse kept for private use, **25**,
  506
Horse racecourse
approval by Levy Board, **2**, 1557
betting track, *see* BETTING
bookmakers, facilities for, **2**, 1557
certification of, **2**, 1557
pool betting on, **2**, 1557, 1564
Horse racing
historical background, **19**, 1203
licence, **19**, 1238
profits from, income tax, **19**, 1297
See also HORSERACE BETTING LEVY BOARD; HORSE
  RACECOURSE
Horsedrawn vehicles
drivers, duty of care, **2**, 163
road, on—
  child driving, **20**, 706
  generally, **20**, 706
  load inadequately secured, **20**, 706
  reckless driving, **20**, 706
Horseflesh
sold for human consumption, **11**, 432
Horsekeeper
employment in mine, **14**, 1665, 1667

Horserace Betting Levy Board
approval of tracks by, **2**, 1577
creation of, **2**, 1553
functions of, **2**, 1553
levy—
  application of, **2**, 1553
  assessment—
    appeal against, **2**, 1555
    interim, **2**, 1555
    notice of, **2**, 1554
  certificate of payment, **2**, 1554
  failure to pay, **2**, 1554
  liability for, **2**, 1553
  payment on account, **2**, 1554
  scheme—
    contributions by Totalisator Board, **2**, 1556
    powers as to, **2**, 1554
Horserace Totalisator Board
general betting duty, **7**, 1081
Horticultural producer
Agricultural and Horticultural Co-operation
  Scheme, **12**, 617
fuel, excise duty relief, **7**, 1069
Horticulture
plant and seed protection rights, **6**, 602
trade descriptions, **6**, 121
Hosepipe
restriction of use, **25**, 529
Hospital
administrative authorities, **11**, 1402
birth in, **19**, 1442
boards of management, **11**, 1402
building, accommodation of persons displaced by
  development of, **11**, 1489
building control—
  authorisation of works, **11**, 1537, 1538
    application for, **11**, 1538
  designation of area, **11**, 1539
  inspectors, appointment of, **11**, 1540
  notification of building work, **11**, 1536
  offences in relation to, **11**, 1541
  planning permission, **11**, 1536
controlled premises, **11**, 1536*n*.11.1539, 1540
controlled works, **11**, 1537, 1537*n*, 1540
death in, **19**, 1459
default, in, **11**, 1409
expenses for attending, **11**, 1490, 1517
  companion's expenses, **11**, 1490, 1517
food supplied by, **11**, 342*n*
functions, failure to carry out, **11**, 1409
hospital care, purchase by general practitioners,
  11, 1401
infected persons—
  detention in, **19**, 453
  removal to, **19**, 452
infectious diseases, for, construction or extension,
  19, 15
land ownership, income from, **3**, 1134
mentally disordered patient, *see* MENTAL HEALTH;
  MENTALLY DISORDERED PERSON
national health service trust, ownership and
  management by, **11**, 1401
opting out of health authority control, **11**, 1401

Hospital—*continued*
order—
  appeal against, **17**, 906
  court's power to make, **14**, 1452
  effect of, **14**, 1454
  grounds, **14**, 1453
  interim, **14**, 1462; **17**, 905
  mental disorder, convicted person suffering
    from, **17**, 903
  restriction, *see* MENTALLY DISORDERED PERSON
poison, sale of, **14**, 1215
premises—
  goods and services used by contractor or local
    authority, **11**, 1492
  meaning, **11**, 1536*n*
prisoner, removal of—
  sentence, awaiting, **14**, 1463
  trial, awaiting, **14**, 1463
private, *see* PRIVATE HOSPITAL
psychiatric, **22**, 30
  See also MENTAL HEALTH; MENTALLY DISORDERED
    PERSON
regional hospital boards, **11**, 1402
resident medical capacity, experience in, **14**, 1108
residential and practice accommodation, **11**, 1488
Scottish Hospital Trust, **11**, 1424
Secretary of State's duties in connection with, **11**,
  1476–1493, 1540
self-governing, **11**, 1401
social work department, provision of services in,
  22, 9
State—
  accommodation, provision of, **11**, 1476
  constitution, **14**, 1472
  correspondence of patient in, **14**, 1473
valuation for rating, **24**, 667
water meter charges, **25**, 536
Hospital Endowments Commission
nationalisation, duties with regard to, **11**, 1404,
  1406
Hostage
extradition in relation to crimes involving, **12**,
  508, 532
hostage-taking—
  offences relating to, **6**, 867
International Convention against the Taking of,
  12, 508, 532
Hostage order
breach of, **12**, 187
generally, **12**, 216
prevention of terrorism, **12**, 117, 135
Hostel
counselling by social workers within probation
  hostel, **22**, 34
education authorities' duty to provide, **8**, 729
hotel distinguished, **11**, 1706
housing benefit, **21**, 1105
local authority provision, **19**, 347
meaning, **11**, 1701*n*, 1905*n*
social work department, provision, probationers,
  for, **22**, 34
staff, liability at, **11**, 1742
valuation for rating, **24**, 612, 668
water meter charges, **25**, 536

Hostis humani generis
pirates perceived to be, **19**, 601*n*
Hoswick Whale case
udal law, **24**, 313, 329–400
Hot pursuit, right of
high seas, on, **21**, 44
Hot water
discharge, building controls, **3**, 208
Hotchpot
principle of, **25**, 611
Hotel
accommodation, **11**, 1721
  prices, **6**, 81; **11**, 1785–1787
  refusal of, **11**, 1723
  VAT invoice basis, **7**, 1358
alcoholic liquor—
  occasional licence for, **2**, 25
  offences as to licence, **2**, 80
  permitted hours, **2**, 11, 18, 19
  restricted licence, **2**, 12
  sales permitted by licence, **2**, 11
  six-day licence, **2**, 21
aliens, accommodation of, **11**, 1723, 1730*n*
animals, regulations as to, **11**, 1748, 1757
arrestment of goods by, **8**, 282
bill, payment, burden of proof, **15**, 872
bookings, **11**, 1723–1727
  offer and acceptance, **11**, 1725
  voluntary code of practice, **11**, 1726
brochures, **11**, 1783
classification, **11**, 1812
consumer protection, **11**, 1779–1780
contract—
  breach of, **11**, 1727
  hotelkeeper and guest, between, **11**, 1724–1727
corporate bodies, offences by, **11**, 1788
custody, deposit and restoration, **11**, 1751
development, financial assistance for—
  extensions and alterations, **11**, 1807
  fixed equipment, **11**, 1808
  generally, **11**, 1805
  grants, generally, **11**, 1809
  loans, **11**, 1810
  new hotels, **11**, 1806
dogs, **11**, 1723, 1739, 1739*n*
duties of hotelkeeper, *see* HOTELKEEPER
dwelling house distinguished, **24**, 612
employment, conditions of, **11**, 1790–1792
eventide home distinguished, **11**, 1714
exclusion of establishments, **11**, 1789
fire certificate, **10**, 1453
fire precautions, **11**, 1732–1736
food, offences relating to sale of, **11**, 1779–1781
food hygiene certificate, **2**, 46
gaming held in, person under eighteen on premises, **3**, 1230
generally, **11**, 1701–1703
goods, safe deposit of, **11**, 1751
grading, **11**, 1812
guests—
  acts of, liability for, **11**, 1739
  behaviour of, **11**, 1729
  contact between hotelkeeper and, **11**, 1724–1727
  discontinuance of status as, **11**, 1718

Hotel—*continued*
guests—*continued*
  ejection of, **11**, 1729
  hotelkeeper—
    duty towards guests, **11**, 1719–1723
    See also HOTELKEEPER
    relationship with, **11**, 1717
  lodger distinguished, **11**, 1717, 1718
  luggage, *see* LUGGAGE
  meaning, **11**, 1717
  negligence of, **11**, 1745
  non-paying, **11**, 1717
  property of, hotelkeeper's liability—
    edictal liability, **11**, 1702, 1741
    exceptions from, **11**, 1745–1751
    extent of, **11**, 1744
    generally, **11**, 1741–1744
    hospitium, property within, **11**, 1743
    how arising, **11**, 1741
    limitation of, **11**, 1748–1751
    persons to whom not applied, **11**, 1742
    theft within hotel, **11**, 1744
  refusal to receive, **11**, 1723, 1753
  registration, **11**, 1730
  remedies of—
    damages, action for, **11**, 1753
    declarator of rights of travellers, action for, **11**, 1752
    loss or damage to property, action for, **11**, 1754
  safe keeping, goods deposited for, **11**, 1751
  safety of, **11**, 1738
  traveller, as, **11**, 1716, 1717
    See also TRAVELLER
health and safety at work, **11**, 1737
hostel distinguished, **11**, 1706
hotel records—
  generally, **11**, 1730
  guests' duty to supply information, **12**, 184
  hoteliers' duty to maintain, **12**, 184
  Secretary of State's powers in relation to, **12**, 184
hydropathic establishment, **11**, 1708, 1709
hygiene, **11**, 1780
keeper, *see* HOTELKEEPER
lease, **13**, 197
liability—
  hotelkeepers', *see* HOTELKEEPER
  occupiers', **11**, 1731
  proprietors', **6**, 103
licensing—
  alterations to premises, **11**, 1778
  appeal against refusal of licence, **11**, 1769
  application for—
    generally, **11**, 1765
    grant of licence, **11**, 1767
    hearing, **11**, 1766
    plans and notices, **11**, 1765
    refusal of licence, **11**, 1768
  entertainment licence, **11**, 1761*n*
  generally, **11**, 1760–1778
  hotel licence, **11**, 1763
    restricted, **11**, 1764
  licensing authorities, **11**, 1761, 1762

Hotel—*continued*
licensing—*continued*
  licensing boards, **11**, 1762
  permitted hours, **11**, 1775
    extension of, **11**, 1776, 1777
  premises, reconstruction or alteration, **11**, 1778
  refreshment licence, **11**, 1761*n*
  renewal of licence, **11**, 1770
  seasonal licences, **11**, 1774
  suspension of licence, **11**, 1773
  transfer of licence—
    permanent, **11**, 1771
    temporary, **11**, 1772
  See also ALCOHOLIC LIQUOR
lodging house distinguished, **11**, 1710
luggage, *see* LUGGAGE
meals, liquor sales as ancillary to, **2**, 12
meaning, **2**, 11; **11**, 1706, 1709, 1763
  See also LICENSED PREMISES
motel, **11**, 1711
name, passing off, **18**, 1377
negligence, guest, of, **11**, 1745
place of business, as, **11**, 1706
prices, **11**, 1785–1787
private, **11**, 1709
property of guest, *see* guests *above*
public house distinguished, **11**, 1712
refreshment room distinguished, **11**, 1713
refreshments—
  provision of, **11**, 1720
  refusal to provide, **11**, 1723
registration of visitors, **11**, 1730
residence in, as element of domicile, **4**, 30
residential, **11**, 1709
restaurant distinguished, **11**, 1713
safety provisions, **11**, 1731–1737
Secretary of State's powers, **11**, 1789
sleeping accommodation—
  price, display of, **6**, 81
  requirement as to, **2**, 11
Sunday opening—
  control, **22**, 817
  local licensing board, **22**, 817
temperance hotel, **11**, 1708
third persons, acts of, **11**, 1739
trade descriptions, offences relating to, **11**, 1782
travellers received in, *see* TRAVELLER
valuation for rating, **24**, 668
value added tax, accommodation costs, **11**, 1786
wages, **11**, 1790–1792
water meter charges, **25**, 536
weights and measures, **11**, 1784
See also HOTELKEEPER; LICENSED PREMISES
Hotelkeeper
accommodation, refusal of, **11**, 1723
bookings—
  offer and acceptance, **11**, 1725
  voluntary code of practice, **11**, 1726
case law, **11**, 1704
contract between guest and—
  bookings, offer and acceptance, **11**, 1725
  breach of, **11**, 1727
  generally, **11**, 1724
  voluntary code of booking practice, **11**, 1726

Hotelkeeper—*continued*
duties—
  accommodation, to provide, **11**, 1721, 1723
  generally, **11**, 1719
  luggage, **11**, 1722
  refreshments, provision of, **11**, 1720, 1723
edictal liability, **11**, 1702
English law compared, **11**, 1705, 1707
guest, relationship with, **11**, 1717
liability—
  death and personal injury, **11**, 1738
  debts, guest's, **11**, 1740
  deposit of goods for safe keeping, **11**, 1751
  edictal, **11**, 1702, 1741
  guest—
    act of, **11**, 1739
    property of, *see* HOTEL
  limitation—
    animals, **11**, 1748
    circumstances excluding, **11**, 1750
    deposit of goods for safe keeping, **11**, 1748
    generally, **11**, 1748
    motor car, **11**, 1722, 1748, 1748*n*
    statutory notice, by, **11**, 1749
  notice of limited liability, **11**, 1749
  reasonable care, duty of, **11**, 1738
  third persons, acts of, **11**, 1739, 1740
licensing, *see* HOTEL
lien, right of, **11**, 1757; **13**, 95
luggage, *see* LUGGAGE
meaning, **11**, 1715
nautae, caupones, stabularii edict, **11**, 1702
origin of Scots law, **11**, 1701
private hotels, **11**, 1709
records to be kept by, **11**, 1730
refreshments, refusal of, **11**, 1723
rejection of traveller by, **11**, 1723
remedies of, guests, actions against, **11**, 1756
residential hotels, **11**, 1709
sale of goods left at hotel, **11**, 1758, 1759
statutory provisions, **11**, 1703
strict liability, **15**, 147
  damnum fatale, defence of, **15**, 148
  defences, **15**, 148
  edictal, **15**, 144, 147
  exceptions to, **15**, 148
  goods deposited with innkepper for safe custody, **15**, 149
  Hotel Proprietors Act 1956, effect, **15**, 149
  limitation, **15**, 149
  negligence by traveller, where, **15**, 148
  Queen's enemies, act of, **15**, 148
  Roman law, **15**, 144, 147
  sleeping accommodation, requirement as to, **15**, 149
  statutory notice, display, **15**, 149
  time limits, **15**, 149
  vehicles, live animals, etc, **15**, 149
See also HOTEL
Hour
de momento in momentum, **22**, 820, 823
meaning, **22**, 816

Hour—*continued*
naturalis computatio, period calculated in, **22**, 819,
    820, 831
Hours of work
adult males—
    mining, in, **9**, 68
    night bakeries, in, **9**, 70
    sheet-glass works, in, **9**, 70
    transport, in, **9**, 69
child, employment of, **9**, 74
generally, **9**, 67
mining—
    adult males in, **9**, 68
    generally, **14**, 1667
    lowering and raising workers, **14**, 1669
    suspension on control of hours of work, **14**, 1668
    women in, **9**, 71; **14**, 1666
    young person in, **9**, 71; **14**, 1666, 1671
restrictive labour practices, **4**, 1153
shop assistant, of, **9**, 73
week's pay, calculation of, **9**, 59
women—
    factories, in, **9**, 72
    mining, in, **9**, 71; **14**, 1666
young persons—
    factories, in, **9**, 72
    mining, in, **9**, 71; **14**, 1666, 1671
See also EMPLOYMENT
House
See DWELLING HOUSE; HOUSING
House loan
See LOAN
House of Commons
access to Crown, **7**, 723
Advocate Depute ineligible for membership, **13**,
    1329
allowances, **5**, 380
burgh members, **15**, 1007
Chairman of Ways and Means, **5**, 381
Chairmen's Panel, **5**, 449
Chiltern Hundreds, appointment to stewardship
    of, **5**, 379
Committees of Whole House—
    Bills—
        amendments to, **5**, 401
        committal of, **5**, 400
        report of, **5**, 404
    clauses, **5**, 402
    functions, **5**, 398
    history, **5**, 399
    schedules, **5**, 402
    sittings, **5**, 403
    subsequent proceedings, **5**, 404
constituencies, *see* CONSTITUENCIES
constituency, **15**, 1037
disqualifying offices, **15**, 1064
election candidate, disclaimer of peerage by, **16**,
    1316
elections to, *see* PARLIAMENT
franchise, *see* FRANCHISE
generally, **6**, 810, 819
legislation, *see* LEGISLATION
Manor of Northstead, appointment to stewardship
    of, **5**, 379

House of Commons—*continued*
Members of Parliament—
    advocate as, **13**, 1345
    bankruptcy, **15**, 1059
    ceasing to be member, **5**, 379
    citizenship, requirements as to, **15**, 1058
    disputes regarding qualification, **5**, 379
    disqualification—
        affirmation of allegiance, failure to take, **15**,
            1060
        bankruptcy, **5**, 379; **15**, 1059
        citizenship, **5**, 379; **15**, 1058
        clergy, **5**, 379; **15**, 1061
        common law, **15**, 1055
        mental disability, **5**, 379; **15**, 1055
        non-age, **5**, 379; **15**, 1056
        oath of allegiance, failure to take, **15**, 1060
        office, by virtue of, **5**, 379; **15**, 1064
        peerage, **5**, 379; **15**, 1062
        prisoners, **5**, 379; **15**, 1063
        sequestration, **15**, 1059
        sitting member ineligible for any other, **15**,
            1057
    eligibility for, **5**, 379
        age limit, **3**, 1214; **5**, 379
    evidence of, **10**, 624
    excluded categories—
        aliens, **5**, 379
        bankrupts, **5**, 379; **15**, 1059
        clergy, **5**, 379; **15**, 1061
        convicted person, **5**, 379; **15**, 1063
        office-holders, **5**, 379; **15**, 1064
        peers and peeresses in own right, **5**, 379; **15**,
            1062
        persons under twenty-one years of age, **5**, 379
        unsound mind, those of, **5**, 379; **15**, 1055
    immigration cases, representations concerning,
        12, 329, 370–376
        administrative removal, in respect of, **12**, 376
        after entry cases, **12**, 375
        deportation decisions, in respect of, **12**, 376
        entry, where refusal of, **12**, 374
        entry clearance, where refusal of, **12**, 373
        generally, **12**, 370, 372
        Home Office guidelines, **12**, 371
    interests of, **5**, 380, 442
    legal disability, under, **15**, 1055, 1056
    register of electors, supply to, **15**, 1114
    resignation, **5**, 379
    sequestration, **15**, 1059
    succeeding to peerage, **16**, 1316
    taking seats—
        by-election, after, **5**, 383
        meeting of new Parliament, at, **5**, 382
    witness, as, **10**, 527
origin of, **6**, 803
parliamentary private secretaries, **5**, 386
pay, **5**, 380
powers, generally, **6**, 817
Prime Minister must have seat in, **5**, 306
Scottish business in, **5**, 384
Scottish Grand Committee, *see* standing
    committees *below*
Scottish questions, **5**, 391

House of Commons—*continued*
Scottish representation, **15**, 1006, 1007
second reading committees, **5**, 421
select committees—
    Chairmen's Panel, **5**, 449
    classification of, **5**, 431
    Committee of Privileges, **5**, 439
    Committee of Selection, **5**, 446
    Consolidation &c Bills, Joint Committee on, **5**, 438
    Court of Referees, **5**, 448
    department-related—
        current, **5**, 433
        generally, **5**, 432
        membership, **5**, 435
        reports, debates on, **5**, 434
    domestic, **5**, 442–449
    European Legislation, on, **5**, 426, 441
    generally, **5**, 428–431
    hybrid Bills, **19**, 129
    legislation, relating to, **5**, 439–441
    Liaison Committee, **5**, 445
    members' interests, on, **5**, 442
    membership, **5**, 429
    Parliamentary Commissioner for Administration, on, **5**, 437
    powers of, **5**, 430
    proceedings, **5**, 430
    Public Accounts Committee, **5**, 436, 596
    public business, relating to, **5**, 439–441
    public corporations, control of, **19**, 226
    Scottish Affairs, **5**, 532
    services, on, **5**, 443
    sound broadcasting, on, **5**, 444
    Standing Orders Committee, **5**, 447
    Statutory Instruments, Joint Committee on, **5**, 440
    statutory reports, examining, **5**, 436–438
shire members, **15**, 1007
Speaker, **7**, 723
    election of, **5**, 381
    impartial position of, **5**, 381
    powers, **5**, 381
    responsibilities, **5**, 381
Speaker's Panel, **5**, 381
standing committees—
    allocation of business to, **5**, 407
    Bills—
        committee stage of, **5**, 412
        report, on, consideration of, **5**, 422
        Scottish Grand Committee, **5**, 415
    chairmen, **5**, 408
    committee stage of Bills, **5**, 412
    details, **5**, 411–427
    European Community documents, on, **5**, 426
    general procedure, **5**, 405–410
    history, **5**, 405
    meaning, **5**, 405
    membership of, **5**, 406
    Northern Ireland, **5**, 420
    other procedure, **5**, 409
    regional affairs, on, **5**, 423
    Scottish, **5**, 413

House of Commons—*continued*
standing committees—*continued*
    Scottish Grand—
        Bills—
            consideration on report, **5**, 418
            referred to committee, **5**, 415
        estimates, **5**, 416
        generally, **5**, 334, 414
        matters relating exclusively to Scotland, **5**, 417
        second reading, **5**, 421
        sittings, **5**, 410
        special, **5**, 427
        statutory instruments, on, **5**, 425
        Welsh Grand, **5**, 419
statements in, absolute privilege, **15**, 517
statutory instruments—
    debates in House on, **5**, 424
    Joint Committee on, **5**, 440
    standing committees on, **5**, 425
United Kingdom parliamentary elections—
    order for inspection of ballot papers, **15**, 1357
unparliamentary language, **5**, 387
House of Lords
advocate appearing before, dress, **13**, 1323
Appellate Committees, **5**, 368; **6**, 828, 834, 835
    report to whole House, **22**, 278
appellate jurisdiction, **6**, 801, 825
    abuse of original procedure, **6**, 818
    appeals originating in inferior courts, **6**, 818
    Appellate Jurisdiction Act 1876..., **6**, 821, 822, 826, 827
    competency, **6**, 829
    competency of appeal, **6**, 829
    constitution for, **6**, 826
    Court of Chancery, **6**, 803
    Court of the Lord Lyon, from, **6**, 1010, 1020
    Court of Session, from, **5**, 637; **6**, 801, 811–812, 818, 825, 829, 836, 920; **22**, 602, 635
    Courts-Martial Appeal Court, from, **6**, 884, 893
    Exchequer Court, **6**, 810
    generally, **6**, 825; **22**, 270–285
    interlocutory judgments, **6**, 829
    judicial precedent, effect of, **6**, 833
    Lands Tribunal for Scotland, from, **6**, 1154
    leave required, when, **6**, 829
    no appeal from High Court of Justiciary, **5**, 644; **6**, 801, 813, 829
    points not raised in lower court, **6**, 832
    replacement with Imperial Court of Appeal, proposals for, **5**, 349
    schemes for restructuring, **6**, 821
    Scottish views, **6**, 811
    sittings, **6**, 834
    Supreme Court of Judicature Act 1873..., **6**, 821
    Treaty of Union 1707..., **6**, 811; **22**, 602
    tribunals, appeals from, **6**, 829
audience—
    advocate's right of, **13**, 1325
    appeal to, signature of petition, **13**, 1326
    solicitors' right of, **13**, 1152, 1180
balanced constitution, and, **6**, 817

House of Lords—*continued*
civil legal aid, **13**, 1034, 1045
committees of—
  Committee for Privileges, *see* HOUSE OF LORDS
    COMMITTEE FOR PRIVILEGES
  domestic committees—
    Committee of Selection, **5**, 463
    generally, **5**, 462–466
    Leave of Absence Committee, **5**, 462
  select committees, *see* select committees *below*
  Whole House, committees of—
    functions, **5**, 398
    generally, **5**, 450
composition, **16**, 1307
constitution of, **6**, 823
court, development as, **5**, 341; **6**, 801; **22**, 270–
  285, 323
Court of Session, appeal from, civil legal aid, **13**,
  1034
historical development—
  Claim of Right 1689..., **6**, 809
  court of equity, determination of dispute, **6**,
    812
  Treaty of Union 1707..., **6**, 810, 811
Irish peers, **16**, 1307, 1307*n*
judicial precedent—
  computerised law reports, effect of, **22**, 263
  Court of Exchequer, decisions binding on, **22**,
    322
  generally, **22**, 270–285, 302–304
  imposition of principles of English law, **22**, 276
  Lands Tribunal for Scotland, decisions binding
    on, **22**, 324
  Lands Valuation Appeal Court, decisions not
    binding on, **22**, 323
  Lyon Court, decisions binding on, **22**, 325
  nineteenth century, influence in, **22**, 255
  non-Scottish decisions, effect of, **22**, 277, 279–
    282
    'cross-border' precedents, **22**, 277
  own decisions, authority of, **6**, 833; **22**, 257,
    270, 273, 274, 277, 279, 283–285, 323
  Registration of Voters Appeal Court, decisions
    binding on, **22**, 326
  Restrictive Practices Court, decisions binding
    on, **22**, 327
  Scottish Land Court, decisions binding on, **22**,
    321
  sheriff court, decisions binding on, **22**, 297
  stare decisis doctrine, **22**, 255
  tribunals, decisions binding on, **22**, 328–333
jurisdiction—
  appellate jurisdiction, *see* appellate jurisdiction
    above
  England, in, **6**, 802, 803, 825
  human rights, challenge to decision on, **5**, 357
  Northern Ireland, in, **6**, 825
  original, **6**, 823
  questions of fact, on, **6**, 830
  questions of law, **6**, 831
  Scottish—
    balanced constitution, and, **6**, 817
    Court of Exchequer in Scotland, **6**, 810, 814
    establishment of, **6**, 801

House of Lords—*continued*
jurisdiction—*continued*
  Scottish—*continued*
    extent, **6**, 813–816
    history of, **6**, 801–822
    Jury Court, **6**, 815
    Teind Court, **6**, 816
legislation, role in progress of, **5**, 390
Lord Chancellor—
  appointment of, **5**, 370
  functions of, **5**, 370, 510; **6**, 817, 826, 828
  Keeper of Great Seal, as, **5**, 370
  member of Cabinet, as, **5**, 370
  office of, **5**, 510
  official seat of, **5**, 379
  Roman Catholic Church, office tenable by
    adherent to, **5**, 370
  senior judge, as, **5**, 370
  Speaker of House of Lords, as, **5**, 370
Lords Spiritual, **15**, 1062; **16**, 1307, 1307*n*
membership—
  generally, **5**, 365; **6**, 823
  hereditary peers, **5**, 367
  See also PEERAGE
  life peers, **5**, 639; **16**, 1312
  Lord Chancellor, *see* Lord Chancellor *above*
  Lords of Appeal in Ordinary, *see* LORDS OF
    APPEAL IN ORDINARY
  Lords Spiritual, **5**, 366; **6**, 823
  Lords Temporal, **6**, 823
  own composition may be determined by, **5**,
    367
  Scottish law officers, seat in, **5**, 306, 371; **22**,
    602
peeresses in own right, **5**, 374, 379
peers—
  abolition of right to trial by, **6**, 823
  expenses, entitlement to, **16**, 1308
  hereditary, **6**, 817, 823
  Irish, **16**, 1307, 1307*n*
  lay, **6**, 817, 819, 820, 826
  life, **6**, 823; **16**, 1312
  membership of House of Commons, exclusion
    from, **5**, 379
  privileges, **16**, 1308
  representative Scottish, **16**, 1307
  Scottish, **16**, 1307
  voting in election, disqualification from, **5**, 374
  See also PEERAGE
precedence, **16**, 2010
  ecclesiastical, **16**, 2016
privileges—
  Committee for, *see* HOUSE OF LORDS COMMITTEE
    FOR PRIVILEGES
  generally, **16**, 1308
procedure in appeals, **6**, 835–846
  costs, **6**, 846
  cross-appeal, **6**, 837
  effect of appeal on execution, **6**, 843
  hearing of appeal, **6**, 844
  incidental petitions, **6**, 842
  judgment, **6**, 845
  leave to appeal, **6**, 836
  lodgment of case, **6**, 840

House of Lords—*continued*
procedure in appeals—*continued*
  lodgment of documents, **6**, 841
  petition of appeal, **6**, 836, 837
  rules of, **6**, 835
  security for costs, **6**, 838
reforms of, **5**, 369
Scottish peers, **16**, 1307
  present-day position, **15**, 1008
  representative Scottish peers, **15**, 1008; **16**, 1307
Scottish representation, **15**, 1006, 1008
select committees—
  Bill of Rights, **5**, 313
  Committee for Privileges, **5**, 367, 455
  Consolidation Bills, Joint Committee on, **5**, 438, 454
  European Communities, on, **5**, 458; **10**, 75
  generalised order of reference, with, **5**, 453
  generally, **5**, 452
  Hybrid Instruments, **5**, 457; **19**, 129
  legislation, relating to, **5**, 455–461
  offices, **5**, 465
  Personal Bills Committee, **5**, 460
  Private Bills Committee, **5**, 460; **19**, 98
  Procedure of the House Committee, **5**, 464
  public business, relating to, **5**, 455–461
  public corporations, control of, **19**, 226
  Science and Technology Committee, **5**, 453
  sound broadcasting, **5**, 466
  Standing Orders Committee, **5**, 461
  Statutory Instruments, Joint Committee on, **5**, 440, 456
  statutory reports, examining, **5**, 454
statements in, absolute privilege, **15**, 517
work of, **5**, 372
House of Lords Committee for Privileges
peerage claims—
  attendance by public, **16**, 1319*n*
  claimant's case, **16**, 1319
  claimant's petition, **16**, 1319
  evidence, **16**, 1319
  generally, **16**, 1319
  hearing, **16**, 1319
  Lord Lyon, interlocutor or findings of, **16**, 1320
  reference to, **16**, 1319
  report to House of Lords, **16**, 1319
  rival claimants, **16**, 1319*n*
Houseboat
housing benefit, **21**, 1105
matrimonial home, as, **10**, 857
no place to moor constituting homelessness, **11**, 2048
VAT zero-rating, **7**, 1453
Housebreaking
diminished responsibility, **7**, 150
intent to steal, with, **7**, 164*n*, 347
  firearm or imitation firearm possessed during, **10**, 1565
motive, **7**, 92
theft by—
  definition of breaking, **7**, 341
  generally, **7**, 339, 340

Household
private, exemption from discrimination, **9**, 348
Household insurance
excess clause, **12**, 891
indemnity insurance, as, **12**, 804
Household waste
collection of, **9**, 1165
dustbins, **9**, 1166
privies, emptying of, **9**, 1167
Housing
acquisition and disposal of land, **11**, 1907, 1908
action areas, *see* HOUSING ACTION AREA
administration in Scotland—
  central, **11**, 1902
  local authorities, **11**, 1903–1919
amenity—
  central government contribution to improvement of, **11**, 2034
  improvement of, grants for, **11**, 2033, 2034
  standard, **11**, 2023
association, *see* HOUSING ASSOCIATION—
  co-operative housing association
authority, **11**, 1903–1919
  rehousing by, **5**, 189
  See also HOUSING AUTHORITY
background, **14**, 609
benefits, **14**, 862
capital expenditure, **14**, 613
children, priority housing needs, **11**, 2051, 2053
cleansing and disinfection of premises and contents, **19**, 366, 448
closing order, *see* CLOSING ORDER
common property, **19**, 355
communal—
  residential establishments, **24**, 610*n*, 615
  sheltered housing, **24**, 610*n*, 615
compulsory purchase orders—
  'cleared site value', **6**, 1141
  compensation for, **6**, 1141
  'owner occupier's supplement', **6**, 1141
conditions and needs of each district, **19**, 347
cooking facilities, **11**, 1979
curtilage, **11**, 1937, 1945
damp, **11**, 1979
demolition, housing action areas, **11**, 1996, 1998
demolition order, *see* DEMOLITION
development corporations, **11**, 1920, 1935
distribution of responsibilities, **14**, 610
drainage, **11**, 1979
dwelling house, *see* DWELLING HOUSE
expenditure programme, **5**, 581
finance—
  capital expenditure and receipts, **11**, 1919
  generally, **11**, 1909; **14**, 613
  housing revenue accounts, **11**, 1916, 1917
  housing support grants, **11**, 1910–1914
    aggregate amount of grants, **11**, 1911
    apportionment, **11**, 1913
    housing support grant orders, **11**, 1912
    payment of, **11**, 1914
  local authorities, housing accounts of, **11**, 1915
  slum clearance revenue account, **11**, 1918
fire escapes, **11**, 2028–2030
first-time buyers, assistance for, **11**, 2016

Housing—*continued*
furniture, fittings and conveniences, local authority provision, **11**, 1906
generally, **11**, 1901
grants, *see* GRANT
homelessness, *see* HOMELESSNESS
house, definition, **11**, 1901
house loans, *see* LOAN
houses part of, or within curtilage of, certain other buildings, **11**, 1945
housing accommodation, provision of, **11**, 1905
housing associations, *see* HOUSING ASSOCIATION—co-operative housing association
housing conditions and needs, **11**, 1904
housing list, *see* HOUSING LIST
housing and tenancy court, fairness of methods employed by, **12**, 60
human habitation, fitness for, landlord's obligations as to, **13**, 260
improvement area, *see* IMPROVEMENT AREA
improvement grant, *see* IMPROVEMENT GRANT
improvement order, *see* IMPROVEMENT ORDER
infected—
　ceasing to occupy, **19**, 451
　cleansing and disinfection, **19**, 366, 448
　letting of, **19**, 450
insulation grants, *see* THERMAL INSULATION
lease, *see* LEASE-LEASING
local authority loans, **13**, 1773
local authority powers and duties—
　acquisition and disposal of land, **11**, 1907, 1908
　administration of housing—
　　agreements with other authorities, **11**, 1905
　　ancillary powers, **11**, 1906
　　design and planning considerations, **11**, 1905
　　generally, **11**, 1903
　　housing accommodation, provision of, **11**, 1904, 1905
　　　methods of, **11**, 1905
　　housing finance, capital expenditure and receipts, **11**, 1919
　　　generally, **11**, 1909
　　　housing accounts, **11**, 1915
　　　housing revenue account, **11**, 1916, 1917
　　　housing support grants, **11**, 1910, 1911–1914
　　　slum clearance revenue account, **11**, 1918
　　impending changes, **11**, 1903
　　land, acquisition and disposal of, **11**, 1907, 1908
　　notice by Secretary of State, **11**, 1904
　　planning and amenities, **11**, 1905
　　provision and maintenance of housing, **11**, 1902, 1905
　　regional councils, limited powers of, **11**, 1903
　　remission to district and islands councils, **11**, 1903
　　Wheatley Royal Commission, **11**, 1903
　allocation of housing, **11**, 1935
　alteration, enlargement or improvement of any house or building, **11**, 1905
　ancillary powers, **11**, 1906
　conversion of any buildings to houses, **11**, 1905

Housing—*continued*
local authority powers and duties—*continued*
　erection of houses, **11**, 1905
　furniture, fittings and conveniences, provision of, **11**, 1906
　homelessness, obligations in respect of, *see* LOCAL AUTHORITY
　house loans, *see* LOCAL AUTHORITY
　houses, acquisition of, **11**, 1905
　housing accommodation, provision of, **11**, 1905
　housing accounts, **11**, 1915
　housing action areas, *see* HOUSING ACTION AREA
　housing conditions and needs, **11**, 1904
　housing finance, **11**, 1909–1919; **14**, 613
　improvement grants, *see* IMPROVEMENT GRANT
　overcrowding—
　　licence to exceed limit, **11**, 2002
　　powers and duties as to, **11**, 2003
　　seasonal increases, **11**, 2002
　protected tenant, repossession by landlord, **13**, 709–711
　　certificate of equivalence, **13**, 709, 710
　provision, generally, **19**, 346, 347
lodgers, *see* LODGER
lodging house, *see* LODGING HOUSE
main powers and duties, **14**, 612
mobile homes, sheriff court jurisdiction, **6**, 1099
mobility, grants towards, **11**, 1935
multiple occupation, houses in—
　control orders, **11**, 2009
　generally, **11**, 2004, 2008; **19**, 467
　management code, **11**, 2006
　overcrowding, *see* overcrowding *below*
　registration schemes, **11**, 2005
　works, powers to require, **11**, 2007
　　appeals, **11**, 2007
　　enforcement, **11**, 2007
　　wilful failure to comply, **11**, 2007
new towns, **11**, 1920
NHBC house purchaser's agreement, **3**, 116
organisation, **14**, 611
overcrowding—
　amounting to homelessness, **11**, 2045, 2049
　calculation of areas, **11**, 2001
　endangering health of occupants, **11**, 2049
　generally, **11**, 2000, 2008; **19**, 336
　homelessness, and, **11**, 2049
　house, **19**, 336
　　meaning, **11**, 1901*n*
　local authority licence to exceed limit, **11**, 2002
　meaning, **11**, 2001
　multiple occupation, *see* multiple occupation, houses in *above*
　offences, **11**, 2002
　　exceptions to rule, **11**, 2002
　powers and duties of local authorities, **11**, 2003
　public sector housing list, affecting, **11**, 1935
　room standard, **11**, 2001
　seasonal increases allowed, **11**, 2002
　secure tenancies, **11**, 1947
　space standard, **11**, 2001
policy, determination of, **11**, 1902
post–war measures, **14**, 609
public health legislation, **19**, 305, 346–348

Housing—*continued*
public sector—
  lease, generally, **13**, 121
  regulation of provision, **13**, 121
public sector tenancies, *see* PUBLIC SECTOR
  TENANCY
reform, **14**, 48
rehousing—
  caravan site, displacement from, **5**, 189
  local housing authority, obligations of, **5**, 189
repair notices—
  appeals, **11**, 1994
  generally, **11**, 1993, 1995, 2015
repairs grant, *see* REPAIRS GRANT
revenue expenditure, **14**, 613
road, environmental impact of new, **20**, 675
road bonds, meaning, **20**, 650
sanitary conveniences, *see* SANITARY CONVENIENCE
scope of title, **11**, 1901
Scottish Homes, *see* SCOTTISH HOMES
Scottish Special Housing Association, **11**, 1921
secure tenants, *see* SECURE TENANT
sheriff court jurisdiction, **6**, 1099, 1108
short tenancy, compulsory acquisition, **5**, 185
slum clearance, **11**, 1918, 1996
sound insulation work, **20**, 675
standard amenities, **11**, 2023
structural stability, tolerable standard, **11**, 1979
sub-standard, *see* SUB-STANDARD HOUSING
subsidies, **14**, 613
support grant, **14**, 833
tenant, *see* TENANT-TENANCY
thermal insulation, grants for, *see* THERMAL
  INSULATION
tolerable standard—
  homelessness, and, **11**, 2037
  housing, of, **11**, 1978, 1979
  improvement orders, **11**, 1990
  underground rooms, **11**, 1981, 1982*n*
underground dwellings, infectious disease
  regulations, **19**, 468
underground rooms, **11**, 1981, 1982*n*
unfit for human habitation, concept of tolerable
  standard, replaced by, **11**, 1979
washing facilities, *see* WASHING FACILITIES
Housing action area
control of occupation, **11**, 1999
declaration of, **11**, 1996, 1997
demolition, area for, **11**, 1996, 1998
demolition and improvement, area for, **11**, 1996
generally, **11**, 1996, 1999
house loans, **11**, 2015
improvement, area for, **11**, 1996
improvement grants, **11**, 2031
improvement orders, **11**, 1992
land, acquisition of, **11**, 1998
local authority—
  execution of works by, **11**, 1999
  loans, **11**, 1992
  powers, **11**, 1999
notice, service of, **11**, 1997
powers, generally, **11**, 1999
procedure, **11**, 1997
repairs grants, **11**, 2032

Housing action area—*continued*
revocation of order, application for, **11**, 1999
sub-standard housing, **11**, 1978
types of, **11**, 1996
See also DWELLING HOUSE
Housing association
accounts and audit, **1**, 94; **11**, 1929
allocation of houses, **11**, 1935
assets, freezing of, **11**, 1931
assured tenancy status affected by, **13**, 650
building society's power to invest in and support,
  3, 369
central association, **11**, 1933
change of landlord, **11**, 1924
co-operative, **11**, 1924, 1927
  as landlord, assured tenancy status excluded, **13**,
    636, 647
  See also CO-OPERATIVE HOUSING ASSOCIATION
committee members, **11**, 1928
community-based, designation of, **11**, 1927
community benefit society, as, **12**, 609
definition, **11**, 1924
disposal of land, **11**, 1926
dissolution, **11**, 1928; **12**, 652*n*
expenses, **11**, 1927
extraordinary audit ordered, **11**, 1931
fees, **11**, 1927
finance, **11**, 1932
fully mutual, **11**, 1924
generally, **11**, 1924
housing lists, **11**, 1935
housing society, status as, **12**, 617
inquiries into affairs of, **11**, 1931
members—
  appointment, **11**, 1928
  becoming insolvent, **11**, 1928
  control of payments to, **11**, 1927
  incapacity due to mental disorder, **11**, 1928
  removal or suspension, **11**, 1931
misconduct or mismanagement of affairs, **11**, 1931
objects of, **11**, 1925
payments to members, control of, **11**, 1927
registration, **11**, 1925
  admission to, **11**, 1925
  eligibility for, **11**, 1925
  removal from register, **11**, 1925
    appeals against, **11**, 1925
restriction on transactions, **11**, 1931
right to buy, restrictions on, **11**, 1955
rules, **11**, 1928
  amendment, **12**, 616*n*
Scottish Homes, *see* SCOTTISH HOMES
security of tenure, **11**, 1955
self-build society, **11**, 1924
sheltered housing, **11**, 1955
special, Scottish Special Housing Association, **11**,
  1921
special categories of tenant, **11**, 1947, 1955
sub-standard, *see* SUB-STANDARD HOUSING
supplies to, VAT zero-rating, **7**, 1449
tenancies after 1988..., **11**, 1936, 1955
trading for profit prohibited, **11**, 1925
transfer of land to Scottish Homes or other
  association, **11**, 1931

Housing association—*continued*
voluntary disposal, **11**, 1924
See also DWELLING HOUSE; INDUSTRIAL AND
   PROVIDENT SOCIETY
Housing authority
generally, **11**, 1903–1919
handicapped person, co-ordination of services to
   provide suitable, **22**, 24
homeless person, statutory duty to, **22**, 13
local authority, duty to co-operate with, advice
   etc, to homeless person, **22**, 9, 13
rehousing, duty of, **5**, 189
social work departments, co-ordination to adapt
   housing for handicapped persons, **22**, 9, 24
Housing benefit
administration, **21**, 1101, 1101*n*
appeal, no right of, **21**, 1118
applicable amount, meaning, **21**, 1115
application for, **21**, 1104
bed and breakfast accommodation, **21**, 1105
benefit period, **21**, 1116
calculation—
   weekly basis, on, **21**, 1111
capital restrictions, **21**, 1108
caravan site charge, **21**, 1105
charges not covered by, **21**, 1113
definition, **21**, 1101
eligible rent, **21**, 1113
entitlement—
   conditions—
      capital restrictions, **21**, 1108
      earnings, **21**, 1110
      income—
         assessment, **21**, 1111
         earnings, **21**, 1110
         restrictions, **21**, 1109
      liability for payments, **21**, 1105
      occupation, **21**, 1107
      student, **21**, 1112
      unreasonably high rent, **21**, 1106, 1113
   determination, **21**, 1113–1117
      applicable amount, **21**, 1115
      non-dependants, deductions for, **21**, 1114
fair, **21**, 1106
family, **21**, 1104
fuel charges, **21**, 1113
   communal areas, **21**, 1113
   fixed, **21**, 1113
funding, **21**, 1101
historical development, **21**, 1102
hostel accommodation, **21**, 1105
houseboat payments, **21**, 1105
income—
   assessment, **21**, 1111
   disregards, **21**, 1110
   earnings, **21**, 1110
   restrictions, **21**, 1109
   tariff, **21**, 1108, 1109
income support, interaction with, **21**, 1075, 1104
large or expensive accommodation, **21**, 1106
legislation, **21**, 1103
liable for payments, claimant must be, **21**, 1105
married or cohabiting couple, **21**, 1104
maximum, **21**, 1117

Housing benefit—*continued*
means-tested benefit, as, **21**, 1101
mobile home site charge, **21**, 1105
moving home, where claimant, **21**, 1107
non-dependants, deductions for, **21**, 1114
Northern Ireland, **21**, 1101
regulations, **21**, 1101
review—
   boards, **21**, 1120
   judicial, **21**, 1122
   local authority, **21**, 1119
   scope for, **21**, 1118
   setting aside decision, **21**, 1121
self-employed earners, **21**, 1111
service charges, **21**, 1113
shared accommodation, **21**, 1104
single person, **21**, 1104
social security benefits, disregarded, **21**, 1110
student, **21**, 1112
sub-tenant, **21**, 1105
tariff income, **21**, 1108, 1109
two homes, in respect of, **21**, 1107
unreasonably high rent, **21**, 1106, 1113
violence, home unoccupied through fear of, **21**,
   1107
Housing Corporation
functions of Scottish sector assumed by Scottish
   Homes, **11**, 1921
Housing list
generally, **11**, 1935
   rules for admitting applicants to, **11**, 1935
housing associations, **11**, 1935
priority of applicants, **11**, 1935
publication of rules governing admission to, **11**,
   1935
reasonable preference to be given to certain
   categories, **11**, 1935
tenant selection, **11**, 1935
Housing support grants
aggregate amounts, **11**, 1911, 1912
apportionment, **11**, 1913
generally, **11**, 1910
housing support grant order, **11**, 1912
payment of, **11**, 1914
Housing treatment areas
housing action areas replacing, **11**, 1996
Housing trust
building society's power to invest in and support,
   3, 369
Hovercraft
Athens Convention not applicable to, **21**, 727
carriage of goods by, **21**, 720
collision regulations, **21**, 332
conduct committed in, extradition procedure, **12**,
   515, 568
legislation for, powers of, **1**, 410
maritime lien, giving rise to, **1**, 413
meaning, **21**, 720
motor vehicle, treatment as, **20**, 409
movement, control, **7**, 1240
noise, **9**, 1287
salvage subject, as, **21**, 439
ships, treated as, **1**, 410
stores for, VAT zero-rating, **7**, 1436

Hovercraft—*continued*
suppression of broadcasting from, **17**, 9
telecommunications apparatus, **16**, 1928
temporarily within United Kingdom, patented product in, **18**, 865
wreck from, **18**, 557
Hovering
'hovering' Acts, **21**, 35
innocent passage and, right of, **21**, 6
Hughes Commission
Law Society control of legal aid, criticism of, **13**, 1006
summary cause, **6**, 168
Human body and organs
donation, **8**, 616
transplant, for, **3**, 509
Human habitation, fitness for
landlord's obligations as to, **13**, 260
Human Immunodeficiency Virus (HIV)
legislation as to, **19**, 508, 509
Human remains
ownership of not recognised, **7**, 463, 465
theft of, **7**, 333
See also VIOLATION OF SEPULCHRES
Human rights
aliens' rights, **12**, 6
apartheid, **12**, 5
armed forces, freedom of, **12**, 83
arrest or detention—
alcoholic, of, **12**, 29
arbitrary, freedom from, Universal Declaration of Human Rights, **12**, 4*n*
compensation for wrongful, **12**, 29
compulsory residence, **12**, 40
detention—
deportation, prior to, **12**, 38
end of detention period, what constitutes, **12**, 32
extradition, prior to, **12**, 37
indeterminate length, **12**, 35
lawfulness to be decided speedily, **12**, 33
minors, of, **12**, 39
parole, life prisoners, **12**, 35
setting off against custodial sentence, **12**, 34
unsound mind, persons of, **12**, 41
vagrancy, **12**, 42
voluntary surrender to, **12**, 42
without trial, **12**, 32
wrongful, **15**, 435
drug addict, of, **12**, 29
files, access to, **12**, 36
general rules, **12**, 29
infectious diseases, to prevent spread of, **12**, 29
legitimate detention, what constitutes, **12**, 29, 30
minor, of, **12**, 29
reasons for, obligation to give, **12**, 29
remand, prolonged detention on, **12**, 32
right to be brought before judicial person or body, **12**, 29, 30
promptness, **12**, 30, 32
trial within reasonable time, entitlement to, **12**, 32, 46, 47
unauthorised entrants, **12**, 29

Human rights—*continued*
arrest or detention—*continued*
unsound mind, persons of, **12**, 29
vagrant, of, **12**, 29
artistic expression, freedom of, **12**, 73
audi alteram partem, **10**, 95
See also NATURAL JUSTICE
background, **5**, 315; **12**, 2, 3
capital punishment, **12**, 6, 26
child care, **3**, 1344; **12**, 64
civil and political, **12**, 6
International Covenant on Civil and Political Rights, **12**, 4
Conference on Security and Co-operation in Europe, **12**, 4
conscience, freedom of, **12**, 4, 4*n*, 6, 72, 73, 78–84
corporal punishment, **12**, 26, 90, 91
correspondence, private, **12**, 6, 62
court, right of access to, **12**, 44
cultural life, right to participation in, **12**, 4*n*
International Covenant on Economic, Social and Cultural Rights, **12**, 4
declaration of—
entrenched, cannot be, **5**, 313
international, **5**, 315
legal effect, lack of, **5**, 314
discrimination, *see* DISCRIMINATION; RACIAL DISCRIMINATION; SEX DISCRIMINATION
education, right to, **12**, 4*n*, 87, 89–92
elections, right to free, **12**, 87, 93
employment, **12**, 5, 7
European Commission of Human Rights, *see* EUROPEAN COMMISSION OF HUMAN RIGHTS
European Convention for the Protection of Human Rights and Fundamental Freedoms—
adoption of, **5**, 315, 317; **7**, 737; **12**, 6
effect of, **12**, 6, 94–96
enforcement, **12**, 6, 10
generally, **10**, 2, 2*n*
historical background, **5**, 315; **12**, 2, 3
national law, relationship with, **5**, 313–316, 357; **10**, 2, 4, 316; **12**, 6, 8, 94–96; **19**, 652, 656
petitions under, *see* EUROPEAN COURT OF HUMAN RIGHTS
prospectivity of criminal law, **7**, 4; **12**, 6, 61
source of European law, as, **10**, 74
supervision of, **12**, 13, 94
European Social Charter, **12**, 7
euthanasia, **12**, 25
exile, arbitrary, **12**, 4*n*
expression, freedom of, **12**, 4*n*, 6, 73, 74, 78–84; **18**, 1454
extradition, **12**, 26, 37
family and family life, **12**, 4*n*, 6, 7, 62, 63, 65, 71, 78–84
financial means, discrimination as to, **12**, 86
forced labour, **12**, 5, 6, 28
freedom, restrictions, **12**, 78–84
freedom of association, **12**, 6, 73, 75–77
fundamental, as general principle of Community law, **10**, 94, 95
genocide, **12**, 5

Human rights—*continued*
hearing, right to fair and public—
  defence—
    interpreter, assistance of, **12**, 43, 51
    legal assistance, **12**, 43, 52
    preparation of, **12**, 43
    witnesses, examination of, **12**, 43, 55–59
  extra-judicial assurances, **12**, 60
  fair, public trial as guarantee of, **12**, 49
  fair and public, entitlement to—
    European Convention on Human Rights, **12**, 43–60
    interpreter, right to services of, **12**, 51
    legal assistance, **12**, 52
    Universal Declaration of Human Rights, **12**, 4n
    witnesses, **12**, 55–59
  in absentia, **12**, 50
  independence and impartiality, **12**, 48
  innocence, presumption of, **12**, 43, 53
  interpreter, use of, **12**, 43, 51
  judge, impartiality, **12**, 48
  judicial review, right to, **12**, 54
  legal assistance, **12**, 43, 52
    payment for, **12**, 43
    person not wishing to defend himself, **12**, 52
  press, exclusion from judgment, **12**, 43
  public—
    exclusion from judgment, **12**, 43
    first hearing, **12**, 50
    questions of law, **12**, 50
    trial, as guarantee of fair, **12**, 49
  within reasonable time, right to, **12**, 32, 46
    commencement of period, **12**, 46
    reasonableness, what constitutes, **12**, 47
  witnesses, examination of, **12**, 43, 55–59
home, **12**, 6, 62, 68, 70
homosexuality, **12**, 66
illegitimacy, discrimination as to, **12**, 86
immigration, **12**, 65
innocence, presumption of, **12**, 4n, 43, 53
international efforts to guarantee, **12**, 5
international law, **19**, 694
judicial review, right to, **12**, 54
judiciary, impartiality, **12**, 48, 82
justice, fair administration, **12**, 6
language, discrimination as to, **12**, 85, 86
law—
  accessible and foreseeable, **12**, 79
  'legitimate aim', **12**, 80
legal aid, **12**, 15, 19, 44, 52
legal assistance, right to, **10**, 95; **12**, 43, 52
liberty, **12**, 4n, 6, 29–42
life, right to, **12**, 4n, 6, 25
marry, right to, **12**, 6, 71
meaning, **12**, 1
medical assistance, **12**, 7
minority groups, **12**, 2, 2n, 85
movement, freedom of, **12**, 4n; **16**, 1205n
nationality, freedom of, **12**, 4n
natural justice, *see* NATURAL JUSTICE
non bis in idem, **10**, 95

Human rights—*continued*
opinion and expression, **12**, 4n, 6
passports, proposed reform, **16**, 1234
peaceful assembly—
  association, and, **12**, 73, 75–84
  right to, **12**, 6
policing, **12**, 83; **16**, 1806
political opinion, discrimination as to, **12**, 85
press, freedom of, **12**, 73, 74
private life, respect for, **12**, 6, 62, 63, 66–70
prisoners' rights, **12**, 69; **16**, 1495
property, rights as to, **12**, 4n, 87, 88
public emergency, times of, **12**, 31
punishment, **12**, 5, 26, 27
records, confidential personal, access to, **12**, 63
religious toleration, **3**, 1635n, 1676, 1677; **12**, 4, 4n, 6, 72, 73, 78–86
residence, freedom of, **12**, 4n
rest and leisure, right to, **12**, 4n
security of person, right to, **12**, 4n, 29–42
self-incrimination, protection from, **10**, 95
servitude or slavery, freedom from, **12**, 2, 4n, 6, 8
slavery, freedom from, **12**, 2, 4n, 6, 8
social and economic, **12**, 7
Steering Committee for, **12**, 13
surveillance and intelligence storage, **16**, 1802
telephone—
  private—
    conversations, **12**, 68
    unlawfully obtained used as evidence, **12**, 60
  tapping, **12**, 68
thought, freedom of, **12**, 4, 4n, 6, 72, 73, 78–84
torture, *see* TORTURE
trade union—
  closed shop agreements, **12**, 77
  freedom of association, **12**, 76
  membership, discrimination, **12**, 86
transsexuality, **12**, 67
trial, fair, **12**, 43, 49–51, 54
Universal Declaration of Human Rights, **12**, 4
war, in time of, **12**, 31
work, right to, **12**, 4n
Hume, Baron David
'authoritative writings'—
  inclusion in canon, **22**, 441
commencement, calculation by *naturalis computatio*, **22**, 820
Commentaries, **7**, 2; **22**, 441
  attempt, **7**, 161, 162, 164, 168
  breach of the peace, **7**, 442
  coercion, **7**, 202
  Declaratory Power, **7**, 6–9, 11, 12
  dole, **7**, 58–60
  extortion, **7**, 398
  fireraising, **7**, 415, 417
  insanity, **7**, 119
  intoxication, **7**, 126
  mens rea, **7**, 58–60
  mobbing and rioting, **7**, 424, 425, 427, 432, 441
  murder, the intention to cause harm, **7**, 269
  necessity, **7**, 200
  omissions, **7**, 38
  superior orders, defence of acting on, **7**, 206
  theft, **7**, 321
delict, **15**, 216

Hume, Baron David—*continued*
equity and criminal law, declaratory power of court to designate an action criminal, **22**, 423, 424
Lectures on the Law of Scotland, **18**, 1, 4; **22**, 441
negotiorum gestio, **15**, 112, 113
real rights, on, **18**, 3
special authority of writings, **22**, 437, 440
treatment of property law, **18**, 1
validity of acts performed on Sunday, **22**, 817
Hunter Report, **13**, 591
Hunting
Day Trespass Act, application to, **11**, 821
Husband and wife
adherence, **10**, 839
agency, **10**, 843
aliment, *see* ALIMENT
bigamy, *see* BIGAMY
breach of confidence, **18**, 1466
delict proceedings against spouse, **10**, 844
disqualification between, **25**, 674
divorce, *see* DIVORCE
domicile of married woman, **17**, 197, 200
donation between, **8**, 603, 608, 645
   inter virum et uxorem, **8**, 602, 604, 608
   presumption against, **8**, 626
duty to protect spouse, implied, **7**, 41
engagement—
   effect of, **10**, 80
   property disputes, **10**, 803
foreign decrees, recognition of, **17**, 210
harbouring, treatment of offence, **7**, 562
heritable security granted by wife, **20**, 221
inheritance tax, **25**, 56
judicial separation, *see* JUDICIAL SEPARATION
jurisdiction, **17**, 210
litigation between wife and third party, expenses of, **10**, 843
marriage, *see* MARRIAGE
married couple's allowance, **19**, 1518
matrimonial home, *see* MATRIMONIAL HOME
name, wife's, **10**, 842
rape, marital, **7**, 294, 302
reset, whether wife guilty of, **7**, 392; **10**, 841
residence, **10**, 838
taxation—
   advantages, **10**, 891
   blind person's relief, **10**, 891
   capital gains tax, **10**, 892
      disadvantage of marriage, **10**, 892
   generally, **19**, 1517
   husband only earning, **10**, 894n
   income tax, **10**, 891
   independent taxation, **10**, 890, 891
   inheritance tax, **10**, 893; **25**, 56
      transfers between spouses, **10**, 893
   loan interest, provisions as to, **10**, 891
   married couple's allowance, **10**, 891; **19**, 1518
   partially transferable allowance, **10**, 890, 894
   pre-1990 situation, **10**, 890, 890n
   property held in common, **10**, 891
   reform, **10**, 890–894
   wife only earning, **10**, 894n
wife's income, deceased's liability to tax, **25**, 972

Husband and wife—*continued*
wills and succession—
   courtesty and terce, abolition of, **25**, 702
   witness, spouse of party to action as, **10**, 845
See also MARRIAGE; SPOUSE; WIFE
Hybrid Bill
amendment, made hybrid by, **19**, 130
Examiners of Petitions for Private Bills, **19**, 125
   reference to, **19**, 125
identification, **19**, 125
meaning, **19**, 2, 124
Parliamentary procedure, **19**, 124–130
petitions against, **19**, 128, 129
select committees, **19**, 129
Standing Orders—
   compliance with, **19**, 126
   non-compliance with, **19**, 127
Hybrid instrument
application of procedure, **19**, 131
Hybrid Instruments Committee, **19**, 132
Hydro-electric installation, *see* ELECTRICITY
Hydrocarbon oil
excise duty—
   aviation gasoline, **7**, 1067
   coal tar, **7**, 1067n
   deferred payments, **7**, 1088
   drawback, **7**, 1070
   duty-free oil, **7**, 1068
   fishing boat, fuel for, **7**, 1069
   furnace fuel, **7**, 1069
   generally, **19**, 1543
   horticultural producers, used by, **7**, 1069
   Hydrocarbon Oil Duties Act (1979), **7**, 1067
   lifeboat, fuel for, **7**, 1069
   light and heavy oils, **7**, 1067
   manufacturing ingredient, hydrocarbon oil used as, **7**, 1070
   meaning, **7**, 1067n
   mixed oils, **7**, 1067
   petrol substitutes, **7**, 1067
   petroleum, **7**, 1067n
   power methylated spirits, **7**, 1067n
   rebates, duty, **7**, 1069
   regulations concerning, **7**, 1071
   reliefs on duty, **7**, 1069
   road fuel gas, **7**, 1067
   ships in home waters, fuel for, **7**, 1069
   unleaded petrol, **7**, 1069
exportation, drawback of duty, **7**, 1070
meaning, **7**, 1067n
mixed, **7**, 1067
shipment as stores, **7**, 1070
warehousing for use as stores, **7**, 1070
Hydrochloric acid gas
alkali works, emission from, **9**, 1112
Hydropathic establishment
hotel, regarded as, **11**, 1708
Hygiene
food, *see* FOOD
private markets, **14**, 526
Hypnotic phenomena
public entertainment, for—
   age limit, **3**, 1232
public entertainment, for, licensing, **14**, 523

Hypothec
bottomry, bond of, **20**, 102; **21**, 479
conventional, **21**, 479
delivery not required by, **13**, 1759
distinguishing features, **20**, 7, 101
landlord, of, operation of, **5**, 903; **8**, 377, 378,
   see also LANDLORD
lien distinguished, **20**, 68, 101
maritime, **20**, 101*n*; **21**, 479
   ship, arrest *in rem*, **8**, 322
maritime lien, *see* MARITIME LIEN
meaning, **20**, 7; **21**, 479
moveable property, as security over, **20**, 101
nature of, **20**, 101
pledge compared, **20**, 101
possession, **20**, 3
   creditor, by not required, **20**, 101
preference, right of in insolvency, distinguished,
   20, 101
respondentia bond, **20**, 102; **21**, 479
right in security implied by law, **20**, 7

Hypothec—*continued*
rights of, **11**, 1108
Scots law, limited acceptance in, **20**, 102
solicitor's, **13**, 1193, 1195; **20**, 102
   action abandoned or settled by client, **20**, 107
   compensation not pleadable by party liable for
      expenses, **20**, 105
   enforcement, **20**, 104
   expenses awarded to client, confined to, **20**,
      103
   generally, **20**, 103
   implied agreement as basis of, **20**, 103
   implied assignation as basis of, **20**, 103
   right of solicitor to be sisted as party to action,
      20, 107
   sequestration of solicitor, **20**, 103
   statutory order for satisfaction, **20**, 106
   where court decision reversed on appeal, **20**, 103
tacit, **21**, 479
Hypothetical tenancy
See VALUATION FOR RATING

I

Ice
pavement on, liability for, **20**, 700n
roads authority duties as to, **20**, 665
Ice clause
time charterparty, **21**, 640
voyage charterparty, **21**, 618
ICE Conditions
building contracts, **3**, 12, 23, 27, 60, 124, 168
Ice cream
advertisements for, **11**, 364
choc ice or bar, **11**, 362
composition, **11**, 364
heat treatment of, **11**, 354
labelling, **11**, 364
manufacture of, **11**, 364
Parev ice, **11**, 364
premises and vehicles used for sale, registration,
   11, 364
Iceberg
peril of the sea, as, **21**, 551
Iceland
Code of Magnus 'the Law-Mender', **24**, 303
Grågås law code, **24**, 303
seabed and foreshore, ownership of, **24**, 316
Idea
copyright in does not exist, **18**, 941, 942
patent not grantable in respect of, **18**, 825
Identification
See EVIDENCE
Identification parade
automatic legal aid, **13**, 1054
criminal legal aid, **13**, 1052
   duty solicitor, **13**, 1053
defence, preparation of, **17**, 655
irregularity, police, by, **7**, 496
personal search, **16**, 1797
procedure, **17**, 606
refusal to take part in, **17**, 606
Identity
detention on arrival for identification, **12**, 167
examination on arrival to establish, **12**, 162
Idiot
disqualification for parliamentary candidature, **15**,
   1055
meaning, **14**, 1401; **15**, 1055
mental disorder, meaning, **14**, 1401
Ignorantia juris neminem excusat
unjust enrichment, **15**, 17–20
Illegal entrant
administrative removal, **12**, 195, 198
control of departure decisions, limits on appeals
   relating to, **12**, 341
deportation order, **12**, 202
illegal entrant, definition, **12**, 198
illegal entry, offence as, **12**, 185
Illegitimacy
abolition of status of, **12**, 1268; **25**, 664, 699
decree of declarator, **19**, 1430
discrimination, **12**, 86

Illegitimacy—*continued*
executor, duties of, **25**, 1106
illegitimate child—
   adoption, **10**, 1191
   aliment, **10**, 1177, 1235–1239
   British citizenship, **10**, 1186
   children's hearing, attendance of parents at, **3**,
      1321
   citizenship of, **10**, 1186
   class gift to, **25**, 843
   coat of arms of, differences in, **11**, 1618
   consanguinity and capacity to marry, **10**, 817
   curators, **10**, 1085, 1089
   custody, **10**, 1178
      at common law, **10**, 1277
      statutory intervention, **10**, 1278
   decree of declarator, **19**, 1430
   discharge of obligation, **10**, 1236
   domicile and nationality, **10**, 1223
   domicile of origin, **10**, 1186
   duration of obligation, **10**, 1238
   father of, position of, **10**, 1187
   filius nullius, **10**, 1176
   financial support, liability for, **22**, 6
   generally, **10**, 1147, 1148, 1177; **11**, 1617, 1618
   historical development of illegitimacy, **10**,
      1174–1184
   international law, **10**, 1183
   legal equality of legitimate and illegitimate
      children, **10**, 1185–1186
   legitim right to, **25**, 699, 788
   legitimated, **19**, 1443
   marriage, prohibited degrees, **10**, 817, 1180,
      1219
   meaning, **10**, 1174
   modern position, **10**, 1185–1187
   parents, obligations of, **10**, 1235
   public disabilities, **10**, 1175
   quantification, **10**, 1237
   reform of law, **10**, 1181–1184; **22**, 690
   registration of birth, **19**, 1439
   relationship by illegitimate link—
      incest, **10**, 1180
      marriage, bar to, **10**, 817, 1180, 1219
   relatives other than parents, non-liability, **10**,
      1239
   succession by, **10**, 1179, 1220; **25**, 663
incidental finding of, jurisdiction of sheriff court,
   4, 5
legitimation, **19**, 1443
matriculation of father's coat of arms, **11**, 1617
reform of law, **22**, 690
registration of birth, **19**, 1439
status, action relating to, **4**, 68
trust created by person of illegitimate birth, **24**, 14
Illiterate testator
notarial execution, **25**, 725
Illustrator
public lending right, **13**, 1508

Immigration

abode, right of, *see* ABODE

administrative removal, *see* ADMINISTRATIVE
  REMOVAL

admission—
  meaning, **12**, 146
  temporary, **12**, 119, 146, 168, 169
    authority for, **12**, 168
    breach of conditions, **12**, 187
    refusal of leave to enter, following, **12**, 170
  in temporary capacity, **12**, 146

adoption, settlement, family reunion or creation
  by, **12**, 279

amnesty, illegal entrant, for, **12**, 112

appeals—
  adjudicators, **12**, 331
  after entry cases, representation by member of
    Parliament, **12**, 375
  aliens, aplication to, **12**, 329
  appealable decisions, **12**, 336–343
    notice of, **12**, 345
  Commonwealth citizens, application to, **12**,
    329
  control after entry decisions, limits on, **12**, 340
  control before entry decisions, limits on, **12**,
    338
  control on entry decisions, limits on, **12**, 339
  departure decisions, limits on, **12**, 341–343
  deportation orders, limits on control of
    departure decisions, **12**, 342
  discretion of Secretary of State or officer,
    against, **12**, 333
  first stage appeals, **12**, 345–356
    burden of proof, **12**, 354
    determination, **12**, 351, 356
    evidence, **12**, 353
    explanatory statement, respondent, by, **12**,
      349
    grounds for, **12**, 333
    hearing, **12**, 352
      in absence of a party, **12**, 355
    nature of, **12**, 333
    notice of, **12**, 346
      appealable decision, **12**, 345
    parties to, **12**, 347
    preliminary issues, **12**, 350
    record of proceedings, **12**, 356
    summary determination, **12**, 351
    time limits, **12**, 348
  forgery as limit on, **12**, 337
  further appeals—
    determination, **12**, 363, 366
    disposal of application, **12**, 360
    evidence, **12**, 365
    hearing, **12**, 364
      determination without, **12**, 363
    Immigration Appeal Tribunal, to, **12**, 357
    leave for, **12**, 358
    nature of, **12**, 334
    notice of application, **12**, 361
    parties to, **12**, 362
    summary determination, **12**, 363
  illegal entrants, limits on control of departure
    decisions, **12**, 341

Immigration—*continued*
appeals—*continued*
  Immigration Appeal Tribunal, *see* IMMIGRATION
    APPEAL TRIBUNAL
  members of Parliament, representations by, **12**,
    329, 370–376
    administrative removal, in respect of, **12**, 376
    after entry cases, **12**, 375
    deportation, in respect of, **12**, 376
    entry, where refusal of, **12**, 374
    entry clearance, where refusal of, **12**, 373
    Home Office guidelines, **12**, 371
  non-appealable decisions, **12**, 344
  procedure—
    burden of proof, **12**, 354
    determination—
      first stage appeals, **12**, 351, 356
      further stage appeals, **12**, 363, 366
    evidence—
      first stage appeals, **12**, 353
      further stage appeals, **12**, 365
    explanatory statement by respondent—
      first stage appeals, **12**, 349
    first stage appeals, **12**, 345–356
    further appeals, **12**, 357–366
    hearing—
      absence of a party—
        first stage appeals, **12**, 355
      determination without—
        first stage appeals, **12**, 351
        further appeals, **12**, 363
      first stage appeals, **12**, 352
      further stage appeals, **12**, 364
    notice—
      appealable decisions, **12**, 345
      first stage appeals, **12**, 345, 346
      time limits, **12**, 348, 359
    preliminary issues—
      first stage appeals, **12**, 350
    record of proceedings—
      first stage appeals, **12**, 356
    Secretary of State, on reference from, **12**, 367
    'security' deportation cases—
      criticisms of, **12**, 369
      'Three Wise Men', representations to, **12**,
        368
    summary determination—
      first stage appeals, **12**, 351
      further stage appeals, **12**, 363
    time limit—
      first stage appeals, **12**, 348
      further appeal, **12**, 359
  refusal of entry cases, representation by
    member of Parliament, **12**, 374
  refusal of entry clearance cases, representation
    by member of Parliament, **12**, 373
  removal destination, limits on control of
    departure decisions, **12**, 343
  requirement to depart, variation, **12**, 329
  'security' deportation cases, **12**, 335, 368, 369
  success rate, **12**, 329
  system—
    appellate authorities, **12**, 330
    criticism of, **12**, 329

Immigration—*continued*
appeals—*continued*
  system—*continued*
    leave to enter or remain, effects of appeal,
      12, 329, 332
    personnel, **12**, 331
    Three Wise Men, *see* THREE WISE MEN
    wrong identity as limit on, **12**, 337
arrest, constable or immigration officer, by, **12**,
  168
arrival—
  detention on—
    bail, **12**, 169
    examination, for, **12**, 167
  examination on, **12**, 162
    conduct of, **12**, 164
    detention for, **12**, 167
    documents, declaration of, **12**, 162
    failure to comply with requirements, **12**, 166
    medical, **12**, 165
    search warrant and arrest, **12**, 168
  meaning, **12**, 146
artists, **12**, 149, 151, 154, 175, 254, 255, 256, 257
asylum, *see* ASYLUM
au pairs, **12**, 149, 151, 154, 175, 291, 310–313
authorisation, meaning, **12**, 146
border controls, prevention of terrorism powers,
  12, 133
British citizen, abode, right of, **12**, 118
British Dependent Territories citizen, **12**, 107,
  120, 121, 132
British National (Overseas), **12**, 120, 121, 132,
  220*n*
British Overseas citizen, **12**, 107, 120, 121, 132
British protected person, **12**, 120, 132
British subject, leave to enter, **12**, 120, 120*n*, 121
businessmen, **12**, 175, 250–253
child—
  adoption, family reunion by settlement, **12**, 279
  born in United Kingdom who are not British,
    12, 127
    entry clearance, **12**, 151
    Immigration Rules, **12**, 149
    settlement, family reunion or creation by,
      12, 284
  dependant, as, **12**, 264
  deportation of parent, **12**, 208
  European Union law, 'primary right' holder,
    of, **12**, 223
  illegitimate, family reunion by, **12**, 279
  meaning, **12**, 279
  parent, meaning, **12**, 279
  polygamous wives and widows, of, **12**, 118*n*
  settled Commonwealth citizen, of, **12**, 125
  settlement, family reunion or creation by, *see*
    SETTLEMENT (IMMIGRATION)
citizenship, acquisition—
  naturalisation, by, **12**, 121
  registration, by, **12**, 121
citizenship status matched with legal rights, **14**,
  1903
common law—
  generally, **12**, 108
  nineteenth-century, **12**, 105

Immigration—*continued*
common travel area—
  exclusions from, Secretary of State's powers,
    12, 122
  journeys outwith—
    leave to enter, **12**, 119
    prevention of terrorism powers, **12**, 133
    ships and aircraft, **12**, 133
  local journeys, **12**, 122
  meaning, **12**, 122
Commonwealth citizen, rights of, **14**, 1902, 1903
  See also COMMONWEALTH CITIZEN
consuls and their families, **12**, 130
control—
  adjudicators, appointment of, **12**, 139
  airports, **12**, 161
  bail, application for, **12**, 169
  breach of conditions and requirements, **12**, 186,
    187
    deportation following, **12**, 205
  central, **12**, 138–140
  declaration of, **12**, 162
  definitions, **12**, 146, 147
  departure, of, *see* DEPARTURE
  deportation, *see* DEPORTATION
  detention on arrival—
    bail, **12**, 169
  documents—
    search for, **12**, 162
  entry clearance, *see* ENTRY CLEARANCE
  entry clearance officers, **12**, 141
  entry requirements, **12**, 161
  examination on arrival, **12**, 162
    identification, **12**, 167
    non-disclosure of material facts, **12**, 166
  examining officers, **12**, 145
  government departments, role of, **12**, 140
  groups exempted from—
    air crew, **12**, 129
    armed forces, members of certain, **12**, 131;
      14, 1905
    consuls, **12**, 130
    deportation orders, **12**, 132
    diplomats, **12**, 130; **14**, 1905
    international acts, covered by, **12**, 130, 130*n*
    leave to enter, **12**, 128
    passports relevant to, **12**, 132
    seamen, **12**, 129
    settlement, relationship to, **12**, 128
    statutory instrument, by, **12**, 128
    unlawful entry, **12**, 132
  Home Office, powers of, **12**, 138
  hotel records, **12**, 184
  identification of passenger, **12**, 167
  identity, establishment of, **12**, 162
  illegal entry, **12**, 185
  Immigration Appeal Tribunal, *see* IMMIGRATION
    APPEAL TRIBUNAL
  immigration officers, **12**, 142
  Immigration Rules, issue of, **12**, 138
    See also IMMIGRATION RULES
  institutions of, **12**, 138–145
  landing card, requirement to complete, **12**, 163
  local, **12**, 141–145

Immigration—*continued*
control—*continued*
  Lord Chancellor, role of, **12**, 139
  medical inspectors, **12**, 143
  nationality, establishment of, **12**, 162
  overstaying, **12**, 186
    tracing overstayers, **12**, 188
  passport or travel document, **12**, 162
    endorsement, **12**, 120
  phases of, **12**, 148
  police, **12**, 144
    Home Office control, **12**, 138
  ports, **12**, 161
  post-entry controls, **12**, 185–191
    employment, **12**, 191
    generally, **12**, 189
    'passport raids', **12**, 190
    police checks, **12**, 190
    unofficial, **12**, 189
    welfare state facilities, **12**, 191
  private security firms, contracts with, **12**, 138
  Secretary of State, primary responsibility of, **12**, 138
  sponsorship, **12**, 160
  temporary admission, **12**, 119, 168, 169
  temporary release, **12**, 146, 169, 187
court decisions, **12**, 113
criminal record, refusal of leave to enter due to, **12**, 171
deception, refusal of leave to enter following, **12**, 171
dentists in postgraduate training, **12**, 292, 295, 298, 300
departure—
  control of, **12**, 147, 148
    administrative removal, *see* ADMINISTRATIVE REMOVAL
    curtailment of stay, **12**, 215
    embarkation, place and manner of, requirements as to, **12**, 192
    embarkation card, requirements as to, **12**, 192
    extradition, *see* EXTRADITION
    hostage order, *see* HOSTAGE ORDER
    mental patient, removal of, **12**, 216
    passport, endorsement of, **12**, 193
    safety order, *see* SAFETY ORDER
    supervised departure, **12**, 215
    voluntary departure, **12**, 215
deportation, *see* DEPORTATION
detention—
  administrative removal, for, **12**, 199
  arrival, on, **12**, 167, 169
  deportation decision, following, **12**, 211, 213
  release, temporary, **12**, 146, 169, 187
diplomat, **12**, 130; **14**, 1905
  family of, **12**, 130
  servants and staff, **12**, 247
discretion of Secretary of State or officer, appeal against, **12**, 333
doctors in postgraduate training, **12**, 292, 295, 298, 300
employment—
  breach of conditions, **12**, 188
  businessmen, permit exemption, **12**, 154

Immigration—*continued*
employment—*continued*
  change of, **12**, 248
    artists, **12**, 256
    businessmen, **12**, 252
    self-employed, **12**, 252
    writers, **12**, 256
  entry clearance, liability for, **12**, 151
  Immigration Rules, **12**, 149
  leave to enter, conditions imposed by, **12**, 174
  leave to remain, **12**, 140
  migration for reasons of, **12**, 102
    'replacement labour', **12**, 102
  permit-free—
    artists, **12**, 254–257
    businessmen, **12**, 250–253
    change of employment, **12**, 248
    entry clearance, **12**, 151, 246
    extension of leave, **12**, 249
    Immigration Rules, **12**, 149, 246–249
    independent means, persons of, **12**, 258–260
    meaning, **12**, 247
    police registration conditions, **12**, 175
    self-employed, **12**, 250–253
    writers, **12**, 254–257
  post-entry control, **12**, 191
  self-employed—
    entry clearance, **12**, 151
    Immigration Rules, **12**, 149
    work permit exemption, **12**, 154
  students, **12**, 296
    dependants of, **12**, 302
  visitors, **12**, 305
  work permit, *see* WORK PERMIT
enter, leave to—
  appeal, effect of, **12**, 332
  appeals system, effect of, **12**, 329, 332
  asylum, grant of, **12**, 318
  authorisation by Secretary of State, **12**, 119
  breach of conditions, **12**, 188
  Channel Islands or Isle of Man, entry via, **12**, 123
  children, family reunion or creation by settlement, **12**, 280
  conditions, **12**, 119
    variation of, *see* variation *below*
  curtailment, general considerations for, **12**, 181
  deception, obtained by, **12**, 119
  departure—
    nullifying, **12**, 120
    outwith common travel area, **12**, 119
    returning resident status, **12**, 120
  deportation order, **12**, 119
  duration, **12**, 119
    extension, **12**, 119
    removal of time limit, **12**, 119
    restriction, **12**, 119
  employment—
    conditions, imposition of, **12**, 174
    restrictions, **12**, 119
  fiancé or fiancée, **12**, 274–277
    variation after marriage, **12**, 277
  grant of, **12**, 170
  groups exempted from immigration control, **12**, 128

Immigration—*continued*
enter, leave to—*continued*
  Immigration Rules, **12**, 170, 240
  indefinite, **12**, 120, 173, 177
    absences and re-entry, **12**, 120
    deportation order, **12**, 120, 177
    prevention of terrorism, **12**, 177
    restrictions, **12**, 120
  lapse, **12**, 176, 177
  limited, **12**, 173
    police registration, **12**, 175
  offences in relation to, refusal following, **12**, 171
  police registration, **12**, 119, 175, 183, 236
  Prevention of Terrorism Act, subject to, **12**, 119
  refugee—
    appeal against refusal, **12**, 322
    seeking in different capacity, **12**, 317, 319
  refusal of, **12**, 170
    administrative removal, **12**, 197
    entry clearance—
      person holding, **12**, 172
      person not holding, **12**, 170
    refugee, **12**, 322
    work permit holders, **12**, 242
  Republic of Ireland, entry via, **12**, 124
  returning residents, **12**, 176
  settled, meaning, **12**, 120
  settlement—
    family reunion or creation by, **12**, 270, 280
    variation for, **12**, 182
  sponsorship, **12**, 160
  spouse, family reunion or creation by settlement, **12**, 270
  temporary absences, **12**, 119
  temporary admission distinguished, **12**, 119
  time limit, **12**, 173
    variation, **12**, 177
  variation, **12**, 119, 149, 175, 177
    appeals, **12**, 329
    application for, **12**, 178
    decision to be given in writing, **12**, 178
    lapse, **12**, 179
    marriage, after, **12**, 277
    outside the rules, **12**, 177, 318
    refusal of, general considerations, **12**, 181
    settlement, for, **12**, 182
    sponsorship, **12**, 160
    without application, **12**, 180
  visitors, **12**, 307
  work permits, **12**, 154, 244
entry, meaning, **12**, 146
entry, right of—
  Commonwealth citizens, **12**, 125
  European Union nationals, **12**, 225, 236
    families of, **12**, 236
    police registration, **12**, 236
    'primary right' holders, **12**, 236
    'secondary right' holders, **12**, 236
entry clearance—
  application for, **12**, 152
  artists, **12**, 254, 255
  burden of proof, **12**, 152, 153

Immigration—*continued*
entry clearance—*continued*
  businessmen, **12**, 250, 251
  categories leading to settlement, **12**, 241
  certificate of entitlement, **12**, 153
  certificate of patriality, **12**, 153
  change of circumstances since issue, **12**, 172
  children, family reunion or creation by settlement, **12**, 280
  Commonwealth citizens with UK ancestry, **12**, 261
  dependants, **12**, 264, 265
  false representation, **12**, 172
  family reunion and creation by settlement, **12**, 268
  fiancés or fiancées, **12**, 274
  form of, **12**, 150
  Immigration Rules categories, **12**, 240
  independent means, persons of, **12**, 151, 258, 259
  material fact, failure to disclose, **12**, 172
  meaning, **12**, 150
  passenger holding, refusal of leave to enter, **12**, 172
  passenger not holding, refusal of leave to enter, **12**, 171
  permit-free employment, **12**, 246
  refugee travel document, **12**, 151*n*
  refusal of entry, grounds for, **12**, 150
  refusal of, **12**, 152
    representations by member of Parliament, **12**, 373
  right of abode, **12**, 151, 153
    proof of, **12**, 153
  self-employed, **12**, 250, 251
  settlement, family reunion or creation by, **12**, 270, 280
  special vouchers holders, **12**, 159
  spouse, family reunion or creation by settlement, **12**, 270
  students, **12**, 292–294
  validity, **12**, 150
  visitors, **12**, 305
  who needs, **12**, 151
  work permit operating as, **12**, 244
  writers, **12**, 254, 255
EU citizens, *see* EUROPEAN UNION
EU law, **12**, 219*ff*
European Convention on Human Rights, **12**, 65
examination on arrival—
  conduct of, **12**, 164
  detention for, **12**, 167
  documents—
    declaration of, **12**, 162
    search for, **12**, 162
  failure to comply with requirements, **12**, 166
  medical, **12**, 165
  search warrant and arrest, **12**, 168
extradition, *see* EXTRADITION
family unification, **12**, 102
foreign workers, **12**, 101
Hong Kong citizens, **12**, 101
identity, establishment of, **12**, 162
illegal entry, **12**, 185
  amnesty, grant of, **12**, 112

Immigration—_continued_
Immigration Act, sponsor under, income support, **21**, 1070
Immigration Appeal Reports, **12**, 113
Immigration Appeal Tribunal, _see_ IMMIGRATION APPEAL TRIBUNAL
Immigration Rules, _see_ IMMIGRATION RULES
independent means, person of—
  entry clearance, **12**, 151, 258, 259
  extension of leave, **12**, 260
  Immigration Rules, **12**, 149
  police registration conditions, **12**, 175
  work permit exemption, **12**, 154
international law—
  Convention on the Status of Refugees, **12**, 116
  European Convention on Human Rights, **12**, 115
  International Convention on the Elimination of all Forms of Discrimination, **12**, 116
  International Covenant on Civil and Political Rights, **12**, 116
  international customary law, **12**, 116
  International Labour Organisation Resolutions, **12**, 116
  Universal Declaration of Human Rights, **12**, 116
Ireland, from, **12**, 101
Irish Potato Famine, **12**, 101
Jewish, **12**, 101
leaving United Kingdom, rights as to, **16**, 1205, 1205_n_
marriage, **10**, 836
medical examination—
  after entry, **12**, 165
  breach of conditions, **12**, 187
  generally, **19**, 510–512
  immigration control, **12**, 165
  referral for, **12**, 165
  refusal of leave to enter following, **12**, 171
  vaginal, no longer allowed, **12**, 165
  who may make, **12**, 165
medical inspector—
  appointment, **12**, 138, 143
  instructions to, **12**, 111
  powers, **12**, 143
medical treatment—
  visitor seeking, **12**, 305
    conditions for entry, **12**, 306
    visitors' dependants, **12**, 309
ministerial discretion, **12**, 110, 112
MP, representations concerning immigration cases, _see_ MEMBER OF PARLIAMENT
naturalisation, requirements for, **14**, 1920
non-national document, **12**, 151
offence, refusal of leave to enter following, **12**, 171
officers, _see_ IMMIGRATION OFFICER
overstaying, **12**, 186, 188
  acquittal of offence, **12**, 205
  deportation following, **12**, 204, 205
  ignorance no defence, **12**, 205
  offence, as, **12**, 186, 205
  tracing overstayers, **12**, 188
passport, _see_ PASSPORT

Immigration—_continued_
patrials, **12**, 107, 118_n_
political offence, _see_ POLITICAL OFFENCE
polygamous wives and widows, **12**, 118_n_, 269
  children of, **12**, 118_n_
postgraduate training, for, **12**, 175
protected status, groups with, **12**, 125–127
public funds, **12**, 160, 160_n_
public good, exclusion conductive to, **12**, 171
racial tension, and, **12**, 102
reform, **14**, 1903
refugees, **12**, 101, 102. _See also_ REFUGEE
remain, leave to—
  appeals system, **12**, 329, 332
    effect of appeal, **12**, 332
  breach of conditions, **12**, 188
  Department of Employment approval, **12**, 140
  extension—
    artists, **12**, 257
    businessmen, **12**, 253
    Commonwealth citizens with UK ancestry, **12**, 262
    dependants, **12**, 266
    independent means, persons of, **12**, 260
    self-employed, **12**, 253
    writers, **12**, 257
  generally, **12**, 119
  Immigration Rules categories, **12**, 240
  indefinite, **12**, 120
    absences and re-entry, **12**, 120
    deportation, **12**, 120
    restrictions, **12**, 120
    work permit holders, **12**, 244
  lapse, **12**, 176
  marriage after admission for purpose other than, **12**, 278
  refugees—
    appeal against refusal, **12**, 322
    exceptional leave to remain, **12**, 320, 322
  Secretary of State's powers, **12**, 138
  settlement, family reunion or creation by—
    children, **12**, 280
    spouse, **12**, 270
  work permit holders, **12**, 244
  See also enter, leave to _above_
removal, meaning, **12**, 147
removal destination, control of departure decisions, limits on appeals relating to, **12**, 343
'replacement labour', **12**, 102
Republic of Ireland, _see_ REPUBLIC OF IRELAND
restricted returnability, **16**, 1205_n_
  meaning, **12**, 171
  refusal of leave to enter due to, **12**, 171
  visitors, **12**, 305
restriction direction, civil prisoner subject to, **14**, 1468
returning resident—
  British Overseas citizen, **12**, 120
  entry clearance, **12**, 151
  leave to enter, **12**, 120
  readmission as, **12**, 176
search warrant, issue of, **12**, 168
self-employed, **12**, 250–253

Immigration—*continued*
servant, private, **12**, 247
settlement, *see* SETTLEMENT (IMMIGRATION)
special voucher—
    allocation, **12**, 159
    entry clearance, **12**, 159
    generally, **12**, 158
    number and distribution, **12**, 112
    refusal, **12**, 159
        no appeal against, **12**, 344
    who is covered, **12**, 159
sponsorship, **12**, 160
statute law—
    generally, **12**, 109
    twentieth-century immigration law, **12**, 106, 107
temporary admission, **12**, 119, 168, 169
temporary release, **12**, 146, 169, 187
tourists, immigration controls, **12**, 101, 102
transfer direction, civil prisoner subject to, **14**, 1468
tribunal decisions, **12**, 113
United Kingdom, immigration to, historical background, **12**, 101–107
    common law, **12**, 105
    nineteenth century, **12**, 104, 105
    statute law, **12**, 106, 107
    twentieth-century, **12**, 102, 106, 107
    until the Union, **12**, 103
visitors to UK, *see* VISITOR, UK, TO
welfare state facilities, post-entry control, **12**, 191
work permit, *see* WORK PERMIT
writers, **12**, 149, 151, 154, 175, 254, 255, 256, 257
wrongful identity, **12**, 337
Immigration Appeal Tribunal
appeal to, generally, **12**, 357
appointment of, **12**, 139
generally, **12**, 330; **23**, 902, 911
members, **12**, 331
president, **12**, 331
Immigration officer
appointment, **12**, 138, 142
arrest by, **12**, 168
conduct of examination, **12**, 164, 170
controls on entry, duties as to, **12**, 161–170
enter, grant or refusal of leave to, **12**, 170
instructions to, **12**, 111
meaning, **16**, 1205*n*
powers, **12**, 142; **16**, 1206
temporary admission, authority given for, **12**, 168
temporary release and bail, **12**, 169
Immigration Rules
adoption, child entering for, **12**, 279
appeals against, **12**, 333
artists, **12**, 254–257
asylees, **12**, 320
asylum, **12**, 149
au pairs, **12**, 149, 291, 310–313
businessmen, **12**, 250–253
categories—
    artists, **12**, 254–257
    au pairs, **12**, 291, 310–313
    businessmen, **12**, 250–253

Immigration Rules—*continued*
categories—*continued*
    change of, **12**, 240
        au pairs, **12**, 313
    children, admission of, **12**, 279–285
    Commonwealth citizens—
        United Kingdom ancestry, with, **12**, 261, 262
        working holidaymakers, **12**, 241, 263
    dependants, **12**, 264–266
    employment, persons in, **12**, 241–249
    EU law, entrants under, **12**, 219–239
    fiancés and fiancées, **12**, 274–277
    generally, **12**, 149
    grandparents, admission of, **12**, 285–290
    independent means, persons of, **12**, 258–260
    marriage, **12**, 278
        family reunion and creation by settlement, **12**, 267–273
        fiancés and fiancées, **12**, 274–277
    parents, admission of, **12**, 285–290
    political asylees, **12**, 315–323
    refugees, **12**, 314, 316–323
    role of, **12**, 240
    self-employment, **12**, 250–253
    settlement—
        family reunion and creation by, **12**, 267–273
        leading to, **12**, 241
    students, **12**, 291, 292–300
        dependants of, **12**, 301–304
    United Kingdom passport holders, **12**, 324–328
    visitors, **12**, 291, 305–308
        dependants of, **12**, 309
    writers, **12**, 254–257
children born in UK but not UK citizens, **12**, 149
Convention on the Status of Refugees, **12**, 116
employment or business, passengers coming for, **12**, 149
enter, grant or refusal of leave to, **12**, 170
EU law as mediated by—
    entry, **12**, 236
    remain after employment, right to, **12**, 239
    residence, **12**, 237
        permits, **12**, 237
        termination of right to reside, **12**, 238
    United Kingdom and EU law, relationship between, **12**, 235
European Union nationals, **12**, 114, 134, 149, 221
    families of, **12**, 134
independent means, passengers of, **12**, 149
issue of, **12**, 138
marriage, passengers coming for, **12**, 149
outside the Rules, Secretary of State's power to decide, **12**, 110, 112, 149, 177, 318
reissue, **12**, 110
requirement for, **12**, 110
settlement, passengers coming for, **12**, 149
sexually dicriminatory nature, **12**, 267
status, **12**, 110
students, **12**, 149
temporary purposes, passengers coming for, **12**, 149
transitional provisions, **12**, 110
visitors, **12**, 149

Immigration Rules—*continued*
work permits, passengers on, **12**, 149
writers, **12**, 254–257
Immissio **principle**
digest in, **14**, 2007, 2009
Immunisation
See VACCINATION AND IMMUNISATION
Immunity
Crown, **19**, 233–236
diplomatic, **19**, 679, 681–684
    agents and mission personnel, **19**, 682
    consular staff, **19**, 684
    mission premises, **19**, 683
    public service, **19**, 682
    social security payments, **19**, 682
    taxes, **19**, 682
foreign governments, **19**, 235
military obligations, **19**, 682
restricted, **19**, 680
sovereign, **19**, 679, 680
statutory, **19**, 237
waived, may be, **19**, 680
Impalement
husband and wife, **11**, 1627
meaning, **11**, 1627
official coats of arms impaled with personal, **11**, 1627
Impeachment
House of Lords jurisdiction, **6**, 823
Imperial law
common law, overseas migration of, **5**, 713
constitutional law, **5**, 719
delict, **5**, 718
financial law, **5**, 717
generally, **5**, 711
jurisdiction, **5**, 714
mercantile law, **5**, 717
military law, **5**, 715
naturalisation, **5**, 716
pretensions of English law as, **5**, 711–719
public international law, **5**, 712
Impersonation
constable, of—
    generally, **16**, 1809
    Ministry of Defence Police, **16**, 1816
heirs or legatees, of, **11**, 748, 759
Implement
common interest, as remedy for breach of, **18**, 366
real burden, breach of, **18**, 423
Implied revocation
See WILL
Implied terms
contract, essentials of, **14**, 1037
contract, in, *see* CONTRACT (TERMS)
contract of sale for moveable property, *see* SALE AND SUPPLY OF GOODS
sale contract, in, prohibition of exclusion, **6**, 34
Implied trust
operation of law, by, **24**, 12
private trust, as, **24**, 16
Import procedure
abandonment of goods to Exchequer, **7**, 1136
air, goods imported by, **7**, 1141

Import procedure—*continued*
breaches of importation rules, **7**, 1139
cancellation of duty, **7**, 1145
Community customs territory, importation into, **7**, 1130, 1131
correction of duty, **7**, 1145
customs office, conveyance of goods to, **7**, 1132
customs-approved treatment or use, allocation, **7**, 1131, 1136
    time limits, **7**, 1138
destruction of goods, **7**, 1136
duty, attempted avoidance, **7**, 1151
economic impact, customs procedures with, **7**, 1137
entry requirements, failure to comply with, **7**, 1150
European Union law—
    breaches of import rules, **7**, 1139
    customs office, conveyance of goods to, **7**, 1132
    customs supervision, duration, **7**, 1131
    customs-approved treatment or use, allocation, **7**, 1131, 1133, 1136
        time limits, **7**, 1138
    economic impact, customs procedures with, **7**, 1137
    effect, **7**, 1129
    European Union customs territory, importation into, **7**, 1130
    local clearance procedure, **7**, 1137
    other Community member state, importation from, **7**, 1140
    presentation of goods, **7**, 1133
    summary declaration, **7**, 1134
    temporary storage, **7**, 1135
    treatment of goods, **7**, 1131
illegally imported goods, **7**, 1151
inward processing, *see* CUSTOMS AND EXCISE
land boundary, goods imported across, **7**, 1141
local clearance procedure, **7**, 1137
payment of duty, **7**, 1148
    non-payment for warehousing, transit or temporary importation, **7**, 1149
pipe-line, goods imported by, **7**, 1141
postponed entry, **7**, 1143
postponed payment of duty, **7**, 1143
presentation of goods, **7**, 1133
prohibitions, attempted avoidance, **7**, 1151
Queen's warehouse, removal of goods to, **7**, 1147
re-exportation, **7**, 1136
re-importation, **7**, 1148
restrictions, attempted avoidance, **7**, 1151
sea, goods imported by, **7**, 1141
simplified entries, **7**, 1144
summary declaration, **7**, 1134
surplus stores of ship or aircraft, **7**, 1147
temporary importation, **7**, 1149
temporary storage, **7**, 1135, 1149
time of importation, establishing, **7**, 1141
transit or transhipment, goods imported for, **7**, 1149
warehousing, goods imported for, **7**, 1149
Importation
animals, of, *see* ANIMAL; ENDANGERED SPECIES
antiques, **7**, 1120

Importation—*continued*
buy-national policy, European Union prohibition between member states, **7**, 1019
certificate or licence, European Union prohibition between member states, **7**, 1019
child or young person, works likely to corrupt, **7**, 1203
Common Customs Tariff (CCT), *see* COMMON CUSTOMS TARIFF
controlled drugs, **14**, 1236
copyright, infringing copies, **7**, 1199
customs duty, charge to, generally, **7**, 1001, 1037, 1040
dangerous goods, control of, **6**, 58
drug, prescribed, **7**, 1195
EC mark, **6**, 262
European Union quantitative restrictions—
generally, **7**, 1018, 1019
imports other than from specified third countries, **7**, 1027, 1028
specified third countries—
imports from, **7**, 1029
feeding stuff, **1**, 725; **11**, 317
foodstuffs, **7**, 1201
free zones, *see* FREE ZONE
grandfather clause, European Union prohibition between member states, **7**, 1019
hazardous substances, restrictions on, **9**, 1203
import ban or quota, European Union prohibition between member states, **7**, 1019
import duty reliefs, **7**, 1099–1122
Import of Goods (Control) Order (1954), **7**, 1193
import levies—
advance fixing procedure, **1**, 920
beef and veal, on, **1**, 933
customs duties, and, **1**, 919
goatmeat, on, **1**, 936
legal nature of, **1**, 919
live sheep and goats, on, **1**, 936
purpose of, **1**, 920
sheepmeat, on, **1**, 936
world and Community prices, difference between, **1**, 914, 919
indecent materials, **7**, 1203
legatee, goods imported by, **7**, 1314
licence, **7**, 1019, 1193, 1202
animals, importation of, **2**, 206
atomic energy materials, relating to, **9**, 924
lottery advertisement or notice of, **7**, 1203
meat, **1**, 933, 936; **11**, 414, 416
misleading advertising, **6**, 95
obscene materials, **7**, 1203
offence, **14**, 1843
outward processing, **7**, 1188–1191
permanently imported goods, excise duty relief, **7**, 1113
postal, **7**, 1198, 1445
price-regulatory measure, European Union prohibition between member states, **7**, 1019
prison outwith European Union, goods produced in, **7**, 1203
prizes and honours awarded abroad, **7**, 1120
procedure, *see* IMPORT PROCEDURE

Importation—*continued*
re-importation—
outward processing, **7**, 1188–1191
standard exchange system, **7**, 1191
VAT exemption, **7**, 1314
regulated packages, **6**, 259
standard exchange system, **7**, 1191
storage—
free zones, *see* FREE ZONE
warehouse, *see* WAREHOUSE
temporary importation—
availability, **7**, 1187
duration, **7**, 1187
export following, **7**, 1194
generally, **7**, 1149, 1187
goods applicable to, **7**, 1187
supplies outside scope of VAT, **7**, 1290
trade descriptions, **6**, 132
transit or transhipment, for, **7**, 1149
unlawful, **7**, 1040
VAT, charge to, **7**, 1312–1316, 1400
conditional relief, **7**, 1315
input tax, **7**, 1372
reliefs, **7**, 1313–1316
valuation of imported goods, **7**, 1316
zero-rating, **7**, 1457
warehousing, for, **7**, 1149
Importer
excise duty, liability to pay, **7**, 1054
occasional, meaning, **7**, 1058
registered excise dealers and shippers (REDS), **7**, 1057
Impotency
voidable marriages, **10**, 827–829
personal bar, **10**, 829
Impounding
water, of, **25**, 328
Imprisonment
civil—
debt, for, **8**, 101
officers of court, exercise by, **8**, 105
competent sentence, **17**, 797
court conviction, following, **15**, 437
criminal offence, in cases of, **8**, 349
debt, for, *see* DEBT
judicial order, following, **15**, 441, 442
offence punishable by, deportation recommendation following conviction, **12**, 206
prison breaking, *see* PRISON BREAKING
rates, recovery of, **14**, 848
unlawful, **7**, 554
wrongful—
malicious prosecution, following, **15**, 447
See also DETENTION, WRONGFUL
See also CONVICTED PERSON; PRISONER
Improvement area
amenities, improvement of, **14**, 653
building—
conversion, **14**, 654
improvement, **14**, 654
procedure for declaring, **14**, 652
Improvement grant
amount of, **11**, 2021
additional amounts, **11**, 2021

Improvement grant—*continued*
application for—
approval, **11**, 2020
matters to be specified in, **11**, 2020
rateable value restriction, **11**, 2020
refusal, **11**, 2020
restriction on, **11**, 2020
central government contributions, **11**, 2034
conditions, **11**, 2024
disabled occupant, house for, **11**, 2019, 2020
drainage works, **25**, 372
earlier grant, effect of, **11**, 2021
enforcement of conditions, **11**, 2024
generally, **11**, 2018, 2019
historic interest, buildings of, **11**, 2021
housing action areas, **11**, 2031
improvement, meaning, **11**, 2019
improvement orders, *see* IMPROVEMENT ORDER
local authority house loans, and, **11**, 2015
mandatory, **11**, 1981, 1992
maximum amount, **11**, 2021
payment of, **11**, 2022
repairs grant additional to, **11**, 2021, 2025
repayment, **11**, 2024
standard amenities, grants for, **11**, 2023
statutory provisions, **11**, 2018
sub-standard housing, **11**, 1981
works for which made, **11**, 2019
Improvement notice
See HEALTH AND SAFETY AT WORK
Improvement order
appeals, **11**, 1991
compulsory acquisition of property, **11**, 1992
drainage works, **25**, 369
generally, **11**, 1990, 1992
housing action areas, **11**, 1996
improvement grant towards cost, **11**, 1992
local authority acquisition, **11**, 1992
local authority loan, **11**, 1992, 2015
mandatory improvement grants, **11**, 1992
notice of, **11**, 1991
owner of property, works to be done by, **11**, 1990
power to make, when exercisable, **11**, 1990
sub-standard housing, **11**, 1978, 1981
time for completion of works, **11**, 1990
In re mercatoria
guarantee—
effect, **3**, 875
meaning, **3**, 875
writings—
documentary evidence, as, **10**, 602
meaning, **10**, 602
In rixa
statements made, defamation, **15**, 546
Incapacity
beneficiary, **24**, 79
buy, capacity to, **20**, 816
court's powers relating to, **17**, 808
criminal responsibility, age of, **11**, 1202*n*
ground for removal of trustee, **24**, 168
guardian, of, **14**, 1445
incapax—
curator bonis to, *see* CURATOR
welfare and benefit of, **11**, 1206, 1208

Incapacity—*continued*
legal protection of persons under, **11**, 1201, 1202
curators, *see* CURATOR
minority, status of, **11**, 1205
minor's contracts, reduction of, **11**, 1205
pupillarity, status of, **11**, 1203
tutors, *see* TUTOR
marriage, age of capacity, **11**, 1202*n*
pupil, of, **24**, 128
reduction on grounds of, **13**, 44
sell, capacity to, **20**, 816
types of, **11**, 1202
witness, of—
contempt of court, when, **10**, 532
mental incapacity, **10**, 532
oath and affirmation, **10**, 548
physical incapacity, **10**, 533
self-induced, **10**, 532
See also INCAPAX
Incapax
contract, capacity to enter, **13**, 1780
curator bonis, *see* CURATOR
debts owing to, recovery of, **11**, 1225
deed granted by, **12**, 1229
foreign, with property in Scotland, **11**, 1223
rights of, **11**, 1075
welfare and benefit of, **11**, 1206, 1208
writs and titles owing to, recovery of, **11**, 1225
See also INCAPACITY
Incest
abuse of trust, **7**, 318
actus reus, **7**, 315
adoptive relationships, **7**, 314, 315; **10**, 1191,
1227
age limits, parties to act, **3**, 1238; **22**, 695
assault with intent to commit, **7**, 236
Biblical prohibition, **7**, 314
child abuse, as, **7**, 4
child in danger of, **3**, 1330, 1331
consent, **7**, 316
defences to charge of, **7**, 316; **10**, 1227
High Court of Justiciary jurisdiction, **6**, 867
historical background, **7**, 314
illegitimate link, relationship through, **10**, 1180
jurisdiction, **6**, 867; **7**, 319; **17**, 516
knowledge of relationship, requirement, **7**, 316
legal control, generally, **7**, 294
meaning, **7**, 315
mens rea, **7**, 316
onus of proof, **7**, 316
penalties, **7**, 319
person in position of trust, **22**, 695
prohibited relationships, **7**, 315; **10**, 1227
public morality, offence against, **7**, 295
relationships to which confined, **22**, 695
Scottish Law Commission review, **22**, 695
sexual intercourse—
acts falling short of, **7**, 315
requirement for, **7**, 315
statutory offence, **22**, 695
step-children, **3**, 1238, 1244; **7**, 317; **10**, 1227; **22**,
695
step-parents, **3**, 1238, 1244; **10**, 1227; **22**, 695
unmarried relationships, **7**, 315

Inchoate crime
attempt, *see* ATTEMPT
conspiracy, *see* CONSPIRACY
generally, **7**, 160
incitement, *see* INCITEMENT
instigation, **7**, 160
meaning, **7**, 160
mens rea, **7**, 162, 168
preliminary act criminal, where, **7**, 167
stages, **7**, 160
Inchoate instrument
bill of exchange, conversion of bill into, **4**, 117
Incitement
attempted, **7**, 176
controlled drugs, offence relating to, **14**, 1250
generally, **7**, 173, 175
impossible objective, where, **7**, 176
inchoate crime, as, **7**, 160
mens rea, **7**, 174
Income
accumulation of, *see* ACCUMULATION OF TRUST
    INCOME
concept of money central to, **14**, 1801
dividends, *see* DIVIDENDS
security of, **25**, 130
shareholder, rights of, **25**, 14
yield, selection of, **25**, 19
Income support
abroad, person from, **21**, 1081
adjudication, **21**, 1149
age of claimant, **21**, 1064, 1065, 1067
alone, claimant living, **21**, 1068
assumed weekly income, **21**, 1072
available for work—
    groups not required to be, **21**, 1067
    requirement as to, generally, **21**, 1067
blind claimant, **21**, 1065, 1067
British scheme, as, **21**, 1064
calculation—
    bedding, **21**, 1073
    capital, **21**, 1072, 1077, 1078
        disregards, **21**, 1079
        income treated as, **21**, 1080
        notional, **21**, 1080
    clothing, **21**, 1073
    community charge, **21**, 1073
    computation, **21**, 1072
    disability premium, **21**, 1074, 1077
    family premium, **21**, 1074
    gifts, **21**, 1077
    housing costs, **21**, 1072, 1075
    income, **21**, 1077
    lone parent premium, **21**, 1074, 1077
    pensioner premium, **21**, 1074, 1077
        higher, **21**, 1074
    personal allowances, **21**, 1072, 1073
    premiums, **21**, 1072
        meaning, **21**, 1074
    residential care, costs of, **21**, 1076
    urgent cases, **21**, 1081
capital, **21**, 1072
    business assets, **21**, 1079
    calculation, **21**, 1078
    child, of, **21**, 1078

Income support—*continued*
capital—*continued*
    company, sole owner, **21**, 1080
    disposal, **21**, 1080
    disregards, **21**, 1079
    dwelling house, **21**, 1079
    failure to avail oneself of, **21**, 1080
    income tax refund, **21**, 1080
    income treated as, **21**, 1080
    life assurance policy, **21**, 1079
    notional, **21**, 1080
    partner, of, **21**, 1078
    personal possessions, **21**, 1079
    sale of dwelling house, proceeds of, **21**, 1079
    tariff income, **21**, 1077
carer aged less than eighteen, **21**, 1065
charitable work, claimant undertaking, **21**, 1077
child under sixteen—
    child benefit not payable, **21**, 959
    generally, **21**, 1069
    liability to maintain, **21**, 1070
    maintenance order, **21**, 1070
    personal allowance, **21**, 1072
cohabitation rule, **21**, 1068
community charge payments, **21**, 1082
comprehensive nature, **21**, 1061
court attendance, claimant required for, **21**, 1067
debts, direct payments to repay, **21**, 1082
deductions, **21**, 1082
definition, **21**, 1061
direct payments, **21**, 1082
    gas and electricity billa, **21**, 1082
disability premium—
    earnings disregards, **21**, 1077
    generally, **21**, 1074, 1077
    qualification for, **21**, 1074
    severe, **21**, 1074
disabled claimant, **21**, 1065, 1067
dwelling house, calculation of capital, **21**, 1079
earnings in kind, **21**, 1077
education, claimant in, **21**, 1065
entitlement—
    abroad, where claimant, **21**, 1064
    conditions—
        age, **21**, 1064, 1065
        employment—
            availability for, **21**, 1067
            claimant in, **21**, 1066
            claimant not in full-time, **21**, 1066
        family circumstances, **21**, 1068
        household—
            children, **21**, 1069
            cohabiting couple, **21**, 1069
            married couple, **21**, 1069
            meaning, **21**, 1069
            separate, **21**, 1069
        liability to maintain, **21**, 1070
        link with Great Britain, **21**, 1064
        trade dispute disqualification, **21**, 1066, 1071
    European Union, claimant from, **21**, 1064
    Norway, claimant from, **21**, 1064
    Sweden, claimant from, **21**, 1064
    visitor to Britain, **21**, 1064
        urgent cases payment, **21**, 1064

Income support—*continued*
family circumstances—
   generally, **21**, 1068
family premium, **21**, 1074
foster child, single person looking after, **21**, 1065, 1067
fuel board, direct payment to, **21**, 1082
hardship categories, claimant under eighteen, **21**, 1065
historical background, **21**, 1062
holiday from paid employment, claimant on, **21**, 1066
household, what constitutes, **21**, 1069
housing benefit, **21**, 1104
housing costs, **21**, 1072, 1075
   capital element of repayment arrangement, **21**, 1075
   direct payments, **21**, 1082
   excessive, **21**, 1075
   mortgage interest, **21**, 1075
Immigration Act, sponsor under, **21**, 1070
incapable of work, claimant, **21**, 1065, 1067
income—
   benefits, **21**, 1077
   boarder or tenant, income from, **21**, 1077
   calculation, generally, **21**, 1077
   earnings, **21**, 1077
      disregards, **21**, 1077
   educational and training payments, **21**, 1077
   maintenance payments, **21**, 1077
   notional, **21**, 1077
   tariff, **21**, 1077
   trade dispute disqualification, **21**, 1077
income due but not yet paid, where, **21**, 1081
legal custody, claimant in, **21**, 1067
legislation, **21**, 1063
liability to maintain, **21**, 1070
lone parent, **21**, 1065, 1067
   lone parent premium, **21**, 1074, 1077
maintenance order, requirement as to, **21**, 1070
Northern Irish scheme, **21**, 1064
Open University student, **21**, 1067
orphaned claimant, **21**, 1065
overpayments, **21**, 1014
parentage, disputes as to, **21**, 1070
pension supplemented by, **21**, 1201
pensioner premium, **21**, 1074, 1077
   higher, **21**, 1074
personal allowance, **21**, 1072, 1073
pregnant woman, **21**, 1065, 1067
premiums, **21**, 1072, 1074, 1077
prisoner, discharged, **21**, 1067
rates, national determination, **21**, 1062
refugees, **21**, 1067
remunerative work, claimant in, **21**, 1066
rent, **21**, 1075
   direct payment, **21**, 1082
residential care, costs of, **21**, 1076
seasonal worker, **21**, 1081
severe hardship, **21**, 1065
signing on, **21**, 1067
sixty, claimant over, **21**, 1067
social fund, interaction with, **21**, 1123, 1124, 1125
   See also SOCIAL FUND

Income support—*continued*
social work department, payment from, **21**, 1079
social fund payment, **21**, 1079
state retirement pension, recipient of, **21**, 1221
student, **21**, 1077
trade dispute, claimant engaged in, **21**, 1066, 1071, 1077
training scheme, claimant on, **21**, 1065, 1067, 1077
unmarried couple, **21**, 1068
urgent cases, **21**, 1081
visitor to Britain, **21**, 1064
youth training, trainee undergoing, **21**, 1077
Income tax
administration and collection generally, **19**, 1544
advertising appearances, income obtained by, **19**, 1306
agriculture, **19**, 1572, 1573
amateur sportsmen, **19**, 1312
assessment of liability, **19**, 1544
backward spreading, **18**, 1586, 1593, 1594
beneficiaries' liability—
   annuitants, **25**, 984
   generally, **25**, 983
   non-residuary legatees, **25**, 984
   other interests, **25**, 987
   residue—
      absolute interests in, **25**, 986
      limited interests in, **25**, 985
benefit and testimonial matches, income from, **19**, 1302
bookmakers' profits, **19**, 1298
business expansion scheme relief, **25**, 48
capital allowances against, **19**, 1300, 1314
cautionary obligations, treatment of, **3**, 1001
charity, treatment of, *see* CHARITY (INCOME TAX)
child, taxation of, **19**, 1517
clubs, liability of, **2**, 821
cohabitees, **10**, 1008
completion of administration for purposes of, **19**, 1648
copyright—
   author, tax treatment, **18**, 1585–1589
      backward spreading, **18**, 1586
      forward spreading, **18**, 1587
   purchaser, tax treatment, **18**, 1590, 1591
covenanted payment or donation to charity, *see* CHARITY (income tax)
damages, interest on, **12**, 1034
deceased's estate, income arising during administration of—
   beneficiaries, payments to, **25**, 980
   completion, **25**, 981
   executors' expenses, **25**, 979
   foreign estates, **25**, 982
   generally, **25**, 974
   investment income, **25**, 978
   receipts—
      deceased's employment, attributable to, **25**, 975
      deceased's profession, attributable to, **25**, 976
      deceased's trade, attributable to, **25**, 976
      post-cessation, **25**, 977

Income tax—*continued*
deceased's liability—
annuities, **25**, 969
business expansion scheme, withdrawal of relief, **25**, 970
copyright, **25**, 971
dividends, **25**, 969
executor, liability of, **25**, 963
interest—
bank, **25**, 967
building society, **25**, 967
government securities, **25**, 967
loans, **25**, 967
securities, **25**, 968
stocks, **25**, 968
land, income from, **25**, 966
patents, **25**, 971
pensions, **25**, 964
personal relief, **25**, 973
profession, income from, **25**, 965
relief—
business expansion scheme, **25**, 973
personal, **25**, 973
trade, income from, **25**, 965
trust income, **25**, 969
wages, **25**, 964
wife's income, **25**, 972
deduction at source, **19**, 1296, 1304–1308
design right, payments in respect of, **18**, 1593
director, **25**, 57
divorce, and—
existing obligations—
election to have treated as new, **10**, 996
payments made under, **10**, 994
maintenance payments, Finance Act 1988—effect, **10**, 992
new obligations, payments made under, **10**, 995
registration for preservation and execution, **10**, 993
remarriage of recipient spouse, **10**, 997
donations, **8**, 654
double taxation agreements, **19**, 1516
employee, **25**, 57
employment, income and benefits from, **19**, 1514
enterprise zone, **14**, 647
expenses allowable against, **19**, 1303, 1513, 1514
financial year, **22**, 811
foreign estates, **25**, 982, 989
forward spreading, **18**, 1587, 1593
friendly societies, exemption, **12**, 687, 689, 690
grazing rights, **19**, 1573
husband and wife, **10**, 891
blind person's relief, **10**, 891
generally, **19**, 1517
loan interest, **10**, 891
married couple's allowance, **10**, 891
property held in common, **10**, 891
inheritable securities, **19**, 1518
investment income, **19**, 1517
know-how—
purchaser, tax treatment, **18**, 1583, 1584
seller, tax treatment, **18**, 1580–1582
legal rights, interest on, **25**, 796
leisure and recreation businesses, **19**, 1319–1321

Income tax—*continued*
maintenance payments—
existing obligations—
election to have treated as new, **10**, 996
new obligations, **10**, 995
payments made under, **10**, 994
registration for preservation and execution, **10**, 993
remarriage of recipient spouse, **10**, 997
market gardening, **19**, 1665, 1667
married couple's allowance, **19**, 1518
non–cash benefits, **19**, 1514
non-resident beneficiaries, **25**, 988
non-resident legatee, **25**, 984
non-resident sportsmen, **19**, 1296, 1304–1308
occupational pension scheme—
approved scheme—
generally, **21**, 1313
taxation of payments from, **21**, 1316
See also PENSION (occupational)
exempt approved scheme, **21**, 1313, 1314
free-standing additional voluntary contribution scheme, **21**, 1313
higher-rate tax payers, **21**, 1313
net pay arrangement, **21**, 1313
tax-free investment income, **21**, 1314
unapproved scheme, **21**, 1325–1333
partnership, liability—
basis of assessment, **16**, 1126
calculation of tax, **16**, 1129
change in composition of partnership, **16**, 1128
dissolution of partnership, where, **16**, 1132
generally, **16**, 1124; **19**, 1586
income other than trading profits, **16**, 1130
opening and closing years, **16**, 1127
payment of tax, **16**, 1129
retirement annuities, **16**, 1131
trading profits, **16**, 1125
patents—
capital allowances, **18**, 1576
deduction of tax at source, **18**, 1577
foreign patents, **18**, 1579
licensee, tax treatment, **18**, 1575, 1576
licensor, tax treatment, **18**, 1572–1574
non-resident, payments to, **18**, 1578
Pay As You Earn (PAYE) system, **19**, 1515
pensioners, **19**, 1518
personal allowance, **19**, 1518
personal pension schemes, **19**, 1518
polygamous marriage, effect of, **17**, 216
prize money, **19**, 1298
professional sportsmen, **19**, 1297–1308
promotional activities, income obtained by, **19**, 1298, 1306
Provisional Collection of Taxes Act 1968 ..., **19**, 1504*n*
public lending right, payments under, **18**, 1592
racing tips, regular income obtained by supplying, **19**, 1298
rates, **19**, 1518
recovery of, **19**, 1550
refund, calculation of income support, **21**, 1080
registered design right, payments in respect of, **18**, 1593

Income tax—*continued*
reliefs and allowances, **19**, 1511
residence in United Kingdom, **19**, 1516
retirement annuity schemes, **19**, 1518
retirement benefit schemes, **19**, 1518
royalties, **18**, 1572, 1575, 1577
   copyright, in respect of, **18**, 1585, 1591
   deduction of tax at source, **18**, 1577
   know how, in respect of, **18**, 1580–1584
schedules, **19**, 1512; **25**, 57
self-employed sportsmen, **19**, 1297, 1298–1303
sheriff court jurisdiction, **6**, 1109
single parents, **19**, 1518
state retirement pension, **21**, 1221
third persons, payments to, **19**, 1307
trade and service marks, income in respect of—
   licensee, tax treatment, **18**, 1598, 1599
   owner, tax treatment, **18**, 1595, 1596
   purchaser, tax treatment, **18**, 1598, 1599
trading profits, **19**, 1513
transfers (provision of goods and services), **19**, 1305, 1305n, 1307
travelling expenses, **19**, 1514
trust funds, payments into, **19**, 1312
tuition fees, **19**, 1298
unearned income, **19**, 1297, 1515
unregistered design rights, income from, **18**, 1593
widows with dependent children, **19**, 1518
wife, taxation of, **19**, 1517
woodlands, **11**, 642–648
   abolition of previous system, **11**, 644
   capital allowances, **11**, 646
   election to be charged under Schedule D, **11**, 643
   former taxation under Schedule B, **11**, 642
   transitional provisions, **11**, 645; **19**, 1510
works of art, income from sale by artist, **18**, 1594
year of assessment, **19**, 1504, 1511
Inconvenience
harm arising from, **14**, 2047
Incorporated company
partnership distinguished, **4**, 318
Incorporation
Act of Parliament, by, **4**, 303, 314
artificial legal person, creation of, **4**, 317
certificate of—
   company has no legal existence before date on, **4**, 317
   partnership does not require, **4**, 302
contractual authority for, **9**, 34
non-profit purposes, for, **4**, 302
piercing veil of, **4**, 317–319, 370
pre-incorporation contract, **4**, 432
proposed memorandum and articles of association, registration of, **4**, 304
Registrar of Companies, registration with, **4**, 314
registrar's certificate relating to, **4**, 332
royal charter, by, **4**, 303, 314
Incorporation of Goldsmiths of the City of Edinburgh
generally, **18**, 1412
Incorporeal property
assignation of voluntary obligations, **11**, 766
bank notes, **14**, 1806

Incorporeal property—*continued*
bank notes as, **14**, 1806
cheques, **11**, 768
corporeal property distinguished, **18**, 11
destruction, meaning, **18**, 9
documents of title, **11**, 769
donation, as, **8**, 601
generally, **6**, 591; **11**, 765; **25**, 825
heritable bonds, **11**, 770
incorporeal heritable property—
   adjudication, **18**, 13
   future time, rights with tract of, **18**, 14
   generally, **18**, 13
   goodwill, **18**, 14
   inhibition, **18**, 13
   land, real rights in, **18**, 14
      personal rights to, **18**, 14
      uncompleted, **18**, 14
   meaning, **18**, 13
   personal bond, **18**, 14
   titles of honour, **18**, 14
incorporeal moveable property—
   arrestment, **8**, 247, 261; **18**, 13
   contract of deposit, may not be subject of, **8**, 4
   copyright as, **18**, 1005
   document relating to, contract of deposit, **8**, 4
   donation, delivery, **8**, 636
   generally, **18**, 13
   intellectual property as, **18**, 802
   lex situs, **8**, 130
   meaning, **18**, 13
   patent, **18**, 811, 878
   poinding, **18**, 13
   real conditions, **18**, 353
meaning, **18**, 11, 16, 652
negotiable instruments, **11**, 767
personal rights, **18**, 11
   See also RIGHT
possession, generally, **18**, 120
promissory notes, **11**, 767
real rights, **18**, 11, 11n, 16
   See also REAL RIGHT
security over, **13**, 1759
separate tenement, *see* LANDOWNERSHIP
share certificates, **11**, 771
transfer of ownership—
   abstract basis of transfer, **18**, 611
   alimentary in nature, where right is, **18**, 652
   assignation—
      delivered but unintimated assignation, **18**, 658
      execution and delivery, **18**, 654
      express prohibition, where, **18**, 652
      generally, **18**, 653
      obligation, of, **18**, 662
   assignatus utitur jure auctoris rule, **18**, 660, 688, 688n
   contract of sale, **18**, 653, 654
   death of assignee, **18**, 659
   death of cedent, **18**, 659
   delectus personae, right involving, **18**, 652
   failure of contract, effect, **18**, 612
   future rights, **18**, 652
   generally, **4**, 102; **18**, 605

Incorporeal property—*continued*
transfer of ownership—*continued*
  incapable of transfer, property which is, **18**, 652
  insolvency of assignee, **18**, 659
  insolvency of cedent, **18**, 659
  intimation, **18**, 653, 656
    acknowledged letter, by, **18**, 656
    court action or diligence, by, **18**, 656
    importance of, **18**, 658
    performance, by, **18**, 656
    registration, by, **18**, 656
  meaning, **18**, 652
  obligation, assignation of, **18**, 662
  personal rights—
    assignation, **18**, 660
    assignatus utitur jure auctoris rule, **18**, 660, 688
    generally, **18**, 652
    intimation, **18**, 653, 656, 658
    meaning, **18**, 656
    obligation in debtor, **18**, 656
    real rights, in competition with, **18**, 688, 688*n*
    real rights accompanying, **18**, 657
  possession, **18**, 653, 657
    requirement for, **18**, 657
  real rights—
    generally, **18**, 652
    personal rights, in competition with, **18**, 688, 688*n*
    personal rights accompanying, **18**, 657
    possession, **18**, 653, 657
    registration, **18**, 653, 657
  registration, **18**, 653, 657
  retrocession, **18**, 661
  rights as constituents of, **18**, 605
  spes successionis, **18**, 652
  stages of transfer—
    evaluation, **18**, 658
    generally, **18**, 653
  statutory prohibition, where, **18**, 652
  two or more separate rights, contract conferring, **18**, 652
  void transfers, **18**, 652
  warrandice, *see* WARRANDICE
warrandice, *see* WARRANDICE
Incorporeal right
conveyancing, **12**, 1244
theft of document incorporating, **7**, 325
Incrimination
adultery, **10**, 675
criminal offences, **10**, 671–674
furth of Scotland, liability to prosecution, **10**, 674
generally, **7**, 173; **10**, 670
privilege, statutory restrictions on, **10**, 672
spouse, of, **10**, 673
Indecency
gross and shameless, homosexual acts, **7**, 312
nuisance *contra bonos mores*, **14**, 2083
shameless, child, towards, **3**, 1235, 1236
Indecent act
acts amounting to, **7**, 223
young person, with, **7**, 309, 310
Indecent assault
body part involved, **7**, 306
circumstances of indecency, **7**, 306

Indecent assault—*continued*
consent, **7**, 307
  relevancy, **7**, 93, 97, 220, 223
corporal punishment, **7**, 306
definition, **7**, 305
generally, **7**, 217, 223
man, committed by, **7**, 305
requirements of, **7**, 305
same sex, victim of, **7**, 305
sexual assault, as, **7**, 295
sleeping or unconscious woman, **7**, 298
woman, committed by, **7**, 305
Indecent display
statotory control, **7**, 488
Indecent exposure
actus reus, **7**, 474
circumstances of exposure, importance, **7**, 473, 474
generally, **7**, 473
male genital organs, exposure of, **7**, 473, 474
mens rea, **7**, 475
private person, to, **7**, 474
public, **7**, 474
shamelessly indecent conduct, as, **7**, 83, 468
woman, by, **7**, 474
Indecent material
import to United Kingdom, **7**, 1203
postal packet, enclosed in, **16**, 1909
publication, restrictions on, **17**, 40
Indecent message
telecommunications, sent by, **16**, 1959
Indecent remarks or suggestions
breach of the peace, as, **7**, 453
Indemnity
action for, European Union law, **10**, 67
building contracts, *see* BUILDING CONTRACT
contract of, cautionary obligation distinguished, **3**, 844
directors' liabilities, for, **4**, 417
health and safety inspector, of, **9**, 494
registration of title, *see* REGISTRATION OF TITLE
security, as, **5**, 908
Indemnity clause
contract, in, **15**, 718
  statutory control, **15**, 726
definition, **15**, 718
Indemnity insurance
contribution, *see* INSURANCE
cover note, **12**, 825
fire insurance, **12**, 804
household and property cover, **12**, 804
insurable interest, time of loss, **12**, 855
marine cover, **12**, 804
meaning, **12**, 804
motor insurance, **12**, 804
partnership agreement provisions, **16**, 1009
recoverable loss, **12**, 885, 886
renewable contracts—
  cover notes, **12**, 825
  notice of renewal, **12**, 825
subrogation, *see* INSURANCE
temporary cover, **12**, 818, 825
uncertainty, event insured against must contain element of, **12**, 804

Independence of judiciary
See JUDICIARY
Independent Broadcasting Authority
advertisements, publication of, **17**, 45
  misleading advertising, **6**, 95
Channel Four, **17**, 7
direct broadcasting by satellite, **17**, 7
election matter, transmission of, **17**, 43
functions, **17**, 7
ITV, **17**, 7
programmes provided by, regulation of, **17**, 8
regulation, generally, **17**, 2, 7, 8
services provided by, **17**, 7
teletext services, **17**, 8
Independent International Law Association
law clarification, **19**, 650
Independent Living Fund
payments from, effect on income support, **21**, 1077
Independent Order of Odd Fellows
generally, **12**, 679, 679*n*
Independent school
characteristics, notification of changes in, **8**, 811
complaints regarding, **8**, 812
  independent schools tribunal, powers, **8**, 813
  notice of complaint, **8**, 812
disqualification—
  premises, of, **8**, 813, 814
  proprietor, of, **8**, 813, 814
  teacher, of, **8**, 813, 814
fees, **8**, 818
generally, **8**, 701
independent schools tribunal—
  composition, **8**, 813
  powers, **8**, 813
  referral to, **8**, 813
meaning, **8**, 810
Registrar of Independent Schools in Scotland, **8**, 811
registration, **8**, 811
  application for, **8**, 811
technology academy, *see* TECHNOLOGY ACADEMY
Independent Schools Tribunal
Scottish Committee, supervision by, **23**, 911*n*
sheriff's duties in respect of, **6**, 1046
Independent Tribunal Service
constitution, **21**, 1174
generally, **21**, 1174
president, powers and functions of, **21**, 1174
Indexed rental
commercial lease, **13**, 71
India
personal law, domicile as indicator of, **17**, 188
Indictment
actus reus, **7**, 31
conclusion, **7**, 13*n*
innominate offence, **7**, 24
major proposition, **7**, 13*n*
  syllogistic form, **7**, 13*n*
minor proposition, **7**, 13*n*
nominate offence, **7**, 24
specimen charges, **7**, 31
Individual
business name, registration and use of, **4**, 321
domicile of, **4**, 30

Individual—*continued*
duties of in public international law, **19**, 695
harm, sensitivity to, **14**, 2061
meaning, **5**, 806
procedural capacity of, **19**, 696
rights of, **19**, 694
See also PERSONS–PERSONALITY; PRIVATE CITIZEN
Individual resale price maintenance
See RESALE PRICE MAINTENANCE
Indivision
England, **25**, 642
France, **25**, 642
Germany, **25**, 642
Indorsee
meaning, **4**, 134
Indorsement
delivery, completed by, **4**, 143
meaning, **4**, 134, 143
Indult
meaning, **3**, 1656*n*
quattor abhinc annos, **3**, 1656
Industrial action
ballot—
  action done by trade union, meaning, **23**, 871
  constituency, **23**, 873
  generally, **23**, 869
  procedure, **23**, 874
  relevant industrial action, **23**, 870
  without support of ballot, meaning, **23**, 872
benefits obtained as a result of, **23**, 854
contract of employment, and, **9**, 129–133
criminal law, and, **9**, 131
direct interest, meaning, **21**, 872
dismissal in case of, **9**, 226
forms of, **9**, 132; **21**, 865
go-slow, **9**, 132
immunities—
  contemplation or furtherance of trade dispute, meaning, **23**, 857, 862
  dispute, meaning, **23**, 858
  legal liability, **23**, 713
  picketing, **23**, 879, 880
  proper parties, **23**, 859
  proper purpose, **23**, 860
  secondary action, **23**, 864, 866
  specific delicts, **23**, 856
  statutory, **23**, 855
  subject matter, **23**, 860
  trade dispute, matters of, **23**, 861
income support, disqualification for, **21**, 1071, 1077
legal regime, **23**, 848
non-recognition supplier, aimed at, **23**, 877
picketing, *see* PICKETING
place of employment, meaning, **21**, 866
recognition-only practice, in support of—
  general, **23**, 875
  membership grounds, primary action on, **23**, 878
  non-recognition supplier, action aimed at, **23**, 877
remedies—
  authorisation of action, **23**, 886
  damages, **23**, 885–888

Industrial action—*continued*
remedies—*continued*
  endorsement of action, **23**, 886
  general, **9**, 133; **23**, 883
  interim interdict, **23**, 884
  vicarious liability, rules on, **23**, 889
reparation, liability in—
  breach of contract, **23**, 851, 852
  conspiracy, **23**, 850
  delictual wrong, **23**, 849
  economic duress, **23**, 854
  intimidation, **23**, 853
  sit-in, **23**, 854
  unlawful means, concept of, **23**, 854
  work-in, **23**, 854
secondary, **23**, 865–868
statutory protection, **9**, 130; **23**, 863
stoppage, meaning, **21**, 863
strike, *see* STRIKE
supplier of goods or services, aimed at, **23**, 876
trade dispute—
  employees, between, **21**, 864
  meaning, **21**, 864
  seamen and their employers, **21**, 275
  social fund payments, **21**, 1124, 1125
  unemployment benefit, disqualification for—
    causation, **21**, 869
    claimant leaving employment prior to dispute, where, **21**, 867
    claimant prevented from taking up employment by existence of dispute, **21**, 867
    demarcation disputes, **21**, 864
    duration, **21**, 871
    employees, disputes between, **21**, 864
    end of stoppage—
      generally, **21**, 870
      onus of proof, **21**, 870
    existence of dispute, what constitutes, **21**, 865
    generally, **21**, 863
    loss of employment by reason of stoppage, **21**, 867
    more than one issue, dispute involving, **21**, 872
    no direct interest in dispute, claimant with, **21**, 863, 871, 872
    onus of proof, **21**, 863
    place of employment, **21**, 863, 866
    re-employment of claimant during stoppage—
      elsewhere, **21**, 873
      with same employer, **21**, 873
    redundancy termination employment during dispute, **21**, 871
    stoppage ceasing to be trade dispute, where, **21**, 869
    termination of employment contract during, **21**, 868
    withdrawal of labour, **21**, 874
unfair dismissal, claim for, **9**, 214, 225, 226
union-only practice, in support of—
  general, **23**, 875
  membership grounds, primary action on, **23**, 878

Industrial action—*continued*
union-only practice, in support of—*continued*
  non-recognition supplier, action aimed at, **23**, 877
  supplier of goods or services, action aimed at, **23**, 876
vicarious liability for, rules on, **23**, 889
working to rule, **9**, 132
Industrial assurance
collecting societies, **12**, 682
Industrial death benefit
overlapping benefits, **21**, 1001, 1002, 1003
Industrial derating
See VALUATION FOR RATING
Industrial design, protection of
architectural designs, **18**, 1155
artistic craftsmanship, works of, **18**, 1155
author—
  commission, works designed in pursuance of, **18**, 1163
  computer-generated works, **18**, 1163, 1221
  employee, works designed by, **18**, 1163
  who is, **18**, 1163
Berne Convention provisions, **18**, 1151
commissioned works—
  author, **18**, 1163
  semiconductor topographies, **18**, 1245, 1246
  unregistered design right, ownership, **18**, 1221
copyright—
  artistic character, articles of, **18**, 1158
  artistic works, **18**, 1155–1157
    character merchandising, **18**, 1157
    design documents, **18**, 1155
    exploitation by industrial process and marketing, **18**, 1156
    generally, **18**, 1153
    originality, **18**, 1153
  calculations, **18**, 1153
  character merchandisng, and, **18**, 1157
  computer, material stored on, **18**, 1153
  corresponding registered design, where, **18**, 1193
  design documents, **18**, 1154, 1155
    restriction of copyright, **18**, 1154
  direct copying, **18**, 1153
  drawings, **18**, 1153
  generally, **18**, 1151
  indirect copying, **18**, 1153
  literary character, articles of, **18**, 1158
  models, **18**, 1153, 1154
  originality, **18**, 1153
  quality, no requirement of, **18**, 1153
  registration, things done in reliance on, **18**, 1159
  restrictions—
    artistic work, exploitation by industrial process, where, **18**, 1156
    character merchandising, **18**, 1157
    design documents, **18**, 1154, 1155
    excluded articles, **18**, 1158
    models, **18**, 1154
  surface decoration applied to industrial product, **18**, 1155
  things done in reliance on registration, **18**, 1159

Industrial design, protection of—*continued*
copyright—*continued*
  transitional provisions, **18**, 1152, 1160, 1161
  typefaces, **18**, 1134, 1159, 1160
  verbal ideas, **18**, 1153
  when copyright exists, **18**, 1153
  where right will exist, **18**, 1153
design, meaning, **18**, 1214
design documents, **18**, 1220
  definition, **18**, 1154
  production of as infringement of unregistered
    design right, **18**, 1230, 1231
  restriction of copyright, **18**, 1154
design right, *see* unregistered design right *below*
direct copying, **18**, 1153
employee, designs by—
  semiconductor topographies, **18**, 1245, 1246
  unregistered design right, ownership, **18**, 1221
European Community legislation—
  franchises, **18**, 1662
  generally, **18**, 1615, 1617
  licensing, **18**, 1660
  spare parts, supply, **18**, 1662
generally, **18**, 1151
history, **18**, 1151
indirect copying, **18**, 1153
International Convention for the Protection of
  Industrial Property, **18**, 801, 865, 865*n*, 891,
  1151, 1168
  application for registration, and, **18**, 1168
legislation, **18**, 1151
models, **18**, 1220
originality, unregistered design rights, **18**, 1215
ownership—
  author, meaning, **18**, 1163
  commission, works designed on, **18**, 1163
  employee, works designed by, **18**, 1163
prototypes, **18**, 1220
registered designs—
  account of profits, order for following
    infringement, **18**, 1209
  appeal to and judgment by eye—
    appearance not material to customer, where,
      18, 1178
    functionality combined with, **18**, 1176
    general prnciple, **18**, 1171, 1176
    noticeability, **18**, 1177
  application for registration—
    amendment of design during, **18**, 1167
    appeals, **18**, 1166
    contentious applications, **18**, 1166
    convention applications, **18**, 1168
    division of earlier application, **18**, 1167
    modifications, Registrar may insist on, **18**,
      1166
    registrability, **18**, 1171
  article, design must be applied to—
    generally, **18**, 1173
    meaning of article, **18**, 1173
    sets of articles, **18**, 1174
  assignation, **18**, 1197
    tax treatment, **18**, 1593
  associated designs, expiry, **18**, 1194
  buildings, exclusion of, **18**, 1173

Industrial design, protection of—*continued*
registered designs—*continued*
  certificate of registration, **18**, 1167
    infringement predating issue, **18**, 1208
  colour in relation to novelty, **18**, 1190
  construction method or principle, **18**, 1180
  corresponding copyright design, where, **18**,
    1193
  criminal offences, **18**, 1169, 1195
    body corporate, by, liability, **18**, 1169
  Crown use—
    provisions allowing, **18**, 1201
    third party rights, **18**, 1202
  damages for infringement, **18**, 1209
  dealings in—
    assignation, **18**, 1197
      tax treatment, **18**, 1593
    generally, **18**, 1197
    licence—
      compulsory, **18**, 1200
      Crown use of design and third party
        rights, **18**, 1202
      defender in infringement proceedings
        undertaking to take, **18**, 1210
      generally, **18**, 1197, 1203
      order for, **18**, 1199
    Monopolies and Mergers Commission
      report, **18**, 1199
    unregistered design rights, and, **18**, 1198
  delivery up, order for following infringement,
    18, 1209
  Designs Registry, **18**, 1162
  distasteful designs, **18**, 1171
  duration of right, **18**, 1191
    expiry—
      associated designs, **18**, 1194
      copyright expiry, following, **18**, 1193
      late extension application following, **18**,
        1192
      marking design as registered after, **18**,
        1195
    extensions, **18**, 1191
      late application, **18**, 1192
    renewal fee, **18**, 1191
  European Community legislation—
    free movement of goods, **18**, 1637–1639
    lawful marketing of goods without consent,
      18, 1639
    national laws, and, **18**, 1638
    specific subject matter, **18**, 1637
  excluded categories, **18**, 1173
  expiry, *see* duration of right *above*
  falsely claiming design is registered, **18**, 1169
  features of shape, configuration, pattern or
    ornament, **18**, 1171, 1172, 1203
  functionality—
    exclusion on grounds of, **18**, 1176, 1779
    generally, **18**, 1179
    method or principle of construction, **18**, 1180
    'must match' exception, **18**, 1181
    no 'must fit' exception, **18**, 1182
  generally, **18**, 1162
  industrial process, design must be applied by,
    18, 1175

Industrial design, protection of—*continued*
registered designs—*continued*
infringement—
committed before date of certificate, where, **18**, 1167
defences, **18**, 1211
design applied to different article, **18**, 1203
direct, **18**, 1204
eye, judgment to be made by, **18**, 1204
general principles, **18**, 1203
interdict following, **18**, 1209
kits, **18**, 1206
licence of right, undertaking to take, **18**, 1210
making something which enables infringing article to be made, by, **18**, 1205
not all features of design taken, **18**, 1203
novelty, concept of, **18**, 1204
ownership, and, **18**, 1207
predating issue of certificate of registration, **18**, 1208
remedies, **18**, 1209
test for, **18**, 1204
threat of infringement proceedings—
generally, **18**, 1213
groundless, **18**, 1212, 1213
title to sue, **18**, 1207
law, design contrary to, **18**, 1171
licence—
compulsory, **18**, 1200
Crown use of design and third party rights, **18**, 1202
defender in infringement proceedings undertaking to take, **18**, 1210
generally, **18**, 1197, 1203
no title to sue conferred by, **18**, 1207
order for, **18**, 1199
tax treatment, **18**, 1593
licence of right—
order for, **18**, 1199
terms, **18**, 1199
models, **18**, 1220
Monopolies and Mergers Commission report, Registrar's powers in respect of, **18**, 1199
morality, design contrary to, **18**, 1171
novelty requirement—
colour and novelty, **18**, 1190
generally, **18**, 1162, 1171, 1172, 1183
immaterial difference, **18**, 1188
infringement, and, **18**, 1204
international agreement, communication made under, **18**, 1187
known features, combinations of, **18**, 1189
'obviousness' test, **18**, 1189
prior publication, **18**, 1184, 1186
prior registration, **18**, 1184, 1185
problems arising, **18**, 1183
source common to all mankind, design taken from, **18**, 1184
substantial novelty, **18**, 1188
test, **18**, 1183
trade variations, **18**, 1188
ownership, infringement, title to sue, **18**, 1207
payments in respect of, tax treatment, **18**, 1593, 1600, 1602

Industrial design, protection of—*continued*
registered designs—*continued*
pre-registration transactions, **18**, 1165
printed matter, **18**, 1173
prior registration, where, **18**, 1184, 1185
proprietor, rights, **18**, 1203
prototypes, **18**, 1220
publication prior to registration, **18**, 1184, 1186
Register of Designs, **18**, 1162
application to register, **18**, 1162
amendment of design, **18**, 1162
applicant's right to be heard, **18**, 1162
death of applicant, **18**, 1162
design applied to more than one article, **18**, 1162
errors in application, correction, **18**, 1162
novelty, statement of, **18**, 1162, 1172, 1183–1190
owner of design, to be made by, **18**, 1163
reasonable cause, requirements for, **18**, 1162
specimens, **18**, 1162
time limit for completion, **18**, 1162
computer, may be kept on, **18**, 1162
contents, **18**, 1162
criminal offences in relation to, **18**, 1169
false entry, making, **18**, 1169
public inspection, open to, **18**, 1162
writing, need not be in, **18**, 1162
registrability, **18**, 1171
Registrar, **18**, 1162
registration—
application, *see* registered designs (Register of Designs) *above*
cancellation—
appeal against, **18**, 1196
application for, **18**, 1196
grounds for, **18**, 1196
Registrar's decision as to, **18**, 1196
generally, **18**, 1167
manufacture of article prior to, **18**, 1219
rights conferred by, **18**, 1203
replacement parts, **18**, 1174
rights conferred by registration, **18**, 1203
set of articles, in respect of, **18**, 1174
three-dimensional forms and patterns or ornamentation, **18**, 1172
unregistered design right, where subsisting, **18**, 1164
registration, **18**, 1151
semiconductor topographies, *see* SEMICONDUCTOR TOPOGRAPHIES
specific subject matter—
European Community legislation, **18**, 1637
surface decoration applied to industrial product, **18**, 1155, 1214
three-dimensional article copied from two-dimensional design document, **18**, 1154
transitional provisions, **18**, 1152, 1161
typefaces, **18**, 1159
unregistered design right—
aesthetic designs, **18**, 1219
appearance of product, emphasis on, **18**, 1214

Industrial design, protection of—*continued*
unregistered design right—*continued*
  assignation, **18**, 1227
    tax treatment, **18**, 1593
  author, **18**, 1221
  commissioned works, semiconductor top-
    ographies, **18**, 1245, 1246
  Comptroller, jurisdiction, **18**, 1225
  construction, methods or principals of, exclu-
    sion from protection, **18**, 1214
  copyright, interaction with, **18**, 1233
  Crown rights, **18**, 1228
  dealings in—
    assignation, **18**, 1227
      tax treatment, **18**, 1593
    generally, **18**, 1227
    joint ownership, where, **18**, 1127
    registered design rights, and, **18**, 1198
    testamentary disposition, **18**, 1127
  design, meaning, **18**, 1214
  design documents, **18**, 1220
  disputes, Comptroller's jurisdiction, **18**, 1225
  duration, **18**, 1223, 1224
    disputes as to, jurisdiction, **18**, 1225
  employee, designs by, semiconductor top-
    ographies, **18**, 1245, 1246
  expiry, **18**, 1223
  free-standing articles, **18**, 1219
  functional articles, **18**, 1214, 1219
  generally, **18**, 802, 1151, 1214
  infringement—
    accounting of profits, **18**, 1234
    copyright, interaction of unregistered design
      right with, **18**, 1233
    damages, **18**, 1234
    delivery up, order for, **18**, 1234
    design documents, reproduction of, **18**,
      1230, 1231
    disposal of infringing articles, order for, **18**,
      1234
    groundless threats of infringement
      proceedings, remedy for, **18**, 1238
    innocent, **18**, 1236
    interdict, **18**, 1234
    licence of right, infringer undertaking to
      take, **18**, 1237
    licensee, exclusive, position of, **18**, 1235
    primary—
      causal link must exist, **18**, 1230
      generally, **18**, 1230
      innocent, **18**, 1236
    remedies, **18**, 1234
    reproduction—
      commercial purposes, for, **18**, 1230
      meaning, **18**, 1230
    secondary, **18**, 1232
      innocent, **18**, 1236
  joint designs, **18**, 1222
  kits, **18**, 1214
  'must match' and 'must fit' exceptions, **18**, 1218
  licence—
    right, of—
      infringer undertaking to take, **18**, 1237
      provision for, **18**, 1224

Industrial design, protection of—*continued*
unregistered design right—*continued*
  licence—*continued*
    tax treatment, **18**, 1593
    terms, **18**, 1229
  licensee, exclusive, position of, **18**, 1235
  models, **18**, 1220
  Monopolies and Mergers Commission report,
    powers following, **18**, 1229
  monopoly right, unregistered design right—
    is not, **18**, 1230
  'must fit' exception, **18**, 1216–1218
  'must match' exception, **18**, 1216–1218
  non-functional articles, **18**, 1219
  originality, requirement for, **18**, 1215
  ownership—
    commissioned works, **18**, 1221
    computer-generated works, **18**, 1221
    employee, works designed by, **18**, 1221
    first, **18**, 1221
      subsistence, disputes as to, jurisdiction, **18**,
        1225
    joint, **18**, 1127, 1222
    semiconductor topographies, **18**, 1245, 1246
    test, **18**, 1221
  patents, and, **18**, 1214
  payments in respect of, tax treatment, **18**, 1600,
    1602
  prototypes, **18**, 1220
  qualification for protection, **18**, 1226
  qualifying country, connection with, **18**, 1226
  qualifying person, connection with, **18**, 1226
  reciprocity, **18**, 1226
  registration of design in which subsisting,
    application for, **18**, 1164
  replacement pieces in sets, **18**, 1218
  Secretary of State's power to order grant, **18**,
    1229
  semiconductor topographies, *see* SEMICONDUCTOR
    TOPOGRAPHIES
  spare parts exception, **18**, 1216–1218
  subsistence, disputes as to, jurisdiction, **18**,
    1225
  surface decoration, exclusion from protection,
    18, 1214
  tax treatment, **18**, 1593
  testamentary disposition, **18**, 1127
  three-dimensional design, emphasis on, **18**,
    1214
  transmission, **18**, 1127
  unregistrable designs, **18**, 1151
Industrial development
certificate, repeal of provisions, **23**, 205
generally, **14**, 637
local authority, powers of, **14**, 638
reform, **14**, 46
Industrial injuries benefits
absent from Great Britain, claimant, **21**, 1024
accident—
  abroad, **21**, 1027
  causation, **21**, 968
  employment, causal link with, **21**, 977, 978
  meaning, **21**, 969
adjudication, **21**, 989, 1164, 1166

Industrial injuries benefits—*continued*
byssinosis, **21**, 992, 997
cigarette smoking, accident caused by, **21**, 978, 979
claimant contravening employment regulations, where, **21**, 979
deafness, occupational—
  definition, **21**, 993
  disablement benefit, **21**, 995
  prescribed disease, as, **21**, 992
  prescribed occupations in respect of, **21**, 994
  time limits for claims, **21**, 996
diffuse mesothelioma, **21**, 997
disablement benefit, entitlement, **21**, 966, 980n
disablement questions, **21**, 989
disease, prescribed, in respect of—
  generally, **21**, 966, 991
  meaning, **21**, 992
  See also PRESCRIBED DISEASES
disease due to nature of employment abroad, **21**, 1027
employment—
  accident arising in course of, **21**, 966, 970–973
  accident arising out of, **21**, 966, 970, 977
  commencement of, what constitutes, **21**, 972
  interruptions in, accident occuring during, **21**, 974
  on call, employee, **21**, 971
  recreational activity, accident occuring during, **21**, 971, 973
  sporting activity, accident occuring during, **21**, 973
  travelling to work, accident occuring during, **21**, 975
  work break, accident occuring during, **21**, 972–974
employment premises, employee not on, **21**, 972
entitlement, **21**, 801
  generally, **21**, 966
general risks, **21**, 978
invalidity pension, **21**, 1001
misconduct, accident caused by, **21**, 979
pain or increase in pain, **21**, 967
peripatetic employee, accident while travelling, **21**, 975
personal injury—
  artificial limb or prosthesis, damage to, **21**, 967
  causation, **21**, 968
  generally, **21**, 966, 967
  meaning, **21**, 967
physiological injury, **21**, 967
pneumoconiosis, **21**, 992, 997
psychological injury, **21**, 967
public highway, accident occuring on, **21**, 978
reduced earnings allowance, entitlement, **21**, 966
risk created or added to by claimant, where, **21**, 979
risk encountered by general public as well as employee, where, **21**, 978
road accident, **21**, 978
sickness benefit, entitlement, **21**, 966
skylarking, accident caused by, **21**, 979
Social Security Commissioner, appeal to, **21**, 1182
specific event or number of events, injury must arise from, **21**, 969

Industrial injuries benefits—*continued*
successive industrial accidents, **21**, 990
temporary place of work, accident occuring on journey to, **21**, 975
time period involved, **21**, 969
time when symptoms emerged, **21**, 969
travelling in course of employment, accident during, **21**, 975, 978
travelling to work, accident occuring during, **21**, 975
  employee obliged to use particular means of transport, where, **21**, 975
  employee obliged to use particular route, where, **21**, 975
  express or implied persmission of employer to travel as passenger, **21**, 976
  facts and circumstances, importance of, **21**, 976
  particular task for employer, employee performing, **21**, 975
tuberculosis, **21**, 992
unforeseen aggravation, where, **21**, 989
Industrial injury
See DISABLEMENT BENEFIT; INDUSTRIAL INJURIES BENEFITS
Industrial pollution
See POLLUTION; SMOKE
Industrial process
design applied by, registration, **18**, 1175
manufacture of articles by, limitation of artistic copyright, **18**, 1157
Industrial property
meaning, **18**, 801
See also INDUSTRIAL DESIGN, PROTECTION OF; INTELLECTUAL PROPERTY
Industrial and provident society
accounts—
  annual return, **12**, 634
  balance sheet, **12**, 632, 655
  generally, **1**, 90
  group accounts, **12**, 633
  publication, **12**, 635
  requirement to keep, **12**, 630
  revenue account, **12**, 631
  year of account, **12**, 630
agricultural supply or marketing society, agricultural charge, **12**, 641
amalgamations, **12**, 648
Assistant Registrar for Scotland, **12**, 604, 610
books, inspection of, powers as to, **12**, 644, 645
cancellation or suspension of registration by, **12**, 611
disputes, settlement by, **12**, 647
duties, **12**, 604
industrial and provident society rules, **12**, 612–616
  amendment, **12**, 616
inspectors, appointment of, **12**, 646
qualifications for appointment, **12**, 604
registration by, **12**, 610
special meeting called by, **12**, 646
audit, **12**, 613
auditors—
  appointment, **12**, 639
  disqualification from appointment as, **12**, 638
  qualification, **12**, 637

Industrial and provident society—*continued*
audit—*continued*
  auditors—*continued*
    removal, **12**, 639
    reports of, **12**, 640
  exemption from, **12**, 636
  requirement for, **12**, 636
balance sheet, **12**, 632
  deliberate falsification, **12**, 655
bank customer, as, **2**, 1249
banking business, **12**, 622
body corporate, as, **12**, 606
books, inspection of, **12**, 615
  members, by, **12**, 643
  order, by, **12**, 644
  production of documents, **12**, 645
  restrictions on, **12**, 642
borrowing powers, **12**, 613
building society investment in or support of, **3**, 366
building society member, as, **3**, 379
byelaws, **12**, 612
co-operative society, **12**, 607
committee, **12**, 613
committee of management, **12**, 619
  duties, **12**, 620
  good faith, **12**, 620
  liability, **12**, 620
  obligations of, **12**, 620
community benefit society, **12**, 609
company—
  conversion from, **12**, 651
  conversion into, **12**, 650
constitution, **12**, 612
credit unions, *see* CREDIT UNION
current legislation, **12**, 603
  non-compliance with, **12**, 611
debt recovery, **12**, 625
deposits, **12**, 613
disputes, regulation of settlement, **12**, 615
disputes, settlement of, **12**, 647
dissolution, **12**, 652
  advertisement, **12**, 652
  disadvantages, **12**, 652
  offences in relation to, **12**, 655
finance—
  advances to members, **12**, 623
  banking business, carrying on, **12**, 622
  debt recovery, **12**, 625
  investments by societies, **12**, 624
  loans, **12**, 622
  shareholdings, **12**, 606, 618, 621
    capital duty, avoidance of, **12**, 621
    interest on, **12**, 621
    maximum, **12**, 613, 621
    minimum, **12**, 621
    nomination, **12**, 613, 620, 626–629
    redeemable, **12**, 606
    repayment of capital on termnation of membership, **12**, 618
    share holding prerequisite of membership, **12**, 606
    transferable, **12**, 606, 613
    withdrawable, **12**, 613

Industrial and provident society—*continued*
floating charge, **12**, 641
  registration provisions, **12**, 641
formed by two or more societies joining, **12**, 606
fraud, proceedings in case of, **12**, 620
friendly society category, proposal for, **12**, 684
funds—
  investment, **12**, 613, 624
  in possession of officers, security for, **12**, 615, 619, 620
historical development, **12**, 602
illegal purpose, existing for, **12**, 611
inspection of affairs, **12**, 646
inspector—
  appointment, **12**, 646
  powers, **12**, 646
instrument needed to carry out objectives of society, **12**, 615
investment by, **12**, 613, 624
lending powers, **13**, 1776
limited liability, **12**, 613
liquidation, **12**, 653
  certificate of transfer of assets, **12**, 653
loans, **12**, 613, 622
managers, **12**, 613
meetings, procedure at, **12**, 613
member—
  advances to, **12**, 615, 623
  death of—
    with a nomination, **12**, 627
    without a nomination, **12**, 628
  debt due from, **12**, 625
  mental disorder of, **12**, 629
membership—
  age restriction, **12**, 615
  formed by two or more societies joining, **12**, 606
  intestate member, **12**, 620
  mental incapacity of member, **12**, 618, 620
  minimum, **12**, 606
    number falling below, **12**, 611
  necessary requirements, **12**, 618
  register of, **12**, 618
  rights of members, **12**, 618
  shareholdings, **12**, 618
    maximum and minimum, **12**, 613, 621
    prerequisite to membership, as, **12**, 606
  termination, **12**, 613, 618
  terms of admission, **12**, 613
name—
  offences in relation to, **12**, 655
  rules as to, **12**, 613
nomination, **12**, 613, 620
  death, on, **12**, 627
  meaning, **12**, 626
  mental disorder of member, **12**, 629
objects of, **12**, 613
offences—
  dissolution of society, in relation to, **12**, 655
  duration, **12**, 654
  false returns, making, **12**, 655
  falsification of documents, **12**, 655
  generally, **12**, 655
  inadequate information, provision of, **12**, 655

Industrial and provident society—*continued*
offences—*continued*
 name, in relation to, **12**, 655
 officers, liability, **12**, 654
 penalties, **12**, 654, 655
 rules, fraudulent issue, **12**, 655
 society property, in relation to, **12**, 655
officers, **12**, 613, 619
 appointment, **12**, 619
 dismissal, **12**, 619
 funds, in possession of, **12**, 615, 619
 offences, liability for, **12**, 654
 powers, **12**, 619
 qualification, **12**, 619
ownership or tenancy of land, prohibition on, **12**, 615
profits of, application, **12**, 613
property, offences in relation to, **12**, 655
property held in trust for society, **12**, 610
purpose, **12**, 601
receivership unavailable to, **12**, 641
registered office, **12**, 613
registrar, abuse of discretion, **12**, 610
registration, **12**, 604, 606, 610
 acknowledgement, **12**, 610
 cancellation, **12**, 611
  appeal against, **12**, 611
 documents to be lodged, **12**, 610
 fraud, by, **12**, 611
 mistake, by, **12**, 611
 property held in trust for society, **12**, 610
 recording requirements, **12**, 610
 refusal, appeal against, **12**, 610
 registrable society, **12**, 607
 requirements for, **12**, 610
 signatories, **12**, 610
 society no longer qualified for, **12**, 611
 suspension, **12**, 611
  appeal against, **12**, 611
registration area, **12**, 605
rules, **12**, 612–617
 amendment, **12**, 616
 audit, **12**, 613
 books, inspection of, **12**, 615
 borrowing powers, **12**, 613
 committee, **12**, 613
 constitution and byelaws, **12**, 612
 copies to be given on request, **12**, 614
 disputes, regulation of settlement, **12**, 615
 fourteen points, **12**, 612, 613
 fraudulent issue of, **12**, 655
 funds in possession of officers, security for, **12**, 615, 620
 instrument needed to carry out obejectives of society, **12**, 615
 investment of funds, **12**, 613
 managers, **12**, 613
 meetings, procedure, **12**, 613
 members—
  advances to, **12**, 615, 623
  age restriction, **12**, 615
  termination of membership, **12**, 613
  terms of admission, **12**, 613
 model, **12**, 612

Industrial and provident society—*continued*
rules—*continued*
 name, **12**, 613
 objects, **12**, 613
 officers, **12**, 613
 ownership or tenancy of land, **12**, 615
 preparation, **12**, 612
 profit, application of, **12**, 613
 registered office, **12**, 613
 registrar, negotiation with, **12**, 612
 seal, use of, **12**, 613
 shareholdings, **12**, 613
seal, use of, **12**, 613
secretary, **12**, 619
shareholdings, **12**, 606, 613, 618, 621
society no longer meeting its original description, **12**, 611
source and meaning of title, **12**, 606*n*
special meeting, call for, **12**, 646
sponsoring organizations, model rules supplied by, **12**, 612
subsidiary companies or societies—
 group accounts, **12**, 633
 meaning, **12**, 633
supervision, **12**, 606
supervisory functions, **12**, 604
transfer of engagements to another society, **12**, 649
Industrial rationalisation scheme
exemption, **4**, 1158
Industrial relations
collective bargaining, **9**, 7
general characteristics, **9**, 5
statute law, role of, **9**, 8
union membership, **9**, 6
See also COLLECTIVE AGREEMENT; COLLECTIVE BARGAINING; TRADE UNION
Industrial scholarship
award of, **8**, 708
Industrial school
local authority library service loans to inmates, **13**, 1505
Industrial training board
enterprise zone, liability of, **14**, 647
Industrial tribunal
appeal from, **6**, 961, 963, 992*ff*
appeal to—
 generally, **9**, 326
 improvement notice, against—
  burden of proof, **9**, 508
  decisions, review of, **9**, 509
  effect of, **9**, 507
  judicial review, **9**, 510
  jurisdiction, **9**, 504
  procedure, **9**, 505
  relevant factors, **9**, 506
 prohibition notice, against—
  burden of proof, **9**, 508
  decisions, review of, **9**, 509
  effect of, **9**, 507
  judicial review, **9**, 510
  jurisdiction, **9**, 504
  procedure, **9**, 505
  relevant factors, **9**, 506

Industrial tribunal—*continued*
award, enforcement of, **9**, 328
commencement of proceedings, **9**, 314
conciliation, **9**, 315
constitution, **9**, 303
decision—
  generally, **9**, 324
  review of, **9**, 325
Employment Appeal Tribunal, *see* EMPLOYMENT
  APPEAL TRIBUNAL
equal pay claim, procedure on, **9**, 327
establishment of, **6**, 981; **9**, 302
exclusions, **9**, 331
further information, **9**, 317
hearing—
  evidence, **9**, 322
  expenses, **9**, 323
  notice of, **9**, 322
  preliminary, **9**, 320
  witnesses, **9**, 322
jurisdiction—
  common law, **9**, 305
  contract of employment, existence of, **9**, 308
  dismissal, need for, **9**, 306
  employment outside Great Britain, **9**, 312
  extension of, **6**, 981
  fixed-term contract, **9**, 311
  generally, **9**, 330
  limits of, **9**, 304
  preservation of, **6**, 982
  qualifying period, **9**, 310
  statutory provisions, **9**, 305
  territorial, under procedural regulations, **9**, 313
  time limits, **9**, 307
legal aid, **9**, 329
local authority solicitors, participation in, **13**, 1447
miscellaneous powers, **9**, 316
pre-hearing assessment, **9**, 321
precedent, as binding authority, **22**, 328, 330
redundancy payments, **6**, 981
supervision of by Scottish Committee, **23**, 911*n*
unfair dismissal, **6**, 981
wages, complaints relating to deductions from, **9**, 65
witness orders, **9**, 318
written representations, **9**, 319
Industrial waste
collection of, **9**, 1169
Industry
balanced distribution of, Monopolies and Mergers
  Commission regard for, **4**, 563
commerce, *see* COMMERCE
enterprise zone, *see* ENTERPRISE ZONE
equipment—
  government grants and investment schemes, **14**,
    1006
  taxation allowances, **14**, 1006
expenditure programme, **5**, 579
financial assistance to, **14**, 312, 639, 640
industrial—
  lands and heritages, valuation roll, **24**, 432
  major accident hazard, control of, **9**, 533
  plant, handling hazardous substances, **9**, 1201
  pollution, **19**, 303
    See also POLLUTION

Industry—*continued*
industrial—*continued*
  promotion—
    aims, **14**, 631
    code of practice, **14**, 636
    development powers, relationship with
      enactments conferring, **14**, 635
    district council, powers of, **14**, 634
    islands council, powers of, **14**, 633
    limitations on powers, **14**, 632
    regional council, powers of, **14**, 633
  loan—
    building, erection of, **14**, 639
    interest, **14**, 639
    land, acquisition of, **14**, 639
    security for advance, **14**, 639
  pollution, *see* POLLUTION; SMOKE
Industry Department for Scotland
assistance for financial institutions by, **2**, 1282
ministerial responsibilities, **14**, 102
Scottish Office, Legal Civil Service, **13**, 1401
Inescutcheon
meaning and effect, **11**, 1629
Inevitability doctrine
due care and diligence, proof of, **14**, 2112
limits of, **14**, 2112
Infancy
meaning, **10**, 1050
Infant
See CHILD-CHILDREN
Infanticide
Scots law, generally, **7**, 258
Infection
fear of, **14**, 2082
Infectious disease
See DISEASE
Infeftment
clauses excluding assignees before, **6**, 524
granter of feu grants, of, **6**, 475
meaning, **18**, 93
public, **18**, 93
without entry, **18**, 93, 102
Inferior courts
meaning, **6**, 1155
summary procedure, **6**, 1155
trial without jury, **17**, 560
Infertility treatment
databank information on, limitation on access to,
  18, 1541
See also ARTIFICIAL INSEMINATION
Infestation
food, of, **11**, 317
Infirm person
contributory negligence by, **15**, 406
Inflammable substances or materials
conveyance—
  road, by, **19**, 388–391
  water, by, **19**, 392–394
disused containers, **19**, 399
gas, prevention of ignition, **14**, 1650
inspection, testing and seizure, **19**, 405 411
  inspectors, appointment of, **19**, 405
  obstruction, **19**, 408, 411
  samples, purchase of, **19**, 406

Inflammable substances or materials—
continued
inspecting, testing and seizure—*continued*
  search warrants, **19**, 409, 411
  written notice of tests, **19**, 407
labelling, **19**, 395, 396
packaging, **19**, 396
petroleum, *see* PETROLEUM-PETROLEUM-SPIRIT
public health legislation, **19**, 383–411
  enforcement, **19**, 386
  scope, **19**, 383
storage, **14**, 1661; **19**, 383, 383*n*, 397
transport, **19**, 383
See also HAZARDOUS SUBSTANCES; NOXIOUS
  SUBSTANCES
Inflation
capital gains tax allowance for, **19**, 1528
fire insurance, **25**, 144
price agreement as counter-inflationary device, **4**,
  1163
Ingleby Committee, 22, 4
Inherent condition of the right
See REAL BURDEN
Inheritance tax
accumulation of income, **24**, 38
administration and collection, **19**, 1544
agricultural property relief, *see* AGRICULTURE
annual exemption, **19**, 1533
appeals, **25**, 1022
assessment, **25**, 1021
bequests, attribution of value to, **25**, 1018
business property relief, **19**, 1533; **25**, 56
calculation of, **25**, 1016
capital gains tax—
  interaction with, **19**, 1600
  value of asset binding for, **25**, 55
capital transfer tax replaced by, **25**, 624
charge of, generally, **19**, 1616
chargeable transfer, **19**, 1532; **25**, 624
  meaning, **8**, 652
charitable gift, **25**, 1010
charity, treatment of, *see* CHARITY (inheritance
  tax)
cumulative gifts, **8**, 652
cumulative total of transfers, **19**, 1532
death, charge on, **19**, 1532
debts preferred to, **25**, 847
deceased's estate, charge on—
  generally, **25**, 1003
  property included in, **25**, 1004
  valuations—
    certain types of property, of, **25**, 1006
    debts, deduction of, **25**, 1008
    expenses, deduction of, **25**, 1008
    generally, **25**, 1005
    property left out of account, **25**, 1007
deeds of family arrangement, **25**, 1028
disclaimers, **25**, 1028
discretionary trust, transfers into—
  partnerships, **16**, 1137
disposition, **8**, 652
donations *inter vivos*, **8**, 652
donations *mortis causa*, **8**, 652
donee, **8**, 652

Inheritance tax—*continued*
donor, **8**, 652
excluded property, **19**, 1534
executors—
  discharge of, **25**, 1027
  lifetime transfers, liability for, **25**, 1002
exemptions, **8**, 652
  charities, gifts to, **25**, 1010
  generally, **19**, 1533
  national heritage property, **19**, 1533; **25**, 1011
  public bodies, gifts to, **25**, 1010
  spouses, transfers between, **25**, 1009
expenses, deduction of, **25**, 1008
extra, **19**, 1616
fiscal distinguished from real market values, **25**, 67
gifts, lifetime—
  cash, made with, **19**, 1606
  charities, to, **19**, 1533
  chattels, **19**, 1610
  cheque, made by, **19**, 1606
  contract, preceded by, **19**, 1602
  corporeal moveable property, **19**, 1604
  exemptions and reliefs, **19**, 1533
  general principles, **19**, 1532, 1601, 1618
  heritable property, **19**, 1603
  incorporeal moveable property, **19**, 1605
  joint bank account, money in, **19**, 1612
  joint and common property, **19**, 1611, 1619
  marriage, in consideration of, **19**, 1533
  national body, to, **19**, 1533
  normal expenditure of income, **19**, 1533
  reservation, subject to, **19**, 1532, 1607–1610
  small, **19**, 1533
  spouses, between, **19**, 1533
  time of completion, **19**, 1601–1606
  tracing of property, **19**, 1608
  trustee's heirs, destination to, **19**, 1609
gifts with reservation, **8**, 652
husband and wife, **10**, 893; **19**, 1533, 1574, 1575,
  1577, 1578
separate taxation, **25**, 56
transfers between spouses, **25**, 1009
incidence of, **25**, 1017
Inland Revenue charge, property subject to, **25**,
  1025
intellectual property rights, payments in respect
  of, **18**, 1601
introduction of, **24**, 17
inventory, delivery of, **25**, 1019
land, valuation for, **6**, 1141, 1149
legal rights—
  generally, **25**, 1029
  potential claimant for, **25**, 790
liability for—
  acceptance of property in satisfaction, **25**, 1024
  meaning, **25**, 1020
  persons liable, **25**, 1020
liferents, **19**, 1640
lifetime gifts—
  partnerships, **16**, 1137
lifetime transfers, **19**, 1310
  executors' liability, **25**, 1002
  exempt, **25**, 999
  gift subject to reservation, **25**, 1001

Inheritance tax—*continued*
lifetime transfers—*continued*
  liabilities in respect of, **25**, 999–1002
  seven years before death, within, **25**, 1000
maintenance payments—
  capital transfers, **10**, 999
  lump sums, **10**, 998
  periodical payments, **10**, 998
maintenance payments and transfers of property
  on matrimonial breakdown—
  capital transfers, **10**, 999
  lump sums, **10**, 998
  periodical payments, **10**, 998
measure of charge, **19**, 1532
minor's property, **19**, 1583
national heritage property, **19**, 1533; **25**, 1011
occupational pension scheme—
  generally, **21**, 1334
  Inheritance Act 1984 ..., **21**, 1335
  payments made by schemes, **21**, 1334, 1337
  payments made to schemes, **21**, 1334, 1336
  sponsored superannuation scheme, **21**, 1335
  ten-yearly and exit charges on settlements, **21**,
    1334, 1338
partner, death of—
  liability for payment of tax, **16**, 1139
  valuation of estate, **16**, 1139
  valuation of interest in partnership, **16**, 1140
partnership, **19**, 1588–1591
  partnership property, generally, **16**, 1073, 1124
  transfer of value by, **16**, 1138
  value of partnership shares, **19**, 1596
partnership share, on value of, **16**, 1137; **19**, 1596
  instalments, payment in, **16**, 1137
payment of, **25**, 1023
potentially exempt transfer, **8**, 652; **19**, 1533; **25**,
  56
prior rights, exemption of property passing by,
  19, 1623
professional sportsmen, **19**, 1310
property—
  Inland Revenue charge, subject to, **25**, 1025
  liability, acceptance in satisfaction of, **25**, 1024
  situated outside United Kingdom, **19**, 1534
  transfer of, **19**, 1598, 1599, 1600
pupil's property, **19**, 1582
qualifying sale of shares, **25**, 56
rate, **19**, 1532
recovery of, **25**, 1026
reliefs—
  agricultural property, *see* AGRICULTURE
  assets from deceased's estate, sale of, **25**, 1015
  business property, **19**, 1533; **25**, 1012
  generally, **19**, 1533
  quick succession, **25**, 1014
house, *see* husband and wife *above*; DIVORCE,
  EFFECT OF
succession, generally, *see* SUCCESSION
survivorship clauses, **25**, 1030
transfer of property, generally, **19**, 1598–1600
transfer of value, **19**, 1532; **25**, 56
trusts—
  accumulation and maintenance, **19**, 1533
  transfers into and out of, **19**, 1532, 1533

Inheritance tax—*continued*
valuations, and, **25**, 56
  land, **6**, 1141, 1149
vitious intromitter, liability of, **25**, 637
woodlands, **11**, 651–654
  deferral of tax, **11**, 651
  advantages of, **11**, 653
  agricultural land, **11**, 654
  subsequent disposal, **11**, 652; **19**, 1510
zero band, **19**, 1532
Inhibition
assignation, **8**, 186
attachment—
  inhibition after attachment, **8**, 181
  inhibition after floating charge but before
    attachment, **8**, 180
bill and letters, **8**, 138
  fiated, **8**, 138
  procedure without, **8**, 139
caveat, **8**, 147
child support liability order, **8**, 134
company administration, and, **8**, 183
consistorial causes—
  inhibition in security, **8**, 135, 136
Court of Session jurisdiction, **4**, 8
creation—
  bill and letters, **8**, 138
    procedure without, **8**, 139
  date from which inhibition effective, **8**, 142
  Land Register of Scotland, **8**, 144
  notice, **8**, 143
  registration, **8**, 141
  renewal, **8**, 145
  Sasine Register, **8**, 144
  service, **8**, 140
date from which effective, **8**, 142
death of debtor, **8**, 127, 153
death of inhibitor, **8**, 153, 186
debt, passing automatically with, **8**, 186
debt contracted by debtor after, **8**, 133
dependence, on the, *see* INHIBITION ON THE
  DEPENDENCE
diligence, as, **8**, 101
Diligence Register, **8**, 141*n*
discharge, **8**, 146
  grounds for, **8**, 148
  partial, **8**, 146
document of debt, on, **8**, 134
effects, **8**, 133
  debtor barred from sale or disposal of heritable
    estate, **8**, 161
  debts contracted by debtor after inhibition, **8**,
    163
  generally, **8**, 155, 159
  granting of security over heritable estate barred,
    8, 162
  multiplepoinding, **8**, 171
  no real right, **8**, 160
  reduction, **8**, 168
    further procedure, **8**, 170
    when not required, **8**, 169
  security, inhibition as, **8**, 166
  where no debts or deeds, **8**, 167
execution, in, **8**, 134

Inhibition—*continued*
expenses—
  generally, **8**, 187
  liability for, **8**, 131
extinction—
  caveat, **8**, 147
  death of debtor, **8**, 153
  death of inhibitor, **8**, 153
  discharge, **8**, 146
    grounds for, **8**, 148
  interdict, **8**, 147
  nimiety, **8**, 149
  oppression, **8**, 149
  prescription, **8**, 154
  recall—
    expenses for application, **8**, 152
    generally, **8**, 147
    grounds for, **8**, 148
    ineffectiveness, for, **8**, 151
    third party, **8**, 150
  restriction, **8**, 146
floating charges, and—
  generally, **8**, 178
  inhibition after floating charge but before
    attachment, **8**, 180
  inhibition prior to floating charge, **8**, 179
future voluntary debts and deeds—
  debtor barred from sale or disposal of heritable
    estate, **8**, 161
  generally, **8**, 159, 161–165, 167
  granting of security over heritable estate barred,
    8, 162
generally, **8**, 133
grant, **8**, 133
heritable property, **18**, 13
heritable securities—
  after inhibition, **8**, 173
  future advances, security for, **8**, 174
  heritable creditor, inhibition against, **8**, 175
  prior to inhibition, **8**, 172
insolvency procedures and, **8**, 176–183
interdict, **8**, 147
jurisdiction, **4**, 8; **8**, 133
Land Register of Scotland, **8**, 144
letters of, **8**, 120
liquidation, and, **8**, 182
meaning, **8**, 133
multiplepoinding, **8**, 171
nature of, **8**, 133
nimiety, **8**, 149
no real right vested by, **8**, 160
non-adjudgeable lease, **8**, 155
notice of, **8**, 143
officers of court, exercise by, **8**, 105
oppression, **8**, 149
pecuniary, claim must be, **8**, 137
  exceptions to rule, **8**, 137
Personal Register, **8**, 141*n*
prescription, **8**, 154
property law, and—
  acquirenda, **8**, 156
  acquisata, **8**, 156
  generally, **8**, 155
  heritable property, **8**, 155

Inhibition—*continued*
property law, and—*continued*
  joint and common property, **8**, 158
  property affected by inhibition, **8**, 155
  trust property, **8**, 157
ranking processes, **8**, 133
re-inhibition, **8**, 154
recall, **8**, 133
  expenses for application, **8**, 152
  generally, **8**, 147
  grounds for, **8**, 148
  ineffectiveness, for, **8**, 151
  third party, **8**, 149
receivership, and, **8**, 178
reduction—
  contraventions, of, **8**, 133
  further procedure, **8**, 170
  generally, **8**, 168
  when not required, **8**, 169
Register of Inhibitions and Adjudications, **8**, 141
registration, **8**, 141
renewal, **8**, 145
restriction, **8**, 146
sale, transfer by barred by, **8**, 133
Sasine Register, **8**, 144
searches—
  clear search, **8**, 185
  length of search, **8**, 184
security, in—
  consistorial causes, **8**, 135, 136
  debtor *meditatione fugae*, **8**, 135
  debtor *vergens ad inopiam*, **8**, 135
  meaning, **8**, 135
  recall, **8**, 135
security, inhibition as, **8**, 166
security over property barred by, **8**, 133
sequestration, and, **8**, 176
service, **8**, 140
sheriff court jurisdiction, **4**, 8
summary diligence, by way of, **8**, 134
third party recall, **8**, 149
title to heritage, implement of obligation to grant,
  8, 137
transfer of property barred by, **8**, 133
trust deeds for behoof of creditors, **8**, 177
types, **8**, 134
use on dependence of action, **8**, 120
winding up, effect of, **4**, 844
wrongous, damages for, **8**, 188
Inhibition on the dependence
abuse of process, **15**, 465
civil legal aid, urgency, situation of, **13**, 1048
discharge and recall, **8**, 147
  expenses of application, **8**, 152
  grounds for, **8**, 148
generally, **8**, 134
nimiety, **8**, 149
oppression, **8**, 149
recall, caution, requirement for, **3**, 997
Inhibitions and Adjudications, Register of
access to, **19**, 878
awards recorded in, **2**, 1338, 1340

Inhibitions and Adjudications, Register of—
continued
entry in—
deferment of debtor's discharge, **2**, 1439
effect of, **2**, 1340
error or omission in, **6**, 766
generally, **6**, 465, 707; **19**, 820, 840
keeper of, court orders to be sent to, **2**, 1340
matters to be recorded, **2**, 1340; **13**, 66
notice of reduction, **13**, 66
rectification and reduction, recording, **13**, 66
registration in, **8**, 141, 193, 195
searches, **6**, 465, 641; **8**, 184, 185; **19**, 851
title sheets, Register entries to be listed in, **6**, 707
Inhibitor
death of, **8**, 153, 186
discharge of inhibition by, **8**, 146
Injunction
interlocutory remedy, *see* INTERDICT (INTERIM)
See INTERDICT
Injurious affection
basis of assessment, **5**, 172
compensation for, **5**, 33; **25**, 520, 522
injury to land, **5**, 171
land taken and land retained, link between, **5**, 170
no land taken, where—
construction of works—
damage arising from, **5**, 177
damage caused by, **5**, 173
interest in land, damage to, **5**, 176
land, damage to, **5**, 176
right of action but for Act, **5**, 175
three propositions, **5**, 174
use of works, claims—
generally, **5**, 182
works whose use gives rise to, **5**, 180
damage caused by, **5**, 173
effects of works, mitigation of, **5**, 184
entitlement to compensation, **5**, 179
generally, **5**, 178
interests qualifying for compensation, **5**, 181
severance distinguished from, **5**, 169
short tenancy, **5**, 185
water supply, in relation to, **25**, 520, 522
See also DAMAGE
Injury
animals, by, *see* ANIMAL
competition, legitimate, **15**, 575
Criminal Injuries Compensation Scheme *see* CRIMINAL INJURIES COMPENSATION SCHEME
culpa as proximate cause, **11**, 1019
culpably and recklessly, **7**, 82, 247
derivative or parasitic economic loss, **15**, 574
economic loss, **15**, 574
non-relational, **15**, 574
economic relationship, to, *see* ECONOMIC RELATIONSHIP
failure to protect others from, **7**, 40
family relationship, to, *see* FAMILY RELATIONSHIP
fireman, to—
firemen's pension scheme, **10**, 1448
liability of occupier, **10**, 1475
interference with honour and reputation, *see* HONOUR AND REPUTATION, INTERFERENCE WITH

Injury—*continued*
interference with liberty, *see* DETENTION, WRONGFUL; LIBERTY
obligation of reparation, **11**, 1032
personal, *see* PERSONAL INJURY
pure economic loss, **15**, 574
questions of, legal advice and assistance, **13**, 1028
radiation, from, compensation for, **9**, 1198
reporting of, **9**, 534
verbal, *see* VERBAL INJURY
Inland Revenue
accountant dealing with, **1**, 100
charge, property subject to, **25**, 1025
collection and administration of taxes, **19**, 1545
disclosure of information to, by Commissioners of Customs and Excise, **7**, 1283
extra-statutory concessions—
contrast with statements of practice, **22**, 243
legality, **22**, 242
quasi-legislative, **22**, 241
inventory, delivery of, **25**, 1019
preferential debts, **4**, 853
Share Valuation Division, recent values agreed with, **25**, 51
special powers, **8**, 128
Inland Revenue Board (Scotland)
legal staff, **13**, 1411
Solicitor (Scotland), duties, **13**, 1411
Inland Revenue Commissioners
administration and collection of taxes, **19**, 1544
appeals from, **19**, 1502
charitable tax exemption, claim for, **3**, 1101
Inland Revenue Pension Schemes Office (PSO)
occupational pension scheme, approval of, **21**, 1284, 1285
See also PENSION (OCCUPATIONAL)
Inland Revenue Superannuation Funds Office
generally, **21**, 1284
Inland waters
control of, **14**, 686
generally, **21**, 112
meaning, **11**, 5*n*
salvage operations, **21**, 440
Inland waterways
Convention on the Contract for the International Carriage of Goods by Road (CMR), **3**, 646
EU transport policy, **3**, 731
See CANALS AND INLAND WATERWAYS
Inland Waterways Amenity Advisory Council
constitution, **19**, 1118
functions, **19**, 1119
Inn
English law compared, **11**, 1705, 1707, 1715
essential requirement, **15**, 147, 149
innkeeper, *see* INNKEEPER
meaning, **11**, 1707
public house, deemed to be, **2**, 9
See also PUBLIC HOUSE
Inner House
See COURT OF SESSION

Inner London Education Authority
elections, **14**, 62
functions, **14**, 60
Inner urban area
action, special arrangements for determining, **14**, 655
designated district, **14**, 649
different expenditure powers, relationship between, **14**, 660
generally, **14**, 648
grant—
amenities, improvement of, **14**, 653
building, conversion or improvement, **14**, 654
co-operative enterprise, establishment of, **14**, 651
common ownership, establishment of, **14**, 651
urban programme, eligibility for, **14**, 661
improvement area, **14**, 652
loan—
amenities, improvement of, **14**, 653
building, conversion or improvement, **14**, 654
co-operative enterprise, establishment of, **14**, 651
common ownership, establishment of, **14**, 651
designated district authority, by, **14**, 650
ministerial initiatives, **14**, 655
Secretary of State's powers, **14**, 655
special area—
generally, **14**, 656
loan—
interest, grant towards, **14**, 659
site preparation, for, **14**, 657
rent, grant towards, **14**, 658
Innkeeper
game, sale of, **11**, 836
general objection of, **11**, 1705
generally, *see* HOTELKEEPER
lien—
extent of, **20**, 91
extinction, **20**, 92
nature of, **20**, 90
possession, **20**, 92
right of, **13**, 95
sale, power of, **20**, 93
medieval law, **19**, 202, 202*n*
strict liability, **15**, 147
damnum fatale, defence of, **15**, 148
defences, **15**, 148
edictal, **15**, 144, 147
exceptions, **15**, 148
goods deposited with innkepper for safe custody, **15**, 149
Hotel Proprietors Act 1956, effect, **15**, 149
limitation, **15**, 149
modern position, **15**, 147
negligence by traveller, where, **15**, 148
Queen's enemies, act of, **15**, 148
Roman law, **15**, 144, 147
sleeping accommodation, requirement as to, **15**, 149
statutory notice, display, **15**, 149
time limits, **15**, 149
vehicles, live animals, etc, **15**, 149
See also INN

Innocence
presumption of, **10**, 754
European Convention on Human Rights, **12**, 43, 53
Universal Declaration of Human Rights, **12**, 4*n*
rebuttable presumption in favour of, **10**, 750
Innocent misrepresentation
See MISREPRESENTATION
Innocent passage, right of
territorial sea, *see* TERRITORIAL SEA
Innocent publication
defences, **17**, 30
Innominate offence
generally, **7**, 24
indictment, **7**, 24
Innuendo
actions, by, **15**, 496
defamation—
circumstances of statement, **15**, 495
examples, **15**, 499
generally, **15**, 495
matters of fact and law, **15**, 498
pursuer's onus, **15**, 496
reasonable man test, **15**, 497
definition, **15**, 495
foreign language, in, **15**, 496
words, by, **15**, 496
Input tax
See VALUE ADDED TAX
Inquest
England and Wales, **17**, 975
See also FATAL ACCIDENT INQUIRY
Inquiry
Commissioners of Customs and Excise, held by, **7**, 1213
electricity, in connection with, **9**, 658
generating station, into, **9**, 629
fatal accident, *see* FATAL ACCIDENT INQUIRIES
Health and Safety Commission, by—
See HEALTH AND SAFETY COMMISSION
local, *see* LOCAL INQUIRY
public local inquiry, *see* PUBLIC LOCAL INQUIRY
railway accident, into, **19**, 1003, 1004, 1071
reasons for decision, giving, **1**, 291
review of proceedings, person applying for, **1**, 315
sport or recreation, matters connected with, **19**, 1207
Inquiry Reporters' Unit
clerk, attendance at public local inquiry of, **23**, 927
functions of, **23**, 920*n*
planning law—
examination in public, **23**, 263
functions, **23**, 4
Insanity
alcoholism, **7**, 133
alienation, requirement for, **7**, 114, 121, 122, 127
American Law Institute test, **7**, 117
automatism, *see* AUTOMATISM
bank account of insane person, **2**, 1258
bar of trial, as plea in, **7**, 125
subsequent fitness to plead, **7**, 125
battered woman syndrome, **7**, 147
burden of proof, **7**, 124, 125; **10**, 747, 756

Insanity—*continued*

capacity of testator, challenge to, **25**, 762

Cardle v Mulrainey, **7**, 122

cognition of insane person, **11**, 1232

Courts-Martial Appeal Court powers, **6**, 890

criteria—
    causal tests, **7**, 115, 118, 120
    cognitive tests, **7**, 115, 116, 119, 120, 122
    control tests, **7**, 115, 117

defence of, **7**, 34, 92, 125
    chronic alcoholism, **7**, 133
    strict liability, where, **7**, 108

depression, **7**, 147

development of Scots law on, **7**, 119, 120

diminished responsibility, *see* DIMINISHED
    RESPONSIBILITY

donation, incapacity to make, **8**, 611

ground for removal of trustee, **24**, 133, 168

hearsay evidence, statement by insane person as,
    10, 711

Hume's view, **7**, 119

incapacity, **11**, 1053, 1067
    dole, for, **11**, 1054
    donation, as to, **8**, 611

intoxication, **7**, 113, 127–130

legal, **7**, 113

lunatics, care of, **14**, 35

meaning, **7**, 113, 114
    current definition, **7**, 121

medical, **7**, 113

mens rea, **7**, 123, 129

mental disease or defect, **7**, 114, 121

mental disorder, meaning, **14**, 1401

mental illness, **7**, 114, 121

mental incapacity due to external factor, **7**, 124

M'Naghten Rules, **7**, 116, 117, 120, 121, 122,
    155

natural incapacity, **24**, 128

offence, at time of commission of, **14**, 1461

offeree or offeror, of, effect, **15**, 616, 652

personality disorders, **7**, 144

plea in bar of trial, **7**, 125; **17**, 688, 896

poor relief, **14**, 34, 35

pre-menstrual syndrome, **7**, 146

presumption of sanity, **7**, 124

promisor or promisee, of, **15**, 616

psychopathy, **7**, 144, 145

special defences, **17**, 553, 895, 902

strict liability, and, **7**, 123

trial, in bar of, **14**, 1460; **17**, 896

unsoundness of mind, **7**, 114, 121

voluntary obligation, insane person's capacity to
    enter, **15**, 661

See also MENTAL HEALTH; MENTALLY DISORDERED
    PERSON

Inshore fishing

See FISHERIES

Insider dealing

civil remedies, potential, **12**, 1535

communication of information to others who
    may deal, **12**, 1502, 1518

company, meaning, **12**, 1506

company securities, legislation aimed at, **12**,
    1501

Insider dealing—*continued*

confidentiality of information, **12**, 1509

contemplated transactions, **12**, 1511

counselling or procuring others to deal, **12**, 1502,
    1517

creation of offence, **4**, 305

deal—
    meaning, **12**, 1510
    outside United Kingdom, **12**, 1502

debentures, **12**, 1510

defences to, **12**, 1527

director, **12**, 1501, 1505, 1506, 1507
    body corporate as, **12**, 1506
    shadow director, **12**, 1506

employee of company or related company, **12**,
    1507

European Community directive, **12**, 1536

facilitating the completion or carrying out of
    transaction, **12**, 1530

individual connected with a company—
    dealings by, **12**, 1502
        in securities of another company, **12**, 1511
        in securities of same company, **12**, 1503–
            1510
    who is regarded as, **12**, 1505

information obtained in official capacity, abuse of,
    12, 1519–1522

insider information must be held as a result of
    connection with company, **12**, 1509

investigation by Department of Trade, **4**, 309

investigations into, **12**, 1533

jobber, **12**, 1529

knowingly connected, individual must be, **12**,
    1508

liquidator, action in good faith by, **12**, 1528

loss, thing done other than to avoid, **12**, 1527

manager, **12**, 1507, 1507*n*

market maker, **12**, 1529

meaning, **12**, 1501

off-market deals, **12**, 1502, 1523, 1524
    deals outside Great Britain, **12**, 1525

permitted actions, **12**, 1526

personal representative, permitted actions by, **12**,
    1532

price stabilisation, **12**, 1531

primary insider, **12**, 1501
    off-market deals outside Great Britain, **12**, 1525
    prohibitions on, **12**, 1502

profit, thing done other than to make, **12**, 1527

prohibited dealings, generally, **12**, 1503

public servant, **12**, 1501, 1502, 1519–1522
    tippee rules, **12**, 1522

punishment of offences, **12**, 1534

receiver, action in good faith by, **12**, 1528

recognised stock exchange, dealing on, **12**, 1502

reform, proposals for, **12**, 1536

related company, meaning, **12**, 1506, 1507

secondary insider (tippee), **12**, 1501, 1509
    off-market deals outside Great Britain, **12**, 1525
    prohibitions on, **12**, 1502, 1512, 1513
    public servant, information obtained from, **12**,
        1522

secretary, company, **12**, 1507, 1507*n*

securities, meaning, **12**, 1510

Insider dealing—*continued*
shares, **12**, 1510
SIB Core Conduct of Business Rules, **12**, 1387
statutory codes relating to, **4**, 306, 307
statutory offences, **12**, 1501
takeover offers, and, **12**, 1502, 1514, 1515
  Panel on Takeovers and Mergers, members and staff, **12**, 1520
  tippee from individuals contemplating takeover offers, **12**, 1516
tippee, *see* secondary insider *above*
trustee, permitted actions by, **12**, 1532
trustee in bankruptcy, action in good faith by, **12**, 1528
unpublished price sensitive information, **12**, 1509
  meaning, **12**, 1504
wilful blindness, **12**, 1508

Insignia of office
generally, **11**, 1610
grant of additaments, **11**, 1610, 1621
lieutenancy, **5**, 562
Lord Justice-General, **11**, 1610
messenger-at-arms, of, **14**, 1502, 1503

Insolvency
absolute—
  meaning, **2**, 1390
  presumption or proof, **2**, 1390
adjudication rendering debtor apparently, **8**, 201
administration, *see* ADMINISTRATION
apparent—
  adjudication, **8**, 221
  body corporate, **2**, 1324
  circumstances constituting, **2**, 1323
  claim by creditor not met, **2**, 1323
  duration of, **2**, 1325
  effect, **4**, 848
  equalisation of arrestments, **8**, 291
  establishment, necessity for, **2**, 1322
  meaning, **2**, 1322
  partnership, **2**, 1324
  poinding, **8**, 244
  real poinding, **8**, 368
  sequestration, constituted by, **2**, 1323
  sequestration for rent, **8**, 386
  tenant, of, **13**, 414
  time limits as to, **2**, 1332
cautionary obligations—
  cautioner—
    principal debtor insolvent, where, **3**, 953–956
    principal debtor solvent, where, **3**, 948–950
  co-cautioner, **3**, 942
  principal debtor—
    cautioner insolvent, where, **3**, 953–956
    cautioner solvent, where, **3**, 951, 952
company fraud, **7**, 380
contract, of party to—
  administrators, **15**, 823
  contractual provisions as to, **15**, 819
  effect on title to sue, **15**, 819
  generally, **15**, 817, 819
  liquidators, **15**, 821
  receivers, **15**, 822

Insolvency—*continued*
contract, of party to—*continued*
  sequestration—
    delectus personae, **15**, 819
    trustee in, **15**, 820
contract, termination of—
  receiver, appointment of, **9**, 146
  sequestration, **9**, 145
  winding-up, **9**, 145
conventional incapacity, **24**, 128
Cork Report, **4**, 308
corporate, solicitor's lien, **20**, 100
corporeal moveable property, **11**, 778
court outwith Scotland, order or judgment made by, **8**, 544*ff*
  discharge of bankrupt by foreign order, **8**, 551
  mutual assistance scheme, **8**, 549
  recognition, **8**, 550
  UK reciprocal enforcement scheme, *see* UK reciprocal enforcement scheme *below*
debtor's, right in security as safeguard against, **20**, 1
discharge in—
  court outwith Scotland, order or judgment made by, **8**, 551
  UK reciprocal enforcement scheme, **8**, 548
donor, of, **8**, 648
electricity supply, disconnection in respect of, **9**, 701
employer of—
  statutory maternity pay, payment provisions, **21**, 901
  statutory sick pay, payment provisions, **21**, 917
foreign, arrestment and, **8**, 298
fraud or unfairness in relation to, **11**, 776
fraudulent preferences, **11**, 781
generally, **9**, 144
gratuitous alienations, **11**, 780
historical summary, **2**, 1301–1303
insolvency practitioner, *see* INSOLVENCY PRACTITIONER
interim trustee, duties, **2**, 1309
jurisdiction, **8**, 431, 435
lessee, of, **13**, 185
  termination on breach, **14**, 1063
lessor, of, **13**, 159, 351
Northern Ireland, judgment made in, **8**, 546
occupational pension scheme, need for independent trustee, **21**, 1266–1272
preferential claims—
  national insurance, **9**, 150
  pension contributions, **9**, 150
  preferred debts, payments out of Redundancy Fund, **9**, 149
  salaries, for, **9**, 148
  statutory provisions, **9**, 147
  wages, for, **9**, 148
preferential rights, hypothec distinguished, **20**, 101
proceedings—
  enforcement of—
    foreign corporate insolvency proceedings, **4**, 945
    within UK, **4**, 944
  foreign corporate, recognition and enforcement in Scotland, **4**, 945

Insolvency—*continued*
proceeding—*continued*
  recognition of—
    foreign corporate insolvency proceedings, **4**,
      945
    within UK, **4**, 944
  sederunt book, maintenance of, **4**, 839
proprietor of, standard securities, **20**, 165
public lending right transferred on, **13**, 1509
receivership, *see* RECEIVERSHIP
Redundancy Fund—
  claim from—
    generally, **9**, 151
    nature of, **9**, 155
    pension contributions, **9**, 156
    presentation of, **9**, 153
    subrogation, **9**, 157
  preferred debts, **9**, 149
  range of employees protected, **9**, 154
  scope of, **9**, 152
Register of—
  awards to be registered in, **2**, 1338
  contents, **2**, 1339
  maintenance of, **2**, 1339
retailer, of, **9**, 774
shareholder participating in management, liability,
  4, 319
tenant, of, **13**, 414
  irritancy, **13**, 415
transactions in fraud of creditors, **11**, 779
trustee's—
  apparent insolvency not ground for removal,
    24, 167
  beneficiaries' rights on, **24**, 50
  position as, **24**, 130
UK reciprocal enforcement scheme—
  discharge in insolvency, effect, **8**, 548
  effect given to UK insolvency order, **8**, 546
  generally, **8**, 484, 545
  limitation, **8**, 546
  mutual assistance provisions, **8**, 547
  scope of, **8**, 545
voluntary obligations, **11**, 777
winding up—
  insolvent company, **17**, 353
  termination of contract, **9**, 140, 145
  voluntary, provisions as to arbitration, **2**, 412
  See also BANKRUPTCY; WINDING UP
Insolvency practitioner
caution, **4**, 950
  regulations, generally, **3**, 994
  requirement for, **3**, 994
competent authority, authorisation by, **4**, 951
disqualifications, **2**, 1308; **4**, 948
Insolvency Practitioners Tribunal, **4**, 952; **23**,
  911*n*
interim, qualifications, **2**, 1308
only individual may be, **4**, 318
permanent trustee, as, **2**, 1314
position prior to 1985 reforms, **4**, 946
qualifications to act as, **2**, 1308
requisite qualifications, **4**, 949
scope of provisions as to, **4**, 947
security, **4**, 950

Inspector of Constabulary
appointment, **16**, 1733
assistant inspectors, **16**, 1733
duties, **16**, 1733
establishment, **16**, 1709
finance specialists, **16**, 1733
reports, **16**, 1733
role, **16**, 1733
staff officers, **16**, 1733
Inspector of salmon fisheries for Scotland
appointment, **11**, 32
functions, **11**, 32
Instalment credit
leasing, potential for, **14**, 1006
Instigation
art and part liability, **7**, 179, 183
  withdrawal of instigation, **7**, 184
attempted, **7**, 170, 176
generally, **7**, 160, 174
impossible objective, where, **7**, 176
Institute
conditional, **25**, 892
meaning, **25**, 891
substitute compared with, **25**, 891
testator's intention, **25**, 893
Institute of Actuaries
authorisation by, **12**, 1313
**Institute of Chartered Accountants in
  England and Wales**
authorisation by, **12**, 1313
origins, **1**, 8
**Institute of Chartered Accountants in
  Northern Ireland**
authorisation by, **12**, 1313
**Institute of Chartered Accountants of
  Scotland**
authorisation by, **12**, 1313
discipline, enforcing, **1**, 26
Ethical Guide, **1**, 33
generally, **1**, 8
joint disciplinary scheme, **1**, 27, 28
membership, education and training for, **1**, 15
practical experience, requiring, **1**, 16
See also ACCOUNTANT
**Institute of Cost and Management
  Accountants**
disciplinary arrangements, **1**, 35
generally, **1**, 9
Institute of Internal Auditors
generally, **1**, 10
Institution (place)
child born in, **19**, 1441
death occurring in, **19**, 1459
food supplied by, **11**, 342*n*
resident medical capacity, experience in, **14**, 1108
Institutional writers
'authoritative writings' as, **22**, 438–441
Bankton, Andrew McDouall, Lord, *see* BANKTON,
  ANDREW MCDOUALL, LORD
Bell, Professor George Joseph, *see* BELL, PROFESSOR
  GEORGE JOSEPH
canon of, **22**, 441
citation in court as authority, **22**, 538

Institutional writers—*continued*
Craig of Riccarton, Sir Thomas, *see* CRAIG OF
   RICCARTON, SIR THOMAS
criteria for entry into category, **22**, 538
custom, **22**, 364–369
   juristic treatment, **22**, 32, 33, 43, 530
   See also CUSTOM
description as, significance of, **22**, 438
Erskine, *see* ᶜRSKINE, ᴿOFESSOR ᴼHN
European context, **22**, 434
formal source of Scots law, as, **22**, 501, 534–538
Hume's *Commentaries* whether institutional
   writing, **22**, 537
'institutional', meaning, **22**, 439
judicial recognition, **22**, 439, 440
judiciary and, **22**, 259
Justinian's *Institutes*, **22**, 434, 534
Kames, *see* KAMES, HENRY HOME, LORD
Mackenzie, *see* MACKENZIE OF ROSEHAUGH, SIR
   GEORGE
meaning, **22**, 438, 534
modern judicial reference to, **22**, 259
Practicks, digest, **22**, 251
precedent, **22**, 251, 259, 543
primary source of law, as, **22**, 433, 439–441
relevance today, **22**, 259
Stair, *see* STAIR, SIR JAMES DALRYMPLE, VISCOUNT
   OF
stare decisis doctrine of, **22**, 538, 541, 542
terminology, **22**, 438
Union legislation as fundamental law, **22**, 147
vernacular, as opposed to Latin writing, **22**, 534
writers of institutional works distinguished, **22**,
   534
Institutions (incorporeal)
existence of entities through time, **11**, 1113
institutional fact, **11**, 1114
Insulation
noise, **9**, 1296
thermal, *see* THERMAL INSULATION
Insulting language
breach of the peace, whether, **7**, 454
Insurable interest
advantage or benefit, **12**, 849, 850
   expectation of, **12**, 850
carrier or custodier of goods, **12**, 852
child's life, in, **12**, 853
common law, **12**, 848
definition, **12**, 849
essential element of insurance contract, as, **12**,
   848
factual expectation test, **12**, 850*n*
heritable subjects, interest in passing to purchaser,
   12, 850, 850*n*, 900
hirer of goods, **12**, 852
indemnity insurance, **12**, 855
leases of property, **12**, 852
life assurance, **12**, 853
marine insurance, **12**, 855
nature of, **12**, 849–857
prerequisite to insurance contract, as, **12**, 802
property, **12**, 849, 851
   possession of, **12**, 852
statutory provisions, **12**, 848

Insurable interest—*continued*
tenant under lease, **12**, 852
time and—
   insuring, time of, **12**, 856
   loss, time of, **12**, 855, 856
   prospective cover, **12**, 857
   retrospective cover, **12**, 857
   when policy effected, **12**, 854
Insurance
advertising—
   annuity policy, **12**, 810
   linked long-term insurance, **12**, 810
advocate, indemnity insurance, practice rules, **13**,
   1322
agreed value policy, meaning, **12**, 888
annuity policy—
   advertisement of, **12**, 810
   Financial Services Act, application, **12**, 807
   friendly society, **12**, 810
assignation—
   assignatus utitur jure auctoris, **12**, 846
   donatio mortis causa, **12**, 847
   form and wording, **12**, 847
   intimation to insurer, necessity for, **12**, 847
   life policy, **12**, 854
   policy, of, **12**, 845, 846
   rights under policy, of, **12**, 845, 846
   subrogation compared, **12**, 894
   valid, prerequisites of, **12**, 847
   written, must be, **12**, 847
Association of British Insurers (ABI), *see*
   ASSOCIATION OF BRITISH INSURERS
average rule, insured's duty to account, **12**, 903
banker as insurance intermediary, **12**, 811
bankruptcy, Third Party (Rights Against Insurers)
   Act 1930, **12**, 904–910
bonus or commission paid to intermediary, **12**,
   812
broker—
   advertising by, **1**, 533
   code of conduct, **12**, 813
   complaints against, investigation of, **12**, 813
   disciplinary conmmittee, **12**, 813
   duty of care, **15**, 278
   entitlement to term, **12**, 813
   financial criteria to be satisfied, **12**, 813
   independent intermediary or broker, **12**, 806,
      811, 812
      code of practice, **12**, 815
   Insurance Brokers Registration Council, **12**,
      809
   list of thoses carrying on business as, **12**, 813
   negligence, compensation fund for victims of,
      12, 813
   partnership, as, **16**, 1011
   professional rules, contravention, **16**, 1017
   qualifications required, **12**, 813, 813*n*
   register of, **12**, 813
   regulation , **12**, 813
   temporary cover, authority to supply, **12**, 825
   title of, entitlement to use, **12**, 811
building contracts, *see* BUILDING CONTRACT
building society as insurance intermediary, **12**,
   811

Insurance—*continued*
capital redemption contract, Financial Services Act, **12**, 807
carrier or custodier of goods, **12**, 852
cash, premium payment by, **12**, 833
cattle insurance society, *see* CATTLE INSURANCE SOCIETY
causation, recovery dependent on, **12**, 879
cheque, premium payment by, **12**, 833
child, parents' insurable interest in life of, **12**, 853
claim—
    agreed value policy, **12**, 888
    assessment, services in connection with, **7**, 1421
    average clause, **12**, 893
    causation, and, **12**, 879
    excess clause, **12**, 891
    franchise clause, **12**, 892
    general principles, **12**, 880
    loss—
        betterment, allowance for, **12**, 886
        indemnity principle, **12**, 885, 886
            contractual variation, **12**, 887–893
        limit on, **12**, 886
            value of item lost higher than, **12**, 886
        notification of—
            by whom made, **12**, 883
            place for notification to be given, **12**, 882
            time limits, **12**, 881
        partial, **12**, 886
        particulars and proof of, **12**, 884
        recoverable—
            generally, **12**, 885, 886
            repairs, cost of, **12**, 886
    marine insurance, causation, **12**, 879
    reinstatement clause, **12**, 890
    replacement value policy, **12**, 889
    sale of goods repossessed under, **7**, 1290
    subrogation, *see* subrogation *below*
    time limit, **12**, 881
classification, **12**, 803–805
cold-calling to promote, **12**, 812
commercial lease, insurance clause, **13**, 580
company, *see* INSURANCE COMPANY
complaints, Insurance Ombudsman Bureau, **12**, 816
consumer protection—
    insurance intermediaries other than registered brokers, **12**, 815
    Insurance Ombudsman Bureau, **12**, 816
    Personal Insurance Arbitration Service, **12**, 817
    Policyholders Protection Board, **12**, 814
contract, **4**, 55, 56, 57; **12**, 802
    agreed value policy, **12**, 888
    average clause, **12**, 893
    basis of contract clause, **12**, 823
    breach of warranty, **12**, 835
    consensus in idem, **12**, 818
    counter-offer, **12**, 818
    cover dependent upon payment of first premium, **12**, 818, 834
    disclosure, duty of, *see* misrepresentation and non-disclosure *below*
    double insurance—
        terms excluding or limiting liability, **12**, 916
        terms requiring notification of, **12**, 915

Insurance—*continued*
contract—*continued*
    duration of cover, agreement as to, **12**, 818
    enforcement of, **12**, 807
    excess clause, **12**, 891
    formation of—
        cancellation, rules for, **12**, 819, 821
        cover note, **12**, 825
        Insurance Companies Regulations 1981 ..., **12**, 819, 820
        law of contract, generally, **12**, 818
        proposal form, **12**, 822–824
        statutory notices and cooling-off periods, **12**, 819–821
    franchise clause, **12**, 892
    illegality, **12**, 835
    indemnity principle, contractual variation, **12**, 887–893
    insurable interest, requirement of, **12**, 848
    insurer unauthorised, where, **12**, 835
    investment, as, **12**, 1308, 1308*n*
    jus quaesitum tertio, **15**, 841
    material facts—
        disclosure of, **12**, 823, 824
        non-disclosure of, **12**, 835
        See also misrepresentation and non-disclosure *below*
    material terms, agreement as to, **12**, 818
    misrepresentation, *see* misrepresentation and non-disclosure *below*
    non-disclosure, *see* misrepresentation and non-disclosure *below*
    non-renewable, duration of duty of disclosure, **12**, 863
    offer and acceptance, **12**, 818
        basis of contract clause, **12**, 823
    oral, **12**, 828
    premium, agreement as to, **12**, 818
    prospective cover, **12**, 857
    protection policies, **12**, 1308
    reinstatement clause, **12**, 890
    renewable—
        duration of duty of disclosure, **12**, 863
        premiums, payment of, **12**, 834
    replacement value policy, **12**, 889
    risk—
        risk to be covered, agreement as to, **12**, 818
        unjust enrichment, doctrine of, **12**, 835
    sum insured, agreement as to, **12**, 818
    suspensive condition, **12**, 818
    term assurance, **12**, 1308
    term descriptive of risk, **12**, 878
    uberrimae fidei, as contract of, **3**, 852, 899; **12**, 802, 858
    unauthorised insurance business, **12**, 807
        enforcement of, **12**, 807
    void—
        return of premium, **12**, 835
        void ab initio, **12**, 835
    voidable, return of premium, **12**, 835
    warranty, *see* warranty *below*

Insurance—*continued*
contribution—
  double insurance—
    generally, **12**, 913
    liability, contract terms excluding or limiting, **12**, 916
    notification of, contract terms requiring, **12**, 915
    prerequisites for contribution, **12**, 914
  effect, **12**, 912
  indemnity insurance, **12**, 912
  issue between two or more insurers, as, **12**, 912
  prerequisites for, **12**, 914
  same risk and interest, policies must cover, **12**, 914
  valid and enforceable, policies must be, **12**, 914
cooling-off periods, **6**, 157; **12**, 819–821
cover note, *see* COVER NOTE
definition, **12**, 802
direct debit, premium payment by, **12**, 833
direct obligation imposed by, **12**, 802
documents as to terms of, **4**, 254
double—
  generally, **12**, 913
  liability, contract terms excluding or limiting, **12**, 916
  marine insurance, **12**, 913*n*
  notification of, contract terms requiring, **12**, 915
  prerequisites for contribution, **12**, 914
employer's liability—
  approved policies, **15**, 351
  generally, **15**, 350
English law and practice, influence of, **12**, 801
excepted perils clause—
  effect, **12**, 837
  subrogation, **12**, 909
excess clause, meaning, **12**, 891
exchange, as type of, **12**, 801, 801*n*
exclusion clauses, judicial hostility to, **14**, 1057
fidelity bond contract, insurance business, as, **12**, 802
fidelity guarantee, *uberrimae fidei* contract, as, **12**, 802
finance lease, contractual terms in, **14**, 1057
Financial Intermediaries, Managers and Brokers Regulatory Association (FIMBRA), **12**, 809, 812
Financial Services (Cancellation) Rules 1988 …, **12**, 819, 821
fire, valuation for—
  inflation, provision for, **25**, 144
  other considerations, **25**, 145
  two bases, **25**, 143
fire insurance, **12**, 804, 890
fireraising to defraud insurer, **7**, 418
first-party cover, **12**, 805
franchise clause, **12**, 892
friendly society—
  child under ten years, insurance relating to death of, **12**, 692, 724
  insurance benefits offered by, **12**, 686
  restrictions on, **12**, 687
full repairing and insuring lease, **13**, 556, 557, 563, 580, 581

Insurance—*continued*
general business—
  classes of, **12**, 807
  company insolvency, **12**, 814
gift to insured from party responsible for loss, **12**, 902
goods, money as, **14**, 1808
goods in transit, of, **3**, 628
government agreements for classes of people, **22**, 246
heritable property, **12**, 890, 900
historical development in Scotland, **12**, 801
honour policy, marine insurance, **12**, 848
household—
  excess clause, **12**, 891
  indemnity insurance, as, **12**, 804
hypothetical tenancy, **24**, 618
indemnity insurance, *see* INDEMNITY INSURANCE
independent intermediary or broker, **12**, 806, 811, 812
  code of practice, **12**, 815
insurable interest, *see* INSURABLE INTEREST
intermediary—
  accountant, as, **12**, 811
  banker, as, **12**, 811
  bonus or commission paid to, disclosure of, **12**, 812
  broker, *see* broker *above*
  building society, as, **12**, 811
  cold-calling, **12**, 812
  independent, **12**, 811
    code of practice, **12**, 815
    volume commission or bonus received by, **12**, 812
  Insurance Brokers (Registration) Act 1977 in relation to, **12**, 813
  other than registered broker, code of practice, **12**, 815
  polarisation, **12**, 811, 812
  regulation—
    Financial Services Act 1986, under, **12**, 812
    general, **12**, 806, 811–813
    Insurance Brokers (Registration) Act 1977, under, **12**, 81
  solicitor, as, **12**, 811
  tied agent, **12**, 806, 811
    appointed representative of authorised principal, **12**, 812
    breach of rules by, responsibility for, **12**, 812
    code of practice, **12**, 815
investment business, **12**, 807, 812
investment fraud, **12**, 810
law, generally—
  disclosure of, **22**, 655
  Law Commission (England and Wales)—
    recommendations, **22**, 655
  Law Reform Committee for Scotland 1957 report, **22**, 654
  married women's policies of assurance, **22**, 689
    Scottish Law Commission recommendations, **22**, 689
  material terms of contract, **22**, 654
life assurance, *see* LIFE ASSURANCE
local authority as own insurer, **14**, 1057

Insurance—*continued*
long-term business—
 classes of, **12**, 807
 statutory notice in respect of, **6**, 157
loss—
 claim for, *see* claim *above*
 gift to insured from responsible party, **12**, 902
 indemnification for—
  compensation for distinguished, **12**, 903
  subrogation as measure of, **12**, 900–903
 subrogation, *see* subrogation *below*
manufacturers' guarantee compared, **12**, 802
marine, *see* MARINE INSURANCE
market manipulation, **12**, 810
marketing of insurance products, **12**, 809, 810, 812
misleading statements, **12**, 810
misrepresentation and non-disclosure—
 basis of contract clause, **12**, 823
 disclosure, duty of—
  continuing, **12**, 863
  duration, **12**, 863
  material facts, **12**, 864
  new material fact, discovery of—
   after completion of proposal form, **12**, 863
   after policy issued, **12**, 863
   renewable contracts, **12**, 863
  positive duty of both parties, **12**, 858
 generally, **12**, 858
 immaterial facts, warranties, **12**, 873
 See also warranty *below*
 information which is not requested, **12**, 858
 materiality—
  ABI statements of practice, **12**, 867
  doubtful, **12**, 865
  expert evidence as to, **12**, 864
  immaterial facts, **12**, 865
  material facts, **12**, 864
  waiver of disclosure, **12**, 866
  test of, **12**, 864
   ABI statements of practice, **12**, 872
   generally, **12**, 868
   marine insurance, **12**, 869
   motor vehicle insurance, **12**, 869
   reasonable insured, of, **12**, 871
   reasonable insurer, of, **12**, 870
   statutory, **12**, 869
 misrepresentation—
  actionable, **12**, 859
  as basis of contract clause, **12**, 823
  contract induced by, **12**, 859
  insurer, by, **12**, 859
  material, **12**, 859
  meaning, **12**, 858*n*
 non-disclosure—
  common law, **12**, 860
  disclosure to intermediary not passed on, **12**, 862
  extent of, **12**, 860
  life assurance, **12**, 860
  marine insurance, **12**, 860
  meaning, **12**, 858*n*
  motor vehicle insurance, **12**, 860
  statements of opinion, **12**, 861
 remedy for, **12**, 858

Insurance—*continued*
money or money's worth, benefit received must be, **12**, 802
Motor Insurers' Bureau, **22**, 246
motor vehicle, *see* MOTOR VEHICLE INSURANCE
nationalised industry as own insurer, **14**, 1057
non-disclosure, *see* misrepresentation and non-disclosure *above*
outwith insurer's control, event insured must be, **12**, 802
overinsurance—
 contribution, *see* contribution *above*
 double insurance, **12**, 913
person carrying on business of, whether moneylender, **13**, 1770
personal accident, recoverable loss, **12**, 885
Personal Insurance Arbitration Service, **12**, 817
policy—
 agreed value, **12**, 888
 ambiguity in, **12**, 837, 842
 arrestment, **8**, 277, 284
 assignation, *see* ASSIGNATION
 average clause, **12**, 893
 cancellation before stipulated date of expiry, **12**, 836
 classification, **12**, 829
 constitution and proof, **12**, 828
 construction and interpretation—
  accident, meaning of, **12**, 844
  ambiguities, **12**, 837, 842
  construing policy as a whole, **12**, 843
  context of words, **12**, 837, 840
  excepted perils clause, **12**, 837
  generally, **12**, 837
  grammar, **12**, 837, 841
  ordinary meaning of word, **12**, 837, 838
  technical words, **12**, 837, 839
 contents, **12**, 827
 duration, **12**, 836
 embodiment of terms on which contract provided, as, **12**, 826
 estate, as part of, **19**, 1621
 excepted perils clause, **12**, 837
 excess clause, **12**, 891
 expiry, **12**, 836
 franchise clause, **12**, 892
 married women's assurance, **19**, 1580; **24**, 33
 oral contract, **12**, 828
 premium, *see* premium *below*
 printer's imprint not required, **17**, 3
 proceeds, payment of, **14**, 1057
 reinstatement clause, **12**, 890
 replacement value, **12**, 889
 rights under, rights in security, **20**, 43
 terms—
  immediate notice, requiring, **12**, 825
  unusual, contained in, **12**, 825
 trust deemed to be, **24**, 10
 unvalued, **12**, 829, 831
 valued, **12**, 829, 830
 warranty, **12**, 874
 See also warranty *below*
 writing, whether in, **12**, 828
Policyholders Protection Board, **12**, 814

Insurance—*continued*
prejudicial arrangements, against, **24**, 80
premium—
    agreement as to, **12**, 818
    cash or cheque, payment by, **12**, 833
    cover dependent upon payment of first, **12**, 818, 834
    days of grace, **12**, 834
    direct debit, payment by, **12**, 833
    duration of policy, **12**, 836
    form of, **12**, 833
    instalments, payment by, **12**, 833
    insurer's obligation to pay, **12**, 832
    promissory note, payment by, **12**, 833
    renewable cover, **12**, 834
    repayment, **12**, 835
        breach of warranty, where, **12**, 835
        illegal contract, where, **12**, 835
        insurer unauthorised, where, **12**, 835
        void or voidable contract, **12**, 835
        where insurer ran no risk, **12**, 835
    standing order, payment by, **12**, 833
    time for payment, **12**, 834
premiums, **14**, 329
proceeds, payment of policy, **14**, 1057
promissory note, premium payment by, **12**, 833
promotion of insurance products, **12**, 809, 810, 812
proposal form—
    Association of British Insurers statements of insurance practice, **12**, 824
    basis of the contract clause, **12**, 823
    form and content, **12**, 822
    misrepresentation and non-disclosure, *see* misrepresentation and non-disclosure *above*
    warranty, *see* warranty *below*
provision of services—
    generally, **12**, 806
    independent intermediary or broker, **12**, 806, 811, 812
    regulation, **12**, 806–808
    statutory controls, **12**, 806
    tied agent, **12**, 806, 811, 812, 815
    See also intermediary *above*
purpose of, **12**, 802
reasonable precautions clause, **12**, 910
recognised professional bodies, **12**, 809, *see also* RECOGNISED PROFESSIONAL BODIES
reinstatement clause, **12**, 890
reinsurance, VAT exemption, **7**, 1421
renewal notice, temporary cover, **12**, 825
renewal and repair fund, **14**, 329
replacement value policy, **12**, 889
residual value, **14**, 1057
retrospective cover, **12**, 857
risk allocation, other forms distinguished, **12**, 802
risk categories—
    damage caused by equipment, **14**, 1056
    risk to equipment, **14**, 1057
schemes intended to confer benefit on others, **12**, 802
Securities and Investments Board, marketing regulated by, **12**, 809

Insurance—*continued*
self-regulatory organisations (SROs), **12**, 809, 812
separate, **14**, 1057
standard securities, **20**, 160
standing order, insurance premium payment by, **12**, 833
statutory controls, **12**, 806
statutory notices, **12**, 819–821
subrogation—
    ambiguous subrogation clause, **12**, 901
    assignation compared, **12**, 894
    company insured, where, **12**, 905, 906
    contract silent as to, **12**, 901
    control of litigation, **12**, 899
    corollary of indemnity principle, as, **12**, 894
    enforceability, **12**, 897
    excepted perils clause, **12**, 909
    individual insured, where, **12**, 905
    insured must not prejudice right of, **12**, 898
    knock for knock agreement, **12**, 897, 897*n*
    life assurance, no application to, **12**, 894
    measure of indemnity, as—
        basic principle, **12**, 900
        contractual variation of principle, **12**, 901
        gifts, **12**, 902
        insured's duty to account, **12**, 903
    motor vehicle insurance, **12**, 911
    'pay to be paid' clause, **12**, 907
    purpose of, **12**, 895
    reasonable precautions clause, **12**, 909
    right arising automatically, **12**, 894
    right dependent on settlement of claim, **12**, 896
    statutory—
        contracting out, **12**, 907
        generally, **12**, 904
        insured, existence of, **12**, 906
        insurer, defences available to, **12**, 909
            restrictions on, **12**, 910
        insurer and insured, arrangements between, **12**, 908
        motor vehicle insurance, third party rights, **12**, 911
        Third Parties (Rights against Insurers) Act 1930, application of, **12**, 905–910
    windfall profits, **12**, 900, 901, 901*n*
    written notice of accident or claim, requirement to give, **12**, 909
subsidiary powers, **14**, 329
temporary cover—
    indemnity insurance, **12**, 825
    life assurance, **12**, 825
third party—
    claim, **14**, 329
    insured's right to sue, **12**, 898
    motor vehicle insurance, **12**, 911
    subrogation, *see* subrogation *above*
    third-party cover, meaning, **12**, 805
tied agent, **12**, 806, 811
    appointed representative of authorised principal, **12**, 812
    breach of rules by, responsibility for, **12**, 812
    code of practice, **12**, 815
uncertainty, event insured must contain element of, **12**, 802

Insurance—*continued*
under-insurance, **12**, 893, 903
undervaluation, **12**, 903
Unfair Contract Terms Act, exclusion of
    insurance contracts from, **12**, 802
unjust enrichment, doctrine of, **12**, 835
VAT exemption, **7**, 1421
warranty—
    ABI statements of insurance practice, **12**, 877
    breach of, **12**, 875
        return of premium, **12**, 835
    categories, **12**, 876
    creation of, **12**, 874
    effect, **12**, 875
    future facts, **12**, 876
    immaterial facts, non-disclosure of covered by,
        12, 873
    implication, arising by virtue of, **12**, 874
    marine insurance, **12**, 874
    opinion, of, **12**, 876
    past or present facts, **12**, 876
    policy, in, **12**, 874
    proposal form, **12**, 874
    purpose of, **12**, 873
    terms descriptive of risk distinguished, **12**, 878
    use of term, **12**, 878
    whole life policy, **12**, 804
Insurance Brokers Registration Council
authorisation by, **12**, 1313
recognised professional body, as, **12**, 809
Insurance company
advertising by, **1**, 533
assets must be sufficient to meet liabilities, **12**, 807
authorisation, **12**, 807
    conditions for, **12**, 807
    failure to commence business after, **12**, 807
    Financial Services Act 1986, under, **12**, 1315,
        1316
    necessity for, **12**, 802
    revocation, **12**, 807
bond of caution, issue of, **14**, 1502
building society's power to invest in and support,
    3, 369
cautionary obligation granted by, **3**, 985
collapse, consequences of, **12**, 806
controllers, **12**, 807
Department of Trade and Industry supervision,
    12, 1316
exempt agreement, **5**, 821
financial services, **2**, 1266; **12**, 1315, 1316
general business—
    long-term business finances to be kept separate,
        12, 807
head office outside EEC member states, **12**, 807
insolvency, Policyholders Protection Board
    powers, **12**, 814
Insurance Companies Act, failure to comply with,
    12, 807
intervention by Department of Trade and
    Industry, **12**, 808
investment business, **12**, 812
    authorisation to carry on, **12**, 807
liquidation, **12**, 807
loan by, **20**, 231

Insurance company—*continued*
long-term business—
    company liquidation, **12**, 807
    general business finances to be kept separate,
        12, 807
    investment business, **12**, 807
margin of solvency, requirement to maintain, **12**,
    807
regulation, **12**, 807, 808
    statutory controls, **12**, 806
Secretary of State, winding up petition by, **4**, 740
Securities and Investments Board Core Conduct
    of Business Rules, **12**, 1399
self-regulating organisation, membership, **12**,
    1316
share capital, **12**, 807
shares, interest in, exclusion relating to, **4**, 346
unauthorised business, conduct of, **12**, 807
Insurance Ombudsman Bureau
awards made by, **12**, 816
decision binding on insurer, **12**, 816
fair and commonsense conclusion, **12**, 816
good insurance practice, obligation to take into
    account, **12**, 816
who may complain to, **12**, 816
Integrated circuit
See SEMICONDUCTOR TOPOGRAPHIES
Integrity (copyright)
See COPYRIGHT (MORAL RIGHTS)
Intellectual property
assignation, transfer by, **18**, 802
breach of confidence, *see* BREACH OF CONFIDENCE
copyright, *see* COPYRIGHT
data protection, *see* DATA PROTECTION
definition, **18**, 801, 1452
design rights, *see* DESIGN RIGHTS
European Union legislation—
    biotechnology, **18**, 1611
    competition law—
        articles 85 and 86 of EEC Treaty, position
            under, **18**, 1647, 1648, 1656
        broadcasting, **18**, 1663, 1664
        collecting societies, **18**, 1661
        'comfort letter', issue of, **18**, 1648
        exemption, European Commission grant, **18**,
            1648
        film distribution, **18**, 1664
        generally, **18**, 1647–1649
        licensing of intellectual property, and, **18**,
            1647, 1649–1660
            copyright licensing, **18**, 1660
            design licensing, **18**, 1660
            franchise agreements, **18**, 1658, 1659
            know-how, **18**, 1653
            patents, **18**, 1650–1652, 1656
            research and development, **18**, 1654
            trade marks, **18**, 1657, 1658
        negative clearance, **18**, 1648
        spare parts, supply of, **18**, 1662
    computer programs, **18**, 1611
    copyright, **18**, 1611, 1615, 1616, 1618
        broadcasting, **18**, 1643, 1644
        cable programmes, **18**, 1643, 1644
        commercial exploitation, **18**, 1643

Intellectual property—*continued*
European Union legislation—*continued*
  copyright—*continued*
    disparity in national laws, **18**, 1634
    dramatic works, **18**, 1643
    exhaustion of rights, **18**, 1633
    films, **18**, 1643
    import from outside European Community, **18**, 1636
    musical works, **18**, 1643
    performance rights, **18**, 1643
    recording rights, **18**, 1643
    right to reward, **18**, 1635
    services, provision of, **18**, 1643–1645
    specific subject matter, **18**, 1632
  data protection, **18**, 1611
  European Economic Community Treaty, **18**, 801, 1612
  franchising, **18**, 1611
  free movement of goods, *see* free movement of goods *above*
  generally, **18**, 801, 805, 1611, 1613, 1643
  industrial and commercial property, generally, **18**, 801
  industrial designs, **18**, 1615, 1617
  know-how, **18**, 1611
    licensing agreement block exemption, **18**, 1653, 1655
    member states, organisation of individual systems of property rights, **18**, 1612
  origin, appellations of, **18**, 1615
  parallel importing, **18**, 1613
  passing off, **18**, 1617, 1640–1642
  patents—
    common origin, **18**, 1629
    Community patent—
      exhaustion, and, **18**, 1631
      generally, **18**, 1631
    compulsory licences, **18**, 1628
    consent—
      compulsory licences, **18**, 1628
      first marketing, to, exhaustion by, **18**, 1627
    different national laws, effect, **18**, 1630
    European Patent Convention (1973), *see* PATENT (INTERNATIONAL LAW)
    exhaustion—
      Community patent, and, **18**, 1631
      consent to first marketing, by, **18**, 1627
      free movement of goods, **18**, 1625–1631
      generally, **18**, 891, 1615, 1650–1652, 1656
    reform of law, **18**, 815
    specific subject matter—
      definition, **18**, 1625
      exhaustion by consent to first marketing, **18**, 1627
      generally, **18**, 1625
      patentee's right to reward as part of, **18**, 1626
    See also PATENT
  plant varieties, rights in, **18**, 1611, 1650
  protection, generally, **18**, 801, 865, 865*n*, 891, 1151, 1168
  registered design rights—
    free movement of goods, **18**, 1637–1639

Intellectual property—*continued*
European Union legislation—*continued*
  registered design rights—*continued*
    lawful marketing of goods without consent, **18**, 1639
    national laws, and, **18**, 1638
    specific subject matter, **18**, 1637
  rental rights, **18**, 1611
  research and development, **18**, 1611
    licensing block exemption, **18**, 1654, 1655
  right unknown in other states, grant by member state, **18**, 1618
  semiconductor topographies, **18**, 1611
  service marks, **18**, 1615
  services, provision of, **18**, 1643–1646
    copyright, and, **18**, 1643–1645
    free movement of goods, and, **18**, 1645
    passing off, and, **18**, 1646
    trade marks, and, **18**, 1646
  source, indications of, **18**, 1615
  trade marks, **18**, 1611, 1615, 1619–1624
    specific subject matter, **18**, 1619
    trade names, **18**, 1615
    unfair competition—
      case law, **18**, 1641
      generally, **18**, 1615, 1617, 1640
    utility models, **18**, 1615
expiry of term, **18**, 9
features of, **18**, 802
franchising schemes, **18**, 802
General Agreement on Trade and Tariffs (GATT), **18**, 804
generally, **18**, 801
hallmarking, *see* HALLMARKING
incorporeal moveable property, as, **18**, 802
industrial designs, *see* INDUSTRIAL DESIGNS, PROTECTION OF
infringement—
  accountings of profits from, **18**, 803
  copyright, *see* COPYRIGHT
  criminal offence, where, **18**, 803
  damages, **18**, 803
  delivery up of infringed objects, **18**, 803
  disclosure of information, **18**, 803
  innocent, **18**, 803
  interdict, **18**, 803
  patent, *see* PATENT
  policy towards, generally, **18**, 803
  remedies, generally, **18**, 803
  unjustified threats of legal action, **18**, 803
international aspects—
  developed and underdeveloped countries, **18**, 804
  European Community, **18**, 805
  General Agreement on Trade and Tariffs (GATT), **18**, 804
  generally, **18**, 804
  Trade-Related Aspects of Intellectual Property Rights (TRIPS), **18**, 804, 931
  World Intellectual Property Organisation (UN), **18**, 801
licensing, **4**, 1160
licensing schemes, **18**, 802
meaning, **18**, 801

Intellectual property—*continued*
moveable property, as, **18**, 14
parallel importing, effect of, **18**, 1613
passing off, *see* PASSING OFF
patent, *see* PATENT
performance, rights in, *see* RIGHTS IN PERFORMANCES
plant breeders' rights, *see* PLANT BREEDERS' RIGHTS
plant varieties, protection of, *see* PLANT BREEDERS' RIGHTS
real right in, whether, **18**, 5
recording rights, *see* RECORDING RIGHT
registration, **18**, 802
rights in, creation, **18**, 802
royalties, *see* ROYALTIES
self incrimination, privilege against, **18**, 1452
semiconductor topographies, protection of design rights, *see* SEMICONDUCTOR TOPOGRAPHIES
trade mark, *see* TRADE MARK
trade secret, *see* TRADE SECRET
Trade-Related Aspects of Intellectual Property Rights (TRIPS), **18**, 804, 931
transfer, assignation, by, **18**, 802
World Intellectual Property Organisation (UN), **18**, 801
Intelligence gathering and storage
police powers, **16**, 1802
Intelligence services
statutory basis, **7**, 732
Intent
assault, **7**, 232
    constructive intention, **7**, 233
    evil intent, **7**, 231
crime, to commit, **7**, 68, 70
proof of, **7**, 87
transferred *mens rea*, **7**, 89
wilfulness, **7**, 70
Intentional killing
culpable homicide, **7**, 272
mens rea of murder, **7**, 266, 267
Intentionally
recklessly and—
    proof of intent, **7**, 88
    recklessly compared, **7**, 82
use of term, **7**, 76, 78
Inter regalia minora
salmon fishing rights as, **11**, 4
Inter vivos
contract, revocation of, **25**, 737
gifts—
    foundations, to, **24**, 118
    See also GIFT
transfer of property, *see* PROPERTY
Inter vivos **settlement**
interpretation, **12**, 1214, 1262
Inter vivos **trust**
accumulation of income, **24**, 40, 41, 46
ascertainment of trust estate, **24**, 191
avoidance of legal rights, **25**, 811
comparative law, **24**, 121
completion of title, **24**, 148, 149
death of trustee, **24**, 162
declaration, trust created by, **24**, 115
deeds, **24**, 40, 41

Inter vivos **trust**—*continued*
generally, **24**, 13, 16
irrevocable, **24**, 63
    conditions for, **24**, 61
    variation under, **24**, 79
judicial variation, **24**, 75
minor, created by, **24**, 14
repugnancy, **24**, 73
revocation, **24**, 60
third parties, for, **24**, 60
Interdict
ab ante against anticipated nuisance, **14**, 2146
abuse of process—
    generally, **15**, 461
    interim interdict, **15**, 461
        continuing possession, **15**, 464
        discretionary nature, **15**, 461
        inverting possession, **15**, 463
    perpetual interdict, **15**, 461, 462
actions which court might have prohibited by, specific implement, **13**, 11
appeal against interlocutor granting or refusing, **17**, 1257
arrestment prevented by, **8**, 300
breach by landlord, as remedy against, **13**, 283
breach by tenant, as remedy against, **13**, 276
breach of confidence, where, **18**, 1452, 1478, 1488
breach of—
    committal for, treatment of prisoner, **16**, 1426
    contempt of court, whether, **6**, 322
    generally, **13**, 20
building contracts—
    remedy for breach, **3**, 104
    remedy for nuisance, **3**, 155
burden of proof, **14**, 2107
civil legal aid, urgency, situation of, **13**, 1048
common interest, as remedy for breach of, **18**, 366
company meeting, member's right to requisition, **4**, 476
copyright, infringement, where, **18**, 803, 1086, 1087
    moral rights, **18**, 1140
Crown, against, **1**, 328; **7**, 748, 748*n*; **13**, 23
custody orders, **8**, 516
damages claimed along with, **14**, 2150
declarator as appropriate remedy in lieu of, **14**, 2149
defence of existing possession, as remedy for, **18**, 140
dicta on, **14**, 2155
duration, **13**, 22
encroachment, against, **18**, 178
enforcement of statutory duty by, **1**, 334
equitable remedy, as, **13**, 17
fiar's right to remedy of, **13**, 1660
fixed rights, **14**, 2147
generally, **1**, 327; **14**, 2145
infringement of rights, protection from, **13**, 18
intellectual property—
    industrial design, infringement, where—
        registered design, **18**, 1209
        unregistered design right, **18**, 1234

nterdict—*continued*
interim, **1**, 329, 342; **4**, 44, 1194; **13**, 19; **18**, 803
  breach of order for, **13**, 20
  civil legal aid, urgency, situation of, **13**, 1048
  Crown, against, **13**, 23
  periculo petentis, **13**, 19
  dicial discretion, **14**, 2147
nd, recovery of founded on right to possession—
  attractions of remedy, **18**, 155
  competency, **18**, 155
  ejection, as subsidiary crave in action of, **18**, 155
  generally, **18**, 152, 155
  purpose, **18**, 155
meaning, **13**, 16*n*
mortgagee's powers as to, **21**, 179
natural possession, protection of, **18**, 138
negative, **13**, 21
negative prescription of objection by way of, **14**, 2123
o. nary action, remedy in, **4**, 962
passing off, where, **18**, 1398, 1399
patent, infringement, where, **18**, 858
perpetual, **13**, 22
  authority to breach, **13**, 22
petition for, rights of minority shareholders, **4**, 470
plant breeders' rights, infringement, where, **18**, 915
public interest, restrictions contrary to, **4**, 1189, 1194
purpose, **15**, 461
real burden, breach of, **18**, 423
recovery of possession, action for, **18**, 140, 151, 159
remedial measures, **14**, 2147
servitude right, as to, **18**, 482
special jurisdiction, **4**, 44
statutory body carrying out functions of Crown, against, **7**, 748, 753
support, right to, where breach of, **18**, 262
suspension, combination with, **13**, 16
tenant returning or threatening to return after dispossession, **13**, 470
tenant's right to sue third party, **13**, 290
terms, **14**, 2148
third party alleging right to use subject of lease, **13**, 470
trespass, against, **18**, 182
wrongful dismissal, opportunities in case of, **9**, 195

Interest
arbitration award, on, **12**, 1035
beneficiary, directions for payment to, **25**, 924
bill payable with, **4**, 113
business charges, **12**, 1011
compound, **12**, 1038
  contractual stipulation, **12**, 1002
  generally, **12**, 1038
compulsory acquisition of land, **5**, 194
concept of money central to, **14**, 1801
contract, breach of, interest as damages for, **12**, 1018–1020

Interest—*continued*
contractual stipulation, **12**, 1001
  agreed rate, where, **12**, 1037
  contract rate or legal rate of interest, **12**, 1003
  express contract, interest due by, **12**, 1002
  fluctuating rates of interest, **12**, 1004
  implied contract term—
    credit, as to, **12**, 1011
    general law, on basis of, **12**, 1007
    heritage, sales of, **12**, 1010
    interest due by, **12**, 1005
    moveable property, sales of, **12**, 1009
    particular facts, on basis of, **12**, 1006
    types of implied term, **12**, 1005
  loans, **12**, 1008
  sale, contracts of, **12**, 1009
    heritage, sales of, **12**, 1009, 1010
    moveable property, **12**, 1009
  terms of, **12**, 1002
damages, on, **22**, 653
  date allowable from, **12**, 1032
  death or personal injury, awarded for, **12**, 1034
  discretion of court, **12**, 1032
  generally, **12**, 1032
  interest on interest, **12**, 1032
  lump sum damages, **12**, 1033
  taxation of, **12**, 1034
date from which due, **12**, 1001
  contractual stipulation, **12**, 1002
  damages and decrees, **12**, 1032
  judicial demand, **12**, 1015
debts, on, **4**, 832
deceased's liabilities—
  bank, **25**, 967
  building society, **25**, 967
  government securities, **25**, 967
  loans, **25**, 967
  securities, **25**, 968
  stocks, **25**, 968
decrees, on, **12**, 1032
delayed payment, as result of, **12**, 1001
due *ex lege*, **12**, 1001; **14**, 1827
due *ex mora*, **12**, 1001; **14**, 1828
due *ex pacto*, **12**, 1001; **14**, 1826
error, sum paid in, interest on, **12**, 1012, 1012*n*
executry funds, **12**, 1031
extortionate agreement, **14**, 1826
fixed—
  contractual stipulation, **12**, 1002
formal demand for payment, **12**, 1014–1017
general principles, lack of, **14**, 1825
grounds for which awarded, **12**, 1001
interest on, **12**, 1032
interest rates, levels of, **25**, 31
intimation to debtor, **12**, 1014, 1016
judicial demand for payment, **12**, 1014, 1015
legacy, on, **25**, 852
legal, **14**, 1826
legal rights in succession, on—
  generally, **12**, 1001; **25**, 795
  income tax, **25**, 796
loans, interest on general implied, **12**, 1002
meaning, **12**, 1001

Interest—*continued*
moveable property—
  contracts of sale, **12**, 1009
  deprivation of, interest payable for, **12**, 1021
open account, **12**, 1011
payment of, prescription, **16**, 2116
pecuniary crave, on, **17**, 1185
principal sum—
  calculation of—
    contractual stipulation, **12**, 1002
    decree for payment, **12**, 1003
    judicial demand, **12**, 1015
    parasitic upon claim for, **12**, 1001
property assets, valuation of, **25**, 104
rate, **12**, 1001
  appropriately calculated, **12**, 1037
  contract rate or legal rate, **12**, 1003
  contractual agreement, where, **12**, 1037
  court, fixed by, **12**, 1037
  express contract, interest due by, **12**, 1002
  fluctuating, **12**, 1004
    contractual stipulation, **12**, 1002
  intimation to debtor, **12**, 1016
  legal, **12**, 1037
  trust funds, **12**, 1023
  variation or substitution, **12**, 1003
rules as to, **12**, 1001
statute, by operation of, **12**, 1001, 1012
tax-deductible, **14**, 1014
tribunal award, on, **12**, 1036
trust funds, **12**, 1001
  advances to beneficiaries, **12**, 1022, 1030
    ultra vires, **12**, 1030
  delay in payment, **12**, 1029
  failure of trust, **12**, 1029
  rate specified, **12**, 1023
  right to interest, implied, **12**, 1023
  trust deed, interest due by, **12**, 1022, 1023
  trustees' liability for interest, **12**, 1022, 1024–1029
    terms of deed impossible to carry out, **12**, 1023
wrongful withholding of sum, due to, **12**, 1001
  breach of contract, interest as damages for, **12**, 1018–1020
  contractual debts, **12**, 1012
  date payable from, **12**, 1012
  formal demand, constituted by, **12**, 1017
  formal demand for payment, **12**, 1014–1017
  generally, **12**, 1012
  justifiable withholding, **12**, 1013
  'open accounts', **12**, 1014, 1016
  quantum meruit, sums due, **12**, 1012
  rent, **12**, 1012
  rules, **12**, 1012
  statute, debts due under, **12**, 1012
  sums paid in error, on, **12**, 1012, 1012*n*
  wrongful withholding, what constitutes, **12**, 1013, 1014
Interest in land
See LAND
Interest in lease
See LEASE-LEASING

Interest in possession
deceased having had, **19**, 1620
definition, **24**, 17
trusts conferring, **24**, 16, 17
Interest in shares
disclosure and registration, **4**, 346
meaning, **4**, 346
Interest warrant
negotiable instrument, as, **4**, 103
Interference
course of justice, with, *see* ADMINISTRATION OF JUSTICE (OFFENCES AGAINST)
honour and reputation, with, *see* HONOUR AND REPUTATION, INTERFERENCE WITH
lessor, obligations of, **14**, 1040
nuisance, as—
  personal comfort of occupier, with, **14**, 2044
  single, **14**, 2053
  temporary, **14**, 2052
Interim decree
Court of Session procedure, **17**, 1394
sheriff court procedure, **17**, 1066
Interim liberation
warrant for, **6**, 865
Interim orders
arrestment—
  jurisdiction, to found, **17**, 1119
  meaning, **17**, 1113
  security, in—
    arrestee, **17**, 1116
    dependence of action, **17**, 1114
    recall of, **17**, 1118
    subjects of, **17**, 1117
    warrant, execution of, **17**, 1115
custody, **17**, 1128
evidence, debate on, **17**, 1183
generally, **17**, 1103
interim interdict—
  appeal, **17**, 1111
  application for—
    effect of, **17**, 1107
    generally, **17**, 1106
  caution, **17**, 1109
  caveat, **17**, 1105
  children, proceedings concerning, **17**, 1112
  Court of Session procedure, **17**, 1420
  duration of, **17**, 1110
  grant of, **17**, 1108
  historical background, **17**, 1104
  recall, **17**, 1111
matrimonial home, relating to—
  cohabiting couple, **17**, 1124
  duration, **17**, 1123
  enforcement of, **17**, 1125
  exclusion orders, **17**, 1122
  generally, **17**, 1120
  non-entitled spouse, rights of, **17**, 1121
  poinding, protection from, **17**, 1126
  procedure, **17**, 1127
  recall of, **17**, 1123
  variation, **17**, 1123
opposing, civil legal aid, urgency, situation of, **13**, 1048

Interim payment
appeal against interlocutor for, **17**, 1258
Interim trustee
See BANKRUPTCY
Interlocutor
civil proceedings, in, as documentary evidence, **10**, 585
judicial record, as, **10**, 582
Interlocutory judgments
no appeal to House of Lords allowed, **6**, 829
Internal combustion engine
petrol for use in, **19**, 398
Internal private law
choice of law—
  compatibility of, **17**, 131
  distinction between, **17**, 130
  statutory provisions, spheres of operation of, **17**, 132
meaning, **17**, 108; **25**, 721*n*
private international law distinguished from, **17**, 108
renvoi, **17**, 155
Internal Taxation Directorate
generally, **7**, 1282
Internal valuer
meaning, **25**, 116
Internal waters
meaning, **21**, 112
International Accounting Standards Committee
generally, **1**, 73
International Air Transport Association
summary of provisions as to, **2**, 907
International Auditing Practices Committee
establishment of, **1**, 74
International Bank
employees of, **12**, 130*n*
International Chamber of Commerce Model Guarantee
cautionary obligation, as, **3**, 991
generally, **3**, 991
International Civil Aviation Organisation
establishment and purposes, **2**, 906
International Co-ordinating Committee of the Accountancy Profession
establishment of, **1**, 71
International Congress of Accountants
generally, **1**, 71
International contract
indexation, **14**, 1824
International Court of Justice
access to, **19**, 726
advisory opinions, **19**, 739
assessors, **19**, 724
breach of international law, remedies for, **19**, 746
Calvo Clause, **19**, 742
case law, **19**, 636
  recourse to, **19**, 646
company, claims on behalf of, **19**, 743
contentious cases—
  jurisdiction in, **19**, 728
  procedure, **19**, 737
  experts, **19**, 724

International Court of Justice—*continued*
forum prorogatum, **19**, 729
functioning of, **19**, 727
General List of cases, **19**, 725
general principles of law, **19**, 645
individuals, espousal of claims on behalf of, **19**, 740
interim measures, **19**, 735
international character, **19**, 721
international organisations, **19**, 726
intervention by third party, **19**, 734
judges, **19**, 722
  appointment, **19**, 722
  diplomatic privileges and immunities, **19**, 722
  dismissal, **19**, 722
judgments—
  construction of, **19**, 736
  publication, **19**, 725
  revision, **19**, 736
jurisdiction, **19**, 728
  appellate, **19**, 738
  article 36(1), under, **19**, 730
  article 36(2), under, **19**, 731
  contentious cases, **19**, 728
  incidental, **19**, 737
  optional clause, under, **19**, 731, 736
  states not recognising, **19**, 729
local remedies, exhaustion of, **19**, 744
lump sum agreements, **19**, 745
nationality of claims rule, **19**, 741
no appeal from, **19**, 736, 737
non-United Nations members, **19**, 726
optional clause, jurisdiction under, **19**, 731, 736
preliminary objections, **19**, 733
President and Vice President, **19**, 722, 737
private interests, proceedings as to, **19**, 726
procedure—
  in camera, **19**, 737
  majority decisions, **19**, 737
  oral proceedings, **19**, 737
  public, hearings in, **19**, 737
  written proceedings, **19**, 737
Registrar and Deputy Registrar, **19**, 725
Registry of, **19**, 725
reparation, **19**, 747
Rules of Court, **19**, 721
seat of, **19**, 721
shareholders, claims on behalf of, **19**, 743
states, **19**, 726
statute, **19**, 721
treaties, disputes as to validity, **19**, 636
United Nations Security Council recommendation, **19**, 730
voluntary nature of jurisdiction, **19**, 603*n*
International Development Association
employees of, **12**, 130*n*
International disputes
arbitration, **19**, 719
  compromis, **19**, 720, 720*n*
  consent to, **19**, 720
commissions of inquiry, **19**, 714, 717
conciliation commissions, **19**, 714, 718
good offices, **19**, 714, 715

International disputes—*continued*
judicial settlement, **19**, 713–747
mediation, **19**, 714, 716
negotiation, resolved by, **19**, 714
third party settlement, **19**, 714, 714*n*
International Federation of Accountants
generally, **1**, 72
management accounting, defining, **1**, 52
International Finance Corporation
employees of, **12**, 130*n*
International Headquarters
immunity and privileges, **2**, 787
visiting forces provisions applied, **2**, 787
International Labour Organisation
law clarification, **19**, 650
resolutions of, **12**, 116
International law
accretion and avulsion, territory acquired by, **19**,
    670
agents of state, responsibility for acts of, **19**, 645
air space, **19**, 673
alternative reference, rules of, **17**, 126
arbitration tribunals, **19**, 636
breach of, remedies for, **19**, 746
circumstantial evidence, **19**, 645
conflict of laws, **19**, 604
conquest of territory, **19**, 688, 700*n*
conservation of salmon in the North Atlantic, **11**,
    101–105
copyright, **18**, 931
customary, **19**, 603, 637–644
    amendment, **19**, 641
    criticism of, **19**, 641
    diplomatic relations, **19**, 681
    dissenting states, **19**, 640
    material element, **19**, 638, 639
    meaning, **19**, 637, 637*n*, 652
    minority groups, **12**, 2
    modification, **19**, 641, 644
    opinio juris sive necessitatis, **19**, 643, 643*n*
    oral statements, **19**, 636, 636*n*
    piracy, **19**, 601*n*, 695
    psychological element, **19**, 638
    self-defence, **19**, 702
    state practice, evidence of, **19**, 642
    treaty law, and, **19**, 643, 644
    United Kingdom approach, **19**, 654
    Universal Declaration of Human Rights, **12**, 4
    usage distinguished, **19**, 638
damage, reparation for, **19**, 645
Declaration concerning Friendly Relations and
    Co-operation, **19**, 685
definition, **19**, 601, 613
dissenting states—
    customary law, from, **19**, 640
    later opposition, **19**, 640
    opposition must be expressed, **19**, 640
domestic law, relationship with—
    conflicting legislation, **19**, 655
    dualist approach, **19**, 652
    'Fitzmaurice Compromise', **19**, 602, 603, 613,
        652–656
    monist approach, **19**, 652, 652*n*
    treaty law, **19**, 656

International law—*continued*
draft conventions, **19**, 650
effects principle, **19**, 677
equity, principles of, **19**, 645
estoppel, **19**, 645
European Community Common Fisheries Policy,
    see COMMON FISHERIES POLICY
exclusive economic zone, **11**, 116
extradition, **12**, 503, 506
    Commonwealth countries, to, **12**, 518
    Republic of Ireland, to, **12**, 525
    treaties, **12**, 503
extradition procedure, **12**, 26
factors differentiating, **19**, 603
fisheries, *see* FISHERIES
force, use or threat of, **19**, 668
    Declaration concerning Friendly Relations and
        Co-operation, **19**, 685
foreign nationals, **19**, 686
foreign relations law, and, **19**, 605
general principles of law, **19**, 645
genocide, **19**, 678, 698
governments, recognition of, **19**, 660
Hague Convention on Recognition of Divorces
    and Legal Separations—
    ratification, **22**, 693
high seas, *see* HIGH SEAS—
    maritime law
humanitarian law, **19**, 706–708
immigration, **12**, 115, 116
immunity—
    diplomatic, **19**, 679, 681–684
    restricted, **19**, 680
    sovereign, **19**, 679, 680
    waived, may be, **19**, 680
incorporation, doctrine of, **19**, 654, 654*n*
individuals—
    duties of, **19**, 695
    procedural capacity of, **19**, 696
    rights of, **19**, 694
intellectual property—
    European Union law, *see* EUROPEAN UNION
    generally, **18**, 804, 1611
international agreements, **19**, 615
International Court of Justice, *see* INTERNATIONAL
    COURT OF JUSTICE
International Law Commission, *see* INTERNATIONAL
    LAW COMMISSION
international personality, *see* INTERNATIONAL
    PERSONALITY
intertemporal law, doctrine of, **19**, 668, 668*n*
judicial decisions, **19**, 646
judicial writings, **19**, 630, 634, 647, 651
maritime law, *see* ADMIRALTY; HIGH SEAS;
    MARITIME LAW; TERRITORIAL SEA
marriage, implications for municipal law, **22**,
    693
migratory species, **11**, 65
military force, taken by, **19**, 668
modern interest in, **19**, 612
monistic and dualistic approaches, **12**, 8, 8*n*
municipal law compared, **19**, 602, 603, 613
nationality principle, **19**, 675
natural resources, **19**, 671

International law—*continued*
need for legal framework, **11**, 65
occupatio (occupation), doctrine of, **18**, 558
occupation of territory, **19**, 667
opinio juris sive necessitatis, **19**, 643, 643*n*
outer space, **18**, 198; **19**, 674
par in parem non habet imperium principle, **19**, 680
passive personality principle, **19**, 676
patents, international recognition, *see* PATENT
peace, international law of, **19**, 657–696
plant breeders' rights, **18**, 911
polar regions, **19**, 672
private—
    public distinguished, **19**, 604
    See also PRIVATE INTERNATIONAL LAW
public, **5**, 712
renvoi, *see* renvoi
reparation for damage, **19**, 645, 747
right to leave a country, **16**, 1205*n*
Scottish influence, **19**, 607
Scottish Law Commission Reports—
    jointly with the Law Commission (England and
        Wales), **22**, 693
sea, of—
    development, **21**, 2
    generally, **21**, 1
    multilateral treaties, **21**, 1–4
self-defence, force used in, **19**, 668
semiconductor topographies, design rights
    protection, **18**, 1244, 1253
sources, **19**, 613*ff*
    custom, **19**, 603
    formal, **19**, 614–645
    international agreements, **19**, 615
    International Law Commission, **19**, 650
    judicial decisions, **19**, 646
    judicial writings, **19**, 647
    jus cogens, **19**, 651
    material, **19**, 614, 646, 647
    regional organisations, **19**, 649
    treaties, **19**, 603, 615–636
    United Nations resolutions, **19**, 648
state practice, evidence of, **19**, 642, 647
    international obligations, non-fulfilment of, **19**,
        652
    primary concern, as, **19**, 603, 604, 658
    recognition of, **19**, 659–663
    war, duties in time of, **19**, 688
subjugation of territory, **19**, 668
territorial jurisdiction, **19**, 675–684
    exceptions to, **19**, 679–684
territorial sea, *see* TERRITORIAL SEA
treaties, *see* TREATIES
United Kingdom approach, **19**, 653, 654
United Nations Conferences on the Law of the
    Sea, **11**, 65, 70, 73, 76, 80
United Nations Convention on the Law of the
    Sea, **11**, 82, 84, 106–109
universality principle, **19**, 678
usage, **19**, 637, 638
Vienna Convention on the Law of Treaties, **19**,
    616, 617
war, of, *see* WAR

International law—*continued*
waters off Scotland—
    before 1976, **11**, 92
    North-East Atlantic Fisheries Commission, **11**,
        92–96
    Northwest Atlantic Fisheries Commission, **11**, 92
International Law Commission
constitution, **19**, 650*n*
Draft Articles on State Responsibility, 689*n*; **19**, 689
establishment, **19**, 650*n*
international law, as source of, **19**, 650
law of the sea, **21**, 2
state liability, nature of, **19**, 690
International lease, *see* CROSS-BORDER LEASING
**International Maritime Consultative
Organisation (IMCO)**
generally, **21**, 117
International Maritime Organisation (IMO)
abandoned or disused installations on continental
    shelf, **21**, 33
constitution, **21**, 117
establishment, **21**, 104, 117
function, **21**, 117
International Convention for the Safety of Life at
    Sea (1974), **21**, 195
purpose, **21**, 104
safety, conventions relating to, **21**, 194
International Military Tribunal,, **19**, 695
Charter of, **19**, 700*n*
International Monetary Fund
employees of, **12**, 130*n*
special drawing right, introduction of, **14**, 1832
International organisation
employees of, **12**, 130*n*, 247
member of—
    goods imported for, **7**, 1314
    inland purchases by, **7**, 1290
relevant service, **14**, 1916
International Patent Co-operation Union,
    18, 892
International personality
determination, **19**, 658
generally, **19**, 660*n*, 664
international organisation as, **19**, 692
nature of, **19**, 657
United Nations, as, **19**, 693
International private law, *see* PRIVATE
    INTERNATIONAL LAW
**International Regulations for Preventing
Collisions at Sea**
See SHIPPING (COLLISION REGULATIONS)
International relations
external public policy rule, **17**, 170
International trade
early, references to, **4**, 104
letters of credit, background to, **4**, 218
negotiable instruments, origin of use of, **4**, 104
Interpretation
conveyance, of, *see* CONVEYANCE
deed, of, *see* DEED
distance, measurement of, **12**, 1209
gender, rules as to, **12**, 1207
generally, **12**, 1206
heritable security, of, *see* HERITABLE SECURITY

Interpretation—*continued*
lease, of, *see* LEASE-LEASING
number, rules as to, **12**, 1207
person, meaning of, **12**, 1211
post, service by, **12**, 1208
powers and duties, continuity of, **12**, 1210
question of law, as, **12**, 1214
statute, of, *see* STATUTE
will, of, *see* WILL
Interpreter
court examination, for, **10**, 551
  oath taken by, **10**, 551
court hearing, at, **12**, 43, 51
pre-trial proceedings, **12**, 51
Intertemporal law
doctrine of, **19**, 668, 668*n*
Intervention Board for Agricultural Produce
delegation of powers, **1**, 984
establishment of, **1**, 983
European Union law, **19**, 243
levies, collecting, **1**, 875
Ombudsman system, **19**, 242
provisions on, **1**, 875
Intestacy
administration, **25**, 1036
adopted person—
  generally, **25**, 713
  succession by, **25**, 714
aliment, surviving spouse's right to, **25**, 711
avoidance of, **25**, 822
choice of law rules, **17**, 342
common law—
  general scheme of succession, **25**, 676
  heritable estate, *see* HERITABLE ESTATE
  history, **25**, 676–685
  moveable estate, *see* MOVEABLE ESTATE
croft, intestate succession to, **1**, 807, 808
  near relative by, **1**, 791
  notice to landlord of acquisition of lease, **1**, 790
  notice to quit on successor, **1**, 791–794
  objection by landlord, **1**, 790
  procedure, **1**, 789
  successor, position of, **1**, 791
  time limit, **1**, 789
  transfer of tenant's interest, **1**, 789
default, **25**, 630
England, **25**, 631
executors, position of, **1**, 795
France, **25**, 632
generally, **25**, 675
Germany, **25**, 633
history, **25**, 676–685
intestate succession as specialised concept of law, **11**, 1005
lease, *see* LEASE-LEASING
lease rights, succession, *see* TENANT-TENANCY (SUCCESSION)
legal rights in, **25**, 781
meaning of intestate, **25**, 689*n*
modern law—
  courtesy, abolition of, **25**, 702
  dwelling house—
    interest in, dispute as to, **25**, 692
    prior rights, **25**, 690

Intestacy—*continued*
modern law—*continued*
  furniture, **25**, 691
    value, dispute as to, **25**, 692
  heritable estate, assimilation of, **25**, 701
  moveable estate, assimilation of, **25**, 701
  plenishing—
    prior rights, **25**, 691
    value, dispute as to, **25**, 692
  radical changes, **25**, 688
  surviving spouse—
    executor, appointment as, **25**, 694
    prior rights—
      dwelling house, **25**, 690
      financial provision, **25**, 693
      furniture, **25**, 691
      generally, **25**, 689
      partial intestacy, **25**, 707
      plenishings, **25**, 691
  terce, abolition of, **25**, 702
mournings, widow's right to, **25**, 712
partial—
  bank account, **25**, 708
  building society account, **25**, 708
  dispute relating to, **25**, 710
  remainder of estate, distribution of, **25**, 709
  residue of estate, **25**, 706
  surviving spouse, prior rights of, **25**, 707
  when arising, **25**, 705
presumption against, **12**, 1267
prior rights, **12**, 1264
reform of, **25**, 686, 687
rights of succession—
  assimilation of heritable and moveable property, **25**, 701
  calculation of, **25**, 703
  collaterals, **25**, 698
  courtesy, abolition of, **25**, 702
  division among those having right, **25**, 696
  division of estate on or after 8 December 1986—
    examples, **25**, 704
  generally, **25**, 695
  legitim—
    division of, **25**, 700
    illegitimate child, right of, **25**, 699
    representation in, **25**, 700
  representation, **25**, 697
  terce, abolition of, **25**, 702
  See also SUCCESSION
rules, **25**, 613
sheriff court jurisdiction, **4**, 5
tenancy passing on, repossession, **13**, 749, 756, 781
testacy, as negative of, **25**, 630
udal law, **24**, 308
ultimus haeres state as, **17**, 343; **25**, 681
universal successor distinguished from singular successor, **25**, 675
See also SUCCESSION
Intestate estate
meaning, **25**, 689*n*
Intimidation
economic delict of, **15**, 580

Intimidation—*continued*
public procession, caused by, **14**, 1326
witness, of, **10**, 637
Intoxication
alcoholic liquor, generally, *see* ALCOHOLIC LIQUOR
alienation, and, **7**, 127
assault by intoxicated person, **7**, 228, 231, 234
capacity, and, **7**, 112
chronic alcoholism, **7**, 133
contempt of court, as, **6**, 319
criminal behaviour, link with, **14**, 1221
culpable homicide, murder reduced to, on
    grounds of, **7**, 271
defence, as, **7**, 112, 130, 131
diminished responsibility, **7**, 128–130, 133, 135,
    148
generally, **7**, 126
Hume's view, **7**, 126
insanity, plea of, **7**, 113, 127–130
intention to commit crime taken before
    intoxication, **7**, 126
involuntary, **7**, 134
mens rea, **7**, 127, 134
passenger in vehicle where driver intoxicated, **15**,
    395, 402
recklessness, **7**, 129, 130
social policy, effect of, **14**, 1220
therapeutic drugs, induced by, **7**, 132
See also DRUNKENNESS
Intra vires
byelaws must be, **14**, 291
Intromission
See VITIOUS INTROMISSION
Invalid care allowance
absent from Great Britain, claimant, **21**, 1025
age of claimant, **21**, 952
attendance allowance, person in receipt of, **21**,
    949
dependent adult, increase where, **21**, 1017
dependent child, increase where, **21**, 1015
disability living allowance, person in receipt of,
    21, 949
engaged in care rule, **21**, 949, 951
entitlement, **21**, 801, 949
    exclusions, **21**, 952
gainful employment, claimant in, **21**, 949, 950
generally, **21**, 949
overlapping benefits, **21**, 998
residence and presence in Great Britain, condition
    as to, **21**, 952
severely disabled person, meaning, **21**, 949
Invalid carriage
age limit for licence holder, **20**, 448
definition, **20**, 407
exclusion from definition of motor car, **20**, 406
licence to drive, age limit, **3**, 1229
provision of, **11**, 1486
vehicle excise licence exemptions, **20**, 463
wings, **20**, 483
Invalidity allowance
entitlement, **21**, 890, 891
invalidity pension, claimant receiving, **21**, 891
pension, invalidity addition, **21**, 1217
rates, **21**, 890

Invalidity benefit
absent from Great Britain, claimant, **21**, 1021,
    1022
contribution record, **21**, 941
disability appeal tribunal, member, **21**, 896
disqualification, **21**, 888, 892
entitlement, **21**, 801
generally, **21**, 890
incapacity for work, **21**, 892
income support—
    disability premium, **21**, 1074
    pensioner premium, **21**, 1074
invalidity allowance—
    entitlement, **21**, 890, 891
    pension, invalidity addition, **21**, 1217
    rates, **21**, 890
    See also INVALIDITY ALLOWANCE
invalidity pension—
    entitlement, **21**, 890
    rates, **21**, 890
    See also INVALIDITY PENSION
severe disablement allowance, interaction with,
    21, 941
sickness benefit, interaction with, **21**, 890
statutory sick pay, interaction with, **21**, 894
Invalidity pension
dependent adult, increase where, **21**, 1017
dependent child, increase where, **21**, 1015
entitlement, **21**, 890
invalidity allowance, interaction with, **21**, 891
rate, **21**, 890
statutory sick pay, interaction with, **21**, 912
Invasion
prerogative powers of Crown, **7**, 726
Invasion of interest
See INTEREST
Invention
copyright, **9**, 128
immoral behaviour, likely to encourage, **18**, 827,
    843
made after May 1978 ..., **9**, 127
made before June 1978 ..., **9**, 126
patent, *see* PATENT
Inventory
confirmation, *see* ADMINISTRATION OF ESTATE
deceased's estate of, **25**, 1019
judicial factor's duty to prepare, **24**, 245
sale, on, necessity for, **6**, 555
Inverness, Earldom of
generally, **7**, 704*n*
Inverse quantum
comparative principle, **24**, 532
Invest
meaning, **24**, 205
Investigation
Commission for Racial Equality, by, **9**, 390
Commissioner for Local Administration, by, *see*
    COMMISSIONER FOR LOCAL ADMINISTRATION IN
    SCOTLAND
Equal Opportunities Commission, by—
    power to conduct, **9**, 380
    terms of reference, **9**, 381
fatal accident inquiry, **17**, 965
Health and Safety Commission, by, **9**, 416

Investigation—*continued*
health and safety inspector, by, **9**, 490
police, **17**, 547
pre-trial, **17**, 544
Investiture
feudal law—
    improper investiture, **18**, 96
    proper investiture, **18**, 96
    renewal of investiture, **18**, 94, 106, 108
liferent, **18**, 74
See VESTING
Investment
advice—
    newspaper or magazine, given in, **12**, 1307
    sound, television or cable broadcast, **12**, 1307
business, *see* INVESTMENT BUSINESS
collective investment scheme, *see* COLLECTIVE
    INVESTMENT SCHEME
dealing in, **12**, 1307
fraud, **7**, 381
growth potential, **25**, 37
heritage, in, **25**, 810
income, taxation of—
    capital allowances, **14**, 1009
    generally, **19**, 1514; **25**, 978
industrial and provident society, by, **12**, 624
interest in, **12**, 1308
investment agreement, meaning, **12**, 1332*n*
investor protection, *see* INVESTOR PROTECTION
meaning, **12**, 1308; **25**, 69
Over the Counter Market (OTC), **12**, 1303
return, **25**, 44, 45
rights to, **12**, 1308
transactions—
    between companies in same group or
        enterprise, **12**, 1307
    designed to acquire more than 75 per cent of
        shares in body corporate, **12**, 1307
    employees' share schemes, **12**, 1307
    excluded from investment business, **12**, 1307
    industrial or commercial concern, arranged in
        connection with, **12**, 1307
    international securities self-regulating
        organisation, **12**, 1307
    trustee or personal representative by or for, **12**,
        1307
trust, *see* INVESTMENT TRUST
trustees' duty, *see* TRUSTEE
trustees' responsibility, **24**, 194, 204*ff*
unit trust scheme, *see* UNIT TRUST SCHEME
valuation, method of assessment, **25**, 123
Investment business
accounting records, **12**, 1408
advice offered by, **12**, 1307
adviser—
    agents on behalf of clients, **12**, 1353, 1362
    principals dealing with customers, **12**, 1353,
        1362
    SIB statements of principle, **12**, 1353
agent—
    on behalf of clients, **12**, 1353, 1362
    fiduciary duties of, **12**, 1354
appointed representative, *see* FINANCIAL SERVICES
assets, management by, **12**, 1307

Investment business—*continued*
authorisation—
    automatic, **12**, 1309
    European Community member state—
        collective investment scheme from, **12**,
            1318
        persons authorised in other, **12**, 1320
    generally, **12**, 1315
    insurance company, **12**, 1316
    registered friendly society, **12**, 1317
    Secretary of State, granted by, **12**, 1319
    fit and proper person, applicant must be, **12**,
        1310, 1311, 1338
    necessity for, **12**, 1309
    recognised professional body, member of, **12**,
        1309, 1313
    refusal and revocation of recognition, **12**,
        1314
    refusal, **12**, 1311
    routes to, **12**, 1309
    self-regulating organisation, member—
        generally, **12**, 1309, 1310
        refusal and revocation of recognition, **12**,
            1314
    SIB, by, **12**, 1309, 1312
        withdrawal, **12**, 1311
    suspension, **12**, 1311
    withdrawal, **12**, 1311
authorised person, *see* FINANCIAL SERVICES
bodies carrying on, winding up petition by
    Secretary of State, **4**, 741
carried on by unauthorised or unexempted
    person—
    interdict, **12**, 1324
    restitution order, **12**, 1324
cessation of business, SIB Core Conduct of
    Business Rules, **12**, 1396
Chinese walls, **12**, 1358, 1395
clients' money, protection of, **12**, 1409
communications, fair and clear, must be, **12**, 1371
complaints procedure, **12**, 1394
compliance with regulatory rules, **12**, 1393
conduct of—
    advertising, restrictions on, **12**, 1337
        exceptions to rules, **12**, 1337*n*
        extra-territorial application, **12**, 1337
        investment advertisement, meaning, **12**,
            1337*n*
    authorised person, *see* FINANCIAL SERVICES
    cancellation—
        notice of, effect, **12**, 1336
        provisions as to, **12**, 1336
        rules as to, **12**, 1340
        shortfall, **12**, 1336
    cold-calling—
        agreement entered after, effect of, **12**, 1334
        permitted, **12**, 1335
        prohibition on, **12**, 1333
            extra-territorial application, **12**, 1333
            power to lift, **12**, 1335
        public statement as to misconduct, **12**, 1339
        regulations, **12**, 1335
        rules as to, **12**, 1340
    concealment of facts, **12**, 1332

Investment business—*continued*
conduct of—*continued*
  Conduct of Business Rules, **12**, 1331
  conflicts of interest, **12**, 1348
  cooling-off periods, **12**, 1336
  customers—
    assets of, **12**, 1349
    information about, **12**, 1346
    information for, **12**, 1347
  disqualification direction, **12**, 1338
  financial resources, **12**, 1350
  integrity, **12**, 1343
  internal organisation, **12**, 1351
  market practice, **12**, 1345
  misconduct, public statement as to, **12**, 1339
  misleading statements and practice, **12**, 1332
    defences to, **12**, 1332*n*
    overseas person, by, **12**, 1332
    penalty for, **12**, 1332
    restitution order following, **12**, 1332
  notification of events, **12**, 1340
  prohibited person, employment of, **12**, 1338
    public statement as to, **12**, 1339
  regulators, relations with, **12**, 1352
  rules—
    cancellation, **12**, 1340
    clients' money, as to, **12**, 1340
    compensation fund, establishment of, **12**, 1340
    conduct of business, **12**, 1340
    contravention, public statement as to misconduct, **12**, 1339
    financial resources, **12**, 1340, 1350
    indemnity, **12**, 1340
    notification regulations, **12**, 1340
    Secretary of State's power to make, **12**, 1331
    SIB power to make, **12**, 1331
  SIB statements of principle, *see* SECURITIES AND INVESTMENTS BOARD
  skill, care and diligence, **12**, 1344
  unsolicited calls—
    agreement entered after, effect of, **12**, 1334
    permitted, **12**, 1335
    prohibition on, **12**, 1333
      extra-territorial application, **12**, 1333
      power to lift, **12**, 1335
    public statement as to misconduct, **12**, 1339
    regulations, **12**, 1335
    rules as to, **12**, 1340
customer, *see* FINANCIAL SERVICES
customer agreements, **12**, 1375
dealing in investments, **12**, 1307
exclusions from, **12**, 1307
exempted person, *see* FINANCIAL SERVICES
financial supervision, SIB rules—
  accounting records, **12**, 1404, 1408
  auditors, appointment of, **12**, 1405
  disapplication, where, **12**, 1402
  financial resources of firm, **12**, 1403
  generally, **12**, 1402, 1408
  internal controls and systems, **12**, 1407
  reports, publication of, **12**, 1404, 1406
independence, SIB Core Conduct of Business Rules, **12**, 1357–1362

Investment business—*continued*
inducements, giving or receiving, **12**, 1357
information and advice, supply—
  firm, about, **12**, 1364
  packaged products, about, **12**, 1363, 1365
liability, SIB Core Conduct of Business Rules, **12**, 1376
material interest in transaction, with, **12**, 1358
meaning, **12**, 1307, 1308; **25**, 69
misconduct, public statement as to, **12**, 1339
packaged products, **12**, 1360
professional rules, contravention, **16**, 1017
public, issues to, **4**, 360
remedies against, *see* FINANCIAL SERVICES (investors' remedies)
SIB Core Conduct of Business Rules, application, **12**, 1399
  See also SECURITIES AND INVESTMENTS BOARD
soft commission, **12**, 1359
volume overriders, **12**, 1357
written description of, SIB Core Conduct of Business Rules, **12**, 1392
Investment exchange
function, **12**, 1322
recognised—
  application for recognition order, **12**, 1322
  exempted person under Financial Services Act 1986, as, **12**, 1322
register, **12**, 1415
Investment grant
generally, **14**, 1009
Investment lease
generally, **13**, 210
Investment Management Regulatory Organisation (IMRO)
recognised self-regulating organisation, as, **12**, 1312
Investment trust
Business Start-Up Scheme, **2**, 1277
comparative law, **24**, 119
Estate Duties Investment Trust, **2**, 1276
nature of, **2**, 1274
private companies, investment in, **25**, 48
trust concept, **24**, 11
unit trust distinguished, **2**, 1275
Investor protection
See FINANCIAL SERVICES; INSIDER DEALING
Invitation to treat
advertisements, **15**, 624
auction sales, **15**, 625
generally, **15**, 620
offer distinguished, **15**, 620
quotation, **15**, 626
self-service display, **15**, 622
shop window displays, **15**, 621
tenders, **15**, 626
vending machines, **15**, 623
Invoice
documentary evidence, as, **10**, 602
information to be stated on, **16**, 1025
letter of credit, consistent with description goods in, **4**, 253
Inward processing
See CUSTOMS AND EXCISE

Ionising radiations
safety from, at work, **9**, 914
IOU
interest, whether payable, **13**, 1752
loan, as evidence of, **13**, 1731
meaning, **12**, 1008
non-negotiability of, **4**, 103
repayment, **12**, 1008
Ireland
Church of Ireland, disestablishment, **5**, 688
competition rules, application, **4**, 1304
European Union customs territory, **7**, 1010
immigration from, **12**, 101
incorporation into UK, **5**, 361
Irish peers, **16**, 1315
    House of Lords, **16**, 1307, 1307*n*
land legislation—
    Irish Land Commission, **6**, 954
    resettlement of populations, **6**, 954
    Scottish legislation compared, **6**, 953, 954
partition of, **5**, 361
Potato Famine, **12**, 101
proportional representation, **5**, 378
Republic of, *see* REPUBLIC OF IRELAND
VAT customs union, **7**, 1281
See also NORTHERN IRELAND; REPUBLIC OF IRELAND
Irish Sea
continental shelf delimitation agreement, **21**, 30
Ironworks
valuation for rating, **24**, 669
Irradiation
food, of, **11**, 357
Irrebuttable presumptions
exclusion of evidence, **10**, 520
Irrigation
abstraction of water, **25**, 330
spray, **25**, 331, 389
Irritancy
breach by tenant, as remedy against, **13**, 275, 276
clause in lease, generally, **12**, 1251
commercial lease, **13**, 559, 560, 584
contract, in, *see* CONTRACT
conventional, **13**, 584
    generally, **13**, 426
    grounds for, **13**, 427–430
    meaning, **13**, 423
    non-payment of rent, **13**, 427
    prohibited assignation or sublease, **13**, 428
    purging—
        common law, **13**, 431
        monetary breach, **13**, 433
        non-monetary breach, **13**, 434
        statute law, **13**, 432
    rescission compared, **13**, 426
disclamation, casualty of, **18**, 83
extinction of real right, **18**, 9
feudal law—
    casualty or remedy, classification as, **18**, 85
    lessee, in favour of, **18**, 85
    superior, in favour of, **18**, 85
euduty, **18**, 69
irritant and resolute clauses, **6**, 525
ease, of—
    insolvency, on, **13**, 415

Irritancy—*continued*
legal—
    common law, **13**, 424
    meaning, **13**, 423
    purging, **13**, 425
    statute law, **13**, 424
pactional, **13**, 584
penal, **13**, 584
procedure, **6**, 534
recognition, casualty of, **18**, 82
remedy of, **6**, 533
reserved power of possession compared, **13**, 446
severity of remedy, **13**, 584
termination of lease by—
    conventional irritancy, *see* conventional *above*
    enforcement—
        effect, **13**, 437
        generally, **13**, 435
        procedure, **13**, 436
    extraordinary removing, **13**, 466
    generally, **13**, 423
    irritancy clause, **13**, 423
    legal irritancy, *see* legal *above*
    procedure, **13**, 436
Ish
fixed date not necessary, **13**, 302
lease, in, necessity for, **13**, 597
meaning, **13**, 103
notice of termination, **13**, 468
real rights, and, **13**, 108, 301–303
removings, notice must be prior to, **13**, 475
security of tenure, and, **13**, 317
tacit relocation following, **13**, 450
tenancy, as prerequisite for, **13**, 613
tenant not moving out at, ordinary removing, **13**, 466
very long lease, **13**, 303
Island
alluvion, formation by, **18**, 594
building, supply of water to, **25**, 531
council, *see* ISLANDS AREA; LOCAL AUTHORITY
description of, **6**, 482
loch, in, ownership, **18**, 303
river, in—
    avulsion, formed by, **18**, 278
    ownership, **18**, 278
sea, in—
    artificial, construction in high seas, **21**, 41
    continental shelf of, **21**, 25
    straits formed by island belonging to mainland state, international navigation, **21**, 10
    territorial sea, baselines, **21**, 12
Islands area
corporate personality, **14**, 2
council—
    aerodrome, powers relating to, *see* AERODROME
    art gallery authority, **14**, 688, 689
    byelaws, *see* BYELAWS
    community council, scheme for establishing, **14**, 74
    concerted action, **14**, 80
    Convention of Scottish Local Authorities, representation on, **14**, 84
    drainage works, **25**, 373

Islands area—*continued*
council—*continued*
  education authority, as, **8**, 712
  ferries, powers in relation to, *see* FERRY
  fire services, *see* FIRE SERVICES
  floods—
    control powers, **25**, 377
    prevention, *see* FLOOD
    warning system, **25**, 379
  Food and Drugs (Scotland) Act, administration
    of, **11**, 329
  functions—
    concurrent, **14**, 79
    sole, **14**, 78
  harbour, acquisition of, **14**, 444
  housing—
    allocation of, **11**, 1935
    See also HOUSING
  industrial promotion, **14**, 633
  inter-authority relationships—
    concerted action, **14**, 80
    concurrent functions, **14**, 79
    generally, **14**, 77
    sole functions, **14**, 78
  library authority, **14**, 687, 689
  licences, powers relating to, *see* LICENCES
  litigation, **14**, 118
  museum authority, **14**, 688, 689
  name, change of, **14**, 71
  new structure, **14**, 64
  pier, acquisition of, **14**, 444
  private legislation, promotion of, **14**, 306
  public health matters, **19**, 308, 308*n*
  public procession, *see* PUBLIC PROCESSION
  public transport, *see* PUBLIC TRANSPORT
  registration, powers relating to, *see* REGISTRATION
  river purification, **14**, 477
  social work, *see* SOCIAL WORK
  tourism, promotion of, **14**, 662
  water authority, *see* WATER AUTHORITY
education, responsibility for, **14**, 36
electoral divisions, **15**, 1039
highways, responsibility for, **14**, 33
map, **14**, 64
meaning, **15**, 1039
Islands or district council
allotments—
  duties in relation to, **13**, 531

Islands or district council
allotments—*continued*
  provision of, **13**, 535
  common pasture, land acquired for, **13**, 534, 541
  landlord, as, assured tenancy status excluded, **13**,
    636, 647
  library service, **13**, 1504
Isle of Man
adoption order made in, **8**, 535
civil jurisdiction, **4**, 23
Commissioners of Customs and Excise—
  disclosure of information to, **7**, 1283
  recovery proceedings, **7**, 1283
common travel area, **12**, 122; **16**, 1208
competition rules, application, **4**, 1304
copyright legislation, **18**, 935
deportation order made by, **12**, 123
entry to United Kingdom via, **12**, 123
  restrictions on, **12**, 123
EU law rights, **12**, 220
European Union customs territory, **7**, 1010
Immigration Act, application to, **12**, 123
Independent Broadcasting Authority, functions
  of, **17**, 7
inland bill, nature of, **4**, 120
Manx herring fishing licences, **11**, 114
overseas company, **4**, 315
patient absent without leave, custody of, **14**, 1423
service Acts applying, **2**, 613
territorial sea, **11**, 76
VAT customs union, **7**, 1281
visiting forces in, **2**, 786
Issue
birth, effect on vesting subject to defeasance, **25**, 935
meaning, **4**, 138; **12**, 1268; **13**, 1627; **25**, 877
original share, application of *conditio*, **25**, 901
  See also CHILD–CHILDREN
Italy
civil jurisdiction, contracting state, as, **4**, 22
competition rules, application, **4**, 1304
constitutional amendments, **5**, 307
European Union customs territory, **7**, 1010
Itinerancy
special jurisdiction, **4**, 35
ITV
Independent Broadcasting Authority, provision
  by, **17**, 7
Ius, *see* JUS

J

Jack Report
government response to, **4**, 105, 191
Jacobite rebellions
peerages forfeited on, **16**, 1313
policing, effect on, **16**, 1706, 1707
Jacobites
presbyterianism and episcopacy, **3**, 1611–1613
Japan
cross-border leasing, **14**, 1094
Jason clause
generally, **21**, 704*n*
See also NEW JASON CLAUSE
Jeffrey principle
succession to armorial dignities, **11**, 1619
Jenkins Report
case law since, **4**, 480
implementation of proposals, **4**, 305, 479, 481
Jersey
inland bill, nature of, **4**, 120
Jersey cattle
milk, regulations as to, **11**, 466
Jetsam
meaning, **21**, 511
wreck, when classed as, **21**, 511
Jetty
lease, **13**, 205
Jewellery
carriage of, **3**, 610
Jewish faith
barbers' business, Sunday opening, **3**, 1681
Beth Din, **3**, 1675
civil courts, interaction with, **3**, 1675, 1675*n*
burial grounds, **3**, 531
burial society, **12**, 694*n*
Chief Rabbi, jurisdiction, **3**, 1675
clergy, special status, **3**, 1687
confined mourning, friendly society registered to
secure payments during, **3**, 1686
Court of the Chief Rabbi, **3**, 1675
disabilities attaching to Jews, **3**, 1676, 1677
discrimination, protection of Jews against, **3**,
1676
Edinburgh Hebrew Congregation, **3**, 1673
factory or business owned by Jew, employment of
young persons on Sunday, **3**, 1682
Glasgow Jewish community, **3**, 1673
historical background, **3**, 1673
immigration of Jews, **12**, 101
Jew, who is, **3**, 1675, 1675*n*
kosher food, **3**, 1675
marriage, **3**, 1675, 1683
Orthodox, **3**, 1675
Passover, **22**, 808
Reform congregation, **3**, 1675
religious instruction or observance in schools,
right to withdraw from, **3**, 1679
religious toleration, **3**, 1676
ritual slaughter of animals, **3**, 1675, 1680
status of Jews, **3**, 1677

Jewish faith—*continued*
statutory recognition, **3**, 1678–1683
Sunday employment, **22**, 817
synagogues—
affiliation in Scotland, **3**, 1675
charitable status, **3**, 1684
number in Scotland, **3**, 1675
voluntary churches, as, **3**, 1674
trust deed, condition as to faith in, **3**, 1685
voting rights and Jews, **3**, 1678
will, condition as to faith in, **3**, 1685
Jobber
insider dealing rules, **12**, 1529
Joint Contracts Tribunal (JCT)
building contracts, **3**, 10
Joint Legal Committee
establishment, **13**, 1139
generally, **13**, 1139, 1140
Joint property
See CO-OWNERSHIP
Joint purchase agency
European Union, in, **4**, 1389
Joint sales agency
European Union, in, **4**, 1370
Joint stock company
legal personality, **4**, 303
memorandum of association, alteration of, **4**, 320
registrar, *see* REGISTRAR OF JOINT STOCK COMPANIES
South Sea Company, formation of, **4**, 303
Joint title
trust title as, **24**, 162
Joint venture
choice as business medium, **16**, 1004
collective investment scheme categorisation,
exclusion from, **12**, 1325
contract of—
building contracts, **3**, 9
lease distinguished, **13**, 117
European Union aspects, **4**, 1391
Jointure
settlement of, **25**, 611
Journalist
copyright of written work by, **18**, 997
information, disclosure of sources, **6**, 316
Securities and Investments Board Core Conduct
of Business Rules, **12**, 1399
Joy-riding
charges against joyrider, **7**, 336
meaning, **20**, 444
offence of, **20**, 444
Judge
See JUDICIARY *and under names of particular courts*
Judge Admiral
office of, **1**, 403
Judge Advocate
army and air force—
appointment, **2**, 714, 716
duties, **2**, 727
summing up by, **2**, 727

Judge Advocate—*continued*
Fleet, of—
    deputy, **2**, 675
    functions, **2**, 675
    office, constitution of, **2**, 675
    reference of courts-martial findings, **2**, 675
naval—
    appointment, **2**, 695
    duties, **2**, 695
    summing up by, **2**, 704
Judge Advocate General
appointment, **2**, 676
duties, **2**, 676
Vice JAG, **2**, 676
Judgments, recognition and enforcement
comity and reciprocity, theory of, **8**, 400
decree conform, **8**, 401, 403, 405, 413, 415
diligence, *see* DILIGENCE
European institutions, of, **8**, 565–568
European judgments in civil and commercial
    matters—
    appeals—
        diligence during period of, **8**, 464, 466
        further appeal, **8**, 459
        generally, **8**, 457, 458, 478
        protective measures—
            generally, **8**, 460, 463
            maintenance judgments, in respect of, **8**,
                467
        restrictions during period of, **8**, 459
        warrant issued before application for registra-
           tion, **8**, 465
    authentic instrument, **8**, 474
    court settlement, **8**, 474
    decree and warrant—
        period for service, **8**, 462
        registration, **8**, 468
    enforcement, application for—
        Court of Session, to, **8**, 453
        court to which made, **8**, 451
        generally, **8**, 455
        grant of, effect, **8**, 457
        maintenance judgments, **8**, 454
        procedure, **8**, 452
        refusal, **8**, 440–448, 456
        sheriff court, to, **8**, 454
        title to apply, **8**, 450
    excluded topics, **8**, 431, 437
    exclusive jurisdiction of, **8**, 410, 439
    execution of registered judgments, **8**, 469
    expenses, recovery of, **8**, 470
    generally, **8**, 428, 429, 475
    interest, recovery of, **8**, 470
    legal aid, **8**, 471
    recognition—
        effect, **8**, 480
        procedure for, **8**, 479
    Scottish judgment, enforcement outwith UK,
        8, 473
    security for costs, **8**, 472
    types of judgment covered by, **8**, 438
foreign—
    administration of estates, **8**, 552, 553

Judgments, recognition and enforcement—
    continued
foreign—*continued*
    Administration of Justice Act 1920—
        application for registration, **8**, 414, 415
        Court of Session, procedure in, **8**, 416
        geographical extent, **8**, 411
        refusal of recognition, grounds for, **8**, 417
        registration, effect of, **8**, 418
        scope, **8**, 412
    adoption orders, **8**, 534–538. *See also* ADOPTION
    arbitral awards—
        Arbitration Act 1950—
            awards within scope of, **8**, 558
            enforcement, mode and effect, **8**, 559
            foreign award, conditions for enforcing, **8**,
                560
        Arbitration Act 1975—
            effect, **8**, 562
            enforcement, **8**, 562
            refusal, grounds for, **8**, 563
            scope, **8**, 561
        Arbitration (International Investment) Disputes
           Act 1933 ..., **8**, 557
        common law, at, **8**, 554
    authority from Scottish court, **8**, 401
    common law, at—
        arbitration, **8**, 554
        challenge, grounds for, **8**, 404–409
        decree conform, by, **8**, 401, 403, 413, 415
        generally, **8**, 402
    custody order, **8**, 504–533. *See also* CUSTODY
        ORDER
    death, presumption of, **8**, 542
    European Union, of, *see* European judgments
        above
    Foreign Judgments (Reciprocal Enforcement)
        Act 1933—
        extent, **8**, 420
        judgments to which provisions apply, **8**, 421
        registration—
            effect, **8**, 426
            objection to, **8**, 423
            procedure, **8**, 422
            setting aside, **8**, 424, 425
    grants of arms, **8**, 543
    insolvency, **8**, 544, 549–551; **17**, 351
    maintenance order, *see* MAINTENANCE ORDER
    matrimonial decrees, *see* MATRIMONIAL DECREES
    mentally disordered person, curator appointed
        by foreign court—
        custody, power of, **8**, 540
        generally, **8**, 539
        property, power over, **8**, 541
    registration—
        refusing or setting aside, **8**, 417, 424, 425
inter-UK civil judgments—
    arbitral awards, **8**, 555
    certificate or certified copy of, **8**, 485–487
    costs or expenses of registration, **8**, 487, 488
    excluded matters, **8**, 484
    money and non-money provisions, **8**, 485
    nature and extent, **8**, 481
    procedure, **8**, 485, 486

Judgments, recognition and enforcement—
continued
inter-UK civil judgments—*continued*
  recognition, **8**, 491
  scope, **8**, 483
  setting aside registration, **8**, 490
  sisting execution, **8**, 489
Lugano or Parallel Convention, **8**, 429
matrimonial decrees, *see* MATRIMONIAL DECREES
Protection of Trading Interests Act 1980,
  judgment affected by, **8**, 404, 409, 425
Scottish judgments—
  enforcement outwith UK, **8**, 419, 427, 473
status of foreign decrees, **8**, 400
vested rights theory, **8**, 400
See also CHOICE OF LAW; CIVIL JURISDICTION
Judicial arrangement
Judgments Convention, exclusion from scope of,
  4, 74; **8**, 431
Judicial bonds of caution
See CAUTIONARY OBLIGATION
Judicial Committee of the Privy Council
See PRIVY COUNCIL
Judicial decision
See CASE LAW
Judicial decree
deed, as, **16**, 2109
servitudes, creation, **18**, 448
Judicial examination
new-style, **17**, 643
old form, **17**, 646
pre-trial procedure, **17**, 546
record of—
  generally, **17**, 647
  trial diet, **17**, 757
  verification of, **17**, 648
Judicial factor
Accountant of Court, role and duties of, **6**, 937;
  22, 694; **24**, 237, 246, 250, 253, 255, 265
administration by, reasons for, **24**, 237
administration of property in dispute, **13**, 24
appointment, **4**, 14, 70, 487, 999; **17**, 1424; **24**, 9,
  13, 190, 202
  administration/management of trust estate, **24**,
    158
  common law, at, **24**, 158
  deceased debtor's estate, for, **2**, 1451
  failure where no caution found, **24**, 242
  jurisdiction to appoint, **24**, 238
  matters to be presented to court, **2**, 1334
  nobile officium as basis of, **24**, 238
  persons eligible, **24**, 241
  petition for, **2**, 1332; **24**, 240
  power to appoint, **2**, 1318
  procedure for, **24**, 240
  sheriff court powers, **6**, 1072
caution granted for—
  amount required, **3**, 993
  generally, **3**, 993
  institution, by, **3**, 986
  intromissions of—
    amount of, generally, **24**, 242
    duty to find, **24**, 242, 243
    failure to appoint where not found, **24**, 242

Judicial factor—*continued*
caution granted for—*continued*
  intromissions of—*continued*
    liability of cautioner, **24**, 242
    sufficiency of, **24**, 242
    time for finding, **24**, 242
Church of Scotland ministers, **24**, 241
classes of, **24**, 237*n*, 239, 268–281
commission, entitlement to, **24**, 252
common property, on, **24**, 278
company, on estate of, **24**, 239, 276
curator bonis, **4**, 14, 70; **24**, 239, 265, 270, 271
deceased person, on estate of, **24**, 239, 274
defaulting solicitor, on estate of, **24**, 239, 277
definition, **3**, 993*n*; **24**, 237
delict—
  defender, as, **15**, 234
  title and interest to sue, **15**, 234
duties—
  accounts, submission of, **24**, 246
  administration of estate, **24**, 246, 253
  administration of sequestration by, **2**, 1320; **24**,
    273
  auctor in rem suam, not to be, **24**, 170, 246
  breach of, **24**, 250
  care, skill and diligence, **24**, 248
  cash holdings, limitation on, **24**, 246
  caution, to find, **24**, 242, 243
  conservation of estate, **24**, 244, 247
  fiduciary, **24**, 172, 246
  generally, **24**, 243
  ingathering of estate, **24**, 244
  inventory, preparation of, **24**, 245
  not to delegate, **24**, 249
  skill, **24**, 248
  statutory, **24**, 246
fee *in pendente*, **24**, 281
female, **24**, 241
gratuitous alienation, challenge of, **2**, 1318
historical origins, **24**, 238
ineligibility—
  bankrupt, **24**, 241
  limited company, **24**, 241
  partnership, **24**, 241
judicial conveyance in relation to, **18**, 664
Judicial Factors Act, applications under—
  alienation of property, **24**, 260
  business, to carry on, **24**, 259
  capital, encroachment on, **24**, 261
  election in succession, **24**, 256
  generally, **24**, 255
  heritage, to purchase, **24**, 258
  special powers, for, **24**, 255
  third parties, allowances to, **24**, 257
lessee, as, **13**, 187
lessor, as, **13**, 154, 167
liability generally, **24**, 264
loco absentis, **4**, 14, 70; **24**, 239, 272
loco tutoris, **4**, 14, 70; **24**, 239, 269
minors, damages for, **24**, 279
negligent investment, **24**, 250
partnership estate, **24**, 239, 275
pending litigation, **24**, 280

Judicial factor—*continued*
personal injury, as pursuer in action relating to,
    16, 2150, 2168
petition for appointment, **24**, 240
powers—
    administration of estate, **24**, 253
    alienation, **24**, 253
    discretionary, **24**, 253
    generally, **24**, 251
    investment, **24**, 253
    restriction on, **24**, 253
    sequestrated trust estate, **24**, 273
    special, **24**, 254, 255, 263, 264, 273
        retrospective grant, **24**, 263
    usual, **24**, 253
property, transfer of, **24**, 266
pupils, damages for, **24**, 279
removings, action of, **13**, 497
remuneration, **24**, 190, 202
resignation, **24**, 164, 165
responsibilities of, effect, **24**, 237
rights, **24**, 251
Scottish Law Commission recommendations, **22**,
    694
sequestrated estates, **2**, 1320; **24**, 273
supervision by Accountant of Court, **24**, 237, 250
termination and discharge, **24**, 267
trust estates, on, **24**, 239, 273
trustee, as, **24**, 128
Trusts (Scotland) Acts, applications under, **24**, 255
width and flexibility of office, **24**, 268
Judicial functions
nature of, **1**, 210
quasi-judicial, use of term, **1**, 212
sheriff, of, **1**, 210
Judicial officer
abuse of power, **7**, 549
bribery, **7**, 405, 547
delict committed by, liability, **15**, 242
neglect of duty, **7**, 551
oppression by, **7**, 548–551
Judicial precedent
American Legal Realism, **22**, 263
appellate jurisdiction, generally, **22**, 265–333, 544
authoritative writings in Scots law, effect, **22**, 440
binding element—
    generally, **22**, 111, 334–354
    ratio decidendi, **22**, 334–345
        See also ratio decidendi below
broad principles of formulation by judge, **22**, 256
case law—
    appellate jurisdiction—
        generally, **22**, 265–333
        principle of binding precedent, **22**, 265
    binding custom, as—
        commercial contracts, **22**, 260
        Mackenzie, **22**, 251
        Stair, citation of cases in *Institutions*, **22**, 251
    changing conceptions of, **22**, 256
    English, influence of, **22**, 264, 544
    European Court of Justice, **22**, 268
    international law, as source of, **19**, 646

Judicial precedent—*continued*
case law—*continued*
    Scottish—
        citation in legal argument, **22**, 264
        reference in legal writing, **22**, 264
    trusts, case law relating to, **17**, 337
College of Justice—
    establishment, **22**, 249, 251
    Senator of, Court of Session decisions recorded
        by, **22**, 251
computerised databases—
    effect on application of precedent, **22**, 263
    House of Lords, views, **22**, 263
    Lexis, **22**, 263
        See also DATABASE
Court of Exchequer, **22**, 322
Court of Session, **22**, 251, 254, 257, 286–292,
    294, 295, 298, 541, 544
    See also COURT OF SESSION
criminal courts, **22**, 302–320
    See also CRIMINAL COURTS
custom and, **22**, 257, 260, 543
effect of, **6**, 833
European Community law, **10**, 80, 82, 83; **22**,
    266–269
    See also EUROPEAN COMMUNITY LAW; EUROPEAN
        COURT OF JUSTICE
flexibility or rigidity of operation, **22**, 257, 259
generally, **11**, 1011; **22**, 247–354
hierarchy of the courts, **22**, 265–333
High Court of Justiciary, **22**, 302–312
    See also HIGH COURT OF JUSTICIARY
historical outline—
    College of Justice, **22**, 249, 251
    generally, **22**, 249–256
    nineteenth century, **22**, 252–256
    pre-sixteenth century, **22**, 250
    sixteenth and seventeenth centuries, **22**, 251
House of Lords, **22**, 263, 270, 273, 274, 277, 279,
    283–285, 323, 544
    See also HOUSE OF LORDS
institutional writers, **22**, 251, 259
Judicial Committee of the Privy Council, advice
    on appeals from jurisdictions not based on
    English law, **22**, 278
    See also PRIVY COUNCIL
juristic writing, **22**, 259
justification, **22**, 248, 542
Lands Tribunal for Scotland, **22**, 324
    See also LANDS TRIBUNAL FOR SCOTLAND
Lands Valuation Appeal Court, **22**, 323
    See also LANDS VALUATION APPEAL COURT
law reporting—
    databases, **22**, 263
    generally, **22**, 261–263
    influence, **22**, 545
    modern, **22**, 263
    nineteenth century improvements, **22**, 253
    reported cases, **22**, 261
    unreported cases, **22**, 262
    See also LAW REPORTING
'legislating' through, judicial policy decisions, **22**,
    258
legislation contrasted, **22**, 110–115, 258

Judicial precedent—*continued*
Lexis, inclusion of Scottish material, **22**, 263
Lord Advocate's references, **22**, 319
Lyon Court, **22**, 325
  See also LYON, COURT OF THE LORD
meaning, **22**, 247
nature, **22**, 247, 248
obiter dicta—
  legal principle, statements contained in, **22**, 343
  ratio decidendi distinguished, **22**, 343
obsolescence and desuetude compared, **22**, 256
other sources of law, in context of, **22**, 257–260
overruling prior decisions—
  House of Lords, own, **22**, 270, 274, 283–285, 323
  policy decisions, judges, **22**, 258
Practicks—
  Court of Session decisions, **22**, 539
  digest—
    Balfour, Sir James, **22**, 251, 540, 609, 627
    contents, **22**, 540
    Hope, Sir Thomas, **22**, 540
    Spottiswoode, Sir Robert, **22**, 540, 605
ratio decidendi—
  consistency with actual determination by court, **22**, 340
  discovery, **22**, 337
  dissenting judicial opinions in case determined by plurality of judges, **22**, 342
  Donoghue v Stevenson, **22**, 339
  generally, **22**, 334–345
  Goodhart's theory, **22**, 344
  hierarchy of courts, **22**, 345
  identifying issue in earlier case crucial to formulation, **22**, 344
  judges differ, where, **22**, 342
  limited by context of general law, **22**, 338
  meaning, **22**, 335
  narrow and wide *rationes*, **22**, 339
  obiter dicta distinguished, **22**, 343
  opinions of the judges in prior case, **22**, 341
  proposition of law, as, **22**, 336
  Scottish courts, in relation to actual practices, **22**, 335
  search for, **22**, 339
reasons for not following prior decisions—
  age of prior case, **22**, 350
  case with no clear *ratio*, **22**, 348
  defective reporting of prior case, **22**, 352
  different issues, respective cases, **22**, 347
  generally, **22**, 346–354
  key point of law not argued in prior case, **22**, 351
  lack of reliance on old case, **22**, 350
  not binding in terms of *stare decisis* hierarchy of courts and *ratio decidendi*, **22**, 345
  point of law conceded in prior case, **22**, 351
  prior decision—
    not consistent with existing authority, **22**, 348
    per incuriam, **22**, 349
Registration of Voters Appeal Court, **22**, 326
Restrictive Practices Court, **22**, 327
Scottish Land Court, **22**, 321

Judicial precedent—*continued*
Sheriff of Chancery, **22**, 301
sheriff court—
  civil jurisdiction, **22**, 296–301
  criminal jurisdiction, **22**, 313–318
  See also SHERIFF COURT
sheriff principal, **22**, 299, 300
source of law, as, **22**, 501, 539–545
Stair, citation of cases in *Institutions*, **22**, 251
stare decisis—
  Court of Session decision, **22**, 252, 440
  development of doctrine in Scotland, **22**, 252, 255, 440, 538, 541, 542
  hierarchy of courts and *ratio decidendi*, **22**, 252, 255
  House of Lords, influence on development in Scots law, **22**, 255
  modern rules, **22**, 544
  narrow sense of precedent, **22**, 247
  specialised sense influenced by English law, **22**, 247
  war pension cases, **22**, 332
statute and—
  generally, as sources of law, **22**, 134–143
  precedent as gloss on, **22**, 135, 136
  valid, compared with binding precedent, **22**, 111
statutory abrogation—
  common law principles, **22**, 143
  generally, **22**, 141–143
  rule of law emerging from judicial decision, **22**, 141
statutory derogation, common law principles, **22**, 142
statutory endorsement—
  concept, **22**, 137
  doctrine, **22**, 138, 139
  presumption, **22**, 140
tribunals, generally, **22**, 328–333
trusts, case law relating to, **17**, 337
wide and narrow sense of, **22**, 247, 248
See also PRECEDENT
Judicial proceedings
copyright—
  acts done for purposes of proceedings, **18**, 1122
  report of proceedings, **18**, 1122
quasi-judicial proceeding, statement made in, absolute privilege, **15**, 524
reports of, qualified privilege, **15**, 533, 534
statements in—
  absolute privilege, **15**, 518–522, 533
  civil proceedings, **15**, 518, 523
  court officers, **15**, 518
  qualified privilege, **15**, 523, 535
Judicial records
challenge of, **10**, 582
convictions, as, **10**, 582
correction of entries, **10**, 582
decrees, **10**, 582
documentary evidence, as—
  bail orders, **10**, 588
  civil proceedings, decrees and verdicts in, **10**, 585

Judicial records—*continued*
documentary evidence, as—*continued*
  criminal convictions, **10**, 584
  decrees in absence, **10**, 586
  foreign courts, decrees of, **10**, 587
  generally, **10**, 582
  judicial warrants, **10**, 589
  notes of evidence, **10**, 590
  subsequent proceedings, use in, **10**, 583
history of, **19**, 801, 856
interlocutors, **10**, 582
Lord Clerk Register, **19**, 801–807
meaning, **10**, 582
proof of, **10**, 582
verdicts, as, **10**, 582
Judicial remedies
See REMEDIES
Judicial review
absence or inadequacy of reasons for decision, where, **1**, 293
acts of Community institutions, **10**, 85
application for—
  declarator, when sought, **1**, 326
  first order, **1**, 346
  generally, **14**, 125
  interdict, when sought, **1**, 327
  new procedure, **1**, 324, 345
  orders on, **1**, 346
  procedure, **1**, 346
  reduction, when sought, **1**, 325
  scope and extent of, **1**, 348
compulsory purchase of, **1**, 296
contract of employment, application to, **9**, 40
Court of Justice powers, **4**, 1366
Court of Session—
  powers of, **14**, 126
  procedure, **17**, 1419
discretion, of exercise of—
  extent of, **1**, 234
  generally, **14**, 1959
  grounds for, **1**, 236
  relevant considerations, on basis of, **1**, 237
  unreasonableness, on grounds of, **1**, 240
English law, comparison with, **1**, 345
errors, correction of, **1**, 247, 285
European Union legislation, obligation to give reasons facilitating, **22**, 202
exclusion of court's power, **1**, 306; **13**, 32
  arbitration, **13**, 34
  statutory, **13**, 33
extension of, **5**, 330
failure to act, **1**, 302
grounds of, **1**, 213; **5**, 331; **14**, 124
illegality, defence of, **1**, 331
improvement notice, of, **9**, 510
jurisdictional grounds, on, **1**, 306
legal rights on death of spouse, **19**, 1624
nationality, discretionary decisions as to, **14**, 1959
nature of, **5**, 331; **14**, 124
Order in Council, exercise of powers conferred on Minister by, **22**, 173
planning decisions, of, **23**, 243, 268, 277–278
powers on application, **14**, 126
prerogative powers, **1**, 234; **7**, 720, 720*n*, 721, 721*n*

Judicial review—*continued*
procedure—
  English, **5**, 668
  Scottish, **5**, 669; **14**, 123
prohibition notice, of, **9**, 510
reduction, Court of Session, **13**, 28
relief, forms of, **1**, 347
Revenue cases, **19**, 1549
right to, **12**, 54
scope, **1**, 248
statutory remedies to be exhausted before, **1**, 305, 346
supervisory jurisdiction, **1**, 248
Takeover Panel decisions, **4**, 542
title and interest, establishment of, **1**, 308, 346
  actions involving Crown, in, **7**, 751
ultra vires doctrine, and, **1**, 216
Union Agreement of 1707 ..., **5**, 347; **22**, 150
See also COURT OF SESSION; JUDICIAL CONTROL
Judicial separation
action of—
  jurisdiction, **4**, 5, 39; **8**, 432
  status, **4**, 68
court decree, **10**, 934
custody of children, **10**, 1317
defences and bars, **10**, 936
effects, **10**, 937
generally, **10**, 934
grounds, **10**, 935
homeless persons, **10**, 934
recognition of decree—
  Family Law Act 1986—
    British Islands, decrees granted in, **10**, 943
    generally, **10**, 942
    overseas, decrees granted, **10**, 944–947
religious reasons, used for, **10**, 934
separation agreement, **10**, 934, 939
  expenses, **10**, 939
stepchildren, aliment for, **10**, 1246
termination, **10**, 938
See also MATRIMONIAL DECREES
Judicial slander
defamation, **15**, 523
  meaning, **15**, 523
  qualified privilege, **15**, 529, 535
Judicial warrant
documentary evidence, as, **10**, 589
Judiciary
absolute privilege, **15**, 519
appointment, **13**, 1259
authority and impartiality, maintenance of, **12**, 8?
bribe, **7**, 547
  attempt to, **5**, 667; **7**, 547
compulsory retirement age, **5**, 664
defamation by, **15**, 519
delict, title and interest to sue, **15**, 227
function of, **5**, 622
immunity from suit—
  judges of, **5**, 665
  public prosecutor, **5**, 666
impartiality, **12**, 48
independence of, **5**, 663–667
judical slander, **15**, 523

Judiciary—*continued*
judicial appointments—
  data held in connection with, limitation on access to, **18**, 1532
  Faculty of Advocates, from, **13**, 1259
killing, treason, as, **7**, 569
liability—
  malicious prosecution, **15**, 448
  wrongful detention, **15**, 441–443
Lord Chancellor as senior judge, **5**, 370
murmuring judges, **5**, 667
neglect of duty, **7**, 551
oath or affirmation of allegiance, **6**, 1041; **7**, 706
offence against—
  assault, **7**, 545
  defamation, **7**, 501, 546
  generally, **7**, 491
offence by, **7**, 491
oppression, generally, **7**, 548
precedence, **16**, 2020
  international courts, **16**, 2020
qualified privilege, **15**, 519
removal from office, **5**, 664
role of—
  basic constitution, and, **5**, 360
  emancipation legislation, **5**, 359
  legality of legislation, **5**, 358
separation of powers, doctrine of, **5**, 341, 623
solicitor appointed as, **13**, 1186
See also under names of particular courts
Jungholz
European Union customs territory, **7**, 1010
Junk yard
unaesthetic sight, as, **14**, 2084
Jurisdiction
meaning, **4**, 1
monetary value of claim, civil proceedings, **4**, 12–19
multiple, criminal, **17**, 591
subject matter—
  civil proceedings, **4**, 3–11
  criminal proceedings, **17**, 592
territorial—
  civil, **4**, 2
  criminal, **17**, 589
    extra-territorial, **17**, 590
See also under names of particular courts; JUDGMENTS, ENFORCEMENT OF
Jury
absolute privilege, **15**, 522
address to, **17**, 762
age limit for jury service, **3**, 1214
charge to, solemn trial procedure, **17**, 557
clergy, jury service, **3**, 1571, 1632*n*, 1669, 1687
deliberations of, **17**, 764
empanelling, **17**, 747
examination of real evidence by, **10**, 618, 619
fatal accident inquiry, **17**, 955, 959
improper conduct by juror, inquiry into, **10**, 529
jury service—
  advocate ineligible for, **13**, 1329
  generally, **17**, 542
  minister excusable from, **3**, 1571, 1632*n*
  peer excusable from, **16**, 1308

Jury—*continued*
jury service—*continued*
  police exempt from, **16**, 1749
  solicitor ineligible for, **13**, 1172
management of, **17**, 749
oral evidence by juror, **10**, 529
protection of deliberations, **6**, 315
questioning by, **10**, 559; **17**, 754
sheriff's duties in respect of jurors, **6**, 1046
trial by—
  Court of Session, **17**, 1412; **22**, 635
  development of, **17**, 542
Trial of Pyx, **14**, 1821
trial without, **17**, 560
verdict once case remitted to, **17**, 748
veterinary surgeons excluded from jury service, **25**, 206
Jury Court
assimilation by Court of Session, **6**, 815, 915
creation, **6**, 815
House of Lords appellate jurisdiction, **6**, 815
jurisdiction, **6**, 915
Jus ad rem
beneficiary's right as, **24**, 7
generally, **11**, 1099
Lord Chancellor as senior judge, **5**, 370
obligation, creditor in, **15**, 1
prosecutor, relationship to, **17**, 583
public duties, enforcement of, **11**, 1024
role of—
  basic constitution, **5**, 360
  emancipation legislation, **5**, 359
  legality of legislation, **5**, 358
Scottish judges, attendance in House of Lords, **5**, 640
separation of powers, **5**, 341, 623
special legal powers, **11**, 1062
valid law, implementation of, **11**, 1002
Jus administrationis, **24**, 648
Jus cogens
meaning, **19**, 651
source of international law, as, **19**, 651
validity of treaty, and, **19**, 630, 634, 651
Jus crediti
beneficiary's right as, **24**, 7, 12
Jus in personam
See RIGHT (PERSONAL)
Jus in re
entitlement of person vested with, **15**, 1
See RIGHT (THINGS, IN)
Jus in re aliena
meaning, **8**, 111
Jus in rem
See RIGHT (THINGS, IN)
Jus mariti, **22**, 648
Jus primae noctis
casualty of, feudal law, **18**, 77
Jus quaesitum tertio, *see* CONTRACT (TITLE TO SUE)
Jus relictae vel relicti
claim to, **25**, 785
inheritance tax, and, **19**, 1624
Jus relicti
obligation to satisfy, **16**, 2116

Just and equitable rule
petition to wind up based on, *see* WINDING UP
unfair prejudice remedy, history of, **4**, 478
Justice
attempt to pervert course of, **6**, 314
fair administration, **12**, 6
meaning, **7**, 1083*n*
Justice ayres
generally, **6**, 851; **16**, 1705
Justice Clerk
Officer of State, **7**, 790, 791, 792, 800
Justice General
origin of office, **17**, 505
Justice of the peace
administrative duties, **14**, 27
appointment of, **6**, 1159, 1162; **14**, 513
compulsory removal of child, social worker's duty
    in relation to, **22**, 18
court, *see* JUSTICE OF THE PEACE COURT
district court, **6**, 1162
duties, **6**, 1159
eighteenth century, **16**, 1706
gentleman, designation as, **16**, 2023
highways, responsibility for, **14**, 33
history of term, **17**, 502
instruction and training, **6**, 1164, 1168
introduction of, **14**, 27; **16**, 1705
judicial duties, **14**, 27
justices' committees, **6**, 1164
liability in cases of wrongful detention, **15**, 442,
    443, 448
local authority, member of, **14**, 513
Lord Lieutenant, duties with regard to, **5**, 552
nomination, **6**, 1162, 1163
office of, **6**, 1159
place of safety warrant, **22**, 22
poor relief, **14**, 34
prison, right to visit and inspect, **16**, 1422
removal from office, **6**, 1164
retirement, **6**, 1164
Scottish, powers of, **6**, 1159
selection, **6**, 1163
solicitor as, **6**, 1164
supplemental list, **6**, 1164
transmission of records, **19**, 853, 859
Justice of the peace court
abolition, **6**, 1160; **17**, 517, 519
antecedent of district court, **6**, 1155
appeal hearings, **6**, 1159

Justice of the peace court—*continued*
court of quarter sessions, **6**, 1159, 1160
criminal jurisdiction, **6**, 1159
generally, **6**, 1159
history, **17**, 519
inferior court, as, **6**, 1155
lawburrows, warrant of, **13**, 902, 905, 906
quorum of justices, **6**, 1159
small debt court, **6**, 1159, 1160
summary procedure, **6**, 1155
territorial jurisdiction, **17**, 519
Justiciar
administrative function, **6**, 903
areas, division of Scotland into, **6**, 848
ayres or period circuits, **22**, 507
deficiencies of Justiciar's court, **6**, 854
earliest record of, **6**, 848
feudal jurisdiction, **22**, 507
generally, **22**, 520
jurisdiction, **6**, 849; **17**, 508
Justices-Depute, **6**, 850
king, jurisdiction exercised in name of, **6**, 850
matters reserved to courts of, **22**, 507, 508
office of, **16**, 1704
    origins of, **6**, 848; **17**, 505
    reformation of, **6**, 848
Officer of State, **7**, 790
progression to office of Lord Justice-General, **6**,
    849
qualifications, **17**, 506
seventeenth century criminal business, **22**, 25
sixteenth century, criminal jurisdiction, **22**, 520
See also LORD JUSTICE-GENERAL
Justification
defamation, *see* DEFAMATION (*veritas* AS DEFENCE)
Justinian
Corpus Iuris Civilis, **18**, 1, 530
    ius scriptum distinguished from custom, **22**, 356
    pattern for 'institutional writing' in Scotland,
        22, 434
unjust enrichment, **15**, 11, 32
Juvenile court
care and protection, children needing, **3**, 1280
criminal jurisdiction, **3**, 1280
Kilbrandon Committee recommendations, **22**, 5
Juvenile delinquent
Kilbrandon Committee report, **22**, 5
Juvenile friendly society
generally, **12**, 729

K

Kames, Henry Home, Lord
'authoritative writing',—
    inclusion in canon, **22**, 441
criminality, criteria, **22**, 442
Dictionary of Decisions, **22**, 542
equity and common law, **22**, 537, 546, 547
Historical Law-Tracts, **22**, 547
nobile officium, **22**, 429, 430
precedent, **22**, 251, 542
Principles of Equity, **22**, 411–416, 422, 429, 430,
    437, 440, 441, 537, 546
special authority of writings, **22**, 437, 440
Stair, assessment, **22**, 440
Keeper of the Great Seal
Lord Chancellor as, **5**, 370
office of, **7**, 804, 805, 864, 877
Keeper of Holyroodhouse
office of, **7**, 820, 823
Keeper of the Privy Seal
office of, **7**, 790, 792, 800, 806, 866, 880
Keeper of the Records
former office of, **19**, 811
Keeper of the Records of Scotland
administrative records, **19**, 845
appointment, **19**, 819
care and custody of records, statutory responsibility,
    19, 864
court records, transmission to, **19**, 856
functions, **19**, 818, 865
loan of records by, **19**, 873
miscellaneous records, **19**, 844
origin of office, **19**, 816
petition for commission lodged with, **14**, 1502
preservation of records, **19**, 871
records not transmitted to, **19**, 845
Scottish Record Office, use of term, **19**, 848, 849
service of petition for variation of trust, **24**, 83
transmission of records to, **19**, 842, 853, 854, 860
voluntary transmissions to, **19**, 862
Keeper of the Registers of Scotland
abolition of earlier office of, **19**, 816
appointment, **19**, 819
functions, **19**, 817
General Register of Sasines, **19**, 820, 821
historical origins of office, **19**, 812–815
Land Register of Scotland, **19**, 821, 842
    See also LAND REGISTER OF SCOTLAND
land registration joint consultative committee, **19**,
    822
Lands Tribunal for Scotland, **19**, 821
other registers held by, **19**, 820
title sheet, refusal or failure to enter information,
    6, 772
Keeper of the Signet
office of, **7**, 887; **19**, 805, 807
Keith, Arthur Berriedale
international law, writings on, **19**, 611
Kellogg-Briand Pact, **19**, 698n

Kelp shore
lease, **13**, 206
valuation for rating, **24**, 734
Kelt
meaning, **11**, 18
offences in relation to, **11**, 18
Kenning
feudal law, generally, **18**, 110
meaning, **18**, 74
Kilbrandon Committee
appointment, **3**, 1278
recommendations, **22**, 5, 6
    juvenile court, abolition, **22**, 5
    juvenile delinquent, **22**, 5
    young people, provision of facilities for, **22**, 21
report, **3**, 1278–1280, 1380
Kindly tenancy
feudal law, generally, **18**, 72, 72n
registration of title, **6**, 714, 777
Roll of Kindly Tenants, **6**, 777
Kindly Tenants of Lochmaben
generally, **13**, 212
King
See CROWN; MONARCHY; ROYAL COURTS; SOVEREIGN
Kingdom
sovereignty of, **5**, 354
King's Bench
emergence of, **6**, 803
King's Bill
abolition, **7**, 871
King's Council
See Curia Regis
King's officer
sheriff, assistance for, **14**, 1501
King's tradesmen
generally, **7**, 819, 850
Kinross
water authority, as, **25**, 505
Kirk
land and property—
    type of tenure, **18**, 47, 66, 68, 70; **24**, 307
    See also CHURCH OF SCOTLAND
Kirk session
accounts, annual attestation, **3**, 1512
church officer, **3**, 1510
clerk, **3**, 1510
communion plate, alienation by sale or gift, **3**,
    1508
Communion Roll, duties in relation to, **3**, 1508
composition, **3**, 1507
congregational funds, appeal for outwith
    congregation or parish, **3**, 1508
court of first instance, as, **3**, 1512
disciplinary powers, **3**, 1512
ecclesiastical buildings, duties in regard to, **3**,
    1508
elders—
    admission, form of, **3**, 1507
    appointment, **3**, 1507

Kirk session—*continued*
elders—*continued*
  elect, **3**, 1507
  election, **3**, 1507
  Formula, subscription to, **3**, 1507
  generally, **3**, 1507
  minister, dissatisfaction with, **3**, 1512
  minister as elder, **3**, 1507
  number required, **3**, 1507
  objections to life or doctrine of, **3**, 1507
  resignation, **3**, 1507
  roll of, **3**, 1507
  ruling, **3**, 1507
  teaching, **3**, 1507
establishment, **3**, 1501
generally, **3**, 1501, 1502, 1505
hours of worship, fixing, **3**, 1508
meetings—
  private, held in, **3**, 1509
  provisions as to, **3**, 1509
minister—
  appointment, **3**, 1511
  elder, as, **3**, 1507
  as member, **3**, 1507
  vacancy, duties during, **3**, 1511
minutes—
  annual submission, **3**, 1512
  extract, issue, **3**, 1510
  generally, **3**, 1510
  record, **3**, 1510
moderator—
  casting vote, **3**, 1507
  interim, **3**, 1507
  meetings, duty to call, **3**, 1509
  minister as *ex officio*, **3**, 1563
  minutes, duty in relation to, **3**, 1510
officers, **3**, 1510
precentor, appointment and dismissal, **3**, 1510
presbytery, access to, **3**, 1512
property register, annual attestation, **3**, 1512
ranking, **3**, 1506
records, submission, **3**, 1512
register of baptisms, annual attestation, **3**, 1512
responsibilities, **3**, 1508
roll of baptised persons, annual attestation, **3**, 1512
services, fixing number held, **3**, 1508
spiritual oversight of church members, **3**, 1508
superior courts, review and directions by, **3**, 1506
Supplementary Roll, duties in relation to, **3**, 1508
treasurer, **3**, 1510
visitation of congregation, presbytery, **3**, 1523
voting—
  casting vote, **3**, 1507
  elders, election, **3**, 1507
Kirkyard
See BURIAL GROUND; CHURCHYARD
Kit
design in kit form—
  registered industrial design, infringment, **18**, 1206

Kit—*continued*
design in kit form—*continued*
  unregistered design right—
    generally, **18**, 1214
    'must match' and 'must fit' exceptions, **18**, 1218
Kites
flying near aerodrome, **2**, 973
orders, exemption from, **2**, 981
Knacker
knacker's yard—
  animal slaughtered in, **11**, 404, 407, 413, 498
  licence, **11**, 501
  methods of slaughter, **11**, 503
  product purchased from, **11**, 404
licensing of, **19**, 381
meaning, **19**, 373n
qualification and licence, **11**, 513
Knight Marischal
Officer of the Crown, as, **7**, 812, 817
Knock for knock agreement
subrogation, **12**, 897, 897n
Know-how
bilateral agreement for exchange of, **4**, 1160
blacklists clause, **18**, 1458n
breach of confidence, **18**, 1455
  generally, **18**, 1452
capital asset, treatment as, **18**, 1582, 1584
definition, **18**, 1580
EU competition rules, **10**, 162
European Community legislation, **18**, 1611
  licensing agreement block exemption, **18**, 1653, 1655
exempt agreement, **4**, 1176
lump sum payments in respect of, tax treatment, **18**, 1580, 1582, 1584
patented product, licence, **18**, 1452
purchaser, tax treatment—
  lump sum payments, **18**, 1584
  royalties, **18**, 1583
royalties in respect of, tax treatment, **18**, 1580, 1581, 1583
seller, tax treatment—
  generally, **18**, 1580
  lump sum payments, **18**, 1582
  royalties, **18**, 1581
whitelists clause, **18**, 1458n
Knowingly
element of crime, as, **7**, 79
See also MENS REA
Knowledge
acquiescence, and, **16**, 1615
proof of, **7**, 90
relevancy as evidence, **10**, 624
relevancy to facts at issue, **10**, 624
Korea, North
imports, European Union regulations, **7**, 1029
Kosher food
provision, **3**, 1675
Krugerrands
goods, whether, **14**, 1808

L

Labelling
dangerous substances, of, **9**, 851
explosives, **10**, 1617
food, of, *see* FOOD
gunpowder, **10**, 1605
gunpowder, conveyance of, **10**, 1608
medicinal products, **6**, 12, 79
milk, of, *see* MILK
poison, supply of, **14**, 1217
preservatives, food containing, **11**, 377
vessels containing petroleum-spirit, of, **9**, 850
Laboratory
infectious disease, provision to control, **19**, 499
medicine—
    qualifications, **14**, 1106
technician—
    medical, employment of, **11**, 1500
Labour Party
annual conference, **5**, 393
constituency party, **5**, 393
organisation of, **5**, 393
work of, **5**, 393
Laddergang
servitude, **6**, 515*n*
Lade
See MILL LADE
Lading
bill of, *see* BILL OF LADING
Laesae majestatis
See TREASON (high)
Lagan
meaning, **21**, 511
wreck, when classed as, **21**, 511
Lairages
animals awaiting slaughter, **11**, 503
meaning, **11**, 505
Laird
peerage, and, development of, **16**, 1304
Lanark
Court of Four Burghs, **14**, 13
See also CLYDESDALE
Lancaster, Duchy of
parliamentary Bill affecting prerogative or
    interest, **7**, 744
Land
accession, *see* ACCESSION
acquisition of—
    afforestation, for, **11**, 634
    compulsory acquisition, *see* COMPULSORY
        ACQUISITION
    concurrent proceedings in respect of special
        and trunk roads schemes and orders, **20**,
        714
    electricity, relating to, **9**, 656
    fire authority, by, **10**, 1421; **14**, 502
    flood prevention, for, **14**, 464
    gas, relating to, **9**, 874
    housing action areas, **11**, 1998
    light railway construction, for, **19**, 1086

Land—*continued*
acquisition of—*continued*
    local authority, by, **11**, 1907, 1908; **14**, 316
        loan for, **14**, 639
    public recreation, for, from heir to entail, **14**,
        322
    railway construction, for, **19**, 1018, 1086
    roads authority, by—
        adverse environmental effects, mitigation of,
            20, 709
        agreement, by, **20**, 708, 710, 713
        compulsory, **20**, 708, 712
        generally, **20**, 708
        local, **20**, 711
        special, **20**, 711
    Secretary of State, by, **20**, 711
    tramway undertakers, by, **19**, 1129, 1131
    transfer and vesting for rights of statutory
        undertakers, **20**, 608
    water authority, by, **25**, 518
    See also ACQUISITION OF LAND (AUTHORISATION
        PROCEDURE) (SCOTLAND) ACT 1947;
        COMPULSORY ACQUISITION
advertising on, **14**, 335
agent, functions of, **25**, 136
    partnership, **16**, 1011, 1012
agricultural, *see* AGRICULTURAL LANDS AND
    HERITAGES; AGRICULTURE; VALUATION FOR
    RATING
alien permitted to hold, **14**, 1901
allegiance, effect of owing, **14**, 1901
allodial—
    meaning, **18**, 646
    transfer of ownership, **18**, 646
    udal law, generally, **18**, 44
allotment, *see* ALLOTMENT
alluvion, *see* ALLUVION
annual rent, right of, **20**, 110
appropriation of by local authority, **14**, 319
auction, sale by, **20**, 904
avulsion, *see* AVULSION
blight, subject to, *see* BLIGHT
boundaries, *see* BOUNDARIES; HERITABLE PROPERTY
British Railways Board development, **19**, 1018
British Waterways Board, development by, **19**,
    1105, 1106
building society powers, *see* BUILDING SOCIETY
    (land)
burdens, presumed free from perpetual, **18**, 349
capital item, as, **7**, 1380
carriage by—
    carrier, *see* CARRIER
    consignee, *see* CARRIAGE
    consignor, *see* CARRIAGE
    forwarding agent, **3**, 618
    generally, **3**, 601
    nature of contract, **3**, 601
    passenger, *see* PASSENGER
    sources of law, **3**, 602

Land—*continued*

certificate, *see* REGISTRATION OF TITLE

Church of Scotland, owned by, *see* CHURCH OF SCOTLAND (property and endowments)

Clauses Act, *see* LANDS CLAUSES CONSOLIDATION (SCOTLAND) ACT

cleansing of, **19**, 365

coast protection works, powers relating to, **25**, 384

common, *see* COMMON LAND

commonty, **18**, 37

compensation—
    damage, for, **25**, 513, 522
    loss, for, *see* COMPULSORY ACQUISITION
    nuisance, in relation to, **14**, 2115
    payment by one local authority to another, **14**, 323

compulsory acquisition, *see* COMPULSORY ACQUISITION

compulsory grant of rights to PTO—
    compensation, **16**, 1957
    generally, **16**, 1957

compulsory purchase, *see* COMPULSORY PURCHASE

conjunct fees, co-ownership, **18**, 18

corporeal moveable property attached to, **18**, 12

Court, *see* SCOTTISH LAND COURT

credit union, ownership, lease or disposal by, **12**, 667, 678

crop—
    accession by fruits, **18**, 570, 595, 596
    industrial growing, **18**, 12, 596

Crown, application of Roads (Scotland) Act 1984 ..., **20**, 719

damage to—
    compensation for, **25**, 513, 522
    public telecommunications operator, by, **16**, 1956

deceased's income from, liability to tax, **25**, 966

deeds, registration of, *see* DEED

development of, *see* TOWN AND COUNTRY PLANNING

disposal of—
    common good, forming part of, **14**, 321
    local authority, by, **11**, 1907, 1908; **14**, 320, 321

dominant tenement—
    generally, **18**, 7
    lease, **18**, 351
    standard security, **18**, 351
    superiority, **18**, 351

dominium, *see* DOMINIUM

donation, **8**, 638
    local authority, by, **8**, 615

drainage, *see* DRAINAGE; DRAINAGE WORK

dwelling house let with, protected tenancy status affected by, **13**, 635

electricity, use in connection with—
    compensation, **9**, 657
    compulsory purchase, **9**, 656
    surveys, **9**, 655

encroachment—
    Act of Parliament, encroachment authorised by, **18**, 177
    building, by, **18**, 175
    common gables, where, **18**, 177

Land—*continued*

encroachment—*continued*
    consent as defence, **18**, 176
        express grant, where, **18**, 176
        implied by actings, where, **18**, 176
        successors to land, where bound by consent, **18**, 176
    defence of possession against, **18**, 175–179
        harm, no need to prove, **18**, 175
    definition, **18**, 175
    examples, **18**, 175
    exercise of a right as defence, **18**, 177
        extrajudicial remedies, **18**, 179
        judicial remedies, **18**, 178
    negative prescription as defence, **18**, 177
    ownership of encroaching thing, **18**, 179

entry on—
    game, in pursuit of, **11**, 803, 817
    Lands Clauses Act, under, **5**, 19
    right of, **5**, 49

escape of dangerous agencies from—
    culpa, importance in Scots law, **15**, 190–195
    damnum fatale, **15**, 193
    defences, **15**, 193
    English law, **15**, 188
    fault, **15**, 193–195
        specification, **15**, 194
    natural use cases, **15**, 191
    occupier's liability, generally, **15**, 187
    Scottish law, **15**, 189, 190
    stream, diversion, **15**, 195
    strict liability—
        generally, **15**, 187

excambion, contract of, **20**, 921

exchange of, **20**, 921

expiry of the legal, declarator of, **13**, 6

expulsion of offenders by local authority, **14**, 300

fencing, responsibility for, **20**, 611

feudal system, *see* FEUDAL LAW

flood prevention, **14**, 464; **19**, 324

forestry, for, **11**, 633–635; **23**, 88

friendly society, ownership of, **12**, 702

fruits, accession by, **18**, 570, 595, 596

game—
    damage caused to neighbouring land, **11**, 894
    entry on land in pursuit of, **11**, 803, 817

gas—
    acquisition relating to, **9**, 874
    development relating to, **9**, 877

glebe, *see* GLEBE

ground annual, *see* GROUND ANNUAL

heritable property, as, **18**, 11, 12

heritable security, *see* HERITABLE SECURITY

hire of, **14**, 1002

industrial growing crops—
    goods, as, **20**, 805
    meaning, **20**, 805

interest in—
    as capital item, **7**, 1380
    destination, subject to, **6**, 709
    enforceable real right, **6**, 707, 708
    fixing interests, **5**, 117
    grant, assignation or surrender, charge to VAT, **7**, 1288

Land—*continued*
interest in—*continued*
  heritable securities over, **6**, 707
  indemnity, exclusion of, **6**, 707
  information as to, **9**, 1229
  land certificate, **6**, 713
  meaning, **6**, 707*n*; **23**, 329*n*
  positive prescription, **16**, 2105, 2109
  Register of Inhibitions and Adjudications
    entries, **6**, 707
  registered, **6**, 715
  subsisting real burden or condition, **6**, 707
  title sheet, *see* TITLE SHEET
  unregistered, **6**, 714
  valuation, *see* VALUATION
  voluntary obligations, constitution, **15**, 668
  voluntary registration, **6**, 716
interference with use or enjoyment, **14**, 2046
international law, duties of state to, **19**, 687
intersected, **5**, 20
landholder, *see* LANDHOLDER; SMALLHOLDING
landowner, *see* LANDOWNER; LANDOWNERSHIP
Lands Clauses Consolidation Act, *see* LANDS
  CLAUSES CONSOLIDATION (SCOTLAND) ACT
lease, *see* LEASE; LEASE-LEASING
lease, security over, *see* LEASE-LEASING
local authority—
  acquisition by, **11**, 1907, 1908; **14**, 316, 464
  advertising, **14**, 325
  appropriation by, **14**, 319
  disposal of, forming part of common good, **14**,
    321
  expulsion of offenders by, **14**, 300
  loan for purchase of, **14**, 639
  title to, **14**, 318
  works on, **14**, 325
major interest in, meaning, **7**, 1449
meaning, **6**, 707*n*; **23**, 64
measures, udal law, **24**, 311
missives of sale, *see* MISSIVES
motorway service area, acquisition of land for, **20**,
  628
neighbouring, damage caused by game from, **11**, 894
noise—
  compensation in case of, **9**, 1295
  valuation, effect of, **9**, 1297
nuisance—
  compensation, **14**, 2115
  interference with use or enjoyment, **14**, 2046
  physical damage to, **14**, 2044, 2045
  private, use and enjoyment of land—
    aircraft, **14**, 2086
    ball games, **14**, 2085
    defences, *see* NUISANCE
    harm, *see* HARM
    infection, fear of, **14**, 2082
    liability, *see* LIABILITY; NUISANCE
    nuisance *contra bonos mores*, **14**, 2083
    personal injury, **14**, 2080
    reasonable tolerability, test of, *see* NUISANCE
    recreational interests, **14**, 2081
    rifle range, **14**, 2085
    unaesthetic sight, **14**, 2084
    water pollution, **14**, 2079

Land—*continued*
nuisance—*continued*
  social value of use, **14**, 2055
  support, rights of, **14**, 2029
  transfer of, occupier's liability after, **14**, 2143
  See also NUISANCE
obligations—
  meaning, **6**, 496
  See also REAL BURDENS; REAL CONDITIONS
occupancy, periodical sum due under, prescription,
  16, 2116
occupier, *see* OCCUPIER
occupiers' liability, *see* OCCUPIER S LIABILITY
'option to tax', **7**, 1420
ownership, *see* LANDOWNERSHIP
pars soli, **18**, 578*n*
parts and pertinents, *see* LANDOWNERSHIP
physical damage to, **14**, 2044, 2045
pipe-lines, discharge of oil into sea from, **9**, 1209
planning law—
  enforcement notice, effect of, **23**, 303
  material change of use, *see* USE
  previous planning permission, **23**, 314
  relevant powes, meaning, **23**, 320*n*
  simplified planning zone scheme, exclusion
    from, **23**, 119
  See also TOWN AND COUNTRY PLANNING
pollution, control of, **19**, 303
  See also POLLUTION
possession—
  defence of, **18**, 174
  natural, protection of, **18**, 138
  See also POSSESSION
preservation, custody or detention, court powers
  in relation to, **13**, 24
private road over, owner's responsibilities, **20**, 614
property law—
  history of treatment, **18**, 1
provisional order—
  affecting, deposited plans, **19**, 24
  books of reference, **19**, 25
  compulsory acquisition or use, **19**, 12, 12*n*, 15,
    19, 25
  improvement charge, **19**, 19, 25
  proposing to take, **19**, 11
railway, adjoining—
  access to, **19**, 1019, 1026
  accommodation works, **19**, 1041–1045
  compensation in lieu of accommodation works,
    19, 1042
  fire damage to land or crops, **19**, 1056
  powers of entry to extinguish fires, **19**, 1056
railway, development for, **19**, 1018
rating, valuation areas and authorities, **24**, 404–406
real burdens and conditions transmitted with, **12**,
  1245
real conditions, *see* LAND OBLIGATIONS; REAL
  CONDITION
real right in, **18**, 14
  imprescriptive right, as, **16**, 2126
  uncompleted, **18**, 14
reclamation, accession, **18**, 593
recovery founded on right to possession—
  buildings, removal of, **18**, 157

Land—*continued*
recovery founded on right to possession—
    continued
    ejections, **18**, 152, 153, 154
    generally, **18**, 152
    interdict, **18**, 152, 155
    removings, **18**, 152, 153
    seizure without consent, **18**, 152
    self-help, **18**, 152, 156
    title to sue, **18**, 152
recovery of possession, action for, generally, **18**, 151
recreational purposes, access for, **25**, 358
regulation of development, *see* TOWN AND
    COUNTRY PLANNING
right held in one piece of land by persons in their
    capacity as owner of another piece of land,
    18, 7
right of way, *see* RIGHT OF WAY
road, adjoining—
    dangerous site on, **20**, 611
        private road, **20**, 614
    environmental impact on, **20**, 675
    flood prevention works, roads authority
        contributions towards, **20**, 681
    ploughing on unenclosed, **20**, 682
    trees and shrubs on, **20**, 673
        planting, **20**, 672
    water or other matter, prevention of flow onto
        road, **20**, 700
roads authority, powers of entry, **20**, 716
sale of, *see* HERITABLE CONVEYANCING; MISSIVES
sasine, *see* SASINE
Scottish Land Court, *see* SCOTTISH LAND COURT
seizure without consent, **18**, 152
separate tenements, *see* LANDOWNERSHIP
servient tenement, **18**, 7
servitudes, *see* SERVITUDE
social value of use, **14**, 2055
special road, acquisition to build or improve, **20**,
    626
spuilzied property, natural possession, protection
    of, **18**, 140
standard security, *see* HERITABLE SECURITY
support, right of, *see* SUPPORT, RIGHTS OF
tenure—
    burgage, **6**, 586
    sheriff court jurisdiction, **6**, 1111
things attached to or forming part of, contract of
    sale, **20**, 805
timeshare agreement, **18**, 39
title deed, pledge ineffectual, **20**, 15
title or interest in, imprescriptive rights, **16**, 2104,
    2105, 2126
title to, registration of, **19**, 821–822
    See also REGISTRATION OF TITLE
transfer of interest in, **6**, 714
transfer of—
    occupier's liability after, **14**, 2143
    singular successors, **18**, 598
    universal successors, **18**, 598
    warrandice, *see* WARRANDICE
    See also TRANSFER OF OWNERSHIP
trespass, *see* TRESPASS

Land—*continued*
uninfeft proprietor—
    meaning, **18**, 645
    transfer of land by, **18**, 645
use, periodical sum due under, prescription, **16**,
    2116
use of, **11**, 635
valuation, *see* VALUATION; VALUATION FOR RATING
VAT exemption—
    election to waive, **7**, 1420
    exceptions, **7**, 1419
    general, **7**, 1418–1420
VAT input tax, **7**, 1381
wadset, **20**, 109
warrandice, *see* WARRANDICE
waste, control of pollution by, *see* waste
water authority—
    damage caused by, **25**, 513, 522
    development by, **25**, 517
works, **14**, 325
    prevention of damage by animals or birds, **11**,
        859
See also CORPOREAL HERITABLE PROPERTY; HERITABLE
    CONVEYANCING; HERITABLE PROPERTY; MISSIVES
Land Court
See SCOTTISH LAND COURT
Land-locked states
rights on high seas, **11**, 87
rights of, **21**, 41
Land Register of Scotland
adjudication, completion of title, **8**, 194
appeals against decision of Keeper, **6**, 756
areas covered by, **6**, 470
boundaries, alteration, **18**, 219
burden or condition in, inability to enforce, **6**,
    763
coast protection works schemes, **25**, 383
competing titles, rule as to, **18**, 685
control and management, **6**, 705
creation, **6**, 705
Crown title, no register of, **18**, 48
Department of the Registers of Scotland, as part
    of, **19**, 850
disposition, registration of, **6**, 579; **18**, 640, 643
drainage works, agreements relating to, **25**, 373
effect of registration in, **6**, 726
establishment and purpose of, **6**, 470
fees, registration of, **6**, 787
fraud or carelessness, rectification resulting from,
    6, 769
heritable right or title, **19**, 821
indemnity excluded by keeper, where, **16**, 2110
indemnity not excluded by keeper, where, **16**
    2110
information wrongly inserted, **6**, 768
inhibitions, record in, **8**, 144
inspection, **6**, 705
interests in land, as register of, **16**, 2105, 2110
Keeper of, *see* KEEPER OF THE REGISTERS OF
    SCOTLAND
land certificates—
    generally, **6**, 713
    issue of, **6**, 470

Land Register of Scotland—*continued*
land registered in—
    determination of ownership, **18**, 194
    horizontal limits of estate, **18**, 197
    possession, proof of right of, generally, **18**, 141, 147
Lands Tribunal for Scotland, *see* LANDS TRIBUNAL FOR SCOTLAND
lease, effect of registration under, **18**, 9
multiple occupation control orders, recording in, **11**, 2009
non-payment of stamp duty, **19**, 1536
occupancy rights in matrimonial homes, **6**, 783
operational areas, **6**, 703, 704
Ordnance maps, use of, **6**, 731
positive prescription, and, **16**, 2105, 2106, 2110
public records, and, **19**, 842
ranking of titles, **6**, 785
real burden—
    failure to appear, effect, **18**, 437
    registration of, **18**, 386, 389
real condition, registration of, **18**, 349
real and personal rights, registration, **18**, 657
recording of deeds—
    qualified conveyancer, by, **13**, 1228
    solicitor, by, **13**, 1228
rectification, **13**, 71
    generally, **6**, 750
    indemnity for loss through—
        carelessness, **6**, 769
        death, presumed, **6**, 759
        documents defectively expressed, **6**, 771
        dominant proprietor in servitude, **6**, 767
        exclusion of right to, **6**, 756–771
        fraud, **6**, 769
        generally, **6**, 753
        ground annual creditor, **6**, 768
        heritable security, claim relating to, **6**, 770
        'insurance' principle, **6**, 753
        mines and minerals, **6**, 762
        overriding interest, loss arising through, **6**, 764
        prevailing title, loss arising through, **6**, 757
        real burden, inability to enforce, **6**, 763
        reduction or setting aside of title, **6**, 758
        right to, **6**, 755
        Scottish and English systems contrasted, **6**, 754
        superior not entitled, **6**, 768
        title sheet, incorrect entry in, **6**, 761
        trusts, **6**, 765
    initiation, **6**, 751
    prejudice to possession, where, **18**, 116
    proprietor in possession, to prejudice of, **6**, 752
registration of leases, **13**, 318, 324
    commercial lease, **13**, 558, 585
        recording dues, **13**, 587
rule-making authority, **19**, 821
rules, forms appended to, **6**, 728
Sasine Register—
    contrasted, **6**, 452, 706
    operation in tandem with, **6**, 452, 703
    supersedes, **6**, 705
scheme of operation, **6**, 768

Land Register of Scotland—*continued*
seal, **6**, 705
servitude rights—
    registration, generally, **18**, 451, 477
    variation or discharge by Lands Tribunal, registration of orders, **18**, 477
subjects, description of, **6**, 730
sublease, registration, **13**, 380
title sheet, *see* TITLE SHEET
uninfeft proprietors, **18**, 645
Landholder
common grazings, sharing, **1**, 853
compensation to—
    compulsory acquisition, for, **6**, 1141
    improvements, for, **1**, 842
    incoming landholder, paid by, **1**, 842
    Opencast Coal Act, under, **1**, 842
    resumption, following, **1**, 840
    tenant of agricultural holding, same rights as, **1**, 843
compulsory acquisitions, compensation for, **6**, 1141
crofters renamed, **6**, 956
defects in system, **6**, 965
drainage works carried out by, **25**, 363
Landholders Holdings Book, **1**, 851
legatee as, **1**, 847
meaning, **1**, 837
original jurisdiction relating to holdings of, **6**, 963, 964
overriding interests of, **6**, 741
protection of, **1**, 838
removal of, **1**, 839; **6**, 964
renunciation of holding, **1**, 841
security of tenure, **1**, 838, 839
small, **6**, 956
statutory small tenancies, **1**, 837; **6**, 956, 964
subsidiary occupation, using holding for, **1**, 839
See also CROFTER; SCOTTISH LAND COURT; SMALLHOLDING
Landing
card—
    details required, **12**, 163
    requirement to complete, **12**, 163
meaning, **12**, 146
Landlord
adjacent land retained by, **13**, 241, 250, 253
agricultural tenant, relationship with—
    common law, **11**, 887–889
    compensation, tenant's right to, **11**, 889, 890, 892–894
    increase of game, **11**, 889
    landlord's rights, **11**, 887
    tenant's rights, **11**, 888
allotment, of, rights and duties, **13**, 542
assignable lease, conditions running with lands, **13**, 239–243
assignation—
    completion of assignee's title, **13**, 370
    consent to, **13**, 345
        unreasonably withheld, **13**, 359, 360
assignee, acceptance of, **13**, 363
assured tenancy, market rent, determination, **13**, 672–676

Landlord—_continued_

bequest by tenant, acceptance or repudiation, **13**, 401, 402

board, payments to including payment for, **13**, 628

building standards, entry into building to comply with, **3**, 244

change of, secure tenancies—
  acquisition of house, acceptance, notice of, **11**, 1975
    application for, **11**, 1973
    refusal of application, **11**, 1976
    variation of conditions, **11**, 1974
  generally, **11**, 1971
  right to acquire, **11**, 1972
  subsequent disposals, **11**, 1977
  tenant's 'right to choose', **11**, 1971

commercial lease, _see_ LEASE-LEASING

delictual liability, defences, **15**, 395, 396, 397

derogation from grant, **13**, 241, 250, 253

destination by tenant, acceptance or repudiation, **13**, 401, 402

fair rent—
  certificate, **13**, 652
  registration, **13**, 652
  See also RENT

fences, maintenance of, **11**, 904

game tenant, relationship with—
  normal clauses of, **11**, 899–904
  shooting lease—
    granters of, **11**, 898
    nature of, **11**, 895–897

harassment by, _see_ HARASSMENT

heritable creditor as, **13**, 164

hypothec, **13**, 201, 275
  bankruptcy, and, **13**, 523
  breach of sequestration, **13**, 521
  Crown rights, preference of, **13**, 523
  deathbed and funeral expenses of tenant, preference of, **13**, 523
  fishings and sporting leases, **13**, 202
  feuduty, superior's hypothec for, **13**, 523
  generally, **5**, 903; **13**, 201, 275, 513
  heritable creditor, **13**, 514
  in manibus curiae, inventoried goods as, **13**, 521
  invecta et illata, **13**, 513, 516, 519
  inventory, **13**, 520, 521
  landlord's sequestration, and, **13**, 523
  loss of right, **13**, 522
  meaning, **13**, 513
  mineral lease, **13**, 199
  other diligences, relationship with, **13**, 523
  parties entitled to exercise right of, **13**, 514
  plenish subject, tenant's obligation to, **13**, 271
  plenishing order, **13**, 518, 582
  procedure, **13**, 520
  purchaser of hypothecated goods, **13**, 523
  rent, for, **8**, 377, 378; **13**, 515; **14**, 1812
  right of retention, enforcement, **13**, 519
  sequestration, and, **13**, 523
  subjects affected, **13**, 513
  sublease, where, **13**, 517
  tacit or legal hypothec, as, **13**, 513

Landlord—_continued_

interest of—
  acquisition—
    cottar, by, **13**, 335
    crofter, by, **13**, 335
    tenant-at-will, by, **13**, 334
  transfer—
    adjudication, by, **13**, 348
    bankruptcy, as result of, **13**, 348, 351
    death, by succession on, **13**, 348, 350
    generally, **13**, 348
    heritable security, by enforcement of, **13**, 348, 352
    inter vivos deed, by, **13**, 348
    infeftment, **13**, 349
    purchaser, **13**, 349
    singular successor, purchaser as, **13**, 349
    superior lease, assignation of tenancy under, **13**, 349
    voluntary, **13**, 349

irritancy clause, _see_ IRRITANCY

Lands Tribunal, references to, **11**, 1976

leased goods, rights over, **14**, 1070

long lease—
  acquisition of landlord's interest, **13**, 334, 335
  failure to renew, **13**, 336
  meaning, **13**, 103

memoranda by, as evidence of lease, **13**, 134

negotiating strength, **13**, 562

neighbouring land, damage caused by game from, **11**, 894

obligations—
  derogation from grant, **13**, 253
  full possession, to give—
    degree of possession, **13**, 250
    generally, **13**, 249
  generally, **13**, 248
  maintain tenant in possession, to—
    generally, **13**, 251
    limitations on obligation, **13**, 252
  repair, to keep subjects in—
    avoidance, **13**, 602
    rural subjects—
      implied repairs provision, **13**, 262
    urban subjects—
      common law, **13**, 257, 258
      exclusions, **13**, 258
      fitness for human habitation, **13**, 260
      generally, **13**, 257, 259
      implied repairs provision, **13**, 261
      statute law, **13**, 259–261
  tenantable condition, as to—
    generally, **13**, 254
    rural subjects, **13**, 256
    urban subjects, **13**, 255

occupiers' liability, **15**, 311, 317, 320

owner occupier, **13**, 594

repossession on grounds of—
  assured tenancy, **13**, 749, 750
  protected tenancy, **13**, 736, 737, 748

personal circumstances to be disregarded in decisions as to fair rent, **13**, 660–662

public sector tenancies, _see_ PUBLIC SECTOR TENANCIES

Landlord—*continued*
'reasonable landlord', **13**, 562
rei interventus, actings amounting to, **13**, 140
remedies available to—
  conventional irritancy, **13**, 276
  damages, **13**, 276
  generally, **13**, 274
  interdict, **13**, 276
  monetary breaches, where, **13**, 275
  rescission, **13**, 276
  specific implement, **13**, 276
  terminal conditions in lease, **13**, 276
  termination of lease, **13**, 276
  whole contract breached, where, **13**, 274
removings, action of, *see* REMOVINGS
rent—
  hypothec for, **8**, 377, 378; **14**, 1812
  recovery of, **13**, 513
  sequestration for, *see* SEQUESTRATION FOR RENT
rent book, duty to provide, **13**, 694
renunciation, lease of—
  generally, **13**, 438
  See also LEASE-LEASING
repairs, obligations as to, *see* obligations *above*
repossession by, *see* TENANT-TENANCY
resident, **13**, 593, 594
  assured tenancy, **13**, 636, 645
  Part VII contract, **13**, 629
  protected tenancy, **13**, 629
resumption of possession, reserved power, **13**, 445, 446
sequestration for rent by, *see* SEQUESTRATION FOR RENT
services—
  provision, **13**, 600
  withholding, **13**, 701, 702
sheriff court jurisdiction as to landlord and tenant, **6**, 1112
sublease—
  consent to, **13**, 345
    unreasonably withheld, **13**, 359
  principal landlord, position of, **13**, 378
  principal tenant, relationship with, **13**, 381
  remedies available to landlord, **13**, 384
  subtenant, acceptance of, **13**, 636
  tenant, relationship with, **13**, 383
  See also SUBLEASE
substantial attendance, provision by, rent including, **13**, 627
succession, repossession by, **25**, 718
successor, **13**, 103
tacit relocation, *see* TACIT RELOCATION
tenancy-at-will, acquisition of landlord's interest, **13**, 334
tenant, nuisance created by, liability for, **14**, 2140
termination of lease, *see* LEASE-LEASING
third party rights, and, **13**, 289, 290
threats and intimidation by, **13**, 702
title to sue, **14**, 2133
trustee in sequestration, acceptance of, **13**, 419
unlawful eviction by, *see* EVICTION
valuation for rating, and, **24**, 444, 521
violent profits, title to, **13**, 505

Landlord—*continued*
warrandice, **13**, 251
See also LEASE-LEASING; LESSOR; TENANT-TENANCY
Landownership
a coelo usque ad centrum principle, **18**, 196, 198, 207, 228, 647
  separate tenements, **18**, 198
access, whether inherent right of, **18**, 454, 457
airspace, **18**, 198
alien owning Scottish land, common law doctrine, **18**, 53, 53*n*
boundary wall or fence—
  alteration, **18**, 219–221, 225
    March Dykes Act 1669, by, **18**, 221
  common boundary, on, **18**, 217
  common gables, **18**, 218, 225, 229, 233, 272
  estate, within, **18**, 215, 215*n*
  generally, **18**, 214
  March Dykes Act 1661 ... 216
  March Dykes Act 1669, alteration of boundary by, **18**, 221
  ownership and maintenance—
    ad medium filum, wall owned, **18**, 226
    agreement as to maintenence, **18**, 226
    alteration, **18**, 225
    in common, wall owned, **18**, 226
    contracting out, **18**, 224
    local authority powers, **18**, 226
    March Dykes Act 1661 ... 226
    real burden, where title contains, **18**, 226
    wall or fence on both sides of boundary, **18**, 223
    wall or fence on one side of boundary, **18**, 222
break-off conveyance, **18**, 197, 205
capacity, **18**, 599
charity as owner, income tax exemption, **3**, 1103, 1134
deer, **11**, 926
determination—
  General Register of Sasines, land recorded in, **18**, 194
  Land Register of Scotland, land registered in, **18**, 194
  unregistered land, **18**, 194
dominium directum, *see* FEUDAL LAW
dominium utile, *see* FEUDAL LAW
duty of care in delict, trespassers, **18**, 184
feudal system, *see* FEUDAL LAW
flatted property, **18**, 196, 198
General Register of Sasines, land to which deeds recorded in, **18**, 194, 197
ground game, **11**, 854
  concurrent right to take or kill, **11**, 852
Gulathing law, **24**, 307, 308
heritable property, **18**, 196
horizontal limits of estate, **18**, 196, 197
  vertical limits of estate, **18**, 197, 198
Land Register of Scotland, land to which title registered in, **18**, 194, 197
mineral rights, **18**, 198
  generally, **18**, 196
moveable property, **18**, 196
pars soli principle, **18**, 198

Landownership—*continued*
parts and pertinents—
  deed, wording in, **6**, 489
  generally, **12**, 1242; **18**, 196, 199, 200, 647
  parts—
    meaning, **18**, 200
  pertinents—
    alveus of non-tidal waters, **18**, 202
    common passage and stair, **18**, 202
    commonty, **18**, 37
    contiguous and discontiguous land, **18**, 203
    creation of, **18**, 203, 204
    invariable, **18**, 201
    meaning, **18**, 200
    prescription, **18**, 205
    separate tenements, **18**, 206, 209
    valuation for rating, **24**, 502, 580
physical limits of estate, **18**, 196–198
prescription—
  negative, **18**, 9
  positive, **18**, 9
regalian rights, **18**, 207, 210
rights of landowner—
  absolute nature, **18**, 195
  exclusive nature, **18**, 195
  generally, **18**, 195
  pertinents, *see* pertinents *above*
  possession, **18**, 195
  restrictions on, **18**, 195
  sub-grants of land, **18**, 195
  subordinate real rights, grant of, **18**, 195
sasine, *see* SASINE
scattald, **24**, 310
seizure, powers of, **11**, 812
separate tenements—
  ancillary real rights, subject to, **18**, 208
  boundaries of tenement, cannot cross, **18**, 208,
    578*n*, 585
  coal rights, **18**, 209, 211, 212
  conventional, **18**, 206, 209, 212
  corporeal, **18**, 207, 212
    creation, **18**, 209
  creation, **18**, 209
  ferry, right of, **18**, 319, 334
  feudal nature, **18**, 208
  flatted property, **18**, 207, 212
  generally, **18**, 198, 207
  incorporeal, **18**, 10, 207
  independent thing, treatment as, **18**, 208
  landowner holding, **18**, 209
  law, arising by, **18**, 209
  legal, **18**, 209, 210, 211
  meaning, **18**, 196, 207
  mineral rights, **18**, 207, 209, 212, 578*n*., 585
  mussels, right to gather, **18**, 318, 319, 332, 332*n*
  no accession across, **18**, 585
  oysters, right to gather, **18**, 318, 319, 332, 332*n*
  pertinent, and, **18**, 206, 209
  port, right of, **18**, 319, 334
  regalian rights, **18**, 209
    generally, **18**, 207
  reintegration with land, capacity for, **18**, 209
  salmon fishings, **18**, 10, 280, 318, 319
  support, right to, *see* SUPPORT, RIGHTS OF

Landownership—*continued*
separate tenements—*continued*
  teinds, **18**, 209, 211
  transfer of ownership, **18**, 647
  warrandice, **18**, 703, 703*n*
  wreck (wrak), **18**, 213, 213*n*
  tenement building, **18**, 196, 198
  timeshare agreement, **18**, 39
  trout fishing rights as incident of, **11**, 48, 49
  udal law, **24**, 306, 307, 308
  Union with England Act 1707 ..., **19**, 206
  unregistered land, **18**, 194
  water and water rights, **25**, 301
Landrail
game, as, **11**, 802
Lands Clauses Consolidation (Scotland) Act
application of, **5**, 14
common land, **5**, 21
compensation, application of, **5**, 17
compulsory purchase code, incorporation into, **5**, 40
conveyances—
  forms of, **5**, 18, 31
  generally, **5**, 18
criticism of, **5**, 12
entry on land, **5**, 19
general vesting declaration, application to, **5**, 48
interests omitted to be purchased, **5**, 26
intersected land, **5**, 20
leases, land subject to, **5**, 25
modern relevance of, **5**, 13
mortgage, lands in, **5**, 22
notices, **5**, 28
penalties, recovery of, **5**, 29
purchase of lands—
  agreement, by, **5**, 15
  notice to treat, **5**, 16
  otherwise than by agreement, **5**, 16
rentcharges, land subject to, **5**, 24
scope of, **5**, 11
Special Act, access to, **5**, 30
superfluous land, sale of, **5**, 27
unfit house, heritable security relating to,
  modification of terms, **5**, 23
Lands Tribunal for Scotland
administration, **6**, 1153
agricultural tenants, notice of entry compensation,
  6, 1141
allocation, order for, **6**, 531
appeal from, **6**, 1154
  Court of Session, to, **6**, 924
  Lands Valuation Appeal Court, to, **6**, 943; **24**,
    494, 495
applications, **6**, 1148
ascertainment of facts, **6**, 1152
blight, **6**, 1141, 1149
  blight-notice, reference of, **5**, 102; **23**, 321
capital gains tax, valuation of land for, **6**, 1141,
  1149
casting vote, **6**, 1140
civil legal aid, **6**, 1152*n*; **13**, 1034
common interest, variation or discharge, **18**, 374
compensation, **6**, 1141
compulsory acquisition of land, **6**, 1141
  compensation for, valuation date, **5**, 120

Lands Tribunal for Scotland—*continued*
conduct of hearing, **6**, 1151
contempt, **6**, 1151
corporation tax, appeals against assessments, **6**, 1149
crofters, notice of entry compensation, **6**, 1141
depreciation in value of land, compensation for, **6**, 1141
disputed compensation claims, **5**, 195; **11**, 618
disturbance payments, **6**, 1141
documents to be produced prior to hearing, **6**, 1149
enforcement, **6**, 1154
establishment of, **5**, 657
expenses, **5**, 196; **6**, 1151
failure to comply with requirements imposed by, **6**, 1151
farm loss payments, **6**, 1141
harbours, dredging of, **6**, 1141
hearsay evidence, **6**, 1152
housing legislation, compensation under, **6**, 1141
inheritance tax, valuation of land for, **6**, 1141, 1149
inspection of land or buildings, **6**, 1152, 1153
interest awarded by, **5**, 194
jurisdiction, **5**, 195, 657; **6**, 943, 1141
land obligations—
    inspection of land or buildings, **6**, 1152
    jurisdiction to vary or discharge, **6**, 1142, 1146, 1149
legal aid, **6**, 1152*n*; **13**, 1034
legal staff, **13**, 1413
listed buildings—
    refusal to allow alteration or extension, **6**, 1141
    revocation or modification of consent, **6**, 1141
location, **6**, 1153
long lease, variation of land obligations, **13**, 338
majority decisions, **6**, 1140
membership, **5**, 195; **6**, 1140
origin, **6**, 1139
particulars of case, power to ask for, **6**, 1150
party litigants, **6**, 1148, 1152
peripatetic nature, **6**, 1153
planning permission, revocation or modification of, **6**, 1141
precedent—
    English decisions, **22**, 324
    own decisions binding, **22**, 324
    superior Scottish courts, binding decisions, **22**, 324
President, **6**, 1140
previous system, **6**, 1139
procedure—
    decisions, **5**, 196
    expenses, **5**, 196
    generally, **6**, 1147–1154
    hearing—
        notice of, **5**, 196
        oral, **5**, 196
        witnesses, **5**, 196
    institution of proceedings, **5**, 196
    legal aid, **5**, 196
public sector tenants, house sales to, **6**, 1144
    landlord's unreasonable conditions, **6**, 1144

Lands Tribunal for Scotland—*continued*
purpose, **6**, 1139
quarrying or mining operations stopped, compensation for, **6**, 1141
rating, appeals in valuation for, **6**, 1145, 1149
    acceptance of referral, **24**, 494
    application for, **24**, 492
    generally, **24**, 491
    notification of decision, **24**, 493
    referral by valuation appeal committee, **24**, 493
    refusal of referral, **24**, 494
real burden, variation or discharge, **18**, 395, 426, 438
recovery of documents, power to order, **6**, 1150
redevelopment of land previously acquired, compensation for, **6**, 1141
register of land, **19**, 821
registration of title, **6**, 1143
    rectification of register, **6**, 1143
reporting of decisions, **6**, 1139
restrictions on new developments, compensation for, **6**, 1141
rules, **6**, 1147, 1149
servitude rights, jurisdiction as to, **18**, 477, 478, 480
severance cases, **6**, 1141, 1146
simpler cases, **6**, 1140
stop notice ceasing effect, **6**, 1141
supervision of by Scottish Committee, **23**, 911*n*
tenant at will, application to purchase land by, **6**, 1143
tenants' rights, **6**, 1146
    right to buy, powers in relation to, **11**, 1964
        appeal from, **11**, 1964
        specific performance, decree of, **11**, 1964
test with regard to land obligations, **6**, 512, 513
unallocated feuduties, **6**, 1142, 1149
valuation, **6**, 1139, 1141
voluntary acquisitions of land, **6**, 1141
witnesses—
    placed on oath, **6**, 1151
    power to require attendance, **6**, 1150
    statement of evidence by expert, **6**, 1152

Lands Valuation Appeal Court
advocate's right of audience, **13**, 1325
appeals to, **6**, 941–950
    Lands Tribunal for Scotland, from, **6**, 1145; **24**, 494, 495
    subject matter of, **6**, 950
authority of decisions, **6**, 947
civil legal aid, **13**, 1034
comparative principle, **24**, 534
constitution and sittings, **24**, 427
Court of Session jurisdiction, **6**, 949
court's powers, **24**, 499
expenses, **6**, 948; **24**, 499
facts of appeal, **24**, 498
form of appeal, **24**, 497
function, **6**, 945; **22**, 323
generally, **24**, 495
grounds of appeal, **24**, 498
introduction of, **6**, 938
judges, **6**, 925, 928; **24**, 427
jurisdiction, **6**, 943, 949

Lands Valuation Appeal Court—*continued*
no appeal to House of Lords, **6**, 829
origin, **6**, 941, 942
powers, **6**, 946; **24**, 499
precedent—
    flexibility, **22**, 323
    House of Lords, decisions, no basis for binding
        force, **22**, 323
    power to overrule own decisions, **22**, 323
procedural timetable, **6**, 944
records of valuation appeal committee proceedings,
    24, 485
scope of questions of value, **24**, 496
time limits, **24**, 497
valuation appeal committee decisions, **24**, 495
Lane
boundary on, **12**, 1239
use of term replaced by road, **20**, 501, 609
Language
assistants and work permits, **12**, 247
discrimination, **12**, 85, 86
educational considerations, **12**, 89
election nomination papers—
    English, **15**, 1260
    Gaelic, **15**, 1260
    Welsh, **15**, 1260
naturalisation, requirements for, **14**, 1920
unparliamentary, **5**, 387
Latin
charters, **6**, 405, 412
Faculty of Advocates—
    examination in, former requirement for
        admission, **13**, 1301
    original use of, **6**, 412
Launderette/laundry business
public health nuisance, as, **19**, 336n
water supply, not for domestic use, **25**, 506
Laundry services
disabled person, person caring for, **22**, 14, 24
discretionary, **22**, 26
elderly person, **22**, 26
eligibility, **22**, 14
facilities, local authority provision, **11**, 1906
home help, ancillary to, **22**, 14, 24, 26
Law
agent, *see* SOLICITOR
general principles recognition in international
    law, **19**, 645
history of Scots law—
    burgh court, **17**, 518
    central control, **17**, 502
    Committees of Whole House, **5**, 399
    Dark Ages, **22**, 513–515
    early, **17**, 502
    environmental law, development of, **9**, 1102
    feudal Scotland, **22**, 505–512
        See also FEUDAL LAW
    generally, **22**, 503–522
    health and safety legislation, of, **9**, 404
    hire contract, of, **14**, 1001–1004
    interim interdict, **17**, 1104
    justice of peace court, **17**, 519
    leasing, of, **14**, 1006
    lieutenancy, of, **5**, 544–547

Law—*continued*
history of Scots law—*continued*
    Lord Advocate, office of, **17**, 527
    medieval procedure, **17**, 541
    modern era, **22**, 516–522
    'peace', **17**, 502
    police court, **17**, 518
    pre-feudal Scotland, Celtic law, **25**, 503–505
    seventeenth century onwards, **17**, 503
    small claims procedure, **17**, 1337
    standing committees, **5**, 405
    trial by jury, **17**, 542
    wills, statutory regulation of, **25**, 501–506
international, *see* INTERNATIONAL LAW; PRIVATE
    INTERNATIONAL LAW
knowledge of, presumption as to, **7**, 95, 96
maxims of, **19**, 645
operation of, trust resulting from, **24**, 12
private international law, guides to—
    articles, **17**, 117
    casebooks, **17**, 116
    Law Commission reports, **17**, 119
    papers, **17**, 119
    reference works, **17**, 118
    textbooks—
        branches of private law, on, **17**, 115
        conflict, on, **17**, 114
    See also PRIVATE INTERNATIONAL LAW
reform *see*, LAW REFORM
sources of—
    Acts of Parliament, *see* ACT OF PARLIAMENT
    Adjournal, Acts of, *see* ACT OF ADJOURNAL
    appellate jurisdiction, *see* HOUSE OF LORDS;
        JUDICIAL COMMITTEE OF THE PRIVY
        COUNCIL; JUDICIAL PRECEDENT
    assythment, action of, **22**, 354
    authoritative writings, *see* INSTITUTIONAL
        WRITERS; LEGAL LITERATURE
    bible, *see* BIBLE
    brieve system, *see* BRIEVE SYSTEM
    byelaws, *see* BYELAWS
    canon law, **22**, 548, 557–586
        See also CANON LAW
    Celtic law, *see* CELTIC LAW
    codes of practice, *see* CODES OF PRACTICE
    common law, *see* COMMON LAW
    constitutional law, *see* CONSTITUTIONAL LAW
    criminal law, *see* CRIMINAL LAW
    custom, *see* CUSTOM
    Dutch influence—
        education of Scottish law students, **22**, 604
        Faculty of Advocates library, collections, **22**,
            606
        historical sources of Scots law, **22**, 603, 604,
            606, 607
        Leyden, University of, **22**, 604
        Roman law influence on Scots law through,
            22, 604, 606
        trade as basic link, **22**, 603
        Utrecht, University of, **22**, 604
    economic conditions, **22**, 502
    English influence, **22**, 597–602
    equity, *see* EQUITY

Law—*continued*
sources of—*continued*
  European Community, *see* EUROPEAN UNION—
    European Parliament, *see* EUROPEAN
      PARLIAMENT
  European Court of Justice, *see* EUROPEAN
    COURT OF JUSTICE
  feudal law, *see* FEUDAL LAW
  formal, **22**, 501
  French influence—
    'Auld Alliance' as basic link, **22**, 603
    Bourges, University, humanist lawyers, **22**,
      604
    customary law, **22**, 605
    education of Scottish law students, **22**,
      604
    historical sources of Scots law, **22**, 603, 604,
      605, 607
    legal literature in Scotland, **22**, 605
    Orléans law school, **22**, 604
    Roman law, **22**, 604, 605
  German influence, **17**, 111
  historical, meaning, **22**, 502
  history of Scots law distinguished, **22**, 502
  international law, *see* INTERNATIONAL LAW;
    PRIVATE INTERNATIONAL LAW
  judicial precedent, *see* JUDICIAL PRECEDENT
  judicial review, *see* JUDICIAL REVIEW
  law merchant, **22**, 608–610
    See also MERCANTILE LAW
  law reform, *see* LAW REFORM
  law reporting, *see* LAW REPORTING
  legal method, *see* LEGAL METHOD
  legislation, *see* LEGISLATION
  natural law, *see* NATURAL LAW
  Parliament, *see* PARLIAMENT
  positive law, *see* POSITIVE LAW
  reference works, **17**, 118
  Roman law, **22**, 502, 548–556
    See also ROMAN LAW
  Scottish Law Commission, *see* SCOTTISH LAW
    COMMISSION
  Sederunt, Acts of, *see* ACT OF SEDERUNT
  servitudes, *see* SERVITUDES
  statutory, *see* STATUTORY SOURCES OF SCOTS
    LAW
  statutory instruments, *see* STATUTORY
    INSTRUMENTS
  Union Agreement, *see* UNION AGREEMENT OF
    1707
  universities, *see* UNIVERSITY
  usage, *see* USAGE

Law Commission
See LAW REFORM; SCOTTISH LAW COMMISSION

Law merchant
See MERCANTILE LAW

Law Officers of Crown
generally, **5**, 535
historical background, **5**, 536
Lord Advocate, *see* LORD ADVOCATE
preclusion from private practice, **13**, 1342
Solicitor General for Scotland, *see* SOLICITOR
  GENERAL FOR SCOTLAND

Law and order
expenditure programme, **5**, 583
licences, *see* LICENCES
police, *see* POLICE
preservation of—
  common law, **5**, 608
  enforcement, **5**, 612
  generally, **5**, 605, 613
  Northern Ireland, **5**, 609, 610
  options available to government, **5**, 607
  threat, when arising, **5**, 606
registration, *see* REGISTRATION
terrorism, **5**, 611

Law reform
1832 to mid-twentieth century—
  departmental committees, **22**, 637, 638
  entail, law of, **22**, 646
  family law, **22**, 648, 649
  generally, **22**, 637–649
  land law, **22**, 646, 647
  mercantile law, **22**, 640–645
  royal commissions, **22**, 637, 638
  sources of reform, **22**, 637
aims, generally, **22**, 623
aliment, sheriff court , 1957 report, **22**, 657
animals, civil liability for loss etc caused by, 1963
  report, **22**, 662
Benthamism, responses to, **22**, 624
Blue Books, meaning, **22**, 638
codification, by, **22**, 626, 627, 643, 644
damages, in actions for fatal or personal injuries,
  22, 653, 656, 660, 675, 676
  See also DAMAGES
dangerous agencies escaping from land, 1964
  report, **22**, 663
departmental committees—
  Blue Books, **22**, 638
  definition, **22**, 637
  generally, **22**, 624
  Lord Advocate, of, **22**, 637
  nineteenth century, **22**, 637
  royal commission distinguished, **22**, 637
desuetude, doctrine of, reform, **22**, 626
  See also DESUETUDE, DOCTRINE OF
diligence of goods, 1964 report, **22**, 664
divorce law, **22**, 649
ejection and removing actions, 1957 report, **22**,
  652
employee, injury to, employer's right to recover
  damages for, **22**, 661
family law, **22**, 648–649
  See also FAMILY LAW
generally, **22**, 623–704
Green Papers, definition, **22**, 639
insurance law, 1957 report, **22**, 654
interest on damages, 1957 report, **22**, 653
jury trial, introduction to Court of Session, **22**,
  635
land law, **22**, 646–647
  See also CONVEYANCING; ENTAIL
Law Commissions—
  consultation among Commissions—
    statutory requirements, **22**, 666
  delict, memorandum on, **17**, 301

Law reform—*continued*
Law Commissions—*continued*
  domicile, reforms relating to, **17**, 207–209
  European Communities law, harmonisation, **22**, 625
  foreign currency, on, **14**, 1831
  international law considerations, **22**, 625
  jurisdiction to which functions extend, **22**, 665
  Mercantile Law Commission 1856 ..., **22**, 640
  nineteenth century, generally, **22**, 639, 640
  personnel, **22**, 625
  philosophy of, **22**, 625
  political pressures, **22**, 625
  purpose, **22**, 665
  reports, generally, **17**, 119
  requirement to consider codification, **22**, 626
  royal commission 1834 ..., **22**, 637
  Scottish, *see* SCOTTISH LAW COMMISSION
  statutory basis, **22**, 625, 626
Law Reform Committee for Scotland—
  constitution, **22**, 650
  generally, **22**, 650–664
  Lord Advocate—
    institution by, **22**, 650
    remittal of matters for consideration by, **22**, 650
  membership, **22**, 650
  purpose, **22**, 650
  reports—
    aliment, action of, **22**, 657
    animals, civil liability for loss etc caused by, **22**, 662
    damages for fatal injuries, **22**, 660
    dangerous agencies escaping from land, **22**, 663
    diligence of goods not belonging to debtor, **22**, 664
    employer's right to recover damages for injury to employee, **22**, 660
    insurance law, **22**, 654
    maintenance orders, reciprocal enforcement, **22**, 655
    occupier's liability, **22**, 651
    removing and ejection, actions of, **22**, 652
    security over moveable property, floating charges, **22**, 658
    taxation of damages, **22**, 656
    trustees, powers of, **22**, 659
    trusts, variation of, **22**, 659
legislation as main instrument, **22**, 623
Lord Advocate—
  Law Reform Committee for Scotland—
    institution, **22**, 650
    remittal of matters for consideration to, **22**, 650
maintenance orders, reciprocal enforcement, 1956 report, **22**, 655
marriage law, **22**, 649
medieval times to the Union of, **8**, 1707
  Balfour's *Practicks*, **22**, 540, 609, 627
  commission of 1425 ..., **22**, 627
  generally, **22**, 627–629
  James VI and I, projects for unification, **22**, 628
  legislative landmarks, **22**, 629
  Scottish Privy Council, **22**, 627

Law reform—*continued*
medieval times to the Union of—*continued*
  unification, Scots and English law, proposals—
    Charles II, **22**, 628
    Cromwell, **22**, 628
    James VI and I, **22**, 628
  mercantile law, **22**, 640–645
  methods, generally, **22**, 623, 637
  occupier's liability, 1957 report, **22**, 651
  procedural law, **22**, 652, 657
  repeal of obsolete law, **22**, 626
  royal commissions—
    Blue Books, **22**, 638
    Command Papers, **22**, 637
    conveyancing, 1837 ..., **22**, 647
    definition, **22**, 637
    departmental committee distinguished, **22**, 637
    divorce, 1850 ..., **22**, 649, 655
    generally, **22**, 624
    marriage, **22**, 649, 655
    mercantile law, 1853, **22**, 640
    nineteenth century, **22**, 637, 640, 647, 649, 655
  security over moveable property and floating charges, 1960 report, **22**, 658
  socio-legal research, **22**, 615
  sources—
    Scottish Law Commission, *see* SCOTTISH LAW COMMISSION
  taxation of damages, 1957 report, **22**, 656
  trusts, variation of, 1960 report, **22**, 659
  Union of 1707 to 'reform Acts' of, **0**, 1832
    bankruptcy legislation, **22**, 633
    Court of Session, **22**, 635
    employment legislation, **22**, 632
    entail law, **22**, 634
    generally, **22**, 630–636
    imposition of policies of government in London, legislation reflecting, **22**, 630
  Whig policies, post-Union, **22**, 635, 636
  White Paper—
    definition, **22**, 638
    purpose, **22**, 638
Law reporting
American Legal Realism, **22**, 263
case law, effect on attitudes towards, **22**, 253
computerised databases—
  effect on application of precedent in Scotland, **22**, 263
  House of Lords, views, **22**, 263
criminal cases, **22**, 262
Crown Office circulars as source of case law, **22**, 262
defective, **22**, 352
delay in publication, **22**, 262
eighteenth century examples, **22**, 253
Faculty of Advocates, collections, **22**, 253
Lexis, **22**, 263
Morison's *Dictionary of Decisions*, **22**, 253
nineteenth century improvement, **22**, 253
Practicks, development from, **22**, 253
precedent—
  databases, **22**, 263
  modern reporting, **22**, 263
  reported cases, **22**, 261

Law reporting—*continued*
precedent—*continued*
unreported cases, **22**, 262
reliability in Scotland, **22**, 262, 263
reports, generally, *see* LAW REPORTS
Session Cases, **22**, 253
unreported cases—
criteria for decision, **22**, 262
deficiencies in system, **22**, 262
Law reports
citation, **22**, 261
commencement, **22**, 545
defects in, **22**, 352
Faculty of Advocates *Collection*, **22**, 545
Faculty of Advocates *Decisions*, **22**, 545
Forbes, William, **22**, 545
precedent, influence on development, **22**, 545
reporting, generally, *see* LAW REPORTING
Session Cases, **22**, 545
Stair's *Reports*, **22**, 545
status, **22**, 261
Law Society of Northern Ireland
authorisation by, **12**, 1313
Law Society of Scotland
Arbitration Rules of—
adoption by parties, **2**, 443
application of, **2**, 508
purposes of, **2**, 443
text of, **2**, 508
arbitration services, **2**, 419
authorisation by, **12**, 1313
Council, **13**, 1145
ad hoc committees, **13**, 1149
complaints, investigation of, **13**, 1202
complainer, qualified privilege, **13**, 1205
Complaints Committees, **13**, 1203, 1205, 1207, 1208
consistency between, **13**, 1204
Complaints Supervisory Committee, **13**, 1204
inadequate professional services, complaints concerning, **13**, 1203
obligations as to, **13**, 1203
procedure, **13**, 1205
professional misconduct, complaints concerning, **13**, 1203
written report, obligation to make, **13**, 1205
disciplinary powers, **13**, 1199
duties, **13**, 1150, 1152
legal training, powers as to, **13**, 1151
meetings, **13**, 1148
membership, **13**, 1145
appointment, **13**, 1145
elected, **13**, 1145
ex officio, **13**, 1145
expenses, **13**, 1145
notaries, admission to or removal from register, **13**, 1151
Officers, **13**, 1146
powers, **13**, 1150, 1151
discretionary nature, **13**, 1151
practice certificate—
issue of, **13**, 1159
rules as to, **13**, 1151
withdrawal, **13**, 1192

Law Society of Scotland—*continued*
Council—*continued*
President, **13**, 1146
Roll of Solicitors, striking off—
notaries public, **13**, 1218
Scottish Solicitors' Discipline Tribunal, complaints to, **13**, 1206
secretariat, **13**, 1147
solicitors' fees, powers in relation to, **13**, 1192
standing committees, **13**, 1149
establishment, **13**, 1149
expenses, **13**, 1149
Vice-President, **13**, 1146
creation, **13**, 1003
disciplinary powers, **13**, 1151
examinations—
generally, **13**, 1162
qualification for candidature, **13**, 1162
functions, **13**, 1144
Law Reform Committee for Scotland, representation on, **22**, 650
legal aid, Law Society control, **13**, 1003, 1006, 1008
Master Policy, **13**, 1198
membership, **13**, 1144
honorary members, **13**, 1144
non-practising members, **13**, 1144
obligations—
court, to, **13**, 1200
profession, to, **13**, 1201
organisation of solicitors' profession, **13**, 1144
precedence, **16**, 2004, 2020
Roll of Solicitors in Scotland—
inspection, **13**, 1152
maintenance, **13**, 1152
solicitor's right to practice dependent on inclusion on, **13**, 1159
Scottish Law Commission, proposals for reform by Society to, **22**, 666, 694
solicitors, control over admission of persons as, **13**, 1160
'troubleshooters' scheme, **13**, 1209
use of arms of, **11**, 1614
Lawbooks
Udal law, **24**, 303
Lawburrows
action of—
expenses, **13**, 919
future actions, designed to prevent, **13**, 921
when competent, **13**, 901, 920–922, 925
witnesses, **13**, 918, 919
appeal by stated case, **13**, 907
Books of Court, caution acted in, **13**, 907
case law, **13**, 911, 912, 916, 917
since 1882, **13**, 920–922
caution, **13**, 901
amount, **13**, 907
bond without, **13**, 907
Books of Court, acted in, **13**, 907
crave, **13**, 907
defender failing to find, **13**, 901, 907
caption and imprisonment following, **13**, 901, 903, 907, 918
forfeiture, **13**, 901

Lawburrows—*continued*
Civil Imprisonment (Scotland) Act 1882—
  actions regulated by, **13**, 902, 906
  procedural reforms instigated by, **13**, 918
  restriction in scope of lawburrows, **13**, 918
contravention—
  defender, by—
    contravention action, **13**, 901
      Procurator Fiscal, concurrence of required,
        13, 901
    forfeiture of caution, **13**, 901
  delict, **15**, 216
criminal breach, civil remedy delayed until
  criminal case decided, **13**, 912
criminal proceedings, ancillary or complementary
  to, **13**, 915
decline in use of remedy, **13**, 908
defender—
  bond without caution granted by, **13**, 907
  caution, failure to find, **13**, 901, 907
    imprisonment following, **13**, 901, 903, 907,
      918
  contravention by, **13**, 901
  criminal breach, civil remedy delayed until
    criminal case decided, **13**, 912
  poor, **13**, 912
district court, actions in, **13**, 906
frankpledge compared, **13**, 908
historical background—
  cases, **13**, 911, 912, 916, 917, 920–922
  Claim of Right, **13**, 914
  Covenanters, use of lawburrows against, **13**,
    913, 914
  decline in use of remedy, **13**, 908
  early examples, **13**, 909
  early legislation, **13**, 910
  entire community, involving, **13**, 911, 915
  Lawburrows Acts, **13**, 910
  lawburrows between 1689 and 1882 ..., **13**,
    915–917
  origins, **13**, 908
  other legal systems compared, **13**, 908
justice of the peace court, action in, **13**, 902, 905,
  906
meaning, **13**, 901, 908
modern actions—
  cases, evaluation of, **13**, 920–922
  matrimonial disputes, **13**, 924
  rarity, **13**, 923
  recent cases, **13**, 925
  survival of lawburrows, **13**, 926
  usefulness of remedy, **13**, 924
neighbours, disputes between, **13**, 911, 925
petition, **13**, 918
poor defenders, **13**, 912
procedure—
  appeal by stated case, **13**, 907
  initial writ, **13**, 907
  prior to 1882—
    Court of Session, warrant obtained from, **13**,
      902, 903
    generally, **13**, 902
    High Court of Justiciary, warrant obtained
      from, **13**, 902, 903

Lawburrows—*continued*
procedure—*continued*
  prior to 1882—*continued*
    justice of the peace court, warrant obtained
      from, **13**, 902, 905
    sheriff court, warrant obtained from, **13**, 902,
      904
  reform, **13**, 918
  since 1882—
    cases, **13**, 920–922
    district court action, **13**, 906
    forum, **13**, 906
    generally, **13**, 907
    justice of the peace court, warrant obtained
      from, **13**, 902, 905
    sheriff court action, **13**, 906, 907
proof of grounds of dread, **13**, 920–922
property rights, disputes over, **13**, 915
pupil may not be compelled to find, **13**, 912
remedy, generally, **13**, 901
restriction in scope, **13**, 918
sheriff court, actions in, **13**, 902, 904, 906
spouses, disputes between, **13**, 911, 916, 924
survival of, **13**, 926
warrant of, procedure prior to 1882, **13**, 902–905
witnesses to a diet of proof, **13**, 918, 919
Lawful business
assault with intent to prevent, **7**, 236
Lawyer
See ADVOCATE; LEGAL PROFESSION; SOLICITOR
Lay-by
tent, pitching in, **20**, 692
whether part of road, **20**, 612
Lay days
See LAYTIME
Lay-off
redundancy, effect on, **9**, 165
Lay precedence
generally, **16**, 2003
Laytime
berth charterparty, **21**, 672, 675
bill of lading, performance of contract, **21**, 585
commencement—
  arrival at destination, **21**, 671, 672
  express terms, **21**, 675
  generally, **21**, 671
  quarantine restrictions, **21**, 673
  readiness, **21**, 671, 673
    legal requirements of port, **21**, 673
    notice of, **21**, 671, 674
  seaworthiness, **21**, 673
conditions preventing, **21**, 666
consecutive days, meaning, **21**, 670
conventional days, meaning, **21**, 670*n*
damages for detention, liability for, **21**, 681*n*
days, meaning, **21**, 670
demurrage, *see* DEMURRAGE
despatch money (despatch), **21**, 666, 689
detention of ship beyond, **21**, 666
  demurrage, *see* DEMURRAGE
  reason for, **21**, 666, 668
deviation, **21**, 615
dock charterparty, **21**, 672
end of operation, **21**, 681

Laytime—*continued*
exceptions—
   clause, protection by, **21**, 666, 668
   fault of shipowner, delay caused by, **21**, 677, 677*n*
   general exceptions clause, **21**, 676
expiry, **21**, 681
fixed, where—
   charterer's obligation, nature of, **21**, 668
   separate loading and discharging periods, **21**, 669
   time periods, **21**, 670
generally, **21**, 666
holiday periods, **21**, 676, 679
lightening, cargo removed before discharge for, **21**, 670*n*
loading and discharging rate, reference to, **21**, 670
matters outwith charterer's control, delay caused by, **21**, 676
meaning, **21**, 666
moving berth, delay caused by, **21**, 676
not fixed, where, **21**, 667, 676*n*
per hatch per day, rate, **21**, 670, 670*n*
port charterparty, **21**, 672, 675
reachable on arrival clause, **21**, 675
running days, meaning, **21**, 670, 670*n*
second and subsequent loading ports, **21**, 674
strike action, delay caused by, **21**, 676, 677, 680
tanker charterparty, disconnection of hoses, **21**, 681*n*
total period for both loading and discharging, **21**, 669
unreasonably detaining ship where laytime not expired, **21**, 681, 681*n*
voyage charterparty, **21**, 612, 618, 622*n*, 666
weather, exceptions clause, **21**, 676, 678
weather permitting, meaning, **21**, 670*n*
weather working days, meaning, **21**, 670
working days, meaning, **21**, 670, 670*n*

Lead
petrol, in, EEC directives on, **9**, 1144
poisoning, damages against water authority, **25**, 508
restriction on use in food, **11**, 381
water authorities' duties, **25**, 508
work, at, control of, **9**, 527

League of Nations
aggression, use of term, **19**, 700
convention on territorial waters, **21**, 2
Covenant, **19**, 698
establishment, **19**, 601*n*
member states, **19**, 698*n*
minority treaties, **12**, 2

Learned profession
member of, designation as gentleman, **16**, 2023

Lease-leasing (heritable property)
abandonment, renunciation distinguished, **13**, 438
acceptance by lessee, effect, **13**, 154
accretion, **18**, 677
actings unequivocally referable to, *rei interventus*, **13**, 138
adjudication, **8**, 197, 198
   decree of, effect on lease, **13**, 158
   lease, of, **13**, 184

Lease-leasing (heritable property)—*continued*
agent, grant by, removings, action of, **13**, 498
agreement between two parties, as, **13**, 123
agreement to lease, form of writing, **13**, 124
agricultural, **6**, 639
   liquidated damages clause, **15**, 800
allotment—
   land acquired for use as, **13**, 539
   See also ALLOTMENT
arable, **13**, 215
arbitration—
   clause, **13**, 234
   commercial lease, **13**, 558
articles of, form of writing, **13**, 125
assedation, meaning, **13**, 103
assignation—
   express prohibition, where, **18**, 652
   See also ASSIGNATION
assured tenancy, *see* TENANT-TENANCY
attendance, payments in respect of, **13**, 627
bankruptcy—
   lessor, of, **13**, 159
   tenant, of, **13**, 414
bequest, lease, of—
   power of—
      express, **13**, 397
      express exclusion, **13**, 398
      generally, **13**, 395
      implied, **13**, 396
      implied exclusion, **13**, 399
      landlord—
         acceptance by, **13**, 401
         repudiation by, **13**, 402
      legatee, repudiation by, **13**, 402
      whether made, **13**, 400
   where none made—
      executor, selection of successor by, **13**, 404
      generally, **13**, 403
board, payments in respect of, **13**, 628
bowing (cows), **13**, 219
breach, lease, of—
   monetary, **13**, 275
   redding-up condition, **13**, 276
   remedies—
      landlord's, **13**, 274–276
      tenant's, **13**, 277–284
   terminal condition, of, **13**, 276
building, **13**, 209
building society leasing facilities, *see* BUILDING SOCIETY
business premises, furnishings, **13**, 217
cardinal elements, **13**, 104
categories, **13**, 102, 207–220
chattel leasing agreement, **4**, 619
choice of law, **13**, 228
commercial lease, **13**, 210
   adverse rent review clause, effect, **13**, 561
   arbitration, **13**, 558
   assignation, **13**, 583
   assignee, **13**, 564
   clean and tidy condition, tenant's obligation to keep premises in, **13**, 588
   conditions, tenant's failure to observe, **13**, 584

Lease-leasing (heritable property)—*continued*
commercial lease—*continued*
  dangerous, offensive, highly combustible or
    highly inflammable items, introduction
    onto premises, **13**, 588
  decorative order of premises, clauses relating
    to, **13**, 586
  defects, tenant's duty to inform landlord, **13**,
    588
  delectus personae, doctrine of, **13**, 357
  destruction of or damage to property, **13**, 579,
    581
  documentation, **13**, 558
  expenses incurred in drawing up, **13**, 153, 587
  extension, **13**, 560
  fixtures, **13**, 566, 588
  floors, overloading, **13**, 269, 588
  frustration of contract, **13**, 579
  'full repairing and insuring lease', **13**, 556, 580,
    581
  generally, **13**, 210, 525, 563
  'good covenant', meaning, **13**, 562
  indemnification of landlord against legal
    liability, **13**, 588
  insurance clause, **13**, 580
  irritancy, **13**, 559, 560, 584
  landlord, **13**, 564
    fees and outlays of, payment, **13**, 587
    obligations, **13**, 58
  local government requirements, compliance
    with, **13**, 588
  maintenance and repair obligation, **13**, 578
  missives, **13**, 558
  nature, **13**, 555
  negotiation—
    importance of, **13**, 560
    relative negotiating strengths, **13**, 562
  noise, excessive, **13**, 588
  notices, tenant's duty to inform landlord, **13**, 588
  noxious effluents, **13**, 588
  parties to, **13**, 564
  planning legislation, **13**, 588
  plenishing order, **13**, 517, 582
  quiet possession, tenant must be allowed, **13**, 58
  'reasonable landlord', **13**, 562
  registration, **13**, 558, 585
    recording dues, **13**, 587
  rei interitus, **13**, 579, 581
  removal on termination, **13**, 588
  rent—
    advance, payment in, **13**, 567
    adverse rent review clause, effect, **13**, 561
    calculation, **13**, 567
    indexed rental, **13**, 71
    initial, **13**, 567
    irritancy, **13**, 584
    negotiation, **13**, 560, 567
    peppercorn, **13**, 567
    quarter days, payment on, **13**, 567
    requirement for, **13**, 567
    review—
      arbitration—
        clause, **13**, 574–576
        mechanism, **13**, 575

Lease-leasing (heritable property)—*continued*
commercial lease—*continued*
  rent—*continued*
    review—*continued*
      assumptions relevant to, **13**, 573
      clause, generally, **13**, 572
      generally, **13**, 569, 570
      interval between reviews, **13**, 571
      object, **13**, 573
      procedure, **13**, 573
      valuation process, **13**, 573
      willing landlord and willing tenant, **13**,
        573
    royalty rental, **13**, 71
    turnover rental, **13**, 71
    value added tax, **13**, 568
  review—
    arbitration, payment of rent during, **13**, 577
    formal memorandum, **13**, 577
    lowering of rent, clause preventing, **13**, 577
  Scottish and English leases distinguished, **13**,
    558
  securities over, **13**, 585
  security, tenant's obligations as to, **13**, 588
  service roads, tenant's obligations as to, **13**, 588
  servitudes, tenant's obligations as to, **13**, 588
  signs, landlord's approval, **13**, 588
  stamp duty, **13**, 587
  statutory regulation, **13**, 559
  statutory requirements, compliance with, **13**,
    588
  subject—
    description, **13**, 565
    range of, **13**, 563
  sublease, **13**, 583
  subtenant, **13**, 564
  tenant, **13**, 564
    assignees and subtenants, **13**, 564
    cautioner, **13**, 564
    guarantor, **13**, 564
    successors, **13**, 564
  termination, **13**, 588
  title, **13**, 558
  title conditions, tenant's duty to observe, **13**,
    588
  trade fixtures, **13**, 566
  use of premises, user clause, **13**, 582
  value added tax, **13**, 568, 587
  warrant at all hands and against all mortals, **13**,
    58
commercial property, **6**, 639
common law—
  cardinal elements of lease, **13**, 104
  consensus in idem, **13**, 104, 105
  consideration, **13**, 107
  generally, **13**, 101
  heritable subjects, occupation of, **13**, 106
  period of lease, **13**, 108
common property, **18**, 23, 28, 28n
compulsory acquisition of land subject to, **5**, 25
  53
conditions running with lands, **13**, 239
confusion, **13**, 231
consensus in idem, **13**, 104, 105

Lease-leasing (heritable property)—*continued*
consent of parties, **13**, 222
consideration—
  annual sum based on percentage of capital expended on property, **13**, 107
  annuity, **13**, 107
  cardinal element, as, **13**, 104
  debt, set off against, **13**, 107
  discharge, **13**, 107
  elusory, **13**, 107
  fruits, in form of, **13**, 107
  interest, set off against, **13**, 107
  nominal, **13**, 107
  services, in form of, **13**, 107, 242
constitution and proof, **13**, 122–141
  expenses of preparation, **13**, 142, 143
  informal leases, **13**, 130–134
  rei interventus, **13**, 130, 135–141
  writing—
    form of, **13**, 123–126
    leases for not more than one year, **13**, 122, 127–129
    necessity for, **13**, 122
continuing obligations—
  conditions running with lands, **13**, 239
  option of renewal, **13**, 150–153, 243
  personal conditions, meaning, **13**, 242
  real conditions—
    generally, **13**, 239, 240
    meaning, **13**, 241
contra proferentem, to be construed, **13**, 227
contract, lease as, **13**, 101, 104
  arbitration clause, **13**, 234
  bilateral contract, form of writing, **13**, 123
  choice of law, **13**, 228
  confusion, **13**, 231
  consent, **13**, 222
  construction, principles of, **13**, 227
  contract of location, **13**, 103
  error, **13**, 223
  frustration, **13**, 226
  generally, **13**, 221
  homologation, **13**, 224
  illegality, **13**, 225
  jurisdiction, **13**, 228
  management conditions, **13**, 237, 238
  misrepresentation, **13**, 223
  mutuality, **13**, 232
  other contracts distinguished, **13**, 109–121
  penalties, **13**, 238
  personal bar, **13**, 224
  prescription, **13**, 230
  rent, payment of, **13**, 229, 596, 598
  resolutive conditions, **13**, 236
  suspensive conditions, **13**, 236
  unity of contract, **13**, 233
  warrandice, **13**, 235
Cost of Leases Act 1958 ..., **13**, 153
date of entry, **13**, 244
definition of lease, **13**, 103, 555
delectus personae, doctrine of, **13**, 355–357, 583
destination, special, **13**, 394
diligence, effect, **13**, 158
dominant interests, **18**, 351, 352

Lease-leasing (heritable property)—*continued*
drafts and copies as evidence of, **13**, 133
dwelling house—
  generally, **13**, 595
  tenancy and other contracts, **13**, 595
entry—
  date of, **13**, 244, 245, 246
  lease signed after, **13**, 244
  refusal to take, as remedy available to tenant, **13**, 280
  term days, **13**, 245
error, reduction on, **13**, 223
expenses of lease preparation, **13**, 142, 143
expiry, **18**, 9
family settlement or arrangement, whether lease, **13**, 113
feu contract compared, **13**, 110, 602
finance, *see* FINANCE LEASE
fishings, **13**, 205
foregift, meaning, **13**, 103
fraud, obtained by, **13**, 469
frustration of lease, **13**, 226
'full repairing and insuring lease', **13**, 556, 557, 563, 580, 581
furnishings, **13**, 195, 217
generally, **18**, 3
grantee, *see* LESSEE; TENANT-TENANCY
granter, *see* LANDLORD; LESSOR
grassum—
  meaning, **13**, 103
  rei interventus, amounting to, **13**, 140
ground, **13**, 209
headlease, **13**, 103
heritable right, as, **18**, 14
heritable subject, **13**, 194
  occupation, **13**, 106
hire contract distinguished, **13**, 103
historical background, **13**, 101
homologation, **13**, 224
human habitation, fitness for, landlord's obligations as to, **13**, 260
illegal or immoral purpose, to promote, **13**, 225
impugn lease, singular successor's right to, **13**, 314
informal lease—
  constitution, **13**, 130
  drafts and copies, **13**, 133
  memoranda by landlord, **13**, 134
  oral, **13**, 129
    proof, **13**, 131
  proof, **13**, 131
  rei interventus, **13**, 136, 138, 144
  verbal, **13**, 129
    proof, **13**, 131
  writ as evidence of agreement, **13**, 132
inhibition, **8**, 155; **13**, 184
inhibition of proprietor, effect, **13**, 158
insolvency or apparent insolvency of tenant, **13**, 414
insolvency of lessor, **13**, 159
interest in—
  land of lessee, positive prescription, **16**, 2107
  lease—
    decisions in respect of, **25**, 720
    landlord, repossession by, **25**, 718

Lease-leasing (heritable property)—*continued*
interest in—*continued*
  lease—*continued*
    succession to, **25**, 716
    termination of, **25**, 717
    vesting of, **25**, 715
interposed lease—
  competence, **13**, 387
  effect, **13**, 388
  grant, **13**, 387
  historical background, **13**, 386
  sublease, **13**, 379
interpretation and construction—
  cardinal elements, **12**, 1252
  casualty, payment of, **12**, 1251
  consensus in idem, **12**, 1252
  construed as a whole, lease must be, **12**, 1251
  contra proferentem, **12**, 1251
  definite period of let, **12**, 1252
  English form, lease drawn up in, **12**, 1251
  extraneous evidence, **12**, 1251
  extrinsic evidence, **13**, 144–146
  general principles, **12**, 1251
  heritable subject, **12**, 1252
  irritancy clause, **12**, 1251
  long lease, **12**, 1251
  parole evidence—
    generally, **13**, 144, 147
    when admissible, **13**, 145
  parole proof, **12**, 1251
  prior communings excluded, **13**, 146
  rent, **12**, 1252
  Rent (Scotland) Act 1984 ..., **12**, 1253
  subsequent alteration of written contract—
    general rule, **13**, 147
    innovation, **13**, 148
    proof of reduction of rent, **13**, 149
  termination, **12**, 1251
investment lease, **13**, 210
irritancy, **18**, 9
  agricultural leases, **15**, 808
  bankruptcy of tenant, on, **15**, 809
  conventional, **15**, 809
  generally, **15**, 802
  legal, **15**, 808
  long leases, **15**, 808
  residential leases, **15**, 808
  right to irritate, **15**, 807
  Scottish Law Commission report, **22**, 681
irritancy clause—
  conventional—
    generally, **13**, 423, 426
    grounds for, **13**, 426–430
    purging—
      common law, **13**, 431
      monetary breaches, **13**, 433
      non-monetary breaches, **13**, 434
      statute law, **13**, 432
  enforcement—
    effect, **13**, 437
    generally, **13**, 435
    procedure, **13**, 436
  generally, **13**, 423

Lease-leasing (heritable property)—*continued*
irritancy clause—*continued*
  legal—
    common law, **13**, 424
    generally, **13**, 423
    purging, **13**, 425
    statute law, **13**, 424
ish—
  meaning, **13**, 103
  necessity for, **13**, 597
  notice of termination, **13**, 468
  real rights, and, **13**, 108
  security of tenure, and, **13**, 317
  tacit relocation following, **13**, 450
joint tenancy, *see* TENANT-TENANCY
joint venture contract distinguished, **13**, 117
jus relictae, **13**, 412
jus relicti, **13**, 412
Kindly Tenants of Lochmaben, **13**, 212
landlord, *see* LANDLORD
landowner, grant by, **18**, 195
Lands Clauses Acts, application of, **5**, 25
lease-purchase agreement, *see* LEASE-PURCHASE
  AGREEMENT
leasehold interest, meaning, **19**, 1614
Leases Act 1449 ..., **13**, 101
legitim, **13**, 412
lessee, *see* LESSEE; TENANT-TENANCY
lessee's right under recorded, imprescriptive right,
  as, **16**, 2126
lessor, *see* LANDLORD; LESSOR
lex loci situs, **13**, 228, 389
licence agreement, **12**, 1252
licence distinguished, **12**, 1252; **13**, 596–598
licence to occupy—
  lease compared—
    exclusivity of possession, **13**, 597
    generally, **13**, 596
    rent, provisions for, **13**, 598
  meaning, **13**, 596
liferent, and, **13**, 114, 393
liquidation of tenant, **13**, 414
location, *see* LEASE-HIRE (MOVEABLES)
long lease—
  building lease, **13**, 209
  definition, **13**, 340
  disadvantages to tenant, **13**, 317
  feu—
    conversion into—
      agreement, by, **13**, 333
      Long Lease (Scotland) Act 1954, under,
        13, 332
    inferior to, **13**, 327
  generally, **13**, 208, 317
  grant of, **6**, 776
  ground lease, **13**, 209
  interest in land in, grant of, **6**, 714
  landlord's interest, acquisition of—
    cottars, **13**, 335
    crofters, **13**, 335
    tenancies-at-will, **13**, 334
  meaning, **6**, 707*n*
  nature of, **13**, 327
  private dwelling house, meaning, **13**, 341

Lease-leasing (heritable property)—*continued*
long lease—*continued*
  real conditions in assignations, creation of, **13**, 337
  registration, **6**, 776
    assignation, **13**, 321
    effect, **13**, 322
    generally, **13**, 318
    improbative lease, **13**, 319
    Land Register of Scotland, in, **13**, 318, 324
    nature of long leasehold, and, **13**, 327
    positive prescription, **13**, 326
    Register of Sasines, in, **13**, 101, 318, 325
    requirements, **13**, 319
    securities, leasehold, **13**, 330
    sublease, **13**, 380
    title, of, **13**, 324
    whether necessary, **13**, 323
    writs registrable, **13**, 320
  renewal—
    failure by landlord to renew, **13**, 336
    Sheriff's powers in relation to, **13**, 336
  residential use of property let by, limitations—
    ancillary provisions, **13**, 346
    breach of prohibition, **13**, 344
    conventional prohibition, **13**, 342
    defences, **13**, 345
    definition of long lease, **13**, 340
    generally, **13**, 339
    private dwelling house, **13**, 341
    protected tenancy, **13**, 343
    statutory tenancy, **13**, 343
    sublease, effect, **13**, 347
  securities, leasehold, **13**, 328–331
  statutory provisions affecting, **13**, 317–347
  termination, **6**, 776
  variation of land obligations, **13**, 338
lordship—
  meaning, **13**, 103
  mineral lease, **13**, 199
management conditions, **13**, 237, 238
marine fish farms, **11**, 61
matrimonial home, **13**, 174, 193
  spouse, rights of, **13**, 193
matters affecting conveyancer, **6**, 639
meaning, **18**, 5
memoranda by landlord as evidence of lease, **13**, 134
mineral—
  generally, **6**, 780
  sale, or, **13**, 111
  trustees as lessor, **13**, 165
misrepresentation—
  damages in respect of, **13**, 223
  fraudulent, **13**, 223
  innocent, **13**, 223
  negligent, **13**, 223
  reduction on, **13**, 223
missives of, as deed of trust, **24**, 27
mutuality, **13**, 232
nature, **13**, 555
nemo dat quod non habet rule, **18**, 669
new lease, implied renunciation resulting from, **12**, 1235

Lease-leasing (heritable property)—*continued*
for not more than one year—
  constitution, **13**, 122, 127
  proof, **13**, 128
occupation, **13**, 216
operating, *see* OPERATING LEASE
oral—
  duration, **13**, 129
  proof, **13**, 131
oral agreement, subsequent alteration by—
  general rule, **13**, 147
  innovation, **13**, 148
  interpretation, **13**, 147–149
  proof of reduction of rent, **13**, 149
order for possession, **12**, 1253
owner may not hold over own property, **18**, 9
Part VII contract distinguished, **13**, 626
pastoral, **13**, 215
penalties, **13**, 238
period of lease—
  indefinite, **13**, 108
  perpetuity, in, **13**, 108
  term of endurance, necessity for, **13**, 108
  until occurence of particular event, **13**, 108
periodical sum due under, prescription, **16**, 2116
personal bar, **13**, 224
personal conditions—
  generally, **13**, 240
  meaning, **13**, 242
personal licence distinguished, **13**, 120
plenishing order, landlord's hypothec, **13**, 517, 582
possession—
  defence of, generally, **18**, 174
  effect, **13**, 141
  exclusivity, **13**, 597
  right to, **18**, 127, 151
  See also POSSESSION
precarious possession distinguished, **13**, 119
preparation, expenses, **13**, 142, 143
prescription, **13**, 230
  negative, **18**, 9
  positive, **18**, 9
prior communings, **13**, 146
private sector residential tenant, protection, *see* TENANT-TENANCY
profit rental, **13**, 569
proof, **13**, 122–141
property under, insurable interest, **12**, 852
prorogation—
  meaning, **13**, 150
  real rights, and, **13**, 312
  right of, **13**, 153
  tacit relocation compared, **13**, 450
protected tenancy, *see* TENANT-TENANCY
public sector housing, **13**, 121
purchaser—
  knowledge of lease, **13**, 315
  protection of tenant, **13**, 314–316
  questions for, **13**, 315
  tenant compared, **13**, 602
real condition—
  dominant property, **18**, 350
  generally, **13**, 239, 240; **18**, 349, 351, 352

Lease-leasing (heritable property)—*continued*
real condition—*continued*
   meaning, **13**, 241
   See also REAL CONDITION
real right, lease as—
   commercial lease, registration, **13**, 585
   generally, **18**, 5
   historical background, **13**, 292, 293
   ish, requirements as to, **13**, 108, 301–303
   land, subject must be—
      generally, **13**, 296
      sporting lease, **13**, 297
   Leases Act 1449 ..., **13**, 293
   parties against whom protection given, **13**, 294
   possession, requirements as to, **13**, 308–313
   protection—
      parties against whom given, **13**, 294
      requisites for, **13**, 295
   purchaser, questions with, **13**, 314–316
   rent, requirements as to, **13**, 107, 304–307
   writing, when lease required in, **13**, 298–300
   See also REAL RIGHT
redding-up condition, breach, **13**, 276
reduction, sublease, where, **13**, 379, 380
registered—
   generally, **6**, 639
   imprescriptible nature, **18**, 9
registration—
   assignation, **13**, 321
   commercial lease, **13**, 558, 585
      recording dues, **13**, 587
   effect, **13**, 322
   generally, **13**, 318
   Land Register of Scotland, **13**, 318, 324
   long lease, *see* long lease *above*
   long leasehold, nature of, **13**, 327
   positive prescription, **13**, 326
   real conditions in assignations, creation of, **13**, 337
   Register of Sasines, **13**, 318, 325
   renunciation of registered lease, **13**, 436
   requirements, **13**, 319
   securities, leasehold, **13**, 328–331
   sporting lease, **13**, 202
   title, of, **13**, 324
   variation of land obligations, **13**, 338
   whether necessary, **13**, 323
   writs registrable, **13**, 320
Registration of Leases (Scotland) Act 1857 ..., **13**, 101
rei interventus, *see* REI INTERVENTUS
relocation, option to renew in relation to, **13**, 153
removings, *see* TENANT-TENANCY
renewal of lease—
   granter, questions with, **13**, 151
   meaning, **13**, 150
   option for, **13**, 153, 243
   real rights and, **13**, 312
   singular successors—
      generally, **13**, 243
      questions with, **13**, 152
   tacit relocation compared, **13**, 450
rent, *see* RENT
rent books, **6**, 639

Lease-leasing (heritable property)—*continued*
renunciation—
   abandonment distinguished, **13**, 438
   acceptance, **13**, 441
   capacity of parties, **13**, 444
   discharge of claims, **13**, 442
   effects, **13**, 443
   executor's statutory power to terminate distinguished, **13**, 438
   form, **13**, 436
   generally, **13**, 438
   implied, **13**, 440
   informal lease, **13**, 436
   meaning, **13**, 438
   new lease following, **13**, 443
   registered lease, **13**, 436
   sublease, **13**, 443
   verbal, **13**, 436
resident landlord, where, **13**, 629
resolutive conditions, **13**, 236
restriction, meaning, **4**, 1136
right in, incorporeal property, as, **18**, 652
right of occupation distinguished, **13**, 118
right in security, test for, **13**, 116
royalty—
   meaning, **13**, 103
   mineral lease, **13**, 199
rural lease, **13**, 213–215, 217
   arable lease, **13**, 215
   assignability, **13**, 356
   delectus personae, doctrine of, **13**, 356
   pastoral lease, **13**, 215
   repairs—
      landlord's obligations, **13**, 256, 262
      tenant's obligations, **13**, 270
   subjects, **13**, 214
   tenantable condition, landlord's obligations, **13**, 256
   urban lease distinguished, **13**, 213
sale contract distinguished, **13**, 111
salmon fishings, **11**, 9
   singular successors, protection against claim by, **11**, 9
Scottish jurisdiction, **13**, 228
search, expenses, **13**, 142
seasonal, tacit relocation not applicable, **13**, 452
secure tenancy, **11**, 1950
secured lease, arrears of rent, **18**, 14
security over—
   assignment, **20**, 257
   cash credits, **20**, 257
   discharge, **20**, 257
   dwelling house, private, **20**, 177, 178, 181, 18 261
   enabling rights, **20**, 257, 258
   land registration, **20**, 262
   poinding the ground, **20**, 259
   possession, **20**, 257
      original necessity of, **20**, 256
   prescription, **20**, 260
   recording—
      effect of, **20**, 259
   Registration of Lease (Scotland) Act 1857 . **20**, 257

Lease-leasing (heritable property)—*continued*
security over—*continued*
   renunciation, **20**, 257, 258
   translation, **20**, 257
   wife and children, provision for, **20**, 257
separate tenement as subject of, **18**, 208
sequestration—
   lessor, of, effect, **13**, 159
   tenant, of, effect, **13**, 414
     renunciation of lease, **13**, 438, 439
service occupancy compared, **13**, 115, 601
services, provision of, **13**, 195, 218
   tenant, by, **13**, 107, 242
servient interests, **18**, 352
set, meaning, **13**, 103
shared occupation rights distinguished, **13**, 112
shared property, **13**, 599
'Shogun', *see* CROSS-BORDER LEASING
shop, of, *see* SHOP
short lease—
   meaning, **6**, 776; **18**, 657*n*
   overriding interest, **6**, 739, 776
   possession, requirement for, **18**, 657
singular successor—
   enforcement against, **13**, 101
   impugn lease, right to, **13**, 314
   lease valid against, **13**, 101, 102
   option to renew, and, **13**, 152, 243
special destination, **13**, 394
sporting rights, assignability, **13**, 356
stamp duty, exemption of charitable bodies, **3**, 1164
standard security, **20**, 150
   destruction of lease, **18**, 9
   private dwelling house, protection on leasehold
     subjects, **20**, 177, 178, 181, 182
   redemption—
     agricultural holding, **20**, 179
     contracting out of statutory provisions
       forbidden, **20**, 184
     croft, **20**, 179
     limit in amount recoverable on, **20**, 183
     private dwelling house, **20**, 177, 178, 181,
       182, 261
     protected tenancy, **20**, 180
     secure tenancy, **20**, 180
     smallholding, **20**, 179
     statutory tenancy, **20**, 180
steelbow, **13**, 217, 220
subject—
   allotment, *see* ALLOTMENT
   buildings, **13**, 194
   business premises, **13**, 197
   caravan, **13**, 194
   care, tenant's obligation to use reasonable, **13**,
     269
   commodities, **13**, 198
   destruction—
     effect, **13**, 287
     commercial lease, **13**, 579–581
     negligence or fault of party, caused by, **13**,
      288
     partial, **13**, 286
     rei interitus, **13**, 285, 287
     commercial lease, **13**, 579, 581

Lease-leasing (heritable property—*continued*
subject—*continued*
   ferry, **13**, 206
   feuduty, **13**, 206
   fishings, **13**, 194, 202
   foreshore, **13**, 194, 205
   furnished house, **13**, 195
     degree of possession, **13**, 253
     services, provision of, **13**, 195, 218
   game, **13**, 194, 202
   generally, **13**, 194
   glebe lands, **13**, 204
   heritable property, **13**, 106, 194
   kelp shore, **13**, 206
   land—
     allodial tenure, **13**, 194
     feudal tenure, **13**, 194
     subject must be, **13**, 296, 297
   lodgings, **13**, 196
   mill, **13**, 206
   minerals, **6**, 780; **13**, 194, 199
   mines royal, **13**, 200
   mobile home, **13**, 194
   moveable property, **13**, 194
   multure, **13**, 206
   plenish, tenant's obligation to, **13**, 271, 582
   rabbits, **13**, 202, 203
   railway, **13**, 206
   rent, **13**, 206
   repair—
     landlord's obligation to keep in, **13**, 256, 262
     rural subjects, **13**, 256, 262
     urban subjects, **13**, 257–261
     tenant's obligations as to, **13**, 270
   rural—
     repair—
       landlord's obligation to keep in, **13**, 256,
       262
       tenant's obligations as to, **13**, 270
   sale of, removings, action of, **13**, 495
   seabed, **13**, 194, 205
   shootings, **13**, 202
   shop, *see* SHOP
   sporting lease, **13**, 202, 297
   tenantable condition, landlord's obligations—
     generally, **13**, 254
     rural subjects, **13**, 256
     urban subjects, **13**, 255
   timber, **13**, 194, 201
   toll, **13**, 206
   urban—
     repair, landlord's obligation to keep in, **13**,
      257–261
     repair, tenant's obligations as to, **13**, 270
     tenantable condition, landlord's obligations,
      13, 255
   water, **13**, 194
sublease, *see* SUBLEASE
subsequent alteration of written contract—
   generally, **13**, 147
   innovation, **13**, 148
   proof of reduction of rent, **13**, 149
succession, *see* TENANT-TENANCY
suspensive conditions, **13**, 236

Lease-leasing (heritable property)—*continued*
tacit relocation, *see* TACIT RELOCATION
Tenancy of Shops (Scotland) Acts, **13**, 197
tenancy-at-will, **13**, 211
  landlord's interest, acquisition of, **13**, 334
tenant, *see* TENANT-TENANCY
term days, definition, **13**, 245
term of lease, meaning, **19**, 1614
termination of lease—
  agreement, by, renunciation, *see* renunciation *above*
  allotment, **13**, 544
    rights of parties on, **13**, 546, 547
  allotment garden, **13**, 545
    rights of parties on, **13**, 548–554
  bankruptcy, by, **13**, 414
  break at instance of either party, **13**, 446–449
  commercial, **13**, 588
  ejection—
    removings distinguished, **13**, 467
    wrongous, **13**, 471
  generally, **18**, 6
  harassment, **13**, 472
  interdict, **13**, 470
  irritancy, by, *see* IRRITANCY
  landlord, as remedy available to, **13**, 276
  notice, **13**, 468
  procedural matters—
    assured tenancy, **13**, 763–767
    inclusion of grounds in lease, **13**, 767
    notice of proceedings for possession—
      contents, **13**, 764
      duration, **13**, 766
      minimum period, **13**, 765
    protected tenancy, **13**, 762
  reform, need for, **13**, 462
  removings—
    court action, necessity for, **13**, 469–472
    defender—
      assignee, **13**, 502
      joint tenants, **13**, 501
      subtenant, **13**, 502
        notice, **13**, 503
      violent profits, caution for, **13**, 504, 505
    ejection distinguished, **13**, 467
    extraordinary, **13**, 464, 466
      notice to quit, whether neccessary, **13**, 468
      violent profits, **13**, 505, 507, 512
    irritancy, termination of lease by, **13**, 466
    ish, tenant not moving out at, **13**, 466
    landlord, recovery of possesion by, **13**, 466
    meaning, **13**, 463, 467
    notice—
      calculation, **13**, 480
      common law, **13**, 476
      form, **13**, 481–489
      ish, must be prior to, **13**, 475
      joint tenants, to, **13**, 501
      lapsed, **13**, 491
      period of, **13**, 475–480
      quit, notice to, **13**, 475
      Removal Terms (Scotland) Act 1886 ...,
        13, 477
      Rent (Scotland) Act 1984 ..., **13**, 479

Lease-leasing (heritable property)—*continued*
termination of lease—*continued*
  removings—*continued*
    notice—*continued*
      service and evidence, **13**, 490
      subtenant, to, **13**, 503
      timeous, **13**, 475
      withdrawn, **13**, 491
    notice of termination of lease, **13**, 468
    ordinary, **13**, 465, 466, 470
      forms, **13**, 474
      violent profits, **13**, 505, 506
    reform, need for, **13**, 462
    solemn, **13**, 466, 466n
    summary, **13**, 466, 466n
    summary cause, **13**, 466, 473
    title to sue—
      agent, lease granted by where, **13**, 498
      generally, **13**, 492
      heritable securities, **13**, 499
      joint proprietors, where, **13**, 496
      limited owners, where, **13**, 497
      missives, effect, **13**, 495
      principal tenant, **13**, 500
      pursuer lessor, where, **13**, 493
      pursuer not lessor, where, **13**, 494
      subtenant, **13**, 500
    violent profits, caution for, **13**, 505
    warning or letter of removal, **13**, 475
  resumption of possession by landlord, **13**, 445
  security of tenure—
    generally, **13**, 696
  Sheriff Courts (Scotland) Act 1907 ..., **13**, 462
  summary cause for recovery of heritable
    property, **13**, 470
  tacit relocation—
    following, **13**, 451
    security of tenure, relationship with, **13**, 696
  unlawful eviction, **13**, 472
third party—
  alleging right to use subject, interdict, **13**, 470
  landlord and tenant, rights of, **13**, 290
  rights, **13**, 289
  tenant and superior, relationship between, **13**, 291
time-sharing contract distinguished, **13**, 112
title—
  accretion, **13**, 156
  bad, **13**, 154
  generally, **13**, 154
  incomplete, granter holding, **13**, 155
  infeftment, **13**, 155, 156
  limited, **13**, 157
  registered, **13**, 155
transfer of ownership, and, **18**, 604
trout fishing, of, **11**, 49
trust deed, grant of, effect, **13**, 414
trustees' powers, **24**, 202
tutor, management by, **11**, 1225
two or more tenants holding distinct *pro indivis*
  shares, **13**, 189
types of, **25**, 715
unilateral obligations, probative, **13**, 126
unity of contract, **13**, 233

Lease-leasing (heritable property)—*continued*
unregistered, overriding interest, as, **13**, 315
urban lease, **13**, 213, 216, 217
  arable lease distinguished, **13**, 213
  assignability, **13**, 357
  landlord's hypothec, **13**, 513
  occupation lease, **13**, 216
  removings, notice, **13**, 482
  repair—
    landlord's obligation as to, **13**, 257–261
    tenant's obligations as to, **13**, 270
    tenantable condition, landlord's obligations, **13**, 255
user clause, commercial lease, **13**, 582
valuation of leased subjects, **24**, 416
verbal, **13**, 129
  proof, **13**, 131
violent profits, *see* VIOLENT PROFITS
warrandice, **13**, 235
  sale of property, in, **13**, 316; **18**, 704, 718
  whether contract amounts to, determination, **13**, 595–602
writ as evidence of, **13**, 132
writing—
  form of, **13**, 123–126
  more than one year, lease for, **13**, 300
  necessity for, **13**, 122
  one year or less, lease for, **13**, 122, 127–129, 298, 299

Lease/hire (moveables)
advantages—
  100 per cent financing of cost, **14**, 1016
  capital, limited authority to spend, **14**, 1016
  certainty, **14**, 1016
  fixed assets, capital not tied up in, **14**, 1016
  generally, **14**, 1015, 1018
  individual lessee needs, tailoring for, **14**, 1016
  obsolescence of equipment, **14**, 1016
  off-balance sheet finance, **14**, 1016
  revenue budget, expenditure of, **14**, 1016
  taxation, impact of, **14**, 1016
  writing-down allowance, **14**, 1016
bailment, as, **14**, 1007
common law—
  essentials—
    generally, **14**, 1033
    implied terms, **14**, 1037
    parties, consent of, **14**, 1036
    rent, **14**, 1035
    things let, **14**, 1034
  lessee's obligations—
    delivery, **14**, 1044
    generally, **14**, 1043
    proper care, **14**, 1047
    purpose for which hired, used for, **14**, 1046
    rent, **14**, 1045
  lessor's obligations—
    defects, warranty that thing let is free from, **14**, 1042
    delivery, **14**, 1039
    enjoyment, **14**, 1040
    generally, **14**, 1038
    interference, **14**, 1040

Lease/hire (moveables)—*continued*
common law—*continued*
  lessor's obligations—*continued*
    repair, **14**, 1041
    restoration, **14**, 1048
computer industry, **14**, 1006
conditional sale agreement distinguished, **14**, 1007
consent of parties, **14**, 1036
contract, **14**, 1003
delivery, obligations as to, **14**, 1039, 1044, 1058
development of leasing, **14**, 1005–1007
disadvantages—
  expense, **14**, 1017
  fixed term of lease, **14**, 1017
  generally, **14**, 1015, 1018
  grants, **14**, 1017
  residual value of asset, loss of, **14**, 1017
  restrictions on use, **14**, 1017
display of goods for, **15**, 621
double depreciation, **14**, 1096
double dip, **14**, 1096
equipment of, **14**, 1006
fixed term, **14**, 1017
full pay-out, meaning, **14**, 1005
hire, contract of—
  basis of, **14**, 1022, 1023
  caravan or mobile home, **13**, 194
  commercial vehicles, **14**, 1022
  common law, at—
    essentials—
      generally, **14**, 1033
      implied terms, **14**, 1037
      parties, consent of, **14**, 1036
      rent, **14**, 1035
      thing let, **14**, 1034
    lessee's obligations—
      delivery, **14**, 1044
      generally, **14**, 1043
      proper care of thing hired, **14**, 1047
      purpose for which hired, use for, **14**, 1046
      rent, **14**, 1045
      restoration of thing hired, **14**, 1048
    lessor's obligations—
      defects, warranty that thing let is free from, **14**, 1042
      delivery, **14**, 1039
      enjoyment, **14**, 1040
      generally, **14**, 1038
      interference, **14**, 1040
      repair, **14**, 1041
consumer hire agreement, *see* CONSUMER HIRE AGREEMENT
control order, **14**, 1053
damage, liability for, **14**, 1003
duration of, **22**, 827
exclusion clauses, **6**, 101
furniture in leased, furnished house, **13**, 195
harm, liability for, **14**, 1003
history—
  contract of location, classification of, **14**, 1001
  generality of definition, **14**, 1002
  nominate consensual contract, **14**, 1004
  principle, importance of, **14**, 1003

Lease/hire (moveables)—*continued*
hire, contract of—*continued*
  insurable interest of goods under, **12**, 852
  lease compared, **13**, 103
  leasing distinguished from, **14**, 1006
  locatio conductio operarum, **14**, 1004
  locatio conductio rei, **13**, 1783; **14**, 1004
  locatio custodiae, **14**, 1004
  locatio operis, **14**, 1004
  lodgings, furniture in, **13**, 196
  nominate consensual contract, as, **14**, 1004
  novation, **14**, 1029
  obsolescence of equipment, **14**, 1016
  purpose, fitness for, **14**, 1003
  restitution of goods, **15**, 46, 49
  Scottish Law Commission proposals, **14**, 1054
  standard form, meaning, **14**, 1052
  sub-hire—
    generally, **14**, 1089
    lessee, powers of, **14**, 1091
    lessor, security for, **14**, 1093
    possession, sub-hirer's right to, **14**, 1092
    sub-lessee, liability of, **14**, 1090
  supplier—
    lessor and, **14**, 1069, 1085
    obligation, failure to perform, **14**, 1069
  termination due to lessee's breach, **14**, 1067
  termination of hire period, specific implement
    for possession on, **13**, 12
  third-party involvement, **14**, 1083
  unfair contract terms, **14**, 1052
leveraged, **14**, 1018, 1096
location, contract of—
  caravan, holiday rental of, **14**, 1002
  company director, employment of, **14**, 1002
  equipment—
    100 per cent financing, **14**, 1016
    lessor, involvement in contract, **14**, 1027,
      1028
    obsolescence, **14**, 1016
    use, restrictions on, **14**, 1017
  general classification, **14**, 1001, 1007
  generality of definition, **14**, 1002
  meaning, **14**, 1001
  motor car, holiday rental of, **14**, 1002
  moveables, not limited to, **14**, 1002
meaning, **14**, 1005
minors, soliciting for business with, **3**, 1220
mutuum, contrasted with, **13**, 1706
novation, **14**, 1029
operating lease, **14**, 1020
owner's title, **18**, 534
pre-lease contract, **14**, 1032
products—
  big ticket, **14**, 1025
  contract hire, **14**, 1022
  finance lease, **14**, 1019
  hire agreement, **14**, 1023
  lease purchase, **14**, 1024
  operating lease, **14**, 1020
  rental agreement, **14**, 1023
  sales-aid leasing, **14**, 1021
  small ticket, **14**, 1025
restoration of thing hired, **14**, 1048

Lease/hire (moveables)—*continued*
reverse double dip, **14**, 1096
sales aid, leasing as, **14**, 1021
ship, of, *see* CHARTERPARTY
taxation—
  allowances—
    first year capital—
      introduction of, **14**, 1009
      phasing out, **14**, 1009
    impact of, **14**, 1006, 1008
    lessor, benefit obtained by, **14**, 1011
    writing-down, **14**, 1010
  cross-border leasing, **14**, 1096
  impact of, **14**, 1016
  interest, **14**, 1014
  non-recourse financing, **14**, 1014
  rentals, **14**, 1014
  telephone, lease of, **14**, 1006
  writing down allowance, **14**, 1010, 1013, 1016
trade fixtures, tenant's, **14**, 1074
Lease-purchase agreement
assignation, **14**, 1030
hire-purchase distinguished from, **14**, 1024
Leasehold interest
meaning, **19**, 1614
Leasing-making (crime of)
generally, **7**, 595
meaning, **7**, 595
Leave to enter
See IMMIGRATION (enter, leave to)
Leave to remain
See IMMIGRATION (remain, leave to)
Legacy
abatement, **25**, 856
ademption, **25**, 848, 854
aliment, for, **25**, 847
alimentary use, for, directions relating to, **25**, 834,
  836
assignation of, **6**, 596
concept of money central to, **14**, 1801
conditions attached to—
  accumulations, **25**, 868
  arms, assumption of, **25**, 871
  casual and potestative distinguished, **25**, 862
  employment, **25**, 869
  generally, **25**, 861
  immoral, **25**, 865–873
  impossible, **25**, 875
  marriage, **25**, 864, 866
  name, assumption of, **25**, 871
  potestative, **25**, 862
  public policy, against, **25**, 865–873
  residence, **25**, 870
  resolutive, **25**, 862
  spouses, separation of, **25**, 867
  suspensive, **25**, 862
  trustee, acceptance of office as, **25**, 863
  uncertain, **25**, 874
  unenforceable, **25**, 864
cumulative—
  generally, **25**, 857
  more than one deed, **25**, 858
  one deed, **25**, 859
debts, payment of, **25**, 847

Legacy—*continued*
demonstrative—
   abatement, **25**, 856
   nature of, **25**, 849, 853
donation *mortis causa* compared, **8**, 607
forfeiture of, **25**, 872
funeral expenses, payment of, **25**, 847
general, **25**, 850, 853, 856
interest on, **25**, 852
legatee, *see* LEGATEE
legitim, held as surrogate for, **25**, 925
meaning, **25**, 693*n*, 707
mournings, for, **25**, 847
pecuniary, **25**, 850, 853
portion, satisfaction of, **25**, 611
rei alienum, **25**, 855
relationship, must be motivated by, application of
   conditio, **25**, 900
residual, **25**, 851
special, **25**, 848, 853
specific, **25**, 848, 853
substitutional—
   conditions, **25**, 860
   generally, **25**, 857
   limitations, **25**, 860
   more than one deed, **25**, 858
   one deed, **25**, 859
tense use in wording, **25**, 926
types, **25**, 846–852
value, attribution of, **25**, 1018
verbal, **25**, 730
wills, *see* WILL
Legal advice and assistance
agreement, making, **13**, 1030
ancillary work, **13**, 1031
application form, completion by solicitor, **13**,
   1025
assistance by way of representation (ABWOR)—
   criminal cases, **13**, 1052, 1067
      financial eligibility, **13**, 1068
   generally, **13**, 1020, 1023, 1030
   introduction, **13**, 1010
   meaning, **13**, 1021
categories of work for which available, **13**, 1030,
   1031
charges—
   assessment, **13**, 1027
   recovery, **13**, 1027
   scale, **13**, 1027
   time basis, **13**, 1027
citizenship dues, **13**, 1031
civil cases, **13**, 1052
civil litigation, and, **5**, 541
claim, settlement of, **13**, 1030
confidentiality of information supplied in
   connection with, **13**, 1081
content, **13**, 1028–1031
counsel—
   fee, **13**, 1031
   provision by, **13**, 1021
criminal cases, **13**, 1052
debt, questions of, **13**, 1028
defamation, **13**, 1024
definition, **13**, 1021

Legal advice and assistance—*continued*
disposable income and capital, computation, **13**,
   1025
   spouse's income, **13**, 1025
divorce applications, **13**, 1024
doctor's fee, **13**, 1031
executry services, in relation to, **13**, 1022
expenditure limit, **13**, 1026
false information furnished by applicant, **13**, 1082
financial limits, **13**, 1025
   £80 or less, costing, **13**, 1031
free, Poors Counsel Act 1424 ..., **13**, 1132, 1132*n*
generally, **13**, 1004, 1020
hire purchase, questions of, **13**, 1028
inquiry agent, costs incurred by, **13**, 1030, 1033
keycard, **13**, 1025
law, advice of, **13**, 1029
Legal Advice and Assistance Act 1972 ..., **13**, 1004
legal capacity, age limit, **3**, 1215
legislation, and, **5**, 539
marriage, questions of, **13**, 1024, 1028, 1033
matrimonial work, **13**, 1033
   investigations by inquiry agent, costs incurred,
      13, 1030, 1033
money recovered or preserved for client,
   payments out of, **13**, 1027
nature, **13**, 1029
neighbours, over, **13**, 1028
passport dues, **13**, 1031
reasonableness test, **13**, 1031
recording dues, **13**, 1031
recovered money or property, **13**, 1027
restrictions, **13**, 1022, 1031
scope, **13**, 1028
   potential for expansion, **13**, 1024
Scottish Legal Aid Board control, **13**, 1031
Scottish Legal Aid Board functions in relation to,
   13, 1011
search, **13**, 1031
solicitor—
   account, payment of, **13**, 1027
   provision by, **13**, 1021
stamp duty, **13**, 1031
steps which client may take, **13**, 1030
survey, cost of, not recoverable, **13**, 1031
transaction, making, **13**, 1030
will, making, **13**, 1030
Legal adviser
communications with clients, confidentiality of,
   10, 505
prisoner, to—
   correspondence with prisoner, **16**, 1461
   visits to prisoner, **16**, 1460
Legal aid
access, obtaining report, urgency, situation of, **13**,
   1048
adjustments to—
   court powers, **13**, 1084
   Secretary of State's powers, **13**, 1083
administration, **13**, 1004
   Scottish Legal Aid Board, **13**, 1008, 1009
   See also SCOTTISH LEGAL AID BOARD
adoption freeing order, urgency, situation of, **13**,
   1048

Legal aid—*continued*

advice and assistance, *see* LEGAL ADVICE AND ASSISTANCE

aliment, minute, lodging, urgency, situation of, **13**, 1048

answers, lodging, urgency, situation of, **13**, 1048

appeals, **17**, 816, 840

appearance, entering, urgency, situation of, **13**, 1048

appellate proceedings, urgency, situation of, **13**, 1048

arrest, power of, urgency, situation of, **13**, 1048

assistance by way of representation (ABWOR), *see* LEGAL ADVICE AND ASSISTANCE

Auditor of the Court of Session, **6**, 936

child cases, **13**, 1070

children, proceedings relating to, **13**, 1070

children's hearing, **10**, 1130

  appeal, **3**, 1353, 1361

civil cases, **13**, 1020

  abroad, individual resident, **13**, 1036

  application for, **13**, 1041

    processing, **13**, 1042

  assisted person—

    party becoming during dependence of cause, **13**, 1044

    procedural aspects, **13**, 1044

  availability of, **13**, 1034

  contributions by legally-assisted persons, **13**, 1040

  counsel, approval of, **13**, 1045

  courts in which available, **13**, 1034

  decision *in re sua*, **13**, 1043

  disposable income and capital, computation, **13**, 1039

  distinct proceedings, **13**, 1034

  eligibility, **13**, 1036

    financial, **13**, 1039

    foreign origin, person of, **13**, 1036

  emergency, **13**, 1047

  expenses, exceptional, **13**, 1046

  expert witnesses, approval of, **13**, 1045

  financial eligibility, **13**, 1039

  legal aid certificate—

    generally, **13**, 1045

    lodging, **13**, 1044

    work outwith scope of, **13**, 1045

  litigant, procedural aspects, **13**, 1044

  meaning, **13**, 1035

  probable cause, **13**, 1042

    applicant must show, **13**, 1037, 1038, 1039

    urgency, situation of, **13**, 1048

  procedural aspects of grant, **13**, 1044

  property or money, recovery or preservation, **13**, 1075

  provision of services by persons who have acquired rights to conduct litigation or rights of audience, **13**, 1034

  reasonableness, **13**, 1038, 1039

    urgency, situation of, **13**, 1048

  refusal of legal aid, review procedure, **13**, 1080

  urgency, situation of, **13**, 1048

    eighteen steps, **13**, 1048, 1049

    where legal aid granted, **13**, 1050

    where legal aid refused, **13**, 1051

Legal aid—*continued*

civil cases—*continued*

  urgency, situation of special, **13**, 1048

    where legal aid granted, **13**, 1050

    where legal aid refused, **13**, 1051

  when grantable, **13**, 1011

confidentiality of information supplied in connection with, **13**, 1081

consistency in grant or refusal, **13**, 1012

consumer redress, **6**, 168

contempt of court, in respect of, **13**, 1020, 1071

counsel—

  choice of, **13**, 1072

  exclusion by Faculty of Advocates, **13**, 1389

  exclusion from selection, **13**, 1072

  fees and expenses, **13**, 1074

  fees in legally aided cases, **13**, 1384, 1386, 1390

    civil proceedings, **13**, 1390

    criminal proceedings, **13**, 1390

    Table of Fees, **13**, 1390

  refusal to act, **13**, 1072

  relationship with client not affected by grant of, **13**, 1389

  selection of, **13**, 1389

court, right of access to, **12**, 44

Court of Justice of the European Communities, **10**, 293

Courts-Martial Appeal Court, **6**, 895

criminal cases, **13**, 1080

  appeals, **13**, 1069

  automatic, **13**, 1053, 1054

  availability, **13**, 1052

    automatic, **13**, 1052

    restrictions on, **13**, 1052

  bail appeals or review, duty solicitor, **13**, 1053

  conflict of interest, **13**, 1065

  contribution not payable, **13**, 1052

  counsel, representation by, **13**, 1052

  distinct proceedings—

    separate application, **13**, 1057

  duty solicitor, **13**, 1053

    duties of, **13**, 1053

    eligibility, **13**, 1053

    fees, **13**, 1053

    over- or under-provision, **13**, 1053

    where legal aid withdrawn, **13**, 1053

  extension to, **13**, 1005

  financial eligibility, **13**, 1058

  generally, **13**, 1020

  homicide, duty solicitor, **13**, 1053

  identification parade, **13**, 1052

    automatic availability of legal aid, **13**, 1054

    duty solicitor, **13**, 1053

  justice, interests of—

    assessment, **13**, 1060

    factors determining, **13**, 1059

  mental status of accused, proof concerning, duty solicitor, **13**, 1053

  murder or attempted murder, duty solicitor, **13**, 1053

  new prosecution—

    automatic availability of legal aid, **13**, 1054

  plea in bar of trial, duty solicitor, **13**, 1053

  preliminary plea, duty solicitor, **13**, 1053

Legal aid—*continued*
criminal cases—*continued*
preliminary steps in criminal proceedings, **13**, 1052
provision of services by persons who have acquired rights of audience, **13**, 1052
provision of services by persons who have acquired rights to conduct litigation, **13**, 1052
sanction for expert witnesses, **13**, 1064
solicitor—
duty, *see* duty solicitor *above*
representation by, **13**, 1052
solemn procedure—
appeals, **13**, 1069
application for criminal legal aid, **13**, 1055
automatic availability of legal aid, **13**, 1054
person in custody under, duty solicitor, **13**, 1053
sanction for counsel, **13**, 1063
summary procedure, **13**, 1052
appeals, **13**, 1069
application for criminal legal aid, **13**, 1055, 1056, 1057
automatic availability of legal aid, **13**, 1054
distinct proceedings, separate applications, **13**, 1057
financial eligibility, **13**, 1058
generally, **13**, 1056
person in custody under, duty solicitor, **13**, 1053
sanction for counsel, **13**, 1063
special urgency, **13**, 1066
termination of aid, **13**, 1065
trial verdict set aside by High Court, where, **13**, 1055
when grantable, **13**, 1011
work covered by, **13**, 1062
custody—
obtaining report, urgency, situation of, **13**, 1048
urgency, situation of, **13**, 1048
defence, lodging, urgency, situation of, **13**, 1048
denial of, **12**, 52
discharge on diet of proof, **13**, 1048
district court, **6**, 1157
divorce, lodging minute for award on, **13**, 1048
European Commission of Human Rights, **12**, 15, 19
European Court of Human Rights, **12**, 19
expenses—
effect on, **17**, 1198
indemnity against, **13**, 1079
recovery—
indemnity, adaptation of rights to, **13**, 1079
legally-aided litigant, by, **13**, 1076
unassisted party, by, **13**, 1077
false information furnished by applicant, **13**, 1082
nature of, **13**, 1085
historical background—
generally, **13**, 1001
Poor's Roll, **13**, 1002
House of Lords, **6**, 836, 839
industrial tribunal, representation before, **9**, 329

Legal aid—*continued*
introduction of system, **13**, 1003
Lands Tribunal for Scotland, **5**, 196; **6**, 1152*n*
Law Society of Scotland, role of, **13**, 1004, 1006, 1008
Legal Advice and Assistance Act 1972 ..., **13**, 1004
Legal Aid (Scotland) Act 1967 ..., **13**, 1004
Legal Aid (Scotland) Act 1986—
generally, **13**, 1008
principal changes introduced by, **13**, 1010
transitional provisions, **13**, 1009
Legal Aid in Scotland consultation paper, **13**, 1007
Legal Aid and Solicitors (Scotland) Act 1949 ..., **13**, 1003, 1141
legal capacity, age limit, **3**, 1215
non-Scottish judgments, enforcement, **8**, 471
probabilis causa litigandi, **13**, 1037, 1038, 1039, 1042, 1048
property or money, recovery or preservation—
exceptions to provisions, **13**, 1078
expenses, **13**, 1076, 1077, 1079
generally, **13**, 1075
rights to indemnity, adaptation, **13**, 1079
successful unassisted party, by, **13**, 1077
proposed re-examination, **13**, 1007
refusal, review procedure, **13**, 1080
reponing urgency, situation of, **13**, 1048
restriction of availability until, **13**, 1010
Scottish Legal Aid Board, *see* SCOTTISH LEGAL AID BOARD
Scottish Legal Aid Fund, *see* SCOTTISH LEGAL AID FUND
sheriff court jurisdiction, **6**, 1113
sheriff principal, appeal to, **13**, 1034
sist—
generally, **17**, 1056
opposing motion to recall, **13**, 1048
solicitor—
choice of, **13**, 1072
exclusion from selection, **13**, 1072
fees and expenses, **13**, 1074
refusal to act, **13**, 1072
statutory concept, **13**, 1020
supplementing, **13**, 1073
suspension, urgency, situation of, **13**, 1048
terminology, **13**, 1020
time bar, action about to be barred, **13**, 1048
unassisted party, recovery of expenses by, **13**, 1077
urgency, situation of, **13**, 1048
Legal assistance
fundamental human right, Community law, **10**, 95
Legal capacity
See CHILD-CHILDREN; YOUNG PERSON
Legal certainty
principle of in EC law, **10**, 96
Legal Civil Service
Civil Service Commission General Regulations 1988 ..., **13**, 1393
code of conduct, **13**, 1398
complaints procedure, **13**, 1399
Crofters Commission, **13**, 1414

Legal Civil Service—*continued*
Crown Office, **13**, 1410
Deputy Solicitor, **13**, 1395
Diplomatic Service, **13**, 1392, 1393
disclosure of information, restrictions relating to, **13**, 1396
division of responsibility for areas of law, **13**, 1400
Divisional Solicitor, **13**, 1395
entrance conditions and requirements, **13**, 1393
  nationality of candidate, **13**, 1394
European Commission, service with—
  generally, **13**, 1419, 1421
  qualifications for appointment, **13**, 1420
European Community exchange schemes, **13**, 1424
European Council of Ministers, service with, **13**, 1419, 1422
European Court of Justice, service with, **13**, 1419, 1421, 1423, 1424
European Parliament, service with, **13**, 1419, 1422
Foreign and Commonwealth Office, **13**, 1392, 1393
functions, **13**, 1417
recruitment, eligibility for, **13**, 1416
generally, **13**, 1392
grades, **13**, 1395
Inland Revenue Board (Scotland), **13**, 1411
Lands Tribunal for Scotland, **13**, 1413
Legal Officer, **13**, 1395
Lord Advocate, departments under responsibility of, **13**, 1400
Lord Advocate's Department—
  generally, **13**, 1403
  Legal Secretaries to the Lord Advocate, **13**, 1403, 1404
  Scottish consolidation bills, drafting, **13**, 1405
  Scottish Parliamentary Counsel, **13**, 1403, 1405
nationality of candidates for, **13**, 1394
Office of the Solicitor to the Secretary of State for Scotland—
  conveyancing work, **13**, 1402
  functions, **13**, 1402
  generally, **13**, 1400, 1401
  litigation work, **13**, 1402
  primary legislation, preparation, **13**, 1402
  secondary legislation, preparation, **13**, 1402
Official Secrets Act, **13**, 1396
Overseas Development Administration, **13**, 1418
political activities, restrictions relating to, **13**, 1397
Principal Legal Officer, **13**, 1395
Red Deer Commission, **13**, 1415
Scottish Courts Administration—
  functions, **13**, 1406
  Lord Advocate's functions exercised by, **13**, 1406
  officials, **13**, 1406
  Secretary of State's functions exercised by, **13**, 1406
Scottish Land Court, **13**, 1412
Scottish Law Commission—
  functions, **13**, 1408
  law reform in Scotland, generally, **13**, 1407, 1408

Legal Civil Service—*continued*
Scottish Law Commission—*continued*
  legal staff, **13**, 1409
  ministerial responsibility, **13**, 1407
Secretary of State for Scotland, departments under responsibility of, **13**, 1400, 1401
Senior Principal Legal Officer, **13**, 1395
Solicitor, **13**, 1395
Legal education
admissions, growth in, **13**, 1122
aims and objectives, **13**, 1119–1121
canon law, influence of, **22**, 552
curriculum, future changes, **13**, 1123
Dark Ages, **22**, 514
Dutch influence, **22**, 603, 604, 606, 607
French influence, **22**, 603, 604, 605, 607
future changes, **13**, 1122–1125
generally, **13**, 1101
historical background—
  advocates—
    BL and LLB degrees, **13**, 1282
    educational requirements, **13**, 1262
    generally, **13**, 1260
    professional, **13**, 1261
    Roman law, **13**, 1261
  Bar, **13**, 1102
  Faculty of Advocates, **13**, 1102, 1103, 1244, 1248, 1256
  solicitors, **13**, 1103
  university law courses in Scotland, **13**, 1102, 1104, 1244, 1257, 1278, 1279, 1281–1283
  Writers to the Signet, **13**, 1103, 1104
Joint Standing Committee on Legal Education, **13**, 1163, 1164
judges, requirement of legal qualification, **22**, 630
landowners' duty to educate heirs, **22**, 514
Law Society of Scotland, powers, **13**, 1151
solicitor—
  Diploma in Legal Practice, **13**, 1164
  Law Society examinations, **13**, 1162
  training contract—
    assignment, **13**, 1170
    generally, **13**, 1169
    on-Diploma, **13**, 1165, 1168
    period of service under, **13**, 1165
    post-Diploma, **13**, 1165, 1167
    pre-Diploma, **13**, 1162, 1165, 1166
    registration, **13**, 1170
  university degree, **13**, 1161
technology, application of, **13**, 1124, 1125
university chairs of law, **13**, 1244
university law courses in Scotland, **13**, 1102, 1104, 1244, 1257, 1278, 1279, 1281–1283
  admissions, **13**, 1107
    disadvantaged applicants, **13**, 1113, 1114
    numbers, **13**, 1112
  applications, **13**, 1108
  BL and LLB degrees, **13**, 1282
  ethnic origins of intrants, **13**, 1110
  gender of intrants, **13**, 1111
  generally, **13**, 1107
  historical background, **13**, 1102, 1104
  research and teaching, **8**, 1007
  social composition, **13**, 1109

Legal education—*continued*
vocational training—
    contracts of training, **13**, 1117
    Diploma in Legal Practice, **13**, 1116, 1118
    fluctuations in numbers, **13**, 1118
    generally, **13**, 1115
See also UNIVERSITY
Legal and equitable estates
not recognised in Scots law, **24**, 2, 7
Legal literature
authoritative writings in Scots law—
    anomolous restrictions on acceptance, **22**, 443
    'authoritative'—
        meaning, **22**, 439
        canon of, **22**, 441
        generally, **22**, 439–441
        institutional writers, accuracy of description,
            22, 439
        judicial precedent in development of
            recognition, **22**, 440
        judicial recognition, **22**, 439, 440
        primary source of law, as, **22**, 439–441
    authority, meaning, **22**, 438–441
Bankton, *see* BANKTON, ANDREW MCDOUALL, LORD
Bell, *see* BELL, PROFESSOR GEORGE JOSEPH
cases, use in legal argument and legal writing, **22**,
    264
Craig, *see* CRAIG OF RICCARTON, SIR THOMAS
criteria for evaluation, **22**, 445
Erskine, *see* ERSKINE, PROFESSOR JOHN
feudal period, **22**, 512
formal source of Scots law, as, **22**, 433–445
French influence, **22**, 605
historical development in Scotland, **22**, 437
Hume, *see* HUME, BARON DAVID
institutional writers, *see* INSTITUTIONAL WRITERS
institutional writing—
    'authoritative writing' as preferred description,
        22, 439–441
    description, significance of, **22**, 433
    European context, **22**, 434
    'institutional', meaning, **22**, 439
    judicial recognition, **22**, 439, 440
    Justinian's *Institutes*, **22**, 434, 534
    primary source of law, **22**, 433, 439–441
    See also INSTITUTIONAL WRITERS
judicial precedent, effect on authoritative
    writings, **22**, 440
judicial recognition—
    authoritative writing in Scots law, **22**, 439, 440
    South African law, compared, **22**, 440
Kames, *see* KAMES, HENRY HOME, LORD
lawyers, meaning in context of, **22**, 438
learned journals, **22**, 445
Mackenzie, *see* MACKENZIE OF ROSEHAUGH, SIR
    GEORGE
Practicks of the Court of Session, **22**, 251, 253
primary source of law, **22**, 433
Quoniam Attachiamenta, **22**, 512, 627
Regiam Majestatem, **22**, 512, 627
Roman Dutch law, affinity with Scots law, **22**,
    436
Roman law, influence of, **22**, 554
scholarship, works of, **22**, 444

Legal literature—*continued*
secondary source of law, anomalous restrictions
    on acceptance, **22**, 443
Skene's *Auld Lawes and Constitutions of Scotland*,
    22, 627
source of law, as, **22**, 435, 623
South African law, judicial and statutory
    acceptance of 'Old Writers', **22**, 436, 440
Stair, *see* STAIR, SIR JAMES DALRYMPLE, VISCOUNT OF
textbooks, **22**, 443–445
Legal method
appeal to principle view—
    Dworkin, idea of legal principle, **22**, 620
    traditional emphasis of Scots law, **22**, 620
consistency, coherence and consequences,
    requirements of, **22**, 622
deductive reasoning, view, **22**, 618, 620
evidence, rules of, limitations on fact-finding, **22**,
    616
facts, and, **22**, 616
generally, **22**, 615–622
indeterminate law view, **22**, 619
law, and, **22**, 617
meaning, **22**, 615
public interest view, **22**, 621
reasoning, concept of—
    appeal to principle view, **22**, 621
    deductive, **22**, 618, 622
    indeterminate law view, **22**, 619
    legal system, in, **22**, 616
    public interest view, **22**, 621
Legal nuisance
See NUISANCE
Legal person/personality
children, of, **10**, 1014
donations, capacity to make and receive, **8**, 611
status or legal capacity, application of Judgments
    Convention, **8**, 432
Legal privilege
European Union, **4**, 1347
Legal profession
Act of Union 1707 ..., **13**, 1135
advocate, *see* ADVOCATE; FACULTY OF ADVOCATES
College of Justice, **13**, 1129, 1241
conveyancer, *see* CONVEYANCER
executry practitioner, *see* EXECUTRY PRACTITIONER
Joint Legal Committee, **13**, 1139, 1140
judge, *see* JUDGE
Law Society of Scotland, *see* LAW SOCIETY OF
    SCOTLAND
Legal Civil Service, *see* LEGAL CIVIL SERVICE
legal education, *see* LEGAL EDUCATION
local government, lawers in, *see* LOCAL
    GOVERNMENT
non-lawyer, *see* NON-LAWYER
notary public, *see* NOTARY PUBLIC
precedence, **16**, 2020
Procurator Fiscal Service, *see* PROCURATOR FISCAL
    SERVICE
professional immunity, **6**, 68
public service, in, **13**, 1392
Scottish Conveyancing and Executry Services
    Board, *see* SCOTTISH CONVEYANCING AND
    EXECUTRY SERVICES BOARD

Legal profession—*continued*
Scottish Law Commission, *see* SCOTTISH LAW
  COMMISSION
solicitor, *see* SOLICITOR
Legal Profession in Scotland
Consultation Paper 1989 ..., **13**, 1453
Legal representation
accused, rights of, **17**, 550
European Community law, fundamental human
  rights in, **10**, 95
sheriff court, in, **17**, 1003
small claims procedure, **17**, 1344
summary causes, **17**, 1299
Legal rights
See SUCCESSION
Legal sources
See FORMAL SOURCES OF LAW
Legal tender
bank notes, *see* BANK NOTES
coins, *see* COINS
creditor, payment of, **14**, 1823
demonitisation, **14**, 1819
generally, **14**, 1815
indexation, **14**, 1824
money, and, **14**, 1816
Scots currency, **14**, 1818
Scottish bank notes, **14**, 1817
statutory provisions, **14**, 1815
what constitutes, **13**, 1753
See also MONEY
Legal time
See TIME
Legate
precedence, **16**, 2014
Legatee
goods imported by, **7**, 1314
impersonation of, **11**, 748, 759
non-residuary, income tax, **25**, 984
Legis actio
system of procedure, **13**, 1128
Legislation
Acts of Parliament—
  operation, generally, **22**, 153–170
  See also ACT OF PARLIAMENT; STATUTE
Adjournal, Acts of, High Court of Justiciary—
  See also ACT OF ADJOURNAL
authority, **22**, 111
autonomic or autonomous, subordinate legislation,
  as, **22**, 194
British legislative ethos—
  consequences, **22**, 117
  Scots common law contrasted, **22**, 116
Church, amendment of, **5**, 687
concept—
  generally, **22**, 101–115
  legislation and contract, compared, **22**, 103–105
consolidation—
  1949 procedure for consolidation Bills, **22**, 699
  generally, **22**, 698–704
  meaning, **22**, 698
  on proposals of Law Commissions, **22**, 700
  repeal combined in single Bill with, **22**, 702
  Statute Law Committee, **22**, 698

Legislation—*continued*
consolidation—*continued*
  Statute Law (Repeals) Acts, **22**, 703
  Statute Law Revision Acts, **22**, 703
contract and—
  comparison, generally, **22**, 103–105
  contractual simulation of legislation, **22**, 106–
    108
  formal differences, **22**, 104
  generality of norms, **22**, 105
  parallel, **22**, 103
creation of, **5**, 385
Crown, historical role of, **22**, 523
custom contrasted, **22**, 109
definition, **22**, 101, 102, 523
delegated—
  debates in House on, **5**, 424
  generally, **22**, 523
  Standing Committees on, **5**, 425
  See also DELEGATED LEGISLATION
desuetude, doctrine of—
  ius commune recognition, **22**, 526
  post-Union statutes, whether applicable, **22**,
    526
  tacit repeal, pre-Union statutes, **22**, 526
drafting of, **5**, 540
duration, **2**, 605
earliest, **2**, 1
emancipation, *see* EMANCIPATION LEGISLATION
entrenchment of fundamental law by—
  elective dictatorship, **5**, 355
  human rights, **5**, 357
ersatz—
  bases, **22**, 225–228
  circulars, government—
    legality of guidance, **22**, 239, 240
    variety, **22**, 238
  coercion to enforce, **22**, 232
  consensus, **22**, 228
  coverage, **22**, 230, 231
  discretion—
    government departments, administration of
      laws, **22**, 227
    'quasi-legislative' character, **22**, 236
  economic policy, **22**, 226, 230
  generally, **22**, 223–246
  government contracts, **22**, 234–235
    See also CONTRACT
  government policy, **22**, 223, 224
  incomes policy, social contracts as vehicle, **22**,
    245
  Inland Revenue extra-statutory concessions
    22, 241–243
  insurance, government agreements as social
    contracts, **22**, 246
  legitimacy, public opinion, **22**, 233
  purpose, **22**, 224
  social contracts, **22**, 244–246
  'soft' law in international relations compared
    22, 224
  weakness, **22**, 229–233
European Communities—
  binding legislation, **22**, 523
  directives, **5**, 324

Legislation—*continued*
European Communities—*continued*
  generally, **5**, 324; **22**, 202–222
  implementation in United Kingdom, **22**, 221, 222
  Parliamentary control of—
    defects of, **5**, 326
    generally, **5**, 325
    regulations, **5**, 324
    Select Committee on, **5**, 426, 441
  See also EUROPEAN UNION LAW
foreign expropriatory, scope of application of, **17**, 333
form of Acts of Parliament, **22**, 116–119
  See also ACT OF PARLIAMENT
formal source of Scots law, as, **22**, 523–528
fundamental law entrenched by—
  elective dictatorship, **5**, 355
  human rights, **5**, 357
  generally, **22**, 501
  ipsissima verba, **22**, 113
  judicial review, **22**, 150
  justification, **22**, 112
  law and, **5**, 530
Law Commissions, *see* LAW REFORM; SCOTTISH LAW COMMISSION
legal advice and, **5**, 539
legality of, **5**, 358
Parliament—
  Scottish legislation, arrangements for, **5**, 531
  sovereignty of, **22**, 120
pre-Union—
  characteristics, **22**, 526
  generally, **22**, 525, 526
  repeal by desuetude, **22**, 526, 626
precedent contrasted, **22**, 110–115
prerogative—
  Act of Parliament, power to override or supersede, **22**, 171
  authority, **22**, 171
  delegation, subordinate legislation, **22**, 175
  generally, **22**, 523
  Order in Council, **22**, 171
  overlapping Act of Parliament, supersession by statute, **22**, 174
  primary legislation, as, **22**, 171, 173
  reviewability, **22**, 173
  scope, **22**, 172
  supersession by statute, **22**, 174
primary—
  Acts of Parliament, **22**, 153–170
  prerogative, **22**, 171–174
private, *see* PRIVATE LEGISLATION
private international law, legislation as source of, **17**, 112
progress of—
  amendments, admissibility of, **5**, 390
  House of Lords, in, **5**, 390
  information on, **5**, 390
  standing committee, **5**, 390
rationalisation—
  corpus of statutes, **22**, 118
  structure of individual statutes, **22**, 119
repeal, tacit, by desuetude—
  pre-Union statutes, **22**, 526

Legislation—*continued*
representations on, **5**, 385
retrospective, **5**, 311
revision, Law Commission responsibility, **22**, 704
royal charter, powers conferred on self-governing bodies corporate, **22**, 194
Scottish Law Commission recommendations resulting in, **22**, 696
Scottish Privy Council before 1707 ..., **22**, 524
Sederunt, Acts of—
  consolidation, **22**, 528
  Court of Session, origin of powers, **22**, 528
  supersession by Rules of Court 1936 ..., **22**, 528
  See also ACT OF SEDERUNT
select committees relating to, **5**, 439–441, 455–461
service law—
  civilians subject to, **2**, 614
  nature of, **2**, 605
specific contracts governed by, **17**, 289
statute—
  contract and—
    contracting out—
      avoidance distinguished, **22**, 122
      express conditions, **22**, 123
      implications of legislative intention, **22**, 124–128
      object of statute, implication from, **22**, 128
      public interest criterion, **22**, 125
  custom and—
    desuetude, doctrine of, **22**, 129
    generally, **22**, 129–133
    ius cogens and *ius dispositivum*, **22**, 121
    sources of law, as—
      Bankton, **22**, 131
      Erskine, **22**, 132
      Mackenzie, **22**, 130
      Stair's view of primacy of custom, **22**, 129
  generally, **22**, 523
  precedent and—
    Bankton, **22**, 136
    precedent as gloss on statute, **22**, 135, 136
    sources of law, generally, **22**, 134–143
    statutory abrogation, **22**, 141–143
    statutory endorsement, **22**, 137–140
  primary source of law, as, **22**, 523
  qualified presumption, **22**, 124, 126
  sources of Scots law, as, **22**, 525–528
  supremacy, **22**, 120
  wording of statute, implication from, **22**, 127
  See also ACT OF PARLIAMENT; STATUTE; STATUTORY SOURCES OF SCOTS LAW
Statute Law Committee, consolidation, **22**, 698
statutory abrogation of precedent—
  common law principles, **22**, 143
  generally, **22**, 141–143
  rule of law emerging from judicial decision, **22**, 141
statutory derogation of precedent—
  common law principles, from, **22**, 142
statutory endorsement of precedent—
  concept, **22**, 137
  doctrine, **22**, 138, 139
  presumption, **22**, 140

Legislation—*continued*

subordinate—

byelaws, *see* BYELAWS

codes of practice, statutory, **22**, 195–201

   See also CODES OF PRACTICE, STATUTORY

delegated powers, **22**, 175

European Communities legislation, implementation by, **22**, 221

generally, **22**, 175–201

meaning, **22**, 175

repeal of enabling Act, effect, **22**, 160

statutory instruments, **22**, 176–187

   See also STATUTORY INSTRUMENT

subordinate instruments not statutory instruments—

   autonomic/autonomous legislation, **22**, 194

   byelaws, **22**, 189–193

     See also BYELAWS

   status, **22**, 188

See also DELEGATED LEGISLATION

trading standards, **14**, 593

Union—

fundamental law, as—

   academic logic, **22**, 152

   assertion and proof, **22**, 151

   difficulties, Universities (Scotland) Act 1853 ..., **22**, 149

   generally, **22**, 144–146

   judicial review, competence, **22**, 150

   objections to thesis of—

     Dicey, **22**, 148

     institutional writers, **22**, 147

     political realism, **22**, 152

   treaty of 1707—

     application of legislation in Scotland, **22**, 527

     Union Agreement as constituent document, **22**, 145

   intention, **22**, 146

validity, **22**, 111

vested rights approach, **17**, 124

See also ACT OF PARLIAMENT; STATUTE

Legitim

division of, **25**, 700, 787

generally, **25**, 786

illegitimate child, right of, **25**, 699, 788

legacy held as surrogate for, **25**, 925

obligation to satisfy, **16**, 2116

potential claimant—

   provision for, **25**, 789

   statutory code, **25**, 790

reform, **25**, 1113

representation in, **25**, 700

tax planning device, as, **25**, 776

voluntary lifetime discharge, **25**, 807

See also LEGAL RIGHTS; SUCCESSION

Legitimacy

action of declarator of, Court of Session jurisdiction, **4**, 5

children, of—

   adultery of parents, **10**, 1167

   birth, at, **17**, 239

   generally, **10**, 1165

   immoveable property, exception relating to, **17**, 241

Legitimacy—*continued*

children, of—*continued*

   presumption of, **10**, 1166

   putative marriages, children of, **10**, 1168

   rape, child conceived as result of, **10**, 1169

   void marriages, children of, **10**, 1168

   voidable marriages, children of, **10**, 1170

decree of declarator, **19**, 1430

incidental finding of, sheriff court jurisdiction, **4**, 5

legitimation, *see* LEGITIMATION

status, action relating to, **4**, 68

Legitimate expectation

fairness, related to, **1**, 267

Legitimation

adopted child, of, **10**, 1167

generally, **10**, 1171

incidental finding of, jurisdiction of sheriff court, **4**, 5

letters of, **10**, 1172

per subsequens matrimonium, **10**, 1173

Scottish Law Commission recommendations, **22**, 691

status, action relating to, **4**, 68

Leisure

expenditure programme, **5**, 585

facilities, byelaws as to, **14**, 277

Leisure centres

See AMUSEMENT ARCADE

Leith

educational provision, **14**, 36

Lending body

building society's power to invest in and support, **3**, 369

Lenocinium

defence to charge of adultery, as, **10**, 917

meaning, **10**, 917

Lesion

reduction on grounds of, **13**, 44

Lessee

acceptance of lease, effect, **13**, 154

assignation, **14**, 1030, 1085

assignation of lease, **13**, 184

bankruptcy of, effect, **13**, 185

capital allowances, entitlement to, **14**, 1011

child as, **13**, 188

co-lessees, *jus quaesitum tertio*, **15**, 850

collateral contract, establishment of, **14**, 1087

compensation, entitlement to, **5**, 113

corporate body as, **13**, 190

curator as, **13**, 187

damages, termination when entitled to, **14**, 1065

delivery, obligations, of, **14**, 1044

diligence on, effect, **13**, 184

equipment becoming heritable, enforcement of obligations, **14**, 1072

executor as, **13**, 187

factor as, **13**, 187

heritable property affected by provisional order, **19**, 15

individual needs, tailoring lease to meet, **14**, 1016

insolvency of, effect, **13**, 185

joint lessees, **13**, 189

judicial factor as, **13**, 187

Lessee—*continued*
lessor, assignation of rights, **14**, 1085
meaning, **19**, 15*n*
novation, **14**, 1029
obligations of—
  delivery, **14**, 1044
  generally, **14**, 1043
  proper care of thing hired, **14**, 1047
  purpose for which hired, use for, **14**, 1046
  rent, payment of, **14**, 1045
  restoration of thing hired, **14**, 1048
overriding interest of, **6**, 739, 740
partnership as, **13**, 192
principal, **13**, 103
protection of, real rights, *see* REAL RIGHT
purchaser from, **14**, 1080
sequestration of, effect, **13**, 185
spouse as, **13**, 193
sub-hire, power to, **14**, 1091
sublease, of, **13**, 103
supplier—
  dealings with, **14**, 1083
  delictual liability, **14**, 1084
tax-deductible rentals, **14**, 1014
termination of contract—
  breach, common law rights of lessor, **14**, 1067
  damages, **14**, 1065
  insolvency, **14**, 1063
  minimum hiring clause, **14**, 1063
third party, involvement with—
  collateral contract, **14**, 1087
  delict, **14**, 1084
  generally, **14**, 1077
  ius quaesitum tertio, **14**, 1088
  lessor, **14**, 1085–1086
  liability of lessor, **14**, 1082
  lien, **14**, 1079
  purchaser from lessee, **14**, 1080
  remedies, **14**, 1081
  reputed ownership, **14**, 1078
  supplier, **14**, 1083
trust deed, grant by, **13**, 185
trustee as, **13**, 186
tutor as, **13**, 187
two or more tenants holding distinct *pro indiviso*
  shares, **13**, 189
unincorporated body as, **13**, 191
See also TENANT-TENANCY
Lessor
administrator for proprietor, as, **13**, 154
affixation to heritage—
  affixed goods, protection in respect of, **14**, 1076
  equipment becoming heritable—
    lessee's obligations, enforcement of, **14**, 1072
    relevant factors, **14**, 1073
    generally, **14**, 1071
    interests of other parties, **14**, 1075
    trade fixtures, **14**, 1074
agent as, **13**, 183
assignation of rights, **14**, 1085
attorney as, **13**, 154, 183
bankruptcy of, effect, **13**, 159
capital allowances, benefit obtained from, **14**,
  1011

Lessor—*continued*
child as, **13**, 168
contract, involvement in—
  assignation, **14**, 1030
  equipment already ordered, **14**, 1028
  equipment not yet ordered, **14**, 1027
  generally, **14**, 1026
  novation, **14**, 1029
  sale and lease-back, **14**, 1031
corporate body as, **13**, 177
Crown as, **13**, 181
curator as, **13**, 167
debtor as—
  bonds and dispositions in security, under, **13**,
    160, 162
  ex facto absolute disposition, under, **13**, 161
  generally, **13**, 160
  heritable creditors, **13**, 164
  standard security, under, **13**, 163
delivery—
  common law obligations, exclusion of, **14**, 1058
  obligations as to, **14**, 1039
derogation from grant, **13**, 241, 250, 253
diligence, effect, **13**, 158
executor as, **13**, 166
fiar as, **13**, 171
fiduciary fiar as, **13**, 170
fitness for purpose—
  common law obligations, exclusion of, **14**,
    1059
  obligations as to, **14**, 1042
guardian as, **13**, 167
heir of entail as, **13**, 172
heritable securities, effect, **13**, 160
insolvency of, effect, **13**, 159
joint proprietors as, **13**, 173
judicial factor as, **13**, 154, 167
leased goods, landlord's rights over, **14**, 1070
liferenter as, **13**, 154, 169
local authority as, **13**, 182
matrimonial home, entitled and non-entitled
  spouses, **13**, 174
new town development corporation as, **13**, 182
obligations of—
  delivery, **14**, 1039
  enjoyment, **14**, 1040
  fitness for purpose, **14**, 1042
  generally, **14**, 1038
  interference, **14**, 1040
  repair, **14**, 1041
partnership as, **13**, 180
pro indiviso proprietors as, **13**, 173
receiver as, **13**, 178
removings, action of, *see* REMOVINGS
repossession, right to effect, **14**, 1064
sale contract, enforcement of, **14**, 1086
sequestration, effect, **13**, 159
singular successors, *see* SINGULAR SUCCESSOR
supplier, failure to perform obligations, **14**, 1069
tax-deductible interest, **14**, 1014
tenant, as, **13**, 154
termination of contract—
  damages, **14**, 1066
  lessee's breach, due to, **14**, 1067

Lessor—*continued*
third party, involvement with—
  heritage, affixation to, **14**, 1071–1076
  landlord's nights, **14**, 1070
  lessee, parties who have dealt with, **14**, 1077–1082
  liability to, **14**, 1082
  remedies against, **14**, 1081
title—
  accretion, **13**, 156
  bad, **13**, 154
  generally, **13**, 154
  incomplete, granter holding, **13**, 155
  infeftment, **13**, 155, 156
  limited, **13**, 157
  registered, **13**, 155
  trustee as, **13**, 154, 165, 166, 170
  trustee for creditors, **13**, 176
  trustee in sequestration, **13**, 175
  tutor as, **13**, 167
  unincorporated body as, **13**, 179
See also LANDLORD
Letter
meaning, **16**, 1905*n*
overseas, meaning, **16**, 1905*n*
personal conveyance and delivery by sender, personal friend or messenger, **16**, 1905
Post Office monopoly over conveying—
  duties of Post Office, **16**, 1904
  exceptions, **16**, 1905
  exclusive privilege, **16**, 1905
  statutory position, **16**, 1904
private postal network, **16**, 1905
See also MAIL; POSTAL PACKET
Letter box
offences in relation to, **16**, 1911
Letter of comfort
binding, whether, **3**, 992
generally, **3**, 992
meaning, **3**, 992
Letter of consent
application procedure, **16**, 1239
entry clearance, as, **12**, 150; **16**, 1238
Letter of credit
acceptance, **4**, 238
anticipatory credit, **4**, 229, 233
application for, **4**, 222
autonomy, principle of, **4**, 244
back-to-back credit, **4**, 229, 231
background, **4**, 218
bill of exchange attached to, negotiation of, **4**, 218
buyer, *see* parties *below*
confirmation, **4**, 228
credit procedure—
  application, **4**, 222
  generally, **4**, 221
  issue, **4**, 223
  presentation, **4**, 224
  settlement, **4**, 225
deferred payment, **4**, 237
documents—
  banker's pledge, **4**, 258
  false, **4**, 257
  security of, **4**, 258

Letter of credit—*continued*
document—*continued*
  tender of—
    bills of lading—
      clean bills, **4**, 249
      description, **4**, 251
      other requirements, **4**, 252
      received for shipment bills, **4**, 250
      rules for, **4**, 248
      shipped bills, **4**, 250
    certificate of quality, **4**, 255
    false documents, **4**, 257
    generally, **4**, 247
    insurance documents, **4**, 254
    invoices, **4**, 253
    other documents, **4**, 256
generally, **3**, 989
indemnity, **4**, 245
irrevocable credits—
  confirmation, **4**, 228
  nature of, **4**, 227
  revocable credits distinguished from, **4**, 226
issue, **4**, 223
issuing bank, *see* parties *below*
meaning, **4**, 220
negotiation credit, **4**, 239
non-negotiability of, **4**, 103
parties—
  autonomy, **4**, 244
  buyer—
    issuing bank, relationship with, **4**, 241
    seller, relationship with, **4**, 240
  confirming bank, **4**, 243
  indemnity, **4**, 245
  issuing bank—
    buyer and, **4**, 241
    intermediary bank, relationship with, **4**, 242
    seller, relationship with, **4**, 243
  other relationships, **4**, 246
  payment under reserve, **4**, 245
  seller—
    buyer, relationship with, **4**, 240
    confirming bank, relationship with, **4**, 243
    issuing bank, relationship with, **4**, 243
payment—
  acceptance, **4**, 238
  deferred, **4**, 237
  generally, **4**, 235
  negotiation credit, **4**, 239
  sight, **4**, 236
payment under reserve, **4**, 245
presentation, **4**, 224
revocable credits—
  irrevocable credits distinguished from, **4**, 226
  nature of, **4**, 226
revolving credit, **4**, 229, 232
seller, *see* parties *above*
settlement, **4**, 225
sight payment, **4**, 236
standby letters of credit, **3**, 989; **4**, 229, 234
transferable credit, **4**, 229, 230
Uniform Customs and Practice for Documentary Credits—
  adoption of, **4**, 219

Letter of credit—*continued*
Uniform Customs and Practice for Documentary
 Credits—*continued*
 bills of lading, **4**, 248–252
 insurance documents, on, **4**, 254
 invoices, on, **4**, 253
 payment, rules on, **4**, 235
 standby credits covered by, **4**, 234
 standby letters of credit, rules on, **4**, 234
 tender of documents, on, **4**, 247
 transferable credit governed by, **4**, 230
Letter of intent
building contracts—
 effect, **3**, 22
 tendering, in relation to, **3**, 22
 work done by contractor on faith of, **3**, 22, 23
Letter of respectability
See LETTER OF COMFORT
Letters of attorney
printer's imprint, requirement not applicable, **17**, 3
Letters patent
armorial bearings, grant of, **6**, 1017
deed of trust, as, **24**, 27
Great Seal of Scotland, **7**, 874
Great Seal of the United Kingdom, **7**, 856, 859, 871
peerage, creation, **16**, 1305, 1309, 1312
 line of descent, statement of, **16**, 1309
uses, **7**, 859
Leucotomy
consent to, **14**, 1425
Level crossings
accommodation works, **19**, 1042
 maintenance of, **19**, 1033
barriers, **19**, 1032, 1034, 1034*n*
common law obligations at, **19**, 1035
construction, **19**, 1033
foggy conditions, **19**, 1035
footpaths, over, **19**, 1031
footways, over, **19**, 1031
gates, **19**, 1030, 1032*n*, 1033, 1034
 erection and maintenance, **19**, 1030
 gatekeeper, **19**, 1030, 1033, 1034
generally, **20**, 645
Level Crossings Act 1983 ..., **19**, 1034
lighting, **19**, 1032, 1035
lodges, **19**, 1033, 1034
maintenance, **19**, 1033
negligence, gatekeeper, by, **19**, 1033
person crossing, common law obligations, **19**,
 1035
private roads, over, **19**, 1031
protection, safety and convenience of users, order
 for, **19**, 1034
protective equipment, **19**, 1034, 1034*n*
public carriageways, over, **19**, 1030, 1032, 1033
shunting over forbidden, **19**, 1033
signs, **19**, 1032, 1034
speed of crossing trains, **19**, 1034, 1035
statutory provisions applying to British Railways
 Board, **19**, 1032
Leveraged lease
development, **14**, 1018
principles of, **14**, 1096
structure of, **14**, 1096

Lewd, indecent and libidinous practices
boy under eighteen, **7**, 309
child under puberty, towards, **3**, 1235, 1236; **7**,
 309, 310
child under seventeen, Schedule 1 offences, **3**, 1251
girl under sixteen, **7**, 309
Lewd performance
shamelessly indecent conduct, **7**, 83
Lex causae
ascertainment of, **17**, 146
changes in, **17**, 186
characterisation by, **17**, 140, 143
connecting factor, **17**, 122
lex fori, application of mandatory provisions of,
 17, 182, 183
limitations on application, **17**, 167
meaning, **17**, 110
polygamous marriage, and, **17**, 218
recharacterising property under, **17**, 318
renvoi, **17**, 155–157
Lex domicilii
capacity to marry, **17**, 140
meaning, **17**, 110
Lex fori
characterisation by—
 application of, **17**, 141, 166
 exceptions, **17**, 142
connecting factor, **17**, 147
evidence, governs matters of, **17**, 359
mandatory provisions, rule requiring application
 of—
 formal validity of contract, **17**, 259
 generally, **17**, 181
 illustrations of, **17**, 182
 limits of rule, **17**, 183
meaning, **17**, 110
procedure, governs matters of, **17**, 359, 361
renvoi, **17**, 156
unlawfulness by, **17**, 262
Lex loci celebrationis
capacity to marry, **17**, 140
formal validity of marriage prescribed by, **17**, 226
meaning, **17**, 110
nature of, **17**, 120
renvoi, **17**, 158
vested rights type approach, **17**, 124
Lex loci contractus
application of, **17**, 257
connecting factor, **17**, 146
meaning, **17**, 110
nature of, **17**, 120
vested rights approach, **17**, 124
Lex loci delicti commissi
meaning, **17**, 110
renvoi, **17**, 158
sea, delict at, **17**, 299
vested rights type approach, **17**, 124
Lex loci rei situs
meaning, **17**, 110
Lex loci situs
lease, application to, **13**, 228, 389
Lex loci solutionis
meaning, **17**, 110
unlawfulness by, **17**, 267

Lex patriae
meaning, **17**, 110
renvoi, **17**, 153
Lex situs
meaning, **17**, 110
moveables and immoveables distinguished, **17**, 314–317
nature of, **17**, 120
property, transfer of, **17**, 319, 330
transfer of ownership of moveables governed by, **17**, 138
vested rights type approach, **17**, 124
Lex ultimi domicilii
connecting factor, **17**, 146
meaning, **17**, 110
Liability
art and part, *see* ART AND PART
boarding house, **11**, 1742
  luggage, for, **11**, 1710
British Waterways Board, **19**, 1108–1110
canal undertaker, **19**, 1109
capacity-responsibility, **11**, 1054–1058
causation, *see* CAUSATION
civil—
  duty and, **11**, 1016
  health and safety at work, **9**, 538, 547
common law contempt of court, **6**, 323
concurrent and cumulative, **15**, 9
consumer protection, delictual liability, **15**, 196
corporate, *see* CORPORATE LIABILITY
councillor, of, **14**, 223
counsel, of, **13**, 1380
delictual—
  fraud for, **11**, 785
  generally, **14**, 1084, 2097
  third person, to, **9**, 903
discrimination, for, *see* EMPLOYMENT
edictal, **11**, 1702, 1741
employer, of, **9**, 904; **14**, 1507
  See also EMPLOYER
European Community directive, **6**, 39
exclusion clauses, **6**, 97–103
fault—
  categories of—
    conduct, **14**, 2087
    intent, **14**, 2087
    malice, **14**, 2087
    negligence, **14**, 2087
    recklessness, **14**, 2087
  wrong distinguished from, **14**, 2090
feuar, of, **14**, 2141
garage, **11**, 1742
harm—
  generally, **14**, 1003
  intentional, **14**, 2105
  negligent, **14**, 2106
  types of conduct creating, **14**, 2089
health and safety, *see* HEALTH AND SAFETY AT WORK
hotels—
  dog belonging to guest, act of, **11**, 1739, 1739*n*
  hotelkeeper, *see* HOTELKEEPER
  occupier of hotel, **11**, 1731
  private, **11**, 1709
landlord, of, for tenant's nuisance, **14**, 2140

Liability—*continued*
legal, capacity for, **11**, 1057
lessor, of, to third party, **14**, 1082
man-made nuisance, **14**, 2099
manufacturer, of—
  agricultural products, **6**, 40
  damaged products, **6**, 43
  dangerous or defective products, **6**, 37, 39, 41, 43, 44
  defences, **6**, 42
  development risk defence, **6**, 42
  economic loss, claim for, **6**, 38
  guarantees, **6**, 36
  limitation of actions, **6**, 44
  prescription of obligations, **6**, 44
messenger-at-arms, of, **14**, 1507
mineral lease, under, **14**, 1688
mines, manager of, **14**, 1608, 1609
non-contractual—
  European Community institution, actions against—
    fault, liability for, **10**, 225
    generally, **10**, 222
    grounds, **10**, 223
    loss, necessity of, **10**, 228
    loss and act, causal link between, **10**, 229
    maladministration, **10**, 226
    national authorities, claims against, **10**, 230
    time limit, **10**, 231
    without fault liability, **10**, 224
    wrongful legislative measures, **10**, 227
nuisance, **14**, 2017; **19**, 1245
  balancing process, determination as, **14**, 2040
  basis of, **14**, 2087
  intentional, **14**, 2095
  man-made, **14**, 2099
  owner's failure to abate, **14**, 2139
  several defenders contributing to, **14**, 2137
  source arising naturally, **14**, 2098, 2100
  strict liability, *see* STRICT LIABILITY
  tenant's nuisance, landlord's liability, **14**, 2140
  third person, created by, **14**, 2098
occupier, of—
  failure to abate, for, **14**, 2139
  hotel, of, **11**, 1731
  third person, nuisance by, **14**, 2142
  transfer of land, after, **14**, 2143
  See also OCCUPIER'S LIABILITY
participation, by—
  art and part liability, **7**, 177, 178
  generally, **7**, 177
  victim, art and part liability, **7**, 177, 178
power, and, **11**, 1087
private hotels, **11**, 1709
professional, *see* PROFESSIONAL LIABILITY
prohibition of exclusion or restriction of, **6**, 34
public house, **11**, 1742
railway undertaker, **19**, 1023
refreshment room, **11**, 1742
residential hotels, **11**, 1709
restaurant, **11**, 1742
Securities and Investments Board Core Conduct of Business Rules, **12**, 1376
sewer, inadequate, for, **14**, 2122

Liability—*continued*
sporting disasters, **19**, 1244
staff hostels, at, **11**, 1742
strict, *see* STRICT LIABILITY
sub-lessee, of, **14**, 1090
tenant, nuisance created by, **14**, 2140
third person, failure to abate nuisance created by,
    14, 2098
trade descriptions, **6**, 128
unregistered medical practitioner, of, **14**, 1104
vicarious—
    absolute and continuing obligation, **14**, 1618
    breach of instructions, **7**, 195
    company incurring, **4**, 318
    due diligence, defence of, **7**, 197
    employer, of, **7**, 194–197
    generally, **11**, 1055
    meaning, **7**, 194
    mens rea, **7**, 196
    owner cannot be absolved from, **14**, 1619
    statute law, **7**, 194
    statutory defences, **7**, 197
    vicarious responsibility, **7**, 194
weighing process, determination as, **14**, 2040
wrong, fault distinguished, **14**, 2090
wrongful act of constable, for, **14**, 493
Liaison Committee
appointment of, **5**, 445
functions of, **5**, 445
membership, **5**, 445
Libel
agreement or discrepancy with evidence, **10**, 746
Liberal Party
annual conference, **5**, 394
leader of, **5**, 394
organisation of, **5**, 394
Social Democratic Party, special relationship
    with, **5**, 394
Liberty
crime, detention on suspicion of, **15**, 438
European Convention on Human Rights, **15**, 435
interference with—
    child, removal from parent or guardian, **15**, 596
    wrongful detention, *see* DETENTION, WRONGFUL
legal protection, generally, **15**, 435
loss of—
    damages in respect of, **15**, 435
    detention, what constitutes, **15**, 436
    personal injury, **15**, 435
    time limit for actions, **15**, 435
right to—
    European Convention on Human Rights, **12**,
        6, 29–42
        arrest or detention, *see* ARREST OR DETENTION
        general rules, **12**, 29
        judicial person or body, right to be brought
            before, **12**, 30
    Universal Declaration of Human Rights, **12**, 4*n*
    rights contrasted, **11**, 1085
    state, deprivation by, **12**, 39
    voluntary limitation, **15**, 437
Liberum maritagium
feudal law, generally, **18**, 73
wardholding, as form of, **18**, 73

Library
copies of publications to be delivered to, **17**, 2, 5
copyright, permitted acts—
    export condition, copies required to be made
        as, **18**, 1119
    generally, **18**, 1115
    other librarians, making and supplying copies
        to, **18**, 1118
    published material, **18**, 1116
    replacement copies, making, **18**, 1119
    research and private study, making and
        supplying copies for, **18**, 1116, 1117
    unpublished material, **18**, 1117
expenditure programme on libraries, **5**, 585
libraries authority, **14**, 687, 689
local authority, *see* LOCAL AUTHORITY (library
    service)
National Library of Scotland, *see* NATIONAL
    LIBRARY OF SCOTLAND
penal establishment, in, **16**, 1457
public lending right, *see* PUBLIC LENDING RIGHT
reform of library provision, **14**, 51
university, compensation for lost privilege, **13**,
    1503
Licence
alcoholic liquor, *see* ALCOHOLIC LIQUOR
animal, premises used for, **14**, 524
    See also ANIMAL
atomic energy materials, *see* ATOMIC ENERGY AND
    RADIOACTIVE SUBSTANCES
attempts to transplant to Scots law, **13**, 771
betting licence, *see* BETTING
child in theatre, **9**, 1052
circuses, **9**, 1034
civic code—
    additional activities, **14**, 566
    appeal to sheriff, **14**, 544
    application—
        disposal of, **14**, 534
        grant, **14**, 532
        objections, **14**, 533
        register of, **14**, 542
        renewal, **14**, 532
        representations, **14**, 533
        successive, restriction on, **14**, 535
    boat hire, **14**, 560
    decisions—
        notification of, **14**, 543
        reasons, giving of, **14**, 543
    duration, **14**, 537
    generally, **14**, 529
    indoor sport, **14**, 563
    late hours catering, **14**, 564
    licensing authority—
        discharge of functions, **14**, 531
        generally, **14**, 530
    mandatory provisions, **14**, 548
    metal dealer, **14**, 559
    notification of changes and alterations, **14**, 538
    offences, **14**, 546, 547
    optional provisions, **14**, 549
    premises—
        entry, powers of, **14**, 545, 546
        inspection of, **14**, 545

Licence—*continued*
civic code—*continued*
  premises—*continued*
    licence holder, of, **14**, 545
    unlicensed, **14**, 546
    private hire car, *see* PRIVATE HIRE CAR
    private market, **14**, 562
    second-hand dealer, **14**, 558
    street trader, **14**, 561
    surrender, **14**, 541
    suspension, **14**, 540
    taxi, *see* TAXI
    temporary licence, **14**, 536
    variation, **14**, 539
    window cleaner, **14**, 565
  coal working, **14**, 1606
  commercial cinema, **9**, 1020
  copyright, *see* COPYRIGHT
  driving, *see* DRIVING LICENCE
  English term, **13**, 596, 626
  entertainment licence—
    appeal, **9**, 424
    public entertainment licence distinguished, **9**, 1020
  excise licence duty, **7**, 1001
    mechanically propelled vehicles, **7**, 1073–1078
    trade licence, **7**, 1074
    vehicle excise licence, **7**, 1074
  explosives, **14**, 520
  fishing boat, **11**, 195
  game, licence to deal in, *see* GAME
  game, licence to kill, *see* GAME
  gaming, *see* GAMING LICENCE
  gaming machine licence, **7**, 1080, 1085
  goods vehicles operator's, **20**, 494
  knacker's, **11**, 501, 513
  landowner, grant by, **18**, 195
  large goods vehicles driver's, **20**, 495
  lease distinguished, **12**, 1252
  liquor, *see* ALCOHOLIC LIQUOR
  local authority powers, generally, **14**, 515
  lotteries, **14**, 517
  meaning, **13**, 771
  milk, *see* MILK
  music and dancing, **9**, 1038
  nuclear installation, *see* NUCLEAR INSTALLATION
  oil production, *see* OIL
  Part VII protection, **13**, 771
  passenger-carrying vehicles driver's, **20**, 492
  personal—
    lease distinguished, **13**, 120
    meaning, **13**, 120
  petroleum-spirit, **9**, 847; **14**, 522
  prisoner, release on, **17**, 563
    See also PAROLE
  public entertainment, *see* PUBLIC ENTERTAINMENT
  public house, *see* LICENSED PREMISES; PUBLIC HOUSE
  public service vehicle driver's, *see* PUBLIC SERVICE VEHICLE
  public service vehicle operator's, *see* PUBLIC SERVICE VEHICLE
  refreshment, *see* REFRESHMENT LICENCE
  restaurant, *see* RESTAURANT
  road transport deregulation, **14**, 422

Licence—*continued*
  sea trout, dealing in, **14**, 566
  seals, *see* SEALS
  seamen's canteen *see* SEAMEN S CANTEEN
  sex shop, **14**, 119, 527
  slaughtermen, **11**, 513
  sports premises, **14**, 563; **19**, 1254
  sports requiring, **19**, 1238
  spray irrigation, **25**, 331
  taxi, *see* TAXI
  tree-felling, *see* TREES
  vehicle excise, *see* MOTOR VEHICLE
  venison, to deal in, *see* VENISON
  waste disposal, *see* WASTE
  whaling ships and whale oil factories, **11**, 237
  wild birds, killing or taking, **11**, 883
Licence agreement
  lease of dwelling house, **12**, 1252
Licence duties
  revenue, as, **19**, 1510
Licensed areas
  valuation for rating, **24**, 670
Licensed premises
  alteration—
    consent required, **2**, 64
    control of, **2**, 36
    material changes, **2**, 36
    offences in respect of, **2**, 71
    order by board for, **2**, 64, 71
  applications—
    types of, **2**, 32
  assured tenancy, exclusion from, **13**, 636, 640
  betting and gaming in, **2**, 76
  categories of, **2**, 8
  child or young person on, **3**, 1227
  children not admitted, **2**, 74
  closure order—
    board, by, **2**, 63
    grounds for, **2**, 63
    period of, **2**, 63, 67
    power to make, **2**, 63
    sheriff, by, **2**, 67
  conduct of, controlling, **2**, 98
  containers, presumption as to contents, **2**, 83
  controls—
    introduction and development, **2**, 1
    war-time, **2**, 1
  criminal activities in, **2**, 76
  early morning opening, **2**, 24
  emergency supply of alcohol outwith, **2**, 96
  employees, minimum age, **2**, 74
  entry—
    generally, **14**, 545, 546
    police powers, **2**, 68
  excisable liquor, for, tenure of, **11**, 1937, 1943
  exclusion orders, **2**, 82
  fire safety provisions, **2**, 48; **10**, 1473
  food hygiene certificate for, **2**, 46
  hours of opening, *see* ALCOHOLIC LIQUOR (permitted hours)
  meter charges, **25**, 536
  new towns, in, **2**, 17; **23**, 370
  noise, soundproofing, **2**, 47, 98
  orders by board respecting, **2**, 64

Licensed premises—_continued_
permitted hours, _see_ ALCOHOLIC LIQUOR
planning permission—
    certificate of, **2**, 44
    not required, when, **2**, 44
plans, lodging of, **2**, 38
police officers—
    drinking by, **2**, 78
    entry, powers of, **2**, 68
reconstruction—
    carrying on business during, **2**, 34
    consent required, **2**, 36
restriction orders, _see_ permitted hours _above_
sale etc, transfer of licence, **2**, 35
sale of liquor to young persons, **2**, 74
site only licence, **2**, 33, 38
special roads, on, **2**, 95
structural alterations order, **2**, 71
suitability, certificate of, **2**, 43
Sunday opening—
    control, **22**, 817
    local licensing board, powers, **22**, 817
tenancy of, **11**, 1937, 1943
valuation for rating, **24**, 671
See also PUBLIC HOUSE
Licensing authority
administrative nature of, **1**, 211
natural justice, observing rules of, **1**, 259
right to be heard before, **1**, 259
See also LICENCE
Lieber Code
war conduct, **19**, 707
Liechtenstein
reception of trust law in civil law jurisdiction, **24**, 125
Lieges
expenses, service on, **14**, 1504
messenger-at-arms, refusal to serve, **14**, 1504
sheriff officer, duty of, **14**, 1511
Lien
animals, no right over, **11**, 1757
auctioneer's, **20**, 896
breach or threatened breach of contract, cases of, **20**, 66
carrier's—
    British Railways Board powers, **3**, 700
    generally, **3**, 629
    luggage, over, **3**, 672
classes, **20**, 75
contract of deposit, and, **8**, 15, 15n
contract of sale not rescinded by, **20**, 881
custody—
    possession distinguished, **20**, 70
    relinquished by lien-holder, **20**, 67
decree obtained for price of goods, **20**, 877
expiry with loss of possession, **20**, 67, 74
extent of right given by, **20**, 73
extinction, **20**, 74
general, **13**, 1759
    advertisement, resting on, **20**, 78
    banker's lien, **20**, 81–85
        See also BANKER
    businesses and trades where recognised, **20**, 79
    characteristics, **20**, 78

Lien—_continued_
general—_continued_
    common law, **20**, 78
    express contract condition, **20**, 78
    factor's lien, **20**, 86–89
        See also FACTOR
    innkeeper's lien, **20**, 90–93
        See also INNKEEPER
    limits, **20**, 80
    meaning, **20**, 75
    solicitor's lien, **20**, 94–100
        See also SOLICITOR
    trade usage, **20**, 78
hotelkeeper's—
    generally, **11**, 1757
    true owner, against, **11**, 1757
hypothec distinguished, **20**, 68, 101
insolvency, cases of, **20**, 66
instalment contracts, **20**, 876
luggage, over, **11**, 1757
maritime, _see_ MARITIME LIEN
meaning, **20**, 7, 66, 872
motor vehicle—
    no right of lien over, **11**, 1757
    property left in, **11**, 1757
negotiable instument, seller accepting, **20**, 874
part delivery, **20**, 876
pledge distinguished, **20**, 14, 67, 84
possession—
    custody distinguished, **20**, 70
    expiry with loss of, **20**, 67, 74
    foundation of, **20**, 69
    lien incompatible with contract under which possession obtained, **20**, 71
    person obtained from must have real or apparant right to transfer property, **20**, 72
    right to, **18**, 127
    seller must be in possession of goods, **20**, 875
    what constitutes, **20**, 67
possessory—
    failure to relinquish where adequate security offered, **21**, 480
    maritime lien, priority of, **21**, 479, 479n
    priority over ships' mortgage, **21**, 185
    salvor's, **21**, 480
    shipowner's—
        bill of lading, express terms, **21**, 546
        breach of contract, where, **21**, 719
        demurrage, **21**, 686, 686n, 688
        freight, **21**, 656, 656n, 665
        general average contribution, **21**, 711
        time charterparty, **21**, 640, 664
        voyage charterparty, **21**, 612, 618, 688
    subsequent to maritime lien, **21**, 392
    whether _negotiorum gestor_ has right to, **15**, 128
property held for lien-holder by another, **20**, 67
ranking of, **20**, 309, 310
retention distinguished, **20**, 66
right of—
    effect, **13**, 95
    meaning, **13**, 95
    when exercisable, **13**, 95
right in security implied by law, **20**, 7
security for loan, as, **13**, 1759

Lien—*continued*
seller's right of, **20**, 870, 873
shares, over, **4**, 364
ship—
 common law, **20**, 299–303
 generally, **20**, 273, 297
 maritime lien, *see* MARITIME LIEN
 possessory lien over—
  common law, **20**, 299–303
  damage caused to British property by foreign ship, **20**, 297
  harbour authority, exercised by, **20**, 298
  ranking, **20**, 309
  salvage, for, **20**, 302
  ship repairer's lien, **20**, 300
   voluntary surrender of, **20**, 301
  statutory, **20**, 297, 298
  towage, for, **20**, 303
 statutory lien, **20**, 304–307
  arrest under, **20**, 304
  categories of dispute giving rise to claim under, **20**, 305
  creditor's rights compared, **20**, 306
ship engineer's lien, **20**, 77
solicitor's, **13**, 1193, 1194
special, **13**, 1759
 characteristics, **20**, 76
 circumstances in which invoked, **20**, 76
 meaning, **20**, 75
 specific instances of, **20**, 77
statutory, **21**, 482n
stoppage in transit—
 distinguished, **20**, 873
 seller's lien resumed by, **20**, 878
sub-sales, effect of, **20**, 880
surrender of part of property, **20**, 74
termination of, **20**, 877
waiver, **16**, 1638; **20**, 877
Lieutenancy
appointment of Lieutenant, **5**, 558
clerks of, **5**, 560
creation of office, **5**, 558
Deputy Lieutenant, **5**, 559
English background, **5**, 546
flag, **5**, 562
generally, **5**, 544
history, **5**, 544–547
insignia, **5**, 562
legislative background, **5**, 564
list of—
 Borders Region, **5**, 565
 Central Region, **5**, 565
 Dumfries and Galloway Region, **5**, 565
 Fife Region, **5**, 565
 generally, **5**, 565
 Grampian Region, **5**, 565
 Highland Region, **5**, 565
 Islands Areas, **5**, 565
 Lothian Region, **5**, 565
 Strathclyde Region, **5**, 565
 Tayside Region, **5**, 565
modern—
 establishment of, **5**, 548–565
 evolution of, **5**, 547

Lieutenancy—*continued*
modern—*continued*
 structure of, **5**, 548–565
pre-Union, in Scotland, **5**, 545
processions, **5**, 561
uniform, **5**, 562
See also LORD LIEUTENANT
Life
rebuttable presumption in favour of, **10**, 750
right to—
 difficulty of defining, **11**, 1092
 European Convention on Human Rights, **12**, 6, 25
 Universal Declaration of Human Rights, **12**, 4n
Life assurance
annuity contract, **12**, 807
assignation of policies, **6**, 594; **12**, 846, 847, 854
capital redemption contract, **12**, 807
company, appointed representative of, **12**, 1361
company insolvency, **12**, 814
contingency insurance, as, **12**, 804
contract, *jus quaesitum tertio*, **15**, 841
cover dependent on payment of first premium, **12**, 818
debtor's life insured by creditor, **12**, 854
disclosure, duration of duty of, **12**, 863
endowment policy, **12**, 804
 meaning, **12**, 804
Financial Services Act, application of, **12**, 804
friendly society, **12**, 686
generally, **12**, 854
income support, whether policy affecting, **21**, 1079
insurable interest, **12**, 853, 854
 requirement of, **12**, 848
investment business, **12**, 807
investments linked to, **12**, 804
marketing, regulation, **12**, 812
non-disclosure, **12**, 860
recoverable loss, **12**, 885
reduction of policy, **13**, 37
security subject, as—
 assignation, **20**, 61, 63
 contingent security, **20**, 61
 creditor, taken out by, **20**, 61
 existing policy, precautionary measures, **20**, 62
 independent security, **20**, 61
 insurable interest in life assured, **20**, 64
 ownership of policy on debtor's life, **20**, 65
taxation of gain under, **21**, 1329
temporary cover, **12**, 825; **21**, 1329
uncertainty, event insured against must contain element of, **12**, 804
whole life policy, meaning, **12**, 804
Life Assurance and Unit Trust Regulatory Organisation (LAUTRO)
generally, **12**, 1312
promotion and marketing of insurance products, **12**, 809
recognised self-regulating organisation, as, **12**, 1312
regulation of insurance intermediaries, **12**, 812

Life expectancy
missing person, **25**, 648
Life peerage
baron, **16**, 1312
child of life peer, mode of address, **16**, 1322
degrees of rank, **16**, 1312
former peer, conferred on, **16**, 1314
generally, **16**, 1312
House of Lords, attendance at, **16**, 1312
See also HOUSE OF LORDS; PEERAGE
Life sentence
discretionary, **16**, 1477
prisoner serving, **16**, 1447
   release on compassionate grounds, **16**, 1471
Lifeboat
fuel, excise duty relief, **7**, 1069
provision of, regulations as to, **21**, 216, 217
vehicle, excise duty exemption, **7**, 1073
wreck endangering, power to remove, **21**, 514
Lifeboatman
salvage award, entitlement to claim, **21**, 460
Liferent
agricultural land, **13**, 1639
alimentary, **12**, 1264; **24**, 80
   adopted child, **13**, 1656
   constitution, **13**, 1617
   death of liferenter, **13**, 1655
   estate must be beyond control of liferenter, **13**, 1617
   excessive endowment, **13**, 1617
   failure, **13**, 1656
   loss of alimentary nature, **13**, 1656
   meaning, **13**, 1611
   refusal, **13**, 1655
   renunciation, **13**, 1655
   revocation, **13**, 1655; **24**, 81, 82
   termination, **13**, 1655
   trustees, **13**, 1617
   variation, **24**, 81, 82
allernarly, **13**, 1629
ambiguity of deed, **13**, 1618–1621
annuity distinguished, **13**, 1606
ante-nuptial, date of deed, **13**, 1631
beneficial liferenter, **18**, 93
beneficiary's right to, **24**, 45, 53
classification, **13**, 1607–1611
confusion, termination on, **13**, 1647, 1650
consolidation, termination on, **13**, 1647, 1650
constituent—
   meaning, **13**, 1603
   proper liferent, **13**, 1608
constitution—
   alimentary liferent, **13**, 1617
   formalities, **13**, 1612
   proper liferent, **13**, 1613–1615
   trust liferent, **13**, 1616
conventional, **13**, 1607
courtesy, **13**, 1607; **18**, 74
   abolition, **13**, 1607
   meaning, **13**, 1607
creation—
   generally, **25**, 770
   registered interest in land, over, **6**, 714
date of deed, **13**, 1631

Liferent—*continued*
date of operation of deed, **13**, 1632
death, termination on, **13**, 1647, 1648, 1654*n*, 1655
destinations—
   children, to—
      allernarly liferent, **13**, 1629
      Dobie's table, **13**, 1622
      generally, **13**, 1626
      legatees, descriptive terms, **13**, 1627
      unascertainable heir, **13**, 1628, 1629
      unborn children, **13**, 1628, 1629
   confusio, doctrine of, **13**, 1624
   Dobie's table, **13**, 1622
   joint liferent, **13**, 1622–1624
   spouses, to—
      Dobie's table, **13**, 1622
      generally, **13**, 1625
   strangers, to, **13**, 1622–1624
      Dobie's table, **13**, 1622
division per stirpes, **25**, 890
divorce, termination on, **13**, 1658
duration, **13**, 1605
escheat, **18**, 84
extension, **13**, 1621
fealty, and, **18**, 74
fee, meanings, **13**, 1603
feudal law, reservation, **18**, 55
fiar, *see* FIAR
general law of, **13**, 1610
historical background, **13**, 1601, 1601*n*
improper, **18**, 5, 74, 93
infeft, man dying, **18**, 74
investiture, **18**, 74
   renewal, **18**, 74
joint or conjunct—
   destinations, **13**, 1622–1624
   spouses, destinations to, **13**, 1625
landlord's hypothec, **13**, 514
lease, and, **13**, 114, 393
legal, **13**, 1607; **18**, 74
   abolition, **13**, 1607
liferenter, *see* LIFERENTER
limitation, **13**, 1621
marriage settlement, liferent created by—
   termination, **13**, 1658
meaning, **13**, 1601, 1602; **18**, 74
mortis causa—
   date of deed, **13**, 1631
   date of operation of deed, **13**, 1632
   death-bed estate, proportion covered by liferent, **13**, 1637
possession—
   defence of, generally, **18**, 174
   right to, **18**, 127, 151
prescription, termination on, **13**, 1647, 1653
proper, **13**, 1601, 1607; **18**, 74; **19**, 1639, 1640
   ambiguity in construction, **13**, 1618
   ambiguity of deed, **13**, 1618–1621
      'Cochrane's rules', **13**, 1619, 1621
   assignation of income, **13**, 1646
   bipartite legal interest in, **13**, 1603
   'Cochrane's rules', **13**, 1621
   constitution, **13**, 1613–1615

Liferent—*continued*
proper—*continued*
destination, **13**, 1618
fiar—
full fee going to, **13**, 1634
rights of, **13**, 1660
general law of liferent, **13**, 1610
heritable property, rights of liferenter, **13**, 1639
inter vivos deed, creation by, **13**, 1608
interpretation, **13**, 1618
joint liferenters, **13**, 1624
legal relationships constituted by, **13**, 1608
liferenter, rights of, **13**, 1634
mortis causa deed, creation by, **13**, 1608
parties to, **13**, 1608
real right, as, **18**, 5
reservation, by, **13**, 1608
constitution, **13**, 1615
restriction on creation, **13**, 1631
simple, **13**, 1608
constitution, **13**, 1614
delivery, **13**, 1614, 1614*n*
subject matter, **13**, 1614
termination—
confusion or consolidation, by, **13**, 1647, 1650
death, on, **13**, 1647, 1648
destruction of subject, on, **13**, 1647, 1652
event, on occurrence of, **13**, 1647, 1651
prescription, by, **13**, 1647, 1653
renunciation, by, **13**, 1647, 1649
title to sue, liferenter's right, **13**, 1635
twin interests model, **13**, 1608
property subject to—
agricultural property relief, **19**, 1562
variation of distribution of estate, **19**, 1639
real right, as, **11**, 1110
renunciation, **13**, 1647, 1649, 1655, 1657
restrictions on creation—
anti-accumulation provisions, **13**, 1633
deed executed on or after 25 November 1968 ..., **13**, 1632
deed executed before 25 November 1968 ..., **13**, 1631
generally, **13**, 1630
right of occupancy distinguished, **13**, 1606
servitude granted by liferenter, **18**, 449
subject matter—
accidental damage to, **13**, 1645, 1645*n*
bipartite legal interest in, **13**, 1603
competent and incompetent, **13**, 1604, 1604*n*
destruction of, termination of liferent on, **13**, 1647, 1652
enjoyment of subject must not reduce, diminish or destroy it, **13**, 1604
heritable property, **13**, 1639
legal ownership in trust liferent, **13**, 1603
liability of liferenter, **13**, 1645
liferenter's right of enjoyment, **13**, 1638
moveable property, **13**, 1640
proper liferent, **13**, 1603
simple proper liferent, **13**, 1614
subject matter, **13**, 1604
wear and tear, **13**, 1645, 1645*n*

Liferent—*continued*
subordinate real right, as, **18**, 534
successive, restraints on, **25**, 770
superiority—
including, **13**, 1639
liferenter, **18**, 74
tenancy, tacit relocation not applicable, **13**, 452
terce, **13**, 1607; **18**, 74
abolition, **13**, 1607
kenning, **18**, 74
meaning, **13**, 1607
termination—
alimentary liferent, **13**, 1655
confusion or consolidation, by, **13**, 1647, 1650
death, on, **13**, 1647, 1648, 1654*n*, 1655
destruction of subject, on, **13**, 1647, 1652
divorce, on, **13**, 1658
event, on occurrence of, **13**, 1647, 1651
marriage settlement, liferent created by, **13**, 1658
prescription, by, **13**, 1647, 1653
proper liferent, **13**, 1647–1653
refusal, by, **13**, 1655
renunciation, by, **13**, 1647, 1649, 1655, 1657
revocation, by, **13**, 1655
specified event, on, **13**, 1605
trust liferent, **13**, 1654
trust, **13**, 1601, 1607; **18**, 5
alimentary, **13**, 1611
ambiguity of deed, **13**, 1618–1621
anti-accumulation provisions, **13**, 1633
assignation of income, **13**, 1646
'Cochrane's rules', **13**, 1621
constitution, **13**, 1616
construction, ambiguity of deed, **13**, 1618
death, by, **13**, 1654*n*
delivery, **13**, 1616
destination, **13**, 1618
execution, **13**, 1616
failure of purposes, **13**, 1654
fiar, **13**, 1609
rights of, **13**, 1662
general law of liferent, **13**, 1610
heritable property, rights of liferenter, **13**, 1639
imprescriptable nature, **13**, 1654
interpretation, **13**, 1618
joint liferenters, **13**, 1624
legal ownership of subject matter, **13**, 1603
legal relationships constituted by, **13**, 1609
liferenter, **13**, 1609
rights of, **13**, 1634
restriction on creation, **13**, 1631
termination, **13**, 1654
generally, **13**, 1654
title to sue, liferenter's right, **13**, 1636
transfer, **13**, 1616
trust *simpliciter* compared, **13**, 1610
trustees, **13**, 1603, 1609
action against raised by liferenter, **13**, 1636
dominium vesting in, **13**, 1636
twin interests model, **13**, 1608
written deed, necessity for, **13**, 1612
Liferenter
accumulation of income, **24**, 37
acquiescence by, **16**, 1616

Liferenter—*continued*
beneficial, **18**, 93
capital, encroaching on to benefit, **25**, 923
civil possession by, **18**, 121
conceived after deed comes into operation, **13**, 1632
death—
  alimentary liferent, termination by, **13**, 1655
  before termination of liferent, **13**, 1605
  joint liferenter, rights of, termination on, **13**, 1623
disappearance of, **24**, 71
fixtures fitted by, ownership, **18**, 582
joint, right of, termination on death, **13**, 1623
jus habendi, **13**, 1619
lessor, as, **13**, 154, 169
liabilities of, **13**, 1645
meaning, **13**, 1603
must be alive at date of deed, **13**, 1631
possession through, **16**, 2108
proper, **13**, 1634
  heritable property, **13**, 1639
  title to sue, **13**, 1635
proper liferent, **13**, 1608
proprietor, as, **24**, 444
real burden, liability for, **18**, 413
rights of—
  assignation of income, **13**, 1646
  bank deposits, enjoyment of, **13**, 1641
  business profits, enjoyment of, **13**, 1643
  death-bed estate, proportion covered by liferent, **13**, 1637
  general nature, **13**, 1634
  heritage, enjoyment of, **13**, 1639
  liferented subject, enjoyment of, generally, **13**, 1638
  literary works, enjoyment of, **13**, 1643
  moveables, enjoyment of, **13**, 1640
  real right, **13**, 1603, 1608
  stocks and shares, enjoyment of, **13**, 1642
  title to sue—
    proper liferent, **13**, 1635
    trust liferent, **13**, 1636
servitude granted by, **18**, 449
shooting lease by, **11**, 898
superiority, **18**, 74
trust, **13**, 1601, 1609, 1634
  action raised against trustees, **13**, 1636
  heritable property, **13**, 1639
  title to sue, **13**, 1636
Lift
affixation to heritage, **14**, 1071
belonging, test of, **14**, 1013
telecommunications apparatus installed in, **16**, 1949
Light
access to, no natural right to, **14**, 2032
building work blocking, **3**, 155
res communes, as, **18**, 282
right of, **11**, 1109
right to—
  building abutting public road, **18**, 359, 359*n*
  law of the tenement, **18**, 236
  tenement buildings, **18**, 359, 486
  urban servitude, as, **18**, 483, 486

Lighter, mechanical
excise duty, **7**, 1097
Lightering
carrier utilised for, liability, **21**, 560
Lighters
discharge of cargo into, **21**, 632, 632*n*
  laytime, **21**, 670*n*
Lighthouse
Commissioners of the Northern Lights, **11**, 1322
sheriff's duties in respect of, **6**, 1046
Lighthouse authority
salvage award, entitlement to claim, **21**, 459
wreck, removal of, **21**, 514
Lighting
plant, whether, **14**, 1012
tolerable standard, **11**, 1979
wild birds or animals taken or killed with artificial lighting, **11**, 880, 884
Limitation of actions
acquiescence, *mora* and taciturnity, **16**, 2207
alteration in designation of defender, **16**, 2185
carriage of persons and property—
  air, by, **16**, 2200
  generally, **16**, 2134
  rail, by, **16**, 2201
  road, by, **16**, 2202, 2203
  sea, by, **16**, 2204, 2205
decree passed against defender, **16**, 2133
defamation and related actions—
  accrual of right of action, **16**, 2174
  application of provisions, **16**, 2173
  commencement, **16**, 2172, 2175
  convicium, **16**, 2173
  death of defamed party, **16**, 2174
  defamation, definition, **16**, 2173
  disregard provisions, **16**, 2175
  executor as pursuer, **16**, 2174
  limitation period—
    computation, **16**, 2172, 2175
    generally, **16**, 2172
    judicial discretion to override, **16**, 2176–2185
  malicious falsehood, **16**, 2173
  nonage, **16**, 2172, 2175
defender, plea must be taken by, **16**, 2133
delictual claim, **17**, 297
discharge of contract, **17**, 276
European Commission, **4**, 1355
historical background, **16**, 2134
hotelkeeper's liability, of, *see* HOTELKEEPER
ignorance of right to raise proceedings, **16**, 2185
justification for rules, **16**, 2135
manufacturers' liability, **6**, 44
meaning, **16**, 2133
mora—
  defence, as, **16**, 2206
  mora, taciturnity and acquiescence, **16**, 2207
negative prescription distinguished, **16**, 2133
personal injury, rules relating to—
  alteration to pleading—
    adjustment, **16**, 2156
    amendment, **16**, 2157, 2159, 2160
    basis of case, change in, **16**, 2161
    generally, **16**, 2155
    Pompa's Trustees, principles in, **16**, 2158

Limitation of actions—*continued*
personal injury, rules relating to—*continued*
  alteration to pleading—*continued*
    radical incompetence, where, **16**, 2160
    substitution by right defender, **16**, 2159
    technical irregularity, where, **16**, 2160
    trivial error in designation, where, **16**, 2159
  causation of injury, **16**, 2152
  commencement of action, **16**, 2146
  contraction date impossible to determine,
    where, **16**, 2137
  date injury sustained—
    determination, **16**, 2148
    generally, **16**, 2147
    no clearly defined date, where, **16**, 2148
  date of knowledge, determination, **16**, 2149
    test, **16**, 2150
  death of injured party, where—
    curator as pursuer, **16**, 2168
    executor as pursuer, **16**, 2165, 2168
    extinction of right, **16**, 2171
    generally, **16**, 2137, 2138, 2162, 2163
    judicial factor as pursuer, **16**, 2168
    legal disability, pursuer under, **16**, 2162, 2170
    limitation period, **16**, 2162
      commencement, **16**, 2167–2169
    product liability actions, **16**, 2192–2197
    relative—
      meaning, **16**, 2164
      pursuer, as, **16**, 2168
      rights of, **16**, 2165
    relevant facts, **16**, 2169
    solatium, damages by way of, **16**, 2165
    time bar, **16**, 2171
  defender, identity, **16**, 2153
  delay in proceedings where improvement
    hoped for, **16**, 2151
  disregard provisions, **16**, 2154, 2170
  evolution—
    generally, **16**, 2134, 2136
    Law Reform (Limitation of Actions, etc) Act
      1954: **16**, 2137
    Prescription and Limitation (Scotland) Act
      1973: **16**, 2139
    Scottish Law Commission report 1965 ...,
      16, 2138
    Scottish Law Commission report 1983 ...,
      16, 2140
    Scottish Law Commission report 1989 ...,
      16, 2141
  generally, **16**, 2134
  judicial discretion, **16**, 2139
  justifiable ignorance, injured party in state of,
    16, 2149
  justification, **16**, 2135
  legal disability, injured party under, **16**, 2137,
    2138, 2141, 2142, 2154
  limitation period—
    commencement, **16**, 2146–2153
    commencement of action, **16**, 2146
    computation, **16**, 2142, 2145
    duration, **16**, 2145, 2146
    judicial discretion to override time limits, **16**,
      2176–2185

Limitation of actions—*continued*
personal injury, rules relating to—*continued*
  personal injury, definition, **16**, 2143
  Prescription and Limitation (Scotland) Act
    1973—
    generally, **16**, 2139
    section 17, application, **16**, 2142
  pursuer—
    assignation of claim by, **16**, 2150
    curator *ad litem* as, **16**, 2150
    executor as, **16**, 2150
    generally, **16**, 2144
    injured party as, **16**, 2150
    judicial factor as, **16**, 2150
  seriousness of injury, **16**, 2151
  terminus a quo, **16**, 2137
  time bar, **16**, 2137, 2151, 2171
    judicial discretion to override, **16**, 2176–2185
  who may bring action, **16**, 2144
prescription, and, **16**, 2101
prescription distinguished, **16**, 2133
private international law, **16**, 2198, 2199
product liability defects—
  application of limitation provisions, **16**, 2187,
    2192
  commencement, **16**, 2189, 2194
  death—
    defect not resulting in, **16**, 2187–2191
    defect resulting in, **16**, 2192–2197
  disregard provisions, **16**, 2190, 2195
  extinction of right of action, **16**, 2196
  generally, **16**, 2186
  legal disability, pursuer under, **16**, 2190, 2195
  liability, **16**, 2186
  limitation period—
    duration, **16**, 2188, 2193
    extension of time limit, **16**, 2191, 2197
Scottish Law Commission recommendations, **22**,
  672
solicitor, failure to commence action within time
  limit, **16**, 2182, 2184
taciturnity, *mora*, and acquiescence, **16**, 2207
time bar, **16**, 2137, 2151, 2171
  judicial discretion to override—
    alternative remedy, where, **16**, 2182, 2184
    appeal, right of, **16**, 2183
    application of discretionary power, **16**, 2177
    facts before the court, decision to be reached
      on, **16**, 2181
    generally, **16**, 2176, 2178, 2182, 2185
    interests of both parties, **16**, 2180
    onus of proof, **16**, 2179
    pursuer deriving title from injured party, **16**,
      2177
    when discretion exercisable, **16**, 2185
  solicitor failing to commence action within, **16**,
    2182, 2184
Limitation clause
contract, in, **15**, 718
definition, **15**, 718
Limited company, see COMPANY
Limited partnership
assignation of share by, **16**, 1119
bankruptcy of partner, **16**, 1120

Limited partnership—*continued*
body corporate as, **16**, 1113, 1120
changes in—
  advertisement, **16**, 1117
  liability of partners, change in, **16**, 1116
  notice of, **16**, 1116
  registration, **16**, 1116
choice as business medium, **16**, 1004
constitution, **16**, 1111–1113
dissolution, *see* PARTNERSHIP (dissolution)
firm name, **16**, 1114
formation, **16**, 1111–1114
general partner, **16**, 1113
  limited partner, becoming, **16**, 1116, 1117
  powers, **16**, 1118
general partners, **16**, 1113, 1116, 1117
generally, **16**, 1110, 1113, 1116, 1117
limited partner, **16**, 1113
  assignation of share of, **16**, 1117
  disposal of interest by, tax treatment, **16**, 1142
  general partner, becoming, **16**, 1116, 1117
  powers, **16**, 1118
    dissolution, as to, **16**, 1120
management—
  assignation of share by limited partner, **16**, 1119
  differences arising between partners, settlement, **16**, 1118
  powers, generally, **16**, 1118
mental disorder of partner, **16**, 1120
mental incapacity of partner, **16**, 1120
number of partners, **16**, 1112
powers, **16**, 1118
  dissolution, as to, **16**, 1120
private company as alternative to, **16**, 1110
registration, **16**, 1115
  false statements, **16**, 1115
  fee, **16**, 1115
  firm name, change in, **16**, 1114
  notice of changes, **16**, 1116
  records to be kept, **16**, 1115
sequestration, **2**, 1321, 1486
statutory provisions, **16**, 1110
tax treatment, **16**, 1142
Lindsay on the Mount, Sir David
armorial by, **11**, 1602
Liner
meaning, **21**, 524
Liner conference
Convention on a Code of Conduct for Liner Conferences, **21**, 118
generally, **21**, 118
meaning, **21**, 527
Linlithgow
Court of Four Burghs, **14**, 13
Linseed oil
weights and measures legislation, **6**, 244
Liquidated damages clause
contractually stipulated, *see* CONTRACT
Liquidation
adjudication and, **8**, 211
administration, comparison with, **4**, 612
administration order, *see* COMPANY
arrestment and, **8**, 294

Liquidation—*continued*
background in Scotland, **4**, 308
Bankruptcy (Scotland) Act 1985 ..., **4**, 308
building contractor, of, **3**, 162n
building society, of, **3**, 392
capital profits, relating to, **25**, 41
claim in, **14**, 257
committee, *see* LIQUIDATION COMMITTEE
Companies Act 1989 ..., **4**, 310
continuous employment, effect on, **9**, 49
contract, effect on—
  no automatic termination, **4**, 859
  repudiation, right of, **4**, 860
  rescission, right of, **4**, 860
Cork Committee, **4**, 308
court, winding up by, *see* WINDING UP
Court of Session, jurisdiction of, **4**, 15
Crown preferences for tax, **8**, 129
diligence distinguished, **8**, 106
expenses, **17**, 1190
floating charge, *see* FLOATING CHARGE
hope value, **25**, 23
inhibition and, **8**, 182
Insolvency Act 1985 ..., **4**, 308
international dimension, **4**, 311
irritancy following, **13**, 584
legislation, **4**, 307
liquidator, *see* LIQUIDATOR
maills and duties, and, **8**, 399
occupational pension scheme, need for independent trustee, **21**, 1266–1272
poinding and, **8**, 239
principal debtor, of, **3**, 922
real poinding, and, **8**, 370
receiver, *see* RECEIVER
sequestration for rent, and, **8**, 388
shareholder, rights of, **25**, 13
sheriff court, jurisdiction of, **4**, 15
Third Party (Rights Against Insurers) Act 1930, application, **12**, 904–910
transmission of claim on, **15**, 606
trustee's, beneficiaries' rights, **24**, 49, 50
vesting of company property in liquidator, judicial conveyance, as, **18**, 664
voluntary, **4**, 380
voluntary arrangement, *see* COMPANY
voluntary winding up, *see* VOLUNTARY WINDING UP
winding up, *see* WINDING UP
Liquidation committee
establishment, **4**, 778
functions, **4**, 778
powers, **4**, 778
Liquidator
actions, power to bring or defend, **4**, 765
administrator, relationship with, **4**, 638
associate, transactions with, **4**, 895
bankrupt estate, trustee on, powers of, **4**, 769
bill of exchange, powers relating to, **4**, 127
committee, powers exercisable with sanction of, **4**, 770
company cannot be appointed, **4**, 318
corrupt inducement affecting appointment of, **4**, 922

Liquidator—*continued*
court—
 general control by, **4**, 767
 powers exercisable with sanction of, **4**, 770
debtor's contracts, title to sue, **15**, 821
delict, title and interest to sue, **15**, 230
financial markets, operation of, **4**, 771
functions, **4**, 763
getting in company's property, **4**, 768
insider dealing rules, **12**, 1528
interim—
 administration, following, **4**, 761
 appointment of, **4**, 759
 contributories, first meeting of, **4**, 760
 creditors, first meeting of, **4**, 760
 early dissolution, order for, **4**, 762
 voluntary arrangement, following, **4**, 761
joint appointments, **4**, 774
member's liability, enforcement of, **4**, 343
owner, as, **14**, 1602
personal bar, **16**, 1607
personal rights, and, **18**, 694
powers exercisable without sanction, **4**, 766
provisional liquidator—
 appointment, **4**, 746
 functions, **4**, 748
 qualification, **4**, 747
 remuneration, **4**, 749
 termination of appointment, **4**, 750
public examination of officers, **4**, 773
receiver, relationship with, **4**, 709
release, **4**, 777
removal from office, **4**, 776
remuneration, **4**, 775, 814
restrictions on powers of, **4**, 771
sale of, **4**, 850
statement of affairs, requirement relating to, **4**, 772
style, **4**, 764
submission to arbitration, in, **2**, 412
title, **4**, 764
vacation of office, **4**, 776, 793
validity of acts, **4**, 774
voluntary arrangement proposed by—
 another insolvency practitioner as nominee, **4**, 586
 liquidator as nominee, **4**, 585
voluntary winding up, *see* VOLUNTARY WINDING UP
winding up by court, *see* WINDING UP
Liquor
See ALCOHOLIC LIQUOR
Liquor licence
See ALCOHOLIC LIQUOR
Lis pendens
plea, basis of, **4**, 65
Listed building
advertisement on, control of, **23**, 196
alteration of, **23**, 180
appeals against refusal of listed building consent, **23**, 184
building preservation notice, **23**, 181
dangerous structure, declared to be, **23**, 181
demolition of, **11**, 1983; **23**, 73, 180

Listed building—*continued*
development of, **23**, 180
emergency works, **23**, 181
enforcement notice, **23**, 187
extension of, **23**, 180
grants and loans, **23**, 183
listed building consent—
 application for, **23**, 180
 Crown land, **23**, 105, 107, 180
 meaning, **23**, 180*n*
 purchase notice, giving rise to, **5**, 95; **23**, 185, 311
 refusal of—
  appeals against, **23**, 184
  compensation for, **23**, 186
 when required, **23**, 180
listing of buildings, generally, **23**, 179
meaning, **23**, 179
offences, **23**, 188, 283
penalties, **23**, 188
repair of, **23**, 182
Listed security
fraudulent misrepresentation in prospectus, **11**, 783
Literary work
anonymous or pseudonymous, **18**, 995, 996, 1032
author—
 meaning, **18**, 980
 See also COPYRIGHT
breach of confidence in relation to, **18**, 1452, 1456
computer programs, **18**, 950, 954
copyright—
 adaptation, **18**, 1065
 aesthetic or intellectual quality, no requirement for, **18**, 941, 943
 audio-visual recording, **18**, 949
 computer, storage on, **18**, 949
 Crown copyright, term of, **18**, 1034, 1037
 educational establishment performing, showing or playing, **18**, 1112
 employment by another, work made in course of, **18**, 997–999
 generally, **18**, 931, 933, 949
 infringement by public performance, **18**, 1060, 1061
 moral rights, *see* COPYRIGHT (MORAL RIGHTS)
 originality, **18**, 941
 parliamentary, term of, **18**, 1036, 1037
 public readings and recitations, **18**, 1127
 published editions, **18**, 933, 936, 977, 984
  infringement, **18**, 1056
  originality, **18**, 948
  term of copyright, **18**, 1041
 recording without permission, **18**, 949
 term of copyright, **18**, 1029, 1030
 writing, meaning, **18**, 949
databases, **18**, 953
definition, **18**, 950
developing but unfinished ideas, **18**, 1452
examples, **18**, 951
liferenter's rights, **13**, 1644
performance, rights in, *see* RIGHTS IN PERFORMANCES

Literary work—*continued*
public lending right, tax treatment of payments
    under, **18**, 1592
spoken works, **18**, 950
sung works, **18**, 950
tables and compilations, **18**, 950, 952, 953
Literature
society promoting, **12**, 694n
Lithography
in writing, meaning, **4**, 109
Lithuania
imports, European Union regulations, **7**, 1029
Litigation
abuse of process—
    breach of contract, **15**, 460
    generally, **15**, 458
    malice and want of probable cause, **15**, 459
conduct of—
    advocate's duties—
        at hearing, **13**, 1358–1362
        before hearing, **13**, 1356, 1357
    counsel failing to attend, **13**, 1358
Crown, involving—
    Crown privilege, **7**, 750
    delict, **7**, 745
    English and Scots law compared, **7**, 745, 751
    generally, **7**, 734
    judicial review, **7**, 751
    Law Officers of Crown, intervention, **7**, 752
    liabilities of crown in proceedings, **7**, 749
    Officers of State, role, **7**, 801
    personal capacity of Crown, **7**, 746
    procedure, **7**, 747
    public interest immunity, **7**, 750
    remedies against Crown, **7**, 748, 748n
    rights of Crown in proceedings, **7**, 749
    special position of Crown, **7**, 746
    title and interest, **7**, 751
curator *ad litem*, appointment, **3**, 1215
legal capacity, age limit, **3**, 1215
negotiorum gestor, intervention by, **15**, 96, 101
no counsel attending on either side, **13**, 1358
non-lawyer, conduct by—
    application for right, **13**, 1454
        consideration of, **13**, 1455
    complaints procedure, **13**, 1460
    draft schemes, **13**, 1454–1457
    exercise of, **13**, 1458
    Lord President, responsibilities of, **13**, 1454–
        1457, 1463
    offences in relation to, **13**, 1461
    order of precedence, **13**, 1459
    review of schemes, **13**, 1463
    revocation, **13**, 1463
    Secretary of State, responsibilities of, **13**, 1454–
        1457, 1463
    surrender of rights, **13**, 1462
Litigiosity
effect of diligence, **8**, 116
meaning, **8**, 116, 286
nexus, and, **8**, 116
Litter
abatement notice, **20**, 678
bins, **9**, 1174

Litter—*continued*
deposit of, **19**, 327
offences, **9**, 1173
provisions as to, **19**, 328
responsibility for clearing, **20**, 677
roadside bins, provision of, **20**, 680
street litter control notice, **20**, 679
throwing down, dropping or depositing, **20**, 677
Liverpool Freeport
free zone, as, **7**, 1164n
Livery colours
generally, **11**, 1604
heraldic terms, **11**, 1604n
Livestock
animals attacking, **2**, 168, 169
beekeeping, **24**, 571
buildings, **24**, 432, 570, 571
carriage by road—
    domestic, **3**, 625
    international, **3**, 654
diseases, *see* ANIMAL HEALTH
duties relating to, **2**, 163
exportation of, *see* ANIMAL
lost or abandoned, ownership, **18**, 547n, 549
medical operations on, **2**, 246
prevention of damage to, **11**, 859, 883, 886
protection of, **2**, 168
straying—
    detention of, **2**, 167
    duty to prevent, **2**, 163
trespass by, *see* ANIMAL
valuation for rating, and, **24**, 570, 571
Lloyds underwriters
authorisation, **12**, 807
exempted person under Financial Services Act
    1986 ..., **12**, 1321
generally, **21**, 119
Register of Shipping, **21**, 120
Standard Form of Salvage Agreement, *see* SALVAGE
taxation of, **19**, 1544
Load
overhanging or projecting, lighting, **20**, 479
Load lines
deck cargo, **21**, 230
offences in relation to, **21**, 230
pleasure vessel in commercial use, **21**, 230
regulations, generally, **21**, 230, 230n
Loan
bank, unrestricted-use credit agreement, as, **5**, 809
borrower—
    commodatum contract, **13**, 1784, 1789
    loan repayment, proof of, **13**, 1747
    money, proof of loan of, **13**, 1715, 1716
        formal bond to repay, **13**, 1720
    mutuum contract—
        agreement of, **13**, 1706
        fungible, delivery to, **13**, 1706
        liability, **13**, 1709
        obligations under, **13**, 1709
        as owner of thing lent, **13**, 1709
bridging facilities, building society, *see* BUILDING
    SOCIETY
building, erection of, **14**, 639
building society, *see* BUILDING SOCIETY

Loan—*continued*
business charges, **12**, 1008
cash advance, as, **12**, 1008
clog on redemption, **13**, 1762
  whether unlawful, **13**, 1762
commercial undertakings, **14**, 640
commodatum, see COMMODATUM
community council, to, **14**, 73*n*
company, to, **13**, 1774
consumption, for, *see* MUTUUM
credit union, by, **12**, 659, 661, 666, 669, 670; **13**,
  1777
deposit—
  improper, contract of, **13**, 1705
  loan compared, **13**, 1705
  locatio custodiae, **13**, 1783
  See also deposit-taking *below*
deposit-taking—
  deposit-taking business, meaning, **13**, 1765
  inducement by false, deceptive or misleading
    statement or forecast, **13**, 1765
  material fact, concealment of, **13**, 1765
  unauthorised person, by, **13**, 1765
director, to—
  generally, **4**, 426
  public companies, **4**, 427
disaster, relating to, **14**, 327
discharge of, **6**, 637
emergency, relating to, **14**, 327
extortionate credit bargain or transaction, **13**,
  1771
friendly society, by, **12**, 720; **13**, 1775
gambling bet, to make or pay, **13**, 1761
gambling losses, money lent on, **13**, 1761
goods held on, restitution, **15**, 46, 49
government—
  lending and borrowing by, **13**, 1772
  Treasury control of borrowing, **13**, 1782
harbour authority, to, **14**, 446
hire compared, **13**, 1706
house—
  amount of principal not to exceed value of
    subject, **11**, 2012
  building society or other recognised body,
    agreement made with, **11**, 2017
  conditions relating to, **11**, 2012
  first-time buyers, assistance for, **11**, 2016
  generally, **11**, 2010, 2011, 2017
  heritable security, secured by, **11**, 2012
  homesteading scheme, **11**, 2017
  housing action area, houses in, **11**, 1992, 2015
  improvement grant, where, **11**, 2015
  improvement order, in respect of, **11**, 1995,
    2015
  interest, rates of, **11**, 2013
  local authority owes no duty of care, **11**, 2012,
    2017
  purposes for which available, **11**, 2011
  repair notice, in respect of, **11**, 1995, 2015
  repairs grant, where, **11**, 2015
  right to buy, tenant exercising, **11**, 1961, 2014
  Scottish Homes, power to make, **11**, 1923
  Secretary of State, advice given by, **11**, 2011
  valuation must precede, **11**, 2012

Loan—*continued*
illegal purpose, made for, **13**, 1760
incapax, by or to—
  curator bonis, **13**, 1780
  void transactions, **13**, 1780
industrial and provident society, by, **13**, 1776
industrial and provident society, to, **12**, 622
industrial undertakings, **14**, 640
inner urban area, to, *see* INNER URBAN AREA
interest, **12**, 1008; **14**, 639
  contractual stipulation, **12**, 1002
  deceased's liability to tax, **25**, 967
  general implication, **12**, 1002, 1007, 1008
  relief for, married couples, **19**, 1574
IOU, treatment of, **12**, 1008
land, acquisition of, **14**, 639
landlord or agent, demand by, prohibition, **13**, 690
lender—
  commodatum contract, **13**, 1784, 1788
  money, proof of loan of, **13**, 1716
  mutuum contract—
    agreement of, **13**, 1706
    fungible, delivery by, **13**, 1706
    liability, **13**, 1709
  writ of, as evidence of loan, **13**, 1734
local authority, lending and borrowing by, **13**,
  1773
locatio conductio rei, **13**, 1783
  compared, **13**, 1706
locatio custodiae, **13**, 1783
  compared, **13**, 1705
meaning, **12**, 1008
minor—
  advancement to, **3**, 1220
  soliciting for business with, **3**, 1220
money, of—
  bank overdraft, **13**, 1713
  bill of exchange, by, **13**, 1713
  cash transfer, by, **13**, 1713
  cheque, by, **13**, 1713
  debentures, issue of, **13**, 1713
  delivery, loan constituted on, **13**, 1713
  disproof of—
    oath, **13**, 1748
    onus of proof of repayment, **13**, 1747
    parole evidence, **13**, 1749
    writ, **13**, 1748
      extrinsic evidence to contradict, **13**, 1750
  general rules of contract, **13**, 1714
    application, **13**, 1721–1725
  heritable property, for purchase of, standard
    security, **13**, 1758
  interest on—
    exceptions to general rule, **13**, 1752
    generally, **13**, 1701, 1704, 1712, 1751
    IOU, where loan evidenced by, **13**, 1752
    Roman law, **13**, 1751
  method of constitution, **13**, 1713
  mutuum, **13**, 1712
  obligations, **13**, 1714
    Paterson v Paterson, law in, **13**, 1716
    proof of, *see* proof of loan *below*
    testing, requirement for, **13**, 1716
    writing, requirement to be in, **13**, 1716

Loan—*continued*
money, of—*continued*
  perfection of contract, **13**, 1713
  proof of loan—
    current account, transactions between
      principal and agent, **13**, 1723
    evidence—
      bill of exchange as, **13**, 1732
      consumer credit agreement, **13**, 1746
      consumer hire agreement, **13**, 1746
      debtor's books do not constitute, **13**, 1738
      express acknowledgment, **13**, 1728
      indorsed cheque does not constitute, **13**,
        1735
      IOU as, **13**, 1731
      judicial admission, **13**, 1730, 1740–1745
      oath, **13**, 1718, 1720, 1740–1745
        bankrupt, of, not constituting, **13**, 1736
        borrower of, **13**, 1715
      parole, **13**, 1726
      solicitor's business books do not
        constitute, **13**, 1737
      unqualified acknowledgment, **13**, 1729
      what constitutes, **13**, 1728–1734
      writ, **13**, 1718, 1719, 1740–1745, 1746
        agent, of, **13**, 1733
        borrower, of, **13**, 1715
        lender, of, **13**, 1734
    formal bond to repay, **13**, 1720
    generally, **13**, 1713, 1715
    judicial admission, **13**, 1722
    loan incidental to other relationship, where,
      13, 1724
    loan not exceeding £100 Scots, **13**, 1712,
      1715, 1716, 1721
      proof *prout de jure*, **13**, 1721
    loan one of a series, where, **13**, 1725
    Paterson v Paterson, law in, **13**, 1716
    reform of rule, **13**, 1717
    restriction of proof to be pled, **13**, 1727
    testing, requirement for, **13**, 1716
    writing, requirement to be in, **13**, 1716
  repayment—
    foreign currency, payable in, **13**, 1754
    form of, **13**, 1753
    interest, *see* interest on *above*
    prescription—
      debt extinguished by, **13**, 1756
      quinquennial, **13**, 1755
    proof of loan by, **13**, 1748
    proof of—
      general rule, **13**, 1747
      oath, **13**, 1747
      onus of proof, **13**, 1747
      parole evidence, **13**, 1747
      writ, **13**, 1747
        extrinsic evidence to contradict, **13**, 1750
  Roman law, **13**, 1712
  security for—
    bill of exchange, deposit of, **13**, 1759
    bottomry bond, **13**, 1759
    cargo, *respondentia* on, **13**, 1759
    debenture, **13**, 1759
    delivery, **13**, 1759

Loan—*continued*
money, of—*continued*
  security for—*continued*
    floating charge, **13**, 1759
    general lien, **13**, 1759
    hypothec, **13**, 1759
    incorporeal property, over, **13**, 1759
    lien, **13**, 1759
    negotiable instrument, deposit of, **13**, 1759
    pledge, **13**, 1759
    special lien, **13**, 1759
    standard, **13**, 1758
    stamp duty, liability to, **13**, 1757
    stipulato contract, **13**, 1712
    unlawful—
      clog on redemption, **13**, 1762
      gaming contract, **13**, 1761
      illegal contract, **13**, 1760
  moneylending—
    extortionate credit bargain or transaction, **13**,
      1771
    meaning of moneylender, **13**, 1770
  mutuum, *see* MUTUUM
  National Loans Fund, **13**, 1772
  nationalised industry, government loan to, **13**,
    1772
  offences—
    advertising—
      building society, by, **13**, 1766
      infringement of regulations relating to, **13**,
        1769
      minor, document inviting borrowing sent to,
        13, 1767
      misleading advertisement, **13**, 1768
    building society advertising, in relation to, **13**,
      1766
    deposit-taking, **13**, 1765
      inducing deposit, **13**, 1765
    minor, in relation to, **13**, 1767
    undischarged bankrupt obtaining credit, **13**,
      1764
  owner retaining title and civil possession, **18**, 534
  personal, unrestricted-use credit, as, **5**, 809
  precarium, *see* PRECARIUM
  proof of, evidence—
    admission of receipt, **13**, 1739
    bill of exchange, **13**, 1732
    consumer credit agreement, **13**, 1732
    consumer hire agreement, **13**, 1736
    debtor's books do not constitute, **13**, 1738
    endorsed cheque does not constitute, **13**, 1735
    express acknowledgment, **13**, 1728
    IOUs, **13**, 1731
    judicial admission, **13**, 1730
    oath, **13**, 1718, 1720, 1740–1745
      bankrupt, of, does not constitute, **13**, 1736
      borrower, of, **13**, 1715
    parole evidence, **13**, 1726
    restriction of proof to be pled, **13**, 1727
    solicitor's business books do not constitute, **13**,
      1737
    unqualified acknowledgment, **13**, 1729
    what constitutes evidence, **13**, 1728

Loan—continued

proof of, evidence—continued

    writ, **13**, 1718, 1719, 1740–1745, 1746

        agent, of, **13**, 1733

        borrower, of, **13**, 1715

        lender, of, **13**, 1734

public authority, **13**, 1781

Public Works Loans Commissioners, **13**, 1772

pupil, capacity to contract, **13**, 1779

quasi-loan, **4**, 427

reciprocal obligations, **13**, 1704

repayment, proof of, parole evidence, **13**, 1749

reserved functions, **14**, 236

Roman law, **13**, 1702–1704

Scots law, generally, **13**, 1704

secured—

    arrears of interest, **18**, 14

    estate, on, **24**, 202

security for advance, **14**, 639

security for, money, *see* money *above*

standard security and conditions, **6**, 633–637

subject matter, delivery, contract completed by, **13**, 1703

to or by trustee, **24**, 180

Treasury, control of borrowing by, **13**, 1782

unfair contract terms, **13**, 1763

    commodatum contracts, **13**, 1790

    Mutuum contracts, **13**, 1710

    precarium contracts, **13**, 1790

unilateral obligations, **13**, 1704

unlawful—

    clog on redemption, **13**, 1762

    gaming contract, **13**, 1761

    illegal contract, **13**, 1760

use, for, *see* COMMODATUM

Loan security

building contract, assignation, **3**, 32

Loan stock

investment, as, **12**, 1308

Lobsters

prohibition on taking and sale of certain, **11**, 168

public right to take, **18**, 521, 521n

Local administration

local government, replacement of term, **14**, 1

services, development of, **14**, 31

Local authority

accommodation, assistance in finding, **11**, 2040

accounts, *see* ACCOUNTS

administration—

    co-ordinating and servicing role of lawyers, **13**, 1445

    district courts, responsibility for, **13**, 1448

    lawyers and, **13**, 1445

    legal services sections or departments, **13**, 1446

    licensing boards, **13**, 1449

    public inquiries, **13**, 1447

adoption agencies, **10**, 1199

advice—

    advisory functions, appointment of committee with, **14**, 239

    consumer, **14**, 594

agenda, **14**, 263

airports, *see* AIRPORT

Local authority—continued

allotments, provision of—

    duties in relation to, **13**, 531, 542

    generally, **13**, 535

    landlord, as, **13**, 542

    lease, generally, **13**, 541

    rights in relation to, **13**, 542

    termination of tenancy, **13**, 544, 545

allowances—

    approved duties, **14**, 224

    attendance, **14**, 225

    code of conduct, **14**, 232

    conference, attendance at, **14**, 228

    financial loss, **14**, 226

    meetings, attendance at, **14**, 228

    police constable, **14**, 488

    regulation-making powers, **14**, 231

    special responsibility, **14**, 230

    subsistence, **14**, 227

    travelling, **14**, 227

    See also expenses *below*

alteration, enlargement or improvement of any house or building, **11**, 1905

amenities, provision of, **11**, 1906

appeal from decision of, **1**, 337

application to assume parental rights, legal aid, **13**, 1070

    urgency, situation of, **13**, 1048

art gallery authority, **14**, 688, 689

assistance in kind, discretion to provide, **22**, 13

badges, **11**, 1631

bank—

    customer of, as, **2**, 1247

    overdrafts etc, **2**, 1248

banning sporting activities, **19**, 1226

bias, rule applying to, **1**, 253

borrowing by—

    borrowing powers, **2**, 1248; **20**, 223

    generally, **13**, 1773

    purposes of Food and Drug (Scotland) Act 1956, for, **11**, 436

boundary walls and fences, statutory powers in relation to, **18**, 226

budget, revenue, **14**, 838

building control, **3**, 203; **14**, 629

    class warrant, role in relation to, **3**, 218

    dangerous building, powers as to, *see* BUILDING AND BUILDING CONTROLS (dangerous buildings)

    existing building, power to require conformity, **3**, 215

    appeals, **3**, 236

    inspection prior to, **3**, 237

    relaxation, application for, **3**, 215

    expenses incurred by authority, recovery, **3**, 243, 244

    fees, prescribed, **3**, 242

    inspection and testing—

        notice of, **3**, 237

        obstruction, **3**, 237, 241

        powers as to generally, **3**, 237, 239

        warrant for inspection, **3**, 238

    records, **3**, 240

Local authority—*continued*
building control—*continued*
  register of applications—
    inspection, must be available for, **3**, 240
    requirement to keep, **3**, 240
  See also BUILDING AND BUILDING CONTROLS
building regulations, power to relax, **3**, 211, 212
building warrant—
  application for, **3**, 220, 221
  building constructed in contravention of, **3**, 228, 229
  building constructed without, **3**, 228, 229
  building remaining in existence in contravention of, **3**, 228, 229
  refusal to grant, **3**, 221, 222
  Secretary of State, where application referred to, **3**, 222
  See also BUILDING AND BUILDING CONTROLS
buildings authority jurisdiction and functions transferred to, **3**, 201
buildings and building control, **19**, 350, 352
burial grounds, transfer to, **3**, 519, 520
burial of persons in care at time of death, **22**, 15
byelaws, **19**, 1220
  confirmation of, **1**, 300
  milk and dairies, in relation to, **11**, 322, 492
  power to make, **11**, 1902
  slaughterhouses, **11**, 502
'cabinet' system, **14**, 94
capacity to contract, **3**, 26
capital expenditure—
  central government loan, **22**, 16
care, burial or cremation of person who dies in, **22**, 15
central government loan to, **22**, 16
chairman, **3**, 1306
charges—
  community, *see* COMMUNITY CHARGE
  revenue expenditure, **14**, 828
  services, discretionary, **22**, 14
chief executive—
  duties and responsibilities, **13**, 1443, 1444
  role of, **13**, 1440
  whether lawyer, **13**, 1440, 1441
child minding and day care—
  child-minders, duty to monitor, **22**, 2
  provision, **3**, 1259
  registers, **3**, 1259
children—
  adoption agencies, **10**, 1199
  advice, guidance and assistance of child and family, **3**, 1261, 1287
  assistance in kind or cash, **3**, 1261
  case of—
    rights and duties in respect of, **11**, 1238
    visits to, payments for, **22**, 15
  children's officer, appointment of, **22**, 2
  duty to, **22**, 17–13
    See also CHILD-CHILDREN; CHILD IN CARE; residential care facilities *below*
  foster children, duties in relation to, **3**, 1260
  Scottish custody order committing to care or supervision, **8**, 508
  secure accommodation for, registration, **22**, 33

Local authority—*continued*
children's committee, **22**, 2
children's hearings—
  decision—
    implementation of decision, **3**, 1355
    notification as to, **3**, 1295
  duties, **22**, 21
  See also CHILDREN S HEARINGS
children's panel—
  accommodation and facilities for, duty to provide, **3**, 1303
  duty to form, **3**, 1303, 1305
  reporter, appointment of, **14**, 110, 249
  training, **3**, 1307
children's panel advisory committee, obligation to form, **3**, 1306
cinema, licensing provisions, **9**, 1020
civic amenities—
  countryside, *see* COUNTRYSIDE
  libraries, *see* LIBRARIES
  recreation, *see* RECREATION AND SPORT
  reform, **14**, 51
  tourism, *see* TOURISM
cleansing, duty as to, **19**, 364–367
  public health, **14**, 706
  road, **14**, 411
clerk, instruction of advocate by, **13**, 1298
clerk of the peace, appointment of, **6**, 1164
closing order—
  appeals, **11**, 1986
  consequences of, **11**, 1988
  generally, **11**, 1981, 1982
  powers of acquisition, **11**, 1987
  revocation, **11**, 1984
  service of, **11**, 1985
  suspension, **11**, 1984
  vacation, notice requiring, **11**, 1988
coast protection, *see* COAST PROTECTION
cold stores provided by, **11**, 405
committees—
  admission, public right of, **14**, 1327, 1328
  appointment of, **14**, 238, 239
  attendance at, **17**, 14
  cabinet system, **14**, 94
  chairmanship, **14**, 93
  code of conduct, **14**, 232
  departmentalism, encouragement of, **14**, 237
  education, *see* EDUCATION
  fire authority, **14**, 499
  functions—
    authority, reserved to, **14**, 236
    discharge of, arrangement for, **14**, 234
  joint—
    discharge of functions, **14**, 235
    disqualification for membership, **14**, 244
    expenses, **14**, 242
    joint board compared with, **14**, 243
    report, **14**, 267
    return, **14**, 267
  majority party, position of, **14**, 91
  meeting, member's right to attend, **14**, 220
  membership—
    body, membership of, **14**, 246
    cessation of, **14**, 240

Local authority—*continued*

committees—*continued*

  membership—*continued*

    court, membership of, **14**, 246

    disqualification for, **14**, 244

    statutory provisions, **14**, 91

    minority party, position of, **14**, 92

    need for, **14**, 233

    public, attendance of, **14**, 92

    river purification, relating to, **14**, 476

    roads, **14**, 406

    sewerage, powers relating to, **14**, 456

    social work, *see* SOCIAL WORK

    special provisions, **14**, 241

    standing orders, **14**, 234

    statutory, **14**, 237

    statutory provisions, **14**, 91

    sub-committee, *see* MEETING

    voting—

      absent, **14**, 91

      free, **14**, 91

      pecuniary interest, disability because of, **14**, 245

      proxy, **14**, 91

    water authority, **14**, 453

common good fund, **19**, 1223

common pasture, land acquired for, **13**, 534, 541

community service order, duty to provide supervision, **22**, 38

compensation—

  flood prevention operation, land depreciated by, **14**, 466

  payment by one local authority to another, **14**, 323

compulsory purchase by, **14**, 1680

constitution—

  central government, control by, **14**, 101

  elections, timing of, **14**, 202

  electoral areas, **14**, 203

  franchise, **14**, 201

  returning officers, **14**, 204

consultation—

  non-domestic ratepayers with, **14**, 839

  planning authority, with, **14**, 618

consumer protection, **6**, 12

  See also CONSUMER PROTECTION

contracts, **14**, 326

convener, **14**, 6*n*

Convention of Scottish Local Authorities, *see* CONVENTION OF SCOTTISH LOCAL AUTHORITIES

coronets, special designs, **11**, 1607

corporate personality, **14**, 2

council housing, sale of, **13**, 1446

councillor, qualified privilege, **15**, 528

county clerk, **13**, 1443, 1443*n*

cremation—

  functions in respect of, **14**, 699

  person dying in care, of, **22**, 15

curator bonis petition to court for appointment of, **14**, 1478

dairies and dairymen—

  inspection of dairies, **11**, 444, 445

  registration, **11**, 494

day care facilities, provision of, **22**, 16

Local authority—*continued*

dead bodies, duties in relation to—

  corpse killed by infectious disease, **3**, 510

  disposal, **3**, 512

    costs, recovery, **3**, 512

    cremation, **3**, 512

    death in local authority care, **3**, 512

decision of, reduction, **13**, 36

deeds, execution of, **14**, 260

defamation, title to sue, **15**, 477

default order—

  Court of Session, powers of, **14**, 127

  Secretary of State, power to make, **14**, 117

delegation of general duty, **22**, 13

delict, title and interest to sue, **15**, 223

delictual liability, **3**, 151

demolition order, **11**, 1981, 1983, 1988, 1989

  appeals, **11**, 1986

  consequences of, **11**, 1988

  demolition by local authority, **11**, 1988

  revocation, **11**, 1984

  service of, **11**, 1985

  suspension, **11**, 1984

  vacation, notice requiring, **11**, 1988

depots for sale of milk to children, **11**, 451

designation orders, **14**, 304

direct labour organisations—

  accounts, **14**, 910

  annual balance sheet, **14**, 911

  annual report, **14**, 914

  construction or maintenance work, meaning, **14**, 903

  contract, non-commercial requirements and conditions of, **14**, 909

  exemptions, **14**, 902

  functional work—

    competition, **14**, 917

    meaning, **14**, 904

    regulation of, **14**, 907

  generally, **14**, 901

  lowest tender, non-acceptance of, **14**, 908

  rate of return on capital, **14**, 912

  reserve funds, **14**, 811

  sanctions, **14**, 913

  types of work covered, **14**, 904

  works contract—

    competition, **14**, 916

    limitations on, **14**, 906

    local authority functions, **14**, 326

    meaning, **14**, 904

    regulation, **14**, 905

director of administration—

  assistant, **13**, 1445

  depute, **13**, 1445

  duties and responsibilities, **13**, 1444

  Society of Directors of Adminstration, **13**, 145?

director of social work, duty to appoint, **22**, 8

disease, prevention and mitigation of, *see* DISEASE

district council, *see* DISTRICT

donation of land by, **8**, 615

drains, duties and powers in relation to, **19**, 330, 332

duties, **1**, 305; **14**, 1474; **22**, 13, 14, 16, 21, 23–3?, 33, 38

Local authority—*continued*
education—
ad hoc authorities, **14**, 36
authority—
discharge of functions, **14**, 597
general functions, **14**, 603
generally, **14**, 595
legal action by, **13**, 1446
bus—
permit for use of, **14**, 423
school, use to carry fare-paying passenger, **14**, 438
college council—
disqualification, **14**, 600
duty to appoint, **14**, 598
membership, **14**, 599
committee—
disqualification, **14**, 600
membership, **14**, 596
powers, **14**, 36
special provisions, **14**, 241
development of service, **14**, 36
director of, **14**, 249, 601
reform, **14**, 47
school council, **14**, 598–600
secondary, **14**, 36
sub-committee, disqualification from member-ship, **14**, 600
teachers, **14**, 602
See also EDUCATION
elderly persons, duty to, **22**, 25–29
elections, *see* ELECTIONS
electricity, generation and supply of, by, **9**, 714
emergency procedures—
compulsory care order for elderly person, **22**, 29
expenditure and grants, **14**, 327
mental disorder, person with, compulsory admission to hospital, **14**, 1417; **22**, 30
employee, **9**, 38
See also staff *below*
enforcing authority, default when acting as, **9**, 485
enterprise zone, *see* ENTERPRISE ZONE
entry, powers of—
countryside, **14**, 685
flood prevention, **14**, 465
licence holder, premises of, **14**, 545
sports ground, **14**, 580
unlicensed premises, **14**, 545
environmental health, *see* ENVIRONMENTAL HEALTH
equipment, insurance of, **14**, 329
excise licence, issue and regulation, **7**, 1245
exempt agreement, **5**, 821
expenditure, *see* PUBLIC EXPENDITURE
expenses—
capital, meaning, **14**, 805
code of conduct, **14**, 232
Commission for Local Authority Accounts in Scotland, **14**, 885
Commissioner for Local Administration, of, **14**, 135
contributions towards, **19**, 1218
courtesy visit, **14**, 229

Local authority—*continued*
expenses—*continued*
district court, **14**, 514
generally, **14**, 834
joint committees, of, **14**, 242
local authority, how met, **14**, 834
local inquiry, **14**, 116
members, of, **14**, 224–230
official and courtesy visits, **14**, 229
explosives, administration as to, **10**, 1622
facilities outside area of, **19**, 1218
failure to abate nuisance, **14**, 2102
ferry, powers in relation to, *see* FERRY
fiduciary duty, **14**, 132
film censorship, **9**, 1027
finance, *see* LOCAL GOVERNMENT
fire escapes, grants for, **11**, 2028–2030
amount of grant, **11**, 2029
procedural and other provisions, **11**, 2030
fire precautions, loans for, **10**, 1469
fire services—
authority—
functions, **14**, 502–504
generally, **14**, 497
combined areas, **14**, 498
committees, **14**, 499
discipline, **14**, 501
establishment schemes, **14**, 500
finance, **10**, 1416
firemaster, appointment of, **14**, 501
functions, **14**, 502–504
generally, **10**, 1406–1409
London, **14**, 62
other ranks, appointment of, **14**, 501
reform, **14**, 49
Secretary of State, functions of, **14**, 505
See also FIRE SERVICES
flood prevention, *see* FLOOD
fluoridation of water supply, **25**, 509
food—
examination and seizure of unfit, **11**, 397
food and drugs, enforcement of provisions, **11**, 329
acquisition of land by local authority, **11**, 332
default of local authority, **11**, 331
legislation, generally, **11**, 308–310
regulations, appeal against, **11**, 434
footpaths, sporting events on, **19**, 1284
foster children, duties in relation to, **3**, 1260
functions, *see* LOCAL GOVERNMENT
furniture, fittings and conveniences, provision of, **11**, 1906
furniture and furnishings, filling materials for, enforcement of regulations as to, **19**, 431–443
gifts of property to, **14**, 328
government distinguished from administration, **14**, 1
grants, *see* GRANT
grants of arms to, **11**, 1604
guardian, as—
amicus curiae, appointment of, **11**, 1230
care provisions, **11**, 1231
discharge from, **14**, 1449
disputes, resolution of, **11**, 1230

Local authority—*continued*
guardian, as—*continued*
  generally, **11**, 1229
  Mental Health Act guardians, **11**, 1241
  notices, **11**, 1230
  parental rights and powers, vesting of, **11**, 1230
  reception into—
    application for, **14**, 1435
    duties, **14**, 1441
    special duties of local authorities which are, **14**, 1476
  statutory provisions, **11**, 1229, 1230
  welfare of child as criterion, **11**, 1229
gunpowder factories and magazines, licensing of, **10**, 1593
gunpowder stores, licensing of, **10**, 1597
handicapped person, duty to, **22**, 13
harbour, powers in relation to, **14**, 443
harbour authority, as, **11**, 1302
health and safety at work legislation, responsibility for enforcing, **19**, 342
health service joint liaison committees, **11**, 1412
heritable security granted by, **20**, 223
homelessness, obligations in respect of—
  advice and assistance, **11**, 2070
  applications, **11**, 2039, 2073
    appeals against decisions, **11**, 2073
  change in statutory duty to homeless person, **22**, 13
  charging for accommodation, **11**, 2071
  Code of Guidance, **11**, 2037, 2040, 2044, 2053, 2054
  generally, **11**, 2037
  homes not reaching tolerable standard, **11**, 2037
  inquiries into application, **11**, 2040
  intentional homelessness, **11**, 2057–2067
  interim accommodation, **11**, 2068, 2071
  permanent accommodation, **11**, 2069, 2071
  priority need, **11**, 2051–2056
    limitation of obligation, **11**, 2057
  protection of property, **11**, 2072
  temporary accommodation, provision, **13**, 636, 648
hospitality, code of conduct, **14**, 232
hostel provision, **19**, 347
house loans—
  amount of principal not to exceed value of subject, **11**, 2012
  authority owes no duty of care, **11**, 2012
  building society or other recognised body, agreement made with, **11**, 2017
  conditions relating to, **11**, 2012
  first-time buyers, assistance for, **11**, 2016
  generally, **2**, 1267; **11**, 2010, 2011
  homesteading scheme, **11**, 2017
  interest, rates of, **11**, 2013
  privately let accommodation, **11**, 2017
  purposes for which available, **11**, 2011
  Secretary of State, advice given by, **11**, 2011
  secured by heritable security, **11**, 2012
  tenants exercising right to buy, loans to, **11**, 2014
  valuation must precede, **11**, 2012
housing, *see* HOUSING

Local authority—*continued*
improvement of amenity grants, **11**, 2033
improvement grants, *see* IMPROVEMENT GRANT
improvement orders, **11**, 1990–1992
independents, position of, **14**, 92
inflammable substances, inspection, testing and seizure, **19**, 405–411
inspection—
  accounts, of, **14**, 888
  agenda, of, **14**, 263
  background paper, of, **14**, 263
  central government powers, **14**, 113
  documents, of, **14**, 263–265
  list of officers, of, **14**, 254
  minutes, of, **14**, 263
  report, of, **14**, 263
  residential facilities, of, **22**, 16
  sports grounds, of, **14**, 580
insurance by, **14**, 329
inter-authority relationships—
  concerted action, **14**, 80
  concurrent functions, **14**, 79
  generally, **14**, 77
  sole functions, **14**, 78
investigation of, *see* COMMISSIONER FOR LOCAL ADMINISTRATION IN SCOTLAND
islands area council, *see* ISLANDS AREA
joint board—
  joint committee compared, **14**, 243
  report, **14**, 267
  return, **14**, 267
joint committee, *see* committees *above*
justices of the peace, nomination of, **6**, 1162, 1163
land—
  acquisition of—
    agreement, by, **14**, 316
    loan for, **14**, 639
    public recreation, for, from heir to entail, **14**, 322
  advertising on, **14**, 335
  appropriation of, **14**, 319
  common good, forming parts of, disposal of, appeal, **14**, 119
  compensation, payment by one local authority to another, **14**, 323
  compulsory acquisition, **14**, 317, 502
    See also COMPULSORY ACQUISITION
  disposal of, **14**, 320–321
  disposition to by heir of entail, for recreation, **20**, 246
  expulsion of offenders, application of management rules, **14**, 300
  flood prevention, acquisition for, **14**, 464
  police, **14**, 489
  purchase money, **14**, 323
  title to, **14**, 318
  valuation, **14**, 804
  works, **14**, 325
land transactions, *see* LAND
landlord, as, assured tenancy status excluded, **13**, 636, 647
laundry service, facilities for, **11**, 1906; **22**, 14

Local authority—*continued*
lawyers in—
  administrative functions—
    district courts, responsibility for, **13**, 1448
    future role, **13**, 1452
    generally, **13**, 1445
    legal service sections or departments, **13**,
      1446
    licensing boards, **13**, 1449
    public inquiries, **13**, 1447
  chief executive, **13**, 1440
    duties and responsibilities, **13**, 1443, 1444
  competition from other professionals, **13**, 1441,
    1445
  competitive tendering, **13**, 1443, 1444, 1452
  director of administration—
    duties and responsibilities, **13**, 1444
  distinctive features of local government work,
    13, 1442
  duties and responsibilities—
    chief executive, **13**, 1443, 1444
    director of administration, **13**, 1444
  financial rewards, **13**, 1452
  future role, **13**, 1452
  political dimension to work, **13**, 1442
  Public Service and Commerce Group, **13**, 1451
  representative bodies, **13**, 1451
  Society of Directors of Adminstration, **13**, 1451
  special skills needed by, **13**, 1442
  specialisation, **13**, 1450
  statute-based nature of work, **13**, 1442
legal proceedings, by or against, **1**, 322; **14**, 256
legal profession, historical relationship with, **13**,
  1438
legal services sections or departments, **13**, 1446
legislative powers, **14**, 3, 269
leisure and recreational activities, committee with
  responsibility for, **19**, 1219
lending by, **13**, 1773
lessor, as, **13**, 182
library service—
  authority for purpose of Public Libraries
    (Scotland) Acts, **13**, 1504
  books—
    purchase of, **13**, 1505
    sale or exchange, **13**, 1505
  buildings, powers in relation to, **13**, 1505
  byelaws, **13**, 1506
  contributions towards expenses of other library,
    13, 1505
  duty to provide, **13**, 1505
  education service, cooperation with, **13**, 1505
  financial provision, **13**, 1507
  furniture and fittings, provision, **13**, 1505
  management, **13**, 1505
  newspapers and periodicals, purchase of, **13**,
    1505
  other lending authorities, cooperation with, **13**,
    1505
  public lending right, *see* PUBLIC LENDING RIGHT
  reading rooms, **13**, 1505
  statutory provisions, **13**, 1504
  tapes, records and films, purchase of, **13**, 1505
  who may borrow, **13**, 1505

Local authority—*continued*
licensing, *see* LICENCE; LICENSING
light railways, construction and working of, **19**,
  1076, 1081
litter, duties as to, **20**, 677
local roads authority, *see* ROADS AUTHORITY
Lord Provost, **14**, 6n
McBoyle Committee recommendations, **22**, 4
management—
  countryside, agreement relating to, **14**, 679
  financial, **14**, 801
  rules—
    evidence of, **14**, 229
    exclusion order, **14**, 301
    general scope, **14**, 296
    offender, expulsion of, **14**, 300
    procedure for making, **14**, 297
    publication, **14**, 298
meals, facilities for obtaining, **11**, 1906
meaning, **11**, 329n
meetings—
  access to, *see* MEETING
  adjourned, **14**, 1319
  agenda—
    availability of, **14**, 1322
    background papers, inspection of, **14**, 1324
    deposit of, **14**, 263
    documents, inspection of, **14**, 1324
    inspection of, **14**, 263, 1323
    issue of, **14**, 1320
    order of business, **14**, 1321
    reports, inspection of, **14**, 1323
  attendance—
    allowance, **14**, 228
    summary of rights, **14**, 264
  chairman—
    code of conduct, **14**, 232
    committee, **14**, 93
    statutory office, appointment to, **14**, 91
    sub-committee, **14**, 93
  co-opted members, **14**, 1308
  COSLA, *see* CONVENTION OF SCOTTISH LOCAL
    AUTHORITIES
  debate—
    chairman, duties of, **14**, 1342
    members, behaviour of, **14**, 1344
    motion to terminate, **14**, 1340
    order of, **14**, 1319
    order of speaking, **14**, 1341
    point of order, **14**, 1345
    stewards, **14**, 1343
  essentials—
    co-opted members, **14**, 1308
    convening formal meeting, **14**, 1307
    purpose, **14**, 1306
    quorum, **14**, 1305
  exclusion from, **14**, 1319
  expenses—
    capital expenses, meaning, **14**, 805
  failure to attend, **14**, 211, 1319
  formal—
    co-opted members, **14**, 1308
    convening, **14**, 1307
    purpose, **14**, 1306

Local authority—*continued*
meetings—*continued*
  full council, member's right to attend, **14**, 219
  informal, **14**, 1306
  member's right to requisition, **14**, 221
  minutes, *see* MEETING
  motion, *see* MEETING
  ordinary, *see* MEETING
  place of, **14**, 1313
  press privileges at, **17**, 13
  private meeting, classed as, **14**, 1304
  public right to attend, **17**, 12
  purpose, **14**, 1306
  quorum, *see* MEETING
  right of requisition, **14**, 221
  right to attend, **14**, 1335–1337; **17**, 12
  special, **14**, 1310, 1319
  standing orders, **14**, 1316–1319
  statutory, **14**, 1311, 1319
  sub-committee, *see* MEETING
  time of, **14**, 1312
  types of—
    ordinary, **14**, 1309
    special, **14**, 1310
    statutory, **14**, 1311
  validity—
    notice, **14**, 1315
    summons, **14**, 1315
    what constitutes, **14**, 1314
  voting, *see* MEETING
  See also MEETING
members—
  corruption, **7**, 406, 408
  declaration of interests, **7**, 408
  subsistence allowance, **14**, 227
membership—
  age limit, **3**, 1214
  allowances—
    approved duties, **14**, 224
    attendance, **14**, 225
    conference, attendance at, **14**, 228
    financial loss, **14**, 226
    meetings, attendance at, **14**, 228
    regulation-making powers, **14**, 231
    special responsibility, **14**, 230
    subsistence, **14**, 227
    travelling, **14**, 227
  casual vacancies, **14**, 212
  code of conduct, **14**, 232
  council facilities, code of conduct as to use of, **14**, 232
  disqualification—
    effect of, **14**, 208
    grounds for, **14**, 206
    proceedings for, **14**, 207
  expenses—
    courtesy visit, **14**, 229
    official visit, **14**, 229
  general rights and duties, **14**, 218
  information, right of access to, **14**, 222
  justice of peace, appointment of, **14**, 513
  meetings—
    allowance for attending, **14**, 228
    committee, right to attend, **14**, 220

Local authority—*continued*
membership—*continued*
  meetings—*continued*
    full council, right to attend, **14**, 219
    requisition, right to, **14**, 221
    sub-committee, right to attend, **14**, 220
  officer, prohibition of appointment as, **14**, 252
  pecuniary interests—
    code of conduct, **14**, 232
    declaration of, **14**, 213
    disability—
      exclusion of, **14**, 215
      removal of, **14**, 217
      voting, **14**, 245
    disclosure—
      officers, **14**, 253
      recording of, **14**, 216
    general notice, **14**, 216
    indirect, **14**, 214
  personal liability, **14**, 223
  qualifications, **14**, 205
  register of members, **14**, 209
  resignation, **14**, 210
  vacation of office, **14**, 211
  voting, restrictions on—
    disability—
      exclusion of, **14**, 215
      removal of, **14**, 217
    pecuniary interest—
      declaration of, **14**, 213
      general notice, **14**, 216
      indirect, **14**, 214
      offence, **14**, 213
      recording of disclosure, **14**, 216
mental disorder, person with, duty to, **11**, 1241; **22**, 13, 30, 31
mental health officers—
  appointment of, **14**, 1475
  duty to provide sufficient number, **22**, 30
mentally handicapped person—
  duty to, **22**, 13, 23, 24, 31
  occupation, provision of, **14**, 1477
  training, provision of, **14**, 1477
milk, purveyors of, registration, **11**, 495
Milk and Dairies (Scotland) Act 1914, compliance of consigning authority, **11**, 446
minutes of proceedings as documentary evidence, **10**, 595
multiple occupation, housing in—
  control orders, **11**, 2009
  directions to prevent or reduce overcrowding **11**, 2008
  limits fixed by local authority, **11**, 2008
  management code, **11**, 2006, 2007
  powers to require works, **11**, 2007
  registration schemes, **11**, 2005
museums and art galleries—
  functions of museum and art gallery authorities **13**, 1519
  provision, generally, **13**, 1520
music and dancing, support for, **9**, 1036
musical nuisance, control of, **9**, 1039
navigation, publc right of, powers as to, **18**, 520

Local authority—*continued*
nearest relative, special duties of local authority vested with, **14**, 1476
negligence by, **3**, 151
noise—
　byelaws, **9**, 1293
　execution of works, **9**, 1268
　periodical inspections, **9**, 1248
non-tidal lochs, powers in relation to, **18**, 308
non-tidal river, powers as to, **18**, 281
offences—
　byelaws, contravention of, **14**, 288, 289
　generally, **14**, 572
　licensing, **14**, 546, 547
　pecuniary interests, relating to, **14**, 213
　public procession, **14**, 572
　sports ground, safety certificate for, **14**, 581
office—
　casual vacancies, **14**, 212
　resignation, **14**, 210
　vacation by failure to attend meetings, **14**, 211
officers—
　appointment, **14**, 110
　code of conduct, **14**, 232
　dismissal, **14**, 110
　district court, **14**, 512
　lists of, **14**, 254
　member of local authority, prohibition of appointment, **14**, 252
　pecuniary interests, disclosure of, **14**, 253
　registration, **14**, 584
　rewards, acceptance of, **14**, 253
　river purification, relating to, **14**, 476
　roads, responsibility for, **14**, 407
　security taken in relation to, **14**, 251
　sewerage, powers relating to, **14**, 456
　statutory, appointment of, **14**, 249
　water authority, **14**, 453
order made by—
　closing, **14**, 305
　default, *see* default order *above*
　demolition, **14**, 305
　designation, **14**, 304
　exclusion, **14**, 301
　generally, **14**, 302–305
　public procession, regulation of, **14**, 305
　traffic regulation, **14**, 303
overcrowding—
　licence to exceed limit, **11**, 2002
　powers and duties as to, **11**, 2003
　seasonal increases allowed, **11**, 2002
parental rights, assumption of—
　access rights, **3**, 1270
　duties in exercise of rights, **3**, 1270
　effect of resolution, **3**, 1269
　generally, **3**, 1265
　grounds for, **3**, 1266, 1267
　　procedure, **3**, 1268
　objections, procedure, **3**, 1268
　proposed changes in law and procedure, **3**, 1271
　reviews, **3**, 1272
　special duties of local authorities vested with, **14**, 1476
　termination of assumption resolution, **3**, 1273

Local authority—*continued*
parole, duty to provide service for, **22**, 35
permit—
　betting agency, **14**, 517
　bookmaker, of, **14**, 517
　bus, *see* BUS
　gaming machine, **14**, 517
　generally, **14**, 515
　public charitable collection, **14**, 119, 528
persons in need, duties under, Social Work (Scotland) Act 1968 ..., **22**, 13
physically handicapped person—
　duty to, **22**, 23, 24
　　See also DISABLED PERSON
pier, powers in relation to, *see* PIER
port local authorities, **19**, 309–313
　constitution, **19**, 309
　debts, **19**, 312
　delegation of powers, **19**, 311
　expenses, **19**, 312
　jurisdiction, **19**, 310
　ships within, **19**, 313
powers—
　administration, limited to, **14**, 1
　assistance in kind, provision, **22**, 13
　burial or cremation, persons in care at time of death, **22**, 15
　central government control, **14**, 3
　delegation of, **1**, 224
　excess, exercising, **1**, 218
　laundry service, provision, **11**, 1906; **22**, 14
　limits on, **1**, 220
　miscellaneous, **22**, 15
　public rights, interfering with, **1**, 219
　sources of, **1**, 220
　subsidiary, **14**, 309
　visits to child in care, payment, **22**, 15
premises, licensing of, **2**, 95
procurator fiscal, reference of case to, **17**, 531
provisional order—
　promoted by local authority, **19**, 20, 35*n*
　proposals, notification of, **19**, 19
public analysts, appointment of, **11**, 330
public conveniences, provision of, **19**, 368, 369
public corporation, as, **19**, 201, 213
public health nuisance—
　duties and powers in relation to, **19**, 337, 338
　entry, powers of, **19**, 338
public health officers, appointment of, **19**, 314
public health responsibilities—
　district councils, **19**, 308, 308*n*
　islands councils, **19**, 308, 308*n*
　port local authorities, **19**, 309–313
　regional councils, **19**, 308, 308*n*
public service vehicle run by, **20**, 493
public transport, *see* PUBLIC TRANSPORT
radioactive waste, disposal of, **9**, 1190
records—
　access to, **19**, 882
　held by Scottish Record Office, **19**, 849
　retransmission, **19**, 872
　transmission, **19**, 853, 864
recreation centres, **19**, 1225

Local authority—*continued*

recreation and sport, role as to, **19**, 1218–1226
  advisory bodies, **19**, 1222
  district councils, **19**, 1218
  islands councils, **19**, 1218
  regional councils, **19**, 1218
reform, *see* LOCAL GOVERNMENT
regional council, *see* REGIONAL COUNCIL
registration of births, marriages and deaths, authority for, **14**, 32
remand accommodation, duty to provide, **22**, 33
repair notice, *see* REPAIR NOTICE
repairs grant, *see* REPAIRS GRANT
report, **14**, 267
reporter to children's panel—
  accommodation and facilities, provision, **3**, 1283
  appointment, **3**, 1283
  staff, provision, **3**, 1283
representative nature of, **14**, 6
residential care facilities—
  advice to children formerly in care, **3**, 1274
  duty to provide—
    delegation to voluntary organisations, **22**, 10, 13, 16, 28
    generally, **22**, 13, 16, 21, 24, 28
  keeping child in care, **3**, 1263
  parent or guardian—
    child abandoned by, **3**, 1262
    incapacity etc, of, **3**, 1262
    position of, **3**, 1263, 1264
  provision of, **3**, 1261; **22**, 16
  receiving child into care, **3**, 1262
  registration of, **22**, 16, 28
  religious persuasion of child, **3**, 1263
  reviews, **3**, 1272
  special measures needed, where, **3**, 1330
  See also CHILD IN CARE
returns, **14**, 267
revenue, rents and charges, from, **14**, 828
right or interest of, over land, **6**, 743
right of way, creation of public, **18**, 502
roads—
  cleansing, duties as to, **20**, 618, 620, 665, 677
  detrunking, **20**, 622
  new, consultations over, **20**, 616
  provisional order relating to, **19**, 22
  provisional orders relating to, **19**, 22
  repair and maintenance of, **20**, 618
  roads and footpaths, sporting events on, **19**, 1284
  trunking, **20**, 621
  See also ROAD
roads authority, *see* ROADS AUTHORITY
seal, use of, **14**, 260
secure accommodation, registration by Secretary of State, **22**, 33
  young person, for, duty to provide, **22**, 16
separate departments providing social services within—
  co-ordination, growth, **22**, 3, 4
  historical background, **22**, 2
servants, corruption, **7**, 406
sewerage, functions relating to, **14**, 456, 457; **19**, 330, 332

Local authority—*continued*

slaughterhouses—
  byelaws as to, **11**, 502
  functions in relation to, **11**, 509
  powers of entry, **11**, 515
  provision of, **11**, 499, 499n
smoke control order, power to make, **9**, 1133
social work, *see* SOCIAL WORK
social work department, *see* SOCIAL WORK DEPARTMENT
sovereign powers, lack of, **14**, 3
specific implement against, **13**, 11
sponsorship of sporting activities by, **19**, 1218
staff—
  appointment, **14**, 247
  Commissioner for Local Administration, **14**, 135
  competent, selection of, employer's duty as to, **9**, 77
  indemnity, **14**, 248
  secondment, **14**, 250
  security taken in relation to, **14**, 251
  statutory officers, appointment of, **14**, 249
  treasurer, appointment of, **14**, 249
standing orders, **14**, 234, 326
statute, powers circumscribed by, **14**, 3
statutory regulation, **25**, 501, 502
stipendiary magistrates, appointment, **6**, 1164
sub-committees, **3**, 1306
sub-standard housing, *see* SUB-STANDARD HOUSING
subordinate legislation, *see* BYELAWS—
  delegated legislation
subsidiary powers, **14**, 309
tendering by, **3**, 16
thermal insulation, grants for, **11**, 2036
title and interest to sue, **1**, 319
tourism, powers and duties, **11**, 1793–1795
  collaboration between districts, **11**, 1795
  financial assistance, **11**, 1794
  promotion of tourism, **11**, 1793
trading standards, *see* TRADING STANDARDS
tramways—
  position in relation to, **19**, 1129, 1131, 1139n, 1140
  regulations, power to make, **19**, 1135
transfer of functions to new authority, **19**, 864, 864n
travel concessions, **14**, 420; **20**, 493
travelling people, provision for, **19**, 349
trustee, as, **24**, 134, 135
ultra vires principle, application of, **14**, 131
  See also ULTRA VIRES DOCTRINE
unstable tip, powers in respect of, **14**, 1696
use of health service premises, goods or services, **11**, 1492
vermin, control of, **19**, 444
veterinary inspectors, appointment of, **11**, 444, 444n
voluntary organisations—
  discretion to assist, **22**, 10
voting, **14**, 91
waste collection and disposal, **19**, 361–363
water supply, fluoridation of, **25**, 509
works, **14**, 325, 326, 904–906, 916

Local authority—*continued*
young person, duty to, **22**, 17–22
    See also YOUNG PERSON
See also LOCAL GOVERNMENT
Local byelaws
See BYELAWS
Local courts
feudal system, **6**, 897, 908
Local elections
See ELECTION
Local government
administration—
    government and local government
        distinguished, **14**, 1
    parish, **14**, 24
    rural—
        commission of supply, **14**, 25, 29
        constable, **14**, 25, 28
        county, **14**, 23
        justice of peace, **14**, 25, 27
        parish, **14**, 24
        sheriff, **14**, 25, 26
    services, development of, **14**, 31
administrative county, England and Wales, **14**, 6
advice—
    central government, **14**, 104
    Convention of Scottish Local Authorities
        (COSLA), **14**, 86
area—
    boundary order by Secretary of State, **14**, 70
    change of name, **14**, 71
    enterprise zone, designation of, **14**, 643
    islands, see ISLANDS AREA
    local inquiry, **14**, 69
    passenger transport, see PUBLIC TRANSPORT
    police, **14**, 478
    report, **14**, 69
    repositories, **14**, 586
    review—
        direction, **14**, 68
        electoral arrangements, **14**, 67
        periodic, **14**, 66
        powers, **14**, 65
        procedural arrangements, **14**, 68
area tourist board, **14**, 664
assistant chief constable, appointment, **14**, 483
audit—
    auditors, general duties, **14**, 886
    completion of, **14**, 890
    controller, issues raised with, **14**, 897
    report, **14**, 891, 892
borrowing—
    foreign, **14**, 820
    purposes of, **14**, 814
    reserved functions, **14**, 236
    sources of, **14**, 815
burgh, see BURGH
byelaws, see BYELAWS
central government—
    controls—
        appellate powers, **14**, 112
        approval, **14**, 105
        byelaws, confirmation of, **14**, 109
        consent, **14**, 105

Local government—*continued*
central government—*continued*
    controls—*continued*
        default powers, **14**, 117
        direct, **14**, 105
        financial relationship with, **5**, 572, 573; **14**, 114
        generally, **14**, 101
        inspection, powers of, **14**, 113
        intervention, powers of, **14**, 106
        local inquiry, power to order, **14**, 116
        ministerial responsibilities, **14**, 102
        officers, appointment and dismissal, **14**, 110
        regulation-making powers, **14**, 107
        relaxation of, **14**, 115
        removal of, **14**, 115
        veto, powers of, **14**, 108
    education, responsibility for, **14**, 36
    executive authority, **14**, 3
    expenditure guidelines, **14**, 875
    influence, **14**, 103, 104, 111
    local government compared with, **14**, 1, 94
    Parliament, answerable directly to, **14**, 3
    poor relief, responsibility for, **14**, 34
charter—
    burgh, **14**, 10
    Crown, **14**, 10
    feu-ferme, **14**, 11
civil defence, see CIVIL DEFENCE
coast protection, see COAST PROTECTION
code of conduct, **14**, 232
commerce—
    burgh, privileges of, **14**, 12
    enterprise zone, see ENTERPRISE ZONE
    financial assistance to, **14**, 312
    loan, **14**, 639
Commissioner for Local Administration in Scotland, see COMMISSIONER FOR LOCAL ADMINISTRATION IN SCOTLAND
competition, **14**, 915–920
Convention of Scottish Local Authorities, see CONVENTION OF SCOTTISH LOCAL AUTHORITIES
council—
    burgh, **14**, 14, 16
    community, see COMMUNITY COUNCIL
    county, see COUNTY COUNCIL
    district, see DISTRICT COUNCIL
    facilities, use of, code of conduct, **14**, 232
    full, meetings of, member's right to attend, **14**, 219
    islands area, see ISLANDS AREA
    regional, see REGIONAL COUNCIL
councillor—
    code of conduct, **14**, 232
    disqualification, appeal to sheriff, **14**, 119
    election, see ELECTION
    personal liability, **14**, 223
    qualified privilege, **15**, 528
countryside, see COUNTRYSIDE
default powers, **14**, 117
development—
    nineteenth century, **5**, 567
    to end of 1939–45 War, **5**, 568
district, see DISTRICT

Local government—*continued*
documents—
  deposit of, **14**, 263
  inspection of, **14**, 263, 264, 265
  local elections, **14**, 90
  photographic copies, **14**, 266
  seal, use of, **14**, 260
elections, *see* ELECTION
emergency, **14**, 327
England and Wales, in, **14**, 60–62
  See also ENGLAND AND WALES
enterprise zone, *see* ENTERPRISE ZONE
expenditure, *see* PUBLIC EXPENDITURE
expenses, *see* LOCAL AUTHORITY
external controls—
  central government, *see* CENTRAL GOVERNMENT
  Commissioner for Local Administration, *see*
    COMMISSIONER FOR LOCAL ADMINISTRATION
    IN SCOTLAND
  judicial, *see* JUDICIAL CONTROL
  ultra vires doctrine of, *see* ULTRA VIRES DOCTRINE
  veto, powers of, **14**, 108
finance—
  borrowing, reserved functions, **14**, 236
  burgh, liability of, **14**, 11
  capital expenditure, *see* expenditure *above*
  central government, control by, **14**, 101
  commerce, aids to, *see* commerce *above*
  Convention of Scottish Local Authorities, **14**, 87
  general fund, **14**, 803
  housing, **14**, 613
  industry, aids to, *see* industry *below*
  management, **14**, 801
  planning system, **14**, 806
  public transport, assistance for, **14**, 417
  revenue expenditure, *see* expenditure *above*
  Secretary of State, powers reserved to, **14**, 114
  sewerage, powers relating to, **14**, 458
  See also PUBLIC EXPENDITURE
financial controls, **14**, 114
fire services, *see* FIRE SERVICES; LOCAL AUTHORITY
flood prevention, *see* FLOOD
functions—
  administration of, **13**, 1439
  allocation of, **14**, 402
  civic amenities, *see* civic amenities *above*
  committee, discharge by, *see* MEETING
  concerted action, **14**, 80
  concurrent, **14**, 79
  discharge of, **14**, 8
  education, *see* education *above*
  environmental health, *see* ENVIRONMENTAL
    HEALTH
  examination of, **14**, 45
  generally, **14**, 401
  housing, *see* HOUSING
  individual, **14**, 403
  parliament, control by, **14**, 101
  planning, *see* TOWN AND COUNTRY PLANNING
  poor relief, **14**, 34
  registration, *see* REGISTRATION
  reserved, **14**, 236
  sole, **14**, 78
  Stodart Committee, influence of, **14**, 59

Local government—*continued*
functions—*continued*
  transportation, *see* TRANSPORT
  urban development corporation, exercise by,
    14, 668
  vagrancy, **14**, 34
  Wheatley Report, effect of, **14**, 58, 59
fundamental concepts—
  corporate personality, **14**, 2
  discharge of functions, **14**, 8
  government distinguished from administration,
    14, 1
  legislative powers, **14**, 3
  local dimension, **14**, 5
  representative nature, **14**, 6
  Scottish dimension, **14**, 4
  sovereign powers, **14**, 3
  taxing powers, **14**, 7
  generally, **5**, 566
grants, *see* GRANT
guidance—
  central government, **14**, 104
  planning, **14**, 626
history of—
  burgh, *see* BURGH
  housing, **14**, 609
  provision of services, **22**, 2
  roots of system, **14**, 9
  rural administration—
    commission of supply, **14**, 25, 29
    constable, **14**, 25, 28
    county, **14**, 23
    justice of peace, **14**, 25, 27
    main institutions, **14**, 25
    parish, **14**, 24
    sheriff, **14**, 25, 26
improvement area, *see* IMPROVEMENT AREA
industrial promotion, **14**, 631–636
industry—
  enterprise zone, *see* ENTERPISE ZONE
  financial assistance to, **14**, 312, 639, 640
  loan, **14**, 639
information—
  access to—
    member's right of, **14**, 222
    public's right of, **14**, 334
  code of conduct, **14**, 232
  collection of, **14**, 331
  generally, **14**, 330
  provision of, **14**, 332
  publication, **14**, 333
  research, **14**, 331
  road safety, **14**, 412
inner urban area, *see* INNER URBAN AREA
insurance, **14**, 329
islands area, *see* ISLANDS AREA
licensing, *see* LICENCE; LICENSING
loan—
  administration, **13**, 1446
  building, erection of, **14**, 639
  capital, *see* expenditure *above*
  commercial undertakings, **14**, 640
  community council, to, **14**, 73*n*
  disaster, relating to, **14**, 327

Local government—*continued*
loan—*continued*
  emergency, relating to, **14**, 327
  harbour authority, to, **14**, 446
  industrial undertakings, **14**, 640
  inner urban area, to, *see* INNER URBAN AREA
  interest, **14**, 639
  land, acquisition of, **14**, 639
  reserved functions, **14**, 236
  security for advance, **14**, 639
local administration, replacement of term, **14**, 1
meaning, **14**, 5
meeting, *see* LOCAL AUTHORITY; MEETING
ministerial responsibility, **14**, 102
monitoring officer, **13**, 1444
National Code of Local Government Conduct,
  14, 232
nineteenth century developments, **5**, 567
official visits, expenses of, **14**, 229
orders—
  boundary, **14**, 70
  closing, **14**, 305
  demolition, **14**, 305
  designation, **14**, 304
  exclusion, power to make, **14**, 301
  local authority, made by, **14**, 302–305
  public procession, regulation of, **14**, 305
  standing, *see* STANDING ORDER
  traffic regulation, **14**, 303
parish, *see* PARISH
physical renewal, years of, **5**, 570
planning, *see* TOWN AND COUNTRY PLANNING
police, *see* POLICE
political dimension—
  cabinet system, **14**, 94
  committees—
    appointment of, **14**, 91
    chairmanship, **14**, 93
    majority party, position of, **14**, 91
    minority party, position of, **14**, 92
  generally, **13**, 1442; **14**, 89
  independent members, **14**, 92
  internal organisation and operations, **14**, 91
  local elections, **14**, 90
  majority parties, **14**, 91
  minority parties, **14**, 92
  publicity, prohibition of, **14**, 314, 336
  Widdicombe Report, **14**, 95
post-war period, **5**, 569
private interests, code of conduct, **14**, 232
public health legislation, **19**, 305
public inquiries, **13**, 1447
public transport, *see* PUBLIC TRANSPORT
rates, *see* RATES
reform—
  1929, in, **14**, 38–40
  1973, in—
    functions, examination of—
      amenity functions, **14**, 51
      areas, examination of, **14**, 53
      communities, examination of, **14**, 53
      community council, **14**, 57
      conclusions, **14**, 52
      districts, **14**, 56

Local government—*continued*
reform—*continued*
  1973, in—*continued*
    functions, examination of—*continued*
      environmental services, **14**, 50
      generally, **14**, 45
      housing, **14**, 48
      personal social services, **14**, 47
      planning and associated services, **14**, 46
      protective services, **14**, 49
      regions, **14**, 55
      structure, conclusions on, **14**, 54
      tiers—
        first, **14**, 55
        second, **14**, 56
    move for reform, **14**, 41
    need for reform, **14**, 43
    objectives, **14**, 44
    Stodart Committee, influence of, **14**, 59
    Wheatley Commission, **14**, 42
    Wheatley Report, effect of, **14**, 58
  burghal, **14**, 21
  county council, **14**, 30
  education, **14**, 36
  England and Wales, **14**, 61
  late nineteenth century, **14**, 30–37
  lunacy, **14**, 35
  objectives, **14**, 44
  poor relief, **14**, 34
  public health, **14**, 37
  registration, **14**, 32
  roads, **14**, 33
  services, development of, **14**, 31
  vagrancy, **14**, 34
regional council, *see* REGIONAL COUNCIL
regional planning authority, *see* REGIONAL
  PLANNING AUTHORITY
regulations, Secretary of State's powers, **14**, 107
reorganisation, **5**, 502
  implementation of, **5**, 571
  planning for, **5**, 571
  and the reporter service, **3**, 1302
  See also structure of *below*
report—
  chief constable, **14**, 485
  Commissioner for Local Administration,
    investigation by, **14**, 143
  deposit of, **14**, 263
  inspection of, **14**, 263
  joint board, **14**, 267
  joint committee, **14**, 267
  local authority, **14**, 267
  review by Local Government Boundary
    Commission, **14**, 69
  See also REPORT
rural administration, *see* RURAL ADMINISTRATION
Secretary of State, power of veto, **14**, 108
sewerage, functions as to, *see* LOCAL AUTHORITY;
  SEWAGE
sheriff court jurisdiction, **6**, 1115
social facilities, *see* SOCIAL FACILITIES
structure of—
  boundary orders, **14**, 70
  central government, control by, **14**, 101

Local government—*continued*
structure of—*continued*
  community councils—
    amendment of schemes, **14**, 76
    elections, **14**, 75
    functions, **14**, 72
    resources, **14**, 73
    schemes for establishment, **14**, 74
    status, **14**, 72
  district council—
    change of name, **14**, 71
    new structure, **14**, 64
  districts, **14**, 56
  inter-authority relationships—
    concerted action, **14**, 80
    concurrent functions, **14**, 79
    generally, **14**, 77
    sole functions, **14**, 78
  islands area council—
    change of name, **14**, 71
    new structure, **14**, 64
  local inquiry, **14**, 69
  regional council—
    change of name, **14**, 71
    new structure, **14**, 64
  regions, **14**, 55
  reorganisation—
    district councils, **14**, 64
    generally, **14**, 63; **25**, 502
    implementation of, **5**, 571
    islands area councils, **14**, 64
    planning for, **5**, 571
    regional councils, **14**, 64
  review—
    directions, **14**, 68
    electoral arrangements, **14**, 67
    Local government Boundary Commission, **14**, 65
    periodic, **14**, 66
    procedural requirements, **14**, 68
    report, **14**, 69
  tiers—
    first, **14**, 55
    second, **14**, 56
  Wheatley Commission conclusions, **14**, 54
tourism, *see* TOURISM
town clerk, **13**, 1443, 1443*n*
trading standards department, local authority, **6**, 95
Wales, in, *see* ENGLAND AND WALES
water authority, *see* WATER AUTHORITY
Wheatley Report, **11**, 1903; **14**, 41–58; **23**, 9
Widdicombe Report, **14**, 94, 95
wide-ranging role, **13**, 1442
See also LOCAL AUTHORITY
Local journey
common travel area, **12**, 122
meaning, **12**, 122
Local plan
See TOWN AND COUNTRY PLANNING
Local statutory provision
in force on 16 May 1975 ..., **14**, 307
general repeal, **14**, 308
meaning, **14**, 307

Locatio conductio rei
contract of, generally, **3**, 601
loan compared, **13**, 1706
meaning, **13**, 1783
Locatio custodiae
contract of, **8**, 3
loan compared, **13**, 1705
Locatio mercium vehendarum
nature of contract, **3**, 601
Locatio operis faciendi
contract of, **8**, 3
locatio mercium vehendarum, as, **3**, 601
Location, contract of
See LEASE/HIRE OF MOVEABLES
Loch
alveus, *see* ALVEUS
drainage, **25**, 338
generally, **25**, 337
inland, **21**, 112; **25**, 337
  salvage operations, **21**, 440
islands—
  formation of, **18**, 59, 593
  ownership, **18**, 303
more than one proprietor owning surrounding land, **11**, 48
navigable, ownership, **18**, 304, 304*n*
navigation, **25**, 337
non-tidal—
  a coelo usque ad centrum, *alveus* owned, **18**, 303
  alveus, **18**, 303
  banks, local government powers as to, **18**, 308
  common interest, doctrine of, **18**, 305, 307, 359
  fishing rights, **18**, 306, 307
    over-fishing, where danger of, **18**, 306
  fundus, **18**, 303
  islands, ownership, **18**, 303
  local government powers as to, **18**, 308
  navigation, public right of, *see* NAVIGATION
  nuisance, regulations as to, **18**, 308
  overflowing legal boundary, riparian proprietors' rights, **18**, 306
  ownership—
    a coelo usque ad centrum, **18**, 303
    alveus, **18**, 275–277
    common, **18**, 305
    generally, **18**, 304
    islands, **18**, 303
    loch bordering on more than one estate, **18**, 304
    loch wholly within one estate, **18**, 304
    presumption as to, **18**, 304
    riparian proprietor, **18**, 304, 305
    several, **18**, 305
    stagnum lochs, **18**, 304
    water, of, **18**, 304
  pollution, regulations as to, **18**, 308
  riparian proprietor, **18**, 303, 305
    fishing rights, **18**, 306
    obligations in common interest, **18**, 307
    restrictions on use, **18**, 306–308
    right to enter that part of *alveus* which is not his, **18**, 306
    sailing rights, **18**, 306
    use of loch, **18**, 306

Loch—*continued*
non-tidal—*continued*
   sailing rights, **18**, 306, 307
   salmon fishings, **18**, 306
   seasonal variations, **18**, 303
   servitudes, **18**, 308
non-tidal waters, **21**, 112
overflow, where no perennial, **18**, 303
pollution, **25**, 338
public rights over—
   generally, **18**, 514
   navigation, *see* NAVIGATION
sea, **25**, 337
   ownership, **18**, 309
shared, **25**, 339
stagnum, **18**, 307
   drainage rights, **18**, 340, 341
   meaning, **18**, 303
   ownership of water in, **18**, 304
surface water, whether heritable or moveable
   property, **18**, 273
tidal—
   adjacent proprietors, rights of, **18**, 312
   alienation to subject proprietors, **18**, 311
   Crown ownership, **18**, 309
     nature of, **18**, 310
   trespass on, **18**, 180
   See also TRESPASS
valuation for rating, **24**, 672
water pollution, **14**, 2079
within one property, **25**, 338
Lochaber
population, **14**, 64
Lochmaben
Kindly Tenants of, **13**, 212
Lockfast place
opening, with intent to steal, **7**, 348
theft by opening, **7**, 339, 342
Lock-out
continuous employment, effect on, **9**, 46
loss or damage resulting from, carrier not liable,
   21, 603
redundancy payment, effect on, **9**, 182
Locomotive
heavy, **20**, 407
light, **20**, 407
operation of, **14**, 1640
weight, **20**, 476
Locus standi
private Bill, petitioner against, **19**, 85, 86
   objection to, **19**, 87
provisional order, petitioner against, **19**, 49, 51,
   54
Lodger
multiple occupation registration schemes, **11**, 2005
not occupier, **24**, 447*n*
police force, member of taking in, **16**, 1749, 1754
public sector housing, **11**, 1951
Lodging house
boarding house distinguished, **11**, 1710
common, meaning, **19**, 454*n*
hotel distinguished, **11**, 1710
infectious diseases, regulations in relation to, **19**,
   469–472

Lodging house—*continued*
infectious persons in, **19**, 454
inspection, **19**, 469
keeper of—
   duties, **19**, 472
   meaning, **19**, 454*n*
liability, **11**, 1742
lodger, generally, *see* LODGER
meaning, **11**, 1710
public health provisions, **19**, 306, 454
registration of, **19**, 469–471
Lodgings
advance booking, **13**, 196
lease, **13**, 196
residence in, as element of domicile, **4**, 30
tenancy excluded from protected tenancy status,
   13, 630
Lomé Convention
generally, **10**, 74
signatories to, CCT preferential trade agreement,
   7, 1016
London Convention (1976)
limitation of liability, *see* SEA, CARRIAGE BY
   (limitation of liability)
London Dumping Convention
abandoned or disused installations on continental
   shelf, **21**, 33
London Gazette
documentary evidence, as, **10**, 593
notice of provisional order in, **19**, 7
London International Financial Futures
   Exchange
investment exchange, as, **12**, 1322
London Options Clearing House
investment exchange, as, **12**, 1322
London Regional Transport
functions, **14**, 62
Loosing
arrestment, **8**, 307
Lord
administration of justice, **22**, 509
feudal tenure of land, **22**, 509
franchisal justice, grant to, **22**, 509
free tenants, disputes within powers of lord's
   court, **22**, 509
right to hold court for tenants, **22**, 509
unfree tenants, judicial powers in relation to, **22**,
   509
Lord Advocate
absolute privilege, **15**, 444, 448, 449, 526
advisory role, **13**, 1403
appeals, consideration of, **13**, 1434
appointment of, **17**, 529, 578
Attorney General in England, analogous power of
   reference, **22**, 319
consultation of Lord President, **6**, 930
Conveyancing (Departmental) Committee, law
   reform, **22**, 637, 646, 647
criminal prosecutions brought by, **7**, 26; **13**, 1430
Crown Office, **13**, 1410
department of, **5**, 509
functions, **17**, 578
great officer of state, as, **6**, 862
history of office, **17**, 527

Lord Advocate—*continued*
House of Lords, customarily has seat in, **5**, 306,
   371
indictment in name of, **6**, 872
judiciary, relationship to, **17**, 583
Law Reform Committee for Scotland, **9**, 1954
   institution by, **22**, 650
   referral of matters by Lord Advocate to, **22**,
      650
   secretariat provided from Lord Advocate's
      Department, **22**, 650
law reform as duty of, **6**, 1051
legal advice—
   civil litigation, and, **5**, 541
   legislation, and, **5**, 539
legal ministerial functions, **5**, 538
legislation—
   drafting of, **5**, 540
   legal advice and, **5**, 539
litigation, intervention in, **7**, 752
Lord Advocate's Department, *see* LEGAL CIVIL
   SERVICE
'Master of instance', as, **6**, 872
miscellaneous functions, **5**, 542
modern status of office, **17**, 529
Officer of State, **7**, 800, 804, 808
police, relationship to, **17**, 584
precedence, **16**, 2020
private prosecutors and, **17**, 528
procurator fiscal, links with, **17**, 534
Procurator Fiscal Service, **13**, 1410, 1425
prosecution of crime in Scotland, **6**, 872; **7**, 26;
   13, 1403, 1410
public interest, acting in, **1**, 323
public prosecutor, as, **17**, 578
questions to, **5**, 391
reference to High Court—
   generally, **17**, 830
   point of law, **22**, 319, 320
   Thomson Committee on Criminal Appeals in
      Scotland, recommendation, **22**, 319
Scottish Courts Administration, discharge of
   functions by, **13**, 1406
Scottish Law Commission—
   annual report by Commissioners to, **22**, 666
   appointment of Commissioners, **22**, 665
   duty to lay Commission's programme before
      Parliament, **22**, 666
   responsibility for, **13**, 1407
Secretary of State for Scotland, continuing
   relationship with, **5**, 537
sheriff court, powers in relation to, **6**, 1051
solicitors to, **17**, 539
solemn procedure, duties, **13**, 1432
specific performance of statutory duty, applying
   for, **1**, 336
staff, **17**, 537
sudden, suspicious or unexplained death, report
   by procurator fiscal, **13**, 1435
Lord Auditors
hearing and disposition of petitions and
   complaints by, **6**, 902
jurisdiction, **6**, 902

Lord Chamberlain
office of, **7**, 774
Lord Chancellor
appointment and functions, **5**, 370, 510
appointment of Scottish, **13**, 1300
House of Lords, as member of, **6**, 817, 821, 826,
   828
killing, treason, as, **7**, 569
office of, **7**, 774, 864
   functions of, **5**, 510
See also HOUSE OF LORDS
Lord Chief Baron
office of, **7**, 804
Lord Clerk Register
appointment, **19**, 802, 805
Commissioner for the Regalia, **19**, 805, 807
Deputy Clerk Register, *see* DEPUTY CLERK
   REGISTER
duties devolved to Deputy Clerk Register, **19**, 809
functions of, **19**, 807
history of office, **19**, 801–807
   after the Union, **19**, 805
   before the Union, **19**, 804
   Court of Session judge, sitting as, **19**, 804
   Deputy Keepers, **19**, 806
   early records, keeping of, **19**, 803
   elections of Scottish representative peers, **19**,
      805, 807
   jurisdiction, **19**, 801
   origins, **19**, 802
   Register of Sasines, **19**, 804, 810
Keeper of the Signet, **19**, 805, 807
miscellaneous records, **19**, 844
Officer of State, **7**, 804, 807
oldest surviving officer of state, **19**, 801
precedence, **19**, 807
register, meaning, **19**, 802, 802*n*
titular dignity, as, **19**, 801, 805
Lord High Admiral
Officer of the Crown, as, **7**, 812, 816
Lord High Chancellor of Great Britain
See HOUSE OF LORDS; LORD CHANCELLOR
**Lord High Commissioner to the General
   Assembly of the Church of Scotland**
precedence, **16**, 2006
Lord High Constable of Scotland
armorial additaments or insignia, **11**, 1610, 1621
Great Officer of royal household, as, **7**, 820, 821
Officer of the Crown, as, **7**, 812, 814
precedence, **16**, 2006
Lord High Treasurer
killing, treason, as, **7**, 569
Lord Justice-Clerk
bail appeals, **6**, 862
Court of Session, **6**, 862, 923, 926, 929, 930, 931
deputes, appointment of, **17**, 506
functions and duties, **6**, 862, 931; **17**, 506; **22**, 520
great officer of state, as, **6**, 862
origin of office, **6**, 862
sheriff court, duties in relation to, **6**, 1052
status, **6**, 862
Lord Justice-General
Court of Session, **6**, 903, 911, 923
criminal business, seventeenth century, **22**, 520

Lord Justice-General—*continued*
early history, **6**, 848*ff*.849
functions, **6**, 862
great officer of state, as, **6**, 862
High Court records, disposal of, **19**, 866
insignia of office, **11**, 1610
Justiciar, progression of office from, **6**, 849
Lord President, merger of office with, **6**, 903
origin of office, **17**, 506
paroled prisoners, **6**, 862
President of High Court of Justiciary, as, **6**, 862, 864; **22**, 520
Queen's Counsel, appointment of, **6**, 862
subordinate legislation, responsibility for, **6**, 862
See also JUSTICIAR; LORD PRESIDENT
Lord Lieutenant
appointment of, **5**, 548
Association of Lieutenants of Counties and Custodes Rotulorum, **5**, 563
deputy, **5**, 559
duties of—
    armed forces, **5**, 550
    civil functions, **5**, 556
    generally, **5**, 548
    honours, recommendations for, **5**, 551
    justices, **5**, 552
    matters of general concern, **5**, 554
    medals, presentation of, **5**, 551
    protocol, **5**, 555
    royal visits, **5**, 549
    social functions, **5**, 556
    tax commissioners, **5**, 553
    visiting heads of state, **5**, 549
lieutenant, appointment of, **5**, 558
vice, **5**, 557
See also LIEUTENANCY
Lord Lyon
See LYON KING OF ARMS, LORD
Lord of the Isles
heir to Crown as, **7**, 704, 704*n*, 786
Lord Ordinary
See COURT OF SESSION
Lord President
appointment, **6**, 930
casting vote, **22**, 254
court records, disposal of, **19**, 866
Court of Session, **6**, 903, 911, 913, 923, 926, 927, 929, 930, 934
functions, **6**, 930
historical background, **22**, 517
merger with office of Lord Justice-General, **6**, 903
non-lawyers, consideration of draft scheme proposals as to rights of audience or conduct of litigation, **13**, 1455–1457
Private Office, **6**, 934
sheriff court, duties in relation to, **6**, 1052
Lord President of the Council
office of, **7**, 774, 799
Officer of State, **7**, 792, 793
Lord Privy Seal
office of, **7**, 774, 792, 866
Lord Provost, **14**, 6*n*
Lords, House of, *see* HOUSE OF LORDS

Lords of Appeal in Ordinary
appointment, **6**, 927
functions, **5**, 368
House of Lords, **6**, 821, 822, 823, 826, 827, 828
number of, **5**, 368; **6**, 827
oath of allegiance, **6**, 827
precedence, **16**, 2018, 2020
qualification, **6**, 827
removal from office, **6**, 827
retirement, **6**, 827
Scottish, **5**, 368
Lords Commissioners of Justiciary
Court of Session, **6**, 923; **22**, 520
Lords of Council and Session
Court of Session, **6**, 903, 904
jurisdiction, **6**, 903
Lords of Regality
Courts of Regality, **6**, 897
Lords of Session
early history, **6**, 851
Lords Spiritual
House of Lords, **5**, 366; **6**, 823
precedence, **16**, 2016
Lords in Waiting
appointment, **7**, 774
Lordship
mineral lease, **13**, 103, 199
Lorimer, James
international law, writings on, **19**, 610
Lorry
contract for carriage by, **3**, 601
Loss
annoyance, arising from, **14**, 2047
discomfort, arising from, **14**, 2047
economic—
    claim against manufacturer, **6**, 38
    damages for, **14**, 2153
    duty of care, *see* CARE, DUTY OF
    generally, *see* ECONOMIC LOSS
farm, of, *see* FARM LOSS PAYMENT
home, of, *see* HOME LOSS PAYMENT
inconvenience, arising from, **14**, 2047
obligation of reparation, **11**, 1032
process, of, **17**, 1041
Scottish Arts Council guarantee against, **9**, 1007
unfair dismissal, award for, *see* UNFAIR DISMISSAL
Loss adjuster
partnership, number of partners allowed, **16**, 1011
Lost property
See PROPERTY (lost or abandoned)
Lothian Region
population, **14**, 64
structure, **14**, 64
transport undertakings, operation of, **14**, 419
Lottery
advertisement or notice of, importation, **7**, 1203
advertisement of, **1**, 531
appeal to sheriff relating to, **17**, 1249
Art Union Draw, **2**, 1658
'free lotteries', **2**, 1661
history of, **2**, 1658
illegality, **2**, 1662
legislation, current, **2**, 1659

Lottery—*continued*
Lex fori application of mandatory provisions of, **17**, 183
licensing, **14**, 517
local—
  expenses of running, **2**, 1676
  frequency of, **2**, 1674
  general provisions, **2**, 1674
  meaning, **2**, 1671
  price of tickets, **2**, 1675
  prizes, limitation of, **2**, 1676
  proceeds, application of, **2**, 1672
  purposes of, **2**, 1672
  schemes for—
    approval of, **2**, 1671
    registration of, **2**, 1673
    residual powers of Minister, **2**, 1677
lottery duty, **7**, 1080, 1086
meaning, **2**, 1660
National Lottery, **7**, 1080, 1086
nature of, **2**, 1658
newspaper competitions, **2**, 1661
offences—
  defences to, **2**, 1664
  summary of, **2**, 1663
premium savings bond, **2**, 1658
private—
  conditions for, **2**, 1666
  meaning, **2**, 1666
promotional lotteries, **2**, 1661
Scottish law, **2**, 1660
sheriff court jurisdiction, **6**, 1082; **17**, 1249
small, conditions of, **2**, 1665
society's lottery—
  expenses of running, **2**, 1676
  frequency of, **2**, 1674
  general provisions, **2**, 1674
  legality, **2**, 1668
  meaning, **2**, 1667
  price of tickets, **2**, 1675
  prizes, limitation of, **2**, 1676
  proceeds, application of, **2**, 1668
  registration of society—
    application for, **2**, 1669
    refusal of, **2**, 1669
  returns to be made of, **2**, 1670
VAT exemption, **7**, 1423
Louisiana
Trust Code, **24**, 126
Lowest low-water mark
meaning, **12**, 1239
Loyal Order of Ancient Shepherds
generally, **12**, 679*n*
Lozenge
arms of ladies depicted on, **11**, 1604, 1614
device displayed on, **11**, 1613
Lubricants
weights and measures legislation, **6**, 237
Lucratus
recompense, and, **15**, 62, 63, 64
Lugano Convention
generally, **8**, 429

Luggage
air, carriage by—
  baggage checks, **3**, 745
  destruction, loss or damage to, **3**, 751
    contributory negligence, where, **3**, 754
boarding house keeper's liability, **11**, 1710
carrier's lien, **3**, 672
dangerous, **11**, 1722
generally, **11**, 1743
hotel's duty to receive, **11**, 1722
hotelkeeper's duty to receive, **11**, 1722
liability of hotelkeeper—
  extent of, **11**, 1744
  limitation, **11**, 1748–1751
lien over, **3**, 672; **11**, 1757
meaning, **11**, 1722; **21**, 727*n*
rail—
  domestic carriage by, **3**, 709, 724
    articles left on Board's premises or trains, **3**, 709
    left luggage offices and lockers, **3**, 725
  international carriage by, **3**, 728, 729
road—
  domestic carriage by, **3**, 686
  international carriage by, **3**, 691
sale of goods left at hotel, **11**, 1759
sea, carriage by—
  cabin—
    meaning, **21**, 727*n*
  contract for carriage of—
    Athens Convention—
      application, **21**, 725
        notification, carrier's duty as to, **21**, 728
      burden of proof, **21**, 732
      generally, **21**, 724
      interpretation, **21**, 726
      jurisdiction, **21**, 731
      limitation of actions, **21**, 737
      scope, **21**, 727
    generally, **21**, 721
    late re-delivery to passenger, pecuniary loss following, **21**, 727*n*
    liability of carrier, **21**, 730, 733
      exclusion and limitation of liability, **21**, 729, 733, 755, 755*n*
      court powers, **21**, 735
      loss of, **21**, 734
      servants and agents, for, **21**, 736
    loss of or damage to luggage, **21**, 727, 730
    nuclear damage, **21**, 738
    valuables, **21**, 728, 733
      deposit with carrier, **21**, 733
      limitation of liability, **21**, 557
    vehicles, **21**, 728
theft of, **11**, 1744, 1745
unreasonable, **11**, 1722
Luminibus non officiendi
servitude right of, **18**, 486
Luminous tube sign
meaning, **19**, 357*n*
regulations as to, **19**, 357
Lump labour
generally, **3**, 7

Lunatic
disqualification for parliamentary candidature, **15**, 1055
meaning, **15**, 1055
mental disorder, meaning, **14**, 1401
statutory provisions, **14**, 1403
See also INSANITY; MENTALLY DISORDERED PERSON
Lunatic asylum
mental disorder, meaning, **14**, 1401
Lures
illegal, **11**, 12
Secretary of State, powers as to, **11**, 23
Luxembourg
European Union customs territory, **7**, 1010
Luxembourg Compromise, **10**, 42
veto introduced by, **10**, 14, 17
Luxembourg Conference, **10**, 24
Lyon, Court of the Lord
abuses of heraldic law, **6**, 1014
administrative and ministerial functions, **6**, 1017
advocate appearing before, dress, **13**, 1323
appeals from—
   Court of Session, to, **6**, 1010, 1020; **22**, 325
   House of Lords, to, **6**, 1010, 1020; **22**, 325
armorial bearings—
   aliens, **6**, 1017
   attributed to wrong person, **6**, 1021
   Commonwealth citizens, **6**, 1017
   Crown interests, **6**, 1019
   deletion, **6**, 1021
   failure to record, **6**, 1017
   grant of, **6**, 1017
   judicial determination of claims, **6**, 1018
   matriculation of, **6**, 1018
   petition initiated by private individual, **6**, 1019
   restoration of, **6**, 1017
   unregistered, **6**, 1021
   wrongful assumption of, **6**, 1014
baronets—
   judicial functions in relation to, **6**, 1018
   Official Roll of, **6**, 1017
constitution, **6**, 1010
Court of Session—
   appeal to, **22**, 325
   jurisdiction to review proceedings, **22**, 325
crest badges, unlicensed manufacture, **11**, 1631
deed of resignation recorded in, **11**, 1622
display of arms without authority, **11**, 1633
enforcement of decrees, **6**, 1021
escheat or arrestment, **6**, 1021
Exchequer dues payable in, **6**, 1014
herald as advocate, **13**, 1323
heraldic decisions, **6**, 1010
heralds and pursuivants, **6**, 1013, 1021
High Court of Chivalry, comparison, **22**, 325
   jurisdiction to reduce own decrees, **22**, 325
House of Lords—
   appeal to, **6**, 1010; **22**, 325
   writ of summons to attend, **6**, 1018
judicial functions, **6**, 1018
judicial titles designated by, **6**, 929
jurisdiction, **5**, 658; **22**, 325
letters of horning, issue of, **6**, 1021

Lyon, Court of the Lord—*continued*
Lord Lyon King of Arms—
   administrative and ministerial duties, **6**, 1010
   appointment, **6**, 1011
   baton, **6**, 1011
   coronation, duties at, **6**, 1010
   late medieval position, **6**, 1010
   oath of allegiance, **6**, 1011
   oath *de fideli administratione*, **6**, 1011
   origin of style and title, **6**, 1011
   pre-feudal Celtic position, **6**, 1010
   presides over court, **6**, 1010
   qualifications for office, **6**, 1011
   retirement, **6**, 1011
   royal appointment, **6**, 1011
Lyon Clerk and Keeper of the Records—
   appointment, **6**, 1012
   commission, petition for, **14**, 1502
   duties, **6**, 1012
   retirement, **6**, 1012
Macer of the Lyon Court, **6**, 1015
money penalties payable to Crown, **6**, 1021
name and change of name, **6**, 1018
order of precedence, definition, **6**, 1017
origins, **6**, 1010
pedigree, proof of, **11**, 1623
peerage claim, hearing in connection with, **16**, 1320, 1320n
   appeals, **16**, 1320n
precedent—
   binding decisions—
      Court of Session, **22**, 325
      High Court of Justiciary, **22**, 325
      House of Lords in Scottish appeals, **22**, 325
   power to distinguish decisions inconsistent with authority, **22**, 325
prescription of decrees of, **11**, 1624
preservation of armorial records, **11**, 1602
procedure, **6**, 1019
Procurator Fiscal of the Lyon Court, **6**, 1021
   appointment, **6**, 1014
   duties, **6**, 1014
protection of armorial rights, **11**, 1633
public ceremonies, **6**, 1017
Public Register of All Arms and Bearings in Scotland, **6**, 1012, 1014, 1018; **11**, 1602
Public Register of All Genealogies and Birthbrieves in Scotland, **6**, 1012
records of, **19**, 842
recovery of documents, commission and diligence for, **6**, 1019
registers, official, **19**, 801
right already vested in another, **6**, 1017
right of audience—
   advocates, **6**, 1013
   enrolled solicitors, **6**, 1013
   heralds of England, **6**, 1013
   members of Scottish peerage, **6**, 1013
   Scottish officers of arms, **6**, 1013
Roll of Officers of Arms and Messengers-at-Arms, **6**, 1012
royal proclamations, execution of, **6**, 1017
Scottish honours, dignities and ceremonies, **6**, 1017

Lyon, Court of the Lord—*continued*
Seal, **7**, 885
state ceremonies, **6**, 1017
state trumpeters, **6**, 1016
statutory offences, **6**, 1014
supporters and other additaments, **6**, 1017, 1018
territorial designations, **6**, 1018
ultra vires acts, **6**, 1017
Lyon King of Arms, Lord
banner sizes laid down by, **11**, 1609
change of name granted by, **19**, 1428
commission of herald, issue of, **14**, 1501
confirmation of arms, **11**, 1616
control exercised by, **14**, 1506
coronet designs, assignment of, **11**, 1607
Court, *see* LYON, COURT OF THE LORD
devices amounting to armorial bearings, **11**, 1613
differences, matriculation of, **11**, 1617, 1620, 1621
Earl Marshal of England, authority of compared,
    22, 325
foreign grants of arms, recognition of, **11**, 1625

Lyon King of Arms, Lord—*continued*
messenger-at-arms—
    appointment, **14**, 1502
    control, **14**, 1501
Officer of the Crown, as, **7**, 812, 818
official arms impaled by personal, **11**, 1627
petitions to, **11**, 1615
powers more extensive than English Kings of
    Arms, **11**, 1615
precedence, judicial role, **16**, 2008
precedency, **16**, 2011, 2013
prerogatives to grant arms, **11**, 1615
refusal to grant arms, **11**, 1615
royal household, as member of, **7**, 833
supporters, grant of, **11**, 1608
titles of honour, role in respect of, **16**, 1321
trade marks jurisdiction, **11**, 1630
wrongful use of arms, *see* LYON, COURT OF THE
    LORD
Lyon Macer
petitioner, examination of, **14**, 1502

M

McBoyle Committee
generally, **22**, 4, 6
Macdonald, John A H
Practical Treatise on the Criminal Law of Scotland, **7**,
2, 6, 13, 268, 272
Macer
appointment and duties, **6**, 935
College of Justice, **6**, 904
Court of Session, **6**, 935
Falkland, **6**, 935
Her Majesty's officers-of-arms, corps of, **14**, 1501
High Court of Justiciary, **6**, 878, 935
Lyon Court, of, **6**, 1015
Macfarlane Trust
payments from, effect on income support, **21**, 1077
MacGibbon, I C
international law, writings on, **19**, 611
Machine tools
plant, as, **14**, 1012
Machinery
See PLANT AND MACHINERY
Mackenzie of Rosehaugh, Sir George
criminal law—
crime against natural or positive law,
distinction, **22**, 421
equity, part in development, **22**, 421
custom and statute, **22**, 130
customary law, **22**, 365, 367
desuetude, doctrine of, **22**, 130
heraldry, law of, **11**, 1612
Institutions of the Law of Scotland, **22**, 434, 441,
538, 543
precedent, view of, **22**, 251
special authority of writings, **22**, 437, 441
*The Laws and Customs of Scotland in Matters
Criminal*, **7**, 58, 161, 162, 168; **22**, 461, 537
written and unwritten law, **22**, 365
Mackerel
fishing licences, **11**, 114
pressure stocks, **11**, 115
Mackintosh Committee
intestate succession, report on, **25**, 686, 687
Magazines
copies to be delivered to certain libraries, **17**, 5
investment advice, publication, **12**, 1307
Magistrate
breach of duty, **6**, 867
judgments of, whether enforceable in Scotland, **8**,
484
lay—
future of, **6**, 1168
generally, **6**, 1160–1168
training, **6**, 1163, 1168
liability in cases of wrongful detention, **15**, 442,
443, 448
office of, **6**, 1156
stipendiary, **6**, 1158, 1160, 1167
appointment, **6**, 1164
temporary, **6**, 1164

Mail
acceptance of offer by post, **15**, 644
communication by post, contract law, **15**, 644,
647, 648
induciae commencement of action *naturalis
computatio* from time of posting, **22**, 820
interception of communications, *see*
COMMUNICATIONS
interception of, police surveillance activities, **16**,
1802
inviolability, **16**, 1912
postal packet, import and export, regulation, **7**,
1198
receiving stolen or secreted, **7**, 395
service by post, Interpretation Act 1978 rules as
to, **12**, 1208
theft of, **7**, 339, 343
transit of goods via post, **7**, 1169, 1172
unlawful dealing in, **7**, 345
See also COMMUNICATIONS; POSTAL PACKET
Mail order
advertising, **6**, 84
information in, **1**, 535
Mailing list
data protection register, exemption from
registration in, **18**, 1519
Maills and duties
action of, **20**, 115, 265
effect on lease, **13**, 158
transfer of landlord's interest, **13**, 351
adjudger of leased subjects, use by, **8**, 305
common law procedure, **8**, 397
company administration, and, **8**, 399
competence, **8**, 397
competition, **8**, 399
creditor, rights of, **8**, 398
debitum fundi, holder of, **8**, 394
defender, **8**, 397
enforcement of secured debts, **8**, 101
floating charge, and, **8**, 399
heritable creditor, **8**, 305
intimation, **8**, 397
liquidation of debtor, unaffected by, **8**, 399
nature of, **8**, 393
parties available to, **8**, 394
procedure, **8**, 397
sequestration of debtor, unaffected by, **8**, 399
service, **8**, 397
standard security, enforcement of direct payment,
8, 396
statutory procedure, **8**, 397
Maintenance
actions for recovery of, **6**, 1062
advances to beneficiaries for, **24**, 76, 203
counterclaim for, **17**, 1048, 1233
current maintenance arrestment, **8**, 248
family credit, entitlement to affected by, **21**, 1090
income support, calculation, **21**, 1077
liability for payment, calculation of period, **22**, 827

Maintenance—*continued*
order—
 continuing periodical obligation to pay, **8**, 569
 enforcement—
  common law, under, **8**, 570
   foreign legal system, and, **8**, 569
  foreign legal system, under—
   common law, **8**, 569, 570
   generally, **8**, 569
   statutory schemes, **8**, 569
  non-UK order—
   bilateral arrangements, **8**, 583
   generally, **8**, 580
   Maintenance Orders (Reciprocal Enforce-
    ment) Act (1972)—
    generally, **8**, 577
    scope and extent of provisions, **8**, 578
   provisional order procedure, **8**, 581
   registration under one UK legal system, **8**,
    571
   United Nations Convention for the
    Recovery Abroad of Maintenance, **8**,
    582
  Scottish order—
   beyond UK, **8**, 579
   elsewhere in UK, **8**, 571
  UK order—
   beyond UK—
    bilateral agreements, **8**, 583
   elsewhere in UK—
    aliment, orders for, **8**, 571
     discharge, **8**, 575
     generally, **8**, 574
     Maintenance Orders Act (1950),
      extent and scope, **8**, 571
     Northern Ireland, **8**, 571
    registration of order—
     application for, **8**, 572
     cancellation, **8**, 574, 576
     generally, **8**, 571
     transmission of order, **8**, 573
    variation, **8**, 575
   generally, **8**, 579
   Judgments Convention—
    application, **8**, 432, 454, 455, 467
    overlap with other schemes, **8**, 585
    procedure, generally, **8**, 586
    scope, **8**, 584
   Maintenance Order (Reciprocal Enforce-
    ment) Act (1972)—
    generally, **8**, 577
    scope and extent of provisions, **8**, 578
   provisional order procedure, **8**, 581
   United Nations Convention for the
    Recovery Abroad of Maintenance, **8**,
    582
 meaning, **8**, 569
 parent on income support, **21**, 1070
special jurisdiction, **4**, 39
succession, meaning, **25**, 616
See also ALIMENT
Mair
sheriff, assistance for, **14**, 1501
sheriff officer, replacement by, **14**, 1508

Majority
age of, **10**, 1049
attainment of—
 naturalis computatio calculation by, **22**, 820, 824
 European Convention on the Calculation of
  Time Limits, **22**, 827
meaning, **12**, 1218, 1268
Mala in se
strict liability, **7**, 107
use of term, **7**, 25
Mala prohibita
strict liability, **7**, 107
use of term, **7**, 25
Male
heritable succession, **25**, 678
preference of, abolition of, **25**, 687
Malice
appeal, grounds for, **17**, 846
averment, judicial remedies against actings of
 voluntary church, **3**, 1652
averment of, sufficiency, **15**, 456
conduct causing invasion, **14**, 2069
defamation—
 damages, award of, **15**, 552
 generally, **15**, 470, 479, 500
diligence, **15**, 465
evidence, in, inference of, **10**, 744
liability, *see* LIABILITY
litigation, **15**, 459
malicious mischief, *see* MALICIOUS MISCHIEF
malicious motives, *see* AEMULATIO VICINI
malicious prosecution, *see* MALICIOUS PROSECUTION
meaning, **15**, 454
non-natural person, **15**, 479
prior, towards victim of assault, **7**, 236
publication privileged unless made with, **17**, 20
qualified privilege—
 generally, **15**, 527, 537
 proof of, **15**, 538
use of term, **7**, 69
wrongful detention, **15**, 439, 443
Malicious falsehood
defamation, as, **16**, 2173
English law, **15**, 557
limitation of actions, **16**, 2173
Malicious mischief
contractual duties, **9**, 123
definition, **7**, 410
entitlement to act, defence of, **7**, 412
explosive substances, use of, **7**, 413
firearm or imitation firearm possessed during, **10**,
 1565
fireraising, *see* FIRERAISING
malicious, meaning, **7**, 411
more than one mental element, where, **7**, 85
scope of offence, **7**, 410
ship, destroying or sinking, **7**, 421
vandalism, **7**, 410, 410*n*, 414
Malicious prosecution
averments, sufficiency, **15**, 456
generally, **15**, 444, 447
liability—
 generally, **15**, 448
 person providing information, **15**, 452

Malicious prosecution—*continued*
liability—*continued*
    private prosecutor, **15**, 451
    prosecuting agency, **15**, 448–451
    solemn procedure, **15**, 449
    summary procedure, **15**, 450
malice—
    averments, sufficiency, **15**, 456
    generally, **15**, 453
    meaning, **15**, 454
    requirement to show, **15**, 447
prosecuting agencies, protection, **15**, 447
summary procedure, **15**, 450
want of probable cause—
    averments, sufficiency, **15**, 4567
    generally, **15**, 453
    meaning, **15**, 455
wrongful imprisonment following, **15**, 447
Maliciously
use of term, **7**, 76, 80
Mall
as part of shopping centre, valuation for rating, **24**, 673
Malta, Sovereign Order of
international personality, **19**, 664
Malus animus
use of term, **7**, 69
Management accounting
activities of, **1**, 53
financial market theory, and, **1**, 53
International Federation of Accountants, definition by, **1**, 52
meaning, **1**, 52
profit forecasts, rules on, **1**, 54
securities market, regulation of, **1**, 54
standards, **1**, 52
Management and Personnel Office
establishment of, **5**, 492
responsibilities of, **5**, 492
Managers' association
standard contract agreed between entertainers' unions and, **9**, 1006
Managing director
status of, **4**, 412
Mandatary/mandatory
death of mandatary, **24**, 6
delict, title and interest to sue, **15**, 235
mandatary holds as agent, **24**, 9
powers and duties of mandatary, **1**, 665
sisting of mandatary, **17**, 1076
termination of relationship, **1**, 665
Mandate
meaning, **1**, 665
negotiorum gestio, and, **15**, 91
performance of—
    agent, obligations of, **1**, 630
    defective, etc, liability for, **1**, 632
    reimbursement of expenses, **1**, 640
powers implied in contract of, **1**, 665
proof of, **1**, 665
supersession by commercial agency, **1**, 665
trusts compared, **24**, 6, 9

Mandatory enactment
effect, **12**, 1175
generally, **12**, 1176
permissive enactment mandatory in effect, **12**, 1175
statutory requirement held to be discretionary, **12**, 1178
statutory requirement held to be mandatory, **12**, 1177
where consequence of non-compliance not declared, **12**, 1175
Mandatum
root of trust law, as, **24**, 112
Manor of Northstead
appointment to stewardship of, **5**, 379
Manpower Services Commission
codes of practice issued by, **9**, 11
discrimination, liability for, **9**, 346
unemployed, temporary employment and training for, **14**, 630
Manpower taxes, **19**, 1531
Manrent
personal vassalage, **18**, 43*n*
Manse
allodial land, whether, **18**, 47
allowance in lieu of, **3**, 1560
consent to minister residing elsewhere, **3**, 1560
death of minister, vacation of manse by family, **3**, 1560
feudal law, generally, **18**, 68*n*, 70
minister's right to occupy, **3**, 1560
parliamentary—
    historical position, **3**, 1589
    post-1925 position, **3**, 1590
quoad omnia parish—
    historical position, **3**, 1579, 1591
    New Parishes (Scotland) Act 1844, erected under, **3**, 1591
    post-1925 position, **3**, 1580, 1591
quoad sacra parish—
    historical position, **3**, 1583
    non-statutory endowments, **3**, 1586
    post-1925 position, **3**, 1584
    statutory endowments, **3**, 1585
sale of congregational properties and endowments, **3**, 1607–1609
situation, requirement as to, **3**, 1580
size, requirements as to, **3**, 1580
See also CHURCH OF SCOTLAND (property and endowments)
Mansholt Plan
proposals in, **1**, 971
Mantling
colour rules, **11**, 1605
generally, **11**, 1605
officers of state, **11**, 1605
peers, **11**, 1605
Sovereign's, **11**, 1605
Manufacturer
article for use at work, duties as to—
    generally, **9**, 455
    information, provision of, **9**, 459
    installation, **9**, 460
    meaning, **9**, 456

Manufacturer—*continued*

article for use at work, duties as to—*continued*
   research, **9**, 458
   suppliers, **9**, 457
   supply, **9**, 462
   transfer of responsibility, **9**, 461
   users, **9**, 457
duty of care, **6**, 37
economic loss, claim for, **6**, 38
food, of, notification of sampling, **11**, 338
liability of, *see* LIABILITY
manufacturer's guarantee, **6**, 36, 101, 154
production, restrictions on volume or range of, **4**, 1143

Manure

public health nuisance, **19**, 336
removal of, **19**, 367

Map

builders' developments, **6**, 734, 736
copyright, **18**, 958
documentary evidence, as, **10**, 604, 607
Keeper of Registers, prepared by, **6**, 733
map, chart or topographical plan—
   VAT zero-rating, **7**, 1447
Ordnance, **6**, 708, 731, 732

Marathon

prohibiting or restricting traffic, **19**, 1285

March (boundary)

meaning, **18**, 214
boundary between, **12**, 1239
stones, **18**, 214
See also BOUNDARY

March (walk)

common law rights, **14**, 1325

Margarine

advertisement, **11**, 365
composition, **11**, 365
early legislation, **11**, 301
labelling, **11**, 365

Marine insurance

agreed value policy, **12**, 888
assignation of policy, **12**, 846, 846*n*, 847
average principle, **12**, 893
claims—
   causation, **12**, 879
   proximate clause, **12**, 879
double insurance, **12**, 913*n*
follow London clause, **17**, 290
generally, **21**, 101, 119
historical development, **12**, 801, 801*n*
'honour' policy, **12**, 848
hull and machinery, relating to, perils of the sea, **21**, 551
indemnity insurance, as, **12**, 804
insurable interest—
   must exist at time of loss, **12**, 855
   not existing when contract made, **12**, 855
   requirement of, **12**, 848
interest or no interest policy, **12**, 848
loss—
   betterment, **12**, 886*n*
materiality, test of, **12**, 869
non-disclosure, **12**, 860
policies proof of interest (ppi), **12**, 835, 848

Marine insurance—*continued*

ratification of contract, **1**, 628
uberrimae fidei doctrine, **12**, 858, 858*n*
valued policies, **12**, 830
warranty, **12**, 874
writing, must be in, **12**, 828

Marine mammals

protection of, **11**, 215
res conveniens, as, **11**, 215
salmon fishing rights, **11**, 5, 5*n*
seals, **11**, 215, 216–225
trout fishing rights, **11**, 48
whales, **11**, 215, 226–240

Marine structures

suppression of broadcasting from, **17**, 9

Marine works

definition, **11**, 1311
exempted works, **11**, 1311
pier, *see* PIER

Mariner

See SEAMAN

Marischal

Earl Marischal, **7**, 815
Knight Marischal, **7**, 817
Officer of State, **7**, 790

Maritime arrestment

See ARRESTMENT

Maritime casualty

high seas, on, power to take avoidance measures, **21**, 46

Maritime cause

cases constituting, **1**, 411
maritime law applying to, **1**, 411
sheriff court jurisdiction, **4**, 18
territorial jurisdiction, **4**, 2

Maritime hypothec

generally, **20**, 101*n*

Maritime law

Admiralty Court, **22**, 519, 609
   See also ADMIRALTY
Balfour's *Practicks*, **22**, 609
basic concepts in shipping and navigation law, **21**, 105
bills of lading etc, **22**, 609
common law, **21**, 102, 102*n*
Court of Admiralty applying, **1**, 403
English courts—
   generally, **21**, 739
   influence of, **21**, 102
   law reports, **21**, 740
English and Scottish laws, relationship between, **21**, 102
fishing—
   freedom of, **19**, 608
   zones, **19**, 608
   See also FISHERIES
formal authority, modern, **22**, 609
general average, **21**, 700
general and international nature, effect of, **1**, 402
historical source, **22**, 609
international conventions, **21**, 104
   implementation within UK law, **21**, 104
international co-operation, **21**, 101, 104
judicial decisions, **19**, 636

Maritime law—*continued*
lien, *see* MARITIME LIEN
manuscript sources, **22**, 609
mare clausum and *mare liberum*, **19**, 608
marine insurance, **22**, 609
maritime custom—
   administration in Scotland, **22**, 609
   Consulato del Mare, **22**, 609
   law merchant, **22**, 608, 609
   Scotland, medieval influence, **22**, 609
   statutory collection, **22**, 609
   written code, Mediterranean ports, **22**, 609
Merchant Shipping Acts, **21**, 103
navigation, freedom of, **19**, 608; **21**, 39, 41
open seas doctrine, **19**, 608
Reddie's writings on, **19**, 609
sources, **21**, 101, 102, 102*n*
United States courts, **21**, 739
   law reports, **21**, 740
Welwod (Welwood)'s writings on, **19**, 608; **22**, 609

Maritime lien
action *in personam*, **21**, 393, 393*n*, 394, 394*n*, 481, 482
action *in rem*, executed by, **1**, 414; **21**, 393, 393*n*, 394, 394*n*, 481, 482
bottomry, bond of, **20**, 6, 26, 281, 305; **21**, 260, 392, 479
cargo, over, **21**, 479
caution, security in form of, **21**, 479*n*
change in ownership of property, **21**, 479
character, **20**, 275
collision damage, **21**, 260, 479
condemnation by Prize Court, **21**, 479
consignation, security in form of, **21**, 479*n*
constitution, **21**, 479
creditors' claims, priority over, **21**, 392
creditor's statutory rights distinguished, **20**, 306
Crown, vessel owned by, **21**, 479, 479*n*
damage—
   generally, **21**, 392
   ranking, **21**, 392
definition, **20**, 286
delivery to or possession by creditor not necessary, **21**, 479
events giving rise to, **20**, 277*ff*
extinction, **20**, 286; **21**, 479
factors extinguishing, **21**, 479
foreign sovereign, vessel owned by, **21**, 479, 479*n*
freight, over, **21**, 479
generally, **20**, 101*n*, 273
historical development, **20**, 274
hypothec, as, **21**, 479
judicial sale of property, **21**, 479
jurisdiction, **21**, 393
   earlier cognate proceedings in non-Scottish court, **21**, 393, 393*n*
legal process, carried into effect by, **20**, 285
liability, limitation of, **20**, 284
limitation period, **21**, 479*n*
   expiry, **21**, 479
maritime hypothec, **21**, 479

Maritime lien—*continued*
master's remuneration and disbursements, **20**, 280, 305, 313
liabilities made or incurred by him, and, **21**, 260, 392, 479
matters giving rise to, **1**, 413
meaning, **1**, 413; **21**, 479
nature of, **20**, 286
necessaries, claims for, priority over, **21**, 392
priority over ship's mortgage, **21**, 185
privileged claim, **20**, 276
ranking, **1**, 413; **20**, 308–315; **21**, 185, 260, 479, 479*n*
respondentia bond, **20**, 281; **21**, 260, 479
revival—
   generally, **21**, 479, 479*n*
   retrieval of ship from apparent destruction, on, **21**, 479*n*
salvage, **20**, 278, 312; **21**, 260, 392
   conditions for, **21**, 479
   generally, **21**, 479
   priority over other claims, **21**, 479, 479*n*
   ranking claims, **21**, 479, 479*n*
   seamen's wages, **21**, 479
salvage award, payment or settlement of, **21**, 479
seaman's wages, for, **20**, 279, 305, 313; **21**, 260, 392, 479, 479*n*
service rendered to vessel, **20**, 277
ship, over, **21**, 479
ship's mortgage, priority over, **21**, 392
statutory, **21**, 479
subsequent possessory, **21**, 392
vessel, damage by, **20**, 282, 283, 284, 311
vessels subject to, **1**, 413

Maritime security
Brussels international convention on maritime law, **20**, 273
ranking of claims—
   generally, **20**, 308
   liens—
      damage, **20**, 311
      maritime, **20**, 308–310
      possessory, **20**, 309
      salvage, **20**, 311, 312
      statutory, **20**, 315
      wages and disbursements, **20**, 311, 313
   mortgages, **20**, 314
Scots law, generally, **20**, 273
ship, mortgage, *see* MORTGAGE
statutory lien—
   Administration of Justice Act 1956—
      arrest of ship under, **20**, 304
      categories of dispute giving rise to claim under, **20**, 305
      creditor's rights and lien compared, **20**, 306
   arrest of ship—
      Administration of Justice Act 1956, under, **20**, 304
      Civil Jurisdiction and Judgments Act 1982, under, **20**, 307
      creditor's rights compared, **20**, 306
      priority of, **20**, 315

Maritime telecommunications services, provision
regulatory control, **16**, 1923
Market
generally, **14**, 695
operator, **14**, 119, 562
provision of, functions in relation to, **14**, 696
right to hold—
 regalian right, as, **18**, 210
 separate tenement, as, **18**, 210
valuation for rating, **24**, 673
Market garden-gardening
income tax, **19**, 1572
landlord's hypothec, **13**, 513
valuation for rating—
 agricultural buildings, **24**, 565
 mushroom growing, **24**, 560
Market in shares
fixed price transfer, **25**, 52
less regular, **25**, 48
market maker—
 insider dealing rules, **12**, 1529
 off-exchange, Securities and Investments Board
  Core Conduct of Business Rules, **12**, 1389
 soft commission, **12**, 1359
 turn, **12**, 1359
market manipulation—
 offence of, **4**, 541
market practice—
 Securities and Investments Board statement of
  principle, **12**, 1345
market transactions—
 nature of, **25**, 7
 shares, valuation of, **25**, 7
marketability, degree of, **25**, 46
non-existent, **25**, 49
occasional, **25**, 49
over counter market, **25**, 47
overseas—
 secondary markets, **25**, 47
 stock exchanges, **25**, 47
price by contract, **25**, 52
ready, **25**, 47
recent sales, **25**, 51
recognised, **25**, 47
restrictions, **25**, 50
Stock Exchange Third Market, **25**, 47
unlisted securities market, **25**, 47
Marketing
artistic copyright, limitation, **18**, 1157
Marketing of Investments Board (MIB)
establishment, **12**, 1305
Financial Services in the United Kingdom ... white
 paper, **12**, 1305
merger with Securities and Investments Board,
 12, 1305
Organising Committee (MIBOC), **12**, 1305
Marking
coins, of, **14**, 1820
notes, of, **14**, 1820
Marklands
udal law, **24**, 311
Marquess
daughter of, mode of address, **16**, 1322

Marquess—*continued*
eldest son, courtesy title, **16**, 1311
mode of address, **16**, 1322
title, generally, **16**, 1311
younger son, mode of address, **16**, 1322
Marriage
adherence, **10**, 839
adoption, relationships by, **10**, 817
adultery, **10**, 840
 child of parents who have committed, **10**, 1167
 divorce cases, *see* DIVORCE
affinity, relationship by, **10**, 817, 1219
after admission to UK for purpose other than, **12**,
 278
age of capacity, **3**, 1235, 1241; **11**, 1202*n*
agency, and, **10**, 843
aliment, *see* ALIMENT
annulment, recognition of decree, common law,
 10, 941
 See also ANNULMENT OF MARRIAGE
antenuptial settlement—
 incidental order in divorce proceedings, **10**,
  955
banns of—
 parish registers, **19**, 1401
 transmission of records, **19**, 853
bars to—
 consanguinity or affinity, **10**, 817, 1219
 illegitimate link, relationship through, **10**, 1180
 step-parent and stepchild, **10**, 1217
Bible, law of the, post-Reformation influence,
 22, 612–614
bigamy, *see* BIGAMY
breach of promise actions no longer competent,
 11, 786
breakdown—
 separation of property on, **25**, 602
 valuation of property on, **25**, 9
British Dependent Territories citizenship, **14**,
 1938
British subject, **14**, 1950
canon law—
 dispensation etc, *Sacra Penitentiaria Apostolica*,
  archival material, **22**, 573, 574
 as law of pre-Reformation Scotland, **22**, 580
capacity to marry, **17**, 140
 remarriage, **17**, 224
casualty of, feudal law, **18**, 76
Celtic customs, **22**, 504
change of name following, **19**, 1428
children, status of, **10**, 846
 See also CHILD-CHILDREN
choice of law rules relating to, **17**, 129; **22**, 693
church courts, powers to resolve matters relating
 to, **22**, 511
Church of Scotland minister, solemnisation by, **3**,
 1564
citizenship, and, **10**, 836
civil, **10**, 808; **14**, 589
civil jurisdiction, **4**, 26
civil preliminaries, **10**, 805–807
cohabitation with habit and repute, by, **10**, 811,
 814, 819; **19**, 1574
 tax consequences, **19**, 1574

Marriage—*continued*
Commissary Court—
  matrimonial jurisdiction, **22**, 585
  post-Reformation powers, **22**, 519
company cannot marry, **4**, 318
conditions as to, **25**, 864, 866
conflict of laws, relevance to, **17**, 140, 213
consanguinity, relationships by, **10**, 817, 1219
consent—
  absence of, **10**, 826
  exchange of consents, survival of principle, **22**, 581, 612
  requirement of, **17**, 229
contract—
  discharge of legal rights, **25**, 799, 806
  interpretation, **12**, 1262
  legal capacity to enter, **10**, 843
  notary public, execution by, **13**, 1221
contract trust—
  alimentary restrictions, **24**, 81
  antenuptial, **24**, 18, 60, 69, 80, 81, 84
    where revocable, **24**, 62, 69
  generally, **4**, 41; **24**, 4, 16, 18
  judicial variation, **24**, 80
  postnuptial, **24**, 18, 60, 69, 81
  prejudicial arrangements, **24**, 80
  revocability, **24**, 69
  rights conferred—
    children of marriage, on, **24**, 69
    third parties, on, **24**, 69
convenience, of—
  deportation order, **12**, 207
  meaning, **12**, 207*n*
court order, advantages over separation
  agreement, **19**, 1579, 1581
death—
  declarator of, **10**, 819, 833, 834
  presumption of, **10**, 833, 834
  termination on, **10**, 801
declarator of, **13**, 4
  action for, **10**, 830
  Court of Session jurisdiction, **4**, 5
declarator of freedom and putting to silence, **10**, 832
declarator of nullity of, **10**, 831; **19**, 1420, 1467
deemed valuable consideration, **6**, 714*n*
delict proceedings against spouse, **10**, 844
desertion, *see* DIVORCE
dissolution of—
  choice of law on, **17**, 235, 328
  exclusion from scope of Judgments
    Convention, **8**, 432
  generally, **19**, 1430
divorce, *see* DIVORCE
domicile, **10**, 837
engagement—
  effect of, **10**, 802, 803
  not legally enforceable contract, **10**, 802
  property disputes, **10**, 803
  rings, **10**, 803
entrapment, **11**, 787
error, vitiated by, **10**, 823
errors as to identity or quality of contracting
  party, **11**, 788

Marriage—*continued*
evidence, spouse, competence to give, **10**, 845
exclusion orders, **10**, 863–865, 902
family relationships, **11**, 1068
fideicommissum, **24**, 4
force or fear, consent obtained by, **10**, 824
formalities of—
  general rule, **10**, 804
  irregular marriages, **10**, 811–814
  regular marriages, **10**, 805–810
fraudulent misrepresentation, **11**, 787, 788
freedom, declarator of, **10**, 832
friendly society endowments on, **12**, 686
future married name, postdated passport issued in,
    16, 1223
gifts in consideration of—
  future marriage, **8**, 648
  inheritance tax exemption, **19**, 1533
girl under sixteen, **3**, 1235
goods imported on occasion of, **7**, 1100, 1113
Hague Convention on Recognition of Divorces
  and Legal Separations, Scottish Law
  Commission recommendations, **22**, 693
heritage, **10**, 881–884
homosexual, **10**, 818
immigration, importance in relation to, **10**, 836
Immigration Rules, **12**, 149
impediment to, **10**, 806*n*
impotency of partner or partners, **10**, 827–829
  personal bar, **10**, 829
institution of, generally, **10**, 801
international law—
  constitution of—
    capacity to marry, **17**, 221
    capacity to remarry, **17**, 224
    consent, **17**, 229
    exceptions, **17**, 222–224
    foreign marriage, **17**, 227
    formal validity, **17**, 226
    generally, **17**, 220
    intended matrimonial home, **17**, 225
    local forms cannot be observed, **17**, 228
    penal exception, **17**, 222
    public policy exception, **17**, 222
    reducible marriage, **17**, 230
    Sottomayer v De Barros (No 2) exception, **17**, 223
    voidable marriage, **17**, 230
  duration of, **17**, 214
  external public policy rule, **17**, 170, 171
  fragmentation of rules, **17**, 124
  Law Commissions, recommendations, **22**, 693
  personal consequences of—
    changes in, **17**, 234
    generally, **17**, 232
  proprietary consequences of—
    delimitation of field, **17**, 325
    dissolution of marriage, **17**, 328
    husband and wife, **17**, 211
    immoveables, **17**, 327
    moveables, **17**, 326
  reducible, **17**, 230
intoxication of party, marriage void as result, **10**, 822

Marriage—*continued*
irregular, **10**, 811–814
  abolition, **22**, 649
irregularities, effect of, **10**, 810
irretrievable breakdown, **10**, 840
Jewish form, validity, **3**, 1683
judicial separation, *see* JUDICIAL SEPARATION
law reform, **22**, 649
legacy, as condition of, **25**, 864, 866
legal capacity, and, **10**, 843
legal effects, **10**, 835–889
  aliment, **10**, 847–853
  creditors, spouses and, **10**, 887–889
  generally, **10**, 835
  heritage, **10**, 881–884
  married women's policies of assurance, **10**, 886
  occupancy rights, **10**, 845–870
  personal effects, **10**, 836–846
  property, **10**, 871–880
  tenancies, **10**, 885
  violence, protection from, **10**, 863–865, 869, 870
legal impediments to, **10**, 806
legitimation *per subsequens matrimonium*, **10**, 1173
lex loci celebrationis must conform to, **10**, 804
marriage contract trust, **4**, 41
marriage notice—
  affinity, degree of, **10**, 805
  birth certificate, **10**, 805
  divorce or nullity, decree or declarator of, **10**, 805
  domicile abroad, **10**, 805
  fee, **10**, 805
marriage schedule, **10**, 807
married women's policies of assurance, **19**, 1580
matrimonial decrees, *see* MATRIMONIAL DECREES
matrimonial home, *see* MATRIMONIAL HOME
meaning, **11**, 1209*n*
mental illness or defect of contracting party, **10**, 821
minimum age, **10**, 1080
minor, of, **10**, 843, 1040, 1080, 1100
modern Scots law—
  canonist attitudes to impediments reflected in, **22**, 581, 584, 585
name, wife's, **10**, 842
nationality, and, **10**, 836
notice, **10**, 807
nullity—
  canonical law, **22**, 613
  Court of Session jurisdiction, **4**, 5
  declarator of, **10**, 831; **19**, 1420, 1467
  exclusion from scope of Judgments Convention, **8**, 432
  generally, **11**, 788
  matter derived from nullity proceedings, restriction on publication, **17**, 41
  recognition of decree, **10**, 941
  register of declarations of, **19**, 857
  second marriage, notice of, **10**, 805
objections to, **10**, 806
occupancy rights—
  arrest—
    consequences of, **10**, 869
    powers of, **10**, 868

Marriage—*continued*
occupancy rights—*continued*
  cohabitees, **10**, 854, 870
  division and sale, **10**, 866
  ejection, **10**, 866
  entitled and non-entitled spouses, **10**, 856, 859, 860, 866
  exclusion orders, **10**, 863–865
  furniture and plenishings, **10**, 858
  generally, **10**, 854, 855
  interdicts, **10**, 868
  matrimonial homes, **10**, 857
  protection, generally, **10**, 860
  remedies, **10**, 860–862
  subsidiary and consequential rights, **10**, 859
  tenants, special provisions relating to, **10**, 867
  See also MATRIMONIAL HOME
officials' courts, matrimonial jurisdiction transferred to Commissary Courts, **22**, 575
per verba de futuro subsequente copula, **10**, 811, 813
per verba de praesenti, **10**, 811, 812
personal Bill enabling, **19**, 111, 115
polygamous, **12**, 118*n*, 269
  adultery, and, **10**, 899
  choice of law, and, **17**, 219
  conflict of laws, and, **17**, 217
  determination whether marriage is, **17**, 233
  domestic law, and, **17**, 216
  generally, **10**, 846
  legitimacy at birth, **17**, 239
  lex causae and, **17**, 218
  meaning, **17**, 215
  potentially, **17**, 215
    Scottish Law Commission recommendation, **22**, 693
  potentially polygamous, **12**, 269
post-Reformation Scotland—
  canon law as law of Scotland, **22**, 580, 581
  canon law and procedure, indirect influence, **22**, 580
postnuptial settlement—
  incidental order in divorce proceedings, **10**, 955
prior subsisting marriage, **10**, 819
prohibited degrees—
  adopted children, **10**, 1191
  consanguinity and affinity, **10**, 817, 1219
  generally, **22**, 573, 612
promise to marry, **17**, 212
proof of, **10**, 933
property—
  acquired before marriage, **10**, 803
  assurance, married women's policies of, **10**, 886
  bank accounts, **10**, 880
  corporeal moveable, **10**, 877–880
  creditors, rights of, **10**, 888, 889
  creditors, spouses and, **10**, 887–889
    rights of creditors, **10**, 888
    rights of non-debtor spouses, **10**, 889
  deeds, rules relating to, **10**, 876
  deposit receipts, **10**, 880
  divorce, financial provision on, *see* DIVORCE
  donation between spouses, **10**, 873
    trust, overlap with, **10**, 875

Marriage—*continued*

property—*continued*
  fairness, **10**, 884
  generally, **10**, 871
  gifts between spouses, **10**, 873
  heritage, **10**, 881–884
    fairness and separate property rules, **10**, 884
    infeftment, position prior to, **10**, 881
    registration—
      position on or after, **10**, 882
      position prior to, **10**, 881
    title not exclusively in name of purchasing spouse, **10**, 883
  household goods, **10**, 877
  infeftment or registration, **10**, 881, 882
  married women's policies of assurance, **10**, 886
  matrimonial home, *see* MATRIMONIAL HOME
  separate property rule, **10**, 872, 881, 884
  separation of on breakdown, **25**, 602
  tenancies, **10**, 885
  title not exclusively in name of purchasing spouse, **10**, 883
  transfer—
    on divorce, on, **10**, 952, 953
    spouses, between, **10**, 879
  trusts, **10**, 874
    between spouses, **10**, 874
    donation, and, **10**, 875
  valuation of on breakdown, **25**, 9
  wedding presents, **10**, 878
  See also MATRIMONIAL PROPERTY
putative, children of, **10**, 1168
  legitimacy of, **17**, 239
questions of, legal advice and assistance, **13**, 1024, 1028, 1033
rape within, **10**, 840
records, transmission of, **19**, 853
reform of law, **17**, 112; **22**, 649
Reformation, effect on canonical law, **22**, 612
registration, *see* MARRIAGES, REGISTRATION OF
regular marriages, **10**, 805–810
religious, **10**, 809; **14**, 589
  authorised celebrant, **10**, 809, 809n
remarriage, capacity, **17**, 224
reset, **10**, 841
residence, **10**, 838
restraint on, **25**, 866
right not to marry, **12**, 71
right to marry—
  European Convention on Human Rights, **12**, 6, 71
  Universal Declaration of Human Rights, **12**, 4n
same sex, partners of, **10**, 818
schedule, **10**, 807, 810
  falsified or forged, **10**, 810
secular, Celtic legal origin, **22**, 530
separation, *see* DIVORCE; JUDICIAL SEPARATION
separation agreement, taxation consequences, **19**, 1579, 1581
settlement, family reunion or creation by, *see* SETTLEMENT (IMMIGRATION)
settlement—
  liferent created by, termination, **13**, 1658
  variation of, **25**, 617

Marriage—*continued*

sexual intercourse, **10**, 840
  refusal of, **10**, 906
sham, **10**, 825
spouse, *see* HUSBAND AND WIFE; SPOUSE; WIFE
status, action relating to, **4**, 68
status relation, as, **11**, 1068
step-parent and stepchild, **10**, 1217
taxation, separation on, **19**, 1579, 1581
transfer of interest in land in consideration of, **6**, 714
transsexuals, **10**, 818; **11**, 1038
unreasonable behaviour, *see* DIVORCE
valid, actions related to existence of, **10**, 830–832
violence, protection from, **10**, 854, 863–865, 868
  arrest—
    consequences of, **10**, 869
    powers of, **10**, 868
  cohabitees, **10**, 870
  exclusion orders, **10**, 863, 864
  interdicts, **10**, 868
void—
  absence of consent, **10**, 826
  adoption, relationship by, **10**, 817
  affinity, relationship by, **10**, 805, 817
  capacity to marry, **10**, 816–819
  children of, **10**, 831, 1168
  consanguinity, **10**, 817
  consent, absence of, **10**, 826
  declarator of nullity, **10**, 831
  defective consent, **10**, 820–826
  error, as result of, **10**, 823
  forbidden degrees of relationship, **10**, 817
    adoption, relationship by, **10**, 817
    affinity, **10**, 817
    consanguinity, **10**, 817, 1219
  force or fear—
    consent obtained by, **10**, 824
    marriage contracted under, **10**, 824
  found or declared, **19**, 1465
  generally, **10**, 815
  homosexuals, between, **10**, 818
  intoxication, incapacity as result of, **10**, 822
  legitimacy of children, **10**, 831
  mental illness or defect, incapacity as result of, **10**, 821
  non-age, **10**, 806n, 816
  parental rights, **10**, 1266
  prior subsisting marriage, **10**, 806n, 819
  same sex, partners of, **10**, 806n, 818
  sham marriages, **10**, 825
  wilfully inducing, **11**, 787
voidability, exclusion from scope of Judgments Convention, **8**, 432
voidable—
  children of, **10**, 831, 1170
  declarator of nullity, **10**, 831
  generally, **10**, 827–829; **17**, 230; **19**, 1575
  impotency of partner or partners, **10**, 827–829
    incurable impotency, **10**, 828, 829
    personal bar to remedy, **10**, 829
  legitimacy of children, **10**, 831
  meaning, **10**, 827
  parental rights, **10**, 1266

Marriage—*continued*
voidable—*continued*
personal bar, **10**, 829
will revoked by, **17**, 348; **25**, 611
witnesses, **10**, 808, 809
See also HUSBAND AND WIFE; LEX LOCI
CELEBRATIONIS; SPOUSE; WIFE
Marriages, registration of
certificate, failure to deliver, **19**, 1474
citizenship by, **14**, 1917
civil marriages, **19**, 1462
cohabitation with habit and repute, marriage by,
19, 1463
declaration *de praesenti* by, **19**, 1463
district registrar, **19**, 1406
attendance at registration offices, **19**, 1408
returns, **19**, 1431
salary, allowances and compensation, **19**, 1407
districts and authorities, **19**, 1405
documentary evidence, register as, **10**, 591
extracts—
authentication, **19**, 1420
misuse of, **19**, 1474
fees, collection and accounting of, **14**, 588; **19**,
1410
forged documents, **19**, 1472
General Register Office, **19**, 1402, 1404
generally, **10**, 808–810, 810*n*; **19**, 305, 809, 811,
828, 842
historical background, **19**, 1401, 1402
hours fixed for, **19**, 1408
information, failure to give, **19**, 1474
irregular marriages, **19**, 1463
local authority duty, **14**, 588, 589
marriage schedule, **19**, 1461, 1462
failure to deliver, **19**, 1476
falsification, **19**, 1475
forgery, **19**, 1475
offences, **19**, 1477
certificate, failure to deliver, **19**, 1474
destruction of entry, **19**, 1473
duplication of entry, **19**, 1473
failure to deliver up registers, **19**, 1471
false information, **19**, 1472
forged documents, **19**, 1472
information, failure to give, **19**, 1474
marriage certificate, in relation to, **19**, 1475,
1476
misuse of extract certificate, **19**, 1474
organisation, **19**, 1401–1410
outside United Kingdom, ceremony performed,
19, 1464
parish registers, **19**, 1401, 1411–1413
procedure, **19**, 1461–1465
promise *subsequente copula* by, **19**, 1463
records, safe custody of, **19**, 1408
area repositories, **19**, 1409
registers, **19**, 1466
authentication of extracts, **19**, 1420
cancellation of entry in, **19**, 1465
correction of, **19**, 1414, 1421, 1422–1424
change of name or status, **19**, 1425–1430
clerical errors, **19**, 1423
destroyed, **19**, 1402*n*, 1417

Marriage registration of—*continued*
registers—*continued*
destruction of entry, **19**, 1473
duplication, **19**, 1415
of entry, **19**, 1473
examination, **19**, 1416
failure to deliver up, **19**, 1471
illegible, **19**, 1402*n*, 1417
indexes of, **19**, 1418, 1419
information required from, **19**, 1431, 1432
lost, **19**, 1402*n*, 1417
mutilated, **19**, 1402*n*, 1417
parochial, **19**, 1401, 1411–1413
provision, **19**, 1415
replacement, **19**, 1417
reproductions of, **19**, 1416
statutory control, **19**, 1414
Registrar General, **19**, 1402, 1403
registration authority, **14**, 32
registration offices, **19**, 1408
religious marriages, **19**, 1461
salary, allowances and compensation for officers,
19, 1407
second marriage ceremony, following, **19**, 1464
sheriff, supervision by, **19**, 1402
sheriff court jurisdiction, **6**, 1127
United Kingdom citizenship, **14**, 1917
void, marriage found or declared, **19**, 1465
Married woman
domicile, **17**, 197, 200
national insurance contributions, **21**, 1047
policies of assurance—
Scottish Law Commission recommendations,
22, 6, 9
trusts arising under, **24**, 21, 29, 33
state retirement pension scheme, **21**, 1204
contracted-out employment, **21**, 1226
non-contributory pension, **21**, 1220
status, **22**, 648
Marriott, Oliver
The Property Boom, **13**, 556, 569
Marsh
See STAGNUM
Marshalling
arms, of, **11**, 1626
Martial law
prerogative powers of Crown, **2**, 605; **7**, 726
Mascot
motor vehicle, carried by, restrictions on use, **20**,
443
Master (mode of address)
use of term, **16**, 1322
Master and servant
contract of employment—
spread of, **9**, 2
statute, and, **9**, 3
early law, **9**, 1
employment law, reduction of, **9**, 4
servant's powers of seizure, **11**, 812
Master Carver
office of, **7**, 819, 828
Master of the Household
office of, **7**, 820, 822

Master of Requests
Officer of State, **7**, 792, 798
Master of the Wardrobe
office of, **7**, 800
Master Printer
office of, **7**, 819, 851
Matches
excise duty, **7**, 1097
Maternity
care, *see* MIDWIFERY, MATERNITY AND CHILD CARE
establishment of, *see* PARENTAGE
home—
   meaning, **11**, 1525*n*
   nursing home, as, **11**, 1525
Maternity allowance
absent from Great Britain, claimant, **21**, 1021, 1022
behavioural rules, failure to observe, **21**, 899
confinement—
   early, where, **21**, 898
   meaning, **21**, 898
death of claimant, where, **21**, 899
dependent adult, increase where, **21**, 1017
disqualification, **21**, 899
employed earner, **21**, 898
entitlement, **21**, 801, 898
medical examination, failure to attend, **21**, 899
national insurance contributions, **21**, 1042
period for which payable—
   commencement, **21**, 898
   generally, **21**, 898
self-employed earner, **21**, 898, 899
statutory maternity pay, interaction with, **21**, 898
statutory sick pay, interaction with, **21**, 912
work carried out during payment period, **21**, 899
Maternity pay
adjudication, **21**, 1149, 1170
   appeals, **21**, 1170
administration, **21**, 801
confinement—
   early, where, **21**, 901, 902, 904
   meaning, **21**, 901*n*
contract of service—
   ended solely or mainly for purpose of avoiding
     liability, **21**, 905
   week during which claimant works under, **21**,
     902, 902*n*
contracting-out, **21**, 905
contractual remuneration, effect on right to, **21**,
   906
day of unemployment, whether day classed as, **21**,
   906
duty to give, **21**, 904
earnings, as, **21**, 1031
entitlement, **21**, 801, 901
incapacity for work, day of, whether day classed
   as, **21**, 906
insolvency of employer, where, **21**, 901
invalidity pension, interaction with, **21**, 906
liability for payment, **21**, 901, 905
   contracting-out, **21**, 905
lower earnings limit, **21**, 901
maternity allowance, interaction with, **21**, 898

Maternity pay—*continued*
maternity pay period—
   commencement, **21**, 902
   end, **21**, 902
   meaning, **21**, 902
   payable during, **21**, 902
notice of absence, form, **21**, 904
payment, **21**, 801
rates, **21**, 903
Social Security Commissioner, appeal to, **21**, 1182
Maternity rights
ante-natal care, time off for—
   introduction of, **9**, 96
   refusal of, remedy for, **9**, 103
   remuneration, **9**, 102
   right to, **9**, 100, 101
expenses from social fund, **21**, 1123, 1127
generally, **9**, 99
pregnancy—
   absence due to—
     generally, **9**, 104
     maternity pay, right to, **9**, 106
     qualifications, **9**, 105
   dismissal because of—
     automatically unfair, **9**, 115
     generally, **9**, 114
     incapability, **9**, 116
     remedy, **9**, 117
     sex discrimination, whether, **9**, 358
     unfair, **9**, 227
   return to work—
     confinement, after, **9**, 107, 220
     contractual right, **9**, 110
     exceptions, **9**, 113
     interruption of work, effect of, **9**, 109
     postponement of, **9**, 108
     redundancy situation, **9**, 112
     same job, right to return to, **9**, 111
     statutory right, **9**, 110
principal rights, **9**, 99
See also PREGNANCY
Mathematical theory or method
patent not grantable, **18**, 824
Matriculation
adopted child, **11**, 1617
differences, **11**, 1617
illegitimate child, **11**, 1617
prescription, **11**, 1624
progress, by, **11**, 1617
reasons for, **11**, 1617
rematriculation, **11**, 1617, 1621
tailzied arms, **11**, 1620
value of, **11**, 1617
'with insignia appropriate', **11**, 1612
Matrimonial decrees
British Islands, granted in—
   civil courts, recognition limited to decrees
     granted by, **8**, 492
   recognition—
     duty to recognise, **8**, 493
     exceptions to, **8**, 493–495
    res judicata, decrees rendered, **8**, 494
    where no prior subsisting marriage, **8**, 495

Matrimonial decrees—*continued*
British Isles, granted in—
    civil courts, recognition limited to decrees
        granted by, **8**, 492
    recognition—
        limited to decrees by civil courts, **8**, 492
non-judicial proceedings, divorce or annulment
    arising as result of, **8**, 492
overseas, recognition—
    conversion of legal separation into divorce, **8**, 502
    cross-proceedings, where, **8**, 498
    generally, **8**, 496
    grounds for, **8**, 498, 500
    overseas divorce, annulment or legal separation,
        meaning, **8**, 496
    proceedings—
        decrees obtained by means of, **8**, 497–499
            refusal of recognition, **8**, 499
        decrees obtained without, **8**, 497
            grounds for recognition, **8**, 500
            refusal of recognition, **8**, 501
        meaning, **8**, 497
    proof of facts, **8**, 503
    refusal of, **8**, 499, 501
See also ANNULMENT OF MARRIAGE
Matrimonial home
acquisition of, wife's contribution to, **25**, 611
alteration or repair—
    co-owner's right to carry out, **18**, 27
    expenditure, apportionment, **18**, 27
caravan as, **10**, 857
cohabitees, **10**, 1005
common property—
    division and sale, **18**, 27, 32
    generally, **18**, 27
conveyance to third party of *pro indiviso* share, **18**,
    27
definition, **18**, 27
division and sale, **10**, 866; **18**, 27, 27*n*
divorce, fair sharing of net value of matrimonial
    property, **10**, 957–962
ejection, **10**, 866
exclusion orders, **10**, 863; **17**, 1122, 1241
    duration, **10**, 865
    making effective, **10**, 864
freedom of testation, **25**, 601
generally, **17**, 1240
houseboat as, **10**, 857
incidental order as to, **10**, 955
intended, **17**, 225
interim order—
    cohabiting couple, **17**, 1124
    duration of, **17**, 1123
    enforcement of, **17**, 1125
    exclusion order, **17**, 1122
    generally, **17**, 1120
    non-entitled spouse, rights of, **17**, 1121
    poinding, protection from, **17**, 1126
    procedure, **17**, 1127
    recall of, **17**, 1123
    variation of, **17**, 1123
lease, **13**, 174, 193
    non-entitled spouse's consent, **13**, 174
    rights of spouses, **13**, 174, 193

Matrimonial home—*continued*
meaning, **10**, 857
notary public, declaration made before, **13**, 1223
occupancy rights—
    arrest—
        consequences of, **10**, 869
        powers of, **10**, 868
    children, **10**, 855
    cohabitees, **10**, 870
    court order as to, **18**, 27
    creditor under secured loan, **10**, 860
    creditors of entitled spouse, rights of, **18**, 10
    entitled and non-entitled spouses, **10**, 856, 859,
        860, 863, 866
    exclusion orders, **10**, 863–865
    furniture and plenishings, **10**, 858
    generally, **6**, 783; **10**, 854, 855
    gift, transfer of property by, **18**, 10
    inhibition, unaffected by, **8**, 155
    interdicts, **10**, 868
    nature of right, **18**, 10
    non-entitled spouse, **18**, 10
    protection, **10**, 860
    remedies, **10**, 860, 862
        regulation, by way of, **10**, 861
    renunciation of, **6**, 568; **10**, 860
    sale of property, **18**, 10
    spouse owner or joint owner, **10**, 855; **22**, 687
    spouse tenant, **10**, 855; **22**, 687
    subsidiary and consequential rights, **10**, 859
    third party, rights of, **10**, 860
overriding interest of spouse, **6**, 747
overseas divorce or annulment proceedings, **10**,
    947
possession of, actionable nuisance interfering
    with, **14**, 2134
rights relating to, **17**, 1121
rights of spouses, **6**, 568; **10**, 855; **22**, 687
sheriff court jurisdiction, **6**, 1100
standard security or other dealing in, grant in
    relation to *pro indiviso* share, **18**, 27
tenancy, transfer of, **10**, 867
transfer following separation, capital gains tax, **10**,
    1002
Matrimonial property
fair sharing of net value on divorce—
    conduct of parties, **10**, 962
    gifts from third parties, **10**, 960
    meaning of matrimonial property, **10**, 960
    meaning of net value, **10**, 958
    principle, generally, **10**, 957, 961
    property bought before marriage, **10**, 960
    relevant date, **10**, 959, 960
freedom of testation, restriction on, **25**, 601
law reform, **22**, 648, 688
rights in, exclusion from Judgments Convention,
    8, 431, 433
See also MARRIAGE (PROPERTY); MATRIMONIAL HOME
Maundy money
standards for, **14**, 1821
Mauritius
emancipation legislation, **5**, 353
Maxwell Committee
recommendations, **4**, 25

May Report
recommendations, **16**, 1493
Mayonnaise
advertisement, **11**, 367
composition, **11**, 367
labelling, **11**, 367
Meals
countryside, provision in, **14**, 680
facilities for obtaining, local authority provision, **11**, 1906
Measles
vaccination against, **11**, 1446
Measured Terms Contract, Scottish
generally, **3**, 11
Meat
carcases, inspection of, **11**, 413
classification, **11**, 432
cold stores, **11**, 405
distribution of, **11**, 416
export, for—
　inspection of meat for, **11**, 417
　slaughterhouses, **11**, 510, 511
handlers, hygiene regulations, **11**, 415
horseflesh sold for human consumption, **11**, 432
hygiene, *see* FOOD
imported, **11**, 414
inspection of—
　animals slaughtered, **11**, 507, 508
　carcases, **11**, 413
　inspectors, **11**, 507, 507*n*, 512
knacker's yard, animals slaughtered in, **11**, 404, 407, 413, 498
labelling, **11**, 432
markets, hygiene regulations, **11**, 412
marking, **11**, 432
Meat and Livestock Commission, **1**, 984; **11**, 432
pigmeat, **1**, 937, 938
poultry, hygiene regulations, **11**, 418
products—
　composition, **11**, 366
　ingredients, list of, **11**, 366
　labelling, **11**, 366
　meat content, declaration of, **11**, 366
　raw and unprocessed, substances added to, **11**, 374, 374*n*
sheepmeat, **1**, 934–936
slaughter of animals, *see* ANIMALS; KNACKER; SLAUGHTERHOUSES
uncooked products, **11**, 358
unfit for human consumption, **11**, 407
unwrapped, distribution of, **11**, 416
venison, sale of, **11**, 433
wrapped, distribution of, **11**, 416
Meat and Livestock Commission
classification, marking and labelling of meat, **11**, 432
powers delegated to, **1**, 984
Mechanically propelled vehicle
meaning, **20**, 405
motor vehicle, term of to be replaced by, **20**, 414*n*
Medal
hallmarking, whether exempt, **18**, 1413
presentation by Lord Lieutenant, **5**, 551

Medical appeal tribunal
appeal against decision of, **21**, 1179
appeal to, **21**, 1179
　notice of, **21**, 1179
　time limit, **21**, 1179
chairman, powers of, **21**, 1179
constitution, **21**, 1174
generally, **21**, 1148
jurisdiction, **21**, 1179
majority decision, where, **21**, 1179
organisation, **21**, 1174
proceedings before, **21**, 1179
referral to, **21**, 1179
review of decisions of, **21**, 1171
Social Security Commissioner, appeal to, **21**, 1182, 1183
Medical authority
meaning, **14**, 1134
registration, **14**, 1134
Medical equipment
temporary importation, **7**, 1187
Medical laboratory technician
Council for Professions Supplementary to Medicine, **15**, 1516–1521
Medical list, *see* DOCTOR
Medical officer
designated, **11**, 1502
guardianship, discharge of patient from, **14**, 1449
hospital, discharge of patient from, **14**, 1427, 1428
Medical practitioner
care, standard of, **14**, 1126, 1128
complaints against, **11**, 1520–1524
　appeals, **11**, 1520
conduct—
　advertising, **14**, 1124
　appeal against committee decision, **14**, 1117
　care, standard of, **14**, 1126, 1128
　causation, **14**, 1129
　committee structure, *see* GENERAL MEDICAL COUNCIL
　criminal conviction, **14**, 1114, 1119
　dishonesty, **14**, 1124
　experience, **14**, 1128
　immediate suspension, **14**, 1116
　judgment, errors of, **14**, 1127
　misdiagnosis, **14**, 1127
　negligence, **14**, 1125
　professional misconduct—
　　finding of, consequences of, **14**, 1114
　　neglect of duty, **14**, 1123
　　patient, sexual involvement with, **14**, 1122
　　serious, **14**, 1120
　　unethical behaviour, **14**, 1121
　proof, burden of, **14**, 1129
　unfitness to practise, **14**, 1115
disqualification of, **11**, 1521
food poisoning, duties as to, **11**, 406
fund-holding practice, application for recognition as, **11**, 1401
health boards, powers of, **11**, 1401
health service facilities—
　contractors, use by, **11**, 1492
　private practice, used for, **11**, 1496
health service staffing, **11**, 1497, 1498

Medical practitioner—*continued*
ophthalmic, **11**, 1464
  complaints against, **11**, 1520
  ophthalmic list, *see* OPHTHALMIC SERVICES
overseas—
  dentistry, **14**, 1135, 1136
  European Economic Community—
    dentistry, **14**, 1135
    member state, qualification from, **14**, 1109
    qualification from state outwith, **14**, 1109
    registration, **14**, 1105, 1109
penal establishment, appointment to, **16**, 1418
registration—
  generally, **14**, 1103*ff*
  health visitor, *see* HEALTH VISITOR
  nurse, *see* NURSE-NURSING
  optician, **14**, 1166
  pharmaceutical chemist, **14**, 1160, 1162
  supplementary professions, **14**, 1174
  temporary, for visiting practitioner, **14**, 1110
reporter, referral of child to, **3**, 1287
Scottish Medical Practices Committee, *see*
  SCOTTISH MEDICAL PRACTICES COMMITTEE
sexual act with patient, **14**, 1122
trainee, **11**, 1447*n*
unfitness to practice, **14**, 1115
unregistered—
  civil liability, **14**, 1104
  criminal liability, **14**, 1104
  holding-out provisions, **14**, 1103
visiting, temporary registration, **14**, 1110
See also DOCTOR; GENERAL MEDICAL COUNCIL;
  MEDICAL PROFESSION
Medical profession
control over, scope of, **14**, 1101
criminal convictions, **14**, 1114, 1119, 1169
discipline—
  hearing aid dispenser, **14**, 1172
  optician, **14**, 1168
  pharmaceutical chemist, **14**, 1163
  supplementary professions, **14**, 1176
duty of care, **6**, 68
Medical Appeal Tribunal, **23**, 902, 911
negligence—
  burden of proof, **14**, 1129
  causation, **7**, 264; **14**, 1129
  duty, neglect of, **14**, 1123
  errors of judgment, **14**, 1127
  misdiagnosis, **14**, 1127
  patient's remedies, **14**, 1125
partnership as business medium, **16**, 1004
professional misconduct, **14**, 1140, 1169
professions supplementary to, **14**, 1174–1176
qualifications—
  dental, supervision of granting of, **14**, 1135
  experience, **14**, 1108
  health visitor, *see* HEALTH VISITOR
  midwife, *see* MIDWIFE, MATERNITY AND CHILD CARE
  nurse, *see* NURSE-NURSING
  registration, for—
    primary, **14**, 1107
    training, **14**, 1106
  supplementary profession, **14**, 1175
  dentistry, graduate or licentiate in, **14**, 1134

Medical profession—*continued*
registration—
  health visitor, *see* HEALTH VISITOR
  hearing aid dispenser, **14**, 1171
  limited, **14**, 1105, 1109
  medical practitioner, **14**, 1103
  midwife, *see* MIDWIFE, MATERNITY AND CHILD
    CARE
  nurse, *see* NURSE-NURSING
  optician, **14**, 1166
  overseas practitioner, **14**, 1105, 1109
  pharmaceutical chemist, **14**, 1160, 1162
  primary qualifications, **14**, 1107
  provisional, **14**, 1105, 1109
  qualifications, refusal to register, **14**, 1105
  register—
    overseas list, **14**, 1105
    principal list, **14**, 1105
    visiting EEC practitioners list, **14**, 1105
    visiting overseas doctors list, **14**, 1105
  retired practitioner, **14**, 1105
  supplementary profession, **14**, 1174
  temporary, for visiting practitioner, **14**, 1110
  training for, **14**, 1106
sexual act with patient, **14**, 1122
supplementary profession—
  discipline, **14**, 1176
  organisation, **14**, 1173
  qualifications, **14**, 1175
  registration, **14**, 1174
suspension of, **14**, 1116
training, **14**, 1144, 1148, 1149
unethical behaviour, **14**, 1121
unfitness to practice, **14**, 1115
Medical school
visitor, **14**, 1106
Medical supplies
control of prices for, **11**, 1509
VAT exemption, **7**, 1426
Medical treatment
assault, as, **7**, 222
child's capacity to consent, **3**, 1207, 1211
consent to, **15**, 393*n*
damages for injury, **11**, 1073
general medical services—
  accommodation for provision of, **11**, 1476
  adequacy of services, **11**, 1431
  administrative authorities, **11**, 1402
  ambulances, provision of, **11**, 1485
  application to provide, **11**, 1429
  blood supplies, **11**, 1485
  complaints against practitioners—
    appeals, **11**, 1520
    disqualification of practitioners, **11**, 1521
    generally, **11**, 1520
  developments, persons displaced by, **11**, 1489
  doctor, *see* DOCTOR
  educational and research facilities, **11**, 1487
  executive councils, **11**, 1402
  family planning, *see* FAMILY PLANNING
  health boards—
    administration by, **11**, 1410
    duty to provide general medical services, **11**
      1427

Medical treatment—*continued*
general medical services—*continued*
    health education, **11**, 1482
    infectious disease, control of spread, **11**, 1483
    invalid carriages, provision of, **11**, 1486
    meaning, **11**, 1427
    medical list, *see* DOCTOR
    practice—
        exchange of, **11**, 1434
        sale of prohibited, **11**, 1435
        vacant, succession to, **11**, 1433
    remuneration for, **11**, 1510
    residential and practice accommodation, **11**, 1488
    schools health service, **11**, 1410, 1450, 1479
guardianship, patients under, *see* GUARDIAN-GUARDIANSHIP
hospital, patient in, *see* HOSPITAL
improper, causation in relation to, **7**, 54
negligent, and causation of homicide, **7**, 264
obligation of reparation, **11**, 1032
parents' right to determine, **11**, 1208
personate existence, commencement of, **11**, 1037
right to, European Social Charter, **12**, 7
transactional capacity, **11**, 1059
transplant surgery, **11**, 1038, 1039
Medicinal product
abolition of distinctions, **14**, 1201
adulteration of, **14**, 1210
advertising, **1**, 536; **14**, 1211, 1212; **17**, 45
background of legislation, **14**, 1201
categories, **14**, 1201
clinical trial, *see* CLINICAL TRIAL
general sale list, **14**, 1208, 1209
licence—
    exemptions, **14**, 1203
    generally, **14**, 1203
    granting of, **14**, 1204
    manufacturer, of, **14**, 1203
    new product, **14**, 1206
    offences, **14**, 1203
    product, **14**, 1203
    revocation, **14**, 1205
    suspension, **14**, 1205
meaning, **6**, 79; **14**, 1202
medicinal poison, **14**, 1213
    See also POISON
new product, testing, **14**, 1206
offences—
    advertising, relating to, **14**, 1212
    confiscating order relating to, **14**, 1255
    controlled drugs, *see* DRUGS
    licences, in connection with, **14**, 1203
    medicinal product, quality of, **14**, 1210
    restraint order relating to, **14**, 1256
packaging, **14**, 1211
poisons, *see* POISON
prescription, supplied by, **14**, 1209
presentation, control of, **14**, 1210
quality, control of, **14**, 1210
radioactive substances, **14**, 1201
regulatory framework, **14**, 1201
representation in respect of, **14**, 1212

Medicinal product—*continued*
sale or supply—
    general sale list, **14**, 1208
    product not on general sale list, **14**, 1209
scope of legislation, **14**, 1201
veterinary drugs, **14**, 1201
See also MEDICINE
Medicinal purpose
legal control, **14**, 1220
meaning, **14**, 1202
Medicine
advertising, **6**, 73, 79
clinical, **14**, 1106
community medicine specialist—
    employment of, **11**, 1498
    meaning, **11**, 1498
drug, meaning of, **11**, 311
labelling and packaging, **6**, 12, 79
licence—
    exemptions, **14**, 1203
    granting of, **14**, 1204
    manufacturer, **14**, 1203
    new product, **14**, 1206
    offences, **14**, 1203
    product, **14**, 1203
    revocation, **14**, 1205
    suspension, **14**, 1205
public health regulations, **19**, 473
radioactive substances, safety regulations, **9**, 916
safety regulations, **6**, 63
sheriff court jurisdiction, **6**, 1117
trade descriptions, **6**, 121
VAT zero-rating, **7**, 1456
weights and measures, **6**, 185*n*
See also MEDICINAL PRODUCT
Medicine, professions supplementary to
professional bodies, membership and elections, **15**, 1516–1521
Medicines Commission
powers, **14**, 1201
statute, established by, **14**, 1201
Medieval documents
collection of, **19**, 849
Medieval law
public corporations, **19**, 202–205
Medium filum
deliniation of, **25**, 317
salmon fishing rights, **11**, 5, 5*n*
trout fishing rights, **11**, 48
Meeting
access to—
    common law rights, **14**, 1325
    confidential information—
        exclusion, **14**, 1330
        statutory provisions, **14**, 1329
    exclusion—
        confidential information, **14**, 1330
        disorderly conduct, due to, **14**, 1334
        exempt information, **14**, 1331
        improper, **14**, 1333
        procedure, **14**, 1332
    exempt information, **14**, 1331
    law prior to 1961, **14**, 1327

Meeting—*continued*
access to—*continued*
  members—
    exclusion, **14**, 1336
    right to know principle, **14**, 1337
    rights of, **14**, 1335
  public body, **14**, 1328
  statutory control, **14**, 1326
  statutory provisions, **14**, 1304, 1322
adjourned, **14**, 1319
advertisement, **14**, 1311
agenda, **14**, 1322–1324
annual, **14**, 1309
attendance—
  allowance, **14**, 228
  summary of rights, **14**, 264
background papers, inspection of, **14**, 1324
business, order of—
  agenda, **14**, 1321
  standing orders, **14**, 1319
categories, **14**, 1303
chairman—
  casting vote, **14**, 1347
  debate, duties as to, **14**, 1342
  points of order, **14**, 1345
  standing orders, **14**, 1319
club, private meeting in, **14**, 1303
company, *see* COMPANY
co-opted members, **14**, 1308
COSLA, *see* CONVENTION OF SCOTTISH LOCAL
  AUTHORITIES
debate—
  chairman, duties of, **14**, 1342
  members, improper behaviour of, **14**, 1344
  motion to terminate, **14**, 1340
  order of, **14**, 1319
  order of speaking, **14**, 1341
  points of order, **14**, 1345
  stewards, **14**, 1343
disorderly conduct, **14**, 1334
dissent, standing orders, **14**, 1319
documents—
  inspection of, **14**, 1324
  right to know principle, **14**, 1337
exempt information, **14**, 1331
failure to attend, vacation of office by, **14**, 211
formal—
  co-opted members, **14**, 1308
  convening, **14**, 1307
  purpose, **14**, 1306
full council, member's right to attend, **14**, 219
gathering, meeting as, **14**, 1301
general, shareholders' rights, **25**, 13
goods for display or use at, temporary
  importation, **7**, 1187
improper exclusion, **14**, 1333
information, access to—
  agenda, **14**, 1323
  background papers, **14**, 1324
  confidential, **14**, 1329
  documents, **14**, 1324
  exclusion—
    confidential, **14**, 1330
    disorderly conduct, due to, **14**, 1334

Meeting—*continued*
information, access to—*continued*
  exclusion—*continued*
    exempt, **14**, 1331
    improper, **14**, 1333
    procedure, **14**, 1332
  reports, **14**, 1323
  statutory provisions, **14**, 1322
  legal, must be, **14**, 1302
local authority, *see* LOCAL AUTHORITY
meaning, **14**, 1301
members—
  conduct of, **14**, 1319, 1344
  improper behaviour of, **14**, 1334
  meeting, right to attend, **14**, 1335–1337
  requisition, right to, **14**, 221
minutes—
  amendment, **14**, 1350
  common law, **14**, 1348
  form of, **14**, 1349
  inspection, **14**, 1351
  reduction, **13**, 37
  standing orders, **14**, 1319
motion—
  formal, **14**, 1340
  moving, **14**, 1338
  notice of, **14**, 1319
  original, **14**, 1339
  procedural, **14**, 1340
notice—
  agenda included in, **14**, 1320
  motion, of, **14**, 1319
  standing orders—
    alteration of, **14**, 1317
    content of, **14**, 1319
  validity of meeting, **14**, 1314, 1315
numbers present at, **14**, 1301
ordinary—
  cost, **14**, 1309
  election, before, **14**, 1309
  notice of, **14**, 1315
  standing orders, **14**, 1319
place of—
  local authority, **14**, 1313
  private, **14**, 1303
  public, **14**, 1303
  standing orders, **14**, 1316
points of orders, **14**, 1345
political uniforms, **14**, 1343
private legislation, statutory meeting relating to,
  14, 1311
private meeting—
  admission, public right of, **14**, 1328
  club, **14**, 1303
  company, **14**, 1303
  control, **14**, 1303
  local authority meeting classed as, **14**, 1304
  meaning, **14**, 1303
  private premises, held on, **14**, 1303
  trade union, **14**, 1303
public, **14**, 1303
public bodies, of, **17**, 15
quorum—
  local authority meeting, **14**, 1305

Meeting—*continued*
quorum—*continued*
    standing orders, **14**, 1316, 1319
    validity of meeting, **14**, 1314
reports, inspection of, **14**, 1323
shouting at, **7**, 454
special meeting, **14**, 1310, 1319
standing orders, **14**, 1316-1319
statutory, **14**, 1311, 1319
stewards, **14**, 1343
sub-committee—
    chairmanship, **14**, 93
    code of conduct, **14**, 232
    education, disqualification for membership, **14**, 600
    majority party, position of, **14**, 91
    meeting, member's right to attend, **14**, 220
    membership, **14**, 91
    minority party, position of, **14**, 92
    public, attendance of, **14**, 92
    statutory provisions, **14**, 91
unnecessarily long speech, making, **7**, 454
validity of, **14**, 1314, 1315
voting—
    chairman's casting vote, **14**, 1347
    method of, **14**, 1346
    standing orders, **14**, 1319
Member of European Parliament
See EUROPEAN PARLIAMENT
Member of Parliament
See HOUSE OF COMMONS
Memorandum of association
alteration of, **4**, 320
amended, copy of, **4**, 320
construction, and charitable status, **3**, 1115
copy of, **4**, 320
correct company name, use of, **4**, 321
effect of, **4**, 330
form of, **4**, 320
incorporation, fundamental conditions for, **4**, 314
interpretation of, **4**, 330
limited company, **4**, 312
membership—
    rights and obligations, **4**, 343
    shares—
        class rights—
            generally, **4**, 347
            variation of, **4**, 348, 349
        disclosure of interests in, **4**, 346
        registration of interests in, **4**, 346
name clause, **4**, 321
objects clause, **4**, 322
proposed, incorporation by registering, **4**, 304
registered office, **4**, 320, 435
signature, **4**, 320
    witness, **4**, 314
statutory forms of, technical reform relating to, **4**, 306
subscriber, **4**, 314, 320
subscription clause—
    final, **4**, 320
    signature to, **4**, 344
ultra vires doctrine—
    associate and, **4**, 328

Memorandum of association—*continued*
ultra vires doctrine—*continued*
    charitable company and, **4**, 327
    Companies Act 1989 and, **4**, 326
    director and, **4**, 328
    European Communities Act 1972 and, **4**, 325
    generally, **4**, 323
    traditional, **4**, 324
Menacing character, message of
telecommunications, sent by, **16**, 1959
Mens rea
absence of words importing, **7**, 100
actus reus, and, **7**, 34
aiding and abetting, **7**, 102
allowing, **7**, 103
animus pirandi, **7**, 63
assault, **7**, 213, 224
    constructive intention, **7**, 233
    evil intention, **7**, 231, 234
    generally, **7**, 230
    intention, **7**, 232
    motive as aggravation, **7**, 236
    proof, **7**, 235
    recklessness, **7**, 234
attempted crime, **7**, 162, 168
automatism, **7**, 158
bigamy, **7**, 481
blameworthiness, **7**, 64
breach of the peace, **7**, 460
capacity, **7**, 112
causal link independent of, **7**, 49
causing, **7**, 103
consent of victim, **7**, 93
conspiracy, **7**, 171
corporate liability, **7**, 110, 111
crimen dolo contrahitur, **7**, 61
criminal responsibility, **7**, 64
cruelty, **7**, 104
culpably and recklessly, **7**, 82
dole—
    generally, **7**, 58, 61, 66, 73
    Gordon on, **7**, 59
    Hume on, **7**, 58, 60
embezzlement, **7**, 353
English law, use of term in, **7**, 57
error, person labouring under, **7**, 95–98
error, reckless, **7**, 98
error of fact, **7**, 95, 97
error of law, **7**, 95, 96
falsely, **7**, 76, 77
fireraising, **7**, 416
fraud, **7**, 365, 371
fraudulently, **7**, 76, 77
generally, **7**, 29, 57, 62
gravity of crime, **7**, 107
guilty intention, **7**, 67
Hume's commentaries, **7**, 58–60
immoral lifestyle of accused, irrelevancy, **7**, 94
implication in criminal charge, **7**, 74
incest, **7**, 316
incitement, **7**, 174
indecent exposure, **7**, 475
insanity, **7**, 123, 129
intent, **7**, 68, 76, 78, 82

Mens rea—continued
intoxication, **7**, 112, 127, 134, 231
involuntary intoxication, **7**, 134
knowingly, **7**, 79
  proof of knowledge, **7**, 90
malice, **7**, 69, 76, 80
malus animus, **7**, 69
mobbing, **7**, 441
more than one mental element, where, **7**, 85
motive, relevancy, **7**, 92
murder, **7**, 266
negligently, **7**, 81
non-age, **7**, 159
non-insane automatism, defence of, **7**, 34
objective, **7**, 86
permitting, **7**, 103
possession, **7**, 101
proof—
  generally, **7**, 86
  intent from recklessness, of, **7**, 88
  intention, of, **7**, 87
  knowledge, of, **7**, 90
  objective *mens rea*, **7**, 86
  recklessness, of, **7**, 91
  subjective *mens rea*, **7**, 86
  transferred *mens rea*, **7**, 89
rape, **7**, 303
reckless error, **7**, 98
recklessly, **7**, 76, 82, 98
  assault, **7**, 234
  proof of recklessness, **7**, 91
requirement for, **7**, 28, 61, 99
reset, **7**, 391
Scots criminal law, generally, **7**, 28, 61
Scots law, use of term, **7**, 57, 60, 62, 70, 73
shamelessly, **7**, 83
significant words, **7**, 76–84
strict liability, relationship with, **7**, 99–108
subjective, **7**, 86
suspicion, **7**, 105
terminology, **7**, 62–84
terms importing no mental element, **7**, 106
terms specifically denoting, **7**, 74–84
text writings, **7**, 58–61, 74
theft, **7**, 336–338
transferred, **7**, 89
uttering, **7**, 377
uttering threats, **7**, 251
vicarious liability, **7**, 196
violation of sepulchres, **7**, 466
voluntary conduct, **7**, 34
wilfully, **7**, 70, 76, 84
words of style, **7**, 75
See also MENTAL ELEMENT
Mental act
patent may not be granted in respect of, **18**, 825
Mental criminality
use of term, **7**, 70
Mental defective
statutory provisions, **14**, 1404
Mental disability
See MENTALLY DISORDERED PERSON; MENTAL HEALTH
Mental element
crime, in, *see* MENS REA

Mental health
brain tissue, surgical operation to remove, **14**, 1425
code of practice, Secretary of State's powers, **14**, 1487
cognition of the insane, **11**, 1232
curator bonis, see *curator bonis*; mentally disordered person
electro-convulsive therapy, **14**, 1425
furious person, **14**, 1401
General Board of Control for Scotland, **14**, 1405
guardianship, *see* GUARDIAN-GUARDIANSHIP
hormone implantation, **14**, 1425
hospital, *see* MENTALLY DISORDERED PERSON
idiot, **14**, 1401
ill-treatment of patient, **14**, 1480
insanity, *see* INSANITY
leucotomy, **14**, 1425
local authority—
  duties—
    curator bonis petition court for appointment of, **14**, 1478
    generally, **14**, 1474; **22**, 30
    mentally handicapped person—
      occupation, provision of, **14**, 1477
      training, provision of, **14**, 1477
    special—
      guardian, **14**, 1476
      nearest relative, vested with functions of, **14**, 1476
      parental rights, vested with, **14**, 1476
  mental health officer, appointment of, **14**, 1475
lunatic, **14**, 1401, 1403
lunatic asylum, **14**, 1401
medical officer, **14**, 1427, 1428, 1449
mental defective, **14**, 1404
mental disorder, *see* MENTALLY DISORDERED PERSON
mental handicap, *see* MENTAL HANDICAP—
  mentally handicapped person
mental illness, **14**, 1401
mental impairment, **14**, 1402
Mental Welfare Commission for Scotland, *see*
  MENTAL WELFARE COMMISSION FOR SCOTLAND
officer, *see* MENTAL HEALTH OFFICER
public health regulations, **19**, 302
Secretary of State, powers of, **14**, 1487, 1488
sheriff court jurisdiction, **6**, 1073, 1118
State hospital, **14**, 1472, 1473
statutory provisions, **14**, 1406
See also MENTALLY DISORDERED PERSON
Mental health officer
appointment of, **14**, 249, 1475
competence, proof before appointment, **22**, 30
compulsory admission to psychiatric hospital by, **22**, 30
consent, emergency compulsory admission person to psychiatric hospital, **22**, 30
functions, **22**, 30
guardianship application made by, **14**, 1435, 1437; **22**, 31
legal status, **22**, 3
local authority duty to provide sufficient number, **22**, 30
qualifications, **22**, 11

Mental health officer—*continued*
report on patient's social circumstances, submission, **22**, 30
social worker as, **22**, 30
training, **22**, 11
Mental illness
domicile of mentally ill person, **4**, 30
dominus negotii suffering from, **15**, 141
early provisions, **14**, 35
generally, **7**, 121
local authority responsibility for mentally ill, **14**, 35
meaning, **7**, 114
mental handicap distinguished from, **14**, 1401
nervous shock, *see* CARE, DUTY OF
psychiatric injury, strict liability, **15**, 204
voluntary obligation, mentally incapacitated person's capacity to enter, **15**, 661
woman suffering from, rape, **7**, 301
See also INSANITY; MENTALLY DISORDERED PERSON
Mental impairment
meaning, **14**, 1402
severe, meaning, **14**, 1402
Mental Welfare Commission for Scotland
compulsory admissions or detentions in psychiatric hospital, reports to Commission, **22**, 30
constitution, **14**, 1407
discharge of patient by, **14**, 1427, 1429
duties, **14**, 1408, 1409
establishment of, **14**, 1406
functions, **14**, 1408, 1409
guardianship—
  discharge, order for, **14**, 1449
  duration of authority, **14**, 1446
  private mental hospitals, inspection of, **11**, 1535
transfer of patient, notification of, **14**, 1424
Mentally disordered person
after-care services, provision for, **22**, 30
aggravation by external factor, **7**, 156
common law definition, **14**, 1401
compulsory admission/detention in psychiatric hospital, **22**, 30
contract, capacity to, **15**, 661
correspondence of, **14**, 1421
court proceedings, unfitness to plead—
  generally, **17**, 895
  insanity in bar of trial, **17**, 896
  proceedings commenced, procedure where, **17**, 898
  prosecutor's decision to take no proceedings, **17**, 897
  recovery of accused, proceedings on, **17**, 901
  restriction orders, **17**, 900
  sentence, determination of appropriate, **17**, 907
  trial diet, mental disorder not discovered until, **17**, 899
Criminal Injuries Compensation Scheme, **7**, 652.3
curator bonis
  administrative costs, **11**, 1236
  appointment, **11**, 1232, 1233
  death of, **11**, 1235
  discharge of, **11**, 1235
  duties, **11**, 1234

Mentally disordered person—*continued*
curator bonis—*continued*
  exercise of office, problems with, **11**, 1236
  foreign court, appointed by, recognition in Scotland, **8**, 540, 541
  more than one curator appointed, **11**, 1233
  petition for, **11**, 1233
  reappointment, **11**, 1235
  recovery of ward, **11**, 1235
  reform, proposals for, **11**, 1237
custody, in, **14**, 1447
detention, **12**, 41
diminished responsibility—
  battered woman syndrome, **7**, 147
  depression, **7**, 147
  intoxication, **7**, 148
  personality disorders, **7**, 144
  pre-menstrual syndrome, **7**, 146
  psychopathy, **7**, 144, 145
  requirement as to, **7**, 140–142
  strict legal formula, application, **7**, 143
disability living allowance, **21**, 929, 934, 937, 939, 1097–1100
disablement benefit, **21**, 980
domicile of, **4**, 30
dominus negotii suffering from, **15**, 141
driving licence application, declaration in, **20**, 450
early provisions, **14**, 35
external factor, due to, **7**, 124
guardianship of—
  age limit of guardian, **11**, 1238
  appointment, **11**, 1240; **17**, 904; **22**, 31
  community care, as aspect of, **11**, 1240
  death of guardian, **14**, 1445
  discharge from, **14**, 1448–1451
  duration of authority for, **14**, 1446–1447
  duties, **11**, 1240, 1241; **22**, 31
  generally, **11**, 1238–1241
  guardianship order—
    appeal against, **17**, 906
    court's power to make, **14**, 1452; **17**, 904
    review, **22**, 31
  hospitalised patients—
    absence without leave, **14**, 1443
    generally, **11**, 1240
    transfer of, **14**, 1444
House of Commons, excluded from, **5**, 379
incapacity of, **14**, 1445
industrial injuries benefit, **21**, 967
industrial and provident society, member of, **12**, 618, 620
local authority as guardian—
  duties of, **14**, 1441, 1476
  duties to, **11**, 1241
  reception, application for, **14**, 1435
mentally handicapped person over 16 years, for, **22**, 31
proposed reform, **11**, 1237
pupil, of, **11**, 1238
reception into—
  application, **14**, 1435–1440
  grounds for, **14**, 1434
retention under, duration of authority, **14**, 1446
tutors dative, **11**, 1239

Mentally disordered person—*continued*
hospital—
  absence without leave from, **14**, 1423
  admission—
    application for, **14**, 1412–1416
    emergency, **14**, 1417
    general requirements, **14**, 1411
    medical recommendations, **14**, 1413, 1416
  care, general provisions for, **14**, 1413
  correspondence, **14**, 1421
  detention—
    duration of authority, **14**, 1426
    general requirements, **14**, 1411
  discharge from, **14**, 1427–1431
  information, **14**, 1419
  leave of absence, **14**, 1422
  naturalisation of person in, **14**, 1920
  private, **11**, 1494–1496, 1533–1535
  psychiatric, **22**, 30
  transfer between, **11**, 1491; **14**, 1424
  treatment in, **14**, 1418, 1425
  See also patient *below*
hospital order—
  appeal against, **17**, 906
  court's power to make, **14**, 1452; **17**, 903
  effect of, **14**, 1454
  grounds, **14**, 1453
  interim, **14**, 1462; **17**, 905
  restriction, *see* restriction order *below*
legal representation, exclusion from scope of
  Judgments Convention, **8**, 432
local government candidate, disqualification as,
  15, 1071
mental health officer, *see* MENTAL HEALTH OFFICER
mentally handicapped person, **14**, 1401; **22**, 31
  See also MENTALLY HANDICAPPED PERSON
offences against, **14**, 1482, 1483
  absence without leave, relating to, **14**, 1483
  false statement, **14**, 1479
  ill-treatment of patient, **14**, 1480
  insanity at time of commission, **14**, 1461
  mentally disordered patient, against, **14**, 1482
  mentally handicapped female, against, **7**, 301;
    14, 1481
  obstruction, **14**, 1484
parliamentary candidate, disqualification as, **15**,
  1055
partner—
  dissolution of partnership, grounds for, **16**,
    1013, 1087
  limited partnership, **16**, 1120
patient—
  conditionally discharged, **14**, 1459
  correspondence of, **14**, 1421, 1473
  ill-treatment of, **14**, 1480
  money held on behalf of, **14**, 1420
  place of safety, removal to, **14**, 1485, 1486
  property, of, **14**, 1420; **22**, 30
  removal from UK, **12**, 216; **14**, 1470, 1471
  transfer of, notification to nearest relative, **14**,
    1424
  See also hospital *above*
person in need, as, **22**, 13

Mentally disordered person—*continued*
place of safety, removal to, **14**, 1485, 1486
prisoner, removal from hospital of, **14**, 1463
psychiatric injury, strict liability, **15**, 204
rape of woman suffering from, **7**, 301
relative of—
  discharge of patient by, **14**, 1427, 1432
  guardianship, duties in relation to, **14**, 1451
  information to be given to, **14**, 1419
  local authority, special duties vested with, **14**,
    1476
  meaning, **14**, 1412
  notification of discharge, **14**, 1433
residential care, provision of, **22**, 30
restriction direction—
  appeal, **14**, 1466
  civil prisoner subject to, **14**, 1468
  convicted prisoner subject to, **14**, 1467
  Secretary of State, by, **14**, 1465
restriction order—
  appeal—
    conditionally discharged patient, **14**, 1459
    generally, **17**, 906
    insanity—
      offence, at time of commission of, **14**,
        1461
      trial, in bar of, **14**, 1460
    rights of, **14**, 1456
    Secretary of State, powers of, **14**, 1458
    sheriff, powers of, **14**, 1457
  court's power to make, **14**, 1455
  special restrictions, **14**, 1455
  unfitness to plead, **17**, 900
State hospital, **11**, 1476; **14**, 1472, 1473
statutory definition, **14**, 1402
statutory sick pay, **21**, 908
transfer direction—
  civil prisoner subject to, **14**, 1468
  convicted prisoner, relating to, **14**, 1464, 1467
  restriction direction by Secretary of State, **14**,
    1465
transfer order, prisoner, **14**, 1463
treatment, types of, **14**, 1425
trust, may not create, **24**, 14
voting rights—
  disqualification, **15**, 1082
  European Union election, in, **15**, 1124
  generally, **15**, 1149
  registration for, **15**, 1121
  residence of person detained, **15**, 1081
Mentally handicapped person
community services, **22**, 31
day-care facilities, **22**, 10, 24, 31
definition, statutory, **22**, 31
education authority, duty to inform, **22**, 31
family of, facilities provided for, **22**, 31
female, offence against, **14**, 1481
guardian—
  person over 16 years, social work department
    application to sheriff, **22**, 31
  persons who may be named, **22**, 31
  powers vested in, **22**, 31
  See also GUARDIAN-GUARDIANSHIP
home-help services, **22**, 23

Mentally handicapped person—*continued*
housing, adaptation, **22**, 24
laundry services, **22**, 23
mental impairment, meaning, **14**, 1402
mentally disordered person distinguished, **14**, 1401
occupation, local authority's duty to provide, **14**, 1477
occupational therapists, **22**, 2
parent, education authority's duty to, **22**, 31
person in need, as, **22**, 13, 23
practical assistance, provision of, **22**, 10, 24, 31
residential care, **22**, 10, 24, 31
severe mental impairment, meaning, **14**, 1402
sheltered accommodation, **22**, 31
sheltered employment, local authority provision, **22**, 31
training, local authority's duty to provide, **14**, 1477; **22**, 31
transport provision, **22**, 31
voluntary organisations—
co-ordination, statutory services, **22**, 24
transport, provision of, **22**, 31
Mercantile agent
broker distinguished, **20**, 849
lien, right of, **13**, 95; **20**, 87
meaning, **20**, 849
title, acquisition through, **20**, 849
title conferred by under Factors Acts, **18**, 671
Mercantile law
assimilation of Scots and English law, **22**, 600, 601, 633, 640, 644
bankruptcy, *see* BANKRUPTCY
bills of exchange, *see* BILL OF EXCHANGE
debt recovery, **22**, 645
See also DEBT RECOVERY
diligence, **22**, 664, 679
See also DILIGENCE
English influence on development after the Union, **22**, 600, 601, 633, 640, 644
European Communities, assimilation within, **22**, 625
good faith, doctrine of, not in Scots law, **22**, 610
imperial law, English law as, **5**, 717
inland trade, usages of—
fair, right to hold a court, **22**, 610
generally, **22**, 608, 610
negotiable instruments, origin, **22**, 610
law merchant—
historical sources of Scots law, as, **22**, 608–610
inland trade, usages of, **22**, 608, 610
maritime custom, **22**, 608
origins, **22**, 608
maritime custom—
administration in Scotland, **22**, 609
Consulato del Mare, **22**, 609
law merchant, **22**, 608, 609
maritime law, influence on, **22**, 609
Scotland, medieval influence, **22**, 609
statutory collection, **22**, 609
written code, Mediterranean ports, **22**, 609
negotiable instruments, origin, **22**, 610
partnerships—
nineteenth-century reform, **22**, 642
Scots law, extent to which English legislation assimilated, **22**, 642

Mercantile law—*continued*
reform—
1832 to mid-twentieth century, **22**, 640–645
Bell *Principles* and *Commentaries*, **22**, 640
bills of exchange, **22**, 641
law of sale, attempts to assimilate Scots and English law, **22**, 640, 643
Mercantile Law Commission 1853 ..., **22**, 640
sale of goods—
Sale of Goods Act, **7**, 1893
assimilation, Scots and English law, **22**, 643
common law of sale in Scotland, **22**, 640, 643
criticism as method of law reform, **22**, 643
English terminology, **22**, 643
exemption clauses, Scottish Law Commission recommendations, **22**, 670
Faculty of Advocates, revision of Bill, **22**, 643
implied terms, Scottish Law Commission recommendations, **22**, 670
problem of interpretation in Scotland, **22**, 643
Society of Solicitors, revision of Bill, **22**, 643
Writers to the Signet, revision of Bill, **22**, 643
Scottish Law Committee recommendations, **22**, 670
Unfair Contract Terms Act 1977 ..., **22**, 670
See also MARITIME LAW
Mercantile sequestration
See SEQUESTRATION
Mercantile transactions
writings *in re mercatoria*, **6**, 443
Mercenary
British subject as, rules applicable to, **16**, 1205*n*
definition, **19**, 709
status, **19**, 709
Merchandise
meaning, **24**, 603
Merchant bank
nature of, **2**, 1105
Scotland, in, **2**, 1124
services provided by, **2**, 1105
takeover bid, steps before making of, **4**, 544
Merchant guild
creation, **14**, 14
exclusive privilege, **18**, 5
Merchant marine
contractual duties reinforced by criminal law, **9**, 125
industrial tribunal, jurisdiction of, **9**, 331
Merchant Navy Established Service Scheme
abolition, **21**, 241
Merchant seaman
residence, **15**, 1081
Merchant ship
homosexual acts between crew members, **7**, 313
register of merchant ships, **21**, 131*n*
Merchant Shipping Acts
generally, **21**, 103
Merchant Shipping Notices (M Notices)
generally, **21**, 377
requirement for ship to carry, **21**, 229*n*
towage contract, implied terms, **21**, 404

Merchantable quality
contract for sale, implied terms, **20**, 824
meaning, **20**, 824
Mercy
prerogative of, **7**, 727, 727n; **17**, 833
Merger
balance of payments, effect on, **4**, 1284
City Code on Takeovers and Mergers—
   employee concerns, basis of, **4**, 537
   Rules Governing Substantial Acquisitions of
      Shares, **4**, 550
   self-regulation, **4**, 542, 543
conflict between UK and EU law, **4**, 1118
conglomerate, investigation of, **4**, 1287
countervailing benefits, **4**, 1281
creeping, **4**, 1271
Director General, *see* DIRECTOR GENERAL OF FAIR
   TRADING
efficiency, effect on, **4**, 1286
EU competition rules, **10**, 165
foreign takeovers of domestic companies, controls
   used to prevent, **4**, 1107
generally, **4**, 1270
governmental control of—
   Anderson case, **4**, 567
   Elders case, **4**, 569
   Fair Trading Act 1973, investigation under, **4**, 562
   Hiram and Highland case, **4**, 564
   Lonrho case, **4**, 565
   Royal Bank case, **4**, 566
   Scottish interests, operation of policy on, **4**,
      563
   undertakings as alternative to merger reference,
      4, 568
horizontal, **4**, 1279
international competition, effect on, **4**, 1282
investigation, *see* MONOPOLIES AND MERGERS
   COMMISSION
meaning, **4**, 536, 558, 1271
Mergers Panel, role of, **4**, 1273
minority shareholders, judicial attitudes towards,
   4, 561
newspaper, **4**, 1269
other issues, **4**, 1288
overseas companies, with, **4**, 1285
panel, *see* PANEL ON TAKEOVERS AND MERGERS
policy, operation of, **4**, 563
regulation of—
   self-regulation, **4**, 542, 543
   statutory, **4**, 541
Secretary of State, role of, **4**, 1274
statutory mechanisms for—
   Companies Act 1985 ss 425–427 ..., **4**, 560
   generally, **4**, 558
   Insolvency Act 1986 ..., **4**, 559
   minority shareholders, judicial attitudes towards,
      4, 561
   undertakings as alternative to merger reference, **4**,
      568
vertical, **4**, 1280
Messenger-at-arms
admission, **14**, 1502
Advisory Council of Messengers-at-Arms and
   Sheriff Officers, **14**, 1504

Messenger-at-arms—*continued*
appointment, **14**, 1502
apprenticeship, **14**, 1502
baton, function, **14**, 1503
bond of caution, **14**, 1502
caution granted for—
   generally, **3**, 1000
   institution, by, **3**, 986
   requirement for, **3**, 1000
cautioner—
   bankruptcy of, **14**, 1502
   death of, **14**, 1502
   liability of, **14**, 1507
   reparation, liability in action of, **14**, 1504
child, custody of, **14**, 1504
commission, **14**, 1501, 1502
control, **14**, 1506
deprivation, **14**, 1504, 1506
diligence, and, **14**, 1505, 1507
distribution, **14**, 1501
duties, **14**, 1504
generally, **16**, 1901
insignia, **14**, 1502, 1503
instructions, acknowledgment of receipt of, **14**,
   1504
jurisdiction, **14**, 1504
liability, **14**, 1507
lieges, service of, **14**, 1504
misconduct, **14**, 1506
numbers, **14**, 1501, 1502
oath, **14**, 1501, 1502
office, **14**, 1501
powers, **14**, 1501
professional qualification, **14**, 1502
qualifications of, **14**, 1502
rates, recovery of, **14**, 1504
regulation of office, **14**, 1504
remuneration, **14**, 1505
reparation, liability in action of, **14**, 1504
roll, signing of, **14**, 1502
sheriff court, position in relation to, **14**, 1504
summary cause procedure, **14**, 1504
suspension, **14**, 1506
tax, recovery of, **14**, 1504
value added tax, recovery of, **14**, 1504
warrant, authority to execute, **14**, 1504
Messina Conference, **10**, 8
Metal dealer
licensing, **7**, 45; **14**, 119, 559
Metals
heraldic, **11**, 1604n
precious, Crown ownership, **6**, 491
Meters
electricity, *see* ELECTRICITY
gas, **9**, 885
water, *see* WATER SUPPLY
Methane drainage licence
natural gas, application to, **9**, 730
Methyl alcohol
excise duty, **7**, 1061n, 1062
Methylated spirits
excise duty, **7**, 1061n, 1062
meaning, **3**, 1224n

Methylated spirits—*continued*
sale of, **14**, 526
  person under age of fourteen, to, **3**, 1224
Metrication
European Community average system, **6**, 176, 256, 259
information on imperial equivalent, **6**, 186
sale of goods, quantity marking, **6**, 194
voluntary nature of change, **6**, 176
Metropolitan Sees
Roman Catholic Church, **3**, 1655
Mice
discouragement and destruction of, **19**, 326
mine, freedom from, **14**, 1664
Micro organism
patent of invention requiring use of, **18**, 828, 837
Microfilm and microfiche
evidence, as, **10**, 607
records on, **19**, 846, 847, 849
Midwife
controlled drugs, possession of, **14**, 1259
domestic tribunal for regulation of, **23**, 917
licensing system, exemption from, **14**, 1203
male, **14**, 1154*n*
professional conduct, **14**, 1148, 1149
qualifications—
  obtained outside UK, **14**, 1152
  United Kingdom, **14**, 1154
register—
  preparation and maintenance of, **14**, 1150
  removal from, **14**, 1158
registration—
  eligibility for, **14**, 1152
  periodic, **14**, 1151
  renewable, **14**, 1151
regulation, framework of, **14**, 1147
restrictions on practice, **14**, 1156, 1157
training, **14**, 1148, 1149
  immigration rules, **12**, 292, 293
See also MIDWIFERY, MATERNITY AND CHILD CARE
Midwifery, maternity and child care
area nursing and midwifery committee, **11**, 1423
health boards, administration by, **11**, 1410
maternity medical services—
  doctors' obligations as to, **11**, 1446
  termination of, **11**, 1440
midwives, *see* MIDWIFE
national nursing and midwifery consultative committee, **11**, 1419
non-designated services, **4**, 1177*n*
Migration
reasons for, **12**, 102
Milan Summit, **10**, 24
Milestone
railway, **19**, 1039
Military aid
emergency regulations—
  making of, **5**, 601
  powers conferred by, **5**, 602
generally, **5**, 598
other authorities, **5**, 604
proclamations of emergency—
  generally, **5**, 599
  parliamentary consideration of, **5**, 600

Military aid—*continued*
servicemen, temporary employment of, **5**, 603
Military equipment
export, **7**, 1194
Military law
civilians, trial of, **2**, 605
imperial law, English law as, **5**, 715
See also COURTS-MARTIAL; SERVICE LAW
Military personnel
domicile, **4**, 30
UK, right to enter, **16**, 1208
See also ARMED FORCES
Milk
additives, **11**, 442
advertising, **11**, 469
  skimmed milk, **11**, 480
analysis of samples, **11**, 336
  automatic machine, purchase of sample from, **11**, 338*n*
  division and disposal of samples, **11**, 338
bottles and cap colouring, **11**, 471
bovine disease—
  diseased cow, milk of, **11**, 317
  persons suffering from, **11**, 448
  precautions against spread of, **11**, 447
buttermilk, **11**, 443
byelaws, **11**, 322; **14**, 710
cattle, inspection of—
  dairies, in, **11**, 444, 444*n*
  elsewhere, **11**, 445
Channel Islands breeds, **11**, 466
children, milk prepared for, depots for sale of, **11**, 451
composition and treatment of, regulations as to, **11**, 352
condensed—
  colouring matter not permitted, **11**, 372
  generally, **11**, 442, 443
  ingredients, **11**, 486
  labelling, **11**, 485
  meaning, **11**, 483
  offences, penalties and exemptions, **11**, 487
  preparation, **11**, 486
  restriction on use of description, **11**, 484
  sale, **11**, 486
  skimmed, **11**, 480, 481
consigning authority, securing compliance by, **11**, 446
cow's, meaning, **11**, 443
cream, *see* CREAM
customers, lists of, **11**, 450
dairy byelaws, **11**, 492
  model, **11**, 492, 493
dairy produce quotas—
  administration of, **1**, 930
  establishing, **1**, 926
  exchange and reallocation, **1**, 927
  generally, **1**, 925
  levy where quota exceeded, **1**, 929
  quota reserves, **1**, 928
dealer's licence, **11**, 459, 459*n*
dealer's supplementary licence, **11**, 459, 459*n*
definition, **11**, 438

Milk—*continued*
dried, **II**, 442, 443
  colouring matter not permitted, **II**, 373
  ingredients, **II**, 486
  labelling, **II**, 485
  meaning, **II**, 483
  offences, penalties and exemptions, **II**, 487
  preparation, **II**, 486
  restriction on use of description, **II**, 484
  sale, **II**, 486
  skimmed, **II**, 480, 481
drinking milk—
  composition, **II**, 472
  enforcement, **II**, 473
  labelling, **II**, 473
  meaning, **II**, 472*n*
  records, **II**, 473
  sale of, **II**, 472
early legislation, **II**, 301, 302
education authority, provision by, **8**, 850
European Union—
  dairy price quota, **I**, 925–930
  levies system, **I**, 924
  Milk Marketing Boards, **I**, 931
  New Zealand dairy products, **I**, 932
  pilot and assimilated products, **I**, 923
evaporated, **II**, 443
functions relating to, **14**, 710
goat's, **II**, 438
Guernsey breed, **II**, 466
historical background, **II**, 441
Jersey breed, **II**, 466
labelling, **II**, 383, 468–471, 485
  bottles, **II**, 471
  bulk containers, **II**, 469
  cap colouring, **II**, 471
  condensed milk, **II**, 485
  containers, **II**, 468
  dried milk, **II**, 485
  drinking milk, **II**, 473
  marks, location of, **II**, 469
  offences and proceedings, **II**, 470
  skimmed milk, **II**, 480, 481
local authority, enforcement of provisions by, **14**, 710
marketing board, *see* MILK MARKETING BOARD
meaning, **II**, 352*n*, 443
milk licence, **II**, 452; **14**, 526
  appeals, **II**, 463
  application for, **II**, 459
  conditions, **II**, 457
    breach of, **II**, 457
  dealer's licence, **II**, 459, 459*n*
    supplementary, **II**, 459, 459*n*
  duration, **II**, 460
  grant of, **II**, 459
  pasteurised milk, **II**, 459
  revocation, refusal or suspension, **II**, 458, 461–463
  samples, taking of, **II**, 464
  sterilised milk, **II**, 459
  types of, **II**, 459
  ultra heat treated milk, **II**, 459
pasteurised, **II**, 459

Milk—*continued*
price control, **II**, 467
processor, meaning, **II**, 482, 482*n*
products, *see* MILK PRODUCTS
quotas, *see* dairy produce quotas *above*
raw milk, **II**, 472*n*
reconstituted, **II**, 442
regulations, power to make, **II**, 306
sale of, **II**, 440
  dealer's licence and dealer's supplementary licence, **II**, 459, 459*n*
  historical background, **II**, 441
  labelling, **II**, 468–471
  place where milk sold, **II**, 454
  registration of purveyors of milk, **II**, 495
  skimmed milk, **II**, 480–482
  special designations, **II**, 452–467
sampling, **II**, 336, 338, 338*n*, 464
Secretary of State's powers in relation to, **II**, 321
semi-skimmed, **II**, 472*n*, 482
separated, **II**, 443
  added to unseparated, **II**, 442
sheep's, **II**, 438
skimmed, **II**, 443, 472*n*, 480–472*n*, 482
  with non-milk fat, **II**, 480
South Devon breed, **II**, 466
special designations—
  licence authorising, **II**, 452, 457–463
  milk from elsewhere in United Kingdom, **II**, 465
  power to prescribe, **II**, 452
  specified area, **II**, 453, 455
  use of, **II**, 453
specified area, **II**, 453
  establishment of, **II**, 455
statutory provisions, **14**, 710
sterilised, **II**, 459
stoppage of milk supplies, **II**, 449
suppliers, lists of, **II**, 450
surplus production, **I**, 924
target price, **I**, 923
treatment of, provision of facilities for, **II**, 456
ultra heat treated, **II**, 459
welfare, **II**, 432, 432*n*
whole milk, **II**, 472*n*
See also DAIRIES

Milk marketing boards
areas of, **I**, 703
EEC, allowed to function within, **I**, 704, 931
Intervention Board for Agricultural Produce exercise of functions of, **I**, 929
intervention functions, **I**, 985
powers delegated to, **I**, 984
rights of, **I**, 931
Secretary of State, discharging function of, **I**, 930
trading functions, **I**, 706

Milk products
assimilated products, prices for, **I**, 923
co-responsibility levy, **I**, 904, 924
common organisation—
  milk marketing boards, role of, **I**, 985
  quality standards, **I**, 968
dairy produce quota system, **I**, 925
Dairy Produce Quota Tribunals, **I**, 925, 930

Milk products—*continued*
export refunds, **1**, 923
guarantee thresholds, **1**, 924
income support, **1**, 924
intervention prices, **1**, 923
levy—
    annually, paid, **1**, 929
    collection of, **1**, 929
    proceeds, use of, **1**, 929
    quota exceeded, where, **1**, 929
    regions, division of territory into, **1**, 925
    scheme for, **1**, 925
New Zealand dairy products, import of, **1**, 932
pilot products, prices for, **1**, 923
production quota system, **1**, 924
quotas—
    administration of system, **1**, 930
    development claims, **1**, 926
    direct sales, **1**, 925
    establishment of, **1**, 926
    exceeding, levy on, **1**, 929
    exchange of, **1**, 927
    reallocation of, **1**, 927
    reserves, **1**, 928
    Scotland, division of, for, **1**, 926
    small producer provision, **1**, 926
    wholesale, **1**, 925
target price, **1**, 923
See also MILK; MILK MARKETING BOARDS
Mill
diversion or detention of non-tidal river by
    proprietor, **18**, 292, 293, 295
lease, **13**, 206
sasine, symbols of, **18**, 90
servitude of aqueduct, **25**, 353
thirlage, **18**, 90*n*
Mill lade
diversion of water, **25**, 327
examination of, **11**, 25
meaning, **11**, 25*n*
obstruction of passage of salmon, **11**, 19
Secretary of State's powers, **11**, 23
water pollution, **14**, 2079
Millar, Professor John, **18**, 1*n*, 4, 4*n*
Miller
right of lien, **20**, 77
Miller's Trustees v Miller
principle of, **24**, 72, 73
Milner Holland Committee
recommendations, **13**, 698
Minches
internal waters, as, **11**, 78
Mine
pertinent, as, **12**, 1242
royal, Crown hereditary revenue derived from, **7**,
    769
Mineclearance operation, vessel engaged in
restricted manoeuvrability, vessel with, lights and
    shapes to be displayed, **21**, 365
Minerals
a coelo usque ad centrum principle, **6**, 491; **12**, 1243;
    18, 198
ings, **6**, 495

Minerals—*continued*
coal, **6**, 491
common law provisions, modification of, **6**, 493
conveyance separately from land, **6**, 780; **12**, 1243
Crown, belonging to, **6**, 491
deposits, public health nuisance, **19**, 226*n*
hydrocarbons, food containing, **11**, 375
lease—
    assignability, **13**, 356
    duration, **13**, 199
    generally, **6**, 780; **13**, 111, 194, 199
    landlord's hypothec, **13**, 199, 513
    liability under, **14**, 1688
    liferenter as lessor, **13**, 169
    lordship or royalty, **13**, 103, 199
    minerals and surface under separate ownership,
        13, 199
    payments for, **13**, 71, 103, 199
    surface let separately, **13**, 199
    trustees as lessor, **13**, 165
meaning, **6**, 492; **14**, 1601; **24**, 677
metals, **6**, 491
mines royal, **13**, 200; **18**, 210
pertinent, as, **12**, 1242
petroleum and gas, **6**, 491
power to work, **6**, 493
refuse, public health nuisance, **19**, 336
registration of leases, **6**, 780
reservation of, **6**, 491–493
rights—
    a coelo usque ad centrum principle, **6**, 491; **12**,
        1243; **18**, 198
    foreshore, **18**, 318
    liferenter's rights, **13**, 1639
    ownership, **18**, 198
    registration of, **6**, 491–493, 762, 780
    separate tenement, as, **6**, 780; **18**, 207, 209, 212
    servitude rights in relation to, **18**, 491
    superior, reservation by, **6**, 491, 493, 762; **12**,
        1243; **18**, 60, 703, 703*n*
    support, right to, *see* SUPPORT, RIGHTS OF
sheriff court jurisdiction, **6**, 1119
short and long leases, **6**, 780
significance of, in property agreements, **6**, 494
statutory control of rights to work, **14**, 1681
undertakings—
    going concern, as, **25**, 141
    value of, **25**, 142
valuation—
    capital, redemption of, **25**, 139
    rating, for, **24**, 676, 678, 682
    risk factor, **25**, 140
    types of, **25**, 141
working of—
    power to, **6**, 493
    railway, near, **14**, 1692
    statutory control of, **14**, 1681
Mines
access—
    electrical apparatus, to, **14**, 1650
accident—
    notification of, **14**, 1659
    shaft unavailable through, **14**, 1621

Mines—*continued*

animals—
  care of, **14**, 1665
  horse, employment of, **14**, 1665
apparatus—
  breathing, **14**, 1662
  electrical, **14**, 1650
  gas—
    construction, **14**, 1647
    installation, **14**, 1647
    maintenance, **14**, 1647
  haulage, **14**, 1625
  inspection, **14**, 1645
  steam—
    construction, **14**, 1647
    installation, **14**, 1647
    maintenance, **14**, 1647
  testing, **14**, 1645
  winding, *see* winding apparatus *below*
  See also machinery *below*
blasting materials—
  compressed air blasting shells, use of, **14**, 1651
  maintenance, **14**, 1651
  quarry, in, **14**, 1706
  use, **14**, 1651
breakdown, shaft unavailable through, **14**, 1621
breathing apparatus, provision of, **14**, 1662
British Coal Corporation—
  constitution, **14**, 1604
  financial directions, **14**, 1604
  functions, **14**, 1603
  grants, **14**, 1604
  licence to work coal, **14**, 1606
  minerals, statutory control of rights to work, **14**, 1681
  National Coal Board, interests transferred from, **14**, 1603
  opencast coal mining—
    compulsory rights orders, **14**, 1699
    rights of way, suspension of, **14**, 1698
    statutory control, **14**, 1697
  pneumoconiosis compensation scheme, **14**, 1678
  policy, **14**, 1603
  subsidence damage, obligations in respect of, **14**, 1694
  support, right to withdraw, **14**, 1685
building—
  support, *see* support *below*
  surface, safety of, **14**, 1624
canal, support of land purchased for construction, **14**, 1690
care, duty of—
  common law, **14**, 1616
  statutory, **14**, 1617
charitable trust, coal industry beneficiaries, representation for, **14**, 1677
cigarette, employee striking match to light, **14**, 1649
coal, licence to work, **14**, 1606
Coal Industry Social Welfare Organisation—
  functions, **14**, 1677
  local welfare committees, transfer of functions, **14**, 1677

Mines—*continued*

common law, care, duty of, **14**, 1616
compensation—
  opencast coal mining, **14**, 1700
  pneumoconiosis, for, **14**, 1678
  support, relating to, **14**, 1689
  working facilities, grant of, **14**, 1683
construction—
  gas apparatus, **14**, 1647
  roads, of, **14**, 1630
  shaft, of, **14**, 1621
  steam apparatus, **14**, 1647
contractor—
  owner, as, **14**, 1602
  tunnelling, required to employ support rules, **14**, 1637
conveyor—
  operation of, **14**, 1640
  signalling rules, **14**, 1641
Court of Session, charitable trusts, amendment of, **14**, 1677
damages—
  firedamp, explosion occurring after, **14**, 1656
  injury suffered by breach of provision, **14**, 1619
  redundancy payments, effect of, **14**, 1679
  subsidence damage, for, **14**, 1694
  support, loss of, **14**, 1686
  working place, fall into, **14**, 1633
danger—
  fall, duty to avoid, **14**, 1702
  hours of work, exemption from control, **14**, 1668
  official, duty to report to, **14**, 1657
  overhang, duty to avoid, **14**, 1702
  removal of, **14**, 1657
  workman, withdrawal of, **14**, 1657, 1707
defence, impracticability of, **14**, 1620
deputy—
  appointment, **14**, 1611
  hours of work, **14**, 1667
  inspection, duties relating to, **14**, 1612
  lamps, use of, **14**, 1612
  qualifications, **14**, 1611
  statutory duties, **14**, 1612
discipline—
  breaches of, **14**, 1674
  statutory control of, **14**, 1673
district—
  deputy, duties of, **14**, 1612
  size, **14**, 1612
disused part of, entrance to, **14**, 1623
Domestic Coal Consumers' Council, duties, **14**, 1605
doors, ventilation, must be self-closing, **14**, 1655
drinking water, supply of, **14**, 1664
dust—
  accumulation of, **14**, 1658
  control of, **14**, 1658
  quarry, in, **14**, 1706
egress, means of—
  emergency, scheme for, **14**, 1629
  outlet, *see* outlet *below*
  shaft, *see* shaft *below*

Mines—*continued*
electrical apparatus—
   access to, **14**, 1650
   installation, **14**, 1650
   use, **14**, 1650
   working space, adequacy of, **14**, 1650
electricity—
   inflammable gas, prevention of ignition, **14**, 1650
   installation, **14**, 1650
   insulation, **14**, 1650
   quarry, in, **14**, 1705
   use, **14**, 1650
emergency—
   egress, scheme for, **14**, 1629
   hours of work, exemption from control, **14**, 1668
   portable lamp for use in, **14**, 1648
   ventilation, interruption of, **14**, 1655
employee—
   cigarette, striking match to light, **14**, 1649
   danger, duty to withdraw from, **14**, 1657, 1707
   fire, withdrawal in case of, **14**, 1662
   first aid, provision of, **14**, 1663
   health, **14**, 1664
   protection of, **14**, 1643
   redundancy payments, **14**, 1679
   welfare, **14**, 1664
employment—
   child, of, **3**, 1257
   women, of, **14**, 1666
   young person, of, **14**, 1666
   See also hours of work *below*
entrance—
   disused part of mine, to, **14**, 1623
   outlet, to, **14**, 1628
   shaft, to, **14**, 1628
   staple pit, to, **14**, 1628
escape, fire, in case of, **14**, 1660
explosion, firedamp, occurring after, **14**, 1656
explosives—
   care of, **14**, 1652
   conveyance, **14**, 1651
   statutory control, **14**, 1651
   storage, **14**, 1651
   use, **10**, 1620; **14**, 1652
fall, danger from, duty to avoid, **14**, 1702
fan worker, hours of work, **14**, 1667
fencing—
   disused shaft, of, **14**, 1626
   exposed machinery, **14**, 1646
fire—
   breathing apparatus, **14**, 1662
   central rescue station, availability of, **14**, 1662
   escape, means of, **14**, 1660
   inflammable material, storage of, **14**, 1661
   precautions, **14**, 1661
   rescue equipment, **14**, 1662
   workmen, withdrawal of, **14**, 1662
firedamp—
   detectors, provision of, **14**, 1655
   explosion occurring after, **14**, 1656
fireman, *see* deputy *above*

Mines—*continued*
first aid—
   equipment, provision of, **14**, 1663
   facilities, provision of, **14**, 1663
   manager, duty of, **14**, 1663
foot passenger, transport road, in, safety of, **14**, 1631
furnace worker, hours of work, **14**, 1667
gas apparatus—
   construction, **14**, 1647
   installation, **14**, 1647
   maintenance, **14**, 1647
gas inflammable, *see* inflammable gas *below*
grants, British Coal Corporation, to, **14**, 1604
gunpowder, statutory control, **14**, 1651
haulage apparatus—
   employee, protection of, **14**, 1643
   rope—
      operation of, **14**, 1640
      signalling rules, **14**, 1641
   shaft, in, **14**, 1625
Health and Safety Commission, discharge of functions, **14**, 1615
health and welfare—
   drinking water, provision of, **14**, 1664
   employee, of, **14**, 1664
   legislation, **19**, 344
   mice, freedom of mine from, **14**, 1664
   rats, freedom of mine from, **14**, 1664
   sanitary convenience, provision above and below ground, **14**, 1664
highways, *see* roads *below*
horse—
   care of, **14**, 1665
   meaning, **14**, 1665n
horsekeeper—
   appointment of, **14**, 1665
   hours of work, **14**, 1667
hours of work—
   deputy, **14**, 1667
   exemption from control, **14**, 1668
   fan worker, **14**, 1667
   furnace worker, **14**, 1667
   horsekeeper, **14**, 1667
   lowering, times of, **14**, 1669
   mechanic, **14**, 1667
   pump-minder, **14**, 1667
   raising, times of, **14**, 1669
   shift worker, **14**, 1667
   surveyor, **14**, 1667
   suspension of control, **14**, 1668
   young person, **14**, 1671
impracticability, defence of, **14**, 1620
inflammable gas, ignition, prevention of, **14**, 1650
inflammable material, storage of, **14**, 1661
information—
   Health and Safety Commission, power to obtain, **14**, 1615
ingress, means of—
   disused part of mine, entrance to, **14**, 1623
   outlet, *see* outlet *below*
   shaft, *see* shaft *below*
inrush—
   inspection, manager's duty of, **14**, 1639

Mines—*continued*
inrush—*continued*
    manager, duty to prevent, **14**, 1638
    notification, **14**, 1639
inspection—
    apparatus, **14**, 1645
    daily, **14**, 1613
    inrush, manager's duty relating to, **14**, 1639
    machinery, **14**, 1645
    manager, duty of, **14**, 1609
    monthly, **14**, 1614
    outwith deputies' districts, **14**, 1613
    pre-shift, **14**, 1612
instruction, competent, duty to provide, **14**, 1672
lamps—
    deputy, use by, **14**, 1612
    provision of, **14**, 1648
land, support, *see* support *below*
lease, liability under, **14**, 1688
liability—
    manager, of, **14**, 1608, 1609
    mineral lease, under, **14**, 1688
    roof and sides, duty to secure, **14**, 1635
    vicarious—
        absolute and continuing obligation, **14**, 1618
        owner cannot be absolved from, **14**, 1619
licence, coal working, **14**, 1606
lighting—
    provision of, **14**, 1648
    quarry, in, **14**, 1706
liquidator as owner, **14**, 1602
local authority—
    compulsory purchase by, **14**, 1680
    unstable tip, powers in respect of, **14**, 1696
locomotive, operation of, **14**, 1640
lowering, times of, **14**, 1669
machinery—
    exposed, fencing of, **14**, 1646
    inspection, **14**, 1645
    installation, **14**, 1645
    maintenance, **14**, 1645
    quarry, in, **14**, 1705
    testing, **14**, 1645
maintenance—
    gas apparatus, **14**, 1647
    machinery, **14**, 1645
    roads, **14**, 1630
    steam apparatus, **14**, 1647
    winding apparatus, **14**, 1627
manager—
    age, **14**, 1608
    appointment, **14**, 1608
    dust, duty relating to, **14**, 1658
    duties, **14**, 1609
    first aid, duty relating to, **14**, 1663
    inrush, duty to prevent, **14**, 1638, 1639
    inspection, duties relating to, **14**, 1609
    jurisdiction, **14**, 1608
    liability, **14**, 1608, 1609
    owner as, **14**, 1608
    plan of working, duty to keep, **14**, 1610
    qualifications, **14**, 1608
    roof, duty to secure safety of, **14**, 1633
    sole, **14**, 1608

Mines—*continued*
manager—*continued*
    substitute, appointment of, **14**, 1608
    under-, *see* under-manager *below*
    ventilation, duty relating to, **14**, 1655
meaning, **14**, 1601
mechanic, hours of work, **14**, 1667
medical examination, young person, **14**, 1666
mice, freedom of mine from, **14**, 1664
miner, working place, duty to secure, **14**, 1636
minerals—
    interest in, **6**, 762
    lease, liability under, **14**, 1688
    meaning, **14**, 1601
    railway, working near, **14**, 1692
    statutory control of rights to work, **14**, 1681
Miners' Welfare Commission—
    dissolution, **14**, 1677
    transfer of functions, **14**, 1677
mining code, *see* MINING CODE
mining operations, planning permission, **14**, 1680
misfire, procedure to be adopted after, **14**, 1654
name, change in, notification of, **14**, 1615
National Coal Board, *see* British Coal Corporation *above*
negligence, support rules, as to, **14**, 1637
notification—
    accident, of, **14**, 1659
    electrical apparatus, installation of, **14**, 1650
    inrush, of, **14**, 1639
    name, change in, **14**, 1615
    new operations, of, **14**, 1615
    owner, change of, **14**, 1615
    railway, minerals lying under area of protection, **14**, 1691
    waterworks, minerals lying under area of protection, **14**, 1691
nuisance—
    mine, use of land as, **14**, 1616
    quarry, use of land as, **14**, 1616
offence—
    absolute and continuing obligation, **14**, 1618
    discipline, breach of, **14**, 1674
    impracticability, defence of, **14**, 1620
    penalties, **14**, 1676
    smoking materials, **14**, 1649
    summary, **14**, 1675
official, danger, duty to report, **14**, 1657
opencast coal mining—
    compensation, **14**, 1700
    compulsory rights orders, **14**, 1699
    rights of way, suspension of, **14**, 1698
    statutory control, **14**, 1697
operations, new, notice of, **14**, 1615
outlet—
    entrance to, **14**, 1628
    provision of, **14**, 1621
    surface surrounding or adjacent to, **14**, 1601
    unwalkable, **14**, 1621
    way to, provision of, **14**, 1622
    winding apparatus, **14**, 1621
overhang, danger from, duty to avoid, **14**, 1702

Mines—*continued*
owner—
  additional—
    liquidator as, **14**, 1602
    receiver as, **14**, 1602
  British Coal Corporation as, **14**, 1603
  change of, notification of, **14**, 1615
  contractor as, **14**, 1602
  manager, appointment as, **14**, 1608
  meaning, **14**, 1602
  powers of, **14**, 1602
  trespasser, duty to, **14**, 1708
  vicarious liability, **14**, 1619
passenger, foot, safety on transport road, **14**, 1631
pertinent, as, **12**, 1242
pipe-lines, right of support, **14**, 1693
plan—
  tip, of, **14**, 1695
  working, of, manager's duty to keep, **14**, 1610
planning permission—
  local authority, compulsory purchase by, **14**, 1680
  mining operations, **14**, 1680
  rescinding of, **14**, 1680
pneumoconiosis, compensation scheme, **14**, 1678
public works, support of land purchased for construction, **14**, 1690
pump-minder, hours of work, **14**, 1667
quarry distinguished, **14**, 1601
railway—
  moving train, protection of employee, **14**, 1643
  support—
    mining codes, **14**, 1690
    notices, **14**, 1691
    working minerals, **14**, 1692
  surface, **14**, 1644
raising, times of, **14**, 1669
rats, freedom of mine from, **14**, 1664
receiver, owner, as, **14**, 1602
redundancy payments—
  damages for personal injury, calculation of, **14**, 1679
refuge hole—
  obstruction, **14**, 1632
  provision, **14**, 1632
regulations, current, **14**, 1607
remedial works, subsidence damage, execution in case of, **14**, 1694
rescue—
  central station, availability of, **14**, 1662
  fire, in case of, **14**, 1662
rights of way, suspension of, **14**, 1698
roads—
  clearances, **14**, 1632
  construction, **14**, 1630
  diversion, **14**, 1684
  foot passengers, safety of, **14**, 1631
  maintenance, **14**, 1630
  refuge holes, **14**, 1632
  stopping up, **14**, 1684
roof—
  securing safety of—
    damages for injuries, **14**, 1633
    liability for breach, **14**, 1635
    manager, duty of, **14**, 1633, 1634

Mines—*continued*
roof—*continued*
  support rules, **14**, 1637
rope haulage apparatus, *see* haulage apparatus *above*
royal, Crown hereditary revenue derived from, **7**, 769
running away, meaning, **14**, 1642
safety—
  absolute and continuing obligation, **14**, 1618
  accident, *see* accident *above*
  building on surface, of, **14**, 1624
  care, duty of—
    common law, **14**, 1616
    statutory, **14**, 1617
  danger, duty of workmen to withdraw from, **14**, 1657, 1707
  dust, control of, **14**, 1658
  electricity, *see* electricity *above*
  explosives, *see* explosives *above*
  fire, *see* fire *above*
  first aid, *see* first aid *above*
  foot passengers, of, **14**, 1631
  gas apparatus, *see* gas apparatus *above*
  haulage apparatus, *see* haulage apparatus *above*
  impracticability, defence of, **14**, 1620
  inrush—
    inspection, **14**, 1639
    manager's duty to prevent, **14**, 1638
    notice, **14**, 1639
  lamps, provision of, **14**, 1648
  lighting, provision of, **14**, 1648
  machinery, *see* machinery *above*
  object of provisions, **14**, 1619
  quarry, in, **14**, 1703
  roads, *see* roads *above*
  roof, *see* roof *above*
  shaft, of, *see* shaft *below*
  smoking materials, **14**, 1649
  steam apparatus, *see* steam apparatus *below*
  structure on surface, of, **14**, 1624
  vehicle, device for, **14**, 1642
  ventilation, *see* ventilation *below*
sanitary convenience, provision of, **14**, 1664
Secretary of State, British Coal Corporation, powers relating to, **14**, 1604
sewers, support, right of, **14**, 1693
shaft—
  accident, unavailable through, **14**, 1621
  breakdown, unavailable through, **14**, 1621
  construction, **14**, 1621
  disused, fencing of, **14**, 1626
  entrance to, **14**, 1628
  haulage apparatus, **14**, 1625
  number, **14**, 1621
  provision of, **14**, 1621
  safety of, **14**, 1626
  surface surrounding or adjacent to, **14**, 1601
  way to, provision of, **14**, 1622
  winding apparatus, **14**, 1621, 1625
shelter—
  misfire, procedure to be adopted after, **14**, 1654
  proper, meaning, **14**, 1653
  shot firing, **14**, 1653

Mines—_continued_
sheriff court jurisdiction, **6**, 1119
shift—
    lowering, times of, **14**, 1669
    meaning, **14**, 1667
    raising, times of, **14**, 1669
    worker, hours of work, **14**, 1667
shot firing—
    damages, **14**, 1653
    misfire, procedure to be adopted after, **14**, 1654
    proper shelter, meaning, **14**, 1653
    shot hole, charging of, **14**, 1653
sides—
    securing safety of—
        damages for injuries, **14**, 1633
        liability for breach, **14**, 1635
        manager, duty of, **14**, 1633, 1634
    support rules, **14**, 1637
signalling—
    conveyor, **14**, 1641
    rope haulage apparatus, **14**, 1641
    winding apparatus, **14**, 1627
smoking materials—
    cigarette, employee striking match to light, **14**, 1649
    offence, **14**, 1649
stables, construction and use, **14**, 1665
staple pit, entrance to, **14**, 1628
statutory control—
    regulations, **14**, 1607
    statutes, **14**, 1607
steam apparatus—
    construction, **14**, 1647
    installation, **14**, 1647
    maintenance, **14**, 1647
structure, surface, safety of, **14**, 1624
subsidence—
    damage—
        British Coal Corporation, obligations of, **14**, 1694
        damages, **14**, 1694
        dwelling house, provision of alternative accommodation, **14**, 1694
        remedial works, **14**, 1694
supervision, duty to provide, **14**, 1672
support—
    canals, **14**, 1690
    compensation clauses, **14**, 1689
    counter-notice, service of, **14**, 1691
    loss of, assessing damages for, **14**, 1686
    mineral lease, liability under, **14**, 1688
    mining codes, **14**, 1690
    notice, service of, **14**, 1691
    pipe-lines, **14**, 1693
    public works, **14**, 1690
    railways, **14**, 1690
    right to, **14**, 1685
    sewers, **14**, 1693
    waterworks, **14**, 1690
    withdrawal of, **14**, 1687
    working minerals, **14**, 1692
surface—
    building, safety of, **14**, 1624
    railway, **14**, 1644

Mines—_continued_
surface—_continued_
    sanitary convenience, provision of, **14**, 1664
    structure, safety of, **14**, 1624
surveyor, hours of work, **14**, 1667
testing—
    apparatus, **14**, 1645
    machinery, **14**, 1645
time checker, appointment, **14**, 1670
tip—
    cessation of use, **14**, 1695
    plan of, **14**, 1695
    security of, **14**, 1695
    unstable, **14**, 1696
train, employee, protection of, **14**, 1643
transport roads, _see_ roads _above_
treasury, British Coal Corporation, powers relating to, **14**, 1604
trespasser, quarry owner's duty to, **14**, 1708
trust, welfare, _see_ welfare _below_
under-manager—
    absolute and continuing obligation, **14**, 1618
    age, **14**, 1608
    appointment, **14**, 1608
    qualifications, **14**, 1608
    substitute, appointment of, **14**, 1608
underground water, **18**, 343, 343_n_; **25**, 347
valuation for rating—
    apportionment, **24**, 683
    buildings and plant, of, **24**, 681
    derating, **24**, 682
    generally, **24**, 679
    meaning of mine, for, **24**, 682
    prescribed valuation formula, **24**, 547
    valuation, **24**, 680, 681
        reduction of, **24**, 684, 685
vehicle—
    employee, protection of, **14**, 1643
    quarry, in, **14**, 1704
    running away, meaning, **14**, 1642
    safety device, **14**, 1642
ventilation—
    adequate, duty to secure, **14**, 1655
    breach of provisions, **14**, 1655
    fans, provision of, **14**, 1655
    interruption of, **14**, 1655
    manager, duties of, **14**, 1655
    mechanically operated apparatus, **14**, 1655
    self-closing doors, **14**, 1655
    See also firedamp _above_
vicarious liability, _see_ liability _above_
water pollution, **14**, 2079
waterworks, support of land purchased for construction, **14**, 1690
welfare—
    charitable trusts, representation for coal industry beneficiaries, **14**, 1677
    Coal Industry Social Welfare Organisation, **14**, 1677
    local committees, transfer of functions, **14**, 1677
    Miners' Welfare Commission, **14**, 1677
    pneumoconiosis compensation scheme, **14**, 1678
    redundancy payments, **14**, 1678
    See also health and welfare _above_

Mines—*continued*
winding—
  lowering, times of, **14**, 1669
  raising, times of, **14**, 1669
  time checkers, **14**, 1670
winding apparatus—
  maintenance, **14**, 1627
  operation, **14**, 1627
  shaft, in, **14**, 1621, 1625
  signalling, **14**, 1627
  unwalkable outlet, in, **14**, 1621
women, employment, conditions of, **14**, 1666
working, plan of, manager's duty to keep, **14**, 1610
working facilities—
  grant of—
    application for, **14**, 1682
    compensation, **14**, 1683
  minerals, statutory control of rights to work, **14**, 1681
  roads, stopping up or diversion, **14**, 1684
working place—
  fall into, damages for injuries, **14**, 1633
  miner's duty to secure, **14**, 1636
  roof and sides, duty to secure safety of, **14**, 1633, 1634
  See also roof *above*; sides *above*
workman, *see* employee *above*
young person—
  employment, conditions of, **14**, 1666
  hours of work, **14**, 1671
  medical examination, **14**, 1666
Minimum Lending Rate
money obligations linked to, **14**, 1824
Mining code
compulsory purchase order, and, **5**, 34
Minister of the Crown
absolute privilege, **15**, 526
access to Crown, **7**, 723
appointment of, **5**, 481
cabinet, **5**, 480
categories of, **5**, 480
challenging ministerial action, **5**, 484
delict, title and interest to sue, **15**, 226
functions, **1**, 210
meaning, **5**, 479
ministerial responsibility, doctrine of, **5**, 482; **7**, 852
Parliament, in, **5**, 482
parliamentary secretary as, **5**, 480
precedence, **16**, 2014
prerogative powers exercised by, **7**, 719, 723
prerogative powers exercised by Queen on advice of, **7**, 719, 723
public duties, enforcement of, **11**, 1024
special legal powers, **11**, 1062
statutory executive powers, **7**, 719, 723
statutory executive powers of Crown on advice of, **7**, 719
statutory quasi-judicial powers, **7**, 719
subordinate legislative powers, **7**, 719
Treasury, **5**, 496
Minister for Health and Home Affairs
penal establishments, function in relation to, **16**, 1412

Ministerial responsibility
doctrine of, **5**, 482; **7**, 852
Ministry of Defence Police
appointment to, **16**, 1816, 1818
Defence Police Federation, **16**, 1816
establishment, **16**, 1816
impersonation of member of, **16**, 1816
jurisdiction, **16**, 1816
powers, **16**, 1816
privileges, **16**, 1816
Minor
acquiescence by, **16**, 1616
actings of—
  curators, and, **10**, 1105, 1108, 1109
  exceptions to full legal capacity, **10**, 1107
  generally, **10**, 1105
  minors without curators, **10**, 1106
  reform of law, **10**, 1109
adoption of, **10**, 1196
age of majority, **10**, 1041
age of minority, **11**, 1202
aliment for, **19**, 1581
application for curatory, **10**, 1316
apprenticeship, contract of, **10**, 1078
approval of variation on behalf of, **24**, 79
arbiter, acting as, **2**, 416
arbitration, limitations as to, **2**, 407
assignee of, enorme lesion, plea of, **10**, 1110
bank account, opening, **2**, 1232
British subject, registration as, **14**, 1950
building society member, as, **3**, 379, 414
business, contract in course of, **10**, 1079
capacity of, **9**, 25
  buy and sell, to, **20**, 816
  cautionary obligations, in relation to, **3**, 859
  exclusion from scope of Judgments Convention, **8**, 432
cautionary obligations, **2**, 1234
circular to, **5**, 834
classification, proposed reform, **11**, 1243
contracts—
  capacity to enter, **12**, 1229, 1231
  contracts reducible on majority, **2**, 1233
  contractual power of minors, **11**, 1204
  reduction of minor's contracts, **11**, 1205
contractual capacity, **2**, 1232
conventional incapacity, **24**, 128
creation of trust by, **24**, 14
creditor of, enorme lesion, plea of, **10**, 1110
curator—
  actings of minors, **10**, 1105, 1108, 1109
  appointment—
    court, by, **10**, 1095
    generally, **2**, 1235
    testamentary, **10**, 1087
  control of minor's person—
    education, **10**, 1118
    generally, **10**, 1117
    medical treatment, **10**, 1119
    reform of law, **10**, 1120
  curator bonis to, **24**, 239, 270
  father as, **10**, 1084–1987
  generally, **10**, 1083
  illegitimate children, **10**, 1085

Minor—*continued*
curator—*continued*
  legitimate children, **10**, 1084
  married children, **10**, 1086
  minor's choice, **10**, 1092
    statutory erosion of, **10**, 1093
  mother as, **10**, 1088, 1089
  parents as, **10**, 1090
  role of, **10**, 1096
    respective roles of tutor and, **10**, 1073
  termination of curatory, **10**, 1097
  testamentary, **10**, 1094
    appointment of, **10**, 1087, 1091
  tutor compared, **10**, 1056, 1073, 1083
deed, capacity to grant deed, **12**, 1229, 1231
definition, **24**, 36
detention of, **12**, 39
domicile of dependence, **4**, 30
dominus negotii, as, **15**, 137, 141
donation *inter vivos*, incapacity to make, **8**, 611
donation *mortis causa*, **8**, 611
employment, contract of, **10**, 1078
enorme lesion—
  exclusion of plea, **10**, 1114
  generally, **10**, 1110
  meaning, **11**, 1205
  onus of proof, **10**, 1112
  presumption and proof, **10**, 1113; **11**, 1205
  quadriennium utile, **10**, 1111
  reform of law, **10**, 1115
  to whom plea available, **10**, 1110
executor dative, entitled to be deemed, **24**, 129
factors for damages for, **24**, 279
forisfamiliation—
  doctrine of, generally, **1**, 602; **10**, 1097, 1098; **25**, 808
  education, by, **10**, 1103
  effect of, **10**, 1104
  generally, **10**, 1097, 1098
  independent residence, by, **10**, 1102
  marriage, on, **10**, 1100
  nature of concept, **10**, 1098
  setting up business, by, **10**, 1101
  unilateral act of minor, by, **10**, 1099
fraudulent misrepresentation by, **10**, 1116
friendly society membership, **12**, 704
gender in relation to—
  generally, **10**, 1039
  marriage of minor, **10**, 1040
heir of, enorme lesion, plea of, **10**, 1110
heritable property burdened by, **20**, 219
hours of work, **9**, 74
judicial factor, appointment of, **4**, 14
legal capacity, **10**, 1073, 1144–1146; **19**, 1581
  exceptions to full, **10**, 1107
  legal relations, capacity to enter, **10**, 1074, 1083
legal recognition, **10**, 1050
legitim, entitlement to, **19**, 1628
liable for breach of trust, **24**, 129
loan, documents advertising or relating to sent to for financial gain, **13**, 1767
marriage of, **10**, 843, 1040, 1080
  forisfamiliation following, **10**, 1100
meaning, **10**, 1049, 1073; **24**, 36, 270

Minor—*continued*
medical treatment, **10**, 1119
minority, **24**, 36
National Savings account for, **2**, 1230
necessaries, supply of, **11**, 1205
nonage, **10**, 1139–1140; **24**, 129
  See also NONAGE
obtaining necessaries—
  common law, at, **10**, 1075
  sale of goods legislation, under, **10**, 1076
  scope of doctrine, **10**, 1077
partner, as, **16**, 1012
party to contract, **19**, 1233
pawn, articles taken in, **20**, 41
property of—
  capital gains tax, **19**, 1583
  inheritance tax, **19**, 1583
reform of law, **10**, 1082, 1141–1146
registration, **14**, 1913, 1936
status of, **11**, 1204
  exclusion from scope of Judgments Convention, **8**, 432
trade, contract in course of, **10**, 1079
transactions on behalf of, **11**, 789
trustee, as, **24**, 129
  sequestrated estate, **24**, 129
  void in English trusts, **24**, 129
vassal, as, feudal law, **18**, 75
voluntary obligation, capacity to enter, **15**, 660
will, power to make, **10**, 1081
See also CHILD-CHILDREN; YOUNG PERSON
Minor Works Contract, Scottish
generally, **3**, 11
Minority
reduction on grounds of, **13**, 44
Minority groups
customary international law before 1945 ..., **12**, 2
minority treaties, **12**, 2, 2*n*
national minorities, discrimination, **12**, 85
Minority shareholder
See SHAREHOLDER
Mint
See ROYAL MINT
Minute (time)
meaning, **22**, 816
Mirrors
wild birds or animals taken or killed with, **11**, 880, 884
Mischief
Heydon's Case, **12**, 1115
remedy of, by statute, rule as to, **12**, 1115
Misconduct
dental practitioner, by, **14**, 1140
dismissal, reason for, **9**, 255
frequenters of premises, of, **2**, 62
licensee, of, **2**, 62
medical practitioner, by, *see* MEDICAL PRACTITIONER
messenger-at-arms, by, **14**, 1506
optician, by, **14**, 1169
railway property, on, **19**, 1064
rebuttable presumption against, **10**, 750
redundancy payment, effect on, **9**, 182
sheriff officer, by, **14**, 1506
ultra vires doctrine, application, **4**, 324

Misdiagnosis
negligence, as, **14**, 1127
Misleading statements and practices
investors' remedies, **12**, 1410
Misprision of treason
generally, **7**, 584
Scots law, incorporation into, **7**, 566, 568
Misrepresentation
agent, by, **1**, 638
cautionary obligation, *see* CAUTIONARY OBLIGATION
fraudulent—
    active concealment, **11**, 711
    appearance of goods constituting, **11**, 710
    bankers' documentary credits, **11**, 772, 773
    company prospectus, **11**, 782, 783
    concealment, deliberate, **11**, 711
    conduct, by, **11**, 710
    corporeal moveables obtained by, **11**, 761–764
    creditworthiness, as to, **11**, 706
    false statements, **11**, 709, 717
    identity, as to, **11**, 706
    incorporeal property, in relation to, 11, 765–770
    inducement of innocent party, **11**, 713
    inducing contract by, **15**, 683
    insolvency, **11**, 776–781
    marriage, **11**, 787, 788
    material error, inducement of, **11**, 713
    minor, by, **10**, 1116
    non-disclosure, **11**, 712
    parties, **11**, 724
    positive acts, **11**, 710
    proof of, **11**, 729
    remedies for, **11**, 714
    representor, position of, **11**, 709, 717
    what constitutes, generally, **11**, 723
innocent—
    doctrine of, generally, **11**, 715
    false statement of fact essential, **11**, 709, 717
    generally, **11**, 718
    inducing contract by, **15**, 685
    materiality of error, **11**, 716
    reduction of contract on grounds of, **11**, 715
    rescission for, **11**, 715
    restitutio in integrum, **11**, 717
insurance claims, *see* INSURANCE (misrepresentation and non-disclosure)
negligent—
    competency of action for, **11**, 732
    generally, **11**, 732
    inducing contract by, **15**, 589, 684
    liability for, **11**, 732
    reversal of rule in *Manners* reforming legislation, **22**, 673
    Scottish Law Commission recommendation, **22**, 673
partnership—
    dissolution on grounds of, distribution of assets, **16**, 1100
    person induced into, by, **16**, 1057, 1078
passing off, *see* PASSING OFF
supplier, by, **5**, 871–872
Missile
designed to explode on or immediately before impact, **10**, 1517

Missing person
death, proof of—
    background to legislation, **25**, 649
    common law, presumption under, **25**, 647
    declarator of death—
        jurisdiction, **25**, 652
        seven-year rule, **25**, 651
    generally, **25**, 646
    life expectancy, **25**, 648
    seven-year rule, **25**, 651
    statutory provisions, **25**, 650
reappearance of—
    information, disclosure of, **25**, 654
    property rights order, **25**, 653
    variation order, **25**, 653
Mission church
sale of congregational properties and endowments, **3**, 1607
Missionary
Church of Scotland—
    corresponding membership of General Assembly, **3**, 1543
    supervision, **3**, 1534
lay, dwelling house held for occupation by, repossession—
    assured tenancy, **13**, 749, 754
    protected tenancy, **13**, 736, 742
permit-free employment status, **12**, 247
Missives
acceptance, **6**, 572
binding contract, as, **6**, 553
breach of obligations under—
    damages, measure of, **6**, 576
    purchaser, failure of, **6**, 575
    seller, failure of, **6**, 574
caveat emptor, **6**, 566
commercial lease, **13**, 558
common terms in, **20**, 912
conclusion, evaluation, **18**, 644
conclusion of, **6**, 572, 573
contents—
    alterations to property, **6**, 565
    Builders Council certificate, **6**, 567
    entry, date of, **20**, 913
    feu duty, **6**, 562; **20**, 917
    fixtures and fittings, **6**, 558
    local authority notices, **6**, 560
    matrimonial home, **6**, 568
    minerals, where reserved to third party, **6**, 564
    moveable items included in price, **6**, 558
    non-supersession clause, **6**, 566
    obligations of seller, **6**, 561
    price, **6**, 557; **20**, 914
    prior communings superseded by, **6**, 566
    rates, **6**, 562; **20**, 917
    roads and footpaths, warranty of, **6**, 563
    sewers, warranty of, **6**, 563
    suspensive clauses, **6**, 570
    title—
        conditions of, **6**, 559
        marketable, **20**, 918
        vacant possession, **20**, 916
contract, and, **18**, 640, 641
death of transferee, where, **18**, 649

Missives—*continued*
death of transferor, where, **18**, 648
definition, **6**, 553
destruction of property after completion of, **6**, 569
disposition, normally superseded by, **6**, 579
essential constituents, **6**, 554
form, **6**, 555; **18**, 641
general, **6**, 553; **20**, 904
holograph letters as common form, **6**, 554
homologation, **6**, 573
insolvency of transferee, where, **18**, 649
insolvency of transferor, where, **18**, 648
Law Society of Scotland standard clauses, **18**, 641
matters covered by, **18**, 641
meaning, **18**, 640, 641
no interest passes under, **6**, 553
offer to purchase, **18**, 641
    commercial property, **18**, 641
'one contract rule', **6**, 566
purpose, **18**, 640
purpose and use of, generally, **6**, 552
reduction, **13**, 37
rei interventus, **6**, 573
requisites, **6**, 554
right of purchaser under, nature of, **18**, 14
risk, passing of, **6**, 569
roup, articles of, **18**, 641
rule in *Winston v Patrick*, **6**, 566
'subject to contract', **20**, 905
time limit, **6**, 566
    limitation clauses, **6**, 571
warrandice, **18**, 702, 708
    enforcement, **18**, 710, 711
    extinction, **18**, 714
    missives kept in force beyond disposition, where, **18**, 710, 714

Mistress
former, payment of aliment to, **15**, 767

Misuse of drugs
See DRUG ABUSE

Mittelberg
European Union customs territory, **7**, 1010

Mixed condition
meaning, **15**, 6

M'Naghten Rules
generally, **7**, 116, 117, 120, 122, 155
influence, **7**, 116, 122
objections to, **7**, 116, 120, 121

Mobbing and rioting
actus reus, **7**, 424, 426
    breach of public peace, **7**, 432–434
    common purpose, **7**, 428–431, 439
    extended concept of guilt, **7**, 438–440
    membership of mob, **7**, 435–437
    number of persons assembled, **7**, 427
art and part liability, **7**, 438–440
    common purpose, **7**, 439
assemblage by design, **7**, 427
breach of the peace, and, **7**, 429, 433, 434, 448, 456
    disturbance and commotion, **7**, 432, 433
    establishment of sufficient disturbance, **7**, 434
    generally, **7**, 432, 456

Mobbing and rioting—*continued*
common purpose—
    agreement and establishment, **7**, 428, 430
    arrest and conviction, matters arising, **7**, 431
    art and part liability, **7**, 439
    essential element, as, **7**, 428
    generally, **7**, 427, 428
    mens rea, and, **7**, 441
    specific crime as purpose, **7**, 440
    specific purpose, **7**, 429
    spontaneously, arising, **7**, 430
    unlawful, must be, **7**, 428, 429
crowd originally gathered for another purpose, **7**, 430
definition, **7**, 424, 424*n*
elections, affecting, **15**, 1229, 1301, 1316, 1376
firearm or imitation firearm possessed during, **10**, 1565
generally, **7**, 425
levying war compared, **7**, 574
loss or damage, carrier's liability, **21**, 603
membership of mob, **7**, 435
    voluntary withdrawal, **7**, 437
mens rea, **7**, 441
number of persons required, **7**, 427
presence at, **7**, 424, 426, 435–437
severity of crime, **7**, 426
smaller groups, mob splitting into, **7**, 427
sports-related violence, **19**, 1267

Mobile home
accession, considerations as to, **18**, 584
lease, **13**, 194
no place to park amounting to homelessness, **11**, 2045, 2048
sheriff court jurisdiction, **6**, 1099
site charge, housing benefit, **21**, 1105
VAT zero-rating, **7**, 1453

Mobility allowance
See DISABILITY LIVING ALLOWANCE

Mock auction
meaning, **6**, 155
offence of holding, **6**, 156

Model
copyright, **3**, 139; **18**, 1153
    restriction, **18**, 1153
European Community legislation, generally, **18**, 1615

Model Building Byelaws
generally, **3**, 201

Model Deed of Constitution
Church of Scotland, **3**, 1508, 1515, 1563

Moderator of the General Assembly of the Church of Scotland
designation, **16**, 2016
Moderator-Elect, **3**, 1545
precedence, **16**, 2006, 2016
See also GENERAL ASSEMBLY OF THE CHURCH OF SCOTLAND

Moles
requirement notice to control, **11**, 860–863

Molestation
delict, **15**, 216

Molesting police officer
offence of, **16**, 1807
Molluscs
continental shelf, on, rights of coastal state, **21**, 19
Molony Report (1962)
consumer protection, **6**, 8, 9, 51, 104, 111, 126, 159
Monaco
European Union customs territory, **7**, 1010
Monarchy
Church, relations with, **5**, 686
constitutional, UK as, **7**, 701
power vested in, **7**, 701
restraints on power, *see* SOVEREIGN (RESTRAINTS ON POWER)
royal prerogative, *see* ROYAL PREROGATIVE
special legal powers, **11**, 1062
See also CROWN; ROYAL COURTS; SOVEREIGN
Monetary transaction
VAT exemption, **7**, 1424
Money
action for payment of, **17**, 1322
bank, in, donation, **8**, 637
bank account without charge, placed in, **13**, 1705
bank notes, *see* BANK NOTE
Carriers Act (1830), **3**, 610
coins, *see* COIN
commodity, contract for sale as, enforcement of, **14**, 1814
consideration mixture of money and goods, **20**, 899
contract of deposit, as subject matter, **8**, 7, 10
contract of sale must involve, **20**, 801, 818
corporeal moveable property, as, **14**, 1804, 1805
counterfeit currency, **14**, 1843
decree for payment of, suspension of, **4**, 13
diligence, exempted from, **8**, 229, 229n
diligence against, **14**, 1812
fluctuations in cost, rental variation clause, **14**, 1056
foreign, *see* FOREIGN CURRENCY
foreign currency, loan repayment in, **13**, 1754
function of—
  deferred payment, standard for, **14**, 1803
  law, in, **14**, 1804
  medium of exchange, as, **14**, 1803
  store of value, as, **14**, 1803
  unit of account, as, **14**, 1803
fungible, as, **13**, 1707
goods, exclusion from term, **14**, 1808
inherent difficulties, **14**, 1801
legal tender—
  what constitutes, **13**, 1753
  See also LEGAL TENDER
loan of, *see* LOAN
meaning, **4**, 113; **14**, 1802; **25**, 880
mutuum proper, **13**, 1707
not classified as goods, **20**, 805
notion of, **14**, 1801
obligation, enforcement of, **14**, 1813
offences relating to, generally, **14**, 1834
patient, held on behalf of, **14**, 1420
periodical payments, obligation to pay, negative prescription, **16**, 2116

Money—*continued*
printer's imprint, requirement not applicable, **17**, 3
receiver, distribution by—
  order of, **4**, 704
  right to consign, **4**, 705
Sale of Goods Act, not covered by, **20**, 805
security, cannot be subject of, **14**, 1811
stolen—
  recovery of, **14**, 1810
  restitution not applicable, **15**, 52
sum certain in money, meaning, **4**, 105, 113
term, use of, **14**, 1802
theft, generally, **7**, 324
value, as store of, **14**, 1803
See also CURRENCY
Money laundering
generally, **7**, 1261
meaning, **7**, 1261
penalties, **7**, 1261
Money market institutions
exempted under Financial Services Act 1986 ..., **12**, 1321
Moneylending
extortionate credit bargain or transaction, **13**, 1771
moneylender, meaning, **13**, 1770
negotiorum gestor, by, **15**, 133
regulation of moneylenders, **2**, 1268
repeal of legislation, **5**, 801
Mongolia
imports, European Union regulations, **7**, 1029
Monopolies
behavioural—
  exports, in relation to, **4**, 1226
  goods, in relation to, **4**, 1222
  monopoly situation, meaning, **4**, 1229
  services, in relation to, **4**, 1223
Commission, *see* MONOPOLIES AND MERGERS COMMISSION
competition contrasted with, **4**, 1103
consumer protection, **6**, 13, 15
deadweight loss attributable to, **4**, 1103
objection to, **4**, 1103
situation, *see* MONOPOLY CONTROL
structural—
  exports, in relation to, **4**, 1225
  goods, in relation to, **4**, 1221
  monopoly situation, statutory definition of, **4**, 1230
  services, in relation to, **4**, 1223
toll roads, **20**, 645
welfare cost of, **4**, 1103
Monopolies and Mergers Commission
airport charges references to, **2**, 927
anti-competitive practices, *see* COMPETITION LAW
functions, **4**, 1122
Hiram and Highland case, **4**, 564
investigation by—
  competitive structure of market, impact on, **4**, 1278
  generally, **4**, 1275
  importance of competition in, **4**, 1283
  manner of, **4**, 1238

Monopolies and Mergers Commission—
continued
investigation by—*continued*
  monopoly situation—
    exploitation of, **4**, 1245
    maintenance of, **4**, 1246
  no criticism, **4**, 1249
  oligopoly, **4**, 1248
  practice of Commission, **4**, 1239
  procedure, **4**, 1275
  public interest, consideration of, **4**, 1237
  public interest letter, preparation of, **4**, 1239
  qualification for, **4**, 1272
  report, *see* report *below*
  scope of, **4**, 1236
  services sector, restrictive trade practices in, **4**, 1247
  structure of market, **4**, 1244
  undertakings following, **4**, 1166
membership, **4**, 1122
merger policy, operation of, **4**, 563
panels, investigations carried out by, **4**, 1122
permanent staff, **4**, 1122
practice of, **4**, 1239
professions, investigation into, **6**, 64
public corporations, **19**, 224, 224*n*, 241
reference to, **9**, 805
referral to, **4**, 562
registered industrial design, report in respect of, **18**, 1199
reports—
  1965 report, **9**, 806
  1979 report, **9**, 811
  action following, **4**, 1276
  analysis of, **4**, 1277
  Anderson case, **4**, 567
  consequences of—
    agreements, **4**, 1243
    public interest—
      harm to, **4**, 1242
      no harm to, **4**, 1241
    publication of report, **4**, 1240
    recipients of report, **4**, 1240
    undertakings, **4**, 1243
  Elders case, **4**, 569
  Hiram and Highland case, **4**, 564
  Lonrho case, **4**, 565
  publication of, **4**, 1240
  recipients, **4**, 1240
  Royal Bank case, **4**, 566
  scope of, **4**, 1236
Secretary of State, reference by, **4**, 1124, 1274
structure of market, **4**, 1244
UK authorities, attitude of, **4**, 1119
unregistered design right, report in respect of, **18**, 1229
semiconductor topographies, **18**, 1248
See also MONOPOLY CONTROL
Monopoly control
complex monopolies, investigation of, **4**, 1230
general references, **4**, 1234
generally, **4**, 1219

Monopoly control—*continued*
Monopolies and Mergers Commission, investigation by, *see* MONOPOLIES AND MERGERS COMMISSION
monopoly reference, types of, **4**, 1233
monopoly situation—
  Director General of Fair Trading, duties and powers of, **4**, 1121, 1232
  exploitation of, **4**, 1245
  exports, in relation to—
    behavioural monopolies, **4**, 1226
    generally, **4**, 1224
    structural monopolies, **4**, 1225
  gathering information about, **4**, 1232
  goods, in relation to—
    behavioural monopolies, **4**, 1222
    generally, **4**, 1220
    structural monopolies, **4**, 1221
  local, **4**, 1227
  maintenance of, **4**, 1246
  meaning, **4**, 1219
  non-economic meaning, **4**, 1229
  parts of UK, in, **4**, 1227
  registrable agreement, **4**, 1228
  services, in relation to—
    behavioural monopolies, **4**, 1223
    place of supply, **4**, 1223
    structural monopolies, **4**, 1223
  statutory definition of—
    behavioural monopoly, **4**, 1230
    jurisdictional division, **4**, 1231
    non-economic meaning, **4**, 1229
    structural monopoly, **4**, 1230
  supplementary provisions, **4**, 1228
  supply, form of, **4**, 1228
  uncompetitive practices, meaning, **4**, 1232*n*
references—
  general, **4**, 1234
  limited to facts, **4**, 1233
  restricted public-interest reference, **4**, 1233
  restrictive labour, **4**, 1235
  types of, **4**, 1233
restrictive labour references, **4**, 1235
Montevideo Convention
states, characteristics of, **19**, 658, 664, 665
Month
calendar month, duration, **22**, 813
definition, **22**, 813
European Convention on the Calculation of Time-Limits, **22**, 829
evolution of concept, **22**, 801
fraction of, **22**, 829
Julian calendar, **22**, 803
leap year, **22**, 813
lunar—
  definition, **22**, 813
  incompatibility with solar day/tropical year, **22**, 801, 802
lunation as foundation, **22**, 801, 813
meaning, **4**, 112; **12**, 1171
  common law, at, **22**, 813
Roman Republican calendar, **22**, 801, 802
Scotland, statutory interpretation—
  England, definition distinguished, **22**, 813

Month—*continued*
solar, **22**, 813
termination, **22**, 813
Montreal Protocols
air, carriage by, **3**, 739, 739*n*
Montserrat Island
British Dependent Territories citizenship, **14**, 1932
Monument
ancient, *see* ANCIENT MONUMENT
erection, **14**, 2084
preservation and maintenance, **3**, 519
provision, **14**, 703
right to erect, **3**, 524
unaesthetic sight, **14**, 2084
Moor game
eggs, protection of, **11**, 802, 843
Game (Scotland) Act 1832 ..., **11**, 815
Poaching Prevention Act 1832 ..., **11**, 843
trespass in search of, **11**, 817
Mooring
fixed, natural harbours, in, **11**, 1304
lease, **13**, 205
valuation for rating, **24**, 686
Moorland
ground game, right to take and kill, **11**, 853
Moped
age limit for licence holder, **20**, 448
definition, **20**, 407
licence to drive, age limit, **3**, 1229
Mora
abandonment, presumption, **16**, 1624
acquiescence, interaction with, **16**, 1613, 1621–1625
annulment of voidable obligation barred by, **15**, 672
culpable delay, **16**, 1621
delay alone insufficient, **16**, 1622
heritable title, **16**, 1625
limitation of actions—
generally, **16**, 2206
mora, taciturnity and acquiescence, **16**, 2207
meaning, **16**, 1621
modern division of judicial opinion, **16**, 1623
Mortensen v Peters, **19**, 602, 655
plea in bar of trial, **17**, 692
taciturnity, interaction with, **16**, 1621–1625
Moral character, imputations on
defamation, **15**, 490
Morals
See PUBLIC MORALS
Morass
See stagnum
Moratorium
administration order, on, **4**, 611
Moray
local roads authority, **14**, 404
population, **14**, 64
Moray Firth
excluded from internal waters, **11**, 78
More burgi
feudal law, generally, **18**, 109
meaning, **18**, 65

Mormaer
title of, **16**, 1303
Mortar
prohibited weapon, as, **10**, 1506*n*
Mortgage
advance secured by, **3**, 347
aircraft, *see* AIRCRAFT
chattels—
finance lease as, **14**, 1007
plant and machinery, ownership of, **14**, 1013
English law, as concept of, **21**, 172
finance rights, acquisition, **3**, 378
fishing boat, of, **11**, 128
fixed security, as, **21**, 172
income support payments towards, **21**, 1075
direct payments, **21**, 1082
second mortgage, **21**, 1075
lands in, **5**, 22
meaning, **5**, 908; **21**, 172
registered fishing vessel or share, of, **11**, 194
regulation of, **14**, 816
residual mortgage debt, acquisition, **3**, 378
rights of, **11**, 1108
security, as, **5**, 908
See also HERITABLE SECURITY
ship's—
British registered ship, instrument of mortgage, **20**, 287
certificate of—
abolition, **21**, 161*n*
removal from register, effect, **21**, 161
discharge of, **20**, 288
dispute over, **20**, 305
entry of discharge, **21**, 180
equitable, **21**, 173, 173*n*, 174*n*
foreclosure, **21**, 173
form, **21**, 175, 175*n*
generally, **20**, 28, 273, 287
legal, **21**, 173, 173*n*
lien taking priority over, **21**, 185, 392, 479
mortgagee, **21**, 172
duties and liabilities, **21**, 177
legal position, **21**, 177
possession, in, **20**, 292–295
power of sale, **20**, 296
rights of, **20**, 293
rights of third parties, and, **20**, 295
taking, **20**, 292
possession of ship, taking, **21**, 179
power of sale, **20**, 296
protection afforded to, **21**, 178
remedies available to, **21**, 179
rights of, **20**, 291
sale, power of, **21**, 179
second and subsequent, restrictions on rights of, **21**, 179
status of, **20**, 290
mortgagor, **21**, 172
default by, **21**, 177
legal position, **21**, 178
obligation to pay sums due, **21**, 178
origins, **21**, 172
Part I of the Merchant Shipping Act 1894, under, **21**, 174–182

Mortgage—*continued*
ship's—*continued*
  power to grant, **21**, 174
  priority between mortgages, **20**, 289; **21**, 183, 184
  ranking, **20**, 314
  redemption, right of, **21**, 173
  registration, **21**, 174
  removal from register, effect, **21**, 161
  Scots law—
    generally, **21**, 172
    problems arising, **21**, 173
  share in ship, of, **21**, 174*ff*
  ship owned by registered company, **21**, 172
  statutory, **21**, 174
  subject—
    apparel and equipment, **21**, 176
    cargo, **21**, 176
    generally, **21**, 176
  transfer, **21**, 181
  transmission, **21**, 182
  unregistered mortgages, **21**, 173, 174*n*, 184*n*
    priority between, **21**, 184
    priority of registered mortgages, **21**, 184
  unregistered ships, **21**, 173
valuation, report of, **25**, 82
See also HERITABLE SECURITY; STANDARD SECURITY
Mortgage indemnity funding body
building society's power to invest in and support,
  3, 369
Mortgage indemnity insurance body
building society's power to invest in and support,
  3, 369
Mortification
beneficial public purposes, for, **24**, 3
feudal law, generally, **18**, 66, 68*n*, 70
public or charitable trusts, **24**, 3
souls of deceased, for benefit of, **24**, 3
subinfeudation, and, **18**, 58
***Mortis causa* trust**
generally, **24**, 16
judicial variation, **24**, 80
prejudicial arrangements, **24**, 80
Mortmain
feudal law, generally, **18**, 66*n*
Morton Committee
recommendations, generally, **3**, 1277
Mortuary
conveyance of body to, **3**, 526
provision, burial authority, by, **3**, 526
provision of, **19**, 465
Moslem
personal law, domicile as indicator of, **17**, 188
MOT certificate
vehicle excise licence, production to obtain, **20**, 463
Motel
hotel distinguished, **11**, 1711
keepers' liability, **11**, 1715
meaning, **11**, 1711
Motion roll appearance
ex parte statements made at bar, **13**, 1360
Motive
defence, as, **7**, 92
insane, **7**, 92
relevancy, **7**, 92

Motor bicycle
definition, **20**, 407
Motor car
definition, **20**, 406
heavy, definition, **20**, 407
See also MOTOR VEHICLE
Motor cycle
age limit for licence, **3**, 1229; **20**, 448
brakes, **20**, 478
definition, **20**, 407
exclusion from definition of motor car, **20**, 406
helmet, VAT zero-rating, **7**, 1460
helmets, safety provisions, **6**, 62
licence to drive, age limit, **3**, 1229; **20**, 448
noise, EU measures on, **9**, 1301
number of persons allowed on, **20**, 438
plates, **20**, 477*n*
protective headgear—
  offences in relation to, **20**, 438
  required standards, selling or offering for sale
    helmet failing to meet, **20**, 438
  requirement to wear, **20**, 438
  safety provisions, generally, **6**, 62
safety provisions, **6**, 62; **20**, 438
three-wheeled, **20**, 407
wings, **20**, 483
See also MOTOR VEHICLE
Motor fuels
See OIL (marketing)
Motor tractor
definition, **20**, 407
Motor trader
trade licence, **7**, 1074
vehicle excise trade licence, **20**, 465
Motor vehicle
abandoned, ownership, **18**, 552
abandoned on road or land forming part of road,
  20, 691
accession, law of, **18**, 576, 576*n*
accident, *see* ROAD ACCIDENT
advertising on, **1**, 532; **14**, 335
alteration, **20**, 467
  vehicle excise licence, effect on, **7**, 1076; **20**, 464,
    467
bird or animal, used in pursuit of, **11**, 880, 884
brakes—
  construction and use regulations, **20**, 478
  parking, **20**, 478
broken up or destroyed, **20**, 467
car parks, *see* CAR PARKS
car-sharing arrangement, **20**, 488
car tax, *see* EXCISE LICENCE *below*
careless driving, *see* CARELESS DRIVING
cars for sale, details displayed on, **6**, 82
change of ownership—
  notification of, **20**, 467
  registration document, delivery on, **20**, 467
charge of, in, definition in relation to drink
  driving offences, **20**, 420
commercial, temporary importation, **7**, 1315
conditional sale agreement, subject to, sale, **15**, 52, 64
confiscation by customs officials, **7**, 1225
construction and use regulations—
  brakes, **20**, 478

Motor vehicle—*continued*
construction and use regulations—*continued*
  dimensions, **20**, 475
  engine emissions, **20**, 485
  European Union directives and regulations, **20**, 473, 473*n*, 474
  generally, **20**, 473
  horns, **20**, 481
  lighting, **20**, 479
  plates, **20**, 477
  silencers, **20**, 484
  speedometers, **20**, 486
  type approval schemes, **20**, 474
  tyres, **20**, 482
  under-runs, **20**, 483
  vision, **20**, 480
  weight, **20**, 476
  wings, **20**, 483
contract for carriage by sea, Athens Convention, **21**, 728
contract hire, **14**, 1022
dangerous driving, *see* DANGEROUS DRIVING
deer, driving with, **11**, 941, 942
definition, **20**, 405
delict committed by driver who is not owner, liability, **15**, 242, 244
detention, customs' officers power of, **7**, 1240
dimensions, construction and use regulations, **20**, 475
disabled people, for, excise duty exemption, **7**, 1073
documents, falsification, **20**, 472
door, opening, offences in relation to, **20**, 443
drink driving offences, *see* ALCOHOLIC LIQUOR
drink or drugs, in charge while under influence of, **7**, 33
driver, *see* DRIVER
driving deer with, **11**, 941, 942
driving off the road, **20**, 434
driving offence in, owner's art and part liability, **7**, 182
drought, water used to wash motor vehicle during, **25**, 529, 530
drug related offences, *see* DRUGS
drunken driver, passenger, *volenti non fit injuria*, **15**, 395, 402
dynamo, fitted with, **20**, 408
electrically propelled, excise duty exemption, **7**, 1073
emission from—
  EU directives—
    diesel engine, on, **9**, 1143
    lead in petrol, on, **9**, 1144
    petrol-driven vehicle, on, **9**, 1142
    UK measures implementing, **9**, 1145
    United Kingdom measures supplementing, **9**, 1145
  generally, **9**, 1141; **19**, 303
  requirements as to, generally, **20**, 485
employee, used by, **7**, 1290
excise licence—
  alteration of, **20**, 466
  alteration of nature of vehicle, **7**, 1076; **20**, 464, 467

Motor vehicle—*continued*
excise licence—*continued*
  application for, false or misleading statement in, **7**, 1077; **20**, 466
  calculation of duty, **20**, 409
  duplication, **20**, 466
  duty to licence, **20**, 464
  engine removed, vehicle where, **7**, 1073
  exempted vehicles, **7**, 1073, 1077; **20**, 463
  forgery, **7**, 1077; **20**, 466
  fraudulent use, **7**, 1077; **20**, 466
  generally, **7**, 1073; **19**, 1543; **20**, 463
  lending or allowing to be used, **7**, 1077
  mechanically propelled vehicles, **7**, 1073
  MOT certificate, **20**, 463
  offences in relation to, **7**, 1077; **20**, 466
  penalties for keeping unlicensed vehicle, **20**, 464
  proceedings in relation to, **7**, 1078
  public road, vehicle used or kept on, **7**, 1073
  rates, **7**, 1073
  registration mark, issue and display, **20**, 464
  surrender and refund, **20**, 464
  temporary, **7**, 1074; **20**, 464
  trade licence, **7**, 1074, 1077; **20**, 465
  use of vehicle, alteration, **7**, 1076
  using or keeping vehicle without, **7**, 1075
  vehicle classification, **7**, 1073
  Vehicle Excise and Registration Act (1994), **7**, 1073
expansion chamber, fitted with, **20**, 484
fire service vehicles, **10**, 1476
firearm or imitation firearm possessed while taking, **10**, 1565
food sold from—
  entry, powers of, **11**, 340
  hygiene regulations, **11**, 408, 409, 411
fuel, private use, available for, Class 1A national insurance contributions, **21**, 1036
gift of, **7**, 1298
goods, *see* GOODS VEHICLE
handicapped person, hire or sale to, **7**, 1456
hire—
  acquired for, **7**, 1382
  hire or sale to handicapped person, **7**, 1456
  supplied by, **7**, 1382
hire purchase agreement, subject to—
  nemo dat quod non habet rule, exception to, **18**, 683
  sale, **15**, 52, 64
hired car, **3**, 601, 684
holiday rental, **14**, 1002
horn, construction and use regulations, **20**, 481
hosepipe, restrictions on use for private vehicle, **25**, 529
hotelkeeper's duty to receive, **11**, 1722
hotelkeeper's liability, **11**, 1722, 1748, 1748*n*
housing and maintenance of road vehicles, valuation for rating, **24**, 646, 647
importation, VAT, **7**, 1382
inconsiderate driving, **7**, 449
injury sustained by, Criminal Injuries Compensation Scheme, **7**, 9
insurance, *see* MOTOR VEHICLE INSURANCE

Motor vehicle—*continued*
invalid carriage, *see* INVALID CARRIAGE
joy-riding, offence of, **20**, 444
keeper of vehicle must provide information as to
    driver, **20**, 436
legislation, generally, **20**, 401
licence for, *see* DRIVING LICENCE
lighting, construction and use regulations, **20**,
    479
load, overhanging or projecting, **20**, 479
local-authority owned, advertising on, **14**, 335
locks, **3**, 626
lost or abandoned property on, **16**, 1819*n*
mascots, restrictions on use of, **20**, 443
mechanically propelled vehicle, term to replace,
    20, 414*n*
mirrors, construction and use regulations, **20**, 480
motor cycle, *see* MOTOR CYCLE
no right of lien over, **11**, 1757
noise, *see* NOISE
occupier's liability, **15**, 322
odometer, alteration of, **6**, 114, 119, 171
operating lease, **14**, 1020
owner's change of address, **20**, 467
ownership, change of, **20**, 467
parking—
    darkness, during hours of, **20**, 443
    illegally, obstructively or dangerously parked
        vehicles—
        immobilisation, **20**, 439
        removal of, **20**, 439
    meters, **20**, 439
    motor vehicle, of, offences in relation to, **20**,
        439
    places, provision of, **20**, 439
        countryside, in, **14**, 681
    servitude rights and, **18**, 491
    traffic warden, powers and duties, **20**, 510
    See also CAR PARK
passenger in, delictual liability towards, **15**, 395,
    402
pedestrian crossings, regulations as to, **20**, 440
petrol for use in, **9**, 852
petrol-driven, EC directives on, **9**, 1142
plant, as, **14**, 1012
plates, construction and use regulations, **20**, 477
police, **14**, 489; **16**, 1714
private hire car, *see* PRIVATE CAR HIRE
private use, available for, Class 1A national
    insurance contributions, **21**, 1036
public service, *see* PUBLIC SERVICE VEHICLE
qualifying motor car, meaning, **7**, 1382
race or trial, unauthorised, **20**, 434
registration document—
    alteration, **20**, 468
    change of ownership, delivery on, **20**, 467
    defacing or mutilating, **20**, 468
    falsification, **20**, 472
    issue of, **20**, 468
road, housing and maintenance of, **24**, 646, 647
road fuel, input tax, **7**, 1376
road traffic offence, used to commit, **20**, 459
roadworthiness, liability, **3**, 606, 615, 625
    latent defect, **3**, 626

Motor vehicle—*continued*
safety provisions—
    domestic carriage of passengers by road, **3**, 674
    generally, **6**, 62
sanitary arrangements attached to, **20**, 443
search, customs officers' powers of, **7**, 1228
seat belt, offences in relation to, **20**, 438
security alarms, radios etc, **3**, 626
self-supply, **7**, 1301, 1302
sent permanently out of Great Britain, **20**, 467
sign on, **14**, 554
silencer, construction and use regulations, **20**, 484
siren, equipped with, **20**, 481
small passenger vehicle, age limit for licence
    holder, **20**, 448
spare parts, supply of, **6**, 72
special appliance or apparatus, fitted with, **20**, 408
specific legacy, **25**, 848
speed restrictions—
    offences in relation to, **20**, 442
    radar device, evidence of, **20**, 442
    restricted road, on, **20**, 442
    variation of, **20**, 442
    vehicles exempt from, **20**, 442
    weight of vehicle, relevance of, **20**, 409
speedometer, construction and use regulations,
    20, 486
stolen, driving, **20**, 444
stopping, offences in relation to, **20**, 443
supplied to person departing from Community
    member states, **7**, 1441
supply, VAT, **7**, 1382
tachograph, **20**, 497, 498
taking and driving away, **7**, 337; **20**, 444
taking and using, **7**, 345
telecommunications apparatus, **16**, 1928
television, installation and use in, **20**, 443
temporarily within United Kingdom, patented
    product in, **18**, 865
test certificate—
    age of vehicle, **20**, 470
    exemptions from requirement for, **20**, 470
    failure to have, **20**, 470
    false particulars, **20**, 472
    falsification, **20**, 472
    goods vehicle, **20**, 496
    inspector, impersonation of, **20**, 472
    parked vehicles, **20**, 470
    police power to require production, **20**, 436
    production on demand, **20**, 472
    roadside test, **20**, 471
theft, **7**, 336
tow, in—
    insurance of, **20**, 461
    person directing or steering, whether driver,
        20, 410
    whether still motor vehicle, **20**, 405
trade descriptions, **6**, 108, 114, 117, 119
traffic directions and signs, compliance with, **20**,
    435
    failure, prosecution, **20**, 446
transfer, **8**, 635
tyres, *see* TYRES
unattended, regulations as to, **20**, 443

Motor vehicle—*continued*
under-run, construction and use regulations, **20**, 483
upholstery, **19**, 421
  premises used for, **19**, 421
van, *see* VAN
VAT margin scheme for used goods, **7**, 1363
VAT zero-rating, **7**, 1441, 1444
vehicle excise duty, *see* EXCISE LICENCE *above*
vision, construction and use regulations, **20**, 480
vulnerable locality, leaving in, **3**, 626, 627
washing, **25**, 506, 529, 530
weapon, used as, Criminal Injuries Compensation Scheme, **7**, 9
weight—
  alteration, **20**, 409
  ballast, **20**, 409
  calculation of, **20**, 409
  construction and use regulations, **20**, 476
  goods vehicles, plating certificate, **20**, 496
  laden, **20**, 409
  loose equipment, **20**, 409
  unladen, **20**, 409
welding plant, fitted with, **20**, 408
wheel-clamping—
  extortion, **7**, 400
  theft by appropriation, as, **7**, 332, 337
windscreen and windows, **20**, 480
windscreen wipers, **20**, 480
wings, **20**, 483
wrecking yard as unaesthetic sight, **14**, 2084
Motor vehicle insurance
bankrupt, insured person becoming, **20**, 461
certificate—
  delivery to insured, **20**, 460
  falsification, **20**, 472
  form, **20**, 460
  production—
    demand, on, **20**, 472
    police powers to require, **20**, 436
excess clause, **12**, 891
generally, **14**, 329
indemnity insurance, as, **12**, 804
insurer's duties, **20**, 462
knock for knock agreement, **12**, 897, 897*n*
limited company, **20**, 461
materiality, test of, **12**, 869
non-disclosure, **12**, 860
owner allowing or giving permission for vehicle to be used, **20**, 460
parked vehicle, of, **20**, 461
person charged with having no, **20**, 461
police power to determine whether or not vehicle being driven without, **20**, 436
policy, who may issue, **20**, 462
reinstatement clause, **12**, 890
renewal notice, **12**, 825
subrogation, **12**, 911
temporary cover, **12**, 818
third party rights, **12**, 911; **15**, 841; **20**, 818
use to which vehicle put, **20**, 461
voidable contract of, **20**, 461
winding up of insured company, **20**, 461
See also INSURANCE

Motor vehicle tester
vehicle excise trade licence, **20**, 465
Motoring event, race or trial
dangerous driving regulations, **20**, 413
off the road, **20**, 434
unauthorised, **20**, 434
  obligatory disqualification following conviction, **20**, 453
Motorway
filling stations, **9**, 808
road authority for, **20**, 624
service area, **20**, 624
  access to, **20**, 628
  facilities provided by, **20**, 626
  hours of opening, **20**, 626
  intervals beween, **20**, 626
  land, acquisition to build, **20**, 628
  operation, control of, **20**, 628
  standards for, **20**, 626
signs on, **20**, 624
special road, as, **20**, 624
See also SPECIAL ROAD
Motto
battle cry (slughorn), **11**, 1611
entitlement to, **11**, 1611
positioning, **11**, 1611
Motu proprio
Ecclesia Dei, **3**, 1656
meaning, **3**, 1656*n*
Mountain farming
EC Directive on, **1**, 971, 972
Mournings
inheritance tax, **25**, 1008
legacy for, **25**, 847
widow's right to, **25**, 712
Moveable estate
administration—
  heritable estate, distinction between, abolition of, **25**, 1038
  historical development, **25**, 1035, 1038
collation *inter haeredes*, **25**, 683
general scheme of succession, **25**, 676
heritable estate—
  assimilation of, **25**, 687, 701
  distinction between, **25**, 682
legal rights—
  heritable and moveable property distinguished, **25**, 778
  quantification of, **25**, 783
surviving spouse, succession to, **25**, 680
ultimus haeres, **25**, 681
vesting, **25**, 685
Moveable property
accession, *see* ACCESSION
adjudication, **8**, 197, 200
arrestment of, **4**, 42; **8**, 101, 247; **14**, 1812; **17**, 1364
assignation, **6**, 592*ff*
  basic pattern of, **6**, 593
  copyright, **6**, 600
  debts, **6**, 595
  design registration, **6**, 602
  generally, **6**, 592
  goodwill, **6**, 598

Moveable property—*continued*
assignation—*continued*
  intimation of, **6**, 593
  legacies, **6**, 596
  life insurance policies, **6**, 594
  mode of, **6**, 593
  patents, **6**, 599
  plant and seed protection rights, **6**, 602
  service marks, **6**, 601
  stocks and shares, transfer of, **6**, 597
  trade marks, **6**, 601
  trusts, interests under, **6**, 596
beneficial interest, meaning, **4**, 42
bona vacantia, **24**, 313
child's passive capacity, **3**, 1203
completion of title, **24**, 148, 157
contract of location not limited to, **14**, 1002
contract of sale, interest implied, **12**, 1009
conveyancing, aspects of, **6**, 591
  foreign deeds, privileged, **6**, 442
copyright, **18**, 14
corporeal, *see* CORPOREAL MOVEABLE PROPERTY
delivery of, *see* SALE AND SUPPLY OF GOODS
deprivation of, interest payable for, **12**, 1021
diligence, **18**, 13
disposal, **4**, 43
ejusdem generis, **25**, 825
executor-creditor, confirmation as, **8**, 355
floating charges, conditions in, **18**, 353
goods, meaning, **20**, 805
goodwill, **18**, 14
heritable property—
  conversion to, **18**, 15
  distinguished, **18**, 11
Hume's *Lectures*, **18**, 1
immoveables distinguished from, **17**, 313
incorporeal, *see* INCORPOREAL PROPERTY
insolvent, conveyance to, **11**, 778
intellectual property rights, **18**, 14
lease, **13**, 194
lex situs transfer of ownership governed by, **17**, 138
lien, right of, **13**, 95
liferent—
  liferenter's rights, **13**, 1640
  restriction on creation, **13**, 1631, 1632
  simple proper, **13**, 1614
long negative prescription, **16**, 2121, 2121*n*, 2122
marriage, proprietary consequences of, **17**, 326
meaning, **18**, 11
mussels, **18**, 331
negative prescription, **16**, 2121
oysters, **18**, 331
patent, **18**, 14
personal bond, **18**, 14
poinding, **8**, 101
real conditions, **18**, 344, 349, 353
removal from or inclusion in price, **6**, 558
rights in security, *see* RIGHT IN SECURITY
rights therein, **4**, 43
sale of—
  generally, **20**, 802
  pre-1979 cases, **20**, 803
  Sale of Goods Act 1893 ..., **20**, 803

Moveable property—*continued*
sale of—*continued*
  Sale of Goods Act 1979 ..., **20**, 803, 804
  Scots common law, **20**, 802, 802*n*, 804, 809
  security over goods, **20**, 815
  See also SALE AND SUPPLY OF GOODS
security over, *see* RIGHT IN SECURITY
ship as, **21**, 101, 131
situation of, **4**, 42
specific implement to restore possession, **13**, 12
term money held to cover, **14**, 1802
transfer of, **4**, 102
trust beneficiary, interest of, **18**, 14
trusts, **24**, 27
udal law, **24**, 307
water, when classified as, **18**, 273
Movement
freedom of, **12**, 4*n*
Mud
road, on, responsibility for, **20**, 702
Mugging
robbery, as, **7**, 358
Muir fowl
close season, **11**, 806
custody of, by unqualified person, **11**, 807
Muirburning
control of, **11**, 924
damage caused by, **11**, 924
hill farming improvement scheme, **11**, 923
moor game must breed on site, **11**, 916
negligence in operation, **11**, 925
notice of place and extent, **11**, 921, 924
prohibition of, at certain times, **11**, 917–919
regulation of, **11**, 924
Secretary of State's powers, **11**, 918, 922
tenant's right to make muirburn, **11**, 920
Multiple occupation
housing in, *see* HOUSING
Multiplepoinding
arrestment, **8**, 284, 318
Court of Session procedure, **17**, 1408
equivalent to formal intimation of assignation, as, **20**, 49
holder's right of action, **4**, 148
inhibition, **8**, 172
sheriff court, actions in, **17**, 1199, 1246, 1323
trusts, powers granted by court, **24**, 203, 210
Multure
lease, **13**, 206
Mumps
vaccination against, **11**, 1446
Municipal banks
Scotland, in, **2**, 1125
Municipal law
extradition—
  Commonwealth country, to, **12**, 519
  Republic of Ireland, to, **12**, 525
See DOMESTIC LAW
Munus publicum
holder of, termination of contract, **9**, 142
Murder
abortion, death during course of, **7**, 270
act, by, **7**, 266
actus reus, **7**, 30

Murder—*continued*

assault, and, **7**, 243, 244
assault with intent to, **7**, 236
attempted, **7**, 168
   child, of, **3**, 1250
   person charged with, duty solicitor, **13**, 1053
bail in case of, **17**, 551
capital punishment, **17**, 562
child under eighteen convicted of, **3**, 1218; **16**, 1432
coercion unavailable as defence, **7**, 202
committed outside United Kingdom, **6**, 867
concealment of pregnancy, *see* CONCEALMENT OF PREGNANCY
consent of victim, where, **7**, 93
constructive, **7**, 270
contract killing, **7**, 80
corporate liability, **7**, 110
criminal homicide, as, **7**, 253
criminal jurisdiction, **6**, 867; **17**, 516
culpable homicide, reduction to, grounds for, **7**, 271
death or suicide of victim following assault, **7**, 227
defences—
   diminished responsibility, **7**, 135, 136, 138, 139, 149, 150, 242, 253
   provocation, **7**, 241, 253
definition, **7**, 266
fireraising, death during course of, **7**, 270
foetus, of, **10**, 1030
forfeiture rule, adjudication, **21**, 1169, 1186
High Court of Justiciary jurisdiction, **6**, 867
intention to cause harm, **7**, 266, 269
intentional killing, **7**, 78, 168, 266, 267, 272
malice, **7**, 80
meaning, **7**, 253
mens rea, **7**, 168, 266
more than one mental element, where, **7**, 85
motive, **7**, 92
novus actus interveniens, **7**, 51
omission, by, **7**, 266
participation, art and part liability, **7**, 187, 188
person charged with, duty solicitor, **13**, 1053
pre-trial investigations, **17**, 544
previous malice, statements inferring, **10**, 744
proof of cause of death, **7**, 50
rape, death during course of, **7**, 270
recklessness, **7**, 82, 168
result-crime, as, **7**, 32, 46
revenge, acts of, **7**, 272, 274
robbery, killing during course of, **7**, 270
sheriff court jurisdiction, **17**, 516
sporting events, in the course of, **19**, 1264, 1266
succession, disqualification of killer, *see* SUCCESSION
victim's request, killing at, **7**, 255
wicked recklessness, **7**, 266, 268, 282
See also CULPABLE HOMICIDE; HOMICIDE

Museums and galleries

Dunblane Cathedral, provisions relating to, **13**, 1514
firearms licences for, **10**, 1548

Museums and galleries—*continued*

local authority—
   functions of museum and art gallery authorities, **13**, 1519
   provision by, generally, **13**, 1520
museum authority—
   generally, **14**, 688
   powers and duties, **14**, 689
National Galleries of Scotland—
   accounts, **13**, 1513
   board of trustees, **13**, 1511, 1512
      appointment, **13**, 1512
      Crown immunity not enjoyed by, **13**, 1512
      historical background, **13**, 1511
      membership, **13**, 1512
      powers, **13**, 1512
      property of as Crown property, **13**, 1512
      purpose, **13**, 1512
   buildings, **13**, 1514
      maintenace and repair, **13**, 1514
      purposes for which used, **13**, 1514
   collections, **13**, 1514
      acquisitions, **13**, 1514
   Director, appointment, **13**, 1513
   employees, appointment, **13**, 1513
   Gallery of Modern Art, **13**, 1514
   historical background, **13**, 1511
   meaning, **13**, 1514
   National Gallery, **13**, 1514
   National Portrait Gallery, **13**, 1514
   reports, **13**, 1513
   Royal Institution, **13**, 1514
   Royal Scottish Academy, **13**, 1514
      Diploma Collection, **13**, 1514
National Museums of Scotland—
   acquisitions, **13**, 1518
   board of trustees—
      accounts, **13**, 1518
      allowances, **13**, 1518
      Crown immunity not enjoyed by, **13**, 1518
      director, appointment of, **13**, 1518
      expenses, **13**, 1518
      membership, **13**, 1518
      powers and functions, **13**, 1517, 1518
   disposals, **13**, 1518
   establishment, **13**, 1517
   meaning, **13**, 1517
   National Museum of Antiquities of Scotland, **13**, 1516
   purpose, **13**, 1517
   Royal Scottish Museum, **13**, 1515

Music

dancing, and—
   busking, **9**, 1040
   copyright, **9**, 1037
   licences, **9**, 1038
   nuisance, **9**, 1039
   pop festivals, **9**, 1041
   professional performers, **9**, 1036
sheet music, VAT zero-rating, **7**, 1447
society promoting, **12**, 694*n*

Musical band

name, passing off, **18**, 1377

Musical instrument
noise caused by, **9**, 1298
Musical work
anonymous or pseudonymous, **18**, 995, 996, 1032
author—
 meaning, **18**, 980
 See also COPYRIGHT
composer, *see* COPYRIGHT
copyright, **18**, 931, 933, 956
 adaptation, **18**, 1065
 audio-visual recording, **18**, 949
 computer, storage on, **18**, 949
 Crown copyright, term of, **18**, 1034, 1037
 educational establishment performing, showing
  or playing, **18**, 1112
 employment by another, work made in course
  of, **18**, 997–999
 European Community legislation, **18**, 1643
 folksongs, **18**, 996
  archive recordings, **18**, 1120
 generally, **18**, 949
 incidental inclusion, **18**, 1108
 infringement by public performance, **18**, 1060,
  1061
 moral rights, *see* COPYRIGHT (MORAL RIGHTS)
 originality, **18**, 941
 parliamentary, term of, **18**, 1036, 1037
 published editions, **18**, 933, 936, 977, 984
  infringement, **18**, 1056
  originality, **18**, 948
  term of copyright, **18**, 1041
 tape-recording, **18**, 949
 term of copyright, **18**, 1029, 1030
 writing, meaning, **18**, 949
 See also COPYRIGHT
meaning, **18**, 956
performance, rights in, *see* RIGHTS IN
 PERFORMANCES
record of performance of, offence relating to, **9**,
 1006
Musk rats
importation, **2**, 218
licence to keep, **2**, 218
Mussels
early legislation, **11**, 118, 122
heritable or moveable property, whether, **18**, 331
inter regalia minora, as, **18**, 521
lease of mussel bed, **13**, 205
Mussel Fisheries (Scotland) Act 1847 ..., **11**, 122
ownership, **18**, 331
right to gather—
 acquisition, **18**, 332
 foreshore, in relation to, **18**, 318
 public rights, **18**, 333
 regalian right, as, **18**, 210

Mussels—*continued*
right to gather—*continued*
 separate tenement, as, **18**, 210, 319, 332, 332*n*
 statutory regulation, **18**, 332
Mustard
food standard, **11**, 353
Mutiny
armed forces by, incitement, **7**, 597
Mutuum
agreement of lender and borrower, **13**, 1706
borrower, *see* BORROWER
commodatum compared, **13**, 1702
contract of, money as subject matter, **8**, 7
contract *stricti juris*, as, **13**, 1702
definition, **13**, 1705
fungible, delivery to borrower, **13**, 1706
gratuitous contract, as, **13**, 1701, 1706
hire compared, **13**, 1706
lender, *see* LENDER
locatio conductio rei compared, **13**, 1706
meaning, **13**, 1701, 1783
money, loan of, **13**, 1701, 1704, 1712
 See also MONEY
nature of, **13**, 1703
nexum replaced by, **13**, 1703
proper—
 constitution of contract, **13**, 1708
 essential elements, **13**, 1706
 meaning, **13**, 1706
 obligations under contract, **13**, 1709
  prescription, **13**, 1711
 prescription, **13**, 1711
 proof of contract, **13**, 1708
 proof of loan, **13**, 1708
 steelbow, **13**, 1707
 subject matter, **13**, 1707
real contract, as, **13**, 1702
Roman law, **13**, 1702
subject matter—
 borrower as owner, **13**, 1709
 corporeal moveable property, **13**, 1708
 damage or loss, borrower's obligations, **13**, 1709
 defective, lender's liability, **13**, 1709
 delivery, contract completed by, **13**, 1703
 fungibles, **13**, 1707
 mutuum proper, **13**, 1707
 non-fungibles, **13**, 1707
 ownership—
  mutuum proper, **13**, 1707
  transfer of, **13**, 1702
 proof of loan, **13**, 1708
 steelbow, **13**, 1707
unfair contract terms, **13**, 1710
Myxomatosis
spreading, **11**, 877

N

Nails
weights and measures legislation, **6**, 243
Nairn
local roads authority, **14**, 404
population, **14**, 64
Name
business, *see* BUSINESS
Certificate of Official Recognition of Change of, **6**, 1018
change of, **19**, 1428
   child under sixteen, **19**, 1426
   legacy, as condition of, **25**, 871
   Lord Lyon King of Arms, granted by, **19**, 1428
   marriage, following, **10**, 842; **19**, 1428
   person over sixteen, **19**, 1427
   restrictions on, **19**, 1426–1428
   will, settlement or deed requiring, **19**, 1428
   within twelve months of date of birth, **19**, 1425
child, of, parental rights as to, **10**, 1305
English equivalent to non-English name, **19**, 1428
firm of, *see* PARTNERSHIP
passing off—
   business names, **18**, 1377
      non-distinctive elements, **18**, 1377
   generally, **18**, 1374
   geographical names, **18**, 1376
   personal names, **18**, 1376, 1377
Nanny
exclusion from child minder provisions, **3**, 1259
Napier Commission
report, **6**, 955, 966
National Audit Office
control of expenditure, **7**, 766
creation of, **5**, 595
functions of, **5**, 595
National Board of Scotland
constitution, **14**, 1149
functions, **14**, 1149
National body
inheritance tax, exemption on gifts to, **19**, 1533
National Coal Board
See BRITISH COAL CORPORATION
National Consultative Committee of Scientists in Professions Allied to Medicine
duty of, **11**, 1419
National Consumer Council
consumer protection, **6**, 1, 9, 25
reports, **6**, 25
National Enterprise Board
establishment, **19**, 211
National Federation of Consumer Groups
activities of, **6**, 27
consumer protection, **6**, 9
National Film Finance Corporation
dissolution of, **9**, 1028
establishment of, **9**, 1028
National Galleries of Scotland
See MUSEUMS AND GALLERIES

National Giro Bank
establishment, **2**, 1111
services provided by, **2**, 1111
National health service
administrative authorities, **11**, 1402
charges—
   clinics, goods supplied at, **11**, 1515
   dental appliances and treatment, **11**, 1514
   drugs, medicines, appliances and pharmaceutical services, **11**, 1512
   evasion of, **11**, 1519
   expensive supplies, **11**, 1516
   generally, **11**, 1511
   optical appliances, **11**, 1513
   overseas visitors, to, **11**, 1518
   remission, repayment or reduction of, **11**, 1517
   repairs and replacements, for, **11**, 1516
Common Services Agency, **11**, 1411, 1506, 1508, 1522–1524
management committee, **11**, 1401
dentists, *see* DENTIST
doctors, *see* DOCTOR; MEDICAL PRACTITIONER
endowments—
   nationalisation, arrangements made during, **11**, 1404
   Scottish Hospital Endowments Research Trust, **11**, 1424
establishment of, **14**, 37
expenditure, control over, **5**, 529
general dental services, *see* DENTISTRY
general medical services, *see* MEDICAL CARE
general ophthalmic services, *see* OPHTHALMIC SERVICES
health boards, *see* HEALTH BOARDS
Health Service Commissioner, *see* HEALTH SERVICE COMMISSIONER FOR SCOTLAND
Hospital Endowments Commission, **11**, 1404, 1406
hospitals, *see* HOSPITAL
joint liaison committees, **11**, 1412
land, purchase and disposal of, **11**, 1504, 1505
local health authorities, **11**, 1403
medical list, *see* DOCTOR
medical supplies, control of prices for, **11**, 1509
mentally ill, responsibility for, **14**, 35
   See also MENTAL HEALTH; MENTALLY DISORDERED PERSON
national consultative committees, **11**, 1419
   prospective abolition, **11**, 1401
National Health Service (Scotland) Act 1947—
   aims, **22**, 2
nationalisation, **11**, 1401–1406
Ombudsman system, **19**, 242
ophthalmic services, *see* OPHTHALMIC SERVICES
origins of, **11**, 1401
overnight accommodation expenses, payment of, **11**, 1517
pharmaceutical services, *see* PHARMACEUTICAL SERVICES

National health service—*continued*
property, purchase of, **11**, 1504
reform, **14**, 47
reorganisation—
co-operation of organisations, **11**, 1412
Common Services Agency, **11**, 1411, 1413
dissolution of former administrative authorities, **11**, 1414
health boards, **11**, 1412, 1413
Health Service Commissioner for Scotland, **11**, 1426
joint liaison committees, **11**, 1412
local advisory bodies, **11**, 1420
local consultative committees, **11**, 1423
local health councils, **11**, 1421
university liaison committees, **11**, 1420, 1422, 1506*n*
national advisory bodies, **11**, 1417
national consultative committees, **11**, 1401, 1419
national health service trusts, *see* NATIONAL HEALTH SERVICE TRUSTS
Scottish Dental Practices Board, **11**, 1416
Scottish Health Service—
infectious diseases, report on, **19**, 486
Planning Council, *see* SCOTTISH HEALTH SERVICE PLANNING COUNCIL
Scottish Hospital Endowments Research Trust, **11**, 1424
Scottish Hospital Trust, **11**, 1424
Scottish Medical Practices Committee, **11**, 1415
Secretary of State—
default of health board etc, **11**, 1409
emergency powers, **11**, 1409
general duty, **11**, 1407
inquiries, **11**, 1409
specific duties, **11**, 1408
Tribunal, **11**, 1425
Scottish Health Service Planning Council, *see* SCOTTISH HEALTH SERVICE PLANNING COUNCIL
staffing—
community medicine specialists, **11**, 1498
conditions of service, **11**, 1497
consultants, **11**, 1498
designated medical officers, **11**, 1502
employment, generally, **11**, 1497
health visitors, **11**, 1499
injury benefits, **11**, 1503
premature retirement, **11**, 1497
redundancy, **11**, 1497
remuneration, **11**, 1497
speech therapists, **11**, 1501
superannuation, **11**, 1503
supplementary professions, **11**, 1500
transfer and vesting of property, **11**, 1405
endowments, **11**, 1406
travelling expenses, payment of, **11**, 1490, 1517
companion's expenses, **11**, 1490, 1517
Tribunal, **11**, 1425
appeals against decisions, **11**, 1521
chairman, **11**, 1425
disqualification of practitioners, **11**, 1521
expenses, **11**, 1506

National health service—*continued*
Tribunal—*continued*
inquiries, **11**, 1521
members, **11**, 1425
powers, **11**, 1521
publication of decisions, **11**, 1521
supervision of, Scottish Committee, by, **23**, 911*n*
trusts, *see* NATIONAL HEALTH SERVICE TRUSTS
Working for Patients White Paper, **11**, 1401
National health service trusts
establishment, **11**, 1401
hospitals, ownership and management of, **11**, 1401
powers, **11**, 1401
staff, employment by, **11**, 1401
transfer of property, liabilities and obligations to, **11**, 1401
National Heritage Memorial Fund
company donation to, **3**, 1155
functions of, **9**, 1220
stamp duty, exemption from, **3**, 1164
tax treatment, **3**, 1166
National heritage property
inheritance tax exemption, **19**, 1533; **25**, 1011
National House Builders Council
membership and activities, **6**, 567
new houses, certificate of warranty, **6**, 567
National Industrial Relations Court
abolition, **6**, 982
basis of Employment Appeal Tribunal, **6**, 981, 982
former constitution and membership, **6**, 982
National insurance contributions
age, determination of, **19**, 1584
benefits where entitlement dependent on payment of, **21**, 801, 1034
benefits where entitlement not dependent on payment of, **21**, 801
Class 1 ..., **21**, 1035
lower earnings limit, **21**, 1035
married woman, **21**, 1047
primary, **21**, 1035
secondary, **21**, 1035
state retirement pension, **21**, 1203
upper earnings limit, **21**, 1035
Class 1A ..., **21**, 1036
Class 2 ..., **21**, 1037
married woman, **21**, 1047
state retirement pension, **21**, 1203
Class 3 ..., **21**, 1038
state retirement pension, **21**, 1203
Class 4 ..., **21**, 1039
classes, generally, **19**, 1530
credits, **21**, 1046
diplomatic immunity, **19**, 682
earnings factor—
calculation, **21**, 1045
credits, **21**, 1046
generally, **21**, 1045
earnings limits, **19**, 1530
employed earner, **21**, 1048
employment category, **21**, 1048
generally, **19**, 1510, 1530
insolvency, preferential claim in case of, **9**, 150

National insurance contributions—*continued*
introduction of, **12**, 679
married woman, **21**, 1047
partner, payment by, **16**, 1124
payroll deduction scheme, **3**, 1153
preferential debts, **4**, 855
self-employed, **21**, 1048
state retirement pension—
    contribution conditions, **21**, 1203
    See also PENSION
tax week, meaning, **21**, 1035*n*
tax year, meaning, **21**, 1035*n*
voluntary, **21**, 1038
National Library of Scotland
accounts, **13**, 1502
Advocates' Library, **13**, 1501
board of trustees, **13**, 1501
    chairman, **13**, 1502
    common seal, **13**, 1501
    constitution, **13**, 1502
    expenses, **13**, 1502
    functions, **13**, 1502
    membership, **13**, 1502
        appointment, **13**, 1502
        ex-officio members, **13**, 1502
    perpetual succession, **13**, 1501
    power to sue and be sued, **13**, 1501
    property, power to acquire and hold, **13**, 1501
    service on, **13**, 1501
books, delivery of copies to, **17**, 5
delivery of books to, **13**, 1503
    failure to deliver, **13**, 1503
disposal of duplicate or otherwise unwanted
    books etc., **13**, 1502
establishment, **13**, 1501
Faculty of Advocates, Law Library, interchange of
    books with, **13**, 1502
gifts and bequests, **13**, 1502
loans from, **13**, 1502
purpose, **13**, 1501
register of electors, supply to, **15**, 1114
staff, appointment, **13**, 1502
National Library of Wales
books, delivery of copies to, **17**, 5
National Loans Fund, **13**, 1772
government expenditure and borrowing, **7**, 766
Public Works Loans Commissioners, **13**, 1772
National Medical Consultative Committee
duty of, **11**, 1419
National Museum of Antiquities of Scotland,
    13, 1516
National Museums of Scotland
see MUSEUMS AND GALLERIES
**National nursing and midwifery consultative
    committee**
duty of, **11**, 1419
National optical consultative committee
duty of, **11**, 1419
**National paramedical (therapeutic) consult-
    ative committee**
duty of, **11**, 1419
**National pharmaceutical consultative
    committee**
duty of, **11**, 1419

National Playing Fields Association (NPFA),
    19, 1210, 1219
National Portrait Gallery, **13**, 1514
National Research Development Corporation
establishment, **19**, 211
National Savings Bank
business, regulation of, **2**, 1163
deposit accounts—
    annual statement of, **2**, 1162
    bodies which may open, **2**, 1164
    death of depositors, **2**, 1165
    deposits to, **2**, 1164
    kinds of, **2**, 1160
    management of, **2**, 1162
    maximum sum for, **2**, 1163
    withdrawals from, **2**, 1164
deposits with, **2**, 1110
establishment, **2**, 1110
investment deposits—
    maximum, **2**, 1161
    payment to National Loans Fund, **2**, 1161
minor, account in name of, **2**, 1230; **3**, 1219
nominations, **25**, 733
Scotland, development in, **2**, 1123
services, provision of, **2**, 1110, 1159
National Savings certificate
nominations, **25**, 733
National security
data held for purpose of safeguarding, **18**, 1515
National treasures, protection
European Union customs law, **7**, 1022
National Trust for Scotland
conveyance of croft land, **1**, 830
disposal of land owned by, **8**, 615
land held inalienably by—
    compulsory purchase order exemption, **11**, 634
    felling directions and, **11**, 623
Nationalised and regulated industries
archives and records of, **19**, 849, 862
canals, **19**, 1103
coal, **6**, 162
consumer or consultative councils, **6**, 159, 166;
    19, 240, 241, 242*n*
consumer protection, **19**, 240–242
electricity, **6**, 160; **9**, 605
European Community provisions, **19**, 244
foreign propriatory claims, **17**, 329
gas, **6**, 161, 857
generally, **6**, 159, 166; **19**, 209, 209*n*, 210*n*, 211,
    222, 227
insurance by, **14**, 1057
ministerial control, **19**, 227*n*
mixed enterprise, **19**, 211
Monopolies and Mergers Commission investiga-
    tion, **19**, 224, 224*n*
National Health Service, **11**, 1401–1406
postal services, **6**, 164
Public Accounts Committee, **19**, 224
railways, **6**, 163; **19**, 1001, 1088
special legal powers conferred on boards, **11**, 106
telecommunications, **6**, 165
Nationality
children, domicile and, **10**, 1223
citizenship, *see* CITIZENSHIP

Nationality—*continued*
concept of, **14**, 1901
discrimination on grounds of—
  European Union law, **12**, 221
early legislation, **14**, 1902
EU law rights, **12**, 220, 220*n*
evidence, **14**, 1957
examination on arrival to establish, **12**, 162
fishing vessels, jurisdiction of flag state over, **11**, 88
freedom of, **12**, 4*n*
International Court of Justice rule as to, **19**, 741
Ireland, separation of, effect of, **14**, 1901
Judgments Convention, exclusion from scope of, **8**, 432
judicial review, **14**, 1959
marriage, **10**, 836
offences, **14**, 1958
ordinarily resident, meaning, **14**, 1905
personal law, indicator of, **17**, 189
proceedings, **14**, 1958
registration, *see* CITIZENSHIP
Scottish, pre-Union legislation, **22**, 275
settled, meaning, **14**, 1905
ship, of, *see* SHIP
status—
  categories, **14**, 1904
  generally, **11**, 1069
trials which may be prejudiced by, extradition procedure, **12**, 516, 532, 534
Natural accession
restitution, obligation of, **15**, 54
Natural Environment Research Council
borehole, proposal to sink, **25**, 345
well, proposal to sink, **25**, 345
Natural gas
rights—
  regalian right, as, **18**, 210
  separate tenement, as, **18**, 210
See GAS
Natural harbour
anchorage, **11**, 1304
common law, **11**, 1304
Crown rights, **11**, 1304
foreshore, use of, **11**, 1304
generally, **11**, 1304
navigation, right of, **11**, 1304
statutory provisions, **11**, 1304
Natural History Museum
company donation to, **3**, 1155
tax treatment, **3**, 1166
Natural justice
adjournment of proceedings, need for, **1**, 275
administrative decisions, applying to, **1**, 230
appeal, no right of, **1**, 282
audi alteram partem, see right to be heard *below*
bias, rule against—
  arbiter, of, **1**, 252
  criteria for finding, **1**, 257
  decision-making process, in, **1**, 256
  exemption from disqualification for, **1**, 258
  generally, **1**, 251
  improper procedure, arising from, **1**, 255
  interest, arising from, **1**, 251

Natural justice—*continued*
bias, rule against—*continued*
  licensing authority, of, **1**, 254
  likelihood of, establishing, **1**, 257
  local government matter, in, **1**, 253
  minister, application of principle to, **1**, 253
  object to, waiver of, **1**, 258
  one member of body, of, **1**, 257
  pecuniary interest, **1**, 251
  public interest, decisions taken in, **1**, 253
  reasonable suspicion of, **1**, 257
breach, remedy for, **1**, 284
contract of employment, application to, **9**, 39
development of, **1**, 250
duty to observe—
  administrative bodies, by, **1**, 210
  disciplinary proceedings, during, **1**, 210
  failure, challenge for, **1**, 205
  licensing board, of, **1**, 211
evidence—
  observation of rules of, **1**, 280
  right to know, **1**, 276
failure to observe, **1**, 284
fair procedure, principles of, **1**, 250
fairness, and, **1**, 249, 283
findings to be supported by evidence, requirement of, **1**, 280
interpreter, requiring provision of, **1**, 282
justice to be seen to be done, **1**, 249
legal representation, right to, **1**, 279
legitimate expectation, **1**, 267
licensing authorities observing, **1**, 259
material held by public authority, right to know, **1**, 277
national security considerations excluding, **1**, 265
observation of, **1**, 249
origin of principles, **1**, 249
procedural requirements arising from, **1**, 230
proceedings, right to have notice of, **1**, 274
proceedings of tribunal, in, **1**, 276
reasons for decision, no requirement of, **1**, 281
revocation of decision, in, **1**, 297
right to be heard—
  alien, on deportation of, **1**, 264
  application of principle, **1**, 259
  disciplinary powers, on exercise of, **1**, 268
  dismissal from office or employment, before, **1**, 269
  fair hearing, obligation to have, **1**, 272
  fundamental human right, as, **10**, 95
  hearing, nature of, **1**, 278
  hearing making no difference, where, **1**, 270
  investigation, in, **1**, 262
  legislative powers, in exercise of, **1**, 263
  legitimate expectation, where existing, **1**, 267
  national security, considerations of, **1**, 265
  notice of proceedings, **1**, 274
  particular circumstances, in, **1**, 261
  person hearing, decision by, **1**, 273
  preliminary inquiry, at, **1**, 262
  privilege, on withdrawal of, **1**, 266
  procedural requirements, **1**, 278
  procedural rules, interpretation of, **1**, 271
  representation, right of, **1**, 279

Natural justice—*continued*
right to be heard—*continued*
  statute, excluded by, **1**, 271
  statutory provisions, effect of, **1**, 271
  when arising, **1**, 260
rules of, **1**, 249
Scottish and English law on, **1**, 250
sports discipline, **19**, 1240
Natural law
authority of equity in, **22**, 406
Bankton, equity as synonym for law of nature, **22**, 409
criminal law—
  Kames, **22**, 422
  Mackenzie, **22**, 421
  mala in se and *mala prohibita* distinction, **22**, 420
divine law and, **22**, 401
Erskine, positive and natural law, **22**, 410
fundamental law, acceptance as, **5**, 339
Kames's *Principles of Equity*, **22**, 411–416
Stair's jurisprudence—
  equity as a source of law, **22**, 400, 401, 406, 408
  meaning, **22**, 401
  principles identical with those of equity, **22**, 401
survival of, **5**, 340
unjust enrichment, **15**, 11
Natural person
artificial legal personality of company, difficulty of attributing characteristics to, **4**, 318
company enters contract and acquires property on same basis as, **4**, 318
donation, incapacity to make, **8**, 611
status or legal capacity, exclusion from scope of Judgments Convention, **8**, 431, 432
Natural resources
availability of water as natural resource, **25**, 301
continental shelf, **21**, 15, 18, 19
Convention on the Continental Shelf, **11**, 82–85
deep sea bed, **21**, 47, 49
exclusive economic zone, *see* EXCLUSIVE ECONOMIC ZONE
exploitation of, **11**, 85; **19**, 671, 687
exploration and exploitation interfering with navigation, fishing or conservation, **11**, 85
expropriation of property, **19**, 671, 671*n*
foreign investment in, **19**, 671
meaning, **11**, 84
nationalisation of property, **19**, 671
rights to, **11**, 83
state sovereignty over, **19**, 671
territorial jurisdiction over exploitation, **4**, 2
transnational corporations, **19**, 671
Naturalisation
British Dependent Territories citizenship, **14**, 1937
citizenship, acquisition by, **12**, 121
requirements of—
  character, **14**, 1920
  employment, **14**, 1920
  future home, **14**, 1920
  language, **14**, 1920
  residence, **14**, 1920

Naturalisation—*continued*
Secretary of State, functions of, **14**, 1904
Secretary of State's discretion, at, **12**, 121
settlement as precondition, **12**, 121
spouse of British citizen, of, **14**, 1921
Nature Conservancy Council
functions of, **9**, 1234
nature reserves, **9**, 1237
planning system, role in, **23**, 19, 169
Nature reserve
management of, **9**, 1237
provision of, **14**, 671
Nautae, caupones, stabularii
edict, **11**, 1702
Naval forces
components of, **2**, 606
composition, **2**, 606
discipline—
  regulations, **2**, 606
legal basis of, **2**, 606
meaning, **2**, 607
Naval Discipline Act, *see* NAVY
pay etc, authority for, **2**, 607
personnel, **2**, 607
women's services, status of, **2**, 612
Naval Reserve
authority for, **2**, 607
call out for service etc, **2**, 745
composition, **2**, 743
departments of, **2**, 743
officers—
  organisation, **2**, 743
  period of service, **2**, 744
  qualifications, **2**, 744
training, call out for, **2**, 745
women's sections, **2**, 743
Naval ship
civilian employees on, **2**, 614
foreign jurisdiction, **2**, 606
hazarding etc, **2**, 653
Navigable river
See RIVER
Navigation
anchorage, right of, **18**, 520
anchoring, **21**, 380
ancillary rights, **18**, 520
background to legislation, generally, **21**, 101
basic concepts in shipping and navigation law, **21**, 105
canals, navigable waters, as, **21**, 112
collision, *see* SHIPPING
confined areas, **21**, 379
construction or alteration, **19**, 19*n*
dangerous areas and weather, **21**, 379
error made in emergency situation, **21**, 314
exclusive economic zone, **11**, 107
fairway, *see* FAIRWAY
freedom of, **19**, 608; **21**, 41
  exclusive economic zone, **21**, 39
generally, **18**, 494
getting under way, **21**, 379
high seas, rights on, **11**, 87
ice endangering, master's duty to report, **21**, 210

Navigation—*continued*
interference with rights, **11**, 7
  exploration and exploitation of natural resources, caused by, **11**, 85
launching operations, **21**, 381
local byelaws to control, **25**, 307
loch, **25**, 337
meaning, **18**, 519, 520; **21**, 108*n*
Merchant Shipping Notices (M Notices), **21**, 229*n*, 377
mooring rights, **18**, 520
narrow channel—
  collision regulations—
    generally, **21**, 347
  features forming, **21**, 347
  fishing vessel in, **21**, 347
  navigation and management rules, **21**, 379
  overtaking in, **21**, 351
  turning in, **21**, 347*n*
natural harbours, in, **11**, 1304
navigable river, *see* RIVER
navigable waters, meaning, **21**, 112
navigational equipment—
  duty to use properly, **21**, 340, 341
  instruction and maintenance manual, requirement to carry, **21**, 229*n*
  safety regulations, **21**, 218
navigational watch arrangements, **21**, 340
negligent—
  damages, liability for, **21**, 390
  responsibility, Hague-Visby Rules, **21**, 603
  See also SHIPPING (collision; negligence)
non-navigable waters, meaning, **21**, 112
owner's duty to ensure safe, **21**, 378
pilotage, *see* PILOT; PILOTAGE
prohibited places, **25**, 307
proof of fault following collision, **21**, 319
public right of—
  ancillary rights, **18**, 520
  byelaws, power to make, **18**, 520
  Crown ownership, **18**, 514
  extinction, **18**, 517
  fishing rights, and, **18**, 280
  foreshore, **18**, 318, 524, 525
    Crown or private ownership of foreshore, **18**, 524
  foreshore or bank, ancillary rights exercisable on, **18**, 520
  generally, **18**, 514
  navigation, **18**, 514
  non-tidal waters—
    acquisition of right, **18**, 516
    establishment as navigable, **18**, 523
    generally, **18**, 522, 523
    lochs, **18**, 308, 523
    measure of right, **18**, 523
    physical navigability, **18**, 523
    private ownership subject to public right of, **18**, 522
    rivers, **18**, 281, 523
  pilotage, **18**, 520
  public right to gather white fish and shellfish, and, **18**, 515
  right of way, not classified as, **18**, 497

Navigation—*continued*
public right of—*continued*
  river banks, use of, **18**, 528
  salmon fishings must not interfere with, **18**, 326
  tidal waters—
    generally, **18**, 518, 519
    navigable waters, meaning, **18**, 519
    navigation, meaning, **18**, 519, 520
public rights—
  exercise of right, **25**, 307
  non-tidal river, **25**, 314, 315
  theoretical base, **25**, 306
real right, right of navigation as, **18**, 5, 7
submarine cables and pipelines, **21**, 380
territorial sea, *see* TERRITORIAL SEA
tidal river, public rights, **25**, 310
transit passage, **21**, 10
trout fishing, and, **11**, 50
unlawful impeding of, **25**, 312
wreck endangering, power to remove, **21**, 514
Navigational aids
damage to, limitation of liability, **21**, 755
Navy
aliment—
  deductions from pay, **2**, 768
  process, service of, **2**, 769
authority for, **2**, 602
billeting, authority for, **2**, 770
complaints—
  procedure, **2**, 637
  redress, **2**, 637
court-martial, *see* COURTS-MARTIAL
discipline—
  arrest, powers of, **2**, 689
  arrested persons rights of, **2**, 690
  civil court trial, effect of, **2**, 622
  civilians, application to, **2**, 614
  court-martial, *see* COURTS-MARTIAL
  custody—
    close, period of, **2**, 690
    forms of, **2**, 690
  desertion—
    offence of, **2**, 649
    waiver of trial, **2**, 666
  disciplinary courts—
    constitution, **2**, 713
    procedure of, **2**, 713
    restitution, order for, **2**, 707
  duration of, **2**, 605
  offences under—
    award of punishment, **2**, 669
    civilians, against, **2**, 668
    election for court-martial, **2**, 668, 687
    evidence etc in, **2**, 669
    jurisdiction, scope of, **2**, 668
    procedure, **2**, 669
    restitution order, **2**, 707
    subsequent trial barred, **2**, 669
    summary punishment, **2**, 687
  personnel subject to, **2**, 607, 630
  reserve forces subject to, **2**, 607
  Royal Marines subject to, **2**, 610
  spying, arrest for, **2**, 689
  summary punishment, **2**, 687

Navy—*continued*
discipline—*continued*
    territorial application, **2**, 613
    women's services subject to, **2**, 612
enlistment regulations, **2**, 606
licensing requirements exemption, **2**, 784
naval forces, *see* NAVAL FORCES
naval ship, *see* NAVAL SHIP
pay, deductions from—
    aliment payments, **2**, 768, 769
    court order, by, **2**, 768
    maintenance arrears, **2**, 768
personnel—
    arrest of, **2**, 689
    arrested persons, rights of, **2**, 690
    provost marshal, appointment, **2**, 696
Reserve, *see* NAVAL RESERVE
wills, validity, **2**, 780
See also ARMED FORCES
Nearest relative
See RELATIVE
Necessity
defence of, **15**, 420, 421
    coercion compared, **7**, 198
    defence of justification, as, **7**, 198
    examples, **7**, 199
    generally, **7**, 199
    Hume's views, **7**, 200
    limits of defence, **7**, 201
    Scots law, **7**, 200
Negative prescription
contracting out, prohibition on, **16**, 2115, 2130
de die in diem, **22**, 823
definition, **16**, 2115
generally, **11**, 1624; **16**, 2115; **22**, 672
historical background, **16**, 2115
imprescriptible rights and obligations, **16**, 2126
interruption of prescriptive period, **16**, 2124
limitation distinguished, **16**, 2133
long—
    bill of exchange, obligation under, **16**, 2121
    extension, **16**, 2122
    generally, **16**, 2115
    heritable property, **16**, 2121, 2122
    imprescriptible rights and obligations, **16**, 2126
    introduction, **16**, 2102
    moveable property, **16**, 2121, 2121*n*, 2122
    period, **16**, 2121
    promissory note, obligation under, **16**, 2121
    public rights of way, **16**, 2121, 2122
    relevant acknowledgement, **16**, 2121
        interruption by, **16**, 2125
    reparation, obligation to make, **16**, 2121
    servitudes, **16**, 2121, 2122
    terminus a quo, **16**, 2121, 2122
    wrongdoers, obligation to make contributions
        between, extinction, **16**, 2123
meaning, **16**, 2104
no relevant claim, requirement as to, **16**, 2124
obligation or right must subsist for appropriate
    period, **16**, 2124
relevant claim, **16**, 2124
short—
    accounting, obligation of, **16**, 2116

Negative prescription—*continued*
short—*continued*
    appropriate date, **16**, 2117, 2117*n*, 2118
        specified obligations, in respect of, **16**, 2119
    bill of exchange, obligation under, **16**, 2116
    breach of contract or promise, obligation
        arising from, **16**, 2116
    computation of prescriptive period, **16**, 2117
    generally, **16**, 2115, 2121
    imprescriptible rights and obligations, **16**, 2126
    money, periodical payments, obligation to pay,
        16, 2116
    negotiorum gestia, obligation arising from, **16**,
        2116
    obligations extinguished by, **16**, 2116
    operation, **16**, 2117
    promissory note, obligation under, **16**, 2116
    recompense, obligation of, **16**, 2116
    relevant acknowledgement, interruption by, **16**,
        2125
    reparation, liability to make, obligation arising
        under, **16**, 2116
    repetition, obligation of, **16**, 2116
    restitution, obligation of, **16**, 2116
    statutory check list, **16**, 2120
    terminus a quo, **16**, 2118
    time bar, **16**, 2118, 2120
    unjustified enrichment, redress, obligation
        based on, **16**, 2116
trust estate, **16**, 2125, 2125*n*
two or more persons bound jointly by obligation,
    16, 2125
Negative value
valuer, duties of, **25**, 110
Neglect of duty
culpable and reckless, **7**, 82
Negligence
accountant or auditor, of, **1**, 25
adjoining proprietor, occupier's duty to, **15**, 151
agent, by, **1**, 632, 652
animal, owner's liability for, **15**, 179, 185
breach of duty, **15**, 311
breach of statutory duty, **15**, 171, 175
building contracts, *see* BUILDING CONTRACT
burden of proof, **14**, 1129
canal undertaker's liability, **19**, 1109, 1124, 1125
care, tenant's obligation to use reasonable, **13**, 269
carelessness, **15**, 255, 256
causation, **14**, 1129
    See also CAUSATION
company law—
    state of mind of company, means of
        determining, **4**, 318
    ultra vires doctrine, application, **4**, 324
contributory—
    agony rule, **15**, 408
    appeal, reconsideration on, **15**, 409
    apportionment, **15**, 409, 410
    causation, **15**, 403, 407, 408, 415, 432
        test, **15**, 403
    child, by, **15**, 406
    common law, **15**, 403, 417
    criminal conduct, pursuer participating in, **15**,
        411

Negligence—*continued*
contributory—*continued*
    damnum fatale, **15**, 412–415
    defence, as, **15**, 403*ff*
    delict, as defence in case of, **15**, 403*ff*
    dilemma principle, **15**, 408
    disabled or infirm person, by, **15**, 406
    effect of defence, **15**, 403
    employment, breach of statutory duty, **15**, 405
    ex turpi causa non oritur actio, **15**, 411
    exceptions, **15**, 408
    fires, **15**, 414
    floods, **15**, 413
    generally, **15**, 403
    inevitable accident, **15**, 415
    instinctive behaviour, **15**, 408
    justification, **15**, 418
    meaning, **15**, 403*n*
    multiple defenders, **15**, 410
    necessity, **15**, 21, 420
    novus actus interveniens, **15**, 403*n*, 407
    onus of proof, **15**, 403
    provocation, **15**, 419
    reduction of damages where, **15**, 929
    self-defence, **15**, 420
    standard of care, **15**, 403, 404
    statutory authority, **15**, 416
    volenti non fit injuria, **15**, 403*n*
culpable homicide, **7**, 282
damages, reduction on proof of pursuer's contributory negligence, **13**, 80
defamation, negligent, **15**, 280
delict—
    liability in, **14**, 1084
    negligence and, **15**, 217
Donoghue v Stevenson, importance, **15**, 258
duty—
    neglect of, **14**, 1123
duty of care, and, **15**, 255–257
    See also CARE, DUTY OF
economic loss—
    derivative, **15**, 273
    development of law, **15**, 274
    pure, **15**, 273
    See also CARE, DUTY OF; ECONOMIC LOSS
elements, **15**, 311
employer's liability, *see* EMPLOYER (liability)
errors of judgment, **14**, 1127
exclusion clause in contract, **15**, 720
family relationship, injury to—
    destroying relationship, **15**, 598–602
    disenhancing relationship, **15**, 597
    undermining relationship, **15**, 596
fault—
    culpa, **15**, 254
    definition, **15**, 252
    dolus, **15**, 253
    generally, **15**, 252
    intentional injury, **15**, 253
    unintentional injury, **15**, 254
fire authorities' liability for, **10**, 1474
fire services vehicles, injuries caused by, **10**, 1476
fireman, by, **10**, 1474, 1475
gatekeeper of level crossing, **19**, 1033

Negligence—*continued*
harm, **14**, 2106; **15**, 311
historical background, **15**, 257
hotels, in, **11**, 1745
intent to cause injury, and, **15**, 255
intentional harm, **15**, 257
meaning, **15**, 255, 256
misdiagnosis, **14**, 1127
misrepresentation, negligent, **15**, 589, 684
misstatement, economic loss caused by, **15**, 555, 556
nervous shock, **15**, 284
    See also CARE, DUTY OF
novus actus interveniens, **15**, 431, 434
nuisance contrasted with, **14**, 2041
obligation of reparation, **11**, 1032
occupiers' liability, *see* OCCUPIER S LIABILITY
patient's remedies, **14**, 1125
professional liability, *see* PROFESSIONAL LIABILITY
railway construction, **19**, 1024
recreational and sporting activities, **19**, 1241–1244
relational economic loss and—
    duty of care, **15**, 586, 588
    existing contract—
        negligent interference, **15**, 592
        negligent performance, **15**, 590, 593
    general duty, **15**, 587
    generally, **15**, 586, 588, 594
    Henderson v Merrett Syndicates Ltd, decision in, **15**, 586, 587
    Junior Books Ltd v Veitchi Co Ltd, decision in, **15**, 592, 594
    misrepresentation, negligent, **15**, 589
    prospective contract—
        inducing, **15**, 589
        preventing, **15**, 591
remoteness of damage—
    concept, generally, **15**, 257
    See also DAMAGE
sheriff officer, liability of, **14**, 1511
support rules, as to, **14**, 1637
tax loss due to, partnerships, **19**, 1594
taxpayer, by, **19**, 1544
traffic offences—
    reckless driving, **20**, 412
    skids, **20**, 414
tramway undertakers, **19**, 1137
veterinary surgeon, position of, **25**, 214
Negligent misrepresentation
liability for, **11**, 732
Negligently
use of term, **7**, 81
Negotiable instrument
arrestment, **8**, 278
assignation of debt compared, **20**, 56
assignation of debts, **4**, 102
capacity, **4**, 125
cash, payable to, **4**, 192
cheque, *see* CHEQUE
Consumer Credit Act 1974, provisions of, **20**, 42
delivery, requirement of, **4**, 102
deposit of, as security, **13**, 1759
execution, requirement of, **4**, 102
forged, **11**, 767

Negotiable instrument—*continued*
full canon of law on, development of, **4**, 104
historical background, **4**, 104
holder in due course, title of, **18**, 676
inhibition, **8**, 134
less than 100p, made for, **4**, 113
meaning, **4**, 105
'mere personal defences', meaning, **4**, 150
negotiability—
    customary commercial usage, arising from, **4**, 103
    formal requirements of, **4**, 103
    free transfer as feature of, **4**, 103
    instrument should stand alone, requirement that, **4**, 103
    law merchant, description of, **4**, 103
    quality of, **4**, 103
    recognition of, **4**, 103
    statutory recognition, arising from, **4**, 103
    time of payment, importance of, **4**, 111
nemo dat quod non habet rule, exception to, **18**, 676
non-financial obligations, **4**, 103
pledge, **20**, 15, 57
pledgee—
    favourable position of, **20**, 58
    power to deal with instrument as owner, **20**, 60
promissory notes, *see* PROMISSORY NOTES
reform, proposals for, **4**, 105
Sale of Goods Act, not covered by, **20**, 805
Scottish and English law, overlap between, **4**, 104
security provided by, **20**, 56, 59
seller accepting, effect on rights of lien, **20**, 874
stolen, restitution not applicable, **15**, 52
third party rights, **15**, 848
transfer, **8**, 636
    bearer instrument, **18**, 653
    order instrument, **18**, 653
transfer of debts, generally, **4**, 102
types, **4**, 103
value—
    holder for, rights of, **4**, 150
    meaning, **4**, 144
See also BILL OF EXCHANGE; SECURITIES

Negotiorum gestio
absence, ignorance or incapacity of *dominus*, **15**, 95, 107–109, 122
actio negotiorum gestorum contraria, **15**, 123, 124
actio negotiorum gestorum directa, **15**, 123, 124
acts amounting to, **15**, 95, 96
    factual, **15**, 96
    physical, **15**, 96
administration of another's affairs, **15**, 95, 103, 110
    against express wishes of *dominus*, **15**, 137, 138, 139
    assessment of utility, **15**, 121
    by *gestor* in bona fide belief they are his own, **15**, 137, 140
    by *gestor* for his own benefit, **15**, 137, 138
    dominus and *gestor* both interested in affair, where, **15**, 104
    failure of *dominus* to object, **15**, 109
    fault in, liability, **15**, 136
    initial utility of management, **15**, 117–122
    minor or pupil, *dominus* as, **15**, 137, 141
    necessity and utility, **15**, 120

Negotiorum gestio—*continued*
administration of another's affairs—*continued*
    presumable wishes of *dominus*, **15**, 122
    ultimate result, **15**, 121
    utiliter, requirement as to, **15**, 118
    utility at time of intervention, **15**, 121
agency of necessity, English doctrine of, **15**, 94
aliment, provision of, **15**, 98, 116
amount recoverable—
    exceeding amount by which *dominus* enriched, **15**, 89
    limitation of liability, **15**, 115
animus negotia aliena gerendi, **15**, 95, 110–116
auctor in rem suam, **15**, 134, 135
cautionary obligation, incurring, **15**, 96
completion, *gestor's* duty as to, **15**, 129, 130
contract, *gestor* must not be bound by, **15**, 91
contrary actions, **15**, 123
definition, **15**, 87
direct actions, **15**, 123
division and sale of common property, availability, **15**, 104
domino prohibente, **15**, 137, 138, 139
dominus negotii, *see* DOMINUS NEGOTII
donation, presumption against, **15**, 116
elements—
    absence, ignorance or incapacity of *dominus*, **15**, 95, 107–109
    administration of another's affairs, **15**, 95, 103, 104
    animus negotia aliena gerendi, **15**, 95, 110–116
    essential element lacking, effect, **15**, 137
    forms of *negotiorum gesta*, **15**, 96–102
    generally, **15**, 95
    initial utility of management, **15**, 95, 117–122
    intention of *gestor*, **15**, 95, 110–116
    negotium utiliter coeptum, **15**, 95, 117–122
    unauthorised and voluntary character of administration, **15**, 95, 105, 106
enrichment of *dominus*, limitation of *gestor's* claims, **15**, 137–141
forms, **15**, 96–102
future development, **15**, 86
future and past losses of *gestor*, **15**, 127
gains, surrender by *gestor*, **15**, 129, 133
gestor, *see* NEGOTIORUM GESTOR
health, preservation of, **15**, 102
impure, **15**, 137
initial utility of management, **15**, 95, 117–122
    assessment, **15**, 121
    necessity and utility, **15**, 120
    presumable wishes of *dominus*, **15**, 122
    role of initial utility, **15**, 117
    time of intervention, utility at, **15**, 121
    ultimate result of intervention, **15**, 121
    utiliter—
        meaning, **15**, 119
        requirement to manage affairs *utiliter*, **15**, 118
institutional writers, **15**, 112
intention of *gestor*, **15**, 95, 110–116
    family duty, presumption as to, **15**, 116
    generally, **15**, 110
    gestor's intent to benefit *dominus*, **15**, 113
    gestor's motive to benefit self as well as *dominus*, **15**, 114

Negotiorum gestio—continued
intention of *gestor—continued*
  institutional writers, **15**, 112
  ius commune, **15**, 111
  limitation of liability to expenses, **15**, 115
  presumption against donation, **15**, 116
  Roman law, **15**, 111
interest on capital, **15**, 133, 135
intromissions, duty to account, **15**, 129, 132
ius commune, **15**, 111
life or limb, rescue of, **15**, 102
litigation, intervention by *gestor*, **15**, 96, 101
loss, prevention of, **15**, 100
mandate, and, **15**, 91
  implied mandate, **15**, 91
maritime hypothec, not giving rise to, **15**, 94
meliorations, **15**, 96
money-lending, *gestor*, by, **15**, 133
necessity and utility, **15**, 120
negotiorum gestor, see NEGOTIORUM GESTOR
negotium utiliter coeptum, **15**, 95, 117–122
obligation arising from, prescription, **16**, 2116
obligations arising from, **15**, 90
origins, **15**, 88
possessory lien—
  whether *gestor* has, **15**, 128
  whether giving rise to, **15**, 94
prescriptive period in action arising from, **15**, 72
preservation of propery, **15**, 96, 99
pro-curatory distinguished, **15**, 92
pro-tutory distinguished, **15**, 92
profit, loss of, prevention, **15**, 100
property of *dominus* used in trade or business of
  gestor, **15**, 135
quantum of recovery, **15**, 89
reasonableness, concept of, **15**, 119
reciprocal rights, duties and remedies—
  actio negotiorum gestorum contraria, **15**, 123, 124
  actio negotiorum gestorum directa, **15**, 123, 124
  contrary actions, **15**, 123
  direct actions, **15**, 123
  duties of *gestor*, **15**, 129–136
  generally, **15**, 123
  rights of *dominus*, **15**, 129–136
  rights of *gestor* against *dominus*, **15**, 125–128
  transmissibility, **15**, 124
recompense, relationship with, **15**, 83
repairs, **15**, 95, 96
restoration of property, **15**, 129, 133
Roman law, **15**, 88, 111
salvage distinguished, **15**, 93
single isolated act, **15**, 96
standard of care, **15**, 136
sui lucri causa, **15**, 137, 138
three-party cases, **15**, 142, 143
ultimate result of intervention, **15**, 121
unauthorised character of administration, **15**, 95,
  105, 106
unjust enrichment, **15**, 2, 12, 65, 83
  distinguished, **15**, 89
use of term, **15**, 87
voluntary or spontaneous character of administration, **15**, 95, 105, 106, 122

Negotiorum gestor
animus negotia aliena gerendi, **15**, 95, 110–116
cautionary obligation, incurring, **15**, 96
death of—
  obligations of representatives, **15**, 130
  transmissibility of actions, **15**, 124
debts due by or to *dominus*, payment or
  collection, **15**, 96, 97
donation, presumption against, **15**, 116
duties—
  auctor in rem suam, **15**, 134, 135
  completion of *gestio*, **15**, 129, 130
  gains, surrender, **15**, 129, 133
  generally, **15**, 129
  intromissions, to account for, **15**, 129, 132
  negative duties, **15**, 134, 135
  not to commence new business or affair, **15**,
    131
  restoration of property, **15**, 129, 133
  standard of care, **15**, 136
enrichment claim, **15**, 94
enrichment of *dominus*, limitation of *gestor's*
  claims, **15**, 137–141
expenses and outlays incurred by, **15**, 89, 93, 126
  future and past losses, **15**, 127
  interest accrued, right to claim, **15**, 126
  limitation of liability to, **15**, 115
  unjustified enrichment of *dominus*, **15**, 137–141
general factor, acting as, **15**, 130
indemnity, **15**, 126
intention of—
  benefit *dominus*, to, **15**, 113
  benefit self as well as *dominus*, to, **15**, 114
  family duty, presumption of, **15**, 116
  generally, **15**, 95, 110
  institutional writers, **15**, 112, 112*n*
  ius commune, **15**, 111
  limitation of liability to expenses, **15**, 115
  presumption against donation, **15**, 116
  Roman law, **15**, 111
labour and services, no right to recompense for,
  15, 126
liability—
  fault in management, for, **15**, 136
  several *gestor's*, where, **15**, 130, 132
litigation, intervention in, **15**, 101
management of another's affairs—
  in bona fide belief they are *gestor's* own, **15**,
    137, 140
  dominus and *gestor* both interested, where, **15**,
    104
  dominus minor or pupil, where, **15**, 137, 141
  express wishes of *dominus*, against, **15**, 137, 138,
    139
  fault in, liability, **15**, 136
  generally, **15**, 95, 103
  impure *gestio*, **15**, 137
  for own benefit, **15**, 137, 138
mandate, must act without, **15**, 91
meaning, **15**, 87
money-lending by, **15**, 133
obligation to *dominus*, **15**, 90
possessory lien, whether possessing, **15**, 128
pro-curator compared, **15**, 92

Negotiorum gestor—continued
pro-tutor compared, **15**, 92
relief from obligations, **15**, 127
rights against *dominus*—
    generally, **15**, 125
    indemnity of *gestor*, **15**, 126
    possessory lien, **15**, 128
    relief from obligations, **15**, 127
several *gestor's*, where, **15**, 130, 132
three-party cases, **15**, 142, 143
unjustified enrichment of *dominus*, **15**, 137–141
voluntary or spontaneous character of administra-
    tion, **15**, 95, 105, 106, 122
Negotium utiliter coeptum
negotiorum gestio, **15**, 117–122
Neighbours
legal advice and assistance over, **13**, 1028
Nemo dat quod non habet
See TRANSFER OF OWNERSHIP
Nemo debet locupletari ex aliena jactura
unjustified enrichment, **15**, 60, 60n, 65, 74
Nephew
deceased specified relative, as, **15**, 602
Nervous shock
See CARE, DUTY OF
Net charterparty
generally, **21**, 534n
Net and coble
annual close time, **11**, 15
bag net, **11**, 11
coble, meaning, **11**, 3n
definition, **11**, 11
fly net, **11**, 11
lease of fishings, **11**, 9
River Tweed, **11**, 43
salmon fishing, **11**, 3, 5, 11, 188; **18**, 326
stake net, **11**, 11
Netherlands
Civil Code, **24**, 124
civil jurisdiction, contracting state, as, **4**, 22
competition rules, application, **4**, 1304
European Union customs territory, **7**, 1010
no-passport excursions to, **12**, 132
sources of private international law, **17**, 111
Neutral goods
contraband, as, **17**, 419
droits of Crown, as, **17**, 407
Neutral ship
blockade, attempting to break, **17**, 413
capture, **17**, 412
contraband carried to enemy in, **17**, 414
droits of Crown, as, **17**, 407
Neutrality
declaration of, **7**, 857
New Jason clause
bill of lading, express terms, **21**, 546
general average, **21**, 704n
time charterparty, **21**, 640
voyage charterparty, **21**, 618
New Licht
generally, **3**, 1637
seceders, **3**, 1636
New Roads by New Means **Green Paper**, **20**, 607

New town
annual grant, **11**, 1920
burial grounds, in, **23**, 376
churches, in, **23**, 376
creation of, **23**, 359
designated area, reduction of, **23**, 364
designation of site of, procedure for, **23**, 363
development corporation, *see* NEW TOWN
    DEVELOPMENT CORPORATION
future of, **23**, 384
generally, **23**, 359
legislation, **23**, 360, 361, 386
licensed premises in, **2**, 17; **23**, 370
open spaces, **23**, 376
planning control in, **23**, 368
proposed, designation of site, **23**, 362
rental income, **11**, 1920
roads authority, acquisition of land by, **20**, 715
special development orders, **23**, 369
New town development corporation
accounts, **23**, 383
advances to, **23**, 380
annual reports, **23**, 383
building, provision of, **23**, 378
enterprise zone, establishment of, **23**, 114
general powers of, **11**, 1920; **23**, 367
grants, **23**, 380
information to be supplied by, **23**, 383
land—
    acquisition of, **23**, 371
    compulsory acquisition of, **23**, 372, 373, 374
    disposal of, **23**, 377
    roads, acquisition for, **23**, 375
lessor, as, **13**, 182
local authority, co-operation with, **23**, 379
members, appointment and conduct of, **23**, 366
objects of, **23**, 367
operations, provision of, **23**, 378
Parliamentary Commissioner for Administration,
    investigation by, **23**, 367
planning system, role in, **23**, 19
Secretary of State, payment to, **23**, 382
Treasury guarantees, **23**, 381
winding up of, **23**, 385
New Zealand
constitutional amendments, **5**, 307
Newspaper
advertisement—
    election campaign, **15**, 1242
    notice of provisional order, **19**, 11, 12, 13
copies to be delivered to certain libraries, **17**, 5
investment advice, publication, **12**, 1307
limits on authors' and directors' rights of
    identification, **18**, 1134
meaning, **15**, 536; **17**, 20n
merger, consent to, **17**, 2
merger, control, **4**, 1269
racing tips supplied to, **19**, 1298
reports, qualified privilege, **15**, 536
representative of, **12**, 247
VAT zero-rating, **7**, 1447
Next of kin
body, entitlement to arrange disposal of, **3**, 503,
    506

Next of kin—*continued*
common law concept, **25**, 1045
debts of, **25**, 1058
meaning, **12**, 1268; **13**, 1627; **25**, 879
Next Step Agency
generally—
chief executive, **7**, 755
status, **7**, 755
United Kingdom Passport Agency, **16**, 1214, 1214n
Nexum
meaning, **13**, 1703
mutuum, replacement by, **13**, 1703
Nexus
arrestment, **8**, 285, 286
effect of diligence, **8**, 115
litigiosity, and, **8**, 116
meaning, **8**, 115, 286
Nicotinic acid
meat, added to, **11**, 374n
Niece
deceased specified relative, as, **15**, 602
Night
oil, transfer of, **9**, 1211
poaching, *see* POACHING
shooting—
deer, **11**, 934–936, 940
ground game, **11**, 828, 872
Night bakeries
adult males in, **9**, 70
Nightworker
unemployment benefit, calculation of entitlement
to, **21**, 813
Nitrate mixture
explosive, as, **10**, 1588
Nitro-compound
explosive, as, **10**, 1588
Nitro-glycerine
explosive, as, **10**, 1586
Nitrogen dioxide
air quality, **9**, 1148
Nobile officium
arbitration, and, **6**, 924
children's hearing, application in respect of, **3**, 1386
common law power of intervention, **6**, 870
Court of Session jurisdiction, **4**, 4, 26, 28, 1000
generally, **1**, 332; **6**, 924, 926; **22**, 426–430, 547, 583
High Court of Justiciary, **6**, 870
modern exercise of, **22**, 431
officium ordinarum distinguished, **22**, 426–430
petition to, **6**, 865, 870; **17**, 883
pre-nineteenth century exercise of, **22**, 430
reduction, action of, **1**, 325, 331; **6**, 924, 1060
remedy of, **13**, 86
use of, **1**, 332
when power available, **6**, 870
Noise
abatement notice—
appeal against, **9**, 1250
contravention of, **9**, 1251
local authority, service by, **9**, 1249
abatement order, making of, **9**, 1259
abatement zone, designation of, **9**, 1258

Noise—*continued*
aerodromes—
charges, fixing by reference to noise and
vibration, **2**, 1023
damage caused by, **2**, 1020
generally, **9**, 1283
insulation grant schemes, **2**, 1022
military aerodromes, **2**, 1022
noise certificates, **2**, 1025; **9**, 1280–1282
nuisance, **2**, 1021
planning controls, **9**, 1285
regulation of, **2**, 933, 1042; **9**, 1283
sound-proofing buildings, **2**, 1022; **9**, 1284
vibration, **9**, 1283
aircraft—
aircraft operator's duties as to, **9**, 1278
certificate—
generally, **2**, 1025; **9**, 1280
issue of, **9**, 1281
offences in relation to, **9**, 1282
rules of, **9**, 1281
damage caused by, **2**, 1020
military, **9**, 1286
navigation, **9**, 1279
quiet areas, control in, **9**, 1276
regulation of, **9**, 1277
vibration—
aircraft operator's duties as to, **9**, 1278
regulation of, **9**, 1277
appeal—
abatement notice, against, **9**, 1250
construction site, notice as to, **9**, 1254
reduction notice, against, **9**, 1264
Secretary of State, to, **9**, 1269
building construction work caused by, as
nuisance, **3**, 155
byelaws, control by, **25**, 359
codes of practice for minimising, **9**, 1270
construction site, on—
appeal against notice as to, **9**, 1254
generally, **9**, 1253
prior consent for work—
appeal as to, **9**, 1256
generally, **9**, 1255
control of, **2**, 47, 98
degree, matters of, **14**, 2051
EU measures on—
directives on other subjects, **9**, 1302
general, **9**, 1299
motor cycle, **9**, 1301
motor vehicle, **9**, 1300
general regulation of, **9**, 1245
heavy industrial drop hammer, from, action to
interdict, **14**, 2039
hovercraft, **9**, 1287
insulation, **9**, 1296
land—
compensation, **9**, 1295
valuation, effect on, **9**, 1297
level—
contravention of requirements, **9**, 1262
exceeding registered level, **9**, 1261
new buildings, for, **9**, 1266
register, **9**, 1260

Noise—*continued*
local authority—
  byelaws, **9**, 1293
  execution of works by, **9**, 1268
  periodical inspection by, **9**, 1248
meaning, **9**, 1244
motor cycle, **9**, 1301
nuisance, constituting, **9**, 1246
occupational—
  codes of practice, **9**, 1289
  deafness, social security benefit for, **9**, 1291
  exposure, **9**, 1288
  factories, in, **9**, 1290
occupier of premises, summary application by, **9**, 1252
planning controls, **9**, 1294
plant and machinery, from, **9**, 1267
playing instruments, from, **9**, 1298
pollution—
  See POLLUTION
radios, from, **9**, 1298
reduction notice—
  appeal against, **9**, 1264
  contravention of, **9**, 1265
  generally, **9**, 1263
roads, on, **9**, 1257
singing, from, **9**, 1298
statute, regulation by, **9**, 1247
statutory defence, **9**, 1292
temporary interference caused by, **14**, 2052
time of day, effect on gravity of harm, **14**, 2054
traffic, **9**, 1271
vehicle—
  construction of vehicle, **9**, 1273
  EC measures on, **9**, 1300
  generally, **9**, 1272
  quiet areas, control in, **9**, 1276
  roads, use of vehicle on, **9**, 1274
  type approval of vehicle, **9**, 1275
Nom de plume
passing off, **18**, 1397
Nomen juris
identification of crime by, **7**, 74
Nomenclature Committee
European Union Common Customs Tariff (CCT), **7**, 1015
Nominate consensual contract
contract of sale as, **14**, 1004
hire contract as, **14**, 1004
Nominate offence
meaning, **7**, 24
Nomination
See ADMINISTRATION OF ESTATES
Non-administrative receiver
See RECEIVER
Non aedificandi
servitude, **6**, 515; **18**, 486
Non bis in idem
fundamental human right, as, **10**, 95
Non-fungible property
commodatum, contract of, **13**, 1785
meaning, **13**, 1707
mutuum contract, **13**, 1707

Non officiendi luminibus
servitude, **6**, 515
Non valens agere cum effectu
prescription, as defence against, **16**, 2127
Nonage
capacity, and—
  challenge to capacity, **25**, 761
  contract or grant deed, capacity to enter, **12**, 1229, 1231
  generally, **7**, 112, 159
  incapacity, **11**, 1053
defence, as, **7**, 112
  strict liability, where, **7**, 108, 159
generally, **10**, 1139, 1140
minors, of, **10**, 1139, 1140; **24**, 129
plea in bar of trial, **17**, 687
variation of trust because of, **24**, 78
Norroy and Ulster King of Arms, **11**, 1625
Norske Veritas, **21**, 120
North Atlantic Salmon Conservation Organisation (NASCO), **11**, 67, 104, 105
North Atlantic Salmon Convention, **11**, 103
North Atlantic Treaty Organisation
forces consignments, transit, **7**, 1169, 1172
generally, **19**, 702, 702*n*
NATO countries—
  service jurisdiction in, **2**, 619
  waiver of jurisdiction, **2**, 619
representatives, precedence, **16**, 2014
North Channel
innocent passage, right of, **21**, 10
North of Scotland Hydro-Electric Board
incorporation, **19**, 201, 209
North Sea Fisheries Act 1893 ..., **11**, 129
North-East Atlantic Fisheries Commission (NEAFC), **11**, 67, 89, 92
after 1981 ..., **11**, 94
before 1982 ..., **11**, 93
enforcement, **11**, 96
powers, **11**, 95
North-East Atlantic Fisheries Convention, **11**, 89
Northern Ireland
committee, **5**, 420
company carrying on business in, maintenance of overseas branch register,, **4**, 345
designated milk brought from, **11**, 465
enforcement of provisions, **5**, 612
exclusion orders, **12**, 134
housing benefit, **21**, 1101
income support, **21**, 1064
land boundary—
  goods exported across, **7**, 1155
  goods imported across, **7**, 1141
law and order, preservation of, **5**, 609, 610
mentally disordered patient absent without leave, **14**, 1423
Northern Ireland Office, **5**, 511
overseas company, **4**, 315
part of United Kingdom, as, **4**, 28
proportional representation, **5**, 378
proscribed organisations, *see* TERRORISM
representation at Westminster, **5**, 373

Northern Ireland—*continued*
terrorism—
    failure to disclose information as to, **7**, 625
    prejudicing investigation, **7**, 626, 626*n*
    prevention of, **5**, 611
    See also TERRORISM
Northwest Atlantic Fisheries Commission (NAFC), **11**, 67, 89, 92, 97–100
Northwest Atlantic Fisheries Organisation, **11**, 99
Norway
'annual of Norway', **24**, 302
Hebrides ceded to Scotland, **24**, 302, 304
law codes—
    Borgathing, **24**, 303
    Frostathing, **24**, 303, 315
    Gulathing, **24**, 303
    Heidsaevisthinglaw (Eidsivathinglaw), **24**, 303
political authority in Orkney and Shetland, **24**, 302
seabed, ownership of, **24**, 316
Notarial execution
blind testator, **25**, 725
docquet to be holograph, **6**, 432
illiterate testator, **25**, 725
meaning, **6**, 431
notary to have no interest, **6**, 431
procedure, **6**, 432
Notarial instrument
deed, as, **16**, 2109
Notarial protocols
See PUBLIC REGISTERS
Notary public
breach of fiduciary duty, reduction on grounds of, **13**, 44
Clerk to the Admission of Notaries Public, transfer of functions, **13**, 1151
contradiction of notarial deed, **13**, 1223
evidential quality of notarial act, **13**, 1223
functions—
    affidavit divorce procedure, **13**, 1223
    bill of exchange, protest of, **13**, 1223
    bonds of debenture, drawing for repayment, **13**, 1223
    company registration overseas, **13**, 1223
    conveyancing, **13**, 1220
    entry of person overseas, **13**, 1223
    generally, **13**, 1219
    maritime matters, protests in, **13**, 1223
    Matrimonial Homes (Family Protection) (Scotland) Act 1981, under, **13**, 1223
    modern day, **13**, 1223
    notarial instruments, **13**, 1221
    notarial protocol, **13**, 1221
        See also PUBLIC REGISTERS
    oaths, administration of, **13**, 1222, 1223
    powers of attorney for use abroad, attestation of authentication, **13**, 1223
historical background, **13**, 1212–1216
    Law Agents (Scotland) Act 1873 ..., **13**, 1215
    Law Agents (Scotland) Amendment Act 1896 ..., **13**, 1216
international recognition, **13**, 1212
noting, procedure for, **4**, 161

Notary public—*continued*
probativity of notarial act, **13**, 1223
Register of Notaries Public—
    admission to, **13**, 1217
    removal from, **13**, 1218
    restoration to, **13**, 1218
    transfer of functions, **13**, 1151
registration, **13**, 1151
Notice
blight, *see* BLIGHT
constructive, doctrine of, **4**, 326
deemed, doctrine of, **4**, 335
health and safety, *see* HEALTH AND SAFETY AT WORK
prescribed form, **12**, 1178
purchase, *see* PURCHASE NOTICE
termination of contract, *see* CONTRACT OF EMPLOYMENT
treat, to, *see* TREAT, NOTICE TO
Notice reference
meaning, **4**, 1261
See also COMPETITION LAW (anti-competitive practices)
Noting
procedure for, **4**, 161
Notour bankruptcy
See BANKRUPTCY; INSOLVENCY (apparent)
Nova Scotia, baronetage of
generally, **11**, 1621
precedence, **16**, 2005, 2019
Novation
assignation, advantages over, **14**, 1029
cautionary obligation, **3**, 850
discharge of contract in international law, **17**, 277
extinction of contractual obligation by, **15**, 865, 874
lessor, involvement of, **14**, 1029
Novel dissasine
remedy of, **15**, 215
***Novodamus*, charter of**
feudal conveyance, **18**, 94, 95
generally, **6**, 530
real burden extinguished by, **18**, 426
Novus actus interveniens
causation, and, **7**, 51
contributory negligence, **15**, 403*n*, 407
improper medical treatment, **7**, 54
legal causation, **15**, 431, 434
special susceptibility of victim, **7**, 55
third party intervention, **7**, 56
victim, act or omission by, **7**, 52
Noxious fumes or vapour
degree, matters of, **14**, 2051
physical damage caused by, **14**, 2045
Noxious gas or liquid
alkali works, escape of noxious gases from, **9**, 1113
ammunition containing, **10**, 1517
weapons designed for discharge of, **10**, 1516
Noxious substance
fishing with, **11**, 12, 21
food, as ingredient of, **11**, 325
industrial premises, emission from, **9**, 1114
postal packet, enclosed in, **16**, 1909
tenant's obligation regarding, **13**, 588

Noxious substance—*continued*
water, prevention of pollution from, **25**, 407
See also HAZARDOUS SUBSTANCE
Nuclear damage
liability—
  Athens Convention, **21**, 738
  Hague-Visby Rules, **21**, 611
  limitation, **21**, 757
Nuclear Industry Radioactive Waste Executive (NIREX)
responsibilities of, **9**, 1191
Nuclear installation
foreign operator, duty of, **9**, 1199
licensing—
  excepted matter, **9**, 1197
  generally, **9**, 1195
  licensee's liability, **9**, 1196
radiation, compensation for injury from, **9**, 1198
See also ATOMIC ENERGY AND RADIOACTIVE SUBSTANCES
Nuclear weapons
multilateral agreements on, **19**, 712
Nuclear Test Ban Treaty, **19**, 712
Nuisance
abatement—
  meaning, **14**, 2039
  noise, of, *see* NOISE
  potential, duty of occupier, **14**, 2041
  self-help, **14**, 2144, 2158
abatement by person affected, **13**, 92
absolute, **14**, 2006
acquiescence, **16**, 1617
  objection to nuisance lost by, **14**, 2128
  public place, invasion of interest in use and enjoyment, **14**, 2168
annoyance, *see* ANNOYANCE
architectural, **14**, 2014
building works, in relation to, **3**, 155
  delictual liability, **3**, 143
  generally, **3**, 155
  loss of business, **3**, 155
  remedies, **3**, 155
byelaws for preventing, **25**, 362
care, standard of—
  onus of proof, **14**, 2107
  subjectively measured, **14**, 2102
common, meaning, **14**, 2015
conduct causing invasion—
  aemulatio, **14**, 2070
  character of locality, suitability to—
    development plan, **14**, 2075
    evaluation of, **14**, 2074
  illegal motive, **14**, 2071
  liability, *see* LIABILITY
  malice, **14**, 2069
  object of, **14**, 2068
  onus of proof, **14**, 2107
  positive, liability for, **14**, 2103, 2136
  public interest, **14**, 2073
  relevant factors in evaluating, **14**, 2067
  remedial measures—
    failure to take, **14**, 2077
    practicability of, **14**, 2076, 2077
    reasonable care, **14**, 2076

Nuisance—*continued*
conduct causing invasion—*continued*
  social utility, **14**, 2072
  source of invasion, **14**, 2078
culpa, necessity for, **14**, 2005
damage—
  direct and consequential distinguished, **14**, 2010
  discomfort distinguished from, **14**, 2048, 2049
  physical, **14**, 2045, 2050
  remoteness of, **14**, 2156
damages for, **19**, 1245
defence to action for—
  abnormal danger, special use creating, **14**, 2109
  acquiescence, **14**, 2128, 2168
  contributory fault—
    common law, **14**, 2129
    statute, **14**, 2130
  general rule, **14**, 2109
  ineffectual, **14**, 2132
  legal and ultimate burdens distinguished, **14**, 2109
  prescription—
    continuous period, **14**, 2125
    declarator, **14**, 2123
    interdict, **14**, 2123
    limits on, **14**, 2124
    public place, invasion of interest in use and enjoyment, **14**, 2168
    reparation, **14**, 2123
    succession of interests, **14**, 2126
  public place, invasion of interest in use and enjoyment, **14**, 2168
  statutory authorisation—
    exoneration clause, **14**, 2116
    four rules, **14**, 2117–2121
    generally, **14**, 2110
    inadequate sewer, liability for, **14**, 2122
    inevitability of nuisance, **14**, 2112
    land compensation, **14**, 2115
    nature of, **14**, 2111
    negligence, absence of, **14**, 2117–2121
    non-exoneration clause, **14**, 2116
    nuisance clause, **14**, 2116
    public place, invasion of interest in use and enjoyment, **14**, 2168
    rejection of defence, **14**, 2113
    statutory powers and duties, **14**, 2116
    upholding of defence, **14**, 2114
  strict liability, **14**, 2131
  very high standard of care, imputed fault derived from, **14**, 2109
  volenti non fit injuria, **14**, 2127
earliest references to, **14**, 2001
encroachment—
  highway, on, **14**, 2164
  meaning, **14**, 2027
  nuisance distinguished, **14**, 2027
  ownership, vertical extent of, **14**, 2028
  tree, of, **14**, 2028
English doctrine—
  common nuisance, **14**, 2015
  comparison with Scots law—
    generally, **14**, 2018
    highways, **14**, 2166

Nuisance—*continued*
English doctrine—*continued*
  comparison with Scots law—*continued*
    identity of principle, **14**, 2025
    prescription, **14**, 2022
    public nuisance, **14**, 2020
    remedies, **14**, 2024
    scope, **14**, 2019
    title to sue, **14**, 2023
    unintentional harm, **14**, 2021
    private nuisance, **14**, 2015
    public nuisance, **14**, 2015
    Scots law, reception in, **14**, 2016
enjoyment of land, *see* PUBLIC PLACE
etymological derivation, **14**, 2001
factual, **14**, 2004
fault—
  categories of—
    conduct, **14**, 2087
    intent, **14**, 2087
    malice, **14**, 2087
    negligence, **14**, 2087
    recklessness, **14**, 2087
  contributory—
    common law, **14**, 2129
    statute, **14**, 2130
  wrong distinguished from, **14**, 2090
generally, **9**, 1107
harm, causing, *see* HARM
historical origins—
  aemulatio vicini doctrine of, **14**, 2007, 2008
  architectural nuisance, **14**, 2014
  burgh, application within, **14**, 2012
  direct and consequential damage distinguished, **14**, 2010
  English doctrine—
    common nuisance, **14**, 2015
    private nuisance, **14**, 2015
    public nuisance, **14**, 2015
    Scots law, reception in, **14**, 2016
  generally, **14**, 2007
  immissio principle in Digest, **14**, 2007, 2009
  neighbourhood, **14**, 2011
  public police, **14**, 2011
  sheriff, jurisdiction of, **14**, 2013
independent contractor, created by, **14**, 2138
industrial pollution, complaint of, **9**, 1117
inflammable materials, storage of, **19**, 383*n*
inherent ambiguity of term, **14**, 2001
invasion of interests, as, **14**, 2002, 2068–2073
legal, **14**, 2004
liability, **14**, 2017; **19**, 1245
  balancing process, determination as, **14**, 2040
  basis of, **14**, 2087
  delictual, **14**, 2097
  fault—
    categories of—
      conduct, **14**, 2087
      intent, **14**, 2087
      malice, **14**, 2087
      negligence, **14**, 2087
      recklessness, **14**, 2087
    wrong distinguished from, **14**, 2090
  feuar, of, **14**, 2141

Nuisance—*continued*
liability—*continued*
  harm—
    intentional, **14**, 2105
    negligent, **14**, 2106
    types of conduct creating, **14**, 2089
  inadequate sewer, for, **14**, 2122
  incidence of, **14**, 2135
  independent contractor, creation by, **14**, 2138
  infection, fear of, **14**, 2082
  land, source of nuisance arising naturally on, **14**, 2100
  landlord, of, for tenant's nuisance, **14**, 2140
  man-made nuisance, **14**, 2099
  nature, failure to abate nuisance created by, **14**, 2098
  occupier, of—
    failure to abate, for, **14**, 2139
    third person, nuisance by, **14**, 2142
    transfer of land, after, **14**, 2143
  onus of proof, **14**, 2107
  other grounds, **14**, 2108
  owner, of, for failure to abate, **14**, 2139
  policy considerations, **14**, 2091
  positive conduct creating nuisance, for, **14**, 2103, 2136
  reasonable tolerability, test of, **14**, 2037
  several defenders contributing to nuisance, **14**, 2137
  strict—
    abnormally dangerous thing or activity, doctrine of, **14**, 2093
    defences, **14**, 2131
    foreseeability, **14**, 2094
    highway, premises in disrepair near, **14**, 2101
    intentional nuisance, confusion with higher standard or care in, **14**, 2095
    interdict cases, **14**, 2094, 2096
    nuisance giving rise to, reasons for idea, **14**, 2092
    reference to, **14**, 2088
    reparation action, **14**, 2096
  summary of principles, **14**, 2104
  superior, of, **14**, 2141
  tenant, nuisance created by, **14**, 2140
  third person, failure to abate nuisance created by, **14**, 2098
  uncertainty as to principles, **14**, 2017
  weighing process, determination as, **14**, 2040
loose legal usage, **14**, 2001
meaning, **14**, 2001–2006
medieval assize, origins in, **14**, 2001
mine, use of land as, **14**, 1616
musical, **9**, 1039
negligence contrasted with, **14**, 2041
noise constituting, **9**, 1246
  See also NOISE
non-tidal loch, application of law, **18**, 308
non-tidal river, application to, **18**, 281
noxious fumes, as, **14**, 2045, 2051
occupier's enjoyment, infringement of, **14**, 2032
offensive trades, **19**, 378
open spaces, private, **19**, 356
origin of, **14**, 2078

Nuisance—*continued*
per accidens, **14**, 2006
per se, **14**, 2006
police powers, **16**, 1785, 1785*n*
pollution, *see* POLLUTION
private, **14**, 2015
protective measures—
    complainer, burden on, **14**, 2064–2066
    extent of, **14**, 2066
    want of, **14**, 2065
public, **14**, 2015, 2020, 2159
public health, **19**, 305, 306, 335–341
    anticipated, **19**, 339
    author of, **19**, 335
    entry, powers of, **19**, 338
    essential elements, **19**, 335
    flats, **19**, 341
    local authority duties and powers, **19**, 337, 338
    meaning, **19**, 336
    natural rights, infringing, **19**, 335
    public as sufferer, **19**, 335
    sheriff court proceedings, **19**, 340
    sufferer, **19**, 335
    tenements, **19**, 341
public place, defences to nuisance in, **14**, 2168
quarry, use of land as, **14**, 1616
railway byelaws concerning, **19**, 1015
reasonable care, **14**, 2076
reasonable tolerability—
    abatement of nuisance, meaning, **14**, 2039
    balancing process, determination as, **14**, 2040
    evidential aspects, **14**, 2042
    heavy industrial drop hammer, action to
        interdict noise and vibrations, **14**, 2039
    liability for nuisance, nature of test for, **14**,
        2037
    maxim alienum non laedas, **14**, 2038
    noxious vapours, physical damage caused by,
        14, 2039
    objective standpoint, assessment from, **14**, 2041
    water pollution, action to interdict, **14**, 2039
    weighing process, determination as, **14**, 2040
recreational nuisance, **19**, 1245
relative, **14**, 2006
remedial measures—
    failure to take, **14**, 2077
    practicability of, **14**, 2076, 2077
    reasonable care, duty to take, **14**, 2076
remedies for—
    comparison of Scots and English law, **14**, 2024
    damages, *see* DAMAGES
    generally, **14**, 2144
    interdict, *see* INTERDICT
    order *ad factum praestandum*, **14**, 2157
    self-help abatement, **14**, 2144, 2158
repossession, as grounds for—
    assured tenancy, **13**, 725, 733
    protected tenancy, **13**, 714, 716
road traffic, application to, **20**, 401
smoke emission from railway locomotives, **19**, 1052
source of, conduct of defender, **14**, 2078
statutory, **9**, 1108
statutory provision relating to, proposal to alter or
    repeal, **19**, 15

Nuisance—*continued*
support, right of, **14**, 2029; **18**, 256, 256*n*
tenement buildings, **18**, 243
tree—
    encroachment of, **4**, 2028
    felled to abate, **11**, 617
trespass, **14**, 2027, 2028
unprotected interests, **14**, 2032
variety of meanings, **14**, 2003
water rights, **14**, 2031
Nulla poena sine crimine, nullum crimen sine lege
principle of, **11**, 1012
Nullity of marriage
See MARRIAGE
Number
Interpretation Act 1978 rules as to, **12**, 1207
Nuncio
precedence, **16**, 2014
Nuremberg Principles
generally, **19**, 700*n*
Nuremberg Tribunal
war crimes, **19**, 695
Nurse-nursing
area nursing and midwifery committee, **11**, 1423
domestic tribunal, regulation by, **23**, 917
health boards, administration of nursing care, **11**,
    1410
legal control, scope of, **14**, 1101
licensing system, exemption from, **14**, 1203
midwife, *see* MIDWIFE—
    midwifery, maternity and child care
national nursing and midwifery consultative
    committee, **11**, 1419
non-designated services, **4**, 1177*n*
nursing services, provision of, **11**, 1476
professional conduct, **14**, 1148, 1149
qualifications—
    obtained outside UK, **14**, 1152
    United Kingdom, **14**, 1153
register—
    preparation and maintenance, **14**, 1150
    removal from, **14**, 1158
registration—
    eligibility for, **14**, 1152
    periodic, **14**, 1151
    renewable, **14**, 1151
regulation, framework of, **14**, 1147
restrictions on practice, **14**, 1156
sheriff court jurisdiction, **6**, 1116
training, **14**, 1148, 1149
training in, immigration rules, **12**, 292, 293
Nursery garden
landlord's hypothec, **13**, 513
Nursery school
appointment of teachers, **8**, 823
ineligibility for self-governing status, **8**, 779
registration, **22**, 2
statutory provisions, **22**, 2
Nursing home
birth in, **19**, 1442
Christian Science house, **11**, 1531
conduct of, **11**, 1530
death in, **19**, 1459

O

Oath
administration by notary public, **13**, 1222, 1223
allegiance, of, *see* OATH OF ALLEGIANCE
bankrupt, of, not evidence of loan, **13**, 1736
Coronation, **7**, 708, 709
Employment Appeal Tribunal proceedings, **6**, 989
evidence—
   form of, **10**, 548
   generally, **6**, 989
   interpreters, **10**, 551
   reference to, **10**, 621
   refusal to swear, **6**, 317
   witnesses, examination in court, **10**, 548
evidence on, generally, **6**, 989
executors, oath of confirmation, **25**, 1075-1077
false, taking, **7**, 512
False Oaths (Scotland) Act (1933)—
   generally, **7**, 516
   offences under, **7**, 516-520
false statement on, making, **7**, 517-520
form, **7**, 505
judicial, sheriffs to take, **6**, 1041
Lands Tribunal for Scotland, **6**, 1151
loan repayment, proof by, **13**, 1748
messenger-at-arms, taken by, **14**, 1501, 1502
perjury, **7**, 505, 512
proof of agreement by, **3**, 886
proof by, generally, **17**, 1132
proof of contract by, **13**, 1718, 1720
   bankrupt, oath of, **13**, 1736
   qualification—
      general rule, **13**, 1740
      intrinsic, must be, **13**, 1744
      not negativing loan, **13**, 1743
      oral, **13**, 1742
      parole evidence not to disprove, **13**, 1745
      written, **13**, 1741
religion other than Christianity, **7**, 505
sheriff officer, taken by, **14**, 1509
trust proved by, **24**, 13
Oath of allegiance
affirmation in place of, **7**, 706
breach, **7**, 506
form, **6**, 1041
Lord Lyon King of Arms, **6**, 1011
Lords of Appeal in Ordinary, **6**, 827
Member of Parliament failing to take, **15**, 1060
obligation to take, **7**, 706
sheriffs, **6**, 1041
Oath *de fideli administratione*
Lord Lyon King of Arms, **6**, 1011
Oath of verity
Poaching Prevention Act 1832..., **11**, 845
Obedience
employee's duty as to, **9**, 83
principle of equity, as, **11**, 1125
Obligation
ad factum praestandum, **15**, 7
adoption, **16**, 1643

Obligation—*continued*
antecedent, **11**, 757
building contract, *see* BUILDING CONTRACT
causation, *see* CAUSATION
cautionary obligations—
   disclosure—
      duty of, **11**, 775
      voluntary, **11**, 774
   induced by fraud, **11**, 774
   writing, must be in, **11**, 774
classification, **15**, 1-4
concept of, **11**, 1028
conditional, *see* CONDITIONAL OBLIGATION
conditions, fulfilment, **15**, 5
contingent, *see* CONDITIONAL OBLIGATION
contract, arising from—
   breach of contract, **15**, 3
   conventional obligation, as, **15**, 11
   generally, **15**, 1
   meaning of contract, **15**, 4
   voluntary obligations, **15**, 4
   See also CONTRACT
contract as, **11**, 1031
conventional, **15**, 1, 11
conveyancing, *see* CONVEYANCING
creditor, *see* OBLIGEE
debtor, *see* OBLIGOR
defamation, *see* DEFAMATION
delectus personae, where, **15**, 7
delict, *see* DELICT
derivation, **15**, 1
economic relationships, injuries to, **15**, 574-594
event, dependent on occurrence of, **15**, 5
family relationships, injuries to, **15**, 595-603
force of law, arising from, **15**, 1, 2
   negotiorum gestio, *see* NEGOTIORUM GESTIO
   strict liability, *see* STRICT LIABILITY
   unjust enrichment, *see* UNJUST ENRICHMENT
fraudulent preference, payment by, **11**, 781
frustration, *see* FRUSTRATION
future, **15**, 5
insolvency and bankruptcy, **11**, 776-781
interference with honour and reputation, *see*
   HONOUR AND REPUTATION, INTERFERENCE WITH
law of property and law of obligations, **18**, 1
liability, concurrent and cumulative, **15**, 9
non-voluntary, **11**, 1032
obediential, **15**, 1, 3, 4, 11
   unjust enrichment, *see* UNJUST ENRICHMENT
object of—
   act as—
      generally, **15**, 8
      obligee must have patrimonial interest, **15**, 8
      performance must be possible, **15**, 8
   ceased to exist, where, **15**, 8
   existence in doubt, where, **15**, 8
   generally, **15**, 8
   personal agreement not enforceable, **15**, 8

Obligation—*continued*
object of—*continued*
thing as, **15**, 8
yet to come into existence, **15**, 8
obligatory, meaning, **11**, 1027
obligee and obligor, **11**, 1029
parties to—
death of, **15**, 7
generally, **15**, 7
jus quaesitum tertio, **15**, 7
multiple obligors, where, **15**, 7
personal element in obligation, where, **15**, 7
persons other than parties not bound, **15**, 7
See also OBLIGEE; OBLIGOR
personal agreement compared, **15**, 8
personal element, effect, **15**, 7
personal right, as, **15**, 1
prescription and limitation, **11**, 1033
prevention of constitution of, **11**, 705, 706
promise, arising from—
generally, **15**, 1, 4
meaning of promise, **15**, 4
property, law of distinguished from law of, **11**, 756, 762
pure, **15**, 5
quasi ex delicto, **15**, 2
quasi-contractual, **15**, 2
quasi-delictual, **15**, 2, 3
real right distinguished, **15**, 1
simple (pure), **15**, 5
trust, breach of, **15**, 3
unconditional (pure), **15**, 5
unjust enrichment, *see* UNJUST ENRICHMENT
verbal injuries, *see* VERBAL INJURY
void, object of obligation ceasing to exist, where, **15**, 8
voluntary, *see* VOLUNTARY OBLIGATION
Obligee
death of, effect, **15**, 7
generally, **15**, 7
right of action against debtor, **15**, 1
Obligor
creditor's right of action against, **15**, 1
death of, effect, **15**, 7
generally, **15**, 7
joint and several liability, **15**, 7
liability, multiple obligors, where, **15**, 7
multiple—
in solidum liability, **15**, 7
pro rata liability, **15**, 7
representative of, creditor's right of action against, **15**, 1
Obscene material
import to United Kingdom, **7**, 1203
postal packet, enclosed in, **16**, 1909
publication—
children, protection of, **3**, 1242
publication, restrictions on, **17**, 40
Obscene message
telecommunications, sent by, **16**, 1959
Obscenity
broadcasting obscene material, **7**, 486
criminal, **7**, 486
deprave and corrupt, material calculated to, **7**, 487

Obscenity—*continued*
film shown to consenting adults in private, **7**, 13, 83
having or keeping obscene material, **7**, 486
Indecent Displays (Control) Act (1981), **7**, 488
indecent remarks and suggestions as breach of peace, **7**, 453
obscene article—
deprave or corrupt, liable to, **7**, 470
selling or exposing for sale, **7**, 13, 83, 469, 486
warehousing, **7**, 469
obscene material, meaning, **7**, 487
play, public performance of, **9**, 1044
printing etc. obscene material, **7**, 486
See also PORNOGRAPHY
Obstruction
armed forces, of, **7**, 602
building, as—
demolition of, **11**, 1989
meaning, **11**, 1989
enforcing officer, of, **11**, 29
examination of, **11**, 25
highway, on, **14**, 2165
offence, **14**, 1484
police, of *see* POLICE (resisting or obstructing)
police powers, **16**, 1785, 1785*n*
railway official, of, **19**, 1062
regulations as to, **11**, 32
road, of, *see* ROAD
salmon, obstructing passage of, **11**, 14, 19, 23
trees felled to remove, **11**, 617
Occupancy
right of—
liferent distinguished, **13**, 1606
matrimonial home, of, *see* MATRIMONIAL HOME
presumption in favour of, **13**, 1620
***Occupatio* (occupation)**
doctrine of, *see* OWNERSHIP
Occupation
liferent, **13**, 114
multiple, *see* HOUSING
occupancy agreement, **13**, 771
personal licence, **13**, 120
precarious possession, **13**, 119
right of, gratuitous, **13**, 118
shared, lease distinguished, **13**, 112
workplace, of, **9**, 124
Occupation lease
generally, **13**, 216
Occupational noise
See NOISE
Occupational pension
See PENSION
Occupational therapist
Council for Professions Supplementary to Medicine, **15**, 1516-1521
employment of, **11**, 1500
functions, **22**, 9
handicapped person, visits, **22**, 24
Occupier
common property, of, **19**, 355
heritable property affected by provisional order, **19**, 15

Occupier—*continued*
hotel, of—
  fire certificate, duties pending, **11**, 1734*n*
  liability, **11**, 1731
land, of—
  ground game—
    authorisation of other person to kill, **11**, 850
    rabbit clearance orders, **11**, 869
    right to take and kill, **11**, 850, 855
  seizure, powers of, **11**, 812
meaning, **19**, 15*n*; **24**, 447
personal comfort, interference with, **14**, 2044
potential nuisance, abatement of, **14**, 2041
premises, of—
  drains and sewers, rights and duties in relation
    to, **19**, 331
  inspection of, duty of, **14**, 2041
valuation for rating—
  'actual state' rule, **24**, 508
  generally, **24**, 447
  rateable occupation, **24**, 448
  rival occupancy, **24**, 451, 453
  subjects—
    actual use, **24**, 449
    permanent use, **24**, 450
    unoccupied, **24**, 450, 452
  unit of use, **24**, 451
  valuation roll, **24**, 432
Occupier's liability
actio de effusis vel dejectis, **15**, 151-153
actio de positis vel suspensis, **15**, 151-153
acts and omissions, **15**, 317, 323
adjoining proprietor, occupier's duty to, **15**, 151
burden of proof, **15**, 326
categories of person to whom duty owed, **22**, 651
compulsory purchase order, effect, **15**, 319
control of premises, **15**, 311, 319
Crown, application to, **15**, 330
culpa principle, **22**, 651
dangers protected against, **15**, 324
duty of care—
  extent, **15**, 325
  generally, **15**, 311, 317, 319
  hazards and dangers covered by, **15**, 324
  higher duty, where law has imposed, **15**, 328
  interests protected by, **15**, 323
  modification, **15**, 327
  nature, **15**, 325
English law compared, **15**, 313
entry at own risk, **15**, 329
escape of dangerous agencies from land, **15**, 187
exclusion, powers of, **15**, 319
failure to abate, **14**, 2139
fire in premises, for, **10**, 1475
footpath, public, **15**, 321
generally, **15**, 311, 312
historical background—
  Dumbreck, decision in, **15**, 314
  importance, generally, **15**, 312
  post-*Dumbreck*, **15**, 315
  pre-*Dumbreck*, **15**, 313, 318
hotels, **11**, 1731
interests protected, **15**, 323
land, **15**, 311, 319, 321

Occupier's liability—*continued*
landlord, liability, **15**, 311, 317, 320
Law Reform Committee for Scotland, 1957
  report, **22**, 651
liability, generally, **15**, 311
'mechanical jurisprudence', superimposition, **15**,
  314
modification, **15**, 327
negligence at common law, **15**, 318, 319
neighbour, no liability to, **15**, 311
non-occupier, liability, **15**, 311
occupation of premises, **15**, 311, 319
occupier, persons amounting to, **15**, 319
Occupiers' Liability (Scotland) Act 1960—
  effect, **15**, 316, 318
  enactment, reasons for, **15**, 316
  generally, **15**, 311, 317
passer-by, no liability to, **15**, 311
person, damage to, **15**, 323
premises—
  control, **15**, 311, 319
  generally, **15**, 317
  meaning, **15**, 321
  moveable property as, **15**, 317, 322
  notional, **15**, 317, 322
  occupation, **15**, 311, 319
property, damage to, **15**, 323
public right of way, where, **15**, 319, 321
pursuer's own fault, injury due to, **15**, 329
road, public, **15**, 321
standard of care, **22**, 651
statute law imposing higher duty, where, **15**, 328
sub-tenancy, where, **15**, 320
tenancies, **15**, 311, 317, 320
third party, nuisance by—
  consent to, **14**, 2142
  failure to prevent, **14**, 2142
third person, nuisance by, **14**, 2142
transfer of land, after, **14**, 2143
trespassers, **15**, 314
volenti non fit injuria, **15**, 329
Odal
See UDAL LAW
Odalsrett
See UDAL LAW
Odometer
alteration of reading, **6**, 114, 119, 171
OECD
See ORGANISATION FOR ECONOMIC CO-OPERATION
  AND DEVELOPMENT
Oeno Island
British Dependent Territories citizenship, **14**,
  1932
Off-market deals
insider dealing, **12**, 1502, 1523, 1524
  deals outside Great Britain, **12**, 1525
off-market dealer, meaning, **12**, 1524
Off-market purchase
own shares, purchase by company, **4**, 366
Off-sale licence
application for, **2**, 38
authorisation given by, **2**, 10
increase in, **2**, 9
permitted hours, **2**, 18, 19

Off-sale licence—_continued_
premises—
  alterations to, **2**, 36
  drinking in, forbidden, **2**, 79
  special trading hours for, **2**, 80
Sunday trading barred, **2**, 18
supermarkets, **2**, 10
trading hours, **2**, 18, 80
Offal
distribution, **11**, 416
imported, **11**, 416
public health nuisance, **19**, 336
Offence
arrest without warrant for, **17**, 598
bail, **17**, 634
charge, nature and case of accusation to be given in
  language understood by accused, **12**, 43
counselling, **7**, 183
crime distinguished, **12**, 1140
defence—
  legal assistance, **12**, 43, 52
    payment for, **12**, 43
  preparation of, **12**, 43
  witnesses, examination of, **12**, 43, 55–59
dismissal, reason for, **9**, 256
innocence, presumption of, **12**, 43, 53
instigation, _see_ INSTIGATION
meaning, **17**, 501
participation in commission—
  concert, acting in, **7**, 189
  degree of, **7**, 187, 188
  pre-involvement actions, **7**, 190
  unintended consequences, liability for, **7**, 191–
    193
police officer, committed by, **16**, 1771
  allegation of commission, **16**, 1777
  defence costs, **19**, 1777
  investigation of complaints as to, **16**, 1773, 1777
  punishment, **16**, 1776
presence at, art and part liability, **7**, 180-182
preventive powers of police, **16**, 1785
supply of materials or information, art and part
  liability, **7**, 185, 186
use of term, **7**, 23
Offender
after-care, young offender, for, **22**, 36
bail, **22**, 32
  See also BAIL
child or young person in adult court, **22**, 32, 33
community service order, **22**, 38
  See also COMMUNITY SERVICE ORDER
compensation, payment of, **17**, 803
detention, sentence—
  person under 21 years, **22**, 32
  requirements before imposition, **22**, 32
fine supervision, **22**, 36
  See also FINES
first time offender, **16**, 1403
  custodial sentencing, restrictions, **16**, 1435
  mandatory social inquiry report, **22**, 32
imprisonment—
  restrictions on court powers to impose, **16**,
    1403
  sentence, restrictions, **22**, 32

Offender—_continued_
parole, **22**, 35
  See also PAROLE
parolee as further, **22**, 35
probation, **22**, 34
  See also PROBATION
rehabilitation, **16**, 1483; **17**, 812
restitution, requirement to make, **17**, 803
social inquiry report—
  copy, requirement to provide for parent/
    solicitor, **22**, 32
  generally, **22**, 32
under twenty-one, **16**, 1403, 1404
  custodial sentencing, restrictions, **16**, 1438
  custody and treatment, generally, **16**, 1434
  female, **16**, 1434
  male, **16**, 1434
  young offenders institution, _see_ YOUNG
    OFFENDERS INSTITUTION
  Young Offenders (Scotland) Rules 1965, **16**,
    1406
young, _see_ CHILD–CHILDREN; YOUNG OFFENDER
Offensive trade
smells from, **9**, 1120
Offensive weapon
firearm as, **10**, 1506
meaning, **10**, 1506_n_
public place, use in, **14**, 1326
Offer
acceptance, **15**, 627
  agreement, and, **15**, 619
  agreement without offer and, **15**, 655
  battle of forms, **15**, 636
  communication—
    contract of cautionry, **15**, 642
    late, **15**, 645
    need for, **15**, 641
    post or telegram, by, **15**, 644
    what amounts to, **15**, 643
  conduct—
    implied or inferred from, **15**, 631, 633, 638,
      641
  counter-offers, **15**, 635
  definition, **15**, 631
  express, **15**, 631
  generally, **15**, 631
  identical cross-offers, where, **15**, 634
  ignorance of offer, in, **15**, 633
  implied, **15**, 616, 631, 633, 638
  mode prescribed by offeror, **15**, 637
  qualified, **15**, 635, 636
  silence—
    acceptance not implied from, **15**, 639
    amounting to acceptance, **15**, 640
  'subject to contract', **15**, 635
  time limit for, **15**, 648
  what constitutes, **15**, 631-640
  who may accept, **15**, 616, 632
  words, in, **15**, 631
  See also MISSIVES
addressee—
  class as, **15**, 627
  general public as, **15**, 627
  individual as, **15**, 627

Offender—*continued*
advertisements, **15**, 624
agreement without offer and acceptance, **15**, 655
auction sales, **15**, 625
communication—
    delivery, sufficiency, **15**, 629
    instantaneous, **15**, 629
    irregular, **15**, 630
    time of, **15**, 628
    unauthorised, **15**, 630
contract—
    offer ripening into, **15**, 631
    offers and invitations to treat, *see* CONTRACT
counter-offers, **15**, 635
cross-offers, identical, **15**, 634
delivery, sufficiency, **15**, 629
invitation to treat distinguished, **15**, 620
lapse, **15**, 616
meaning, **15**, 620
offeree—
    bankruptcy, **15**, 616, 653
    death, **15**, 616, 651
    insanity, **15**, 616, 652
    position of, generally, **15**, 616
    rejection by, **15**, 654
offeror—
    bankruptcy, **15**, 616, 653
    death, **15**, 616, 651
    insanity, **15**, 616, 652
    mode of acceptance prescribed by, **15**, 637
    position of, generally, **15**, 616
post or telegram, communication by, **15**, 644, 647, 648
promise distinguished, **15**, 615, 616
quotations, **15**, 626
revocation, **15**, 628, 647
self-service displays, **15**, 622
shop window displays, **15**, 621
tenders, **15**, 626
termination—
    bankruptcy, on, **15**, 616, 653
    death, on, **15**, 616, 651
    generally, **15**, 646
    insanity, on, **15**, 616, 652
    lapse of time, **15**, 648
    material change of circumstances, **15**, 650
    occurrence of condition, **15**, 649
    rejection by offeree, **15**, 654
    revocation, **15**, 628, 647
    withdrawal, **15**, 628, 647
unilateral promise to keep open, **15**, 616, 617
vending machines, **15**, 623
withdrawal, **15**, 628, 647
See also MISSIVES

Office of Fair Trading
booklets, **4**, 1121
codes of conduct, agreeing, **1**, 547
codes of practice, **6**, 23, 72, 158
competition policy, **6**, 13
conduct detrimental to consumers' interests, **6**, 16
consumer protection legislation, **6**, 13-24
Director General, *see* DIRECTOR GENERAL OF FAIR
    TRADING
establishment, **4**, 1121

Office of Fair Trading—*continued*
estate agents, **6**, 22
European Commission, liaison with, **4**, 1121
information and assistance, **6**, 24
licensing, **6**, 21
misleading advertising, **6**, 95
number of agreements sent to, **4**, 1155
OECD, liaison with, **4**, 1121
registration of agreements, **4**, 1180
staff, **4**, 1121; **6**, 14
traders' assurances, **6**, 18, 19, 20
UK authorities, attitude of, **4**, 1119
unfair conduct, meaning, **6**, 17
Office holder
Crown, servant of, **9**, 38
local authority, person employed by, **9**, 38
meaning, **9**, 38
membership of House of Commons, exclusion
    from, **5**, 379
termination of contract, **9**, 142
time off for, **9**, 94
Office premises
fire certificates, **10**, 1454
health and safety at work legislation, **14**, 705; **19**, 343
railway premises, of, valuation for rating, **24**, 725
tenancy not secure, **11**, 1937, 1943
valuation for rating, **24**, 687
Office of Telecommunications (OFTEL)
generally, **16**, 1923
licences granted, lists, publication, **16**, 1927
Officer of court
administration of property in dispute, **13**, 24
Officer of the law
evading police, **7**, 542
meaning, **7**, 539
resisting or obstructing, **7**, 539-541
See also POLICE
Officers of the Crown
Earl Marischal, **7**, 812, 815
generally, **7**, 811, 812
Great Chamberlain, **7**, 812, 813
Great Steward of Scotland, **7**, 812
heritable and non-heritable offices, **7**, 812
Knight Marischal, **7**, 812, 817
Lord High Admiral, **7**, 812, 816
Lord High Constable, **7**, 812, 814
Lord Lyon King of Arms, **7**, 812, 818
meaning, **7**, 811
Officers of State, *see* OFFICERS OF STATE
Parliament, attendance at, **7**, 81
Union, effect, **7**, 81
Officers of State
absolute privilege, **15**, 526
Advocate, **7**, 790, 792, 800
Chamberlain, **7**, 790, 800
Chancellor, **7**, 790, 791, 792, 793, 794
Clerk Register, **7**, 790, 792, 800
Clerk of the Rolls, **7**, 790
Collector-General of the thirds of benefices, **7**, 791
Comptroller, **7**, 790, 791, 792
Constable, **7**, 790
definition, **7**, 789

Officers of State—*continued*
Justice Clerk, **7**, 790, 791, 792, 800
Justiciar, **7**, 790
Keeper of the Great Seal, **7**, 804, 805, 864, 877
Keeper of the Privy Seal, **7**, 790, 792, 800, 804, 805, 866, 880
litigation involving Crown, role in, **7**, 801
Lord Advocate, **7**, 808
Lord Clerk Register, **7**, 804, 807
Lord High Chancellor, **7**, 804
Lord High Treasurer, **7**, 804
Lord Justice-Clerk, **7**, 804
Lord Justice-General, **7**, 804
Lord President, **7**, 804
Lord Privy Seal, **7**, 792, 866
Marischal, **7**, 790
Master of Requests, **7**, 792, 798
nomination, **7**, 792
oath or affirmation of allegiance, **7**, 706
officers of Crown, as, **7**, 791
Parliament, right to sit in, **7**, 791, 792
precedency, **7**, 793
present day, **7**, 805–810
President of the Council, **7**, 792, 793, 799
Privy Council, **7**, 790, 792
Regalia, safe keeping, repair and preservation, **7**, 804
Secretary, **7**, 790, 791, 792, 797
Steward, **7**, 790
Treasurer, **7**, 790, 791, 792, 793, 795
Treasurer-depute, **7**, 791, 792, 796
Union, after—
    effect of Union, **7**, 801
    generally, **7**, 789
    nineteenth century, **7**, 803
    present day, **7**, 804
    seventeenth and eighteenth centuries, **7**, 802
Union, before—
    early history, **7**, 790
    fifteenth and sixteenth centuries, **7**, 791
    generally, **7**, 789
    precedency, **7**, 793
    sixteenth and seventeenth centuries, **7**, 792
use of term in Scotland, **7**, 789
Vice-Admiral, **7**, 804
Official documents
documentary evidence, as, **10**, 594
Official Gazettes
documentary evidence, as, **10**, 593
Official notification
meaning, **4**, 333*n*
registrar, powers of, **4**, 333
Official Receiver
none in Scotland, **4**, 718
Official Roll of Baronets
Court of the Lord Lyon, **6**, 1017
Official secrets legislation
attempted offence, **7**, 637
crime and special investigation, in relation to, **7**, 638, 643
Crown servant, **7**, 639–647
defence, in relation to, **7**, 636, 641
disclosure—
    confidential information, of, **7**, 638
    foreign state, information entrusted to, **7**, 646

Official secrets legislation—*continued*
disclosures—*continued*
    information, safeguarding against, **7**, 644, 647
    lawful authority, without, **7**, 639
    protected information, **7**, 645
enemy, information useful to, **7**, 630
foreign agent, communications with, **7**, 631, 633
foreign embassy, offence by member of, **7**, 627
generally, **7**, 565, 627
government contractor, **7**, 639–647
incitement to commit offence, **7**, 637
intelligence services, member or former member, **7**, 638, 640
international relations, in relation to, **7**, 638, 642
Official Secrets Act (1911), **7**, 627–637
Official Secrets Act (1920), **7**, 628–637
Official Secrets Act (1989), **7**, 627, 638–647
penalties, **7**, 563
preparatory acts, **7**, 637
prohibited place—
    approaching or entering, **7**, 629, 632
    fraudulent means, gaining admission by, **7**, 634
    meaning, **7**, 629
    obstruction of guards, **7**, 635
sabotage, **7**, 628
safety or interests of state, purpose prejudicial to, **7**, 632
    proof, **7**, 633
security services, member or former member, **7**, 638, 640
spy, harbouring, **7**, 636
spying, **7**, 628
who may commit offence, **7**, 627
Offshore employment
discrimination, genuine occupational qualification as defence to, **9**, 368
industrial tribunal, jurisdiction of, **9**, 312, 331
Offshore installation
continental shelf, transboundary fields, **21**, 30
control of, **9**, 731–733
Court of Session, territorial limits, **4**, 2
employment of, **9**, 733
manager, **9**, 732
meaning, **9**, 732; **24**, 688
oil production, **9**, 731–733
police jurisdiction, **16**, 1804
sheriff court, territorial limits, **4**, 2
valuation for rating, exclusion from, **24**, 688
Offshore natural gas
consent for liquefaction of, **9**, 901
Oil
abandonment, **9**, 751
appraisal, **9**, 747
bidding agreements, **9**, 739
consortia, **9**, 738
continental shelf, transboundary fields, **21**, 30
conveyance, **9**, 845
derelict petrol tanks, **9**, 848
development, **9**, 749
discharge of, liability for, **6**, 1212; **11**, 1327
enterprise, excluded jurisdiction, **4**, 83
exploration, **9**, 746

Oil—*continued*
financing—
  generally, **9**, 752, 762
  licence, **9**, 755
  oilfield itself, **9**, 753
  operating agreement, **9**, 756
  other property, **9**, 760
  participation agreement, **9**, 759
  platform, **9**, 754
  securities, **9**, 761
  unitisation agreement, **9**, 758
generally, **9**, 721
generating station, oil-fired, **9**, 630
heating—
  operational safety, **3**, 208
  storage tank, **3**, 208
  VAT rating, **7**, 1461
joint operating agreements—
  assignment clauses, **9**, 744
  cash calls under, **9**, 742
  exploration, **9**, 746
  generally, **9**, 739
  operator under, **9**, 741
  sole risk clauses, **9**, 743
  unitisation, **9**, 748
  withdrawal clauses, **9**, 745
legislation, **9**, 723
licences—
  exploration, **9**, 727
  financing, **9**, 755
  generally, **9**, 726
  methane drainage, **9**, 730
  petroleum production, licensees' rights in respect
    of, **9**, 725
  production—
    landward areas, for, **9**, 728
    seaward areas, for, **9**, 729
marketing—
  competition law, *see* COMPETITION LAW
  exclusive purchasing—
    company-owned filling stations, **9**, 767
    motor fuels, **9**, 765
    petroleum products, application to, **9**, 766
  filling station—
    clauses, **9**, 776
    company-owned—
      advertising, restriction of, **9**, 794
      agreements not assignable, **9**, 798
      See also COMPETITION
      gallonage clauses, **9**, 801
      generally, **9**, 789
      hours of trading, **9**, 800
      licence—
        agreements, **9**, 790
        fee, **9**, 796
        typical conditions, **9**, 792
        undertakings in relation to, revision of,
          9, 791
      licensees—
        codes of practice for, **9**, 802
        position in Scotland, **9**, 804
      maintenance, **9**, 795
      motor-fuels, pricing of, **9**, 797
      operating conditions, **9**, 800

Oil—*continued*
marketing—*continued*
  filling station—*continued*
    company-owned—*continued*
      owner—
        obligations to supply, **9**, 799
        sanctions available on breach of code
          by, **9**, 803
        rent, **9**, 796
        repairs, **9**, 795
        sales promotion, **9**, 801
        solus agreement, **9**, 767
        solus tie condition, **9**, 793
        tenancies, typical conditions of, **9**, 792
    effect of invoking, **9**, 777
    EU law applicable to, **9**, 822-833
    financial loans, **9**, 787
    generally, **9**, 780
    heritable security, **9**, 788
    insolvency of retailer, **9**, 774
    meaning, **9**, 764
    motorway, **9**, 808
    petrol prices, indication of, **9**, 854
    privately-owned—
      cash advances, **9**, 787
      equipment—
        assignation, **9**, 786
        heritable or moveable, **9**, 785
        loan of, typical conditions for, **9**, 781
        products used with, solus tie restriction
          on, **9**, 782
        termination by lender, **9**, 784
      supply agreement—
        consideration, **9**, 769
        continuation clause, **9**, 772
        death of retailer, **9**, 773
        duration of tie, **9**, 770
    purchasing obligations, suspension of, **9**, 778
    solus obligation, nature of, **9**, 771
    solus tie condition, **9**, 768
    supplier's obligation to supply, **9**, 775
    supply obligations, suspension of, **9**, 778
    time of delivery, **9**, 779
    write-off period, **9**, 783
  motor fuels—
    meaning, **9**, 764
    solus trading in, general background to, **9**, 765
  restraint of trade between motor fuel suppliers
    and retailers—
    compulsory trading obligation, **9**, 839
    English decisions on, application in Scotland,
      9, 843
    generally, **9**, 838, 841
    petrol tie agreements—
      conveyances, restrictions in, **9**, 836
      duration of petrol tie, **9**, 834
      lease and lease back transactions, **9**, 837
      leases, restrictions in, **9**, 836
      loans, relating to, **9**, 835
      present regime of controls affecting, **9**, 844
      supply, **9**, 835
    positive trading obligation, **9**, 839
    resale price maintenance, **9**, 840
    selective price support in relation to, **9**, 842

Oil—*continued*
marketing—*continued*
  retail petrol suppliers, undertaking regarding, **9,**
    855
  scope of section, **9,** 763
  solus agreements—
    company-owned filling stations, **9,** 767
    motor fuels, **9,** 765
    other petroleum products, **9,** 766
North Sea reserves, **11,** 1302
offshore installations, **9,** 732; **21,** 30
offshore operations, **9,** 731
offtake, **9,** 750
petroleum-spirit, *see* PETROL-PETROLEUM-SPIRIT
pipe-lines—
  onshore, **9,** 735
  submarine, **9,** 734
pollution of sea—
  damage—
    civil liability, **9,** 1215
    compensation for, international fund for, **9,**
      1216
    limitation of liability, **21,** 757
  exploration operations, **9,** 1209
  generally, **9,** 1208
  harbour, discharge into, **9,** 1212
  land pipe-lines, discharge from, **9,** 1209
  night, transfer at, **9,** 1211
  oil records, **9,** 1214
  ship, from, **9,** 1210
  shipping casualties, **9,** 1213
rig, plant, as, **14,** 1012
rig or platform, ship, whether, **21,** 108*n*, 110
state participation—
  British National Oil Corporation, **9,** 736
  Oil and Pipelines Agency, **9,** 737
storage, **9,** 845
taxation, **19,** 1544
unitisation, **9,** 748
Oil market
Securities and Investments Board Core Conduct
  of Business Rules, **12,** 1399
Oil and Pipelines Agency
participation by, **9,** 737
Oil platform
action for recovery of possession, **18,** 159
securities over—
  common law, **20,** 266–270
  controlled waters, within, **20,** 271
  foreshore, platform on, common law, **20,** 268
  generally, **20,** 272
  land, platform on—
    common law, **20,** 267
    pipelines, servitudes for, **20,** 267
  licence to search for and get petroleum, **20,** 271
  offshore petroleum, meaning, **20,** 271
  pipeline—
    controlled, **20,** 271
    servitudes for, **20,** 267
  sea bed, platform on—
    common law, **20,** 269, 270
    sea, meaning, **20,** 271
    territorial waters, platform within, **20,** 269, 271
  statutory provisions, **20,** 271

Oil platform—*continued*
securities over—*continued*
  territorial waters—
    definition, **20,** 271
    platform outwith—
      common law, **20,** 270
      statutory provisions, **20,** 271
    platform within—
      common law, **20,** 269
      statutory provisions, **20,** 271
  ship, whether, **21,** 108*n*, 110
Oil tanker
disconnection of hoses, laytime, **21,** 681*n*
Old Extent
franchise based on, **15,** 1010
Old people's home society
friendly societies legislation, **12,** 601
friendly society, as, **12,** 679*n*, 685
generally, **12,** 694
valuations exemption, **12,** 717
Old Session
See AULD SESSION
Oligopoly
Monopolies and Mergers Commission, investigation
  by, **4,** 1248
Olive oil
composition, **11,** 370
Olympic Games, 19, 1205
Ombudsman
See COMMISSIONER FOR LOCAL ADMINISTRATION IN
  SCOTLAND
Omission
assault, when, **7,** 218
duty of care, *see* CARE, DUTY OF
element of crime, as *see* CRIME (elements)
meaning, **7,** 38
statute, in, not to be inferred, **12,** 1107–1110
Oneris ferendi
servitude, **6,** 515; **18,** 484
Onus reale
See REAL BURDEN
Open account
meaning, **12,** 1011
Open-ended investment company
meaning, **12,** 1325
shares or securities in, **12,** 1308
See also COLLECTIVE INVESTMENT SCHEME
Open market
concept, **25,** 60
meaning, **25,** 10, 60
tax purposes, valuation for, **25,** 10
value—
  articles of association, provisions of, **25,** 63
  meaning, **25,** 73
Open network provision (ONP)
EU telecommunications strategy, **16,** 1967, 1969
  ONP directive, **16,** 1973, 1974
Open University
funding, **8,** 1015
purpose and operation, **8,** 993
student, income support, **21,** 1067
Opencast coal mining
See MINES

Operating lease
bulk purchase, **14**, 1020
buy-back arrangement, **14**, 1020
car, **14**, 1020
computer, **14**, 1020
development, **14**, 1005
maintenance service, **14**, 1020
obsolescence risk, **14**, 1020
period of, **14**, 1020
product knowledge, **14**, 1020
profit, **14**, 1020
rentals, **14**, 1020
traditional lease, similar to, **14**, 1020
Ophthalmic services
accommodation, provision for, **11**, 1476
administrative authorities, **11**, 1402
area optical committee, **11**, 1423
arrangements for, **11**, 1463
charges for optical appliances, **11**, 1513
complaints, **11**, 1520
contractor—
    deputies, **11**, 1465, 1465n, 1467
    duties, **11**, 1467
    records of, **11**, 1467
diabetes, treatment of person suffering from, **11**, 1463n
disqualification of practitioner, **11**, 1521
doctor, referral to, **11**, 1467
executive councils, **11**, 1402
health boards, administration by, **11**, 1410
national optical consultative committee, **11**, 1419
non-designated, **4**, 1177n
obtaining, **11**, 1466
ophthalmic list, **11**, 1465
    application for inclusion, **11**, 1465
    copies of, **11**, 1465
    medical practitioners, **11**, 1465
    opticians, **11**, 1465
    reinstatement, application for, **11**, 1521
    removal from, **11**, 1465, 1521
    Tribunal, inquiry by, **11**, 1425
    withdrawal from, **11**, 1465
ophthalmic medical practitioners, qualifications of, **11**, 1464
Ophthalmic Qualifications Committee, **11**, 1464
opthalmic service committee, **11**, 1520
patients, services to, **11**, 1467
payments for, **11**, 1468
prescriptions, **11**, 1467
private practice, health service facilities used for, **11**, 1496
remuneration for, **11**, 1510
specified examinations, **11**, 1467
    written statements as to, **11**, 1467
testing of sight, **11**, 1466
use of health service premises, goods or services, **11**, 1492
Opiates/opium
controlled drug, as, **14**, 1224
offences relating to, **14**, 1248
opiates as controlled drugs, **14**, 1224
Opinio juris sive necessitatis
international law, effect upon, **19**, 643, 643n

Oppression
abuse of power, **7**, 549
generally, **7**, 501, 548
meaning, **4**, 478n, 479
Optical appliances
charges for, **11**, 1513
Optician
complaints against, **11**, 1520
criminal convictions, **14**, 1169
discipline, **14**, 1168
disqualification of, **11**, 1521
domestic tribunal, regulation of, **23**, 917
legal control, scope of, **14**, 1101
misconduct, **14**, 1169
ophthalmic list, *see* OPHTHALMIC SERVICES
organisation of profession, **14**, 1165
registration, **14**, 1166
restrictions on practice, **14**, 1167
Options
generally, **12**, 1303
investment, as, **12**, 1308
London Options Clearing House, **12**, 1322
VAT zero-rating, **7**, 1433
Oral evidence
approach to witness, **10**, 535
bankers, **10**, 537
citation, appearance without, **10**, 536
civil cases, **10**, 538
compellability, **10**, 525
competence, **10**, 524
criminal cases, rules in—
    accused, generally, **10**, 539
    defence witness when co-accused, **10**, 542
    defence witness when tried alone, **10**, 541
    generally, **10**, 539-546
    oral testimony, principle of, **17**, 568
    persons not named in list, by, **10**, 546
    prosecution witness, as, **10**, 540
    prosecutors, **10**, 545
    socii criminis, **10**, 544
    spouse of accused, **10**, 543
diplomatic immunity, **10**, 526
examination of witnesses, *see* WITNESS
generally, **10**, 522, 523
incapacity of witness—
    mental, **10**, 532
    physical, **10**, 533
judge, by, **10**, 528
judge's function, **10**, 568
jurors, **10**, 529
meaning, **10**, 503, 523
member of Parliament, by, **10**, 527
objections to evidence, **10**, 567
parole evidence, *see* PAROLE EVIDENCE
party to case, **10**, 538
presence of witness in court, **10**, 534
privilege to withhold, **10**, 668
solicitor to party, **10**, 538
Sovereign as witness, **10**, 526
spouses, **10**, 538
written statement in lieu of—
    civil proceedings, **10**, 570

Oral evidence—*continued*
written statement in lieu of—*continued*
  criminal proceedings, **10**, 571
  general rules, **10**, 569
See also WITNESS (examination in court)
Oral message
conveyance of, contractual form, **16**, 1902
Oral statements
customary international treaty law, **19**, 636
Oral testimony
principles of, **17**, 568
Orchard
felling trees in, **11**, 617
pertinent, as, **12**, 1242
rating relief, **24**, 560
Ordeal
trial by, **17**, 541
Order *ad factum praestandum*
appeal against interlocutor making, **17**, 1253
competence of, **14**, 2157
Order in Council
announcement, **7**, 857
documentary evidence, as, **10**, 576
judicial review—
  exercise, ministerial powers conferred by, **22**, 173
prerogative legislation, **22**, 171
Privy Council—
  by and with advice of, **22**, 171
royal proclamations contrasted, **22**, 171
Order of the Thistle
Usher of the Green Rod, **7**, 829
Ordinarily resident
meaning, **14**, 1905
Ordinary causes
appeals—
  Court of Session, to—
    abandonment of, **17**, 1286
    effect of, **17**, 1283
    form of, **17**, 1284
    generally, **17**, 1280
    right of, **17**, 1281
    scope of, **17**, 1285
    time for, **17**, 1282
  sheriff principal, to—
    abandonment of, **17**, 1272
    decree, **17**, 1274
    expenses, **17**, 1271
    final judgment, against, **17**, 1256
    generally, **17**, 1254
    interlocutor, against—
      effect of, **17**, 1267
      form of, **17**, 1266
      hearing, form of, **17**, 1268
      incompetent interlocutor, **17**, 1265
      interdict, granting or refusing of, **17**, 1257
      interim payment, for, **17**, 1258
      leave, with, **17**, 1263, 1264
      order *ad factum praestandum*.for making, **17**, 1258
      proof, as to mode of, **17**, 1260
      reponing note, refusal of, **17**, 1261
      scope of, **17**, 1269
      sisting action, **17**, 1259
      time for, **17**, 1262, 1264

Ordinary causes—*continued*
appeals—*continued*
  sheriff principal, to—*continued*
    powers of sheriff principal, **17**, 1270
    right of appeal, **17**, 1255
    simplified divorce procedure, action under, **17**, 1275
  statutory applications and appeals—
    betting, gaming and lotteries, **17**, 1249
    firearms, **17**, 1250
    generally, **17**, 1248
    licensing, **17**, 1252
    race relations, **17**, 1253
    sex discrimination, **17**, 1251
    See also SHERIFF COURT
betting, relating to, **17**, 1249
decree—
  days of charge, **17**, 1205
  default, by, **17**, 1204
  extract, **17**, 1206
  grant of, effect of, **17**, 1203
defended—
  abandonment of cause—
    common law, **17**, 1080
    offer to, **17**, 1079
  closing record—
    joint motion, by, **17**, 1084
    procedure after, **17**, 1085
    sheriff, by, **17**, 1084
    stating preliminary pleas, **17**, 1086
    time for, **17**, 1083
  counterclaim—
    abandonment where lodged, **17**, 1047
    access to child, for, **17**, 1048
    civil jurisdiction convention, under, **17**, 1049
    custody of child, for, **17**, 1048
    lodging, **17**, 1046
    maintenance, for, **17**, 1048
  decree by default—
    generally, **17**, 1081
    reponing, **17**, 1082
  defences—
    form of, **17**, 1043
    lodging outside party, **17**, 1044
    order to be lodged, **17**, 1042
    skeleton, **17**, 1045
  expenses—
    interim—
      condition precedent, payment as, **17**, 1071
      generally, **17**, 1069
    security for—
      defender, **17**, 1074
      limited company, **17**, 1073
      mandatory, sisting of, **17**, 1076
      order to find caution for, **17**, 1072
      procedure, **17**, 1075
  interim decree—
    consignation of fund, **17**, 1067
    damages, **17**, 1068
    expenses—
      condition precedent, payment as, **17**, 1071
      interim, **17**, 1069
      reserved, **17**, 1070
    grant of, **17**, 1066

Ordinary causes—*continued*
defended—*continued*
   notice of intention to defend—
      aliment, minute relating to, **17**, 1035
      defences, necessity to lodge, **17**, 1034
      lodging, **17**, 1033
   pleadings—
      adjustment of—
         admissions, **17**, 1064
         alteration of sum sued for, **17**, 1061
         averments, **17**, 1065
         deleted admissions, **17**, 1065
         implied admissions, **17**, 1063
         procedure for, **17**, 1060
         purpose of, **17**, 1059
         pursuer, by, **17**, 1062
         roll, **17**, 1058
      amendment of—
         creditors, not to prejudice, **17**, 1094
         criteria for, **17**, 1091
         generally, **17**, 1087
         leave to amend, **17**, 1088
         parties, of, **17**, 1093
         procedure for, **17**, 1092
         proposal for, **17**, 1089
         time for, **17**, 1090
      preliminary pleas—
         competency, to, **17**, 1096
         generally, **17**, 1095
         no jurisdiction, **17**, 1101
         relevancy, to, **17**, 1097-1100
         res judicata, **17**, 1102
         statement of, **17**, 1086
   pleas-in-law, **17**, 1010
   process—
      borrowing, **17**, 1040
      custody, **17**, 1040
      documents, loss or destruction of, **17**, 1041
      lodging, **17**, 1039
   protestation, **17**, 1038
   sisting of proceedings—
      effect of, **17**, 1057
      generally, **17**, 1055
      legal aid, **17**, 1056
      recall of, **17**, 1057
   tabling—
      cause not tabled, **17**, 1037
      generally, **17**, 1036
   third party procedure, **17**, 1050
      grant of decree, **17**, 1053
      jurisdiction, **17**, 1054
      notice, **17**, 1052
      raising claim, **17**, 1051
   time to pay direction, application for, **17**, 1078
   unopposed motions, **17**, 1077
divorce, *see* DIVORCE
firearms, relating to, **17**, 1250
interim orders, *see* INTERIM ORDERS
licensing, relating to, **17**, 1252
mandatory, sisting of, **17**, 1076
multiplepoinding, **17**, 1199, 1246
proof, *see* PROOF
race relations, relating to, **17**, 1253
remitted from sheriff court, **17**, 1287

Ordinary causes—*continued*
rolls, remits between summary cause rolls and, **17**, 1310
sex discrimination, relating to, **17**, 1251
summary causes brought as, and vice versa, **17**, 1292
summary suspension of charge, **17**, 1247
time to pay—
   directions—
      generally, **17**, 1208
      lapse of, **17**, 1209
      recall, **17**, 1209
      variation, **17**, 1209
   generally, **17**, 1207
   orders—
      generally, **17**, 1210
      lapse of, **17**, 1211
      recall, **17**, 1211
      variation, **17**, 1211
undefended—
   decree in absence—
      amendment of writ, **17**, 1027
      direction, application for time to pay, **17**, 1024
      divorce, **17**, 1023
      extract of, **17**, 1025
      finality of, **17**, 1026
      granting, **17**, 1025
      minute for, **17**, 1021
      parentage, action affecting, **17**, 1023
      parental rights, **17**, 1022
      separation, **17**, 1023
   reponing—
      consignation, **17**, 1029
      Crown, special provision in decree against, **17**, 1032
      expenses, **17**, 1029
      grounds for, **17**, 1031
      method of, **17**, 1028
      sisting of diligence, **17**, 1030
      time of, **17**, 1028
writ—
   citation—
      certificate of, **17**, 1018
      form of, **17**, 1015
      generally, **17**, 1012
      period of notice, **17**, 1014
      simplified divorce procedure, in, **17**, 1019
      warrant of, **17**, 1013
   form of—
      backing, **17**, 1011
      condescendence, **17**, 1009
      crave, **17**, 1008
      generally, **17**, 1004
      heading, **17**, 1006
      instance, **17**, 1007
      pleas-in-law, **17**, 1010
      prescribed, **17**, 1005
      signature, **17**, 1011
   service—
      irregularity in, **17**, 1020
      outwith Scotland, **17**, 1017
      period of notice, **17**, 1014
      in Scotland, **17**, 1016

Ordinary deposit receipt
non-negotiability, **4**, 103
Ordnance maps
limitations of, **6**, 732
use of, **6**, 708, 731
Organisation
business, as, **7**, 1295
Organisation of American States
copyright, **18**, 1004
international law, as source of, **19**, 649*n*
Organisation for Economic Co-operation and Development (OECD)
accounting standards, group on, **1**, 76
Office of Fair Trading, liaison with, **4**, 1121
relation of European Community with, **10**, 299
Orkney
Act of 1611 abolishing foreign laws, **24**, 304, 319, 320
allodial land, transfer of ownership, **18**, 646
Code of Magnus 'the Law-Mender' (*Gulathing* law), **24**, 303, 304
customary law—
    distinction from common law of Scotland, **22**, 387
    reasonableness *Bruce v Smith*, **22**, 385-388
    udal rights—
        Bankton *Institutes*, **22**, 368
        Erskine *Institutes*, **22**, 367
        modern cases, **22**, 385-388
        Stair's *Institutions*, **22**, 366
earls of—
    laws enforceable by, **24**, 306
    relationship with Norwegian king, **24**, 302
    title granted by king, **24**, 306
feudal system—
    charters, **24**, 308
    infeftments, **24**, 307
foreshore, **24**, 314, 320
impignoration to Scotland, **24**, 301, 304, 317, 326
land measures, **24**, 311
landownership, udal law, **24**, 306
lawbooks, **24**, 303, 304
Lawman of, **24**, 303, 317
Norwegian Crown, political authority of, **24**, 302
population, **14**, 64
salmon fishings, **18**, 321; **24**, 315
scat, *see* SCAT
scattald, *see* SCATTALD
Scots law, application of, **24**, 301, 325
Scottish Crown's claim to, **24**, 302, 326, 327
Scottish influence, **24**, 317
seabed, ownership of, **18**, 310, 317; **24**, 316
sovereignty, **24**, 305
    Scottish, **24**, 326-400
    transfer from Norway to Scotland, **24**, 305, 326, 327
udal law, generally, **18**, 44, 47
urislands, **24**, 310
water authority, as, **25**, 505
weights and measures, **24**, 312
See also UDAL LAW
Orthoptist
Council for Professions Supplementary to Medicine, **15**, 1516-1521
employment of, **11**, 1500

Oslo Commission
abandoned or disused installations on continental shelf, **21**, 33
Otterboards
illegal use in trout fishing, **11**, 54
Ouncelands (eyrislands)
udal law, **24**, 311
Outer House
See COURT OF SESSION
Outer space
activities—
    licence—
        grant of, **2**, 1070
        requirement for, **2**, 1070
        transfer of, **2**, 1070
    meaning, **2**, 1070
    Scotland, provisions as to, **2**, 1070
international law, **18**, 198
leasing, **14**, 1095
treaty regime, **19**, 674
Output tax
See VALUE ADDED TAX
Over the Counter Market (OTC)
generally, **12**, 1303
market maker, value given by, **25**, 47
Overcrowding
alternative accommodation offered to protected tenant, **13**, 713
factory, **19**, 336
housing, *see* HOUSING
protected tenancy, of, as ground for repossession, **13**, 714, 724
Overdraft facility
building society, by—
    corporate body, for, **3**, 355
    power to make, **3**, 355
    to whom available, **3**, 357
local authority borrowing by way of, **14**, 817
unrestricted-use credit agreement, as, **5**, 809
Overflight
exclusive economic zone, **11**, 107
Overhead lines
See ELECTRICITY
Overriding interests
See REGISTRATION OF TITLE
Overseas company
See COMPANY
Overseas Development Administration
legal staff, **13**, 1418
Overseas secondary market
market maker, value given by, **25**, 47
Overseas stock exchange
market maker, value given by, **25**, 47
Overseas visitor
charges for medical services and supplies, **11**, 1518
Oversman
See ARBITER
Ovum donation
databank information on donors, limitation on access to, **18**, 1541
establishing maternity, **10**, 1150
Owner-occupier
home loss payment, entitlement to, **5**, 186
meaning, **5**, 189*n*

Owner-occupier—*continued*
supplement—
 first owner, payment to, **5**, 192
Owner-occupier
 unfit house, paid in respect of, **5**, 190, 192
 well-maintained payment, effect of payment of,
  5, 191
Ownership
abandoned property, **18**, 541
 See also CORPOREAL MOVEABLE PROPERTY
absolute right, as, **18**, 531
accession—
 nemo dat quod non habet rule, **18**, 676
 original acquisition, as, **18**, 597
 See also ACCESSION
accretion—
 heritable property, **18**, 677
 legal fiction, working by, **18**, 677
 meaning, **18**, 677
 moveable property, **18**, 678
 ratification by principal of transfer by agent, **18**,
  679
acquisition—
 corporeal moveable property, *see* CORPOREAL
  MOVEABLE PROPERTY
 derivative—
  meaning, **18**, 597
  See also TRANSFER OF OWNERSHIP
 original, **18**, 597
alienation, right of, **18**, 533, 535
allodial, *see* ALLODIAL OWNERSHIP
appropriation, *occupatio* (occupancy), and, **18**, 541,
 541*n*
capacity for, **18**, 599
co-ownership, *see* CO-OWNERSHIP
commixtion, **18**, 539, 564
 accession compared, **18**, 571*n*
 original acquisition, as, **18**, 597
common property, *see* CO-OWNERSHIP
confusion, **18**, 539, 564
 accession compared, **18**, 571*n*
 original acquisition, as, **18**, 597
corporeal moveable property—
 abandonment, **18**, 568
 destruction, **18**, 568
 extinction, **18**, 568
 presumption of, arising from possession, **18**,
  114
 See also CORPOREAL MOVEABLE PROPERTY
definition, **18**, 531
derivative, **18**, 539
derivative acquisition—
 meaning, **18**, 597
 See also TRANSFER OF OWNERSHIP
dominium, *see* DOMINIUM
encroachment on land, ownership of encroaching
 thing, **18**, 179
English law compared, **18**, 531, 531*n*
fact and law, as matter of, **18**, 114
feudal system, *see* FEUDAL LAW
inalienable property, **18**, 600
insurable interest, **12**, 851
joint property, *see* CO-OWNERSHIP
land, of, *see* LAND; LANDOWNERSHIP

Ownership—*continued*
lost and abandoned property, **18**, 568
 nemo dat quod non habet rule, **18**, 676
 See also CORPOREAL MOVEABLE PROPERTY
nemo dat quod non habet rule, *see* TRANSFER OF
 OWNERSHIP
nullius est fit domini regis, **18**, 540
occupatio (occupation)—
 acquisition of title by, **19**, 667
 appropriation, **18**, 541, 541*n*
 game and game legislation, **18**, 541, 544, 545
 international law, **18**, 558
 meaning, **18**, 539, 540
 original acquisition, as, **18**, 597
 royal fish, **18**, 541, 542, 543
 scope, **18**, 540
 terra nullius, title to, **19**, 667
 things never owned, **18**, 540
 things once owned but no longer having
  owner, **18**, 540
 things which can be acquired, **11**, 1102; **18**, 542
 trespass, law of, in relation to, **18**, 541
 wildlife conservation, **18**, 546
original, **18**, 539
ownerless property, Crown ownership, **18**, 540,
 547
ownership may not be owned, **18**, 652
possession—
 benefit of ownership, as, **18**, 130
 corporeal moveable property, **18**, 531, 565
  positive prescription, **18**, 539, 565, 566
 defence of, generally, **18**, 174
 ownership distinguished, **18**, 114
 possession signifies ownership, presumption as
  to, **18**, 130
 prerequisite to ownership, where, **18**, 116
 right to, **18**, 127, 151
pre-emption, property subject to right of, **18**, 600
prescription—
 corporeal moveable property—
  generally, **18**, 565
  loss of ownership rights by, **18**, 569
  negative, **18**, 567
  positive, **18**, 539, 565, 566
 positive, original acquisition, as, **18**, 597
pro indiviso—
 defining characteristic, **18**, 17
 See also CO-OWNERSHIP
registration of title, original acquisition, as, **18**, 597
reputed, **18**, 532
right, holder of, owner, as, **18**, 16
right of, content, **18**, 533
rights carried by, **18**, 114
Scots law, generally, **18**, 531
specificatio (specification)—
 accession compared, **18**, 571*n*
 case law, **18**, 562
 common property, original acquisition, **18**, 22*n*
 definition, **18**, 559
 institutional writers, **18**, 561
 meaning, **18**, 539, 559
 nemo dat quod non habet rule, **18**, 676
 original acquisition, as, **18**, 597
 Roman law, **18**, 560

Ownership—*continued*
specificatio (specification)—*continued*
   Scottish Law Commission proposals, **18**, 563
spuilzie, and, **18**, 162
subordinate rights, grant of, **18**, 533, 534
traditio, **18**, 116
traditionibus non nudis pactis dominia rerum transferuntur rule, **18**, 606
transfer of, *see* TRANSFER OF OWNERSHIP
treasure, **18**, 553
unititular nature of Scots law, **18**, 603, 644
wreck—
   common law, **18**, 554
   Merchant Shipping Acts, **18**, 555, 556
   title to wreck, **18**, 556
   unclaimed, **18**, 556
See also DOMINUIM

Oysters
bed, lease, **13**, 205
heritable or moveable property, whether, **18**, 331
inter regalia minora, as, **18**, 521
ownership, **18**, 331, 331*n*
Oyster Fisheries (Scotland) Act 1840..., **11**, 121
oyster rights, dredging of harbours, **6**, 1141
prohibition on sale of, **11**, 167
right to gather—
   acquisition, **18**, 332
   foreshore, in relation to, **18**, 318
   public rights, **18**, 333
   regalian right, as, **18**, 210
   separate tenement, as, **18**, 210, 319, 332, 332*n*
   statutory regulation, **18**, 332
Sea Fisheries Act 1883..., **11**, 125
valuation for rating, **24**, 661

P

Package deal contract
building contracts, **3**, 9
Packaged goods
checking and quality control, **6**, 259
codes of practice, **6**, 260
EU average system, **6**, 176, 256, 259
EU mark, **6**, 262
inadequate packages, **6**, 261
multipacked food, **6**, 206
package, meaning, **6**, 257
packers' and importers' duties, **6**, 259
predetermined constant quantity, **6**, 258
prepacked—
    food, **6**, 227, 228, 253
    meaning, **6**, 194
    offences relating to sale of, **6**, 251
    required to be, **6**, 248
prescribed goods, meaning, **6**, 257
See also LABELLING; PACKAGING
Packaging
dangerous substances, of, **9**, 851
explosives, **10**, 1617
gunpowder, **10**, 1605, 1608
medicinal product of, **14**, 1211
temporary importation, **7**, 1187
trade marks, *see* TRADE MARK
See also PACKAGED GOODS
Packer
food, of, notification of sampling, **11**, 338
right of lien, **20**, 79
Packet switching technology
telecommunication system, use by, **16**, 1934*n*
Pacta de quota litis
advocate or solicitor, between, **15**, 769
Pacta illicita
See CONTRACT
Pacta sunt servanda **rule**
treaties, **19**, 621
Paid-up shares
meaning, **4**, 351
Paint
weights and measures legislation, **6**, 243, 244
Paint removers and thinners
weights and measures legislation, **6**, 244
Painter and Limner
royal household, **7**, 847
Painting
copyright, **18**, 931, 958
Panel on Takeovers and Mergers
declaratory order by court into decision of, **4**, 542
judicial review of decisions of, **4**, 542
self-regulation, **4**, 541, 542
Parachuting, **19**, 1287
Parade
circus, **9**, 1033
identification, *see* IDENTIFICATION PARADE
Parallel Convention
generally, **8**, 429

Paramedical services
national paramedical (therapeutic) consultative
    committee, **11**, 1419
VAT exemption, **7**, 1426
Pardon
effect of, **17**, 885
pre-trial procedure, **17**, 554
royal, **7**, 727, 727*n*
solemn appeals, **17**, 833
Parent
access, rights of, where child in local authority
    care, **3**, 1270
adopted children, **10**, 1147
alcoholic, **3**, 1267
behavioural problem, with, **3**, 1350
child appearing in adult court, social inquiry
    reports, **22**, 32
children's hearing—
    appeal against decision of, **3**, 1358
    attendance at, **3**, 1321
        adopted child, parent of, **3**, 1321
        exclusion from, **3**, 1320
        expenses, reimbursement, **3**, 1322
        guardian, **3**, 1321
        illegitimate child, parent of, **3**, 1321
        non-attendance, offence, as, **3**, 1321
        persons believed by child to be parents, **3**,
          1321
        presence dispensed with, where, **3**, 1321
        unmarried parents, **3**, 1321, 1322
        who qualifies as parent, **3**, 1321
    discussion, **3**, 1344
    grounds of referral, statement of, **3**, 1292
    involvement with, **3**, 1279
    notification of decision, **3**, 1353
    notification of hearing, **3**, 1291
    referral of child by parent, **3**, 1287
    representation at, **3**, 1322
    right to be present at, **3**, 1321, 1344
    statement of reasons, entitlement to see, **3**,
      1294
curators, as, **11**, 1209
death of, **11**, 1211
    guardian's allowance where both parents dead,
      21, 953
    nationality at time of, **14**, 1909
    surviving parent, **11**, 1214
    tutors testamentar or nominate, **11**, 1214
delict by child, responsibility, **15**, 603
disputes, **11**, 1209
divorce, effect of, **11**, 1210
duty of care, **11**, 1015; **15**, 299
    duty to rescue child, **15**, 304
estate of child, management of, **11**, 1214
family relationships, **11**, 1068
father and mother, equal rights of, **11**, 1209
guardians, as, **11**, 1208-1213
immediate family, as, **15**, 601
insolvent, **11**, 1214

Parent—*continued*
legitimacy and illegitimacy, **10**, 1147, 1148
liability of, **11**, 1225
meaning, **12**, 279
mental disorder, with, **3**, 1267
mentally handicapped person of, duty of education department to inform, **22**, 31
moveable succession, **25**, 682
non-voluntary obligations, **11**, 1032
parentage, *see* PARENTAGE
parental rights, *see* PARENTAL RIGHTS
permanent disability, with, **3**, 1267
private international law, rights of—
    custody, **17**, 237
    generally, **17**, 236
    property, **17**, 238
    will, revocation of, **17**, 348
reporter, referral of child to, **3**, 1287
status, concept of, **11**, 1068
trans-sexual, **11**, 1038
tutors, as, **11**, 1209
tutors testamentar or nominate, appointment of, **11**, 1214
undue influence, **25**, 764
unmarried parents, child of, **11**, 1209
See also CHILD-CHILDREN
Parentage
action affecting, **17**, 1023
blood test evidence, **10**, 1163
corroboration by false denial, abolition of, **10**, 1160
declarator of, action for, **10**, 1160-1164
disputes over, generally, **10**, 1160
DNA fingerprinting, **10**, 1164
establishing maternity—
    generally, **10**, 1149
    ovum donation, **10**, 1150
    surrogacy, **10**, 1151, 1152
        contracts, **10**, 1153
        custody of surrogate child, **10**, 1154
establishing paternity—
    artificial insemination, **10**, 1159
    pater est quem nuptiae demonstrant presumption, **10**, 1155
        rebuttal of, **10**, 1156
    registration as father of child, **10**, 1158
    statutory presumption, **10**, 1157
gestation periods, **10**, 1161
incidental finding of, sheriff court jurisdiction, **4**, 5
non-parentage, action for, **10**, 1160-1164
    jurisdiction, **4**, 5, 68; **10**, 1160
physical resemblance, **10**, 1162
rebuttable presumption in favour of, **10**, 750
status, action relating to, **4**, 68
surrogacy, **10**, 1151-1154
Parental rights
abduction of child, **10**, 1225, 1342
access—
    adopted children, **10**, 1296
        adoption orders, **10**, 1303
    Hague Convention on the Civil Aspects of International Child Abduction, **10**, 1341
    how applications arise, **10**, 1298
    illegitimate children, **10**, 1295

Parental rights—*continued*
access—*continued*
    Law Reform (Parent and Child) (Scotland) Act 1986—
        under, **10**, 1298-1302
    legitimate children, **10**, 1294
    nature of right, **10**, 1293
    stepchildren, **10**, 1297
    welfare of child—
        assessment of, **10**, 1299
        child's views, **10**, 1302
        emotional, **10**, 1301
        physical, **10**, 1300
adopted children, custody of, **10**, 1279
adoption, agreement to, **10**, 1202
    agreement dispensed with, **10**, 1202
    freeing orders, **10**, 1202, 1203
        criterion for, **10**, 1204
        effect, **10**, 1204
    parent or guardian—
        abandoning or neglecting child, **10**, 1209
        failing to discharge parental duties, **10**, 1208
        ill-treating child, **10**, 1210, 1211
        incapable of agreeing, **10**, 1206
        protection of child from abuse or neglect, **10**, 1212
        withholding agreement unreasonably, **10**, 1207
    withdrawal of, **10**, 1202, 1205
aliment, parental right of, abolition, **10**, 1259, 1261, 1262
application for, **10**, 1267; **11**, 1209
assessing child's welfare, **10**, 1284
court's powers, **10**, 1273; **11**, 1212
criteria for court's decision, **10**, 1272
curator, *see* CURATOR
custody, **10**, 1259
    adopted children, **10**, 1279
    assessing child's welfare, **10**, 1284
    behaviour of applicant, **10**, 1291
    child's views, **10**, 1287
    criteria for resolution, **10**, 1283
    emotional welfare of child, **10**, 1286
    gender of child, **10**, 1289
    illegitimate children, **10**, 1277, 1278
    imaginative custody decisions, **10**, 1292
    Law Reform (Parent and Child) (Scotland) Act 1986—
        under, **10**, 1281-1292
    legitimate children, **10**, 1275, 1276
    local authority duties as to, **14**, 1476
    nature of right to, **10**, 1274
    physical possession of child, and, **10**, 1306
    physical welfare of child, **10**, 1285
    procedural issues, **10**, 1281
    spiritual welfare of child, **10**, 1290
    statutory intervention, **10**, 1276, 1278
    stepchildren, **10**, 1280
    tender years doctrine, **10**, 1288
    third persons, applications by, **10**, 1282
decision-making, in—
    chastisement of child, **10**, 1312

Parental rights—*continued*
decision-making, in—*continued*
  chastisement of child, **10**, 1312
  education, **10**, 1307, 1308
  generally, **10**, 1304
  name of child, **10**, 1305
  physical possession of child, **10**, 1306
  religion, **10**, 1309-1311
  residence, place of, **10**, 1306
development of, **10**, 1260
duration of, **11**, 1213
education, rights and duties as to—
  attendance of child at school—
    commencement of, **8**, 889
      dates for, **8**, 890
    exemption from, **8**, 892
    leaving date, **8**, 891
    migrants, children of, **8**, 893
    travelling persons, children of, **8**, 893
  choice of school—
    generally, **8**, 874
    parental wishes, **8**, 874
    placing request—
      catchment area, and, **8**, 875
      generally, **8**, 875
      refusal—
        appeal against—
          appeal committee, **8**, 878, 881, 885
          appeal against decision of, **8**, 887
          combined hearing, **8**, 883
          decisions, **8**, 885, 886
          generally, **8**, 877
          jurisdiction, **8**, 879
          persons entitled to be present, **8**, 884
          procedure, **8**, 882
          self-governing schools, **8**, 880
        grounds for, **8**, 876
        review of related cases, **8**, 888
  consultation and consent over changes in certain educational matters, **8**, 724
  education, duty to provide, **8**, 874
  no obligation to send child to school, **8**, 874
  non-attendance at school—
    enforcement procedures, **8**, 896-901
    failure to attend without reasonable excuse, **8**, 894, 895
  parental involvement, school board, promotion by, **8**, 771
  parents' meetings, school boards duties in relation to, **8**, 772
  pupils to be educated in accordance with parents' wishes, **8**, 702
  school board, **8**, 749, 751
    membership of—
      generally, **8**, 736, 737, 738
  self-governing school board of managment, membership of, **8**, 787
  special needs, children with—
    assessment, **8**, 911
    recording children, **8**, 912-915
      appeal and review procedure, **8**, 916-921
 xercise of, **10**, 1269

Parental rights—*continued*
 father, **10**, 1222, 1266
  illegitimate child, of, **10**, 1187
 history of, **10**, 1261-1264
 local authority—
  assumption by—
    child in care, where, **3**, 1266
    generally, **3**, 1265
    statutory grounds, **3**, 1267
  special duties of, **14**, 1476
 loss of, **10**, 1268
 meaning, **4**, 69; **10**, 1260
 mother, **10**, 1222, 1266
 nature of, **10**, 1259
 obedience, right to, **10**, 1263, 1264
 plagium, **10**, 1225, 1342
 private international law—
  common law jurisdiction, **10**, 1314, 1315
  Court of Session jurisdiction, **10**, 1314
  generally, **10**, 1313
  sheriff court jurisdiction, **10**, 1315
  statutory jurisdiction, **10**, 1316, 1317
 punishment of child, **10**, 1224
 regulation, **10**, 1265
 rights which might be applied for, **10**, 1271
 step-parents, **10**, 1217
  aliment, **10**, 1220
  incest, **10**, 1227
  succession, **10**, 1220
 third party, defence against, **10**, 1259
 tutor—
  father as, **10**, 1058
  mother as, **10**, 1059
  parents as, **10**, 1060
 undefended action relating to, **17**, 1022
 void or voidable marriages, **10**, 1266
 who may apply for, **10**, 1270
 See also CHILD-CHILDREN
Parish
 abolition, **14**, 24
 boundaries, **14**, 24
  alteration, **3**, 1522
 burghal, **15**, 1025
 Church of Scotland—
  boundaries, alteration, **3**, 1522
  parochial charge, *see* MINISTER OF RELIGION (Church of Scotland)
  quoad sacra et civilia (quoad omnia), **3**, 1508, 1508*n*
  quoad sacra tantum, **3**, 1508*n*
  reappraisal, **3**, 1522, 1525
  union and linking of congregations, **3**, 1527
 community, identification of, **14**, 53
 council—
  abolition, **15**, 1025
  burial grounds, transfer to, **3**, 520
  election and franchise, **15**, 1025
  history, **15**, 1025
 creation, **14**, 24
 education, responsibility for, **14**, 36
 functions, **14**, 24
 kirk door donations, **14**, 34
 landward, **15**, 1025
 local authority elections, **15**, 1021, 1025

Parish—*continued*
parochial charge—
  eligibility for, **3**, 1557
  jus devolutum, **3**, 1526, 1558
  settlement in, **3**, 1557, 1559
  tenure, **3**, 1559
  termination, **3**, 1559
poor relief, **14**, 34
public corporation, as, **19**, 208
public health, responsibility for, **14**, 37
quoad sacra et civilia (*quoad omnia*), **3**, 1508,
  1508*n*
  churches—
    historical position, **3**, 1578, 1591
    New Parishes (Scotland) Act 1844, erected
      under, **3**, 1591
    post-1925 position, **3**, 1580, 1591
  glebes—
    historical position, **3**, 1581
    post-1925 position, **3**, 1582
  manses—
    historical position, **3**, 1579, 1591
    New Parishes (Scotland) Act 1844, erected
      under, **3**, 1591
    post-1925 position, **3**, 1580, 1591
  sale of congregational properties and endow-
    ments, **3**, 1607
quoad sacra tantum, **3**, 1508*n*
  properties and endowments—
    historical position, **3**, 1583
    non-statutory, **3**, 1586
    post-1925 position, **3**, 1584
    statutory, **3**, 1585
  sale of congregational properties and endow-
    ments, **3**, 1607
reappraisal, **3**, 1522, 1525
union and linking of congregations, **3**, 1527
records—
  local examiner, powers of, **14**, 32
  transmission of, **19**, 842, 853
registers—
  banns of marriage, publication of, **19**, 1401
  baptisms, records of, **19**, 1401
  burials, records of, **19**, 1401
  correction of entries, **19**, 1413
  historical background, **19**, 1401
  searches and extracts, **19**, 1412, 1420
  transmission of, **19**, 1411
Roman Catholic Church, **3**, 1655
See also RELIGION, MINISTER OF (Church of
  Scotland)
Park
country, **9**, 1239; **14**, 676; **25**, 360
countryside, **9**, 1239
keeper—
  tobacco or tobacco products, seizure from
    young person, **3**, 1225
meaning, **24**, 689
parks police, *see* PARKS POLICE
private, valuation for rating, **24**, 690
public, exemption from valuation roll, **24**, 689
regional, **9**, 1240; **14**, 677; **25**, 360
Parking
See CAR PARK; MOTOR VEHICLES

Parks police
control, **16**, 1817
jurisdiction, **16**, 1817powers, **16**, 1817
privileges, **16**, 1817
Parliament
absolute privilege, **17**, 19
Act of, *see* ACT OF PARLIAMENT; STATUTE
antecedent limitations of, **5**, 343
appeal from Court of Session to—
  after Union, **5**, 639
  before 1707, **5**, 638
arrest, Parliamentary privilege, **6**, 867
bicameral nature, **6**, 803, 810
Bill, copyright, **18**, 1001
broadcasting, qualified privilege conferred on, **17**,
  19
burghal representation, **14**, 15
central government answerable directly to, **14**, 3
central and local government, essential difference
  between, **14**, 94
Chairman of Committees—
  division of Bills between Houses, **19**, 84
  Examiners of Petitions' reports, **19**, 30
  General Order, application for dispensation of,
    19, 31
  generally, **19**, 5, 7, 7*n*
  recommendations of, **19**, 59
Chairman of Ways and Means, **19**, 5, 7, 7*n*
  division of Bills between Houses, **19**, 84
  Examiners of Petitions' reports, **19**, 30
  General Order, application for dispensation of,
    19, 31
  recommendations of, **19**, 59
challenging ministerial action, **5**, 484
Clerk of the House of Commons, **7**, 757
Clerk of Parliaments, **7**, 757
Cohen Committee recommendations, **4**, 471
Committee for Privileges, *see* HOUSE OF LORDS
  COMMITTEE FOR PRIVILEGES
committees—
  advocate appearing before, dress, **13**, 1323
  classification of, **5**, 398
  Committee on Unopposed Bills in the
    Commons, **19**, 95
  committees of Whole House, **5**, 398
  establishment of, **5**, 398
  House of Lords select committees on private
    Bills, **19**, 98
  Hybrid Instruments Committee, **19**, 132
  judicial business, dealing with—
    ad causas et querelas, **22**, 515
    ad iudicia contradicta, **22**, 515
    competence, duration, **22**, 515
  opposed private Bill committees, **19**, 96-100
  procedure, **5**, 397
  Public Bill, *see* HOUSE OF LORDS
  report stage in Commons, **19**, 100
  select *see* HOUSE OF COMMONS; HOUSE OF LORDS
  standing, *see* HOUSE OF COMMONS
community legislation, control of—
  defects in, **5**, 326
  generally, **5**, 325
confirmation Act, printing of, **19**, 79
  confirmation Bill, **19**, 64-77

Parliament—*continued*
confirmation Bill
  House of Lords, **19**, 68, 72
  introduction of, **19**, 69, 70
  joint committee proceedings, **19**, 74-77
  suspension of, **19**, 78
consent of, requirement for, **7**, 702, 702*n*
constituency—
  burghal, **15**, 1002, 1007, 1015, 1016
  county, **15**, 1015, 1016
constitutional monarchy, **7**, 701, 702
Crown, powers of, **6**, 817
Dark Ages, development, **22**, 515
demise of Crown, effect, **7**, 714
designation of, **5**, 361
dissolution, **7**, 713, 713*n*, 857; **15**, 1041
division of Bills between Houses, **19**, 84
duration, **15**, 1041
educational administration, **14**, 36
elections—
  act or omission in breach of election law, **15**, 1441
  boundaries—
    Boundary Commission, **15**, 1029
    historical background, **15**, 1028, 1029
  by-election—
    expenses, maximum amount, **15**, 1414
    statutory timetable, **15**, 1225
    timing, **15**, 1041, 1219
  combined poll, **15**, 1360
  corrupt or illegal practice—
    candidate guilty of, **15**, 1072-1074
    election agent, duties, **15**, 1052
    election petition, **15**, 1233
    proceedings as to, **15**, 1019
  count, *see* COUNT—
    disposal of documents, after, *see* ELECTION
    (documents)
  counting agent, **15**, 1244
  demise of Crown, where, **7**, 714; **15**, 1418
  deposit, payment by candidate, **15**, 1287
  dispute as to, legal proceedings, **15**, 1019
  disqualification, *see* HOUSE OF COMMONS
    (members of parliament)
  early medieval period, **15**, 1002
  election agent, **15**, 1051
    duties, **15**, 1052
    sub-agent, **15**, 1053
  Election of Commissioners Act 1681 ..., **15**,
    1005, 1006, 1010
  election court, **6**, 928; **15**, 1472
  election expenses—
    county and burghal constituencies, **15**, 1037
    election agent, duties, **15**, 1052
    limitation, **15**, 1018-1020
    maximum amount, **15**, 1414
    meaning, **15**, 1405
    personal expenses, **15**, 1407
    returning officer, role, **15**, 1435
    time provisions, **15**, 1220
  election petition, **15**, 1438, 1474
    amendment, **15**, 1233
    presentation, **15**, 1233
  'Election Writ and Return', **15**, 1353

Parliament—*continued*
elections—*continued*
  elector, meaning, **15**, 1277
  electoral corruption, Union Agreement,
    following, **15**, 1009-1011
  fifteenth century, **15**, 1003
  financial aspects—
    advance on account of charges to returning
      officer, **15**, 1396
    combined poll, **15**, 1388-1393
    consideration in respect of writ, **15**, 1394
    recovery of charges, **15**, 1395
    rendering accounts, **15**, 1401
    superannuation, **15**, 1400
    taxing of accounts, **15**, 1399
  generally, **15**, 1035
  illegal practice, *see* corrupt or illegal practice
    above
  local elections compared, **14**, 6
  meaning, **15**, 1032
  nineteenth-century reforms, **15**, 1011-1017
  notification, **15**, 1240, 1241, 1247
  Parliamentary Elections Act 1742 ..., **15**, 1010
  patient's declaration, **15**, 1128
  personal expenses of candidate, **15**, 1407, 1409
  plural voting, **15**, 1018
  postal election address, **15**, 1019, 1020
  public notice—
    form, **15**, 1243
    generally, **15**, 1240, 1241, 1244
    meaning, **15**, 1240
    statutory, **15**, 1245
  questioning—
    election petition, **15**, 1438
    generally, **15**, 1436
    method, **15**, 1438
  register of electors, **15**, 1019, 1104, 1105
  Representation of the People Act 1949 ..., **15**,
    1020
  restriction on publication of election matter,
    17, 43
  returning officer, **15**, 1048
  Scottish Parliament, **15**, 1002-1006
  secret ballot, **15**, 1027
  service declaration, **15**, 1137
  sheriff clerk, role, **15**, 1355-1358
  sixteenth and seventeenth centuries, **15**, 1004
  statutory notices and notifications, **15**, 1245, 1247
    misnomer or inaccurate description, **15**, 1249
    mode, **15**, 1248
  statutory timetable, **15**, 1225
  time, provisions as to, generally, **15**, 1217,
    1219-1222
  timing, **15**, 1041
  twentieth-century reforms, **15**, 1018-1020
  Union Agreement, effect, **15**, 1006, 1009
  voting—
    modes, **15**, 1152
    person, in, **15**, 1153
  writ, consideration in respect of, **15**, 1394
  See also ELECTION
European, *see* EUROPEAN PARLIAMENT
European Communities, restriction by, **5**, 329
expiry, **15**, 1041

Parliament—*continued*
feudal system, **6**, 802, 803, 850, 901; **22**, 506
   Parliament as feudal court, **22**, 506, 616
Finance Acts, enactment of, **19**, 1503
freedom of speech and debate, **7**, 710
frequency of Parliaments, **7**, 710
future, cannot bind itself for, **5**, 312, 352
General Orders, **19**, 11
government departments, authority for, **5**, 477
Great Britain, of, **15**, 1006
historical development, **7**, 702
House of Commons, *see* HOUSE OF COMMONS
House of Lords, *see* HOUSE OF LORDS
hung, **7**, 712*n*, 713
hybrid Bills, **19**, 124-130
   amendment, made by, **19**, 130
   petitions against, **19**, 128
   select committees, **19**, 129
hybrid instruments, **19**, 131, 132
   Hybrid Instruments Committee, **19**, 132
in parliamento sitting of King's Council, **22**, 506
King or Queen in, **5**, 364; **6**, 901
legislative framework, **5**, 364; **19**, 223; **22**, 524
legislative supremacy—
   critical scrutiny—
      European Communities, United Kingdom
         accession to, **22**, 120, 214
      fundamental postulate, **22**, 120
      Union of England and Scotland, **22**, 120
local authority functions, control of, **14**, 101, 306
Lords Auditors, **6**, 902
medieval role, **22**, 524
ministerial responsibility, **19**, 223, 225, 227, 227*n*
ministers in, **5**, 482
modern cabinet government, **6**, 819
Officers of the Crown, attendance by, **7**, 81
Officers of State, **7**, 791, 792
Official Report ('Hansard'), **19**, 70
origins of, **5**, 361
papers for use of, printer's imprint, **17**, 3
parliamentary copyright—
   acts done for purposes of, **18**, 1122
   generally, **18**, 979, 980, 1001
   literary, dramatic, musical or artistic works—
      generally, **18**, 1036
      transitional provisions, **18**, 1037
   moral rights, **18**, 1134, 1136
   report of proceedings, **18**, 1122
   reproduction of copyright material, permission
      for, **18**, 1028
peer, entitlement to attend, **16**, 1301, 1304, 1307
   expenses, reimbursement, **16**, 1307
personal Bills, **19**, 111-116
   Commons proceedings, **19**, 116
   first reading, **19**, 115
   Personal Bills Committee, **19**, 112-115
   second reading, **19**, 115
political parties, *see* POLITICAL PARTIES
political reorganisation, **5**, 356
precedence—
   determination, **16**, 2009
   generally, **16**, 2004
   House of Lords, **16**, 2010, 2016

Parliament—*continued*
private Bills—
   deposit of, **19**, 81
   first reading, **19**, 88
   function in relation to, **19**, 2
   late Bills, **19**, 81, 107
   opposed, **19**, 96-100
   petition for, **19**, 81
      additional provision, **19**, 106, 107
   presentation, **19**, 88
   report stage in Commons, **19**, 100
   royal assent, **19**, 105
   second House—
      amendments, **19**, 104
      examination, **19**, 90
   second reading, **19**, 89
   substituted Bills, **19**, 108-110
   suspension of, **19**, 105
   third reading—
      in Commons, **19**, 101
      in Lords, **19**, 103
   unopposed, **19**, 95
      provision in Lords, **19**, 102
private business—
   deferred, **19**, 66
   opposed, **19**, 67
   unopposed, **19**, 65
privilege from arrest, **6**, 867
proclamation of emergency, consideration of, **5**, 600
Public Accounts Committee, **19**, 224
public Bills—
   function in relation to, **19**, 2
   Public Bill Office, **19**, 125
public corporations, Parliamentary control, **19**, 223-227
public expenditure, supervision of, **19**, 223, 224
questions, **5**, 391
representation post-Union, **5**, 469
Royal assent, **7**, 715
Scottish—
   abolition of, **19**, 805
   attendance at, allowance, **15**, 1004
   Claim of Right 1689 ..., **6**, 809
   committees, **6**, 806
   constitution, **16**, 1306
   Court of Session, and, **6**, 808
   customary law, confirmation, **22**, 361
   General Council, **6**, 804, 805
   judicature, as, **6**, 804, 808, 809, 850, 898
      'falsing the doom', **6**, 806, 808, 850, 898, 902
   legal status, **15**, 1006
   location of, **6**, 907*n*
   no court of appeal to replace, **6**, 810
   origins, **15**, 1002
   peers, **16**, 1304, 1306
   powers of judicature, **6**, 804
   precedence, **16**, 2003
   representation in—
      burghal, **15**, 1002
      early medieval period, **15**, 1002
      Election of Commissioners Act 1681 ..., **15**, 1005, 1006, 1010
      fifteenth century, **15**, 1003
      sixteenth and seventeenth centuries, **15**, 1004

Parliament—*continued*
Scottish—*continued*
supreme feudal court, as, **6**, 850, 901
treason trials, **6**, 850
Union Agreement, effect, **15**, 1006
Scottish representation, **15**, 1006, 1007, 1028
select committees, *see* HOUSE OF COMMONS; HOUSE
OF LORDS
self-limitation by—
emancipation legislation, **5**, 353
European Communities, accession to, **5**, 354
reformulation, **5**, 352
sovereignty of, *see* SOVEREIGNTY OF PARLIAMENT
special proceedings orders, **19**, 120-123
Standing Orders, **19**, 11
statements in, absolute privilege, **15**, 517
state's international obligations, non-fulfilment of,
19, 652*n*
statute, *see* ACT OF PARLIAMENT; LEGISLATION;
STATUTE
suffrage, extension of, **14**, 21
summons, **7**, 857
supremacy, recent constraints on, **5**, 363
treason felony against, **7**, 585
Under Clerk of Parliaments, **7**, 757
Union Agreement—
effect, **15**, 1006, 1009
generally, **6**, 810, 811
implications of, **5**, 362
legislation in Scotland, effect on application,
22, 527
origins founded in, **5**, 361
university members, **15**, 1016, 1018, 1019, 1028
voting by, **5**, 588-589, 592
Westminster, after the treaty of Union 1707 ...,
22, 601
See also CONSTITUENCY; HOUSE OF COMMONS;
HOUSE OF LORDS
Parliamentary agent
generally, **19**, 9, 9*n*
instruction of advocate by, **13**, 1298
non-designated services, **4**, 1177*n*
Parliamentary burgh
police burgh distinguished from, **17**, 518
Parliamentary church
sale of congregational properties and endowments, **3**, 1607
**Parliamentary Commissioner for Admin-
istration**
areas of investigation, **1**, 207
challenging ministerial action, **5**, 484
Commissioner for Local Administration,
consultation with, **14**, 145
development corporation, investigation of, **23**, 367
investigation by, **19**, 242
passports, jurisdiction as to, **16**, 1231
planning appeals, role in, **23**, 281
select committee on, **5**, 437
Parliamentary election
See PARLIAMENT
Parliamentary journals
documentary evidence, as, **10**, 594
Parliamentary powers
obtaining, **19**, 1

Parliamentary private secretary
appointment of, **5**, 386
duties of, **5**, 386
Parliamentary report
absolute privilege, **15**, 525, 532
qualified privilege, **15**, 532
Parliamentary secretary
minister, as, **5**, 480
private, **5**, 386
Parliamentary sovereignty
See SOVEREIGNTY OF PARLIAMENT
Parochial records
See PARISH
Parole
criteria, **16**, 1478
discretionary life sentence prisoner, **16**, 1477
generally, **16**, 1473
introduction, **16**, 1403
licence, **16**, 1479; **17**, 563; **22**, 35
life parolee, **22**, 35
life prisoners, **12**, 35
local authority duty to parolee, **22**, 35
mandatory indeterminate sentence, where, **16**, 1476
meaning, **22**, 35
offence committed during, **16**, 1474; **22**, 35
prisoner sentenced after October 1993, **16**, 1473,
1475
prisoner sentenced before October 1993, **16**,
1473, 1474
recall of parolee to prison, Secretary of State's,
discretion, **22**, 35
remission system, **16**, 1447
report on home circumstances, **22**, 35
social worker, **22**, 35
statistics, **16**, 1480
statutory provisions, **16**, 1403; **22**, 35
Parole (oral) agreement
proof of, **15**, 666-669
rei interventus, **16**, 1620
Parole Board for Scotland
advice to Secretary of State as to release of young
offender from detention, **22**, 33
criteria used by, **16**, 1478
establishment and function, **16**, 1473
generally, **16**, 1471, 1473
guidelines to supervising officers, **22**, 35
report to, social work department, **22**, 33
Senators of the College of Justice, **6**, 923
Parole evidence
contract—
commodatum proved by, **13**, 1786
deposit proved by, **8**, 10
lease, parole evidence generally incompetent,
13, 144, 146, 147
exceptions, **12**, 1251; **13**, 145, 149
proof of generally, **15**, 666-668
deeds, **12**, 1222, 1223, 1225
donation, and, **13**, 1749
loan—
collateral agreement, **13**, 1750
judicial admission, **13**, 1739
qualification of, **13**, 1739, 1745
proof by writ or oath, **13**, 1727, 1748
writ, contradiction of, **13**, 1726, 1750

Parole evidence—*continued*
negotiable instruments, and, **4**, 185
trust, proof of, **24**, 26–28

Part exchange
contract, classification of, **14**, 1802
goods given in, cancellation, consequences of, **5**, 870

Partial intestacy
See INTESTACY

Participation, liability by
See LIABILITY (participation, by)

Partner-partnership
abroad, controlled, tax treatment, **16**, 1144
accountancy partnership, number of partners allowed, **16**, 1011, 1112
accounting for, **1**, 103
accounts—
  partners refused access, **16**, 1090
  refusal to keep proper, **16**, 1090
  whose members are all limited companies, **16**, 1003
actions raised by and against, **16**, 1027
acts binding on, **16**, 1031
actuary partnership, number of partners allowed, **16**, 1011
admission by, **16**, 1033
advances, right to interest on, **16**, 1065
advantages, **16**, 1005
agency—
  act apparently outwith ordinary course of business, **16**, 1032
  actual authority—
    partner acting outwith, **16**, 1032
    partner acting with, **16**, 1029
  admissions, **16**, 1033
  apparent authority, partner acting with, **16**, 1030
  firm, acts binding on, **16**, 1031
  generally, **16**, 1028
  implied authority, **16**, 1029
  indemnity, partner's right to, **16**, 1063
  informally executed writings, **16**, 1031
  liability, *see* liability *below*
  non-trading firm, **16**, 1029
  notice to partner, **16**, 1034
  partner exceeding authority, **16**, 1028
  partners, acts binding on, **16**, 1031
  representations, **16**, 1033
  trading firm, **16**, 1029
agent, partner as, **1**, 606
agreement, *see* PARTNERSHIP AGREEMENT
agreement to enter, specific implement inappropriate, **13**, 9
agricultural property relief, **19**, 1558-1560, 1589
alien as, **16**, 1014
alien enemy as, **16**, 1014
apparent insolvency, **2**, 1324
arbitration—
  agreement for, **2**, 424
  disputes, of, **2**, 413
  powers as to, **2**, 411
assets—
  conveyance on sale, stamp duty, **16**, 1124
  disposal, capital gains tax, **16**, 1124, 1133

Partner-partnership—*continued*
assignation of interest, **20**, 45
auctioneer partnerships, number of partners allowed, **16**, 1011, 1112
audit, **1**, 96
bank account—
  agreement providing for, **2**, 1250
  bankruptcy, effect of, **2**, 1254
  death of partner, effect of, **2**, 1254
  honouring cheques, **2**, 1251
  letter of authority, **2**, 1251
  medical partnership, **2**, 1252
  overdraft—
    death etc, effect of, **2**, 1253
    facilities for, **2**, 1252
  stopping operations on, **2**, 1253
banking partnerships—
  partnership agreement, provisions in, **16**, 1009
  professional rules, contravention, **16**, 1017
bankruptcy—
  claims against partners, **16**, 1109
  dissolution of firm on, **16**, 1083
  effect, **16**, 1098
  generally, **16**, 1106
  liability for debts and obligations of firm, **16**, 1037, 1038
  limited partner, of, **16**, 1120
  partners remaining solvent, where, **16**, 1106, 1109
  position, generally, **16**, 1106, 1108
  sequestration—
    firm and partners, of, **16**, 1108
    limited partnership, of, **16**, 1123
    partner, of, **16**, 1123
    petition for, **16**, 1107
  termination of lease by, **13**, 414
bequest, creation by, **25**, 823
bill of exchange—
  acceptance of, **4**, 139*n*
  authority relating to, **4**, 128
  capacity relating to, **4**, 128
  signature on, **4**, 123
  when binding, **16**, 1031
bookmaking partnerships, contravention of professional rules, **16**, 1017
borrowing requirements, **16**, 1005
breach of obligations to other partners, remedies, **16**, 1070
building design partnerships, number of partners allowed, **16**, 1011
business name, registration and use of, **4**, 321
Business Names Act, application, **16**, 1025
business premises, information to be displayed, **16**, 1025
capacity to become partner—
  alien, **16**, 1014
  alien enemy, **16**, 1014
  company, **16**, 1015
  corporation, **16**, 1015
  mental incapacity, **16**, 1013, 1087
  minor, **16**, 1012
capacity to contract, **3**, 26
capital gains tax liability—
  asset-owning ratio, change in, **16**, 1134
  generally, **19**, 1587

Partner-partnership—*continued*
capital gains tax liability—*continued*
 partnership assets, disposal, **16**, 1124, 1133
 partnership composition, change in, **16**, 1135
 partnership share, gift or bequest, **16**, 1124, 1136
 roll-over relief, **16**, 1133
cautionary obligation—
 capacity to enter, **3**, 865
 liability of partner, **3**, 866, 919
  joint and several, **3**, 866
 undertaken by, **3**, 920
 undertaken for, **3**, 919
 undertaken to, **3**, 919
certificate of incorporation not required, **4**, 302
change in constitution, effect on cautionary
  obligations, **3**, 983
cheques, signature, **16**, 1009, 1031
choice as business medium—
 alternative forms, **16**, 1004
 factors influencing, **16**, 1005
 generally, **16**, 1004
 professions demanding partnership form, **16**,
  1004
claims against partners, **2**, 1412
co-ownership, **16**, 1021
co-partners—
 interpretation of contract, **12**, 1261
 joint and several liability, **16**, 1046
 loss or injury to, liability, **16**, 1044
 wrongful act or omission done with authority
  of, **16**, 1043
collective investment scheme categorisation,
  exclusion from, **12**, 1325
common interest in stock or estate, **16**, 1001
company, **4**, 312
company distinguished, **4**, 302
company as partner, **4**, 318; **16**, 1006, 1015
 tax treatment, **16**, 1143
compete with firm, duty not to, **16**, 1060
conduct destroying mutual confidence, **16**, 1090
conduct prejudicial to business, **16**, 1089
consensual contract, based on, **16**, 1007
constitution—
 change in—
  capital gains tax, **16**, 1135
  income tax treatment, **16**, 1128
  revocation of cautionary obligation, **16**, 1039
  termination of contracts on, **16**, 1040, 1098
  illegality in, dissolution on, **16**, 1085
constitution of, changes in, effect, **3**, 919
constructive trusts, **24**, 30
consulting engineers', number of partners
  allowed, **16**, 1011
contract of employment, change in constitution
  of firm, effect, **16**, 1040
contract of, third party rights, **15**, 851
corporation as, **16**, 1015
covenanted payments by—
 authority to execute, **3**, 1150
 change of partners, where, **3**, 1150
 tax treatment, **3**, 1150
creation of trust by, **24**, 14
crime, partnership established for purpose of
  committing, **16**, 1017

Partner-partnership—*continued*
death of partner—
 business continued in old firm name, **16**, 1052
 dissolution of firm on, **16**, 1040, 1082
 distribution of assets, **16**, 1103, 1104
 inheritance tax—
  generally, **16**, 1139
  liability for payment of tax, **16**, 1139
  valuation of estate, **16**, 1139
  valuation of interest in partnership, **16**, 1140
 liability of estate, **16**, 1037, 1038, 1047
 limited partner, of, **16**, 1120
 partnership continuing in business, post-
  dissolution profits, **16**, 1102
 taxation considerations, **16**, 1009
 valuation of estate, **16**, 1071
 valuation of share on, **19**, 1595
debt, liability of partner for—
 bankruptcy of partner, where, **16**, 1037
 death of partner, where, **16**, 1037
 existence of partnership, determination, **16**,
  1020
 generally, **16**, 1035
 incoming partners, **16**, 1036
 joint and several liability, **16**, 1035
 retirement, obligations incurred after, **16**, 1038
 retiring partners, **16**, 1037
deed, whether binding on, **16**, 1093
defamation—
 partnership as defender, **15**, 480
 partnership as pursuer, **15**, 475
dentists', **16**, 1004, 1017
directorship fees, income tax treatment, **16**, 1130
disability, partnership agreement provisions, **16**,
  1009
disclosure, duty of, **16**, 1058
discrimination, liability for, **9**, 343
dishonesty, conviction for, **16**, 1089
dissolution—
 action of declarator, **16**, 1093
 application for, **16**, 1086
 consequences—
  authority of partners, effect on, **16**, 1098
  contracts, effect on, **16**, 1098
  partner's right to give notice of dissolution,
   16, 1097
  rights of persons dealing with firm, **16**, 1096
 continuing authority of partners, **16**, 1098
 contract entered prior to, **16**, 1098
 contracts of employment, whether affected by,
  16, 1098
 court, by—
  application for, **16**, 1086
   limited partnerships, **16**, 1121
  circumstances in which dissolution decreed,
   16, 1086
  grounds for, **16**, 1087-1092
  procedure, **16**, 1093
 death of partner, on, **16**, 1040, 1082
 deceased partner's share, **16**, 1103, 1104
 declarator, action of, **16**, 1093
 delectus personae, contract involving, **16**, 1098
 distribution of assets, **16**, 1099
  partners' rights, **16**, 1099, 1100

Partner-partnership—*continued*
dissolution—*continued*
  final settlement of accounts, distribution of assets, **16**, 1105
  fixed term, partnership entered into, **16**, 1081
  fraud, for, distribution of assets, **16**, 1100
  generally, **4**, 76, 302
  goodwill, sale on, **16**, 1076
  income tax treatment, **16**, 1132
  limited partnership, of—
    application to court, **16**, 1121
    events giving rise to, **16**, 1120
    limited partner, powers of, **16**, 1120
    procedure on, **16**, 1122
    sequestration, **16**, 1123
  misrepresentation, for, distribution of assets, **16**, 1100
  notice of change, **16**, 1096
  notice of, partner's right to give, **16**, 1097
  partner leaving firm, where, **16**, 1077
    dissolution to enforce, **16**, 1061
  partnership agreement, **16**, 1009
    events specified in agreement, on, **16**, 1077
  partnership at will, **16**, 1080
  petition for, **16**, 1093
  premiums, return, **16**, 1101
  professional negligence, prior to, **16**, 1098
  profits made after, **16**, 1102
  reasons for—
    arbitration clause, **16**, 1079
    breach of partnership agreement, **16**, 1090
    charge for separate debt, **16**, 1084
    conduct destroying mutual confidence, **16**, 1090
    conduct prejudicial to business, **16**, 1089
    death of partner, **16**, 1040, 1082
    expiry of term, **16**, 1081
    generally, **16**, 1077
    illegality, **16**, 1085
    just and equitable, **16**, 1092
    loss, business carried on at, **16**, 1091
    mental incapacity of partner, **16**, 1087
    partnership at will, notice of, **16**, 1080
    permanent incapacity of partner, **16**, 1088
    rescission of partnership agreement, **16**, 1078
    sequestration of partner, **16**, 1083
  retiring partner's share, **16**, 1103, 1104
  right to give notice of, **16**, 1097
  sequestration of dissolved partnership, **16**, 1107
  sequestration of partner, on, **16**, 1083
  termination of contract by, **9**, 139
  use of term, **16**, 1077
  winding up—
    dissolution on, generally, **16**, 1077
    procedures—
      banking partnership, **16**, 1095
      financial services partnership, **16**, 1095
      insurance partnership, **16**, 1095
      unregistered company, **16**, 1094
doctors' partnership, **16**, 1004, 1017
drawings on account, partnership agreement, **16**, 1009

Partner-partnership—*continued*
duration—
  express or implied term, **16**, 1018
  partnership at will, **16**, 1019
employment, contract of—
  change in constitution of firm, effect, **16**, 1040
  dissolution of partnership, effect, **16**, 1098
estate, appointment as judicial factor, **24**, 275
estate agents', **16**, 1011, 1017, 1112
estate managers', **16**, 1011, 1112
existence, determination—
  conduct, inferred from, **16**, 1020
  statutory rules, **16**, 1020-1023
expulsion—
  clause, **16**, 1061
  generally, **16**, 1061
  majority of partners, by, **16**, 1061
  partnership agreement provisions, **16**, 1009
fiduciary duty, partner's, **24**, 172, 181
firm, meaning, **16**, 1024
firms reality over and above partners, **11**, 1042
fixed term—
  constituted for, **16**, 1009
  continuance after, **16**, 1067
  dissolution after, **16**, 1081
forcing partner to leave firm, **16**, 1061
formation, **4**, 312
fraud by, **16**, 1043, 1089
good faith—
  compete with firm, duty not to, **16**, 1060
  duty of disclosure, **16**, 1058
  expulsion clauses, **16**, 1061
  private profit, duty not to make, **16**, 1059
  requirement of good faith, generally, **16**, 1057
  retired partners, **16**, 1060
  separate business run by partner or former partner, **16**, 1060
goods, restrictive agreement as to, **4**, 1137
goodwill—
  individual trading under firm name, **16**, 1010
  partnership agreement, provisons in, **16**, 1009
  partnership property, as, **16**, 1074, 1076
  sale—
    dissolution of firm, on, **16**, 1076
    firm name, effect on choice of, **16**, 1024
    payment by share in future profits, **16**, 1023
gross returns, sharing, **16**, 1021
guarantor for firm, as, **16**, 1046
historical development of law—
  English law, influence, **16**, 1002
  generally, **16**, 1001
  Roman law, influence, **16**, 1001, 1026
  statutory regulation, **16**, 1001, 1003
holding out to be—
  death of partner, effect on firm, **16**, 1052
  knowingly suffering representation as partner, **16**, 1049, 1051
  liability—
    delict, in, **16**, 1054
    firm, of, **16**, 1055
    generally, **16**, 1049
    retired partner, **16**, 1053, 1055
    words or conduct, **16**, 1049, 1050
illegal activity, deriving profit from, **16**, 1017

Partner-partnership—*continued*
illegality—
    dissolution on, **16**, 1085
    generally, **16**, 1017
illness, partnership agreement provisions, **16**, 1009
implied authority, **16**, 1029
incapacity, permanent, **16**, 1088
income tax liability—
    basis of assessment, **16**, 1126
    calculation of tax, **16**, 1129
    change in composition of partnership, **16**, 1128
    dissolution of partnership, where, **16**, 1132
    generally, **16**, 1124; **19**, 1586
    income other than trading profits, **16**, 1130
    opening and closing years, **16**, 1127
    payment of tax, **16**, 1129
    retirement annuities, **16**, 1131
    trading profits, **16**, 1125
incoming—
    consent to, **16**, 1062
    liability for wrongful acts, **16**, 1047
    taxation considerations, **16**, 1009
incorporated (or quasi-), concept of, **4**, 512
incorporated company distinguished, **4**, 319
indemnity, right to, **16**, 1063
individual trading under firm name, **16**, 1010
informally executed writings, **16**, 1031
inheritance tax liability—
    death of partner, where—
        generally, **16**, 1139
        valuation of estate, **16**, 1139
        valuation of interest in partnership, **16**, 1140
    discretionary trust, transfers into, **16**, 1137
    generally, **19**, 1588, 1591
    lifetime gifts, **16**, 1137
    partnership property, generally, **16**, 1073, 1124
    partnership share, on value of, **16**, 1137
        instalments, payment in, **16**, 1137
    reliefs, **19**, 1589
    transfer of value by partnership, **16**, 1138
insurance brokers', number of partners allowed, **16**, 1011
interest in, legacy of, **25**, 848
joint tenancy, **13**, 192
judicial factor, ineligible as, **24**, 241
land agents', number of partners allowed, **16**, 1011, 1112
land and other feudalised real rights, ownership, **18**, 599
lawyers', number of partners allowed, **16**, 1011
legal person distinct from individual members, as, **4**, 302
legal *persona*, **3**, 823
lessee, as, **13**, 192
lessor, as, **13**, 180
liability—
    act apparently outwith ordinary course of business, **16**, 1032
    bankruptcy of partner, where, **16**, 1037, 1038
    co-partners, **16**, 1046
    death of partner, where, **16**, 1037, 1038, 1047
    debts of firm, partner's liability for—
        benefit of discussion, **3**, 825
        benefit of division, **3**, 825

Partner-partnership—*continued*
liability—*continued*
    debts of firm, partner's liability for—*continued*
        capacity of partner to enter cautionary obligation, **3**, 865
        caution, partner's relationship with firm as one of, **3**, 823
        cautioner and partner contrasted, **3**, 824
        dicharge of one partner, where, **3**, 826
        generally, **3**, 822, 823, 827, 866
        giving of time to principal debtor, **3**, 826
    generally, **16**, 1028, 1035
    guarantors for firm, partners as, **16**, 1046
    holding out to be partner, person, **16**, 1049-1055
    incoming partner, **16**, 1036, 1047
    joint and several partners, **16**, 1035, 1046
        English law, **16**, 1046
        value added tax, **16**, 1141
    limited, **16**, 1003
    loss or injury to co-partners, **16**, 1044
    nature of, **16**, 1046
    partner, for acts of, **16**, 1028
    prior acts of firm, **16**, 1036
    retiring partner, **16**, 1037, 1047
        debts and obligations incurred after retirement, **16**, 1038
    trust property, for improper use of, **16**, 1048
    wrongful act or omission of partner, for—
        authority of co-partners, act done with, **16**, 1041, 1043
        fraud, **16**, 1043
        generally, **16**, 1041
        judicial slander, **16**, 1043
        loss or injury to co-partner, where, **16**, 1044
        misapplication of money or property, **16**, 1045
        ordinary course of business, act done in, **16**, 1041, 1042
        professional negligence, **16**, 1042
        statutory offence, **16**, 1042
    See also agency *above*
liability of partners—
    unlimited, **4**, 302
limit of twenty-five members on, **4**, 303
limited, *see* LIMITED PARTNERSHIP
limited company—
    accounts, publication, **16**, 1003
    conversion to, **16**, 1040
    members limited companies, where, **16**, 1003
loss, business carried on at, **16**, 1091
loss adjusters', number of partners allowed, **16**, 1011
majority, power to act contrary to minority's wishes, **16**, 1009
management by partners, **4**, 302
management flexibility, **16**, 1005, 1017
management of partnership affairs—
    advances, interest on, partner's right to, **16**, 1065
    arbitration, provision for, **16**, 1069
    breach of partners' obligations to one another, remedies, **16**, 1070
    continuance of partners' rights and duties, **16**, 1067

Partner-partnership—*continued*
management of partnership affairs—*continued*
  generally, **16**, 1062
  indemnity, partner's right to, **16**, 1063
  partnership at will, termination, **16**, 1068
  partnership books, right of access to, **16**, 1066
  remuneration of partners, **16**, 1064
  right to manage, generally, **16**, 1062
  rights and duties of partners, **16**, 1062
meaning, **16**, 1006
medical profession, **16**, 1004
mental incapacity, **16**, 1013
  dissolution of partnership, as grounds for, **16**, 1087
minor as, **16**, 1012
misapplication of money or property by, **16**, 1045
misrepresentations, person induced into partnership by, **16**, 1057, 1078
modern, features of, **4**, 302
name—
  death of partner, effect, **16**, 1052
  generally, **16**, 1024
  goodwill, sale of, affecting, **16**, 1024
  individual trading under, **16**, 1010
  limited partnership, **16**, 1114
  partnership agreement, **16**, 1009
  passing off, **16**, 1024; **18**, 1377
  restrictions on, **16**, 1024, 1025
names, partners', stationery, to be printed on, **16**, 1025
names and addresses of partners, display, **16**, 1025
national insurance contributions, liability to pay, **16**, 1124
nature, **4**, 312; **16**, 1006
new partner, consent to, **16**, 1062
notice to partner, effect, **16**, 1034
number of partners—
  limitation, **16**, 1003, 1011
    limited partnership, **16**, 1112
  maximum, **16**, 1011
  two or more persons, **16**, 1010
obligation under contract of partnership, **16**, 2116, 2119
obligations, liability of partners—
  bankruptcy of partner, where, **16**, 1037
  death of partner, where, **16**, 1037
  generally, **16**, 1035
  incoming partners, **16**, 1036
  joint and several liability, **16**, 1035
    value added tax, **16**, 1141
  prior acts, for, **16**, 1036
  retirement, obligations incurred after, **16**, 1038
  retiring partners, **16**, 1037
outgoing partner—
  goodwill, **16**, 1009
  partnership agreement, **16**, 1009
  payments to, **16**, 1009
  taxation considerations, **16**, 1009
  See also death of partner *above*; retirement of partner *below*
partner's contribution to partnership, form, **16**, 1074
partner's share, assignee of, position, **16**, 1062
partnership agreement, *see* PARTNERSHIP AGREEMENT

Partner-partnership—*continued*
partnership at will, termination, **16**, 1068
partnership books, partner's right of access to, **16**, 1066
partnership contract, rights and obligations between partners, **16**, 1056
partnership property—
  arrestment, **8**, 269
  asset-owning ratio, change in, capital gains tax, **16**, 1134
  co-ownership—
    existence of partnership, determination, **16**, 1021
    generally, **18**, 18, 18*n*
  diligence, **8**, 128
  goodwill, **16**, 1074, 1076
  heritable, **16**, 1072, 1073
  inheritance tax, **16**, 1073, 1124
  interest in, **16**, 1073
  partners' interest in, **16**, 1009
    nature of, **16**, 1073
    succession, **16**, 1073
  partner's name, property held in, **16**, 1072
  partner's share—
    assignation, **16**, 1075
    equality, presumption of, **16**, 1074
    extent, **16**, 1074
    transfer to third party, **16**, 1075
  partnership agreement, **16**, 1009
  partnership money, property bought with, **16**, 1071
  separate debt, charge for, dissolution on, **16**, 1084
  share in—
    assignation, **16**, 1075
    equality, presumption of, **16**, 1074
    extent, **16**, 1074
    transfer to third party, **16**, 1075
  statutory provisions, application, **16**, 1071
  succession, **16**, 1073
  what constitutes, **16**, 1071, 1072
  winding up, distribution of assets, **16**, 1099
    deceased partner's share—
      ascertainment, **16**, 1104
      treatment, generally, **16**, 1103
    final settlement of accounts, on, **16**, 1105
    fraud, partnership dissolved for, **16**, 1100
    misrepresentation, partnership dissolved for, **16**, 1100
    partners' rights, **16**, 1099, 1100
    post-dissolution profits, **16**, 1102
    premiums, return of, **16**, 1101
    retiring partner's share—
      ascertainment, **16**, 1104
      treatment, generally, **16**, 1103
partnership share—
  assignee of, position, **16**, 1062
  gift or bequest, **16**, 1136, 1137
    capital gains tax, **16**, 1124, 1136
partnership tenancies, **19**, 1568, 1590
  dissolved on death, **19**, 1570
  landlord as partner, **19**, 1571
  not dissolved on death, **19**, 1569

Partner-partnership—*continued*
patent agents', number of partners allowed, **16**,
    1011, 1017
persona—
    actions raised by and against firm, **16**, 1027
    bankruptcy laws, application, **16**, 1106
    consequences, **16**, 1026
    corporation persona, and, **16**, 1026
    liability of partners for wrongs, **16**, 1046
    quasi persona, **16**, 1026
    recognition of legal personality, **16**, 1026
    separate, **16**, 1001
    separate legal personality, **19**, 1585
personal responsibility of partners, **16**, 1001
praepositus negotiis societatis, **16**, 1028
precedent, **16**, 1129
premises, **24**, 30
premium paid by, return on dissolution, **16**, 1101
privacy, generally, **16**, 1005
private Bill—
    giving powers to partnership, **19**, 91-94
    promoted by partnership, **19**, 91-94
private profit, partner's duty not to make, **16**,
    1059
professional negligence—
    by partner, **16**, 1042
    dissolution of partnership, effect, **16**, 1098
professional rules, contravention, **16**, 1017
profit—
    definition, **16**, 1022
    division, partnership agreement, **16**, 1009
    gross returns, sharing, **16**, 1022
    income tax, *see* income tax liability *above*
    participation in, and determination of existence
        of partnership, **16**, 1023
    partnership must be carried on with view to, **4**,
        302
profit-sharing terms, person lending money on,
    16, 1057
promissory note, when binding, **16**, 1031
provisional order relating to, **19**, 23, 23*n*
quasi-partnership, *see* QUASI-PARTNERSHIP
racial discrimination—
    choice of partners, in, **16**, 1016
    expulsion of partners, in, **16**, 1061
registration, **16**, 1003
relation, constitution, **16**, 1007-1023
relations between partners—
    conduct destroying mutual confidence, **16**,
        1090
    express and implied terms, **16**, 1056
    generally, **16**, 1056
    good faith principle—
        compete with firm, duty not to, **16**, 1060
        duty of disclosure, **16**, 1058
        expulsion clause, **16**, 1061
        generally, **16**, 1057
        misrepresentations, person induced into
            partnership by, **16**, 1057, 1078
        private profit, duty not to make, **16**, 1059
    management of partnership affairs—
        advances, right to interest on, **16**, 1065
        arbitration, provision for, **16**, 1069
        breach of obligations, remedies, **16**, 1070

Partner-partnership—*continued*
relations between partners—*continued*
    management of partnership affairs—*continued*
        fixed term, continuance after, **16**, 1067
        indemnity, partner's to, **16**, 1063
        partnership books, right of access to, **16**,
            1066
        remuneration, presumption against right to,
            16, 1064
        rights as to, generally, **16**, 1062
        termination of partnership at will, **16**, 1068
    partnership contract, **16**, 1056
    rights and obligations of partners, **16**, 1056
remuneration of partner, presumption against
    right to, **16**, 1064
representation made by partner, **16**, 1033
representation of partnership by partner, **16**,
    1028-1034
resignation of partner, **19**, 1595
    valuation of share on, **19**, 1595
retirement annuity paid to, income tax treatment,
    16, 1131
retirement of partner—
    competitive business carried on by, restrictive
        covenant as to, **16**, 1060
    continuing liability, **16**, 1037, 1038
    debts and obligations incurred after, **16**, 1038
    distribution of assets, **16**, 1103, 1104
    holding out, doctrine in relation to retired
        partners, **16**, 1053, 1055
    liability of retiring partner, **16**, 1037, 1047
    partnership agreement provisions, **16**, 1009
rights and duties—
    continuance after fixed term, **16**, 1067
    determination, **16**, 1062
royal charter, partnership does not require, **4**, 302
salary, partner's, **16**, 1023
    partnership agreement, **16**, 1009
separate business carried on by, **16**, 1060
separate legal personality, as, **19**, 1585
    consequences of, **19**, 1585
sequestration—
    Court of Session jurisdiction, **2**, 1333
    dissolution of firm on, **16**, 1083
    dissolved partnership, of, **16**, 1107
    firm and partners, of, **16**, 1108
    jurisdiction for purposes of, **4**, 72
    limited partnerships, **2**, 1321, 1486
    petition for, **16**, 1107
sexual discrimination—
    choice of partners, in, **16**, 1016
    expulsion of partners, in, **16**, 1061
shares—
    assignation, **16**, 1009
    conveyance on sale, stamp duty, **16**, 1124
sheriff court jurisdiction, **6**, 1120
ship owned by, registration, **21**, 133
slander by, **16**, 1043
sleeping partner, **16**, 1006
    limited liability, **4**, 302*n*
sole partner, **16**, 1010
solicitors', **16**, 1011, 1017, 1112
stamp duty, liability for, **19**, 1593
state, requires no recognition from, **4**, 302

Partner-partnership—*continued*

stationery, **16**, 1025, 1038, 1096
statutory offence by, **16**, 1042
statutory regulation, **16**, 1001, 1003
stock exchange, as member of, **16**, 1011, 1112
subscription by partners, **6**, 417
surveyors', number of partners allowed, **16**, 1011, 1112
tax advantage as predominant purpose, **16**, 1006
tax considerations, **16**, 1005
tax loss due to fraud, wilful default or neglect, **19**, 1594
termination of partnership at will, **16**, 1068
trades description legislation, subject to, **6**, 109
trading in share of partner, impossibility, **4**, 302
transfer of ownership, capacity, **18**, 599
transfer of value by, **16**, 1138
trust property, improper use, **16**, 1048
trustees' liability, **24**, 229
two or more persons, meaning, **4**, 1137
unlawful, nature of business becoming, **16**, 1085
upper limit on size of, **4**, 302
value added tax liability—
    assessment served on, **7**, 1405
    changes in partnership composition, **16**, 1141
    generally, **16**, 1124; **19**, 1592
    input tax, **16**, 1141
    joint and several liability, **16**, 1141
    output tax, **16**, 1141
    registration, **16**, 1141
value added tax registration provisions, **7**, 1345
    deemed partnership, **7**, 1346
value of partnership share, **19**, 1595
    inheritance tax consequences, **19**, 1596
    under contract of co-partnery, **19**, 1595
valuers', number of partners allowed, **16**, 1011, 1112
vassal, incapacity as, **18**, 61
vicarious admissions or confessions, **10**, 726
vicarious liability, **15**, 246
will, at, *see* PARTNERSHIP AT WILL
winding up, *see* WINDING UP (partnership, of)
wrongful act or omission by, liability—
    co-partners, act done with authority of, **16**, 1041, 1043
    co-partners, where loss or injury to, **16**, 1044
    fraud, **16**, 1043
    generally, **16**, 1041
    judicial slander, **16**, 1043
    misapplication of money or property, **16**, 1045
    ordinary course of business, partner acting in, **16**, 1041, 1042
    professional negligence, **16**, 1042
    statutory offences, **16**, 1042
See also MERCANTILE LAW
Partnership agreement
arbitration, provisions as to, **16**, 1009, 1069, 1079
authority of partner, provisions as to, **16**, 1029
banking, provisions as to, **16**, 1009
breach, **16**, 1090
    penalty for, **16**, 1009
capital, provisions as to, **16**, 1009
cheques, provisions as to, **16**, 1009
conduct of partnership affairs, **16**, 1009
consensual contract, based on, **16**, 1007

Partnership agreement—*continued*
contents, **16**, 1009
dissolution—
    events specified in, on, **16**, 1077
    provisions as to, **16**, 1009
drawings on account, provisions as to, **16**, 1009
duration of partnership, provisions as to, **16**, 1018, 1019
expulsion—
    expulsion clause, **16**, 1061
    power of, **16**, 1009
firm name, **16**, 1009
formal, use of, **16**, 1008, 1009
goodwill, provisions as to, **16**, 1009
indemnity insurance, **16**, 1009
losses, division, **16**, 1009
nature of business, description, **16**, 1009
partner's share, assignation, **16**, 1009
partnership at will, **16**, 1009
partnership property, **16**, 1009
    definition, **16**, 1071
profits, division, **16**, 1009
rescission, dissolution on, **16**, 1078
restrictive covenants, **16**, 1009
retiral, provisions as to, **16**, 1009
salaries, provisions as to, **16**, 1009
taxation considerations, **16**, 1009
Partnership at will
dissolution, **16**, 1080
partnership agreement, **16**, 1009
terminate, partner's right to, **16**, 1068
when arising, **16**, 1019
Partnership property
See PARTNER-PARTNERSHIP
Partridge
close season, **11**, 806
custody of, by unqualified person, **11**, 807
eggs, protection of, **11**, 802, 843
game, as, **11**, 802
Game (Scotland) Act 1832 ..., **11**, 815
Poaching Prevention Act 1832 ..., **11**, 843
trespass in search of, **11**, 817
Parts and pertinents
See LANDOWNERSHIP
Party political association
community benefit society, as, **12**, 609
Passage
common, *see* CO-OWNERSHIP
innocent, through territorial waters, *see* TERRITORIAL SEA
right of, and sovereignty, **19**, 687
straits used for international navigation, **21**, 10
    alternative routes, **21**, 10
transit, meaning, **21**, 10
way, or, right of, *see* RIGHT OF PASSAGE OR WAY
Passage money
meaning, **21**, 721*n*
salvage subject, as, **21**, 437
Passage and pasturage
servitude right of, **18**, 487
Passenger
air, carriage by—
    contributory negligence by, **3**, 754
    death, carrier's liability, **3**, 750

Passenger—*continued*
air, carriage by—*continued*
  delay, liability for, **3**, 752
  personal injury, carrier's liability, **3**, 750
  tickets, **3**, 740, 745
bus station, safety, **3**, 671
common carrier, of, **3**, 604
contract carriage, **3**, 684
death, liability and damages for, **3**, 683, 689, 750
delay, liability and damages for, **3**, 682, 752
domestic carriage by rail—
  accidents and collisions, **3**, 722, 723
  alight—
    invitation to, **3**, 714
    time allowed for alighting, **3**, 714
    track, passenger alighting on, **3**, 714
  British Railways Board—
    duty of care, **3**, 715
    ex contractu duties, **3**, 709
    ex lege duties, **3**, 709
    generally, **3**, 709
  carriage doors, shutting, **3**, 718
  Conditions of Carriage, **3**, 709
  crowd control, **3**, 712
  disorderly conduct etc, **3**, 719
  driving, duty as to, **3**, 721
  drunken passenger, **3**, 712, 714
  guard's van, travelling in, **3**, 717
  head, putting out of window, **3**, 718
  hired carriages, **3**, 709
  injury by another passenger, **3**, 719
  left luggage offices and lockers, **3**, 725
  line, provisions as to, **3**, 720
  luggage, **3**, 724
  overcrowding, **3**, 716
  permanent way, provisions as to, **3**, 720
  platforms, provisions relating to, **3**, 711-713
  prospective passengers, **3**, 710
  signalling, provisions as to, **3**, 720
  station safety, **3**, 711-713
  tickets, **3**, 709
  timetables, issue and alteration, **3**, 709
domestic carriage by road—
  accidents and collisions, **3**, 677, 678
  alighting, passenger injured while, **3**, 680
  boarding, passenger injured while, **3**, 680
  bus station safety, **3**, 671
  carrier's duty of care, **3**, 670
  contract carriage, **3**, 684
  death, personal injury for, **3**, 683
  delay, damages for, **3**, 682
  delict, claim in, **3**, 670
  drunken or dangerous passenger, **3**, 681
  fares, **3**, 672
  generally, **3**, 670
  handling of vehicle, **3**, 676
  luggage, **3**, 686
  overcrowding, **3**, 675, 681
  overturning, **3**, 677
  passenger injured by another passenger, **3**, 681
  personal injury, damages for, **3**, 683
  public service vehicle, *see* PUBLIC SERVICE
    VEHICLE
  skidding, **3**, 677

Passenger—*continued*
domestic carriage by road—*continued*
  speed of journey, **3**, 673
  stopping and starting, vehicle, **3**, 679
  taxi, *see* TAXI
  time of journey, **3**, 673
  vehicle safety, **3**, 674
driver's duty of care, **3**, 676
drunken or dangerous—
  domestic carriage by rail, **3**, 712, 714
  domestic carriage by road, **3**, 681
fare-paying, use of school bus for, **14**, 438
fares, **3**, 672
foot, in transport road, safety of, **14**, 1631
injury—
  by one passenger to another, **3**, 681
  liability and damages for, **3**, 683, 689, 750
  while boarding or alighting, **3**, 680
international carriage by rail—
  Convention concerning ... (COTIF), **3**, 727
  death, liability and damages for, **3**, 728, 729
  extinction of claims, **3**, 730
  International Convention concerning ...
    (CIV), **3**, 726, 727
  limitation of claims, **3**, 730
  loss, liability and damages for, **3**, 728, 729
  luggage, **3**, 727, 728, 729
    See also LUGGAGE
  personal injury, liability and damages for, **3**,
    728, 729
  tickets, **3**, 727
international carriage by road—
  carrier's liability—
    personal injury or death, for, **3**, 689, 690
  Convention on ... (CVR)—
    contracting out void, **3**, 694
    generally, **3**, 687
  death, liability for, **3**, 689
  generally, **3**, 690
  jurisdiction, **3**, 692
  limitation periods, **3**, 693
  luggage and effects, **3**, 691
  personal injury, liability for, **3**, 689
  transport documents, **3**, 688
land, carriage by, **3**, 601
luggage, *see* LUGGAGE
meaning, **3**, 687*n*
personal injury, damages for, **3**, 683
private hire car, carriage at separate fare, **14**, 440
refusal to take on board—
  proper fare in legal tender, for refusal to pay, **3**,
    673
sea, carriage by—
  Athens Convention—
    application, **21**, 725
      notification, carrier's duty as to, **21**, 728
    burden of proof, **21**, 732
    domestic carriage, **21**, 725
    exclusion or limitation of liability, **21**, 722,
      755, 755*n*
      loss of limitation, **21**, 734
    force of law, **21**, 724
    generally, **21**, 724
    interpretation, **21**, 726

Passenger—*continued*
sea, carriage by—*continued*
  Athens Convention—*continued*
    jurisdiction, **21**, 731
    liability of carrier, **21**, 730, 733
    scope, **21**, 727
  confinement by master, **21**, 723
  contract of passage, meaning, **21**, 721*n*
  death of, inquiry into, **21**, 240
  death of passenger, **21**, 727, 730
    limit for claims, **21**, 761
    limitation of liability, **21**, 755, 755*n*
  detention for examination, **12**, 167
  drunkenness, master's powers in relation to, **21**, 723
  duty of care towards, **21**, 721
  exclusion and limitation of liability, **21**, 722, 729, 733, 734, 755, 755*n*
    aggregation of claims, **21**, 762
  generally, **21**, 721
  immigration laws, **21**, 721
  luggage, *see* LUGGAGE
  master's disciplinary powers, **21**, 723
  meaning, **21**, 727*n*
  misconduct, master's powers in relation to, **21**, 723
  passage money, meaning, **21**, 721*n*
  passenger ship, *see* SHIP
  personal effects not salvage subject, **21**, 436
  personal injury, **21**, 727, 730
    limit for claims, **21**, 761
    limitation of liability, **21**, 755, 755*n*
  safety regulations—
    bridge visibility on passenger ships, **21**, 233
    emergency information, **21**, 233
    passenger counting and recording systems, **21**, 233
  safety of ship and those on board, passenger may be compelled to work for, **21**, 723
  salvage award, entitlement to claim, **21**, 456
  services and facilities, provision of, **21**, 721
  shipowner or operator's duties, **21**, 721
  transport, provision of, **21**, 721
standing, **3**, 676
taxi, carriage at separate fare, **14**, 440
ticket, *see* TICKET
Passenger conveyor
building controls, **3**, 208
Passenger transport
See PUBLIC TRANSPORT
Passenger transport authority
function of, **20**, 493
Passenger transport executive
function of, **20**, 493
railway closures, **19**, 1098
Passing off
advertising, **18**, 1381
  comparative, **18**, 1394
  insert, **18**, 1383, 1393
altered, repaired, modified or deteriorated goods, **18**, 1393
basis of action, **18**, 1364

Passing off—*continued*
business of another trader—
  actual damage caused to, **18**, 1362
  misrepresentation calculated to injure, **18**, 1362
business context, **18**, 1363
business name, **18**, 1377
  non-distinctive elements, **18**, 1377
cause of action, characteristics of, **1**, 507
character merchandising, **18**, 1382
characteristics, **18**, 1362
charity, action brought by, **18**, 1363
common field of activity, parties must both trade in, **18**, 1386
company directors, personal liability, **18**, 1401
company name, **18**, 1377
confusion—
  common field of activity, parties must both trade in, **18**, 1386
  evidence of, **18**, 1385
  likelihood of, **18**, 1384
  test for, **18**, 1385
consumer, misrepresentation to, **18**, 1362
customers—
  existence of, **18**, 1365
  misrepresentation to prospective, **18**, 1362
definition, **18**, 1362
  English, **18**, 1362
delict, **15**, 255
descriptive class designation, improper use, **18**, 1396
device associated in market with another party or parties, use of, **18**, 1361
devices protectable, **18**, 1374-1382
endorsement, application to cases on, **1**, 521
English law, **18**, 1361
essential features, **18**, 1362
European Community legislation, **18**, 1617, 1640-1642, 1646
  free movement of goods, **18**, 1640
foreseeable consequence, presence of, **18**, 1362
fraud not essential, **18**, 1387
future damage, **18**, 1362
generally, **18**, 1361
get-up, product, **18**, 1380, 1385
goodwill—
  actual damage caused to, **18**, 1362
  cessation of business, effect, **18**, 1370
  character merchandising, **18**, 1366
  customers, existence of, **18**, 1365
  damage, **18**, 1372
    prospective, **18**, 1362, 1366, 1373
  device, in, **18**, 1366
  duration, **18**, 1366
  existence of must be established, **18**, 1364
  foreign, **18**, 1367
  franchise operation, **18**, 1371
    foreign, **18**, 1368
  identity of trader need not be known, **18**, 1366
  meaning, **18**, 1365
  misrepresentation, and, **18**, 1383
  misrepresentation calculated to injure, **18**, 1362
  necessity to show, **18**, 1362, 1363, 1365
  product, **18**, 1365
  product launch, prior to, **18**, 1366

Passing off—*continued*
goodwill—*continued*
   prospective damage, **18**, 1362, 1366, 1373
   regional, **18**, 1369
   shared, **18**, 1365, 1366, 1371
   transfer of business, effect, **18**, 1370
intellectual property, in relation to, **18**, 801
intent to cause injury, **15**, 255
intermediary, by, **18**, 1390
inverse, **18**, 1392
letters, group of, **18**, 1379
liability, **18**, 1401
mark, **18**, 1374
misrepresentation—
   descriptive class designation, improper use, **18**, 1396
   as essence of passing off, **18**, 1374
   foreign market, in, **18**, 1389
   fraud not essential, **18**, 1387
   generally, **18**, 1362, 1364, 1383
   goodwill, and, **18**, 1383
   intermediary, by, **18**, 1390
   meaning, **18**, 1383
   quality, as to, **18**, 1393
   statement true in some respects, **18**, 1388
   substitution selling, **18**, 1390
name, **18**, 1374
   authorship and personality, **18**, 1376, 1397
   descriptive of goods or services offered, **18**, 1388
   geographical, **18**, 1376
   nom de plume, **18**, 1397
   personal, **18**, 1376
   surname as business name, **18**, 1388
numbers, group of, **18**, 1379
occurrences of, **1**, 507
partnership name, **16**, 1024; **18**, 1377
professional association—
   misleading indication of membership, **18**, 1395
   name of, **18**, 1377
prospective damage, **18**, 1362, 1366, 1373
quality of goods or services, **18**, 1393
quia timet action, **18**, 1362
remedies—
   accounting of profits, **18**, 1400
   damages, **18**, 1400
   generally, **18**, 1398
   interdict, **18**, 1398
    interim, **18**, 1398, 1399
reputation, trading, existence of must be established, **18**, 1364
right of property, invasion by misrepresentation, **18**, 1364
second-hand goods sold as new, **18**, 1393
services, **18**, 1362
shape of product, **18**, 1380
spin off merchandising, **18**, 1382
statement other than trade name, **18**, 1362
statement true in some respects, **18**, 1388
substantial damage to plaintiff's property, **18**, 1362
   likelihood of, **18**, 1362
substitution selling, **18**, 1390
supply of goods by one party, whether leading to passing off by another, **18**, 1391

Passing off—*continued*
title of publication or event, **18**, 1378
trade association, action brought by, **18**, 1363
trade mark, **18**, 1361, 1374
trade name, **18**, 1362
trader in course of trade, by, **18**, 1362
trading context, **18**, 1363
unfair competition, in relation to, **18**, 801, 1364
words, **18**, 1374, 1375
   generic, words which become, **18**, 1375
   invented or fancy, **18**, 1375
Passing and tendering
offences, **14**, 1837
Passport
British citizens, **12**, 121
British Dependent Territories citizens, **12**, 121
British Excursion document, **16**, 1225
British Nationals (Overseas), **12**, 121
British Overseas citizens, **12**, 121
British subjects, **12**, 121
British Visitor's passport—
   child under eight, **16**, 1224
   child under sixteen, **16**, 1224
   eligibility to hold, **16**, 1224
   fee, **16**, 1224
   generally, **16**, 1207, 1224
   issue, **16**, 1224
   purpose, **16**, 1224
collective, **12**, 132; **16**, 1225, 1236
common travel area, **16**, 1208
criminal offences in relation to, **16**, 1226
diplomatic, **16**, 1236
diplomatic protection, as aid in seeking, **16**, 1203, 1212, 1213
endorsement, **16**, 1244
   on departure, **12**, 193
immigration control of British subjects, **12**, 120
enter, right to—
   international carrier, passenger of, **16**, 1205
European Union marking, **16**, 1218
examination on arrival, **12**, 162
extra-long passports, **16**, 1218
failure to hold, **12**, 171
false, use of, **16**, 1226, 1226*n*
false information to obtain, giving, **16**, 1226
foreign, entry into UK by holder, **16**, 1208-1211
forged, uttering, **16**, 1226, 1226*n*
function, **16**, 1203
historical background, **16**, 1202, 1214
immigration control exemptions, **12**, 132
importance, **16**, 1201
issue—
   amendment of current passport, **16**, 1222
   appeal, no mechanism for, **16**, 1216, 1234
   British Excursion document, **16**, 1225
   British Visitor's passport, **16**, 1224
   Central Records Unit, **16**, 1215
   collective passport, **16**, 1225
   computerisation, **16**, 1215, 1218
   documentary evidence, requirement for, **16**, 1217
   eligibility, **16**, 1217
   European Union law, **16**, 1233
   extra-long passports, **16**, 1218

Passport—*continued*
issue—*continued*
  false information to obtain, giving, **16**, 1226
  family passport, **16**, 1220
  fee, **16**, 1217
  forms of standard UK passport, **16**, 1218
  future married name, postdated passport in, **16**,
    1223
  generally, **16**, 1215, 1216
  historical background, **16**, 1214
  judicial review, **16**, 1216, 1232, 1232*n*, 1234
  legal controls—
    European Union law, **16**, 1233
    generally, **16**, 1229
    judicial review, **16**, 1216, 1232, 1232*n*
    ministerial responsibility, **16**, 1230
    Parliamentary Commissioner for Administra-
      tion, **16**, 1231
    reforms, proposed, **16**, 1229, 1234
  ministerial responsibility, **16**, 1230
  over sixteen, to person aged, **16**, 1219, 1221
  Passport Issuing and Management Information
    System (PIMIS), **16**, 1215, 1218
  photographs, **16**, 1217
    recent, addition, **16**, 1222
  postdated, **16**, 1223
  refusal, grounds for, **16**, 1227
  regional offices, **16**, 1215
  royal prerogative, under, **16**, 1216
  under eight, child aged, **16**, 1224
  under five, child aged, **16**, 1221
  under sixteen, child aged, **16**, 1219, 1220, 1221,
    1224
  United Kingdom Passport Agency, **16**, 1214,
    1215, 1230
leaving UK—
  European Union law, **16**, 1205
  foreign national's right to leave, **16**, 1205,
    1205*n*
  generally, **16**, 1204, 1205, 1205*n*
  Immigration Act, powers under, **16**, 1205
  international carrier, passenger of, **16**, 1205
  right to leave, **16**, 1205, 1205*n*
machine-readable, **16**, 1218
modern development, **16**, 1203
'Next Steps' programme, **16**, 1214, 1214*n*
no-passport excursions, **12**, 132
origins, **16**, 1202
'passport raids', **12**, 190
photographs, **16**, 1217
possession, implications—
  international travel, control and facilitation, **16**,
    1204-1211
  protection and allegiance, **16**, 1203, 1212, 1213
'returnability' of bearer, **16**, 1203, 1203*n*
royal prerogative, issue under, **16**, 1216
service passport, **16**, 1236
services, provision, **16**, 1214, 1214*n*
settlement, **12**, 121
significance, **16**, 1203
travel document—
  passport as, **16**, 1201
  See also TRAVEL DOCUMENT

Passport—*continued*
United Kingdom—
  amendment, **16**, 1222
  blue-coloured, **16**, 1218, 1222
  British citizen, **16**, 1201
  British Dependent Territories citizen, **16**, 1201
  British Excursion document, **16**, 1225
  British National (Overseas), **16**, 1201
  British Overseas citizen, **16**, 1201
  British protected person, **16**, 1201
  British subject, **16**, 1201
  British Visitor's passport, **16**, 1224
  burgundy-coloured, **16**, 1218
  collective passport, **16**, 1225
  criminal offences in relation to, **16**, 1226
  Crown property, as, **16**, 1216, 1228
  Crown's prerogative, EU law and, **16**, 1233
  duration, **16**, 1219
  eligibility for, **16**, 1217
  European Union law, **16**, 1233
  European Union marking, **16**, 1218
  false information to obtain, giving, **16**, 1226
  family passport, **16**, 1220
  forms, **16**, 1218
  future married name, postdated passport issued
    in, **16**, 1223
  holder—
    entry into UK, **16**, 1207
    not eligible to hold EU passport, **16**, 1218
    impoundment by third party, **16**, 1216, 1228
  issue, *see* issue *above*
  machine-readable, **16**, 1218
  meaning, **16**, 1207*n*
  ministerial responsibility, **16**, 1230
  name change, where, **16**, 1222
  over sixteen, issue to person aged, **16**, 1219, 1221
  Parliamentary Commissioner for Administration,
    jurisdiction, **16**, 1231
  postdated, **16**, 1223
  refusal, **16**, 1216, 1227
    European Union rules, **16**, 1233
    judical review, **16**, 1232
  retention by third party, **16**, 1216, 1228
  revocation, **16**, 1216, 1227
    European Union rules, **16**, 1233
    judicial review, **16**, 1232
    legal controls, **16**, 1229
  right to, reform proposals, **16**, 1234
  security for private debt, may not be used as,
    16, 1228
  under eight, child aged, **16**, 1224
  under five, child aged, **16**, 1221
  under sixteen, child aged, **16**, 1219, 1220, 1221,
    1224
  validity, **16**, 1219
  warrant for arrest of applicant or holder, where,
    16, 1227
  who may hold, **16**, 1201
United Kingdom Passport Agency, generally, **16**,
  1214, 1230
United Kingdom passport holders, **12**, 324-328
  immigration control, subject to, **12**, 120
Vatican passport *per l'estero*, **16**, 1236
visa, *see* VISA

Passport Issuing and Management Information System (PIMIS)
generally, **16**, 1215, 1218

Pasteurisation
cream, **11**, 355, 479
ice cream, **11**, 354
liquid egg, **11**, 356
milk, **11**, 459

Pastoral lease
generally, **13**, 215

Pasturage
rights of, as real condition, **13**, 241
servitude right of—
generally, **6**, 515; **18**, 483, 488
passage and pasturage, right of, **18**, 487
utilitas test, **18**, 488

Pasture
prevention of damage by injurious animals or birds, **11**, 859

Patent
aircraft—
exempted, **18**, 865
temporarily within United Kingdom, **18**, 865
amendment—
application to Court of Session, **18**, 863
infringement proceedings, during, **18**, 870, 873
specification, **18**, 855, 857
typographical errors, **18**, 855, 856
animal variety, not grantable in respect of, **18**, 828
appeal procedure—
European patent, **18**, 901
pre-grant stage—
Court of Session, appeal to, **18**, 854
external appeals, **18**, 852
foreign or convention patent, **18**, 853
generally, **18**, 852, 853
internal appeals, **18**, 852
Scotland, proceedings in, **18**, 853
application—
adequacy of application, **18**, 833
appeal in pre-grant stage, **18**, 852-854
application process—
generally, **18**, 832
drawings, submission, **18**, 840
employee, invention by, **18**, 829, 830
entitlement to patent, generally, **18**, 829
European patent—
appeals, **18**, 901
examination and grant, **18**, 898
generally, **18**, 896
opposition procedures, **18**, 899, 900
proceedings, **18**, 897
examination—
appeal against decision of examiner, **18**, 841
European patent, **18**, 898
preliminary, **18**, 840, 841
substantive, **18**, 845
appeals against decision, **18**, 845
fee, **18**, 845
formal request, **18**, 845
time limit, **18**, 845
examiner's report, **18**, 841
expenditure incurred, tax treatment, **18**, 1574

Patent—*continued*
application—*continued*
fees—
tax treatment, **18**, 1574
filing date, **18**, 838
filing fee, **18**, 832, 838
form, **18**, 829, 832
formal requirements, **18**, 840, 840*n*
initial investigations, **18**, 841
joint applications, **18**, 829
micro-organism, invention requiring use of, **18**, 837
non-inventor, by, **18**, 831
overseas resident, by, **18**, 829
Patent Office, role, **18**, 839
person other than inventor, by, **18**, 831, 840
priority date, **18**, 838, 840
priority rights in Paris Convention signatories, **18**, 891
procedure—
failure to comply, **18**, 839
generally, **18**, 839
preliminary examination and search, **18**, 840
publication, **18**, 842
effect, **18**, 844
scrutiny, **18**, 833, 841
similar application, submission of, **18**, 842
specification, **18**, 834
amendment, **18**, 846-848
construction, **18**, 836
publication, **18**, 843
statement of claim, **18**, 835
construction, **18**, 836
two or more linked inventions, **18**, 841
United Kingdom national, by, **18**, 829
who may make, **18**, 829
withdrawal by applicant, **18**, 842
written representations concerning validity, **18**, 844
notification of applicant, **18**, 844
reply by applicant, **18**, 844
assignation, **6**, 599; **18**, 811; **20**, 55
application for patent by assignee, **18**, 829
registration, **18**, 812
award, *see* grant *below*
Banks Committee on the British Patent System, **18**, 815, 825
breach of confidence, relationship with patent protection legislation, **18**, 1452, 1460
business method, patent may not be granted in respect of, **18**, 825
commercial exploitation, **18**, 855
common origin, European Community legislation, **18**, 1629
Comptroller of Patents, **18**, 812
certificate of contested validity, **18**, 875
declaration on non-infringement, **18**, 875
jurisdiction, **18**, 858
legal proceedings before, **18**, 858, 860
advantages and disadvantages, **18**, 859
agreement of all parties concerned, **18**, 860
appeal against, **18**, 859
Comptroller declining to deal with matter, **18**, 860

Patent—*continued*

Comptroller-General of Patents, Designs and Trade Marks—
certificate granted by, **18**, 814

computer program, patent may not be granted in respect of, **18**, 825

consent—
European Community legislation—
compulsory licences, consent and, **18**, 1628
first marketing, exhaustion by consent to, **18**, 1627

construction, methods or principles of, **18**, 1214

Convention for the European Patent for the Common Market (Community Patent Convention), **18**, 815, 815*n*, 902, 1611, 1611*n*

Convention on the Grant of European Patents (European Patent Convention), *see* international law *below*

Convention for the Protection of Industrial Property (Paris Convention), **18**, 801, 865, 865*n*, 891

copyright, relationship with, **18**, 826

Court of Session jurisdiction, **6**, 924

Crown right to use patented invention without royalty, **7**, 763

Crown use of patented invention—
compensation for, **18**, 888
disputes concerning, **18**, 877
emergency powers, **18**, 889
rights of proprietor, **18**, 887

data processing system, patent not grantable in respect of, **18**, 825

dealings in—
generally, **18**, 878
holograph writing, by, **18**, 878
licences, *see* licence *below*
probative writing, by, **18**, 878

death of patent holder, **18**, 811

deceased's liability to tax, **25**, 971

developments not classed as invention, **18**, 816

discovery, **18**, 824

duration of rights, **18**, 851
lapse, **18**, 851
renewal, **18**, 851
fee for, **18**, 851
resubmission fee, **18**, 851

earlier patent, improved version of, **18**, 812

effect, generally, **18**, 812

employee, invention by, **18**, 829, 830

entitlement to, generally, **18**, 829

European Union legislation, **18**, 1611
common origin, **18**, 1629
Community patent, **18**, 1631
consent—
compulsory licences, and, **18**, 1628
first marketing, to, exhaustion by, **18**, 1627

Convention for the European Patent for the Common Market (Community Patent Convention), **18**, 815, 815*n*, 902, 1611, 1611*n*

Convention on the Grant of European Patents (European Patent Convention), *see* international law *below*

Patent—*continued*

European Union legislation—*continued*
different national laws, effect, **18**, 1630
exhaustion—
Community patent, and, **18**, 1631
consent to first marketing, by, **18**, 1627
free movement of goods, **18**, 1625-1631
generally, **18**, 1615
licensing, **18**, 1650-1652
block exemption, **18**, 1651, 1652
specific subject matter—
generally, **18**, 1625
patentee's right to reward as part of, **18**, 1626
See also international law *below*

examiners, **18**, 840, 841
appeal against decision of, **18**, 841
preliminary examination, **18**, 840, 841
substantive examination, **18**, 845

exclusion from patent protection—
discovery, **18**, 824
materials excluded, generally, **18**, 823
mathematical theory or method, **18**, 824
scientific theory, **18**, 824

exclusive jurisdiction, **4**, 58, 59, 60

exhaustion—
European Union legislation—
Community patent, and, **18**, 1631
consent to first marketing, by, **18**, 1627

foreign, tax treatment, **18**, 1579

game, patent may not be granted in respect of, **18**, 825

generally, **18**, 814

grant—
amendment prior to, **18**, 847
amendment subsequent to, **18**, 848
certificate of, **18**, 849
generally, **18**, 849
legal proceedings subsequent to, *see* legal proceedings subsequent to grant *below*
publication, **18**, 849, 850, 851
specification, amendment, **18**, 855, 857
subsequent matters arising, **18**, 855-857
time limit, **18**, 849
typographical errors, amendment, **18**, 855, 856

idea, patent not grantable in respect of, **18**, 825

incorporeal moveable property, as, **18**, 14, 811, 878

individual resale price maintenance for patented article, **4**, 1204

industrial application, patented article must be have, **18**, 816, 822

industrial exploitation, capacity for, **18**, 816

infringement—
action for—
generally, **18**, 855, 864, 865
petition, by, **18**, 864
summons, by, **18**, 864
acts considered to constitute, **18**, 865
amendment of specification following, **18**, 848
conversion process constituting, **18**, 866
damages, award in respect of, **18**, 858, 867, 868
declarator, issue of, **18**, 858, 875, 877
delivery up of infringing products, order for, **18**, 867

Patent—*continued*
infringement—*continued*
  groundless threats of infringement proceedings,
    18, 877
  indirect, **18**, 865
  innocent, **18**, 870, 871
  interdict, issue, **18**, 858
  lapsed patent, **18**, 870
  order for delivery up of infringing copies, **18**,
    858
  order for destruction of infringing copies, **18**,
    858
  permitted acts, **18**, 865
  proceedings, **18**, 866-873
    amendment of patent during, **18**, 870, 873
    defence to, **18**, 877
    groundless threat, remedy for, **18**, 874
  profits made as result, order to account for, **18**,
    858, 867, 869, 870
  proof, **18**, 866
  remedies, **18**, 867
  rights of patent holder, **18**, 865
intellectual property, as, **18**, 801
international law—
  Convention for the European Patent for the
    Common Market (Community Patent
    Convention) (1975), **18**, 815, 815*n*, 902,
    1611, 1611*n*
  Convention on the Grant of European Patents
    (European Patent Convention) (1973)—
    Administrative Council, **18**, 894
    appeals, **18**, 901
    application for European patent, **18**, 896
    European Patent Bulletin, **18**, 898
    European Patent Office, **18**, 894, 896, 897
      opposition division, proceedings before,
        18, 900
    European Patent Organisation, **18**, 894
    examination of application, **18**, 898
    generally, **18**, 815, 815*n*, 891, 894, 1611*n*
    grant of patent, **18**, 898
      criteria for, **18**, 895
    language of application, **18**, 896
    opposition—
      grounds for, **18**, 899
      proceedings, **18**, 899, 900
    proceedings, investigative nature, **18**, 897
    signatories, **18**, 894
    substantive law, **18**, 895
    third party intervention, no provision for,
      18, 899
  Convention for the Protection of Industrial
    Property (Paris Convention), **18**, 801, 865,
    865*n*, 891
  generally, **18**, 890
  International Patent Co-operation Union, **18**, 892
  Patent Co-operation Treaty (1970), **18**, 891,
    892, 893
  See also European Union legislation *above*
  International Patent Co-operation Union, **18**, 892
inventions qualifying for protection—
  generally, **18**, 816
  industrial exploitation, capacity for, **18**, 816,
    822

Patent—*continued*
inventions qualifying for protection—*continued*
  invention already created, **18**, 819
  invention readily deducible from available
    information, **18**, 819
  inventiveness, invention must display, **18**, 816,
    820, 821
  meaning of invention, **18**, 816
  novelty, invention must display, **18**, 816, 817-
    819, 842
inventiveness—
  criteria of, application, **18**, 820, 842
  novelty distinguished, **18**, 820
  product must display, **18**, 816, 820, 821
legal proceedings subsequent to grant—
  amendment of specification during, **18**, 870,
    873
  choice of forum, **18**, 859
  Comptroller, before, **18**, 858, 860
    advantages and disadvantages, **18**, 859
    agreement of all parties concerned, **18**, 860
    appeal against decision, **18**, 859
    Comptroller declining to deal with matter,
      18, 860
  Court of Session, before—
    amendment of patent, application for, **18**,
      862
    generally, **18**, 861
    infringement, proceedings for, **18**, 864, 865
    Patent Office inquiry, order for, **18**, 861
    revocation of patent, application for, **18**, 863
  courts, before, **18**, 858
  Crown use of patented invention, disputes
    concerning, **18**, 877
  damages, award of, **18**, 858, 867, 868, 870
  declaration on non-infringement, **18**, 875
  declarator, issue of, **18**, 858
  England, in, **18**, 859
  generally, **18**, 858
  innocent infringement, **18**, 871
  interdict, issue, **18**, 858
  order for delivery up of infringing copies, **18**,
    858, 867
  order for destruction of infringing copies, **18**,
    858
  patent holder, action instituted by, **18**, 858
  profits made as result, defender ordered to
    account for, **18**, 858, 869, 870
  revocation of patent following, **18**, 858
  Scotland, in, **18**, 860
  third party, institution by, **18**, 858
  validity—
    certificate of contested, **18**, 876
    challenge by third party, **18**, 858
    proceedings challenging, **18**, 877
licence—
  bilateral agreement for exchange of, **4**, 1160
  compulsory—
    European Union legislation, **18**, 1628
    general principles for award, **18**, 885
    generally, **18**, 879, 882
    grant, **18**, 886
      objection to, **18**, 884
    grounds for award, **18**, 883

Patent—*continued*
licence—*continued*
  compulsory—*continued*
    onus of proof, **18**, 883
    Paris Convention, **18**, 891
    procedure, **18**, 884
    time limit, **18**, 882
    European Union legislation, **18**, 1628, 1650-1652
      block exemption, **18**, 1651, 1652
    generally, **18**, 879
    grant—
      third party, to, **18**, 855
    right, of, **18**, 881
    tying arrangements, **18**, 880
    voluntary, **18**, 880
    expiry, **18**, 880
licensee—
  tax treatment—
    deduction of tax at source, **18**, 1577
    lump sum payments, capital allowances, **18**, 1576
    royalties, charges on income, **18**, 1575
licensor—
  tax treatment—
    deduction of tax at source, **18**, 1577
    lump sum receipts, **18**, 1573
    non-resident licensor, **18**, 1578
    periodic payments, **18**, 1572
    royalties, **18**, 1572
lump sum payment in respect of, tax treatment, **18**, 1573
mathematical theory or method, **18**, 824
mental act, patent may not be granted in respect of, **18**, 825
micro organism, invention requiring use of, **18**, 828, 837
nature of patent rights, **4**, 1173; **18**, 811
novelty—
  conduct of applicant affecting, **18**, 817, 818
  invention already created, **18**, 819
  invention must display, **18**, 816, 817-819
  invention readily deducible from available information, **18**, 819
  inventiveness distinguished, **18**, 820
  publication in journal or correspondence prior to application for registration, **18**, 818
  sale or demonstration prior to application for registration, **18**, 818
number, attachment to product, **18**, 871
offensive, immoral or anti-social behaviour, invention considered likely to encourage, **18**, 827, 843
Official Journal, **18**, 848*n*, 849, 851
Patent Co-operation Treaty (1970), **18**, 804, 815, 891, 892, 893
  same invention, application for registration in signatory state, **18**, 838
Patent Office, **18**, 812
  examiners, *see* examiners *above*
  inquiry into questions of fact or opinion, Court of Session order for, **18**, 861
  role, **18**, 839
payments in respect of, tax treatment, **18**, 1572, 1576, 1600, 1602

Patent—*continued*
period for which effective, **18**, 812
plant variety, not grantable in respect of, **18**, 828
prior use of patented invention, **18**, 872
proprietor failing to exploit patent, compulsory licence, *see* licence *above*
publication—
  patent application, of, **18**, 842
  specification, of, **18**, 843
reform of law, **18**, 815
Register of Patents—
  compulsory licence, where granted, **18**, 886
  failure to register, **18**, 812
  generally, **18**, 812, 850
  licence of right, entry indicating availability, **18**, 886
  publication of specification, **18**, 850
  record by Comptroller of Patents, **18**, 812
  registered agreement or patent, priority over unregistered, **18**, 812, 850
  transfer of patent rights to third party, **18**, 812
renewal, **18**, 851
  fee—
    licence of right, where, **18**, 881
  lapsed, infringement during, **18**, 870
resubmission, **18**, 851
revocation, **18**, 858
  action seeking, **18**, 833
  application to Court of Session, **18**, 863
  proceedings seeking, **18**, 877
rights in, disposal of, *see* dealings in *above*
rights in security, **20**, 43
royal prerogative, and, **18**, 814
royalties—
  tax treatment, **18**, 1572, 1576, 1602
    non-residents, payments to, **18**, 1578
  trading income, when treated as, **18**, 1572
same invention, application for registration in respect of, **18**, 838
scientific theory, **18**, 824
Scots law, generally, **18**, 814
security, rights in, **18**, 811
  registration, **18**, 812
special jurisdiction, **4**, 48
specific subject matter—
  definition, **18**, 1625
  European Union legislation—
    generally, **18**, 1625
    patentee's right to reward, **18**, 1626
  exhaustion by consent to first marketing, **18**, 1627
specification, **18**, 834
  ambiguity in, **18**, 866
  amendment, **18**, 855, 857
    alleged infringement, following, **18**, 848
    generally, **18**, 846
    legal proceedings, during, **18**, 870, 873
    patent holder, at request of, **18**, 848
    prior to grant, **18**, 847
    subsequent to grant, **18**, 848
  construction, **18**, 836
  proof of infringement, and, **18**, 866
  publication—
    effect, **18**, 843
    generally, **18**, 843, 850

Patent—*continued*
statement of claim, **18**, 835, 835*n*
  construction, **18**, 836
succession, rights on, **18**, 811
third party licensed to use, **18**, 811
transfer of ownership, **18**, 653
transfer of patent rights to third party, **18**, 812
two or more linked inventions, **18**, 841
university teacher, patentable invention made by, **8**, 1022
unregistered, **18**, 812
validity—
  certificate of contested, **18**, 875
  challenge of, **18**, 833, 877
    third party, by, **18**, 855, 858
  prior use of patented invention, **18**, 872
Patent agent
instruction of advocate by, **13**, 1298
non-designated services, **4**, 1177*n*
partnership, number of partners allowed, **16**, 1011
professional rules, partnership contravening, **16**, 1017
restrictive trade practices, **4**, 1247
Patent Co-operation Treaty 1970, **18**, 891, 892, 893
Patent Office, **19**, 219
Paternity
decree of, **19**, 1430
establishment of, *see* PARENTAGE
findings of, as evidence, **10**, 502
real evidence in questions of, **10**, 620
statutory declaration acknowledging, **19**, 1430
Paternity (copyright)
See COPYRIGHT (moral rights)
Path
See PUBLIC PATH
Patient
definition, **11**, 1445
dental services, **11**, 1456
doctors' duty to attend and treat, **11**, 1446
doctors' list—
  application for acceptance on, **11**, 1436
  limitation of persons in, **11**, 1439
  removal from, **11**, 1438, 1443
  revision, **11**, 1438
  schools and residential institutions, **11**, 1443
  transfers, **11**, 1438
holidays for, **11**, 1491
hospital—
  attendance at, expenses incurred, **11**, 1490
  return from outside British Isles, **11**, 1491
  transfer within British Isles, **11**, 1491
ill-treatment of, **14**, 1480
medical card, failure to produce, **11**, 1450
mentally ill, *see* MENTAL HEALTH; MENTALLY DISORDERED PERSON
negligence, remedies in case of, **14**, 1125
ophthalmic services, **11**, 1467
pharmaceutical services for, **11**, 1472
police station, doctor attending and examining at, **11**, 1450
private—
  fees for treating, **11**, 1450
  health service facilities used for, **11**, 1496

Patient—*continued*
private—*continued*
  national health service accommodation and services used for, **11**, 1494, 1495
  records on, **11**, 1446
  return from outside British Isles, **11**, 1491
  sexual involvement with, **14**, 1122
  transfer within British Isles, **11**, 1491
  undue influence, **25**, 764
  valuables held on behalf of, **14**, 1420
  See also HOSPITAL; MENTAL HOSPITAL
Patient's declaration
See ELECTIONS
Patrial
abode, right of, **12**, 118*n*
meaning, **12**, 107, 118*n*
wives of, **12**, 107
Patronage
sasine, symbols of, **18**, 90
Pavement
fouling by dogs, **19**, 371
ice on, liability for, **20**, 700
See also FOOTPATH
Pawnbroker
goods disposed by, to pawner, **7**, 1290
moneylender, not classed as, **13**, 1770
Pawnbroking
Consumer Credit Act 1974, provisions in, **20**, 41
failure to redeem, **20**, 41
firearms requiring firearm certificate, **10**, 1519, 1520, 1555*n*
minors, **20**, 41
offences, generally, **20**, 41
pawn-receipt, **20**, 41
  lost or unavailable, **20**, 41
pledge, contract of, **20**, 14
realisation, **20**, 41
repeal of legislation, **5**, 801
return of property in, **20**, 41
See also PLEDGE
Pay
See REMUNERATION; WAGES
Pay As You Earn (PAYE)
charities, payments to, **3**, 1153
income tax, **19**, 1514
Payment
concept of money central to, **14**, 1801
consumer credit agreements—
  agreement exempt by reference to number of, **5**, 822
  appropriation of payments, **5**, 881
  cancellation, recovery on, **5**, 867
  variation of payments, **5**, 882
decree for, **13**, 10
due course, in, **4**, 176
fixed future time, at, **4**, 111
honour, for, **4**, 177
letter of credit, *see* LETTER OF CREDIT
on demand or at fixed or determinable future time, meaning, **4**, 111
shareholder's right to, **25**, 13
water authorities, between, as to supply, **25**, 516
Payroll
data, exempted from registration, **18**, 1520

Payroll—*continued*
deductions—
  charities, payments to, **3**, 1153
  income tax, **19**, 1514
taxes, abolition, **19**, 1531
Peace
breach of, *see* BREACH OF THE PEACE
crimes against, **19**, 695
early history, **17**, 502
international law of, **19**, 657–696
justice of the, *see* JUSTICE OF THE PEACE
Peaceful assembly and association
freedom of, restrictions on, **12**, 78–84
right of, **12**, 73, 75–77
trade union freedom, **12**, 76
  closed shop agreements, **12**, 77
Peafowl
Games Acts, **11**, 496*n*
Peat
right to cut, valuation for rating, **24**, 691
rights to take, personal and real conditions, **13**, 241
Pecuniary legacy
abatement, **25**, 856
nature of, **25**, 850, 853
Pecuniary real burden
assignment, **18**, 383
competence, **18**, 383
confusion with real burden, **18**, 385, 385*n*
creation, **18**, 388*n*
ground annual, contract of, **18**, 383, 383*n*
heritable security, as, **18**, 383
meaning, **18**, 375, 383
obsolete nature, **18**, 383
real burden compared, **18**, 380, 383, 385, 391*n*
Pedestrian crossing
alteration, **20**, 440
controlled, **20**, 440
establishment, **20**, 440
pelican, **20**, 440
removal, **20**, 440
school crossing, **20**, 441
uncontrolled, **20**, 440
zebra, **20**, 440
Pedigree
proof of, in armorial succession, **11**, 1623
recording, **11**, 1623
Pedlars
sheriff court jurisdiction, **6**, 1135
Peerage
access to Crown, **7**, 723
advocate, peer as, **13**, 1346
'blank' charter or patent, **16**, 1305
child of peer, franchise, **15**, 1082
civil action against peer, **16**, 1308
claims—
  Court of Session, in, **16**, 1318
  House of Lords Committee for Privileges, before, **16**, 1319
  House of Lords jurisdiction, **6**, 823
  Lyon Court hearings in connection with, **16**, 1320
constitution, as part of, **16**, 1301

Peerage—*continued*
creation—
  ceremonial, **16**, 1305
  coronation, on, **16**, 1309
  dissolution of Parliament, on, **16**, 1309
  generally, **16**, 1309
  letter patent, by, **16**, 1305, 1309, 1312
  New Year, at, **16**, 1309
  Parliamentary scrutiny, **16**, 1301
  personal merit, on grounds of, **16**, 1309
  political expediency, for reasons of, **16**, 1309, 1309*n*
  Political Honours Committee, **16**, 1309
  regrant, **16**, 1305, 1305*n*
  resignation *in favorem*, **16**, 1305, 1305*n*, 1310
  royal charter, by, **16**, 1305, 1309
  safeguards and advice, **16**, 1309
  sovereign as 'fount of honour', **16**, 1309
  sovereign's birthday, on, **16**, 1309
degrees of rank—
  baron, **16**, 1311, 1311*n*
  duke, **16**, 1311
  earl, **16**, 1311
  hereditary peerages, **16**, 1311
  life peerages, **16**, 1312
  lord, **16**, 1311
  marquess, **16**, 1311
  viscount, **16**, 1311
deprivation, **16**, 1313
disclaimer, **15**, 1062, 1082
  courtesy title, use following, **16**, 1314*n*
  devolution on death of disclaimer, **16**, 1314
  effect, **16**, 1314
  generally, **16**, 1314
  life peerage subsequently conferred, **16**, 1314
  MP or Parliamentary election candidate, by, **16**, 1316
  succession, **16**, 1315
dormant, **16**, 1317
  right to claim, **16**, 1317
England, of, peer of Scotland holding, **16**, 1307
European Parliament—
  candidature, **15**, 1065
  franchise, **15**, 1076, 1082, 1091
  overseas elector, qualify as, **15**, 1146, 1147
extinct, **16**, 1317
  proof of extinction, **16**, 1317
female, devolution on, **16**, 1310, 1310*n*
forfeiture, **16**, 1313
  restoration, **16**, 1313
franchise, **15**, 1023
  European parliamentary elections, **15**, 1076, 1082
    registration, **15**, 1084, 1105
  local government elections, **15**, 1082
  overseas electors, **15**, 1123
  United Kingdom Parliamentary elections, **15**, 1082
generally, **16**, 1301
Great Britain, of, peer of Scotland holding, **16**, 1307
hereditary—
  degrees of rank, **16**, 1311
  recent creations, **16**, 1312

Peerage—*continued*
hereditary—*continued*
  succession, *see* succession *below*
  See also HOUSE OF LORDS
historical background—
  Celtic influence, **16**, 1303
  generally, **16**, 1302
  House of Lords, **16**, 1307
  later development, **16**, 1304-1306
  origins, **16**, 1303
  records, **16**, 1302
  Scottish Parliament, **16**, 1304, 1306
homage, Coronation, at, **7**, 706
House of Commons, disqualification from
  candidature for, **15**, 1062
House of Lords, *see* HOUSE OF LORDS
lands, title identifiable with, **16**, 1304
life, **16**, 1312, 1314, 1322
Master, **16**, 1322
modes of address, **16**, 1322
origin of term, **16**, 1301
Parliament—
  Scottish peers, present-day position, **15**, 1008
  summons to, **16**, 1301, 1307
    expenses, entitlement to, **16**, 1307
personal right, as, **24**, 15
precedence—
  children—
    esquire, entitlement to rank as, **16**, 2022
    generally, **16**, 2018, 2019
    peerage disclaimed, where, **16**, 2018
    Scale of General Precedence, **16**, 2013
  Decreet of Ranking, **16**, 2010, 2018
  determination, **16**, 2010
  disclaimed peerages, **16**, 2018
  generally, **16**, 2018
  Lords of Appeal in Ordinary, **16**, 2018
  Parliament, **16**, 2004, 2010
  Scots peerage, **16**, 2010, 2018
  statutory control, **16**, 2005
  wives, **16**, 2007
    divorced, **16**, 2007
    husband deceased, where, **16**, 2007
    peerage disclaimed, where, **16**, 2018
    Scale of Precedence for Ladies, **16**, 2013
privileges, **16**, 1301
  arrested in course of civil action, peer may not
    be, **16**, 1308
  attendance of House of Lords, **16**, 1308
    expenses, entitlement to, **16**, 1308
  court of law, right to sit covered in, **16**, 1308
  jury service, peer excusable from, **16**, 1308
  recognition by courts, **16**, 1301
records, judgments based on incomplete, **16**, 1302
regrant, **16**, 1305, 1305*n*
resignation *in favorem*, **16**, 1305, 1305*n*, 1310
Scottish Parliament, **15**, 1002, 1003; **16**, 1306
subscription, **6**, 417
succession—
  'blank' charter or patent, **16**, 1305
  female, peerage capable of devolving on, **16**,
    1310, 1310*n*
  Great Seal Register, **16**, 1310

Peerage—*continued*
succession—*continued*
  heir male, meaning, **16**, 1310
    of the body, destination to, **16**, 1310
    extinction, **16**, 1317
  heirs, nomination where no issue, **16**, 1305
  heirs of tailzie, **16**, 1310
  inquiry as to pedigree, **16**, 1301
  letter patent, statement in, **16**, 1309
  original charter or patent lost, where, **16**, 1310
  Parliamentary scrutiny, **16**, 1301
  peerage disclaimed, where, **16**, 1314
  presumption in law, **16**, 1310
  resignation *in favorem*, **16**, 1310
  second marriage, heirs of, **16**, 1310
  special destination, peerage granted with, **16**,
    1310
title of honour, *see* TITLE OF HONOUR
United Kingdom, of, peer of Scotland holding,
  16, 1307
unwarranted assumption of dignity, **16**, 1301
wife of peer, franchise, **15**, 1082
will, dignity cannot be assumed at, **16**, 1301
See also BARON; DUKE; EARL; HOUSE OF LORDS;
  MARQUESS; VISCOUNT
Peeress
franchise, **15**, 1082
House of Commons, disqualification from
  candidature for, **15**, 1062
mode of address, **16**, 1322
Pelican crossing
meaning, **20**, 440
Penal establishment
administration—
  chaplains, **16**, 1417
    See also PRISON (chaplain)
  Chief Inspector of Prisons, **16**, 1423
  civilian staff, **16**, 1416
  governors, *see* PRISON (governor)
  justice of the peace, inspection by, **16**, 1422
  medical officers, *see* medical officer *below*
  Minister for Health and Home Affairs, role, **16**,
    1412
  police cell, use as prison, **16**, 1424
  Scottish Prison Service, **16**, 1413
    See also SCOTTISH PRISON SERVICE
  Secretary of State for Scotland, role, **16**, 1411
  sheriff, inspection by, **16**, 1422
  social workers, **16**, 1419
  teachers, **16**, 1420
  visiting committee, *see* PRISON (visiting
    committee)
alternatives to committal to, development, **16**, 1500
complaints procedure, **16**, 1469
conditions, inspection and report, **16**, 1423
courts, intervention by, **16**, 1486
current practice—
  future changes, **16**, 1485-1493
  generally, **16**, 1484
dental officer, **16**, 1418
escape from, assisting or effecting, **16**, 1468
future changes—
  contemporary penological theory, **16**, 1491
  courts, intervention by, **16**, 1486

Penal establishment—*continued*
future changes—*continued*
  English influence, **16**, 1487
  generally, **16**, 1485
  justice model, **16**, 1491, 1492
  May Report, **16**, 1493
  pressure groups, effect, **16**, 1489
  prison staff, calls for change by, **16**, 1490
  public pressure as to, **16**, 1488
historical background, **16**, 1401–1403
inspection, **16**, 1411, 1423
justice model, **16**, 1491, 1492
legal regulation, desirability, **16**, 1497
maintenance, **16**, 1411
matron, appointment, **16**, 1411
medical officer—
  admission of new prisoner, duty on, **16**, 1441
  appointment, **16**, 1411, 1418
  cellular confinement, prisoner in, visits to, **16**, 1464
  death of prisoner, duty on, **16**, 1482
  responsibility, **16**, 1464
  restraint, prisoner under, examination, **16**, 1453
nursing staff, **16**, 1418
objectives of custodial sentencing, **16**, 1436
offences in relation to, **16**, 1468
offenders under twenty-one, **16**, 1404
parole, *see* PAROLE
prescribed activity, meaning, **16**, 1453*n*
prison officer, *see* PRISON OFFICER
prisoner, *see* PRISONER
release from, *see* PRISONER (release)
remission system, **16**, 1447
request procedure, **16**, 1469
treatment model, **16**, 1491
unauthorised property, introduction into, **16**, 1452
welfare provision, **16**, 1463
work, *see* PRISONER
See also PRISON; PRISONER
Penal reform
alternatives to committal, development, **16**, 1500
contemporary penological theory, **16**, 1491
courts, role of, **16**, 1486
English influence, **16**, 1487
generally, **16**, 1485, 1498
justice model, **16**, 1491, 1492
legal regulation—
  desirability, **16**, 1497
  re-ordering, **16**, 1499
May Report recommendations, **16**, 1493
outside pressure groups, **16**, 1489
prison officers, role, **16**, 1490
public awareness, effect, **16**, 1488
Penalties
contractually stipulated, *see* CONTRACT
cumulo, **17**, 791
custodial, **17**, 563
fines, **17**, 621, 799, 810
fixed—
  competent sentence, **17**, 810
  prosecutor's discretion to offer, **17**, 620
generally, **17**, 561
inventory, failure to deliver, **25**, 1019

Penalties—*continued*
non-custodial, **17**, 563
notice, **17**, 709
offences, for, **5**, 965
recovery of, Land Clauses Consolidation (Scotland) Act 1845 ..., **5**, 29
stamp duty, **25**, 1031
Penitent
privilege in relation to communications with clergyman, **10**, 685
Pennylands
udal law, **24**, 311
Penological theory
contemporary, **16**, 1491
Pension
Appeal Tribunal, *see* PENSION APPEAL TRIBUNAL
arrestment of, **8**, 331
building society scheme, **3**, 328, 374
claimant absent from Great Britain, **21**, 1023
company director, of, **4**, 418
contributions, preferential claim in case of insolvency, **9**, 150, 156
Crown servants, **7**, 762
damages, effect on scale of, **15**, 930
deceased, of, income tax, **25**, 964
disablement benefit, *see* DISABLEMENT BENEFIT
final salary scheme, **21**, 1210
  revaluation of preserved benefits, **21**, 1236
Firemen's Pension Scheme—
  contents, **10**, 1445
  development of, **10**, 1444
  Fire Brigade Pensions Act (1925), **10**, 1442
  generally, **10**, 1443
  injury awards, **10**, 1448
  ordinary pensions, **10**, 1446
  review, **10**, 1449
  state benefits, relationship to, **10**, 1450
  widow's pensions, **10**, 1447
friendly society, **12**, 689
fund—
  building society power to invest in, **3**, 369
  shares in, disclosure requirements, **4**, 305
  takeover, position on, **4**, 538
heritable property, as, **18**, 14
invalidity, *see* INVALIDITY PENSION
money purchase scheme, **21**, 1210, 1211, 1213
  cash equivalent, **21**, 1239
  meaning, **21**, 1250*n*
  revaluation of preserved benefits, **21**, 1237
national insurance contributions, **21**, 1044
occupational—
  approved, **21**, 1255
    Inland Revenue Pension Schemes Office (PSO), **21**, 1284, 1285
    See also taxation *below*
  Barber judgment, **21**, 1222, 1223, 1276
  capital gains tax relief, exempt approved scheme, **21**, 1315
  cash equivalent, right to—
    conditions to be met, **21**, 1238
    exercising right in relation to, **21**, 1240
    generally, **21**, 1238
    meaning, **21**, 1239

Pension—*continued*
occupational—*continued*
collective investment scheme categorisation, exclusion from, **12**, 1325
deductions, employee's wages, from, **21**, 1274
disclosure of information, requirements as to, **21**, 1241
employee leaving pensionable service before normal penson age, preserved benefit—
affected schemes, **21**, 1228
generally, **21**, 1228
long service benefit, **21**, 1228, 1229, 1231
preservation requirements, **21**, 1231
revaluation—
final salary benefits, **21**, 1236
generally, **21**, 1235
money purchase benefits, **21**, 1237
short service benefit, **21**, 1230, 1231
eligibilty, **21**, 1232
employer, payments to, **21**, 1321
employer-related investments, limit on—
legislative provisions, **21**, 1253
five per cent limit, **21**, 1256
schemes outside, **21**, 1255
less than twelve members, scheme with, **21**, 1255
meaning of employer-related investments, **21**, 1253
overriding provisions, **21**, 1254
employer's contributions, tax relief on—
exempt approved scheme, **21**, 1312
unapproved scheme, **21**, 1326
equal treatment between sexes—
Barber judgment, **21**, 1222, 1223, 1276
different normal pension ages, where, **21**, 1280
equal treatment principle, **21**, 1278
exemptions from, **21**, 1279
generally, **21**, 1278
family leave, treatment of, **21**, 1281
levelling up, compulsory, **21**, 1282
maternity absence, paid, **21**, 1281
non-compliance of scheme, **21**, 1282
Occupational Pension Board's power to modify schemes, **21**, 1283
Social Security Act 1989 ..., **21**, 1222, 1277
frozen, **21**, 1255
guaranteed minimum pension (GMP), **21**, 1211, 1226
anti-franking, **21**, 1233, 1234
revaluation addition, **21**, 1234
revaluation of preserved benefits, **21**, 1235-1237
in-house voluntary contributions, **21**, 1290, 1319
independent trustee, need for—
court order requiring appointment, scheme member obtaining, **21**, 1267
employer sole trustee, where, **21**, 1272
fees and expenses of independent trustee, **21**, 1270
generally, **21**, 1266, 1267
independent of employer, meaning, **21**, 1268
restrictions on scheme rules provisions, **21**, 1270

Pension—*continued*
occupational—*continued*
independent trustee, need for—*continued*
rights of independent trustees, **21**, 1270
statutory provisions ceasing to apply, where, **21**, 1271
trustee ceasing to be independent, **21**, 1269
when provisions applicable, **21**, 1266
Inland Revenue Pension Schemes Office (PSO), **21**, 1284, 1285
investment income, tax-free, exempt approved scheme, **21**, 1314
investments, employer-related, *see* employer-related investments, limit on *above*
levy, Department of Social Security's power to levy, **21**, 1265
limited price-indexing (LPI), **21**, 1244-1247, 1249
manager, disclosure of information by, **21**, 1241
member—
disclosure of information, **21**, 1241
voluntary nature of membership, **21**, 1242
member's contributions—
repayment during his lifetime, **21**, 1317
tax relief on—
approved scheme, **21**, 1313
exempt approved scheme, **21**, 1313
free-standing additional voluntary contribution scheme, **21**, 1313, 1319
higher-rate tax payers, **21**, 1313
net pay arrangement, **21**, 1313
unapproved scheme, **21**, 1328
Occupational Pensions Board—
cost of, levy towards, **21**, 1265
sex discrimination, powers in relation to, **21**, 1283
payments—
annual increase—
earlier service component, **21**, 1247
fund moneys paid to employer, **21**, 1249
generally, **21**, 1245
limited price-indexing (LPI), **21**, 1244-1247, 1249
later service component, **21**, 1246
retail price index, increase in line with, **21**, 1244
when payable, **21**, 1248
Pensions Ombudsman, *see* PENSIONS OMBUDSMAN
pension scheme—
collective investment scheme, not, **12**, 1325
generally, **21**, 1224–1227
Pensions Schemes Register—
cost of, levy towards, **21**, 1265
failure to supply required information to registrar, **21**, 1264
generally, **21**, 1262
purpose, **21**, 1262
registrable scheme, **21**, 1263
Secretary of State's powers in relation to, **21**, 1262
trustees, duty to supply information, **21**, 1264
perpetuities, rule against, **21**, 1273
retail price index, increase in line with, **21**, 1244

Pension—*continued*
occupational—*continued*
  sex discrimination, *see* SEX DISCRIMINATION
  state earnings-related pension scheme—
    contracting out—
      date from which payable, **21**, 1227
      generally, **21**, 1225
      guaranteed minimum pension (GMP), **21**,
        1226
        anti-franking, **21**, 1233, 1234
        preserved benefits, **21**, 1235-1237
        revaluation addition, **21**, 1234
      incentive payments, **21**, 1225
      protected rights, **21**, 1227
      rebates, **21**, 1225
  surpluses, reduction of, **21**, 1322-1324
  tax-approved, **21**, 1255
  tax-free lump sum, scheme approved by PSO,
    21, 1308
  taxation—
    administrator of retirement benefits scheme,
      meaning, **21**, 1296
    annual remuneration, meaning, **21**, 1290
    commutation on grounds of ill-health, **21**,
      1318
    earnings cap, **21**, 1291, 1299
    evolution of relevant tax legislation, **21**,
      1286-1293
    favourable tax treatment, generally, **21**, 1284
    Finance Act 1970 ..., **21**, 1286
    Finance Act 1986 ..., **21**, 1289
    Finance (No 2) Act 1987 ..., **12**, 1290
    Finance Act 1989 ..., **12**, 1291
      changes in practice following, **21**, 1293
    inheritance tax—
      generally, **21**, 1334
      payments made by scheme, **21**, 1334, 1337
      payments made to scheme, **21**, 1334, 1336
      section 151, Inheritance Act 1984 ..., **21**,
        1335
      sponsored superannuation scheme, **21**,
        1335
      ten-yearly and exit charges on settlements,
        21, 1334, 1338
    life assurance policy, taxation of gain under,
      21, 1329
    overriding provisions, **21**, 1292
    post-1970 changes, **21**, 1288
    pre-1970 scheme, **21**, 1287
    retirement benefits scheme, meaning, **21**,
      1294
      width of definition, **21**, 1295
    saving provisions, **21**, 1292
    scheme approval by Inland Revenue Pension
      Schemes Office (PSO), **21**, 1284, 1285
      alterations to approval scheme, **21**, 1306
      consequences, **21**, 1307-1309
      consideration of other retirement benefits,
        21, 1304
      continuation of approval, **21**, 1305
      discretionary approval—
        power to grant, **21**, 1302
        width of power, **21**, 1303

Pension—*continued*
occupational—*continued*
  taxation—*continued*
    scheme approval by Inland Revenue Pension
      Schemes Office (PSO)—*continued*
      exempt—
        actuarial valuations, **21**, 1289, 1322
        capital gains tax relief, **21**, 1315
        contributions, **21**, 1290
        employer's contributions, tax relief, **21**,
          1312
        generally, **21**, 1285, 1287, 1310
        investment income, tax-free, **21**, 1314
        member's contributions, tax relief, **21**,
          1313
        payment of moneys to employer, **21**,
          1289
        repayment of member's contributions,
          21, 1317
        surpluses, reduction of, **21**, 1322-1324
        tax advantages, **21**, 1310, 1311
      irrecoverable trust, established under, **21**,
        1310
      mandatory approval—
        anti-avoidance provisions, **21**, 1300
        conditions for, **21**, 1297, 1298
        continuation of approval, **21**, 1305
        earnings cap, **21**, 1291, 1299
        generally, **21**, 1285, 1301
      meaning, **21**, 1310
      no tax charge on member of, **21**, 1307
      tax-free sum on retirement, **21**, 1308
      taxation of payments from, **21**, 1316
      unapproved and approved existing
        alongside, **21**, 1304
    tax-free lump sum, **21**, 1285
      final remuneration used to determine, **21**,
        1290
    trivial pensions, **21**, 1318
    unapproved scheme—
      emerging benefits, taxation of—
        funded unapproved schemes, **21**, 1331
        gains, taxation of, **21**, 1333
        generally, **21**, 1330
        unfunded unapproved schemes, **21**,
          1332
      employer's contributions, tax relief on, **21**,
        1327
      generally, **21**, 1325
      life assurance policy, taxation of gain
        under, **21**, 1329
      member, tax charge on, **21**, 1326
      member's contributions, tax relief on, **21**,
        1328
      unapproved and approved schemes
        existing alongside, **21**, 1304
    value added tax—
      generally, **21**, 1339
      not reclaimable by employer, **21**, 1341
      reclaimable by employer, **21**, 1340
      trustees reclaiming value added tax, **21**,
        1342
  trustee, disclosure of information by, **21**, 1241

Pension—*continued*
occupational—*continued*
  unapproved scheme—
    generally, **21**, 1325
    taxation, **21**, 1326-1333
  unauthorised payments from, **21**, 1320
  unemployment benefit—
    abatement, **21**, 1275
    effect on, **21**, 833
  voluntary contribution scheme—
    free-standing, **21**, 1290, 1313, 1319
    in-house, **21**, 1290, 1319
  voluntary contributions, right to pay, **21**, 1243
  voluntary nature of membership, **21**, 1242
  wages, pension payments to retired employee not to be treated as, **21**, 1274
  Wages Act 1986, provisions in, **21**, 1274
  winding-up scheme, debt due from employer—
    determining amount of debt, **21**, 1252
  winding-up schemes, debt due from employer—
    legislative provisions, **21**, 1250, 1251
occupational pension scheme, contributions to, as preferential debts, **4**, 856
pension fund, private companies' investment in, **25**, 48
pension rights, donation, **8**, 615
pension scheme, avoidance of legal rights, **25**, 814
pensionable age—
  male and female, **21**, 1202
  meaning, **21**, 1202
  proof of, **21**, 1202
  state retirement pension dependent on, **21**, 1201, 1202
Pensions Ombudsman, *see* PENSIONS OMBUDSMAN
personal scheme—
  appropriate, **21**, 1212
  contracting out of SERPS, **21**, 1210, 1212
  generally, **19**, 1518, **21**, 1201
  inflation, **21**, 1213
  levy, Department of Social Security's power to, **21**, 1265
  voluntary contributions, **21**, 1212
police, *see* POLICE
retirement benefits scheme—
  administrator, meaning, **21**, 1296
  meaning, **21**, 1294
    width of definition, **21**, 1295
rights, loss of, compensatory award for unfair dismissal, **9**, 274
state, arrestment, **8**, 280
state earnings-related pension scheme (SERPS)—
  contracting out, **21**, 1210
    additional pension entitlement, **21**, 1213
    contracted-out rebate, **21**, 1211
    contracting-out certificate, **21**, 1211
    final salary scheme, **21**, 1210, 1211
      revaluation of preserved benefits, **21**, 1236
    generally, **21**, 1225
    guaranteed minimum pension (GMP), **21**, 1211, 1213, 1226
      calculation, **21**, 1213
      widow or widower, **21**, 1214

Pension—*continued*
state earnings-related pension scheme (SERPS)—
  continued
  contracting out—*continued*
    money purchase scheme, **21**, 1210, 1211, 1213
      cash equivalent, **21**, 1239
      revaluation of preserved benefits, **21**, 1237
    voluntary contributions, **21**, 1211, 1212
    See also occupational *above*
  generally, **21**, 1224
  introduction, **21**, 1201, 1224
state retirement—
  additional earnings-related—
    age addition, **21**, 1218
    best twenty years rule, **21**, 1224
    calculation, **21**, 1208
    Category A, **21**, 1208
    Category B, **21**, 1209
    Christmas bonus, **21**, 1201, 1219
    contracted-out scheme, **21**, 1213
    contracting out, **21**, 1210
      See also occupational *above*
    contribution conditions, **21**, 1208
    deferred claim—
      claim procedure, **21**, 1221
      increments for, **21**, 1216
    entitlement to, **21**, 1208
    generally, **21**, 1224
    graduated pension, **21**, 1215
    guaranteed minimum pension, **21**, 1213
    increases in, **21**, 1224
    introduction, **21**, 1224
    invalidity addition, **21**, 1217
    occupational scheme, **21**, 1211
    personal pension scheme, **21**, 1212
    surviving spouse, **21**, 1224
    widow, **21**, 1209, 1214, 1224
    widower, **21**, 1209, 1214, 1224
  age addition, **21**, 1201, 1218
  basic—
    Category A, **21**, 1203
    Category B, **21**, 1204-1207
    composite, **21**, 1204
    divorced person, **21**, 1207
    married woman, **21**, 1204
    widow, **21**, 1205
    widower, **21**, 1206
  Category A, **21**, 1201, 1202, 1221
    additional earnings-related pension, **21**, 1208, 1209
    contribution conditions, **21**, 1203, 1203*n*
    deferred claim, increments for, **21**, 1216
    entitlement—
      calculation, **21**, 1203
      child or incapacitated person, where claimant has cared for, **21**, 1203
      generally, **21**, 1203
      self-employed, **21**, 1203
      voluntary contributions, **21**, 1203
    widow, **21**, 1205
    widower, **21**, 1206
  Category B, **21**, 1201, 1221
    additional earnings-related pension, **21**, 1209
    deferred claim, increments for, **21**, 1216

Pension—*continued*
state retirement—*continued*
  Category B—*continued*
    divorcee, **21**, 1207
    married woman, **21**, 1204
    widow, **21**, 1205
    widower, **21**, 1206
  Category C, **21**, 1201, 1220, 1221
  Category D, **21**, 1201, 1220, 1221
  Christmas bonus, **21**, 1201, 1219
  claim procedure, **21**, 1221
  composite, **21**, 1201, 1204
  contribution conditions, **21**, 1201
  deferred—
    claim procedure, **21**, 1221
    increments for, **21**, 1201
  dependants, increases for, **21**, 1201
  divorcee, **21**, 1207
  earnings-related supplement, **21**, 1201
  employed person, entitlement, **21**, 1201
  entitlement—
    generally, **21**, 1201
    pensionable age, recipient must be over, **21**, 1201, 1202
  flat-rate, **21**, 1201
  funding, **21**, 1201
  generally, **21**, 1201
  graduated retirement benefit, **21**, 1201, 1215
    widow or widower, **21**, 1215
  guaranteed minimum pension (GMP), **21**, 1211, 1213
    deferred claim, increments for, **21**, 1216
  income support, interaction with, **21**, 1201, 1221
  income tax, subject to, **21**, 1221
  introduction, **21**, 1201
  invalidity addition, **21**, 1201, 1217
  legislation, generally, **21**, 1201
  life, payable for, **21**, 1221
  married woman, **21**, 1204
  non-contributory, **21**, 1201, 1220
  payment, **21**, 1221
  pensionable age, recipient must be over, **21**, 1201, 1202
  rates, **21**, 1221
  widow, **21**, 1205
    forfeiture rule, **21**, 1205
  widower, **21**, 1206
widow's, *see* WIDOW
Pension Appeal Tribunal
Court of Session, appeal to, **6**, 924
precedent, binding authority, **22**, 332
supervision of, Scottish Committee by, **23**, 911*n*
war pension cases *stare decisis* doctrine, application, **22**, 332
Pensioner
attendance allowance, *see* ATTENDANCE ALLOWANCE
disability living allowance, **21**, 928
income support—
  pensioner premium, **21**, 1074
    higher, **21**, 1074
income tax allowance, **19**, 1518
invalid care allowance, **21**, 952
severe disablement allowance, **21**, 943, 944
travel concession, local authority, **20**, 493

Pensions Ombudsman
appointment, **21**, 1257
authorised complainant, **21**, 1258, 1259
cost of, levy towards, **21**, 1265
decision of final as to fact, **21**, 1261
disputes of fact and law, investigation, **21**, 1258
hearings, **21**, 1258
jurisdiction, **21**, 1258
  exclusions from, **21**, 1258
maladministration, alleged injustice in connection with, **21**, 1258
pre-1991 complaints, **21**, 1257
procedure, **21**, 1260
Pensions Schemes Register
See PENSION (occupational)
Pentland Firth
innocent passage, right of, **21**, 10
territorial sea, **11**, 76
***Per saltum* grant**
meaning, **7**, 904
Percolating water
feudal title, **25**, 342
generally, **25**, 342
rights regarding, **25**, 343
underground, **25**, 344
Percussion caps
explosives, as, **10**, 1586
licensing exemption, **10**, 1620
Perduellion
See TREASON (high)
Performance
contract, of, *see* CONTRACT
copyright not applicable, **18**, 1431
meaning, **18**, 1432
recording in relation to—
  meaning, **18**, 1432
rights in, *see* RIGHTS IN PERFORMANCE
Performance bond
building contract, *see* BUILDING CONTRACT
contract, insurance business, as, **12**, 802
Performer
personal name, protection by passing off action, **18**, 1376, 1397
Performing animals
bulls, involving, **2**, 269
cruelty to, **9**, 1031
  training, in, **2**, 267
dangerous, **9**, 1029
generally, **6**, 1078
horses, offences as to, **2**, 269
inspection etc, powers of, **2**, 268
protection from, **9**, 1029
protection of, **9**, 1030
sheriff, powers of, **2**, 267
trainer or exhibitor—
  certification of, **2**, 266
  disqualification, **2**, 267
  inspection of register, **2**, 266
  offences, **2**, 267
  premises, power of entry, **2**, 268
  registration, necessity for, **2**, 266; **14**, 523
Performing Right Society
generally, **18**, 1013
musical copyright, **9**, 1037

Performing Right Tribunal
See COPYRIGHT TRIBUNAL
Perfumery
weights and measures legislation, **6**, 241
Perils of the sea
bills of lading, **21**, 551
burden of proof, **21**, 551, 551*n*
carrier not liable for, **21**, 603
charterparty contracts, **21**, 551
deviation to avoid, **21**, 615
marine insurance policies, **21**, 551
meaning, **21**, 551
piracy, as, **21**, 550*n*, 551
terrorist acts, as, **21**, 550*n*
Periodical
limits on authors' and directors' rights of identification, **18**, 1134
VAT zero-rating, **7**, 1447
Peritoneal dialysis
sickness benefit where claimant receiving, **21**, 880
Perjury
accused, by, **7**, 504
affirmation, evidence given under, **7**, 505
art and part guilt, **7**, 513
breach of oath of office, **7**, 506
competent judicial proceedings, must be made at, **7**, 506
conduct-crime, as, **7**, 32
contempt of court, as, **7**, 501
corruptly, accused must act, **7**, 511
declaration, evidence given under, **7**, 505
definite and unequivocal, statement must be, **7**, 510
definition, **7**, 504
evidence—
    competent, **7**, 507, 508
    relevant, **7**, 507
exculpatory evidence at own trial, **7**, 26
false, statement must be, **7**, 510
false statement not amounting to, **7**, 511
generally, **7**, 489, 490, 491
mental element, **7**, 511
oath—
    evidence given under, **7**, 505
    taking false, **7**, 512
precognitions, **7**, 509
    what amounts to, **7**, 509
public nature, **7**, 26
seriousness of crime, **7**, 503
subornation, **7**, 490, 491
    attempted, **7**, 515
    contempt of court, and, **7**, 501
    generally, **7**, 514
    inducements and threats amounting to, **7**, 514, 523
    meaning, **7**, 514
tribunal, at, **7**, 506
wilfully, accused must act, **7**, 84, 511
Permanent Court of International Justice, **19**, 721
Permanent trustee
See BANKRUPTCY
Permitted developments
agricultural buildings, works and uses, **23**, 147

Permitted developments—*continued*
amusement park, **23**, 159
caravan site, **23**, 157
change of use, **23**, 145
conditions attached to, **23**, 137
conditions require to be fairly and reasonably related to, **23**, 241
conditions restricting, **23**, 135
curtilage—
    building, of, erection within, **23**, 141
    dwelling house, of, development within, **23**, 139
    enclosure, of, erection within, **23**, 141
directions restricting, **23**, 134
dwelling house, **23**, 139, 140
forestry buildings and works, **23**, 148
industrial purposes, development for, **23**, 149
interpretation of classes, of, **23**, 133
land drainage, **23**, 150
local Act, development under, **23**, 151
local authority, development by, **23**, 152
mineral workings, **23**, 155
nature of, **23**, 133
oil storage tank, erection of, **23**, 143
peat, **23**, 156
physical limitations on, effect of exceeding, **23**, 138
private Act, development under, **23**, 151
private street, **23**, 150
satellite antenna, installation of, **23**, 142
scope of—
    Class I ..., **23**, 139
    Class I para (1) ..., **23**, 140
    Class I para (2) ..., **23**, 141
    Class I para (3) ..., **23**, 143
    Class II ..., **23**, 144
    Class III ..., **23**, 145
    Class IV ..., **23**, 146
    Class V ..., **23**, 147
    Class VI ..., **23**, 148
    Class VII ..., **23**, 149
    Class VIII ..., **23**, 150
    Class IX ..., **23**, 150
    Class X ..., **23**, 151
    Class XI ..., **23**, 152
    Class XII ..., **23**, 152
    Class XIII ..., **23**, 150
    Class XIV ..., **23**, 152
    Class XIX ..., **23**, 153
    Class XV ..., **23**, 153
    Class XVI ..., **23**, 155
    Class XVII ..., **23**, 155
    Class XVIII ..., **23**, 156
    Class XX ..., **23**, 152
    Class XXI ..., **23**, 157
    Class XXII ..., **23**, 157
    Class XXIII ..., **23**, 154
    Class XXIV ..., **23**, 154
    Class XXV ..., **23**, 155
    Class XXVI ..., **23**, 155
    Class XXVII ..., **23**, 158
    Class XXVIII ..., **23**, 159
services, **23**, 150
statutory undertaker, development by, **23**, 153

Permitted developments—*continued*
sundry minor operations, **23**, 144
telecommunications development, **23**, 154
temporary buildings, **23**, 146
temporary uses, **23**, 146
warehouse, **23**, 158
Permitting
mens rea, **7**, 103
use of term, **7**, 103
Perpetuities
statutory limitation, **13**, 1630
Person
See PERSONS AND PERSONALITY
Person in need
meaning under Social Work (Scotland) Act 1968
..., **22**, 13, 23, 27, 30
Personal accident insurance
recoverable loss, **12**, 885
Personal bar
acquiescence, *see* ACQUIESCENCE
adoption—
    generally, **16**, 1642
    holding out, **16**, 1644
    ratification, **16**, 1643
appeal, failure to exercise right of, **1**, 304
applicability, **16**, 1607-1611
authority, abuse of power by, **1**, 296
bodies subject to, **1**, 296
buyer in possession, where, **18**, 682
concept of, **1**, 294
contract, as part of law of, **16**, 1601
Crown, pleas against, **16**, 1610
definition, **16**, 1601, 1602
development, **16**, 1603
equitable doctrine, as, **16**, 1603
estoppel, English law of, compared, **16**, 1602; **18**, 680
evidence, as part of law of, **16**, 1601
exclusions, **16**, 1607-1611
exclusivity, **16**, 1604
generally, **16**, 1601
good faith, and, **11**, 1133
homologation, **16**, 1601
importance, **16**, 1603
incorporated company, **16**, 1607
latent claims, **16**, 1612
limitation on, **1**, 294
liquidator, **16**, 1607
mora—
    culpable delay, **16**, 1621
    delay alone insufficient, **16**, 1622
    heritable title, **16**, 1625
    judicial opinion, modern, **16**, 1623
    meaning, **16**, 1621
    presumption of abandonment, **16**, 1624
motor vehicle subject to hire purchase, statutory
    exception as to, **18**, 683
nemo dat quod non habet rule, exclusion from, **18**, 680-683
non-negotiable instrument, **16**, 1608
notice, by, **16**, 1612
owner's conduct precluding him from denying
    seller's authority to sell, **18**, 680
planning law, in, **1**, 295; **23**, 171

Personal bar—*continued*
plea in bar of trial, **17**, 691
pled by party, must be, **16**, 1604
principal not barred by actings of agent, **16**, 1607
rei interventus, *see* REI INTERVENTUS
representation, **16**, 1613
sale of goods, **18**, 668; **20**, 852
seller in possession, where, **18**, 681
statutes, applicability to, **16**, 1609
taciturnity—
    generally, **16**, 1621
    heritable title, **16**, 1625
    judicial opinion, modern, **16**, 1623
    mora, interaction with, **16**, 1621, 1622
    presumption of abandonment, **16**, 1624
trustee, **16**, 1607
ultra vires—
    act by statutory body, **16**, 1611
    contract, **16**, 1606
waiver—
    alteration of position by partner alleging, **16**, 1629, 1630
    definition, **16**, 1629
    delay as evidence, **16**, 1633
    examples, **16**, 1640
    express, **16**, 1628
    generally, **16**, 1626
    implied, **16**, 1628
    inconsistent actings, **16**, 1636
    insurance law, **16**, 1641
    lien, of, **16**, 1638
    more than statement of intention required, **16**, 1631
    payment without deduction, whether amounting to, **16**, 1639
    personal bar, as aspect of, **16**, 1626, 1632
    plea of no jurisdiction, as, **16**, 1634
    prejudice suffered, **16**, 1629
    relationship between, **16**, 1627
    reliance, and, **16**, 1629, 1630
    requirements of waiver, **16**, 1628
    right, waiver must be of, **16**, 1628, 1635
    ultra vires actings, **16**, 1637
    use of term, **16**, 1628
    what amounts to, **16**, 1628
who may plead—
    generally, **16**, 1607
    successor, **16**, 1607
writing, requirement of, rule as to, **16**, 1605
Personal Bill
Commons proceedings, **19**, 116
entail cases, **19**, 114
estate Bill, **19**, 5, 5*n*, 111
first reading, **19**, 115
marriage enabling, **19**, 111, 115
meaning, **19**, 2, 3, 111
Personal Bills Committee, **19**, 112, 113, 115
    proceedings in, **19**, 114
petition for, **19**, 111
reference to judges, **19**, 113
second reading, **19**, 115
settled estate, regulating and varying, **19**, 111
Standing Orders, **19**, 3

Personal bond
moveable or heritable, whether, **18**, 14
Personal effects
specific legacy, **25**, 848
Personal equity plan
building society powers, **3**, 374
building society shares held by, **3**, 328
collective investment scheme categorisation, exclusion from, **12**, 1325
Personal injury
action for damages, uncorroborated evidence, **10**, 502
British Railways Board liability, **19**, 1013
cause of action in nuisance, whether giving, **14**, 2044
damages, **14**, 2080, 2152. *See also* DAMAGES
damages, interest on, **12**, 1034
hotelkeeper's liability, **11**, 1738
industrial injuries benefits, *see* INDUSTRIAL INJURIES BENEFITS
limitation of actions—
  alteration to pleading—
    adjustment, **16**, 2156
    amendment, **16**, 2157, 2159, 2160
    basis of case, change in, **16**, 2161
    Pompa's Trustees, principles in, **16**, 2158
    radical incompetence, where, **16**, 2160
    substitution by right defender, **16**, 2159
    technical irregularity, where, **16**, 2160
    trivial error in designation, where, **16**, 2159
  causation of injury, **16**, 2152
  commencement of action, **16**, 2146
  contraction date impossible to determine, where, **16**, 2137
  date injury sustained—
    determination, **16**, 2148
    generally, **16**, 2147
    no clearly defined date, where, **16**, 2148
  date of knowledge, determination, **16**, 2149
    actual knowledge, **16**, 2149
    constructive knowledge, **16**, 2149
    test, **16**, 2150
  death of injured party, where—
    curator as pursuer, **16**, 2168
    executor as pursuer, **16**, 2165, 2168
    extinction of right, **16**, 2171
    generally, **16**, 2137, 2138, 2162, 2163
    judicial factor as pursuer, **16**, 2168
    legal disability, pursuer under, **16**, 2162, 2170
    limitation period, **16**, 2162
      commencement, **16**, 2167-2169
      judicial discretion to override, **16**, 2176-2185
    product liability actions, **16**, 2192-2197
    relative—
      meaning, **16**, 2164
      pursuer, as, **16**, 2168
      rights, **16**, 2165
    relevant facts, **16**, 2169
    solatium, damages by way of, **16**, 2165
    time bar, **16**, 2171
  defender, identity, **16**, 2153
  delay in proceedings where improvement hoped for, **16**, 2151

Personal injury—*continued*
limitation of actions—*continued*
  disregard provisions, **16**, 2154, 2170
  evolution of rules—
    generally, **16**, 2134, 2136
    Law Reform (Limitation of Actions, etc) Act 1954: **16**, 2137
    Prescription and Limitation (Scotland) Act 1973: **16**, 2139
    Scottish Law Commission report 1965: **16**, 2138
    Scottish Law Commission report 1983: **16**, 2140
    Scottish Law Commission report 1989: **16**, 2141
  generally, **16**, 2134, 2155
  judicial discretion, **16**, 2139
  justifiable ignorance, injured party in state of, **16**, 2149
  justification for rules, **16**, 2135
  legal disability, injured party under, **16**, 2137, 2138, 2141, 2142, 2154
  limitation period—
    commencement, **16**, 2147-2153
    commencement of action, **16**, 2146
    computation, **16**, 2142, 2145
    duration, **16**, 2145, 2146
  personal injury, definition, **16**, 2143
  Prescription and Limitation (Scotland) Act 1973—
    section 17, application, **16**, 2142
  pursuer, **16**, 2144
    assignation of claim by, **16**, 2150
    curator *ad litem* as, **16**, 2150
    executor as, **16**, 2150
    injured party as, **16**, 2150
    judicial factor as, **16**, 2150
  seriousness of injury, **16**, 2151
  terminus a quo, **16**, 2137
  time bar, **16**, 2137, 2151, 2171
    judicial discretion to override, **16**, 2176-2185
  who may bring action, **16**, 2144
reparation, obligation to make, **16**, 2116
Personal Insurance Arbitration Service
decisions of, **12**, 817
membership, **12**, 817
Personal Register
See INHIBITIONS AND ADJUDICATIONS, REGISTER OF
Personal representative
duties, **25**, 635
insider dealing rules, **12**, 1532
investment transactions arranged by or for, **12**, 1307
obligation, death of party to, **15**, 7
outsider mistakenly usurping function of, **25**, 637
powers, **25**, 635
property passes intact to, **25**, 606
transmission of estate—
  acceptance to act, **25**, 637
  generally, **25**, 635
unwilling person, burdens cannot be imposed on, **25**, 637
unwillingness to act, **25**, 637
Personal right
See RIGHT

Personalty
meaning, **25**, 607
realty distinguished from, **25**, 607
Personation
creditor, of, reduction on grounds of, **13**, 50
electoral malpractice, **7**, 409
See also ELECTION
fraud, **7**, 388
Persons and personality
active and passive aspects of personateness, **11**, 1035
capacity—
 act, to, **11**, 1057
 acted upon with legal effect, to be, **11**, 1049
 active, **11**, 1052-1058
  capacity-responsibility, **11**, 1052, 1054
  nature of, **11**, 1053
  passive and active capacity, personality involving, **11**, 1051
  pure, **11**, 1051*n*
  transactional, **11**, 1052
 beneficiary of the law, identifying, **11**, 1046
 beneficiary in private law, **11**, 1048
 capacity-determining features, **11**, 1053
 capacity-responsibility, **6**, 1054-1058; **11**, 1051*n*, 1052
  act, capacity to, **11**, 1057
  harm occasioned by others, responsibility for, **11**, 1056
  legal liability, capacity for, **11**, 1057
  nature of, **11**, 1054
  vicarious liability, **11**, 1055
 corporations, of, **11**, 1064-1066
 dole, for, **11**, 1054
 family relationships, **11**, 1068
 harm, to suffer, **11**, 1035, 1041
 insanity, **11**, 1053
 interests, to have, **11**, 1035, 1041
 legal rights, enforcement of, **11**, 1050
 legal wrong, to suffer, **11**, 1047
 liability, **11**, 1054
  capacity for, **11**, 1057
  vicarious, **11**, 1055, 1056
 mens rea, **11**, 1054
 nonage, **11**, 1053
 passive, **11**, 1045-1051
  capacity-responsibility, **11**, 1054
  nature of, **11**, 1045
  passive and active capacity, personality involving, **11**, 1051
  passive transactional capacity, **11**, 1048-1051
  pure passive capacity, **11**, 1045-1047
  pupils, **11**, 1051*n*
  rational and intentional action, for, **11**, 1035, 1041
  status, *see* STATUS
  transactional, **11**, 1052, 1059-1063
   legal powers, exercise of, **11**, 1060-1063
   nature of, **11**, 1059
   passive, **11**, 1048-1051
corporate actings, **11**, 1041-1043
corporate personality, **11**, 1041-1043
 artificial legal person, creation of, **4**, 317
 body corporate, constitution of, **4**, 317

Persons and personality—*continued*
corporate personality—*continued*
 firms, quasi-personality of, **11**, 1042
 legal, **11**, 1044
 legal existence, termination of, **4**, 317
 member's legal personality distinct from, **4**, 319
corporations, capacity of, **11**, 1064-1066
 active, **11**, 1065
 transactional, **11**, 1065
death, ascertainment of, **11**, 1039
European Community, free movement within, **10**, 112, 131-150
firms, **11**, 1042
fraud and the law of—
 delictual liability, **11**, 785
 entrapment, **11**, 787
 generally, **11**, 784
 marriage, **11**, 788
  void, fraudulently inducing, **11**, 787
 minors, **11**, 789
 pupils, **11**, 789
 seduction, **11**, 786
human identity, survival of, **11**, 1038
includes company, **6**, 109
international, *see* INTERNATIONAL PERSONALITY
legal principles and rules, necessity for, **11**, 1040
meaning, **6**, 109
 Interpretation Act 1978, under, **12**, 1211
natural person, **4**, 318
nature of personality, **11**, 1041
personal status, *see* STATUS
personate existence—
 commencement, **11**, 1037
 termination, **11**, 1039
quasi-personality, **11**, 1042
rights—
 legal, enforcement of, **11**, 1050
 recognition of active, **11**, 1078
 vesting in, **11**, 1073
social collectivity, attitude of law to, **11**, 1042
 non-personification of certain types, **11**, 1042
split personalities, **11**, 1038
status, *see* STATUS
time—
 continuity of persons in, **11**, 1036
  consciousness of, **11**, 1036
 existence of entities through, **11**, 1113
 overall well-being of person through, **11**, 1036
trans-sexuals, **11**, 1038
transplant surgery, **11**, 1038, 1039
unborn or unconceived foetus, **11**, 1037
See also INDIVIDUAL; PRIVATE CITIZEN
Perth and Kinross
local roads authority, **14**, 404
population, **14**, 64
Pertinents
See LANDOWNERSHIP (parts and pertinents)
Pertussis
vaccination against, **11**, 1446
Perverting the course of justice
See ADMINISTRATION OF JUSTICE (offences against)
Pesticides
EEC directive on, **9**, 1207
meaning, **11**, 319*n*

Pesticides—*continued*
powers as to import, sale and use of, **11**, 319
UK legislation on, **9**, 1206
Pests
animals or birds, removal of, **1**, 721
control of, **1**, 719
destruction of, **19**, 326
meaning, **1**, 719
pesticides, *see* PESTICIDES
protection of trees and forest products from, **11**, 608, 608n
rabbit clearance orders, **1**, 721
sheriff court jurisdiction, **6**, 1124
Pet animals
selling or keeping—
  market stalls etc, at, **2**, 121
  meaning, **2**, 119
  persons under 12 years, to, **2**, 121
shops, *see* PET SHOP
Pet food
VAT zero-rating, **7**, 1445
weights and measures legislation, **6**, 243, 246
Pet shop
definitions respecting, **2**, 119
disqualification for keeping, **2**, 123
generally, **19**, 1295
inspection of, **2**, 122
keeping—
  meaning, **2**, 119
  when not deemed to be, **2**, 119
licence, **14**, 119, 524; **19**, 1295
  conditions for granting, **2**, 120
  requirement for, **2**, 120
market stall etc as, **2**, 121
pet foods, weights and measures legislation, **6**, 243, 246
sale of animals, offences, **2**, 121
unlicensed, offence of keeping, **2**, 120
Petrifying fluid
weights and measures legislation, **6**, 244
Petrol tie agreements
conveyances, restrictions in, **9**, 836
duration of petrol tie, **9**, 834
lease and lease back transactions, **9**, 837
leases, restrictions in, **9**, 836
loans, relating to, **9**, 835
present regimes of controls affecting, **9**, 844
supply, **9**, 835
Petroleum/petroleum-spirit
conveyance of, **9**, 849; **19**, 388-394
Crown, rights of, **6**, 491; **9**, 724
derelict petrol tanks, **9**, 848
disused containers, **19**, 399
enforcement of legislation, **19**, 386
excise duty, **7**, 1067, 1067n, 1069
financing, **9**, 757
inspection, testing and seizure, **19**, 405-411
internal combustion engines, for, **19**, 398
labelling of containers, **9**, 850, 851; **19**, 395
lead in, EU directives, **9**, 1144
licence to keep petroleum spirit, **9**, 847; **14**, 522; **19**, 400-404
  appeals, **19**, 404
  contravention of conditions, **19**, 402

Petroleum/petroleum-spirit—*continued*
licence to keep petroleum spirit—*continued*
  grant of, **19**, 401
  meaning, **19**, 400
  transfer of, **19**, 403
licence to search for and get, **20**, 271
licensees, rights of, **9**, 725
meaning, **9**, 722, 846; **19**, 384, 385
motor vehicles, for use in, **9**, 852
offences, punishment of, **19**, 387
oil platform, securities over, *see* OIL PLATFORM
packaging of, **9**, 851
petrol tie agreements, *see* PETROL TIE AGREEMENTS
pollution, control of, **9**, 853
price marking, regulation of, **1**, 538; **6**, 81
production from below sea bed, **24**, 670
revenue tax, *see* PETROLEUM REVENUE TAX
rights—
  regalian right, as, **18**, 210
  separate tenement, as, **18**, 210
scope of legislation, **19**, 383
storage, **19**, 397
unleaded petrol, **7**, 1069
valuation for rating—
  licensed areas, exclusion from, **24**, 670
  offshore installations, **24**, 688
  petrol station, **24**, 663
See also INFLAMMABLE SUBSTANCES; OIL
Petroleum revenue tax, **19**, 1510
administration and collection, **19**, 1544n
Provisional Collection of Taxes Act 1968 ..., **19**, 1504n
Pharmaceutical chemist
animal, medical test on, **14**, 1206
carrying on business of, **14**, 1161
complaints against, **11**, 1520
contraceptive substances and appliances, supply of, **11**, 1471
controlled drugs, use of, **14**, 1258
Council of the Pharmaceutical Society of Great Britain, **15**, 1514
discipline of profession, **14**, 1163; **23**, 917
disqualification of, **11**, 1521
infringement of patent rights, **18**, 865
legal control, scope of, **14**, 1101
licensing system, exemption from, **14**, 1203
not employed at health centre—
  payment of, **11**, 1474
  services by, **11**, 1473
organisation of profession, **14**, 1159
pharmaceutical list—
  reinstatement, **11**, 1521
  removal from, **11**, 1521
pharmaceutical services for patients, **11**, 1472
records, duty to keep, **11**, 1471
register, grounds for removal, **14**, 1164
registration—
  premises, **14**, 1162
  qualification for, **14**, 1160
services supplied by, VAT exemption, **7**, 1426
Statutory Committee, **14**, 1163
supplemental services, supply of, **11**, 1471
terms of service, **11**, 1471
unregistered person, description by, **25**, 203

Pharmaceutical services
accommodation, provision for, **11**, 1476
administrative authorities, **11**, 1402
area pharmaceutical committee, **11**, 1423, 1472
arrangements for, **11**, 1469
charges for, **11**, 1512
chemist, *see* PHARMACEUTICAL CHEMIST
complaints, **11**, 1520
drugs and medicines—
    proper and sufficient supply of, **11**, 1469
    See also DRUGS
executive councils, **11**, 1402
health boards—
    administration by, **11**, 1410
    duties as to, **11**, 1469
meaning, **11**, 1469
national pharmaceutical consultative committee, **11**, 1419
patients, for, **11**, 1472
pharmaceutical list—
    reinstatement, application for, **11**, 1521
    removal from, **11**, 1521
pharmaceutical service committee, **11**, 1520
private practice, health service facilities used for, **11**, 1496
remuneration for, **11**, 1510
Tribunal, inquiry by, **11**, 1425
use of health service premises, goods or services, **11**, 1492
Pharmacist
See PHARMACEUTICAL CHEMIST
Pheasant
close season, **11**, 806
custody of, by unqualified person, **11**, 807
eggs, protection of, **11**, 802, 843
game, as, **11**, 802
Game Acts, **11**, 496*n*
Game (Scotland) Act 1832 ..., **11**, 815
Poaching Prevention Act 1832 ..., **11**, 843
trespass in search of, **11**, 817
Phillimore Committee
contempt of court, report on, **6**, 304, 305, 315
statutory departure from recommendations of, **6**, 304
Phonographic Performance Limited, **18**, 1013, 1024
musical copyright, **9**, 1037
Photocopying
copyright, and—
    generally, **18**, 1020
    licensing schemes, **18**, 1020
        certified, **18**, 1021
        compulsory, **18**, 1022
        Copyright Tribunal, licence terms, determination, **18**, 1022
        right, licences of, **18**, 1022
Photograph
aircraft, taken from, **14**, 2086
copyright, **18**, 931, 933, 957, 958, 960
commissioners' right to privacy, **18**, 1130, 1139
evidence as, **10**, 607
film, and, **18**, 970
identification by, **10**, 667
indecent, child, of, **3**, 1251

Photograph—*continued*
police surveillance activities, **16**, 1802
wild bird or animals, photography of, **11**, 883, 886
in writing, meaning, **4**, 109
Physicians to the Queen in Scotland
generally, **7**, 841
Physiological function
medicinal purpose, meaning, **14**, 1202
Physiology
discrimination, genuine occupational qualification as defence to, **9**, 361
Physiotherapist
Council for Professions Supplementary to Medicine, **15**, 1516-1521
domestic tribunal, regulation by, **23**, 917
employment of, **11**, 1500
non-designated services, **4**, 1177*n*
veterinary practice by, **25**, 203
Picketing
criminal liability, and, **23**, 882
immunity, **23**, 879, 880
secondary action, and, **23**, 881
See also INDUSTRIAL ACTION
Picnic facilities
provision of, **20**, 612, 623
roads authority, provision by, **20**, 503
Picric acid and picrates
explosives, as, **10**, 1587*n*
Picture
defamatory, **15**, 483
Pier
acquisition of—
    district council, by, **14**, 445
    islands council, by, **14**, 444
    regional council, by, **14**, 444
byelaws, **11**, 1317
constables, undertaker's power to appoint, **16**, 1818
construction or alteration, **11**, 1310, 1311; **19**, 19*n*
damage to, **11**, 1327
free port, in, **11**, 1306
harbour master's duties, **11**, 1320
lease, **13**, 205
local authority, functions of, **14**, 443, 447
low water mark, development above and below, **11**, 1310
permitted development of, **23**, 153
private, **11**, 1307
    Crown grant, when required, **11**, 1307, 1310
    dues, payment of, **11**, 1307
    generally, **11**, 1307
    public rights, consideration of, **11**, 1307
safety, **11**, 1321
sheriff court jurisdiction, **6**, 1106
statute law, **11**, 1308, 1310, 1311, 1326
valuation for rating—
    ferry, occupied with right of, **24**, 693
    generally, **24**, 598, 692, 694
    meaning of pier, **24**, 599
works, acquisition of powers for, **11**, 1311
wrecks and obstructions, removal of, **11**, 1322
Pigeons
categories of, **2**, 108

Pigeons—*continued*
dovecot, special rules, **2**, 108
Games Acts, **11**, 496*n*
property in, **2**, 108
protection of, **2**, 108
Pigmeat
accession compensatory amounts, **1**, 937
basic price, **1**, 938
cereal market, parallel legislation to, **1**, 937
common organisation, **1**, 938
export refunds, **1**, 938
sluice-gate price, **1**, 938
Pignus
See RIGHT IN SECURITY
Pigs
footpath, footway or cycle track, on, **20**, 706
operations on, **2**, 246
pigmeat, *see* PIGMEAT
slaughter, methods of, **11**, 503
Pilot (shipping)
authorisation, **21**, 297
    revocation or suspension, **21**, 297
authorised—
    meaning, **21**, 770*n*
    rights of, **21**, 304
delict committed by, liability, **15**, 242
drink or drugs, under influence of, **21**, 307
duties, **21**, 306
    breach of, **21**, 307
employment, **21**, 297, 298
ladders and hoists, regulations as to provision, **21**, 221
liability, **15**, 242; **21**, 306
    vicarious, of shipowner, **21**, 308
licensed, **21**, 297*n*
limitation of liability, **21**, 751, 753*n*, 770, 770*n*, 772
meaning, **21**, 292, 770*n*
misconduct by, endangering ship or persons on board, **21**, 307
pilot vessel, *see* PILOTAGE
pilotage dues, time charterparty, **21**, 640
salvage award, entitlement to claim, **21**, 455
seaworthiness in relation to, **21**, 614*n*
unauthorised, **21**, 297, 297*n*, 304, 304*n*
Pilotage
accounts relating to, publication, **21**, 296
administration—
    agents, delegation of harbour authority functions to, **21**, 295
    authorisaton of pilots and pilot boats, **21**, 297-299
    duplication of functions, **21**, 293
    generally, **21**, 293, 294
    inefficiency, **21**, 293
    joint arrangements, **21**, 295
charges, **21**, 296
compulsory, **25**, 307
    effect, **21**, 303
    exemption certificate, **21**, 302
    generally, **21**, 300
    pilotage direction, **21**, 301
    unauthorised pilot, **21**, 304
dispute over, **20**, 305

Pilotage—*continued*
fees, general average, **21**, 710
generally, **21**, 291
history, **21**, 291
maritime lien, whether giving rise to, **1**, 413
meaning, **21**, 292
order, river subject to, **25**, 307
pilot vessel—
    authorisation, **21**, 299
    construction and survey, **21**, 212, 212*n*
    lights and shapes to be displayed, **21**, 367
    sound signals, **21**, 374
port and harbour authorities, functions in relation to, **21**, 291, 293-297
services, VAT zero-rating, **7**, 1452
sheriff court jurisdiction, **6**, 1131
Trinity Houses, **21**, 291
Pilotage authority
agent of, limitation of liability, **21**, 771, 771*n*, 772
limitation of liability, **21**, 753*n*, 771, 771*n*, 772
Pin-table
game of chance, whether, **9**, 1010
Pinsel
clan chiefs, grant to, **11**, 1609
Pipe
accession to wall, **18**, 238
communication, *see* COMMUNICATION PIPES
gas, *see* GAS
law of the tenement, **18**, 238, 239, 241
operations not constituting development, **23**, 68
valuation for rating, **24**, 695-698, 714
water—
    service, meaning, **25**, 524
    servitudes, **25**, 348
    supply, meaning, **25**, 524
    temporary discharge of water, **25**, 333
    water fittings, as, **25**, 527
Pipe-lines
controlled, definition, **20**, 271
gas, **9**, 876
goods exported by, time of exportation, **7**, 1155
goods imported by, time of importation, **7**, 1141
movement of goods in, control, **7**, 1240
oil, discharge into sea, **9**, 1209
onshore, **9**, 735
search of land adjacent to, customs officers' powers, **7**, 1228
servitude for, **20**, 267
sheriff court jurisdiction, **6**, 1125
submarine, **9**, 734
    continental shelf, laying and maintenance rights and duties, **21**, 31
    exclusive economic zone, laying and maintenance rights, **21**, 39
    high seas, freedom to lay in, **21**, 41
submarine, navigation rules, **21**, 380
support, right of, **14**, 1693
Piracy
act of, exclusion or limitation of liability, **21**, 550*n*, 551
aircraft, against, **6**, 867
common law, **7**, 362
customary international law, **19**, 695
elements of, **7**, 362

Piracy—*continued*
High Court of Justiciary jurisdiction, **6**, 867
hijacking, **7**, 364
hostis humani generis pirates perceived as, **19**, 601*n*
international law, **7**, 363
jurisdiction on high seas, **21**, 44, 45
meaning, **7**, 362
robbery, as, **7**, 362
Pirate radio stations
advertising, **1**, 539
suppression of, **17**, 9
Pistol
machine, **10**, 1516
pistol club—
  inspection of premises, **10**, 1575
  possession of firearms, generally, **10**, 1538
  prohibited weapon, as, **10**, 1506*n*
Pit
right to sink as real condition, **13**, 241
Pit and gallows
right of, **17**, 522
Pitcairn Island
British Dependent Territories citizenship, **14**, 1932
Place of safety
court, committal, young person to, **22**, 33
custody in, **17**, 892
meaning, **17**, 892; **22**, 33
mentally disordered person, removal of, **14**, 1485, 1486
registration of secure accommodation as by Secretary of State, **22**, 33
warrant—
  child abuse, where risk of, **22**, 22
  children's hearing, time limit after issue, **22**, 22
  reporter, children's hearings, notification, **22**, 22
young person, committal by court to, **22**, 33
Place of work
redundancy, effect on, **9**, 167
safety, employer's duty as to, **9**, 79, 441, 442
safety representative, right to inspect, **9**, 473
unfair dismissal, effect on, **9**, 210
Placing request
See EDUCATION
Plagium
child, theft of, **3**, 1242
generally, **7**, 328; **10**, 1225, 1342
See also CHILD ABDUCTION
Plague
death by, cremation following, **3**, 565
Plan
conveyancing, **12**, 1240
copyright, **3**, 139; **18**, 958
Planning
See TOWN AND COUNTRY PLANNING
Planning application
acknowledgment, **23**, 160
agricultural tenant, notification to, **23**, 163
bad neighbour development, **23**, 164
conservation area, **23**, 164
consultation, **23**, 169
Court of Session, statutory appeal to, **6**, 924:, **23**, 276

Planning application—*continued*
district planning authority, to, **23**, 160
drawings, **23**, 160
fees, **23**, 165
form, **23**, 160
general planning authority, to, **23**, 160
generally, **23**, 160
listed building, **23**, 164
material considerations in determination of, **23**, 172
neighbouring land, meaning, **23**, 164
notifiable interest, meaning, **23**, 164
notification—
  agricultural tenant, to, **23**, 163
  owner, to, **23**, 163
  Secretary of State, to, **23**, 166
outline planning permission, **23**, 161
owner, notification to, **23**, 163
plans, **23**, 160
publicity, **23**, 164
reference of—
  regional planning authority, to, **23**, 168
  Secretary of State, to, **23**, 167
regional planning authority, reference of application to, **23**, 168
reserved matters, **23**, 161
Secretary of State—
  consultation, **23**, 169
  notification to, **23**, 166
  reference to, **23**, 167
variations to, **23**, 162
Planning authority
bias by, **23**, 112
development by—
  bias, **23**, 112
  deemed planning permission accompanying another statutory consent, **23**, 111
  environmental impact assessment, need for, **23**, 110
  generally, **23**, 109
  notice of intention to develop, **23**, 109
  statutory consent, deemed planning permission accompanying, **23**, 111
development plan, required to produce, **23**, 22
district, *see* DISTRICT PLANNING AUTHORITY
environmental impact assessment, decision relating to, **23**, 130
general, *see* GENERAL PLANNING AUTHORITY
hydro-electric development, notification of, **9**, 636
inter-relationship between different authorities, **14**, 617
internal organisation, **23**, 16
jurisdiction, **23**, 12
local plan, adoption of, **23**, 56
meaning, **23**, 108*n*, 122*n*
public path created by, **14**, 405
public right of way, establishment and maintenance, **18**, 502, 504, 506
purchase notice, service of, **5**, 92
reformed local government structure, in, **23**, 11
regional, *see* REGIONAL PLANNING AUTHORITY
Scottish Office, relationship with, **23**, 6, 7
section 50 agreement fettered by discretion of, **23**, 258

Planning blight
See BLIGHT
Planning permission
application for, *see* PLANNING APPLICATION
building or works—
    meaning, **23**, 177*n*
    removal of, **23**, 177
    time limits, **23**, 251
caravan site, for, **23**, 329
conditions, **5**, 197
construction of, **23**, 174
Crown land, *see* CROWN LAND
deemed, accompanying another statutory consent,
    23, 111
development not requiring, **23**, 101
development order, by—
    general order, **23**, 132
    generally, **23**, 131
    hazardous substances, **23**, 136
    modification of, **5**, 201
    permitted development, **23**, 133-138
    resumption of use after, **23**, 103
    special order, **23**, 132
    time limits, **23**, 251
    withdrawal of, **5**, 201
discontinuance of use, **5**, 200; **23**, 177
enforcement notice, resumption of lawful use
    after service of, **23**, 104
environmental impact assessment, *see* TOWN AND
    COUNTRY PLANNING
full, environmental impact assessment, **23**, 127
hospital building control, **11**, 1536
implementation of, **23**, 175
licensed premises, **2**, 44
limitations, **23**, 133
limited period, for, resumption of use after, **23**,
    102
mining operations, **14**, 1680
modification of, **23**, 176, 213
outline—
    environmental impact assessment, **23**, 127
    meaning, **23**, 161
    reserved matters, **23**, 161
    time limits, **23**, 251
refusal, right of appeal, **1**, 337
reserved matters, **23**, 251
resumption of use after—
    development order, planning permission by,
    23, 103
    enforcement notice, service of, **23**, 104
    limited period, planning permission for, **23**, 102
revocation of, **5**, 200; **23**, 176, 213
roads, in respect of, **20**, 720
serious personal hardship resulting from refusal of,
    23, 225
specified operation, meaning, **23**, 251
time limits for expiration of, conditions imposing,
    23, 251
Use Classes Order, limitation of, **23**, 93
valuation of land, effect of, **5**, 128
variations to, **23**, 162
when required, **23**, 100
whether required, application to determine, **23**, 170

Plant and machinery
accession, law of, **18**, 576, 576*n*, 580, 581, 582
belonging, test of, **14**, 1013
employer's duty as to, **9**, 78, 430-433
employer's liability, **15**, 346, 347
fencing of—
    civil action, causation and, **9**, 547
    construction of, **9**, 548
    duty to fence—
      generally, **9**, 539
      nature of, **9**, 545
    exceptions, **9**, 550
    extraneous objects, dangers arising from, **9**, 542
    foreseeability, questions of, **9**, 544
    maintenance of, **9**, 548
    materials—
      dangers arising out of use of, **9**, 541
      ejection of, **9**, 543
    in motion or use, meaning, **9**, 549
    part of any machinery, meaning, **9**, 540
    safe to every person, meaning, **9**, 546
functional test, **14**, 1012
hired, **3**, 2
insurance, **14**, 329
local authority powers, **14**, 329
machine tools, **14**, 1012
machinery, meaning, **14**, 1012
maintenance of, **9**, 432
meaning, **9**, 433
noise from, **9**, 1267
plant, meaning, **14**, 1012
prefabricated timber-framed unit, **14**, 1012
provision of, **9**, 431
unfenced, **9**, 551-600
valuation, method of, **24**, 715
valuation for rating, **24**, 441
    classes of, **24**, 703
    electric motors used in trade process, **24**, 708
    extent of plant and machinery, **24**, 711
    external plant and machinery, **24**, 712
      removal, **24**, 713
    inclusive provisions, **24**, 703-706
    machinery within buildings, **24**, 709
    meaning, **24**, 700
      whether heritable or moveable, **24**, 699
    mobility, test of, **24**, 710
    moveable plant, classes of, **24**, 707
    pipes, **24**, 714
    statutory provisions, **24**, 699-702
      application and construction of definition,
      24, 701, 702
      fixed or attached, valuation generally, **24**,
      699
valuation roll, **24**, 441
writing-down allowance, **14**, 1010
Plant breeders' rights
application—
    incorrect information in, **18**, 921
    refusal, appeal, **18**, 912
assignment, **18**, 920
conditions—
    attached to licence, breach, **18**, 915
    limitations or restrictions, imposition on
      assignment, **18**, 920

Plant breeders' rights—*continued*
Convention for the Protection of New Varieties of Plants (1961), **18**, 911
dealing in, **18**, 920
designation of variety, **18**, 912
duration, **18**, 912
England, **18**, 912
EU legislation, **18**, 911, 1611, 1650
false representation offences, **18**, 917
genetic variants, **18**, 912
grant—
  application for, **18**, 912, 921
  conditions for, **18**, 913
    distinctiveness, **18**, 913
    stability, **18**, 913
    uniformity, **18**, 913
  previous commercialisation, **18**, 913
  refusal of, appeal, **18**, 912
grapevine varieties, **18**, 912
infringement—
  accounting of profits, **18**, 915
  Crown, by, **18**, 914
  damages in respect of, **18**, 915
  generally, **1**, 723; **18**, 914
  innocent, **18**, 915
  interdict, **18**, 915
  name of variety, **18**, 916, 917
  remedies, **18**, 915
intellectual property, as, **18**, 801
licence—
  compulsory, **18**, 922
  grant by breeder, **18**, 920
name of variety—
  infringement, **18**, 916, 917
  register, **18**, 912
  selection, **18**, 912
nature, **18**, 914
Northern Ireland, **18**, 912
Plant Variety Rights Office, **18**, 911
  Controller, **18**, 911, 912
priority rights—
  applications made outside United Kingdom, **18**, 912
  within United Kingdom, **18**, 912
protection of plant varieties—
  generally, **18**, 911
  international legislation, **18**, 911
  United Kingdom legislation, **18**, 912
reproductive material—
  breeders' duty to maintain, **18**, 918
  definition, **18**, 919
  other variety, of, **18**, 914
  production for sale, **18**, 914
  sale—
    buyer's rights, **18**, 920
    generally, **18**, 914
    outside United Kingdom, **18**, 914
    what constitutes, **18**, 914
sale of parts or products of variety, other than reproductive material, **18**, 914
Scotland, **18**, 912
succession, **18**, 912
surrender, **18**, 921

Plant breeders' rights—*continued*
termination by Controller, **18**, 921
  appeal, **18**, 918, 921
  conditions leading to, **18**, 918
tree varieties, **18**, 912
varieties for which rights may be granted, **18**, 912
Wales, **18**, 912
wild plant, discovery of, **18**, 912
Plant Varieties and Seeds Tribunal
functions, **23**, 902
Scottish Committee, supervision by, **23**, 911*n*
Plants and seeds
accession by fruits, **18**, 595, 596
health—
  generally, **14**, 711
  promotion of, **1**, 719
information as to, **1**, 724
patent not grantable in respect of, **18**, 828
plant breeders' rights, *see* PLANT BREEDERS' RIGHTS
plant propagation, means of, VAT zero-rating, **7**, 1445
plant-based product, exemption from licensing system, **14**, 1203
protection rights, **6**, 602
weeds, removal of, **1**, 720
weights and measures legislation, **6**, 243, 245
Plasmapheresis
sickness benefit where claimant receiving, **21**, 880
Platforms and raised structures
safety of, **19**, 354
Plating certificate
goods vehicle, **20**, 496
Platinum
false trade description, **18**, 1418, 1418*n*
hallmarking, *see* HALLMARKING
plated articles, **18**, 1419
Play
amateur performances, **9**, 1048
meaning, **9**, 1043
obscene performances, **9**, 1044
professional performances, **9**, 1048
prosecutions in respect of performance of, **9**, 1048
school, **9**, 1052
See also DRAMATIC WORK; PERFORMANCE; THEATRE
Playground
road used as, prohibition of traffic on, **20**, 441
supervision—
  education authorities' duty to provide, **8**, 865
Pleading
absolute privilege, in, **15**, 520
advocate's duties as to, **13**, 1363
copyright, **13**, 1326
signature, **13**, 1326
written, conduct of litigation before hearing, **13**, 1356
Pleas-in-law
Court of Session procedure, **17**, 1374
evidence, debate on, **17**, 1182
writ, prescribed form of in ordinary causes, **17**, 1010
Pleas of the Crown
criminal jurisdiction, **17**, 508, 516
fireraising, **17**, 516
incest, **17**, 516

Pleas of the Crown—*continued*
murder, **17**, 516
rape, **17**, 516
robbery, **17**, 516
Pleasure craft
definition, **21**, 211*n*
Pleasure fair
amusement arcade distinguished from, **9**, 1008
meaning, **9**, 1008
Pledge
actual delivery, need for, **20**, 17, 18
bill of lading, transfer in security, **20**, 19, *19*
common property, of, **18**, 28
Consumer Credit Act 1974, provisions in, **20**, 41
creation, **20**, 17
debts for which pledge may be retained, **20**, 16
generally, **5**, 912
incorporeal moveable property, **20**, 15
jus in re aliena, where, **8**, 111
land title deeds, of, **20**, 15
lien distinguished, **20**, 14, 67, 84
nature of contract of, **20**, 14
negotiable instrument, **20**, 15
pawn, **20**, 14
    agreement to take article in, **5**, 913
    delivery of, **5**, 917
    failure to redeem, consequences of, **5**, 918
    realisation of, **5**, 919
    receipt, loss of, **5**, 916
    redemption—
        period, **5**, 914
        procedure, **5**, 915
pledgee—
    civil possession by, **18**, 121
    obligations of, **20**, 24
    power of sale invested in, **20**, 14
    real right, delivery essential to completion of, **20**, 8, 14
    surrender of possession by, **20**, 14
    title of—
        pledge by agent, **20**, 21
        pledge neither authorised nor protected by statute, where, **20**, 22
pledgor, title of, and personal bar, **20**, 23
possession, right to, **18**, 127
possessory right in security, creation at common law, **20**, 8
right in security, as, **18**, 5
rights of, **11**, 1108
sale on expiry of redemption period, **20**, 854
security, as, **5**, 908; **13**, 1759
sub-pledge, power to, **20**, 25
subjects which may be pledged, **20**, 15
transfer of property on *ex facie* absolute title compared, **20**, 20
Plenishing order
commercial lease, **13**, 582
landlord's hypothec, **13**, 517, 582
Plenishings
intestate succession—
    prior rights, **25**, 691
    value, dispute as to, **25**, 692
meaning, **25**, 691*n*

Plimsoll lines
See LOAD LINES
Ploughing
unenclosed land, on, **20**, 682
Pneumoconiosis
compensation scheme, **14**, 1678
Pneumoconiosis and Byssinosis Benefit Scheme, **21**, 1002
prescribed diseases regulations, **21**, 992, 997
Poaching
brown trout, **11**, 51
day, **18**, 182
deer, **11**, 938
detention of suspected persons, **11**, 844
evidence of, **11**, 846
firearm, discharge at poachers, **10**, 1573
forfeiture of fish or other articles, **11**, 11, 27
freshwater fish, **11**, 10
game laws, generally, **10**, 1583
gang poaching, **11**, 939
justice of the peace court, **6**, 1159
night, **18**, 182
    agricultural tenant, by, **11**, 810*n*
    apprehension, powers of, **11**, 812
    company of person with net or gun, being in, **11**, 810, 813
    entering on land with nets or guns, **11**, 810
    group offences, **11**, 813
    meaning, **11**, 811
    Night Poaching Acts 1828 and 1844 ..., **11**, 810-814
    prosecutions, **11**, 814
    public road, highway or path, taking game on, **11**, 810
    seizure, powers of, **11**, 812
    taking or destroying game by, **11**, 810
oath of verity, **11**, 845
offence of, generally, **7**, 333
Poaching Prevention Act 1832 ..., **11**, 843-847
salmon, **11**, 10, 11
search, powers of, **11**, 844
seizure, powers of, **11**, 844
Poinding
abuse of process, **8**, 124; **15**, 465
arrestment, competition with, **8**, 290
attachment, as, **8**, 286
certificate of execution, **8**, 222
charge—
    days of, **8**, 218
    error or omission in, **8**, 218
    execution, **8**, 219
    expiry, **8**, 221
    jurisdiction, **8**, 220
    nature of, **8**, 218
    officer serving having personal interest, **8**, 218
    overstatement of sum due, **8**, 218
    partner, against, **8**, 218
    preceding poinding, **8**, 218
    prescription, **8**, 218
    re-charge, **8**, 218
    regulation, **8**, 218
    report of, **8**, 219
    service, **8**, 219
        keyhole, **8**, 219

Poinding—*continued*
charge—*continued*
  suspension *quoad excessum*, **8**, 218
  warrant to, extract decree, as, **8**, 218
child support liability order, **8**, 217
common, goods owned in, **8**, 223
common and statute law, **8**, 217
company administration, and, **8**, 241
conjoined, **8**, 225, 244
control of poinded goods, **8**, 233
corporeal moveable property, attaching to, **8**, 217, 229
creditor, ownership transferred to, **8**, 243
death of debtor, effect, **8**, 127
decree for payment, **8**, 119, 217
delict, **8**, 124
diligence—
  effect of winding up on, **4**, 845, 846
  poinding as, **8**, 101
duration, **8**, 227
equalisation, **8**, 244
  proposed reforms, **8**, 104
execution, **8**, 222
expenses, **8**, 237
floating charges, and, **8**, 240
forcible entry, powers of, **8**, 222
ground, of, *see* POINDING OF THE GROUND
inventory, **8**, 222
judicial discretion, **8**, 126
landlord's hypothec, and, **8**, 387
liquidation, and, **8**, 239
messenger-at-arms, duty as to, **14**, 1504
moveable property, **8**, 107; **18**, 13
nature of, **8**, 217
negligent officer, liability of, **14**, 1507
officers of court, exercise by, **8**, 105
ownership, **8**, 243
  presumptions as to, **8**, 232
poinder, proceeds of sale paid to, **8**, 217
poinding of the ground compared, **8**, 362
power of sale conferred by, **18**, 667
property of wrong person, **8**, 124
protection from, **17**, 1126
public authority, use by, **8**, 217, 245
ranking, **8**, 244
real, *see* POINDING OF THE GROUND
real right, as, **8**, 243
recall, **8**, 228
receivership, and, **8**, 240
redemption of poinded items, **8**, 224
release, **8**, 228
report of, **8**, 226
sale—
  boat, gear or catch of, **11**, 174
  proceeds of, **8**, 217
  recovery of tax by, **19**, 1550
  undervalue, at, **8**, 124
schedule of poinding, **8**, 222
security, real right of, **8**, 243
sequestration, and, **8**, 238
sequestration for rent, competition with, **8**, 387
subject matter—
  common law, subjects poindable at, **8**, 229
  common ownership, goods in, **8**, 231

Poinding—*continued*
subject matter—*continued*
  control, **8**, 233
  corporeal moveable property, **8**, 217, 229
  exemptions from poinding, **8**, 229, 230
  ownership, presumptions as to, **8**, 232
  reacquired by debtor, **8**, 229
  removal of goods, **8**, 233
  sale to bona fide purchaser, **8**, 233
  statute law, under, **8**, 230
  third party rights, **8**, 231
  warrant sale, **8**, 234
summary warrant, on, **8**, 217, 245
third party rights, **8**, 231
time limit for execution, **8**, 222
time to pay direction, and, **8**, 242
time to pay order, and, **8**, 242
unduly harsh, where sale would be, **8**, 228
valuation, **8**, 223
warrant for, **8**, 119
warrant sale, **8**, 234
  cancellation, **8**, 234
  conduct of, **8**, 234
  expenses, **8**, 237
  goods sold at less than appraised value, **8**, 234
  place of, **8**, 234
  proceeds of, **8**, 235
  refusal, sheriff's power of, **8**, 234
  removal of goods for, **8**, 233
  report of, **8**, 236
  reserve prices, **8**, 234
  roup, conduct by, **8**, 234
  unsold items, **8**, 234
  warrant, service of, **8**, 234
  who may bid, **8**, 234
warrant to poind, **8**, 222
wrongous charges, **8**, 246
Poinding of the ground
action of, **8**, 362, 366
adjudger, **8**, 364
adjudication on a *debitum fundi* following, **8**, 373
administration, and, **8**, 371
compared, **8**, 362
creditor—
  competence, **8**, 362, 364
  debitum fundi, must hold, **8**, 364
  generally, **8**, 360
  heritably secured, must be, **8**, 362
  infeft, must be, **8**, 364
creditor's rights, **20**, 117
debtor, **8**, 365
  death of, effect, **8**, 127
defender, **8**, 365
effect, **8**, 368
enforcement of secured debts, **8**, 101
generally, **14**, 1812
ground annual, **20**, 265
heritable creditor, **8**, 364
let subjects, **8**, 361, 365
liquidation, and, **8**, 370
long lease, creditor holding security over, **8**, 364
moveables, attachment of, **20**, 117
nature of, **8**, 360
officers of court, exercise by, **8**, 105

Poinding of the ground—*continued*
owner of goods, **8**, 365
personal poinding compared, **8**, 362
prior decree for payment not required, **8**, 362
procedure, **8**, 366, 367
reason for use, **8**, 363
receivership, and, **8**, 371
security over lease, **20**, 259
sequestration, and, **8**, 369
standard security holder, **8**, 364
subjects attachable, **8**, 361, 362
    exemptions, **8**, 361, 367
    ordinary poinding compared, **8**, 362
    owner of, **8**, 365
superior, **8**, 364
Poison
fish farms, controlling pollution from, **11**, 62
fishing with prohibited, **11**, 12, 21
illegal use in trout fishing, **11**, 54
inspection, **14**, 1219
killing of animals with, control provisions, **11**, 864
    wild birds or animals, **11**, 880, 884
meaning, **14**, 1213
medicinal, **14**, 1213
non-medicinal, **14**, 519
possession, control of, **25**, 407
sale of—
    business purposes, for, **14**, 1215
    containers, **14**, 1217
    export sale, **14**, 1215
    governmental purposes, for, **14**, 1215
    labelling, **14**, 1217
    licensing, **14**, 520
    Poisons Book, recording in, **14**, 1214
    professional sale, **14**, 1215
    public hospital, to, **14**, 1215
    regulation, generally, **14**, 519
    restrictions, **14**, 1216
    scientific purposes, for, **14**, 1215
    wholesale transaction, **14**, 1215
sheriff court jurisdiction, **6**, 1117
storage, **14**, 1218
transport, **14**, 1218
water system, prevented from entering, **25**, 407
Poisoning
Criminal Injuries Compensation Scheme, **7**, 1
Poisons Board
functions, **14**, 1213
Poisons List
contents, **14**, 1213
Polar regions
international law, **19**, 672
Police
abuse of power, **7**, 549
accommodation, *see* housing *below*
accountability, **16**, 1701
additional police services, provision, **16**, 1719
adequate force, provision, **16**, 1714
administration, **16**, 1710
agreement—
    collaboration, **14**, 490
    premises, watching of, **14**, 491
alcoholic liquor, discreditable behaviour in relation, **16**, 1771

Police—*continued*
allowances, *see* pay and allowances *below*
amalgamation scheme—
    appointments and promotions, **16**, 1751
    chief constable, **16**, 1757, 1757*n*
    effect, **16**, 1757
    generally, **14**, 480
    joint police committee, **16**, 1757
    local government reorganisation, on, **14**, 481
    pecuniary loss due to, **16**, 1757, 1757*n*
    proposals for, **16**, 1720
        inquiry into, **16**, 1726
    Secretary of State's power to approve or require, **16**, 1725, 1757
    transfer of constables, **16**, 1757
    transfer of property, rights and liabilities, **16**, 1757
animal, slaughter without owner's consent, **25**, 206
appointments, **16**, 1737
    amalgamation scheme, where, **16**, 1751
    chief constables' powers, **16**, 1737
    constables, **16**, 1747
        discrimination, **16**, 1747, 1747*n*
        qualification for, **16**, 1747
    senior ranks, **16**, 1748
apprehension of accused, **17**, 543
area, *see* POLICE AREA
arrest, *see* ARREST
assault against, **7**, 541; **16**, 1807; **19**, 1266
    real or imitation firearm possessed during, **10**, 1565
Association of Chief Police Officers, **16**, 1763
Association of Scottish Police Superintendents, **16**, 1763
authority, *see* POLICE AUTHORITY
beat—
    generally, **16**, 1741
    meaning, **16**, 1771*n*
body prints, *see* FINGERPRINTS AND OTHER IMPRESSIONS
body samples, taking, **16**, 1797
breach of the peace, preventive powers, **16**, 1785, 1786
bribe, officer accepting, **16**, 1767
British Transport Police, *see* BRITISH TRANSPORT POLICEF
bugging, surveillance activities, **16**, 1802
buildings, **14**, 489
burgh, **14**, 21
business interest, member of force holding, **16**, 1747, 1748
byelaws, **14**, 272
cadet—
    appointment, **16**, 1737, 1746
    control, **16**, 1737, 1746
    dismissal, **16**, 1737
    employer, **16**, 1746
    number, approval by police authority, **16**, 1714
    purpose of police cadet scheme, **16**, 1746
    qualification for appointment, **16**, 1746
    regulations, Secretary of State's power to make, **16**, 1723
    resignation, **16**, 1746
    training, **16**, 1737

Police—continued
canvassing, offence under discipline code, **16**, 1771
causing disaffection amongst, **7**, 604
caution of police officer—
  breach of discipline code, following, **16**, 1776
  senior officer, of, **16**, 1780
central government funding—
  generally, **16**, 1714, 1714n
  payment to police authorities, **16**, 1734
  power to withhold, **16**, 1734
central government involvement, **16**, 1710, 1711
central government supervision—
  generally, **16**, 1709
  police authorities, supervision, **16**, 1713
centralisation, **16**, 1710
chief constable, *see* CHIEF CONSTABLE
chief inspector—
  appointment, **16**, 1748
  rank structure, **16**, 1742
chief superintendant, **16**, 1742
child, custody of, **14**, 1504
children's hearing—
  decision of, notification as to, **3**, 1295
  stand-by at, **3**, 1346
citation, service and execution, **16**, 1784
citizen, intervention in crime prevention by, **16**, 1701, 1701n
civilian support staff—
  employment—
    number employed, Secretary of State's powers, **16**, 1724
    responsibility for, **16**, 1714
  generally, **16**, 1708
collaboration scheme—
  chief constables' power to create, **16**, 1738
  expenditure, meeting, **16**, 1726
  generally, **16**, 1714
  Secretary of State's power to require, **16**, 1726, 1738
commission of supply, duties of, **14**, 29
committee, *see* POLICE COMMITTEE
common police services—
  expenditure on, **16**, 1732
  provision, **16**, 1732
  secondment to, **16**, 1732
complaints system—
  complaints book, **16**, 1772
  complaints procedure, **16**, 1772
  false complaints, **16**, 1772
  falsification, discipline code, **16**, 1771
  generally, **14**, 494; **16**, 1770
  hearing—
    application to vary election, **16**, 1775
    evidence, **16**, 1775, 1779
    finding, communication to complainer, **16**, 1775
    legal assessor, **16**, 1775
    non-senior officer, **16**, 1775
    private, held in, **16**, 1775
    record of proceedings, **16**, 1775, 1779
    representation at, **16**, 1775, 1778, 1779
    senior officer, complaint against, **16**, 1779
    witnesses, **16**, 1775, 1779
      cross-examination, **16**, 1775, 1779

Police—continued
complaints system—*continued*
  non-senior officers, complaints against—
    application to vary election, **16**, 1775
    criminal offence, allegations of, **16**, 1773, 1777
    discipline form, **16**, 1774, 1775
    hearing, **16**, 1775
    investigating officer—
      appointment, **16**, 1773
      responsibilities, **16**, 1774
    investigation, **16**, 1773, 1774
    legal representation, **16**, 1774, 1775
    no charge brought, where, **16**, 1774
    punishment, **16**, 1776
    representation at hearing, **16**, 1775
    warning, constable served with, **16**, 1774
  police authority duty as to, **16**, 1720
  procurator fiscal in relation to, **13**, 1437
  punishment—
    non-senior officers, **16**, 1776
    senior officers, **16**, 1780
  reform proposals, **16**, 1770, 1783
  senior officers, complaints against—
    appeal to Secretary of State, **16**, 1781
    discipline form, **16**, 1778
    hearing, **16**, 1779
    independent solicitor, **16**, 1778, 1779
    inquiry by sheriff principal, **16**, 1781, 1782
    investigation, **16**, 1778
    legal representation, **16**, 1778
    punishment, **16**, 1780
    representation at hearing, **16**, 1778
  suppression of complaints, discipline code, **16**, 1771
  suspension from duty, **16**, 1772
conditions of service, attention must be drawn to, **16**, 1749
conduct—
  discreditable, **16**, 1771
  prejudicial to discipline, **16**, 1771
  unlawful or unnecessary exercise of authority, **16**, 1771
consent or coercion, policing by, **16**, 1701
constable—
  allowances, **14**, 488
  appointment, **16**, 1747
    conditions of service, attention must be drawn to, **16**, 1749
    declaration, requirement to make on, **16**, 1747
    qualification for, **16**, 1747
    sexual or racial discrimination, **16**, 1747
  assault, *see* assault against *above*
  bribe, acceptance, **16**, 1767
  business interests, **16**, 1747, 1749
  chief constable's duty of care, **16**, 1769
  complaint about, privileged, **15**, 528
  conditions of service, attention must be drawn to, **16**, 1749
  constabulary independence, **16**, 1703
  crime committed by another officer, presence at, **16**, 1767
  criminal offence, committed by, **16**, 1755, 1767, 1771

Police—continued

constable—continued

criminal responsibility, **16**, 1767
  immunity from, **16**, 1768
  self-defence, **16**, 1767
  undercover work, **16**, 1768
damages or expenses awarded against or incurred by, **16**, 1765
disaffection, causing, **16**, 1747
discipline, *see* discipline *below*; discipline code *below*
disclosure of information by, **16**, 1767, 1803
dismissal, **16**, 1755
duties, **16**, 1784
  neglect or violation, **16**, 1767
  wilful absence from, **16**, 1767
duty of care, failure to discharge, **16**, 1766
equipment, *see* equipment *below*
examinations, **16**, 1751, 1751*n*
exceeding powers, **16**, 1766
family, business interests of, **16**, 1749
fingerprints, register of, **16**, 1752
  destruction, **16**, 1755
hindering, **16**, 1807
historical background, **16**, 1705, 1706
hours of duty, **16**, 1753
inducement or reward, offering to, **16**, 1807
jurisdiction, scope, **16**, 1804
jury service, exemption from, **16**, 1749
law—
  application to constable, **16**, 1703
  responsibility to, **16**, 1703
leave, **16**, 1753
legal responsibility, *see* legal responsibility of police officers *below*
meaning, **16**, 1742
number appointed, determination, **16**, 1742
off duty—
  discipline code, application, **16**, 1703, 1749
  status of constable while, **16**, 1703
office of, generally, **16**, 1703
other than regular police force, **16**, 1813-1818
  discipline, **16**, 1813
  duties and responsibilities, **16**, 1813
  enabling legislation, **16**, 1818
  powers, **16**, 1813
  privileges, **16**, 1813
overseas service, **16**, 1758
overtime, **16**, 1753
pain or suffering, intentional infliction by act or omission, **16**, 1767
pay, **14**, 488
pension, *see* pension *below*
personal record—
  contents, **16**, 1752
  destruction, **16**, 1755
  generally, **16**, 1752
  inspection, right of, **16**, 1752
  punishments, record of, **16**, 1752
  transfer of officer, where, **16**, 1752
police authority, relationship with, **16**, 1703
politics, active part in disallowed, **15**, 1019; **16**, 1749, 1749*n*
powers, *see* powers *below*

Police—continued

constable—continued

prisoner, visits to, **16**, 1460
probationary service, **16**, 1750
  discharge of probationer, **16**, 1750
promotion, **16**, 1751, 1751*n*
  temporary, **16**, 1751
public holidays, **16**, 1753
rank structure, **16**, 1742
regular, **16**, 1742, 1744
  definition, **16**, 1744
remuneration, **16**, 1708
residence—
  approval, **16**, 1749, 1754
  lodger in, **16**, 1749
  sub-letting, **16**, 1749
  See also housing *below*
resignation, **16**, 1755
retirement, **16**, 1755
Royal Ulster Constabulary, service in, **16**, 1758
servant of justice, as, **16**, 1784
special, **16**, 1742, 1744
status, **16**, 1703
suspension from duty, **16**, 1755, 1772
temporary, **16**, 1742, 1744
threats, making, **16**, 1767
travelling time, duty, calculation as, **16**, 1753
uniform, *see* uniform *below*
wrongdoing by—
  criminal responsibility, **16**, 1767
  delictual liability, **16**, 1766
  malice, proof of, **16**, 1766
  operational policy, and, **16**, 1769
  undercover work, **16**, 1768
  vicarious liability, **16**, 1765
wrongful act of, liability for, **14**, 493
constabulary independence, **16**, 1701
construction works, extra policing at, **14**, 492; **16**, 1738
control and accountability, **16**, 1701
crimes, investigatory powers, generally, **16**, 1787
criminal offence, officer committing—
  generally, **16**, 1771
Crown servants, when operating as, **7**, 757
custody—
  powers as to, **16**, 1788
  treatment of prisoners, **16**, 1767
debt, constable refusing or neglecting to discharge, **16**, 1749
deer, offences in relation to, powers, **11**, 957, 958
Defence Police Federation, **16**, 1816
deforcement, **7**, 540
deliverance, service and execution, **16**, 1784
departmental circulars—
  contents, **16**, 1721*n*
  issue, **16**, 1721, 1721*n*
  status, **16**, 1721*n*
Desborough Committee report, **16**, 1708, 1708*n*
detention, *see* DETENTION
disaffection—
  causing among constables, **16**, 1808
  constable causing, **16**, 1747
discipline—
  accessory to disciplinary offence, **16**, 1771

Police—_continued_
discipline—_continued_
  authority of chief constable, **16**, 1737
  code, _see_ discipline code _below_
  complaints system, _see_ complaints system _above_
  conduct prejudicial to, **16**, 1771
  criminal offence, police officer, committed by, **16**, 1755, 1767, 1771
  deputy chief constables' responsibilities, **16**, 1743
  discipline book, **16**, 1772
  reform proposals, **16**, 1770, 1783
  Secretary of State's functions in relation to, **16**, 1731
  special constabulary, **16**, 1745
  statutory control, **16**, 1741
  suspension from duty, **16**, 1755, 1772
discipline code—
  breach, **16**, 1755
    caution following, **16**, 1776
    investigation, **16**, 1770
    punishment, **16**, 1776
  breach of confidence, **16**, 1771
  complaints procedure, **16**, 1772
  corrupt practice, **16**, 1771
  generally, **16**, 1770
  off duty activities and behaviour, **16**, 1703, 1749
  specified offences, **16**, 1771
disclosure of information, officer, by, **16**, 1767, 1803
dismissal—
  breach of discipline code, for, **16**, 1776
  generally, **16**, 1755
  senior officer, of, **16**, 1780
  temporary service overseas, while on, **16**, 1758
  unfair dismissal legislation not applicable, **16**, 1755
division, **16**, 1741
drinking etc in licensed premises, **2**, 78
driver or cyclist, powers in relation to, **20**, 436
driving licence, production to, **20**, 436
drunken person, powers as to, **16**, 1787
duties, **16**, 1784
  generally, **16**, 1784
  wilful or careless neglect, **16**, 1771
enforcement of legislation, authority as to, **11**, 24
entry, powers of, **11**, 25
  generally, **11**, 25
  licensed premises, **2**, 68
equipment, **14**, 489
  ownership, **16**, 1754
  Police Negotiating Board powers, **16**, 1760
  provision by police authority, **16**, 1714
  regulations as to, power to make, **16**, 1724
  Secretary of State's powers in relation to supply, **16**, 1724
  special constable, **16**, 1745
  supply, **16**, 1754
  uniform, _see_ uniform _below_
EU co-operation on policing, **16**, 1805
European Convention on Human Rights—
  policing and, **16**, 1806
  surveillance and intelligence-storage, **16**, 1802

Police—_continued_
Europol, **16**, 1805
evading, **7**, 542
  assisting evasion, **7**, 542
evidence—
  attendance at court to give, **16**, 1784
  generally, **16**, 1784
  illegally obtained, **16**, 1802
  interception of communications, to obtain, **16**, 1802
examinations, **16**, 1751, 1751n
expenses, reimbursement, **16**, 1714
fabrication of evidence, **7**, 496
failure to prevent crime, art and part liability, **7**, 39, 182
false reporting to—
  generally, **7**, 529, 533
  Kerr v Hill, decision in, **7**, 529
  mental element, **7**, 531
  setting investigation in motion, **7**, 529, 532
  wasting police time, **7**, 530
falsehood, making wilful or careless, **16**, 1771
fine following breach of discipline code, **16**, 1776
fingerprints, _see_ FINGERPRINTS AND OTHER IMPRESSIONS
firearms, acquisition and possession of, **10**, 1543, 1580
  police permits, **10**, 1544
fishing, powers in connection with, **11**, 25, 26
force, establishment of, **14**, 487
freedom of, **12**, 83
functions—
  interference with—
    assault on police officer, **16**, 1807
    attempting to pervert the course of justice, **16**, 1811
    custody, assisting escape of person in, **16**, 1807
    disaffection, causing, **16**, 1808
    hindering police duty, **16**, 1807
    impersonation of police constable, **16**, 1809
    inducement or reward, offering constable, **16**, 1807
    liquor licensing, offences in relation to, **16**, 1812
    molesting police officer, **16**, 1807
    obstruction, **16**, 1807
    resistance, **16**, 1807
    wasting police time, **16**, 1810
giving false information to, **7**, 496
grant, **14**, 496
hindering police officer, **7**, 541; **16**, 1807
historical development—
  central government supervision, **16**, 1709
  early framework, **16**, 1704
  eighteenth century, **16**, 1706
  feudal system, **16**, 1704
  first police forces, **16**, 1707
  justiciar, introduction, **16**, 1704
  reigns of James I to James VI, **16**, 1705
  rogue money, **16**, 1707
  twentieth century, **16**, 1708
  watch and ward, **16**, 1705

Police—*continued*
hours of duty—
  Police Negotiating Board powers, **16**, 1760
  regulations, generally, **16**, 1753
housing—
  allowance, **16**, 1754
  approval, **16**, 1749, 1754
  free, provision of, **16**, 1754
  lodger, member of force taking in, **16**, 1749,
    1754
  provision, generally, **16**, 1724, 1754
  sub-letting by member of force, **16**, 1749, 1754
ill-health gratuity, **16**, 1756*n*
immigration controls—
  Home Office control, **12**, 138
  illegal immigrants, guide to treatment of, **12**,
    190, 190*n*
  leave to enter, grant of, police registration
    conditions, **12**, 175, 183, 236
  'passport raids', **12**, 190
  post-entry control by, **12**, 190
  private security firms, contracts with, **12**, 138
  registration of aliens, **12**, 144
  search warrant and arrest, **12**, 168
impersonating constable, **16**, 1809, 1816
industrial tribunal, jurisdiction of, **9**, 331
injury award, **16**, 1756*n*
insecure premises, protection, **16**, 1785, 1785*n*
inshore fishing, powers as to, **11**, 142
inspector, *see* chief inspector *above*
Inspector of Constabulary, *see* INSPECTOR OF
    CONSTABULARY
insubordination, discipline code, **16**, 1771
inter-force co-operation, **16**, 1709, 1710
international organisation of forces, **16**, 1741
interrogation, *see* questioning *below*
investigation—
  false statement in course of—
    generally, **7**, 533, 535
    inducing another to make, **7**, 534
    statutory provisions, **7**, 536-538
  pre-trial procedure, **17**, 547
jurisdiction, scope, **16**, 1804
jury service exemption, **16**, 1749
justifiable homicide in line of duty, **7**, 254
land and buildings for use by, provision and
    maintenance, **14**, 489; **16**, 1714, 1724
leave—
  entitlement to, **16**, 1753
  Police Negotiating Board powers, **16**, 1760
legal responsibility of police officers—
  criminal responsibility, **16**, 1767
  delictual liability, **16**, 1766
  generally, **16**, 1764
  law enforcement, **16**, 1768
  operational policy, for, **16**, 1769
  undercover work, **16**, 1768
  vicarious liability, **16**, 1765
liberation of person in custody by, **17**, 609
licensing—
  consultation with board, **2**, 48
  objection notice by, **2**, 50
local forces, system of, **16**, 1702
local government reorganisation, **16**, 1710

Police—*continued*
local policing—
  advice as to, **16**, 1715
  tradition, **16**, 1710-1712
lodger, taking in, **16**, 1749, 1754
London, **14**, 62
lost or abandoned property—
  care and custody, **16**, 1819
  claim made on, **16**, 1820
  disposal, **16**, 1820
  dog, stray, **16**, 1819*n*, 1820*n*
  person taking possession of, duty, **16**, 1819,
    1819*n*
  police functions, generally, **16**, 1819
  property classified as, **16**, 1819
  record of, **16**, 1819
  reward, claimant ordered to make, **16**, 1820
  transport undertaking, found on, **16**, 1819*n*
  unclaimed, **16**, 1820
mail, interception, **16**, 1802
maintenance of force, requirement as to, **16**, 1712
malingering, discipline code, **16**, 1771
Ministry of Defence, *see* MINISTRY OF DEFENCE
    POLICE
molesting police officer, offence of, **16**, 1807
mutual aid—
  chief constables' application for, **16**, 1738
  Secretary of State's power to require scheme,
    16, 1726, 1738
neglect of duty, **7**, 551
number of forces, **16**, 1708, 1708*n*, 1710
oath of verity (poaching prevention), **11**, 845
obstruction of police officer, *see* resisting or
    obstructing *below*
officer, *see* constable *above*
offshore installation, police jurisdiction, **16**, 1804
operational control, **16**, 1702
operational support units, **16**, 1741
oppression, **7**, 548
  discipline code, **16**, 1771
organisation—
  generally, **16**, 1710
  standardisation, **16**, 1708
outwith Scotland, action, **16**, 1804
overseas—
  temporary service overseas, **16**, 1758
  discipline code, **16**, 1771
overtime, **16**, 1753
parks, *see* PARKS POLICE
Parliament, Secretary of State's responsibility to,
    in police matters, **16**, 1735
passport, retention by, **16**, 1228
pay and allowances—
  clothing, **16**, 1754
  determination, **16**, 1754
  escort duty, **16**, 1754
  generally, **16**, 1708
  housing allowance, **16**, 1754
  medical charges, **16**, 1754
  payment, **16**, 1714
  Police Negotiating Board powers, **16**, 1760
  reduction in, following breach of discipline
    code, **16**, 1776
  refreshment and subsistence, **16**, 1754

Police—*continued*
pay and allowances—*continued*
  removal allowance, **16**, 1754
  rewards, **16**, 1754
  special area undermanning, **16**, 1754
  statutory control, **16**, 1741
  suspension, officer on, **16**, 1772
  transportation, **16**, 1754
pension—
  appeals, **16**, 1756
  assignment, **16**, 1756
  charge on, **16**, 1756
  dependant, payable to, **16**, 1756
  forfeiture, **16**, 1756, 1756*n*
  former police officer, payment to, **16**, 1720
  ill-health, **16**, 1756*n*
  ill-health gratuity, **16**, 1756*n*
  injury award, **16**, 1756*n*
  payment, **16**, 1756
  police force, **16**, 1756
    transfer, where officer makes, **16**, 1756
  Police Negotiating Board powers, **16**, 1760
  short service, **16**, 1756*n*
  widow, payable to, **16**, 1756
personal record—
  contents, **16**, 1752
  destruction, **16**, 1755
  generally, **16**, 1752
  inspection, right of, **16**, 1752
  punishments, record of, **16**, 1752
  transfer of officer, procedure on, **16**, 1752
personation of constable, **7**, 388
pervert course of justice, attempt to, **7**, 496
photographs, surveillance activities, **16**, 1802
physical force in execution of duty, use of, **7**, 238
Poaching Prevention Act 1832—
  powers under, **11**, 844
Police Advisory Board for Scotland, **16**, 1761
police authority, *see* POLICE AUTHORITY
police committee, *see* POLICE COMMITTEE
police custody, escape and rescue from, **7**, 560, 561
police property, wilful or careless damage to, **16**, 1771
police/public relations, fostering good, **16**, 1713
policing, inquiry into, **16**, 1728
political pressure, protection of force from, **16**, 1702
powers—
  apprehension of suspects, **16**, 1787-1793
  arrest and detention, **16**, 1788-1793
  arrest without warrant, **16**, 1790-1792
  data, storage and protection, **16**, 1802, 1803
  detention, **16**, 1794-1796
  drunken person, as to, **16**, 1787
  generally, **16**, 1701, 1701*n*, 1784
  intelligence gathering, **16**, 1802, 1803
  investigative, **16**, 1789, 1796-1801
  lost or abandoned property, in relation to, *see* lost or abandoned property *above*
  personal search, **16**, 1797
  premises, entry to and search of, **16**, 1798, 1799
  preventive, *see* preventive powers *below*
  questioning, of, **16**, 1800

Police—*continued*
powers—*continued*
  search, *see* SEARCH, POLICE POWERS
  surveillance, **16**, 1802
  terrorist activities, person suspected of, in relation to, **16**, 1801
pre-emptive policing, **16**, 1802
preventive powers—
  entry, powers of, **16**, 1799
  generally, **16**, 1701, 1701*n*, 1784, 1785
  public peace—
    disturbance, prevention, **16**, 1786
    preservation of, **16**, 1785
procurator fiscal and, relationship between, **13**, 1431, 1432; **17**, 615
probationary service, **16**, 1750
promotion—
  amalgamation scheme, where, **16**, 1751
  basis of selection, **16**, 1751
  chief constables' powers, **16**, 1737
  examinations, **16**, 1751, 1751*n*
  qualification for, **16**, 1751
  standardisation, **16**, 1751
  statutory control, **16**, 1741
  temporary, **16**, 1751
prosecutor, relationship to, **17**, 584
public, fostering good relations with, **16**, 1718
public assembly, police power to impose conditions, **16**, 1786, 1786*n*
public procession, police powers, **14**, 569; **16**, 1738, 1786, 1786*n*
public safety, **19**, 1278
punishment—
  complaints system, **16**, 1776, 1779
  discipline code, for breach of, **16**, 1776
  European Convention on Human Rights, **16**, 1806
questioning—
  answers, whether required, **16**, 1800
  European Convention on Human Rights, **16**, 1806
  failure to answer truthfully, **16**, 1800
  police powers as to, **16**, 1796, 1800
  tape-recording interviews, **16**, 1800
racial discrimination in appointments to force, **16**, 1747, 1747*n*
rank, reduction in, following breach of discipline code, **16**, 1776
rank structure—
  generally, **16**, 1703, 1742
  special constabulary, **16**, 1745, 1745*n*
  statutory control, **16**, 1741
records, data protection, **16**, 1803
reform, **14**, 49
remuneration, *see* pay and allowances *above*
reporter—
  meetings with, **3**, 1285
  referral of child to, **3**, 1287
  report to, **3**, 1287
representative organisations, **16**, 1759-1763
reprimand—
  breach of discipline code, following, **16**, 1776
  senior officer, of, **16**, 1780

Police—*continued*
resignation—
  generally, **16**, 1755
  requirement to resign—
    breach of discipline code, following, **16**, 1776
    senior officer, **16**, 1780
resisting or obstructing—
  authorisation to act, police must have, **7**, 539
  common law, **7**, 539
  deforcement, **7**, 540
  evading police, **7**, 542
  generally, **7**, 540, 543; **11**, 29; **16**, 1807
  obstruction of police officer, **16**, 1807
  statute law, **7**, 541, 543, 544
retirement—
  age, **16**, 1755
  generally, **16**, 1755
Royal Commission on the Police (1962)—
  police discipline, consideration of, **16**, 1783
  report, **16**, 1708, 1708*n*, 1711
Royal Ulster Constabulary, service in, **16**, 1758, 1771
Scottish Crime Squad, **16**, 1709, 1732
Scottish Police College, **16**, 1751
Scottish Police Federation, **16**, 1753
search, powers of, *see* SEARCH, POLICE POWERS
Secretary of State's functions in relation to, *see* SECRETARY OF STATE FOR SCOTLAND
section, **16**, 1741
seizure, powers of, **16**, 1787
senior officers—
  appointment, **16**, 1713, 1716
  discipline, **16**, 1713, 1716
  dismissal, **16**, 1717
  removal, **16**, 1713, 1716
  resignation, **16**, 1717
  retirement, **16**, 1717
sergeant—
  probationary service, **16**, 1750
  promotion, **16**, 1751
  rank structure, **16**, 1742
services at sports grounds, payment for, **19**, 1277
sexual discrimination in appointments to force, **16**, 1747, 1747*n*
sheriff court jurisdiction, **6**, 1121
sheriff's duties in respect of, **6**, 1046
special Branch, **16**, 1741
special constable, *see* SPECIAL CONSTABLE
special legal powers, **11**, 1062
specialised units, **16**, 1741
standardisation of provision, **16**, 1708
statements made to—
  arrest, after, **10**, 732
  generally, **10**, 729
  inadmissible confession, admissibility of evidence obtained as result of, **10**, 734
  initial investigation, **10**, 730
  questioning, circumstances and manner of, **10**, 733
  stage of suspicion, **10**, 731
  tape-recorded interviews, **10**, 735
station, medical examination at, **11**, 1450
sub-division, **16**, 1741

Police—*continued*
superintendent—
  appointment, **16**, 1748
  Association of Scottish Police Superintendents, **16**, 1763
  business interests, **16**, 1748
  rank structure, **16**, 1742
surveillance, **16**, 1802
  under agreement with occupier, **16**, 1738
suspension from duty—
  generally, **16**, 1755, 1772
  pay and allowances, **16**, 1772
  senior officers, **16**, 1772
  termination, **16**, 1772
telephone-tapping, **16**, 1802
temporary constable—
  appointment, **16**, 1737
  generally, **16**, 1742, 1744
  list of constables, **16**, 1737, 1744
  training, **16**, 1737
terrorist, suspected, powers as to, **16**, 1801
threat, police officer making, **16**, 1767
trade union membership barred, **16**, 1749, 1759, 1763
traffic regulation, by, pedestrian contravening, **7**, 544
undercover work, **16**, 1768
  entrapment, **7**, 203–205
unfair dismissal, **9**, 211
uniform—
  failure to return, **16**, 1767
  impersonating constable, **16**, 1809, 1816
  ownership, **16**, 1754
  Police Negotiating Board powers, **16**, 1760
  special constable, **16**, 1745
  supply, **16**, 1754
uniformity in provision, **16**, 1741
unlawful arrest and detention, **7**, 550
warrant, *see* WARRANT
wasting police time, **7**, 530; **16**, 1810
Police Advisory Board for Scotland
purpose, **16**, 1761
Police area
amalgamations, **16**, 1712, 1713, 1720
  Secretary of State's power to approve or require, **16**, 1725
beats, **16**, 1741
division, **16**, 1741
generally, **14**, 478
meaning, **16**, 1712
police authority for, **16**, 1712
sections, **16**, 1741
sub-division, **16**, 1741
Police authority
cadet, as employer of, **16**, 1746
chief constables' reports, **16**, 1715
composition, **16**, 1713
constabulary independence, and, **16**, 1703
damages or expenses awarded against or incurred by constable, **16**, 1765
efficiency, **16**, 1714
functions, **14**, 482
  additional police services, provision, **16**, 1719
  adequate police force, provision, **16**, 1713, 1714

Police authority—*continued*
functions—*continued*
  administrative nature, **16**, 1714
  advice, **16**, 1713
  amalgamation schemes, proposals for, **16**, 1720
  cadets, approval of number, **16**, 1714
  civil defence training, as to, **16**, 1720
  civilian support staff, employment, **16**, 1714
  clothing and equipment, provision, **16**, 1714
  complaints against police, with regard to, **16**, 1720
  discharge, central government control, **16**, 1713
  generally, **16**, 1713, 1720
  land and buildings, provision and maintenance, **16**, 1714
  local policing, advising on, **16**, 1715
  number of officers in force, determination, **16**, 1714
  pensions and rewards, payment of, **16**, 1720
  police committee, delegation to, **16**, 1713
  police officers' salary and allowances, payment, **16**, 1714
  police/public relations, as to, **16**, 1713, 1718
  prison, declaration that premises are, **16**, 1720
  reimbursement of police expenses, **16**, 1714
  senior officers—
    appointment, **16**, 1713, 1716
    discipline, **16**, 1713, 1716
    removal, **16**, 1713, 1716
    resignation, **16**, 1717
    retirement, **16**, 1717
  traffic wardens, appointment, **16**, 1720
  vehicles, provision, **16**, 1714
generally, **14**, 479
landlord, as, **11**, 1937, 1944
local policing, tradition of—
  central and local government, relationship with, **16**, 1711
  generally, **16**, 1710
  police areas, **16**, 1712
  police forces, **16**, 1710, 1712
police area, meaning, **16**, 1712
political pressure, protection of force from, **16**, 1702
regional or islands council, **16**, 1712, 1713
system, generally, **16**, 1702
wrongful act of constable, liability for, **14**, 493
Police burgh
parliamentary burgh distinguished from, **17**, 518
Police cell or other premises
detention in, **16**, 1822
prison, declaration that cells are, **16**, 1720, 1822
prison, use as, **16**, 1424
Police committee
appointment, **16**, 1713, 1713*n*
composition, **16**, 1713
function, **16**, 1713, 1713*n*
special provisions, **14**, 241
Police Complaints Authority
establishment, **16**, 1783
Police constable
See POLICE (constable)
Police court
Aberdeen Police Court, **6**, 1157, 1158
abolition, **6**, 1160; **17**, 517

Police court—*continued*
antecedent of district court, **6**, 1155
burgh court distinguished, **6**, 1156
classes, **6**, 1157
competency, **6**, 1157
Dundee Police Court, **6**, 1157, 1158
Edinburgh Police Court, **6**, 1156, 1157, 1158
Glasgow Police Court, **6**, 1157, 1158
Greenock Police Court, **6**, 1157, 1158
history, **17**, 518
inferior court, as, **6**, 1155
judges, **6**, 1157
summary procedure, **6**, 1155, 1157
Police Federation for Scotland
establishment, **16**, 1759
expenses incurred in connection with, **16**, 1762
membership, generally, **16**, 1749, 1763
purpose, **16**, 1759, 1762
Secretary of State's powers in relation to, **16**, 1762
Police National Computer
data protection, **16**, 1803
Police Negotiating Board for the United Kingdom
chairman, **16**, 1760
deputy chairman, **16**, 1760
establishment, **16**, 1759
powers, **16**, 1760
recommendations, **16**, 1722*n*
Policyholders Protection Board
establishment and purpose, **12**, 814
insolvent company's business, arrangements for, **12**, 814
powers, **12**, 814
Poliomyelitis
vaccination against, **11**, 1446
Polish
weights and measures legislation, **6**, 245
Political asylee
See ASYLUM
Political Honours Committee
function, **16**, 1309
Political offence
extradition, restrictions on, **12**, 516
  1870 procedure, **12**, 532
  1989 procedure, **12**, 533
    variations, **12**, 534
  generally, **12**, 531
  Republic of Ireland, in relation to, **12**, 535
See also STATE, OFFENCES AGAINST; TERRORISM; TREASON
Political opinion
discrimination, **12**, 85
right to, assault in attempt to prevent, **7**, 236
trials which may be prejudiced by, extradition procedure, **12**, 516, 532, 534
Political organisation
business, whether carrying on, **3**, 1162
Conservative Party, **5**, 392
generally, **5**, 388
groups—
  meetings of, **5**, 389
  organisation into, **5**, 389
independent, position of, **14**, 92

Political organisation—*continued*
Labour Party, **5**, 393
legislation, progress of, **5**, 390
Liberal Party, **5**, 394
local authority prohibited from promoting, **14**, 314, 336
majority, position of, **14**, 91
minority, position of, **14**, 92
questions, **5**, 391
Scottish National Party, **5**, 396
Social Democratic Party, **5**, 395
Poll tax
See COMMUNITY CHARGE
Pollution
abstraction of water, **25**, 330
acquiescence, **16**, 1617
air, **19**, 315-317, 687
    alkali, **19**, 317
    smoke, *see* SMOKE
alveus operations on, **25**, 322
atmospheric, harmful emission into, **9**, 453, 454
canal or inland waterway, of, **19**, 1125
control, generally, **9**, 853; **19**, 303, 329; **25**, 394, 395, 425, 428
Convention on Long-range Transboundary Air Pollution, **19**, 687
damages for, **21**, 390
duty of persons in control of premises, **9**, 453, 454
fauna and flora, protection of—
    disposal of polluting material, **25**, 424
    generally, **25**, 422
    removal of polluting material, **25**, 424
    review of consent, **25**, 423
fish farms, **11**, 62
gas, with regard to, **9**, 878
hazardous substances, *see* HAZARDOUS SUBSTANCES
high seas, power to take avoidance measures, **21**, 46
industrial—
    alkali works—
        best practicable means, meaning, **9**, 1116
        generally, **19**, 317
        hydrochloric acid gas, emission of, **9**, 1112
        noxious gas, escape of, **9**, 1113
        offensive gases, escape of, **9**, 1113
        registration of, **9**, 1115
    cable burning, **9**, 1119
    control of, generally, **9**, 1111
    European Economic Community, and, **9**, 1121
    generally, **19**, 303
    hydrochloric acid gas, emission from alkali works, **9**, 1112
    Industrial Pollution Inspectorate, consultation with, **23**, 129
    noxious substances, emission from industrial premises, **9**, 1114
    nuisance, complaint of, **9**, 1117
    offences, prosecution of, **9**, 1118
    offensive trades, smells from, **9**, 1120
    registration of works, **9**, 1115
    smoke, *see* SMOKE
    water, pollution of, **14**, 2079
international awareness of problems, **9**, 1104
international crime, as, **19**, 687

Pollution—*continued*
legislation—
    development of, **9**, 1109
    relevant, **9**, 1110
loch, of, **25**, 338
long-range transboundary pollution, **19**, 687
meaning, **9**, 1105
nitrogen dioxide, **9**, 1148
noise, **19**, 303, 318
    See also NOISE
non-tidal loch, **18**, 308
non-tidal river—
    common interest, doctrine of, **18**, 299
    defences to action, **18**, 300
    domestic sewerage, by, **18**, 300
    generally, **18**, 281
    negative prescription, defence of, **18**, 300
    private law, **18**, 298
    public law, **18**, 298
    salmon fishings, rights of proprietors, **18**, 298
    nuisance, as, **18**, 298
oil pollution of sea, *see* OIL
pollutant, entry into water—
    circumstances where not unlawful, **25**, 403
    control, generally, **25**, 401
    good agricultural practice, **25**, 405
    noxious material, control of possession of, **25**, 407
    poisonous material, control of possession, **25**, 407
    possession, control of, **25**, 407
    prohibition of, **25**, 402
    solid waste, **25**, 404
    stream—
        deposits in, **25**, 406
        vegetation in, **25**, 406
power stations, emissions from, **9**, 668
public health, protection of, **25**, 427
radioactive substances, *see* ATOMIC ENERGY AND RADIOACTIVE SUBSTANCES
rivers, **11**, 6; **14**, 2079; **19**, 321-323; **25**, 397
    See also RIVER PURIFICATION AUTHORITY
sea, discharge of oil into, *see* OIL
sewage effluent, *see* SEWAGE EFFLUENT
sheriff court jurisdiction, **6**, 1099
shipping, jurisdiction generally, **21**, 101
smoke, *see* SMOKE
Stockholm Declaration on the Human Environment, **19**, 687
sulpher dioxide—
    gas oil, from—
        EEC directions on, **9**, 1146
        United Kingdom controls, **9**, 1147
    smoke, and, **9**, 1148
territorial sea, in, **21**, 7
trade effluent, *see* TRADE EFFLUENT
vehicle, emission from—
    EEC directives—
        diesel engines, **9**, 1143
        lead in petrol, **9**, 1144
        petrol-driven vehicles, **9**, 1142
        United Kingdom measures implementing, **9**, 1145
    generally, **9**, 1141

Pollution—*continued*
waste, *see* WASTE
water—
  abstraction of, **25**, 330
  agreements as to, **25**, 426
  byelaws, **25**, 426, 528
  common law control, **25**, 395
  consent system—
    application—
      consideration of, **25**, 416
      procedure, **25**, 414
    consent to discharge—
      conditions, **25**, 417
      duration, **25**, 418
      review, **25**, 419
  dust, *see* DUST
  flora and fauna, **25**, 423
  generally, **25**, 413
  information, **25**, 421
  registers, **25**, 420
  Secretary of State, powers of, **25**, 415
  fluoridation, **19**, 320
  generally, **19**, 319-323; **25**, 335
  high seas, power to take avoidance measures, **21**, 46
  industrial works, by, **14**, 2079
  offences, **25**, 428
  sewage, **14**, 2079
  statutory control, **25**, 396
  supply, closure of, **25**, 526
  territorial sea, in, **21**, 7
  wholesome, provision of, **19**, 319
  See also WATER
Polychlorinated biphenyls
EEC directives on, **9**, 1177
Polygamy
consistorial action, for, **17**, 1225
polygamous wives and widows—
  abode, right of, **12**, 118*n*
  children of, **12**, 118*n*
  generally, **12**, 269
Pomponius
unjust enrichment, **15**, 11, 16, 74
Pontage
funeral procession, exemption, **3**, 526
Pony
exportation—
  examination before, **2**, 222
  restrictions on, **2**, 221
  welfare provisions, **2**, 222
public performances, in, **2**, 269
Pool
public health nuisance, as, **19**, 336
surface water, whether heritable or moveable property, **18**, 273
swimming, *see* SWIMMING POOL
Pool betting
accountant—
  annual report by, **2**, 1566
  powers, duties etc, **2**, 1565
  statement by promoter to, **2**, 1566
  supervisory role, **2**, 1565
charitable competitions, **2**, 1568
dog tracks, on, **2**, 1564

Pool betting—*continued*
duty—
  assessment for, **2**, 1646
  collection of, **2**, 1647
  liability for payment, **2**, 1646
  rate of, **2**, 1646
excise duty, **7**, 1080, 1082
  exemptions, **7**, 1082
  rate, **7**, 1082
football pools, **2**, 1587
lottery distinguished, **2**, 1563
meaning, **2**, 1513, 1563
off-track, **2**, 1565
operation of, **2**, 1564
promoter—
  registration—
    effect of, **2**, 1514
    procedure on, **2**, 1516
  reports to be made by, **2**, 1566
racecourses, on, **2**, 1557, 1564
sponsored, **7**, 1081
Poor relief
charitable purpose, as, **3**, 1108, 1116, 1118
early provisions concerning, **14**, 34
historical development, **21**, 1062; **22**, 1
kirk-session obligation to provide, **19**, 208
poor, definition, **3**, 1118
state centralisation, **19**, 210
Pop festivals
illegal, **9**, 1041
illegal behaviour at, **9**, 1041
meaning, **9**, 1041
open country, in, **9**, 1041
planning permission, **9**, 1041
public entertainment licence, **9**, 1041
sports stadium, in, **9**, 1041
Population
district councils, **14**, 64
regional councils, **14**, 64
Populous place
burgh, establishment of, **14**, 21
Porch
exemptions from building regulations, **3**, 209
Pornography
broadcasting, **7**, 486
child, **7**, 311
deprave or corrupt, liable to, **7**, 470
film shown to consenting adults in private, **7**, 13, 83, 468
having or keeping obscene material, **7**, 486
Indecent Displays (Control) Act (1981), **7**, 488
obscene material, meaning, **7**, 487
printing etc, **7**, 486
selling or exposing for sale, **7**, 13, 83, 469, 486
warehousing obscene material, **7**, 469
Porpoise
occupancy, no right of acquisition by, **18**, 543*n*
Port
approved, Commissioners' powers in relation to, **7**, 1239
construction or alteration, **19**, 19*n*
control areas, **12**, 161
controls, prevention of terrorism powers, **12**, 133
designated, **12**, 133, 161

Port—_continued_
development of, **23**, 123, 153
dockyard, _see_ DOCKYARD PORT
free, _see_ FREE PORT
lightening ship to enter, **21**, 621_n_, 632, 632_n_
local authority, _see_ PORT LOCAL AUTHORITY
meaning, **11**, 1303
pilotage, _see_ PILOT; PILOTAGE
port charterparty, **21**, 672
express terms, **21**, 675
sheriff, jurisdiction of, **4**, 2
time charterparty—
loading port, preliminary voyage to, **21**, 640
safe port—
express terms, **21**, 640
implied terms, **21**, 639, 640
voyage charterparty—
discharge port, **21**, 620, 621
express terms, **21**, 618
impediment preventing ship's entry, **21**, 622
loading port—
delay in naming, **21**, 620
generally, **21**, 620, 621
preliminary voyage to, **21**, 618, 619
safe port, **21**, 618, 621
unsafe port, nomination, **21**, 621_n_
water sports and recreation, **19**, 1283
Port, right of
acquisition, **18**, 334
land ownership, and, **18**, 335
obligations of, **18**, 335
public rights as to, **18**, 529
regalian right, as, **18**, 210
rights conferred by, **18**, 335, 336
separate tenement, as, **18**, 210, 319, 334
Port local authority
administration of Food and Drugs Act, **11**, 329
constitution, **19**, 309
debts, **19**, 312
delegation of powers, **19**, 311
expenses, **19**, 312
jurisdiction, **19**, 310
ships within, **19**, 313
pilotage, **21**, 291, 293-297
powers and responsibilities, **21**, 114
salvage award, entitlement to claim, **21**, 459
Port of London
warehouse warrants in, as negotiable instrument, **4**, 103
Portugal
competition rules, application, **4**, 1304
European Union customs territory, **7**, 1010
Positive law
equity, principles of natural law distinguished, **22**, 402
Erskine, positive and natural law, foundation of relationship, **22**, 410
Kames's _Principles of Equity_, **22**, 411-416
meaning, **22**, 402
natural law, distinction, **22**, 402
Scots law as, **22**, 403
Stair's _Institutions_, **22**, 402-408
theological foundations, **22**, 405

Positive prescription
allodial land, interest in, **16**, 2107
continued and unequivocal possession, **16**, 2105
Crown, against, **16**, 2102, 2107
decennalis et triennalis, **16**, 2108
deed—
forged, **16**, 2106, 2107
interest founded on, **16**, 2109
interest recorded in, **16**, 2106
invalid, **16**, 2106, 2107
foreshore, **16**, 2102, 2107
generally, **6**, 782
heritable property, **16**, 2105
introduction, **16**, 2102
judicial interruption, **16**, 2108, 2113
land—
general interest in, **16**, 2106
interest in, **16**, 2105
title to interest in, **16**, 2104, 2105
Land Register of Scotland, **16**, 2105, 2106, 2110
lease, interest in land of lessee, **16**, 2107
legal disability, person against whom prescription pled under, **16**, 2113
meaning, **16**, 2104
original acquisition, as, **18**, 597
period, **16**, 2102
computation, **16**, 2114
positive servitude, **16**, 2105, 2111
possession—
civil, **16**, 2105, 2108
founded, must be, **16**, 2106
nature of, **16**, 2108
openly and peaceably, **16**, 2108, 2113
public right of way, **16**, 2105, 2111, 2112
registration of interest, **16**, 2106
salmon fishings, **16**, 2102, 2107
ten years, title and possession for, **16**, 2106
title, clear and distinct, **16**, 2105
twenty years, title and possession for, **16**, 2107
Possession
acquisition—
animus, **18**, 117
See also animus below
corpus, **18**, 117
See also corpus below
action for recovery—
necessity for court action, **13**, 469-472
ordinary removing, forms, **13**, 474
summary cause, **13**, 473
See also TENANT–TENANCY
animo solo, retention by, **18**, 122
animus—
animus possidendi, **18**, 123
generally, **18**, 117, 123
intention to exercise control, **18**, 123, 124
intention to hold as one's own, **18**, 123, 125
presumption from _corpus_, **18**, 123
assured tenancy, and, **13**, 613-615
body, act of, _see corpus below_
bona fide—
actual knowledge, **18**, 133
constructive knowledge, **18**, 134
error must be of fact, not law, **18**, 131
generally, **18**, 131

Possession—*continued*
bona fide—*continued*
  gratuitous possessor, **18**, 136
  interpretation of knowledge, **18**, 135
  litiscontestation, loss at, **18**, 137
  meaning of *bona fide* possessor, **18**, 131, 131*n*
  meaning of good faith, **18**, 132
  recovery of possession, defence to claim arising from, **18**, 171
  termination of good faith, **18**, 137
civil, **18**, 121, 123, 127
  positive prescription, **16**, 2105, 2108
co-ownership, *see* CO-OWNERSHIP
competing claims, **18**, 118
concealed objects, **18**, 124
concept of, generally, **18**, 114
constructive transfer of, **4**, 137
corporeal moveable property—
  defence of possession, **18**, 174
  detention, **18**, 119
  possession presumed to be lawful, **18**, 129
  presumption of ownership arising from possession, **18**, 114
  recovery founded on right to possession—
    action of delivery, **18**, 158
      ejection, **18**, 159
      interdict, **18**, 159
      self-help, **18**, 160, 161
      spuilzie, **18**, 160
  reputed ownership, **18**, 532
corpus—
  animus presumed from, **18**, 123
  civil possession, **18**, 121
  continuing detention, **18**, 122
  corpus possidendi, **18**, 123
  generally, **18**, 117
  incorporeal property, **18**, 120
  initial detention, **18**, 119
criminal law, **18**, 123
defence of—
  corporeal moveable property, **18**, 174
    applicable rules, **18**, 192
    generally, **18**, 191
  encroachment—
    defences to—
      Act of Parliament, encroachment authorised by, **18**, 177
      common gables, **18**, 177
      consent, **18**, 176
      exercise of a right, **18**, 177
      negative prescription, **18**, 177
      ownership of encroaching thing, **18**, 179
    definition, **18**, 175
    examples, **18**, 175
    extrajudicial remedies, **18**, 179
    generally, **18**, 175
    harm, no need to prove, **18**, 175
    intrusion compared, **18**, 175
    judicial remedies, **18**, 178
    things, encroachment must be by, **18**, 175
  exclusivity, based on, **18**, 174
  generally, **18**, 174
  land, **18**, 174
  lease, **18**, 174

Possession—*continued*
defence of—*continued*
  liferent, **18**, 174
  ownership, **18**, 174
  remedies, **18**, 140
  title to sue, **18**, 140
  trespass, *see* TRESPASS
detention—
  animo solo, retention by, **18**, 122
  body, act of, **18**, 119, 122
  civil possession, **18**, 121
  continuing, **18**, 122
  corporeal moveable property, **18**, 119
  incorporeal property, **18**, 120
  initial, **18**, 119
  mind, act of, **18**, 123
  for own use, **18**, 125
  physical control, **18**, 119
  requirement for, generally, **18**, 119
dispossession, rights against, **18**, 115
  lost property, rules as to, **18**, 115
dual, **18**, 118, 130
employee, through, **16**, 2108
encroachment—
  possessor, rights of, **18**, 115
  See also defence of *above*
exclusivity—
  in detemining whether contract amounts to lease, **13**, 597
  as essence of possession, **18**, 118
fact, as matter of, **18**, 114
feudal grant, civil possession, **18**, 121
fruits of—
  accounting for in action of recovery, **18**, 151
  generally, **15**, 55
gratuitous possessor, **18**, 136
incorporeal property, detention, problems arising, **18**, 120
inversion—
  examples, **13**, 266
  tenant's obligations, **13**, 265-268
jura ad rem, **18**, 128
jura possessionis—
  generally, **18**, 115
  meaning, **18**, 114
jus possidendi, **18**, 114
  holder of, recovery of possession, **18**, 151
  pro indiviso holders, **18**, 118, 130
  title to sue, **18**, 141, 142
landlord's obligations—
  full possession, to give, **13**, 249, 250
  maintain tenant in possession, to, **13**, 251-253
lawful, presumption of, **18**, 129
licence to, **18**, 128
liferenter, through, **16**, 2108
loss of, liability for restitution or repetition, **15**, 55
lost or abandoned property, **18**, 124
meaning, **4**, 137; **18**, 5
mens rea, **7**, 101
mercantile agent entrusted with, transfer of ownership by, **18**, 671
mind, act of, *see animus above*
natural accession, by, **15**, 55

Possession—*continued*
natural possession, **18**, 127
  protection of—
    defence of possession, **18**, 174-192
    petitory and possessory remedies, **18**, 139
    recovery of possession, **18**, 151-173
    spuilzied property, **18**, 140
    title to sue, **18**, 138-150
nature of, **16**, 2108
ownership—
  possession as benefit of, **18**, 130
  possession distinguished, **18**, 114
  presumption that possession signifies, **18**, 130
peaceful use of property free from intrusion, possesser's entitlement to, **18**, 174
personal right of, **18**, 127
positive prescription, **16**, 2105
possessor—
  out of possession, where, **18**, 127
  recovery of possession by, **18**, 127
possessory judgment—
  effect on bona fide possessor, **18**, 133, 133*n*
  right to, **18**, 116
precario (precarious), **18**, 128
presumption of ownership, and, **8**, 634; **20**, 852
pro indiviso proprietors, **18**, 118, 130
title to sue, **18**, 141
proof of right—
  corporeal moveable property—
    defence of possession, actions in, **18**, 149
    generally, **18**, 141, 148
    recovery of possession, actions for, **18**, 150
  derivative right, where, **18**, 142, 144
  independent right, defender averring, **18**, 142, 145
  jus possidendi, title to sue, **18**, 141, 142
  Land Register land, generally, **18**, 141, 147
  no right averred by defender, where, **18**, 142, 143
  Sasine land, generally, **18**, 141, 142
  seven-year possessory judgment, **18**, 145, 146
  short lease, **18**, 147
  uninfeft proprietor, **18**, 142
public right of way, **18**, 126*n*
real right, as, **18**, 5, 127
real rights affected by—
  exclusive possession, **13**, 313
  generally, **13**, 308
  lease in question, must be under, **13**, 311
  manner of possession, **13**, 310
  prorogation, **13**, 312
  renewal, **13**, 312
  time possession taken, **13**, 309
recovery, action for—
  accounting for fruits of possession, **18**, 151, 168
  bona fide possession, defence of, **18**, 167, 171
  brevi manu repossession, **18**, 156
  claims arising on—
    ordinary profits, **18**, 167, 168, 171
    party from whom possession recovered, by—
      improvements, expenditure on, **18**, 173
      maintenance, expenditure on, **18**, 172
    party recovering possession, by—
      generally, **18**, 167

Possession—*continued*
recovery, action for—*continued*
  corporeal moveable property, **18**, 151
    action of delivery, **18**, 158
    ejection, **18**, 159
    generally, **18**, 150
    interdict, **18**, 159
    self-help, **18**, 160
    spuilzie, **18**, 160
  damage to property while in defender's possession, where, **18**, 170
  damages under breach of contract, **18**, 170
  delict, **18**, 170
  delivery, **18**, 151
  economic loss, **18**, 170
  ejection, **18**, 151
  generally, **18**, 127, 151, 168
  good faith, relevance of, **18**, 151
  improvements to property, claim by party from whom possession recovered, **18**, 173
  interdict, **18**, 151
  judicial remedies, **18**, 151
  jus possidendi, holder of, **18**, 151
  land, **18**, 151
  lease, **18**, 151
  liability of outgoing possessor, **18**, 151
  liferent, **18**, 151
  maintenance of property, claim by party from whom possession recovered, **18**, 151, 173
  ordinary profits—
    meaning, **18**, 167
  ownership, **18**, 151
  remedies, **18**, 140
  removing, **18**, 151
  self-help as alternative to judicial remedies, **18**, 151, 156, 159, 160
  spuilzie, action of, **18**, 151, 156
  title to sue, **18**, 140, 151
  violent profits—
    bona fide possession as defence, **18**, 171
    entitlement to, **18**, 151
    generally, **18**, 167, 169, 171
    meaning, **18**, 167
    spuilzie, **18**, 165, 169
  vitious dispossession, claim based on, **18**, 151, 156
registration, requirement for, **18**, 142
rei interventus, in relation to, **13**, 140, 141
remedies—
  natural possession, in relation to—
    classification by result sought, **18**, 138
    title to sue—
      classification by, **18**, 139
      right in property, **18**, 141
  recovery, action for, **18**, 140
removings, *see* REMOVINGS
repossession by lessor, *see* TENANT-TENANCY
requirement for, **18**, 142
resumption of, by landlord, reserved power, **13**, 445, 446
right to—
  generally, **18**, 126
  importance of concept, **18**, 127
  lawful possession, presumption of, **18**, 129

Possession—*continued*

right to—*continued*

personal right, **18**, 126, 128

possession signifies ownership, presumption as
to, **18**, 130

real right, **18**, 126, 127

rights of possessor, **18**, 114

encroachment, as to, **18**, 115

jura possessionis, **18**, 114, 115

rights for which possession a prerequisite—

delict, right to claim in, for economic loss,
18, 116

generally, **18**, 114, 116

possessory judgment, right to, **18**, 116

real rights, acquisition of, **18**, 116

rectification of Land Register, protection
against, **18**, 116

trespass, as to, **18**, 115

salmon fishing rights, **11**, 4

sasine, *see* SASINE

security of tenure, **13**, 696, 697

servitudes, **18**, 120*n*, 126*n*

seven-year possessory judgment, **18**, 145, 146

spuilzie, *see* SPUILZIE

sublease, **13**, 380

succession, in relation to, **13**, 787

suspension, as remedy available to tenant, **13**, 281

symbolic delivery, **18**, 119, 119*n*

tenancy, as prerequisite for, **13**, 613

tenant—

obligations of—

not to invert possession, **13**, 265-268

to remain in possession, **13**, 264

to take possession, **13**, 263

possession through, **16**, 2108

remaining in after termination of lease—

removings, *see* REMOVINGS

summary cause for recovery of heritable
property, **13**, 470

returning or threatening to return after
dispossession—

interdict, **13**, 470

third party, through, **16**, 2108

title to sue—

classification of remedies—

result sought, by, **18**, 138

title to sue, by, **18**, 139

defence of existing possession, **18**, 140

possession as, **18**, 140

recovery of possession, for, **18**, 140

right in property as, **18**, 141

sasine land—

generally, **18**, 142

traditio, **18**, 116

trespass, possessor, rights of, **18**, 115

uncompleted title, where, **18**, 127

uninfeft proprietor, protection of possession,
action for, **18**, 142

unlawful, **18**, 5

use of term, **7**, 101

vassal, through, **16**, 2108

vi aut clam, vitious dispossession, and, **18**, 164

violent or illegal, **13**, 505

violent profits, *see* VIOLENT PROFITS

Post

See MAIL; POSTAL PACKET

Post mortem examination

anatomical examination not allowed where
likelihood of, **3**, 507

cremation following, **3**, 559

defence, preparation of, **17**, 656

procurator fiscal, preliminary inquiries by, **17**, 613

provision of premises for, **19**, 466

Post Office

agent of sender, as, **16**, 1902

business—

inciting obstruction or molestation, **16**, 1911

obstruction, **16**, 1911

person engaged in, obstruction, molestation,
etc, **16**, 1911

contractual relationship, whether, **16**, 1908

control and regulation, **16**, 1906

Crown, not servant or agent of, **16**, 1904

Development of the Single Market Postal Services,
Green Paper, **16**, 1913

duties, generally, **16**, 1904

exclusive privilege, **16**, 1905, 1905*n*

licence to perform Post Office activities, **16**,
1906

Future of Postal Services, Green Paper, **16**, 1906,
1906*n*

inviolability of mails, **16**, 1912

legislation governing, generally, **16**, 1903

liability in postal service provision—

delict, in, **16**, 1907

generally, **16**, 1908

licence to perform Post Office activities—

duration, **16**, 1906

fee, **16**, 1906

grant, **16**, 1906

renewal, **16**, 1906

mail, *see* MAIL

monopoly over conveyance of letters—

exceptions to, **16**, 1905

exclusive privilege, **16**, 1905, 1905*n*

statutory position, **16**, 1904

offences—

inviolability of mails, **16**, 1912

letter box, in relation to, **16**, 1911

property and premises, concerning, **16**, 1911

stamps, concerning, **16**, 1910

things sent through the post, **16**, 1909

postal services, provision, **16**, 1904

powers, **16**, 1906

property and premises, offences concerning, **16**,
1911

public authority, as, **16**, 1904

stamp, *see* STAMP

telegram service, **16**, 1916

telephone service—

acquisition, **16**, 1918, 1919

deregulation, **16**, 1920

telepost services, provision, **16**, 1904, 1920, 1920*n*

transport by, VAT zero-rating, **7**, 1452

words 'letter box', use of, **16**, 1911

words 'post office', use of, **16**, 1911

Postal order

non-negotiability, **4**, 103

Postal packet
air, carriage by, **3**, 744
dangerous, noxious etc substance, enclosing, **16**,
    1909
destruction or disposal by Post Office, **16**, 1912
detention, **16**, 1912
Her Majesty's Service, wrapper implying packet
    sent on, **16**, 1909
human sexual techniques, unsolicited mail
    describing, **16**, 1909
imitation post office mark or stamp, **16**, 1909
indecent or obscene material, enclosing, **16**, 1909
injury, likely to cause, **16**, 1909
inviolability of mails, **16**, 1912
living creature, enclosing, **16**, 1909
meaning, **16**, 1909*n*
offences, generally, **16**, 1909
opened by Post Office, when package may be, **16**,
    1912
See also MAIL
Postal services
consumer protection, **6**, 164; **19**, 241, 241*n*
contractual duties reinforced by criminal law, **9**,
    125
historical background, **16**, 1901–1903
Post Office Users' Councils, **6**, 164
private postal network, establishment, **16**, 1905
radioactive materials, transport by, **9**, 921
state centralisation, **19**, 210
VAT exemption, **7**, 1422
Posthumous child
See CHILD-CHILDREN
Postmaster General
former position of, **16**, 1904
incorporation, **19**, 209
Potato Marketing Board
EEC Treaty, compatibility with, **1**, 704
Great Britain, covering, **1**, 703
Potato starch
monetary compensatory amounts on, **1**, 940
Potatoes
production refund, **1**, 940
Potestative condition
meaning, **15**, 6
Poulterer
office of, **7**, 831
Poultry
accession compensatory amounts, **1**, 937
ante- and post-mortem inspections, **11**, 418
cereal market, parallel legislation to, **1**, 937
cutting premises, **11**, 418
diseases, meaning, **2**, 178
evisceration, **11**, 418
export refunds, **1**, 938
exportation control, **2**, 219
houses, as agricultural buildings for valuation for
    rates, **24**, 566
importation, birds or eggs—
    control of, **2**, 205
    licence requirement, **2**, 213
    quarantine provisions, **2**, 213
    veterinary inspector's powers, **2**, 213
imported, destruction of, **2**, 213
inspectors, powers of, **2**, 232

Poultry—*continued*
meaning, **2**, 177; **11**, 878*n*
meat, hygiene regulations, **11**, 418
minor procedures on, **25**, 203
not wild birds, **11**, 878
public health legislation, **19**, 477
slaughter, **14**, 698
    enforcement of provisions, **11**, 519
    entry, powers of, **11**, 518
    generally, **11**, 418, 496, 498, 516–520
    hygiene, **11**, 520
    Jewish method, **11**, 517
    method of, **11**, 517
    Muslim method, **11**, 517
sluice-gate price, **1**, 938
Pound (weight)
definition, **6**, 179
Poverty
See POOR RELIEF
Power of appointment
discretionary trust distinguished, **24**, 55
fraud, on, **11**, 754
Power of attorney
attestation by notary public, **13**, 1223
contract of agency, as, **1**, 604
forged, **3**, 334
interpretation, **12**, 1262
Power station
atmospheric emissions from, **9**, 668
Practicks
See JUDICIAL PRECEDENT
Pre-menstrual syndrome
diminished responsibility, **7**, 146
Pre-trial diet
See TRIAL
Precarium
commodatum compared, **13**, 1791
meaning, **13**, 1791
prescription, **13**, 1792
unfair contract terms, **13**, 1790
Precatory bequest
construction, **25**, 823
Precatory trust
creation, **24**, 10
meaning, **24**, 19
Precedence
academic, **16**, 2024
advocates, **16**, 2020
ambassadors, **16**, 2014
Attorney General, **16**, 2020
baronage, **16**, 2021
baronetage, **16**, 2019
chargé d'affaire, **16**, 2014
claims, determination, **16**, 2008
clan chiefs, **16**, 2021, 2022
College of Justice, **16**, 2020
Commonwealth High Commissioner, **16**, 2014
Commonwealth Secretariat, **16**, 2014
company board meetings, at, **16**, 2002
consular, **16**, 2014, 2015
corporations, **16**, 2025
Decreet of Ranking, **16**, 2010, 2018

Precedence—*continued*
determination—
    claims, of, **16**, 2008
    Parliamentary precedence, of, **16**, 2009
diplomatic, **16**, 2014
earlier creation, creation of dignity with
    precedence over, **16**, 2004
ecclesiastical, **16**, 2003, 2016
English personages and officials, ranking with
    Scots, **16**, 2011
envoys, **16**, 2014
esquires, **16**, 2022
foreign personages and officials, **16**, 2012
    diplomatic and consular precedence, **16**, 2014,
        2015
gentry, **16**, 2023
grant, how effected, **16**, 2005
hereditary official, **16**, 2006
historical background, **16**, 2003
House of Lords, **16**, 2010, 2016
judiciary, **16**, 2020
ladies, **16**, 2007, 2013
Law Society of Scotland, **16**, 2004, 2020
lay, **16**, 2003
legal profession, **16**, 2020
legates, **16**, 2014
Lord Advocate, **16**, 2020
Lord High Commissioner to the General
    Assembly, **16**, 2006
Lords of Appeal in Ordinary, **16**, 2018, 2020
Lords Spiritual, **16**, 2016
ministers, **16**, 2014
Moderator of the General Assembly, **16**, 2006,
    2016
nature of, **16**, 2001
nuncios, **16**, 2014
official—
    English officials, **16**, 2011, 2012
    examples, **16**, 2006
    hereditary, **16**, 2006
    ladies, **16**, 2007
    personal precedence, interaction, **16**, 2006
official act, as result of, **16**, 2002
Parliamentary, **16**, 2004, 2009, 2010, 2016
peerage, *see* PEERAGE
personal—
    English personages, **16**, 2011, 2012
    official precedence, interaction, **16**, 2006
petition for royal warrant to declare, **16**, 2004
professional, **16**, 2024
Queen's counsels, **16**, 2020
regional council, **16**, 2002
right to, **16**, 2005
    statutory, **16**, 2005
royal, **16**, 2017
royal grant, as result of, **16**, 2002
royal prerogative, arising from, *see* ROYAL
    PREROGATIVE
Scale of General Precedence in Scotland, **16**, 2013
Scots personages and officials outwith Scotland,
    16, 2011, 2012
Senators of the College of Justice, **16**, 2020
United Kingdom, within, **16**, 2011
United Nations representatives, **16**, 2014

Precedence—*continued*
universities, **16**, 2024
wives, **16**, 2007
    divorced, **16**, 2007
    husband deceased, where, **16**, 2007
Precedent
See JUDICIAL PRECEDENT
Precious metals
carriage of, **3**, 610
false trade description, **18**, 1418, 1418n
hallmarking, *see* HALLMARKING
Precognition
defence, preparation of, **17**, 659
perjury, **7**, 509
pre-trial procedure, **17**, 545
witness, of, generally, **10**, 523; **17**, 1142
Preference shares
See SHARES
Preferential creditor
See CREDITOR
Preferential payments
common law, at, **2**, 1419
executor's expenses, **2**, 1419
fraudulent preference, **11**, 781
pension contributions, **2**, 1430
petitioning creditor's expenses, **2**, 1420
remuneration—
    interim trustee, of, **2**, 1417
    permanent trustee, of, **2**, 1418
statutory, **2**, 1416
unfair preference, **11**, 781n
Preferred debts
categories, **2**, 1426
common law, at, **2**, 1419, 1426
Crown debts, **2**, 1426
customs and excise, **2**, 1426
deceased's estate, **2**, 1419; **25**, 1057
employees' remuneration, **2**, 1431
fraudulent preference, **11**, 781
funeral etc expenses, **2**, 1419
gaming duties, **2**, 1428
generally, **2**, 1426
inadequate funds to meet, **2**, 1426
Inland Revenue debts, **2**, 1427
national insurance, **2**, 1421; **9**, 150
ordinary debts, ranking, **2**, 1422
pension contributions, **2**, 1430; **9**, 149
petitioning creditor, **2**, 1420
post-sequestration interest, **2**, 1423
Redundancy Fund, payments out of, **9**, 149
salaries, **9**, 148
social security contributions, **2**, 1429; **9**, 150
statutory, ranking of, **2**, 1416, 1421
statutory provisions, **9**, 147
taxes, **2**, 1427
trustee's remuneration, **2**, 1417, 1418
unfair preference, **11**, 781n
value added tax, **2**, 1428
wages, **9**, 148
Pregnancy
abortion, *see* ABORTION
concealment, *see* CONCEALMENT OF PREGNANCY
dismissal on grounds of, *see* dismissal
maternity allowance, *see* MATERNITY ALLOWANCE

Pregnancy—*continued*
priority housing needs, **11**, 2051, 2052
right to return to work following, **6**, 999
sickness benefit—
  single or separated woman, **21**, 888
  whether entitlement to, **21**, 879
statutory maternity pay, *see* MATERNITY PAY
statutory sick pay, effect on entitlement to, **21**, 912
wrongful—
  abortion, failed, **15**, 305, 306
  'consent-based' negligence actions, **15**, 307
  contractual negligence, **15**, 307
  damages to compensate for upbringing, **15**, 309
  failure to inform, **15**, 307
  generally, **15**, 305
  negligent failure to warn, **15**, 308
  Scottish position, generally, **15**, 310
See also MATERNITY RIGHTS

Premises
cleansing and disinfection of, **19**, 306, 448
controlled drugs, use of, **14**, 1247
definition, **19**, 336*n*
diplomatic mission, **19**, 683
electricity supply to, termination on consumer quitting, **9**, 706
entry and inspection of, by Health and Safety Commission inspector, **9**, 417
expulsion of offenders, local authority powers, **14**, 300
food prepared, where, **11**, 407
food sold, where, **11**, 407
health and safety—
  harmful emissions into atmosphere, duties as to—
    best practicable means, **9**, 454
    generally, **9**, 453
  person concerned with, duty of—
    bearers of duty, **9**, 450
    nature of, **9**, 448
    non-domestic premises, **9**, 449
    recipients of duty, **9**, 451
highway, in disrepair near, **14**, 2101
housing, *see* HOUSING
immoral or illegal purpose, used for—
  generally, **13**, 225
  repossession, as grounds for—
    assured tenancy, **13**, 725, 733
    protected tenancy, **13**, 714, 716
insecure, police protection, **16**, 1785, 1785*n*
licence holder, of, **14**, 545
licensed, *see* LICENSED PREMISES
liquor licensing, **14**, 516
  See also ALCOHOLIC LIQUOR
neighbouring, *Maloco v Littlewoods Organisation Ltd*, decision in, **15**, 302, 318
occupier of, summary application as to noise, **9**, 1252
occupiers' liability, *see* OCCUPIER'S LIABILITY
overcrowded, **19**, 336
  See also HOUSING
police constable, watching by, **14**, 491

Premises—*continued*
police powers of entry—
  entry and search—
    European Convention on Human Rights, **16**, 1806
    generally, **16**, 1798
    warrant for, **16**, 1798
  preventive measure, as, **16**, 1799
police surveillance, **16**, 1802
price display, meaning, **9**, 854
private supplier, of, right to enter, **9**, 719
public entertainment, used for, **9**, 1002
public health nuisance, becoming, **19**, 335, 336
railway, **19**, 343
revenue trade provisions, **7**, 1246-1248
search, customs officers' powers—
  generally, **7**, 1228
  revenue trader, premises of, **7**, 1252
search of, **17**, 607
sports, **19**, 358
unlicensed, **14**, 546
unoccupied, relief from rates, **14**, 864
valuation for rating, **24**, 627
watching under agreement with occupier, **16**, 1738

Premium
insurance, *see* INSURANCE
rent, *see* RENT

Prentice Report
recommendations, **4**, 326
ultra vires doctrine, Companies Act 1989 and, **4**, 326

Prepacked
meaning, **6**, 195

Prerogative legislation
See LEGISLATION

Prerogative orders
English law, in, **1**, 204

Prerogative powers
Bill affecting, Queen's consent, **7**, 744
case law, **7**, 740
definition, **7**, 720
excess, curbing, **7**, 720
exercised by Crown alone, **7**, 719, 723
exercised by Queen on advice of ministers, **7**, 719, 723
extent—
  Bible, regulation of printing, **7**, 731, 851
  committees of inquiry, appointment, **7**, 728
  criminal injuries compensation, **7**, 729
  emergency or war, during, **7**, 726
  enlarged, powers may not be, **7**, 722, 735
  European Convention on Human Rights, **7**, 737
  foreign affairs, **7**, 720, 724, 736
  generally, **7**, 723
  intelligence services, **7**, 732
  interception of communications, **7**, 733
  international obligations, and, **7**, 736, 737
  litigation, in, **7**, 734
  martial law, **7**, 726
  mercy, prerogative of, **7**, 727, 727*n*
  novel situations, **7**, 722, 735
  royal commissions, appointment, **7**, 728
  security services, **7**, 732

Prerogative powers—_continued_
extent—_continued_
treaties, ratification, **7**, 725, 738
wrongful conviction and detention, compensation, **7**, 730
generally, **7**, 716, 720
international relations, **7**, 720, 724, 736
judicial review, **7**, 720, 720n, 721, 721n
mercy, prerogative of, **7**, 727, 727n
national security, **7**, 720
Officers of State, nomination, **7**, 792
public law, subject to, **7**, 720, 722
royal prerogative, **7**, 716, 720
Presbyterian Church
measures to secure, **5**, 361
See also CHURCH OF SCOTLAND
Presbytery, Church of Scotland
appellate functions—
appeal, generally, **3**, 1535, 1536
court of review, as, **3**, 1535
dissent and complaint, **3**, 1535, 1537
petition from lower court, **3**, 1535, 1538
reference from lower court, **3**, 1535, 1538
scope of reviews, **3**, 1540
auxiliary ministers, supervision, **3**, 1534, 1573
bounds, creating, uniting and disjoining, **3**, 1518
clerk, **3**, 1520
commissioners to General Assembly, election, **3**, 1543
congregation—
assessors, **3**, 1523
changed circumstances, in, **3**, 1529
dissolution, **3**, 1528
jus devolutum, **3**, 1526, 1558
minister and, dissolution of pastoral tie, **3**, 1524
superintendence committee, **3**, 1523
union and linking, **3**, 1527
unsatisfactory state, in, powers in relation to, **3**, 1523, 1524
vacant, **3**, 1525
visitation, **3**, 1523
court of review, as, **3**, 1535
creation, **3**, 1518
deacons and deaconesses, supervision, **3**, 1534
ecclesiastical buildings, powers in relation to, **3**, 1508
England, of, **3**, 1518
establishment, **3**, 1501
Europe, of, **3**, 1518
fabric committee, **3**, 1523, 1606
functions, **3**, 1522
furth of Scotland, **3**, 1518
generally, **3**, 1501, 1502, 1505
Jerusalem, of, **3**, 1518
kirk session—
access to, **3**, 1512
review of and directions to, **3**, 1506
licentiates, supervision, **3**, 1533
meetings—
open court, as, **3**, 1521
date and place, **3**, 1521
in hunc effectum, **3**, 1521
private, sitting in, **3**, 1521
pro re nata, **3**, 1521

Presbytery, Church of Scotland—_continued_
meetings—_continued_
quorum, **3**, 1521
membership, **3**, 1519
corresponding member, **3**, 1519
ministers—
death of minister, procedure on, **3**, 1570
demission of charge by minister, **3**, 1569
discipline, **3**, 1531, 1567
mental incapacity of minister, procedure on, **3**, 1568
ministerial certificate, grant and renewal, **3**, 1530
supervision, **3**, 1530, 1567-1569
termination of tenure, **3**, 1529
missionaries, supervision, **3**, 1534
moderator, **3**, 1520
number, **3**, 1518
officer, **3**, 1520
officials, **3**, 1520
precentor, **3**, 1520
probationers, supervision, **3**, 1533
readers, supervision, **3**, 1534
records, **3**, 1520
Standing Orders of General Assembly, adoption, **3**, 1547
students of divinity, powers and duties in relation to, **3**, 1522, 1532
title to sue in civil courts, **3**, 1522
treasurer, **3**, 1520
Presbytery of Relief
generally, **3**, 1636
Prescribed diseases
adjudication in prescribed diseases cases, **21**, 1165, 1166
byssinosis, **21**, 992
diffuse mesothelioma, **21**, 997
industrial injuries benefits, generally, **21**, 991
medical appeal tribunal, referral of cases to, **21**, 1179
occupational deafness—
definition, **21**, 993
disablement benefit, **21**, 995
generally, **21**, 992
time limit for claims, **21**, 996
onus of proof, **21**, 992
pneumoconiosis, **21**, 992, 997
prescribed occupations, **21**, 992
regulations, **21**, 992
tuberculosis, **21**, 992
what constitutes a prescribed disease or injury, **21**, 991
Prescription
arrestment, **8**, 308
bad faith, **16**, 2104
cautionary obligation, of, **3**, 984
clergyman, _decennalis et triennalis_ prescription, **16**, 2108
commencement, prescriptive period, **22**, 823
comparison of Scots and English law, **14**, 2022
consolidation of interests by, **6**, 782
Consumer Protection Act 1987, obligations under, **16**, 2128
contracting out, prohibition on, **16**, 2130

Prescription—*continued*
corporeal moveable property—
  negative prescription, **18**, 567
    loss of ownership rights by, **18**, 569
  positive prescription, **18**, 539, 565, 566
    loss of ownership rights by, **18**, 569
  Scottish Law Commission proposals, **18**, 566
  whether applicable, **18**, 5656
criminal law, **16**, 2131
custom and, **22**, 391
decennalis et triennalis, **16**, 2108
delictual claim, **17**, 297
discharge of contract, **17**, 276
disposition *a non domino*, **6**, 782
doctrine, **22**, 391
extinction of contractual obligation by, **15**, 865, 890
extinction of real right, **18**, 9
extrajudicial interruption, **16**, 2124, 2125
heritable property, **16**, 2105, 2121, 2122, 2132
historical background, **16**, 2102
imprescriptible rights and obligations, **16**, 2126
judicial interruption, **16**, 2108, 2124
legal certainty, Community law, **10**, 96
legislation, **22**, 823
lex rei sitae, **16**, 2132
liferent, termination on, **13**, 1647, 1653
limitation, and, **16**, 2101, 2133
Lyon Court decrees, of, **11**, 1624
meaning, **16**, 2104
naturalis computatio calculation of period by, **22**, 820, 823
negative, *see* NEGATIVE PRESCRIPTION
negotiorum gestio, obligation arising from, **15**, 72
period, interruption, **16**, 2124
positive, *see* POSITIVE PRESCRIPTION
private international law, **16**, 2132
public law, **16**, 2131
public place, invasion of interest in use and enjoyment, **14**, 2168
public rights, application to, **22**, 391
quinquennial, **16**, 2102
recent developments, **16**, 2103
recompense, and, **15**, 70
registration of title, **6**, 782
replies to plea of—
  imprescriptible rights and obligations, **16**, 2126
  non valens agere cum effectu, **16**, 2127
  relevant acknowledgment, **16**, 2125
  relevant claim, **16**, 2124
right acquired/lost by lapse, prescriptive period, **22**, 823, 825
role of, in registration of title, **6**, 782
running of—
  methods of computation, **22**, 823, 825
salmon fishing rights, **11**, 4
savings, **16**, 2129
Scottish Law Commission recommendations, **22**, 672
septennial, **16**, 2102
servitudes—
  prescriptive period, **22**, 392
sexennial, **16**, 2102
statutory basis in modern Scots law, **22**, 391

Prescription—*continued*
statutory provision, **11**, 1624; **16**, 2101, 2103
triennial, **16**, 2102
two or more persons bound jointly by obligation, **16**, 2125
uniformity, reforming legislation, **22**, 672
unjustified enrichment, action based on, **15**, 72
vicennial, **16**, 2102
warrandice, negative prescription, **18**, 714
Preservatives
early legislation, **11**, 301
food containing, **11**, 377
Preserves
food standard, **11**, 353
President of Industrial Tribunals for Scotland
powers of, **9**, 303
President of United States
office limited to two terms, **5**, 306
Press and broadcasting
administration of justice—
  active proceedings, **17**, 29
  contempt of court, publication in, **17**, 33
  defences, **17**, 30
  generally, **17**, 27
  proceedings—
    active, **17**, 29
    reports of, **17**, 31
  public affairs, **17**, 32
  public interest, **17**, 32
  publication harmful to, **17**, 34
  strict liability rule, **17**, 28
advertisements, restrictions on publication, **17**, 45
agreements, printer's imprint, requirement not applicable, **17**, 3
aircraft, suppression of broadcasting from, **17**, 9
auction, particulars of sales, requirement as to printer's imprint, **17**, 3
bank notes, printer's imprint, requirement not applicable, **17**, 3
betting, advertisements, restrictions on, **17**, 45
bills of exchange, printer's imprint, requirement not applicable, **17**, 3
bills of lading, printer's imprint, requirement not applicable, **17**, 3
Bodleian Library, Oxford, delivery of copies to, **17**, 5
bonds, printer's imprint, requirement not applicable, **17**, 3
book—
  copies, delivery to certain libraries, **17**, 5
  meaning, **17**, 5*n*
British Broadcasting Corporation—
  charter, regulation by, **17**, 2, 6
  election matter, transmission of, **17**, 43
  government control, **17**, 6
  home services—
    finance, **17**, 6
    meaning, **17**, 6*n*
  licences, revenue from, **17**, 6
  primary duty, **17**, 6
  Secretary of State, powers of, **17**, 6
British Code of Advertising Practice, **17**, 45
Broadcasting Complaints Commission, **17**, 2, 10

Press and broadcasting—*continued*
business cards, printer's imprint, requirement not applicable, **17**, 3
cable programme services—
 licensing, **17**, 9
 special qualified privilege, **17**, 20
Cambridge University Library, delivery of copies to, **17**, 5
Channel Four, **17**, 7
Channel Islands, Independent Broadcasting Authority, functions of, **17**, 7
child—
 adoption, advertisement relating to, **17**, 45
 care, advertisement relating to, **17**, 45
 fostering, advertisement relating to, **17**, 45
 horror comics, access to, **17**, 39
 identity of—
  children's hearings, **17**, 37
  civil proceedings, **17**, 36
  criminal proceedings, **17**, 35
  fatal accident inquiries, **17**, 38
 meaning, **17**, 37
children's hearings—
 attendance at, **3**, 1326
 identity of child, **17**, 37
 privileges relating to, **17**, 17
civil proceedings—
 active, **17**, 29
 child, identity of, **17**, 36
comic, horror, falling into hands of child, **17**, 39
confidence—
 breach of, **17**, 44
 obligation of, publication in breach of, **17**, 44
consumer credit, advertisements, restrictions on, **17**, 45
contempt of court—
 broadcasting, effect on activities of those concerned with, **17**, 1
 defences, **17**, 30
 non-disclosure, **17**, 23
 press, effect on activities of those concerned with, **17**, 1
 publication in, **17**, 33
 strict liability rule, **17**, 28
contract—
 broadcasting, effect on activities of those concerned with, **17**, 1
 press, effect on activities of those concerned with, **17**, 1
copies—
 libraries, delivery to, **17**, 2, 5
 preservation of, **17**, 2, 4
copyright—
 broadcasting, effect on activities of those concerned with, **17**, 1
 matter protected by, **17**, 26
 press, effect on activities of those concerned with, **17**, 1
court—
 contempt of, *see* contempt of court *above*
 documents, printer's imprint, **17**, 3
 proceedings, privileges relating to, **17**, 16

Press and broadcasting—*continued*
criminal proceedings—
 active, **17**, 29
 child, identity of, **17**, 35
damages—
 confidence, breach of obligation of, **17**, 44
 defamatory matter, claim resulting from publication, **17**, 25
deeds, printer's imprint, requirement not applicable, **17**, 3
defamation—
 Act of 1952 generally, **17**, 20
 action, defence to, **17**, 18
 broadcasting, effect on activities of those concerned with, **17**, 1
 generally, **17**, 18
 non-disclosure, **17**, 23
 parliamentary papers, **17**, 19
 press, effect on activities of those concerned with, **17**, 1
 qualified privilege—
  extent of, **17**, 22
  matters enjoying, **17**, 21
  reports enjoying, **17**, 21
defamatory matter, damages, publication may result in claim for, **17**, 25
defences—
 contempt of court, **17**, 30
 copyright, action relating to, **17**, 26
 defamation action, **17**, 18
 innocent publication, **17**, 30
 strict liability rule, **17**, 30
direct broadcasting by satellite, **17**, 7
disclosure, **17**, 23
dividend warrants, printer's imprint, requirement not applicable, **17**, 3
divorce proceedings, matter derived from, restriction on publication, **17**, 41
drugs, advertisements, restrictions on, **17**, 45
encyclopaedia, certain libraries, delivery of copies to, **17**, 5
exempt information, exclusion from meeting, **14**, 1331
fatal accident inquiry, child, identity of, **17**, 38
food, advertisements, restrictions on, **17**, 45
freedom of—
 breach of confidence, and, **18**, 1473
 generally, **12**, 73, 74
gaming, advertisements, restrictions on, **17**, 45
goods, receipts for, printer's imprint, **17**, 3
horror comic, child, falling into hands of, **17**, 39
hovercraft, suppression of broadcasting from, **17**, 9
indecent matter, publication, restrictions on, **17**, 40
Independent Broadcasting Authority—
 advertisements, publication of, **17**, 45
 Channel Four, **17**, 7
 direct broadcasting by satellite, **17**, 7
 election matter, transmission of, **17**, 43
 functions, **17**, 7
 ITV, **17**, 7
 programmes provided by, regulation of, **17**, 8
 regulation, **17**, 2, 7, 8

Press and broadcasting—*continued*
Independent Broadcasting Authority—*continued*
  services provided by, **17**, 7
  teletext services, **17**, 8
innocent publication, defences, **17**, 30
insurance policies, printer's imprint, requirement
  not applicable, **17**, 3
Isle of Man, Independent Broadcasting Authority,
  functions of, **17**, 7
ITV, **17**, 7
letters of attorney, printer's imprint, requirement
  not applicable, **17**, 3
libraries, copies, delivery of, **17**, 2, 5
local authority—
  committees, attendance at, **17**, 14
  meetings—
    press privileges at, **17**, 13
    public right to attend, **17**, 12
local government, election matter, restriction on
  publication, **17**, 43
magazines, certain libraries, delivery of copies to,
  17, 5
malice, publication privileged unless made with,
  17, 20
marine structures, suppression of broadcasting
  from, **17**, 9
medicinal products, advertisements, restrictions
  on, **17**, 45
meetings—
  committees, **17**, 14
  local authority—
    press privileges at, **17**, 13
    public right to attend, **17**, 12
  public bodies, of, **17**, 15
money, printer's imprint, requirement not
  applicable, **17**, 3
National Library of Scotland, delivery of copies
  to, **17**, 5
National Library of Wales, delivery of copies to,
  17, 5
negligent statement—
  broadcasting, effect on activities of those
    concerned with, **17**, 1
  press, effect on activities of those concerned
    with, **17**, 1
newspapers—
  certain libraries, delivery of copies to, **17**, 5
  meaning, **17**, 20*n*
non-disclosure, generally, **17**, 23
nullity proceedings, matter derived from,
  restriction on publication, **17**, 41
obscene material, publication, restrictions on, **17**,
  40
offences—
  copyright, relating to, **17**, 26
  printer's imprint, relating to, **17**, 3
  racial hatred, publication of matter likely to stir
    up, **17**, 42
parliament—
  absolute privilege, **17**, 19
  broadcasting, qualified privilege conferred on,
    17, 19
  election matter, restriction on publication, **17**, 43
  papers for use of, printer's imprint, **17**, 3

Press and broadcasting—*continued*
personal cards, printer's imprint, requirement not
  applicable, **17**, 3
pirate radio stations, suppression of, **17**, 9
Press Council, regulation by, **17**, 2
printer's imprint—
  name and address, **17**, 3
  offences, **17**, 3
  prosecutions, **17**, 3
  regulation, **17**, 2, 3
privilege—
  generally, **17**, 11
  meetings—
    committees, **17**, 14
    local authority—
      press privileges at, **17**, 13
      public right to attend, **17**, 12
    public bodies, of, **17**, 15
  proceedings—
    children's hearings, **17**, 17
    court, **17**, 16
  qualified, **17**, 21, 22
  statements—
    subject to explanation or contradiction, **17**,
      21
    without explanation or contradiction, **17**, 21
proceedings—
  active, **17**, 29
  children's hearings, *see* CHILDREN'S HEARINGS
  civil, *see* civil proceedings *above*
  court, privileges relating to, **17**, 16
  criminal, *see* criminal proceedings *above*
  reports of, **17**, 31
promissory notes, printer's imprint, requirement
  not applicable, **17**, 3
prosecutions, printer's imprint, relating to, **17**, 3
public affairs, publication made as part of
  discussion, **17**, 32
public boards, papers printed by authority of,
  requirement for imprint, **17**, 3
public interest, publication in, **17**, 32
public officers, papers printed by authority of,
  requirement for imprint, **17**, 3
publication—
  administration of justice—
    active proceedings, **17**, 29
    contempt of court, **17**, 33
    defences, **17**, 30
    generally, **17**, 27
    harm to, **17**, 34
    proceedings—
      active, **17**, 29
      reports of, **17**, 31
    public affairs, **17**, 32
    public interest, **17**, 32
    strict liability rule, **17**, 28
  advertising matter, **17**, 45
  child, restrictions relating to, *see* CHILD-
    CHILDREN
  confidential matter, **17**, 44
  contempt of court, in, **17**, 33
  copyright, matter protected by, **17**, 26
  defamatory matter, **17**, 25
  divorce proceedings, matter derived from, **17**, 41

Press and broadcasting—*continued*
publication—*continued*
  election matter, **17**, 43
  indecent matter, of, **17**, 40
  innocent, defence of, **17**, 30
  nullity proceedings, matter derived from, **17**, 41
  obscene material, of, **17**, 40
  performers' rights, matter protected by, **17**, 26
  racial hatred, matter likely to stir up, **17**, 42
  restrictions generally, **17**, 24
  separation proceedings, matter derived from, **17**, 41
racial hatred, matter likely to stir up, restriction on publication, **17**, 42
receipts, printer's imprint, requirement not applicable, **17**, 3
regulation—
  British Broadcasting Corporation, of, **17**, 2, 6
  copies—
    libraries, delivery to, **17**, 2, 5
    preservation of, **17**, 2, 4
  generally, **17**, 2
  Independent Broadcasting Authority, of, **17**, 2, 7, 8
  newspaper merger, prohibition of, **17**, 2
  Press Council, by, **17**, 2
  printer's imprint, **17**, 2, 3
report—
  proceedings, of, **17**, 31
  qualified privilege, **17**, 21
satellite, direct broadcasting by, **17**, 7
Satellite Broadcasting Board, **17**, 7
secretary of state—
  British Broadcasting Corporation, powers relating to, **17**, 6
  newspaper merger, consent to, **17**, 2
securities, printer's imprint, requirement not applicable, **17**, 3
separation proceedings, matter derived from, restriction on publication, **17**, 41
sex discrimination, advertisements, restriction on, **17**, 45
share transfers, printer's imprint, requirement not applicable, **17**, 3
ships, suppression of broadcasting from, **17**, 9
strict liability rule—
  contempt of court, **17**, 28
  defence, **17**, 30
surrogacy, advertisements relating to arrangements, **17**, 45
teletext services, **17**, 8
territorial waters, suppression of broadcasting from outside, **17**, 9
trade descriptions, false, advertisements containing, **17**, 45
Trinity College, Dublin, library, delivery of copies to, **17**, 5
Prestwick Freeport
free zone, as, **7**, 1164*n*
Presumptions of law
See EVIDENCE
Preventative medicine
arrangements for, **11**, 1477
health boards, administration by, **11**, 1410

Preventive medicine—*continued*
research into, **11**, 1487
Preventive offence
attempt, and, **7**, 164*n*
generally, **7**, 164*n*
Price
agreement to recommend, **4**, 1141
concept of money central to, **14**, 1801
fixing, **4**, 1140, 1369
inflation, capacity of competition to dampen, **4**, 1107
price agreement as counter-inflationary device, **4**, 1163
sale of goods, **14**, 1802
Priest
jury service, excused from, **3**, 1571, 1632
Roman Catholic—
  confessional, seal of, **3**, 1658, 1667
  declining number, **3**, 1656
  deprivation of office, **3**, 1658
  dismissal from clerical state, **3**, 1658
  House of Commons, disabled from sitting in, **3**, 1662
  privilege, **3**, 1667
    confessional, of, **3**, 1667
Scottish Episcopal Church—
  generally, **3**, 1614
Primary liability
contract of, cautionary obligation distinguished, **3**, 844
existence of, generally, **3**, 846
necessity for, **3**, 846
reference to, essential nature of, **3**, 887
Primary school
appointment of teachers, **8**, 822
compulsory testing, education authorities' function, **8**, 859
Prime Minister
appointment, **7**, 712, 712*n*
first Lord of Treasury, as, **5**, 494
House of Commons, must have seat in, **5**, 306
office of, **5**, 306
  establishment, **7**, 702
precedence, **16**, 2006, 2007
Queen acts in public affairs on advice of, **5**, 306
Scottish, **7**, 702
Primogeniture
introduction to Orkney and Shetland, **24**, 308
rule of, abolition of, **25**, 687
Primus
Scottish Episcopal Church—
  designation, **3**, 1619
  election, **3**, 1619
  functions, **3**, 1619
Prince and Great Steward of Scotland
Prince's Seal, **7**, 890
Sovereign's eldest son as, **7**, 704, 704*n*, 786
succession to title of, **5**, 707
title of, **5**, 708
where no eldest son, **7**, 786
Prince's Seal
generally, **7**, 890

Prince's Seal—*continued*
Register of—
Department of Registers, kept in, **19**, 820
generally, **6**, 461
Principal (agency)
agent's rights against—
lien against goods, **1**, 643
reimbursement, **1**, 640
remuneration, **1**, 602, 641
counterclaim against third party by, **1**, 620
defective instructions, giving, **1**, 632
delay by, **1**, 632
delegation, consent to, **1**, 633
exception clauses, bound by, **1**, 622
foreign, **1**, 659
frustration of contract by, **1**, 642
improper intromission with property, claim for,
1, 655
losses of, agent claiming, **1**, 645
ratification of agent's acts by, *see* AGENT
recompense, liability on principle of, **1**, 627
shipping agent, of, **1**, 614
third party—
duties and liabilities to—
agent's authority, scope of, **1**, 649
authority, agent acting within, **1**, 650
fraud by agent, where, **1**, 651
limit on agent's authority, where, **1**, 653
negligence by agent, where, **1**, 652
rights against, **1**, 655
unauthorised contract, taking benefit of, **1**, 627
undisclosed—
agent elected as debtor where, **1**, 657
bankruptcy, effect of, **1**, 619
contractual rights, **1**, 622
damages, suing for, **1**, 618
disclosure of, **1**, 616, 617
inquiry, duty of, **1**, 623
marine insurance contract, in, **1**, 628
price of goods, suing for, **1**, 619
purchaser, as, **1**, 618
ratification, and, **1**, 625
recompense, liability on principle of, **1**, 627
rights and duties, crystallisation of, **1**, 619
seller, as, **1**, 619
set-off, effect on, **1**, 621
third party, liability of agent to, **1**, 635, 637
third party, right to sue, **1**, 655
usual authority, agent acting within, **1**, 626
vicarious liability, **15**, 243-246
Printer, Master
office of, **7**, 819, 851
Printer's imprint
name and address, **17**, 3
offences, **17**, 3
prosecutions, **17**, 3
regulation, **17**, 2, 3
Prior communings rule
building contracts, **3**, 28
Prior rights
See SPOUSE
***Prior tempore potier jure* rule**, **8**, 106

Prison
accommodation, rules as to, **16**, 1442
administration, *see* PENAL ESTABLISHMENT
alternatives to committal, development, **16**, 1500
breaking, *see* PRISON BREAKING
cell—
design regulations, **16**, 1442
female prisoners, separate from male prisoners,
16, 1427
over-crowding, **16**, 1442
police, use as prison, **16**, 1424
silent, confinement in, **16**, 1453
two or more prisoners in, **16**, 1442
untried prisoners, **16**, 1426
changing attitude to imprisonment, **16**, 1410
chaplain—
appointment, **16**, 1417
Church of Scotland, **3**, 1668; **16**, 1411, 1417,
1458
denominations other than Church of Scotland,
16, 1411, 1417, 1458
generally, **16**, 1417
hours of attendance, **16**, 1456
influence of, decline, **16**, 1403
Roman Catholic, **3**, 1668; **16**, 1458
Chief Inspector of Prisons, **16**, 1423
civilian staff, **16**, 1416
conditions, inspection and report, **16**, 1411, 1423
control—
centralisation, **16**, 1401
Secretary of State's role, **16**, 1401, 1402
counselling provision, **16**, 1454, 1456
dental officer, **16**, 1418
discipline—
appeal—
finding of breach of discipline, against, **16**,
1450
punishment imposed, against, **16**, 1450
'awards', **16**, 1450
judicial comment on, **16**, 1451
breach of—
charge of, **16**, 1448
inquiry into, **16**, 1448, 1450
prisoner, full opportunity to present own
case, **16**, 1450
proof beyond reasonable doubt, **16**, 1450
punishment, **16**, 1450
subsequent behaviour, **16**, 1450*n*
co-operation in control of other prisoners,
enlisting, **16**, 1446
criminal law, offences against, **16**, 1449
disciplinary procedure, **16**, 1450
judicial comment, **16**, 1451
prison rules, availability to prisoners, **16**, 1441
prisoners not to be employed in disciplinary
capacity, **16**, 1446
remission system, and, **16**, 1447
responsibility for, **16**, 1446
restraints, **16**, 1453
silent cell, confinement in, **16**, 1453
educational provision, **16**, 1454, 1456
employees, **16**, 1415
escape from, assisting or effecting, **16**, 1468
exercise, provisions as to, **16**, 1465

Prison—*continued*

fire certificates not required for, **10**, 1470

governor—
  admission of new prisoner, duty on, **16**, 1441
  appointment, **16**, 1411, 1414
  deputies and assistants, **16**, 1414
  directives to, **16**, 1409
  duties, **16**, 1414
    discipline, as to, **16**, 1446, 1448-1451
    generally, **16**, 1414
    statutory responsibilities, **16**, 1414
    training, **16**, 1414

historical background—
  pre-1877, **16**, 1401
  from 1877 to 1950, **16**, 1402
  recent developments, **16**, 1403
  offenders under twenty-one, **16**, 1404

imprisonment, restrictions on court powers to impose, **16**, 1403

inspection, **16**, 1411

inspector, appointment, **16**, 1411

justice of the peace, inspection by, **16**, 1422

justice of peace court powers, **6**, 1159

legal framework—
  changing attitude to imprisonment, **16**, 1410
  circular instructions, **16**, 1408
  directives to governors, **16**, 1410
  Prisons (Scotland) Act 1989, **16**, 1405
  Prisons and Young Offenders Institutions (Scotland) Rules 1994, **16**, 1406
  standing orders, **16**, 1407, 1408

legal regulation, desirability, **16**, 1497

letters, *see* mail *below*

library, **16**, 1457

mail—
  censorship, **16**, 1461
  courts, correspondence with, **16**, 1461, 1461*n*
  entitlement to, **12**, 69; **16**, 1459, 1461
  extra letters, **16**, 1461
  illegal enclosures, **16**, 1461
  legal adviser, correspondence with, **16**, 1461, 1461*n*
  Member of Parliament, to, **16**, 1461
  restrictions as to, **16**, 1461
  rules as to, generally, **16**, 1459, 1461
  writing materials, provision of, **16**, 1461*n*

maintenance, **16**, 1411

medical officer, *see* PENAL ESTABLISHMENT

objectives of custodial sentencing, **16**, 1436

offences in relation to, **16**, 1468

outwith European Union, goods produced in, **7**, 1203

outwith Scotland, transfer to or from, **16**, 1440

parole, *see* PAROLE

pay-telephones, **16**, 1459, 1462

police cells, use as prison, **16**, 1424

police cells declared, **16**, 1720, 1822

prescribed activity, meaning, **16**, 1453*n*

prison officer, *see* PRISON OFFICER

prisoner, *see* PRISONER

prohibited article, introduction into, **16**, 1452, 1468

purchase of prisons or land, **16**, 1411

release from, *see* PRISONER (release)

Prison—*continued*

religious provision, **16**, 1441, 1458

rules, information concerning, provision, **16**, 1445

sale of prisons or land, **16**, 1411

Scottish Prison Service, **16**, 1413
  See also SCOTTISH PRISON SERVICE

sheriff, inspection by, **16**, 1422

silent cell, **16**, 1453

social work department—
  provision of services, generally, **22**, 9
  social worker, link role, **22**, 36

social workers, **16**, 1419

staff—
  appointment, **16**, 1403
  training, **16**, 1403

teachers, **16**, 1420

unauthorised property, introduction into, **16**, 1452

visiting committee—
  appointment, **16**, 1421
    termination, **16**, 1421
  clerk, stipend, **16**, 1421
  expenses, reimbursement, **16**, 1421
  historical background, **16**, 1402
  young offenders institutions, **16**, 1421

visits—
  duration, **16**, 1460
  family, by, **16**, 1460
  foreign prisoner, **16**, 1460
  general practice, **16**, 1460
  legal adviser, by, **16**, 1460
  minimum entitlement, **16**, 1460
  national or international authorities, by, **16**, 1460
  number, discretion of governor as to, **16**, 1459
  refusal of entry to certain persons, **16**, 1459, 1460
  rules as to, generally, **16**, 1459
  termination, **16**, 1459, 1460
  transfer of prisoner to facilitate, **16**, 1460
  unused allowance, accumulated, **16**, 1460
  young prioner, entitlement to, **16**, 1460*n*

welfare provision, **16**, 1463

work, *see* PRISONER

young offenders institution, transfer from, **16**, 1434

See also PENAL ESTABLISHMENT

Prison breaking

civil prisoner, **7**, 554

definition, **7**, 553

escape, means of, **7**, 555

generally, **7**, 489, 491, 552

lawfully confined, prisoner must be, **7**, 553, 554

prison, meaning, **7**, 556

real or imitation firearm possessed during, **10**, 1565

remand, prisoner on, **7**, 554

Prison officer

accommodation, **16**, 1415

appointment, **16**, 1411

apprehension of offenders, **16**, 1468

conditions of employment, action as to, **16**, 1490

control of prisoners, **16**, 1446

disciplinary code, **16**, 1415

Prison officer—*continued*
generally, **16**, 1414, 1415
minimum entry age, **16**, 1415
physical force in execution of duty, use of, **7**, 238
press, unauthorised contact with, **16**, 1415
preventive powers, **16**, 1468
promotion, **16**, 1415
recruitment, **16**, 1415
retirement, **16**, 1415
rules and orders, conformity with, **16**, 1415
search of, **16**, 1415
training, **16**, 1414, 1415
Prison service
See SCOTTISH PRISON SERVICE
Prisoner
absconding, **7**, 557
accommodation, **16**, 1442
admission to prison, **16**, 1441
after-care, provision, **22**, 36
aftercare, **16**, 1463
age, effect on allocation, **16**, 1439
alien, **16**, 1430
    diplomatic services representative, visit by, **16**, 1460
allocation, **16**, 1437-1439
assisting escape of, **7**, 559
awaiting sentence, treatment, **16**, 1426
baby of female prisoner, **16**, 1427, 1441
breach of interdict, committed for, **16**, 1426
cell, special or silent, confinement in, **16**, 1453
child—
    Criminal Procedure (Scotland) Act 1975, sentenced under, **16**, 1432
    disentitlement to child benefit, **21**, 962
    educational provision, **16**, 1456
    unruly or depraved, **16**, 1431
Christmas and summer leave, **16**, 1471, 1471*n*
civil—
    negligent officer, liability of, **14**, 1507
    restriction direction, subject to, **14**, 1468
    transfer direction, subject to, **14**, 1468
    treatment, **16**, 1432
    See also CIVIL PRISONER
classification, **16**, 1437, 1438
clothing—
    prisoner's own clothing, use of, **16**, 1443
    suitable clothing, **16**, 1443, 1443*n*
Commonwealth citizen, **16**, 1430
complaints procedure, **16**, 1469
confinement, Secretary of State's powers, **16**, 1411
consecutive sentences, serving, **16**, 1447
contempt of court, committed for, **16**, 1426
convicted—
    restriction direction, subject to, **14**, 1467
    transfer direction, subject to, **14**, 1464, 1467
correspondence, **12**, 69
court, right of access to, **12**, 44
death—
    procedure on, **16**, 1482
    public inquiry into, **16**, 1482
    report, **16**, 1414
discharge, *see* release *below*
discharged, income support, **21**, 1067

Prisoner—*continued*
discipline and control, *see* PRISON (discipline)
educational provision, **16**, 1454, 1456
escape, assisting or effecting, **16**, 1468
exercise, provisions as to, **16**, 1465
family—
    notification on death of prisoner, **16**, 1482
    visits by, **16**, 1459
    welfare provision, **16**, 1463
female, **16**, 1434, 1442
    baby of, **16**, 1427, 1441
    male and female accommodation to be separate, **16**, 1442
    pregnant, **16**, 1427
    under twenty-one, **16**, 1434
fine and compensation defaulters, treatment, **16**, 1428, 1433*n*
fingerprints, requirement to take, **16**, 1441
food and drink, provisions as to, **16**, 1444
franchise, disqualification, **15**, 1082
hair, beard and moustache, regulations as to, **16**, 1445
half-way house, as unaesthetic sight, **14**, 2084
House of Commons, disqualification from candidature for, **15**, 1063
leave, **16**, 1471, 1471*n*
legal action by, **16**, 1470
length of sentence, effect on allocation, **16**, 1439
letters, *see* PRISON (mail)
licence, release on *see* PAROLE
life sentence, serving, **16**, 1447
long home leave, **16**, 1471, 1471*n*
mail, *see* PRISON (mail)
mandatory indeterminate sentence, **16**, 1476
medical services, **16**, 1464
Member of Parliament, access to, **16**, 1470
naturalisation requirements, **14**, 1920
number, fluctuations, **16**, 1403
offence, effect on allocation, **16**, 1439
parole, *see* PAROLE
pay-telephone, access to, **16**, 1459, 1462
petition Crown, right to, **16**, 1470
photograph of, requirement to take, **16**, 1441
police custody—
    escape and rescue from, **7**, 560, 561
    treatment, in, **16**, 1767
pre-parole or pre-life licence leave, **16**, 1471, 1471*n*
pre-Training for Freedom leave, **16**, 1471, 1471*n*
previous convictions, effect on allocation system, **16**, 1439
prison breaking, *see* PRISON BREAKING
privileges—
    allocation, **16**, 1494
    determination, **16**, 1407
    generally, **16**, 1466, 1495
    legal regulation, desirability, **16**, 1497
property—
    cash, **16**, 1467
    cell, entitlement to keep in, **16**, 1467
    record of, **16**, 1467
    safe storage, **16**, 1467
records, **16**, 1441
recreation, **16**, 1457

Prisoner—*continued*
refractory, restraint, **16**, 1453
release—
  calculation of date, **16**, 1472
  compassionate grounds, on, **16**, 1464, 1471
  discharge grant, **16**, 1481
  discretionary life sentence prisoner, **16**, 1477
  licence, on, **16**, 1479
  mandatory indeterminate sentence, where, **16**, 1476
  parole, **16**, 1473
    criteria, **16**, 1478
    licence, **16**, 1479
    statistics, **16**, 1480
    See also PAROLE
  permanent, **16**, 1472
  prisoner sentenced after October 1993 ..., **16**, 1473, 1475
  prisoner sentenced before October 1993 ..., **16**, 1473, 1474
  recall, **16**, 1471, 1472, 1473
  Secretary of State's powers, **16**, 1411
  temporary, **16**, 1471
religious service, attendance at, **16**, 1458
remission system, **16**, 1447
requests procedure, **16**, 1469
restraints, **16**, 1453
search on admission, **16**, 1441
security categories, **16**, 1438
sentence, awaiting, removal to hospital of, **14**, 1463
sentenced prisoner, treatment, **16**, 1433
sex, effect on allocation, **16**, 1439
social relations, **16**, 1463
social security payments payable in respect of, **21**, 1020
social worker, link role, **22**, 36
solitary confinement, rules as to, **16**, 1453
statutory sick pay, **21**, 912
transfers—
  other UK establishments, to or from, **16**, 1440
  Scottish institutions, between, **16**, 1440
  visits, to facilitate, **16**, 1460
treatment—
  accommodation, **16**, 1442
  admission, **16**, 1441
  allocation system, **16**, 1437-1439
  complaint by prisoner, **16**, 1469
  discipline and control, *see* PRISON (discipline)
  inspection and report, **16**, 1423
  legal action by prisoner, **16**, 1470
  objective, **16**, 1436
  rules as to—
    accommodation, **16**, 1442
    aliens, **16**, 1430
treatment
  children—
    Criminal Procedure (Scotland) Act 1975, sentenced under, **16**, 1432
    unruly or depraved, **16**, 1431
  civil prisoners, **16**, 1426
  Commonwealth citizens, **16**, 1430
  courts-martial, persons sentenced by, **16**, 1429
  exercise, **16**, 1465

Prisoner—*continued*
treatment—*continued*
  rules as to—*continued*
    fine and compensation order defaulters, **16**, 1428
    food and drink, **16**, 1444
    generally, **16**, 1425
    hygiene, **16**, 1445
    medical services and facilities, **16**, 1464
    sentence, prisoners awaiting, **16**, 1427
    sentenced prisoners, **16**, 1433
    under twenty-one, persons, **16**, 1434
    untried prisoners, **16**, 1426
    welfare, **16**, 1463
  Secretary of State's powers, **16**, 1411
  security categories, **16**, 1438
  transfers, **16**, 1440, 1460
trial, awaiting, removal to hospital, **14**, 1463
under twenty-one, aged—
  allocation, **16**, 1439
  treatment, rules as to, **16**, 1434
  untried prisoners, treatment, **16**, 1426
unescorted exceptional day release, **16**, 1471, 1471*n*
untried—
  innocence, presumption of, **16**, 1426
  meaning, **16**, 1426, 1426*n*
  medical or dental practitioner of own choice, visits by, **16**, 1464
  privileges, **16**, 1466
  security category, **16**, 1438
  treatment, **16**, 1426
  under twenty-one, aged, **16**, 1426
  visitors, **16**, 1459
  work, **16**, 1455
violent, restraint, **16**, 1453
visitors, **16**, 1459, 1460
war, of—
  assisting escape, **7**, 611
  See also PRISONER OF WAR
welfare, **16**, 1463
work—
  civil prisoners, **16**, 1455
  maximum working week, **16**, 1455
  payment for, **16**, 1455
  requirement to work, exceptions, **16**, 1445*n*
  rest day, **16**, 1445
  rules as to, **16**, 1455
  untried prisoners, **16**, 1455
Prisoner of war
assisting escape, **7**, 611
Geneva Red Cross Conventions, **19**, 708, 709*n*
statements by as hearsay evidence, **10**, 711
Privacy
aemulatio vicini answer to allegation of, **14**, 2036
discrimination, genuine occupational qualification as defence to, **9**, 362
no natural right to, **14**, 2032
right to, difficulty of defining, **11**, 1094
Private Act
meaning, **12**, 1202
strict interpretation, **12**, 1203, 1204
Private authority
borrowing powers, **20**, 225

Private Bill
additional provision, petitions for, **19**, 106, 107
alternatives to private Bill procedure, **19**, 4
area and interests involved, **19**, 2
association, promoted by, **19**, 91-94
commercial companies—
　giving powers to, **19**, 91-94
　promoted by, **19**, 91-94
　Wharncliffe orders, **19**, 92
company—
　powers, giving to, **19**, 91-94
　promoted by, **19**, 91-94
confirmation Bill, **19**, 64-77
deposit of, **19**, 81
division of Bills between Houses of Parliament,
　19, 84
Examiners of Petitions, **19**, 82, 83
　hybrid Bill, **19**, 125
extending inside and outside Scotland, **19**, 80, 108
factors determining whether Bill should proceed
　as private, **19**, 2
first reading, **19**, 88
government may not introduce, **19**, 2
hybrid Bill, *see* HYBRID BILL
late Bill, **19**, 81, 107
marriage enabling Bill, *see* PERSONAL BILL
non-compliance with Standing Orders, **19**, 82, 83
objection to, **19**, 2
opposed—
　Parliamentary committees, **19**, 38
　substituted Bills, **19**, 109
Parliament—
　function of, **19**, 2
　late Bill, **19**, 107
　passage through, **19**, 88-105
　substituted Bill, **19**, 108-110
Parliamentary committees—
　constitution, **19**, 96
　House of Lords select committees, **19**, 98
　powers, **19**, 99
　report stage in Commons, **19**, 100
　sittings, **19**, 97
　unopposed Bills, **19**, 95
particulars to be made available, **19**, 81
partnership, promotion by, **19**, 91-94
personal Bill, *see* PERSONAL BILL
petitions against, **19**, 85
　locus standi of petitioner, **19**, 85-87
petitions for, **19**, 81
　additional provision, for, **19**, 106, 107
　deposit of, **19**, 2
presentation to Parliament, **19**, 88
primary purpose, **19**, 1*n*
private legislation, promotion by, **19**, 1
promoter, **19**, 2
provisional order confirmation, exceptions to, **19**, 80
public Acts amended or repealed by, **19**, 2
public Bill distinguished, **19**, 2
public matter as main object, **19**, 2
public policy affected by, **19**, 2
representation for one enactment, **19**, 7
second House—
　amendments, **19**, 104
　examination, **19**, 90

Private Bill—*continued*
second reading, **19**, 89
settled estate, regulating and varying, *see*
　PERSONAL BILL
society, promotion by, **19**, 91-94
substituted Bill, **19**, 80, 108-110
　limitations on, **19**, 110
　opponents, notice to, **19**, 109
　orders objected to by Chairman, **19**, 108
suspension of, **19**, 105
third reading in Commons, **19**, 101
third reading in Lords, **19**, 103
unopposed—
　amendments to, **19**, 95
　Committee on Unopposed Bills in the
　　Commons, **19**, 95
　provision in Lords, **19**, 102
Wharncliffe orders, **19**, 92
See also PRIVATE LEGISLATION
Private citizen
arrest without warrant by, **17**, 597
crime prevention, intervention by, **16**, 1701,
　1701*n*
institution of proceedings by, **17**, 585
search of, **17**, 604
See also INDIVIDUAL; PERSONS AND PERSONALITY
Private documents
documentary evidence, as, **10**, 599-613
privileged writings, **10**, 600-602
Private dwelling house
See DWELLING HOUSE
Private enterprise
historical development, **5**, 8
Private hire car
application relating to, appeal to sheriff, **14**, 119
civic code licence—
　conditions, **14**, 553
　driver, **14**, 552
　generally, **14**, 550, 551
　signs on vehicle, **14**, 554
separate fare, carriage of passengers at, **14**, 440
Private hospital
meaning, **11**, 1525*n*
mental hospitals—
　control of, **11**, 1535
　inspection, **11**, 1535
　registration, **11**, 1532, 1533
　　application for, **11**, 1533
　　cancellation, **11**, 1534
　　certificate of registration, display of, **11**, 1533
Private hotel
keeper not subject to strict liability, **11**, 1709
Private international law
agreements under, *see* ARBITRATION AGREEMENT
choice of law, *see* CHOICE OF LAW
contract—
　alternative reference, rules of, **17**, 126
　characterisation, **17**, 360
　choice of law clause distinguished from
　　unilateral choice of law provisions, **17**, 133
　commercial, formation of, **17**, 254
　connecting factor, **17**, 122, 125
　construction, **17**, 270
　current approach, evolution of, **17**, 246

Private international law—*continued*
contract—*continued*
  discharge of—
    compensation, **17**, 275
    delegation, **17**, 277
    general rule, **17**, 274
    limitation, **17**, 276
    novation, **17**, 277
    prescription, **17**, 276
    set-off, **17**, 275
  EEC Convention on Contractual Obligations—
    background, **17**, 278
    evasion, prevention of, **17**, 284
    generally, **17**, 285
    governing system, ascertainment of, **17**, 280
    presumption, advantages and disadvantages of, **17**, 283
    proper law, **17**, 281, 282
    scope, **17**, 279
  formation of—
    agreement, **17**, 269
    capacity, **17**, 254, 255
    consent, **17**, 269
    formal validity—
      formalities, **17**, 256
      lex fori, mandatory rules of, **17**, 259
      lex loci contractus, application of, **17**, 257
      proper law, application of, **17**, 258
    legality—
      external public policy rule, **17**, 263
      foreign law, general rules excluding, **17**, 261
      foreign revenue claim, **17**, 264
      penal claim, **17**, 264
      unlawful contract, specific rules on, **17**, 265
      unlawfulness, **17**, 260, 262, 266, 267, 268
    residual category, **17**, 268
  fragmentation of rules, **17**, 124
  general approach, **17**, 245
  interpretation of, **17**, 270
  most closely connected system—
    application of, **17**, 252
    factors relevant to determine, **17**, 253
  overlap with private international law, **17**, 107
  parties, obligations of—
    foreign currency, payment in, **17**, 273
    generally, **17**, 271
    proper law, exceptions to application of, **17**, 272
  penalty clause in, **17**, 177
  proper law of—
    autonomy approach, **17**, 249
    evasion, **17**, 250
    formal validity, **17**, 258
    general approach, **17**, 245
    implied choice of, **17**, 251
    most closely connected system—
      application of, **17**, 252
      factors relevant to determine, **17**, 253
    parties, selection by, **17**, 249
    putative, **17**, 248
    relevance of, **17**, 248
  scope, **17**, 244

Private international law—*continued*
contract—*continued*
  self-denying statutes, **17**, 134
  separate treatment of conflict rules, reasons for, **17**, 109
  sources of law, **17**, 247
  specific—
    ascertaining proper law, **17**, 290
    divisibility, **17**, 287
    examples, **17**, 286
    international conventions, governed by, **17**, 288
    legislation, governed by, **17**, 289
  transfer of property *inter vivos*, **17**, 320
  unlawful, specific rules on, **17**, 265
    agreement void for, **17**, 260
    lex fori, by, **17**, 262
    lex loci solutionis, by, **17**, 267
    proper law, by, **17**, 266
  See also LEX LOCI CONTRACTUS
conventions as source of, **17**, 112
definition of subject, **17**, 106
delict—
  aircraft, involving, **17**, 300
  alternative reference, rules of, **17**, 126
  characterisation, **17**, 360
  double delict rule—
    defences, **17**, 295
    English law, differences with, **17**, 293
    general rule, **17**, 292
    limitation, **17**, 297
    matters of substance in delict, **17**, 296
    place of delict, **17**, 298
    prescription, **17**, 297
    proper law exceptions, **17**, 294
  evolution of choice of law rules, **17**, 123
  flexible connecting factors, **17**, 125
  Law Commissions' memorandum on, **17**, 301
  overlap with private international law, **17**, 107
  reforms—
    anomalies in present law, **17**, 302
    case for, **17**, 301-306
    forum shopping, **17**, 305
    injustice, present law leads to, **17**, 303
    proposed, **17**, 307-309
    uncertainty of present law, **17**, 304
  sea, at, **17**, 299
  separate treatment of conflict rules, reasons for **17**, 109
  writings on topic, **17**, 291
  See also LEX LOCI DELICTI COMMISSI
diligence, **8**, 130
dispute with foreign element—
  characterisation—
    approaches to, **17**, 141
    autonomous concepts, by, **17**, 144
    choice of law rules, uncertainty as to, **17**, 14
    connecting factor, interpretation of—
      law of country, **17**, 147
      process, **17**, 146
    foreign expropriatory claim—
      applicable choice of law rules, **17**, 329
      legislation, scope of application, **17**, 333

Private international law—*continued*
dispute with foreign element—*continued*
  characterisation—*continued*
    foreign expropriatory claim—*continued*
      lex situs, transfer of property governed by,
        17, 330
      penal, **17**, 331
      public law, **17**, 332
    foreign law, proof of—
      ascertainment of law, **17**, 163
      exceptions, **17**, 161
      expert evidence, **17**, 160, 162
      general rule, **17**, 159
      previous case, in, **17**, 164
    general limiting rules—
      external public policy rule—
        choice of law rules, exceptions to, **17**,
          172
        formulation of, **17**, 170
        generally, **17**, 168
        purpose, **17**, 169
        relative nature of test, **17**, 171
      foreign penal claim—
        apparent exceptions rule, **17**, 175
        defining scope of rule, **17**, 174
        expropriatory, **17**, 331
        external public policy, effect of, **17**, 178
        legality of contract, **17**, 264
        marriage, constitution of, **17**, 222
        penalty clause in contract, **17**, 177
        rule, **17**, 173, 176
        utility of rule, **17**, 180
      foreign public law claim—
        apparent exceptions to rule, **17**, 175
        defining scope of rule, **17**, 174
        expropriatory, **17**, 332
        rule, **17**, 173, 179
        utility of rule, **17**, 180
      foreign revenue claim—
        apparent exceptions to rule, **17**, 175
        defining scope of rule, **17**, 174
        legality of contract, **17**, 264
        rule, **17**, 173
        utility of rule, **17**, 180
    lex causae, application of, **17**, 167
    lex fori, rule requiring application of
        mandatory provisions of—
      generally, **17**, 181
      illustrations, **17**, 182
      limits of, **17**, 183
  incidental question, **17**, 184, 185
  jurisdiction, **17**, 139
  lex causae, by, **17**, 143
  lex fori, by—
    application of, **17**, 141
    exceptions, **17**, 142
    rule of law, **17**, 166
  process of, **17**, 140
  relevant processes, **17**, 138
  renvoi—
    causes of, **17**, 153
    foreign court theory, **17**, 157
    internal law theory, **17**, 155
    nature of, **17**, 152

Private international law—*continued*
dispute with foreign element—*continued*
  characterisation—*continued*
    renvoi—*continued*
      partial theory, **17**, 156
      Scotland, **17**, 158
      solutions to, **17**, 186
    rule of law—
      lex fori, by, **17**, 166
      process of, **17**, 165
    time factor, **17**, 186
    unrecognised government—
      development of more sophisticated
        approach, **17**, 150
      pragmatic approach, **17**, 151
      problems of, **17**, 148
      traditional approach, **17**, 149
  external public policy rule—
    duress, **17**, 171
    exceptions to choice of law rules, **17**, 172
    formulation of, **17**, 174
    generally, **17**, 168
    legality of contract, **17**, 263
    penal rule and, **17**, 178
    purpose of, **17**, 169
    relative nature of test, **17**, 171
    transfer of property *inter vivos*, **17**, 324
  foreign expropriatory claim—
    applicable choice of law rules, **17**, 329
    legislation, scope of application, **17**, 333
    lex situs, transfer of property governed by, **17**, 330
    penal, **17**, 331
    public law, **17**, 332
  foreign law—
    ascertainment of, **17**, 163
    establishment of fact—
      admission, by, **10**, 653
      remit to foreign counsel, by, **10**, 653
      skilled evidence, by, **10**, 653
      statutory ascertainment, by, **10**, 653
    general rules excluding, **17**, 261
    proof of—
      exceptions, **17**, 161
      expert evidence, **17**, 160, 162
      general rule, **17**, 159
      previous case, in, **17**, 164
    refusal to apply, **17**, 159
  formal validity of will, **25**, 721
  immoveables—
    legitimacy, exception relating to, **17**, 241
    marriage, proprietary consequences of, **17**, 327
    moveables distinguished from, **17**, 313
  incidental questions, **17**, 184, 185, 322
  internal private law distinguished from, **17**, 108
  jurisdiction—
    adoption, **17**, 242
    alternative reference, rules of, **17**, 126
    bankruptcy, **17**, 351
    dispute with foreign element, **17**, 139
    husband and wife, **17**, 210
    rules of—
      choice of law rules, relationship with, **17**,
        135, 136
      generally, **17**, 103

Private international law—*continued*
limitation of actions, **16**, 2198, 2199
names, **17**, 101
overlap with other branches of legal system, **17**, 107
personal law—
  generally, **17**, 187
  indicators of, **17**, 188-190
prescription, **16**, 2132
processes relevant in, **17**, 138
property—
  characterisation of—
    lex causae, recharacterising under, **17**, 318
    lex situs, **17**, 314-317
    moveables and immoveables distinguished, **17**, 313
  child, rights of, **17**, 238
  foreign expropriatory claim—
    choice of law rules, **17**, 329
    legislation, scope of application, **17**, 333
    lex situs, transfer of property governed by, **17**, 330
    penal, **17**, 331
    public law, **17**, 332
  marriage consequences of—
    delimitation of field, **17**, 325
    dissolution of marriage, **17**, 328
    immoveables, **17**, 327
    moveables, **17**, 326
  parent, rights of, **17**, 238
  transfer *inter vivos*—
    contract, **17**, 320
    conveyance, **17**, 320
    external public policy, **17**, 324
    incidental question, **17**, 322
    lex situs, governed by, **17**, 319
    securities over moveables, **17**, 323
    time factor, **17**, 321
quasi-contract, **17**, 310-312
reform—
  bankruptcy, **17**, 354
  domicile, **17**, 207-209
renvoi, see RENVOI
scope of field, **17**, 102
separate treatment of rules, reasons for, **17**, 109
sources—
  continental jurists, influence of, **17**, 111
  contract, **17**, 247
  conventions, **17**, 112
  English law, influence of, **17**, 111
  harmonisation, **17**, 113
  legislation, **17**, 112
textbooks, **17**, 114
theories, importance of, **17**, 128
unrecognised government—
  development of more sophisticated approach, **17**, 150
  enforceability of law, current approach to, **17**, 129
  pragmatic approach, **17**, 151
  problem of, **17**, 148
  traditional approach, **17**, 149
  validity of laws, **17**, 107

Private land
See LAND
Private law
internal, **17**, 108
international, *see* PRIVATE INTERNATIONAL LAW
public law, and, **1**, 205
textbooks on branches of, **17**, 115
Private legislation
confirmation Bill, **19**, 64-77
England and Wales, effect in, **19**, 1
having effect beyond Scotland, **19**, 5, 5*n*, 6, 108
historical development, **5**, 9
hybrid Bill, *see* HYBRID BILL
hybrid instruments, *see* HYBRID INSTRUMENT
local statutory provisions—
  in force on 16 May 1975 ..., **14**, 307
  general repeal, **14**, 308
  meaning, **14**, 307
meaning, **19**, 1
opposition to, **14**, 306
primary purpose of Bill, **19**, 1*n*
private Bill, promotion by, **19**, 1
  See also PRIVATE BILL
promotion of, **14**, 306
Scotland, effect in, **19**, 1
statutory meeting relating to, **14**, 1311
See also PRIVATE BILL
Private life
respect for—
  access to confidential personal records, **12**, 63
  correspondence, **12**, 6, 62, 68
    prisoners', **12**, 69
  European Convention on Human Rights, **12**, 6, 62
  home, **12**, 6, 62, 68, 70
  homosexuality, **12**, 66
  telephone conversations, **12**, 68
Private market operator
licensing, **14**, 119, 562
Private nuisance
See NUISANCE
Private prosecution
assault, **17**, 528
game, relating to, **17**, 531
Lord Advocate, concurrence of, **17**, 528
public prosecutor, concurrence of, **17**, 528
rape, **17**, 528
salmon fisheries, relating to, **17**, 531
Private records
public records distinguished, **19**, 843
Scottish Record Office, held in, **19**, 849
Private river
public river distinguished from, **25**, 305
Private road
construction consent, **20**, 649
  appeals, **20**, 649
  application for, **20**, 649
  construction without, **20**, 649
  lighting, provisions as to, **20**, 663
  road bonds, **20**, 650
  time limit, **20**, 649, 649*n*
emergency work, **20**, 648
entry on valuation roll, **24**, 732

Private road—*continued*
frontagers' duties and responsibilities, **20**, 648
  service of notice of, **20**, 648
generally, **20**, 411, 608
level crossing over, **19**, 1031
lighting, provision on, **20**, 663
local roads authority—
  maintenance work by, **20**, 648
  powers of, **20**, 648
meaning, **14**, 405; **20**, 501, 609, 648
private access distinguished, **20**, 609
public right of passage, **20**, 648
public road, alteration of status to, **20**, 648, 649
  application for, **20**, 648
responsibility to road users, **20**, 614
road bonds, **20**, 650
  completion time, alteration, **20**, 650
  construction consent, **20**, 650
  disputes, determination of, **20**, 650
  offences, **20**, 650
  purpose of, **20**, 650
toll, future policy as to, **20**, 607
Private secretary
See PARLIAMENTARY PRIVATE SECRETARY
Private trust
appointment of trustees at common law, **24**, 158
banks and insurance companies as trustees, **24**, 134
classification, **24**, 16
conferring interest in possession, **24**, 16, 17
creditors, for, **24**, 16, 20
discretionary, **24**, 16, 17
enforcing performance, **24**, 89
inter vivos, **24**, 16
interest in possession, conferring, **24**, 16, 17
judicial variation, **24**, 76
marriage contract trust, *see* MARRIAGE
meaning, **24**, 10
mortis causa, **24**, 16
power to nominate trustees, **24**, 155
precatory, **24**, 16, 19
public trust distinguished, **24**, 85, 86
regulation, **24**, 85
Private will
formal validity, **25**, 722
France, **25**, 628
Germany, **25**, 628
signing, **25**, 724
special cases, **25**, 722
testamentary intention, test of, **25**, 765
Privatisation
gas industry, of, **9**, 867; **19**, 209*n*
governmental functions, of, **7**, 756
governmental powers, **19**, 212
public corporations, of, **19**, 212
Privative jurisdiction
generally, **6**, 1061
limit to be raised, **6**, 1061*n*
Privilege
protection of certain communications, *see* DEFAMATION (privilege)
right to withhold information from court, *see* EVIDENCE (privilege)

Privileged will
England, **25**, 628*n*
France, **25**, 628
Privileged writings
deeds not of great importance, **6**, 435
'envelope cases', **6**, 441
foreign deeds, **6**, 442
generally, **6**, 433
holograph writings, **6**, 436-440
statute, privileged by, **6**, 434
writings *in re mercatoria*, **6**, 443
Privileges
See COMMITTEE FOR PRIVILEGES; COMMITTEE OF PRIVILEGES
Privy (latrine)
emptying of, **9**, 1167
public health nuisance, as, **19**, 336
Privy Council
abolition in Scotland, **6**, 811; **19**, 805
advocate appearing before, dress, **13**, 1323
appellate jurisdiction, replacement with Imperial Court of Appeal, **5**, 349
audience—
  advocate's right of, **13**, 1325
  solicitors' right of, **13**, 115, 1180
before the Union, **7**, 790, 792
Cabinet, replaced by, as principal organ of executive government, **5**, 306
College of Justice, and, **6**, 904
Commonwealth, judicial function extending to, **7**, 778
Curia Regis, development from, **6**, 898
development, **7**, 702
Judicial Committee of—
  appeal to, **14**, 1117
    overseas, from, **5**, 659; **22**, 278
  constitution, **5**, 661
  dissenting opinions, **5**, 662
  generally, **6**, 820, 821
  jurisdiction, **5**, 659, 660
legal commencement of year, ordinance, **22**, 806
President, **7**, 774, 799
ranking within, **7**, 793
Privy Purse
generally, **7**, 771
Privy Seal Bill
abolition, **7**, 871
Privy Seal of Scotland
desuetude, **7**, 881, 905
generally, **7**, 855, 878, 897, 898, 901
history, **7**, 878
Keeper, **7**, 880
uses, **7**, 879
Privy Seal of the United Kingdom
generally, **7**, 855, 865
history, **7**, 865
Keeper, **7**, 866
Prize
abroad, awarded, customs and excise relief, **7**, 1120
admiralty—
  droits of, **17**, 407
  jurisdiction—
    abolition of, **17**, 405
    challenges to, **17**, 405

Prize—*continued*
admiralty—*continued*
  prize law, **17**, 404
aircraft—
  prize jurisdiction extended to, **17**, 401, 402
  salvage, payment of, **17**, 426
American colonies—
  vessels, prize law extended to, **17**, 401
appeal, decree of prize court, from, **17**, 430
appearance, rules relating to, **17**, 424
blockade—
  close, **17**, 413
  neutral ship attempting to break, **17**, 413
  purpose of, **17**, 413
booty—
  meaning, **17**, 401
  prize jurisdiction, **17**, 401
capture—
  blockade, **17**, 413
  contraband, penalty for carrying, **17**, 414
  enemy goods, **17**, 418
  enemy ship, **17**, 411
  lawful, **17**, 409
  neutral goods as contraband, **17**, 419
  neutral ship, **17**, 412
  outbreak of war, may be effected from, **17**, 409
  ownership of goods, **17**, 421
  pre-emption, **17**, 422
  ransom, **17**, 416
  requisition, **17**, 415
  unjustified seizure, claims for, **17**, 420
  wrongful, **17**, 417
cause, disposal of, **17**, 425
certification—
  condemnation, of, **17**, 429
  restitution, of, **17**, 429
  sale, of, **17**, 429
compensation, wrongful capture, for, **17**, 417
condemnation—
  copy to be produced on registration, **21**, 150,
    150n
  decree of, **17**, 428
  enforcement, **17**, 428
  sentence, effect of, **17**, 427
contraband—
  neutral goods as, **17**, 419
  penalty for carrying, **17**, 414
Court of Admiralty jurisdiction, **1**, 406
Crown—
  droits of, **17**, 407
  wrongful capture, compensation for, **17**, 417
decree—
  appeal, **17**, 430
  condemnation, of, **17**, 428
  enforcement, **17**, 428
  restitution, of, **17**, 428
domicile, enemy character, means of determining,
  17, 410
droits—
  Admiralty, of, **17**, 407
  Crown, of, **17**, 407
economic sanctions, increasing support for
  concept of, **17**, 431

Prize—*continued*
enemy character—
  domicile, effect of, **17**, 410
  ship's flat, determined by, **17**, 411
enemy goods—
  capture, **17**, 418
  droits of Crown, as, **17**, 407
enemy ship—
  capture, **17**, 411
  droits of Crown, as, **17**, 407
enforcement, condemnation, decree of, **17**, 428
England, prize court, law applied by, **17**, 406
English courts, **21**, 739
future of prize, **17**, 431
goods—
  enemy, *see* enemy goods *above*
  ownership, **17**, 421
  requisition, **17**, 415
  salvage, payment of, **17**, 426
jurisdiction—
  abolition of, **17**, 405
  aircraft, extension to, **17**, 401, 402
  booty subjected to, **17**, 401
  challenges to, **17**, 405
  Court of Admiralty, **1**, 406
  private interest, **17**, 403
  prize court, **17**, 408
meaning, **17**, 401, 402
neutral goods—
  contraband, as, **17**, 419
  droits of Crown, as, **17**, 407
neutral ship—
  blockade, attempting to break, **17**, 413
  capture, **17**, 412
  contraband carried to enemy in, **17**, 414
  droits of Crown, as, **17**, 407
ownership of goods, date of seizure, determined
  with reference to, **17**, 421
penalty for carrying contraband, **17**, 414
pre-emption, capture of goods, **17**, 422
private interest, prize jurisdiction, **17**, 403
prize court—
  appeal from decree of, **17**, 430
  jurisdiction, **17**, 408
  law applied by, **17**, 406
procedure—
  appeal, **17**, 430
  appearance, **17**, 424
  certification, **17**, 429
  condemnation of prize, **17**, 427
  decree, **17**, 428
  disposal of cause, **17**, 425
  enforcement, **17**, 428
  institution of proceedings, **17**, 423
  pleading, **17**, 424
  prize salvage, **17**, 426
ransom, meaning, **17**, 416
requisition, belligerent has qualified right to, **17**, 415
salvage—
  amount of, **17**, 426
  payment of, **17**, 426
seizure—
  ownership determined with reference to date
    of, **17**, 421

Prize—*continued*
seizure—*continued*
  unjustified, claims for, **17**, 420
ship—
  capture—
    blockade, **17**, 413
    contraband, penalty for carrying, **17**, 414
    enemy ship, **17**, 411
    neutral ship, **17**, 412
    ransom, **17**, 416
    requisition, **17**, 415
    wrongful, **17**, 417
  droits of Admiralty, as, **17**, 407
  enemy, *see* enemy ship *above*
  flag, enemy character determined by, **17**, 411
  meaning, **17**, 402
  requisition, **17**, 415
  salvage, payment of, **17**, 426
  significance of prize, **17**, 402
technology, implications of, **17**, 431
war, capture may be effected from outbreak of,
  17, 409
world wars, effect of, **17**, 431
wrongful capture, compensation for, **17**, 417
Prize competitions
newspapers, run by, **2**, 1661
position of, **2**, 1678
Prizes
amusement arcades, chance provided at, **9**, 1008
food offered as, **11**, 400
non-mechanical amusements with, permits for, **9**,
  1014
sponsiones ludicrae, not constituting, **15**, 768
See also AMUSEMENTS WITH PRIZES
***Pro hac vice* employment**
vicarious liability, **15**, 249
***Pro indiviso* proprietor**
lessor, as, **13**, 173
Probabilis causa litigandi
civil legal aid, **13**, 1037, 1038, 1039, 1042
  urgency, situation of, **13**, 1048
Probation
competent sentence, **17**, 803
mental disorder, person suffering from, **17**, 907
non-custodial sentence, **17**, 563
order—
  breach, **22**, 34
  child subject to, moving to Scotland, **3**, 1384
  community service order supervision contrasted,
    22, 38
  conditions, **22**, 34
  copies, social worker's duty, **22**, 34
  definition, **22**, 34
  discharge, **22**, 34
  generally, **17**, 803
  good behaviour, application for discharge, **22**,
    34
  hostels, provision by social work department,
    22, 34
  social work department, duties, **22**, 34
  suitability of offender for, social inquiry report,
    22, 32

Probation—*continued*
order—*continued*
  unpaid work by offender—
    report on suitability, **22**, 34
    supervision, **22**, 38
  warrant for arrest, probationer, breach of order,
    22, 34
Probative writings
See DEED
Procedural law
brieve system—
  Anglo-Norman influence on Scots law, **22**,
    598, 599
    See also BRIEVE SYSTEM
canon law, influence, **22**, 582, 584
damages for personal injuries claims—
  Court of Session, **22**, 676
  Scottish Law Commission recommendations,
    22, 676
  sheriff court, **22**, 676
reform—
  Law Reform Committee for Scotland—
    actions of removing and ejection, **22**, 652
  Scottish Law Commission—
    damages for personal injuries claims, **22**, 676
removing and ejection, actions of—
  Law Reform Committee for Scotland 1957
    report, **22**, 652
royal courts *Regiam Majestatem*, **22**, 512
terminology, derivation from rotal terminology,
  22, 582
Procedure
See CRIMINAL PROCEDURE *and under names of
individual courts and actions*
Procession
See PUBLIC PROCESSION
Proclamation, royal
Great Seal of the United Kingdom, **7**, 856, 857
meaning, **7**, 857
publication, **7**, 731
Procurator
canonical procedure, **13**, 1130, 1131
use of term, **13**, 1126
Procurator fiscal
absolute privilege, **15**, 444, 448, 449, 526
  summary procedure, **15**, 450
accountability, Lord Advocate, to, **13**, 1425
accused, bringing before court, **17**, 624
alternative action, discretion to take, **17**, 619
appointment, **6**, 1033; **13**, 1425; **17**, 532
assistant, **13**, 1430
autopsy, attendance at, **13**, 1432
central position, **13**, 1425
charge, discretion as to nature of, **17**, 622
child, custody of, **14**, 1504
control of, **17**, 535
criminal prosecutions brought by, **7**, 26
death investigated by, **19**, 1458
decision whether or not to prosecute, **17**, 617
depute, **13**, 1430
development of office, **17**, 530
duties, generally, **6**, 1034
expenditure, **17**, 533
fiscal, meaning, **17**, 530

Procurator fiscal—*continued*
fiscal fines, **17**, 621
fixed penalty, discretion to offer, **17**, 620
functions of, **17**, 530, 581
immunity, **15**, 227
incidents of office, **6**, 1033
income, **17**, 533
judicial examination, **17**, 546
judiciary, relationship to, **17**, 583
lawburrows, action of contravention, **13**, 901
liability of, **15**, 450
Lord Advocate, links with, **17**, 534
Lyon Court, of, **6**, 1021
   appointment, **6**, 1014
   duties, **6**, 1014
   unwarrantable use of armorial bearings, **6**, 1019
modern status of office, **17**, 531
murder, scene of suspected, attendance at, **13**, 1432
no further proceedings, discretion to order, **17**, 618
number, **13**, 1430
origin of office, **17**, 530
precognitions, **17**, 545
preliminary inquiries by—
   court, incidental applications to, **17**, 616,
   experts, use of, **17**, 612
   police, instructions to, **17**, 615
   post mortem dissections, **17**, 613
   productions, **17**, 614
   sources of information, **17**, 611
prisoner, visits to, **16**, 1460
privileged position, **13**, 1425
proceedings in court, discretion as to form of, **17**, 623
procurator, meaning, **17**, 530
prosecuting duties, **17**, 530
prosecutor in public interest, as, **6**, 1033
public prosecutor, as, **17**, 581
quasi-judicial role, **13**, 1425
removal from office, **17**, 535
reporter, meetings with, **3**, 1285
responsibilities, **17**, 581, 582
senior depute, **13**, 1430
sheriff, appointment by, **17**, 532
tenure of office, **6**, 1033
title to sue, **14**, 2161
use of term, **13**, 1427
warn, discretion to, **17**, 619
See also PUBLIC PROSECUTOR
Procurator Fiscal Service
administrative, clerical and support staff, **13**, 1430
appeals, **13**, 1434
civil service, assimilation into, **17**, 536
criminal prosecution in Scotland—
   generally, **13**, 1430
   Lord Advocate, function of, **13**, 1430
duties—
   appeals, **13**, 1434
   common law duty to investigate all crime in district, **13**, 1431
   solemn procedure, **13**, 1432
   summary procedure, **13**, 1433
exchequer, and, **13**, 1436

Procurator Fiscal Service—*continued*
generally, **13**, 1410, 1425
historical background—
   generally, **13**, 1426
   nineteenth century, **13**, 1429
   seventeenth and eighteenth centuries, **13**, 1428
   term 'procurator fiscal', **13**, 1427
police—
   complaints against, functions in relation to, **13**, 1437
   relationship with, **13**, 1431, 1432
Queen's and Lord Treasurer's Remembrancer, **13**, 1436
solemn procedure, **13**, 1432
staff, **13**, 1425
sudden, suspicious or unexplained death, investigation, **13**, 1435
summary procedure, **13**, 1433
   discretionary powers, **13**, 1433
   report of cases to procurators fiscal, **13**, 1433
supervision of, **17**, 540
Procurators of the council
generally, **13**, 1241
Procuring
offences in relation to, **3**, 1239
   Schedule 1 offences, **3**, 1244
Producer
meaning, **6**, 39*n*
Product
dangerous or defective, **6**, 37, 39, 41, 43
meaning, **6**, 39*n*
medicinal, *see* MEDICINAL PRODUCT
products liability, *see* CONSUMER PROTECTION
safety, *see* SAFETY
Profanity
offence, validity of acts performed on Sunday, **22**, 817
Professional association
authorisation under Financial Services Act 1986 by, **12**, 1313
   recognition order, application for, **12**, 1313
discrimination, liability for, **9**, 343
meaning, **12**, 1313
member of, instruction of advocate by, **13**, 1298, 1348
membership subscriptions, VAT exemption, **7**, 1428
misleading indication of membership, **18**, 1395
name, passing off, **18**, 1377
reinstatement on roll, fairness of method, **12**, 60
Professional competence or conduct, imputations against
defamation, **15**, 492
Professional Conduct Committee
General Dental Council, **14**, 1132, 1138
General Medical Council, *see* GENERAL MEDICAL COUNCIL
Professional equipment
temporary importation, **7**, 1187
Professional liability
contractual, **15**, 353, 354, 357
disappointed beneficiary cases, **15**, 358
duty of care—
   advice, negligent, **15**, 355, 356

Professional liability—*continued*
duty of care—*continued*
  economic loss—
    generally, **15**, 355, 356
    physical loss distinguished, **15**, 355
  foreseeability, **15**, 354
  generally, **15**, 278
  misstatements, **15**, 356
  physical loss, injury or damage, **15**, 354
    economic loss distinguished, **15**, 355
  services, negligent provision, **15**, 355, 357
  third parties, to, **15**, 358
exclusion clauses, **15**, 357
generally, **15**, 353
professional status, general considerations, **15**, 354
regulatory bodies—
  generally, **15**, 353
standard of care—
  common practice, **15**, 372, 374, 375
  generally, **15**, 359, 361
  leading cases, **15**, 360
  ordinariness and standard practice, **15**, 360, 361
  reasonable care, **15**, 372
  'reasonable man' test, **15**, 359-361
third parties, duties to, **15**, 358
See also under names of individual professions
Professional skill
restraint of trade, protectable interests, **15**, 773
Professional sportsmen
capital gains tax, **19**, 1309
income tax, **19**, 1297-1308
inheritance tax, **19**, 1310
non-resident, **19**, 1304-1308
prize money, taxation of, **19**, 1298
promotional activities, income from, **19**, 1298, 1306
retirement age, **19**, 1300n
Profit
capital profits, **25**, 41
company's financial record, **25**, 32
definition, **16**, 1022
net, assessment of, **24**, 540
operating lease, **14**, 1020
shareholder's right to participate in, **25**, 13
Profit rental
meaning, **13**, 569
Profit-sharing terms
partnership, money lent to, **16**, 1057
Profitability
share value, effect on, **25**, 1
valuation for rating, **24**, 511
Profits à prendre
English law of, **18**, 440n
Profits of justice
sheriff, duties of, **17**, 510
Prohibited place
See OFFICIAL SECRETS LEGISLATION
Prohibited weapons
See FIREARMS
Prohibition notice
sports ground, **14**, 579
See also HEALTH AND SAFETY AT WORK

Promise
breach, obligation arising from, prescription, **16**, 2116, 2121
breach of, obligation arising from, **15**, 3
jus quaesitum tertio, **15**, 827
meaning, **15**, 4
obligation arising from—
  generally, **15**, 1, 4
  meaning of promise, **15**, 4
unilateral, *see* UNILATERAL PROMISE
unilateral transaction, as, **3**, 1202
Promissory note
dishonoured, creditor holding, **8**, 121
documentary evidence, as, **10**, 602
indorsement, **4**, 217
inducement to sign by fraudulent misrepresentation, **11**, 767
insurance premium payment by, **12**, 833
interest due *ex lege*, **14**, 1827
joint and several notes, **4**, 216
liability of parties, **4**, 217
made on or after 15 February 1971 ..., **4**, 113
meaning, **4**, 214
nature of, **4**, 214
negotiable instrument, as, **4**, 103
obligation under, prescription, **16**, 2116
parole evidence in questions relating to, **15**, 760
partner, when binding, **16**, 1031
partnership, when binding, **16**, 1031
presentment for payment, **4**, 217
printer's imprint, requirement not applicable, **17**, 3
quinquennial prescription not applicable, **13**, 1755
required form, **4**, 215
See also NEGOTIABLE INSTRUMENT
Proof
answer, before, **17**, 1131
burden of, **17**, 565
  extradition from United Kingdom, **12**, 562
closure of, **17**, 1172
concessions in course of, **17**, 1140
conduct of—
  closure of proof, **17**, 1172
  cross-examination, **17**, 1167
  examination-in-chief, **17**, 1166
  failure to attend, **17**, 1163
  leading at proof, **17**, 1162
  objections to evidence, **17**, 1170
  opening proof, **17**, 1164
  re-examination, **17**, 1169
  recording evidence, **17**, 1161
  witnesses—
    hostile, **17**, 1168
    leading, **17**, 1165
    privilege, claims of, **17**, 1171
Court of Session procedure, **17**, 1389, 1411
cross-examination, **17**, 1167
evidence—
  commission, on—
    conduct of, **17**, 1156
    form of, **17**, 1155
    generally, **17**, 1154
  competency, **17**, 1143
  facts, establishment of, **17**, 1141

Proof—*continued*
evidence—*continued*
  objections to, **17**, 1170
  preparation of, **17**, 1141-1143
  recording, **17**, 1161
  relevancy, **17**, 1143
  to lie *in retentis*, **17**, 1153
  witnesses, precognition of, **17**, 1142
  examination-in-chief, **17**, 1166
  failure to attend, **17**, 1163
  habili modo, **17**, 1133
  identity of persons, disclosure of, **17**, 1152
  inspection, **17**, 1151
  issues for—
    admissions—
      direct, **17**, 1137
      implied, **17**, 1138
      minutes of, **17**, 1139
    concessions, **17**, 1140
    generally, **17**, 1136
  large, at, **17**, 1130
  leading at, **17**, 1162
  modes of—
    answer, before, **17**, 1131
    appeal against interlocutor as to, **17**, 1260
    generally, **17**, 1129
    habili modo, **17**, 1133
    large, at, **17**, 1130
    oath, by, **17**, 1132
    preliminary, **17**, 1135
    prout de jure, **17**, 1130
    restricted proof, **17**, 1134
    writ, by, **17**, 1132
  oath, by, **17**, 1132
  opening, **17**, 1164
  preliminary, **17**, 1135
  preparation for—
    citation—
      duration of, **17**, 1159
      witnesses, of, **17**, 1157
    witnesses—
      citation of, **17**, 1157
      failure to attend, **17**, 1158
      marshalling, **17**, 1160
  preservation, **17**, 1151
  productions—
    commission, recovery by, **17**, 1149
    court, dispensing powers of, **17**, 1147
    diligence—
      executing, **17**, 1150
      recovery by, **17**, 1149
    documents—
      founded upon, **10**, 557; **17**, 1145
      party, recovery from, **17**, 1148
    evidential, **17**, 1146
    generally, **17**, 1144
  prout de jure, **17**, 1130
  re-examination, **17**, 1169
  restricted, **17**, 1134
  sampling, **17**, 1151
  small claims procedure, **17**, 1342
  standard of, **17**, 565
  summary causes, **17**, 1317

Proof—*continued*
witnesses—
  hostile, **17**, 1168
  leading, **17**, 1165
  privilege, claims of, **17**, 1171
  writ, by, **17**, 1132
PROP (National Prisoners Movement)
prisoners' rights group, **16**, 1489
Propaganda
control of, **5**, 377
Proper law
contract, of *see* CONTRACT
double delict rule, **17**, 294
Property
abandonment, **18**, 568
  See also lost or abandoned *below*
accessio, **18**, 2
accession, *see* ACCESSION
acquisition—
  latent claims and personal bar, **16**, 1612
  personal bar by notice, **16**, 1612
assets, valuation of, *see* VALUATION
breach of confidence, *see* BREACH OF CONFIDENCE
co-ownership, *see* CO-OWNERSHIP
common, *see* CO-OWNERSHIP
copyright, *see* COPYRIGHT
corporeal, *see* CORPOREAL PROPERTY
corporeal moveable, *see* CORPOREAL MOVEABLE
  PROPERTY
criminal damage—
  fireraising—
    actus reus, **7**, 416
    culpable and reckless, **7**, 415
    defences, **7**, 419
    generally, **7**, 415
    insurers, to defraud, **7**, 418
    mens rea, **7**, 417
    wilful, **7**, 415, 417
  malicious mischief—
    definition, **7**, 410
    entitlement to act, defence of, **7**, 412
    explosive substances, use of, **7**, 413
    malicious, meaning, **7**, 411
    scope of offence, **7**, 410
    vandalism, **7**, 410, 414
data protection, *see* DATA PROTECTION
defence of, self-help, **13**, 90
deposit, on, negative prescription, **18**, 566
derivative acquisition—
  meaning, **18**, 597
  See also TRANSFER OF OWNERSHIP
design rights, *see* DESIGN RIGHTS
destruction, **18**, 568
devolution on death, *see* SUCCESSION
diligence and property law—
  catholic securities, **8**, 117
  co-ownership, **8**, 110
  generally, **8**, 107
  jura in re aliena, **8**, 111
  litigiosity, **8**, 116
  nexus, **8**, 115
  personal diligence, **8**, 118
  personal rights, **8**, 112
  real diligence, **8**, 118

Property—*continued*
diligence and property law—*continued*
  secondary securities, **8**, 117
  third party rights, **8**, 108
  trust rights, **8**, 113, 114
  where debtor has no title, **8**, 109
disposal, right of, **12**, 88
dominium, **18**, 2
donation, **8**, 601
English and Scots law compared, **18**, 2
extinction, **18**, 568
feudal law, **18**, 1, 2
  See also FEUDAL LAW
German and Scots law compared, **18**, 2
gratuitous alienation, **11**, 780
heritable, *see* HERITABLE PROPERTY
history of Scots law, **18**, 1, 2
inalienable, **18**, 600
  donation, **8**, 615
incorporeal, *see* INCORPOREAL PROPERTY
indemnity insurance, **12**, 804
industrial, **18**, 801
industrial or commercial, protection, **7**, 1022
inhibition and property law—
  acquirenda, **8**, 156
  acquisata, **8**, 156
  adjudgeable by creditor, must be, **8**, 155
  generally, **8**, 155
  heritable property, **8**, 155
  joint and common property, **8**, 158
  trust property, **8**, 157
Inland Revenue charge, subject to, **25**, 1025
insurable interest in, **12**, 849, 851, 852
intellectual, *see* INTELLECTUAL PROPERTY
Japanese and Scots law compared, **18**, 2
joint—
  inhibition, **8**, 158
  will, importance of, **6**, 480
  See also CO-OWNERSHIP
joint or common, **19**, 1619
  common interest in, **6**, 781
land, *see* LAND; LANDOWNERSHIP
land law, **18**, 1
litigiosity, **8**, 116
lost or abandoned—
  abandoned property, definition, **18**, 547
  appeals, **18**, 551
  care and custody, **16**, 1819; **18**, 548
  claim made on, **16**, 1820
  claimant, rules as to, **18**, 549
  Crown ownership, **18**, 540, 547
  disposal, **16**, 1820; **18**, 549
    chief constable, responsibility of, **18**, 549
  dog, stray, **16**, 1819*n*, 1820*n*; **18**, 552
  employer of finder, duty of, **18**, 548
  finder, duty of, **18**, 548
  living creatures, **18**, 547*n*, 549
  lost property, definition, **18**, 547
  motor vehicle, **18**, 552
  negotiorum gestor, **18**, 547, 547*n*
  owner of land where property discovered, duty of, **18**, 548
  person taking possession of, duty, **16**, 1819, 1819*n*

Property—*continued*
lost or abandoned—*continued*
  police functions, generally, **16**, 1819
  property classified as, **16**, 1819
  public sector tenant, abandoned by, **18**, 552
  public transport undertaking, abandoned on premises of, **18**, 552
  quod nullius est fit domini regis, **18**, 540, 547
  records, **16**, 1819
    chief constable's duty to keep, **18**, 550
  restitution, **15**, 46, 47
  reward, claimant ordered to make, **16**, 1820
  stray dog, **16**, 1819*n*, 1820*n*; **18**, 552
  title to, **18**, 550
  transport undertaking, found on, **16**, 1819*n*
  unclaimed, **16**, 1820
  waifs and strays, **18**, 547*n*
matrimonial, *see* MATRIMONIAL PROPERTY
money as, **14**, 1808
moveable, *see* MOVEABLE PROPERTY
obligations, law of, and, **18**, 1
original acquisition, **18**, 597
ownerless, right to acquire, **18**, 5
ownership—
  insurable interest, **12**, 851
  passing of, **19**, 1597, 1598
  See also OWNERSHIP
partnership—
  asset-owning ratio, change in, capital gains tax, **16**, 1134
  co-ownership, existence of partnership, determination, **16**, 1021
  goodwill, **16**, 1074, 1076
  heritable, **16**, 1072, 1073
  inheritance tax, **16**, 1073, 1124
  partners' interest in, **16**, 1009
    nature of, **16**, 1073
    succession, **16**, 1073
  partner's name, property held in, **16**, 1072
  partner's share—
    assignation, **16**, 1075
    equality, presumption of, **16**, 1074
    extent, **16**, 1074
    transfer to third party, **16**, 1075
  partnership agreement, **16**, 1009
  partnership's money, property bought with, **16**, 1071
  separate debt, charge for, dissolution on, **16**, 1084
  statutory provisions, application, **16**, 1071
  what constitutes, **16**, 1071, 1072
  winding up, distribution of assets, **16**, 1099
    deceased partner's share—
      ascertainment, **16**, 1104
      treatment, generally, **16**, 1103
    final settlement of accounts, on, **16**, 1105
    fraud, partnership dissolved for, **16**, 1100
    misrepresentation, partnership dissolved for, **16**, 1100
    partners' rights, **16**, 1099, 1100
    post-dissolution profits, **16**, 1102
    premiums, return of, **16**, 1101
    retiring partner's share—
      ascertainment, **16**, 1104

Property—*continued*
partnership—*continued*
  winding up, distribution of assets—*continued*
    retiring partner's share—*continued*
      treatment, generally, **16**, 1103
passing off, *see* PASSING OFF
patent, *see* PATENT
peaceful enjoyment of, **12**, 88
performers' rights, *see* PERFORMERS' RIGHTS
plant breeders' rights, *see* PLANT BREEDERS' RIGHTS
police property, wilful or careless damage to, **16**, 1771
possession, **18**, 1, 2
  See also POSSESSION
pre-emption, subject to right of, **18**, 600
preservation, custody or detention, court powers in relation to, **13**, 24
private, alternative to, **11**, 1112
purchase and sale, *see* VALUATION
real, *see* REALTY
real or personal, specific implement to restore possession, **13**, 11
real rights, **18**, 2
  See also RIGHTS
realising gains and losses, **19**, 1600
right to own, **12**, 87, 88
  Universal Declaration of Human Rights, **12**, 4*n*
rights, generally, **11**, 1097, 1099-1112
rights in things, *see* RIGHTS
Roman law as source of Scots law, **18**, 2
slander of, *see* SLANDER
sources of property law, **18**, 2
specialised concept of law, as, **11**, 1005
stolen, right to recover, imprescriptible nature, **18**, 566
tax liability, acceptance in satisfaction of, **25**, 1024
taxation of, **19**, 1597-1615
  conveyancing as, **6**, 401
  death, on, *see* DEATH
  See also TAXATION
theft—
  destruction, by, **7**, 410
  See also THEFT
things, generally, **18**, 3, 3*n*, 11
trade mark, *see* TRADE MARK
traditio, **18**, 2
transfer of—
  capital gains tax, **19**, 1598, 1600
  contract of sale, in pursuance of, **19**, 1598
  English law compared, **19**, 1597, 1598
  gifts, lifetime, *see* INHERITANCE TAX
  inheritance tax, *see* INHERITANCE TAX
  unilateral promise, in pursuance of, **19**, 1598
transfer of ownership—
  generally, **18**, 1
  See also TRANSFER OF OWNERSHIP
trust, *see* TRUST
unabandoned property, position of finder, **8**, 2
use of, state control, **12**, 88
water, *see* WATER
Property rights order
missing person, reappearance of, **25**, 653

Proportional representation
additional member system, **5**, 378
alternative vote system, **5**, 378
generally, **15**, 1028, 1343
party list system, **5**, 378
proposals for introduction of, **5**, 378
single transferable vote, **5**, 378
Proprietor
joint—
  action of removing, **13**, 496
  generally, **13**, 173
  landlord's hypothec, **13**, 514
prescription of rights, **16**, 2104
pro indiviso proprietors as lessors, **13**, 173
Proscribed organisation
See TERRORISM
Prosecution
court, by, **17**, 586
Crown agent, by, **17**, 580
Crown counsel, by, **17**, 579
Crown office, by, **17**, 580
generally, **7**, 26; **17**, 577
judiciary, and, **17**, 583
Lord Advocate, by, **17**, 578
malicious, *see* MALICIOUS PROSECUTION
officials, by, **17**, 587
procurator fiscal, by, **6**, 1033; **17**, 581, 582
  See also PROCURATOR FISCAL; PROCURATOR FISCAL SERVICE
private individuals, by, **17**, 585
  liability of, **15**, 451
police, and, **17**, 584
public, **7**, 26; **17**, 577
public bodies, by, **17**, 587
Solicitor General, by, **17**, 579
Prospect
right to, urban servitude, as, **18**, 483, 486
Prostitute-Prostitution
generally, **7**, 484
importuning person in public place, **7**, 484
lease misused for purposes of, **13**, 225
loitering in public place, **7**, 484
male prostitute, criminal activity by, **7**, 484, 485
offences in relation to, **3**, 1239, 1244
parent or guardian who is, **3**, 1267
sexual immorality, contract promoting, **15**, 763, 767
soliciting in public place, **7**, 484
Protected persons
Convention relating to, **19**, 695*n*
Protected tenancy
See TENANT-TENANCY
Protection and Indemnity Clubs (P & I Clubs)
generally, **21**, 119
Protection racket
extortion by, **7**, 396
Protective services
civil defence, *see* CIVIL DEFENCE
expenditure programme, **5**, 583
fire services, *see* FIRE SERVICES
police, *see* POLICE
sports ground, safety of, *see* RECREATION AND SPORT
trading standards, *see* TRADING STANDARDS

Protestant religion
measures to secure, **3**, 1501; **5**, 361
See also CHURCH OF SCOTLAND
Protests
form of, **4**, 163
procedure for, **4**, 161
Register of, **6**, 455; **19**, 820
Protocol
Lord Lieutenant, duties with regard to, **5**, 555
notarial, *see* PUBLIC REGISTERS
Prototype
unregistered design right, **18**, 1220
Prout de jure
contract of deposit proved, **8**, 10
trust proved, **24**, 13
Province of St Andrews and Edinburgh
Roman Catholic Church, **3**, 1655
Proving tenor
action of, exclusive to Court of Session, **4**, 11; **6**,
  924
Provisional order
advertisements, proof of, **19**, 28
alternative to private Bill, as, **19**, 4
association, relating to, **19**, 23, 23*n*
books of reference, **19**, 25
buildings—
  compulsory acquisition, **19**, 19
  improvement charge on, **19**, 19
canal affected by, **19**, 15
company, relating to, **19**, 23, 23*n*
company as promoter—
  consents of members and directors, **19**, 27
compliance with General Orders—
  complaints of non-compliance, **19**, 29
  proof of, **19**, 28
compulsory acquisition or use of land, **19**, 12, 12*n*
confirmation Acts, printing of, **19**, 79
confirmation Bill, suspension of, **19**, 78
Counsel to Secretary of State, report of, **19**, 41
'D' copy, **19**, 37-40
declarations, where required, **19**, 19
deposit of documents, **19**, 11
  draft orders, copies of, **19**, 11
  estimates, **19**, 20
  local authorities, copies for, **19**, 19
  March deposit, **19**, 18-23
  mode of, **19**, 17
  November deposit, **19**, 18-23
  personal delivery, **19**, 17
  plans, **19**, 24
  post, by, **19**, 17
  public offices, copies for, **19**, 20
  sections, **19**, 26
drafting of, **19**, 9
electricity supply maps, **19**, 19
estimates, **19**, 20
European Union grant, **19**, 10
Examiners of Petitions—
  appointment, **19**, 28
  functions, **19**, 28
  referral to, **19**, 28-30
  report, **19**, 30
exceptions to system, **19**, 80
fees, **19**, 57

Provisional order—*continued*
filled-up order, **19**, 32, 39-41, 48
financial memorandum, **19**, 10
fish, obstructing passage of, **19**, 22
form of, **19**, 9
General Orders—
  dispensation with, **19**, 31
  not previously inquired into, **19**, 61
government department observations, **19**, 36
government grant, **19**, 10
heritable property, affecting, **19**, 15
inquiry into opposed, **19**, 43-58
  action after, **19**, 60
  arrangements for, **19**, 55
  commissioners, **19**, 44-47
    appointment, **19**, 44
    decision of, **19**, 54
    declaration of, **19**, 46
    report to, **19**, 53
  confirmation Bill, **19**, 73
  expenses, **19**, 56, 58
  filled-up order, **19**, 48
  locus standi, **19**, 49
  non-appearance of petitioners, **19**, 51
  notice of, **19**, 45
  procedure, **19**, 52
  shorthand notes, **19**, 56
  sittings, **19**, 47
  when may be directed, **19**, 43
  withdrawal of petition, **19**, 50, 51
issue of, **19**, 59, 60
land—
  compulsory acquisition or use, **19**, 12, 12*n*, 15,
    19
  improvement charge on, **19**, 19
  proposal to take, **19**, 11
light railway, **19**, 1079, 1080
local authority as promoter, **19**, 20, 35*n*
locus standi, **19**, 49, 51, 54
March deposit, **19**, 8*n*, 12, 12*n*, 13, 18-23
  petitions against, **19**, 32
modified, **19**, 59
  alteration of works, **19**, 62
  companies' orders, alterations to, **19**, 63
  examination of, **19**, 61-63
notice of proposals, **19**, 11-16
  Edinburgh Gazette in, **19**, 13
  mode of giving, **19**, 16
  newspaper advertisement, by, **19**, 11, 12, 13
  occasions for, **19**, 15
  personal service, by, **19**, 11, 16
  post, by, **19**, 11, 16
  poster, by, **19**, 11
November deposit, **19**, 8*n*, 12, 12*n*, 13, 18-23
  petitions against, **19**, 32
opposed, **19**, 43-58
  confirmation Bill, **19**, 73-77
opposition to, **19**, 32-40
  'D' copy, **19**, 37-40
  filled-up order, **19**, 32, 39-41
  government department observations, **19**, 36
  negotiations between petitioner and promoter,
    19, 33
  petitions against, **19**, 32-35, 43

Provisional order—*continued*
opposition to—*continued*
  Scottish Office observations, **19**, 36
  subsequent amendment opposed, **19**, 32
  withdrawal of petition, **19**, 34
partnership, relating to, **19**, 23, 23*n*
petition against, **19**, 32-35, 43
  mode of, **19**, 32
  Scottish Office observations, **19**, 37
  time of, **19**, 32
  withdrawal of, **19**, 50, 51
petition for—
  deposit of, **19**, 2
  form of, **19**, 9
  Secretary of State, to, **19**, 8, 9
  withdrawal of, **19**, 8, 8*n*, 50
promoter, **19**, 2
  expenses, liability for, **19**, 58
  fees payable by, **19**, 57
  memorandum, **19**, 39, 41
  parliamentary agent, **19**, 9, 9*n*, 39, 40
promotion of tramway undertaking by, **19**, 1129
proof of unopposed orders, **19**, 41, 42
public Bill distinguished, **19**, 2
railway, in connection with, **19**, 14, 15
representation for one enactment, **19**, 7
road—
  interference with, **19**, 22
  powers to alter or disturb road surface, **19**, 14
Scotland, in, **19**, 4, 5
Scottish Office observations, **19**, 36, 37
sewage, discharge into river, **19**, 22
sittings, **19**, 47
society, relating to, **19**, 23, 23*n*
subsequent amendment, **19**, 32
tidal lands, plan and section of, **19**, 19
tramroad, in connection with, **19**, 14, 15
tramway, in connection with, **19**, 14, 15, 19
trolley vehicle system, in connection with, **19**, 14,
  15, 19
unopposed—
  confirmation Bill, **19**, 71, 72
  inquiry, **19**, 43-58
  proof of, **19**, 41, 42
water—
  impounded from non-navigable stream, **19**, 15
  removal from river, **19**, 22
  supply maps, **19**, 19
Provocation
adultery, **7**, 273
assault, mitigatory plea in case of, **7**, 237, 241
battered woman syndrome, **7**, 275
culpable homicide, murder charge reduced to, **7**,
  272-277
homicide, **7**, 253
immediacy, requirement of, **7**, 274
physical, **7**, 273
revenge, acts of, **7**, 272, 274
self-defence, and, **7**, 277
verbal, **7**, 273
Proxy
See VOTE
Psalms
metrical version, copyright, **18**, 1002

Psychiatric hospital
See MENTALLY DISORDERED PERSON; MENTAL HEALTH;
  MENTAL HOSPITAL
Psychiatric injury
nervous shock, *see* CARE, DUTY OF
strict liability, **15**, 204
Psychiatrist
children's hearing, attendance at, **3**, 1327
Psychologist
children's hearing, attendance at, **3**, 1327
Psychopath
crime committed by, **7**, 114
diminished responsibility, **7**, 144, 145
Ptarmigan
See TARMARGAN
Puberty
age of—
  boys, **3**, 1234
  girls, **3**, 1234
Public
access—
  ancient monuments, to, **9**, 1224
  countryside, to, **9**, 1235
  court, to, **17**, 750, 776
  meeting, to, *see* MEETING
assembly, *see* ASSEMBLY
disorder, procession resulting in, **14**, 1326
documents, inspection of, **14**, 263, 264, 265
endangering, culpable and reckless, **7**, 248
information, right of access to, **14**, 334
list of officers, inspection of, **14**, 254
local authority meetings, right to attend, **14**, 92;
  17, 12
procession, *see* PUBLIC PROCESSION
public body, admission to meeting of, **14**, 1304
recreation, *see* RECREATION AND SPORT
Public Accounts Committee
appointment of, **5**, 436
functions of, **5**, 436, 596
public corporations expenditure, **19**, 224
Public Act
private Bill amending or repealing, **19**, 2
Public analyst
appointment, **11**, 330; **14**, 249, 709
certificates given by, **11**, 333
certification of substance as not complying with
  regulations, **11**, 352
deputy analyst, **11**, 330
fees, **14**, 709
remuneration, **11**, 330, 333
report, **11**, 330
samples—
  analysis of, generally, **11**, 333-338
  obligation to analyse, **11**, 333
  procuring of, **11**, 334
  who may submit, **11**, 224, 333
Public authority
act of, reduction of, **13**, 36
byelaws, unreasonable, **1**, 299
capital gains tax, liability for, **19**, 1525
compensation for maladministration by, **1**, 333
corporation created by, **14**, 2
court proceedings, institution by, **17**, 587
damages against, **1**, 333

Public authority—*continued*
delictual liability, **3**, 151
dismissal by, right to be heard before, **1**, 269
duties, failure to perform, **1**, 302
enforcement of duties, **1**, 302
error of law by, **1**, 286
excess of power, exercising, **1**, 218
failure to act, **1**, 302
fair, procedures to be, **1**, 230
gift to, **25**, 1010
implied powers, exercising, **1**, 217
individual rights, action infringing, **1**, 333
judicial control of administrative law, falling
    outside, **1**, 205
legal capacity to act, **1**, 215
loan to, **14**, 821
material held by, right to know, **1**, 277
meeting of, public right to access to, **14**, 1304
negligence by, **3**, 151
obligations and property, governed by law of, **1**, 203
personal bar, concept of, **1**, 294
powers—
    action coming within, whether, **1**, 221
    allocation between bodies, **1**, 215
    benefits, to confer, **1**, 215
    delegation of, **1**, 223
    economic and commercial activities, to regulate,
      1, 215
    homolgation of exercise of, **1**, 226
    incorrect procedure in exercising, **1**, 227
    overlapping, **1**, 222
    person exercising, relevance of, **1**, 223
    rights and liberties, infringing, **1**, 215
prerogative powers, sources of, **1**, 202
prior representation, acting without regard to, **1**,
    296
revenue, power to raise, **1**, 215
scrutiny of acts of, **1**, 201
statutory duty, breach of—
    bad faith, **15**, 177
    duty of care, **15**, 178
    economic loss, harm in form of, **15**, 178
    generally, **15**, 157, 177
statutory duty, discretion in exercising, **1**, 235
statutory powers—
    interpretation of, **1**, 219
    misuse of, **1**, 333
tendering by, **3**, 17
title and interest to sue, **1**, 308
ultra vires, acting, **1**, 215
unlawful acts by employees or officials, **1**, 333
See also PUBLIC CORPORATION
Public Bill
alternative to private Bill, as, **19**, 4
Parliament, function of, **19**, 2
private Bill distinguished, **19**, 2
public legislation, as, **19**, 1
Public Bill Committees
See HOUSE OF LORDS
Public character, aspersions against
defamation, **15**, 494
Public charitable collection
permit, **14**, 119, 528
war charity, **14**, 518

Public clock
illumination, **14**, 701
maintenance, **14**, 701
Public company
See COMPANY
Public convenience
disabled persons, for, **19**, 369
licensing, **14**, 526
local authority duties, **14**, 526
provision of, **14**, 707; **19**, 368, 399
public health, **14**, 707
regulation, **14**, 526
Public corporation
accounts of, **1**, 91
administrative, **19**, 221
audits, **19**, 224
classification, **19**, 221
commercial, **19**, 221
consumer protection, **19**, 240-242
Contingencies Fund, **19**, 224
control, **19**, 201, 222-227
    audits, **19**, 224
    consumer, **19**, 239-242
    Council on Tribunals, **19**, 239
    courts, role of, **19**, 238
    Crown immunities, **19**, 233-237
    Crown privilege, **19**, 236
    efficiency and costs, **19**, 224
    European Community law, **19**, 243-249
    expenditure procedures, **19**, 224
    factual background, **19**, 232
    foreign government immunity, **19**, 235
    judicial, **19**, 228-238
    legislative background, **19**, 231
    ministerial responsibility, **19**, 225, 227, 227*n*
    Ombudsman system, **19**, 239, 242
    Parliamentary, **19**, 223-227
    'province of government' criterion, **19**, 233,
      234
    state aid, **19**, 244
    state monopolies, **19**, 245
    statutory immunities, **19**, 237
    where duties not enforceable, **19**, 231
corporate personality, **19**, 214-219
    'Bubble Act', **19**, 217
    burghs, **19**, 215, 216
    civilian example, **19**, 216*n*
    concession theory, **19**, 214
    Crown, **19**, 208
    fiction theory, **19**, 214
    individual liability, **19**, 229
    internal organisation, **19**, 218
    juristic, **19**, 205
    medieval law, **19**, 205
      burgh charters, **19**, 215
    official capacity, possession of, **19**, 204
    privileges by prescription, **19**, 218
    'public bodies lacking', **19**, 219
    realist theory, **19**, 214
    relations with others, **19**, 218
    Scottish statutes, **19**, 217
    theories of, **19**, 214
corporation sole, concept of, **19**, 206, 208, 209
Crown immunities, **19**, 233-237

Public corporation—*continued*
cultural or educational objective, **19**, 247
definition, **19**, 213
delict, title and interest to sue, **15**, 223
dominium governmental exercise of, **19**, 222
duties, where not enforceable, **19**, 231
economic intervention, **19**, 211, 212
economic objects, having, **19**, 247
efficiency and costs, **19**, 224
European Union law, **19**, 243-249
  allocation of functions, **19**, 244
  consequences of membership, **19**, 243
  direct control, **19**, 243
  exceptions from, **19**, 248, 249
  general interest principle, **19**, 249
  performance of functions, **19**, 247
  rules contrary to EEC Treaty, enactment of,
    19, 246
  State monopolies, **19**, 245
expenditure, **19**, 224
functions, **19**, 221, 222
  resource utilisation, **19**, 238
  statutory allocation, **19**, 238
history, **19**, 202-212
  corporate status, **19**, 208
  departmental government, **19**, 210
  economic intervention, **19**, 211-212
  juristic personality, **19**, 205
  king, position of, **19**, 203, 204, 207
  medieval law, **19**, 202-205
  modern state, **19**, 206-209
  privatisation, **19**, 212
  Reformation, effect of, **19**, 206
  Revolution Settlement, **19**, 207
imperium governmental exercise of, **19**, 222
industrial, **19**, 221
judicial control, **19**, 228-238
liability, individual, **19**, 229
'making' or 'erecting', **19**, 217
managerial-economic, **19**, 221
managerial-social, **19**, 221
meaning, **19**, 201
ministerial power, **19**, 210, 210*n*
ministerial relations, **19**, 225
Monopolies and Mergers Commission, **19**, 224,
  241
nationalised industries, **19**, 211, 222
non-departmental bodies, **19**, 222
operational, **19**, 221
Parliamentary debates concerning, **19**, 225
private interests, impact on, **19**, 222
privatisation, **19**, 212
Public Accounts Committee, **19**, 224
'public bodies lacking corporate personality', **19**,
  219
public control or ownership, **19**, 213
public or private, **19**, 213, 213*n*, 220, 221, 230
  distinguished, **19**, 220
  functions, **19**, 221
quasi-corporation, as, **19**, 218, 219
regulatory, **19**, 221
regulatory-social, **19**, 221
resource utilisation functions, **19**, 238
sex discrimination, **19**, 247

Public corporation—*continued*
social service, **19**, 221
state aid, **19**, 248
  European Union restrictions, **19**, 244
state intervention, **19**, 211, 212
statutory basis for activities, **19**, 223
statutory incorporation, **19**, 223
subjection to ordinary law, **19**, 230
supervisory bodies, **19**, 221
trading functions, body with, **19**, 221
ultra vires doctrine, **19**, 229, 230, 238
Public documents
documentary evidence, as, **10**, 591-598
inspection of, **14**, 263-265
Public duties
code of conduct, **14**, 232
time off for, **9**, 94
See also OFFICE HOLDER
Public emergency
See EMERGENCY POWERS
Public entertainment
application relating to, appeal to sheriff, **14**, 119
licence, **14**, 523
  conditions attached to, **9**, 1002
  entertainment licence distinguished from, **9**,
    1005
  grant of, **9**, 1003
  offences, **9**, 1002
  pop festivals, **9**, 1041
  renewal of, **9**, 1003
  revocation, **9**, 1002
  safety precautions, **9**, 1002
  suspension, **9**, 1002
  temporary, **9**, 1004
  variation, **9**, 1002
place of—
  meaning, **9**, 1002
  performance constituting infringement of
    copyright, permitting use for, **18**, 1079
water meter charges, **25**, 536
Public expenditure
allocation of resources—
  consultation concerning, **5**, 527
  discretion over, **5**, 526
  recent years, in, **5**, 525
Comptroller and Auditor General, **7**, 766
Consolidated Fund, **7**, 766
control of—
  appropriation accounts, **5**, 594
  Committee of Public Accounts, **5**, 596
  generally, **7**, 766
  local authority, **5**, 528
  National Audit Office, **5**, 595
  national health service, **5**, 529
  supply estimates—
    generally, **5**, 588
    supplementary, **5**, 591
  votes—
    account, on, **5**, 592
    cash limited, **5**, 589
    generally, **5**, 588
generally, **5**, 574-587
Goschen formula, **5**, 524
importance in Scottish economy, **5**, 575

Public expenditure—*continued*
local government expenditure—
  capital—
    bearer bonds, **14**, 819
    bills, **14**, 818
    block allocations, **14**, 806
    bonds, **14**, 816
    borrowing—
      foreign, **14**, 820
      purposes of, **14**, 814
      sources of, **14**, 815
    consent to incur, **14**, 805
    consolidated loans funds, **14**, 813
    financing of, **14**, 807
    funds, **14**, 810
    generally, **14**, 803
    grants, **14**, 809
    interest, **14**, 822, 823
    loan, **14**, 821, 822
    meaning, **14**, 805
    mortgage, **14**, 816
    other local authorities, loans to, **14**, 821
    overdraft, **14**, 817
    principal, procedure on default of payment, **14**, 823
    private sector housing, **14**, 613
    public body, loan to, **14**, 821
    public sector housing, **14**, 613
    renewal fund, **14**, 811
    repair fund, **14**, 811
    revenue, contributions from, **14**, 808
    securities, **14**, 816, 819
    social work departments, by, **22**, 16
    stock, **14**, 816
    temporary loan, **14**, 817
    temporary use of funds, **14**, 812
  charitable fund, contributions to, **14**, 313
  commerce, assistance to, **14**, 312, 639, 640
  control over, **5**, 528
  defraying, **14**, 311
  disaster, relating to, **14**, 327
  emergency, relating to, **14**, 327
  Free Twopence, **14**, 310
  general application of power, **14**, 310
  industry, assistance to, **14**, 312, 639, 640
  not otherwise authorised, limitation on, **14**, 315
  procurator fiscal, of, **17**, 533
  publication of material, **14**, 314
  revenue—
    capital, contributions to, **14**, 808
    charges, **14**, 828
    fees, **14**, 828
    financing, **14**, 825
    generally, **14**, 803, 824
    government grant, *see* GRANT
    guidelines, **14**, 875
    housing, **14**, 613
    rates, *see* RATES
    rents—
      generally, **14**, 826
      house, **14**, 827
      other, **14**, 828
  meaning, **5**, 574
  monarch's recommendation, on, **7**, 767

Public expenditure—*continued*
money Bills, passage through Parliament, **7**, 768
National Audit Office, **7**, 766
National Loans Fund, **7**, 766
programmes—
  agriculture, fisheries and food, **5**, 578
  arts, **5**, 585
  education, **5**, 584
  employment, **5**, 579
  energy, **5**, 579
  generally, **5**, 577
  health, **5**, 586
  housing, **5**, 581
  industry, **5**, 579
  law, **5**, 583
  leisure, **5**, 585
  libraries, **5**, 585
  order, **5**, 583
  other environmental services, **5**, 582
  other public services, **5**, 587
  protective services, **5**, 583
  recreation, **5**, 585
  social work, **5**, 586
  tourism, **5**, 579
  trade, **5**, 579
  transport, **5**, 580
Scotland, in, **5**, 523
survey, **5**, 576
Public finance
sheriff court jurisdiction, **6**, 1123
Public hatred, contempt and ridicule
convicium, **15**, 558
meaning, **15**, 568
requirements for actionability, **15**, 564
series of statements, **15**, 565
solatium, **15**, 567, 569
unpopular sentiments, attributions, **15**, 566
verbal injury, generally, **15**, 558, 564
Public health
annoying and offensive behaviour, **19**, 370-372
buildings and building controls, **19**, 350-358
byelaws, **14**, 273
caravan sites, **19**, 349
central government responsibility, **19**, 307
clean air, **19**, 315-317
cleansing, **14**, 706
cleansing and disinfection of premises, **19**, 306, 448
coast protection, **19**, 325
common lodging houses, **19**, 306, 454
conservation of environment, **19**, 303
dangerous or annoying creatures, **19**, 372
defecation, **19**, 370
Department of Agriculture and Fisheries, **19**, 307*n*
development of service, **14**, 37
disease, *see* DISEASE
ditches, **19**, 336, 367
dogs, fouling by, **19**, 371
environment, *see* ENVIRONMENT
environmental health, **19**, 301
European Community regulations, **19**, 307
factories, **14**, 705
flood prevention, **19**, 324, 325
food, regulations as to, *see* FOOD

Public health—*continued*
furniture and furnishings, **19**, 420-443
gas, with regard to, **9**, 878
generally, **14**, 704
health and safety at work legislation, 342-345; **19**, 304
   See also HEALTH AND SAFETY AT WORK
health services compared, **19**, 302, 305
historical background, **19**, 301
hospital services, responsibility for, **14**, 37
housing, **19**, 346-348
   cleansing of house and contents, **19**, 366
immunisation, *see* VACCINATION AND IMMUNISATION
infectious diseases, *see* DISEASE
inflammable substances, **19**, 383-411
   enforcement of legislation, **19**, 386
   inspection and testing, **19**, 405-409
   labelling, **19**, 395, 396
   packaging, **19**, 395, 396
   petroleum and petroleum spirit, meaning, **19**, 384, 385
   petroleum spirit licences, **19**, 400-404
   punishment of offences, **19**, 387
   road, conveyance by, **19**, 388-391
   scope of legislation, **19**, 383
   seizure, **19**, 410, 411
   storage, **19**, 395-399
   water, conveyance by, **19**, 392-394
knackers, **19**, 373*n*, 381
land, cleansing of, **19**, 365
licensing, **14**, 526
litter—
   deposit of, **19**, 327
   provisions as to, **19**, 327, 328
local authority responsibility, **19**, 308, 314
   officers, appointment of, **19**, 314
   port local authorities, **19**, 309-313
local government responsibility, **19**, 308, 308*n*
lodging houses, **19**, 306
manure, removal of, **19**, 367
meaning, **19**, 302
mental health, **19**, 302
National Health Service, *see* NATIONAL HEALTH SERVICE
noise—
   control, **19**, 303
   pollution, **19**, 318
nuisance, **19**, 306, 335-341, 378, 383*n*
offensive or dangerous trades, *see* TRADE
officers, appointment of, **19**, 314
offices, **14**, 705
open spaces, private, **19**, 356
pests, destruction of, **19**, 326
physical health, **19**, 302
platforms and raised structures, safety of, **19**, 354
pollution, *see* POLLUTION
port local authorities, **19**, 309-313
   constitution, **19**, 309
   debts, **19**, 312
   delegation of powers, **19**, 311
   expenses, **19**, 312
   jurisdiction, **19**, 310
     ships within, **19**, 313

Public health—*continued*
prevention and control of disease, **19**, 302
   See also DISEASE
protection, national and EU law, where disparity between, **7**, 1021
protection of, **25**, 427
public convenience—
   disabled persons, for, **19**, 369
   licensing, **14**, 526
   local authority duties, **14**, 526
   provision of, **14**, 707; **19**, 368, 369
   regulation, **14**, 526
rag flock and other filling materials, **19**, 420-443
responsible authorities, **19**, 307-314
   central government, **19**, 307
   local authorities, **19**, 308, 314
   officers, appointment of, **19**, 314
   port local authorities, **19**, 309-313
river pollution, **19**, 321-323
roads, cleansing of, **19**, 364
sanitary conditions, *see* SANITARY CONDITIONS, CREATION OF
scope of title, **19**, 306
Scottish Development Department, **19**, 307*n*
Scottish Home and Health Department, **19**, 307*n*
sheriff court jurisdiction, **6**, 1124
shops, **14**, 705
slaughterhouses, **19**, 373, 379-382
special inquiries, **19**, 307
sports grounds and premises, **19**, 358
town and country planning, **19**, 359, 360
travelling people, **19**, 349
urinating, **19**, 370
vaccination, *see* VACCINATION AND IMMUNISATION
vermin control, **19**, 326, 444
waste collection and disposal, **14**, 706; **19**, 361-363
water—
   environmental health, powers in respect of, **25**, 526
   fluoridation, **19**, 320; **25**, 509
   water rights, acquisition of, **25**, 519
   wholesome, provision of, **19**, 319*n*; **25**, 508
wild birds or animals killed or taken in interests of, **11**, 881, 885
Public house
amusements with prizes, **14**, 517
child or young person in, generally, **3**, 1227
gaming held in, person under eighteen on premises, **3**, 1230
hotel distinguished, **11**, 1712
inn deemed to be, **2**, 9
innkeepers' strict liability not applicable to, **15**, 147
lease, **13**, 197
liability, **11**, 1742
licence—
   airports allowed to hold, **2**, 8
   authorisation given by, **2**, 9
   restaurants holding, **2**, 13
meaning, **2**, 9, 18; **11**, 1712
part of hotel, as, **11**, 1712
permitted hours, *see* ALCOHOLIC LIQUOR

Public house—*continued*
Sunday opening—
    control, **22**, 817
    local licensing board, **22**, 817
See also ALCOHOLIC LIQUOR; INN; INNKEEPER;
    LICENSED PREMISES
Public inquiry
generating station, into, **9**, 629
local, *see* PUBLIC LOCAL INQUIRY
local authority solicitors, participation in, **13**, 1447
planning matters, **23**, 197, 265
statement made in, absolute privilege, **15**, 524
Public interest
conceptions of, **22**, 125
conduct causing invasion, **14**, 2073
Crown privilege lies in, **19**, 236
fair comment as defence against defamation, **15**,
    539, 540, 544
harm to, consequences of Commission's report, **4**,
    1242
hearing, **4**, 1239
immunity, concept of, **7**, 750
media right to discuss matters of, **6**, 313
Monopolies and Mergers Commission, investigation
    by, **4**, 1237
no harm to, consequences of Commission's
    report, **4**, 1241
public interest letter, preparation of, **4**, 1239
publication in, **17**, 32
reasonableness in, **4**, 1211
restraint of trade doctrine, scope of, **4**, 1213
restrictions contrary to—
    agreement to like effect, **4**, 1190
    declaration, **4**, 1187
    interdicts, **4**, 1189
    interim injunction, **4**, 1194
    interim interdict, **4**, 1194
    provisional validity, **4**, 1193
    severance, **4**, 1188
    suspension of court's order, **4**, 1192
    trade association, **4**, 1191
    undertakings, **4**, 1189
restrictions not contrary to, **4**, 1186
restrictive labour practices, **4**, 1235
Public international law
individuals, **19**, 694-696
state, self-determination of, **19**, 665
war of self-determination, **19**, 708
Public law
application to particular person, **19**, 221
prescription, **16**, 2131
private law, and, **1**, 205
Public legislation
meaning, **19**, 1
Public lending right
ascertainment, **13**, 1510
author—
    disposal of right by, **13**, 1509
    eligible and ineligible, **13**, 1509
authors, **13**, 1508
books eligible for, **13**, 1508
calculation, **13**, 1510
disposal by author, **13**, 1509
duration, **13**, 1509

Public lending right—*continued*
illustrators, **13**, 1508
payment, **13**, 1510
payments under, tax treatment, **18**, 1592
Public Lending Right Scheme 1982 ..., **13**, 1508
register—
    application for registration, **13**, 1509
    application for transfer of registered interest,
        13, 1509
    maintenance, **13**, 1509
Registrar, **13**, 1509
sampling points, **13**, 1510
transfer, **13**, 1509
    insolvency, on, **13**, 1509
translators, **13**, 1508
Public life
standards in, Royal Commission on, **5**, 380
Public local inquiry
adjournment, **23**, 931
administrative decision, **23**, 918
alternative procedure—
    hearing, **23**, 940
    written submission, **23**, 941
alternative site, **12**, 924
appeal—
    grounds of, **23**, 946
    making of, **23**, 920
    person aggrieved, meaning, **23**, 945
    right to, **23**, 945
appearance—
    order of, **23**, 929
    right to appear, **23**, 927
conduct of, **23**, 919
delegation, **23**, 922
disruptive behaviour, **23**, 932
evidence—
    nature of, **23**, 930
    new, **23**, 938
expenses, **14**, 116; **23**, 934
fact, variations in findings of, **23**, 938
government department, statement of, **23**, 928
hearing, **23**, 940
information, advance exchange of, **23**, 923
initial procedure—
    delegation, **23**, 922
    making appeal or objection, **23**, 920
    right to be heard, **23**, 921
judicial review, **23**, 944
legal proceedings, questioning validity of decision
    in, **23**, 943
local authority, statement of, **23**, 928
non-compliance with relevant requirement, **23**,
    947
notice of, **23**, 923
objection, making of, **23**, 920
post-inquiry procedure—
    fact, variations of findings of, **23**, 938
    new evidence, **23**, 938
    reporter's decision—
        letter, by, **23**, 935
        persons entitled to be notified of, **23**, 936
    Secretary of State—
        decision of, **23**, 939
        determination of case by, **23**, 937

Public local inquiry—*continued*
procedure at—
  adjournment, **23**, 931
  appearance—
    order of, **23**, 929
    right to appear, **23**, 927
  disruptive behaviour, **23**, 932
  evidence, nature of, **23**, 930
  expenses, **23**, 934
  right to appear, **23**, 927
  site inspection, **23**, 933
procedure before—
  alternative site, **23**, 924
  information, advance exchange of, **23**, 923
  notice of inquiry, **23**, 923
  technical assessor, **23**, 926
  witness, citation of, **23**, 925
quashing of decision, **23**, 948
report's decision—
  letter, by, **23**, 935
  persons entitled to be notified of, **23**, 936
right to appear, **23**, 927
Secretary of State—
  decision of, challenging, **23**, 942-948
    post-inquiry procedure, **23**, 939
    quashing, **23**, 948
  delegation, **23**, 922
  determination of case by, **23**, 937
section 26 parties, meaning, **23**, 923*n*
site inspection, **23**, 933
technical assessor, **23**, 926
witness, citation of, **23**, 925
written submission, **23**, 941
See also TRIBUNAL
Public meeting
access to, **14**, 1325
candidacy in election, for purposes of advancing, **5**, 375
meaning, **14**, 1303
private premises, held on, **14**, 1303
Public nuisance
comparison of Scots and English law, **14**, 2020
meaning, **14**, 2015, 2159
See also NUISANCE
Public open space
meaning, **11**, 617*n*
trees growing on, felling licence not required, **11**, 617
Public order, crimes against
bigamy, *see* BIGAMY
blasphemy, **7**, 476
breach of the peace, *see* BREACH OF THE PEACE
homosexual offences, **7**, 485
indecent exposure, *see* INDECENT EXPOSURE
mobbing and rioting, *see* MOBBING AND RIOTING
obscenity, criminal, **7**, 486
  Indecent Displays (Control) Act (1981), **7**, 488
  obscene material, meaning, **7**, 487
  See also OBSCENITY
prostitution, **7**, 484
rioting, *see* MOBBING AND RIOTING
shamelessly indecent conduct, *see* SHAMELESSLY
  INDECENT CONDUCT

Public order, crimes against—*continued*
soliciting, **7**, 484
violation of sepulchres, *see* VIOLATION OF
  SEPULCHRES
Public path
creation and maintenance of, **14**, 674
generally, **9**, 1239
long distance route, **14**, 675
Public peace
disturbance, police powers as to, **16**, 1786
preservation, police powers as to, **16**, 1785, 1787
See also BREACH OF THE PEACE
Public place
drink driving offences, definition in relation to, **20**, 420
nuisance in—
  defences—
    acquiescence, **14**, 2168
    prescription, **14**, 2168
    statutory authorisation, **14**, 2168
  liability—
    adjoining property causing harm, **14**, 2167
    general principles, **14**, 2163
    highway—
      adjoining property causing harm to users, **14**, 2167
      danger on, **14**, 2165
      encroachment on or over, **14**, 2164
      obstruction on, **14**, 2165
    scope, **14**, 2163
    Scots and English law compared, **14**, 2166
  place of safety, removal of mentally disordered person, **14**, 1486
  public nuisance, meaning, **14**, 2159
  title to sue—
    generally, **14**, 2160
    procurator fiscal, powers of, **14**, 2161
    statutory entitlement, **14**, 2162
Public police
cases, **14**, 2011
procurator fiscal, powers of, **14**, 2161
Public policy
beneficiary, statutory exclusion on grounds of, **25**, 621
'cross-border' precedents, **22**, 277
European Union customs law, **7**, 1022
external, *see* PRIVATE INTERNATIONAL LAW
marriage, constitution of, **17**, 222
private Bill affecting, **19**, 2
testamentary provisions contrary to, **25**, 771
vesting, rules of law of, **25**, 906
Public procession
civic code, **14**, 573
common law rights, **14**, 1325
conditions—
  council, imposed by, **14**, 568
  police, imposed by, **14**, 569; **16**, 1738, 1786, 1786*n*
enforcement, **14**, 572
intimidation, **14**, 1326
notification, **14**, 567
offences, **14**, 572, 1326
offensive weapon, use of, **14**, 1326

Public procession—*continued*
order relating to, appeal to sheriff court, **14**, 119, 571
permission not required, **14**, 570
prohibition, order for, **14**, 305, 568
public disorder, resulting in, **14**, 1326
regulation, order for, **14**, 305
statutory control, **14**, 1326
Public prosecution
See PROSECUTION
Public prosecutor
absolute privilege, **15**, 444, 448, 449
chief constable, directions to, **16**, 1740
concept, emergence of, **17**, 526
Crown Agent, *see* CROWN AGENT
Crown counsel, *see* CROWN COUNSEL
Crown Office, *see* CROWN OFFICE
death penalty, concurrence to, **17**, 528
district court, in, **17**, 538
generally, **17**, 577
judiciary, relationship to, **17**, 583
police, relationship to, **17**, 584
preliminary inquiries, duties at end of—
    accused, bringing before court, **17**, 624
    alternative action, discretion to take, **17**, 619
    charge, discretion as to nature of, **17**, 622
    decision whether or not to prosecute, **17**, 617
    fiscal fines, **17**, 621
    fixed penalty, discretion to offer, **17**, 620
    no further proceedings, discretion to order, **17**, 618
    proceedings in court, discretion as to form of, **17**, 623
    warn, discretion to, **17**, 619
procurator fiscal, *see* PROCURATOR FISCAL
Solicitor General, *see* SOLICITOR GENERAL FOR SCOTLAND
Public records
access to, **19**, 874-882
    closure periods, **19**, 875-877
    confidence, information supplied in, **19**, 875, 876
    disclosure, prohibitions on, **19**, 877
    distress or danger caused by, **19**, 875
    exceptionally sensitive papers, **19**, 875
    motives of inquirer, **19**, 879
    personal information, **19**, 875, 876
administrative, **19**, 845
adoption processes, access to, **19**, 879
area depositories, **19**, 1409
arranging, **19**, 871
calendars of, **19**, 871, 874
catalogues of, **19**, 871, 874
church court records, **19**, 849
cleaning, **19**, 871
confidence, information supplied in, **19**, 875, 876
copyright, **18**, 1122; **19**, 874, 881
criminal registers, access to, **19**, 879
data protection, **19**, 847, 875
departmental records, transmission to Scotland, **19**, 861
disposal of records—
    court records, of, **19**, 869
    limiting date for, **19**, 864, 867

Public records—*continued*
disposal of records—*continued*
    regulations as to, **19**, 866
    review for, **19**, 870
    transfer, by, **19**, 868, 871
early Scottish records, **19**, 861, 861*n*
engrossing, **19**, 846
exceptionally sensitive papers, **19**, 875
extracts from, **19**, 880, 881
facsimiles, **19**, 846
form of, **19**, 846
functions—
    Keeper of the Records of Scotland, **19**, 865
    selection and disposal of records, **19**, 866-870
gifts of, **19**, 849, 863
government departments, of, **19**, 849
    access to, **19**, 874, 875
handwritten, **19**, 846
heritors' records, **19**, 849
indexes of, **19**, 871, 874
loan, records on, **19**, 849, 863
loan of records, **19**, 873
local authority records, **19**, 849
    transmission of, **19**, 864
maintenance of, **19**, 871-873
meaning in Scotland, **19**, 842, 849
microcopying, **19**, 846
nationalised undertakings, records and archives of, **19**, 849, 862
nature and form in Scotland, **19**, 842-847
non-departmental government bodies, records of, **19**, 849
non-departmental public bodies, records of, **19**, 862
non-paper form, **19**, 846, 847, 849
parochial registers, *see* PARISH REGISTERS
preservation of records, **19**, 871, 874
private hands, in, **19**, 844
private records distinguished, **19**, 843
Public Records (Scotland) Act 1937, scope of, **19**, 854
public registers separated, **19**, 860
purchases by Keeper, **19**, 849, 863
records, meaning, **19**, 846
recovery of, **19**, 844
    limitation period, **19**, 844
registration offices, custody in, **19**, 1408
repairing, **19**, 871
Scottish Office records, **19**, 849
Scottish Record Office, *see* SCOTTISH RECORD OFFICE
Scottish Records Advisory Council, **19**, 823, 824
state, records of, **19**, 843
    transmission to Scotland, **19**, 861
statute-barred, **19**, 877
transfer, disposal by, **19**, 868
transmission of, **19**, 853-864
    Keeper of the Records of Scotland, to, **19**, 842
    regulation, **19**, 860
    retransmission, **19**, 872
typewritten, **19**, 846
valuation rolls, **19**, 849

Public Register of All Arms and Bearings in Scotland
arms, recording, **11**, 1625
coats of arms, recording of, **11**, 1614
generally, **11**, 1602
heirs, references to, **11**, 1615
pedigrees, recording of, **11**, 1623
preservation in Lyon Court, **11**, 1602
royal arms recorded in, **6**, 1012, 1014, 1018; **11**, 1632
Public Register of All Genealogies and Birth Brieves in Scotland
Lyon Clerk's duties, **6**, 1012
pedigrees recorded in, **11**, 1623
Public registers
access to, **19**, 878
court records, **19**, 830
  Books of Council and Session, **19**, 839
  church courts, registration in, **19**, 836
  legal fiction, registration as, **19**, 837
  Register of Appraising, **19**, 841
  Register of Hornings, **19**, 840
  Register of Inhibitions, **19**, 840
  Subscription of Deeds Act 1584 ..., **19**, 838
Department of the Registers of Scotland, **19**, 850
  Chancery Office, **19**, 850
  Deeds Office, **19**, 850
  family agreements, **19**, 850
  finance, **19**, 852
  Horning Office, **19**, 850
  land, deeds for, **19**, 850
  Land Register of Scotland, **19**, 850
  official searches, **19**, 851
  private searches, **19**, 851
  Sasine Office, **19**, 850
  state appointments, deeds, **19**, 850
  succession, deeds relating to, **19**, 850
  trusts, deeds relating to, **19**, 850
notarial protocols, **19**, 830-835
  notarial instruments, **19**, 831
  notary, classes of, **19**, 832
  protocol books as registers, **19**, 833
  register of sasines, *see* SASINES
origins, **19**, 830-841
public records separated, **19**, 860
sasines, *see* SASINES
searches—
  official, **19**, 851
  private, **19**, 851
transmission of, **19**, 860
Public right
action to enforce, **1**, 309
Attorney-General, enforced by, **1**, 323
navigation, *see* NAVIGATION
right of way, *see* PUBLIC RIGHT OF WAY
tidal area, in, **25**, 310
tidal river, in, **25**, 310, 312
Public right of passage or way
See RIGHT OF PASSAGE; RIGHT OF WAY
Public river
See RIVER
Public road
meaning, **14**, 405; **20**, 501, 609

Public school
corporal punishment, **8**, 903
denominations, must be open to all, **8**, 856
exclusion from as disciplinary measure, **8**, 905-907
land ownership, income from, **3**, 1134
Public sector tenancy
abandoned, ownership of property left on premises, **18**, 552
agricultural premises, **11**, 1937, 1943
allocation of houses, **11**, 1935
business premises, **11**, 1937, 1943
change of landlord provisions, **11**, 1934
contract of employment, premises occupied under, **11**, 1937, 1938
fire authority as landlord, **11**, 1937, 1944
generally, **11**, 1934; **13**, 121
homeless persons, accommodation for, **11**, 1937, 1942
  See also HOMELESSNESS
houses part of, or within curtilage of, certain other buildings, **11**, 1937, 1945
housing lists, **11**, 1935
  priority of applicants, **11**, 1935
  publication of rules governing admission to, **11**, 1935
  rules for admission to, **11**, 1935
  tenant selection, **11**, 1935
inspection of house, **11**, 1934
local authority powers, **11**, 1934
police authority as landlord, **11**, 1937, 1944
private sector landlord, disposal to, **11**, 1908
right to buy, *see* SECURE TENANT
sale of houses to, **6**, 1144
  See also SECURE TENANT
secure tenancy, **11**, 1903, 1934, 1936
  abandonment of tenancy, **11**, 1948
  after 1988 ..., **11**, 1936
  assignation, **11**, 1951
  assured tenancy, conversion into, **11**, 1936
  creation of, **11**, 1936
  disposal by local authority of houses let on, **11**, 1908
  exceptions, **11**, 1937-1945
  improvements, **11**, 1952
  landlords of, **11**, 1936
  lease must be in writing, **11**, 1950
  lodgers, **11**, 1951
  meaning, **11**, 1936
  possession, proceedings for, **11**, 1947
  repairs, **11**, 1952, 1953
  right to buy, *see* SECURE TENANT
  security of tenure, **11**, 1946
  subletting, **11**, 1951
  succession to, **11**, 1949
  variation of terms, **11**, 1950
  See also SECURE TENANT
temporary letting—
  during works, **11**, 1937, 1941
  pending development, **11**, 1937, 1940
  person seeking accommodation, to, **11**, 1937, 1939
Public security
European Union customs law, **7**, 1022

Public servant
insider dealing, **12**, 1502, 1519-1522
    primary insider, as, **12**, 1501
    tippee rules, **12**, 1522
meaning, **12**, 1520
Public service vehicle
bus shelters, provison of, **20**, 667
car-sharing arrangement distinguished, **20**, 488
certificate of fitness, **20**, 489, 490
    equivalents of, **20**, 490
common carrier, operator as, **3**, 670
conductor, conduct of, **20**, 492
damage to, notification, **20**, 491
deregulation, **20**, 489n
driver—
    conduct of, **20**, 492
    hours of work, **20**, 497, 499
    licence, **20**, 489, 492
    foreign, **20**, 499
    driver's hours of work, **20**, 499
generally, **3**, 670
handling of vehicle, **3**, 676
inspection, **20**, 489
local authority, run by, **20**, 493
luggage, **3**, 686
meaning, **20**, 488
operator—
    duties of, **20**, 491
    licence, **20**, 489
        alteration, **20**, 491
        application for, **20**, 491
        assignable, not, **20**, 491
        conditions imposed by, **20**, 491
        curtailment, **20**, 491
        disqualification from holding, **20**, 491
        disc, display on vehicles, **20**, 491
        duration, **20**, 491
        forgery, **20**, 491
        grant of, **20**, 491
            objections to, **20**, 491
        more than one, operator holding, **20**, 491
        necessity for, **20**, 491
        number of vehicles covered by, **20**, 491
        offences in relation to, **20**, 491
        refusal of application, **20**, 491
        restricted, **20**, 491
        revocation, **20**, 491
        standard, **20**, 491
        suspension, **20**, 491
overcrowding, **3**, 675, 681
passenger, conduct of, **20**, 492
public passenger service, requirements of, **20**, 489
regulation of road use by, **20**, 508
road service licence, former requirement for, **20**, 489n
safety of vehicle, **3**, 674
travel concessions, local authority, **20**, 493
weight, **20**, 476
See also BUS
Public services
expenditure programme, **5**, 587
investigation into irregularity of conduct, admissibility as hearsay evidence, **10**, 737

Public supply contract
local authority functions, **14**, 326
Public telecommunications operator (PTO)
class licence and, mutual exclusivity, **16**, 1948
competitive environment—
    apparatus, production of, **16**, 1944
    charges, publication, **16**, 1941
    creation, generally, **16**, 1935, 1940
    cross subsidies, **16**, 1942
    exclusive dealing—
        generally, **16**, 1945
        international services, **16**, 1946
    separate accounts, provision, **16**, 1943
    terms and conditions, publication, **16**, 1941
confidentiality of customer information, **16**, 1937, 1938
connection into British Telecom system, **16**, 1934-1936
consumers, service and support for—
    generally, **16**, 1937
    testing of apparatus, **16**, 1938
    wiring, **16**, 1939
damage to corporeal moveable by, **16**, 1956
directory information services, provision, **16**, 1937, 1937n
disabled persons, provision for, **16**, 1933, 1933n
emergency services, provision, **16**, 1923, 1932, 1932n
equal access, principle of—
    connection to other systems, **16**, 1936
    generally, **16**, 1934
    interconnection, agreement for, **16**, 1935
itemised information, provision of, **16**, 1937
licence—
    common features, **16**, 1931-1947
    equal access, provisions as to, **16**, 1934-1936
    individual licence, **16**, 1929
    notice, requirement as to, **16**, 1930
    objections or representations, consideration, **16**, 1930
    permissible conditions, **16**, 1929
    revocation, **16**, 1931, 1931n
    service and support for users, provisions as to, **16**, 1937-1939
long line, **16**, 1934, 1934n
maintenance services, provision, **16**, 1937, 1937n
maritime services, provision, **16**, 1932, 1932n
metering, **16**, 1937, 1937n
non-discrimination, **16**, 1933, 1933n, 1940
numbering arrangements, **16**, 1937, 1937n
OSI standard, **16**, 1938, 1938n
priority fault repair service, **16**, 1937, 1937n
private circuits, provision, **16**, 1940
public call box services, provision, **16**, 1923, 1932, 1932n, 1933
rural areas, services in, **16**, 1933, 1933n
testing apparatus, provisions as to, **16**, 1938, 1938n
universal service, provision, **16**, 1932
value added services, **16**, 1950
wiring, provisions as to, **16**, 1939
Public tranquility
offences against, *see* BREACH OF THE PEACE
Public transport
air services, **14**, 451

Public transport—*continued*
ancillaries, provision of, **14**, 418
bus—
  permit—
    community, **14**, 424
    educational body, use by, **14**, 423
    religious body, use by, **14**, 423
    social welfare, for, **14**, 423
    school, use to carry fare-paying passenger, **14**, 438
  station, **14**, 431
  undertakings—
    company, transfer to, **14**, 426, 429
    regional council, exclusion of power of, **14**, 428
co-ordination, **14**, 416
company, **14**, 430
concessionary fares—
  apart from scheme, **14**, 435
  scheme—
    eligible persons, **14**, 433
    eligible service, **14**, 434
    establishment of, **14**, 433
    participation in, **14**, 434
    particulars of, **14**, 433
  superseded provisions, **14**, 420
deregulation, **14**, 422
financial assistance, **14**, 417
grants—
  facilities, **14**, 436
  rural area, service in, **14**, 437
  services, **14**, 436
Greater Glasgow Passenger Transport Authority, **14**, 415
infectious person, prohibition on conveyance, **19**, 458, 459
local authorities generally, **14**, 413
other areas, functions of local authority in, **14**, 427
ownership of abandoned property left on premises of, **18**, 552
private hire car, carriage of passenger at separate fare, **14**, 440
service subsidies, **14**, 432
Strathclyde Passenger Transport Area, **14**, 419, 425, 426
taxi—
  local service, special licence for providing, **14**, 439
  separate fare, carriage of passenger at, **14**, 440
Transport Act 1985—
  changes effected by, **14**, 421
undertakings, operation of, **14**, 414, 419
Public trust
beneficial interest, special features of, **24**, 86
beneficiaries, disputes on, **24**, 89
certainty of description, **24**, 90
charitable purposes, **24**, 87, 91
charitable trust and, **24**, 102
cy-près, doctrine of, **24**, 7, 101-111
enforcement, **24**, 86, 89
executors, disputes on, **24**, 89
meaning, **24**, 10
mortifications, **24**, 3

Public trust—*continued*
nomination of trustees, **24**, 155
private trusts distinguished, **24**, 85, 86
public purposes, meaning, **24**, 87
real subrogation, doctrine of, **24**, 7
regulation, **24**, 85
trustees' discretion, **24**, 88
validity, disputes on, **24**, 89
variation of trust purposes, **24**, 76
Public works
authorised, service of purchase notice in case of, **5**, 95
construction of, injurious affection resulting from, *see* INJURIOUS AFFECTION
home acquired for, *see* HOME LOSS PAYMENT
injurious affection resulting from use of, *see* INJURIOUS AFFECTION
support of land published for construction, **14**, 1690
Public Works Loans Commissioners
powers, **13**, 1772, 1781
Publication
administration of justice—
  active proceedings, **17**, 29
  contempt of court, **17**, 33
  defences, **17**, 30
  generally, **17**, 27
  harm to, **17**, 34
  proceedings—
    active, **17**, 29
    reports of, **17**, 31
  public affairs, **17**, 32
  public interest, **17**, 32
  strict liability rule, **17**, 28
advertising matter, **17**, 45
book—
  delivery to certain libraries, **13**, 1503; **17**, 5
  meaning, **17**, 5*n*
  talking, supply of, **3**, 1163; **7**, 1448
  trade descriptions, **6**, 122
byelaws, of, **14**, 284
child, restrictions relating to, *see* CHILD-CHILDREN
confidential matter, **17**, 44
contempt of court, in, **17**, 33
  delayed publication, order for, **6**, 312
  distribution, **6**, 306
  innocent publication, defence of, **6**, 331; **17**, 30
copyright—
  generally, **17**, 26
  typeface, in, **18**, 1134, 1154, 1155, 1160
  typographical arrangement, in, **18**, 933, 936, 977, 984
country of first, **18**, 938
defamatory matter, **17**, 25
definition, **18**, 939
divorce proceedings, matter derived from, **17**, 41
election matter, **17**, 43
indecent matter, of, **17**, 40
information, of, **14**, 333
libraries, delivery to specified, **13**, 1503; **17**, 5
local authority, expenditure on material, **14**, 314
management rules, of, **14**, 298
nullity proceedings, matter derived from, **17**, 41
obscene material, of, **17**, 40

Publication—*continued*
performers' rights, matter protected by, **17**, 26
public lending right, *see* PUBLIC LENDING RIGHT
racial hatred, matter likely to stir up, **17**, 42
restrictions generally, **17**, 24
separation proceedings, matter derived from, **17**, 41
VAT zero-rating, **7**, 1447
Publicity
prejudicial, plea in bar of trial, **17**, 693
press, prohibition on, **17**, 751
smoke control order, for, **9**, 1136
trial diet, **17**, 751, 776
Publisher
Securities and Investments Board Core Conduct of Business Rules, **12**, 1399
Pump
public, provision of, **25**, 526
Pundlar case
udal law, **24**, 312, 321, 324
Punishment
capital, *see* CAPITAL PUNISHMENT
corporal, *see* CORPORAL PUNISHMENT
European Convention on Human Rights, **12**, 6, 26
inhuman or degrading treatment, **12**, 26
   European Convention for the Prevention of Torture and Inhuman or Degrading Treatment or Punishment, **12**, 27
international conventions on, **12**, 5
Pupil
abduction of, **10**, 1342
adoption of, **10**, 1196
age of pupillarity, **11**, 1202
alienation of heritage, **11**, 1225
aliment for, **19**, 1581
application for tutory, **10**, 1316
bank account, opening, **2**, 1229
beneficial transactions, **10**, 1052
capacity to enter contract, **2**, 1229; **10**, 1052, 1053, 1055; **11**, 1203; **12**, 1229; **13**, 1779; **20**, 816, 816n
capacity to grant deed, **12**, 1229
capacity to make will, **25**, 761
cautionary obligations, **2**, 1234
contracts reducible on majority, **2**, 1233
domicile of dependence, **4**, 30; **17**, 201
dominus negotii, as, **15**, 137, 141
donation, incapacity to make, **8**, 611
factor *loco tutoris*, **10**, 1069
factors for damages for, **24**, 279
female, **10**, 1049
financial obligations, **2**, 1231
gender and pupillarity, **10**, 1039
guardian, acting through, **13**, 1779
heritable property burdened by, **20**, 219
judicial factor, appointment, **4**, 14
lawburrows, may not be compelled to find, **13**, 912
legal incapacity, **10**, 1051; **24**, 128
legal recognition, **10**, 1050
liability for necessaries, **10**, 1054
male, **10**, 1049
mental disability, pupil suffering from, **11**, 1238

Pupil—*continued*
National Savings Bank account, **2**, 1230
necessaries, supply of, **11**, 1203
nonage, **24**, 129
reciprocity, **10**, 1053
reduction, action of, **13**, 26
reform of law, **10**, 1082, 1141-1146; **11**, 1243
relevance in modern context, **10**, 1055
status of pupillarity, **11**, 1203
taxation—
   capital gains tax, **19**, 1582
   inheritance tax, **19**, 1582
transactions on behalf of, **11**, 789
trust, may not create, **24**, 14, 128
trustee, cannot accept office as, **24**, 129
tutor—
   administration of pupil's estate, **10**, 1056, 1071
   appointment of, **2**, 1235
   at law, **10**, 1064-1066
   control of pupil's person, **10**, 1056, 1070
   curator compared, **10**, 1056, 1073, 1083
   dative, **10**, 1065, 1067-1069
   factors *loco tutoris*, **10**, 1069
   father as, **10**, 1058
   function of, **10**, 1056
   history of tutory, **10**, 1057
   mother as, **10**, 1059
   parents as, **10**, 1060
   role of, **10**, 1070, 1071, 1073
   termination of tutory, **10**, 1072
   testamentary, **10**, 1015, 1061-1063
vassal, as, feudal law, **18**, 75
voluntary obligation, capacity to enter, **15**, 660
welfare and benefit of *incapax*, **11**, 1206
Puppet
defamatory, **15**, 483
Purchase notice
adverse planning decision giving rise to, **23**, 310, 311
compensation after, **5**, 96
counter-notice, service of, **5**, 93
land with restricted use, **23**, 314
Secretary of State, options of, **5**, 94; **23**, 313
service of—
   authorised buildings or works, in case of, **5**, 95
   authorised use, **5**, 95
   form of, **5**, 92
   grounds for, **5**, 92
   listed building consent, in case of, **5**, 95; **23**, 185
   local planning authority, on, **5**, 92
   planning permission—
      granted subject to conditions, in case of, **5**, 92
      modification of, in case of, **5**, 95
      refusal of, in case of, **5**, 92
      revocation of, in case of, **5**, 95
   procedure following, **23**, 312
   regional planning authority, on, **5**, 92
Purchase tax
relief for traveller from outwith European Union, **7**, 1112
Pure obligation
meaning, **15**, 5

Q

Quadriennium utile
reduction of minor's contract within, **11**, 1205
Quail
game, as, **11**, 802
Game Acts, **11**, 496*n*
slaughter of, **11**, 516
Quaker burial ground, **3**, 531
Qualified chapels
assimilation, **3**, 1616
generally, **3**, 1616, 1616*n*, 1617, 1631
Qualified privilege
See DEFAMATION (privilege)
Quantity surveyor
appointment by architect, **3**, 130
contract, **3**, 127
generally, **3**, 2, 142
position of, generally, **3**, 127
sub-contracted, **3**, 127
Quantum meruit
wrongful withholding of sums due, interest
    payable on, **12**, 1012
Quarantine
laytime, effect on, **21**, 673
restraint of princes, as, **21**, 550
restrictions, loss or damage resulting from, carrier
    not liable, **21**, 603
Quarry
blasting materials, **14**, 1706
child employed in, **3**, 1257
danger—
    falls, from, **14**, 1702
    overhangs, from, **14**, 1702
    workmen, withdrawal of, **14**, 1707
dust, **14**, 1706
electricity in, **14**, 1705
explosives for use in, **10**, 1620
falls, duty to avoid danger from, **14**, 1702
health and safety at work legislation, **19**, 344
lighting, **14**, 1706
long lease, right to quarry stone, **13**, 241
machinery in, **14**, 1705
meaning, **14**, 1601
mine distinguished from, **14**, 1601
mining lease, landlord's hypothec, **13**, 513
overhangs, duty to avoid danger from, **14**, 1702
permitted development of, **23**, 241
roads authority powers as to, **20**, 661
safety, **14**, 1703
servitude right to quarry sand, gravel or stone, **18**,
    491
statutory control, **14**, 1607
statutory provisions, **14**, 1701
trespasser, duty of owner to, **14**, 1708
valuation for rating, **24**, 679, 684, 685
    prescribed formula, **24**, 547
vehicles in, **14**, 1704
Quarter (time)
definition, **22**, 812

Quarter (time)—*continued*
duration, **22**, 812
quarter days—
    England, **22**, 812
    Scotland, **22**, 812
rent, payment due quarterly, **22**, 812
tenancy, duration determined by, **22**, 812
value added tax, for purpose of, **22**, 812
Quarter Seal
administration of justice, **7**, 884
custody, **7**, 893
design, **7**, 893
generally, **7**, 855, 897, 903, 905
history, **7**, 891
Register of, **6**, 460; **19**, 820
uses, **7**, 884, 892
white wax, use of, **7**, 891
Quarter sessions, court of
abolition, **6**, 1160
former functions, **6**, 1159
Quartering (Heraldry)
principal quarter used alone, **11**, 1628
rematriculation, **11**, 1628
representation affected by, **11**, 1628
Quasi-contractual obligation
force of law, arising by, **15**, 2
meaning, **15**, 2
unjust enrichment, **15**, 2, 11
Quasi-corporation
Scots law, **19**, 208, 218, 219
Quasi-delict
special jurisdiction, **4**, 37
use of term, **15**, 2, 3
Quasi-judicial proceeding
statement made in, absolute privilege, **15**, 524
Quasi-partnership
application of principle in Scotland, **4**, 514
concept of, **25**, 15
elements which characterise, **25**, 15
identification of, **4**, 513
larger public company distinguished from, **4**, 487
meaning, **4**, 513
shares, valuation of, **25**, 15
unfair prejudice, **25**, 16
unfairly prejudicial conduct and—
    generally, **4**, 486
    receiver, appointment of, **4**, 487
Quay
construction or alteration, **19**, 19*n*
valuation for rating, **24**, 599
Quebec
Civil Code, **24**, 126
Queen
Council, in—
    prerogative powers, **7**, 719
    subordinate legislative powers, **7**, 719
public affairs, acting in, **5**, 306

Queen—*continued*
See also CROWN; KING; MONARCHY; ROYAL COURTS;
  SOVEREIGN
Queen's Award to Industry
false representations as to, **6**, 133
Queen's Bodyguard
generally, **7**, 836
Queen's Counsel
application to become, **13**, 1317
dress, **13**, 1323

Queen's Counsel—*continued*
generally, **13**, 1273, 1274, 1317
letters patent of commission, **7**, 874
precedence, **16**, 2020
precedence at Bar, **13**, 1273, 1274
Scottish Roll, creation of, **13**, 1273, 1274
Queen's and Lord Treasurer's Remembrancer
procurator fiscal and, **13**, 1436
Queen's warehouse
See WAREHOUSE

R

Rabbits
agricultural executive committee powers, **11**, 851
agricultural tenant—
    permission to kill given by, **11**, 818
    rights of, **11**, 888
breeding places and cover, destruction of, **11**, 862
clearance orders, **1**, 721
common grazing, **11**, 858
common law right to kill, **11**, 854
concurrent right to take and kill, **11**, 852
control of, **11**, 859–865
damage caused by, **11**, 851
forests, prevention of damage to, **11**, 866, 867
game, as, **11**, 802
Game Acts, **11**, 496*n*
land occupier's right to take and kill, **11**, 850
landowner, taken or destroyed by, **11**, 830
legal proceedings, who may institute, **11**, 857
moorland, **11**, 853
myxomatosis, **11**, 877
night—
    shooting, **11**, 872
    taking or destroying by, **11**, 810–814
physical damage caused by, **14**, 2045
Poaching Prevention Act 1832 ..., **11**, 843
rabbit clearance areas, **11**, 851, 862, 868, 869
rabbit clearance orders, **11**, 868–871
    failure to comply with, **11**, 871
    liability of authorised person, **11**, 870
    occupiers' duties, **11**, 869
requirement notice to control, **11**, 860–863
right to shoot or trap, lease, **13**, 202, 203
shooting lease, clauses in, **11**, 900
spring traps—
    approved, **11**, 874
    inspection of, **11**, 875
    open trapping of, **11**, 876
    use, sale and possession of, **11**, 873
trespass in search of, **11**, 817
unenclosed land, **11**, 853
Rabies
infected places—
    disinfection, **2**, 191
    entry of premises in, **2**, 192
    inquiries as to, **2**, 192
    rules pertaining to, **2**, 191
    sporting etc activities in, **2**, 194
    wild animals in, destruction, **2**, 193
inspector, inquiries by, **2**, 192
isolation of infected animals, **2**, 191
notification, **2**, 190
offences—
    generally, **2**, 195
    seizure of animals for, **2**, 230
    unlawfully landing animals, **2**, 229
    virus, relating to, **2**, 196
prevention of spread—
    import controls, by, **2**, 209

Rabies—*continued*
prevention of spread—*continued*
    samples, power to take, **2**, 192
    seizure of animals for, **2**, 230
public health legislation, **19**, 476
separation of animal with, **2**, 190
virus, control of, **2**, 196
wild animals, destruction of, **2**, 193
Race, motor
off the road, **20**, 434
unauthorised, **20**, 434, 453
Race Relations Board
corporate personality, **19**, 219, 219*n*
Racecourse
dog, pool betting on, **2**, 1564
horse, *see* HORSE RACECOURSE
valuation for rating, **24**, 746
Racial discrimination
advocate, instruction of, **13**, 1347
carrier, by, **3**, 615
Commission for Racial Equality, **9**, 388–391; **17**, 1253
complaints and appeals, **6**, 996
conciliation in case of claim, **9**, 315
employment, in, **9**, 332ff
European Convention on Human Rights, **12**, 6, 85, 86
incapacity as argument for, **11**, 1053
international conventions on, **12**, 5
Jews, discrimination against, **3**, 1676
Office of Fair Trading licensing, **6**, 21
partner, expulsion, **16**, 1061
partnership, in offer of, **16**, 1016
police force, appointments to, **16**, 1747, 1747*n*
private clubs, practised by, **19**, 1260
sheriff court jurisdiction, **6**, 1128; **17**, 1253
sport, in, **19**, 1259–1261
sporting representatives, **19**, 1261
status, and, **11**, 1071
trials which may be prejudiced by, extradition procedure, **12**, 516, 532, 534
unfair dismissal, **9**, 231, 357
Racial hatred
incitement to, in public performance of play, **9**, 1045
matter likely to stir up, restriction on publication, **17**, 42
Racial tension
immigration control, **12**, 102
Radar (shipping)
collision regulations, **21**, 341
duty to use radar properly, **21**, 340, 341, 344
equipment, provision and maintenance, safety requirements, **21**, 218
observers, regulations as to, **21**, 246, 247
plotting, regulations as to, **21**, 247
reflector, small ships, **21**, 378*n*
vessel with operational, safe speed, **21**, 343, 343*n*

Radiation
compensation for injury from, **9**, 1198
Radical Alternatives to Prison (RAP)
pressure group, **16**, 1489
Radio
blind person, provided for, **7**, 1448
election broadcasts, restriction, **15**, 1020, 1231
noise from, **9**, 1298
shipping—
   radio certificate, **21**, 222; **21**, 222*n*
   radio equipment—
      provision and maintenance, **21**, 215, 218
      surveys, **21**, 222
   radio operators, **21**, 215, 246, 247
   signals list, requirement to carry, **21**, 229*n*
   survival craft, equipment in, **21**, 216
   watch, requirement to keep, **21**, 215, 247
Radio broadcast
See BROADCAST
Radioactive substances
See ATOMIC ENERGY AND RADIOACTIVE SUBSTANCES
Radiographer
Council for Professions Supplementary to
   Medicine, **15**, 1516–1521
domestic tribunal, regulation by, **23**, 917
employment of, **11**, 1500
Radiological protection
international bodies, **9**, 1182
UK administrative bodies, **9**, 1181
Radiotherapy
sickness benefit where claimant receiving, **21**, 880
Rag flock
See FURNITURE AND FURNISHINGS
Rags or bones
public health nuisance, **19**, 336
Railing
road, provision on, **20**, 660
Railway Freight Convention
generally, **3**, 704
Railway Savings Banks
maintenance etc of, **2**, 1166
Railways
abandoned property left on railway premises,
   ownership, **18**, 552
access to land adjoining railway, **19**, 1019
accidents, **19**, 1068–1073
   communication in carriages, **19**, 1053
   compensation, **19**, 1073
   employees, to, **19**, 1068
   inquiries into, **19**, 1003, 1004, 1071
   investigation, **19**, 1071
   notice of, **19**, 1070
   passengers, to, **19**, 1072
   Prevention of Accidents Rules, **19**, 1069
   undertaker's liability, **19**, 1068, 1072
accommodation works, **19**, 1025, 1041–1045
   additional, obligations for, **19**, 1044
   arches, **19**, 1042
   bridges, **19**, 1042
   cattle—
      protection of, **19**, 1042
      provision of water for, **19**, 1042
   culverts, **19**, 1042
   disputes, settlement of, **19**, 1043, 1044

Railways—*continued*
accommodation works—*continued*
   drains, **19**, 1042
   failure to shut and fasten gates, **19**, 1033
   fences, **19**, 1042
   gates, **19**, 1042
   maintenance, **19**, 1041, 1042, 1043
   needs of owners and occupiers, **19**, 1042
   passages, **19**, 1042
   provision of, **19**, 1041, 1042
   rights of way, **19**, 1045
   stiles, **19**, 1042
administration, **19**, 1001
   regional railway boards, **19**, 1007
agricultural land or crops, damage to, **19**, 1056
alcohol—
   byelaws relating to, **19**, 1272
   football trains etc, on, **19**, 1066
alteration, **19**, 19*n*, 24
area transport users consultative committees, **19**,
   1092–1094
authorisation, statutes relating to, **19**, 1001
boiler gauge glasses, **19**, 1069
brake vans, **19**, 1069
brakes, **19**, 1054, 1069
bridges—
   accommodation crossing, **19**, 1025
   construction, **19**, 1024, 1025
   inspection and survey, **19**, 1026
   maintenance, **19**, 1025, 1026
   navigable tidal waters, over, **19**, 1025
   over railway not owned by British Railways
      Board, **19**, 1028
   roads on or over—
      responsibility for maintenance, **19**, 1027
      roads authorities' duties, **19**, 1026
British Rail General Conditions—
   generally, **3**, 696
   liability for loss, damage or delay, **3**, 697
   unfair contract terms, **3**, 701
British Railways Board, *see* BRITISH RAILWAYS
   BOARD
British Transport Police, *see* BRITISH TRANSPORT
   POLICE
byelaws, **19**, 1015, 1016, 1272
carriage by—
   generally, **3**, 601, 617
   limitation of actions—
      goods, loss or damage to, **16**, 2201
      luggage, loss or damage to, **16**, 2201
      passenger, death or personal injury, **16**, 2201
   solid fuel, carriage of, **6**, 236
   See also domestic carriage of goods *below*;
      domestic carriage of passengers *below*;
      international carriage of goods *below*;
      international carriage of passengers *below*
carriages, **19**, 1050
   communication in, means of, **19**, 1053
   exclusion of persons from, **19**, 1060
   liability of owners, **19**, 1051
   regulations as to, **19**, 1050
   upholstered fittings for, **19**, 421
Central Transport Consultative Committee for
   Great Britain, **19**, 1092

Railways—*continued*
charges, scheme of, **19**, 1013
closure, **19**, 1096–1100
    consent to, **19**, 1096, 1099
    experimental services, of, **19**, 1100
    notice of, **19**, 1096
    objections to, **19**, 1096
    passenger services, of, **19**, 1096
    passenger transport executives, special provisions,
        19, 1098
    procedure, **19**, 1096
    Secretary of State's consent, **19**, 1096, 1097,
        1099
communication in carriages, **19**, 1053
    passenger using without sufficient cause, **19**,
        1053
compensation for death or injury, **19**, 1073
construction, **19**, 19*n*, 24, 1017–1025
    acquisition of land, **19**, 1018, 1019
    Act, special, **19**, 1017
    aqueducts, **19**, 1024
    arches, **19**, 1024
    Bill, promotion through Parliament, **19**, 1021
    book of reference, deposit of, **19**, 1021
    bridges, **19**, 1024, 1025
    buildings, **19**, 1024, 1036
    canals, alteration of course, **19**, 1024
    compensation payments, **19**, 1024
    cuttings, **19**, 1024
    drains, **19**, 1024
    electricity generating stations, **19**, 1046
    embankments, **19**, 1024
    fences, **19**, 1024
    lateral deviation, **19**, 1022
    negligence, **19**, 1024
    omissions, misstatements or erroneous descrip-
        tions, **19**, 1021
    passages, **19**, 1024
    piers, **19**, 1024
    plan of works, deposit of, **19**, 1021
    private road or land, entry and use of, **19**, 1020
    rivers, alteration of course, **19**, 1024
    roads, **19**, 1024
    section of works, deposit of, **19**, 1021
    stations, **19**, 1036
    statutes relating to, **19**, 1001
    statutory authority for, **19**, 1017
    subsoil, use of, **19**, 1037
    trial borings, **19**, 1024
    tunnels, **19**, 1024, 1037
    undertaker's statutory powers, **19**, 1024
    vertical deviation, **19**, 1022
consultative committees, **19**, 1092, 1093
    appointment, **19**, 1092
    constitution, **19**, 1092
control, **19**, 1001
creditors, rights of, **19**, 1101, 1102
damages for offences committed on, **19**, 1065
derating, **24**, 730
development of, **23**, 123, 153
diversion, **19**, 24
domestic carriage of goods—
    British Rail General Conditions, **3**, 696

Railways—*continued*
domestic carriage of goods—*continued*
    British Railways Board—
        common carrier, not regarded as, **3**, 695
        duty of care, **3**, 702, 703
        position, generally, **3**, 695
    charges, **3**, 690
    consignment note, **3**, 696
    damage, liability for, **3**, 697
    dangerous goods, **3**, 698
    decline goods, Board's power to, **3**, 695
    delay, liability for, **3**, 697
    generally, **3**, 695
    lien, **3**, 700
    loss, liability for, **3**, 697
    sub-contract, Board's power to, **3**, 696
    unfair contract terms, **3**, 701
    visitors to railway premises, **3**, 702
    water, goods partly carried by, **3**, 696
domestic carriage of passengers—
    accidents and collisions, **3**, 722, 723
    alighting—
        invitation to alight, **3**, 714
        time allowed, **3**, 714
        track, on, **3**, 714
    British Railways Board—
        ex contractu liability, **3**, 709
        ex lege liability, **3**, 709
        generally, **3**, 709
        passengers, duty of care to, **3**, 715
        visitors to premises, duty of care to, **3**, 710
    carriage doors, shutting, **3**, 718
    Conditions of Carriage, **3**, 709
    crowd control, **3**, 712
    disorderly conduct etc by passenger, **3**, 719
    driving, provisions as to, **3**, 721
    drunken passenger, **3**, 712, 714
    generally, **3**, 709
    guard's van, travelling in, **3**, 717
    head, passenger putting out of window, **3**, 718
    hired carriages, **3**, 709
    invitation to board or alight, **3**, 714
    left luggage offices and lockers, **3**, 725
    lines, state of, **3**, 720
    luggage, **3**, 724
        Conditions of Carriage, **3**, 709
        premises or train, left on, **3**, 709
    overcrowding, **3**, 716
    passenger injured by another passenger, **3**, 719
    permanent way, state of, **3**, 720
    platforms, provisions as to, **3**, 711, 712
        crossings between platforms, **3**, 713
        lighting, **3**, 712
        train short of or overshooting platform, **3**,
            714
    prospective passengers, **3**, 710
    signalling system, duty of care, **3**, 720
    station approaches and exits, **3**, 711
    stations, safety in, **3**, 711–713
    tickets, **3**, 709
    timetables, issue and alteration, **3**, 709
    unattended child, **3**, 718
electricity boards, supply by, **9**, 622

Railways—*continued*
electrification, **19**, 1046–1048
  authorisation, **19**, 1046
  generating stations, construction and maintenance, **19**, 1046
  objections to, **19**, 1047
  opening electrified lines, **19**, 1048
  order, procedure for, **19**, 1047
  safety, **19**, 1046
employees—
  Criminal Injuries Compensation Scheme, **7**, 3, 10, 14
  liability for accidents to, **19**, 1068
  offences by, **19**, 1067
  physical force in execution of duty, use of, **7**, 238
  share schemes, **19**, 1008
engines, **19**, 1049
  approval of, **19**, 1049
  brakes, **19**, 1069
  fires caused by, **19**, 1055–1056
  liability of owners, **19**, 1051
  steam, **19**, 1055
  unfit for use, **19**, 1049
equipment, **19**, 1049–1057
EU transport policy, **3**, 731
experimental services, closure of, **19**, 1100
explosives, carriage of, **19**, 1015
explosives for use on—
  byelaws as to, **10**, 1610, 1620
  inspections, **10**, 1621
fares, evasion of payment, **19**, 1015
fencing, **19**, 1040, 1042
fires caused by engines, **19**, 1055–1056
  agricultural land or crops damaged, **19**, 1056
  sub-surface stations, fire prevention at, **19**, 1057
football trains, **19**, 1066
goods—
  international carriage, **19**, 1014
  receipt and delivery of, **19**, 1015
government responsibility, **19**, 1002
ground levers, **19**, 1069
harbours, railway property in, **24**, 727
historical development, **5**, 6
hotels, **24**, 721
independent, **19**, 1088–1091
  abandonment, **19**, 1091
  byelaws, **19**, 1089
  company accounts, **19**, 1090
  company meetings, **19**, 1090
  duties, **19**, 1088
  functions, **19**, 1088
  meaning, **19**, 1088
  statutory provisions, application of, **19**, 1088
  winding up, **19**, 1091
industry, **6**, 163
inspectors—
  accidents, inquiry into, **19**, 1003
  appointment, **19**, 1003
  powers, **19**, 1003
interference with working of, **19**, 1015
international carriage of goods—
  Additional Convention, **3**, 704
  consignment note, **3**, 704

Railways—*continued*
international carriage of goods—*continued*
  Convention concerning International Carriage by Rail (COTIF), **3**, 705, 706, 727
  Convention on the Contract for the International Carriage of Goods by Road (CMR), **3**, 646
  damage to goods, **3**, 707
  EU transport policy, **3**, 731
  generally, **3**, 704
  International Convention concerning the Carriage of Goods by Rail (CIM), **3**, 704, 705*n*
  liability of railway, **3**, 707
  loss of goods, **3**, 707
  Railway Freight Convention, **3**, 704
  responsibility for carriage, **3**, 706
  Uniform Rules, **3**, 706, 707
international carriage of passengers—
  Convention concerning International Carriage by Rail (COTIF), **3**, 727
  customs requirements, **3**, 727
  death, liability and damages, **3**, 728, 729
  extinction of claims, **3**, 730
  International Convention concerning … (CIV), **3**, 726, 727
  limitation of claims, **3**, 730
  live animals, **3**, 727
  loss or damage, liability and damages, **3**, 728, 729
  luggage, **3**, 727
    loss or damage, **3**, 728, 729
  personal injury, liability and damages, **3**, 728, 729
  tickets, **3**, 727
  Uniform Rules, **3**, 727
international carriage of passengers and goods, **19**, 1014
lease, **13**, 206
level crossings, *see* LEVEL CROSSINGS
light, **19**, 1001, 1074–1087
  acquisition by other bodies, **19**, 1084
  authorisation methods, **19**, 1075
  buildings, acquisition of, **19**, 1086
  classes of, **19**, 1074
  conditions, contravention of, **19**, 1082
  dissolution, **19**, 1087
  financial provisions, **19**, 1083
  land, acquisition of, **19**, 1086
  licensing procedure, **19**, 1075
  local authority, **19**, 1081
  maintenance, **19**, 1074
  management, **19**, 1074
  managing body, constitution of, **19**, 1083
  meaning, **19**, 1074
  order, **19**, 1075
    amendment of, **19**, 1085
    applicant for, **19**, 1076
    application for, **19**, 1077
    consideration by Secretary of State, **19**, 1078
    contents, **19**, 1080
    grant, grounds for, **19**, 1079
    provisional, **19**, 1079, 1080
    refusal, grounds for, **19**, 1079
  public roads, lines laid along, **19**, 1074

Railways—*continued*
light—*continued*
    regulations, contravention of, **19**, 1082
    statutory code, **19**, 1074
    tramway, of nature and status of, **19**, 1084, 1084*n*, 1130
    winding up, **19**, 1087
malicious damage to, **19**, 1064
milestones, **19**, 1039
    damage to, **19**, 1039
mineral railway, **24**, 678
Minister of Transport, **19**, 1002
misconduct on, **19**, 1064
narrowing, **19**, 24
nationalisation, **19**, 1001, 1088
nuisance—
    prevention of, **19**, 1015
    smoke, **19**, 1052
obstruction—
    of railway, **19**, 1015
    of railway officials, **19**, 1062
offences—
    alcohol on football trains etc, **19**, 1066
    damages in addition to penalty, **19**, 1065
    malicious damage, **19**, 1064
    misbehaviour by passenger, **19**, 1060
    misconduct, **19**, 1064
    obstruction of railway officials, **19**, 1062
    operation of railways, connected with, **19**, 1001
    prosecution of, **19**, 1060–1067
    railway employees, by, **19**, 1067
    railway undertakers' enforcement powers, **19**, 1060–1067
    ticket, **19**, 1060, 1061
    trespass on railway property, **19**, 1063
    wrong class of carriage, travel in, **19**, 1060, 1061
officials, obstruction of, **19**, 1062
organisation, **19**, 1001
passenger transport areas, authorities and executives, **19**, 1095
passengers, **19**, 1072
    accidents to, **19**, 1072
    British Railways Board liability towards, **19**, 1013
    international carriage, **19**, 1014
    permitted to cross on the level, **19**, 1035
    safety of, responsibility for, **15**, 298
point rods, **19**, 1069
premises—
    fire certificates, **10**, 1454
    health and safety at work legislation, **19**, 343
provisional order in connection with, **19**, 15, 26
railway services, closure of, **19**, 1096–1100
refreshments, provision of, **19**, 1005
regional railway boards, **19**, 1007
    corporate status, **19**, 1007
regulations for working, **19**, 1001
relaying and repair gangs, safety of, **19**, 1069
right of way, severing, **19**, 1045
roads, crossing, **19**, 1025, 1026
    bridge, by, **20**, 645
        construction costs, **20**, 645
        liability for, **20**, 645
        not owned by railway operator, where, **20**, 645
    See also LEVEL CROSSINGS

Railways—*continued*
rolling stock, meaning, **19**, 1102*n*
safety—
    access to adjoining land, **19**, 1019
    additional land required for, **19**, 1019
Scottish historical railways records, **19**, 853
Scottish Transport Group, **19**, 1094
sheriff court jurisdiction, **6**, 1125
shunting, **19**, 1069
signal wires, **19**, 1069
smoke, **9**, 1126; **19**, 1052
smoking, byelaws as to, **19**, 1015
sporting events, designated, journey to or from, **19**, 1066
stations—
    approaches and exits, **3**, 711
    byelaws regulating, **19**, 1015
    construction, **19**, 1036
    crowd control, **3**, 712
    exclusion of persons from, **19**, 1060
    platforms—
        crossings between, **3**, 713
        lighting, **3**, 712
        provisions as to, **3**, 711, 712
        signposting, **3**, 712
        train short of or overshooting, **3**, 714
    sub-surface, prevention of fires at, **19**, 1057
stock and plant—
    diligence, exclusion from effects of, **19**, 1101
    distress for rent, exclusion from, **19**, 1102
sub-surface stations, prevention of fires at, **19**, 1057
support—
    mining codes, **14**, 1690
    notices, **14**, 1691
    working minerals, **14**, 1692
surface, **14**, 1644
tickets—
    byelaws concerning, **19**, 1015
    platform, **19**, 1015
    ticket offences, **19**, 1060, 1061
trees, removal of, **19**, 1038
trespass on railway property, **19**, 1063
    injury sustained through, Criminal Injuries Compensation Scheme, **7**, 1, 3, 14
tunnels—
    cattle-grids over or near, **19**, 1029
    land over, **19**, 1037
    underground, **19**, 14
underground stations, prevention of fires at, **19**, 1057
undertaker—
    exemption from liability, **19**, 1023
    statutory powers, **19**, 1024
valuation for rating of railway lands and heritages, **24**, 719–728
wagons, **19**, 1050
    brake levers, **19**, 1069
    labelling, **19**, 1069
widening, **19**, 24
See also PASSENGER
Rainbow trout, **11**, 52
fish farms, **11**, 58

Rainfall
flood warning system, **25**, 379
shortage, leading to serious deficiency, **25**, 516
Raising powder
food standard, **11**, 353
Rallying
regulations as to, **19**, 1284, 1286
Ramps
building controls, **3**, 208
Ramsay, Allan
poem on arbitration, **13**, 576*n*
Ramsay principle
tax avoidance schemes, **19**, 1508, 1509
Rankine, Sir John
Law of Leases in Scotland, **13**, 596
Ransom
meaning, **17**, 416
Rape
actus reus, **7**, 35
art and part liability, **7**, 177, 180
assault, and, **7**, 215, 236, 243
character of victim, admissibility of facts as to, **10**, 634
child, of, **3**, 1250; **7**, 4
child conceived as result of, **10**, 1169
    Criminal Injuries Compensation Scheme, **7**, 1, 7, 11
cognitive element, **7**, 79
cohabitee, of, **10**, 1010
consent, relevancy, **7**, 93
Criminal Injuries Compensation Scheme, **7**, 1, 7
criminal jurisdiction, **17**, 516
criminal registers concerning, access to, **19**, 879
death during course of, **7**, 270
definition, **7**, 296, 297
drugged or intoxicated victim, **7**, 297, 299
    administration of drugs or alcohol, **7**, 299
enticement to leave spouse, **15**, 596
error of fact, **7**, 97
evidence, admissibility of, **10**, 502
firearm or imitation firearm possessed during, **10**, 1565
fraudulent misrepresentation, **7**, 297, 300
girl under age of sixteen, sexual intercourse with, **3**, 1235
girl under age of twelve, sexual intercourse with, **3**, 1235
High Court of Justiciary jurisdiction, **6**, 867
'homosexual', **7**, 296
husband, by, **7**, 294, 302
incest, and, **7**, 316
man may not be raped, **7**, 296
marriage, within, **10**, 840
mens rea, **7**, 97, 303
mentally defective woman, **7**, 301
more than one mental element, where, **7**, 85
overcoming of the will, **7**, 296, 297
penalties, **7**, 296
penetration, degree, **7**, 296
physical requirements, **7**, 296
presence at, **7**, 39
private prosecution, **7**, 26; **17**, 528
recklessness, **7**, 303, 304
reform of law, **7**, 294

Rape—*continued*
resistance, woman's, **7**, 297
semen, emission, **7**, 296
sexual assault, as, **7**, 295
sleeping or unconscious woman, **7**, 297, 298
threats or force, sue of, **7**, 297
under-age girl, **3**, 1235; **7**, 301, 304, 308
willing woman withdrawing consent, **7**, 297
Rat
discouragement and destruction, **19**, 326
freedom of mine from, **14**, 1664
ship, holes in made by, **21**, 551*n*
Rateable value
See VALUATION FOR RATING
Ratepayer
fiduciary duty owed by local authority, **14**, 132
Rates
bond and disposition in security, liability of creditor for, **20**, 116
compulsory reduction in, **14**, 878
Crown bodies, **7**, 753
demand, defences to, **14**, 850
determination of rate—
    duty, **14**, 835
    mode, **14**, 836
    non-domestic ratepayers, consultation with, **14**, 839
    prescribed date, **14**, 837
    revenue budget, **14**, 838
domestic, replacement by community charge, **19**, 1538
'domestic subjects'—
    abolition of, **24**, 610, 617
electricity boards, paid by, **9**, 626
enterprise zone, exemption for, **14**, 646
expenses of local authority, how met, **14**, 834
fixing, **14**, 7
heritable securities, competition with, **20**, 249
levying of—
    assessment roll, **14**, 842
    collection, **14**, 845
    demand note—
        appeal against, **14**, 844
        issue of, **14**, 843
        supporting information, **14**, 843
    rating authorities, **14**, 840
    recovery, **14**, 845
    subjects on which levied, **14**, 841
    valuation for, *see* VALUATION FOR RATING
messenger-at-arms, recovery by, **14**, 1504
non-domestic sewerage, **14**, 859
partial residential subjects, **24**, 611
poinding on summary warrant, **8**, 245
prescribed classes of domestic subjects, **24**, 613–615
rate support grant—
    estimated aggregate, redetermination of, **14**, 879
    expenditure guidelines, **14**, 875
    general abatement, **14**, 879
    generally, **14**, 832
    reduction of element of, **14**, 876
rate-capping—
    procedure, timetable for, **14**, 881

Rates—*continued*
rate-capping—*continued*
    rate levels, order controlling, **14**, 880
    taxing powers, **14**, 7
rateable value, *see* VALUATION FOR RATING
rebate—
    generally, **14**, 860
    housing benefits, **14**, 862
    revaluation, **14**, 865
recovery of—
    appeal, **14**, 849
    generally, **14**, 845
    imprisonment, **14**, 848
    ordinary process, **14**, 846
    priority of claims, **14**, 852
    rate demand, defence to, **14**, 850
    summary warrant, **14**, 847
    supplementary powers, **14**, 851
redetermination by local authority, **14**, 877
reliefs—
    charities, **14**, 861
    disabled person, **14**, 863
    generally, **14**, 860
    unoccupied premises, **14**, 864
reserved functions, **14**, 236
revaluation, **14**, 865
roads, valuation and rating, **20**, 722
sale of heritage, **20**, 917
sheriff court jurisdiction, **6**, 1126
statutory meeting to fix, **14**, 1311
telecommunications operator, **16**, 1954
valuation for rating, *see* VALUATION FOR RATING
valuation roll as basis for levying, **6**, 939–941; **24**,
    436
    See also VALUATION ROLL
water—
    collection, **14**, 860
    direct charge, **14**, 856
    domestic, **14**, 855; **25**, 533
    generally, **14**, 853; **25**, 532
    levy, **14**, 860
    non-domestic, **14**, 858; **25**, 535
    public, **14**, 854

Ratification
actings of person acting without authority, of, **16**,
    1644

Rating authority
meaning, **14**, 840
special powers, **8**, 128

Real burden
ambiguous expressions read *contra proferentem*, **18**,
    416, 419
benefit conferred, **18**, 407
breach, remedies, **18**, 423, 424
character, restrictions on, **18**, 391
charter of novodamus—
    extinction by, **18**, 426
    new burdens imposed by, **18**, 426
    registration, **18**, 426
co-disponees—
    implied rights, **18**, 404
    interest of must be established, **18**, 430
    mutuality principle, **18**, 435

Real burden—*continued*
co-feuars—
    creation of, **18**, 399
    dominant, **18**, 400
    enforcement by, **18**, 429
    enforcement *inter se*, **18**, 415
    feuing plan enforceable by, **18**, 401
    implied rights, and, **18**, 399
    interest of must be established, **18**, 430
    interest to enforce lying with, **18**, 408
    juridical basis of co-feuars' rights, **18**, 402
    jus quaesitum tertio, rights as, **18**, 402
    mutuality principle, **18**, 435
    notice to servient, method of giving, **18**, 400
    praedial nature of rights, **18**, 402
    rights of enforcement, whether reciprocal, **18**,
        400
    separate properties held subject to same burden,
        where, contravention by one property, **18**,
        429
    successive grants by superior, **18**, 400, 401
    superior compared, **18**, 408
common property, **18**, 23, 26
compulsory purchase, effect, **18**, 436
consolidation, extinction by, **18**, 432
content, restrictions as to, **18**, 385*n*, 386, 391
contra proferentem rule, **18**, 390, 419
contravention—
    acquiescence—
        completed contravention, **18**, 428
        generally, **18**, 427
        prospective contravention, **18**, 429
    separate properties held subject to same burden,
        where, **18**, 429
conveyance—
    creation in, **6**, 497; **18**, 386, 387, 388
    feu, grant in, where, **18**, 387
    ordinary disposition, where, **18**, 387
    subsequent, repetition in, **18**, 396
creation—
    conveyance, in, **18**, 386, 387, 388
    deed of conditions, in, **18**, 386, 387, 388
    only principal deed may be consulted, **18**, 388
deed of condition, creation in, **18**, 386, 387, 388
deed creating, dominant tenement, specification,
    18, 397
default in performance, irritancy clause, *see*
    irritancy *below*
discharge, *see* extinction *below*
disponee—
    co-disponee—
        implied rights, **18**, 404
    co-disponees—
        enforcement *inter se*, **18**, 415
disponer—
    implied rights, **18**, 403
    interest to enforce, **18**, 407, 408
    irritancy action by, **18**, 424
    property reverting to original in irritancy
        action, **18**, 424, 424*n*
    superior compared, **18**, 408
dominant proprietor, **18**, 383
    acquiescence by, **18**, 427

Real burden—*continued*
dominant proprietor—*continued*
contravention by servient proprietor, implied consent or acquiescence to, **18**, 427–429
agent, knowledge by, **18**, 427
discharge of burden by, **18**, 426
interpretation against, **18**, 415, 416
title and interest, must be able to show, **18**, 397
two or more—
implied consent or acquiesence by one, **18**, 427
unreasonable withholding of consent, **18**, 416, 422
See also superior *below*
dominant tenement—
deed, specified in, **18**, 397
disponer, **18**, 403
division, **18**, 409
dominium utile as, **18**, 409
enforcement, *see* enforcement *below*
implied, **18**, 397
co-feuars, **18**, 399
obligation imposed for benefit of, **18**, 386, 387, 391
physical changes affecting, extinction by, **18**, 434
requirement for, **18**, 386, 387
right to enforce, generally, **18**, 397
servient tenement coming into same ownership, **18**, 433
single grant followed by sub-division, **18**, 401
subdivision, **18**, 387
successive grants, **18**, 400, 401
superior, **18**, 403
superiority, **18**, 398, 409
two or more, **18**, 387
dominium utile—
consolidation or irritancy, **18**, 432
subdivision, **18**, 409, 414
superiority coming into same ownership, **18**, 433
draftsmanship, rules of, **18**, 390
Edinburgh New Town cases, **18**, 376–379
emergence as separate category, **18**, 385
enforcement—
co-disponees, enforcement *inter se*, **6**, 507; **18**, 415
co-feuars—
enforcement *inter se*, **18**, 415
generally, **6**, 506; **18**, 408, 429
rights of, juridical basis, **18**, 402
defences, **18**, 425
disponer, **18**, 407, 408
division of dominant tenement, effect, **18**, 409
express rights, **18**, 405
heritable creditor, no right of, **18**, 406
implied rights—
co-disponees, **18**, 404
co-feuars, **18**, 399–402
disponer, **18**, 403
superior, **18**, 398
interest to enforce, **18**, 397, 407, 408
establishment of interest, **18**, 430
loss of, **6**, 508; **18**, 430

Real burden—*continued*
enforcement—*continued*
interest to enforce—*continued*
patrimonial, whether, **18**, 407, 408
presumption of interest, **18**, 430
title, may be uncoupled from, **18**, 408
irritancy, **18**, 424, 424n
non-owner, rights of, **18**, 406
original parties to grant, between, **18**, 415
reciprocity, **18**, 400
remedies, **18**, 423
irritancy clause, default, **18**, 424
rules for, **18**, 384
single grant followed by subdivision, **18**, 401
successive grants, **18**, 400
successors, against, **18**, 384
superior, **6**, 505; **18**, 407, 408, 429
tenant, rights of, **18**, 406
title to enforce, **18**, 397
interest, may be uncoupled from, **18**, 408
trivial burdens and interests, **18**, 407
exhibited plans, whether enforceable, **18**, 378, 379
express rights, **18**, 405
extent, restriction as to, **18**, 391
extinction—
acquiescence, **6**, 509, 510; **18**, 427
completed contravention, **18**, 428
charter of *novodamus*, **18**, 426
completed contravention, **18**, 428
compulsory purchase, effect of, **18**, 436
consolidation of feu, **18**, 432
deed of discharge, **18**, 426
dominant and servient tenement coming into single ownership, **18**, 433
express consent, **18**, 426
failure to appear on Land Register, **18**, 437
heritable property, agreement relating to, **18**, 426
implied consent, **18**, 427
informal consent, **18**, 426
irritancy of feu, **18**, 432
loss of interest to enforce, **18**, 430
minute of waiver, **18**, 426
mutuality principle, **18**, 435
negative prescription, **18**, 431
partial, **18**, 426
payment in exchange for discharge, **18**, 426
physical changes affecting either tenement, **18**, 434
prospective contravention, **18**, 429
variation and discharge by Lands Tribunal, **6**, 511–513; **18**, 426, 438
extrinsic evidence, **18**, 390
failed—
incapable of rescue, **18**, 392
original parties bound by, **18**, 392
feudal condition—
compared, **18**, 380, 382
model, as, **18**, 393
relationship with, **18**, 385, 385n, 393
feudal grant, **18**, 398
co-feuars, **18**, 399
consolidation or irritancy, **18**, 432

Real burden—*continued*
feudal grant—*continued*
  negative prescription, whether subject to, **18**, 431
  real burden compared, **18**, 376
  See also FEUDAL LAW
feuing plan put into words, as, **18**, 379, 379n
freedom, presumption for, **18**, 416
heritable security (pecuniary real burden), **18**, 375
immediated connection with estate, **18**, 391n
implied, **18**, 378
implied rights—
  co-feuars, **18**, 399
  disponer, **18**, 403
  superior, **18**, 398
imprecise obligation, failure of, **18**, 416
in rem, **18**, 344
interest to enforce, *see* enforcement *above*
interpretation—
  ambiguous expressions read *contra proferentem*, **18**, 416, 419
  consent of dominant proprietor not to be unreasonably withheld, **18**, 416, 422
  freedom, presumption for, **18**, 416
  generally, **18**, 415
  imprecise obligation, failure of, **18**, 416
  objects rule, **18**, 416, 420
  precision, requirement for, **18**, 416, 418
  structure and use of buildings, **18**, 416, 421
  words cannot be implied, **18**, 416, 417
introduction, **18**, 375
irritancy—
  clause—
    effect, **18**, 424
    generally, **18**, 390, 424
    purpose, **18**, 424
  clauses irritant and resolutive, **18**, 424n
  disponer—
    action by, **18**, 424
    property reverting to original, **18**, 424, 424n
  entails, **18**, 424n
  express provision, necessity for, **18**, 424
  extinction by, **18**, 432
  purgation, **18**, 424
  superior, action by, **18**, 424
juristic basis, **18**, 380
lands, running with, **18**, 387, 391
  importance of drafting obligation, **18**, 390
Lands Tribunal, variation or discharge by, **18**, 395
legal, must be, **18**, 391
liability—
  division of servient tenement, where, **18**, 414
  failure where imprecise, **18**, 416–418
  identification of servient tenement, **18**, 410
  indefinite sum, for, **18**, 418
  interpretation, *see* interpretation *above*
  liferenter, **18**, 413
  maintenance, obligation as to, **18**, 418
  maintenance costs, for, **18**, 418
  mutuality principle, **18**, 435
  non-owner, **18**, 413
  pro indiviso shares as servient tenements, **18**, 411
  servient proprietor, **18**, 412
  tenant, **18**, 413

Real burden—*continued*
liability—*continued*
  time limit for, **18**, 418
  transferee, **18**, 412
  transferor, **18**, 412
maintenance, obligation as to, **18**, 418
  maintenance costs, liability for, **18**, 418
  rebuilding obligation included in, **18**, 418
  standard of performance, **18**, 418
  where property to be maintained not part of servient tenement, **18**, 418
meaning, **18**, 344n, 375, 383, 386
mutuality principle, **18**, 435
negative prescription, **18**, 431
  change in ownership during period, **18**, 431
  relevant period, **18**, 431
  subdivision of dominant or servient tenement, where, **18**, 431
neighbourhood, change in nature of, **18**, 430
non-feudal—
  dominant property, **18**, 350
non-owner, rights of, **18**, 406
nuisance clauses, **18**, 418
objects rule, **18**, 416, 420
origins and early history, **18**, 376–379
patrimonial benefit must be conferred, **18**, 407, 408
pecuniary real burden—
  compared, **18**, 380, 383, 391n
  confusion with, **18**, 385, 385n
perpetual personal obligation, as, **18**, 383
personal bond compared, **18**, 391n
physical distance between tenements, **18**, 407
praedial, must be, **18**, 391, 397
praedial benefit, **18**, 407
praedial nature, co-feuar's rights, **18**, 402
precision, requirement for, **18**, 416, 418
property and proprietary rights, limitations repugnant to, **18**, 391
prototypes for—
  feudal condition, **18**, 380, 382, 384, 385
  pecuniary real burden, **18**, 380, 383, 384, 385
  servitude, **18**, 380, 381, 384, 385
public policy, must not be contrary to, **18**, 391
purpose, **18**, 375
real condition, as, **18**, 344, 375, 381, 387
registration, **18**, 386, 389
  limited period for, creation of, **18**, 389, 389n
  position before, **18**, 389
remedies—
  damages, **18**, 423
  implement, **18**, 423
  interdict, **18**, 423
  irritancy clause, default, **18**, 424
restraints imposed, **18**, 407
restriction must match facts as they appear on the ground, **18**, 388
rules of constitution, **18**, 380, 384, 386–392
  content, as to, **18**, 386, 391
  conveyance or statutory deed of conditions, burden must be contained in full in, **18**, 386, 388
  dominant and servient tenement, **18**, 386, 387
  failure to comply with, **18**, 392

Real burden—*continued*
rules of constitution—*continued*
form, as to, **18**, 386, 390
generally, **18**, 386
mandatory nature, **18**, 392
patrimonial (praedial) benefit must be conferred, **18**, 407, 408
registration, **18**, 386, 389
separate properties held subject to same burden, where—
contravention by one property, **18**, 429
servient proprietor, **18**, 383
contravention—
implied consent by dominant proprietor, **18**, 427–429
agent, knowledge by, **18**, 427
infeft or uninfeft, **18**, 412
interpretation in favour of, **18**, 415, 416
liability, **18**, 412
pro indiviso shares as servient tenements, **18**, 411
transferee, liability, **18**, 412
transferor, liability, **18**, 412
servient tenement—
conveyance or deed must relate to, **18**, 388
conveyance of, **18**, 387
deed of conditions made with reference to, **18**, 387
division, **18**, 414
feudal, **18**, 414
physical, **18**, 414
dominant tenement coming into same ownership, **18**, 433
dominium utile, **18**, 414
identification, **18**, 410
non-owner, liability, **18**, 413
notice of change of ownership, **18**, 412
obligation imposed on owner of, **18**, 386, 387, 391
physical changes affecting, extinction by, **18**, 434
pro indiviso shares as, **18**, 411
requirement for, **18**, 386, 387
subdivision of, **18**, 387
superiority, **18**, 414
tenant, liability, **18**, 413
two or more, **18**, 387
servitude compared, **18**, 380, 381
single act, obligation to perform, **18**, 390, 390*n*
structure and use of buildings, as to, **18**, 416, 421
style of building, description of, **18**, 418
sub-division—
clearly not intended by superior, where, **18**, 401
express prohibition on, **18**, 401
single grant followed by, **18**, 401
subsequent disposition, created by, consolidation and irritancy, **18**, 432
successive grants, **18**, 400
co-disponees, **18**, 404
superior—
co-feuar compared, **18**, 408
consent not to be unreasonably withheld, **18**, 422
discharge of burden by, **18**, 426

Real burden—*continued*
superior—*continued*
disponer compared, **18**, 408
enforcement by, **18**, 429
interest may be uncoupled from title, **18**, 408
interest of presumed, **18**, 430
interest to enforce, **18**, 407, 408
irritancy action by, **18**, 424
notification of change of vassal, **18**, 412
obligations burdening, **18**, 394, 394*n*
mutuality principle, **18**, 435
oppressive or capricious actions, **18**, 408
See also dominant proprietor *above*
superiority—
consolidation or irritancy, **18**, 432
dominium utile coming into same ownership, **18**, 433
subdivision, whether capable of, **18**, 409, 409*n*
Tailors of Aberdeen v Coutts, decision in, **18**, 384, 384*n*, 385, 386
tenant, rights of, **18**, 406
time limits, **18**, 418
transfer of ownership, and, **18**, 604
unassignable nature, **18**, 383
unenforceable, burden proving to be, **18**, 389
unlawful construction, **18**, 423
variation or discharge by Lands Tribunal, **18**, 395, 438
warrandice, obligation of, **18**, 705, 705*n*
wording, importance of, **18**, 390
Real condition
benefit conferred must be praedial, **18**, 348
benefited proprietor, **18**, 344*n*
burdened proprietor, **18**, 344*n*
characteristics, **18**, 344
common interest, *see* COMMON INTEREST
common property, **18**, 23, 26
conditions *in personam*, **18**, 344, 346, 347
conditions *in rem*, **18**, 344, 347
constitution, rules of, **18**, 349
content, rules as to, **18**, 344, 348
dominant property—
condition must benefit, **18**, 348
existence presupposed by existence of real condition, **18**, 349
more than one, where, **18**, 345
second interest in servient property as, **18**, 349, 351
separate land as, **18**, 349, 350
servient property need not be contiguous, **18**, 348
sub-division of, **18**, 345, 345*n*
two or more people owning, **18**, 345
dominant proprietor—
enforcement *in personam* against servient proprietor, **18**, 346
meaning, **18**, 345
two or more, where, **18**, 345
dominant tenement—
generally, **18**, 344
lease, in, **18**, 351, 352
right to enforce derived from ownership of, **18**, 344, 345
standard security, in, **18**, 351

Real condition—*continued*
dominant tenement—*continued*
  superiority, **18**, 351
  use of term, **18**, 344*n*
enforcement, right of, **18**, 344, 345
floating charges, **18**, 353
heritable property, **18**, 344, 349
in personam, **18**, 344
in rem, **18**, 344
invariable pertinent as, **18**, 201
land presumed free from perpetual burdens, **18**, 349
lease, assignation of, **18**, 351, 352
long lease, creation of real conditions in assignations, **13**, 337
meaning, **18**, 344, 375
moveable property, **18**, 344, 349, 353
property law, as part of, **18**, 346
real burden, meaning, **18**, 344, 381, 387
  See also REAL BURDEN
registration, **18**, 349
servient property—
  condition must regulate, **18**, 348
  dominant property need not be contiguous, **18**, 348
  dominium utile of land, as, **18**, 349
  existence presupposed by existence of real condition, **18**, 349
  generally, **18**, 344
  land, as, **18**, 349
  lease, in, **18**, 352
  lease, right of, as, **18**, 349
  real right over, **18**, 344, 347
  second interest in same piece of land, **18**, 349, 351
  separate land as, **18**, 349, 350
  servient tenement, use of term, **18**, 344*n*
  sublease, right of, as, **18**, 349
servient proprietor—
  enforcement *in personam* against, **18**, 346
  personal right against, **18**, 344, 346
servitude, **18**, 344, 381
standard security, in, **18**, 351
superiority, in, **18**, 351
things, functions of in relation to, **18**, 346
third parties, no independent rights of enforcement, **18**, 345
transfer of ownership, adverse real conditions, **18**, 604
two pieces of property, existence of as fundamental feature, **18**, 344
who may hold, **18**, 344
See also LAND OBLIGATIONS
Real estate
loan on security of, *see* HERITABLE SECURITY
meaning, **25**, 607
Real evidence
See EVIDENCE
Real injury
general principle of, **7**, 13
Real lien
See REAL BURDEN
Real property
See REALTY

Real right
air, right to, **18**, 5
ancillary personal right, warrandice, **18**, 718
assignation, **18**, 8
civil possession, title to sue, **18**, 141
classification—
  dominium and subordinate rights, **18**, 6
  holder of right, by reference to, **18**, 7
common interest, right of, **18**, 7, 290
competing titles—
  'offside goals', rule against—
    antecedent contract or other obligation—
      breach, **18**, 698
      generally, **18**, 696
      remedies, **18**, 700
    bad faith, **18**, 699
    double grant, where, **18**, 697
    generally, **18**, 695
    personal rights competing with real rights, **18**, 690, 693, 694
    reduction of prohibited grant, **18**, 700
    remedies, **18**, 700
    value, absence of, **18**, 699
    warrandice, breach of, **18**, 697
  personal rights competing with real rights—
    grant in breach of trust, **18**, 691
    grantee not bound by personal obligations of author, **18**, 688
    granter's power to grant unimpaired by personal obligations, **18**, 689
    'offside goals', rule against, **18**, 690, 693, 694
    secured creditors, **18**, 693
    unsecured creditors, **18**, 694
    voidable title, grant by one holding, **18**, 692
  real right competing with real right—
    first completion, rule of, **18**, 684
    Land Register titles, **18**, 685
    last completion, rule of, **18**, 685
    rights in security, competing, **18**, 686
    subordinate real rights, transferee affected by, **18**, 687
confusion, doctrine of, **18**, 9
contract, originating in, **18**, 8
creation, **18**, 8
destruction of the thing, **18**, 9
disposition, **18**, 8
dominium, **18**, 4, 5
  See also DOMINIUM; OWNERSHIP
double grant—
  compatible and incompatible grants, **18**, 697
  'offside goals', rule against, **18**, 697
enforcement, **18**, 3
exclusive privilege, **18**, 4, 5
expiry of term, **18**, 9
extinction, **18**, 9
fishing rights, **18**, 5
foreshore, public rights in, **18**, 5
grant in breach of pre-existing contract or other obligation, **18**, 695
held in one piece of land by persons in their capacity as owner of another piece of land, **18**, 7
incorporeal property, **18**, 11
intellectual property, **18**, 5

Real right—*continued*
irritancy, **18**, 9
jura ad rem, possession, **18**, 128
jurae in re aliena, **18**, 6
jus possidendi, title to sue, **18**, 141
land, in—
  heritable right, as, **18**, 14
  uncompleted, **18**, 14
landowner, grant by, **18**, 195
lease, *see* LEASE-LEASING
lease as—
  historical background, **13**, 292–294
  ish, requirements as to, **13**, 301–303
  land, subject must be—
    generally, **13**, 296
    sporting lease, **13**, 297
  Leases Act 1449 ..., **13**, 293
  parties against whom protection given, **13**, 294
  possession, requirements as to, **13**, 308–313
  protection—
    parties against whom given, **13**, 294
    requisites for, **13**, 295
  purchaser, questions with, **13**, 314–316
  rent, requirements as to, **13**, 304–307
  writing, when lease required in, **13**, 298–300
liferent, *see* LIFERENT
list, **18**, 5
loch, public rights in, **18**, 5
meaning, **18**, 4, 5, 16
more than one in respect of same thing, **18**, 6
navigation rights, **18**, 5
negative prescription, **18**, 9
nemo dat quod non habet rule, **18**, 669, 677
occupatio, doctrine of, **18**, 5
ownerless property, right to acquire, **18**, 5
ownership, **18**, 4, 5
  See also DOMINIUM; OWNERSHIP
personal, assignation, **18**, 718
personal right, **18**, 14
  conversion from, possession and, **13**, 141
positive prescription, **18**, 9
possession, **18**, 126, 127
  civil possession, **18**, 127
  generally, **18**, 5
  natural possession, **18**, 127
  prerequisite, where, **18**, 116
  uncompleted title, where, **18**, 127
  See also POSSESSION
power distinguished, **11**, 1083, 1105, 1106
proper liferent as, **18**, 5, 74
property law, and, generally, **18**, 3
public, rights held by, **18**, 4, 5, 7, 693
real conditions, **18**, 7
registration, **18**, 8
  commercial lease, of, **13**, 585
renunciation, **18**, 9
right in security, *see* RIGHT IN SECURITY
right of way, public, *see* PUBLIC RIGHT OF WAY
rights resembling, **18**, 10
river, public rights in, **18**, 5
sea, public rights in, **18**, 5
security, *see* RIGHT IN SECURITY
servitude, *see* SERVITUDE
standard security, **18**, 8

Real right—*continued*
subordinate—
  creation of, *nemo dat quod non habet* rule, **18**, 669, 677
  generally, **18**, 6
  incorporeal thing, real right granted in respect of, **18**, 16
  warranties, **18**, 704, 704*n*
temporary, **18**, 6
things, in, as right to, **18**, 3, 3*n*, 4, 11, 16
transfer of ownership—
  adverse real rights, **18**, 604
  publicity, requirement for, **18**, 602
  subordinate real rights, grant of, **18**, 605
  See also TRANSFER OF OWNERSHIP
unsecured creditor, and, **18**, 694
which may be held without restriction, **18**, 7
Real subrogation
doctrine of, **24**, 7
Realty
meaning, **25**, 607
personalty distinguished from, **25**, 607
Rebus sic stantibus
See VALUATION FOR RATING
Receipt
information to be stated on, **16**, 1025
stamp duty, **13**, 1757
Receiver
additional statutory powers, **4**, 679
administrative, concept of, **4**, 650, 671
administrator, relationship with, **4**, 636, 708
agent of company, as, **4**, 684
alienation, reduction of, **4**, 680
appointment of, **4**, 76
  chargeholder, by, **4**, 674
  court, by—
    application for, **4**, 675
    circumstances justifying, **4**, 673
  floating charge holder, by, **4**, 672
  generally, **4**, 445
  notice of, **4**, 695
  other parts of UK, in, **4**, 683
  power to appoint, **4**, 671
  quasi-partnership and, **4**, 487
bill of exchange, powers relating to, **4**, 127
care, duty of, **4**, 693
company may not be appointed, **4**, 318
contract—
  employment, of—
    adoption of, **4**, 690
    consultation, **4**, 688
    guaranteed claim, **4**, 689
    no automatic termination, **4**, 687
    preferential claim, **4**, 689
    re-engagement, **4**, 691
    transfer of undertakings, **4**, 692
  entered into by receiver, **4**, 685
  pre-existing, **4**, 686
court, powers of, **4**, 681
debtor's contracts, title to sue, **15**, 822
delict, title and interest to sue, **15**, 230
directions, application for, **4**, 681
directors, relationship with, **4**, 706

Receiver—*continued*
disposal of interest in property—
    authority to dispose, **4**, 711
    effect of, **4**, 710
distribution of money—
    order of, **4**, 704
    right to consign, **4**, 705
duties of—
    care, duty of, **4**, 693
    company's statement of affairs, relating to, **4**, 696
    creditors—
        committee of, **4**, 700
        report to, **4**, 697
        secured, meaning, **4**, 697*n*
    directors' conduct, report on, **4**, 699
    notice of appointment, relating to, **4**, 695
    payments, abstract of, **4**, 698
    receipts, abstract of, **4**, 698
    Registrar of Companies, report to, **4**, 697
    returns, enforcement of duty to make, **4**, 701
    sederunt book, **4**, 703
    specific statutory, **4**, 694
    VAT bad debt certificate, **4**, 702
functions of, **4**, 676
further reform, **4**, 649
insider dealing rules, **12**, 1528
lessor, as, **13**, 178
liquidator, relationship with, **4**, 709
money, distribution of—
    order of, **4**, 704
    right to consign, **4**, 705
other receivers, relationship with, **4**, 707
position after 1961 and before 1972 , **4**, 648
position before 1961, **4**, 647
powers of—
    additional statutory, **4**, 679
    generally, **4**, 677
    power to sue, **4**, 678
pre-existing contracts, **4**, 686
preference, reduction of, **4**, 680
primary function, **4**, 676
property, disposal of interest in—
    authority to dispose, **4**, 711
    effect of, **4**, 710
reflotation after termination, **4**, 715
reform of law relating to, **4**, 308
Registrar of Companies, notice to, **4**, 714
removal of, **4**, 713
remuneration, right to, **4**, 682
resignation of, **4**, 712
specific statutory duties, **4**, 694
termination of receivership—
    reflotation, **4**, 715
    Registrar of Companies, notice to, **4**, 714
    removal, **4**, 713
    resignation, **4**, 712
    vacation of office, **4**, 712
vacating office, **4**, 614, 636, 712
winding up petition by, **4**, 730, 737
See also FLOATING CHARGE
Receiver of wreck
See WRECK

Receivership
adjudication and, **8**, 212
arrestment and, **8**, 295
building contractor, of, **3**, 162*n*
diligence distinguished, **8**, 106
industrial and provident societies, unavailable to, **12**, 641
inhibition and, **8**, 178
irritancy following, **13**, 584
poinding and, **8**, 240
real poinding, and, **8**, 371
sequestration for rent, and, **8**, 389
Receiving stolen property
See RESET
Reckless conduct
result-crime, as, **7**, 46
Reckless cycling
charge of, **20**, 413
warning or notice of intended prosecution, **20**, 446
Reckless driving
causing death by, **20**, 412
    aiding and abetting offence of, **20**, 412
    alcohol consumption, and, **20**, 412
    connection between driving and death must exist, **20**, 412
    disqualification following conviction, **20**, 412, 413, 453
    licence, endorsement of, **20**, 412, 413
dangerous driving, offence to be replaced by, **20**, 412, 413
death not involved, where, **20**, 413
disqualification following conviction, **20**, 453
liege, danger of, **20**, 413
meaning, **20**, 412
necessity, whether defence to, **20**, 413
negligence, **20**, 412
penalties for, **20**, 413
prosecution, warning or notice of intended, **20**, 446
what constitutes, **20**, 413
Reckless error
generally, **7**, 98
Recklessly
assault, **7**, 234, 249
    culpable and reckless endangering of public, **7**, 248, 249
    culpable and reckless injury, **7**, 82, 247, 249
attempted murder, **7**, 168
culpably and recklessly, **7**, 82
intention and—
    intention compared, **7**, 82
    proof of intent, **7**, 88
intoxication, and, **7**, 129, 130, 234
murder, wicked recklessness, **7**, 266, 268, 269, 282
proof of recklessness, **7**, 91
rape, **7**, 303, 304
reckless supply of dangerous substances, **7**, 13, 30, 85
use of term, **7**, 76, 82, 98
Reclamation
lease, **13**, 205

Recognised professional body (RPB)
Insurance Brokers Registration Council, **12**, 809
investment business, relations with, **12**, 1352
promotion and marketing of insurance products,
    regulation of, **12**, 809
register, **12**, 1415
Recognition
casualty of, feudal law, **18**, 82, 82*n*
non-Scottish judgments, of, *see* JUDGMENTS
Recompense
annulment of contract, where, **15**, 66
Bankton's view, **15**, 59
breach of contract, **15**, 67
contract related situations, **15**, 66, 67
    valid subsisting contract, where, **15**, 67, 70
definition, **15**, 60
donation, whether intention of, **15**, 61–63
elements, **15**, 60–63, 82, 83
equitable doctrine, as, **15**, 68
error in fact or in law, **15**, 61–63
examples, **15**, 64–67
future development, **15**, 86
gain, defender must have, **15**, 61, 63
general enrichment action, as, **15**, 73, 82, 83, 86
    objections to, **15**, 85
generally, **15**, 59
hire purchase, sale of goods held on, **15**, 64
improvements made in belief property is one's
    own, **15**, 65
in suo actings by party seeking, **15**, 61–63, 83
loss, pursuer must have suffered, **15**, 61–63, 83
nature of remedy in Scots law, **15**, 82
negotiorum gestio, relationship with, **15**, 65, 83
nemo debet locupletari ex aliena jactura, **15**, 60, 60*n*,
    65, 74
origins of term, **15**, 59
other legal remedies, relationship with, **15**, 68–71
prescription, and, **15**, 70
requirements, **15**, 60–63, 82, 83
resale, profit on, **15**, 64
    liability for, **15**, 57, 64
restitution and repetition distinguished, **15**, 28, 82
service or services, provision of, **15**, 82
Stair's view, **15**, 59
stolen money or negotiable instrument, **15**, 52
subsidiarity, relationship with, **15**, 61, 63, 68–71, 82
unjust enrichment (*lucratus*), **15**, 2, 11, 12, 28, 62,
    63, 64
void contract, where, **15**, 66
Recorded pupil
See SPECIAL EDUCATION
Recording
performance of dramatic or musical work, of,
    offences relating to, **9**, 1006
rights—
    assignation, **18**, 1438
    consent in relation to, **18**, 1436
    copyright—
        Copyright Tribunal, matters which may be
            brought before, **18**, 1436
        European Community legislation, **18**, 1643
    criminal offences, **18**, 1442, 1443
    infringement, **18**, 1442
        remedies for, **18**, 1438

Recording—*continued*
rights—*continued*
    more than one performer, consent of all
        required, **18**, 1436
    permitted acts, **18**, 1439
    re-recordings of earlier performances, **18**, 1437
    rights in performance, and, **18**, 1432, 1435
    transmission, **18**, 1438
trade descriptions, **6**, 122
Recourse agreement
cautionary obligation, whether, **3**, 833, 834
generally, **3**, 816, 833
Recreation
See RECREATION AND SPORT
Recreation and sport
access agreement or order, **25**, 359
access to land for recreational purposes, **25**, 358
alcohol and related offences, **19**, 1269–1272
amenity, improvement of, **25**, 362
animals, involving, **19**, 1292–1295
    criminal law relating to, **19**, 1274, 1275
aviation, **19**, 1287–1291
banning, **19**, 1202, 1226
betting at sporting event, *see* BETTING
boating, **25**, 359
breach of the peace, **19**, 1268
byelaws, **14**, 277, 278; **19**, 1220
canals and inland waterways, **19**, 1106*n*
Central Council for Physical Recreation, **19**,
    1209, 1211
clubs—
    alcoholic liquor, sale of, **19**, 1229
    capital allowances, **19**, 1314
    corporation tax, **19**, 1313, 1314
    incorporated, **19**, 1228
    private—
        racial discrimination practised by, **19**, 1260
        sex discrimination practised by, **19**, 1257
    unincorporated, **19**, 1227
    value added tax, **19**, 1315–1318
contracts of employment, **19**, 1231–1237
    covenants in restraint of trade, **19**, 1235
    dismissal, **19**, 1237
    freedom of contract, **19**, 1236
    inducement of breach, **19**, 1234
    interference with performance of, **19**, 1234
    minors, **19**, 1233
    retention and transfer system, **19**, 1235, 1236
country park, **25**, 360
criminal law relating to, **19**, 1263–1279
    alcohol and related offences, **19**, 1269–1272
    animals, offences involving, **19**, 1274, 1275
    assault, **19**, 1265, 1266
    blood sports, **19**, 1275
    breach of the peace, **19**, 1268
    bribes, **19**, 1273
    conspiracy, **19**, 1273
    crowd control, **19**, 1276–1278
    culpable homicide, **19**, 1264, 1266
    fraud, **19**, 1273
    mobbing, **19**, 1267
    murder, **19**, 1264, 1266
    offences against the person, **19**, 1264–1266
    public tranquility, offences against, **19**, 1267, 1268

Recreation and sport—*continued*
criminal law relating to—*continued*
  rioting, **19**, 1267
  Sundays, control of sport on, **19**, 1279
  supporters, violence among, **19**, 1266
  unintentional killing, **19**, 1264
crowd control, **19**, 1276–1278
discrimination in—
  racial discrimination, **19**, 1259–1261
  religious discrimination, **19**, 1262
  sex discrimination, **19**, 1255–1258
district council, powers and duties, **14**, 690–692
domestic tribunals, **19**, 1239
duty of care, **19**, 1241
  damages, **19**, 1243
  employees, **19**, 1241
  participants, **19**, 1241
  spectators, **19**, 1241
  sporting disasters, **19**, 1244
  third parties, **19**, 1241
  volenti non fit injuria, **19**, 1242
education authorities' duty as to, **19**, 1224
establishment in Scotland, **19**, 1203
expenditure programme, **5**, 585
facilities for—
  byelaws, **14**, 277, 278
  district council, powers and duties, **14**, 690–692
  indoor, licensing of, **14**, 563; **19**, 1254
  islands council, powers and duties, **14**, 690–692
  regional council, financial contributions by, **14**, 693
  sports ground, *see* sports ground *below*
financial assistance, **19**, 1206
fire precautions, **19**, 1253
firearms—
  gunbearers, position in relation to firearm certificates, **10**, 1536
  licence, sports requiring, **19**, 1238
  starters, as, **10**, 1507*n*, 1537
Forestry Commission, facilities provided by, **11**, 610
generally, **25**, 358
grants—
  common good funds, **19**, 1223
  local authority powers, **19**, 1218, 1223
historical background, **19**, 1201–1205
indoor sports premises, **19**, 1254
international sport, **19**, 1208
islands council, powers and duties, **14**, 690–692
land acquired for, from heir to entail, **14**, 322
leisure businesses, taxation of, **19**, 1319–1324
licence of indoor premises, **19**, 1254
licensing, **19**, 1238
local government, role of, **19**, 1218–1226
mobbing, **19**, 1268
National Playing Fields Association, **19**, 1210, 1219
negligence, **19**, 1241–1244
noise, control of, **25**, 359
nuisance—
  interference with recreational interests as legal, **14**, 2081
  liability for, **19**, 1245
open air, improvement of waterways for, **14**, 683

Recreation and sport—*continued*
participation in, **19**, 1205
police, payment for services of, **19**, 1277
postponement of match, **19**, 1278
prizes, sex discrimination, **19**, 1258
professional sportsmen, *see* PROFESSIONAL SPORTSMEN
public safety, guarantee of, **19**, 1278
public rights—
  foreshore, **18**, 318
  generally, **18**, 494
  swimming, **18**, 518
recreation centres, **19**, 1225
recreation grounds, *see* RECREATION GROUND
recreational provision generally, **19**, 305
reform, **14**, 46
regional council, financial contributions by, **14**, 693
regional park, **25**, 360
regulation—
  autonomous governing bodies, **19**, 1204, 1205, 1206
  central government, by, **19**, 1206–1208
  domestic tribunals, **19**, 1239
  inquiries, **19**, 1207
  international sport, **19**, 1208
  local government, **19**, 1218–1226
  ministerial responsibility, **19**, 1206
  natural justice, **19**, 1240
  non-governmental, **19**, 1205, 1209–1217
  sports-governing institutions, **19**, 1205, 1239
representatives of country, place or area, **19**, 1261
rioting, **19**, 1268
roads and vehicles, **19**, 1284–1286
savings, **14**, 694
Scottish Sports Association, **19**, 1217
sheriff court jurisdiction, **6**, 1098
sporting disasters, **19**, 1244
Sports Council, *see* SPORTS COUNCIL
sports councils, local, **19**, 1221
sports grounds, **19**, 1246–1254
  alteration or extension, **14**, 578; **19**, 1251
  capital allowances for expenditure on, **19**, 1296
  enforcement of provisions, **14**, 580; **19**, 1252
  entry, **14**, 580
  extension of, **14**, 578
  fire precautions, **6**, 1098; **10**, 1471, 1472; **19**, 1253
  inspection, **14**, 580
  large, **14**, 574
  licensing of indoor premises, **19**, 1254
  modification orders, **19**, 1248
  offence, **14**, 581
  prohibition notice, **14**, 579
  safety at, **19**, 305, 358, 1246
  safety certificates, **19**, 1247–1250
    amendment, **14**, 576
    appeal, **14**, 577; **19**, 1250
    application, **14**, 575; **19**, 1249
    cancellation, **14**, 576
    generally, **14**, 574
    modification orders, **19**, 1248
    replacement, **14**, 576
    stands, **14**, 582

Recreation and sport—*continued*

sports grounds—*continued*

safety certificates—*continued*

terms and conditions, **19**, 1247, 1248

transfer, **14**, 576

standard of care, **19**, 1242

statutory bodies, facilities provided by, **25**, 361

stewarding, **19**, 1276

Sundays, control of sport on, **19**, 1202, 1279

taxation—

clubs and associations, *see* clubs and associations *above*

generally, **19**, 1296

leisure businesses, *see* leisure businesses *above*

sportsmen of, *see* PROFESSIONAL SPORTSMAN

tickets, forgery of, **19**, 1273

trusts, **19**, 1230

valuation for rating, **24**, 746

venue for, meaning, **10**, 1471*n*

water authority, provision of facilities by, **14**, 684

water sports and recreation, **19**, 1218, 1280–1283

See also SPORT

Recreation ground

local authority provision of, **11**, 1906

valuation for rating, of, **24**, 689, 690

Red Cross

International Committee of, **19**, 708

Red Deer Commission

See DEER

Red fish

meaning, **11**, 2*n*

Redcliffe-Maud Commission

appointment, **14**, 41

recommendations, **14**, 61

Reddendo

form of clause, **6**, 528

Reddie, James

maritime law, writings on, **19**, 609

Redemption

clauses of, **6**, 521

feu duties, of—

financial provisions upon, **6**, 536

generally, **6**, 535

Halliday Committee recommendations, **6**, 535

notice of, **6**, 536

statutory terms, summary of, **6**, 535

valuable consideration, on sale for, **6**, 537

shareholder, rights of, **25**, 13

Redemption of pawn

See PLEDGE

Redress, substitutory

See DAMAGES

Reduced earnings allowance

entitlement to, generally, **21**, 966

imprisonment of claimant, **21**, 1020

Reduction

actings, **13**, 36

action of, **1**, 325, 331; **6**, 924, 1060

ad hunc effectum, **13**, 64; **18**, 664

arrestment, of, **8**, 300

auditor's certificate, **13**, 37

bars to—

delay, **13**, 60

generally, **13**, 53

Reduction—*continued*

bars to—*continued*

mora, **13**, 60

no purpose or benefit produced by reduction, **13**, 62

prescription, **13**, 61

singular successors, rights of, **13**, 54

third party rights—

generally, **13**, 54

heritable rights, **13**, 55

personal rights, **13**, 59

sales of corporeal moveables, **13**, 58

void deeds and decrees, **13**, 56

voidable deeds and decrees, **13**, 57

catholic, **18**, 664

citation, execution of, **13**, 37

conveyance, **13**, 37

Court of Session—

decrees, **13**, 38

financial agreement by spouses, **13**, 30

jurisdiction, **4**, 6

decree, **13**, 35, 38

in absence, **13**, 40

adoption, of, **13**, 42

extracted, **13**, 39

grounds for reduction, generally, **13**, 43

in foro, **13**, 41

void and voidable, **13**, 35, 56, 57

deed or writing, **13**, 37

grounds for reduction, **13**, 43

informal, **13**, 37

multilateral, **13**, 37

mutual, **13**, 37

null, **13**, 35

probative, **13**, 37

unilateral, **13**, 37

void, **13**, 35

voidable, **13**, 35

defences to—

homologation, **13**, 35

personal bar, **13**, 35

third party rights, **13**, 35

defender—

general interest in action, **13**, 27

patrimonial interest, **13**, 27

production of deed or writing under reduction, **13**, 67

title and interest, **13**, 27

deposit receipt, **13**, 37

donation, of, **13**, 36

effect, **13**, 64

ex capite inhibitionis, **13**, 65

ope exceptionis, **13**, 65

retroactivity, **13**, 64

whether catholic, **13**, 64

electoral decision, **13**, 37

equitable remedy, as, **13**, 25

ex capite inhibitionis, **13**, 44

effect, **13**, 65

ex capite lecti, **13**, 44

exclusion of review—

arbitration, **13**, 34

generally, **13**, 32

statutory, **13**, 33

Reduction—*continued*
feu contract deed plan, **13**, 37
generally, **13**, 25
grounds for—
  action dismissed *ex proprio motu*, **13**, 47, 48
  alienation, **13**, 44
  applicable in exercise of court's ordinary
    jurisdiction, **13**, 44
  auctor in rem suam, **13**, 52
  bad faith, **13**, 44
  bankrupt, alienation or unfair preference by,
    13, 44
  blundered expression, **13**, 44
  court acting in excess of jurisdiction, **13**, 48
  decrees, reduction of, **13**, 43, 45–52
  divorce, transaction designed to defeat claims
    for financial provision on, **13**, 44
  error, **13**, 44, 47
    agent, by, **13**, 47
  ex capite inhibitionis, **13**, 44
  facility and circumvention, **13**, 44
  fiduciary duty, breach of, **13**, 44
  force and fear, **13**, 44
  forgery, **13**, 44
  fraud, **13**, 44
    on the court, **13**, 50
  generally, **13**, 43
  incapacity, **13**, 44
  irregularities in original process, **13**, 49
  minority and lesion, **13**, 44
  omission by party or agent, **13**, 47
  res judicata, **13**, 45, 50
  res noviter, **13**, 51
  review, reduction as mode of, **13**, 46, 47
  spouses, financial agreement between, **13**, 44
  statutory formalities, want of, **13**, 44
  uberrimae fidei contract, **13**, 44
  ultra vires, court acting, **13**, 44, 47, 48
  undue influence, **13**, 44
  whitebonnet, **13**, 44
heritable right, affecting, **13**, 66
heritable security, **13**, 37
incidental procedure, **13**, 66, 67
inter vivos trust, **13**, 37
judicial abandonment, of, **13**, 36
judicial conveyance, involuntary transfer of
  ownership by, **18**, 664
jurisdiction—
  generally, **4**, 6; **13**, 28
  ope exceptionis, **13**, 29
    effect of reduction, **13**, 65
life assurance policy, **13**, 37
local authority decision, of, **13**, 36
meaning, **13**, 25
minutes of meeting, **13**, 37
missive, **13**, 37
nullity, and, **13**, 35
ope exceptionis, **13**, 26, 29, 35
  effect, **13**, 31, 65
  refusal, **13**, 29
  sheriff court, **13**, 31
ordinary action, remedy in, **4**, 960
partial—
  decree arbitral, of, **13**, 63

Reduction—*continued*
partial—*continued*
  generally, **13**, 63
  granted *quoad* award in excess of amount
    sought, **13**, 63
production of deed or writing under, **13**, 67
pupil not properly made defender, **13**, 26
pursuer—
  objecting *ope exceptionis*, **13**, 26
  patrimonial interest, **13**, 26
  title and interest, **13**, 26
rectification by, **13**, 70
remedies akin to, **13**, 69–71
rescissory action, as, **13**, 25, 43
retroactive effect, **13**, 64
review, **13**, 25, 43, 47
  advocation, **13**, 68
  suspension, **13**, 68
  where other modes available, **13**, 46
roup, articles of, **13**, 37
roup sale, **13**, 37
several deeds or writings in one cause, **13**, 26
share transfer, **13**, 37
sheriff court—
  decrees, **13**, 38
  financial agreement by spouses, **13**, 30
  generally, **13**, 30
  objector ordered to find caution or make
    consignation, **13**, 31
  ope exceptionis, **13**, 31
  principal action, as, **13**, 30
sheriff court jurisdiction, **4**, 6
spouses, financial agreement between, **13**, 30, 44
testamentary writing, **13**, 37
title and interest, **13**, 26, 27
  civil right, infringement of, **13**, 26
  contingent, **13**, 26
  jus quaesitum tertio, constituted by, **13**, 26
  patrimonial interest, **13**, 26, 27
  pecuniary interest, **13**, 26
  person not party to decree, reduction by, **13**, 26
town council action, of, **13**, 36
voidable deeds or writings, **13**, 35
Reduction of Intermediate Nuclear Forces
generally, **19**, 712
Redundancy
bumping, **9**, 171
business—
  franchise, transfer of, **9**, 180
  meaning, **9**, 166
  parts of, transfer of, **9**, 181
  tenancy, transfer of, **9**, 180
  transfer of, **9**, 177
  what constitutes, **9**, 179
collective, influence of Community directives, **9**,
  15
complaints and appeals relating to, **6**, 998
dismissal—
  meaning, **9**, 160
  reasons for, **9**, 166, 246, 258
  selection for, **9**, 230
  time for, **9**, 164
  unfair, **9**, 230, 269
employer's reasons, **23**, 765

Redundancy—*continued*
Fund, *see* REDUNDANCY FUND
generally, **9**, 158
impending, consultation in respect of, **4**, 863
lay-off, **9**, 165
lock-out, payment in case of, **9**, 182
meaning, **9**, 246; **23**, 763
misconduct, payment in case of, **9**, 182
notices, **9**, 159
offer—
  different terms, of, **9**, 174
  same terms, of, **9**, 173
payment—
  age, reduction for, **9**, 190
  calculation of, **9**, 189
  claim for, **9**, 187
  damages for personal injury, calculation of, **14**, 1697
  exclusion from—
    agreement, by, **9**, 185
    domestic service by relatives, **9**, 184
    miscellaneous, **9**, 186
    working abroad, **9**, 184
  industrial tribunal, jurisdiction of, **6**, 981; **9**, 306
  lock-out, in case of, **9**, 182
  misconduct, in case of, **9**, 182
  onus of proof, **9**, 188
  rebates, **9**, 191, 192
  renewal of employment contract, effect, **9**, 172
  strike, in case of, **9**, 182
  unfair dismissal, effect on basic award, **9**, 267
place of employment, **9**, 167
re-engagement, effect of, **9**, 172
renewal, of employment contract, effect, **9**, 172
reorganisation—
  bumping, **9**, 171
  shift work, effect on, **9**, 170
shift work, effect of reorganisation on, **9**, 170
short time, **9**, 165
special circumstances, **23**, 766
strike, payment in case of, **9**, 182
suitable employment—
  factors bearing on suitability of, **9**, 176
  reasonable refusal and, **9**, 176
termination—
  earlier, employee's notice of, **9**, 161
  implied, **9**, 162
  trade union consultation on, **6**, 995
trade union, consultation with, **23**, 763–766
transfer of undertakings, **9**, 178
trial period, commencement of, **9**, 175
volunteers for, **9**, 163
work of particular kind—
  changing job skills, **9**, 169
  functions, **9**, 169
  generally, **9**, 168
  reorganisation, **9**, 170
Redundancy Fund
claim from—
  presentation of, **9**, 153
  range of employees protected, **9**, 154
  subrogation, **9**, 157, 192
control of, **9**, 192

Redundancy Fund—*continued*
generally, **9**, 151
preferred debts, **9**, 149
rebates, **9**, 192
scope of, **9**, 152
Reed beds
rating relief, **24**, 560, 731
Reformation
commissary courts, **6**, 918
Crown as corporation, **19**, 206–208
Teind Court, **6**, 921
Reformatory
local authority library service loans to inmates, **13**, 1505
Refreshment licence
effect of, **2**, 14
generally, **11**, 1761*n*
introduction of, **2**, 14
permitted hours, **2**, 18
premises—
  admission of children, **2**, 14
  child or young person on, **3**, 1227
  eligibility of, **2**, 14
unpopularity of, **2**, 14
Refreshment room
hotel distinguished, **11**, 1713
liability, **11**, 1742
part of hotel, as, **11**, 1713
Refreshments
countryside, provision in, **14**, 680
hotelkeeper's duty to provide, **11**, 1720
provision of, **11**, 1720
  refusal to provide, **11**, 1723
refreshment licence, *see* REFRESHMENT LICENCE
refreshment room, *see* REFRESHMENT ROOM
See also FOOD
Refrigeration
supply, charge to VAT, **7**, 1288, 1320
Refugee
appeals, **12**, 322
asylum—
  applicants for, removal of, **12**, 318
  claimed for, **12**, 318
  eligibility for, **12**, 318
  grant of, **12**, 318
  Immigration Rules, **12**, 320
control, application of—
  after entry, **12**, 320
  before entry, **12**, 317
  departure, of, **12**, 321
  on entry, **12**, 318, 319
Convention and Protocol Relating to the Status of Refugees, **12**, 116, 314
definition, **12**, 314
denial of asylum to, **12**, 315
deportation, **12**, 203, 321, 322
  judicial review of decision, **12**, 322
entry clearance, **12**, 151*n*
European Union law, **12**, 222
exceptional leave to remain, **12**, 318, 320, 322
immigration, **12**, 101, 102
  Immigration Acts, **12**, 316
  Immigration Rules, **12**, 116, 316–323

Refugee—*continued*
leave to enter, **12**, 171, 318
   appeal against refusal, **12**, 322
   outside the Rules, **12**, 318
   sought in different capacity, **12**, 317, 319
leave to remain—
   appeal against refusal, **12**, 322
refugee status—
   loss of, **12**, 314
   no appeal against refusal, **12**, 344
   refusal of, **12**, 322
removal, judicial review of decision, **12**, 322
restricted returnability, **12**, 323
rights to be given to, **12**, 314
tactics used to gain entry, **12**, 317
travel documents, **12**, 151*n*, 314, 323; **16**, 1236
   Home Office travel document, **16**, 1237
   visa national holding, **16**, 1210
undertaking course in English, income support,
   21, 1067
United Kingdom law, **12**, 316–323
Refuse
collection—
   explosives, **10**, 1628
   generally, **14**, 706
food businesses, **11**, 408, 410
public health nuisance, as, **19**, 336
tip, theft from, **7**, 333
See also WASTE
Regalia
safe keeping, repair and preservation, **7**, 804
treasure as, **18**, 553
Regalian right
alienation, **18**, 207
fairs and markets, right to hold, **18**, 210
ferry, right of, **18**, 210
forestry, **18**, 213
generally, **18**, 207, 210
heritable jurisdiction, **18**, 213
mineral rights, **18**, 210
mussels, right to gather, **18**, 210
oysters, right to gather, **18**, 210
petroleum and natural gas, rights to, **18**, 210
port, right of, **18**, 210
salmon fishings, **18**, 207, 210
separate tenement by legal implication, as, **18**, 209
wreck (wrak), **18**, 213, 213*n*
Regality
feudal law, generally, **18**, 54
jurisdiction, **18**, 54
Regality, Courts of
abolition, **17**, 504, 525
criminal jurisdiction, **17**, 521
feudal system, **6**, 897
officers, **17**, 521
Regent
choice of, **7**, 705
circumstances requiring, **7**, 705
functions exercised by, **7**, 705
Region
community, identification of, **14**, 53
corporate personality, **14**, 2
education, responsibility for, **14**, 36
highways, responsibility for, **14**, 33

Region—*continued*
map, **14**, 64
structure of, **14**, 55
Regional council
aerodrome, powers relating to, *see* AERODROME
allocation of functions, **14**, 402
bus undertaking, exclusion of power to run, **14**,
   428
byelaws, *see* BYELAWS
civil defence, **14**, 506, 507
coast protection, *see* COAST PROTECTION
concerted action, **14**, 80
Convention of Scottish Local Authorities,
   representation on, **14**, 84
education authority, as, **8**, 701, 712
electoral divisions, **15**, 1036, 1039
employees, election staffing, **15**, 1317
ferries, powers in relation to, *see* FERRY
fire services, *see* FIRE SERVICES
flood prevention, *see* FLOOD PREVENTION
functions—
   concurrent, **14**, 79
   sole, **14**, 78
harbour, acquisition of, **14**, 444
housing, *see* HOUSING
industrial promotion, **14**, 633
inter-authority relationships—
   concerted action, **14**, 80
   concurrent functions, **14**, 79
   generally, **14**, 77
   sole functions, **14**, 78
landlord, as, assured tenancy status excluded, **13**,
   636, 647
library authority, **14**, 687, 689
library service, **13**, 1504
licences, powers relating to, *see* LICENCES
litigation, **14**, 118
name, change of, **14**, 71
new structure, **14**, 64
permit, powers relating to, **14**, 515
pier, acquisition of, **14**, 444
police authority, as, **16**, 1708, 1712, 1713
precedence, **16**, 2002
private legislation, promotion of, **14**, 306
public health matters, **19**, 308, 308*n*
public procession, *see* PUBLIC PROCESSION
public transport, *see* PUBLIC TRANSPORT
regional planning authority, as, **23**, 11
registration, powers relating to, *see* REGISTRATION
registration officer, appointment, **15**, 1083
roads authority, as, **20**, 608
social work, *see* SOCIAL WORK
tourism, promotion of, **14**, 663
trading standards, *see* TRADING STANDARDS
ultra vires principle, application of, **14**, 131
water authority, *see* WATER AUTHORITY
Regional park
provision of, **25**, 360
Regional planning authority
call-in power, recommendations of Stodart
   Committee, **23**, 14
district planning authority, and, **23**, 13
enforcement by, **23**, 286
local plans, reserve powers regarding, **23**, 48

Regional planning authority—continued
meaning, **23**, 11
planning application, reference of, **23**, 168
regional planning functions, **23**, 11
regional report, preparation of, **23**, 26
Regional water boards
establishment, **25**, 502
transfer of functions, **25**, 502
Register House
Edinburgh Castle, records deposited in, **19**, 826, 843
history, **19**, 825–829
  first recorded, **19**, 826
Laigh Parliament House, records deposited in, **19**, 826, 843
Meadowbank House, **19**, 828
meaning of term, **19**, 827
New Register House, **19**, 828
Old Register House, **19**, 827, 828
purpose of, **19**, 827
Registry of Births, Deaths and Marriages, **19**, 828
trustees, **19**, 827
West Register House, **19**, 829
Register of Designs
See INDUSTRIAL DESIGN, PROTECTION OF
  (REGISTERED DESIGNS)
Register of electors
additions to, inspection, **15**, 1237
appeals, **15**, 1119
applications, sending of, **15**, 1150
arrangement, **15**, 1107
claims, **15**, 1110, 1117, 1237
  appeals, **15**, 1119
  disposal, **15**, 1118
  inclusion, for, **15**, 1117, 1237
  notice, **15**, 1117
  objections, **15**, 1237
  sending of, **15**, 1150
  signing of, **15**, 1151
combined poll, **15**, 1375
conclusive nature, **15**, 1111
copies, supply, **15**, 1109, 1237
  polling station, **15**, 1312
correction, **15**, 1110, 1237
duration, **15**, 1237
effect, **15**, 1111
election expenses, calculation of allowable, **15**, 1415
electoral areas, **15**, 1106
  copies to be available in, **15**, 1109
electoral divisions, **15**, 1106
European parliamentary electors, **15**, 1104, 1105, 1113
generally, **15**, 1035, 1103, 1104
inaccurate description, effect of, **15**, 1112
inclusion in, claim for, **15**, 1237
information as to, supply, **15**, 1113
inspection, **15**, 1109
introduction, **15**, 1019
labels, supply of, **15**, 1115
local government electors, **15**, 1104, 1105
mental disorders, persons suffering from, **15**, 1149
misnomer, effect of, **15**, 1112
notice, sending of, **15**, 1150

Register of electors—continued
objections, **15**, 1110, 1117, 1237
  appeals, **15**, 1119
  disposal, **15**, 1118
  sending of, **15**, 1150
  signing of, **15**, 1151
overseas electors, **15**, 1113, 1123
overseas electors' declaration—
  attestation, **15**, 1142
  cancellation, **15**, 1144
  contents, **15**, 1141
  effect, **15**, 1143
  evidential value, **15**, 1143
  generally, **15**, 1113
  notification requirements, **15**, 1145
  qualification as overseas elector, **15**, 1140
  qualification of a peer as overseas elector, **15**, 1146, 1147
  requirements, **15**, 1141
patient's declaration—
  attestation, **15**, 1126
  cancellation, **15**, 1129
  content, **15**, 1125
  effect, **15**, 1127
  generally, **15**, 1113
  local government elections, **15**, 1128
  notification requirements, **15**, 1130
  requirements, generally, **15**, 1125
  United Kingdom parliamentary elections, **15**, 1128
peers entitled to vote in European elections, **15**, 1084, 1105
polling districts, **15**, 1106
preparation, **15**, 1108
publication, **15**, 1108, 1109
purpose, **15**, 1104
registration expenses, payment of, **15**, 1086
relevant citizens of the Union—
  applications by, **15**, 1148
  conditions in respect of, **15**, 1124
  declarations, **15**, 1148
  entitled to vote in European elections, **15**, 1105
  meaning, **15**, 1076
relevant data—
  meaning, **15**, 1115
  supply of, **15**, 1115
right to be registered—
  generally, **15**, 1120
  overseas electors, **15**, 1123
  relevant citizens of the Union, **15**, 1124
  service qualification, **15**, 1122
  voluntary mental patients, **15**, 1121
sale, copies of, **15**, 1116
service declaration—
  attestation, **15**, 1135
  cancellation, **15**, 1138
  contents, **15**, 1133
  effects, **15**, 1136
  generally, **15**, 1113
  local government elections, **15**, 1137
  notification requirements, **15**, 1139
  provisions, generally, **15**, 1132, 1134
  service qualification, **15**, 1131
  United Kingdom parliamentary elections, **15**, 1137

Register of electors—*continued*
service qualification, **15**, 1122
statutory provisions, **15**, 1493
structure, **15**, 1106
supply, **15**, 1114
 data and labels, **15**, 1115
time provisions, **15**, 1108
types of register, **15**, 1105
United Kingdom parliamentary electors, **15**, 1104, 1105
voluntary mental patients, **15**, 1121
voting age, voters attaining, **15**, 1113
wards, **15**, 1106
Register of Inhibitions and Adjudications
See INHIBITIONS AND ADJUDICATIONS, REGISTER OF
Register of Patents
See PATENT
Register of Sasines
See GENERAL REGISTER OF SASINES
Register of Sheriff's Commissions, 6, 463; **19**, 820
Registered club
See CLUB
Registered design
See INDUSTRIAL DESIGN, PROTECTION OF (REGISTERED DESIGNS)
Registered   excise   dealer   and   shipper (REDS)
excise duty, liability to pay, **7**, 1054, 1057
generally, **7**, 1057
goods consigned to, excise duty point, **7**, 1053
importation by, **7**, 1056, 1057
introduction, **7**, 1057
meaning, **7**, 1053*n*
records to be kept, **7**, 1057
regulations as to, power to make, **7**, 1244
Registers
births, *see* BIRTHS, REGISTRATION OF
byelaws, of, **14**, 286
Commonwealth list, **25**, 204
community charges, **14**, 871
deaths, *see* DEATHS, REGISTRATION OF
Department of Registers of Scotland, *see* REGISTERS OF SCOTLAND, DEPARTMENT OF
Inhibitions and Adjudications, *see* INHIBITIONS AND ADJUDICATIONS, REGISTER OF
insolvencies, of, *see* INSOLVENCY
Keeper of, *see* KEEPER OF THE REGISTERS OF SCOTLAND
marriages, *see* MARRIAGES, REGISTRATION OF
members of local authority, **14**, 209
public, *see* PUBLIC REGISTERS
Register of Protests, **6**, 455; **19**, 820
river purification authority, maintained by, **25**, 420
stillbirths, *see* STILLBIRTHS, REGISTRATION OF
veterinary surgeons, **25**, 204, 205
 removal of names from, **25**, 212
 restoration of names to, **25**, 213
See also REGISTRATION
Registers of Scotland, Department of
Chancery Office, **19**, 850
Deeds Office, **19**, 850
duties, **19**, 850
family agreements, deeds relating to, **19**, 850

Registers of Scotland, Department of—*continued*
finance, **19**, 852
Horning Office, **19**, 850
land, deeds relating to, **19**, 850
Land Register of Scotland, **19**, 850
official searches, **19**, 851
private searches, **19**, 851
Sasine Office, **19**, 850
state appointments, deeds relating to, **19**, 850
succession, deeds relating to, **19**, 850
trusts, deeds relating to, **19**, 850
Registrar General for Scotland
annual report, **19**, 1432
Deputy, **19**, 1403
duties, **19**, 1403*n*
indexes of births, marriages and deaths, **19**, 1419
local examiner, appointment of, **14**, 32
offices of, **19**, 1402, 1403
powers, **19**, 1403*n*
Registrar-General of Shipping and Seamen
appointment and duties, **21**, 113
Registrar of births, deaths and marriages
appointment, **7**, 757
dismissal, **7**, 757
status, **7**, 757
Registrar of Companies
annual return, **4**, 334
certificate of—
 change of name, authentication of, **4**, 332
 incorporation of company, authentication of, **4**, 332
 public company's entitlement to commence business, authentication of, **4**, 332
 registration of charge, authentication of, **4**, 332
 re-registration of company, authentication of, **4**, 332, 341
company secretaries, register of, **4**, 434
creation of separate office of, **4**, 303
deemed notice, **4**, 335
director, appointment of, **4**, 404
documents presented to effect registration, **4**, 314
incorporation by registration with, **4**, 314
office of, **4**, 331
official notification, **4**, 333
receivership, termination of, notice of, **4**, 714
returns to, **4**, 834
Registrar   of   Independent   Schools   in Scotland
duties, **8**, 811
Registrar of Joint Stock Companies
incorporation with, **4**, 303, 304
office of, creation, **4**, 303
Registrar of Restrictive Trading Agreements
transfer of functions, **4**, 1126
Registration
alkali works, of, **9**, 1115
child born in UK, **14**, 1912
 See also BIRTHS, REGISTRATION OF
community charge, *see* COMMUNITY CHARGE
day care establishment, **14**, 521
death, *see* DEATH (registration of)

Registration—*continued*
decree of, **8**, 122
deeds, of, *see* DEED
dentistry, graduate or licentiate in, **14**, 1134
district registrar, appointment of, **14**, 249
documents, of, notarial protocols, *see* PUBLIC
    RECORDS
health visitor, *see* HEALTH VISITOR
hearing aid dispenser, **14**, 1171
local examiner, appointment of, **14**, 32
local government duties—
    area repositories, **14**, 586
    authorities, **14**, 583
    census, **14**, 590
    day care establishment, **14**, 521
    deaths, marriages and births, **14**, 32, 589
    district, **14**, 583
    district registrar, appointment, **14**, 249
    fees, **14**, 587
    marriage, **14**, 589
    officers and offices, **14**, 584, 585
    parochial records, **14**, 32
    registers, **14**, 588
    registrar, **14**, 584
    returns, **14**, 588
    senior registrar, appointment, **14**, 249
    war charity, **14**, 518
marriage, *see* MARRIAGES, REGISTRATION OF
medical and allied professions, *see* MEDICAL
    PRACTITIONER
midwife, *see* MIDWIFE
mobile radioactive apparatus, of, **9**, 1187
nationality and citizenship, *see* CITIZENSHIP
noise levels, **9**, 1260
nurse, *see* NURSE–NURSING
optician, **14**, 1166
parochial records, **14**, 32
performing animal, exhibiting or training, **14**, 523
pharmaceutical chemist, **14**, 1160, 1162
radioactive materials, users of, **9**, 1185
residential care establishment, **14**, 521
Royal College of Veterinary Surgeons, **25**, 201,
    206
social work establishment, **14**, 521
title, of, *see* REGISTRATION OF TITLE
war charity, **14**, 518
See also REGISTERS
Registration Appeal Court
Court of Session judges, **6**, 928; **15**, 1119, 1175
judicial precedent, **22**, 326
stated case, **17**, 1454
Registration of title
appeals as to, **6**, 786
boundaries—
    discrepancies in, **6**, 734
    physical objects, in relation to, **6**, 735
builders' developments, **6**, 736
burden—
    title sheets, **6**, 707, 711
    whether entitled to, **6**, 763
common interest, **6**, 781
compulsory, **6**, 714, 715
description of subjects, **6**, 729, 730
effect of, **6**, 726

Registration of title—*continued*
English system compared, **6**, 726
entry guaranteed by state, **6**, 701
examples, **6**, 573
first registration—
    application for, **6**, 721
    completion, **6**, 724
    conveyancing procedure leading to, **6**, 720
    effect, **6**, 726
    forms and reports, **6**, 727, 733
    further information, **6**, 722
    generally, **6**, 718
    non-acceptance of application, **6**, 723
    subsequent dealings in land, **6**, 725
    when transaction occurs, **6**, 719
floating charges, **6**, 775
foreshore, **6**, 778
generally, **19**, 821, 822
Henry Committee Report, **6**, 410, 411, 702
heritable securities, **6**, 774
history in Scotland, **6**, 702
indemnity—
    claims for, generally, **6**, 753
    exclusion of right to, **6**, 756*ff*
    right to, **6**, 755
    Scottish and English registers contrasted, **6**, 754
introduction of, **19**, 821
joint or common property, **6**, 781
kindly tenancy, **6**, 777
land certificate—
    generally, **6**, 470
    interpretation, **12**, 1259
    meaning, **6**, 713
land register, *see* LAND REGISTER OF SCOTLAND
Lands Tribunal for Scotland, **6**, 1143
leases, **6**, 776
maps, **6**, 731, 733
matrimonial homes, occupancy rights, **6**, 783
minerals, **6**, 780
'mirror' principle, **6**, 737
nature of, **6**, 701
operational areas, **6**, 703
'or thereby' rule, **6**, 732
Ordnance map, use of, **6**, 731, 733
overriding interests—
    common property or interest, **6**, 749
    cottar, **6**, 741
    crofter, **6**, 741
    Crown, right or interest of, **6**, 743
    error or omission in noting of, **6**, 764
    floating charge, holder of, **6**, 745
    generally, **6**, 737
    government department, right or interest of, **6**,
        743
    land in relation to, **6**, 749
    landholder, **6**, 741
    lease other than long lease, **6**, 739
    local authority, right or interest of, **6**, 743
    long lease, lease under possession of subjects
        under, **6**, 740
    matrimonial home, **6**, 747, 783
    meaning, **6**, 738
    public authorities, **6**, 743
    rights of way, **6**, 746

Registration of title—*continued*
overriding interests—*continued*
  servitude, dominant proprietor in, **6**, 742
  short lease, **6**, 739, 776
  small tenants, **6**, 741
  spouse, non-entitled, **6**, 747
  telecommunications operator, **6**, 744
  title sheets, noted in, **6**, 711
  unrecorded or unregistered rights, **6**, 748
perfection of missives by, **6**, 573
prescription, **6**, 782
rectification of register, **6**, 750–752, 1143
  See also LAND REGISTER OF SCOTLAND
registration fees, **6**, 787
salmon fishings, **6**, 779
Sasines Register taken over, **6**, 703, 704
Secretary of State may require registration, **6**, 703
servitude, **6**, 784
sheriff court jurisdiction, **6**, 1090
straddling plots, **6**, 717
title sheet, *see* TITLE SHEET
titles, ranking of, **6**, 777, 785
transfer of interest in land, **6**, 714
udal tenure, **6**, 777
unregistered interests, **6**, 148, 714
voluntary, **6**, 716
Registration officer (elections)
absent voting application, grant or refusal, **15**, 1160–1174
  appeals, **15**, 1175
adjudge person's mental capacity, **15**, 1149
appointment, **15**, 1083
data user, as, **15**, 1115
decision of, appeal against, **15**, 1237
discharge of registration duties, **15**, 1085
duties and powers, timetable in respect of, **15**, 1225–1232, 1236, 1237
electors lists—
  alterations and corrections, **15**, 1094, 1095
  claims and objections, **15**, 1097–1102
  preparation and publication, **15**, 1088–1092
  supply, **15**, 1092
expenses of registration, **15**, 1086
functions, **15**, 1084
list of proxies, duty to keep, **15**, 1188
notices and notifications by, **15**, 1150, 1247
  misnomer or inaccurate description, **15**, 1249
  mode, **15**, 1248
official duty, breach of, **15**, 1087
postal votes, records, **15**, 1183–1187
proxy—
  appointment, **15**, 1180
  records, **15**, 1183
register of electors, preparation and publication, **15**, 1106*ff*
Regulated tenancy
generally, **13**, 610
Rehabilitation of offenders
contractual rights and duties, **9**, 118
principle of, **17**, 563
provisions as to, **16**, 1483
Rehabilitation of Offenders Act 1974—
  child, effect on, **3**, 1337

Rehabilitation of offenders—*continued*
spent convictions, **17**, 812
unfair dismissal, **9**, 229
Rehousing
caravan site, displacement from, **5**, 189
local housing authority, obligations of, **5**, 189
Rei interitus
commercial lease, **13**, 579, 581
effect on lease, **13**, 285
frustration of building contract by, **3**, 96
Rei interventus
abstention from action, consisting of, **13**, 135
abstention from looking for other accommodation, **13**, 140
acquiescence, interaction with, **16**, 1613
actings—
  amounting to, **13**, 140
  application of *rei interventus*, **13**, 136
  consisting of, **13**, 135
  known to and permitted by obligor, **13**, 137
  landlord, by, **13**, 140
  unequivocally referable to a lease, **13**, 138
application, **13**, 136
conditions to be satisfied, **13**, 135
constitution and proof, **13**, 130, 135–141
contract, construing, **16**, 1619
definition, **13**, 135
doctrine of—
  averments, **3**, 885
  effect, **3**, 885
  examples, **3**, 885
  imperfections of constitution, where, **3**, 885
  inferred, where, **3**, 885
  obligation not in writing, proposed reforms, **3**, 880
  offer and acceptance, **3**, 883
  proof of cautionary obligation, **3**, 885
  sale of heritage, **20**, 910
  writing subscribed by cautioner, necessity for, **3**, 871, 874
  written documents, **3**, 874
elements of, **13**, 135
grassum, payment of, **13**, 140
increased rent, payment of, **13**, 140
informal lease, **13**, 144
informality—
  actings unequivocally referable to lease, **13**, 138
  agreement not binding where, **13**, 136
loss or inconvenience, **13**, 139
mistaken assumption negotiations have reached point of completion, **13**, 136
nature of, **13**, 135
obligor, actings known to and permitted by, **13**, 137
parole agreement, **16**, 1619
personal bar, and, **16**, 1601
possession—
  effect of, **13**, 140, 141
  generally, **13**, 140
  improvements or alterations, expenditure by tenant on, **13**, 140
sublease in relation to, **13**, 140
tenant, by, **13**, 140
verbal or informally executed agreement perfected by, **13**, 135

Reinstatement clause
meaning, **12**, 890
Reinstatement order
compliance with, **9**, 264
factors to be considered, **9**, 263
generally, **9**, 261
Related actions
conflicts of jurisdiction, **4**, 65
Relative
death of family member—
damages in respect of—
death of claiming relative, **15**, 934
deceased's claim, **15**, 599
derivative claim, **15**, 935
funeral expenses, **15**, 937
generally, **15**, 598
immediate family, **15**, 601, 936
loss of support, **15**, 937
relatives dependent, **15**, 598, 599, 600
specified relatives, **15**, 602
disposal of body, entitlement to arrange, **3**, 503, 506
family relationship, injury to, see FAMILY
RELATIONSHIP
meaning, **15**, 597; **16**, 2164
personal injuries case, as pursuer in—
generally, **16**, 2168
judicial discretion to override time limits, **16**, 2177
legal disability, pursuer under, **16**, 2162, 2170
meaning of relative, **16**, 2164
nature of rights, **16**, 2165
product liability defect, case arising from, **16**, 2192, 2195
Relative nuisance
absolute nuisance distinguished from, **14**, 2006
Relevium
casualty of, feudal law, **18**, 79
Relief
casualty of, feudal law, **18**, 79, 80
Relief Church
generally, **3**, 1636
Religion
advancement of, see CHARITABLE PURPOSE
discrimination on grounds of—
European Convention on Human Rights, **12**, 85, 86
sport, in, **19**, 1262
feudal system, and, **18**, 42
freedom of—
generally, **12**, 73
human right, as, **12**, 4, 4n, 6
restrictions on, **12**, 78–84
instruction in—
arrangements for, generally, **3**, 1665
denominational education, see EDUCATION
discontinuance, **3**, 1665
education authorities' duties as to—
denominational schools, **8**, 857
generally, **8**, 856
local authority schools, **10**, 1311
parental rights as to, **8**, 856
promotion—
education committees' duty in relation to, **8**, 717, 718
historical background, **8**, 701

Religion—*continued*
instruction in—*continued*
right to withdraw from, **3**, 1679
withdrawal of pupil from, **8**, 856
minister of—
Church of Scotland—
age limit, **3**, 1559
appointment, **3**, 1511
jus devolutum, **3**, 1526, 1558
presbytery, **3**, 1526
presbytery advisory committee, **3**, 1525
auxiliary, **3**, 1534, 1573
women, **3**, 1573
Baptisms, choice of time for administering, **3**, 1508
beadle, direction of, **3**, 1565
choirmaster, direction of, **3**, 1565
church officer, direction of, **3**, 1565
complaints as to life and doctrine of, **3**, 1531
conduct and discharge of professional duties, **3**, 1522
congregation in unsatisfactory state, **3**, 1524
congregational official, direction, **3**, 1565
death—
procedure on, **3**, 1525, 1570
vacation of manse by family, **3**, 1560
decennalis et triennalis possessor non tenetur docere de titulo, **3**, 1572
tenant, possession constituted through, **3**, 1572
definite charge, not intending to proceed to, **3**, 1556
demission of charge, **3**, 1569
deposed, reponing, **3**, 1531, 1567
disability, **3**, 1571
discipline, **3**, 1531, 1567
disqualifications, **3**, 1571
dissatisfaction with, **3**, 1512, 1529
duties and functions, **3**, 1563
bounds of parish must be within, **3**, 1563
ecclesiastical buildings, use of, **3**, 1605
elder, as, **3**, 1507
election, **3**, 1511, 1557, 1558
congregation's right to elect, **3**, 1504, 1557, 1558
eligibility, **3**, 1553
women, **3**, 1553, 1573
employment outside Church, taking up, **3**, 1530, 1571
Formula, subscription to, **3**, 1556
Fund for the Maintenance of the Ministry, **3**, 1562
funding, **3**, 1562
generally, **3**, 1552
glebe—
entitlement to, **3**, 1581
See also GLEBE
House of Commons, may not become member of, **3**, 1571
induction, **3**, 1522, 1556
interim moderator, **3**, 1507, 1525
judicatory, member of, **3**, 1571

Religion—*continued*
minister of—*continued*
  Church of Scotland—*continued*
    jury service—
      eligibility for, **3**, 1669
      ministers excusable from, **3**, 1571, 1632*n*, 1669
    kirk session, **3**, 1507
    licentiate, **3**, 1554, 1555
      generally, **3**, 1554
      supervision, **3**, 1533, 1555
    listed expenses, **3**, 1562
    local authority etc, member of, **3**, 1571
    manse—
      allowance in lieu of, **3**, 1560
      living elsewhere than, **3**, 1560
      right to occupy, **3**, 1560
    marriages, solemnisation, **3**, 1564
    mental incapacity, **3**, 1568
    ministerial certificate, grant and renewal, **3**, 1530
    ministerial commissioners to General Assembly, election, **3**, 1543
    misdemeanour by, termination of tenure, **3**, 1559
    notarial execution by, **3**, 1566
    ordination, **3**, 1533, 1556
    organist, direction of, **3**, 1510, 1565
    oversight by presbytery, **3**, 1522
    parochial charge—
      eligibility for, **3**, 1557
      settlement in—
        generally, **3**, 1557
        jus devolutum, **3**, 1526, 1558
    physical fitness, **3**, 1553
    possession of title, **3**, 1572
    precentor, direction of, **3**, 1510, 1565
    preparation for ministry, **3**, 1553–1556
    presbytery, membership, **3**, 1519
    prison chaplains, appointment, **3**, 1668
    Probationer—
      generally, **3**, 1555
      supervision, **3**, 1533
    prohibitions, **3**, 1571
    public office, as, **3**, 1563
    Sacrament of Lord's Supper, appointment of time and place for, **3**, 1508
    stipend—
      allocation, **3**, 1592
      appropriate, **3**, 1562
      determination, **3**, 1522, 1562
      extinction, **3**, 1596
      Fund for the Maintenance of the Ministry, **3**, 1562
      generally, **3**, 1562
      historical position, **3**, 1592
      kind, payment in, **3**, 1592
      listed expenses, **3**, 1562
      Minimum Stipend Fund, **3**, 1562
      payment, **3**, 1562, 1592, 1593
      post-1925 position, **3**, 1593
      review, **3**, 1592
      sale of properties originating in pre-1929 Church of Scotland, **3**, 1607

Religion—*continued*
minister of—*continued*
  Church of Scotland—*continued*
    stipend—*continued*
      standard value, **3**, 1594, 1596
      standardisation, **3**, 1593, 1595
      teinds, as burden on, **3**, 1592
        See also TEINDS
      victual, standard value, **3**, 1594
    supervision, **3**, 1530, 1567
    tenure, **3**, 1559
      ad vitam aut culpam, **3**, 1559
      security of, **3**, 1559
      termination—
        culpa, on grounds of, **3**, 1559
        generally, **3**, 1529, 1559
    training, **3**, 1553
      Exit Certificate, **3**, 1554
      length, **3**, 1553
    trials, **3**, 1554
    vacancy, kirk session duties, **3**, 1511
    vacant congregations, **3**, 1525
    visitation of congregation, presbytery, **3**, 1523
    women, eligibility for ministry, **3**, 1553, 1573
  dwelling house held for occupation by, repossession—
    assured tenancy, **13**, 749, 754
    protected tenancy, **13**, 736, 742
  non-designated services, **4**, 1177*n*
  privilege, **10**, 685
  unfair dismissal, **9**, 211
  work permit not required, **12**, 247
parental right to determine, **10**, 1309, 1310; **11**, 1208
toleration of—
  European Human Rights Convention, **3**, 1635*n*
  Jews, of, **3**, 1676
  non-Christian bodies, **3**, 1635
  voluntary churches, **3**, 1635, 1635*n*
See also CHURCH OF SCOTLAND; ROMAN CATHOLIC CHURCH

Religious community
charitable or mutual improvement function, whether, **3**, 1130
enclosed, charitable status, **3**, 1643
supplies of goods and services by, **7**, 1426

Religious order, member of
permit-free employment status, **12**, 247

Religious Society of Friends
burial grounds, **3**, 531

Remain, leave to
See IMMIGRATION

Remand centre
establishment, **16**, 1411
young person, committal, **22**, 33

Remedial gymnast
employment of, **11**, 1500

Remedial statute
interpretation, **12**, 1186

Remedial works
subsidence damage, execution in case of, **14**, 1694

Remedies

account, obligation to, **13**, 88

account—
  payment of, entitlement to, **13**, 88
  statement of, entitlement to demand and
    receive, **13**, 88

actings, reduction, **13**, 36

action taken without prior judicial sanction, **13**, 1

citation, execution, reduction, **13**, 37

classification, **13**, 2

common law, at, **1**, 324*ff*

compensation, **13**, 96

compensatory—
  damages, *see* DAMAGES
  recompense—
    factors required for remedy of, **13**, 83
    negotorium gestio, **13**, 84
    repetition, **13**, 85

count reckoning and payment, **13**, 88

damages, award of, **1**, 333
  See also DAMAGES

declarator, *see* DECLARATOR

decree, *see* DECREE

England and Scotland, in, **1**, 203

European Community directives, **13**, 87

generally, **13**, 1

interdict, *see* INTERDICT

legal right as counterpart, **13**, 2

nobile officium, **13**, 86

preservation, custody or detention of property,
  13, 24

preventive—
  administration of property in dispute, **13**, 24
  generally, **13**, 24
  interdict—
    breach of order, **13**, 20
    Crown, against, **13**, 23
    duration, **13**, 22
    equitable remedy, as, **13**, 17
    infringement of rights, protection from, **13**,
      18
    interim, **13**, 19
      breach of order, **13**, 20
    negative, **13**, 21
    suspension, combination with, **13**, 16
  suspension—
    definition, **13**, 15
    function, **13**, 15
    interdict, combination with, **13**, 16

recompense—
  contract, where parties' relations regulated by,
    13, 83
  defender must have incurred benefit, **13**, 83
  factors required for remedy of, **13**, 83
  negotiorum gestio, **13**, 84
  nemo debet locupletari ex aliena jactura, **13**, 83
  pursuer must have incurred loss, **13**, 83

reduction, *see* REDUCTION

remedium, meaning, **13**, 2

self-help—
  animals, defence of or against, **13**, 91
  defence of persons or property, **13**, 90
  nuisance, abatement of, **13**, 92
  trespass, against, **18**, 182, 184

Remedies—*continued*

specific implement, *see* SPECIFIC IMPLEMENT

statutory—
  duty to exhaust, **1**, 304, 305
  generally, **1**, 303, 337*ff*

statutory restriction of—
  aims of legislation, **1**, 306
  current practice, **1**, 307
  exclusion clause, **1**, 306, 307

ubi jus ibi remedium, **13**, 2

Remission (private international law)

See renvoi

Remission of offence

prerogative of mercy, **7**, 727, 727*n*

Remits

See SHERIFF COURT

Remoteness of damage

See DAMAGE

Removing

availability of remedy, **18**, 153

ejection distinguished, **18**, 153

land, recovery of founded on right to possession,
  18, 152, 153

preliminary notice, requirement for, **18**, 153

Remuneration

ante-natal care, time off for, **9**, 102

damages, effect on scale of, **15**, 930

deductions—
  cash shortages, for, **9**, 64
  general restrictions on, **9**, 63
  remedies in case of, **9**, 65
  stock deficiencies, for, **9**, 64

equal pay, *see* EQUAL PAY

guarantee payments, **9**, 60

industrial action, withheld as result of, **9**, 133

itemised pay statements, **9**, 66

maternity pay, right to, **9**, 106

medical grounds, payment when suspended on, **9**,
  61

messenger-at-arms, of, **14**, 1505

sheriff officer, of, **14**, 1511

statute, under, **9**, 58–66

unjust enrichment, *see* RECOMPENSE

Wages Act 1986—
  effect of, **9**, 62

week's pay, **9**, 59

See also WAGES

Remuneratory grant or donation

generally, **8**, 606

meaning, **8**, 608

Renfrew

Baron of—
  heir to Crown as, **7**, 704, 704*n*, 786

population, **14**, 64

Rent

abatement—
  real and personal conditions, **13**, 241
  remedy available to tenant, as, **13**, 279

agricultural holdings—
  appeal, **1**, 771
  arbitration, reference to, **1**, 769
  arrears, action for, **1**, 737
  basis for fixing, **1**, 770
  due dates, **1**, 753

Rent—*continued*
agricultural holdings—*continued*
  failure to pay, **1**, 752, 753
  non-payment, termination of tenancy by, **1**, 772
  open market, **1**, 770
  scarcity value, inflation by, **1**, 770
  Scottish Land Court jurisdiction, **6**, 969, 970
  statutory small tenant, paid by, **1**, 770
  variation of, **1**, 768, 769
allotment or allotment garden, **13**, 541
apportionment of, land subject to lease, **5**, 53
arrears—
  repossession on grounds of—
    assured tenancy, **13**, 725, 730, 749, 757
    protected tenancy, **13**, 714, 715
assignation of, **6**, 539
backhand, **13**, 246
caution for, permitting tenant to take possession, **3**, 885
cautioner for, landlord's hypothec, **13**, 514
clause of assignation, implied terms, **12**, 1235
commercial lease, **13**, 560
  advance, payment in, **13**, 567
  adverse rent review clause, effect, **13**, 561
  calculation, **13**, 567
  indexed rental, **13**, 71
  initial, **13**, 567
  irritancy, **13**, 584
  maintenance and repair obligation, **13**, 578
  negotiation, **13**, 567
  peppercorn, **13**, 567
  quarter days, payment on, **13**, 567
  requirement for, **13**, 567
  review—
    arbitration—
      arbiter, **13**, 576, 576*n*
      clause, **13**, 574–576
      independent expert, **13**, 576
      mechanism, **13**, 575
    arbitration, payment of rent during, **13**, 577
    assumptions relevant to, **13**, 573
    clause, generally, **13**, 572
    formal memorandum, **13**, 577
    generally, **13**, 569, 570
    interval between reviews, **13**, 571
    lowering of rent, clause preventing, **13**, 577
    object, **13**, 573
    procedure, **13**, 573
    valuation process, **13**, 573
    willing landlord and willing tenant, **13**, 573
  royalty rental, **13**, 71
  turnover rental, **13**, 71
  value added tax, **13**, 568
control—
  classification of tenancy affecting, **13**, 651
  deposit, payment of, **13**, 693
  fair rent—
    assessment, **13**, 659
    certificate, **13**, 652
    change in conditions following decision, **13**, 669
    disrepair, tenant's failure to abide by lease, due to, **13**, 661, 663

Rent—*continued*
control—*continued*
  fair rent—*continued*
    duration of decision, **13**, 669
    excess charges, **13**, 670
    furnishings, matters affecting fair rent decisions, **13**, 661, 663, 664
    improvements and repairs, tenant, carried out by, effect, **13**, 661, 664
    increase of rent, **13**, 669
    personal circumstances to be disregarded, **13**, 660–662
    protected tenancy, **13**, 604
    registration, **13**, 652
      amount to be registered, **13**, 668
      furnishings, payments in respect of, **13**, 668
      procedure, **13**, 653
      services, payments in respect of, **13**, 668
    rent assessment committees, *see* rent assessment committees *below*
    rent officers, *see* rent officers *below*
    scarcity deduction, **13**, 666
    statutory direction, lack of clear, **13**, 667
    supply and demand, assumption of equilibrium, **13**, 666
    systems, generally, **13**, 652
    uniformity, **13**, 667
    written notice of decision as to, **13**, 657
  furnishings, **13**, 661, 663, 664, 668
  generally, **13**, 651
  market rent, determination—
    assumptions, **13**, 678
    assured tenancy, **13**, 672–676
    disregards, **13**, 679
    generally, **13**, 672
    rent assessment committees—
      criteria for fixing rent, **13**, 677–679
    rent increase proposals—
      notice of, **13**, 675
  premium, payment of, *see* premium *below*
  reasonable rent—
    Part VII tenancy, **13**, 671
    registration, **13**, 671
  rent assessment committees, *see* rent assessment committees *below*
  short assured tenancy—
    determination, date of effect, **13**, 687
    non-determinations under—
      duplication, avoidance, **13**, 684
      pool of comparables, **13**, 685
      significantly higher rent, tenant must be paying, **13**, 686
    rent assessment committees, role, **13**, 683
    disapplication, **13**, 688
  statutory increase mechanism—
    avoidance, **13**, 682
    rent assessment committees, and, **13**, 681
  tenancy in existence on 2 January 1989 ..., **13**, 652
  where no provision for rent increase in rent agreement, **13**, 674, 675, 682
crofter, paid by, *see* CROFT
definite, real rights affected by, **13**, 304–307

Rent—*continued*
deposit, premium distinguished, **13**, 693
distress for, railway stock and plant, **19**, 1102
elusory, must not be, **13**, 305
failure to pay punctually, penalty conditions, **13**, 238
fair rent, *see* control *above*
farm—
  apportionment, **13**, 247
  payment, **13**, 246
fixing—
  Rent Act 1965 ..., **13**, 592
  Rent Act 1974 ..., **13**, 593
foregift, meaning, **13**, 103
forehand, **13**, 246
form, **13**, 306
generally, **14**, 826
grassum, meaning, **13**, 103
growth, **25**, 129
hire contract, essential of, **14**, 1035
house, **14**, 827
housing benefit, *see* HOUSING BENEFIT
income support payments towards, **21**, 1075
  direct payments, **21**, 1082
landlord, recovery by, **13**, 513
landlord's hypothec—
  arrears of rent, **13**, 515
  breach of sequestration, **13**, 521
  generally, **8**, 377, 378; **13**, 513; **14**, 1812
  invecta et illata, **13**, 513, 516, 519
  loss of right, **13**, 522
  other rights, relationship with, **13**, 523
  parties entitled to exercise right, **13**, 514
  plenishing order, where, **13**, 518
  procedure, **13**, 520
  rent securable, **13**, 515
  retention, right of, **13**, 519
  subjects where remedy available, **13**, 513
  sublease, where, **13**, 517
  time limit, **13**, 515, 522
  See also LANDLORD
lease, **13**, 206
  as cardinal element of, **12**, 1252
  essential of, **14**, 1035
  existence dependent upon payment of rent, **13**, 596, 598
lessee, obligations of, **14**, 1045
level, **25**, 128
low—
  assured tenancy, excluded tenancies, **13**, 636, 638
  protected tenancy status affected by, **13**, 630, 631
maills and duties, *see* MAILLS AND DUTIES
market, *see* control *above*
meaning, **13**, 103
no provision made for, where, **13**, 107
non-payment—
  irritancy clause, **13**, 427
  remedies available to landlord, **13**, 275
other, **14**, 828
Part VII contract, **13**, 624
payment—
  apocha trium annorum, **13**, 229
  entitlement to receive, **13**, 229

Rent—*continued*
payment—*continued*
  farm rent, **13**, 246
  generally, **13**, 229, 596
  increase after natural end of lease, **13**, 140
  necessary to existence of lease, **13**, 596, 598
  permanent change in payment method as real condition, **13**, 241
  premature, **13**, 229
  tenant, by, **13**, 229
  tenant's obligations as to, **13**, 272, 273
  terms of, **13**, 246
peppercorn, commercial lease, **13**, 567
percentage of capital expenditure, as, **13**, 306
persistent delay in payment, repossession, **13**, 725, 729
premium—
  assured tenancy, **13**, 689–692
  deposit distinguished, **13**, 693
  furnishings, excessive price charged for, **13**, 692
  meaning, **13**, 689
  penalty for offences in relation to, **13**, 689
  prohibition on charge, **13**, 689
  protected tenancy, **13**, 690–692
prescription, **16**, 2116
profit rental, **13**, 569
protected tenancy, **13**, 630, 631
provision for, **13**, 107
real rights, and, **13**, 107, 304–307
reduction, proof of, **13**, 149
registration—
  registration service, **13**, 593
  short tenancy, **13**, 594
Rent Acts, **13**, 590*ff*
  attempts to avoid, **13**, 595, 596
  deferred/rental purchase, **13**, 772
rent assessment committees—
  constitution, **13**, 655
  criteria for fixing rent, **13**, 677
    assumptions, **13**, 678
    disregards, **13**, 679
  criticisms of, **13**, 655
  decisions, delivery, **13**, 655
  duplication of references to, **13**, 680
  fair rent—
    assessment of rents, **13**, 659
    challenges to decisions, **13**, 667
    generally, **13**, 652, 653, 655, 658
    matters to be regarded and disregarded, **13**, 660–662, 679
    Part VII contract, **13**, 624, 671
  functions, **23**, 902
  generally, **13**, 593, 652, 653
  market rent, criteria for fixing, **13**, 677–679
  market rent, determination, **13**, 673
  president and vice-president, **13**, 655
  procedure, **13**, 658
  short assured tenancy, **13**, 683, 688
  statutory increase mechanism, **13**, 681, 682
rent book—
  landlord's duty to provide, **13**, 694
  provisions relating to, **13**, 694
rent officers—
  appointment, **13**, 654

Rent—*continued*
rent officers—*continued*
  fair rent—
    assessment of rents by, **13**, 659
    generally, **13**, 652, 653, 654, 656, 657
    matters to be regarded and disregarded by, **13**, 660–662
    objection to decision of, **13**, 658
    generally, **13**, 652, 653
    procedure, **13**, 656
    written notice of decision, **13**, 657
rent tribunal, **23**, 902, 911*n*
retention by lessee, **13**, 273, 278, 307
review—
  Rent Act 1965 ..., **13**, 592
  Rent Review Board, **12**, 60
  rent review clause, **13**, 304
sequestration for, *see* SEQUESTRATION FOR RENT
services, in form of, **13**, 306
sheriff, duties of, **17**, 570
short tenancy, **13**, 594
social fund crisis loan, **21**, 1125
special area, in, grant towards, **14**, 658
tenancy, as prerequisite for, **13**, 613
tenant's obligations as to, **13**, 272, 273
tribunal, **13**, 593
  rent assessment committee, transfer of jurisdiction to, **13**, 593
valuation for rating—
  comparative principle, **24**, 524
  consideration other than, **24**, 520
variable, **13**, 304
where no provision made for, **13**, 107
where none paid, protected tenancy status affected by, **13**, 630, 631
wilful non-payment, **11**, 2057
wrongful withholding of sums due, interest payable on, **12**, 1012
See also TENANT-TENANCY
Rentals
agreement, basis of, **14**, 1023
finance lease, contractual terms in, **14**, 1056
operating lease, **14**, 1020
sub-lease, *see* SUB-HIRE
tax-deductible, **14**, 1014
valuation, duties of valuer, **25**, 109
variation clause—
  capital allowances, **14**, 1056
  cost of money fluctuations, **14**, 1056
  grants, **14**, 1056
  taxation, changes in, **14**, 1056
Rentcharge
compulsory acquisition of land subject to—
  general vesting declaration, acquisition by way of, **5**, 52
  Lands Clauses Act, application of, **5**, 24
Renunciation
extinction of real right, **18**, 9
instrument of, notary public, execution by, **13**, 1221
lease, of, *see* LEASE-LEASING
liferent, termination on, **13**, 1647, 1649
minute of—
  interpretation, **12**, 1262

Renvoi
causes of, **17**, 153
connecting factor, **17**, 146
evolution of choice of law rules, **17**, 123
foreign court theory, **17**, 155
meaning, **17**, 110, 152
partial theory, **17**, 156
Scotland, in, **17**, 158
solutions to, **17**, 154
total, **17**, 157
Repair notice (housing)
appeals, **11**, 1994
arrangement and execution of works by local authority, **11**, 1995
generally, **11**, 1993, 1995
local authority loan, **11**, 1995, 2015
power to serve, **11**, 1993
repair grant, *see* REPAIRS GRANT
serious disrepair, house in, **11**, 1993
tenant bearing expense, **11**, 1995
time for execution of works, **11**, 1993
Repairs
coast protection works, **14**, 474; **25**, 387
defective, **6**, 69
drainage works, damage caused by, **25**, 370
highway, premises in disrepair near, **14**, 2101
lessor, obligations of, **14**, 1041
possession of customer's goods to effect, **6**, 70
repair funds, local government, **14**, 811
repair notice, *see* REPAIR NOTICE
repairs grant, *see* REPAIRS GRANT
secure tenancy, **11**, 1952, 1953
valuation for rating—
  'actual state' rule, **24**, 506
  hypothetical tenancy, **24**, 521, 618
Repairs grant
additional to improvement grant, **11**, 2021, 2025
amount, **11**, 2026
application for, **11**, 1995, 2025
approval, **11**, 2025
central government contributions, **11**, 2034
generally, **11**, 1978–1981, 2025
housing action areas, **11**, 2032
local authority duty, **11**, 1980
local authority house loans, and, **11**, 2015
procedural and other provisions, **11**, 2027
specific functions of local authorities, **11**, 1981
Reparation
action for—
  ball games, **14**, 2085
  Court of Session procedure, **17**, 1375, 1405
  Dean of Guild, jurisdiction of, **14**, 2017
  negative prescription of obligation, **14**, 2123
  plea to relevancy in, **17**, 1098
  process of, **17**, 524
  rifle range, **14**, 2085
concept of money central to, **14**, 1801
delict, **15**, 216
  defences, *see* DELICT (defences)
fault as fundamental principle, **15**, 252
international law, **19**, 747
liability in action of, **14**, 1504

Reparation—*continued*
liability to make, **15**, 2, 4*n*
obligation to make, prescription, **16**, 2121
obligations of, **11**, 1032–1034
Roman law, **15**, 214
Repatriation
public expense, at, **16**, 1227
Repayment trader
meaning, **7**, 1342*n*
Repetition
condictio causa data causa non secuta—
　Bankton's view, **15**, 33
　breach of contract, **15**, 34, 38, 39, 42
　classification in Scots law, **15**, 34
　contractual framework, operation within, **15**, 34
　examples, **15**, 33
　frustration of contract, **15**, 34, 36, 37, 42
　generally, **15**, 15, 31
　goods and corporeal moveables, **15**, 31, 31*n*, 86
　meaning, **15**, 32
　money, **15**, 31, 86
　operation outwith contract, **15**, 34, 35
　problems arising, **15**, 41–43
　Stair's view, **15**, 33
　void contract, **15**, 34, 40
　voidable contract, **15**, 34, 40
condictio indebiti—
　equitable, must be, **15**, 16, 27
　error of fact, payment arising from, **15**, 17–26
　error of law, payment arising from, **15**, 17–26
　generally, **15**, 15, 16
　goods and corporeal moveables, **15**, 16, 31
　ignorantia juris maxim, **15**, 17–20
　scope, **15**, 16
condictio ob causam finitam, **15**, 15
condictio ob turpem vel injustam causam, **15**, 15
condictio sine causa, **15**, 15
loss of possession, after, **15**, 55
money, recovery of, **15**, 14, 16
payment made in error, obligation of recipient, **15**, 4*n*
remedy of, **13**, 85
restitution, and, **15**, 86
restitution and recompense distinguished, **15**, 14, 28, 82
unjust enrichment, **15**, 2, 12, 28
　categories of repetition, **15**, 15
　scope of remedy, **15**, 14
Replacement value policy
insurance, meaning, **12**, 889
Reponing
See SHERIFF COURT
Repossession of goods
distinction between rights in England and Scotland, **14**, 1064
entry for repossession of goods, **5**, 892
financial relief for hirer on, **5**, 928
landlord, rights of, **14**, 1070
lessor's right to effect, **14**, 1064
protected goods, **5**, 891
sale of goods repossessed under finance agreement, **7**, 1290

Representation as to credit
See CREDIT
Reprography
copyright, and—
　educational establishment, use by, **18**, 1114
　generally, **18**, 1020
　licensing schemes—
　　certified, **18**, 1021
　　compulsory, **18**, 1022
　　Copyright Tribunal, licence terms, determination, **18**, 1022
　　educational establishment, **18**, 1114
　　right, licences of, **18**, 1022
meaning, **18**, 1020
Republic of Ireland
alien, citizen not regarded as, **14**, 1901
arrival in UK from or through—
　generally, **16**, 1208
　restrictions on, **16**, 1208*n*
British subject, **14**, 1950, 1955
citizen of, **14**, 1955
　deportation, protection against, **12**, 125
　treason by, **7**, 580
civil jurisdiction, contracting state, as, **4**, 22
common travel area, **12**, 122; **16**, 1208
entry to United Kingdom via, **12**, 124
　appeal against refusal, **12**, 124
　European Union citizens, **12**, 124
　restrictions, **12**, 124
extradition, **12**, 510, 581, 582
　authority to proceed, **12**, 555
　contumacy, **12**, 537
　double punishability, **12**, 548
　extradition crime, **12**, 528
　from United Kingdom—
　　authentication of documents, **12**, 567
　　hearing and committal, **12**, 564
　　order by Secretary of State, not applicable, **12**, 576
　　review, **12**, 572, 573
　　warrants, **12**, 558, 561
　international law, **12**, 525
　liability for, **12**, 527
　municipal law, **12**, 526
　'own nationals' exemption not applicable, **12**, 549
　political offence exemption, **12**, 535
　previous acquittal or conviction, **12**, 539
　prima facie rule, **12**, 547
　restrictions on, **12**, 529
　speciality, **12**, 543
immigration control exemptions, **12**, 132
leave to enter, where required, **12**, 124
meaning, **16**, 1208*n*
separation of, effect of, **14**, 1901
See also IRELAND
Repudiation
building contracts—
　extinction of obligations, **3**, 95
　remedy for breach, **3**, 104, 105, 107
Repugnancy
will, interpretation and construction of, **12**, 1109, 1269

Reputation
interference with—
  See HONOUR AND REPUTATION, INTERFERENCE
    WITH
trading, passing off, see PASSING OFF
Requisition
belligerent has qualified right to, **17**, 415
foreign expropriatory claim, **17**, 329
restraint of princes, as, **21**, 550
Res conveniens
marine mammals, **11**, 215
Res gestae
statements forming part of, as hearsay evidence,
  10, 710
Res ipsa loquitur
rebuttable presumption arising from, **10**, 750
Res judicata
estoppel, **16**, 1602
exclusion of evidence, **10**, 521
plea in bar of trial, **17**, 689
plea of, **17**, 1102
Res merae facultatis
examples of rights which are, **16**, 2126
imprescriptive right, as, **16**, 2121, 2126
Res nullius
game, as, **11**, 803
generally, **18**, 531
salmon, **11**, 3
trout, **11**, 47, 51
Resale price maintenance
collective—
  enforcement, **4**, 1201
  generally, **4**, 1199
  unlawfulness of, **4**, 1200
EU law and, **4**, 1382
individual—
  enforcement, **4**, 1207
  exemption, **4**, 1206
  generally, **4**, 1202
  patented articles, **4**, 1204
  supplementary provisions, **4**, 1205
  unlawfulness of, **4**, 1203
nature of, **4**, 1198
outline of UK law, **4**, 1110
Rescission
breach by tenant, as remedy against, **13**, 275, 276
breach of contract, remedy for, **14**, 1063
building contracts—
  extinction of obligations, **3**, 95
  remedy for breach, **3**, 104, 106, 107
contract, of—
  when available, **13**, 93
  where restitution no longer possible, **13**, 93
  wrongful attempt to rescind, **13**, 93
Court of Session jurisdiction, **4**, 6
equitable remedy, as, **13**, 93
fraud, lease obtained by, **13**, 469
irritancy compared, **13**, 426
notice of, **5**, 906
Rescissory actions
meaning, **13**, 25
Rescue
duty of care, and, **15**, 304

Rescuer
delict, *volenti non fit injuria*, **15**, 395, 396, 401
Research and development
articles for use at work, on, **9**, 458
European Community legislation, **18**, 1611
  licensing block exemption, **18**, 1654,
    1655
information, **14**, 331
joint agreement for, EU aspects, **4**, 1388
provision, VAT exemption, **7**, 1425
research and development agreements, European
  Union rules on competition, **10**, 162
scientific, see SCIENTIFIC PURPOSE
Reservoir
abandoned, **25**, 329
alteration of, **19**, 19n, 24; **25**, 329
construction of, **19**, 19n, 24; **25**, 329
  in relation to hydro-electric development, **9**,
    640
large raised, **25**, 329
raised, **25**, 329
recreational or sporting use, **19**, 1218
registers of, **25**, 329
sources of supply, **25**, 515
temporary discharge of water, **25**, 333
water pollution, **14**, 2079
Reset
analogous statutory offences, **7**, 395
child, of, **7**, 393
cognitive element, **7**, 79
cohabitee, whether guilty of, **10**, 841
company, by, **7**, 392
connivance, **7**, 390
definition, **7**, 389
documentary evidence, as, **10**, 594
evidence as to, **7**, 394
guilty knowledge, **7**, 391
innocently obtained goods, **7**, 390
intention to detain goods, **7**, 391
mens rea, **7**, 390, 391
person other than thief, goods obtained from, **7**,
  390
police court jurisdiction, **6**, 1157
possession—
  accused not in possession, where, **7**, 390
  control of accused, goods in, **7**, 390
  duration, **7**, 390
  meaning, **7**, 390
sale of goods, proceeds passed to third party, **7**,
  393
what may be resetted, **7**, 389, 393
who may be guilty of, **7**, 392
wife, exemption from conviction, **7**, 392
wife, whether guilty of, **10**, 841
wilful blindness to character of goods, **7**, 391
Residence
British Dependent Territories citizenship, **14**,
  1938
company, of, **17**, 356
domicile, as element of, **4**, 30
domicile of choice, acquisition of, **17**, 204
electoral registration, and, **5**, 374
foreign, trustee, **24**, 137
freedom of, **12**, 4n

Residence—*continued*
habitual, **4**, 39, 68; **17**, 190
meaning, **4**, 30
naturalisation, requirements for, **14**, 1920
ordinarily resident, **14**, 1905; **17**, 190
parents' right to determine place of, **11**, 1208
permit—
   European Union nationals, **12**, 237
     curtailment, **12**, 238
registration, **14**, 1916, 1938
requirement—
   breach of conditions, **12**, 187
right of—
   European Union nationals, **12**, 226
     termination, **12**, 227
second residence, household effects, European
   Union import duty relief, **7**, 1100
settled, meaning, **14**, 1905
spouse—
   failure to reside with, **10**, 838
   freedom of, **10**, 838
transfer from third country, import duty relief, **7**,
   1100, 1113
will, conditions as to, **25**, 870
Residential care
after-care on release, child detained at direction
   of, Secretary of State, **22**, 36
appeal against refusal of registration, **22**, 16
capital expenditure, central government loan, **22**,
   16
child—
   in care, local authority duty to provide
     facilities, **22**, 17
     visiting, regulation, **22**, 17
   detained at direction of Secretary of State,
     after-care on release, **22**, 36
   referral from children's panel, role of social
     worker, **22**, 21
   voluntary organisations, provision, **22**, 13
costs of, income support, **21**, 1076
elderly persons, **22**, 25, 28
financing—
   capital expenditure, central government loan,
     22, 16
   elderly persons, in privately owned accom-
     modation, **22**, 28
handicapped persons, **22**, 24, 31
income support payments towards, **21**, 1076
inspection by local authority, **22**, 16
legislation, early, **22**, 2
local authority, *see* LOCAL AUTHORITY
mentally handicapped persons, **22**, 24, 31
regulations by Secretary of State, **22**, 16
residential care establishment—
   abscondment from, **3**, 1373
   children's hearing supervision requirement, **3**,
     1349, 1352
   harbouring absconder from, **3**, 1374
   meaning, **3**, 1349*n*
   registration, **14**, 521; **22**, 16, 28
   religious persuasion of child, **3**, 1352
   voluntary sector, **3**, 1380, 1380*n*
standards, **22**, 16
voluntary organisations, **22**, 10, 13, 16, 28

Residential hotel
keeper not subject to strict liability, **11**, 1709
Residential school
reform proposals, **3**, 1380
Resignation
ad remanentiam perpetuam, **18**, 97
feudal conveyance, generally, **18**, 97, 103
in favorem, **18**, 97
***Respondentia* bond**
conventional hypothec, as, **21**, 479
generally, **20**, 6, 27, 281
jurisdiction, generally, **21**, 101
maritime lien, **1**, 413; **21**, 260, 479
Responsibility
capacity-responsibility, legal concept of, **11**,
   1054–1058
   capacity to act, **11**, 1057
   harm occasioned by others, **11**, 1056
   legal liability, capacity for, **11**, 1057
   nature of, **11**, 1054
   vicarious liability, **11**, 1055
See also LIABILITY
Rest and leisure
right to, **12**, 4*n*
Restaurant
age for drinking in, **2**, 13
alcohol licence, **2**, 1
bars in, **2**, 13
food hygiene certificate, **2**, 46
hotel distinguished, **11**, 1713
innkeepers' strict liability not applicable to, **15**,
   147
lease, **13**, 197
liability, **11**, 1742
licence—
   effect of, **2**, 13
   premises eligible for, **2**, 13
name, passing off, **18**, 1377
occasional licence for, **2**, 25
part of hotel, as, **11**, 1713
permitted hours, **2**, 18
planning permission, **2**, 44
public house licence for, **2**, 13
Sunday opening—
   control, **22**, 817
   local licensing board, **22**, 817
water meter charges, **25**, 536
Restitution
annulment of contract, subsequent, goods
   delivered where, **15**, 46, 50
Bankton's view, **15**, 59
civil claim for, **4**, 38
compensation distinguished from, **17**, 803
conditio causa data causa non secuta, **15**, 33, 45, 46
conditio indebiti, **15**, 45, 46
continuing liability, **15**, 56
corporeal moveables, recovery of, **15**, 14
dare, **15**, 82
delivery of goods by mistake, **15**, 46, 48
deposit, goods held on, **15**, 46, 49
examples, **15**, 46
fruits, liability for, **15**, 54
   bona fide consumption, **15**, 54
future development, **15**, 86

Restitution—*continued*
goods, recovery of, **15**, 14, 86
hire, goods held on, **15**, 46, 49
immoral situations, **15**, 53
interim possessor—
    good faith, where not in, **15**, 56
    negligent, where, **15**, 56
loan, goods held on, **15**, 46, 49
loss of possession, liability after, **15**, 55
lost goods, **15**, 46, 47
mislaid or straying goods, **15**, 46, 47
money, recovery of, **15**, 14, 86
natural accession, liability for, **15**, 54
offender required to make, **17**, 803
pirates, things recovered from, **15**, 45
recompense, liability in, **15**, 57
repetition, and, **15**, 14, 28, 82, 86
repetition and recompense distinguished, **15**, 14, 28, 82
resale, profit made on, **15**, 57
scope of remedy, **15**, 44
specification—
    interim possessor, liability, **15**, 56
    strict liability as result of, **15**, 58
Stair's view, **15**, 45
stolen goods, **15**, 45, 46, 51, 52
straying, goods, **15**, 45, 46, 47
thieves or robbers, things recovered from, **15**, 45
turpis causa transactions, **15**, 53
unjust enrichment, **15**, 2, 11, 12, 28, 46
See also UNJUSTIFIED ENRICHMENT
Restitution order
Financial Services Act 1986, under—
    Court of Session powers, **12**, 1411, 1413
    investment business carried on by unauthorised or unexempted person, where, **12**, 1324
    misleading statement or practice, following, **12**, 1333
Restraint of trade
ambit, **15**, 774
bargaining power, inequality of, **4**, 1107
contemporary law, doctrine as part of—
    horizontal agreement, **4**, 1216
    residual role, **4**, 1215
    trade associations, **4**, 1218
    trade unions, **4**, 1218
    vertical agreement, **4**, 1217
content of doctrine—
    generally, **4**, 1208
    interest meriting protection, **4**, 1209
    parties, reasonableness between, **4**, 1210
    reasonableness—
        parties, between, **4**, 1210
        public interest, in, **4**, 1211
covenant in, **19**, 1235
duration, **15**, 774
extent, **15**, 774
limitations of doctrine—
    public interest, **4**, 1213
    scope, **4**, 1212
    third parties, **4**, 1214
meaning, **15**, 770
opening door test, **4**, 1212
parties accepting, where, **15**, 774

Restraint of trade—*continued*
protectable interests, **15**, 773
public interest requirement, **15**, 775
reasonableness, **15**, 772
    onus of proof, **15**, 776
    parties, between, **15**, 774
    public, with regard to, **15**, 775
severability of unreasonable restraints, **15**, 778
terms, interpretation, **15**, 777
unenforceability of contracts, **15**, 763, 770–772
Restraint order
drugs-related offence, relating to, **14**, 1256
Restraints of princes
carrier not liable for, **21**, 603
exclusion or limitation of liability, **21**, 550
meaning, **21**, 550
Restriction direction
See MENTALLY DISORDERED PERSON
Restriction order
See MENTALLY DISORDERED PERSON
Restrictive agreement
See RESTRICTIVE TRADE PRACTICES ACT
Restrictive covenant
See COMPETITION LAW
Restrictive practices
See COMPETITION LAW; RESTRICTIVE TRADE PRACTICES ACT 1976
Restrictive Practices Court
agreement not referred to—
    EU law, regard to, **4**, 1181
    filleted agreement, **4**, 1183
    Secretary of State, discretion of, **4**, 1184
    terminated agreement, **4**, 1182
civil legal aid, **13**, 1034
decisions binding on, **22**, 327
functions of, **4**, 1123
institution, **22**, 327
reference to—
    gateways, **4**, 1185
    order of court—
        agreement 'to like effect', **4**, 1190
        declaration, **4**, 1187
        interdict—
            interim, **4**, 1194
            power to make, **4**, 1189
        interim injunction, **4**, 1194
        interim interdict, **4**, 1194
        provisional validity, **4**, 1193
        public interest—
            restrictions contrary to, **4**, 1187–1194
            restrictions not contrary to, **4**, 1186
        severence, **4**, 1188
        suspension of, **4**, 1192
        trade association, relating to, **4**, 1191
        undertaking—
            interim, **4**, 1194
            power to make, **4**, 1189
        variation of court's decision, leave to apply for, **4**, 1186
    tailpiece, **4**, 1185
registration of agreements, **4**, 1180
Senator of the College of Justice, **6**, 923
suspension of court's order, **4**, 1192
traders' unfair conduct, **6**, 19

Restrictive Trade Practices Act 1976
background, **4**, 1126
enforcement provisions—
    failure to register, **4**, 1197
    generally, **4**, 1195
    investigation, powers of, **4**, 1196
goods—
    information agreement as to—
        agreements covered, **4**, 1170
        control of, **4**, 1171
        generally, **4**, 1127, 1169
    restrictive agreement as to—
        agreement, meaning, **4**, 1129, 1133
        arrangements, meaning, **4**, 1130, 1131
        carrying on business within UK, meaning, **4**, 1138
        disregarded provisions—
            approved standards, **4**, 1152
            coal producers, **4**, 1149
            extension of, **4**, 1155
            financing terms, **4**, 1154
            generally, **4**, 1148
            judicial decisions, **4**, 1151
            restrictive labour practices, **4**, 1153
            steel producers, **4**, 1149
            vertical restraints, **4**, 1150
        duration irrelevant, **4**, 1168
        exempt agreements—
            agriculture, agreement affecting, **1**, 704; **4**, 1165
            coal, agreement affecting, **4**, 1165
            Crown agreement, **4**, 1167
            exclusive distribution agreement, **4**, 1159
            export agreement, **4**, 1161
            express authorisation, **4**, 1157
            fisheries, agreement affecting, **4**, 1165
            forestry, agreement affecting, **4**, 1165
            generally, **4**, 1156
            industrial rationalisation schemes, **4**, 1158
            intellectual property, licensing of, **4**, 1160
            merger investigation, undertaking following, **4**, 1166
            monopoly investigation, undertaking following, **4**, 1166
            prices, agreement to keep down, **4**, 1163
            section 29 agreement, **4**, 1162
            steel, agreement affecting, **4**, 1165
            wholesale co-operative agreements, **4**, 1164
        generally, **4**, 1127
        legislation, **4**, 1128
        recent decisions, **4**, 1132
        restrictions—
            implied, **4**, 1135
            leases, meaning of restriction in, **4**, 1136
            markets, division of, **4**, 1144
            meaning, **4**, 1134, 1136
            price fixing, **4**, 1140
            prices, agreement to recommend, **4**, 1141
            range of production, on, **4**, 1143
            relevant, meaning, **4**, 1197n
            section 6, relating to matters specified in, **4**, 1139

Restrictive   Trade   Practices   Act   1976—
    continued
goods—*continued*
    restrictive agreement as to—*continued*
        restrictions—*continued*
            terms and conditions, agreement relating to, **4**, 1142
            volume of production, on, **4**, 1143
        supplementary provisions—
            compliance, benefits for, **4**, 1146
            generally, **4**, 1145
            non-compliance, penalties for, **4**, 1146
            trade associations, **4**, 1147
        time element, **4**, 1168
        two or more persons—
            bodies corporate, **4**, 1137
            partnerships, **4**, 1137
        two persons carrying on business, **4**, 1138
historical development, **4**, 1126
information agreements—
goods, as to, *see* goods *above*
    services, as to, **4**, 1127, 1178
outline of UK law, **4**, 1110
registrable agreements—
    categories, **4**, 1127
    crossover problem, **4**, 1179
    cumulative basis, agreement not registrable on, **4**, 1179
    definitions, **4**, 1127
    information agreements—
goods, as to, *see* goods *above*
    services, as to, **4**, 1127, 1178
    restrictive agreements—
goods, as to, *see* goods *above*
    services, as to, *see* services *below*
registration—
    Director General of Fair Trading, duties of, **4**, 1180
    failure to register, enforcement on, **4**, 1197
    Office of Fair Trading, powers of, **4**, 1180
    Restrictive Practices Court, *see* RESTRICTIVE PRACTICES COURT
review of, **4**, 1289
services—
    control—
        agreement brought under, **4**, 1173
        agreement potentially subject to, **4**, 1178
    information agreement as to, **4**, 1127, 1178
    restrictive agreement as to—
        control, agreement brought under, **4**, 1173
        designated, **4**, 1177
        disregarded provisions, **4**, 1175
        exemptions, **4**, 1176
        generally, **4**, 1127, 1172
        services order, **4**, 1177
        supplementary provisions, **4**, 1174
Resumption
crofters' land by landlord—
    authorisation, **6**, 959, 963
    compensation, assessment of, **6**, 959, 967
    de-crofting compared, **6**, 967
    generally, **1**, 809; **6**, 967

Retail sale
meaning, **6**, 195
shops, *see* SHOP
Retail shop
See SHOP
Retailer
meaning for VAT, **7**, 1366
notice or statement made by, **6**, 154
oil, *see* OIL MARKETING
Retainers
general, **13**, 1349, 1351
meaning, **13**, 1349
non-recoverable from opponent on taxation, **13**, 1349
purpose, **13**, 1349
special, **13**, 1349, 1350
Retention
building contracts, remedy for breach, **3**, 104
equitable remedy, as, **13**, 94
Retention of title agreement
administrator, powers of, **4**, 619
meaning, **4**, 619
Retirement
age, professional sportsmen, **19**, 1300*n*
discrimination, provisions in relation to, **9**, 349
Retirement annuity
partner, payment to, income tax treatment, **16**, 1131
Retirement benefit or annuity scheme
building society shares held by, **3**, 328
graduated, overlapping benefits, **21**, 999, 1003
income tax relief, **19**, 1518
Retirement home
lessor's, repossession of protected tenancy on grounds of, **13**, 736, 738, 748
Retroactive legislation
non-retroactivity as principle of Community law, **10**, 96
Retrocession
transfer of incorporeal property, **18**, 661
Retrospective criminality
European Convention on Human Rights, **12**, 6, 61
Returning officer
act or omission in breach of election law, **15**, 1441
advance on account of charges, **15**, 1396
appointment of, **14**, 204
ballot boxes, issue, **15**, 1312
ballot papers, issue, **15**, 1312
combined poll, **15**, 1363
  accountability, **15**, 1388
  count, **15**, 1384, 1385
    disposal of documents, after, **15**, 1378, 1386
count—
  attendance, **15**, 1330
  combined poll, **15**, 1384, 1385
  doubtful papers, decisions as to, **15**, 1335
  order, maintenance, **15**, 1332
  secrecy, duty to give notice of requirement as to, **15**, 1331
declaration of candidate elected, **15**, 1230, 1352
deposit, payment by candidate, **15**, 1287–1290

Returning officer—*continued*
duties—
  election expenses, in relation to, **15**, 1435
  equality of votes, where, **15**, 1230, 1339
  timetable in respect of, **15**, 1239
election expenses, functions in relation to, **15**, 1435
equality of votes, where, decision by lot, **15**, 1230, 1339
equipment, issue, **15**, 1312
European parliamentary election timetable, **15**, 1226, 1227, 1232
European parliamentary elections, **15**, 1049, 1226, 1227
retention of documents, **15**, 1355
expenses, payment, **15**, 1018
forwarding of documents, after count, **15**, 1355
functions, **14**, 204
income tax, liability to, **15**, 1403
local government election—
  generally, **15**, 1047
  timetable, **15**, 1232
national insurance contributions, liability for, **15**, 1402
nomination of candidates, role—
  publication of—
    notice of poll, **15**, 1303
    statement of persons nominated, **15**, 1302
  validity of nomination paper, as to, **15**, 1250–1258
  whether candidate nominated, determination, **15**, 1250, 1258
  procedure on decisions, **15**, 1299
nomination paper, rejection of, **5**, 375
poll cards, dispatch, **15**, 1309
polling districts, determination, **15**, 1304
polling station staff, appointment, **15**, 1317
postal ballot, issue and receipt (opening), **15**, 1197
postal voting documents, forwarding, **15**, 1213
presiding officer, acting as, **15**, 1317
public notices, publication, **15**, 1240, 1241
  statutory notices, **15**, 1245, 1246
    misnomer or inaccurate description, **15**, 1249
    mode, **15**, 1248
re-counts, powers as to, **15**, 1338
recovery of charges, **15**, 1395
register of electors, supply to, **15**, 1114
rendering accounts, **15**, 1401
responsibilities of, **5**, 374
return name of candidate elected, **15**, 1352, 1353
sealing up of ballot papers, **15**, 1354
secrecy, maintenance, **15**, 1318
staff employed or required by, **15**, 1337
  income tax, **15**, 1403
  national insurance contributions, **15**, 1402
superannuation, **15**, 1400
time and place of count, notification, **15**, 1334
timetable—
  generally, **15**, 1239
  local government elections, **15**, 1228–1230
United Kingdom Central Council for Nursing, Midwifery and Health Visiting, **15**, 1497
United Kingdom parliamentary election, **15**, 1048, 1225, 1227
  timetable, **15**, 1225, 1227, 1232

Returning officer—_continued_
verification of ballot paper accounts, **15**, 1328
verifying officer, acting as, **15**, 1317, 1328
Revalorisation
good faith, on principle of, **14**, 1823
Revenue trader
accounts, regulations as to, **7**, 1254
duty—
   goods taken in default, **7**, 1251
   liability for, **7**, 1249
   payment and collection, **7**, 1250
entry and search regarding, powers of, **7**, 1252
entry as to premises or articles, **7**, 1246–1248
meaning, **7**, 1249
noxious or detrimental sustances etc, use of, **7**, 1253
'specimen' document, **7**, 1253
Reverse compulsory acquisition
blight—
   notice—
      compensation after, **5**, 104
      effect of, **5**, 103
      interests qualifying for protection, **5**, 99
      land which may be subject to, **5**, 98
      Lands Tribunal, reference to, **5**, 102
      service of—
         counter-notice, service of, **5**, 101
         grounds for, **5**, 100
      when arising, **5**, 97
generally, **5**, 91
purchase notice—
   compensation after, **5**, 96
   counter-notice, service of—
      contents, **5**, 93
      time limit, **5**, 93
   Secretary of State, options of, **5**, 94
   service of—
      authorised buildings or works, in case of, **5**, 95
      authorised use—
         conditions imposed as to continuation of, in case of, **5**, 95
         discontinued, in case of, **5**, 95
      form of, **5**, 92
      grounds for, **5**, 92
      listed building consent, in case of, **5**, 95
      local planning authority, on, **5**, 92
      planning permission—
         granted subject to conditions, in case of, **5**, 92
         modification of, in case of, **5**, 95
         refusal of, in case of, **5**, 92
         revocation of, in case of, **5**, 95
      regional planning authority, on, **5**, 92
relevant legislation, **5**, 91
when arising, **5**, 91
Reverse engineering or analysis
confidential information, discovery by, **18**, 1472
Reversionary company
loan by, **20**, 232
Reversionary interest
meaning, **19**, 1614
Review Body on Top Salaries
examination of judicial salaries, **6**, 863

Review Committee on Banking Services
cheques, proposals for reform of, **4**, 191
reforms proposed by, **4**, 105
Revolution
fundamental law and, **5**, 340
Revolution Settlement
Church of Scotland, **3**, 1610, 1611
king's governmental and personal capacities, **19**, 207
Scottish Episcopal Church, **3**, 1610, 1611
Reward
advertisement offering, **1**, 503
food offered as, **11**, 400
local government officer, acceptance by, **14**, 253
police officer, payment to, **16**, 1720
Rhine Manifest
transit of goods under, **7**, 1169, 1172
Riddell, John, **16**, 1302, 1302_n_
Riding establishment
health etc of horses, provisions for, **2**, 126
inspection of, **2**, 128
insurance, requirement for, **2**, 125
keeping—
   disqualification from, **2**, 130
   meaning, **2**, 124
licence, **14**, 524
   age limit for obtaining, **2**, 125
   appeals respecting, **2**, 125
   applicant, suitability of, **2**, 126
   conditions, subject to, **2**, 125
   duration, **2**, 125
   matters specified in, **2**, 125
   provisional, **2**, 127
   requirement for, **2**, 124
   transmission on death, **2**, 125
meaning, **2**, 124
offences, **2**, 129
person in charge, minimum age, **2**, 125
protection of horses, **2**, 129
registration, **19**, 1294
safety requirements, **2**, 126
sheriff court jurisdiction, **6**, 1135
veterinary practitioner—
   inspection of premises, **2**, 128
   report by, **2**, 126
Rifle
See FIREARM
Right in security
accessory and principal property, **18**, 578
accessory right, as, **20**, 1
agreement, need for more than, **20**, 4, 6, 7
assignation, creation by—
   arrestment, effect of, **20**, 47
   assignee, **20**, 46
      competition between assignees, **20**, 47
      duty to account to cedent, **20**, 54
      intimation, **20**, 47
      necessary to complete right of, **20**, 47
      management of security subjects, duties as to, **20**, 54
   cedent, **20**, 46
      assignee's duty to account, **20**, 54
      intimation by, **20**, 47
      safeguard of interests of, **20**, 54
      warrandice granted by, **20**, 54

Right in security—*continued*
assignation, creation by—*continued*
  completion, **20**, 55
  confirmation, effect of grant of, **20**, 47
  copyright, assignation of, **20**, 55
  debt owed by more than one person, **20**, 47
  effect of, **20**, 46
  ex facie absolute, **20**, 53
  floating charge, effect of, **20**, 47
  form of, **20**, 46
  generally, **20**, 46
  goodwill, assignation of, **20**, 55
  granted in security, **20**, 53
  intimation—
    assignatus utitur jure auctoris rule, **20**, 51, 52
    completion by, **20**, 55
    effect, **20**, 53
    equivalents of formal, **20**, 49
    methods, **20**, 48
    necessity for, **20**, 53
    necessity to complete right of assignee, **20**, 47
    requirement for, effects of, **20**, 50, 51
    restrictive effect of requirement for, **20**, 50
  patent, assignation of, **20**, 55
  requirements for, **20**, 46
  rights of parties *inter se*, **20**, 54
  sequestration, effect of, **20**, 47
  shares, transfer of, **20**, 55, 55*n*
  trade mark, assignation of, **20**, 55
  unintimated assignation, **20**, 47
  warrandice, **20**, 54
    express, **20**, 54
    implied, **20**, 54
  winding up, effect of, **20**, 47
bottomry, bond of, **20**, 6, 26, 281, 305
cautionary obligation, counterpart or correlative of, **20**, 2
classes, **20**, 2
common law, creation under—
  bottomry, bonds of, **20**, 6, 26, 281, 305
  contractual non-possessory rights in security at common law, **20**, 26, 27
  nature of rights, **20**, 8
  ownership, transfer from debtor to secured creditor, **20**, 8
  pledge, **20**, 8, 14–25
  possession of security subjects, **20**, 8–13
  respondentia, bonds of, **20**, 6, 27
  traditionibus, non nudis pactis, dominia rerum transferuntur maxim, **20**, 8
common property, *pro indiviso* shares, **18**, 28
competing titles, rule as to, **18**, 686
debt, secured—
  payment or other satisfaction, **20**, 1
  as safeguard against personal failure of debtor, **20**, 1
English law contrasted, **20**, 5
express discharge, **18**, 9
fittings, **18**, 578
fixtures, **18**, 578
floating charge, **18**, 5
general nature, **20**, 1
heritable property, as, **18**, 14

Right in security—*continued*
heritable security, *see* HERITABLE SECURITY
historical background, **20**, 3
hypothec, **18**, 534
  distinguishing features, **20**, 7, 101
  lien distinguished, **20**, 68, 101
  maritime, **20**, 101*n*
  meaning, **20**, 7
  moveable property, **20**, 101
  nature of, **20**, 101
  pledge compared, **20**, 101
  possession by creditor not required, **20**, 101
  right in security implied by law, as, **20**, 7
  Scots law, limited acceptance in, **20**, 102
incorporeal property, as, **18**, 652
law, implied by, **20**, 2, 7, 66
  hypothec, *see* hypothec *above*
  lien, *see* LIEN
lease distinguished, **13**, 116
legal hypothec, **20**, 7
maritime lien, *see* LIEN
meaning, **18**, 5; **20**, 1
moveable property—
  agreement, constitution by, **20**, 2
  common law, creation under, *see* common law, creation under *above*
  corporeal—
    bill of lading, **20**, 12
    Consumer Credit Act 1974, transactions affected by—
      cancellation or termination, **20**, 40
      failure to comply with requirements, **20**, 38
      generally, **20**, 36
      information, creditor's duty to give, **20**, 39
      negotiable instruments, **20**, 42
      pledges, **20**, 41
      securities—
        realisation of, **20**, 40
        related, enforcement of, **20**, 40
        requirements as to, **20**, 37
    delivery—
      actual, **20**, 9, 10
      attempted evasion of requirement for, **20**, 13
      constructive, **20**, 9, 11
      possession resulting from, **20**, 9–12
      symbolical, **20**, 9, 12
    hire purchase—
      instalment, payment only possible by, **20**, 35
      lump sum, payment of whole price by, **20**, 35
      motor vehicle, of, **20**, 35
      owner of goods, protection of, **20**, 35
      resale of goods by buyer, **20**, 35
      sale, contract of, distinguished, **20**, 34
    nature of possession required, **20**, 9–13
    negotiable instruments, **20**, 15, 42
    pledge—
      actual delivery, need for, **20**, 17, 18
      agent, by, and title of pledgee, **20**, 21
      bill of lading, transfer in security, **20**, 19
      Consumer Credit Act 1974, provisions of, **20**, 41
      creation, **20**, 17

Right in security—*continued*
moveable property—*continued*
  corporeal—*continued*
    pledge—*continued*
      debts for which pledge may be retained, **20**, 16
      delivery essential to completion of pledgees's real right, **20**, 8, 14
      Hamilton v Western Bank of Scotland, **20**, 17, 18
      lien distinguished, **20**, 14
      nature of contract, **20**, 14
      negotiable instruments, **20**, 15, 42
      pawn, **20**, 14, 41
      pledgee—
        obligations of, **20**, 24
        real rights, **20**, 8, 14
        surrender of possession by, **20**, 14
        title of, **20**, 21, 22
      possessory right in security, creation at common law, **20**, 8
      sub-pledge, power to, **20**, 25
      subjects which may be pledged, **20**, 15
      title—
        pledgee, of, **20**, 21, 22
        pledgor, of, **20**, 23
      transfer of property on *ex facie* absolute title compared, **20**, 20
    possession, creditor taking, **20**, 4, 6, 8
      bill of lading, **20**, 12
      delivery—
        actual, **20**, 9, 10
        appropriate to security subject, must be, **20**, 9
        attempted evasion of requirement for, **20**, 13
        constructive, **20**, 9, 11
        physically impossible, where, **20**, 10
        symbolical, **20**, 9, 12
      nature of possession required, **20**, 9–13
    statutory powers, creation under, *see* statutory powers, creation under *below*
    title—
      retention on sale by seller—
        all-sums retention of title clause, **20**, 32, 32*n*
        generally, **20**, 29
        insolvency of buyer, **20**, 31
        nature of retention clauses, **20**, 30
        seller's rights, generally, **20**, 32, 32*n*, 33
        subjects of sale resold by buyer, **20**, 31
      Romalpa clause—
        meaning, **20**, 29
        nature of, **20**, 30
        seller's right to retain title, generally, **20**, 32, 32*n*, 33
        subject of sale no longer held by buyer, where, **20**, 31
  diligence, acquisition by use of, **20**, 2
  generally, **6**, 626, 627; **18**, 14; **20**, 2
  hypothec, **20**, 101
  incorporeal—
    alimentary funds, **20**, 43, 44

Right in security—*continued*
moveable property—*continued*
  incorporeal—*continued*
    assignation, creation by—
      arrestment, effect of, **20**, 47
      assignation in security, **20**, 53
      assignee, **20**, 46
        competition between assignees, **20**, 47
        duty of care, **20**, 54
        intimation by, **20**, 47
        intimation necessary to complete right of, **20**, 47
        obligation to account to cedent, **20**, 54
      cedent, **20**, 46, 51
        intimation by, **20**, 47
        obligations of assignee to, **20**, 54
        warrandice granted by, **20**, 54
      company shares, **20**, 55, 55*n*
      completion, **20**, 55
      copyright, **20**, 55
      debt owed by more than one person, **20**, 47
      effect of, **20**, 46
      ex facie absolute, **20**, 53
      floating charge, effect of, **20**, 47
      form of assignation, **20**, 46
      generally, **6**, 627; **20**, 46
      goodwill, **20**, 55
      grant of confirmation, effect of, **20**, 47
      intimation—
        assignatus utitur jure auctoris rule, **20**, 51, 52
        completion by, **20**, 55
        effect, **20**, 53
        equivalents to formal, **20**, 49
        methods, **20**, 48
        necessity for, **20**, 53
        necessity to complete right of assignee, **20**, 47
        requirement for, effects of, **20**, 50, 51
      patents, **20**, 55
      requirements for, **20**, 46
      rights of parties *inter se*, **20**, 54
      sequestration, effect of, **20**, 47
      trade marks, **20**, 55
      unintimated assignation, **20**, 47
      warrandice—
        express, **20**, 54
        grant of, **20**, 54
        implied, **20**, 54
      winding up, effect of, **20**, 47
    claims, **20**, 43
    company shares, **20**, 43
    copyright, **20**, 43
    creation—
      assignation, by, **20**, 46–55
      negotiable instrument, in, **20**, 56–60
    debts, **20**, 43
    delectus personae, element of, **20**, 43, 45
    future performance of contractual obligation, **20**, 45
    future rights, **20**, 43, 50
    goodwill, **20**, 43
    hypothec, **20**, 101

Right in security—*continued*
moveable property—*continued*
  incorporeal—*continued*
    insurance policy, rights under, **20**, 43
    life assurance policy as security subject—
      assignation, **20**, 61, 63
      contingent security, as, **20**, 61
      independent security, as, **20**, 61
      insurable interest in life assured, **20**, 64
      ownership, **20**, 65
      precautionary measures, **20**, 62
    methods of constituting, **20**, 46–60
    negotiable instrument, creation in—
      assignation of debt compared, **20**, 56
      characteristics of negotiable instrument,
        20, 56
      pledged, negotiable instrument may be,
        20, 57
      pledgee—
        favourable position of, **20**, 58
        power to deal with instrument as
          owner, **20**, 60
      security provided by negotiable
        instrument, **20**, 56, 59
    partnership, assignation of interest, **20**, 45
    patents, **20**, 43
    right personal to grantee, **20**, 45
    skill, talent or other personal characteristic,
      right enjoyed because of, **20**, 43
    trade marks, **20**, 43
    where right may be created—
      generally, **20**, 43
  law, implied by, **20**, 2, 7
  hypothec, *see* hypothec *above*
  lien, *see* LIEN
  pledge—
    delivery essential to completion of pledgees's
      real right, **20**, 8, 14
  possession, creditor taking, **20**, 4, 6, 8
  transfer *inter vivos*, *lex situs*, **17**, 323
nemo dat quod non habet rule, **18**, 669
overt act making right's existence known to third
  parties, **20**, 4, 7
owner may not hold over own property, **18**, 9
passing of property, **18**, 637
patent, **18**, 811
  registration, **18**, 812
pledge, **18**, 5, 534
pledge, lien distinguished, **20**, 67, 101
possession, **20**, 3
  creditor taking, **20**, 4, 6, 8
  mortgage substituted for, **20**, 28
  registration substituted for, **20**, 6, 28, 55
  right to, **18**, 127
preferential right, **20**, 2
principal debtor to cautioner, given, transfer, **3**,
  938
purpose, **20**, 1
real estate, loan on security of, *see* HERITABLE
  SECURITY
real right, as, **18**, 4, 5, 693; **20**, 2
renunciation, **18**, 9
requirements under Scots law, **20**, 4–7
  English law contrasted, **20**, 5

Right in security—*continued*
respondentia bond, **20**, 6, 27, 281
Roman law, influence of, **20**, 3
ship—
  maritime lien, *see* MARITIME LIEN
standard security, **18**, 5
statutory powers, creation under—
  aircraft, mortgage over, **20**, 28
  floating charge, **20**, 28
  ship, mortgage over, **20**, 28
subordinate real right, as, **18**, 534
termination of right, **18**, 6
third parties, existence must be known to, **20**, 4, 7
transfer of ownership, and, **18**, 604
Right of passage or way (servitude)
agricultural or market garden purposes, limited
  to, **18**, 460
alteration of line or course, **18**, 469, 487
dangerous animal kept on, **18**, 487
diversion of line or course, **18**, 469, 487
drove road, **18**, 487
express provision, creation by, **18**, 487
foreshore, **18**, 526
generally, **6**, 515; **18**, 487
locked gate or door, **18**, 487
maintenance of passage or way, **18**, 487
obstruction—
  generally, **18**, 487
  judicial proceedings, **18**, 482
particular purpose, restricted to, **18**, 487
passage and pasturage, right of, **18**, 487
pedestrian, **18**, 487
prescription, creation by, **18**, 487
public—
  built-up area, road in, **20**, 612
  private road, **20**, 648
    owner's responsibility for, **20**, 614
  requirements for, **20**, 612
  Secretary of State's powers, **20**, 616
public right of way—
  compared, **18**, 492, 495
  See also RIGHT OF WAY (PUBLIC)
replacement, **18**, 487
Roman law, **18**, 487
servitude, as, **6**, 515; **18**, 483, 487
third parties, use by, **18**, 345
vehicular use, **18**, 487
width, reduction of, **18**, 487
Right of way (public)
building contracts, and, **3**, 159
custom, and, **22**, 380, 391, 393
foot, on, **20**, 653
opencast mining, suspension of right of way, **14**,
  1698
order extinguishing, **5**, 42
overriding interest, as, **6**, 746
public—
  acquiescence—
    establishment by, **16**, 1616
    loss by, **16**, 1616
  alteration, **18**, 509
  benefit of public generally, existence for, **18**,
    495
  bridleway, **18**, 503

Right of way (public)—_continued_
public—_continued_
  bull kept on, **18**, 507
  compulsory acquisition of land, effect, **18**, 511
  creation, **18**, 494
    express written provision, **18**, 498
    judicial proceedings, title to sue, **18**, 512
    prescription, by—
      generally, **18**, 499
      possession, requirements of, **18**, 501
      registration, no requirement for, **18**, 501
      statutory provisions, **18**, 500
      tolerance, possession should not be
        attributable to, **18**, 501
      user, requirements of, **18**, 501
    statutory authority, under—
      Countryside Acts, **18**, 503
      local government legislation, **18**, 502
      town and country planning legislation, **18**,
        504
  creation of, **6**, 746
  custom, and, 'time immemorial', **22**, 380, 393
  dedication, creation by, **18**, 498
  direction notices, erection and maintenance,
    18, 506
  disputes as to, **18**, 497
  diversion, **18**, 508_n_, 509
  encroachments, responsibility for removal, **18**,
    506
  enforcement, **18**, 494
  establishment, **18**, 506
  express grant or dedication, constitution by,
    traffic types, and, **18**, 505
  extinction—
    compulsory acquisition of land, on, **18**, 511
    non-use, by, **18**, 510
      prescriptive period, **18**, 510
    statutory provisions or powers, by, **18**, 511
  fences, **18**, 495
  foreshore, on, **18**, 497, 526
  gates, **18**, 495, 508
  generally, **6**, 517; **18**, 7, 494
  grant, creation by, **18**, 498
  guide posts, erection and maintenance, **18**, 506
  judicial proceedings—
    action of declarator, **18**, 512, 513
    effect of judgment, **18**, 513
    establishment, proceedings for, **18**, 512
    form of procedure, **18**, 513
    title to sue, **18**, 512
  landowner—
    judicial proceedings instigated by, **18**, 512
    liability, **18**, 507
    no obligation to repair or maintain way, **18**, 506
    rights and obligations, generally, **18**, 495
    rights of ownership, effect of right of way,
      18, 508
  limitations of, **18**, 497, 501
  maintenance, responsibility for, **18**, 495, 506
  meaning, **22**, 393
  negative prescription, **16**, 2121, 2122
  obstruction, **18**, 508
    responsibility for removal of obstruction, **18**,
      506

Right of way (public)—_continued_
public—_continued_
  occupier's liability, **15**, 319
  pedestrian, **18**, 505
  planning authority, rights and duties of, **18**, 506
  plough, landowner's right to, **18**, 508, 508_n_
  positive prescription, **16**, 2105, 2111, 2112
  possession, rights of, **18**, 126_n_
  prescription—
    application of doctrine, **22**, 391, 393
    constitution by—
      prescriptive period, **18**, 494
      traffic types, and, **18**, 505
  private land, over, **18**, 495
  properties situated on route, as access to, **18**,
    497
  public highway or street distinguished, **18**, 495
  public path creation agreement, **18**, 503, 508_n_
  public path creation order, **18**, 503, 508_n_, 510
  public path diversion order, **18**, 503, 508_n_, 509
  public place, meaning, **18**, 496
  real right, as, **18**, 5, 494
  repairs, responsibility for, **18**, 506
  rights and duties as to—
    alteration of route, **18**, 509
    diversion of route, **18**, 509
    establishment of way, **18**, 506
    maintenance, **18**, 506
    occupier's liability, **18**, 507
    ownership rights, affect on, **18**, 508
    traffic types which may use way, **18**, 505
  route or connection between public places, as,
    18, 495–497, 501
  servitude right of passage or way—
    co-existing over same road or path, **18**, 487,
      487_n_
    distinguished, **16**, 2112; **18**, 492, 495
    See also RIGHT OF PASSAGE OR WAY
  solum remaining property of landowner, **18**,
    495
  stiles, **18**, 495, 508
  track, whether visible, **18**, 497
  traffic types, **18**, 505
  vehicular traffic, **18**, 505
railway, land severed by, **19**, 1045
registration—
  prescription, right of way created by, **18**, 501
  statutory authority, right of way created under,
    18, 503
Rights
abortion, right to procure, **11**, 1095
absence of legal requirements, and, **11**, 1082
abstract states of affairs, **11**, 1098
abstract things, **11**, 1096–1098
acquired, respect for, **10**, 96
acting 'within one's rights', **11**, 1084, 1085
active—
  conjoined with passive, **11**, 1088
  'liberty', **11**, 1081
  'privilege', **11**, 1081
  recognition of, **11**, 1078
  'right of action', **11**, 1081, 1085, 1091, 1095
association, rights of, **11**, 1095
'claims' or 'claim-rights', **11**, 1079

Rights—*continued*
conduct—
  personal, **11**, 1081
  rights bearing on, **11**, 1079
consequential rights and powers, **11**, 1105, 1106
contract of employment, within, *see* CONTRACT OF
    EMPLOYMENT
correlative, **11**, 1080
divestment, **11**, 1107
event giving rise to, **11**, 1100
'faculty'—
  'choice' or 'will' theory, **11**, 1073, 1077, 1090
  fixed or limited terms, **11**, 1108
  freedom contrasted, **11**, 1085
future time, with tract of, **18**, 14
good faith as precondition, **11**, 1128, 1132
heritable, **18**, 13, 14
holder and right, relationship between, **18**, 16
hypothec, **11**, 1108
incapax of, **11**, 1076
incorporeal separate tenements, **18**, 10
incorporeal thing, as, **18**, 11*n*, 16
jus ad rem, **11**, 1099
jus in personam, *see* personal *below*
jus in re, *see* REAL RIGHT
jus in rem, *see* REAL RIGHT
liability and power, **11**, 1087
liberty contrasted, **11**, 1085
life, right to, **11**, 1092, 1096
mortgage, **11**, 1108
nature of, **11**, 1073
non-divestability, **11**, 1089
occupancy, of non-entitled spouse, **18**, 10
'of recipience', **11**, 1079
ownership, and, **18**, 16
passive, **11**, 1080, 1091, 1095
  capacity to have, **11**, 1075
  conjoined with active, **11**, 1088
performance, in, *see* RIGHTS IN PERFORMANCES
personal—
  ancillary—
    warrandice, **18**, 718
  assignation, **18**, 8*n*
    warrandice, **18**, 717
  assignatus utitur jure auctoris, **13**, 59
  competition with real right, where—
    grant in breach of trust, **18**, 691
    grantee not bound by personal obligations of
      author, **18**, 688
    granter's power to grant unimpaired by
      personal obligation, **18**, 689
    'offside goals', rule against, **18**, 690, 693, 694
    secured creditors, **18**, 693
    unsecured creditors, **18**, 694
    voidable title, grant by one holding, **18**, 692
  delict, contractual right arising under, *see* DELICT
  enforcement, **18**, 3
  feudal tenure, **18**, 42
  incorporeal property, **18**, 11
  meaning, **18**, 3
  negative prescription, **18**, 9
  obligation as, **15**, 1
  possession, **18**, 126, 127, 128
    jura ad rem, **18**, 128

Rights—*continued*
personal—*continued*
  real right, conversion to, possession and, **13**,
    141
  real right in land, to, **18**, 14
  secured creditor, and, **18**, 693
  third party interests, reduction, and, **13**, 59
  trusts, **24**, 15
  trusts and, **24**, 15
  unsecured creditor, and, **18**, 694
personal conduct, and, **11**, 1081
pledges, **11**, 1108
power—
  liability and, **11**, 1087
  powers distinguished, **11**, 1083
presumption against enactment taking away, **12**,
    1131
privacy, **11**, 1094, 1096
privilege contrasted, **11**, 1085
public, *see* PUBLIC RIGHTS
real, *see* REAL RIGHT
real security, **11**, 1108
relevant duty, depends on, **11**, 1074
remedies distinguished, **11**, 1077
right to buy, *see* SECURE TENANT
rights in rights, **18**, 16
riparian, *see* RIPARIAN RIGHTS
security, in, *see* RIGHT IN SECURITY
self-defence, right to, **11**, 1095
servitudes, **11**, 1109, 1110
  praedial, **11**, 1109, 1110
shareholders, of, *see* SHAREHOLDER
speech, rights as to, **11**, 1095
standard security, **11**, 1108
states of affairs, in regard to, **11**, 1091–1098
states of being, in regard to, **11**, 1091–1098
stricto sensu, **11**, 1079
succession, legal rights, *see* SUCCESSION
surrender, **11**, 1090
termination, **11**, 1107
things, in (real rights), **11**, 1101, 1111
  beneficial legal relations, as, **11**, 1104
  consequential rights and powers, **11**, 1105
    variation, **11**, 1106
  derivative modes of acquisition, **11**, 1103
  divestitive and terminative provisions, **11**, 1107
  liferent, **11**, 1110
  meaning of real rights, **11**, 1101
  obligations distinguished, **15**, 1
  occupatio act of, **11**, 1102
  ownership, **11**, 1101, 1110
  private property, alternative to, **11**, 1112
  property, rights of, **11**, 1107
    imprescriptive, **16**, 2126
  real security, **11**, 1101, 1110
  servitude, **11**, 1101, 1109, 1110
  tenancy, **11**, 1101, 1108, 1110
  title to, **11**, 1102
  types of, **11**, 1110
things, to, **11**, 1099, 1100, 1197
  abstract things, **11**, 1096–1098
    abstract states of affairs distinguished, **11**,
      1098
  corporeal, **11**, 1097

Rights—*continued*
things, to—*continued*
  durability, **11**, 1097
  heritability, **11**, 1097
  incorporeal, **11**, 1097
title, **11**, 1101
transfer, **11**, 1090, 1107; **18**, 16
  unrecorded or unregistered, **6**, 748
trust beneficiary, of, **18**, 10
trusts, constitution of, **24**, 12, 15
waiver, **11**, 1090
work, right to, **11**, 1091, 1093
Rights in performances
assignation, **18**, 1438
breach of statutory duty, **18**, 1438
consent in relation to—
  generally, **18**, 1436
  lack of sufficient, **18**, 1442
copyright licensing, interaction with, **18**, 1437
Copyright Tribunal, matters which may be
  brought before, **18**, 1436
criminal offences, **18**, 1442, 1443
death, transfer on, **18**, 1441
duration, **18**, 1440
European Union legislation, **18**, 1643
exceptions, **18**, 1439
generally, **18**, 1431
infringement—
  acquisition of illicit recording, **18**, 1438
    innocent, **18**, 1438
  broadcast or cable programme, illicit recording,
    18, 1438
  damages for, **18**, 1438
  delivery up, order for, **18**, 1438, 1442
  generally, **18**, 1434
  remedies, **18**, 1438
  seizure of illicit copies, **18**, 1438
more than one performer, consent of all required,
  18, 1436
performance, meaning, **18**, 1432
performer's rights, generally, **18**, 1434
permitted acts, **18**, 1439
qualification for statutory protection, **18**, 1433
re-recordings of earlier performances, **18**, 1437
reciprocal countries, qualification for protection,
  18, 1433
recording—
  illicit, acquisition, **18**, 1438
  meaning in relation to performance, **18**, 1432
  recording rights, and, **18**, 1432, 1435
transmission, **18**, 1441
Rioting
See MOBBING AND RIOTING
Riotous assemblies
sheriff court jurisdiction, **6**, 1091
Riparian rights
abstraction of water, **25**, 330
addition of water, **25**, 332
bank, constraint on operation on, **25**, 324
generally, **25**, 316
meaning, **25**, 304
tidal area, above, **25**, 311
water, operations directly affecting—
  categories of action, **25**, 325

Riparian rights—*continued*
water, operations directly affecting—*continued*
  consumption, **25**, 334
  flow, *see* RIVER
  pollution, **25**, 335
See also LOCH; RIVER
River
abstraction of water from, **11**, 6
access to exercise salmon fishing right, **11**, 8
alteration of course—
  common interest, doctrine of, **18**, 284, 285
  salmon fishings, **18**, 326
alveus, see ALVEUS
aquaehaustus, servitude of, **18**, 281, 287, 288, 295
artificial channel, water in, **18**, 302
bank—
  alluvion, **18**, 593
  building on, common interest, and, **18**, 297
  constraint on operation on, **25**, 324
  maintenance, obligations as to, **18**, 281
  public right of navigation, ancillary rights, **18**,
    528
barriers prohibited, **11**, 14
bridge, construction over, **20**, 638, 639, 644
channel, whether obligation to scour, **18**, 281,
  284
common interest, doctrine of—
  alveus, building on, **18**, 296
  artificially introduced water, **18**, 286
  development of doctrine, **18**, 282
  dominant and servient proprietors, **18**, 283
  enforcement, **18**, 290
  ex adverso proprietors, **18**, 282
  generally, **18**, 281, 359
  loch, river flowing from, **18**, 307
  mineral rights, **18**, 282
  natural flow of water, preservation, **18**, 284,
    289, 291–294, 295
  natural servitude, as, **18**, 355
  pollution, **18**, 298, 299
  real right, as, **18**, 290
  res communes, running water as, **18**, 282
  riparian proprietor, obligations, **18**, 281
  scope, **18**, 284
  sources feeding into river or stream, **18**, 286
  superior and inferior heritors, **18**, 284
  variation and discharge, **18**, 290
  weir or dam, construction of, **18**, 296
consumption of water, *see* WATER
dams, **11**, 19, 25, 25*n*
  Secretary of State's powers, **11**, 23
different proprietor on each bank—
  salmon fishing, **11**, 5
  trout fishing, **11**, 48
diversion of watercourse, **25**, 327
Esk, *see* RIVER ESK
estuary, *see* ESTUARY
fish, obstructing passage of, **11**, 14, 19; **19**, 22
fish passes, **11**, 19
flood prevention, **19**, 324
flooding, seasonal—
  barrier against as interference with natural flow,
    18, 297

River—*continued*
flow—
  abstraction of water, **25**, 330
  addition of water, **25**, 332
  categories of action, **25**, 326
  dam, construction of, **25**, 329
  diversion of water, **25**, 327
  impounding water, **25**, 328
  reservoir, construction of, **25**, 329
  spray irrigation, **25**, 331
  storage of water, **25**, 328
  superior proprietor, rights of, **25**, 336
  temporary discharge, **25**, 333
inland water, as, **21**, 112
island in—
  formation, **18**, 278, 593
  ownership, **18**, 278
lateral boundary, **12**, 1239
limits of, **11**, 32
local authority powers, **18**, 281
loch, flowing from, common interest, **18**, 307
meaning, **18**, 286; **25**, 302
medium filum, **11**, 5, 48
  marking, **18**, 278
  ownership, and, **18**, 278
  salmon fishing rights, and, **18**, 327, 329
mill lades, **11**, 19, 25, 25*n*
  Secretary of State's powers, **11**, 23
natural flow of water—
  flood barrier, interference by, **18**, 297
  meaning, **18**, 285
  preservation, **18**, 284, 289, 291–294, 295
  salmon fishings must not intefere with, **18**, 326
  seasonal flooding, **18**, 297
  upper proprietors' obligation not to interfere
    with, **18**, 355
navigable—
  diversion, widening or narrowing, **19**, 24
  navigability, **25**, 306
  navigation—
    exercise of right, **25**, 307
    public rights—
      extinction, **25**, 308
      revival, **25**, 308
    rights, generally, **11**, 7
  non-navigable river distinguished from, **25**, 305
  public river, use of term, **18**, 277
  right to sail on, **16**, 2126
  riparian rights, *see* RIPARIAN RIGHTS
  valuation, not subject to, **24**, 600
navigation rights, *see* NAVIGATION
new schemes, **25**, 516
non-navigable—
  meaning, **12**, 1239
  navigable river distinguished, **25**, 305
non-tidal, **21**, 112
  alveus, see alveus
  anchoring in, **25**, 307
  bed, ownership of, **25**, 317
  meaning, **25**, 313
  medium filum, **25**, 317
  navigability, **25**, 314
  navigation, right of, **25**, 315
nuisance, application of law, **18**, 281

River—*continued*
obstruction of salmon, **11**, 14, 19
  Secretary of State's powers, **11**, 23
ownership—
  alveus, **18**, 275–278
    a coelo ad centrum, **18**, 278
    Crown ownership, **18**, 275
    generally, **18**, 278
    private ownership, **18**, 275
    tidal and non-tidal waters, **18**, 275, 276
  boundary between estates, river on, **18**, 278
  medium filum, **18**, 278
  one estate, river within, **18**, 278
  riparian proprietor, *see* riparian proprietor *below*
  several consecutive estates, river within, **18**, 278
pilotage, *see* PILOT (shipping); PILOTAGE
pollution—
  common interest, doctrine of, **18**, 298, 299
  defences to action, **18**, 300
  negative prescription, defence of, **18**, 300
  private law, action taken under, **18**, 298
  public law, **18**, 298
  restrictions on, generally, **18**, 281
  See also POLLUTION
private, public river distinguished from, **25**, 305
promotion of cleanliness, **19**, 322
provisional order affecting, **19**, 21
public, use of term, **18**, 277
public rights over, generally, **18**, 5, 494
purification, *see* RIVER PURIFICATION
railway construction affecting, **19**, 1024
riparian proprietor, **25**, 303
  agricultural purposes, water consumption for,
    18, 282, 287, 288
  alveus, building on, **18**, 296
  bank, building on, **18**, 297
  bank, of, but not of *alveus*, **18**, 283
  common interest, doctrine of, *see* common
    interest, doctrine of *above*
  domestic purposes, water consumed for, **18**,
    279, 282, 287
  dominant, **18**, 283
  entitlement to receive water of same quality as
    that bestowed by nature, **18**, 299
  fishing rights, **18**, 279, 280
  industrial uses, water may not be used for, **18**,
    279, 287, 288
  insignificantly small section of *alveus* owned by,
    18, 279
  meaning, **18**, 278
  primary purposes, water consumption for, **18**,
    287
  removal of water by pipe or other mechanical
    means, **18**, 287
  restrictions on use, **18**, 281
  rights as to use of water, **18**, 279
    restrictions, **18**, 281
  sailing rights, **18**, 279
  servient, **18**, 283
  servitudes, **18**, 281
  surplus water, return of, **18**, 287
riparian rights, *see* RIPARIAN RIGHTS
river purification authority, *see* RIVER PURIFICATION
  AUTHORITY

River—*continued*
running water as *res communes*, **18**, 282
salmon fishing rights, *see* SALMON-SALMON
    FISHERIES
salvage operations, **21**, 440
servitudes—
    generally, **18**, 281
    grant of, **25**, 349
sewage discharged into, **19**, 22
sheriff, jurisdiction of, **4**, 2
sources feeding into, whether part of river, **18**,
    286
spray irrigation, **19**, 323
statutory restrictions, generally, **18**, 281
superior proprietor, rights of, **25**, 336
territorial sea, baselines, **21**, 12
tidal—
    adjacent proprietors, rights of, **18**, 312
    alienation to subject proprietors, **18**, 311
    Crown rights, **18**, 309, 310; **25**, 310, 312
    dredging, **25**, 312
    foreshore, alienation of, **25**, 310
    meaning, **25**, 309
    navigation—
        public rights, **25**, 310
        unlawful impeding of, **25**, 312
    public rights, **25**, 310, 312
    tidal area—
        Crown rights in, **25**, 310
        public rights in, **25**, 310
        riparian rights above, **25**, 311
tidal navigable, meaning, **12**, 1239
tidal parts, whether sea, **21**, 112
transboundary, **19**, 687
trespass on, **18**, 180
    See also TRESPASS
tunnel, construction under, **20**, 638, 644
Tweed, *see* RIVER TWEED
underground water, **18**, 301
water pollution, **14**, 2079
water rights, acquisition of, **25**, 519
water sports and recreation, **19**, 1280
water wheels, Secretary of State's powers as to,
    11, 23
River Esk
administration, **11**, 39
close time—
    annual, **11**, 46
    weekly, **11**, 46
poaching, **11**, 46
salmon fishing, regulation of, **11**, 46
River purification
authority, *see* RIVER PURIFICATION AUTHORITY
board, **14**, 475
committee, **14**, 476
generally, **25**, 397
officers, **14**, 476
reform, **14**, 46
River purification authority
constitution, **25**, 399
duties and functions, **14**, 477; **25**, 398
establishment, **25**, 399
generally, **19**, 321, 324; **25**, 398
information required by, **25**, 421

River purification authority—*continued*
planning application, consultation over, **23**, 169
pollution, control of, *see* POLLUTION
powers, **25**, 398
spray irrigation, **25**, 331, 389
waters controlled by, **25**, 400
River purification board
See RIVER PURIFICATION AUTHORITY
River Tweed
Acts, **11**, 40, 43
    enforcement, **11**, 41
administration, **11**, 39
    salmon fisheries, **11**, 40, 41
bag net, regulations as to, **11**, 43
baits and lures, regulations as to, **11**, 43
close time—
    annual, **11**, 42, 43
    weekly, **11**, 42, 43
Commissioners, **11**, 39, 40, 41
    water bailiffs appointed by, **11**, 42
Council, **11**, 40, 41
    annual general meeting, **11**, 41
    application to Secretary of State to make
        regulations, **11**, 43
    chairman, **11**, 41
    constitution, **11**, 41
    powers and duties, **11**, 41
    proprietary commissioners, **11**, 41, 41*n*
    proxy votes, **11**, 41
    representative commissioners, **11**, 41
    voting, **11**, 41
enforcing officers' powers of arrest, **11**, 28
exemption of offences, **11**, 43
fixed nets or engines prohibited, **11**, 42
fly net, regulations as to, **11**, 43
freshwater fishing, legislation relating to, **11**, 10
limits, **11**, 40
meaning, **11**, 40
net and coble, regulations as to, **11**, 43
obstruction of enforcing officer, **11**, 29
obstruction of fish, **11**, 19*n*
salmon fisheries—
    legislation relating to, **11**, 10
    regulation of, **11**, 42
    salmon fishery districts, **11**, 33
Secretary of State's powers, **11**, 23*n*
stake net, regulations as to, **11**, 42, 43
weekly close time, **11**, 17
Ro-ro passenger ship
meaning, **21**, 213*n*
safety requirements, **21**, 213
Road
access to—
    prevention of, **20**, 660
    private, stopping up, **20**, 653
accident, *see* ROAD ACCIDENT
alteration, **20**, 616
    roads authority, powers of, **20**, 646, 660
animals on—
    dogs, *see* dog on *below*
    generally, **20**, 506, 706
    horses and carts, **20**, 706
    liability for accident caused by, **15**, 185
    straying on road, **20**, 707

Road—*continued*

apparatus, laying under—
    not belonging to statutory undertakers, **20**, 687
    roads authority control, **20**, 683
arches under, maintenance of, **20**, 664
authority, *see* ROADS AUTHORITY
barbed wire fence dangerous or injurious to
    person using, **20**, 697
barrier—
    protective, provision of, **20**, 660
    wilful damage to, **20**, 704
boundary, on, **12**, 1239
breaking open of, **25**, 519
bridge, *see* BRIDGE
bridleway, **20**, 610
    footpath, conversion into, **20**, 676
British Railways Board, transport by, **19**, 1005
building, projections from, **20**, 694, 695
building materials deposited on, **3**, 201; **20**, 684
built-up area, in, public right of passage, **20**, 612
bus shelter, provision of, **20**, 612, 667
camber, alteration, **20**, 660
capital resources, allocation of, **20**, 615
carriage by—
    bus, *see* BUS; PUBLIC SERVICE VEHICLE
    generally, **3**, 601, 617
    limitation of actions—
        goods, carriage of, **16**, 2203
        luggage, loss or damage, **16**, 2202
        passenger, death or personal injury, **16**, 2202
    passengers, *see* PASSENGER
    solid fuel, carriage of, **6**, 236
    taxi, *see* TAXI
carriageway—
    division, **20**, 660
    meaning, **14**, 405; **20**, 501
    when road classed as, **20**, 610
cattle grid—
    notice of proposed, **20**, 669
    objections to, **20**, 669
    over or near railway tunnel, **19**, 1029
    provision and maintenance of, **20**, 503, 618,
        669
cellar under, maintenance of, **20**, 664
central reservation, provision of, **20**, 660
classification, **20**, 615
cleaning—
    generally, **9**, 1172; **14**, 411; **19**, 364
    responsibility for, **20**, 616, 618, 665, 677
    trunk roads, **20**, 620
clearances, **14**, 1632
committee, **14**, 406
compulsory acquisition of land—
    motorway service area, for, **20**, 628
    provision of buildings or facilities to service or
        construct, **20**, 620
    roads authority, by, **20**, 708, 712
    special road, for, **20**, 626
construction, **14**, 1630; **20**, 617
    local roads authority, by, **20**, 646
    special roads, **20**, 626
    toll road, **20**, 636
    trunk roads, **20**, 620
    water diversion whilst road under, **20**, 608

Road—*continued*

creation, provision for, **20**, 608
Crown land, application of Roads (Scotland) Act
    1984 ..., **20**, 720
cutting, environmental impact assessment, **20**, 671
cycle racing, **19**, 1284, 1286
cycle track—
    meaning, **14**, 405
    when classed as, **20**, 501, 610
damage to—
    extraordinary expenses in repairing, **20**, 703
    fire, caused by, **20**, 704
    generally, **20**, 506
    heavy or extraordinary vehicles, responsibility
        for, **20**, 703
    offences as to, **20**, 704
    regulation of, **20**, 608
danger created by, responsibility for, **20**, 611
dangerous buildings, **20**, 696
dangerous condition, in—
    fencing off, **20**, 611
    responsibility for, **20**, 611
    stopping up, **20**, 652
dangerous site next to—
    private road, **20**, 614
    roads authorities duties as to, **20**, 611
defence, stopping up or diverting road for
    purposes of, **20**, 657
defence manoeuvres, effect of, **20**, 659
definition, **20**, 411, 501, 609
    drink driving offences, in relation to, **20**, 420
design, toll road, **20**, 636
development order, affected by, **20**, 654
developments, permitted—
    standard conditions as to, **23**, 137
ditches, where source of danger, **20**, 698
diversion, **14**, 1684
    aviation purposes, for, **20**, 657
    defence purposes, for, **20**, 657
    development order, road affected by, **20**, 654
dog on—
    collars, requirement to wear, **2**, 174
    control of, **2**, 173
    generally, **2**, 173, 174
    liability for accident caused by, **15**, 185
    where lead necessary, **20**, 439
    See also animals on *above*
domestic carriage of goods by—
    carrier—
        delivery to, **3**, 620
        types, **3**, 619
    charge for, **3**, 629
    consignee's duty, **3**, 634
    crew, sufficiency of, **3**, 626
    damage in transit, **3**, 640
    dangerous goods, **3**, 623
    delay in transit, **3**, 636–639
        expenses caused by, **3**, 637
        loss of market or customers caused by, **3**, 638
    delivery to consignee, **3**, 633
        delivery not taken, where, **3**, 635
    dispatch and delay, **3**, 632
    duration of transit, **3**, 642
    insurance of goods in transit, **3**, 628

Road—continued

domestic carriage of goods by—*continued*
  labelling, consignor's duty, **3**, 621
  livestock, **3**, 625
  loss in transit, **3**, 640
  misdelivery, **3**, 633, 640
  operator's licence, **3**, 619
  packing, consignor's duty, **3**, 621
  perishable goods, **3**, 624
  precautions en route, **3**, 627
  route, provisions as to, **3**, 630
  Scottish Transport Group, **3**, 619
  stoppage in transit, **3**, 641–644
  stowage, **3**, 622
  sub-contracting, **3**, 631
  vehicle, sufficiency of, **3**, 626
domestic carriage of passengers by—
  accidents and collisions, **3**, 677, 678
  alighting, passenger injured while, **3**, 680
  boarding, passenger injured while, **3**, 680
  bus, *see* BUS; PUBLIC SERVICE VEHICLE
  bus station safety, **3**, 671
  carrier's duty of care, **3**, 670
  contract carriage, **3**, 684
  death, damages for, **3**, 683
  delay, damages for, **3**, 682
  delict, **3**, 670
  fares, **3**, 672
  generally, **3**, 670
  handling of vehicle, **3**, 676
  luggage, **3**, 686
  overcrowding, **3**, 675, 681
  overturning, **3**, 677
  passenger injured by another passenger, **3**, 681
  personal injury, damages for, **3**, 683
  public service vehicle, *see* PUBLIC SERVICE VEHICLE
  safety of vehicle, **3**, 674
  skidding, **3**, 677
  speed of journey, **3**, 673
  starting and stopping, vehicle, **3**, 679
  taxi, *see* TAXI
  time of journey, **3**, 673
drainage system—
  generally, **20**, 503, 662
  roads authority contribution to, **20**, 681
electric lines in, **9**, 652
electrified fence, dangerous or injurious to person using, **20**, 697
embankment, environmental impact assessment, **20**, 671
England, carriage to or from, *see* international carriage of goods by *below*
environmental aspects of—
  adjoining land, effect on, **20**, 675
  bridleway, conversion of road into, **20**, 676
  cleansing, duties in respect of, **20**, 677
    See also cleansing, responsibility for *above*
  drainage or flood prevention works, **20**, 681
  environmental impact assessment, **20**, 671
  footpath, conversion of road into, **20**, 676
  landscaping, **20**, 674
  litter—
    abatement notice, **20**, 678
    duties in respect of, **20**, 677

Road—continued

environmental aspects of—*continued*
  litter—*continued*
    roadside bins, provision of, **20**, 680
    street litter control notice, **20**, 679
  ploughing on unenclosed land, **20**, 682
  trees and shrubs, planting, **20**, 672, 673
equipment and materials, deposit under, proposed charge for, **20**, 607
EU transport policy, **3**, 731
excavations—
  consent for, **20**, 683
  dangerous, **20**, 683
  marking, fencing and lighting obstructions, **20**, 686
  roads authority control over, **20**, 683
explosives, byelaws as to, **10**, 1612
fence—
  barbed wire, **20**, 697
  electrified, **20**, 697
  provision of, **20**, 660
  wilful damage to, **20**, 704
fire on or near, **20**, 506, 704
flood prevention works, **20**, 660, 681
floodlight at or near, **20**, 697
foot, public right of way on, **20**, 653
foot bridge, provision of, **20**, 660
foot passage, control of, **20**, 504
foot passengers, safety of, **14**, 1631
footpath—
  conversion into, **20**, 676
  meaning, **14**, 405; **20**, 610
  when road described as, **20**, 501
  See also FOOTPATH
footway—
  meaning, **14**, 405; **20**, 610
  provision of, **20**, 660
  when road described as, **20**, 501
frontagers, notification of changes to, **20**, 646
future roads policy, **20**, 607
grass, planting and maintenance, **20**, 672, 674
grit, receptacles for, **20**, 503
gritting, **20**, 620
haulage contractor, **3**, 619
heavy or extraordinary vehicles, responsibility for damage by, **20**, 703
hedge overhanging, **20**, 505, 696
history of road development—
  eighteenth-century developments, **20**, 604
  generally, **5**, 5; **20**, 601
  Macadam roads, **20**, 604
  medieval developments, **20**, 602
  nineteenth-century developments, **20**, 605
  Roads (Scotland) Act 1984, consolidation of legislation by, **20**, 606, 608
  Roman occupation, **20**, 601
  seventeenth-century developments, **20**, 603
  twentieth-century developments, **20**, 606
hole in—
  roads authorities, responsibilities as to, **20**, 611
  shallow, **20**, 611
horse on, provisions as to, **20**, 706
horses and carts, provisions as to, **20**, 706
house numbers, **14**, 410

Road—*continued*
hump—
  generally, **20**, 503, 668
  obstruction, when not classed as, **20**, 689
ice on, roads authority duties as to, **20**, 665
improvement, **20**, 616
  experiments or trials for, **20**, 615
  provision for, **20**, 608
  roads authority, powers of, **20**, 646, 660
  Secretary of State's powers, **20**, 615
  special roads, **20**, 626
  water diversion whilst, **20**, 608
inflammable substances conveyed by, **19**, 388–391
injurious weeds, land occupier's duty in respect
  of, **20**, 660
interference with, regulation of, **20**, 608
international carriage of goods by—
  arbitration, **3**, 665
  carrier's liability, **3**, 653
    exceptions from, **3**, 654
  carrier's responsibility, **3**, 649
  compensation—
    calculation, **3**, 656
    declaration of value, where, **3**, 657
    extra-contractual claims, **3**, 659
    interest on, **3**, 658
    payment, generally, **3**, 656, 661
    wilful misconduct or default, where, **3**, 660
  consignment note, **3**, 647
  contract, **3**, 647
  Convention on the Contract for … (CMR), **3**,
    646
    contrary stipulations, **3**, 668
    jurisdiction, **3**, 662, 663
  declaration of value, **3**, 657
  delay, liability for, **3**, 653
  delivery—
    Cash on Delivery terms, where, **3**, 653
    liability to deliver, **3**, 651
    provisions as to, **3**, 661
    time of, **3**, 652
  disposal, right of, **3**, 650
  EU transport policy, **3**, 731–735
  extra-contractual claims, **3**, 659
  generally, **3**, 645
  international road haulage permit, **20**, 500
  jurisdiction, **3**, 662, 663
  limitation periods, **3**, 664
  loss, liability for, **3**, 653
  perishable goods, **3**, 669
  permits, quota, **3**, 734
  rate bracket system, **3**, 733
  regulations, generally, **20**, 500
  sender's liability, **3**, 655
  sender's responsibility, **3**, 648
  sovereign immunity, **3**, 666
  stoppage in transit, **3**, 650
  successive carriers, carriage by, **3**, 667
  system of law, **3**, 663
international carriage of passengers by—
  carrier's liability—
    generally, **3**, 690
    personal injury or death, for, **3**, 689

Road—
international carriage of passengers by—*continued*
  Convention on …(CVR), **3**, 687
    contracting out void, **3**, 694
    contrary stipulations, **3**, 694
    jurisdiction, **3**, 692
  death, liability for, **3**, 689
  generally, **3**, 690
  jurisdiction, **3**, 692
  limitation periods, **3**, 693
  luggage and effects, **3**, 691
  personal injury, liability for, **3**, 689
  transport documents, **3**, 688
land, acquisition of, *see* compulsory acquisition of
  land *above*
land adjoining—
  environmental impact of road, **20**, 675
  flood prevention works, roads authority
    contributions towards, **20**, 681
  notification of changes to frontagers, **20**, 646
  ploughing on unenclosed, **20**, 682
  prevention of flow of water or other matter
    onto road, **20**, 700
  trees and shrubs on—
    notice for removal, **20**, 673
    planting, **20**, 672
landscaping, **20**, 674
landslide, protection from, **20**, 660
lane, term replaced by road, **20**, 501, 609
lay-by as part of, **20**, 612
level, alteration, **20**, 660
  environmental impact, **20**, 675
level crossings, *see* LEVEL CROSSINGS
light railway laid along, **19**, 1074
lighting—
  building, power to fix on, **20**, 663
  compensation for damage caused by execution
    of works, **20**, 663
  generally, **20**, 663
  private road, on, **20**, 663
  provision and maintenance of, **20**, 663
  roads authorities, powers and duties, **20**, 611
litter, **20**, 677, 678, 679, 680
  abatement notice, **20**, 678
  offences in relation to, **20**, 677
  responsibility for clearing, **20**, 677
  roadside bins, provision of, **20**, 680
  street litter control notice, **20**, 679
local authority—
  ancillaries, provision of, **14**, 418
  functions, **14**, 408, 409
  generally, **14**, 404
maintenance, **14**, 1630
  history of responsibility for, **14**, 33; **20**, 601–
    607
  not 'development', **23**, 68
  organisation, **20**, 617
  responsibility for, **20**, 608, 611, 618, 646, 660
  Secretary of State's duties, **20**, 616, 618
  trunk roads, **20**, 620
management of, responsibility for, **20**, 611
markers, provision of, **20**, 660
meaning, **9**, 1172; **14**, 405
motor, construction or alteration, **19**, 19*n*

Road—*continued*

motor racing, **19**, 1284, 1286
motor vehicle, abandoned, **20**, 692
motorway, *see* MOTORWAY; SPECIAL ROAD
mud or offensive matter, flow onto, **20**, 506
mud or other materials, responsibility for, **20**, 702
names, **14**, 410
new—
   construction of, **20**, 616, 617
     local authority, consultation with, **20**, 616
   design, **20**, 617
   objections to, **20**, 616, 668
new town, in, acquisition of land for, **23**, 375
noise on, **9**, 1257
obstruction—
   accidental, **20**, 690
   consent for, **20**, 689
   door, by, **20**, 695
   gate, by, **20**, 695
   general restrictions, **20**, 689
   hedge, by, **20**, 696
   marking, fencing and lighting, **20**, 686
   motor vehicle, abandoned, **20**, 691
   notice, **20**, 701
     objection to, **20**, 701
   offences in relation to, **20**, 689
   overhead dangers, **20**, 693
   power to remove, **20**, 689, 690, 692
   projections, **20**, 694
   refuse, abandonment of, **20**, 691
   removal of obstruction, **20**, 505
   road humps, **20**, 689
   road users' view, of, **20**, 701
   roads authorities, responsibilities as to, **20**, 611
   shrub, by, **20**, 696
   tree, by, **20**, 696
   window, by, **20**, 695
occupation of public, charges for, **20**, 688
occupier's liability, **15**, 321
offences relating to, provisions regarding, **20**, 607
officers, **14**, 407
overhead cables, **20**, 693
overhead dangers, **20**, 693
overhead pipes, **20**, 693
overhead wires, **20**, 693
painting or marking, **20**, 506
painting on, **20**, 704
parking offences, **20**, 439
passenger transport, *see* PUBLIC TRANSPORT
pavement light, maintenance of, **20**, 664
paving, provision of, **20**, 660
pedestrian crossing, **20**, 440, 441
petroleum-spirit, conveyance of, **9**, 849
picnic facilities, provision of, **20**, 503, 612, 623
pillars, **20**, 660
planning permission, requirement for, **20**, 720
ploughing, unenclosed land, on, **20**, 682
private, *see* PRIVATE ROAD
private access, stopping up, **20**, 653
private land and houses served by it, relationship
   between, **18**, 362, 362*n*
private toll roads, future policy as to, **20**, 607
prohibition, **20**, 507, 508
projections onto, removal of, **20**, 694

Road—*continued*

protection of, **20**, 503
protective barriers, provision of, **20**, 660
provision of, **20**, 668
provisional order relating to, **19**, 22, 26
public, **20**, 608
   building abutting, right to light, **18**, 359
   construction or alteration, **19**, 19*n*
   diversion, widening or narrowing, **19**, 24
   meaning, **14**, 405; **20**, 501, 609
   Night Poaching Acts, **11**, 810
   provisional orders, **19**, 26
   rateable, not, **14**, 732
   solum, rights of, **20**, 613
   vesting, **20**, 613
public carriageways, level crossings over, **19**, 1030
public gas supplier, power to break up, **9**, 875
public health nuisance, becoming, **19**, 336
public right of passage, **20**, 612, 614, 616, 648
public service vehicle, regulation of use by, **14**,
   421, 422; **20**, 508
public use, acquiescence by land owner, **16**, 1616
purpose, **20**, 668
radioactive substances, carriage of, **9**, 1194
rail, provision of, **20**, 660
railway bridge—
   road on, **19**, 1027
   roads authorities' duties, **19**, 1026
railway crossing, **20**, 645
   bridges, **19**, 1025, 1026
   roads authorities' duties, **19**, 1026
rating, **20**, 722
reconstruction, **20**, 616
   local roads authority, by, **20**, 646
   roads authority, powers of, **20**, 660
reform, **14**, 46
refuge, provision of, **20**, 660
refuge holes, **14**, 1632
renewal, **20**, 616
   roads authority, powers of, **20**, 660
repair—
   history of responsibility for, **14**, 33; **20**, 601–
     607
   justice of the peace court, **6**, 1159
   local authority, by, **20**, 618
   organisation, **20**, 617
   responsibility for, generally, **20**, 611
   Secretary of State's duties, **20**, 616, 618
restricted, meaning in relation to speed limits, **20**,
   442
restriction, **20**, 507, 508
road humps, *see* ROAD HUMP
road-making materials, roads authority's power to
   quarry for, **20**, 661
road signs, *see* TRAFFIC DIRECTIONS AND SIGNS
road traffic, *see* ROAD TRAFFIC
roads authority, *see* ROADS AUTHORITY
Roads Directorate, **20**, 617
roadside structure or works, damage to, **20**, 506
rope, wire or other apparatus placed on, **20**, 506
roundabout, provision of, **20**, 660
safety—
   information, **14**, 412
   training, **14**, 412

Road—*continued*
scaffolding, erection on, **3**, 201; **20**, 684
school crossing, **20**, 441
Secretary of State for Scotland, powers and duties, **20**, 615–617
service area, *see* MOTORWAY; SERVICE AREA
sewer gratings, responsibility for, **20**, 611
sewerage system, agreements in respect of, **25**, 437
sheriff court jurisdiction, **6**, 1129, 1130
side, **20**, 651
skip, right to deposit on, **3**, 201
slippery, responsibility for, **20**, 611
snow and ice—
    roads authorities duties in relation to, **20**, 503
    roads authority duties as to, **20**, 665
    snow gates, provision of, **20**, 503, 666
solum, rights of, **20**, 613
special, *see* SPECIAL ROAD
speed restrictions, *see* MOTOR VEHICLE
sport on, **19**, 1284–1286
    local authority authorisation, **19**, 1284
    prohibiting or restricting traffic, **19**, 1285
statutory undertaker, *see* STATUTORY UNDERTAKER
stopping up—
    aviation purposes, for, **20**, 657
    dangerous or unnecessary road, **20**, 652
    defence purposes, for, **20**, 657
    development order, road affected by, **20**, 654
    generally, **14**, 1684; **20**, 608
    private access, of, **20**, 653
    side road order, **20**, 651
street cleansing, responsibility for, **20**, 665
substitute, temporary provision, **20**, 608, 655
subway, provision of, **20**, 660
surface—
    powers to alter or disturb, **19**, 14
    slight inequalities in, **20**, 611
survey, powers of entry in relation to, **20**, 716
taxi, carriage by, *see* TAXI
telecommunication apparatus—
    inspection, **16**, 1955
    installation under, over, on, along or across, **16**, 1955
    maintenance and repair, **16**, 1955
    works, execution, **16**, 1955
Telecommunications Code, **16**, 1955, 1958
temporary closure, public right of passage not affected by, **20**, 612
temporary restrictions or prohibitions, **20**, 655
    substitute road, temporary provision, **20**, 608, 655
    temporary route, provision of, **20**, 655
tent, pitching in, **20**, 692
through traffic, national system of routes for, **20**, 615, 619
    Secretary of State's duty to keep, **20**, 620
toll, *see* TOLL ROAD
trading on or near public, **20**, 506, 699
traffic, *see* ROAD TRAFFIC
traffic sign, *see* TRAFFIC DIRECTIONS AND SIGNS
tramway
    constructed on road, **20**, 721
    laying, **19**, 1132
    See also TRAMWAY

Road—*continued*
transport of radioactive substances by, **9**, 920
trees and shrubs, **20**, 503, 505, 672–674
trunk, *see* TRUNK ROAD
tunnel, *see* TUNNEL
turnpike, **14**, 33
types of, **20**, 610
underpass, construction of, **20**, 611
unenclosed land next to, ploughing, **20**, 506
unnecessary, stopping up, **20**, 652
valuation and rating, **20**, 722
vault under, maintenance of, **20**, 664
vehicle, upholstered fittings for, **19**, 421
verge—
    inclusion in definition of road, **20**, 609
    injurious weeds on, **20**, 660
    scrub and tall plants on, **20**, 660
vesting, **20**, 613
view, obstruction of, **20**, 701
wall, provision of, **20**, 660
warranty as to, **6**, 563
waste paper, receptacles for, **20**, 503
water, prevention of flow onto, **20**, 506, 700
water mains, power to lay, **25**, 520
watering to allay dust, **20**, 616
widening, **20**, 616
    local roads authority, by, **20**, 646
    roads authority, powers of, **20**, 660
works—
    accident caused by, **20**, 611
    animals adversely affected by, **20**, 611
    consent for, **20**, 683
    control of, **20**, 608
    dangerous, **20**, 683
    marking, fencing and lighting obstructions, **20**, 686
    roads authority—
        control, powers of, **20**, 683
        duties as to, **20**, 611
works carried out on or near, **20**, 508
writing on, **20**, 704
See also HIGHWAY; LEVEL CROSSING
Road accident
arising out of presence of vehicle on road, **20**, 437
driver—
    breath test of, following, **20**, 422
    See also BREATH TEST
    duties on, following, **20**, 437
    stop, duty to, **20**, 437
emergency treatment at, **11**, 1450
failure to report, **7**, 45
failure to stop following, **7**, 45
industrial injuries benefits, entitlement to, **21**, 978
property damaged by, **20**, 437
report of, requirements as to, **20**, 437
roadside test of vehicle following, **20**, 471
Road traffic
control, generally, **20**, 504, 608
dangerous driving, **7**, 82*n*
driver, *see* DRIVER
driving licence, *see* DRIVING LICENCE
European Union directives and regulations, **20**, 402

Road traffic—*continued*
experimental traffic orders, **20**, 507
failure to stop when so required by police, **7**, 544
false information or statement, giving, **7**, 537, 538
foot passage on roads, control of, **20**, 504
fraud, **7**, 386
Highway Code, **20**, 433
inconsiderate driving, as breach of the peace, **7**, 449
information to be given under, statutory provisions, **7**, 537
offences—
  accident, duties on drivers following, **20**, 437
  aiding and abetting offender, **20**, 445
  careless driving, *see* CARELESS DRIVING
  dangerous driving, *see* DANGEROUS DRIVING
  disqualification following, *see* DRIVER
  drink related, *see* ALCOHOLIC LIQUOR
  driving off a road, **20**, 434
  driving vehicles, generally, **20**, 443
  drugs related, *see* DRUGS
  endorsement of driving licence, *see* DRIVING LICENCE
  fixed penalties and conditional offers, **20**, 458
  forfeiture of property used or intended to be used for, **20**, 459
  generally, **20**, 433
  Highway Code, **20**, 433
  joy-riding, **20**, 444
  official records, use in proceedings, **20**, 446
  parking and related offences, **20**, 439
  pedestrian crossings, in relation to, **20**, 440
  penalty points, **20**, 456, 457
  playgrounds, in relation to, **20**, 441
  police powers in relation to, **20**, 436
  prosecution, warning or notice of intended, **20**, 446
  protective headgear, in relation to, **20**, 438
  race and trials, unofficial, **20**, 434
  reckless driving, *see* RECKLESS DRIVING
  school crossings, in relation to, **20**, 441
  seat belts, in relation to, **20**, 438
  speed limits, in relation to, **20**, 442
  stopping vehicles, generally, **20**, 443
  summary proceedings, **20**, 446
  taking and driving away motor vehicle without consent, **20**, 444
  traffic directions and signs, **20**, 435
  vehicle used to commit, **20**, 459
pedestrian crossing, **20**, 440, 441
reckless driving, **7**, 82, 82*n*
regulation—
  generally, **20**, 508
  traffic regulation order, **20**, 507
regulation and management, **14**, 409
roadside test—
  preliminary breath test, **20**, 418
  test certificate, **20**, 471
Scots and English law, **20**, 402
sources of law, **20**, 401
speed restrictions, *see* MOTOR VEHICLE
territorial application of law, **20**, 402
traffic wardens, **20**, 510
See also DRIVER; DRIVING; MOTOR VEHICLE; ROAD

Roads authority
acquisition of land, powers as to—
  adverse environmental effects, for mitigation of, **20**, 709
  agreement, by, **20**, 708, 710, 713
  compensation, **20**, 713
  compulsory, **20**, 708, 712
  concurrent proceedings in respect of special and trunk roads schemes and orders, **20**, 714
  generally, **20**, 708
  land which may be compulsorily acquired, **20**, 712
  local roads authority, **20**, 711
  new towns, **20**, 715
  Secretary of State, by, **20**, 711
  special roads authority, **20**, 711
action against, onus of proof, **20**, 611
alteration, road, powers as to, **20**, 646, 660
bridge—
  construction over navigable water, **20**, 638
  revocation or variation of order for, **20**, 644
  responsibilities as to, **20**, 611
cattle grid—
  notice of proposed, **20**, 669
  objections to, **20**, 669
  provision and maintenance, **20**, 667, 669
damage caused by works of, **20**, 660
damages, liability for, **20**, 611
danger created by road, responsibility for, **20**, 611
dangerous road, fencing off, **20**, 611
dangerous site adjoining road, duties as to, **20**, 611
disabled or blind persons, duty of care towards, **20**, 660, 670
drainage systems, **20**, 662, 681
duty of, generally, **20**, 503, 611
entry, powers of, **20**, 506, 716
  inspection, for, **20**, 716
    expenses incurred by authority, **20**, 716
  notice of entry, **20**, 716
  refusal of entry, **20**, 716
experimental traffic order, **20**, 507
flood prevention works, contributions towards, **20**, 681
grass, planting and maintenance, **20**, 672
ice, duties as to, **20**, 665
improvement, road, powers as to, **20**, 646, 660
inspections by, **20**, 611
  frequency of, **20**, 611
land, acquisition by, **20**, 506
land adjoining road, duty in relation to, **20**, 660
landscaping work by, **20**, 674
liability of, **20**, 611
lighting, powers as to, **20**, 611, 663
local, **20**, 502
  acquisition of land, **20**, 711
  alteration and improvement of roads by, **20**, 646
  bridges, responsibility for, **20**, 647
  construction of roads by, **20**, 646
  developer, agreement with, **20**, 646
  discharge of functions, **20**, 646
  footpath, taking responsibility for, **20**, 648
  frontagers, notification of changes to, **20**, 646

Roads authority—*continued*
local—*continued*
   list of roads managed and maintained by, duty
     to keep, **20**, 646
   private roads, powers in relation to, **20**, 648
   reconstruction of roads by, **20**, 646
   road maintenance expenditure, **20**, 646
   roads for which responsible, **20**, 646
   special road order, power to make, **20**, 626
   statutory undertakers' rights, **20**, 717
   Transport Policy and Programme documents,
     20, 646
   widening of roads by, **20**, 646
maintenance of road, responsibility as to, **20**, 611,
   646, 660
management of road, responsibility as to, **20**, 611,
   646
meaning, **20**, 502
motorways, for, **20**, 624
obstructions to road, power to remove, **20**, 505,
   689, 690, 691
overhead dangers, control over, **20**, 693
pavement lights, powers as to, **20**, 664
privately-owned bridge, agreement with owner,
   20, 641
property of, taking away or displacing, **20**, 660,
   661
protection of roads by, **20**, 503
public right of passage, duties in relation to, **20**,
   612
quarrying, powers as to, **20**, 661
reconstruction and renewal of road, powers as to,
   20, 646, 660
repair of road, responsibility as to, **20**, 611
road humps, construction of, **20**, 646, 668
road-making materials, powers to ontain by
   quarrying, **20**, 661
road users, responsibility to, **20**, 611
scaffolding, erection on road, consent for, **20**, 684
Secretary of States for Scotland, as, **20**, 616
   local authorities carrying out work on behalf
     of, **20**, 618
sewer gratings, responsibility for, **20**, 611
skip—
   permission for use of, **20**, 685
   removal or reposition, order for, **20**, 685
snow, duties as to, **20**, 503, 620, 660, 665
snow gates, provision of, **20**, 503, 666
solum, rights of, public roads, **20**, 613
special, **20**, 624
   bridge on, **20**, 643
   statutory undertakers' rights, **20**, 717, 718
special road authority, **20**, 625
   payments to, **20**, 626
temporary restrictions or prohibitions, power to
   make, **20**, 655
   substitute road, temporary provison, **20**, 655
   temporary route, provision of, **20**, 655
toll road—
   amount of toll, **20**, 631
   collection of toll, **20**, 631
   construction, contract for, **20**, 636
   design, contract for, **20**, 636

Roads authority—*continued*
toll road—*continued*
   order, **20**, 629
     assignation of rights under, **20**, 630
     extension, **20**, 631
   toll period, **20**, 631
traffic control, **20**, 504
traffic regulation, **20**, 508
   traffic regulation order, **20**, 507
traffic signs, powers and duties in respect of, **20**,
   509
tramway constructed on road operated by, **20**,
   721
trees and shrubs, planting and maintenance, **20**, 672
trunk roads, **20**, 619
tunnel—
   construction under navigable water, **20**, 638
     revocation or variation of order for, **20**, 644
   under road, powers as to, **20**, 664
vault or cellar under road, powers as to, **20**, 664
vesting of public roads, **20**, 613
view, obstruction of, powers as to, **20**, 701
water diversion, powers as to, **20**, 640
who may be, **20**, 608, 609, 616
widening, road, powers as to, **20**, 646, 660
works and excavations, control over, **20**, 683
Roads Directorate
engineering division, **20**, 617
purpose and functions, **20**, 617
technical division, **20**, 617
Robbery
armed, **7**, 358
assault, and, **7**, 243, 245, 359, 360
assault with intent to perpetrate, **7**, 215, 236
constructive violence, **7**, 245
definition, **7**, 357
drugging, forcible, **7**, 358
extortion distinguished, **7**, 397
firearm or imitation firearm possessed during, **10**,
   1565
force as element of, **7**, 357, 358, 359
hijacking, **7**, 364
intent to rob, **7**, 359
intimidation, by, **7**, 361
killing during course of, **7**, 270
mugging, **7**, 358
piracy—
   common law, **7**, 362
   elements of, **7**, 362
   hijacking, **7**, 364
   international law, **7**, 363
   meaning, **7**, 362
sheriff court jurisdiction, **17**, 516
theft, as, **7**, 357
violence as element of, **7**, 357, 358
   intent, **7**, 359
   threat to commit violence, **7**, 361
   threat to third person, **7**, 361
Robens Committee
findings of, **9**, 406
recommendations of, **9**, 406
self-regulation, role of, **9**, 405
Rochdale Society of Equitable Pioneers
generally, **12**, 607, 607*n*

Rockall
Convention on the Continental Shelf, **11**, 82
ownership, **18**, 48
Scottish claim to, **18**, 558
territorial sea, **11**, 76
Rockall-Faroes plateau
continental shelf, claims to, **21**, 25, 30
Rocket
designed to explode on or immediately before
    impact, **10**, 1517
explosive, as, **10**, 1586
launcher—
    prohibited weapon, as, **10**, 1506n
station—
    exemption from explosives regulations, **10**, 1589
Rod and line
annual close time, **11**, 15, 16
baits, **11**, 23
freshwater fish, **11**, 11
lease of fishings, **11**, 9
lures, **11**, 23
salmon fishing, **11**, 5, 5n, 11
    rights, **11**, 3; **18**, 326
trout fishing, **11**, 54
weekly close time, **11**, 17
See also FISHING
Rodents
See VERMIN
Roe
buying, selling or possessing, **11**, 20
Rogue money
levy, **16**, 1707
***Romalpa* clause**
constructive delivery, **24**, 24, 113
generally, **18**, 638
meaning, **20**, 29
nature of, **20**, 30
seller's right to retain title, generally, **20**, 32, 32n,
    33
subject of sale no longer held by buyer, where,
    20, 31
validity, **18**, 628
Roman Catholic Church
archdioceses, **3**, 1655
Birmingham Tribunal, **3**, 1658
bishops, *see* BISHOP (Roman Catholic)
churches, chapels and other buildings—
    planning, **3**, 1671
    rates, **3**, 1671
    valuation, **3**, 1671
clergy, disqualification for parliamentary election,
    15, 1061
clergy of, exclusion from membership of House
    of Commons, **5**, 379
Code of Canon Law, *see* CODE OF CANON LAW
Codex Iuris Canonici, *see* CODE OF CANON LAW
courts, **3**, 1658
Decretals of Gregory IX, **3**, 1658
dioceses, **3**, 1655
disabilities of church and members—
    civil disabilities, **3**, 1660
    penal statutes, **3**, 1659
    present-day, **3**, 1660, 1662
    relief, **3**, 1661

Roman Catholic Church—*continued*
estimated Catholic population of Scotland, **3**,
    1656
First Vatican Council, **3**, 1657
indult, meaning, **3**, 1656n
jurisdiction—
    civil courts, interaction with, **3**, 1658
    Code of Canon Law, *see* CODE OF CANON LAW
    first instance cases, **3**, 1658
    limitation, **3**, 1658
    penal discipline, *see* penalties *below*
    Pope, position of, **3**, 1658, 1659
    procedural law, **3**, 1658
    second instance cases, **3**, 1658
    third instance cases, **3**, 1658
laity, involvement, **3**, 1656
Latin, use of, **3**, 1656
liturgy, **3**, 1656
Mass—
    Novus ordo missae, **3**, 1656
    percentage attending, **3**, 1656
    Tridentine—
        generally, **3**, 1656
        legality, **3**, 1656
Metropolitan Sees, **3**, 1655
motu proprio, meaning, **3**, 1656n
offences, **3**, 1658
office of Lord Chancellor tenable by adherent to,
    5, 370
parishes, **3**, 1655
penal statutes against, **3**, 1659
    relief, **3**, 1661
penalties—
    automatically incurred, **3**, 1658
    deprivation of office, **3**, 1658
    dismissal from clerical state, **3**, 1658
    excommunication, **3**, 1658
    ferendae sententiae, **3**, 1658
    interidct, **3**, 1658
    latae sententiae, **3**, 1658
    poenae expiatoriae, **3**, 1658
    poenae medicinales, **3**, 1658
    specific sentence, imposed by, **3**, 1658
    suspension, **3**, 1658
priests, *see* PRIEST (Roman Catholic)
prison chaplains, **3**, 1668; **16**, 1458
provinces, **3**, 1655
religious toleration, **3**, 1635
Sacrae discipinae leges, **3**, 1657
Sacred Roman Rota, **3**, 1658
schools, state-supported, *see* SCHOOL
Scottish National Tribunal, **3**, 1658
Second Vatican Council, consequences, **3**, 1656,
    1657
Suffragan Sees, **3**, 1655
tribunals, **3**, 1658
voluntary church, as, **3**, 1633n; **5**, 702
Roman Dutch law
Scots law, affinity, **22**, 436, 440
South African law, **22**, 440
Roman law
advocates, use of arguments based on, assisting
    reception into Scots law, **22**, 553
bankruptcy legislation, effect, **22**, 629

Roman law—*continued*

canon law—

  admixture, **22**, 549

  influence of Roman law in Scotland through, **22**, 551

commodatum, **13**, 1702, 1703

contract, law of, generally, **13**, 1702

contract law, influence traceable in, **22**, 556

Corpus Iuris Civilis, **22**, 549

decline of influence, **22**, 555

direct influence, development, **22**, 551

Dutch influence, entry into Scots law through, **22**, 604, 606

English property law, influence on, **18**, 2

feudal law, admixture, **22**, 549

French influence, entry into Scots law through, **22**, 604

generally, as source, **22**, 502

guardian and ward, law of, influence traceable in, **22**, 556

historical source of Scots law, as, **22**, 502, 548–556

ius commune of Europe, origins, **22**, 549

Justinian's *Institutes*, **22**, 534, 548, 554

legal literature, importance in content/presentation, **22**, 554

medieval Europe, arrival in Scotland through development in, **22**, 549

money, loan of, **13**, 1712

  interest on, **13**, 1751

mutuum, **13**, 1702, 1703

property law, influence traceable in areas of, **22**, 556

ratio scripta influence on Scottish courts in default of other guidance, **22**, 553

real contracts, **13**, 1702

reception in Europe, **22**, 550

reception in Scotland—

  canon law, influence through, **22**, 551

  imperio rationis, **22**, 548

  ius commune of Europe, as, **22**, 551

  practice of the courts, through, **22**, 553

  professional lawyers, through influence, **22**, 551

Scots property law, as source of, **18**, 2

terminology, different meanings in Scots law, **22**, 556

universities—

  continental, **22**, 552

  Scottish, **22**, 552

  See also UNIVERSITY

Romano-canonical procedure

representation, **13**, 1130, 1131

Rome, Treaties of

generally, **10**, 8

Ronaldsway Airport

free zone, as, **7**, 1164*n*

Roof

law of the tenement, **18**, 230, 231

securing safety of—

  damages for injuries, **14**, 1633

  liability for breach, **14**, 1635

  manager, duty of, **14**, 1633, 1634

support rules, **14**, 1637

Ross, Earl of

Sovereign's second son, entitlement to title of, **7**, 788

Rothesay, Duke of

arms, **7**, 787

heir to Crown as, **7**, 704, 704*n*, 786

Rotuli Scotiae

documentary evidence, as, **10**, 577

Roundabout

provision of, **20**, 660

Roup

articles of, **18**, 641; **20**, 904, 919

  contents, **6**, 577

  reduction, **13**, 37

bidding, rules for, **6**, 577

common property, sale by, **18**, 33

meaning, **6**, 577

minute of enactment and preference, **6**, 578

retraction of bid, **20**, 896

sale by, reduction, **13**, 37

title 'as it stands', **20**, 919

Roxburgh

Court of Four Burghs, **14**, 13

population, **14**, 64

Royal Air Mail

improper use of term, **16**, 1911

Royal approval

false representations as to, **6**, 133

Royal arms

ensigns of sovereignty, as, **11**, 1632

improper use as treason, **11**, 1632

no portion to be granted without royal warrant, **11**, 1632

persons with power to display, **11**, 1632

United Kingdom and Scottish forms, **11**, 1632

Royal assent

generally, **7**, 715

judicial control of Assembly legislation—

  after, **5**, 337

  before, **5**, 336

Royal Bank of Scotland

bank notes, issue of, **14**, 1817

competition with other bank, **2**, 1116

functions etc, **2**, 1104

mergers with, **2**, 1119

royal charter, grant of, **2**, 1116

stock, adjudication, **8**, 200

Royal burgh

See BURGH

Royal charter

incorporation by, **4**, 303, 314

peerage, creation, **16**, 1305, 1309

powers conferred by, **22**, 194

Royal College of Veterinary Surgeons

charters, **25**, 201

Commonwealth list, **25**, 204

conduct of profession, powers relating to, **25**, 201

Council—

  constitution, **25**, 207

  disciplinary powers, **25**, 210

  duties, **25**, 208

  elections, **15**, 1532, 1533

Royal College of Veterinary Surgeons—
continued
Council—*continued*
  members—
    appointed, **15**, 1531
    elected, **15**, 1531, 1533
    President, **15**, 1531
    Vice-Presidents, **15**, 1531
Disciplinary Committee, **25**, 210
discipline, powers, **25**, 209
education, powers relating to, **25**, 201
foreign list, **25**, 204
general list, **25**, 204
Preliminary Investigation Committee, **25**, 210
qualifications, **25**, 204
register—
  commonwealth list, **25**, 204
  foreign list, **25**, 204
  general list, **25**, 204
  removal of names from, **25**, 212
  restoration of names to, **25**, 213
  supplementary, **25**, 205
  temporary list, **25**, 204
registration, **25**, 201, 206
royal charter, **25**, 201
supplementary register, **25**, 205
temporary list, **25**, 204
Royal commission
appointment, **7**, 728
call to serve on, **7**, 728
copyright—
  acts done for purposes of proceedings, **18**, 1122
  report of proceedings, **18**, 1122
Royal Commission on the Court of Session
report of, **13**, 1297
Royal Commission on Friendly Societies and Benefit Building Societies
generally, **12**, 602
Royal Commission on Legal Services in Scotland
establishment and report of, **13**, 1142
report of, **13**, 1297
Royal Company of Archers
royal bodyguard, as, **7**, 836
Royal courts
contrast in administration with church courts, **22**, 511
Curia Regis description, **22**, 506
procedure *Regiam Majestatem*, **22**, 512
Royal Faculty of Procurators in Glasgow
Joint Legal Committee, **13**, 1139
origins, **13**, 1135
precedence, **16**, 2020
Royal family
precedence, **16**, 2017
Royal household
Almoner, **7**, 837, 839
apothecaries, **7**, 843
Armour-Bearer, **7**, 820, 824
Astronomer Royal, **7**, 849
Bearer of the National Flag of Scotland, **7**, 820, 826
Bearer of the Royal Banner, **7**, 820, 825
Chaplains in Ordinary, **7**, 837
Dean of the Chapel Royal, **7**, 837, 838

Royal household—*continued*
Dean of the Thistle, **7**, 837
development, **7**, 774
ecclesiastical offices, **7**, 837–839
generally, **7**, 774, 819
Geographer Royal, **7**, 844
Governor of Edinburgh Castle, **7**, 834
Great Officers, **7**, 820–826
heralds, **7**, 833
hereditary offices, **7**, 819, 820–831
historical background, **7**, 819
Historiographer Royal, **7**, 819, 844, 845
Keeper of Holyroodhouse, **7**, 820, 823
Keepers of palaces and castles, **7**, 830, 835
King's Botanist, **7**, 846
King's tradesmen, **7**, 819, 850
learning and the arts, patronage of, **7**, 844–849
Lord High Constable, **7**, 820, 821
Lord Lyon King of Arms, **7**, 833
Master carver, **7**, 819, 828
Master of the Household, **7**, 820, 822
Master Printer, **7**, 819, 851
medical offices, **7**, 840–843
non-hereditary offices, **7**, 819, 832–849
Painter and Limner, **7**, 847
physicians or mediciners, **7**, 841
Poulterer, **7**, 831
pursuivants, **7**, 833
Queen's Bodyguard, **7**, 836
Sculptor, **7**, 847
superior officers, **16**, 2022
surgeons, **7**, 842
Usher of Exchequer, **7**, 829
Usher of the Green Rod, **7**, 829
Usher of the Royal Chapel, **7**, 829
Usher of the White Rod, **7**, 829
Royal Incorporation of Architects in Scotland
building contracts, **3**, 141
Royal Institute of British Architects
building contracts, **3**, 141
Royal Institute of Chartered Surveyors
background papers, **25**, 122
building contracts, **3**, 142
guidance notes, **25**, 121
Royal Mail
improper use of term, **16**, 1911
See also MAIL
Royal Marines
authority over, **2**, 610
laws applicable to, **2**, 610
legal basis for, **2**, 610
pay, deductions from, **2**, 768
Reserve—
  calling out, **2**, 747
  maintenance, **2**, 747
status, **2**, 608
Royal Mint
coins produced by, as legal tender, **14**, 1816
Trial of Pyx, **14**, 1821
Royal officer
functions, **17**, 504
Royal Park Constabulary
generally, **16**, 1817

Royal Parks Botanic Gardens Constabulary
generally, **16**, 1817
Royal prerogative
court-martial convictions, **6**, 883
government departments established by, **5**, 476
passports issued under, **16**, 1216
precedence arising from—
    earlier creation, creation of dignity with precedence over, **16**, 2004
    generally, **16**, 2002, 2004
    petition for royal warrant to declare, **16**, 2004
See also PREROGATIVE POWERS
Royal proclamation
documentary evidence, as, **10**, 577
Prerogative Order in Council contrasted, **22**, 171
Royal Scottish Academy, **13**, 1514
Royal Scottish Museum, **13**, 1515
Royal Standard
form used, **7**, 711, 711*n*
Royal Ulster Constabulary
constables or other assistance, provision to, **16**, 1758
discipline code, **16**, 1771
Royal visits
Lord Lieutenant, duties of, **5**, 549
Royalties
commercial lease, **13**, 71
copyright, in respect of—
    Copyright Tribunal powers and duties, **18**, 1019
    fixing royalties, **18**, 1019
    generally, **18**, 1005
    tax treatment, **18**, 1585, 1591
        foreign royalties, **18**, 1589
        non-resident, payment to, **18**, 1589
    variation of royalties, **18**, 1019
Crown use of registered industrial design, in respect of, **18**, 1201
generally, **18**, 802

Royalties—*continued*
know how, in respect of, tax treatment, **18**, 1580, 1581, 1583
mineral lease, **13**, 71, 103, 199
minerals, valuation of, **25**, 141
patent, in respect of—
    tax treatment, **18**, 1572, 1575
        deduction of tax at source, **18**, 1577
        non-residents, payments to, **18**, 1578
trade or service mark, in respect of, tax treatment, **18**, 1595, 1598
value added tax, **18**, 1602
Rubbish
See WASTE
Rubella
vaccination against, **11**, 1446
Rugby Union
sports-governing institutions, **19**, 1205
Runrig
meaning, **1**, 822
Rural administration
commission of supply, **14**, 25, 29
constable, **14**, 25, 28
county, **14**, 23
England and Wales, **14**, 62
justice of peace, **14**, 25, 27
parish, **14**, 24
sheriff, **14**, 25, 26
Rural area
designated, **11**, 1972
public passenger transport service, grant for, **14**, 437
telecommunications services, provision in, **16**, 1923, 1933, 1933*n*
Rural borough
England and Wales, **14**, 62
Rural environment
See COUNTRYSIDE
Rust remover
weights and measures legislation, **6**, 244

S

Saavedra Lamas Treaty
generally, **19**, 698*n*
Sabbath
profanation of, **6**, 1159
Sabotage
crime of, **7**, 628
Safe custody/safekeeping
deposit of goods for, **11**, 1751
proof of deposit and restoration, **11**, 1751
Safeguarder
appointment—
conflict between interests of child and parent,
where, **3**, 1362
duration, **3**, 1362
generally, **3**, 1362
children's hearing, role at, **3**, 1344
documents to be sent to, **3**, 1288, 1362
introduction, **3**, 1362
more than one child, where, **3**, 1362
presence at children's hearing, **3**, 1323, 1362
remuneration, **3**, 1362
report, **3**, 1288
sheriff, where appeal to, **3**, 1362
statement of reasons, entitlement to see, **3**, 1294
training, **3**, 1362
Safety
absolute and continuing obligation, **14**, 1618
accident, *see* ACCIDENT
atmospheric emissions, **9**, 668
atomic energy and radioactive substances—
codes of practice, **9**, 923
educational establishments, **9**, 915
food, **9**, 916
ionising radiations at work, **9**, 914
medicine, **9**, 916
notes of guidance, **9**, 923
social security, **9**, 922
transport of—
air, by, **9**, 917
post, by, **9**, 921
rail, by, **9**, 919
road, by, **9**, 920
sea, by, **9**, 918
building on surface, of, **14**, 1624
care, duty of—
common law, **14**, 1616
statutory, **14**, 1617
child in theatre, of, **9**, 1052
cinema, of, **9**, 1021
committee—
establishment of, **9**, 476, 477
general functions of, **9**, 476
specific functions, **9**, 478
consumer, **6**, **9**, 31
contract of sale for moveable property, **20**, 827
electricity supply, of, **9**, 675
employer's duty as to, **9**, 75
explosives, *see* EXPLOSIVES

Safety—*continued*
Factories Act 1961—
effect of, **9**, 665
fire, *see* FIRE
foot passengers, of, **14**, 1631
gas, relating to, **9**, 884
health and safety at work, *see* HEALTH AND
SAFETY—
health and safety at work
machinery, *see* PLANT AND MACHINERY
mine, in, *see* MINES
occupiers' liability, generally, **11**, 1731
place of work, employer's duty as to, **9**, 79
product—
aerosol dispensers, **6**, 63
dangerous goods and substances, **6**, 51, 58, 61
defective, **6**, 41
defences, **6**, 53, 57
due diligence, defence of, **6**, 57
failure to comply, **6**, 52, 54
forfeiture of unsafe goods, **6**, 59
general requirement, **6**, 52, 53
imported goods, **6**, 58
legislation, **6**, 51, 54
motor cycle helmets, **6**, 62
motor vehicles, **6**, 62
non-flammable or flame-resistant textiles, **6**, 63
notice to warn, **6**, 51, 55
prohibition notice, **6**, 51, 55
prohibition order, **6**, 51
regulations, **6**, 54
requirements imposed by enactments or
Community obligations, **6**, 52
statutory duty, breach of, **6**, 60
suspension notice, **6**, 56
public entertainment licence, conditions attached
to, **9**, 1002
quarry, in, **14**, 1703
representatives—
appointment of, **9**, 469
general functions of, **9**, 471
information, right to, **9**, 475
inspection—
dangerous occurrence, following, **9**, 474
documents, of, **9**, 475
notifiable accident, following, **9**, 474
notifiable disease, following, **9**, 474
workplace, of, **9**, 473
number of, **9**, 470
specific functions of, **9**, 472
time off for, **9**, 97, 479–481
workplace, right to inspect, **9**, 473
roads, *see* ROAD
roof, *see* ROOF
smoking materials, **14**, 1649
sports ground, certificate for, *see* RECREATION AND
SPORT
statutory controls, **14**, 1051
system of work, employer's duty as to, **9**, 76

Safety fuses
licensing exemption, **10**, 1620
sale, records of, **10**, 1607
special powers in relation to, **10**, 1590
Safety order
breach of, **12**, 187
generally, **12**, 117, 136, 216
Sailing rights
non-tidal loch, **18**, 306, 307
riparian proprietor, **18**, 279
Sailing rules
See SHIPPING (collision regulations, steering and
  sailing rules)
St Helena and Dependencies
British Dependent Territories citizenship, **14**, 1932
St Mary's Music School
aided places, **8**, 819
St Ninian's Isle Treasure case
udal law, **24**, 304, 313, 321, 322, 324–327, 329–400
St Olav's law
See CODE OF MAGNUS 'THE LAW-MENDER'
St Silas's Church, Glasgow
position with Scottish Episcopal Church, **3**, 1617
Salad cream
advertisement, **11**, 367
composition, **11**, 367
labelling, **11**, 367
Sale and lease-back
delivery, requirement of, **14**, 1031
health and safety, **14**, 1051
hire-purchase transaction, application to, **14**, 1031
removal of disincentive, **14**, 1031
title, passing of, **14**, 1031
Sale and supply of goods
advertising, *see* ADVERTISING
agreement to sell—
  conditional contract of sale, **20**, 810
  creation of, **20**, 809
  meaning, **20**, 809
  sale, becoming, **20**, 809
all sums clause, **18**, 638
appearance, contract of sale for moveable
  property, **20**, 827
arrestment or poinding, repeal of remedy, **20**, 870
ascertained goods, statutory classification, **20**, 807
bargain and, **20**, 809
barter, *see* BARTER
buyer—
  acceptance by—
    duty to accept, **20**, 858
    generally, **20**, 866, 868
  duty to pay, **20**, 858, 870
  insolvency, **20**, 870
  non-acceptance by, **20**, 866
  remedies of, **20**, 885–891
cash, consumer sales for, **18**, 631
coins, of, **14**, 1807
conditional sale agreements, **20**, 814
consumer goods, meaning, **6**, 52
consumer protection, **6**, 1, 32
contract, sale of goods, as, **18**, 625
contract of sale—
  agreement to sell, **18**, 625; **20**, 809
  sale, becoming, **20**, 809

Sale and supply of goods—*continued*
contract of sale—*continued*
  ascertained goods, **20**, 807
  assignation, **14**, 1030
  barter, evolution from, **20**, 801
  building contract—
    contract of location distinguished, **3**, 6
    generally, **3**, 6
  classification, **14**, 1802
    importance of correct, **20**, 801
  commodity, sale of money as, enforcement of,
    14, 1814
  consumer contract, meaning, **6**, 33
  credit, where purchaser given, **20**, 858, 874
  exchange distinguished, **20**, 801, 899
  exclusion or restriction of obligations not
    prohibited, **6**, 35
  existing goods, **20**, 806
  failure by seller to perform material part, **20**,
    820
  future goods, **20**, 806
  generally, **6**, 32, 50; **15**, 612; **18**, 625
  generic goods, **20**, 808
  goods, meaning, **20**, 805
  heritage, sale of, *see* HERITABLE PROPERTY
  hire purchase agreements, **20**, 813
  immoveable property, *see* HERITABLE PROPERTY
  includes provision of services, **6**, 66
  instalment contract, seller's right of retention,
    20, 872
  interest stipulated by, **12**, 1007, 1009, 1010
  ius quaesitum tertio effect of, **14**, 1088
  judicial sales, **20**, 853
  lease distinguished, **13**, 111
  lessor, enforcement by, **14**, 1086
  meaning, **20**, 809, 809*n*
  money, price must be in, **20**, 801, 818
  moveable property—
    absolute sale, **20**, 809
    auction, sale by—
      auctioneer's lien, **20**, 896
      completion of transaction, **20**, 896
      conduct of, **20**, 897
      generally, **20**, 896
      mock auctions, **20**, 898
      reserve price, **20**, 896
      retraction of bid, **20**, 896
      right to bid expressly reserved, **20**, 896
      seller's right to withdraw item from sale,
        20, 896
      upset price, **20**, 896
    bargaining positions of parties, relevance of
      strength, **20**, 831
    breach of—
      buyer's remedies, **20**, 885–891
      reform, proposals for, **20**, 890, 891
      seller's remedies, **20**, 870–884
      term, of, remedy for, **20**, 888
    bulk, goods sold in, **20**, 835
    buyer—
      breach, remedies for, **20**, 885–891
      examination by, **20**, 868, 893
      non-acceptance by, damages for, **20**, 884

Sale and supply of goods—*continued*
contract of sale—
  moveable property—*continued*
    buyer—*continued*
      obliged to account for resale profits, where, **20**, 815
      partial rejection by, **20**, 889
      rights of, **20**, 885–891
        in personam, **20**, 810
    capacity to buy, **20**, 816
    capacity to sell, **20**, 816
    condition precedent, **20**, 810
    conditional contract, **20**, 810
      buyer, right of, *in personam*, **20**, 810
      remedy against, **20**, 810
    conditional sale, **20**, 809, 810, 814
    conduct, contract implied by, **20**, 817
    conformity of goods, lack of, international sales, **20**, 893
    consideration mixture of money and goods, **20**, 899
    corporeal, **20**, 802
    credit sale agreement, **20**, 814
    customer's knowledge of terms, **20**, 831
    deliverable state, meaning, **20**, 836–839
    delivery of goods—
      actual, **20**, 860
      bill of lading, transfer of, **20**, 860
      buyer—
        acceptance of goods by, **20**, 868
        duties of, **20**, 866
        possession taken by, **20**, 859
        right of rejection, **20**, 867
      carrier, to, **20**, 861, 878, 879
      constructive, **20**, 860
      different description, goods of, **20**, 864
      documents of title, transfer of, **20**, 860
      expenses of, **20**, 859
      generally, **20**, 858, 859
      immediate, buyer's entitlement to, **20**, 858
      instalment, by, **20**, 863
      late, **20**, 862
      meaning of delivery, **20**, 837*n*, 859
      payment as concurrent condition, **20**, 858
      place of, **20**, 859
      quantity tendered, **20**, 864
      reasonable hour, must be made at, **20**, 859
      reform, proposals for, **20**, 865, 869
      seller—
        duty as to delivery, **20**, 858
        goods sent by, **20**, 859
        third person, where goods in possession of, **20**, 859
      time for not fixed, where, **20**, 859
    examination by buyer, **20**, 868, 893
    failure to contract, **20**, 818
    form of contract, **20**, 817
    goods identified and agreed on at the time of contract, **20**, 807
    heritage, small items of, **20**, 817
    hire purchase contract, **20**, 855
    implied terms—
      appearance and finish, **20**, 827
      business, goods sold in course of, **20**, 823

Sale and supply of goods—*continued*
contract of sale—*continued*
  moveable property—*continued*
    implied terms—*continued*
      conditions and warranties, **20**, 820, 821
      description, as to, **20**, 822
      durability, **20**, 827
      exclusion of, **20**, 830
      fitness for purpose, as to, **20**, 823–827
      generally, **20**, 819
      quality, as to, **20**, 819, 823, 824, 826, 827
        acceptable or satisfactory quality, **20**, 827
      reasonableness guidelines, **20**, 831
      safety, **20**, 827
      sample, sale by, **20**, 823*n*, 828, 829
      title, as to, **20**, 821
      warrandice, **20**, 819, 821
      where none, **20**, 823
    inducements, customer receiving, **20**, 831
    intention of parties, ascertaining, **20**, 836–840
    international sales—
      examination of goods by buyer, **20**, 893
      fundamental breach, **20**, 893
      lack of conformity in goods, **20**, 893
      offer and acceptance, **20**, 893
      Uniform Laws on International Sales Act 1967 ..., **20**, 892, 893
      Vienna Convention, **20**, 894, 895
    liability, terms restricting, **20**, 831
    lien, *see* LIEN
    lost and abandoned, sale by chief constable, **20**, 856
    mercantile agent, **20**, 849
    neglect or refusal to deliver by seller, **20**, 885
    part owners, between, **20**, 809
    payment for, *see* SALE AND SUPPLY OF GOODS
    performance, **20**, 858–869
    perished goods, **20**, 807
    in possession of persons taken into custody, sale by chief constable, **20**, 857
    pre-1893 conditions, **20**, 809
    pre-1979 cases, **20**, 803
    price—
      fixing of, **20**, 818
      reasonable, **20**, 818
    private individuals for private purposes, between, **20**, 823
    resale, seller's right of, **20**, 870, 873, 881
    rescission, **20**, 881
    reservation of title, **20**, 842
    resolutive condition, **20**, 810
    retention, seller's right of, **20**, 872
    Sale of Goods Act 1893 ..., **20**, 803
    Scots common law, **20**, 802, 802*n*, 804, 809
    security over goods, **20**, 815
    seller—
      breach, remedies for, **20**, 870–884
      rights of, **20**, 870–884
    special order, goods manufactured, processed or adapted to, **20**, 831
    specific goods, **20**, 807
    specific performance, **20**, 887

Sale and supply of goods—*continued*
contract of sale—*continued*
  moveable property—*continued*
    stoppage in transit, *see* STOPPAGE IN TRANSIT
    suspensive condition, **20**, 810
    trade customs, **20**, 831
    unascertained goods, **20**, 834, 835
    unpaid seller—
      meaning, **20**, 871
      remedies of, **20**, 871, 872
    word of mouth, contract by, **20**, 817
    work and materials, contract for, distinguished, **20**, 812
    written contracts, **20**, 817
    See also PROPERTY
  negotiable instrument, seller accepting, **20**, 874
  nemo dat quod non habet rule, **20**, 847, 852
  nominate consensual contract, as, **14**, 1004
  perished goods, **20**, 807
  personal bar, **20**, 852
  pledged goods, **20**, 854
  possession and presumption of ownership, **20**, 852
  prohibition of exclusion or restriction of liability, **6**, 34
  purpose of, **20**, 832
  Roman law, **20**, 801
  seller with voidable title, **13**, 58
  seller's authority to sell, **20**, 847
  shortfall or excess of goods, **15**, 866
  specific goods, **20**, 807
  unascertained goods, **20**, 808
contractual arrangement with consequences in property law, as, **18**, 625
credit or charge card, consumer sales for, **18**, 631
credit sale agreements, **20**, 814
dangerous or defective products, **6**, 39, 41, 43, 44, 51, 56, 58, 61
definition, **20**, 809
delivery—
  acceptance by buyer, **20**, 866, 868
  actual, **20**, 860
  approval, delivery on, **20**, 840
  bill of lading, transfer of, **20**, 860
  buyer—
    acceptance of goods by, **20**, 866, 868
    duties of, **20**, 858, 866
    examination of goods by, **20**, 868
    international sales, **20**, 893
    non-acceptance by, **20**, 866
    rejection, right of, **20**, 867
    taking possession, **20**, 859
  carrier, to, **20**, 861, 878, 879
  constructive, **20**, 860
  delayed delivery and risk, **20**, 846
  deliverable state, meaning, **20**, 836–839
  delivery, meaning, **20**, 837*n*
  different description, goods of, **20**, 864
  documents of title, transfer of, **20**, 860
  expenses of, liability for, **20**, 859
  generally, **20**, 809
  immediate, buyer's entitlement to, **20**, 858
  instalment, by, **20**, 863
  lien, effect on rights of, **20**, 876

Sale and supply of goods—*continued*
delivery—*continued*
  late, **20**, 862
  lien, *see* LIEN
  moveable property—
    exchange, contracts of, **20**, 900
    performance, **20**, 901
  neglect or refusal to deliver by seller, **20**, 885–888
  non-acceptance by buyer, **20**, 866
  non-delivery, damages for, **20**, 885–888
  payment—
    concurrent condition, as, **20**, 858
    credit, where purchaser given, **20**, 858
  place of, **20**, 859
  postponement of, **20**, 837
  quantity—
    less than seller contracted to sell, **20**, 864
    more than seller contracted to sell, **20**, 864
  reasonable hour, must be made at, **20**, 859
  reform of law, proposals for, **20**, 865, 869
  rejection, buyer's right of, **20**, 867
  sale and delivery, generally, **20**, 809
  sale or return, on basis of, **20**, 840
  sea transit, involving, **20**, 861
  seller—
    duty of, **20**, 858
    right to withhold delivery, **20**, 870, 872
  stoppage in transit, *see* STOPPAGE IN TRANSIT
  third person, goods in possession of, **20**, 859, 860
  within reasonable time, **6**, 35; **20**, 859
description, contract of sale for moveable property, implied terms, **20**, 822
document, goods accompanied by, **6**, 250
existing goods, statutory classification, **20**, 806
fitness for purpose, *see* FITNESS FOR PURPOSE
food, of, *see* FOOD
foreign currency, of, **14**, 1809
free gifts, **6**, 126
future goods, statutory classification, **20**, 806
generally, **14**, 1802
generic goods, as unascertained goods, **20**, 808
goods—
  definition—
    common law, **20**, 805
    statutory, **20**, 805
  statutory classification—
    ascertained goods, **20**, 807
    existing goods, **20**, 806
    future goods, **20**, 806
    specific goods, **20**, 807
    unascertained goods, **20**, 808
heritage, sale of, *see* HERITABLE PROPERTY
hire-purchase agreement, *see* HIRE-PURCHASE AGREEMENT
hotel, sale of goods left at, **11**, 1758, 1759
implied terms, **6**, 34
instalment, delivery by, **20**, 863
liquor, sale of—
  offences relating to, **2**, 79
  Sunday, on, **2**, 15
  theatres, in, **2**, 26
  weights and measures legislation, *see* ALCOHOLIC LIQUOR

Sale and supply of goods—*continued*
manufacturers' liability, *see* LIABILITY
medicinal product, *see* MEDICINAL PRODUCT
metric packs, **6**, 194
money as commodity, contract for, enforcement
    of, **14**, 1814
notes, of, **14**, 1807
part owners, contract of sale between, **20**, 809
payment—
    action for price, **20**, 882
    buyer's duty to pay, **20**, 858, 870
    concurrent condition to delivery, as, **20**, 858
    credit, where purchaser given, **20**, 858
    damages for non-acceptance, **20**, 884
    interest, seller's right to recover, **20**, 883
    postponement of, **20**, 837
    seller's action for price, **20**, 882
    unpaid seller—
        meaning, **20**, 871
        remedies of, **20**, 871, 872
perished goods, **20**, 807
    without fault by buyer or seller, **20**, 807
personal bar, *see* PERSONAL BAR
poison, of, *see* POISON
prepacked, *see* PACKAGED GOODS
price, **20**, 818
    failure to contract, **20**, 818
    reasonable, **20**, 818
price marking—
    misleading, **6**, 141–145
    regulation of, **6**, 81
product safety, *see* SAFETY
property—
    buyer in possession, **20**, 851
    conditional sale agreements, **20**, 855
    heritable, sale of, *see* HERITABLE PROPERTY
    hire purchase contracts, **20**, 855
    lost and abandoned, sale by chief constable, **20**,
        856
    passing between buyer and seller—
        approval, delivery on, **20**, 840
        bills of lading, **20**, 843
        goods bought in bulk, **20**, 835
        bulk, goods sold in, **20**, 835
        buyer's remedies for breach, **20**, 885–891
        delayed delivery and risk, **20**, 846
        deliverable state, meaning, **20**, 836–839
        delivery, *see* SALE AND SUPPLY OF GOODS
        generally, **20**, 832–834
        intention of parties, ascertaining, **20**, 836–
          841
        judicial sales, **20**, 853
        mercantile agents, **20**, 849
        nemo dat quod non habet rule, **20**, 847, 852
        payment—
          postponement of, **20**, 837
        pledged goods, **20**, 854
        precise time of, **20**, 833
        reservation of title, **20**, 842
        risk—
          delayed delivery, and, **20**, 846
          determination of liability for, **20**, 844–846
        sale or return, delivery on basis of, **20**, 840

Sale and supply of goods—*continued*
property—*continued*
    passing between buyer and seller—*continued*
        seller—
          authority to sell, **20**, 847
          bound to particular action, where, **20**,
            838, 839
          in possession after sale, **20**, 850
          remedies for breach, **20**, 870–884
        unascertained goods, **20**, 834, 835, 841
        unconditional contract, **20**, 837
        voidable title, **20**, 848
    in possession of persons taken into custody, sale
        by chief constable, **20**, 857
    Sale of Goods Act 1979 ..., **20**, 832
    third parties and, **20**, 832
        brokers, **20**, 849
        buyer in possession, **20**, 851
        conditional sale agreements, **20**, 855
        goods found in possession of certain persons,
          sale by chief constable, **20**, 857
        hire purchase agreements, **20**, 855
        judicial sales, **20**, 853
        lost and abandoned goods, sale by chief
          constable, **20**, 856
        mercantile agents, **20**, 849
        nemo dat quod non habet rule, **20**, 847, 852
        personal bar, **20**, 852
        pledge, **20**, 854
        seller in possession after sale, **20**, 850
        voidable title, **20**, 848
        warrant sales, **20**, 853
    title to, *nemo dat quaod non habet* rule, **20**, 847, 852
purity of goods, **6**, 4
purpose of sale transaction, **18**, 625
pyramid selling, *see* PYRAMID SELLING
quality—
    contract of sale for moveable property—
        generally, **20**, 819
        implied terms, **20**, 823, 824
          acceptable or satisfactory quality, **20**, 827
          merchantable quality, **20**, 824
          reform, proposals for, **20**, 826
          sample, sale by, **20**, 828
quantity—
    by, **6**, 254
    marking, **6**, 194
reasonableness, contract of sale for moveable
    property, **20**, 831
resale—
    buyer obliged to account for resale profits,
        where, **20**, 815
    seller's right of, **20**, 870, 873, 881
retail sale, meaning, **6**, 194
risk—
    liability for, where property passing between
        buyer and seller, **20**, 844–846
    delayed delivery, in cases of, **20**, 846
    passing, **18**, 639
Romalpa clause, **18**, 628, 638
Sale of Goods Act 1979, under—
    approval, delivery of goods on, **18**, 634
    ascertainment of goods, **18**, 627
    dominium, **18**, 625, 628

Sale and supply of goods—*continued*
Sale of Goods Act 1979, under—*continued*
  express provision, absence of, **18**, 629
  generally, **18**, 624, 626
  intention as test of passing of property, **18**, 613,
    628, 636, 637
  purpose of sale transaction, **18**, 625
  reversion of title, **18**, 638
  risk, passing of, **18**, 639, 639n
  sale or return, delivery on basis of, **18**, 634
  section 18 rules, **18**, 630–635
  security, sales intended to operate in, **18**, 637
  specific act, where sale dependent on, **18**, 632
  unascertained or future goods, sale of, **18**, 635,
    636
  unconditional contract, by, **18**, 631, 631n
  weighing, measuring or testing, where sale
    dependent on, **18**, 633, 633n
sample, by, **20**, 828, 829
security over goods, **20**, 815
self-service stores, **6**, 254
seller—
  duty to deliver, **20**, 858, 859
  remedies of, **20**, 870–884
services, *see* SERVICES
specific goods, **20**, 807
  statutory classification, **20**, 807
superfluous land, of, **5**, 27
supermarket or cash and carry, sale in, **18**, 630
suspension notices served on dangerous goods, **6**,
  56
title to goods, reservation, **18**, 638; **20**, 842
trading in, **6**, 49
trading stamps, **6**, 146, 147
unascertained goods, statutory classification, **20**, 808
unsevered portions of larger goods, identified
  quantity of, **20**, 808
unsolicited goods and services—
  generally, **6**, 151
  human sexual techniques, relating to, **6**, 153
  protection of persons receiving, **6**, 152
vending machines, **6**, 248
weighing in customer's presence, **6**, 254
weights and measures legislation—
  abbreviation of units, **6**, 194
  agricultural liming materials, **6**, 239
  agricultural salt, **6**, 239
  alcoholic liquor, **6**, 193, 196–199
  capacity measurement, goods sold by or
    marked with, **6**, 244, 245, 249
  cement mortar, ready-mixed, **6**, 238
  concrete, ready-mixed, **6**, 238
  food, *see* FOOD
  generally, **6**, 193
  inorganic fertilisers, **6**, 239
  length, goods sold by or marked with, **6**, 242
  liquid fuel, **6**, 237
  lubricants, **6**, 237
  metric quantities, **6**, 194
  net weight, goods sold by or marked with, **6**,
    243, 245
  number, sold by, **6**, 246
  offences, **6**, 248–250
    defences to, **6**, 251, 253

Sale and supply of goods—*continued*
weights and measures legislation—*continued*
  perfumery, **6**, 241
  prepacked goods, **6**, 193, 195
  quantity marking, **6**, 194
  quantity to be stated in writing, **6**, 249
  sand and ballast, **6**, 229
  soap, **6**, 241
  solid fuel, **6**, 231–236
  toilet preparations, **6**, 241
  wood fuel, **6**, 240
  See also WEIGHTS AND MEASURES
See also CONTRACT; MERCANTILE LAW; TRANSFER OF
  OWNERSHIP
Salmon-salmon fisheries
access, right of—
  generally, **18**, 327, 328
  rights and duties of servient proprietor, **18**, 464
  servitude, as, **18**, 443
act or omission exempted by Secretary of State,
  11, 13
administration of fishings, **11**, 31–39
  Commissioners, **11**, 32
  district boards, **11**, 32, 32n
  early history, **11**, 32
  Fishery Board for Scotland, **11**, 32
  inspector of salmon fisheries for Scotland, **11**,
    32
  mandatories, **11**, 37
  proprietors, **11**, 34
  salmon fishery districts, **11**, 33, 36
alveus operations on, **25**, 321
authority to enforce legislation, **11**, 24
baits, **11**, 23
barriers, prohibition against, **11**, 14
black fish, meaning, **11**, 2n
byelaws, enforcement of, **11**, 38
close season, buying, selling or exposing for sale
  during, **11**, 312
close time—
  annual, **11**, 14–16, 23, 32
  River Tweed, **11**, 42
  weekly, **11**, 2, 14, 17, 23, 32
conservation, **11**, 89
  North Atlantic, in, **11**, 101–105
  stock improvement and, acts carried out for,
    11, 13, 43
  United Nations Convention on the Law of the
    Sea, **11**, 102
Crown, provisions binding on, **11**, 39
cruives, fishing by, *see* CRUIVES
dead, unlawfully taking or removing, **11**, 21
dealers in, licensing of, **11**, 23; **14**, 566
district salmon fishery boards, *see* DISTRICT
  SALMON FISHERY BOARDS
dragging, **11**, 11n
eggs—
  act or omission relating to, **11**, 13
  importing live, **11**, 20
  introduction into inland waters, **11**, 20, 63
  non-native fish, **11**, 20
estuary limits—
  fixing, **11**, 23
  order, **11**, 23

Salmon-salmon fisheries—*continued*
farmed salmon, ownership, **18**, 320
farming rights included in salmon fishing rights, **18**, 321
fish farms, **11**, 5*n*, 58
  concessions to, **11**, 10, 12*n*
  derating of, **11**, 64
  exceptions and exemptions for, **11**, 63, 64
  inland, **11**, 57, 59, 60
  marine, **11**, 61
  meaning, **11**, 57*n*
  pollution control, **11**, 62
fish pass—
  prevention of passage through, **11**, 19
  taking fish at prohibited, **11**, 12
Fisheries Committee, **11**, 39
fishery assessments, **11**, 38
fishery districts, *see* SALMON FISHERY DISTRICTS
fishing without title, **18**, 326
fishings—
  agricultural lands and heritages, deemed, **24**, 660
  conveyance of for valuable consideration, **6**, 714*n*
  lease, **11**, 9; **13**, 202, 205, 296
  ownership, positive prescription, **16**, 2102, 2107
  protection of rights, **25**, 519
  registration of, **6**, 779
  rights, **24**, 658
  valuation roll, entry in, **24**, 432, 658, 660
fixed engines, fishing by, **18**, 326
forfeiture of illegally taken fish, **11**, 3, 22, 27
history of regulation, **11**, 2
illegal fishing, **11**, 21
import of live, **11**, 20
inland waters, **11**, 5
  introduction into, **11**, 20
  permitted fishing methods, **18**, 326
Inspector of salmon fisheries for Scotland, **11**, 432
inter regalia minora, salmon as, **18**, 521
juvenile—
  obstruction of passage of, **11**, 19
  protection of, **11**, 20
kelt, **11**, 18
leaping at falls, nets or engines to catch, **11**, 12
lease of salmon fishings, **11**, 9; **13**, 202, 205, 296
lower proprietors, **11**, 32, 34, 35
lures, **11**, 23
mandatory, **11**, 37
meaning, **11**, 1
net and coble, fishing by—
  annual close time, **11**, 15
  bag net, **11**, 11
  coble, meaning, **11**, 3*n*
  definition, **11**, 11
  fly net, **11**, 11
  lease of fishings, **11**, 9
  River Tweed, **11**, 43
  salmon fishing, **11**, 3, 5, 11, 188; **18**, 326
  stake net, **11**, 11
non-native fish, importing, keeping or releasing, **11**, 20
non-tidal lochs, **18**, 306

Salmon-salmon fisheries—*continued*
North Atlantic Salmon Conservation Organisation, **11**, 67, 104, 105
North Atlantic Salmon convention, **11**, 103
obstruction of, **11**, 19, 32
  Secretary of State's powers, **11**, 23
obstruction preventing free passage of fish, **18**, 330
occupancy, no right of acquisition by, **18**, 543
occupation, doctrine of, **18**, 320
open sea, permitted fishing methods, **18**, 326
ownerless status of wild salmon, **18**, 320
ownership of salmon fishings, positive prescription, **16**, 2102, 2107
pertinent, salmon fishery as, **12**, 1242
poaching, **11**, 10, 11
pollution, proprietor's rights in cases of, **18**, 298
private prosecutions relating to salmon fisheries, **17**, 531
proprietors, definition, **11**, 34
prosecution of offences, **11**, 38, 39
protection of rights, **25**, 519
public right to gather white fish and shellfish, and, **18**, 515
red fish, meaning, **11**, 2*n*
regulation of salmon fishing, **11**, 10–30
  electricity generating stations, effect on stocks, **11**, 10
  exemptions from prosecution, **11**, 13
  fish farmers, concessions to, **11**, 10, 12*n*
  passage of salmon, **11**, 23
  permitted methods of fishing, **11**, 11
  poaching, **11**, 10
  River Esk, **11**, 46
  River Tweed, **11**, 10
  Solway Firth, **11**, 10
  statutory basis, **11**, 10
res nullius, salmon as, **11**, 3; **18**, 320
restocking, **11**, 39
River Esk, *see* RIVER ESK
River Tweed, *see* RIVER TWEED
rod and line, fishing by, **11**, 3, 5, 11; **18**, 325, 326
  annual close time, **11**, 15, 16
  baits and lures, **11**, 23
  Crown right of salmon fishing, **18**, 321
  lease of fishings, **11**, 9
  meaning, **11**, 5*n*
  weekly close time, **11**, 17
roe—
  act or omission relating to, **11**, 13
  buying, selling or possessing, **11**, 20
salmon fishery districts, *see* SALMON FISHERY DISTRICTS
salmon fishing rights—
  access to water, **11**, 8
  acquisition—
    express grant, by, **18**, 322, 323
    generally, **11**, 4
    prescription, by, **18**, 322, 324, 325
    subject proprietor, by, **18**, 322
  adjacent dry land, rights over, **18**, 327, 328, 443, 464
  alteration in course of water, **18**, 326
  ancillary rights, **11**, 8; **18**, 327–330

Salmon-salmon fisheries—*continued*
salmon fishing rights—*continued*
  common interest obligations, **18**, 326, 359
  Crown, vested in, **11**, 3, 3*n*; **18**, 321
  definite boundaries, acquisition where, **18**, 323
  district salmon fishery boards, policing by, generally, **18**, 326
  dominium utile, **18**, 10
  drawing and drying salmon nets, **11**, 8
  exercise of, **18**, 326
  express grant from Crown, **11**, 4
  extent of right, **11**, 5
  foreshore, in relation to, **18**, 318
  free passage of salmon, right to, **18**, 327, 330
  generally, **18**, 319, 320
  history of, **11**, 2
  imprescriptible nature, **18**, 326
  indefinite boundaries, acquisition where, **18**, 323
  inland waters—
    generally, **11**, 5, 5*n*
    permitted fishing methods, **18**, 326
  inter regalia minora, **11**, 4
  land adjoining water in different ownership, **11**, 5, 8
  land ownership, not incident of, **11**, 4
  leases of salmon fishings, **11**, 9
  medium filum—
    rights across, **18**, 327, 329
    rules regarding, **11**, 5, 5*n*
  nature of, **11**, 3; **18**, 320
  open sea, permitted fishing methods, **18**, 326
  other fish, right to catch, **18**, 326
  prescriptive possession, **11**, 4
  public right of navigation, and, **18**, 515*n*
  regalian right, as, **18**, 210
  restrictions, **11**, 6; **18**, 326
  right in existence on 10 May 1951 ..., **11**, 5, 11
  rights of navigation and, **11**, 7
  riparian proprietor's fishing rights, and, **18**, 280
  river banks vested in different proprietors, **11**, 5
  salmon farming rights included in, **18**, 321
  sea fishing, **11**, 8
  separate feudal estate, as, **11**, 4
  separate heritable right, **11**, 5
  separate tenement, as, **18**, 10, 210, 280, 319
  statutory protection, **11**, 2
  trout fishing rights—
    included in, **11**, 5, 48
    yield to, **18**, 326
scientific purposes, acts carried out for, **11**, 13, 18, 43
screens in off-takes from internal waters, **11**, 23
sea fish, as, **11**, 183*n*
Sea Fish (Conservation) Act 1967 ..., **11**, 144
sea fishing, **11**, 8, 144
Secretary of State's powers, **11**, 32, 38
sniggering, **11**, 11*n*
Solway Firth, *see* SOLWAY FIRTH
spawning beds, disturbance of, **11**, 20
stake nets, fishing by, **18**, 326
statutory protection, **11**, 31
  fishing rights, of, **11**, 2

Salmon-salmon fisheries—*continued*
stocks, protection of, **11**, 20, 21
  arrest, powers of, **11**, 28
  dead salmon, unlawful taking or removal, **11**, 21
  enforcement of legislation, **11**, 24
  entry, powers of, **11**, 25
  forfeiture, **11**, 22
  illegal fishing, **11**, 21
  obstruction of enforcing officer, **11**, 29
  packages containing salmon, **11**, 21
  possession of illegal substances or instrument, **11**, 21
  search, powers of, **11**, 26
  Secretary of State—
    powers of, **11**, 23
    powers of persons appointed by, **11**, 24, 30
  seizure, powers of, **11**, 27
  trawls or other moving gear, **11**, 21
  wardens appointed by Secretary of State, **11**, 24
  water bailiffs, **11**, 24
temporary discharge of water, **25**, 333
unclean—
  buying, selling or exposing for sale, **11**, 18
  meaning, **11**, 18, 18*n*
  taking or fishing for, **11**, 18
United Nations Convention on the Law of the Sea, **11**, 102
unlawful methods of fishing, **11**, 12
unseasonable, **11**, 18
upper proprietors, **11**, 32, 34, 35
water, abstraction of, **11**, 6
water bailiffs, *see* WATER BAILIFF
water pollution injuring salmon fishing, **14**, 2079
wild salmon, status of, **18**, 320
Salmon fishery districts
administration of salmon fisheries by, **11**, 33
extent, **11**, 33
meaning, **11**, 33
River Tweed, **11**, 33
Secretary of State's powers, **11**, 33
sole proprietor in, **11**, 36
Salmonella
testing of poultry for, **19**, 477
Salt
raw and unprocessed meat, added to, **11**, 374*n*
Salvage
action *in personam*, **21**, 481, 482
  competing claims, **21**, 482
action *in rem*, **21**, 481, 482
agreement excluding right to, circumstances vitiating, **21**, 478
aircraft, **2**, 1065, **17**, 426, **21**, 439
amount of, **17**, 426
armed forces, member of, entitlement to claim salvage award, **21**, 458
assistance, duty to give, **21**, 209
award, *see* salvage award *below*
bill of lading, express terms, **21**, 546
Brussels Convention on Salvage 1910, **21**, 431*n*, 440*n*
cargo put at risk by salvage operation, **21**, 447
civil, **21**, 431*n*
coastguard, entitlement to claim salvage award, **21**, 459

Salvage—*continued*

compensation, when payable, **21**, 464

concealment by master of serious damage or valuable cargo, **21**, 478, 478n

contract—

agreement excluding right to salvage, circumstances vitiating, **21**, 478, 478n

agreement fixing amount of salvage award, **21**, 478

amount payable, agreement as to, **21**, 477

contract not necessary, **21**, 477

fixed price, agreement as to, **21**, 478, 478n

independent law of salvage, relationship with, **21**, 477

inequality of bargaining power, **21**, 478, 478n

labour and materials, to provide, **21**, 477

law of contract, relevance, **21**, 433

less remunerative basis, agreement for services to be paid on, **21**, 478

Lloyd's form, *see* Lloyd's Standard Form of Salvage Agreement *below*

rendering of services on salvage basis, agreement excluding, **21**, 477

right to, independent of contract, **21**, 433

rights and obligations of parties, **21**, 477

salvage services, to provide, **21**, 477

service agreed not salvage service, where, **21**, 477

type of service rendered, **21**, 477

types of agreement, **21**, 477

vitiating elements, **21**, 478

contractual, **21**, 433

Crown, entitlement to claim salvage award, **21**, 457

Crown servant, entitlement to claim salvage award, **21**, 458

danger—

actual, **21**, 441

apprehended, **21**, 441

assessment of salvage award, **21**, 469

contractual liability, risk of, as danger, **21**, 442

degree of danger—

disputes as to, **21**, 441

requirements as to, **21**, 432

delictual liability, risk of incurring, as danger, **21**, 442

human life, to, assessment of salvage award, **21**, 469

inferred, **21**, 441

non-physical, **21**, 442

property, to, assessment of salvage award, **21**, 469

property rights in ship etc., danger to, **21**, 442

salvaged property must be in position of, **21**, 431, 432, 441

demise charter, earned by, **21**, 534

elements, **21**, 432

expenses incurred—

damages for, **21**, 386, 390

fuel consumption, **21**, 386

International Convention on Salvage (1989), **21**, 431, 431n

international law, **21**, 431

jurisdiction, **21**, 101, 102n, 481

Salvage—*continued*

lien, **20**, 77, 278, 311, 312

maritime, **21**, 392

possessory, **20**, 303

ranking, **20**, 311, 312

statutory, **20**, 305

lifeboatman, entitlement to claim salvage award, **21**, 460

limitation of liability, **21**, 755, 757

Lloyd's Standard Form of Salvage Agreement—

arbitration—

appeal, **21**, 495, 496

appearance at, **21**, 491

award, **21**, 495

cargo interests, **21**, 493

costs, **21**, 497

evidence, admission of, **21**, 493

generally, **21**, 488

initiation, **21**, 490

interim award, **21**, 493, 494, 498

overpayment, **21**, 498

payment, **21**, 498

procedural rules, **21**, 492

procedure at, **21**, 493

procedure prior to, **21**, 492

salvage award, **21**, 494

arbitrator—

appointment, **21**, 490

powers, **21**, 493

cargo interests, **21**, 493

conclusion, **21**, 484

contractor, obligations of, **21**, 485

costs and fees, orders as to, **21**, 493

Council of Lloyd's, liability, **21**, 499

cross-appeal, **21**, 496

documents, exchange of, **21**, 492

English law, governed by, **21**, 485, 488

generally, **21**, 483

master and crew, claims on behalf of, **21**, 498

origins, **21**, 483

parties to, **21**, 484

payment on account, **21**, 494

pre-contractual services, **21**, 487

realisation of security if sum not paid, **21**, 498

salvage award—

fixing, generally, **21**, 494

interest payable on, **21**, 495

interim, **21**, 493, 494, 498

salved property owner, obligations of, **21**, 486

security, provisions as to, **21**, 489

sub-contractor, servant or agent, claims on behalf of, **21**, 498

written pleadings, **21**, 492

maritime cause, as, **1**, 411

maritime lien—

conditions for, **21**, 479

generally, **1**, 413; **21**, 479

priority over claim for necessaries, **21**, 479n

priority over other claims, **21**, 479, 479n

master of salved vessel—

apportionment of salvage award, **21**, 473, 474

claim on behalf of, **21**, 498

concealment of serious damage or valuable cargo by, **21**, 478, 478n

Salvage—*continued*
master of salved vessel—*continued*
  duty to salvors, **21**, 465, 466
  owner renouncing salvage, position where, **21**, 454
  voyage charterparty master's power to enter salvage agreement, **21**, 629
  whether entitled to claim salvage award, **21**, 452, 454
meaning, **21**, 431
military, **21**, 431*n*
moral duties, irrelevance of, **21**, 448
negotiorum gestio, concept of, **21**, 431
  distinguished, **15**, 93
origins, **21**, 431
owner renouncing, position of master and crew, **21**, 454
owner of salvaged property, duty to, **21**, 449
owner of salved vessel, duty to salvors, **21**, 465, 466
passenger, entitlement to claim salvage award, **21**, 456
payment, generally, **17**, 426
pilot, entitlement to claim salvage award, **21**, 455
place of—
  generally, **21**, 431, 440
  inland waters, property in, **21**, 431*n*, 432, 440
  sea, property in, **21**, 432, 440
  tidal waters, property in, **21**, 440
port or lighthouse authority, entitlement to claim salvage award, **21**, 459
private law, as branch of, **21**, 468
prize, **17**, 426; **21**, 431*n*
reward, *see* salvage award *below*
salvage award—
  agreement fixing, circumstances vitiating, **21**, 478
  apportionment, **21**, 432
    differents sets of salvors, between, **21**, 475
    owners, master and crew, between, **21**, 473, 474
    plurality of salvors, where, **21**, 473–475
  assessment—
    amount of award, **21**, 472
    appeals, **21**, 472
    cargo, valuation, **21**, 469*n*
    environmental damage, **21**, 469*n*
    factors relevant to, **21**, 469
    falls in value of money, **21**, 471
    freight, valuation, **21**, 469*n*
    guidance from other cases, **21**, 470
    interest, award of, **21**, 471
    International Convention on Salvage criteria, **21**, 469
    public interest, element of, **21**, 468
    public policy, **21**, 468
    risks run by salvors, **21**, 469*n*
  coastguards, port and lighthouse authorities, entitlement to claim, **21**, 459
  compensation as alternative to, **21**, 464
  crew of salved vessel, **21**, 451, 454, 473, 474, 498
  diminution on fault or misconduct of salvors, **21**, 469

Salvage—*continued*
assessment—*continued*
  entitlement to claim, **21**, 444
  foreign currency, made in, **21**, 469
  liability to pay, **21**, 432
    value, contribution in proportion to, **21**, 476
    life salvage, contribution to, **21**, 476
  Lloyd's Standard Form of Salvage Agreement, **21**, 494
  lost opportunity, in respect of, **21**, 463
  master of salved vessel, whether entitled to claim, **21**, 452, 454
  meaning, **21**, 431
  right to, establishing, **21**, 432
  statutory duties, whether precluding claim, **21**, 450
salvage contract—
  duty and fault of salvors, **21**, 465–467
  express and implied terms, **21**, 465
salvage service, definition, **15**, 93
salvage services—
  expense incurred, assessment of salvage award, **21**, 469
  general average, **21**, 710
  generally, **21**, 443
  loss incurred, assessment of salvage award, **21**, 469
  meaning, **21**, 431, 432
  rendered against will of salved property, **21**, 441*n*
  responsibilities incurred, assessment of salvage award, **21**, 469
  voyage charterparty, rendered to, **21**, 630
salvor, *see* SALVOR
services, VAT zero-rating, **7**, 1452
sheriff court jurisdiction, financial limits, **4**, 18
ship, meaning, **21**, 107
ship or cargo threatening environment, where, **21**, 464, 469*n*
subject—
  aircraft, **21**, 439
    prize salvage, as, **17**, 426
  cargo, **21**, 434, 436
  derelict, **21**, 434
  fixed or floating platforms or drilling units not classed as, **21**, 434
  flotsam, **21**, 434
  freight, **21**, 434, 437
  generally, **21**, 107, 431*n*, 432
  hovercraft, **21**, 439
  jetsam, **21**, 434
  lagan, **21**, 434
  life, **21**, 438, 439, 469
    salvage award, contribution, **21**, 476
  maritime lien, ranking, **21**, 479*n*
  passage money, **21**, 437
  recognised, **21**, 434
  ship, **21**, 107, 434, 435
    prize salvage, as, **17**, 426
  ships' apparel, **21**, 434, 435
  wreck, **21**, 434
success—
  contributions to, award in respect of, **21**, 462, 463
  dismissal and supersession of salvors, **21**, 463

Salvage—*continued*
success—*continued*
   exceptions to rule, **21**, 464
   rule as to, generally, **21**, 432, 461
tidal, waters must be, **21**, 112*n*
validity of claim, determining, **21**, 432
voluntariness, requirement of—
   coastguard, position of, **21**, 459
   crew of salved vessel, whether entitled to claim
      award, **21**, 451, 454
   Crown right to claim salvage award, **21**, 457
   Crown servant, position of, **21**, 458
   generally, **21**, 431, 448
   lifeboatman, position of, **21**, 460
   lighthouse authority, position of, **21**, 459
   master of salved vessel, whether entitled to
      claim award, **21**, 452, 454
   member of armed forces, position of, **21**, 458
   moral duties, irrelevance of, **21**, 448
   passenger, position of, **21**, 456
   pilot, position of, **21**, 455
   port authority, position of, **21**, 459
   statutory duties, and, **21**, 450
   tug under towage contract, **21**, 453
      cargo on board tow, **21**, 453
voyage charterparty master's power to enter
   salvage agreement, **21**, 629
who may claim, **21**, 432
wreck of historical, archaeological or artistic
   importance, **21**, 515
Salvor
breach of duty by, **21**, 463
breach of obligations, assessing, **21**, 465
bribery by, **21**, 467
charterer as, **21**, 444, 446
compensation payable to, as alternative to salvage
   award, **21**, 464
completion of services, contractual obligations as
   to, **21**, 463
conduct of, relevance, **21**, 469
contract, under—
   dismissal, **21**, 463
   express and implied terms, **21**, 465
contractual, **21**, 477, 478
contributions to salvage, award in respect of, **21**,
   462, 463, 475
dismissal, **21**, 463
   assessment of salvage award where, **21**, 475
duty, generally, **21**, 465
entitlement to claim salvage award, **21**, 444
fault by—
   assessment, **21**, 465
   consequences, **21**, 466
   diminution of salvage award by reason of, **21**,
      469
   generally, **21**, 465
forcible ejection of prior salvors, **21**, 467
   assessment of salvage award, **21**, 475
limitation of liability, **21**, 751, 754, 754*n*
   London Convention, **21**, 753
lost opportunity, award in respect of, **21**, 463
misconduct by, **21**, 467
   diminution of salvage award by reason of, **21**,
      469

Salvor—*continued*
negligence, public policy towards, **21**, 468
owner of property other than ship as, **21**, 444, 447
owner of salvaged property, duty to, **21**, 449
personal services, person rendering, as, **21**, 444,
   445
plurality of, where, apportionment of salvage
   award, **21**, 473–475
right of lien, **20**, 77
salvage award, factors relevant to assessment, **21**,
   469
shipowner as, **21**, 444, 446
skill of, relevance, **21**, 469
supersession, **21**, 463
   assessment of salvage award where, **21**, 475
theft by, **21**, 467
vandalism by, **21**, 467
voluntariness, requirement for, *see* SALVAGE
San Marino
European Union customs territory, **7**, 1010
Sand
weights and measures legislation, **6**, 229
Sandwich
labelling, **11**, 388
Sanitary conditions, creation of
annoying and offensive behaviour, **19**, 370–372
buildings and building controls, **19**, 350–358
caravan sites, **19**, 349
cleansing, **19**, 364–367
dangerous and annoying creatures, **19**, 372
dogs, fouling by, **19**, 371
drains, **19**, 330–334
health and safety at work, **19**, 342–345
housing, **19**, 346–348
nuisances, public health, **19**, 335–341
public conveniences, **19**, 368, 369
public health legislation, generally, **19**, 306, 330–
   372
sewers, **19**, 330–334
town and country planning, **19**, 359, 360
urinating and defecation, **19**, 370
waste collection and disposal, **19**, 361–363
Sanitary convenience
building controls, **3**, 208
improvement grants, **11**, 2023
mines and quarries, in, **14**, 1664
multiple occupation, housing in, **11**, 2005
public, **11**, 1979
See also PUBLIC CONVENIENCE; WATERCLOSET
Sanitary inspector
appointment of, **14**, 249
food unfit for human consumption, **11**, 402
Sark
inland bill, nature of, **4**, 120
Sasine
clare constat, **18**, 108, 109
   writ of, **6**, 605
Crown, of, **18**, 48
description of subjects, **6**, 729
fealty, oath of, **18**, 89
feu charter, **18**, 96
feudal law, generally, **18**, 89, 99
General Register of, *see* GENERAL REGISTER OF
   SASINES

Sasine—*continued*
giving of, **6**, 402; **18**, 89
  equivalents to, **18**, 92
instrument of—
  deed, as, **16**, 2109
  execution by notary public, **13**, 1221
history of, **18**, 89, 91
investiture, **18**, 89
  renewal of, **18**, 108
meaning, **18**, 89, 93
notarial instrument, **18**, 89, 89*n*, 92, 96, 99
nulla sasina nulla terra rule, **18**, 644
precepts of, **18**, 96, 101, 109
recording, **18**, 96, 99
registration—
  generally, *see* GENERAL REGISTER OF SASINES
  historical, **18**, 91
service procedure, **18**, 108, 109
symbols of, **18**, 90
udal law, and, **24**, 308
Sasine Department
generally, **19**, 851
searching department transferred to, **19**, 851
Satellite
broadcast, copyright in, **18**, 972
communications, regulation of, **16**, 1924*n*
cross-border leasing, **14**, 1095
direct broadcasting by, **17**, 7
dish, tenement on, **18**, 238
installation of antenna, permitted development, **23**, 142
Satellite Broadcasting Board
direct broadcasting by satellite, **17**, 7
Saturday
bill due and payable on, **4**, 112
European Convention on the Calculation of Time-Limits, **22**, 830
Sausage
skin, **11**, 358
Savings bank
first, opening of, **2**, 1120
historical background, **2**, 1120
meaning, **2**, 1157
National Savings Bank, *see* NATIONAL SAVINGS BANK
nature of, **2**, 1157
railway, deposits in, **2**, 1166
Scottish—
  development of, **2**, 1120
  historical background, **2**, 1120
  statutory provisions, **2**, 1120
trustee, *see* TRUSTEE SAVINGS BANK
Savings society
generally, **12**, 694*n*
Sawmill
public health nuisance, **19**, 336*n*
whether entitled to rating relief, **24**, 560
Scaffolding
occupier's liability, **15**, 322
road, erection on, **3**, 201; **20**, 684
Scarecrow
agricultural tenant's rights, **11**, 888
Scat
acknowledgment of royal authority, **24**, 327
compulsory purchase of land, **24**, 309

Scat—*continued*
conveyance for valuable consideration, land passed by, **24**, 309
effect of 1611 Act, **24**, 320
failure to deliver, **24**, 309
meaning, **24**, 309
nature of, **24**, 309
no new scats to be created, **24**, 309
non-payment of, **24**, 308
origin, **24**, 309
Orkney, **24**, 309
payment of, **24**, 306, 307, 309
redeemed, **24**, 309
right secured by prescription, **24**, 307
scattald, *see* SCATTALD
Shetland, **24**, 309
translated into fixed cash payments, **24**, 309
variable, **24**, 309
Scattald
effect of 1611 Act, **24**, 320
enclosure and division of lands, **24**, 310
foreshore rights, **24**, 310
meaning, **24**, 310
members' privileges, **24**, 310
Schedule A Conveyance
See STATUTORY CONVEYANCE
Schism
Roman Catholic Church, *latae sententiae* offence, **3**, 1658
Schizophrenic
crime committed by, **7**, 113
Scholarship
education authorities' power to award, **8**, 844
industrial—
  award of, **8**, 708
School
amalgamation, ineligibility for self-governing status, **8**, 779
board, *see* SCHOOL BOARD
burgh, **14**, 36
catchment area—
  change in, consultation and consent, **8**, 724
  determination, **8**, 875
  placing requests, and, **8**, 875
  pupil attending school outside, travelling expenses, **8**, 851
  self-governing school, restriction on changes, **8**, 794
cleansing of, **19**, 366*n*
combined, interim school board, **8**, 752
community involvement, promotion by school board, **8**, 771
dental services—
  administration, **11**, 140
  provision of, **8**, 861; **11**, 1479
discontinuance, ineligibility for self-governing status, **8**, 779
education, *see* SCHOOL EDUCATION
education authorities' duty to provide, **8**, 729
educational endowment, **8**, 839
food supplied by, **11**, 342*n*
grant-aided, *see* GRANT-AIDED SCHOOL
health and safety standards, compliance with, **8**, 734

School—*continued*

holidays, occasional, school board's power to fix, **8**, 774

independent, *see* INDEPENDENT SCHOOL

maintenance, charitable purpose, as, **3**, 1119

management committees, **14**, 36

meaning, **8**, 843*n*

medical services—
  administration, **11**, 140
  provision of, **8**, 861; **11**, 1479

parish, **14**, 36

parliamentary, **14**, 36

premises, use outside school hours, school board's power in relation to, **8**, 773

privately-run, **14**, 36

proposed discontinuance, **8**, 726

provision of new, consultation and consent, **8**, 724

public, charitable status, **3**, 1134

public health nuisance, **19**, 336

Roman Catholic, state-supported—
  change to non-denominational school, **3**, 1664
  closure, **3**, 1664, 1665
    compensation, **3**, 1664, 1665
  Education (Scotland) Act 1872, effect, **3**, 1663
  Education (Scotland) Act 1918, effect, **3**, 1664
  Education (Scotland) Act 1980, effect, **3**, 1665
  Education (Scotland) Act 1981, effect, **3**, 1665
  generally, **3**, 1656
  new, provision, **3**, 1664
  religious instruction, arrangements for, **3**, 1665
  Self-Governing Schools etc (Scotland) Act 1989, effect, **3**, 1666
  site, changing, **3**, 1665
  teachers, approval by Church representatives, **3**, 1664, 1665, 1666
  transfer of Catholic schools to local school board, **3**, 1663, 1664, 1665

safety provisions, educational authorities' duties, **8**, 734

secondary, **14**, 36

self-governing, *see* SELF-GOVERNING SCHOOL

side, **14**, 36

site, proposed change, **8**, 726

special education, *see* SPECIAL EDUCATION

teachers, *see* HEADTEACHER; TEACHER

technology academy, *see* TECHNOLOGY ACADEMY

transfer from primary to secondary, change in, consultation and consent, **8**, 724

valuation for rating, **24**, 733

water meter charges, **25**, 536

See also EDUCATION; SCHOOL EDUCATION

School board

allowances for members, **8**, 741
  terms of office, **8**, 742

appointment committee—
  assistant headteacher, appointment of, **8**, 760, 763
    short leet procedure, **8**, 766
  denominational school, appointment of teachers in, **8**, 761
  deputy headteacher, appointment of, **8**, 760, 763
    short leet procedure, **8**, 766

School board—*continued*

appointment committee—*continued*
  Director of Education, role of, **8**, 765
  headteacher, appointment of, **8**, 760, 762
    short leet procedure, **8**, 766
  membership, **8**, 764
    expenses, **8**, 768
  short leet procedure, **8**, 766
  voting procedure, **8**, 767

appointment of teachers, **8**, 821

chairman—
  casting vote, **8**, 753
  election, **8**, 745

clerk to, **8**, 746

combined schools, **8**, 752

delegation of functions by education authority, **8**, 776

disestablishment, **8**, 751

disqualification from membership, **8**, 745

education authority—
  co-operation with, **8**, 736
  delegation of duties by, **8**, 725

elections to—
  chairman, **8**, 745
  education authority, duties of, **8**, 747
  electoral roll, **8**, 749
  generally, **8**, 747
  scheme of arrangements, **8**, 748
  vice-chairman, **8**, 745
  voting procedure, **8**, 750

establishment, **8**, 701, 751

financing, **8**, 777

generally, **8**, 736

interim, **8**, 752

introduction of, **8**, 736

meetings—
  agenda, **8**, 754
  committees, formation of, **8**, 758
  director of education or officer, attendance by, **8**, 759
  education authorities' duty to advise, **8**, 759
  headteacher, attendance and advice of, **8**, 759
  minutes, **8**, 754, 757
  non-members, attendance and advice of, **8**, 759
  private business, **8**, 755
  public access to, **8**, 755
  quorum, **8**, 756
  regulation of proceedings, **8**, 756
  reports, **8**, 754
  voting procedure, **8**, 753

member of staff parent of pupil at same school, where, **8**, 749

membership, **8**, 701
  chairman, election of, **8**, 745
  classes of members, **8**, 737
  co-opted members, **8**, 737, 740
  parent members, **8**, 736, 737, 738, 749, 751
    meaning of parent, **8**, 738
  staff members, **8**, 737, 739, 749
    formed without, **8**, 737
    single-teacher school, **8**, 737
    visiting teachers, **8**, 737
  vice-chairman, election of, **8**, 745

School board—*continued*
parental involvement—
  board designed to increase, **8**, 736
  generally, **8**, 701
powers and duties—
  books and materials, approval of expenditure on, **8**, 769
  delegation of functions by education authority, **8**, 776
  financial powers, **8**, 775
  information and reports, education authority's duty to provide, **8**, 770
  occasional holidays, power to fix, **8**, 774
  parental and community involvement, promotion of, **8**, 771
  parents' meetings, in relation to, **8**, 772
  premises, control of use, **8**, 773
powers transferred to, **8**, 701
removal from office, **8**, 743
self-governing status, acquisition by school, **8**, 779–783
size, **8**, 737
vice-chairman—
  casting vote, **8**, 753
  election, **8**, 745
School crossing
failure to comply with requirement to stop at, **20**, 441
patrol uniform, **20**, 441
patrolling, **20**, 441
School education
assembly, **14**, 36
attendance at school—
  commencement, **8**, 889
    dates for, **8**, 890
  exemption from, **8**, 892
  leaving date, **8**, 891
  migrants, children of, **8**, 893
  non-attendance—
    attendance order, **8**, 897
      amendment, **8**, 898
      appeal against, **8**, 897
      failure to comply, **8**, 900
      period of operation, **8**, 899
      revocation, **8**, 898
    education authority powers, **8**, 896
    failure to attend without reasonable excuse, **8**, 894, 895
    generally, **3**, 1330, 1343, 1379
    prosecution following, **8**, 901
    sickness, due to, **8**, 895
    travelling arrangements, **8**, 895
  travelling persons, children of, **8**, 893
attendance records, **8**, 907
attendance registers, **8**, 858
books and equipment—
  education authorities' duty to provide, **8**, 847
  provision of, generally, **8**, 769, 847
  school board's powers, **8**, 769
catchment area, *see* CATCHMENT AREA
child guidance services, provision of, **8**, 864
cleanliness, education authorities' power to ensure, **8**, 862
closure of school on medical advice, **8**, 863

School education—*continued*
clothing—
  allowance, **8**, 849
  provision where inadequate, **8**, 848
  school uniforms, education authorities powers and duties, **8**, 849
compulsory testing in primary schools, education authorities' function, **8**, 859
corporal punishment—
  action which teacher may take, **8**, 903
  grant-aided schools, **8**, 820
  private schools, **8**, 903
  public schools, **8**, 903
  self-governing schools, **8**, 903
dental care, provision of, **8**, 861
detention, punishment by, **8**, 904
discipline—
  confiscation of property, **8**, 908
  corporal punishment, **8**, 820
  grant-aided schools, **8**, 820
  detention, **8**, 904
  exclusion from public school—
    action following, **8**, 906
    attendance records, record in, **8**, 907
    generally, **8**, 905
  generally, **8**, 902, 908
  lines, **8**, 908
  withdrawal of privileges, **8**, 908
discretionary payment of allowances to defray expenses, **8**, 846
education authorities. *see* EDUCATION
equipment, *see* books and equipment *above*
fees—
  scholarships, award of, **8**, 844
  where chargeable, **8**, 844
food, provision of, **8**, 850
free education, education authorities' duty to provide, **8**, 844
homework—
  education authorities' duties as to, **8**, 860
  publication of information as to policy, **8**, 860
infectious disease—
  child having, **19**, 456
  teacher or other employee having, **19**, 457
meaning, **8**, 843, 843*n*
medical care, provision of, **8**, 861
medical examination of schoolchildren, **19**, 480
medical services, fees for, **11**, 1450
milk, provision of, **8**, 850
parental involvement, promotion by school board, **8**, 771. *See also* EDUCATION (parental rights and duties)
placing request, *see* EDUCATION
playground supervision, provision of, **8**, 865
progress records, **8**, 858
provision elsewhere than at educational establishment, **8**, 845
purchase of books and materials, powers of school board, **8**, 769
religious instruction, *see* RELIGIOUS INSTRUCTION
reporter—
  referral of child to, **3**, 1287
  report to, **3**, 1287

School education—*continued*
school uniforms, education authorities powers and duties, **8**, 849
special education, *see* SPECIAL EDUCATION
teachers, *see* HEADTEACHER; TEACHER
transport, provision of—
  admission examination, attendance at, travelling expenses, **8**, 852
  bicycles, provision of, **8**, 851
  education authority policy, **8**, 843
  exceptional cases, **8**, 854
  generally, **8**, 851
  interviews, travelling expenses for attendance at, **8**, 852
  more than one facility offered to same pupil, **8**, 851
  non-attendance at school due to lack of transport, **8**, 895
  pupil attending school in area of other authority, **8**, 851
  pupil attending school outside catchment area, **8**, 851
  self-governing school, pupil attending, **8**, 855
  travelling expenses, **8**, 851
  walking distance, **8**, 851, 853
    meaning, **8**, 851, 853
travel concession, **20**, 493
welfare provisions, education authorities' duties as to, **8**, 861–865
See also SCHOOL
Schoolchildren
cleanliness, education authorities' power to ensure, **8**, 862
employment of—
  byelaws, education authorities' power to make, **8**, 869
  generally, **8**, 866
  offences in relation to, **8**, 869
  performances, in—
    dangerous nature, performance of, **8**, 872, 873
    generally, **8**, 870
    licences for children under fourteen, **8**, 871, 873
    power of entry in respect of, **8**, 873
  restrictions on, **8**, 868
  work experience, **8**, 867
entry clearance (immigration), **12**, 291, 292
special educational needs, with, *see* SPECIAL EDUCATION
Schumann Declaration, **10**, 6, 6*n*, 9, 348, 348*n*
Science
society promoting, **12**, 694*n*
Scientific evidence
identification, as to, **10**, 662
Scientific interest
special, sites of, **9**, 1241, 1242
Scientific materials
European Union import duty relief, **7**, 1100
temporary importation, **7**, 1187
Scientific purpose
act or omission relating to salmon, salmon roe or salmon eggs, **11**, 13, 43
poison, sale of, **14**, 1215

Scientific purpose—*continued*
research—
  exclusive economic zone, **11**, 107
  high seas, freedom of, in, **21**, 41
  international co-operation, **11**, 68
taking or killing wild birds or animals in interests of, **11**, 883, 886
unclean or unseasonable salmon, taking or fishing for, **11**, 18
whaling, permits for, **11**, 230, 238
Scientific research association
company donation to, **3**, 1155
scientific research, meaning, **3**, 1165
tax treatment, generally, **3**, 1165
Scotland
Principality of—
  erection of, **5**, 706
  Prince and Great Steward of Scotland, title of, **5**, 708
  revenues of, **5**, 709
  seal of, **5**, 710
United Kingdom Act extending to, **12**, 1101, 1187
  older Acts, **12**, 1187
  uniform application, **12**, 1188
VAT customs union, **7**, 1281
Scotsman
England, in, status of, **14**, 1901
Scott, Sir Walter
Ballantynes Bank, personal liability for debts of, **4**, 302
Scottish Arts Council
grant-aid provided by, **9**, 1007
guarantees against loss offered by, **9**, 1007
music and dancing, support for, **9**, 1036
Scottish Assembly
judicial control of legislation—
  after royal assent, **5**, 337
  before royal assent, **5**, 336
legislative power, devolution of, **5**, 335
Scottish Association of Children's Panels (SACP), **3**, 1313
Scottish Ballet
music and dancing, contribution made by, **9**, 1036
Scottish Boundary Commission
draft Order in Council—
  approval of, **5**, 373
  validity of, **5**, 373
general review of constituencies, **5**, 373
membership of, **5**, 373
notice of recommendations, **5**, 373
objections, **5**, 373
report to Secretary of State, **5**, 373
Scottish Building Contracts Committee (SBCC)
constituent bodies, **3**, 10
generally, **3**, 10
standard contract, **3**, 10
Scottish Building Control Organisation
constitution, **3**, 245
establishment and function, **3**, 218, 245
type approval scheme—
  administration, **3**, 245
  application for type approval, **3**, 246

Scottish Building Control Organisation—
continued
type approval scheme—*continued*
  buildings to which applicable, **3**, 245
  generally, **3**, 245
  type approval certificate, **3**, 247
Scottish central institutions (higher education)
academic boards, **8**, 970
academic matters, responsibility for, **8**, 970
administrative arrangements, **8**, 981
admissions, **8**, 981
board of governors, **8**, 970, 981
colleges accorded status of, **8**, 967, 968
corporate personality—
  limited companies, **8**, 969
  statutory corporations, **8**, 969
courses run by, **8**, 976
Credit Accumulation and Transfer Scheme (CATS), **8**, 976
degrees awarded by, **8**, 976
funding, **8**, 966, 972, 981
  proposed reforms, **8**, 977, 978
  Scottish Higher Education Funding Council, **8**, 977, 978
future role, **8**, 980
Glasgow Polytechnic, structure and powers, **8**, 981
management, **8**, 970
meaning, **8**, 966
powers, example, **8**, 981
Privy Council powers in relation to designated institutions, **8**, 979
proposed reforms, **8**, 965, 977–980
research projects, **8**, 975
staff, **8**, 981
  non-academic, **8**, 974
  staff student ratio, **8**, 974
structure, **8**, 971
  example, **8**, 981
student numbers, **8**, 973
students' association, **8**, 981
use of term, **8**, 966
vocational nature of courses, **8**, 976
Scottish Chamber Orchestra
music and dancing, contribution made by, **9**, 1036
Scottish Charities Office
establishment and purpose, **3**, 1107
Scottish Committee
chairman, **23**, 910
Parliamentary Commissioner for Administration as member of, **23**, 910
tribunals under supervision of, **23**, 911*n*
Scottish Confederation of British Industry
regular contact between political parties and, **5**, 389
Scottish Confession of Faith
generally, **3**, 1627
Scottish Consumer Council
establishment and activities, **6**, 1, **9**, 25
Scottish Conveyancing and Executry Services Board
appointments to, **13**, 1224
constitution, **13**, 1224
expenses, **13**, 1225

Scottish Conveyancing and Executry Services Board—*continued*
functions, **13**, 1225
intervention, powers of, **13**, 1237
powers, **13**, 1225, 1237
qualified conveyancers, register of, **13**, 1227
register of executry practitioners, **13**, 1232, 1233
regulatory responsibilities—
  disclosure of documents, **13**, 1238
  inadequate professional services, **13**, 1236
  independent qualified conveyancers, regulation of, **13**, 1230
  professional misconduct, **13**, 1236
Scottish Council for Civil Liberties
penal reform, role as to, **16**, 1489
Scottish Counties of Cities Association
replacement by Convention of Scottish Local Authorities, **14**, 81
Scottish Courts Administration
constitution and functions, **13**, 1406
functions, **6**, 1049
Scottish Credit Accumulation and Transfer Scheme (SCOTCATS), **8**, 976
Scottish Crime Squad
establishment, **16**, 1709
officer temporarily seconded to, **16**, 1732
Scottish Criminal Record Office
generally, **16**, 1732*n*
Scottish Criminal Records Cards
introduction, **16**, 1709
Scottish Criminal Records Computer
data protection, **16**, 1803
Scottish Dental Practice Board
alleged failure by, investigation into, **11**, 1522–1524
chairman, **11**, 1416
Common Services Agency, service by, **11**, 1411
default, in, **11**, 1409
expenses, **11**, 1506
functions, **11**, 1416
  failure to carry out, **11**, 1409
investigation of complaints as to, **11**, 1426
members, **11**, 1416
Scottish Development Agency
business of, **2**, 1283
Hiram and Highland case, **4**, 564
ministerial supervision, **19**, 210
planning system, role in, **23**, 19
public corporation, as, **19**, 201
Scottish Development Department
functions, **5**, 512
ministerial responsibilities, **14**, 102
public health matters, **19**, 307*n*
public local inquiry, guidance for, **23**, 919
town and country planning, and—
  circulars, **23**, 3
  conditions, legality of, **23**, 239
  Crown land, consultation regarding, **23**, 106
  Development in Countryside and Green Belts, **23**, 230
  development planning, purposes of, **23**, 22
  development plans, Skeffington Report on, **23**, 24
  land use planning, responsibility for, **23**, 4

Scottish Development Department—*continued*
town and country planning, and—*continued*
  local plan, purpose of, **23**, 42
  negative conditions, approval of use of, **23**, 244
  non-statutory material, **23**, 3
  occupancy, conditions restricting, **23**, 242
  Parliamentary Under-Secretary of State, responsibilities of, **23**, 4
  Royal Commission, evidence to, **23**, 9
  structure plan, purpose of, **23**, 27
Scottish Ecclesiastical Commissioners
creation and discharge, **3**, 1577
orders made by, **3**, 1577
Scottish Economic and Planning Department
assistance, areas for, **2**, 1282
Scottish Education Department
functions of, **5**, 512
ministerial responsibilities, **14**, 102
Scottish Ensemble
music and dancing, contribution made by, **9**, 1036
Scottish Enterprise
exempted person under Financial Services Act 1986, as, **12**, 1323
Scottish Episcopal Church
Anglican Communion, relationship to, **3**, 1614, 1617
Articles of Agreement, **3**, 1615
baptism, **3**, 1629
bishops, *see* BISHOP
Church of England, relationship to, **3**, 1617
Code of Canons, **3**, 1615
  alteration and amendments, **3**, 1625, 1625n, 1628
  contract of association, **3**, 1624
  fundamental nature, **3**, 1627
  generally, **3**, 1615, 1625
  implementation, **3**, 1620
College of Bishops, **3**, 1618, 1619
communicants, **3**, 1629
Communicants' Roll, **3**, 1629
constitution—
  alteration, **3**, 1626, 1628
    limitations on, **3**, 1628
  Code of Canons, **3**, 1625
  contract of association, **3**, 1623, 1624
  fundamental elements, **3**, 1627
  membership, **3**, 1629
  voluntary status, **3**, 1623
contract of association, **3**, 1623, 1624
  alteration, **3**, 1626, 1628
  fundamental elements, **3**, 1627
courts—
  jurisdiction, **3**, 1623
  secular courts, relationship with, **3**, 1623
deacons/deaconesses, *see* DEACON/DEACONESS (Scottish Episcopal Church)
dioceses, **3**, 1618
diocesan synod, **3**, 1621
ecclesiastical character, **3**, 1614
eighteenth-century development, **3**, 1615
Episcopal Synod, **3**, 1618, 1619
General Synod, **3**, 1620
  exempted person under Financial Services Act 1986, as, **12**, 1323

Scottish Episcopal Church—*continued*
Holy Catholic or Universal Church, as part of, **3**, 1614
Jacobitism, **3**, 1611–1613
jurisdiction—
  civil courts, recourse to, **3**, 1630, 1631
  generally, **3**, 1623
legislation—
  General Synod, **3**, 1620, 1628
  Primus, **3**, 1619
liturgy, **3**, 1612
meeting house, definition, **3**, 1613
membership—
  baptism, **3**, 1629
  communicants, **3**, 1629
  contract of association, **3**, 1623, 1624
  generally, **3**, 1629
oath of abjuration, **3**, 1613
oath of allegiance, **3**, 1613
organisation—
  bishops, **3**, 1618
  College of Bishops, **3**, 1618, 1619
  dioceses, **3**, 1618
  diocesan synod, **3**, 1621
  Episcopal Synod, **3**, 1618, 1619
  finance, **3**, 1620
  General Synod, **3**, 1620, 1628
  Primus, **3**, 1619
origins, **3**, 1610
penal laws, **3**, 1613
  repeal, **3**, 1613
priests, **3**, 1614
Primus, *see* PRIMUS
prison minister, **16**, 1458
qualified chapels, **3**, 1616, 1616n, 1617, 1631
religious toleration, **3**, 1635
Representative Church Council, **3**, 1630
Revolution Settlement, **3**, 1610, 1611
Scottish Confession of Faith, **3**, 1627
state, relations with, history, **3**, 1610
Thirty-nine Articles of the Church of England, **3**, 1627
Toleration Act 1712 ..., **3**, 1612, 1612n, 1613
voluntary Church, as, **5**, 703
voluntary status, **3**, 1623, 1633n; **5**, 703
  civil courts, jurisdiction, **3**, 1631
Scottish Examination Board
appeals from examination results, **8**, 957
assessors, **8**, 955
duties, **8**, 950
education authorities' duty to provide information to, **8**, 949
establishment, **8**, 948
finance, **8**, 956
functions and powers, determination, **8**, 948
membership, **8**, 953
  allowances for members, **8**, 954
  disqualification of member, **8**, 953
powers, **8**, 951
purposes, **8**, 948, 949
reports, **8**, 952
Secretary of State's powers in relation to, **8**, 948
staff and agents, appointment, remuneration and pension arrangements, **8**, 948

Scottish Exchequer
records, **19**, 849
Scottish Executive
executive powers, devolution of, **5**, 335
Scottish Food Hygiene Council
abolition, **11**, 328
Scottish Grand Committee
Bills, **5**, 415
consideration of Bills on report, **5**, 418
estimates, **5**, 416
generally, **5**, 414
matters relating exclusively to Scotland, **5**, 417
setting up of, **5**, 334
Scottish Health Board
Acquired   Immune   Deficiency   Syndrome
    (AIDS)—
    duties as to, **19**, 508, 509
Human Immunodeficiency Virus (HIV)—
    duties as to, **19**, 508, 509
Scottish Health Service
infectious disease, report of, **19**, 486
Scottish Health Service Planning Council
annual report, **11**, 1418
chairman, **11**, 1418
constitution, **11**, 1418
expenses, **11**, 1506
members, **11**, 1418
national consultative committees, role of, **11**,
    1419
National Health Service reorganisation, **11**, 1417
prospective abolition, **11**, 1401
Secretary of State, duty to advise, **11**, 1418
Scottish Higher Education Funding Council
membership, **8**, 978
proposed establishment and functions, **8**, 977,
    978, 1015
Quality Assessment Committee, **8**, 978
Secretary of State—
    information and advice to be given to, **8**, 978
    powers in relation to, **8**, 978
Scottish Home and Health Department
consumer protection, **6**, 11
fire services, duties in relation to, **10**, 1413
functions of, **5**, 512
infectious disease, report of, **19**, 486
ministerial responsibilities, **14**, 102
police matters, role in oversight of, **16**, 1721
public health matters, **19**, 307n
Scottish Homes
accounts, **11**, 1923
acquisition on change of landlord, **11**, 1972–1977
allocation of housing, **11**, 1935
annual report, **11**, 1923
appointments to, **11**, 1922
chairman, appointment of, **11**, 1922
community-based associations, designation of, **11**,
    1927
constitution, **11**, 1922
creation of, **11**, 1921
establishment, **11**, 1921
functions, **11**, 1923
housing associations, **11**, 1924
    admission and removal of associations from
        register, **11**, 1925

Scottish Homes—_continued_
housing associations—_continued_
    control of payments by, **11**, 1927
    extraordinary audit, order of, **11**, 1931
    finance, powers as to, **11**, 1932
    guidance of, **11**, 1930
    inquiries into affairs of, **11**, 1931
    management guidelines, **11**, 1930
    operation of, **11**, 1928
    registration of, **11**, 1925
    remedial measures, powers as to, **11**, 1931
investigation into action of, **11**, 1922
landlord, as, assured tenancy status excluded, **13**,
    636, 647
membership, **11**, 1922
powers, **11**, 1923
proceedings, **11**, 1922
remuneration and allowances, **11**, 1922
Secretary of State's powers in relation to, **11**,
    1923
**Scottish Hospital Endowments Research
    Trust**
duty, **11**, 1424
Scottish Hospital Trust
duty, **11**, 1424
**Scottish Joint Negotiating Committee for
    Teaching Staff in School Education**
arbitration, reference to, **8**, 835
chairman, **8**, 832
membership, **8**, 832
remit, **8**, 831
resolutions, **8**, 833
settlements, **8**, 834
vice-chairman, **8**, 832
Scottish Land Court
advocate's dress when appearing before, **13**, 1323
agricultural holdings—
    improvements to—
        approving,
        valuing, **1**, 842
antecedents, **6**, 953
appeal from, **6**, 829, 958
Board of Agriculture, duties and powers, **6**, 957
Chairman, **6**, 958, 960
    precedence, **16**, 2020
civil legal aid, **13**, 1034
common seal, **6**, 958
crofting—
    acquisition of croft land, authorisation, **1**, 828
    compensation for improvements, determination,
        1, 811
    compensation on resumption, determination, **1**,
        809
    conveyance of land, powers on, **1**, 830
    counties and parishes, **6**, 955
    Crofters Commission, **6**, 955, 956, 966
        appeal from, **1**, 815
    crofters renamed 'landholders', **6**, 956
    fair rent, fixing, **1**, 802
    jurisdiction, **6**, 965–968
    legislation, **6**, 955
    record of, making, **1**, 803
    reference of nature of tenure, **1**, 800
    removal of crofter, ordering, **1**, 810

Scottish Land Court—*continued*
crofting—*continued*
  resumption, authorisation of, **6**, 967
  site of dwelling house, ordering conveyance of,
    1, 829
  tenure, jurisdiction over, **1**, 829
delegation of powers, **6**, 961
Divisional Courts as delegation of, **6**, 961
duties, **6**, 958, 959
English courts, persuasive authority, **22**, 321
establishment of, **5**, 656; **6**, 952, 958
evidence, **6**, 972
Gaelic, conduct of cases in, **6**, 960
Highland Land League, **6**, 953
investigating powers, **6**, 972
Irish legislation as model for Scottish, **6**, 954
judicial nature of, **6**, 952, 959, 980
jurisdiction—
  agricultural holdings, **6**, 967, 970
  crofts, **6**, 965–968
  generally, **5**, 656; **6**, 958, 962
  landholders' holdings, **6**, 963, 964, 968
  subject matter of, **6**, 967
jurisdiction in relation to, **6**, 969, 970
legal assessors, **6**, 961
legal staff, **13**, 1412
legatee, declaration as tenant, **1**, 788
litigation, other courts compared, **6**, 959
membership, **5**, 656; **6**, 960
Napier Commission, **6**, 955, 966
notice to quit, consent to operation of—
  conditions attached to, **1**, 747
  failure to remedy breach, where, **1**, 756
  fair and reasonable landlord not insisting on
    possession, withholding for, **1**, 746
  grounds of, **1**, 745
  requirement of, **1**, 744
  resort to, ways in which arising, **1**, 757
notice to quit not requiring consent of, **1**, 748*ff*
objection by landlord, hearing—
  intestate succession, on, **1**, 790
  legatee, to, **1**, 788
precedent, binding decisions, **22**, 321
procedure, **6**, 971
  agricultural expertise of court, **6**, 973
  documentation, **6**, 975
  evidence, **6**, 972
  expenses, **6**, 978
  facts, ascertainment of, **6**, 972
  location of hearing, **6**, 974
  orders, enforcement, **6**, 977
  process, **6**, 976
  regulation of own, **6**, 971
  rehearing, **6**, 979
  representation, **6**, 974
quorum, **6**, 961
record of holding, preparation of, **1**, 844
records—
  access to, **19**, 879
  transmission of, **19**, 858
report on management of land by, **1**, 712
resumption, authorisation of, **6**, 967
review of determination under delegation, **6**, 961
Rules, **6**, 972

Scottish Land Court—*continued*
seaweed, peat and thatching materials, regulation
  of use, **1**, 843
small landholders, **6**, 956
special case, statement of, **6**, 958
statutory provisions, result of, **6**, 959
statutory small tenancies, **6**, 956
succession, jurisdiction on questions of, **1**, 796
Taylor Commission, **6**, 965, 966
two-level nature of system, **6**, 961
Scottish Law Agents Society
incorporation, **13**, 1139*n*
Joint Legal Committee, **13**, 1139
precedence, **16**, 2020
Scottish Law Commission
animals, civil liability in relation to, **22**, 662
assimilation of Scots and English law, **22**, 625
bankruptcy law reform, **22**, 633, 678
codification, statutory requirement to consider,
  22, 625
Commissioners—
  disqualification from membership, House of
    Commons, **22**, 665
  qualifications, **22**, 665
  term of appointment, **22**, 665
confidence, law on breach, consideration by, **22**,
  674
consolidating statutes—
  1949 procedure for consolidating bills, **22**, 699
  generally, **22**, 698–704
  meaning, **22**, 698
  Statute Law Commission, **22**, 698
  See also LEGISLATION
consolidation on proposals of the Law
  Commissions, **22**, 700, 701
constitution, **22**, 665
consultation with other Law Commissions,
  statutory requirement, **22**, 666
consultative memoranda—
  generally, **22**, 666, 679, 688, 697
  list, **22**, 697
contract of hire, proposals on, **14**, 1054
contract law, **22**, 670
damages for personal injuries, **22**, 676
  See also DAMAGES
diligence, recommendations as to, **22**, 679
draftsmen, **13**, 1405
duties, statutory, **22**, 666
evidence, recommendations—
  presumption of death, **22**, 669
  sexual offences, **22**, 668
Faculty of Advocates, proposals of reform by, **22**,
  666
family law, recommendations, **22**, 682–692
  See also FAMILY LAW
floating charges, recommendations implemented
  in legislation, **22**, 680
foreign currency, on, **14**, 1831
functions, **13**, 1408
generally, **22**, 665–697
Hunter, Lord, views on codification, **22**, 625
international law, considerations, **22**, 625
judicial factors, exercise of statutory powers,
  recommendations, **22**, 694

Scottish Law Commission—*continued*
Law Commission (England and Wales) contrasted, **6**, 665*n*
law reform in Scotland, generally, **13**, 1407, 1408
Law Society of Scotland, proposals of reform by, **22**, 666
leases, irritancies in—
  recommendations implemented in legislation, **22**, 681
legal staff, **13**, 1409
legislative basis, **22**, 665
Lord Advocate—
  annual report by Commission to, **22**, 666
  appointment of Commissioners, **22**, 665
  duty to lay Commission's programme before Parliament, **22**, 666
mercantile law, assimilation within European Union, **22**, 625
ministerial responsibility, **13**, 1407
ministers, proposals of reform by, **22**, 666
negligent misrepresentation, reversal of rule in *Manners* recommended, **22**, 673
poinding, on, **14**, 1812
policy considerations in creation, **22**, 625
prescription and limitation, recommendations as to modernisation of law, **22**, 693
private international law, joint reports with the Law Commission (England and Wales), **22**, 693
  See also INTERNATIONAL LAW
products liability, Council of Europe draft Convention, attitude, towards, **22**, 677
programmes of law reform, **22**, 666
proof of survivorship, proposed reform, **25**, 659
purpose, **22**, 665
rectification of documents, **22**, 671
reforms recommended by Commission—
  consultative memoranda, **22**, 697
  enforcement of rights, **22**, 678–681
  evidence, **22**, 668, 669
  family law, **22**, 682–692
  generally, **22**, 667–697
  incest, **22**, 695
  judicial factors, powers, **22**, 694
  obligations, **22**, 670–677
  private international law, **22**, 693
  statutory provisions resulting from, **22**, 696
  wills and succession, **25**, 1111–1121
review of law—
  prescribed methods, **22**, 666
revision of legislation—
  joint responsibility with the Law Commission (England and Wales), **22**, 704
Scottish consolidation bills, drafting, **13**, 1405
sheriff's duties in respect of, **6**, 1046
socio-legal research, recognition of need, legal method, **22**, 615
statutory provisions resulting from proposals— list, **22**, 696
Whitehall departments, attempts to assert influence, **22**, 625
Scottish Legal Aid Board
administration of legal aid system, **13**, 1008
advice, power to give Secretary of State, **13**, 1017

Scottish Legal Aid Board—*continued*
advice and assistance, control, **13**, 1031
chairman, **13**, 1011
civil legal aid, applications for, **13**, 1041
  application, process of, **13**, 1042
  decisions *in re sua*, **13**, 1043
conduct of business, **13**, 1015
constitution, **13**, 1011
contract or agreement, power to enter into, **13**, 1017
corporate plan, **13**, 1017
creation, **13**, 1008, 1010
criminal legal aid—
  appeals, applications for aid, **13**, 1069
  conflict of interests, **13**, 1065
  interests of justice—
    assessment, **13**, 1060
    factors determining, **13**, 1059
  sanction for counsel, **13**, 1063
  sanction for expert witnesses, **13**, 1064
  termination of aid, **13**, 1065
duties, **13**, 1017
  duty solicitor, in relation to, **13**, 1053
  Scottish Legal Aid Fund, establishment and maintenance, **13**, 1018
establishment, **13**, 1011
functions, **13**, 1011
  delegation, **13**, 1015, 1016
  inquiries or investigations into, **13**, 1017
  publication of information as to discharge of, **13**, 1017
  publicity relating to, **13**, 1017
independence, **13**, 1017
information furnished to, confidentiality, **13**, 1081
land, acquisition or disposal, **13**, 1017
membership, **13**, 1011
  appointment, **13**, 1011
  remuneration, **13**, 1011
  status, **13**, 1013
  tenure, **13**, 1011
  termination, **13**, 1011
money, power to invest, **13**, 1017
powers, **13**, 1017
proceedings, regulation of, **13**, 1015
refusal of legal aid, review procedure, **13**, 1080
Secretary of State—
  guidance from, **13**, 1017
  information to be furnished to, **13**, 1017
  powers, **13**, 1017
solemn procedure, application for criminal legal aid, **13**, 1055
staff, **13**, 1014
status, **13**, 1013
summary criminal cases, application to for legal aid, **13**, 1056, 1057
transition from Law Society of Scotland, **13**, 1009
Scottish Legal Aid Fund
advice and assistance, solicitor's claim for payment, **13**, 1027
demand-led nature, **13**, 1019
establishment and maintenance, **13**, 1018
payments from, **13**, 1018
payments into, **13**, 1019
  assisted person, contributions payable by, **13**, 1019

Scottish Legal Aid Fund—*continued*
payment into—*continued*
  civil legal aid, by persons granted, **13**, 1040
  property or money recovered or preserved in
      favour of assisted person, **13**, 1019, 1075
  exceptions to provisions, **13**, 1078
  sum recovered under award of court, **13**, 1019
  sums paid or determined by Secretary of State,
      13, 1019
Scottish Legal Profession: The Way Forward
paper 1989 ..., **13**, 1453
Scottish Legal Services Ombudsman
advocate ineligible for appointment as, **13**, 1329
advocates, investigation of complaints regarding,
    13, 1378
annual report, **13**, 1211
appointment, **13**, 1211
function, **13**, 1211
solicitor, ineligible for appointment as, **13**, 1172
who may become, **13**, 1211
Scottish Medical Practices Committee
chairman, **11**, 1415
Common Services Agency, service by, **11**, 1411
default, in, **11**, 1409
expenses, **11**, 1506
functions, **11**, 1409
medical list, consideration of applications for
    membership, **11**, 1415
members, **11**, 1415
Scottish National Building Code
building contracts, **3**, 10
Scottish National Orchestra
music and dancing, contribution made by, **9**, 1036
Scottish National Party
annual national conference, **5**, 396
formation of, **5**, 396
National Council, **5**, 396
organisation of, **5**, 396
Scottish National Tribunal
Roman Catholic Church, **3**, 1658
Scottish Nuclear Ltd
exempted person under Financial Services Act
    1986, as, **12**, 1323
Scottish Office
advice, **14**, 104
civil servants, role of, **5**, 521
development of, **5**, 512
establishment, **14**, 4
Finance Division, ministerial responsibilities, **14**,
    102
functions of, **5**, 512
future, **5**, 534
generally, **5**, 516
guidance, **14**, 104
history, **5**, 516
junior ministers—
    introduction of, **5**, 518
    role of, **5**, 520
law and legislation, **5**, 530
ministerial responsibilities, **14**, 102
modern evolution, **5**, 517
operational considerations, **5**, 533
organisation of, **5**, 512; **14**, 4
provisional orders, observations on, **19**, 36, 37

Scottish Office—*continued*
records, **19**, 849
statutory duties, **5**, 512
strengths of, **5**, 522
weaknesses of, **5**, 522
See also SECRETARY OF STATE FOR SCOTLAND
Scottish Opera
music and dancing, contribution made by, **9**, 1036
Scottish peerage
see PEERAGE
Scottish Police College
special course, selection for, **16**, 1751
Scottish Police Federation
attendance at, **16**, 1753
Scottish Prison Service
agency status, move towards, **16**, 1413
aspects outwith control, **16**, 1403
Chief Executive, **16**, 1413
generally, **16**, 1413
headquarters, **16**, 1413
position papers, publication, **16**, 1403, 1403*n*
Prisons Board, **16**, 1413
Scottish Privy Council
equitable jurisdiction of the Crown, exercise
    before 1707 ..., **22**, 547
law reform commissions, **22**, 627
legislative role before 1707 ..., **22**, 524
Scottish Record Office
divorces, register of, **19**, 857
gifts, records given as, **19**, 849, 863
Justiciary records, **19**, 801
loan, records on, **19**, 849, 863
maps and plans, **19**, 849
microfilm records, **19**, 849
private records, **19**, 849
purchase of records, **19**, 849, 863
records held by, **19**, 849
Register House, **19**, 828
role of, **19**, 848
shipbuilding records, **19**, 849
Scottish Records Advisory Council
chairmanship, **19**, 823, 824
constitution, **19**, 823
functions, **19**, 824
origins, **19**, 823
Scottish Register Office
Liaison Division, **19**, 829
National Register of Archives (Scotland), **19**, 829
Scottish Rifles
formation of, **2**, 601
Scottish Solicitors' Discipline Tribunal
appeal to Court of Session from, **23**, 917
complaint to—
    appeal against decision, **13**, 1206
    powers, **13**, 1206
    professional misconduct, following, **13**, 1206,
        1207
    publication of findings, **13**, 1206
    who may make, **13**, 1206
establishment, **13**, 1206
membership, **13**, 1206
Scottish Solicitors Guarantee Fund
generally, **13**, 1196, 1197

Scottish Special Housing Association
functions of assumed by Scottish Homes, **11**, 1921
Scottish Sports Association, 19, 1217
Scottish Standing Committees
appointment, **5**, 413
membership, **5**, 413
procedure, **5**, 413
Scottish Stock Exchange
'Big Bang', **2**, 1270
City Code on Take-overs, **2**, 1273
complaints of, **2**, 1272
floor of, **2**, 1269
historical background, **2**, 1269
investors, protection of, **2**, 1272
members of, **2**, 1270
nature of, **2**, 1270
reform of, **2**, 1270
rules of, **2**, 1273
Securities and Investment Board, **2**, 1271
self-regulation, **2**, 1271
Unlisted Securities Market, **2**, 1273
Scottish Tourist Board
exempted person under Financial Services Act
    1986, as, **12**, 1323
See TOURISM
Scottish Trades Union Council
regular contact between political parties and, **5**,
    389
Scottish Traffic Area
generally, **20**, 487
Scottish Transport Group
domestic carriage of goods by road, **3**, 619
public corporation, as, **19**, 201, 1094
**Scottish Universities Committee of the
Privy Council, 8**, 992
Scottish Universities Council on Entrance
establishment and purpose, **8**, 1006
Scottish Valuation Advisory Council
chairman, **24**, 428
constitution, **24**, 428
expenses and allowances, **24**, 428
functions, **14**, 804; **24**, 429
membership, **24**, 428
reports, **24**, 430
**Scottish Vocational Education Council
(SCOTVEC)**
central institutions, degrees awarded by, **8**, 976
generally, **8**, 927
Scottish and Welsh Development Agencies
establishment of, **19**, 211
Script
meaning, **9**, 1047
public performance of play, as evidence of, **9**,
    1047
Sculptor
royal household, **7**, 847
Sea
artificial barriers against, erection, **18**, 318
    damage caused by, **18**, 318
beach, meaning, **12**, 1239
bed, *see* SEA BED
carriage by, *see* SEA, CARRIAGE BY
coast, protection of, *see* COAST PROTECTION
common law of, **1**, 402

Sea—*continued*
contiguous zone, *see* CONTIGUOUS ZONE
continental shelf, *see* CONTINENTAL SHELF
Convention on the Contract for the International
    Carriage of Goods by Road (CMR), **3**, 646
delict at, **17**, 299
disposal of waste at, **9**, 1164
European Union transit procedures, **7**, 1173
exclusive economic zone, *see* EXCLUSIVE
    ECONOMIC ZONE
fisheries, *see* SEA FISHERIES
foreshore, *see* FORESHORE
goods exported by, time of exportation, **7**, 1155
goods imported by, time of importation, **7**, 1141
high, *see* HIGH SEAS
innocent passage, right of, *see* TERRITORIAL SEA
international law of the—
    development, **21**, 2
    generally, **21**, 1
    multilateral treaties, **21**, 1–4
lateral boundary, **12**, 1239
law, *see* MARITIME LAW
meaning, **12**, 1239; **14**, 470*n*; **21**, 112
offences committed at, **6**, 867
oil pollution of—
    avoidance measures, power to take, **21**, 46
    damage—
        civil liability, **9**, 1215
        compensation for, international fund for, **9**,
            1216
    exploration operations, **9**, 1209
    generally, **9**, 1208
    harbour, discharge into, **9**, 1212
    land pipe-lines, discharge from, **9**, 1209
    night, transfer at, **9**, 1211
    oil records, **9**, 1214
    ship, from, **9**, 1210
    shipping casualties, **9**, 1213
ownership, udal law, **18**, 310
perils of, *see* PERILS OF THE SEA
pollution, control of, **19**, 303
products taken from—
    European Union import duty relief, **7**, 1103
    United Kingdom import duty relief, **7**, 1106
public rights over—
    Crown ownership, **18**, 514
    generally, **18**, 5, 7, 494, 514
right to sail on, **16**, 2126
rock or sand outcrops, **18**, 313
salmon fishing, **11**, 8, 144
    access, **11**, 8
    drawing and drying salmon nets, **11**, 8
shipping, *see* SHIP; SHIPPING
shore, *see* FORESHORE
swimming, public right of, **18**, 518
territorial—
    adjacent proprietors, rights of, **18**, 312
    alienation of subject proprietors, **18**, 311
    foreshore, *see* FORESHORE
    meaning, **18**, 309
    ownership, **18**, 309, 310
    See also TERRITORIAL SEA
transport of radioactive material by, **9**, 918
trout, dealing in, licensing, **14**, 566

Sea—*continued*
udal law, territorial rights, **24**, 315
UNCLOS, *see* UNITED NATIONS CONFERENCE ON
    THE LAW OF THE SEA
water sports and recreation, **19**, 1280
wreck, *see* WRECK
See also MARITIME LAW
Sea bed
continental shelf—
    natural resources, rights in, **21**, 19
    Truman Proclamation, **21**, 15
Crown rights in, **11**, 61, 1304; **21**, 11; **24**, 316
deep—
    customary law, **21**, 4
    Enterprise, **21**, 48
    international legal regime, **21**, 4
    International Sea Bed Authority, **21**, 48
    legal approach to, generally, **21**, 47
    natural resources, **21**, 47, 49
    UK position on deep sea mining, **21**, 49
    UNCLOS III, **21**, 48
    United Nations General Assembly Declaration
        of Principles Governing the Sea Bed and
        the Ocean Floor, **21**, 47, 48
exploration, territorial jurisdiction, **4**, 2
lease, **13**, 194, 205
marine fish farms, **11**, 61
oil platform on—
    common law, **20**, 269, 270
    controlled pipeline, definition, **20**, 271
    controlled waters, **20**, 271
        definition, **20**, 271
    licence to search for and get petroleum, **20**, 271
    offshore petroleum, meaning, **20**, 271
    sea, meaning, **20**, 271
    statutory provisions, **20**, 271
    territorial waters—
        definition, **20**, 271
        outwith, **20**, 270, 271
        within, **20**, 269, 271
planning controls, absence of, **23**, 12
submarine cable or pipeline—
    continental shelf, laying and maintenance rights
        and duties, **21**, 31
    exclusive economic zone, laying and
        maintenance rights, **21**, 39
    high seas, freedom to lay in, **21**, 41
    navigation rules, **21**, 380
territorial sea, of, legal status, **21**, 11
udal law, **24**, 316
Sea, burial at
ashes, scattering, **3**, 539
coffins, suitable, **3**, 540
directions of deceased, **3**, 506
generally, **3**, 538
historical background, **3**, 501
land, person who dies on, **3**, 538
letters of authorisation, **3**, 539
sites, suitable, **3**, 540
statutory regulation, **3**, 502
Sea, carriage by
Athens Convention, *see* PASSENGER
authoritative texts, **21**, 523
bill of lading, *see* BILL OF LADING

Sea, carriage by—*continued*
breach of contract, *see* CONTRACT
cargo, *see* CARGO
cargo liner, meaning, **21**, 524
charterparty, *see* CHARTERPARTY
common and statute law, **21**, 521
competition law, **4**, 1177
container, carriage by, generally, **21**, 526
contract—
    affreightment, of, **21**, 521*n*
    carriage by sea, for, as contract for services and
        custody, **21**, 613, 613*n*
    insurance, freight (cif) contract, **21**, 524*n*
    law of, generally, **21**, 521
    sale of ship subject to existing contract, **21**,
        718
crew, *See* SEAMAN
damages for detention—
    calculation, **21**, 685
    entitlement to, **21**, 717
    general ship, carriage by, **21**, 585
    generally, **21**, 387, 387*n*, 685
    liability—
        action, **21**, 688
        charterparty, **21**, 686
        general ship, **21**, 687
        generally, **21**, 682
        lien, **21**, 688
        unreasonably detaining ship where laytime
            not expired, **21**, 681*n*
    loss of profits, **21**, 387, 387*n*
    voyage charterparty, **21**, 612, 624*n*, 633
dangerous goods—
    bill of lading, express terms, **21**, 546
    fire protection regulations, **21**, 214
    Hague-Visby Rules, **21**, 607, 617
    meaning, **21**, 617*n*
    notice of danger given to shipowner, **21**, 617
    reasonably foreseeable danger, **21**, 617, 617*n*
    safety regulations—
        generally, **21**, 231
        non-compliance with, **21**, 231
    shipowner knows or ought to know danger,
        where, **21**, 617
    time charterparty, express and implied terms,
        21, 639, 643
    voyage charterparty, implied terms, **21**, 617,
        617*n*
    wrongful loading, **21**, 717
delict, action for, **21**, 719
demise charter, *see* CHARTERPARTY
demurrage, *see* DEMURRAGE
deviation—
    clauses allowing, **21**, 615
    implied terms as to, **21**, 615
    justifiable, **21**, 615
    laydays and demurrage, effect on, **21**, 615
    'liberty to call at any ports', **21**, 615
    material breach, as, **21**, 615*n*
    reasonable, **21**, 615
    sacrifice or expenditure as result of, general
        average, **21**, 704, 704*n*

Sea, carriage by—*continued*
deviation—*continued*
    saving or attempting to save life or property at
        sea—
        Hague-Visby Rules, **21**, 605
        implied terms, **21**, 615
    time charterparty, **21**, 615*n*, 639
    unintentional, **21**, 615
    unjustified, liability, exclusion or limitation of,
        21, 547, 547*n*
    voyage charterparty—
        express terms, **21**, 618
        implied terms, **21**, 615, 615*n*
        master's powers in relation to, **21**, 629
electronic data interchange, contract involving,
    21, 532
English law, relationship with Scots law, **21**, 522,
    522*n*
environmental damage, ship owner and master,
    duty, **21**, 465
fire, liability for, **21**, 603
forwarding agent, **21**, 524*n*
freight—
    action in claim for, **21**, 665
    advance, **21**, 612, 653, 659, 659*n*
        non-delivery of cargo following, **21**, 659
    arrestment, salvage actions, **21**, 482*n*
    back, **21**, 653*n*, 656*n*, 661
    bill of lading, **21**, 653, 653*n*
        calculation, express terms as to, **21**, 546
        declaration of value, express terms as to, **21**,
            546
        liability for freight, **21**, 662
        recalculation, express terms, **21**, 546
        to whom payable, **21**, 664
    calculation, **21**, 527, 654, 654*n*
        bill of lading, express terms, **21**, 546
        oil tanker freight, **21**, 654*n*
        shrinkage or expansion of freight in transit,
            21, 654*n*
    collection, **21**, 664
    conferences, **21**, 527
    contract, insurance, freight (cif) contract, **21**, 524*n*
    dead, **21**, 612, 625, 653*n*, 660, 717
    declaration of value, bill of lading, express
        terms, **21**, 546
    deemed earned, **21**, 659*n*
    delivery, necessity for, **21**, 656, 656*n*
    earned, **21**, 659*n*
    freight forwarder, **21**, 524*n*
    general average, *see* GENERAL AVERAGE
    jurisdiction, **21**, 665
    liability for—
        bill of lading, **21**, 662
        voyage charterparty, **21**, 663
    lien for, **21**, 665
        voyage charterparty, **21**, 635–637
    lien over, **21**, 479, 656, 656*n*, 665
    liner conferences, **21**, 527
    loss of, general average, *see* GENERAL AVERAGE
    lump sum, **21**, 612, 653, 655, 655*n*, 657, 657*n*
    meaning, **21**, 524*n*, 527
    non-payment or late payment, shipowners'
        lien, **21**, 665

Sea, carriage by—*continued*
freight—*continued*
    part delivery of cargo only, **21**, 656
    payment—
        bill of lading, express terms, **21**, 546
        generally, **21**, 656
        to whom payable, **21**, 664
    performance of contract, carriage by general
        ship, **21**, 585
    pro rata (freight *pro rata itineris*), **21**, 653, 656*n*,
        658
    rate, fixing, **21**, 527
    recalculation, bill of lading, express terms, **21**,
        546
    salvage, generally, **21**, 434, 437
        valuation in assessment of salvage award, **21**,
            469*n*
    voyage charterparty, **21**, 612, 618, 633, 653, 653*n*
        liability for freight, **21**, 663
        to whom payable, **21**, 664
freight forwarder, **21**, 524*n*
general average, *see* GENERAL AVERAGE
general cargo, **21**, 524, 524*n*
general ship, *see* GENERAL SHIP
generally, **21**, 521
Hague Rules, **21**, 586, 587
Hague-Visby Rules, **21**, 586–611
Hamburg Rules, **21**, 586, 586*n*
law, development of, **21**, 521
lay/can spread, meaning, **21**, 691*n*
laytime (lay days), *see* LAYTIME
limitation of actions—
    goods, carriage of, **16**, 2205
    luggage, loss or damage, **16**, 2204
    passenger, death or personal injury, **16**, 2204
limitation of liability—
    actual fault concept, **21**, 752, 758*n*
    aggregation of claims, **21**, 762
    Athens Convention, **21**, 722, 734, 755, 755*n*,
        761, 761*n*
        court powers, **21**, 735
        limitation and exclusion clauses, invalidity,
            21, 729
        servants and agents, **21**, 736
    basin, damage to, **21**, 755
    canal owner, **21**, 753*n*, 769, 769*n*
    cargo—
        claims, generally, **21**, 753*n*
        destruction, loss resulting from, **21**, 756
        harmless, loss resulting from rendering, **21**,
            756
        removal, loss resulting from, **21**, 756
    carrier, **21**, 606, 753*n*
    categories of limits, **21**, 760, 760*n*
    charterer, **21**, 751
    charterparty, *see* CHARTERPARTY
    conduct barring limitation, **21**, 758, 758*n*
        burden of proof, **21**, 758*n*
        test for, **21**, 758*n*
    consequential loss, **21**, 755
    conservancy authority, **21**, 753*n*, 769, 769*n*
    Convention on Limitation of Liability for
        Maritime Claims, *see* London Convention
        below

Sea, carriage by—*continued*
limitation of liability—*continued*
 counterclaims, **21**, 759, 759*n*
 defence, pled as, **21**, 763
 delay, loss resulting from, **21**, 756
 dock owner, **21**, 753*n*, 769, 769*n*
 establishing right to limit, **21**, 763
 excepted claims, **21**, 757, 757*n*
 general average, **21**, 757
 general ship, contract for carriage in, *see* GENERAL SHIP
 generally, **21**, 751
 harbour authority, **21**, 751, 753*n*, 769, 769*n*
 harbour works, damage to, **21**, 755
 history, **21**, 751, 752
 limitation action, **21**, 763
 limitation fund—
  advantage of establishing, **21**, 763
  bar to other actions, **21**, 768
  constitution, **21**, 763, 765, 766, 769
  distribution, **21**, 765, 767, 769
  generally, **21**, 763
  without constitution of fund, **21**, 764
 London Convention—
  application, **21**, 753
  categories of limits, **21**, 760, 760*n*
  claims excepted from limitation, **21**, 757, 757*n*
  claims subject to limitation, **21**, 755, 755*n*, 756
  conduct barring limitation, **21**, 758, 758*n*
  counterclaims, **21**, 759, 759*n*
  generally, **21**, 753
  interpretation, generally, **21**, 753
  limitation fund, *see* limitation fund *above*
  persons entitled, **21**, 754
  travaux préparatoires, **21**, 753, 758*n*
  United Kingdom, force of law in, **21**, 753, 753*n*
 loss of life, **21**, 755, 755*n*, 760, 761
 master, **21**, 557, 751
 navigational aids, damage to, **21**, 755
 negligent navigation or management, damage resulting from, **21**, 755*n*
 nuclear damage, **21**, 757
 oil pollution damage, **21**, 757
 operator, **21**, 751
 owner, **21**, 751, 753*n*, 754
 passenger claims, limit, **21**, 761
 personal injury, **21**, 755, 755*n*, 760, 761
 pilot, **21**, 751, 753*n*, 770, 770*n*, 772
 pilotage authority or agent, **21**, 753*n*, 771, 771*n*, 772
 privity of person seeking to limit, **21**, 758*n*
 property, injury, loss of or damage to, **21**, 755, 755*n*
 rights, infringement of, loss resulting from, **21**, 756
 salvage operations, **21**, 755, 757
 salvor, **21**, 753*n*, 754, 754*n*
 servant of shipowner or salvor, claim by, **21**, 736, 757
  heirs, dependents etc. of servant, **21**, 757
 shipmaster, **15**, 144; **21**, 557, 751

Sea, carriage by—*continued*
limitation of liability—*continued*
 shipowner, **1**, 481; **21**, 558
 shipper, **21**, 606
 Warsaw Convention, **21**, 758*n*
 waterway, damage to, **21**, 755
 wreck-raising expenses, **21**, 756, 756*n*
liner, meaning, **21**, 524
mixed cargos, **21**, 526, 526*n*
navigation, *see* NAVIGATION
non-negotiable receipt for goods, use of, **21**, 525
overloading ship, damages for negligence, **21**, 719*n*
passenger, *see* PASSENGER
quarantine, *see* QUARANTINE
reasonable despatch, implied terms, **21**, 616
received for shipment bill, **21**, 524*n*, 526*n*, 528*n*, 571*n*, 572
safety, law relating to, *see* SHIPPING (safety)
sea waybill, *see* SEA WAYBILL
seaworthiness, *see* SEAWORTHINESS
ship's delivery order, **21**, 530
shipper—
 act or omission of, carrier not liable, **21**, 603
 exceptions in favour of, Hague-Visby Rules, **21**, 604
 indemnification of carrier by, **21**, 597
 registered excise, *see* REGISTERED EXCISE DEALER AND SHIPPER (REDS)
 title to sue—
  demise charterer, **21**, 578
  Dunlop v Lambert, rule in, **21**, 582
  shipowner, **21**, 578
shipping line, meaning, **21**, 524
time charterparty, *see* CHARTERPARTY
towage, *See* TOW
tramp ship, **21**, 526, 526*n*
transfer of rights and liabilities—
 bills of lading, *see* BILL OF LADING
 sea waybills, **21**, 575
 ship's delivery orders, **21**, 574
tug, *See* TUG
tug and tow, *See* TOW
unseaworthiness, *see* SEAWORTHINESS
waybill, third party rights, **15**, 847
voyage charterparty, *see* CHARTERPARTY
York-Antwerp Rules—
 bill of lading, express terms, **21**, 546
 general average, **21**, 700, 700*n*
  expenditure, **21**, 710
  fault, where, **21**, 704, 704*n*
 time charterparty, **21**, 640
 voyage charterparty, **21**, 618
Sea Fish Industry Authority, **11**, 212
grants and loans by, **2**, 1289
Sea fisheries
British fishery limits, **11**, 172
compensation for damage, **11**, 176
conduct of fishing operations, regulation of, **11**, 170
conservation of sea fish, **11**, 144–154
Convention on Fishing and Conservation of the Living Resources of the High Seas, **21**, 2
damages, offence, relating to, **4**, 38

Sea fisheries—*continued*
European Union rules and measures—
 conservation, **11**, 180
 enforcement, **11**, 178–182
 quota measures, **11**, 181
exclusive economic zone, *see* EXCLUSIVE
 ECONOMIC ZONE
fines, recovery of, **11**, 174
high seas, in, freedom of, **21**, 41
North Sea Convention, **11**, 126
officers—
 Convention for Regulating the Police of the
  North Sea Fisheries, **11**, 126
 designated persons, categories of, **11**, 171
 enforcement of statutory provisions, **11**, 24,
  126, 127
 foreign, **11**, 171
 generally, **11**, 171
 meaning, **11**, 126*n*
 obstruction or assault of, **11**, 126, 141, 174, 176
 powers—
  boarding of boats, **11**, 126
  British boats, **11**, 126
  convention enforcement, **11**, 173
  detention of boats, **11**, 172
  fishing boats, **11**, 126, 185, 186
  foreign boats, **11**, 126
  generally, **11**, 126, 154, 172
  inshore fishing, **11**, 141
  premises on land, in relation to, **11**, 186
  seizure of fish, nets and gear, **11**, 141
 protection, **11**, 126
products of, European Union import duty relief,
 7, 1103
prosecution of offenders, **11**, 174, 175
salmon, **11**, 8, 144
sea fish, meaning, **11**, 144
sea fish industry—
 financial assistance for, **11**, 213, 214
 fish farming, **11**, 214
 herring, **11**, 210
  Herring Industry Board, abolition of, **11**,
   210, 211
 Sea Fish Industry Authority, **11**, 212
 white fish, **11**, 209
  White Fish Authority, abolition of, **11**, 209,
   211
statistics, **11**, 177
statute law, **11**, 123–128, 144
 Sea Fish (Conservation) Act 1967 ..., **11**, 144
 Sea Fisheries Act 1868 ..., **11**, 123
 Sea Fisheries Act 1968 ..., **11**, 169
 Sea Fishing Boats (Scotland) Act 1886 ..., **11**,
  128
territorial sea, fishing in, as non-innocent activity,
 21, 7
third countries, fishing by, **11**, 182
United Kingdom laws—
 compensation for damage, **11**, 176
 European Community rules and measures,
  enforcement of, **11**, 178–182
 fines, recovery of, **11**, 174
 prosecution court, **11**, 175
 regulation of fishing operations, **11**, 170

Sea fisheries—*continued*
United Kingdom laws—*continued*
 sea fisheries—
  sea fishery officers, *see* officers *above*
  sea fishery statistics, **11**, 177
Sea-greens
foreshore, not included in, **18**, 313
meaning, **18**, 313
Sea-letter
generally, **16**, 1202
Sea trout
close season, buying, selling or exposing for sale
 during, **11**, 312
licence to deal in, **14**, 566
River Tweed, **11**, 40
Sea waybill
chartered ship, generally, **21**, 690
definition, **21**, 531
electronic data interchange, contract involving,
 21, 532
generally, **21**, 521*n*, 531
Hague and Hague-Visby Rules, application, **21**,
 547*n*
non-negotiable document, as, **21**, 525, 531, 690
rights and liabilities, transfer of, **21**, 575
third party rights, **15**, 847
title to sue, **21**, 575, 578, 578*n*, 579
Seal
advantages of use, **7**, 910
Cachet, *see* CACHET SEAL
Casset, *see* CACHET SEAL
company—
 obligation to have, **4**, 437
 registered name shown on, **4**, 321
Court of Exchequer, of, **7**, 885
Court of Session, of, **7**, 885
Crown—
 Act of Union, effect, **7**, 855
 English, **7**, 855
 generally, **7**, 852
 intention and authority of Sovereign, as
  expression of, **7**, 852
 law and custom governing use, **7**, 852
 Scottish, **7**, 855
Crown writ, **7**, 852, 853
customs and excise, interference with, **7**, 1237
evidence, as, **7**, 853
Great, Keeper of, **5**, 370
Great Seal, *see* GREAT SEAL OF SCOTLAND; GREAT
 SEAL OF THE UNITED KINGDOM
High Court of Justiciary, of, **7**, 886
historical background, **7**, 854
keepers of, **7**, 852
Lyon Court, of, **7**, 885
meaning, **7**, 853
obsolescence, **7**, 912
Order of Chancery in Scotland, **7**, 897–907
Order of Chancery of the United Kingdom, **7**,
 870–872
Prince's, **7**, 890
Principality, of, **5**, 710
Privy Seal, *see* PRIVY SEAL OF SCOTLAND; PRIVY
 SEAL OF THE UNITED KINGDOM
Quarter Seal, *see* QUARTER SEAL

Seal—*continued*
royal signature, **7**, 853
royal succession, striking of new seals on, **7**, 896
seal and counter-seal, **7**, 853
seal matrix, **7**, 853
Secretaries of State, **7**, 868, 869
Secretary of State for Scotland, of—
    design, **7**, 889
    history, **7**, 888
    Keeper, **7**, 889
    use, **7**, 888
signatures, **7**, 853
Signet, *see* SIGNET OF SCOTLAND; SIGNET OF UNITED
    KINGDOM
standing orders, **14**, 1319
United Kingdom seals—
    Great Seal, *see* GREAT SEAL OF THE UNITED
        KINGDOM
    Order of Chancery, **7**, 870–872
    Privy Seal, *see* PRIVY SEAL OF THE UNITED
        KINGDOM
    Signet, *see* SIGNET OF UNITED KINGDOM
use of, **14**, 260
White Wax, *see* QUARTER SEAL
writ, execution, **7**, 853
Seals
Behring Sea Award Act 1894 ..., **11**, 217
carcases, ownership, **2**, 310
cessation of seal killing, **11**, 225
close season, **2**, 305; **11**, 216, 217
Conservation of Seals Act 1970 ..., **11**, 220
entry, powers of, **2**, 310; **11**, 223
generally, **11**, 215
licence to kill, **11**, 22
    acts done by virtue of, **2**, 306
    grant of, **2**, 307
    purposes of, **2**, 307
    revocation, **2**, 307
offences—
    defences, **2**, 306
    forfeiture, order for, **2**, 308
    generally, **2**, 305
    jurisdiction as to, **2**, 309
    sea, at, **2**, 309
police powers, **2**, 308
protection, exceptions to, **11**, 221
res conveniens, **11**, 215
scientific advice, **11**, 224
Seal Fisheries (North Pacific) Acts, **11**, 218, 219
Seal Fishery Act 1875 ..., **11**, 216
seizure of articles, **2**, 308
Slaughter of Animals (Scotland) Act 1980 not
    applicable to, **11**, 496
suspect, stopping and search, **2**, 308
taking or killing—
    circumstances for, **2**, 306
    close season, during, **2**, 305
    firearms for, **2**, 305
    poisonous substances, use of, **2**, 305
    prohibit, power to, **2**, 305
udal law, **24**, 314
Seaman
administrative matters relating to, **21**, 113
barratry, acts of, **21**, 551*n*, 554

Seaman—*continued*
breach or neglect of duty, **21**, 208*n*
cancellation or suspension of certificate, **21**, 238,
    239
canteen, *see* SEAMEN'S CANTEEN
civil liability for misconduct, **21**, 271
claim by, limitation of liability, **21**, 757
contract of employment, **21**, 241, 261
    Employment Protection (Consolidation) Act
        (1978) and related legislation, **21**, 244
cooks, regulations as to, **21**, 245, 247
crew agreement—
    account of wages, **21**, 255
    admissibility in evidence, **21**, 228
    discharge, record of, **21**, 252
    disputes about wages, **21**, 256
    enforcement of regulations as to, **21**, 251
    form, **21**, 250
    generally, **21**, 250
    inspection, **21**, 228
    meaning, **21**, 250
    provision, **21**, 250
    ship, must be carried on, **21**, 226, 250
    subordinate legislation, **21**, 251
    wages, provisions as to, **21**, 255
crimping, **21**, 249
dangerous conduct by, **21**, 269
death of—
    burial or cremation expenses, **21**, 268
    inquiry into, **21**, 240
discharge, **21**, 252
    book, **21**, 252
    record of, **21**, 252
    ship ceasing to be registered in UK, where, **21**,
        253
discipline, **21**, 270
disobedience, **21**, 269
doctors, regulations as to, **21**, 245, 247
drink or drugs, under influence of, **21**, 208, 269,
    269*n*
employment—
    crew agreement, *see* crew agreement *above*
    generally, **21**, 241
    restrictions on making employment arrange-
        ments, **21**, 249
Employment Protection (Consolidation) Act
    (1978) and related legislation, **21**, 244
engine operators, **21**, 246
English language, knowledge of, **21**, 246
functions, **21**, 243
impeding voyage or navigation, **21**, 269
injury to, reparation for, **21**, 261
insolvency of employer, **21**, 244
liability—
    civil, **21**, 271
    limitation, **21**, 557
lien for wages, **20**, 279, 305
    priority of, **20**, 313
manning—
    dangerously unsafe ship, **21**, 206
    requirements as to, **21**, 245, 247, 313, 313*n*, 378
        enforcement, **21**, 248
master not treated as, **21**, 242
meaning, **21**, 242

Seaman—*continued*
medical certificate, when required, **21**, 246
Merchant Navy Established Service Scheme, abolition, **21**, 241
misconduct by, **21**, 269–271
  endangering ships, structures or individuals, **21**, 208, 208n
nationality, conditions as to, **21**, 245
neglect of duty, **21**, 269
offences by, **21**, 269–271
officer—
  cancellation or suspension of certificate, **21**, 236, 237, 239
  deck, **21**, 246
  engineer, **21**, 246
  fitness or conduct of, inquiry into, **1**, 409; **21**, 237, 239
  misconduct or negligence by, marine accident investigations, **21**, 236
  physical force in execution of duty, use of, **7**, 238
  qualifications, requirements as to, **21**, 245, 246
    enforcement, **21**, 248
  radio, **21**, 215, 246
personal effects not salvage subject, **21**, 436
qualifications, requirements as to, **21**, 245, 246
  enforcement, **21**, 248
  grading, **21**, 246
radar observers, **21**, 246, 247
radio and radiotelephone operators, **21**, 246, 247
redundancy—
  generally, **21**, 244, 244n
  payment, right to, **21**, 244, 244n
repatriation on total loss of ship, damages claim in respect of, **21**, 385
rights, generally, **21**, 244
safety, health and welfare—
  accommodation, **21**, 267, 267n
  contract of service, **21**, 261
  embarkation and disembarkation, **21**, 261
  general duty incumbent on employer, **21**, 261
  generally, **21**, 191
  Health and Safety at Work etc Act (1974), **21**, 262
  medical, dental or optical treatment and supplies, **21**, 245, 247, 268
  Merchant Shipping Act (1979), regulations under, **21**, 265
  Merchant Shipping (Health and Safety: General Duties) Regulations (1984), **21**, 264
  provisions and water, **21**, 267
  safe working practices code, **21**, 266
  seaworthiness of vessel, **21**, 261
  Secretary of State's powers in relation to, **21**, 261, 263
  sources of law, **21**, 192
salved vessel, of, whether entitled to claim salvage award, **21**, 451, 454
seaworthiness in relation to, **21**, 614, 614n
statutory jurisdiction, **21**, 241, 244
tug hired with or without crew, **21**, 403, 405
wages—
  account of, **21**, 255
  allotment, **21**, 258
    note, **21**, 257, 258

Seaman—*continued*
wages—*continued*
  arrestment, **21**, 257
  assignment, restriction on, **21**, 257
  attachment, **21**, 257
  bonus payments, **21**, 255
  crew agreement, *see* crew agreement *above*
  deductions, **21**, 255
    Child Support Act, under, **21**, 257
  disputes, **20**, 305; **21**, 256
  forfeiture of right to, repeal of law, **21**, 254
  general average, **21**, 710, 712
  generally, **21**, 254
  jurisdiction, **21**, 101
  lien for, **20**, 279, 305, 313
  loss of ship, where, **21**, 254
  maritime lien, **21**, 260, 392, 479, 479n
  payment, time for, **21**, 255
  rights and obligations, **21**, 254
  sale of ship, on, **21**, 259
  sums expended by authorities on maintenance of seamen's dependents, **21**, 255
  wreck or loss of ship, on, **21**, 259
Seamanship
proof of fault following collision, **21**, 319
Seamen's canteen
licence—
  breach of conditions, **2**, 70
  conditions, power to attach, **2**, 16
  grant and effect of, **2**, 16
meaning of canteen, **2**, 16
permitted hours, **2**, 18
provision of, **2**, 16
statutory provision for, **2**, 16
Seaplane
collision regulations, **21**, 332n, 333, 356
collisions, prevention of, **2**, 1066
lights and shapes to be displayed, **21**, 369
meaning, **21**, 332n
Search
arrest, following, unjustified, **15**, 440
child, for, **14**, 1504
controlled drugs, relating to, **14**, 1252
customs officers' powers, **7**, 1228
district registrars' index, of, **19**, 1418
explosives, offences in connection with, **10**, 1632
failure to warn police of dangerous object, **7**, 43
females, search of, **11**, 26
firearms and ammunition—
  control over movement of, **10**, 1581
  stop and search powers, **10**, 1574
  warrant, search with, **10**, 1575
generally, **17**, 603
intimate, **7**, 1228
parochial registers, of, **19**, 1412
person, of, **17**, 604
petroleum and inflammable materials, **19**, 409, 411
Poaching Prevention Act 1832 ..., **11**, 844
police powers—
  European Convention for the Protection of Human Rights and Freedoms, **16**, 1806
  generally, **11**, 26; **16**, 1787
  obstructing etc police, **16**, 1807

Search—*continued*
police powers—*continued*
'on the street', **16**, 1795
personal search—
    arrest, following, **16**, 1797
    body samples, **16**, 1797
    danger to searcher, **7**, 43
    detainee, of, **16**, 1797
    fingerprints and other impressions, **16**, 1797
    generally, **16**, 1797
    identification parades, **16**, 1797
    person not arrested, of, **16**, 1797
    probes beyond the skin, **16**, 1797
    terrorism, person suspected of involvement in, **16**, 1801
    warrant, **16**, 1794
        without, **16**, 1794, 1797
premises—
    generally, **16**, 1798
warrant—
    person, to search, **16**, 1794
premises, of, **17**, 607
customs officers' powers, **7**, 1228
revenue traders, premises of, **7**, 1252
Registrar General's index, of, **19**, 1419
rub-down, **7**, 1228
salmon fishing offences, **11**, 26
strip, **7**, 1228
unlicensed premises, **14**, 546
Search warrant
databank information, search of—
    Data Protection Registrar's power to apply for, **18**, 1555
    intentional obstruction of execution, **18**, 1550
generally, **16**, 1790
infringement of copyright, issue in relation to, **18**, 1096
warrant for entry and search, **16**, 1798
Searches (in registers)
General Register of Sasines, **6**, 641
Register of Charges, **6**, 641
Register of Inhibitions and Adjudications—
    clear search, **8**, 185
    generally, **6**, 641
    length of search, **6**, 641; **8**, 184
Seashore
See FORESHORE
Seasonal worker
income support, **21**, 1081
Seasons
cycle, **22**, 801
duration, determination, **22**, 801
tropical year, cycle of seasons as, **22**, 801
vernal equinox—
    Easter, to fix date, **22**, 808
    recurrence as measurement, **22**, 801, 804, 806
Seat belt
exemptions on requirement to wear, **20**, 438
medical examination in connection with, **11**, 1450
obligation to wear, **11**, 1027
offences in relation to, **20**, 438
Seaward areas
oil production licence for, **9**, 729

Seaware
servitude right to take, **18**, 318, 491
Seaweed
right to gather, valuation, **24**, 734
servitude right to take, **18**, 318, 491
udal law, **24**, 314
Seaworthiness
absolute obligation of carrier as to, **21**, 593, 593*n*
burden of proof, **21**, 614
cargo—
    fitness to receive and carry, **21**, 614
    protection of, **21**, 628, 628*n*
cargo-worthiness, *see* CARGO-WORTHINESS
common law obligation of owner as to, **21**, 542
contracting out, non-negotiable receipts, **21**, 602
dangerously unsafe ship, **21**, 206, 206*n*
defect normally rectified after sailing, **21**, 614
deviation to remedy unseaworthiness, **21**, 615
documentation, **21**, 614
duty to maintain ship in seaworthy state, **21**, 378
equipment, **21**, 614, 614*n*
fuel supply, **21**, 614
Hague-Visby Rules, **21**, 593, 593*n*
latent defect, **21**, 603, 614*n*
laytime, commencement, **21**, 673
manning, **21**, 614
meaning, **21**, 614
perils differing throughout voyage, **21**, 614
pilotage, **21**, 614*n*
safety of crew, implied obligation of owner as to, **21**, 261
stowage, **21**, 614*n*
time charterparty, **21**, 614, 639, 645
    express terms, **21**, 640, 644
trivial defects, **21**, 614*n*
unseaworthiness—
    arising on voyage, **21**, 614*n*, 628*n*
    liability, exclusion or limitation of, **21**, 547, 547*n*
    not cause of loss, where, **21**, 614
voyage charterparty, **21**, 614, 614*n*
    express terms, **21**, 618
Seceders
Anti-Burghers, **3**, 1636
Associate Synod, **3**, 1636
Auld Lichts, **3**, 1636, 1637
Burghers, **3**, 1636
Church of Scotland, from, **3**, 1636
General Associate Synod, **3**, 1636
legal status, **3**, 1637
New Lichts, **3**, 1636, 1637
Second (Time)
meaning, **22**, 816
Secondhand dealer
licensing, **14**, 119, 558
Secret
theft of, **7**, 326
Secret Intelligence Service (SIS)
statutory basis, **7**, 732
Secretary
Officer of State, **7**, 790, 791, 792, 797
Secretary of State
authorisation to carry on investment business of individual or organisation, **12**, 1319

Secretary of State—*continued*
authority of, **5**, 478
development of office, **7**, 774, 797, 868
investment business, investigatory powers as to, **12**, 1415
meaning, **5**, 478*n*
powers of, **5**, 478
provisional orders, **19**, 7, 7*n*, 38, 39, 41
   petition for issue, **19**, 8, 9
representation for one enactment, **19**, 6
signets and seals, **7**, 868
telecommunications, functions in relation to, **16**, 1922
   apparatus, requirements, power to make, **16**, 1951
   grants, power to make, **16**, 1922
   licensing authority, role as, **16**, 1921, 1922, 1926
Secretary of State for Defence
incorporation, **19**, 209
property, rights etc transferred to, **2**, 603
responsibility of, **2**, 603
Secretary of State for Employment
codes of practice issued by, **9**, 10
Health and Safety Commission, control of, **9**, 413
health and safety regulations, duties as to, **9**, 523
industrial tribunals, responsibility for, **9**, 302
Secretary of State for Energy
incorporation, **19**, 209
Secretary of State for the Environment
canals and inland waterways, **19**, 1103, 1113–1117
Secretary of State for Industry
incorporation, **19**, 209
Secretary of State for Scotland
consumer protection, **6**, 11
delict, title and interest to sue, **15**, 223
education, powers in relation to, *see* EDUCATION
Lord Advocate, continuing relationship with, **5**, 537
Office of the Solicitor to the Secretary of State for Scotland, *see* LEGAL CIVIL SERVICE
parliamentary private secretary to, **5**, 386
police, powers in relation to—
   amalgamation schemes—
      approval, **16**, 1725
      power to require, **16**, 1725
   appeal to, following disciplinary hearing, **16**, 1781
   authority in relation to police force, **16**, 1709
   central grant, payment to police authorities, **16**, 1734
   civilian staff, number employed, as to, **16**, 1724
   common police services, provision, **16**, 1732
   departmental circulars, issue, **16**, 1721, 1721*n*
   disciplinary matters, as to, **16**, 1731
   generally, **14**, 495; **16**, 1721, 1721*n*
   information on policing matters, power to call for, **16**, 1727
   inquiry, power to cause, **16**, 1728
   Inspector of Constabulary, as to, **16**, 1733
   material resources, powers as to, **16**, 1724
   mutual aid and collaboration schemes, power to require, **16**, 1726, 1738
   number of constables employed, powers as to, **16**, 1724

Secretary of State for Scotland—*continued*
police, powers in relation to—*continued*
   oversight of police matters, generally, **16**, 1721
   Parliament, responsibility to, **16**, 1735
   Police Federation for Scotland, **16**, 1762
   regulations, power to make—
      generally, **16**, 1721
      police cadets, for, **16**, 1723
      police government and administration, **16**, 1722, 1722*n*
   reporting of criminal statistics, **16**, 1729
   Scottish Home and Health Department, role, **16**, 1721
   senior police officers, as to, **16**, 1730, 1736
prisons, functions in relation to—
   appointments, power to make, **16**, 1411
   confinement of prisoners, **16**, 1411
   directives to governors, **16**, 1409
   discharge of prisoners, **16**, 1411
   generally, **16**, 1401, 1402, 1407, 1411
   governors, **16**, 1414
   maintenance of buildings, **16**, 1411
   prisoner, petition by, **16**, 1469
   purchase and sale of land and buildings, **16**, 1411
   regulation and management of prisons, rules as to, power to make, **16**, 1406
   remand centre, **16**, 1411
   reports to Parliament, **16**, 1411
   Scottish Prison Service, relationship with, **16**, 1413
   standing orders, power to make, **16**, 1407
   treatment of prisoners, **16**, 1411
   young offenders institution, **16**, 1411
public expenditure, **5**, 523
questions to, **5**, 391
register of electors, supply to, **15**, 1114
responsibilities of, **5**, 516, 519
Scottish Courts Administration, discharge of functions by, **13**, 1406
Seal of—
   design, **7**, 889
   history, **7**, 888
   Keeper, **7**, 889
   use, **7**, 888
Secretary for Scotland—
   creation of post, **13**, 1270
   elevation of office to Secretary of State, **5**, 334
   revival of office of, **5**, 334
See also SCOTTISH OFFICE
Secretary of State for Trade and Industry
competition law, powers, **4**, 1124
incorporation, **19**, 209
Monopolies and Mergers Commission, reference to, **4**, 1124, 1274
Restrictive Practices Court, agreement not referred to, **4**, 1184
Secretary of State for Transport
light railway—
   application, consideration of, **19**, 1078
   authorisation of, **19**, 1075
railways—
   closure of, **19**, 1097
   Prevention of Accidents Rules, **19**, 1069
   responsibility for, **19**, 1002, 1006

Secretary of State for War
incorporation, **19**, 209

Secure tenant
abandonment of tenancy, **11**, 1948
after 1988 ..., **11**, 1936
agricultural premises, **11**, 1937, 1943
annoyance or nuisance, conduct amounting to, **11**, 1947
assignation, **11**, 1951
assured tenancy—
  conversion into, **11**, 1936
  generally, **13**, 696, 697
  repossession, grounds for—
    discretionary—
      alternative accommodation, provision of, **13**, 725, 727
      annoyance, **13**, 725, 733
      breach of tenancy obligations, **13**, 725, 731
      deterioration in condition of house or furnishings, **13**, 725, 732, 734
      establishment, **13**, 726
      ex-employee as tenant, **13**, 725, 735
      generally, **13**, 725
      immoral or illegal purpose, premises used for, **13**, 725, 733
      notice to quit, withdrawal by tenant, **13**, 725, 728
      nuisance, **13**, 725, 733
      rent—
        persistent delay in payment, **13**, 725, 729
        unpaid, **13**, 725, 730
    mandatory—
      demolition or construction work, house required for, **13**, 749, 755
      educational body, non-student let by, **13**, 749, 753
      heritable security default, **13**, 749, 751
      intestacy, tenancy passing on, **13**, 749, 756, 781
      lay missionary, house held for occupation by, **13**, 749, 754
      minister, house held for occupation by, **13**, 749, 754
      off-season holiday let, **13**, 749, 752
      owner occupier, landlord as, **13**, 749, 750
      rent arrears, **13**, 749, 757
      will, tenancy inherited under, **13**, 749, 756, 781
  status affected by secure tenancy, **13**, 650
avoidance devices—
  bed and breakfast, **13**, 770
  company let, **13**, 773
  deferred purchase agreement, **13**, 772
  generally, **13**, 768
  holiday let, **13**, 769
  non-exclusive occupation agreement, **13**, 771
  rental purchase agreement, **13**, 772
business premises, **11**, 1937, 1943
change of landlord—
  acceptance, notice of, **11**, 1975
  application for, **11**, 1973
    refusal of, **11**, 1976
  generally, **11**, 1971
  Lands Tribunal, references to, **11**, 1976

Secure tenant—*continued*
change of landlord—*continued*
  public sector landlord, from, **11**, 1972
  subsequent disposals, **11**, 1977
  tenant's 'right to choose', **11**, 1971
  variation of condition, **11**, 1974
contract of employment, tenancy held under, **11**, 1937, 1938, 1947
creation of, **11**, 1936
demolition or substantial works, **11**, 1947
disposal by local authority of houses let on, **11**, 1908
exceptions, **11**, 1937–1945
false statement, landlord induced to grant tenancy by, **11**, 1947
fire authorities as landlord, **11**, 1937, 1944
furnished lease, **13**, 696
generally, **11**, 1903, 1934, 1936; **13**, 696
harassment—
  generally, **13**, 698, 701
  intention, **13**, 702
  landlord or agent, provisions only applicable to, **13**, 703
  peace and comfort of occupier, acts likely to interfere with, **13**, 702, 703
  penalties for, **13**, 702, 703
  residential occupier, meaning, **13**, 690
  services, withholding, **13**, 701, 702
  threats and intimidation, **13**, 702
homeless persons, accommodation for, **11**, 1937, 1942
houses part of, or within curtilage of, certain other buildings, **11**, 1937, 1945
housing associations, **11**, 1947
immoral or illegal purposes, house used for, **11**, 1947
improvements to property, **11**, 1952
ish, **13**, 317
islands council houses held for education authority purposes, **11**, 1947, 1972
joint tenant, **13**, 697
landlords, **11**, 1936
lease must be in writing, **11**, 1950
Leases Act 1449 ..., **13**, 293
lodgers, **11**, 1951
meaning, **11**, 1936
new towns, tenants of, **11**, 1920
obligations of tenancy broken, **11**, 1947
overcrowding, **11**, 1947
Part VII contract, **13**, 696
  1 December 1980—
    contracts entered on or after, **13**, 761
    contracts entered before, **13**, 760
  generally, **13**, 759
police authorities as landlord, **11**, 1937, 1944
possession, proceedings for, **11**, 1947
  conduct grounds, **11**, 1947
  management grounds, **11**, 1947
  service of notice, **11**, 1947
  transfer of secure tenancy to spouse etc, **11**, 1947
principal home, ceasing to occupy as, **11**, 1947
protected tenancy, **13**, 696
  agreement by tenant to give up statutory rights, **13**, 708

Secure tenant—*continued*
protected tenancy—*continued*
  repossession, grounds for—
    discretionary—
      alternative accommodation, provision, **13**, 709–713
      annoyance, **13**, 714, 716
      assignation, **13**, 714, 720
      breach of tenancy agreement, **13**, 714, 715
      dangerous structure, property designated, **13**, 709
      deterioration in condition of house or furnishings, **13**, 714, 717, 718
      employee of landlord, house required for, **13**, 714, 721
      family member of landlord, house required for, **13**, 714, 722
      generally, **13**, 708
      immoral or illegal purpose, premises used for, **13**, 714, 716
      landlord, house required for occupation by, **13**, 714, 722
      local authority, property acquired by, **13**, 709
      notice to quit, withdrawal, **13**, 714, 719
      nuisance, **13**, 714, 716
      occupancy, determination of, **13**, 708
      overcrowding, **13**, 714, 724
      rent arrears, **13**, 714, 715
      spouse or cohabitee, occupancy exercised by, **13**, 708
      sublease, **13**, 714, 720, 723
      two houses, tenant with, **13**, 708
    mandatory—
      agricultural worker, dwelling house held for, **13**, 736, 743
      armed forces, landlord member of, **13**, 736, 747, 748
      educational body non-student let, **13**, 736, 740
      farm—
        amalgamation of farms, **13**, 736, 744
        occupation, **13**, 736, 745
      generally, **13**, 708, 736
      minister or lay missionary, dwelling house held for, **13**, 736, 742
      notice requirement, waiver, **13**, 748
      off-season holiday let, **13**, 736, 739
      owner occupier requiring house as residence, **13**, 736, 737, 748
      retirement home, owner's, **13**, 736, 738, 748
      short tenancy, **13**, 736, 741
      special needs, dwelling house adapted for, **13**, 736, 746
public sector tenancies, *see* PUBLIC SECTOR TENANCY
redemption of standard securities, **20**, 180
Rent Act 1974 ..., **13**, 593
repairs—
  repairing obligations, **11**, 1952
  right to repair, **11**, 1953
right to acquire, **11**, 1972
  exclusions from, **11**, 1972

Secure tenant—*continued*
right to buy—
  amenity housing, **11**, 1958
  application to purchase, **11**, 1957
  conditions of sale, landlord's powers, limitation of, **11**, 1958
  defective housing, **11**, 1969
  discount, basic, **11**, 1956
  exceptions, **11**, 1955
  generally, **11**, 1934, 1954, 1955, 1970
  housing associations, restrictions affecting tenants of, **11**, 1955
  landlord, duties of, **11**, 1966
  Lands Tribunal for Scotland, powers of, **11**, 1964
    appeal from, **11**, 1964
    specific performance, decree of, **11**, 1964
  lessee, where landlord is, **11**, 1968
  loans to tenants to assist purchase, **11**, 1961, 2014
  maximum, **11**, 1956
  neighbours, protection of rights of, **11**, 1959
  occupation, meaning, **11**, 1955
  offer to sell, landlord's—
    generally, **11**, 1957
    not following, **11**, 1957
    notice of acceptance by tenant, **11**, 1960
  pre-emption, right of, **11**, 1958
  prescribed form, **11**, 1957
  price, calculation of, **11**, 1956
    fixed price option, **11**, 1962
  prior occupation by tenant, **11**, 1955
  prohibitions, **11**, 1958
  reasonable, must be, **11**, 1958
  recoverability of, **11**, 1965
  refusal of, **11**, 1963
  regional council as landlord, **11**, 1903
  restrictions, **11**, 1955
  Secretary of State, powers of, **11**, 1967
  statutory conditions, to be satisfied, **11**, 1955
  statutory requirements, compliance with, **11**, 1958
  variation, **11**, 1959
  voluntary disputes, **11**, 1970
security of tenure, generally, **11**, 1946; **13**, 696
services, provision of, **13**, 600
sheltered housing, **11**, 1947
short assured tenancy, **13**, 696
  repossession, grounds for, **13**, 758
special needs, house adapted for, **11**, 1947
subletting, **11**, 1951
succession to, **11**, 1949
tacit relocation, relationship with, **13**, 696
temporary letting—
  during works, **11**, 1937, 1941
  pending development, **11**, 1937, 1940
  person seeking accommodation, to, **11**, 1937, 1939
termination of tenancy—
  generally, **13**, 696
  tacit relocation, **13**, 696
unlawful eviction—
  damages in respect of, **13**, 704, 705
    amount, **13**, 707
    defences to damages action, **13**, 706

Secure tenant—*continued*
unlawful eviction—*continued*
   generally, **13**, 698, 700
   residential occupier, meaning, **13**, 690
variation—
   of conditions, **11**, 1959
   of terms, **11**, 1950
waste, neglect or default by tenant, **11**, 1947
Securities
advertising, controls on, **1**, 533
cautionary obligation, *see* CAUTIONARY OBLIGATION
consumer credit—
   meaning of securities for, **5**, 908
   realisation of, **5**, 922
deceased's liability to tax on interest on, **25**, 968
floating charges, *see* COMPANY
generally, **18**, 3
government, **25**, 967
heritable, **6**, 627
in solidum or *pro rata*, **6**, 626
inhibition as, **8**, 166
interest on, deceased's liability to tax, **25**, 968
law of, principles, **6**, 626
leasehold securities—
   creditor's remedies, **13**, 331
   effect of registration, **13**, 330
   generally, **13**, 328
   writs registrable, **13**, 329
meaning, **12**, 1510
money, as subject of, **14**, 1811
money, for loan of, **13**, 1758, 1759
moveable property, over, **6**, 627; **17**, 323
obsolescent, **6**, 626–632
open-ended investment company, in, **12**, 1308
overt and covert, **6**, 626
pledge, *see* PLEDGE
printer's imprint, requirement not applicable, **17**, 3
ranking, **6**, 626
regulation of, **14**, 819
Securities Association, **12**, 1312
Securities and Futures Association, **12**, 1312
standard, *see* STANDARD SECURITY
sub-lease rental, over, **14**, 1093
transactions with, VAT exemption, **7**, 1424
See also HERITABLE SECURITY
Securities Association (TSA)
recognised self-regulating organisation, as, **12**, 1312
Securities and Futures Association (SFA)
recognised self-regulating organisation, as, **12**, 1312
Securities and Investments Board Ltd
Court of Session, proceedings brought in, **12**, 1305
establishment, **12**, 1305
proceedings arising out of act or omission of, **12**, 1305
See also SECURITIES AND INVESTMENTS BOARD
Securities and Investments Board (SIB)
authorisation by, **12**, 1309, 1310
   application for, **12**, 1310
   compliance orders, **12**, 1314
   disqualification direction, **12**, 1339
   fit and proper person, applicant must be, **12**, 1310, 1311, 1338

Securities and Investments Board (SIB)—*continued*
authorisation by—*continued*
   grant of, **12**, 1310
   refusal, withdrawal or suspension, **12**, 1310, 1311, 1314
   self-regulating organisation, of, **12**, 1312
     refusal or revocation, **12**, 1314
cancellation, rules covering, **12**, 1336
central compensation fund, **12**, 1408
clearing house, application for recognition as, **12**, 1322, 1322n
clients' money regulations, **12**, 1409
collective investment schemes, powers as to, **12**, 1328
   interventions, **12**, 1329
   investigations, **12**, 1330
compensation scheme, **12**, 1420, 1421
   claims under, **12**, 1422
cooling-off period, rules covering, **12**, 1336
Core Conduct of Business Rules, **12**, 1356
   administration, rules on, **12**, 1391–1401
   advertising, rules on, **12**, 1366–1370
     overseas businesses, **12**, 1369, 1370
   allocation—
     fair, **12**, 1383
     timely, **12**, 1382
   application, **12**, 1399
   appointed representatives, **12**, 1361, 1378
   cessation of business, **12**, 1396
   charges, fairness of, **12**, 1374
   Chinese walls, **12**, 1395
   churning, **12**, 1385
   complaints procedure, **12**, 1394
   compliance, **12**, 1393
   confirmations, **12**, 1377
   contingent liability transactions, **12**, 1386
   customer—
     classes of, **12**, 1398
     customer agreements, **12**, 1375
     customer order priority, **12**, 1379
     customers' rights, **12**, 1376
     customers' understanding, **12**, 1372
     dealing with, **12**, 1379–1386
     information, disclosure to, **12**, 1377
     investments of, safeguarding, **12**, 1391
     non-private, **12**, 1362
     relationship with, **12**, 1371–1378
   derivative transactions, **12**, 1386
   execution—
     best, **12**, 1359, 1381
     timely, **12**, 1380
   fair and clear communications, **12**, 1371
   independence, rules on, **12**, 1357–1362
   inducements, **12**, 1357, 1362
   information and advice, rules on, **12**, 1363–1365
     disclosure to customers, **12**, 1377
   insider dealing, **12**, 1387
   investment firm, information about the, **12**, 1364
   market integrity, rules on, **12**, 1387–1390
   material interest, **12**, 1358, 1362
   off-exchange market makers, **12**, 1389

Securities and Investments Board (SIB)— *continued*
Core Conduct of Business Rules—*continued*
  packaged products—
    information about, **12**, 1363
    standards of advice on, **12**, 1365
  polarisation, **12**, 1360
  problems arising, **12**, 1362
  publication, dealing ahead of, **12**, 1384
  reliance on others, rules as to, **12**, 1397
  remuneration, fairness of, **12**, 1374
  reportable transactions, **12**, 1390
  scope of business, regarding, **12**, 1392
  soft commission, **12**, 1359, 1362
  stabilisation of securities, **12**, 1388
  suitability, **12**, 1373
  switching, **12**, 1385
  time, application as to, **12**, 1401
establishment, **12**, 1305
Financial Services Tribunal—
  references to, **12**, 1417
  report of, **12**, 1419
Financial Services in the United Kingdom ... white
  paper, **12**, 1305
financial supervision rules—
  ad hoc reporting requirements, **12**, 1406
  auditors, appointment of, **12**, 1405
  disapplied, where, **12**, 1402
  financial resources of investment firm, **12**, 1403
  generally, **12**, 1402, 1408
  internal controls and systems, **12**, 1407
  records and reporting, **12**, 1404
information and investigations, powers as to, **12**,
  1415
intervention, powers of, **12**, 1414
investment business, relations with, **12**, 1352
investment exhange, application for recognition
  as, **12**, 1322, 1322*n*
investors' remedies, *see* INVESTORS' REMEDIES
merger with Marketing of Investments Board, **12**,
  1305
misconduct by investment business, public
  statement as to, **12**, 1339
professional body, application for recognition
  order, **12**, 1313, 1313*n*
  refusal or revocation, **12**, 1314
promotion and marketing of insurance products,
  regulation of, **12**, 809
register, **12**, 1415
rules—
  adequacy test, **12**, 1341
  cancellation rules, **12**, 1340
  compensation fund, establishment of, **12**, 1340
  contravention, public statements concerning,
    12, 1339
  core, **12**, 1341
    See also Core Conduct of Business Rules
     above
  damages, restriction on right to sue for, **12**,
    1341
  financial resources rules, **12**, 1340, 1350
  financial supervision rules, *see* financial
    supervision rules *above*
  holding clients' money, as to, **12**, 1340

Securities and Investments Board (SIB)— *continued*
rules—*continued*
  indemnity rules, **12**, 1340
  'new settlement' approach, **12**, 1341
  notification regulations, **12**, 1340
  rule-making powers, generally, **12**, 1340
  statements of principle, *see* statements of
    principle *below*
  statutory changes, **12**, 1341
statements of principle—
  advisers, classification of, **12**, 1353
  authorised person, conduct and financial
    standing of, **12**, 1342
  conflicts of interest, **12**, 1348, 1355
  customer assets, statement on, **12**, 1349
  failure to comply with, **12**, 1342
  fiduciary duties, and—
    classification of adviser, **12**, 1353
    conflicts of interest, **12**, 1348, 1355
    generally, **12**, 1356
    nature of fiduciary duties, **12**, 1354
  financial resources, statement on, **12**, 1350
  generally, **12**, 1342
  information about customers, statement on, **12**,
    1346
  information for customers, statement on, **12**,
    1347
  integrity, statement on, **12**, 1343
  internal organisation, statement on, **12**, 1351
  issue of, **12**, 1342
  market practice, statement on, **12**, 1345
  modification to adapt to particular
    circumstances, **12**, 1342
  purpose of, **12**, 1342
  relations with regulators, statement on, **12**,
    1352
  skill, care and diligence, statement on, **12**, 1344
unit trust scheme, authorisation of, **12**, 1327
  revocation, **12**, 1327
unsolicited calls regulations, power to make, **12**,
  1335
Securities market
regulation of, **1**, 54
Security guard
failure to prevent crime, **7**, 39
Security of person
right to—
  European Convention on Human Rights, **12**,
    29–42
  Universal Declaration of Human Rights, **12**, 4*n*
Security of tenure
See TENANT-TENANCY
Security, right in
See RIGHT IN SECURITY
Security services
statutory basis, **7**, 732
Sederunt, Acts of
See ACT OF SEDERUNT
Sedition
aggravated, **7**, 593
conspiracy, and, **7**, 594
crime against state, as, **7**, 589
form, **7**, 588

Sedition—*continued*
freedom of speech, and, **7**, 591
generally, **7**, 564, 587
incitement, **7**, 593
meaning, **7**, 587
mental element, **7**, 593
political climate, influence, **7**, 592
real, **7**, 588
seditious tendency, **7**, 590
treason, and, **7**, 587
treason felony, and, **7**, 585
verbal, **7**, 588
written or spoken words, uttering, **7**, 587, 588
Seduction
action for, **11**, 786
Seeds
See PLANTS AND SEEDS
Seeking business
See BUSINESS
Seisin
See SASINE
Seizure, police powers
generally, **16**, 1787
Select committees
See HOUSE OF COMMONS; HOUSE OF LORDS
Self-build society
housing associations, **11**, 1924
Self-defence
defence of, **15**, 420
defence to charge of assault, as, **7**, 240
provocation and, **7**, 277
right to, **11**, 1095
United Nations Charter, **19**, 702
Self-employed
family credit, **21**, 1093
  business expenses, **21**, 1094
housing benefit, **21**, 1111
immigration—
    change of employment, **12**, 252
    entry clearance required by, **12**, 250, 251
    extension of leave, **12**, 253
income support, business assets, **21**, 1079
liability for independent contractor, **15**, 335
maternity allowance, entitlement to, **21**, 898, 899
national insurance contributions, **21**, 1048
person other than employee, duty to, **9**, 445–447
social security contributions, **19**, 1530
    Class 2, **21**, 1037
    Class 4, **21**, 1039
sportsmen, *see* PROFESSIONAL SPORTSMEN
unemployment benefit, entitlement to, **21**, 804
    no work no wages rule, **21**, 806
    sleeping partner, **21**, 804
Self-governing dominions
nationality laws, **14**, 1902
Self-governing school
admission to, parental rights, **8**, 809
articles of constitution, **8**, 785
articles of management, **8**, 786
ballot to determine self-governing status, **15**, 1534
board of management—
    community use of school, promotion of, **8**, 791
    composition, **8**, 778
    contracts entered into by, **8**, 791

Self-governing school—*continued*
board of management—*continued*
    direct funding, **8**, 778
    discontinuance of school by, **8**, 804
    execution of documents, **8**, 790
    generally, **8**, 778, 784
    interest groups, **8**, 778
    membership, **8**, 701, 787
      appointed members, **8**, 787
      disqualification from, **8**, 788
      headteacher, **8**, 787
      parent members, **8**, 787
      staff members, **8**, 787
    operation, **8**, 789–792
    parental and community involvement,
        promotion of, **8**, 791
    powers and duties, generally, **8**, 791
    proceedings, **8**, 789
    Secretary of State, powers of in relation to, **8**,
        792
    transfer of property to—
      commissioner for school assets, **8**, 799
      generally, **8**, 800
      procedure for, **8**, 801
catchment area, restriction on changes in, **8**, 794
characteristics—
    changes in, **8**, 808
    meaning, **8**, 808
    nature of, **8**, 808
    publication, **8**, 808
closure—
    discontinuance by board of management, **8**,
        804
    winding-up order, **8**, 806
    withdrawal of grant by Secretary of State, **8**,
        805
commissioner for school assets—
    appointment, **8**, 799
    function, **8**, 799
    reduction or prevention of unauthorised
        property deals, **8**, 802, 803
community use of school, promotion of, **8**, 791
corporal punishment, **8**, 903
denominations, must be open to all, **8**, 856
duties, failure to discharge, **8**, 701
education authority—
    interaction with, **8**, 807
    restrictions on, **8**, 793–797
eligible schools, **8**, 779
exclusion of pupil from, appeals, **8**, 809
financing—
    generally, **8**, 798
    interim payments, **8**, 798
    recorded pupils, where provision for, **8**, 798
    recurrent grants, **8**, 798
    Secretary of State's role, **8**, 798
    special schools, **8**, 798
funding, **8**, 701, 778
government of—
    articles of constitution, **8**, 785
    articles of management, **8**, 786
    board of management, *see* board of manage-
        ment *above*
grant to, withdrawal by Secretary of State, **8**, 805

Self-governing school—*continued*
ineligible schools, **8**, 779
management, **8**, 701
parental rights, admissions and exclusions, as to, **8**, 809
placing request, appeals, **8**, 880
property—
   holding of, **8**, 796
   transfer of assets to board of management—
      commissioner for school assets, **8**, 799
      procedure, **8**, 801
      property to be transferred, **8**, 800
   unauthorised disposal of—
      prevention, **8**, 803
      reduction of transactions, **8**, 802
      repudiation of agreements, **8**, 803
restriction in changes in educational matters, **8**, 794
Roman Catholic state-supported schools, **3**, 1666
school property, transfer of, **8**, 778
Secretary of State's powers and duties in relation to, **8**, 778, 783
self-governing status—
   acquisition of—
      ballot, **8**, 780
         rules for, **8**, 781
      effect of initiating procedure, **8**, 793–797
      eligibility, **8**, 779
      initial procedure, **8**, 780
      publication of proposals, **8**, 782
      Secretary of State's powers, **8**, 783
   effect, **8**, 778
   school attaining, **8**, 701
   Secretary of State's powers, **8**, 701
   service of resolution to acquire, **8**, 793
staff—
   appointment, **8**, 795
   transfer, **8**, 778
transport, education authority provision, **8**, 855
winding-up order, **8**, 806
Self-Governing Schools Appeal Committee
Scottish Committee, supervision by, **23**, 911*n*
Self-regulating organisation (SRO)
Financial Intermediaries Managers and Brokers Regulatory Association, **12**, 1312
Financial Services in the United Kingdom ... white paper, **12**, 1305
international securities, investment transactions by, **12**, 1307
investment business, relations with, **12**, 1352
Investment Management Regulatory Organisation, **12**, 1312
Life Assurance and Unit Trust Regulatory Organisation, **12**, 1312
meaning, **12**, 1312
member of, automatic authorisation, **12**, 1312
promotion and marketing of insurance products, regulation of, **12**, 809
recognition—
   application for, **12**, 1312
   grant or refusal of, **12**, 1312
regulation of insurance intermediaries, **12**, 812
Securities Association (TSA), **12**, 1312
Securities and Futures Association (SFA), **12**, 1312

Self-regulating organisation (SRO)—*continued*
unsolicited calls regulations, **12**, 1335
See also FINANCIAL INTERMEDIARIES, MANAGERS AND BROKERS REGULATORY ASSOCIATION; LIFE ASSURANCE AND UNIT TRUST REGULATORY ORGANISATION
Self-service display
invitation to treat, as, **15**, 622
Semiconductor topographies
definition, **18**, 1240
derivative works, as, **18**, 1243
designer, determination, **18**, 1247
European Union legislation as to, **18**, 1611
materials, **18**, 1240
unregistered design right, protection by—
   assignation, **18**, 1248
   commissioned works, **18**, 1245
   conditions for existence of right, **18**, 1243
   dealings in right, **18**, 1248
   derivative works, **18**, 1250
   design 'must not be commonplace', **18**, 1243
   designer, determination, **18**, 1247
   employee, works designed by, **18**, 1245
   European Union Directive, **18**, 1240
   General Agreement on Trade and Tariffs (GATT), **18**, 1253
   generally, **18**, 1214, 1239
   history, **18**, 1241
   infringement—
      commercial purposes, for, **18**, 1250
      future developments, **18**, 1253
      non-commercial aims, reproduction for, **18**, 1250
      possession for commercial purposes, **18**, 1252
      primary, **18**, 1250
      sale or hire in course of business, **18**, 1252
      secondary, **18**, 1252
      substantial reproduction, **18**, 1251
   legislation, **18**, 1239, 1241
   international, **18**, 1253
   licence—
      grant of, **18**, 1248
      of right, **18**, 1248
   Monopolies and Mergers Commission report in repect of right, **18**, 1248
   originality, **18**, 1243
   ownership of design, **18**, 1245, 1246
   qualification for protection, **18**, 1244
      commissioned works, **18**, 1244
      employee, design by, **18**, 1244
      generally, **18**, 1244
      reciprocity, **18**, 1244
   term, **18**, 1249
   testamentary disposition, **18**, 1248
   transfer of right, **18**, 1248
   transitional provisions, **18**, 1242
   Treaty on Intellectual Property in Respect of Integrated Circuits, **18**, 1253
Senator of the College of Justice
Court of Session, **6**, 906*n*, 923; **8**, 929, 930
Employment Appeal Tribunal, **6**, 923
former recording of decisions of, **22**, 251
generally, **6**, 860

Senator of the College of Justice—*continued*
nomination, **6**, 811
Parole Board, **6**, 923
Restrictive Practices Court, **6**, 923
See also COURT OF SESSION
Sentence
absolute discharge, **17**, 806
adjournment prior to, **17**, 786
admonition, **17**, 805
alteration of, **17**, 790
appeal against conviction and sentence—
  solemn procedure—
    abandonment, **17**, 819
    bringing appeal, **17**, 818
    determination of, **17**, 821
    disposal of, **17**, 827
    grounds of appeal, **17**, 822–826
    hearing of, **17**, 820
  summary procedure—
    disposal of, **17**, 865
    grounds of, **17**, 843–849
    hearing, **17**, 863
    procedure, **17**, 851–862
    prosecutor, by, **17**, 850
    remit to court of first instance, **17**, 864
    stated case, by, **17**, 839–842
appeal against sentence alone—
  solemn procedure, **17**, 828, 829
  summary procedure—
    disposal of, **17**, 870
    generally, **17**, 866
    grounds for, **17**, 867
    hearing of note of, **17**, 869
    manner of, **17**, 868
    time of, **17**, 868
capital punishment, **17**, 562, 796
caution, **17**, 801
community service, **17**, 802
compensation orders, **17**, 800
consecutive, **17**, 792
court's discretion, **17**, 793
cumulo penalties, **17**, 791
custodial penalties, **17**, 563
death penalty, **7**, 567; **17**, 796
deferment of—
  generally, **17**, 787
  mental disorder, person suffering from, **17**, 907
  period of, **17**, 804
deportation, **17**, 809
detention, **17**, 798
disqualifications, **17**, 808
expenses, **17**, 811
factors affecting, **17**, 793
fines, **17**, 799
  imprisonment for default, **16**, 1428
fixed penalties, **6**, 1165; **17**, 620, 810
forfeiture, **17**, 807
hard labour, abolition of, **17**, 563
High Court of Justiciary, jurisdiction of, **17**, 571
imprisonment, **17**, 797
incapacities, **17**, 808
interruption of proceedings for, **17**, 788
mitigation, plea of *de minimis non curat lex*, **7**, 27
murder, for, **17**, 562

Sentence—*continued*
non-capital punishment, **17**, 562
non-custodial penalties, **17**, 563
plea in mitigation, **17**, 795
preliminary procedure, **17**, 785
previous convictions, **17**, 794
prisoner awaiting, removal to hospital of, **14**, 1463
probation, **17**, 803
  See also PROBATION
pronouncing, **17**, 789
recording, **17**, 789
rehabilitation of offender, **17**, 812
restrictions on, **22**, 32
solemn procedure, **17**, 640
spent convictions, **17**, 812
summary procedure, **17**, 640
See also PENALTIES
Separate tenement
See LANDOWNERSHIP
Separation
See JUDICIAL SEPARATION
Separation of powers
doctrine of, **1**, 206; **5**, 341
Septic tank
emptying of, **25**, 431
Sequestration
abuse of process, **15**, 469
accretion, prevention of, **18**, 677
act and warrant of trustee in, judicial conveyance, as, **18**, 664
adjudication and, **8**, 210
adjudication on a *debitum fundi*, and, **8**, 375
alienation of property, *see* DEBTOR'S ESTATE
arbitration provisions, **2**, 413
arrestment and, **8**, 292
award of—
  action of reduction, **2**, 1362
  appeal against, **2**, 1337, 1359
  assignation defeated by, **20**, 47
  cause shown against, **2**, 1336
  conditions for, **2**, 1336
  creditor's petition, on, **2**, 1336
  debtor's petition, on, **2**, 1336
  delay in process after, **2**, 1336
  finality of, **2**, 1359
  Gazette notices of, **2**, 1341
  publicity requirement, **2**, 1338
  refusal to grant, **2**, 1337
  speed essential in, **2**, 1359
bankruptcy, *see* BANKRUPTCY
bill of exchange, holder's rights in, **4**, 145
body corporate, **2**, 1321, 1326; **4**, 72
borrower's estate, of, *commodatum* property, **13**, 1789
cessio distinguished, **22**, 645
civil jurisdiction, generally, **4**, 78
claim in, **14**, 257
Commissioners, *see* SEQUESTRATION COMMISSIONERS
concurrent proceedings, **2**, 1334
condition relating to, **25**, 873
confirmation as executor-creditor, and, **8**, 357
conflicts of jurisdiction, **4**, 76
contracts made prior to, **2**, 1378

Sequestration—*continued*
Court of Session jurisdiction, **2**, 1333, 1335; **6**, 924
creditors, involvement of, **2**, 1326
Crown preferences for tax, **8**, 129
date of, ascertaining, **2**, 1336, 1339
death of petitioner, **2**, 1329
debtor's contracts, right to adopt, **15**, 820
debtor's estate, *see* DEBTOR'S ESTATE
debtors subject to, **2**, 1302
deceased debtor, **2**, 1332, 1450; **4**, 72
decree, effect on diligence, **2**, 1395
deduction from earnings order, and, **8**, 346
diligence distinguished, **8**, 106
disabilities on—
    criminal penalties, **2**, 1477
    directorship of company, **2**, 1475
    generally, **2**, 1472
    insolvency practitioner, acting as, **2**, 1476
    justice of the peace, as, **2**, 1473
    local government, **2**, 1473
    parliamentary, **2**, 1473
    receiver, acting as, **2**, 1475
    solicitor, suspension of, **2**, 1474
discharge, *see* DEBTOR
estates subject to—
    generally, **2**, 1319
    particular individuals, **2**, 1320
exempted person rules, **12**, 1323
expenses, **17**, 1190
family home of debtor, **13**, 417
feuduty, for, **8**, 392
generally, **15**, 469
inhibition and, **8**, 176
insolvency provisions, *see* INSOLVENCY
insolvent defunct, estate of, **8**, 350
    advantages of confirmation as executor-
        creditor, **8**, 350
interim administration, **2**, 1309
interim procedure—
    general powers of trustee, **2**, 1342
    preservation of estate, **2**, 1342–1344
judicial factor, appointment of, **24**, 273
jurisdiction of Scottish courts—
    concurrent, **2**, 1335
    conflicting with other countries, **2**, 1334
    Court of Session, **2**, 1333
    rules, criticism of, **2**, 1333
    sheriff courts, **2**, 1333
landlord's, *see* SEQUESTRATION FOR RENT
landlord's hypothec—
    breach, **13**, 521
    generally, **13**, 520
    ordinary sequestration, relationship with, **13**, 523
lessee, of, **13**, 185
lessor, of, **13**, 159
limited partnership, **2**, 1321, 1486; **4**, 72
living debtor, **4**, 72
local authority, **2**, 1321
local government candidate, **15**, 1068
maills and duties, and, **8**, 399
Member of Parliament, **15**, 1059
minor not to be appointed on sequestrated estate,
    24, 129
minors, **2**, 1320

Sequestration—*continued*
modified procedure—
    appointments under, **2**, 1355
    circumstances for, **2**, 1354
    conducted under, **2**, 1344
    effect of, on Accountant, **2**, 1344
    examination of debtor, **2**, 1356
    historical note, **2**, 1353
    introduction of, **2**, 1354
    trustee under, *see* BANKRUPTCY
non-traders, in case of, **2**, 1319
notice, renewal of, **8**, 145
objects of, **2**, 1416
offences, *see* DEBTOR
other entities, **4**, 72
partner, of, **16**, 1083
partnership—
    bankruptcy of, **16**, 1107, 1108
        limited partnership, **16**, 1123
    generally, **2**, 1321, 1326; **4**, 72
person under disability, **2**, 1326
petition for, **4**, 16
    body corporate, of, **2**, 1326
    creditors, by, *see* CREDITORS
    death of party, **2**, 1329
    debtor, by, **2**, 1322, 1326
    executor, by, **2**, 1326, 1332
    limited partnership, of, **2**, 1332
    notice to Accountant, **2**, 1305
    partnership, of, **2**, 1326
    trustee estate, for, **2**, 1326
    trustees, by, **2**, 1328
poinding and, **8**, 238
preferential payments, *see* PREFERENTIAL PAYMENTS
procedure, defects in, **2**, 1480
property excluded, **2**, 1385
real poinding, and, **8**, 369
recall of award—
    circumstances for, **2**, 1361
    discretion of court, **2**, 1361
    effect of, **2**, 1364
    expenses in connection with, **2**, 1365
    grounds for, **2**, 1361
    order for, effect of, **2**, 1366
    pending, continuation of sequestration, **2**, 1363
    petition for—
        answers to, **2**, 1363
        exclusive jurisdiction in, **2**, 1359
        Gazette notice of, **2**, 1360
        grant of, effect, **2**, 1364
        grounds of, **2**, 1359
        service of copies, **2**, 1360
        spouse of debtor, by, **2**, 1377
        time for presenting, **2**, 1362
        who may present, **2**, 1360
    reinvesting of property on, **2**, 1366
    spouse's occupancy rights, to defeat, **2**, 1361
    summary as to, **2**, 1359
    vexatious petition for, **2**, 1365
recall of, **4**, 76
record, sederunt book for, **2**, 1380
reforming procedures, **22**, 645
Register of Inhibitions and Adjudications, *see*
    INHIBITIONS AND ADJUDICATIONS, REGISTER OF

Sequestration—*continued*
regulations, **2**, 1483
removal of trustee, **24**, 130
rent, for, *see* SEQUESTRATION FOR RENT
requirements, failure to comply with, **2**, 1480
Schedule 5 of 1982 Act, **4**, 77
Schedule 8 of 1982 Act, **4**, 71, 72
sequestrated estate, removal of trustee, **24**, 130
sheriff court—
  jurisdiction, **22**, 645
  remission to, **2**, 1335
solicitor, examination of, **13**, 1190
solicitor's lien, in relation to, **20**, 98
  ranking of liens, **20**, 99
stamp duties, exemption, **2**, 1485
statistical report, **2**, 1305
summary procedure, **2**, 1353
tenant, of, **13**, 414
  renunciation of lease, **13**, 438, 439
termination of contract, **9**, 140, 145
trust, **4**, 72
trust estate, **2**, 1320, 1326
trustee in—
  abuse of process, **15**, 469
  beneficiaries' rights, **24**, 49, 50
  as lessor, **13**, 175
  personal rights, and, **18**, 694
unincorporated body, **2**, 1321; **4**, 72
wills, conditions relating to sequestration, **25**, 873
Sequestration Commissioners
absence of, duties in, **2**, 1305
advisory functions, **2**, 1315
clerk to, **2**, 1317
consultation by permanent trustee, **2**, 1317
default in duties, **2**, 1316
election—
  general provisions, **2**, 1316
  new or additional commissioners, **2**, 1316
  statutory meeting, at, **2**, 1348
expenses etc, **2**, 1317
functions, **2**, 1317, 1352
meetings—
  convening, **2**, 1317, 1350
  duty to hold, **2**, 1352
  record of, **2**, 1317
modified procedure, effect of, **2**, 1355
number of, **2**, 1316
offences by, suspected, reporting, **2**, 1316
proceedings of, **2**, 1352
qualification to be, **2**, 1316, 1352
removal of, **2**, 1316
resignation, **2**, 1316
supervisory functions, **2**, 1317
Sequestration for rent
adjudger against landlord, by, **8**, 379
advantages, **8**, 377
breach, **8**, 385
  good faith as defence to, **8**, 385
  third party, in, **8**, 385
company administration, and, **8**, 390
competence, **8**, 380
debtor, service of action on, **8**, 380
defences, **8**, 381
effect, **8**, 386

Sequestration for rent—*continued*
enforcement of secured debts, **8**, 101
execution, in, **8**, 384
floating charges, and, **8**, 389
future rent, in security of, **8**, 380
generally, **8**, 377; **13**, 351; **14**, 1063; **17**, 1328
goods subject to, **8**, 377
heritable creditor of landlord, by, **8**, 379
hypothec—
  enforcement of, **8**, 377
  goods covered by, **8**, 378
  meaning, **8**, 378
  real right, as, **8**, 377, 378, 387
landlord, by, **8**, 379
liquidation, and, **8**, 388
mercantile sequestration compared, **8**, 377
nature of, **8**, 377
officers of court, exercise by, **8**, 105
ordinary action, **8**, 380
personal action combined, **8**, 380
poinding, competition with, **8**, 387
procedure—
  further, **8**, 382
  initial, **8**, 380
recall, **8**, 382
receivership, and, **8**, 389
roup, **8**, 382
security, in, **8**, 384
summary cause, **8**, 380
three-month rule, **8**, 383, 384
time to pay orders and directions, and, **8**, 391
undefended action, **8**, 382
warrant, **8**, 380
warrant for sale, **8**, 382
who may sequestrate, **8**, 379
Servant
See DOMESTIC SERVICE; MASTER AND SERVANT
Service, contract of
day of employment in relation to, **21**, 805
director—
  generally, **4**, 422
  payments relating to, **4**, 422
obligation, personal element, **15**, 7
See also CONTRACT OF EMPLOYMENT
Service and Heirs, Register of
Department of Registers, kept in, **19**, 820
Service area
motorway, *see* MOTORWAY
special road, on, **20**, 624
valuation for rating, **24**, 663
Service law
civilians subject to, **2**, 614
criminal offences under, **2**, 664
NATO countries, in, **2**, 619
nature of, **2**, 605
Service lines
electricity supply, **9**, 643
Service mark
assignation, **6**, 601
capital gains tax on payments in respect of, **18**, 1600
European Community legislation, generally, **18**, 1615

Service mark—*continued*
licensee—
  tax treatment—
    lump sum payments, **18**, 1599
    periodic payments, **18**, 1598
    royalties, **18**, 1598
owner—
  tax treatment—
    lump sum payments, **18**, 1596
    periodic payments, **18**, 1595
    royalties, **18**, 1595
purchaser—
  tax treatment—
    lump sum payments, **18**, 1599
    periodic payments, **18**, 1598
    royalties, **18**, 1598
royalties, **18**, 1595, 1598
Service occupancy
ejection, action of, **13**, 469
lease compared, **13**, 115, 601
tenant, **11**, 1948
Service of documents
constable's duties in respect of, **16**, 1784
civil proceedings—
  citation, **17**, 1012–1016
    certificate of, **17**, 1018
    irregularity in, **17**, 1020
    outwith Scotland, **17**, 1017
    simplified divorce procedure, **17**, 1019
criminal proceedings—
  citation, **17**, 712
    custody, where accused in, **17**, 718
    failure to appear after, **17**, 720
    outwith Scotland, **17**, 713
messenger-at-arms, by, **16**, 1504; **17**, 1016
post, by—
  solicitor, by, **14**, 1504; **17**, 1016
  statutory interpretation rules as to, **12**, 1208
sheriff officers, by, **14**, 1504; **17**, 1016
Service Pensions Instrument
overlapping benefits, **21**, 1002
Service pipe
water supply, **25**, 524
Servicemen
See ARMED FORCES
Services
competition law, *see* COMPETITION LAW
contract for, distinguished from contract of employment, **9**, 18
director's contract of, and for, **4**, 422
free movement within European Union, **10**, 112, 131–150; **12**, 114, 221
House of Commons, Select Committee on, **5**, 443
legal categories, **6**, 65, 66
payments in respect of, fair rent decisions, **13**, 668
price advertising, **6**, 142
provision of—
  furnished house, lease, **13**, 195
  lease, generally, **13**, 218
  lodgings, **13**, 196
  tenancy excluded from protected tenancy status, **13**, 630, 632
  tenant, by, **13**, 107, 242
restrictive trade practices, **4**, 1247

Services—*continued*
supply of—
  codes of practice, **6**, 72
  consumer protection, **6**, 67–72
  contract for work and materials, **6**, 66
  exclusion clauses, **6**, 71
  legal profession, **6**, 68
  medical profession, **6**, 68
  possession of goods to effect repairs, **6**, 70
  professional services, **6**, 64, 65
  range available, **6**, 64
  trades and vocations, **6**, 69
trade descriptions of, **6**, 126–130
unsolicited—
  generally, **6**, 151
  protection of persons receiving, **6**, 152
Servitude
access, right of—
  alteration of diversion, **18**, 469
  implied, on division of property, **18**, 452–456
  landlocked property, **18**, 454, 457
  least interference or inconvenience to servient proprietor, must cause, **18**, 464
  obstruction, judicial proceedings, **18**, 482
  See also RIGHT OF PASSAGE OR WAY
agreement of, **18**, 450
agreement or undertaking to grant, **18**, 450
altius non tollendi, **6**, 515; **18**, 486
aquae educendae, **25**, 354
aquaeductus, **6**, 515; **18**, 490; **25**, 353
aquaehaustus, **6**, 515; **18**, 281, 287, 288, 490; **25**, 352
aqueduct, **6**, 515; **18**, 490; **25**, 353
authentication, **18**, 450
bleaching and drying of clothes, as to, **18**, 491
bond of, **18**, 450
building contracts, **3**, 159
buildings, affecting, *see* urban *below*
categories, **25**, 350
cattle, watering of, **18**, 469
change of use, **18**, 464
classification, generally, **18**, 483
common interest—
  compared, **18**, 357, 445
  natural servitude, as, **18**, 355
common property, **18**, 23, 26, 28
compulsory acquisition of land—
  creation of servitude on, **18**, 448, 468
  loss of servitude on, **18**, 479
construction, **18**, 450
content, rules as to, **18**, 348
contravention, acquiescence by dominant tenement, **16**, 1616
conveyance, creation in, **18**, 450
creation—
  acquiescence, actings constituting, **18**, 450
  acquiescence, by, **18**, 448, 462
  agreement, bond or grant of servitude, **18**, 450
  compulsory acquisition of land, **18**, 448, 463
  conveyance, in, **18**, 450
  defective drafting, **18**, 450
  express constitution, contract, as, **18**, 469
  generally, **6**, 515; **18**, 448; **25**, 348
  improbative document, **18**, 450

Servitude—*continued*
creation—*continued*
  inference or implication, by, **18**, 448, 452–457
  judicial decree, **18**, 448
  negative servitudes, **18**, 448
  positive servitudes, **18**, 448
  prescription, by, **18**, 448, 458–461, 464
  questions of right, title and capacity affecting, **18**, 449
  rei interventus, actings constituting, **18**, 450
  statutory authority, by, **18**, 463
  verbal agreement, **18**, 450
  written provision, **18**, 448, 450, 451, 464
customary law and, **22**, 392
damages as remedy, **18**, 482
damhead, **18**, 295; **25**, 353
declarator, action of, **18**, 482
defective drafting in deed, **18**, 450
discharge, **6**, 784; **18**, 470
division of property, implied grant or reservation on, **18**, 452–455
  essential to enjoyment of property, right must be, **18**, 453, 454
  single property disposed of in parts, **18**, 455
  where limited right expressly provided, **18**, 453
divot, **6**, 515; **18**, 489
  extent of right, **18**, 464
  restriction of area to which access allowed, **18**, 469
dominant proprietor—
  overriding interests of, **6**, 742
  rights and duties—
    civiliter, servitude rights must be exercised, **18**, 464
    communication to third party, **18**, 464
    damage caused to servient tenement by maintenance works, **18**, 466
    discontinuance or renunciation of right, **18**, 466
    diversion of rights, **18**, 464
    division of dominant tenement, effect, **18**, 465
    extension of rights, **18**, 464
    feuar, exercise by, **18**, 464
    least interference or inconvenience to servient proprietor, must cause, **18**, 464
    maintenance, responsibility for, **18**, 466
    more than one dominant tenement held over same servient tenement, where, **18**, 467
    solely for benefit of dominant tenement, exercise must be, **18**, 464
    tenant, exercise by, **18**, 464, 470
  title and interest to sue, **18**, 481
  whether entitled to indemnity for loss, **6**, 767
dominant tenement—
  benefit to, servitude must constitute, **18**, 444, 464
  division, effect, **18**, 465
  generally, **18**, 7, 350
  heritable property, must be, **18**, 443
  identification in deed, **18**, 451
  more than one held over same servient tenement, where, **18**, 467
  ownership, **18**, 443, 449

Servitude—*continued*
dominant tenement—*continued*
  particular category of persons as, **18**, 443
  party expected to acquire, **18**, 449
  physical changes affecting, **18**, 475
  positive servitude, **18**, 441
  public body as, **18**, 443
  right to obtain substances must be exercised to meet only requirements of, **18**, 444, 464
  rights and duties, enlargement of use or exercise of servitude, **18**, 464
  salmon fishings, **18**, 443, 464
  servient tenement coming into same ownership, **18**, 476
  singular successors, **18**, 440
  what constitutes, **18**, 443
drainage, **18**, 460
easement compared, **18**, 440, 440*n*
eavesdrop, **6**, 515; **18**, 485; **25**, 351
endurance, **18**, 446
English law compared, **18**, 2
exclusive possession, right of, distinguished, **18**, 445
existence of, effect on notice to treat, **5**, 115
expressio unius est exclusio alterius, **18**, 453
extinction, *see* restriction, suspension or extinction *below*
extinguishing, **25**, 348
feal, **18**, 489
fee, **18**, 439
feudal tenure, land held on, **18**, 449
feuing conditions, where conflict with, **18**, 449
fishing rights, whether constituting, **18**, 492
form, **18**, 450
fowling rights, whether constituting, **18**, 492
freedom from restrictions, presumption of, **18**, 450
fuel, **18**, 489
  extent of right, **18**, 464
  generally, **18**, 489
  restriction of area to which access allowed, **18**, 469
fuel, feal and divot, **6**, 515; **18**, 489
generally, **6**, 514, 515; **18**, 439, 440; **19**, 687; **25**, 348
golfing rights, **18**, 491
grant—
  agreement or undertaking as to, **18**, 450
  generally, **18**, 450; **25**, 349
  heritable properties, operative between, **18**, 443
heritable right, as, **18**, 14
identification of respective tenements, **18**, 451
implication—
  creation by, **18**, 448, 452–457
  restriction, suspension or extinction by, **18**, 474
implied, **18**, 257, 452–455
in personam, **18**, 344
in rem, **18**, 346
increase in use, **18**, 464
  level not contemplated when right constituted, to, **18**, 464, 465
infeftment, **18**, 440
inference, creation by, **18**, 448, 452–457
infringement, onus of proof, **18**, 469
interdict, action of, **18**, 482

Servitude—*continued*
interpretation, **12**, 1262
judicial proceedings—
    jurisdiction, generally, **18**, 480
      procedure and forms of action, **18**, 482
    title and interest to sue, **18**, 481
laddergang, **6**, 515*n*
land, running with, **18**, 446
landowner, grant by, **18**, 195
Lands Tribunal for Scotland, jurisdiction, **18**, 480
let properties, **18**, 449
liferent, **18**, 439
liferenter, grant by, **18**, 449
limitation to established uses and restraints, **18**, 440, 447
luminibus non officiendi, **18**, 486
maintenance of facilities, responsibility for, **18**, 466, 484
meaning, **18**, 5; **19**, 687
mineral workings, in relation to, **18**, 491
natural, **25**, 343, 347
    doctrine of common interest, and, **18**, 282
natural property rights distinguished, **18**, 442
nature and origin, **18**, 439, 440
negative, **18**, 347, 441, 444
    creation, **18**, 448, 452
    inapplicability of implication to, **18**, 456
    negative prescription, operation of, **16**, 2121, 2122; **18**, 471
    prescription, no creation by, **18**, 458
    real burden compared, **18**, 381
    unregistered, **18**, 451
no fixed term, **18**, 6
non aedificandi, **6**, 515; **18**, 486
non officiendi luminibus, **6**, 515
obligation to recognise, **16**, 2116
oil pipeline, for, **20**, 267
oneris ferendi, **6**, 515; **18**, 484
overriding interests, as, **6**, 742, 784
ownership, dominant and servient tenements comng into same, **18**, 476
parking, rights as to, **18**, 491
passage, right of, *see* RIGHT OF PASSAGE OR WAY
passage and pasturage, right of, **18**, 487
passive nature, **18**, 468
passive obligations, **18**, 347
pasturage, right of, **6**, 515; **18**, 488
personal, **18**, 7
    acquiescence, creation by, **18**, 462
    generally, **6**, 514
    meaning, **18**, 439
    praedial servitude distinguished, **18**, 439
    rights in Scotland, **6**, 514
pertinents, and, **12**, 1242; **18**, 201
physical changes—
    subsistence of servitude right, whether affecting, **18**, 475
    for which neither party responsible, **18**, 464
positive, **18**, 347, 441
    creation, **18**, 448
    deed, possession following execution, **16**, 2111
    express grant, creation by, **16**, 2111
    implied right where single property disposed of in parts, **18**, 453, 455

Servitude—*continued*
positive—*continued*
    inference, creation by, **18**, 452
    negative prescription, operation of, **18**, 471
    positive prescription, **16**, 2105, 2111; **18**, 458–461
    public right of way distinguished, **16**, 2112
    rural servitudes as, **18**, 483
    unregistered, **18**, 451
possession, **18**, 120*n*, 126*n*
possessory right or remedy, **18**, 461
praedial, **11**, 1109, 1110; **18**, 7
    characteristics—
      dominant tenement, servitude must benefit, **18**, 444
      natural rights of property distinguished, **18**, 442
      positive or negative form, **18**, 441
      restriction to established uses and restraints, **18**, 440, 447
      running with land without transmission, **18**, 446
      separate ownership of tenements, **18**, 443, 449
      servient tenement, heritable property, **18**, 445
    meaning, **18**, 440
    personal servitude distinguished, **18**, 439
    positive and negative, **6**, 515
    rural, **6**, 515
    urban, **6**, 515
prescription—
    creation by—
      drainage, servitude for, **18**, 460
      essential elements, **18**, 458
      increase in change of use of servitude, **18**, 464
      infeftment in quasi-dominant tenement, **18**, 460
      negative servitudes, not applicable to, **18**, 458
      positive servitudes, **18**, 458
      possession—
        actual, **18**, 458
        apparent, **18**, 458
        civil, **18**, 460
        continuous—
          extra-judicial interruption, **18**, 460
          judicial interruption, **18**, 460
          requirement as to, **18**, 460
        physical, **18**, 460
        possession or use for less than prescriptive period, **18**, 461
      prescriptive period, **18**, 459, 460
        possession or use for less than, **18**, 461
      requirements, generally, **18**, 460
      statutory provisions, **18**, 459
    deed, execution following prescriptive period, **18**, 459
    defect in servitude based on express grant, where, **18**, 458
    negative, **18**, 458, 460
      contracting out not permitted, **18**, 472
      express provision for servitude, where, **18**, 472
      negative servitudes, **18**, 471

Servitude—*continued*
prescription—*continued*
  negative—*continued*
    positive servitudes, **18**, 471
    prescriptive period, **18**, 472; **22**, 392
    res merae facultatis, exclusion of servitudes
      from, **18**, 473
    statutory provisions, **18**, 472
  prescriptive period, **18**, 472; **22**, 392
  pro indiviso owners, **18**, 443, 449
  proprietary interest distinguished, **18**, 445
  public rights of way, **6**, 517
  public undertakings, rights of, **18**, 493
  quasi-servitude, **25**, 348
  rateable value, whether affecting, **18**, 445
  real, **18**, 7
  real burden compared, **18**, 380, 381, 385
  real condition, as, **18**, 7, 344, 375, 381
  real right, as, **11**, 1101, 1109, 1110; **18**, 5, 347
  registration—
    effectiveness not dependent on repetition in
      subsequent transmissions of property, **18**,
      451
    generally, **18**, 451
    no requirement for, **18**, 447, 451
  requirements of, **18**, 381
  restriction, suspension or extinction—
    change of circumstances, following, **18**, 457,
      476
    creditors, consent of, **18**, 470
    discharge of servitudes, **18**, 470
    express writing, by, **18**, 470
    generally, **18**, 6; **25**, 348
    implication from actings, by, **18**, 474
    negative prescription, by operation of, **18**, 471–
      473
    prescriptive period, **18**, 472
    statutory provisions or powers, **18**, 477–479
    tenant of dominant tenement, consent of, **18**,
      470
    uninfeft proprietor, **18**, 470
  restriction to known types, **18**, 381
  rights or burdens not regarded as, **18**, 444
  rights resembling but not constituting, **18**, 492,
    493
  riparian ownership burdened by, **18**, 281
    aquaehaustus, **18**, 281, 287
  Roman law, derivation from, **18**, 440
  rural—
    aquaeductus, **18**, 490
    aquaehaustus, **18**, 281, 287, 490
    classification, generally, **18**, 483
    divot, **6**, 515; **18**, 489
    feal, **6**, 515; **18**, 489
    fuel, **6**, 515; **18**, 464, 469, 489
    meaning, **18**, 483
    pasturage, right of, **18**, 488
    positive servitudes, as, **18**, 483
    right of passage or way, *see* RIGHT OF PASSAGE
      OR WAY
    water on land, rights in relation to, **18**, 490
  sand, gravel or stone, right to quarry, **18**, 491
  seaware and seaweed, right to take, **18**, 318, 491

Servitude—*continued*
servient proprietor—
  no positive obligation on, **18**, 441, 468
  ownership, rights of—
    exercise of, **18**, 469
    retention, **18**, 469
  title and interest to sue, **18**, 481
servient tenement—
  burden on—
    exclusive possession, right of, distinguished,
      18, 445
    proprietary interest distinguished, **18**, 445
  dominant   tenement   coming   into   same
    ownership, **18**, 476
  generally, **18**, 7
  heritable property, must be, **18**, 443
  identification in deed, **18**, 451
  negative servitude, **18**, 441
  ownership, **18**, 443, 449
  physical changes affecting, **18**, 475
  singular successors, **18**, 440
  servitus in faciendo consistere nequit principle, **18**,
    441, 484
severance of property, implied servitude created
  on, **18**, 452–455
  where   limited   right   of   access   expressly
    provided, **18**, 453
significance of, in conveyancing, **6**, 516
singular successors—
  dominant tenement, **18**, 440
  servient tenement, **18**, 440
sinks, of, **25**, 351
sporting rights, whether constituting, **18**, 492
stillicide, right of, **6**, 515; **18**, 485; **25**, 351
substances, right to take—
  fuel, feal and divot, **6**, 515; **18**, 464, 489
  must be exercised to meet only requirements of
    dominant tenement, **18**, 444
  sand, gravel or stone, **18**, 491
  seaware and seaweed, **18**, 491
successors in ownership, **18**, 446
superiority, whether qualifying, **18**, 443
support, right of, **18**, 254, 257, 258
  generally, **18**, 483, 484
  oneris ferendi, **18**, 484
  tigni immittendi, **18**, 484
suspension,   *see*   restriction,   suspension   or
  extinction *above*
suspension and interdict, action of, **18**, 482
tenant, may not be created in favour of, **18**, 449
thirlage, whether constituting, **18**, 492
tigni immittendi, **6**, 515; **18**, 484
transfer of ownership, and, **18**, 604
transmission, no requirement for, **18**, 446
trustees' power to grant, **18**, 449
urban—
  categories, **18**, 483
  classification, generally, **18**, 483
  eavesdrop, right of, **18**, 485
  light and prospect, protection of, **18**, 483, 486
  meaning, **18**, 483
  stillicide, right of, **18**, 485
  support, right of, generally, **18**, 483, 484
  water disposal, facilities affecting, **18**, 483, 485

Servitude—*continued*
validity resting upon its being known to the law, **18**, 451
variation or discharge, Lands Tribunal for Scotland, jurisdiction and powers, **18**, 477, 478
warrandice, obligation of, **18**, 705, 705*n*
water—
  discharge onto servient tenement, rights as to, **18**, 491
  disposal from buldings, urban servitude right, **18**, 483, 485
  servitude rights, generally, **18**, 483, 490; **25**, 343, 347, 348–354
water-gang, **25**, 353
way, right of, *see* RIGHT OF PASSAGE OR WAY
wayleaves, **6**, 517; **18**, 493
Set (let)
meaning, **13**, 103
Set and sale, action of
ship as subject, **21**, 107
  private treaty, sale by, **21**, 138
  public roup, sale by, **21**, 138
  ship in co-ownership, where, **21**, 137, 138
Set-off
agent and third party, between, **1**, 621
characterisation, **17**, 360
discharge of contract, **17**, 275
Settlement (immigration)
advantage over naturalisation, **12**, 121
dependants, **12**, 266
employment, **12**, 174
entry clearance, **12**, 151
excluded categories, **12**, 241
  change from, **12**, 241
family relationship, on grounds of, **12**, 268
family reunion or creation by, **12**, 267
  aunt, **12**, 289, 290
  brother, **12**, 289, 290
  child, **12**, 267, 268
    adoption, child entering for, **12**, 279
    adoptive parents, **12**, 279
    born in UK who is not British citizen, **12**, 284
    children, **12**, 279
    conditions of admission, **12**, 281, 282
    entry clearance, **12**, 280
    generally, **12**, 279
    leave to enter or remain, **12**, 280
    maintenance and accommodation requirements, **12**, 283
    meaning, **12**, 279
    parent, meaning, **12**, 279
    'serious and compelling family or other considerations', **12**, 281
    'sole responsibility' of parent, **12**, 281
    step-parents, **12**, 279
    welfare of primary consideration, **12**, 279
  entry clearance, **12**, 268
  fiancé or fiancée, **12**, 267, 268, 274–277
    entry clearance, **12**, 274
    leave to enter, **12**, 274
      conditions of, **12**, 274, 276
      variation after marriage, **12**, 277

Settlement—*continued*
fiancé or fiancée—*continued*
  family reunion or creation by—*continued*
    maintenance and accommodation, consideration of, **12**, 276
    nature of marriage, **12**, 274
    'primary purpose' rule, **12**, 274
    variation of leave after marriage, **12**, 277
  grandparent, **12**, 285–288
    eligibility, **12**, 286
    maintenance, accommodation and dependency requirements, **12**, 287, 288
  homosexual relationships, **12**, 269*n*
  leave to enter and remain, **12**, 271
  marriage after admission for other purposes, **12**, 278
  nature of marriage—
    fiancé or fiancée, **12**, 275
    spouse, **12**, 271
  parent, **12**, 285–288
    eligibility, **12**, 286
    maintenance, accommodation and dependency requirements, **12**, 287, 288
  'primary purpose' condition—
    fiancé or fiancée, **12**, 275
    spouse, **12**, 272
  proof of marriage, **12**, 273
  sexually discriminatory nature of rules, **12**, 267
  sister, **12**, 289, 290
  spouse, **12**, 267, 269–273
    entry clearance, **12**, 270
      conditions for, **12**, 271–273
    leave to enter and remain, **12**, 270
    maintenance and accommodation, consideration of, **12**, 272
    marriage after admission for other purpose, **12**, 278
    meaning, **12**, 269
    nature of marriage, **12**, 271
    'primary purpose' rule, **12**, 271
      burden of proof, **12**, 271
    proof of marriage, **12**, 273
  uncle, **12**, 289, 290
generally, **12**, 121
groups exempted from immigration control, **12**, 128
Immigration Rules categories leading to, **12**, 241
leave to enter—
  indefinite, **12**, 173
  variation, **12**, 182
nationality not affected by, **12**, 121
naturalisation following, **12**, 121
passengers coming for, Immigration Rules, **12**, 149
passports, **12**, 121
settled Commonwealth citizen, wife and children of, **12**, 125
special vouchers, **12**, 158
work permit holder, **12**, 244
Seven-year rule
declarator of death, action for, **6**, 1062; **25**, 652
missing person, **25**, 651
Several fishery, grant of right of
See SHELLFISH
Severance
See COMPULSORY ACQUISITION

Severe disablement allowance
absent from Great Britain, claimant, **21**, 1021, 1022
adjudication, **21**, 989, 1164, 1166
age of claimant, **21**, 942, 943
age related addition, **21**, 948
child receiving, disentitlement to child benefit, **21**, 962
contribution record of claimant, **21**, 941
dependent adult, increase where, **21**, 1017
dependent child, increase where, **21**, 1015
disablement questions, **21**, 989
entitlement, **21**, 801, 942
   disqualification, **21**, 947
   incapacity for work, **21**, 947
   pensionable age, claimant of, **21**, 943, 944
   previous entitlement, where, **21**, 945
exclusions, **21**, 943
extent of disability, **21**, 942
full-time education, claimant receiving, **21**, 943
generally, **21**, 941
incapacity for work, **21**, 947
income support—
   disability premium, **21**, 1074
   pensioner premium, **21**, 1074
overlapping benefits, **21**, 998
pensionable age, claimant of, **21**, 943, 944
rate, **21**, 941
statutory sick pay, interaction with, **21**, 912
successive industrial accidents, **21**, 990
unforeseen aggravation, where, **21**, 989
Sewage
authority—
   discharge by, **25**, 412
   expenses, **25**, 430
   powers, **25**, 430
committee, **14**, 456
compensation, **25**, 439
control, generally, **25**, 429
discharge into river, **19**, 22
domestic, pollution of non-tidal river by, **18**, 299
effluent—
   discharge—
      consent to, **25**, 417
      lawful, **25**, 411
      prohibition of, **25**, 410
      sewage authority, by, **25**, 412
   generally, **25**, 408
   meaning, **25**, 409
   water, pollution of, **14**, 2079
facilities, agreements in respect of, **25**, 438
finance, **14**, 458
flood prevention scheme, **14**, 467
local authority, functions of, **14**, 456, 457
non-domestic rate, **14**, 859
officers, **14**, 456
physical damage caused by, **14**, 2045
reform, **14**, 46
roads, agreements in respect of, **25**, 437
sewage farm, construction or extension, **19**, 15
sewage treatment works—
   agreement in respect of, **25**, 438
   construction, **19**, 15

Sewage—_continued_
system—
   maintenance, **25**, 434, 435
   public sewers, provision of, **25**, 432
   septic tanks, **25**, 431
   use of, **25**, 440
   vesting of, **25**, 433
trade effluent, _see_ TRADE EFFLUENT
water pollution, **14**, 2079
Sewer
alteration, **19**, 19_n_
construction, **19**, 19_n_; **25**, 436
exemption from rating, **24**, 735
exemptions from building regulations, **3**, 209
inadequate, liability for, **14**, 2122
junctions with, **19**, 332
local authority duties and powers, **19**, 330
matter or substance prejudicial to health, **19**, 334
meaning, **24**, 735
owners' and occupiers' rights and duties, **19**, 331
private, **19**, 332
public, provision of, **25**, 432
public health nuisance, as, **19**, 305
support, right of, **14**, 1693
trade effluents discharged into, **19**, 330, 333, 334
treatment works, **19**, 332
   private, **19**, 332
vesting in local authorities, **19**, 332
warranty as to, **6**, 563
Sex change
See GENDER
Sex discrimination
advertisements, restriction on, **17**, 45
advocate, instruction of, **13**, 1347
carrier, by, **3**, 615
complaints and appeals, **6**, 994, 996
conciliation in case of claim, **9**, 315
EEC law, **9**, 14; **10**, 154, 171, 172
European Convention on Human Rights, **12**, 6, 85, 86
incapacity as argument for, **11**, 1053
international conventions on, **12**, 5
lawful and unlawful distinguished, **19**, 1256
occupational pension schemes—
   Barber judgment, **21**, 1222, 1223, 1276
   different normal pension ages, **21**, 1280
   equal treatment principle, **21**, 1278
      exemptions from, **21**, 1279
   generally, **21**, 1222, 1276
   legislative provisions, **21**, 1222, 1277
   levelling up, compulsory, **21**, 1282
   maternity and family leave provisions, **21**, 1281
   non-compliance, **21**, 1282
   Occupational Pension Board's power to modify schemes, **21**, 1283
Office of Fair Trading licensing, **6**, 21
partner, expulsion, **16**, 1061
partnership, in offer of, **16**, 1016
police force, appointments to, **16**, 1747, 1747_n_
private clubs, **19**, 1257
prizes, **19**, 1258
sheriff court jurisdiction, **6**, 1128; **17**, 1251
sport, in, **19**, 1255–1258

Sex discrimination—*continued*
status, concept of, **11**, 1068, 1071
unfair dismissal, **9**, 231, 357
Sex education
European Convention on Human Rights, **12**, 92
Sex shop
licensing, **14**, 119, 527
residential area, in, **14**, 2083
Sexual behaviour
breach of the peace, **7**, 455
consensual, **7**, 294
legal control, generally, **7**, 294
Sexual immorality
contract promoting, **15**, 763, 767
Sexual offence
abuse of trust, **7**, 318
anal penetration, **7**, 296, 312
art and part liability of victim, **7**, 178
assault, **7**, 217, 223, 295
bestiality, **7**, 295, 320
buggery, **7**, 4
categorisation, **7**, 295
child victims—
    generally, **10**, 1136
    heterosexual offences, **10**, 1043
    homosexual offences, **10**, 1044
    See also CHILD-CHILDREN (sexual activities);
      CHILD ABUSE
complainers, identification in court, **10**, 552
Criminal Injuries Compensation Scheme, **7**, 2, 4,
    7, 9, 11
evidence in cases of, **10**, 502, 508
    character of victim, admissibility of facts as to,
      10, 634
    Scottish Law Commission recommendations,
      22, 668
homosexual *see* HOMOSEXUAL ACT
'homosexual rape', **7**, 296
incest, *see* INCEST
indecent assault, *see* INDECENT ASSAULT
indecent exposure, *see* INDECENT EXPOSURE
legal control, generally, **7**, 294
non-consensual activity, **7**, 294
oral penetration, **7**, 296
public display of sexuality, **7**, 294
public morality, against, **7**, 295
rape, *see* RAPE
sexual intercourse—
    assault, when, **7**, 217, 223
    mentally defective woman, with, **7**, 301
    under-age girl, with, **7**, 301, 304, 308
shamelessly indecent conduct, **7**, 83, 295, 472
step-parent and stepchild, **10**, 1217
vaginal penetration, **7**, 296
young person, against—
    boys, **7**, 310
    child pornography, **7**, 311
    generally, **7**, 295
    girls—
      acts falling short of sexual intercourse, **7**, 13, 309
      sexual intercourse, **7**, 301, 304, 308
Shamelessly indecent conduct
accused must be aware of indecency or obscenity,
    7, 470

Shamelessly indecent conduuct—*continued*
actus reus, **7**, 37
child, towards, **3**, 1235, 1236
corrupt and deprave, must be liable to, **7**, 470
elements of, **7**, 470
film shown to consenting adults in private, **7**, 13,
    83, 468
generally, **7**, 83, 467
gross and shameless indecency, **7**, 312
homosexual acts, **7**, 312, 467, 468
incestuous relationships, **7**, 315
indecent exposure, *see* INDECENT EXPOSURE
limited company, by, **7**, 471
moral or social repugnancy, **7**, 472
obscene article, selling or exposing for sale, **7**, 469
proof of knowledge, **7**, 90
public morality, offence against, **7**, 295
shamelessly, use of term, **7**, 83
Watt v Annan, decision in, **7**, 13, 83, 468
young person, with, **7**, 309, 310
Shannon
free zone, as, **7**, 1164
Share capital
authorised minimum, of public company, **4**, 355
calls, **4**, 361
certificate as to, failure to obtain, **4**, 723
company having, admission as member, **4**, 344
company limited by shares, in, **4**, 351
function of, **4**, 350
government control of raising of, **4**, 350
groups of companies, **4**, 370
lien over shares, **4**, 364
limited company, reduction by, **4**, 359
permissible capital payment, **4**, 367
redeemable shares, **4**, 365
redemption, procedure after, **4**, 368
reduction of—
    limited company, by, **4**, 359
    variation of capital other than, **4**, 358
unlimited company, **4**, 312
variation of, other than reduction, **4**, 358
Share certificate
fraud, obtained by, **11**, 771
generally, **4**, 371
non-negotiability, **4**, 103
Share fisherman
industrial tribunal, jurisdiction of, **9**, 331
unemployment benefit, eligibility for—
    absence of fish, failure to work due to, **21**, 861
    conditions, **21**, 860, 861
    generally, **21**, 860
    good cause ground, **21**, 861, 862
    intention of further fishing with vessel ceased,
      where, **21**, 861, 861*n*
    repairs and maintenance, failure to work due
      to, **21**, 861
    weather, failure to work due to, **21**, 861
unfair dismissal, **9**, 211
Share scheme
employees, investment transactions for, **12**, 1307
Shared ownership agreement
assured tenancy status excluded, **13**, 636, 649
Shareholder
advance corporation tax, **19**, 1521

Shareholder—*continued*
aggrieved, petition by, **4**, 996
assets of company, no direct interest in, **25**, 12
cash, right to receive dividend in, **4**, 468
farming company, controlling shareholding in, **19**, 1555
International Court of Justice claims, **19**, 743
liability, petition granting relief from, **4**, 995
management, participating in, liability on insolvency, **4**, 319
members referred to as, **4**, 344
minority—
  action for reduction, **4**, 470
  disputes, resolution of, **25**, 29
  expectations of, **25**, 28
  influence, **25**, 28
  position of, **25**, 28
  protection—
    class rights, variation of, right to object to—
      court, powers of, **4**, 522
      minority, rights of, **4**, 521
    Foss v Harbottle, rule in—
      company in question, meaning, **4**, 462
      exceptions, **4**, 464
      interests of justice, **4**, 469
      origins, **4**, 463
      right of majority to, **4**, 462
  investigation—
    affairs of company, of, *see* AFFAIRS OF COMPANY
    interests in shares, into, right to requisition—
      concert party agreement, **4**, 515
      generally, **4**, 515
      minorities, rights of, **4**, 516
      notice, failure to comply with, **4**, 518
      preparation of report, **4**, 517
  just and equitable rule, petition to wind up based on—
    Companies Act 1985 s59, relationship to, **4**, 499
    company, position of, **4**, 502
    contingent creditors, position of, **4**, 504
    contributory, position of, **4**, 503
    court's powers, **4**, 501
    deadlock in management, **4**, 511
    directors, position of, **4**, 504
    general basis for petition, **4**, 505
    illegality of purpose, **4**, 508
    impossibility of purpose, **4**, 508
    incorporated partnership, **4**, 512
    older Scottish decisions, **4**, 507
    petitioner's conduct, reasonableness of, **4**, 500
    preliminary consideration, **4**, 506
    primary purpose of company, ascertainment of, **4**, 509
    quasi-partnership—
      application of principle in Scotland, **4**, 514
      generally, **4**, 512
      identifying, **4**, 513
    right to present, **4**, 498
    substratum of company, failure of, **4**, 510
    unfair prejudice remedy, history of, **4**, 478

Shareholder—*continued*
minority—*continued*
  protection—*continued*
    meetings of members, *see* MEETINGS OF MEMBERS
    objects clause, alteration in, right to object to—
      court, powers of, **4**, 520
      minority, rights of, **4**, 519
    rights of minority shareholders—
      company in question, meaning, **4**, 462*n*
      Foss v Harbottle, rule in—
        company in question, meaning, **4**, 462
        exceptions, **4**, 464
        interests of justice, **4**, 469
        origins, **4**, 463
        recognised branches of, **4**, 462
      fraud on minority, **4**, 467
      illegal acts, **4**, 465
      interests of justice exception, **4**, 469
      modern developments, **4**, 471
      personal right of shareholder, infringement of, **4**, 468
      procedural aspects, **4**, 470
      qualified majority, irregularity in resolution requiring, **4**, 466
      ultra vires acts, **4**, 465
      unfairly prejudicial conduct, **4**, 482–497; **25**, 16
  representative action, **4**, 470
  rights, **25**, 28
opposing, ordinary action, **4**, 956
personal right of, infringement of, **4**, 464, 468
qualified majority, resolution requiring, irregularity in, **4**, 466
qualified privilege of, **4**, 396
rights—
  capital, share of, **25**, 13
  capital assets, participation in, **25**, 14
  development of, **25**, 14
  general meetings, relating to, **25**, 13
  income, relating to, **25**, 14
  net worth, share of, **25**, 13
  payment, **25**, 13
  profits, participation in, **25**, 13
  public registers, access to, **25**, 13
  recent developments, **25**, 3
  security of repayment, **25**, 14
  shareholding, distinguished from rights attaching to, **25**, 14
  variation, valuation on, **25**, 9
  voting power, **25**, 13
sale of control, general offer relating to, **4**, 549
scheme of arrangement, petition for, **4**, 984
takeover, analysis of interests on, **4**, 538
See also COMPANY (members)
Shares
allotment, consideration for, **4**, 356
arrestment, **8**, 269, 284
articles of association, and, **25**, 50, 52, 63, 68
  pre-emption rights under, **4**, 377
assignation, *see* transfers *below*
bank, of, banker's lien over, **20**, 85
bearer share warrants, **4**, 371

Shares—*continued*
'bed and breakfasting', **19**, 1600
building society, *see* BUILDING SOCIETY
capital, *see* SHARE CAPITAL
certificates, *see* SHARE CERTIFICATE
charity, held by, **3**, 1103
class rights—
    articles, provision in, **4**, 347
    class, meaning, **4**, 347
    memorandum, no provision made in, **4**, 347
    variation of, right to object to—
        court, powers of, **4**, 522
        minority's right to object, **4**, 521
classification, **25**, 46
company, rights in security, **20**, 43
company limited by, *see* COMPANY (limited)
director—
    dealings by, **4**, 425
    interests in, **4**, 428
employee shares, rights relating to, **4**, 347
financial assistance for share acquisition, **4**, 369
forfeiture of, **4**, 362
holding company, in, held by subsidiary, **4**, 370
insider dealing, *see* INSIDER DEALING
interests in—
    concert parties, arrangements for notifying, **4**, 346
    disclosure of, **4**, 346
    exclusions, **4**, 346
    information, failure to respond to company's request for, **4**, 346
    interest, meaning, **4**, 346
    investigation by company into, right to requisition—
        generally, **4**, 515
        minorities, rights of, **4**, 516
        notice, failure to comply with, **4**, 518
        preparation of report, **4**, 517
    matters included in, **4**, 515*n*
    registration of, **4**, 346
investment, as, **12**, 1308
investment transactions designed to acquire more than 75 per cent in body corporate, **12**, 1307
issue of—
    agreement to take shares, **4**, 352
    authority for, **4**, 353
    directors acting *ultra vires*, **4**, 352
    offers of shares, **4**, 352
    public, to, **4**, 360
    unfairly prejudicial conduct, as, **4**, 490
issued, variation of class rights, **4**, 349
lien over, **4**, 364
listed, **25**, 66
market in, *see* MARKET IN SHARES
meaning, **25**, 5
negotiable instrument, as, **4**, 103
open-ended investment company, in, **12**, 1308
ordinary—
    class rights, **4**, 347
    pre-emption rights, **4**, 354
own, purchase by company, **4**, 366
    funding, **4**, 367
    procedure, **4**, 368
paid-up, **4**, 351

Shares—*continued*
pre-emption rights, **4**, 354, 377
preference—
    class rights, **4**, 347
    dividends, special rights in relation to, **4**, 461
    pre-emption rights, **4**, 354
    redeemable, class rights, **4**, 347
purchase of, winding up following, **4**, 735
quoted, **25**, 58
redeemable, **4**, 365
redeemable preference, rights relating to, **4**, 347
redemption of, winding up following, **4**, 735
registration, refusal of, **4**, 377
renounceable allotment letter, issued on, renunciation of, **4**, 377
restrictions on, **4**, 534
retention over, **4**, 364
rights in security, **20**, 43
Sale of Goods Act, not covered by, **20**, 805
share capital, *see* SHARE CAPITAL
shareholders, *see* SHAREHOLDER
speculation on, **15**, 768
surrender of, **4**, 363
transfer of shares—
    agreement to, **4**, 373
    assignation, **6**, 597; **20**, 55, 55*n*
    form of, **4**, 374
    generally, **4**, 372
    pre-emption rights under articles, **4**, 377
    reduction, **13**, 37
    registration, refusal of, **4**, 377
    restrictions on, **25**, 63
    right to transfer, **4**, 377
    share transfer, printer's imprint not required, **17**, 3
    stamp duty on, **4**, 375
transmission of shares, **4**, 372, 376
trust—
    calls on shares, **24**, 230
    shares held in, **4**, 357
unissued, variation of class rights, **4**, 348
unquoted—
    hypothetical willing purchaser, **25**, 62
    hypothetical willing seller, **25**, 61
    specific provisions, **25**, 59
valuation—
    articles of association, governed by, **25**, 8
    asset value, **25**, 22
    assets, **25**, 21
    commercial transactions, **25**, 7
    composition of shareholding, **25**, 42
    constitutional documents, governed by, **25**, 8
    contract law, **25**, 6
    custom and practice, importance of, **25**, 3
    date, **4**, 497
    discounted cash flow basis, **25**, 24
    disputes, resolution of, **25**, 29
    dividends, **25**, 18
    earnings, **25**, 20
    fair values, **25**, 8
    financial position of company, **25**, 30–43
    general principles, **25**, 12–29

Shares—*continued*
valuation—*continued*
  holdings—
    controlling, **25**, 27
    minority, **25**, 28
    non-controlling, **25**, 28
  hope value, **25**, 23
  inter-relationship of factors, **25**, 11
  market—
    actual or assumed, **25**, 46–52
    open, **25**, 10, 60
    transactions, **25**, 7
  notional disposal, **25**, 64
  parties—
    rights, alteration of, **25**, 9
    status, alteration of, **25**, 9
  practice, evolution of, **25**, 3
  principal factors, **25**, 17
  property—
    alteration of rights in or to, **25**, 9
    passing, meaning, **25**, 12
  purpose, **25**, 2
  quasi-partnership, **25**, 15
  risk and return, **25**, 44, 45
  sale at arm's length, **25**, 5
  Scottish legal tradition, **25**, 4
  share, meaning, **25**, 5
  shareholder, rights of, *see* SHAREHOLDER
  shareholding, *see* SHAREHOLDING
  statute law, **25**, 6
  tax liability, for purpose of computing, **25**, 53
  trade custom, **25**, 25
  transfers, printer's imprint, requirement not applicable, **17**, 3
  unfair prejudice, **25**, 16
  unfairly prejudicial conduct, and, **4**, 496, 497
  yield, selection of, **25**, 19
value, factors influencing—
  current market forces, **25**, 1
  custom and practice, **25**, 1
  economic conditions, **25**, 1
  expected future market behaviour, **25**, 1
  legal requirements, **25**, 1
  profitability of company, **25**, 1
winding up following redemption or purchase of, **4**, 735
Sheep
Chernobyl accident, affected by, **2**, 227
dipping, orders for, **2**, 182
exportation of, **2**, 227
meat, *see* SHEEPMEAT
milk, **11**, 438
obligation to take over stock left by tenant, **13**, 241
operations on, **2**, 246
stocks bound to land, **1**, 777
Sheepmeat
aid and intervention systems, **1**, 934
annual ewe headage payment, **1**, 935
basic prices, **1**, 934
export refunds, **1**, 936
import levy, **1**, 936
reference prices, **1**, 934
variable slaughter premium, **1**, 935

Sheet-glass works
adult males in, **9**, 70
Shell
See EXPLOSIVES
Shellfish
cleansing of, **11**, 403
continental shelf, on, rights of coastal state, **21**, 19
crabs—
  prohibition on taking and sale of certain, **11**, 145*n*, 168
  size limits, **11**, 145*n*
disease, powers in relation to, **11**, 163, 166
early legislation, **11**, 118, 121, 122
fish farms, **11**, 57, 60
food, preparation and sale as, **11**, 312
importation, powers in relation to, **11**, 164, 165
lobsters, prohibition on taking and sale of certain, **11**, 168
meaning, **11**, 57*n*, 155; **18**, 521
mussels, *see* MUSSELS
oysters, *see* OYSTERS
protection of shellfish fisheries, **11**, 161
public fisheries, disease or pests at, **11**, 166
public right to take, *see* FISHING
regulations as to, **11**, 407
restoration of shellfish fisheries, grants and loans for, **11**, 162
sea fish, as, **11**, 183*n*
Sea Fisheries (Shellfish) Act 1967 ..., **11**, 155
several fishery, grant of right of, **11**, 155, 157
  cesser of rights, **11**, 160
  effect, **11**, 158
  licensing powers in relation to, **11**, 159
  making and maintaining beds, **11**, 157
  time limit, **11**, 157
white fish, as, **11**, 209
Sheltered housing
restriction on right to buy, **11**, 1955
secure tenant's right to acquire, exclusion from, **11**, 1972
security of tenure, **11**, 1947
Sheriff
antiquity of office, **5**, 645; **6**, 1022
appointment, **6**, 1038; **22**, 508
Chancery, of, *see* SHERIFF OF CHANCERY
children's hearing—
  appeals, **3**, 1275, 1300, 1358, 1361, 1362
  finding as to grounds, **3**, 1293, 1333, 1334
  remit of court case to, **3**, 1378
children's panel reporters' right to conduct proceedings before, **3**, 1284
county administration, role in, **14**, 23, 26
court, *see* SHERIFF COURT
depute, *see* SHERIFF DEPUTE
disqualification, **6**, 1042
duties, **6**, 1046, 1054; **17**, 510
fitness for office, investigation into, **6**, 1051
floating sheriffs, **6**, 1048
hereditary office, **6**, 1023, 1024; **14**, 508
  abolition of, **17**, 513; **22**, 521
history, **5**, 645–647; **6**, 1022, 1028; **14**, 23, 26; **22**, 507, 508, 521, 581
honorary sheriffs, **6**, 1048
illness or incapacity, **6**, 1049

Sheriff—*continued*
judicial functions, **1**, 210; **17**, 511
lawburrows, powers in relation to, **13**, 901
leave, **6**, 1044, 1053
oath—
 of allegiance, **6**, 1041
 judicial, **6**, 1041
pension, **6**, 1040
placing request appeals, **8**, 887
precedence, **6**, 1045
principal, *see* SHERIFF PRINCIPAL
prison, right to visit and inspect, **16**, 1422
procurator fiscal, appointment of, **17**, 532
protection from proceedings, **2**, 81
qualification for office, **6**, 1042; **22**, 521
removal from office, **6**, 1042, 1049
residence, **6**, 1043
retirement, **6**, 1040
safeguarder, appointment, **3**, 1362
salary and allowances, **6**, 1039
sheriff clerk, *see* SHERIFF CLERK
sheriff principal, *see* SHERIFF PRINCIPAL
sheriff substitutes, *see* SHERIFF SUBSTITUTE
sheriffdom, *see* SHERIFFDOM
special educational needs, children with, decisions
 on, **8**, 920
statutory functions, **1**, 208
suspension from office, **6**, 1048
temporary sheriffs—
 floating, **6**, 1048
 honorary, **6**, 1048
 principal, **6**, 1047, 1049
travelling expenses, **6**, 1039
warrant, execution of, **14**, 1501
Sheriff clerk
appointment, **6**, 1032
deputation, grant of, **6**, 1032
duties, **6**, 1032, 1054
exempted person under Financial Services Act
 1986, as, **12**, 1323
history of office, **6**, 1032
removal, **6**, 1032
security of tenure, **6**, 1032
service of petition for variation of trust, **24**, 83
Sheriff court
advocate appearing before, dress, **13**, 1323
appeal to—
 local government action, against, **1**, 338; **14**,
  119–121
 statutory appeals and applications, *see* statutory
  applications and appeals *below*
appropriate, meaning, **4**, 41, 70
arrestment—
 arrest of ship, jurisdiction, **8**, 322
 service of, **8**, 258
authentic instruments, **8**, 474
caution for expenses, **3**, 996
civil legal aid, **13**, 1034, 1045
civil procedure—
 ordinary causes, *see* ORDINARY CAUSES
 small claims, *see* SMALL CLAIMS
 summary causes, *see* SUMMARY CAUSES
confirmation as executor-creditor, jurisdiction, **8**,
 351

Sheriff court—*continued*
court house and offices, **6**, 1037
Court of Session, appeal to, **6**, 924; **17**, 1463
criminal legal aid, **13**, 1052
criminal procedure, *see* CRIMINAL PROCEDURE—
 solemn procedure—
  summary procedure
diligence, exercise by sheriff officers, **8**, 105
districts, **5**, 649; **6**, 1025, 1049
fatal accident inquiries, *see* FATAL ACCIDENT
 INQUIRY
first proceedings, civil legal aid, **13**, 1034
foreign enforcement of judgments made in, **8**, 427
High Court of Admiralty, merger of jurisdiction
 with, **4**, 2
historical background, **5**, 645; **6**, 1022–1024; **17**,
 509–516
inhibition, **8**, 133
inhibition on the dependence, **8**, 134
Judgment Convention judgments, **8**, 454, 455
judicial precedent—
 civil jurisdiction, generally, **22**, 296–301
 Court of Session, binding decisions of, **22**, 298
 criminal jurisdiction, generally, **22**, 313–318
 English criminal courts, **22**, 318
 High Court of Justiciary, **22**, 314, 315
 historical background, **22**, 296
 House of Lords, decisions of binding, **22**, 297
 sheriff court decisions, **22**, 299, 300, 316
 sheriff principal, binding decisions of, **22**, 299
 sheriff and sheriff principal, decisions
  distinguished, **22**, 299, 300
 stare decisis, doctrine of, **22**, 544
jurisdiction—
 administrative, general, **1**, 204, 208, 210
 adoption of children, **6**, 1064
 aliment, action of, **6**, 1062; **22**, 657
 appellate, **17**, 1248; **22**, 508
 arbitration, **6**, 1065
 bankruptcy, **6**, 1066
 civil jurisdiction, **5**, 651; **6**, 1059–1062
 clubs, licensing and gaming, **6**, 1067
 commissary business, **6**, 1068
 common property, division and sale of, **6**, 1062
 company, winding up, **6**, 1069
 consumer redress, **6**, 168, 169
 contempt proceedings, **6**, 309
 criminal jurisdiction generally, **5**, 654; **6**, 1056;
  17, 516
 declarator, actions of, **6**, 1062; **25**, 642
 decrees of court, action for suspension of, **6**,
  1062
 excluded, matters, **6**, 1060
 firth, **4**, 2
 generally, **6**, 1027
 heritable, **5**, 646; **6**, 1055, 1062; **17**, 513
 heritable securities, **6**, 1071
 judicial factors, **6**, 1072; **24**, 237, 238
 maintenance, actions for recovery of, **6**, 1062
 maritime, **1**, 407
 meaning, **4**, 1
 mental health—
  application for admission to hospital,
   approved by, **14**, 1414

Sheriff court—*continued*
jurisdiction—*continued*
  mental health—*continued*
    discharge of patient by, **14**, 1427, 1430
    generally, **6**, 1073, 1118
    guardianship, and, **14**, 1438, 1446, 1480; **22**,
      31
    restriction order, powers on appeal to, **14**,
      1457
  nuisance, **14**, 2013
  private, **4**, 19
  privative, **6**, 1061
  recovery of tax, **19**, 1550
  separation, actions for, **6**, 1062
  sequestration, **2**, 1335; **22**, 645
  social work, **6**, 1074
  statute ousting or adding to, **12**, 1129
  subject matter—
    adjudication, **4**, 7
    consistorial proceedings, **4**, 5
    generally, **4**, 3
    inhibition, **4**, 8
    reduction, **4**, 6
    trusts, **4**, 9
  suspension of charges, **6**, 1062
  territorial, **4**, 2; **6**, 1055, 1056; **17**, 572
  value—
    bankruptcy, **4**, 16
    death, presumption of, **4**, 17
    generally, **4**, 12
    judicial factor, appointment of, **4**, 14
    liquidation, **4**, 15
    maritime proceedings, **4**, 18
    private jurisdiction, **4**, 19
    suspension, **4**, 13
lawburrows, action of, **13**, 906, 907
  prior to 1882, **13**, 902, 904
location of courts, **6**, 1027
maills and duties, action of, **8**, 397
maintenance order made by, application for
  registration, **8**, 572, 573
Ordinary Court Rules, **17**, 1002
organisation and administration—
  administrative directors, **6**, 1049, 1053
  division and disposal of business, **6**, 1053
  general superintendence, **6**, 1049–1052
  generally, **6**, 1025–1027; **22**, 296
  Ordinary Cause Rules, **17**, 1002
  particular superintendence, **6**, 1053
  Rules Council, **6**, 930, 1049–1052
  Scottish Courts Administration, **6**, 1049
  sheriff principal, **6**, 1053
    See also SHERIFF PRINCIPAL
  sheriffdom, *see* SHERIFFDOM
  territorial organisation, **6**, 1025–1027
other courts and tribunals, contrasted with, **4**, 1
personnel—
  auditor of court, **6**, 1035
  messenger-at-arms, **6**, 1036
    See also MESSENGER-AT-ARMS
  procurator fiscal, **6**, 1033, 1034
  sheriff, *see* SHERIFF
  Sheriff of Chancery, *see* SHERIFF OF CHANCERY
  sheriff clerk, *see* SHERIFF CLERK

Sheriff court—*continued*
personnel—*continued*
  sheriff depute, *see* SHERIFF DEPUTE
  sheriff officer, *see* SHERIFF OFFICER
  sheriff principal, *see* SHERIFF PRINCIPAL
  sheriff substitute, *see* SHERIFF SUBSTITUTE
petition for suspension, **3**, 998
public right of way, proceedings relating to, **18**,
  513
recall of arrestment on dependence, caution,
  requirement for, **3**, 997
records—
  access to, **19**, 879
  disposal of, **19**, 869
  retransmission, **19**, 872
  sheriff court books, **6**, 468; **19**, 839
  transmission, **19**, 855, 859, 860
reduction—
  decree, of, **13**, 38
  generally, **13**, 30
  objector ordered to find caution or make
    consignation, **13**, 31
  ope exceptionis, **13**, 31
  principal action, as, **13**, 30
  spouses, financial agreements between, **13**, 30
reform, **22**, 521, 581, 630
registration of foreign judgments, **8**, 468
representation in, **17**, 1003
Rules Council—
  functions and duties, **6**, 1050
  members, appointment of, **6**, 930, 1050, 1052
  qualification, **6**, 1050
  Secretary of State's duty, **6**, 1049
Scottish judgment, enforcement in overseas
  contracting state, **8**, 473
sequestration for rent, **8**, 380
servitude rights, actions concerning, **18**, 480
sessions, **6**, 1053
statutory appeals and applications—
  agriculture, **6**, 1076
  alcoholic liquor, **2**, 81; **6**, 1077; **17**, 1252
  animals, **6**, 1078
  arbitration, **6**, 1079
  armed forces, **6**, 1080
  aviation, **6**, 1081
  betting, **6**, 1082; **17**, 1249
  births, registration of, **6**, 1127
  building, **6**, 1083
  building societies, **6**, 1084
  burial, **6**, 1085
  business names, **6**, 1120
  canals, **6**, 1125
  capital gains tax, **6**, 1109
  children, **6**, 1086
  Church of Scotland, **6**, 1087
  coast protection and flooding, **6**, 1088
  compulsory acquisition, **6**, 1089
  consumer credit, **5**, 924; **6**, 1107
  conveyancing, **6**, 1090
  corporation tax, **6**, 1109
  cremation, **6**, 1085
  criminal law, **6**, 1091
  customs and excise, **6**, 1092
  data protection, **6**, 1128

Sheriff court—*continued*

statutory appeals and applications—*continued*

deaths, registration of, **6**, 1127

debtors, **6**, 1097

docks, **6**, 1106

drugs, **6**, 1117

economic controls, **6**, 1123

education, **6**, 1093

elections, **6**, 1094

employment, **6**, 1095

energy, **6**, 1096

enforcement, **6**, 1097

entertainment, **6**, 1098

environment, **6**, 1099, 1124

explosives, **6**, 1102

family law, **6**, 1100

fire services, **6**, 1101

firearms, **6**, 1102; **17**, 1250

fisheries, **6**, 1103

food, **6**, 1104

friendly and provident societies, **6**, 1105

gaming, **2**, 1592; **6**, 17, 1082, 1249

generally, **1**, 338; **6**, 1075; **17**, 1248

harbours, **6**, 1106

health service, **6**, 1132

housing, **6**, 1108

income tax, **6**, 1109

land drainage, **6**, 1110

land tenure, **6**, 1111

landlord and tenant, **6**, 1112

lawyers and notaries, **6**, 1113

legal aid, **6**, 1113

local government, **6**, 1115

lotteries, **6**, 1082; **17**, 1249

marriages, registration of, **6**, 1127

matrimonial homes, **6**, 1100

medicines, **6**, 1117

mental health, **6**, 1118

mining and minerals, **6**, 1119

nurses, **6**, 1116

partnerships, **6**, 1120

piers, **6**, 1106

pipelines, **6**, 1125

poisons, **6**, 1117

police, **6**, 1121

public finance, **6**, 1123

public health, **6**, 1124; **19**, 340

racial discrimination, **6**, 1128; **17**, 1253

railways, **6**, 1125

rating, **6**, 1126

registration of title, **6**, 1090

road traffic, **6**, 1129

roads and bridges, **6**, 1130

sex discrimination, **6**, 1128; **17**, 1251

shipping, **6**, 1131

social security, **6**, 1132

succession, **6**, 1133

telecommunications, **6**, 1122

town and country planning, **6**, 1134

trade, **6**, 19, 1135

trusts, **6**, 1136; **24**, 160

water, **6**, 1137

weights and measures, **6**, 1138

young persons, **6**, 1086

Sheriff court—*continued*

summary application, proceedings by way of, **4**, 19

suspension as mode of review, **13**, 68

vacation courts, **6**, 1053

Sheriff depute

appointment, **14**, 26; **17**, 514

commission of supply, duties with regard to, **14**, 29

death, effect on sheriff substitute, **17**, 515

generally, **5**, 647

history of office, **6**, 1028

legal qualifications, **6**, 1028; **17**, 511

numbers of, **17**, 514

payment by Crown, **17**, 514

substitute, *see* SHERIFF SUBSTITUTE

Sheriff of Chancery

judicial precedent, and, **22**, 301

service of heirs by, **6**, 1031

transfer of jurisdiction, **6**, 1031

Sheriff officer

Advisory Council of Messengers-at-Arms and Sheriff Officers, **14**, 1504

appointment, **14**, 1509

caution granted for—

generally, **3**, 1000

institution, by, **3**, 986

requirement for, **3**, 1000

commission, **14**, 1509

Court of Session, authority to act given by, **14**, 1504

damages, liability for, **14**, 1511

debt collection, **14**, 1512

duties, **6**, 1036; **14**, 1511

local officer of Crown, as, **14**, 1508

messenger-at-arms, appointment as, **6**, 1036; **14**, 1502

misconduct by, **14**, 1506

negligence, liability for, **14**, 1511

oath, **14**, 1509

office of, **14**, 1508

remuneration, **14**, 1511

supervision, **14**, 1510

suspension or removal, **6**, 1036

value added tax, liability for, **14**, 1511

Sheriff principal

appeal to—

appellate function, evolution of, **6**, 924, 1028, 1029

binding authority of decisions, **22**, 299, 300

civil legal aid, **13**, 1034

generally, **5**, 650; **6**, 1028, 1029; **17**, 514

history of office, **6**, 1028

numbers of, **17**, 514

ordinary causes—

abandonment of, **17**, 1272

decree, error in, **17**, 1274

expenses, **17**, 1271

final judgment, against, **17**, 1256

generally, **17**, 1254

interlocutor, against—

effect of, **17**, 1267

form of, **17**, 1266

hearing, form of, **17**, 1268

Sheriff principal—*continued*
appeal to—*continued*
  ordinary causes—*continued*
    interlocutor, against—*continued*
      incompetent interlocutor, **17**, 1265
      interdict, granting or refusing, **17**, 1257
      interim payment, for, **17**, 1258
      leave, with, **17**, 1263, 1264
      order *ad factum praestandum* for making, **17**, 1258
      powers of sheriff principal, **17**, 1270
      proof, as to mode of, **17**, 1260
      reponing note, refusal of, **17**, 1261
      right of appeal, **17**, 1255
      rules, relief from failure to comply with, **17**, 1273
      scope of, **17**, 1269
      simplified divorce procedure, action under, **17**, 1275
      sisting action, **17**, 1259
      time for, **17**, 1262, 1264
    summary application—
      generally, **6**, 1029; **17**, 1276, 1277
      meaning, **17**, 1276
      sheriff's decision final, **17**, 1278
      statute making no provision for appeal, **17**, 1279
    summary causes, **17**, 1333
chief constable, directions to, **16**, 1740
inquiry into disciplinary hearing, **16**, 1781, 1782
precedent, binding authority of decisions of, **22**, 299, 300
private practice, engaging in, **13**, 1345, 1345*n*
sheriff officer, supervision of, **14**, 1510
sheriff and sheriff principal, decisions distinguished, **22**, 299
title, **17**, 514
Sheriff substitute
appointment, **17**, 515; **22**, 521
death of sheriff depute, effect of, **17**, 515
dismissal, **17**, 515
qualifications, **17**, 515
Sheriffdom
boundaries, alteration of, **4**, 2
criminal jurisdiction, territorial extent, **6**, 1056
establishment, **14**, 23; **22**, 508
existing, abolition of, **4**, 2
new, formation of, **4**, 2
reorganisation, **6**, 1025–1027; **14**, 1509
Sheriffs' Commissions
Register of, **6**, 463; **19**, 820
Shetland
Act of 1611 abolishing foreign laws, **24**, 304
allodial land, transfer of ownership, **18**, 646
Code of Magnus 'the Law-Mender' (*Gulathing* law), **24**, 303, 304
customary law—
  distinction from common law of *Scotland*, **22**, 387
  reasonableness *Bruce v Smith*, **22**, 385–388
  udal rights—
    Bankton *Institutes*, **22**, 368
    Erskine *Institutes*, **22**, 367
    modern cases, **22**, 385–388
    Stair's *Institutions*, **22**, 366

Shetland—*continued*
feudal system—
  charters, **24**, 308
  infeftments, **24**, 307
foreshore, **24**, 314, 320
impignoration to Scotland, **24**, 301, 304, 318, 326
land measures, **24**, 311
landownership, udal law, **24**, 306
lawbooks, **24**, 303, 304
Norwegian Crown, political authority of, **24**, 302
population, **14**, 64
salmon fishings, **18**, 321; **24**, 315
scat, *see* SCAT
scattald, *see* SCATTALD
Scots law, application of, **24**, 301, 325
Scottish Crown's claim to, **24**, 302, 326, 327
Scottish influence, **24**, 318
seabed, ownership of, **18**, 310, 317; **24**, 316
sovereignty, **24**, 305
  Scottish, **24**, 326–400
  transfer from Norway to Scotland, **24**, 305, 326, 327
sysselman laws enforceable by, **24**, 306
udal law, *see* UDAL LAW
water authority, as, **25**, 505
weights and measures, **24**, 312
See also UDAL LAW
Shield
banners and flags, display on, **11**, 1609
barons and persons of higher rank, **11**, 1604
chapeau, depiction of, **11**, 1607
charges, **11**, 1604, 1618*n*
conventional devices, **11**, 1601, 1604
coronet, depiction of, **11**, 1607
corporations and local authorities, **11**, 1604
crest, addition of, **11**, 1606
generally, **11**, 1604
gentleman's entitlement, **11**, 1604
helmet above, rules as to, **11**, 1605
ladies, arms of, **11**, 1604, 1606
livery colours and metals, **11**, 1604*n*
lozenge, **11**, 1604
mantling, **11**, 1605
oval, **11**, 1604
roundel, **11**, 1604
shape, variation of, **11**, 1604
square, **11**, 1604
supporters, **11**, 1608
tincture, **11**, 1604
wreath, **11**, 1605
Shift work
reorganisation involving introduction of, **9**, 170
Ship
abandoned *sine spe revertendi* or *sine spe recuperandi*, **21**, 511
acquisition, financing, generally, **21**, 101
action for recovery of possession, **18**, 159
administrative removal, procurement for, **12**, 200
aground, vessel—
  lights and shapes to be displayed, **21**, 368
  sound signals, **21**, 374
amended Jason clause, *see* AMENDED JASON CLAUSE
anchor, stowing, **21**, 378

Ship—*continued*
anchored vessel—
   lights and shapes to be displayed, **21**, 368
   sound signals, **21**, 374
amended Jason clause, *see* AMENDED JASON CLAUSE
anchoring—
   emergency, in, **21**, 379
   narrow channel or fairway, in, **21**, 347
   navigation rules, **21**, 380
approved port, **7**, 1239
arrest—
   maritime lien distinguished, **20**, 306
   statutory, **20**, 304, 305, 307
arrestment, *see* ARRESTMENT (ship, of)
automatic pilot—
   duty to use properly, **21**, 340
   prohibitions on use, **21**, 219
   provision and maintenance, safety requirements,
      21, 219
bell, **21**, 372
beneficial interest—
   dealings with registered owner, and, **21**, 134
   enforcement against third party, **21**, 133*n*
   legal title distinguished, **21**, 133
berth, *see* BERTH
bill of lading, *see* BILL OF LADING
bill of sale, **21**, 151, 167
birth on board, **21**, 226
boarding, customs officers' powers, **7**, 1240
boarding station, **7**, 1239
bottomry bond, dispute over, **20**, 305
bridge, manning, **21**, 340
broadcasting from, suppression of, **17**, 9
builder's certificate, retention by registrar, **21**,
      151
capture—
   blockade, **17**, 413
   contraband, penalty for carrying, **17**, 414
   enemy ship, **17**, 411
   neutral ship, **17**, 412
   ransom, **17**, 416
   requisition, **17**, 415
   wrongful, **17**, 417
cargo, *see* CARGO
cargo liner, **21**, 524
cargo ship—
   equipment survey, **21**, 223
   load lines, **21**, 230, 230*n*
   radio certificate, **21**, 222, 222*n*
   radio installations, requirements as to, **21**,
      215
cargo-worthiness—
   generally, **21**, 614*n*
   time charterparty—
      express terms, **21**, 640, 644
   voyage charterparty, **21**, 618
carriage by sea, *see* SEA, CARRIAGE BY
carriage of goods by, dispute over, **20**, 305
certificate of registry—
   delivery on request, **21**, 153
   detention, **21**, 153
   generally, **21**, 153
   lost, **21**, 153, 154
   offences in relation to, **21**, 153, 153*n*

Ship—*continued*
certificate of registry—*continued*
   provisional, **21**, 154, 155
   temporary pass, provision of, **21**, 156
chartering—
   generally, **21**, 101
   See also CHARTERPARTY
charts, duty to equip with up-to-date, **21**, 227,
   378
classification for safety purposes, **21**, 211, 211*n*
co-ownership, **18**, 18
coasting, **7**, 1241
coastwise traffic, customs powers relating to, **7**,
   1241
collision—
   assistance, duty to give, **21**, 209
   avoidance action—
      collision regulations—
         generally, **21**, 345
         obedience to rule, **21**, 346
      damage caused by, **21**, 311
   both to blame collision clause—
      bill of lading, **21**, 546
      cargo damage, **21**, 584, 584*n*
      time charterparty, **21**, 640
      voyage charterparty, **21**, 618
   cargo damage—
      both to blame clause, **21**, 584, 584*n*
      claims—
         generally, **21**, 584
         restriction on extent of, **21**, 584
      damages in respect of, **21**, 391
   collision with third ship following, **21**, 318,
      318*n*
   crew of damaged ship, duty following collision,
      21, 318
   damage caused by—
      action *in personam*, **21**, 393, 394, 394*n*, 481,
         482
      damage sustained after collision, where, **21**,
         327
      jurisdiction, **21**, 393
      liability for, **21**, 321
         apportionment, **21**, 322, 323
            damage covered by statutory apportion-
               ment rule, **21**, 325
            damage sustained after collision, where,
               21, 327
            raising issue of, **21**, 326
            two or more vessels must be involved,
               21, 324
            type of loss, **21**, 325
      maritime lien, generally, **21**, 479
      title to sue, **21**, 320
      towage, in cases of, **21**, 409
   delict, law of—
      application, **21**, 312
      generally, **21**, 311
   Department of Transport inspectors, **21**,
      204
   details of vessel and port to which bound etc.,
      master's duty to give, **21**, 209, 209*n*
   different flags, collision between vessels of, **21**,
      46

Ship—*continued*
collision—*continued*
  duty of master or person in charge of vessel, **21**, 209
  failure to display lights or shapes, following, **21**, 358
  fault after, **21**, 318
  generally, **21**, 311
  investigation of marine accidents—
    Department of Transport, by, **21**, 235
    formal, **21**, 236
  jurisdiction, generally, **21**, 46
  negligence—
    breach of collision regulations as evidence of, **21**, 331
    causation and damage, **21**, 317
    contributory, **21**, 316, 316*n*, 322*ff*
    emergencies, **21**, 314
    error made in emergency situation, **21**, 314
    failure of good seamanship or maritime skill, **21**, 313
    failure to exercise skill and care of reasonably competent seaman, **21**, 313
    fault after collision, **21**, 318
    inevitable accident, **21**, 315
    liability for collision damage, **21**, 321
    proof of fault, **21**, 319
    standard of care, **21**, 313
    title to sue, **21**, 320
    two or more ships to blame for collision, **21**, 317
  persons on board, loss or damage caused to, **21**, 321, 325
  pollution caused by, damages in respect of, **21**, 390
  property other than ship, damage to, **21**, 311
  regulations, *see* COLLISION REGULATIONS
  risk, determining, **21**, 344
  territorial jurisdiction, **4**, 2
  two or more ships to blame, **21**, 317
collision regulations—
  application, **21**, 332
  breach as evidence of fault or negligence, **21**, 331
  crossing situations, steering and sailing rules, **21**, 352
  detention, powers of, **21**, 331
  distress signals, **21**, 331, 375, 376
  enforcement, **21**, 331, 333
  generally, **21**, 104
  give-way vessel, action by, **21**, 354
  head-on situations, steering and sailing rules, **21**, 352
  history, **21**, 331
  hovercraft, **21**, 332
  international—
    application, **21**, 336
    exemption from, **21**, 335
    generally, **21**, 331, 332
    interpretation, **21**, 334
    object, **21**, 334
    scheme, **21**, 335
    signals, **21**, 371
    special circumstances, where, **21**, 336

Ship—*continued*
collision regulations—*continued*
  international—*continued*
    steering and sailing rules—
      applicable in any condition of visibility, **21**, 338–348
      generally, **21**, 335, 337
      vessels in restricted visibility, **21**, 357
      vessels in sight of one another, **21**, 349–356
    vessel held to be at fault by not departing from, where, **21**, 336
  light signals, **21**, 335
    See also lights and shapes *below*
  lights and shapes—
    aground, vessel, **21**, 368
    anchored vessel, **21**, 368
    compliance, **21**, 359
    darkness, hours of, **21**, 358
    daylight hours, **21**, 358, 359
    equipment for, safety regulations, **21**, 220
    exemptions, **21**, 370
    failure to display, **21**, 358
    fishing vessel, **21**, 364
    generally, **21**, 335, 358
    manoeuvrability, vessel with restricted, **21**, 365
    oars, vessel under, **21**, 363
    pilot vessel, **21**, 367
    power-driven vessel—
      towing or pushing, **21**, 361
      underway, **21**, 360
    purpose of display, **21**, 358
    pushed, vessel being, **21**, 362
    restricted visibility, conditions of, **21**, 359
    sailing vessel underway, **21**, 363
    seaplane, **21**, 369
    technical requirements, **21**, 359, 359*n*
    towed, vessel being, **21**, 362
    towing or pushing vessel, **21**, 361
    towing vessel, **21**, 361
    vessel constrained by its draught, **21**, 366
    vessel not under command, **21**, 365
  look-out, **21**, 339–342
  meaning of ship for purpose of, **21**, 109
  narrow channels and fairways, **21**, 347, 347*n*, 351, 351*n*
  overtaking, **21**, 351
  penalties, **21**, 331
  responsibilities between vessels, **21**, 356
  risk of collision, determining, **21**, 344
  safe speed—
    determining, **21**, 343
    generally, **21**, 342
    meaning, **21**, 342
    radar, vessel with operational, **21**, 343
  sailing rules, *see* steering and sailing rules *below*
  seaplane, **21**, 332*n*, 333, 356
  shapes, *see* lights and shapes *above*
  signals—
    attention, to attract, **21**, 375
    distress, **21**, 376
    failure to use, **21**, 371
    generally, **21**, 371

Ship—*continued*
collision regulations—*continued*
  signals—*continued*
    improper, making, **21**, 371
    international regulations, **21**, 371
    light, **21**, 335, 371, 373, 375
      See also lights and shapes *above*
    manoeuvrability, vessel with restricted, **21**, 374
    manoeuvring, **21**, 373
    restricted visibility, in, **21**, 374
    sailing vessel, **21**, 374
    shapes, *see* lights and shapes *above*
    sound, **21**, 335, 371, 374, 375
      equipment for, **21**, 372
      restricted visibility, in, **21**, 374
    vessel constrained by its draught, **21**, 374
    vessel not under command, **21**, 374
    warning, **21**, 373
  stand-on vessel, action by, **21**, 355
  steering and sailing rules—
    action to avoid collision—
      generally, **21**, 345
      obedience to rule, **21**, 346
    applicable to vessels in any conditions of visibility, **21**, 338–348
    crossing situation, in, **21**, 353
    generally, **21**, 337
    give-way vessel, action by, **21**, 354
    head-on situation, in, **21**, 352
    look-out—
      aural, **21**, 341, 371
      bridge, manning, **21**, 340
      generally, **21**, 339
      navigational watch arrangements, **21**, 340
      radar watch, **21**, 341
      visual, **21**, 341
    narrow channel or fairway, in, **21**, 347
      overtaking, **21**, 351
    overtaking, **21**, 351
      application of rule, **21**, 351*n*
    responsibility between vessels, **21**, 356
    risk of collision, determining, **21**, 344
    safe speed—
      determining, **21**, 343
      generally, **21**, 342
      meaning, **21**, 342
      purpose, **21**, 342
    stand-on vessel, action by, **21**, 355
    traffic separation scheme, **21**, 348
    vessels in restricted visibility, **21**, 357
    vessels in sight of one another, **21**, 349–356
      meaning, **21**, 349
  traffic separation scheme, **21**, 348
  UK law, **21**, 331, 332
  visibility—
    restricted, steering and sailing rules, **21**, 357
    vessels in sight of one another, steering and sailing rules, **21**, 349–356
common travel area, journeys outwith, **12**, 133, 568
compass, provision and maintenance, **21**, 218
competition, policy formulation as to, responsibility for, **21**, 113

Ship—*continued*
condemnation—
  dispute over, **20**, 305
  restraint of princes, as, **21**, 550
condition of—
  negligence, and, **21**, 313
  See also CARGO-WORTHINESS; SEAWORTHINESS
conduct committed on, extradition procedure, **12**, 515
conferences, **21**, 118
confiscation by customs officials, **7**, 1225
construction, dispute over, **20**, 305
contract for carriage, *jus quaesitum tertio*, **15**, 847
cook, ship's, regulations as to, **21**, 245, 247
corporeal moveable property, as, **21**, 101, 131
crew, *see* SEAMAN
crew agreement, *see* SEAMAN
crimping, restrictions on, **21**, 249
customs and excise—
  powers of boarding, **7**, 1240
  report, **7**, 1142
damage done or received by, **20**, 305
damage to, general average, **21**, 709
damages—
  apportionment—
    appeals, **21**, 329
    assessment, **21**, 327
    basic rule, **21**, 323
    effect, **21**, 330
    generally, **21**, 322
    raising issue of, **21**, 326
    sub-apportionment, **21**, 327
    three or more ships involved, where, **21**, 328
  breach of contract of carriage, for, *see* CONTRACT (breach of)
  cargo—
    damage to—
      generally, **21**, 391
      measure of damages, **21**, 716
    discharge of, in respect of, **21**, 390
  causation and damage, **21**, 317
  claim for, arrestment, **21**, 394
  dead freight, **21**, 717
  detention, for, *see* damages for detention *below*
  dock charges or dues, **21**, 386
  dry docking expenses, **21**, 386
  England or Northern Ireland, proceedings commenced in, **21**, 394, 394*n*
  European Union, proceedings commenced in, **21**, 394, 394*n*
  expenses ancillary to actual repairs, **21**, 386
  fuel consumption resulting from damage, costs of, **21**, 386, 386*n*
  fuel oil pollution, **21**, 390
  harbour charges or dues, **21**, 386
  jurisdiction, **21**, 393
    Court of Session, **21**, 394
    sheriff court, **21**, 394
  laid up, expenses incurred in having ship, **21**, 386
  legal principles relating to, generally, **21**, 383
  loss of profits—
    damages for detention, **21**, 387, 387*n*
    detention period must be reasonable, **21**, 387, 387*n*

Ship—*continued*
damages—*continued*
  loss of profits—*continued*
    determination, **21**, 387, 387*n*
    fishing vessels, **21**, 389
    future engagements, loss of, **21**, 387, 387*n*
    generally, **21**, 387
    profit-earning item of property, damaged ship must be, **21**, 387
    proof of, **21**, 387, 387*n*
    unreasonable desire to have repairs carried out in certain port, **21**, 387*n*
  management of ship, negligent, liability as result of, **21**, 390
  navigation, negligent, liability as result of, **21**, 390
  negligence, damage caused by, *see* negligence *below*
  new vessel, costs of obtaining after total loss, **21**, 385
  non-profit making vessel, loss of, **21**, 387
  other repairs carried out during detention period, effect, **21**, 388
  overloading ship, damages for negligence, **21**, 719*n*
  port of repair, expenses of proceeding to, **21**, 386
  possessory lien, failure to relinquish where adequate security offered, award on, **21**, 480
  proceedings *in personam*, **21**, 394
  proceedings *in rem*, **21**, 394
  remoteness precluding recovery, **21**, 390
  repair costs, **21**, 386
    duty to mitigate costs, **21**, 386*n*
  repatriation of crew, cost of, **21**, 385
  salvage expenses, **21**, 386
  temporary repairs, **21**, 386
  title to sue, collision damage, **21**, 320
  total loss—
    actual, **21**, 384*n*
    ascertaining, costs of, **21**, 385
    constructive, **21**, 384, 384*n*
      falling short of, **21**, 386
    falling short of, **21**, 386
    hire of substitute vessel, **21**, 385, 385*n*
    meaning, **21**, 384
    measure of damages, **21**, 385
    ship, of, **21**, 383–385
    use of vessel, loss of, **21**, 385
    wreck-raising expenses, **21**, 385
  towage—
    charges, **21**, 386
    damage caused by tow or flotilla, **21**, 409
  value of ship, measure, **21**, 385
    future engagements lost, damages for, **21**, 385, 385*n*
  wreck-raising expenses, **21**, 385, 386
dangerously unsafe, **21**, 206
death on board, **21**, 226
definition—
  common law meaning, **21**, 107
  definition of vessel, and, **21**, 106, 108, 109
  Hague-Visby Rules, for purpose of, **21**, 109, 587

Ship—*continued*
definition—*continued*
  navigability, **21**, 108
  need for, **21**, 106
  Oxford English Dictionary, **21**, 107*n*
  statutory, **21**, 108
    consequences of being within or outwith, **21**, 111
  structures other than ship or vessel, and, **21**, 110
delict, *see* DELICT
delivery order—
  chartered ship, generally, **21**, 690
  definition, **21**, 530
  document of title, treatment as, **21**, 574
  generally, **21**, 530
  jus quaesitum tertio, **15**, 847
  non-negotiable document, as, **21**, 690
  title to sue—
    generally, **21**, 578, 578*n*, 579
    transfer of, **21**, 574
  transfer of rights and liabilities, **21**, 574
demurrage, *see* DEMURRAGE
deportee, removal by, **12**, 212
derelict, *see* DERELICT
despatch money (despatch), **21**, 666, 689
destroying or sinking—
  common law, **7**, 421
  insurer, with intent to defraud, **7**, 421
  malicious mischief, **7**, 421
  statute law, **7**, 422
  vandalism, **7**, 421
detention—
  customs' officers power of, **7**, 1240
  generally, **1**, 417
  wrongful, as breach of contract, **21**, 717
direction finder, provision and maintenance, **21**, 218
distress, in, international duty in respect of, **21**, 43
distress signal—
  collision regulations, **21**, 331, 375, 376
  duty on receipt of, **21**, 209
  equipment, safety regulations, **21**, 220
diving operation, vessel engaged in, **21**, 365
division and sale, action of, **21**, 137, 138
dock charges, dispute over, **20**, 305
dock dues, dispute over, **20**, 305
documentation—
  birth or death on board, as to, **21**, 226
  change of master, procedure on, **21**, 227
  charts, **21**, 227, 229, 229*n*, 378
  crew agreements, **21**, 226
    See also SEAMAN
  crew list, **21**, 226, 228
  evidence, admissibility in, **21**, 228
  evidence, as, **10**, 592
  inspection, **21**, 228
  log book, **21**, 224, 640
  nautical publications, **21**, 228*n*, 229
  operations book, **21**, 224
  seaworthiness, in relation to, **21**, 614
dracone—
  meaning, **21**, 362*n*
  towed or pushed, lights, **21**, 362

Ship—*continued*
dredging operation, vessel engaged in, **21**, 365
droits of Admiralty, as, **17**, 407
echo sounder, provision and maintenance, **21**, 218
embargo as restraint of princes, **21**, 550
English courts—
    law reports, **21**, 740
    maritime law cases, **21**, 739
entry, powers of, in relation to Food and Drugs (Scotland) Act 1956 ..., **11**, 340
entry control requirements, **12**, 161
environmental damage, duty of ship owner and master, **21**, 465
equipment—
    adequately equipped, ship must be, **21**, 378
    cargo damage caused by defect in, **21**, 632
    dangerously unsafe ship, **21**, 206
    dispute oer, **20**, 305
    duty to use safely, **21**, 378
    failures in, notification, **21**, 340
    jettison of or damage to, general average, **21**, 709
    navigational, duty to use properly, **21**, 340, 341
    negligence in relation to, **21**, 313
    provision and maintenance, safety requirements, **21**, 191, 212, 213
        automatic pilot, **21**, 219
        cargo ship safety equipment survey, **21**, 223
        compass, **21**, 218
        direction finder, **21**, 218
        echo sounder, **21**, 218
        life saving appliances—
            generally, **21**, 216, 216*n*
            passenger ships, **21**, 217
        lights, **21**, 220
        navigational equipment, **21**, 218
        pilot ladders and hoists, **21**, 221
        radar equipment, **21**, 218
        radio equipment, **21**, 215, 215*n*, 218
            survey of, **21**, 222
        shapes, equipment for, **21**, 220
        signalling equipment, **21**, 220
        steering gear, **21**, 219
    seaworthiness in relation to, **21**, 614, 614*n*
    sound signalling, **21**, 372
    stowing, **21**, 378
    time charterparty, **21**, 640, 646
European Union—
    policies pursued by, **21**, 115
    transit procedures, **7**, 1173
examination of goods loaded into, **7**, 1214
explosives—
    byelaws as to, **10**, 1609, 1610, 1613
    exemptions from regulations, **10**, 1589
Export of Goods (Control) Order 1994 ..., **7**, 1194
export procedure, clearance outwards, **7**, 1161
fairway, *see* FAIRWAY
fire damage, limitation of liability, **21**, 557
firearms and ammunition as part of equipment, **10**, 1541
firearms transported to and from, **10**, 1581
fitting, foreign state at war with friendly state, for, **7**, 610

Ship—*continued*
fixed platform, destroying or endangering, **7**, 422
flag—
    enemy character determined by, **17**, 411
    flags, generally, **21**, 113, 140, 140*n*
    refusal to show, **21**, 45
flag of convenience, policy formulation as to, **21**, 113
flag state, jurisdiction of, **21**, 43-45
flotilla—
    command, **21**, 408
    manned or unmanned, **21**, 408
    relationship to third parties, **21**, 401
flotsam, **21**, 511
foreign—
    damage caused to British property by, **20**, 297
    possessory lien over, **20**, 297
forfeiture, dispute over, **20**, 305
fuel—
    excise duty relief, **7**, 1069
    seaworthiness in relation to, **21**, 614, 614*n*
    stops for, prior agreement, **21**, 614
    time charterparty, **21**, 640, 647
    voyage charterparty, **21**, 614
general average, *see* GENERAL AVERAGE
general ship, *see* GENERAL SHIP
gong, **21**, 372
goods exported by, time of exportation, **7**, 1155
goods imported by, time of importation, **7**, 1141
grounded, wreck compared, **21**, 511
Hamburg Rules, **21**, 586, 586*n*
Her Majesty, goods supplied to, excise duty relief, **7**, 1115
hijacking, **7**, 362
hire agreement, dispute over, **20**, 305
hot pursuit, right of, **21**, 44
hovercraft, *see* HOVERCRAFT
hovering, **21**, 6, 35
husband—
    appointment, **21**, 139
    authority of, **21**, 139
    duty to account, **21**, 139
    generally, **21**, 139
    meaning, **21**, 139*n*
    registration, **21**, 139
    remuneration, **21**, 139
hypothecation, dispute over, **20**, 305
illegally enlisted person, taking or engaging on, **7**, 609
immersion suits, provision of, **21**, 216
immigrants, entry of, **19**, 510, 512
infected persons, prohibition on conveyance of, **19**, 458, 459
infectious disease, regulations as to, **19**, 491, 492, 494, 496
inflammable substances, conveyance by, **19**, 393
insurance, marine—
    generally, **21**, 101, 119
    hull and machinery, relating to, **21**, 551
interaction, **21**, 351*n*
international co-operation on legislation covering, **21**, 101
International Code of Signals, **21**, 229*n*

Ship—*continued*
International Convention for the Safety of Life at
  Sea, **21**, 195
International Maritime Consultative Organisation
  (IMCO), **21**, 117
International Maritime Organisation (IMO), *see*
  INTERNATIONAL MARITIME ORGANISATION
jetsam, **21**, 511
jettison of part, general average, **21**, 709
lagan, **21**, 511
launching operation, **21**, 381
lay/can spread, **21**, 619*n*
laytime (lay days), *see* LAYTIME
leading marks—
  bill of lading, **21**, 595
    express terms, **21**, 546
    generally, **21**, 562, 565
  Hague-Visby Rules, **21**, 595
legal title, beneficial interest distinguished, **21**,
  133
lex loci celebrationis of marriage celebrated on, **17**,
  226
lien—
  Administration of Justice Act 1956, under,
    categories of dispute giving rise to claim,
    20, 305
  creditor's rights compared, **20**, 306
  maritime, *see* MARITIME LIEN
  shipowner's, *see* LIEN (POSSESSORY)
  statutory, **20**, 304–307
lifeboat, *see* LIFEBOAT
lifebuoy, provision of, **21**, 216, 217
lifejacket, provision of, **21**, 216, 217
liferaft, provision of, **21**, 216, 217
light signals and lights and shapes to be displayed,
  see collision regulations *above*; lights *below*
lightering, carrier utilised for, liability, **21**, 560
lighters, **21**, 632, 632*n*, 670*n*
lights—
  all-round, **21**, 360*n*
  collision regulations, *see* collision regulations
    (lights and shapes) *above*
  display of, while underway, **21**, 363
  flashing, **21**, 360*n*
  masthead, **21**, 360*n*
  sidelight, **21**, 360*n*
  signals—
    collision regulations, **21**, 371
    equipment for, safety regulations, **21**, 220
  sternlight, **21**, 360*n*
  towing, **21**, 361*n*
line throwing appliances, provison of, **21**, 216
liner, **21**, 524
liner conferences, **21**, 118, 527
Lloyd's, **21**, 119
load lines, **21**, 230, 230*n*
local rules, duty to equip ship with up-to-date,
  21, 378
log book, **21**, 224
look-out—
  aural, **21**, 341, 371
  duty to maintain, **21**, 339
  generally, **21**, 339
  navigational watch arrangements, **21**, 340

Ship—*continued*
look-out—*continued*
  no appropriate look-out being kept, **21**, 371
  radar, *see* RADAR
  visibility conditions, **21**, 339*n*
  visual, **21**, 341
  See also watch *below*
loss, total, **21**, 383–385, 384*n*
loss or damage to, general average, *see* GENERAL
  AVERAGE
loss of life in consequence of defect in, **20**, 305
maintenance, rules as to, **21**, 378
management—
  dangerously unsafe ship, **21**, 206, 206*n*
  Merchant Shipping Notices (M Notices), **21**,
    377
  negligent—
    liability for damages as result of, **21**, 390
    responsibility, Hague-Visby Rules, **21**, 603
    unsafe navigation, leading to, **21**, 313
manning—
  dangerously unsafe ship, **21**, 206
  duty to ensure proper, **21**, 378
  inadequate, **21**, 313
  requirements as to, **21**, 245, 247, 313*n*
    enforcement, **21**, 248
  See also master *below*; SEAMAN
manoeuvrability—
  collision regulations, responsibility between
    vessels, **21**, 356
  safe speed, determining, **21**, 343
  vessel with restricted—
    lights and shapes to be displayed, **21**, 365
    sound signals, **21**, 374
    warning broadcasts by, **21**, 379
manoeuvring, signalling, **21**, 373
marine fuel, import, VAT regulations, **7**, 1314
marine insurance, **21**, 119
mariners handbook, **21**, 229*n*
maritime hypothec, **21**, 479
maritime lien, *see* MARITIME LIEN
maritime telecommunications services, provision,
  16, 1923
marking—
  offences in relation to, **21**, 148
  regulations as to, **21**, 148
master—
  barratry, acts of, **21**, 551*n*, 554
  breach or neglect of duty, **21**, 208*n*
  change of, handing over ship's documentation,
    21, 227
  collision, duties when involved in, **21**, 209,
    209*n*
  contract of employment, **21**, 241
    Employment Protection (Consolidation) Act
      (1978) and related legislation, **21**, 244
  dangerous conduct by, **21**, 269
  dangerously unsafe ship, liability, **21**, 206
  death of, inquiry into, **21**, 240
  disbursements and liabilities made or incurred
    by, maritime lien, **21**, 260, 392, 479
  disciplinary powers, **21**, 270
    passengers, over, **21**, 723
  distress signal etc, duty on receipt of, **21**, 209

Ship—*continued*
master—*continued*
  drink or drugs, under influence of, **21**, 208,
    269, 269*n*
  employment, generally, **21**, 241
  Employment Protection (Consolidation) Act
    (1978) and related legislation, **21**, 244
  environmental damage, duty as to, **21**, 465
  freight, payment to, **21**, 664
  ice endangering navigation, duty to report, **21**,
    210
  insolvency of employer, **21**, 244
  liability, limitation, **21**, 557, 751
  Lloyd's Standard Form of Salvage Agreement,
    21, 484
  misconduct endangering ships, structures or
    individuals, **21**, 208, 208*n*
  navigational warnings, duty to give, **21**, 210
  property of traveller, strict liability for, **15**, 144
  qualifications, requirements as to, **21**, 245
    enforcement, **21**, 248
  redundancy—
    generally, **21**, 244
    redundancy payment, right to, **21**, 244
  remuneration and disbursements, **20**, 280, 305
    priority of maritime lien, **20**, 313
  rights, generally, **21**, 244
  safety, health and welfare, *see* SEAMAN
  salved vessel, of—
    duty to salvors, **21**, 465, 466
    whether entitled to claim salvage award, **21**,
      452, 454
  seaman, not treated as, **21**, 242
  statutory jurisdiction, **21**, 241
  voyage charterparty—
    agent of charterer, whether, **21**, 629
    agent of shipowner, as, **21**, 629
    authority of master, **21**, 629
  wages and disbursements, maritime lien, **21**,
    260, 392, 479, 479*n*
mate's receipt, **21**, 562
meaning, **8**, 322; **17**, 402
measurement, **21**, 147
merchant—
  Merchant Shipping Acts, **21**, 103
  Merchant Shipping Notices (M Notices), **21**,
    229*n*, 377, 404
  register of merchant ships, **21**, 131*n*
mineclearance operation, vessel engaged in, **21**,
  365
mortgage of, *see* MORTGAGE
moveable property, as, **21**, 101, 131
name—
  change of, **21**, 148*n*
  choice of, **21**, 148*n*
  marking, **21**, 148
  requirements as to, generally, **21**, 148*n*
nationality—
  British nationality—
    acquisition and possession, **21**, 141
      national colours, requirements as to, **21**,
        141, 141*n*
      unregistered ships, **21**, 141
    false claim to, **21**, 141

Ship—*continued*
nationality—*continued*
  concealing, **21**, 141
  deceiving inquiry into, **21**, 141
  documentation, requirement for, **21**, 140
  flag, requirement to fly, **21**, 140, 140*n*
  international requirement for, **21**, 131, 140
  jurisdiction and, **21**, 140
  two flags, ship sailing under, **21**, 140
  UK customs and excise regulations, **21**, 140
nautical almanac, requirement to carry, **21**, 229*n*
navigation, *see* NAVIGATION
navigational equipment, damage or destruction, **7**,
  422
negligence—
  apportionment of liability, **21**, 322–330
  collision—
    fault after, **21**, 318
    See also collision *above*
  collision regulations, breach as evidence of, **21**,
    331
  contributory, **21**, 316, 316*n*, 322*ff*
  damage caused by avoidance action, **21**, 311
  damages, *see* DAMAGES
  delict, application of law, **21**, 311, 312
  emergency situation, in, **21**, 314
  heavy swell, raising, **21**, 311
  inevitable accident, **21**, 315
  liability, exclusion or limitation of, **21**, 547, 556
  management of ship, in, **21**, 313
  manning levels, **21**, 313
  personal injury—
    collision causing, **21**, 321, 325
    ship causing, **21**, 311
  proof of fault in navigation and seamanship, **21**,
    319
  property other than ship, damage to, **21**, 311
  reasonably foreseeable event, failure to guard
    against, **21**, 551*n*
  salvor, by, public policy, **21**, 468
  ship, common law meaning, **21**, 107
  signals, failure to comply with collision
    regulations, **21**, 371
  standard of care, **21**, 313
new Jason clause, *see* NEW JASON CLAUSE
non-passenger, classification for safety purposes,
  21, 211
notices to mariners, requirement to carry, **21**,
  229*n*
notification of infectious diseases, **19**, 490
number, marking, **21**, 148
oars, vessel under, **21**, 363
occupier's liability, **15**, 322
offences committed on, **6**, 867
officer, *see* SEAMAN
oil, discharge into sea, **9**, 1210, 1213
oil rigs and other structures, whether classed as,
  21, 108*n*
operations book, **21**, 225
outward entry, **7**, 1160
overtaking, **21**, 351
owner—
  beneficial interest amounting to beneficial
    ownership, **21**, 133

Ship—*continued*

owner—*continued*

breach of contract by, **21**, 716

British ship, of, qualification for—

generally, **21**, 144

non-qualified person owning interest in British ship, **21**, 144

Scottish partnership not qualified, **21**, 133

civil liability, **21**, 261

co-ownership—

co-owners' authority to bind one another to contracts, **21**, 136

concept of, generally, **21**, 135

disclaim participation, minority interest's ability to, **21**, 137, 137*n*

disputes between co-owners, **21**, 137

sale of ship, as to, **21**, 137

managing owner, appointment of, **21**, 139

small ships register, **21**, 132, 132*n*

declaration of ownership, requirement on registration, **21**, 150

disposal, powers of, **21**, 134

dispute as to ownership, **20**, 305

employer as, general duties owed to seamen, **21**, 261

environmental damage, duty as to, **21**, 465

evidence as to ownership, **21**, 150

freight, payment to, **21**, 664

joint owners—

generally, **21**, 135

registration, **21**, 132

set and sale or division and sale at instance of one joint owner, **21**, 138

small ships register, **21**, 132, 132*n*

liability—

damage caused by acts or omissions of owner, **21**, 321

dangerously unsafe ship, **21**, 206

limitation of—

charterparty, in, **21**, 558

generally, **1**, 418

See also SEA, CARRIAGE BY (limitation of liability)

pilot, fault by, vicarious liability of shipowner, **21**, 308

unsafe operation of ship, **21**, 207

managing—

authority of, **21**, 139

commercial, not legal term, as, **21**, 139*n*

duty to account, **21**, 139

generally, **21**, 139

qualification to be, **21**, 139

registration, **21**, 139

remuneration, **21**, 139

maximum number of owners allowed to register, **21**, 132

mortgagee as, **21**, 177

organisations designed to promote interests of owners, **21**, 118

owners in common—

generally, **21**, 135

set and sale and division and sale, actions of, **21**, 137, 138

passenger, duties as to, **21**, 721

Ship—*continued*

owner—*continued*

Protection and Indemnity Clubs (P & I Clubs), **21**, 119

registered, dealing with, **21**, 134

registered company, as, ship's mortgage where, **21**, 172

right to sue shipowner, **21**, 576–582

salvaged property, of, duty of salvor to, **21**, 449

salved vessel, of, duty to salvors, **21**, 465, 466

salvor, shipowner as, **21**, 444, 446

seaworthiness of vessel—

implied terms, **21**, 614

obligation as to, **21**, 542

ship, failure to provide, **21**, 716

ship ceasing to be British owned, **21**, 159

ship's mortgage, power to grant, **21**, 174

unsafe operation of ship, duty as to, **21**, 207

owners, liability of, **12**, 161

ownership, declaration of, retention by registrar, **21**, 151

parts and equipment, VAT zero-rating, **7**, 1452

passage money, **21**, 437, 721*n*

passenger, *see* PASSENGER

passenger ship—

classification for safety purposes, **21**, 211, 211*n*

definition, **21**, 211*n*

life saving appliances, provision of, **21**, 217

newly converted, fire protection regulations, **21**, 214, 214*n*

passenger certificate, **21**, 222, 222*n*

ro-ro—

meaning, **21**, 213*n*

safety requirements, **21**, 213

perils of the sea, *see* PERILS OF THE SEA

person born on, acquisition of British citizenship, **14**, 1908

personal injury in consequence of defect in, **20**, 305

pilotage, dispute over, **20**, 305

piracy, *see* PIRACY

plant, as, **14**, 1012

Plimsoll lines, *see* load lines *above*

port, *see* PORT

port local authority, within jurisdiction of, **19**, 313

possession, dispute over, **20**, 305

possessory lien over, *see* LIEN

power-driven vessel—

collision regulations, **21**, 356

lights and shapes to be displayed while underway, **21**, 360

towing or pushing, **21**, 361

restricted manoeuvrability, with, lights and shapes to be diplayed, **21**, 365

prevention of terrorism powers, **12**, 133

property rights in, danger to, salvage, **21**, 442

Protection and Indemnity Clubs (P & I Clubs), **21**, 119

purchase, *see* sale of *below*

pushed, vessel being, **21**, 361, 362, 374

quarantine, *see* QUARANTINE

radar, *see* RADAR

radio, *see* RADIO

Ship—*continued*
rat, holes made by, **21**, 551*n*
received for shipment bill, **21**, 524*n*, 526*n*, 528*n*, 571*n*, 572
registered—
    beneficial interest, **21**, 133
    legal title, **21**, 133
registered British—
    shares, transfer of, **8**, 635
    transfer of, **8**, 635
registration—
    application for, **21**, 149
    bad faith, obtained in, **21**, 134
    British registers—
        admissibility in evidence of information in, **21**, 145
        certificate of registry, **21**, 153–156
        copy, right to obtain, **21**, 145
        first registration, **21**, 146–151
        forgery in relation to, **21**, 145
        form of documents, **21**, 145
        generally, **21**, 145
        inspection, right of, **21**, 145
        refusal and termination of registration, **21**, 157–161
        small ships register, **21**, 162
    British ships—
        generally, **21**, 142
        previous overseas registration, where, **21**, 152
        ships registered in UK overseas territories, **21**, 131*n*, 143
    certificate of registry—
        bad faith, obtained in, **21**, 134
        delivery on request, **21**, 153
        detention, **21**, 153
        generally, **21**, 153
        importance, **21**, 153
        lost, **21**, 153, 154
        offences in relation to, **21**, 153, 153*n*
        provisional, **21**, 154, 155
        temporary pass, provision of, **21**, 156
    documents, retention by registrar, **21**, 151
    first—
        application for registry, **21**, 149
        declaration of ownership, **21**, 150
        evidence as to, **21**, 150
        documents to be furnished, **21**, 151
        generally, **21**, 146
        marking of ship, **21**, 148
        new ships, **21**, 146
        particulars to be furnished, **21**, 151
        previous overseas registration, where, **21**, 152
        second-hand ships, **21**, 146
        survey and measurement of ship, **21**, 147
    fishing vessels, register of, **21**, 131*n*
    international requirement for, **21**, 131
    managing owner, **21**, 139
    maximum number of owners allowed to register, **21**, 132
    merchant shipping, **21**, 131*n*
    overseas—
        termination on registration in UK, **21**, 152

Ship—*continued*
registration—*continued*
    reasons for, **21**, 142
    refusal of application, **21**, 157
    registrars—
        duties, **21**, 145
        liability, **21**, 145
    ship becoming entitled to registration while abroad, **21**, 155
    small ships register—
        application for registration, **21**, 162
        generally, **21**, 131*n*, 162
        joint and co-ownership, **21**, 132, 132*n*
        offences, **21**, 162
        qualification for registration, **21**, 162
        termination of registration, **21**, 162
    termination—
        lost ships, **21**, 159
        mortgage, effect on, **21**, 161
        removal from register, **21**, 158
        safety, on grounds of, **21**, 158
        ship ceasing to be British owned, **21**, 159
        small ships register, **21**, 162
        UK registration, of, discharge of seamen where, **21**, 253
        voluntary, **21**, 160
    transfer of title, registration, **21**, 167
repair, dispute oer, **20**, 305
requisition, **17**, 415
restraint of princes, as, **21**, 550
respondentia bond, **21**, 101, 260, 479
restoration after seizure, **20**, 305
restraints of princes, **21**, 550, 603
Rhine Navigation Convention, **21**, 393
right in security, where no delivery to security holder, **21**, 131
safety—
    assistance, duty to give, **21**, 209, 209*n*
    bridge visibility on passenger ships, **21**, 233
    certificate of compliance, **21**, 202
        alteration or cancellation, **21**, 202
    classification of ships for purposes of, **21**, 211, 211*n*
    closure of openings, **21**, 234
    construction of ships, **21**, 191
        cargo ships, **21**, 212, 212*n*
        construction certificate, **21**, 212, 213
        fire protection, **21**, 214
        passenger ships, **21**, 213, 213*n*
    crew and passengers, health and safety of, **21**, 191
    criminal offences in relation to, **21**, 201
    danger to navigation, master's duty to report, **21**, 210
    dangerous goods, carriage of, **21**, 231
    dangerously unsafe ship, **21**, 206, 206*n*
    detention of ship in interests of, **21**, 200
    distress signal etc, duty on receipt of, **21**, 209
    enforcement of safety legislation, **21**, 200–205
    environmental aspects, **21**, 191
    equipment of ship, provision and maintenance, **21**, 191, 206, 212, 213
        automatic pilot, **21**, 219
        cargo ship safety equipment survey, **21**, 223

Ship—*continued*
safety—*continued*
  equipment of ship, provision and maintenance—
    continued
    compass, **21**, 218
    direction finder, **21**, 218
    echo sounder, **21**, 218
    life saving appliances—
      generally, **21**, 216, 216n
      passenger ships, **21**, 217
    lights, **21**, 220
    navigational equipment, **21**, 218
    pilot ladders and hoists, **21**, 221
    radar equipment, **21**, 218
    radio, **21**, 215–217, 215n, 218
      equipment surveys, **21**, 222, 222n
    shapes, **21**, 220
    signalling equipment, **21**, 220
    steering gear, **21**, 219
  exemption from specified provisions, **21**, 202
    alteration or cancellation, **21**, 202
  fire protection, **21**, 214
    exceptions from regulations, **21**, 214
  flares, provision of, **21**, 216, 217
  grain, carriage of, **21**, 232
  immersion suits, provision of, **21**, 216
  improvement notice, **21**, 203
  inquiries and investigations, **21**, 235–240
  inspector—
    appointment, **21**, 204
    functions, **21**, 204
    offences in relation to, **21**, 205, 205n
    powers, **21**, 204
    unnecessarily preventing procedure of voyage,
      21, 204
  international conventions—
    generally, **21**, 193
    implementation, **21**, 196, 197
    International Convention for the Safety of
      Life at Sea (1974), **21**, 195
    modern, **21**, 194, 195
  life saving appliances, provision of—
    generally, **21**, 216
    passenger ships, **21**, 217
  lifeboats and craft, regulations as to, **21**, 216, 217
  lifebuoys, regulations as to, **21**, 216, 217
  lifejackets, regulations as to, **21**, 216, 217
  line throwing appliances, provision of, **21**, 216,
    217
  maintenance of ships, **21**, 191
  misconduct endangering ships, structures or
    individuals, **21**, 208, 208n
  navigational warnings, duty to give, **21**, 210
  passenger, provisions as to, **21**, 233
  pilotage—
    compulsory, **21**, 300
    misconduct by pilot endangering ship or
      persons on board, **21**, 307
    See also PILOT; PILOTAGE
  procedures, regulations as to, **21**, 234
  prohibition notice, **21**, 203
  property and persons other than ship and crew,
    of, **21**, 191, 208
  rocket parachute flares, provision of, **21**, 216, 217

Ship—*continued*
safety—*continued*
  signalling equipment, **21**, 216, 217
  sources of law, **21**, 192
  statute law, **21**, 193
  subordinate legislation, **21**, 193, 196
    consultation, **21**, 198
    enabling powers to make, **21**, 197–199
    modification and repeal, **21**, 199
  survey—
    cargo ships, **21**, 212, 212n
    certificate, **21**, 212, 213
    passenger ships, **21**, 213, 213n
  unsafe operation of ship, **21**, 207
safety of those on board, responsibility for, **15**,
  298, 304
sailing directions, **21**, 229n, 378
sailing vessel, *see* SAILING VESSEL
sale of—
  common law meaning, **21**, 107
  contract for, form, **21**, 165, 166
  court order, by, **21**, 168
  disputes between co-owners as to, **21**, 137
  generally, **21**, 101, 131
  mortgagee's remedies, in relation to, **21**, 179
  wages, crew's right to, **21**, 259
  See also title *below*
Saleform 1983 ...., **21**, 165, 166
salvage, *see* SALVAGE
salvor, *see* SALVOR
saving or attempting to save life at sea, loss or
  damage resulting from, **21**, 603, 605
scale showing water draught, **21**, 148, 148n
sea waybill, *see* SEA WAYBILL
seaman, *see* SEAMAN
search, customs officers' powers of, **7**, 1228
seaworthiness, *see* SEAWORTHINESS
services in connection with, VAT zero-rating, **7**,
  1452
set and sale, action of, **21**, 107, 137, 138
shapes, display—
  equipment for, safety regulations, **21**, 220
  see also collision regulations (lights and shapes)
    above
share in—
  dispute over ownership, **20**, 305
  division into shares, **21**, 132
  joint owners, **21**, 135
  majority interest, meaning, **21**, 144n
  mortgage, **21**, 174ff
  owner, *see* owner *above*
  registration, maximum number of owners
    allowed, **21**, 132
  transfer, *see* title *below*
  transmission, *see* title *below*
sheriff court jurisdiction, **6**, 1131
shipbuilding records, **19**, 849
ship's delivery order, *see* SHIP'S DELIVERY ORDER
ship's husband, *see* SHIP'S HUSBAND
signals—
  attention, to attract, **21**, 375
  collision regulations, generally, **21**, 371
  distress, **21**, 209, 220, 331, 375, 376
  failure to use, **21**, 371

Ship—*continued*
signals—*continued*
  improper, making, **21**, 371
  light, **21**, 373, 375
    collision regulations, *see* collision regulations *above*
    equipment and maintenance, **21**, 220, 229*n*
  manoeuvring, **21**, 373
  requirement for ship to carry publications containing, **21**, 229*n*
  shapes—
    collision regulations, *see* collision regulations *above*
    equipment for, **21**, 220
  signalling equipment, safety regulations, **21**, 220
  sound, **21**, 375
    equipment for, **21**, 220, 372
    restricted visibility, in, **21**, 374
  warning, **21**, 373
slave trade, engaged in on high seas, jurisdiction, **21**, 44, 45
small—
  concept of, **21**, 106*n*
  radar reflector, **21**, 378*n*
  small ships register, **21**, 131*n*
    joint and co-ownership, **21**, 132, 132*n*
  traffic separation scheme, **21**, 348
  unregistered, British nationality, **21**, 141
sound signals, *see* SIGNALS
stateless, rights of interference with, **21**, 44, 45
steering gear, **21**, 219
steering rules, *see* collision regulations (steering and sailing rules)
stevedore, *see* STEVEDORE
stores—
  export, **7**, 1194
  surplus, import procedure, **7**, 1147
  VAT zero-rating, **7**, 1436
stowage—
  bad—
    negligence, as, **21**, 551*n*
    unseaworthiness, when amounting to, **21**, 614*n*
  bill of lading, express terms, **21**, 546
  Hague-Visby Rules, **21**, 594
  performance of contract, **21**, 585
  time charterparty, **21**, 640
  voyage charterparty, **21**, 626
    equipment, provision of, **21**, 626
    express terms, **21**, 618
    liability for improper, **21**, 626
stowaway, **21**, 270
submarine, *see* SUBMARINE
subsidies, policy formulation as to, responsibility for, **21**, 113
supply, VAT zero-rating, **7**, 1452
supply of goods and materials to, disputes over, **20**, 305
survey, **21**, 147
  cargo ships, **21**, 212, 212*n*
  generally, **21**, 147
  passenger ships, **21**, 213, 213*n*
surveyor's certificate, retention by registrar, **21**, 151

Ship—*continued*
temporarily within United Kingdom, patented product in, **18**, 865
temporary importation, **7**, 1194
threat to destroy or endanger ship, platform etc, **7**, 404
tidal stream atlas, **21**, 229*n*
tide tables, **21**, 229*n*
title—
  legal—
    beneficial interest distinguished, **21**, 133
  sue, to—
    bill of lading—
      contract contained in, **21**, 576, 579, 579*n*
      implied contract, **21**, 581
      transfer of, **21**, 570–572
    charterparty, contract evidenced by, **21**, 576, 577
    collision damage, in respect of, **21**, 320
    contract law, **21**, 576, 576*n*
    delict, **21**, 576, 576*n*
      title to sue shipowner, **21**, 580
    Dunlop v Lambert, rule in, **21**, 582
    negligence, **21**, 320, 576
    shipowner, right to sue, generally, **21**, 576
    transfer of—
      bill of lading, **21**, 570–572
      sea waybill, **21**, 575, 578, 578*n*, 579
      ship's delivery order, **21**, 574, 578, 578*n*, 579
transfer of—
  bill of lading, **21**, 566
  bill of sale, **21**, 167
  contract, form of, **21**, 165, 166
  court order, sale by, **21**, 168
  court power to prohibit, **21**, 169
  declaration of transfer, **21**, 167
  disputes between co-owners as to, **21**, 137
  formalities relating to registered ships, **21**, 167–169
  generally, **21**, 101, 131, 163, 164
  registration, **21**, 167
  sale, common law meaning, **21**, 107
  Saleform 1983 ..., **21**, 165, 166
  share in ship, **21**, 163–169
  ships' mortgage, title to, **21**, 181
transmission of—
  bankruptcy or liquidation of owner, on, **21**, 170
  death of owner, on, **21**, 170
  generally, **21**, 163, 170
  share in ship, **21**, 170, 171
  ships' mortgage, title to, **21**, 182
  unqualified persons, to, **21**, 171
  unregistered ships, **21**, 170
towage, *see* TOW
trades description legislation, **6**, 112
traffic density—
  safe speed, determining, **21**, 343
  traffic separation scheme, **21**, 348
traffic separation scheme—
  fishing vessels, **21**, 348
  generally, **21**, 348
  inshore zone, **21**, 348

Ship—*continued*
traffic separation scheme—*continued*
  object, **21**, 348
  safety zones, **21**, 348
  separation zone, **21**, 348
  small vessels, **21**, 348
tramp, meaning, **21**, 526, 526*n*
transhipment—
  carrier utilised for, liability, **21**, 560
  clause, bill of lading, **21**, 546
  voyage charterparty, **21**, 618, 629, 630
transire, **21**, 140, 140*n*
transit passage, **21**, 10
tug, *see* TUG
tug and tow, *see* TOW
UK registered ship in dangerously unsafe
  condition, **21**, 206, 206*n*
unauthorised person on board, **21**, 269*n*, 270
UNCLOS, *see* UNITED NATIONS CONFERENCE ON
  THE LAW OF THE SEA
underwater operation, vessel engaged in, **21**, 365
underway, meaning, **21**, 356*n*
unregistered, **21**, 132
  beneficial interest, **21**, 133
  legal title, **21**, 133
unseaworthiness, *see* SEAWORTHINESS
upholstered fittings for, **19**, 421
valuables on board—
  limitation of liability in respect of, **21**, 557
  luggage, contract for carriage of, **21**, 728, 733
vessel—
  definition, **21**, 106, 108, 109, 111, 211*n*
  navigability, **21**, 108
  not under command, **21**, 365, 374
  oil rigs and other structures, whether classed as,
    21, 108*n*
visibility—
  restricted—
    lights, display of, collision regulations, **21**,
      359
    meaning, **21**, 357*n*
    sound signals, **21**, 374
    steering and sailing rules, **21**, 357
  safe speed, determining, **21**, 343
  vessels in sight of one another—
    meaning, **21**, 349
    steering and sailing rules, **21**, 349–356
voyage, definitions, **21**, 211*n*
warship—
  high seas, on, jurisdiction, **21**, 44
  innocent passage, right of, through territorial
    sea, **21**, 9
watch—
  navigational watch arrangements—
    bridge, manning, **21**, 340
    generally, **21**, 340
    officer in charge, **21**, 340
  radio, **21**, 247
  See also look-out *above*
watchkeeping arrangements, regulations as to, **21**,
  247
weather—
  dangerous, duty as to, **21**, 210, 379
  favourable, definition, **21**, 211*n*

Ship—*continued*
whistle, **21**, 372
wreck, *see* WRECK
See also PRIZE; SHIPPING
Ship agent, **1**, 614
Ship engineer
right of lien, **20**, 77
Shipbroker
meaning, **21**, 533
Shipbuilding
foreign state at war with friendly state, for, **7**, 610
Shipbuilding Industry Board
establishment of, **19**, 211
Shipping
authorities and organisations concerned with, **21**,
  113–121
Baltic Exchange, **21**, 120
barratry, **21**, 551*n*, 554
basic concepts in shipping and navigation law, **21**,
  105
blockade as restraint of princes, **21**, 550
bottomry, **21**, 101
bottomry bond—
  conventional hypothec, as, **21**, 479
  maritime lien—
    giving rise to, **21**, 392, 479
    priority, **21**, 479*n*
Bureau Veritas, **21**, 120
cargo, *See* CARGO
carriage by sea, *see* SEA, CARRIAGE BY
classification societies, **21**, 120
coastguard, *see* COASTGUARD
Shipping agent
appointment, voyage charterparty, **21**, 618
Shipping casualty
jurisdiction over, **1**, 408
Shipping conference
generally, **21**, 118
Shipping line
contract, insurance, freight (cif) contract, **21**, 524*n*
liner conferences (conferences), **21**, 527
meaning, **21**, 524
Shire
community, identification of, **14**, 53
Shogun lease
See CROSS-BORDER LEASING
Shooting gallery
exemption from firearm certificates, **10**, 1539
Shooting lease
assignation, **11**, 902
control of game, clauses in respect of, **11**, 900
conveyance of shooting rights, **11**, 897
exclusive, **11**, 903
fences, **11**, 904
generally, **13**, 202
granters of, **11**, 898
joint proprietors, where, **11**, 898
landlord indemnified against agricultural tenant's
  claims, **11**, 901
landlord's hypothec, **13**, 513
Leith case, **11**, 896
liferenters and trustees, by, **11**, 898
nature of, **11**, 895–897
normal clauses, **11**, 899–904

Shooting lease—*continued*
right to kill game, clauses in respect of, **11**, 900
subletting, **11**, 902
transmitted by agricultural lease, when, **11**, 897
Shooting rights
buildings, **11**, 908
exclusive, **11**, 903
foreshore, on, **20**, 268
house, attached to, **11**, 914
lands and heritage, meaning, **11**, 905
unlet, **11**, 912
valuation, **11**, 905–915
 buildings, **11**, 908
 carcases, **11**, 915
 entry of, **11**, 906
 extra commercium subjects, **11**, 912
 house, shooting rights attached to, **11**, 914
 net annual value, **11**, 907
 rateable value, **11**, 909; **24**, 736–740
 reduction in value, **11**, 911
 shootings used for other purposes, **11**, 910
 unlet sporting rights, **11**, 913
Shop
assured tenancy, exclusion from, **13**, 636, 639
charitable purpose, run for, **3**, 1123
fire certificates, **10**, 1454
health and safety at work legislation, **19**, 343
hours of work, **9**, 73
lease, **13**, 197
 'full repairing and insuring lease', **13**, 556, 557,
  563, 580, 581
 landlord's hypothec, **13**, 513
 meaning of shop, **13**, 525
 renewal—
  application for, **13**, 527
  effect, **13**, 527
 Tenancy of Shops (Scotland) Act 1949 ...—
  subject of lease, **13**, 525
local authority provision, **11**, 1906
meaning, **13**, 525
public health, **14**, 705
shop hours, **6**, 11
tenancy—
 landlord, **13**, 526
 parties to, **13**, 526
 protection, extent of, **13**, 527
 renewal, application for—
  expenses, award of, **13**, 530
  further applications, **13**, 529
  procedure, **13**, 530
  refusal, **13**, 528
 security of tenure, generally, **11**, 1937, 1943;
  13, 524
 Tenancy of Shops (Scotland) Acts—
  generally, **13**, 197, 524
  subjects applicable to, **13**, 525
 tenant, **13**, 526
trading stamps, **6**, 146
valuation for rating, **24**, 741
 comparative principle, **24**, 529
 excluded from industrial derating, **24**, 640
 meaning, **24**, 641
 repair work, meaning, **24**, 641
 shopping malls, **24**, 673

Shop club
registration, **12**, 680*n*
Shop window display
invitation to treat, as, **15**, 621
Short assured tenancy
See TENANT-TENANCY
Short tenancy
acquiring authority, powers of, **5**, 185
agricultural holding, service of notice to quit, **5**,
 185
break clause, existence of, **5**, 185
duration, **13**, 594
fair rent, registration, **13**, 594
features, **13**, 594
injurious affection, **5**, 185
introduction, **13**, 594
just allowance, **5**, 185
loss or injury sustained, **5**, 185
meaning, **5**, 185
notification to tenant, **13**, 594
repossession, **13**, 736, 741
severance, **5**, 185
unexpired term, value of, **5**, 185
Short time
redundancy, effect on, **9**, 165
Shot firing
damages, **14**, 1653
misfire, procedure to be adopted after, **14**, 1654
proper shelter, meaning, **14**, 1653
shot hole, charging of, **14**, 1653
Shot gun
adapted to have non-detachable magazine, **10**, 1520
antique, **10**, 1520
carrying in public place, **10**, 1567
child or young person, sale to, **3**, 1223
children and young persons, possession by, **3**,
 1223; **10**, 1553
component parts, **10**, 1520
control, generally, **10**, 1512
definition, **10**, 1520
drunk in possession in public place, **10**, 1567
firearm certificates, **10**, 1520
prohibited weapons, as, **10**, 1515*n*
shortening, **10**, 1572
shot gun certificates, **10**, 1520
 applications, **10**, 1529
  details to be included, **10**, 1529, 1530
  photographs may be required, **10**, 1529, 1530
  verification of, **10**, 1530
 artificial target shooting, **10**, 1549
 borrowed gun on private premises, **10**, 1549
 conditions prescribed by Secretary of State, **10**,
  1529
 dealers and their employees, **10**, 1555
 duration, **10**, 1529
 exemptions, **10**, 1549
 false, **10**, 1520
 false entries, **10**, 1520
 grant, **10**, 1529
 Northern Ireland, issued in, **10**, 1549
 personation of person to whom made, **10**, 1520
 production of, powers to demand, **10**, 1576
 refusal of application, **10**, 1529
 renewal, **10**, 1529

Shot gun—*continued*
shot gun certificates—*continued*
  revocation, **10**, 1529
  signature, **10**, 1529
visitors' permits, **10**, 1531, 1546
  group applications, **10**, 1531, 1546
Shouting
breach of the peace, as, **7**, 454
Show
See PLEASURE FAIR
Shroud
unlawful removal, **3**, 505
Shrub
overhanging road, **20**, 505, 696
planting alongside road, **20**, 672–674
roads authority, provision by, **20**, 503
Shynd bills
udal law, **24**, 307
Sick pay
contract, under, express or implied, **9**, 54
earnings, as, **21**, 1031
statutory—
  adjudication, **21**, 1149, 1170
    appeals, **21**, 1170
  administration, **21**, 801
  armed forces, members of, **21**, 920
  claimant unable to act, where, **21**, 918
  contract of service—
    ended solely or mainly for purpose of avoiding liability, **21**, 905
    where more than one, **21**, 924
  contractual remuneration, **21**, 923
  contributions conditions, **21**, 894
  Crown employment, **21**, 920
  deductions from, **21**, 921
  disablement, incapacity by way of, **21**, 908
  earnings, as, **21**, 1031
  entitlement, **21**, 907
    commencement, **21**, 911
    exclusion, **21**, 912
    generally, **21**, 801
    maximum, **21**, 915
    period of, **21**, 910
  first day of employment, employee sick on, **21**, 912
  fixed term contract, employee under, **21**, 912
  generally, **21**, 907
  incapacity for work—
    day of—
      meaning, **21**, 908
      Sundays, **21**, 909
    generally, **21**, 907
    period of—
      calculation, **21**, 909
      meaning, **21**, 909
      Sundays, **21**, 909
  interruption of employment, **21**, 912
  invalidity benefit, interaction with, **21**, 894
  invalidity pension days, **21**, 912
  legal custody, employee in, **21**, 912
  liability for, **21**, 916
    appeal against, **21**, 917
    avoidance, **21**, 913
    insolvency of employer, where, **21**, 917

Sick pay—*continued*
statutory—*continued*
  lower earnings limit, **21**, 912
  maternity allowance, **21**, 912
  mental disablement, incapacity by way of, **21**, 908
  payment, **21**, 801
    commencement, **21**, 914
    form, **21**, 917
    generally, **21**, 917
  pensionable age, employee over, **21**, 912
  pregnant employee, **21**, 912
  prison, employee in, **21**, 912
  qualifying conditions, **21**, 907
  qualifying days—
    first three, **21**, 914
    meaning, **21**, 914
    regulations as to, **21**, 914
  rates, **21**, 917, 917*n*
    daily rate, **21**, 917
  recovery by employer of amounts paid, **21**, 919
  severe disablement allowance, **21**, 912
  sickness benefit, **21**, 912
    entitlement to precluded by receipt of statutory sick pay, **21**, 878, 922
  social security benefits, relationship with, **21**, 922
  Social Security Commissioner, appeal to, **21**, 1182
  specific disease, incapacity by way of, **21**, 908
  trade dispute at place of employment, **21**, 912
Sickness benefit
absence of claimant from place of residence, **21**, 888
absent from Great Britain, claimant, **21**, 1021, 1022
alcoholism, **21**, 888
behaviour calculated to retard recovery, **21**, 888
change of occupation, whether claimant might be expected to make, **21**, 883
contribution record, **21**, 941
convalescence, **21**, 886
criminal proceedings, relevance of, **21**, 889
cytotoxic drugs, claimant receiving chemotherapy with, **21**, 880
dependent adult, increase where, **21**, 1017
dependent child, increase where, **21**, 1015
disease, meaning, **21**, 879
disqualification, **21**, 888
doctor's certificate, **21**, 881
entitlement—
  generally, **21**, 801, 878, 966
  self-employed, **21**, 878
  unemployed, **21**, 878
gainful occupation, meaning, **21**, 882*n*
haemodialysis, regular weekly treatment for, **21**, 880
incapacity for work, **21**, 878, 881
  agoraphobia, **21**, 881, 881*n*
  alcoholism, **21**, 879
  bodily disablement, **21**, 878, 879
  change of occupation, whether claimant might be expected to make, **21**, 883
  character defects, **21**, 879

Sickness benefit—*continued*
incapacity for work—*continued*
  claimant unable to work properly, **21**, 881
  claimant unable to work without injury to
    health, **21**, 881
  deemed—
    convalescence, **21**, 886
    generally, **21**, 884
    infectious disease, carrier of, **21**, 886
    work done, **21**, 885
  definition, **21**, 882
  degree of incapacity, **21**, 881
  doctor's certificate, **21**, 881
  extraneous factors, **21**, 882
  fact, as question of, **21**, 881
  hospital in-patient, **21**, 881
  medical evidence, **21**, 881
  mental disablement, **21**, 878, 879
  misconduct of claimant, caused by, **21**, 888
  notification of, **21**, 916
  onus of proof, **21**, 881, 884
  particular doctor's opinion not conclusive, **21**,
    881
  pregnancy, **21**, 879
  previous claims record of claimant, **21**, 881
  psychological state of claimant, **21**, 879
  self-certificate, **21**, 881
  short-term, **21**, 883
  specific disease, **21**, 878, 879
    causation, knowledge of not required, **21**,
      879
    meaning, **21**, 879
  training course, claimant attending, **21**, 887
  travel, claimant unable to, **21**, 881
  work, definition, **21**, 882
industrial injury, generally, **21**, 966
infectious disease, carrier of, **21**, 886
interruption of employment, period of, **21**, 878,
  880
invalidity benefit, interaction with, **21**, 890
limited importance of, **21**, 878
medical or other examination, failure to attend,
  21, 888
medical or other treatment, failure to submit to,
  21, 888
misconduct of claimant causing incapacity, **21**,
  888
national insurance contributions, **21**, 1041
notification of incapacity, **21**, 916
period for which payable, **21**, 890
peritoneal dialysis, claimant receiving, **21**, 880
plasmapheresis, treatment for, **21**, 880
pregnancy, single or separated woman, **21**, 888
previous claims record of claimant, **21**, 881
radiotherapy, claimant receiving, **21**, 880
self-certificate, **21**, 881
self-employed, entitlement to, **21**, 878
severe disablement allowance, interaction with,
  21, 941
statutory sick pay, interaction with, **21**, 878, 912,
  922
training course, claimant attending, **21**, 887
unemployed, entitlement to, **21**, 878
venereal disease, **21**, 888

Sickness benefit—*continued*
work, definition, **21**, 882
work undertaken—
  disqualification where, **21**, 888
  generally, **21**, 885
  medical supervision, under, **21**, 885, 888
  medical treatment, as part of, **21**, 888
Sight
testing, *see* OPHTHALMIC SERVICES
Sighting device
wild birds or animals taken or killed with, **11**,
  880, 884
Signalling device
firearm certificates, **10**, 1522*n*, 1541*n*
Signature
attested will, **25**, 724
cautionary obligation, of, **3**, 855
foot of writ, whether signature must be at, **3**, 877
holograph will, **25**, 724
lack of signed writ, proof of agreement, where, **3**,
  886
passing of seals, **7**, 897, 898
royal, **7**, 853
  Cachet Seal, **7**, 853
superscribing, **6**, 416
valid subscription, what constitutes, **3**, 876
who may sign, **3**, 878
will, in, what constitutes, **25**, 724
witnesses, of, **6**, 421
writ, prescribed form of, **17**, 1011
See also DEED OR WRITING
Signet Bill
abolition, **7**, 871
Signet Office
former existence, **7**, 887
Signet of Scotland
Court of Session summonses, **7**, 883, 884
design, **7**, 882
generally, **7**, 855, 882, 897, 900
history, **7**, 882, 883
Keeper, **7**, 887
multiplicity, **7**, 882
new Sovereign, accession, **7**, 882
uses, **7**, 883
Signet of the United Kingdom
Cachet Seal, **7**, 868, 869
generally, **7**, 855, 867
Greater, **7**, 868, 869
Keeper, **7**, 868
Lesser, **7**, 868, 869
Secretaries of State, **7**, 868
Signposting
trunk roads, **20**, 620
Silicon chip
See SEMICONDUCTOR TOPOGRAPHIES
Silos
agricultural buildings, as, **24**, 562
Silver
articles or coin, Carriers Act (1830), **3**, 610
false trade description, **18**, 1418, 1418*n*
hallmarking, *see* HALLMARKING
mines royal, **13**, 200
plated articles, **18**, 1419

Singing
noise from, **9**, 1298
Single Administrative Document (SAD)
customs warehousing, **7**, 1174
European Union customs documentation, **7**,
  1124, 1125, 1154
Single parent
income tax allowance, **19**, 1518
Single prices
See COMMON AGRICULTURAL POLICY
Singular successor
acquiescence of author, bound by, **16**, 1616,
  1616*n*
acquisition of title by, reduction barred by, **13**, 54
contravention of servitude, whether bound by,
  16, 1616
impugn lease, right to, **13**, 314
landlord's interest, transfer on, **13**, 348, 350
lessor, of—
  accretion, **13**, 156
  continuing obligations—
    generally, **13**, 239
  lessee's protection against—
    historical background, **13**, 101
    lease, categories of, **13**, 102
  limited title, **13**, 157
  personal conditions, **13**, 240, 242
  real conditions, **13**, 239–241
  tenant's option to renew, **13**, 152, 243
meaning, **25**, 675
salmon fishings leases protected from claims by,
  11, 9
universal successor distinguished from, **18**, 598;
  25, 675
Sink
public health nuisance, as, **19**, 336
water fittings, as, **25**, 527
Sinks
servitude of, **25**, 351
Siren
motor vehicle equipped with, **20**, 481
Sister
deceased specified relative, as, **15**, 602
division of estate on or after 8 December 1986—
  examples, **25**, 704
heritable succession, **25**, 679
moveable succession, **25**, 682
settlement, family reunion or creation by, **12**,
  289, 290
Skating
historical background, **19**, 1203
Skip
builder's—
  control, **3**, 201
  road, deposit on, **3**, 201
owner's name, telephone number and address to
  be marked on, **20**, 685
police powers in relation to, **20**, 685
removal, order for, **20**, 685
removal of unauthorised, **20**, 505
repositioning, order for, **20**, 685
responsibility for, **20**, 685
road, permission for use on, **20**, 685
vehicle carrying, dimensions, **20**, 475

Slander
judicial, **15**, 523, 529, 535
partner, by, liability, **16**, 1043
third party—
  Broom v Ritchie & Co, decision in, **15**, 571
  examples, **15**, 570
  generally, **15**, 570
title, goods or business, of—
  absolute privilege, **15**, 559
  business, slander of, **15**, 563
  comparative advertising, in, **1**, 515
  defences, **15**, 559
  falsity of statement, **15**, 560
  generally, **15**, 559
  loss, remarks must have caused, **15**, 560
  malicious, statement must be, **15**, 560
  property, slander of, **15**, 561
  requisites for actionability, **15**, 559, 560
  title, slander of, **15**, 562
Slaughter
See ANIMALS; KNACKER; SLAUGHTERHOUSE
Slaughterhouse
byelaws and regulations, **11**, 502
ceilings, **11**, 505
cleansing, **11**, 505
confinement and treatment before slaughter, **11**,
  503
construction, **11**, 505
diseases, persons handling meat, of, **11**, 506
drainage, **11**, 505
early legislation, **11**, 303, 304
entry, powers of, **11**, 515
equipment, **11**, 505
export, animals slaughtered for, **11**, 510, 511
first aid materials, **11**, 506
floors, **11**, 505
generally, **14**, 697
humane conditions, **19**, 382
hygiene, **11**, 504, 506
infestation, prevention of, **11**, 505
inspection of meat, **11**, 507
interdict *ab ante*, **14**, 2146
Jewish slaughter, **11**, 503, 513
knacker's yard, *see* KNACKER
lighting, **11**, 505
local authorities, functions of, **11**, 509
local authority provision, **11**, 499, 499*n*
meaning, **11**, 404*n*, 499*n*; **19**, 380
meat inspector, **11**, 507, 507*n*
methods of slaughter, **11**, 503
Muslim slaughter, **11**, 503, 513
offences, **11**, 514
offensive and dangerous trades, regulation of, **19**,
  373, 373*n*, 379–382
poultry, **14**, 698
private, **11**, 500
  certificate of registration, **11**, 500
  confinement of animals, separate premises used
    for, **11**, 500
  registered person, **11**, 500
public, **11**, 499
  disposal of, **11**, 499
  employees, **11**, 499
  plant and apparatus, **11**, 499

Slaughterhouse—*continued*
public health provisions, **19**, 305, 373, 379–382, 474
Secretary of State's powers in relation to, **11**, 321
slaughtering instruments and ammunition, possession of, **10**, 1535
unregistered premises used as, **11**, 500
ventilation, **11**, 505
veterinary meat inspector, **11**, 507, 507*n*
walls, **11**, 505
water supply, **11**, 505
Slaughtermen
qualification and licensing, **11**, 513; **19**, 381
Slavery
customary international law before 1945 …, **12**, 2
European Convention on Human Rights, **12**, 6, 28
International Convention for the Suppression of the White Slave Traffic, **12**, 508
ship engaged in slave trade, jurisdiction, **21**, 44, 45
Universal Declaration of Human Rights, **12**, 4*n*
Sleeping policeman
See road (hump)
Slughorn
grant of, **11**, 1611
shouter, **11**, 1611
Slum clearance
revenue account, **11**, 1918
slum clearance areas replaced by housing action areas, **11**, 1996
Small claims procedure
appeals, **17**, 1348
book of small claims, **17**, 1346
civil legal aid, when not available, **13**, 1034
claim—
initiation of, **17**, 1340
response to, **17**, 1340
consumer redress, **6**, 169
decree, **17**, 1343
expenses, **17**, 1345
goals, **17**, 1336
historical background, **17**, 1337
nature of scheme, **17**, 1339
preliminary hearing, **17**, 1341
proof, **17**, 1342
reform, movement towards, **17**, 1338
remitting cases, **17**, 1347
representation, **17**, 1344
Small tenant
See STATUTORY SMALL TENANT
Smallholding
adjoining land owners, right of pre-emption of, **1**, 845
agricultural holding, constituting, **1**, 727
assignation of, **1**, 845
bequest of, **1**, 847
enlargement of, **1**, 849
excluded land, **1**, 836
existing, **1**, 836
extent and value, **6**, 956
landholder, *see* LANDHOLDER
long lease, standard securities, **20**, 179
meaning, **1**, 836

Smallholding—*continued*
new, registration of, **1**, 836
record of, **1**, 844
register of, **1**, 852
registration, abortive scheme for, **6**, 956, 964
renunciation of, **1**, 841
residence on, **1**, 839
resumption by landlord, **1**, 840
statutory small tenancies, **6**, 956, 964
statutory small tenant of, *see* STATUTORY SMALL TENANT
subjects of, **1**, 836
subletting, **1**, 846
succession on intestacy, **1**, 848
vacant, dealing with, **1**, 850
See also AGRICULTURAL HOLDING
Smallpox
death by, cremation following, **3**, 565
infection, fear of, **14**, 2082
Smell
factory, from, action to interdict, **14**, 2039
offensive trade, from, **9**, 1120
Smith, Adam
Lectures on Jurisprudence, **18**, 4, 4*n*
Smith, Sir Thomas, **25**, xi–xiii
Smoke
control area—
designation order, **14**, 304
emission in, **9**, 1134
non-smokeless unauthorised fuel, use of, **9**, 1139
control orders—
local authority, powers of, **9**, 1133
publicity for, **9**, 1136
Secretary of State, direction by, **9**, 1135
Crown premises, emission from, **9**, 1137
dark—
emission of, **9**, 1123
meaning, **9**, 1122
railway engine, from, **9**, 1126
vessel, from, **9**, 1127
emission of—
chimney of domestic building, from, **9**, 1124
defence to charge of, **9**, 1124, 1125
generally, **19**, 316
industrial premises, from, **9**, 1125
railway locomotives, from, **19**, 1052
trade premises, from, **9**, 1125
fireplace, grant to adapt, **9**, 1138
furnaces, from—
dust—
emission of, **9**, 1129
equipment to arrest—
exemption from requirement, **9**, 1131
provision of, **9**, 1130
generally, **9**, 1128
grit—
emission of, **9**, 1129
equipment to arrest—
exemption from requirement, **9**, 1131
provision of, **9**, 1130
height of chimneys, **9**, 1132
meaning, **9**, 1122
pollution, **19**, 303, 316

Smoke—*continued*
sulphur dioxide and, **9**, 1148
trade secrets under Clean Air Acts, disclosure of, **9**, 1140
wild birds or animals taken with, **11**, 880, 884
Smoking
meat and food handlers, hygiene regulations, **11**, 415
person under age of sixteen, by, in public place, **3**, 1225
railway byelaws concerning, **19**, 1015
sale of smoking materials—
   person under age of sixteen, to, **3**, 1225
   regional and islands council duties, **3**, 1225
Smuggling
armed, **7**, 1235
barratry, **21**, 554*n*
drug, detention relating to, **7**, 1230
sale of smuggled goods, **7**, 1236
signals connected with, **7**, 1234
small ships, regulations regarding, **7**, 1233
Snare
deer taken or killed with, **11**, 940
wild birds or animals taken or killed with, **11**, 880, 884
Sniggering
salmon fishing by, **11**, 11*n*
Snipe
custody of, by unqualified person, **11**, 807
game, as, **11**, 802
Game Acts, **11**, 496*n*
nets or springs, taken by, **11**, 830
Poaching Prevention Act 1832 ..., **11**, 843
trespass in search of, **11**, 817
Snow
gates, provison of, **20**, 503
road, protection from, **20**, 660
roads, on—
   roads authority duties, **20**, 665
   snow gates, provision of, **20**, 666
   trunk roads, **20**, 620
roads authorities' duties as to, **20**, 503
Snuff
meat and food handlers, hygiene regulations, **11**, 415
Soap
weights and measures legislation, **6**, 241
Socage (soccage)
feudal law, generally, **18**, 70
Social Democratic Party
Council for Scotland, **5**, 395
Liberal Party, special relationship with, **5**, 395
organisation of, **5**, 395
regional committee, **5**, 395
Social facilities
byelaws, **14**, 277
district council, powers and duties, **14**, 690–692
islands council, powers and duties, **14**, 690–692
regional council, financial contributions by, **14**, 693
Social fund
appeals, **21**, 1123, 1130
budgeting loan, **21**, 1123, 1124
budgets, management of, **21**, 1123

Social fund—*continued*
cash limits, **21**, 1123
cold weather payment, **21**, 1123, 1129
community care grant, **21**, 1123, 1125, 1126
crisis loan, **21**, 1123, 1125
definition, **21**, 1123
directions and guidance on issue of payments, **21**, 1123
discretionary nature, **21**, 1062
discretionary provisions, **21**, 1124–1126
eligible loans, **21**, 1124
excluded items, **21**, 1124
funeral expense payment, **21**, 1123, 1128
   adjudication, **21**, 1149
income support, interaction with, **21**, 1079, 1123, 1124, 1125
maternity expense payment, **21**, 1123, 1127
   adjudication, **21**, 1149
purpose, **21**, 1123
rent, crisis loan towards, **21**, 1125
review, **21**, 1123
Social Fund Commissioner, **21**, 1149
Social Fund Manual, **21**, 1123
trade dispute, claimant involved in, **21**, 1124, 1125
Social reformers
Hill, Octavia, **22**, 1
Shaftesbury, Lord Ashley, Earl of, **22**, 1
Social security
absent from Great Britain, claimant or dependant, **21**, 1020–1029
   continental shelf, employment on, **21**, 1026
   temporary, **21**, 1021, 1022
adjudication—
   adjudication officer, *see* ADJUDICATION OFFICER
   alteration of decisions—
      correction, **21**, 1173
      review—
         powers of, **21**, 1171
         provisions governing, **21**, 1172
         scope, **21**, 1172
         setting aside, **21**, 1173
   appeals—
      appeal tribunals, generally, **21**, 1141
      disability appeal tribunal, *see* DISABILITY APPEAL TRIBUNAL
      error in decision, correction, **21**, 1173
      exclusions, **21**, 1175
      generally, **21**, 1149, 1151
      medical appeal tribunal, *see* MEDICAL APPEAL TRIBUNAL
      pre-1980 structure, **21**, 1144
      setting aside decision, **21**, 1173
      social security appeal tribunal, *see* SOCIAL SECURITY APPEAL TRIBUNAL
   advice, duty of Department of Social Security to give, **21**, 1160
   assessors, assistance by, **21**, 1150
   attendance allowance, **21**, 1167, 1171
   availability for employment cases, **21**, 1171
   disability appeal tribunal, **21**, 1152
   disability living allowance, **21**, 1167, 1168, 1171
   disability working allowance, **21**, 1168, 1171

Social security—*continued*
adjudication—*continued*
  error in, correction, **21**, 1173
  European Court of Justice, references to, **21**, 1188
  experts, referral to, **21**, 1150
  finality of decisions, pre-1980 structure, **21**, 1145
  forfeiture rule question, **21**, 1169, 1186
  generally, **21**, 1141
  Health and Social Services and Social Security Adjudications Act 1983 ..., **21**, 1148
  historical background—
    changes up to 1986 ..., **21**, 1146–1149
    Disability Living Allowance and Disability Working Allowance Act 1991 ..., **21**, 1152
    pre-1980 structure, **21**, 1142–1145
    Social Security Act 1989 ..., **21**, 1150
    Social Security Act 1990 ..., **21**, 1151
    Social Security Administration Act 1992 ..., **21**, 1153
  Independent Tribunal Service, **21**, 1174
  industrial injuries benefits, **21**, 1164, 1166
  initial, **21**, 1141
  claim—
    delay in due to ill health, **21**, 1158
    deliberately refraining from, **21**, 1157
    generally, **21**, 1154
    delegation, **21**, 1161
    ignorance of entitlement, **21**, 1156
    medical appeal tribunal, referral to, **21**, 1179
    official misinformation, where, **21**, 1160
    reliance on advice as to entitlement, **21**, 1159
    responsibility for, **21**, 1162
    time limit, extension for good cause, **21**, 1155
  investigative nature, **21**, 1141
  medical appeal tribunal, *see* MEDICAL APPEAL TRIBUNAL
  medical authorities—
    industrial injuries benefits, **21**, 1164, 1166
    prescribed diseases, **21**, 1165, 1166
    severe disablement allowance, **21**, 1164, 1166
  medical practitioner, by, review of decisions, **21**, 1171
  prescribed diseases cases, **21**, 1165, 1166
  reports, **21**, 1145
  review, *see* alteration of decisions *above*
  Secretary of State for Social Security—
    function, **21**, 1141, 1149, 1154
    questions reserved to, **21**, 1163
  setting aside decision, **21**, 1173
  severe disablement allowance, **21**, 1164, 1166
  Social Security Act 1979 ..., **21**, 1146
  Social Security Act 1980 ..., **21**, 1147
  Social Security Act 1986 ..., **21**, 1149
  social security appeal tribunal, *see* SOCIAL SECURITY APPEAL TRIBUNAL
  Social Security Commissioner, *see* SOCIAL SECURITY COMMISSIONER
  statutory adjudicating authorities, **21**, 1141
  statutory maternity pay, **21**, 1170
  statutory sick pay, **21**, 1170

Social security—*continued*
adjudication—*continued*
  supplementary benefit, **21**, 1147
  tribunals, constitution, **21**, 1146
  tribunals or bodies outwith courts, vesting in, **21**, 1143
  victim of accident etc, compensation sum falling to, **21**, 1150
attendance allowance, *see* ATTENDANCE ALLOWANCE
benefits—
  arrestment, **8**, 280
  classification, **21**, 801
  damages, effect on scale of, **15**, 930
  definition, **21**, 801
  donation, receipt of effecting, **8**, 658
  means tested, **21**, 1061*ff*
  national insurance contributions—
    where entitlement dependent on, **21**, 801
    where entitlement not dependent on, **21**, 801
  non-means tested, **21**, 801*ff*
  not assignable, **8**, 615
  occupational deafness, cases of, **9**, 1291
child benefit, *see* CHILD BENEFIT
Christmas bonus, pensioners', **21**, 1201
claim—
  additional information, requirement for, **21**, 1154
  adjudication, *see* adjudication *above*
  approval of form, **21**, 1154
  condition of right to benefit, as, **21**, 1154
  delay in—
    deliberately refraining from claiming, **21**, 1157
    English language, ignorance of, **21**, 1156, 1159
    ignorance of entitlement, where, **21**, 1156
    ill health, due to, **21**, 1158
    illiteracy of claimant, **21**, 1156
    official misinformation, following, **21**, 1160
    reliance on advice as to entitlement, **21**, 1159
    time limit, **21**, 1154
    extension for good cause, **21**, 1155, 1156
  delegation, **21**, 1161
  manner of, **21**, 1154
  time limit, **21**, 1154
    extension for good cause, **21**, 1155, 1156
cohabitation rule, **21**, 1068
contributions, *see* NATIONAL INSURANCE CONTRIBUTIONS
Court of Appeal, appeals to, **21**, 1187
Court of Session, appeals to, **21**, 1187
dependants, increases for—
  absent from Great Britain, dependant, **21**, 1020, 1028
  adult—
    allocation of contributions, **21**, 1019
    child, person having care of, **21**, 1017
    common conditions, **21**, 1018
    disqualification, **21**, 1018
    family fund test, **21**, 1019
    generally, **21**, 1017
    spouse, **21**, 1017

Social security—*continued*

dependants, increase for—*continued*
  allocation of contributions, **21**, 1019
  child, **21**, 1015, 1016
    allocation of contributions, **21**, 1019
    conditions to be met, **21**, 1015
    family fund test, **21**, 1019
  family fund test, **21**, 1019
  legal custody, dependant in, **21**, 1020
  prison, dependant in, **21**, 1020
disability living allowance, *see* DISABILITY LIVING
  ALLOWANCE
Disability Living Allowance and Disability
  Working Allowance Act 1991 ..., **21**, 1152
disability working allowance, *see* DISABILITY
  WORKING ALLOWANCE
disablement benefit, *see* DISABLEMENT BENEFIT
earnings—
  accommodation, **21**, 1032
  amount, meaning, **21**, 1031
  amount to which entitled but not received, **21**,
    1030
  calculation, **21**, 1030, 1032
  Christmas bonus, **21**, 1032
  deductions, **21**, 1033
  estimation, **21**, 1030, 1032
  expenses—
    account to be taken of, **21**, 1032
    incurred prior to employment relationship,
      21, 1033
    payments to reimburse, **21**, 1031
  food or produce, **21**, 1032
  generally, **21**, 1030
  meal vouchers, **21**, 1032
  meals, **21**, 1032
  meaning, **21**, 1030
  self-employed, **21**, 1030
  sick pay, **21**, 1031
  statutory maternity pay, **21**, 1031
employment protection ceasing on retirement, **21**,
  1201
European Union, freedom of movement within,
  10, 139
European Social Charter, **12**, 7
family credit, *see* FAMILY CREDIT
forfeiture rule, **21**, 1169, 1186, 1205
guardian's allowance, *see* GUARDIAN'S ALLOWANCE
Health and Social Services and Social Security
  Adjudications Act 1983 ..., **21**, 1148
housing benefit, *see* HOUSING BENEFIT
immigrants, access to, **12**, 102
income support, *see* INCOME SUPPORT
industrial injuries benefits, *see* INDUSTRIAL
  INJURIES BENEFITS
invalid care allowance, *see* INVALID CARE
  ALLOWANCE
invalidity allowance, *see* INVALIDITY ALLOWANCE;
  INVALIDITY BENEFIT
invalidity benefit, *see* INVALIDITY BENEFIT
invalidity pension, *see* INVALIDITY BENEFIT;
  INVALIDITY PENSION
Judgments Convention, exclusion from scope of,
  4, 26; **8**, 431, 436
jurisdiction in, **4**, 26; **6**, 1132; **8**, 431, 436
legal custody, claimant or dependant in, **21**, 1020

Social security—*continued*

maternity allowance, *see* MATERNITY ALLOWANCE
medical appeal tribunal, *see* MEDICAL APPEAL
  TRIBUNAL
occupational pension, *see* PENSION
overlapping benefits—
  attendance allowance, **21**, 999, 1001
  contributory and non-contributory benefits, **21**, 999
  deemed entitlement, **21**, 1007
  dependency benefits, **21**, 998
    child benefit, **21**, 1005
    generally, **21**, 1002
    meaning, **21**, 998
    personal benefits, and, **21**, 1003
    training allowance, **21**, 1004
  disability living allowance, **21**, 999, 1001
  double adjustment, prevention of, **21**, 998
  earnings-related additions, **21**, 999
  earnings-related supplements, **21**, 999
  generally, **21**, 998
  graduated retirement benefit, **21**, 1003
  guardian's allowance, **21**, 1002
  industrial death benefit, **21**, 1001, 1002, 1003
  industrial injuries benefits, **21**, 1001
  invalid care allowance, adjustment, **21**, 998
  invalidity pension, **21**, 1000
  lump sum grants, **21**, 999
  personal benefits, **21**, 998
    adjustment, **21**, 999
    dependency benefits and, **21**, 1003
    meaning, **21**, 998
  Personal Injuries Scheme, **21**, 1002
  Pneumoconiosis and Byssinosis Benefit
    Scheme, **21**, 1002
  priority between persons entitled to increase,
    21, 1006
  retirement benefit, graduated, **21**, 999
  Service Pensions Instrument, **21**, 1002
  severe disablement allowance, adjustment, **21**, 998
  training allowance, **21**, 1003, 1004
  unemployability supplement, **21**, 1003
  War Injuries Scheme, **21**, 1002
  war pension death benefit, **21**, 1001, 1003
  weekly and other bases, benefits payable on,
    21, 999
  widow's benefits, **21**, 1000
overpaid benefits—
  bank account, credited to, **21**, 1014
  causation, **21**, 1013
  claimant could not reasonably expect to realise
    overpayment made, where, **21**, 1008*n*
  detection, **21**, 1008
    death of claimant, on, **21**, 1008*n*
    unified test, **21**, 1008
  disclosure—
    casual or incidental, **21**, 1010
    constructive, **21**, 1011
    duty to disclose, **21**, 1009, 1010
    failure to disclose, **21**, 1010, 1013
    innocent misrepresentation or non-dis-
      closure, **21**, 1010
    material facts, of, **21**, 1008, 1009
    misrepresentation, **21**, 1010, 1013

Social security—*continued*
overpaid benefits—*continued*
  disclosure—*continued*
    onus of, **21**, 1010
    requirements of, **21**, 1009, 1011
    statutory test, **21**, 1009, 1013
    to whom made, **21**, 1009, 1012
  family credit, **21**, 1014
  generally, **21**, 1008
  income support, **21**, 1014
  misrepresentation, following, **21**, 1008, 1010, 1013
  onus of proof, **21**, 1008, 1008*n*
  recovery—
    death of claimant, on, **21**, 1008*n*, 1014
    deductions, by, **21**, 1014
    enforcement, **21**, 1014
    generally, **21**, 1008, 1008*n*, 1014
    unified test, **21**, 1008
pension schemes, *see* PENSION
Pensions Ombudsman, *see* PENSIONS OMBUDSMAN
prescribed diseases, *see* PRESCRIBED DISEASES
prison, claimant or dependant in, **21**, 1020
qualifying periods for benefit, European Convention on the Calculation of Time-Limits, **22**, 827
radiation, person developing disease connected with, **9**, 922
reduced earnings allowance, **21**, 966
severe disablement allowance, *see* SEVERE DISABLEMENT ALLOWANCE
sheriff court jurisdiction, **6**, 1132
sickness benefit, *see* SICKNESS BENEFIT
social fund, *see* SOCIAL FUND
social security appeal tribunal, *see* SOCIAL SECURITY APPEAL TRIBUNAL
Social Security Commissioner, *see* SOCIAL SECURITY COMMISSIONER
state retirement pension, *see* PENSION
statutory maternity pay, *see* MATERNITY PAY
statutory sick pay, *see* SICK PAY
tribunals—
  precedent, binding authority, **22**, 328, 331
  statutory reform, **22**, 331
underpayments, **21**, 1008, 1014
unemployment benefit, *see* UNEMPLOYMENT BENEFIT
Universal Declaration of Human Rights, **12**, 4*n*
victim of accident etc, compensation sum falling to, **21**, 1150
widowed mother's allowance, **21**, 896
widow's payment, **21**, 895
widow's pension, **21**, 897
Social security appeal tribunal
absence of member, **21**, 1176
adjournment of hearing, **21**, 1176
appeal to, generally, **21**, 1178
assessors, use of, **21**, 1177
casting vote of chairman, **21**, 1176
constitution, **21**, 1174
decisions, **21**, 1178
  error in, correction, **21**, 1178
decisions binding on, **21**, 1178
experts, referral to, **21**, 1177

Social security appeal tribunal—*continued*
form of appeal, **21**, 1175
functions, **23**, 902
generally, **21**, 1148
hearsay evidence, **21**, 1178
jurisdiction, **21**, 1175
misconduct, employment lost through, adjudication of claim, **21**, 841, 842
oral hearings, **21**, 1176
organisation, **21**, 1174
person other than claimant, appeal by, **21**, 1175
postponement of hearing, **21**, 1176
precedent, binding authority, **22**, 328, 331
referral of cases to, **21**, 1162
review of decision of, **21**, 1171
Scottish Committee, supervision by, **23**, 911*n*
setting aside decision of, **21**, 1178
social fund payment, appeal against decision, **21**, 1130
Social Security Commissioner, appeal to, **21**, 1182
statement made in, absolute privilege, **15**, 524
statutory reform, **22**, 331
striking out application, **21**, 1176
time limit for appeal, **21**, 1175
Social Security Commissioner
appeal from decision of, **21**, 1187
appeal to—
  grant or refusal of, **21**, 1182
    judicial review, **21**, 1182
  investigative nature, **21**, 1183
  leave to appeal, **21**, 1182
  notice of, **21**, 1183
  procedure, **21**, 1183
  restriction, **21**, 1149
  time limit, **21**, 1183
appeal to Court of Session, **6**, 924
appointment, **21**, 1181
decision-making powers, **21**, 1186
deputy, **21**, 1181
European Court of Justice, reference to, **21**, 1188
forfeiture rule questions, **21**, 1169, 1186
generally, **21**, 1141
jurisdiction in appeals, **21**, 1182
legal assistants to—
  appointment, **21**, 1184
  powers, **21**, 1184
oral hearings, **21**, 1185
  amicus curiae, **21**, 1185
  legal aid not available, **21**, 1185
powers of, **21**, 1186
review of decision of, **21**, 1171
social fund payment, appeal against decision, **21**, 1130
Social welfare services
European Social Charter, **12**, 7
Social work
authorities, **14**, 604
committee—
  functions, **14**, 606; **22**, 8
  membership, **14**, 606
  registration of residential facilities, functions with regard to, **22**, 16
  special provisions, **14**, 241

Social work—*continued*
committee—*continued*
  statutory basis, **22**, 8
  sub-committees, **22**, 8
  term of office, **14**, 606
department, *see* SOCIAL WORK DEPARTMENT
director—
  appointment, **14**, 110, 249, 605
  dismissal, **14**, 110, 605
  functions, **14**, 605
establishment, registration of, **14**, 521
expenditure programme, **5**, 586
function, **14**, 608
other delegations, **14**, 607
reform, **14**, 47
reports—
  adoption proceedings, **22**, 19
  after-care supervision, **22**, 36
  children's hearing, **22**, 21
  community service order, **22**, 38
  custody proceedings, **22**, 20
  medical, court proceedings, for, **22**, 32
  mental disorder, person with, compulsory admission or detention in psychiatric hospital, **22**, 30
  Morison Report, social inquiry reports, guidelines, **22**, 32
  parole, report on home circumstances before release on, **22**, 35
  Parole Board of Scotland, for, **22**, 33
  probation order, connected with, **22**, 34
  remission of case from adult court to children's hearing, **22**, 33
  social inquiry—
    access of social worker to subject for preparation, **22**, 32
    See also BAIL
    adjournment of court for preparation, **22**, 32
    contents, **22**, 32, 33
    copy, requirement to provide for parent or solicitor of offender, **22**, 32
    court proceedings, for, generally, **22**, 32
    discretion of court to call for, **22**, 32
    first offender, **22**, 32
    format, **22**, 32
    mandatory, **22**, 32
    opinion evidence in, **22**, 32
  Streatfield Report, **22**, 32
  young person, adult court appearance, **22**, 33
sheriff court jurisdiction, **6**, 1074, 1115
social worker, *see* SOCIAL WORKER
Social work department
administration, **22**, 9
adoption services, **22**, 18, 19
  See also ADOPTION
advice/guidance/assistance—
  discretion, **22**, 13–16
  duty, **22**, 13–16
after-care, *see* AFTER-CARE
assistant director, **22**, 9
child—
  abuse, guidance notes for staff, **22**, 22
  duty to, **22**, 17–22
    See also CHILD-CHILDREN

Social work department—*continued*
child—*continued*
  rights relating to, **17**, 1236
child in care—
  decisions relating to—
    criteria, **22**, 18
    evidence to support, **22**, 18
co-ordination of services—
  central advisory services, **22**, 7
  child at risk, **22**, 4
  geographical organisation, **22**, 8, 9
  historical perspective, **22**, 1
  internally, **22**, 9
  Kilbrandon Committee recommendations, **22**, 5
  local authority, departments within, development, **22**, 3
  McBoyle Committee recommendations, **22**, 4
  proposals, generally, **22**, 6
  Social Work (Scotland) Act 1968 ..., **22**, 8, 9, 12
  Social Work Services Group, **22**, 7
  voluntary organisations and state provision, **22**, 10
community service order, supervision, **22**, 34, 38
compulsory care, elderly person, **22**, 29
counselling services, **22**, 13, 30, 34
custody proceedings, **22**, 20
  See also CHILD-CHILDREN
day facilities, *see* DAY FACILITIES
depute director, **22**, 9
development of services—
  aim of early services, **22**, 1
  central advisory services, **22**, 7
  child at risk—
    generally, **22**, 1
    McBoyle Committee recommendations, **22**, 4
  environmental focus, early services, **22**, 1
  generally, **22**, 1–12
  health service, early legislation, **22**, 2
  historical perspective, **22**, 1
  income maintenance service, statutory provision, **22**, 2
  individual social work services, **22**, 1
  Ingleby Committee in England and Wales, **22**, 4
  Kilbrandon Committee report, **22**, 5
  legislative regulation, early statutes, **22**, 2
  local authority, within, **22**, 3
  McBoyle Committee recommendations, **22**, 4
  social reformers—
    Hill, Octavia, **22**, 1
    Shaftesbury, Lord Ashley, Earl of, **22**, 1
  social work departments, **22**, 9
  state provision of services—
    historical prespective, **22**, 1
    problems, **22**, 1
  welfare departments, **22**, 2
director—
  appointment, **14**, 110; **22**, 8
  assistant director, functions, **22**, 9
  depute director, functions, **22**, 9
  dismissal, **14**, 110
  functions, **22**, 8
  qualifications, **22**, 8
  Secretary of State, powers, **22**, 8

Social work department—*continued*
disabled person, duties to, **22**, 23, 24
  See also DISABLED PERSON
education authority, duty to notify of mental
  handicap, **22**, 31
elderly person—
  duty to provide services to, **22**, 25–29
  removal to compulsory care, **22**, 29
families of mentally handicapped person,
  provision of facilities to, **22**, 31
geographical organisation, **22**, 8, 9
guardian, as, mentally handicapped person over
  16 years, **22**, 31
handicapped person, duties to, **22**, 23, 24, 31
historical background, **22**, 1–9
home meals service, **22**, 9, 27
home-help service, **22**, 26
  See also HOME HELP SERVICE
hospital, provision of services in, **22**, 9
hostels, provision for probationers, **22**, 34
housing authorities, co-ordination with, **22**, 9, 13,
  24
laundry services, **22**, 14, 24, 26
local authority, exercise of powers and duties
  through, **22**, 13–16
  See also LOCAL AUTHORITY
manager of miscellaneous services, **22**, 9
mentally handicapped person, duties to, **22**, 23,
  24, 31
occupational therapist, visits to handicapped
  persons, **22**, 24
organisation, **22**, 9
payments, whether affecting income support
  claim, **21**, 1079
police, duties to, where court appearance by child
  or young person, **22**, 33
powers and duties, generally, **22**, 12
prison, provision of services in, **22**, 9
probation order, supervision, **22**, 34
registration of privately owned residential home,
  22, 16, 28
release of young offender from detention, duties,
  22, 33
residential care, *see* RESIDENTIAL CARE
residential facilities, advice and support, **22**, 16,
  28, 31
review, children's hearing, delegated power to
  recommend, **22**, 8
social inquiry reports, **22**, 32
statutory requirements, **22**, 9
structure, **22**, 9
team social work, **22**, 9
voluntary organisations—
  adoption services, **22**, 19
  after-care services, persons with mental
    disorder, co-operation with local authority
    to provide, **22**, 30
  co-operation with local authority, **22**, 10, 30
  counselling services, **22**, 13
  day facilities, provision, delegation by local
    authority, **22**, 16, 28
  definition, for purposes of social work
    legislation, **22**, 10
  education departments, discretion to assist, **22**, 10

Social work department—*continued*
voluntary organisations—*continued*
  grants to, **22**, 10
  health service premises, goods or services, use
    of, **11**, 1493
  historical perspective, provision of services, **22**,
    1
  loans to, **22**, 10
  local authority—
    discretion to assist, generally, **22**, 10
    funding by, **22**, 10
  National Health Service nationalisation, **11**,
    1401
  occasional permissions for, **2**, 25
  residential care—
    elderly persons for, financing, **22**, 28
    local authority duty, delegation, **22**, 13, 28
  Secretary of State, powers to make grants/loans
    to, **22**, 10
young person, duty to, **22**, 17–22
  See also YOUNG PERSON
Social Work Services Group
administration function, **22**, 7
central advisory service, as, **22**, 7
formation, **22**, 7
Secretary of State, powers, vested in, **22**, 7
Social worker
access to offender for preparation of social inquiry
  report, **22**, 32
adoption—
  procedures, role, **22**, 18
  report, **22**, 19
after-care, young offender—
  statutory duty, **22**, 36
  supervisory role, generally, **22**, 36
child—
  abuse, duty to investigate report, **22**, 22
  appearing in adult court, **22**, 33
  care, planning, **22**, 18
  custody of, report, **22**, 20
  decision relating to, **22**, 18
children's hearing—
  attendance at, **3**, 1327
  evidence, compulsory removal of child,
    application, **22**, 18
  reports, **22**, 21
  supervision, child requiring care, **22**, 21
community service order—
  discretion when offender fails to comply, **22**,
    38
  supervision, **22**, 38
  supervisory role contrasted with probation
    supervision, **22**, 38
court proceedings, power to initiate—
  probation order, breach, **22**, 34
decision relating to child—
  compulsory removal of child, **22**, 18
  criteria, **22**, 18
  evidence, **22**, 18
elderly person, compulsory care—
  application, court order, **22**, 29
  duties—
    person/relatives, to, **22**, 29
    protection, person's property, **22**, 29

Social worker—_continued_
fine supervision, **22**, 37
justice of the peace, application to for compulsory removal of child, **22**, 18
laundry services, _see_ LAUNDRY SERVICES
legal basis of child's care, requirement to consider, **22**, 18
mental disorder, counselling service as part of psychiatric hospital team, **22**, 30
mental health officer, as, **22**, 11, 30
    See also MENTAL HEALTH OFFICER
occupational therapist, **22**, 9, 24
offender, access to—
    bail, on—
        condition of bail, as, **22**, 32
        problems, **22**, 32
opinion evidence, social inquiry report, **22**, 32
parole—
    licence, issue to, **22**, 35
    service to parolee, **22**, 35
    See also PAROLE; PAROLE BOARD FOR SCOTLAND
place of safety warrant, applicant, **22**, 22
prison work, role, **22**, 36
probation order—
    copy of order as evidence of probationer's contract, duty to retain, **22**, 34
    hostel, counselling to inmates, **22**, 34
    power to initiate court proceedings for breach, **22**, 34
    supervisory duties, generally, **22**, 34
    See also PROBATION
professional training—
    generally, **22**, 11
    historical perspective, **22**, 1
    specialised, **22**, 11
psychiatric hospital, counselling service, **22**, 30
public criticism, **22**, 1
qualifications, **22**, 11
reporter—
    referral of child to, **3**, 1287
    report to, **3**, 1287
reports, **22**, 19, 20, 21, 30, 32, 33, 34, 38
    See also SOCIAL WORK
risks, personal, **22**, 1
Secretary of State, after-care, duties in relation to, **22**, 36
sheriff, application to, for compulsory removal of child, **22**, 18
social work report, discussion with child and family, **3**, 1289
stresses, personal, of profession, **22**, 1
supervision by, **22**, 21, 33
supervision of, **22**, 9
training, **22**, 11
    Younghusband Report, **22**, 11
Societas Europaea
proposed, **16**, 1004
Society of Accountants and Auditors
incorporation, **1**, 9
Society of Advocates in Aberdeen
Joint Legal Committee, **13**, 1139
origins, **13**, 1135
Society of Incorporated Accountants
chartered institutes, integration with, **1**, 9

Society of Solicitors in the Supreme Courts in Scotland
Joint Legal Committee, **13**, 1139
origins, **13**, 1103, 1104, 1134
precedence, **16**, 2020
Society of Writers to Her Majesty's Signet
Joint Legal Committee, **13**, 1139
origins, **13**, 1133
Socii criminis
meaning, **10**, 544
    plea in bar of trial, **17**, 690
    witness, as, **10**, 544
Sodomy
consensual, **3**, 1237
criminal offence, as, **3**, 1237; **7**, 312, 485
intimation in case of, **17**, 1225
Schedule 1 offences, **3**, 1250
Soil-pans
water fittings, as, **25**, 527
Soil preservation
statutory control of, **1**, 711
Solatium
assignation of claim, **15**, 605
award of, **5**, 108
damages in delict, measure—
    generally, **15**, 922
    loss of amenity, etc, **15**, 924
    pursuer's awareness, relevance, **15**, 923
death, transmission on, **15**, 934
honour and reputation, interference with, **15**, 446, 567, 569, 571
meaning, **5**, 108
prohibition of payment, **5**, 109, 133
right to damages by way of, deceased's executor, **16**, 2165
Soldier
testamentum militare, **25**, 731
    See also ARMED FORCES; ARMY; VISITING FORCES
Sole trader
charity, covenanted payment to, **3**, 1151
choice as business medium, **16**, 1004
Solemn Declaration of Stuttgart, **10**, 22
Solemn procedure
appeals in, **6**, 874
appearance in private—
    examination—
        first, **17**, 642
        further, **17**, 644
        new-style judicial, **17**, 643
        full committal, **17**, 645
        generally, **17**, 641
bail, **17**, 629
criminal legal aid—
    appeals, **13**, 1069
    application for, **13**, 1055
    automatic criminal legal aid, **13**, 1054
defence—
    preparation of—
        Crown productions, examination of, **17**, 657
        documents, recovery of, **17**, 658
        generally, **17**, 654
        identification parade, **17**, 655
        post mortem, **17**, 656

Solemn procedure—*continued*
defence—*continued*
  preparation of—*continued*
    witness—
      examination of, **17**, 657
      precognoscing, **17**, 659
    requirements of—
      generally, **17**, 671
      preliminary pleas, **17**, 673
      productions—
        examination, **17**, 674
        lists of, **17**, 672
        recovery of, **17**, 674
      witnesses—
        Crown, objections to, **17**, 675
        lists of, **17**, 672
    special—
      fair notice, requirement of, **17**, 678
      lodging of, **17**, 676
      meaning, **17**, 677
      withdrawal of, **17**, 679
  documentation, **17**, 639
  early plea of guilty—
    court, procedure in, **17**, 653
    section 102 indictment, **17**, 650, 652
    withdrawal of, **17**, 651
  generally, **6**, 1155; **17**, 637
  indictment—
    form of, **17**, 666
    generally, **17**, 665
    productions—
      additional, **17**, 669
      lists of, **17**, 667
    record copy, lodging of, **17**, 670
    service of, **17**, 668
    witnesses—
      additional, **17**, 669
      list of, **17**, 667
  initial steps, **17**, 638
  judicial examination—
    appearance in private, **17**, 643
    extraneous matters, delection of, **17**, 649
    new-style, **17**, 643
    old form, **17**, 646
    record of, **17**, 647
    verification of record, **17**, 648
  preliminary diet—
    appeal from, **17**, 683
    charge, separation of, **17**, 694
    competency, **17**, 685
    notice of, **17**, 681
    plea in bar of trial—
      generally, **17**, 686
      insanity at time of trial, **17**, 688
      mora, taciturnity and delay, **17**, 692
      nonage, **17**, 687
      personal bar, **17**, 691
      prejudicial publicity, **17**, 693
      res judicata, **17**, 689
      socius criminis, **17**, 690
    pleading, **17**, 680
    procedure at, **17**, 682
    procurator fiscal, duties, **13**, 1432
    relevancy, **17**, 685

Solemn procedure—*continued*
  preliminary diet—*continued*
    trial—
      conjoining of, **17**, 695
      generally, **17**, 680
      postponement of, **17**, 684
      record of proceedings, **17**, 766
      separation of, **17**, 694
      See also TRIAL
  sentencing powers, **17**, 640
  time limits—
    eighty-day rule, **17**, 662
    extension of, **17**, 664
    generally, **17**, 660
    hundred-and-ten-day rule, **17**, 661
    one-year rule, **17**, 663
  trial, *see* TRIAL
Soliciting
public place, in, **7**, 484
Solicitor
absolute privilege, **15**, 520
access to, **13**, 1155
accounts, **1**, 92
  duties as to, **13**, 1191
  rules as to, **13**, 1152
admission as solicitor in Scotland, **13**, 1159, 1160
  non-Scottish jurisdictions, from, **13**, 1162
  prerequisites, **13**, 1160
  procedure for, **13**, 1171
advertising, **13**, 1201
advice and assistance provided by, **13**, 1021
  payment for, **13**, 1027
agent, as, **1**, 613
  inquiry, duty of, **1**, 623
  law, **1**, 613; **13**, 1138, 1139
  lien over client's property, having, **1**, 643
  undue influence of, **25**, 764
audience, right of—
  Bill Chamber, before, **13**, 1325
  generally, **13**, 1178
  lists of solicitors with, **13**, 1152
  rules as to, **13**, 1152
Bill Chamber, right of audience before, **13**, 1325
body corporate, practice as, **13**, 1201
books, duties as to, **13**, 1191
borrowing processes, restriction on, **13**, 1181
breach of fiduciary duty, reduction on grounds of, **13**, 44
business books of, not evidence of loan, **13**, 1737
chambers, practice in, **13**, 1182
children's hearing, acting as representative at, **3**, 1322
client—
  acceptance of instructions from, **13**, 1188
  client's money, obligations as to, **13**, 1191
  conflict of interests, **13**, 1188
  criminal activity, communications amounting to advice on, **13**, 1190
  duty to, **13**, 1173
  information embarrassing or detrimental to, **13**, 1190
  legacy bequeathed to solicitor, **13**, 1189
  obligations to, *see* obligations *below*

Solicitor—_continued_
client—_continued_
  statutory protection, **13**, 1196
    professional indemnity insurance, **13**, 1196, 1198
    Scottish Solicitors Guarantee Fund, **13**, 1196, 1197
client account—
  bank's liability for, **2**, 1241
  composite rate tax, effect of, **1**, 663
  death, operation on, **2**, 1243
  incorporated practice, of, **2**, 1242
  meaning, **2**, 1240
  overdrawing, **2**, 1240
  payments to be made to, **2**, 1240
  striking off etc, effect of, **2**, 1242
Code of Conduct, **13**, 1180
complaints—
  complainer, qualified privilege, **13**, 1205
  Complaints Committees, **13**, 1203, 1205
    consistency between, **13**, 1204
  Complaints Supervisory Committee, **13**, 1204
  Council of Law Society of Scotland, investigation by, **13**, 1202–1205
  inadequate professional services, concerning, **13**, 1203
  negligence, **13**, 1206, 1209
  practising certificate, grant or refusal following, **13**, 1210
  procedure on, **13**, 1205
  professional misconduct, concerning, **13**, 1203, 1206, 1207
  Scottish Legal Services Ombudsman, **13**, 1211
  'troubleshooters' scheme, **13**, 1209
  unprofessional behaviour, **13**, 1206, 1207, 1208
  writing, must be made in, **13**, 1205
confidentiality, duty of, **13**, 1190
  continental legal systems, **13**, 1190
  contractual, **13**, 1190
  criminal proceedings, in relation to, **13**, 1190
  exceptions, **13**, 1190
  information embarrassing or detrimental to client, **13**, 1190
  legal professional privilege, **13**, 1190
  post litem motam, **13**, 1190
  privileged communications, **13**, 1190
confirmation, **13**, 1182, 1184
conflict of interests, **13**, 1188
conveyancing, **13**, 1182, 1183, 1185
counsel's fees, obligations as to, **13**, 1384
counsel's opinion, acting upon, **13**, 1188
Court of Session—
  controls over solicitors, **13**, 1160, 1171, 1199
  disciplinary powers, **13**, 1199
  right of audience before, **13**, 1180
criminal legal aid duty solicitor—
  bail appeals or review, **13**, 1053
  duties, **13**, 1053
  eligibility, **13**, 1053
  fees, **13**, 1053
  over- or under-provision, **13**, 1053
  where legal aid withdrawn, **13**, 1053
defaulting, factor on estate of, **24**, 277

Solicitor—_continued_
disciplinary proceedings, complaints, _see_ complaints _above_
distribution of solicitors and firms, **13**, 1156, 1157
district court, right of audience before, **13**, 1180
duty of care, **13**, 1189; **15**, 200
  generally, **15**, 278
  potential beneficiaries of will-making clients, **15**, 281–283, 358
embezzlement by, **7**, 352, 356
Faculty of Procurators and Solicitors in Dundee, **13**, 1139
fees—
  calculation, **13**, 1192
  excessive, **13**, 1192
  extra-judicial (non-judicial), **13**, 1192
  hypothec, **13**, 1193, 1195
  judicial, **13**, 1192
  Law Society Table of Fees, **13**, 1192
  lien, **13**, 1193, 1194
  multi-disciplinary practices, **13**, 1192
  no win, no fee basis, **13**, 1192
  obligations as to, **13**, 1192
  offences in relation to, **13**, 1192
  pactum de quota litis, **13**, 1192
  scale, abolition, **13**, 1192
  speculative, **13**, 1192
fiduciary relationship and duty of care, **13**, 1189
functions, **13**, 1153
General Council of Solicitors in Scotland, **13**, 1140
High Court of Justiciary, right of audience before, **13**, 1180
historical background, **13**, 1103
  Act of Union 1707 ..., **13**, 1135
  Civil law, **13**, 1128
  College of Justice, establishment, **13**, 1129
  designation 'solicitor', **13**, 1126
  eighteenth century, **13**, 1135
  fifteenth century, **13**, 1132
  Joint Legal Committee, **13**, 1139
  Law Agents (Scotland) Act 1873 ..., **13**, 1138, 1139
  Legal Aid and Solicitors (Scotland) Act 1949 ..., **13**, 1141
  procurator's mandate, **13**, 1131
  Procurators (Scotland) Act 1865 ..., **13**, 1136
  representation, right of, **13**, 1127
  Romano-canonical procedure, **13**, 1130
  Royal Commission 1870 ..., **13**, 1137
  Scottish feudal law, **13**, 1129
  Society of Solicitors in the Supreme Courts, **13**, 1134
  Society of Writers to Her Majesty's Signet, **13**, 1133
  Solicitors (Scotland) Act 1933 ..., **13**, 1140
  twentieth century, **13**, 11389
House of Lords, right of audience before, **13**, 1180
hypothec, **13**, 1193, 1195
  action abandoned or settled by client, **20**, 107
  compensation not pleadable by party liable for expenses, **20**, 105
  enforcement, **20**, 104

Solicitor—*continued*
hypothec—*continued*
   expenses awarded to client, confined to, **20**, 103
   implied agreement as basis of, **20**, 103
   implied assignation as basis of, **20**, 103
   right of solicitor to be sisted as party to action, **20**, 107
   sequestration of solicitor, **20**, 103
   statutory order for satisfaction, **20**, 106
independence of profession—
   ability to act without regard to consequences, **13**, 1177
   generally, **13**, 1173
   government interference, independence from, **13**, 1174
   government money, independence by not taking, **13**, 1175
   self-governance, **13**, 1176
insurance intermediary, **12**, 811
Joint Legal Committee, **13**, 1139, 1140
judge, appointment as, **13**, 1186
jury service, ineligibility for, **13**, 1172
justice of the peace, as, **6**, 1164
knowingly assisting unlawful financial services transactions, **13**, 1188
Law Society of Scotland, *see* LAW SOCIETY OF SCOTLAND
legacy bequeathed by client, **13**, 1189
legal aid—
   choice of counsel, **13**, 1072
   conflict of interests, **13**, 1065
   criminal, generally, **13**, 1052
   exclusion from selection, **13**, 1072
   fees and expenses, **13**, 1074
      regulation, **13**, 1074
   refusal to act, **13**, 1072
Legal Aid and Solicitors (Scotland) Act 1949 ..., **13**, 1141
Legal Civil Service, *see* LEGAL CIVIL SERVICE
legal education—
   historical background, **13**, 1103
   modern, **13**, 1105
lien, **13**, 1193, 1194
   bankruptcy of solicitor, passing on, **20**, 94
   corporate insolvencies, **20**, 100
   death, passing on, **20**, 94
   debts for which claimed, **20**, 95
   generally, **20**, 94
   persons other than qualified solicitors, **20**, 94
   possession—
      loss of, **20**, 94
   ranking, with other unsecured creditors, **20**, 99
   restrictions on exercise of, **20**, 96
   right of, **13**, 95
   sequestration of client's estate, consequences of, **20**, 98
   termination, **20**, 94
   third party, exercise against, **20**, 94, 97
Lord Advocate, to, **17**, 539
multi-disciplinary practices—
   fees, **13**, 1192
   meaning, **13**, 1192*n*
negligence by, **13**, 1206, 1209
   third party claims, **15**, 843, 844

Solicitor—*continued*
notary public, *see* NOTARY PUBLIC
numbers practising, **13**, 1154, 1156
obligations—
   accounts, as to, **13**, 1191
   books, duty to keep, **13**, 1191
   client, to—
      care, duty of, **13**, 1189
      client's money, as to, **13**, 1191
      confidentiality, **13**, 1190
      conflict of interests, **13**, 1188
      diligently and efficiently, obligation to act, **13**, 1188
      fiduciary relationship, **13**, 1189
      generally, **13**, 1188
      instructions, acceptance of, **13**, 1188
      professional indemnity, **13**, 1198
      Scottish Solicitors Guarantee Fund, **13**, 1197
      solicitors' fees, **13**, 1192
      solicitors' hypothec, **13**, 1193, 1195
      solicitors' lien, **13**, 1193, 1194
      statutory protection for client, **13**, 1196
   court, to, **13**, 1200
   diligently and efficiently, obligation to act, **13**, 1188
   generally, **13**, 1187
   officer of court, solicitor as, **13**, 1199
   profession, to, **13**, 1201
officer of court, as, **13**, 1199
   English position compared, **13**, 1199
organisation of profession by Law Society of Scotland, **13**, 1144
pacta de quota litis, **15**, 769
partnership, number of partners allowed, **16**, 1011, 1112
practice management course, attendance, **13**, 1201
practising certificate, **13**, 1159
   grant or refusal following complaint over solicitor's conduct, **13**, 1210
   rules as to, **13**, 1151
   withdrawal, **13**, 1192
principal in private practice, **13**, 1201
privileges, *see* rights and privileges *below*
Privy Council, right of audience before, **13**, 1180
professional indicators, **13**, 1173
professional liability, *see* PROFESSIONAL LIABILITY
professional misconduct—
   Court of Session powers, **13**, 1199
   meaning, **13**, 1206, 1207
professional rules, partnership contravening, **16**, 1017
qualification—
   Diploma in Legal Practice, **13**, 1163, 1164
   generally, **13**, 1159
   Law Society examinations, **13**, 1162
   non-Scottish jurisdictions, admissions from, **13**, 1162
   Pre-Diploma training contract, **13**, 1162
   training contract—
      assignment, **13**, 1170
      generally, **13**, 1169
      non-Diploma, **13**, 1165, 1168
      period of service under, **13**, 1165
      post-Diploma, **13**, 1165, 1167

Solicitor—*continued*
qualification—*continued*
  training contract—*continued*
    pre-Diploma, **13**, 1165, 1166
    registration, **13**, 1170
    university degree, **13**, 1161
rights and privileges—
  audience, rights of, **13**, 1178
  Bill Chamber, right of audience before, **13**, 1325
  case law, arising from, **13**, 1178
  custom, arising from, **13**, 1178
  generally, **13**, 1172, 1178
  judge, appointment as, **13**, 1186
  monopolies, **13**, 1185
  practice before the courts, **13**, 1179
  practice in chambers, **13**, 1182
  superior courts, right of audience before, suspension or revocation, **13**, 1199
  supreme courts, right of audience before, **13**, 1180, 1325
Roll of Solicitors in Scotland, **13**, 1152
  maintenance of name on, **13**, 1159
  striking off, **13**, 1199
Royal Commission on Legal Services in Scotland, report of, **13**, 1142
Royal Faculty of Procurators in Glasgow, **13**, 1135, 1139
Scottish Law Agents Society, **13**, 1139, 1139n
Scottish Legal Services Ombudsman, ineligible for appointment as, **13**, 1172
Scottish Solicitors' Discipline Tribunal, **6**, 930; **13**, 1206, 1207
Scottish Solicitors Guarantee Fund—
  award of compensation by, **13**, 1151
  control and management, **13**, 1151
self-regulatory status of profession, **13**, 1151, 1173
sequestration, effect of, **2**, 1474
sequestration proceedings, examination in, **13**, 1190
sheriff court, right of audience before, **13**, 1180
sheriff court jurisdiction, **6**, 1113
size of legal firms, **13**, 1158
social inquiry report, social worker's requirement to provide copy of, **22**, 32
Society of Advocates in Aberdeen, **13**, 1135, 1139
Society of Solicitors in the Supreme Courts in Scotland, **13**, 1134, 1139
Society of Writers to Her Majesty's Signet, **13**, 1133, 1139
Solicitors Account Rules, failure to comply, **13**, 1151
solicitors in practice, analysis of, **13**, 1154
Solicitors (Scotland) Act 1980 ..., **13**, 1143
Solicitors of the Supreme Court, **13**, 1103, 1104
specialisation, **13**, 1153
supreme courts, right of audience before, **13**, 1325
  generally, **13**, 1180
  writ, signature of, **13**, 1326
suspension from practice, **13**, 1199
undue delay in completion of client's business, **13**, 1210
unprofessional behaviour, **13**, 1206, 1208, 1287

Solicitor—*continued*
witness—
  interview of potential, **13**, 1357
  solicitor called as, **10**, 538; **13**, 1190
Writers to the Signet, **13**, 1103
  officers of court, as, **13**, 1199
Solicitor General for Scotland
appointment, **17**, 579
criminal prosecution in Scotland, functions as to, **13**, 1430
functions, **5**, 543; **13**, 1430; **17**, 537
historical development, **5**, 543
House of Lords, customarily has seat in, **5**, 306, 371
judiciary, relationship to, **17**, 583
origins of, **5**, 543
prosecution conducted by, **6**, 872; **13**, 1430
public prosecutor, as, **6**, 872; **13**, 1430; **17**, 579
Scottish questions answered by, **5**, 391
Solum
law of the tenement, **18**, 228, 231, 233, 241
rights to, road, of, **20**, 613
Solus agreement
restraint of trade doctrine, scope of, **4**, 1212
See also OIL MARKETING
Solvents
abuse—
  driving after, **20**, 417
child, supply to, **3**, 1226
drug abuse, patterns of, **14**, 1222
food containing, **11**, 378
meaning, **11**, 378n
Solway Firth
administration, **11**, 39
definition, **11**, 44
fixed engines, **11**, 45
limits, **11**, 32, 44
paidle nets, **11**, 45
privileged fixed engines, fishing by, **11**, 11
regulation of salmon fisheries, **11**, 45
salmon and freshwater fishing, legislation relating to, **11**, 10
Somnambulism
treatment in Scots law, **7**, 151, 157
Son
ancestral land, share in, **25**, 608
heritable succession, **25**, 678
Son-in-law
immediate family, as, **15**, 601
Sonic boom
damage caused by, building contracts, **3**, 89
Sorn Report
Lands Valuation Appeal Court, **6**, 942
Sound broadcasting
Select Committee on, **5**, 444, 466
Sound insulation
building controls, **3**, 208
Sound recording
copyright, **18**, 933, 967, 968, 1024, 1025
  author, meaning, **18**, 979, 981
  Crown copyright, **18**, 1039
  educational establishment playing, **18**, 1112
  European Union legislation, **18**, 1643

Sound recording—*continued*
copyright—*continued*
  infringement, **18**, 1055
    playing in public, by, **18**, 1062–1064
    supply of copies, **18**, 1081
  needletime, **18**, 1024
  originality, **18**, 948
  permitted acts, **18**, 1126
  rental rights, **18**, 1059
  term of copyright, **18**, 1038, 1039
  joint authorship, **18**, 987
live bird or animal attracted by, **11**, 880, 884
live performance, of, **18**, 1432
meaning, **18**, 969
South Africa
sporting links with, **19**, 1208*n*
trust law, **24**, 126
South Devon cattle
regulations as to, **11**, 466
South Sea Company
joint stock company, as, **4**, 303
Southampton Freeport
free zone, as, **7**, 1164*n*
Sovereign
Accession Declaration, **7**, 708, 709
allegiance to, *see* ALLEGIANCE
arms, **7**, 785
assault on, **7**, 586
Church of England, must be in communion with, **7**, 703*n*
Church of Scotland, position in relation to, **3**, 1501
coins, monopoly over making of, **14**, 1834
Commonwealth—
  executive powers, exercise, **7**, 777
  succession to throne, **7**, 776
  title in, **7**, 775, 775*n*
constitutional conventions, **7**, 711, 711*n*
courts, participation in work of, **5**, 624
death, compassing or imagining, **7**, 569, 570, 571
death, Parliament, whether affecting, **7**, 714
deposing, **7**, 571
discretionary powers, exercise, **7**, 711–713, 723
dissolution of Parliament, **7**, 713, 713*n*
eldest son and heir—
  arms, **7**, 787
  compassing or imagining death of, **7**, 569, 570
  Scottish titles, **7**, 704, 704*n*, 786
  style and title, **7**, 786
  treason, protection by law of, **7**, 704
  violating wife of, **7**, 569, 572
eldest unmarried daughter—
  protection by law of treason, **7**, 704
  violation, **7**, 569, 572
'fount of honour', as, **16**, 1309
government and parliamentary activity, reporting to, **7**, 711
heir, *see* eldest son *above*
injure or depose, compassing to, **7**, 571
Jewish faith, person of, disabilities, **3**, 1677
King's wife—
  compassing or imagining death of, **7**, 569, 570
  violation, **7**, 569, 572

Sovereign—*continued*
leasing-making, **7**, 595
levying war against, **7**, 569, 571, 573, 574
maiming, imprisoning etc sovereign or heirs, **7**, 569
political activity, **7**, 711
political impartiality, **7**, 711
power—
  authority of court derives from, **4**, 1
Prime Minister, appointment, **7**, 712, 712*n*
restraints on power—
  Church of England, relationship with, **7**, 708, 709
  Church of Scotland, relationship with, **7**, 708, 709
  constitutional conventions, **7**, 711, 711*n*
  Coronation Oath, **7**, 708, 709
  generally, **7**, 707
  statutory, **7**, 710
Roman Catholic faith, person of, disabilities, **3**, 1662
royal arms, **7**, 785
Royal assent, **7**, 715
royal family, **7**, 704, 704*n*
royal style and titles—
  consent to, **7**, 703, 703*n*
  generally, **7**, 784
  present, **7**, 703, 703*n*, 784
  Scottish, **7**, 704, 704*n*
second son, style and title, **7**, 788
succession, *see* CROWN
treason, protection by law of, **7**, 704
treason felony against, **7**, 585
witness, as, **10**, 526
See also CROWN; KING; MONARCHY; QUEEN
Sovereignty
air space, **19**, 673
concept of—
  international, **19**, 666
  state, within, **19**, 666
Crown as focus of national, **7**, 701
jurisdiction, **19**, 675–684
natural resources, over, **19**, 671, 687
occupation of territory, **19**, 667
outer space, **19**, 674
Parliament, *see* SOVEREIGNTY OF PARLIAMENT
Scottish, Orkney and Shetland, **24**, 326–400
states enjoy rights inherent in, **19**, 666
udal law—
  dimensions of, **24**, 327
  dominium.and, **24**, 327, 328
  property rights, and, **24**, 329
Sovereignty of Parliament
Act of Union, **5**, 309; **6**, 810
apparent qualifications of, **5**, 342
auto organisation, power of, **5**, 354
community international agreements, restriction by, **5**, 328
concept of, **5**, 362
emergence of doctrine of, **5**, 340
future, Parliament cannot bind itself for, **5**, 312
limitation of—
  European Communities Act 1972—
    by, **5**, 310
  Union Agreement between Scotland and England, by, **5**, 309; **6**, 810

Sovereignty of Parliament—*continued*
meaning, **5**, 308
retrospective legislation, **5**, 311
separation of powers, **5**, 341
Spain
competition rules, application, **4**, 1304
European Union customs territory, **7**, 1010
Spare parts
European Union legislation, **18**, 1662
registered industrial design, **18**, 1174
unregistered design rights, **18**, 1216–1218
Spawning beds
disturbance of, **11**, 20
Speaker
See HOUSE OF COMMONS
Spears
fishing with, **11**, 12
Special area
See INNER URBAN AREA
Special Branch
establishment, **16**, 1741
Special Commissioners (Revenue)
appeal to, **19**, 1544, 1547
appointment, **19**, 1546
meaning, **19**, 1544*n*
supervision of, Scottish Committee, by, **23**, 911*n*
Special constable
appointment, **16**, 1745
discipline, **16**, 1745
generally, **16**, 1742, 1744
number employed, determination, **16**, 1714
powers, duties and privileges, **16**, 1745
qualification for appointment, **16**, 1745, 1745*n*
resignation, **16**, 1745
retirement, **16**, 1745
special constabulary—
history, **16**, 1745
promotion, **16**, 1745
purpose, **16**, 1745
rank structure, **16**, 1745, 1745*n*
uniform and equipment, **16**, 1745
Special defence
See CRIMINAL PROCEDURE
Special destination
heritable conveyance, in—
generally, **6**, 480
revocation, **6**, 481
wills—
acquisition after will executed, **25**, 758
alteration of, **25**, 739
confirmation, procedure for obtaining, **25**, 1072
evacuation, **25**, 755
executor, vesting of estate in, **25**, 1109
former prominence, **25**, 755
heritable property, **25**, 677
legal rights, avoidance of, **25**, 815
meaning, **25**, 732
reform, **25**, 1120
revocation—
generally, **25**, 755
implied, **25**, 757
power to revoke, **25**, 756

Special destination—*continued*
wills—*continued*
revocation—*continued*
testamentary disposition executed on or after 10 September 1964 ..., **25**, 757
title to property, insertion in, **25**, 739
will substitute, as, **25**, 732
Special drawing right
advantages of, **14**, 1832
concession of, **1**, 418
International Monetary Fund, introduction by, **14**, 1832
Special education
education authorities' duty to provide, **8**, 909
fees and costs, **8**, 920
future provision for recorded children, **8**, 922
placing requests, and, **8**, 916, 919, 920
provision—
generally, **8**, 909, 913
outwith UK, **8**, 924
special educational needs, children with—
appeals against education authority decisions—
appeal committee—
duties of, **8**, 917
generally, **8**, 916
powers, **8**, 919
generally, **8**, 918
grounds for, **8**, 916
procedure, **8**, 916
sheriff, to, **8**, 920
assessment of needs—
parents, duties of, **8**, 911
procedure, generally, **8**, 911
duties of education authority, generally, **8**, 909
education authority functions in relation to, **8**, 843, 911*ff*
meaning, **8**, 910
record of—
continuance beyond school age, **8**, 923
decision to record, **8**, 912
destruction, **8**, 915
disclosure of records, **8**, 914
discontinuance, **8**, 915
generally, **8**, 913
preservation, **8**, 915
review of recording decisions, **8**, 921
self-governing school providing for, financing, **8**, 798
special school—
appointment of teachers, **8**, 825
self-governing—
financing, **8**, 798
Special legacy
abatement, **25**, 856
nature of, **25**, 848, 853
Special needs
dwelling house adapted for, repossession, **13**, 736, 746
housing adapted for, **11**, 1947
Special procedure order
alternative to private Bill, as, **19**, 4
application in Scotland, **19**, 117–119
Bill in lieu of, **19**, 120
bringing into effect, **19**, 123

Special procedure order—*continued*
fees, **19**, 119
inquiry, shorthand notes of evidence at, **19**, 118
Parliamentary proceedings, **19**, 120–123
    joint committee on petitions, **19**, 122, 123
    orders laid before Parliament, **19**, 121
statutory provisions, **19**, 117
Special road
access to, special road orders, **20**, 626
acquisition of land, **20**, 711
advertisement of opening, **20**, 624
authorisation, **20**, 625
bridge, **20**, 643
    navigable water over—
        authority to construct, **20**, 638
        revocation or variation of order for, **20**, 644
classes of traffic, **20**, 624
cleansing, **20**, 677
construction, **20**, 626
Edinburgh Outer City Bypass, **20**, 624
generally, **20**, 501, 608
improvement, **20**, 626
land, acquisition to build or improve, **20**, 626, 711, 714
litter, **20**, 677
meaning, **20**, 624
order, **20**, 626
    revocation, **20**, 627
    variation, **20**, 627
private access, stopping up, **20**, 653
regulation of use, **20**, 508
road crossing or entering, special road order, **20**, 651
scheme, **20**, 625
    advertising, **20**, 626
    notification, **20**, 626
    objections to, **20**, 626
    revocation, **20**, 627
    variation, **20**, 627
Secretary of State's powers and duties as to, **20**, 615, 616, 624, 626
service area, *see* MOTORWAY
side road order, **20**, 651
signs on, **20**, 624
special road authority, **20**, 624, 625
    payments to, **20**, 626
special road order, **20**, 651
statutory undertakers, rights of, **20**, 717
toll road order, **20**, 629
    assignation of rights under, **20**, 630, 631, 634
traffic regulations governing, **20**, 624
tunnel, navigable water under—
    authority to construct, **20**, 638
    revocation or variation of order for, **20**, 644
Special Telecommunications Action for Regional Development (STAR) programme
European Union telecommunications deregulation, **16**, 1966
Specific implement
action for, agreement to pay money not enforceable by, **14**, 1813
actions which court might have prohibited by interdict, **13**, 11

Specific implement—*continued*
breach by landlord, as remedy against, **13**, 283
breach by tenant, as remedy against, **13**, 276
building contracts, **3**, 104
continuing performance, securing, **13**, 14
contractual performance, **13**, 8–10
decree of, **13**, 8
    alternative remedies, **13**, 10
    exceptions, **13**, 9
defender's refusal to implement obligation, **13**, 13
fiar's right to remedy of, **13**, 1661
interim, **13**, 14
local authority, against, **13**, 11
non-contractual circumstances, in—
    court powers, **13**, 11
    moveable property, **13**, 12
ordinary action, remedy in, **4**, 961
restoration of possession of moveable property, **13**, 12
restoration of possession of real or personal property, **13**, 11
substituted performance, **13**, 13
***Specificatio* (specification)**
doctrine of, *see* OWNERSHIP
Specification
restitution—
    generally, **15**, 58
    interim possessor, liability, **15**, 56
Speech therapist
employment of, **11**, 1501
Speed restriction
obligation to observe, **11**, 1027
Speedometer
construction and use regulations, **20**, 486
Sperm donor
databank information on, limitation on access to, **18**, 1541
Spin off merchandising
passing off, **18**, 1382
Spitting
assault, whether amounting to, **7**, 217
meat and food handlers, **11**, 415
prohibited in premises where food sold, **11**, 407
Sponsio
Roman law and development of law of caution, **3**, 806, 808
***Sponsiones ludicrae* contracts**
betting and wagering contracts, **15**, 768
Sponsors' mark
generally, **18**, 1417
meaning, **18**, 1417, 1417*n*
unhallmarked articles, **18**, 1418*n*
Sport
competition entry fees, VAT exemption, **7**, 1429
injury sustained during, when assault, **7**, 220, 221
membership fees and subscriptions, VAT exemption, **7**, 1429
participant in, delictual liability towards, **15**, 395, 400
society promoting, **12**, 694*n*
spectator at, delictual liability towards, **15**, 395, 399
See also RECREATION AND SPORT

Sporting facilities
See RECREATION AND SPORT

Sporting lease
categories of rights, **13**, 202
delectus personae, doctrine of, **13**, 356
generally, **13**, 202
landlord's hypothec, **13**, 513
real right, when qualifying as, **13**, 297
registration, **13**, 202

Sporting purposes
lands and heritages kept or preserved for, **24**, 561

Sporting rights
servitude rights, whether constituting, **18**, 492
tenant, not extending to, **1**, 765

Sporting tenant
See TENANT

Sports Council
financial assistance made through, **19**, 1206
functions, **19**, 1214, 1216
generally, **19**, 1209
members, **19**, 1213
Scottish, **19**, 1212, 1215, 1216
staff, **19**, 1213

Sports grounds
See RECREATION AND SPORT

Spouse
adherence, **10**, 839
alimentary liferent, see LIFERENT
antenuptial trust, **24**, 62
bigamy, **15**, 596
British citizen, of, naturalisation of, **14**, 1921
communications between spouses—
    privilege, **10**, 669
        civil proceedings, **10**, 678
        criminal proceedings, **10**, 679
        general rules, **10**, 677
        marital intercourse, privilege concerning, **10**, 680
    rules of evidence, **10**, 505
death by common calamity, interpretation of will following, **12**, 1266
death of—
    declarator, **10**, 833
    injury, as result of, **15**, 601
    presumption of, **10**, 833, 834
    rights on, **25**, 602
delict by other spouse, responsibility, **15**, 603
delict committed by, liability, **15**, 242
delict proceedings against, **10**, 844
deportation, **12**, 208
destination of liferent property to—
    conjunct liferent and fee, **13**, 1625
    Dobie's table, **13**, 1622
dispute between spouses, action of lawburrows, **13**, 911, 916, 924
divorce, see DIVORCE
divorced, deceased specified relative, as, **15**, 602
donation, **8**, 603, 608, 645
    inter virum et uxorem, **8**, 602, 604, 608
    presumption against, **8**, 626
duty to protect implied by relationship, **7**, 41
dwelling house occupied by, as heritable security, **20**, 221
employed, unfair dismissal, **9**, 211

Spouse—continued
enticement to leave, **15**, 596
entrapment, **15**, 596
European Union law, 'primary right' holder, of, **12**, 223
financial agreement between spouses, reduction, **13**, 30, 44
immediate family, as, **15**, 601
income tax, **19**, 1517, 1518
incrimination of, privilege against, **10**, 673
inheritance tax exemption, **19**, 1533, 1574, 1575, 1577, 1624
joint appointment of, genuine occupational qualification, **9**, 369
judicial discretion—
    applicant for, **25**, 616
    exercise of, **25**, 617
judicial separation, see JUDICIAL SEPARATION
jus relicti vel relictae, claim for, interest on sum, **12**, 1031
marriage after admission to UK for other purpose, **12**, 278
matrimonial home, see MATRIMONIAL HOME
meaning, **12**, 269
of party to action as witness, **10**, 845
property, see MARRIAGE
public sector secure tenancy transferred to, **11**, 1947
residence of, **10**, 838
separation—
    agreements, **19**, 1579
    benefit enduring during, **25**, 867
separation of property, **25**, 602
settlement—
    family relationship, on grounds of, **12**, 268
    family reunion or creation by, **12**, 267, 269–273
        age limit, **12**, 269
        entry clearance, **12**, 270
            conditions for, **12**, 271–273
            proof of marriage, **12**, 273
        extra-judicial divorces, **12**, 269
        meaning, **12**, 269
        polygamous marriages, **12**, 269
        potentially polygamous, **12**, 269
surviving—
    aliment, right to, **25**, 711
    division of estate on or after 8 December 1986—
        examples, **25**, 704
    executor, appointment as, **25**, 694
    executor dative, appointment of, **25**, 1046
    heritable estate, **25**, 680
    life assurance policy, benefit under, **25**, 734
    moveable estate, **25**, 680
    other claimants distinguished from, **25**, 611
    prior rights—
        dwelling house, **25**, 690
        financial provision, **25**, 693
        furniture, **25**, 691
        generally, **16**, 2116; **25**, 689
        partial intestacy, **25**, 707
        plenishings, **25**, 691
        reform, **25**, 1112

Spouse—*continued*

surviving—*continued*

  succession of lease affected by, **13**, 413

taxation, *see* HUSBAND AND WIFE

title to sue, **14**, 2134; **15**, 603

transfers between, **25**, 1009

truster and trustee, relationship between, **24**, 25

will or other testamentary writing, legal rights, **12**, 1264

witness, as, **10**, 845

  civil cases, **10**, 538

  competence, generally, **10**, 502

  criminal cases, **10**, 543

See also HUSBAND AND WIFE; MARRIAGE; WIFE

Spray irrigation

control order, **25**, 331

licence, **25**, 331

river purification authority, responsibility of, **25**, 331, 389

Spuilzie

actual possession, right to possession must be accompanied by, **18**, 163

both natural and civil possessor, where, **18**, 164

dispossession under judicial warrant does not amount to, **18**, 164

ejection, **18**, 154, 161

modern law, place in, **18**, 161, 166

ownership, and, **18**, 162

possession—

  animo solo, **18**, 163

  quality of pursuer's, **18**, 163

  title to sue, as, **18**, 140

possessory action, as, **18**, 162

remedies, **18**, 165

  restoration of property, **18**, 165

  value of property, entitlement to, **18**, 165

  violent profits, entitlement to, **18**, 165, 169

remedy of, **15**, 215

spoliatus ante omnia restituendus rule, **18**, 162

title of pursuer, **18**, 162

vitious dispossession, **18**, 156, 164

  recovery founded on, generally, **18**, 161

  scope, **18**, 164

Spying

acts amounting to, **7**, 628

approaching or entering prohibited place, **7**, 629, 632

attempted offence, **7**, 637

communications with foreign agents, **7**, 631, 633

enemy, meaning, **7**, 630

gaining admission to prohibited place by fraudulent means, **7**, 634

harbouring spies, **7**, 636

inciting offence, **7**, 637

information useful to enemy, **7**, 630

obstruction of guards in prohibited place, **7**, 635

official secrets legislation, gnerally, **7**, 628

proof of purpose, **7**, 633

purpose prejudicial to safety or interests of state, **7**, 632, 633

spy, wartime status of, **19**, 709

Squatter

dwelling houses occupied by, **6**, 967

not qualified as proprietor, **24**, 444

possession, exercise of right, **18**, 5

Squirrels

forests, prevention of damage to, **11**, 866n

Sri Lanka

personal law, domicile as indicator of, **17**, 188

Trust Ordinance, **24**, 126

Stabilisers

food, in, **11**, 373

Stable

construction and use, **14**, 1665

factory or workshop premises, **24**, 637, 646

public health nuisance, as, **19**, 336

Stable-keeper

strict liability—

  present position, **15**, 150

  Roman law, **15**, 144, 150

Stag hunting, **19**, 1275

Stagnum

meaning, **25**, 340

owner of land containing, rights of, **25**, 341

stagnum loch, meaning, **18**, 303

Stair, Sir James Dalrymple, Viscount of

acts performed on Sunday, validity of, **22**, 817

assessment by other authoritative writers, **22**, 440

biographical details of, **1**, ix, x

cautionary obligations, **3**, 813

citation as authority during lifetime, **22**, 437

common law, custom as, **22**, 366

critiques of fundamental legal philosophy, **22**, 408

custom as formal source of law, **22**, 129, 366, 375

custom and statute distinguished, **22**, 529

customary law, **22**, 529–533, 543

delict, **15**, 216

desirable end of all law, **22**, 529

duties and rights, **15**, 12

equity as formal source of law—

  positive and natural law, distinction, **22**, 400–408

Institutions of the Laws of Scotland, **22**, 536, 537, 543, 574, 584, 627, 628

  canon of 'authoritative writings'— inclusion, **22**, 441

  citation of cases in, **22**, 251

  editorial errors once impairing, **22**, 441

  formal source of law, as, **22**, 434

  reliable edition, **22**, 441

  special authority, **22**, 437, 441

legislation, definition, **22**, 523

lex and *consuetudo* distinction, **22**, 366

natural law, **22**, 401

negotiorum gestio, **15**, 112

nobile officium, **22**, 427, 430

obligation as personal right, **15**, 1

positive law, **22**, 402

pre-eminence as special authority—

  Court of Session, nineteenth century, **22**, 440

  evaluation of other institutional writers related to recognition as, **22**, 437

precedent, view of, **22**, 251

real rights, on, **18**, 3n

recompense, **15**, 59

Regiam Majestatem, attitude to, **22**, 360

sources of civil law in Scotland, **22**, 366, 400–408

special authority of writings, **22**, 437, 440

Stair, Sir James Dalrymple, Viscount of—
continued
Union legislation as fundamental law, objection
to thesis, **22**, 147
unjust enrichment, **15**, 11, 12, 33, 45, 59, 86
Stairs
building controls, **3**, 208
common, *see* TENEMENT
Stake net
salmon fishing by, **11**, 11
salmon fishing rights, exercise of, **18**, 326
Stall
food sold from, hygiene regulations, **11**, 408, 409,
411
Stamp
Post Office—
fictitious—
equipment for making, **16**, 1910
making, uttering, dealing in or selling, **16**,
1910
meaning, **16**, 1910*n*
imitation, **16**, 1909
offences concerning, **16**, 1910
Stamp duty
ad valorem duty, **19**, 1535
adjudication, **6**, 447
administration and collection, **19**, 1544*n*
assessment, **6**, 447
cautionary obligations, treatment of, **3**, 1003
certificate, **6**, 549
charge to, **25**, 54
charitable body, exemption, **3**, 1164
commercial lease, **13**, 587
conveyances on sales, **19**, 1535
deeds, on, **6**, 447
donations, **8**, 655
duty *ad valorem*, **25**, 1031
feu grants, **6**, 476
generally, **25**, 54, 1031
gifts, abolition of charge relating to, **25**, 54
instruments—
chargeable—
duty to, **25**, 1031
exemption, **25**, 1031
in respect of, **19**, 1535
land, transfer of, **18**, 643
late payment, **19**, 1536
lease, conveyance on, **19**, 1535
moveable items, not payable on, **6**, 558
partnership assets or shares, conveyance on sale,
16, 1124
partnerships, **19**, 1593
penalties, **19**, 1536; **25**, 1031
receipts, **13**, 1757
reserve tax, **19**, 1504*n*, 1537
share transfers, **4**, 375
stock transfers, **19**, 1535, 1537
time allowed for, **6**, 447
valuation, generally, **25**, 1031
value, meaning, **25**, 54
voluntary disposition *inter vivos*, **19**, 1510; **25**, 54
winding up by court, consequences, **4**, 755
writs, **13**, 1757

Standard amenities
meaning, **11**, 2023
Standard charge
generally, **18**, 211
Standard (Heraldic)
grant of and display, **11**, 1609
meaning, **11**, 1609
Standard of proof
See PROOF
Standard security
accretion, **18**, 677
advantages, **20**, 148
agricultural holding, **20**, 179
alteration, **20**, 172
assignation, **6**, 637; **20**, 169, 170
deduction of title by granter, **20**, 174
effect, **20**, 170
prescribed form, **20**, 170
proprietor's rights and obligations, of, **20**, 194
transfer by, **20**, 170
availability, **20**, 148
bondholder, application by, **20**, 217
building society, taken by, **20**, 228
contents, **20**, 230
deed of variation of standard conditons, **20**, 229
calling-up, **20**, 163
amount due, statement of, **20**, 188
interest, statement of amount due, **20**, 188
notice, **20**, 185
creditor's rights on debtor's default, **20**, 191–
194
dispensing with period of, **20**, 189
duration, **20**, 190
form, **20**, 185
person served with, **20**, 186
service—
mode of, **20**, 187
proof of, **20**, 187
principal, statement of amount due, **20**, 188
commercial lease, over, **13**, 585
common property, *pro indiviso* shares, **18**, 28
contract, originating in, **18**, 8
conveyance *ex facie* absolute, already granted by
granter, **20**, 157
creditor—
assignation by, **20**, 170
clause undertaking to make payments to, **20**,
151
debtor's obligations, right to perform, **20**, 162
deduction of title, **20**, 174
default by debtor—
application for remedies on, **20**, 199–201
calling-up notice, in complying with, **20**,
191–194
possession on, **20**, 166
powers on, **20**, 166
service of notice of, **20**, 195–198
foreclosure, power of, generally, **20**, 206
let subject, power to, **20**, 166
planning notice or order, particulars of to be
given to, **20**, 159
possession, power to enter into, **20**, 166
redemption, entitlement to, **20**, 175
sale of subject by, **20**, 166, 192, 202–205

Standard security—*continued*
creditor—*continued*
  subject let by, **20**, 193
  title of, protection after foreclosure, **20**, 214
  variation of standard conditions by, **20**, 155
croft, **20**, 179
debenture conditions unaffected by, **20**, 254
debt—
  contracted after recording of security, **20**, 148
  fixed amount, **20**, 148
  indefinite amount, **20**, 148
  meaning, **20**, 147*n*
debtor—
  default—
    calling-up notice, in complying with, creditor's
      rights, **20**, 166, 191–194, 199–201
    creditor's powers on, **20**, 166
    service of notice of, **20**, 195–198
    when held to be in, **20**, 164
  foreclosure, decree of, **20**, 207, 209
  insurance, obligation as to, **20**, 160
  liability for expenses, **20**, 168
  obligations, **20**, 158–162
    creditor's right to perform, **20**, 162
  planning notice or order received by, **20**, 159
  redemption, right of, **20**, 167, 175
  variation of standard conditions by, **20**, 155
debtor under, as lessor, **13**, 163, 164
deduction of title, **20**, 156
  form, **20**, 157
default—
  certificate of, **20**, 201
  debtor's, **20**, 164, 199–201
    creditor's rights and powers on, **20**, 166,
      191–194, 199–201
  notice of, **20**, 195–198
    duration, **20**, 196
    effect, **20**, 195
    objections to, **20**, 197, 198
    service, **20**, 195, 196
      rights and duties after, **20**, 198
  where debtor not in, **20**, 200
delivered but not yet registered, **18**, 14
discharge, **6**, 637; **20**, 169, 173
  deduction of title by granter, **20**, 174
  partial, **20**, 171
dominant interests, **18**, 351
enabling powers, **20**, 150–157
enforcement, **6**, 636
  ejection, **18**, 154
expenses, debtor's liability for, **20**, 168
fixed amount, payment to creditor, clause undertaking to make, **20**, 151
fluctuating amount, payment to creditor, clause
  undertaking to make, **20**, 151
foreclosure—
  application for decree of, **20**, 207
    court's power on, **20**, 209
    service, **20**, 209
  creditor—
    power of foreclosure, generally, **20**, 206
    title after foreclosure, protection of, **20**, 214
  debtor's personal obligation, recourse against,
    20, 213

Standard security—*continued*
foreclosure—*continued*
  decree of—
    application for, **20**, 207, 209, 210
    contents of, **20**, 211
    generally, **20**, 211
    recording, effect of, **20**, 212
    registration, effect of, **20**, 212
  statement of amount due, **20**, 208
forms, **6**, 633; **20**, 149, 157
generally, **13**, 160, 1758; **18**, 5
ground annual, **20**, 150
holder's right to enforce direct payment, **8**, 396
income support payments towards, **21**, 1075
insurance, obligation as to, **20**, 160
insurance company, taken by, **20**, 231
interest in land—
  grant over, **20**, 150
  meaning, **20**, 150
introduction, **20**, 147
jurisdiction, **20**, 215
law of, **6**, 633
lease, over, destruction of lease, **18**, 9
lease, registered, **20**, 150
maills and duties, action of, **8**, 396
matrimonial home, grant in relation to *pro indiviso*
  share, **18**, 27
non-monetary obligation, for, **20**, 157
payment to creditor, clause undertaking to make,
  20, 151
procedure, **20**, 216
proprietor—
  assignation of rights and obligations, **20**, 194
  notice of default, service on, **20**, 195–198
  redemption, entitlement to, **20**, 175
  service of application for decree of foreclosure
    on, **20**, 209
  when deemed insolvent, **20**, 165
real conditions, **18**, 351
redemption—
  amount recoverable, **20**, 183
  contracting out of statutory provisions for-
    bidden, **20**, 184
  forms, **20**, 175
  generally, **20**, 175
  notice, **20**, 175
  person entitled unable to obtain discharge, **20**,
    176
  private dwelling house, protection on leasehold
    subjects, **20**, 177, 178, 181, 182
  residential use not permitted, where, **20**, 182
registration for execution—
  clause consenting to, **20**, 153
restriction, **6**, 637; **20**, 169, 171
  deed of, deduction of title by granter, **20**, 174
reversionary company, taken by, **20**, 232
right in security, as, **18**, 5
rights of, **11**, 1108
sale, exercise of power of, **20**, 166, 202–205
  advertisement of sale, **20**, 202
  application of proceeds, **20**, 205
  creditor's power, generally, **20**, 202
  disponee, nomination by purchaser of another,
    20, 204

Standard security—_continued_
sale, exercise of power of—_continued_
  disposition by creditor on sale, **20**, 203
  exposure to sale, by, **20**, 202
  foreclosure, application for decree of following, **20**, 207
  private bargain, by, **20**, 202
separate tenement as subject of, **18**, 208
smallholding, **20**, 179
specialised concept of law, as, **11**, 1005
standard conditions—
  alteration, **20**, 172
  alteration of subject, **20**, 158, 166
  calling up standard security, **20**, 163
  creditor—
    planning notice or order, particulars of to be given to, **20**, 159
    powers on default by debtor, **20**, 166
    right to perform debtor's obligations, **20**, 162
  debtor—
    default—
      creditor's powers on, **20**, 166
      when held to be in, **20**, 164
    insurance, obligation as to, **20**, 160
    liability for expenses, **20**, 168
    obligations, **20**, 158–162
      creditor's right to perform, **20**, 162
    planning notice or order received by, **20**, 159
    redemption, right of, **20**, 167
  demolition of subject, **20**, 158
  expenses, debtor's liability for, **20**, 168
  generally, **20**, 154
  insurance, obligation as to, **20**, 160
  maintenance of subject, **20**, 158
  planning notices and orders, **20**, 159
  repair of subject, **20**, 158, 166
  sub-letting, **20**, 161
  subject—
    alteration of, **20**, 158, 166
  variation, **20**, 155, 157, 172
subject—
  burdened by other standard security or heritable security, **20**, 157
  description of, **20**, 157
  let by creditor, **20**, 193
sub-letting, **20**, 161
summary application, procedure by, **20**, 216
title, deduction of, **20**, 156, 174
transfer by assignation, **20**, 170
variation, **20**, 169, 172
warrandice clause—
  importance of, **20**, 152
warrandice in sale of property, **18**, 704
See also HERITABLE SECURITY
Standard time
British Standard Time, **22**, 810
Greenwich mean time as species, **22**, 809
Standing civilian court
appeal from, **2**, 742
compensation, order to pay, **2**, 740
constitution, **2**, 738
courts-martial—
  appeal to, powers of, **2**, 742
  election for, **2**, 739

Standing civilian court—_continued_
establishment, **2**, 738
evidence—
  generally, **2**, 677
  rights as to, **2**, 679
findings—
  petition against, **2**, 742
  review of, **2**, 741
magistrate, appointment, **2**, 738
purposes of, **2**, 738
restitution orders, **2**, 740
sentence—
  categories of, **2**, 740
  powers as to, **2**, 740
  procedure, **2**, 740
  promulgation of, **2**, 741
  review of, **2**, 741
trial, procedure, **2**, 739
Standing Committees
See HOUSE OF COMMONS
Standing Council of Scottish Chiefs
licences to manufacture badges, **11**, 1631
Standing order
code of conduct, **14**, 232
commencement, **14**, 1319
Committee, _see_ STANDING ORDERS COMMITTEE
compliance with, **14**, 1318
content, **14**, 1319
contract of local authority, **14**, 326
financial, **14**, 1316
force of law, whether having, **14**, 1316
generally, **14**, 1316
hybrid Bills—
  compliance with, **19**, 128
  non-compliance with, **19**, 127
insurance premium payment by, **12**, 833
personal Bill, **19**, 3
place of meeting, **14**, 1316
private Bill, non-compliance with, **19**, 82, 83
proceedings, **14**, 1316
quorum, **14**, 1316
revocation, **14**, 1317
suspension, **14**, 1319
terms, **14**, 1316
third party, effect on, **14**, 1316
variation, **14**, 1317
Standing Orders Committee
appointment of, **5**, 461
functions of, **5**, 447
membership of, **5**, 447
powers of, **5**, 461
**Stare decisis**
See JUDICIAL PRECEDENT (_stare decisis_)
State
arbitration, consent to, **19**, 720
ceasing to exist, **19**, 660_n_
characteristics, **19**, 658, 658_n_
Church and—
  See CHURCH AND STATE
crime committed abroad, **19**, 675, 676
Declaration concerning Friendly Relations and Co-operation, **19**, 685
duties of, **19**, 685–688

State—*continued*
education, shifting relationship with church over, **5**, 346
equality between, **19**, 680
international disputes, *see* INTERNATIONAL DISPUTES
jurisdiction, **19**, 675–684
    adjudicate, right to, **19**, 675
    claimed in concurrence with other state, 19, 675
    diplomatic immunity, **19**, 679, 681–684
    effects principle, **19**, 677
    enforce, right to, **19**, 675
    exceptions to territorial jurisdiction, **19**, 679–684
    international law, and, **19**, 675
    nationality principle, **19**, 675
    passive personality principle, **19**, 676
    prescribe, right to, **19**, 675
    sovereign immunity, **19**, 679, 680
    universality principle, **19**, 678
liability, nature of, **19**, 690
new, legal effects of creation of, **5**, 343
offences against, *see* STATE, OFFENCES AGAINST
officials, responsibility for acts of, **19**, 689
par in parem non habet imperium principle, **19**, 680
partnership requires no recognition from, **4**, 302
primary concern of international law, **19**, 603, 604, 658
procedural capacity, **19**, 692
recognition, **19**, 659, 659*n*
    de facto, **19**, 662, 663
    de jure, **19**, 662–664
    effect on United Kingdom municipal law, **19**, 663
    implied, **19**, 661, 661*n*
    importance, **19**, 662
    modes of, **19**, 661
    recognition of governments distinguished, **19**, 660
    territory necessary prerequisite, **19**, 666
    United Kingdom practice, **19**, 662–664
responsibility, **19**, 689–693
    Draft Articles on, **19**, 689, 689*n*
rights and duties of, **19**, 666*ff*
    Declaration concerning Friendly Relations and Co-operation, **19**, 685
    environment, duties as to, **19**, 687
    foreign nationals, duties to, **19**, 686
    jurisdiction, **19**, 675–684
    land, duties as to, **19**, 687
    sovereignty, **19**, 666–674
    war, duties in time of, **19**, 688
self-determination, **19**, 665
sovereignty, **19**, 666
    natural resources, over, **19**, 671, 687
state territory, meaning, **19**, 666*n*
territory, *see* TERRITORY
two nations in one, continuation after Union, **5**, 346
State aid
control, **4**, 1111
European Economic Community rules, **10**, 152, 167
State earnings-related pension scheme (SERPS)
See PENSION

State hospital
constitution, **14**, 1472
correspondence of patient in, **14**, 1473
fire certificates not required for, **10**, 1470
provision of accommodation at, **11**, 1476
State, offences against
armed forces, in respect of—
    aliens, incitement, **7**, 599
    dealings with enemy, **7**, 605–608
    desertion—
        assisting, **7**, 601
        incitement, **7**, 596
    disaffection, incitement, **7**, 598
    foreign enlistment, **7**, 609
    interference with duty, **7**, 602
    malingering, aiding, **7**, 603
    mutiny, incitement, **7**, 597
    prisoners of war, assisting escape, **7**, 611
    shipbuilding etc., offences, **7**, 610
conspiracy, **7**, 594
generally, **7**, 563
historical background, **7**, 564
leasing-making, **7**, 595
misprision, **7**, 566, 568, 584
modernisation of law, **7**, 565
official secrets legislation, *see* OFFICIAL SECRETS LEGISLATION
peace, during, **7**, 565
political nature, **7**, 563
sabotage, **7**, 628
sedition, *see* SEDITION
seriousness, **7**, 563
spying, **7**, 628
terrorism, *see* TERRORISM
treason, *see* TREASON
war, during, **7**, 565
State retirement pension
See PENSION
Stated case
appeal by way of, **17**, 1453–1458
Stateless person
British citizenship, acquisition of, **14**, 1906
citizenship status, acquisition of, **14**, 1951
European Union law, **12**, 222
registration, **14**, 1952
resident in UK, Home Office travel document, **16**, 1237
Statements of Standard Accounting Practice
generally, **1**, 45
local authority accounts, applying to, **1**, 47
Stationery
business, **4**, 436
change in particulars printed on as notice of change in firm, **16**, 1038, 1096
company, registered name shown on, **4**, 321
partnership, **16**, 1025
self-supply, **7**, 1301, 1303
    VAT input tax, **7**, 1374
weights and measures legislation, **6**, 246
Statue
maintenance of, **14**, 703
Status
action relating to, **4**, 68
change of, registration, **19**, 1429

Status—*continued*
concept of—
  adulthood, **11**, 1067
  bankruptcy, **11**, 1067
  capacity, **11**, 1067
  childhood, **11**, 1067
  citizenship, **11**, 1069
  commoner, **11**, 1069
  corporate, **11**, 1072
  decline in importance of, **11**, 1070
  differences in status, **11**, 1067
  elections—
    candidature for election, **11**, 1069
    capacity to vote at, **11**, 1069
  family relationships, **11**, 1068
  nationality, **11**, 1069
  nobility, **11**, 1069
  prisoners, **11**, 1069
  public law, **11**, 1069
  sex, differences of, **11**, 1068
  unsound mind, persons of, **11**, 1067
  weaker parties, protection of, **11**, 1071
persons, of—
  church courts, powers to resolve matters relating to, **22**, 511
  Commissary Courts, post-Reformation, powers, **22**, 519
Status of Forces Agreement
provisions of, **2**, 619
signatories to, **2**, 619
Statute
deeds, effect of statute on interpretation, **12**, 1218
desuetude, **12**, 1201
Great Britain Bill, Scotland included in, **12**, 1101, 1187
in pari materia, **12**, 1156
interpretation and construction—
  absurdity, avoidance of, **12**, 1109, 1124, 1125
  Act not to be extended beyond object, **12**, 1111–1113
  ambiguities, **7**, 21; **12**, 1113, 1114, 1163
  casus omissus not to be supplied by courts, **12**, 1107
  consolidating Acts, **12**, 1148, 1158
  construction—
    application of principle, **12**, 1120
    application of rule to scheme of Act, **12**, 1122
    external aids to, *see* external aids to construction *below*
    internal aids to, *see* internal aids to construction *below*
    limit to principle, **12**, 1121
    not to make Act invalid, **12**, 1123
  contemporanea expositio—
    ancient statutes, **12**, 1112
    modern statutes, **12**, 1113
  Crown, application of enactments to, **12**, 1212
  de minimus non curat praetor, **12**, 1170
  declaratory acts, **12**, 1193
  desuetude, Acts falling into, **12**, 1201
  dictionary as aid to, **12**, 1152
  directory enactments, **12**, 1175, 1180
  discretionary enactments, **12**, 1175, 1179, 1180

Statute—*continued*
interpretation and construction—*continued*
  distance, measurement of, **12**, 1209
  duties, continuity of, **12**, 1210
  ejusdem generis rule—
    generally, **12**, 1166
    inapplicability of rule, **12**, 1168
    rule of construction, as, **12**, 1167
  European Union legislation, **12**, 1205
  expressio unius est exclusio alterius, **12**, 1165
  extending to more than one part of United Kingdom, **12**, 1188
  external aids to construction—
    administrative practice, **12**, 1162
    analogy, **7**, 20
    common sense, **7**, 18, 22
    consolidating Acts, **12**, 1148, 1158
    conventions, **12**, 1153, 1154
    conveyancing practice, **12**, 1161
    dictionaries, **12**, 1152
    earlier enactments, **12**, 1155–1159
    explanatory memoranda, **12**, 1149, 1150
    generally, **12**, 1143
    historical setting, **12**, 1144–1146
    international conventions, **12**, 1153
    later enactments, **12**, 1155, 1160
    legislative history, **12**, 1147
    modern decisions, **12**, 1146
    modifications, **12**, 1159
    official reports, **12**, 1149
    older decisions, **12**, 1145
    Parliamentary history, **12**, 1147, 1148
    policy consideration, **7**, 20
    re-enactments, **12**, 1159
    statutes construed with other statutes, **12**, 1157
    statutes *in pari materia*, **12**, 1156
    statutory instruments, **12**, 1164
    textbooks, **12**, 1151
    travaux préparatoires, **12**, 1154
    uniform decisions, **12**, 1163
    usage, **12**, 1163
  faultiness of expression, correction, **12**, 1108
  gender, rules as to, **12**, 1207
  general principles, **7**, 4, 16, 18; **12**, 1101, 1206
  golden rule, **12**, 1109
    limitations to, **12**, 1110
  grammar, rules of, **12**, 1103, 1106, 1109
  Heydon's Case, rule in, **12**, 115
  inconsistency, golden rule, **12**, 1109
  injustice, duty of courts to avoid, **12**, 1114
  intent, according to—
    conflicting approaches, illustrations of, **12**, 1117
    generally, **12**, 1116
    object of section, **12**, 1118, 1120
  intention of Parliament, **12**, 1102
  internal aids to construction—
    generally, **12**, 1134
    headings, **12**, 1138
    interpretation sections, **12**, 1140
    preamble, **12**, 1136
    provisos, **12**, 1139
    punctuation, **12**, 1142

Statute—*continued*
interpretation and construction—*continued*
  internal aids to construction—*continued*
    rubric of section, **12**, 1137
    schedules, **12**, 1141
    short and long title, **12**, 1135
    side note of section, **12**, 1137
  literal reading, unintelligible result produced by, **12**, 1108
  literal rule, **12**, 1103–1106
  mandatory enactments, **12**, 1175–1178
  meaning clear, where, **12**, 1103–1113
  meaning not clear, where, **12**, 114–1125
  mischief rule, **12**, 1115
  number, rules as to, **12**, 1207
  omissions not to be inferred, **12**, 1107–1110
  penal statutes, **12**, 1184
  permissive enactments, **12**, 1175, 1180
  person, meaning, **12**, 1211
  post, service by, **12**, 1208
  powers, continuity of, **12**, 1210
  pre-Union Scots Acts—
    desuetude, **12**, 1201
    generally, **12**, 1200
  presumptions—
    against change in law and practice, **12**, 1126, 1127
    burdens, against imposing, **12**, 1131
    common calamity, cases of, **12**, 1266
    common law, against change of, **12**, 1126
    conditio si institutus sine liberis decesserit, **12**, 1265
    conditio si testator sine liberis decesserit, **12**, 1265
    correct use of words, **12**, 1133
    division *per capita*, **12**, 1268
    falsa demonstratio non nocet, **12**, 1268
    intestacy, against, **12**, 1267
    jurisdiction, in relation to—
      sheriff courts, **12**, 1129
      superior courts, **12**, 1128
      supervisory power of, **12**, 1130
    legality, of, **12**, 1267
    popular construction, in favour of, **12**, 1132
    retrospectivity, **12**, 1191
    rights, against taking away, **12**, 1131
    rules of practice and procedure, against change of, **12**, 1127
  private Acts—
    generally, **12**, 1202
    meaning, **12**, 1202
    strict interpretation, **12**, 1203, 1204
  rank, words of, **12**, 1169
  remedial statutes, **12**, 1186
  repeals—
    delegated legislation, **12**, 1196
    desuetude, Acts falling into, **12**, 1201
    effect of, generally, **12**, 1194
    implied repeal, **12**, 1198
    prevailing practice as to, **12**, 1199
    re-enactment, **12**, 1196
    repealing enactment, repeal of, **12**, 1197
    revival of previously repealed act, **12**, 1197
    special acts, **12**, 1198
    subordinate legislation, **12**, 1196
    substituted provisions, **12**, 1195

Statute—*continued*
interpretation and construction—*continued*
  repugnancy, golden rule, **12**, 1109
  retrospection—
    declaratory acts, **12**, 1193
    generally, **12**, 1189
    legality of past transactions, **12**, 1190
    presumption against, rebuttal, **12**, 1191
    procedure, alterations in form of, **12**, 1192
    vested rights, **12**, 1190
  rules—
    golden rule, **12**, 1109
      limitations to, **12**, 1110
    literal rule, **12**, 1103–1106
    necessity for, **12**, 1101
    paramount, **12**, 1102
    special, enactments to which applicable, **12**, 1200–1205
  Scotland, drafting difficulties, **12**, 1101
  section—
    interpretation sections, **12**, 1140
    meaning of, determination by reference to general scheme of Act, **12**, 1122
    object of, **12**, 1118, 1120
    rubric of, **12**, 1137
    side note of, **12**, 1137
  service, interpretation of term, **12**, 1208
  statutes construed with other statutes, **12**, 1157
  statutory duties—
    absolute, **12**, 1181, 1182
    qualified, **12**, 1181, 1183
  taxing statutes, **12**, 1185
  technical words, **12**, 1103
  territorial extent, **12**, 1187
  time, computation of, **12**, 1171–1174
  unambiguous words, **12**, 1105, 1112
  uniform application of Acts extending to Great Britain, **12**, 1188
  ut res magis valeat quam pereat, **12**, 1123, 1124
  whole, statute to be read as, **12**, 1119–1122
invalid, construction not to make Act, **12**, 1123
long title, **12**, 1135
object of, interpretation not to extend, **12**, 1111–1113
penal, interpretation, **12**, 1184
personal bar, applicability, **16**, 1609
pre-Union Scots Acts, interpretation, generally, **12**, 1200, 1201
private legislation, *See* PRIVATE BILL; PRIVATE LEGISLATION
remedial, interpretation, **12**, 1186
repeal—
  decisions made under previous legislation, **12**, 1194
  delegated legislation under repealed enactment, **12**, 1196
  implied repeal, **12**, 1198
  practice prevailing under repealed statute, **12**, 1199
  re-enactment, **12**, 1196
  repealing enactment repealed by, **12**, 1197
  subordinate legislation under repealed enactment, **12**, 196
  substituted provisions, **12**, 1195

Statute—*continued*
short title, **12**, 1135
source of law, as—
Adjournal, Acts of, High Court of Justiciary, **22**, 528
desuetude, tacit repeal by, pre-Union legislation, **22**, 526, 626
See also DESUETUDE, DOCTRINE OF
post-Union, **22**, 525, 527, 528
pre-Union—
characteristics, **22**, 526
generally, **22**, 525, 526
repeal by desuetude, **22**, 526, 626
records, before 1707 ..., **22**, 525
Sederunt, Acts of, **22**, 528
Union, Treaty of 1707, application of legislation in Scotland, effect, **22**, 527
statutory requirement—
discretionary, held to be, **12**, 1178, 1180
mandatory, held to be, **12**, 1177
summary diligence, exclusion by, **4**, 184
taxing, interpretation, **12**, 1185
See ACT OF PARLIAMENT; LEGISLATION
Statute-barred information
executive act made under, declaration, **7**, 857
public records, in, **19**, 877
Statute of Westminster
Commonwealth, generally, **7**, 781, 782
royal succession and style and titles, consent to, **7**, 703, 703*n*
Statutory certificate
documentary evidence, as, **10**, 597
Statutory Committee of the Pharmaceutical Society of Great Britain
constitution, **15**, 1515
elections, **15**, 1515
functions, **15**, 1515
Statutory conveyance
compulsory purchase—
benefits accruing to promoter by use of, **5**, 84
difficulties, **5**, 83
generally, **5**, 81
recording, **5**, 85
style, **5**, 84
third party rights, **5**, 86–88
creation, **6**, 588
form and effect, **6**, 588
Statutory declaration
interpretation, **12**, 1262
Statutory duty
breach of, *see* STRICT LIABILITY
Statutory endorsement
concept of, **22**, 137
doctrine of, **22**, 138, 139, 140
Statutory formality
want of, reduction on grounds of, **13**, 44
Statutory instrument
Adjournal, Acts of, as statutory instruments, **22**, 187
See also ACT OF ADJOURNAL
affirmative procedures, **22**, 180
annulment, subject to, provision of parent Act, **22**, 178

Statutory instrument—*continued*
citation, **22**, 186
classification, **22**, 176
codes of practice brought into force by, **22**, 197
commencement, **22**, 177, 179, 180
date of issue, **22**, 184
debates in House on, **5**, 424
definition, **22**, 176
documentary evidence, as, **10**, 576
draft to be laid before Parliament—
time limits, **22**, 179
expiry of temporary, **22**, 182
fishery Acts implemented by, **11**, 117
Hybrid Instruments Committee, **5**, 457
Joint Committee on, **5**, 440, 456
lapse, parent Act, repeal, **22**, 182
preparation of, role of Office of the Solicitor to the Secretary of State for Scotland, **13**, 1402
prerequisites to commencement, **22**, 177
promulgation, **22**, 184
proof, **22**, 185
revocation—
effect on validity of acts done under, **22**, 178
procedure, **22**, 181
Sederunt, Acts of, **22**, 187
See also ACT OF SEDERUNT
Standing Committees on, **5**, 425
subordinate legislation, concept, **22**, 175
use in construction of Act, **12**, 1164
See also DELEGATED LEGISLATION
Statutory jurisdiction
authority exercising, **16**, 2116
Statutory maternity pay
See MATERNITY PAY
Statutory offence
arrest without warrant for, **17**, 598
initiating proceedings for, **17**, 697
Statutory office
appointment to, **14**, 91, 249
Statutory presumption of survivorship
See SURVIVORSHIP
Statutory reports
select committees examining, **5**, 436–438, 454
Statutory sick pay
See SICK PAY
Statutory small tenant
assignation of lease, **1**, 859
bequest of tenancy, **1**, 859
buildings, maintenance of, **1**, 855
joint, **1**, 854
meaning, **1**, 837, 854
overriding interests of, **6**, 741
removal of, **1**, 858
rent, fixing, **1**, 856
resumption of holding, **1**, 858
rights and obligations of, **1**, 854
security of tenure, **1**, 854, 857
subletting, **1**, 859
succession, rights of, **1**, 859
vacant tenancies, dealing with, **1**, 860
Statutory tenancy
generally, **13**, 609
Statutory trust
See TRUST

Statutory undertaker
acquisition, transfer and vesting of land for rights of, **20**, 608
proposed charges to, **20**, 607
rights of—
    extinguishment of, **20**, 718
    generally, **20**, 717
    special roads, **20**, 717, 718
side road order, protection of rights under, **20**, 651

Steam
discharge, building controls, **3**, 208

Steam-engine
order *ad factum praestandum*, **14**, 2157

Steel industry
competition law, **4**, 858, 1149, 1165, 1308
consumer protection, **19**, 240

Steelbow
lease, **13**, 217, 220
meaning, **13**, 1707
mutuum contract, **13**, 1707

Steering Committee for Human Rights, **12**, 13

Stepchild
aliment, **10**, 1220
conditio si institutus sine liberis decesserit application of, **25**, 896
immediate family, as, **15**, 601
incest with, **3**, 1238, 1244
succession, **10**, 1220

Step-parent
custody of stepchildren, **10**, 1280
incest, **10**, 1227
legal position of, **10**, 1217

Sterilisation (food)
cream, **11**, 355, 479
ice cream, **11**, 354
milk, **11**, 459

Sterilisation (human)
wrongful pregnancy—
    'consent-based' negligence actions, **15**, 307
    generally, **15**, 305
    negligent failure to warn, **15**, 308

Sterling
See CURRENCY; MONEY

Stevedore
employment of, liability, **21**, 560, 560n
time charterparty, **21**, 640
voyage charterparty, **21**, 618

Steward
Officer of State, **7**, 790

Stewartry
population, **14**, 64

Stewartry court
abolition, **17**, 504, 525
jurisdiction, **6**, 1022; **17**, 523

Stillbirth
burial of stillborn child, **19**, 1449
cremation of stillborn child, **3**, 566
meaning, **19**, 1446n
registration of—
    certificate of registration of stillbirth, **19**, 1448
    certificate of stillbirth, **19**, 1447
        informant's declaration, **19**, 1447

Stillbirth—*continued*
registration of—*continued*
    correction of errors, **19**, 1442
    issue of extracts from, **19**, 1418, 1418n
    local authority duty, **14**, 588
    register of stillbirths, **19**, 1446
    registration district, **19**, 1433
    requirement to keep, **19**, 1433

Stillicide
cognate of, **25**, 351
servitude, **6**, 515; **18**, 485; **25**, 351
variations of, **25**, 351

Stipend
payment of, generally, **18**, 211
See RELIGION, MINISTER OF (Church of Scotland)

Stipendiary magistrate
appointment of, **14**, 512

Stipulatio
Roman law and development of law of caution, **3**, 806, 809

Stirling
Court of Four Burghs, **14**, 13
population, **14**, 64

Stirling Castle
keeper of, **7**, 830

Stock deficiencies
wages, deductions from, **9**, 64

Stock Exchange
investment exchange, as, **12**, 1322
listing, regulations on, **1**, 54
partnership as member, number of partners allowed, **16**, 1011, 1112
quotation, standards imposed as condition of obtaining, **4**, 305
takeover bid, steps before making of, **4**, 544
TAURUS scheme, transfer of shares by, **4**, 372
See also SCOTTISH STOCK EXCHANGE

Stock Exchange Third Market
market maker, value given by, **25**, 47

Stock market
contract for differences, **15**, 768
general outlook, **25**, 31

Stockbroker
agent, as, **1**, 603, 615
appointment by trustee of, **24**, 190
lien, right of, **1**, 643; **20**, 78, 87
proper conclusion of contract by, **1**, 631

Stockholm Declaration on the Human Environment, **19**, 687

Stocks
calls on, **24**, 230
insider dealing, *see* INSIDER DEALING
investment, as, **12**, 1308
regulation of, **14**, 816
shares, and—
    liferent, liferenter's rights, **13**, 1642
transfers—
    assignation, **6**, 597
    stamp duty, **19**, 1535, 1537

Stodart Committee of Inquiry
community councils, evidence on, **23**, 17
housing, recommendations as to, **11**, 1903
influence of, **14**, 59

Stodart Committee of Inquiry—*continued*
planning authority, internal organisation of, **23**, 16
terms of reference, **23**, 14
Stolen property
imprescriptive rights and obligations, **16**, 2126
money, **15**, 52
  recovery of, **14**, 1810
motor vehicle subject to hire-purchase or conditional sale agreement, sale, **15**, 52
negotiable instrument, **15**, 52
original owner's right to reclaim, **15**, 51
possession of, *see* RESET
recompense, **15**, 52
resale, profit made on, **15**, 57
restitution, **15**, 45, 46, 51
  exceptions to rule, **15**, 52
  money or negotiable instrument, **15**, 52
vitium reale, **15**, 51
Stone of Destiny
Coronations, **7**, 709*n*
Stoppage in transit
air, carriage by, **3**, 748
contract of sale, effect on, **20**, 878, 881
  property already passed to buyer, where, **20**, 878
Convention on the Contract for International Carriage of Goods by Road (CMR), **3**, 650
duration or extent of transit, **20**, 878
goods rejected by buyer, where, **20**, 878
how effected, **20**, 879
insolvency of buyer, **20**, 878
lien distinguished, **20**, 873
part delivery of goods already made, where, **20**, 878
purpose of, **20**, 878
rescission and resale by seller, **3**, 644
seller's right of, **20**, 870, 872, 878, 879
ship chartered by buyer, goods delivered to, **20**, 878
sub-sales, effect of, **20**, 880
unpaid seller's right of, **3**, 641–644
when goods deemed to be in transit, **20**, 878
Storage
import procedure, **7**, 1135
oil, of, **9**, 845
poison, **14**, 1218
premises, exclusion from derating, **24**, 643
underground, of gas—
  authorisation order, **9**, 895–896
  protective areas, operations in, **9**, 897
  storage areas, operations in, **9**, 897
valuation for rating, meaning for, **24**, 643
water, of, **25**, 328
Storage heaters
rating relief in respect of, **24**, 578
Storekeeper
right of lien, **20**, 77
Stowage
See SHIP
Stowaway
statutory offences directed at, **21**, 270

Straits
international navigation, used for—
  innocent passage, right of, **21**, 10
  overflight, no right of, **21**, 10
  straits formed by island belonging to mainland state, **21**, 10
  submarines, **21**, 10
  transit passage, **21**, 10
Straits of Dover
innocent passage, right of, **21**, 10
Stranger
destination of liferent property to—
  common property, **13**, 1623
  confusio, **13**, 1624
  Dobie's table, **13**, 1622
  joint property, **13**, 1622–1624
transfer of arms to, **11**, 1622
Strategic Arms Limitation Talks, **19**, 712
Strategic Arms Reduction Talks, **19**, 712
Strategic planning
See TOWN AND COUNTRY PLANNING
Strathclyde Region
passenger transport, **14**, 419, 425, 426
population, **14**, 64
structure, **14**, 64
water authority, as, **25**, 505
Stream
addition of water, **25**, 332
artificial—
  generally, **25**, 355
  permanent, **25**, 356
  temporary, **25**, 357
bank, constraints on operations on, **25**, 324
common interest, doctrine of—
  generally, **18**, 286
  See also COMMON INTEREST; RIVER
consumption of water, **25**, 334
deposits in, **25**, 406
diversion, strict liability for consequences, **15**, 195
flow, *see* RIVER
industrial purposes, use for, **25**, 519
loch, flowing from, common interest, **18**, 307
meaning, **25**, 302, 400*n*
navigability, **25**, 306
new schemes to impound, **25**, 516
pollution, *see* POLLUTION
riparian proprietor, *see* RIVER
servitudes, grant of, **25**, 349
sources feeding into, whether part of stream, **18**, 286
stagnum, addition of water from, **25**, 341
time immemorial, use for, **25**, 306
underground, **25**, 344
vegetation in, **25**, 406
water rights, acquisition of, **25**, 519
See also RIVER; WATERCOURSE
Street
cleaning, **9**, 1172
construction or alteration, **19**, 19*n*
public, public right of way distinguished, **18**, 495
use of term replaced by road, **20**, 501, 609
Street trader
child engaged in street trading, **3**, 1255
licensing, **14**, 119, 561

Strict liability
abnormally dangerous thing or activity, doctrine
    of, **14**, 2093
actio de effusis vel dejectis—
    application in Scotland, **15**, 152
    case law, **15**, 153
    generally, **15**, 151
    institutional writers, **15**, 152
    meaning, **15**, 151
actio de positis vel suspensis—
    application in Scotland, **15**, 152
    case law, **15**, 153
    generally, **15**, 151
    institutional writers, **15**, 152
    meaning, **15**, 151
aiding and abetting, **7**, 102
allowing, **7**, 103
animal, injury or damage caused by, *see* ANIMAL
art and part liability, **7**, 177
automatism, **7**, 158
carrier, of, **21**, 543, 544
causing, **7**, 103
consumer protection, *see* CONSUMER PROTECTION
contempt of court, **6**, 306; **17**, 28
cruelty, **7**, 104
defences, **7**, 108; **14**, 2131; **17**, 30
delegation, **7**, 103
edictal—
    common carriers, **15**, 144, 145, 146
    historical background, **15**, 144
    innkeepers, **15**, 144, 147–149
    institutional writers, **15**, 144
    shipmasters, **15**, 144
    stable-keepers, **15**, 144, 150
foreseeability, **14**, 2094
generally, **7**, 99; **12**, 1181, 1182
gravity of crime, **7**, 107
highway, premises in disrepair near, **14**, 2101
identification criteria, **7**, 107
identification of strict liability offences, **7**, 100
insanity and, **7**, 123
intentional nuisance, confusion with higher
    standard of care in, **14**, 2095
interdict cases, **14**, 2094, 2096
knowledge of facts, proof, **7**, 177
land, escape of dangerous agencies from—
    culpa, importance in Scots law, **15**, 190–195
    damnum fatale, **15**, 193
    defences, **15**, 193
    English law, **15**, 188
    fault, **15**, 193–195
        specification, **15**, 194
    generally, **15**, 187
    Kerr v Earl of Orkney, decision in, **15**, 189, 190
    natural use cases, **15**, 191
    occupier's liability, generally, **15**, 187
    Rylands v Fletcher, decision in, **15**, 188–192
    Scottish law, **15**, 189, 190
    stream, diversion, **15**, 195
mala prohibita, **7**, 107
mala in se, **7**, 107
mens rea, and, **7**, 99–108
non-age, **7**, 108, 159
nuisance giving rise to, generally, **14**, 2092

Strict liability—*continued*
onus to require, **7**, 99
permitting, **7**, 103
possession, **7**, 101
reference to, **14**, 2088
reparation action, **14**, 2096
statutory duty, breach—
    animal, injury or damage caused by, **15**, 155,
        180–186
    bad faith, **15**, 177
    causation—
        establishment, **15**, 166
        omission, breach taking form of, **15**, 167
        problems arising, **15**, 167
    civil court actions, generally, **15**, 154–156
    class intended to benefit, **15**, 160–162
        duty owed to persons generally, where, **15**,
            161
        pursuer must belong to, **15**, 160, 162
    consumer protection, *see* CONSUMER PROTECTION
    contractor, **15**, 159
    contributory factors, **15**, 168
    contributory negligence, **15**, 162, 175
    damages—
        express statement as to, where, **15**, 155
        requisites for claim, **15**, 158
        statute silent, where, **15**, 156
    damnum fatale, defence of, **15**, 175
    defences, **15**, 175
    duty—
        defender's failure to perform, **15**, 158, 163
        delegation to employee, where, **15**, 170
        delegation to pursuer, where, **15**, 170
        extent as question of construction, **15**, 172
        harm, and, establishing causal link, **15**, 166
        imposition on defender, **15**, 159
        standard of, **15**, 163
        statutory standard, **15**, 172
    economic loss, harm involving, **15**, 157, 178
    employee—
        contributory negligence by, **15**, 175
        delegation of duty to, **15**, 170, 175
        hired out to work for others, **15**, 159
    generally, **15**, 154, 157, 169
    harm—
        breach of duty and, causal link, **15**, 166
        breach must have caused, **15**, 158
        economic loss, **15**, 157
        type of, questions arising, **15**, 164
    Health and Safety at Work etc Act 1974 …, **15**,
        155, 155*n*, 159
    nature of action, **15**, 171
    negligence, and, **15**, 171, 175
    occupier, duties enforceable against, **15**, 159
    omission, breach taking form of, **15**, 167
    practicable or reasonably practicable steps,
        where defender took, **15**, 173, 174
    public authority as defender, **15**, 157, 176–178
        bad faith, **15**, 177
        discretionary power, where, **15**, 177
        duty of care, **15**, 178
    pursuer—
        act of, as real cause, **15**, 162, 168
        delegation of duty to, **15**, 170

Strict liability—*continued*
statutory duty, breach—*continued*
  reasonable care, standard of, **15**, 171
  statute must be viewed as a whole, **15**, 169, 172
  statutory purpose, interpretation, **15**, 165
  statutory standard, **12**, 1181–1183; **15**, 172
  volenti non fit injuria, **15**, 175
suspicion, **7**, 105
Strike
building contracts, provisions as to, **3**, 48
charterparty or bill of lading, strikes exception, **21**, 555
continuous employment, effect on, **9**, 46
contractual rights and duties, **9**, 132
evidence of dispute, as, **23**, 858
loss or damage resulting from, carrier not liable, **21**, 603
meaning, **9**, 132; **21**, 555
redundancy payment, effect on, **9**, 182
See also INDUSTRIAL ACTION; PICKETING
Strychnine
special restrictions, **14**, 1216
Student
au pair, change of category to, **12**, 297
change of category, **12**, 297
collective passport, issue, **16**, 1225
dependants of—
  conditions for entry, **12**, 302
  earnings, **12**, 299
  employment of, **12**, 303
  extension of leave, **12**, 304
  Immigration Rules, **12**, 301–304
  meaning of dependant, **12**, 301
employment, **12**, 154, 296
family credit, **21**, 1090
grant, payment to, **8**, 701, 708
housing benefit, **21**, 1112
immigration controls—
  entry clearance, **12**, 292–294
  extension of leave, **12**, 299
    doctor or dentist in postgraduate training, for, **12**, 300
  police registration conditions, **12**, 175
Immigration Rules, **12**, 149, 291, 292–300
income support, qualification for, **21**, 1077
letting—
  assured tenancy status, exclusion from, **13**, 636, 643
  protected tenancy status, exclusion from, **13**, 630, 633
meaning, **12**, 292
migration by, **12**, 102
spouse, change of category to, **12**, 297
university—
  academic performance, **8**, 1026, 1027
  bursary, award of, **8**, 1029
  copyright of, **8**, 1023
  disciplinary powers over, **8**, 1028
  duty of care owed to, **8**, 1025
  examinations, **8**, 1026
  freedom of speech, right of, **8**, 1031
  grant, payment to, **8**, 701, 708, 1030
  legal relations with university, **8**, 1024, 1024*n*
  occupation of university premises by, **8**, 1032

Student—*continued*
university—*continued*
  prizes, award of, **8**, 1029
  scholarship, award of, **8**, 1029
  sending down, **8**, 1027
  students' societies, **8**, 1031
  students' union, **8**, 1031
  suspension, **8**, 1027
work permit, grant of, **12**, 157
young Commonwealth working holidaymaker, change of category to, **12**, 297
Stultifying or stupifying substance
wild birds or animals taken or killed with, **11**, 880, 884
Sturgeon
occupancy, no right of acquisition by, **18**, 543*n*
Subfeuing
prohibition against, **6**, 523
Subinfeudation
transfer of ownership, and, **18**, 650
Sublease
amounting to *rei interventus*, **13**, 140
assignability, **13**, 354
assignation distinguished, **13**, 353
commercial lease, **13**, 564, 583
consent, landlord's, unreasonably witheld, **13**, 359
covert form, in, **13**, 361
delectus personae, doctrine of, **13**, 355–357, 583
duration, **13**, 379
effect—
  assignation and sublease, competition between, **13**, 385
  landlord and principal tenant, between, **13**, 381
  landlord and subtenant, between, **13**, 383
  landlord's remedies, **13**, 384
  tenant and principal tenant, between, **13**, 382
expiry, **13**, 379
express exclusion, **13**, 358–362
  enforceability, **13**, 362
  evasion, **13**, 361
express power to assign, **13**, 364
form, **13**, 378
generally, **13**, 154, 345
head lease, **13**, 583
inhibition, **13**, 184
insolvency or bankruptcy of lessee, **13**, 185
interposed lease—
  competence, **13**, 387
  effect, **13**, 388
  grant, **13**, 387
  historical background, **13**, 386
  principal lease as, **13**, 379
joint tenancy compared, **13**, 599
landlord—
  acceptance of subtenant by, **13**, 363
  consent of, **13**, 345
  hypothec, **13**, 517
  interest of, transfer, **13**, 349
  principal, **13**, 378
  principal tenant, relationship with, **13**, 381
  remedies available to, **13**, 384
  subtenant, relationship with, **13**, 383
lessee, principal, **13**, 103
lessor, **13**, 154

Sublease—*continued*
limitations, **13**, 379
long lease, limitations on residential use of
    property let by, **13**, 347
meaning, **13**, 103, 353
mutual contract, as, **13**, 380
nature of, **13**, 377
police force, sub-letting by member of, **16**, 1749,
    1754
possession, seal of real, **13**, 380
prescription, **13**, 230
principal landlord, **13**, 378
principal lease—
    break, **13**, 380
    irritancy, **13**, 380
    power of resumption, **13**, 380
    reduction, **13**, 379, 380
    renunciation, **13**, 443
principal lessee, **13**, 103
principal tenant, **13**, 103, 378
    landlord, relationship with, **13**, 381
    obligations in favour of, **13**, 378
    obligations of, **13**, 378
    position of, **13**, 353
    removings, action of, **13**, 500
    shared property, **13**, 599
    subtenant, relationship with, **13**, 382
profit rental, **13**, 569
prohibited, irritancy, **13**, 428
protected tenancy, repossession, **13**, 714, 720, 723
real conditions attached to, **18**, 349
registered, **13**, 380
rei interventus, amounting to, **13**, 140
removings, action of, **13**, 500
standard security, **20**, 161
subject—
    extent of subjects grantable, **13**, 379
    whole or part of principal lease, may be, **13**,
        377
sublessee, **13**, 103
subtenant, **13**, 103
    acceptance by landlord, **13**, 363
    assured tenancy, **13**, 613, 621
    completion of rights, **13**, 380
    generally, **13**, 103, 353, 378
    housing benefit, receiving, **21**, 1105
    landlord, relationship with, **13**, 383
    principal tenant, relationship with, **13**, 382
    removings, action of, **13**, 469, 500, 502
        notice, **13**, 503
    rights which may be granted, **13**, 379
tacit relocation, effect, **13**, 459
termination, **13**, 379
unlawful, renunciation of principal lease, **13**, 443
warrandice, **13**, 378
Submarine
passage—
    straits used for international navigation, **21**, 10
    territorial sea, **21**, 7
Submarine pipelines and cables
exclusive economic zone, **11**, 107
Subordinate legislation
See BYELAWS; DELEGATED LEGISLATION; STATUTORY
    INSTRUMENT

Subornation of perjury
reduction of decree on grounds of, **13**, 50
Subrogation
insurance claims, *see* INSURANCE
real, doctrine of, **24**, 7
Subscription
electoral documents, **15**, 1151
    claims, **15**, 1151
    objections, **15**, 1151
meaning, **15**, 1275
nomination paper—
    electoral numbers of subscribers, **15**, 1280
    European parliamentary election, **15**, 1276–
        1278, 1280
    local government election, **15**, 1276–1278,
        1280
    restrictions, **15**, 1278
    United Kingdom parliamentary election, **15**,
        1276–1278, 1280
    valid signatures, **15**, 1279
See also DEED OR WRITING; SIGNATURE
Subsidence
support, right to, *see* SUPPORT, RIGHTS OF
Subsidiarity
recompense, relationship with, **15**, 61, 63, 68–71
Sub-standard housing
closing order, *see* CLOSING ORDER
demolition order, *see* DEMOLITION
generally, **11**, 1978
improvement grants, **11**, 1981
improvement orders, **11**, 1981
local authorities—
    general duties, **11**, 1980
    powers as to, **11**, 1978–1981
    specific function, **11**, 1981
public health, **19**, 348
tolerable standard, **11**, 1978, 1979
underground rooms, **11**, 1981
Substitute will
See WILL
Substituted Bill
generally, **19**, 80
Substitutional legacy
See LEGACY
Substitutory redress
See DAMAGES
Subtenant
See SUBLEASE
Subway
construction or alteration, **19**, 19*n*
provision of, **20**, 660
Succession
active succession—
    discretionary provisions—
        court orders, **25**, 617
        generally, **25**, 614, 615
        judicial decisions, **25**, 618
        judicial discretion, classes of applicant for, **25**,
            614, 616
    England, **25**, 614
    France, **25**, 614
    Germany, **25**, 614
administration of estate—
    choice of law rules, **17**, 129, 349, 350

Succession—_continued_
administration of estate—_continued_
  taxation, on, **19**, 1642–1648
  See also ADMINISTRATION OF ESTATE
adopted person, succession by, **10**, 1191; **25**, 713, 714
agricultural tenancies—
  common law, at, **1**, 786
  generally, **1**, 848
  Land Court, jurisdiction of, **1**, 796
  liferent lease, no right to, **1**, 787
  right of, **1**, 727
  statutory small tenancy, to, **1**, 859
  taxation, **19**, 1666
  testate—
    acceptance by legatee, **1**, 788
    assignees, exclusion of, **1**, 787
    bequest, power of, **1**, 787
    heirs, by, **1**, 788
    null and void bequest declared, **1**, 788
    objection to legatee, **1**, 788
alienation, **18**, 535
  trust property, **18**, 535
assured tenancy—
  generally, **13**, 781
  original tenant, **13**, 782
  successor tenant, **13**, 783
beneficiary, _see_ BENEFICIARY (WILLS AND SUCCESSION)
canon law as law of pre-Reformation Scotland, **22**, 580
capital gains tax, **19**, 1636, 1641
case law—
  family, meaning, **13**, 785
  only or principal home, meaning, **13**, 786
choice of law, current approach to, **17**, 129
civil jurisdiction, Convention not applicable, **4**, 26
collateral—
  division of estate on/after 8 December 1986—
    examples, **25**, 704
    heritable succession, **25**, 679
    intestate succession, **25**, 698
    moveable succession, **25**, 682
collation—
  doctrine of, **25**, 808
  inter haeres, **25**, 683
Commissary Clerk of Edinburgh, transfer of functions to, **22**, 581
Commissary Courts, canonical procedure, retention, **22**, 581
copyright, moral rights, **18**, 1141
croft, to, **1**, 808
Crown, _see_ CROWN
death—
  presumption of, **25**, 653
  proof of, _see_ DEATH
  tax consequences, **19**, 1616, 1631
debts—
  deceased, due to, **25**, 1064
  deduction of, inheritance tax, **25**, 1008
  diligence, forming basis of, **25**, 1054
  generally, **25**, 665
  heir, liability of, **25**, 637
  heritable, **25**, 667

Succession—_continued_
debts—_continued_
  inheritance tax, preferred to, **25**, 847
  legal rights, **25**, 782, 791, 792
  moveable, **25**, 667
  next of kin, of, **25**, 1058
  payment of, **25**, 666, 847
  preference of, **25**, 1057
  privileged, **25**, 666, 847
devolution—
  clause, destination over distinguished from, **25**, 917
  intestacy, on—
    England, **25**, 631
    France, **25**, 632
    generally, **25**, 630
    Germany, **25**, 633
  intestacy, upon, _see_ INTESTACY
  kinds of succession—
    active, **25**, 614
    passive, **25**, 613
  terminology, **25**, 612
  voluntary and statutory, balance between, **25**, 629
discharge of rights, **11**, 746
disclaimers, **19**, 1639
distribution—
  administration prior to—
    in division and partition, **25**, 642
    English law, **25**, 640
    establishment of estate, **25**, 638
    France, in, **25**, 639
    Germany, in, **25**, 639
    statutory trusts, **25**, 641
  England, **25**, 605
  executor, duties of, **25**, 1105
  France, **25**, 605, 639
  Germany, **25**, 605, 639
  partial intestate estate, remainder of, **25**, 709
election, reduction of deed of, **11**, 747
election in, by judicial factor, **24**, 256
England and Wales—
  active succession, **25**, 614
  death, property passing on—
    competent beneficiaries, **25**, 621
    future property, **25**, 622
    generally, **25**, 619
    spouse of, rights on, **25**, 602
  devolution, **25**, 606
  disqualification under common law, **25**, 670
  distribution of property, **25**, 605
  executor, acceptance to act, **25**, 637
  family property, **25**, 608
  freedom of testation, **25**, 601
  identification of property, **25**, 605
  intestate succession, **25**, 631
  joint tenancy, **25**, 640
  partition, **25**, 642
  privileged will, **25**, 628_n_
  reassembly of estate, **25**, 611
  species of property, distinction of, **25**, 607
  transmission, **25**, 635
  trust for sale, **25**, 641
entails, _see_ ENTAIL, LAW OF

Succession—*continued*
estate, reassembly of, **25**, 609–611
executors, confirmation and duties, canon law
    influences in modern Scots law, **22**, 581, 584
family property, **25**, 608
female—
    heritable succession, **25**, 678
    male, preference of, abolition of, **25**, 687
France, in, *see* FRANCE
fraud in relation to, generally, **11**, 743
future property, transfer of, **25**, 622
general scheme of, **25**, 676
Germany, in, *see* GERMANY
heirs, impersonation of, **11**, 748, 759
heritable, *see* HERITABLE ESTATE
heritable and moveable property, **18**, 11, 11*n*
identification of property, **25**, 605
illegitimate child, *see* ILLEGITIMACY
inheritance tax, incidence of, **19**, 1637–1639
    See also INHERITANCE TAX
interest on sum due as legal rights in, **12**, 1031
intestate—
    accession, **18**, 576
    former rules as to, **18**, 11
    See also INTESTACY
Judgments Convention, exclusion from scope of,
    4, 26; **8**, 431, 434
Land Court, jurisdiction of, **1**, 796
legal rights—
    alternative to provision in will, as, **25**, 774
    amount of—
        spouse but no children, person survived by,
            25, 773
        spouse and children, person survived by, **25**,
            773
    avoidance of—
        generally, **25**, 809
        heritage, investment in, **25**, 810
        inter vivos trust, **25**, 811
        life policy, **25**, 813
        outright lifetime gift, **25**, 812
        pension scheme, **25**, 814
        special destination, property subject to, **25**,
            815
    calculation of, **25**, 703
    claim for—
        effect of, **25**, 779
        forfeiture of provision in will, **25**, 780
        intestacy, **25**, 781
    confirmation, **19**, 1627
    conversion, **25**, 816
    courtesy, abolition of, **25**, 702, 778
    date of death, property owned at—
        actual realised values, **25**, 794
        capital gains tax, **25**, 797
        interest—
            generally, **25**, 795
            income tax, **25**, 796
        quantification of, **25**, 784
        values, **25**, 793
    debts, **25**, 782, 791, 792
    descendant's claim—
        legitim—
            division of, **25**, 787

Succession—*continued*
legal rights—*continued*
    descendant's claim—*continued*
        legitim—*continued*
            generally, **25**, 786
            illegitimate child, **25**, 788
        potential claimant—
            provision for, **25**, 789
            statutory code, **25**, 790
    discharge of—
        effect of, **25**, 773
        generally, **25**, 775, 798
        marriage contract, under, **25**, 799
        spouse, renunciation by, **25**, 800
    election in respect of, **25**, 777
    equitable compensation—
        income, accumulation of, **25**, 804
        issue, provision for, **25**, 805
        principle, **25**, 803
    explicit lifetime discharge—
        collation, **25**, 808
        forisfamiliation, **25**, 808
        generally, **25**, 806
        marriage contract, **25**, 806
        voluntary, **25**, 807
    family protection, as, **25**, 772
    generally, **11**, 745
    heritable property, **25**, 778
    inheritance tax, **25**, 1029
    interest on, **12**, 1031
    intestacy, **25**, 781
    jus relictae, **19**, 1624
    jus relictae vel relicti claim to, **25**, 785
    jus relicti, **19**, 1624
    legitim, **19**, 1625–1630
    meaning, **17**, 340; **19**, 1625
    minor children—
        election, **19**, 1629
        generally, **19**, 1628
        unresolved problems, **19**, 1630
    moveable property, **25**, 778
    nature of, **25**, 791
    possibility of claiming, **25**, 774
    prior, of surviving spouse, *see* SPOUSE
    prior rights contrasted, **14**, 340
    quantification of—
        date of death, property owned at, **25**, 784
        debts, **25**, 782
        heritable property, **25**, 783
        moveable property, **25**, 783
    reform, **25**, 1113
    relevant choice of law rules, **17**, 341
    renunciation, **19**, 1626
    spouse—
        prior claim by surviving, *see* SPOUSE
        renunciation by, **25**, 800
    tax planning device, legitim as, **25**, 776
    terce, abolition of, **25**, 702, 778
    valuation for claim, **25**, 4
    See also legitim *below*
legatees, impersonation of, **11**, 748, 759
legitim—
    division of, **25**, 700, 787
    generally, **25**, 786

Succession—*continued*
legitim—*continued*
    illegitimate child, right of, **25**, 699, 788
    legacy held as surrogate for, **25**, 925
    potential claimant—
        provision for, **25**, 789
        statutory code, **25**, 790
    reform, **25**, 1113
    representation in, **25**, 700
    tax planning device, **25**, 776
    taxation, **19**, 1625–1630
    voluntary lifetime discharge, **25**, 807
    See also legal rights *above*
legitimate children, **10**, 1220
liferent lease, no right to, **1**, 787
lifetime gifts to or by deceased, **19**, 1618
    See also INHERITANCE TAX
moveable, *see* MOVEABLE ESTATE; MOVEABLE PROPERTY
moveables distinguished from immoveables, **17**, 313
nasciturus principle—
    application to succession, **10**, 1016
    meaning, **10**, 1015
    modern reproductive techniques, **10**, 1017–1020
    stepchildren, **10**, 1220
passive, **25**, 613
patent rights, **18**, 811
peerage, *see* PEERAGE
post-Reformation law of Scotland—
    canon law, procedure, indirect influence, **22**, 580, 581
posthumous child, *see* CHILD-CHILDREN
preliminary comments, **17**, 339
private international law, overlap with, **17**, 107
property—
    passing of—
        competent, beneficiaries, **25**, 621
        death, presumption of, **25**, 620
        distribution, generally, **25**, 605
        family property, **25**, 608
        future property, **25**, 622
        generally, **25**, 604, 605, 619
        identification, **25**, 605
        Inland Revenue charge, **25**, 1025
        reassembly of estates, **25**, 609–611
        transmission of—
            '1964' method, **6**, 611
            clare constat,.writ of, **6**, 605
            disposition, **6**, 610
            executor's title, completion of, **6**, 608
            general service, decree of, **6**, 607
            generally, **6**, 603
            heirs title of heritage, completion of, **6**, 604
            notice of title, **6**, 613
            owners domiciled outwith Scotland, **6**, 612
            special service decree of, **6**, 606
            trustees, conveyance to, **6**, 609
reform—
    discretionary family provisions, **25**, 1114
    divorce, revocation on, **25**, 1117

Succession—*continued*
reform—*continued*
    killer, disqualification of, **25**, 1119
    legal rights, **25**, 1113
    legitim, **25**, 1113
    presumptions on survivorship, **25**, 1119
    prior rights, **25**, 1112
    Scottish Law Commission proposals, **25**, 1111–1121
    special destinations, **25**, 1121
    will—
        miscellaneous reforms, **25**, 1118
        rectification of, **25**, 1116
        validity of, **25**, 1115
renunciations, **19**, 1639
renvoi, **17**, 153
reserved property—
    free estate—
        calculation of, **25**, 625
        France, **25**, 625
        Germany, **25**, 626
    generally, **25**, 623
    gift—
        purposes of, **25**, 627
        valid, formalities required for, **25**, 628
    heir, rights of, **25**, 626
    voluntary provision, **25**, 624
    voluntary and statutory devolution, balance between, **25**, 629
    will—
        purposes of, **25**, 627
        valid, formalities required for, **25**, 628
secure tenancy, to, **11**, 1949
separate treatment of conflict rules, reasons for, **17**, 109
sheriff as commissary, moveable succession jurisdiction, **22**, 581
sheriff court jurisdiction, **6**, 1133
simulate *inter vivos* disposition, **11**, 745
singular successor, *see* SINGULAR SUCCESSOR
species of property, **25**, 607
special destination, **25**, 677
statutory small tenancy, to, **1**, 859
survivorship, proof of, *see* SURVIVORSHIP
taxation, liability to—
    administration of estate, **19**, 1642–1648
    agricultural tenancies, **19**, 1666
    business expansion scheme, **25**, 970
    capital gains tax, **19**, 1636, 1641; **25**, 995
    death, on, **19**, 1616, 1631
    disclaimers, **19**, 1639
    estate, generally, **19**, 1617–1623
    inheritance tax—
        agricultural property, **25**, 1013
        business property, **25**, 1012
        deceased's estate, sale of assets from, **25**, 1015
        quick succession, **25**, 1014, 1015
    interest in possession, deceased, held by, **19**, 1620
    joint or common property, **19**, 1619
    jus relictae and *jus relicti*, **19**, 1624
    legitim, **19**, 1625–1630
    lifetime gifts to or by decrease, **19**, 1618
    pecuniary legacy, **19**, 1633

Succession—*continued*
taxation, liability to—*continued*
    personal taxation, **25**, 973
    residue, gift of, **19**, 1634
    settled property, life interest in, **19**, 1635
    specific legacy, **19**, 1632
    survivorship, interests passing on, **19**, 1619
    testamentary expense, tax not treated as, **19**, 1638
    unadministered estate, interest in, **19**, 1631–1636
testamentary, to moveable property, canon law as law of pre-Reformation Scotland, **22**, 580
testamentary expense, tax not treated as, **19**, 1638
testate—
    agricultural holdings, **1**, 787, 788
    capacity to test, **17**, 344
    wills—
        construction of, **17**, 347
        essential validity, **17**, 346
        formal validity, **17**, 345
        fraudulent inducement to sign, **11**, 744
        generally, **11**, 744
        innocent beneficiary, position of, **11**, 744
        revocation of, **17**, 348
        undue influence, made under, **11**, 744
        See also WILL
universal succession—
    Roman concept of, **25**, 606
universal successor—
    distinction between singular successor and, **18**, 598
    meaning, **25**, 675
variation order on reappearance of missing person, **24**, 653
vesting, *see* VESTING ESTATE
vitious intromission, *see* VITIOUS INTROMISSION
See also HERITABLE PROPERTY; TENANT-TENANCY
Succession to arms
heir of line and male heir, **11**, 1619
Jeffrey principle, **11**, 1619
Successor
personal bar, plea of, **16**, 1607
universal, distinguished from singular successor, **25**, 675
Sue
title and interest to, *see* TITLE AND INTEREST TO SUE
Suet
food standard, **11**, 353
Sufficiency of evidence
See EVIDENCE
Suffragan Sees
Roman Catholic Church, **3**, 1655
Sugar
Commonwealth Sugar Agreement, imports under, **1**, 939
production quotas, **1**, 939
products—
    dextrose, **11**, 369
    labelling, **11**, 369
    white, use of word, **11**, 369
Sugar Board
dissolution of, **1**, 875

Suicide
aiding, **7**, 255
attempt—
    breach of peace, as, **7**, 255, 455
    dominus negotii, by, **15**, 102*n*
crime, whether, **7**, 255
encouraging, **7**, 255
homicide, and, **7**, 255, 263
pact, **7**, 255
threat, breach of peace, as, **7**, 455
Suitability
of investment to client, **12**, 1373
Sulphur dioxide
gas oil, from—
    EC direction on, **9**, 1146
    UK regulations to control, **9**, 1147
smoke, and, **9**, 1148
Sum certain in money
meaning, **4**, 105
Summar roll
petitions to revoke or vary trusts, **24**, 83
Summary application
proceedings by way of, **4**, 19; **6**, 1075*ff*
Summary causes
appeals—
    Court of Session, to, **17**, 1334
    sheriff principal, to, **17**, 1333
    time to pay direction, relating to, **17**, 1335
charge, **17**, 1331
classes of action, **17**, 1293
competent actions, **17**, 1293, 1294
conduct of proceedings—
    abandonment, **17**, 1319
    arrestment on dependence, **17**, 1297
    citation, **17**, 1301
    counterclaim, **17**, 1308
    decree—
        default, by, **17**, 1314
        recall of, **17**, 1306
    defence, **17**, 1307
    documents lost or destroyed, **17**, 1312
    first calling, **17**, 1305
    general rules, **17**, 1295
    generally, **17**, 1320
    havers, **17**, 1315
    incidental applications, **17**, 1316
    non-appearance, dismissal for, **17**, 1314
    period of notice, **17**, 1298
    productions, **17**, 1311
    proof, **17**, 1317
    recall of, **17**, 1306
    remits—
        person of skill, to, **17**, 1318
        summary and ordinary cause rolls, between, **17**, 1310
    representation, **17**, 1299
    re-service, **17**, 1302
    sheriff court, **6**, 168
    summons—
        alteration of, **17**, 1313
        generally, **17**, 1296
        return of, **17**, 1304
    time to pay directions, **17**, 1300
    transfer to another court, **17**, 1309

Summary causes—*continued*
conduct of proceedings—*continued*
variation of, application for, **17**, 1332
warrant of concurrence not required, **17**, 1303
witnesses, **17**, 1315
decree—
abandonment, **17**, 1319
arrestment on dependence, **17**, 1297
citation, **17**, 1301
counterclaim, **17**, 1308
decree—
default, by, **17**, 1314
recall of, **17**, 1306
defence, **17**, 1307
documents lost or destroyed, **17**, 1312
first calling, **17**, 1305
general rules, **17**, 1295
generally, **17**, 1320
havers, **17**, 1315
incidental applications, **17**, 1316
non-appearance, dismissal for, **17**, 1314
period of notice, **17**, 1298
productions, **17**, 1311
proof, **17**, 1317
recall of, **17**, 1306
remits—
person of skill, to, **17**, 1318
summary and ordinary cause rolls, between,
17, 1310
representation, **17**, 1299
re-service, **17**, 1302
summons—
alteration of, **17**, 1313
generally, **17**, 1296
return of, **17**, 1304
time to pay directions, **17**, 1300
transfer to another court, **17**, 1309
variation of, application for, **17**, 1332
warrant of concurrence not required, **17**, 1303
witnesses, **17**, 1315
development of, **17**, 1289
diligence, **17**, 1330
bills of exchange, on, **4**, 116
cheques, not competent on, **4**, 184, 192
foreign bills, on, **4**, 104
inland bills, on, **4**, 104
expenses, **17**, 1321
first calling, **17**, 1305
jurisdiction—
generally, **17**, 1290
privative, **17**, 1291
Lyon Court decrees, enforcement of, **6**, 1021
messenger-at-arms, role of, **14**, 1504
ordinary cause brought as, and *vice versa*, **17**, 1292
rolls, remits between ordinary cause rolls and, **17**,
1310
sheriff court procedure, **6**, 168
small claims procedure—
appeals, **17**, 1348
book of small claims, **17**, 1346
claim—
initiation of, **17**, 1340
response to, **17**, 1340
decree, **17**, 1343

Summary causes—*continued*
small claims procedure—*continued*
expenses, **17**, 1345
goals, **17**, 1336
historical background, **17**, 1337
nature of scheme, **17**, 1339
preliminary hearing, **17**, 1341
proof, **17**, 1342
reform, movement towards, **17**, 1338
remitting cases, **17**, 1347
representation, **17**, 1344
special actions—
aliment of small amount, **17**, 1329
count reckoning and payment, **17**, 1325
delivery, **17**, 1327
furthcoming, of, **17**, 1324
heritable property, recovery of possession of,
17, 1326
money, payment of, **17**, 1322
multiplepoinding, **17**, 1323
rent, sequestration for, **17**, 1328
trial procedure—
form of petition for, **17**, 1432
generally, **17**, 1431
procedure on, **17**, 1433
value of cause, **17**, 1294
writ, *see* WRIT
Summary procedure
appeals arising from—
abandonment of, **17**, 861
adjustments, **17**, 857
advocation, bill of, **17**, 880–882
appellant in custody, **17**, 852
bail, **17**, 841
conviction, against, **17**, 839–865
conviction and sentence, against, *see* SENTENCE
sentence alone, against, *see* SENTENCE
sentence by prosecutor, appeal against, **17**, 850
setting aside conviction, consent to, **17**, 853
stated case—
application for, **17**, 851
content of, **17**, 855
draft, **17**, 854
final, **17**, 858
form of, **17**, 842
restrictions on procedure, **17**, 843
suspension, bill of, **17**, 871–879
assistance by way of representation (ABWOR),
13, 1067
financial eligibility, **13**, 1068
bail, **17**, 631
complaint—
amendment of, **17**, 708
answering, **17**, 718
citation—
accused, of, **17**, 711
furth of Scotland, **17**, 713
manner of, **17**, 712
documents, service of, **17**, 710
form of, **17**, 707
generally, **17**, 705
heading of, **17**, 706
penalty notices, **17**, 709
previous convictions, schedules of, **17**, 709

Summary procedure—*continued*
criminal legal aid, **13**, 1056
  appeals, **13**, 1069
  application for, **13**, 1056, 1057
  automatic, **13**, 1054
  financial eligibility, **13**, 1058
  special urgency, cases of, **13**, 1066
defence—
  preparation of—
    documents, recovery of, **17**, 701
    generally, **17**, 700
    intermediate diets, **17**, 703
    preliminary pleas, **17**, 704
    witnesses, **17**, 702
  requirements on—
    generally, **17**, 714
    rights of defence, **17**, 715
    special defences, **17**, 716
documentation, **17**, 639
generally, **6**, 1155; **17**, 637
malicious prosecution, liability, **15**, 450
pre-trial diet—
  acceleration of diet, **17**, 724
  answering complaint, **17**, 718
  bail, **17**, 719
  calling case, **17**, 717
  failure to answer, **17**, 720
  intermediate diet, **17**, 728
  plea—
    adjournment without, **17**, 723
    continuation without, **17**, 723
    guilty, **17**, 727
    not guilty, **17**, 726
    preliminary, **17**, 725
  postponement of diet, **17**, 724
  remit to another court, **17**, 722
  trial in absence of accused, **17**, 721
prescription of crime, **17**, 569
procurators fiscal, duties, **13**, 1433
sentencing powers, **17**, 640
sheriff court, **6**, 1155; **17**, 573
time limits—
  common law proceedings, **17**, 696
  computation of time, **17**, 698
  statutory offences, **17**, 697
  subsequent to taking proceedings, **17**, 699
trial—
  conduct of—
    Crown case, **17**, 779, 780
    defence case, **17**, 781
    evidence, objections to, **17**, 778
    generally, **17**, 777
    no case to answer, **17**, 780
    record of proceedings, **17**, 784
    speeches, **17**, 782
    verdict, **17**, 783
  diet—
    accused, absence of, **17**, 769
    adjournment of, **17**, 770
    calling, **17**, 767
    complaint, amendment of, **17**, 775
    desertion—
      pro loco et tempore, **17**, 771
      simpliciter, **17**, 772

Summary procedure—*continued*
trial—*continued*
  diet—*continued*
    parties, presence of, **17**, 768
    pleading—
      generally, **17**, 773
      not guilty plea, **17**, 774
    postponement of, **17**, 770
    public access to court, **17**, 776
    publicity, **17**, 776
  without jury, **17**, 560
Summary trial
See SUMMARY PROCEDURE
Summary warrant
poinding on, **8**, 245
rates, recovery of, **14**, 847
Summer time
British Standard Time, as, **22**, 810
daylight saving, historical background, **22**, 810
description, **22**, 810
European Union, harmonisation, **22**, 810
Greenwich mean time, variant, **22**, 810
legal time, as—
  generally, **22**, 810
  purposes for which not legal time, **22**, 810
statutory basis, **22**, 809, 810
Sunday
alcoholic liquor—
  hotel licence, premises, opening on, **22**, 817
  licensed premises—
    extension of hours, **2**, 20
    opening, generally, **2**, 1, 55; **22**, 817
    permitted hours, **2**, 18
  public house, **22**, 817
  refreshment licence, **22**, 817
  sale of, **2**, 15
calculation of time limits, **22**, 815, 817
common law maxim, **22**, 817
employment—
  contract of employment providing for, **9**, 24
  statutory prohibitions, **22**, 817
European Convention on the Calculation of Time-Limits, **22**, 830
expiry day of given period for act, performance, following day, **22**, 817
invalid acts performed on, **22**, 817
Jews, exemptions from prohibitions, **22**, 817
judicial acts, validity, **22**, 817
private acts, validity, **22**, 817
profanity, offence, **22**, 817
prohibition of specific activities on, **22**, 817
recreation and sport, **19**, 1202, 1279
salmon fishing close time, **11**, 17
shooting of game on, **11**, 804
statutes, extant, affecting prohibition, specific activities, **22**, 817
termination of period on—
  measured in days, **22**, 825
  qualification to principle of exclusion, **22**, 825
validity, steps in a judicial process, **22**, 817
within a period—
  calculation, total period, **22**, 825
woman, employment, **22**, 817

Sunday—_continued_
worker—
  unemployment benefit, calculation of
    entitlement to, **21**, 814, 816
young person, employment, **22**, 817
Sunday Observance Law
Bible, law of the, Post-Reformation influence,
  22, 614
Superior
See FEUDAL LAW
Superior orders
defence of acting under—
  case law, **7**, 207
  Hume's views, **7**, 206
Superiority
See FEUDAL LAW
Supermarket
off-sale licences, **2**, 10
sale by, passing of property, **18**, 630
Supervision order
child subject to, moving to Scotland, **3**, 1384
Supervision requirement
abscondment from control of person imposed by,
  3, 1372–1374
access to child, conditions as to, **3**, 1350
centre, requiring attendance at, **3**, 1350
child benefit, disentitlement to, **21**, 962
child reaching eighteen, **3**, 1356
child reaching sixteen, **3**, 1295
child subject to deemed to be in local authority
  care, **3**, 1355
children's hearing's power to make, **3**, 1349
clinic, requiring attendance at, **3**, 1350
conditions attached to—
  generally, **3**, 1350
  national standards, proposed development, **3**, 1380
  placement in household outwith child's own
    home, **3**, 1351
  placement in residential establishment, **3**, 1352
  secure accommodation, as to, **3**, 1376
  variation, **3**, 1357
effect, when taking, **3**, 1353
harbouring absconder from, **3**, 1375
home supervision requirement, **3**, 1380
implementation, **3**, 1355
postponement, **3**, 1353
Rehabilitation of Offenders Act (1974), effect, **3**,
  1337
religious persuasion of child, **3**, 1672
remit of court case to children's hearing, **3**, 1378
requirements of, **3**, 1349
residential establishment, **3**, 1349, 1349n, 1352
review, **3**, 1296, 1356, 1357
  automatic, **3**, 1357
  child and parent's right to call for, **3**, 1357
  period, **3**, 1357
  reform proposals, **3**, 1380
secure accommodation, placement in, _see_
  CHILDREN'S HEARING
suspension, application for, **3**, 1290
termination, Secretary of State's powers, **3**, 1385
variation, **3**, 1356, 1357
Supplementary benefit
generally, **21**, 1062

Supplementary benefit—_continued_
sheriff court jurisdiction, **6**, 1132
unfair dismissal, recoupment in case of award—
  calculation, method of, **9**, 299
  future loss, **9**, 301
  general principles, **9**, 298
  regulations, effect of, **9**, 300
Supplementary revenue tax
Provisional Collection of Taxes Act 1968 ..., **19**,
  1504n
Supplementary Roll
Church of Scotland, **3**, 1508
Supplementary Statistical Declaration (SSD)
European Union customs documentation, **7**, 1124
Support, rights of
adjacent support, **18**, 253
  buildings, **18**, 272
  land, **18**, 263
buildings—
  adjacent support, **18**, 272
  building to building, **18**, 271, 272
  land to land support, generally, **18**, 258, 260
  mineral rights sterilised by building, **18**, 260
  obligation to support—
    acquisition, **18**, 260
    generally, **18**, 260
  weight of building partly responsible for
    subsidence, where, **18**, 258
canals, **14**, 1690
common gables, **18**, 233, 272
common interest, **18**, 254, 255, 258
common walls, **18**, 252, 272
compensation clauses, **14**, 1689
contracting in, **18**, 264
contracting out, **18**, 265
contractor's duties, **14**, 1637
counter-notice, service of, **14**, 1691
damages, **18**, 253
delict, **18**, 254, 256, 258
evaluation, **18**, 258
generally, **3**, 159; **11**, 1109; **14**, 1685; **18**, 252,
  483, 484
implied servitude, **18**, 257
land to land, **18**, 253ff.
law of the tenement, **18**, 233
legal basis, **18**, 254
liability, **18**, 253, 261, 262
loss of, assessing damages for, **14**, 1686
mineral lease, liability under, **14**, 1688
Mines (Working Facilities and Support) Act 1966
  ..., 267, 268, 270
mining codes, **14**, 1690
mining operations, **18**, 252
  break-off conveyance, **18**, 264, 265
  coal mining—
    generally, **18**, 252
    liability, **18**, 262
    variation, **18**, 267
  contracting in and out, **18**, 264, 265
natural obligation, **18**, 259–263, 268
natural right, as, **18**, 254, 258, 259
negative obligation, as, **18**, 253
  legal basis, **18**, 254
notice, service of, **14**, 1691

Support, rights of—*continued*
nuisance, **18**, 256, 256*n*
nuisance distinguished, **14**, 2029
obligation not to withdraw support, **18**, 259
oneris ferendi, **18**, 484
pipe-lines, **14**, 1693
public works, **14**, 1690
railways, **14**, 1690
remedies—
　damages, **18**, 262
　interdict, **18**, 262
removal of support, building contracts, **3**, 155
servitude right—
　express, **18**, 269
　generally, **18**, 268, 269
　implied, **18**, 254, 258, 269
　positive servitude, as, **18**, 269
sewers, **14**, 1693
subjacent support, **18**, 253
subsidence caused by building works, **18**, 252
sued, who may be, **18**, 262
tenanted land, liability where, **18**, 262, 262*n*
tenement building, **18**, 233, 271
tigni immittendi, **18**, 484
variation—
　juridicial basis, **18**, 266
　statute, by, **18**, 267
　title, by, **18**, 264, 265
waterworks, **14**, 1690
withdrawal of, **14**, 1687
working minerals, **14**, 1692
Surety
English law, **3**, 801*n*, 803, 804
person cannot act as surety for himself, **3**, 835
rights, guarantees under Consumer Credit Act
　1974 ..., **5**, 857
Surface water
See WATER
Surgeon
veterinary, *see* VETERINARY SURGEON
Surgeons to the Queen in Scotland
generally, **7**, 842
Surrogacy
See CHILD-CHILDREN
Surrogatum sapit naturam surrogati
doctrine of, **24**, 7
Surveillance
aircraft, carried on from, **14**, 2086
police powers, **16**, 1802
Survey
dual-purpose survey and valuation, **25**, 83
electricity, land suitable for use, **9**, 655
Expert Committee, response of, **25**, 80
full structural, **25**, 85
multiple survey problem, **25**, 79, 86
powers of entry in relation to, **20**, 716
structural, **25**, 78
traditional private, **25**, 84
valuation, **25**, 77
valuation roll, **24**, 459
water supply, development of new sources, **25**,
　517
Surveyor
chartered, **3**, 142

Surveyor—*continued*
duty of care, **15**, 278
non-designated services, **4**, 1177*n*
partnership, number of partners allowed, **16**,
　1011, 1112
professional organisation, **3**, 142
quantity, *see* QUANTITY SURVEYOR
restrictive trade practices, **4**, 1247
Survivorship
clause, inheritance tax, **25**, 1030
interests passing on, **19**, 1619
presumption of, proposed reform, **25**, 1119
proof of—
　common law, **25**, 656
　generally, **25**, 655
　proposed reform, **25**, 659
　statutory presumption—
　　generally, **25**, 657
　　nature of, **25**, 658
spouse, *see* SPOUSE
Suspect
arrest—
　rights on, **16**, 1793
　See also ARREST
charge, **16**, 1793
custody, detention in, *see* CUSTODY
detention, *see* DETENTION
questioning, police powers, **16**, 1800
search, *see* SEARCH, POLICE POWERS
seizure, police powers, **16**, 1787
terrorism, person suspected of involvement in, **16**,
　1801
Suspension
charges, of, **4**, 13
decrees, of, **4**, 13
definition, **13**, 15
function, **13**, 15
interdict—
　combination with, **13**, 16
　meaning, **13**, 16*n*
petition for—
　caution, requirement for, **3**, 998
　types, **3**, 998
review, as mode of, **13**, 68
Suspension, bill of
appropriateness, **17**, 873
competency, **17**, 872
Court of Session procedure, **17**, 1420
disposal of, **17**, 879
generally, **17**, 871
grounds for, **17**, 874
hearing, **17**, 877
procedure, **17**, 876
remits, **17**, 878
time for appeal, **17**, 875
Suspicion
mens rea, **7**, 105
use of term, **7**, 105
Sutherland
population, **14**, 64
Sweeteners
food containing, **11**, 379
Swans
Game Acts, **11**, 496*n*

Swans—*continued*
property in, **2**, 109
Swimming pools
education authority, establishment by, **19**, 1224
valuation for rating, **24**, 746
Swine
See PIGS
Synagogue
affiliation in Scotland, **3**, 1675
charitable status, **3**, 1684
number in Scotland, **3**, 1675
voluntary church, as, **3**, 1674
Synod
Associate, **3**, 1636

Synod—*continued*
Church of Scotland—
  abolition, **3**, 1541
  establishment, **3**, 1501
  generally, **3**, 1501, 1502, 1505
General Associate, **3**, 1636
Scottish Episcopal Church—
  constitution, **3**, 1620
  diocesan, **3**, 1621
  Episcopal, **3**, 1618, 1619
  General—
    functions, **3**, 1620
    legislation, **3**, 1628
    legislative power, **3**, 1620
    supremacy, **3**, 1628

T

Table meal
meaning, **11**, 1764
Tabling
defended ordinary action—
cause not tabled, **17**, 1037
generally, **17**, 1036
Tachograph
offences in relation to, **20**, 498
requirement for, **20**, 497
exemption from, **20**, 497, 498
Tacit relocation
agricultural holding, **13**, 453
assured tenancy, **13**, 673
consent, based on, **13**, 450
contracting out, **13**, 453
death of party to claim, **13**, 454
effect, **13**, 451
exclusion, **13**, 455, 460
generally, **18**, 6, 9
meaning, **13**, 450
notice of termination, **13**, 455
formality, **13**, 456
objection to, exclusion, **13**, 461
parties to, **13**, 454
plurality of tenants or landlords, where, **13**, 454,
457
proposed reforms, **13**, 458
prorogation compared, **13**, 450
renewal compared, **13**, 450
seasonal lease, **13**, 452
security of tenure, relationship with, **13**, 696
silence of parties, **13**, 450
subject, effect of, **13**, 452
subtenant, where, **13**, 459
termination following, **13**, 451
terms on which lease continues, **13**, 451
where not applicable, **13**, 452
Taciturnity
acquiescence, interaction with, **16**, 1621–1625
annulment of voidable obligation barred by, **15**,
672
delay, along with, **16**, 1622
heritable title, in relation to, **16**, 1625
meaning, **16**, 1621
modern division of judicial opinion, **16**, 1623
mora, interaction with, **16**, 1621–1625
plea in bar of trial, **17**, 692
presumption of abandonment, **16**, 1624
Tack
meaning, **13**, 103
Tacksman
meaning, **13**, 103
Tailzie
arms subject to, generally, **11**, 1620
feudal conveyance, generally, **18**, 111
heir of, **18**, 111
peerage granted with destination to, **16**, 1310
matriculation of appropriate arms, **11**, 1620
name and arms conditions, **11**, 1620

Tailzie—*continued*
prescription of tailzied arms, **11**, 1624
See also ENTAIL, LAW OF
Takeover (company)
activity, **4**, 535
bid—
advertisements, control of, **4**, 553, 556
competition law, defences under, **4**, 555
control, sale of—
nature of control, **4**, 548
rapid acquisition of control, **4**, 550
shareholders, general offer to, **4**, 549
defensive tactics in—
advertisements, control of, **4**, 553, 556
competition law, defence against bid on
grounds of, **4**, 555
financial information, disclosure of, **4**, 554, 556
media, influence of, **4**, 553
preparing to meet bid, **4**, 552
target company, response of, **4**, 551
effect of, **4**, 540
financial data, updating of, **4**, 552
financial information, disclosure of, **4**, 554, 556
media influence, **4**, 553
merchant bank, by, **4**, 544
offer—
document—
contents of, **4**, 546
responsibility statement, **4**, 546
time periods relating to, **4**, 545
firm intention to make, announcement of, **4**,
545
misstatements, liability for, **4**, 547
omissions, liability for, **4**, 547
takeover offer, meaning, **4**, 557
target offeree board, put to, **4**, 545
preparing to meet, **4**, 552
secrecy, **4**, 544
shareholdings, geographical breakdown of, **4**,
552
steps before making of, **4**, 544
target company, response of, **4**, 551
trading data, updating of, **4**, 552
capital profits, leading to, **25**, 41
City Code on Takeovers and Mergers—
employee concerns, basis of, **4**, 537
Rules Governing Substantial Acquisitions of
Shares, **4**, 550
self-regulation, **4**, 542, 543
declaratory order, Takeover Panel, decision of, **4**,
542
dissenting minority, acquisition of shares of, **4**,
557
employee concerns, basis of, **4**, 537
Fair Trading Act 1973, investigation under, **4**, 562
hope value, **25**, 23
insider dealing, **12**, 1502, 1514, 1515
Panel on Takeovers and Mergers, members and
staff of, **12**, 1520

Takeover (company)—*continued*
legal regulation, **4**, 570
management, position of, **4**, 539
market manipulation, offence of, **4**, 541
meaning, **4**, 536
minority shareholders—
    dissenting, acquisition of shares of, **4**, 557
    judicial attitudes towards, **4**, 561
Monopolies and Mergers Commission, reference
        to, *see* MONOPOLIES AND MERGERS COMMISSION
Panel, *see* PANEL ON TAKEOVERS AND MERGERS
pension fund, position of, **4**, 538
petition relating to, **4**, 990
prospectus, form and content of, **4**, 541
regulation—
    legal, **4**, 570
    self-regulation, **4**, 542, 543, 570
    statutory, **4**, 541
self-regulation, **4**, 542, 543, 570
shareholder, rights of, **25**, 13
shareholders' interests, analysis of, **4**, 538
statutory mechanisms—
    Company Act 1985, ss 425 to 427 ..., **4**, 560
    generally, **4**, 558
    Insolvency Act 1986, s 110 ..., **4**, 559
    minority shareholders, judicial attitudes towards,
        4, 561
statutory regulation, **4**, 541
unit trust manager, position of, **4**, 538
Taking and using
copyright, **7**, 345
motor vehicle, **7**, 345
without owner's consent, **7**, 344, 345
Taking title
See TITLE (TO PROPERTY)
Taking up dittay
pre-trial procedure, **17**, 548
Tallyman
extortion by, **7**, 396
Tank
exemptions from building regulations, **3**, 209
fuel, building regulations, **3**, 208
Tanker
chemical, construction and survey, **21**, 212, 212*n*
fire protection regulations, **21**, 214
meaning, **21**, 212*n*
oil, disconnection of hoses, laytime, **21**, 681*n*
Tap
water fitting, as, **25**, 527
Tape recording
contempt of court in relation to, **6**, 315
evidence, as, **10**, 572, 607
police interview, of, **10**, 735
Taric
European Union Common Customs Tariff (CCT),
    7, 1015, 1015*n*
Tariff and non-tariff barriers
Common Customs tariff, **10**, 129
free circulation of goods within European
    Economic Community, **10**, 116
Tarmargan (ptarmigan)
close season, **11**, 806
custody of by unqualified person, **11**, 807
game, as, **11**, 802

Tattooing
age limit, **3**, 1231
TAURUS Scheme
transfer of shares by, **4**, 372
Taxation
additional personal allowance on divorce, **10**, 991
advice—
    building society providing, **3**, 374
agent—
    composite rate tax, **1**, 663
    non-resident, of, **1**, 662
avoidance, **19**, 1507–1509
betting tax, *see* BETTING AND GAMING DUTIES
bill of exchange, transactions involving, **4**, 189
capital gains tax, *see* CAPITAL GAINS TAX
capital transfer tax, *see* CAPITAL TRANSFER TAX
car tax, **19**, 1504*n*, 1510; **20**, 469
charitable, meaning, **24**, 91, 92
child, additional personal allowance in respect of,
    10, 991
classification of taxes, **19**, 1510
cohabitees, of, **10**, 1003, 1008
collection, **19**, 1544
community charge, *see* COMMUNITY CHARGE
composite rate tax and agency, **1**, 663
concept of money central to, **14**, 1801
Consolidated Fund, **7**, 766
corporation tax, *see* CORPORATION TAX
Crown bodies, **7**, 753
Crown preferences, **8**, 129
Crown revenues, *see* CROWN REVENUES
customs and excise duties, *see* CUSTOMS AND EXCISE
damages, interest on, **12**, 1034
databank information—
    access to information principle, exception, **18**,
        1530
    disclosure to aid collection of assessment, **18**,
        1526
death, liability arising out of, **25**, 962, 973
diligence, effect of winding up on, **4**, 849
diplomatic immunity from, **19**, 682
divorce, on—
    additional personal allowances, **10**, 991
    capital gains tax—
        assets other than dwelling house, **10**, 1001
        generally, **10**, 1000
        matrimonial home, transfer of, **10**, 1002
        transfers after separation, **10**, 1001
    children, additional personal allowances in
        respect of, **10**, 991
    income tax—
        existing obligations—
            election to have treated as new, **10**, 996
            payments made under, **10**, 994
        Finance Act 1988—
            effect of, **10**, 992
        new obligations, **10**, 995
        registration for preservation and execution,
            10, 993
        remarriage of recipient spouse, **10**, 997
    inheritance tax—
        capital transfers, **10**, 999
        lump sums, **10**, 998
        periodical payments, **10**, 998

Taxation—*continued*

divorce, on—*continued*

maintenance payments and transfers of property, **10**, 992–997

married couple's allowance, **10**, 990

remarriage, **10**, 991

single person's allowance, **10**, 989

electricity boards, of, **9**, 626

European Union rules—

application, **10**, 169

Community assets and revenues, exemption from, **10**, 296

customs duties, **10**, 118

fiscal barriers to trade, **10**, 170

generally, **10**, 168

evasion, **19**, 1507

false statements and representations, **19**, 1552

family law, **19**, 1574ff

feudal law, **18**, 42

Finance Acts, annual, **19**, 1503

Finance Bill, **7**, 765

financial year, **22**, 811

forestry, income from—

abolition of previous system, **11**, 644

capital allowances, **11**, 646

election to be charged under Schedule D, **11**, 643

former taxation under Schedule B, **11**, 642

transitional provisions, **11**, 645

Forestry Commission exempt from, **11**, 641

generally, **25**, 53

goods and services, on, **19**, 1510

grant of right to fell and removed timber, **11**, 650

husband and wife—

advantages, **10**, 891

blind person's relief, **10**, 891

capital gains tax, **10**, 892

generally, **19**, 1517

husband only earning, **10**, 894n

income tax, **10**, 891

inheritance tax, **10**, 893

loan interest, provisions as to, **10**, 891

married couple's allowance, **10**, 891

partially transferable allowance, **10**, 890

pre-1990 situation, **10**, 890

reform of, **10**, 890–894

advantages and disadvantages, **10**, 894

wife only earning, **10**, 894n

imposition of, **19**, 1503–1505

income tax—

cohabitees, of, **10**, 1008

divorce, and—

existing obligations—

election to have treated as new, **10**, 996

payments made under, **10**, 994

maintenance payments—

Finance Act 1988—

effect of, **10**, 992

new obligations, payments made under, **10**, 995

registration for preservation and execution, **10**, 993

remarriage of recipient spouse, **10**, 997

financial year, **19**, 1504; **22**, 811

See also INCOME TAX

Taxation—*continued*

indirect, European Union proposals for harmonisation, **7**, 1033, 1034

information, agent giving, **1**, 661

inheritance tax, *see* INHERITANCE TAX

intellectual property, taxation aspects—

artist, sale of works by, **18**, 1594

capital gains tax, **18**, 1600

capital returns, **18**, 1571

copyright—

author, tax treatment, **18**, 1585–1589

generally, **18**, 1571

purchaser, tax treatment, **18**, 1590, 1591

generally, **18**, 1571

income, **18**, 1571

inheritance tax, **18**, 1601

know how—

purchaser, tax treatment of, **18**, 1583–1584

seller, tax treatment of, **18**, 1580–1582

patents—

deduction of tax at source, **18**, 1577

foreign, payments in respect of, **18**, 1579

general principle, **18**, 1571

licensee, tax treatment, **18**, 1575, 1576

licensor, tax treatment, **18**, 1572–1574

non-resident, taxation of payments made to, **18**, 1578

periodic payments made in respect of, **18**, 1572

royalties earned in respect of, **18**, 1572

public lending right, payments under, **18**, 1592

registered design rights, **18**, 1593

service marks, **18**, 1595–1599

trade marks, **18**, 1595–1599

unregistered design rights, **18**, 1593

value added tax, **18**, 1602

interpretation of statutes, **19**, 1506–1510

lease, *see* LEASE-LEASING

licence duties, **19**, 1510

local, **14**, 7

location, *see* LEASE-LEASING

married couple's allowance on divorce, **10**, 990

monarch, payment of tax by, **7**, 773

open market concept, **25**, 60

open market valuation, **25**, 10

overdue, interest on, **19**, 1544

overlap with private international law, **17**, 107

partnership—

choice of partnership as business medium, **16**, 1005

controlled abroad, **16**, 1144

corporate partner, with, **16**, 1143

generally, **16**, 1124; **19**, 1585–1596

limited partnership, **16**, 1142

NIC, partner's liability, **16**, 1124

partnership agreement, framing, **16**, 1009

stamp duty, **16**, 1124

penalties—

for non-disclosure, **19**, 1544

for offences, **19**, 1554

personal pension scheme, *see* PENSION (OCCUPATIONAL)

petroleum revenue tax, *see* PETROLEUM REVENUE TAX

Taxation—*continued*
poinding on summary warrant, **8**, 245
profit, on, **19**, 1510
property, on, **19**, 1510
property, transfer of—
    capital gains tax, **19**, 1600
    gifts—
        cheques and cash, **19**, 1606
        contract, preceded by, **19**, 1602
        corporeal moveable property, **19**, 1604, 1610
        general principles, **19**, 1601
        heritable property, **19**, 1603
        incorporeal moveable property, **19**, 1605
    heritable property, **19**, 1613–1615
    inheritance tax, **19**, 1599, 1601
    joint and common, **19**, 1611, 1612
    ownership, interpretation of, **19**, 1567, 1598
prosecution for offences, **19**, 1553
public trusts, **24**, 87
quoted shares, **25**, 58
Ramsay principle, **19**, 1508, 1509
rates, domestic, *see* COMMUNITY CHARGE; RATES;
    VALUATION FOR RATING
recovery of, **19**, 1550
    arrestment and forthcoming by, **19**, 1550
    Crown's priority, **19**, 1550
    messenger-at-arms, by, **14**, 1504
    sheriff court, in, **19**, 1550
return, agent required to make, **1**, 660
Scottish administration, **19**, 1544–1554
    appeals, **19**, 1544, 1547, 1548
    application of legislation, **19**, 1502
    assessments, **19**, 1544
    collection, **19**, 1544
    criminal proceedings, **19**, 1551–1554
    General and Special Commissioners, appoint-
        ment of, **19**, 1546
    investigations, **19**, 1551–1554
    judicial review, **19**, 1549
    recovery of tax, **19**, 1550
sheriff, former duties of, **17**, 510
single person's allowance on divorce, **10**, 989
social security contributions, *see* SOCIAL SECURITY
sportsman, *see* PROFESSIONAL SPORTSMAN
stamp duty, *see* STAMP DUTY
tax planning legitim as device for, **25**, 776
tax year, **19**, 1504; **22**, 811
terminology, **19**, 1614
tuition fees, of, **19**, 1298, 1311
unearned income, of, **19**, 1515
unquoted shares—
    hypothetical willing purchaser, **25**, 62
    hypothetical willing seller, **25**, 61
    specific provisions, **25**, 59
value added tax, *see* VALUE ADDED TAX
vehicle excise licence, *see* MOTOR VEHICLE
Ways and Means resolutions, **7**, 765
woodlands—
    death of owner, **11**, 651
    inheritance tax deferment, **11**, 652–654
    purchase and sale of, **11**, 647
        capital gains tax, **11**, 649
        income tax, **11**, 648
wrongful dismissal, award of damages for, **9**, 199

Taxation—*continued*
'year of assessment', **22**, 811
See also CAPITAL GAINS TAX; INCOME TAX;
    INHERITANCE TAX; VALUE ADDED TAX
Taxi
application relating to, appeal to sheriff, **14**, 119
civic code licence—
    conditions, **14**, 553
    driver, **7**, 45; **14**, 552
    fares, **14**, 556
    generally, **14**, 550, 551
    operation outside area, **14**, 555
    stances, **14**, 557
common carrier, operator as, **3**, 670, 685
contract for carriage by, **3**, 601
duty of care, **3**, 685
fares, **3**, 672, 685
generally, **3**, 670
handling of vehicle, **3**, 676
local service, special licence for providing, **14**,
    439
luggage, **3**, 686
passenger carried at separate fare, **14**, 440
passengers sharing fare, **20**, 488
regulation, **3**, 685
safety of vehicle, **3**, 674
Taxidermy
taking or killing wild birds, **11**, 883
Taxing statute
interpretation, **12**, 1185
Tayside Region
population, **14**, 64
structure, **14**, 64
transport undertakings, operation of, **14**, 419
water authority, as, **25**, 505
Tea
colouring matter not permitted, **11**, 372
Teacher
adequate, education authority's duty to employ,
    8, 821
appointment—
    appointment committee nominees, **8**, 821
        education authority refusing to appoint, **8**,
        821
    assistant headteacher, **8**, 821
    denominational schools, **8**, 826
    deputy headteacher, **8**, 821
    headteacher, **8**, 821
    nursery schools and classes, **8**, 823
    primary departments and schools, **8**, 822
    procedure, generally, **8**, 821
    secondary departments and schools, **8**, 824
    special schools and classes, **8**, 825
    where no suitably qualified registered teacher
        available, **8**, 821
children's hearing, attendance at, **3**, 1327
dismissal, **8**, 829; **14**, 602
    education authority powers, **8**, 723
    education committee, decision taken by, **8**, 821
education committee, representation on, **8**, 717,
    719, 720
employment terms and conditions, Scottish Joint
    Negotiating Committee for Teaching Staff in
    School Education, **8**, 831–835

Teacher—*continued*
exchange scheme, **12**, 247
General Teaching Council for Scotland—
   Disciplinary Committee—
      appeals from decisions of, **8**, 828
      powers and duties, **8**, 828
   duties, **8**, 827
   establishment, **8**, 827
   Investigating Committee—
      dismissal of teachers, **8**, 829
      powers and duties, **8**, 828
   register, **8**, 827
headteacher, *see* HEADTEACHER
housing provided for, **8**, 731
   purchase, right of, **8**, 733
prison, provision in, **16**, 1420
register—
   General Teaching Council for Scotland, **8**, 827
   removal of name from, **8**, 827, 828
remuneration, Scottish Joint Negotiating
   Committee for Teaching Staff in School
   Education, **8**, 831–835
resignation, character or conduct leading to, **8**,
   829
retirement, **8**, 830
right to punish child, **10**, 1224
Roman Catholic state-supported schools, **3**, 1664,
   1665, 1666
school board, membership of, **8**, 737, 739
Scottish Joint Negotiating Committee for
   Teaching Staff in School Education—
   arbitration, reference to, **8**, 835
   membership, **8**, 832
   remit, **8**, 831
   resolutions, **8**, 833
   settlements, **8**, 834
self-governing school, membership of board of
   managment, **8**, 787
special provisions, **14**, 602
university, academic freedom, **8**, 985, 1020
See also EDUCATION; SCHOOL
Technology academy
curriculum, **8**, 815
establishment, **8**, 815
funding, **8**, 816
independent status, **8**, 815
introduction, **8**, 701
meaning, **8**, 815
purpose, **8**, 701
Teeth-marks
identification by, **10**, 662
Teind
allocation, **3**, 1592
canon law, surviving influence, **22**, 584
Clerk of Teinds, **3**, 1595
free, **18**, 211
historical position, **3**, 1592
kind, payment in, **3**, 1592
meaning, **18**, 211
post-1925 position, **3**, 1593
review, **3**, 1592
sasine, symbols of, **18**, 90
separate tenement, as, **18**, 209, 211
standard charge, **18**, 211

Teind—*continued*
stipend as burden on, **3**, 1592
   See also RELIGION (minister of) (Church of
      Scotland)
teind roll, **3**, 1595
Teind Court
continued existence, **6**, 921
Court of Session as, **6**, 921
House of Lords appellate jurisdiction, **6**, 816
judges, **6**, 921
jurisdiction, **6**, 816, 921
records of, **19**, 801
transmission of records, **19**, 858
Telecommunication system
definition, **16**, 1924
domestic purposes, run for, **16**, 1928
in-house, **16**, 1928
licensing, *see* TELECOMMUNICATIONS (LICENSING
   SYSTEM)
public telecommunications operator (PTO), *see*
   PUBLIC TELECOMMUNICATIONS OPERATOR
running, meaning, **16**, 1926
unconnected to any other system, **16**, 1928
vehicle, vessel, aircraft or hovercraft, on, **16**, 1928
Telecommunications
apparatus—
   Branch System General (BSG) Licence, **16**, 1949
   contractors, approval, **16**, 1951
   cross subsidies, prohibition on, **16**, 1942
   designation or approval, **16**, 1951
   disabled persons, for use by, **16**, 1922, 1949
   meaning, **16**, 1922*n*
   meters, approval, **16**, 1951
   safety and integrity, **16**, 1951
   testing by PTO, licensing provisions, **16**, 1938,
      1938*n*
apparatus, valuation for rating, **24**, 415, 744
Branch System General (BSG) Licence, **16**, 1948,
   1949
British Telecom, *see* BRITISH TELECOMMUNICATIONS
   PLC
charges—
   avoidance, **16**, 1959
   EU tariffing guidelines, **16**, 1974
closed circuit television system, **16**, 1928
Code, *see* TELECOMMUNICATIONS CODE
competition, regulatory controls, **16**, 1923
*Competition and Choice: Telecommunications Policy
   for the 1990s,* White Paper, **16**, 1924
competitive environment, EU provision, **16**, 1970
computer-controlled services, **16**, 1950
Conference of European Post and Telecommunications Administrations (CEPT), **16**, 1974
confidentiality of customer information, **16**, 1937,
   1938
consumer—
   information and advice for, publication, **16**, 1923
   interests of, promotion, **16**, 1923
consumer protection, **6**, 165
deregulation, **16**, 1920
   EU strategy, *see* European Union *below*
*Development of the Common Market for
   Telecommunications Services and Equipment,*
   Green Paper, **16**, 1966, 1967, 1973

Telecommunications—*continued*

Director General of, *see* DIRECTOR GENERAL OF TELECOMMUNICATIONS

Directorate-General for Telecommunications, Information Industries and Innovation (DG XIII), **16**, 1966

directory information services—
charges for, **16**, 1937*n*
printed directories, **16**, 1937*n*
provision, **16**, 1923, 1924, 1937, 1937*n*

disabled persons—
lift, telecommunications apparatus in, **16**, 1949
PTO licence requirements as to, **16**, 1933, 1933*n*
research and development of apparatus for use by, **16**, 1922

emergency services, provision, **16**, 1923, 1932, 1932*n*

EU strategy—
antitrust guidelines—
aim, **16**, 1971
application, **16**, 1975
articles 85 and 86, application, **16**, 1972, 1974
basic and enhanced services, **16**, 1973
generally, **16**, 1971
issue, **16**, 1971
relevant market, **16**, 1973
scope, **16**, 1972
tariffing, **16**, 1974
common standards, establishment, **16**, 1968
competitive environment, **16**, 1970
Conference of European Post and Telecommunications Administrations (CEPT), **16**, 1974
criteria, **16**, 1966
Development of the Common Market for Telecommunications Services and Equipment, Green Paper, **16**, 1966, 1967, 1973
Directorate-General for Telecommunications, Information Industries and Innovation (DG XIII), **16**, 1966
European Telecommunications Standards Institute (ETSI), **16**, 1968
generally, **16**, 1966
harmonised network, development, **16**, 1969
leased lines, **16**, 1969, 1970
open network provision (ONP), **16**, 1967, 1969, 1972, 1974
single European network, **16**, 1966, 1971
strategy, main elements, **16**, 1967
European Telecommunications Standards Institute (ETSI), **16**, 1968

historical background—
controls, **16**, 1916, 1918
generally, **16**, 1914, 1917
Post Office role, **16**, 1919
postal service, brought within, **16**, 1916
public funds, allocation, **16**, 1917
telegraph, **16**, 1915, 1916
telephonic communications, development, **16**, 1917

interception of communications—
generally, **7**, 733
See also COMMUNICATIONS

Telecommunications—*continued*

international transit services—
meaning, **16**, 1923*n*
provision, **16**, 1923

itemised information, provision of, **16**, 1937

land—
compulsory grant of rights, **16**, 1957
compulsory purchase, **16**, 1917, 1956

licensing system—
class licence—
Branch System General (BSG) Licence, **16**, 1948, 1949
generally, **16**, 1929, 1948
PTO licence and, mutual exclusivity, **16**, 1948
Value Added and Data Services (VADS) Licence, **16**, 1948, 1950
conditions, permissible, **16**, 1927
duration, **16**, 1926
exceptions to requirement for licence, **16**, 1928
generally, **16**, 1921
grant of licence, generally, **16**, 1926
individual licence, **16**, 1929
licensing authority, **16**, 1921, 1922, 1926
offences, **16**, 1925
OFTEL lists of licences granted, **16**, 1927
payments, conditions as to, **16**, 1927
public telecommunication system—
British Telecom, price control, **16**, 1947
class licence, **16**, 1929, 1948–1950
common features, **16**, 1931
competitive environment, creation of, **16**, 1940–1946
conditions, permissible, **16**, 1929
equal access, **16**, 1934–1936
form, **16**, 1931
individual licence, **16**, 1929
non-discrimination, **16**, 1933, 1933*n*, 1940
notice, requirement for, **16**, 1930
revocation, **16**, 1931, 1931*n*
service and support for users, **16**, 1937–1939
universal service, provision, **16**, 1932, 1932*n*
public telecommunications operator (PTO), *see* PUBLIC TELECOMMUNICATIONS OPERATOR
writing, licence must be in, **16**, 1926

light, messages conveyed by, **16**, 1928

line—
inspection and works, compulsory grant of rights, **16**, 1957
land—
compulsory grant of rights, **16**, 1957
compulsory purchase, **16**, 1956
leased, **16**, 1969, 1970
road, under, over, on, along or across, **16**, 1955
tree, obstruction or interference by, **16**, 1957
maintenance service, provision, **16**, 1937, 1937*n*
maritime services, provision, **16**, 1923, 1932, 1932*n*
metering, **16**, 1937, 1937*n*
monopolies, investigation, **16**, 1923
nationalisation, **16**, 1916
numbering arrangements, **16**, 1937, 1937*n*
offences—
assaulting or obstructing operator, **16**, 1959
charge, avoidance, **16**, 1959

Telecommunications—*continued*
offences—*continued*
  false message, sending, **16**, 1959
  interception of communications, *see* INTER-
     CEPTION OF COMMUNICATIONS
  menacing message, sending, **16**, 1959
  obtaining service dishonestly, **16**, 1959
  offensive, indecent or obscene message,
     sending, **16**, 1959
  public, committed by, **16**, 1959
  telecommunications operator, committed by,
     16, 1960
  unlicensed telecommunications system, running,
     16, 1925
Office of Telecommunications (OFTEL)—
  generally, **16**, 1923
  licences granted, lists, publication, **16**, 1927
Open network provision (ONP), **16**, 1967, 1969,
     1973, 1974
operator—
  assaulting or obstructing, **16**, 1959
  disclosure of intercepted message, by, **16**, 1960
  interception of communications—
     generally, **16**, 1961
     safeguards, **16**, 1963
     unlawful, **16**, 1960
     warrant, **16**, 1961, 1962
     See also COMMUNICATIONS
  offence committed by, **16**, 1960
  prescribed valuation formula, **24**, 547
  public (PTO), *see* PUBLIC TELECOMMUNICATIONS
     OPERATOR
  rating, **16**, 1954
overriding interests of operator, **6**, 744
packet switching technology, **16**, 1934*n*
planning controls—
  British Telecom, privileges, **16**, 1953
  compulsory grant of rights, **16**, 1957
  compulsory purchase, **16**, 1956
  generally, **16**, 1952
  road works, **16**, 1955
  Telecommunications Code, **16**, 1958
priority fault repair service, **16**, 1937, 1937*n*
private circuits, **16**, 1940, 1949
privatisation, **4**, 1125
public call services, provision, **16**, 1923, 1932,
     1932*n*, 1933
public telecommunications operator (PTO), *see*
     PUBLIC TELECOMMUNICATIONS OPERATOR
regulatory framework—
  Director General of Telecommunications,
     functions, **16**, 1921, 1923
  generally, **16**, 1921, 1952
  information and advice to consumers, as to, **16**,
     1923
  international transit services, promotion, **16**,
     1923
  licensing authority, **16**, 1921, 1922
  licensing system, **16**, 1921
  monopolies, investigation, **16**, 1923
  planning controls, **16**, 1952–1958
  regulatory agency, **16**, 1921, 1923
  Secretary of State, functions, **16**, 1921, 1922
  Telecommunications Code, **16**, 1958

Telecommunications—*continued*
research and development, regulatory controls,
     16, 1922, 1923
road, apparatus under, over, on, along or across—
  inspection, **16**, 1955
  installation, **16**, 1955
  maintenance and repair, **16**, 1955
  Telecommunications Code, **16**, 1955, 1958
  works, execution, **16**, 1955
rural areas, provision in, **16**, 1923, 1933, 1933*n*
satellite communications, regulation, **16**, 1924*n*
service, meaning, **16**, 1924
sheriff court jurisdiction, **6**, 1122
supplies, winding up, position relating to, **4**, 867
tariffing, EU guidelines, **16**, 1974
telecommunication system, *see* TELECOMMUNICA-
     TION SYSTEM
testing apparatus, provisions as to, **16**, 1938
value added services, **16**, 1950
visual images, coveyance, **16**, 1924
wireless telegraphy, system using, **16**, 1928
wiring—
  British Telecom, **16**, 1939
  PTO, licence provisions, **16**, 1939
Telecommunications Code
application, **16**, 1958
compulsory grant of rights, **16**, 1957
conditions, **16**, 1958
environment, protection, **16**, 1958
exceptions, **16**, 1958
generally, **16**, 1958
liabilities arising from exercise, **16**, 1958
road works, **16**, 1955, 1958
Telegram
acceptance of offer by, **15**, 644
communication by, contract law, **15**, 644, 647,
     648
disclosure of information given for conveyance,
     16, 1916
payment for, **16**, 1916
postal service, brought within, **16**, 1916
Telegraph
controls over telegraphic services, **16**, 1916
development, **16**, 1914, 1915
disclosure of information given for conveyance,
     16, 1916
meaning, **16**, 1915*n*
nationalisation, **16**, 1916
postal service, brought within, **16**, 1916
railway companies, and, **16**, 1914–1916
See also TELECOMMUNICATIONS
TELEMATIQUE programme
European Union telecommunications deregulation,
     16, 1966
Telephone
cold-calling, investor protection, *see* INVESTOR
     PROTECTION
development, **16**, 1917
  public funds, allocation, **16**, 1917
leasing, commencement of, **14**, 1006
legislative controls, development, **16**, 1918
metering, **12**, 68
nationalisation, **16**, 1916
Post Office role, **16**, 1918, 1919

Telephone—*continued*
private conversations, **12**, 68
  unlawfully obtained used as evidence, **12**, 60
tapping, **12**, 68
  police surveillance activities, **16**, 1802
See also TELECOMMUNICATIONS
Telepost service
meaning, **16**, 1904*n*
Post Office provision, **16**, 1904
provision, **16**, 1920*n*
Teletext services
Independent Broadcasting Authority, provision by, **17**, 8
Television
aerial, on tenement, **18**, 238
cinema, effect on, **9**, 1018
closed circuit, whether licence required, **16**, 1928
freedom of expression, **12**, 73
installation and use in motor vehicle, **20**, 443
licensing, **7**, 45; **12**, 73
See also BROADCAST; CABLE PROGRAMME
Telex
value added service, as, **16**, 195
Temperance hotel
generally, **11**, 1708
Temperance polls
limited provisions as to, **2**, 97
Tenancy at will
application to purchase land by, **6**, 1143
compulsory purchase, rights as to, **18**, 72
feudal law, generally, **18**, 72
house, sale of, **13**, 211
landlord's interest, acquisition of, **13**, 334
meaning, **13**, 211
Tenant-in-chief
Scottish Parliament, representation in, **15**, 1002, 1004
Tenant netsmen
district salmon fisheries boards, **11**, 35, 37
Tenant-tenancy
Accommodation Agencies Act 1953 ..., **13**, 695
agreement, necessity for, **13**, 613
agricultural, **6**, 1141
  angling rights, **11**, 49
  bird scarers and scarecrows, **11**, 888
  family or servants of, taking game, **11**, 818
  fixed term, **19**, 1565
  Game (Scotland) Act 1832 ..., **11**, 818
  game taken or frightened away by, **11**, 887
  ground game, **11**, 888
  inheritance tax, **19**, 1564–1567
  muirburn, right to make, **11**, 920
  neighbouring lands, damage caused by game from, **11**, 894
  Night Poaching Acts, conviction under, **11**, 810*n*
  notice of entry, compensation, **6**, 1141
  notice to terminate, **19**, 1564
  partnership tenancies, **19**, 1587–1571, 1590
  permission to kill rabbits or hares, given by, **11**, 818
  relationship with landlord—
    common law, **11**, 887–889
    compensation for damage by game, **11**, 889–894

Tenant-tenancy—*continued*
agricultural—*continued*
  relationship with landlord—*continued*
    increase of game, **11**, 889
    landlord's rights, **11**, 887
    tenant's rights, **11**, 888
  security, **11**, 1937, 1943
  succession, **19**, 1622
  tacit relocation, **19**, 1564–1566
  transferred during lifetime of tenant, **19**, 1567
  valuation of, **19**, 1564–1567
  See also AGRICULTURAL HOLDING
allotment, tenant of, rights and duties, **13**, 543
assignable lease—
  conditions running with lands, **13**, 239–243
    personal conditions, **13**, 240, 242
    real conditions, **13**, 239–241
assignation of lease by tenant, **13**, 184, 345, 353
assured tenancy—
  actual exclusive occupation, **13**, 614
  assignation, payment of premiun or loan on, prohibition, **13**, 691
  caravan, **13**, 615
  definition, **13**, 612
  flat, **13**, 615
  generally, **11**, 1936; **13**, 594, 611
  house—
    meaning, **13**, 615
    separate dwelling, let as, **13**, 616
  individual, tenant must be, **13**, 612, 617
  joint tenants, **13**, 612, 615, 618
  land, house rented along with, **13**, 619
  loan, landlord or agent, demand by, prohibition, **13**, 689–691
  main purpose of let, **13**, 619
  market rent, determination, **13**, 672–676
    generally, **13**, 672
    rent assessment committees, by, **13**, 673, 674
    rent increase proposals, **13**, 675
      preventing, **13**, 676
    where no provision for rent increase made in rent agreement, **13**, 674
  only or principal home of tenant, house must be, **13**, 612, 618
  premium, landlord or agent, demand by, prohibition, **13**, 689–692
  protection of tenant, **13**, 594
  qualifying conditions, **13**, 612
  repossession—
    discretionary grounds for—
      alternative accommodation, provision of suitable, **13**, 725, 727
      annoyance, **13**, 725, 733
      deterioration in condition of house or furnishings, **13**, 725, 732, 734
      ex-employee as tenant, **13**, 725, 735
      generally, **13**, 725
      immoral or illegal purpose, premises used for, **13**, 725, 733
      notice to quit, withdrawal by tenant, **13**, 725, 728
      nuisance, **13**, 725, 733

Tenant-tenancy—*continued*
assured tenancy—*continued*
 repossession—*continued*
  discretionary grounds for—*continued*
   rent—
    breach of tenancy obligations, **13**, 725, 731
    persistent delay in payment, **13**, 725, 729
    unpaid, **13**, 725, 730
  mandatory grounds for—
   demolition or construction work, house required for, **13**, 749, 755
   educational body, non-student let by, **13**, 749, 753
   generally, **13**, 749
   heritable security default, **13**, 749, 751
   intestacy, tenancy passing on, **13**, 749, 756, 781
   lay missionary, house held for occupation by, **13**, 749, 754
   minister, house held for occupation by, **13**, 749, 754
   off-season holiday let, **13**, 749, 752
   owner occupier, landlord as, **13**, 749, 750
   rent arrears, **13**, 749, 757
   will, tenancy inherited under, **13**, 749, 756, 781
 requirements for, **13**, 600
 security of tenure, **13**, 696, 697
 shared accommodation, **13**, 615, 620
  subtenant, with, **13**, 621
 shared property, **13**, 599
 short—
  definition, **13**, 623
  fair rent—
   determination—
    comparables, pool of, **13**, 685
    date effect taken, **13**, 687
    duplication, avoidance, **13**, 684
    significantly higher rent, tenant must pay, **13**, 686
   registration, **13**, 622
  generally, **13**, 622
  possession, landlord, regained by, **13**, 623
  rent assessment committees, role, **13**, 683, 684
  repossession, grounds for, **13**, 758
  security of tenure not provided by, **13**, 696
 single room, **13**, 615
 statutory rent increase mechanism, avoidance, **13**, 682
 subtenant, **13**, 613, 621
 succession—
  cohabitee, **13**, 781
  generally, **13**, 781
  original tenant, to, **13**, 782
  spouse, **13**, 781
  successor tenant, to, **13**, 783
 tenancies excluded from—
  agricultural holding, tenancy of, **13**, 636, 642
  agricultural land, tenancy of, **13**, 636, 641
  Crown tenancy, **13**, 636, 646
  generally, **13**, 636

Tenant-tenancy—*continued*
assured tenancy—*continued*
 tenancies excluded from—*continued*
  holiday let, **13**, 636, 644
  homeless person, temporary accommodation for, **13**, 636, 648
  housing association, tenancy under, **13**, 650
  licensed premises, tenancy of, **13**, 636, 640
  low rent, tenancy at, **13**, 636, 638
  protected tenancy, **13**, 650
  public sector tenancy, **13**, 636, 647
  resident landlord, where, **13**, 636, 645
  secure tenancy, **13**, 650
  shared ownership agreement, **13**, 636, 649
  shop, tenancy of, **13**, 636, 639
  student, letting to, **13**, 636, 643
  tenancy entered before 2 January 1989 ..., **13**, 636, 637
 tenancy, meaning, **13**, 613
 termination, procedure, **13**, 763–767
bankruptcy, irritancy of lease on, **15**, 809
bankruptcy of tenant—
 agricultural holding, **13**, 414
 debtor's family home, **13**, 417
 generally, **13**, 414
 growing crops, **13**, 422
 irritancy, **13**, 415
 trust deed for creditors, **13**, 418
 trustee—
  abandonment by, **13**, 421
  acceptance by landlord, **13**, 419
  adoption by, **13**, 420
  vesting in, **13**, 416
building contracts—
 collateral warranty, **3**, 158
 prospective tenant, interests of, **3**, 2
business, transfer of, **9**, 180
civil possession by, **18**, 121
co-tenants, *jus possidendi, pro indiviso* holders of same right to, **18**, 118
cohabitee, succession, **10**, 1005; **13**, 776
commercial lease, *see* LEASE-LEASING
common interest, doctrine of, **18**, 363, 364
contract of employment, premises occupied under, **11**, 1937, 1948
controlled, **13**, 603
Crown, assured tenancy status, exclusion from, **13**, 636, 646
damage by other tenants, **13**, 289
death of tenant—
 delectus personae, doctrine of, **13**, 355
 succession, *see* succession *below*
delectus personae, doctrine of, **13**, 355–357, 583
delict committed by, liability, **15**, 242
deposit, payment of, **13**, 693
diligence on tenant, effect, **13**, 184
disturbance payment, *see* COMPULSORY ACQUISITION
domestic, rent owed by tenant, **8**, 126
education authority, of, right to buy, **8**, 733
elements for creation, **13**, 613
eviction—
 damages for, **13**, 251
 partial, **13**, 251
 third party, by, **13**, 251

Tenant-tenancy—*continued*
extortion by tenant, **7**, 403
extortion from tenant, **7**, 403
fair rent—
    registration, **13**, 652
    See also RENT
family member, succession by, **13**, 777–780, 785
feudal law, **18**, 47
fixtures fitted by tenant, ownership, **18**, 574, 574*n*, 575, 582, 586
free, lord, power to hold courts to settle disputes, **22**, 509
furnished lease, security of tenure, **13**, 696
game tenant—
    relationship with landlord—
        entry, right of, **11**, 895
        Leith case, **11**, 896
        shooting lease—
            granters of, **11**, 898
            nature of, **11**, 895–897
            normal clauses, **11**, 899–904
'good covenant', meaning, **13**, 562
harassment of tenant, **7**, 403
    protection against, **13**, 593
holiday let, **13**, 604, 634, 636, 644
home loss payment, entitlement to, **5**, 186
housing and tenancy court, fairness of methods employed by, **12**, 60
improvements, alterations or repairs—
    lessee, by—
        fair rent decisions, **13**, 661, 664, 669
        irritancy, **13**, 415
        market rent, determination, **13**, 679
        obligation to compensate as real condition, **13**, 241
        possession, and, **13**, 140
        retention of rent for, **13**, 307
    See also repairs *below*
income from, calculation of income support, **21**, 1077
insolvency or apparent insolvency, **13**, 415
    irritancy, **13**, 415
insurable interest of, **12**, 852
ish, necessity for, **13**, 613
joint tenancy—
    accretion to survivors, **13**, 189
    assured tenancy, **13**, 612, 615, 618
    bankruptcy of one tenant, **13**, 189
    default by one tenant, **13**, 599
    English law, **25**, 640
    generally, **13**, 599
    liability of tenants, **13**, 189, 599
    meaning, **13**, 189
    moveable items, ownership, **13**, 189
    one lessee not occupying subject, **13**, 189
    partnership, **13**, 192
    removings, action of, **13**, 501
    security of tenure, **13**, 697
    sequestration of one tenant, **13**, 189
    subtenant and joint tenant compared, **13**, 599
    survivorship clause, **13**, 189
    tacit relocation, obligations arising as result of, **13**, 189
    transmission of interest, **13**, 189

Tenant-tenancy—*continued*
joint tenancy—*continued*
    two or more tenants holding distinct *pro indiviso* shares, **13**, 189
kindly tenancy, **18**, 72, 72*n*
    registration of title, **6**, 714, 777
    Roll of Kindly Tenants, **6**, 777
landlord, *see* LANDLORD
landlord's hypothec, *see* LANDLORD (RENT, HYPOTHEC FOR)
Lands Tribunal for Scotland, **6**, 1146
lease, *see* LEASE–LEASING
leased dairy, alterations to, **11**, 491
leased goods, landlord's rights over, **14**, 1070
lessor, tenant as, **13**, 154
loan, landlord or agent, demand by, prohibition, **13**, 690, 691
lodgings, **13**, 630, 632
long lease—
    disadvantages, **13**, 317
    See also LEASE–LEASING
matrimonial home, transfer of, **10**, 867
meaning of tenant, **13**, 103
negotiating strength, tenant's, **13**, 562
netsmen, **11**, 37
nuisance created by, landlord's liability for, **14**, 2140
obligations, tenant's—
    breach, landlord's remedies—
        generally, **13**, 275, 276
        monetary breach, **13**, 276
    plenish subject, to, **13**, 271
    possession—
        not to invert, **13**, 265–268
        to remain in, **13**, 264
        to take, **13**, 263
    reasonable care, to use, **13**, 269
    rent, payment of, **13**, 272, 273
    repair of subject, **13**, 270
occupiers' liability, **15**, 311, 317, 320
    sub-tenancy, **15**, 320
Part VII contract—
    attendance, payments in respect of, **13**, 627
    board, payments in respect of, **13**, 628
    contracts covered by, **13**, 625
    English equivalent, **13**, 625
    lease distinguished, **13**, 626–629
    licensee, **13**, 771
    meaning, **13**, 624
    occupancy rights, contract giving, **13**, 625
    reasonable rent, **13**, 671
    rent, variation, **13**, 624
    rent assessment committees, **13**, 624, 671
    resident landlord, **13**, 624, 629
    security of tenure, **13**, 696, 759–761
personal circumstances to be disregarded in decisions as to fair rent, **13**, 660–662
possession—
    inversion—
        examples, **13**, 266
        obligations, generally, **13**, 265, 267, 268
    landlord's obligation to maintain in—
        derogation from grant, **13**, 253
        generally, **13**, 251
        limitations on obligation, **13**, 252

Tenant-tenancy—*continued*
possession—*continued*
  necessity for, **13**, 613
  obligations as to—
    inversion of possession, **13**, 265–268
    remaining in possession, **13**, 264
    taking possession, **13**, 263
  order for, **12**, 1253
  unjustifiable retention, violent profits, **13**, 505
possession through, **16**, 2108
premium, *see* RENT
principal, **13**, 103
proprietor, as, **24**, 444
protected tenancy—
  assignation, payment of premiun or loan on, prohibition, **13**, 691
  assured tenancy status affected by, **13**, 650
  board, payments in respect of, **13**, 628
  building let partly for business purposes, **13**, 607
  dwelling house, must be let as, **13**, 605, 606
  establishment of system, **13**, 604
  fair rent—
    failure to register, **13**, 604
    registration, **13**, 604
    generally, **13**, 604
  loan, landlord or agent, demand by, prohibition, **13**, 690, 691
  long lease, **13**, 343
  premium, landlord or agent, demand by, prohibition, **13**, 690–692
  qualifying conditions, **13**, 605
  rateable value, **13**, 605, 608
  redemption of standard securities, **20**, 180
  repossession—
    discretionary grounds for—
      alternative accommodation—
        assured tenancy, replacement by, **13**, 711
        equivalent, **13**, 709–711
        housing authority certificate, **13**, 709, 710
        landlord, provision by, **13**, 709–713
        overcrowding, **13**, 713
        suitability, **13**, 709–713
      annoyance, **13**, 714, 716
      assignation, **13**, 714, 720
      breach of tenancy obligations, **13**, 714, 715
      deterioration in condition of house or furnishings, **13**, 714, 717, 718
      employee of landlord, house required for, **13**, 714, 721
      family member of landlord, house required for, **13**, 714, 722
      generally, **13**, 708
      harassment, considerations as to, **13**, 709
      immoral or illegal purposes, premises used for, **13**, 714, 716
      landlord—
        house required as residence for, **13**, 714, 722
        onus on, **13**, 708
      notice to quit, withdrawal, **13**, 714, 719
      nuisance, **13**, 714, 716

Tenant-tenancy—*continued*
protected tenancy—*continued*
  repossession—*continued*
    discretionary grounds for—*continued*
      occupancy—
        spouse, by, **13**, 708
        statutory rights, agreement by tenant to give up, **13**, 708
        two houses, tenant with, **13**, 708
        what constitutes, **13**, 708
      overcrowding, **13**, 714, 724
      rent arrears, **13**, 714, 715
      sublease, **13**, 714, 720, 723
    mandatory grounds for, **13**, 708
      agricultural worker, dwelling house required for, **13**, 736, 743
      armed forces, landlord member of, **13**, 736, 747, 748
      educational body non-student let, **13**, 736, 740
      farm—
        amalgamation of farms, **13**, 736, 744
        occupation, **13**, 736, 745
      generally, **13**, 736
      minister or lay missionary, dwelling house held for occupation by, **13**, 736, 742
      off-season holiday let, **13**, 736, 739
      owner occupier requiring house as own residence, **13**, 736, 737, 748
      retirement home, owner requiring house as, **13**, 736, 738, 748
      short tenancy, **13**, 736, 741
      special needs, dwelling house adapted for, **13**, 736, 746
  resident landlord, position where, **13**, 629
  security of tenure, **13**, 696
  separate dwelling, must constitute, **13**, 605, 607
  statutory tenancy following, **13**, 609
  substantial attendance, rent including, **13**, 627
  succession—
    death of tenant, on, **13**, 775
    first successor who succeeded prior to 2 January 1989, death, **13**, 780
    member of tenant's family, by, **13**, 777–780, 785
    new tenancy, grant to successor, **13**, 779
    second successor, **13**, 778
    surviving cohabitee, by, **13**, 776
    surviving spouse, by, **13**, 776, 778
  tenancies excluded from—
    dwelling house let with land and other premises, **13**, 630, 6345
    generally, **13**, 630
    holiday let, **13**, 630, 634
    lodgings, **13**, 630, 632
    rent, non-existent or low, **13**, 630, 631
    service letting, **13**, 630, 632
    student tenancy, **13**, 630, 633
  termination, procedure, **13**, 762
protection of tenant—
  private sector residential—
    assured tenancy, *see* assured tenancy *above*
    controlled tenancy, **13**, 603
    furnished property, **13**, 594

Tenant-tenancy—*continued*
protection of tenant—*continued*
   private sector residential—*continued*
      furnished tenancy, **13**, 593
      generally, **13**, 590–594
      historical background, **13**, 590, 591
      owner occupier as landlord, **13**, 594
      protected tenancy, **13**, 604–608
      regulated tenancy, **13**, 610
      rent—
         assessment committee, **13**, 593
         fixing, **13**, 592, 593
         registration service, **13**, 593
         review, **13**, 592
         tribunal, **13**, 593
      Rent Act 1965 ..., **13**, 592
      Rent Act 1974 ..., **13**, 593
      resident landlord, **13**, 593, 594
      Scottish legislation—
         generally, **13**, 592
      security of tenure, **13**, 594
      short tenancy, **13**, 594
      shorthold tenancy, **13**, 594
      statutory tenancy, **13**, 609
      tenancy—
         attempts to avoid contract involving, **13**, 595
         other rights of occupancy in relation to, **13**, 595–602
      Tenants' Rights Etc (Scotland) Act 1980 ..., **13**, 594
      unfurnished tenancy, **13**, 593
   real rights, *see* REAL RIGHT
public sector tenancy—
   assured tenancy status, exclusion from, **13**, 636, 647
   property abandoned by, ownership, **18**, 552
   See PUBLIC SECTOR TENANCY
purchase of furniture, tenancy agreement requiring, **7**, 403
questions of, legal advice and assistance, **13**, 1028
real burden—
   dominant tenement, no right of enforcement, **18**, 406
   liability for, **18**, 413
reasonable care, tenant's obligation to use, **13**, 269
regulated tenancy, **13**, 610
rei interventus, actings amounting to, **13**, 140
remedies available to tenant—
   abandonment, **13**, 282
   damages, **13**, 284
   entry, refusal to take, **13**, 280
   generally, **13**, 277
   interdict, **13**, 283
   possession, suspension, **13**, 281
   rent—
      abatement, **13**, 279
      retention, **13**, 278
   rescission, **13**, 282
   specific implement, **13**, 283
removings—
   commercial lease, **13**, 588
   court action, necessity for, **13**, 469–472
   ejection distinguished, **13**, 467

Tenant-tenancy—*continued*
removings—*continued*
   extraordinary, **13**, 464
      notice to quit, whether neccessary, **13**, 468
      violent profits, **13**, 505, 507, 512
   irritancy, termination of lease by, **13**, 466
   ish, tenant not moving out at, **13**, 466
   landlord, recovery of possession by, **13**, 466
   meaning, **13**, 463, 467
   notice—
      agricultural subjects, **13**, 483
      common law, **13**, 476
      contents, **13**, 484
      description of subject, **13**, 486
      dwelling house, **13**, 483
      form—
         generally, **13**, 481
      generally, **13**, 475
      ish, must be prior to, **13**, 475
      lapsed, **13**, 491
      lease, reference to, **13**, 487
      ordinary removing, **13**, 483
      parties, specification, **13**, 488
      period of, **13**, 475–480
         calculation, **13**, 480
      prescribed information, **13**, 489
      quit, notice to, **13**, 475
      Removal Terms (Scotland) Act 1886 ..., **13**, 477
      Rent (Scotland) Act 1984 ..., **13**, 479
      service and evidence, **13**, 490
      Sheriff Courts (Scotland) Act 1907 ..., **13**, 478
      term, specification, **13**, 485
      timeous, **13**, 475
      title to sue—
         agent, lease granted by, **13**, 498
         generally, **13**, 492
         heritable securities, **13**, 499
         joint proprietors, where, **13**, 496
         limited owners, where, **13**, 497
         missives, effect, **13**, 495
         principal tenant, **13**, 500
         pursuer lessor, where, **13**, 493
         pursuer not lessor, where, **13**, 494
         subtenant, **13**, 500
         urban subjects, **13**, 482
      withdrawn, **13**, 491
   ordinary, **13**, 465, 470
      forms, **13**, 474
      notice, form, **13**, 483
      notice of termination, **13**, 468
      violent profits, **13**, 505, 506
   reform, need for, **13**, 462
   service tenancy, **13**, 469
   Sheriff Courts (Scotland) Act 1907 ..., **13**, 462
   solemn, **13**, 466, 466*n*
   solemn causes, **13**, 466
   subtenant, **13**, 469
   summary, **13**, 466, 466*n*
   summary cause, **13**, 466, 473
   violent profits, caution for, **13**, 505
   warning or letter of removal, **13**, 475

Tenant-tenancy—*continued*
rent—
    necessity for, **13**, 613
    payment of, generally, **13**, 229
    retention of, **13**, 273
    sequestration for, *see* SEQUESTRATION FOR RENT
    tenant's obligation to pay, **13**, 272
    See also RENT
Rent Acts, **13**, 590*ff*
Rent (Scotland) Act 1984 ..., **12**, 1253
renunciation, lease of—
    generally, **13**, 438
    See also LEASE-LEASING
repair notice, bearing expense of, **11**, 1995
repairs—
    commercial lease—
        destruction of or damage to property, **13**,
            579–581
        maintenance and repair obligation, **13**, 578
        'full repairing and insuring lease', **13**, 556, 557,
            563, 580, 581
    landlord's obligations as to—
        avoidance, **13**, 602
        rural subjects, **13**, 262
        urban subjects—
            common law, **13**, 257, 258
            statute law, **13**, 259–261
    obligations as to, generally, **13**, 270
    tenant's obligations as to, **13**, 270
right to buy, *see* SECURE TENANT
secure, *see* SECURE TENANT
separate dwelling, **13**, 599
service occupancy, **11**, 1948; **13**, 601
services, provision of, **13**, 600, 630, 632
servitude—
    exercise of, **18**, 464, 470
    may not be created in favour of, **18**, 449
    over let property, creation, **18**, 449
shared property, **13**, 599
    separate dwelling, **13**, 599
shop, of, *see* SHOP
short assured tenancy—
    definition, **13**, 623
    fair rent—
        determination, **13**, 683
            comparables, pool of, **13**, 685
            date effect taken, **13**, 687
            duplication, avoidance, **13**, 684
            significantly higher rent, tenant must pay,
                13, 686
        non-determination, **13**, 684
        registration, **13**, 622
    generally, **13**, 622
    possession, landlord, regained by, **13**, 623
    rent assessment committees, role, **13**, 683, 684
        disapplication, **13**, 688
    repossession, grounds for, **13**, 758
    security of tenure not provided by, **13**, 696
short tenancy, *see* SHORT TENANCY
shorthold, **13**, 594
small tenant, *see* STATUTORY SMALL TENANT
sporting—
    agricultural tenant's rights, **11**, 888
    ground game, **11**, 852, 854

Tenant-tenancy—*continued*
spouse, succession by, **13**, 776, 778
statutory, redemption of standard securities, **20**,
    180
statutory protection of tenant, generally, **13**, 101
statutory small tenant, *see* STATUTORY SMALL
    TENANT
statutory tenancy, **13**, 609
    long lease, **13**, 343
steelbow contract, **13**, 1707
student, granted by specified educational
    institution, **13**, 633, 636, 643
sublease, *see* SUBLEASE
subtenant, *see* SUBLEASE
succession—
    bequest of lease—
        landlord—
            acceptance by, **13**, 401
            repudiation by, **13**, 402
        legatee, repudiation by, **13**, 402
        power of, **13**, 395–397
            exclusion, **13**, 398, 399
        statutory rights, **13**, 390
        whether made, **13**, 400
    case law—
        residing with, meaning, **13**, 784
        so long as he or she retains possession,
            meaning, **13**, 787
    choice of law, **13**, 389
    excluded, where, **13**, 392, 393
    executor—
        role—
            breach of conditions, **13**, 408
            termination—
                compensation for, **13**, 407
                provision for, **13**, 406
                renunciation distinguished, **13**, 438
            vesting, **13**, 405
        selection of successor by, **13**, 404
    family member, by—
        meaning of family, **13**, 785
        protected tenancy, **13**, 777–780, 785
        residing with, meaning, **13**, 784
    generally, **13**, 391
    jus relictae, **13**, 412
    jus relicti, **13**, 412
    lease, where regulated in, **13**, 394
    legal rights, **13**, 412
    legatee, **13**, 409
    legitim, **13**, 412
    liferent lease, **13**, 393
    no bequest, where—
        executor, selection of successor by, **13**, 404
        generally, **13**, 403
    prior rights, **13**, 413
    special destination, **13**, 394
    statutory—
        generally, **13**, 390
        lease rights—
            generally, **13**, 774
            intestacy, on, **13**, 774
            will, by, **13**, 774
        protected tenancy—
            death of tenant, on, **13**, 775

Tenant-tenancy—*continued*
succession—*continued*
  statutory—*continued*
    protected tenancy—*continued*
      first successor who succeeded prior to 2
        January 1989, death, **13**, 780
      member of tenant's family, by, **13**, 777
      new tenancy, grant to successor, **13**, 779
      second successor, **13**, 778
      surviving spouse, by, **13**, 776, 778
    statutory successor, **13**, 410
    taking up lease, **13**, 409–411
    termination on death of tenant, **13**, 392, 393
    ultimus haeres, **13**, 411
superior, tenant's relationship with, **13**, 291
support, right to, of tenanted land, **18**, 262, 262n
tacit relocation, *see* TACIT RELOCATION
temporary lettings—
  pending development, **11**, 1937, 1940
  person seeking accommodation, to, **11**, 1937,
    1939
  works, during, **11**, 1937, 1941
tenancy rights, **11**, 1101, 1108, 1110
tenant at will, **6**, 1143
termination, *see* LEASE-LEASING
termination by adandonment of possession, **12**,
  1235
third party rights, and, **13**, 289–291
tied, **11**, 1948, 2057
title to sue, **14**, 2133
title to sue third party, **13**, 290
trout fishing lease, **11**, 49
two or more, holding distinct *pro indiviso* shares,
  13, 189
udal tenure, registration of title, **6**, 714, 777
unfree, lord, powers regarding, **22**, 509
unpaid rent, poinding of the ground, **8**, 361
valuation roll, **24**, 432
violent profits, caution for, removings, action of,
  13, 504
when occupier, **24**, 447n
wrongous ejection, damages for, **13**, 471
See also LEASE-LEASING; LESSEE; RENT
Tender
building contracts, *see* BUILDING CONTRACT
definition, **21**, 211n
legal, *see* LEGAL TENDER
offer, as, **15**, 626
Tendering
offence, **14**, 1837
Tenendas
Form of clause, **6**, 527
Tenement
separate, *see* LANDOWNERSHIP
Tenement building
a coelo usque ad centrum principle, **18**, 228
alienation of *pro indiviso* share, **18**, 242
alterations to—
  dormer windows, **18**, 245
  parts owned by individual proprietors, **18**, 245
  parts owned in common, **18**, 244
back green, **18**, 228, 241
  combustible substances, **18**, 242
  open space, as, **18**, 246

Tenement building—*continued*
back green—*continued*
  ordinary and extraordinary use, **18**, 242
  statutory duty of common owners, **18**, 246
ceilings, **18**, 229
chimneys—
  generally, **18**, 230
  right to use chimney vents, **18**, 237
co-ownership, **18**, 18
combustible substances, passage, stair and back
  green to be kept free from, **18**, 242
common gables—
  right of support, **18**, 233
common interest—
  boundaries of individual tenements, whether
    rights extend accross, **18**, 232
  chimney vents, right to use, **18**, 237
  common property, relationship with, **18**, 232,
    356, 357
  doctrine of, generally, **14**, 2030; **18**, 232, 350,
    355, 357n, 358, 359, 361
  down pipes, right to use, **18**, 238
  drains, right to install, **18**, 239
  implication of law, arising by, **18**, 232, 358
  light and air, right to, **18**, 236, 359, 361, 486
  limits of positive obligations, **18**, 235
  natural servitude, as, **18**, 355
  pipes—
    right to install, **18**, 239
    right to use, **18**, 238
  reciprocal nature of rights, **18**, 232
  satellite dish, right to place, **18**, 238
  scope, **18**, 232
  shelter, right to, **18**, 234, 235
  support, right of, **18**, 233, 235
    common gables, **18**, 233
    lower flats, **18**, 233
    solum, **18**, 233
  television aerial, right to erect, **18**, 238
  title and interest to enforce, **18**, 363
common law rules, **18**, 227
common ownership, parts in—
  alterations, **18**, 244
  cleanliness, statutory duty as to, **18**, 247
  generally, **18**, 24
  repairs, **18**, 246
  use, **18**, 242
    ordinary and extraordinary use, **18**, 242
common passage and stair—
  co-ownership, **18**, 18
  combustible substances, **18**, 242
  generally, **18**, 24, 26, 202, 228, 231, 241
  obstruction, **18**, 242
  ordinary and extraordinary use, **18**, 242
  paint or decorate, requirement to, **14**, 278n
  presumed pertinent, as, **18**, 202
  roof above, **18**, 230, 231
  solum, **18**, 228, 231
common property, **18**, 26
converted buildings, **18**, 227
deeds dealing with, **6**, 584
definition, **6**, 584; **18**, 227
destruction—
  demolition costs, **18**, 249

Tenement building—*continued*
destruction—*continued*
  disposal of *solum*, **18**, 250, 251
  generally, **18**, 235
  rebuilding, **18**, 250
division and sale, **18**, 242
dormer window, construction in roof, **18**, 245
drains, right to install, **18**, 239
electricity supply to, **9**, 651
flat, as a separate tenement, **18**, 207, 212
floors, **18**, 229
individual proprietors, parts owned by, **18**, 247
law of the tenement, generally, **6**, 584; **18**, 227
light and air, common interest right to, **18**, 236,
  359, 361, 486
maintenance costs, **18**, 241
nuisance, law of, **18**, 243; **19**, 34
obstruction of parts in common ownership, **18**,
  242
ownership, **18**, 196, 198
pertinents, **18**, 202, 205
pipes, **18**, 241
  down pipes, **18**, 238
  right to install, **18**, 239
  right to use, **18**, 238
rebuilding—
  airspace, encroachment of, **18**, 250
  consent of all affected proprietors required, **18**,
    250
  requirement, where, **18**, 250
reconstruction of building, **18**, 235
repair—
  local authority powers to require, **18**, 248
  parts owned in common, **18**, 246
rhone, **18**, 241
roof, **18**, 230
  dormer window, construction by top floor
    proprietor, **18**, 245
roof space, **18**, 241
  dormer windows, **18**, 245
  top floor proprietor extending into, **18**, 245
satellite dish, right to install, **18**, 238
shelter—
  common interest right of, **18**, 359
  generally, **18**, 234, 235
  obligation of, **18**, 355, 357n, 361
solum, **18**, 228, 241
  disposal on demolition, **18**, 250, 251
  right of support, **18**, 233
  stair and passage, beneath, **18**, 228, 231
support, right of, **18**, 233, 235, 355, 357n, 359,
  361
television aerial, right to install, **18**, 238
title deeds, variation—
  examples, **18**, 241
  method, **18**, 240
use—
  parts owned by individual proprietors, **18**, 243
  parts owned in common, **18**, 242
walls—
  accession, **18**, 241
  common gables, **18**, 229
  common stair and passage, of, **18**, 231
  external, **18**, 229

Tenement building—*continued*
walls—*continued*
  internal—
    between flats, **18**, 229
    within flat, **18**, 229
Tennis
club professionals, **19**, 1231
sports-governing institutions, **19**, 1205
Tent
lay-by, pitching in, **20**, 692
road, pitching in, **20**, 692
Tenure
land, *see* LAND TENURE
Terce
abolition of, **25**, 702
feudal law, generally, **18**, 110
heritable securities, former competition with, **20**,
  248
kenning, **18**, 74
legal liferent, as, **18**, 74
obligation to satisfy, **16**, 2116
Term days
definition, **13**, 245
Terminal markets
VAT zero-rating, **7**, 1433
Territorial Army
additional duties, **2**, 760
associations—
  expenses, **2**, 765
  facilities provided by, **2**, 765
  powers and duties, **2**, 765
attachment to other forces, **2**, 760
calling out—
  billeting, obtaining, **2**, 763
  civil power, to aid, **2**, 764
  home defence service, for, **2**, 762
discharge, delivering up property on, **2**, 758
discipline, **2**, 634
government etc, **2**, 757
home defence service by, **2**, 762
Home Service Force—
  composition, **2**, 757
  sphere of service, **2**, 757
legal basis for, **2**, 611
maintenance, **2**, 757
requisitioning powers, **2**, 763
training—
  annual, **2**, 760
  notice to attend for, **2**, 761
  preliminary, **2**, 759
Territorial designations
Court of the Lord Lyon, **6**, 1018
Territorial sea
baseline system, **11**, 74, 76, 76n, 77
  bays, **11**, 78
  fishery limits, **11**, 130
  generally, **21**, 12, 112
  internal waters, **11**, 79
  'normal' baselines, **21**, 12
  straight baselines, **11**, 78; **21**, 12
  United Kingdom practice, **11**, 78–91
British fisheries, access to, **11**, 131, 132
conflicts between international and municipal
  law, **11**, 75

Territorial sea—*continued*
contiguous zone, *see* CONTIGUOUS ZONE
continental shelf, *see* CONTINENTAL SHELF
criminal jurisdiction, **21**, 8
    outward bound vessels, **21**, 8
Crown property rights, **21**, 11
division with high seas, origin of, **11**, 71
exclusive economic zone, **11**, 107
exclusive fishery zone, **11**, 80, 81, 86, 92, 107
Fisheries Convention 1964 ..., **11**, 81
fishing limits, **1**, 943
fishing in as non-innocent activity, **21**, 7
generally, **11**, 76; **21**, 2, 35, 36
innocent passage, right of—
    anchoring, **21**, 6
    generally, **21**, 6
    hovering, **21**, 6
    meaning, **21**, 6, 7
    non-innocent activities, **21**, 7
    right to deny, **21**, 8
    stopping, **21**, 6
    straits used for international navigation, **21**, 10
        alternative routes, **21**, 10
    submarines, **21**, 7
    suspension, rights as to, **21**, 8
    warships, **21**, 9
internal waters, **11**, 79
international law, **11**, 71–77
land-kenning, **11**, 73
League of Nations convention on territorial waters, **21**, 2
limits, **11**, 73, 74; **21**, 5
    history, generally, **21**, 5
    outer, **11**, 77
    United Kingdom practice, **11**, 78–91
mare liberum and *mare clausum*, **11**, 72
meaning, **21**, 112
natural resources, **11**, 82–85
salvage operations, **21**, 440
sea bed, legal status of, **21**, 11
straits used for international navigation, **21**, 10
subsoil, legal status of, **21**, 11
UK practice, **21**, 5
uninhabited islands, **11**, 76
United Nations Conferences on the Law of the Sea, **11**, 65, 70, 73, 76, 80
United Nations Convention on the Law of the Sea, *see* UNITED NATIONS CONVENTION ON THE LAW OF THE SEA
weapons exercises, **21**, 7
See also TERRITORIAL WATERS
Territorial waters
Court of Session, jurisdiction of, **4**, 2
definition, **20**, 271
extent, **20**, 271
jurisdiction of harbour authorities, **11**, 1302
offences committed in, **6**, 867
oil platform outwith, **20**, 270, 271
oil platform within, **20**, 269, 271
oil reserves in, **11**, 1302
seabed, Crown rights in, **11**, 1304
suppression of broadcasting from outside, **17**, 9
See also TERRITORIAL SEA

Territory
accretion, **19**, 670
air space, **19**, 673
avulsion, **19**, 670
cession, **19**, 669
conquest, **19**, 668, 700*n*
crimes against, **19**, 695
earldoms, **16**, 1303
occupation, **19**, 667
polar regions, **19**, 672
self-defence, force used in, **19**, 668
servitudes, **19**, 687
state, meaning, **19**, 666*n*
state recognition, prerequisite to, **19**, 666
subjugation, **19**, 668
terra nullius, **19**, 667
territorial designations, **6**, 1018
territorial integrity, respect for, **19**, 666
territorial jurisdiction, **19**, 675–684
    diplomatic immunity, **19**, 679, 681–684
    effects principle, **19**, 677
    exceptions to, **19**, 679–684
    nationality principle, **19**, 675
    passive personality principle, **19**, 676
    sovereign immunity, **19**, 679, 680
    universality principle, **19**, 678
territorial sovereignty, **19**, 666
territorial waters, see TERRITORIAL SEA; TERRITORIAL WATERS
Terrorism
act of, peril of the sea, as, **21**, 550*n*
arms, training in use of, **7**, 612
definition, **7**, 616
deterritorialism of criminal jurisdiction, **12**, 503
drilling, unlawful, **7**, 612
European Convention on the Suppression of, **12**, 508, 532; **19**, 695*n*
failure to disclose information as to, **7**, 625
financial assistance, for, **7**, 620, 621
high seas, acts on, **21**, 44
hostage order, **12**, 135
International Convention against the Taking of Hostages, **12**, 508, 532
offences relating to, **6**, 867
omission as *actus reus*, **7**, 45
outside UK, act, **7**, 621
penalties, **7**, 563
person suspected of involvement, police powers, **16**, 1801
political offence, not regarded as, **12**, 532, 532*n*
prejudicing investigation, **7**, 626, 626*n*
prevention of, **5**, 611
    exclusion order, **12**, 107, 117, 122, 134
    indefinite leave to enter, and, **12**, 177
    leave to enter, **12**, 119
    leave to remain, **12**, 119
    legislation, **7**, 565, 615–626
    port and border controls, **12**, 133
    Prevention of Terrorism (Temporary Provisions) Act, operation of, **12**, 138
proscribed organisations—
    display of public support, **7**, 619

Terrorism—*continued*
proscribed organisations—*continued*
  financial assistance—
    giving or receiving, **7**, 620
    soliciting, **7**, 620
  generally, **7**, 617
  meetings, **7**, 618
  membership, **7**, 618
    defence, **7**, 618
    outside Northern Ireland, **7**, 617
  support, **7**, 618
  terrorist funds—
    disclosure of information as to, **7**, 623, 624
    retention, control etc, **7**, 622
public order offences, **7**, 613, 614
quasi-military organisations, **7**, 613
safety order, **12**, 136
terrorist funds—
  disclosure of information as to, **7**, 623, 624
  failure to disclose information as to, **7**, 624
  meaning, **7**, 622
  retention, control etc., **7**, 622
uniform, wearing—
  generally, **7**, 614
  what constitutes, **7**, 614
Test certificate
see MOTOR VEHICLE
Testacy
adopted person—
  generally, **25**, 713
  succession by, **25**, 714
aliment, surviving spouse's right to, **25**, 711
intestacy as negative of, **25**, 630
lease, *see* LEASE-LEASING
mournings, widow's right to, **25**, 712
testate succession as specialised concept of law, **11**, 1005
Testament
term will used in preference to, **25**, 612
Testamentary capacity
child, of, **3**, 1208
exercise, **3**, 1202, 1211
young person, of, **3**, 1211
Testamentary freedom
See WILL
Testamentary trust
appointment of trustees, **24**, 140
ascertainment of trust estate, **24**, 191
comparative law, **24**, 120
completion of title, **24**, 148, 149
death of trustee, **24**, 162
death of truster, **24**, 21
delivery, **24**, 21
establishment of, **24**, 13
irrevocable nature, **24**, 75
judicial variation, **24**, 80
minor, created by, **24**, 14
revocation, **24**, 58
Testamentary writings
adoption orders, **12**, 1218
date born by, **12**, 1218
deed—
  exclusion of day of making when computing survivorship of granter, **22**, 822

Testamentary writings—*continued*
deed—*continued*
  expiry, sixty-day period, law of deathbed, **22**, 823
disposition—
  copyright, transmission by, **18**, 1027
  unregistered design right, semiconductor topographies, **18**, 1248
donation or disposition in contemplation of imminent death, **12**, 1263
donations, and, **8**, 601, 609
falsa demonstratio non nocet, **12**, 1268
interpretation, object of, **12**, 1214
latter-will, **12**, 1263
legal rights, **12**, 1264
parish minister, execution by, **3**, 1566
prior rights, **12**, 1264
rectification, recommendations as to, **13**, 71
reduction, **13**, 37
restrictions affecting, **12**, 1264
subscription, **6**, 415, 719
subsequent to probative will, **12**, 1263
testing clauses, **6**, 416
validation of doubtful, **6**, 416
words with testamentary intention, **12**, 1263
See also WILL
Testamentum militare
special latitude to, **25**, 731
Testation
See WILL
Testator
blind, notarial execution, **3**, 1566; **25**, 725
capacity of—
  circumvention, **25**, 763
  essential requirements, **25**, 761
  facility, **25**, 763
  insanity, **25**, 762
  intention to test, **25**, 765
  nonage, **25**, 761
  undue influence, **25**, 764
death, beneficiary must be known and in existence at or prior to, **25**, 934
direction of, destruction at, **25**, 745
facts material to construction of will, extrinsic evidence to prove knowledge of, **25**, 831
illiterate, notarial execution, **25**, 725
intention of—
  conditio application of, **25**, 899
  conditional institution, relating to, **25**, 893
  proof of, **25**, 833
    testator's intention to revoke will, **25**, 742
  substitution, relating to, **25**, 893
  vesting, suspension of, **25**, 932
revocation of will, *see* WILL
undue influence on, effect, **25**, 764
vesting—
  acceleration of, **25**, 955
  intention to suspend, **25**, 932
  phrases, **25**, 910
  punctuation, **25**, 910
  terms, **25**, 910
Tetanus
vaccination against, **11**, 1446

Tetrachloroethylene
content in olive oil, **11**, 370, 370*n*
Textile printer
right of lien, **20**, 78
Textiles
non-flammable or flame-resistant, safety
regulations, **6**, 63
Thalidomide
teratogenic effects, **14**, 1201
Thallium salts
special restrictions, **14**, 1216
Thane
title of, **16**, 1303
Theatre
actors, employment of, **9**, 1051
alcoholic liquor sold in, **2**, 26
children in—
    education, **9**, 1052
    licences, **9**, 1052
    safety, **9**, 1052
    school plays, **9**, 1052
    welfare, **9**, 1052
controls over, **9**, 1042
licensing, **6**, 1159; **9**, 1049; **14**, 523
    appeal to sheriff court, **14**, 119
meaning, **9**, 1043
obscenity in, **9**, 1044
order in, **9**, 1050
peace, provocation of breach of, **9**, 1046
play, meaning, **9**, 1043
prosecutions, **9**, 1048
racial hatred, incitement to, **9**, 1045
script—
    evidence of what was performed, as, **9**, 1047
    meaning, **9**, 1047
sheriff court jurisdiction, **6**, 1098
valuation for rating, **24**, 745
See also PLAY
Theft
abandoned property, **7**, 333
actus reus, **7**, 35
aggravated—
    generally, **7**, 339
    housebreaking, theft by, **7**, 339, 340, 341
    lockfast place, by opening, **7**, 339, 342
    mail, theft of, **7**, 339, 343
amotio, **7**, 329
appropriation, **7**, 322, 331, 332
    intention to appropriate must be proved, **7**, 336
    without owner's consent, must be, **7**, 335
barratry, **21**, 554*n*
capable of being stolen, object must be, **7**, 323
child, of, **7**, 328
Civic Government (Scotland) Act (1982),
    provisions under, **7**, 349
claim of right, **7**, 96
consent, relevancy, **7**, 93
destruction, by, **7**, 410
development of law, **7**, 321, 322
diminished responsibility, **7**, 150
electricity, of, **7**, 327
embezzlement, and, **7**, 350, 352
    embezzlement distinguished, **7**, 356
entitlement, defence of, **7**, 338

Theft—*continued*
finding, by, **7**, 330
firearm or imitation firearm possessed during, **10**,
    1565
furtum usus, **7**, 337, 344
guest's property, of, liability for, **11**, 1744, 1745
hired goods, of, **7**, 322
historical background, **7**, 321, 322
housebreaking, **7**, 339, 340, 341, 347
incorporeal right, document incorporating, **7**, 325
intent to commit, firearm or imitation firearm
    possessed during, **10**, 1565
intent to deprive, **7**, 78
joy-riding, **20**, 444
lockfast place, opening, **7**, 339, 342
    with intent to steal, **7**, 348
mail, of, **7**, 339, 343
mens rea—
    entitlement, defence of, **7**, 338
    furtum usus, **7**, 337
    generally, **7**, 336
money, of, **7**, 324
motor vehicle—
    taking and driving away, **20**, 444
    theft of, **7**, 336
ownership—
    fish, **7**, 333
    ownerless goods, **7**, 333
    vested in another person, must be, **7**, 334
    wild animals, **7**, 333
    without owner's consent, appropriation must
        be, **7**, 335
police court jurisdiction, **6**, 1157
presence on premises property, **7**, 349
preventive offences, **7**, 346–349
preventive powers of police, **16**, 1785, 1785*n*
refuse tip, from, **7**, 333
robbery as, **7**, 357
    See also ROBBERY
secret, of, **7**, 326
self-service store, from, **7**, 329
stolen property, right to recover, imprescriptible
    nature, **18**, 566
taking, by, **7**, 329
taking and using without owner's consent, **7**, 344,
    345
tool or other object, possession, **7**, 349, 395
transfer of ownership, in relation to, **18**, 618
trout, of, **11**, 47, 51
wheel-clamping, **7**, 332, 337
Theological college
copyright, permitted acts, *see* EDUCATION
Thermal insulation
current order, scheme and directions, **11**, 2036
finance, **11**, 2036
grants for, **11**, 2035, 2036
homes insulation scheme, **11**, 2035
Thessaloniki
free zone, as, **7**, 1164
'Thin skull' rule
criminal law, **7**, 261
Things
classification, **18**, 11
corporeal, **18**, 11

Things—*continued*
existence of entities through time, **11**, 1113
heritable, **18**, 11, 16
incorporeal, **11**, 1113; **18**, 11, 16
moveable, **18**, 11
property law as law of, **18**, 3, 3*n*, 11
rights in, *see* REAL RIGHT
rights in, property law as law of, **18**, 16
rights in and to, *see* RIGHTS
Thirlage
generally, **18**, 90*n*
servitude right, whether constituting, **18**, 492
Thoroughfare
use of term replaced by road, **20**, 609
Thought
freedom of, **12**, 73
   European Convention on Human Rights, **12**, 6, 72
   restrictions on, **12**, 78–84
   Universal Declaration of Human Rights, **12**, 4, 4*n*
Threat
assault, when amounting to, **7**, 215
breach of the peace, **7**, 398, 446, 447, 452
criminal, **7**, 251
extortion, *see* EXTORTION
firearm or imitation firearm possessed during, **10**, 1565
police officer making, **16**, 1767
uttering, **7**, 250, 251
   demands, aggravation by, **7**, 251
violent crime, to commit, Criminal Injuries Compensation Scheme, **7**, 5
Three Wise Men
appointment, **12**, 331
generally, **12**, 330
'security' deportation cases, **12**, 368
Thrift society or club
generally, **12**, 694*n*
registration, **12**, 680*n*
Ticket
air, carriage by, **3**, 740, 745
conditions, containing, **3**, 714
contractual nature, whether of, **15**, 703
rail—
   domestic carriage, **3**, 709
   international carriage, **3**, 727
road—
   domestic carriage, **3**, 672
   international carriage, **3**, 688
Tidal lands
provisional orders, **19**, 19
Tide tables
requirement for ship to carry, **21**, 229*n*
Tied accommodation
contract of employment, under, **11**, 1938; **13**, 115
intentional homelessness and, **11**, 2057
lease compared, **13**, 115
Tigni immittendi
servitude rght of, **6**, 515; **18**, 484
Tilbury Freeport
free zone, as, **7**, 1164*n*
Timber
curator bonis refused permission to fell, **24**, 247

Timber—*continued*
deterioration after refusal of felling licence, **11**, 618
felled, **18**, 12
fiar, rights of, **13**, 1660
float of, damage to harbours by, **11**, 1327
growing—
   poinding not competent against, **8**, 107, 229
   whether heritable or moveable, **18**, 12
lease, **13**, 194, 201
liferenter's rights, **13**, 1639
meaning, **11**, 608*n*
ownership of, **11**, 608
right to fell and remove, grant of, **11**, 650
sale, **11**, 608
standing, purchase of, **11**, 608
utilisation, **11**, 608
Time
'at a time', **22**, 822, 826
'at least' a specified period must elapse, **22**, 826
bills of exchange, in relation to, **4**, 112
building contracts, in, **3**, 47
clear days, meaning, **22**, 822, 823, 826
commencement of period of time—
   bankruptcy law, **22**, 822, 823
   civilis computatio, **22**, 820, 821, 822
   'commencing from (date)', **22**, 822
      See also DAY; DATE
   dies inceptus principle, **22**, 822, 823
   exceptions to general rule, **22**, 822
   exclusion *dies a quo* and *dies ad quem*, **22**, 819, 821, 822
   inclusion *dies a quo* and *dies ad quem*, **22**, 819, 821
   naturalis computatio, **22**, 820, 821
   prescriptive period, legislation, **22**, 823
complaint of unfair dismissal out of, **9**, 213
computation of—
   ambiguous phrases, **22**, 822
      See also DAY
   bankruptcy proceedings, **22**, 822
      See also BANKRUPTCY
   civilis computatio—
      commencement of period, **22**, 822
      European Convention on the Calculation of Time-Limits, **22**, 828, 831
      generally, **22**, 819, 820, 821, 822
      naturalis computatio distinguished, **22**, 820
      termination of period, **22**, 823
   commencement of period, **22**, 819, 820, 821, 822
      See also COMMENCEMENT OF PERIOD
   construction of expressions, judicial, **22**, 826
      See also DAY
   criminal procedure, **22**, 817, 819, 822
      See also CRIMINAL PROCEDURE
   date, **22**, 822, 826
      See also DATE
   day, **22**, 801–803, 815–826
      See also DAY
   development of law, **22**, 819
   dies inceptus pro completo habetur, **22**, 819, 823
   European Convention on the Calculation of Time-Limits, **22**, 828, 831

Time—*continued*
computation of—*continued*
  first day, exclusion/inclusion, **22**, 819, 820,
    821, 822
  forthwith, **12**, 1174
  last day—
    exclusion/inclusion, generally, **22**, 819, 820,
      821, 822
    part, inclusion, **22**, 819, 822
  method, **22**, 819
  naturalis computatio—
    age of majority, **22**, 820, 824
    civilis computatio distinguished, **22**, 820
    de momento in momentum, **22**, 820, 823
    generally, **22**, 819, 820, 831
    induciae commencement, **22**, 820
    prescription, **22**, 820, 823
  prescriptive periods, **22**, 823, 825
    See also PRESCRIPTION
  retroactive calculation, limits, **22**, 827, 831
  statute, in construction of, **12**, 1171–1174
    financial year, **12**, 1171
    forthwith, meaning of, **12**, 1174
    month, **12**, 1171
    period of time after, or from, event, **12**, 1173
    period of time before event, **12**, 1172
    week, **12**, 1171
  statutory provision, desirability, **22**, 819
  termination of period, **22**, 819–823, 825
  total charge for credit, of—
    annual percentage rate, **5**, 819
    generally, **5**, 818
  year and a day, **22**, 823
    See also YEAR
continuity of persons in, **11**, 1036
custom—
  'time immemorial', **22**, 372, 379, 380
  tract of time, **22**, 379–382
date—
  distinguished, **22**, 822
  See also DATE
day, *see* DAY
dies ad quem meaning, **22**, 828, 829
dies a quo meaning, **22**, 828, 829
dismissal, time of, **9**, 164
European Convention on the Calculation of
  Time-Limits—
  attainment of majority, **22**, 827
  bankruptcy law, **22**, 827
  business hours, **22**, 828
  civilis computatio, **22**, 828, 831
  contract—
    acceptance/offer, **22**, 828
    duration—
      hire/lease/employment, **22**, 827
  definitions, problems, **22**, 827
  dies ad quem definition, **22**, 828, 829
  dies a quo definition, **22**, 828, 829
  generally, **10**, 2, 2n, 4; **22**, 827–831
  limitations on scope, **22**, 827, 831
  maintenance payments, period of liability, **22**,
    827
  month, calculation, **22**, 829
  purpose, **22**, 827

Time—*continued*
European Convention on the Calculation of
  Time-Limits—*continued*
  ratification by United Kingdom, **22**, 827, 839
  retroactively calculated time limits, **22**, 827
  Scotland, effect on ratification, **22**, 830
  signatories, **22**, 827
  social security benefits, qualifying periods, **22**,
    827
  Sundays, principle of counting, **22**, 830
  week, calculation, **22**, 829
  year, calculation, **22**, 829
existence of entities through, **11**, 1113
fixed future time, meaning, **4**, 111
gap, between crime and result, **7**, 47
goods, restrictive agreement as to, **4**, 1168
Greenwich Mean Time, *see* GREENWICH MEAN TIME
holidays, *see* HOLIDAY
hour, *see* HOUR
human arrangements and, **11**, 1114
human identity, survival of, **11**, 1038
institutive rules, **11**, 1118
legal arrangements and, **11**, 1115
legal time—
  Greenwich mean time, **22**, 809
  summer time, **22**, 810
local authority meeting, of, **14**, 1312
meaning, **22**, 822
month, *see* MONTH
obligation, time span of, **11**, 1030
overall well-being of person through, **11**, 1036
prescriptive period, servitudes, **22**, 392
protest, of, **4**, 162
quarter, *see* QUARTER
retroactive calculation, limits, **22**, 827, 831
standard time, **22**, 809, 810
Summer time, *see* SUMMER TIME
Sunday, *see* SUNDAY
termination of contract by passage of, **9**, 141
termination of period—
  bankruptcy law, **22**, 823
  business hours etc, defined by, **22**, 823
  civilis computatio, **22**, 823
  contract, as term, **22**, 823
  dies inceptus principle, **22**, 823
  generally, **22**, 819, 820, 821, 822, 823
  holiday, on, **22**, 825
  last day, exclusion, **22**, 823, 825
  naturalis computatio, *de momento in momentum*,
    22, 823
  prescriptive period, where right to be
    acquired/lost by lapse, **22**, 823, 825
  presumption, **22**, 823
  right to be acquired/lost by lapse of
    prescriptive period, where, **22**, 823, 825
  Sunday, on, **22**, 825
terminative rules, **11**, 1117, 1118
time, meaning, **22**, 822
week, *see* WEEK
'within' a specified time, **22**, 826
year, *see* YEAR
zone time, **22**, 809
Time charterparty
See CHARTERPARTY

Time to pay direction or order
adjudication and, **8**, 214
arrestment and, **8**, 297
poinding and, **8**, 242
sequestration for rent unaffected by, **8**, 391
Timeshare agreement
creation, methods of, **18**, 39
generally, **18**, 39
joint proprietors, **11**, 34
lease distinguished, **13**, 112
Tincture
shield background, **11**, 1604
Tindemans Report, **10**, 378
Tinsel
generally, **15**, 804; **18**, 85
superiority, of, **18**, 86
Tippee
insider dealing, **12**, 1509, 1512, 1513
    prohibitions, **12**, 1502
meaning, **12**, 1501
off-market deals outside Great Britain, **12**, 1525
takeover offers, and, **12**, 1502, 1516
Title of honour
change of, **16**, 1304
choice, **16**, 1304, 1321
courtesy titles, **16**, 1322
divorced wife, use by, **16**, 2007
foreign, use in Scotland, **16**, 1301, 1301*n*
heritable property, as, **18**, 14
lands, identifiable with, **16**, 1304
may not be donated, **8**, 615
modern usage, **16**, 1321
modes of address, **16**, 1322
territory, associated with, **16**, 1301, 1301*n*, 1321
wife of deceased husband, use by, **16**, 2007
See also PEERAGE
Title and interest to sue
broadcasting, relating to, **1**, 317
categories of, **1**, 310
corporation, members having, **1**, 318
electors having, **1**, 316
judicial review, on, **1**, 346
licensing, in, **1**, 313
litigant having, **1**, 308
negligence claims, **3**, 154
neighbour having, **1**, 314
nuisance in—
    comparison of Scots and English law, **14**, 2023
    landlord, **14**, 2133
    other persons, **14**, 2134
    owner, **14**, 2133
    public place, invasion of rights—
        generally, **14**, 2160
        procurator fiscal, powers of, **14**, 2161
        statutory entitlement, **14**, 2162
    spouse, **14**, 2134
    tenant, **14**, 2133
persons not having, **1**, 321
planning law, under, **1**, 314
professional interests, **1**, 312
property damage, in respect of, proprietary or
    possessory interest, **3**, 154
prosecute, title to, *see* TITLE TO PROSECUTE
public rights, action to enforce, **1**, 309

Title and interest to sue—*continued*
ratepayers having, **1**, 319
statutory decision, person aggrieved by, **1**, 315
taxpayer having, **1**, 320
trading and commercial interests, **1**, 311
unincorporated association, members having, **1**,
    318
See also TITLE TO SUE
Title sheet
amendment of, **6**, 713
application for, **6**, 712
Burdens Section, **6**, 707, 711
Charges Section, **6**, 707, 710
description of land, **6**, 708
enforceable real right, **6**, 707, 708
incorrect entry in, **6**, 761
interest in land, of, **6**, 707
land certificate, **6**, 713
office copy, **6**, 712
overriding interests, **6**, 711
plan of land involved, **6**, 708
Property Section, **6**, 707, 708
Proprietorship Section, **6**, 707, 709
Title to property
all sums clause, **18**, 638
'as it stands', buyer's agreement to accept
    heritage, **20**, 919
building contract, and—
    common interests, **3**, 159
    private or public rights affecting site, **3**, 159
    real burden or conditions, **3**, 159
    rights of way, **3**, 159
    servitudes, **3**, 159
    support, right of, **3**, 159
competing—
    'offside goals', rule against—
        antecedent contract or obligation, where, **18**,
            696
        breach, **18**, 698, 700
        remedies, **18**, 700
    bad faith, **18**, 699
    double grants, **18**, 697
    equity, founded on, **18**, 700
    generally, **18**, 695
    personal rights in competition with real
        rights, **18**, 690, 693, 694
    remedies, **18**, 700
    value, absence of, **18**, 699
    warrandice, breach of, **18**, 697, 697*n*
real rights—
    competition with personal rights—
        grant in breach of trust, **18**, 691
        grantee not bound by personal obligations
            of author, **18**, 688
        granter's power to grant unimpaired by
            personal obligations, **18**, 689
        'offside goals', rule against, **18**, 690, 693,
            694
        secured creditors, **18**, 693
        unsecured creditors, **18**, 694
        voidable title, grant by one holding, **18**, 692
    competition with real rights—
        first completion, rule of, **18**, 684
        Land Register of Scotland titles, **18**, 685

Title to property—*continued*
competing—*continued*
  real rights—*continued*
    competition with real rights—*continued*
      last completion, rule of, **18**, 685
      rights in security, **18**, 686
      subordinate real rights, transferee affected
        by, **18**, 687
completion, feudal law, **18**, 93
compulsory purchase, taking title on—
  disposition in common form, by, **5**, 81
  general vesting declaration, *see* GENERAL
    VESTING DECLARATION
  generally, **5**, 81–90
  methods, **5**, 81
  notarial instrument, by, **5**, 81, 89
  statutory conveyance, by, **5**, 83–88
  See also STATUTORY CONVEYANCE
conditional sale agreement, **20**, 855
*decennalis et triennalis possessor non tenetur docere de
  titulo*, **3**, 1572
deed of land, pledge of, ineffectual, **20**, 15
defects of title—
  force and fear, **4**, 150
  fraud, **4**, 150
document of—
  contract of deposit, **8**, 4
  meaning, **18**, 621*n*
  transfer, **18**, 621
    equivalent to delivery, as, **20**, 860
    from buyer on seller's remedies for breach,
      effect, **20**, 880
feudalisation, **18**, 93
guarantee, *see* WARRANDICE
heritable property, to—
  common title to, **6**, 713
  compulsory purchase, *see* compulsory purchase
    above
  land certificate as title deed, **6**, 713
  local authority title to, **14**, 318
  notice of, **6**, 613
  ranking, **6**, 785
  recorded, disposition by person without, **6**, 589
hire purchase contract, **20**, 855
implied terms as to, contract of sale for moveable
  property, **20**, 821
incapax of, recovery, **11**, 1225
incorporeal property, fraudulent transfer of title
  deeds, **11**, 769
marketable, seller's duty to give, **20**, 918
mercantile agent, acquisition through, **20**, 849
moveable property, to, in truste estate, **24**, 148,
  157
nemo dat quod non habet rule, *see* TRANSFER OF
  OWNERSHIP
publication or event, of—
  passing off, **18**, 1378
registration—
  competing titles—
    rule of first completion, **18**, 684
    rule of last completion, **18**, 685
  original acquisition, as, **18**, 597
See also REGISTRATION OF TITLE
reservation of, **18**, 638; **20**, 842

Title to property—*continued*
reversion of—
  property held by education authority, **8**, 735
  School Sites Act 1841 ..., **8**, 839
Romalpa clause, **18**, 628, 638
sheet, *see* TITLE SHEET
sheriff court, jurisdiction of, **4**, 6
subsistent, *nemo dat quod non habet* rule, **18**, 669
sue, title and interest to, *see* TITLE AND INTEREST
  TO SUE
transfer of ownership—
  nemo dat quod non habet rule, *see* TRANSFER OF
    OWNERSHIP
  personal rights, **18**, 669
  subordinate real rights and conditions, **18**, 669
transmission of on death, **6**, 608–613
  confirmation, restriction to executry estate, **25**,
    1071
  disposition, by, **6**, 610
  executor's, completion of, **6**, 608, 611
  owners domiciled outwith Scotland, **6**, 612
  protection of persons acquiring on, **25**, 1110
trust, completion of title in estate—
  generally, **24**, 147
  heritable property, **6**, 609; **24**, 149, 157
  moveable property, **24**, 148, 157
void, **18**, 601
  real vice, where, **18**, 614
voidable, **18**, 601, 607; **20**, 848
  avoidance, **18**, 692
  grant of, competing titles, **18**, 692
  holder of, legal position, **18**, 692
  meaning, **18**, 692
  nemo dat quod non habet rule, *see* TRANSFER OF
    OWNERSHIP
  reduction, **18**, 692
  vice of consent, where, **18**, 614
warrandice, *see* WARRANDICE
Title to prosecute
Crown Agent—
  procurator fiscal service, supervision of, **17**, 540
  solicitors to Lord Advocate, as, **17**, 539
Crown counsel, **17**, 537
Lord Advocate, *see* LORD ADVOCATE
private prosecution, **17**, 526
procurator fiscal, *see* PROCURATOR FISCAL
public prosecution, **17**, 526
public prosecutor, *see* PUBLIC PROSECUTOR
Solicitor General, **17**, 537
Tlatelco Treaty, 19, 712
Tobacco
advertising, **1**, 547
British Code of Advertising Practice, **6**, 93
child, purchase by, **3**, 1225; **10**, 1126
duty, tobacco products, **19**, 1543
manufactured—
  chewing tobacco, **7**, 1072*n*, 1097
  cigarette, length, **7**, 1072
  duty—
    calculation, **7**, 1072
    rates, **7**, 1072
    remission or repayment, **7**, 1072
  European Union excise law, **7**, 1035, 1036
  hand-rolling tobacco, **7**, 1072*n*

Tobacco—*continued*
manufactured—*continued*
  imported, **7**, 1072
  tobacco products—
    manufactured in UK, **7**, 1072
    meaning, **7**, 1072*n*
    medical advice as to use, **11**, 1446
    regional and islands council duties, **3**, 1225
    sale to person under age of sixteen, **3**, 1225
    Tobacco Products Duty Act 1979 ..., **7**, 1072
meat and food handlers, hygiene regulations, **11**, 415
prisoner, supply to, **16**, 1452, 1466
weights and measures legislation, **6**, 246

Tocher
feudal law, avail of marriage, **18**, 76

Toilet preparations
weights and measures legislation, **6**, 241

Toll
bridge, **14**, 33
  generally, **20**, 607
  valuation for rating, **20**, 722; **24**, 580, 581
canal byelaws, **19**, 1107
funeral procession, exemption, **3**, 526
lease, **13**, 206

Toll road
access, **20**, 633
amount of toll, **20**, 632
collection of toll, **20**, 632
  suspension, **20**, 632
construction, contract for, **20**, 636
  report on, by Secretary of State, **20**, 637
crossings, **20**, 633
design, contract for, **20**, 636
  report on, by Secretary of State, **20**, 637
evasion of toll payment, **20**, 632
exemptions from liability for toll, **20**, 632
extension toll order, **20**, 631
failure to pay toll, **20**, 632
major crossing, **20**, 633
  meaning, **20**, 633*n*
maximum toll chargeable, **20**, 632
monopolies, **20**, 645
order, **20**, 629
  assignation of rights under, **20**, 630, 631, 634
  crossings, **20**, 633
  objections to, **20**, 629
  report on, by Secretary of State, **20**, 637
  revocation, **20**, 634
  variation, **20**, 634
private, future policy as to, **20**, 607
rating, exemption from, **20**, 629
report on, by Secretary of State, **20**, 637
special roads, **20**, 629
toll period, **20**, 631
turnpike roads, **14**, 33
valuation and rating, **20**, 722

Tomato ketchup
food standard, **11**, 353

Tombstones
historical background to use, **3**, 501
preservation and maintenance, **3**, 519
right to erect, **3**, 524

Tort
See DELICT

Torture
Convention against, **19**, 695*n*
definition, **12**, 26
European Convention on Human Rights, **12**, 6, 26; **16**, 1806
European Convention for the Prevention of Torture and Inhuman or Degrading Treatment or Punishment, **12**, 27
inhuman and degrading treatment distinguished, **12**, 26
international conventions on, **12**, 5

Totalisator Board
contributions to levy scheme, **2**, 1556
levy on, *see* HORSERACE BETTING LEVY BOARD

Tourism
area tourist board, scheme for, **14**, 664
British Tourist Authority—
  duty of, **11**, 1802
  establishment, **11**, 1797
  financial assistance for tourist projects, **11**, 1803
  functions and powers, **11**, 1798
  membership, **11**, 1797
  promotion of tourism, **11**, 1796, 1798
collaboration between districts, **11**, 1795
district council, powers of, **14**, 662
expenditure programme, **5**, 579
financial assistance to aid, **11**, 1794, 1805–1810
Forestry Commission, provision of facilities by, **11**, 610
immigration controls, **12**, 101, 102
islands council, powers of, **14**, 662
local authorities' powers and duties, **11**, 1793–1795
promotion of, **11**, 1793, 1796, 1797
recreation, **14**, 46
regional council, power to make financial contributions, **14**, 663
registration of tourist accommodation, **11**, 1811
Scottish Tourist Board—
  assistance provided by, **2**, 1285
  co-operation with other bodies, **11**, 1801
  duties, **11**, 1802
  establishment, **11**, 1797
  expenditure by, financial provision in respect of, **11**, 1814
  functions, **11**, 1798
  powers, **11**, 1799–1804
  promotion of tourism by, **11**, 1796, 1798
  tourist projects, execution of, **11**, 1804
tourist boards, generally, **11**, 1796, 1797

Tow
collision regulations, more than one vessel, **21**, 362
contract, generally, **21**, 401
damage claim by third party, responsibility for, **21**, 409
delict, generally, **21**, 401
dispute over, **20**, 305
duties of, **21**, 407
fit to be towed, must be, **21**, 407
flotilla—
  command of, **21**, 408
  relationship to third parties, **21**, 401

Tow—*continued*

general average in situation of tug and tow, **21**, 703

goods under, salvage subject, **21**, 436, 453

implied terms as to, in towage contract, **21**, 407

manned, **21**, 408

motor vehicle in, *see* MOTOR VEHICLE

possessory lien for, **20**, 303

pushing, definition of towage, **21**, 402

restricted manoeuvrability, vessel with, lights and shapes to be diplayed, **21**, 365

towage—

  actions in respect of, **21**, 423

  charges, damages claims, **21**, 386

  contract—

    charterparty, when expressed as, **21**, 403, 403*n*

    classification, **21**, 403

    contract to perform towage—

      command of flotilla, **21**, 408

      duties of tow, **21**, 407

      express terms, **21**, 410

      implied terms, **21**, 406

      manning and equipment implied terms, **21**, 406

      named or unnamed tug, whether, **21**, 406

      reasonable care, implied term, **21**, 406

      responsibility for damage caused, **21**, 409

    crew, **21**, 403

    delict, law of, **21**, 404

    demise charterparty, **21**, 403

    express terms—

      where no, **21**, 403, 404

    hire of tug, for, **21**, 403, 405, 406

    implied terms, **21**, 404

    oral, **21**, 403

    parties to, **21**, 413

    performance of towage, for, **21**, 403, 406

    tug under, whether entitled to salvage award, **21**, 453

    written, **21**, 403

  definition, **21**, 402

  generally, **21**, 401

  maritime cause, as, **1**, 411

  maritime lien, whether giving rise to, **1**, 413

  performance of towage, for—

    implied terms, **21**, 406

    named or unnamed tug, **21**, 406

  services, VAT zero-rating, **7**, 1452

towing, definition, **21**, 412

towing light, **21**, 361*n*

tug—

  relationship with, express terms, **21**, 410

  See also TUG

tugowner—

  liability, **21**, 411, 414–417

    limitation, **21**, 420

United Kingdom Standard Towing Conditions (UKSTC)—

  choice of law, **21**, 422

  exclusion clauses, **21**, 411

  exemption clause, **21**, 415

    where not applicable, **21**, 416

  generally, **21**, 411, 411*n*

Tow—*continued*

United Kingdom Standard Towing Conditions (UKSTC)—*continued*

  indemnity provisions, **21**, 411, 418

  jurisdiction, **21**, 422

  liability of tugowner and tow owner, **21**, 411, 414–417

    limitation, **21**, 420

  parties to contract, **21**, 413

  pro hac vice employment clause, **21**, 411, 414

  salvage, right to, **21**, 420

  scope of operations, **21**, 412

  substitution clause, **21**, 419

  tugowner's employees, protection, **21**, 421

unmanned, **21**, 408

vessel under, collision regulations, **21**, 361, 362

  sound signals, **21**, 374

whilst towing, definition, **21**, 412

Town clerk

appointment of, **14**, 249

Town and country planning

action area, **23**, 30, 45

administration—

  central government—

    Scottish Office, relationship between planning authorities and, **23**, 7

    Secretary of State for Scotland, powers of, **23**, 4–6

    See also Secretary of State *below*

  EC legislation, effects of, **23**, 20, 325

  local government—

    community council, establishment of, **23**, 17

    district planning authority, *see* district planning authority *below*

    Montgomery Committee, **23**, 15

    planning authority, **23**, 12–17

      See also PLANNING AUTHORITY

    reform, **23**, 8, 10

    regional planning authority, *see* regional planning authority *below*

    Stodart Committee, **23**, 14

    two-tier division, origins, **23**, 9

  public sector agencies, **23**, 18–19

adverse planning decision—

  appeal, *see* appeal *below*

  Court of Session, appeal to—

    generally, **6**, 924; **23**, 270

    non-statutory challenge, **23**, 277–279

    statutory application to quash, **23**, 271–276

  development plan, **23**, 261

  examination in public, **23**, 263

  generally, **23**, 259

  inquiry, **23**, 264–265

  maladministration, **23**, 280–282

  natural justice, **23**, 268

  private hearing, **23**, 267

  procedure rules, **23**, 268

  public inquiry, **23**, 265

  purchase notice, *see* purchase notice *below*

  quicker decisions, **23**, 269

  Secretary of State, role of, **23**, 260

  written submissions, **23**, 266

advertisement, *see* ADVERTISEMENT

aerodrome, planning controls, **9**, 1285

Town and country planning—*continued*
aggrieved person, meaning, **23**, 63, 272
agricultural land, meaning, **23**, 147
agricultural tenant, notified of planning
    application, **23**, 163
amenity, **23**, 226
ancillary and incidental uses, **23**, 76
appeal—
    administrative—
        appealable decisions, **23**, 262
        Commissioner for Local Administration in
            Scotland, **23**, 282
        development plan, **23**, 261
        examination in public, **23**, 263
        generally, **23**, 259
        inquiry, **23**, 264, 265
        natural justice, **23**, 268
        Parliamentary Commissioner for Admin-
            istration, **23**, 281
        private hearing, **23**, 267
        procedure rules, **23**, 268
        public inquiry, **23**, 265
        quicker decisions, **23**, 269
        Secretary of State, role in respect of adverse
            planning decision, **14**, 112; **23**, 266
        written submission, **23**, 266
    advertisement, control of, **23**, 197
    Court of Session—
        adverse planning decision, **23**, 270–279
        development plan, **23**, 63
        enterprise zone scheme, **23**, 114
        planning authority, consideration of bias by,
            23, 112
        simplified planning zone, **23**, 118
    enforcement notice, against, *see* enforcement
        notice *below*
    listed building, relating to, **23**, 184
    non-statutory material, decisions made by
        Secretary of State as, **23**, 3
    similar pending application, effect on, **23**, 224
    See also adverse planning decision *above*
associated services, **14**, 46
bad neighbour development, **23**, 164
blight notice, *see* BLIGHT NOTICE
British Coal Corporation, role in, **23**, 19, 169, 231
building operations, *see* BUILDING AND BUILDING
    CONTROLS
building preservation notice, **23**, 181
caravan/caravan site, *see* CARAVAN
codes of practice, **23**, 34, 263, 264, 266
compensation—
    advertisement, control of, **23**, 200
    blight notice, *see* BLIGHT NOTICE
    conditions relating to, **23**, 246
    entitlement to, **23**, 309
    established development value, unexpended
        balances of, **23**, 324
    European Convention on Human Rights,
        arising under, **23**, 325
    listed building, relating to, **23**, 186
    minerals, controls relating to, **23**, 218
    new development, **23**, 323, 324
    planning permission, revocation or modifi-
        cation, **23**, 176

Town and country planning—*continued*
compensation—*continued*
    prohibition order may give rise to, **23**, 215
    purchase notice, *see* PURCHASE NOTICE
    stop notice, arising from, **23**, 307
    tree preservation order, **23**, 203
compulsory purchase—
    general vesting declaration, **5**, 46–49
    generally, **5**, 44, 45
    leases, land subject to, **5**, 53
    notice to treat, restriction on power to
        withdraw, **5**, 50
    rentcharges, land subject to, **5**, 52
    severance, **5**, 51
    statutory undertakers, land acquired by, **5**, 55
    title, person retaining documents, **5**, 54
conditions—
    breach of condition notice, **23**, 290*n*
    developer, requiring contribution from, **23**, 246
    discharge of, **23**, 250
    existing use rights, interference with, **23**, 245
    invalid, severance of, **23**, 249
    legality of, **23**, 239
    occupancy, restricting, **23**, 242
    permitted development, **23**, 135, 137, 241
    planning purpose, required to be imposed for,
        23, 240
    reasonableness, **23**, 243
    site licence, of, **23**, 334, 336
    statutory power to impose, **23**, 238
    time limits, imposing, **23**, 251
    uncertain, **23**, 248
    unenforceable, **23**, 244
    unnecessary, **23**, 247
conservation area, *see* CONSERVATION AREA
Crown land, *see* CROWN LAND
development—
    cessation of use, **23**, 80–83
    details of, **23**, 233
    economic viability of, **23**, 232
    General Development Order, *see* GENERAL
        DEVELOPMENT ORDER
    impact of, **23**, 226
    land, meaning, **23**, 64
    meaning, **14**, 614; **23**, 64, 208
    need for, **23**, 230
    new, **23**, 323, 324
    non-agricultural, **23**, 230
    operational, *see* OPERATIONAL DEVELOPMENT
    operations not constituting, **23**, 68
    order, *see* DEVELOPMENT ORDER
    permitted, *see* PERMITTED DEVELOPMENT
    planning permission for, *see* PLANNING
        PERMISSION
    significance of, **23**, 65
    siting of, **23**, 231
    statutory definition, **23**, 64
    use, *see* USE
development control—
    decision-making, **23**, 16
    development plan, importance of, **23**, 22
    legal framework of—
        advertisement, control of, *see* ADVERTISEMENT
        conservation area, *see* CONSERVATION AREA

Town and country planning—_continued_
development control—_continued_
  legal framework—_continued_
    Crown land, see CROWN LAND
    enterprise zone, see ENTERPRISE ZONE
    environmental impact assessment, see
      environmental impact assessment _below_
    hazardous substances consent, see HAZARDOUS
      SUBSTANCES
    industrial development certificate, **23**, 205
    listed building control, see LISTED BUILDING
    minerals, additional controls relating to, see
      minerals _below_
    office development permit, **23**, 206
    permitted development, see PERMITTED
      DEVELOPMENT
    planning authority, development by, see
      PLANNING AUTHORITY
    planning permission, see PLANNING PERMISSION
    simplified planning zone, see simplified
      planning zone _below_
    tree preservation, **23**, 190, 202, 203
    waste land, **23**, 204
  development order, see also General Development
    Order _below_
  development order—
    general, **23**, 132
    planning permission by—
      general order, **23**, 132
      generally, **23**, 131
      hazardous substances, **23**, 136
      permitted development, **23**, 133–138
      resumption of use after, **23**, 103
      special order, **23**, 132
      time limits, **23**, 251
    special, **23**, 132, 369
  development plan—
    administrative appeal, **23**, 261
    Court of Session, application to, **23**, 63
    Crown land may be included in, **23**, 105
    default powers of Secretary of State, **23**, 61
    development control process, importance in,
      23, 22
    directions, Secretary of State's power to give,
      23, 62
    local plan, see local plan _below_
    material considerations taken into account, **23**,
      222
    meaning, **23**, 21
    new-style, transition from old-style develop-
      ment plan to, **23**, 25
    objections to decision, **23**, 261
    old-style, transition to new-style development
      plan, **23**, 25
    planning authority required to produce, **23**, 22
    public participation in preparation of, **23**, 23
    questioning validity of, **23**, 63
    reform, **23**, 23
    regional report, **23**, 26
    regulations, Secretary of State's power to make,
      23, 62
    role of, **23**, 22
    Secretary of State, additional powers of, **23**, 61,
      62

Town and country planning—_continued_
development plan—_continued_
  Skeffington Report, **23**, 24
  structure plan, see STRUCTURE PLAN
  validity of, **23**, 63
district planning authority, **14**, 615; **23**, 11, 16
district planning functions, **23**, 11
dwelling house, see DWELLING HOUSE
electricity, planning controls on developments in
  connection with, **9**, 659–661
enforcement—
  advertisement, control of, **23**, 198
  generally, **23**, 283
  interdict and, **23**, 308
  listed building, provisions relating to, **23**, 187
  minerals, controls relating to, **23**, 217
  notice, see enforcement notice _below_
  proceedings, see ENFORCEMENT PROCEEDINGS
  regional planning authority, by, **23**, 286
  Secretary of State, by, **23**, 285
  unenforceable conditions, **23**, 244
enforcement notice—
  appeal against, **23**, 294–297
  content of, **23**, 290
  court proceedings, challenging in, **23**, 300
  defective service of, **23**, 292
  defects in, **23**, 293
  form of, **23**, 290
  land, effect on, **23**, 303
  meaning, **23**, 104n
  non-compliance with, **23**, 283n, 301, 302
  register of, **23**, 304
  resumption of lawful use after service of, **23**,
    104
  Secretary of State, challenging decision of, **23**,
    299
  service of, **23**, 291, 292
  stop notice, **23**, 305–307
enforcement proceedings—
  commencement of, **23**, 284
  Crown land, development on, **23**, 105
  established use certificate, **23**, 288, 289
  immunity from, **23**, 287
  power to commence, **23**, 284
enterprise zone, see ENTERPRISE ZONE
environmental impact assessment—
  aerodrome, **23**, 123
  agriculture, **23**, 124
  Annex 1 development, **23**, 123
  Annex 2 development, **23**, 124
  asbestos installation, **23**, 123
  cast-iron works, **23**, 123
  chemical industry, **23**, 124
  chemical installation, **23**, 123
  crude-oil refinery, **23**, 123
  effects, meaning, **23**, 125n
  energy industry, **23**, 124
  enterprise zone established after 1 July 1988 ...,
    23, 114
  environmental information, meaning, **23**, 122n
  environmental statement, **23**, 125–129
  extractive industry, **23**, 124
  food industry, **23**, 124
  full planning permission, **23**, 127

Town and country planning—_continued_
environmental impact assessment—_continued_
  generally, **23**, 121
  glass making, **23**, 124
  infrastructure project, **23**, 124
  inland waterway, **23**, 123
  leather industry, **23**, 124
  metal processing, **23**, 124
  nature of, **23**, 121
  need for, **23**, 110
  neighbouring land, meaning, **23**, 128n
  other projects, **23**, 124
  outline planning permission, **23**, 127
  paper industry, **23**, 124
  planning authority—
    decision by, **23**, 130
    meaning, **23**, 122n
  planning permission—
    full, **23**, 127
    outline, **23**, 127
    specified categories of development for, **23**, 122
  publicity for, **23**, 110n
  radioactive waste installation, **23**, 123
  railway line, **23**, 123
  reporter, meaning, **23**, 122n
  road, **23**, 123
  rubber industry, **23**, 124
  steel works, **23**, 123
  textile industry, **23**, 124
  thermal power station, **23**, 123
  trading port, **23**, 123
  waste-disposal installation, **23**, 123
  wood industry, **23**, 124
established use—
  certificate of, **23**, 288, 289
  nature of, **23**, 80
General Development Order—
  effect of, **23**, 99
  existing use rights, interference with, **23**, 245
  hazardous substances, **23**, 136
  planning authority, development by, **23**, 109
  statutory undertaker, development by, **23**, 18
  See also PERMITTED DEVELOPMENT
general vesting declaration, **5**, 46–49
green belt—
  listed building, _see_ LISTED BUILDING
  occupancy, conditions restricting, **23**, 242
  simplified planning zone scheme, exclusion from, **23**, 119
guidelines, **23**, 3
harbour, development of, **11**, 1316; **23**, 153
hazardous substances, **23**, 219–220
  See also HAZARDOUS SUBSTANCES
Health and Safety Executive, consultation with, **23**, 169
Historic Buildings Council for Scotland, inspection of listed building, **23**, 183
historical background, **23**, 1
industrial development certificate, repeal, **23**, 205
Industrial Pollution Inspectorate, consultation regarding environmental statement, **23**, 129
industrial process, **23**, 95, 149

Town and country planning—_continued_
industrial undertaker, **23**, 149
legislation, **5**, 44, 45; **23**, 2
listed building, _see_ LISTED BUILDING
local plan—
  action area plan, **23**, 45
  adoption of, **23**, 56
  alteration of, **23**, 60
  approval of, **23**, 57
  consultation, **14**, 618; **23**, 50
  content of, **23**, 43
  form of, **23**, 43
  index map, **23**, 59
  inquiry—
    code of practice, **23**, 263, 264
    generally, **23**, 53
    procedure, **23**, 264
    procedure where none held, **23**, 54
  nature of, **23**, 42
  non-statutory policies embodied in, **23**, 223
  objections to, **23**, 52
  preparation of—
    procedure following, **23**, 51
    structure plan, in advance of, **23**, 47
  proposed modifications, **23**, 55
  public inspection, **23**, 58
  publicity requirements, **23**, 23, 50
  purpose of, **23**, 22, 42
  regional planning authority, powers of, **14**, 620, 621; **23**, 48
  street authorisation map adopted as, **23**, 25
  structure plan, **23**, 9, 46, 47
  subject plan, preparation of, **23**, 44
  survey, **23**, 49
  validity of, **23**, 63
local planning and strategic planning distinguished, **23**, 9
maladministration, **23**, 280–282
material change of use, _see_ USE
minerals—
  compensation, **23**, 218
  development, meaning, **23**, 208
  discontinuance of use, **23**, 214
  enforcement, **23**, 217
  meaning, **23**, 71
  periodical review of workings, **23**, 212
  planning permission, **23**, 209–213
  prohibition order, **23**, 215
  Stevens Report, **23**, 207
  suspension order, **23**, 216
  Use Classes Order, operation of, **23**, 91
national planning guidelines—
  decision-making influenced by, **23**, 234
  Scottish Development department, issued by, **23**, 3
  Secretary of State, informal powers of, **23**, 6
national scenic area—
  meaning, **23**, 142n
  planning application, notification of, **23**, 166
  satellite antenna, installation of, **23**, 142
  simplified planning zone scheme, exclusion from, **23**, 119

Town and country planning—*continued*
Nature Conservancy Council—
  planning application, consultation over, **23**, 169
  planning system, role in, **23**, 19
new town, *see* NEW TOWN
New Town Development Corporation, *see* NEW
  TOWN DEVELOPMENT CORPORATION
noise, planning control and, **9**, 1284; **23**, 233
operational development—
  building, meaning, **23**, 69
  building operations, **23**, 69
  demolition, **23**, 73
  development, meaning, **23**, 64
  engineering operations, **23**, 70
  material change of use distinguished from, **23**,
    66
  meaning, **23**, 67
  means of access, meaning, **23**, 70
  mining operations, **23**, 71
  operations not constituting development, **23**,
    68
  other operations, **23**, 72
  rebuilding operations, **23**, 69
  structural operations, **23**, 69
  structure or erection, **23**, 69
permitted development, *see* PERMITTED
  DEVELOPMENT
person aggrieved, meaning, **23**, 63, 272
pier, development of, **23**, 153
planning application, *see* PLANNING APPLICATION
planning authority, *see* PLANNING AUTHORITY
planning permission, *see* PLANNING PERMISSION
public health, planning controls, **19**, 305, 359, 360
regional planning authority—
  call-in powers, **14**, 621; **23**, 14
  default powers, **14**, 622
  district planning authority and, **14**, 615; **23**, 13
  enforcement by, **23**, 286
  local plans, reserve powers regarding, **14**, 620;
    23, 14
  meaning, **23**, 11
  planning application, reference to, **23**, 168
  regional planning functions, **14**, 615; **23**, 11, 13
  regional report, **23**, 26
right of way, creation of public, **18**, 504
Scottish Development Department, *see* SCOTTISH
  DEVELOPMENT DEPARTMENT
Secretary of State for Scotland—
  adverse planning decision, role in respect of,
    23, 260
  appeal, **14**, 628
  approval required, **14**, 627
  circulars, issue of, **14**, 626; **23**, 6
  default powers, **14**, 627; **23**, 5, 61
  development plan, additional powers relating
    to, **14**, 624; **23**, 61, 62
  directions, power to give, **14**, 625; **23**, 5, 62
  enforcement by, **23**, 285
  enforcement notice, challenging decision in
    appeal against, **23**, 299
  local plan, approval of, **23**, 57
  minister, meaning, **23**, 328
  national planning guidelines, issues of, **14**, 626;
    23, 6

Town and country planning—*continued*
Secretary of State for Scotland—*continued*
  new town development corporation, payments
    by, **23**, 382
  notice of intention to develop, procedure on
    receipt of, **23**, 109
  permitted development, directions restricting,
    23, 134
  planning application, **23**, 166–169
  powers of, generally, **14**, 623; **23**, 5, 6
  structure plan, and, **14**, 619, 627; **23**, 32–36
servitude rights, and, **18**, 480
sheriff court jurisdiction, **6**, 1134; **23**, 354
simplified planning zone—
  generally, **23**, 116
  meaning, **23**, 117
  scheme, **23**, 116–120
structure plan—
  action area, designation of, **23**, 30
  alteration of, **23**, 39–41
  approval by Secretary of State, **14**, 105, 627
  calling-in powers, **14**, 621
  consultation, **14**, 618; **23**, 31, 40
  contents of, **23**, 29
  default powers, **14**, 622
  examination in public, **14**, 619; **23**, 34
  index map, **23**, 38
  local plan, **23**, 9, 46, 47
  nature of, **23**, 27
  objections, **14**, 619
  old development plan conflicting with, **23**, 25
  public inspection of, **23**, 37
  publicity, **23**, 31, 40
  purpose of, **23**, 22, 27
  regional report, basis of, **23**, 26
  regional survey, **23**, 28
  register, **23**, 38
  sale of, **23**, 37
  Secretary of State, **14**, 619, 627; **23**, 32–36
  submission of, **14**, 619; **23**, 32
  validity of, **23**, 63
tree preservation, **23**, 202–203
waste land, **23**, 204
Wheatley Report, **23**, 8, 9
  See also WHEATLEY REPORT

Town lands
compulsory acquisition or use, **19**, 12, 19
meaning, **19**, 12*n*

Township reorganisation scheme
enlargement of croft by, **1**, 799
provisions in, **1**, 820

Toxic waste
EEC directives on, **9**, 1178

Tractor
agricultural—
  licence to drive, **20**, 447
    age limit, **20**, 448
  whether motor vehicle, **20**, 405
licence to drive, age limit, **3**, 1229; **20**, 448
motor, **20**, 407

Trade
association, *see* TRADE ASSOCIATION
burgh, privileges of, **14**, 12
charity, carried on by, taxation, *see* CHARITY

Trade—*continued*
custom, **25**, 25
deceased, of, receipts attributable to, **25**, 976
deceased's income from, liability to tax, **25**, 965
description, *see* TRADE DESCRIPTIONS
effluent—
  consent, **25**, 417
    appeal in respect of, **25**, 445
    review, **25**, 446
  discharge—
    consent to, **25**, 417
    existing—
      meaning, **25**, 447
      new discharge distinguished, **25**, 441
    lawful, **25**, 411
    new—
      agreements relating to, **25**, 443
      consent to, **25**, 444
      existing discharge distinguished, **25**, 441
      meaning, **25**, 442
    prohibition of, **25**, 410
    sewers, into, **9**, 330, 333, 334
  generally, **25**, 408
  meaning, **25**, 409
  See also POLLUTION
established business, meaning, **19**, 374
expenditure programme, **5**, 579
fixtures, **14**, 1074
marks, *see* TRADE MARK
meaning, **4**, 1315
offensive or dangerous—
  celluloid and cinematograph film, **19**, 412–419
  established without sanction, **19**, 376
  inflammable or dangerous substances, **19**, 383–411
  meaning of offensive trade, **19**, 373
  nuisance, complaints as to, **19**, 378
  public health provisions, **19**, 306, 373–443
  rag flock and other filling materials, **19**, 420–443
  regulation, **19**, 377
  sanction to establish, **19**, 375
  slaughterhouses, **19**, 373, 379–382
  smells from, **9**, 1120
premises—
  emission of smoke, defence to charge of, **9**, 1125
  meaning, **5**, 832
  meter charges, **25**, 536
  off, canvassing, **5**, 832
public health nuisance, **19**, 336
records, evidence, as, **10**, 502, 603, 605, 608
restraint of, *see* RESTRAINT OF TRADE
royal burgh, monopoly of, **14**, 12, 19
supplies in course of, charge to VAT, **7**, 1295
United Nations Commission on International Trade Law, **19**, 650
waste, collection of, **9**, 1168
Trade and Industry, Department of
consumer protection, **6**, 11, 69
creation of, **5**, 513
EU company law proposals, regular bulletin on progress in, **4**, 311*n*
functions of, **5**, 513

Trade and Industry, Department of—*continued*
insider dealing, power to investigate, **4**, 306
investigation, consideration of potential cases for, **4**, 523
provisional order, copies of, **19**, 20
shares, beneficial ownership of, power to investigate, **4**, 357
Supply of Beer Orders, **4**, 1119
Trial of Pyx, **14**, 1821
weights and measures standards, **6**, 181
See also SECRETARY OF STATE FOR TRADE AND INDUSTRY
insurance company—
  authorisation, **12**, 807
  intervention into business of, **12**, 808
Trade association
agreement, activities deemed to give rise to, **4**, 1129
company limited by guarantee, formation of, **4**, 312
consumer redress, dispute resolution, **6**, 172
discrimination, liability for, **9**, 343
goods, restrictive agreement as to, **4**, 1147
meaning, **4**, 1147
passing off action brought by, **18**, 1363
public interest, restrictions contrary to, **4**, 1191
restraint of trade doctrine, **4**, 1218
standard form contract, **4**, 1142
supplementary provisions, **4**, 1174
Trade descriptions
accommodation, **6**, 126, 142
advertising, in—
  generally, **6**, 105, 123, 124, 135
  price advertising, **6**, 142
animals, **6**, 120
brochures, **11**, 1783
'by-pass' provision, **6**, 138
commercial counterfeiting, **6**, 118
composition, as to, **6**, 116
criminal offences, **6**, 105
defences—
  due diligence, **6**, 135, 136, 137
  generally, **6**, 135
definition of terms, **6**, 105
disclaimers, relevance of, **6**, 114
enforcement of legislation, **6**, 104, 139
exceptions, **6**, 121
facilities, of, **6**, 126, 142
false—
  advertisements containing, **17**, 45
  applying, **1**, 510
  meaning of, **6**, 113, 127
  prohibition of, **6**, 106
false representations—
  Queen's Award to Industry, **6**, 133
  royal approval, **6**, 133
false statement—
  made during course of business, **6**, 129
  when communicated, **6**, 124
fault of another person, offences due to, **6**, 138
fitness for purpose, as to, **6**, 117
food, in relation to, **11**, 316
fraud, **7**, 382

Trade descriptions—*continued*
free gifts, **6**, 126
generally, **6**, 104; **11**, 1782
goods, meaning, **6**, 112
hallmarking, **18**, 1418, 1418*n*
imported goods, **6**, 132
'in the course of ordinary trade or business', **6**, 107
liability, **6**, 128
limited companies subject to legislation, **6**, 109
manufacture, details of, **6**, 118
marking orders, **6**, 131
meaning, **6**, 115
mens rea, **6**, 128
misleading claims, **6**, 5
Molony Committee recommendations, **6**, 104, 111, 126
obstruction of enforcement officer, **6**, 140
offences, **11**, 1782
oral, **6**, 111
origins, misleading statements on, **6**, 118
other history, **6**, 119
partnerships subject to legislation, **6**, 109
passing off, *see* PASSING OFF
penalties, **6**, 140
previous ownership or use, **6**, 119
private individuals, **6**, 138
purchases, offences arising from, **6**, 108
scope of term, **6**, 122
services, of, **6**, 126–130, 142
statements of fact and statements as to future conduct, **6**, 130
supply of goods or services, **6**, 134
trading standards officers' powers, **6**, 139
when applied, **6**, 110
Trade dispute
See INDUSTRIAL ACTION; PICKETING; STRIKE
Trade-in
contract, classification of, **14**, 1802
Trade mark
armorial in character, **11**, 1630
artificial market partitioning, **18**, 1620
assignation, **6**, 601; **20**, 55
bilateral agreement for exchange, **4**, 1160
comparative advertising infringing, **1**, 514
Comptroller-General of Patents, Designs and Trade Marks, **18**, 814
European Union legislation—
  artificial market partitioning, **18**, 1620
  Community trade mark, **18**, 1624
    exhaustion, and, **18**, 1624
  exhaustion of rights—
    common origin, by, **18**, 1622, 1623
    Community trade mark, and, **18**, 1624
    generally, **18**, 1621
  free movement of goods, **18**, 1619–1624
  generally, **18**, 1611, 1615, 1646
  licensing—
    exclusive distribution and franchising agreements, **18**, 1658, 1659
    generally, **18**, 1657
  specific subject matter, **18**, 1619
exclusive jurisdiction, **4**, 58, 59, 60

Trade mark—*continued*
exhaustion of rights—
  common origin, by, **18**, 1622, 1623
  Community trade mark, and, **18**, 1624
  generally, **18**, 1621
franchising scheme, **18**, 802, 1658, 1659
infringement, **1**, 508
intellectual property, as, **18**, 801
International Convention for the Protection of Industrial Property 1883 ..., **18**, 801
licensee—
  tax treatment—
    lump sum payments, **18**, 1599
    periodic payments, **18**, 1598
    royalties, **18**, 1598
Madrid Agreements, **18**, 804
may not be substituted for real name of food, **11**, 384
meaning, **1**, 508
owner—
  tax treatment—
    lump sum payments, **18**, 1596
    periodic payments, **18**, 1595
    royalties, **18**, 1595
packaging—
  artificial market partitioning, **18**, 1620
  specific subject matter, **18**, 1619
passing off, *see* PASSING OFF
payments in respect of, tax treatment, **18**, 1595, 1596, 1598, 1599, 1600
purchaser—
  tax treatment—
    lump sum payments, **18**, 1599
    periodic payments, **18**, 1598
    royalties, **18**, 1598
recording, **11**, 1614
registration, **1**, 508
rights in security, **20**, 43
royal arms, restraint on use of, **11**, 1632
royalties, tax treatment, **18**, 1595, 1598
special jurisdiction, **4**, 48
specific subject matter, European Community legislation, **18**, 1619
use in Scotland, **11**, 1614
Trade name
European Community legislation, generally, **18**, 1615
Trade-Related Aspects of Intellectual Property Rights (TRIPS)
intellectual property, **18**, 804
Trade secret
breach of confidence, **18**, 1455, 1470, 1471
Clean Air Act, disclosure under, **9**, 1140
employee's duty of confidence, **9**, 85
intellectual property, as, **18**, 801
meaning, **18**, 1471
restraint of trade, protectable interests, **15**, 773
restrictive covenant, protection by, **18**, 1470
reverse engineering or analysis, **18**, 1472
Trade union
accounts of, **1**, 95
action short of dismissal—
  appropriate time and activities, **9**, 89; **23**, 721–723
  complaint of, **23**, 725

Trade union—*continued*
action short of dismissal—*continued*
  employer's consent, **23**, 724
  generally, **23**, 720
  interim relief, **23**, 726
  limits on protection, **23**, 722
  membership and activities, **9**, 88
activities of—
  freedom of association protection, **23**, 721
  independence, privileges of, **23**, 795
  meaning, **23**, 721
  time off for, **23**, 755
administration, legal framework of—
  ballots, **23**, 828–833
  certification officer, *see* CERTIFICATION OFFICER
  common law, at, **23**, 825–827
  dissolution, **23**, 805
  members, rights of, *see* membership *below*
  secession, **23**, 804
  status, *see* status *below*
  statutory definition, *see* statutory definition
    below
advertisement, indicating unlawful conditions, **23**,
  719
Advisory, Conciliation and Arbitration Service, *see*
  ADVISORY, CONCILIATION AND ARBITRATION
  SERVICE
amalgamation, *see* merger *below*
annual returns, **23**, 797
anti-discrimination, **23**, 819
association, *see* freedom of association *below*
audits, **23**, 796
authorisation, **12**, 807
ballot, **15**, 1495
  constituency, **23**, 873
  employer's premises, on, **6**, 1001; **23**, 831
  executive elections, **23**, 832–837
  industrial action, **23**, 869–873
  merger of trade union, **23**, 801
  political fund, **23**, 844
  state subsidy for, **23**, 828–831
  types of payment, **23**, 830
  See also election *below*
bank customer, as, **2**, 1255
benefits—
  disclosure of information on, **23**, 749
  industrial action, obtained as result of, **23**, 854
building society shares held by, **3**, 328
candidates, executive election, **23**, 836
certificate of independence—
  Certification Officer's test, **23**, 794
  listing as prerequisite for application for, **23**, 791
  meaning, **23**, 792
  privileges of independence, **23**, 795
  procedure, **23**, 793
Certification Officer, *see* CERTIFICATION OFFICER
check-off arrangements, **23**, 847
closed shop agreements, **12**, 77; **23**, 719
code of practice, **9**, 241; **23**, 749, 752
collective agreement, *see* COLLECTIVE AGREEMENT
collective bargaining, *see* COLLECTIVE BARGAINING
Commissioner for Rights of Trade Union
  Members, **23**, 838–840

Trade union—*continued*
consultation with—
  redundancy on, **6**, 995; **23**, 763–766
  right to, generally, **23**, 757
  safety representative, rights of, **23**, 758
  transfer of undertakings, **23**, 759–762
contract—
  breach of, **23**, 851, 852
  collective agreement, as, **23**, 736
  lack of, effect on admission, **23**, 808
  trade union's capacity to make, **23**, 781
  unlawful means, indirect interference by, **23**,
    852
criminal liability and picketing, **23**, 882
Crown employment, access to, **23**, 719n
debtor, as, **8**, 128
defamation, **15**, 476
discipline—
  bias, absence of, **23**, 817
  contract of membership, right based on, **23**, 806
  fair notice, **23**, 815
  fair opportunity, **23**, 816
  internal remedies, exhaustion of, **23**, 818
  intervention, basis for, **23**, 810
  misapplication of rules, **23**, 811, 812
  natural justice, **23**, 814
  reasonableness of decision, **23**, 813
  trade dispute, matters of, **23**, 861
  unjustifiable, **23**, 822–824
discrimination on grounds of race or sex, **9**, 343;
  23, 819
dismissal for reasons concerning—
  appropriate time, **9**, 239
  compensatory award, **9**, 286; **23**, 727
  fair, **9**, 234, 285
  generally, **9**, 232
  membership agreement, **9**, 233
  protected employee, **9**, 238
  third party, payment to, **9**, 237
  unfair, generally, **9**, 236
dissolution, **23**, 805
Donovan Commission, **23**, 708, 709
election—
  executive membership, for, **15**, 1495
  independent scrutineer, eligibility as, **15**, 1495
  independent scrutiny, **15**, 1495
Employment Appeal Tribunal, *see* EMPLOYMENT
  APPEAL TRIBUNAL
establishment, meaning, **23**, 764
excluded employment, **23**, 719n
executive, election to, **23**, 832–837
  See also BALLOT
expulsion—
  bias, absence of, **23**, 817
  fair notice, **23**, 815
  fair opportunity, **23**, 816
  intervention, basis for, **23**, 810
  meaning, **23**, 821
  misapplication of rules, **23**, 811, 812
  natural justice, **23**, 814
  reasonableness of decision, **23**, 813
freedom of association, **12**, 76
  action short of dismissal, **23**, 720–726
  activities of independent trade union, **23**, 721

Trade union—_continued_
freedom of association—_continued_
  dismissal, **23**, 722–727
  employment, access to, **23**, 718
  European Convention on Human Rights, **23**, 717
  general, **23**, 717
  history, **23**, 702
  International Labour Organisation, convention, **23**, 717
  right not to join, **23**, 718
health and safety at work, representatives, **23**, 758
  See also HEALTH AND SAFETY AT WORK
historical development—
  abstention, period of, **23**, 707
  collective rights, **23**, 712
  common law, development of, **23**, 705
  Conspiracy and Protection of Property Act 1875 ..., **23**, 704
  current legislative provision, **23**, 714
  Donovan Commission, **23**, 709
  employment legislation, deregulation of, **23**, 715
  freedom of association, **23**, 702
  Industrial Relations Act 1971 ..., **23**, 710
  parliamentary reaction, **23**, 706
  period to 1906 ..., **23**, 703
  politics, trade union and, **23**, 841
  renewed legal intervention, **23**, 708
  Social Contract era, **23**, 711
  trade union immunities, **23**, 713
  union power, reduction in, **23**, 716
incorporation of, **23**, 737, 738
independent trade union, meaning, **23**, 792
  See also CERTIFICATION OFFICER
industrial action, _see_ INDUSTRIAL ACTION
industrial relations, meaning, **23**, 753
industrial tribunal, _see_ INDUSTRIAL TRIBUNAL
legal personality, **15**, 476
membership—
  agreement, **9**, 233
  Certification Officer's test, **23**, 794
  declarator as to, **13**, 4
  discrimination, **12**, 86
  freedom of association, _see_ freedom of association _above_
  generally, **9**, 6
  independence, privileges of, **23**, 795
  primary action on grounds of, **23**, 878
  rights of members—
    admission, **23**, 808, 809
    anti-discrimination, **23**, 819
    discipline, **23**, 810–818
    Employment Act 1980 ..., **23**, 820, 821
    Employment Act 1988 ..., **23**, 822–824
    expulsion, **23**, 810–818
    judicial intervention, legal basis for, **23**, 806, 807
    race legislation, **23**, 819
    sex discrimination, **23**, 819
merger—
  amalgamation as form of, **23**, 798
  ballot, **23**, 801
  Certification Officer, powers of, **23**, 798–803

Trade union—_continued_
merger—_continued_
  complaints, **23**, 803
  forms of, **23**, 798
  instrument setting out terms of, **23**, 800, 802
  procedure, **23**, 799
  transfer of engagements as form of, **23**, 798
picketing, **23**, 879–882
police force, members barred from membership, **16**, 1749, 1759, 1763
political fund—
  ballot, **23**, 844
  creation of, **23**, 842
  exempted members, rights of, **23**, 846
  management of, **23**, 845
  political objects, **23**, 843
politics and—
  check-off arrangements, **23**, 847
  exempted members, rights of, **23**, 846
  history, **23**, 841
  legislative functions, **23**, 842
  political fund, _see_ political fund _above_
  political objects, **23**, 843
public sector, in, **23**, 744–746
recognition—
  ACAS, reference of issue to, **23**, 712, 743
  International Labour Organisation, **23**, 743
  meaning, **23**, 763
  recognition-only practices, action in support of, **23**, 875–878
redundancy, _see_ REDUNDANCY
refusal to join, redundancy following, unemployment benefit, **21**, 836, 849
refusal to leave, redundancy following, unemployment benefit, **21**, 836, 849
restraint of trade doctrine, scope of, **4**, 1212, 1218
secondary action, _see_ INDUSTRIAL ACTION
sheriff court jurisdiction, **6**, 1135
status of—
  common law, at—
    restraint of trade, **23**, 775
    title to sue, **23**, 783
  current, **23**, 781
  employers' association, **23**, 787
  judicial interpretation, **23**, 779
  jurisdiction of court, **23**, 777
  legal entity, meaning, **23**, 779
  ownership of property, **23**, 785, 786
  restraint of trade—
    purposes in, **23**, 775
    purposes not in, **23**, 776
    Trade Union and Labour Relations Act 1974—
      provisions of, **23**, 782
  Scottish position, **23**, 780
  statutory quasi-corporation, meaning, **23**, 780
  title to sue, **23**, 783, 784
  Trade Union Act 1871 ..., **23**, 776–780
  Trade Union and Labour Relations Act 1974 ..., **23**, 781, 782
  voluntary registration, **23**, 778
strike—
  as evidence of dispute, **23**, 858
  See also INDUSTRIAL ACTION; PICKETING; STRIKE

Trade union—*continued*
subscriptions, VAT exemption, **7**, 1407
sue and be sued, ability to, **15**, 476
time off—
   case law, **23**, 753
   pay, with, **23**, 752
   reasonable, right to, **23**, 754
   remedies, **23**, 756
   trade union activities, for, **9**, 93; **23**, 755
transfer of undertakings—
   consultation, duties relating to, **23**, 761
   duty to inform, **23**, 760
   recognition rights, application of, **23**, 747
   regulations, **23**, 759
   relevant transfer, meaning, **23**, 747
   remedies, **23**, 762
union-only practices, action in support of, **23**,
   876–878
voluntary obligation, capacity to enter, **15**, 664
Trade usage
interpretation of deeds affected by, **12**, 1215
Trader
business disclosure in advertisements, **6**, 83
conduct detrimental to consumers' interests, **6**, 16
consumer redress, *see* CONSUMER REDRESS
notice to warn, **6**, 51, 55
Office of Fair Trading licensing, **6**, 21
product safety, **6**, 51
prohibition notice, **6**, 51, 55
prohibition order, **6**, 51
revenue, *see* REVENUE TRADER
service supplied by, **6**, 69
suspension notice, **6**, 56
unfair conduct, assurances to cease, **6**, 18, 19, 20
United Kingdom, when deemed to belong to, **7**,
   1294
unlicensed, enforceability of agreements made by,
   5, 953
value added tax—
   default surcharge, **7**, 1416
   dishonest conduct in relation to, **7**, 1408, 1410
   goods acquired or imported by trader, **7**, 1375
   liability to registration, **7**, 1324, 1325, 1329,
     1333
   persistent misdeclarations, **7**, 1411
   records, inspection and verification, **7**, 1401
   records, notice requiring, **7**, 1283
   recovery proceedings against trader, **7**, 1413
   serious misdeclaration as to, **7**, 1409, 1410
   taxable person, trader as, **7**, 1324
Trades and vocations
consumer protection, **6**, 69
Trading
fraudulent, *see* FRAUDULENT TRADING
roadside, control of, **20**, 699
wrongful, *see* WRONGFUL TRADING
Trading company
borrowing, **4**, 438; **13**, 1774
Trading corporation
functions, **19**, 221
   public concern, **19**, 221
public corporation—
   distinguished, **19**, 220
   treated as trading corporation, **19**, 221

Trading fund
delegation of powers through, **7**, 756
Trading interests
protection of, excluded jurisdiction, **4**, 84
Trading loss
corporation tax, **19**, 1520
Trading name
bill of exchange, signature on, **4**, 123
misleading, **5**, 942
Trading practices
codes of practice, **6**, 158
consumer's rights, statements as to, **6**, 154
control of—
   exclusion clauses, **6**, 97–103
   generally, **6**, 96
insurance business, long-term, **6**, 157
misleading prices—
   code of practice, **6**, 144
   defences, **6**, 143
   enforcement of provisions, **6**, 145
   generally, **6**, 141
   price advertising regulation, **6**, 141
mock auctions, **6**, 155, 156
notices, control of display, **6**, 154
notices and statements made by retailers, **6**, 154
pyramid selling—
   control of, **6**, 149
   meaning, **6**, 148
   penalties for offences, **6**, 150
statements, restrictions on, **6**, 154
statutory control, **6**, 158
trade descriptions, *see* TRADE DESCRIPTIONS
trading stamps, **6**, 146, 147
unsolicited goods and services—
   generally, **6**, 151
   human sexual techniques, relating to, **6**, 153
   protection of persons receiving, **6**, 152
Trading profit
taxation of, **19**, 1513
Trading stamps
control of issue, **6**, 146
display of notices, **6**, 154
issue outside scope of VAT, **7**, 1290
redemption of, **6**, 147
VAT invoice basis, **7**, 1358
Trading standards
consumer advice, **14**, 594
fair trading, **14**, 593
generally, **14**, 591
legislation, **14**, 593
weights and measures, **14**, 592
Traditio
transfer of ownership, completion by, **18**, 116
*Traditionibus, non nudis pactis, dominia rerum
   transferuntur*
rights in security, **20**, 8
Traffic
areas, **20**, 487
local authority functions, **14**, 409
noise, **9**, 1271
regulation order, **14**, 303
Traffic Commissioner, supervision of, **23**, 911*n*
See also ROAD; MOTOR VEHICLE

Traffic commissioners
generally, **20**, 487
Traffic directions and signs
compliance with, **20**, 435, 446
conformity with description in regulations, **20**, 435
damaging or painting, **20**, 506, 704
lawful placing on road, **20**, 435
prescribed types, **20**, 509
roads authority's powers and duties in respect of, **20**, 509
Secretary of State, directions by, **20**, 509
special road, on, **20**, 624
trunk roads, **20**, 620
wilful damage to, **20**, 704
Traffic lights
compliance with, **20**, 435
pedestrian crossing, at, **20**, 440
Traffic regulation orders
special roads, **20**, 624
Traffic warden
employment of, **20**, 510
functions of, **20**, 510
powers of, **20**, 510
Trailer
brakes, **20**, 478
definition, **20**, 408, 408n
dimensions, **20**, 475
door, opening, offences in relation to, **20**, 443
drawing unit, **20**, 408
lighting, **20**, 479
plates, **20**, 477
restriction on number drawn by one vehicle, **20**, 408
semi-trailer, definition, **20**, 408
tyres, **20**, 482
weight, **20**, 476
calculation of, **20**, 409
wings, **20**, 483
Train
See RAILWAYS
Trainee
work permit holder, **12**, 241
extension of leave, **12**, 245
Training
allowance—
overlapping benefits, **21**, 1003, 1004
course—
claimant attending, sickness benefit not payable, **21**, 887
unemployment benefit—
claimant failing to apply for place on, **21**, 856
claimant on, **21**, 810, 811
vocational—
disabled persons, **12**, 7
European Social Charter, **12**, 7
Tramcar
definition, **19**, 1128
excise duty exemption, **7**, 1073
Tramp ship
meaning, **21**, 526, 526n
Tramroad
construction or alteration, **19**, 19n, 24
diversion, widening or narrowing, **19**, 24

Tramroad—*continued*
meaning, **19**, 14n
provisional orders in connection with, **19**, 14, 15, 26
Tramway
advantages and disadvantages, **19**, 1127
alteration, **19**, 19n
byelaws, **19**, 1135
carriages, **19**, 1133
charges, **19**, 1134
construction, **19**, 19n, 1132; **20**, 721
application for, **20**, 721
breaking up roads in connection with, **20**, 721
objections to, **19**, 1132
obstructing, **19**, 1136
damage—
passenger to, **19**, 1137
tramway to, **19**, 1136
dangerous goods brought onto, **19**, 1136
definition, **19**, 1128
discontinuance of undertaking, **19**, 1140
employee, injury to, **19**, 1138
fares, **19**, 1134
avoidance of, **19**, 1136
historical background, **19**, 1127
indemnification of roads authority by operator, **20**, 721
injury—
employee, to, **19**, 1138
passenger, to, **19**, 1137
insolvency of undertaking, **19**, 1141
land, acquisition of, **19**, 1129, 1131
liability of undertakers, **19**, 1137, 1138
light railway of the nature of, **19**, 1084, 1084n, 1130
local authorities, position of, **19**, 1129, 1131, 1139n, 1140
maintenance, **19**, 1132; **20**, 721
military, **19**, 1142
use by public, **19**, 1143
motive power, **19**, 1133
naval, **19**, 1142, 1143
negligence, **19**, 1137
obstructing or hindering, **19**, 1136
offences, penalties for, **19**, 1135, 1136
opening up road over which tramway laid, **20**, 721
operation, **19**, 1132–1134
passenger—
injury or damage to, **19**, 1137
offences by, **19**, 1136
promotion of tramway undertakings, **19**, 1129–1131
Light Railways Act 1896—
under, **19**, 1130
provisional order, by, **19**, 1129, 1132
Tramways Act 1870—
under, **19**, 1131
provisional orders in connection with, **19**, 14, 15, 19
rails, **19**, 1133
regulations, **19**, 1135
removal of undertaking, **19**, 1140
repair, obstruction of, **19**, 1136

Tramway—*continued*
road traffic legislation, application of, **19**, 1136,
  1144
safety hazard, **19**, 1127
sale of undertaking, **19**, 1139
undertakers' liability, **19**, 1137, 1138
winding up undertaking, **19**, 1141
Tranquillisers
controlled drug, as, **14**, 1230
Transfer of arms
inter vivos, **11**, 1622
stranger, to, **11**, 1622
Transfer of ownership
abstract basis of transfer, **18**, 608–613
adverse real rights and conditions, **18**, 604
all sums clause, **18**, 638
approval, delivery of goods on, **18**, 634
ascertainment of goods, **18**, 627, 627n, 628, 635,
  639
assignatus utitur jure auctoris—
  intrinsic conditions, **18**, 660, 688
  relationship of cedent to debtor, **18**, 660
bankruptcy, on, involuntary transfer, as, **18**, 597,
  613
capacity—
  company, of, **18**, 599
  corporation, of, **18**, 599
  partnership, of, **18**, 599
  transferee, of, **18**, 599
  transferor, of, **18**, 599
  trustees, of, **18**, 599
causal basis of transfer, **18**, 608–613
company—
  capacity of, **18**, 599
competing titles, *see* TITLE
compulsory purchase, on, involuntary transfer, as,
  18, 597, 613
contract—
  conveyance, preceding, **18**, 606
  interdependence, **18**, 608
  failure—
    abstract basis of transfer, **18**, 608–613
    causal basis of transfer, **18**, 608–613
    conveyance, effect on, **18**, 608
    corporeal moveables, **18**, 609
      Sale of Goods Act 1979, under, **18**, 610
    incorporeal property, **18**, 612
    justa causa traditionis, **18**, 608
    land, **18**, 611
  generally, **18**, 606
  subsequent to passing of property, **18**, 628
  voidable, **18**, 607
conveyance—
  as act of transfer itself, **18**, 606
  contract, effect of, **18**, 606
  contract preceding, **18**, 606
    failure of, **18**, 608
    interdependence, **18**, 608
  generally, **18**, 606
  intention as part of—
    consent of transferor and transferee, **18**, 613
    error, **18**, 614, 617
    force and fear, **18**, 614, 615
    fraud, **18**, 614, 616

Transfer of ownership—*continued*
conveyance—*continued*
  intention as part of—*continued*
    real vices, **18**, 614
    theft, **18**, 618
    vices of consent, **18**, 614
    voidable title, where, **18**, 607
corporation, capacity of, **18**, 599
corporeal heritable property—
  nemo dat quod non habet rule, **18**, 669
  warrandice, *see* WARRANDICE
corporeal moveable property, *see* CORPOREAL
  MOVEABLE PROPERTY
death, on, involuntary transfer, as, **18**, 597, 613
delivery—
  causal or abstract basis of transfer, **18**, 608–612
  definition, **18**, 609
  generally, **18**, 613
  symbolical—
    feudal law, **18**, 640
derivative acquisition, as, **18**, 597
disposition, unregistered, **18**, 645
dominium, **18**, 625, 628, 637
error—
  error in causa, **18**, 617
  error in corpore, **18**, 617
  error in dominio, **18**, 617
  error in negotio, **18**, 617
  error in persona, **18**, 617
  error in pretio, **18**, 617
  void or voidable title following, **18**, 614, 617
feudal tenure—
  alienation—
    generally, **18**, 59, 59n
    objections to, **18**, 59
  breach, sanctions for, **18**, 62
  casualty, **18**, 63, 63n
  confirmation, charter of, **18**, 58
  conquest, **18**, 56
  conveyance *a me*, **18**, 58
  destination *et assignatis suis*, **18**, 59
  dispone, power to, **18**, 59
  disposition, **18**, 58
  disposition *a me*, **18**, 58, 59
  grant *de me*, **18**, 58
  heritage, **18**, 56
  inheritability, **18**, 55
  mineral rights, **18**, 60
  reddendo, **18**, 63
  subinfeudation—
    burgage tenure, **18**, 58
    confirmation, charter of, **18**, 58
    double manner of holding, where, **18**, 58
    feu charter, **18**, 58
    feu contract, **18**, 58
    feu disposition, **18**, 58
    feufarm, grant in, **18**, 58
    grant *de me*, as, **18**, 58
    grassum, **18**, 58
    meaning, **18**, 57
    midsuperiors, **18**, 57
    mortification, **18**, 58
    pre-emption clause, where, **18**, 58
    present-day position, **18**, 58

Transfer of ownership—*continued*
feudal tenure—*continued*
  subinfeudation—*continued*
    prohibition of subinfeudation, where, **18**, 58
    wardholding, land held by, **18**, 58
    superior, position of, **18**, 60
    vassal, who could be, **18**, 61
    wardholding, land held by, **18**, 58
force or fear, void or voidable title following, **18**, 614, 615
fraud, voidable title following, **18**, 614, 616
future goods, sale of, **18**, 627, 635
  meaning of future goods, **18**, 627*n*
future rights, incorporeal property, **18**, 652
generic goods, sale of, **18**, 627
heritable property—
  accretion, **18**, 677
  acquiescence, not inferred from, **16**, 1614
  'offside goals', rule against, *see* 'offside goals', rule against *below*
inalienable property, **18**, 600
  pre-emption, property subject to right of, **18**, 600
incorporeal property, *see* INCORPOREAL PROPERTY
instantaneous and absolute nature, **18**, 603, 644
intention as requirement for passing of goods, **18**, 613, 628, 636, 637
international trade—
  generally, **18**, 638, 638*n*
  risk, passing of, **18**, 639
involuntary—
  Act of Parliament, transfer by, **18**, 663, 665
  compulsory purchase of land, **18**, 663, 666
  creditor, sale by, **18**, 667
  death of transferor, where, **18**, 663
  generally, **18**, 597, 613, 663
  insolvency of transferor, where, **18**, 663
  judicial conveyance—
    adjudication, **18**, 664
    company property, liquidator, vesting in, **18**, 664
    confirmation of executors, **18**, 664
    forfeiture as criminal penalty, **18**, 664
    generally, **18**, 663, 664
    judicial factor, appointment of, **18**, 664
    power to effect transfer, **18**, 664
    power to order transfer, **18**, 664
    reduction—
      ad hunc effectum, **18**, 664
      catholic, **18**, 664
      generally, **18**, 664
    trustee, appointment by court, **18**, 664
    trustee in sequestration, act and warrant of, **18**, 664
  meaning, **18**, 663
  nemo dat quod non habet rule, **18**, 663, 668
    buyer in possession, where, **18**, 682
    estoppel, English law on, **18**, 680
    generally, **18**, 672
    motor vehicle subject to hire purchase, statutory exception as to, **18**, 683
    owner's conduct precluding him from denying seller's authority to sell, **18**, 680
    personal bar in sale of goods, **18**, 680
    seller in possession, where, **18**, 681

Transfer of ownership—*continued*
involuntary—*continued*
  personal bar in sale of goods, **18**, 668
  refusal to pay debt due, where, **18**, 663
judicial conveyance, *see* involuntary *above*
land—
  abstract basis of transfer, **18**, 611
  accretion, **18**, 677
  allodial land, **18**, 646
  assignation, **18**, 645, 645*n*
  contract for sale—
    missives of sale, *see* MISSIVES OF SALE
    non-supersession clause, **18**, 641
    prescription, **18**, 641
  death of transferee, **18**, 649
  death of transferor, **18**, 648
  disposition, **18**, 645, 645*n*
    execution and delivery, **18**, 640, 642
    meaning, **18**, 640
    registration, **18**, 640
    See also DISPOSITION
  failure of contract, effect, **18**, 611
  feudal tenure, transfer of, **18**, 640
  generally, **18**, 602
  grant and registration of disposition, **18**, 613
  incorporeal tenement, **18**, 647
  insolvency of transferee, **18**, 649
  insolvency of transferor, **18**, 648
  missives of sale—
    conclusion, **18**, 640
    transfer preceded by, **18**, 640, 641
    See also MISSIVES OF SALE
  modern law—
    generally, **18**, 640
    old law, definition by reference to, **18**, 640
  nemo dat quod non habet rule, **18**, 669
  passing of ownership, **18**, 640
  personal rights, **18**, 647
  real rights and conditions, transferee takes land subject to, **18**, 647
  registration, **18**, 640
    General Register of Sasines, **18**, 640
    Land Register of Scotland, **18**, 640
    uninfeft proprietor, where, **18**, 645
  risk, passing of, **18**, 651
  roup, sale by, **18**, 641
    articles of roup, **18**, 641
  sasines—
    nulla sasina nulla terra rule, **18**, 644
  separate tenements—
    generally, **18**, 647
    warrandice, **18**, 703, 703*n*
  stages of—
    evaluation, **18**, 644
    generally, **18**, 640
  stamp duty, **18**, 643
  subinfeudation, **18**, 650
  subordinate real rights, warrandice, **18**, 704, 704*n*
  substitution, classification as, **18**, 650
  uninfeft proprietor, **18**, 645
  warrandice, *see* WARRANDICE
lease, where, **18**, 604
mercantile agent under Factors Acts, title conferred by, **18**, 671

Transfer of ownership—*continued*
negotiable instrument, **18**, 653
nemo dat quod non habet rule—
  agent of transferor, transfer by, **18**, 670
  application, **18**, 669
  assignatus utitur jure auctoris rule, **18**, 660
  exceptions—
    accretion, **18**, 672, 677
    generally, **18**, 669, 672
    involuntary transfer, **18**, 672, 680
    original acquisition—
      accession, acquisition by, **18**, 676
      generally, **18**, 672
      lost and abandoned property acquired
        from police, **18**, 676
      negotiable instrument, holder in due
        course, **18**, 676
      positive prescription—
        heritable property, **18**, 674
        moveable property, **18**, 675
      registration in Land Register, **18**, 673
      specification, acquisition by, **18**, 676
  extrinsic conditions, **18**, 660, 688
  generally, **18**, 669; **20**, 447, 852
  hire, deposit or loan, goods held on, **15**, 49
  involuntary transfers, **18**, 663, 668
  mercantile agent under Factors Acts, title
    conferred by, **18**, 671
  personal bar, doctrine of, **18**, 670, 670*n*
  personal rights, **18**, 669
  relationship of cedent to right being assigned,
    18, 660
  subordinate real rights and conditions, **18**, 669,
    677
  subsistent title, and, **18**, 669
non-owner (*non domino*), by, *nemo dat quod non
  habet* rule, **18**, 672, 677
'offside goals', rule against—
  antecedent contract or other obligation—
    application, generally, **18**, 698
    breach of, **18**, 698
      remedies, **18**, 700
    double grant, generally, **18**, 697
    generally, **18**, 696
    pre-emption, rights of, **18**, 698
    reduction, rights of, **18**, 698
    trust rights, **18**, 698
  application, **18**, 695
  bad faith, **18**, 699
  double grants, **18**, 697
  fraud, and, **18**, 695, 695*n*
  generally, **18**, 695
  personal right in competition with real right,
    where, **18**, 690, 693, 694
  recent developments, **18**, 695
  reduction, **18**, 698, 700
  remedies, **18**, 700
  value, absence of, **18**, 699
  warrandice, breach of, **18**, 697
partnership, capacity of, **18**, 599
passing of property—
  approval, delivery of goods on, **18**, 634
  cash, consumer sales for, **18**, 631
  contract subsequent to, **18**, 628

Transfer of ownership—*continued*
passing of property—*continued*
  credit or charge charge card, consumer sale
    using, **18**, 631
  deliverable, where seller bound to take action
    to make goods, **18**, 632
  express provision, absence of, **18**, 629, 630
  future goods, **18**, 627, 635
  intention of parties, based on, **18**, 613, 628, 636
  risk, passing of, **18**, 639
    international trade, **18**, 639
  Sale of Goods Act 1979, section 18 rules, **18**,
    630–635
  sale or return, delivery of goods on, **18**, 634
  supermarket or cash and carry, sale in, **18**, 630
  timing of passing, based on, **18**, 628
  unascertained goods, **18**, 627, 628, 635, 639
  unconditional contract for sale of specified
    goods in deliverable state, **18**, 631
  weighing, measuring or testing, sale dependent
    on, **18**, 633
personal bar, *see* PERSONAL BAR
personal rights, **18**, 652
  generally, **18**, 669
  See also incorporeal property *above*
personal rights do not run with property, **18**, 604
positive act, necessity for, **18**, 613
pre-emption, property subject to right of, **18**, 600
publicity, requirement for, **18**, 602
quasi-specific goods, **18**, 639
real burden, where, **18**, 604
real rights, *see* incorporeal property *above*
right in security, where, **18**, 604, 637
rights—
  running with property, **18**, 604
  transfer of, *see* incorporeal property *above*
risk, passing of, **18**, 639
  corporeal heritable property, **18**, 651
  frustration of contract, and, **18**, 639
  insurable interest, **18**, 639
  transit, whilst goods in, **18**, 639
Romalpa clause, **18**, 628, 638
sale of goods, Anglicised nature of law, **18**, 606
Sale of Goods Act 1979, under—
  dominium, **18**, 625, 628
sale or return, delivery of goods on, **18**, 634
servitude, where, **18**, 604
singular successors, meaning, **18**, 598
specific goods, meaning, **18**, 628*n*
spes successionis, **18**, 652
subordinate real rights and conditions—
  competing titles, where, **18**, 687
  generally, **18**, 604, 669
  grant of, **18**, 605
theft, void title following, **18**, 614, 618
title—
  competing titles, *see* TITLE
  guarantee, *see* WARRANDICE
  subsistent, *nemo dat quod non habet* rule, **18**, 669
  voidable, **18**, 607
    nemo dat quod non habet rule, **18**, 669
traditio, completion by, **18**, 116
*traditionibus non nudis pactis dominia rerum
  transferuntur* rule, **18**, 606

Transfer of ownership—*continued*
transferee—
  age of, **18**, 599, 599*n*
  capacity of, **18**, 599
  intention, **18**, 613, 628, 636, 637
transferor—
  capacity of, **18**, 599
  intention, **18**, 613, 628, 636, 637
trust property—
  capacity of trustees, **18**, 599
unascertained goods, risk, passing of, **18**, 639
unidentified goods, sale of, **18**, 627
unititular nature of Scots law, **18**, 603
universal successors, **18**, 598
void and voidable titles, **18**, 601
voluntary, **18**, 597
See also SALE AND SUPPLY OF GOODS
Transfer of undertakings
community law, influence of, **9**, 16
continuous employment, **9**, 48
redundancy, effect on, **9**, 178
unfair dismissal, **9**, 228
Transhipment
carrier utilised for, liability, **21**, 560
clause, bill of lading, **21**, 546
goods imported for transit or, **7**, 1149
voyage charterparty, **21**, 618, 629, 630
Transire
meaning, **21**, 140*n*
nationality of ship, requirement for, **21**, 140
Transit
stoppage in, *see* STOPPAGE IN TRANSIT
Transit passage
meaning, **21**, 10
Translator
public lending right, **13**, 1508
Transmission
See RENVOI
Transnational corporations
natural resources, **19**, 671
Transplant
human organ—
  meaning of organ, **3**, 509*n*
  offences in relation to, **3**, 509
Transport
aerodromes, *see* AERODROME
air services, **14**, 451
airport, *see* AIRPORT
British Transport Commission, **19**, 1001
British Transport Police, *see* BRITISH TRANSPORT POLICE
capital resources allocation to, **20**, 615
competition law, **4**, 1311
contract of, **4**, 56
England and Wales, **14**, 62
European Union, freedom of movement within, **10**, 150
expenditure programme, **5**, 580
ferry, *see* FERRY
food in transit, examination of, **11**, 401
harbour, *see* HARBOUR
hazardous substances, of, **9**, 1202
industry, consumer protection, **19**, 241, 241*n*
liability, restrictions on limitation, **6**, 103

Transport—*continued*
lost or abandoned property on, **16**, 1819*n*
meat, of, hygiene regulations, **11**, 416, 417
new means of, VAT zero-rating, **7**, 1444
pier, *see* PIER
poison, of, **14**, 1218
public, *see* PUBLIC TRANSPORT
radioactive material, of, *see* ATOMIC ENERGY AND RADIOACTIVE SUBSTANCES
reform, **14**, 46
roads, *see* ROAD
ship, *see* SHIP
supervision of by Scottish Committee, **23**, 911*n*
'ticket' cases, **6**, 98
tribunal, **22**, 333
VAT rating, **7**, 1452
water rights, acquisition of, **25**, 519
See also PASSENGER
Transport, Department of
creation of, **5**, 514
functions of, **5**, 514
Marine Accident Investigations Branch, **21**, 113, 235, 235*n*
Marine and Ports Directorate, **21**, 113
shipping, functions in relation to, **21**, 113
Shipping Directorate, **21**, 113
Transport industry
consumer protection, **19**, 241, 241*n*
Transport policies and programmes
capital resources, allocation of, **20**, 615
Trans-sexual
See GENDER
Trap
freshwater fishing by, **11**, 11
gin, prohibition of, **11**, 879, 880
spring, **11**, 880
  approved, **11**, 873, 874
  hares, open trapping of, **11**, 876
  inspection, **11**, 875
  possession, **11**, 873
  rabbits, open trapping of, **11**, 876
  sale, **11**, 873
  use, **11**, 873
taking or killing deer with, **11**, 940
Travaux préparatoires
aid to construction of statute, as, **12**, 1154
Travel agent
licence, requiring, **1**, 542
Travel concession
local authority grant, **20**, 493
qualified persons, **20**, 493
Travel document
certificate of entitlement to right of abode, **16**, 1242
Certificate of Identity, **16**, 1237
collective passport, **16**, 1225, 1236
Declaration of Identity, **16**, 1237
entry certificate, **16**, 1238
entry clearance—
  application procedure, **16**, 1239
  legal controls, **16**, 1240
  types, **16**, 1238
European Union *laissez-passer*, **16**, 1236
European Union nationals, **12**, 233

Travel document—*continued*
failure to hold, **12**, 171
foreign, holder entring UK, **16**, 1208–1211
French foreign legion identity card, **16**, 1236
German Democratic Republic, **16**, 1236, 1236*n*
Home Office, **16**, 1237
identity card, **16**, 1206, 1236
letter of consent, **16**, 1238
military identity card, **16**, 1236
non-national, supply to, **16**, 1201
passport, *see* PASSPORT
primary travel formalities, **16**, 1235–1237
refugee, issued to, **16**, 1210, 1236
    Home Office travel document, **16**, 1237
refugees, **12**, 314, 323
seaman's book, **16**, 1236
secondary travel formalities, **16**, 1238–1244
stateless person resident in UK, issue to, **16**, 1237
United Nations *laissez-passer*, **16**, 1236
Vatican passport per l'estero, **16**, 1236
visa, *see* VISA
Travel services
VAT zero-rating, **7**, 1452
Traveller
declarator of rights of travellers, action for, **11**, 1752
discontinuance of status as, **11**, 1718
early statutes, **11**, 1701
excise duties—
    European Union, traveller from outwith, **7**, 1112
    European Union, traveller from within, **7**, 1111
guest, *see* HOTEL
hotelkeeper's duty towards, **11**, 1719–1723
    See also HOTELKEEPER
luggage, *see* LUGGAGE
meaning, **11**, 1716, 1716*n*
possessions of, customs officers' powers in relation to, **7**, 1222
refusal to receive, **11**, 1723, 1753
Travelling people
children of, school attendance, **8**, 893
public health legislation, **19**, 349
sites for, provision of teachers at, **8**, 893
Trawler
lights and shapes to be displayed, **21**, 364
Trawling
beam or otter, **11**, 112
Treason
abrogation of Scots law, Westminster legislation after the Union, **22**, 601, 630
adhering to sovereign's enemies, **7**, 569, 575, 609, 611
    aid and comfort, intention to give, **7**, 576
    overt act, **7**, 575
allegiance—
    aliens, **7**, 581, 582
    British citizens, **7**, 579
    British subjects not British citizens, **7**, 580
    generally, **7**, 578
art and part guilt, **7**, 583
assault on sovereign, **7**, 586
bail in case of, **17**, 551
capital offence, as, **7**, 567

Treason—*continued*
capital punishment, **17**, 562
coercion, defence of, **7**, 577
committed abroad, **6**, 867
conspiracy, **7**, 594
constructive—
    forms, **7**, 571
    levying war, **7**, 559, 571, 573, 574
death penalty, **7**, 563
deposing sovereign, **7**, 571
felony, **7**, 571, 585
    sedition, and, **7**, 585
forms, **7**, 569
high, **7**, 566, 568
High Court of Justiciary jurisdiction, **6**, 867
historical background, **7**, 564
inciting invasion, **7**, 571
injure or depose sovereign, compassing to, **7**, 571
insurrection, **7**, 573
judge, killing, **7**, 545, 569
King's wife—
    compassing or imagining death of, **7**, 569, 570
    violation, **7**, 569, 572
leasing-making, **7**, 595
levying war, **7**, 569, 571, 573, 574
    outside realm, **7**, 573
    riot compared, **7**, 574
Lord Chancellor, killing, **7**, 569
Lord High Treasurer, killing, **7**, 569
maiming, imprisoning etc sovereign or heirs, **7**, 569
misprision, **7**, 566, 568, 584
peace, during, **7**, 565
peerage, forfeiture on, **16**, 1313
petit, **7**, 568
procedure, **7**, 567
royal family, protection, **7**, 704
Scots law, replacement with English law, **7**, 566
sedition and, **7**, 587
sovereign's death, compassing or imagining, **7**, 569, 570, 571
sovereign's eldest son and heir—
    compassing or imagining death of, **7**, 569, 570
    violating wife of, **7**, 569, 572
sovereign's eldest unmarried daughter, violation, **7**, 569, 572
succession to Crown, attempting to hinder, **7**, 569
summons, Great Seal, passed under, **7**, 874
time limits, **7**, 567
Treason Act (1351), **7**, 568
trials for, history, **6**, 850
war, during, **7**, 565
Treasure
Crown hereditary revenue derived from, **7**, 769
Crown's right to, **18**, 553; **24**, 313, 324, 329
    regalia, as, **18**, 553
definition, **18**, 553; **24**, 313
disposal, **18**, 553
finder—
    duty of, **18**, 553
    reward, payment to, **18**, 553
ownership, **18**, 553; **24**, 313
udal law, **24**, 313
valuation, **18**, 553

Treasurer
Officer of State, **7**, 790, 791, 792, 795
Treasurer-depute
Officer of State, **7**, 791, 792, 796
Treasurer of the Household
office of, **7**, 774
Treasurer of Public Charities
incorporation, **19**, 209
Treasury
breaking up, authority for, **14**, 1842
British Coal Corporation, powers relating to, **14**, 1604
coins, making or issuing without authority, offence, **14**, 1841
control of borrowing by, **13**, 1782
denomination, approval for, **14**, 1823
exportation, consent for, **14**, 1843
financial control exercised by, excluded agreements, **4**, 1177
functions of, **5**, 497
importation, consent for, **14**, 1843
loan capital, control of raising of, **4**, 438
Lords of, **5**, 494
meaning, **5**, 493
melting down, licence for, **14**, 1842
metal used as token for money, restriction on, **4**, 109
ministers, **5**, 496
organisation of, **5**, 498
Review Committee on Banking Services set up by, **4**, 105
share capital, control of raising of, **4**, 438
Trial of Pyx, **14**, 1821
Treasury bill
negotiable instrument, as, **4**, 103
Treat, notice to
meaning, **5**, 16
notice of entry served simultaneously with, **5**, 80
restriction on power to withdraw, **5**, 50
service of, **5**, 16
servitude, effect of existence of, **5**, 115
Treaties, **19**, 615–636
acceptance, **19**, 617
accession, **19**, 617
agreements relating to, **19**, 622
amendment, **19**, 623
approval, **19**, 617
binding force, **19**, 621
bipartite (bilateral), **19**, 615, 624
black letter law, as, **19**, 615
capacity to enter, **19**, 617
cession of territory, pertaining to, **19**, 656n
change of circumstances, fundamental, **19**, 632, 632n
competence to conclude, **19**, 626
conflict with peremptory norm, in, **19**, 630, 634, 651
consent to be bound by, **19**, 617
consular relations between parties, severance of, **19**, 632
context, **19**, 622
customary international law, and, **19**, 643, 644
definition, **19**, 616
diplomatic relations between parties, severance of, **19**, 632

Treaties—*continued*
domestic and international law, relationship between, **19**, 652
enabling Act, **19**, 656
error in, **19**, 627
executive act, as, **19**, 617
extension of context, **19**, 622
impossibility of performance, **19**, 632
instruments relating to, **19**, 622
international—
    Great Seal of the United Kingdom, **7**, 856, 860
international law—
    relevant to, **19**, 622
    as source of, **19**, 603, 615–636
international organisation, creating, **19**, 615
international—
    incorporation into domestic law, **7**, 736
    making, prerogative powers, **7**, 724, 724n, 736
    EC law, effect, **7**, 738
    ratification, **7**, 725
interpretation, **19**, 622
    objective approach, **19**, 622
    supplementary means, **19**, 622
    teleological approach, **19**, 622
    travaux préparatoires, **19**, 622
    two or more languages, authenticated in, **19**, 622
    ut res magis valeat quam pereat, **19**, 622n
invalidity—
    acts performed before invalidity invoked, **19**, 633
    consequences of, **19**, 633, 634
    suspension of operation, **19**, 635
later treaty concluded, **19**, 632
law-making (*traité-lois*), **19**, 615
material breach, **19**, 632, 632n
meaning, **19**, 652
modification, **19**, 624
multipartite (multilateral), **19**, 615
    amendment, **19**, 623
    modification, **19**, 624
municipal law, effect upon, **19**, 605
non-signatories, **19**, 615
obligation to incorporate, **19**, 656
oral statements, **19**, 636
pacta sunt servanda rule, **19**, 621
Ponsonby Rule, **19**, 656n
prior publicity, **19**, 656n
ratification, **19**, 617
rebus sic stantibus doctrine, **19**, 632
regional organisations with treaty-making competence, **19**, 649
reservations to, **19**, 615, 615n, 618
    acceptance of, **19**, 619
    international law of, **19**, 618
    legal effects, **19**, 620
    meaning, **19**, 618
    null and void, **19**, 618n
    objection to, **19**, 619, 620
    other parties, effect upon, **19**, 620
signature, **19**, 617
source of international law, as, **19**, 603
special international regime, establishing, **19**, 615
state practice, as evidence of, **19**, 642

Treaties—*continued*
states, recognition of, **19**, 661
subsequent agreements and practices, **19**, 622
suspension of operation, **19**, 632
  consequences, **19**, 635
termination, **19**, 631, 632
treaty contracts (*traité-contrats*), **19**, 615
two or more languages, authenticated in, **19**, 622
United Kingdom—
  domestic law, incorporation into, **19**, 656
  position, **19**, 617
  procedures, **19**, 605
validity, **19**, 625
  coercion, **19**, 629
  competence to conclude, **19**, 626
  corruption, **19**, 628
  disputes relating to, **19**, 636
  error in, **19**, 627
  fraud, **19**, 628
  international law, conflict with, **19**, 630, 634
  jus cogens, **19**, 630, 634, 651
Vienna Convention on Law of Treaties, **19**, 605,
  616, 617, 718*n*
void—
  acts performed before invalidity invoked, **19**,
    633
  established as, **19**, 633
written agreements, **19**, 636
Treating
corrupt practice, as, **15**, 1445
elector, by, **15**, 1445
electoral malpractice, **7**, 409
proxy, by, **15**, 1445
what constitutes, **15**, 1445
Treaty of Union
See UNION AGREEMENT OF 1707
Tree
accession by fruits, **18**, 595, 596
conservation area, preservation in, **23**, 190
cutting, wayleave agreement, rights contained in,
  9, 650
encroachment on neighbour's land—
  generally, **18**, 179
  ownership, **18**, 179
felling of—
  danger, to prevent, **11**, 617
  enforcement of provisions as to—
    committee of reference, **11**, 629
    compliance notice, **11**, 628
    expenses of, **11**, 630
    identification of trees, **11**, 631
    service of documents, **11**, 632
  felling directions—
    agricultural interests to be considered, **11**,
      623
    committee of reference, **11**, 629
    farm or dwelling house, interests to be
      considered, **11**, 623
    Forestry Commission's power to direct, **11**,
      623
      restrictions of, **11**, 624
    identification of trees, **11**, 631
    interests to be considered, **11**, 623
    persons adversely affected by, **11**, 626

Tree—*continued*
felling of—*continued*
  felling directions—*continued*
    proceedings in respect of, **11**, 627
    review of, **11**, 624–626
    statement of grounds to be given, **11**, 623
  felling licence—
    application for, **11**, 616
    committee of reference, **11**, 629
    conditional, **11**, 619
      review of conditions, **11**, 619
    enforcement, **11**, 628–632
    exemption from requirement, **11**, 617
    felling without authority of, **11**, 622
    generally, **11**, 612, 616
    identification of trees, **11**, 631
    preservation orders, trees subject to, **11**, 621
    public open space, trees growing on, **11**, 617
    refusal to grant—
      compensation for, **11**, 618
      deterioration of timber after, **11**, 618
      review of, **11**, 621
  nuisance, to abate, **11**, 617
  obstruction, to remove, **11**, 617
  restocking notice, *see* FORESTRY
  unauthorised, **11**, 622
lopping, **11**, 617
obstruction or interference of telecommunications
  line by, **16**, 1957
overhanging boundary, **14**, 2028
overhanging road, **20**, 505, 673, 696
pertinents, as, **12**, 1242
preservation order, **11**, 620; **23**, 203
prevention of damage by injurious animals or
  birds, **11**, 859
removal, service of notice for, **20**, 673
restocking notice, *see* FORESTRY
road, planting alongside, **20**, 672–674
roads authority, provision by, **20**, 503
roots shooting into neighbour's ground, **14**, 2028
topping, **11**, 617
tree preservation order, subject to, **20**, 696
Trespass
aggravated, **7**, 345
agricultural tenant, by, **11**, 818
aircraft, by, liability for, **2**, 1020
airspace, in, **18**, 180
animal, by, **18**, 180
  straying animals—
    damages in respect of, **18**, 190
    detention of, **18**, 188
    generally, **18**, 183, 186
    interdict, **18**, 183, 187
    killing or injuring, **18**, 189
apprehension of trespassers, **11**, 820
assault by trespasser, **11**, 823
building contracts, **3**, 161
constructive, **11**, 819
criminal offence, whether, **18**, 182
damages in respect of, **18**, 182, 185
  straying animals, **18**, 190
Day Trespass Act, **11**, 815–824
  daytime, meaning, **11**, 816

Trespass—*continued*
defences—
  Act of Parliament, intrusion authorised by, **18**, 181
  consent, **18**, 181
  exercise of a right, **18**, 181
  judicial warrant, intrusion authorised by, **18**, 181
  public interest, intrusion in, **18**, 181
definition, **18**, 180
disguised or with blackened face, **11**, 817
dogs sent onto land, **11**, 819
duty of care in delict, landowner's, **18**, 184
explosives, law in relation to, **10**, 1626
firearm, with, **10**, 1568, 1583
fishing, as, **18**, 280
future, interdict against, **18**, 182, 183
game, in search or pursuit of, **11**, 803, 817
  damage caused by, **11**, 803
  landowners' remedies, **11**, 803
heritage, on, **7**, 345
hunting, application to, **11**, 820, 821
injury as result of, whether, **18**, 180
interdict, future trespass, against, **18**, 182, 183
land, on, **18**, 180
landowner's rights, **18**, 195
loch, on, **18**, 180
lodging or encamping on private property, **18**, 182
meaning, **11**, 819; **14**, 2027
nuisance distinguished from, **14**, 2027
obstruction by trespasser, **11**, 823
occupier's liability, *Dumbreck*, decision in, **15**, 314
ownership, vertical extent of, **14**, 2028
person, by, **18**, 180
poaching—
  day, **18**, 182
  night, **18**, 182
possession, defence of, **18**, 140, 141n
private property, meeting held on, **14**, 1303
prosecution under Day Trespass Act, **11**, 824
quarry, in, **14**, 1708
railway property, on, **19**, 1063
remedies, **18**, 182
river, on, **18**, 180
self-help against, **18**, 182, 184
  straying animals, killing or injuring, **18**, 189
tenant farmers, **11**, 818
thing, by, **18**, 180
trout fishing, **11**, 50
what qualifies as, **18**, 180
wild animal, in pursuit of, **18**, 541
Trial
absence of accused, in, **17**, 721
combat, by, **17**, 541
compurgation, by, **17**, 541
conjoining of, **17**, 695
defence, *see* CRIMINAL PROCEDURE
diet—
  generally, **17**, 680
  mental disorder not discovered until, **17**, 899
  postponement of, **17**, 684
  See also solemn procedure *below*

Trial—*continued*
fair—
  publicity as guarantee of, **12**, 49
  right to, *see* COURTS
hearing, right to fair and public, *see* HUMAN RIGHTS
in absentia, **12**, 50
insanity in bar of, **14**, 1460
interpreter, right to services of, **12**, 43, 51
  pre-trial proceedings, **12**, 51
judge, misdirection by, **17**, 824
judicial review, right to, **12**, 54
jury, by—
  Court of Session procedure, **17**, 1412
  development of, **17**, 542
length of, **17**, 555
new, motion for—
  generally, **17**, 1449
  Inner House, powers of, **17**, 1451
  procedure, **17**, 1450
ordeal, by, **17**, 541
plea in bar of—
  generally, **17**, 686
  insanity at time of trial, **17**, 688, 896
  mora taciturnity and delay, **17**, 692
  nonage, **17**, 687
  personal bar, **17**, 691
  prejudicial publicity, **17**, 693
  res judicata, **17**, 689
  socius criminis, **17**, 690
pre-trial procedure, *see* CRIMINAL PROCEDURE
prisoner awaiting, removal to hospital of, **14**, 1463
separation of, **17**, 694
solemn procedure—
  adjournments, **17**, 558
  charge to jury, **17**, 557
  diet—
    accused—
      absence of, **17**, 736
      body corporate, **17**, 737
      evidence for, **17**, 759
    adjournment of, **17**, 738
    calling, **17**, 734
    desertion—
      pro loco et tempore, **17**, 739
      simpliciter, **17**, 740
    documentation, **17**, 766
    evidence—
      accused, for, **17**, 759
      additional, **17**, 760
      commission, on, **17**, 757
      replication, in, **17**, 761
    indictment, amendment of, **17**, 746
    judge—
      charge of, **17**, 763
      death of, **17**, 741
      illness of, **17**, 741
      questioning by, **17**, 754
    judicial examination, record of, **17**, 757
    jury—
      addresses to, **17**, 762
      deliberations of, **17**, 764
      empanelling, **17**, 747

Trial—*continued*
solemn procedure—*continued*
  diet—*continued*
    jury—*continued*
      management of, **17**, 749
      questioning by, **17**, 754
      verdict once case remitted to, **17**, 748
      See also JURY
    misdescriptions, **17**, 742
    misnomers, **17**, 742
    no case to answer, **17**, 758
    parties, presence of, **17**, 735
    pleading—
      generally, **17**, 743
      not guilty plea, **17**, 745
      refusal to plead, **17**, 744
    preliminary matters, **17**, 752
    press publicity, prohibition on, **17**, 751
    public access to court, **17**, 750
    verdict—
      delivery of, **17**, 765
      recording of, **17**, 765
    witnesses—
      contempt by, **17**, 756
      Crown, examination for, **17**, 753
      prevarication by, **17**, 756
      recall of, **17**, 755
  evidence, **17**, 556
  length of trial, **17**, 555
  period, commencement of, **9**, 175
  sheriff court, **17**, 573
  speeches, **17**, 557
  verdicts, **17**, 559
summary—
  form of petition for, **17**, 1432
  generally, **17**, 1431
  procedure on, **17**, 1433
without jury, **17**, 560
Trial of Pyx
provisions relating to, **14**, 1821
Tribunal
administrative, meaning, **23**, 901
appeal—
  appeal from or review of decision, **4**, 85
  case stated, by way of, **23**, 905
  Court of Session, to, **23**, 907, 917
  enforcement notice, against, **23**, 920
  generally, **1**, 339
  superior tribunal, to, **23**, 905
award, interest on, **12**, 1036
chairman, selection of, **23**, 907
contempt proceedings, **6**, 309
Council on, *see* COUNCIL ON TRIBUNALS
decision, judicial review of, **23**, 905
Director General of Fair Trading as, **5**, 803
domestic—
  jurisdiction, **23**, 916
  Privy Council, appeal to, **23**, 917
  setting up, **23**, 901, 916
  statutory regulation, **23**, 917
evidence, whether bound by, **10**, 501*n*
generally, **23**, 901
industrial, *see* INDUSTRIAL TRIBUNAL
Insolvency Practitioners, **4**, 952

Trial—*continued*
jurisdiction, deciding on, **1**, 246
order, obligation to recognise or obtemper, **16**, 2116
Parliament, set up by, **23**, 901
perjury, **7**, 506
reasons for decision, giving, **1**, 291
Scottish Committee, under supervision of, **23**, 911*n*
statement made in, absolute privilege, **15**, 524
statutory—
  chairman, selection of, **23**, 907
  jurisdiction, subject matter of, **23**, 904
  member, appointment of, **23**, 903
  membership, termination of, **23**, 907
visit to, by Council on Tribunals, **23**, 915
Trieste
free zone, as, **7**, 1164
Trinity College, Dublin
library, copy of publications to be delivered to, **17**, 5
Trinity Houses
pilotage, generally, **21**, 291
Triple-dip lease
cross-border leasing, **14**, 1096
Troll or long-line
fishing with prohibited, **11**, 12
Trolley vehicle
definition, **19**, 1128
system—
  meaning, **19**, 14*n*
  provisional orders in connection with, **19**, 14, 15, 19
Trout
annual close time, **11**, 53
artificially introduced, **11**, 47
brown—
  fish farms, **11**, 58
  regulation of fishing, *see* regulation of brown trout fishing *below*
  right to fish for, **11**, 5, 48
  salmon fishing rights include, **11**, 5, 48
bull trout, **11**, 40
close season, buying, selling or exposing for sale during, **11**, 312
definition, **11**, 47
fish farms—
  brown trout, **11**, 58
  derating of, **11**, 64
  inland, **11**, 57, 59, 60
  marine, **11**, 61
  meaning, **11**, 57*n*
  pollution control, **11**, 62
  rainbow trout, **11**, 58
fishing rights, **11**, 49
  extent of, **11**, 50
  lease of, **11**, 49
  private water, **11**, 50, 51
  public, **11**, 50
  salmon fishing rights, and, **18**, 326
fishings—
  lease, **13**, 296, 297
  pertinents, as, **12**, 1242
  valuation for rating, **24**, 661
fishpond, in, **11**, 47

Trout—*continued*
illegal fishing methods, **11**, 54
loch, more than one proprietor owning surrounding land, **11**, 48
meaning, **11**, 5*n*
otterboards, **11**, 54
permission to fish, where required, **11**, 50
permitted methods of fishing, **11**, 11
protection orders, **11**, 55
    wardens to enforce, **11**, 56
purchase, sale or exposure for sale during close time, **11**, 53
rainbow, **11**, 52, 58
regulation of brown trout fishing, **11**, 51
    annual close time, **11**, 53
    illegal fishing methods, **11**, 54
    protection orders, **11**, 55, 56
    statutory controls, **11**, 52
res nullius as, **11**, 47, 51
right to fish for, incident of land ownership, **11**, 48, 49
rod and line fishing, **11**, 54
salmon fishing rights include trout fishing rights, **11**, 5, 48
sea fish, as, **11**, 183*n*
Sea Fish (Conservation) Act 1967 ..., **11**, 144
sea fishing, **11**, 144
sea trout, River Tweed, **11**, 40
stank, in, **11**, 47
theft, **11**, 47, 51
'True and fair view'
concept of, **1**, 42, 67
consolidated accounts, for, **1**, 68
meaning, **1**, 43
Truman Proclamation on the continental shelf
generally, **21**, 15, 18, 27
significance, **21**, 16
Trunk road
bridge—
    navigable water over—
        authority to construct, **20**, 638
        revocation or variation of order, **20**, 644
    ownership, **20**, 642
cleansing, **20**, 620, 677
construction, **20**, 620
creation, **20**, 615, 620
    objections to, **20**, 620
    trunk road order, advertising, **20**, 620
    trunking local authority road, **20**, 621
definition, **20**, 619
detrunking, **20**, 615, 620, 622
generally, **20**, 501, 608, 619
gritting, **20**, 620
junction layout, alteration, **20**, 620
land, compulsory purchase, **20**, 620, 714
litter, **20**, 677
local authority road, trunking, **20**, 621
maintenance, responsibility for, **20**, 620
order—
    advertising, **20**, 620
    objections to, **20**, 620
    revocation, **20**, 620
    variation, **20**, 620

Trunk road—*continued*
picnic sites, provision of, **20**, 623
Railways Board, bridge belonging to, transfer to Secretary of State, **20**, 642
reconstruction, **20**, 620
responsibility for, **20**, 619
roads authority for, **20**, 619
Secretary of State's powers and duties, **20**, 619, 620
signposting, **20**, 620
snow clearance, **20**, 620
surface treatments, **20**, 620
through traffic, national system of routes for, **20**, 615, 619
    Secretary of State's duty to keep, **20**, 620
tunnel, navigable water under—
    authority to construct, **20**, 638
    revocation or variation of order for, **20**, 644
Waterways Board, bridge belonging to, transfer to Secretary of State, **20**, 642
Trust
accommodation, provision for beneficiary of, **24**, 202
accumulation of income, *see* ACCUMULATION OF TRUST INCOME
accumulation and maintenance, **24**, 17
accumulation trusts, **19**, 1659
    adult beneficiaries, **19**, 1660
    appointment, deed of, **19**, 1663
    intermediate income, right to, **19**, 1662
    liferents, **19**, 1663
    minor beneficiaries, **19**, 1661
    statutory restrictions, **19**, 1663
    tax treatment, **19**, 1661
    See also ACCUMULATION OF TRUST INCOME
acts at variance with purpose of, **24**, 203
administration—
    ascertainment of trust estate, **24**, 191
    debts and expenses, **24**, 193
    general duties of trustees, **24**, 189, 190
    international law in, **17**, 337, 338
    majority or quorum, action as, **24**, 192
    practical, **24**, 191*ff*
    revocation of trusts for, **22**, 59
    trust for, **24**, 59
agricultural property relief, **19**, 1561–1563
alienation of trust property, **18**, 535; **24**, 49, 247, 260, 266
aliens, **22**, 14, 132
alimentary liferent, **12**, 1264
Anglo-American influences, **24**, 112, 114, 115, 116
annuities, **12**, 1264; **24**, 54
arrestee, as, **8**, 259
arrestment, interaction with, **8**, 271
asset, **24**, 12
assignation of interests under, **6**, 596
beneficial interest, **24**, 63, 179
beneficiaries, *see* BENEFICIARY (OF TRUST)
breach of, **11**, 1015
    obligation arising from, **15**, 3
case law relating to, **17**, 337
categories, **24**, 115
Chancery jurisprudence not applicable, **24**, 1

Trust—*continued*
charitable, *see* CHARITABLE TRUST
classification, **24**, 10
closest and most real connection, **4**, 41
commercial, **24**, 11, 115
companies, *see* COMPANY
comparative law, **24**, 112–127
  civil law solutions corresponding to trusts, **24**, 117
  commercial operations, **24**, 119
  contractual devices, **24**, 122
  corresponding civil law solutions, **24**, 117
  foundations, **24**, 118
  generally, **24**, 112–127
  inter vivos benefactions, **24**, 121
  Netherlands, **24**, 124
  reception of trust law in civil law jurisdiction, **24**, 125
  testamentary provisions, **24**, 120
  trusts in 'mixed jurisdiction', **24**, 126
  unjustified enrichment, **24**, 123
concept of, in Scots and English law, **19**, 1654
constitution, **11**, 750; **24**, 12–20
construction, **17**, 337, 338
constructive—
  creation, **19**, 1655; **24**, 10, 29
  doctrine of, **19**, 1654; **24**, 7, 115
  English law, **19**, 1654
  meaning, **24**, 10, 30
  taxation, **19**, 1654, 1655
constructive delivery, **24**, 23, 24
continuing, conveyance to trustees, **25**, 905
conveyancing device, as, **24**, 5
Court of Session jurisdiction, **4**, 9; **6**, 924, 926; **17**, 1426; **24**, 83, 203
creation, **19**, 1655
  by legal implication, **24**, 10
  created expressly, **24**, 10
creditors, for, **24**, 16, 20
deed—
  behoof of creditors, for, **8**, 177
  condition as to Jewish faith in, **3**, 1685
  construction—
    affecting termination, **24**, 71
    effect on revocability, **24**, 64
  creditors, for, arrestment and, **8**, 293
  definition, **24**, 13
  delivery, **24**, 12, 21–25
  language of, **24**, 68
  lessee, grant by, **13**, 185
  requirements, **24**, 27
  transfer of, **24**, 21
  voluntary, interpretation, **12**, 1262
  what may constitute, **24**, 27
definition, **24**, 9
delivery, **24**, 12, 21–25
  accumulation and maintenance trust, **24**, 17
  class of persons must be certain, **24**, 55
  generally, **24**, 16, 55
  meaning, **24**, 55
  power of appointment distinguished, **24**, 55
  private trust, as, **24**, 16, 17
deposit compared, **24**, 6, 9
diligence, interaction with, **8**, 113, 114

Trust—*continued*
discretionary, **24**, 23, 24
  charitable purposes, payment for, **3**, 1152
  transfers into, **16**, 1137
domicile, **4**, 33, 41
donation, capacity to receive, **8**, 611
donation by means of—
  capacity to make donation, **8**, 611
  delivery, **8**, 631
  revocability, **8**, 632
effects of, **17**, 337, 338
enforceability, **24**, 86, 89
English law—
  contrasted, **24**, 12
  influence of, **24**, 7, 112–115
essential principles, **24**, 9
establishment as legal term, **24**, 1
estate, negative prescription of obligations, **16**, 2125, 2125*n*
ex lege, **24**, 115
expenses of administration, **24**, 193
express, **24**, 16
extended meaning, **24**, 2
failure of, **12**, 1029
family relationships, **24**, 25
feudal conveyancing techniques, **24**, 5
fideicommissum, **24**, 4
fiduciary fee, **24**, 10, 21, 29, 32
form of words, **24**, 13
fraud, proof of, **11**, 750
freedom of testation, restriction on, **25**, 601
fund—
  interest due on, **12**, 1001
    advances to beneficiaries, **12**, 1022, 1030
      ultra vires, **12**, 1030
    delay in payment, **12**, 1029
    rate specified, **12**, 1023
    trust deed, interest due by, **12**, 1022, 1023
    trustees' duty to invest, **12**, 1025
    trustees' liability for interest, **12**, 1022, 1024–1029
  loss by *ultra vires* actions, trustees' liability, **12**, 1026
  no trust funds available for investment, where, **12**, 1025
  right to interest, implied, **12**, 1023
  taxation of payments into, **19**, 1312
  trustees' liability for interest—
    co-trustees, liability for, **12**, 1028
    terms of deed impossible to carry out, **12**, 1023
  trustees using for own purposes, **12**, 1027
future acquirenda, **24**, 12
generally, **11**, 749; **17**, 334
gift to charity by, inheritance tax treatment, **3**, 1161
heir-at-law, **24**, 162
heir of provision in, **24**, 162
history, **24**, 1–7, 112, 115
human beneficiaries, **24**, 115
implied, **24**, 12, 16
income, deceased's liability to tax, **25**, 969
indemnity, whether entitlement to, **6**, 765
independent origins of Scots law, **24**, 1

Trust—*continued*
'institutional formulation', **24**, 6
inter vivos, see INTER VIVOS TRUST
interests in possession, **19**, 1656–1658
international law, in, **17**, 335–337, 338
investment trust, **24**, 11, 119
irrevocability—
    conditions for, **24**, 61
    intimation creating, **24**, 22
joint title, **24**, 162
judicial variation—
    advances for beneficiaries maintenance, **24**, 76
    alimentary liferent, **24**, 81, 82
    alimentary rights, **24**, 75
    application for, **24**, 198
    approval on behalf of those who cannot assent, **24**, 79
    authorisation—
        alimentary liferent, in case of, **24**, 81
        conditions for, **24**, 82
    charitable trusts, **24**, 104
    common law jurisdiction, **24**, 76
    consent granted by court, **24**, 79
    denudation in favour of living beneficiaries, **24**, 76
    divorce, on, **24**, 84
    drafting amendments, **24**, 79
    enlargement of investment powers, **24**, 79
    incapacity, **24**, 78, 79
    insurance to protect interests, **24**, 80
    inter vivos trusts, **24**, 75
    irrevocability, effect of declaration of, **24**, 79
    mortis causa trusts, **24**, 80
    nonage, **24**, 78, 79
    prejudicial arrangements, proviso against, **24**, 80
    private trusts, **24**, 76
    procedure, **24**, 83
        Court of Session jurisdiction, **6**, 924, 926; **24**, 83
        curator *ad litem* appointment, **24**, 83
        documents, **24**, 83
        petition—
            appendix to, **24**, 83
            crave to be included in, **24**, 83
            disposal on summar roll, **24**, 83
            presentation of, **24**, 83
            service, **24**, 83
    public trusts, **24**, 76
    purposes of trust, **24**, 75
    retainer of fund for remoter beneficiaries, **24**, 80
    revocable trusts, **24**, 75
    statutory jurisdiction prior to 1961 ..., **24**, 77
    tax position, improvement of, **24**, 78
    trustees' powers, **24**, 75
    Trusts (Scotland) Act 1961—
        jurisdiction under, **24**, 78
    unborn person, court's approval on behalf of, **24**, 79
juristic acts—
    capacity of, **17**, 335
    formal validity, **17**, 335
    substantive validity, **17**, 336

Trust—*continued*
jus crediti or *jus ad rem* beneficiary's right as, **24**, 7, 12
jus quaesitum tertio compared, **15**, 832
lapsed, **24**, 88
    completion of title, **24**, 198
Latin America—
    reception of trust law in, **24**, 125
'legal' and 'equitable' estates not recognised, **24**, 2, 7
legal personality, does not have, **4**, 41
liferent, *see* LIFERENT
limited meaning, **24**, 2
litigation in connection with, **24**, 235, 236
mandate compared, **24**, 6, 9
marriage contract, *see* MARRIAGE
Married Women's Policies of Assurance (Scotland) Act 1880—
    created by, **24**, 21, 29, 33
    meaning, **24**, 2, 9, 14
minor—
    accumulation of trust income, **24**, 36
    approval or variation of trust, **24**, 79
    creation of trust, **24**, 14
    incapacity, **24**, 128
    liability for breach of trust, **24**, 129
minorities, periods involving, **24**, 36
mixed funds, **24**, 51, 52
mortifications, **24**, 3
mortis causa, **24**, 16, 80
nature of, **24**, 8–11
objects and purposes of, **24**, 57
operation of law, arising from, **24**, 12, 29–33
parties to, **24**, 14
power, fraud on a, **11**, 702, 754
precatory, **24**, 10, 19
prejudicial arrangements—
    insurance against, **24**, 80
    mortis causa trust, **24**, 80
    proviso against, **24**, 80
    retained funds as protective measure, **24**, 80
    where not required, **24**, 80
private, *see* PRIVATE TRUST
prohibition—
    extent of, **24**, 37
    statutory, **24**, 35
proof of, **24**, 26–28
    parole evidence, by, **24**, 26, 27, 28
    prout de jure, **24**, 13
    writ or oath, by, **24**, 13
property—
    alienation of, **24**, 49, 247, 260, 266
    beneficial interest in, **18**, 34
    co-ownership, **18**, 18
    common, judicial factor appointed on, **24**, 278
    delivery of, **24**, 12, 21–25
    foreign heritage, **24**, 14
    generally, **19**, 1651; **24**, 15
    identifiability, **24**, 50
    immoveable and incorporeal, **24**, 6
    imprescriptive rights and obligations, **16**, 2126
    improper use by partnership, liability, **16**, 1048
    inhibition, **8**, 157

Trust—*continued*
property—*continued*
  joint property, as, **18**, 20, 34, 35, 536, 538
    management, rules of, **18**, 36, 36*n*
    See also CO-OWNERSHIP
  missives of sale of, **24**, 13
  moveable, **24**, 266
  ownership—
    generally, **18**, 39, 691
    passing on death or resignation, **18**, 20
    transfer—
      capacity of trustees, **18**, 599
  personal rights, **24**, 15
  prescription, no right to acquire by, **18**, 566
  purchase—
    company, by, **24**, 177
    generally, **24**, 202
    other fiduciaries, by, **24**, 178
    relatives, by, **24**, 176
    trustee, by, **24**, 176, 177
  registrable title, with, **24**, 23
  representing trust property, **24**, 52
  'special range', **24**, 207
  title to, **18**, 34
  transfer of, **24**, 266
  trust, **24**, 15
  trust proved property, **24**, 13
  trustees' legal title to, **24**, 12
  type of, relevance, **24**, 23
  unity of title, **18**, 20
  unsecured creditors, competition of title, **18**, 694, 694*n*
public, *see* PUBLIC TRUST
religious purposes, **24**, 96, 157
repugnancy, **24**, 73
residue clause, **24**, 46
resulting—
  creation, **24**, 10, 29
  doctrine of, **24**, 7, 115
  meaning, **24**, 10, 31
retention of title clauses, **24**, 21
revocation—
  alimentary liferent, **24**, 81
  antenuptial trust, **24**, 62
  beneficial interest, **24**, 63
  beneficiaries, **24**, 67
  construction of deed, **24**, 64
  existence of beneficiary, **24**, 62
  inter vivos trusts for third parties, **24**, 60
  irrevocability, declaration of, **24**, 64
  judicial variation, **24**, 75
  language of deed, **24**, 67
  marriage contract trusts, **24**, 69
  nature of subjects conveyed, **24**, 65
  procedure, **24**, 83
  testamentary trusts, **24**, 58
  trustees' power, **24**, 66
  trusts for administration, **24**, 59
'*Romalpa*' clauses, **24**, 24
Roman Catholic charitable, **3**, 1670
roots of Scots law, **24**, 1–7
sale, for, **25**, 641
secret, **24**, 13
sequestration of trust estate, **4**, 72; **24**, 273

Trust—*continued*
settlements and settled property, **19**, 1653–1655
settlor, action against, **4**, 41
shares held in, **4**, 357
sheriff court for action, appropriate, **4**, 41
sheriff court jurisdiction, **4**, 9; **6**, 1136
simple, **24**, 10, 16
simpliciter, trust liferent compared, **13**, 1610
special, **24**, 10, 16
special jurisdiction, **4**, 41
specific gift, **24**, 45
sporting and recreational purposes, **19**, 1230
spouses, between, **10**, 874, 875
statute, created by, **24**, 10
statutory—
  forms of, **25**, 641
  trust for sale, **25**, 641
subject, nature of, **24**, 65
tax considerations, **19**, 1649–1652
termination—
  beneficiaries, by, **24**, 70–74
  beneficiary's vested right to property, **24**, 71
  contingent right in unborn issue, **24**, 70
  debts, retention for payment of, **24**, 74
  refusal to denude on grounds of minority or incapacity, **24**, 72
  repugnancy, **24**, 73
terminology of tax statutes, **19**, 1652
testamentary, *see* TESTAMENTARY TRUST
title—
  conveyance of to trustees, **6**, 609
  joint, **24**, 162
'tracing' trust assets, **24**, 7
transactions in breach of, **11**, 753
transfer of trust deed, **24**, 21
trust estate, judicial factor on, **24**, 273
trustee, *see* TRUSTEE
truster, *see* TRUSTER
variation of purposes, Law Reform Committee for Scotland 1960 report, **22**, 659
verbal, **24**, 13
vesting, **19**, 1664
  class gifts, **19**, 1669
  future interest, of, **19**, 1667
  right to income, of, **19**, 1666
  subject to defeasance, **19**, 1668
  whole interest, of, **19**, 1665
voluntary church property—
  charitable status, **3**, 1643
  Craigdallie case, **3**, 1645
  Free Church Union Case, **3**, 1646
  generally, **3**, 1642
  gift or subscription, **3**, 1642
  heritage, title to, **3**, 1642
  particular religious beliefs of congregation, **3**, 1645, 1646
  recognition, **3**, 1642
  religious purposes, trusts for, **3**, 1643
    public trust, as, **3**, 1643
voluntary obligations, constitution, **15**, 668
wills creating, **24**, 115
winding up, **18**, 35
words, form of, **24**, 13
writing, where necessary, **24**, 12, 13

Trust corporation
no established Scottish counterpart, **24**, 135, 135n
Trustee
acceptance of office, **24**, 141–143, 156; **25**, 863
  express, **24**, 142
  implied, **24**, 143
accounting, **24**, 195
actings of, personal bar, **16**, 1607
action against, **4**, 41
administration primary function, **24**, 3
agent as, **24**, 2
alien status, **24**, 132
alleged, **24**, 27
also appointed executor, **24**, 165
appointment, **24**, 139–143
  acceptance, **24**, 141–143
  at common law, **24**, 158
  charitable trusts, **24**, 198
  court appointments, generally, **24**, 161
  inaccuracies relating to, **24**, 139
  nomination, **24**, 139
  procedure, **24**, 160
  testamentary, **24**, 140
  under statute, **24**, 159
  where none surviving or capable of acting, **24**, 158
arbitration, reference to by, **2**, 408
assumption, power of, **24**, 153, 154
auctor in rem suam precluded from becoming, **11**, 751; **24**, 2
bank account—
  fiduciary positions, persons in, **2**, 1239
  liability of bank, **2**, 1238
  payments into, **2**, 1237
bankrupt estate, on, powers, **4**, 769
bankrupt tenant, estate of—
  abandonment by, **13**, 421
  acceptance by landlord, **13**, 419
  adoption by, **13**, 420
  vesting, **13**, 416
bankruptcy, **24**, 130
  See also BANKRUPTCY
beneficiaries' rights against, **18**, 691; **24**, 49–52
beneficiary as, **24**, 9, 138
bill of exchange, party to, **4**, 129, 130
breach of fiduciary duty, reduction on grounds of, **13**, 44
  See also FIDUCIARY
breach of trust—
  defences, **24**, 224
  duty to account, **24**, 221
  instigation of beneficiary, at, **24**, 224
  investments, **24**, 223
  liability for, **24**, 220
  relief from liability for, **24**, 211
  standard of care, **24**, 222
building society member, as, **3**, 379
capacity to be, **24**, 128–138
  age limit, **3**, 1202
  conventional incapacities, **24**, 128
  natural incapacities, **24**, 128
  nonage, **24**, 129
capital advance to beneficiaries, **24**, 76, 203
care, standard of, **24**, 222

Trustee—*continued*
cessation of trusteeship, **24**, 162–168
  death of trustee, **24**, 162
  removal at common law, **24**, 167
  removal under statute, **24**, 168
chartered company, as, **24**, 135
co-trustees, discharge from, **24**, 196
completion of title, **24**, 147–149
  heritable property, **24**, 149
  moveable property, **24**, 149
consent negativing breach of duty, **24**, 173
continuing trust, conveyance of, **25**, 905
continuous absence abroad, **24**, 137, 168
corporate bodies, as, **24**, 134, 135
court, application to, **24**, 198, 203
court, appointment by, judicial conveyance, **18**, 664
creditor of, **8**, 114
criminal conviction, **24**, 130
Crown as, **24**, 136
curator as, **24**, 2
deadlock among, **24**, 158, 192, 273
death of, **24**, 162
debtor, as, **8**, 113
debts and expenses, payment of, **24**, 193
decisions—
  deadlock, **24**, 158, 192
  majority, **24**, 192
  quorum, **24**, 192
declinature—
  express, **24**, 144, 145
  implied, **24**, 144, 146
  meaning, **24**, 144
definition, **24**, 9
delict—
  defender, as, **15**, 233
  title and interest to sue, **15**, 233
disappearance of, **24**, 168
discharge, **24**, 202
  capacity to, **24**, 217
  construction and effect, **24**, 218
  from co-trustees, **24**, 196
  judicial exoneration, **24**, 219
  method, **24**, 216
  trustee's right to, **24**, 215
disclaimer, **24**, 144–146
distribution of estate, **24**, 196
divorce, payments or transfers of property to trustee in cases of, **10**, 955
duties—
  administrative, **24**, 189, 190
    professional advice, to take, **24**, 190, 224
    to pay at right time, **24**, 212
    to pay to right person, **24**, 209
  duty of care, **15**, 299
ex officio, **24**, 128, 141, 149, 157
executor as, **24**, 2; **25**, 1107
executor distinguished—
  assimilation of powers, **24**, 169
  functions compared, **24**, 169
  generally, **24**, 3, 169
  limitation of liability, **24**, 169
  titles compared, **24**, 169
executor-creditor, confirmation as, **8**, 355

Trustee—*continued*
expenses, **24**, 232–236
express acceptance, **24**, 141, 142
factor, appointment and remuneration, **24**, 190
family relationships, **24**, 25
fees, charging of, **24**, 173
fiduciary duty, **11**, 751
  See also FIDUCIARY
foreign, **24**, 152, 161
foreign residence, **24**, 137
former, liability of, **24**, 221
function of, **24**, 169
heritable security granted by, **20**, 220
immunity clause in favour of, **24**, 224
implied acceptance, **24**, 141, 143
insane, trustee becoming, **24**, 133
insanity disqualifies, **24**, 133
insider dealing rules, **12**, 1532
insolvency, **24**, 130
  beneficiaries' rights, **24**, 49–52
interim, *see* BANKRUPTCY
investment—
  application for directions on, **24**, 203
  appropriation, **24**, 208
  breach of trust, **24**, 223
  categories of, **24**, 207
  common law and statutory powers, **24**, 207
  compensating transfers, **24**, 207
  duty of care, **24**, 205
  funds must be authorised, **24**, 205
  generally, **24**, 194, 204
  inadequate, liability for loss, **24**, 205
  powers under trust deed, **24**, 206
  'special-range property', **24**, 207
  valuation of, **24**, 207
  widening of powers, **24**, 207
investment transactions arranged by or for, **12**, 1307
joint property held by, inhibition, **8**, 158
joint tenancy, **13**, 189
judicial factor, *see* JUDICIAL FACTOR
law agent, appointment and remuneration, **24**, 173, 190
legal title to property, **24**, 12
lessee, as, **13**, 186
lessor, as, **13**, 154, 165
  mineral lease, **13**, 165
  trustees for creditors, **13**, 176
  trustees in sequestration, **13**, 175
liability—
  former trustees, of, **24**, 221
  third parties, to, **24**, 225–231
lien, right of, **13**, 95
litigation by—
  administration, in connection with, **24**, 235
  trust deed, in connection with, **24**, 236
loans to or by, **24**, 180
local authority as, **24**, 134, 135
majority, acting as, **24**, 192
meaning, **24**, 2
  Trusts (Scotland) Act 1921, under, **24**, 128
meaning of 'invest', **24**, 205
minor may be, **24**, 129
multiplepoinding, process of, **24**, 203

Trustee—*continued*
new, **24**, 150–154
  applications for appointment of, **24**, 159
  appointment at common law, **24**, 158
  appointment under statute, **24**, 159
  assumption at common law, **24**, 150
  assumption under statute, **24**, 151
  capacity, **24**, 152
  court appointments, generally, **24**, 161
  exercise of the power of assumption, **24**, 153
  foreign, **24**, 152, 153
  formal title to trust estate, **24**, 153
  formalities of assumption, **24**, 154
  procedure, **24**, 160
  suitability, **24**, 152
nomination, **24**, 139, 155–161
  acceptance of office, **24**, 156
  assumption of survivorship, **24**, 162
  completion of title, **24**, 157
  delegated to third party, **24**, 139
  description, by, **24**, 139
  power to nominate, **24**, 155
  trust deed, **24**, 139
nonage, **24**, 129
number of trustees reduced to one, **18**, 35
obligation of, imprescriptive nature, **16**, 2126
original, **24**, 128–149
  appointment, **24**, 139–143
  capacity to be, **24**, 128–138
  completion of title, **24**, 147–149
  declinature, **24**, 144–146
outlays, **24**, 232–236
ownership may pass to, **24**, 6
payment by—
  ascertainment of whom entitled, **24**, 210
  distribution *in specie*, **24**, 213
  duty to pay at right time, **24**, 212
  duty to pay to right person, **24**, 209
  form of, **24**, 213
  powers to restrict or withhold, **24**, 214
  recovery of payments, **24**, 211
permanent, *see* BANKRUPTCY
powers—
  access agreements, **24**, 202
  affecting revocability, **24**, 66
  amalgamation, **24**, 202
  bankruptcy, **2**, 1235
  court, granted by, **24**, 203
  discretionary, **24**, 201
  generally, **12**, 1272; **18**, 449, 691; **24**, 199
  implied, **24**, 201
  Law Reform Committee for Scotland 1960 report, **22**, 659
  procedure to enlarge, **24**, 83
  statutory, **24**, 202
  trust deed, under, **24**, 200
powers of trustees, **18**, 449, 691
principal, holds as, **24**, 9
professional advice, duty to take, **24**, 190
profits, accountability for, **24**, 174
property, legal title to, **24**, 12
proprietor, as, **24**, 444
public trusts, *see* PUBLIC TRUST
purchase of trust property by, **24**, 176, 177

Trustee—*continued*
quorum, acting as, **24**, 192
reasonable care, duty to exercise, **24**, 189
recovery of payments, **24**, 211
reimbursement—
    generally, **24**, 232
    litigation, **24**, 235, 236
    outlays and expenses, **24**, 233
    professional fees, **24**, 234
relationship with truster, **24**, 25
removal—
    at common law, **24**, 167
    continuous absence abroad, **24**, 137, 168
    disappearance, **24**, 168
    generally, **24**, 198
    grounds for, **24**, 168
    sequestrated estate, **24**, 130
    sole trustee, **24**, 168
    under statute, **24**, 168
removings, action of, **13**, 497
repetition, remedy of, **24**, 211
resignation, **21**, 144*n*, 163; **24**, 141
    cessation of trusteeship, **24**, 163–166
    conflict of interest, **24**, 165
    effect of, **24**, 166
    extra-judicial, **24**, 164
    judicial, **24**, 165
    non-gratuitous, **24**, 164, 165
    sole trustee, **24**, 153, 164, 165
resignation or death, **18**, 35
sequestration petition by, **2**, 1328
servitude, trustee's power to grant, **18**, 449
shooting lease by, **11**, 898
simple, interest in shares, exclusion relating to, **4**, 346
sole—
    death, **24**, 162
    incapax, **24**, 159
    may not be sole beneficiary, **24**, 9
    power of assumption, **24**, 153
    removal, **24**, 168
    resignation, **24**, 153, 164, 165
    unsatisfactory conduct, **24**, 158
special case, submission of, **24**, 203
standard of care, **24**, 222
statutory company as, **24**, 134
summary trial, petition for, **24**, 203
superintendence order, **24**, 197
testamentary, **24**, 140
theft or embezzlement from, **24**, 209
third parties, liability to—
    calls on shares, **24**, 230
    contracts, **24**, 225
    delict, **24**, 231
    litigation, **24**, 226
    partnership, **24**, 229
    truster's contracts, **24**, 228
    warrandice, **24**, 227
title of, proprietary nature, **24**, 169
trading company, as, **24**, 134
transactions by, whether fair and reasonable, **24**, 174
trust beneficiary and, transaction between, **11**, 752

Trustee—*continued*
trust estate, and, **11**, 751
trust funds—
    investment of, **2**, 1236
    proceeds of, **2**, 1237
trustee may be, **24**, 9, 14, 24, 138
truster, relationship with, **24**, 25
tutor as, **24**, 2
variation of powers of, **24**, 75
verbal acceptance, **24**, 141
voluntary nature, **24**, 141
who may be, **24**, 14
wilful breach of trust committed by, **24**, 52
winding up, conveyance to trustees, **4**, 871
written acceptance, **24**, 141
See also FIDUCIARY
Trustee in bankruptcy
See BANKRUPTCY
Trustee Savings Bank
accounts, **1**, 93
assets—
    depositors' claim to, **2**, 1122
    vesting of, **2**, 1158
beginning of, **2**, 1109
Central Board—
    dissolution of, **2**, 1158
    supervisory powers, **2**, 1157
depositors, rights of, **2**, 810
facilities of, **2**, 1121
growth of, **2**, 1121
law relating to, **2**, 1157
legislative background, **2**, 1122
nominations, testamentary arrangements as to, **25**, 733
privatisation of, **2**, 1158
public limited company, as, **2**, 1122, 1158
reorganisation of, **2**, 1158
restructuring of, **2**, 1122
Scottish—
    formation of, **2**, 1158
    reorganisation of, **2**, 1158
statutory control of, **2**, 1109
surplus assets, ownership, **2**, 810
Trustcard, introduction of, **2**, 1157
Truster
beneficiary, may be, **24**, 9
contract entered into by, **24**, 228
death of, **24**, 21
deathbed and funeral expenses, **24**, 193
debts and expenses, **24**, 193, 202
definition, **24**, 9
family relationships, **24**, 25
power to nominate trustees, **24**, 155
relationship with trustee, **24**, 24, 25
trustee—
    as, **24**, 138
    may be, **24**, 9, 14, 24
    relationship with, **24**, 25
who may be, **24**, 14
Tuberculosis
cow suffering from, notification of, **11**, 447
infection, fear of, **14**, 2082
prescribed diseases regulations, **21**, 992

Tug
definition, **21**, 211*n*
flotilla, relationship to third parties, **21**, 401
general average in situation of tug and tow, **21**, 703
hire, towage contract—
  with crew, **21**, 405
  generally, **21**, 403, 405
  gratuitous, **21**, 405
  implied terms, **21**, 405, 406
  onerous, **21**, 405
  performance, **21**, 405
  reasonable fitness, **21**, 405, 406
  seaworthy vessel, obligation to provide, **21**, 405
  specific or named tug, **21**, 405, 406
  unnamed tug, **21**, 405, 406
  without crew, **21**, 405
law applicable to, generally, **21**, 401
liability of tugowner, **21**, 411, 414–417
  limitation, **21**, 420
salvage award, whether tug under towage contract entitled to, **21**, 453
tow, relationship with, express terms, **21**, 410
tugowner—
  liability—
    death or personal injury resulting from negligence, for, **21**, 416
    detention of tow, no liability for, **21**, 417
    exemption clause, **21**, 415, 416
    strikes, disputes, disturbances etc, consequences of, **21**, 417
    war, riots, terrorism etc., consequences of, **21**, 417
  meaning, **21**, 411*n*
  personal failure to exercise reasonable care, **21**, 416
United Kingdom Standard Towing Conditions (UKSTC), *see* TOW
See also TOW

Tunnel
construction or alteration, **19**, 19*n*, 21; **20**, 608
maintenance, responsibility for, **20**, 664
navigable water, under—
  authority to construct, **20**, 638
  revocation or variation of order for, **20**, 644
as part of road, **20**, 609
provisional orders, **19**, 26
road, under, maintenance of, **20**, 664
road passing through, **20**, 411
Secretary of State's powers, **20**, 615

Turkey
slaughter, **11**, 516
  Jewish ritual, **3**, 1680

Turks and Caicos Islands
British Dependent Territories citizenship, **14**, 1932

Turnkey contract
building contracts, **3**, 9

Turnover rental
commercial lease, **13**, 71

Turpentine and turpentine substitute
weights and measures legislation, **6**, 244

Turpis causa **transaction**
ex turpi causa non oritur actio, **15**, 53

Turpis causa **transaction—***continued*
in turpi causa melior est conditio possidentis, **15**, 53
unjust enrichment, **15**, 53

Tutor
action for aliment brought by, **19**, 1581
administration by, **10**, 1071; **11**, 1222, 1223
alienation of heritage, **11**, 1225
application for tutory, **10**, 1316
appointment of, **24**, 9, 132; **25**, 604
at law—
  generally, **11**, 1215
  history of, **10**, 1064
  qualifications, **10**, 1066
  tutor dative, relationship with, **10**, 1065
brieve of tutory, **11**, 1215
control of pupil's person, **10**, 1056, 1070
curator distinguished, **10**, 1056, 1073, 1083; **11**, 1207
dative—
  factor *loco tutoris*, and, **10**, 1069
  generally, **11**, 1216, 1223
  history of, **10**, 1967
  mentally disabled person, of, **11**, 1239
  qualifications, **10**, 1068
  tutor at law, relationship with, **10**, 1065
death of, **10**, 1071
death of parent, on, **11**, 1211
debarred from profiting by office, **24**, 7
deed, grant of, **12**, 1229
eases, communication of, **24**, 7
estate of child, management of, **11**, 1214
expiry of office, **11**, 1218
factor *loco tutoris*, *see* FACTOR
father—
  nomination of testamentary tutor, **10**, 1015, 1061
  as tutor, **10**, 1058; **24**, 128
fiduciary position, **11**, 1222; **24**, 172
functions of, **10**, 1056
generally, **11**, 1202
guardian of pupil child, as, **11**, 1202
history of tutory, **10**, 1057
illegitimate children, **10**, 1057, 1062, 1070
lease, management of, **11**, 1225
legal rights, potential claimant for, **25**, 790
legitim, **11**, 1215
lessee, as, **13**, 187
lessor, as, **13**, 167
liability, standard of, **11**, 1225
mother, **10**, 1059; **24**, 128
moveable property, powers over, **11**, 1225
nominate, **11**, 1214
parent or parents as, **10**, 1060; **11**, 1209
  See also father *and* mother *above*
pro tutor, **11**, 1217
  meaning, **15**, 92
  negotiorum gestio and pro-tutory distinguished, **15**, 92
proposal to abolish office of, **11**, 1243
proprietor, as, **24**, 444
removal by court, **10**, 1071
removings, action of, **13**, 497
resignation of, **10**, 1071

Tutor—*continued*
respective role of curator and, **10**, 1073
Roman law as basis of office, **11**, 1202
statute law, effect of, **11**, 1202
termination of tutory, **10**, 1071
testamentary—
  appointment, **10**, 1062
  appointment while child *in utero*, **10**, 1015
  failure to nominate, **10**, 1064
  generally, **11**, 1214
  history of, **10**, 1061
  legitimate children, **10**, 1062
  nomination by father, **10**, 1015, 1061
  privileged position of, **10**, 1063

Tutor—*continued*
testamentary—*continued*
  qualifications, **10**, 1063
trustee, as, **19**, 1582; **24**, 2, 128
Tweed
See RIVER TWEED
Tweeddale
population, **14**, 64
Typhoid
wholesome water, duty to provide, **25**, 508
Tyres
car hire firm, vehicle owned by, **20**, 482
construction and use regulations, **20**, 482
radial and cross-ply, **20**, 482

U

Uberrimae fidei
contract—
    breach of warranty, reduction on grounds of,
      13, 44
    fraudulent misrepresentation by non-disclosure,
      11, 712
    insurance contract as, **12**, 802, 858
Udal law
absence of feudal hierarchy, **24**, 306
airff (inheritance feast), **24**, 307, 308
allodial nature of land ownership, **24**, 306, 307
allodial ownership, as, **18**, 47*n*
Borgathing Norwegian law code, **24**, 303
Bruce v Smith reasonableness test of custom, **22**,
    385–388
Code of Magnus 'the Law-Mender' (*Gulathing*
    law)
    common land, **24**, 306
    fishings, **24**, 315
    foreshore, **24**, 306
    landownership, **24**, 307
    St Ninian's Isle Treasure case, **24**, 304, 313
    scat, **24**, 309
    udal law, **24**, 301, 303, 308, 318, 321, 325
    whether surviving to modern times, **24**, 304
common land, **24**, 306
common law of Scotland, distinction, **22**, 387
commonty, **24**, 306
compulsory purchase, land, of, scat, **24**, 309
contrary use, doctrine of, whether applicable, **24**,
    304
conveyance of land, scat, **24**, 309
Crown—
    extent of powers, **24**, 306
    scat payable to, **24**, 309
    Scottish, claim to Orkney and Shetland, **24**,
      302
    seabed, claim to, **24**, 316
current status, **24**, 304
custom, **22**, 366, 367, 368, 387, 530
death of udaller, **24**, 307
desuetude doctrine, whether applicable, **24**, 304
dwelling houses, **24**, 308
Eidsivathinglaw Norwegian law code, **24**, 303
eyrislands, **24**, 311
feudal law—
    introduction to Orkney and Shetland, **24**, 308
    tenure, conversion from udal to feudal, **24**, 307
    udal law compared, **24**, 306, 307
feudal tenure, conversion to, **24**, 307
Fiars Courts—
    abolition, **24**, 309
    scat, **24**, 309
fishings—
    salmon-fishings, **24**, 315, 320
    sea fishings, **24**, 315
foreshore—
    definition, **24**, 314
    fishings, **24**, 315

Udal law—*continued*
foreshore—*continued*
    regalia minora as part of, **24**, 314
    seaweed, **24**, 314
    udal law, **24**, 306, 310, 314, 320
    wrecks, **24**, 314
Frostathing Norwegian law code, **24**, 303, 315
generally, **18**, 44, 47
Gragas, Icelandic law code, **24**, 303
Gulathing law, **24**, 307, 308
Hebrides—
    'annual of Norway', **24**, 302
    ceded to Scotland, **24**, 302, 304
Heidsaevisthinglaw (*Eidsivathinglaw*) Norwegian law
    code, **24**, 303
historical background, **24**, 302, 317–320
Hoswick Whale case, **24**, 313, 329–400
Iceland—
    Code of Magnus 'the Law-Mender', **24**, 303
    Gragas law code, **24**, 303
    seabed and foreshore, ownership of, **24**, 316
intestacy, **24**, 308
kinship rights, **24**, 308
kirklands, **24**, 307
land measures, **24**, 311
land ownership, **24**, 307
    conversion to feudal tenure, **24**, 307
    pre-emption on sale or transfer, **24**, 307
    purchased land, **24**, 307
    sale challenged, **24**, 307
    sale and disposal, **24**, 308
    scat, **24**, 309
    scattald, **24**, 310
    succession and kinship rights, **24**, 308
    upgestrie, **24**, 308
'land-kenning', **24**, 315
lawbooks, **24**, 303
lifetime gifts, **24**, 308
marklands, **24**, 311
meaning, **24**, 301
moveables—
    bona vacantia, **24**, 313
    pre-emption on sale or transfer, **24**, 307
naval service or levy, **24**, 306, 309
Norway—
    'annual of Norway', **24**, 302
    Hebrides ceded to Scotland, **24**, 302, 304
    law codes—
      Borgathing, **24**, 303
      Frostathing, **24**, 303, 315
      Gulathing, **24**, 303
      Heidsaevisthinglaw (*Eidsivathinglaw*), **24**, 303
    political authority in Orkney and Shetland, **24**,
      302
    seabed, ownership of, **24**, 316
origin, **22**, 387

Udal law—_continued_
Orkney—
Act of 1611 abolishing foreign laws, **24**, 304,
319, 320
allodial land, transfer of ownership, **18**, 646
Code of Magnus 'the Law-Mender' (_Gulathing_
law), **24**, 303, 304
earls of—
laws enforceable by, **24**, 306
relationship with Norwegian king, **24**, 302
title granted by king, **24**, 306
feudal system—
charters, **24**, 308
infeftments, **24**, 307
foreshore, **24**, 314, 320
impignoration to Scotland, **24**, 301, 304, 317,
326
land measures, **24**, 311
landownership, udal law, **24**, 306
lawbooks, **24**, 303, 304
Lawman of, **24**, 303, 317
Norwegian Crown, political authority of, **24**,
302
salmon fishing rights, **18**, 321
salmon fishings, **24**, 315
scat, _see_ scat _below_
scattald, _see_ scattald _below_
Scots law, application of, **24**, 301, 325
Scottish Crown's claim to, **24**, 302, 326, 327
Scottish influence, **24**, 317
seabed, ownership of, **18**, 310, 317; **24**, 316
sovereignty, **24**, 305
Scottish, **24**, 326–400
transfer from Norway to Scotland, **24**, 305,
326, 327
urislands, **24**, 310
weights and measures, **24**, 312
ouncelands (eyrislands), **24**, 311
pennylands, **24**, 311
primogeniture, introduction to Orkney and
Shetland, **24**, 308
Pundlar case, **24**, 312, 321, 324
recognition, **24**, 321
roithman, **24**, 308
St Ninian's Isle Treasure case, **24**, 304, 313, 321,
322, 324–327, 329–400
St Olav's law, _see_ Code of Magnus 'the Law-
Mender' _above_
salmon-fishings, _see_ fishings _above_
sasines, **24**, 308
scat—
acknowledgment of royal authority, **24**, 327
compulsory purchase of land, **24**, 309
conveyance for valuable consideration, land
passed by, **24**, 309
effect of 1611 Act, **24**, 320
failure to deliver, **24**, 309
meaning, **24**, 309
nature of, **24**, 309
no new scats to be created, **24**, 309
non-payment of, **24**, 308
origin, **24**, 309
Orkney, **24**, 309
payment of, **24**, 306, 307, 309

Udal law—_continued_
scat—_continued_
Orkney, **24**, 309
payment of, **24**, 306, 307, 309
redeemed, **24**, 309
right secured by prescription, **24**, 307
scattald, _see_ scattald _below_
Shetland, **24**, 309
translated into fixed cash payments, **24**, 309
variable, **24**, 309
scattald—
effect of 1611 Act, **24**, 320
enclosure and division of lands, **24**, 310
foreshore rights, **24**, 310
meaning, **24**, 310
members' privileges, **24**, 310
Scottish recognition of, **22**, 387; **24**, 304
sea, territorial rights, **24**, 315
seabed, **24**, 316
seals, **24**, 314
seaweed, **24**, 314
Shetland—
Act of 1611 abolishing foreign laws, **24**, 304
allodial land, transfer of ownership, **18**, 646
Code of Magnus, 'the Law-Mender' (_Gulathing_
law), **24**, 303, 304
feudal system—
charters, **24**, 308
infeftments, **24**, 307
foreshore, **24**, 314, 320
impignoration to Scotland, **24**, 301, 304, 318, 326
land measures, **24**, 311
landownership, udal law, **24**, 306
lawbooks, **24**, 303, 304
Norwegian Crown, political authority of, **24**,
302
salmon fishing rights, **18**, 321
salmon fishings, **24**, 315
scat, _see_ scat _above_
scattald, _see_ scattald _above_
Scots law, application of, **24**, 301, 325
Scottish Crown's claim to, **24**, 302, 326, 327
Scottish influence, **24**, 318
seabed, ownership of, **18**, 310, 317; **24**, 316
sovereignty, **24**, 305
Scottish, **24**, 326–400
transfer from Norway to Scotland, **24**, 305,
326, 327
sysselman laws enforceable by, **24**, 306
weights and measures, **24**, 312
shynd bills, **24**, 307
sovereignty—
dimensions of, **24**, 327
dominium and, **24**, 327, 328
property rights, and, **24**, 327, 329–400
Scottish, Orkney and Shetland, **24**, 326–400
succession, **24**, 308
tenure, registration of title, **6**, 714, 777
territorial sea and fishing, **24**, 315
title, passing of, **24**, 307
treasure trove—
Crown's claim to, **24**, 324, 329–400
generally, **24**, 313
'hidden' and 'precious', **24**, 313

Udal law—*continued*
udal rights—
  Bankton *Institutes*, **22**, 368
  Erskine *Institutes*, **22**, 367
  modern cases, **22**, 385–388
  Stair's *Institutions*, **22**, 366
udal title burdened by feudal deeds, **24**, 307
Urislands, Orkney, **24**, 310
weights and measures, **24**, 312
whales, **24**, 314, 315
wrecks, **24**, 314
Ulster
baronetcies of, **11**, 1621
questionable jurisdiction of English King of Arms,
  11, 1625
Ulster Defence Regiment
calling out, **2**, 752
maintenance of, **2**, 611
Ultimus haeres
confirmation, estate may be made over without,
  25, 1102
Crown as, **13**, 411
heritable succession, **25**, 681
moveable succession, **25**, 681
Ultra heat-treatment
cream, **11**, 479
milk, **11**, 459
Ultra vires **doctrine**
actings, **16**, 1637
actions subject to, **1**, 221
amendment, **4**, 311
application of, **1**, 216
bill of exchange, capacity of company relating to,
  4, 127
charitable company and, **4**, 327
charity, act by, **4**, 413
Companies Act 1989 and, **4**, 326
constitutional principle, operating on grounds of,
  1, 219
damages, action for, **1**, 333
director, constitutional powers of, **4**, 413
employee, delictual act of, company's liability for,
  4, 318
error of law, and, **1**, 286
European Communities Act 1972, and, **4**, 325
excess of power, preventing exercise of, **1**, 218
exercise of administrative powers, relating to, **1**,
  215
generally, **4**, 323
historical development, **1**, 217
jurisdiction, application to, **1**, 216
local authority acting, **14**, 128–132
meaning, **1**, 214
minority shareholders, rights of, **4**, 464, 465
officer, delictual act of, company's liability for, **4**,
  318
personal bar, **16**, 1606, 1611
procedural grounds, operating on, **1**, 227
public corporation, **19**, 229, 230, 238
public policy, operating on grounds of, **1**, 219
reduction on grounds of, **13**, 44
reform of rule, **4**, 310
scope of, **1**, 215
statutory body, act by, personal bar, **16**, 1611

Ultra vires **doctrine**—*continued*
traditional, **4**, 324
unincorporated clubs, etc, applying to, **1**, 216
various versions of reform of, **4**, 301
Uncle
deceased specified relative, as, **15**, 602
division of estate on or after 8 December 1986—
  examples, **25**, 704
settlement, family reunion or creation by, **12**,
  289, 290
Uncompetitive practices
meaning, **4**, 1232*n*
Under Clerk of Parliaments
status, **7**, 757
Underground railway
provisional orders in connection with, **19**, 14
station, prevention of fires at, **19**, 1057
Underground rooms
closing orders, **11**, 1981, 1982*n*
Underground water
See WATER
Underpass
construction of, **20**, 611
Undertakings
competition law—
  agreements between, application of Article
    85(1) ..., **4**, 1319
  anti-competitive practices, preliminary inves-
    tigation, **4**, 1260
  Articles 85 and 86, scope of, **4**, 1312
  breadth of concept, **4**, 1318
  Commission's report, consequences of, **4**, 1243
  decisions by associations of, application of
    Article 85(1), **4**, 1320
  EU law and, **4**, 1393
  merger investigation, entered into following, **4**,
    1166
  merger reference, as alternative to, **4**, 568
  monopoly investigation, entered into following,
    4, 1166
  one or more, dominant position abused by, **4**,
    1330, 1333
  public interest, restrictions contrary to, **4**, 1189
transfer of—
  continuous employment, effect on, **9**, 48
  European law, influence of, **9**, 16
  redundancy, effect on, **9**, 178
  unfair dismissal, **9**, 228
See TRANSFER OF UNDERTAKINGS
Undertakings for Collective Investment in
  Transferable Securities (UCITS)
collective investment schemes, **12**, 1328
operators and trustees, Securities and Investments
  Board Core Conduct of Business Rules, **12**,
  1399
Underwater operation, vessel engaged in
restricted manoeuvrability, vessel with, lights and
  shapes to be diplayed, **21**, 365
Underwriting
building societies, and, **3**, 374
Underwriting agent
innkeepers' strict liability not applicable to, **15**, 147
Undue influence
capacity of testator, effect on, **25**, 764

Undue influence—*continued*
circumvention distinguished from, **25**, 764
doctrine of, **3**, 903, 904
electoral malpractice, **7**, 409
essence of doctrine, **11**, 738
external public policy rule, **17**, 171
facility distinguished from, **25**, 764
generally, **11**, 738
independent advice, absence of, **11**, 741
material or gratuitous benefit to dominant party,
   11, 740
parties, relationship between, **11**, 739
reduction of donation, **8**, 647
reduction on grounds of, **13**, 44
remedies, **11**, 742
trust, relationship of, **11**, 738
will made under, **11**, 744
Unearned income
taxation of, **19**, 1515
Unemployment
benefit, *see* UNEMPLOYMENT BENEFIT
competition law used as instrument of, **4**, 1107
day of, *see* UNEMPLOYMENT BENEFIT
early provisions, **14**, 34
friendly society member, assistance to, **12**, 694*n*
friendly society payments on, **12**, 686
Manpower Services Commission, arrangements
   by, **14**, 630
Unemployment benefit
adverse industrial conditions, effect of, **21**, 820
another part of country, employment opportunity
   arising in, **21**, 858
availability for work—
   actively seeking work—
      claimant must be, **21**, 825, 829
      what constitutes, **21**, 829
   deemed, **21**, 827
   employment given up in just cause, where, **21**,
      851
   generally, **21**, 825
   holiday, claimant taking, **21**, 828, 829
   interview in connection with employment
      prospects, failure to comply with written
      notice of, **21**, 830
   part-time employment, restriction of avail-
      ability to, **21**, 825
   refusal of suitable offers, **21**, 825
   restrictions on type of work acceptable,
      claimant placing, **21**, 825, 826
   terms and conditions of employment standard
      within local area, **21**, 825
casual employment, **21**, 822
charitable work, worker engaged in, **21**, 815, 829*n*
compensation payments—
   consultation, in lieu of, **21**, 832
   duration of disqualification, **21**, 832
   effect of, generally, **21**, 831
   meaning, **21**, 831
conscientious objection to particular job, where,
   21, 858
day of employment, **21**, 805
day of unemployment—
   adverse industrial conditions, effect, **21**, 820
   annually, wages paid, **21**, 809

Unemployment benefit—*continued*
day of unemployment—*continued*
   arrears, wages paid in, **21**, 809
   availability for work, generally, **21**, 825
   commission, worker paid by, **21**, 806
   contract of employment in relation to, **21**, 803,
      805
      allocation of wages, **21**, 809
      arrears, wages paid in, **21**, 809
      commission, worker paid by, **21**, 806
      default in payment of wages, where, **21**, 807
      no work no wages rule, **21**, 806
      partial payment of wages, where, **21**, 808
      succession of short-term contracts, where,
         21, 812
      termination of employment, **21**, 812
      worker on call, **21**, 825
   council meetings, attendance allowance paid in
      respect of, **21**, 809*n*
   day of employment distinguished, **21**, 805
   full extent normal rule, **21**, 816
   holiday, recognised or customary, **21**, 875
      employed earner's employment, must be in
         connection with, **21**, 875, 877
      exceptions to holiday rule, **21**, 876
      meaning, **21**, 875
      non-working days, **21**, 877
      teachers and other employees in educational
         establishments, **21**, 877
   meaning—
      generally, **21**, 803
      nightworkers, **21**, 813
   normal idle day rule, **21**, 821, 822
   payable in respect of, **21**, 802
   period of interruption of unemployment, **21**,
      813
   quarterly, wages paid, **21**, 809
   requalification for benefit in relation to, **21**,
      824
   self-employed person, **21**, 804
      no work no wages rule, **21**, 806
      sleeping partner, **21**, 804
   subsidiary employment, **21**, 815
   Sundays, **21**, 814
      day substituted for, **21**, 814
   training course, claimant on, **21**, 810, 811, 829*n*
   weekly, wages paid, **21**, 809
dependent adult, increase where, **21**, 1017
dependent child, increase where, **21**, 1015
disabled, occupation centre for, attendance at, **21**,
   811
dismissal—
   conduct inviting, **21**, 843
   unilateral change in employment terms,
      following, **21**, 844
   voluntarily leaving employment without just
      cause, relationship with, **21**, 843
disqualification—
   alternative employment should be sought
      before resignation, **21**, 850
   compensation payments, where, **21**, 832
   early retirement scheme, employee leaving
      under, **21**, 845

Unemployment benefit—*continued*
disqualification—*continued*
  employment opportunity—
    failure to avail oneself of reasonable, **21**, 854
    proper notification, what constitutes, **21**, 853
  misconduct, employment lost through—
    adjudication of claim, **21**, 841, 842
    bad workmanship due to limited ability, **21**, 839
    blameworthiness, concept of, **21**, 839, 840
    breach of contract, where, **21**, 840
    connection of misconduct with employment, **21**, 838
    decisions in other proceedings, relevance of, **21**, 842
    generally, **21**, 835, 845
    joining or refusing to join trade union not amounting to, **21**, 836, 849
    mental state of employee, **21**, 839
    negligence amounting to misconduct, **21**, 839
    onus of proof, **21**, 841
    outwith working hours, misconduct committed, **21**, 838
    resign or be dismissed situation, **21**, 837
    resignation, **21**, 837
    temporary suspension from work, **21**, 837
  official recommendations made to assist finding employment, refusal to follow, **21**, 855
  period of—
    commencement, **21**, 859
    factors determining, **21**, 859
    maximum, **21**, 859
    spell of employment during, **21**, 859
  refusal or failure to apply for job, **21**, 853
  resignation—
    employee initiating, **21**, 845
    fundamental breakdown in relations with employer or fellow workers, where, **21**, 847, 849
    generally, **21**, 845
    involuntary, when treated as, **21**, 845
    misconduct, employment lost through, **21**, 837
    resign or be dismissed situation, **21**, 837
    whether alternative employment sought prior to, **21**, 850
  self-induced unemployment, generally, **21**, 834
  trade dispute—
    causation, **21**, 869
    claimant leaving employment prior to stoppage, where, **21**, 867
    claimant prevented from taking up employment by stoppage, where, **21**, 867
    demarcation dispute, **21**, 864
    direct interest in, meaning, **21**, 872
    duration of disqualification, **21**, 871
    end of dispute—
      onus of proof, **21**, 870
    end of stoppage, **21**, 870
    existence of dispute, **21**, 865
    generally, **21**, 863
    loss of employment by reason of stoppage, meaning, **21**, 867
    meaning of trade dispute, **21**, 864

Unemployment benefit—*continued*
disqualification—*continued*
  trade dispute—*continued*
    more than one issue, dispute involving, **21**, 872
    onus of proof, **21**, 863
    place of work, at, **21**, 863, 866
    place of work, not at, **21**, 874
    re-employment elsewhere during, **21**, 873
    re-employment with employer during, **21**, 873
    stoppage, meaning, **21**, 863
    stoppage ceasing to be due to, **21**, 869
    termination of employment contract following, **21**, 868
    withdrawal of labour, **21**, 874
    worker not directly interested in dispute, where, **21**, 863, 872
  unreasonable refusal of employment or training—
    arrival for interview in unacceptable state, **21**, 854
    burden of proof, **21**, 852
    generally, **21**, 852, 854
    good cause, generally, **21**, 857
    good cause for act or omission—
      generally, **21**, 857
      relevant considerations, **21**, 858
    notification of employment opportunity, following, **21**, 853
    refusal or failure to apply for job, **21**, 853
    relevant considerations, **21**, 858
    suitability of work, **21**, 852
    training places, generally, **21**, 856
  voluntarily leaving employment without just cause—
    alternative employment sought prior to resignation, **21**, 850
    availability for employment and, **21**, 851
    circumstances, importance of, **21**, 847
    dismissal—
      amounting to, **21**, 843
      conduct inviting, **21**, 843
    early retirement, **21**, 845, 846
    generally, **21**, 843
    instances of just cause, **21**, 847, 848
    meaning of just cause, **21**, 846
    onus of proof, **21**, 843
    public interest, acting in, **21**, 846
    resignation, **21**, 845
    unilateral change in employment terms, after, **21**, 844
    union membership, cases relating to, **21**, 836, 849
duration, **21**, 823
  requalification, **21**, 824
early retirement scheme, employee leaving under, **21**, 845
earnings, maximum limit allowed, **21**, 815
employment providing inadequate livelihood, resignation where, **21**, 848
entitlement—
  day of unemployment, *see* day of unemployment *above*
  generally, **21**, 801, 802

Unemployment benefit—*continued*
expenses incurred by particular employment opportunity, consideration of, **21**, 858
full extent normal rule—
    fifty per cent test, **21**, 817
    generally, **21**, 816
    normal idle day rule, overlap with, **21**, 821
    one year before test, **21**, 817
    part-time worker, **21**, 816
        stop-gap test, **21**, 819
    particular claimant, position of, **21**, 818
    record of employment, **21**, 817
    rota, pattern of work laid down by, **21**, 816
    short-time, worker on, **21**, 816, 818
        adverse industrial conditions, **21**, 820
        definition, **21**, 820
    stop-gap test, **21**, 819
guide dog for the blind training course, claimant on, **21**, 829n
health, particular employment or training likely to cause serious harm to, **21**, 858
health of employee leading to resignation, where, **21**, 848
interview in connection with employment prospects, failure to comply with written notice of, **21**, 830
mentally disordered, training centre for, attendance at, **21**, 811
national insurance Class 1 contributions, **21**, 1040
nightworkers, **21**, 813
no work no wages rule, **21**, 806
normal idle day rule, **21**, 821, 822
    full extent normal rule, overlap with, **21**, 821
occupational pension, payment of, effect, **21**, 823, 833
Outward Bound course, claimant attending, **21**, 829n
part-time employment, **21**, 816
    stop-gap test, **21**, 819
part-time worker, **21**, 816
pension scheme, refund of contributions made to, **21**, 831
pension scheme payments, occupational, abatement of benefit where, **21**, 1275
redundancy pay, effect, **21**, 831
religious objection to particular job, where, **21**, 858
requalification, **21**, 824
responsibility for care of another member of household interfering with particular employment opportunity, **21**, 858
rota, pattern of work laid down by, **21**, 816
scope, **21**, 802
share fisherman—
    abroad, day of unemployment while, **21**, 862
    absence of fish, failure to work due to, **21**, 861
    eligibility—
        conditions for, **21**, 860, 861
        generally, **21**, 860
    generally, **21**, 860
    good cause ground, **21**, 861, 862
    intention of further fishing with vessel ceased, where, **21**, 861, 861n
    neglect of reasonable opportunity of fishing, **21**, 861

Unemployment benefit—*continued*
share fisherman—*continued*
    repairs and maintenance, failure to work due to, **21**, 861
    weather, failure to work due to, **21**, 861
short-time, worker on, **21**, 816, 818
stop-gap test, **21**, 819
stress, physical or mental, particular employment likely to cause, **21**, 858
subsidiary employment, effect, **21**, 815
Sunday, religious objection to working on, **21**, 858
suspension of employment, **21**, 822
temporary suspension from work, misconduct, following, **21**, 837
termination of employment, **21**, 812, 822
    compensation payments, effect, **21**, 831, 832
    holiday etc pay accrued before, **21**, 832
    payment in respect of period before, **21**, 831
    redundancy pay, effect, **21**, 831
time involved in travelling to particular employment opportunity, **21**, 858
trade dispute—
    contract of employment terminated during, effect, **21**, 868
    unemployment as result of, *see* disqualification *above*
trainee believing himself to be inadequate for the job, resignation where, **21**, 848
training—
    course, claimant on, **21**, 810, 811, 829n
    failure to apply for place on scheme, **21**, 856
travelling expenses and time involved in particular employment opportunity, **21**, 858
unfair dismissal, recoupment in case of award—
    calculation, method of, **9**, 299
    future loss, **9**, 301
    general principles, **9**, 298
    regulations, effect of, **9**, 300
vocational training or study, claimant participating in, **21**, 829n
voluntary work, claimant undertaking, **21**, 829n
waiting days, **21**, 813, 823, 823n

Unenclosed land
ground game, right to take and kill, **11**, 853

Unfair competition
European Union legislation—
    case law, **18**, 1641
    generally, **18**, 1615, 1617, 1640
International Convention for the Protection of Industrial Property (1883), **18**, 801
passing off in relation to, **18**, 1364
See also PASSING OFF

Unfair contract terms
statutory controls, **14**, 1052

Unfair dismissal
benefits, recoupment of—
    calculation, method of, **9**, 299
    future loss, **9**, 301
    general principles, **9**, 298
    regulations, effect of, **9**, 300
complaints and appeals relating to, **6**, 981, 997
conciliation in case of claim, **9**, 315
Crown servants, **7**, 759, 760

Unfair dismissal—*continued*
excluded classes—
  ACAS, exclusion following action by, **9**, 212
  age of applicant, **9**, 205
  complaint out of time, **9**, 213
  contract law, limitations imposed by, **9**, 204
  contracting out, **9**, 207
  dismissal procedures agreement, **9**, 208
  fixed-term contract, **9**, 209
  industrial action, **9**, 214
  length of service, **9**, 206
  place of employment, **9**, 210
  scope of law, **9**, 203
  specific employments, **9**, 211
expenses, **9**, 279
generally, **6**, 997; **9**, 201; **19**, 1237
industrial tribunal, jurisdiction of, **9**, 306
pregnancy, because of, **9**, 115
protection against, loss of, **9**, 281
remedies for—
  basic award—
    age, reduction on grounds of, **9**, 266
    calculation of, **9**, 265
    contribution, reduction for, **9**, 268
    redundancy case, minimum award in, **9**, 269
    redundancy payment, effect of, **9**, 267
  compensatory award—
    assessment—
      methods of, **9**, 276
      principles of, **9**, 275
      summary of, **9**, 277
    benefits, loss of, **9**, 278
    contributory fault, **9**, 284
    expenses, **9**, 279
    fringe benefits, loss of, **9**, 278
    generally, **9**, 270
    just and equitable reductions, **9**, 285
    manner of dismissal, loss arising from, **9**, 280
    mitigation of loss, **9**, 283
    pension rights, loss of, **9**, 274
    principles, **9**, 271
    reduction of, **9**, 282
    statutory limits, **9**, 287
    trade union membership dismissal, **9**, 286
    unfair dismissal, loss of protection against, **9**, 281
    wages—
      future loss, **9**, 273
      immediate loss of, **9**, 272
  generally, **9**, 260, 295
  interim relief—
    claim—
      determination of, **9**, 294
      presentation of, **9**, 293
    continuation of employment, order for, **9**, 296
    grounds, **9**, 292
    variation of order, **9**, 297
  re-engagement—
    factors to be considered, **9**, 263
    generally, **9**, 262
    orders, compliance with, **9**, 264
  reinstatement—
    factors to be considered, **9**, 263

Unfair dismissal—*continued*
remedies for—*continued*
  reinstatement—*continued*
    generally, **9**, 261
    orders, compliance with, **9**, 264
  special award—
    amount of, **9**, 289
    generally, **9**, 288
    reduction of, **9**, 290
  third party, award against, **9**, 291
statutory remedy, **1**, 269
substance of—
  particular situations—
    changes in terms, refusal to accept, **9**, 259
    criminal offences, **9**, 256
    illness, **9**, 257
    incompetency, **9**, 254
    misconduct, **9**, 255
    redundancy, **9**, 258
  reasonableness—
    employee, personal circumstances of, **9**, 253
    generally, **9**, 249
    procedures, **9**, 252
    statutory guidance, **9**, 250
    test to be applied, **9**, 251
  reasons for dismissal—
    capability, **9**, 244
    conduct, **9**, 245
    enactment, contravention of, **9**, 247
    general considerations, **9**, 243
    generally, **9**, 242
    other, **9**, 248
    qualifications, **9**, 244
    redundancy, **9**, 246
termination of contract—
  confinement, woman's right to return after, **9**, 220
  discrimination—
    effect of, **9**, 226
    race, **9**, 231, 357
    sex, **9**, 231, 357
  dismissal, generally, **9**, 215
  effective date of, **9**, 219
  employee, by, **9**, 218
  employer, by, **9**, 216
  fixed-term contract, expiry without renewal of, **9**, 217
  frustration, **9**, 222
  industrial action, **9**, 225
  non-dismissal, **9**, 221
  pregnancy, **9**, 227
  redundancy, selection for, **9**, 230
  rehabilitation of offenders, **9**, 229
  resignation, **9**, 224
  self-dismissal, **9**, 223
  trade union—
    appropriate time, **9**, 239
    code of practice, **9**, 241
    fair dismissal—
      conditions to be met, **9**, 235
      generally, **9**, 234
    generally, **9**, 232, 236
    membership agreement, **9**, 233
    protected employees, **9**, 238, 240

Unfair dismissal—*continued*
termination of contract—*continued*
trade union—*continued*
third party, payment to, **9**, 237
transfer of undertakings, **9**, 228
wrongful dismissal compared, **9**, 202
Unfair preference
challenge, effect of, **4**, 886
challenging, provisions altering rules for, **4**, 307
common law—
generally, **4**, 880
transactions exempt from challenge at, **4**, 881
who may challenge at, **4**, 882
fraudulent preference replaced by, **11**, 781*n*
Insolvency Act 1986 ..., **4**, 884
old law, **4**, 879
reduction, effect of, **4**, 883
statutory challenge, transactions exempt from, **4**, 885
Uniform Customs and Practice for Documentary Credits
See LETTER OF CREDIT
Unilateral promise
acceptance, no requirement for, **15**, 614, 618
assignation of right to benefit, **15**, 616
communication, **15**, 618
consent, no requirement for, **15**, 614, 618
contract compared, **15**, 611, 613
delivery, **15**, 618
English and Scots law compared, **15**, 614
form, **15**, 615
generally, **15**, 613
gratuitous, constitution, **15**, 668
gratuitous nature, **15**, 613
institutional writers, **15**, 614
offer, to keep open, **15**, 616, 617
offer distinguished, **15**, 615, 616
prescription, **15**, 618
promisee—
acceptance by, no requirement for, **15**, 614, 618
assignation of right to benefit by, **15**, 616
bankruptcy, **15**, 616
conduct meeting terms of promise, effect, **15**, 616
death, **15**, 616
failure to seek performance, **15**, 618
insanity, **15**, 616
no knowledge of promise, where, **15**, 611
position of, generally, **15**, 611, 613
rejection by, **15**, 618
promisor—
bankruptcy, **15**, 616
death, **15**, 616
insanity, **15**, 616
offeror compared, **15**, 616
position of, generally, **15**, 613, 614, 616
rejection by promisee, **15**, 618
resile, actings barring right to, **15**, 669
writ or oath, proved by, **15**, 615
writing, constitution in, **15**, 615
Unincorporated association
capacity to contract, **3**, 26
donations, capacity to make and receive, **8**, 611

Unincorporated association—*continued*
members, number of reduced to one, **18**, 35
property—
beneficial interest in, **18**, 34
joint property, as, **18**, 20, 34, 34*n*
characteristics of joint property, **18**, 35
management, rules of, **18**, 36, 36*n*
resignation or death of member, **18**, 35
See also CO-OWNERSHIP
ownership passing on death or resignation, **18**, 20
title to, **18**, 34
unity of title, **18**, 20
winding up, **18**, 35
See also CLUB
Unincorporated body
joint tenancy, **13**, 189
lessee, as, **13**, 189, 191
lessor, as, **13**, 179
Union Agreement of 1707
Act of Settlement, **7**, 783
Acts of Union, generally, **5**, 344, 361; **19**, 206
admiralty jurisdiction, **7**, 816
alterations in law, **7**, 739
amendment of—
judicial review, by, **5**, 347, 350; **22**, 150, 602
legislation, by, **5**, 346, 347, 470; **22**, 149, 601
binding force, **7**, 739
Church of Scotland, **3**, 1501, 1502, 1634; **5**, 348; **7**, 739
constitutional status, **5**, 343–347; **22**, 145, 600
courts and justiciary, **7**, 739
Crown Seals, **7**, 855
customs and excise laws, **7**, 739
electoral system post Union, **22**, 467–470
English influence after, **22**, 597, 600–602
fundamental law, Union legislation as, **5**, 343–351; **22**, 144–146
Great Seal, **7**, 785
historical background, **5**, 344
House of Lords, appellate jurisdiction under, **6**, 810–812; **22**, 602
intention of, **22**, 146
international adjudication, whether applicable, **7**, 739
interpretation of—
English writers, **5**, 351; **22**, 148
institutional writers, **22**, 147
Ireland, Act of Union compared, **5**, 345, 351
nature of, **5**, 343–346
Officers of the Crown after, **7**, 811
Officers of State after, **7**, 801–804
parliamentary representation, **5**, 469
parliamentary sovereignty, and, **5**, 309, 351, 362; **6**, 810; **22**, 144
permanency, **7**, 739
private rights, protection, **7**, 739
Protestant Religion and Presbyterian Church Act, **3**, 1501
ratification, **7**, 739
royal arms, **7**, 785
Scottish courts, provision for, **5**, 349
Scottish legal system, **5**, 350; **13**, 1135

Union Agreement of 1707—*continued*
statutory source of Scots law, as, **22**, 525–527
treaty, as, **7**, 739
Union Européenne des Experts Comptables, Economiques et Financiers
accounting standards, influence on, **1**, 77
Union of Soviet Socialist Republics (USSR)
imports, European Union regulations, **7**, 1029
Unit of account
common, **14**, 1833
debts incurred in, **14**, 1804
function of money, **14**, 1803
Unit trust company
appointed representatives, **12**, 1361
Unit trust scheme
alterations to, notification, **12**, 1327
authorised—
    authorisation, **12**, 1327
    manager, **12**, 1327*n*
        replacement of, **12**, 1327
    meaning, **12**, 1325
    promotion, **12**, 1326
    revocation, **12**, 1327
    Securities and Investments Board powers, **12**, 1327
    trustee, **12**, 1327*n*
        replacement of, **12**, 1327
corporation tax, **19**, 1519
establishment, **12**, 1307
investment trust distinguished, **2**, 1275
Life Assurance and Unit Trust Regulatory Association, **12**, 1312
management, VAT exemption, **7**, 1424
manager, takeover, position on, **4**, 538
meaning, **12**, 1325
nature of, **2**, 1278
operation, **12**, 1307
Prevention of Fraud (Investments) Act 1958 ..., **12**, 1302
register, **12**, 1415
trust concept, **24**, 11
trustee, **12**, 1327
    investment business acting as, **12**, 1307
trustees not partners, **16**, 1006
winding up, **12**, 1307
See also COLLECTIVE INVESTMENT SCHEME
United Free Church
Church of Scotland properties and endowments originating in, **3**, 1600
sale, **3**, 1608
generally, **3**, 1636
union with Church of Scotland, **3**, 1503
United Kingdom
abode, right of, **12**, 107
    See also ABODE
Act extending throughout, **12**, 1101, 1187
    uniform application, **12**, 1188
allocation of jurisdiction within, **4**, 21, 23
British citizens, **12**, 107
British Dependent Territories citizens, **12**, 107
British Overseas citizens, **12**, 107
civil jurisdiction, contracting state, as, **4**, 22
common travel area, **16**, 1208

United Kingdom—*continued*
enter, right to—
    air crews, **16**, 1208
    Commonwealth citizen, **16**, 1211
    Declaration of Identity for Visa Purposes, **16**, 1211
    diplomatic staff, **16**, 1208
    endorsement of passport, **16**, 1244
    entry clearance, *see* entry clearance *below*
    European Union national, **16**, 1206
    foreign passport or other travel document, holder, **16**, 1208, 1208*n*
    generally, **16**, 1206
    identity, requirement to produce evidence of, **16**, 1206
    identity card, EU, production, **16**, 1206
    immigration officer, powers, **16**, 1206
    letter of consent, **16**, 1211
    military personnel, **16**, 1208
    non-UK passport-holder, **16**, 1208–1211
    sea crews, **16**, 1208
    UK passport-holder, **16**, 1207, 1207*n*
    visa, **16**, 1211
    visa national—
        exemptions, **16**, 1210
        generally, **16**, 1209
    Visitor's Card scheme, **16**, 1206
entry clearance—
    appeal, right of, **16**, 1240
    application procedure, **16**, 1239
    Commonwealth citizen, **16**, 1238
    endorsement of passport, **16**, 1244
    entry certificate, **16**, 1238
    legal controls, **16**, 1240
    letter of consent, **16**, 1238
    types, **16**, 1238
    variation of leave to remain, **16**, 1244
    visa, **16**, 1238
    work permit, **16**, 1243
European Union customs territory, **7**, 1010
European Union law, status of, **10**, 84
exclusion order, **12**, 107
extradition to, **12**, 530
implementation of European directives, **10**, 93
institutions, *see* INSTITUTIONS
international law, approach to, **19**, 653, 654
leave, right to—
    British mercenary, rules applicable to, **16**, 1205*n*
    debtor, absconding, **16**, 1205*n*
    foreign national, **16**, 1205, 1205*n*
    international carrier, passenger of, **16**, 1205
    international law, **16**, 1205*n*
    passport, possession, **16**, 1205, 1205*n*
migration to—
    generally, **12**, 101
    nineteenth century, **12**, 104, 105
    twentieth century, **12**, 101, 102, 106, 107
    until the Union, **12**, 103
national, meaning, **12**, 220
outline of competition law, **4**, 1110
Parliament only sovereign legislature, **12**, 1187
part of, meaning, **4**, 28
passport, *see* PASSPORT

United Kingdom—*continued*
passport holders—
  change of category, **12**, 328
  dependants of, **12**, 326, 328
  entry, generally, **12**, 327
  extensions of leave, **12**, 328
  meaning, **12**, 324
  settlement, eligibility for entry for, **12**, 325
    dependants, **12**, 325
patrials, **12**, 107
'replacement labour', **12**, 102
state, recognition of, **19**, 662–664
  domestic law, effect upon, **19**, 663
treaties, position with regard to, **19**, 605, 617
United Kingdom Atomic Energy Authority
legislation relating to, **9**, 913
**United Kingdom Atomic Energy Authority
  constabulary**
appointment to, **16**, 1815, 1818
jurisdiction, **16**, 1815
organisation, **16**, 1815
powers, **16**, 1815
privileges, **16**, 1815
**United Kingdom Central Council for
  Nursing, Midwifery and Health Visiting**
constitution, **14**, 1148; **15**, 1496
election—
  ballot papers, validity, **15**, 1504
  candidates, **15**, 1499
    list, publication, **15**, 1500
    nomination, **15**, 1500
      appeals, **15**, 1501
      invalid, **15**, 1501
    number required, **15**, 1499
    qualification, **15**, 1500
    right to challenge election, **15**, 1506
    willingness to stand, **15**, 1500
    withdrawal, **15**, 1500
  challenging validity, **15**, 1506
  conduct, **15**, 1502
  count, **15**, 1505
  electoral scheme, generally, **15**, 1496, 1497
  notification, **15**, 1498
  postponement, **15**, 1499
  single transferable vote, **15**, 1497, 1502
  voting procedure, **15**, 1503
electoral roll, **15**, 1498
functions, **14**, 1148; **15**, 1496
returning officer, **15**, 1497
United Kingdom Passport Agency
Central Records Unit, **16**, 1215
computerisation, **16**, 1215, 1218
generally, **16**, 1214, 1230
organisation, **16**, 1215
Passport Issuing and Management Information
  System (PIMIS), **16**, 1215, 1218
regional offices, **16**, 1215
**United Kingdom Standard Towing
  Conditions (UKSTC)**
See TOW
United Nations
Charter, **19**, 698*n*, 699
  aggression under, **19**, 700
  collective force, **19**, 704

United Nations—*continued*
Charter—*continued*
  deficiency, **12**, 3
  generally, **12**, 3
  regional security arrangements, **19**, 703
  self-defence, **19**, 702
collective force through, **19**, 704
Commission on International Trade Law, **4**, 105;
  19, 650
copyright, **18**, 1004
Covenant on Civil and Political Rights—
  General Assembly, adopted by, **5**, 315
  municipal law of United Kingdom, not part of,
    5, 316
establishment, **19**, 601*n*
force, use or threat of, **19**, 699–702
  collective force, **19**, 704
  where permissible, **19**, 705
goods produced by, charge to VAT, **7**, 1314
International Court of Justice, *see* INTERNATIONAL
  COURT OF JUSTICE
international disputes, settlement of, **19**, 718*n*
International Maritime Organisation, *see*
  INTERNATIONAL MARITIME ORGANISATION
international peace and security, maintenance of,
  19, 697*n*, 699
laissez-passer, **16**, 1236
member states, **19**, 603, 603*n*, 648
membership requirements, **19**, 603*n*
non-member states, claims against, **19**, 615*n*
peacekeeping forces, **19**, 704
person, international, as, **19**, 693
personality, objective, possessing, **19**, 615*n*
recognition of, **19**, 661
relation of European Community to, **10**, 299, 302
representatives, precedence, **16**, 2014
resolutions, **19**, 603*n*
  challenged, **19**, 648
  legally binding, **19**, 648*n*
  source of international law, as, **19**, 648
Security Council, **19**, 603*n*
shipping policies, generally, **21**, 116
specialised agencies, **19**, 601*n*, 650
  copyright, **18**, 1004
trusteeship system, **12**, 3, 3*n*
Universal Declaration of Human Rights, **12**, 4
veto, permanent members' power of, **19**, 603*n*
World Intellectual Property Organisation, **18**, 801
**United Nations Conference on Human
  Environment**
international awareness promoted through, **9**, 1104
**United Nations Conference on the Law of
  the Sea (UNCLOS)**
generally, **11**, 65, 70, 73, 76, 80
straits used for international navigation, **21**, 10
UNCLOS I, **21**, 2, 5, 47
UNCLOS II, **21**, 2, 5
  exclusive economic zone, **21**, 38
UNCLOS III—
  continental shelf, approach to, **21**, 23, 30
  continental shelf of islands, **21**, 25
  deep sea bed, **21**, 48
  exclusive economic zone, **21**, 38
  generally, **21**, 3

United Nations Conference on the Law of the Sea (UNCLOS)—*continued*
UNICLOS III—*continued*
  problems arising, **21**, 4
  territorial sea, **21**, 5
  transit passage, **21**, 10
United Nations General Assembly Declaration of Principles Governing the Sea Bed and the Ocean Floor
generally, **21**, 47, 48
United Original Secession Synod
Church of Scotland property and endowments originating in, **3**, 1602
United Presbyterian Church
Church of Scotland properties and endowments originating in, **3**, 1597
generally, **3**, 1636
United Secession Church
generally, **3**, 1636
United States courts
law reports, **21**, 740
maritime law, **21**, 739
United States of America
American Treaty on Pacific Settlement, **19**, 698n, 720n
American Uniform Commercial Code, **14**, 1007
anti-trust legislation, **19**, 677, 677n
Chicago School of economists, **4**, 1106
colonies, prize law extended to vessels of, **17**, 401
constitution—
  amendments to, **5**, 307
  background to, **5**, 303
  single document, contained in, **5**, 303
conventions, **5**, 306
European commercial paper may not be transferred to, **4**, 103
leasing of moveables—
  classification of leases, **14**, 1007
  cross-border leasing, **14**, 1094
  development of, **14**, 1006
president of, **5**, 306
retrospective legislation, Congress forbidden to pass, **5**, 311
Sterling commercial paper may not be transferred to, **4**, 103
tort, application of flexible connecting factors, **17**, 125
Universities Central Council on Admissions
establishment and purpose, **8**, 1005
Universities Funding Council
control exercised by, **8**, 1014
establishment, **8**, 1015
grants to, **8**, 1015
members, **8**, 1015
  appointment, **8**, 1015
powers and responsibilities, **8**, 1015
Scottish Higher Education Funding Council, proposed replacement by, **8**, 1015
terms and conditions of grants and payments, **8**, 1015
University
academic freedom, **8**, 985
  generally, **8**, 985
  restraints, **8**, 985

University—*continued*
academic freedom—*continued*
  tenure, and, **8**, 1020
  threats to, **8**, 985
academic performance—
  examinations, **8**, 1026
  sending down due to, **8**, 1027
  suspension due to, **8**, 1027
accounts, **8**, 1016
admissions, **8**, 1005, 1006
Bourges, **22**, 604
Carnegie Trust for the Universities of Scotland, purpose, **8**, 1003
chair, person or body founding or endowing, **8**, 1018
chancellor, **8**, 996, 1008
charities, as, **8**, 1002
colleges, **8**, 988
Committee of Vice-Chancellors and Principals, **8**, 1004
Comptroller and Auditor-General, access to university accounts, **8**, 1014
constitutional structure, **8**, 995
convocation, **8**, 1000
copyright—
  permitted acts, *see* EDUCATION
  staff, of, **8**, 1022
  students', **8**, 1023
corporations, as, **8**, 987, 995
courts—
  assessors, **8**, 996, 997, 999
  co-opted members, **8**, 999
  generally, **8**, 995
  staff as employees of, **8**, 1019
Crown property granted to, **24**, 595
curriculum, **8**, 984
degrees—
  abbreviations, **8**, 1009, 1012
  cancellation of award, **8**, 1010
  Doctor of Philosophy, **8**, 1009
  higher, **8**, 1009
  honoris causa, conferred, **8**, 1009
  meaning, **8**, 1009
  recognised awards, designation as, **8**, 1013
  unrecognised, **8**, 1013
departments, **8**, 991
diplomas, **8**, 1009
duty of care owed to students, **8**, 1025
endowments, **8**, 837
entitlement to, **8**, 986
faculties, **8**, 989
freedom of speech of persons working in or visiting, **8**, 1031
function of, **8**, 984
funding, **8**, 1014
  accounts, **8**, 1016
  central government, **8**, 1015
  history, **8**, 1015
  Scottish Higher Education Funding Council, **8**, 977
  Universities Funding Council, **8**, 1014, 1015
general council, **8**, 1000
government, legal relations with, **8**, 1014
government investigations, **8**, 1014

University—*continued*
graduates—
  graduates' council, **8**, 1000
  legal relations with university, **8**, 1011
  passing off as graduate, **8**, 1012
graduation, **8**, 1009
grant to, Secretary of State's powers, **8**, 708
health services, *see* UNIVERSITY LIAISON COMMITTEE
higher education, as, **8**, 983
incorporated body of scholars, as, **8**, 984
independence, **8**, 1014
lectureship, person or body founding or endowing, **8**, 1018
legal studies, **8**, 1007
Leyden, **22**, 604
liaison committee, *see* UNIVERSITY LIAISON COMMITTEE
libraries, loss of book delivery privilege, **13**, 1503
maintenance of scholar in, charitable purpose, as, **3**, 1119
members, **8**, 1008
nature of, **8**, 984
negligence, liability for, **8**, 1025
older universities, **8**, 987
Open University, **8**, 993
origins, **8**, 982
Orleans law school, **22**, 604
other forms of higher education compared, **8**, 984
Parliamentary representation, **15**, 1016, 1018, 1019
pass-rate of course, **8**, 1025
patentable invention made by teacher at, **8**, 1023
precedence *inter se*, **16**, 2024
principal, **8**, 997
professions, governing bodies of, legal relations with, **8**, 1017
Public Accounts Committee, reports to, **8**, 1014
qualifications granted by, **8**, 1009
rector, **8**, 997
research—
  emphasis on, **8**, 984
  legal studies, **8**, 1007
schools, **8**, 990
Scotland, universities in—
  Aberdeen, **8**, 987
    canon law teaching in, **22**, 575
    foundation, **22**, 552
    William Hay's lectures, sacrament of marriage, **22**, 581
  Dundee, **8**, 987
  Edinburgh, **8**, 987
    foundation, fifteenth century, **22**, 514
  Glasgow, **8**, 987
    canon law teaching in, **22**, 575
    foundation, **22**, 552
  Heriot-Watt University, **8**, 987
  legal education, canon law, limited extent of teaching, **22**, 552, 575, 580
    Dark Ages, **22**, 514
    fifteenth century development, **22**, 552
    revival in eighteenth century, **22**, 552
    Roman law, failure to teach, **22**, 552
  St Andrews, **8**, 987
    canon law teaching in, **22**, 575
    foundation, **22**, 552

University—*continued*
Scotland, universities in—*continued*
  Stirling, **8**, 987
  Strathclyde, **8**, 987
Scottish Universities Committee of the Privy Council, **8**, 992
Scottish Universities Council on Entrance, **8**, 1006
senate, **8**, 995
staff—
  academic freedom, **8**, 985, 1020
  copyright of, **8**, 1022
  disciplinary measures against, **8**, 1019
  dismissal, **8**, 1019
  employment, generally, **8**, 1019
  generally, **8**, 1008
  legal relations between staff and university, **8**, 1018
  non-academic, **8**, 1018
  patentable invention made by, **8**, 1022
  professional faculties, **8**, 1018
  recruitment, **8**, 1019
  suspension from duty, **8**, 1019
  tenure—
    academic freedom and, **8**, 1020
    ending of, **8**, 1021
  titles and grades, **8**, 1018
  vacant chairs, **8**, 1018
students—
  academic performance, **8**, 1026, 1027
  bursary, award of, **8**, 1029
  disciplinary powers over, **8**, 1028
  grants to, **8**, 1030
  legal relations with university, **8**, 1024, 1024*n*
  misconduct by, **8**, 1028
  occupation of premises by, **8**, 1032
  prize, award of, **8**, 1029
  scholarship, award of, **8**, 1029
  sending down, **8**, 1027
  suspension, **8**, 1027
students' representative councils, **8**, 1001
students' societies, **8**, 1031
students' union, **8**, 1031
universities—
  affiliated institutions, **8**, 987, 988
universities' copyright, **18**, 1003
Universities Funding Council, control exercised by, **8**, 1014
University Commissioners, **8**, 1021
Utrecht, **22**, 604
vice-chancellor, **8**, 996
University liaison committee (health services)
function, **11**, 1420, 1422
members, **11**, 1422
Tribunal, **11**, 1506*n*
Unjust enrichment
actio de in rem verso, **15**, 83, 84
applicable law, **17**, 311
breach of contract, **15**, 34, 38, 39
Byzantine law, **15**, 74
capacity to buy and sell, **20**, 816, 816*n*
change of defender's situation, where, **15**, 30
'change of position', **15**, 30
characterisation problems, **17**, 312

Unjust enrichment—*continued*
comparative law, **24**, 123
condictio causa data causa non secuta, **15**, 45, 46
   See also REPETITION
condictio indebiti, **15**, 45, 46
   See also REPETITION
delict, **15**, 11
doctrine of, insurance premiums, **12**, 835
donation, and, **15**, 16, 29
duty to restore, **15**, 12
elements, **15**, 82
employer, by, **3**, 83, 120
English law, **15**, 10
equity, role of, **15**, 11
error of fact, **15**, 17–26, 29
error of law, **15**, 17–26, 29
French law, **15**, 74, 76
frustration of contract, **15**, 34, 36, 37
future development, **15**, 73, 86
general action, search for, **15**, 73–85
generally, **3**, 3; **15**, 10; **17**, 310
German law, **15**, 74, 78
Grotius, **15**, 11, 75
history, **15**, 11–13
ignorantia juris maxim, **15**, 17–20
immoral situation, arising from, **15**, 53
impoverishment, **15**, 82
institutional writers, **15**, 11–13, 86
Italian law, **15**, 77
ius commune, **15**, 75, 83
justification or cause, absence of, **15**, 82
Masters and Seamen of Dundee v Cockerill, decision
   in, **15**, 29
medieval law, **15**, 75
modern law, **15**, 14*ff*
money, recovery of—
   condictio indebiti, **15**, 16
   generally, **15**, 14, 16
negotiorum gestio—
   generally, **15**, 137–141
   unjust enrichment distinguished, **15**, 89
   See also NEGOTIORUM GESTIO
Netherlands, law of, **15**, 74, 75, 80
obediential obligations, **15**, 11
obligation to pay arising under, **3**, 60, 61, 74
prescriptive period, **15**, 72
quasi-contract, **15**, 2, 11
recompense or remuneration, *see* RECOMPENSE
redress, obligation based on, prescription, **16**, 2116
repetition, *see* REPETITION
restitution, *see* RESTITUTION
risk, **15**, 29, 36
Roman law, **15**, 11
South African law, **15**, 79
Stair, **15**, 11, 12, 33, 45, 59, 86
subsidiary character, **15**, 82
taxonomy in Scots law, **15**, 73–86
turpis causa transactions, **15**, 53
void contract, **15**, 34, 40
voidable contract, **15**, 34, 40
Unjustified enrichment
See UNJUST ENRICHMENT
Unlawful entry
immigration control, exempt groups, **12**, 132

Unlawfully
use of term, **7**, 75
Unlisted Securities Market (USM)
generally, **12**, 1303
Unlisted security
fraudulent misrepresentation in prospectus, **11**,
   783
market maker, value given by, **25**, 47
Unoccupied subjects
valuation roll, **24**, 452
Unreasonable behaviour
as ground for irretrievable breakdown of
   marriage, *see* DIVORCE
Unrecognised government
development of more sophisticated approach, **17**,
   150
enforceability of law, current approach to, **17**, 129
pragmatic approach, **17**, 151
problem of, **17**, 148
traditional approach, **17**, 149
validity of laws, **17**, 107
Unruly certificate
child, relating to, **17**, 893
Unsolicited goods and services
generally, **6**, 151
human sexual techniques, relating to, **6**, 153; **16**,
   1959
obligations of recipient, **8**, 2
offences in relation to, **7**, 402
protection of persons receiving, **6**, 152
Unsound mind, person of
See INSANE PERSON; MENTALLY DISORDERED PERSON
Unum quid
comparative principle, **24**, 529
composite subjects, **24**, 504
geographical test, **24**, 502
industrial derating, **24**, 503
Upholstery
filling materials, *see* FURNITURE AND FURNISHINGS
vehicles, for, **19**, 421
Urban administration
England and Wales, **14**, 62
Urban area
See INNER URBAN AREA
Urban development area
designation, **14**, 665
Urban development corporation
application to Scotland, **14**, 670
dissolution, **14**, 669
establishment of, **14**, 666; **20**, 224
general powers, **14**, 667
landlord, as, assured tenancy status excluded, **13**,
   636, 647
local authority functions, exercise of, **14**, 668
object, **14**, 667
transfer of undertakings, **14**, 669
Urban Motorways Committee
home loss payment, recommendation on, **5**, 186
Urinal
order *ad factum praestandum*, **14**, 2157
public health nuisance, as, **19**, 336
Urination
public health nuisance, as, **19**, 370

Urine test
alcohol or drug consumption, for, **20**, 418
  analysis, provision of specimens for, **20**, 424,
    425
  back calculation of accused's alcohol level, **20**,
    429*n*
  breath test in relation to, **20**, 425, 426
  defect in procedure, **20**, 429
  defences to action following, **20**, 429
  failure to provide specimen, **20**, 416*n*, 427
    defence of reasonable excuse, **20**, 427
    disqualification following, **20**, 453
  first and second specimens, **20**, 426
  hospital patients, safeguards for, **20**, 428
  prescribed limit, **20**, 419
  proportion of alcohol in blood, determination,
    20, 421
  time of, **20**, 426
    time limit for making, **20**, 426
  unfairly or improperly obtained evidence from,
    20, 429
  warning of, failure to give, **20**, 429
Urislands
Orkney, **24**, 310
Usage
custom and—
  custom distinguished, **19**, 638; **22**, 372, 374,
    389, 390
  English law, **22**, 372, 374, 389, 390
  Scots law—
    early, as source, **22**, 363, 366–368
    modern, **22**, 389, 390
mercantile, incorporation into common law, **22**,
  375, 390
Use
abandonment of, **23**, 82
authorised, purchase notice served in case of, **5**, 95
cessation of, **23**, 80–83
compatibility, **23**, 227
discontinuance of—
  minerals, winning and working of, **23**, 214
  nature of, **23**, 81
  planning permission, **23**, 177
established, **23**, 80
existing—
  compatibility with, **23**, 227
  interference with rights, **23**, 245
  restrictions on, **5**, 199
  retention, **23**, 228
  use commenced with planning permission
    distinguished from, **23**, 80
extinguishment of, **23**, 83
incidental, **23**, 76
material change of use—
  advertisements, control of, **23**, 86
  ancillary use, **23**, 76
  development, meaning, **23**, 64
  development not involved in, **23**, 87–89
  generally, **23**, 74
  incidental use, **23**, 76
  intensification of use, **23**, 79
  materiality, concept of, **23**, 75
  operational development distinguished from,
    23, 66

Use—*continued*
material change of use—*continued*
  periodic use, **23**, 77
  permitted development, **23**, 145
  planning unit, **23**, 78
  refuse materials, deposit of, **23**, 85
  residential occupation, land and buildings in,
    23, 75
  seasonal use, **23**, 77
  single dwelling house, division of, **23**, 84
  waste materials, deposit of, **23**, 85
meaning, **23**, 66
nuisance, creating, **14**, 2079–2086
resumption of, **23**, 102–104
rights, **23**, 80
temporary, permitted development, **23**, 146
Use Classes Order
assembly, **23**, 98
business, **23**, 94
care, meaning, **23**, 97*n*
change of use under, **23**, 89
Classes 1 to 4 ..., **23**, 94
Classes 12 to 14 ..., **23**, 97
Classes 15 and 16 ..., **23**, 98
distribution, **23**, 96
drink, **23**, 94
existing use rights, interference with, **23**, 245
financial services, **23**, 94
flat, meaning, **23**, 97*n*
food, **23**, 94
General Development Order, effect of, **23**, 99
general industrial use, **23**, 99
hostel/hotel, **23**, 97
house, **23**, 97
incidental use, **23**, 92
industrial use, **23**, 95
leisure, **23**, 98
multiple occupation, meaning, **23**, 97
non-residential institution, **23**, 98
operation of, **23**, 91
planning permission, effect of conditions on, **23**, 93
professional services, **23**, 94
purpose of, **23**, 90
residential institution, **23**, 97
shop, **23**, 94
special industrial use, **23**, 95
storage, **23**, 96
Usher of Exchequer
office of, **7**, 829
Usher of the Green Rod
Order of the Thistle, **7**, 829
precedence, **16**, 2013
Usher of the Royal Chapel
office of, **7**, 829
Usher of the White Rod
office of, **7**, 829
precedence, **16**, 2013
Usufructus
feudal system, and, **18**, 43
personal servitude of, **13**, 1601
Uttering
actus reus, **7**, 30
case of, relevant facts, **10**, 624
conduct-crime, as, **7**, 32

Uttering—*continued*
definition, **7**, 372
defraud, intention to, **7**, 377
false article, **7**, 375
falsely, use of term, **7**, 85
forged document, **7**, 372, 374
forgery, what constitutes, **7**, 373

Uttering—*continued*
fraud, and, **7**, 372
    attempted fraud, **7**, 164*n*
fraudulently, use of term, **7**, 85
generally, **7**, 372
mens rea, **7**, 377
prejudice, must be calculated to lead to, **7**, 376

V

Vacant possession
seller's duty to give, **6**, 640, 641; **20**, 916
Vaccination and immunisation
damage payments, **19**, 502
    conditions of entitlement, **19**, 504
    determination of claims, **19**, 506
    non-statutory remedies, **19**, 507
    third parties, **19**, 503
    vaccinations outside United Kingdom and Isle
        of Man, **19**, 505
    Vaccine Damage Tribunal, **23**, 911n
doctors' obligations as to, **11**, 1446
health boards, administration by, **11**, 1410
infectious disease, immunisation against, **19**, 500
provisions as to, **11**, 1480
public health provisions, **19**, 306
Secretary of State—
    liability of, **19**, 501
    powers, **19**, 500
travel abroad, in connection with, **11**, 1450
voluntary basis, **19**, 500
World Health Organisation recommendation, **19**,
    500
Vagrancy
detention—
    European Convention on Human Rights, **12**, 42
    voluntary surrender to, **12**, 42
early provisions concerning, **14**, 34
Valuation
accountant, role of, **1**, 103, 104
agricultural, *see* AGRICULTURAL LANDS AND
    HERITAGES
appeal committees, *see* VALUATION APPEAL
    COMMITTEES
arbitration includes, **2**, 406
assets, of, **25**, 993
    See also ASSETS
bequest, attribution of value to, **25**, 1018
certificate of value—
    purchase and sale, **25**, 81
    valuer, duties of, **25**, 111
company—
    assets—
        asset value, **25**, 22
        break-up value, **25**, 22
        capital, shareholder's rights relating to, **25**, 14
        company's financial record, **25**, 32
        cover, existence of, **25**, 32
        fixed, purposes of valuation, **25**, 92
        goodwill, **25**, 34
        net, value of, **25**, 21
        security of repayment against, **25**, 14
        shareholder has no direct interest in, **25**, 12
        surplus, existence of, **25**, 32
    capital, **25**, 13
    contingent liabilities, **25**, 33
    custom and practice—
        shares, **25**, 1, 3
        trade, **25**, 25

Valuation—*continued*
company—*continued*
    customers, **25**, 35
    dividends, **25**, 18
    earnings, **25**, 20
    economic background, **25**, 31
    financial record, **25**, 32
    flotation, *see* COMPANY
    general meetings, **25**, 13
    goodwill, **25**, 34
    growth potential, **25**, 37
    individual factors, assessment of, **25**, 43
    labour, **25**, 36
    liquidation, *see* LIQUIDATION
    management, **25**, 39
    net worth, **25**, 13
    political background, **25**, 31
    profits, **25**, 13
    public registers, **25**, 13
    quasi-partnership, **25**, 15
    redemption, **25**, 13
    relative prospects, **25**, 40
    shares, custom and practice, **25**, 1, 3
    size, **25**, 38
    suppliers, **25**, 35
    takeover, *see* TAKEOVER
    valuer, task of, **25**, 30
    yield, selection of, **25**, 19
compulsory acquisition, *see* COMPULSORY ACQUISI-
    TION
contingent liability, existence, **25**, 33
date of death values—
    actual realised, **25**, 794
    capital gains tax, **25**, 797
    generally, **25**, 793
    interest—
        generally, **25**, 795
        income tax, **25**, 796
depreciation—
    depreciated replacement cost, **25**, 94
    development value, in, **5**, 151
    nuisance, caused by, **14**, 2044
    use value, in, **5**, 151
    value of land, in, disregard of, **5**, 150
external valuer, meaning, **25**, 117
fair value, **25**, 8, 68
Financial Services Act 1986—
    effect, **25**, 69
fire insurance, for—
    bases of, **25**, 143
    inflation, provision for, **25**, 144
    other considerations, **25**, 145
fiscal values and real market values distinguished,
    25, 67
forced sale value, **25**, 73
frequency of, **25**, 113
going concern, **25**, 95, 141
growth potential, **25**, 37

Valuation—*continued*
guidance notes—
    property assets, valuation of, **25**, 121
    value of property, **25**, 131
heritable property, *see* HERITABLE PROPERTY
hope value, **25**, 23
information—
    available, **25**, 65
    individual factors, assessment of, **25**, 43
    unpublished price-sensitive, **25**, 66
    verification of, **25**, 112
inheritance tax—
    debts, deduction of, **25**, 1008
    expenses, deduction of, **25**, 1008
    generally, **25**, 1005
    property—
        account, left out of, **25**, 1007
        certain types of, **25**, 1006
investment, **25**, 123
lands and heritages, of—
    effect of noise on, **9**, 1297
    generally, **14**, 804; **24** 439
    head of claim for compensation, **5**, 106, 107
    meaning, **11**, 905; **18**, 578n; **24**, 438
    shooting rights, **11**, 906–915
    See also LANDS TRIBUNAL FOR SCOTLAND
legal philosophy, **25**, 2
minerals, *see* MINERALS
notional disposal, manner and expenses of, **25**, 64
open market value, **25**, 73
poinding, **8**, 223
principal methods—
    comparative, **25**, 71
    contractor's, **25**, 71
    revenue, **25**, 71
property assets—
    background papers, **25**, 122
    fixed asset valuation, **25**, 92
    going concern value, **25**, 95
    guidance notes, **25**, 121
    valuation—
        basis of, **25**, 93
        depreciated replacement cost basis, **25**, 94
    valuer, duties of—
        date of valuation, **25**, 99
        expenses, **25**, 101
        generally, **25**, 96
        instructions, extent of, **25**, 97
        principal matters to consider—
            details of property, **25**, 103
            frequency of valuation, **25**, 113
            generally, **25**, 102
            information, verification of, **25**, 112
            market analysis, **25**, 107
            nature of interest, **25**, 104
            negative value, **25**, 110
            other factors, **25**, 106
            planning requirements, **25**, 105
            rental valuation, **25**, 109
            statutory requirements, **25**, 105
            valuation certificate, **25**, 111
            valuation report, **25**, 108
        properties to be included, **25**, 98

Valuation—*continued*
property assets—*continued*
    valuer, duties of—*continued*
        special assumptions, **25**, 100
        taxation, allowances for, **25**, 101
    years' purchase, **25**, 127
purchase and sale—
    certificate of value, **25**, 81
    Expert Committee—
        certificate of value, on, **25**, 81
        full structural survey, on, **25**, 85
        response of, **25**, 80
    forced sale value, **25**, 73
    generally, **25**, 72
    open market value, **25**, 73
    residential market, **25**, 75
    survey—
        case law, **25**, 89
        current trends, **25**, 87
        disclaimer, **25**, 90
        dual-purpose, **25**, 83
        Expert Committee, response of, **25**, 80
        full structural, **25**, 85
        multiple survey problem, **25**, 79, 86
        problems, **25**, 91
        structural, **25**, 78
        traditional private, **25**, 84
        valuation, **25**, 77
    valuation—
        current trends, **25**, 87
        disclaimer, **25**, 90
        disclosure of report, **25**, 88
        dual-purpose survey and, **25**, 83
        mortgage, **25**, 82
        problems, **25**, 91
        report for lending purposes, **25**, 76
        survey, **25**, 77
        technique of, **25**, 74
rating, for, *see* VALUATION FOR RATING
rights of parties, alteration of, **25**, 9
shares, *see* SHARES
sheriff's duties in respect of, **6**, 1046
status of parties, alteration of, **25**, 9
valuer, *see* VALUER
Valuation appeal committees
agreement reached with assessor, **24**, 481
appeals to, **24**, 479–487, 534
    conduct of, **24**, 485
    time limits, **24**, 479
complaints to, **24**, 488–490
date of hearing, **24**, 482
hearing, generally, **24**, 483
record of proceedings, **24**, 485
supervision of, Scottish Committee, by, **23**, 911n
written statements, **24**, 484
Valuation for rating
abolition of domestic rates, **24**, 402
'actual state' rule—
    demolition, effect of, **24**, 506
    generally, **24**, 505
    occupier, use made by, **24**, 508
    physical and structural condition, **24**, 506
    repairs, burden of, **24**, 506
    restraints, **24**, 509, 510

Valuation for rating—*continued*
'actual state' rule—*continued*
  unfinished buildings, **24**, 506
  use made of lands and heritages, **24**, 507, 508
advertisement boards, **24**, 550–552
agricultural—
  buildings—
    ancillary usage, **24**, 566
    beekeeping, **24**, 571
    co-operatives, buildings occupied by, **24**, 568, 569
    de minimis non curat praetor, **24**, 567
    dwelling houses not included, **24**, 562
      See also DWELLING HOUSE
    greenhouses, **24**, 565
    livestock buildings, **24**, 570, 571
    market gardens, **24**, 565
    meaning, **24**, 562
    merchandising operations excluded, **24**, 566
    need not be adjacent to agricultural lands, **24**, 563
    occupied with agricultural lands and heritages, **24**, 564
    poultry houses, **24**, 566
    silos, **24**, 562
    sole agricultural use, **24**, 566
  dwelling houses, **24**, 553–555
  lands and heritages, **24**, 556–571
  livestock buildings, **24**, 570, 571
airports, **24**, 572
air-raid protection works, **24**, 573
allotments, **24**, 560
appeals, **6**, 941, 1145, 1149
areas, apportionment between, **24**, 549
assessor—
  application for redress to, **24**, 478
  appointment and qualifications, **24**, 407
  depute assessors, **6**, 939; **24**, 409
  documents, power to call for, **24**, 413
  electoral registration officer, as, **24**, 407
  entry, power of, **24**, 413
  independence of, **24**, 408
  office of, generally, **6**, 939; **24**, 407
  removal, **24**, 407
  resignation, **24**, 407
  return, powers in respect of, **24**, 411, 412
  staff, **24**, 410
  terms and conditions of office, **24**, 410
Assessor of Public Undertakings (Scotland)
  appeals, **24**, 421
  appointment, **24**, 414
  directions as to entries on rolls, **24**, 418, 464
  disputes, **24**, 421
  information, obtaining of, **24**, 420
  staff, **24**, 414
  valuation by—
    date of, **24**, 419
    duties in respect of, **24**, 417
    formula, **24**, 547
    lands ceasing to be valued by, **24**, 463
    subjects of, **24**, 415, 416
bings, **24**, 574–577
block storage heaters, **24**, 578
bridges, **24**, 579–581

Valuation for rating—*continued*
canals, **24**, 582–586
car parks, **24**, 587, 614
caravans and caravan sites, **24**, 502, 588–590, 607
cemeteries, **24**, 591
churches, **24**, 592
cinemas, **24**, 745
co-operatives, buildings occupied by, **24**, 568, 569
colleges, **24**, 733
communal housing, **24**, 615
community charge, *see* COMMUNITY CHARGE
comparative principle as basis for—
  area within which made, **24**, 535
  caravans, **24**, 588, 590
  classes and categories of comparative subjects, **24**, 529
  comparisons outwith Scotland, **24**, 536
  comparisons with valuation of comparable subjects, **24**, 534
  dwelling houses, **24**, 621, 622
  inverse quantum, **24**, 532
  large and small subjects, **24**, 532
  particular features, **24**, 533
  quantum allowance, **24**, 532
  unit of comparison, **24**, 530
  valuation of factories and workshops, **24**, 628
  valuation method, as, **24**, 524
  zoning, **24**, 531
composite subjects, **24**, 504
contractor's principle—
  capital value, calculation of effective, **24**, 542
  decapitalisation rate, **24**, 544
  deductions and allowances, **24**, 543
  factories and workshops, valuation of, **24**, 628
  modification of, **24**, 545
  valuation method, **24**, 527, 542–545
convalescent homes, **24**, 667
coups, **24**, 593
Court of Session, proceedings in, **24**, 500
crematoria, **24**, 591
crofters' houses, **1**, 834; **24**, 594
Crown property, **24**, 495–497
date of valuation—
  date to be struck, **24**, 512
  tone of valuation roll, **24**, 513
deer forests, **24**, 736–740
derating—
  canals, **24**, 585
  factories and workshops, **24**, 523
  freight transport lands and heritages, **24**, 523
  industrial—
    apportionment, **24**, 648–651
    excepted purposes, **24**, 637–645
    generally, **24**, 629
    onus of proof, **24**, 631
    qualification of premises, **24**, 630
    road vehicles, housing and maintenance, **24**, 646, 647
    rules, **24**, 503
    stables, **24**, 646, 647
    use as factory or workshop, **24**, 632–636
  meaning, **24**, 523
  qualification of premises for, **24**, 630
disabled persons, **24**, 748

Valuation for rating—*continued*
docks, **24**, 598–606
documents, assessor's power to call for, **24**, 413
domestic subjects—
    abolition of domestic rates, **24**, 610–617
    hotels and hostels, **24**, 612
    meaning, **24**, 610
    partial residential subjects, **24**, 611
    prescribed classes, **24**, 610*n*, 613–617
dwelling houses—
    agricultural, **24**, 553–555
    domestic, **24**, 607–624
    industrial purpose, used for, **24**, 639
    railway property, **24**, 721
effective capital value, **24**, 527
electricity generation, **24**, 415, 547, 625–627
entry, assessor's power of, **24**, 413
factories, **24**, 529, 628–648
    See also FACTORY
ferries, **24**, 652, 653, 693
fish farms, **24**, 654–656
fishings, **24**, 432, 657–662
flats, **24**, 609
formula, valuation by—
    canals, **24**, 582, 583
    generally, **24**, 528, 546, 547
    railways, **24**, 717
freight transport lands and heritages—
    derating, **24**, 523, 729
    dock undertakings, **24**, 605, 606
    railways, **24**, 729
    valuation roll, **24**, 432
garages, **24**, 663
gasworks, **24**, 547, 664, 665
generally, **6**, 938; **24**, 403, 436, 618
gross annual value, **24**, 618–620
halls, **24**, 666
harbours, **24**, 598–606
historical summary, **6**, 938, 939; **24**, 401
hoardings, **24**, 550–552
horses, land used in respect of, **24**, 559
hospitals and homes, **24**, 667
hostels, **24**, 612, 668
hotels, **24**, 612, 668
hypothetical tenancy—
    assessment of rental valuation, **24**, 515
    burdens of insurance and repair, **24**, 618
    consideration other than rent not payable, **24**, 519, 520
    domestic rates, abolition of, **24**, 515
    duration, **24**, 518
    grassum, **24**, 519, 520
    gross annual value, deductions from, **24**, 516
    landlord's services, no account taken of, **24**, 522
    letting from year to year as basis of, **24**, 518
    maintenance burden of, **24**, 521
    net annual value, **24**, 517
    rateable value, **24**, 523, 618
    rates, burden of, **24**, 521
    statutory provisions, **24**, 514–517, 618
    terms of, **24**, 519–522
ironworks, **24**, 669
jetty, **24**, 599

Valuation for rating—*continued*
kelp shores, **24**, 734
Lands Valuation Appeal Court, *see* LANDS
    VALUATION APPEAL COURT
licensed areas and premises, **24**, 670, 671
livestock buildings, **24**, 570, 571
locks, **24**, 672
machinery, **24**, 441, 699–715
malls, **24**, 673
market gardens, **24**, 560, 565
markets, **24**, 674
methods of valuation—
    agreements and understandings, **24**, 548
    apportionment between valuation areas, **24**, 549
    choice of method, **24**, 524–528
    comparative principle, **24**, 524, 529–536
    contractor's principle, **24**, 527, 542–545
    formula valuations, **24**, 528, 546, 547
    revenue principle, **24**, 526, 539–541
    turnover, by, **24**, 525, 537, 538
mineral railways, **24**, 675
minerals, **24**, 676–678
mines, **24**, 679–685
moorings, **24**, 686
offices, **24**, 687, 725
offshore installations, **24**, 688
operational land, **24**, 627
orchards, **24**, 560
parks, **24**, 689, 690
partial residential subjects, **24**, 611
peat cuttings, **24**, 691
petrol stations, **24**, 663
piers, **24**, 598, 692–694
pipes, **24**, 695–698, 714
plant and machinery, **24**, 441, 699–715
poultry farms, **24**, 560
prescribed subjects, **24**, 547
profitability, **24**, 511
proprietor, meaning, **24**, 444
public supply undertakings, **24**, 644
quay, **24**, 599
racing tracks, **24**, 742
railways, **24**, 675, 716–730
    generally—
        assessors, duty of, **24**, 718
        derating, **24**, 730
        formula, valuation by, **24**, 717
        freight-transport lands and heritages, **24**, 729
        historical background, **24**, 716
        method of valuation, **24**, 728
        prescribed formula, **24**, 547
    lands and heritages—
        capable of separate assessment, **24**, 722
        dwelling houses, **24**, 721
        goods, carriage of, **24**, 726
        harbours, **24**, 728
        hotels, **24**, 721
        incidental and supplementary purposes, **24**, 720
        'letting out', **24**, 723
        office premises, **24**, 725
        passengers, carriage of, **24**, 726
        public refreshment, places of, **24**, 721
        statutory powers, occupied under, **24**, 719
rebus sic stantibus, *see* actual state rule *above*

Valuation for rating—*continued*
recreation grounds, **24**, 689, 690
reed beds, **24**, 560, 731
regional assessor, **14**, 249
retail shops, **24**, 640
return—
   assessor's powers in respect of, **24**, 411
   failure to furnish, **24**, 412
revaluation, **14**, 865
revenue principle—
   annual value, calculation of, **24**, 541
   assessing gross revenue, **24**, 539
   assessing net profits, **24**, 540
   canals, **24**, 586
   valuation method, **24**, 526, 539–541
rights of way, **24**, 747
roads, **24**, 732
roll, *see* VALUATION ROLL
salmon-fishings, **24**, 432, 660
sawmills, **24**, 560
schools, **24**, 733
scope of title, **24**, 403
Scottish Valuation Advisory Council, *see* SCOTTISH VALUATION ADVISORY COUNCIL
seaweed gathering rights, **24**, 734
sewers, **24**, 735
shootings, **11**, 909; **24**, 736–740
shops, **24**, 741
slag heaps, **24**, 574–577
sporting purposes, land used for, **24**, 561
sports grounds, **24**, 742
storage premises, **24**, 614, 643
   whisky maturation for, **24**, 643
structure and machinery of system, **24**, 404–430
subjects of, **24**, 501–513
   'actual state' rule, *see* actual state rule *above*
   ascertaining extent, **24**, 501
   composite, **24**, 504
   corporate subjects, **24**, 504
   date of valuation, **24**, 512, 513
   profitability, **24**, 511
   unit of valuation, **24**, 501–503
swimming pools, **24**, 743
telephone and telegraph apparatus, **24**, 744
tenements, **24**, 609
theatres, **24**, 745
unit of valuation—
   ascertaining extent of subjects, **24**, 501
   caravan sites, **24**, 502
   general rule, **24**, 501
   geographical test, **24**, 502
   industrial derating, **24**, 503
   pertinents, **24**, 502
   sublet premises, **24**, 501
unoccupied subjects, **24**, 452
unum quid—
   comparative principle, **24**, 529
   composite subjects, **24**, 504
   geographical test, **24**, 502
   industrial derating, **24**, 503
valuation appeal committees—
   accommodation and services, **24**, 425
   assessor, agreements reached with, **24**, 481
   association with panel members, **24**, 426

Valuation for rating—*continued*
valuation appeal committees—*continued*
   conduct of appeal, **24**, 485
   constitution, **24**, 424
   decision, **24**, 487
   evidence, **24**, 486
   expenses, **24**, 425
   generally, **6**, 940–942; **24**, 422, 479–490
   hearing, **24**, 482, 483
   regulations, **24**, 479
   supervision, **24**, 424
   time limits, **24**, 479
   who may appeal, **24**, 480
   written statements, **24**, 484
valuation areas and authorities—
   apportionment between areas, **24**, 405
   boundaries, **24**, 405, 406
   combination of councils, **24**, 404
   regions and island areas, **24**, 404
valuation panels—
   accommodation and services, **24**, 425
   association with appeal committees, **24**, 426
   constitution, **24**, 423
   expenses, **24**, 425
   generally, **24**, 422
   membership, **24**, 423
valuation system—
   remedies and appeals, **24**, 477–500
   roll, *see* VALUATION ROLL
   structure and administration, **24**, 404–430
vehicles, housing and maintenance, **24**, 646, 647
water undertakings, **24**, 547
waterfalls, **24**, 672
waterworks, **24**, 746
wayleaves, **24**, 747
welfare structures, **24**, 748
wireless stations, **24**, 744
woodlands, **24**, 560
woods, **24**, 750
workshops, **24**, 628–648
zoning, **24**, 531
See also COMMUNITY CHARGE; RATES; VALUATION ROLL
Valuation roll
alteration—
   after coming into force, **24**, 456–476
   appeal, decision following, **24**, 475
   before coming into force, **24**, 454, 455
   complaint, decision following, **24**, 475
   correction of errors, **24**, 457–461
   date of alteration, **24**, 472
   decision, effect of, **24**, 475
   deletions, **24**, 465
   entry of lands and heritages, **24**, 462–464
   grounds for, **24**, 455, 456
   level of value to be applied, **24**, 474
   notification, **24**, 476
   percentage deduction orders, **24**, 473
   values, changes in, **24**, 466–472
annual revaluation, **24**, 431
assessor, application to for redress, **24**, 478
challenge of entries generally, **24**, 437, 477
Court of Session proceedings, **24**, 500
decision following, **24**, 475

Valuation roll—*continued*
annual revaluation—*continued*
    Lands Tribunal for Scotland, referral to, **24**,
      491–494
    Lands Valuation Appeal Court, **24**, 421, 427,
      495–490
    time limits, **24**, 479
    valuation appeal committee, to, **24**, 479–487
arithmetical errors, **24**, 460
basis for levying rates, as, **24**, 435
ceasing to be in force, **24**, 435
challenge of entries generally, **24**, 437, 477
classification, **24**, 459
clerical errors, **24**, 460
complaint, decision following, **24**, 475
complaints to valuation appeal committee, **24**,
    488–490
copies, **24**, 435
Crown property, **24**, 597
delivery to rating authority, **24**, 433
documentary evidence, as, **10**, 592
errors, correction of, **24**, 457–461
exemptions from, **24**, 442
finality of, **24**, 436, 437
fish farms not to be entered on, **11**, 64
fixtures, **24**, 441
form and contents, **24**, 432
heritable subjects to be entered in, **24**, 438
hypothetical tenancy, **24**, 514
inspection, **24**, 435
lands and heritages—
    deleted, **24**, 457
    generally, **24**, 438–442
    not included, **24**, 457
level of value to be applied, **24**, 474
material change of circumstances, **24**, 466–472
measurement, errors of, **24**, 458, 459
moveable and heritable subjects, distinguished,
    24, 440
notice of entries in, **24**, 434
partial revaluation, **24**, 431
percentage deduction orders, **24**, 473
period for which in force, **24**, 431
persons entered in—
    generally, **24**, 443
    occupiers, **24**, 447–453
    proprietors, **24**, 444
    subtenants, **24**, 446
    tenants, **24**, 445
plant and machinery, **24**, 441
preservation, **24**, 435
proprietor, entry in, **11**, 34
rival occupancy, **24**, 451, 453
Scottish Record Office, records held in, **19**, 849
subjects to be entered in, **24**, 438
survey, **24**, 459
tone of roll, **24**, 513
transmission of records, **19**, 853
'year of revaluation', **24**, 431
Value Added and Data Services (VADS)
    Licence
computer-generated services, **16**, 1950
generally, **16**, 1948
value added service, meaning, **16**, 1950

Value added tax
account—
    correction, **7**, 1396
    requirement to keep and maintain, **7**, 1391
accounting period, **19**, 1539
acquisitions—
    VAT, charge to—
      accounting for tax on taxable acquisition, **7**,
        1322
      generally, **7**, 1318
      meaning of acquisition, **7**, 1317
      place of acquisition, **7**, 1319
      relevant acquisition, person making, **7**, 1332–
        1335, 1340, 1341
      time of acquisition, **7**, 1320
      valuation of transaction, **7**, 1321
      zero-rating, *see* zero-rating *below*
administration, **19**, 1542
    Commissioners of Customs and Excise, **7**, 1282
    Community territory, **7**, 1281
    customs union, **7**, 1281
    generally, **7**, 1281
advocate, liability, **13**, 1391
annual accounting scheme, **7**, 1352
    payment of VAT, **7**, 1399
    prescribed accounting period, **7**, 1392
    regulations, generally, **7**, 1352
antiques, margin scheme for used goods, **7**, 1363
appeals to Court of Session, **6**, 924
art works, **7**, 1290, 1363, 1430
assessment—
    failure in law, **7**, 1405
    further assessments, **7**, 1406
    generally, **7**, 1405
    insufficient, **7**, 1405
    notification of taxable person, **7**, 1405
    partnership, served on, **7**, 1405
    time limits, **7**, 1407
    time period of, definition, **7**, 1405
bad debt certificate—
    administrator, duties of, **4**, 634
    receiver, duties of, **4**, 702
broadcasting equipment, temporary importation,
    7, 1187
building, goods installed in new, **7**, 1383
building construction, **19**, 1316
business—
    assets—
      transfer or disposal, **7**, 1296, 1298
        VAT, charge to, **7**, 1288, 1300
      use of as supply of services, **7**, 1289, 1299
    'commercial reality' test, **7**, 1295
    liabilities, disposition, **7**, 1296
    meaning for VAT purposes, **7**, 1295
    termination, action taken in connection with,
      7, 1296
    tests as to whether VAT business exists, **7**, 1295
    transfer as going concern, **7**, 1290, 1296, 1350
    transfer to member of group, self-supply, **7**,
      1305
business entertainment, **7**, 1384
capital items, **7**, 1380, 1390
cash accounting scheme, *see* output tax (invoicing
    requirements) *below*

Value added tax—*continued*

charge to tax—

acquisitions, *see* acquisitions *above*

goods acquired from another community member state—

accounting for tax, **7**, 1322

acquisition, meaning, **7**, 1317

generally, **7**, 1318

place of acquisition, **7**, 1319

taxable acquisitions, **7**, 1318, 1322

time of acquisition, **7**, 1320

triangulation, **7**, 1290, 1317

value, **7**, 1321

goods imported from Community member state—

aircraft, **7**, 1315

commercial vehicles, **7**, 1315

customs or excise warehouse, goods removed to, **7**, 1315

free zone, goods removed to, **7**, 1315

generally, **7**, 1312

re-exportation, **7**, 1315

relief, **7**, 1313

conditional, **7**, 1313, 1315

temporary import, **7**, 1315

transhipment or transit, goods entered for, **7**, 1315

valuation of imported goods, **7**, 1316

VAT not charged, where, **7**, 1314

VAT not collected, where, **7**, 1314

supplies, *see* supplies *below*

triangulation, **7**, 1290, 1317

charities, treatment of, *see* CHARITY (VALUE ADDED TAX)

civil penalties—

assessment, **7**, 1408

dishonest conduct, for, **7**, 1408

generally, **7**, 1415

interest on, **7**, 1412

persistent misdeclaration, where, **7**, 1411

reasonable excuse for conduct, where, **7**, 1410

serious misdeclaration, where, **7**, 1409

clubs, payable by, **2**, 822; **19**, 1315–1318

commercial lease, **13**, 568, 587

compliance—

goods sold under a power, returns, **7**, 1393

prescribed accounting period, **7**, 1392

repayment claims, **7**, 1394

returns, **7**, 1392

control visit, **7**, 1401

credit, tax excluded from, **7**, 1382–1387

credit note, validity, **7**, 1360

customs charge, not having equivalent effect to, **7**, 1012

Customs and Excise, Department of, *see* CUSTOMS AND EXCISE, DEPARTMENT OF

death of trader, and, **25**, 1032

deregistration, *see* taxable person *below*

dishonest conduct, civil penalty for, **7**, 1408

distance sales, **7**, 1328

donations, **8**, 656

enforcement, **7**, 1413–1416

errors, correction, **7**, 1395

evasion, civil penalty for, **7**, 1408

Value added tax—*continued*

exempt supplies, **7**, 1291, 1359, 1385, 1417–1431; **19**, 1317, 1324, 1540

exports, **19**, 1541

fire services, charges for, **10**, 1418

flat-rate scheme for farmers, **7**, 1353

food—

catering, supplied for, **7**, 1445; **11**, 314

price control, **11**, 314

supplies, generally, **19**, 1316

zero-rated, **7**, 1445; **11**, 314

gaming, exemption from, **19**, 1296

gaming machine, on, **9**, 1015

gifts, relief on, **7**, 1314

goods—

acquisition from another Community member state, **7**, 1317–1322

business goods used for non-business purpose, **7**, 1289

import—

Community member state, via, **7**, 1312

following export, **7**, 1312, 1314

third country, from, **7**, 1312–1316

leaving and re-entering United Kingdom, **7**, 1312, 1314

meaning, **7**, 1001

process, application of treatment of, charge to VAT, **7**, 1288

removal from one Community member state to another, **7**, 1288, 1300

removal from United Kingdom, **7**, 1293

removal to United Kingdom, **7**, 1293

supply of, VAT, charge to—

acquired from another Community member state, goods, **7**, 1317–1322

agent, supply through, **7**, 1285

basic tax point, **7**, 1355

conditions for, **7**, 1284

consideration—

alteration, **7**, 1286

receivability, **7**, 1286

supply must be for, **7**, 1284, 1285, 1286, 1287, 1297

what constitutes, **7**, 1286

contract, generally, **7**, 1285

deregistration, goods held at, **7**, 1309

generally, **7**, 1287, 1288

imported from a place outside the Community member states, goods, **7**, 1312–1316

input tax, **7**, 1372

meaning of supply, **7**, 1285

output tax, **7**, 1354

self-supply, **7**, 1301–1308

supply outside United Kingdom, **7**, 1293

tax point, **7**, 1355–1357

taxable person, supplied by, **7**, 1373

United Kingdom, goods supplied in, **7**, 1293

void or illegal contract, where, **7**, 1285

zero-rated transactions, **7**, 1311

transfer of possession, charge to VAT, **7**, 1288, 1289

transfer of undivided share in property of, **7**, 1289

zero-rating, *see* zero-rating *below*

Value added tax—*continued*
goods and services, supply of, **19**, 1539
heating, **7**, 1288, 1320, 1461
imported goods, **7**, 1312–1316; **19**, 1541
input tax, **19**, 1539
   adjustment of attribution, **7**, 1388–1390
   appropriation of supplies for different purpose,
     7, 1389
   attribution, **7**, 1385
     special methods, **7**, 1385, 1387, 1388
     standard method, **7**, 1385, 1386, 1388
   business, goods or services must be used for, **7**,
     1379
   business entertainment, **7**, 1384
   capital items, **7**, 1380, 1390
   Community member state, VAT incurred in, **7**,
     1380
   documentary evidence of supply or
     importation, **7**, 1378
   election to waive exemption, **7**, 1381
   exempt, **7**, 1388
   exempt supplies, **7**, 1385; **19**, 1540
   exports outside European Union, services
     linked to, **7**, 1371
   generally, **7**, 1322, 1371
   goods, **7**, 1372
   imports, **7**, 1372
   land or buildings, **7**, 1381
   meaning, **7**, 1372
   non-taxable person, goods and services supplied
     by, **7**, 1373
   overdeclaration, **7**, 1395, 1396
   overseas VAT system, tax charged under, **7**, 1380
   payment, **7**, 1380
   person outside European Union, services
     supplied to, **7**, 1371
   reliefs, **7**, 1371
   reverse charges, **7**, 1374
   road fuel, **7**, 1376
   self-supplies, **7**, 1374
   services, **7**, 1372
   supplies, **7**, 1372
     made outside United Kingdom, **7**, 1371
   taxable acquisition from Community member
     state, **7**, 1322
   taxable person—
     goods and services supplied by, **7**, 1373
     restriction to, **7**, 1377
     trader ceasing to be, **7**, 1377
     VAT incurred prior to becoming, **7**, 1377
   taxable supplies, **7**, 1371
   trader, goods acquired or imported by, **7**, 1375
   underdeclaration, **7**, 1391, 1392, 1394, 1449
   VAT wrongly charged, where, **7**, 1380
   zero-rated goods, **19**, 1540
intellectual property rights, payments in respect
   of, **18**, 1602
invoicing requirements—
   output tax, *see* output tax (invoicing
     requirements) *below*
leisure and recreation business, **19**, 1322–1324
margin scheme—
   global accounting system for used goods, **7**, 1363
   quantum of output tax on used goods, **7**, 1364

Value added tax—*continued*
margin scheme—*continued*
   tour operators, **7**, 1365
   used goods, **7**, 1363, 1364
messenger-at-arms, liability of, **14**, 1505
misdeclaration—
   civil penalty for, **7**, 1409
   persistent, **7**, 1411
motor cars, **7**, 1382
notice of prices of accommodation, **11**, 1786
occupational pension scheme—
   generally, **21**, 1339
   tax not reclaimable by employer, **21**, 1341
   tax reclaimable by employer, **21**, 1340
   trustees reclaiming value added tax, **21**, 1342
output tax, **19**, 1539
   bad debt relief, **7**, 1370
   credit note, validity, **7**, 1360
   deemed supplies, **7**, 1354
   generally, **7**, 1322, 1354
   invoicing requirements—
     cash accounting scheme, **7**, 1351, 1354, 1362
     margin scheme, *see* margin scheme *above*
     retail scheme, *see* retail scheme *below*
     tour operators, margin scheme for, generally,
       7, 1354
     used goods, margin scheme for—
       generally, **7**, 1354
       goods eligible for scheme, **7**, 1363
       margin, meaning, **7**, 1364
       quantum of output tax, **7**, 1364
       VAT fraction, **7**, 1364
   VAT invoice basis—
     basic tax point, **7**, 1355
     construction industry stage payments, **7**, 1359
     credit note, issue, **7**, 1360, 1361
     date on invoice, **7**, 1357
     food and accommodation supplied to
       employees, **7**, 1358
     generally, **7**, 1354
     hotel accommodation, **7**, 1358
     monetary consideration, where, **7**, 1358
     money's worth, supply given in, **7**, 1358
     obligation to issue VAT invoice, **7**, 1359
     quantum of output tax, **7**, 1361
     self-billing invoice, **7**, 1359
     stamps, tokens or vouchers, **7**, 1358
     tax points, **7**, 1355–1357
     time invoice issued, **7**, 1357
     time of supply, **7**, 1355, 1356
     trading stamp schemes, **7**, 1358
     treatment or process, goods subject to, **7**,
       1358
     valuation of supplies, **7**, 1358
     zero-rated supplies, **7**, 1357
meaning, **7**, 1354
overdeclaration, **7**, 1395, 1396
quantum, **7**, 1361, 1364
rates, **7**, 1354
standard rate, **7**, 1354
taxable acquisition from Community member
   state, **7**, 1322
underdeclaration, **7**, 1395, 1396, 1398, 1404
zero rate, **7**, 1354

Value added tax—*continued*
overclaim, Commissioners of Customs and Excise
    powers, **7**, 1404
overdeclaration, correction, **7**, 1395, 1396
overpayment, **7**, 1395
overseas supplies, person making, **7**, 1338
partnership, liability—
    changes in partnership composition, **16**, 1141
    generally, **16**, 1124; **19**, 1592
    input tax, **16**, 1141
    joint and several liability, **16**, 1141
    output tax, **16**, 1141
    registration, **16**, 1141
payment—
    account, on, **7**, 1399
    annual accounting scheme, where, **7**, 1399
    generally, **7**, 1399
    imported goods, **7**, 1400
place of supply, **19**, 1541
prescribed accounting period, **7**, 1392
professional sportsmen, **19**, 1311
Provisional Collection of Taxes Act 1968 ..., **19**,
    1504*n*
quarter, for purpose of, **22**, 812
rates, **19**, 1316, 1323, 1540
records, inspection and verification, **7**, 1401
recovery, **7**, 1413; **14**, 1504, 1550
reduced rate, **7**, 1461
refunds, **19**, 1539
register of taxable persons, maintenance, **7**, 1282
registration, *see* taxable person *below*
relevant acquisitions, person making, **7**, 1332–
    1335, 1340, 1341
relevant supplies, person making, **7**, 1328–1331,
    1339
repayment—
    claims for, **7**, 1394
    excessive claims, **7**, 1399
    generally, **7**, 1397, 1399
    overpayments, **7**, 1399
    supplement, **7**, 1399
retail scheme—
    calculation of output tax, **7**, 1368
    choice of scheme, **7**, 1367
    generally, **7**, 1354, 1366
    gross takings, **7**, 1367
    liability to output tax, calculation, **7**, 1366
    retailer, definition, **7**, 1366
    VAT invoice, obligation to issue, **7**, 1369
    VAT output tax—
        calculation of output tax, **7**, 1368
        choice of scheme, **7**, 1367
        export relief, **7**, 1368
        generally, **7**, 1354, 1366
        gross takings, calculation, **7**, 1367
        retail pharmacist's relief, **7**, 1368
return, **7**, 1392, 1399
    failure to provide, **7**, 1415
    goods sold under a power, where, **7**, 1393
    inspection, **7**, 1401
    issue, **7**, 1282
    receipt, **7**, 1282
    VAT Central Unit, **7**, 1282
    verification, **7**, 1401

Value added tax—*continued*
security in respect of, requirement for, **7**, 1413
self-supply order—
    change of building use, **7**, 1306
    construction services, **7**, 1301, 1304, 1374
    developers, **7**, 1307
    generally, **7**, 1301
    group member, business transferred to, **7**, 1304
    input tax, **7**, 1374
    motor vehicles, **7**, 1301, 1302
    stationery, **7**, 1301, 1303, 1374
services—
    activities amounting to, **7**, 1289
        business assets, use of, **7**, 1299
    business goods used for non-business purpose,
        7, 1289, 1299
    exchange of reconditioned articles, **7**, 1289
    supply of, VAT, charge to—
        abroad, services received from, **7**, 1308
        agent, supply through, **7**, 1285
        basic tax point, **7**, 1355
        conditions for, **7**, 1284
        consideration—
            alteration, **7**, 1286
            receivability, **7**, 1286
            supply must be for, **7**, 1284–1287, 1297
            what constitutes, **7**, 1286
        contract, generally, **7**, 1285
        generally, **7**, 1287, 1289
        input tax, **7**, 1372
        meaning of supply, **7**, 1285
        output tax, **7**, 1354
        private or non-business purposes, services
           used for, **7**, 1310
        tax point, **7**, 1355–1357
        taxable person, supply by, **7**, 1373
        time of supply, **7**, 1355–1357
        United Kingdom, supply in, **7**, 1294
        VAT invoice basis, **7**, 1355–1361
        void or illegal contract, where, **7**, 1285
        zero-rated transactions, **7**, 1311
        zero-rating, *see* zero-rating *below*
sheriff court jurisdiction, **6**, 1092
sheriff officer, liability of, **14**, 1511
sports clubs and associations, **19**, 1315–1318
sports competitions, exemption from, **19**, 1296,
    1510
supplies—
    agency supplies, **7**, 1373
    appropriate for different purpose, **7**, 1389
    business, supplies must be in course of, **7**, 1291,
        1295, 1296
    business assets, disposition, **7**, 1296, 1298
    conditions for imposition of VAT, **7**, 1284
    consideration—
        alteration, **7**, 1286
        receivability, **7**, 1286
        supply must be for, **7**, 1285, 1286, 1294,
        1297
        what constitutes, **7**, 1286
    deemed supplies—
        abroad, services received from, **7**, 1308
        deregistration, goods held at, **7**, 1309
        disposal of business assets, **7**, 1298

Value added tax—*continued*
supplies—*continued*
  deemed supplies—*continued*
    generally, **7**, 1297
    goods removed to another Community member state, **7**, 1300
    non-business purposes, services used for, **7**, 1310
    output tax, **7**, 1354
    private purposes, services used for, **7**, 1310
    self-supply order, **7**, 1301
      business transferred to group member, **7**, 1305
      change of building use, **7**, 1306
      construction services, **7**, 1301, 1304
      developers, **7**, 1307
      motor vehicle, **7**, 1301, 1302
      stationery, **7**, 1301, 1303
      use of business assets, **7**, 1299
      zero-rated transactions, **7**, 1311
  employees, services of, **7**, 1295
  exempt supplies, **7**, 1291, 1359, 1385, 1417–1431
  goods, supplies of, **7**, 1284
    See also goods *above*
  input tax, **7**, 1372
  investor in passive role, **7**, 1295
  meaning of supply, **7**, 1285
  output tax, **7**, 1354
  overseas supplies, person making, **7**, 1338
  relevant supplies—
    'distance sales', **7**, 1328
    meaning, **7**, 1328
    person making, **7**, 1328–1331, 1339
  'relevant zero-rated supply', meaning, **7**, 1306
  samples, **7**, 1298
  self-supplies, input tax, **7**, 1374
  self-supply order, *see* self-supply order *above*
  services, supplies of, **7**, 1284, 1287, 1289, 1291, 1294
    See also services *above*
  supplies outside scope of VAT, **7**, 1290
  tangible moveable property, **7**, 1287
  taxable person, supply by, **7**, 1373
  taxable supplies, **7**, 1291, 1295
    bad debt relief, **7**, 1370
    person making, **7**, 1324–1327, 1337
    valuation, **7**, 1324
  time of supply, **7**, 1355–1357
  United Kingdom—
    goods removed from, **7**, 1293
    goods removed to, **7**, 1293
    goods supplied outside, **7**, 1293
    services supplied in, **7**, 1294
    territorial extent, **7**, 1292
  VAT invoice basis, **7**, 1355–1361
  voluntary services, **7**, 1295
  zero-rating, *see* zero-rating *below*
tax invoice, date of issue, **19**, 1541
tax point, **19**, 1541
  basic, **7**, 1355, 1356
  meaning, **7**, 1355
  VAT invoice basis, **7**, 1355–1357
tax return, **7**, 1399

Value added tax—*continued*
taxable person—
  annual accounting scheme, **7**, 1352
  bankruptcy, **7**, 1344, 1351, 1352
  cash accounting scheme, **7**, 1351
  death, **7**, 1344, 1351, 1352
  deregistration—
    goods held at date of, **7**, 1309
    relevant acquisitions, person making, **7**, 1335
    relevant supplies, person making, **7**, 1331
    taxable supplies, person making, **7**, 1327
  flat-rate scheme for farmers, **7**, 1353
  goods and services supplied by, **7**, 1373
  incapacity, **7**, 1344, 1351, 1352
  input tax, **7**, 1377
  meaning, **7**, 1291*n*, 1323
  notification of assessment, **7**, 1450
  registration—
    associations, **7**, 1347
    beneficiaries, **7**, 1344
    bodies corporate, **7**, 1323, 1348
    cancellation, **7**, 1327, 1331, 1335
    certificate, **7**, 1323
    clubs, **7**, 1347
    co-owners, **7**, 1344
    date effective from, **7**, 1325
    deemed partnerships, **7**, 1346
    entitlement to register—
      overseas supplies, making, **7**, 1338
      relevant acquisitions, making, **7**, 1340, 1341
      relevant supplies, making, **7**, 1339
      taxable supplies, making, **7**, 1337
    exemption, **7**, 1342, 1343
    generally, **7**, 1323; **19**, 1539
    groups of companies, **7**, 1349
    individuals, **7**, 1344
    liability to register, **7**, 1324, 1325, 1329, 1333
      cessation of liability, notification, **7**, 1326, 1330, 1334
      failure to notify liability, **7**, 1336
      relevant acquisitions, person making, **7**, 1332–1335
      relevant supplies, person making, **7**, 1328–1331
      taxable supplies, person making, **7**, 1324–1327
    organisations, **7**, 1347
    partnerships, **7**, 1345, 1346
    register of taxable persons, maintenance, **7**, 1282
    transfer of registration, **7**, 1350
    trustees, **7**, 1344
    zero-rated acquisitions, **7**, 1343
    zero-rated supplies, **7**, 1342
  relevant acquisitions, person making, **7**, 1332–1335
  relevant supplies, person making, **7**, 1328–1331
  supply to, **7**, 1291
  taxable supplies, person making, **7**, 1324–1327, 1337
  cessation of supplies, **7**, 1326
tour operator, margin scheme for, *see* output tax (invoicing requirements) *above*

Value added tax—*continued*
underdeclaration—
　Commissioners of Customs and Excise, powers,
　　7, 1404
　correction, **7**, 1395, 1396
　voluntary disclosure, **7**, 1398
used goods, **7**, 1363, 1430
　margin scheme for, **7**, 1354, 1363, 1364
valuation, generally, **25**, 1032
Value Added Tax Tribunal, supervision of, **23**,
　911n
VAT account, requirement to keep and maintain,
　7, 1391
VAT Central Unit, responsibilities of, **7**, 1282
VAT invoice basis, *see* output tax (invoicing
　requirements) *above*
zero-rated schedule, **7**, 1311
zero-rating—
　acquisitions, **7**, 1343
　aircraft and connected services, **7**, 1452
　animal feeding stuff, **7**, 1445
　bank notes, **7**, 1455
　blind, talking books and wireless sets for, **7**,
　　1448
　books, talking, **7**, 1448
　books and other printed matter, **7**, 1447
　caravans, **7**, 1453
　charitable building, construction, **7**, 1448
　charity, supplies made by, **7**, 1459
　clothing, **7**, 1460
　commodity transactions, **7**, 1432, 1433
　drugs, medicinal, **7**, 1456
　exports, **7**, 1457
　food and drink, **7**, 1445
　footwear, **7**, 1460
　freight transport services, **7**, 1452
　futures, **7**, 1433
　generally, **7**, 1432; **19**, 1540
　gold and gold coins, **7**, 1454
　goods exported to place outwith European
　　Union—
　　export house, supplies to, **7**, 1438
　　freight containers, **7**, 1437
　　generally, **7**, 1432, 1434
　　motor vehicles, **7**, 1441
　　overseas person, supplies to, **7**, 1439
　　person departing from Community member
　　　states, **7**, 1440, 1441
　　ship, aircraft or hovercraft, stores for, **7**, 1436
　supplier, export by, **7**, 1435
　goods removed to another Community
　　member state—
　　excise duty, goods subject to, **7**, 1443
　　generally, **7**, 1432, 1442
　　person taxable in another Community
　　　member state, supplies, to, **7**, 1442
　　transport, supplies of new means of, **7**, 1444
　goods to be exported outwith European
　　Union, work carried out on, **7**, 1451
　handicapped, aids for, **7**, 1448, 1456
　houseboats, **7**, 1453
　imports, **7**, 1314, 1457
　international services, supply, **7**, 1451
　live animals, **7**, 1445

Value added tax—*continued*
zero-rating—*continued*
　maps, charts and topographical plans, **7**, 1447
　medicines, **7**, 1456
　motor bicycle helmets, **7**, 1460
　music, sheet, **7**, 1447
　newspapers, journals and periodicals, **7**, 1447
　options, **7**, 1433
　pilotage services, **7**, 1452
　Post Office, transport by, **7**, 1452
　protected building, **7**, 1450
　protective clothing, **7**, 1460
　residential building, construction, **7**, 1448
　salvage services, **7**, 1452
　sea-rescue charity, supplies to, **7**, 1452
　seeds and other plant propagation means, **7**,
　　1445
　sewerage services, **7**, 1446
　ships and connected services, **7**, 1452
　supplies, **7**, 1342, 1357, 1359
　　categories, **7**, 1432
　tax-free shops, **7**, 1458
　terminal markets, **7**, 1433
　towage services, **7**, 1452
　trader exempt from registration, when, **7**, 1342,
　　1343
　transactions, **7**, 1311
　transport services, **7**, 1452
　travel services, **7**, 1452
　water, **7**, 1446
　wireless sets for the blind, **7**, 1448
Valuer
additional, **25**, 119
advice from, **25**, 69
agricultural—
　competent, **25**, 132
　duties, **25**, 138
definitions, **25**, 114–120
external, **25**, 117
fair value, calculation of, **25**, 68
Financial Services Act, implications of, **25**, 69
guidance to, **25**, 70
independent, **25**, 120
instructions to, **25**, 97
internal, **25**, 116
joint, **25**, 118
partnership, number of partners allowed, **16**,
　1011, 1112
qualified, **25**, 115
task of, **25**, 30
Valve
water fitting, as, **25**, 527
Van
contract for carriage by, **3**, 601
hired, **3**, 601
supplier delivering goods in own, **3**, 601
unattended, leaving, **3**, 627
Vandalism
firearm or imitation firearm possessed during, **10**,
　1565
more than one mental element, where, **7**, 85
offence of, **7**, 410, 414
ship, destroying or sinking, **7**, 421

Vapour
See NOXIOUS VAPOUR
Varnish and wood preservative
weights and measures legislation, **6**, 244
Vassal
See FEUDAL LAW
Vassalage
See FEUDAL LAW
Vatican
passport *per l'estero*, **16**, 1236
Vault
right to construct, **3**, 524
road, under, maintenance of, **20**, 664
Veal
guide prices, **1**, 933
Vedel Report, **10**, 376
Vegetation
physical damage to, **14**, 2044, 2045
stream, in, **25**, 406
Vehicle
See MOTOR VEHICLE
Vehicle excise licence
See MOTOR VEHICLE
Vehicle repair or recovery services, body providing
insurance authorisation not required, **12**, 807
Vehicle tester
trade licence, **7**, 1074
Vending machine
food sold from, **11**, 396
    labelling, **11**, 338*n*, 383, 388, 390, 396
    soft drinks, **11**, 368
offences, **6**, 248–250
offer and invitation to treat, **15**, 623
Venereal disease
advertising treatment for, **1**, 536
sickness benefit, **21**, 888
Venison
dealing in—
    dealers' records, **11**, 948–951, 954, 955
    inspection, **11**, 948, 955
    licences, **11**, 944–947; **14**, 525
        applications, **11**, 945
        copies and returns, **11**, 947
        disqualification from holding, **11**, 960
        duration, **11**, 946
        grant of, **11**, 944
        offences, **11**, 952–954
        Red Deer Commission, copies and returns to, **11**, 947
    meaning, **11**, 944
    regulations as to preparation and sale, **11**, 312, 433, 496
    selling, offering and exposing for sale, offences as to, **11**, 952–955
    unlawfully killed deer, selling, offering or exposing for sale, **11**, 953
Ventilation
building controls, **3**, 208
supply, charge to VAT, **7**, 1288, 1320
Verbal injury
absolute privilege, **15**, 556, 559
actual injury, **15**, 555, 572
compensation, loss requiring, **15**, 555

Verbal injury—*continued*
convicium, **15**, 558
defamation, and, **15**, 557
falsity of statement, **15**, 555, 557, 560, 572
generally, **15**, 555, 572, 573
intent to injure, **15**, 555, 557, 560, 572
legal aid availability, **13**, 1034
malicious, statement must be, **15**, 555, 557, 560, 572
malicious falsehood, **15**, 557, 559
meaning, **15**, 557
misstatement, economic loss caused by, **15**, 555, 556
Moffat v London Express Newspapers Ltd, decision in, **15**, 573
negligence, **15**, 555, 556
nervous shock, **15**, 284
public hatred, contempt and ridicule—
    convicium, **15**, 558
    generally, **15**, 558, 564
    meaning, **15**, 568
    relevancy, **15**, 568
    requirements for actionability, **15**, 564
    series of statements, **15**, 565
    solatium, **15**, 567, 569
    Steele v Scottish Daily Record and Sunday Mail Ltd, decision in, **15**, 567, 569
    unpopular sentiments, attributions, **15**, 566
slander—
    third party—
        Broom v Ritchie & Co, decision in, **15**, 571
        examples, **15**, 570
        generally, **15**, 570
    title, goods or business, of—
        absolute privilege, **15**, 559
        business, slander of, **15**, 563
        defences, **15**, 559
        falsity of statement, **15**, 560
        generally, **15**, 559
        loss, remarks must have caused, **15**, 560
        malicious, statement must be, **15**, 560
        property, slander of, **15**, 561
        requisites for actionability, **15**, 559, 560
        title, slander of, **15**, 562
See also DEFAMATION; HONOUR AND REPUTATION, INTERFERENCE WITH
Verdict
application to enter, after direction on point of law, **17**, 1466
delivery of, **17**, 765
fatal accident inquiry, **17**, 958
guilty, **17**, 559
judicial record, as, **10**, 582
not guilty, **17**, 559
not proven, **17**, 559
once case remitted to jury, **17**, 748
recording of, **17**, 765
solemn trial procedure, **17**, 559
summary procedure, trial diet in, **17**, 783
unreasonable, appeal on ground of, **17**, 822
Verge
footpath, **20**, 411
fouling by dogs, **19**, 371
heavy commercial vehicle wholly or partially parked on, **20**, 439

Verge—*continued*
injurious weeds on, **20**, 660
as part of road, **20**, 609
scrub and tall plants on, **20**, 660
Veritas
defamation, *see* DEFAMATION
Verity
oath of, **11**, 845
Vermin
control of, **19**, 444
mice and rats, destruction of, **11**, 859, 866; **19**, 326
prevention of damage—
  forests, to, **11**, 866, 867
  generally, **11**, 859
  requirement notice, **11**, 859–865
Versailles, Treaty of
generally, **19**, 698*n*
Vessel
aground, **21**, 368, 374
dark smoke from, **9**, 1127
definition, and definition of ship, **21**, 106, 108, 109, 111
fishing, *see* FISHING BOATS
lost or abandoned property on, **16**, 1819*n*
navigability, **21**, 108
not under command, **21**, 365, 374
occupier's liability, **15**, 322
oil rigs and other structures, whether classed as, **21**, 108*n*
petroleum-spirit, containing, labelling of, **9**, 850
telecommunications apparatus, **16**, 1928
See also SHIP; SHIPPING
Vested right
beneficiary may acquire, **24**, 71
principle of *Miller's Trustees v Miller*, **24**, 72, 73
truster's intention as to, **24**, 71
Vesting
acceleration of—
  accumulations, **25**, 956
  appointment, power of, **25**, 957
  court, powers of, **25**, 954
  generally, **25**, 953
  testator, intention of, **25**, 955
appointment, powers of—
  acceleration of vesting, **25**, 957
  administrative directions, **25**, 960
  class gift, **25**, 961
  general, **25**, 959
  meaning, **25**, 958
  special, **25**, 959
capital—
  liferenter, power to encroach to benefit, **25**, 923
  sums, power to advance, **25**, 922
cardinal rule, **25**, 906
child and issue, gifts over to, distinguished from gifts over to heirs, **25**, 918
clause of devolution distinguished from destination over, **25**, 917
confirmation, deceased's estate vests on, **25**, 1060
continuing trust, conveyance to trustees of, **25**, 905
contradictory provisions in wills, **25**, 909
deed, construction by court, **25**, 907

Vesting—*continued*
defeasance, subject to—
  beneficiary, exercise of rights conferred on—
    conditional beneficiary, restriction on power of disposal, **25**, 949
    forfeiture, modification orders on, **25**, 947
    generally, **25**, 946, 951
    legal ownership, nature of rights of, **25**, 948
    security holders, **25**, 950
    third parties, **25**, 950
  case potentially involving, approach to be adopted, **25**, 952
  classes of case where applicable—
    defeasance event—
      circumstances in which extension applicable, **25**, 943
      extension of, **25**, 942
      generally, **25**, 941
    generally, **25**, 939
    types of gift, **25**, 940
  complete definition, **25**, 932
  conditional bequests, **25**, 915
  definitive exposition, **25**, 932
  doctrine, **25**, 929
  double contingency rule—
    application of, **25**, 938
    generally, **25**, 936
    number of types of contingency, **25**, 937
  Forfeiture Act, **3**, 1982
    example, **25**, 945
    generally, **25**, 944
  gift—
    absolute ownership, given in, **25**, 933
    types of, **25**, 940
  historical background, **25**, 928
  possible birth of issue to particular person, contingency of, **25**, 935
  presumption, rebuttal of, **25**, 930
  security holder, **25**, 350
  suspensive and resolutive conditions distinguished, **25**, 931
  testator—
    death, beneficiary known or in existence at or prior to, **25**, 934
    intention to suspend, **25**, 932
destination over—
  clause of devolution distinguished from, **25**, 917
  generally, **25**, 916
  gift, appended to, **25**, 919
  survivorship clause compared with, **25**, 916
direction, nature of, **25**, 914
early, presumption in favour of, **25**, 911
executor, in—
  entailed property, **25**, 1109
  special destinations, **25**, 1109
  title, protection of person acquiring, **25**, 1110
  whole estate, **25**, 1108
express declaration, **25**, 908
gifts—
  clause of survivorship appended to, **25**, 919
  conditions—
    construction of, **25**, 913
    generally, **25**, 912
  destination over appended to, **25**, 919

Vesting—*continued*
gifts—*continued*
heritage, of, **25**, 684
interest, directions for payment to beneficiary, **25**, 924
leading principle, **25**, 906
lease, interest in, **25**, 715
legacy—
    legitim held as surrogation for, **25**, 925
    tense use in wording, **25**, 926
limited number of persons—
    appointment, power of, **25**, 927
    division among, **25**, 927
Lord Dunedin's guide-posts, **25**, 911–927
meaning, **25**, 902
miscellaneous factors affecting, **25**, 921–927
moveable succession, **25**, 685
ownership, creation of rights of, **25**, 903
period postponed, **25**, 920
person of full age, directions to retain vested right to, **25**, 834, 835
phraseology of, **25**, 910
rules of law, **25**, 906
survivorship clause—
    destination over compared with, **25**, 916
    generally, **25**, 916
    gift, appended to, **25**, 919
taxation—
    class gifts, **19**, 1669
    future interest, of, **19**, 1667
    generally, **19**, 1664
    right to income, of, **19**, 1666
    subject to defeasance, **19**, 1668
    whole interest, of, **19**, 1665
testator—
    phrases used by, **25**, 910
    punctuation used by, **25**, 910
    terms used by, **25**, 910
time of, **25**, 906
vested property, power to dispone, **25**, 904
Veterinary inspector
certificate, evidence of, **2**, 231
inspection by—
    cattle, of, **11**, 444
    exported animals, of, **2**, 219
    health provisions, under, **2**, 179
    imported poultry, of, **2**, 213
Veterinary meat inspector
generally, **11**, 507, 507*n*
qualification, **11**, 512
Veterinary practice
agricultural animal, owner, veterinary practice by, **25**, 203
animal—
    export, certification for, **25**, 206
    owner, veterinary practice by, **25**, 203
    veterinary student, examination by, **25**, 203
    welfare, rights and duties connected with, **25**, 206
blood, infectious disease, taken for diagnosis of, **25**, 203
boarding establishment, inspection of, **2**, 134
canine specialist, unregistered person, description by, **25**, 203

Veterinary practice—*continued*
canine surgery, unregistered person, description by, **25**, 203
civil liability, negligence, **25**, 214
commonwealth, register of veterinary surgeons, **25**, 204
dentist, veterinary practice by, **25**, 203
discipline of profession—
    criminal offence, **25**, 211
    disgraceful conduct, **25**, 211
    domestic tribunal, statutory regulation of, **23**, 917
    negligence, **25**, 214
    procedure, **25**, 210
    register—
        removal of names from, **25**, 212
        restoration of names to, **25**, 213
    Royal College of Veterinary Surgeons, powers of, **25**, 209
doctor, veterinary practice by, **25**, 203
dog breeding premises, inspection of, **2**, 117
drugs—
    medicinal products distinguished, **14**, 1201
    prescription of, **25**, 206
education, Royal College of Veterinary Surgeons, powers of, **25**, 201
experiments, authorised, special provisions for carrying out, **25**, 203
export, certification of animal for, **25**, 206
foreign list, register of veterinary surgeons, **25**, 204
infectious disease, blood taken for diagnosis, **25**, 203
jury service, registered person excluded from, **25**, 206
lay person, veterinary practice by, **25**, 203
negligence, veterinary surgeon, position of, **25**, 214
operation, unregistered person, carried out by, **25**, 203
owner of animal—
    slaughter without consent of, **25**, 206
    veterinary practice by, **25**, 203
pet shop, inspection of, **2**, 122
pharmaceutical and veterinary chemist, unregistered person, description by, **25**, 203
physiotherapist, veterinary practice by, **25**, 203
police officer, slaughter without owner's consent, warrant for, **25**, 206
poultry, minor procedures on, **25**, 203
register—
    Commonwealth list, **25**, 204
    foreign list, **25**, 204
    general list, **25**, 204
    removal of names from, **25**, 212
    restoration of names to, **25**, 213
    supplementary, **25**, 205
    temporary list, **25**, 204
registration, Royal College of Veterinary Surgeons, **25**, 201, 206
riding establishment, inspection of, **2**, 128
Royal College of Veterinary Surgeons—
    charters, **25**, 201

Veterinary practice—*continued*
Royal College of Veterinary Surgeons—*continued*
  Commonwealth list, **25**, 204
  conduct of profession, powers relating to, **25**, 201
  Council—
    constitution, **25**, 207
    disciplinary powers, **25**, 210
    duties, **25**, 208
  Disciplinary Committee, **25**, 210
  discipline, *see* discipline of profession *above*
  education, powers relating to, **25**, 201
  foreign list, **25**, 204
  general list, **25**, 204
  Preliminary Investigation Committee, **25**, 210
  qualifications, **25**, 204
  register, *see* register *above*
  registration, **25**, 201, 206
  royal charter, **25**, 201
  supplementary register, **25**, 205
  temporary list, **25**, 204
slaughter, consent of owner, without, **25**, 206
student, examination of animal, **25**, 203
temporary list, register of veterinary surgeons, **25**, 204
unregistered person, veterinary practice by, **25**, 203
veterinary forge, unregistered person, use of term by, **25**, 203
veterinary inspector, *see* VETERINARY INSPECTOR
veterinary meat inspector, *see* VETERINARY MEAT INSPECTOR
veterinary profession—
  conduct of, **25**, 201
  formal recognition, **25**, 201
  regulation, **25**, 201
veterinary surgeon, *see* VETERINARY SURGEON
Veterinary Surgeons Act 1966 ..., **25**, 201, 202
veterinary surgery, meaning, **25**, 202
warrant, slaughter of animal, **25**, 206
Veterinary practitioner
See VETERINARY PRACTICE; VETERINARY SURGEON
Veterinary Products Committee
functions, **14**, 1204
Veterinary surgeon
alcohol-related offence by, **25**, 211
animal, medicinal test on, **14**, 1206
controlled drugs, use of, **14**, 1258
criminal offence, **25**, 211
cruelty cases, powers in, **2**, 250
discipline, **25**, 209–214
disgraceful conduct, **25**, 211
legal control, scope of, **14**, 1101
licensing system, exemption from, **14**, 1203
negligence, **25**, 214
operations on animals, prohibited, **2**, 246
poison, sale of, **14**, 1215
prescription, medicinal products supplied by, **14**, 1209
register, *see* VETERINARY PRACTICE
See also VETERINARY PRACTICE
Viaduct
provisional orders in connection with, **19**, 26

Vibration
aerodrome, **9**, 1283
  See also NOISE
aircraft, from—
  aircraft operators' duties as to, **9**, 1278
  regulation of, **9**, 1277
  See also NOISE
degree, matters of, **14**, 2051
heavy industrial drop hammer, from, action to interdict, **14**, 2039
land compensation, **9**, 1295
Vicarious liability
See LIABILITY (VICARIOUS)
Vice-Chamberlain
office of, **7**, 800
Vice-Chamberlain of the Household
office of, **7**, 774
Victim
act or omission by, supervening, **7**, 52
art and part liability, **7**, 177, 178
consent of, **7**, 93
Criminal Injuries Compensation Scheme, *see* CRIMINAL INJURIES COMPENSATION SCHEME
special susceptibility, **7**, 55, 261
Victimisation
discrimination in employment by, **9**, 340
Video
cinema, effect on, **9**, 1018
game, **9**, 1016
piracy, **6**, 118
recording—
  identification by, **10**, 667
  See also COPYRIGHT; FILM
Vietnam
imports, European Union regulations, **7**, 1029
View
uninterrupted, no natural right to enjoyment, **14**, 2032
Violation of sepulchres
actus reus—
  disturbance of body, **7**, 464
  elements of crime, **7**, 462
  generally, **7**, 465
  'raising' of body, **7**, 462, 463
body, requirement as to, **7**, 462
cremated remains, **7**, 465
duration of protection, **7**, 463, 464
generally, **7**, 333, 461
historical background, **7**, 461
mens rea, **7**, 466
motive, **7**, 466
non-consecrated site, **7**, 462
rationale of criminality, **7**, 465
vault, body in, **7**, 462
Violent profits
caution—
  form, **13**, 509
  liability to find, **13**, 505
  removing, action of, **13**, 504–507
ejection, action of, **13**, 505, 508, 512
good faith, **13**, 511
landlord, title to, **13**, 505
liability for, **13**, 505, 510
meaning, **13**, 505

Violent profits—*continued*
proposed reform, **13**, 512
recovery of possession, in action for, **18**, 151
removing, action of, **13**, 504–507
spuilzie, claim arising from, **18**, 165
tenant in unjustifiable possession, **13**, 505
urban subjects, **13**, 505
Virgin Islands
British Dependent Territories citizenship, **14**, 1932
Visa
application procedure, **16**, 1239
Declaration of Identity for Visa Purposes, **16**, 1239
entry clearance, as, **12**, 150
exemption endorsement, **16**, 1244
international carrier, passenger of, **16**, 1238
re-entry, **16**, 1239
requirement for, **16**, 1238
visa national—
    earlier leave to remain, resumption, **16**, 1210
    exemptions from status as, **16**, 1210
    meaning, **12**, 151; **16**, 1209
    UK, leave to enter, **16**, 1209
        re-entry, **16**, 1210
    who needs, **12**, 150*n*, 151
Viscount
children of, mode of address, **16**, 1322
title, generally, **16**, 1311
Visit
right of, and high seas jurisdiction, **21**, 45
Visiting forces
civilian component of—
    offences against UK laws, **2**, 789
    trial by Scottish court, **2**, 789
claims against, settlement of, **2**, 786, 790
colonies, in, **2**, 785
coroner's inquests, **2**, 786
deserters etc, arrest of, **2**, 786
disciplinary provisions, **2**, 602, 636
goods imported for, **7**, 1314
inland purchases by, **7**, 1290
jurisdiction—
    service courts, **2**, 788
    UK courts, **2**, 785, 786, 789
members—
    attachment of, **2**, 785
    claims against, **2**, 790
    evidence of being, **2**, 789
    offences against UK laws, **2**, 786, 787, 789
    trial by Scottish court, **2**, 789
service courts—
    death sentence by, **2**, 788
    jurisdiction, **2**, 788
status of, **2**, 613
statutory provisions—
    application of—
        defence organisations, to, **2**, 787
        generally, **2**, 786
        International Headquarters, to, **2**, 787
    forces affected by, **2**, 786
    NATO, application to, **2**, 786
    purposes of, **2**, 785
    summary, **2**, 785
UK law, application of, **2**, 786

Visitor, UK to
business transactions by, **12**, 154, 242, 250, 305
change of category, **12**, 308
conditions of entry, **12**, 306
dependants, **12**, 309
employment, prohibition on, **12**, 305
entry clearance, **12**, 151
    where advisible, **12**, 305
extension of leave, **12**, 307
Immigration Rules, **12**, 149, 291, 305–309
medical treatment, seeking, **12**, 305
    conditions of entry, **12**, 306
restricted returnability, **12**, 305
visitor's card scheme—
    entry to UK, generally, **16**, 1206
work permit granted to, **12**, 157
Vitious dispossession
action for—
    generally, **18**, 151, 156
    meaning, **18**, 161
    possession *vi aut clam*, **18**, 164
    spuilzie—
        generally, **18**, 161
        See also SPUILZIE
Vitious intromission
circumstances of, **25**, 1062
debts due to deceased, **25**, 1064
generally, **25**, 1061
insolvent estate, **25**, 1065
liability for, **25**, 1063
nature of, **25**, 1062
vitious intromitter—
    fiduciary duty of, **24**, 172
    meaning, **25**, 637
Vitium reale
stolen goods, **15**, 51
Vocational training body
discrimination, liability for, **9**, 344
Voice
identification by, **10**, 663
Volenti non fit injuria
breach of statutory duty, **15**, 175, 186
defence of, **14**, 2127
delictual claim, as defence to—
    acceptance of risk, generally, **15**, 396
    contributory negligence, **15**, 403*n*
    duty of care, **15**, 395
    employment cases, **15**, 395, 396, 398
    generally, **15**, 394
    landlord and tenant cases, **15**, 395, 396, 397
    mental capacity, **15**, 396
    passenger cases, **15**, 395, 402
    principal requisites of defence, **15**, 396
    proof of acceptance, **15**, 394
    property cases, **15**, 395, 396, 397
    'rescuer' cases, **15**, 395, 396, 401
    risk, appreciation of, **15**, 396
    sport-related cases, **15**, 395, 399, 400
doctrine of, generally, **19**, 1242
meaning, **15**, 394
Volume overrider
meaning, **12**, 1357
Securities and Investments Board Core Conduct
    of Business Rules, **12**, 1357

Voluntary association
See ASSOCIATION
Voluntary churches
Burgess Oath, **3**, 1636, 1637, 1637*n*
charitable status, **3**, 1632
church, meaning, **3**, 1633
Church of Scotland position compared, **3**, 1634
civil courts, jurisdiction, *see* judicial remedies against actings of *below*
civil right or interest, infringement, *see* judicial remedies against actings of *below*
clergy—
    jury service, excused from, **3**, 1632*n*
    special status, **3**, 1632, 1632*n*
courts—
    civil courts, jurisdiction, *see* judicial remedies against actings of *below*
    status, **3**, 1647
fiscal privileges, **3**, 1632
generally, **3**, 1632
gift or subscription expressly or impliedly for purposes of, **3**, 1642
historical background, **3**, 1636
incorporation—
    companies legislation, under, **3**, 1632*n*, 1638, 1638*n*
    royal charter, under, **3**, 1632*n*, 1638
Jewish faith, **3**, 1674
judicatories, status, **3**, 1505
judicial remedies against actings of—
    actings beyond constitution, **3**, 1653
    actings calculated to affect civil rights of member, **3**, 1653
    actings calculated to affect partrimonial of member, **3**, 1653
    averment of malice, **3**, 1652
    civil right or interest, infringement, **3**, 1648
        proof, **3**, 1651
    consideration, generally, **3**, 1650
    generally, **3**, 1647
    gross irregularity, cases of, **3**, 1653
    limitation, **3**, 1653
    natural justice complaints, **3**, 1649, 1653
    rules purporting to deprive right of appeal to civil courts, **3**, 1653
    submission by member, **3**, 1652
jurisdiction—
    generally, **3**, 1647
legal characteristics, **3**, 1638, 1638*n*
legal existence, generally, **3**, 1636
legal status, **3**, 1637
name, whether *nomen juris*, **3**, 1638, 1641
persona standi before courts, **3**, 1638
property—
    Craigdallie case, **3**, 1645
    destination, **3**, 1643–1645
    Free Church Union case, **3**, 1646
    gift or subscription, **3**, 1642
    schism within church, where, **3**, 1644, 1645, 1646
    trust, held through—
        charitable status, **3**, 1643
        generally, **3**, 1642
        heritage, title to, **3**, 1642

Voluntary churches—*continued*
property—*continued*
    trust, held through—*continued*
        particular religious beliefs of congregation, **3**, 1645, 1646
        recognition, **3**, 1642
        religious purposes, trusts for, **3**, 1643
        union with another church, where, **3**, 1644, 1646
religious toleration, **3**, 1635, 1635*n*
Roman Catholic Church as voluntary church, **3**, 1633*n*
Scottish Episcopal Church as voluntary church, **3**, 1623, 1631, 1633*n*
status—
    charitable, **3**, 1632
    legal, **3**, 1637
sue, title to, **3**, 1638, 1639, 1640
    representative, through, **3**, 1638, 1640
sued, title to be, **3**, 1638, 1639, 1641
synagogues, **3**, 1674
unincorporated voluntary association, treatment as, **3**, 1632
voluntary, meaning, **3**, 1633
Voluntary obligation
annulment, **15**, 671, 672
    See also invalidity, grounds of *below*
assignation, **11**, 766
averring fraud, **11**, 704
capacity to enter—
    associations, **15**, 663
    children and young persons, **15**, 660
    clubs, **15**, 663
    corporate bodies, **15**, 664
    generally, **15**, 659
    influence of alcohol or drugs, person under, **15**, 662
    insane persons, **15**, 661
    minors, **15**, 660
    natural persons, **15**, 659
    pupils, **15**, 660
    trade unions, **15**, 665
consensus, fraud preventing, **11**, 705, 706
consensus in idem, **15**, 691, 692
consent—
    enforced simulation, **15**, 674
    facility and circumvention, **15**, 678
    force and fear, use of, **15**, 673–677
    fraud as factor vitiating, **11**, 707–714
    improper or illegitimate pressure to consent, **15**, 676
    inequality of bargaining power, **15**, 677
    misrepresentation, following, **15**, 680–685
    position of trust, abuse of, **15**, 679
    reluctant expression, **15**, 675
    undue influence, **15**, 679
    weak-mindedness, taking advantage of, **15**, 678
constitution—
    formalities, **15**, 666–669
    fraud as factor preventing, **11**, 705, 706
contract, *see* CONTRACT
creation, **15**, 4
defects or vices of consent, **15**, 670
force and fear, coercion by, **15**, 673–677

Voluntary obligation—*continued*
fraudulent misrepresentation—
  active concealment, made by, **11**, 711
  false statements, made by, **11**, 709
  non-disclosure, made by, **11**, 712
  positive acts, made by, **11**, 710
generally, **11**, 703–718, 777; **15**, 1, 4, 9
holograph, **15**, 666
homologation, **15**, 666, 669, 672
inaccurately recorded, **15**, 695
inducement of material error, **11**, 713
inequality of bargaining power, **15**, 677
informally constituted, **15**, 666, 667
insolvency, **11**, 777
invalidity, grounds of—
  annulment, conditions of, **15**, 672
  defective expression and rectification, **15**, 695
  defects or vices of consent, **15**, 670
  error, **15**, 686–694
    common, **15**, 690
    dissensus, **15**, 691, 692
    essential, **15**, 688
    expression, of, **15**, 686
    generally, **15**, 686
    intention, of, **15**, 686, 688
    known, **15**, 694
    latent irresolvable ambiguity, **15**, 693
    motive, in, **15**, 686, 688, 690
    mutual, **15**, 691
    substantials, in, **15**, 687–690
    transaction, in, **15**, 686, 688, 689, 690
  facility and circumvention, **15**, 678
  force and fear, **15**, 673–677
  inaccurately recorded obligation, **15**, 695
  misrepresentation, **15**, 680–685
  position of trust, abuse of, **15**, 679
  rectification, **15**, 695
  successful challenge, consequences, **15**, 671
  undue influence, **15**, 679
  weak-mindedness, **15**, 678
misrepresentation, inducement to enter by—
  fraudulent misrepresentation, **15**, 683
  generally, **15**, 680
  inaccurate representation of fact, **15**, 681
  innocent misrepresentation, **15**, 685
  method of representation, **15**, 682
  negligent misrepresentation, **15**, 589, 684
null and void, **15**, 671
obligations literis, **15**, 666, 669
probative, **15**, 667
prout de jure, **15**, 666
rectification of defectively expressed document, **15**, 762
rei interventus, **15**, 666, 669
relevant fraudulent conduct, **11**, 708
remedies, **11**, 714
resile, actings barring right to, **15**, 669
self-evidencing, **15**, 667
unilateral promises, *see* UNILATERAL PROMISE
validity—
  challenge, **15**, 670
    consequences of successful, **15**, 671
  grounds of invalidity, *see* invalidity, grounds of *above*

Voluntary obligation—*continued*
variation, formalities, **15**, 667
void, **15**, 671, 690
voidable, **15**, 671, 672
will of obligor, arising from, **15**, 1, 4
writing, in, **15**, 666, 667, 668
wrongful act, arising from, **15**, 1, 3, 9, 213*ff*
Vote
absent voting—
  appeals against decision, **15**, 1175
  application—
    alter choice of voting, **15**, 1169
    appeals, **15**, 1175
    elector, by, **15**, 1157, 1159
      requirements for grant, **15**, 1160–1166
    generally, **15**, 1159
    grant 1160*ff*
      procedure, **15**, 1174
    proxy, by, **15**, 1158, 1159
      requirements for grant, **15**, 1160, 1163, 1164, 1167, 1168, 1172
    refusal, procedure, **15**, 1174
  blindness, eligibility on grounds of, **15**, 1161, 1163
  eligibility—
    electors, **15**, 1176
    generally, **15**, 1153
    proxies, **15**, 1177–1182
    statutory provisions, **15**, 1493
  employment, entitlement by reason of, **15**, 1153, 1156, 1161–1164
  evidence of, **15**, 1359
  generally, **15**, 1152
  manner, statutory provisions, **15**, 1493
  modes, **15**, 1152
    statutory provisions, **15**, 1493
  physical incapacity, eligibility on grounds of, **15**, 1161, 1163, 1164
  records—
    content, **15**, 1184
    inspection, **15**, 1186
    misdescription in, **15**, 1187
    registration officer, duty, **15**, 1183
    removal from, **15**, 1185
    significance, **15**, 1184
  special lists—
    amendment, **15**, 1191
    combined poll, **15**, 1381
    content, **15**, 1190
    copies, supply, **15**, 1193
    duty to keep, **15**, 1188
    form, **15**, 1190
    generally, **15**, 1188
    inspection, **15**, 1192
    misdescription in, **15**, 1194
    publication, **15**, 1192
    registration officer, duty, **15**, 1188
    significance, **15**, 1189
    supply, **15**, 1193, 1237
  time, provisions as to—
    applications and notices, **15**, 1222
    generally, **15**, 1217, 1221
age limit for voting, **3**, 1214
entitlement to vote, statutory provisions, **15**, 1493

Vote—*continued*
equality of votes, where, **15**, 1230
incompetent, scrutiny and re-count, **15**, 1442
person, in—
  allotted polling station, **15**, 1155
    voting elsewhere than, **15**, 1156
  elector, by, **15**, 1153, 1155
  European parliamentary elections, **15**, 1153
  generally, **15**, 1152
  local government elections, **15**, 1153
  procedure, **15**, 1214
  proxy, by, **15**, 1154, 1155
  United Kingdom parliamentary elections, **15**,
    1153
polling district, **15**, 1040
polling place, **15**, 1040
postal—
  alter choice of voting by, **15**, 1169
  application for—
    appeal against disallowal, **15**, 1237
    requirements, **15**, 1160–1162
    time requirements, **15**, 1162
  ballot box—
    combined poll, **15**, 1382
    marking, **15**, 1200, 1382
    opening, **15**, 1211, 1239
    provision, **15**, 1200, 1210
  ballot paper—
    address to be sent to, **15**, 1201
    application to be sent to different address,
      15, 1160, 1172, 1173
    issue—
      attendance at—
        notice, **15**, 1199, 1239
        secrecy, notification of requirement as
          to, **15**, 1198
        who may attend, **15**, 1197
      combined poll, **15**, 1196, 1362, 1379–1383
      counterfoils, sealing, **15**, 1203, 1239
      delivery to post office, **15**, 1204
      generally, **15**, 1196, 1201
      legislation, generally, **15**, 1195, 1196
      local government elections, **15**, 1229
      more than one issue and opening, where,
        15, 1196
      notice, **15**, 1199, 1245, 1246
      notification, **15**, 1239
      procedure, **15**, 1201
      refusal to issue, **15**, 1202
      reissue on return of spoilt paper, **15**, 1205,
        1215
      statutory provisions, **15**, 1493
      unused, **15**, 1203
    number on, check, **15**, 1215
    receipt (opening)
      attendance at—
        notice, **15**, 1199
        secrecy, notification of requirement as
          to, **15**, 1198
        who may attend, **15**, 1197
      combined poll, **15**, 1196, 1362, 1379–1383
      duly returned, **15**, 1207
      equipment for, **15**, 1209
      generally, **15**, 1196, 1206

Vote—*continued*
postal—*continued*
  ballot paper—*continued*
    receipt (opening)—*continued*
      legislation, generally, **15**, 1195, 1196
      more than one issue and opening, where,
        15, 1196
      notice, **15**, 1199
      procedure, **15**, 1208–1210
      statutory provisions, **15**, 1493
    rejected votes, **15**, 1212
    spoilt, **15**, 1205, 1213, 1239
      return and reissue, **15**, 1205, 1215
    unused, **15**, 1203
  ballot paper envelope, **15**, 1201, 1212, 1215
    combined poll, **15**, 1215, 1382
    number on, check, **15**, 1212
  blindness, eligibility on grounds of, **15**, 1160,
    1161, 1176
  combined poll, **15**, 1363
    absent voters list, marking, **15**, 1381
    agents, notice of appointment, **15**, 1380
    amendments to documentation, **15**, 1382
    ballot boxes, labelling of, **15**, 1382
    ballot papers, **15**, 1382
    declaration of identity, **15**, 1215, 1381, 1382
    envelopes, **15**, 1382
    generally, **15**, 1215, 1362, 1379
    postal proxies list, marking, **15**, 1381
    receptacle, labelling of, **15**, 1382
  count, **15**, 1326
  declaration of identity—
    authentication, **15**, 1212, 1215
    check by returning officer, **15**, 1212
    combined poll, **15**, 1215, 1381, 1382
    form, **15**, 1382
    issue, **15**, 1201
    number on, check, **15**, 1212, 1215
    returned ballot paper must be accompanied
      by, **15**, 1207
    signature, **15**, 1212, 1215
    witness, **15**, 1212, 1215
  duly returned, **15**, 1215
  elector, eligibility, **15**, 1176
  electors list—
    preparation, **15**, 1084
    sealing, **15**, 1203, 1239
  employment, entitlement by reason of, **15**,
    1160–1162, 1176
  European parliamentary elections, **15**, 1239
  failure to exercise vote, **15**, 1152
  forwarding of documents, **15**, 1213
  generally, **15**, 1152
  grant, **15**, 1084
    procedure, **15**, 1174
  hand, return by, **15**, 1215
  inability to exercise vote, **15**, 1152
  indefinite period, for—
    application, **15**, 1160, 1161, 1165
    eligibility, **15**, 1176
  introduction, **15**, 1018
  issue, statutory provisions, **15**, 1493
  list of electors entitled to vote by—
    combined poll, **15**, 1381

Vote—*continued*
postal—*continued*
  list of electors entitled to vote by—*continued*
    generally, **15**, 1188
    sealing, **15**, 1203, 1239
  list of proxies entitled to vote by—
    amendment, **15**, 1191
    combined poll, **15**, 1381
    content, **15**, 1190
    copies, supply, **15**, 1193, 1237
    form, **15**, 1190
    generally, **15**, 1188
    inspection, **15**, 1192
    misdescription in, **15**, 1194
    publication, **15**, 1192
    sealing, **15**, 1203, 1239
    significance, **15**, 1189
  overseas voter, **15**, 1176
  particular election, for—
    application, **15**, 1160, 1162, 1166
  physical incapacity, eligibility on grounds of,
    15, 1160, 1161, 1176
  proxy, by—
    application, **15**, 1160, 1165, 1166
  receipt, statutory provisions, **15**, 1493
  records—
    content, **15**, 1184
    generally, **15**, 1183
    inspection, **15**, 1186
    misdescription in, **15**, 1187
    removal from, **15**, 1185
    significance, **15**, 1184
  refusal, **15**, 1084
    appeals, generally, **15**, 1175
    procedure, **15**, 1174
  rejected votes, **15**, 1212
  removal from record, application for, **15**, 1160,
    1170
  return (covering) envelope, **15**, 1201, 1207,
    1208, 1215
    combined poll, **15**, 1215, 1382
    counting, **15**, 1212
    opening, **15**, 1209, 1212
  secrecy, notification of requirement as to, **15**,
    1198
  voting illegally, **15**, 1448
  voting procedure, **15**, 1215
proportional representation, **15**, 1028, 1343
proxy—
  appointment—
    application for, **15**, 1160, 1167, 1168
    cancellation, **15**, 1181, 1182
    duration, **15**, 1181
    eligibility, **15**, 1177, 1179
    methods, **15**, 1180
    registration officer, by, **15**, 1180
  eligibility to vote, **15**, 1178, 1179
  European parliamentary elections, **15**, 1177,
    1178, 1181
  list of proxies—
    combined poll, **15**, 1375, 1381
    preparation, **15**, 1084
    registration officer, duty to keep, **15**, 1188
    sealing, **15**, 1203, 1239

Vote—*continued*
proxy—*continued*
  list of proxies entitled to vote by post—
    amendment, **15**, 1191
    content, **15**, 1190
    copies, supply, **15**, 1193, 1237
    form, **15**, 1190
    generally, **15**, 1188
    inspection, **15**, 1192
    misdescription in, **15**, 1194
    publication, **15**, 1192
    sealing, **15**, 1203, 1239
    significance, **15**, 1189
  local government elections, **15**, 1177, 1178, 1181
  poll card, **15**, 1309
  proxy paper, issue, **15**, 1180
  questions which may be put to, **15**, 1322
  records—
    electors, **15**, 1183
    proxies, **15**, 1183
    registration officer, duty, **15**, 1183
    removal from, **15**, 1185
  refusal to act, **15**, 1182
  removal from record, application, **15**, 1160, 1171
  treating, **15**, 1445
  United Kingdom parliamentary elections, **15**,
    1177, 1178, 1181
  vote—
    alter choice of voting by, **15**, 1169
    application for—
      appeal against disallowal, **15**, 1237
      requirements, **15**, 1160, 1163, 1164, 1172
      time requirements, **15**, 1164
    blindness, eligibility on grounds of, **15**, 1163,
      1176
    elector—
      eligibility, **15**, 1176
      records as to, **15**, 1183–1187
      removal from records, **15**, 1185
    eligibility of elector, **15**, 1176
    employment, entitlement by reason of, **15**,
      1163, 1164, 1176
    generally, **15**, 1152
    grant, **15**, 1084
    procedure, **15**, 1174
    indefinite period, for—
      application, **15**, 1160, 1163
      eligibility, **15**, 1176
    introduction, **15**, 1018
    list of electors entitled to vote by—
      amendment, **15**, 1191
      content, **15**, 1190
      copies, supply, **15**, 1193, 1237
      form, **15**, 1190
      generally, **15**, 1188
      inspection, **15**, 1192
      misdescription in, **15**, 1194
      publication, **15**, 1192
      sealing, **15**, 1203, 1239
      significance, **15**, 1189
    overseas voter, **15**, 1176
    particular election, for—
      application, **15**, 1160, 1164

Vote—*continued*
proxy—*continued*
  vote—*continued*
    person, proxy voting in, **15**, 1152, 1154,
      1155
    physical incapacity, eligibility on grounds of,
      15, 1163, 1164, 1176
    post, by, application, **15**, 1160, 1165,
      1166
    records—
      content, **15**, 1184
      inspection, **15**, 1186
      misdescription in, **15**, 1187
      removal from, **15**, 1185
      significance, **15**, 1184
    refusal, **15**, 1084
      appeals—
        generally, **15**, 1175
        point of law, on, **15**, 1175
        time limit, **15**, 1175
      procedure, **15**, 1174
    removal from record, application for, **15**,
      1160, 1170
    voting illegally, **15**, 1448
  voters list, *see* proxy (list of proxies) *above*
  voting illegally, **15**, 1448
right to, exercise—
  absent voting, **15**, 1152
  generally, **15**, 1152
  modes, **15**, 1152
  person, in, **15**, 1152
secrecy, **15**, 1320
  notification of requirement as to, **15**, 1198
  officer's etc duty to maintain, **15**, 1318
single transferable, **15**, 1028
swallow voter, measures against, **15**, 1018
tendered ballot papers—
  combined poll, **15**, 1375, 1377
tendered votes list, **15**, 1314
  combined poll, **15**, 1375
United Kingdom Central Council for Nursing,
  Midwifery and Health Visiting election, **15**,
  1503

Vote—*continued*
void, scrutiny and re-count, **15**, 1442
voting illegally, **15**, 1448
voting procedure, *see* VOTING PROCEDURE
See also ELECTION; ELECTOR
Voting procedure
authorised question, **15**, 1322
  combined poll, **15**, 1374
    European parliamentary elections, **15**, 1227
    United Kingdom parliamentary elections, **15**,
      1227
ballot paper counterfoil, marking, **15**, 1320
blind or visually handicapped voter, **15**, 1214,
  1321
close of poll, duties of presiding officer, **15**, 1325
combined poll—
  hours of poll, **15**, 1366
delay, duty to vote without undue, **15**, 1214
delivery of ballot paper to voter, **15**, 1320
generally, **15**, 1320
marking ballot paper, **15**, 1320
number, name and address of elector, calling, **15**,
  1320
person, voting in, **15**, 1214
physically handicapped voter, **15**, 1214, 1321
polling clerk, duties, **15**, 1214
post, voting by, **15**, 1215
presiding officer, duties, **15**, 1214
regulation of voters, **15**, 1324
secrecy, officer's etc duty to maintain, **15**, 1318
United Kingdom Central Council for Nursing,
  Midwifery and Health Visiting election, **15**,
  1503
voting illegally, **15**, 1448
Voyage
definition, **21**, 211n
international, definition, **21**, 211n
long international, definition, **21**, 211n
short international, definition, **21**, 211n
Voyage charterparty
See CHARTERPARTY
Vulgar abuse
defamation, as defence to, **15**, 548

W

Wadset
forms of, **20**, 109
heritable security, as source of, **18**, 112
improper, **20**, 109
meaning, **20**, 109
notary public, execution by, **13**, 1221
reverser, **20**, 109
wadsetter—
    generally, **20**, 109
    proprietor, as, **24**, 444
Wagering
contract, enforceability, **15**, 768
joint adventure to share winnings, **15**, 768
See also BETTING; GAMING
Wages
accrual of, **9**, 52
agricultural, **9**, 403
arrears of, meaning, **4**, 862
bank holiday, due on, **22**, 818
common law, payment at, **9**, 51–57
control of, **9**, 62
deceased, of, income tax, **25**, 964
deductions for stock deficiencies, **9**, 64
equal pay, *see* EQUAL PAY
forfeiture of, **9**, 53
generally, **11**, 1790
holiday, **22**, 818
insolvency, preferential claims in case of, **9**, 148
instrument payable to, **4**, 192
itemised statement, employee's entitlement to, **9**, 66
justice of the peace court powers, **6**, 1159
late payment, **9**, 55
non-payment, **9**, 55
regulation of, **11**, 1791
sickness of employee, during, **9**, 54
unfair dismissal, compensatory award for—
    future loss, **9**, 273
    immediate loss, **9**, 272
Wages Act 1986 ..., **11**, 1792
    appeals under, **6**, 1000
wages councils, powers of, **11**, 1792
withholding, **9**, 57
work not available, when, **9**, 56
See also REMUNERATION
Waiver
alteration of position, where, **16**, 1630
definition, **16**, 1629
delay, whether amounting to, **16**, 1633
election, by, **16**, 1632
estoppel, and, **16**, 1632
express, **16**, 1628
implied, **16**, 1628
inconsistent actings, **16**, 1636
insurance law, **16**, 1641
lien, of, **16**, 1638
minute of—
    interpretation, **12**, 1262
    real burden extinguished by, **18**, 426

Waiver—*continued*
more than statement of intention required, **16**, 1631
payment without deduction, **16**, 1639
personal bar—
    relationship with, **16**, 1627, 1631
    waiver as, **16**, 1626, 1632
plea of no jurisdiction, as, **16**, 1634
prejudice as result of, **16**, 1629, 1630
    proof, **16**, 1628
reliance, generally, **16**, 1629, 1630
requirements, generally, **16**, 1628
right, must be of, **16**, 1628, 1635
ultra vires actings, **16**, 1637
use of term, **16**, 1628
Wales
designated milk brought from, **11**, 465
devolution, **5**, 332
disestablishment, **5**, 688
execution on assets in, **4**, 756
local government in, **14**, 60, 61
over-representation at Westminster, **5**, 373
Prince of, Scottish titles, **6**, 461*n*
VAT customs union, **7**, 1281
Welsh Grand Committee—
    consideration of Bills relating exclusively to Wales, **5**, 419
    membership, **5**, 419
Welsh Office—
    creation of, **5**, 515
    responsibilities, **5**, 515
Wall
ad medium filum, owned, doctrine of common interest, **18**, 359
boundary, *see* BOUNDARY
broken glass or spikes, incorporating, **20**, 697
gable, **12**, 1239
mutual, boundary on, **12**, 1239
privacy, maintenance of, **14**, 2036
removal of, physical damage caused by, **14**, 2045
road, provision on, **20**, 660
War
act of, carrier not liable for, **21**, 603
aggression, meaning, **19**, 700
bacteriological methods, **19**, 711
Brussels Declaration, **19**, 707
capture may be effected from outbreak of, **17**, 409
charity, registration of, **14**, 518
chemical weapons, **19**, 711
civilians, protection of, **19**, 708
clause—
    time charterparty, **21**, 640
    voyage charterparty, **21**, 618
conduct of—
    historical development, **19**, 707
    humanitarian law, **19**, 706–708
    Lieber Code, **19**, 707
conscription, **5**, 615
crimes, **19**, 695, 710

War—*continued*
damage—
  liability, **3**, 91
  work arising from, **3**, 45
declaration, **7**, 724, 857; **19**, 706*n*
defence regulations, **5**, 616
derogation from European Convention on
  Human Rights, **12**, 31
efforts to discourage and limit—
  before 1945 ..., **19**, 698
  since 1945 ..., **19**, 699
enemy—
  duty to assist at sea, **21**, 209
  trading with—
    acts amounting to, **7**, 606
    documents, destruction, **7**, 608
    enemy, what constitutes, **7**, 605
    enemy currency, purchasing, **7**, 606
    generally, **7**, 605
    information, failure to produce, **7**, 608
    mental element, **7**, 607
    penalties, **7**, 606
    securities, transfer and allotment, **7**, 608
    supplementary offences, **7**, 608
    vicarious liability, **7**, 607
force, *see* FORCE, USE OR THREAT OF
foreign enlistment, **7**, 609
  inducing, **7**, 609
frustration of contract by, **3**, 96
generally, **5**, 614
Geneva Agreements and Protocols, **19**, 688, 706,
  708, 711
Hague Conventions, **19**, 688, 698*n*, 706, 708, 711
International Committee of the Red Cross, **19**,
  708
international law of, **19**, 697–712
jus ad bellum doctrine, **19**, 697
jus in bellum doctrine, **19**, 706
lawful acts, deaths resulting from, **12**, 25, 31
levying, **7**, 569, 571, 573, 574
  rioting compared, **7**, 574
means and methods of, **19**, 711
memorial, functions in respect of, **14**, 700
mercenaries, **19**, 709
nuclear weapons, multilateral agreements on, **19**,
  712
peace, conclusion of, **7**, 724, 857
pension death benefit—
  overlapping benefits, **21**, 1001, 1003
prerogative powers of Crown, **7**, 726
prisoners of war, **19**, 708, 709*n*
  assisting escape, **7**, 611
reprisals, **19**, 702*n*
retorsion, **19**, 702*n*
risks—
  bill of lading, express terms, **21**, 546
self-defence, **19**, 702
self-determination, of, **19**, 708
shipbuilding and fitting, offences in relation to, **7**,
  610
spies, **19**, 709
state duties in time of, **19**, 688
treasonable offences during, **7**, 565
United Nations peacekeeping forces, **19**, 704

War—*continued*
zone—
  restraints of princes, exclusion or limitation of
    liability, **21**, 550
War Damage Commission
corporate personality, **19**, 219
Ward
See FEUDAL LAW
Wardholding
See FEUDAL LAW
Warehouse
commercial lease, *see* LEASE-LEASING
customs—
  administration, **7**, 1174, 1175
  approval, **7**, 1174, 1175
    termination, **7**, 1179
  benefit, **7**, 1174
  Common Agricultural Policy, goods covered
    by, **7**, 1174
  Community goods, **7**, 1174
  declaration for warehousing, **7**, 1174
  depositor, responsibilities, **7**, 1174
  documentation, **7**, 1174
  goods removed to, VAT regulations, **7**, 1315
  lost or damaged goods, compensation, **7**, 1178
  meaning, **7**, 1174
  missing or deficient goods, **7**, 1177
  non-Community goods, **7**, 1174
  operation, authorisation for, **7**, 1174
  postponement of customs duty payment, **7**,
    1174
  private, **7**, 1174
  procedure, **7**, 1174
  public, **7**, 1174
  records, **7**, 1174
  regulation, **7**, 1176
  Single Administrative Document, **7**, 1174
  storage in, duration, **7**, 1174
  supervision, **7**, 1174
  temporary removal of goods, **7**, 1174
  transfer between, **7**, 1174
  types, **7**, 1174
  United Kingdom provisions, **7**, 1175
  warehoused goods, regulation, **7**, 1176
  warehousekeeper, responsibilities, **7**, 1174
examination of goods in, **7**, 1214
excise, **7**, 1175
  warehousekeeper's responsibilities, **7**, 1054
free—
  Common Agricultural Policy, goods covered
    by, **7**, 1165
  Community goods, **7**, 1165
  consumption or use of goods in, **7**, 1040
  custom debt on importation from, **7**, 1040
  designation, application for, **7**, 1164
  duration of deposit in, **7**, 1164
  entry or departure, checks on, **7**, 1164
  exportation of goods leaving, **7**, 1165
  free zones, *see* FREE ZONE
  generally, **7**, 1164
  goods which may be placed in, **7**, 1164
  meaning, **7**, 1164
  non-Community goods, **7**, 1165
  permitted actions in respect of goods in, **7**, 1164

Warehouse—*continued*
free—*continued*
  re-exportation of goods leaving, **7**, 1165
  stock records, **7**, 1164
landlord's hypothec, **13**, 513
offences in relation to, **7**, 1181
overloading by tenant, **13**, 269, 588
Queen's—
  examination of goods in, **7**, 1214
  meaning, **7**, 1180
  offences in relation to, **7**, 1181
  purpose, **7**, 1180
  removal of goods to, **7**, 1147
  rent payable for goods stored in, **7**, 1180
  sale of goods in, **7**, 1180
  unlawfully removed goods, **7**, 1259
victualing, **7**, 1175
warehousekeeper—
  excise, responsibilities for, **7**, 1054
  exempt from explosives regulations, **10**, 1589
  firearms and ammunition, possession of, **10**, 1534
  lien for freight, preservation and discharge for, **21**, 635–637
  meaning, **21**, 635*n*
  rent, expenses and protection, **21**, 637
  sale of goods by, **21**, 636
warehousing—
  general average, **21**, 710
  goods imported for, **7**, 1149
  offences relating to, **7**, 1181
  value added tax, **7**, 1320
Warrandice
absolute, **6**, 542, 543
assignation, disposition, in, **18**, 642
assignation of incorporeal property, **18**, 655
breach, 'offside goals', rule against, **18**, 697, 697*n*
claims under, **6**, 547
clause of, in old charters, **6**, 405
contract of sale for moveable property, implied terms, **20**, 819, 821
conveyance, implied into, **18**, 701
corporeal heritable property—
  absolutely good title, **18**, 702, 703, 709
  contra omnes mortales, **18**, 709
  contractual date of entry, **18**, 702, 710
  date disposition delivered, **18**, 702, 703*n*
  delayed settlement, enforcement where, **18**, 710
  description of property in missives, **18**, 703
  disposition, **18**, 702
    delivery, **18**, 710
    enforcement, **18**, 710, 712
    missives kept in force beyond delivery, where, **18**, 710
  dispositions, **18**, 709
  enforcement, **18**, 710–714
  express grant, **18**, 702
  extinction, **18**, 714
  future acts prejudicial to title, **18**, 702, 706
  generally, **18**, 701, 702
  implied warrandice, **18**, 702
  judicial eviction, **18**, 707, 707*n*
    extinction in case of, **18**, 714
  lease, property under, **18**, 704

Warrandice—*continued*
corporeal heritable property—*continued*
  mineral rights, **18**, 703, 703*n*
  missives of sale, **18**, 702, 703*n*, 708
    enforcement, **18**, 710, 711
  negative prescription, **18**, 714
    prescriptive period, **18**, 714
  real burdens, **18**, 705, 705*n*
  real conditions, unusual, **18**, 702, 705
  registration of title, **18**, 713
  separate tenements, **18**, 703
  servitudes, **18**, 705, 705*n*
  standard security, property burdened by, **18**, 704
  subordinate real rights, property must not be affected by, **18**, 702, 704
  transaction not proceeding, enforcement where, **18**, 710
corporeal moveable property—
  breach of implied, remedies, **18**, 715
  donation, **18**, 716
  eviction, no requirement for, **18**, 715
  generally, **18**, 715
  remedies for breach, **18**, 715
  sale, **18**, 715
debitum subesse, **18**, 717, 718
definition, **6**, 541
degrees of, **6**, 542
double grant, 'offside goals', rule against, **18**, 697
express grant, **18**, 701
  real rights, assignation of, **18**, 718
fact and deed, from, **6**, 542, 544
generally, **18**, 701
implied, **18**, 701
  corporeal moveable property—
    donation, **18**, 716
    sale, **18**, 715
  incorporeal property, assignation, **18**, 717, 718
implied terms, **12**, 1235
incorporeal property—
  contract of sale, **18**, 719
  personal rights, assignation, **18**, 717
  real rights, assignation, **18**, 718
indemnity and, **6**, 773
landlord's, **13**, 251
lease, application to, **13**, 235
liability, and, **18**, 701
limits to doctrine of, **6**, 543
meaning, **18**, 701
nature of, **6**, 541
personal, **6**, 542
personal contractual obligation, as, **18**, 701
procedure, **6**, 547
qualifications, **6**, 546
quantum of claims under, **6**, 541
questions with purchasers, **13**, 316
real, **6**, 542; **18**, 701, 701*n*
simple, **6**, 542, 545
sublease, **13**, 378
trustees' liability, **24**, 227
Warrant
arrest, for—
  arrest with, **16**, 1790
  person arrested's entitlement to see, **16**, 1790
  petition for, **16**, 1790

Warrant—*continued*
arrest under—
  furth of jurisdiction, **17**, 601
  furth of Scotland, **17**, 602
  generally, **17**, 600
arrest without—
  common law, **16**, 1791
  generally, **16**, 1790
  statute law, **16**, 1792
arrestment, for, execution of, **17**, 1115
authority to execute, **14**, 1504
bearer shares, **4**, 371
body samples, to take, **16**, 1797
building, *see* BUILDING AND BUILDING CONTROLS
charge, service of, **14**, 1505
citation, of, **17**, 1013
concurrence, of, not required, **17**, 1303
demolition, *see* DEMOLITION
entry and search of premises, for, **16**, 1798
extradition from United Kingdom—
  executing the warrant, **12**, 559–561
  provisional warrants, **12**, 556–558
fingerprints, to take, **16**, 1794
firearms and ammunition, search for, **10**, 1575
interception of communications, for, **16**, 1802
investment, as, **12**, 1308
premises, entry of, **19**, 1551
probe beyond the skin, to take, **16**, 1797
scope of jurisdiction, **16**, 1804
search, of, **16**, 1790
search of person, for, **16**, 1794
service and execution, **16**, 1784
sheriff, execution by, **14**, 1501
slaughter of animal, **25**, 206
Warrant sale
rules regarding sales by non-owners not affecting,
  20, 853
Warranty
collateral contract for breach of, **14**, 1087
contract of sale for moveable property, **20**, 820
  implied terms as to, **20**, 821
defects, thing let is free from, **14**, 1042
defence in relation to sale of goods, **6**, 251
National House Builders Council certificate, **6**,
  567
sale of food, in relation to, **11**, 426, 427
Warsaw Pact
generally, **19**, 702, 702*n*
Washing
consumption of water, **25**, 334
domestic use, supply of water for, **25**, 506
facilities—
  improvement grants, **11**, 2023
  improvement orders, **11**, 1990
  multiple occupation, housing in, **11**, 2005
  tolerable standard, **11**, 1979
water unfit for, **14**, 2079
Waste
collection—
  commercial waste, **9**, 1168
  public health regulations, **14**, 706; **19**, 361–363
disposal—
  Control of Pollution Act 1974—
    under, **9**, 1152

Waste—*continued*
disposal—*continued*
  controlled waste—
    dangerous, **9**, 1162
    meaning, **9**, 1163
    unlawful deposit of—
      defences to, **9**, 1155
      exceptions to, **9**, 1155
    unlicensed disposal, **9**, 1154
  disposal authority, by, **9**, 1161
  licence—
    breach of conditions, **9**, 1160
    conditions in, **9**, 1157
    generally, **14**, 526; **19**, 363
    grant of, **9**, 1156
    licensed sites and plants, supervision of, **9**, 1159
    local authority duties, **14**, 526
    transfer of, **9**, 1158
  plans, **9**, 1153
  radioactive substances, *see* ATOMIC ENERGY AND
    RADIOACTIVE SUBSTANCES
  responsibility for, **9**, 1151
  sea, at, **9**, 1164
  special waste, **9**, 1162
  waste which is not controlled waste, **9**, 1163
  water, near, **25**, 377
EEC directives—
  dangerous waste, **9**, 1178
  generally, **9**, 1175
  polychlorinated biphenyls, **9**, 1177
  toxic waste, **9**, 1178
  waste oils, **9**, 1176
electricity from, **9**, 1171
hazardous, *see* HAZARDOUS SUBSTANCES
heat from, **9**, 1171
household, **19**, 361
  collection of, **9**, 1165
  dustbins, **9**, 1166
  privies, emptying of, **9**, 1167
industrial, collection of, **9**, 1169
legislation, **9**, 1150
litter—
  bins, **9**, 1174
  offences, **9**, 1173
meaning, **9**, 1149
oils, EEC directives on, **9**, 1176
public health regulations, **14**, 706; **19**, 361–363
radioactive, *see* ATOMIC ENERGY AND RADIOACTIVE
  SUBSTANCES
reclamation, **9**, 1170
recycling, **9**, 1170
solid, control of entry into water, **25**, 404
street cleaning, **9**, 1172
trade, **19**, 361
  collection of, **9**, 1168
water authority's power to prevent, **25**, 377, 525
whereabouts of goods, information on, **5**, 879
Wasting police time
offence of, **16**, 1810
Watch, clock or timepiece
carriage of, **3**, 610
Water
abstraction—
  canals, abstraction and sale from, **19**, 1105, 1123

Water—_continued_
abstraction—_continued_
  flow, diversion of, **25**, 330
  salmon fishings, **11**, 6
  underground water, of, **14**, 2034, 2035; **25**, 346
adjacent land—
  public rights over—
    herring fisheries, use of uncultivated land for, **18**, 527
    river banks, use of, **18**, 528
advance, alluvion, **18**, 593
aemulatio vicini relevance of, **14**, 2034, 2035
alluvion, _see_ ALLUVION
alteration in course, salmon fishings, **18**, 326
alveus, see ALVEUS
authority, _see_ WATER AUTHORITY
avulsion, _see_ AVULSION
bailiff, _see_ WATER BAILIFF
board, transfer of functions, **14**, 452
bottled, **7**, 1425
boundaries, **24**, 406
byelaws—
  access agreements and orders, **25**, 359
  boating, control of, **25**, 359
  conservation, relating to, **25**, 390
  danger, prevention of, **25**, 362
  drought, relating to, **25**, 390
  navigation, control of, **25**, 307
  noise, control of, **25**, 359
  nuisance, prevention of, **25**, 362
  pollution, control of, **25**, 426
canals and inland waterways, _see_ CANALS AND INLAND WATERWAYS
casual—
  no natural right to, **14**, 2032
  pollution, **14**, 2079
  sub-surface, right to abstract, **14**, 2034
channel—
  alveus, see ALVEUS
  artificial, **18**, 302
  underground, **18**, 301
  water in definite, common interest, **18**, 286
  water outside definite—
    common interest, **18**, 286
    rights of proprietor—
      above surface, water lying, **18**, 337
      below surface, water lying, **18**, 337
      free drainage, right of, **18**, 337, 339, 342, 359, 442
      free use, right of, **18**, 337, 338
charge, _see_ WATER SUPPLY
classification of waters, **21**, 112, 112_n_
  categories A, B, C and D waters, **21**, 112
coast protection, _see_ COAST PROTECTION
common law, modern developments in, **25**, 301
communication pipes—
  escape of water from, compensation for damage, **25**, 513
  meaning, **25**, 524
  wholesome water, supply of, **25**, 508
conservation, **25**, 389–391, 393
consumption—
  drinking, **25**, 334
  primary purposes, **25**, 334

Water—_continued_
consumption—_continued_
  stream, from, **25**, 334
  washing, **25**, 334
controlled waters, meaning, **25**, 400_n_
country park, provision of, **25**, 360
course, _see_ WATERCOURSE
dam, _see_ DAM
development board, _see_ WATER DEVELOPMENT BOARD
discharge onto servient tenement, servitude right as to, **18**, 491
disposal, servitude rights as to, **18**, 483
diversion—
  notice of, **20**, 640
  roads authorities, powers as to, **20**, 640
domestic use—
  buildings, supply of water to, **25**, 531
  non-domestic use, supplies distinguished, **25**, 510
  piped supply, **25**, 507
  water authorities, duties of, **25**, 506
  water rate, **25**, 533
drainage—
  common interest, doctrine of, **18**, 359
  riparian proprietor's obligations, **18**, 281
  servitude of, prescription, creation by, **18**, 460
  surface water—
    common law, **18**, 340
    statute law, **18**, 341
  water running naturally off superior land, obligation to receive, **18**, 337, 339, 342, 359, 442
  See also DRAINAGE
dredging, _see_ DREDGING
drought, _see_ DROUGHT
eavesdrop, right of, **18**, 485
ferry, right of, _see_ FERRY, RIGHT OF
fittings, **25**, 527
flood, _see_ FLOOD; FLOOD PREVENTION
fluoridation—
  domestic use, supply of water for, **25**, 506
  harmful effects, **25**, 509
  health authority powers as to, **19**, 320
  interdict against addition, grounds for, **25**, 509
  supplies abroad, **25**, 509
food, not classed as, **11**, 311
food premises, supply to, **11**, 419
foreshore, _see_ FORESHORE
harbour, right of, _see_ PORT, RIGHT OF
heritable property, when, **18**, 273, 274
hosepipes, restrictions on use, **25**, 529
impounding, provisional order proposing, **19**, 15
inalienable property, when, **18**, 600
inflammable substances, conveyance by, **19**, 392–394
information as to supply, Secretary of State's duties as to, **25**, 503
ingredient in food, where, **11**, 385
inland, _see_ INLAND WATER
internal waters, **21**, 112
intra fauces terrae, **18**, 309
irrigation, _see_ IRRIGATION
land, as part of, **18**, 273

Water—*continued*
lease, **13**, 194, 198
level, flood warning system, as, **25**, 379
local government powers and duties, **14**, 46, 112
loch, *see* LOCH
mains—
    access to, **25**, 523
    burst, compensation for damage, **25**, 513
    meaning, **25**, 521
    non-domestic water, supply of, **25**, 512
    power to lay, **25**, 520
    reasonable notice of proposal to lay, **25**, 520
    wholesome water, supply of, **25**, 508
mineral, labelling, **11**, 383
mining operations, and, **18**, 343
moveable property, when, **18**, 273, 274
moving, moveable property, as, **18**, 273
mussels, right to gather, *see* MUSSELS
natural flow, salmon fishings must not interfere
    with, **18**, 326
navigable—
    meaning, **21**, 112
    tunnels and bridges, authority to construct, **20**,
      638
navigation, *see* NAVIGATION
non-domestic—
    agreement for supply, **25**, 512
    disputes in respect of, **25**, 511
    non-domestic use, generally, **25**, 510
non-navigable, meaning, **21**, 112
non-tidal—
    meaning, **21**, 112
    navigation, public right of, *see* NAVIGATION
    ownership, **18**, 522
    retreat, alluvion, **18**, 593
    See also LOCHS; RIVERS
ownership, **18**, 274
    alveus—
      Crown or private ownership, **18**, 275, 276
      tidal and non-tidal waters, **18**, 275, 276
    determination, **18**, 274
    non-tidal loch, water in, **18**, 304
    private waters, classification as, **18**, 277
    public waters, classification as, **18**, 277
    riparian proprietor, *see* RIVER
    running water, **18**, 279
    stagnum loch, water in, **18**, 304
    water outside definite channel, **18**, 338
oysters, right to gather, *see* OYSTERS
partially smooth waters, **21**, 112
percolating, abstraction of, **14**, 2035
    See also PERCOLATING WATER
pollution—
    abstraction of water, **25**, 330
    action to interdict, **14**, 2039
    alveus, operation on, **25**, 322
    artificial watercourse, **14**, 2079
    canal, **14**, 2079
    casual water, **14**, 2079
    consent system—
      application, **25**, 414, 416
      consent to discharge, **25**, 417–419
      flora and fauna, **25**, 423
      generally, **25**, 413

Water—*continued*
pollution—*continued*
    consent system—*continued*
      information, **25**, 421
      registers, **25**, 420
      Secretary of State, powers of, **25**, 415
    control—
      agreements, **25**, 426
      byelaws, **25**, 426
      common law, **25**, 395
      generally, **25**, 394, 425
      offences, **25**, 428
      public health, protection of, **25**, 427
      river purification, **25**, 397
      statutory, **25**, 396
    Crown rights, **14**, 2079
    ditch, **14**, 2079
    flora and fauna, protection of, **25**, 422–424
    generally, **25**, 335
    increased pollution, **14**, 2079
    industrial effluent, by, **14**, 2079
    loch, of, **14**, 2079; **25**, 338
    mill-lades, **14**, 2079
    mine, water pumped from, **14**, 2079
    new, **14**, 2079
    pollutant, entry into water, **25**, 401–407
    primary purposes, water fit for, **14**, 2079
    reservoir, **14**, 2079
    river, **14**, 2079
    salmon fishing, **14**, 2079
    sewage, by, **14**, 2079
    sewage effluent, *see* SEWAGE EFFLUENT
    trade effluent, *see* TRADE EFFLUENT
    See also POLLUTION; RIVER PURIFICATION
      AUTHORITY
port, right of, *see* PORT, RIGHT OF
private waters, classification as, **18**, 277
public rights over—
    acquired, **18**, 516
    adjacent land, **18**, 514, 515
    creation, **18**, 494
    Crown ownership, **18**, 494, 514
    enforcement, **18**, 494, 515
    extinction, **18**, 517
    ferry, right to use, **18**, 529
    fishing rights, **18**, 515
    foreshore, **18**, 524–526
      dry land beyond, **18**, 527, 528
    generally, **18**, 494
    land adjacent to water, **18**, 527, 528
    navigation, *see* NAVIGATION
    non-tidal waters, **18**, 522, 523
    navigation rights, *see* NAVIGATION
    port, right to use, **18**, 529
    private rights, public rights prevail over, **18**,
      515, 515*n*
    real rights, as, **18**, 494
    regalia majora, **18**, 514
    right to gather white fish and shellfish, *see*
      FISHING
    swimming for recreation, right of, **18**, 518
    tacit, **18**, 516, 518
    tidal waters, **18**, 518–521
public waters, classification as, **18**, 277

Water—*continued*
rates, *see* RATES
regional park, **25**, 360
removal from river, **14**, 2079
rights—
    acquisition of, **25**, 519
    common law—
        drainage works, relating to, **25**, 364
        modern developments, **25**, 301
        pollution, control of, **25**, 395
    draw—
        natural right, as, **18**, 442
        positive servitude, as, **18**, 441
    nuisance distinguished from, **14**, 2031
    riparian proprietor—
        rights of, **18**, 279, 280
        See also RIVER
river, *see* RIVER
river purification, *see* RIVER PURIFICATION
running—
    inalienable property, as, **18**, 600
    moveable property, as, **18**, 273
    ownership, **18**, 273, 274, 279
    res communes, as, **18**, 282
    res nullius, as, **18**, 279
    statutory restrictions, generally, **18**, 281
salmon fishing rights, *see* SALMON-SALMON
    FISHERIES
servitude rights—
    aquaeductus, **18**, 490
    aquaehaustus, **18**, 490
    categories of, **25**, 350–354
    creation, **25**, 348
    disposal of water from buildings, **18**, 483, 485
    extinguishing, **25**, 348
    generally, **25**, 348
    grant of, **25**, 349
    natural, **25**, 343, 347
    rural servitudes, **18**, 483
sewerage, *see* SEWAGE
sheriff court jurisdiction, **6**, 1137
smooth waters, **21**, 112
sports, *see* WATER SPORTS AND RECREATION
stagnum, drainage rights, **18**, 340, 341
standing—
    heritable property, as, **18**, 273, 274
    ownership, **18**, 273, 274
stillicide, right of, **18**, 485
stream, *see* STREAM
supply, *see* WATER SUPPLY
supply and conveyance, servitude rights as to, **18**,
    490
surface—
    definition, **18**, 340
    drainage rights—
        common law, **18**, 340
        statute law, **18**, 341
    generally, **25**, 342
    heritable or moveable property, whether, **18**, 273
    rights regarding, **25**, 343
territorial, *see* TERRITORIAL SEA
tidal—
    bank immediately adjacent to, proprietor of,
        18, 312

Water—*continued*
tidal—*continued*
    Crown ownership—
        adjacent proprietors, rights of, **18**, 312
        alienation to subject proprietors, **18**, 311
        generally, **18**, 518
        nature, **18**, 310
        presumption of, **18**, 309
    ferry, right of, *see* FERRY, RIGHT OF
    foreshore, *see* FORESHORE
    generally, **21**, 112
    lochs, **18**, 309–312
    meaning, **18**, 276; **21**, 112
    mussels, right to gather, *see* MUSSELS
    navigation, public right of, **18**, 518–520
    ownership, **18**, 275, 276
    oysters, right to gather, *see* OYSTERS
    port, right of, *see* PORT, RIGHT OF
    provisional orders and, **19**, 19
    public rights in, **18**, 5, 7
    retreat, alluvion, **18**, 593
    rivers, **18**, 309–312
    salmon fishing rights, *see* SALMON-SALMON
        FISHERIES
    salvage operations, **21**, 440
    territorial sea, **18**, 309–312
    white fish and shellfish, public right to take, **18**,
        521
    See also TERRITORIAL SEA
trade effluent, *see* TRADE EFFLUENT
underground, **18**, 301
    abstraction of, **14**, 2034, 2035; **25**, 346
    attraction from another's land against course of
        nature, **18**, 342
    borehole, procedure for sinking, **25**, 345
    drainage onto servient proprietor's land, **18**,
        342
    generally, **25**, 344
    interception and extraction, **18**, 342
    lawful abstraction, **25**, 346
    mines, **25**, 347
    mining operations, and, **18**, 343
    outside definite channel, **18**, 337, 342
    specified, meaning, **25**, 400*n*
    surface stream, application of rules relating to,
        25, 344
    well, procedure for sinking, **25**, 345
VAT, charge to, **7**, 1288, 1320, 1446
wholesome—
    meaning, **25**, 508
    provision of, **19**, 319; **25**, 508
    water authorities' duties, **25**, 508
Water authority
added areas, **25**, 505
agreements between authorities as to supply, **25**,
    516
byelaws—
    misuse of water, prevention of, **25**, 527
    pollution, prevention of, **25**, 528
    power to make, **14**, 276
catchment area, **25**, 528
combination of, **25**, 502
committee, **14**, 453
default by, **25**, 514

Water authority—*continued*
drainage works, powers relating to, **25**, 373
duties—
  compensation, **25**, 513
  default, **25**, 514
  domestic use, supply of water for, **25**, 506
  fluoridation, **25**, 509
  generally, **25**, 505
  non-domestic use, supply of water for, **25**, 510
  non-domestic water—
    agreement for supply, **25**, 512
    disputes in respect of, **25**, 511
  reasonable cost, supply of water at, **25**, 507
  wholesome water, duty to provide, **25**, 508
establishment, **25**, 505
fire authorities, relationship with, *see* FIRE SERVICES
functions, **14**, 455
meaning, **14**, 276*n*; **25**, 505
Monopolies and Mergers Commission investigation,
  19, 224
officers, **14**, 453
recreational facilities, provision of, **14**, 684
supply, powers relating to—
  agreements, **25**, 516
  day-to-day running, **25**, 525
  entry, right of, **25**, 525
  environmental health, **25**, 526
  land, acquisition of, **25**, 518
  misuse, prevention of, **25**, 525
  new sources, development of, **25**, 517
  sources, **25**, 515
  waste, prevention of, **25**, 525
  water mains—
    access to, **25**, 523
    injurious affection, **25**, 522
    meaning, **25**, 521
    power to lay, **25**, 520
  water pipes, **25**, 524
  water rights, acquisition of, **25**, 519
  watercourses, temporary discharge into, **25**, 525
transfer of functions, **14**, 452
Water bailiff
appointment, **11**, 24*n*, 38
authority to enforce legislation, **11**, 24–28
inshore fishing, powers as to, **11**, 142
meaning, **11**, 24*n*
obstruction of, **11**, 29
powers of entry, search, seizure and arrest, **11**,
  24–28
River Tweed, **11**, 42
Water development board
agreements for supply, **25**, 516
byelaws—
  misuse of water, prevention of, **25**, 527
  pollution, prevention of, **25**, 528
  power to make, **14**, 276
compensation, **25**, 513
drainage works, powers relating to, **25**, 373
establishment, **14**, 455
functions, **25**, 539
mains, power to lay, **25**, 520
meaning, **14**, 276*n*
powers, **25**, 539
water rights, acquisition of, **25**, 519

Water-gang
servitude of, **25**, 353
Water mains
See WATER
Water rates
See RATES
Water sports and recreation
canals, **19**, 1282
harbours, **19**, 1283
inland waterways, **19**, 1218, 1282
ports, **19**, 1283
rivers, **19**, 1281
sea, **19**, 1280
Water supply
access to water main, **25**, 523
advertisement, making of order, **25**, 516
advisory committee, Secretary of State's powers,
  25, 503
agreement—
  free supply, for, prohibition of, **25**, 538
  non-domestic water, supply of, **25**, 512
  water authorities, between, **25**, 516
agriculture, acquisition of water rights, **25**, 519
alveus operations on, **25**, 323
annual payment, non-domestic water, **25**, 512
arbitration—
  compensation for damage, **25**, 513
  non-domestic water, disputes over supply, **25**,
    511
assembly hall, to, **25**, 536
asylum, to, **25**, 536
bath—
  capacity in excess of 100 gallons, **25**, 506
  water fitting, as, **25**, 527
boarding house, meter charges, **25**, 536
buildings, supply to, **25**, 531
business premises, **25**, 536
byelaws, **25**, 527, 528
camp, meter charges, **25**, 536
Central Authority, **25**, 503, 504
central heating, for, **25**, 506
Central Regional Council, as water authority, **25**,
  505
Central Scotland Water Development Board, **25**,
  502, 539
charges—
  community, **14**, 857
  direct, **14**, 856; **25**, 532
  free supply prohibited, **25**, 538
  generally, **25**, 532–537
  meter, **25**, 536
cisterns, **25**, 527
clubs, meter charges, **25**, 536
cocks, **25**, 527
communication pipes—
  escape from, compensation for damage, **25**, 513
  meaning, **25**, 524
  wholesome water, supply of, **25**, 508
community charge, **25**, 534
compensation—
  claim may be time-barred, **25**, 513
  injurious affection, **25**, 520, 522
  water authorities, duties of, **25**, 513
conservation measures, **25**, 503, 525, 527

Water supply—*continued*

consumer, general supply distinguished from supply to, **25**, 521
cooking, domestic, **25**, 506
cost, **25**, 507
county council, statutory regulation, **25**, 501, 502
Court of Session, default powers, **25**, 514
damage, compensation for, **25**, 513, 522
damages, lead poisoning, **25**, 508
domestic use, **25**, 506, 507, 510, 531
drinking fountain, **25**, 526
drinking trough, **25**, 526, 537
drinking water, **25**, 506
fluoridation, *see* fluoridation *below*
drought, during, **25**, 530
dwelling house, **25**, 533, 536
emergency situation, powers of Secretary of State, **25**, 530
entry, right of, **25**, 517, 525
environmental health, powers of water authorities, **25**, 526
ferrules, **25**, 527
finance—
    charge—
        direct, **25**, 532
        meters, **25**, 532, 536
    community charge, **25**, 534
    free supply, prohibition of agreement for, **25**, 538
    terms and conditions, **25**, 537
    water development boards, **25**, 539
    water rate—
        domestic, **25**, 533
        generally, **25**, 532
        non-domestic, **25**, 535
fire fighting, **25**, 536
    See also FIRE SERVICES
fisheries, acquisition of water rights, **25**, 519
fluoridation—
    domestic use, supply of water for, **25**, 506
    harmful effects, **25**, 509
    interdict against addition, grounds for, **25**, 509
    supplies abroad, **25**, 509
free, prohibition of agreement, **25**, 538
garden, **25**, 506, 529, 530
general, supply to consumer distinguished, **25**, 521
health—
    environmental, powers in respect of, **25**, 526
    fluoridation, **25**, 509
    water rights, acquisition of, **25**, 519
    wholesome water, duty to provide, **25**, 508
historical development, **5**, 7; **25**, 501, 502
horse kept for private use, for, **25**, 506
hosepipe, restriction on use, **25**, 529
hospital, **25**, 536
hostel, **25**, 536
hotel, **25**, 536
industrial purposes, steam, use of, **25**, 519
injurious affection, **25**, 520, 522
land—
    acquisition of, **25**, 518
    damage to, compensation for, **25**, 513, 522
    new sources of supply, development of, **25**, 517

Water supply—*continued*

laundry business, **25**, 506
lead poisoning, **25**, 508
licensed premises, **25**, 536
local authority—
    fluoridation of water supply, **25**, 509
    reasonable cost test, **25**, 507
    statutory regulation, **25**, 501, 502
mains, *see* WATER
manufacturing premises, **25**, 536
meters—
    charges, **25**, 532, 536
    terms and conditions, **25**, 537
    water fittings, as, **25**, 527
misuse, prevention of, **25**, 525, 527
motor vehicles, washing, **25**, 529, 530
national code, statutory regulation, **25**, 501
non-domestic use, **25**, 510, 535
non-domestic water—
    agreement for supply, **25**, 512
    disputes in respect of, **25**, 511
nursing home, **25**, 536
objections, **25**, 516
orders, **25**, 516, 530
payments, making or guarantee of, **25**, 516
pipes, **25**, 524, 527
    See also communication pipes *above*
pollution, **25**, 526, 528
privatisation, establishment of special regime following, **4**, 1125, 1126
profession, carried on in house, **25**, 506
provisional orders in connection with, **19**, 19
public entertainment, place of, **25**, 536
public health, *see* health *above*
public institution, meter charges, **25**, 536
public pump, provision of, **25**, 526
rain, shortage leading to serious deficiency, **25**, 516
rates, *see* RATES
regional water boards, **25**, 502
reservoirs, **25**, 515
restaurant, **25**, 536
rivers, powers as to, **25**, 516, 519
roads—
    breaking open, **25**, 519
    water mains, power to lay, **25**, 520
salmon fishing rights, **25**, 519
sanatorium, **25**, 536
sanitary purposes, for, **25**, 506
school, **25**, 536
Secretary of State—
    arbiter of disputes, as, **25**, 504, 507
    authority of, **25**, 504
    Central Authority, as, **25**, 503, 504
    consent of, **25**, 504
    default powers, **25**, 514
    duties, **25**, 503
    emergency situation, powers relating to, **25**, 530
    powers, **25**, 504
    water rights, acquisition of, **25**, 519
service pipes, **25**, 524
servitude rights, **25**, 538
sink, water fitting, as, **25**, 527

Water supply—*continued*
soil-pan, water fitting, as, **25**, 527
sources, **25**, 515
statutory regulation, **25**, 501, 502
streams, powers as to, **25**, 516, 519
supply pipes, **25**, 524
tap, as water fitting, **25**, 527
tolerable standard, **11**, 1979
trade premises, **25**, 536
transport, acquisition of water rights, **25**, 519
typhoid, **25**, 508
valve, as water fitting, **25**, 527
VAT, charge to, **7**, 1288, 1320
washing, supply of water for domestic use, **25**, 506
waste, water authority's power to prevent, **25**, 525
water authorities, *see* WATER AUTHORITY
water authority powers, *see* WATER AUTHORITY
water development board, *see* WATER DEVELOP-
    MENT BOARD
water fittings, **25**, 527
water mains, *see* WATER
water rates, *see* RATES
waterclosets, water fittings, as, **25**, 527
watercourse, temporary discharge of water into,
    25, 525
waterworks—
    construction or alteration of, **19**, 19*n*; **25**, 519
    support of land purchased for construction, **14**,
        1690
    valuation for rating, **24**, 746
well, **25**, 526
wholesome water, **25**, 508
winding up, position relating to, **4**, 867
Watercloset
public health nuisance, as, **19**, 336
water fitting, as, **25**, 527
See also PUBLIC   CONVENIENCE;   SANITARY
    CONVENIENCE
Watercourse
alteration of natural, building contracts, **3**, 155
artificial, *see* ARTIFICIAL STREAM
flow, *see* RIVER
inland waterway deemed, **19**, 1110
meaning, **25**, 302
new, construction of, **25**, 378
overflow on neighbouring property, physical
    damage caused by, **14**, 2045
public health legislation, **19**, 1110, 1110*n*
public health nuisance, becoming, **19**, 336
servitudes, grant of, **25**, 349
temporary discharge of water into, **25**, 525
water pollution, **14**, 2079
See also RIVER; STREAM
Waterway
construction   or   alteration   under   private
    legislation, **19**, 24
damage to, limitation of liability, **21**, 755
meaning, **19**, 20*n*
open air recreation, improvement for, **14**, 683
See also CANALS AND INLAND WATERWAYS
Way
public right of way, *see* RIGHT OF WAY (PUBLIC)
servitude of, *see* RIGHT OF PASSAGE OR WAY
    (SERVITUDE)

Waygoing claims
common law, arising at, **1**, 775
dilapidations, for, **1**, 782
disturbance, compensation for, **1**, 783
dung, for, **1**, 776
fixtures, removal of, **1**, 779
growing crop, for, **1**, 776
improvements, compensation for, **1**, 780
landlord, by, **1**, 775
limitation, **1**, 775
property, passing of, **1**, 778
reorganisation payments, **1**, 784, 785
sheep stocks, valuation of, **1**, 777
special standard of farming, compensation for, **1**,
    781
types of, **1**, 775
waygoing valuations, **1**, 776
Wayleave
agreement—
    consent embodied in, **9**, 644
    retention of rights, **9**, 649
    tree cutting, **9**, 650
incorporeal heritable rights, **24**, 438
meaning, **18**, 493
overriding interest, as, **6**, 744
public undertaking, of, **18**, 493
servitude compared, **6**, 517; **18**, 493
valuation for rating, **24**, 747
Weapon
lethal, **7**, 226
offensive—
    article adapted to cause injury, **7**, 252
    article offensive by intention of carrier, **7**, 252
    carrying, **7**, 250, 252
    classes, **7**, 252
prohibited, *see* FIREARM
Wedding present
recovery under *condictio causa data*, **15**, 33, 35
Weeds
See PLANTS AND SEEDS
Week
commencement, **22**, 814
common law, meaning at, **22**, 814
continuous employment, counting in computing
    period of, **9**, 43
duration, **22**, 801
European Convention on the Calculation of
    Time-Limits, **22**, 829
evolution of concept, **22**, 801
lunation, basis, **22**, 814
meaning, **12**, 1171, 1172
origin, **22**, 814
pay, **9**, 59
termination, **22**, 814
Weekly close time
See CLOSE TIME
Weights and measures
advertising, controls on, **1**, 534
aerosol products, **6**, 247
agricultural materials, **6**, 239
alcohol, *see* ALCOHOLIC LIQUOR
authority, **14**, 592
bread, **11**, 359
collections of articles, **6**, 247

Weights and measures—*continued*
composite goods, **6**, 247
consumer advice, **14**, 549
consumer protection, **6**, 3, 10, 12
control, **6**, 178
defences—
   deficiency, **6**, 253
   due diligence, **6**, 252
   excess, **6**, 253
   reasonable precautions, **6**, 252
   warranty, **6**, 251
development of science, **6**, 173
document, goods accompanied by, **6**, 250
food, sale by weight, measure or number, **11**, 313
   See also FOOD
fraud, **7**, 384
fuel, *see* FUEL
hens' eggs, grading of, **6**, 184
hotels, in relation to, **11**, 1784
importers' duties, **6**, 259
inspectors—
   appointment of, **6**, 264; **14**, 249, 592
   certificate of qualification, **6**, 264
   duties, **6**, 187, 190
   offences by, **6**, 266
   powers of, **6**, 267, 268
      offences in respect of, **6**, 268
   training, **6**, 264
justice of the peace court, **6**, 1159
legal proceedings, **6**, 269
legislation, **6**, 73, 78
local administration—
   fees, **6**, 265
   generally, **6**, 263
local standards, **6**, 173, 182
lubricants, **6**, 237
medicines, **6**, 185*n*
metrication, *see* METRICATION
misrepresentation as to quantity of goods, **6**, 250
National Weights and Measures Laboratory, **6**, 181, 189
offences—
   inspectors, by, **6**, 266
   penalties, **6**, 270–300
   prepacked, goods required to be, **6**, 248
   quantity, relating to, **6**, 248
   in respect of inspectors' powers, **6**, 268
packaged goods—
   checking and quality control, **6**, 259
   codes of practice, **6**, 260
   European Community average system, **6**, 176, 256, 259
   European Community mark, **6**, 262
   importers' duties, **6**, 259
   inadequate packages, **6**, 261
   package, meaning, **6**, 257
   packers' duties, **6**, 259
   prepackaging required, **6**, 248
   prescribed goods, meaning, **6**, 257
penalties, **6**, 270–300
perfumery, toilet preparations and soap, **6**, 241
predetermined constant quantity, **6**, 258

Weights and measures—*continued*
public weighing and measuring equipment—
   offences, **6**, 192
   provision and use, **6**, 191
quantity—
   sale by, **6**, 254
   to be stated in writing, **6**, 249
ready-mixed cement mortar and concrete, **6**, 238
sand and ballast, **6**, 229
Scotland, development in, **6**, 174
self-regulation, **6**, 177
self-service stores, **6**, 254
sheriff court jurisdiction, **6**, 1138
standardisation, **6**, 173, 174, 175
trade, for—
   equipment used—
      approved patterns, **6**, 189
      deemed for trade, **6**, 190
      forfeiture of, **6**, 190
      generally, **6**, 254
      stamping, **6**, 187, 188, 190
      testing, **6**, 187
   European Community stamp, **6**, 187, 188
   exemption from control, **6**, 184
   exports, **6**, 184
   lawful weights and measures, **6**, 185
   metric unit used, **6**, 186
   offences, **6**, 190
   specifications for equipment, **6**, 189
   'use for trade'—
      meaning, **6**, 184
trading standards officers, **6**, 177
transactions in goods, *see* SALE AND SUPPLY OF GOODS
udal law, **24**, 312
United Kingdom, standardisation in, **6**, 175, 180
units and standards of measurement—
   basic units, **6**, 179
   Department of Trade and Industry standards, **6**, 181
   local standards, **6**, 182
   testing equipment, **6**, 183
   United Kingdom primary standards, **6**, 180
   working standards, **6**, 183
weighbridge, public, **6**, 191, 192
weighing in customer's presence, **6**, 254
Weir
building, enlarging or extending, **19**, 22
construction on *alveus*, common interest, and, **18**, 296
Weir Committee
recommendations of, **9**, 604
Welfare services
discrimination, genuine occupational qualification as defence to, **9**, 366
food and milk—
   applications to obtain, **11**, 432
   meaning, **11**, 432*n*
generally, *see* SOCIAL WORK
immigrants, post-entry control, **12**, 191
meaning, **7**, 1426*n*
VAT exemption, **7**, 1426

Well
closure, **25**, 526
injurious or dangerous to health, **19**, 336
provision of, **25**, 526
sinking, procedure for, **25**, 345
Welwod (Welwood)
mare clausum advocated by, **11**, 72
maritime law, writings on, **19**, 608
West Germany
additional member system, **5**, 378
constitution, **5**, 303
West Lothian
population, **14**, 64
West Midlands Freeport
free zone, as, **7**, 1164*n*
Western Isles
population, **14**, 64
water authority, as, **25**, 505
Westminster College
copyright rights conferred on, **18**, 1003
Westminster Confession of Faith
Declaratory Articles, **3**, 1502; **5**, 348, 698–700
generally, **3**, 1627; **5**, 348
modification, **3**, 1504, 1504*n*
opposite opinions, **5**, 699
ratification, **3**, 1501
status, **3**, 1504
Whales
blubber—
    boiling, interdict *ab ante*, **14**, 2146
fast and loose rule, **2**, 103
generally, **11**, 215
International Whaling Commission—
    commercial whaling, **11**, 229
    establishment, **11**, 226
    scientific permits, **11**, 230
    scope, **11**, 227
    zero catch limits, **11**, 229
non-British ships, application of legislation to, **11**, 240
occupancy, no right of acquisition by, **18**, 543, 543*n*
protection for certain classes of, **11**, 236
res conveniens, **11**, 215
scientific purposes, permit to kill for, **11**, 238
udal law, **24**, 314, 315
United Kingdom waters, prohibition of catching or treating whales within, **11**, 235
whale fishery inspectors, powers of, **11**, 239
whale oil factories, licensing of, **11**, 237
whaling ships, licensing of, **11**, 237
Wharf
approved—
    Commissioners' powers in relation to, **7**, 1239
    generally, **7**, 1239
construction or alteration, **19**, 19*n*
explosives, byelaws as to, **10**, 1611, 1620
meaning, **11**, 1303; **24**, 599
Wharfinger
lien for freight, preservation and discharge for, **21**, 635–637
meaning, **21**, 635*n*
rent, expenses and protection, **21**, 637
sale of goods by, **21**, 636

Wharncliffe orders
private Bill, **19**, 92
Wheel-clamping
extortion, **7**, 400
theft by appropriation, **7**, 332
White fish
industry, generally, **11**, 209
meaning, **11**, 209
public right to take, *see* FISHING
White Fish Advisory Council, **11**, 209
White Fish Authority, abolition of, **11**, 209, 211
White Fish Commission, **11**, 209
White Rod, Usher of the
office of, **7**, 829
White Wax
See QUARTER SEAL
Whitebonnet
reduction on grounds of, **13**, 44
Whiting
River Tweed, **11**, 40
Whole life policy
See LIFE ASSURANCE
Wholesale co-operative society
See CO-OPERATIVE SOCIETY
Wickedly
use of term, **7**, 75
Widdicombe Report
central and local government, essential difference between, **14**, 94
recommendations, **14**, 95
terms of reference, **14**, 95
Widow
aliment, right to, **25**, 711
counselling services, voluntary organisations, **22**, 13
dower, uses to bar, **25**, 611
firemen's pension scheme, **10**, 1447
graduated retirement benefit, **21**, 1215
income tax allowance, **19**, 1518
invalidity pension—
    meaning, **21**, 1000*n*
    overlapping benefits, **21**, 1000
jointure, settlement of, **25**, 611
jus relictae, **25**, 773, 785
legal rights—
    forfeiture, **25**, 801
    homologation, **25**, 801
    injurious election, **25**, 802
mournings, right to, **25**, 712
pension, forfeiture rule, **21**, 1205
state retirement pension—
    additional pension, **21**, 1214, 1224
    deferred claim, increments for, **21**, 1216
    generally, **21**, 1205
    non-contributory pension, **21**, 1220
terce, **18**, 74, 110
widow's benefit—
    absent from Great Britain, claimant, **21**, 1023
    entitlement, **21**, 801
widow's payment—
    cohabitation with another man as man and wife at time of husband's death, **21**, 895
    contribution conditions, **21**, 895
    entitlement, **21**, 895

Widow—*continued*
widow's payment—*continued*
  lump sum payment, as, **21**, 895
  national insurance contributions, **21**, 1043
widow's pension—
  cohabitation with another man as husband and
    wife, **21**, 897
  contribution conditions, **21**, 897
  earnings-related supplement, **21**, 1209
  entitlement, **21**, 897
  invalidity pension, **21**, 1000
  national insurance contributions, **21**, 1044
  period for which payable, **21**, 897
  rate, **21**, 897
  remarriage by claimant, **21**, 897
  widowed mother's allowance, interaction with,
    21, 897
widowed mother's allowance—
  artificial insemination, child conceived by, **21**,
    896
  cohabitation with man as husband and wife, **21**,
    896
  contribution conditions, **21**, 896
  dependent child, increase where, **21**, 1015
  earnings-related supplement, **21**, 1209
  entitlement, **21**, 896
  invalidity pension, **21**, 1000
  national insurance contributions, **21**, 1044
  remarriage by claimant, **21**, 896
  widow's pension, interaction with, **21**, 897
Widower
aliment, right to, **25**, 711
courtesy, **18**, 74, 110
graduated retirement benefit, **21**, 1215
jus relicti, **25**, 773, 785
state retirement pension—
  additional pension, **21**, 1209, 1214, 1224
  deferred claim, increments for, **21**, 1216
  generally, **21**, 1206
Wife
dependant, as, **12**, 264
deportation of husband, **12**, 208
polygamous, **12**, 269
  abode, right of, **12**, 118*n*
  deportation of husband, **12**, 208
settled Commonwealth citizen, of, **12**, 125
settlement—
  family relationship, on grounds of, **12**, 268
  family reunion or creation by, *see* SETTLEMENT
    (IMMIGRATION)
See HUSBAND AND WIFE; MARRIAGE; SPOUSE
Wild animal
dangerous—
  court orders, **2**, 170
  disqualification for keeping, **2**, 114
  licence to keep, **14**, 524; **19**, 1295
    age for obtaining, **2**, 112; **3**, 1222
    application for, **2**, 112
    conditions, imposition, **2**, 112
    death of holder, **2**, 112
    duration of, **2**, 112
    failure to have, **2**, 113
    refusal of, **2**, 112

Wild animal—*continued*
dangerous—*continued*
  licence to keep—*continued*
    specification etc of animals, **2**, 112
    who may apply for, **2**, 112
  premises—
    entry of, powers, **2**, 112
    security requirement, **2**, 112
  unlicensed, seizure, **2**, 114
  zoo, circus etc, in, **2**, 113
endangered species, *see* ENDANGERED SPECIES
game, whether, **18**, 545
liberty, regaining, effect of, **2**, 103
meaning, **11**, 878
meat from, **11**, 496
mechanically propelled vehicles used in pursuit
  of, **11**, 884
new species—
  enforcement of provisions, **2**, 314
  prohibition on releasing, **2**, 314
occupatio (occupancy), doctrine of, **18**, 541, 542
offences—
  defences to, **2**, 312
  generally, **2**, 312
ownership, **2**, 103
pigeons deemed to be, **2**, 108
prohibited methods of taking or killing, **2**, 313;
  11, 884
  circumstances permitting, **2**, 312
  defences, **11**, 885
  licences, **11**, 886
property in, **2**, 103
protected—
  offences as to, **2**, 312
  sale of, prohibition, **2**, 311
protection, provisions for, **2**, 311
rabies, prevention of spread, **2**, 193
res nullius, **11**, 803
sheriff court jurisdiction, **6**, 1078
snares etc, prohibition, **2**, 313
taking or killing—
  circumstances permitting, **2**, 312
  prohibited methods, **2**, 313; **11**, 884–886
tame animals, abolition of distinction with wild
  animals recommended, **22**, 662
theft of, **2**, 103
zoo, in, *see* ZOO
See also WILDLIFE; WILDLIFE AND COUNTRYSIDE ACT
  1981
Wild bird
captivity, in—
  cages, size of, **2**, 290
  liberation for shooting, **2**, 291
  registration required, **2**, 289
  ringing of, **2**, 289
close season, meaning, **2**, 283
conservation provisions, **2**, 282; **11**, 883
eggs—
  protection for, **2**, 282; **19**, 1295
  sale of, **2**, 286
exceptions from provisions, **2**, 284
food, preparation and sale as, **11**, 312
game birds, **11**, 878, 878*n*
  pursuing and killing, **19**, 1295

Wild bird—*continued*
injurious, control of, **11**, 859–865
justice of the peace court powers, **6**, 1159
killing etc—
    authorised person, by, **2**, 282
    exceptions to provisions, **2**, 284
    licence authorising, **2**, 292
    prohibited methods, **2**, 285
    suffering, to prevent, **2**, 284
licence—
    acts authorised by, **2**, 292
    false statements to obtain, **2**, 293
meaning, **2**, 878; **9**, 878; **11**, 804*n*, 860
mechanically propelled vehicle used in pursuit of, **11**, 880
nests, protection for, **2**, 282
offences—
    arrest, powers of, **2**, 294
    exceptions as to, **2**, 284
    forfeiture for, **2**, 295
    generally, **2**, 282
    search of suspects, **2**, 294
police powers, **2**, 294
premises, entry and inspection, **2**, 288
prohibited methods of killing or taking, **11**, 880
    defences, **11**, 881
    exemptions, **11**, 882
    licences, **11**, 883
protection of, generally, **19**, 1295
requirement notice to control, **11**, 860–863
ringing or marking, **11**, 883
sale of, an offence, **2**, 286
shooting on Sunday or Christmas Day, **11**, 804, 804*n*
showing of, **2**, 287
statutory protection, **2**, 282
traps etc, prohibition of, **2**, 285
See also WILDLIFE; WILDLIFE AND COUNTRYSIDE ACT 1981

Wildlife
gin traps, prohibition of use, **11**, 879
object of shooting, as, **24**, 470
protection of, **9**, 1243
wild animal, meaning, **11**, 878
wild bird, meaning, **11**, 878
See also WILD ANIMAL; WILD BIRD; WILDLIFE AND COUNTRYSIDE ACT 1981

Wilfully
meaning, **7**, 84
use of term, **7**, 70, 76, 84

Will
abatement, **25**, 856
administration of estate, *see* ADMINISTRATION OF ESTATE; SUCCESSION
alternative reference, rules of, **17**, 126
attested—
    formal validity, **25**, 723
    signing, **25**, 724
beneficiary, *see* BENEFICIARY (WILLS AND SUCCESSION)
building society powers to assist in making, **3**, 376
change of name required by, **19**, 1428
children—
    adopted, **12**, 1268
    conditio si testator sine liberis decesserit, **12**, 1265

Will—*continued*
children—*continued*
    illegitimacy, abolition of status, **12**, 1268
    rights, generally, **12**, 1264
circumvention, **25**, 763
civil jurisdiction, **4**, 26; **8**, 431, 434
company may not make, **4**, 318
construction—
    accretion—
        class—
            ascertaining, **25**, 844
            gifts, **25**, 843
            conditio si institutus sine liberis decesserit, **25**, 838, 842
            destination over, **25**, 839
            futurity, words of, **25**, 845
            principle, **25**, 838
            shares—
                conditio si institutus, taken as result of, **25**, 842
                equal, **25**, 841
                joint, **25**, 840
    ademption, **25**, 848, 854
    annuity provision in favour of beneficiary, **12**, 1264
    benevolent, **25**, 822
    benevolent or charitable, **25**, 822
    bequest—
        charitable, **25**, 822
        precatory, **25**, 823
    cardinal principle, **25**, 819
    charitable and benevolent, **25**, 822
    charitable and religious, **25**, 822
    charity, gifts to, **12**, 1271
    clauses—
        reconciliation of, **25**, 820
        subordinate, **25**, 820
    codicil, reading of, **25**, 820
    conflicting provisions, **25**, 826, 909
    conversion, **25**, 816
    date, *see* date *below*
    division—
        per capita, **25**, 888
        per stirpes, **25**, 888–890
    double provisions, presumptions against, **25**, 832
    ejusdem generis, **25**, 825
    facts material to, extrinsic evidence to prove testator's knowledge of, **25**, 831
    falsa demonstratio non nocet, **25**, 824
    general principles, **12**, 1263, 1264
    generally, **17**, 347; **25**, 817
    golden rule, **12**, 1109
    ineffectual conditions or directions—
        charitable objects, **12**, 1271
        discretionary powers of trustees too wide, where, **12**, 1271
        public policy, conditions contrary to, **12**, 1270
        uncertainty, **12**, 1271
    institute—
        conditional, **25**, 892
        substitute compared with, **25**, 891
        testator's intention, **25**, 893

Will—*continued*
construction—*continued*
  intestacy, avoidance of, **25**, 822
  irreconcilable provisions, **12**, 1263
  legacy, *see* LEGACY
  normal grammatical meaning, **25**, 821
  ordinary meaning of words, **25**, 821
  precatory bequest, **25**, 823
  public or charitable, **25**, 822
  religious, **25**, 822
  repugnancy—
    alimentary use, directions that legacy is given
      for, **25**, 834, 836
    annuity, directions to executors to buy, **25**,
      834, 837
    cases, **25**, 834
    person of full age, directions to retain vested
      right to, **25**, 834, 835
    when arising, **25**, 834
  simplification of wording, factors leading to,
    25, 818
  substitute—
    institute compared with, **25**, 891
    testator's intention, **25**, 893
  whole will to be read, **25**, 820
  words—
    ordinary meaning, **25**, 821
    simplification, factors leading to, **25**,
      818
contract to make—
  jus quaesitum tertio, **15**, 843
  negligence by solicitor, **15**, 843
date—
  codicil, will modified by, **25**, 887
  deed coming into operation before 8 June 1968
    ..., **25**, 883
  execution—
    on or after 1 January 1970 ..., **25**, 885
    on or after 8 December 1986 ..., **25**, 886
    on or after 10 September 1964 ..., **25**, 882
    on or after 25 November 1968 ..., **25**, 884
    generally, **25**, 881
dependant, inadequate provision for, **25**, 611
description terms commonly used in—
  family, **25**, 876
  heir, **25**, 878
  issue, **25**, 877
  money, **25**, 880
  next of kin, **25**, 879
disposition in contemplation of imminent death,
  12, 1263
donation, **8**, 601, 609; **12**, 1263
earlier—
  construction, **25**, 825
  implied revocation of, **25**, 749
extrinsic evidence, interpretation, **12**, 1263
favourable interpretation, **12**, 1263
holograph, declarator as to, **13**, 7
  See also PRIVATE WILL
home-made, **25**, 765
importance of, where property jointly owned, **6**,
  480
injurious election, **25**, 802
international, **17**, 134, 345; **25**, 721

Will—*continued*
interpretation—
  annuity provision in favour of beneficiary, **12**,
    1264
  charity, gifts to, **12**, 1271
  descendants or nephews and nieces, *conditio si*
    institutus sine liberis decesserit, **12**, 1265
  extrinsic evidence—
    admissibility, **25**, 827
    completed testamentary intention, proof of,
      25, 833
    court enabled to read will, **25**, 828
    double provisions, disproof of presumption
      against, **25**, 832
    extrinsic circumstances, words insensible
      without reference to, **25**, 830
    facts material to construction, proof of
      testator's knowledge of, **25**, 831
    general rule, **25**, 827
    more than one person or thing, words
      applicable indifferently to, **25**, 829
    persons named in will, identification of, **25**,
      829
    things named in will, identification of, **25**,
      829
  general principles, **12**, 1263, 1264
  golden rule, **12**, 1109
  illegitimacy, abolition of status of, **12**, 1268
  ineffectual conditions or directions—
    charitable objects, **12**, 1271
    discretionary powers of trustees too wide,
      where, **12**, 1271
    public policy, conditions contrary to, **12**,
      1270
    uncertainty, **12**, 1271
  intention, ascertainment of, **12**, 1263
  jus relicti, **12**, 1264
  liferent in favour of beneficiary, **12**, 1264
  majority, meaning, **12**, 1218, 1268
  object of, **12**, 1214, 1263
  ordinary meaning of words, **25**, 821
  presumptions, **12**, 1268
    adopted children, **12**, 1268
    bequest to number of persons, **12**, 1268
    between, meaning, **12**, 1268
    children, meaning, **12**, 1268
    class, bequest to, **12**, 1268
    common calamity, **12**, 1266
    conditio si institutus sine liberis decesserit, **12**,
      1265
    conditio si testator sine liberis decesserit, **12**, 1265
    dependants, use of word, **12**, 1268
    falsa demonstratio non nocet, **12**, 1268
    intestacy, against, **12**, 1267
    issue, meaning, **12**, 1268
    knowledge of testator, as to, **12**, 1267
    legality, of, **12**, 1267
    majority, meaning, **12**, 1268
    next of kin, meaning, **12**, 1268
  prior rights, **12**, 1264
  repugnancy, **12**, 1269
  restrictions affecting testamentary writings, **12**,
    1264
  vesting, **12**, 1269

Will—_continued_
intestacy, _see_ INTESTACY
Jewish faith, condition as to, **3**, 1685
joint will, France, **25**, 628
jurisdiction, **4**, 26; **8**, 431, 434
latter-will, **12**, 1263
lease rights, succession, _see_ TENANT-TENANCY
legal advice and assistance—
  questions concerning, **13**, 1028
  will, making, **13**, 1030
legal rights, _see_ LEGAL RIGHTS
minor's power to make, **10**, 1081
mutual, **25**, 628
notarial execution, **25**, 725
notary public, execution by, **13**, 1221
parish minister, execution by, **3**, 1566
passing property, context of, **25**, 604–611
pencil, will written in, **12**, 1263
potential beneficiaries of will-making clients, solicitor's duty of care, **15**, 281–283, 358
printed form, **25**, 726
  problems arising from use of, **12**, 1228
private, _see_ PRIVATE WILL
privileged, **25**, 628, 628n
prospective documents, incorporation of, **25**, 727
public, _see_ PUBLIC WILL
purposes of, **25**, 627
rectification of, proposed reform, **25**, 1116
reform, proposals for—
  discretionary family provision, **25**, 1114
  divorce, revocation on, **25**, 1117
  generally, **25**, 1118
  killer, disqualification of, **25**, 1119
  legal rights, **25**, 1113
  legitim, **25**, 1113
  presumptions of survivorship, **25**, 1119
  prior rights, **25**, 1112
  rectification of will, **25**, 1116
  Scottish Law Commission proposals, **25**, 1111–1121
  special destinations, **25**, 1121
  validity of will, **25**, 1115
registration of, **6**, 468
reserved property—
  free estate—
    calculation of, **25**, 625
    France, **25**, 625
    Germany, **25**, 626
    generally, **25**, 623
  gift—
    purposes of, **25**, 627
    valid, formalities required for, **25**, 628
  heir, rights of, **25**, 626
  voluntary and statutory devolution, balance between, **25**, 629
  voluntary provision, **25**, 624
  will—
    purposes of, **25**, 627
    valid, formalities required for, **25**, 628
retrospective documents, incorporation of, **25**, 727
revival of—
  conditional revocation, **25**, 759
  revoking will, revocation of, **25**, 760

Will—_continued_
revocation of—
  clause of—
    express, **25**, 746
    interpretation, **25**, 747
  conditio si testator sine liberis decesserit, **12**, 1265
    after-born child, for benefit of, **25**, 752
    application of, **25**, 753
    principle, **25**, 751
    rebuttal of presumption, **25**, 754
  conditional, **25**, 759
  contract _inter vivos_, **25**, 737
  divorce, on, proposed reform, **25**, 1117
  express—
    destruction—
      direction of testator, at, **25**, 745
      testator, by, **25**, 744
      what constitutes, **25**, 743
    testator—
      destruction by, **25**, 744
      direction of, destruction at, **25**, 745
      insane, **25**, 741
      intention to revoke—
        generally, **25**, 741
        onus of proof, **25**, 742
    types of, **25**, 740
  implied—
    earlier will, **25**, 749
    testator's intention, **25**, 750
    types of, **25**, 748
  mutual will, **25**, 738
  nominations, **25**, 733
  revoking will, **25**, 760
  special destination, _see_ SPECIAL DESTINATION
  testator, freedom to revoke, **25**, 736
  See also SUCCESSION
special destination, _see_ SPECIAL DESTINATION
spouse—
  common calamity, **12**, 1266
  rights of, **12**, 1264
subscription, **6**, 415, 416, 419
substitute—
  donationes mortis causa, **25**, 735
  generally, **25**, 728
  gifts _inter vivos_, **25**, 729
  life assurance policy, benefit under, **25**, 734
  nomination, **25**, 733
  special destination, **25**, 732
  testamentum militare, **25**, 731
  verbal legacy, **25**, 730
tenancy inherited under, repossession, **13**, 749, 756, 781
testamentary intent, need for, **6**, 416
testamentary writing subsequent to, **12**, 1263
testation, freedom of—
  generally, **25**, 601
  restraints on, **25**, 766–771
testing clauses, **6**, 416
transfer to foundation by, **24**, 118
trust, creation of—
  capacity, **17**, 335
  formal validity, **17**, 335
  substantive validity, **17**, 336

Will—*continued*
trustees—
  powers, **12**, 1272
    discretionary, where too wide, **12**, 1271
types of—
  attested will, **25**, 723, 724
  holograph will, **25**, 722, 724
  notarial execution, **25**, 725
  printed will form, **25**, 726
  prospective document, incorporation of, **25**, 727
  retrospective document, incorporation of, **25**, 727
validation of doubtful, **6**, 416
validity of—
  essential—
    capacity to make will, **25**, 761
    circumvention, **25**, 763
    facility, **25**, 763
    insanity, **25**, 762
    intention to test, **25**, 765
    undue influence, **25**, 764
  formal—
    attested will, **25**, 723, 724
    holograph will, **25**, 722
    notarial execution, **25**, 725
    printed will form, **25**, 726
    private international law, **25**, 721
    prospective document, incorporation of, **25**, 727
    reserved property, **25**, 628
    retrospective document, incorporation of, **25**, 727
  reform, **25**, 1115
vesting, *see* VESTING
witnesses, **6**, 421
  beneficiaries, as, **12**, 1263
  printed form will signed without, **12**, 1263
See also SUCCESSION
Williamson Committee
recommendations of, **9**, 603
Winchester College
copyright rights conferred on, **18**, 1003
Winding up
application of procedures, **4**, 719
bona vacantia—
  Crown disclaimer, **4**, 931
  vesting of, in Crown, **4**, 930
calls—
  enforcement of, **4**, 782
  generally, **4**, 824
  power to make, **4**, 781
cautionary obligation, where company party to, **3**, 982
civil jurisdiction, **4**, 78
claims of creditors, *see* creditors *below*
company names, restriction on re-use of, **4**, 866
compensation—
  generally, **4**, 840
  set-off—
    application of right of, **4**, 842
    crown, **4**, 841
compulsory, **4**, 717
contributories—
  arrest, power of, **4**, 783
  bankrupt, **4**, 821

Winding up—*continued*
contributories—*continued*
  calls on—
    enforcement of, **4**, 782
    power to make, **4**, 781
  debts due from, **4**, 780
  deceased, **4**, 821
  financial interest of, **4**, 736
  liability, prescription of, **4**, 822
  list of, **4**, 823
  meaning, **4**, 816
  petition by—
    financial interest of contributory, **4**, 736
    position of contributory relating to, **4**, 503
    restrictions on right to petition, **4**, 734
    shares, redemption or purchase of shares, following, **4**, 735
  powers of court cumulative, **4**, 784
  reports to, **4**, 833
  settlement of list of, **4**, 779
  wishes of, meetings to ascertain, **4**, 787
Convention not applicable, **4**, 26
court, by—
  administration, liquidator following, **4**, 761
  caveat, **4**, 744
  commencement—
    consequences—
      contracts, effect on, **4**, 758
      directors, powers of, **4**, 757
      disposition of property, **4**, 753
      execution on assets in England and Wales, **4**, 756
      pending actions, **4**, 752
      property remains vested in company, **4**, 754
      stamp duty, **4**, 755
    date of, **4**, 751
  commission for receiving evidence, **4**, 789
  contributories—
    arrest, power of, **4**, 783
    calls on—
      enforcement of, **4**, 782
      power to make, **4**, 781
    court cumulative, powers of, **4**, 784
    debts due from, **4**, 780
    first meeting of, **4**, 760
    meetings to ascertain wishes of, **4**, 787
    settlement of list of, **4**, 779
  creditors—
    first meeting of, **4**, 760
    meeting to ascertain wishes of, **4**, 787
    not proving in time, power to exclude, **4**, 785
  defects in procedure, power to cure, **4**, 790
  early dissolution, **4**, 762
  examination of persons, **4**, 788
  final meeting, **4**, 792
  general jurisdiction, **4**, 720
  grounds for—
    debts, inability to pay, **4**, 727
    dormancy, **4**, 725
    general, **4**, 721
    number of members below two, **4**, 726
    old public company, **4**, 724

Winding up—*continued*
court, by—*continued*
  grounds for—*continued*
    security of creditor entitled to floating
      charge in jeopardy, **4**, 729
    share capital, failure to obtain certificate as
      to, **4**, 723
    special resolution, **4**, 722
    winding up just and equitable, **4**, 728
  interim liquidator, **4**, 759
  liquidation committee—
    establishment, **4**, 778
    functions, **4**, 778
    powers, **4**, 778
  liquidator—
    actions, power to bring or defend, **4**, 765
    administration, following, **4**, 761
    bankrupt estate, powers of trustee on, **4**, 769
    company's property, getting in, **4**, 768
    final meeting, **4**, 792
    functions, **4**, 763
    general control by court, **4**, 767
    interim, **4**, 759
    joint appointments, **4**, 774
    powers of—
      financial markets, operation of, **4**, 771
      restrictions on, **4**, 771
      sanction of court or company, exercisable
        with, **4**, 770
    provisional, *see* provisional liquidator *below*
    public examination of officers, **4**, 773
    release, **4**, 777
    removal from office, **4**, 776
    remuneration, **4**, 775
    sanction, powers exercisable without, **4**, 766
    statement of affairs, **4**, 772
    style, **4**, 764
    title, **4**, 764
    vacation of office, **4**, 776, 793
    validity of acts, **4**, 774
    voluntary arrangement, following, **4**, 761
  miscellaneous powers of court, **4**, 791
  petition—
    administrator, by, **4**, 730, 738
    alternative procedures available, **4**, 731
    Bank of England, by—
      authorised institutions, **4**, 742
      former authorised institutions, **4**, 742
    company, by, **4**, 730, 731
    contributory, by—
      financial interest, **4**, 736
      generally, **4**, 730
      position relating to, **4**, 503
      purchase of shares, winding up following,
        4, 735
      redemption of shares, winding up
        following, **4**, 735
      restrictions on right to petition, **4**, 734
    creditors, by—
      contingent creditors, **4**, 730, 732
      discretion of court, **4**, 733
      prospective creditors, **4**, 730, 732
    directors, by, **4**, 730, 731
    intimation of, **4**, 743

Winding up—*continued*
court, by—*continued*
  petition—*continued*
    just and equitable rule, based on, **4**, 501
    powers relating to, **4**, 501
    presentation of, **4**, 730
    receiver, by—
      generally, **4**, 730
      power to petition, **4**, 737
    Secretary of State, by—
      companies generally, **4**, 739
      insurance companies, **4**, 740
      investment business, bodies carrying on, **4**,
        741
    service of, **4**, 743
    who may petition, **4**, 730
  power to stay or sist winding up, **4**, 786
  provisional liquidator—
    appointment, **4**, 746
    functions, **4**, 748
    qualification, **4**, 747
    remuneration, **4**, 749
    termination of appointment, **4**, 750
  remittal between courts, **4**, 745
  voluntary arrangement, liquidator following, **4**,
    761
Court of Session jurisdiction, **6**, 924
credit union, **12**, 677
creditors—
  claims of—
    adjudication of, **4**, 831
    co-obligants, **4**, 830
    contingent debts, **4**, 828
    debts—
      contingent, **4**, 828
      future, **4**, 828
      interest on, **4**, 832
      secured, **4**, 829
    foreign currency, in, **4**, 827
    future debts, **4**, 828
    interest on debts, **4**, 832
    secured debts, **4**, 829
    submission of, **4**, 826
  court, winding up by, *see* court, by, *above*
  not proving in time, power to exclude, **4**, 785
  reports to, **4**, 833
  voluntary winding up, *see* voluntary winding
    up *below*
  wishes of, meetings to ascertain, **4**, 787
debts—
  Customs and Excise, due to, **4**, 854
  Inland Revenue, due to, **4**, 853
  preferential—
    coal and steel production, levies on, **4**, 858
    Customs and Excise, debts due to, **4**, 854
    debts which are, **4**, 852
    Inland Revenue, debts due to, **4**, 853
    occupational pension scheme, contributions
      to, **4**, 856
    priority, right of, **4**, 851
    remuneration of employees, **4**, 857
    social security contributions, **4**, 855
  winding up by court, grounds for, **4**, 727
deception, **4**, 920

Winding up—*continued*
diligence, effect on—
adjudications, **4**, 844
apparent insolvency, effect of, **4**, 848
arrestments, **4**, 845
bankruptcy rules, application of, **4**, 843
Cross-Border provisions, **4**, 847
inhibitions, **4**, 844
poindings, **4**, 845, 846
taxes, **4**, 849
directors—
court, winding up by, **4**, 730, 731
disqualification of—
Company Directors Disqualification Act
1986 ..., **4**, 909
order—
case not necessarily involving insolvency,
4, 911
contravention, consequences of, **4**, 918
effect of, **4**, 912
insolvency, case of, **4**, 910
register of, **4**, 919
Secretary of State, reports to, **4**, 916
section 6, **4**, 6
application to court under, **4**, 917
requirement under, **4**, 914
unfitness under, **4**, 913
unfitness—
determination under, **4**, 915
section 6, under, **4**, 913
disqualified, liability of—
joint and several liability, **4**, 905
personal liability, **4**, 903
relevant debts, **4**, 904
unregistered companies, application to, **4**,
906
personal liability of, **4**, 901, 903
summary remedy against—
Companies Act 1985, comparison with
position prior to, **4**, 908
court, powers of, **4**, 907
unlimited liability, with, **4**, 819
dissolution declared void, **4**, 317
dissolved company—
court's power to declare dissolution void, **4**,
929
reinstatement of, **4**, 929
distribution of assets—
dividends, **4**, 927
pari passu ranking, **4**, 925
priority of claims, order of, **4**, 926
distribution of surplus, **4**, 825
dividends—
distribution of assets, **4**, 927
unclaimed, lodgment of, **4**, 928
employees—
assets, power to make over, **4**, 865
consultation—
impending redundancies, in respect of, **4**,
863
transfer of undertaking, prior to, **4**, 864
contract of employment, effect of winding up
on, **4**, 861
guaranteed payments, **4**, 862

Winding up—*continued*
employees—*continued*
redundancies, impending, consultation in
respect of, **4**, 863
remuneration, ranking of, **4**, 857
excluded jurisdiction, **4**, 73
extortionate credit transactions, *see* void and
voidable transactions *below*
floating charges, *see* void and voidable transactions
below; FLOATING CHARGE
forms of, **4**, 717
fraudulent preferences, *see* void and voidable
transactions *below*
fraudulent trading—
judicial interpretation, **4**, 898
liability of persons party to, **4**, 897
supplementary provisions, **4**, 899
general, **4**, 716
gratuitous alienations, *see* void and voidable
transactions *below*
heritable security, sale of property subject to, **4**, 850
information—
contributories, reports to, **4**, 833
creditors, reports to, **4**, 833
Registrar of Companies, returns to, **4**, 834
insolvent company, **17**, 353
jurisdiction, **8**, 431, 435
just and equitable rule—
generally, **4**, 728
petition based on—
Companies Act 1985, s 59, relationship to, **4**,
499
conduct of petitioner, reasonableness of, **4**, 500
contingent creditors, position of, **4**, 504
contributory, position of, **4**, 503
court's powers, **4**, 501
deadlock in management, **4**, 511
directors, position of, **4**, 504
general basis of petition, **4**, 505
illegality of purpose, **4**, 508
impossibility of purpose, **4**, 508
incorporated partnership, **4**, 512
older Scottish decisions, **4**, 507
position of company, **4**, 502
preliminary consideration, **4**, 506
primary purpose of company, ascertainment
of, **4**, 509
quasi-partnership—
application of principle in Scotland, **4**, 514
generally, **4**, 512
identifying, **4**, 513
right to present petition, **4**, 498
substratum of company, failure of, **4**, 510
liability—
contributory, of, prescription of, **4**, 822
members, of, **4**, 817
past members, **4**, 817, 818
shares redeemed or purchased, in respect of, **4**,
820
unlimited, of directors, **4**, 819
liquidator—
associate, transactions with, **4**, 895
corrupt inducement affecting appointment of,
4, 922

Winding up—*continued*
liquidator—*continued*
  court, winding up by, *see* court, by, *above*
  sale of property by, **4**, 850
  voluntary winding up, *see* voluntary winding
    up *below*
meetings—
  annual, **4**, 835
  corporate representatives, **4**, 838
  other, **4**, 835
  personnel of company, attendance of, **4**, 836
  procedure, **4**, 837
  proxies, **4**, 838
  sederunt book, maintenance of, **4**, 839
members—
  liability of—
    generally, **4**, 817
    past members, **4**, 817, 818
  voluntary winding up, *see* voluntary winding
    up *below*
offences—
  corrupt inducement, **4**, 922
  deception, **4**, 920
  fraud, **4**, 920
  prosecution of, **4**, 921
office-holder, investigative powers of—
  application of provisions, **4**, 868
  co-operation, duty relating to, **4**, 869
  dealings of company, inquiry into, **4**, 870
  office-holder, meaning, **4**, 868
Official Receiver—
  no Official Receiver in Scotland, **4**, 718
partnership, of—
  authority of partners to wind up affairs, **16**,
    1098
  dissolution of partnership on—
    banking partnership, **16**, 1095
    financial services partnership, **16**, 1095
    generally, **16**, 1077
    insurance partnership, **16**, 1095
    unregistered company, **16**, 1094
  distribution of assets—
    deceased partner's share—
      ascertainment, **16**, 1104
      treatment, generally, **16**, 1103
    final settlement of accounts, on, **16**, 1105
    fraud, partnership dissolved for, **16**, 1100
    misrepresentation, partnership dissolved for,
      16, 1100
    partners' rights, **16**, 1099, 1100
    post-dissolution profits, **16**, 1102
    premiums, return, **16**, 1101
    retiring partner's share—
      ascertainment, **16**, 1104
      treatment, generally, **16**, 1103
  exempted person under Financial Services
    1986, rules, **12**, 1323
  limited partnerships, **16**, 1122
receiver, *see* RECEIVER
Registrar of Companies, returns to, **4**, 834
Schedule 5 of 1982 Act, **4**, 77
Schedule 8 of 1982 Act, **4**, 71, 73
share capital, failure to obtain certificate as to, **4**,
  723

Winding up—*continued*
special manager—
  appointment of, **4**, 923
  duties of, **4**, 924
  powers of, **4**, 924
special resolution for, **4**, 722
striking off—
  company not carrying on business, **4**, 932
  Gazette,
publication of notice in, **4**, 934
  liquidation, company in, **4**, 933
  reinstatement after, **4**, 935
termination of contract, **9**, 140, 145
trading—
  fraudulent, *see* fraudulent trading *above*
  wrongful, *see* wrongful trading *below*
unfair preferences, *see* void and voidable
  transactions *below*
unfair prejudice remedy, history of, **4**, 478
unintimated assignation defeated by, **20**, 47
unregistered company, of—
  applicable provisions, **4**, 937
  company having ceased to carry on business, **4**,
    939
  contributory, meaning, **4**, 942
  debts, inability to pay, **4**, 940
  dissolved company, **4**, 939
  floating charge in jeopardy, **4**, 941
  grounds for winding up, **4**, 938
  jurisdiction, **4**, 937
  restraining proceedings, **4**, 943
  sisting proceedings, **4**, 943
  staying proceedings, **4**, 943
  unregistered company, meaning, **4**, 936
utility suppliers, position of—
  electricity, **4**, 867
  gas, **4**, 867
  telecommunication supplies, **4**, 867
  water, **4**, 867
void and voidable transactions—
  committee members and others, dealings by, **4**,
    896
  conveyance to trustees, **4**, 871
  extortionate credit transactions—
    court order—
      circumstances in which made, **4**, 892
      content of, **4**, 894
    extortionate, meaning, **4**, 893
  floating charges—
    fresh consideration, requirement for, **4**, 889
    Insolvency Act 1986 ..., **4**, 888
    old law, **4**, 887
    relevant time, **4**, 890
    solvency test, **4**, 891
  fraudulent preferences—
    challenge, effect of, **4**, 886
    common law—
      generally, **4**, 880
      transactions exempt from challenge, **4**, 881
      who may challenge, **4**, 882
    Insolvency Act 1986 ..., **4**, 884
    old law, **4**, 879
    reduction, effect of, **4**, 883

Winding up—*continued*
void and voidable transactions—*continued*
  fraudulent preferences—*continued*
    statutory challenge, transactions exempt
      from, **4**, 885
    gratuitous alienations—
      abuse of power, **4**, 878
      burden of proof, **4**, 875
      challenge, effect of, **4**, 877
      common law, **4**, 873
      excess of power, **4**, 878
      Insolvency Act 1986 ..., **4**, 874
      old law, **4**, 872
      statutory provisions, application of, **4**, 876
    liquidator and associate, transactions between,
      4, 895
    unfair preferences—
      challenge, effect of, **4**, 886
      common law—
        generally, **4**, 880
        transactions exempt from challenge at, **4**,
          881
        who may challenge at, **4**, 882
      Insolvency Act 1986 ..., **4**, 884
      old law, **4**, 879
      reduction, effect of, **4**, 883
      statutory challenge, transactions exempt
        from, **4**, 885
voluntary—
  circumstances in which wound up, **4**, 794
  compulsory winding up compared with, **4**, 717
  court, powers of, **4**, 815
  creditors, of—
    annual meetings, **4**, 805
    dissolution, **4**, 808
    final meeting, **4**, 808
    liquidation committee, appointment of, **4**,
      802
    liquidator—
      appointment of, **4**, 801
      release of, **4**, 807
      removal of, **4**, 806
      resignation, **4**, 806
      vacation of office, **4**, 806
    meeting of creditors, **4**, 800
    members' voluntary winding up, conversion
      of, **4**, 798
    schemes of arrangement under s 10 ..., **4**,
      803
    stamp duty, **4**, 804
  directors, powers of, **4**, 811
  distribution of property, **4**, 812
  liquidator—
    appointment of, **4**, 796, 801, 809
    creditors' winding up, *see* creditors, of, *above*
    functions of, **4**, 813
    members' winding up, *see* members, of, *below*
    powers of, **4**, 813
    remuneration, **4**, 814
  members, of—
    annual meeting, **4**, 799
    creditors' voluntary winding up, conversion
      to, **4**, 798
    declaration of solvency, **4**, 795

Winding up—*continued*
voluntary—*continued*
  members, of—*continued*
    dissolution, **4**, 799
    final meeting, **4**, 799
    liquidator—
      appointment of, **4**, 796
      removal of, **4**, 796
      resignation, **4**, 796
    schemes of arrangement under s 110 ..., **4**,
      797
    notices required to be given, **4**, 809
    provisions as to arbitration, **2**, 412
    resolutions—
      effect of, **4**, 810
      requirement, **4**, 794
  wrongful trading—
    Cork Committee recommendation, **4**, 900
    directors, personal liability of, **4**, 307, 901
    introduction of concept, **4**, 307, 900
    shadow directors, personal liability of, **4**, 901
    supplementary provisions, **4**, 902
  See also BANKRUPTCY; INSOLVENCY
Window
building controls—
  cleaning, as potential hazard, **3**, 208
  collision with, as potential hazard, **3**, 208
cleaner's licence—
  appeal to sheriff, **14**, 119
  offence to trade without, **7**, 45
  requirement for, **14**, 565
emptying of vessels from, **19**, 301, 336*n*
windscreen—
  windows, and, regulations, **20**, 480
  wipers, regulations, **20**, 480
Wine
excise duty, **7**, 1061, 1061*n*, 1064
  deferred payments, **7**, 1088
made-wine—
  excise duty, **7**, 1061, 1061*n*, 1064
    deferred payments, **7**, 1088
  producers, licence, **7**, 1066
preservatives, **11**, 377
producers, licence, **7**, 1066
sale in off-sales, **2**, 79
tasting, restriction on, **2**, 10
use of word in composite names, **11**, 383, 393,
  395
See also ALCOHOLIC LIQUOR
Wireless
election broadcasts, restriction, **15**, 1020, 1231
set, blind person, provision for, **7**, 1448
station—
  valuation for rating, **24**, 749
telegraphy—
  telecommunications system using, **16**, 1928
See also RADIO
Wires
overhead, roads authority control over construction, **20**, 693
Witness
absolute privilege, **15**, 521, 524
accused as—
  civil cases, **10**, 538

Witness—*continued*
accused as—*continued*
  criminal cases—
    defence witness, as, **10**, 541, 542
    generally, **10**, 539
    prosecution witness, as, **10**, 540
additional, **17**, 669
advocate, professional detachment, **13**, 1357
age, disclosure of, **10**, 552
ambiguities in evidence, **10**, 560
anonymous, **12**, 43, 55, 59
approach to, **10**, 535
attendance of, **10**, 523
avoiding being called, **7**, 496, 522
bankers, **10**, 537
biased, **12**, 43, 55, 57
certification of, **17**, 1178
character, admissibility of evidence as to, **10**, 630,
    635, 636
  criminal cases, **10**, 632, 635, 636
child as, **10**, 502
  admissibility, **3**, 1216
  commissioner, proceedings before, **3**, 1217
  criminal trial, at, **3**, 1217
  evidence, taking, **3**, 1217
  identification in court, **10**, 552
  live television link, use of, **3**, 1217
  memorandum of guidance, **3**, 1217
  oath and affirmation, **10**, 548
  questions as to credibility, **10**, 636
citation—
  appearance without, **10**, 536
  generally, **17**, 1157
civil cases—
  party to case as witness, **10**, 538
  solicitor to party as witness, **10**, 538
  spouse to party as witness, **10**, 538
co-accused, competence as, **10**, 502
compellability, **10**, 525
  civil cases, **10**, 538
  criminal cases, **10**, 539–546
competence, **10**, 524
  civil cases, **10**, 538
  co-accused, **10**, 502
  criminal cases, **10**, 539–546
  spouse, **10**, 502, 538
conduct of, cross-examination as to, **10**, 555
conscience, refusal to answer on grounds of, **10**,
  508
contempt of court by, **6**, 317, 321; **17**, 756
  refusal to answer questions, **10**, 550, 563
  reluctant witness, **10**, 563
  self-induced incapacity through drink or drugs,
    10, 532
  See also CONTEMPT OF COURT
corroboration, *see* CORROBORATION
courts-martial, **2**, 700, 704, 724, 726; **6**, 894
credibility of—
  admissibility of evidence as to, **10**, 630, 635–
    637
    criminal cases, **10**, 632, 635, 636
  cross-examination as to, **10**, 554
  facts relevant to, **10**, 623
  weight of evidence, **10**, 779

Witness—*continued*
criminal cases—
  accused as witness—
    defence witness when co-accused, **10**, 542
    defence witness when tried alone, **10**, 541
    generally, **10**, 539
    prosecution witness, as, **10**, 540
  prosecutor as witness, **10**, 545
  socii criminis, **10**, 544
  spouse to accused as witness, **10**, 543
  witness not named on list, **10**, 546
cross-examination, **13**, 1366
Crown—
  examination for, **17**, 753
  objections to, **17**, 675
deaf or deaf mute, **10**, 333, 551
deed, to, incompetent, **12**, 1229
defence, preparation of, **17**, 657, 659
discretion to call, **10**, 549
divorce cases—
  compellability, **10**, 930
  competency, **10**, 930
documentary evidence identified by, **10**, 572
documents not requiring witnessing, **6**, 434
documents used to refresh memory, **10**, 566
election court, **15**, 1483
Employment Appeal Tribunal, **6**, 986, 988
evidence, *see* EVIDENCE
examination in court—
  civil cases, **10**, 547
  credibility, as to, **10**, 502
  criminal cases, **10**, 547
  cross-examination, **10**, 547, 549
    credibility, as to, **10**, 554
    failure to cross-examine, **10**, 555, 556
    issues, as to, **10**, 555
    leading questions, **10**, 553
    lodging of documents, **10**, 557
    objects of, **10**, 553
    proof of documents, **10**, 557
    recall of witnesses, **10**, 560
    reliability, as to, **10**, 554
    second, following re-examination, **10**, 558, 559
    witness's liability for, **10**, 533
  examination-in-chief, **10**, 547, 549, 552
    adjournments, **10**, 552
    leading questions, **10**, 552
    object of, **10**, 552
    objections to evidence, **10**, 552
    questions by judge, **10**, 552
  generally, **10**, 547; **12**, 43, 55–59
  interpretation, **10**, 551
  judge, questioning by, **10**, 568
  oath and affirmation, **10**, 548
    exceptions, **10**, 548
    form of, **10**, 548
  order of examination, **10**, 549
  proof, conduct of, **17**, 1166
  questions—
    double, **10**, 550
      objections to, **10**, 567
    duty to answer, **10**, 508, 550
    hypothetical, **10**, 550
      objections to, **10**, 567

Witness—_continued_
examination in court—_continued_
  questions—_continued_
    leading, **10**, 550, 552, 553, 558
      objections to, **10**, 567
    objectionable, **10**, 550, 567
    through the court, **10**, 559
    usurping function of court, **10**, 550
      objections to, **10**, 567
  re-examination, **10**, 547, 549, 558; **17**, 1169
    cross-examination following, **10**, 558
    facts not previously referred to, **10**, 558
    objects of, **10**, 558
    subject matter, **10**, 558
exclusion of—
  approach to witness as grounds for, **10**, 535
  presence in court as grounds for, **10**, 534
expert, **10**, 650; **12**, 43, 55, 56
  assessors, **10**, 654
  conflicting opinions, **10**, 650
  court experts, **10**, 655
  documents used by, **10**, 566
  employment in civil legal aid cases, **13**, 1045
  exchange of expert's reports, **10**, 655
  foreign law, establishment of fact, **10**, 653
  handwriting, **10**, 652
  impartiality, **12**, 56
  meaning, **10**, 647
  men of skill, **10**, 654
  sanction for, criminal legal aid, **13**, 1064
  special features of expert evidence, **10**, 651
eye-witness, visual identification by, **10**, 658–661
failure to attend, **17**, 1158
Health and Safety Commission inquiry, at, **9**, 418
hostile, **17**, 1168
identification in court, **10**, 552
identification parades, **10**, 663, 666
incapacity—
  mental, **10**, 532, 533
    oath and affirmation, **10**, 548
  physical, **10**, 533
  self-induced through drink or drugs, **10**, 532
incompetent, **10**, 532
inconsistency in evidence of, **10**, 555
incrimination—
  adultery, **10**, 675
  criminal offences, **10**, 671–674
  furth of Scotland, liability to prosecution, **10**, 674
  generally, **10**, 670
  privilege, statutory restrictions on, **10**, 672
  spouse, of, **10**, 673
industrial tribunal, attendance at hearing, **9**, 318
interference with, **7**, 499
interview before hearing, **13**, 1357
  skilled witness, **13**, 1357
intimidation of, **7**, 496, 523; **10**, 637
judge as, **10**, 528
judge's function in relation to, **10**, 568
jurors, **10**, 529
Lands Tribunal for Scotland—
  attendance, **6**, 1150
  expert, statement by, **6**, 1152
  generally, **5**, 196
  oath, **6**, 1151

Witness—_continued_
lawburrows, action of, **13**, 918, 919
  witnesses to a diet of proof, **13**, 919
leading, **17**, 1165
lists, **17**, 667, 672
  annexed to indictment, **10**, 546
  persons not named on, **10**, 546
malice, statement inferring, **10**, 744
marshalling, **17**, 1160
member of Parliament as, **10**, 527
mental or physical illness affecting reliability of evidence, **10**, 636
non-compellable, **12**, 43, 55, 58
objection to, presence in court as grounds for, **10**, 534
oral evidence, _see_ ORAL EVIDENCE
ordinary—
  meaning, **10**, 647
  opinion, evidence of, **10**, 649
perjury, _see_ PERJURY
precognition, **10**, 523; **17**, 545, 659, 1142
presence in court as grounds for exclusion, **10**, 534
prevarication by, **17**, 756
previous convictions, admissibility of evidence as to, **10**, 635
privilege, _see_ PRIVILEGE
probative writings, **6**, 414, 420, 421
prosecutor, as, **10**, 545
questions—
  duty to answer, **10**, 508, 550
  question which might render liable to prosecution, **10**, 630
  refusal to answer, **10**, 523
recall of, **10**, 568; **17**, 755
  civil cases, **10**, 560
  criminal cases, **10**, 563
reliability—
  cross-examination as to, **10**, 554
  weight of evidence, **10**, 779
reluctant, **10**, 563
signature of, **6**, 421
socii criminis, **10**, 544
solicitor called as, **13**, 1190
solicitor to party, **10**, 538
Sovereign as, **10**, 526
spouse of party to action as—
  civil cases, **10**, 538
  competence generally, **10**, 502, 845
  criminal cases, **10**, 543
summary causes, **17**, 1315
vulnerable, **10**, 502
who may be, **6**, 420
will, to, **12**, 1263
written statement in lieu of oral evidence, **10**, 569–571
See also EVIDENCE; ORAL EVIDENCE
Woman
creation of trust by, **24**, 14
employment of
  conditions of, **14**, 1666
  European Social Charter, **12**, 7
  maternity rights, **12**, 7
factories, in, **9**, 72

Woman—*continued*
former incapacities affecting, **11**, 1053
franchise—
    municipal elections, **15**, 1023, 1024, 1026
    parliamentary elections, **15**, 1016–1018
hereditary peerage, holder of, **6**, 1018
mentally handicapped, offence against, **14**, 1481
mining, in, **9**, 71
mothers, economic and social protection, **12**, 7
sex discrimination, *see* SEX DISCRIMINATION
Women's institute
community benefit society, as, **12**, 609
Women's Royal Naval Reserve
status, **2**, 743
Woodcock
game, as, **11**, 802
nets or springs, taken by, **11**, 830
Poaching Prevention Act 1832 …, **11**, 843
trespass in search of, **11**, 817
Woodlands
amenity woodlands, **24**, 750
broadleaved, grants for, **11**, 644*n*
capital allowances, **11**, 646
commercial, profits and losses arising from, **11**, 644, 645
death of owner, **11**, 651
    deferral of inheritance tax, **11**, 651–654
Forestry Commission schemes, **11**, 644
lands and heritages, as, **24**, 750
pertinent, as, **12**, 1242
purchase and sale, taxation on, **11**, 647
    capital gains tax, **11**, 649
    income tax, **11**, 648
rating relief, **24**, 560
Word
construction of deed—
    foreign languages, **12**, 1217
    generally, **12**, 1219
    local or class usage, **12**, 1220
    popular sense to be followed, **12**, 1215
    technical terms, **12**, 1215, 1217
    verba sunt interpretanda contra proferentem, **12**, 1232
construction of statute—
    grammar, rules of, **12**, 1103, 1106
    literal construction not to prevail if opposed to legislature, **12**, 1106
    literal rule, **12**, 1103
    presumption as to correct usage, **12**, 1133
    technical words, **12**, 1103
    unambiguous words, **12**, 1105
    words of rank, **12**, 1169
defamatory, **15**, 483
passing off—
    generally, **18**, 1374, 1375
    generic, words which become, **18**, 1375
    invented or fancy words, **18**, 1375
Word processing
data protection in relation to, **18**, 1502
Work
confinement, return after, *see* MATERNITY RIGHTS
employer's duties as to—
    provision, **9**, 80
    safe place, **9**, 79
    safe system, **9**, 76

Work—*continued*
equal pay, *see* EQUAL PAY
experience—
    arrangement of, **8**, 867
health and safety at, *see* HEALTH AND SAFETY AT WORK
hours of, *see* HOURS OF WORK
materials—
    contract for, **6**, 69; **20**, 812
particular kind, of—
    changing job skills, effect of, **9**, 169
    functions, effect of, **9**, 169
    generally, **9**, 168
    shift work, reorganisation involving introduction of, **9**, 170
permit—
    allotment, **12**, 155, 156
        skilled workers, **12**, 155
        trainees, **12**, 155
    Commonwealth citizens, **12**, 107
    distribution, **12**, 112
    employment vouchers, **12**, 107
        number and distribution, **12**, 112
    entry clearance, **12**, 151, 244; **16**, 1243
    excluded work categories, **12**, 154
    exemptions, **12**, 154
    generally, **12**, 102
    grant of, **12**, 154
    holders, Immigration Rules—
        change of employment, **12**, 243
        concealment of material facts, **12**, 242
        extension of leave, **12**, 244
            trainees, **12**, 245
        false representations by, **12**, 242
        generally, **12**, 242
        leave to enter or remain, variation of, **12**, 244
        refusal of leave to enter, grounds for, **12**, 242
        settlement, **12**, 244
    Immigration Rules, **12**, 149
    See also holders, immigration rules *above*
    issue, **12**, 140; **16**, 1243
    leave to remain, approval of, **12**, 140
    no appeal against refusal, **12**, 344
    number, type and distribution, **12**, 154
    number issued, **12**, 112
    permanent settlement following, **12**, 154
    police registration conditions, **12**, 175
    refusal of, no appeal against, **12**, 154
    settlement, categories leading to, **12**, 241
    trainees, **12**, 241
    United Kingdom resident, by, **12**, 157
    young Commonwealth citizen on working holiday, **12**, 241
place of—
    health and safety at work legislation, **19**, 304
    infected person, attendance at, **19**, 457
    occupations, **9**, 124
    safe, employer's duties as to, **9**, 79
right to, **11**, 1091, 1093; **12**, 4*n*
shift, **9**, 170
systems of—
    maintenance of, **9**, 432
    meaning, **9**, 434

Work—*continued*
systems of—*continued*
provision of, **9**, 431
safe, employer's duty as to, **9**, 76
time off to look for, **9**, 95
Worker—
meaning, **9**, 62
seasonal, permit-free employment, **12**, 247
See also EMPLOYEE
See also EMPLOYMENT
Working for Patients **White Paper**, **11**, 1401
Working men's club
friendly societies legislation, **12**, 601
friendly society, as, **12**, 679, 679*n*, 685
meaning, **12**, 694
valuations exemption, **12**, 717
Works
local authority, *see* LOCAL AUTHORITY
See also PUBLIC WORKS
World Health Organisation
immunisation recommended by, **19**, 500
World Intellectual Property Organisation
Treaty on Intellectual Property in Respect of
Integrated Circuits, **18**, 1253
World Trade Organisation
generally, **7**, 1009
World War I (1914–1918)
minority treaties, establishment following, **12**, 2,
2*n*
World War II (1939–1945)
international regulation following, **12**, 3
Wrak, *See* WRECK
Wreath
liveries, of, **11**, 1605, 1606
Wreck
abandoned *sine spe revertendi* or *sine spe recuperandi*,
21, 511
above low water mark, **21**, 511
aircraft, **18**, 557
appropriation of ship or cargo, **7**, 333
below low water mark, **21**, 511
boarding vessel without permission, **21**, 513*n*
cargo—
generally, **21**, 511
receiver of wreck, delivery to, **21**, 513
wreck, classed as, **21**, 511
cargo or other articles, **18**, 555
common law, **18**, 554
crime of wrecking, **7**, 333
Crown hereditary revenue derived from, **7**, 769
Crown rights, **18**, 554, 556; **21**, 512
donatories under, **18**, 556, 557
dangerous—
prohibition on approaching, **9**, 1231
provisions as to, generally, **21**, 515
derelict compared, **21**, 511
disposal, **21**, 513*n*
flotsam, jetsam and lagan, **21**, 511
grounded ship compared, **21**, 511
historical, archaeological or artistic importance,
of—
protection, **9**, 1230; **21**, 515
salvage operations, licensing, **21**, 515
hovercraft, **18**, 557

Wreck—*continued*
impeding saving of vessel, **21**, 513*n*
incapable of navigation, must be, **21**, 511
meaning, **21**, 511
Merchant Shipping Acts, **18**, 555, 556
obliterating or defacing marks on, **21**, 513*n*
owner—
claiming wreck, **18**, 555; **21**, 513
delivery by receiver of wreck, **21**, 513
not claiming, **21**, 513*n*
person finding or taking possession, duties, **18**,
555
raising, costs of, damages for, **21**, 385
receiver of—
appointment, **18**, 555; **21**, 513
delivery of wreck or cargo to, **21**, 513
duties, **18**, 555–557
examination of ship which is or has been in
distress, **21**, 513
notification by owner of wreck, **21**, 513
powers and duties, **21**, 513
removal—
authorities, by, **21**, 514
dockyard port, from, **11**, 1319, 1322
right of—
Crown grant, **18**, 213
generally, **18**, 213, 213*n*
sale—
generally, **21**, 513, 513*n*
harbour or conservancy authority, by, **21**, 514,
514*n*
salvage and *negotiorum gestio* distinguished, **15**, 93
search warrant to look for, **21**, 513*n*
secreting, **21**, 513*n*
statutory provisions as to, **21**, 513
taking abroad wreck found in UK, **21**, 513*n*
taking away part of stranded or distressed vessel,
21, 513*n*
theft of, **7**, 333
title to, **18**, 556
udal law, **24**, 314
unclaimed, **18**, 557; **21**, 512
wages, crew's right to, **21**, 259
wreck-raising expenses, limitation of liability, **21**,
756, 756*n*
Wreck and ware
servitude of, generally, **18**, 318
Wrestling
injuries, and assault, **7**, 221
Writ
advocate, signature by, **13**, 1326
advocate drawing up, **13**, 1326
amendment of, decree in absence, **17**, 1027
assignation, disposition, in, **18**, 642
assignation of, **6**, 538
backing writ, prescribed form of, **17**, 1011
blanks in, **12**, 1228
citation—
certificate of, **17**, 1018
form of, **17**, 1015
generally, **17**, 1012
period of notice, **17**, 1014
simplified divorce procedure, in, **17**, 1019
warrant of, **17**, 1013

Writ—*continued*
clause of assignation, implied terms, **12**, 1235
contra proferentem rule, **12**, 1232
copyright, **13**, 1326
Crown, **7**, 852, 853
  authentication in Scots law, **7**, 908
feu, interpretation of, **12**, 1237
form of—
  backing, **17**, 1011
  condescendence, **17**, 1009
  crave, **17**, 1008
  generally, **17**, 1004
  heading, **17**, 1006
  instance, **17**, 1007
  pleas-in-law, **17**, 1010
  prescribed, **17**, 1005
  signature, **17**, 1011
Great Seal of the United Kingdom, **7**, 856, 858
incapax of, recovery of, **11**, 1225
initial, averments contained in, **17**, 1005, 1009
interpretation of, **12**, 1215
lease, as evidence of, **13**, 132
loan repayment, proof by, **13**, 1748
  extrinsic evidence, **13**, 1750
meaning, **7**, 858
objection to, caution, requirement for, **3**, 999
probative—
  as documentary evidence, **10**, 600
  obligation constituted or evidenced by, **16**, 2116
proof by, **17**, 1132
  contract, of, **13**, 1718
    agent, writ of, **13**, 1733
    Consumer Credit Act 1974 ..., **13**, 1746
    lender, writ of, **13**, 1734
    qualified writ—
      general rule, **13**, 1740
      intrinsic, qualification must be, **13**, 1744
      parole evidence inadmissible to disprove
        qualification, **13**, 1745
      when loan not negatived by, **13**, 1743
      written qualification, **13**, 1741
    requirements, **13**, 1719
seal, **7**, 853
service—
  generally, **14**, 1504; **17**, 1012
  irregularity in, **17**, 1020
  outwith Scotland, **17**, 1017
  period of notice, **17**, 1014

Writ—*continued*
service—*continued*
  Scotland, in, **17**, 1016
  signet, under, **14**, 1504
  solicitor, signature by, **13**, 1326
  stamp duty, **13**, 1757
  trust proved by, **24**, 13
  UK parliamentary elections, **15**, 1225, 1353
  unqualified person drawing or preparing, **13**, 1182, 1183
  See also DEED OR WRITING
Writers to the Signet
entail law reform, draft bill, **22**, 634
generally, **7**, 887, 898
historical background, **13**, 1103, 1104
officers of court, as, **13**, 1199
precedence, **16**, 2020
Sale of Goods Bill 1893—
  revision, **22**, 643
Writing
meaning for copyright purposes, **18**, 949
requirements of, **15**, 666–669
Written statement
contract of employment, in, *see* CONTRACT OF EMPLOYMENT
Wrongful act
obligations arising from, *see* DELICT
Wrongful civil proceedings
See DELICT
Wrongful detention
See DELICT; DETENTION, WRONGFUL
Wrongful dismissal
damages—
  benefits arising on breach, effect of, **9**, 200
  generally, **9**, 196
  loss, mitigation of, **9**, 198
  measure of, **9**, 197
  taxation, incidence of, **9**, 199
declarator, action of, **9**, 195
generally, **9**, 193
interdict, opportunities for, **9**, 195
meaning, **9**, 193
remedies, generally, **9**, 194
unfair dismissal compared with, **9**, 202
Wrongful trading
See WINDING UP
Wrongful witholding
See INTEREST

Y

Yard (measurement)
definition, **6**, 179
Year
astral, **22**, 811
astronomical, **22**, 811
benefit year, social security, **22**, 811
birth of Christ, numbering by reference to, **22**, 807
bisextile, **22**, 811
centennial, **22**, 804, 805
commencement, legal—
    discrepancy, Scotland and England—
        duration, **22**, 806
    Gregorian calendar, **22**, 806, 811
    Jewish, **22**, 806, 808
    meaning, **22**, 811
    Privy Council of Scotland—
        Ordinance of 1599 ..., **22**, 806, 811
common, **22**, 804, 805, 811
definition, **22**, 811
duration—
    calendar, compromise, **22**, 801–804
    expiry, time limits, **22**, 823
    modes of measurement, **22**, 811
European Convention on the Calculation of Time-Limits, **22**, 829
financial—
    Consolidated Fund/central taxes etc, **22**, 811
    corporation tax, **22**, 811
    Scottish regional/islands/district, **22**, 811
intercalation of days—
    Julian calendar, **22**, 802
    Roman Republican calendar, **22**, 802
leap, **22**, 804, 805, 811
natural, **22**, 811
numbering—
    birth of Christ, by reference to, **22**, 807
    Gregorian calendar, **22**, 807
sidereal, **22**, 811
solar, **22**, 811
statutory definition, **22**, 811
taxation purposes, for, **22**, 811
tropical—
    cycle of seasons as, **22**, 801
    duration, **22**, 801, 804, 811
    incompatibility with lunar month/solar day, **22**, 801, 802
year of assessment, income/capital gains tax, **22**, 811
year and a day, expiry, time limits, **22**, 823
Yeomen of the Guard, Captain of
office of, **7**, 774
Young offender
children's hearing—
    generally, **3**, 1379
    reform proposals, **3**, 1380
generally, **16**, 1434; **22**, 32, 33, 36

Young offenders' institution
after-care, young offenders subject to statutory, **22**, 36
allocation to, **16**, 1434
custody and treatment of inmates, **16**, 1434
establishment, **16**, 1404, 1411
females, **16**, 1434
generally, **16**, 1434
males, **16**, 1434
persons committed to, **22**, 32
release, obligatory after-care, **22**, 36
report by social worker for, before offender's release, **22**, 36
transfer to prison from, **16**, 1434
visiting committee, **16**, 1421
Young person
adult court, appearance in, social worker's, duties, **22**, 33
after-care, offender, **22**, 36
business, transaction in course of, **3**, 1211
busking, **9**, 1040
care—
    committal to, **12**, 64
    parental access and visitation rights, **12**, 64
    separation of siblings, **12**, 64
    termination of care order, promotion of parent-child relationship, **12**, 64
corporal punishment, **12**, 26, 90, 91
custodial sentence, imposition, **3**, 1218
economic and social protection, **12**, 7
education, *see* EDUCATION
employment, conditions of, **14**, 1666
European Social Charter, **12**, 7
factory, in, **9**, 72
hours of work, **14**, 1671
Kilbrandon Committee recommendations, **22**, 21
legal capacity—
    adoption, **3**, 1209
    age limit, where express, **3**, 1210, 1213, 1221
    generally, **3**, 1202, 1210
    medical procedures, **3**, 1207
    passive, **3**, 1203, 1219
    prejudicial transactions, **3**, 1211
    residual, **3**, 1206
    testamentary capacity, **3**, 1208
    transaction, *see* CHILD–CHILDREN (LEGAL CAPACITY)
medical examination, **14**, 1666
mining, in, **9**, 71
picture book for, VAT zero-rating, **7**, 1447
place of safety, committal by court to, **22**, 33
protection of, **17**, 969
release from detention, **22**, 33
remand for inquiries, local authority provision of accommodation centre, **22**, 33
rights of, international conventions on, **12**, 5
Schedule 1 offences, *see* SCHEDULE 1 OFFENCES

Z

Zebra crossing
meaning, **20**, 440
Zero-rating
See VALUE ADDED TAX
Zinc phosphide
special restrictions, **14**, 1216
Zoo
employees etc, conviction of, **2**, 139
escape from, precautions, **2**, 140
exempted, **2**, 147
inspection of, **2**, 145
insurance, requirement for, **2**, 140
licence, **14**, 524; **19**, 1295
    alteration of, **2**, 142
    appeals respecting, **2**, 143
    application—
        consideration of, **2**, 138
        matters specified in, **2**, 137
        notice of, **2**, 137
    grant of—
        conditions, subject to, **2**, 140
        grounds for refusing, **2**, 139

Zoo—*continued*
licence—*continued*
    grant of—
        objection to, **2**, 138
    holder—
        conviction of, effect, **2**, 142
        death of, transfer on, **2**, 141
    refusal of, **2**, 139
    renewal, **2**, 141
    representations as to, **2**, 138
    requirement for, **2**, 136
    revocation, grounds for, **2**, 142
    surrender of, **2**, 141
    transfer of, **2**, 141
meaning, **2**, 136
Ministerial functions, **2**, 146
offences in respect of, **2**, 144
sheriff court jurisdiction, **6**, 1078
taking or killing wild animals, **11**, 886
welfare of animals, **2**, 137
Zoonoses
public health legislation, **19**, 477

Z